Annotated Bibliography of Ancient Greek Numismatics

William E. Daehn

Classical Numismatic Group, Inc.
Lancaster / London

Copyright © 2012 by William E. Daehn

Cover designed by A. Ferkingstad.
Cover coin photograph by the author.

All photographs by the author except those on pages 51, 207, 416, 454, 467, 496, and 557 which are courtesy of Classical Numismatic Group, Inc., and those on pages 129, 140, 165 and 193 which are in the public domain. Photo editing by the author.

Library of Congress Control Number 2012900483

ISBN: 978-0-9837652-7-1

Published and Distributed by Classical Numismatic Group, Inc.

Lancaster, Pennsylvania and London, England

Printed in the United States of America

All rights reserved. No part of this publication may be reproduced, stored in a retrieval system, or transmitted in any form, or by any means, electronic, mechanical, by photocopying, recording, or otherwise, without the prior permission of the copyright holder.

Permission is granted for free use of the numbering system in advertisements, price lists, auction catalogues, and critical articles. This permission is granted when acknowledgment is made by stating the author and title.

Contents

Preface vi

General Works on Greek Coinage 1

General Works on Hellenistic Greek Coinage 29

Collecting Guides 33

Origins of Coinage 39

Hoards 51

Artistic Aspects of Greek Coinage
    Types and Representations 87
    Art, Engravers, and Stylistic Trends 108
    Portraits 116
    Epigraphy 123

Technical Aspects of Greek Coinage
    The Minting Process 129
    Metallurgy 140
    Metrology 148
    Counterfeits 155

Important Collections
    Public Collections:
        Australia 165
        Belgium 165
        Brazil 166
        Bulgaria 166
        Canada 166
        Croatia 167
        Cyprus 167
        Egypt 167
        France 167
        Germany 167
        Great Britain 168
        Greece 173
        Hungary 174
        India 175
        Israel 175
        Italy 175
        Japan 175
        Jordan 175
        Lebanon 176
        The Netherlands 176
        New Zealand 176
        Portugal 177
        Rhodesia (Zimbabwe) 177
        Romania 177

Scotland 178
　　　South Africa 178
　　　Sudan 178
　　　Switzerland 178
　　　Tasmania 179
　　　Turkey 179
　　　United States of America..179
　　　Yugoslavia 184
　The Sylloge Nummorum Graecorum Series:
　　　American Series 185
　　　Australian Series 185
　　　Austrian Series 185
　　　Belgian Series...186
　　　Brazilian Series...186
　　　British Series 186
　　　Bulgarian Series 187
　　　Danish Series 187
　　　Finish Series 188
　　　French Series 188
　　　German Series 189
　　　Greek Series 190
　　　Hungarian Series 190
　　　Israeli Series 190
　　　Italian Series 190
　　　Polish Series 191
　　　Slovenian Series 191
　　　Spanish Series...191
　　　Swedish Series 191
　　　Swiss Series 191
　　　Turkish Series 192
　Private Collections..193

WESTERN AND CENTRAL EUROPE

　Spain..203
　Celtic Coinage:
　　　General Works..207
　　　Celtic Coinage of Britain..210
　　　Celtic Coinage of Europe 227
　Italy:
　　　General Works..235
　　　Alba 243
　　　Cumae 243
　　　Etruria 243
　　　Heraklea 244
　　　Kaulonia 245
　　　Kroton 245
　　　Laos 246
　　　Locri Epizephyrii..246
　　　Luceria 247
　　　Metapontum..247
　　　Neapolis..248
　　　Pandosia 248
　　　Poseidonia 249
　　　Rhegion 249
　　　Serdaioi 250
　　　Siris...250
　　　Sybaris..250
　　　Taras 251
　　　Terina 253

- Thurii 254
- Velia 254

Sicily:
- General Works 256
- Aitna 263
- Akragas 263
- Eryx 264
- Gela 265
- Himera 265
- Kamarina 267
- Katana 268
- Kentoripai 268
- Leontinoi 268
- Lipara 268
- Morgantina 268
- Naxos 269
- Segesta 269
- Selinus 270
- Siculo-Punic Coinage 271
- Syracuse 274
- Zankle/Messana 282

MAINLAND GREECE AND THE ISLANDS

Macedonia:
- Cities and Tribes 285
- Macedonian Kingdom—General Works 291
- Alexander's Porus Coins/Medallions 311
- The Roman Province of Macedonia 313

Thrace:
- General Works 316
- Coinage of Lysimachos 322
- Abdera 323
- Ainos 324
- Berge 324
- Byzantion 324
- Cabyle 325
- Deultum 325
- Istros 325
- Lete 326
- Maroneia 326
- Mesambria 327
- Olbia 328
- Samothrace 328
- Thasos 329

Northern Greece:
- Aitolia 332
- Akarnania 333
- Corcyra 334
- Epirus 334
- Illyria 335
- Thessaly 337

Central Greece:
- Boeotia 342
- Euboia 344
- Lokris 346
- Phokis 347

Attica:
- General Works 349
- Wappenmünzen 366

New Style Coinage	367
Athenian Coinage Decree	370
Aegina	373
Megaris	376
Corinthia	377

Peloponnesos:

General Works	381
Achaia	382
Argolis	384
Arkadia	385
Elis	386
Ithaka	388
Lakonia	388
Messenia	389
Phliasia	389
Sikyonia	389
Crete	391
Cyclades Islands	396

ASIA MINOR AND THE BLACK SEA REGION

General Works	401
Bosporos	406
Kolchis	410
Pontos	411
Paphlagonia	414
Bithynia	416

Mysia:

Autonomous Cities	417
Pergamene Kingdom	420
Troas	424
Aeolis	426
Lesbos	427
Ionia	429

Ionian Islands:

Chios	436
Samos	437
Caria	439

Carian Islands:

Kalymnos	445
Karpathos	445
Kos	445
Nisyros	446
Rhodos	446
Telos	450
Lydia	451
Phrygia	454
Lycia	455
Pamphylia	459
Pisidia and Lykaonia	461
Cilicia	462
Galatia	467
Cappadocia	468
Cyprus	471

ASIA

General Works	475

Syria:	
Autonomous Cities	477
Seleucid Kingdom	477
Armenia	496
Phoenicia	506
Palestine:	
Judea and "Coins of the Bible"	513
Philistia	531
Samaria	534
Arabia	536
Mesopotamia, Babylonia, and Assyria	544
Parthia	546
Characene	557
Elymais	559
Persia	561
Persis	568
Bactria and Northwest India	570

NORTH AFRICA

General Works	591
Egypt:	
Pre-Ptolemaic Period	593
Ptolemaic Kingdom	595
Zeugitana	608
Cyrenaica	612
Numidia, Mauretania, and Malta	615

CONCORDANCE: CLAIN-STEFANELLI TO DAEHN 617

INDEX OF CITIES, DISTRICTS, KINGDOMS, AND TRIBES 623

INDEX OF AUTHORS 631

INDEX OF REVIEWERS 647

INDEX OF COLLECTORS AND COLLECTIONS 649

Numismatics is not an easy field. Were it so, all would have been known years ago and research long since would have come to an end. The fact that controversy rages, that new theories are set forth and that there is continuing research is ample indication that our field is neither sterile nor complete.

—John E. Hartmann, 1966

Fortunately, numismatics, like some aspects of astronomy and natural history, remains a branch of learning in which the amateur can still do valuable work, and it is on the great collecting public, or rather on that part of it which is interested in the subject at a scientific level, that the progress of numismatic science largely depends.

—Philip Grierson, 1975

Numismatics has moved far beyond the standard reference works, yet its literature, which exists at many levels, is difficult to navigate even for the advanced student.

—William E. Metcalf, 2012

Preface

The subject matter of coins is so infinite and in such a perpetual state of progression and fluctuation, that it is difficult to write anything which in a few years will not become practically obsolete. Fresh coins come every day to light which enlarge, modify, or confute the accepted canons and generalizations of the science a few months back. Again, numismatic literature is very scattered and unsuited for purposes of rapid reference; the best monographs are often buried in back numbers of periodicals which it is not very easy to refer to.

—J. Leicester Warren, 1863

INTRODUCTION

Ancient numismatics is a field of study which appeals to both the serious scholar and the casual hobbyist. Scholars use coins as tools for uncovering the secrets of the world's history and art. Coin collectors look upon coins as tangible links to the remote past. Both scholars and hobbyists have contributed to the vast body of literature that has grown around the study of ancient coinage over the last 200 years, and this body of literature continues to expand.

While guidance in the selection of research material for ancient Greek numismatics is available, it has been both incomplete and scattered, thereby discouraging both the scholar and the hobbyist from making full use of previous research. And the pace of numismatic publishing has not abated since the first edition of this book went to press (*Ancient Greek Numismatics: A Guide to Reading and Research,* Cold Spring: Davisson's Ltd., 2001).

Numismatic research took a great leap forward when Elvira Clain-Stefanelli published her monumental *Numismatic Bibliography* in 1985, listing over 18,000 references on all phases of numismatics. But while it will always remain an indispensable tool for numismatists, this great work is now more than a quarter-century out of date. Although quite comprehensive, its broad scope required that its listings be selective.

Although more recent specialized bibliographies focusing on Greek numismatics exist, they tend to be brief and quite selective, and provide little or no information regarding the content of the listed works. One useful tool is the American Numismatic Society's periodical *Numismatic Literature.* Unfortunately, the reader would need to search through 150 volumes of this publication and still many works would be overlooked. In recent years, online resources have made great strides but are still woefully inadequate.

SCOPE

This book is intended to provide a comprehensive guide to the literature in the field of ancient Greek numismatics. Included are specialty books and scholarly papers from academic journals as well as popular books and articles from the hobby periodicals. Although the first edition was limited to works published in English, this edition also incorporates works in other languages. Though these listings are not as comprehensive as the English listings, all the major works are included.

Most bibliographies are selective in nature—only works deemed to be of importance to future researchers are included. In compiling this guide, my goal was to include as many works as was practical. All phases of archaic, classical, and Hellenistic Greek numismatics fall within the scope of this book. Also included are works on Celtic, Parthian, Indo-Greek, and early Judean coinage. This book does not cover Roman provincial ("Greek Imperial") coinage, Judean coinage during the Herodian dynasty or the period of the Roman Procurators, or coinage of the native rulers of India. Some sales catalogues have been included when they present important collections or when especially useful information is presented in the catalogue. Publications focusing on Greek art or the ancient economy are included when they provide important information for numismatists.

ARRANGEMENT

The arrangement of the book is as follows: general references are listed first, followed by works on special aspects of Greek numismatics, and then those which focus on specific geographic regions. The geographic listings follow the arrangement traditionally used when cataloguing Greek coins (clockwise around the Mediterranean, starting in the northwest). Under each heading or sub-heading, the items are listed alphabetically by the author's last name, and works by the same author are arranged chronologically according to the original date of publication. Critical reviews are noted. Cross-references are provided to Clain-Stefanelli's bibliography, e.g. [CS 1807]. Indices to authors, reviewers, and collectors and collections are included at the back of the book, as well as an index to cities, districts, kingdoms, and tribes.

This edition incorporates numerous improvements in organization and indexing. A quick review of the *Contents* will reveal that the headings and subheadings now provide a finer breakdown of the topical or geographical areas covered by each section, thus making it easier for the researcher to zero-in on the desired works. Also, the *Index of Collectors and Collections* has been separated from the *Index of Authors*, and an *Index of Reviewers* has been added.

An index number has been assigned to each listing. Each published work appears under the heading to which it most closely relates and cross-references have been provided at the end of other groupings to which a work relates. Some works have been reprinted several times since their first appearance and this is noted when applicable. For works appearing in periodicals published outside of the United States or England, the country of publication has been indicated.

The most important feature of this book is the notes which follow each entry. These notes provide a synopsis of the contents and main conclusions of each publication, enabling the researcher to use his time efficiently, and allowing the hobbyist to choose items of particular interest for leisure-time reading. I wrote the majority of these summaries after a personal review of the publication. However, the abstracts which appeared in *Numismatic Literature* have sometimes been relied upon and are quoted here. In these cases, the names of the original abstractors and the appropriate volume numbers of *Numismatic Literature* have been indicated in brackets, e.g. [*NL* 125].

Occasional use has been made of the abstracts appearing in J. R. Jones' *A Numismatic Index to the American Journal of Archaeology and Hesperia*, *A Numismatic Index to the Journal of Hellenic Studies*, and *Analytical Index to the Journal International d'Archéologie Numismatique*. These are noted as follows: [J. R. Jones, *NIAJAH*], [J. R. Jones, *NIJHS*], or [J. R. Jones, *AIJIAN*]. The abstracts provided here are intended to be factual rather than critical. Therefore, no attempt has been made to indicate which articles have been superseded by more recent research. Some very old and obsolete studies are listed here. I must stress the importance of consulting later studies to see whether old theories have been able to withstand the test of time. As noted above, references have been made to critical reviews published by other writers whenever possible.

ACKNOWLEDGEMENTS

This book was made easier by the work of Elvira Clain-Stefanelli whose listings and format provided an important starting point. In compiling this book, I made extensive use of the resources of the O. Meredith Wilson Library at the University of Minnesota in Minneapolis. Other libraries utilized include the library of the American Numismatic Association in Colorado Springs, the Minneapolis Public Library, and the Memorial Library at the University of Wisconsin in Madison. I also made use of the listings found in the ANS' *Numismatic Literature* series. The numismatic literature sale catalogues of George F. Kolbe also proved useful, especially for their listings of scarce early works.

I would like to thank several knowledgeable numismatists who have supported me in this project in various ways. Todd A. Ballen read drafts of the first edition and suggested many additions and corrections. John R. Melville Jones granted permission to utilize some of the abstracts from his *Numismatic Index* publications. Allan Davisson provided me with access to his remarkable numismatic library. Mark E. Tooth and Pete Smith supplied copies of several articles from periodicals that I would have otherwise overlooked. Remy Bourne provided me with access to many books and periodicals that may otherwise have been neglected. And Brad Nelson shared his bibliographic listings related to classical economies which included numerous items that would otherwise have been neglected here. My thanks also go to Andrea Ferkingstad for the cover design.

I especially want to thank Basil Demetriadi who helped considerably by photocopying and mailing to me a large number of less well-known articles and portions of books from his extensive numismatic library. Without his help, this book would have been less complete. I would also like to thank Allan Davisson for publishing the first edition of this book. Without the encouragement that emerged from that publication, this edition would not have become a reality.

And most of all, I would like to thank my wife Maureen who provided encouragement and displayed great patience as I spent countless hours working on this book over the past twenty years.

Despite the relative completeness of this book, it will soon be quite incomplete as the body of numismatic information continues to expand. The best I can hope for is that this book will make yesterday's literature more accessible to tomorrow's researchers.

William E. Daehn
May 2012

GENERAL WORKS ON GREEK COINAGE

Nothing can be well more amusing than to read history, with contemporary coins before you. It brings the actions in a manner, before your eyes; and we sit, as in a theatre, with the actors before us.

—John Pinkerton, 1808

1 **Alfaro, Carmen, Carmen Marcos, and Paloma Otero, eds.** *XIII Congreso Internacional de Numismática, Madrid – 2003, Actas–Proceedings–Actes I.* Madrid: International Numismatic Commission, 2005.
The text of papers presented at a conference covering all areas of numismatics. Those related to ancient Greek numismatics are: "Statistical Analysis of Hoard Data in Ancient Numismatics" by W. Esty [546a], "La Frappe Libre a-t-elle Existé dans l'Antiquité Gréco-Romaine?" by F. de Callataÿ, "L'Hétérogénité des Teneurs en Plomb dans les Monnaies de Bronze Antiques" by A. Deraisme and J.-N. Barrandon, "La Moneda de los Dioses: Monedas y Santuarios en Grecia" by A. Domínguez Monedero, "El Monetario Perromano del Museo Arqueológico-Etnológico Municipal 'Gratiniano Baches': Pilar de la Horadada (Alicante)" by M. Garcia Samper, "Le Monnayage de Paphos au IVe s.: Nouvelles Perspectives" by A. Destrooper [5171a], "Acarnanian Astacus: New Numismatic Evidence" by E. Georgiou [3793a], "Coinage and History of Messenia (Peloponnesus) until the End of the Hellenistic Period" by C. Grandjean [4388a], "The Athenian Coinage Decree: Inscriptions, Coins and Athenian Politics" by A. Hadji and Z. Kantes [4200a], "Les Monnaies Chypriotes d'Or du IVe s. avant J.-C." by E. Markou [5184a], "Coinage of Nikonion: Greek Bronze Cast Coins between Istrus and Olbia" by M. Mielczarek [4512a], "Monete Suberate Magnogreche: le Zecche della Campania" by A. Parente [2687a], "Distribuzione e Funzione della Moneta Bronzes in Sicilia dalla fine del V sec. a.C. all'età Ellenistica" by M. Puglisi, "Du Lacydon à Massalia, les Émissions Grecques en Gaule du Vème Siècle av. J.-C." by J.-C. Richard and J. Chevillon, "The Early Classical Coinage of Siphnos: Some Thoughts on the Influence of Athens" by K. Sheedy [4478], "Problemi Pondometrici della Monetazione Arcaica della Licia: Una Visione d'Insieme" by N. Vismara, "Financing the Poloponnesian War: The Peloponnesian Perspective" by J. Warren [4299a], "Nuevos Datos Sobre la Moneda en la Colonia de Rhode" by M. Campo, "I Bronzo Zeus Hellanios/Aquila e l'Organizzazione dell'Attività Monetaria Siracusana tra Officine Parallele e Concentrazioni Cronologiche" by B. Carroccio, "Coins of the Unknown Mint Apros in Thrace" by D. Draganov [3592a], "The Weight of the Graeco-Bactrian Chalkous" by D. MacDowall [6396a], "Numidian Royal Portrait" by M. Nicolau Kormikiari [6779], "La Monetazione della Colonia Latina di Cales" by S. Pantuliano, "Lopadusa: An Elusive Mint" by F. Rossini [2973a], "Réflexions sur le Monnayage Municipal Séleucide de Bérytos à la Lumière de Nouveaux Documents Numismatiques" by Z. Sawaya, "Counter-stamping Coins in Hellenistic Crete: A First Approach" by M. Stefanakis [4434b], "Monetary Crises in the Early Hellenistic Poleis of Olbia, Chersonesos and Pantikapaion: A Re-Assessment" by V. Stolba [4561a], "A Contribution to Cassander's Bronze Coinage" by C. Valassiadis [3526a], "L'Apport des Isotopes du Plomb à Étude des Monnayages d'Argent Gaulois du Centre de la Gaule" by J.-N. Barrandon and S. Nieto, "Le Monnayage dit Tarusate (Sub-Ouest de la Gaule): Révisions et Perspectives" by L. Callegarin, "Changing Artistic Perspectives on Celtic Coins" by G. Chimirri-Russell [2535a], "Apport des Découvertes Monétaires Faites sur l'Oppidum Celtique du Mont Beuvray" by K. Gruel, "75 Kilogrammes of Celtic Small Coin—Recent Research on the 'Potinklumpen' from Zurich" by M. Nick [2588a], "La Place du Monnayage Arverne dans les Monnayages Gaulois du Centre et du Sud le la Gaule aux IIe et Ier s. av. J.-C.: Étude Numismatique et Analytique" by S. Nieto. Also includes ten papers related to coinage of the Iberian Peninsula (all in Spanish).

1a **Alföldi-Radnoti, Marie.** *Antike Numismatik.* Two parts. Kulturgeschichte der Antiken Welt 2/3. Mainz, 1978. Second edition, 1982. [CS 1626]

 1. *Theorie und Praxis.* 218 pp., 25 pls., 7 maps.
 2. *Bibliographie.* 114 pp., 20 pls.

2 ——— "Die Münze als Historische Quelle-Moderne Methoden der Antiken Numismatik." *Geldgeschichtliche Nachrichten* (Germany) 14, no. 66 (1978): 164-5. [CS 1627]

3 **Alföldi-Radnoti, Marie, ed.** *Methoden der Antiken Numismatik.* Darmstadt, 1989. 406 pp., 53 pls.

4 **Allan, John, Harold Mattingly, and Edward S. G. Robinson, eds.** *Transactions of the International Numismatic Congress Organized and Held in London by the Royal Numismatic Society, June 30-July 3, 1936.* London: B. Quaritch, 1938. 490 pp., 27 pls. [CS 16874]
The text of the papers presented at the Congress held in 1936. Those related to Greek numismatics are: "Fifty Years of Greek Numismatics" by G. Macdonald [150], "The Relation Between Coins and Sculpture" by B. Ashmole [1142], "The Aphlaston, Symbol of Naval Victory or Supremacy on Greek and Roman Coins" by A. Baldwin Brett [890], "Lokale Elemente im Stil Archaischer Griechischer Münzen" by H. A. Cahn [1149], "The Technique of Greek Coin Dies" by S. Casson [1371], "Di due Piccoli Ripostigli di Argenti Cartaginesi e dei Brettii" by by S. L. Cesano [2644], "Wirtschaftshistorische Beiträge zur Klassisch Griechischen und Hellenistischen Münzhortstatistik" by F. Heichelheim [94], "Eine Verschollene Bronzemünze von Syrakus" by P. Lederer [3179], "The Use of Coins for Teaching Greek and Roman History" by J. G. Milne [163], "Two Gold Coins of Tyras" by P. Nicorescu [5627], "Corinthian Hoard from Chiliomodi" by O. Ravel [727], "Ein Fund Archaischer Münzen von Samothrake" by W. Schwabacher [3755], "Diogenes of Sinope, Son of the Banker Hikesias" by C. T. Seltman [4611], "Anmerkung zu Einem Kimonischen Tetradrachmon"

by H. Wiesinger [3213], "British Tin Coinage of the Iron Age" by D. Allen [2223], and "The Beginnings of Coinage in India" by J. Allan [6256]. Also includes papers on other areas of numismatics including Roman, medieval, modern, British, oriental, and medals.

5   **Alpha Bank.** *History of Coins.* Athens: Alpha Bank, 2006. 16 pp., illus.
A short history of the invention and development of coinage during antiquity, illustrated by coins from the Alpha Bank collection.

6   **Amandry, Michel, and Silvia Hurter, eds.** *Travaux de Numismatique Grecque Offerts à Georges Le Rider.* London: Spink, 1999. 450 pp., 50 pls.
This volume, written in honor of Georges Le Rider on the occasion of this seventieth birthday, includes thirty-seven essays including: "Un Trésor de Tétradrachmes Hellénistiques d'Aigeai en Cilicie" by C. Arnold-Biucchi [5074], "The Coinage of Nisyros" by R. Ashton [4930], "Sur des Types Monétaires de Canatha" by C. Augé, "Alexandre, Ménon et les Mines d'Or d'Arménie" by P. Bernard [5473], "Beobachtungen und Überlegungen zu den Ären der Pamphylischen Alexandreier" by C. Boehringer [3328], "Les Monnaies Séleucides de l'Asie Centrale et l'Atelier de Bactres" by O. Bopearachchi [5523], "Regional Coinage in Thrace and Bithynia during the Flavian Period" by A. Burnett, "Artiste ou Magistrat?" by H. Cahn [2641], "Fiscalité et Monnayage dans l'Oeuvre de Georges Le Rider" by F. de Callataÿ, "La Deuxième Guerre de Syrie (ca. 261-255 avant J.-C.) et les Témoignages Numismatiques" by A. Davesne [5262], "Un Trésor de Tétradrachmes aux Types d'Alexandre Trouvé dans la Beqa" by J. Elayi [3351], "Les Dernieres Monnaies d'Argent du Péloponnèse" by C. Grandjean [4293], "The Use of the Macedonian Calendar under Ptolemies V and VI" by R. Hazzard [6608], "A 1992 Hoard of Bronze Coins of Philip II from Beroia in Thrace" by C. Hersh [3382], "A Drachm of Zankle with Pellets Indicating Value in the Museum of Art, Rhode Island School of Design" by R. Holloway [3223], "The Early Seleucid Mint of Laodicea ad Mare (c. 300-246 B.C.)" by A. Houghton [5328], "Zwei Beiträge zur Seleukidischen Münzprägung des 2. Jahrhunderts v. Chr." by D. Klose [5342], "Des Ateliers de Drachmes Pseudo-Rhodiennes en Béotie? Examen de Quelques Hypothèses Récentes" by D. Knoepfler [3906], "A Propos de Quelques Héros de la Légende Troyenne Selon le Témoignage des Monnaies Grecques" by L. Lacroix [990], "MBGY/Menbibî, Moétaire de Transeuphratène avant Alexandre" by A. Lemaire [5767], "Thessalian Countermarks" by C. Lorber [3864], "Dall'obolo alla Litra e il Problema del 'Damareteion'" by G. Manganaro [3181], "Ancient Greek Gold Coinage up to the Time of Philip of Macedon" by J. Melville Jones [116], "A Note on the Coinage of Hierapolis-Bambyce" by L. Mildenberg [6217], "Argent et or Frappés en Babylonie entre 331 et 311 ou de Mazdai à Séleucos" by H. Nicolet-Pierre [6024], "Le Trésor d'Épidaure 1977" by M. Oeconomides [3454], "Un Monnayage Alexandrin Énigmatique: le Trésor d'Alexandrie 1996" by O. Picard [3465], "Le Portrait Monétaire d'Eumène II: Problèmes d'Interprétation et de Datation" by F. Queyrel [4685], "Peut-on Parler d'Une Circulation des Monnaies Impériales Grecques? De Quelques Constatations Effectuées à Antioche sur l'Oronte" by F. Rebuffat, "The Royal Male Head and Cleopatra at Ascalon" by A. Spaer [5898], "Statères d'Alexandre et Statères de Cyzique. Le Trésor du Pirée, 1882 (*IGCH* 47)" by I. Touratsoglou [805], "A New Look at Some Alexander Staters from 'Salamis'" by H. Troxell [3521], "Considerazioni Sulle Emissioni della Lycia Arcaica a Nome di Xinaxa" by N. Vismara [5046], "More on the 'New Landscape' in the Late Hellenistic Coinage of the Peloponnesos" by J. Warren [4298], "Some Comments on a New Hoard from the Balkan Area" by U. Wartenberg and J. Kagan [835], and "Himera: The Coins of Akragantine Type 2, Based on a Catalogue by Kenneth Jenkins" by U. Westermark [3035], and "Sur le Monnayage des Tribus Thraces" by I. Youroukova [3661]. Also includes a bibliography of Le Rider's work written by M. Amandry. [Reviewed by W. Fischer-Bossert in *Sweizerische Numismatische Rundschau* 79 (2000): 179-192].

7   **Amandry, Michel, and Georges Le Rider, eds.** *Trésors et Circulation Monétaire en Anatolie Antique.* Paris, 1994. 138 pp., 34 pls.
Publishes six coin hoards, two studies of monetary circulation, and a paper concerning the mints of Alexander the Great in Asia Minor. The hoards are mainly from Cilicia.

8   **Ambrosoli, Solone.** *Monete Greche.* Milano, 1899. Two volumes. 286 and 64 pp. Illus.

9   **American Numismatic Association.** *Selections from The Numismatist: Ancient and Medieval Coins.* Racine: Whitman Publishing Co., 1960. 318 pp., illus.
A collection of articles reprinted from *The Numismatist*. Abstracts for some of these articles are included elsewhere as indicated. Of interest to the collector of Greek coins are: "The Invention of Coinage" by Bryan O. Burke [382], "A Brief Survey of Media of Exchange" by J. William Decker, "Herodotus, Grandfather of Numismatics" by Oscar H. Dodson, "Some Notes on Collecting Ancient Greek Coins" by Mead B. Kibbey [325], "Coins of the Greek Period of Sicily" by Raymond J. Walker [2983], "Media of Exchange in Ancient Egypt" by James W. Curtis [6541], "Falsifications of Ancient Coins" by John F. Lhotka, Jr. [1687], "Some Notes on Grading Ancient Coins" by Mead B. Kibbey, "Art History on Persian and Phoenician Coinage" by H. David Rodee [1192], "The Career and Egyptian Coinage of Ptolemy Soter" by Harry J. Stein [6687], "Notes on the Drachms of Parthia" by R. H. Swift [6140], "Persian Coins" by A. Quinnell [6090], "Ancient Coins Associated with Christianity" by Charles E. Tuckwood, "The Beginning of Coin Portraiture" by Lawrence Lee Howe [1261], "Hellenistic and Early Roman Coin Portraiture" [1262] by Lawrence Lee Howe, and "Face to Face with the Ancient Greeks and Romans from a Study of Their Coins" by Jeremiah Zimmerman.

10   **American Numismatic Society.** *Greek—General. Educational Slide Program Series, No. 1.* New York: American Numismatic Society, nd. 39 pp., illus., and 36 color slides.
A set of thirty-six color photographic slides illustrating fifty-eight Greek coins, accompanied by a small booklet describing the coins and their historical background.

11   **Anthon, Charles.** *A Classical Dictionary Containing an Account of the Principal Proper Names Mentioned in Ancient Authors of the Greeks and Romans Together with an Account of Coins, Weights, and Measures.* New York: Harper & Brothers. Numerous editions including 1833, 1844, 1848. 1451 pp.
One of the many revisions of J. Lempriere's classic work. Although the fourth edition (1848) is stated to be a completely new work rather than a revision of Lempriere's text. [See Lempriere below].

12   **Appleton, William S.** "A Few Ancient Coins." *American Journal of Numismatics* 14, no. 1 (July 1879): 1-2. 1 pl.
Illustrates and describes six Greek coins of Himera, Hariartus, Amphilochion, Aspendus (2), and Side.

13   **Ashton, Richard, ed.** *Studies in Ancient Coinage from Turkey.* Special Publication No. 29. British Institute of Archaeology at Ankara Monograph, No. 17. London: Royal Numismatic Society, 1996. 168 pp., 69 pls.
A collection of English translations of twenty essays written by Turkish numismatists. Includes reports on seven hoards of Greek and Greek Imperial coins and four hoards of Roman Imperial coins. Also includes information about ancient coins in Turkish museums and private collections, and the catalogues of

several collections. [Reviewed by A. Walker in *Revue Suisse de Numismatique* 75 (1996): 237-44, by A. Burnett in *Numismatic Chronicle* 157 (1997): 253-4, and by W. Metcalf in *American Journal of Numismatics* 2nd ser., 9 (1997): 157-9].

14 **Ashton, Richard, and Silvia Hurter, eds.** *Studies in Greek Numismatics in Memory of Martin Jessop Price.* London: Spink, 1998. 400 pp., 79 pls.

A collection of essays dedicated to the memory of Martin J. Price, one of the world's leading authorities on Greek coinage, who died in 1995. Price was a former Deputy Keeper of the Department of Coins and Medals at the British Museum. This book contains forty-two essays (thirty-five in English) plus a bibliography of Price's work. The essays are listed individually (except for three essays dealing with the Roman period) as follows: "A Propos d'une Monnaie de Sébastè en Phrygie Frappée pour Septime Sévère, Caracalla et Géta en 198" by M. Amandry, "The Pergamene Mint under Lysimachus" by C. Arnold-Biucchi [3662], "Hellenistic Bronze Coins of Abdera with a Male Portrait" by R. Ashton [3686], "Two Goddesses in Samos" by J. Barron [4845], "De l'Or d'Agathocle" by D. Bérend [3116], "Zur Münzgeschichte von Leontinoi in Klassichen Zeit" by C. Boehringer [3050], "Overstrikes at Neapolis and Coinage at Poseidonia-Paestum" by A. Burnett and M. Crawford [2798], "Ionische Damen" by H. Cahn [4750], "The Dinar Hoard of Persian Sigloi" by I. Carradice [6189], "The End of Greek Coinage in Bactria and India and its Evidence for the Kushan Coinage System" by J. Cribb [6307], "Les Monnaies Hellénistique en Argent de Ténédos" by F. Callataÿ [4703], "Dion in Macedonia: A Bronze Coinage of the Classical Period" by V. Demetriadi [3242], "The Coinage of Terone from the Fifth to the Fourth Centuries B.C." by N. Hardwick [3251], "Additions and Corrections to Martin J. Price's *The Coinage in the Name of Alexander the Great and Philip Arrhidaeus*" by C. Hersh [3380], "Aradus, Not Marathus" by A. Houghton [3388], "'The Pixodaros Hoard': a Summary" by S. Hurter [600], "Epidamnus or Ephyre (Elea)" by J. Kagan [4264], "CH 8, 474: Milesian Silver Coinage in the Second Century B.C." by P. Kinns [4779], "The Early Coinage of Kaunos" by K. Konuk [4882], "Silver in Solon's Laws" by J. Kroll [4057], "The Silver Coinage of Kythnos in the Early Fifth Century B.C." by A. Kyrou and D. Artemis [4458], "Les Tétradrachmes Macédoniens d'Alexandre" by G. Le Rider [3400], "A Hoard of Bronze Coins of Alexander the Great" by K. Liampi [3404], "The Coinage of Mithradates III, Pharnakes and Mithradates IV of Pontos" by H. B. Mattingly [4591], "The Value of Electrum in Greece and Asia" by J. R. M. Jones [1586], "Money Supply under Artaxerxes III Ochus" by L. Mildenberg [6215], "Syracusan Bronze Coinage in the Fifth and Early Fourth Centuries B.C." by J. Morcom [3185], "Autour du Décadrachme Athenien Conservé à Paris" by H. Nicolet-Pierre [4079], "The 1979 Tricala Hoard of Alexanders" by M. Oeconomides [3453], "The Coinage of Syracuse in the Early Fifth Century B.C." by N. Rutter [3196], "A Die Count for a Group of Parthian Drachms" by D. Sellwood [6118], "The Dolphins, the Crab, the Sphinx and 'Aphrodite'" by K. Sheedy [4475], "Notes on Early Electrum Coinage and a Die-linked Issue from Lydia" by J. Spier [5003], "Agathopolis: a Mint on the Black Sea Coast" by W. Stancomb [4521], "Alexanders from Soli on Cyprus" by H. Troxell [3519], "Updating (and Downdating) the Autonomous Bronze Coinage of Sikyon" by J. Warren [4395], "Calymna Calumniated—a Nineteenth-Century Misattribution?" by U. Wartenberg [4917], "A New Tetradrachm of Kamarina" by U. Westermark [3039], "Alexander the Great and the Coinages of Western Greece" by J. Williams and A. Burnett [3542], and "Bibliography of Martin Jessop Price" by M. Stefanakis [221]. [Reviewed by A. Walker in *The Celator* 12, no. 4 (April 1998): 32-4, by Antony Wilson in *Spink Numismatic Circular* 106, no. 5 (June 1998): 210-1, and by W. Fischer-Bossert in *Schweizerische Numismatische Rundschau* 77 (1998): 157-73].

15 **Atlan, Sabahat.** *Grek Sikkeleri (Arkaik, Klassik, Hellenistik).* Istanbul, 1993.

16 **Austin, M. M., and P. Vidal-Naquet.** *Economic and Social History of Ancient Greece: An Introduction.* London: Batsford, 1977. Berkeley and Los Angeles: University of California Press, 1977. 397 pp. [CS 1051]

A general history focusing on economic and social aspects of Greek history rather than the traditional political aspects. Part 1 comprises a basic introduction and Part 2 contains a selection of ancient sources. Begins with the Homeric world and proceeds through the classical era. Includes discussions of slavery, origins of coinage, imports and exports, fiscal policies of cities, taxation, and the control of economic activity. Ancient sources cited include Homer, Herodotus, Aristotle, Plato, Thucydides, Plutarch, Demosthenes, Strabo and others. Includes the text of the Athenian coinage decree and an inscription related to the mines at Laurion.

17 **Babelon, Ernest C.** "Revue de la Numismatique Grecque et Romaine." *American Journal of Archaeology* 1 (1885): 387-400.

A summary of important works published in reviews and periodicals.

18 ——— "Review of Greek and Roman Numismatics. II. Recently Published Books." *American Journal of Archaeology* 3 (1887): 75-86.

A continuation of Babelon's earlier paper, this section summarizes important books published in recent years. Begins with a summary of the volumes of the *British Museum Catalogue of Greek Coins*, currently in progress, with extensive comments on the volumes devoted to Central Greece and Crete.

19 ——— *Traité des Monnaies Grecques et Romaines.* Nine volumes. Paris: Ernest Leroux, 1901-33. Reprint, Bologna: Forni, 1965-76. [CS 1809]

1. *Théorie et Doctrine.* 1901. 604 pp., illus. [For an English translation, see Babelon *Ancient Numismatics and its History* below].
2. *Description Historique:*
    1. *Comprenant les Monnaies Grecques depuis les Origines Jusqu'aux Guerres Médiques.* 1907. 836 pp., illus.
    2. *Comprenant les Monnaies de l'Empire des Perses Achéménides, de l'Orient Sémitique et de l'Asie-Mineure au Ve Siècles avant J.-C.* 1910. 782 pp., illus.
    3. *Comprenant les Monnaies de la Grèce Centrale et Méridionale aux Ve et IVe Siècles avant J.-C.* 1914. 572 pp., illus.
    4. *Comprenant les Monnaies de la Grèce Septentrionale aux Ve et IVe Siècles avant J.-C.* 1926-32. 550 pp., illus.
3. *Planches:*
    1. *Planches I a LXXXV.* 1907. 85 pls.
    2. *Album des Planches: Planches LXXXVI a CLXXXV.* 1910. 100 pls.
    3. *Album des Planches: Planches CLXXXVI a CCLXX.* 1916. 85 pls.
    4. *Planches CCLXXI a CCCLV.* 1926-32. 85 pls.

20 ——— *Les Monnaies Grecques: Aperçu Historique.* Paris: Payot, 1921. 160 pp., illus. [CS 1810]

21 ——— *Ancient Numismatics and Its History, Including a Critical Review of the Literature.* Translated by Elizabeth Saville. Studies in the History of Numismatic Literature, No. 2. Crestline and London: G. F. Kolbe and Spink, 2004. 248 pp., illus.

An English translation of Babelon's comprehensive introduction to the history of ancient numismatics, originally published in 1901 (see Babelon *Traité des Monnaies Grecques et Romaines* above). Babelon explores the definition and scope of ancient numismatics, and the utility of numismatics to the study of history. Discusses the many large collections of ancient coins formed by kings and other nobility of Europe since the fifteenth century. He reviews the related literature from the sixteenth through the nineteenth centuries. Includes a listing of sale catalogues of major collections sold in the nineteenth century.

[Reviewed in *The Celator* 18, no. 9 (September 2004): 4. Also reviewed by Oliver D. Hoover in *American Numismatic Society Magazine* 3, no. 3 (winter 2004): 58-60].

22 **Babelon, Jean.** *La Numismatique Antique.* Paris, 1944. Third edition, Paris: Presse Unversitaire de France, 1964. 127 pp., illus. [CS 1630]

23 **Bates, William N.** "The Coinage of the Ancient Greeks." *Numismatic and Antiquarian Society of Philadelphia, Proceedings, 1899-1901.* Pages 73-84.
The text of a paper read before the society on March 1, 1900.

24 **Bauer, George F.** "A Few Fine Coins of Ancient Greece." *The Numismatist* 7 (1894): 64-6, 109-10, 254-5. Illus.
A brief introduction to ancient Greek coins, describing them as works of art. Eleven coin types are described and illustrated.

25 **Benson, Frank Sherman.** "A Cabinet of Greek Coins." *American Journal of Numismatics* 37, no. 3 (January 1903): 86.
A short poem inspired by ancient Greek coins.

26 **Bérend, Denyse.** "Réflexions sur les Fractions du Monnayage Grec." *Studies in Honour of Leo Mildenberg: Numismatics, Art History, Archaeology.* Edited by A. Houghton et al. Wetteren: Editions NR, 1984. Pages 7-30. 2 pls.
On Greek fractional coinage.

27 **Berg, Joseph.** "Ancient Greeks and Their Coinage." *Numismatic Scrapbook Magazine* 24, no. 8 (August 1958): 1781-2. Illus.
Very brief comments on the coinage of the Greeks, focusing on the artistry and the types chosen for the coins.

28 **Borba-Florenzano, Maria Beatriz.** "Measuring Valuables: Coinage in the Greek Polis." *Revue des Archéologie et Historiens d'Art de Louvain* 32 (1999): 103-7.

29 **Borrell, H. P.** "Unedited Autonomous and Imperial Greek Coins." *Numismatic Chronicle* 6 (1844): 115-60.
The author publishes numerous coins, mostly Roman Provincial issues. [Also see W. Wroth "The Santorin Find" under HOARDS].

30 **Boutkowski-Glinka, Alexandre.** "A Few Rare Greek Coins Published Recently." *Spink Numismatic Circular* 1 (May 1893): 195-7. Illus.
Publishes an alliance coin of Kos and Kalymna, a cistophorus of the town of Synnada in Phrygia, and a few other Roman Provincial coins.

31 **Breglia, Laura.** *Numismatica Antica: Storia e Metodologia.* Milan: Feltrinelli Editore, 1967. 312 pp., 46 pls. [CS 1635]

32 **Bringmann, Klaus.** "Grain, Timber and Money: Hellenistic Kings, Finance, Buildings and Foundations in Greek Cities." *Hellenistic Economies.* Edited by Zofia H. Archibald, John Davies, Vincent Gabrielsen, and G. J. Oliver. London/New York: Routledge, 2001. Pages 205-14.
The author argues that the kings generally did not have enough cash to cover benefactions to cities in excess of 100 talents. For more expensive gifts, kings made payment in kind (grain or building materials). [Reviewed by O. D. Hoover in *American Numismatic Society Magazine* 2, no. 2 (summer 2003): 54-7].

33 **Burns, Arthur R.** *Money and Monetary Policy in Early Times.* London: Kegan Paul, Trench, Trubner, & Co.; and New York: A. A. Knopf, 1927. Reprint, New York: Augustus M. Kelly, 1965. 517 pp., 16 pls., map. [CS 1000]
Examines money in Greek and Roman times from an economic perspective. Discusses pre-monetary means of exchange, the introduction and spread of coinage, the prerogative of coining, mint-marks and their importance for controlling the activities of branch mints, the role of monetary unions, coin types, metals, and fineness. An extensive discussion of weight standards—both before and after the introduction of coinage—closely follows the theories of Ridgeway (see Ridgeway *Origin of Metallic Currency* under METROLOGY). Also describes denominations, bimetallism, the use of bronze token coinage, and monetary policy in Asia, the Greek world, the Roman Republic, and the Roman Empire. The appendices contain reviews of the comments of ancient authors regarding the nature of money, and an examination of the relative values of the monetary metals. [An extremely critical review by G. F. Hill appears in *Numismatic Chronicle* 5th ser., 7 (1927): 378-9. Hill criticizes Burns for his limited numismatic knowledge].

34 **Cadalvène, E. de.** *Recueil de Médailles Grecques, Inédites.* Paris: DeBure Frères, 1828. 260 pp., 5 pls.

35 **Cahn, Herbert A.** *Monnaies Grecques Archaïque.* Basel, 1947.

36 **Cahn, Herbert A., and Georges Le Rider, eds.** *Proceedings of the 8th International Congress of Numismatics, New York—Washington, September 1973.* International Association of Professional Numismatists Publication No. 4. Paris, 1976. Two volumes. 683 pp., 77 pls.
The text of the papers presented at the Congress held in 1973. Abstracts for most of the papers concerning Greek numismatics are included elsewhere. These are: "Jewelers' Hoards and the Development of Early Coinage" by M. Balmuth [376], "The Organization of the Parthian Bronze Coinage" by J. Brindley [6041], "Timoleon and Corinthian Coinage in Sicily" by C. Kraay [3177], "Kimon in the Manner of Segesta" by L. Mildenberg [3072], "À Propos du Monnayage d'Argos" by T. Hackens [4330], "Hellenistic Coin Hoards from the Persian Gulf" by O. Mørkholm [683], "The Weight-System of the Coinage of Croesus" by P. Naster [4994], "Antiochus IV at Ake-Ptolemais" by A. Spaer [5439], and "The Finds of Celtic Coins in Slovakia and the Main Problems of the East Celtic Coinage" by E. Kolníková [2574].

37 **Calhoun, George M.** *The Business Life of Ancient Athens.* Chicago: University of Chicago Press, 1926. 175 pages.
"An attempt to give the general reader...an intelligible account of the way in which business and finance were carried on in Athens in the fourth century before Christ." Includes chapters on the Athenian grain trade, banks and bankers, mines and mining.

38 **Cardwell, Edward.** *Lectures on the Coinage of the Greeks and Romans; Delivered in the University of Oxford.* London: John Murray, 1832. 238 pp.

The text of nine lectures, five of which are primarily devoted to Greek coinage: (1) a general discussion of money, coin weights, and metal purity; (2) a discussion of the difficulties of interpreting the evidence provided by coins; (3) comments on the works of the most well-known and skilled counterfeiters, and methods of faking and altering coins; (4) periods of art and metals; (5) the history of Greek coinage. Sections 7, 8, and 9 describe Roman coinage.

39 **Carradice, Ian A.** *Greek Coins.* London: British Museum Press, 1995. Austin: University of Texas Press, 1995. 112 pp., illus.
The author presents an excellent overview of Greek coinage, from its beginnings to the time of the Roman conquests, showing how the coinage reflects Greek history, art, and society. Focuses on the precious metal coinage. Introduces a few basic numismatic terms. Then Carradice describes the characteristics of the coinage, century-by-century. Concludes with a brief discussion of Roman provincial coinage and the influence of Greek coinage on later (including modern) coinages and art. Includes brief comments on the scientific aspects of the study of Greek numismatics. The book is illustrated throughout by outstanding coins from the British Museum collection. [Reviewed by G. Kumpikevicius in *Canadian Coin News* (Canada) 34, no. 13 (October 22 – November 4, 1996): 8, 11, by J. Morcom in *Numismatic Chronicle* 157 (1997): 255-6, and by C. Arnold-Biucchi in *American Journal of Numismatics* 2nd ser., 12 (2000): 239-47].

40 **Carradice, Ian A., and Martin J. Price.** *Coinage in the Greek World.* London: B. A. Seaby, 1988. Reprint, London: Spink, 2004. 154 pp., maps, 24 pls.
A broad survey of Greek coinage. Reviews the history of collecting Greek coins and the development of methods for the scholarly study of Greek numismatics including the interpretation of hoards, the use of die-links, and the development of chronologies. Discusses the introduction of coinage, production of coinage, and the choice of types. Reviews the evolution of coinage during the classical and Hellenistic periods. Explores the circulation of coinage and the use of countermarks. [Also see Warren W. Esty's index which correlates the plates and the text, published in *The Celator* 5, no. 9 (September 1991): 32. Reviewed by H. B. Mattingly in *Numismatic Chronicle* 149 (1989): 228-32].

41 **Carson, Robert A. G.** *Coins: Ancient, Mediaeval and Modern.* London: Hutchinson, 1962. Also published as *Coins of the World.* New York: Harper, 1962. 642 pp., 64 pls. Second revised edition, 1970. [CS 53]
One of the best comprehensive references on coinage in general, this book devotes ninety-six pages and twelve plates to archaic, classical, and Hellenistic Greek coinage. Using a geographic arrangement, Carson gives brief summaries of the coinage of each area. [Reviewed by P. D. Whitting in *Numismatic Chronicle* 7th ser., 3 (1963): 279-81, and by J. J. North in *Spink Numismatic Circular* 70, no. 11 (November 1962): 230. Also reviewed in *Spink Numismatic Circular* 71, no. 2 (February 1963): 29].

42 ——— *Coins of Greece and Rome.* London: Hutchinson & Co., 1970. Reprint, London: Radius Books/Hutchinson, 1971. 189 pp., 25 pls. [CS 1638]
Carson's book, *Coins: Ancient, Mediaeval and Modern* (see above) was re-published in three volumes: Volume 1, *Coins of Greece and Rome;* Volume 2, *Coins of Europe;* and Volume 3, *Coins of America, Africa, Australasia, and Asia.*

43 ——— "Coins." *Civilization of the Ancient Mediterranean. Greece and Rome. Volume 3.* Edited by Michael Grant and Rachel Kitzinger. New York: Charles Scribner's Sons, 1988. Pages 1795-1816. Illus.
An overview of Greek and Roman coinage. Covers archaic, classical, and Hellenistic Greek coinage, illustrating forty-eight coin-types. Also discusses coinage of the Roman Republic, and the periods of the Principate and the Dominate. Fifty-two Roman coin-types are illustrated.

44 "The Catherine Page Perkins Collection of Ancient Coins." *American Journal of Numismatics* 36, no. 4 (April 1902): 118-9.
General comments on the usefulness of ancient coins in the study of history and art, inspired by the display of Greek coins from the Catherine Page Perkins collection at the Museum of Fine Arts, Boston.

45 **Caspari, M. O. B.** "A Survey of Greek Federal Coinage." *Journal of Hellenic Studies* 37 (1917): 168-83.
This survey of the various federal coinage systems attempts to throw light on the relationship of the federal government to the confederate states in the pre-Roman era. Briefly describes both the federal issues and the local issues of the various leagues and federations. Summarizes the six principal stages of federal money systems and gives examples of each.

46 **Clain-Stefanelli, Elvira E.** "Greek Numismatics." *Numismatics: An Ancient Science.* By E. E. Clain-Stefanelli. Contributions from The Museum of History and Technology: Paper 32. Washington, D.C.: U.S. Government Printing Office, 1965. Pages 42-6. Illus. [CS 16925]
A narrative history of the study of Greek numismatics in modern times. Focuses on the contribution of important scholars who have advanced the study of Greek coinage including F. Imhoof-Blumer, E. Babelon, B. V. Head, R. Poole, G. F. Hill, E. S. G. Robinson, W. Schwabacher, and others. Lists some of their most important works.

47 **Cohen, Edward E.** "Elasticity of the Money Supply at Athens." *The Monetary Systems of the Greeks and Romans.* Edited by W. V. Harris. Oxford: University Press, 2008. Pages 66-83.
Shows that the money supply in fourth century B.C. Athens was in fact elastic—it could be (and was) substantially increased through the provision of credit by merchants and through the banks' creation of non-coin money via deposit accounts and other mechanisms.

48 ——— *Dated Coins of Antiquity: A Comprehensive Catalogue of the Coins and How Their Numbers Came About.* Lancaster and London: Classical Numismatic Group, 2011. 652 pp., illus.
A substantially complete catalogue of dated coins struck before the lifetime of Jesus Christ (where a coin series crosses the millennium divide of 1 B.C./A.D. 1, the catalogue continues to its last dated coin in the A.D. era). The coins of antiquity used various kinds of numbers and more than fifty calendar systems for dating. The dates and their numerals on the coins serve as historical markers for early advances in recording time. The book explores how the Greeks, Romans, Phoenicians, Nabataeans and Jews struggled to understand their own numbers as well as those of their competitors or conquerors. Their calendars and notations for numbers varied among cities and even over time in the same city. Starting with the first dated coin struck by Zankle, Sicily in 494/493 B.C., this book lists all coins displaying annual or monthly dates expressed in numbers or words. Nearly 100 issuing states or authorities are represented. The catalogue describes more than 900 different coin types struck in gold, silver and bronze, exceeding 6000 different dated coins, dozens of which are cited in no other catalogue. It corrects the misreading of numerals in dates from earlier references on Ptolemaic Egypt and Alexandrian Sidon using Greek numbers, and early Tyre dated with Phoenician numbers. It also updates the B.C. dating of coins, such as those from Cappadocia, Cyprus, and Elymais, according to current research. Newly reported dates, including photographs, for the shekels and half shekels of Tyre are extensive. The coins are grouped by the type of

dating system used. For each coin listed, dates are given as B.C./A.D. dates, how the date is shown on the coin, the corresponding year of the regnal or local era, and a catalogue reference. An appendix provides a short history of numbers. Maps are included to show cities grouped by the type of numbers used. Concludes with a bibliography. [Reviewed by David Vagi in *The Celator* 25, no. 10 (October 2011): 39, 38, 46. Also see Cohen "Greek Numbers on Coins, Parts 1 and 2" under EPIGRAPHY].

49 **Crawford, Michael H.** "Numismatics." *Sources for Ancient History.* Edited by Michael H. Crawford. Cambridge: University Press, 1983. Pages 185-233. Illus.
A general introduction to how ancient coins can be employed as historical evidence. Discusses the interpretation of coin hoards, die studies, overstrikes and countermarks, minting techniques, weight standards, style and chronology.

50 "Curious Ancient Gold Coin May Be Ferry Fee for Hades. Sale Offers Possible Charon's Obol." *Coin World* (March 18, 1996): 57. Illus.
Describes and discusses the use of a possible "Charon's obol," a thin gold imitation of a Greek coin. These "coins" were intended to be used to pay the ferryman to transport the souls of the dead across the river Styx on their way to the underworld. The piece illustrated, thought to be from the second century B.C., was offered in the March 20, 1996 sale held by Classical Numismatic Group (lot 2693). [For another "Charon's obol," see lot 16 in the Schulman sale of the Thomas Ollive Mabbott collection, October, 1969; see H. Holzer under PRIVATE COLLECTIONS. Also see A. W. Hands "Notes on Charon's Fee" below, J. Déchelette "The Origins of the Drachm and Obolus" under METROLOGY, and Walker "Dioscuri" under TYPES].

51 **Daehn, William E.** "The Greek Numismatic Festschrifts: Storehouses of Information and Sought-After Collectibles." *Remy Bourne Numismatic Literature Specialist, Public Auction 4, October 25-26, 1996.* Minneapolis: Remy Bourne, 1996. Pages 99-100.
Discusses eight major volumes of essays on Greek Numismatics which were published to honor various numismatic scholars. Describes their content, availability, and market value.

52 ——— *Ancient Greek Numismatics: A Guide to Reading and Research.* Cold Spring: Davissons Ltd., 2001. 401 pp.
The first edition of Daehn's extensive bibliography of books and articles related to ancient Greek coinage, limited to works written in English. Lists 4094 items. Most listings include a summary of the contents and conclusions of the work. Includes a concordance to Clain-Stefanelli's *Numismatic Bibliography*, and various indices. Extensively cross-referenced. The most comprehensive bibliography of English works published prior to Daehn's second edition, *Annotated Bibliography of Ancient Greek Numismatics.*

53 **Davies, Glyn.** *A History of Money from Ancient Times to the Present Day.* Cardiff: University of Wales Press, 1994. 696 pp.
An analysis of the development and role of money in many of the world's nations from ancient to modern times. Includes sections on pre-metallic money, pre-coinage metallic money, the invention of coinage, and the development of coinage in Greece and Rome. Includes discussions of the widening circulation of coins, Laurion silver and Athenian coinage, Greek and metic private bankers, the Attic money standard, banking in Delos, Macedonian money and hegemony, and the financial consequences of Alexander the Great. Also discusses early Celtic coinage.

54 **Davies, John K.** "Temples, Credit, and the Circulation of Money." *Money and Its Uses in the Ancient Greek World.* Edited by A. Meadows and K. Shipton. Oxford: University Press, 2001. Pages 117-28.
Examines the ways in which the adoption of coined money by most Greek states affected the economic activity and attitudes of collectives (demes, phratries, poleis, etc.).

55 **Davis, Norman.** *Greek Coins and Cities, Illustrated from the Collection at the Seattle Art Museum.* London: Spink & Son, 1967. 223 pp., illus., maps. [CS 1818]
An introduction to Greek coins illustrated by enlarged photographs. Discusses the origins and spread of coinage. Illustrates coins of various cities and kingdoms, each of which is discussed, incorporating information on the history and mythology of the city. Illustrates 110 coins. Concludes with an eight-page summary of the history of Greek coinage by Colin M. Kraay. [Reviewed by R. A. G. Carson in *Times Literary Supplement* (February 1, 1968): 118. Carson's review was reprinted in *Spink Numismatic Circular* 79 (1971): 287. Also reviewed by Martin J. Price in *Spink Numismatic Circular* 76, no. 1 (January 1968): 12, and by C. W. Hill in *Spink Numismatic Circular* 76, no. 11 (November 1968): 340-1. Also, a very critical review by Anne E. Chapman appeared in *Numismatic Chronicle* 7th ser., 8 (1968): 277-80].

56 **de Callataÿ, François.** "Le Transport des Monnaies dans le Monde Grec." *Revue Belge de Numismatique et de Sigillographie* (Belgium) 152 (2006): 5-14.

57 **Del Mar, Alexander.** *A History of Money in Ancient Countries from the Earliest Times to the Present.* London: George Bell and Sons, 1885. Reprint, Burt Franklin, 1968. 358 pp.
A general overview of coinage history in China, Japan, and India (from ancient through modern times), and in Bactria, Egypt, Persia, Greece (and the Greek colonies), Carthage, and Rome (both Republic and Empire) in ancient times.

58 **de Morgan, Jacques.** *Manuel de Numismatique Orientale et l'Antiquité et du Moyen Age.* Three parts. Paris, 1923-36. Reprint, Chicago: Obol International, 1979. 480 pp., illus. [CS 3026]
The only volume published covered the ancient period. Includes coins of Persia, Phoenicia, Parthia, Syria, Arabia, India, Sasanians, and others.

59 **Dobson, Rosemary.** *Greek Coins: A Sequence of Poems with Line Drawings.* Canberra: Brindbella Press, 1977. 32 pp., illus.
A limited edition of 240 copies.

60 **Dodson, Oscar H.** *Money Tells the Story.* Racine: Whitman Publishing Co., 1962. 64 pp., illus. [CS 174]
A brief history of money based on the collection formed by Nate S. Shapero and later owned by and exhibited at the Money Museum of the National Bank of Detroit. Includes photographs and brief discussions of the origins of coinage, the coins of Aegina, Athens, Syracuse, Alexander the Great, Lysimachus, and Cleopatra. Also includes other coins from around the world from all eras.

Brief discussion of ancient Greek banking and money lending, interest, measures of value, the introduction of coinage, the spread of coinage, coin types and symbols.

——— *A History of Ancient Coinage, 700-300 B.C.* Oxford, 1918. Reprints, Chicago, 1974; New Delhi, 1975. 463 pp., 11 pls. [CS 1826]
Describes Greek trade routes, classes of traders, bankers, early measures of value and the origin of coin weight-standards. Describes the relationship between the precious metals and discusses monetary alliances. Then begins a geographic review of the coins, with much historical information intertwined with numismatic information. Coin-issuing cities are examined in groups, rather than individually, and lines of trade influence are traced from district to district. Covers Greek coinage up to the start of the Hellenistic age. [Reviewed by G. F. Hill in *Journal of Hellenic Studies* 38 (1918): 196-8, and by J. G. Milne in *Numismatic Chronicle* 4th ser., 18 (1918): 127-9].

Giedroyc, Richard F., and Malcolm W. Heckman, eds. "Greek City-States: The Rise and Fall of their Coinage." *Classical Coin Newsletter* (Maplewood, N.J.) 1, no. 6 (February 1982): 1-2, 7.
A very brief introduction to collecting Greek coins. Discusses the periods of coinage, denominations, etc.

——— "The Greek Archaic Period." *Classical Coin Newsletter* (Maplewood, N.J.) 1, no. 12 (August 1982): 1-2, 7.
A brief introduction to the coinage of the archaic period.

Göbl, Robert. *Antike Numismatik.* Two volumes. Munich: Battenberg Verlag, 1978. [CS 1646]
Covers the Greeks, Romans, Celts, and Sasanians:

1. *Einfuhrung Munzkunde, Munzgeschichte, Geldeschichte Methodenlehre, Praktischer Teil.* 283 pp.
2. *Fussnoten Gesamtwerk, Literaturverzeichnis, Stichwortverzekichnis, Katalog, Tafeeln und Tabellen.* 283 pp., 176 pls.

"Gold Coins of the Ancient Greeks." *Spink Numismatic Circular* 100, no. 1 (February 1992): 9.
Announces an exhibition at the British Museum. Comments on the use of gold in Greek coinage.

"Greek Coins." *American Journal of Numismatics* 8, no. 4 (April 1874): 82-5.
A brief summary of the history of Greek coinage and the history of collecting Greek coins. Reprinted from the *London Times*.

Green, Benjamin R. *A Numismatic Atlas, of Ancient History: Comprised in a Series of Twenty-One Plates, Containing a Selection of 360 Grecian Coins of Kings, disposed in Chronological Order, from their Earliest Period to the Beginning of the Fourth Century, from the Works of Havercamp, Pellerin, Duane, Visconti, Combe, Mionnet, &C.* London: Priestley and Weale, 1829. 42 pp., 21 pls.
Includes a table on the frequency of certain symbols on coins and a hand-colored plate of sizes and values of Greek coins. Includes twenty-one hand-colored lithographic plates of coins with descriptive text. In his sale catalogue for Part 3 of *The Harry W. Bass, Jr. Numismatic Library*, G. F. Kolbe states, "There were only 100 subscribers, indicating a relatively small print run. A well-known water color painter, Green published the *Numismatic Atlas* when he was only twenty-one years old."

——— *Atlas Numismatique de L'Histoire Ancienne, Contenant un Choix de 360 Medailles Grecques.* Paris, 1829. 30 pp., 21 pls.
French version of the above.

——— *A Lecture on the Study of Ancient Coins, in Connexion with History, as Delivered Feb. 6, 1829, in the Theatre of the Royal Institution of Great Britain.* London: B. R. Green, 1829. 39 pp., 2 pls.

Guépin, J. P. "Greek Coinage and Persian Bimetallism." *Jaarboek voor Munt-en Penningkunde* 49 (1962): 1-19. [CS 3062]

Hackens, Tony, and Raymond Weiller, eds. *Proceedings of the 9th International Congress of Numismatics, Berne, September 1979. Volume 1: Ancient Numismatics.* Luxembourg: International Association of Professional Numismatists, 1982. 687 pp., 81 pls.
The text of the papers presented at the Congress held in 1979. Abstracts for each of the papers concerning Greek numismatics are included elsewhere. These are: "Results of Coin Striking to Simulate the Mint of Aegina" by L. Beer [1359], "Persian Satraps and Lycian Dynasts: The Evidence of the Diadems" by J. Zahle [6250], "'Symmachic' Coins in Greek Inscriptions" by J. M. Jones [1333], "Some Plated Coins from the Agora at Athens" by A. Walker [1473], "Kataneische Probleme: Silberne Kleinstmünzen" by C. Boehringer [3042], "Pharaonic Imitations of Athenian Tetradrachms" by T. V. Buttrey [6539], "Early Greek Bronze Coinage in Dalmatia and the Skudljivac Hoard: A Reappraisal of *IGCH* 418-420" by P. Visonà [3831], "The End of Thessalian Civic Coinage in Silver: Macedonian Policy or Economic Reality?" by T. R. Martin [3869], "The Solar Cult on the Coins of Ancient Malta" by R. R. Stieglitz [6784], "The 'Behaviour' of Dies in the Hellenistic Period" by O. Mørkholm [1432], and "The Propontis Hoard, 1950" by N. M. Waggoner [825].

Hands, Alfred Watson. "Common Greek Coins." A series of articles in *Spink Numismatic Circular* 12-30 (1904-1922).
A series of articles forming a catalogue of Greek coin types. Reprinted as a series of books (see below).

——— *Common Greek Coins, Vol. 1: The Coinage of Athens, Corinth, Aegina, Boeotian League, Alexander the Great, Achaean League, and Lycian League.* London: Spink & Son, 1907. 170 pp., illus. [CS 1831]
A review of the coinage, reprinted from the series of articles published in *Spink Numismatic Circular*. [Also see individual entries for A. W. Hands under CORINTHIA, AEGINA, CENTRAL GREECE—BOEOTIA, MACEDONIAN KINGDOM, and PELOPONNESOS—ACHAIA].

——— "Notes on Charon's Fee." *Spink Numismatic Circular* 18 (July 1910): 12176-7.
Discusses the practice of burying the dead with a coin in their mouth. The coin is thought to provide protection from evil spirits which enter the body through the mouth. The soul of the dead was also believed to exit the body through the mouth. Examines the origin of the practice among the Greeks, who used the coin (or a thin metal imitation of a coin) to pay the boatman named Charon to ferry them across the river to the underworld. [Also see "Curious Ancient Gold Coin" above, and Walker "Dioscuri" under TYPES].

60a **Drougou, S., D. Evgenidou, Ch. Kritzas, N. Kaltsas, B. Penna, I. Tsourti, M. Galani-Kribou**
ΚΕΡΜΑΤΙΑ ΦΙΛΙΑΣ—Studies in Honour of Ioannis Touratsoglou. Two volumes. Athens: Hellenic Ministry o
Museum, 2009. 603 pp., 631 pp., illus.
Studies written in honor of the director of the Numismatic Museum, Athens. The first volume focuses on numismatics. T
archaeology and related topics. In Greek.

61 **Dumersan, Théophile Marion, and C. P. Landon.** *Numismatique Du Voyage du Jeune Anacharsis ou Médaille
Grece, Accompagne de Descriptions et D'un Essai La Science Des Médailles.* Two volumes. Paris, 1846. 144 pp.,
Includes ninety finely engraved plates depicting the obverse and reverse of choice ancient Greek coins.

62 **Eckhel, Joseph H.** *Doctrina Numorum Veterum.* Eight volumes. Vienna: Joseph Degen, 1792-8 (volumes 3-8 pub
Addenda. Vienna: Steinbüchel, 1826. Second edition, Leipzig, 1826-8. 4000 pp. [CS 1643]
Eckhel has been called "the father of ancient numismatics." Clain-Stefanelli states "for the first time in its history the basic elem
Roman numismatics—metals, ponderal systems, organization of mints, significance of coin-types, coins in their relation to the
discussed. In dealing with ancient Greek numismatics (in the first four volumes of his work), Eckhel adopted a geographical a
alphabetical groupings generally in use up to his time. This system, previously advocated by the French collector and scholar
worked out in detail, remains the foundation of Greek numismatics to the present day." Volumes 1-4 are devoted to Greek
Volumes 5-8 are devoted to Roman coins. The *Addenda* material was taken from Eckhel's original notes.

62a **Flament, Christophe.** *Contribution à l'Étude des Ateliers Monétaires Grecs: Étude Comparée des Conditions
Monnaie à Athènes, dans le Péloponnèse et dans le Royaume de Macédoine à l'Époque Classique.* Études Numism
Neuve: Association de Numismatique Professeur Marcel Hoc, 2010. 154 pp., illus.

63 **Fowler, Harold N.** *Greek Coins.* New York, 1909. Reprint, Chicago: Obol International, 1981. 23 pp., illus.
A basic overview of Greek coinage. Discusses metals and weight standards and the artistic development of the coinage from th
the Hellenistic era. Illustrated by the major coin types.

64 **Fowler, Harold N., and J. R. Wheeler.** "An Introduction to the Archaeological Study of Greek Coins." *North
Numismatics: The Turtle* 6, no. 7 (July 1967): 211-22; no. 8 (August 1967): 233-41. [CS 1822]
A good introduction to Greek numismatics reprinted (with corrections and simplifications) from *Handbook of Greek Archaeol
overview of coinage metals, minting, shapes and designs, weight standards, denominations, the gold-to-silver ratio, the origins of c
representations on coins, inscriptions and symbols. Continues with a discussion of the various periods of artistic development and d
the art of the coinage of Athens, the Demareteion of Syracuse, coins of Naxos, Elis, and Philip II.

65 **Franke, Peter R., and Max Hirmer.** *Die Griechische Münze.* Munich: Hirmer Verlag, 1964. 174 pp., 220 pls. Sec
Hirmer Verlag, 1972. 175 pp., 239 pls. [CS 1823 and 3556]
Contains the same plates as Kraay and Hirmer's *Greek Coins,* but with different text. [See Kraay and Hirmer below].

66 ——— *La Monnaie Grecque.* Paris: Flammarion, 1966. 153 pp., 240 pls. [CS 1824]
A French translation, by Jean Babelon, of *Die Greichische Münze.*

67 **Franklin, C. W.** *A Handbook of American, Greek, and Roman Coins.* Bellevue, Pennsylvania: C. W. Fran
including 15 pls.
Begins with a brief history of coinage covering the invention and spread of coinage, metals used for coinage, sources o
standards, and a brief discussion of counterfeits. This is followed by tables of exchange rates for world currencies, tables of Uni
(including private gold issues) based on auction records, and fifteen plates of Greek and Roman coins.

68 **Gans, Edward.** "Greek Coins and Their Reflection of Art, History, and Trade." *Bulletin of the California Palace of t
16, nos. 11/12 (March/April 1959): unpaged [12 pages]. Illus.
"This illustrated introduction was prepared to accompany the author's exhibition of ancient Greek coins displayed at the California P
Honor, April 25 to June 7, 1959. It covers the whole of the Greek world from Sicily to Bactria as well as the Celts, Etruscans, early R
Carthaginians." [I. Merker, *NL* 49]

69 **Gardner, Percy.** "Numismatic Reattributions: Phanes, Lamia, Electryona." *Numismatic Chronicle* new ser., 18 (1878
pl.
The author suggests reattributions of a few Greek coins: (1) The coin of Phanes published by Newton (see Newton "Electrum Stater" u
reads the inscription slightly differently. He attributes the coin to the Phanes mentioned by Herodotus, who was probably a tyrant of
rare coin of Lamia in Thessaly. He identifies the head on the obverse as Lamia—a lover of Demetrius Poliorcetes. The head had previ
as Apollo (also see Gardner "Lamia" under THESSALY for follow-up comments on this coin). (3) Gardner identifies the head on certain g
of Rhodes as Electryona, rather than Helios. Electryona was a daughter of Helios and the nymph Rhodos. Gardner believes the female
is "unmistakable."

70 ——— "Pollux' Account of Ancient Coins." *Numismatic Chronicle* 3rd ser., 1 (1881): 281-305. [CS 1825]
A translation, with notes, of the chapter of *Onomasticon* by Julius Pollux which deals with ancient coins. Pollux discusses weights, deno
coins, and their purchasing power. Gardner brings together the statements of Pollux with the existing coins and recent research.

71 ——— "Chapter IV: The Money-Market and Coins." *A Manual of Greek Antiquities.* By Percy Gardner and Frank B
York: Charles Scribner's Sons, 1895. Pages 394-403.

86   **Harris, W. V., ed.** *The Monetary Systems of the Greeks and Romans.* Oxford: University Press, 2008. 336 pp.
A collection of essays written for a conference on the nature of ancient money. The papers explore how the Greek and Roman monetary systems worked. Includes "The Monetary Use of Weighed Bullion in Archaic Greece" by John Kroll [131], "What Was Money in Ancient Greece" by David Schaps [206], "Money and Tragedy" by Richard Seaford [214], "The Elasticity of the Money-Supply at Athens" by Edward Cohen [47], "Coinage as 'Code' in Ptolemaic Egypt" by J. G. Manning [6635], and several papers related to Roman coinage.

87   **Harwood, E.** *Populorum et Urbium, Selecta Numismata Graeca ex Aere.* London, 1812. 115 pp., 7 engraved pls.

88   **Head, Barclay V.** *Coins of the Ancients 700 B.C.-A.D. 1: A Guide to the Principal Gold and Silver Coins of the Ancients in the British Museum.* London, 1881. Fifth edition, 1909. Reprint, Chicago: Argonaut, 1968. 128 pp., 70 pls. [CS 1890]
Lists and describes 792 coins selected from the British Museum collection illustrating the most important coinage from the beginnings of coinage through the Roman Republican period. The catalogue is segregated chronologically and each section is preceded by a brief discussion of the numismatic history of the period. Brief comments are provided for most of the coins. This book is a revised and expanded version of the Birtish Museum's exhibition guide that Head originally prepared in 1872 [see Head *Synopsis* under PUBLIC COLLECTIONS—GREAT BRITAIN (LONDON)] and revised in 1880. It was revised again in 1932 (see below).

89   ——— "Ancient Greek Coins." *American Journal of Numismatics* 18, no. 2 (October 1883): 25-30; no. 3 (January 1884): 49-53; no. 4 (April 1884): 73-7. Illus.
A reprint of a series of articles which originally appeared in *The Antiquary*, an English magazine. Discusses the origin of coinage, religious aspects of coin types, and the history of coinage at various cities and kingdoms. Discusses famous die engravers and the use of magistrates' names on coins.

90   ——— *Historia Numorum: A Manual of Greek Numismatics.* Oxford: Clarendon Press, 1887. Second edition, 1911. Reprints, London: Spink & Son, 1963 and 1977; Chicago: Argonaut, 1967; New York: Sanford J. Durst, 1983 and 1998. 966 pp., illus., 5 tables. [CS 1832]
A comprehensive textbook for the field of Greek numismatics. The introductory chapter contains a thorough discussion of weight-standards, lists of magistrate's titles, games and festivals, civic titles, a discussion of coin types, inscriptions, and dating. The main body of the book follows a geographic arrangement. Each section contains detailed historical and numismatic information. Describes the major coin types of each city, giving approximate dates of issue. A few coins are illustrated by drawings. Completely indexed by subject, city, personal names, inscriptions, magisterial titles, and engravers' names. Contains tables of alphabets and an extensive bibliography. [The 1998 Durst reprint includes plates and additional text. The first edition was reviewed by P. Gardner in *Journal of Hellenic Studies* 8 (1887): 313-5, and by J. H. Middleton in *Numismatic Chronicle* 3rd ser., 7 (1887): 273-6. The second edition was reviewed by A. J. Evans in *Journal of Hellenic Studies* 31 (1911): 131-6. Also see Svoronos and Head *The Illustrations of the Historia Numorum* below. Also see Rutter *Historia Numorum* for Volume 1 of the completely revised edition of this standard work].

91   ——— *A Guide to the Principal Coins of the Greeks from circ. 700 B.C. to A.D. 270, Based on the Work of Barclay V. Head.* London: British Museum, 1932. Second edition, 1959. Reprint, 1965. 108 pp., 52 pls. [CS 1889]
G. F. Hill was actually the author of this substantial revision of Head's *Coins of the Ancients* (see above). In this revision, the Roman Republican coins have been excluded, some Roman Provincial coins down to the end of the reign of Gallienus have been added, and some bronze coins have been added. G. K. Jenkins was responsible for the 1959 revision which includes two additional plates, mostly of recent acquisitions by the British Museum. [The second edition was reviewed by C. M. Kraay in *Numismatic Chronicle* 6th ser., 20 (1960): 298-9].

92   ——— "Table of Greek Eras." *Spink Numismatic Circular* 23 (March-April 1915): 179-81.
A reprint of the table of Greek eras from the first edition of Head's *Historia Numorum* (page 944).

93   **Heckel, Waldemar, and Richard Sullivan, eds.** *Ancient Coins of the Graeco-Roman World: The Nickle Numismatic Papers.* Waterloo, Ontario: Wilfrid Laurier University Press, 1984. 307 pp., illus.
A collection of essays presented at a conference held at the Nickle Museum of the University of Calgary, Alberta in 1981. The papers on Greek numismatics are: "Greek Coinage and War" by C. M. Kraay [125], "The Reduced Euboio-Attic Coin Weight Standard" by M. B. Wallace [1623], "The Silver Coinage of Alexander from Pella" by N. Moore [3430], "Lysimachus the Gazophylax: A Modern Scholarly Myth?" by S. M. Burstein [3665], "The So-Called 'Pedigree Coins' of the Bactrian Greeks" by F. Holt [6348], "The Monetary System in the Seleucid Empire after 187 B.C." by O. Mørkholm [5397], "The Coins of the Phoenician World—East and West" by B. Trell [5641], "Royal Coins and Rome" by R. Sullivan [1091], "A Coin Copy of Lysippus's Heracles at Tarentum" by F. Van Keuren [2858], "Foreign Currency in Etruria Circa 400-200 B.C.: Distribution Patterns" by P. Visonà [2754], "Seldom What They Seem—The Case of the Athenian Tetradrachm" by T. V. Buttrey [3989], and "On Cataloguing the McGill University Collection of Greek and Roman Coins: A Progress Report" by G. M. Woloch [1749]. Also includes five other essays and a few abstracts dealing with Roman coinage.

94   **Heichelheim, Fritz M.** "Wirtschaftshistorische Beiträge zur Klassisch Griechischen und Hellenistischen Münzhortstatistik." *Transactions of the International Numismatic Congress Organized and Held in London by the Royal Numismatic Society, June 30-July 3, 1936.* Edited by J. Allan, H. Mattingly, and E. S. G. Robinson. London: B. Quaritch, 1938. Pages 68-78.

95   **Hill, George F.** *A Handbook of Greek and Roman Coins.* New York: Macmillan, 1899. Reprinted as *Ancient Greek and Roman Coins: A Handbook.* Chicago: Argonaut, 1964. 302 pp., illus., 16 pls. [CS 1650]
Covers all aspects of ancient numismatics: the origin and spread of coinage, metals, weight-standards and denominations, monetary theory, state authority over money, magistrates' symbols, fabric and style of coins, types, inscriptions, and dating. Explains the Greek alphabet and contains tables comparing various weight-standards. Covers both Greek and Roman coinage. An invaluable handbook containing information not easily obtainable elsewhere, especially the discussion on sources of metal.

96   ——— "Bibliographical Notes on Greek Numismatics." *Numismatic Chronicle* 3rd ser., 18 (1898): 326-33; 18 (1899): 251-62; 20 (1900): 363-76.
Lists works related to Greek numismatics which appeared in periodicals not exclusively devoted to numismatics. Most listings are arranged geographically, but Part 3 includes some subject headings.

97 **Hill, George F., ed.** *Corolla Numismatica: Numismatic Essays in Honour of Barclay V. Head.* London: Oxford University Press, 1906. 386 pp., 18 pls. [CS 1817 and 17445]
A collection of essays written to honor Barclay V. Head at the time of his retirement as Keeper of Coins at the British Museum. The papers related to Greek numismatics are: "Une Obole au Nom d'Hippias" by E. Babelon [3970], "La Minerve de Massalia" by A. Blanchet, "The Early Coinages of European Greece" by H. B. E. Fox [392], "Zur Chronologie der Autonomen Prägung von Pergamon" by H. von Fritze [4657], "Étude sur la Numismatique de la Perside" by A. de la Füye [6251], "Monete Inedite o Rare del Museo Nazionale di Napoli" by E. Gabrici [1866], "Copies of Statues on Coins" by P. Gardner [943], "The Coinage of Luceria" by H. A. Gruebner [2784], "Dryops at Asine" by G. F. Hill [4312], "Syrakosai—Lysimachos—Derdas" by F. Imhoof-Blumer [3167], "On the Earliest Coins of Thurioi" by C. Jörgenson [2879], "Fixed and Loose Dies in Ancient Coinage" by G. Macdonald [1420], "Trois Contremarques Inédites sur des Tétradrachmes de Sidé" by R. Mowat [5063], "Coins of the Graeco-Indian Sovereigns Agathocleia, Strato I Soter, and Strato II Philopater" by E. Rapson [6439], "The Chronological Sequence of the Coins of Corinth" by C. Oman [4270], "Charaspes" by K. Regling [3628], "Achilles on Thessalian Coins" by T. Reinach [3877], "ΣΦΡΑΓΙΣ ΑΘΗΝΑΙΚΟΥ ΤΕΤΡΑΔΡΑΧΜΟΥ" by J. N. Svoronos [1461], "Rare or Unpublished Coins in My Collection" by H. Weber [2121], "Themistokles als Herr von Magnesia" by R. Weil [4820], and "Minoan Weights and Mediums of Currency, from Crete, Mycenae and Cyprus" by A. J. Evans [1569]. Also includes a few papers on Roman and Byzantine numismatics. [A brief review of this book appears in *Journal of Hellenic Studies* 27 (1907): 139. For a brief account of the ceremony at the British Museum during which this volume was presented to Barclay Head, see *Numismatic Chronicle* 4th ser., 6 (1906): 387-9. Head died in 1914. His obituary, along with a bibliography of his works, appears in *Numismatic Chronicle* 4th ser., 14 (1914): 249-55].

98 ——— *Historical Greek Coins.* London and New York: Archibald Constable & Co., 1906. Reprints, Chicago: Argonaut, 1966; Chicago: Ares Publishers, 1976. 181 pp., illus., 14 pls. [CS 1833]
Discusses 100 Greek coins "which, either by the mere fact that they were issued, or else by information conveyed through their fabric, types, inscriptions or standard...add to our knowledge of the period to which they belong." Significant historical and numismatic information is given for each coin, and each is photographed. Forms an excellent overview of the most important Greek coins. [Also see Kraay "Historical Interpretations" below for comments and corrections to some of Hill's conclusions].

99 **Hobson, Burton.** *Historic Gold Coins of the World.* Garden City: Doubleday & Company, 1971. 192 pp., illus.
Illustrates 244 gold coins from around the world, from ancient times through modern times, all illustrated with enlarged color photographs. Extensive historical and numismatic notes. Includes twelve Greek coins. Most of the specimens were drawn from the collection of the American Numismatic Society.

100 **Houghton, Arthur, Silvia Hurter, Patricia Erhart Mottahedeh, and Jane Ayer Scott, eds.** *Studies in Honour of Leo Mildenberg: Numismatics, Art History, Archaeology.* Wetteren: Editions NR, 1984. 297 pp., 43 pls.
A collection of twenty-five essays on numismatics and art history written in honor of Leo Mildenberg. The papers related to Greek numismatics are: "Some Examples of Lead Currency from the Hellenistic Period" by D. Barag [5651], "Réflexions sur les Fractions du Monnayage Grec" by D. Bérend [26], "Syrakusanischer Münzstempel der Epoche des Agathokles" by C. Boehringer and O. di Floristella [3119], "Stagira in Tel-Aviv" by H. Cahn [3238], "The Seleucid Mint of Mallus and the Cult of Athena Magarsia" by A. Houghton [5307], "Archaischer Silberfund aus dem Antilibanon" by S. Hurter and E. Pászthory [601], "Varia Punica" by G. K. Jenkins [6720], "Un Trésor de Monnaies Séleucides Trouvé dans le Hauran en 1979 ou 1980: Antiochos VI à Ptolemaïs" by G. Le Rider [5353], "One Hundred Ninety Years of Tyrian Shekels" by Y. Meshorer [5619], "Some Pergamene Coins in Copenhagen" by O. Mørkholm [4681], "Croesus or Pseudo-Croesus? Hoard or Hoax? Problems Concerning the Sigloi and Double Sigloi of the Croeseid Type" by M. Price [4999], "Ascalon: From Royal Mint to Autonomy" by A. Spaer [5440], "Paying the Mercenaries" by M. Thompson [3509], "Carians in Miniature" by H. Troxell [4905], "Seal Impressions in the Manner of the Seleucids" by N. Waggoner [1127], and "Some Hoards from Sicily and a Carthaginian Issue of the Second Punic War" by A. Walker [828].

101 **Howgego, Christopher J.** *Ancient History from Coins.* London and New York: Routledge, 1995. 176 pp., 23 pls.
Intended for students and teachers of ancient history who want to know how the study of coinage can be of interest to them. Outlines the major problems of using coins as an historical source. Discusses the development of coinage, mints and coin production, the relationship of coins to state expenditures, trade, and military preparation, size of issues, impact of empires on coinage, political messages on coins, circulation patterns, and changes caused by economic or military crisis. Discusses devaluation and debasement of coins. Includes bibliographical references. [Reviewed by J. H. C. Williams in *Numismatic Chronicle* 156 (1996): 333-5, by R. Weigel in *The Celator* 12, no. 3 (March 1998): 33, by P. M. Bellemare in *The Anvil* (Canada) 9, no. 1 (March 1, 1999): 13-5, and by R. A. Bauslaugh in *American Journal of Numismatics* 2nd ser., 11 (1999): 151-9].

102 ——— *Geld in der Antiken Welt: Was Münzen über Geschichte Verraten.* Stuttgart: Theiss, 2000. Reprint, Wissenschaftliche Buchgesellschaft, 2007. 223 pp.

103 **Hübner, Ulrich, and Ernst A. Knauf, eds.** *Leo Mildenberg. Vestigia Leonis: Studien zur Antiken Numismatik Israels, Palästinas und der Östlichen Mittelmeerwelt.* Novum Testamentum et Orbis Antiquus 36. Freiburg: Universitätsverlag, and Göttingen: Vandenhoeck & Ruprecht, 1998. 400 pp., 72 pls.
A compilation of thirty-four of Leo Mildenberg's articles (20 in English, 13 in German, and 1 in French) originally published from 1947 to 1995. This volume was presented to Mildenberg in honor of his eighty-fifth birthday in 1998. Includes eleven articles on the local coinages of the Palestine area during the Persian period, five articles on Greek subjects, five on Punic and Siculo-Punic coins, and ten on Bar Kochba studies. Also includes an article on numismatic evidence in general, one on the importance of die axes, and one on a rare medieval Goldgulden from the town of Miltenberg. Also includes a bibliography of Mildenberg's writings. The papers are: "Über das Münzwesen im Reich der Achämeniden" [6214], "Nergal in Tarsos: Ein Numismatischer Beitrag", "Baana: Preliminary Studies of the Local Coinage in the Fifth Persian Satrapy. Part 2." [5621], "Notes on the Coin Issues of Mazday" [6213], "Palästinas in der Persischen Zeit", "On the Money Circulation in Palestine from Artaxerxes II till Ptolemy I: Preliminary Studies of the Local Coinage in the Fifth Persian Satrapy, Part 5." [5805], "Yehud: A Preliminary Study of the Provincial Coinage of Judaea" [5804], "Gaza von 420 bis 332 Nach den Sachquellen", "Gaza Mint Authorities in Persian Times. Preliminary Studies of the Local Coinage in the Fifth Persian Satrapy. Part 4." [5893], "The Philisto-Arabian Coins. A Preview. Preliminary Studies of the Local Coinage in the Fifth Persian Satrapy. Part 3." [5892], "Bes on Philisto-Arabian Coins" [5894], "Von der Kunst der Griechischen Kleinmünzen" [1177], "Mithrapata und Perikles" [5032], "Kimon in the Manner of Segesta" [3072], "Über Kimon und Euainetos im Funde von Naro" [3183], "The Cyzikenes: A Reappraisal" [4647], "Les Inscriptions des Monnaies Carthaginians" [6727], "Punic Coinage on the Eve of the First War Against Rome" [3105], "The Mint of the First Carthaginian Coins" [6728], "RSMLQRT" [3106], "Siculo-Punische Münzlegenden" [3107], "Rebel Coinage in the Roman Empire", "Schekel-Fragen," "Numismatische Evidenze zur Chronologie der Bar Kochba-Erhebung," "The Eleazar Coins of the Bar Kochba Rebellion," "The Monetary System of the Bar Kokhba Coinage," "A Bar Kokhba Didrachm," "Bar Kochba in Jerusalem," "Bar Kokhba Coins and Documents," "The Bar Kokhba Wars in Light of the Coins and Document Finds 1947-1982," "Der Bar-Kochba-Krieg

im Lichte der Münzprägungen," "Numismatic Evidence" [161], "Those Ridiculous Arrows: On the Meaning of the Die Position" [1428], and "Florinus Mildenbergensis." [Reviewed by W. Fischer-Bossert in *Revue Suisse de Numismatique* 78 (1999): 169-170].

104 **Humphreys, Henry Noel.** *Ancient Coins and Medals: An Historical Sketch of the Origin and Progress of Coining Money in Greece and her Colonies; its Progress with the Extension of the Roman Empire; and its Decline with the Fall of That Power. Illustrated by Numerous Fac-Simile Examples in Actual Relief and in the Metals of the Respective Coins.* London: Grant and Griffith, 1850. 2nd ed., London, 1851. 207 pp., 10 pls.
Begins with an introduction to numismatics and the purpose of collecting. Describes the various circulating mediums representing wealth before the introduction of coinage. Then discusses the introduction of coinage by the Lydians, the subsequent coinage of gold in Europe, the first silver coins of Europe, the changes in coinage brought about by Philip of Macedon, and the development of the art of coinage in Italy and Sicily. Humphreys then describes the coins illustrated on the plates. The plates give the appearance of actual coins imbedded in cardboard coin holders. Discusses the coinage of Sicily, Carthage, Spain, Gaul, the Hellenistic kingdoms, the Indo-Greeks, and others. Discusses weight standards and the origin and nature of coin types. Also discusses Palestinian coinage, coinage of the Roman Republic, the Roman Empire, and Roman Provincial coinage. Concludes with a discussion of the selection and classification of coins in a collection, and comments on forgeries of ancient coins.

105 **Hurter, Silvia, and Carmen Arnold-Biucchi, eds.** *Pour Denyse: Divertissements Numismatiques.* Bern, Switzerland: Privately published, 2000. 221 pp., 25 pls.
A collection of eighteen essays written to honor Denyse Bérend. Begins with a Preface by Georges LeRider and a one-page bibliography of Bérend's writings. The essays are: "Une Monnaie de la Cité Ionienne d'Airai" by M. Amandry [4740], "Litras en Argent Contremarquées en Sicile et les Fractions de Sélinonte" by C. Arnold-Biucchi [2898], "Ein Lot Silberner Kleinstmünzen aus Karien" by C. Boehringer [4865], "Die Störche von Kroton" by H. Cahn [2771], "Le Monete di Metaponto e l'Influenza di Agatocle" by M. Caccamo Caltabiano [2785], "Some New Fractions from Central and Southern Greece" by V. Demetriadi [3846], "Un Gruppo di Frazioni di Zecche Siciliane" by G. Gorini [2930], "A Group of Argive Coins at Brown University" by R. Holloway [4331], "Das Palladion als Pro-Athenisches Symbol?" by S. Hurter Mani [970], "Apamée en Syrie: Un Chapitre Contestable de E. T. Newell dans WSM" by G. LeRider [5359], "The Goats of 'Aigai'" by C. Lorber [3267], "Über das Kleingeld des 4. Jahrhunderts im Perserreich" by L. Mildenberg [6219], "Some South Italian Questions" by J. Morcom [2681], "Le Trésor de Lentini (Sicile) 1957 (*IGCH* 2117)" by C. Arnold Biucchi and H. Nicolet Pierre [4081], "The Mysterious Segestans" by K. Rutter [3073], "A Partial Hoard of Royal Macedonian Bronzes" by H. Troxell [3522], "The Silver Coins of Sicyon in Leiden" by J. Warren [4396], and "Skylla on the Coins of Akragas" by U. Westermark [3003].

106 **Imhoof-Blumer, Friedrich W.** *Monnaies Grecques.* Paris/Leipzig, 1883. 518 pp., 18 pls. Reprint, Bologna: Forni, 1967 and 1975. [CS 1837]
[Also see Imhoof-Blumer *Choix de Monnaies Grecque* under PRIVATE COLLECTIONS].

107 ——— *Griechische Münzen: Neue Beiträge und Untersuchungen.* Munich, 1890. 274 pp., 14 pls. Reprint, Graz, 1972. 274 pp., 14 pls. [CS 1838]
Greek coinage—new entries and investigations. A catalogue of 817 Greek coins (including some Roman provincial issues), many of which were previously unpublished varieties. Many are from the collection of the author. Includes discussion of the coins and various indices.

108 **Istituto Italiano di Numismatica.** *Le Origini della Monetazione di Bronzo in Sicilia e in Magna Grecia (Atti del VI Convegno del Centro Internazionale di Studi Numismatici, Napoli Aprile 17-22, 1977).* Supplement to *Annali. Istituto Italiano di Numismatica* (Italy) 25 (1979). Rome, 1979. 387 pp., 41 pls.
A collection of papers exploring the origin and development of bronze coinage in Italy and Sicily. Includes: "The Fifth Century Bronze Coinage of Akragas" by U. Westermark [3000], "The Bronze Coinage of Himera and 'Himera'" by C. M. Kraay [3029], "Le Monnayage de Bronze de Ségeste" by D. Bérend [3066], "Selinus" by M. J. Price [3082], "Una Vittoria Navale dei Liparaioi sue Tyrrhenoi e l'Inizio della Monetazione Bronzea a Lipara" by G. Manganaro [3052], "L'Inizio della Monetazione in Bronzo Siracusana" by R. R. Holloway [3163], "Die Frühen Bronzemünzen von Leontinoi und Katane" by C. Boehringer [3050], "The Fifth Century Bronze Coins of Gela and Kamarina" by G. K. Jenkins [3011], "South Italy and Messana" by K. Rutter [2696], "La Circolazione della Moneta Bronzea in Sicilia" by A. Cutroni Tusa [2918], "La Typologie du Bronze par Rapport à Celle de l'Argent" by L. Lacroix [2951], "Il Sistema della Litra Nella Sicilia Antica tra V e IV secolo a.C." by N. F. Parise [2967], "Les Equivalences de Metaux Monetaires: Argent et Bronze en Sicilia au Ve s. av. J.-C." by T. Hackens [2931], and "The Function of Early Greek Bronze Coinage" by M. J. Price [185].

109 **Jenkins, G. Kenneth.** *Ancient Greek Coins.* London: Barrie & Jenkins, 1972. 310 pp. Second edition: London: Seaby, 1990. 182 pp., illus., 8 pls. [CS 1840]
A broad overview of Greek coinage, focusing on the artistic development of the coin types. The first chapter includes discussions of minting techniques and chronology. The body of the book is segregated chronologically and geographically and provides historical and numismatic information for each section, always comparing and contrasting the artistic styles and coin types from the various regions and eras. Illustrated by hundreds of photographs of Greek coins exhibiting a high level of artistic merit. The second edition has been condensed in size primarily through the use of fewer enlarged photographs and fewer color plates. [The first edition was reviewed by J. S. Wilkinson in *Cornucopiæ* 1, no. 5 (1973): 78-82, and by S. Jameson in *Numismatic Chronicle* 7th ser., 14 (1974): 208-10].

110 ——— *Münzen der Griechen.* Translation into German by Harold Küthmann. Munich: Ernst Battenberg Verlag, 1972. 330 pp., 30 pls. [CS 1841]
The German edition of Jenkins' *Ancient Greek Coins.*

111 ——— *Les Monnaies Grecques.* Translation into French by C. Biucchi. Fribourg, 1973. 326 pp., illus. [CS 1842]
The French edition of Jenkins' *Ancient Greek Coins.*

112 **Jenkins, G. Kenneth, and R. A. G. Carson.** "Greek and Roman Numismatics 1940-1950." *Historia* (Germany) 2, part 2 (1953): 214-34. [CS 1622]

An outline of the studies, theories, and conclusions put forward by researchers in the field of Greek and Roman numismatics during the decade covered. The main ideas are presented and each is cross-referenced to the publication in which the theories or conclusions were presented. The section on Greek numismatics was written by Jenkins; the Roman section was written by Carson.

113 **Jevons, F. B.** "Some Ancient Greek Pay-Bills." *The Economic Journal* 6 (1896): 470 ff. Reprint, *Journal of Numismatic Fine Arts* 4, no. 2 (October 1975): 37-40.
Jevons describes records from the building of the Erechtheum (408 B.C.) and of a temple at Eleusis (328 B.C.) which give first-hand accounts of the prices of materials, the rate of wages, and the cost of living.

114 **Jobert, Louis.** *The Knowledge of Medals: Or, Instructions for Those Who Apply Themselves to the Study of Medals, Both Ancient and Modern, from the French.* London: Printed for William Rogers, at the Sun over-against St. Dunstan's Church in Fleetstreet, 1697. 215 pp.
Translated from French by Roger Gale. This book "served as the most popular general reference to coin collecting until superseded by Pinkerton's *Essay on Medals* (see 181) a century later." [G. F. Kolbe]

115 **Jones, John R. Melville.** *Dictionary of Ancient Greek Coins.* London: Seaby, 1986. Reprinted, 1998, 2000. 248 pp., illus., 5 tables.
Defines and explains terms, names, denominations, deities, types, weight systems, and other subjects encountered in the study of Greek numismatics, arranged in an A-Z format. Presents extended entries for metals, minting, weight standards, types, hoards, and collecting Greek coins. Photographs of coins are interspersed, and five tables of early alphabets are included. [Reviewed by J. Warren in *Numismatic Chronicle* 148 (1988): 225-6, by D. K. Nelson in *Spink Numismatic Circular* 97, no. 2 (March 1989): 47, and by G. Le Rider in *Seaby Coin and Medal Bulletin* 843 (September 1989): 205].

116 ——— "Ancient Greek Gold Coinage up to the Time of Philip of Macedon." *Travaux de Numismatique Grecque Offerts à Georges Le Rider.* Edited by M. Amandry and S. Hurter. London: Spink, 1999. Pages 257-75. 1 pl.
Jones examines the use of gold coinage by Greek mints up to the time of Philip II, with the aim of establishing the reasons for its being issued in each case. Gold coinage was issued by a limited number of mints, and only occasionally—it was rare in the Greek world until late in the reign of Philip II. When it was minted, it was usually the result of a special occasion such as a temporary shortage of silver, the payment of mercenaries in a particular campaign, a payment for particular purposes in which the recipient demanded gold, or perhaps as presentation pieces to honor an important person. Dates are suggested for some issues. Authenticity remains a question for some of the coins known from only a very small number of specimens. Jones discusses issues of Lydia, Persia, Abydos, Cumae, Messana, Akragas Syracuse, Gela, Camarina, Athens, Corinth, Siphnos, Pisa, Aenus, Thasos, Amphipolis, Maroneia, Abdera, Olynthus, and Phillipi.

117 **Kerr, David.** "Notes on Famous Coins: Drachma." *Numismatic Scrapbook Magazine* 16, no. 1 (January 1950): 89-90. Illus.
A brief article describing the origin of the term "drachma" and discussing its use as a weight and then as a unit of coinage in ancient and modern times.

118 **Kim, Henry S.** *Greek Fractional Silver Coinage: A Reassessment of the Inception, Development, Prevalence, and Functions of Small Change during the Late Archaic and Early Classical Periods.* M. Phil. thesis. University of Oxford, 1994.

119 ——— "Archaic Coinage as Evidence for the Use of Money." *Money and Its Uses in the Ancient Greek World.* Edited by A. Meadows and K. Shipton. Oxford: University Press, 2001. Pages 7-21. 1 pl.
Draws a distinction between the terms "coinage" and "money." Argues that a "moneyed economy" can operate in the absence of coinage. Discusses the introduction of coinage in Asia Minor and the spread of coinage across the Greek world. Recent hoard evidence points to an earlier and more widespread use of fractional coins than previously thought. This presents a fundamental change in our understanding of how early coins were made—suggesting that when silver coinage began, it had a much broader base of uses and users. Examines the use of uncoined silver as money. Presents evidence to suggest that coins and bullion were used side-by-side as money, and that silver was used as money before coinage began.

120 ——— "Small Change and the Moneyed Economy." *Money, Labour and Land: Approaches to the Economics of Ancient Greece.* Edited by Paul Cartledge, Edward E. Cohen, and Lin Foxhall. London and New York: Routledge, 2002. Page 44-51.
Kim expands on the concepts presented by S. von Reden and L. Kurke. Examines the impact money and coinage had on society and considers how extensively money was being used by posing two questions: (1) When did a moneyed economy develop in the Greek world? (2) What sections of society participated in the growth of money use? Discusses the use of small change and questions whether the middle and lower strata of society were impacted by its use.

121 **Kos, Peter.** *The Monetary Circulation in the Southeastern Alpine Region ca. 300 BC – AD 1000.* Situla 24. Ljubljana: National Museum, 1986. 263 pp., illus., maps, 10 pls.
An analysis of monetary circulation in the region of the southeastern Alps. The coins that circulated in the region are analyzed by denomination and mint.

122 **Kraay, Colin M.** *Greek Coins and History: Some Current Problems.* London: Methuen; New York: Barnes & Noble, 1969. 81 pp., 8 pls. [CS 1847]
Consists of three essays: Historical Interpretations, The Demareteion and Sicilian Chronology, and Hoards and Circulation. The first essay reviews some traditional historical interpretations of Greek coins which have been rejected by recent researchers using analysis of die-links and overstrikes, and the use of hoard evidence. Examines the didrachms of Zacynthus bearing the name Dionos, the cistophori bearing the inscription BA EY which Kraay attributes to Aristonicus, the new-style Athenian tetradrachms bearing the name Mithradates, and the mints of Philip II (see Kraay "Historical Interpretations" below for a more complete abstract). In the second essay, Kraay discusses the "Demareteion" coinage of Syracuse and proposes a revised chronology for fifth century coinage of Sicily. Suggests the Demareteion was a small gold coin rather than a silver decadrachm as is often assumed (see Kraay "Demareteion and Sicilian Chronology" under SICILY—SYRACUSE for a more complete abstract). In the final essay, he discusses the nature of Greek coin hoards and examines some of the difficulties involved in the interpretation of hoard evidence (see Kraay "Hoards and Circulation" under HOARDS for a more complete abstract). [Reviewed by Shelagh Jameson in *Numismatic Chronicle* 7th ser., 11 (1971): 338-44, and by John Scarborough in *Classical Journal* 67, no. 3 (February-March 1972): 288-9].

123 ——— "Historical Interpretations." *Greek Coins and History: Some Current Problems.* London: Methuen; New York: Barnes & Noble, 1969. Pages 1-18. 2 pls.

This essay on coinage as a source of historical knowledge examines some of the interpretations of G. F. Hill in *Historical Greek Coins* (1906) to see if they can still be supported by more recent numismatic evidence. (1) Re-examines the coinage of Zacynthus bearing the inscription ΔΙΩΝΣ which Hill identified as Dion of Syracuse. More recent hoard evidence casts doubt on this conclusion. (2) Discusses a group of cistophoric tetradrachms signed BA EY which Hill attributed to Eumenes II of Pergamum. Points out Robinson's attribution of these coins to Aristonicus (see Robinson "Cistophori of King Eumenes" under Mysia—Pergamene Kingdom). Discusses the consequences of this attribution for the chronology of cistophoric coinage. (3) Examines the coinage attributed by Hill to the period of the revolt of Andriscus of Macedonia. Kraay points to new hoard evidence and re-assigns this coinage to Philip V—leaving Aristonicus of Macedonia with no coinage. (4) Examines the new-style Athenian coins bearing the names King Mithradates and Aristion. Hill believed these coins were struck by Mithradates VI shortly before the capture of the city by Sulla in 86 B.C. Mentions Thompson's study of the new-style coinage which places these coins into the reign of Mithradates V (ca. 150-120 B.C.). New hoard evidence calls into question Thompson's dating. Kraay suggests that Hill's attribution should not be rejected. (5) Discusses the symbols on the reverses of the coins of Philip II of Macedon which Hill accepted as mintmarks. Refutes the theory that Macedonian regal coinage supplanted local coinage in Thessaly after Philip's conquest in 344 B.C. Discusses the output of the mint at Philippi.

124 ——— *Archaic and Classical Greek Coins.* London: Methuen; Berkeley: University of California Press, 1976. Reprint, New York: Sanford J. Durst, 1993. 390 pp., illus., maps, 64 pls. [CS 1848]

A comprehensive survey of Greek coinage from its beginnings down to ca. 300 B.C. illustrated by over 1100 coins. A general discussion of coinage and minting covers types, legends, weights, dies and die-links. This is followed by an analysis of the spread and development of coinage from Lydia and Persia, to the Balkan peninsula and the Aegean islands, South Italy and Sicily, and the peripheral areas of the Greek world. The latest scholarship has been incorporated into the text. Appendices cover weight systems, Solon's coinage reform at Athens, and Samian coinage during the fifth century. Includes a comprehensive bibliography and five maps. A highly regarded standard reference. [For a more complete description of this book, see A. Kleeb's review in *SAN* 8, no. 2 (winter 1977): 29, 33. Also reviewed by M. J. Price in *Spink Numismatic Circular* 85, no. 2 (February 1977): 56-7, by G. K. Jenkins in *Numismatic Chronicle* 139 (1979): 247-52, and by R. T. Williams in *Journal of Hellenic Studies* 99 (1979): 216-7].

125 ——— "Greek Coinage and War." *Ancient Coins of the Graeco-Roman World: The Nickle Numismatic Papers.* Edited by Waldemar Heckel and Richard Sullivan. Waterloo, Ontario: Wilfrid Laurier University Press, 1984. Pages 3-18.

Kraay discusses the effects that war and the preparation for war had on coinage. He uses sixteen examples to illustrate these effects: (1) He comments on Healy's paper on the unique stater of Mytilene (see Healy "Unique Stater" under Lesbos). Suggests the coin was not issued as a declaration of independence, but rather was minted to pay for war supplies from the Black Sea area. The coin is close in fabric and design to the coinage of Cyzicus which was the standard trade coinage in the Black Sea area. (2) Mentions the hoard of coins of Melos found on the island in 1907. Suggests these coins were minted shortly before the Athenian attack on the city in 416 B.C., with a view to purchasing supplies and mercenaries to withstand the anticipated attack. [Also see Milne "Melos Hoard" and Kraay "Melos Hoard Re-examined" under Cyclades].

(3) Discusses the Siculo-Punic coinage and states that "we may assume that all the Siculo-Punic coinages which were designed for circulation in Sicily had a military purpose." Mentions a recently discovered tetradrachm of Akragas overstruck on one of the military Siculo-Punic tetradrachms. The Akragas coin was minted just before 406 B.C. (4) Describes the coinage of the Persian satraps minted at Tarsus as issues designed primarily for military purposes. (5) Briefly discusses the issues of seven different mints which are inscribed ΣΥΝ (meaning "together"). It is generally accepted that this is an abbreviation for ΣΥΝΜΑΞΙΑ (or ΣΥΝΜΑΞΙΚΟΝ), and that it is evidence of a military alliance. Kraay suggests a reading of ΣΥΝ(ΤΑΞΙΣ) or ΣΥΝ(ΤΕΛΕΙΑ), meaning "the agreed contribution of the Ephesians," referring to contributions made in gratitude (rather than out of military need) to Lysander of Sparta by a number of cities. [Also see Cawkwell "Coinage Alliance," Cook "Spartan Coins," Karweise "Lysander," and Tameanko "The Coinage of the 'Herculean Alliance,'" all under Caria].

(6) Suggests the pegasi issued by Ambracia and Anactorium were minted to serve as contributions to Corinth for her interventions in wars involving Epidamnus and Corcyra ca. 435-433 B.C. Also suggests the pegasi marked E and Π may represent the contributions of Ephyre (or Elaus) and Potidaea. (7) Suggests the issues of pegasi by mints in Acarnania, Epirus, Syracuse, Corcyra, Dyrrhachium, and Apollonia were intended to assist the expedition being organized by Timoleon in support of the Greek cities of Sicily against the Carthaginians. (8) Mentions the issues imitative of Athenian new-style coinage, but issued by the Roman questor under Sulla. (9) Mentions Athenian imitative issues minted by cities in Crete for contributions to Rome. (10) Discusses the gold coins issued by Athens in 406 B.C. to finance their fleet at a time when their silver supplies were exhausted.

(11) Mentions the late fifth century B.C. gold coinage in Sicily, minted during periods of siege. (12) Mentions the gold issues of Abdera minted at the time of an invasion, ca. 375 B.C., as well as (13) various other gold issues minted during times of emergency. (14) Discusses the gold coins and the decadrachms of Syracuse, perhaps minted to help in repelling the Carthaginians from Sicily. (15) Some of the gold coins of Philip II were used to hire mercenaries. (16) The bronze coinage of the Bretti in Italy, used during the Second Punic War.

126 ——— "Coinage." Chapter 7d in *The Cambridge Ancient History, Second Edition, Volume 4: Persia, Greece and the Western Mediterranean c. 525 to 479 B.C.* Edited by John Boardman et al. Cambridge: University Press, 1988. Pages 431-45.

Discusses the origins of coinage in mainland Greece and Asia Minor, chronologies, weight standards used, the introduction of gold and silver coins at Lydia, the introduction of coinage in Italy and Sicily, the spread of coinage to other parts of the Greek world, and the reasons for the adoption of coinage. Describes the role of coins in international trade. [Illustrations and further commentary appeared in the *Plates to Volume 4.* See Price "Coinage" below].

127 **Kraay, Colin M., and Max Hirmer.** *Greek Coins.* London: Thames and Hudson; New York: Harry N. Abrams, 1966. 396 pp., 220 pls., 4 maps. [CS 1849]

Noted for the 1329 photographs of 809 of the best specimens of Greek coinage. The photographs, by Max Hirmer, illustrate both the obverse and reverse in many instances, and the majority are enlarged from two to five times actual size. Includes twenty color plates of gold coins. Begins with Kraay's introduction to the origins of coinage, types, symbols, legends, flans, chronology, occasions of issue, and hoards. Within the geographical regions, the coins are then arranged by types, thereby emphasizing changes in style. The four maps show the sites of all the Greek mints represented by the coins described in this book. Includes full notes on each coin illustrated. Where possible, the weight of each coin is given and reference is made either to its location in a major European collection or to its appearance in a major numismatic auction. Provides indices of geographical divisions, personal names, and types. Bibliographies are included for each geographical section and a general bibliography appears at the end. [Reviewed by J. P. Barron in *Numismatic Chronicle* 7th ser., 6 (1966): 337-40, by R. A. G. Carson in *Times Literary Supplement* (February 23, 1967): 140, by J. A. W. Warren in *Journal of Hellenic Studies* 88 (1968): 243-4, and by J. G. F. Hind in *New Zealand Numismatic Journal* 12, no. 3 (January 1968): 119-21].

128 **Kraay, Colin M., and G. Kenneth Jenkins, eds.** *Essays in Greek Coinage Presented to Stanley Robinson.* Oxford: Clarendon Press, 1968. 268 pp., 33 pls., illus. [CS 1820 and 17998]

A collection of essays written to honor E. S. G. Robinson, former Keeper of the Department of Coins and Medals in the British Museum. Includes: "An Interpretation of *Ath. Pol.* ch. 10" by C. M. Kraay [4046], "Electrum Coins from Gordion" by A. R. Bellinger [504], "Observations on the *Wappenmünzen*" by R. J. Hopper [4159], "Problems of the Earliest Owls of Athens" by E. J. P. Raven [4091], "Early Tarentine Chronology" by H. A. Cahn [2842], "The Fifth-Century Diskoboloi of Kos" by J. P. Barron [4922], "Early Greek Bronze Coinage" by M. J. Price [2842], "New Evidence for the Gold-Silver Ratio" by D. M. Lewis [1528], "Lycian Coin Portraits" by W. Schwabacher [5040], "The Trihemidrachms of Corinth" by J. Warren [4286], "Electrum Coinage at Syracuse" by G. K. Jenkins [3169], "The Mints of Lysimachus" by M. Thompson [3682], "Monnaies Hellénistiques de Byzance et de Calcédoine" by H. Seyrig [3677], "A Tyrant of Karystos" by W. P. Wallace [3952], "New Light on the Roman Victoriate" by H. B. Mattingly, "Les Arsinoéens de Crète" by G. Le Rider [4416], and "The Coinages of Ariarathes VIII and Ariarathes IX of Cappadocia" by O. Mørkholm [5139]. Includes a bibliography of Stanley Robinson's works, 1914-1966. [Reviewed by Shelagh Jameson in *Numismatic Chronicle* 7th ser., 9 (1969): 334-8].

129 **Kroh, Dennis.** "Reference Reviews." Series of articles in *The Celator*.
Lists reference books in the field of ancient numismatics. Describes the contents of each book and rates its usefulness using a five-star scale based on clarity, illustrations, and availability. Gives price estimates for each book. Especially useful for listings and comments on non-English language references. The installments related to Greek coinage are:

Handbooks and General References	5, no. 1 (January 1991) 42-4
Published Collections	5, no. 2 (February 1991) 34-7
The Sylloge Nummorum Graecorum series	5, no. 3 (March 1991) 34-6
Ancient Judaic and Biblical coinage	5, no. 6 (June 1991) 36-9
Coinage of Syracuse, Sicily	5, no. 7 (July 1991) 36-8
Coins of the Seleucid Kingdom	5, no. 8 (August 1991) 40-2
Coins of Celtic and Roman Britain	5, no. 10 (October 1991) 40-2
Coins of the Parthian and Sasanian Kingdoms	5, no. 11 (November 1991) 40-2
Coins of Ptolemaic and Roman Egypt	5, no. 12 (December 1991) 45-9
Coinage of the City of Athens	6, no. 1 (January 1992) 40-3
Coinage of the Kings of Macedon	6, no. 2 (February 1992) 34-8
Coins of North Africa	6, no. 4 (April 1992) 36-8
The Coinages of Greek Italy	6, no. 6 (June 1992) 42-5
The Coinages of Greek Sicily	6, no. 8 (August 1992) 48-50
Forgeries and Counterfeits of Ancient Coins	6, no. 9 (September 1992) 48-50
The Coinage of Corinth and Her Colonies	6, no. 12 (December 1992) 44-5
Bactrian, Indo-Greek, and Indo-Scythian Kingdoms	7, no. 1 (January 1993) 40-1
The Greek Mainland	7, no. 7 (July 1993) 48-51
The Minor Hellenistic Kingdoms	7, no. 8 (August 1993) 44-7

130 ——— *Ancient Coin Reference Reviews*. Ormond Beach: Empire Coins, 1993. 107 pages.
A revised compilation of all of the author's "Reference Reviews" columns published in *The Celator* (including those on Roman and Byzantine coins). The reviews are revised and expanded from those originally published. Kroh rates each publication according to its usefulness and availability and provides estimated market prices for each. Includes an index.

131 **Kroll, John H.** "The Monetary Use of Weighed Bullion in Archaic Greece." *The Monetary Systems of the Greeks and Romans*. Edited by W. V. Harris. Oxford: University Press, 2008. Pages 12-37.
Discusses the mention of silver in Solon's laws. Then describes the use of electrum, gold, and silver bullion in western Asia Minor, how electrum was then employed for coinage, and the later introduction of bimetallic coinage that largely replaced weighed bullion. Kroll then discusses silver bullion in Magna Graecia and Sicily and describes the evidence of hoards containing silver ingots. Concludes that weighed bullion was slow to disappear as a transactional medium in the Greek world, both east and west. Therefore, the introduction of coinage may not have been of great significance in itself.

132 **Kuhner, Max H.** *Money through the Ages*. Worcester, Massachusetts: Max H. Kuhner, 1953. 19 pp. including 5 pls.
A brief history of money illustrated by specimens form the author's collection. Includes a number of Greek coins.

133 **Künker, Fritz Rudolf.** *Griechische Münzen: Faszination und Geschichte. Aufzeichnungen eines Sammlers*. Osnabrück, 2005. 697 pp., illus.

134 **Kurke, Leslie.** *Coins, Bodies, Games, and Gold: The Politics of Meaning in Archaic Greece*. Princeton: University Press, 1999. 384 pp.
Kurke analyzes the ideological functions of Greek coinage as one of a number of symbolic practices that arise for the first time in the archaic period. By linking the imagery of metals and coinage to stories about oracles, prostitutes, Eastern tyrants, counterfeiting, retail trade, and games, the author traces the rising egalitarian ideology of the polis, as well as the ongoing resistance of an elitist tradition to that development. She aims to explore the wider symbolic and social orders within which money functions in Greece, and to chart the impact of historical forces on the existing cultural template in the first 150 years of coinage.

135 **Kyrou, Adonis K.** "The Coin and History: The Confirmation of a Page of Herodotus, III 57-59." Μνήμη *Martin Jessop Price*. Translated by M. J. A. Tzamali. Edited by A. P. Tzamalis and M. J. A. Tzamali. Bibliotheca 5. Athens: The Hellenic Numismatic Society, 1996. Pages 42-50. Illus., map.
Kyrou emphasizes the importance of a coin in determining historical events which previously have been impossible to confirm. Herodotus narrated a story of an unsuccessful attempt by Samian oligarchs to overthrow Polykrates, tyrant of Samos at the end of the sixth century B.C. Then, after a brief raid of Miletus, the unsuccessful fugitives headed for the island of Hydra to establish a base of operations for their planned attacks against Aegina. They were soon driven off the island by the Aeginetans. The author presents evidence of the battle between the Samian fugitives and the Aeginetans gathered from the island of Hydra: bronze arrowheads, an archaic diobol of Samos, a coin of Aegina, and a coin of Miletus.

136 **Laing, Lloyd Robert.** *Coins and Archaeology*. London: Weidenfeld and Nicolson, 1969. 336 pp., illus., 28 pls., maps. [CS 1655]

An aid to archaeologists in understanding the applications of numismatics to the field of archaeology. Focuses on Britain, but contains some useful information on ancient numismatics as well. Overview of dies, die alignment, and minting techniques. Introduction to the study of chronologies, die-links, style, epigraphy, and metrology. Includes a chapter on hoards and their value to numismatists and archaeologists. Continues with information on stratigraphy in excavations, cleaning, recording and interpreting coin finds. Overview of scientific methods for studying coins through metallurgical techniques. The rest of the book is an introduction to early British coinage. [Reviewed by R. A. G. Carson in *Times Literary Supplement* (May 14, 1970): 545, and by John Casey in *Spink Numismatic Circular* 78, no. 10 (October 1970): 393. A very negative review by M. H. Crawford appears in *Numismatic Chronicle* 7th ser., 11 (1971): 356].

137 **Lane-Poole, Stanley, ed.** *Coins and Medals: Their Place in History and Art.* London: Elliot Stock, 1885. Second edition, 1892. 286 pp., illus. Third edition, 1894. Reprint, Chicago: Argonaut, 1968. 156 pp., 9 pls. of drawings. [CS 100]
Attempts to show what coins can teach us as historical documents and monuments of art. The discussion of Greek coinage was written by Barclay V. Head (pages 10-41 in the second edition; pages 6-21 in the reprint). It provides a general overview of the development of Greek coinage, focusing on how the coins reflect historical developments.

138 **Lange, Kurt.** *Antike Münzen.* Berlin: Verlag Gebr. Mann, 1947. 50 pp., illus. [CS 1656]
An introduction to Greek and Roman coins, illustrated by fine specimens from the Berlin Museum Collection.

139 **Lempriere, J.** *A Classical Dictionary Containing an Account of the Principal Proper Names Mentioned in Ancient Authors of the Greeks and Romans Together with an Account of Coins, Weights, and Measures.*1788. Many revisions and reprints, including New York, 1816; London: George Routledge, 1911. 667 pp. Bracken Books, 1990. 736 pp.
A dictionary including all of the names appearing in the classic works of Greek and Roman writers from earliest times through the fall of the Western Roman Empire. Later editions include other entries and articles on art, history, literature, and geography. Includes names of classical artists. The mythological entries distinguish between the Greek and Latin names of the characters. In geographic entries, most modern place-names are indicated. Includes discussions of the values of coins, weights, and measures. [Also see Anthon *A Classical Dictionary* above].

140 **Lengyel, Lancelot, Jean Babelon, and Jacques Yvon.** *Collection: Maitres et Oeuvres. Chefs-d'Oeuvres des Monnaies Grecques.* Montrouge: Éditions Corvina, 1952. 38 pp., 48 pls. [CS 3562]
Foreword by Jean Babelon. Includes 48 plates of enlargements of Greek coins (photographs by Lengyel).

141 **Lenormant, Charles.** "Les Graffiti Monétaires de l'Antiquité." *Revue Numismatique* (France) (1874-1877): 325-46.

142 **Lenormant, Charles, ed.** *Tresór de Numismatique: Numismatique des Rois Grecs.* Paris, 1849.

143 **Le Rider, Georges.** "La Numismatique Grecque comme Source d'Historie Économique." *Études Archeologiques* (France) (1963): 175-92. 3 pls. [CS 1851]

144 ——— *Études d'Histoire Monétaire et Financière du Monde Grec. Écrits 1958-1998.* Bibliothèque de la Sociéte Hellénique de Numismatique 6, and École Pratique des Hautes Études, Sciences Historiques et Philologiques I: Hautes Études Numismatiques 3. Edited by E. Papaefthymiou, F. de Callataÿ, and F. Queyrel. Athens: Hellenic Numismatic Society, 1999. Three volumes: 456 pages, 580 pages, 418 pages. 5 maps, plates.
A collection of eighty-one articles written during 1958-1998 by the French numismatist and historian Georges Le Rider. Volume 1 contains a bibliography of Le Rider's works, five essays regarding acquisitions of the Paris cabinet, three on techniques and technology, and thirteen on coinages of the Greek cities. Volume 2 includes twenty-one essays on regal coinages, and twenty-five on coin hoards. Volume 3 includes fourteen essays on financial history and monetary policy, five indices, and five maps. Text in French. [Reviewed by Alan Walker in *The Celator* 15, no. 7 (July 2001): 35-6].

145 **Le Rider, Georges, G. Kenneth Jenkins, Nancy Waggoner, and Ulla Westermark, eds.** *Kraay—Mørkholm Essays: Numismatic Studies in Memory of C. M. Kraay and O. Mørkholm.* Numismatica Lovaniensia 10. Louvain-la-Neuve: Université Catholique de Louvain, 1989. 321 pp., 72 pls.
A collection of thirty essays written in honor of Colin M. Kraay and Otto Mørkholm. Begins with a tribute to Kraay (b. 1918; d. 1982) and Mørkholm (b. 1930; d. 1983) written by Margaret Thompson. Contains a bibliography of Kraay's works by G. K. Jenkins and a bibliography of Mørkholm's works by J. S. Jensen. Photographs of both honorees are included. The essays related to ancient Greek coins are: "Les Tétradrachmes à la Couronne de Feuillage Frappés à Lébedos (Ionie)" by M. Amandry [4739], "The Silver Coins of Samos" by J. P. Barron [4844], "Histoire de Poulpes" by Bérend [3115], "Himera im IV. Jahrhundert v. Chr." By C. Boehringer [3016], "The Last Silver Coins of Velia in the Light of Two Unpublished Hoards" by A. Burnett [2889], "Riconiazioni e Cronologie in Magna Grecia" by S. Garraffo [2654], "The Royal Seleucid Mint of Seleucia on the Calycadnus" by A. Houghton [5314], "Kuprlli und Idã: Ein Neuer Lykischer Stater" by S. Hurter [5025], "Rhodian Plinthophoroi: A Sketch" by G. K. Jenkins [4968], "The Bronze Coinage of Metapontum" by A. Johnston [2789], "Two Studies in the Silver Coinage of Magnesia on the Maeander" by P. Kinns [4777], "À Propos d'un Passage des Poroi de Xénophon: La Question du Change et les Monnaies Incuses d'Italie du Sud" by G. Le Rider [2671], "Coins of King Timarchos from Nea Paphos" by I. Michaelidou-Nicolaou [5187], "Über Kimon und Euainetos im Funde von Naro" by L. Mildenberg [3183], "Les Statères Ciliciens de Pharnabaze et de Datame à Types Communs" by P. Naster [5107], "Monnaies de Pergame" by H. Nicolet-Pierre [4684], "À Propos du Trésor de Lappa (*IGCH* 35)" by M. Oeconomides-Caramessini [703], "Le Lion et le Taureau sur les Monnaies d'Acanthe" by O. Picard [3275], "The Larissa, 1968 Hoard (*IGCH* 237)" by M. Price [719], "Athens and the Western Greeks in the Fifth Century B.C.: the Numismatic Evidence" by K. Rutter [2698], "More on the 'Ptolemaic' Coins of Aradus" by A. Spaer [5441], "Cilicians and Neighbors in Miniature" by H. A. Troxell and J. H. Kagan [5068], "A New Wrinkle in the Hellenistic Coinage of Antioch/Alabanda" by N. Waggoner [4908], "The 1980 Kato Klitoria Hoard" by J. Warren [832], "Remarks on the Regal Macedonian Coinage c. 413-359 B.C." by U. Westermark [3538], and "Le Monnayage du Souverain Thrace Seuthès II" by I. Youroukova [3658]. [Reviewed by R. H. J. Ashton in *Spink Numismatic Circular* 98, no. 4 (May 1990): 124-5].

146 **Leschhorn, Wolfgang, A. V. B. Miron, and A. Miron, eds.** *Hellas und der Griechische Osten: Festschrift für Peter Robert Franke zum 70. Geburtstag.* Studien zur Geschichte und Numismatik der Griechischen Welt. Saarbrücken: SDV Saarbrücer Druckerei und Verlag, 1996. 299 pp., 11 pls.

A collection of papers written in honor of P. R. Franke on the occasion of his 70th birthday. Includes eighteen papers on historical and numismatic topics. The numismatic papers are: "Das Corpus der Obolen und Hemiobolen des Thessalischen Bundes und die Politische Geschichte Thessaliens im 2. Viertel des 5. Jahrhunderts v. Chr." By K. Liampi [3861], "Gamerses: Überlegungen zur Identität eines Lokalen Münzherrn im Achämenidenreich" by M. K. and J. Nolle [4998], "Ein Münzfund aus Eupatoria von 1917 und der Beginn der Prägung von Kerkinitis" by W. Stolba [3641], and "Influences from South Italy on Early Macedonian Bronze Coins" by U. Westermark [3541].

147 **Linders, Tullia.** "Fallen Money and Broken Crowns—or When Is a Coin Not a Coin?" *Florilegium Numismaticum: Studia in Honorem U. Westermark Edita.* Edited by Harald Nilsson. Stockholm: Svenska Numismatiska Föreningen, 1992. Pages 255-8.
In some lists of votive offerings to Greek temples "fallen coins" are mentioned. This does not mean coins which have fallen in value but coins which have fallen to the ground from their place in the temple. Using evidence from Greek temple inventories, the author examines the nature of temple offerings. Temples could receive coins either as (1) fees paid to the temple, or (2) votive offerings. Coins representing fees paid were collected in a box and could be spent on temple administration expenses. Coins dedicated to the god could not be spent and must be retained in the temple. In fact, such coins were no longer regarded as currency. If such a coin fell to the ground from its place in the temple, it would be recast, along with other debris from votive offerings, into a new dedication and thus continue to be sacred to the god.

148 **Lubbock, John.** "Greek Coinage." *American Journal of Numismatics* 14, no. 4 (April 1880): 90-1.
General comments on ancient Greek coins and coin types.

149 **Macdonald, George.** *The Evolution of Coinage.* Cambridge and New York, 1916. Reprint, Chicago: Obol International, 1980. 148 pp., 7 pls. [CS 107]
Discusses the invention and evolution of coinage from its beginnings to the present day. Examines state control over coinage, debasements and coinage reforms, coinage manufacturing techniques, types, legends, dates, and marks of value. [Reviewed in *Numismatic Chronicle* 4th ser., 16 (1916): 411-2].

150 ——— "Fifty Years of Greek Numismatics." *Transactions of the International Numismatic Congress Organized and Held in London by the Royal Numismatic Society, June 30-July 3, 1936.* Edited by J. Allan, H. Mattingly, and E. S. G. Robinson. London: B. Quaritch, 1938. Pages 3-16. [CS 1800]
The author comments on the progress of numismatic research since 1886. He discusses the influence of Barclay Head's *Historia Numorum*, early efforts to publish a corpus of Greek coins, and efforts to publish catalogues of the major museum collections. He then discusses the importance of metrological studies, the documentation of hoards, and die studies, each of which have made recent contributions to numismatic knowledge.

151 **Mackay, James A.** *Greek and Roman Coins.* London: Arthur Barker Limited, 1971. Toronto: McGraw-Hill Ryerson Ltd., 1971. 141 pp., illus. [CS 1661]
A general introduction to coinage from its origins to ca. A.D. 476, along with a summary of related history. [Reviewed by Michael Woloch in *Echos du Monde Classique* (Canada) 18, no. 2 (August 1974): 56. Woloch condemns the book because "it is replete with historical inaccuracies from beginning to end."].

152 **Mackil, Emily, and Peter G. van Alfen.** "Cooperative Coinage." *Agoranomia: Studies in Money and Exchange Presented to John H. Kroll.* Edited by Peter G. van Alfen. New York: American Numismatic Society, 2006. Pages 201-46. 2 pls.
The authors explore the economic motives of individual cities and groups of cities, for arranging cooperative coinage (coinage in which multiple communities operate together in minting and using money). Of prime importance is the fact that the local and regional economies of the Greeks were deeply interconnected. Therefore, practices such as the minting of coinage were simply responses to that fact and did not necessarily imply a political bond or the exercise of hegemony over another. They argue that the joint coinages were not driven by political motives. Rather, the political will to forge the agreements between cities was driven by *economic* advantages to each. They point out that shared coin types and fabrics are not always indicative of a cooperative arrangement. Often, this is merely imitative, or a result of cultural rather than economic ties. The authors next explore two different examples of cooperative coinage: the coinage of Mytilene and Phokaia, and the coinage of Boiotian and the Achaian *koina*. The electrum coinage of Mytilene and Phokaia lacks any apparent political, religious, or military motivations. The authors argue that the coins were produced primarily to generate revenue from coins that were produced as a commodity to be bought and sold. The Boiotian and Achaian coinages facilitated such things as payment of taxes by multiple cities to a common treasury, construction of shared sanctuaries, manning garrisons, and undertaking military campaigns. [Also see Warren *An Essay on Greek Federal Coinage* below].

153 **Martin, Thomas R.** *Sovereignty and Coinage in Classical Greece.* Princeton: University Press, 1985. 331 pp.
Investigates the relationship between sovereignty and coinage in the Greek world of the classical period. The emphasis is on the fourth century B.C. and the Macedonian kings. Studies the coinage of this period and the ancient historical evidence. Reviews the theory that Macedonian kings suppressed autonomous coinage in the fourth century. Shows how this theory was constructed and points out its faults. Rejects the theory after examining the case of Thessaly. Suggests that economic failure leading to financial weakness in the cities in Thessaly was the cause of the end of Thessalian city coinage. Examines Macedonian, Persian, and Greek evidence for strict control of the monetary system. Concludes "the numismatic, historical, documentary, and literary evidence uniformly fails to support the idea that there was operative in the classical Greek world a strongly felt connection between an abstract notion of sovereignty and the right of coinage which implied the necessity to enforce a uniform monetary circulation." Briefly examines this issue at other cities. [Reviewed by R. Billows in *American Journal of Archaeology* 91, no. 4 (October 1987): 622-3, by J. Warren in *Journal of Hellenic Studies* 107 (1987): 256-7, by Andrew Burnett in *Spink Numismatic Circular* 96, no. 4 (May 1988): 119-20, by H. Mattingly in *Numismatic Chronicle* 148 (1988): 231-3, and by E. Will in *Echos du Monde Classiche. Classical Views* (Canada) 32, n.s. 7, no. 3 (1988): 417-20. Also see Meadows "Money, Freedom, and Empire" under GENERAL WORKS—HELLENISTIC].

154 ——— "Coins, Mints and the *Polis*." *Sources for the Ancient Greek City-State. Symposium August 24-27, 1994.* Acts of the Copenhagen Polis Centre 2. Edited by Mogens Herman Hansen. Copenhagen: Munksgaard, 1995. Pages 257-91.
Martin explores the connection between coins, mints, and the Greek polis—how coinage is related to the identity of a community as a polis. Martin has previously argued against the notion that a desire to explore civic independence provides a motive for the minting of Greek coins. The level of complex transactions that are a characteristic of life in a polis made coinage necessary for a number of reasons: to ensure an adequate supply of currency for state payments and smooth trade; to allow landed elites to turn their produce into cash to help them achieve political goals; and to allow the residents of the polis to engage in impersonal transactions with strangers. [Also see Martin "Greek Polis" under ORIGINS OF COINAGE].

155   **Mathews, George D.** *The Coinage of the World: Ancient and Modern.* New York: Scott & Co., 1876. 305 pp., illus.
A general guide to the world's coinage from all eras. Pages 1-32 provide an overview of the coinage of the ancient Greek world. Engraved illustrations of coins throughout.

156   **Mattingly, Harold B.** *From Coins to History: Selected Numismatic Studies.* Ann Arbor: Michigan University Press, 2004. 310 pp., illus.
A collection of seventeen of Mattingly's essays on Greek and Roman coinage written over the previous thirty years. Those related to the Greek period are: "The Damareteion Controversy—A New Approach" [3182], "A New Light on the Early Silver Coinage of Teos" [4793], "A New Light on the Athenian Standards Decree" [4208], "The Beginning of Athenian New Style Silver Coinage" [4182], "The Coinage of Mithradates III, Pharnakes, and Mithradates IV of Pontos" [4591], "The Second Century B.C. Seleucid Countermarks: Anchor and Facing Helios Head" [5369], "Some Problems in Second-Century Attic Prosopography," and "Some Third Magistrates in the Athenian New Style Silver Coinage" [4181].

157   ——— "Circulation Areas of Ancient Coinage." *Numismatic Chronicle* 163 (2003): 433-5. 2 pls.
The Royal Numismatic Society President's Address. Provides general comments on the usefulness of hoard evidence for understanding circulation patterns of ancient coins.

158   **Meadows, Andrew, and Kirsty Shipton, eds.** *Money and Its Uses in the Ancient Greek World.* Oxford: University Press, 2001. 300 pp.
A collection of essays related to (1) monetization, money supply, and the politics of coinage, and (2) money and society. The essays are: "Archaic Coinage as Evidence for the Use of Money" by H.S. Kim [119], "Coinage and Democracy at Athens" by J. Trevett [4143], "The Politics of Coinage: Athens and Antigonus Gonatas" by G. Oliver [4087], "Money, Freedom, and Empire in the Hellenistic World" by A. Meadows [285], "The Politics of Monetization in Third-Century B.C. Egypt" by S. von Reden [6699], "The Coinage of Rhodes 408-c. 190 B.C." by R. Ashton [4950], "Temples, Credit, and the Circulation of Money" by J. Davies [54], "Money and the Élite in Classical Athens" by K. Shipton [220], and "Money Use among the Peasantry of Ptolemaic and Roman Egypt" by J. Rowlandson [295]. [Reviewed by John H. Kroll in *Bryn Mawr Classical Review* 2002.07.24, and by Wolfgang Fischer-Bossert in *Revue Suisse de Numismatique* 82 (2003): 137-46].

159   **Meadows, Andrew, and Richard W. C. Kan.** *History Re-Stored: Ancient Greek Coins from the Zhuyuetang Collection.* 2004. 117 pp., illus., 3 maps.
A good overview of ancient Greek coinage from its origins through the end of the Hellenistic era, illustrated with 126 coins from the "Zhuyuetang Collection" (the private collection of Richard Kan, a Hong-Kong based collector) as exhibited at the Hong Kong Museum of History. The collection contains many fine rarities including a denomination set of the electrum coinage of "Phanes," a Poros decadrachm of Alexander the Great, and an Athenian decadrachm.

159a **Metcalf, William E., ed.** *The Oxford Handbook of Greek and Roman Coinage.* Oxford: Oxford University Press, 2012. 688 pp., illus.
Begins with a general introduction by Metcalf followed by "The Substance of Coinage: The Role of Scientific Analysis in Ancient Numismatics" by Matthew J. Ponting. The subsequent thirty-two chapters, each by a distinguished scholar, begin with the first evidence of coins in Western Asia Minor in the seventh century B.C. and continue up to the transformation of coinage at the end of the Roman Empire. In addition to providing the essential background and current research questions of each of the major coinages, the handbook also includes articles on the application of numismatic evidence to the disciplines of archaeology, economic history, art history, and ancient history. Includes appendices, a glossary of specialized terms, indices of mints, persons, and general topics, and nearly 900 illustrations. The chapters related to the Greek period are: "The Monetary Background of Early Coinage" by John H. Kroll, "Asia Minor to the Ionian Revolt" by Koray Konuk, "The Coinage of the Persian Empire" by Michael Alram, "The Coinage of Athens, Sixth to First Century B.C." by Peter G. van Alfen, "Aegina, the Cyclades, and Crete" by Kenneth Sheedy, "The Coinage of Italy" by N. K. Rutter, "The Coinage of Sicily" by Wolfgang Fischer-Bossert, "Greece and the Balkans to 360 B.C." by Selene Psoma, "Royal Hellenistic Coinages: From Alexander to Mithradates" by François de Callataÿ, "The Hellenistic World: The Cities of Mainland Greece" by Richard Ashton, "The Coinage of the Ptolemies" by Catharine C. Lorber, "The Seleucids" by Arthur Houghton, "Greek Coinage of Palestine" by Oren Tal, and "The Coinage of the Parthians" by Fabrizio Sinisi. Also includes eighteen chapters on Roman coinage.

160   **Michell, Humfrey.** *The Economics of Ancient Greece.* New York: MacMillan Co. Cambridge: University Press, 1940. 415 pp. Second edition, Cambridge: W. Heffner & Sons, 1957. 427 pages. [CS 1061]
This study of ancient economics includes chapters on agriculture, mining and minerals, labor, industry, commerce, trade, piracy, money and banking, and public finance. The chapter on money and banking includes overviews of the introduction, spread, and development of coinage in the Greek world. Discusses monometallism, bimetallism, debasement of the coinage, banking, money-changing, and lending.

161   **Mildenberg, Leo.** "Numismatic Evidence." *Harvard Studies in Classical Philology* 91 (1987): 381-95. Illus. Reprinted in *Leo Mildenberg. Vestigia Leonis: Studien zur Antiken Numismatik Israels, Palästinas und der Östlichen Mittelmeerweit.* Novum Testamentum et Orbis Antiquus 36. Edited by U. Hübner and E. Knauf. Freiburg: Universitätsverlag, and Göttingen: Vandenhoeck & Ruprecht, 1998. Pages 253-62.
Provides examples of factual evidence obtainable from coins using as examples overstrikes, die links, hoards, types and legends, and imitations. Discusses negative evidence (the fact that no coins of a certain issue were found in a given excavation). [Also see Hübner and Knauf *Vestigia Leonis* above].

162   **Milne, Joseph G.** *Greek Coinage.* Oxford: Clarendon Press, 1931. 131 pp., 12 pls. [CS 1854]
A general history of Greek coinage illustrated by a selection of major coin types. Discusses the first use of coins, the spread of coinage to Aegina and Corinth, and Solon's reforms. Includes a survey of coinage before the Persian invasion, Athenian and Aeginetan coinage in the fifth century B.C., Sicilian coinage, fourth-century and Hellenistic coinages.

163   ——— "The Use of Coins for Teaching Greek and Roman History." *Transactions of the International Numismatic Congress Organized and Held in London by the Royal Numismatic Society, June 30-July 3, 1936.* Edited by J. Allan, H. Mattingly, and E. S. G. Robinson. London: B. Quaritch, 1938. Pages 86-95.
Milne suggests ways in which the evidence of coins may be made more useful for the teaching of history. He emphasizes the importance of a coin's bullion value and weight, as opposed to its denomination, during the Greek period. Discusses in general terms the evidence regarding trade patterns which can be gathered from a study of overstruck and counterstruck coins, the copying of the types and symbols of one city by another city, and the use of hoard evidence.

164 ——— *Greek and Roman Coins and the Study of History.* London: Methuen, 1939. Reprints, Westport: Greenwood Press, 1971; Chicago: Obol International, 1980. 128 pp., 16 pls. [CS 1664]
Suggests to teachers of ancient history what kinds of information can be derived from the study of ancient coins. Chapters cover metals, debasement, fabric, dies, art, types, mints, countermarks, weight-standards, and hoards. Each chapter presents basic information related to both Greek and Roman coinage. [Reviewed by John Allan in *Numismatic Chronicle* 5th ser., 19 (1939): 294].

165 **Mionnet, Théodore E.** *Description des Médailles Antiques: Grecques et Romaines.* Seven volumes. Paris, 1806-08. *Supplement.* Nine volumes. Paris, 1819-37. Reprint, Graz: Akademische Druk- und Verlagsanstalt, 1972-73. Sixteen volumes. 192 pls. [CS 1855]

166 **Montgomery, Hugo.** "Silver, Coins and the Wealth of a City-State." *Opuscula Atheniensia* (Sweden) 15, no. 10 (1984): 123-33.
"By comparison between different areas where early Greek coins were minted, the author concludes that the exploitation of gold and silver mines did not in itself convey wealth to a city-state unless the state possessed also the political power and military capacity to increase its influence." [U. Westermark, *NL* 116]

167 **Mørkholm, Otto.** "A History of the Study of Greek Numismatics. 1. c. 1760-1835: The Foundations." and "2. c. 1835-1870: The Period of Consolidation." *Nordisk Numismatisk Årsskrift* (Sweden) (1979-1980): 5-21. "3. c. 1870-1940: The Scientific Organization." *Nordisk Numismatisk Årsskrift* (1982): 7-26.
Mørkholm traces the history of the collecting and studying of Greek coinage. (1) This period was highlighted by the formation and publication of the great museum collections. The author begins with the work of Joseph Pellerin (b. 1684; d. 1782) who was the first to use a geographical arrangement in cataloguing Greek coins. He was also the first scholar to publish a coin hoard as an entity. Discusses Joseph Eckhel's (1792-8) refinement of the system of classification. Discusses the contributions of Sestini, Brøndsted, Cousinéry, Leake, and Mionnet. (2) This period is marked by the appearance of specialized numismatic publications and societies. Discusses the contributions of Burgon, Borrell, Rochette, Lenormant, Beule, Longpérier, Cavedoni, Fiorelli, and Sambon. Discusses the increase in travel to Europe and the advances made by Fox, Cunningham, Fellows, Newton, and Duc de Luynes. Also during this period, the study of metrology began, and numismatic monographs began to be published. Discusses the efforts of Müller. During this period, errors were made in cataloguing and attribution due to the reliance on arguments from analogy or probability. Numismatic studies were lacking in true scientific method. (3) This period saw growth in the general interest in Greek coinage, and benefited from greater means of communication. Highlights were the introduction of photography and greater international cooperation among scholars. In England, this period saw the publication of catalogues of the British Museum collection, the McClean and Weber collections, catalogues by Babelon, and the works of Head emphasizing the importance of style in classifying coins chronologically. Evans made use of hoard evidence. Important work was done by Hill, Seltman, Milne, and Robinson. In Europe, important work was being done by Friedländer, von Sallet, Dressel, von Prokesch-Osten, Mommsen, Imhoof-Blumer, Regling, Schwabacher, Boehringer, Six, Hirsch, Babelon, Gabrici, Rizzo, and Svoronos. Die-links became a focus of research. In the United States, important work was done by Newell, Noe, and Baldwin-Brett. The publication of excavation finds became common.

168 ——— "Some Reflections on the Production and Use of Coinage in Ancient Greece." *Historia* (Germany) 31 (1982): 290-305.
Mørkholm comments on the use of coinage and monetary policies in Athens in the fourth century B.C. Discusses weights, Solon's reforms, the Athenian coinage decree and its implications for our knowledge of the use of coins in the marketplace. Also comments on the use of coinage, countermarks, and changes in the money supply during the Hellenistic period—in Egypt under the Ptolemies, Byzantium and Calchedon ca. 235-220 B.C., the Pergamene Kingdom ca. 175 B.C., and the Seleucid Kingdom in the second century B.C.

169 **Mørkholm, Otto, and Nancy M. Waggoner, eds.** *Greek Numismatics and Archaeology: Essays in Honor of Margaret Thompson.* Wetteren: Numismatique Romaine, 1979. 326 pp., 41 pls. [CS 1828]
A collection of thirty essays written to honor Margaret Thompson upon her retirement as chief curator at the American Numismatic Society. Includes a bibliography of Margaret Thompson's work. The essays related to Greek numismatics are: "Tetradrachms of Aegeae (Cilicia)" by H. Bloesch [5076], "Zu Finanzpolitik und Münzprägung des Dionysios von Syrakus" by C. Boehringer [3117], "The Athenian Coinage Law of 375/4 B.C." by T. V. Buttrey [3987], "Olynthus and Syracuse" by H. A. Cahn [3125], "The Bronze Coinage of Agathocles" by R. R. Holloway [3162], "Der Tissaphernes-Fund" by S. Hurter [6209], "A Tarantine Footnote" by G. K. Jenkins [2848], "Fifteen Turtles and Tortoises" by F. F. Jones [4232], "The Late Cistophori of Apameia" by F. S. Kleiner [5011], "The Isparta Hoard" by C. M. Kraay [632], "A Chronology of Early Athenian Bronze Coinage ca. 350-250 B.C." by J. H. Kroll [4051], "Un Tétradrachme Hellénistique de Cnide" by G. Le Rider [4887], "Yehud: A Preliminary Study of the Provincial Coinage of Jerusalem" by L. Mildenberg [5804], "Un Tétradrachme Athénien du Nouveau Style Découvert en Dacie" by B. Mitrea [4183], "The Portrait Coinage of Ptolemy V: The Main Series" by O. Mørkholm [6646], "Empreintes de Sceaux Hellénistiques de Warka et Monnaies Séleucides" by P. Naster [5398], "Les Monnaies des Deux Derniers Satrapes d'Égypte avant la Conquête d'Alexandre" by H. Nicolet-Pierre [6550], "The 1970 Myrina Hoard of Aeginetan Staters" by M. C. Oeconomides [4242], "On Attributing Alexanders—Some Cautionary Tales" by M. J. Price [3471], "A Numismatic Commentary on the Ptolemaic Cult Oinochoai" by D. B. Thompson [6689], "Winged Carians" by H. A. Troxell [4904], "Tetradrachms from Babylon" by N. M. Waggoner [6028], "On Numismatic Evidence" by G. D. Weinberg and S. S. Weinberg [251], "Overstrikes of Taras on Didrachms of Acragas" by U. Westermark [2866], and "Near Eastern Elements in the Tetradrachms of Alexander the Great: The Eastern Mints" by O. H. Zervos [3547].

170 **Mosher, Stuart.** "The Story of Money as Told by the Knox Collection." *Bulletin of the Buffalo Society of Natural Sciences* 17, no. 2 (1936): 1-77. 18 pls. [CS 1570]
A brief history of coinage. Includes illustrations and a few brief descriptions of Greek coins.

171 **Moucharte, G., M. B. Borba Florenzano, F. de Callataÿ, P. Marchetti, L. Smolderen, and P. Yannopoulos, eds.** *Liber Amicorum Tony Hackens.* Numismatica Lovaniensia 20. Louvain-la-Neuve: Université Catholique de Louvain, 2007. 461 pp., illus.
A festschrift dedicated to Tony Hackens, containing 20 essays in French, 6 in English, 2 in Italian, and 1 in Spanish. The essays are divided into five topics: (1) mint practices, (2) metrology and metal alloys, (3) numismatic iconography, (4) monetary studies, and (5) circulation. The papers related to ancient Greek coinage are: "Studies of Silver Coins of Alexander of Macedon from the Collection of the State Hermitage" by Y. L. Djukov et al. [3341], "The Kainon Coinage" by R. R. Holloway [3166], "Marduk and the Lion: A Hoard of Babylonian Lion Staters" by P. Iossif and C. Lorber [6022], "Le Trésor de Corfu, 1997" by K. Preka and S. Gjongecaj [713], "Le Trésor de Zougra (*IGCH* 261) et la Circulation Monétaire dans le Péloponnèse au IIe Siècle" by M. Oeconomides and M. L. and P. Marchetti [705], "L'Atelier Athénien: Réflexions sur la 'Politique Monétaire' d'Athènes à l'Epoque Classique" by C. Flament [4016], "Arguments pour une Datation (Très) Tardive du Début des Émissions Monétaires en Argent de Phillipe II de Macédoine" by V. Van Driessche [3526], "Sur l'Étalon Monétaire en Usage à Poseidonia" by L. Brousseau [2802], "Remarques Numismatiques à Propos d'un Traite entre Attale Ier de Pergame et la Cité de Malla (Crète)" by C. Doyen [4670], "Méthode de l'Intervalle de Confiance pour l'Étude Comparative des Poids des Émissions

Monétaires" by L. Villagonga [1621], "Le 'Satyre et la Ménade' Thasiens: Étude d'Iconography Numismatique" by D. Paléothodoros [3768], "A Note on the Triskeles as the Badge of Sicily: Territorial Identity in Ancient Greek Coinage" by M. B. Borba Florenzano [2908], "Le Monnayage en Argent d'Oinoanda: Après Apamée (188 av. J.-C.) ou Aprés Mithradate (85-82 av. J.-C.)?" by F. de Callataÿ [5018], and "Origen, Uso y Función de la Moneda en la Sociedad Hispana: Siglos IV-I a.C." by F. Chaves Tristan [2130]. [Reviewed by A. S. Walker in *The Celator* 22, no. 8 (August 2008): 35-7, 40, 56, and by John Morcom in *Spink Numismatic Circular* 117, no. 3 (July 2009): 119-20].

172 **Newton, Charles T.** "Greek Numismatics." Parts 1 and 2. In *Essays on Art and Archaeology*, by C. T. Newton. London: Macmillan & Co., 1880. Pages 404-26.
These two essays are essentially reviews of the recently published first two volumes of the *Catalogue of Greek Coins in the British Museum*, covering Italy and Sicily. Provides general comments on the coinage and the contents of the museum's collection. Comments on the classification and arrangement of the catalogues.

173 **Nicolet-Pierre, Hélène.** *Numismatique Grecque*. Paris: Armand Colin, 2002. 302 pp., illus.
An advanced introductory work on Greek numismatics. [Reviewed by J. H. Kroll in *American Numismatic Society Magazine* 3, no. 1 (spring 2004): 61-2].

174 **Nilsson, Harald, ed.** *Florilegium Numismaticum: Studia in Honorem U. Westermark Edita*. Stockholm: Svenska Numismatiska Föreningen, 1992. 382 pp., illus.
A collection of forty-three essays written in honor of the numismatist and author Ulla Westermark on the occasion of her retirement after more than thirty-five years of service at the Royal Coin Cabinet in Sweden. The essays related to Greek numismatics are: "The Beginnings of Coinage in the West: Archaic Selinus" by C. Arnold-Biucchi [3075], "Some Forgeries of Rhodian Didrachms of the Mid Third Century B.C." by R. Ashton [4943], "Le Lièvre et le Poulpe" by Denyse Bérend [877], "Ehrenrettung Einer Syrakusanischen Goldmünze" by C. Boehringer [3118], "Faut-il Faire Tomber les Foudres?" by F. de Callataÿ and D. Gerin [912], "Late Silver Issues of Rhegium: A Janus Head Type in Rhegium" by E. E. Clain-Stefanelli [2818], "The Coinage of Demetrius I at Ake-Ptolemais" by A. Houghton [5319], "Teos over Tanagra" by S. Hurter [4766], "Philetaerus in Norway: A Recent Acquisition in a Norwegian Private Collection" by H. Ingvaldsen [4674], "Les Tétradrachmes Attalides au Portrait de Philétaire" by G. Le Rider [4679], "Fallen Money and Broken Crowns—or When Is a Coin Not a Coin?" by T. Linders [147], "The Early Facing Head Drachms of Thessalian Larissa" by C. Lorber [3863], "The Mint of the First Carthaginian Coins" by L. Mildenberg [6728], "Les Monnaies d'Argent de Syros" by H. Nicolet-Pierre and M. Amandry [4468], "The *IGCH* 101 Hoard and the Circulation of the Tortoise in the Peloponnesus" by M. Oeconomides [4244], "Die Münzstätte Zone in Thrakien" by E. Schönert-Geiss [3636], "Protesilaos: First to Fall at Troy and Hero in Northern Greece and Beyond" by C. Vermeule [1125], "Petit Trésor de la Deuxième Guerre Punique avec une Drachme des Bruttiens" by L. Villaronga [820], "Eukleidas—Ein Goldschmied?" by M. Alföldi [3113], and "Les Bronzes Chypriotes Représentant une Tête Féminine et une Croix Ansée dans une Couronne Laurée" by A. Destrooper-Georgiades [5171]. Concludes with H. Nilsson's bibliography of the writings of Ulla Westermark. The other essays, written in several languages, deal with Roman and Byzantine numismatics. [Reviewed by Ian Carradice in *Numismatic Chronicle* 153 (1993): 274-5].

175 **Oeconomides, Mando.** "Athens Collection Among Most Important." *Coin World* (October 28, 1981): 44, 46, 49. Illus.
Text of a presentation by Oeconomides, curator of the numismatic collection at the National Archaeological Museum, Athens. Despite the title, this article presents a summary of the history of coinage from its origins through the Byzantine period. Also includes brief comments on engraved gems.

176 ——— *Archaia Nomismata*. Athens: Ekdotike Athenon, 1996. 270 pp., illus.
A review of Greek coinage from the archaic through the Hellenistic period. Includes commentary and a catalogue of 189 coins selected to emphasize an art historical appreciation of the finest Greek coins. The coins are illustrated with color enlargements. [Reviewed by Kenneth A. Sheedy in *Numismatic Chronicle* 159 (1999): 366-7].

177 **Pellerin, Joseph.** *Recueil de Médailles de Peuples et de Villes, Qui n'ont Point Encore été Publiées ou Qui Sont Peu Connues*. 12 parts. Paris, 1762-1778. Engraved illustrations.
Pellerin was the first to classify Greek coins in geographical order, rather than alphabetical order.

178 **Peter, Ulrike, ed.** *Stephanos Nomismatikos: Edith Schönert-Geiss zum 65. Geburtstag*. Berlin: Akademie Verlag, 1998. 700 pp., illus.
A collection of fifty-five essays in ancient history and numismatics written in honor of Edith Schönert-Geiss on the occasion of her 65th birthday. Those related to ancient Greek numismatics are: "A Hoard of Bronze Coins of Lysimachia" by M. Arslan [5233], "The Earliest Coins of Alexandria Troas" by A. Burnett [4702], "Le Derniers Alexandres Posthumes d'Odessos à Lumière d'Une Trouvaille Récente" by F. de Callataÿ [3587], "Beginn und Ende der Münzprägung in Noricum" by G. Dembski [2548], "Un Bronze Surfrappé de Ptolémée Ier/Demétrios Poliorcète Trouvé dans les Fouilles de l'Université d'Arizona à Dali (Chypre)" by A. Destrooper-Georgiades [6575], "*CH* IV 28 et la Chronologie des Monnaies d'Argent d'Histria au 4e Siècle av. J.C." by K. Dimitrov [3708], "Über die Darstellungen von Schild und Schwert auf einem Münztyp des Bosporanischen Königs Leukon II (Zweite Hälfte des 2 Jhs. V. Chr.)" by N. Frolova [4545], "Vth c. B.C. Coin Hoard from Thrace–Örcünlü (1970)" by T. Gökyildirim [571], "Le Monete di Imbros dal Santuario dei Cabiri a Lemno" by G. Gorini [3599], "Zur Chronologie der Thessalischen Koinongrägung im 2 und 1 Jh. v. Chr.: Ein Weiterer Schatzfund aus Südthessalien" by D. Klose [3858], "Ein Frühptolemäischer Bronzeschatz in Deutschem Privatbesitz" by H.-C. Noeski [6660], "Münzen als Zeugnisse für die Geschichte der Hellenisierung Kleinasiens" by J. Nollé [4518], "Ein Neuer Vorschlag zur Chronologie der Koson-Münzen" by C. Preda [3622], "Die Münzen des 2-1 Jhs v. Chr. in der Sammlung des Historischen Museums von Stara Zagora" by I. Prokopov and M. Minkova [1741], "Ein Unbekannter Gegenstempel auf einer Tetradrachme von Side" by H. Schubert [5065], "ΣΑΜΜΑΣ: Zur Prägung eines Bosporanischen Tyrannen" by W. Stolba [4561], "ΓΕΤΑΣ ΗΔΟΝΕΩΝ ΒΑΣΙΛΕΥΣ" by M. Tatscheva [3296], "Bronzemünzen der Amatokos vom Typ Weintraube/Doppelaxt mit Einem Bisher Unbekannten Symbol, dem Kantharos" by S. Topalov [3648], "Bemerkungen zur Chronologie der Keltischen Münzen vom Kapostaler Typ" by M. Torbágyi [2622], "Die Chronologie der Keltischen Münzprägung am Mittelrhein" by D. Wigg and J. Riederer [2626]. Also includes a bibliography of Schönert-Geiss' works.

179 **Petrie, Alfred E. H.** "Early Greek Coins." *The Canadian Numismatic Journal* (Canada) 1, no. 2 (February 1956): 22-5.
In this outline of a talk given to a coin club, Petrie very briefly describes the introduction of Greek coinage and the development of coin-types. Also comments on collecting Greek coins. [The information provided on the origins of coinage is obsolete].

180 **Picard, Olivier.** "La Valeur des Monnaies Grecques en Bronze." *Revue Numismatique* (France) 153, no. 6 (1998): 7-18.

Numismatists don't agree on the identification of the chalkos among Greek bronze coins. In European Greece, the chalkos was the smallest bronze unit in a monetary system. It had no fractions, and the multiples of the chalkos were usually called obols. In the eastern part of the Hellenistic world, the chalkos is usually identified as a heavier coin, divisible into many fractions. Picard explores whether two different bronze systems coexisted.

181 **Pinkerton, John.** *An Essay on Medals, or An Introduction to the Knowledge of Ancient and Modern Coins and Medals; Especially those of Greece, Rome, and Britain.* London: James Dodsley, 1784. 324 pp. Second edition, 2 volumes: London: J. Edwards and J. Johnson, 1789. 302 pp., 3 pls.; 364 pp., 3 pls. Third edition, London: Cadell and Davies, 1808. 376 pp., 3 pls., and 448 pp., 3 pls.
Reviews the literature on ancient coins starting in 1548. Then discusses the knowledge obtainable from the study of coins of all ages and their connection to the study of art. Explains the Greek weight standards, denominations, portraits, reverse types, symbols, and legends. One plate contains engravings of Greek coins. Volume 2 contains tables of abbreviations, eras used in dating at various cities, magistrates' names appearing on coins, games mentioned on coins, and a rarity rating for various coin types arranged by city. These volumes also cover Roman and British coinage.

182 **Porteous, John.** "The Nature of Coinage." *Coins: An Illustrated Survey 650 B.C. to the Present Day.* Edited by Martin J. Price. New York: Methuen, 1980. Pages 7-19. Illus.
The author examines coin-types as a reflection of the age and civilization which made them. Coins are very inter-related. Of all coinage, the Greek coinage has had the widest influence—being the direct ancestor, through Rome, of all western coinage, and through the Seleucids, the Parthians, and the Sassanians, of all Islamic coinage. Porteous briefly describes the characteristics of the world's coinage: Greece, Rome, India, China, Islamic, Sasanian, Byzantine, early European, and later coinages.

183 **Price, Martin J.** *Greek Bronze Coinage c. 450-150 B.C., Its Introduction, Circulation, and Value, with Particular Reference to the Series of Corinth.* Ph.D. dissertation. Cambridge University, 1967.

184 ——— "Early Greek Bronze Coinage." *Essays in Greek Coinage: Presented to Stanley Robinson.* Edited by C. M. Kraay and G. K. Jenkins. Oxford: Clarendon Press, 1968. Pages 90-104. [CS 2046]
Examines the origins and early history of bronze coinage. The earliest datable bronze coins of mainland Greece are those of Archelaus I of Macedon, ca. 413-399 B.C. Either through necessity due to the shortage of silver, a profit motive, or the need for small change for daily transactions, bronze coinage began. The seeds for a token coinage were sown by the frequent over-valuation of electrum and silver coins. The first Greek bronze coins were in the Sicilian cities, ca. 425 B.C. Olbia was producing bronze coinage long before 400. Athens issued bronze coinage during the economic crisis after the Peloponnesian War. These were withdrawn and declared invalid by 393 B.C. Most Greek cities began to strike bronze only after the emergency issue of Athens. By 300 B.C., bronze coinage had spread over the whole of Greek lands. Discusses numerous cities and the chronology of their bronze issues, including the odd-shaped cast bronze pieces of Akragas and the dolphin-shaped issues of Olbia. States that the weights of bronze coins were of little consequence since the coins are of token value only.

185 ——— "The Function of Early Greek Bronze Coinage." *Le Origini della Monetazione di Bronzo in Sicilia e in Magna Grecia (Atti del VI Convegno del Centro Internazionale di Studi Numismatici, Napoli Aprile 17-22, 1977).* Supplement to *Annali. Istituto Italiano di Numismatica* (Italy) 25 (1979) 351-65.
Price examines the appearance of a regular system of very small coin denominations and the phenomenon of overvaluation of bronze coins in relation to their intrinsic value. Very small denominations enabled 'shopping' to take place. Shopping likely was an outgrowth of the introduction of small coins—not the other way around. Mentions the unusual cast bronze coins of the Black Sea area (S. Russia, Olbia, Istros), Akragas, and Selinus, and seeks to understand why they were not made to look like coins. Price previously suggested that the cast pieces of Selinus may have been privately issued tokens (see Price "Selinus" under SICILY—SELINUS). He now proposes that the cities may have rejected the issuance of fiduciary bronze coins and the issuance of impractically large bronze coins (which would be necessary if their intrinsic value were to match their denomination). But if the local shopkeepers were determined to have their tokens, the cities may have insisted that the shape should not closely resemble that of coins. Nonetheless, in Sicily, their denominations were based on the pre-existing division of the litra, but a new denomination was introduced—the uncia. The function of the new bronze pieces was primarily to facilitate retail trade, as one medium within the general barter system. Therefore, it was not thought necessary to make these new barter-pieces coin-like. The later adoption of bronze coinage by the cities reflects a change in the social system of payments. In the questions and answers from the congress participants, Holloway emphasizes that the unusual and clumsy forms of the cast pieces may have been intended to prevent these pieces from leaving the local economy—although Price refutes this theory in his response.

186 ——— "The First Three Centuries of Coinage." *Coins: An Illustrated Survey 650 B.C. to the Present Day.* Edited by Martin J. Price. New York: Methuen, 1980. Pages 26-41. Illus.
An overview of the origin and development of coinage, 650 to 323 B.C. Discusses the effect of silver supplies on coinage, the introduction of fractional denominations, the introduction of bronze coinage, the use of monograms as control marks, and the spread and use of coinage.

187 ——— "The Coinage of the Northern Aegean." *Coinage and Administration in the Athenian and Persian Empires.* BAR International Series 343. Edited by Ian Carradice. Oxford: British Archaeological Reports, 1987. Pages 43-7. 2 pls.
An examination of coinage in northern Greece based upon evidence from the "Decadrachm" hoard (see Carradice *Coinage and Administration* under ATTICA—GENERAL WORKS). Supports the belief that early coinages were used extensively in trade—not just for the payment of taxes and tribute. Combined with evidence from the Asyut hoard (see Price and Waggoner "Asyut Hoard" under HOARDS), this hoard provides evidence for the chronology of the issues of the Greek cities of the northern Aegean. Examples are given for Abdera, Ainos, Acanthus, Mende, and the Macedonian tribes. Concludes that there is no reason to believe that the Athenian Coinage Decree had any effect on the coinages of the north Aegean. Also notes that the large denomination tribal issues disappear in the mid-fifth century B.C. and are replaced by smaller denominations of other cities. Suggests this was caused by the depletion of silver sources rather than by the effects of a coinage decree.

188 ——— "Coinage." Chapter 15 in *The Cambridge Ancient History: Plates to Volume 4, Greece and the Mediterranean c. 525 to 479 B.C.* New edition. Edited by John Boardman. Cambridge: University Press, 1988. Pages 237-48. Illus.
A summary of the history of coinage from its beginnings in the seventh century B.C. to the early fifth century B.C. Briefly discusses the problems surrounding the date of the first coins. Briefly discusses the problems related to the coins inscribed *Walwel*, *Phanes*, and *Kalil*. Illustrates some of the most important coin-types of the period. Mentions some of the most important coin hoards including the Artemisium deposit, the Asyut hoard, and others. Price's emphasis is on establishing the relative chronology of coinage, illustrating its spread from east to west, and illustrating the development of types and fabric. [Also see Kraay "Coinage" above].

189 **Price, Martin J., ed.** *Coins: An Illustrated Survey 650 B.C. to the Present Day.* New York: Methuen, 1980. 320 pp., illus., maps. [CS 122]
Presents the main trends of coinage from its beginnings through modern times illustrated by more than 2000 photographs and accompanied by twenty essays by specialists relating the coins to their cultural and historical background. Of particular interest to the collector of Greek coins are: "The Nature of Coinage" by J. Porteous [182], "Money Before Coinage" by M. Balmuth [377], "The First Three Centuries of Coinage" by M. Price [186], "The Hellenistic Kingdoms and Coinages 323-170 B.C." by I. Carradice [272], "Rome and the Hellenistic World" by A. Burnett [271], "The Celts" by D. Nash [2198], "The Ancient Near East" by D. Sellwood [5217], and "Ancient India" by D. MacDowell [6391].

190 **Price, Martin J., Andrew Burnett, and Roger Bland, eds.** *Essays in Honour of Robert Carson and Kenneth Jenkins.* London: Spink & Son, 1993. 368 pp., 48 pls.
Contains twenty-eight essays dedicated to Carson and Jenkins, former Keepers of the Department of Coins and Medals at the British Museum, on the occasion of their seventy-fifth birthdays. Includes bibliographies of Carson's and Jenkins' published works. Includes the following essays devoted to Greek numismatics: "A New Coin of the Serdaioi(?) at the ANS" by C. Arnold-Biucchi [2826], "Arethusa Soteira" by H. Cahn [3127], "RSMLQRT" by L. Mildenberg [3106], "A Revised Arrangement for the Earliest Coinage of Rhodes" by R. Ashton [4945], "The Staters of Archelaus: A Die Study" by U. Westermark [3539], "More from Memphis and the Syria 1989 Hoard" by M. Price [720], "Antiochos Hierax am Hellespont" by C. Boehringer [5252], "Les Ressources Financières de Séleucos IV (187-175) et le Paiement de l"Indemnité aux Romains" by G. Le Rider [5355], "The Ma'Aret En-Nu'man Hoard, 1980" by Harold B. Mattingly [657], "Towards a Resolution of the Achaian League Silver Coinage Controversy: Some Observations on Methodology" by J. Warren [4318], and "Parthian Mint Operations" by D. Sellwood [6116]. Also includes numerous essays devoted to Roman numismatics. [Reviewed by Silvia Hurter in *Spink Numismatic Circular* 102, no. 7 (September 1994): 308-9, and by T. V. Buttrey in *Spink Numismatic Circular* 103, no. 10 (December 1995): 382-3].

191 **Prime, William C.** *Coins, Medals, and Seals: Ancient and Modern, Illustrated and Described.* New York: Harper & Brothers, 1861. 292 pp., 65 pls. of engravings.
An introduction to numismatics. Begins with the history of coinage during the Greek and Roman periods. Continues with sections on Jewish, British, early American, and early European coinage. Discusses methods of striking coins. Provides advice to young collectors.

192 **Pryer, Charles.** "Early Greek History, as Illustrated by its Coins." *Proceedings of the American Numismatic Society, 1900-1901.* New York: American Numismatic Society. Page 62.

193 **Psoma, Selene, and Dimitra I. Tsangari.** "Monnaie Commune et États Fédéraux. La Circulation des Monnayages Frappés par les États Fédéraux du Monde Grec." *The Idea of European Community in History, Volume 2: Aspects of Connecting Poleis and Ethne in Ancient Greece.* Edited by K. Buraselis and K. Zoumboulakis. Athens: National and Capodistrian University of Athens, 2003. Pages 111-42.

194 **Raoul-Rochette, Désiré.** *Mémoires de Numismatique et d'Antiquité.* Paris: Imprimerie Royale, 1840. 256 pp., 10 engraved plates.
The plates illustrate ancient Greek coins. Also includes a plate of coin inscriptions.

195 **Raper, Matthew A.** *An Inquiry into the Value of the Ancient Greek and Roman Money.* London, 1772. Also in: *Select and Valuable Tracts of Money.* London, 1856. Pages 527-94.

196 **Rawlings, Gertrude B.** *Coins and How to Know Them.* New York: F. A. Stokes, 1908. Third edition, London: Methuen & Co., 1910. Fourth edition, 1924. 374 pp., 35 pls. Reprinted as *Ancient, Medieval, Modern Coins and How to Know Them.* London, 1935. Reprint, Chicago: Ammon Press, 1966. 360 pp., 36 pls. [CS 127 and 127a]
A general introduction to numismatics. Begins with a short introduction to the origins of coinage and weight-standards. The next 115 pages are devoted to Greek coinage. Denominations, types, and art are discussed. Describes the major coin types following a geographical arrangement. Provides a good, concise summary of the field of Greek coinage. Includes seven plates of photographs of Greek coins. Chapters on Roman coinage and medieval British coinage follow, and concludes with short sections on American coinage and tokens. [Reviewed by H. A. Grueber in *Numismatic Chronicle* 4th ser., 8 (1908): 379-80].

197 **Rebuffat, François.** *La Monnaie dans l'Antiquite.* Picard, 1996. 271 pp.
A review of the history of ancient numismatics in Greece, Rome, China, and India. Consideration is given to the history of exchange, its role in society, and the production and organization of coinage.

198 **Regling, Kurt Ludwig.** *Ancient Numismatics: the Coinage of Ancient Greece and Rome.* Translated by Terry Merz. Chicago: Argonaut, 1969. 79 pp. [CS 1668]
A translation of *Münzkunde* published in 1930 in Germany. An overview of ancient coinage from the first coins through the Roman Imperial period.

199 **Reinfeld, Fred, and Burton Hobson.** *Picture Book of Ancient Coins.* London, Melbourne, and Cape Town: The Oak Tree Press, 1966. 63 pp., illus.
This book for beginning collectors introduces the hobby of coin collecting, and then provides descriptions of 117 Egyptian, Greek, Roman Republican, Roman Imperial, and Holy Land coins. Emphasizes the historical background of the coinage. Includes a general guide to market values for 185 coin types by Burton Hobson.

200 **Reppeteau, L. V.** "Have You Checked Head's." *The Asylum* (Numismatic Bibliomania Society) 9, no. 4 (fall 1991): 10-12.
A brief biography of Barclay V. Head, the well-known author of *Historia Numorum* (see Head above) and Keeper of Coins at the British Museum. Lists numerous books and articles authored by Head.

201 **Robert, Louis.** *Études de Numismatique Grecque.* Paris: Collège de France, 1951. 245 pp., maps, 8 pls. [CS 1860]

202 ——— *Monnaies Grecques: Types, Légendes, Magistrats Monétaires, et Geographie.* Hautes Études Numismatiques II. Paris/Geneva, 1967. 149 pp., 4 pls. [CS 1861]

203 **Rosati, Francesco Panvini.** *La Moneta Greca e Romana.* Storia della Moneta I. L'Erma di Bretschneider. 2000. 161 pp., 5 pls.
A series of papers on Greek and Roman money from its earliest use to the fifth century A.D. The chapters in the Greek section examine prehistoric evidence for the use of money, coinage during and at the end of the Persian wars, money in Magna Graecia and Sicily, and in the Hellenistic period. The second section looks at coinage in pre-Roman Italy, the introduction of denarii and other coins from Augustus through the end of the Roman period.

204 **Rutter, Nicholas K.** *Greek Coinage.* Great Britain: Shire Publications, 1983. 56 pp., 15 pls.
Part of the *Shire Archaeology* series, this introduction to Greek numismatics describes the invention of coinage, minting techniques, and coin types. Focuses on the coins of Italy, Sicily, Athens, and the Hellenistic Kingdoms. This introduction is not just for beginners. Illustrates many high quality coins, mostly from the Hunter Coin Cabinet in the University of Glasgow. Includes a list of museums which house collections of Greek coins. [Reviewed by J. Warren in *Numismatic Chronicle* 145 (1985): 273-4].

205 **Schaps, David M.** "The Monetization of the Marketplace in Athens." *Entretiens d'Archéologie de d'Histoire III: Prix et Formation de Prix dans les Économies Antiques.* Edited by J. Andreau, P. Briant, and R. Descat. Saint-Bertrand-de-Comminges: Musée Archéeologique Departemental de Saint-Bertrand-de-Comminges, 1997. Pages 91-104.

206 ——— "What Was Money in Ancient Greece?" *The Monetary Systems of the Greeks and Romans.* Edited by W. V. Harris. Oxford: University Press, 2008. Pages 38-48.
General comments on the concept of money and the transition in Greek thinking from various forms of "money" to coins as money.

207 **Schwabacher, Willy.** "Contribution to Greek Numismatics." *Numismatic Chronicle* 5th ser., 19 (1939): 1-20. 1 pl.
Publishes numerous previously unpublished Greek coins acquired by the author during residence in Greece. Includes coins of Macedon under the Romans, Scione, Methylium, Peirasia, Elis, Tegea, Melos, and others.

208 ——— "Ancient Numismatics." *Swedish Archaeological Bibliography 1939-1948.* Edited by S. Janson and O. Vessberg. Stockholm: Almquist and Wiskell, 1951. Pages 271-8. [CS 1671]
A narrative review of works on Greek and Roman numismatics by Swedish scholars. Cross-referenced to the accompanying bibliography.

209 ——— "Ancient Numismatics." *Swedish Archaeological Bibliography 1949-1953.* Edited by C. Callmer and W. Holmquist. Stockholm: Almquist and Wiskell, 1956. Pages 202-15. [CS 1672]
A narrative review of works on Greek and Roman numismatics by Swedish scholars. Cross-referenced to the accompanying bibliography.

210 ——— "Ancient Numismatics." *Swedish Archaeological Bibliography 1954-1959.* Edited by W. Odelberg and H. Thylander. Stockholm: Almquist and Wiskell, 1965. Pages 191-204.
A narrative review of works on Greek and Roman numismatics by Swedish scholars. Cross-referenced to the accompanying bibliography.

211 **Seaby's.** *Greek Coins from the Sixth Century B.C. to Alexander the Great.*
A booklet and thirty color photographic slides.

212 **Seaford, Richard.** "Tragic Money." *Journal of Hellenic Studies* 118 (1998): 119-39.
Examines the influence of money, including coinage, on the tragic representation of heroic myth through three case studies. Describes the part played by money in the texture of the plays and indicates the relation of this role to its cultural and historical background.

213 ——— *Money and the Early Greek Mind: Homer, Philosophy, Tragedy.* Cambridge: Cambridge University Press, 2004. 370 pp.
Seaford argues that by transforming social relations, monetization contributed to the concepts of the universe as an impersonal system (fundamental to pre-Socratic philosophy) and of the individual alienated from his own kin and from the gods, as found in tragedy. Seaford argues that an important precondition for monetization was the Greek practice of animal sacrifice, as represented in Homeric epic, which describes a premonetary world on the point of producing money.

214 ——— "Money and Tragedy." *The Monetary Systems of the Greeks and Romans.* Edited by W. V. Harris. Oxford: University Press, 2008. Pages 49-65.
Relates the monetization of Athens to the development of polis festivals under the tyrants, and then to the form and content of tragedy which came into being in a polis festival of Dionysos.

215 **Seibert, Robert.** "Ancient Drama Provides Insight into the Use of Coinage by Common Citizens." *The Celator* 5, no. 7 (July 1991): 30-1.
Discusses various Greek coins which are mentioned in the works of the Greek poets. Gives examples of the coins' purchasing power.

216 **Seltman, Charles T.** *Greek Coins: A History of Metallic Currency and Coinage down to the Fall of the Hellenistic Kingdoms.* London: Methuen, 1933. Second edition, 1955. Third edition, 1960. Reprints, London, 1965; London: Spink & Son, 1977. 311 pp., 64 pls., map, illus. [CS 1870]
A comprehensive handbook of Greek coinage. Begins with the invention of money and the introduction of coinage. Briefly describes the techniques of minting and the spread of coinage and weight-standards. Continues with discussions of the coinage of various regions and time periods ending with the Hellenistic monarchies. Includes a chapter on the league coinages. The many plates provide a comprehensive view of Greek coin types. Includes a concordance of the plates to the related pages of text and a good bibliography. [The first edition was reviewed in *Journal of Hellenic Studies* 53 (1933): 128-31. The second edition was reviewed by G. K. Jenkins in *Numismatic Chronicle* 6th ser., 15 (1955): 262-6, by C. M. Kraay in *Spink Numismatic Circular* 63, no. 4 (April 1955): 169-71, by C. C. Vermeule in *American Journal of Archaeology* 59 (1955): 347-9, by J. May in *Journal of Hellenic Studies* 76 (1956): 139-40, and by W. Schwabacher in *Gnomon* (Germany) 29 (1957): 98-103].

217 ——— *A Book of Greek Coins.* London: Penguin Books, 1952. 30 pp., 48 pls., map. [CS 1869]
A general introduction to Greek coinage of the archaic and classical periods. Discusses the first coins, the development of types and stylistic trends. Illustrates 116 superbly artistic coins. [Reviewed by J. M. F. May in *Numismatic Chronicle* 6th ser., 12 (1952): 170-1, and in *Journal of Hellenic Studies* 73 (1953): 232].

218 **Sestini, Domenico.** *Descrizione degli Stateri Antichi, Illustrati con le Medaglie.* Firenze: Dalla Stamperia Piatti, 1817. 118 pp., 9 engraved plates.

219 **Sheedy, Kenneth A., and Charikleia Papageorgiadou-Banis, eds.** *Numismatic Archaeology/Archaeological Numismatics: Proceedings of an International Conference Held to Honour Dr. Mando Oeconomides in Athens 1995.* Oxbow Monographs 75. Oxford: Oxbow Books and The Australian Archaeological Institute at Athens, 1997. 150 pp., 18 pls.
Fourteen papers presented at an international conference focused on the on-going relationship of numismatic research to the wider discipline of archaeology. The conference was held to honor Dr. Mando Oeconomides upon his retirement as Director of the Athens Numismatic Museum. The papers are: "Αρχαιολογικη Νομισματικη / Νομισματικη Αρχαιλογια" by I. Touratsoglou, "Coins and Stratigraphy" by S. Rotroff [755], "Excavation Coins: The Use and Misuse of Numismatic Evidence in Archaeology" by A. Walker [829], "Monnaies de Fouilles et Histoire Grecque: L'Exemple de Thasos" by O. Picard [3771], "Fundmünzen aus Aigeira I: Lokale Prägungen" by M. Hainzmann [579], "The Contribution of the Numismatic Evidence to the Dating of the Seal Impressions from the 'Archives' of the City of Ancient Paphos" by I. Nicolaou [6657], "Coins as Weights in the Temple Records of Didyma" by J. Melville-Jones [1587], "Epigraphie et Numismatique: Quelques Remarques sur les Noms de Monnaies dans les Inscriptions Grecques Archaïques" by H. Nicolet-Pierre [1342], "Η Αρχαικη νομισματοκπια της Κεας: Προβληματα Αποδοσης" by C. Papageorgiadou-Banis, "ΤΡΙΚΚΑΙΩΝ ΑΘΛΑ" by A. Moustaka, "Thisoa by Mount Lykaion: Further Light on an Arkadian Problem" by J. Warren [4352], "Late Archaic Hoards in the Cyclades and Some Thoughts on a Regional Pattern of Trade" by K. Sheedy [772], "Reconstructing the Circulation of Roman Coinage in First Century B.C. Macedonia" by R. Bauslaugh, "Archéologie et Numismatique en Albanie: Remarques sur l'Activité Monétaire au IV-II Siècle" by S. Gjongecaj [3818], "A Bronze Die from Sounion" by P. Kalligas [1409], and an epilogue by M. Oeconomides.

220 **Shipton, Kirsty.** "Money and the Élite in Classical Athens." *Money and Its Uses in the Ancient Greek World.* Edited by A. Meadows and K. Shipton. Oxford: University Press, 2001. Pages 129-44.
Shipton analyzes the effect of coinage on attitudes toward the use of wealth. She explores the role played by the wealthy elite in the cash-based public economy of Athens, and the behavior of the elite when given a choice between using their money to lease mines or lease public land. She concludes that mine leasing is likely to have reinforced the ties between the wealthy elite and the State whereby each profits from the other. The wealthy are seen to play a dominant role in non-landed activity, which had the potential to produce cash profits.

221 **Stefanakis, Manolis I.** "Bibliography of Martin Jessop Price." *Studies in Greek Numismatics in Memory of Martin Jessop Price.* Edited by Richard Ashton and Silvia Hurter. London: Spink, 1998. Pages 395-400.
A listing of 151 published works of Martin J. Price. Includes his monographs, articles, contributions as editor or reviser, and book reviews.

222 **Stevens, Susan T.** "Charon's Obol and Other Coins in Ancient Funerary Practice." *Phoenix* 45, no. 3 (autumn 1991): 215-29.
Greek and Latin literature from the fifth century B.C. to the second century A.D. mentions the custom of placing a coin in the mouth of the deceased as a payment to the boatman Charon for ferrying the soul across the Acheron or Styx into the underworld. Evidence shows that "Charon's obol" was only one manifestation of a much wider funerary use of coins, and suggests a richer and broader context in which it can be understood. Stevens reviews the literary and archaeological evidence.

223 **Sutherland, Carol H. V.** "The Historical Evidence of Greek and Roman Coins." *Greece and Rome* 9, no. 26 (February 1940): 65-80. 3 pls.
A general discussion of the use of coins as historical evidence. Sutherland emphasizes that coins, as products of the state, are wholly official in the information they provide, as opposed to other works of art which are a free expression of individual tendencies. The historical evidence provided by coins is primarily commercial as opposed to political.

224 ——— "Corn and Coin: A Note on Greek Commercial Monopolies." *American Journal of Philology* 64, no. 2 (1943): 129-47. [CS 1874]
In this rebuttal to J. Hasebrook's *Trade and Politics in Ancient Greece*, Sutherland argues that the possession of a reputable coinage was among the first necessities for a vigorous and progressive Greek state, and that a state, once it had established such coinage, immediately engaged in a national commercial policy designed to supply her with the essentials of life. Demonstrates that Greek coins traveled very widely outside their home cities. Traces the steps in the introduction of coinage at Athens, Aegina, and Corinth. Discusses the distribution of coins as shown by hoard evidence and overstrikes. Argues that state control of coinage went hand-in-hand with constant efforts to establish a state monopoly over the corn supply.

225 **Svoronos, Joannes N.** *Istoria Ton Nomismaton.* Athens, 1898. 35 pls.
The plates prepared to accompany Barclay Head's 1898 Greek edition of Historia Numorum. These plates were reprinted in 1968 in Svoronos and Head's *Illustrations of the Historia Numorum: An Atlas of Greek Numismatics* (see below).

226 **Svoronos, John N., and Barclay V. Head.** *The Illustrations of the Historia Numorum: An Atlas of Greek Numismatics.* Edited by Alyce Marie Cresap. Chicago: Argonaut, 1968. Second edition, Chicago: Ares Publishers, 1976. 64 pp., 39 pls. [CS 1875]
The plates from Svoronos' 1911 Greek translation of Head's *Historia Numorum*, with Cresap's text describing the coins. Issued as a companion volume to the 1968 reprint of *Historia Numorum*, this volume provides plates of coins mentioned in Head's text and is keyed to the pages where the coins are discussed by Head. About 400 coins are illustrated.

227 **Tebbs, H. V.** "Greek Coins as Illustrating History and Art." *Portfolio* (February 1878): 26-31; (March 1878): 35-40. Plates.

228 **Tekin, Oguz, ed.** *Ancient History, Numismatics, and Epigraphy in the Mediterranean World: Studies in Memory of Clemens E. Bosch and Sabahat Atlan and in Honor of Nezahat Baydur.* Instanbul: Ege, 2009. 375+ pp.

A collection of forty essays, including three in English dealing with Greek coins: A. R. Meadows, "The Hellenistic Silver Coinage of Clazomenae" [4796], S. Psoma, "Agathokles Son of Lysimachos in Thrace and Asia Minor: The Numismatic Evidence" [3626], and Oguz Tekin, "A Hellenistic Hoard of Lysimachean Bronze Coins with Tyche and Lion Type" [3681].

229   "Three Fine and Rare Greek Coins." *Spink Numismatic Circular* 1 (December 1892): 3.
Briefly describes three coins: a silver octadrachm of the Orrescii in Macedonia, a silver stater of the Arcadian League, and a silver stater of Elis.

230   **Tzamalis, Anastasios P., and Marion J. A. Tzamali.** Μνημη *Martin Jessop Price.* Bibliotheca 5. Athens: The Hellenic Numismatic Society, 1996. 357 pp., illus.
A collection of eighteen essays written in memory of Martin J. Price, former Assistant Keeper of Coins at the British Museum and Director of the British School of Archaeology at Athens, who died in 1995. The essays all relate to Greek numismatics, from the ancient period to the present. Each essay is presented in both Greek and English. The essays related to the ancient Greek period are: "The Coin and History: The Confirmation of a Page of Herodotus, III 57-59" by A. K. Kyrou [135], "Athenian Silver Coins: 6th-3rd Centuries B.C., The Current Interpretation" by J. Theodorou [4127], "Des Monnaies aux Initiales TPIH" by S. Psoma [3280], "Some Early Issues of Philip II" by D. Portolos [3466], "Un Trésor (1995) de 80 Drachmes aux Types d'Alexandre III" by E. Papaefthymiou [3461], "Posthumous Alexander Type Tetradrachms of Chios and Associated Civic Drachms of the Early Second Century B.C." by C. Lagos [3395], "Polichne" by M. Stephanakis [4432], and "Christodoulou Yet Again" by C. Moulakis [1695]. Also includes a tribute to Martin Price by Manolis I. Stephanakis. [Reviewed by A. Walker in *The Celator* 12, no. 4 (April 1998): 32-4, and by Antony Wilson in *Spink Numismatic Circular* 106, no. 5 (June 1998): 210-1].

231   **Vagi, David L.** "Delian Inventories a Treasure Trove of Information." *The Celator* 9, no. 6 (June 1995): 40-1.
Citing records of the contents of the treasuries at Delos, the author provides some of the descriptions of coins from the treasury inventories.

232   ——— "A Greek Coin Refresher Course." Two parts. *The Celator* 11, no. 6 (1997): 22-4; no. 7 (July 1997): 32-4. Illus.
The author presents twelve basic general observations about Greek coinage. The topics are: the origins of coinage, art and the commercial success of a coinage, the size and function of coins, weight standards, denominations, the gold-to-silver ratio, fabric, the development of style, "beware" of style, dates on coins, portraiture, and propaganda.

233   ——— "The 'Other' Greeks." *The Numismatist* 121, no. 10 (October 2008): 69-71. Illus.
A brief introduction to the non-Greek peoples and those on the far fringes of the Greek world who struck coins that are commonly collected along with Greek coins. Includes the Numidians, Scythians, Celts, Phoenicians, and kingdoms of Persis, Elam, Bactria, and others.

234   ——— "Ancient Greek Coinage Spans 10 Centuries: Coins Useful in Tracking Successes, Failures of Societies." *Coin World* (August 9, 2010): 166-70. Illus.
A brief description of general themes in Greek coinage by century, from the seventh century B.C. to the third century A.D.

235   **Vagi, David L.,** ed. "Previously Unpublished Coins or Unrecorded Varieties." *SAN—Journal of the Society for Ancient Numismatics* 20, no. 1 (1997): 20-2. Illus.
Presents photographs and descriptions of seven previously unrecorded coins, including six Greek coins (Apollonia Pontika, Dardanos, Miletos, Ionia uncertain, Chios, Sidon) and one Roman coin (Caracalla). The coins were reported by Vagi, K. Davis, H. Berk, K. Wetterstrom, and R. Freeman.

236   **van Alfen, Peter G.** *Agoranomia: Studies in Money and Exchange Presented to John H. Kroll.* New York: American Numismatic Society, 2006. 271 pp., 14 pls.
A collection of essays written in honor of John H. Kroll upon his retirement from the University of Texas at Austin. Focuses on Greek coinage, exchange, and polis economies from the archaic to the Hellenistic periods. Included in the collection are studies that explore aspects of Homeric and Archaic exchange, the law of sale, and cavalry costs. Other studies examine the social, economic and historical contexts of coinages from Abdera, Athens, "Lete," Lydia, Mylasa, and Side, and present new interpretative approaches to "cooperative" coinage and those from archaeological sites. Essays included are: "Les Talents d'Homère" by H. Nicolet-Pierre, "Argyrnetos: Les transformations de l'Échange dans la Grèce Archaïque" by R. Descat, "KUKALIM, WALWET, and the Artemision Deposit: Problems in Early Anatolian Electrum Coinage" by R. W. Wallace [5006], "Small Change and the Beginning of Coinage at Abdera" by J. H. Kagan [3689], "The 'Lete' Coinage Reconsidered" by S. Psoma [3720], "A Legal Fiction: The Athenian Law of Sale" by E. Cohen, "Athens and Bronze Coinage" by C. Grandjean [4025], "Polis Economies and the Cost of the Cavalry in Early Hellenistic Athens" by G. Oliver, "The Pseudo-Rhodian Drachms of Mylasa Revisited" by R. Ashton and G. Reger [4863], "Amyntas, Side, and the Pamphylian Plain" by A. Meadows [5060], "Greek Coins from Archaeological Excavations: A Conspectus of Conspectuses and a Call for Chronological Tables" by F. de Callataÿ [532], and "Cooperative Coinage" by E. Mackil and P. van Alfen [152]. [Reviewed by Ben Akrigg in *Bryn Mawr Classical Review* 2007.12.04].

237   **Van der Dussen, J. W.** "Fifth Century Greek Wars and Their Numismatic Consequences." *The Celator* 21, no. 12 (December 2007): 6-26. Illus.
Traces the main wars in the Greek world throughout the fifth century B.C. and reviews their impact on the coinage. Discusses the role of money during wartime. Summarizes the changes in coinage at Athens and the impact of the Athenian Coinage Decree of the coinage of Euboia, Delos, Naxos, Aegina, Scyros, Thasos, Beoetia, Samos, Mytilene, Scione, Mende, and Melos. Discusses the role of unofficial Athenian coinage and imitations, countermarked "owls" and later developments.

238   **Van der Werf, Greg, and Paul R. Secord.** *Rulers of the Ancient World.* Pasadena: published by the authors, 1995. 73 pp., illus., maps.
Lists of rulers, with reign dates, of cities and kingdoms of the ancient world prepared as a companion to coin catalogues and studies of ancient history. The book is divided into the following sections: (1) the archaic age, (2) the classical age, (3) the Hellenistic age, (4) the Roman age. Also includes the following appendices: (1) wars, (2) Hellenistic royal names (gives the meanings of honorary titles), (3) Roman Republican moneyers (with the dates they were active), (4) vestal virgins, and (5) religious figures (priests, prophets, and popes). Also includes some timelines of historical events. Various portrait coin illustrations appear throughout.

239   **Vermeule, Cornelius C.** *A Bibliography of Applied Numismatics in the Fields of Greek and Roman Archaeology and the Fine Arts.* London: Spink, 1956. 172 pp. [CS 1624]

A list of 1300 works in which numismatic evidence has been utilized in the fields of classical archaeology and the fine arts. Summaries of contents are given. Arranged by author within broad topics: Archaeology and Art History; Iconography; Geography, Topography, and Architecture; Related Works in the Fields of History, Politics, and Religion.

239a **von Fritze, Hans, and Hugo Gaebler, eds.** *Nomisma: Untersuchungen auf dem Gebiete der Antiken Münzkunde.* 12 volumes. Berlin, 1907-1923. Reprint, Bologna: A. Forni, 2002.

240 **Von Reden, Sitta.** *Exchange in Ancient Greece.* London: Duckworth, 1995. Paperback edition, 2003. 244 pp., 8 pls.
Re-examines the nature of exchange and commerce in ancient Greece. Emphasizes the importance of the city-state in shaping a notion of commerce. Explores the connections between economic and socio-political life. Includes an exploration of coinage and money. The author suggests that coinage was invented as a means of political patronage. [Reviewed by H. S. Kim in *Numismatic Chronicle* 156 (1996): 340-2].

241 ——— "Money, Law and Exchange: Coinage in the Greek Polis." *Journal of Hellenic Studies* 117 (1997): 154-76.
The author looks historically at the development and use of pre-monetary currencies and early coinage in order to draw attention to the wider spectrum of institutions in which coinage was used in late archaic poleis, side-by-side with other tokens of value and media of exchange. Looks at the construction of meanings of money and the problems that arose politically from the fact that all-purpose money was the standard of value and medium of exchange in very different exchange contexts. Discusses the origin of coinage and the transition from exchange of bullion to the use of coins. Presents literary evidence of monetary exchange in difference social contexts (law, marriage, athletic contests).

242 ——— "Money in the Ancient Economy: A Survey of Recent Research." *Klio* (Germany) 84, no. 1 (2002): 141-74.
An introduction to current debates related to the ancient economy from the archaic Greek period to the fourth century A.D., concentrating on broad monetary developments rather than specific coinages. Von Reden discusses credit and banking, estate management and the micro-economics of money use, monetary policy and the macro-economics of money use, monetization and circulation, and the problems of money use in the Greek polis.

243 ——— *Money in Classical Antiquity.* Key Themes in Ancient History. New York: Cambridge University Press, 2010. 237 pp., illus.
A comprehensive analysis of the impact of money on the economy, society, and culture of the Greek and Roman world. Covering a wide range of monetary contexts within the Mediterranean during the period ca. 600 B.C. to A.D. 300, its method is comparative and specific in order to demonstrate that money plays different roles under different social and political circumstances.

244 **Waddingham, Gary.** "Fifth Century Athens: Literary Sources Reveal Buying Power of Drachm." *The Celator* 2, no. 5 (May 1988): 1, 6.
Literary sources are used to determine the typical wages and costs of goods in fifth century B.C. Athens. Concludes that the general pay for a craftsman was one drachm per day. The costs of various items are listed (one obol for a loaf of bread, etc.).

245 **Walker, Obadiah.** *The Greek and Roman History Illustrated by Coins and Medals. Representing their Religions, Rites, Manners, Customs, Games, Feasts, Arts, and Sciences. Together with a Succinct Account of their Emperors, Consuls, Cities, Colonies, and Families. In Two Parts. Necessary for the Introduction of Youth into All the Useful Knowledge of Antiquity.* London: G. Croom, 1692. 360 pp.
According to numismatic literature expert George F. Kolbe, this was the first substantial work on numismatics published in the English language. It includes introductions to Roman coins, Roman medals, and Greek coins. The Greek section lists many of the coin-issuing cities (their names are written in Greek), and includes very brief comments on the nature of common Greek coins. Continues with extensive descriptions of Roman Imperial coins, and historical information on the Roman emperors and their families.

246 **Wallace, William P.** "Greek Coins and Greek History." *The Phoenix* (Canada) supplement to vol. 1 (spring 1947): 30-5. Also in *Canadian Numismatic Journal* 3, no. 11 (November 1958): 330-6. [CS 1877]
A general discussion of the value of coins in the study of Greek history. States that the contribution of coins to historians is "not as valuable, at least, as numismatists often try to suggest, and not nearly as valuable as it some day can and will be." Briefly discusses some of the important historical information that has been gathered from the study of coins. Discusses Athens' large issue of decadrachms and didrachms to facilitate the distribution of the silver of Laurion, coin weight- standards as an indication of a city's commercial relations, and other issues.

247 **Warren, John B. Leicester.** *An Essay on Greek Federal Coinage.* London, 1863. Reprinted as *Greek Federal Coinage.* Chicago: Argonaut, 1969. 73 pp., illus., 4 maps. [CS 1878]
Describes the nature and purpose of federal coinages. Examines the issues of the Achaean, Aetolian, Boeotian, Akarnanian, Thessalian, and Chalkidian Leagues, the Amphictionic Council, and other federal coinages. [Also see Mackil and van Alfen "Cooperative Coinage" above].

248 **Wartenberg, Ute.** *After Marathon: War, Society and Money in Fifth-Century Greece.* London: British Museum Press, 1995. 64 pp. including 16 pls.
Combining numismatic evidence with information from written sources such as the works of Herodotus and Thucydides, building accounts and records of tribute, the first part of this book looks at the relationship between the political and economic situation in fifth-century Greece and the design and use of coinage, whether in everyday transactions at home, in trade with other powers, or to pay for soldiers and ships in time of war. In the second part of the book, 121 coins from the period in the British Museum's collection are fully described and illustrated. [Reviewed by S. Hurter in *Schweizer Münzblätter* (Switzerland) 47, no. 185 (1997): 22-3, and by J. Morcom in *Numismatic Chronicle* 157 (1997): 256-8].

249 ——— "After Marathon: Money, War and Society in Ancient Greece." *Minerva* 7, no. 1 (January/February 1996): 32-4. Illus.
This brief overview of the use of money and coinage of the Athenian empire in the Classical period serves as an introduction to an exhibition at the British Museum. Explores how the cities in the Athenian empire raised the required sums of money to pay their tribute to Athens, focusing on the coinage of the island of Thasos.

250 **Wedig, Harold.** "Denominations Explained: Greek Coins Were Struck in All Shapes and Sizes." *The Celator* 4, no. 1 (January 1990): 22-3.

Explains the various coin denomination systems used by the Greeks. Presents a table of thirty-two denominations with descriptions of each. Another table shows the common denominations and their standard weights for the Attic, Aeginetan, Corinthian, and Syracusan systems.

251 **Weinberg, Gladys Davidson, and Saul S. Weinberg.** "On Numismatic Evidence." *Greek Numismatics and Archaeology: Essays in Honor of Margaret Thompson.* Edited by O. Mørkholm and N. M. Waggoner. Wetteren: Numismatique Romaine, 1979. Pages 281-6. 2 pls.
Coins are used as evidence in interpreting the design found on an unusual clay loomweight ca. 400 B.C. The weight's design includes a carved donkey on one side, and a bull standing in front of a tree on the other side. The bull and tree motif appears on the reverse of a Roman coin minted at Corinth during the reign of Caracalla. A very similar bull is found on coins of Gortyna, Crete, minted 322-300 B.C., suggesting a common prototype. The loomweight is interpreted as a votive offering, perhaps at the classical Palaimonion (the cult center of Melicertes, in whose honor the Isthmian Games were instituted).

252 **Wenger, Otto Paul.** *Griechische Münzen.* Orbis Pictus Band 60. Bern and Stuttgart: Hallwag Verlag, 1974. 48 pp, illus.
A brief introduction to Greek coinage followed by illustrations and descriptions of fifty-six superb Greek coins.

253 **West, Louis C.** "Ancient Money and Modern Commentators." *Museum Notes* 6 (1954): 1-9.
Attempts to eliminate some misconceptions regarding the functions and nature of money. West states, "changes in currency seem never in themselves to have been the initial cause of financial distress." Rather, changes in monetary systems have come as a result of economic pressures. He emphasizes that although mints could fix the value of gold or silver in terms of its value in coin (drachms, denarii, etc.), the purchasing power of the coins remained subject to fluctuation based on economic forces. The bullion value of subsidiary coinage is of no importance as long as such coins remain convertible to higher denomination coins at face value. Clarifies the meaning and cause of "inflation." Also comments on the use and misuse of other monetary terms (e.g., sesterces, depreciation).

254 **Westermark, Ulla.** "General Works." *A Survey of Numismatic Research, 1960-1965. Volume 1: Ancient Numismatics.* Edited by O. Mørkholm. Copenhagen: International Numismatic Commission, 1967. Pages 13-26. [CS 1804]
A narrative bibliography discussing recently published works in the field of Greek numismatics.

255 ——— "Ancient Numismatics." *Swedish Archaeological Bibliography 1960-1965.* Edited by M. Stenberger and A. Hedvall. Stockholm: Almquist and Wiskell, 1968. Pages 225-32.
A narrative review of works on Greek and Roman numismatics by Swedish scholars. Cross-referenced to the accompanying bibliography.

256 ——— "Ancient Numismatics." *Swedish Archaeological Bibliography 1966-1970.* Edited by M. Stenberger and A. Hedvall. Stockholm: Almquist and Wiskell, 1972. Pages 236-9.
A narrative review of works on Greek and Roman numismatics by Swedish scholars. Cross-referenced to the accompanying bibliography.

257 ——— "Ancient Numismatics." *Swedish Archaeological Bibliography 1971-1975.* Edited by S. Janson and H. Thylander. Stockholm: Almquist and Wiskell, 1978. Pages 240-1.
A narrative review of works on Greek and Roman numismatics by Swedish scholars. Cross-referenced to the accompanying bibliography.

258 ——— "Ancient Numismatics." *Swedish Archaeology 1976-1980.* Edited by A. Hyenstrand and P. Hellström. Stockholm: Swedish Archaeological Society, 1983. Pages 77-9.
A narrative review of works on Greek and Roman numismatics by Swedish scholars. Cross-referenced to the accompanying bibliography.

259 ——— "Ancient Numismatics." *Swedish Archaeology 1981-1985.* Edited by A. Carlson et al. Stockholm: Swedish Archaeological Society, 1987. Pages 221-3.
A narrative review of works on Greek and Roman numismatics by Swedish scholars. Cross-referenced to the accompanying bibliography.

260 **Weston, Stephen B. D.** *Historic Notices of Towns in Greece, and in Other Countries That Have Struck Coins.* London, 1826. 164 pp.

261 **Wilkinson, John S.** "History of Coins." *The Canadian Numismatic Journal* (Canada) 1, no. 3 (March 1956): 53-6; no. 4 (April 1956): 77-9; no. 5 (May 1956): 103-6; no. 6 (June 1956): 130-1; no. 8 (August 1956): 161-9; no. 9 (September 1956): 180-4.
The text of a lecture on coin collecting, focusing on the ancient Greek period. Begins with the invention of money and the first coins. Then describes some of the most important Greek cities and their coins. Briefly reviews the coinage of Rome, Byzantium, and early Europe.

262 **Will, Édouard.** "Fonctions de la Monnaie dans les Cités Grecques de l'Époque Classique." *Numismatique Antique: Problèmes et Methods.* Annales de l'Est Mémoire 44. Etudes d'Archéologie Classique IV. Edited by J. Dentzer, P. Gauthier and T. Hackens. Louvain, 1975. Pages 233-46.

263 **Williams, Jonathan, Joe Cribb, and Elizabeth Errington, eds.** "Mesopotamia, Egypt and Greece." Chapter 1 in *Money: A History.* New York: St. Martin's Press, 1997. Pages 16-38. Illus.
This book was published to accompany the opening of a new money gallery at the British Museum. Chapter 1 reviews the monetary use of precious metals in Mesopotamia and Egypt, the introduction of coinage at Lydia, and the spread and development of coinage among the Greek city-states. Discusses money and credit in the Greek world. Discusses and illustrates examples of Hellenistic portraiture on coins.

264 **Xenou, Argyro-Alexandra.** "Ancient Greek Coins: A History." *Motion: Olympic Airways Magazine* (December 1987): 46-51. Illus.
A brief overview of the history of Greek coinage, illustrated by fourteen coins. Text in English and Greek.

265 **Zograph, Alexander N.** *Anitchnye Monety.* Materials and Researches on the Archaeology of the U.S.S.R., No. 16. Moscow and Leningrad: Academy of Sciences of the U.S.S.R., 1951. 198pp., 50 pls. [CS 1679]

For an English translation, see next item.

266 ———— *Ancient Coinage. Part i: The General Problems of Ancient Numismatics.* 169 pp., illus. *Part ii: The Ancient Coins of the Northern Black Sea Littoral.* 250 pp., 50 pls. BAR Supplementary Series, No. 33 (i). Translated by H. Bartlett Wells. Oxford: British Archaeological Reports, 1977. [CS 1680]
Includes a brief biography of the Soviet numismatist Alexander N. Zograph (b. 1889; d. 1942) and a bibliography of his work. Part 1 is a translation of Zograph's *Antichnye Monety* (Moscow and Leningrad, 1951). Begins with a brief history of the science of numismatics. Then describes the technology of coin manufacturing, the organization of mints, weight-standards, and denominations and their place in monetary circulation in Greece and Rome. Continues with an extensive discussion of coin types, symbols and inscriptions, the arrangement of Greek coins in a collection, dating and identification, and the concept of die-links. Part 2 is an examination of the history of the currency and monetary circulation of the Greek cities on the northern Black Sea coast—Tyra, Olbia, Chersonesus, Kerkinitis, and the Kingdom of the Bosporus. [Reviewed by Martin J. Price in *Spink Numismatic Circular* 86, no. 3 (March 1978): 133].

Also see: Anthony "Collecting" under COLLECTING GUIDES; Callataÿ "Greek Coins from Archaeological Excavations" under HOARDS; Daehn "Artemision" under HOARDS; Gardner "Earliest Coins" under ORIGINS OF COINAGE; Gardner *The Types of Greek Coins* under TYPES; Guillaume *Analysis of Reasonings* under BACTRIA; Hoover *Handbook of Greek Coinage* under COLLECTING GUIDES; Klawans *An Outline* under COLLECTING GUIDES; Klawans *Handbook* under COLLECTING GUIDES; Klein *Sammlung von Griechischen* under PRIVATE COLLECTIONS; Kraay "Hoards, Small Change" under ORIGINS OF COINAGE; Jones "Coin Names" under EPIGRAPHY; Lorber "Notes on West Greek Gold" under SICILY—GENERAL WORKS; MacDonald *Guide Book of Overstruck Greek Coins* under THE MINTING PROCESS.

Regling *Die Antike Münze als Kunstwerk* under ART; Rotroff "Coins and Stratigraphy" under HOARDS; Rutter *Historia Numorum* under ITALY—GENERAL WORKS; Sayles *Ancient Coin Collecting 2* under COLLECTING GUIDES; Sayles *Ancient Coin Collecting 6* under COLLECTING GUIDES; Sear "Greek Coins and Their Values" under COLLECTING GUIDES; Stillman "Coinage of the Greeks" under ART; Sutherland "Overstrikes and Hoards" under THE MINTING PROCESS; Tsangari *Hellenic Coinage* under PRIVATE COLLECTIONS; Wallace "After Athens" under ASIA MINOR—GENERAL WORKS; Walker "Excavation Coins" under HOARDS; Ward and Hill *Coins and Their Parent Cities* under PRIVATE COLLECTIONS.

GENERAL WORKS ON HELLENISTIC GREEK COINAGE

Thus over and above their value as money, these royal portrait coins, bearing the king's head, name, dignities and titles, were a necessary communication between the king and his subjects, a continuing proclamation of his royalty and his rule. Otherwise, word of the king and his doings reached the provinces rarely and belatedly as traveler's tales. Such news as did come was of the greatest interest, to be long and eagerly discussed, for the careers of many of these Hellenistic monarchs were stranger and made more romantic telling than imagination could well invent.

—Norman Davis and Colin Kraay, 1973

267   **Baynham, E. J.** "Continuity and Ambition: The Posthumous Philip II Gold Staters from Colophon/Magnesia." *Alexander and the Hellenistic Kingdoms: Coins, Image and the Creation of Identity. The Westmoreland Collection.* Ancient Coins in Australian Collections 1. Edited by K. A. Sheedy. Sydney: Australian Centre for Ancient Numismatic Studies, Macquarie University, 2007. Pages 23-8.
Discusses a posthumous gold stater of Philip II which bears an unusual depiction of Apollo on the obverse. Apollo seems to incorporate facial features of Alexander III or the Herakles image from Alexander's tetradrachms. The author discusses the mint attribution and historical background of the coin. The coin was minted after Alexander's death and may have been intended to recall the image of Philip II. Discusses the various players in the division of Alexander's empire and how coin images may have been used to bolster their claims. [Also see Sheedy *Alexander and the Hellenistic Kingdoms* under PRIVATE COLLECTIONS].

268   **Bellinger, Alfred R.** "Greek Mints under the Roman Empire." *Essays in Roman Coinage Presented to Harold Mattingly.* Edited by R. A. G. Carson and C. H. V. Sutherland. Oxford: University Press, 1956. Pages 137-48.
Examines the changing role of the Greek mints as Roman rule encroached into Greek lands. Bellinger comments on the influence of the Greek mints on Roman coinage.

269   **Boehringer, Christof.** *Zur Chronologie Mittelhellenistischer Münzserien, 220-160 v. Chr.* Two volumes. Antike Münzen und Geschnittene Steine 5. Berlin: W. de Gruyter, 1973. 228 pp., 40 pls. [CS 2304]

270   **Bresson, A.** "Coinage and Money Supply in the Hellenistic Age." *Making, Moving and Managing: The New World of Ancient Economies, 323-31 B.C.* Edited by Z. H. Archibald, J. K. Davies, and V. Gabrielsen. Oxford: Oxbow, 2005, Pages 44-72.

271   **Burnett, Andrew M.** "Rome and the Hellenistic World." *Coins: An Illustrated Survey 650 B.C. to the Present Day.* Edited by M. J. Price. New York: Methuen, 1980. Pages 54-73. Illus.
An overview of the Greek and Roman coinage of the Hellenistic period. The author describes the gradual debasement of the silver coinage of the Greeks, the increasing use of gold as a coinage metal, and the extensive use of bronze, especially by the Romans. Reviews the introduction of brass coinage by the Romans, the first coins of Rome, the spread of Roman coinage and that of her allies and possessions. Describes the introduction of the series of "wreathed" coins by the Greek cities of the east, and the appearance of the cistophori. Ends with the appearance of Roman Imperial coinage.

272   **Carradice, Ian A.** "The Hellenistic Kingdoms and Coinages 323-170 B.C." *Coins: An Illustrated Survey 650 B.C. to the Present Day.* Edited by M. J. Price. New York: Methuen, 1980. Pages 42-53. Illus.
An overview of the coinage of the Hellenistic period. Discusses the rise of the Hellenistic kingdoms, the introduction of portraiture, the use of broader flans, the introduction of dating systems, and various weight standards. Describes the effects of the Roman conquest on the Hellenistic coinages.

273   **Crawford, Michael H.** *Coinage and Money Under the Roman Republic: Italy and the Mediterranean Economy.* Berkeley and Los Angeles: University of California Press, 1985. 355 pp., illus.
An historical overview of the Roman Republican coinage in relation to other coins being struck throughout the Mediterranean. Crawford traces the history of Roman coinage and the spread in its use, within the context of the economy and society of the different areas involved. He assesses the impact of the revolution in the monetary history of the Mediterranean world brought about by Rome. Includes significant discussion of the Greek coinage in use in each area prior to the periods of Roman rule.

274 **Davis, Norman, and Colin M. Kraay.** *The Hellenistic Kingdoms: Portrait Coins and History.* London: Thames and Hudson, 1973. Reprinted in 1980. 296 pp., illus., maps. [CS 1819]
A history of the Hellenistic age focusing on the kings and queens and illustrated by their portrait coins. Includes discussions of Alexander the Great, the Ptolemies of Egypt, the Seleucids of Syria, the Antigonids of Macedonia, the kings of Bactria and India, and the kings of Pergamum, Bithynia, and Pontos. Within each dynasty, each king and queen is discussed individually. Includes genealogical tables and over 200 photographs of portrait coins, including many enlargements emphasizing the portraits. [Also see the very critical review by R. A. Hazzard in *Cornucopiæ* (Canada) 2, no. 2 (1974): 21-32. Also reviewed by M. J. Price in *Numismatic Chronicle* 7th ser., 14 (1974): 212-3, and by M. Thompson in *Archaeology* 29, no. 2 (April 1976): 139].

274a **de Callataÿ, François.** "Un Tétradrachme de Lysimaque Signé au Droit et la Question des Signatures d'Artistes a la Période Hellénistique." *Revue Archéologique* (France) (1995, no. 1): 23-38. Illus.

275 **de Callataÿ, François, Georges Depeyrot, and Leandre Villaronga.** *L'Argent Monnayé d'Alexandre le Grand à Auguste.* Brussels, 1993. 117 pp.

276 **Hadley, Robert A.** *Deified Kingship and Propaganda Coinage in the Early Hellenistic Age: 323-280 B.C. A Dissertation in History Presented to the University of Pennsylvania, 1964.* Ann Arbor: University Microfilms International, 1983. 148 pp.

277 **Holt, Walter C.** "'Alexander-Type' Tetradrachms in the Names of His Successors." *The Celator* 25, no. 1 (January 2011): 26-33, 36-9. Illus.
The author briefly discusses the tetradrachm and drachm coinage with the types of Alexander (Herakles/Zeus seated) struck by his successors. Coins of many different rulers are illustrated.

278 **Jenkins, G. Kenneth.** "The Monetary Systems in the Early Hellenistic Time, with Special Regard to the Economic Policy of the Ptolemaic Kings." *The Patterns of Monetary Development in Phoenicia and Palestine in Antiquity: International Numismatic Convention, Jerusalem, 27-31 December 1963.* Edited by A. Kindler. Tel-Aviv and Jerusalem, 1967. Pages 53-74. 3 pls. [CS 3163]
Jenkins discusses the coinage of the Palestine-Phoenicia region when it was part of Alexander's empire and when the region came under Ptolemaic rule during the third century B.C. Discusses the role of Athenian coins in the region. Alexander's coins differed sharply in both weight standard and in the ratio of gold-to-silver in comparison with the coins of the Persian satraps that had previously circulated in the region. Jenkins describes the system of mints established by Alexander. Discusses the isolationist character of the Ptolemaic economy—it was compulsory for all foreign coins entering Egypt to be surrendered in exchange for Ptolemaic coins. Discusses the finds of Ptolemaic coins outside of Ptolemaic territory and suggests these coins did not leave Ptolemaic lands through normal trade channels, but rather were the result of financial subsidies to those whom the Ptolemies favored in Greek politics. Discusses changes in designs, weight standards, and gold-to-silver ratios under the Ptolemies. Discusses the application of the Ptolemaic monetary system to the dominions outside of Egypt—especially Phoenicia and Palestine. Discusses the gradual replacement of silver coinage by bronze after 241 B.C.

279 **Jidejian, Nina.** *Lebanon: Its Gods, Legends and Myths Illustrated by Coins.* Beirut: Bank Audi, n.d. (1985).
A excellent overview of Hellenistic history and coinage, with a special emphasis on events in the area of ancient Phoenicia. Includes extensive discussions of the Seleukids and Ptolemies. Illustrated by many enlarged photographs of coins from the collection of Michael Eddé, including many rarities. In English and French.

280 **Jones, John R. Melville.** "The Coinage of Alexander and his Successors: A Common Hellenic Coinage?" *Alexander and the Hellenistic Kingdoms: Coins, Image and the Creation of Identity. The Westmoreland Collection.* Ancient Coins in Australian Collections 1. Edited by K. A. Sheedy. Sydney: Australian Centre for Ancient Numismatic Studies, Macquarie University, 2007. Pages 29-32.
Begins with a quote from Plato citing the need among the Greeks for a common "Hellenic money." Jones discusses the nature of Greek coinage and the widespread use of various coins. But he points out that there was no common Hellenic money as envisioned by Plato. Discusses the vast coinage of Alexander which in some ways was close to a common Hellenic money. [Also see Sheedy *Alexander and the Hellenistic Kingdoms* under PRIVATE COLLECTIONS].

281 **Kleeb, Alvin A.** "Coinage and Politics in the Hellenistic Era." *SAN—Journal of the Society for Ancient Numismatics* 6, no. 1 (fall 1974): 9-13.
An overview of the history and coinage of the early Hellenistic period.

282 **Kollgaard, Ron.** "Coinage Played an Important Political Role in Events Surrounding the Battle of Ipsus." *The Celator* 5, no. 2 (February 1991): 16-25.
A detailed review of the history of the period after the death of Alexander the Great. Chronicles the rivalries between his successors culminating at the Battle of Ipsus in 301 B.C. Describes how the results of the war affected the coinage of Seleucus and Lysimachus: Dionysus appeared on the coinage of Seleucus; some western Asia Minor mints came under the control of Lysimachus. Ptolemy replaced the portrait of Herakles with a portrait of Alexander on his coinage. Also discusses the coinage of Antigonus and Cassander.

283 **Kushnir-Stein, Alla.** "Was Late Hellenistic Silver Coinage Minted for Propaganda Purposes?" *Numismatic Chronicle* 161 (2001): 41-52. Illus.
"The author discusses the meaning of silver coinages produced in various parts of the disintegrating Seleucid kingdom from c. 130 B.C. until 64 B.C., arguing that there is no evidence that any of these coins were minted to advertise political status. None of the local kingdoms and principalities struck silver in this period, and Judea, Nabataea, Ituraea and Commagene issued bronze only. Of the thirteen cities which became autonomous under the Seleucids, only seven struck silver before 64 B.C., in a least five cases clearly dictated by practical considerations." [A. Kushnir-Stein, *NL* 146]

284 **Le Rider, Georges.** "Histoire Economique et Monétaire de l'Orient Hellénistique." *Annuaire de Collège de France 1997-1998.* Paris, 1998. Pages 783-809.

285 **Meadows, Andrew.** "Money, Freedom, and Empire in the Hellenistic World." *Money and Its Uses in the Ancient Greek World.* Edited by A. Meadows and K. Shipton. Oxford: University Press, 2001. Pages 53-63. 5 pls.

Thomas Martin (see Martin, *Sovereignty and Coinage in Classical Greece* under GENERAL WORKS—GREEK) concluded that there was not a strong connection between sovereignty and the right of coinage in the classical Greek world—when a polis came under the control of a foreign power, its own coinage did not necessarily cease. Meadows examines whether this holds true in the Hellenistic period. He finds that this freedom began to erode. Seyrig concluded that no state issued coinage in its own name after it came under the control of a monarch [see Seyrig *Monnaies Hellénistiques* (1963) below]. Meadows shows that autonomy and coinage are not causally linked—coinage often began in an area because of the need for it rather than because of the desire of the new ruler of the area. Concludes that wherever Greek cities existed with their own institutions, they were left to their own devices. But the arrival of Rome brought more intrusion into civic affairs.

286 **Metcalf, William E., ed.** *Mnemata: Papers in Memory of Nancy M. Waggoner.* New York: American Numismatic Society, 1991. 115 pp., map, 21 pls.
A collections of papers written to honor Nancy Waggoner, the late Curator of Greek Coins at the American Numismatic Society. Contains a brief biography of Waggoner's career and a bibliography of her writings. Includes six papers, each of which is individually discussed elsewhere: "A Fifth-Century Circulation Hoard of Macedonian Tetrobols" by C. Hersh [3378], "Silver Coins and Public Slaves in the Athenian Law of 375/4 B.C." by T. Martin [4065], "Alexander's Earliest Macedonian Silver" by H. Troxell [3517], "Circulation at Babylon in 323 B.C." by M. Price [6025], "The Antioch Project" by A. Houghton [5317], and "Arabian Alexanders" by C. Arnold-Biucchi [5914]. [Reviewed by Ute Wartenberg in *Numismatic Chronicle* 153 (1993): 275-6].

287 **Mørkholm, Otto.** "The Hellenistic Period: Greece to East." *A Survey of Numismatic Research 1972-1977.* International Association of Professional Numismatists Publication No. 5. Berne: International Numismatic Commission, 1979. Pages 60-97.
A narrative overview of newly published works in the field of ancient numismatics.

288 ———. "Chronology and Meaning of the Wreathed Coinages of the Early Second Century B.C." *Quaderni Ticinesi. Numismatica e Antichità Classiche* (Switzerland) 9 (1980): 145-58. [CS 1856]

289 ———. *Early Hellenistic Coinage from the Accession of Alexander to the Peace of Apamea (336-186 B.C.).* Edited by P. Grierson and U. Westermark. Cambridge: University Press, 1991. 273 pp., 45 pls., 6 maps.
A full study of early Hellenistic coinage. Provides a general history of the coinage of Alexander the Great and his successors, and of the cities of Greece and Asia Minor between 336-188 B.C. Discusses the imitative coinages bearing the names of Philip, Alexander, and Lysimachus. Includes an epilogue by Grierson describing the main features of the coinage after 188 B.C. The text is fully annotated. Covers metals and weight standards, minting techniques and production, functions of coinage, types, inscriptions, and style. Then examines the coinage of Alexander (both lifetime and posthumous issues), Philip III, the Ptolemies, the Seleucids, Macedonia, Asia Minor and Greece. Includes lists of rulers showing reign dates, and chronological tables for the history of the period under discussion. The plates are based mainly on specimens from the Royal Coin Cabinet in Copenhagen, and illustrate over 600 coins including all types struck prior to 188, and a selection of subsequent coinages. Each coin is fully described. Includes a comprehensive bibliography for the Hellenistic period. [Reviewed by Philip Kinns in *Spink Numismatic Circular* 99, no. 8 (October 1991): 264, and by Martin J. Price in *Numismatic Chronicle* 152 (1992): 198-9].

290 **Newell, Edward T.** "A Survey of the Coinage of Alexander's Successors." *The Elder Monthly* 1, no. 3 (May 1906): 8-11.
A brief account of the evolution of coinage under Alexander the Great, the Seleucids, and the Bactrian Kingdom. Discusses changes in artistic styles, coin types, and weight standards.

291 **Oeconomides, Mando.** "From Macedonia and Epirus to the Peloponnese, with the Sporades, Cyclades, and Crete: The Hellenistic Coinages." *A Survey of Numismatic Research, 1978-1984. Volume 1: Ancient, Medieval and Modern Numismatics.* Edited by M. J. Price, et al. International Association of Professional Numismatists Special Publication, No. 9. London: International Numismatic Commission, 1986. Pages 136-49.
A narrative overview of newly published works in the field of numismatics. Summarizes the major findings, with bibliographic references cited in the footnotes.

292 **Rakicic, Mark.** "Search for Alexander the Great Leads to Journey through Time and Adventures in Ancient Babylon." *The Celator* 5, no. 6 (June 1991): 26-8.
Fictional account of a collector traveling back in time to meet Alexander the Great, Ptolemy, and Lysimachus.

293 **Rostovtzeff, Michael I.** "Some Remarks on the Monetary and Commercial Policy of the Seleucids and Attalids." *Anatolian Studies Presented to William Hepburn Buckler.* Publications of the University of Manchester, No. 265. Edited by W. M. Calder and J. Keil. Manchester: University Press, 1939. Pages 277-98. 2 pls.
Examines the evidence of hoards for coin circulation and economics in the Seleucid and Attalid kingdoms of the third and second centuries B.C. Discusses the tendency toward monetary unification during the Hellenistic period. Examines coin circulation patterns and cooperation between the Seleucids and Attalids as shown by their monetary practices.

294 ———. *The Social and Economic History of the Hellenistic World.* Three volumes. Oxford: Clarendon Press, 1941. Reprint, 1998. 1779 pp.
An extensive review of the economy of the Hellenistic age, through the period of Roman domination. Also includes two brief numismatic essays. [See J. G. Milne "Athenian Coins" under ATTICA—GENERAL WORKS, and E. S. G. Robinson "Coins Standards" under EGYPT—PTOLEMAIC KINGDOM].

295 **Rowlandson, Jane.** "Money Use among the Peasantry of Ptolemaic and Roman Egypt." *Money and Its Uses in the Ancient Greek World.* Edited by A. Meadows and K. Shipton. Oxford: University Press, 2001. Pages 145-55.
Rowlandson concludes that, in the context of rural Egypt, money use does not seem to have produced any clearly differentiated category of social relationships or activities, but instead became incorporated within the wider existing patterns of interactions.

296 **Seyrig, Henri.** "Monnaies Hellénistiques." *Revue Numismatique* (France) 6th ser., 5 (1963): 7-64. 7 pls. [CS 2625]

"Deals with a number of problems of Hellenistic chronology and classification." [C. Kraay]. "Includes Bosporus, Paeonia, Macedon, Asia Minor with Ephesus, Magnesia, Aspendos and Side." [E. Clain-Stefanelli]

297 ——— "Monnaies Hellénistiques." *Revue Numismatique* (France) 6th ser., 6 (1964): 7-67. 8 pls.

298 ——— "Monnaies Hellénistiques." *Revue Numismatique* (France) 6th ser., 11 (1969): 36-52. 2 pls. [CS 1871]
"Important for Lysimachus." [E. Clain-Stefanelli]

299 ——— "Monnaies Hellénistiques." *Revue Numismatique* (France) 6th ser., 13 (1971): 7-25. 2 pls. [CS 1872]

300 **Vagi, David L.** "Greek Coins of the Hellenistic Age." *The Celator* 11, no. 8 (August 1997): 18-20. Illus.
A brief discussion of the nature of coinage during the Hellenistic era. Reviews the use of royal portraits on coins, date letters on coins, etc.

301 ——— "Alexander's Legacy on Coinage." *Numismatist* 120, no. 4 (April 2007): 79-81. Illus.
Examines the coinage of Alexander the Great and Lysimachus, focusing on the long series of coinages issued by many authorities and imitated by peoples on the fringes of the Greek world. Many of the later imitations were lighter in weight than posthumous Alexanders. As a result, the heavier coins were often countermarked (between 180-150 B.C.) to distinguish them from the newer, lighter issues.

Also see: Barag "Lead Currency from the Hellenistic Period" under Palestine—Judea; Buckley "An Analysis...Hellenistic" under Metallurgy; Crawford "Trade and Movement" under Hoards; de Callataÿ "Guerres et Monnayages" under Pontos; de Callataÿ *Recueil Quantitatif* under The Minting Process; Holt *Thundering Zeus* under Bactria; Hoover *Handbook of Greek Coinage* under Collecting Guides; Jidejian *Lebanon and the Greek World...Eddé Collection* under Portraits; Jones "Epigraphical Notes" under Epigraphy; Klose and Müseler *Statthalter Rebellen Könige* under Seleucid Kingdom; Kroh "Reference Reviews" under General Works—Greek; Lawton "Hellenistic Coin Portraits" under Portraits; Le Rider et al. *Kraay—Mørkholm Essays* under General Works—Greek.

Metcalf *Oxford Handbook of Greek and Roman Coinage* under General Works—Greek; Mørkholm "Some Reflections" under General Works—Greek; Newell *Royal Greek Portrait Coins* under Portraits; Newell "Some Cypriote Alexanders" under Macedonian Kingdom—General Works; Oliver "Politics of Coinage" under Attica—General Works; Rakicic "Pixodarus" under Caria; Vagi "Later Alexandrine Coinage" under Macedonian Kingdom—General Works; Vagi "A Dozen Gems" under Portraits; Vagi "Greek Monarchs" under Types; Van der Werf and Secord *Rulers* under General Works—Greek; Vermeule "A Ptolemaic Contribution Box" under Egypt—Ptolemaic Kingdom; Warren "The Achaian League, Sparta, Luccullus" under Peloponnesos—Achaia; Widemann *Les Successeurs d'Alexandre* under Bactria and Northwest India.

COLLECTING GUIDES

But to collect, admire, study and revere ancient Greek coins is not a mere hobby, it is an avocation which brings us to a clearer understanding of one of the most interesting parts of mankind's history, which lifts our hearts to the highest peaks of art that humanity has ever produced, which inculcates us with veneration for the past and which in some cases helps us to forget a not too agreeable present.

—Paul S. Szego, 1937

302 **Akerman, John Yonge.** *A Numismatic Manual, or a Guide to the Collection and Study of Greek, Roman and English Coins.* London: Effingham Wilson, 1832. Second edition, London: Taylor & Walton, 1840. 420 pp., illus.
Describes the origins of coinage, discusses mythological representations on Greek and Roman coins, and presents an overview of Greek, Roman, and English coinage. Presents a ninety-four page listing of the cities and kingdoms which issued coins during the Greek period. Includes a table of drawings illustrating examples of Greek autonomous coin types.

303 ——— *An Introduction to the Study of Ancient and Modern Coins.* London: John Russell Smith, 1848. 220 pp., illus.
A general guide providing an introduction to Greek, Roman, British, Scottish, Irish, and European coinage. Pages 1-34 are devoted to Greek coinage. After brief comments on the origins of coinage, the author describes some of the most important coins of the Greek kingdoms and the independent Greek cities. Illustrated by line drawings.

304 **Anthony, John.** *Collecting Greek Coins.* New York: Longman Group, 1983. 301 pp., illus.
A broad introduction to Greek numismatics providing an overview of how to build a collection, a review of minting techniques, an examination of the coinage of various geographical areas and time periods including Jewish, Parthian and Sasanian coins along with the traditional archaic, classical and Hellenistic Greek coins. Several chapters discuss themes for collecting such as religion, monsters, river-gods, and the voyage of the Argo. Includes photographs of the most important coin types. [A very critical review by Martin J. Price appears in *Numismatic Chronicle* 145 (1985): 273].

305 **Askew, Gilbert.** *A Catalogue of Greek Coins.* London: B. A. Seaby, 1951. 124 pp., illus. [CS 1807]
A catalogue of 2185 coin types, illustrated by line drawings. Discusses weight standards, denominations, and dating. Includes indices of cities and kings. Market values are given in British pounds. [For an updated version of this book, see Seaby and Kozolubski below].

306 **Barry, Kevin, and Zachary Beasley.** "Topical Collecting: Getting Your Feet Wet in Greek Silver." *The Celator* 20, no. 6 (June 2006): 44, 46. Illus.
Suggests forming a series of the hemidrachms of Argos—an affordable coin for collectors. Also suggests the drachms of Apollonia and Dyrrachium. Lists some of the classes of these coins as arranged by Dr. Gyula Petrányi.

307 ——— "The Most Popular Ancient Coin." *The Celator* 23, no. 10 (October 2009): 48. Illus.
An overview of the Athenian "owl" tetradrachm—viewed by the authors as the most popular coin among collectors.

308 **Berk, Harlan J.** "Your First 25 Greek Silver Coins: A Basic Collection." *World Coin News* (February 4, 1991): 10, 18, 20. Illus.
Lists twenty-five silver coins that would form a solid foundation for a collection of Greek coins. The goal was to choose a cross-section of Greek coinage for no more than $3000 per coin. The types chosen are illustrated and described.

309 ——— *100 Greatest Ancient Coins.* Atlanta: Whitman Publishing, 2008. 131 pp., illus.
An illustrated listing of one hundred Greek, Roman, and Byzantine coins which the author considers to be of the greatest artistic or historical significance. Each coin is beautifully illustrated and fully described, with historical background and other commentary. Begins with an introduction to collecting ancient coins incorporating discussions of the marketplace, grading, and conservation. Then two pages are devoted to each of the top ten coins. Coins eleven through 100 are each featured on their own page. [Reviewed by David Hendin in *The Celator* 22, no. 7 (July 2008): 30-1, 37. A review article by Michael E. Marotta appears in *The Celator* 22, no. 11 (November 2008): 34-5, 37].

310 **Blamberg, Jan.** "Reflection of Beauty: Greek Art Pervaded Coins." *The Celator* 2, no. 12 (December 1988): 1, 21, 23. Illus.
Suggests themes for building a collection of Greek coins including one coin per century, historical themes, economic and political themes, geographic themes, and symbolism.

311 **Bray, Thom.** "Collecting Greek Coins: Let Your Imagination Become Your Guide." *Coin World* (June 14, 2004): 102. Illus.

In this very brief introduction to Greek coinage, Bray encourages the beginner to collect inexpensive bronze coins.

312 ———— "Carving Up the Ancient World: Part II: Collecting Ancient Greek Coins." *Coin World* (May 14, 2007): 60. Illus.
Brief suggestions of different ways to collect Greek coins.

313 **Brunk, Gregory G.** "A Tentative Index to Modern Numismatic Auction Catalogs and Pricelists: Ancient Coins." *SAN—Journal of the Society for Ancient Numismatics* 10, no. 2 (September 1979): 24-6.
An index to auction catalogues and dealer price lists which contain especially useful information for identifying ancient coins. Over 2500 catalogues issued since World War II were searched. The emphasis is on Greek coinage. The index is divided geographically.

314 **Cahn, Herbert A.** "Coins." Chapter 6 in *Collecting Greek Antiquities* by Herbert Hoffman. New York: Clarkson N. Potter, Inc., 1971. Pages 205-27. Illus.
This introduction to collecting Greek coins begins with a brief discussion of coins as works of art. Next, the ancient minting process is described, followed by an explanation of coin denominations. A concise history of coinage during the Greek period is followed by some basic recommendations for acquiring and storing a coin collection. Concludes with a brief list of significant museum collections throughout the world. Representative samples of Greek coins are illustrated.

315 **Darling, John.** "Dolphins Around: Ancient Coins as Sacred Objects, Carriers of Myth and Personal Totems." *The Celator* 7, no. 7 (July 1993): 40-2. Illus.
This narrative relates the thrill of shopping for an interesting coin and focuses on the collector's fascination with the symbolism of the ancient goddess depicted on the chosen coin.

316 **Davisson, Allan.** "How-to-Guide: Collecting Greek Coins as an Art Form." *The Celator* 1, no. 5 (October/November 1987): 1, 9, 16-17.
Gives advice for collectors on judging artistic style in coins, choosing a dealer, and determining the authenticity of coins. Segregates Greek coinage into six historical periods and describes the general characteristics of coinage for each. Describes sixteen coins which are recommended as a basis for a collection of Greek coins and suggests some collecting themes and basic books.

317 **Giedroyc, Richard.** "A Beginner's Guide to Ancient Coins." *World Coins* (supplement to *Coin World*). March 1987. 52 pp., illus.
A brief introduction to Greek, Roman, and Byzantine coins. Describes the history of coinage during ancient times, recommends basic books, discusses grading, style, collecting themes.

318 ———— "Allure of Ancient Coins Excites Collectors." *Make a Start with Ancients: Special Supplement to Numismatic News, World Coin News, and Bank Note Reporter.* Iola: Krause Publications, 1999. Pages A3-6. Illus.
A general introduction to collecting ancient coins. Includes brief discussions of the origin of coinage, various periods of art in Greek coinage, and Roman coinage.

319 **Goldsborough, Reid.** "The Changing World of Numismatic Literature: Attributing Ancient Greek-Era Coins—Part 1." *The Celator* 21, no. 4 (April 2007): 30-6. "Part 2." The Celator 21, no. 5 (May 2007): 30-1, 34-7.
Part 1 is a list of books commonly used for attributing Greek coins, along with a discussion of attribution and other helpful sources of information. Part 2 is a list of all volumes in the *Sylloge Numorum Graecorum* series.

320 **Hazlitt, William Carew.** *The Confessions of a Collector.* London: Ward and Downey, 1897. 360 pp.
Hazlitt (b. 1834; d. 1913) discusses some of the great coin dealers of the nineteenth century (e.g., Lincoln, Rollin and Feuardent, Spinks) and important collectors (e.g., Hyman Montagu, John Evans, William Greenwell).

321 **Head, Barclay V.** *The Young Collector's Handbook of Greek and Roman Coins.* London: W. Swan Sonnenschein & Co., 1871. Later appeared as a chapter entitled "Greek and Roman Coins" in *English Coins and Tokens, with a Chapter on Greek and Roman Coins*, by Llewellyn F. W. Jewitt. London: W. Swan Sonnenschein & Co., 1888. Pages 95-128. Illus. Reprinted as *Handbook of Greek and Roman Coins*. New York: Attic Books, 1969. 32 pp., illus. [CS 1648]
Provides an introduction to ancient coins for beginners. Introduces the metals, terminology, types, symbols, and inscriptions related to Greek coins. Illustrates and describes the gods and goddesses which appear on Greek coins. Lists the general geographical arrangement used in cataloging Greek coins. Discusses methods of minting and the common denominations. Also contains some basic information on Roman coins.

322 **Hoover, Oliver D., ed.** *The Handbook of Greek Coinage Series.* Lancaster: Classical Numismatic Group, 2009+.
A series of thirteen volumes, each covering a specific area of Greek coinage. Intended as a quick guide to identification, cross-referenced to a major work which will provide more in-depth information about each coin. The catalogues are arranged chronologically for royal issues, and regionally for the civic issues. Within each region, cities are listed directionally. For those rulers or cities that issued coins concurrently in all three metals, these issues are arranged with gold first, followed by silver, and then bronze. Each metal is arranged by denomination, largest to smallest. Known mints for the royal coinage are listed below the appropriate type, making it easy to search for a specific mint. Each entry includes a rarity rating based on the frequency with which they appear in publications, public and private collections, the market, or are estimated to exist in public or private hands. No market valuations are listed, but a website is maintained with current values (www.greekcoinvalues.com). Each volume includes a *Preface* by D. Scott VanHorn and Bradley R. Nelson which provides an overview of the history of Greek coinage, minting methods, denominations, types, epigraphy, and basic information for collectors regarding grading.

1. [Forthcoming]
2. [Forthcoming]
3. [Forthcoming]
4. [Forthcoming]
5. *Handbook of Coins of the Peloponnesos: Achaia, Phleiasia, Sikyonia, Elis, Triphylia, Messenia, Lakonia, Argolis, and Arkadia, Sixth to First Centuries BC,* by Oliver D. Hoover. 2011. lxxiv + 293 pp., illus. [4294]

6. *Handbook of Coins of the Islands: Adriatic, Ionian, Thracian, Aegean, and Carpathian Seas (Excluding Crete and Cyprus), Sixth to First Centuries BC*, by Oliver D. Hoover. 2010. lxxxii + 358 pp., illus. [4454]
7. *Handbook of Coins of Northern and Central Anatolia: Pontus, Paphlagonia, Bithynia, Phrygia, Galatia, Lykaonia and Kappadokia (with Kolchis and the Kimmerian Bosporos), Fifth to First Centuries BC*, by Oliver D. Hoover. 2012. lxxxii + 352 pp., illus. [4501]
8. [Forthcoming]
9. *Handbook of Syrian Coins: Royal and Civic Issues, Fourth to First Centuries BC*, by Oliver D. Hoover. 2009. lxviii + 332 pp., illus. [5296]
10. *Handbook of Coins of the Southern Levant: Phoenicia, Southern Koile Syria (Including Judaea), and Arabia, Fifth to First Centuries BC*, by Oliver D. Hoover. 2010. lxxix + 201 pp., illus. [5210]
11. [Forthcoming]
12. [Forthcoming]
13. [Forthcoming]

323 **Houghton, Arthur, and David Hendin.** "Defining Rarity." *The Celator* 22, no. 6 (June 2008): 28-31; 37.
The authors provide a framework for categorizing Seleucid coins and Jewish coins by rarity. For each, they establish rarity indicators (C, S, R1, R2, R3) and describe the approximate known quantity and frequency of appearance on the market for gold, silver, and bronze coins. The hope is that this framework will result in a more consistent and well-defined terminology for these two coin series. They suggest a similar framework could be established for other groups of ancient coins.

324 **Humphreys, Henry Noel.** *The Coin Collector's Manual, or Guide to the Numismatic Student in the Formation of a Cabinet of Coins.* 2 volumes. London: H. G. Bohn, 1853. London: George Bell & Sons, 1876. 726 pp., illus.
Discusses the earliest coins, then traces the development of coinage throughout Greek lands. Describes artistic developments, weight-standards, denominations, metals, the origins and nature of coin types, inscriptions. Continues with Roman and Greek Imperial coinage. Volume 2 covers the coinage of modern Europe and England. Includes eleven plates of coin illustrations from steel engravings.

325 **Kibbey, Mead B.** "Some Notes on Collecting Ancient Greek Coins." *The Numismatist* 66, no. 12 (December 1953): 1285-7. Reprinted in *Selections from The Numismatist: Ancient and Medieval Coins.* Racine: Whitman Publishing Co., 1960. Pages 30-2.
An introduction to Greek numismatics for the beginner. Defines the scope of Greek coinage, recommends some basic books, and introduces the Greek coin denominations and weight standards.

326 **Klawans, Zander H.** *An Outline of Ancient Greek Coins.* Racine: Whitman Publishing Co., 1959. Second edition, 1964. Reprint, New York: Sanford J. Durst, 1982. 206 pp., illus., maps. [CS 1846]
A basic introduction to Greek coinage with brief discussions of minting techniques, types, denominations, and inscriptions. Several hundred of the principal coin types are photographed and arranged by city. Reviews common persons and deities found on coins, and Greek kings and rulers portrayed on coins. [The Durst reprint contains two additional pages of suggested reading].

327 ———. *Handbook of Ancient Greek & Roman Coins.* Edited by Kenneth E. Bressett. New York: St. Martin's Griffin, 1995. 288 pages, illus.
Klawans' two books, *An Outline of Ancient Greek Coins* (see above) and *Reading and Dating Roman Imperial Coins* are here combined into one book, with an introduction by Ken Bressett.

328 **Koppersmith, Daniel.** "Important Auction Catalogs Offering Archaic and Classical Greek Coins." *The Celator* 21, no. 5 (May 2007): 22-8. Illus.
Lists and describes numerous auction catalogues that are worthwhile additions to a library—primarily those offering a significant number of coins and excellent photographic plates.

329 **Ladd, Raymond.** *The Illustrated Grading Guide to Ancient Numismatics.* Illustrations by D. R. Tupper. Santa Ana: JSD Numismatic Publications, 1977. 48 pp., illus.
An excellent guide for beginners, this book uses line drawings to illustrate the grading of struck and cast ancient coins. Provides the German and French equivalents of the grades. This book goes beyond describing the amount of wear on a coin. It defines the terminology commonly used to grade and describe ancient coins and provides illustrations, including: brockage, corroded dies, counterstamp, crystallization, die breaks, graffiti, horn silver, tooled, and worn dies, and many more. Illustrates a few basic minting tools.

330 **Mabbott, Thomas Ollive.** "What is a Greek Coin?" *Numismatic Review* 1, no. 2 (September 1943): 72-3.
Attempts to define the term "Greek coin" as used by collectors. Suggests that a Greek coin is any ancient coin minted ca. 700 B.C. to A.D. 300 which is not purely Roman, Far Eastern, Indian, or barbarous in character. The author suggests Greek coins are those inspired by Greek culture, regardless of whether they bear Greek inscriptions.

331 **Miller, Michael F.** *Classical Greek and Roman Coins: The Investor's Handbook.* Connecticut: The Altara Group, 1982. 221 pp., illus.
An introduction to ancient coins for the investor. Provides background on the hobby of collecting ancient coins and an introduction to buying and selling coins. Discusses the financial aspects of coin investing: income tax treatment, investment performance, guidelines for successful investing. Provides tips on selecting coin dealers, buying at coin shows and auctions, record keeping, grading, home security, and selling a collection. Describes the qualities of investment-grade coins including style, centering, toning. Contains a glossary of common terms.

332 **Newman, R. W.** "Cleaning Ancient Coins." *The Voice of the Turtle* 4, no. 3 (March 1965): 7-8. Illus.
Describes some practical methods used in the cleaning of ancient coins.

333 **Palmer, Thomas A., Jr.** "Forming a Representative Set of Ancient Coins." *The Numismatist* 103, no. 11 (November 1990): 1773-80, 1831-3.
Describes and illustrates forty Greek, Roman, and Byzantine coins which are affordable and available, and which provide the new collector of ancient coins a good starting point in forming a collection.

334 **Pennington, Paul.** "$100.00 to Spend for Ancient Coins." *Numismatic Scrapbook Magazine* 14, no. 9 (September 1948): 793-7. Illus.
The author attempts to form a representative set of ancient coins by spending just $100. He chooses six coins in Very Fine or better condition which represent some major phases of Greek and Roman coinage. The coins are an incuse stater of Metapontum, an archaic drachm of Cnidus, a tetradrachm of Alexander the Great, a Roman Republican didrachm, a denarius of the Roman Republic, and a Roman Imperial denarius. Describes each coin type and the reasons it was selected.

335 **Raymond, Wayte.** "Obtainable Types of Greek Coins." *Coin Collector's Journal* 1, no. 5 (August 1934): 112-3. 1 pl.; no. 6 (September 1934): 134-5. 1 pl.; no. 7 (October 1934): 154-5. 1 pl.; no. 8 (November 1934): 176-7. 1 pl.; no. 9 (December 1934): 206-7. 1 pl.; no. 10 (January 1935): 228-9. 1 pl.
A listing of sixty-eight Greek coins which the author considers to be readily obtainable by collectors. All are illustrated. These plates were later incorporated into the author's *Ancient Coins* booklet (see below).

336 ——— *Ancient Coins: Greek, Roman and Byzantine. Guide and Price List.* New York: Wayte Raymond, Inc., 1936. 28 pp. including the 13 plates. Revised edition, *Guide to Ancient Coins.* Coin Collectors Series, No. 11. New York: Wayte Raymond, Inc., 1944 and 1950. 28 pp.
This brief collector's guide lists and illustrates the major types of ancient coins, including sixty-eight Greek coins, showing approximate market values, often in two grades.

337 ——— *A Pictorial Introduction to Greek and Roman Coins.* New York: Wayte Raymond, Inc., n.d. 16 pp. including 8 pls.
Illustrates and briefly describes sixty-eight common Greek coin types as well as seventy common Roman denarii. All coins are photographed.

338 **Rynearson, Paul.** *Collecting Ancient Greek Coins: A Guided Tour Featuring 25 Significant Types.* Racine: Whitman, 2009. 256 pp., illus.
Rynearson explains how to get started collecting ancient Greek coins, emphasizing how to evaluate quality and value. Briefly explains the basics of grading ancient coins and reviews how the coins are catalogued. Provides tips on photographing a collection. Discusses types, denominations, classifications, valuations, coin hoards, famous collections and collectors, symbolism, forgeries in the marketplace, and the risks of cleaning coins. He also lists other useful reference books. Concludes with an "action guide" to building a collection, focusing on twenty-five key coin types. Throughout the book, Rynearson guides the reader in selecting quality coins. An excellent starting point for any collector. Don't miss his comments under "Additional References" on page 98! [Reviewed by M. Marotta in *The Celator* 23, no. 3 (March 2009): 44].

339 **Sayles, Wayne G.** *Ancient Coin Collecting.* Iola, Wisconsin: Krause Publications, 1996. 208 pp., illus. Second edition, 2003. 299 pp., illus.
A good introduction to collecting ancient coins including Greek, Roman, Romaion (Byzantine), and non-classical coins. Begins with brief overviews of the ancient world and the history of collecting ancient coins. Continues with information on ancient coin collectors' clubs and societies, recommended periodicals, coin shows, collector's resources on the internet, the market for ancient coins, and numismatic literature. Provides basic information on identifying ancient coins and provides suggestions on how to begin a collection. Includes a glossary and a bibliography. [Reviewed by Alan Walker in *The Celator* 10, no. 11 (November 1996): 50-2. Also see Sayles' follow-up comments to Walker's review in *The Celator* 10, no. 12 (December 1996): 16. Also reviewed by David Vagi in *SAN* 20, no. 1 (1997): 31].

340 ——— "Centering is an Important Aspect of Eye Appeal." *The Celator* 10, no. 5 (May 1996): 40.
The author points out the importance of centering when choosing a coin for one's collection. Discusses the effect on eye appeal of various types of off-center strikes.

341 ——— "Surfaces are an Important Aspect of a Coin's Desirability." *The Celator* 10, no. 6 (June 1996): 18-9.
The author points out the importance of surface condition when choosing a coin for one's collection.

342 ——— *Ancient Coin Collecting 2: Numismatic Art of the Greek World.* Iola, Wisconsin: Krause Publications, 1997. 208 pp., illus. Second edition, 2007. 304 pp., illus.
An interesting introduction to Greek coinage of the archaic, classical, and Hellenistic periods. Begins with brief chapters on the origin and use of coinage, denominations, and dating. Sayles then describes some of the most popular and significant coin-types from each geographical area of the Greek world. Each geographical section includes maps and brief bibliographies. He then examines the artistic aspects of the coinage by discussing engravers, symbolism, Greek dress and hair styles, recurring mythological themes on coinage, and athletic aspects of Greek coinage. The archaic, classical, and Hellenistic periods of art are then treated separately. This is followed by a review of Hellenistic numismatic portraiture. He concludes by illustrating and discussing twenty-six of the masterpieces of Greek numismatic art. Each is illustrated by an enlarged photograph. Includes a brief glossary, table of historical events, a general bibliography, and an index.

343 ——— *Ancient Coin Collecting 6: Non-Classical Cultures.* Iola, Wisconsin: Krause Publications, 1999. 197 pp., illus.
This well-illustrated introduction to the ancient coinage of non-classical cultures includes discussions of the history and coinage of the Celts, Visigoths, Ostrogoths, Vandals, Lombards, Beneventum, Scythian Kings of Thrace, Kingdom of Sophene, the Artaxiads, Armenian Commagene, Media Atropatene, Cilician Armenia, the Persians, Parthians, Sakaraukae, Sasanians, early Central Asian kingdoms, the Huns, China, Indo-Scythians, Indo-Parthians, the Western Kshatrapas, Kushans, Guptas, Persis, Elymais, Characene, Judean coinage (Hasmonean Kings through the Bar Kochba Revolt and city coinage), Arabia and Nabataea, Sabaeans and Katabanians, Himyarites, Islamic Dynasties, Umayyad Caliphate, Abbasid Caliphate, Fatamid Dynasty, the Ayyubids, Turkish Dynasties of Central Asia and Mesopotamia, Mongols in Persia and Asia Minor, Axumites, and Pharaonic Egypt. Includes bibliographies and a section illustrating some masterpieces of non-classical coinage.

344 **Scaros, Dean.** "In Defense of Magic: An Appreciation of Under-Appreciated Coins." *The Celator* 23, no. 6 (June 2009): 34-6. Illus.
Scaros suggests that many coins possess an 'esprit de coin'—a spirit or aspect to their art or appearance that make them attractive to a collector, regardless of their physical faults (wear, corrosion).

345 **Seaby, Herbert A., and Julius Kozolubski.** *Greek Coins and Their Values.* London: B. A. Seaby, 1959. 157 pp., 4 pls. Second edition, 1966. 218 pp., 8 pls. Revised edition, 1975. [CS 1866]
This revised and expanded version of Askew's work (see Askew *A Catalogue of Greek Coins* above) is a collector's guide to Greek coins with introductory material, a catalogue of types, and approximate market values for the coins. The 1975 edition is the same as the 1966 edition except for the addition of a sixteen-page revised valuations list. [The second edition was reviewed by R. A. G. Carson in *Times Literary Supplement* (October 13, 1966): 945]. This book was substantially revised by David R. Sear in 1978 (see Sear *Greek Coins and Their Values* below).

346 **Sear, David R.** *Collecting Greek Coins.* London: Stanley Gibbons Publications, 1977. 32 pp., illus. [CS 1867]
An introduction to Greek coinage covering the origins of coinage, a brief account of Greek history, coin types and denominations, dating, and advice on forming a collection. An appendix lists rulers and reign dates. Illustrated throughout by coin photographs.

347 ——— *Greek Coins and Their Values, Vol. 1: Europe.* London: Seaby, 1978. Reprinted, 1994, 1995, 1997. 357 pp., maps, illus. *Vol. 2: Asia and Africa.* London: Seaby, 1979. Reprinted 1994, 1996. 393 pp., maps, illus. [CS 1868]
The most popular collector's guide to Greek coins. Introductory chapters cover the history and development of Greek coinage, major coin types (including descriptions of the major gods and heroes), weight standards, denominations, and dating. Also includes a bibliography and tables of ancient alphabets. Lists 7957 coins representing all types of Greek coins. Most major types are illustrated with photographs of coins from the British Museum. The coins are arranged geographically and are grouped by metal (precious or base) and period (archaic, classical and Hellenistic). Coins of the Hellenistic monarchies are incorporated into Volume 2. Includes some Celtic coinages as well as early Parthian coinage. Brief historical outlines appear at the beginning of each section. Value estimates in British pounds are given for each coin. A series of maps pinpoint the locations of most of the coin-issuing cities. Well indexed. [These volumes are a revised version of *Greek Coins and Their Values* (1959 and 1966) by Herbert A. Seaby and J. Kozolubski. Also see Szaivert, Szaivert, and Sear below for a German edition. Volume 2 was reviewed by G. Boon in *Seaby Coin and Medal Bulletin* No. 728 (April 1979): 124-5].

348 ——— *Greek Imperial Coins and Their Values: The Local Coinages of the Roman Empire.* London: Seaby Publications, Ltd., 1982. 636 pages, illus., 10 maps.
Although primarily devoted to Roman Provincial coinage, this catalogue provides a supplement to the listings in Sear's *Greek Coins and Their Values* (see above) in that it contains listings of coins issued by authorities independent of direct Roman control or who came within the category of client kingdoms, including the dynastic issues of Celtic Britain up to the time of the Roman conquest, the restored kingdom of Thrace, the kingdoms of Pontus and Bosporus, the Syrian kingdom, and Commagene. Jewish coinage includes issues of the kings of the Herodian dynasty and later coinages. Also includes the coinage of the Parthian Empire, extending down to the Sasanian conquest in A.D. 223. Also includes coins of the Nabataeans, Himyarites, Edessa, Elymais, Characene, Persis, and Mauretania. In all, the book lists 6034 coin types and provides estimated market values for each.

349 **Sherwood, Earle D.** "Ancient Greek Coins: How to Quickly Identify Many of Them." *Numismatic Scrapbook Magazine* 16, no. 7 (July 1950): 561-6. Illus. Reprinted, *Numismatic Scrapbook Magazine* 27, no. 4 (April 1961): 1147-52. Illus.
General comments on the art and types of Greek coins. Includes brief descriptions of popular coin types from some of the major cities of the Greek world.

350 **Spring, John.** *Ancient Coin Auction Catalogues 1880-1980.* London: John Spring (distributed by Spink), 2009. 374 pp., illus.
Lists and describes 886 auction catalogues from England, Europe, and the United States, beginning in 1880 with the first use of photographic plates. Includes every catalogue printed through 1914 that included at least one plate of ancient coins. Includes those with at least two plates of ancients through 1945, and those with at least five plates of ancients through 1980 when the proliferation of dealers greatly expanded the number of catalogues published. The list includes 32 catalogues in which Celtic coins are prominent and 142 sales of Greek coins. The balance of the sales feature Roman aes grave, struck Roman Republican coins, Roman Imperial coins, Roman Provincial coins, Byzantine coins, coins of the Barbarian migrations, or ancient Spain. Includes biographical sketches of many of the significant dealers recounting the history of their firms, as well as biographical information on some of the important collectors who were consignors to the listed sales. The locales in which the major auction houses worked are shown in several photographs. [Reviewed by Oliver Hoover in *Numismatic Chronicle* 169 (2009): 442-4].

351 **Starck, Jeff.** "Coinage of Ancient Greece Doesn't Have to Be Confusing." *Coin World* (March 27, 2006): 16-20. Illus.
An overview of Greek coinage for beginning collectors.

352 **Sutherland, Carol H. V.** *Ancient Numismatics: A Brief Introduction.* New York: American Numismatic Society, 1958. 29 pp. [CS 1676]
The text of a lecture, this booklet delves into the history of coin collecting. After a general discussion, the author comments on the use of coins as historical documents in the study of chronology, economics, politics, and art. [Reviewed by R. A. G. Carson in *Numismatic Chronicle* (1961): 244-5].

353 **Szaivert, Eva, Wolfgang Szaivert, and David R. Sear.** *Griechischer Münzkatalog. Band 1: Europe.* Munich, 1980. *Band 2: Asien und Afrika.* Munich, 1984. [CS 1876]
The German edition of David Sear's *Greek Coins and Their Values* (see above), with some modifications. It is printed in a larger format and features a few extra coins and some auction prices realized. The catalogue is presented chronologically (rather than separating the archaic period pieces and bronze coinage as was done in the English editions). A different numbering system is used, but the coins are cross-referenced to the English edition numbers.

354 **Szego, Paul S.** "Why and How to Collect Ancient Greek Coins." *The Coin Collector's Journal* new series, 3 (January 1937): 206 ff.; (February 1937): 229 ff.; (March 1937): 254 ff. Reprinted as a booklet, *Collecting Greek Coins: Why and How to Collect Ancient Greek Coins. The Way to Form a Small Collection with Limited Means.* New York: Wayte Raymond Inc., 1937. 15 pp., illus.
This is a brief introduction to Greek numismatics written for the collector of limited means. It gives suggestions for beginning a modest collection and provides an overview of the major coin-issuing cities.

355 **Taylor, J. Edward.** "Valuing the Numismatic Legacy of Alexander the Great." *The Celator* 22, no. 1 (January 2008): 6-26. Illus.
Taylor uses statistical methods to examine the factors that influence the auction prices realized for Alexander tetradrachms. Attempts to determine which factors influence the price.

356 **Vagi, David L.** "Collecting with a Higher Purpose." *The Celator* 8, no. 9 (September 1994): 24. Illus.
Suggests the formation of a collection of Greek coins which follows an historical theme, such as coins of cities involved in a certain war.

357 —— "A Collector's *Top Ten* Guide to Successful Buying." *The Celator* 9, no. 4 (April 1995): 16.
Provides sensible guidelines to help the collector build a quality, satisfying collection.

358 —— "Roman and Greek Coins Accessible to Many." *Make a Start with Ancients: Special Supplement to Numismatic News, World Coin News, and Bank Note Reporter.* Iola: Krause Publications, 1999. Pages A7-11. Illus.
In this brief introduction to Greek and Roman coins, Vagi describes the common denominations of silver and bronze coins and comments on the collectability of each.

359 —— "Collect Coins from Many Ancient Cultures—Enormous Parameter: from Britain to India's Border." *Coin World* (November 8, 2010): 150-3. Illus.
In this installment's of Vagi's "Ancients Today" column, he provides a brief and broad overview of the many ancient cultures that struck coins.

360 —— "Coins Mirror Environment of Source Areas: Geographical Collection Can Offer a Lifetime Journey." *Coin World* (December 6, 2010): 134-7. Illus.
In this installment's of Vagi's "Ancients Today" column, he describes the major geographical areas in which a collector might specialize: Western Europe, Italy and Sicily, Central Europe, Greece, the Black Sea, Asia Minor, Syria and the Holy Land, points east, eastern North Africa, and western North Africa.

361 —— "Greek Colonization Ideal Collecting Theme." *Coin World* (March 7, 2011): 198-200. Illus.
Vagi highlights some prominent Greek colonization efforts and the resulting coinage. Includes discussion of the Corinthian colonization of Syracuse, the Spartan founding of Taras, the founding of Sinope by Miletos, the founding of Phocaea by the Athenians, and the Phocaean founding of Lampsacus, Amisos, and Massalia.

362 —— "Collecting Dime-Size Greek Silver Coins: Smaller Sizes Offer Advantages, Including Price." *Coin World* (July 4, 2011): 164, 168, 170. Illus.
Vagi suggests that collectors focus on small silver coins such as drachms and tetrobols, which can be affordable yet offer a nice selection of cities and artistic styles.

363 —— "Collecting Greek Coins." *The Numismatist* (August 2011): 73-5. Illus.
Vagi discusses some ways to collect Greek coins—by city, type, variety, and discusses some factors which may influence a collector's choices.

364 **Van Meter, David.** *Classical Numismatics and Common Sense.* Nashua: Laurion Numismatics, 1990. 84 pages.
This guide to collecting ancient coins discusses the supply and demand for ancient coins, the types of collectors, collecting themes, investing strategies, buying tips, and reviews some of the current controversies in the hobby. Concludes with a short list of ancient coin dealers and hobby publications.

365 —— *Collecting Greek Coins: A Complete Guide to Beginning and Enjoying a Collection of Classical Greek Coins.* Nashua: Laurion Numismatics, 1990. 144 pages, 18 pls.
An introduction to collecting Greek coins, focusing on the silver issues which are most popular with collectors. Discusses the origins of coinage, denominations, grading (includes a few photographs illustrating various levels of condition), factors in pricing coins, and counterfeits. Continues with an overview of the coinage of the major cities of Magna Graecia, Sicily, Northern Greece, the Greek mainland, and the Macedonian kings. Concludes with a brief chapter on market values, with estimated prices given for several dozen major coin types. The plates illustrate 187 coins.

366 **Wear, Ted G.** *Ancient Coins: How to Collect for Fun and Profit.* Garden City: Doubleday and Co., 1965. 152 pp., 16 pls. [CS 1677]
This beginners' guide to ancient coins includes a brief introduction to the Greek gods and nine plates of Greek coins.

367 **Zemke, Jeff.** "A Beginner's Ancient Journey." *The Celator* 18, no. 8 (August 2004): 26-31. Illus.
A beginning collector of ancient coins recounts his experiences.

Also see: Guilluame *Analysis of Reasonings* under BACTRIA; Hoover *Handbook of Syrian Coins* under SYRIA—SELEUCID KINGDOM; Hoover *Handbook of Coins of the Southern Levant* under ASIA—GENERAL WORKS; Shahar "Factors Influencing Auction Estimates" under NORTHERN GREECE—THESSALY; Vagi "Searching for a Pedigree" under SICILY—SYRACUSE; Vagi "Bronzes of Asia Minor" under ASIA MINOR—GENERAL WORKS; Walker "Catalogues and Their Collectors" under PRIVATE COLLECTIONS.

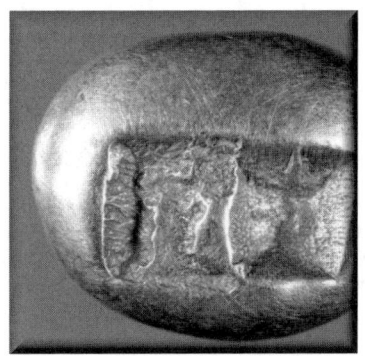

ORIGINS OF COINAGE

Now there is no reason to suppose that the finds from the Artemision do not represent a fair sample of the currency actually in circulation at the time they were laid down; and the high proportion of those pieces (otherwise extremely rare) which represent the stages immediately preceding true coinage compels the conclusion that we are very near in time to its invention. As one passes from the mere dump, through the punched dump, the punched and striated dump, the punched and striated dump with a type cut into it, to the normal coin, and all lying in nearly contemporary deposits, little if at all affected in appearance or weight by wear, one has the feeling of assisting at the very birth of coinage.

—E. S. G. Robinson, 1951

368   **Askew, Gilbert.** "The Origins of Greek Coinage." *Seaby's Coin and Medal Bulletin* 381 (February 1950): 51-3. Illus.
A brief account of the origins of coinage. Discusses early barter and the use of precious metals, the introduction of electrum coinage without types, gold and silver coins with types, and eventually coins bearing inscriptions. Mentions the spread of coinage beyond Asia Minor to Greece.

369   **Babelon, Ernest C.** *Les Origines de la Monnaie Considerés au Point de vue Économique et Historique.* Paris: Didot, 1897. 427 pp. [CS 1464]
[Reviewed by Percy Gardner in *Classical Review* 11, no. 3 (April 1897): 172-3].

370   **Balmuth, Miriam S.** "Epigraphical Intimations of Early Coinage in the Near East." *American Journal of Archaeology* 67, no. 2 (April 1963): 208.
A summary of a paper presented at the 1962 meeting of the Archaeological Institute of America. Inscriptions as early as the eighteenth century B.C. can be interpreted to refer to pre-weighed, recognizable money. These may be the forerunners of coinage.

371   ——— *Forerunners of Coinage: Observations on the Monetary Forerunners of Coinage in the Aegean and the Near East with Special Reference to the Origins of Coinage.* Ph.D. dissertation, Harvard University, 1964.

372   ——— "The Monetary Forerunners of Coinage in Phoenicia and Palestine." *The Patterns of Monetary Development in Phoenicia and Palestine in Antiquity: Proceedings, International Numismatic Convention, Jerusalem, 27-31 December 1963.* Edited by A. Kindler. Tel-Aviv and Jerusalem: Schocken Publishing House, 1967. Pages 25-32. 6 pls. [CS 2894]
Balmuth discusses the transition from money to weighed-metal as a forerunner to the transition from weighed-metal to coinage. Discusses ancient references to the establishment of metal as the measure of value, even though the metal itself was not required for every payment. Discusses the archaeological evidence for the use of metal as currency, including hoards of precious metal ingots and ancient scales and weights.

373   ——— "Remarks on the Appearance of the Earliest Coins." *Studies Presented to George M. A. Hanfmann.* Fogg Art Museum Monographs in Art and Archaeology, No. 2. Edited by D. G. Mitten, J. G. Pedley, and J. A. Scott. Cambridge: Fogg Art Museum, 1971. Pages 1-7. 3 pls. [CS 1465]
Examines the ancient literary evidence related to the earliest coins of Lydia. Discusses a silver ingot with an inscription. Concludes that some North Syrian ingots, which were pre-weighed and marked, meet the definitions of coinage and constitute the earliest use of ingots for the purpose of making payments.

374   ——— "Origins of Coinage." *Survey of Numismatic Research, 1966-1971. Volume 1: Ancient Numismatics.* New York: International Numismatic Commission, 1973. Pages 27-35. [CS 1463]
A narrative bibliography discussing recently published works related to the origins of coinage.

375   ——— "The Critical Moment: The Transition from Currency to Coinage in the Eastern Mediterranean." *World Archaeology* 6, no. 3 (February 1975): 293-8.
Three discs of silver inscribed in Aramaic with the name of Barrekub, a vassal of Tiglath-Pileser, ca. 730 B.C. (found at Zinçirli) illustrate the critical moment when, upon the application of a seal's inscription to the disc, currency acquired the guarantee whereby it became a coin. The use of metal for currency defined by weight, and the use of stone seals for identification, may have been combined in several instances to produce coinage as defined by Aristotle. The transition from currency to coinage has been made at least twice in the first millennium B.C. in the east Mediterranean. The existence of two documented critical moments implies the possibility of others, still unfound or uninterpreted.

376 ——— "Jewelers' Hoards and the Development of Early Coinage." *Proceedings of the 8th International Congress of Numismatics, New York—Washington, September 1973.* Edited by Herbert A. Cahn and Georges Le Rider. International Association of Professional Numismatists Publication, No. 4. Paris/Basel: International Association of Professional Numismatists, 1976. Pages 27-30. 1 pl.

The raw material of a jeweler, even if it were meant originally to supply precious metal for fashioning ornaments, lends itself ideally to monetary transactions by weight. The author describes a jeweler's hoard, found in Israel in 1970, made up of twenty-five kilograms of silver, some of which was worked into finger-rings, nose-rings and earrings. The hoard was stored in five clay pots, three of which bear the inscription "five" in archaic Hebrew letters. Balmuth discusses the nature of this hoard and such hoards in general, and discusses their implications for the history of the development of coinage. Some of the bezels of the rings were flattened into disks which closely resemble coin blanks. The author also notes that seals of identification, often attached to rings, are indicative of precisely the same kind of guarantee as that stamped on coins. Hoards of this type indicate that raw silver still remained the standard in the East even after the appearance of coins in Greece, and that the form and fabric of a coin derived from the bezel, and the type and inscription from the seal.

377 ——— "Money before Coinage." *Coins: An Illustrated Survey 650 B.C. to the Present Day.* Edited by Martin J. Price. New York: Methuen, 1980. Pages 20-5. Illus.

The author traces the evolution of trade, from barter to coinage, from 2000 to 600 B.C. Describes the use of metals, the use of standard weights, and the introduction of inscribed metal as forms of money.

378 ——— "Collection of Material for the Study of the Origins of Coinage." *Proceedings of the 9th International Congress of Numismatics, Berne, September 1979.* Louvain-la-Neuve and Luxembourg: Association Internationale des Numismates Professionels, 1982. Pages 31-5.

The author proposes a joint effort among scholars to work together toward a goal of defining the problems presented by pre-monetary hoards and related matters. She suggests further research on the anthropology of exchange, weight systems, cast copper and bronze, and other topics.

379 **Balmuth, Miriam S., ed.** *Hacksilber to Coinage: New Insights into the Monetary History of the Near East and Greece.* Numismatic Studies 24. New York: American Numismatic Society, 2001. 136 pp., illus.

A collection of eight papers presented at the 99th annual meeting of the Archaeological Institute of America held in 1997. The scholars involved have expertise in archaeology, history, and metallurgical analysis, and in the problems of the background and origins of Greek coinage in antiquity. The papers focus on ancient near eastern hoards of randomly shaped silver, generically called *Hacksilber*, which have increasingly come to be interpreted as pre-coinage currency. The papers draw on new scientific and documentary analyses. The authors explore the important question of how *Hacksilber* gradually evolved into pre-weighed and stamped coinage, the foundation of all modern monetary systems. The papers are "The Silver Hoard from Tel Dor" by Ephraim Stern [458], "The Tel Miqne-Ekron Silver Hoards: The Assyrian and Phoenician Connections" by Seymour Gitin and Amir Golani [569], "The Silver Trail: Response to the Papers of Ephraim Stern and Seymour Gitlin" by William G. Dever [536], "The Impact of the Natural Sciences on Studies of Hacksilber and Early Silver Coinage" by Zofia A. Stos-Gale [1550], "The Conceptual Prehistory of Money and its Impact on the Greek Economy" by David M. Schaps [450], "Observations on Monetary Instruments in Pre-Coinage Greece" by John H. Kroll [419], "Analyzing and Interpreting the Metallurgy of Early Electrum Coins" by Paul T. Keyser and David D. Clark [1522], and "Remarks on the Value and Standards of Early Electrum Coins" by Robert Wallace [1626]. [Reviewed by W. Fischer-Bossert in *Revue Suisse de Numismatique* 81 (2002): 167-72, by Richard Seaford in *Numismatic Chronicle* 162 (2002): 421-4, and by Elizabeth Kosmetatou in *Bryn Mawr Classical Review* 2004.03.16].

380 **Baty, Roger M.** "Numismatology: A Mirror of World Cultures." *SAN—Journal of the Society for Ancient Numismatics* 8, no. 1 (fall 1975): 13-5.

Reviews the evolution of money from primitive forms through coinage. Some aspects of minting technology are described.

381 **Bivar, A. D. H.** "A Hoard of Ingot-Currency of the Median Period from Nush-i Jan, near Malayir." *Iran* (England) 9 (1971): 97-111. 4 pls. [CS 3213]

Discusses a hoard of silver objects in a bronze bowl found at a site which was abandoned ca. 600 B.C. Of over 200 silver objects found in the bowl, some were in the form of jewelry. Suggests that the remaining items were not intended for personal adornment or the manufacture of jewelry, but were rather valued for their bullion content, and are thus of interest for the history of ancient currency prior to the introduction of a formal coinage in the ancient Near East. Describes the objects, including bar-ingots, cut-silver, and ring-money. Discusses the metrology of the ingots. Presents a catalogue of the objects showing their excavation numbers, weights, present location, and a cross-reference to the accompanying plates.

382 **Burke, Bryan O., Jr.** "The Invention of Coins: A Marshaling of Evidence and a Conclusion." *The Numismatist* 72, no. 9 (September 1959): 1059-69. Illus. Reprinted in *Selections from The Numismatist: Ancient and Medieval Coins.* Racine: Whitman Publishing Co., 1960. Pages 9-22. Illus.

"Evidence pertaining to the identification of the first makers of coins is considered under the following topical headings: Forerunners of Coins; Weight System of the Ancients; Historical Evidence of the Invention of Coinage; Methods of Manufacture; China and Rome. No definite conclusion is deemed possible, but the known facts indicate the Lydians as the first issuers of coinage in its accepted modern form. Almost of equal importance with the article itself is its thoroughly extensive and carefully compiled bibliography." [J. Francis, *NL* 51]

383 **Cain, James.** "The Dawn of Coinage: Today's Intricate Coins Sprang from Crude Lumps of Metal Some 2,700 Years Ago." *The Centinel* (Central States Numismatic Society) 58, no. 4 (winter 2010-2011): 22-30. Illus.

A brief introduction to early coinage.

384 **Chiszar, David, and Hobart M. Smith.** "The Influence of Ancient Monetization on Human Psychohistory." *The Celator* 15, no. 7 (July 2001): 19-23.

Discusses the origin of *consciousness*—the awareness of self, especially as a participant in social, political, or other activities. Explains Jaynes' theory of the bicameral mind (J. Jaynes, *The Origin of Consciousness in the Breakdown of the Bicameral Mind*, Boston, 1976). Jaynes suggests the mind has two levels, an executive and a follower. The executive does the planning and decision making, and communicates the resulting directives to the follower. The follower hears the directives as authoritarian voices. After exploring this theory, the authors examine the effects of the introduction of a money-based economy on the functioning of the bicameral mind and the emergence of consciousness. The existence of money may have led to the breakdown in the authoritarian "voices" based on traditional notions of value, as people relied more on an analytical and reflective sense of self nourished by modern money and capitalism. [Also see critical comments by C. Noland and F. Robinson in Letters to the Editor in *The Celator* 15, no. 11 (November 2001): 16, 37, 39, 48. Also see the response by Chiszar and Smith on pages 48-50].

385 **Codrington, K. de B.** "The Origins of Coinage." *Bulletin of the Institute of Archaeology* (University of London) 4 (1964): 1-2. Illus. [CS 1473]
[Reviewed by W. Schwabacher in *Hamburger Beiträge zur Numismatik* 6, no. 18/19 (1964-5): 202-5].

386 **Cook, R. M.** "Speculations on the Origins of Coinage." *Historia* (Germany) 7, no. 3 (July 1958): 257-62. [CS 1474]
Discusses (1) the iron currency spits of the Peloponnese and Pheidon's dedication of the spits to Hera, (2) the original purpose of coinage, and (3) the immediate effects of coinage on society. Suggests that "coinage was invented to make a large number of uniform payments of considerable value in a portable and durable form, and that the person or authority making the payments was the king of Lydia." Cook continues, "the earliest coins were, then, intended only for the single payment and were regarded as bullion. But gradually passed into circulation as money..." He rejects the theory that the introduction of coinage had catastrophic effects on the economy. [Also see Kroll "Observations on Monetary Instruments" below].

387 ———. "The Francis-Vickers Chronology." *Journal of Hellenic Studies* 109 (1989): 164-170.
E. D. Francis and M. Vickers have written numerous papers in recent years promulgating a revised chronology for Greek art from the later Geometric to the early Classical phases. These works are listed here, and their theories are reviewed. Vickers' dating of the coins of Phanes is briefly mentioned on pages 165-6. [Also see Vickers "Early Greek Coinage" below].

388 **Courbin, Paul.** "Dans la Grèce Archaïque: Valeur Comparée du Fer et de l'Argent lors de l'Introduction du Monnayage." *Annales: Économies—Sociétés—Civilisations* 14 (1959): 209-33.
Examines the relative values of iron and silver at the time of the introduction of coinage. [Reviewed by Georges Le Rider in *Revue Numismatique* 6, no. 1 (1958): 205-6].

389 **Daehn, William E.** "Evidence for the Invention of Coinage: Artemision Hoard Launches Debate." *The Celator* 6, no. 1 (January 1992): 18-23.
Discusses the coins found in the foundation of the Temple of Artemis at Ephesus in 1905, and the evidence they provide for the date of the invention of coinage. Summarizes Head's description of the coins, and traces the debate over their interpretation. Presents the arguments of Jacobsthal, Robinson, Kagan, Seltman, Weidauer, Price, and Waggoner for and against the new "low chronology" placing the introduction of coinage near the end of the seventh century B.C.

390 **Dayton, John.** "Money in the Near East before Coinage." *Berytus* (Denmark) 23 (1974): 41-52. Illus.
The author examined the seventy-seven metal rings found during excavations at Ur and Nippur. The rings are overlapped like a modern key ring. The weights of these and other known rings are listed. Dayton tries to find a pattern in their weights. It appears that the rings are based on a system of weights which went up to 180 grains in steps of thirty. Above 180, they progress in steps of sixty. The ring weights are consistent with a weight system with a mina of about 516 grains. The system may be based on the weight of a grain of wheat rather than the more commonly used barley grain. Dayton suggests the rings, which occur in copper, lead, and silver, were a form of money. Mentions the similar Celtic ring money.

391 **Duncan, Charles.** "First Coin Date Remains Unsolved." *Coin World* no. 203 (March 4, 1964): 75, 80. Illus.
"While many numismatists consider the earliest known coins to be those issued in Lydia ca. 652-625 B.C., others believe that the honor may rightly belong to the Chinese, whose spade and knife currency of ca. 680 B.C. apparently bears inscriptions guaranteeing value. The present writer offers a number of arguments in support of his own theory that the first coins may have been produced in India, but admits that proof of this will depend largely upon future discoveries and study. Three early Indian coins are illustrated." [B. Shonnard, *NL* 69]

392 **Earle-Fox, H. B.** "The Early Coinages of European Greece." *Corolla Numismatica: Numismatic Essays in Honour of Barclay V. Head.* Edited by G. F. Hill. London: Oxford University Press, 1906. Pages 34-46. 1 pl.
The author discusses some problems related to the chronology of the earliest coins of the Greek mainland, focusing on the coins of Aegina. He suggests that the change from the sea-turtle to the land-tortoise on Aeginetan coins coincided with the return of the Aeginetan residents in 404 B.C. after their expulsion from the island by Athens in 431. Describes the main types and various classes of the silver coinage of Aegina. Discusses coins with incuse reverse types, and distinguishes between "punch-struck" coins (the reverse was the punch die) and "anvil-struck" coins (the reverse was the anvil die). Points out that the coins of Athens are always punch-struck, while those of her neighbors in the sixth century are anvil-struck. This casts doubt on the Athenian attribution of the Wappenmünzen series. Also discusses the early coins of Eretria in Euboea and the reasons for attributing these to Eretria rather than Athens. Also comments on the chronology of the early coinage of Corinth.

393 **Feuardent, G. L.** "Early Greek Coinage." *American Journal of Numismatics* 13, no. 1 (July 1878): 48.
Points out that Plutarch was wrong in stating that Theseus was the inventor of coins, and in asserting that Solon melted Athenian coinage in order to establish a new system.

394 **Fort, E. Tomlinson.** "The Badge of Phanes: Notes on the Historical and Numismatic Evidence." *The Celator* 10, no. 8 (August 1996): 18-23. Illus.
Examines an electrum stater and a third stater bearing the name Phanes, as well as two 1/12 staters which are uninscribed but similar in style to the Phanes coins. The author reviews the evidence and arguments for the mint city and date of these coins, as well as the evidence for the identity of Phanes. Summarizes the account of a man named Phanes mentioned in Herodotus' *History*. There is little evidence to connect the Phanes of Herodotus to these coins. The author suggests a date in the mid-seventh century B.C. for the coins, and suggests a mint in Western Asia Minor, but admits that this is far from certain. [Also see C. Newton "On an Electrum Stater" under IONIA and Kastner "Phanes" below].

395 **Furtwängler, Andreas E.** "Neue Beobachtungen zur Frühesten Münzprägung." *Revue Suisse de Numismatique* (Switzerland) 65 (1986): 153-65.

396 **Gardner, Percy.** "The Earliest Coins of Greece Proper." *Proceedings of the British Academy, Volume 5, 1911-1912.* London: British Academy, 1914. Pages 161-201. 1 pl. Also printed as a booklet, 41 pp., 1 pl.

The text of an address to the British Academy on June 7, 1911. Examines several electrum coin types attributed to cities in Greece proper and concludes these coins belong to cities in Asia Minor. The first European coins were silver coins struck at Aegina. Examines Pheidon's role in coinage at Aegina. Concludes Pheidon had no authority in Aegina and lived prior to the introduction of coinage. He did reform the Peloponnesian weight system. Discusses the coins of Euboea and the origin of the Euboic weight standard. Discusses early coinage at Corinth and Corcyra. Examines the reforms of Solon at Athens. Compares Aristotle's and Androtion's texts of the Athenian Constitution and analyzes its meaning. Dates the first Athenian owls to the mid-sixth century B.C.

397 **Gerasimov, Theodore D.** "The Origin of Coins and Their Importance as Sources." *Symposium Prez Vekovete.* Sofia, Bulgaria, 1938. Pages 283 ff.

398 **Goldsborough, Reid.** "The Lydian Lion: A Case for the World's First Coin." *Numismatist* 117, no. 5 (May 2004): 50-3. Illus.
The author argues that the Lydian electrum trite with *obv*: lion head, *rev*: incuse punch, is the world's first true coin. He very briefly summarizes other candidates for this distinction. Goldsborough settles on the Lydian trite because the lion motif clearly denotes the coin as an official government issue. Some electrum issues may be earlier, but they may be more properly regarded as privately minted, rather than as government issues. [Also see the "Letter to the Editor" by Jorg Lueke in *Numismatist* 117, no. 8 (August 2004): 17. Also see the expanded version of this article below].

399 ——— "The Lydian Lion: A Case for the World's First Coin." *Journal of the Classical and Medieval Numismatic Society* 2nd ser., 5, no. 3 (September 2004): 111-25. Illus.
An expanded version of the article published in *Numismatist*, including footnotes.

400 **Grierson, Philip.** *The Origins of Money.* London: Athlone Press of the University of London, 1977. 44 pp. [CS 1481]
The revised text of Grierson's Creighton Lecture in History delivered in 1970. Examines factors which led to the development and spread of coins. Discusses primitive money, traditions and law codes regarding money, and the evidence of language for the origin of money. Discusses units of value and the concept of weight as a measure of value. [Reviewed by D. Nash in *Numismatic Chronicle* 138 (1978): 197-8].

401 **Grotefend, G. T.** "What People First Stamped Money? (Welches Volk hat die ersten Münzen Gegrägt?)" *Numismatic Chronicle* 1 (1839): 235-47.
In German and English on alternate pages. Discusses the writings of ancient authors regarding the role of Pheidon in the regulation of weights and measures, dismissing his supposed role in the start of coinage. Mentions Herodotus' claims regarding the Lydians. Also examines numerous other writings of ancient authors which provide evidence for the early use of coinage. Concludes that the Lydians were the first to mint gold coins, the Aeginetans were the first to coin silver, and the Romans the first to coin copper.

402 **Hill, George F.** "Chapter 5: Coinage from its Origin to the Persian Wars." *The Cambridge Ancient History, Vol. 4: The Persian Empire and the West.* Edited by J. B. Bury, S. A. Cook, and F. E. Adcock. Cambridge: University Press, 1926. Revised edition 1930. Reprinted 1939, 1953, 1960, 1964. Pages 124-36.
An overview of the early history of coinage. Begins with a discussion of pre-coinage stages of money. Describes the use of iron spits and the first electrum coins in Lydia and the introduction of gold and silver coins. Describes the westward spread of coinage. Discusses coin weight-standards and theories for their development. Lists the major standards and their areas of use.

403 **Hiller, John.** "The Beginnings of Coinage Were Prompted by the Evolution of the Use and Value of Gold." *The Celator* 5, no. 8 (August 1991): 34-7.
Discusses the geological origins of gold, the first use of gold by man, the mythological accounts of gold, and the eventual development of gold coinage.

404 **Holle, Bruce Fredric.** *Historical Considerations on the Origins and Spread of Greek Coinage in the Archaic Age.* Ph.D. dissertation, University of Michigan, 1978. Ann Arbor: University Microfilms International, 1983. 304 pp., 1 pl.

405 **Holloway, R. Ross.** "The Date of the First Greek Coins: Some Arguments from Style and Hoards." *Revue Belge de Numismatique et de Sigillographie* (Belgium) 130 (1984): 5-18. Illus.
"Recent years have seen both a return to a high chronology for early electrum and proposals to date the first coins within the sixth century, or very shortly before its beginning, and the first silver issues of mainland Greece to about 550 B.C. Central in the new high chronology are arguments based on style. The new low chronology relies on the interpretation of hoards. This paper deals with these two central issues in the debate." [R. Holloway, *NL* 115]

406 **Howe, Laurence Lee.** "Herodotus and the Origin of Coinage." *The Numismatist* 63, no. 5 (May 1950): 253-6.
Reviews the definition of a "coin." Mentions pre-coin money used in Assyria. Points out that Herodotus is sometimes misquoted on the subject of the origin of coinage. Clarifies that Herodotus actually wrote, "And they (the Lydians) were the first men whom we (the Greeks) know to have struck and used gold and silver coins."

407 **Howgego, Christopher J.** "Why Did Ancient States Strike Coins?" *Numismatic Chronicle* 150 (1990): 1-25.
"The author argues against the view that the only reason for the striking of ancient coins was to enable states to make payments. A more complex pattern of motivation is demonstrated (monetary reforms, closed currency systems, renewal of worn coins, standardization, monetary alliances (?), profit, pride, politics, minting for individuals). In particular, it is suggested that there is sufficient ancient evidence to take seriously the possibility that coin was produced to facilitate exchange between individuals, the payment of taxes, and external trade." [C. Howgego, *NL* 126]

408 **Jacobsthal, Paul.** "The Date of the Ephesian Foundation-Deposit." *Journal of Hellenic Studies* 71 (1951): 85-95. 6 pls.
A re-examination of the objects found in the basis deposit of the Temple of Artemis at Ephesus, focusing on the chronological implications for the coins found in the deposit. Discusses the artistic style of pottery, scarabs, figurines, and other objects to determine their approximate dates. Concludes that most all of the objects are from the seventh century B.C. [Also see Robinson "Coins from the Ephesian Artemision" below for a discussion of the dating of the coins. Also see Seltman "The Earliest Hoarded Coins" and D. Williams "The 'Pot-Hoard' Pot" under HOARDS].

409 **Jones, Doran A.** "Collecting Classical Coins: An Introduction." *Numismatic Scrapbook Magazine* 15, no. 3 (March 1949): 209-12.

The first in a planned series of introductory articles on collecting ancient coins. Includes a brief discussion of the origins of coinage and the use of metal as money.

410 **Jones, John R. Melville.** "Revised Datings for the Earliest Greek Coins." *Seaby Coin and Medal Bulletin* 540 (May 1963): 147-8. [CS 1843]
"Suggests that the Aeginetan coinage did not begin until after 600 B.C.; and it is highly unlikely that Corinth began to coin before that date. With Athens, too, it seems that a downward movement of dates is necessary. A recent re-examination of the series, using later evidence available from the hoards, suggests that the Athena/owl tetradrachms did not come into circulation until about 525 B.C. and are to be attributed to Hippias, not Pisistratus, on the occasion of the first Panathenaic Games. With regard to the new datings that are being established for many Greek issues prior to 480 B.C., the writer is of the opinion that none of the revisions is absolutely certain. Cumulatively, however, they strengthen each other, and further hoard discoveries, when datable, may well confirm the revised datings." [*NL* 66]

411 ——— "Why Did the Ancient Greeks Strike Coins?" *Journal of the Numismatic Association of Australia* 17 (2006). [2005 Conference Papers]. Pages 21-30.
A re-examination of theories for the origin of coinage. Summarizes the popular theories and evidence for who struck the first coins and why. Emphasizes that the Greek cities often issued coins for specific reasons (e.g., to finance a war or specific public works) rather than because every community had a need for coins. Many communities never minted coins, some issued coins sporadically, and others issued coins continuously over a long period. Reviews evidence from ancient inscriptions and metallurgical analysis of coins to show that some cities were motivated by the profit to be made from issuing coins. Some coins were clearly commemorative types. Jones also suggests that the use of talented engravers at some cities may have been a defense against counterfeiting—it would be easier to recognize a counterfeit copy of a highly artistic coin.

412 **Kagan, Donald.** "The Dates of the Earliest Coins." *American Journal of Archaeology* 86, no. 3 (July 1982): 343-60.
Challenges the accepted view that the earliest coins were struck in Lydia ca. 630-600 B.C. and that the first coins of Greek lands were struck after 600. Suggests there is no reason to reject the ancient traditions connecting the early Aeginetan coinage with Pheidon of Argos, and the Athenian coinage reforms with Solon. Discusses the controversy over the dating of the Artemision hoard including the arguments of Jacobsthal and Robinson, and the views of Kraay and Weidauer. Reviews the architectural, stylistic, and numismatic evidence for the dating of the Artemision objects. Concludes that the basis deposit was probably closed around the middle of the seventh century B.C. Dates the first coins to ca. 700 B.C. and the first Greek silver coins to ca. 675 B.C. [Also see Kroll and Waggoner "Dating the Earliest Coins" under ATTICA—GENERAL WORKS, Mogelonsky "The Dates" below, and Seltman "The Earliest Hoarded Coins" under HOARDS].

413 **Kagin, Don.** "A Survey of the Origins of Coinage: Its Sources and Implications." *The Numismatist* 88, no. 7 (July 1975): 1459-79. Illus.
Begins with a review of pre-coinage forms of currency and the common weight-standards. Outlines various theories giving the reasons for the introduction of coinage including those of Burgon, Curtius, Ridgeway, Head, Glotz, Seltman, Kraay, and Roebuck. Reviews theories regarding who made the first coins. Then discusses the political, moral, and social effects of the introduction of coinage. Coinage helped to create an international trading network, spurred competition in the marketplace, and widened the pursuit of profit. Describes the spread of coinage to the major cities of the Greek world before 500 B.C. Then, using Athens as an example, examines the economic revolution caused by the introduction of coinage. Mentions Solon's reforms, the introduction of the Athenian owls, and the appearance of bankers.

414 **Kastner, W.** "'Phanes' oder 'Phanos.'" *Revue Suisse de Numismatique* (Switzerland) 65 (1986): 5-10. Illus.

415 **Kern, Jonathan K.** "The Origins of Coinage: Seventh and Sixth Century B.C. Electrum Coins of Ionia." *The Centinel* (Journal of the Central States Numismatic Society) 51, no. 2 (summer 2003): 27-9. Illus.
Kern provides brief comments on the origins of coinage in Asia Minor. He then focuses on the Geometric Series of archaic electrum coins of Ionia, describing the types and denominations.

416 **Kiyonaga, S.** "The Date of the Beginning of Coinage in Asia Minor." *Revue Suisse de Numismatique* (Switzerland) 52 (1973): 5-16.
"The arguments of recent writers concerning the date of the earliest coins are summarized and criticized. E. S. G. Robinson's dating into the late seventh century is preferred." [H. Bloesch, *NL* 99]

417 **Knapp, Robert.** "Greek Mercenaries, Coinage and Ideology." *Eulimene* (Mediterranean Archaeological Society, Rethymno, Greece) 3 (2002): 183-96.
"Dark Age Greece was the starting point for the major changes in Greek culture seen in the Archaic Age. This paper lays out the vast difference between life in Dark Age Greece and in the more advanced cultures of the Near East and Egypt. This contrast serves as a focus for understanding how destabilizing those cultures must have been to Greeks coming into contact with them. While most studies have focused on merchants as the main point of contact, here (the focus is on) the Greek mercenaries whom we know fought in Egypt and throughout the Near East in the late Dark and Archaic Ages. Service as mercenaries not only exposed Greeks to material cultures more sophisticated than their own; that service also served to consolidate ideas of the Hellenic 'ethnicity.' In addition, contact served to heighten the awareness that the inherited status structures based on birth 'back home' could possibly be changed in favor of those who had gained wealth and self-confidence abroad. The author deals especially with the real and symbolic role of coinage in this cultural self-awakening. Whatever the practical advantages of coined money, and whatever the practical relation of the introduction of coinage had to pre-existing monetary systems of western Asia, its symbolic power was to make concrete the centrality of portable wealth in undermining the authority of immobile, land-based wealth. It was a potent symbol, too, of the relativity of power—that money was the actual root of power, no matter what myths existed to validate the continued rule of an adscriptive elite; that as coinage, money was much more visible and obtainable than before; and that as more visible and obtainable, more easily used to destabilize existing elitist intellectual and power structures. In sum, the introduction of coinage is part of the cultural shift influenced by Greek mercenary contact with the civilizations of the Near East and Egypt, and emblematic of the cultural results of Greek experience with those more sophisticated areas." [Robert Knapp, *NL* 147]

418 **Kraay, Colin M.** "Hoards, Small Change, and the Origin of Coinage." *Journal of Hellenic Studies* 84 (1964): 76-91. [CS 3248]
Through an analysis of the contents of coin hoards, Kraay discusses the evidence for the movement of large denomination coins from their areas of origin, and the evidence for the use of fractional coinage. His goal is to gain an understanding of the function of Greek coinage in the sixth and fifth centuries B.C. South Italian and Sicilian coins circulated freely within their respective areas, but played no significant part in international trade. Neither area had an internal source of silver and both wanted to retain their coinage for internal purposes. The Aeginetan coinage had wider circulation during the sixth century, but still did not form a significant part of western currency.

Kraay disputes the widely held view that Corinthian coins provided the source of much of the silver used in Southern Italy. Shows that Corinthian coins did not stray far from their place of origin. The Athenian "owls" however, had become the coins most commonly employed for storing surplus wealth in the east Mediterranean by the end of the fifth century. These coins were regularly dispersed in large numbers to areas far removed from their place of origin. Some of the northern Greek coinages were being dispersed in quantity long before the Athenian owls, and the Athenians may have borrowed the idea from Northern Greece.

Kraay states that the Persian sigloi were strictly a regional currency for use among the Greek subjects of Persia in Western Asia Minor. Emphasizes that coins found in Near Eastern hoards are usually defaced and are considered merely bullion deposits. An examination of small denomination coinage of Western cities shows that there was not enough fractional coinage produced to sustain their general use in retail trade. At Athens however, a full range of fractional denominations was produced in enough quantity that such coins were used in daily transactions at least in the city of Athens itself.

Concludes that most coinages were not exported and that those that were exported were not among the earliest coinages. Therefore, the original intention of coinage was not to facilitate foreign trade. The general lack of small denominations suggests that facilitating retail trade was not the original purpose of coinage either. Rather, coins were intended as a convenience for the government, and the necessity of using local coins in transactions with the government resulted in a premium being attached to the coins locally—thereby discouraging their export. Furthermore, Kraay argues, various factors must have required the continuation of weighing in almost every transaction. Only in rare cases, such as at Athens, where the source of silver was within the state's territory, could coinage be deliberately destined for foreign trade. At Athens, the realization of this purpose led to the replacement of the changing types of the Wappenmünzen by the unchanging owl coinage which clearly proclaims its origin. [Reviewed by W. Schwabacher in *Hamburger Beiträge zur Numismatik* 6, no. 18/19 (1964-5): 205-7. Also see Keyser and Cook "Analyzing and Interpreting the Metallurgy of Early Electrum Coins" under METALLURGY].

419 **Kroll, John H.** "Observations on Monetary Instruments in Pre-Coinage Greece." *Hacksilber to Coinage: New Insights into the Monetary History of the Near East and Greece.* Numismatic Studies 24. New York: American Numismatic Society, 2001. Pages 77-91.
Kroll mentions a find of *Hackgold* in Eretria—an assemblage of gold dumps, ingot fragments, scraps of jewelry, etc. It is identified as a monetary deposit. He suggests that silver became the preferred medium of exchange well before the time of Solon, hence in the 7th century B.C., and this development was probably gradual and was heavily influenced by the increasing availability of silver. Cites Solon's laws which refer to monetary transactions in silver by the government and by private parties. Concludes that the economy of Athens was as monetized at the time of Solon as it was later in the 6th century—after coinage was invented.

Discusses the weight standards in use for the archaic silver coinage of Central Greece and the Peloponnesus. Discusses Solon's reform of weights and Pheidon's involvement with weight systems. Discusses denominational systems. Considers whether the iron spits dedicated by Pheidon of Argos were in fact used as currency in Iron Age Greece. Suggests the spits were related to the ritual cooking of meat and may have been emblematic of wealth and status, but there is little evidence to suggest the spits were monetary in character, and no evidence that they ever were used as currency. The spits may have been used as measure of value, but likely had no exchange value. [Also see Schaps "The Conceptual Prehistory of Money" below].

420 **Leigh, T. Gordon.** "The Contribution of Phanes to the Origin and Concept of the Coin." *The Canadian Numismatic Journal* (Canada) 34, no. 7 (July-August 1989): 264-6. Illus.
A brief review of the famous electrum stater of Ephesus bearing the name Phanes. Describes the transition from a barter and bullion economy to a coin-based economy. Reviews what is known, or can be deduced, about Phanes. [Also see C. Newton "On an Electrum Stater" under IONIA].

421 **Le Rider, Georges.** *La Naissance de la Monnaie: Practiques Monétaires de l'Orient Ancien.* Paris: Presses Universitaires de France, 2001. 274 pp., 8 pls.
Le Rider argues that the opportunity for the state to profit from coinage was one of the primary reasons for the introduction of coinage in the Persian Kingdom. Coinage also provided the kingdom with an opportunity to advertise its power and independence. Le Rider suggests that the gold and silver "Croesids"—the first bi-metallic coinage—may have been minted under Cyrus, rather than Croesus. [Reviewed by J. H. Kroll in *Revue Suisse de Numismatique* 80 (2001): 199-206, by Richard Seaford in *Numismatic Chronicle* 162 (2002): 421-4, and by David M. Schaps in *Bryn Mawr Classical Review* 2003.12.13].

422 **Lindgren, Henry Clay.** "Origin of Money Relates to Psychological Need." Parts 1-3. *The Celator* 3, no. 4 (April 1989): 11, 16; no. 5 (May 1989): 10, 18, 27; no. 6 (June 1989): 10, 19-20.
Explores the psychological reasons for the development of money. Suggests that barter developed partly because it helped satisfy the need of people to interact with others. The introduction of money enabled people to buy and sell more frequently, thus increasing social interaction. Suggests the Egyptians resisted the unsettling novelty of money. The familiarity of Athens' coinage helped to integrate their community. Kings made use of the propaganda value of coinage to remind their subjects they were part of the kingdom. Discusses the use of kings' portraits and the development of lengthy laudatory inscriptions. Suggests that the longer the king's inscription, the shorter and bloodier was his reign. Discusses the introduction of copper fiat money and the resulting abuse and inflation, and the Romans' use of coinage as a propaganda tool.

423 **Linzalone, Joseph.** *Electrum and the Invention of Coinage.* McMillan Scholarly No. 1. No city: Dennis McMillan Publications, 2011. 232 pp., illus.
The plates that make up pages 159-231 provide a good overview of the electrum coin types minted during the archaic and classical periods. Both the color photographs and the illustrated coins are of excellent quality. Brief commentary is provided for each type. The remainder of the book is poorly written and consists primarily of bullet points (without the bullets), haphazardly organized. Although the author attempts to provide an overview of the coinage, most of the commentary is vague, repetitive, and sometimes contradictory. No references are provided to more scholarly works, and little or no new information is provided. [Reviewed by Mike Markowitz in *The Celator* 25, no. 8 (August 2011): 4, 53].

424 **Lipinski, Edouard.** "Les Temples Néo-Assyriens et les Origines du Monnayage." *State and Temple Economy in the Ancient Near East: Proceedings of the International Conference Organized by the Katholieke Universiteit Leuven from the 10th to the 14th of April 1978.* Edited by E. Lipinski. Leuven: Department Oriëntalistiek, 1979. Volume 2, pages 565-88.

425 **Lorber, Catherine C.** "The Origins of Coinage." *Numismatic Fine Arts Winter Mail Bid Sale, December 18, 1987*. Los Angeles: Numismatic Fine Arts, Inc., 1987. Unpaged (5 pp.).
Excellent summary of the development of the earliest coinage. Discusses weight standards and their areas of use, types and die linkages. Examines the evidence provided by the Artemision hoard and compares alternate theories for the date of the earliest coins. Describes possible reasons for the introduction of electrum coinage. This sale catalogue includes portions of the Jonathon P. Rosen collection of archaic fractions, and this essay is accompanied by a two-page table describing the die links among the Rosen coins.

426 **Mabbott, Thomas Ollive.** "The Origins of Coinage." *Numismatic Review* 4, no. 2-4 (April-October 1947): 43-6.
"A brief survey of what little is actually known of the origins of coinage in different parts of the world, pointing out the pattern, recurring almost universally, by which the art progressed from crude pieces of metal to coins designed as such." [A. C. Simpson, *NL 8*]

427 **Madsen, Eardley.** "Some Thoughts on Money and Trade in the Ancient World." *SAN—Journal of the Society for Ancient Numismatics* 12, no. 3 (fall 1982): 52-4.
General comments on the development of coinage as a means of exchange.

428 **Manning, William A.** "The Invention and Spread of Ancient Coinage." *The Anvil* (Canada) 10, no. 1 (March 1, 2000): 1-3, 5-13. Illus.
A summary of the development of coinage. Begins with barter in objects valued in terms of oxen, then describes the use of bronze and gold, and then the striking of coins of uniform weight marked with a design. Examines the reasons for the invention of coinage, the difficulties arising from the multitude of weight standards, the development of weight standards, and the spread of coinage.

429 **Marotta, Michael E.** "Some Questions on the Origin of Coinage." *Classical Numismatic Review* 19, no. 3 (third quarter 1994): 3.
A brief overview of theories explaining the reasons for the introduction of coinage. Supports the "tyrant theory" put forward by P. N. Ure and P. Grierson: the first coins were struck by tyrants for local use in buying the loyalty of mercenaries.

430 ——— "A New Look at the Origins of Coinage." *The Numismatist* 108, no. 8 (August 1995): 956-9, 999-1001. Illus.
Summarizes various theories for why the first coins were struck: (1) the religious theory—coins originated in temples and helped facilitate temple administration and were used to glorify the gods; (2) the commercial theory—coins were invented to facilitate trade; (3) tyrant theory—coins were struck to facilitate payments to mercenaries and to facilitate state administration. No conclusions are drawn, but the author leans toward the latter.

431 ——— "The Origin of Coinage: Evolution of a Theory." *The Celator* 11, no. 10 (October 1997): 32-4.
Marotta reviews various theories which attempt to explain why coins were invented. Provides summaries of the theories of Aristotle, Curtius, Ridgeway, Seltman, Grierson, Ure, Price, and others. The author supports Ure's Tyrant Theory (see Ure "The Origin of the Tyrannis" below).

432 **Martin, Thomas R.** "Why Did the Greek Polis Originally Need Coins?" *Historia* (Germany) 45 (1996): 261-83.
[Also see Martin "Coins, Mints and the *Polis*" under GENERAL WORKS—GREEK].

433 **Meshorer, Ya'akov.** "Means of Payment Prior to Coinage and the First Coinage." *Qadmoniot* (Israel) 9, nos. 2-3 (1976): 34-5 (in Hebrew, pages 51-60).

434 ——— *Ancient Means of Exchange, Weights and Coins.* Haifa: University of Haifa, 1998.

435 **Milne, Joseph G.** *The First Stages in the Development of Greek Coinage.* Oxford: Basil Blackwell, 1934. Reprint, Amherst: Scorpion Publishers. 19 pp.
Milne traces the development of coinage from pre-coin unmarked "dumps" used in trade during Mycenaean times to the widespread use of true coins in the fifth century B.C. He briefly describes the introduction of coins in Ionia, the first use of coins by the Lydians, the first coins of Greece minted at Aegina, the use of iron bar money in the Peloponnesos, the role of Pheidon in coinage, the introduction of coinage at Corinth, and the Solonian reforms at Athens. His chronology would now be considered too early, but Milne provides a good description of the stages in the development of coinage.

436 **Mitchiner, Michael B.** *Ancient Trade and Early Empires.* Two volumes. London: Hawkins, 2004. 692 pp, 728 pp. Illus.
A detailed account of early coinages, incorporating a catalogue of 5900 of the earliest coins of Greece, India, and China, and many peripheral states. Most of the coins are illustrated. Begins with a 190-page account of early migration, metal working, transportation, and trade. This is followed by a detailed account of the world's early coinages including a catalogue and appropriate commentary and observations. The origins of coinage are explored, along with early metrological systems. [Reviewed by Robert Tye in *Spink Numismatic Circular* 113, no. 1 (February 2005): 16-7].

437 **Mogelonsky, Marcia K.** "The Dates of the Earliest Coinage: Some Archaeological Considerations." *ΣΥΝΕΙΣΦΟΡΑ McGill 1: Papers in Greek Archaeology and History in Memory of Colin D. Gordon.* Edited by John M. Fossey. Amsterdam: J. C. Gieben, 1987. Pages 51-63.
The author addresses two different aspects of the Ephesian Artemision deposit: (1) a reconsideration of the archaeological evidence based primarily on Hogarth's publication of the finds from the British Museum excavations, and (2) a discussion of some of the material remains from the Central Basis, including the coins, which have been at the center of numismatic debates since their discovery. Mogelonsky suggests the possibility that the earliest coins found were votive offerings from an earlier temple which were rededicated in the newly constructed Central Basis. She notes similar circumstances observed at the sanctuary of Artemis Orthia at Sparta. She also questions whether the coins can rightly be considered to be a "foundation deposit." Suggest that the four unmarked "dumps" may represent an intermediate step in the production of jewelry rather than the earliest stages of coinage. Urges caution in dating the coins by comparison with other objects from the deposit—only very general dates can be assigned to any artifact. [Also see D. Kagan "Dates of the Earliest Coins" above, and Robinson "Coins from the Ephesian Artemision" below].

438 "The Money of the Iliad and Odyssey: A Theory by M. Svoronos." *The Numismatist* 22, no. 1 (January 1909): 1. Illus.
This brief paper mentions a recent theory advanced by Svoronos that certain thin circular bracteates, ornamented with geometrical patterns, found in the tombs of Mycene by Schliemann are the talents spoken of by Homer, and are consequently the first coined money. The writer disputes this theory.

439 **Mudd, Douglas.** "Timeless Standards: Ancient Coinage Continues to Influence Our Ideas of How Money Should Look and How It is Used." *The Numismatist* 123, no. 5 (May 2010): 87. Illus.
   A brief description of the development of coinage—from weighed metal to early coins

440 **Peacock, M. S.** "The Origins of Money in Ancient Greece: The Political Economy of Coinage and Exchange." *Cambridge Journal of Economics* 30 (2006): 637-50.

441 **Persson, Axel W.** "Contribution à la Question de l'Origine de la Monnaie." *Bulletin de Correspondance Hellénique* (France) 70 (1946): 444-54. [CS 1493]

442 **Price, Martin J.** "Thoughts on the Beginnings of Coinage." *Studies in Numismatic Method Presented to Philip Grierson*. Edited by C. N. L. Brooke et al. Cambridge: University Press, 1983. Pages 1-10.
   Reviews various theories regarding the chronology of the Artemision hoard coins put forward by Head, Hogarth, and others. Discusses theories for the purposes of the first coins including those of Cook and Kraay. Mentions the early coins inscribed *Walwel* and *Kalil*. States that the origin of coin types in general lies in seals as marks of ownership and suggests that early electrum coins could have provided a means for standardizing bonus payments or gifts. The coin-type as the seal of origin represents the source of the bonus. Only when gold and silver coins emerged did coinage become a common medium of exchange.

443 **Quiggin, Alison Hingston.** *A Survey of Primitive Money: the Beginnings of Currency*. London: Methuen & Co., 1949. 344 pp., 34 pls., 4 maps. [CS 1580]
   A detailed survey of the stages which preceded the use of coins as the medium of exchange and the objects coins displaced. Examines cowries and beads, and the pre-coinage means of exchange in Africa, Oceania, Asia, Europe, America, and the West Indies. Illustrated throughout by 143 drawings of objects used as money. Includes thirty-two black and white and two color plates.

444 **Rebuffat, François.** "Phanès: Questions sans Réponses." *Varia Anatolica XII. Mécanismes et Innovations Monétaires dans l'Antiquité Achémenide. Numismatique et Histoire, Actes de la Table Ronde Internationale d'Istanbul, 22-23 Mai 1997*. Paris, 2000. Pages 226 ff.

445 **Richardson, Arthur W.** "Coins of Lydia Dawn of Modern Coinage." *Coin World* (May 5, 1982): 61-2.
   Basic review of the development of coinage beginning with barter and ending with the introduction of coinage in Lydia.

446 **Roberts, P.** "The Origin of Coins." *New Zealand Numismatic Journal* (New Zealand) 6, no. 3 (September 1951-April 1952): 81-2.
   Brief comments on the origin of coinage.

447 **Robinson, Edward S. G.** "The Coins from the Ephesian Artemision Reconsidered." *Journal of Hellenic Studies* 71 (1951): 156-67. 1 pl. [CS 2761]
   A companion to Jacobsthal's paper [see Jacobsthal "Foundation-Deposit" above] which examined various objects from the Artemision foundation hoard found at Ephesus, 1904-1905. This paper re-examines the evidence for the date of the first coinage provided by the hoard coins. Reviews the dates assigned to the burial of the hoard coins by Hogarth, Head, and others. Describes the archaeological contexts of the coins found. Discusses the nose-warts on the lions depicted on some of the coins in relation to similar depictions on other art objects. Robinson believes the "Central Basis" coins are Lydian and date from the third quarter of the seventh century B.C. The "pot hoard" coins he dates to ca. 600 B.C. or slightly later. An appendix lists some of the relevant coins from the hoard, giving find-spots and detailed descriptions. [Also see Mogelonsky "Dates" above and Seltman "The Earliest Hoarded Coins" under HOARDS].

448 ——— "The Date of the Earliest Coins." *Numismatic Chronicle* 6th ser., 16 (1956): 1-8. [CS 2762]
   Reviews the major elements in the controversy over the dating of the Artemision hoard coins. A follow-up to Robinson's 1951 paper (see Robinson "Ephesian Artemision Reconsidered" above) responding to criticisms voiced by Charles Seltman. Seltman argued for an earlier date for the coins. Robinson examines the theories for the destruction of the Temple of Artemis by the Kimmerians. Robinson concludes that the Basis Treasure cannot be Kimmerian debris, and places the beginning of coinage ca. 640-630 B.C.

449 **Robinson, Henry S.** "The Earliest Greek Coins." *The Museum of the University of Oklahoma, Information Series, Circular 4* (March 1948). Norman: University of Oklahoma. Pages 1-8.
   "Descriptive list of twenty-eight Greek coins lent for exhibition from the collection of the author accompanied by brief historical and numismatic commentary." [*NL* 8]

450 **Schaps, David M.** "The Conceptual Prehistory of Money and its Impact on the Greek Economy." *Hacksilber to Coinage: New Insights into the Monetary History of the Near East and Greece*. Numismatic Studies 24. Edited by Miriam S. Balmuth. New York: American Numismatic Society, 2001. Pages 93-103.
   Schaps examines why coinage appeared precisely at the interface of Hellenic and Asiatic culture, and what conditions had been absent in the earlier centuries which were present in the later part of the Greek archaic age. He begins with the use of precious metals of a standard weight and fineness in Mesopotamia in the third millennium B.C. Then he explores the rise of trade in Greece. The invention of coinage was accompanied by an increase in prices and a great increase in retail trade. Coinage made this retail trade more convenient and thus it spread to other areas that wished to join the developing Mediterranean economy. In an *Appendix*, Schaps explores the question: Was there a bullion economy in Athens? He counters Kroll's argument that silver had become the exclusive specie of currency in Athens in the sixth century B.C. Schaps doubts there was a transition from Hacksilber to coinage. Rather, the transition was from spits and cauldrons to coinage. The silver mentioned in Solon's laws should be considered as a standard of value—not a standard of exchange. [Also see Kroll "Observations on Monetary Instruments" above].

451 ——— *The Invention of Coinage and the Monetization of Ancient Greece*. Ann Arbor: University of Michigan Press, 2004. 293 pp., illus.
   Schaps examines the invention and spread of coinage from an historical, economic, and psychological perspective. He examines trade and the concept of money in Greece before the invention of coinage, using the writings of Homer to illustrate how man's thinking about money was very much changed by the invention of coinage. He follows the development of money and exchange through the archaic age and into classical times. Schaps discusses how coins

were used in the marketplace and how monetization of the economy changed society, politics, war, trade, and concepts of wealth. Schaps provides an interesting addition to our understanding of coinage, beyond what is typically found in numismatic books.

452 **Schwabacher, Willy.** "The Origins of Coinage." *A Survey of Numismatic Research, 1960-1965. Volume 1: Ancient Numismatics.* Copenhagen: International Numismatic Commission, 1967. Pages 27-34. [CS 1497]
A narrative bibliography discussing recently published works related to the origins of coinage.

453 **Servet, Jean-Michel.** *Nomismata: État et Origines de la Monnaie.* Lyon: Presses Universitaires de Lyon, 1984. 191 pp., illus.

454 **Sigler, Phares O.** "Did the Lydians Invent Coinage?" *The Numismatist* 63, no. 3 (March 1950): 130-2.
A brief review of the controversy over the invention of coinage. Suggests coinage may have originated in China.

455 **Smith, Sidney.** "A Pre-Greek Coinage in the Near East?" *Numismatic Chronicle* 5th ser., 2 (1922): 176-85. Illus.
Explores whether coinage existed in Assyria prior to Greek times. Quotes an inscription of Sennacherib (ca. 700 B.C.) which mentions the casting of half-shekel pieces. Discusses lead *roundels* of perhaps 1400-1200 B.C. which may have been currency. Quotes a Cappadocian document mentioning lumps of metal, stamped with the official seal of the city, being used to make payments. Concludes there were in circulation in Assyria ca. 720-620 B.C., half-shekel pieces, cast in moulds, similar to the roundels of 1400-1200 B.C. The roundels may themselves have been used as a means of exchange, and thus may be a development of the stamped lumps of lead which were commonly used near Caesarea ca. 2250-2150 B.C.

456 **Starck, Jeff.** "Coinage of Lydia: First Western Coinage Lays Foundation." *Coin World* (September 24, 2007): 86-7. Illus.
This overview of Lydian electrum coinage is marred by its reliance on outdated chronological information, much of it taken from Barclay Head's *Historia Numorum*.

457 **Stecchini, Livio C.** *Origin of Money in Greece.* Ph.D. dissertation. Cambridge: Harvard University, 1946. 172 pp.

458 **Stern, Ephraim.** "The Silver Hoard from Tel Dor." *Hacksilber to Coinage: New Insights into the Monetary History of the Near East and Greece.* Numismatic Studies 24. New York: American Numismatic Society, 2001. Pages 19-26. Illus.
A hoard of silver was found in a clay jug, set in a layer dated to the late 11th or early 10th century B.C. at Dor (Phoenicia). The net weight of the silver was 8.5 kg. The silver was subdivided by units of weight and each unit had been placed in a cloth bag, sealed with a clay bulla, and stamped by a single scarab stamp seal. The hoard was clearly intended as money. The silver may have originated in Spain and may be evidence of trade between the Phoenician coast and southern Spain. [Also see Dever "The Silver Trail" under HOARDS].

459 **Stingl, Timo.** "Barren oder Münzen? Überlegungen zum Beginn der Elektronprägung in Westkleinasien." *Boreas* 23/24 (2001): 35-52.

460 **Strøm, Ingrid.** "Obelos of Pre- or Proto-Monetary Value in Greek Sanctuaries." *Economics of Cult in the Ancient Greek World: Proceedings of the Uppsala Symposium 1990.* Boreas 21. Edited by Tullia Linders and Brita Alroth. Uppsala: Acta Universitatis Upsaliensis, 1992. Pages 41-51.
Examines iron spits (as found at the Argive Heraion)—their primary function and the prerequisites for their use in a monetary-value system. They were originally used for roasting meat and are primarily found in tombs and sanctuaries. Strøm discusses find locations, dates, length, and weight. She then describes their dedication as offerings at Greek sanctuaries, and the transition from use at banquets to a proto-monetary function.

461 **Svoronos, Jean N.** "The Origins of Coinage." *American Journal of Numismatics* 43, no. 2 (1908-1909): 33-45. 1 pl.; no. 3 (1908-1909): 93-101; no. 4 (1908-1909): 141-8. 2 pl.; 44, no. 1 (1910): 14-21. Illus.; no. 4 (October 1910): 145-56. 1 pl.
Part 1 reviews the origins of coinage beginning with barter systems, the use of the ox as a measure of value in Homeric times, and the use of precious metals. Focuses on the use of large copper axe-shaped ingots as money. Part 2 focuses on Homeric talents of gold. Svoronos concludes that the talent did not represent any established value, but only "a definite form, which had no fixed weight." Also discusses the "pelanoi" of Lycurgus—large ingots of iron used as money at Sparta. Part 3 examines the spits (long rods) of iron used as money at Sparta, six of which made a drachm. Part 4 discusses unusual forms of coins including the "anchors" of Cyprus, "fishes" of Olbia, and "hams" of Nemausus. Part 5 discusses the cauldrons and tripods referred to in inscriptions from Crete which some believe relate to the use of cauldrons and tripods as money. Svoronos rejects this theory and instead argues that these were ingots of metal used in exchange before the invention of money, and perhaps their value was equivalent to that of the cauldrons themselves. [Also see Kroll "Observations on Monetary Instruments" above].

462 **Tandy, David W.** "Spits." *Warriors into Traders: The Power of the Market in Early Greece.* Berkeley: University of California Press, 1997. Pages 159-61.
A brief discussion of the iron spits that may have been a pre-coinage form of currency in Argos and other areas. Summarizes various viewpoints regarding the interpretation of the spits, their economic purpose, whether they were indeed a form of currency or merely utilitarian objects. The footnotes provide numerous references to other relevant papers.

463 **Thompson, Christine M.** "Sealed Silver in Iron Age Cisjordan and the 'Invention' of Coinage." *Oxford Journal of Archaeology* 22, no. 1 (February 2003): 67-107.
"Recent finds of hoarded silver in Cisjordan present new material for the consideration of the conceptual history of coined metals. When the fundamental concepts associated with coinage are abstracted from the various objects that express them, it is possible to see that a kind of coined metal existed in Cisjordan and other parts of the Near East prior to the traditional 'invention' of coinage by the Lydians and Greeks ca. 600 B.C. Both hoards and written sources indicate that seals affixed to precious metals at times qualified them in a numismatic sense by guaranteeing weights set to standards as well as controlled composition. What has been characterized as the invention of coinage was rather an adaptation of these same principal concepts. The frequency and size of silver hoards from Cisjordan point to a proliferation in the monetary use of silver in that region during the Iron Age and suggest a relationship to the overwhelming preference for silver among the Greeks." [From an internet posting]

464 **Ure, Percy N.** "The Origin of the Tyrannis." *Journal of Hellenic Studies* 26 (1906): 131-42.

"The early tyrants who rose to power in Greece owed their supremacy to their previous commercial predominance; the invention of coinage, which dates from that age, is a significant factor in this political development." [J. R. Jones, *NIJHS*]

465 **Vagi, David.** "Early Greek Coinage Spread from Ionia to Italy." *The Celator* 8, no. 4 (April 1994): 16. Illus.
A brief description of the spread of coinage from Ionia to the West. Mentions the possible role of Pythagoras in the introduction of the incuse style of coinage in Italy.

466 ——— "Discovering Electrum." *The Numismatist* 121, no. 2 (January 2008): 63-5. Illus.
An overview of the origin and spread of electrum coinage in the Greek world.

467 **van Alfen, Peter.** "Uncoined Money in the Ancient World." *American Numismatic Society Magazine* 2, no. 1 (spring 2003): 16-7. Illus.
Discusses some pre-coinage forms of metallic money (hacksilber) including a round ingot from Egypt (fourth century B.C.), and the dolphin and arrow-shaped bronze "coins" from the Black Sear area.

468 ——— "The Early Electrum Project." *American Numismatic Society Magazine* 4, no. 1 (spring 2005): 32-3. Illus.
Announces a long-term project to conduct metallurgical analysis on early electrum coins in order to better understand their metallic content. Once enough data is gathered, the interpretation of the results may lead to a better understanding of the origins of coinage.

469 **Vickers, Michael.** "Early Greek Coinage: A Reassessment." *Numismatic Chronicle* 145 (1985): 1-44.
A reassessment of the chronology of early Greek coinage citing historical, literary and numismatic evidence supporting a down-dating of many coin issues. Discusses the interpretation of the finds from Persepolis and Ephesos, the Acropolis hoard, the effect on coinage of the destruction of Eretria and Sybaris, and other related matters. Suggests the lion-bull type coins may belong to Darius. Discusses the dating of the Artemision foundation coins. Refutes some of the conclusions of Kagan (see Donald Kagan "Dates of the Earliest Coins" above). Supports a date of ca. 520 B.C. for the building of the Temple and a date of ca. 525-520 B.C. for the Phanes series. Examines the arguments which led to the dating assigned to objects from the Athenian Acropolis excavations. Believes the Wappenmünzen were tribal issues and the owls began ca. 480 B.C. Argues for down dating certain coins of Syracuse and Himera. Suggests ca. 460 B.C. for the burial of the Asyut hoard rather than ca. 475 as suggested by Price and Waggoner. Questions the existence of Solon and argues that the reforms attributed to Solon match the changes which took place in Athens in the 460's B.C. [Also see Root "Evidence from Persepolis" under PERSIA for a rebuttal to Vickers' dating of the early owls and the lion-bull coins. Also see Cook "The Francis-Vickers Chronology" above].

470 **Vismara, Novella.** *Monetazione Arcaica in Elettro dell'Asia Minore nelle Civiche Raccolte Numismatiche: Donazione Winsemann Falghera.* Milan, 1993.
[Also see Vismara *Monetazione Arcaica* under LYCIA].

471 **Wallace, Robert W.** "The Origin of Electrum Coinage." *American Journal of Archaeology* 91, no. 3 (July 1987): 385-97.
Because the inconsistent gold content of electrum made its value uncertain, the carefully standardized weights of early electrum coins imply that coins of similar size were to have a particular value determined by the issuers. Therefore, Wallace argues that coinage served to fix and stabilize the value of electrum. Briefly discusses the invention of coins, the political and intellectual consequences of coinage, and the introduction of silver coinage. [Also see Konuk "The Electrum Coinage of Samos" under IONIAN ISLANDS—SAMOS. Konuk supports Wallace's theory based on evidence from a 1998 hoard. Also see Keyser and Cook "Analyzing and Interpreting the Metallurgy of Early Electrum Coins" under METALLURGY, and R. W. Wallace "Remarks on the Value and Standards" under METROLOGY and R. W. Wallace "KUKALIM, WALWET, and the Artemision Deposit" under LYDIA].

472 **Weidauer, Liselotte.** *Probleme der frühen Elektronprägung.* Typos, Monographen zur Antiken Numismatik, Band 1. Fribourg: Office du Livre, 1975. 114 pp., 29 pls. [CS 2601]
An important examination of early electrum coinage. Begins with a review of the various weight standards used in this coinage. Continues with a discussion of striking techniques, and an examination of the legends on the "Walwel," "Kalil" and "Phanes" issues. Discusses the possible mint attributions. Then discusses the coins from the famous Foundation Deposit at Ephesos. [Reviewed by M. J. Price in *Numismatic Chronicle* 7th ser., 14 (1976): 273-5, and by C. M. Kraay in *Classical Review* new ser. 27, no. 2 (1977): 255-6. Also see R. W. Wallace "KUKALIM, WALWET, and the Artemision Deposit" under LYDIA]. An excellent English translation of this book, by Dane Kurth, was produced in 2009 in a project spearheaded by Reid Goldsborough. The translation was made available in electronic format, without photographs. It retained the same pagination as the original book.

473 ——— "Die Elektronprägung in der Orientalisierenden Epoche Frühgrieschischer Kunst." *Revue Suisse de Numismatique* (Switzerland) 60 (1981): 7-9. Illus.
"Selected specimens of early electrum coins are stylistically analyzed, and the influences of oriental art are studied in great detail. The coins' stylistic features are compared with similar phenomena known from archaeological documents of the 7th century B.C. The author renews the discussion of the beginning of Greek coinage, and is in favor of a date in the first half of the 7th century B.C." [H. Bloesch, *NL* 109]

474 **Will, Édouard.** "De l'Aspect Éthique des Origines Grecques de la Monnaie." *Review Historique* (France) 212 (1954): 209-31. [CS 1501]

475 ——— "Réflexions et Hypothèses sur les Origines du Monnayage." *Revue Numismatique* (France) 5th ser., 17 (1955): 5-23. [CS 1502]

Also see: American Numismatic Association *Selections* under GENERAL WORKS—GREEK; Burns *Money and Monetary Policy* under GENERAL WORKS—GREEK; Cahill and Kroll "New Archaic Coin Finds at Sardis" under HOARDS; Cahn *Monnaies Grecques Archaïque* under GENERAL WORKS—GREEK; Curtis "Media of Exchange" under EGYPT—PRE-PTOLEMAIC PERIOD; Davies *A History of Money* under GENERAL WORKS—GREEK; Dechelette "Les Origines de la Drachme et de l'Obole" under METROLOGY; Evans "Minoan Weights" under METROLOGY; Gitin and Golani "Tel Miqne-Ekon Silver Hoard" under HOARDS; Head "Chapter V: The Coins" under HOARDS; Hendin *Ancient Scale Weights and Pre-Coinage Currency* under METROLOGY; Istituto Italiano di Numismatica *Le Origini della Monetazione* under GENERAL WORKS—GREEK.

D. Kagan "Pheidon's Aeginetan Coinage" under AEGINA; J. Kagan "Small Change and the Beginning of Coinage at Abdera" under THRACE—ABDERA; Karwiese "Artemisium Coin Hoard" under IONIA; Keyser and Cook "Analyzing and Interpreting the Metallurgy of Early Electrum Coins" under METALLURGY; Kim *Greek Fractional Silver Coinage* under GENERAL WORKS—GREEK; Kim and Kroll "A Hoard of Archaic Coins of Colophon" under HOARDS; Kinns "Two Eighteenth Century Studies" under HOARDS; Konuk "The Electrum Coinage of Samos" under IONIAN ISLANDS—SAMOS; Konuk *From Kroisos to Karia* under PRIVATE COLLECTIONS; Kraay "The Asyut Hoard: Some Comments" under HOARDS; Kroll "The Monetary Use of Weighed Bullion" under GENERAL WORKS—GREEK; Kroll and Waggoner "Dating the Earliest Coins" under ATTICA—GENERAL WORKS; Kurke *Coins, Bodies, and Gold* under GENERAL WORKS—GREEK; Macdonald *The Evolution of Coinage* under GENERAL WORKS—GREEK; Marotta "Electrum" under METALLURGY; Meshorer *Ancient Means of Exchange* under PALESTINE—JUDEA; Metcalf *Oxford Handbook of Greek and Roman Coinage* under GENERAL WORKS—GREEK; Newton "On an Electrum Stater" under IONIA.

Papadopoulos "Minting Identity" under ITALY; Price (ed.) *Coins: An Illustrated Survey* under GENERAL WORKS—GREEK; Price "Coinage" under GENERAL WORKS—GREEK; Price "The First Three Centuries" under GENERAL WORKS—GREEK; Price "The Function of Early Greek Bronze Coinage" under GENERAL WORKS—GREEK; Ramage "Golden Sardis" under LYDIA; "Record Price Set" under IONIA; Ridgeway *The Origin of Metallic Currency* under METROLOGY; Root "Evidence from Persepolis" under PERSIA; Rutter "Early Greek Coinage" under ATTICA—GENERAL WORKS; Schaps "The Monetization of the Marketplace" under GENERAL WORKS; Seaford *Money* under GENERAL WORKS; Seltman "The Earliest Hoarded Coins" under HOARDS; Seltman *Greek Coins* under GENERAL WORKS—GREEK; Seltman "Peisistratus" under ATTICA—GENERAL WORKS; Sutherland "Corn and Coin" under GENERAL WORKS—GREEK; Tameanko "Joseph and His Brothers" under PALESTINE—JUDEA; van Alfen, Almagro-Gorbea, and Ripollès "A New Celtiberian Hacksilber Hoard" under SPAIN; Vismara *Monetazione Arcaica* under LYCIA; Von Rheden *Exchange in Ancient Greece* under GENERAL WORKS—GREEK; M. B. Wallace "The First Coins of Greece Proper" under AEGINA; R. W. Wallace "Remarks on the Value and Standards" under METROLOGY; R. W. Wallace "WALWE. and .KALI." under LYDIA; R. W. Wallace "Early Anatolian Electrum" under ASIA MINOR—GENERAL WORKS; Weissl "Zur Datierun des 'Foundation-Deposit' aud dem Artemision" under HOARDS; Wright *Coins from Asia Minor and the East* under ASIA MINOR—GENERAL WORKS.

HOARDS

Through the careful analysis of hoards and the painstaking reconstruction of die sequences the whole chaotic mass of Greek coinage is gradually being arranged with an objective precision which is hardly possible in any other field. Much has still to be done, though important results have already been achieved. The attainment of this chronological classification is the primary task of Greek numismatics today, for, until it is achieved, no full reliable use can be made of the information which Greek coinage provides.

—Colin M. Kraay, 1966

476 **Acar, Özgen, and Melik Kaylan.** "The Hoard of the Century." *Connoisseur* (July 1988) 74-83. Illus. Also appeared in *Coin World* (July 6, 1988): 1 ff.
Tells the story of the famous "Decadrachm Hoard" found in Turkey in 1984. This "expose" describes the discovery of the hoard, its smuggling out of Turkey and sale in Germany and subsequent dispersal. The hoard contained about 2000 Greek silver coins, including fourteen decadrachms. Describes attempts by the Turkish government to recover the coins. [Also see Alexander "Curse," Gibbs "American Returns 'Hoard of the Century,'" Giedroyc "Hoard's Owner Speaks," Meier "Contested Coins," and Vermeule "Athenian Treasury Hoard" below].

477 **Acheilara, L.** "The Messon Sanctuary of Lesbos through the Coin Evidence." *Coins in the Aegean Islands. Proceedings of the Fifth Scientific Meeting, Mytilene, 16-29 September 2006. Volume 1: Ancient Times.* Obolos 9. Edited by Panagiotis Tselekas. Athens: The Friends of the Numismatic Museum, 2010. Pages 201-16.

478 **Adam-Veleni, P.** "Four Hoards from the Hellenistic City at Petres (Florina – West Macedonia)." *Coinage in the Macedonian Region. Proceedings of the 2nd Scientific Meeting.* Obolos 4. Edited by P. Adam-Veleni. Thessaloniki: University Studio Press, 2000.
A paper presented at the 2nd Scientific Meeting held in Thessaloniki in May 1998.

479 **Alexander, David T.** "Curse of the Dekadrachms." *COINage* 35, no. 6 (June 1999): 18-20, 22, 52. Illus.
Recounts the discovery of the Emali hoard, its sale into the collector market, and the return of the coins by William Koch to the Turkish government. [Also see Acar and Kaylan "Hoard" above, and Gibbs "American Returns 'Hoard of the Century,'" Giedroyc "Hoard's Owner Speaks," Meier "Contested Coins," and Vermeule "Athenian Treasury Hoard" below].

480 **Allotte de la Füye, F. M., and R. de Mecquenem.** *Numismatique Épigraphie Grecque. Céramique Élamite.* Mémoires de la Mission Archéologique de Perse, Tome XX, Mission en Susiane. Paris, 1928. 132 pp., 4 pls.
A record of the coins found at Susa. Over half of the text and three of the plates are devoted to coins.

481 **Ariel, Donald T.** "Coins from the Synagogue at Korzim." *The Synagogue at Korazim: The 1962-1964, 1980-1987 Excavations.* Edited by Z. Yeivin. Jerusalem, 2000. Pages 33-49.

482 ——— "The Coins from Khirbet Zemel." *Eretz Zafon: Studies in Galilean Archaeology.* Edited by Z. Gal. Jerusalem, 2002. Pages 119-22.
"Twenty-seven coins (of which only nine were identifiable) were found in the excavations of a small Iturean settlement on the Golan Heights. The coins appear to represent a very restricted period of occupation at the site. Their minimal chronological range is a mere fifteen years. The coins are all Seleucid, from the reign of Demetrius I (159/8) to that of Demetrius II (145-140). The coins include two silver tetradrachms, which were found in the make-up of the earliest floor, just above the bedrock, suggesting that they were placed there for apotropaic reasons, as foundation deposits." [D. Syon, *NL* 146]

483 **Arnold-Biucchi, Carmen, Leslie Beer-Tobey, and Nancy M. Waggoner.** "A Greek Archaic Silver Hoard from Selinus." *Museum Notes* 33 (1988): 1-35. 15 pls.
Analyzes a hoard found in 1985 near Selinus in Sicily. The hoard contained 165 silver coins from eight mints, as well as four silver ingots and a silver dump. The coins are catalogued and a commentary follows each mint listing. The mints included are: Sybaris, Selinus, Aegina, Corinth, Metapontum, Poseidonia, Himera, and Abdera. Die links among the coins are noted. Concludes that the hoard was closed in the last decade of the sixth century B.C. Provides early evidence of the importation of foreign coins into the west, and that the mints of Aegina and Corinth were a possible source of silver for the Sicilian mints one century earlier than previous hoard evidence has allowed. [Also see Beer-Tobey, Gale, Kim, and Stos-Gale "Lead Isotope Analysis" under METALLURGY].

484 **Arslan, Melih, and Chris Lightfoot.** *Greek Coin Hoards in Turkey: The Antalya Archaeological Museum and the C. S. Okray Collection.* Ankara: Melih Arslan and Chris Lightfoot, 1999. 197 pp. including the 75 pls., 2 maps.
A catalogue of 1036 coins which were found in Asia Minor and Thrace. Each coin is illustrated. Includes hoards in the Burdur, Fethiye, and Sinop museums. Also includes 250 coins from the collection of Cafer S. Okray. [Reviewed by Peter A. Clayton in *Spink Numismatic Circular* 107, no. 8 (October 1999): 247].

485 **Arslan, Melih, and Martin J. Price.** "A Hoard from the Durmaz Collection from the Region of Antakya." *Coin Hoards, Volume VIII: Greek Hoards.* Edited by U. Wartenberg, M. J. Price, and K. A. McGregor. London: Royal Numismatic Society, 1994. Pages 80-1. 2 pls.
This report on a hoard (*Coin Hoards VIII*, no. 250) publishes thirty-two coins from a hoard which was said to contain over 200 coins. All are Alexander the Great types with Zeus r./seated Zeus (two are in the name of Seleucus I, and two are in the name of Philip Arrhidaeus). The coins are from a variety of mints, including many from eastern mints. The hoard was found in Antakya and was likely buried ca. 290 B.C.

486 **Ashton, Richard H. J.** "*IGCH* 1289 and 1290 Reconsidered." *Coin Hoards* 2 (1976): 2. 1 pl.
Suggests these hoards may consist of more than two hoards mixed together. *IGCH* 1289 may be comprised of two hoards, one buried ca. 300 and the other ca. 180 B.C. The hoards include Rhodian plinthophoric issues, coins of Mylasa, and others.

487 ——— "Knossos Royal Road South 1971 and 1972 Excavations: The Coins." *Annual of the British School at Athens* 84 (1989): 49-60. 1 pl.
The author records eighty-two coins found during the 1971 and 1972 excavations near Knossos. Includes several coins of Knossos, Gortyn, Itanos, and Rhithymna, and a few non-Cretan Greek mints. The rest of the coins are Roman Provincial, Imperial, Byzantine, or Venetian.

488 ——— "Excavation Coins from Phanagoreia." *Numismatic Chronicle* 163 (2003): 379-85.
A report on a 1996 excavation at Phanagoreia, on the eastern side of the Kimmerian Bosporos. Lists the eighty-four coins found, which are primarily from Pantikapaion, Phanagoreia, and other Black Sea mints.

489 **Ashton, Richard H. J., and Andrew R. Meadows.** "The Letoon Deposit: Lycian League Coinage, Rhodian Plinthophori, and Pseudo-Rhodian Drachms from Haliartos (Yet Again) and Asia Minor." *Numismatic Chronicle* 168 (2008): 111-34.
The Letoon was a Hellenistic temple of Leto near Xanthus in Lycia. The authors discuss the eighty-one coins found during excavations in 1985.

490 **Ashton, Richard H. J., Nicholas Hardwick, Koray Konuk, and Andrew R. Meadows.** "The Pixodarus Hoard (*CH* 9.421)." *Coin Hoards, Volume IX: Greek Hoards.* Edited by A. Meadows and Ute Wartenberg. London: Royal Numismatic Society, 2002. Pages 159-243. 21 pls.
Discusses a hoard found in Bodrum (ancient Halicarnassus) in 1978. The hoard consisted of about 2600 silver coins including some that were previously extremely rare. Most of the coins were taken out of circulation at one time. Burial is placed at 341/0 B.C. Included coins of Thasos, Cyzicus, Colophon, Ephesus (600 tetradrachms), Miletus, 'satrapal' tetradrachms, Chios, Samos, Cnidus, Cos, Rhodes, and over 600 coins of the Hecatomnids (Mausolus, Idrieus, Pixodarus). An extensive discussion of each mint is presented. The hoard was a major addition to the coinage of Thasos—the 29 tetradrachms added to just 32 that were previously known to West (see West, *Fifth and Fourth Century Gold Coins from the Thracian Coast* under THRACE—GENERAL WORKS). The new pieces are combined with those known to West and those in the British Museum, and a full catalogue is included here. The symbols on the coins may indicate annual issues.

The hoard also provided evidence that the mint of Cyzicus had finished minting its Chian-weight coinage by 341/0 B.C. at the latest, and that the reduced ethnic Type 2 tetradrachms were produced between ca. 390-340 B.C. Of the 600 tetradrachms of Ephesus, only three were the early curved-wing type. These, along with the fifty tetradrachms from the Hecatomnus hoard (see Ashton, Kinns, Konuk, and Meadows below), allow a chronology to be proposed for these issues. The full series of tetradrachms is divided into ten classes, dated 390-325 B.C. and the dies and magistrates of each are detailed here. Next, the authors discuss the Royal Achaemenid staters (*obv.*, Persian king kneeling, drawing a bow; *rev.*, rider on a galloping horse, holding a spear). The hoard contained at least sixteen of these previously extremely rare coins.

Lists all the tetradrachms of Chios which have appeared on the market since the discovery of the Pixodarus hoard (it is likely that most of these coins derived from the hoard). Discusses the chronology of the fourth and third century B.C. issues, including the bronze coins. The discussion of the coins of Samos focuses on a newly discovered type with *obv.*, lion's mask, *rev.*, Athena Promachus, with an owl symbol in the field. The coin may indicate a co-existence of Athenians and Samian on the island at the same time (ca. 350 B.C.). Also includes brief comments on the two coins of Cnidus in the hoard.

Next, the 634 coins of the Hecatomnids receive attention, including a new type of Mausolus. The hoard also yielded more than half of all known Apollo-type tetradrachms of Mausolus. The tetradrachms of Idrieus were rare (only 33 known) before the appearance of this hoard. A full die-study of the tetradrachms of Pixodarus is included. At least 74 tetradrachms and 48 didrachms of Cos were in the hoard. The hoard coins are combined with coins from the British Museum to form a partial die-study, allowing the basic pattern and chronology of the fourth century issues to be reconstructed. Four phases of the coinage are identified and a chronology is suggested. Finally, twelve didrachms of Rhodes are catalogued.

491 **Ashton, Richard H. J., Philip Kinns, Koray Konuk, and Andrew R. Meadows.** "The Hecatomnus Hoard (*CH* 5.17, 8.96, 9.387)." *Coin Hoards, Volume IX: Greek Hoards.* Edited by A. Meadows and Ute Wartenberg. London: Royal Numismatic Society, 2002. Pages 95-158. 15 pls.
An analysis of a hoard discovered in 1977 near Söke (between Ephesus and Miletus). It is likely a "circulation" hoard composed of coins in use at the time of burial, which is placed ca. 390-385 B.C. Includes coins of Thasos, Colophon, Ephesus, Chios, Samos, Caunus, Cnidus, Halicarnassus, Idyma, Hecatomnus (77 tetradrachms), Cos, and Rhodes. The hoard included a large number of the otherwise rare ΣYN coinages of Ephesus, Cnidus, and Rhodes, and a full die-study of these three issues is included here. The authors suggest the most likely date for the ΣYN issues is ca. 405 B.C. The Ephesian coins include 50+ tetradrachms (bee/stag) of the early curved-wing variety. The change to straight wings is placed ca. 390-385 B.C. The coins of Samos present in the hoard allow the authors to update Barron's specimen, die, and combination table for the tetradrachms of Samos (see Barron *The Silver Coins of Samos* under IONIAN ISLANDS—SAMOS). Changes to the previously accepted chronology are proposed. The hoard also confirms that Cos began minting before 366 B.C. A catalogue of the hoard coins is provided.

492 **Ashton, Richard, and Jennifer A. W. Warren.** "A Hoard of Western Greek and Pseudo-Rhodian Silver." *Revue Belge de Numismatique et de Sigillographie* (Belgium) 143 (1997): 5-16.
"A hoard of forty-seven Greek silver coins from Corinth, Corcyra, Leukas, Palairos, the Epirote republic, and the Akarnanian league, also containing pseudo-Rhodian drachms is published." [J. van Heesch, *NL* 141]

493 **Babelon, Ernest.** "Trouvaille de Tarente (Juin 1911)." *Revue Numismatique* (France) 4th ser., 16 (1912): 1-40.

494 **Bar, M.** *Monnaies Grecques et Assimilées Trouvées en Belgique.* Brüssel, 1991. 303 pp., 11 pls.

495 **Barnett, R. D.** "The Art of Bactria and the Treasure of the Oxus." *Iranica Antiqua* (Netherlands) 8 (1968): 34-53. 13 pls.
"The latest probable date for the treasure of the Oxus, a collection of gold Bactrian, Persian and Greek objects d'art ranging from the sixth to the second centuries found in Central Asia is discussed. The 1500 coins associated with the treasure are referred to. The coins seem to be of the same provenance as the treasure and date from the early fifth century to 170 B.C. The treasure may be of the period of Euthydemus of Bactria (ca. 180 B.C.) since his are the latest coins found with the treasure. Five coins of Bactria are illustrated." [M. Bates, *NL* 86]

496 **Becker, F.** "Ein Fund von 75 Milesischen Obelen." *Revue Suisse de Numismatique* (Switzerland) 67 (1988): 5-33.

497 **Beckman, Martin.** "Ancient Coins from Shipwrecks." *The Anvil* (Canada) 8, no. 2 (June 1998): 19-23. 2 charts.
A discussion of ancient coins found with ancient shipwrecks. Only a few finds of Greek coins are documented, although it is not uncommon to find Roman coins among the wreckage of Roman-period vessels. Generally, the number of coins is small—limited to the coins owned by the crew. Finding the remains of large shipments of coins is uncommon.

498 **Bell, H. W.** *Publications of the American Society for the Excavation of Sardis, Volume 11: Coins. Part 1, 1910-1914.* Leiden: E. J. Brill, Ltd., 1916. 124 pp., 2 pls.
A catalogue of the coins found during excavations at Sardis, 1910-1914. Includes 419 Greek coins plus many Roman and Byzantine coins. Only sixteen of the Greek coins are pre-Alexandrian; 319 are from the period between Alexander and Augustus. One of the plates primarily illustrates Greek coins. [Reviewed by G. F. Hill in *Numismatic Chronicle* 4th ser., 16 (1916): 199-200].

499 **Bellinger, Alfred R.** *Catalogue of the Coins Found at Corinth, 1925 with a Note on the Cleaning of the Coins.* New Haven and London: Yale University Press and Oxford University Press, 1930. 88 pp., 2 pls.
Lists all the coins which could be identified after cleaning found at Corinth in 1925 by the American School of Classical Studies. Includes Greek, Roman, Byzantine, Frankish, Venetian, Turkish, and modern Greek coins. Only eighteen of the several hundred listed coins are autonomous Greek types. Includes a description of the cleaning process by Charlotte B. Bellinger. [Reviewed by E. T. Newell in *American Journal of Archaeology* 36 (1932): 578-9].

500 ——— "The Coins." *Final report VI of the Excavation at Dura-Europos, conducted by Yale University and the French Academy of Inscriptions and Letters.* New Haven: Yale University Press, 1949. [CS 3211]
The excavations by Yale University at the city of Dura, on the Euphrates river in Northern Mesopotamia, turned up coins of the Seleucid, Parthian, Roman Provincial, and Roman Imperial periods. The author catalogues all of the 14,017 coins discovered at the site. Includes comments on some of the coins, a section on hoards, discussions of denominations and countermarks, a key to the monograms, and indexes of mints and emperors. [Reviewed by G. K. Jenkins in *Journal of Hellenic Studies* 70 (1950): 102-3, and by R. A. G. Carson in *Journal of Roman Studies* 40 (1950): 165-6].

501 ——— "The Coins from the Treasure of the Oxus." *Museum Notes* 10 (1962): 51-67.
After reviewing previous publications which listed parts of the "Oxus Treasure" hoard found in 1877, the author compiles a catalogue summarizing the known coins from the hoard. The coins include issues of several Greek cities as well as many issues of Persia, the Macedonian Kingdom, and Bactria. [Also see Pichikyan "Rebirth of the Oxus Treasure" below].

502 ——— "Electrum Coins from Gordion." *American Journal of Archaeology* 69 (1965): 164.
A brief summary of a paper presented at a conference. "The discovery of twenty-six coins of Lydia (seventh and sixth centuries B.C.) at this site 'adds one more item to the very slight evidence based on provenance.'" [J. R. Jones, *NIAJAH*]

503 ——— "The Thessaly Hoard of 1938." *Congresso Internazionale di Numismatica, Roma 11-16 Settembre 1961. Volume 2.* Rome: Istituto Italiano de Numismatica, 1965. Pages 57-60.
Describes a hoard which included 288 drachms of Alexander II, Philip II, and Lysimachus, 155 drachms of Larissa, 72 old-style Athenian tetradrachms, and other coins. The hoard was probably buried shortly after 250 B.C. Discusses the evidence provided for chronology and monetary circulation.

504 ——— "Electrum Coins from Gordion." *Essays in Greek Coinage Presented to Stanley Robinson.* Edited by C. M. Kraay and G. K. Jenkins. Oxford: Clarendon Press, 1968. Pages 10-5. 1 pl.
Forty-five electrum coins were found by a University of Pennsylvania team during excavations at Gordion in 1963, including 18 twelfths of a stater, one sixth stater, and 26 thirds. Some are countermarked. The types are all the same: the obverse features a lion's head to the right with jaws open; the reverse consists of either a single or double punch. Suggests these coins were the royal money of Lydia, struck at Sardes. Describes the coins found under the Temple of Artemis in Ephesus and discusses the designs and stylistic differences between the Artemision coins and the Gordion coins. Suggests the Gordion hoard coins are neither as early as the earliest Artemision hoard coins, nor as late as the latest Artemision coins. Concludes this hoard covers the years 625-610 B.C., and these coins are the royal currency of Lydia before the reign of Alyattes. Lists the coins and their weights. All are photographed.

505 **Berman, A., and Donald T. Ariel.** "Coins from the Excavations at Giv' at Yasaf (Tel er Ras)." *Atiqot* 37 (1999): 23-4.
"Ten coins found at this site in W. Galilee are described. One is Ptolemaic, two are Seleucid, one is Byzantine (Maurice), one is from the Crusader Period and five are Islamic." [A. Spaer, *NL* 144]

506 **Bingen, J.** "Le Trésor Monétaire Thorikos 1969." *Thorikos* 6 (1973): 7-59.

507   **Bonelou, Elena.** "The Numismatic Circulation from the Private and Public Buildings of the Capital and the Port of Leucas." *Proceedings of the Fourth International Numismatic Congress in Croatia, September 20-25, 2004. Stari Grad (Pharos), the Island of Hvar and M/S Marko Polo, Croatia.* Edited by Julijan Dobrinic. Rijeka: Dobrinic & Dobrinic, 2005.
Reviews the finds from excavations at Leucas to gain an understanding of coin circulation in the city and surrounding area. Suggests that the foreign coins found resulted from either military activity in the region or trade.

508   **Bopearachchi, Osmund, and Philippe Flandrin.** *Le Portrait d'Alexandre le Grand: Histoire d'une Découverte Pour l'Humanité.* Monaco: Éditions du Rocher, 2005. 270 pp., 8 pls.
Provides information on the Mir Zakah Deposit, a massive coin hoard found in 1992 in eastern Afghanistan. Discusses the ransacking of the Kabul Museum in May 1993. Examines the coins of the Mir Zakah Deposit, including a gold double daric with the portrait of Alexander in elephant headdress supposedly minted by Ptolemy I. [Reviewed by W. Fischer-Bossert in *American Numismatic Society Magazine* 5, no. 2 (summer 2006): 62-5, and by M. J. A. Tzamali in *Nomismatika Khronika* (Greece) 24 (2005): 127. Due to gross stylistic flaws, Fischer-Bossert expresses grave doubts regarding the authenticity of the double daric and some other coins in the hoard. Also see Frank Holt, "Ptolemy's Alexander Postscript" under EGYPT—PTOLEMAIC KINGDOM. Holt's article is based on this same, questionable, gold coin].

509   **Broshi, M.** "Excavations at Qumran, Summer of 2001." *Israel Exploration Journal* (Israel) 53, no. 1 (2003): 61-73. Illus.
"Coin finds included a Tyrian silver issue of Antiochus VII, an erased Tyrian half shekel, a coin of Nero struck at Caesarea, one of Alexander Jannaeus, one of the Roman procurator Festus and two coppers of Year 2 of the First Jewish Revolt." [Arnold Spaer, *NL* 147]

510   **Butcher, Kevin.** *Small Change in Ancient Beirut: Coins from BEY 006 and 045.* Berytus Archaeological Studies XLV-XLVI, 2001-2002. Archaeology of the Beirut Souks I. Beirut: Faculty of Arts and Schools, American University of Beirut, 2003. 304 pp., 23 pls.
This edition of the journal *Berytus* is essentially a monograph. Butcher describes and discusses 7000 Persian, Hellenistic, Roman, and Byzantine period coins, nearly all bronze, found during excavations in ancient Beirut conducted by the American University of Beirut and the Archaeological Collaboration of Research and Excavation during 1994-96. [Reviewed by Oliver Hoover in *American Numismatic Society Magazine* 4, no. 3 (winter 2005)].

511   **Buttrey, Theodore V.** "Egypt, Before 1879: Early 5th Century B.C., c. 14 AR." *Coin Hoards, Volume VIII: Greek Hoards.* Edited by U. Wartenberg, M. J. Price, and K. A. McGregor. London: Royal Numismatic Society, 1994. Pages 71-2.
A brief report on a hoard (*Coin Hoards VIII*, no. 57) reported by C. W. King just prior to 1879. Eighteen coins were supposedly found with a mummy. Buttrey discounts the story, but believes some of the coins likely were a hoard.

512   ———. "Part I: The Coins." *The Extramural Sanctuary of Demeter and Persephone at Cyrene, Libya: Final Reports.* Edited by D. White. Philadelphia, 1997.

513   **Buttrey, Theodore V., and R. B. Hitchner.** "The Coins—1976." *Excavations at Carthage Conducted by the University of Michigan, Volume 4.* Edited by J. H. Humphrey. Tunis: Kelsey Museum, University of Michigan, 1978. Pages 99-168.
A report on the 1208 coins found during the 1976 season of excavation at Carthage by the University of Michigan team. They are published in the form of a full catalogue. The attributable coins include 12 Greek, 148 Roman, 124 Vandal, 310 Byzantine, and 3 modern. All but 13 of the finds are bronze. All but 28 of the finds date to the fourth century A.D. or later. The Greek coins were primarily of Cyrene, Alexandria, and Carthage. Also includes J. H. Humphrey's "A Discussion of the Interpretation of the Numismatic Evidence in the Context of the History of the Site" (pages 164-8).

514   **Buttrey, Theodore V., Ann Johnston, Kenneth M. MacKenzie, and Michael Bates.** *Greek, Roman, and Islamic Coins from Sardis.* Archaeological Exploration of Sardis, Monograph 7. Cambridge: Harvard University Press, 1981. 274 pp., 10 pls.
Examines the Lydian, Greek, Roman and Islamic coins found during excavations at Sardis by Harvard and Cornell Universities between 1958 and 1978. Begins with a survey of operational techniques for archaeologists including recording coin finds, cleaning, identification, and production of casts. Briefly describes the archaeological context of the coins found. The discussion of the Greek coins, written by Johnston (see A. Johnston below), covers the pattern of finds, die sharing, and types. Catalogue of 414 Greek and Greek Imperial coins. Discussion of countermarks on Greek Imperial coins. Also includes a chapter on the Byzantine coins found since publication of George Bates' *Sardis, Monograph 1* (1971). [Reviewed by M. Mitchiner in *Seaby Coin and Medal Bulletin* No. 766 (June 1982): 185].

515   **Cahill, Nicholas, and John H. Kroll.** "New Archaic Coin Finds at Sardis." *American Journal of Archaeology* 109, no. 4 (October 2005): 589-617. Illus.
The authors examine the coins found during excavations of the western fortification of Lydian Sardis: a Lydian gold 1/12 stater, a silver 1/12 stater, and a silver 1/24 stater, all of the confronted lion-and-bull 'croesid' type. These coins were in a layer that can be dated to the time of the capture of Sardis by Cyrus the Great in the 540's B.C. The coins provide a much-needed fixed point in the chronology of the archaic coinage of Asia Minor. The authors discuss the excavations, the dating of ceramics, the date of the capture of Sardis, and the coins. The finds confirm that the lion-and-bull series began with Croesus, not in the later Persian period as suggested by Giesecke, Price, and others. This evidence also helps place the introduction of electrum coinage into the second half of the seventh century B.C. [Also see Giesecke *Antike Geldwesen* under METROLOGY, and Price "Croesus or Pseudo Croesus?" under LYDIA].

516   **Cahn, Herbert A.** "Asuit—Kritische Bemerkungen zu Einer Schatzfund Publikation." *Revue Suisse de Numismatique* (Switzerland) 56 (1977): 279-87. [CS 3218]
Comments on the Asyut Hoard. [Also see Kraay "Some Comments on Chronology" below, and Price and Waggoner *Archaic Greek Coinage* below].

517   **Clarke, G. W., P. J. Connor, L. Crewe, B. Frolich, H. Jackson, J. Littleton, C. E. V. Nixon, M. O'Hea, and D. Steele.** *Jebel Khalid on the Euphrates: Report on Excavations 1986-1996. Volume 1.* Mediterranean Archaeology Supplement 5. Sydney, 2002. 335 pp., illus., 59 pls.
Excavation reports on the Hellenistic fortified site of Jebel Khalid. Includes a chapter by Nixon which catalogues the 317 coins found on the site, including many Seleucid issues. [Also see Nixon "The Coins" and "The Coins from Jebel Khalid" below].

518   **Clement, Paul A.** "Chronological Notes on the Issues of Several Greek Mints." *American Journal of Philology* 62 (1941): 157-68.

It is commonly accepted that the site of Olynthus was abandoned in 348 B.C., except for the Northwest Quarter which was abandoned ca. 316. Yet some coins were found in the Olynthus excavations which are thought to have been minted after those dates. Clement's purpose in this paper is: (a) to analyze the numismatic data to determine the odds against the occurrence among the autonomous Greek excavation coins published in *Olynthus IX* (see Robinson and Clement *Excavations at Olynthus, Part 9* below) of pieces later than 348 and of pieces later than ca. 316, and (b) to examine eleven excavation specimens from the autonomous issues of seven Greek mints, conventionally dated between the middle of the fourth and the middle of the third centuries B.C., to find whether such purely numismatic evidence as can at present be used for their chronology supports or contradicts the odds against their conventional date.

519 **Colonna, Giovanni.** "The Sanctuary at Pyrgi in Etruria." *Archaeology* 19, no. 1 (January 1966): 11-23. Illus. [CS 3219]
Describes the archaeological discoveries at Pyrgi in Italy. The most important items found were plaques containing Etruscan and Punic inscriptions. Also found were nine silver tetradrachms of the fifth century B.C. from Athens, Syracuse, Messina, and Leontini—the first to be found in Italy north of the Gulf of Naples.

520 **Cox, Dorothy Hannah.** "The Coins." *Excavations at Gözlü Kule, Tarsus. Volume 1: The Hellenistic and Roman Periods.* Edited by Hetty Goldman. Princeton: Princeton University Press, 1950. Pages 38-83. 6 pls.
Discusses the classical coins found during excavations. With the exception of one bronze coin of Philip II, no coins earlier than Alexander the Great were found. Includes a catalogue of 283 Greek and sixty-two Roman coins. Discusses the significance of the finds.

521 ——— *A Third Century Hoard of Tetradrachms from Gordion.* Museum Monographs of the University Museum. Philadelphia: University of Pennsylvania, 1953. 19 pp., 8 pls., map. [CS 3220]
Describes a hoard of 114 silver tetradrachms found in 1951 at Gordion. The coins were quite crystallized. Primarily included coins of Philip and Alexander and the Seleucid kings. The burial date was ca. 210 B.C. Discusses the evidence provided for the history of Asia Minor in the late third century B.C.

522 ——— *Coins from the Excavations at Curium, 1932-1953.* Numismatic Notes and Monographs, No. 145. New York: American Numismatic Society, 1959. 125 pp., 10 pls. [CS 3221]
Describes the pre-A.D. 1600 coins excavated at Curium on the south coast of Cyprus by the University Museum of Philadelphia. Includes coins from the Greek period through the Venetian occupations. Most of the Greek coins found were Ptolemaic from the mint at Paphos, and these support the attributions made by Svoronos in his work on the Ptolemies. Of the 753 coins listed, 128 are from the Greek period. Provides commentary on the coins. Greek coins are shown on plates 1-5. [Reviewed by J. F. Healy in *Journal of Hellenic Studies* 81 (1961): 229-30, and by G. K. Jenkins in *Numismatic Chronicle* 7th ser., 1 (1961): 237-8].

523 ——— "Gordion Hoards III, IV, V, and VII." *Museum Notes* 12 (1966): 19-55. 19 pls. [CS 3222]
Catalogues the coins founds in four hoards during excavations at Gordian in Asia Minor. Hoard III contained 41 Alexander-type tetradrachms and one Lysimachus-type tetradrachm. The mint of Urianopolis is discussed. Hoard IV contained 50 drachms, all but one being of the Alexander type; one was a Lysimachus type. Hoard V contained 100 tetradrachms, mainly Alexander-types (mostly posthumous) and Seleucid coins; Lysimachus and others make up the rest. Hoard VII contained five gold coins—three Macedonian staters and two rare Seleucid octodrachms.

524 **Crawford, Michael H.** "Trade and Movement of Coinage across the Adriatic in the Hellenistic Period." *Scripta Nummaria Romana: Essays Presented to Humphrey Sutherland.* Edited by R. A. G. Carson and C. M. Kraay. London: Spink and Sons Ltd., 1978. Page 1-11.
Considers the pattern of hoards including Roman coins east of the Adriatic, as well as hoards from Italy including coins from the East. Crawford then considers evidence for the movement of isolated coins across the Adriatic, in both directions.

525 **Curiel, Raoul, and Daniel L. Schlumberger.** "Le Tresor de Mir Zakah Près de Gardez." *Trésors Monétaires d'Afghanistan.* Mémoires de la Délégation Archéologique Française en Afghanistan 14. Edited by R. Curiel and D. Schlumberger. Paris, 1953. Pages 65-99.
Publication of a hoard.

526 **da Costa, Kate, ed.** *Pella in Jordan (1979-1990): The Coins.* Sydney, 2001.
"This volume contains the catalog and associated commentaries for the 1106 coins from the University of Sydney's excavations at Pella in Jordan from 1979 to 1990. The material includes Ptolemaic, Seleucid, Hellenistic city, Jewish, Roman Imperial, Greek Imperial, Byzantine, Umayyad, Abbasid and Mamluk issues. The volume also includes a short introduction to the site and concordances of mints, hoards, findspots and registration numbers to locate the coin corpus within the overall publication plan of the excavation project." [*NL* 144]

527 **Dalton, O. M.** *The Treasure of the Oxus.* London, 1905.
Gives a brief description of some of the coins from the Oxus Treasure, found in 1877.

528 **Dattari, Giovanni.** "Comments on a Hoard of Athenian Tetradrachms found in Egypt." *Journal International d'Archéologie Numismatique* (Greece) 8 (1905): 103-11. 3 pls.
A hoard of Athenian tetradrachms was found near Benha, Egypt, in 1904. Dattari was able to examine 240 pieces (460 of the hoard coins had been melted by jewelers). Ninety-eight of the 239 coins were countermarked with 123 different marks. One of the coins was a coin of Alexander the Great; the others were Athenian tetradrachm types. Sixty-nine of them had a cut on the edge. The coins are of numerous varieties and some appear to not be of Athenian origin—some bear an Aramaic inscription. The author recounts the historical events leading to the reign of Tachos (364 B.C.). Suggests that Tachos minted imitation Athenian tetradrachms in preparation for a war with Persia. Dattari also announces the discovery of a die for imitation Athenian tetradrachms, also found in Egypt. Concludes the die is genuine and was prepared for the purpose of striking coins by order of an Egyptian Pharaoh. Also concludes that 130 of the hoard coins were struck in Egypt.

529 **Davesne, Alain.** "The Medancikkale Hoard." *Trésors et Circulation Monétaire en Anatolie Antique.* Edited by M. Amandry and G. Le Rider. Paris, 1994. Pages 37-43.

530 **Davesne, Alain, and Georges Le Rider.** *Gülnar II: Le Trésor de Meydancikkale (Cilicie Trachée, 1980).* Two volumes. Paris: Éditions Recherche sur les Civilisations, 1989. 377 pp., 157 pls.

An examination of a hoard of 5215 coins found during an archaeological excavation near Gülnar in southern Turkey in 1980. The hoard included 2554 coins of Alexander the Great and many Ptolemaic issues. [Reviewed by Catharine Lorber in *SAN* 18, no. 2 (May 1991): 37-9, and by C. Arnold-Biucchi in *American Journal of Numismatics* 2nd ser., 3-4 (1992): 207-14].

531 **Davidson, G. R., and Dorothy B. Thompson.** "Small Objects from the Pynx, I." *Hesperia, Supplement 7* (1943).
"On pp. 14-29 the coins found in this area are listed and described, together with four lead weights. The list includes a hoard of 243 bronze coins of Athens, ending soon after 90 B.C., some Roman and Byzantine issues, and a few Vandalic, Frankish and Venetian coins." [J. R. Jones, *NIAJAH*]

532 **de Callataÿ, François.** "Greek Coins from Archaeological Excavations: A Conspectus of Conspectuses and a Call for Chronological Tables." *Agoranomia: Studies in Money and Exchange Presented to John H. Kroll*. Edited by Peter G. van Alfen. New York: American Numismatic Society, 2006. Pages 177-200.
Callataÿ highlights J. H. Kroll's summary of coins found in the Athenian agora excavations (Kroll published a table summarizing the counts of coins from each city, indicating the century of minting. See Kroll *The Athenian Agora* under ATTICA—GENERAL WORKS). Callataÿ charts the results of the agora excavation and other excavations to better understand the preponderance of bronze coins, the percentages of local vs foreign coins, and the number of coins by century of minting. He calls for greater use of such statistical compilations, which may reveal important information about coin production, circulation, and patterns of monetization. In an appendix, he lists the archaeological sites for which the Greek coins have been published, including brief counts and other statistics for each.

533 **de Callataÿ, François, and Illya Prokopov.** "The Boljarino Hoard (*IGCH* 975—Near Plovidiv). *Revue Belge de Numismatic et de Sigillographie* (Belgium) 141 (1995): 5-12. Illus.
"The authors publish a hoard found near Plovidiv whose content is chiefly constituted by Thasian imitations along with Athenian 'New Style' tetradrachms and Roman Republican denarii. The burial date is best placed ca. 40/30 B.C. This hoard includes an additional overstrike of a Thasian imitation on Athens (Thompson: ca. 156/5 B.C. = ca. 124/3 B.C.)." [de Callataÿ and Prokopov, *NL* 140]

534 **Destroopers-Georgiades, Anne.** "Le Trésor de Larnaca (*IGCH* 1272) Réexaminé." *Report of the Department of Antiquities Cyprus 1984.* Pages 140-61.

535 ——— "Two Cilician Hoards of the Fourth Century." *Revue Belge de Numismatic et de Sigillographie* (Belgium) 134 (1988): 19-39. Illus. Also appeared in *Numismatic Report* (Cyprus) 22-25 (1991-4): 135-58.
"Two hoards of Cilician origin, already in public cabinets, are analyzed: one in New York at the ANS (*IGCH* 1263) from ca. 1900 (137 coins), the other in Paris at the Cabinet des Médailles (Noe, *Bibliogr GCH* 251) found ca. 1944 (51/52 coins). These hoards are important for the study of the coin emissions and coin circulation between ca. 450 and 370 B.C. Six mints of Cilicia and four of Cyprus are involved." [P. Naster, *NL* 121]

536 **Dever, William.** "The Silver Trail: Response to the Papers of Ephraim Stern and Seymour Gitin." *Hacksilber to Coinage: New Insights into the Monetary History of the Near East and Greece.* Numismatic Studies 24. New York: American Numismatic Society, 2001. Pages 49-51.
In a follow-up to Stern's paper on the Tel Dor hoard (see Stern "The Silver Hoard" under ORIGINS OF COINAGE), Dever points out that the evidence of trade with Spain suggests that the Proto-Canaanite alphabet may have spread to Greece and the Mediterranean world as early as 1100 B.C. The silver hoards also imply a system of weights and balances earlier than previously thought. In a follow-up to Gitin's paper on the Tel Miqne hoard (see Gitin and Golani "The Tel Miqne-Ekron Silver Hoard" below), Dever states that the hoard provides new information on the period of the Assyrian conquests in Palestine and their aftermath.

537 **Dimitrov, Kamen.** "Observations on Several Hoards of Gold Hellenistic Coins from the Balkan Peninsula." *Études Balkaniques* (Bulgaria) 3 (1987): 103-16.

538 ——— "Studies of the Numismatic Material Found at Seuthopolis: Problems, Research Methods and Basic Conclusions." *Museum Notes* 32 (1987): 1-10. 1 pl.
An archaeological study of the early Hellenistic Thracian city of Seuthopolis by the Archaeological Institute and Museum in Sofia from 1948-1954. Coins found at the site included 1300 pre-Roman and thirty Roman pieces. Eight-hundred forty-nine coins were of the ruler Seuthes. Explores the problems related to the chronological limits of the city and the circulation of foreign coins in the region. Concludes that the city was built ca. 320 B.C. and perished ca. 275 B.C. Suggests Adaios was a contemporary of Seuthes III and there was contact between the two kingdoms. Nineteen coins are illustrated.

539 ——— "A Hoard of Gold Staters from Topolovo (*IGCH* 853)." *Bulletin of the Museums in South Bulgaria* (Bulgaria) 15 (1989): 189-207.

540 "Discovery of Ancient Greek Coins." *American Journal of Numismatics* 18, no. 4 (April 1884): 82.
Mentions the discovery of coins near Carystus in Euboea. One of the coins was an Athenian tetradrachm with the name of the *demos* in the inscription rather than the name of an archon.

541 **Dodson, Oscar H., and William P. Wallace.** "The Kozani Hoard of 1955." *Museum Notes* 11 (1964): 21-8. 4 pls. [CS 3225]
Examines a hoard of twenty-seven coins found near Kozani in Southern Macedonia in 1955. The hoard was composed of five drachms of Chalkis, eight tetradrachms of Athens, fourteen tetradrachms of Ptolemy I and II, and one tetradrachm of Aesillas (this coin could not have been originally buried with the others). At least half the Ptolemaic coins seem to be overstrikes and most have punch-marks. Discusses the style of each coin type and the wear evident on each coin. Concludes that the hoard was buried ca. 240-230 B.C. Discusses the locations of other finds of Ptolemaic coins in Greece. This hoard reinforces the fact that most Ptolemaic coins found in Greece were struck by the first two Ptolemies, and extends the area in which they have been found (previous finds have primarily been in the Peloponnesos or in Euboia).

542 **Dreni, Stella.** "The Hoard *IGCH* 137 (Megara 1904)." *Zurück zum Gegenstand. Festschrift für Andreas E. Furtwängler.* Zentrum für Archälogie und Kulturgeschichte des Schwarzmeerraumes, Band 16. Edited by Ralph Einicke et al. Langenweibach: Beier and Beram, 2009.

543 **Dressel, Heinrich A., and Kurt Regling.** "Zwei Ägyptische Funde Altgriechischer Silbermünzen." *Zeitschrift für Numismatik* (Germany) 37 (1927): 1-138. 6 pls.
Includes discussion of the "Zagazig" hoard of 1901 (*IGCH* 1645).

544 **Edwards, Katherine M.** *Corinth: Results of Excavations Conducted by the American School of Classical Studies at Athens. Volume 6: Coins, 1896-1929.* Cambridge: Harvard University Press, 1933. 172 pp., 10 pls.
A catalogue of the coins found at Corinth. Includes ten silver coins and 286 bronze coins of Corinth, as well as many autonomous and provincial coins of other Greek cities. Also includes coins of Corinth as a Roman colony and Roman, Byzantine, and later coins. Most of the types found are illustrated in the plates. The coins now reside in the Numismatic Museum at Athens. [Also see the supplement below].

545 ——— "Report on the Coins Found in the Excavations at Corinth during the Years 1930-1935." *Hesperia* 6 (1937): 241-56.
"This report is a supplement to the account published in volume 6 of the official report on the excavations (dealing with finds up to the end of 1920). A catalogue arranges about sixty thousand coins under the names of the issuing authorities. There is a short discussion of the pattern presented by the coins discovered, and their significance. Among the minor points discussed are the following: It seems clear that coins of the duoviri Capito and Cithero belong to Corinth, not Crete. Bronze coins of Sicyon are very well represented; the legend ΔΗ may stand for Demetrius Poliorcetes, but EY cannot stand for the tyrant Euphron. A bronze of Chios, with magistrate's name Democles, belongs to the first, rather than to the second century B.C. A hoard of the sixth century A.D. included four earlier Greek coins, each cut down to a size of about 10 mm. An early hoard of Romanus I contains a high proportion of coins restruck over issues of Constantine VII." [J. R. Jones, *NIAJAH*]

546 **Ehrhardt, Christopher.** "Greek Treasure Trove: Hoards and Hoarders." *New Zealand Numismatic Journal* (New Zealand) 13, no. 4 (July 1975): 169-73.
The author discusses Greek coin hoards in general, giving some statistics on the distribution of hoards and the percentage of hoards that are properly documented. Ehrhardt's comments are formulated from his analysis of the hoards published by Thompson, Mørkholm, and Kraay in *An Inventory of Greek Coin Hoards* (see below).

546a **Esty, Warren W.** "Statistical Analysis of Hoard Data in Ancient Numismatics." *XIII Congreso Internacional de Numismática, Madrid – 2003: Actas–Proceedings–Actes I.* Edited by Carmen Alfaro, Carmen Marcos, and Paloma Otero. Madrid: International Numismatic Commisson, 2005. Pages 173-7.
It is difficult to prove anything statistically using hoard data because the mathematical assumptions are not under experimental control. Esty provides examples of some of the subtle difficulties of statistical analysis of hoard data and provides suggestions that can make an application of statistics to numismatics more credible.

547 **Evans, J. De Rose.** "Ancient Coins from the Drew Institute of Archaeological Research Excavations of Caesarea Maritima 1971-1984." *Biblical Archaeologist* 58, no. 3 (September 1995): 156-66. Illus.
"This is a preliminary report on the coins found in the excavations, almost all bronzes, dating from the fourth century B.C. to the seventh century A.D. A unique specimen is attributed to the reign of Hadrian, from the mint of Antioch." [J. Evans, *NL* 136]

548 **Evgenidou, Desponia.** "Found underneath a Tree Root…: Ancient Greek Coin Hoards in the Athens Numismatic Museum." *Nomismatika Khronika* (Greece) 28 (2010): 131-2. Illus.
A brief description of an exhibition held at the Athens Numismatic Museum, 2010-2011, which featured ancient Greek coin hoards in the museum's collection. In Greek and English; translated by M. J. A. Tzamali. [Also see Hellenic Ministry of Culture and Tourism below].

549 "Expert Says Black Sea Coins Emergency Issue." *Coin World* (October 31, 1990): 82.
Announces that the International Bureau for the Suppression of Counterfeit Coins has declared the "Black Sea Hoard" coins to be genuine ancient emergency issues struck at a field mint in the general Black Sea area. [The IBSCC later changed their opinion regarding these coins. See Giedroyc "IBSCC Concludes" under COUNTERFEITS. Also see articles by Emory above, and by Flegler, Giedroyc, Sayles, and Wetterstrom under COUNTERFEITS].

550 **Falkland, Warren.** "Notes on Coins Found in Cyprus." *Numismatic Chronicle* 3rd ser., 11 (1891): 140-51. 1 pl.
The author gathered coins while residing in Cyprus for twelve years. The coins found include Greek, Roman Imperial, and Kingdom of Cyprus (twelfth to sixteenth centuries) issues. Suggests the re-attribution to Cyprus of some coins previously given to other cities. Also mentions some Phoenician coins commonly found in Cyprus.

551 **Fisher, Joan E.** "Corinth, 1970: Forum Area. Appendix: Coins." *Hesperia* 40, no. 1 (January-March 1971): 35-51. 2 pls.
"The 270 legible coins consisted of 177 Greek, sixty-nine Byzantine, two Roman Republican and thirteen Roman Imperial, two Latin imitation, one Frankish, two Venetian, one Ottoman and three uncertain coins. In addition there were 303 illegible coins discovered." [*NL* 87]

552 ——— "Corinth, 1971. Forum Area. Appendix: Coins." *Hesperia* 41, no. 2 (April-June 1972): 174-84.
"Excavations in 1971 produced nine Roman, five Byzantine and 373 Greek coins of eighteen mints and Corinth." [*NL* 90]

553 ——— "The Sanctuary of Demeter and Kore on Acrocorinth. Preliminary Report IV: 1969-1970. Appendix: Coins." *Hesperia* 41, no. 3 (July-September 1972): 318-31. 1 pl.
"Of the 153 coins discovered, 4 were silver and the rest bronze. There were 26 Roman Imperial issues, 2 Byzantine, 63 Pegasus-Trident, 5 other Corinthian, 10 of Corinth under the Duoviri, 6 of Corinth under the Empire, 2 Antigonus Gonatas, 2 of Philip V, 16 illegible and the rest of various Greek mints." [*NL* 90]

554 ——— "Corinth, 1972: Forum Area. Appendix II: Coins." *Hesperia* 42, no. 1 (January-March 1973): 34-44. 1 pl.
"The catalogue of 127 issues includes coins of Corinth, Syracuse, Macedonia, Phocis, Boeotia, Salamis, Athens, Sicyon, the Achaean League, Argos, Arcadia, Ptolemy III Euergetes, Nisyros, Paphos, the Roman Empire, William of Villehardouin, Guy II de la Roche, Philip Augustus and Louis VIII or IX of France and Siculo-Punic, Byzantine and uncertain issues." [*NL* 92]

555 ——— "The Sanctuary of Demeter and Kore on Acrocorinth. Preliminary Report V: 1971-1973. Appendix: Coins." *Hesperia* 43, no. 3 (July-September 1974): 292-307. Illus.
"The coins recovered from the Demeter sanctuary during excavations in 1971-1973 total 111 in number: eight silver and 103 bronze, all but eleven of which are legible. The accumulation is marked, as usual, by the relatively low number of individual finds in general, by the predominance of Greek (especially Corinthian) over Roman, Byzantine and later issues, and by the lack both of new coin types and of actual hoards. The coins range in date from Amyntas III of Macedonia, 381-369 B.C. to a Turkish issue of Bayazid II, A.D. 1481, the latest contemporary with the sanctuary itself being a bronze of Arcadius, A.D. 383-408. The Greek coins are discussed in some detail, with emphasis on a large bronze Athena/trident issue of Corinth (no. 340) noteworthy for its comparative rarity and for the chronological significance of its types in relation to the gold coinage of Alexander III." [N. Waggoner, *NL* 95]

556 ——— "Corinth, 1975. Forum Southwest. Appendix: Coins." *Hesperia* 45, no. 2 (April-June 1976): 138-62. Illus. [CS 16137]
Describes the coins found at Corinth during excavations in 1975 including thirty-eight bronze coins of Corinth. Also includes other Greek, Roman, Byzantine, and medieval coins.

557 **Flament, Christophe.** "Un Trésor de Tétradrachmes Athéniens Dispersés suivi de Considérations Relatives au Classement, à Frappe et à l'Attribution des Chouettes à des Ateliers Ètrangers." *Revue Belge de Numismatique et de Sigillographie* (Belgium) 151 (2005): 29-38.

558 **Frenkel, R.** "The Sanctuary from the Persian Period at Mount Mizpe Yahim." *Qadmoniot* (Israel) 30, no. 1 (1997): 46-53.
"Four coins were found during excavations at this site south of Safed: two minor silver coins of Tyre of the Persian period and two Seleucid copper issues of Antiochus IV and V from the mint of Tyre." [A. Spaer, *NL* 139]

559 **Fried, Sallie.** "The Decadrachm Hoard: An Introduction." *Coinage and Administration in the Athenian and Persian Empires.* BAR International Series 343. Edited by Ian Carradice. Oxford: British Archaeological Reports, 1987. Pages 1-10. 5 pls.
An overview of the importance of the so-called Decadrachm hoard containing about 1700 silver coins, mostly uncirculated. The hoard hit the market in 1984. Almost 1000 of the coins are Lycian with the remainder from Athens, northern Greece, the Aegean islands, and Asia Minor. The hoard was probably found in Southern Anatolia. Contained sixty-eight decadrachms of the Bisaltai and 187 Athenian coins. This paper examines the coins from the mints in northern and central Greece, the islands, and Asia Minor. Discusses die-links. Concludes this is neither a commerce nor savings hoard. The lack of fragmentary or mutilated pieces suggests it was not a bullion hoard. It may have come together at one time for a special purpose. Forty-six coins are illustrated. [Also see Carradice *Coinage and Administration* under ATTICA—GENERAL WORKS, and Gibbs "American Returns 'Hoard of the Century,'" Giedroyc "Hoard's Owner Speaks," and Vermeule "The Athenian Treasury Hoard" below].

560 **Fulco, William J., and Fawzi Zayadine.** "Coins from Samaria-Sebaste." *The Hashemite Kingdom of Jordan. Annual of the Department of Antiquities of Jordan* (Jordan) 25 (1981): 197-225; 412-8. Illus.
A report on the excavations conducted at Samaria-Sebaste during 1965-7. Briefly describes the archaeological site, and presents a catalogue of the 346 coins found at the site. Of these, 134 are Greek, Ptolemaic, Seleucid, or Jewish. The rest are Roman Provincial, Roman Imperial, Byzantine, or Islamic. Several of the major types are illustrated.

561 **Gatzolis, Christos.** "Two Hellenistic Hoards from Macedonia." *Coinage in the Macedonian Region. Proceedings of the 2nd Scientific Meeting.* Obolos 4. Edited by P. Adam-Veleni. Thessaloniki: University Studio Press, 2000. Pages 103-26.
A paper presented at the 2nd Scientific Meeting held in Thessaloniki in May 1998.

562 **Gibbs, William T.** "American Returns 'Hoard of the Century.'" *Coin World* (March 22, 1999): 1, 101. Illus.
Reports that William I. Koch has returned 1,661 ancient coins to Turkish authorities. The coins were part of the Emali Hoard, often referred to as the "Hoard of the Century." Recounts the story of the finding of the hoard, its removal to Germany, and its sale to OKS Partners (William I. Koch, Jonathan H. Kagan, and Jeffrey Spier). [Also see Acar and Kaylan "Hoard" above, and Giedroyc "Hoard's Owner Speaks," Meier "Contested Coins," Tompa "Decadrachm Hoard," and Vermeule "Athenian Treasury Hoard" below].

563 **Giedroyc, Richard.** "Hoard's Owner Speaks for the Record." *Coin World* (July 6, 1988): 1 ff.
An interview with William I. Koch, one of the purchasers of the famous "Decadrachm Hoard" found in Turkey in 1984. Includes reaction to the article by Acar and Kaylan (see Acar and Kaylan "Hoard of the Century" above). Refutes some of the statements made by Acar. [Also see Gibbs "American" above].

564 ——— "Coins Found in Caves Near Dead Sea Scrolls Missing Scholars Say." *Coin World* (September 27, 1993): 1, 20.
Reports that most of the 1200 coins found near the caves in which the Dead Sea Scrolls were found are now missing. Most of the coins were Seleucid coins of Syrian mints ca. 125 B.C. and later. Discusses the possible whereabouts of some of the coins. [See Giedroyc "Ancient Coins" below for a related story].

565 ——— "Ancient Coins Associated with Dead Sea Scrolls from Phoenicia. Three Coins on Display at Nixon Library in California." *Coin World* (November 8, 1993): 58.
Reports that three ancient coins associated with the finds in caves where the Dead Sea Scrolls were discovered have been identified as issues of second century B.C. Phoenicia. The coins are on display at the Richard Nixon Library in California. [See Giedroyc "Coins Found Near Cave" above for a related story].

566 **Gitler, Haim.** "A Comparative Study of Numismatic Evidence from Excavations in Jerusalem." *Liber Annuus* (Israel) 46 (1996): 317-62. Illus.
"Statistical analyses and comparison of coins found in excavations at eight different sites in and around the old city of Jerusalem and almost 4000 coins excavated at Massada are included in this article. The coins cover the period from Alexander the Great's death to the Arab conquest. The article includes a catalogue and illustrations of 577 coins found at three of the eight areas dealt with." [A. Spaer, *NL* 139]

567 ——— "A Hacksilber and Cut Athenian Tetradrachm Hoard from the Environs of Samaria: Late Fourth Century BCE." *Israel Numismatic Research* (Israel) 1 (2006): 5-14.

"A hoard from the vicinity of Samaria illustrates that the practice of using cut coins alongside broken pieces of silver ingots and jewelry (Hacksilber) continued into the second half of the fourth century B.C.E. Both the Hacksilber and the cut coins must have circulated as bullion and thus involved weighing in transactions. Prior to this discovery, mixed hoards of this period were composed mainly of uncut coins supplemented by Hacksilber in equal or greater quantities." [Abstract from *INJ*]

568 **Gitler, Haim, and Y. Kahanov.** "The Ascalon 1988 Hoard (*CH* 9.548): A Periplus to Ascalon in the Late Hellenistic Period?" *Coin Hoards, Volume IX: Greek Hoards.* Edited by A. Meadows and Ute Wartenberg. London: Royal Numismatic Society, 2002. Pages 259-68. 1 pl.

Forty-six bronze coins and one diobol were found in 1988 in a late Hellenistic villa in Ascalon. Included coins of Teos, Samos, Knidos, Rhodes, Lycian League, Side, Tyre, Seleucid issues, and Ptolemaic issues. The hoard was concealed ca. 100 B.C. The authors suggest the coins may have been gathered by a crew member aboard a ship sailing along the western coast of Asia Minor. Discusses the ancient trade routes along the sea coast.

569 **Gitin, Seymour, and Amir Golani.** "The Tel Miqne-Ekon Silver Hoard: The Assyrian and Phoenician Connections." *Hacksilber to Coinage: New Insights into the Monetary History of the Near East and Greece.* Numismatic Studies 24. New York: American Numismatic Society, 2001. Pages 27-48. Illus.

Six hoards, comprising 305 pieces of silver, cut silver, and silver ingots have been excavated at Tel Miqne (ancient Ekron), one of the Philistine capital cities. These hoards provide information on the increased use of silver bullion as currency in the ancient Near East during the seventh century B.C. Ekron developed into the largest olive oil production center yet uncovered, and its olive oil production is an example of industrial growth of the seventh century B.C. that would have required the extensive use of silver as currency in international trade. [Also see Dever "The Silver Trail" above].

570 **Göbl, Robert, Georges Le Rider, George Carpenter Miles, and John Walker.** *Numismatique Susienne: Monnaies Trouvées a Suse de 1946 a 1956.* Mémoires de la Mission Archéologique en Iran. Tome XXXVII: Mission de Susiane. Paris: Librairie Orientaliste, 1960. 145 pp, 9 pls.

Describes the coins found during the excavations at Susa, the capital of ancient Persia.

571 **Gökyildirim, Turan.** "Vth c. B.C. Coin Hoard from Thrace–Örcünlü (1970)." *Stephanos Nomismatikos: Edith Schönert-Geiss zum 65. Geburtstag.* Edited by Ulrike Peter. Berlin: Akademie Verlag, 1998. Pages 279-94.

572 **Goodchild, R. G.** "The Greek Coins from Exeter Reconsidered." *Numismatic Chronicle* 5th ser., 17 (1937): 124-34.

A follow-up to a previous article (see Haverfield and Macdonald below) in which finds of Greek and Graeco-Roman coins at Exeter in England were condemned as a modern hoax. Goodchild points out a hoard of such coins found in controlled circumstances and he argues that the earlier finds could be authentic ancient deposits, the earliest Greek coins being deposited in Roman times. On pages 128-34, J. G. Milne agrees that a reconsideration is warranted and discusses some of the possible scenarios in which Greek coins could have come to England.

573 **Gorini, Giovanni.** "The Kupa Hoard." *Coin Hoards* 5 (1979): 34-5.

A hoard of twenty-two coins shows that the coins of Philip II and coins from Cretan mints and Miletus were present in Albania.

574 "Greek Coins from the Gulf of Salonica." *American Journal of Numismatics* 28, no. 1 (July 1893): 14.

Mentions some silver coins "showing the bust of Alexander the Great, holding in one hand a sceptre and in the other a bird, seemingly a falcon." The coins were found by a sponge diver in the harbor of Saloniche.

575 **Greenwell, William (Canon).** "On a Find of Archaic Greek Coins in Egypt." *Numismatic Chronicle* 3rd ser., 10 (1890): 1-12. 1 pl.

Describes twenty-four archaic-period coins from a hoard discovered in the Egyptian delta region circa-1887. Includes coins of Thasos, Lete, Mende, Neapolis, Corinth, Cyzicus, Miletos, Chios, Samos, Cos, Lycia, Cyprus, Tyre, Cyrene, and four coins of uncertain attribution. Also describes another group of coins found in the delta, including issues of Dikaia, Mende, Sermyle, and Athens.

576 ——— "On a Find of Archaic Greek Coins, Principally of the Islands of the Aegean Sea." *Numismatic Chronicle* 3rd ser., 10 (1890): 13-9. 1 pl.

Describes a hoard of coins of the Cyclades and neighboring islands. Includes issues of Aegina, Ceos, Delos (?), Paros, Siphnos, Miletos, Chios, and Cos (?). Discusses each coin. [Also see Sheedy "The Dolphins" under CRETE AND THE CYCLADES ISLANDS].

577 **Haatvedt, Rolfe A., and Enoch E. Peterson.** *Coins from Karanis: The University of Michigan Excavations 1924-1935.* Ann Arbor: Kelsey Museum of Archaeology, 1964. 399 pp., 11 pls. [CS 3234]

Lists 26,796 Greek, Roman, and Byzantine coins found during the excavations in Egypt, including 282 from Ptolemaic Egypt (Ptolemy II to Cleopatra VII). The vast majority of the others are Roman coins from Alexandria. The coins were contained in thirty-eight hoards of varying sizes deposited between 86 B.C. and the first half of the fifth century. [Reviewed by R. A. G. Carson in *Numismatic Chronicle* 7th ser., 4 (1964): 359-60].

578 **Hackens, Tony.** "XVI. Les Monnaies." *L'Îlot de la Maison des Comédiens.* Exploration Archéologique de Délos 27. Edited by P. Bruneau et al. Paris, 1970. Pages 387-419. [CS 3235]

Examines the coins found in the House of the Comedians on the island of Delos.

579 **Hainzmann, Manfred.** "Fundmünzen aus Aigeira I: Lokale Prägungen." *Numismatic Archaeology/Archaeological Numismatics: Proceedings of an International Conference held to Honour Dr. Mando Oeconomides in Athens 1995.* Oxbow Monographs 75. Edited by K. Sheedy and C. Papageorgiadou-Banis. Oxford: Oxbow Books and The Australian Archaeological Institute at Athens, 1997. Pages 40-6. Illus.

580 **Harris, Josephine M.** "Coins Found at Corinth." *Hesperia* 10, no. 2 (April-June 1941): 143-62.

Reports on the 26,521 coins found during excavations at Corinth, 1935-1939. Includes 1101 coins of Corinth (579 are the bronze pegasos/trident issues) and 725 coins of other Greek cities. Tables summarize the coins found. Includes comments on the numismatic history of Corinth.

581 **Haverfield. F., and George Macdonald.** "Greek Coins at Exeter." *Numismatic Chronicle* 4th ser., 7 (1907): 145-55.
Discusses the Greek coins said to have been found at Exeter in England. The authors conclude the finds were the result of a hoax—the coins having been placed in the ground in modern times. [Also see Goodchild "Greek Coins from Exeter Reconsidered" above].

582 **Hazzard, Richard A.** "The Tyre Hoard of 1955: *IGCH* 1591." *Cornucopiæ* (publication of The Ancient Coin Society, Canada) 3, no. 4 (1975): 57-63.
Hazzard publishes a hoard of seventeen Ptolemaic didrachms and three Seleucid staters found at Tyre in 1955. Using Seyrig's field notes, the author corrects the erroneous entry in *IGCH*. He suggests that the silver didrachms were dated from an era of 262 B.C. and entered Coele-Syria with the troops of Ptolemy VI in 147. The author discusses the historical circumstances of the hoard's burial and associates it with the collapse of Ptolemaic authority in 146 B.C.

583 **Head, Barclay V.** "Coins Discovered on the Site of Naukratis." *Numismatic Chronicle* 3rd ser., 6 (1886): 1-18. 1 pl.
The author catalogues and describes the coins found at Naukratis during excavations by the Egypt Exploration Fund, led by Flinders Petrie. The coins include a silversmith's hoard (which included a variety of Greek coins), several Athenian tetradrachms, other Greek coins, coins of the Ptolemies, Roman Imperial coins of Alexandria, and other Roman coins.

584 ——— "Chapter V: The Coins." *British Museum Excavations at Ephesus—The Archaic Artemisia*. Edited by David G. Hogarth. London: Trustees of the British Museum, 1908. Pages 74-93. 2 pls.
A discussion of the ninety-three early electrum coins discovered by David Hogarth during excavations on the site of the temple of Artemis at Ephesos. The coins form the earliest known coin hoard and provide evidence for the date of the first coinage. The coins were turned over to Head for classification and attribution. Discusses the find-spots. Based upon the total weight of the group of coins, Head believes the coins formed a single votive-offering when the first temple was constructed on the site. Lists and describes each coin and assigns tentative dates of issue. The earliest coins he assigns to the reign of Gyges, 687-652 B.C. The hoard included coins inscribed WALWEL which have played an important role in the controversy over the origin of coinage. Discusses the coin-types including primitive issues, goat types, cock types, lion types, inscribed types, and others. [The hoard coins now reside in the Archaeological Museum of Istanbul. Also see R. W. Wallace "KUKALIM, WALWET, and the Artemision Deposit" under LYDIA, and Weissl "Zur Datierung des 'Foundation-Deposit'" below, and Williams "The Pot Hoard Pot" below].

585 **Hellenic Ministry of Culture and Tourism.** *Found Underneath a Tree Root: Ancient Greek Coin Hoards in the Numismatic Museum, Athens.* Athens: Hellenic Ministry of Culture and Tourism, 2010.
Catalogue for an exhibition at the museum, April through December 2010. The exhibit contained twenty-one Greek coin hoards dating between the fifth and first centuries B.C., made up of 3644 electrum, gold, silver, silver-plated, and bronze coins. [Also see D. Evgenidou "Found underneath a Tree Root" above].

586 **Herbert, Sharon C.** "Notes and News—Excavations—Tel Anafa, 1981." *Israel Exploration Journal* (Israel) 32, no. 1 (1982): 59-61.
A summary of the results of excavations in the summer of 1981 at Tel Anafa. A bronze coin of Alexander II Zebina (128-123 B.C.) was found in a bath complex. Twenty-three legible coins were found including five Ptolemaic, seven Seleucid, ten of independent mints of Tyre and Sidon, and one of Herod Philip (found at a Roman level).

587 **Herbert, Sharon C., and Ya'akov Meshorer.** *Tel Anafa I, I. Final Report on Ten Years of Excavations at a Hellenistic and Roman Settlement in Northern Israel.* Journal of Roman Archaeology Suppl. Series 10. Ann Arbor: Kelsey Museum of Archaeology, 1994. Pages 241-60.
"Chapter 4 (pp. 241-260) is a catalogue, partially illustrated, of 319 coins found between 1968 and 1986. The coins cover the period from the late fourth century B.C. to the Ottoman period. Seven are of silver, the rest copper." [A. Spaer, *NL* 133]

588 **Hill, George F.** "A Hoard of Coins from Nineveh." *Numismatic Chronicle* 5th ser., 11 (1931): 160-70.
A catalogue of coins found during excavations at Nineveh in 1929-30. Primarily composed of Roman coins but includes some late Parthian issues.

589 "Hoard of Greek Coins Found." *The Times* (London) (October 6, 1980). Reprinted in *Seaby Coin and Medal Bulletin* 748 (December 1980): 380.
"French archaeologists digging near the town of Gülnar, Taurus Mountains, have discovered some 5200 silver coins dating from the end of the fourth and beginning of the third centuries B.C. Most were struck by Alexander the Great and the ruler of Egypt, Ptolemy Soter." [E. Marles, *NL* 106]

590 **Hohlfelder, Robert L.** *Kenchreai, Eastern Port of Corinth. Results of Investigations by The University of Chicago and Indiana University for The American School of Classical Studies at Athens. Volume III: The Coins.* Leiden: E. J. Brill, 1978. 110 pp., 6 pls., map. [CS 3239]
Presents the results of the excavations at Kenchreai, Greece by the University of Chicago and the University of Indiana, 1963-1966 and 1968. Catalogues the 1315 Greek, Roman, Byzantine, Frankish, and Venetian coins discovered. Most are bronze or copper. Includes 152 late Hellenic and Hellenistic coins. Few are illustrated. [Reviewed by A. Walker in *Numismatic Chronicle* 140 (1980): 217-9. Also see Hohlfelder *Ancient Coins at Indiana University* under PUBLIC COLLECTIONS—UNITED STATES (BLOOMINGTON).]

591 **Holloway, R. Ross.** "Remarks on the Taranto Hoard of 1911." *Revue Belge de Numismatique et de Sigillographie* (Belgium) 146 (2000): 1-8.

592 **Hoover, Oliver.** "Commerce ('Pamphylia or Cilicia' Hoard), 2000 (*CH* 10.292)." *Coin Hoards, Volume X: Greek Hoards.* Edited by Oliver Hoover, Andrew Meadows, and Ute Wartenberg Kagan. New York: Royal Numismatic Society and The American Numismatic Society, 2010. Pages 129-52. 16 pls.
Publication of a hoard of 545 tetradrachms and 205 drachms which appeared on the market in 2000. The find spot is unknown but was likely in Pamphylia or Cilicia. The hoard contained mostly posthumous Alexanders (especially those of Lycia and Pamphylia) as well as Seleucid coins. The

Macedonian coins may have traveled to Anatolia in connection with the Antigonid conquest and administration of Caria between 227 and 210 B.C. The hoard was probably buried ca. 190/189 B.C. A catalogue of the coins is provided.

593 ——— "Northern Israel Hoard, 2002 (*CH* 10.319)." *Coin Hoards, Volume X: Greek Hoards.* Edited by Oliver Hoover, Andrew Meadows, and Ute Wartenberg Kagan. New York: Royal Numismatic Society and The American Numismatic Society, 2010. Pages 227-41.

A hoard of 307 small Seleucid bronze coins appeared on the U.S. market in 2002. The coins were probably buried in northern Israel. Two-hundred seventy-three of the coins were struck at Ptolemais (Ake). The Seleucid coins mainly come from northerly mints. Included a few Ptolemaic coins. A catalogue is presented here. Only a few of the coins were photographed.

594 **Hoover, Oliver, Andrew R. Meadows, and Ute Wartenberg Kagan, eds.** *Coin Hoards, Volume X: Greek Hoards.* New York: Royal Numismatic Society and The American Numismatic Society, 2010. 281 pp., 67 pls.

This volume of the *Coin Hoards* series (see Royal Numismatic Society *Coin Hoards* below) lists 471 hoards containing Greek coins. The contents of each hoard are briefly listed, and each hoard is cross-referenced to other publications that explore the hoard in more detail. Also includes ten articles devoted to the full publication of certain new hoards related to the coinage of the Seleucid Empire: "Commerce ('Seleucus I') Hoard, 2005" by B. R. Nelson [686], "East Arachosia (Quetta) Hoard, 2002" by R. P. Miller [672], "Commerce ('Achaeus') Hoard, 2002" by A. R. Meadows and C. C. Lorber [664], "Commerce ('Pamphylia or Cilicia' Hoard), 2000" by O. D. Hoover [592], "Commerce ('Demetrius I' Hoard), 2003" by C. C. Lorber [650], "The Gaziantep Hoard, 1994" by A. R. Meadows and A. Houghton [663], "Beth Ummar, Israel, 2001" by A. R. Meadows [662], "Northern Israel Hoard, 2002" by O. D. Hoover [593], "Commerce ('Seleucia on the Calycadnus' Hoard), 2002" by C. C. Lorber [5364], and "A Late Seleukid Bronze Hoard, c. 1988" by N. L. Wright [5453]. Includes a concordance of *IGCH* to *CH* 10, a concordance of previous *CH* volumes to *CH* 10, and indices of hoards, mints, and rulers.

595 **Houghton, A. A., and Georges Le Rider.** "Un Trésor de Monnaies Hellénistiques Trouvé Près de Suse." *Revue Numismatique* (France) 6th ser., 8 (1966): 111-27. 8 pls. [CS 3241]

596 **Huber, Christian G.** "Essay on the Classification of Ancient Coins Found in Egypt." *Numismatic Chronicle* new ser., 2 (1862): 160-77.

Discusses the Athenian tetradrachms and Persian coins often found in Egypt. Describes the coinage of Ptolemy I, distinguishing four different series. Describes rare silver obols and half-obols, small bronze coins, coins struck by various Egyptian cities, and the coins of Ptolemaic mints in Cyprus.

597 **Humphris, J. Morineau.** "A Hoard from Thessaly." *Coin Hoards* 3 (1977): 9-17. 2 pls.

Presents a catalogue of a hoard of thirty-eight silver coins found in Thessaly in 1975. The hoard, which includes local and Asiatic currency, was buried ca. 230 B.C.

598 **Hurter, Silvia.** "New Greek Coin Hoard Questioned." *Minerva* 5, no. 4 (July/August 1994): 47. Illus.

An English summary of a previously published review of a book. Examines a hoard of electrum staters with human representations, found in the excavation of Clazomenae at a level dated to before 560 B.C. States that these coins are fake and were planted at the excavation site.

599 ——— "Lions and Lionesses, Eagles and a Few Heads: A New Uncertain Mint in Caria." *Coins of Macedonia and Rome: Essays in Honour of Charles Hersh.* Edited by Andrew Burnett, Ute Wartenberg, and Richard Witschonke. London: Spink, 1998. Pages 109-12. 2 pls.

Publishes part of a hoard of anepigraphic silver obols, probably found in eastern Caria. The coins were probably minted in Caria in the mid-fifth century B.C. No specific mint can be assigned, but Hurter suggests the coins may have all been struck at one mint over the course of a decade. The types include a lion's head, eagle in flight, the mask of a lion, and a female head. Hurter identifies possible proto-types for the designs depicted on the hoard coins.

600 ——— "The 'Pixodaros Hoard': A Summary." *Studies in Greek Numismatics in Memory of Martin Jessop Price.* Edited by Richard Ashton and Silvia Hurter. London: Spink, 1998. Pages 147-53. 3 pls.

Discusses a hoard found in the 1970's. The findspot is unknown. As many as 1200 coins may have been included. A selection of these coins is described and illustrated here. The hoard consisted of tetradrachms and didrachms of Rhodian weight from the major coin-issuing cities of Western Asia Minor, Thasos, and of the Carian satraps. The hoard was probably buried in the mid-330's B.C. Includes brief notes on the coinage of each city and satrap represented. The Pixodaros Hoard shows that the Carian satraps minted on a much larger scale than previously known.

601 **Hurter, Silvia, and Emmerich Pászthory.** "Archaischer Silberfund aus dem Antilibanon." *Studies in Honour of Leo Mildenberg: Numismatics, Art History, Archaeology.* Edited by A. Houghton et al. Wetteren: Editions NR, 1984. Pages 111-25. 4 pls.

602 **Ingvaldsen, Håkon.** "Coin Finds and Sanctuaries: A Case Study from the Island of Kos." *Coins in the Aegean Islands. Proceedings of the Fifth Scientific Meeting, Mytilene, 16-29 September 2006. Volume 1: Ancient Times.* Obolos 9. Edited by Panagiotis Tselekas. Athens: The Friends of the Numismatic Museum, 2010. Pages 481-93.

603 "Israeli Shipwreck Yields 40-kilo Chunk of Ancient Silver Coins from Cyprus." *Coin World* (June 20, 1994): 1. Illus.

Reports that a mass of coins weighing twenty kilograms, as well as 1800 individual coins, all tetradrachms of Ptolemy VII struck at Paphos, Cyprus in 145 B.C., were found off the coast of Haifa.

604 **Jenkins, G. Kenneth.** "Hellenistic Coins from Nimrud." *Iraq* (England) 20, pt. 2 (autumn 1958): 158-68. 1 pl.

Presents the coins found at Nimrud during the excavations of 1957. Includes coins of Alexander the Great, Lysimachus, Seleucus III, Attalus I, Aradus, Alexander I, Antiochus III, and Seleucus IV, both in silver and bronze. Thirteen coins are illustrated. Describes the coins and suggests these were the typical coins in circulation at the time of burial.

605 ——— "Coin Hoards from Pasargadae." *Iran* (England) 3 (1965): 41-52. 4 pls. [CS 3243]

Discusses the coins found in 1962 and 1963 during excavations on Citadel Hill at Pasargadae. Includes coins of Alexander the Great (lifetime and posthumous issues) and coins of Seleucus I of a type minted principally at Persepolis. The coins help to date the destruction of the site.

606 ——— "A Hellenistic Hoard from Mesopotamia." *Museum Notes* 13 (1967): 41-56. 7 pls. [CS 3244]
Discusses a hoard of 100 coins buried ca. 195/190 B.C. and found in Mesopotamia during the period 1914-1918. Shows the wide circulation within the Seleucid empire of other coins struck on the Attic standard. Includes coins of Alexander, Lysimachus, Attalus I, and several Seleucid rulers, all from various mints.

607 **Johnston, Ann.** "The Greek Coins." *Greek, Roman, and Islamic Coins from Sardis*. Edited by T. V. Buttrey et al. Cambridge: Harvard University Press, 1981. Pages 3-89. Illus.
A catalogue of the Greek coins found during excavations at Sardis (see Buttrey et al., *Coins from Sardis* above). "Approximately 1200 Greek coins were found, almost all local Hellenistic and Imperial bronze issues of small denomination (including Seleucid and Macedonian types presumably struck in Western Asia Minor). Previously unpublished types of Miletus, Philadelphia Lydiae and Sardis are illustrated, as is another example of the rare tetradrachm of Achaeus. Various aspects of the Greek Imperials in general and of the coinage of Sardis are discussed in the introduction and the notes to the catalogue." [T. Buttrey, *NL* 109].

608 **Kaenel, Hans-Markus, and Maria R.-Alföldi.** *Coins in Context I: New Perspectives for the Interpretation of Coin Finds*. Studien zu Fundmünzen der Antike, Band 23. Mainz: Philipp von Zabern, 2009. 187 pp.
A collection of eleven papers examining the importance of context when studying coin hoards.

609 **Kagan, Jonathan H.** "The Decadrachm Hoard: Chronology and Consequences." *Coinage and Administration in the Athenian and Persian Empires*. BAR International Series 343. Edited by Ian Carradice. Oxford: British Archaeological Reports, 1987. Pages 21-8.
Examines the chronological implications of the Decadrachm hoard. Correlates this evidence with Starr's and Kraay's dating of Athenian coinage, May's dating for Abdera, and Baron's dating for Samos. Compares the new evidence with that gathered from the Asyut hoard. Suggests a closing date of 465/462 B.C. for the non-Lycian elements of the Decadrachm hoard. Suggests the Athenian/Persian hostilities prevented the free flow of coinage which has existed earlier. [Also see Carradice *Coinage and Administration* under ATTICA—GENERAL WORKS].

610 ——— "*IGCH* 1185 Reconsidered." *Revue Belge de Numismatic et de Sigillographie* (Belgium) 138 (1992): 1-24.

611 ——— "An Archaic Greek Coin Hoard from the Eastern Mediterranean and Early Cypriot Coinage." *Numismatic Chronicle* 154 (1994): 17-52. 9 pls.
"The author studies sixty-seven coins from a partially-recorded bullion hoard from the eastern Mediterranean. The find is dated to the end of the sixth century B.C. While the hoard resembles Egyptian finds of the period of Demanhur (*IGCH* 1637), it is exceptional in its relatively large portion of Cypriot coins (twenty-eight). This allows for a new look at the date of the Cypriot coins in the Persepolis deposit (*IGCH* 1789) and a discussion of the impact of the Ionian Revolt on Cypriot coinage." [J. Kagan, *NL* 134]

612 **Kim, Henry S.** "Electrum Ingot Hoard." *Revue Suisse de Numismatique* (Switzerland) 83 (2004): 5-16. 3 pls.

613 **Kim, Henry S., and John H. Kroll.** "A Hoard of Archaic Coins of Colophon and Unminted Silver (*CH* I.3)." *American Journal of Numismatics* 2nd ser., 20 (2008): 53-103. 15 pls.
The authors examine a sixth century hoard which contained 906 minute silver coins and seventy-seven pieces of unminted silver, over half of which are small, unweighed disks apparently made for monetary exchange. The coins are the earliest coins of Colophon, and the fact that they are smaller than all but three of the pieces of unminted silver suggests that when the hoard was buried the Colophonians were employing what might be termed a bi-specie monetary system: small coins for very low level transactions, and bullion weighed on the balance for transactions involving more substantial sums. Includes a catalogue of the coins.

614 **Kind, H. D., K. J. Gilles, A. Hauptmann, and G. Weisgerber.** "Coins from Faynan, Jordan." *Levant* 37 (2005): 169-95. Illus.
"1395 coins were found at the site, situated about 50 km south of the Dead Sea at the eastern edge of the Wadi Araba rift valley, during extensive studies of ancient copper production in the area in 1963-1997. 1013 of the coins have been identified. Of these 103 were minted from circ. 300 B.C. to A.D. 213. 609 coins are dated between A.D. 312 and the earthquake of A.D. 363. The following 60 years are represented by 643 coins and the next 226 years by only 18 coins. No coins were found for the periods A.D. 656 to 1210 or 1360 to 1800. Eleven Islamic coins date to A.D. 1210-1360. All 1395 coins are listed. Coin no. 77 is a small copper, apparently unpublished, dated to the third century B.C., depicting a bird r. looking backwards on one side and a head (?) on the other." [Arnold Spaer, *NL* 149]

615 **Kindler, Arie.** *Beer Sheba I: Excavations at Tel Beer Sheba, 1969-1971 Seasons*. Edited by Y. Aharoni. Tel Aviv: Tel Aviv University, 1973. 137 pp., 95 pls.
"The eighty coins found are catalogued on pp. 90-96 and pl. 51. The finds cover the period from the fourth century B.C. to the nineteenth century A.D. and include eighteen Ptolemaic issues, two of which are of the silver type now attributed to Aradus, ten Seleucid coins, including three late second century B.C. tetradrachms of Ascalon, and twenty-one Nabataean coins." [A. Spaer, *NL* 104]

616 **Kinns, Philip.** "Two Eighteenth Century Studies of Greek Coin Hoards: Bayer and Pellerin." *Medals and Coins from Bude to Mommsen*. Warburg Institute Surveys and Texts 21. Edited by M. H. Crawford, C. R. Ligota, and J. B. Trapp. London: The Warburg Institute, University of London, 1990. Pages 101-14. Illus.
An examination of the approach taken by eighteenth century numismatists Joseph Pellerin and Gottlieb Siegfried Bayer in the two earliest recognizable publications of hoards of Greek coins. In 1765, Pellerin published the Latakia hoard (*IGCH* 1544). In 1729, Bayer published a hoard of ten coins of Erythrae. Both set standards of hoard publication that would not be matched until well into the nineteenth century. Pellerin was the first to attempt to determine the burial date for a coin hoard. He also tried to date individual coins and to identify which of Alexander's mints struck some of the coins through an examination of symbols and legends. Bayer was one of the first to attempt to determine the date for an undated coin, using modern techniques of die and style analysis. [Reviewed by J. Kagan in *American Journal of Numismatics* 2nd ser., 3-4 (1992): 195-201].

617 **Kleeb, Alvin A.** "Ancient Coins Found in U.S." *SAN—Journal of the Society for Ancient Numismatics* 3, no. 2 (1971-72): 21.
Mentions hoards of ancient coins supposedly found in the United States.

618 **Kleiner, Fred S.** "The 1926 Piraeus Hoard and Athenian Bronze Coinage ca. 86 B.C." *Archaiologikon Deltion* (Greece) 28 (1973): 169-86. Illus.
"In 1926 the Athens Numismatic Collection acquired a hoard of 1716 bronzes found in Piraeus. The contents are generally similar to those of other late second and early first century B.C. Attic bronze hoards. This is the first recorded hoard of bronze coins containing the issue bearing the star between crescents of Mithradates VI of Pontus. The types and symbols of the Athenian bronzes are listed in chronological order. It is possible that some personal crisis led to the burial of the hoard some time in the late 80's B.C., but since there is no coin in the deposit later than the star between crescents issue of 87/86 B.C., the Piraeus hoard may be considered a typical Sullan siege burial." [M. Oeconomides, *NL* 96]

619 ——— "The Giresun Hoard." *Museum Notes* 19 (1974): 3-25. 9 pls.
Publishes a hoard of fifty-five silver coins found in 1933 at Giresun (ancient Cerasus-Pharnaceia) in northern Turkey. The hoard, buried ca. 77 B.C., contains several previously unpublished varieties of tetradrachms of Mithradates VI of Pontus as well as many dated coins. Includes coins of Nicomedes II and III of Bithynia, cistophori of a number of mints, coins of various kings of Cappadocia, and well as Seleucid, Athenian, and Chian coins.

620 **Knaap, Robert C., John D. MacIsaac, and Stephan G. Miller.** *Excavations at Nemea III: The Coins.* Berkeley: University of California Press, 2005. 355 pp., 32 pls.
A detailed presentation of the more than 3000 legible coins from all over the ancient world that have been found during excavations at Nemea (up to 1995) in ancient Corinthia. The coins, which are mostly bronze but show an unusually high proportion of silver, reflect the periods of greatest activity at the site—the late Archaic and Early Classical, the Early Hellenistic, the Early Christian, and the Byzantine. [Reviewed by J. Cargill-Thompson in *Spink Numismatic Circular* 117, no. 2 (May 2009): 56].

621 **Kogan, Howard.** "Variety in Israeli Hoards Caused by Trade and Pilgrims." *The Celator* 4, no. 8 (August 1990): 10, 14, 23, 26.
Discusses the types of coins typically found in hoards in Israel. Mentions copies of Attic tetradrachms minted in Gaza, Alexander the Great tetradrachms, and various coins of the Hellenistic monarchies. Also mentioned are the "Shekels of Tyre" and various Judean, Roman, and Byzantine coins.

622 **Köker, Hüseyin.** "The Greek Coins from the 1952-3 Excavations at Cyzicus." *Numismatic Chronicle* 163 (2003): 385-92.
A report on an excavation which uncovered 193 coins. The 111 Greek coins are catalogued here. Most are from Cyzicus.

623 **Kolitsida-Makri, I.** "O Thesauros Gytheiou *IGCH* 170." *Eulimene* (Mediterranean Archaeological Society, Rethymno, Greece) 2 (2001): 121-8.
"*IGCH* 170 was found at Gythion of Laconia in 1938. It consists of 33 silver coin-issues often occurring in Peloponnesian hoards: 1 drachm of Aegina, 32 triobols of Sikyon, 1 tetradrachm of Antiochus I Soter. The drachm issue, with two incuse dots on the reverse, dates to the second half of the fourth century B.C. The triobols follow the so-called reduced Aeginetan standard, with an average weight of about 2.6 grams each; these can be attributed to the very last years of the fourth up to the first decades of the third century B.C. The tetradrachm of Antiochus I, minted in Seleucia on the Tigris c. 278-274 B.C., is important for the chronology of the find. In a total of 23 coin hoards found in the Peloponnese, buried in the period between the middle of the fourth and the second century B.C., four include Seleucid tetradrachms (17 in all) of which eight were minted in Seleucia-on-the-Tigris. It is probably an emergency hoard connected either with the troubled times of Cleomenes III's war (228-222 B.C.) or the Social War (220-217 B.C.). Thus, the period around the year 220 B.C. is *grosso modo* suggested as the possible burial date. The Gythion find is another important hoard for the dating of the triobols of Sikyon and also provides further evidence for coin circulation in the Peloponnese during the second part of the third century B.C." [I. Kolitsida-Makri, *NL* 147]

624 **Kosmetatou, Elizabeth.** "A Numismatic Commentary of the Inventory Lists of the Athenian Acropolis." *Revue Belge de Numismatique et de Sigillographie* (Belgium) 147 (2001): 11-38.

625 **Kosmidou, Elpida.** "Greek Coins from the Eastern Cemetery of Amphipolis." *Numismatic Chronicle* 166 (2006): 415-31. 2 pls.
A catalogue of coins found including many local mints of the classical and Hellenistic periods.

626 **Kourouniotes, K., and Homer A. Thompson.** "The Pynx in Athens." *Hesperia* 1 (1932): 90-217. Illus.
"On pp. 211-3 fourteen of the bronze coins found on the site are listed and described. They are of common types, from Athens in the fourth century B.C. to coins of Alexius I and William of Villehardouin." [J. R. Jones, *NIAJAH*]

627 **Kourtzellis, I.** "Coins from the Ancient Harbour Installations in the Northern Port of Mytilene." *Coins in the Aegean Islands. Proceedings of the Fifth Scientific Meeting, Mytilene, 16-29 September 2006. Volume 1: Ancient Times.* Obolos 9. Edited by Panagiotis Tselekas. Athens: The Friends of the Numismatic Museum, 2010. Pages 185-200.

628 **Kraay, Colin M.** "The Celenderis Hoard." *Numismatic Chronicle* 7th ser., 2 (1962): 1-15. 2 pls. [CS 3247]
The author reconstructs a hoard found in 1957 in Pamphylia or Cilicia which contained many staters of Celenderis, including nearly all the major types. Also included were coins of Athens, Side, Mallus, Soli, Tarsus, Citium, Lapethus, Paphos, and Salamis. The coins were likely buried ca. 401 B.C.

629 ——— "Hoards and Circulation." *Greek Coins and History: Some Current Problems.* London: Methuen; New York: Barnes & Noble, 1969. Pages 43-63. 3 pls.
Examines certain aspects of the distribution of coin hoards throughout the Greek world. Discusses the declining influence of the coinage of north Aegean mints in the Near East during the sixth and fifth centuries B.C., the growing importance of Athenian coinage, and the imitation of Greek-type coinage by non-Greek peoples. Discusses the 1839 Athos hoard of Persian darics and Athenian tetradrachms, pointing out how the evidence of this hoard had previously been misinterpreted. Examines the import/export of coins into/out of the East and West and how coins were retained in areas which had no local sources of silver. Reviews the overstriking of Athenian and Corinthian coins in Italy and Sicily. Suggests explanations for the prevalence of Corinthian coins in Sicily.

630 ——— "A Note on the Carosino and Ionian Shore Hoards." *Museum Notes* 16 (1970): 23-30.
Attempts to reconstruct the Carosino (1904) and Ionian Shore (1908) hoards found in South Italy. The hoards included coins of Corcyra, Leucas, Corinth, and Ambracia.

631 ——— "The Asyut Hoard: Some Comments on Chronology." *Numismatic Chronicle* 137 (1977): 189-98. 1 pl. [CS 3251]
Discusses the Asyut hoard of nearly 900 archaic period coins, the closing of which Price and Waggoner date to ca. 475 B.C. (see Price and Waggoner *Archaic Greek Coinage: The Asyut Hoard* below). Kraay re-examines some of the coins for which he believes a date later than 475 B.C. is possible, including an octadrachm of Alexander I of Macedon and some Persian sigloi which Kraay suggests may have been added to the hoard between 475-450 B.C. Also discusses the hoard's implications for the early coinage of Athens, the demareteion of Syracuse, and the beginnings of coinage. Rejects Weidauer's theory dating the origin of coinage to ca. 700 B.C.

632 ——— "The Isparta Hoard." *Greek Numismatics and Archaeology: Essays in Honor of Margaret Thompson*. Edited by O. Mørkholm and N. M. Waggoner. Wetteren: Numismatique Romaine, 1979. Pages 131-137. 1 pl.
A catalogue and discussion of a small hoard found near Isparta (in ancient Pisidia). The coins now reside in the Ashmolean Museum. The hoard included sigloi and double sigloi from Aspendus (nine coins) and twenty-five Persian sigloi. All but one of the coins is countermarked, and some of the same marks appear on both series of coins. The countermarks are of seven principal types, and the triskeles is commonly found. Kraay does not speculate on a burial date for the hoard.

633 ——— "Sovana, Italy 1885 (*IGCH* 2041)." *Coin Hoards* 5 (1979): 34.
"The text of *An Inventory of Greek Coin Hoards* no. 1954 [see Thompson, Mørkholm, and Kraay below] is corrected at two points: first, in the first line for 'SSW' read 'SSE;' second, in the final paragraph, for '70,' read '79.' It also seems likely that A. Sambon (*Les Monnaies Antiques d'Italie*) wrote 'Sovana' in error for 'Cecina.'" [E. Marles, *NL* 105]

634 ——— "Near East, 1980." *Coins Hoards* 7 (1985): 38-9. Illus.
Illustrates five coins from a near eastern hoard including coins of Neapolis (Macedonia), Thasos, Naxos, Samos, and Salamis. Kraay notes that the contents bear similarities to the Asyut hoard and suggests that burial may be not far from that of Asyut, ca. 475 B.C.

635 **Kraay, Colin M., and P. R. S. Moorey.** "Two Fifth Century Hoards from the Near East." *Revue Numismatique* (France) 6th ser., 10 (1968): 181-235. 10 pls. [CS 3252]
"These two substantial hoards, buried about 445 B.C. and 425-420 B.C. respectively, illustrate the kinds of coinage being imported from the Greek world into the Near East at a time for which information has been previously somewhat scarce. Among their very varied contents, both hoards contain large issues minted before 480, whereas in the later hoard contemporary issues are dominant. Light is also thrown on the chronology of some Cypriot issues and on the origins of Phoenician coinage; the earlier hoard included an unpublished Macedonian octadrachm as well as an example of the very rare first issue of Tyre. The presence here of a quantity of local jewelry in a dated context is useful in a field in which such chronological information is usually lacking." [C. Kraay and P. Moorey, *NL* 83]

636 ——— "A Black Sea Hoard of the Late Fifth Century B.C." *Numismatic Chronicle* 141 (1981): 1-19. 9 pls.
"The hoard is composed of 102 coins and numerous fragments of jewelry and scrap silver; the only series of coins present in more than isolated examples are Athens (31), Sinope (37), and Persia (20); hitherto unpublished varieties of the Bisaltae and Tarsus are included. Many of the coins have been fragmented, and one of the scraps of silver bears a partial cuneiform inscription naming a king Darius. A burial date of ca. 420 B.C. is suggested. The major part of the hoard (including the scrap silver and jewelry) is preserved in the Ashmolean Museum, Oxford." [Kraay and Moorey, *NL* 108]

637 **Krishnamurthy, R.** "Coins from Greek Islands, Rhodes and Crete Found at Karur, Tamilnadu." *Studies on South Indian Coins* 5 (1995): 29-36.
"The author publishes five copper coins belonging to Rhodes, Crete, Thrace and Thessaly which were found at Karur in Tiruchirapalli district of Tamilnadu." [A. Jha, *NL* 136]

638 **Kroll, John H.** "A Small Find of Silver Bullion from Egypt." *American Journal of Numismatics* 2nd ser., 13 (2001): 1-20. 1 pl.
Examines a hoard residing at the American Numismatic Society consisting of nineteen pieces: 3 round cake ingots, 2 fifth century Athenian tetradrachms, 1 flattened coin-like dump, and 13 irregular pieces of cut silver of various sizes. The hoard was found in Egypt (date found is not known). Kroll dates the hoard to the late fifth to early fourth century B.C. Describes each piece. Compares the contents to similar Egyptian hoards. The flattened dump has the exact weight of an Attic drachm (4.29 gm.). Discusses the controversy over whether such silver hoards represent a form of money or are merely silversmith's or jeweler's hoards. Explores the Egyptian preference for Athenian tetradrachms after silver had become well-established as a form of money. Suggests that the transition from weighed-silver to the use of coins without weighing took a long time, and was not complete until the Ptolemaic era. The hoard also demonstrates that weighed silver was used in small transactions as well as large ones. [Also see Balmuth *Hacksilver to Coinage* under ORIGINS OF COINAGE].

639 **Lagos, Constantine.** "A Hoard of the Chremonidean War." *Numismatic Chronicle* 156 (1996): 272-7. 1 pl.
A catalogue and discussion of a hoard containing five bronze coins, buried ca. 267-262 B.C. in East Attica. The coins are of Attica (two), Chios, Ptolemy III, and Pergamum.

640 **Lambert, C.** "Egypto-Arabian, Phoenician, and Other Coins of the Fourth Century B.C. found in Palestine." *Quarterly of the Department of Antiquities in Palestine* 2, no. 1 (1932): 1-10. 2 pls.
A catalogue of a hoard of sixty-three coins including coins of Alexander the Great, Athenian types, Sidonian types, Tyrian types, Egypto-Arabian and Philisto-Arabian types.

641 **Lang, R. Hamilton.** "On Coins Discovered during Recent Excavations in the Island of Cyprus." *Numismatic Chronicle* new ser., 11 (1871): 1-18. Illus. Also appeared in *Numismatic Report* (Cyprus) 5 (1974): 18-32. Illus.
Publishes two hoards (48 coins and 17 coins) primarily of Cypriot coins, but containing some coins with Phoenician legends, and seven Athenian tetradrachms. Comments on the history of the island during the period of burial.

642 ——— "Treasure-Trove in Cyprus of Gold Staters." *Numismatic Chronicle* new ser., 11 (1871): 229-34. 1 pl.
Discusses a hoard of about 900 coins found in Cyprus, mostly gold staters of Philip II, Alexander III, and Philip III. Some of the varieties found are not listed by Müller.

643 **Le Rider, Georges.** *Deux Trésors de Monnaies Grecques de la Propontide.* Bibliothèque Archéologique et Historique de l'Institut Français d'Archéologie d'Istanbul 18. Paris, 1963. 67 pp., 20 pls. [CS 3253]
"Important for the chronology of many mints in Asia Minor in the fourth century." [C. Kraay]. "Coins of Byzantium, Chalcedon and Chios." [E. Clain-Stefanelli]

644 ——— "Un Trésor Hellénistique de Monnaies d'Argent Trouvé en Syrie en 1971 (*Coin Hoards* II, 81)." *Syria* 75 (1998): 89-96.

645 ——— "Monnaies Trouvées à Mirgissa." *Ètudes d'Historie Monétaire et Financière du Monde Grec. Ècrits 1958-1998.* Bibliotheca of the Hellenic Numismatic Society, No. 6. Athens: Hellenic Numismatic Society, 1999. Pages 1027-35.
A hoard containing forty-three coin blanks and seventeen coins imitating Ptolemaic coins of the years after 180 B.C. proves that a mint was in operation in Mirgissa (near the Sudan/Egypt border) producing imitation bronze Ptolemaic coins.

646 **Lewis, R. B.** "Hoard of Greek Coins from Spain." *Numismatic Chronicle* 7th ser., 2 (1962): 425-7. 1 pl.
Describes and illustrates a hoard of six coins found in Spain. The coins were struck in Italy and Sicily between 485-456 B.C.

647 **Liampi, Katerini.** "NIKA, ΛEIA: Graffiti on Sicyonian and Theban Staters in a New Hoard from Boeotia/Beginning of 2000." *American Journal of Numismatics* 2nd ser., 20 (2008): 209-26. 2 pls.
Graffiti on five coins from a recent hoard present a narrative recording, most likely a dedication of victory spoils to an unknown deity by Macedonians following the Battle of Chaeronea in 338 B.C. The hoard contained at least fourteen coins, dating from 470-338 B.C. Includes a catalogue of the coins (all staters of Sicyon or Thebes). Discusses the use of graffiti on ancient coins. The coins were likely placed in a bronze vessel which was dedicated in a sanctuary in Boeotia.

648 **Liampi, Katerini, and Katerina Peristeri.** "Excavation Coins from the Sanctuary of Dionysus in Kali Vryssi, Prefecture of Drama." *American Journal of Numismatics* 2nd ser., 22 (2010): 1-16. 5 pls.
A report on thirty-four late classical and Hellenistic coins found in the destruction layer of the Sanctuary of Dionysos in Kali Vryssi during the course of excavations in the 1990s. The coins suggest that the sanctuary was operational already in the fourth century B.C. and was destroyed during the Gallic invasion in the early third century B.C. The coins include issues of Philip II, Alexander III, Cassander, and Demetrius Poliorcetes, as well as coins of Gomphoi (Thessaly) and Amphipolis.

649 **Lönnqvist, Kenneth, and Minna Lönnqvist.** "The Numismatic Chronology of Qumran: Fact and Fiction." *Numismatic Chronicle* 166 (2006): 121-65.
Examines the coins found at Qumran along with the Dead Sea Scrolls.

649a **Lorber, Catharine C.** "Thessaly, 1993 Hoard." *Revue Suisse de Numismatique* (Switzerland) 88 (2009): 127-40.

650 ——— "Commerce ('Demetrius I' Hoard), 2003 (*CH* 10.301)." *Coin Hoards, Volume X: Greek Hoards.* Edited by Oliver Hoover, Andrew Meadows, and Ute Wartenberg Kagan. New York: Royal Numismatic Society and The American Numismatic Society, 2010. Pages 153-72. 8 pls.
The hoard comprised 532 coins including 450 tetradrachms and 79 drachms. The largest components were 105 New Style tetradrachms of Athens, 92 Alexanders from Temnus, and 78 bee/stag drachms of Arados. The hoard was likely deposited in 151/0 B.C. in association with the invasion of Syria by Alexander Balas. It also helps to support a low chronology for the New Style tetradrachms. Lorber discusses the Temnus Alexanders, the wreathed tetradrachms of western Asia Minor, the Aradian drachms, seventeen coins of Demetrius I, and several other rare, unpublished, or noteworthy coins (including a tetradrachm of Orophernes of Cappadocia). Includes a catalogue of the coins.

651 **Losada, Luis A.** "The Aetolian Indemnity of 189 and the Agrinion Hoard." *Phoenix* (Canada) 19, no. 2 (summer 1965): 129-33.
The Agrinion Hoard (see M. Thompson below) provides evidence that the introduction of Athenian tetradrachms into Aetolia in quantity and with regularity was exactly contemporary with, and undoubtedly due to, the treaty of 189 B.C. between Rome and Aetolia. In the treaty, the Romans demanded payment in coinage of the Euboic-Attic standard. But the minting of Aetolia's own Attic-weight tetradrachms ceased ca. 225-220 B.C. Losada comments on Roman political policy toward Greece during this period.

652 **MacDowall, David W.** "A Note on the Pre-Islamic Coins from the 1975 Season." *Excavations at Kandahar 1974 and 1975: The First Two Seasons at Shahr-I Kohna (Old Kandahar) Conducted by the British Institute of Afghan Studies.* Edited by Anthony McNicoll and Warwick Ball. BAR International Series 641. Society for South Asian Studies Monograph 1. Oxford: Tempus Reparatum, 1996. Pages 305-11, including 5 pls.
A few Hellenistic coins were found in the excavations at Kandahar, Afghanistan, including copper coins of Antiochus III, Euthydemus I, and Eucratides.

653 **MacIsaac, John D.** "Corinth: Coins, 1925-1926. The Theater District and the Roman Villa." *Hesperia* 56, no. 2 (April-June 1987): 97-157. 5 pls.
Presents a catalogue of the coins found in 1925-1926 during excavations near the main Theater and other places. Six-hundred thirteen Greek coins were found, as well as many Roman, Byzantine, and later coins. Includes many Corinthian pegasos/trident bronzes from contexts that are Roman. Discusses coin loss patterns.

654 **Magen, Y.** "Mt. Gerizim—A Temple City." *Qadmoniot* (Israel) 32, no. 2 (2000): 74-119. Illus.
"On pp. 114-115 and pl. 4 a short reference is made to the approximately 13,000 coins found during eighteen years of excavations at this site in Samaria. Out of this total, less than half have so far been identified. About 3500 are Seleucid issues from Seleucus II to Antiochus VIII including a hoard of 129 tetradrachms struck at Tyre during the period 136-125 B.C. Also included in the finds were 257 pieces of autonomous Ake-Ptolemais and 546 Hasmonean issues." [A. Spaer, *NL* 144]

655 **Martin, Thomas R.** "A Third-Century B.C. Hoard from Thessaly at the ANS. (*IGCH* 168)." *Museum Notes* 26 (1981): 51-77. 7 pls.

Describes a hoard of 571 coins found near Larissa, ca. 1938. Included 155 drachms of Larissa, 72 tetradrachms of Athens, 248 drachms of Alexander III, and other coins. Discusses the contents of this and similar hoards and concludes the coins were buried ca. 250 B.C. Presents tables of the weights of the Athenian tetradrachms and Larissa drachms.

656 **Mattingly, Harold B.** "The Jordan Hoard (*IGCH* 1482) and Kimon's Last Campaign." *Proceedings of the 10th International Congress of Numismatics, London, 1986.* IAPN Publication, No. 11. Edited by I. A. Carradice. London: International Association of Professional Numismatists, 1986. Pages 59-64.
Reviews evidence provided by the Jordan Hoard (buried ca. 445 B.C.) in an attempt to assign a more definite burial date. Suggests a relationship between this hoard and the Athenian general Kimon's attack on the Phoenician city of Kition.

657 ——— "The Ma'Aret En-Nu'man Hoard, 1980." *Essays in Honour of Robert Carson and Kenneth Jenkins.* Edited by M. J. Price, A. M. Burnett, and R. Bland. London: Spink & Son, 1993. Pages 69-86. 3 pls.
Presents a catalogue of a hoard of 536 coins found southeast of Antioch in 1980. Includes Seleucid issues from Antiochus I through Antiochus V, coins of the Pergamene Kingdom, posthumous Alexanders from a variety of mints, posthumous issues of Lysimachos from a variety of mints, and other coins. The author concludes the hoard was buried in 162 B.C. Includes a number of rarities. Mattingly compares the contents of the hoard with similar hoards.

658 ——— "Coin Hoards and History." *Numismatic Chronicle* 161 (2001): 385-8.
The text of the President's Address (Royal Numismatic Society). Mattingly comments on some hoards that, if properly dated, could yield important historical results.

659 **McDowell, Robert H.** *Coins from Seleucia on the Tigris.* University of Michigan Studies, Humanistic Series 37. Ann Arbor: University of Michigan Press, 1935. 248 pp., 6 pls. [CS 3011]
Examines the coins found during excavations at Seleucia on the Tigris, 1927-1932. More than 30,000 coins were found. One-hundred forty-eight coin types are catalogued here, mostly from the Seleucid and Parthian periods. Includes an extensive discussion of the Parthian mint at Seleucia. Discusses the calendar employed, coin types struck, legends, and monograms. [Reviewed by E. T. Newell in *American Journal of Archaeology* 41 (1937): 515-7. Also see McDowell "Models of Seleucid Coins" under SYRIA—SELEUCID KINGDOM].

660 **Meadows, Andrew R.** "The Apadana Foundation Deposit (*IGCH* 1789): Some Clarification." *Numismatic Chronicle* 163 (2003): 342-4.
Provides information not previously published regarding the Apadana Foundation Deposit from the Persian capital of Persepolis. Lists the thirteen coins found along with the weight of each. [Also see Zournatzi "The Apadana Coin Hoards" below].

661 ——— "Systematic Recording: Greek Coin Hoards and the ANS." *ANS Magazine* 9, no. 2 (summer 2010): 38-42. Illus.
Discusses the role of the American Numismatic Society in recording and publishing information on Greek coin hoards, beginning with Sydney Noe's *A Bibliography of Greek Coin Hoards*. Traces the evolution of the recording of hoards through Thompson and Mørkholm's *Inventory of Greek Coin Hoards*, the *Coin Hoards* series, and the development of web-based hoard mapping tools.

662 ——— "Beth Ummar, Israel, 2001 (*CH* 10.315)." *Coin Hoards, Volume X: Greek Hoards.* Edited by Oliver Hoover, Andrew Meadows, and Ute Wartenberg Kagan. New York: Royal Numismatic Society and The American Numismatic Society, 2010. Pages 225-6.
The brief publication of coins found in Israel in 2001 including a run of Tyrian tetradrachms and didrachms from the second reign of Demetrius II. The hoard was likely deposited in 127/6 B.C.—perhaps in connection with the military conflict between Demetrius and Hasmonaean Judaea under John Hyrcanus I.

662a ——— "The Chian Revolution: Changing Patterns of Hoarding in 4th-Century B.C. Western Asia Minor." *Bulletin de Correspondance Hellénique* (France) Supplement 53 (2011).

663 **Meadows, Andrew R., and Arthur Houghton.** "The Gaziantep Hoard, 1994 (*CH* 9.527; 10.308)." *Coin Hoards, Volume X: Greek Hoards.* Edited by Oliver Hoover, Andrew Meadows, and Ute Wartenberg Kagan. New York: Royal Numismatic Society and The American Numismatic Society, 2010. Pages 173-223. 16 pls.
The hoard appeared on the market in several parcels in London, Beirut, and the U.S. in 1994. In total, it comprised 1916 coins including 287 wreathed tetradrachms of Kyme, 383 wreathed tetradrachms of Myrina, 86 Alexanders of Temnus, 119 coins of Magnesia, 110 of Alabanda, and 268 Seleucid coins. Also included coins of Mytilene, Chios, Phaselis, Aspendos, Perge, Side, and Athens (New Style). The hoard evidence suggests that Seleucid coinage was in the minority in the circulation pool in Seleucid Syria in the mid-second century B.C.

664 **Meadows, Andrew R., and Catharine C. Lorber.** "Commerce ('Achaeus' Hoard), 2002 (*CH* 10.277)." *Coin Hoards, Volume X: Greek Hoards.* Edited by Oliver Hoover, Andrew Meadows, and Ute Wartenberg Kagan. New York: Royal Numismatic Society and The American Numismatic Society, 2010. Pages 115-27. 4 pls.
The hoard contained 87 tetradrachms, including 44 tetradrachms of Alexander type from various mints, and 22 Seleucid types including three tetradrachms of the Seleucid usurper Achaeus of which only three specimens were previously known. Includes a catalogue of the coins and commentary. The find spot is unknown but likely was in southwestern Asia Minor. Burial was likely ca. 204-199 B.C.

665 **Meadows, Andrew R., and Ute Wartenberg, eds.** *Coin Hoards, Volume IX: Greek Hoards.* London: Royal Numismatic Society, 2002. 308 pp., 66 pls.
This volume of the *Coin Hoards* series (see Royal Numismatic Society *Coin Hoards* below) lists 744 hoards containing Greek coins (pp. 1-81). The contents of each hoard are briefly listed, and each hoard is cross-referenced to other publications that explore the hoard in more detail. Pages 85-292 are devoted to twelve papers examining various hoards in detail: "A Small Group of Tetradrachms of Alexander I of Macedon" by U. Wartenberg [3532], "The Demirler, Lycia (c. 1972) Hoard" by Spier, Arslan, and Dervisagaoglou [5042], "The Hecatomnus Hoard" by Ashton, Kinns, Konuk, and Meadows [491], "The Pixodarus Hoard" by Ashton, Hardwick, Kinns, Konuk, and Meadows [490], "The 'Myndos' 1996 Hoard" by Zabel and Meadows [4914], "The Tyre, 1987 Hoard of Seleucid Silver" by C. Lorber [5363], "'Thasos'/New Style Hoard, 1996" by A. Meadows [3767], "The

Ascalon 1988 Hoard: A Periplus to Ascalon in the Late Hellenistic Period?" by Gitler and Kahanov [568], "Provenances, Attributions and Chronology of Some Early Italian Coinages" by M. Crawford [2648], "A Hoard of Punic 'Horse and Palm' Billon Tetradrachms" by C. Lorber [6723], "A Hoard of Parthian Coins in Afyon Museum" by Ashton, Sellwood, and Üyümez [6031], and "The Akura Hoard of Parthian Coins" by Z. Sawaya [6094].

666 **Meier, Barry.** "The Case of the Contested Coins: A Modern-Day Battle over Ancient Objects." *The New York Times* (September 24, 1998): section C, pages 1, 23. Illus.
Recounts the discovery of the Emali hoard, its sale into the collector market, and the attempts of the Turkish government to re-gain possession of the coins from William Koch. [Also see Alexander "Curse," Gibbs "American Returns 'Hoard of the Century,'" and Giedroyc "Hoard's Owner Speaks," above, and Tompa "Decadrachm Hoard" and Vermeule "Athenian Treasury Hoard" below].

667 **Meshorer, Ya'akov.** "Coins from Areas A and C." *Excavations at Dor, Final Report. Qedem Reports 1B.* Jerusalem, 1995. Pages 461-71. Illus.
"This is an illustrated catalogue of 116 coins found during these excavations. They begin with Phoenician issues of the Persian period and end with Roman issues up to Constantius II." [A. Spaer, *NL* 136]

668 ——— "The Coins." *Yoqne'am I: The Late Periods. Qedem Reports 3.* Jerusalem, 1996. Pages 239-41. Illus.
"The author describes and illustrates the sixteen coins found during excavations of this Lower Galilee site. They include two Persian-period coins of Sidon, one tetradrachm of Alexander the Great (Sidon), two Seleucid issues, three Roman provincial coins, two fourth-century Roman issues, one Byzantine, two Islamic, one Crusader, and two Ottoman issues." [A. Spaer, *NL* 139]

669 **Michaelidou-Nicolaou, Ino.** "Four Ptolemaic/Roman Hoards from Cyprus." *Numismatic Chronicle* 153 (1993): 11-29. 7 pls.
"These hoards give an idea of the coinage which normally circulated in Cyprus in the Ptolemaic and Roman (first to early second centuries A.D.) periods, and attest to the contacts of the island with neighboring countries, namely Egypt, Palestine, Syria, Asia Minor, and Arabia." [I. Michaelidou-Nicolaou, *NL* 134]

670 **Mielczarek, Mariusz.** *Ancient Greek Coins Found in Central, Eastern and Northern Europe.* Wroclaw-Warsaw-Kraków-Gdansk-Lodz, 1989. 205 pp., illus.
"The Greek coins found in central, eastern and northern Europe are the basis for a study of the inflow of these coins into the vast area in question from the fourth to the late first century B.C. Most of the ca. 180 catalogued finds contained the Hellenistic pieces, while the whole chronological scope of the issues ranged from late seventh to late first century B.C. The Sicilian and South Italian coins made their way to barbarian Europe in the fourth/third centuries B.C. by means of the amber trade. The Macedonian coins, mainly those of Philip II and Alexander the Great, were redistributed by the Celts and similarly the Thracian and Thasos pieces by the Geto-Dacians, mostly in the first century B.C. The coins struck in the northern Black Sea zone crossed the Scythian area. The Seleucid silver and bronze pieces were redistributed partly by the Geto-Dacians and partly by the Roman soldiers. A number of Egyptian bronzes penetrated the Barbaricum from the Roman imperial borderland. The Greek coins in the area in question played a role of a commodity based on their metallic value." Includes a summary in Polish. [A. Mikolajczyk, *NL* 124]

671 **Militký, Jiri.** *Finds of Greek, Roman and Early Byzantine Coins in the Territory of the Czech Republic, I. Bohemia.* Institute of Archaeology, Warsaw University. Wetteren: Moneta, 2010.
The catalogue presents a list of finds of Greek, Roman and early Byzantine coins (fifth century B.C. to seventh century A.D.) from Bohemia. It is a 50,971 square kilometer region corresponding to the present administrative structure without reference to the historical boundary between Bohemia and Moravia. The catalogues are divided into regions. All surviving coins are described in detail and most are illustrated. Each volume includes an index of sites.

   Volume 1. Collection Moneta 107. 290 pp., illus.
   Volume 2. Collection Moneta 108. 196 pp., illus.
   Volume 3. Collection Moneta 109. 206 pp., illus.

672 **Miller, Richard P.** "East Arachosia (Quetta) Hoard, 2002 (*CH* 10.275)." *Coin Hoards, Volume X: Greek Hoards.* Edited by Oliver Hoover, Andrew Meadows, and Ute Wartenberg Kagan. New York: Royal Numismatic Society and The American Numismatic Society, 2010. Pages 105-14. 11 pls.
Miller documents a hoard of 230 Hellenistic tetradrachms found near Quetta in western Pakistan (ancient Arachosia), which included coins from the lifetime of Alexander to the passage of Antiochos III through Ecbatana in 209 B.C. One hundred eighty-three of the coins are catalogued here. The largest component is local imitations of Alexander tetradrachms. Also includes many Seleucid coins. The hoard was likely buried ca. 206 B.C. The hoard provides evidence that Arachosia developed its own distinct patterns of monetization and trade by the third century B.C. The region followed western coin types and designs, rather than those to the north or east.

673 ——— "An Unpublished Imitation Alexander from the East Arachosia 2002 Hoard." *The Celator* 24, no. 11 (November 2010): 24. Illus.
Publishes and illustrates an imitation of a tetradrachm of Alexander the Great from the Arachosia hoard which was not previously published (see Miller "East Arachosia" above). The coin was struck in what is now Pakistan.

674 **Milne, Joseph G.** "A Hoard of Coins from Egypt of the Fourth Century B.C." *Revue Archéologique* (France) 4th ser., 5 (1905): 257-61.
Examines a hoard of Athenian tetradrachms and Phoenician coins found in 1903-1904 at Beni Hasan. Describes the Phoenician coins from Sidon, Gaza, and Tyre. Notes the discrepancy in the state of preservation between the Athenian coins and the others. Suggest this was a silversmith's hoard. [Milne later determined the "Athenian" coins to be local imitations, thus accounting for their well-preserved condition. See Milne "Beni Hasan Coin-Hoard" below. Also see E. S. G. Robinson "A Hoard from 'Sidon'" below].

675 ——— "The Beni Hasan Coin-Hoard." *Journal of Egyptian Archaeology* 19 (1933): 119-21.
Discusses a hoard found in Egypt which, along with the usual cut coins and fragments, included fifty-four mint-state Athenian tetradrachms. Describes some typical hoards found in Egypt and shows that the coins were obviously traded as bullion. Milne suggests that the Athenian tetradrachms in this hoard are the product of a local Egyptian workshop at Beni Hasan which minted the silver collected in the levy of Tachos, the Egyptian rebel leader of 361 B.C. The hoard was probably deposited ca. 360 B.C. [Also see Milne "Hoard of Coins from Egypt" above and E. S. G. Robinson "A Hoard from 'Sidon'" below].

676 ——— *Finds of Greek Coins in the British Isles: The Evidence Reconsidered in the Light of the Rackett Collection from Dorset*. London: Oxford University Press, 1948. 47 pp., 3 maps. [CS 3255]
Discusses the coins found by Rev. Thomas Rackett in England in the nineteenth century, nearly all of which were Greek bronzes of the autonomous period. Begins with a general discussion of the difficulties of interpreting hoard evidence and the knowledge which can be gained from such studies. About 100 coins were found, mainly from the central Mediterranean area, focused on Syracuse and Carthage from the fourth through first centuries B.C. Concludes that the coins were buried in Britain probably within fifty years of their minting. [Reviewed by G. K. Jenkins in *Journal of Hellenic Studies* 69 (1949): 121].

677 **Mirnik, Ivan.** "A Thracian Silver Coin Hoard in the Osijek Slavonian Museum." *Numismatic Chronicle* 153 (1993): 197-200. 5 pls.
"The author discusses a coin hoard from the Osijek collection confiscated at the Croato-Hungarian border in 1968. The provenance (possibly Bulgarian) and data about its completeness remain obscure. The Osijek parcel contains thirty-one tetradrachms of Euboean-Attic standard: eight were struck at Maroneia, one is an imitation, four belong to Thasos, seven are early barbarous imitations of Thasian tetradrachms, and there are eleven later barbarous imitations of the same type. All types belong to the second and early first centuries B.C., permitting the conclusion that burial occurred in the first half of the first century B.C. In the article, the Schönert-Geiss catalogue was used for the Maroneian silver, the *SNG* volumes for Thasos, and Göbl's typology for their imitations." [I. Mirnik, *NL* 134]

678 **Morineau-Humphris, J.** "A Hoard from Thessaly." *Coin Hoards* 3 (1977): 9-17, including 2 pls.
The author comments on a hoard of thirty-eight silver coins found in Thessaly in 1975. Compares the contents of the hoard with the contents of similar hoards. Suggests a burial date of ca. 229-8 B.C. Presents a catalogue of the coins. The hoard contained coins of Macedonia, the Seleucid Kingdom, the Ptolemaic Kingdom, Caria, Ionia, Central Greece, Peloponnesos, and others.

679 **Mørkholm, Otto.** "A South Anatolian Coin Hoard." *Acta Archaeologica* (Denmark) 30 (1959): 184-201. 4 pls., map.
Describes a hoard discovered near Karaman (ancient Laranda in Lycaonia) during 1947-1948. The hoard contained about 1062 coins, 316 of which are catalogued here. Includes coins of Athens, Sinope, Aspendos, Selge, Pharnabazos and Datames (Cilicia).

680 ——— "Greek Coins from Failaka." *KUML. Årbog for Jysk Arkaeologisk Selskah* (Denmark) (1960): 199-207.

681 ——— "Une Trouvaille de Monnaie Grecques Archìque." *Revue Suisse de Numismatique* (Switzerland) 50 (1971): 79-91. 4 pls. [CS 3259]

682 ——— "A Hellenistic Coin Hoard from Bahrain." *KUML. Årbog for Jysk Arkaeologisk Selskah* (Denmark) (1972): 183-202. Illus.
A pot hoard containing 292 Hellenistic silver coins was found in Bahrain in 1970. The author discusses the attribution and chronology of the coins, all of which were imitations of Alexander tetradrachms. The coins supplement other historical information on Arab trade in the Hellenistic period and correct to a certain extent the impression that Ptolemaic Egypt, with its special coin standard and mercantile economy, was able to dominate the trade in oriental luxury articles in this period.

683 ——— "Hellenistic Coin Hoards from the Persian Gulf." *Proceedings of the 8th International Congress of Numismatics, New York—Washington, September 1973.* Edited by Herbert A. Cahn and Georges Le Rider. International Association of Professional Numismatists Publication, No. 4. Paris/Basel: International Association of Professional Numismatists, 1976. Page 123.
An abstract of the paper presented by Mørkholm at the 1973 Congress. Mentions the two known Hellenistic coin hoards from the Persian Gulf. The first, discovered in 1960, contained a tetradrachm of Antiochus III from Susa and twelve imitations of tetradrachms of Alexander the Great. The second, discovered in 1970, contained 292 tetradrachms of two different series of imitations of Alexander. The burial date of the hoard was ca. 230 B.C.

684 ——— "New Coin Finds from Failaka." *KUML. Årbog for Jysk Arkaeologisk Selskah* (Denmark) (1979): 219-36. Illus.
A hoard of sixteen silver coins (ten tetradrachms and six drachms) was found at Failaka, the ancient Ikaras, in 1961. Included five Seleucid coins and eleven imitations of Alexander coins. The author also describes some finds of single coins including three silver and twenty-two bronze coins, primarily Seleucid.

685 **Nash, Daphne.** "The Kuft Hoard of Alexander III Tetradrachms." *Numismatic Chronicle* (1974): 14-30.
"An inventory is made of coins certainly or probably from the hoard of silver tetradrachms of Alexander III, Philip III and Ptolemy I found in ca. 1875 at Kuft in Egypt (*IGCH* 1670). An unpublished inventory compiled by E. T. Newell, the collection of the late J. L. Strachan-Davidson on loan to the Ashmolean Museum, Oxford, and the British Museum collection provided the basis for the present inventory. The contents of the Kuft hoard are compared with those of the first jar of the Phacous hoard (*IGCH* 1678), and conclusions about the economic conditions in Egypt in the late fourth century B.C. drawn by Jenkins on the basis of the Phacous hoard are broadly confirmed." [D. Nash, *NL* 94]. [Also see Zervos "Newell's Manuscript" below for additions and corrections. Also see Jenkins "An Early Ptolemaic Hoard from Phacous" under EGYPT—PTOLEMAIC KINGDOM].

686 **Nelson, Bradley R.** "Commerce ('Seleucus I') Hoard, 2005 (*CH* 10.265)." *Coin Hoards, Volume X: Greek Hoards.* Edited by Oliver Hoover, Andrew Meadows, and Ute Wartenberg Kagan. New York: Royal Numismatic Society and The American Numismatic Society, 2010. Pages 73-104. 5 pls.
A hoard, possibly containing 3000 pieces, appeared on the market in 2005. It consisted of silver tetradrachms and drachms from a wide variety of mints, mostly Hellenistic Royal types. Included probably 1000 issues of Demetrius Poliorcetes (none were recorded). The next largest groups were Seleucid coins of Alexander type, Athena-in-chariot types, some Nike-trophy issues, and lifetime issues of Lysimachus. The groups of coins are discussed and 1721 coins are summarily catalogued. The hoard was likely buried ca. 281 B.C. Nelson discusses the historical events in Asia Minor which may have led to the accumulation and burial of the coins. The hoard was quite possibly part of the Seleucid treasury.

687 **Newell, Edward T.** "A Cilician Find." *Numismatic Chronicle* 4th ser., 14 (1914): 1-33. 4 pls.
Publishes a hoard of 141 coins found in Cilicia. Includes coins of Syracuse, Athens, Byzantion, Kalchedon, Sinope, Miletus, Samos, Aspendos, Side, Tlos, Kelenderis, Soli, Mallos, Issos, satrapal issues of Tiribazos, Salamis, Kition, Aradus, Tyre, Phoenicia, and Persian kings. Three varieties dominate: Athenian owls, Persian "archers," and the issues of certain cities and Persian satraps in Cilicia. Discusses the date of the hoard. Most of the coins were minted ca. 380 B.C. and 114 of the coins bear test cuts.

688 ——— "Egyptian Coin Hoards." *The Numismatist* 37, no. 4 (April 1924): 301-2.
In this interesting brief paper, written in Cairo in January 1924, Newell describes the "practically inexhaustible" supply of ancient coins coming to the market from Egyptian finds. He specifically describes a hoard found in 1919 at the village of Abu Hommos which included 750 tetradrachms of Alexander and 250 of Ptolemy I, and a hoard found near Keneh in 1923 which included 45 gold octodrachms. Also mentions several other hoards. Interestingly, he mentions the complaint of Egyptian dealers that despite the continued abundance of finds, the finds of coins are not as frequent nor as important "as in the old days."

689 ——— *Alexander Hoards 4: Olympia.* Numismatic Notes and Monographs, No. 39. New York: American Numismatic Society, 1929. 27 pp., 4 pls.
Publishes a hoard found near Olympia, ca. 1922. Contains coins of Elis (31), Sicyon (2), Aegina (5), Athens (11), Thebes (4), Opuntian Lokris (1), Alexander types (18), Lysimachus (1), and Ptolemaic types (6). One of the Sicyonian coins is a rare stater bearing a lion rather than a chimera. Newell places the hoard's burial at ca. 250-225 B.C.

690 ——— "Addition to the Delta (Benha El-Asl) Hoard." *Numismatic Chronicle* 5th ser., 11 (1931): 66-8.
Publishes eleven additional coins identified as coming from the "Delta Hoard" published by Robinson in 1930 (see E. S. G. Robinson "A Find of Archaic Greek Coins from the Delta" below).

691 ——— *The Küchük Kohne Hoard.* Numismatic Notes and Monographs, No. 46. New York: American Numismatic Society, 1931. 33 pp., 3 pls.
Describes a hoard of twenty-eight coins found in central Anatolia in the early 1930's. The coins are of Sinope, Amisos, and Tarsos from the late fourth century B.C.

692 ——— *A Hoard from Siphnos.* Numismatic Notes and Monographs, No. 64. New York: American Numismatic Society, 1934. 17 pp., 1 pl.
Describes a hoard of thirty silver coins found on the island of Siphnos in 1930. Lists coins of Siphnos, Athens, Rhodes, and one drachm of Alexander the Great. Discusses the significance of each group.

693 ——— *Five Greek Bronze Coin Hoards.* Numismatic Notes and Monographs, No. 68. New York: American Numismatic Society, 1935. 67 pp., 9 pls.
Describes five hoards of bronze coins from Euboea, Epidaurus, Mytilene, Magnesia ad Maeandrum, and Ptolemaic Egypt. The Euboea hoard contained 184 coins and may have been buried ca. 192-191 B.C. The Epidaurus hoard contained fifty-eight coins and was found in 1934. The coins are catalogued by type. Burial was perhaps ca. 280 B.C. The Mytilene hoard contained 179 bronze coins all of one type. None of the coins had been counterstamped as these coins are commonly found. This hoard was buried shortly after 250 B.C. The Magnesia ad Maeandrum hoard contained forty-six coins and was found in 1933. It was probably buried ca. 200 B.C. The Egyptian hoard contained sixty-nine Ptolemaic bronze coins.

694 ——— "Coins from the Excavations at Beisan (Nysa-Scythopolis, Tel Beth Shean): 1929-1935." *American Journal of Numismatics* 2nd ser., 20 (2008): 1-52. 11 pls.
Describes the coins found during the University of Pennsylvania excavations at Beisan. Includes Greek and later coins. [This paper was discovered and published seventy years after Newell's death. See Witschonke below].

695 **Nicolaou, Ino.** *Paphos 2: The Coins from the House of Dionysos.* Nicosia: Department of Antiquities, Cyprus, 1990. 227 pp., 41 pls.
A sequel to Nicolaou and Mørkholm's work (see Nicolaou and Mørkholm, *Paphos Volume 1* under EGYPT–PTOLEMAIC KINGDOM), this volume presents the coins found during excavations at Nea Paphos, Cyprus. Presents a brief history of Cyprus. Catalogues the coins found during excavations including Cypriot and non-Cypriot coins, and provides commentary. Primarily of importance for the study of the Roman provincial issues of Paphos. [Reviewed by D. Parks in *American Journal of Numismatics* 2nd ser., 3-4 (1992): 222-5, and by K. Butcher in *Numismatic Chronicle* 152 (1992): 199-200].

696 **Nicolet-Pierre, Hélène.** "Monnaies Grecques Trouvées en Afghanistan." *Revue Numismatique* (France) 6th ser., 15 (1973): 35-53.
Discusses eight silver coins acquired by the Cabinet de Médailles (Paris) in 1972. The coins were found in Afghanistan.

697 **Nixon, C. E. V.** "The Coins." *Jebel Khalid on the Euphrates: Report on Excavations 1986-1996. Volume 1.* Mediterranean Archaeology Supplement 5. Edited by G. W. Clarke et al. Sydney, 2002. Pages 291-335.
[Also see Clarke et al *Jebel Khalid* above].

698 ——— "The Coins from Jebel Khalid, a Hellenistic City in Syria." *Journal of the Numismatic Society of Australia* (Australia) 17 (2006): 92-6.
[Also see Clarke et al *Jebel Khalid* above].

699 **Noe, Sydney P.** *Coin Hoards.* Numismatic Notes and Monographs, No. 1. New York: American Numismatic Society, 1920. 47 pp., 6 pls.
A general discussion of the characteristics of coin hoards. Noe begins with an explanation of Gresham's Law (bad money drives out good money), then discusses the factors which contribute to hoarding. Reviews the laws of various countries regulating the ownership of coins found in hoards. Discusses the containers in which coins have been found, and some hiding places for hoards. Briefly comments on the condition of coins found, noting that the degree of preservation will vary with soil conditions. Discusses the dating of hoards and how hoard studies aid in the chronological classification of coins. Discusses the use of coins in the study of patterns of commerce. Concludes with brief comments on various hoards: the Anadol Find (1895; Alexander gold coins), the Auriol Find (1867; 2130 archaic coins), the Boscoe Reale Find (1895; Roman coins), the Vicarello Hoard (1852; Greek and early Roman coins), the Saida Find (1852; 3000 gold coins of Philip II and Alexander III), the Blackmoor Hoard (30,000 coins of Allectus and Carausius), and the Economy Hoard (1878; early American coins).

700 ——— *A Bibliography of Greek Coin Hoards.* Numismatic Notes and Monographs, No. 25. New York: American Numismatic Society, 1925. Second edition, Numismatic Notes and Monographs, No. 78. 1937. 362 pp. [CS 3208]

A comprehensive listing of hoards which contained Greek coins. Each hoard is listed under the name of the place where it was found, and these place-names are arranged alphabetically. The year of finding is given. When a date for burial of a hoard has been assigned, that date is also given. Indicates the number of coins found and their metal. Then lists the cities or rulers whose coins are represented in the hoard along with the number of coins for each. Disposition of the hoard is noted when known. Provides a bibliography of published works related to the hoard. Indexed by mint and by the district of the find locality. The second edition lists 1186 hoards, almost twice as many as the first edition. In the second edition, the hoards have been numbered sequentially, and have been indexed by year of finding and by the name of the author who published the hoard. [The second edition was reviewed by A. R. Bellinger in *American Journal of Archaeology* 42 (1938): 317-9. Also see Thompson, Mørkholm, and Kraay *An Inventory of Greek Coin Hoards* below].

701 ——— "Hoard Evidence and Its Importance." *Hesperia: Supplement 8: Commemorative Studies in Honor of Theodore Leslie Shear.* Athens: American School of Classical Studies, 1949. Pages 235-42. [CS 3262]
Discusses some of the problems and pitfalls involved in the interpretation of hoard evidence: incomplete hoards, accurate knowledge of find-spots, the importance of completely identifying all the coins found, the working of Gresham's law (bad money drives out good) leading to better quality coins (less wear/better metal) being hoarded while lesser quality coins were spent. Warns that the absence of a known debased issue from a hoard does not necessarily mean the hoard was buried prior to the introduction of such coins—the debased coins are unlikely to have been hoarded.

702 ——— "The Corinth Hoard of 1938." *Museum Notes* 10 (1962): 9-41. 11 pls. [CS 3264]
Discusses a hoard of 382 silver coins found at Corinth in 1938. Summarizes the volatile political situation at Corinth, 229-220 B.C., providing a possible motive for the secreting of this hoard. Presents a catalogue of the coins, which include issues of Athens (including 136 fourth-century tetradrachms), the Aitolian League, Ephesos, and Rhodes, as well as Seleucid and Ptolemaic issues. Also includes twenty tetradrachms and ninety drachms of Alexander the Great. Noe concludes the hoard was buried ca. 215 B.C. Alexander-type tetradrachms of Argos and Megalopolis are examined in the Appendices.

703 **Oeconomides, Mando Caramessini.** "À Propos du Trésor de Lappa (*IGCH* 35)." *Kraay—Mørkholm Essays: Numismatic Studies in Memory of C. M. Kraay and O. Mørkholm.* Numismatica Lovaniensia 10. Edited by G. Le Rider, G. K. Jenkins, N. Waggoner, and U. Westermark. Louvain-la-Neuve: Université Catholique de Louvain, 1989. Pages 217-23. 3 pls.
Examines a hoard primarily containing coins of Aegina and Elis.

704 **Oeconomides, Mando Caramessini, and Fred S. Kleiner.** "The Hierapytna Hoard: A Supplement." *Revue Belge de Numismatique et de Sigillographie* (Belgium) 121 (1975): 5-19. Illus.
"Two lots of coins acquired by the Athens Numismatic Collection prior to 1940 are identified as part of the 1933 Hierapytna hoard (*IGCH* 352). The new section comprises forty-four Athenian New Style tetradrachms and thirty cistophoric tetradrachms. A reconstruction of the Athenian and cistophoric sections of the hoard is attempted on the basis of the supplementary coins. The evidence of the new specimens confirms the burial date 44-42 B.C. suggested in *Numismatic Chronicle* 5th ser., 18 (1938): 138-58. The two supplementary lots contain a new Athenian two-magistrate issue (ΜΝΑΣΑΓΟΡΑΣ–ΜΕΝΤΩΡ), two newly-linked late issues, and the seventh known example of a cistophori of Cicero." [M. Oeconomides and F. Kleiner, *NL* 96]. [See Raven "The Hierapytna Hoard" below].

705 **Oeconomides, Mando, M. Lakakis-Marchetti, and Patrich Marchetti.** "Le Trésor de Zougra (*IGCH* 261) et la Circulation Monétaire dans le Péloponnèse au IIe Siècle." *Liber Amicorum Tony Hackens.* Edited by G. Moucharte, M. B. Borba Florenzano, F. de Callataÿ, P. Marchetti, L. Smolderen, and P. Yannopoulos. Numismatica Lovaniensia 20. Louvain-la-Neuve: Université Catholique de Louvain, 2007. Pages 379-433.
Zougra is the site of ancient Pellene. The hoard was found in 1859 and included 9171 silver coins—all hemidrachms. Half were Achaean League issues and others were from a variety of Peloponnesian and Central Greek mints. The authors support the view that the Achaean League coinage ended in 146 B.C. [Extensive review and commentary by Alan Walker in *ANS* 7, no. 3 (winter 2008): 53-8. Walker strongly refutes the suggested date for the end of the League coinage].

706 **Oeconomides, Mando L.** "Searching for Hoards in the Numismatic Museum of Athens." *Nomismatika Khronika* (Greece) 28 (2010): 25-30. Illus.
A reminiscence of the author's efforts to re-assemble hoards from coins in the collection of the museum in an effort to contribute to the compilation of hoards for the *Inventory of Greek Hoards*, during the period 1967-73. [In Greek on pp. 25-7 and English on pp. 28-30; translated by M. J. A. Tzamali].

707 **Olçay, Nekriman, and Otto Mørkholm.** "The Coin Hoard from Podalia." *Numismatic Chronicle* 7th ser., 11 (1971): 1-29. 11 pls.
An analysis of a hoard of about 1600 silver coins of Lycia and Aspendus in Pamphylia. The hoard was discovered in 1957. Turkish authorities recovered 510 of the coins and these are published here, along with a number of other Lycian coins that may have originally been part of the hoard. In all, 488 Lycian coins and 242 coins of Aspendus (40 sigloi and 202 staters) are catalogued here. Includes a review of weights and a discussion of mints and chronology.

708 **Olçay, Nekriman, and Henri Seyrig.** *Le Trésor de Mektepini en Phrygie.* Trésors Monétaires Seleucides Publiés sous la Direction de M. Henri Seyrig, I. Paris: Librarie Orientaliste Paul Geuthner, 1965. 33 pp., 33 pls. [CS 3265]
"Coins of Alexander the Great, Lysimachus, early Seleucids and late Macedonians." [E. Clain-Stefanelli]. [Also see Seyrig *Trésors Monétaires Séleucides* under SYRIA—SELEUCID KINGDOM].

709 **Pemberton, Elizabeth G.** "Ten Hellenistic Graves in Ancient Corinth." *Hesperia* 54, no. 3 (July-September 1985): 271-307. 9 pls.
Discusses the findings from the excavations of Hellenistic graves. Among the many objects found were four silver coins of Corinth, Boeotia, and Leukas. Notes the paucity of coins in these graves. The coins are clearly earlier than the pottery found in the graves.

710 **Petitot-Biehler, Claire Yvonne, and Paul Bernard.** "Trésor de Monnaies Grecques et Greco-Bactriennes Trouveé à Aï Khanoum (Afghanistan): Note sur le Signification Historique de la Trouvaille." *Revue Numismatique* (France) 6th ser., 17 (1975): 23-69. 6 pls. [CS 3267]

711 **Pichikyan, I.** "Rebirth of the Oxus Treasure: Second Part of the Oxus Treasure from the Miho Museum Collection." *Ancient Civilization* 4 (1997): 306-83.
A lost portion of the famous Oxus Treasure is said to be in a Japanese museum. [Also see Bellinger "Coins from the Oxus Treasure" above].

712 **Pollak, Phyllis.** "A Bithynian Hoard of the First Century B.C." *Museum Notes* 16 (1970): 45-56. 10 pls. [CS 3270]
Catalogues and discusses a hoard of fifty-four tetradrachms found in Bithynia in Turkey, ca. 1928. Includes royal issues of the Kingdoms of Pontus and Bithynia and civic issues of Heracleia Pontica and Byzantium.

713 **Preka, Kalliopi, and Shpresa Gjongecaj.** "Le Trésor de Corfu, 1997." *Liber Amicorum Tony Hackens*. Edited by G. Moucharte, M. B. Borba Florenzano, F. de Callataÿ, P. Marchetti, L. Smolderen, and P. Yannopoulos. Numismatica Lovaniensia 20. Louvain-la-Neuve: Université Catholique de Louvain, 2007. Pages 365 ff.
The authors publish a silver hoard from Corfu buried ca. 270 B.C.

714 **Price, Martin J.** "The Coins." *The Sanctuary of Hemithea at Kastabos*. Edited by J. M. Cook and W. H. Plommer. Cambridge: University Press, 1966. Pages 66-71.
A summary of the coins found during the excavation of a Greek sanctuary in the south-west corner of the mainland of Asia Minor opposite Rhodes—once known as the Carian Chersonese. The excavations took place in 1959-1960. This is the first Greek temple of any size uncovered in that part of Asia Minor. Price summarizes the general finds and the 175 coins found in the earth fill below the floor of the cella. The coins suggest a date of deposit around 300 B.C.

715 ——— "Coins from Some Deposits in the South Stoa at Corinth." *Hesperia* 36, no. 4 (October-December 1967): 347-88. 2 pls.
Lists and describes the coins found in five separate deposits from the South Stoa at Corinth. Includes coins from seventy-nine mints and monarchs. The coins provide evidence that Corinth had ceased to issue autonomous coins by ca. 200 B.C., and for the next fifty years, relied considerably on the coins of Sicyon. Presents a full catalogue of the coins.

716 ——— "Greek Coin Hoards in the British Museum." *Numismatic Chronicle* 7th ser., 9 (1969): 1-14. 4 pls. Also appeared in *Numismatic Report* (Cyprus) 6 (1975): 43-51.
"The coins from five hoards are published: the two Dali hoards from Cyprus (*Noe* 297); the Larnaca hoard (*Noe* 600), including supplementary material from Berlin; the Salonica find (*Noe* 898 = *Noe* 631); the Maeander Valley hoard (*Noe* 637); the Urfa hoard (*Noe* 1147), including supplementary material from the American Numismatic Society." [M. Price, *NL* 84]

717 ——— "A Field in Western Thrace." *Coin Hoards* 2 (1976): 7. 1 pl.
Lists ten coins found in Western Thrace, buried ca. 500-480 B.C. Consists of electrum coins of Cyzicus and other uncertain mints.

718 ——— "Mit Rahineh (1860): *IGCH* 1636." *Coin Hoards* 3 (1977): 6-8. 1 pl.
Publishes casts of coins from the Mit Rahineh hoard found in 1860. The hoard was buried perhaps ca. 500 B.C.

719 ——— "The Larissa, 1968 Hoard (*IGCH* 237)." *Kraay—Mørkholm Essays: Numismatic Studies in Memory of C. M. Kraay and O. Mørkholm*. Numismatica Lovaniensia 10. Edited by G. Le Rider, G. K. Jenkins, N. Waggoner, and U. Westermark. Louvain-la-Neuve: Université Catholique de Louvain, 1989. Pages 233-43. 2 pls.
Discusses the "Sitichoro" hoard, actually found at Larissa in 1968. Most of the weight of the hoard was in the form of reduced-weight tetradrachms of King Perseus of Macedonia, and locally struck drachmae imitating the coins of Rhodes, most bearing the name ΕΡΜΙΑΣ. Lists 1092 coins from the hoard, indicating die-links. Price dates the burial of the hoard to ca. 165 B.C.

720 ——— "More from Memphis and the Syria 1989 Hoard." *Essays in Honour of Robert Carson and Kenneth Jenkins*. Edited by M. J. Price, A. M. Burnett, R. Bland. London: Spink & Son, 1993. Pages 31-5. 2 pls.
Publishes a hoard found in Syria in 1989. The most important coins in the hoard are five coins with the inscription "Artaxerxes Pharaoh" in demotic script. The coin types are imitations of the Athenian owl coinage. These coins are connected with the presence in Egypt of Artaxerxes III Ochus following his successful campaign to regain Egypt for the Persian empire in 343 B.C. Another coin in the hoard links the demotic coinage with the Aramaic issues in the name of Sabakes, satrap of Egypt who died at the battle of Issus in 333 B.C. The hoard includes other Athenian owl-type coins—whether they were struck at Athens or are imitations is unknown. The hoard was most likely buried ca. 333 B.C. Concludes with a catalogue of the 164 coins in the hoard.

721 **Price, Martin J., and Nancy M. Waggoner.** *Archaic Greek Coinage: The Asyut Hoard*. London: V. C. Vecchi and Sons, 1975. 143 pp., 36 pls., map. [CS 3272]
Describes a hoard of about 900 silver coins from the archaic period which was discovered in Egypt in 1969. Focuses on the implications of the hoard evidence upon the accepted chronology of early Greek coins. A table and brief discussion summarize the contents and conclusions drawn from other important hoards of archaic coinage. A catalogue of 873 of the Asyut coins follows, arranged by city and incorporating a substantial amount of commentary on the implications of each city's coins on the chronology of Greek coinage in general. Most of the coins are photographed. Concludes with a discussion of the chronological anomalies created by the authors' interpretation of the hoard evidence. A down-dating of the previously accepted chronology is called for in many instances. [Reviewed by C. M. Kraay in *Journal of Hellenic Studies* 97 (1977): 230-1, by L. Breglia in *Annali del Istituto Italiano di Numismatica* 21-22 (1974-75): 231-7, by R. R. Holloway in *Gnomon* 50, no. 6 (October 1978): 597-600, by D. Gerin in *Revue Numismatique* (France) 6th ser., 20 (1978): 175-7, and by J. H. Kroll in *American Journal of Archaeology* 83, no. 3 (July 1979): 359-60. Also see Cahn "Asuit" above, and Kraay "Some Comments on Chronology" above].

722 **Prokopov, Ilya.** "Again on the Kolyo Marinovo Coin Hoard." *Studia in Honorem Alexandri Fo*. Thracia 11. Sofia, 1995. Pages 451-4. Illus.

723 **Prokopov, Ilja, and François de Callataÿ.** "A Late Hellenistic Hoard from South-West Bulgaria (Area of Gotse Deltchev)." *Numismatic Chronicle* 158 (1998): 228-36. 5 pls.
Describes a hoard found in 1995 in South-West Bulgaria containing Athenian New Style tetradrachms and Thasian-type tetradrachms. Forty-eight coins are catalogued here. The hoard was buried ca. 70 B.C.

724   **Prokopov, Ilya, and Dochka Vladimirova-Aladzova.** "On the Problem of Coin Circulation in Dobroudja during the 2nd – 1st Century B.C." *Numismatic and Sphragistic Contributions to Ancient and Mediaeval History of Dobroudja.* Proceedings of the International Symposium in Dobrich/Dobroudja 12. Edited by S. Torbatov and V. Yotov. Dobroudja, 1995. Pages 51-6.

725   **Rahmani, Levi Y.** "Descriptions of the Coins." *Excavations at Ramat Rahel: Seasons 1959 and 1960.* Rome: Centro di Studi Semitici, 1962. Pages 93-100. [CS 3274]
Describes the coins found during excavations by the University of Rome and the Hebrew University of Jerusalem at Ramat Rahel in Israel.

726   ——— "Descriptions of the Coins." *Excavations at Ramat Rahel, Seasons 1961 and 1962.* Rome: Centro di Studi Semitici, 1964. Pages 107-17. [CS 3275]
Describes the coins found during excavations by the University of Rome and the Hebrew University of Jerusalem at Ramat Rahel in Israel. Includes a few Ptolemaic, Seleucid, and Judean coins. Includes coins of Abdissares and Xerxes, kings of Sophene.

727   **Ravel, Oscar E.** "Corinthian Hoard from Chiliomodi." *Transactions of the International Numismatic Congress Organized and Held in London by the Royal Numismatic Society, June 30-July 3, 1936.* Edited by J. Allan, H. Mattingly, and E. S. G. Robinson. London: B. Quaritch, 1938. Pages 98-108. 3 pls.
Discusses a hoard of a large number of late Corinthian staters and drachms, some staters of Leukas, and twenty tetradrachms and twelve drachms of Ptolemy I found in Chiliomodi (south of Corinth). This hoard, combined with the Arta hoard [see Ravel *Corinthian Hoards (Corinth and Arta)* under CORINTHIA], forms almost a complete sequence of the last pegasi of Corinth. Ravel lists the coins, along with an indication of the state of preservation of each. Comments on the sequence and chronology of issues. Concludes that during the Ptolemaic domination, the circulation of the local currency was still normal in Corinth. The Ptolemaic coins were most likely only used to pay the Ptolemaic troops.

728   **Raven, E. J. P.** "The Hierapytna Hoard of Greek and Roman Coins." *Numismatic Chronicle* 5th ser., 18 (1938): 133-58. 1 pl.
Raven discusses a hoard found at Gierapetra (the ancient Hierapytna) in Crete containing Cretan silver coins of the latest period, New Style tetradrachms of Athens, cistophori, and Roman Republican denarii. Presents a catalogue of 363 of the coins. Suggests the hoard was buried between 44-42 B.C. Discusses each group of hoard coins and discusses some Cretan imitations of Athenian coins. [Also see Oeconomides and Kleiner "Hierapytna Hoard" above].

729   **Reade, Julian.** "A Hoard of Silver Currency from Achaemenid Babylon." *Iran* 24 (1986): 79-87.
The author re-examines a hoard found in 1882 in Babylonia (*IGCH* 1747) which included coins, cut coins, and other silver objects, formerly referred to as a "silversmith's hoard." The hoard is dated to the early fourth century B.C. Appendix 1 is "Analysis of Silver and Gold Items in a Hoard Found at Babylon" by M. J. Hughes (pp. 87-8), and Appendix 2 is "Preliminary Note on Analysis of *Sigloi* in a Hoard Found in Babylon" by M. R. Cowell (p. 89).

730   ——— "Three Hoards from Babylonia in the British Museum." *Coin Hoards, Volume VIII: Greek Hoards.* Edited by U. Wartenberg, M. J. Price, and K. A. McGregor. London: Royal Numismatic Society, 1994. Pages 88-9.
Brief description of three hoards (*Coin Hoards VIII*, nos. 90, 552, and 556) excavated in Babylonia, 1879-82, on behalf of the British Museum: (1) c. 385 B.C., 23 silver coins; (2) A.D. 45, 1200 Parthian coins; and (3) c. A.D. 183, 35 Parthian and Sasanian coins.

731   **Robinson, David M.** "A Preliminary Report on the Excavations at Olynthos." *American Journal of Archaeology* 33 (1929): 53-76.
"On pp. 73-5 the coins found in these excavations are listed. More than half were of the Chalcidian League, and the rest included a plated coin of Athens, coins of Cersobleptes and Cetriporis, and a tetradrachm of Sermyle. The worn state of a coin of Antoninus Pius reminds the writer that Napoleon I had to issue an edict against the use of such pieces." [J. R. Jones, *NIAJAH*]

732   ——— *Excavations at Olynthus, Part 3: The Coins Found at Olynthus in 1928.* Studies in Archaeology, No. 11. Baltimore: The Johns Hopkins Press, 1931. 129 pp., 28 pls.
A catalogue of 1187 coins, almost all Greek, mainly from Chalcidic cities and Macedonian kings. Eighty-five of the coins are silver. The coins now reside in the National Numismatic Museum in Athens. [Also see Robinson "Excavations at Olynthus, Part 6" below, and Robinson and Clement "Excavations at Olynthus, Part 9" under MACEDONIAN CITIES AND TRIBES].

733   ——— "The Residential Districts and the Cemeteries at Olynthos." *American Journal of Archaeology* 36 (1932): 118-38. 4 pls.
"On pp. 134-6 the coins discovered in 1931 are briefly described. More than half belonged to the Chalcidian League, one hoard of these coins being discovered still piled up on a table. Others came from a very wide variety of sources, and this indicates the extent of the trade carried on by this city, even as far away as Tarentum. A forgery of a Persian coin is dated to the time of the satrap's revolt." [J. R. Jones, *NIAJAH*]

734   ——— *Excavations at Olynthus, Part 6: The Coins Found at Olynthus in 1931.* Studies in Archaeology, No. 19. Baltimore: The Johns Hopkins Press, 1933. 11 pp., 29 pls.
A catalogue of 1226 coins, eighty-five of which are silver. Includes coins of the cities of the Chalcidice, cities and kings of Macedonia, Thrace, Thessaly, Illyria, Euboea, Attica, the Peloponnese, Asia Minor and the Islands, and Crete. [Also see Robinson "Excavations at Olynthus, Part 3" above, and Robinson and Clement "Excavations at Olynthus, Part 9" under MACEDONIAN CITIES AND TRIBES].

735   ——— "The Third Campaign at Olynthos." *American Journal of Archaeology* 39 (1935): 210-47. Illus.
"On pp. 242-7 and fig. 44 the coins found during this season are briefly described and illustrated. The majority belongs to the Chalcidian League and neighboring cities, which shows that foreign trade did not develop greatly until the Hellenistic period. A group of Chalcidian coins bearing the name of the magistrate Dikaios is defended as being genuine, in spite of their coarse style." [J. R. Jones, *NIAJAH*]

736   ——— "The Fourth Campaign at Olynthos." *American Journal of Archaeology* 43 (1939): 48-77. Illus.
"On pp. 76-7 the coins found during the 1938 season are briefly listed; they include a small hoard of unstruck flans." [J. R. Jones, *NIAJAH*]

737   ——— "The Alexander Hoard of Megalopolis." *Museum Notes* 4 (1950): 13-28. 6 pls. [CS 3279]

The author examines a hoard of forty silver coins found ca. 1947 at Megalopolis. The coins include Alexander tetradrachms from Amphipolis, Pella, Babylon, Megalopolis, Sicyon, Aradus, and some uncertain mints. Also includes tetradrachms of Lysimachus from Sardis (?) and Amphipolis, tetradrachms of Ptolemy II from Tyre and uncertain mints, and two octadrachms of Arsinoe II. The hoard, buried ca. 222 B.C., suggests Egyptian aid was provided to Megalopolis and the Peloponnesos.

738 ——— "A New Peloponnesian Hoard of Alexander and Ptolemaic Silver Coins." *American Journal of Archaeology* 54 (1950): 259.
This brief summary of a paper presented at a conference discusses a hoard discovered at Megalopolis. The hoard was more fully published in *Museum Notes* in 1950. [See Robinson "The Alexander Hoard" above].

739 ——— "An Unpublished Hoard of Silver Coins from Carystus." *American Journal of Archaeology* 55 (1951): 151-2.
A brief summary of a paper presented at a conference. "Describes a hoard in the possession of the author, containing coins of various mints from the fifth to the third century, some of which are briefly discussed." [J. R. Jones, *NIAJAH*]

740 ——— "Chapter 5: Coins from Olynthus and Mecyberna, 1938." *Excavations at Olynthus, Part 14: Terracottas, Lamps, and Coins Found in 1934 and 1938*. Studies in Archaeology, No. 39. Baltimore: The Johns Hopkins Press, 1952. Pages 403-29. 5 pls.
Discusses the 635 coins found in the excavations at Olynthus, including 555 from various cities in Olynthus, 32 from Mecyberna, 34 unidentifiable coins, and 14 blank bronze flans. The evidence of the coins suggests that the port town of Mecyberna was completely abandoned in 316 B.C. The weights and diameters of the flans are listed in a table. Some of the coins are catalogued here.

741 ——— *A Hoard of Silver Coins from Carystus*. Numismatic Notes and Monographs, No. 124. New York: American Numismatic Society, 1952. 62 pp., 6 pls. [CS 3280]
Describes a hoard of ninety-two silver coins found near Mount Ocha, the ancient site of Carystus. Lists thirty-seven coins of Carystus, thirty-seven coins of Euboea, a few coins of Athens and Macedonia, and one Seleucid tetradrachm. Discusses the die sequences for Carystian and Euboean coins. [Reviewed by G. K. Jenkins in *Numismatic Chronicle* 6th ser., 13 (1953): 164-5].

742 **Robinson, Edward S. G.** "A Find of Archaic Greek Coins from the Delta." *Numismatic Chronicle* 5th ser., 10 (1930): 93-106. 2 pls. [CS 3282]
Publishes thirty-nine coins from a hoard found in Egypt including a completely new type (triskeles/floral pattern) of uncertain origin, an octadrachm of Abdera, a fragmentary stater of Terone, a coin bearing the Thraco-Macedonian sphinx, and a stater of Phaselis with its reverse perhaps reminiscent of hieroglyphs. The hoard was probably buried shortly after 485 B.C. [Also see E. Newell "Addition to the Delta Hoard" above and Robinson's "Further Notes" below].

743 ——— "Further Notes on the Delta (Benha El-Asl) Hoard." *Numismatic Chronicle* 5th ser., 11 (1931): 68-71.
Publishes and briefly discusses thirty-one fragmentary coins from the "Delta Hoard" (see above).

744 ——— "Coins of Petra, Etc." *Numismatic Chronicle* 5th ser., 16 (1936): 288-91. 1 pl.
Publishes eleven coins found on the site of Petra. Includes coins of Nabatea (Malichus II and Shaqilath II), Petra (?) (Roman period), and four of uncertain attribution.

745 ——— "A Find of Archaic Coins from South-West Asia Minor." *Numismatic Chronicle* 5th ser., 16 (1936): 265-80. 1 pl.
Discusses a hoard of 144 coins (*IGCH* 1180) found near the Caro-Lycian border. Most of the coins are attributed to Caria (uncertain cities). Some of the coins may belong to Aphrodisias or Olbia. The hoard also contained coins of Phaselis. Robinson concentrates on the problems of attributing the coins. [Also see Troxell "Winged Carians" under CARIA].

746 ——— "Coins from the Excavations at Al-Mina (1936)." *Numismatic Chronicle* 5th ser., 17 (1937): 182-96. 1 pl., illus.
Discusses the coins excavated at Posidium, Syria, in 1936. The coins seem to be representative of those in circulation in the area. Three hoards of silver coins were found, each probably buried ca. 420-375 B.C. The first contained fifty-four fractions of Aradus and Sidon. The second contained thirty-five coins including coins of Aradus and imitations of Athenian coins. The third included forty-three coins of Aradus, Sidon, and Athens, as well as Athenian imitations and two of uncertain origin. Robinson also lists other coins found including Greek bronze coins and later coinages. Also illustrates (line drawings) two bronze coins of Posidium in the British Museum. These are the only two known coins of this city. [Also see Alischan "Posidium in Coele-Syria" and Hill "Posidium in Syria" under SYRIA—AUTONOMOUS CITIES].

747 ——— "A Hoard from 'Sidon' [Beni-Hassan]." *Numismatic Chronicle* 5th ser., 17 (1937): 197-9.
Discusses an early drachm of Athens with a crescent moon on the reverse. The moon is not usually present on these early issues and the author suggests this piece is a local imitation. Also discusses some fragments of silver ingots which probably circulated as a bullion currency. The coin and the bullion were from the Beni-Hasan hoard previously published by J. G. Milne (see Milne "The Beni Hasan Coin-Hoard" above). [Also see Milne "A Hoard of Coins from Egypt" above].

748 ——— "Greek Coins Found in the Cyrenaica." *Numismatic Chronicle* 6th ser., 4 (1944): 105-13. 1 pl.
Publishes a list of 103 coins found in Cyrene in Northern Africa. Discusses a few of the more important pieces.

749 ——— "Greek Coins from the Pyramids." *Numismatic Chronicle* 6th ser., 10 (1950): 298.
"A find from the excavations at Giza consists of an earthenware jar containing two scarabs, stone and gold beads and two coins of Sidon. The last, a double and a half-shekel with the galley and king in car types, are of the fourth century B.C. Since at that time coins as such had no significance in Egypt, their former owner must have valued them as mere bullion." [M. Thompson, *NL* 22]

750 ——— "A 'Silversmith's' Hoard from Mesopotamia." *Iraq* (England) 12 (1950): 44-51. 2 pls.
Discusses objects found during the excavation of what had been described as the shop of a "worker in metals," including coins of Athens, Aegina, Samos, Lycia, Aspendos, Salamis, Arados, Sidon, Tyre, and Persian sigloi. The coins are illustrated and described. Robinson dates the hoard to the first quarter of the fourth century B.C. Suggests this was merely a hoard of currency and bullion rather than raw materials for a craftsman. Lists other hoards of similar coins. Concludes that "coined silver, treated as bullion, was a staple export of Greece to the Persian Empire."

751 ——— "Two Greek Coin Hoards." *Numismatic Chronicle* 6th ser., 20 (1960): 31-6. 1 pl.
Discusses the Smyrna (Bairkali) Hoard and the Delta Hoard. "A hoard of twenty silver coins, from a clay 'lydion' found in a stratified deposit of the early years of the fifth century B.C., contains coins attributed to Smyrna? (1-14), Croeseid types (15-16) and Persian types (17-20). The second hoard of ca. 375-350 B.C., discovered in the Egyptian Delta nearly twenty years ago, is noteworthy because of its provenance and composition: Athenian coins and Persian sigloi are absent. The relative number of Phoenician pieces might suggest that it had belonged to a merchant from the Eastern coastal strip of the Mediterranean." [J. Healy, *NL* 60]

752 ——— "A Hoard of Archaic Greek Coins from Anatolia." *Numismatic Chronicle* 7th ser., 1 (1961): 107-17. 3 pls. [CS 3286]
"The contents of a hoard of thirty-eight silver coins recently acquired by the Ashmolean Museum are listed as follows: one tetradrachm of Zancle (Samians), one Akanthos tetradrachm, one Abdera octadrachm, nineteen Athenian tetradrachms, ten Aeginetan staters, one Pseudaeginetic staters, one Corinthian stater, one Parion drachm, one Chios didrachm, one Carian double siglos (uncertain, possibly Mylasa), one Persian siglos. The hoard was found some years ago not far from the Pamphylian-Cilician border and was probably buried ca. 480 B.C. Its extreme diversity enables the author to comment upon a number of different archaic coinages." [I. Merker, *NL* 65]. [Also see W. Wallace "New Anatolian Hoard" below].

753 ——— "A Hoard of Greek Coins from Southern Anatolia?" *Revue Numismatique* (France) 6th ser., 15 (1973): 229-37. Illus.
"A group of about ten coins dating to the last quarter of the sixth century B.C. may have been found near Adana, in Cilicia; it contained two issues each of Myrcinus(?), Lycia and Cyprus and one each of the Thraco-Macedonian region, Lete, southwestern Anatolia and Dicaea (Thrace)." [E. Robinson, *NL* 94]

754 **Robinson, Henry S.** "Excavations at Corinth, 1960." *Hesperia* 31, no. 2 (April-June 1962): 94-133. 16 pls.
"Included in the report is a brief section, prepared by Robert Stroud, devoted to the coins found during the excavations. The earliest specimen was a diobol of Leucas struck late in the fifth century. There were, as expected, several coins of Corinth; also Roman, Byzantine, early modern pieces and a hoard of 196 minimi (Constantine II to Anastasius) buried before 498. Single finds of Corinthian coins—a bronze issue and two silver obols—were made in three graves on the southern slope of the Acropolis." [I. Merker, *NL* 64]

755 **Rotroff, S. I.** "Coins and Stratigraphy." *Numismatic Archaeology/Archaeological Numismatics: Proceedings of an International Conference held to Honour Dr. Mando Oeconomides in Athens 1995.* Oxbow Monographs 75. Edited by K. Sheedy and C. Papageorgiadou-Banis. Oxford: Oxbow Books and The Australian Archaeological Institute at Athens, 1997. Pages 8-16.
Discusses the usefulness of numismatic evidence in the dating of archaeological sites. Points out that the rarity of gold and silver coins in excavations means that coin evidence is rarely available before the introduction of bronze coinage. And only a small percentage of bronze finds are likely to be identifiable. Nonetheless, coins can sometimes add important information for the dating of a site. Rotroff calls for greater cooperation between archaeologists and numismatists.

756 **Royal Numismatic Society.** *Coin Hoards.* London: Royal Numismatic Society, 1975+. [CS 16126]
This publication recorded new hoards as they entered museums or passed through the coin trade, and provided a bibliography on hoards published or discussed during the previous year. Divided into seven groups: Greek, Celtic, Roman, Byzantine, Oriental, Mediaeval and Modern British and Irish, Mediaeval and Modern Continental. Within each group, hoards are listed chronologically according to the approximate date of the latest coins. Each entry gives the find-spot, the date of the latest coins, brief details of contents, and the present whereabouts of the coins. Includes essays giving extensive commentary on some of the hoards and illustrating some of the coins. After the 1994 volume, annual updates were incorporated into *The Numismatic Chronicle*. Occasional new volumes are published as warranted.

> *Vol. I* (1975). 124 pp. Includes 131 Greek and 19 Celtic hoards.
> *Vol. II* (1976). 161 pp. Includes 154 Greek and 28 Celtic hoards.
> *Vol. III* (1977). 203 pp. Includes 97 Greek and 17 Celtic hoards.
> *Vol. IV* (1978). 180 pp. Includes 86 Greek and 10 Celtic hoards.
> *Vol. V* (1979). 160 pp. Includes 65 Greek and 11 Celtic hoards.
> *Vol. VI* (1981). 188 pp. Includes 56 Greek and 8 Celtic hoards.
> *Vol. VII* (1985). 456 pp. Includes 162 Greek and 25 Celtic hoards.
> *Vol. VIII* (1994). 113 pp., 87 pls. Edited by U. Wartenberg, M. J. Price, and K. A. McGregor. Devoted entirely to hoards of Greek coins. Lists 604 hoards. [See 836 Wartenberg, Price, and McGregor below].
> "Coin Hoards 1995." *Numismatic Chronicle* 155 (1995): 324-5. Includes 11 hoards containing ancient coins.
> "Coin Hoards 1996." *Numismatic Chronicle* 156 (1996): 249-88. Includes 127 hoards containing ancient coins.
> "Coin Hoards 1997." *Numismatic Chronicle* 157 (1997): 213-29. Includes 44 hoards containing ancient coins.
> "Coin Hoards 1998." *Numismatic Chronicle* 158 (1998). Does not list any hoards of Greek coins.
> "Coin Hoards 1999." *Numismatic Chronicle* 159 (1999): 339-57. Does not list any hoards of Greek coins. A few Celtic coins are listed.
> "Coin Hoards 2000." *Numismatic Chronicle* 160 (2000): 309-67. Does not list any hoards of Greek coins.
> "Coin Hoards 2001." *Numismatic Chronicle* 161 (2001): 329-59. Includes 29 hoards containing Greek coins.
> "Coin Hoards 2002." *Numismatic Chronicle* 162 (2002): 385-96. Includes 45 hoards, three of which contained Greek coins.
> *Vol. IX* (2002). 308 pp., 66 pls. Edited by A. Meadows and U. Wartenberg. Devoted entirely to hoards of Greek coins. [See 665 Meadows and Wartenberg above].
> "Coin Hoards 2003." *Numismatic Chronicle* 163 (2003): 335-75. Lists 29 ancient hoards.
> "Coin Hoards 2004." *Numismatic Chronicle* 164 (2004): 249-327. Lists 231 ancient hoards.
> "Coin Hoards 2005." *Numismatic Chronicle* 165 (2005): 301-13. Lists 52 ancient hoards.
> "Coin Hoards 2006." *Numismatic Chronicle* 166 (2006): 365-414. Lists 56 ancient hoards.
> "Coin Hoards 2007." *Numismatic Chronicle* 167 (2007): 243-85. Lists 57 ancient hoards.
> "Coin Hoards 2008." *Numismatic Chronicle* 168 (2008): 383-451. Lists 47 ancient hoards.
> "Coin Hoards 2009." *Numismatic Chronicle* 169 (2009): 331-400. Lists 61 ancient hoards.
> "Coin Hoards 2010." *Numismatic Chronicle* 170 (2010): 407-51. Lists 58 ancient hoards.
> *Vol. X* (2010). 281 pp., 67 pls. Edited by Oliver Hoover, Andrew Meadows, and Ute Wartenberg Kagan. Devoted entirely to hoards of Greek coins. [See 594 Hoover, Meadows, and Kagan above].

757 **Russeva, Boriana.** "Coin Hoard from Rakitovo, the Peshtera District (*IGCH* 827)." *Macedonian Numismatic Journal* (Macedonia) 3 (1999): 17-27. Illus.

"In 1920 the National Archaeological Museum in Sofia purchased for its collection eleven tetradrachms from a hoard from the village of Rakitovo in the area of Peshtera in the Rhodopi mountains. Mentioned in *IGCH* as no. 827, it contains four specimens of Alexander III the Great (two of Amphipolis and one of Marathos and Carne), one of Lysimachus (Heraclea Pontica, ca. 288/7-282/1), one of Demetrius Poliorcetes (Pella, ca. 289-288), one of Antioch I (Seleuceia on the Tigris), two of Seleucus I (Seleuceia on the Tigris, ca. 295-292), Antioch II (Milassa, ca. 197-190), and one of Antiochus III the Great (Tarsus, ca. 197-187). The coin find is similar to a few already published hoards from Asia Minor and Syria with burial dates between 190 and 188 B.C." [B. Russeva, *NL* 143]

758 **Rynearson, Paul.** "Partitioned Coins: Hoard Evidence for Fractional Denominations." *SAN—Journal of the Society for Ancient Numismatics* 12, no. 4 (winter 1981-2): 71-3.
Eleven Greek coins, each of them cut into fractional pieces, are described and pictured. Most are from the Asyut hoard. Weights are given and the denomination they may have represented are listed. The use of cut-coins in commerce as small change is discussed.

759 **Sallery, Robert D. H.** "Some Preliminary Observations on the 'Leontini' Hoard." *Seaby Coin and Medal Bulletin* 825 (November 1987): 308-11. Illus.; 826 (December 1987): 340-2. Illus.
An attempt to "reconstitute" a hoard which was dispersed before it could be documented and studied. Presents some preliminary observations and conclusions based on coins that could be identified as coming from the hoard. The hoard consisted of about 700-800 Sicilian coins, primarily from Leontini and Syracuse. Most of the coins were minted ca. 475-425 B.C.

760 **Saryan, Leon A.** "The Sarnakounk Hoard: Armenia in the First Century B.C." *The Numismatist* 105, no. 4 (April 1992): 497 ff. Illus.
Describes a hoard of silver coins found in Armenia in 1945. Of the 373 coins recovered after dispersal of the hoard, 148 are Hellenistic silver coins and 225 are Roman Republican silver coins. The dates of the coins range from the fourth century B.C. to about 31 B.C., with most of the coins from the first century B.C. The Hellenistic coins include Seleucid, Phoenician, Pergamene, Parthian, Cappadocian, Pontic, and Armenian pieces. Discusses the evidence provided for coin circulation in Armenia and the ancient trade routes, and shows that Armenia had wide international contacts during the Artaxiad period.

761 **Schaeffer, C. F. A.** "Une Trouvaille de Monnaies Archaiques Grecques à Ras Shamra." *Mélanges Syriens Offerts à Monsieur René Dussaud*. Volume 1. Paris: Librairie Orientaliste Paul Geuthner, 1939. Pages 461-78.

762 **Scheers, Simone.** "Catalogue of the Coins." *Sagalassos II*. Edited by M. Waelkens and J. Poblommes. Leuven: Leuven University Press, 1993. Pages 249-60. *III* (1995): 307-23; *IV* (1997): 315-50; *V* (2000): 509-49.

763 **Schwabacher, Willy.** "A Find from the Piraeus." *Numismatic Chronicle* 5th ser., 19 (1939): 162-6. 1 pl.
Discusses fifteen coins found near Piraeus in Attica. Suggests their burial was related to the siege of the Piraeus by Sulla in 87-86 B.C. Includes two coins of Mithradates VI and thirteen Athenian New Style tetradrachms. Lists and discusses the coins.

764 **Sebring, Thomas H.** "Ancient Coins from the Sea." *Numismatist* 116, no. 9 (September 2003): 47-9. Illus.
A general discussion of ancient coins found at the sites of ancient shipwrecks. Illustrates a Ptolemaic tetradrachm recovered from a ship which sank off the Phoenician coast about 77 BC.

765 **Sellers, O. R.** "Coins of the 1960 Excavations at Shechem." *Biblical Archaeologist* 25, no. 3 (September 1962): 87-96. 3 pls.
Ninety Ptolemaic and Seleucid coins were found during the excavations, some of which are illustrated. The coins helped to date the site.

766 **Seltman, Charles T.** *A Hoard from Side*. Numismatic Notes and Monographs, No. 22. New York: American Numismatic Society, 1924. 20 pp., 3 pls.
A hoard of twenty-six silver coins, a ring, and a bracelet was found in 1922 near Side in Pamphylia. Seltman here catalogues ten of the coins as well as the ring and bracelet. The coins represent a circulation hoard and include coins of Athens, Corinth, Side, Aspendos, and Citium, and are primarily fifth century B.C. issues.

767 ———. "A Note on the Survival of Ancient Coins." *Numismatic Chronicle* 5th ser., 5 (1925): 121-4.
A dispute over the purpose of the minting of Athenian decadrachms leads Seltman to comment on possible survival rates of ancient coins.

768 ———. "The Earliest Hoarded Coins." *Spink Numismatic Circular* 63, no. 4 (April 1955): 167-8. [CS 3290]
"The twenty-four electrum coins found together in the British Museum excavations at Ephesus, together with other coins, singly or in groups from the site, appear to have 'faded into oblivion' in the Museum at Istanbul—a fact which seems to confuse the evidence as to whether the base hoard was buried shortly after 652 B.C. or in the reign of King Alyattes (615-560)." [C. Vermeule, *NL* 33]

769 **Seyrig, Henri.** "Trésor Monétaires de Nisibe." *Revue Numismatique* (France) 5th ser., 17 (1955): 87-8, 111-28. 1 pl.
Describes a hoard of 715 copper coins. Six hundred twenty-four of these are attributed to various kings during the period 147-31 B.C.

770 ———. "Monnaies Grecques des Fouilles de Doura et d'Antioche." *Revue Numismatique* (France) 6th ser., 1 (1958): 171-81.

771 **Shear, Josephine P.** "Analytical Table of Coins." *Hesperia* 5 (1936): 123-50.
"10,479 coins from the Agora excavations which had been identified and catalogued by July 1, 1935, are listed. They include not only ancient coins, but a number of Byzantine, Frankish and Venetian ones. Two Attic tetradrachms of the fifth and fourth centuries B.C. were found to be plated. Where necessary the types and symbols occurring on the coins of Athens, her cleruchies and Eleusis, are noted for the sake of identification. As might be expected, there is a high proportion of bronze coinage." [J. R. Jones, *NIAJAH*]. [Also see J. H. Kroll "A Chronology of Early Athenian Bronze Coinage" under ATTICA—GENERAL WORKS. Based on new evidence, Kroll criticizes Shear's dating of Athenian bronze coinage as "arbitrary and unreliable."]

772 **Sheedy, Kenneth A.** "Late Archaic Hoards in the Cyclades and Some Thoughts on a Regional Pattern of Trade." *Numismatic Archaeology/Archaeological Numismatics: Proceedings of an International Conference held to Honour Dr. Mando Oeconomides in*

Athens 1995. Oxbow Monographs 75. Edited by K. Sheedy and C. Papageorgiadou-Banis. Oxford: Oxbow Books and The Australian Archaeological Institute at Athens, 1997. Pages 107-17. 1 pl.

The scale and importance of mercantile activity in the Greek world has been a subject of controversy. Sheedy discusses the appearance of well organized trade routes and the introduction of local silver coinage by a variety of Greek and non-Greek states. He re-examines the archaic coin hoards found in the Cyclades and considers their value as evidence for the existence of a route between the southern Cyclades and southwest Asia Minor. Sheedy proposes a broad division of archaic and early classical hoards on the basis of the origin of the coins they contain: "diversified" and "accordant" hoards. A diversified hoard contains coins from a range of mints in a number of different regions. An accordant hoard mostly contains coins from only one state and a few of its near neighbors, or from several cities within the same region. Summarizes the geographical areas where these two types of hoards are found, and discusses the characteristics of a number of hoards found in the Cyclades. Suggests that the three great Cycladic hoards—the Cycladic Hoard (*IGCH* 6), the Santorin Hoard (*IGCH* 7), and the Melos Hoard (*IGCH* 8)—reflect the existence of trade in marble from Naxos and Paros to Caria and Lycia.

773 **Sheedy, Kenneth A., Robert Carson, and Alan Walmsley.** *Pella in Jordan (1979-1990): The Coins.* Adapa Monograph Series 1. Edited by Kate da Costa. Sydney: Adapa, The Near Eastern Archaeological Foundation, University of Sydney, 2001. 186 pp., 15 pls.

Contains the catalogue and associated commentaries for the 1106 coins from the University of Sydney's excavations at Pella in Jordan from 1979 to 1990. The material includes Ptolemaic, Seleucid, Hellenistic city, Jewish, Roman Imperial, Greek Imperial, Byzantine, Umayyad, Abbasid, and Mamluk issues. The volume also includes a short introduction to the site and concordance of mints, hoards, findspots, and registration numbers to locate the coin corpus within the overall publication plan of the excavation project. [Reviewed by Julian Bowsher in *Numismatic Chronicle* 162 (2002): 450-1].

774 **Sheridan, Walter W.** "From Cyzicus to Tyre: Numismatic Evidence on an Ancient Ship's Trip, circa 400 B.C." *The Numismatist* 84, no. 8 (August 1971): 1127-33. Illus.

The author recounts Alexander's siege of Tyre in 332 B.C. Examines a hoard of thirty-three coins discovered near Beirut in 1966. The coins were all fractions, none exceeding 1/12 stater, and were minted at Tyre, Sidon, Byblos, and other nearby cities. A detailed listing of the coins is provided in tables which accompany the text. The author concludes the coins belonged to a sailor who traveled the Phoenician coast.

775 **Sjöqvist, Erik.** "Excavations at Morgantina (Serra Orlando) 1959: Preliminary Report 4." *American Journal of Archaeology* 64, no. 2 (April 1960): 125-35; and "Excavations at Morgantina (Serra Orlando) 1961: Preliminary Report 6." *American Journal of Archaeology* 66, no. 2 (April 1962): 135-43. [CS 3292]

Describes the excavations undertaken in 1959 and 1961. Finds included a few Syracusan coins (bronze issues of Hieron II). The coins help date some of the other finds. [Also see several related articles by Stillwell below].

776 **Souchleris, L.** "Numismatic Evidence from the City of Hephaistia, Lemnos: New Coin Finds from the Theatre Excavations." *Coins in the Aegean Islands. Proceedings of the Fifth Scientific Meeting, Mytilene, 16-29 September 2006. Volume 1: Ancient Times.* Obolos 9. Edited by Panagiotis Tselekas. Athens: The Friends of the Numismatic Museum, 2010. Pages 59-81.

777 **Spaer, Arnold.** "A Hoard from Jericho." *Numismatic Chronicle* 7th ser., 10 (1970): 23-8. 3 pls.

"The entries in this partial catalogue of a hoard of about 200 Seleucid and Tyrian silver coins found in 1965 at Jericho are descriptive. The hoard covers the period 136-102 B.C. and consists mainly of Tyrian silver of Antiochus VII and Demetrius II (second reign), a few pieces of Cleopatra Thea with Antiochus VIII and Antiochus VIII alone, struck at Ascalon and Ace, and some autonomous issues of Tyre after 125 B.C." [A. Spaer, *NL* 85]. [Also see Spaer "A Hoard…Addenda" below].

778 ———. "A Hoard from the Qazvin Area." *Coin Hoards* 1 (1975): 36-41. 2 pls.

A partial catalogue of a hoard of at least 150 pieces, found near Teheran in 1964 or 1965. Includes many coins from the reign of Seleucus I, many from Ecbatana, and a substantial number of Alexander types. Lists eighty-eight coins, some of which are illustrated.

779 ———. "A Hoard of Seleucid Silver Coins from Jericho: Addenda." *Numismatic Chronicle* 142 (1982): 140-2.

"An additional forty-eight coins from the Jericho hoard are published (see Spaer "A Hoard from Jericho" above). These include forty-five Tyrian silver pieces of Antiochus VII and of Demetrius II, tetradrachms of Antiochus VIII struck in Ashkelon, and a pair of tetradrachms from independent Tyre." [A. Spaer, *NL* 110]

780 ———. "Two Hoards of Minor Silver." *Coins of Macedonia and Rome: Essays in Honour of Charles Hersh.* Edited by Andrew Burnett, Ute Wartenberg, and Richard Witschonke. London: Spink, 1998. Pages 103-7. 2 pls.

Lists and discusses two hoards found in or near Israel. The first contained seven silver obols and hemi-obols, mainly of Alexander types, but including one Philisto-Arabian or Samarian issue. Two of the coins may be local copies of Alexander coins. The hoard is dated to late in Alexander's reign or shortly after. The second hoard included thirty-four coins. One is an Athenian imitation; the others are fractions of what are known as 'lion staters,' generally attributed to Babylon. They may have been struck locally as imitations. The hoard is dated to ca. 320-270 B.C.

781 **Stillwell, Richard.** "Excavations at Serra Orlando 1958: Preliminary Report 3." *American Journal of Archaeology* 63, no. 2 (April 1959): 167-73. 6 pls.

"Among the coins discovered during the third season of excavations at Serra Orlando (ancient Morgantina) were 152 bronze specimens ranging from third century coins of Catana to early second century Roman asses and coins of Hieron II. An additional small hoard of nine silver coins was reported in a Lykion jar in the southern Demeter sanctuary." [*NL* 50]

782 ———. "Excavations at Morgantina (Serra Orlando) 1960: Preliminary Report 5." *American Journal of Archaeology* 65, no. 3 (July 1961): 277-81. 4 pls.

"While digging at Serra Orlando (ancient Morgantina) from April 4 to June 24, 1960, the Princeton Archaeological Expedition to Sicily uncovered the following pieces: two half coins of Hieron II cut between 214 and 211 B.C.; a hoard of eleven Syracusan coins (including one Siculo-Punic specimen) issued during the last quarter of the fourth century; thirty-five coins of the 'Hispanorum' series, and a silver decadrachm of Syracuse with signature of Euainetos." [I. Merker, *NL* 57]. [Also see Holloway "Numismatic Notes from Morgantina 2" under SICILY—SYRACUSE].

783 ——— "Excavations at Morgantina (Serra Orlando) 1966: Preliminary Report 9." *American Journal of Archaeology* 71, no. 3 (July 1967): 245-50. 2 pls. [CS 2204]

Reports on an archaeological excavation at the site of Morgantina in Sicily. A hoard of forty-four gold coins dating from the reign of Philip II to that of Pyrrhos of Epirus was found. Briefly describes the coins, which are illustrated on one of the plates. [Also see Sjöqvist "Excavations at Morgantina" above].

784 **Stillwell, Richard, and Erik Sjöqvist.** "Excavations at Serra Orlando: Preliminary Report." *American Journal of Archaeology* 61, no. 2 (April 1957): 151-9. 8 pls.

During excavations in central Sicily in 1955-1956, the Princeton Archaeological Expedition uncovered 3262 ancient coins, 1030 of which were Syracusan, and struck by Hieron II (270-215 B.C.).

785 **Strauss, Pierre.** "Un Trésor de Monnaies Hellénistique Trouvé près de Suse." *Revue Numismatique* (France) 6th ser., 13 (1971): 109-40. 7 pls. [CS 3293]

786 **Stroud, Ronald S.** "The Sanctuary of Demeter and Kore on Acrocorinth: Preliminary Report 1, 1961-1962." *Hesperia* 34, no. 1 (January-March 1965): 1-24. 11 pls.

One-hundred coins were found during the excavations, mostly bronze, and about one-third were minted at Corinth (most from the pegasos/trident series). Other Hellenistic and Roman coins were found. The evidence suggests the sanctuary had been abandoned by the end of the fourth century.

787 ——— "The Sanctuary of Demeter and Kore on Acrocorinth: Preliminary Report 2, 1964-1965." *Hesperia* 37 (1968): 299-330. 13 pls.

"The total number of coins found during the 1964-1965 excavations is 180. About one-third of the total consists of Corinthian coins struck before 140 B.C. Thirty-nine coins belong to other Greek mints of the same period. The remainder includes seventy-two Roman coins from 31 B.C. to ca. AD 400, two Byzantine bronzes of the eleventh century and one Turkish coin." [*NL* 82]

788 **Sturdivant, H. H.** "The Coins of Dura-Europus." *North American Journal of Numismatics. The Turtle* 6, no. 6 (December 1967): 309-10.

A brief summary of the history of the city of Dura in Northern Mesopotamia along with information on the coin-finds. The city was founded ca. 300 B.C. and thrived until at least AD 260. Excavations by Yale University turned-up over 14,000 Greek, Parthian, and Roman coins. [Also see Bellinger "The Coins" *Final Report VI* above].

789 **Syon, Danny.** "The Coins from Gamala." *Israel Numismatic Journal* (Israel) 12 (1992/3): 34-55. Illus.

"Excavations at this site on the western slopes of the Golan Heights yielded over 6200 coins including 3883 Hasmonean issues, 270 coins of the Herodians and the Roman procurators, 941 autonomous issues, 584 Seleucid ones, 63 others, and 428 unidentified. They are listed and partly illustrated including some rare Herodian types and two of the copper issues of the first Jewish Revolt struck at Gamala." [A. Spaer, *NL* 134]

790 ——— "Khisas." *Hadashot Archaeologioth* 112 (2000): 2-10.

"110 coins were found at this N. Galilean site covering the period from second century B.C. coins of Tyre to Mamluk issues." [A. Spaer, *NL* 144]

791 ——— "Coins from the Excavations at Khirbet esh-Shuhara." *Eretz Zafon: Studies in Galilean Archaeology.* Edited by Z. Gal. Jerusalem, 2002. Pages 122-34.

"The author presents 26 coins from the excavations of a small farm in Upper Galilee. The coins are Seleucid, Hasmonean and autonomous Tyrian issues. In addition a hoard of 22 Seleucid silver coins are described in detail, found at the site many years before the excavations. The coins in the hoard date from 148/7 to c. 140 B.C.E. and include a rare tetradrachm of Tryphon from Akko, dated year 1. The coins are analyzed in their archaeological context and a historical reconstruction of the last phases of the settlement is suggested." [D. Syon, *NL* 146]

792 **Thompson, Homer A.** "The Excavation of the Athenian Agora, Twelfth Season: 1947." *Hesperia* 17 (1948): 149-96. 33 pls., illus.

"On p. 192 the coins discovered during the season are briefly mentioned. Eight "tetrobols" of Histiaea were found together, their weights ranging from 1.47 to 2.05 gr." [J. R. Jones, *NIAJAH*]

793 **Thompson, Margaret.** "A Hoard of Greek Federal Silver." *Hesperia* 8 (1939): 116-54. 10 pls.

Discusses a hoard of 677 silver coins, probably found on the central shores of the Ionian Sea. Includes 429 coins of the twenty-two members of the Achaean League and 119 coins from Peloponnesian cities, all from the third or second centuries B.C. The other coins are from Aetolia and central Greece, from ca. 426 to 300 B.C. Presents a catalogue of the coins and a table of weights. Discusses attributions and chronology.

794 ——— "A Countermarked Hoard from Büyükçekmece." *Museum Notes* 6 (1954): 11-34. 7 pls.

The author examines coins from a hoard found on the Propontis ca. 1952 containing primarily tetradrachms of Byzantium, Calchedon, Demetrius Poliorcetes, Attalos I, early Seleucid kings, and coins with the types of Alexander and Lysimachus. Every coin has a circular countermark on the obverse: head of Apollo, head of Demeter, prow, or monogram. She presents a catalogue of eighty-four coins arranged by countermark variety. The prow mark indicates the mint of Byzantium; others may indicate Calchedon. The countermarks were applied in the later part of the third century B.C. Burial of the hoard is very tentatively placed ca. 220 B.C.

795 ——— "A Hoard from Thessaly." *Museum Notes* 11 (1964): 77-80. 2 pls. [CS 3296]

Publishes three coins—two New Style tetradrachms of Athens and one tetradrachm of Perseus—from a hoard of over 100 coins found in Thessaly in 1961 or 1962. The author determines the original hoard consisted of tetradrachms of Philip V, Thasos, Athens, and Perseus. Based on the evidence from this hoard, the dating of the spread-flan coinage of Thasos may need revision. Concludes the burial occurred during the Third Macedonian War, ca. 168 B.C.

796 ——— "A Hoard from Northern Greece." *Museum Notes* 12 (1966): 57-63. 5 pls. [CS 3297]

Discusses a hoard of thirty-six tetradrachms of the second century B.C. Eighteen are New Style Athenian; others are from Byzantium, Thasos, Philip V, Perseus, and Macedonia under the Romans. The coin of Perseus belongs to the "Andriscus" series and contains a new monogram. Thompson suggests the coin was struck during the later part of the reign of Philip V and she questions the chronology of these issues put forward by Gaebler. [For another discussion of these issues, see MacKay "Numismatic Evidence" under MACEDONIAN KINGDOM].

797 ——— *The Agrinion Hoard.* Numismatic Notes and Monographs, No. 159. New York: American Numismatic Society, 1968. 130 pp., 56 pls. [CS 3298]
Examines a hoard of 1340 silver coins found near Agrinion in western Aetolia in 1959. Included 179 autonomous drachms and hemidrachms of various mints in the Peloponnesos and Central Greece. Included thirty-nine tetradrachms of Athens, 151 hemidrachms of Megalopolis, and 834 hemidrachms of the Achaean League. Thirty-nine Roman Republican denarii were also present in the hoard, but may have been added later. Presents a catalogue of the coins with commentary. The hoard is especially important for the information it provides on the chronology and character of the Achaean League coinage and the evidence for monetary circulation in Aetolia in the second century B.C. Suggests the coins in the hoard were taken from circulation in Aetolia over a short period of time in the second century B.C. Thompson dates the League coinage to the period 196-146 B.C. and places the hoard's burial at ca. 135 B.C. [Extensively reviewed by H. B. Mattingly in *Numismatic Chronicle* 7th ser., 9 (1969): 325-33. Also see Losada "The Aetolian Indemnity" above, and Oeconomides et al "Le Trésor de Zougra" above. Also see Clerk *Catalogue*, Crosby *An Achaean League Hoard*, and J. Warren *The Bronze Coinage* under Peloponnesos—Achaia. Also see the extended discussion by Alan Walker in his review of Warren's book in *ANS* 7, no. 3 (winter 2008): 53-8. Walker points out that the later down-dating of the Athenian New Style series causes the burial date of the Agrinion Hoard to now be lowered to the mid-120s B.C. at the earliest. This makes Thompson's explanation harder to accept for the absence from the hoard of the final League issues].

798 ——— "Hoards and Overstrikes: the Numismatic Evidence." *Expedition* 21, no. 4 (summer 1979): 40-6. Illus.
"Hoards and overstruck coins throw light on trading patterns in the eastern Mediterranean during the fifth century B.C. The evidence points to a steady and unilateral flow of silver coinage and bullion from Aegina, Athens, and the Thraco-Macedonian region into southwest Anatolia, the Levant and Egypt." [M. Thompson, *NL* 104]

799 ——— "The Armenak Hoard (*IGCH* 1423)." *Museum Notes* 31 (1986): 63-106. 21 pls.
Examines the so-called "Armenak" hoard of Hellenistic coins found in Asia Minor in 1927. Lists 968 hoard coins, primarily Alexander and Lysimachus drachms and tetradrachms from twenty-one mints. Comments on the coins and suggests a burial date between 275-270 B.C. (Newell had dated the hoard to ca. 280 B.C.). Coins from the hoard seen but not purchased by Newell are listed in an appendix.

800 **Thompson, Margaret, Otto Mørkholm, and Colin M. Kraay, eds.** *An Inventory of Greek Coin Hoards.* New York: American Numismatic Society, 1973. 408 pp., 3 maps. [CS 3300]
Lists 2387 hoards of Greek coins buried prior to 30 B.C. A revision of Noe's *A Bibliography of Greek Coin Hoards* (see Noe above). The hoards are grouped geographically by circulation areas. Within each geographic division, the sequence is chronological by burial date. Provides a brief description of the hoard contents (number of coins, metal, denomination, disposition of the coins if known). Cites published works related to the hoards. Includes a concordance to Noe and various indexes. [Reviewed by M. J. Price in *American Journal of Archaeology* 78, no. 3 (July 1974): 308-9, by Alan Johnston in *Numismatic Chronicle* 7th ser., 15 (1975): 243-4, and by M. B. Wallace in *Cornucopiæ* 3, no. 3 (1975): 45. For a discussion of these hoards along with some statistics drawn from this work, see C. Ehrhardt "Greek Treasure Trove" above].

801 ——— "An Inventory of Greek Coin Hoards: a Discussion." *Annali. Istituto Italiano di Numismatica* (Italy) 23-24 (1976-7): 319-23.
"A reply is made to the observations on editorial criteria by Laura Breglia published in *Annali. Istituto Italiano di Numismatica* 21-22 (1974-5): 215-22." [S. Sorda, *NL* 104]

802 **Tompa, Peter K.** "Decadrachm Hoard Case Settles." *The Celator* 13, no. 4 (April 1999): 32-3.
Briefly describes the legal case which resulted in the return of the famous "Decadrachm Hoard" coins to the Turkish government. [Also see Gibbs "American Returns Hoard" and Meier "Contested Coins" above].

803 **Touratsoglou, Yannis.** *The Coin Circulation in Ancient Macedonia (ca. 200 B.C.— 268-286 A.D.): The Hoard Evidence.* Translated by Marion J. A. Tzamali. Bibliotheca 1. Athens: Hellenic Numismatic Society, 1993. 88 pp., 13 pls., 2 maps, tables.
A study of coin circulation in ancient Macedonia based on the study of hoards of bronze and precious metal coins covering the period from the beginning of the second century B.C. up to the third quarter of the third century A.D. The hoards are divided into the following categories: grave hoards (the most numerous), savings hoards, coins hoarded owing to force of circumstances, and collectors' hoards. Comments on how hoard patterns reflect historical events. Includes brief notes on coin circulation in Thessaly and Epirus. Includes a map of Roman Macedonia, and a map of Macedonia showing the findspots of coin hoards of the late Hellenistic and Roman periods. Various tables (in Greek only) provide lists of Macedonian hoards and their contents. Other tables record iconographic patterns on Macedonian coins, and illustrate the relationships of overstruck coins. Includes extensive lists of monograms found on coins of Macedonia, Thessaloniki, Pella, and Amphipolis. Text in both Greek and English. [Reviewed by A. Walker in *The Celator* 7, no. 12 (December 1993): 42-3, and in *Nomismatika Khronika* (Greece) 13 (1994): 138-40. Walker's review also appeared in *Spink Numismatic Circular* 102, no. 6 (July 1994). Also see MacDonald "Macedonian Civic Bronze Overstrikes" under Macedonian Cities and Tribes].

804 ——— *Disjecta Membra: Two New Hellenistic Hoards from Greece.* Translated by Marion J. A. Tzamali. Bibliotheca 3. Athens: Hellenic Numismatic Society, 1995. 107 pp. (including the 19 pls.), 7 tables (including 2 maps).
A complete publication of two hoards of the Hellenistic period from Crete and Macedonia/Thessaly, set in the context of Greece and Asia Minor at the time of their concealment. Begins with a chronological comparative table of Hellenistic rulers and a timeline summarizing the main historical events of the period 300 to 222 B.C. Part 1 is "Creta Numismatica: A Study of Cretan Numismatics Prompted by the Central-Southern (?) Crete/1991 Hoard." Summarizes the knowledge gained from the eight known Cretan hoards of the early third century B.C. The hoard evidence reinforces the opinion that there was a clash between north and south, Knossos and Gortyna, a few years before the outbreak of the Chremonidian War (the war lasted from 268-262 B.C.). No Cretan hoards of the second half of the third century B.C. have been found. The hoards of the second century B.C. reflect the diplomatic importance of Crete in the fight between Rome and Perseus, and also carry reverberations from the border clashes between the Cretan cities. The composition of the first century B.C. hoards are either the spoils of war or piratical activity outside the island in the face of Roman expansion and the upheavals of the Mithradatic Wars. Presents a catalogue of the Central-Southern (?) Crete/1991 Hoard.

Part 2 is "Pan and Poseidon: The Confiscated Hoard of Thesprotia/1992; Thoughts on the Numismatics of the Mid and Late Third Century B.C." Eighty-six silver tetradrachms were seized by authorities in 1992. The hoard possibly originated in Northern Thessaly with a concealment date of the late third century B.C. The hoard contained 45 tetradrachms of Antigonus Gonatas, 12 of Lysimachus, 8 of Ptolemy II, 5 of Eumenes, and coins of several other Hellenistic rulers. The hoard contributes to our knowledge of coin circulation in Greece, and it poses again the problem of the identity of the issuer of the tetradrachms with *obv.*, head of Poseidon; *rev.*, Apollo on ship's prow, holding a bow. The coins have been attributed to both Antigonos Gonatas and Antigonos Doson. Summarizes the results of a review of the coinages of Antigonos Gonatas, Antigonos Doson, and Antiochus Hierax. Concludes that the "Poseidon/Apollo on prow" coins belong to Antigonos Doson and were issued on the eve of his campaign in Caria to cover the expenses of this overseas operation. Presents a catalogue of The Confiscated Hoard of Thesprotia/1992. Tables and maps present information on sixty-two related hoards from the Eastern Mediterranean Basin. Text in both Greek and English. [Reviewed by R. Ashton in *Spink Numismatic Circular* 104, no. 1 (February 1996): 9-10].

805 ———— "Statères d'Alexandre et Statères de Cyzique le Trésor du Pirée, 1882 (*IGCH* 47)." *Travaux de Numismatique Grecque Offerts à Georges Le Rider*. Edited by M. Amandry and S. Hurter. London: Spink, 1999. Pages 351-7. 1 pl.

806 ———— "The Price of Power: Drachms in the Name of Alexander in Greece (On the Occasion of the Thessaly (1993) Confiscation)." *Eulimene* (Mediterranean Archaeological Society, Rethymno, Greece) 1 (2000): 91-118.
"The 'hoard' confiscated by the authorities of Attica in 1993 and consisting of tetradrachms of Philip II (1 piece), Alexander III (3 pieces), Lysimachos (1 piece) and Athens (2 pieces), drachms of Alexander III (37 pieces), Philip III (6 pieces), Lysimachos (2 pieces), Larissa (3 pieces) and Pharsalos (1 piece), hemidrachms of Pharsalos (2 pieces), Opontii Locri (3 pieces) and Sikyon (1 piece), as well as diobols of Larisa (1 piece), if compared to the other 'finds' of the period, verifies some observations already made in the past with respect to the coin circulation of the minor peripheral mints in the century that followed the death of Alexander. Once again it proves the local character, not only for most of them but also for other, more important mints. In addition the study of the new "hoard" of assumed Thessalian provenance, verifies the power and the potential of certain, mainly regal, coinages (Athens included) with a panhellenic range of production." [M. I. Stefanakis, *NL* 147]

807 "The Treasure-Trove at Sidon." *American Journal of Numismatics* 4, no. 10 (February 1870): 76-8.
An account of the finding of gold coins of Philip and Alexander in Phoenicia, and general comments on digging for treasure in the Middle East.

808 **Trifiro, Maria Daniela.** "The Hoard Αρκαλοχωρι–Ασιριτσι 1936 (*IGCH* 154)." *Eulimene* (Mediterranean Archaeological Society, Rethymno, Greece) 2 (2001): 143-54.

809 **Troxell, Hyla A., and William F. Spengler.** "A Hoard of Early Greek Coins from Afghanistan." *Museum Notes* 15 (1969): 1-19. 2 pls. [CS 3301]
Examines twenty rare or unique coins from a hoard of mostly Athenian tetradrachms found in Afghanistan in 1966, in an area which was once ancient Bactria. The coins discussed are from Lete, Thraco-Macedonian Tribes, Aegina, Cnidus, Phaselis, Celenderis, Tarsus, Citium, Salamis, and Tyre. Provides evidence for the circulation of early Greek silver coins in this remote area. [Reviewed by H. Nicolet in *Revue Archéologique* (Paris) 2 (1971): 359-61].

810 **Tselekas, Panagiotis.** "Grave Hoards of Greek Coins from Greece." *Numismatic Chronicle* 156 (1996): 249-59.
Lists seventy-nine hoards, all of which were found in graves.

811 **Tsotselia, Medea.** *Coin Finds in Georgia (6th century B.C. – 15th Century A.D.)*. Moneta 112. Wetteren, Belgium: Moneta, 2010. 430 pp., illus.
Describes 1453 coin finds from the region of Georgia. Includes maps of the geographical distribution of finds grouped by time periods.

812 **Ujes, Dubravka.** "Hellenic Impact as a Developing Factor in the Triballian and Dardanian Territories from the 6th to 4th c. B.C. with a Reflection on the Appearance of Coin Findings." *Greek-Roman Antiquity in Yugoslavia and in the Balkans*. Ziva Antika, Monographies 9. Skopje, 1991. Pages 216-21.

813 **van Alfen, Peter G.** "The 'Owls' from the 1973 Iraq Hoard." *American Journal of Numismatics* 2nd ser., 12 (2000): 9-58. 8 pls.
An examination of the Athenian-type tetradrachms in a hoard found in Babylon in 1973. Among the approximately 400 coins in the hoard were 165 Attic owls. Other coins included issues of Alexander III (including Porus types) and "lion" staters of Babylon. The hoard was buried ca. 323 B.C. van Alfen examines the countermarks and test cuts on the owl coins. Only 16 of the coins had countermarks but over half bore test cuts. Those that were clearly Attic issues were less likely to be cut; the imitative issues were more likely to be cut. The Attic issues that were cut were more likely to be cut on the reverse rather than the obverse. This tendency was not as strong with the imitative issues. Presents a table of weights. Divides the owls into stylistic groupings and describes the characteristics of each group. Discusses the controversy over the owls bearing the inscriptions MZDK (Mazakes) and SWYK (Sabakes). Describes variations in the flans that may indicate different flan production methods utilized at different mint locations. Discusses the purposes of the minting of the owl imitations and the lion staters. Includes a full catalogue of the owls.

814 ———— "A New Athenian 'Owl' and Bullion Hoard from the Near East." *American Journal of Numismatics* 2nd ser., 16-17 (2004-2005): 47-61. 8 pls.
A recent hoard containing at least seventy-six Athenian owls, both imitations and authentic types, and two silver "dumps" is catalogued and discussed. The late fourth century B.C. hoard shows remarkable affinity to the owl components of two other late-fourth century hoards, the 1989 Syria and 1973 Iraq hoards.

814a ———— "Asyut (*IGCH* 1644) Additions: Cyrenaica and 'Chalcis.'" *Revue Suisse de Numismatique* (Switzerland) 88 (2009): 141-56.

815 ———— "Curator's Message: Digital Coin Hoards." *ANS* 8, no. 2 (summer 2009): 12-13. Illus.
Discusses the development of digital cataloguing of coin hoards and the potential this has for the advancement of the use of hoard evidence in historical studies.

816 **Vanderpool, Eugene, J. R. McCredie, and Arthur Steinberg.** "Koroni: A Ptolemaic Camp on the East Coast of Attica." *Hesperia* 31, no. 1 (January-March 1962): 26-61. 12 pls.
Coins discovered during excavations at Koroni proved important in the dating and identification of the site. Twenty-four of the thirty-two coins found are Ptolemaic. Considering the rarity of Ptolemaic coins in Athens, the conclusion that the army was Ptolemaic is inescapable. [Summarized from *NL* 62]

817 **Vermeule, Cornelius C.** "The Athenian Treasury Hoard." *The Celator* 13, no. 12 (December 1999): 26-30. Illus.
Discusses the famous "Decadrachm" or "Emali" hoard. Lists the contents of the hoard. Contrasts the contents with other hoards found in Lycia. The coins appear to have been in an Athenian treasury at one time, the result of tribute gathered from various cities. The coins were later paid out by Athenian authorities. Vermeule discusses the date of burial of the hoard. Speculates that the coins may actually have come from two hoards. The author strongly

doubts that the coins were found in Lycia as has been claimed by Turkish authorities. He suggests Crete as a more likely source. [Also see Fried "The Decadrachm Hoard" above].

818 **Vickers, Michael.** "Persépolis, Athènes et Sybaris: Questions de Monnayage et de Chronologie." *Revue des Études Grecques* (France) 99 (1986): 239-69.

819 **Villaronga, Leandre.** "The Tangier Hoard." *Numismatic Chronicle* 149 (1989): 149-62. 10 pls.
A report on a hoard found in Spanish Morocco in the 1920's. Presents a catalogue of the coins which includes the following issues: Spanish-Carthaginian, Italo-Carthaginian, Sicily-Carthaginian, Rome, Tarentum, Dyrrhachium, Amphipolis, Magnesia-on-the-Maeander, Emporion, Iberian, Gades, and Ebusus. After some discussion, the author concludes the hoard was buried ca. 211-210 B.C.

820 ——— "Petit Trésor de la Deuxième Guerre Punique avec une Drachme des Bruttiens." *Florilegium Numismaticum: Studia in Honorem U. Westermark Edita.* Edited by Harald Nilsson. Stockholm: Svenska Numismatiska Föreningen, 1992. Pages 347-50. 1 pl.

821 **Waage, Dorothy B.** *Antioch-on-the-Orontes. Volume 4, Part 2: Greek, Roman, Byzantine, and Crusader Coins.* Princeton: University Press, 1952. 187 pages, 8 pls.
Catalogues all the legible Greek, Roman, Byzantine, and Crusader coins found during the 1932-39 excavations at Antioch and the vicinity and at Seleucia Pieria. Most of the coins are bronze. The Greek sections includes 249 Seleucid coins, a few Alexanders and Ptolemaic coins, and a few other autonomous Greek coins, as well as many Roman Provincial coins. Most of the arrangement was done by E. T. Newell. [Reviewed by G. K. Jenkins in *Journal of Hellenic Studies* 74 (1954): 233, and by H. L. Adelson in *American Journal of Archaeology* 59 (1955): 91-2].

822 **Waage, Frederick O.** *Greek Bronze Coins from a Well at Megara.* Numismatic Notes and Monographs, No. 70. New York: American Numismatic Society, 1935. 42 pp., 3 pls.
Discusses the small bronze coins found in a well in Megara in 1929. Of the 682 coins, 273 are from Megara and 357 are from Sicyon. Most of the known types of Megara were represented. Shows that the weights of the Megara coins declined over the years. Most of the Sicyon coins belong to the Achaean League period. The coins are listed by type. No chronological sequence could be established. Waage suggests the coins were deposited in the well by travelers over a period of several centuries for good luck.

823 **Wace, Alan J. B.** "A Hoard of Hellenistic Coins." *Annual of the British School at Athens* 14 (1907-8): 149-58. 2 pls.
Lists eighty-six silver coins found in a vase during excavations at Sparta in 1908. Includes tetradrachms of Lysimachus, Alexander the Great, Demetrius I, Athens, Laconia, the Seleucid Kingdom (various rulers), and the Ptolemaic kingdom. The hoard was probably buried ca. 222-200 B.C.

824 **Waggoner, Nancy M.** "The Propontis Hoard (*IGCH* 888)." *Revue Numismatique* (France) 6th ser., 21 (1979): 7-29. Illus.
"This hoard of 163 pieces consists entirely of Alexander tetradrachms, most of which are late posthumous issues of Greek cities in Asia Minor. The burial date is discussed because of the presence of a cistophoric countermark of Pergamum and a countermark of Cyzicus which is tied to the wreathed issues of the latter mint. The author suggests lowering by only a few years the date proposed by H. Seyrig: the hoard would have been secreted between 180 and 170, and the Temnus Alexanders should be considered modern intrusions." [N. Waggoner, *NL* 107]

825 ——— "The Propontis Hoard, 1950 (*IGCH* 888)." *Proceedings of the 9th International Congress of Numismatics. Berne, September 1979. Volume 1.* Edited by T. Hackens and R. Weiller. Luxembourg: International Association of Professional Numismatists, 1982. Page 233.
An abstract of a report on the hoard of 163 Alexander tetradrachms from more than twenty-five mints, discovered in the region of the Propontis in 1950. The hoard was buried ca. 180 B.C.

826 **Walker, Alan S.** "Worn and Corroded Coins: Their Importance for the Archaeologist." *Journal of Field Archaeology* 3 (1976): 329-34. Illus.
Points out that in order to obtain all the information that coins can supply, archaeologists must be aware of the ramifications of wear and corrosion. Even exceedingly worn or corroded coins may have a real significance—they can either give a precise date for their contextual assembly, or illuminate the economic and political circumstances of their period of deposition.

827 ——— "Four Æ Coin Hoards in the Collection of the American School of Classical Studies at Athens." *Hesperia* 47, no. 1 (January-March 1978): 40-8. Illus.
Discusses four hoards without any provenance found in storage at the school. One hoard consists of 119 bronze coins of Boeotia and twenty-four of surrounding mints and is dated ca. 200-150 B.C. The second is dated ca. 86 B.C. and contains ninety-eight bronzes (including thirty-eight uncertain, one of Antigonus Gonatas and the rest of Athens). The other two hoards are of later, non-Greek coins.

828 ——— "Some Hoards from Sicily and a Carthaginian Issue of the Second Punic War." *Studies in Honour of Leo Mildenberg: Numismatics, Art History, Archaeology.* Edited by A. Houghton et al. Wetteren: Editions NR, 1984. Pages 269-88. 2 pls.
Walker describes two hoards from Sicily dating to the period of the Second Punic War. The hoards include Greek, Punic, and Roman coins. The hoards throw light on the various Republican coins and their interactions, as well as on the problem with the beginning and extent of the early coinage of Roman denarii. Discusses the bronze coins formerly attributed to Hiempsal II. These are now identified as a Punic issue depicting Triptolemus. Discusses the weight standards and denominations of the hoard coins. The hoards were probably buried ca. 210-9 B.C. and ca. 212-10 B.C. Lists the weights and illustrates the die links of the coins.

829 ——— "Excavation Coins: The Use and Misuse of Numismatic Evidence in Archaeology." *Numismatic Archaeology/Archaeological Numismatics: Proceedings of an International Conference held to Honour Dr. Mando Oeconomides in Athens 1995.* Oxbow Monographs 75. Edited by K. Sheedy and C. Papageorgiadou-Banis. Oxford: Oxbow Books and The Australian Archaeological Institute at Athens, 1997. Pages 17-26.

Walker discusses the ways coins can be useful to archaeologists, but highlights the many pitfalls and errors that can easily be made if the evidence is not carefully considered by a knowledgeable numismatist. He also describes some basic suggestions for classification and storage of coin finds from excavation sites.

830 **Walker, F. G.** "Greek Coins found in England." *Numismatic Chronicle* 4th ser., 8 (1908): 374-5. Illus.
Publishes two bronze coins found in England: (1) a first century B.C. coin of Laconia, and (2) a coin of the Arcadians, ca. A.D. 130.

831 **Wallace, William P.** "Note on the New Anatolian Hoard." *Numismatic Chronicle* 7, no. 2 (1962): 42.
Wallace comments on the hoard published by Robinson (see E. S. G. Robinson "A Hoard of Archaic Greek Coins from Anatolia" above) which contained some early Athenian owls. A coin of Zancle in the hoard can be firmly dated to 489/8 B.C. and is the least worn coin in the hoard. Robinson's dating of the burial (ca. 480) seems to suggest his acceptance of Kraay's dates for the Athenian coins. Wallace believes that the freshness of the Athenian coins suggests a burial date of 500-488 B.C., consistent with Wallace's proposed dating of the Athenian coins. [Also see Wallace "The Early Coinages of Athens and Euboia" under ATTICA—WAPENMÜNZEN, at the end of which this brief note appears].

832 **Warren, Jennifer A. W.** "The 1980 Kato Klitoria Hoard." *Kraay—Mørkholm Essays: Numismatic Studies in Memory of C. M. Kraay and O. Mørkholm.* Numismatica Lovaniensia 10. Edited by G. Le Rider, G. K. Jenkins, N. Waggoner, and U. Westermark. Louvain-la-Neuve: Université Catholique de Louvain, 1989. Pages 291-300. 2 pls.
Describes a pot hoard of eighty-three silver coins found in 1980 in northern Arcadia. Composed of six staters, six hemidrachms, and seventy-one obols of Locris, Phocis, Tanagra, Thebes, Aegina, Sicyon, Pellene, Elis, Argos, the Arcadian League, Alea, Cleitor, Pheneus, and Stymphalus. Suggests the hoard was buried ca. 340/330 B.C. The hoard may indicate that small value silver coins and the recently introduced bronze coinage both circulated freely in an area of the Peloponnesos.

833 ——— "The Vonitsa, Acarnania (1993) Hoard." *Coin Hoards, Volume VIII: Greek Hoards.* Edited by U. Wartenberg, M. J. Price, and K. A. McGregor. London: Royal Numismatic Society, 1994. Page 83. 5 pls.
A brief examination of a hoard (*Coin Hoards VIII*, no. 431) found in Acarnania in 1993. It was likely buried no earlier than 172 B.C. Contained five Alexander tetradrachms, four tetradrachms of Side, some triobols of Argos, a tetradrachm of Athens, and others.

834 **Wartenberg, Ute.** "The Alexander-Eagle Hoard: Thessaly 1992." *Numismatic Chronicle* 157 (1997): 179-88. 7 pls.
The hoard was found in Thessaly in 1992 and contained 35 staters of Philip II, 3 "eagle" tetradrachms of Alexander III, 1 or 2 normal tetradrachms of Alexander III, 57 staters of Thebes, 16 staters of Sicyon, 13 staters of Locris Opuntii, and 1 stater of Larissa. The hoard originally included some Athenian coins as well. This is the first recorded hoard context for the rare Alexander "eagle" coins (*obv.*, head of Zeus; *rev.*, eagle standing). Wartenberg discusses each group of coins. The three Alexander eagle coins bring the number known to eight—all of which are listed here. Includes a catalogue of ninety-four of the hoard coins. The hoard was buried ca. 325-300 B.C. The author voices no opinion on the date of the Alexander eagle coins.

835 **Wartenberg, Ute, and Jonathan H. Kagan.** "Some Comments on a New Hoard from the Balkan Area." *Travaux de Numismatique Grecque Offerts à Georges Le Rider.* Edited by M. Amandry and S. Hurter. London: Spink, 1999. Pages 395-407. 6 pls.
Examines a hoard of ninety-eight silver coins—primarily tetradrachms of Philip II, Alexander III, Demetrius Poliorcetes, Lysimachos, Seleucus I, Eumenes, and Antiochos I. The group also included one extremely rare Alexander-type tetradrachm of King Orsoaltios and one Lysimachos tetradrachm of Calchedon. Most of the coins bear test cuts and over half are countermarked. The find was likely made in Serbia or western Romania. The coin of Calchedon leads to a re-examination of this mint and an assignment of a group of Alexander tetradrachms and staters to this mint, and a revision to the dates for the Lysimachus issues of this mint. Includes a catalogue of the hoard coins and commentary on individual coins. The authors suggest that a group of Alexander tetradrachms formerly given to Callatis actually belong to Calchedon. They also suggest the cuts and countermarks were part of a sophisticated and controlled process.

836 **Wartenberg, Ute, Martin Jessop Price, and Kaelyn A. McGregor.** *Coin Hoards, Volume VIII: Greek Hoards.* London: Royal Numismatic Society, 1994. 113 pp., 87 pls.
Lists 604 hoards which were primarily composed of Greek coins (including five hoards thought to be composed of forgeries). The contents of each hoard are briefly listed, along with the estimated burial date, disposition of the coins, find location (if known), and cross references to other publications regarding each hoard. Includes indices of mints, rulers, and findspots, and a cross reference to earlier volumes of *Coin Hoards* (see Royal Numismatic Society *Coin Hoards* above). Also includes short papers or extensive notes on nine of the hoards: "Egypt, Before 1879: Early 5th Century B.C." by T. V. Buttrey [511], "A Hoard of Sigloi" by K. Butcher [6186], "Bemerkungen zu Einem Fund Kleinasiatischer Obole" by S. Schultz; "A Hoard from the Durmaz Collection from the Region of Antakya" by M. Arslan and M. J. Price [485], "The Mugnano Hoard" by M. Crawford [2647], "The Vonitsa, Arcarnania (1993) Hoard" by J. Warren [833], "The Köycegiz Hoard of Late Rhodian Plinthophoric Drachms" by R. Ashton, M. Arslan, and A. Dervisagaoglu [4956], "Three Hoards from Babylonia in the British Museum" by J. Reade [730], and "A Group of Coins from Colophon" by P. Kinns [4778]. [Reviewed by R. Ashton in *Spink Numismatic Circular* 103, no. 3 (April 1995): 92-3. Also see 4779 P. Kinns "CH 8, 474: Milesian Silver Coinage in the Second Century B.C." under IONIA].

837 **Weber, Hermann.** "On Finds of Archaic Greek Coins in Lower Egypt." *Numismatic Chronicle* 3rd ser., 19 (1899): 269-87. 2 pls.
Describes twenty-eight coins found in Egypt including coins of Dicaea (Thrace), Lete, Neapolis (Macedonia), Aegina, Corinth, Naxos, Paros, Mytilene, Chios, Cyrene, and several uncertain types.

838 **Weber, Shirley H.** *An Egyptian Hoard of the Second Century A.D.* Numismatic Notes and Monographs, No. 54. New York: American Numismatic Society, 1932. 41 pp., 3 pls.
Describes a small hoard of silver coins purchased in Cairo in 1923 which included both Greek and Roman coins. The Greek coins included pieces from the Achaean League, Sicyon, Argos, and Rhodes. The Roman coins dated from Nero through Trajan. Discusses possible reasons for the presence of Greek coins in the hoard. Suggests this hoard was not intended for use in Egypt, but was the property of some resident of Achaea temporarily sojourning in Egypt. Concludes that Greek coins remained in circulation under the Roman Empire longer than previously supposed. Presents a catalogue of the coins. [Reviewed by David M. Robinson in *American Journal of Archaeology* 37 (1933): 177-8].

839 **Weinberg, Saul S.** "Tel Anafa: The Hellenistic Town." *Israel Exploration Journal* (Israel) 21, no. 2 (1971): 86-109. 10 pls.

"On p. 97 Phoenician city coins, chiefly of Tyre and Sidon, Ptolemaic, and Seleucid issues and other coins, in all 111 pieces found during excavations, are mentioned. They date from the early third century B.C. to 75 B.C. except for four, including one Arabic, which are later. On p. 106 is described a clay sealing from about 150 B.C. showing a Greek and West Semitic inscription." [A. Spaer, *NL* 88]

840 **Weir, Robert.** "The Stymphalos Hoard of 1999 and the City's Defenses." *American Journal of Numismatics* 2nd ser., 19 (2007): 9-32. 2 pls.
Examines a hoard of six silver and eight bronze coins found during excavations at the Arkadian city of Stymphalos in the Peloponnese. The coins probably were the contents of a purse. Weir presents a catalogue of the coins which included issues of Macedonia, Boiotia, Phlious, Sikyon, Pheneos, Olympia, Ambrakia, Larissa, Chalkis, Athens, Corinth, and Carthage. Discusses the events surrounding Stymphalos in the late fourth and early third centuries. The hoard was likely buried during the destruction of the city's fortifications ca. 275 B.C.

841 **Weissl, Michael.** "Zur Datierung des 'Foundation-Deposit' aus dem Artemision von Ephesos." *Synergia. Festschrift Friedrich Krinzinger, Band I.* Edited by Barbara Brandt, Verena Gassner, and Sabine Ladstätter. Vienna: Phoibos Verlag, 2005. Pages 363-70.
[Also see Head "Chapter V: The Coins" above].

842 **Westermark, Ulla.** "Notes on the Saida Hoard (*IGCH* 1508)." *Nordisk Numismatisk Årsskrift* (Sweden) (1979-80): 22-35. 3 pls.
Discusses one of the most important hoards of gold staters of Philip II and Alexander the Great. "The three gold hoards from Saida (Sidon), uncovered in 1829, 1852 and 1863 are surveyed. They are components of a single deposit, numbering over 7200 staters dating to ca. 323 B.C. A catalogue of forty-three known coins is established." [J. Jensen, *NL* 110]

843 ——— "Coins from the Swedish Excavations at Asine in Argolis." *Opscula Atheniensia* (Sweden) 13 (1990): 247-54, including 2 pls.
Publishes forty-eight coins which were found during the excavations at Asine in Argolis in 1922-30. The coins are of Argos, Chalkis, Athens, Corinth, Phlios, Pellene, Achaian League, Megalopolis, and Rithymna-Arsinoe. Also includes a few uncertain Greek coins and some later coins. Discusses the coinage of some of these cities and comments on the circulation of coins in the Peloponnese.

844 **Williams, D. J. R.** "The 'Pot-Hoard' Pot from the Archaic Artemision at Ephesus." *Bulletin of the Institute of Classical Studies of the University of London* 38 (1991-93): 98-104.
Examines the pot in which the famous "Artemision Hoard" was found. [Also see Jacobsthal "The Date of the Ephesian Foundation-Deposit" and Robinson "Ephesian Artemision" under Origins of Coinage, and Seltman "Earliest Hoarded Coins" above].

845 **Witschonke, Rick.** "Better Late Than Never: Newell Manuscript Finally Published." *ANS* 7, no. 3 (winter 2008): 33-6. Illus.
Provides a brief background to the excavations at Beisan in Israel which began in 1921. Edward T. Newell wrote a manuscript cataloging the coins found at the site, but it remained unpublished until its appearance in the 2008 volume of the American Numismatic Society's *American Journal of Numismatics*. The manuscript resided in the ANS archives. [See Newell "Coins from the Excavations at Beisan" above].

846 **Wroth, Warwick W.** "The Santorin Find of 1821." *Numismatic Chronicle* 3rd ser., 4 (1884): 269-80. 1 pl.
A large hoard found on the island of Santorini (ancient Thera), consisting of 760 archaic Greek silver coins, was briefly mentioned in an article by H. P. Borrell in 1844 (see Borrell "Unedited Autonomous and Imperial Greek Coins" under General Works—Greek). Here Wroth has put together specimens of all the types indicated by Borrell's memorandum with photographs and descriptions.

847 **Yorke, V. W.** "Excavations at Abae and Hyampolis in Phocis." *Journal of Hellenic Studies* 16 (1896): 291-312. Illus., 1 pl.
"On p. 302 a find of coins from Abae is briefly described (a corrected list appears *Noe²*, no. 1); the 'extraordinary predominance of the coins of Sicyon' is noted." [J. R. Jones, *NIJHS*]

848 **Young, Rodney S.** "Operation Gordion." *Expedition* 11, no. 1 (fall 1968): 16-9. Illus. [CS 3308]
A summary of the University of Pennsylvania's excavations at Gordion in Anatolia which began in 1948. Five coin hoards were found on the site. The hoards may represent the pay of Galatians serving as mercenaries, or loot from their raids. [Also see R. S. Young "The 1963 Campaign at Gordion" under Lydia].

849 **Zervos, Orestes H.** "Newell's Manuscript of the Kuft Hoard." *Museum Notes* 25 (1980): 17-29. 1 pl.
Re-examines the Kuft hoard of Alexander III tetradrachms and a few early Ptolemaic tetradrachms from a wide variety of mints found in Egypt. Most of the coins are countermarked. Provides a new discussion of the hoard based on a review of an unpublished manuscript by E. T. Newell. Provides the facts Newell had gathered and the conclusions he had reached. The hoard was previously published by Nash (see Nash "Kuft Hoard" above) who had some differences of opinion on the composition of the hoard. Provides a revised reconstruction of the inventory of the hoard. The coins fall into two series: (1) locally minted Egyptian issues down to ca. 305 B.C.; (2) Alexanders of foreign mintage down to ca. 310 B.C.

850 ——— "Corinth, 1981: East of the Theater. Appendix: Coins." *Hesperia* 51, no. 2 (April-June 1982): 145-63. Illus.
"A report of the 204 readable coins from the city-block (with row of shops) excavated in spring and summer of 1981 from Corinth." [O. Zervos, *NL* 109]

851 ——— "Corinth, 1982: East of the Theater. Appendix: Coins." *Hesperia* 52, no. 1 (January-March 1983): 33-47. Illus.
"The inventory of 200 pieces includes issues of Corinth, Athens, Aegeira, Patrae, Argos, Alexandria, and the Roman Empire, as well as 'Vandalic' and Byzantine specimens." [O. Zervos, *NL* 111/112]

852 ——— "Corinth, 1984: East of the Theater. Appendix: Coins." *Hesperia* 54, no. 1 (January-March 1985): 81-96. Illus.
"This year's excavations at Corinth yielded 301 coins. They include Greek issues of Dyrrhachium, Corcyra, Athens, Corinth, Phlius, Sicyon, Patrae, Lacedaemon, Argos, Troezen, Tegea, Pheneos, Pergamum, and Rhodes, as well as numerous Roman and Byzantine issues." [O. Zervos, *NL* 114]

853 ——— "Coins Excavated at Corinth, 1978-1980." *Hesperia* 55, no. 2 (April-June 1986): 183-205. 2 pls.
A report on the excavations in the southwest corner and east side of the Corinthian Forum in 1978, 1979, and 1980. Presents a catalogue of 452 coins and a list of the more important stratified finds. The coins are mostly Greek, many of Corinth.

854 ——— "Corinth, 1985: East of Theater. Appendix: Coins." *Hesperia* 55, no. 2 (April-June 1986): 163-75. 1 pl.

A report on the excavations at Corinth in 1985. Presents a catalogue of 157 of the identifiable coins found during the year. Includes Greek, Roman, and later coinages.

855 ——— "Corinth, 1986: Temple E and East of the Theater. Appendix: Coins." *Hesperia* 56, no. 1 (January-March 1987): 33-46. 1 pl.

A report on the excavations near Temple E at Corinth in 1986. Presents a catalogue of 141 of the identifiable coins found during 1986. Most of the coins are bronze. Includes a few Greek, but mostly Roman Provincial, Roman Imperial, and later coinages. Also publishes twenty-one coins found during previous seasons.

856 ——— "Corinth, 1987: South of Temple E and East of the Theater: Appendix. Coins." *Hesperia* 57, no. 2 (April-June 1988): 132-46. 1 pl.

A report on the excavations at Corinth in 1987. Presents a catalogue of 179 of the identifiable coins found during the year. Includes Greek, Roman, and later coinages.

857 **Zournatzi, Antigoni.** "The Apadana Coin Hoards, Darius I, and the West." *American Journal of Numismatics* 2nd ser., 15 (2003): 1-28. 1 pl.

Two foundation deposits were found in 1931 in the corner of the great audience hall (the Apadana) at Persepolis, containing archaic gold and silver coins and inscriptions from Darius I (522-486 B.C.). There is controversy over whether the coins, including coins of Abdera, Aegina, and lion-and-bull staters, held political significance or were selected solely for their metallic content. The author comments on the chronology of the Persian "archer" staters of Type I (half-figure of the king) and Type II (kneeling figure)—the earliest coinage of Darius I. Concludes that no lion-and-bull staters were minted by Darius. Comments on the evidence provided by the coins for dating the foundation deposit. A date around 500 B.C. is likely. Examines Aegina's relationship with Persia in the late sixth century B.C. Comments on Darius I's desire to expand his empire to the west. The coins of the Apadana foundation deposit may have been a symbol of Darius' control of important western economic centers, but this is uncertain. [Also see Meadows "The Apadana Foundation Deposit" above].

Notes:
(1) Hoards consisting primarily of coins from one city or kingdom are listed under the section in this book pertaining to that city or kingdom.
(2) For numerous articles discussing the controversy over the so-called "Black Sea Hoard" coins, see Emory, Flegler, Giedroyc, Hurter, Kovacs, Sayles, Saslow, Vagi, and Wetterstrom under COUNTERFEITS.

Also see: Abgarians and Sellwood "Hoard" under PARTHIA; D. Allen (several items) under CELTIC COINAGE OF BRITAIN; Amandry and Le Rider *Tresors* under GENERAL WORKS—GREEK; Anderson and van Alfen "A Fourth Century BCE Hoard" under ATTICA—GENERAL WORKS; Andrew "Iron Age Find" under CELTIC COINAGE OF BRITAIN; Andrew "Iron Age Gold" under CELTIC COINAGE OF BRITAIN; Apostolou "Three Hoards of the Athenian New Style Coins from Delos" under ATTICA—NEW STYLE COINAGE; Arena "New Acquisitions" under MACEDONIAN KINGDOM—GENERAL WORKS; Arnold-Biucchi *Randazzo Hoard* under SICILY—GENERAL WORKS; Arslan "Kargi Hoard" under CARIAN ISLANDS—RHODOS; Arslan "A Hoard of Bronze Coins of Lysimachia" under SYRIA—SELEUCID KINGDOM; Ashton "A Hoard of Koan Coins" under CARIAN ISLANDS—KOS; Ashton "Hoard of Late Rhodian Plinthophoric Hemidrachms" under CARIAN ISLANDS—RHODOS; Ashton, Arslan, and Dervisagaoglu "Ptolemaic Hoard" under EGYPT—PTOLEMAIC KINGDOM; Ashton, Sellwood, and Üyümez "A Hoard of Parthian Coins" under PARTHIA; Ashton, Arslan, and Derisagaoglu "Köycegiz Hoard" under CARIAN ISLANDS—RHODOS; Ashton, Uyumez, and Hosgören "Five Alexander Hoards" under MACEDONIAN KINGDOM—GENERAL WORKS; Augé et al *Le Début des Tétradrachmes d'Athènes du 'Noveau Style'* under ATTICA—NEW STYLE COINAGE; Balmuth *Hacksilber to Coinage* under ORIGINS OF COINAGE; Balmuth "Jeweler's Hoards" under THE ORIGINS OF COINAGE; Barkay "An Archaic Coin" under CARIA; Beckman "Athenian Coin from Persian Palestine" under PALESTINE—PHILISTIA; Bedoukian *Armenian Coin Hoards* under ARMENIA; Bellinger "Philippi in Macedonia" under MACEDONIAN CITIES AND TRIBES; Bellinger *Two Hoards of Attic Bronze* under ATTICA—GENERAL WORKS; Bellinger *Troy: The Coins* under TROAS; Bellinger "Greek Coins from the Yale Numismatic Collection" (Cyzicus) under PUBLIC COLLECTIONS—UNITED STATES (NEW HAVEN).

Bernard *Fouilles d'Aï Khanoum IV* under BACTRIA; Betancourt "Bronze Coins from Erythrae" under IONIA; Biddle "Ptolemaic Coins from Winchester" under EGYPT—PTOLEMAIC KINGDOM; Biglaki-Sophianou "The Gymnasium of Ancient Samos" under IONIAN ISLANDS—SAMOS; Bivar "The Bactrian Treasure" under BACTRIA; Bivar "Chaman Huzuri Hoard" under BACTRIA; Bivar "Ingot Currency" under ORIGINS OF COINAGE; Bivar "The Qunduz Treasure" under BACTRIA; Boehringer "Group of Rhodian Coins" under CARIA; Bonačić Mandinić *Greek Coins* under PUBLIC COLLECTIONS—CROATIA (SPLIT); Bopearachchi "Coins in the Smithsonian Institution" under NORTHWEST INDIA; Bopearachchi and Flandrin under Kleiner *Le Portrait d'Alexandre* under MACEDONIAN KINGDOM—GENERAL WORKS; Brett "The Cave at Vari" under ATTICA—GENERAL WORKS; Brett "Benha Hoard of Ptolemaic Gold" under EGYPT—PTOLEMAIC KINGDOM; Broneer "Isthmia" under PERSIA; Bulatovich "A Hoard of Cyzicenes" under MYSIA—AUTONOMOUS CITIES; Burnett "Aesillas" under MACEDONIAN KINGDOM—THE ROMAN PROVINCE; Burnett "Enna Hoard" under SICILY—SYRACUSE; Burnett "South Italy Hoard" under ITALY—GENERAL WORKS; Butcher "A Hoard of Sigloi" under PERSIA; Buttrey "Seldom What They Seem" under ATTICA—GENERAL WORKS; Buttrey "Siculo-Punic" under SICILY—SICULO-PUNIC COINAGE; Buttrey et al. *Morgantina Studies* under SICILY—MORGANTINA; Buxton "The Northern Syria 2007 Hoard" under ATTICA—GENERAL WORKS.

Calciati *Hoard of Dionysius Drachms* under SICILY—SYRACUSE; Cancio "Athenian Miscellanea" under ATTICA—GENERAL WORKS; Carradice *Coinage and Administration* under ATTICA—GENERAL WORKS; Carradice "The Regal Coinage" under PERSIA; Carradice "Two Achaemenid Hoards" under PERSIA; Collis "Coin of Ptolemy V from Winchester" under EGYPT—PTOLEMAIC KINGDOM; Crawford "Mugnano Hoard" under ITALY—GENERAL WORKS; Crosby and Grace *Achaean League Hoard* under PELOPONNESOS—ACHAIA; Daehn "Artemision Hoard" under ORIGINS OF COINAGE; Davesne and Lemaire "Trésors Hellénistiques du Proche-Oriente" under EGYPT—PTOLEMAIC KINGDOM; "Decadrachm Sells" under ATTICA—GENERAL WORKS; de Callataÿ "Athenian New Style" under ATTICA—NEW STYLE COINAGE; de Callataÿ and Prokopov "An Overstrike" under THRACE—THASOS; De Jersey "A Hoard" under CELTIC COINAGE OF BRITAIN; Destrooper "Coins from the New York University Excavations" under EGYPT—PTOLEMAIC KINGDOM; Destrooper-Georgiades "Hoard of Soloi" under CYPRUS; Dikaios "Cypriote Staters" under CYPRUS; Dimitrov "Early Hellenistic Hoards" under MACEDONIAN KINGDOM—GENERAL WORKS.

Dimitrov "Development of Thrace" under THRACE—GENERAL WORKS; Dimitrov "The Contracts of Thrace" under THRACE—GENERAL WORKS; Dimitrov "Trésor Avec des Monnaies" under MACEDONIAN KINGDOM—GENERAL WORKS; Dukat and Mirnik "The Hoard of Macedonian Bronze" under MACEDONIAN KINGDOM—GENERAL WORKS; Draganov "Unknown Hybrid" (Gorno Novo Selo hoard) under MYSIA—AUTONOMOUS CITIES; Dundua and Lordkipanidze "Hellenistic Coins" under KOLCHIS; Edwards and Thompson "A Hoard of Gold Coins" under MACEDONIAN KINGDOM—GENERAL WORKS; Elayi "Un Trésor de Tétradrachmes aux Types d'Alexandre Trouvé dans la Beqa" under MACEDONIAN KINGDOM—GENERAL WORKS; Elayi and Elayi "Un Nouveau Trésor de Tétradrachmes Athéniens et Pseudo-Athéniens" under ATTICA; Evans "Hoard of Ancient British Coins" under CELTIC COINAGE OF BRITAIN; Evans *Joint Expedition to Caesarea Maritima* under PALESTINE—JUDEA; Frolova and Ireland "A Hoard of Bosporan Coins" under BOSPOROS; Gardner and Malter *Coinage of Parthia* under PARTHIA; Gargali "Coins from a Hellenistic Cemetery" under CARIAN ISLANDS—KALYMNOS; Geva "Jewish Quarter Excavations" under PALESTINE—JUDEA; Göktürk "Polatli Hoard" under ASIA MINOR—GENERAL WORKS; Grigorakis "A Hoard of Ptolemaic Silver Coins from Chios" under EGYPT—PTOLEMAIC KINGDOM; Grunauer von Hoerschelmann

"Lacedaemonian Tetradrachms" under Peloponnesos—Lakonia; Hackens "L'Influence Rhodienne…le Trésor de Gortyne" under Crete; Haughton "Bajaur Hoard" under Northwest India; Haughton "The Shaikhano Dheri Hoard" under Bactria; Hazzard "Two Hoards" under Egypt—Ptolemaic Kingdom; Hazzard "Review of the Cyprus Hoard" under Egypt—Ptolemaic Kingdom; Head "Sicilian Copper Coins" under Sicily—General Works; Head "Staters of Cyzicus" under Mysia—Autonomous Cities; Heintges "Babylonian (?) Alexander Hoard" under Macedonian Kingdom—General Works; Hersh "Phoenicia 1997 Hoard" under Macedonian Kingdom—General Works; Hersh "Fifth Century…Tetrobols" under Macedonian Kingdom—General Works; Hersh "A 1992 Hoard" under Macedonian Kingdom—General Works.

Hersh and Troxell "A 1993 Hoard" under Macedonian Kingdom—General Works; Hill "A Find of Cistophori" under Asia Minor—General Works; Hill "Cyrenaic Bronze" under Cyrenaica; "Hoard of Electrum" under Mysia—Autonomous Cities; Holloway "Archaic Hoard" under Aegina; Holloway "Monetary Circulation" under Sicily—General Works; Hunter "Hoard from Serbia" under Celtic Coinage—General Works; Hurter "Der Tissaphernes-Fund" under Lycia; Huston and Lorber "A Hoard of Ptolemaic Coins" under Egypt—Ptolemaic Kingdom; Huth "Important Hoard" under Arabia; Huth "Monetary Circulation in South West Arabia" under Arabia; Jacobsthal "Ephesian Foundation-Deposit" under Origins of Coinage; Jenkins "Cordova Hoard" under Spain; Jenkins "Celtiberian Hoard" under Spain; Jenkins "Carthaginian Copper" under Kyrenaica; Jenkins "Early Ptolemaic Hoard" under Egypt—Ptolemaic Kingdom; Jenkins "Mqabba (Malta) Hoard of Punic Bronze Coins" under Zeugitana; M. Jenkins "A Hoard from Elephantine Island" under Egypt—Ptolemaic Kingdom; Jentoft-Nilsen "Tarentine Silver" under Italy—Taras; Johnston "Report of a Discussion on South Italian Chronology" under Italy—General Works.

Kadman "The Monetary Development of Palestine" under Palestine—Judea; Kadman "Temple Dues" under Palestine—Judea; Kagin "A Survey" under Origins of Coinage; Kakhidze et al. "Silver Coins of Black Sea Coastal Cities" under Asia Minor and the Black Sea Region—General Works; Karageorghis and Karageorghis "The Menico Hoard" under Cyprus; Karwiese "Artemisium Coin Hoard" under Origins of Coinage; Kindler "Jaffa Hoard" under Palestine—Judea; Kindler "Ptolemaic Coin Hoard" under Egypt—Ptolemaic Kingdom; Kinns "*CH 8*, 474: Milesian Silver Coinage" under Ionia; Kinns "Group of Coins from Colophon" under Ionia; Kleiner *Greek and Roman Coins in the Athenian Agora* under Attica—General Works; Koch *A Hoard of Coins* under Parthia; Kos *The Monetary Circulation* under General Works—Greek; Kos and Mirnik "Ribnjacka Hoard" under Celtic Coinage of Europe; Kraay "Archaic and Classical" (Larnaca hoard) under Cyprus; Kraay "Catanzaro" under Italy—General Works; Kraay "Corinth and Leucas" under Corinthia; Kraay "Hoards, Small Change" under Origins of Coinage; Kraay "Melos Hoard" under Cyclades; Kraay "Mid-fifth Century Hoard" under Italy—General Works; Kraay "Two Late Fifth Century b.c. Hoards" under Italy—General Works; Krishnamurthy "Coins from Phoenicia" under Phoenicia; Kroll *The Athenian Agora* under Attica—General Works; Kroll "Observations on Monetary Instruments" under Origins of Coinage; Kroll "Piraeus 1902 Hoard" under Attica—General Works; Kroll "Two Hoards" under Attica—General Works.

Kushnir-Stein and Gitler "Numismatic Evidence" (Nabatean) under Arabia; Lagos "Two Second Century b.c. Hoards" under Bosporos; Lambert "Phoenician Coins" under Phoenicia; Liampi "Bronze Coins of Alexander" under Macedonian Kingdom—General Works; Le Rider "Un Trésor de Monnaies Séleucides" under Syria—Seleucid Kingdom; Lloyd "A Recent Find" and "Recently Discovered Hoard" under Sicily—General Works; Lorber "A Hoard of Punic Horse and Palm Billion" under Zeugitana; Lorber "Commerce ('Seleucia on the Calycadnus' Hoard)" under Syria—Seleucid Kingdom; Lorber "Large Ptolemaic Bronzes" under Egypt; Lorber "The Tyre, 1987 Hoard" under Syria—Seleucid Kingdom; Lorber and Houghton "Antiochus III Hoard" under Syria—Seleucid Kingdom; MacDonald *Coins of Aphrodisias* under Caria; Macdonald "On A Find Made in the Islands" under Italy—General Works; MacDonald "Note on *CH VIII*, no. 47" (Teos) under Ionia; Maharian "Shaqed" under Syria—Seleucid Kingdom; Marinescu "Late Cistophori" under Asia Minor—General Works; Martin "Gold Coin Find" under Egypt—Ptolemaic Kingdom; Martin "Indo-Greek Hemidrachms" under Northwest India; Mattingly "Coins and Amphoras" under Ionian Islands—Chios; McFadden "Hoard of Early Multi-Denominational Electrum" under Ionia; Meadows "Thasos/New Style Hoard" under Thrace—Thasos; Meir "Tyrian Sheqels and Half Sheqels with Unpublished Dates from the 'Isifya Hoard'" under Phoenicia; Metcalf "The 'Ain Tab Hoard" under Macedonian Kingdom—General Works; Metcalf "Posthumous Alexanders" under Macedonian Kingdom—General Works; Mielczarek "The Szubin Hoard" under Attica—Wappenmünzen; Milne "Brettian Bronze" under Italy—General Works; Milne "The Currency of Arcadia" under Peloponnesos—Arkadia; Milne "An Elymaic Hoard" under Elymais; Milne *The Melos Hoard* under Cyclades Islands; Milne "Persian Sigloi" under Persia; Milne "Temnos" under Aeolis; Metcalf "Ptolemaic and Roman Coins" under Egypt—Ptolemaic Kingdom.

Mørkholm "The Coinages of Ariarathes VIII and IX" under Cappadocia; Mørkholm "Characene" under Characene; Mørkholm "Cyprus Hoard" under Egypt—Ptolemaic Kingdom; Mørkholm "A Group of Ptolemaic Coins" under Egypt—Ptolemaic Kingdom; Mørkholm "A Greek Coin Hoard from Susiana" under Syria—Seleucid Kingdom; Mosser *Catacombs Hoard* under Public Collections—United States (New York); Mousheghian et al. *History and Coins Finds in Armenia* (two items) under Armenia; Mousheghian *The Coins Hoards of Armenia* under Armenia; Mousheghian "The Armenian Hoard" under Armenia; Moustaka and Tselekas "Coins from the Excavation" under Ionia; Newell various "Alexander Hoards" under Macedonian Kingdom—General Works; Newell *Two Recent Egyptian Hoards* under Egypt—Ptolemaic Kingdom; Newell "A Parthian Hoard" under Parthia; Nicolaou "Paphos Hoard" under Egypt—Ptolemaic Kingdom; Nicolaou "Contribution" under Egypt—Ptolemaic Kingdom; Nicolet-Pierre and Amandry "Un Nouveau Trésor…Pseudo-Atheniennes" under Bactria; Nicolet-Pierre and Arnold-Biucchi "Le Trésor de Lentini" under Attica; Nicolet-Pierre and Barrandon "Monnaies d'Électrum Archaïques" under Ionian Islands—Samos; Noe "A Lycian Hoard" under Lycia; Noe *Mende (Kaliandra) Hoard* under Macedonian Cities and Tribes; Noe *Two Hoards of Persian Sigloi* under Persia; Oddy "Two Putative Coin Hoards from South Arabia" under Arabia; Oeconomides "Contribution" under Attica—General Works; Oeconomides "The *IGCH* 101 Hoard and the Circulation of the Tortoise" under Aegina; Oeconomides "The 1970 Myrina Hoard" under Aegina; Oeconomides "Piraeus Hoard" (two items) under Attica—General Works; Oeconomides "The 1979 Tricala Hoard" under Macedonian Kingdom—General Works; Oeconomides "Le Trésor d'Épidaure 1977" under Macedonian Kingdom—General Works; Özbek "Herakleia Hoard" under Attica—New Style Coinage.

Papaeuthymiou "Un Trésor (1995) de 80 Drachmes" under Macedonian Kingdom—General Works; Parke-Bernet Galleries *Extremely Important Greek Hoard* under Macedonian Kingdom—Cities and Tribes; Paton "Find of Coins near Halicarnassus" under Caria; Picard "Monnaies de Fouilles" under Thrace—Thasos; Picard "Un Monnayage Alexandrin" under Macedonian Kingdom—General Works; Price "A Hoard from Gortyn" under Crete; Price "Mugnano Hoard" under Italy—General Works; Price "Thrace" under Thrace—Abdera; Prokopov "The Circulation of Bronze Coins" under Thrace—General Works; Prokopov and Batchvarov "Trésor Monétaire de Popina" under Thrace—Thasos; Psoma *Olynthe* under Macedonian Cities and Tribes; Psoma "Le Trésor de Gazôros" under Thrace—Lete; Psoma, Karadima, and Terzopoulou *The Coins from Maroneia* under Thrace—Maroneia; Rahmani "A Hoard of Alexander Coins" under Macedonian Kingdom—General Works; Ralli and Kombou "Mytilene: The Hoard of Krene Street" under Lesbos; Ravel *Corinthian Hoards* under Corinthia; Ravel "Uninscribed Agathoclean Pegasi" under Sicily—Syracuse; Robinson "A Find of Coins of Thasos" under Thrace—Thasos; Robinson "Coins from the Ephesian Artemision" under Origins of Coinage; Robinson "Hoard of Persian Sigloi" under Persia; Robinson "Larnaca Hoard" under Cyprus; Robinson "A Hoard of Coins of the Libyans" under Zeugitana; Robinson "The Libyan Hoard (1952): Addenda" under Zeugitana; Robinson "Coins from Lycia and Pamphylia" under Lycia; E. S. G. Robinson "A South Italian Hoard" under Italy—General Works; Robinson "The Tell El-Mashkuta Hoard" under Attica—General Works; Robinson and Clement "Excavations at Olynthus, Part 9" under Macedonian Cities and Tribes; Root "Evidence from Persepolis" under Persia; Rudd "Coins of King Prasutagus" under Celtic Coinage of Britain; Rudd "Celtic Currency Bars" under Celtic Coinage of Britain; Rudd "Huge Druid Hoard" under Celtic Coinage of Britain; Rudd "Brittany" under Celtic Coinage of Europe.

Sawaya "The Akura Hoard" under Parthia; Schwabacher "Ein Fund Archaischer Münzen von Samothrake" under Thrace—Samothrace; Schwabacher "A Hoard of Drachms of Elis" under Peloponnesos—Elis; Schwabacher "An Unrecorded Alexander Hoard" under Macedonian Kingdom—General Works; Seager *A Cretan Coin Hoard* under Crete; Sear "Then and Now: Kunduz" under Bactria; Seldarov "Hellenistic Coin Hoard" under Macedonian Kingdom—General

Works; Seldarov *Kings of Ancient Macedonia* under Macedonian Kingdom—General Works; Sellwood "A Currently Emerging Parthian Hoard" under Parthia; Sellwood "New Parthian Coin Types" under Parthia; Seltman "The 'Katoché' Hoard of Elean Coins" under Peloponnesos—Elis; Seyrig *Trésor Monétaires Séleucides* under Syria—Seleucid Kingdom; J. P. Shear "Excavations in the Athenian Agora" under Attica—General Works; T. L. Shear "The Campaign" under Attica—General Works; T. L. Shear "Sixth Preliminary Report" under Lydia; Sheedy and Papageorgiadou-Banis *Numismatic Archaeology* under General Works—Greek; Sheridan "A Hoard of Rhodian Type Drachms" under Caria; Sotheby & Co. *Catalogue of the Extremely Important Paeonian Hoard* under Macedonian Cities and Tribes; Spaer "A Hoard" under Macedonian Kingdom—General Works; Spagnoli and Mensitieri *Ripostigli dalla Piana Lametina* under Italy—General Works; Spier et al. "The Demirler, Lycia Hoard" under Lycia; Stefanakis "The 'Chania 1922' Hoard" under Crete; Stern "The Silver Hoard from Tel Dor" under Origins of Coinage; Stern "The Dating of Stratum II at Tell Abu Hawan" under Phoenicia.

Sutherland "Overstrikes and Hoards" under The Minting Process; Talbert "Corinthian Silver" under Sicily—Syracuse; Tameanko "Coins Reveal" under Phoenicia; Tameanko "Naucratis" under Egypt—Pre-Ptolemaic Period; Taylor "A Find" under Cappadocia; Tekin "Hellenistic Hoard of Lysimachean Bronze" under Thrace—Lysimachos; Terzian and van Steen "A Hoard of Bronze Coins" under Thrace—Maroneia; Thomas "Sur une Trouvaille" under Numidia; H. Thompson "Athenian Agora" (four items) under Attica—General Works; M. Thompson "A Hoard of Athenian Fractions" under Attica—General Works; M. Thompson "The Beginnings of Athenian New-Style" under Attica—New Style Coinage; Thompson "The Cavalla Hoard" under Macedonian Kingdom—General Works; M. Thompson "A Ptolemaic Bronze Hoard" under Egypt—Ptolemaic Kingdom; Thompson and Bellinger "Greek Coins in the Yale Collection" under Macedonian Kingdom—General Works; Touratsoglou "The Adam Zagliveriou/1983 Hoard" under Attica—New Style Coinage; Touratsoglou "The Gymnasium of Ancient Samos" under Ionian Islands—Samos; Touratsoglou and Tsourti "Contribution…Achaean League Triobols" under Peloponnesos—Achaia; Troxell "A Partial Hoard of Royal Macedonian Bronzes" under Macedonian Kingdom—General Works; Tsakos "Ancient Coins" under Public Collections—Sudan (Khartoum).

van Alfen "Herodotus' 'Aryandic' Silver and Bullion Use" under Egypt—Pre-Ptolemaic Period; van Alfen "The 'Owls' from the 1989 Syria Hoard" under Egypt—Pre-Ptolemaic Period; van Alfen "Two Unpublished Hoards" under Attica—General Works; van Alfen, Almagro-Gorbea, and Ripollès "A New Celtiberian Hacksilber Hoard" under Spain; Van Arsdell "Haslemere Hoard" (several items) under Celtic Coinage of Britain; Van Arsdell "A Statistical Analysis" under Celtic Coinage of Britain; Vaux "Extract of a Letter" under Macedonian Kingdom—General Works; Vermeule "A Ptolemaic Contribution Box" under Egypt—Ptolemaic Kingdom; Vickers "Early Greek Coinage" under Origins of Coinage; Visonà "Carthage" under Zeugitana; Visonà "Punic and Greek Bronze" under Zeugitana; Visonà "Finds of Numidian Coins" under Zeugitana; Visonà "Early Greek Bronze…Skudljivac Hoard" under Northern Greece—Illyria; Visonà "The Two Nehavend Hoards" under Parthia; Visonà "A Hoard of Ptolemaic Bronze" under Egypt—Ptolemaic Kingdom; Visonà "A Hoard of 4th Century Athenian Tetradrachms" under Attica—General Works; Vlachogianni "A Hoard of Coins from Thebes" under Central Greece—Boeotia; Vlasto "On a Recent Find" under Italy—Taras; Vlasto "A Find of Tarentine Nomoi" under Italy—Taras; Vlasto "The Late Mr. E. P. Warren's Hoard" under Italy—Taras.

Warren "A Neglected Hoard of Elean Coins" under Peloponnesos—Elis; Wartenberg "A Small Group" under Macedonian Kingdom—General Works; Weber "A Small Find of Coins of Mende" under Macedonian Cities and Tribes; Welch "An Argive Hoard" under Peloponnesos—Argolis; L. M. Wilson "Demetrios II of Bactria and Hoards from Ai Khanoum" under Bactria; Wright "A Late Seleukid Bronze Hoard" under Syria—Seleucid Kingdom; Young "The 1963 Campaign at Gordion" under Lydia; Zabel and Meadows "Myndos 1996 Hoard" under Caria; Zervos "Additions to the Demanhur Hoard" under Macedonian Kingdom—General Works; Zervos "The Delta Hoard" under Egypt—Ptolemaic Kingdom; Zervos "A Ptolemaic Hoard" under Egypt—Ptolemaic Kingdom; Zervos "Two Early Ptolemaic Hoards" under Egypt—Ptolemaic Kingdom; Zograph "Pegasos Staters" under Corinthia; Zograph "Tooapse Hoard" under Thrace—Coinage of Lysimachos.

Artistic Aspects of Greek Coinage

Types and Representations

To enumerate the various reverses would be infinite and impossible; for there are few objects either of nature, or art, which do not make their appearance on ancient coins.

—John Pinkerton, 1808

858 **Alpha Bank.** *Athena and Phoebus: Representation of Two Gods on Coins from the Alpha Bank Collection.* Athens: Alpha Bank, 2004. 18 pp., illus.
Also printed in French and Greek.

859 **Andrews, Alfred C.** "Plant Symbolism on Greek Coins." *Economic Botany* 17, no. 4 (October-December 1963): 317-8.
Describes how coin types came to be recognized symbols of the cities which issued the coins. Points out that the silphium plant became widely known as a product of Cyrenaica, and that the city of Selinus in Sicily became well-known for the selinon (wild celery) leaf on its coins.

860 **Anson, Leo.** *Numismata Graeca: Greek Coin-Types Classified for Immediate Identification.* Thirteen parts in seven volumes. London: Leo Anson, 1910-16. Reprinted in two volumes, Bologna: A. Forni, 1967 and 1976. 904 pp., 150 pls. [CS 3406]
A comprehensive guide to identifying Greek coins. Anson's original goal was to produce two sections classifying every known Greek or Graeco-Roman coin type under the heading of the type and also of the symbol or symbols represented on the coins. Section 1 covers coin types showing inanimate objects, plants, etc. which occur either alone or as symbols in conjunction with figures, animals, etc. Section 2 was to cover animate objects such as figures of deities, heroes, dynasts, animals, etc., but this section was never published. Section 1 includes 7743 types arranged alphabetically by type. Provides a description of each coin including the city, obverse and reverse types, size, weight, denomination, and cross-references to other collections. The parts of Section 1 are:

    Part 1   *Industry—Vases, Recipients, Tripods, etc.* 1911. 138 pp., 27 pls.
    Part 2   *War—Arms, Weapons, Armours, Standards, etc.* 1911. 112 pp., 25 pls.
    Part 3   *Agriculture—Plants and Trees, Fruits, Flowers, etc.* 1912. 152 pp., 30 pls.
    Part 4   *Religion—Altars, Attributes of Deities, Sacrifice, etc.* 1913. 99 pp., 21 pls.
    Part 5   *Architecture—Buildings, Edifices, Monuments, Temples, etc. Naval and Marine-Galley, Shells, etc.* 1914. 146 pp., 25 pls.
    Part 6   *Science and the Arts—Astronomy, Sculpture, Music, Comedy, etc. Various.* 1916. 108 pp., 22 pls. Includes an additional twenty page "Small Numismatic Dictionary" containing most of the words and abbreviations used in the text in English, French, German, Italian, and Spanish. Also includes a seven page table of auction prices realized for some of the listed coins.
    Part 7   *General Guide—Index of the Six Parts of Section 1.* 1910. 41 pp. An alphabetical index to the types, keyed to the main volumes.

[G. F. Hill wrote a brief and critical review of Parts 1-4 which appears in *Numismatic Chronicle* 4th ser., 11 (1911): 199. Interestingly, Hill warns of the difficulties Anson will encounter when he attempts to publish Section 2 covering coins bearing humans and deities. Apparently Anson took heed of this warning as noted above].

861 **Argyropoulou-Evelpidou, Rena.** "Musical Instruments in Antiquity." *Nomismatika Khronika* (Greece) 8 (1989): 31-4. Illus.
A brief discussion of musical instruments that have appeared on Greek coins including various types of lyre, Pan pipes, guitar, and maracas. In Greek on pages 31-2. In English on pages 33-4. English translation by Marion J. Tzamali.

862 **Askew, Gilbert.** "Greek Coin Types." *Seaby Coin and Medal Bulletin* 382 (March 1950): 98-102. Illus.
Describes some of the common coin types at Athens, the use of heraldic types at various cities, and the introduction of royal portraits. Emphasizes the religious nature of many of the coin types prior to the Hellenistic age.

863 **Baker, Donald G.** "Animals on the Coins of Greek Cities." *Harvard Studies in Classical Philology* 43 (1932): 167-8.
A summary of a Ph.D. dissertation which attempts to discover the motives behind the choice of the types for Greek coins, focusing on coins bearing animals as types or symbols. The dissertation lists 2300 coins bearing these types on which over thirty-five kinds of beasts occur. The author concludes that the motives for most of these types was non-religious. Only one out of ten designs was chosen with a purely religious motive.

864 **Banning, Theodore.** "Amphoras and Ancient Coinage." *Canadian Numismatic Journal* (Canada) 17, no. 12 (December 1972): 455, 459.

"The comparison of ancient coins with amphorae to surviving amphorae for the purposes of dating and identification is discussed." [R. Willey, *NL* 90]

865 **Barry, Kevin, and Zachary Beasley.** "Bear Season…" *The Celator* 20, no. 10 (October 2006): 38-9. Illus.
The author discusses his collection of ancient coins which depict bears, including a fifth century B.C. coin of Mantineia and some Celtic potin coins.

866 ——— "Lions and Tigers and Bears, Oh My!" *The Celator* 22, no. 8 (August 2008): 44, 46. Illus.
This installment of the authors' "Internet Connection" column examines mythological creatures and provides internet links for more information on each.

867 ——— "Lassia Come Home!" *The Celator* 25, no. 8 (August 2011): 44, 46. Illus.
This installment of the authors' "Internet Connection" column discusses dogs depicted on ancient coins including a mastiff on an obol of Pherai, a greyhound on a Corinthian stater and a Roman Republican denarius, a hunting dog on a didrachm of Segesta, and Argos—Odysseus' dog—on a Republican denarius.

868 ——— "Before there was the World Wrestling Federation…" *The Celator* 25, no. 10 (October 2011): 44, 40. Illus.
A brief discussion of wrestling scenes on ancient coins.

869 **Barton, John P.** *A Numismatic Bestiary.* Henniker, N.H.: Owl Ltd (n.d.).
Lists 202 ancient Greek and Roman coins bearing zoological types. Includes an introduction by John Twente.

870 **Baumann, Hellmut.** *Pflanzenbilder auf Griechischen Münzen.* Munich: Hirmer Verlag, 2000. 79 pp., pls.
An examination of the depiction of plants on Greek coins, arranged by plant order. Photographs of the plants are accompanied by representations on coins. The study reveals associations between plants, deities, and animals and the prominence of plants in political crests or motifs. Also includes a listing of Greek and Roman authorities on the subject. Lists and illustrates 27 plants. [Reviewed by Stanley Ireland in *Numismatic Chronicle* 162 (2002): 434-5].

871 **Baur, Paul V. C.** "Coins." *Centaurs in Ancient Art.* 1912. Pages 72-3.

872 **Beazley, J. D.** "Bakchos-Rings." *Numismatic Chronicle* 6th ser., 1 (1941): 1-7. Illus.
A cylindrical object, generally shown lying on its side, is often represented on Hellenistic coins of Athens and Eleusis. Some have suggested it is a kalathos or the cista mystica—sacred baskets used in the cult of Demeter at Eleusis. Beazley concludes these objects are rings which held *bakchoi* together. A bakchos is a bundle of leafy branches, tightly bound at intervals by a series of clasps or rings. It was used in the Eleusinian rites. Illustrates bakchoi on vases and coins.

873 **Bellinger, Alfred R., and Marjorie Alkins Berlincourt.** *Victory as a Coin Type.* Numismatic Notes and Monographs, No. 149. New York: American Numismatic Society, 1962. 68 pp., 13 pls. [CS 3410]
A study of the use of the symbol of victory as a coin type from the Greek Nike of the sixth century B.C. to the Christian angel of the sixth century A.D. Begins with the first appearance of Nike as a coin type ca. 510 B.C. at Olympia. Describes the mythological origins of Nike and her meaning. Continues with a survey of cities which used Nike as a coin type and the reasons and symbolism behind the type. Discusses the use of Nike by the Hellenistic kings and the Romans. [Reviewed by J. F. Healy in *Journal of Hellenic Studies* 84 (1964): 236, and by R. R. Holloway in *American Journal of Archaeology* 68 (1964): 213-4].

874 **Ben-Eli, Arie L., ed.** *Ships and Parts of Ships on Ancient Coins.* Haifa: National Maritime Museum, 1975. 80 pp., illus. [CS 2914 and 3411]
Ancient coins portray ships in great detail and contain a wealth of information about ships, their design and construction, sails and oars. This book catalogues and illustrates a selection of coins showing ships and parts of ships. The introduction, written by Lionel Casson, describes the use of ships as coin types. A short essay by Robert R. Stieglitz, "Maritime History on Jewish Coins," follows. The main section of the book is the catalogue of related coins from the National Maritime Museum's collection, compiled by Ya'akov Meshorer. Includes coins of the Roman Republic and the Roman Empire, as well as Roman Provincial coins, Judean coins, and a few coins of autonomous Greek cities and Hellenistic kingdoms. In Hebrew and English.

875 **Benford, Timothy B.** "This Will Really 'Bug' You: Egad! Those Pesky Cicadas are on Everything, Including Coins." *Coin World* (June 7, 2004): 1, 88. Illus.
Discusses the recent batch of cicadas, which emerge every seventeen years in the United States. Discusses the cicadas and other bugs which appear as coin types, especially on ancient Greek coins.

876 **Benton, Sylvia.** "Cattle Egrets and Bustards in Greek Art." *Journal of Hellenic Studies* 81 (1961): 44-55. 5 pls.
"On pp. 46-8 the birds which appear on several West Greek coins are studied. The so-called 'finch' of Phrygillus which appears at Thurium (more properly 'Thouria') seems to be a marsh bird, which may be a Cattle Egret or a Little Egret. The bird on an earlier coin of Sybaris will be the stone-thrush, *laios*, commemorating the help given to the city by the people of Laos." [J. R. Jones, *NIJHS*]

877 **Bérend, Denyse.** "Le Lièvre et le Poulpe." *Florilegium Numismaticum: Studia in Honorem U. Westermark Edita.* Edited by Harald Nilsson. Stockholm: Svenska Numismatiska Föreningen, 1992. Pages 33-9. 1 pl.
Discusses the hare and octopus on Greek coins. [Also see Bérend "Histoire de Poulpes" under SICILY—SYRACUSE].

878 **Bernhart, Max.** *Aphrodite auf Griechischen Münzen.* Munich, 1936. 68 pp., 9 pls. [CS 3418]
Depictions of Aphrodite on Greek coins.

879 ——— "Dionysos und Seine Familie auf Griechischen Münzen." *Jahrbuch für Numismatik und Geldgeschichte* (Germany) 1 (1949): 1-175. 11 pls. [CS 3420]

880 **Bieber, Margarete.** "A Bronze Statuette in Cincinnati and its Place in the History of the Asklepios Types." *Proceedings of the American Philosophical Society* 101, no. 1 (February 1957): 70-92. Illus.

"Section 3 of this article discusses statues of Asklepios depicted upon Greek coins. Seated statues of Asklepios are shown inside and outside the temple upon the coins of Trikka, perhaps the oldest sanctuary of Asklepios. Such statues also appear upon the coins of Epidauros and Pergamon. The Epidaurian coins were issued from the fourth century B.C. to the Antonine period. The statue represented upon the Epidaurian pieces must have been the work executed by Thrasymedes. The seated statues upon the coins of Pergamon first appeared in the reign of Eumenes. Illustrated are three coins, an Athenian piece, the reverse of which shows a statue of Asklepios, a silver coin of Kos, the reverse of which shows a standing statue of Asklepios, and a bronze coin of Kos, which shows Asklepios and Hygeia within a temple." [*NL* 41]

881   **Bird, Susan.** *Greek Designs.* London: British Museum Press, 2003. 128 pp., illus.
A concise introduction to the historical background of Greek designs as seen on borders framing vase paintings, friezes carved on buildings, emblems placed on coins, and other ornaments. Discusses many themes represented in vase painting, sculpture, architecture, and coinage. Introduction by Susan Woodford.

882   **Bitner, John W.** "A History of the Aegis." *The Celator* 13, no. 6 (June 1999): 6-12. Illus.
Reviews the mythological origins of the use of the severed head of the gorgon Medusa as a protective device mounted on the aegis. The aegis is a leather cloak worn loosely around the shoulders. The aegis with gorgon's head is commonly seen on Greek and Roman coins. Several such coins are illustrated.

883   **Borba-Florenzano, Maria Beatriz.** "Notes on the Imagery of Dionysus on Greek Coins." *Revue Belge de Numismatique et de Sigillographie* (Belgium) 145 (1999): 37-48.

884   **Bosworth, A. B.** "Rider in the Chariot: Ptolemy, Alexander and the Elephants." *Alexander and the Hellenistic Kingdoms: Coins, Image and the Creation of Identity. The Westmoreland Collection.* Ancient Coins in Australian Collections 1. Edited by K. A. Sheedy. Sydney: Australian Centre for Ancient Numismatic Studies, Macquarie University, 2007. Pages 17-22. Illus.
Examines the iconography of an outstanding gold stater of Ptolemy I. The reverse depicts Alexander driving a chariot pulled by four elephants. Bosworth suggests the coin delivers the message that Ptolemy is the best successor to Alexander. He discusses the symbolism of elephants and elephant-scalp headdresses on Ptolemy's coinage, as well as on the tetradrachms of Seleucus. The author compares and contrasts the way each ruler used imagery to promote his messages. [Also see Sheedy *Alexander and the Hellenistic Kingdoms* under PRIVATE COLLECTIONS].

885   **Brauer, George C.** "Horseman Spearing a Fallen Enemy—A Recurrent Coin Type." Parts 1 and 2. *SAN—Journal of the Society for Ancient Numismatics* 5, no. 1 (1973-4): 9-11; *SAN* 5, no. 2 (1973-4): 25-7.
Greek and Roman coins which show a horseman and his enemy are discussed and pictured. Several Greek coins are listed and a tetradrachm of Patraus of Peonia is discussed. The emphasis is on Roman coins.

886   ——— "The Kalpe—An Agonistic Reference on Several Greek Coins?" *SAN—Journal of the Society for Ancient Numismatics* 6, no. 1 (fall 1974): 6-7.
Describes an Olympic event in which horse riders leap off and finish a race by running alongside their horses. Suggests this event is depicted on some coins of Erythrae, Celenderis, and Tarentum. [Also see Madsen "Celenderis" under CILICIA for a description of a similar event shown on a coin of Celenderis].

887   **Breitsprecher, Marc, and Melissa Breitsprecher.** "Elephants in Ancient Numismatic History." *The Celator* 20, no. 9 (September 2006): 6-20. Illus.
Traces the role of elephants throughout ancient history and illustrates numerous Greek and Roman coins on which elephants are depicted.

888   **Brett, Agnes Baldwin.** "Facing Heads on Greek Coins." *American Journal of Numismatics* 43, no. 3 (1908-1909): 113-31. 4 pls. Reprinted as *Facing Heads on Ancient Greek Coins.* Closter, New Jersey: C. H. McSorley, 1968. New York: Sanford J. Durst, 1982. 23 pp., 4 pls. [CS 3425]
Explores the facing head design on Greek coins. States that the facing head, in full-front or three-quarter view, developed independently in many places. Argues that the facing head did not originate in the gorgoneion type as is sometimes claimed. Emphasizes that most of the full-front view coins belong to the archaic period; later coins show the head turned slightly to the left or right. Describes 363 facing-head types, many of which are illustrated. [Also see Erhart *The Development of the Facing Head Motif* below].

889   ——— "Symbolism on Greek Coins." *American Journal of Numismatics* 49 (1915): 89-194. Illus., 6 pls. Reprints, New York, 1916; New York: Sanford J. Durst, 1977. 106 pp., illus., 6 pls. [CS 3424]
Explores the psychological origins for the use of symbols—representations of ideas or concepts. Examines the uses and significance of the swastika, the triskeles, the ankh, and the winged disk in ancient art and coinage. Presents a list of coins bearing these symbols. Includes illustrations of coins and other art works. [Also see Thomas "The Indian Swastika" below].

890   ——— "The Aphlaston: Symbol of Naval Victory or Supremacy on Greek and Roman Coins." *Transactions of the International Numismatic Congress Organized and Held in London by the Royal Numismatic Society, June 30-July 3, 1936.* Edited by J. Allan, H. Mattingly, and E. S. G. Robinson. London: B. Quaritch, 1938. Pages 23-32. 2 pls.
The aphlaston (*aplustre* in Latin) is the curving end of the stern on an ancient war galley which was torn away from an enemy's ship and carried away by the victor in a naval battle. The aphlaston served as a signal-post where the pennants of the ship's captain were hung. The author discusses the symbolic significance of the aphlaston, lists many appearances of the aphlaston on Greek and Roman coins, and attempts to relate the aphlaston's appearance on coins with specific naval victories. Discusses the use of the symbol on coins of Histiaea, Phaselis, Corcyra, Cyzicus, Himera, Syracuse, Rhodes, Leucas, various issues struck on Cyprus, and on coinage of Demetrius Poliorcetes and Ptolemy I. [Also see *Note 10* of B. Emmons "The Overstruck Coinage of Ptolemy I" in *Museum Notes* 6 (1954): 73, for another opinion on some details of the aphlaston's significance].

891   ——— "Athena ΑΛΚΙΔΕΜΟΣ of Pella." *Museum Notes* 4 (1950): 55-72. 3 pls.
Discusses the numismatic depiction of Athena Alkidemos, "Defender or Protector of the People." This fighting Athena usually wields a thunderbolt but sometimes uses a spear, and is sometimes erroneously identified as Athena Promachos. The type was copied from a statue which stood at Pella. It appeared as a symbol on coins of Alexander the Great, and as a type on early Ptolemaic tetradrachms, gold staters of Demetrius Poliorcetes, gold staters of Pyrrhus of Epirus, and tetradrachms of Antigonus Gonatas and Philip V of Macedon, and Menander of Bactria. Discusses the meaning of the type. Barclay Head

suggested it was a symbol of sovereignty over Macedonia; Svoronos believed it to be a symbol of freedom for Greek cities; Brett rejects these theories. She concludes the Athena Alkidemos was a Macedonian symbol and other kings used it to emphasize their connection with Macedonia.

892 **Briggs, Sherry.** "Honest Asclepius vs. Sly Old Hermes?" *The Celator* 17, no. 5 (May 2003): 40-1, 60. Illus.
Briggs discusses the staff of Asclepius and the caduceus of Hermes as symbols of the medical profession. Shows the variations in the symbols and discussions their meanings.

893 **Broneer, Oscar.** "The Isthmian Victory Crown." *American Journal of Archaeology* 66, no. 3 (July 1962): 259-63. 1 pl.
"Early in the fifth century B.C. the pine crowns originally awarded to victors at the Isthmian Games were replaced by wilted celery. In the second century B.C. pine was re-introduced with the celery and from that time until the second century of the present era both types of crown were awarded. Various coins of Corinth illustrate these crowns." [I. Merker, *NL* 62]

894 **Brown, R.** "Constellation Figures as Greek Coin-Types." *Scientific American Supplement* 51 (March 16, 1901): 21083-4.

895 **Brunnsåker, Sture.** *The Tyrant-Slayers of Kritios and Nesiotes.* Dissertation. Lund University (Sweden), 1955.
A discussion of the statues of the famous Tyrant-Slayers in the Agora of Athens. Considers the evidence of their representations on coins and tessarae.

896 **Burgon, Thomas.** "An Inquiry into the Motives Which Influenced the Ancients in Their Choice of the Various Representations which We Find Stamped on Their Money." *Numismatic Journal* 1 (1837): 97-131.
Argues that "from the first striking of money, down to the extinction of the Byzantine Empire, religion was the sole motive of the types of coins." Regarding royal portrait types, Burgon states "no mortal ever appears upon an ancient coin, but in the character of a deity."

897 **Bush, Joseph E.** "Homer's Odyssey and Numismatics." *North American Journal of Numismatics: The Turtle* 6, no. 7 (July 1967): 197-9.
Identifies persons and objects related to Homer's *Odyssey* which may be found on Greek coins.

898 **Cahn, Herbert A.** "Die Löwen des Apollo." *Museum Helveticum* 7, no. 4 (1950): 185-99. [CS 3426]
The lions of Apollo.

899 **Cammann, Jean B.** *Numismatic Mythology.* New York: Wayte Raymond, 1936. 39 pp., illus., map. [CS 3427]
An overview of Greek coinage which focuses on the mythological and legendary stories which relate to the coin types. [Originally published in twelve installments in *The Coin Collector's Journal*, 1934-1936].

900 **Carlton, Walker.** "Ancient Warships 700-31 B.C." Parts 1-4. *SAN—Journal of the Society for Ancient Numismatics* 3, no. 3 (1971-2): 39-41, 52-3; no. 4 (1971-2): 63-6, 70; 4, no. 1 (1972-3): 12-7; no. 2 (1972-3): 23-4.
Discusses the types of ancient warships and their development. Discusses possible arrangements of the rows of oars, and contains diagrams and pictures of ships on ancient coins. Part 2 focuses on the trireme. Part 3 focuses on Hellenistic ships.

901 **Chandler, Tertius.** "Zeus and Hercules: Men or Myth?" *The Celator* 7, no. 8 (August 1993): 32-4. Illus.
Argues that Zeus was a real person—a king who ruled in Greece ca. 1366 B.C. Lists the succession of kings from Zeus to Agamemnon (1202 B.C.). Relates stories connecting Zeus with Moses and Egypt's Akhenaten. Suggests Zeus' son, Hercules, was also a real person. Hercules' battle with the Hydra was in fact a war with Indra in 1358 B.C. Comments on Athena and Geryon, mythical figures which may also have been historical persons. [Also see the strong rebuttals by A. Walker in *The Celator* 7, no. 9 (September 1993): 38-40 and J. Rieske in *The Celator* 7, no. 10 (October 1993): 4].

902 **Cheek, Kevin R.** "Cult Overtones: Helmets on Coins Reflect Militaristic Societies." *The Celator* 3, no. 11 (November 1989): 20.
The use of helmets in war and the depiction of helmets on coins is discussed. Many coins showing a helmet as a symbol of war were minted during the Persian and Peloponnesian wars. The significance of the helmet symbol to the Thraco-Macedonian tribes is explored.

903 **Chiszar, David, and Hobart M. Smith.** "The Caduceus and the Staff of Aesculapius as Symbols of Medicine." *The Celator* 12, no. 2 (February 1998): 14-7. Illus.
The authors explain how the caduceus of Hermes became accepted as a symbol of medicine and healing, in place of the more appropriate staff of Aesculapius. In the nineteenth century, the caduceus was used as a symbol to identify non-combatant military personnel and soon became associated with medical units.

904 **Chiszar, David, William Dunn, and Hobart M. Smith.** "The Relative Absence of Amphibians from Ancient Greek Coins." *The Celator* 11, no. 6 (June 1997): 10-5. Illus.
The authors compare the appearance of animals on Roman coins versus Greek coins. They note the relative scarcity of frogs, toads, salamanders, and caecilians on Greek coins. The authors discuss the attitudes of Aristotle toward frogs and toads, and conclude that they were considered to be killers of bees, a favored animal in the Greek world, and thus were purposely ignored by coin engravers.

905 **Chittenden, Jacqueline.** "The Master of Animals." *Hesperia* 16 (1947): 89-114. 7 pls.
"The earliest representations of Hermes, dating to the Bronze Age, take the form of a heap of stones, which is preserved on coins of Segesta of the fifth century B.C. (p. 94). These coins and others of Pandosia (pp. 103-4) also show that Hermes was associated with hunters and hunting. A selection of coins appears in plate 21." [J. R. Jones, *NIAJAH*]

906 **Clayton, Peter A.** "The Ancient Olympic Games." *Seaby Coin and Medal Bulletin* 744 (August 1980): 250-2.
Briefly describes the ancient Olympic games and some of the Greek and Roman coins related to the games.

907 **Cook, A. B.** "Animal-worship in the Mycenaean Age." *Journal of Hellenic Studies* 14 (1894): 81-169. Illus.
"On p. 115 three Republican coins (Caecilia, Eppia, Coponia) are noted as showing the club of Herakles in the form of a tree-trunk; a coin of Selge shows a club and a tree together. It is suggested that the club was originally the symbol of a tree-god. On p. 124 Cretan coins showing Europa amid the branches are

connected with the myth of her marriage to Zeus beneath a plane tree. On pp. 128-9 the bull on denarii of Caesar is explained as referring to the bull-hunts which he introduced as a spectacle at Rome (Pliny, *NH* 8, 182), and Thessalian coin types showing bull-wrestling scenes are noted. On p. 141 coins of Thelpusa and Phigaleia with Demeter types are claimed to be inspired by the myth of the wooing of Demeter as a mare by Poseidon. On p. 148-9 the coins of Nicaea showing a rider on a horse with human feet are explained as representing the subjugation of the Chthonian horse, the escort of the dead. On p. 151, coins of the Fonteian *gens* showing Cupid on a goat are connected with Aphrodite Pandemos." [J. R. Jones, *NIJHS*]

908 ——— "The Bee in Greek Mythology." *Journal of Hellenic Studies* 15 (1895): 1-24.
"On p. 3 it is agreed that the bee which appears as an emblem on coins of Elyrus, Hyrtacina and Praesus, refers to the myth of the feeding of the infant Zeus with honey. On p. 4, the bee on coins of Melitaea is explained as a reference to a local legend, rather than as a *type parlant*. On p. 13, coins of Smyrna, Erythrae, Aradus and Parium showing the bee as an emblem of Artemis are noted; the theory that the bee is an appropriate emblem for a colony is discounted." [J. R. Jones, *NIJHS*]

909 **Croon, J. H.** "The Mask of the Underworld Daemon." *Journal of Hellenic Studies* 75 (1955): 9-16.
"On pp. 12-2 coins with Gorgon types are discussed. A high proportion of them comes from cities famed for hot springs, and this suggests that they are an echo of local cults connected with the underworld." [J. R. Jones, *NIJHS*]

910 **Cummings, Prentiss.** "Homer and Astronomic Coin-Types." *American Journal of Numismatics* 30, no. 2 (October 1895): 38-40.
Discusses the knowledge of astronomy which is evident in Homer's *Iliad* and *Odyssey* as a supplement to Svoronos' discussion of astronomical coin types (see Svoronos "Significance of Certain Ancient Monetary Types" below). Cummings also comments on the use of cattle as legal tender. [Also see "Cow-Money and Staters" under METROLOGY].

911 **Curtius, Ernst.** "On the Religious Character of Greek Coins." *Numismatic Chronicle* new ser., 10 (1870): 91-111.
Curtius explores the relationship between coins and religious worship. He notes that the deities used on coins are not always the town or state deities. Discusses the use of temples as the first "banks." The temples played a role in the progress of the knowledge of metals. Discusses temples as centers of trade, and reviews coin types and inscriptions referring to religious festivals. [Also see Head "On the Religious Character" below].

912 **de Callataÿ, François, and Dominique Gerin.** "Faut-il Faire Tomber les Foudres?" *Florilegium Numismaticum: Studia in Honorem U. Westermark Edita*. Edited by Harald Nilsson. Stockholm: Svenska Numismatiska Föreningen, 1992. Pages 103-9. 1 pl.
Lightning bolts on Greek coins.

913 **da Costa, Virginia.** "Five Olympian Goddesses: Part I: Aphrodite." *The Celator* 17, no. 9 (September 2003): 6-18. Illus.
The author explores the origins of Aphrodite and describes many variations in her mythology and worship. Aphrodite's depiction on Greek coins is then discussed.

914 **Daehn, William E.** "Mythological Themes Influenced Ancient Greek Coin Designs." *The Celator* 5, no. 1 (January 1991): 30-3.
Discusses the influence of religion and mythology on the designs chosen for ancient Greek coins. Recounts the myths of Artemis, Perseus, and Bellerophon and shows how the legends surrounding them were depicted on coins.

915 **Demeester, Anne, and Bernard Daubersy.** *Les Animaux la Monnaie Grecque: Une Collection Preivee de Petites Monnaies Grecques en Argent a Theme Animalier*. Brussels, n.d. Illus.
Lists 156 Greek silver coins depicting animals. Includes 110 enlargements.

916 **Desneux, Jules.** "Sur Quelques Représentations du 'Lion à la Proie' en Glyptique et en Numismatique Antiques." *Revue Belge de Numismatique et de Sigillographie* (Belgium) 106 (1960): 5-19. 2 pls. [CS 3430]

917 **Dodson, G. Derk.** "Multidimensional Beliefs Fall into Definable Categories." *The Celator* 7, no. 9 (September 1993): 12-4. Illus.
A brief comparison of various types of deities and their interrelationships. Classifies Western gods into four categories: command gods, historical gods, concept gods, and visualization gods. Compares the deities and symbols of Western religions to those of Eastern religions.

918 ——— "Spiritual Energy Served as a Foundation for Mythological Symbols." *The Celator* 8, no. 6 (June 1994): 6-11. Illus.
Explains the material and spiritual meanings behind various ancient symbols: wine, serpents, the protruding tongue (as on Medusa), the colors of the rainbow, fire, the lion, and the owl.

919 **Douglass, Summer.** "For the Birds: Eagles, Owls and Other Fowl made Frequent Appearances on Ancient Coinage." *Coin World* (June 25, 2001): 98. Illus.
Illustrates and describes ancient Greek and Roman coins which depict birds. Discusses the symbolism of the birds and their connection to mythology.

920 **Driega, A. W.** "Ancient Greek Olympic Commemoratives." *The Canadian Numismatic Journal* (Canada) 19, no. 6 (June 1974): 185-6.
Briefly discusses three coins which have Olympic games motifs: the tetradrachm of Messana commemorating Anaxilas' victory in his mule biga, the tetradrachm of Philip II of Macedonia commemorating his victory in a horse race, and the stater of Aspendus showing two wrestlers.

921 **Dunbabin, T. J.** "Bellerophon, Herakles and Chimaera." *Studies Presented to David Moore Robinson on His Seventieth Birthday*. Volume 2. Edited by George E. Mylonas and Doris Raymond. St. Louis: Washington University, 1953. Pages 1164-84. 3 pls.
Discusses the origin and development of the Bellerophon/chimaera myth and examines its depiction on vases, monuments and other art works including coins. Includes a list of pre-fourth century B.C. monuments involved in some part of the Bellerophon story.

922 **Elbers, G. C. A.** "Canting Puns on Ancient Coins." Parts 1-2. *SAN—Journal of the Society for Ancient Numismatics* 15, no. 1 (spring 1984): 15-8; no. 2 (summer 1984): 24-5, 32.

Discusses coins whose type is a reference to the name of the issuing city, such as the melon on the coins of Melos. Twenty-three coins containing canting types are pictured. Alternate translations are given for some Greek words, and etymologies are discussed. The author lists his guidelines for determining if a coin type qualifies as a canting type.

923 **Erhart, Katherine Patricia.** *The Development of the Facing Head Motif on Greek Coins and its Relation to Classical Art.* Outstanding Dissertations in the Fine Arts. New York and London: Garland Publishing, 1979. 523 pp., 21 pls. [CS 3432]
A doctoral dissertation at Harvard University. Erhart discusses the representation of the human face in either a frontal or an oblique view in two-dimensional or low-relief art. Traces the stylistic and iconographic changes in this motif through its five principal periods of development—changes which "revolutionized classical art." Discusses the relationships of facing head types in other art media. Discusses the facing heads of the gorgon, sphinx, gods, and goddesses. Presents a catalogue of facing heads on 116 Greek coins. Plates show enlargements of coins and relevant scenes from vase paintings. Includes a bibliography. [Also see Brett "Facing Heads on Greek Coins" above].

924 **Evans, Arthur J.** "Mycenaean Tree and Pillar Cult and its Mediterranean Relations." *Journal of Hellenic Studies* 21 (1901): 99-204. Illus., 1 pl.
"On pp. 108-9 coins of Tenedos and of Aphrodisias in Caria are quoted as illustrations of the survival of the double axe as a representation of a pair of divinities, most probably solar and lunar." [J. R. Jones, *NIJHS*]. [Also see Rouse "The Double Axe" below].

925 **Evgenidou, Desponia, Elena Glytsi et al., eds.** *Nike-Victoria on Coins and Medals.* Athens: Hellenic Ministry of Culture/Numismatic Museum, 2004. 108 pp. illus.
Examines the depiction of Nike on coins and medals from ancient times through modern times in the Western world. Begins with the Nike on coins of Elis and traces the development of Nike/Victory through the Roman and Byzantine era, which saw the transmutation of the image into an angel, and continuing through the Renaissance, and to the modern European use of Nike on Olympic victors' medals. Also reviews various iconographic types of Victory, including depictions with a wreath, trophy, charioteer, and shield.

926 **Fagerlie, Joan.** "Monies of Antiquity: Coins Commemorate Gods, Fauna, and Civic Pride." *Natural History* 73, no. 1 (January 1964): 20-5. Illus. [CS 3436]
A brief review of some of the animals and plants used as types or symbols on ancient Greek coins. Illustrated by numerous enlarged photographs.

927 **Faintich, Marshall.** *Astronomical Symbols on Ancient and Medieval Coins.* Jefferson, North Carolina: McFarland & Co., 2008. 232 pp., illus.
This work hypothesizes that astronomical symbols on ancient and medieval coins were often used as a way to record actual celestial events. The author provides more than 550 figures and line drawings of coins, maps, and astronomical events to illustrate this hypothesis. Several appendices evaluate the historical accuracy of ancient and medieval coinage and offer additional examples. [Reviewed by M. Marotta in *The Centinel* 58, no. 3 (fall 2010): 50-2, and by Robert S. McIvor in *The Celator* 24, no. 11 (November 2010): 40].

928 **Falter, Reinhard.** "The River as God—The Actuality of the Perception of Antiquity." *The Celator* 15, no. 4 (April 2001): 6-16. Illus.
Examines the history and development of the depiction of river gods in ancient art, primarily their representation on coins. Focuses on the perception of rivers as beings.

929 **Feuardent, Robert.** "Réflexions Relatives au Silphium." *Revue Numismatique* (France) 5th ser., 10 (1947-48): 27-32. Also appeared in *Revue Numismatique* 5th ser., 13 (1951): 13-18. [CS 3437]

930 **Fink, C. M.** "The Greeks Symbolized Gods on Coins." *Numismatic Scrapbook Magazine* 24, no. 11 (November 1958): 2313-6. Illus.
"Mentions the symbols used to designate the various gods and goddesses found on coins of ancient Greece, and includes some references to symbols of countries and cities as well as to the Greek civic, monarchical and Imperial issues." [G. North, *NL 48*]

931 **Forrer, Leonard.** "Le Labyrinthe de Knossos et ses Représentations sur les Monnaies." *Revue Suisse de Numismatique* (Switzerland) 10 (1900): 193-211. [CS 3438]
The labyrinth of Knossos and its depiction on coins.

932 **Franke, Peter R.** "Olympia Antiqua: Münzen und Geschichte." *Haller Münzblätter* (Germany) 2, nos. 1-2 (1976): 3-32. Illus. [CS 3441]
"On Olympic Games on Greek coins." [E. Clain-Stefanelli]

933 **Franke, Peter R., and Irini Marathaki.** *Wine and Coins in Ancient Greece.* Athens: The Hatzimichalis Estate, 1999. 167 pp., illus., map.
A beautifully designed book examining the role of wine in ancient Greece and the depiction of wine-related themes on ancient Greek coins. In Part 1, "Wine and Coins in Ancient Greece," Franke examines the history of wine, wine making, and wine drinking in ancient Greece. Incorporates passages from ancient authors. Discusses the origin, spread, and development of coinage. Provides a general discussion of hoards, die linking, wages and prices, numbers of coins struck, die engraving, artistic styles, and denominations. In Part 2, "Wine and Coins in Ancient Greece: A Stroll," Marathaki examines coins depicting vines, grapes, wine vessels, Dionysus, and other mythological characters related to the cult of Dionysus. Discusses the symbolism exhibited on each coin. Concludes with a bibliography of works on wine, vines, and ancient numismatics. Includes many enlarged color photographs. [Part 2 was translated into English by David Hardy. Reviewed in *The Celator* 14, no. 3 (March 2000): 34-5].

934 **Fraser, Peter M., and Tullia Rönne.** *Boeotian and West Greek Tombstones.* Lund, Sweden, 1957.
In the descriptions of the griffins on the tombstones of Eubolos from Tanagra, Rönne refers to the stylistic development of griffins on Greek coins. She also compares the depictions of helmets on tombstones and coins. Fraser comments on the dating of the early coins of the Acarnanians, and comments on the oak wreaths found on tombstones and coins. [Reviewed by D. Feaver in *American Journal of Archaeology* 64 (1960): 103-5].

935 **Gardiner, E. Norman.** "Wrestling." *Journal of Hellenic Studies* 25 (1905): 14-31, 263-93; 26 (1906): 4-22. Illus., 2 pls.
"On pp. 270-8 of vol. 25, coins of Aspendus, Heracleia Lucaniae, Syracuse and Alexandria (Antoninus Pius) are illustrated, and the holds employed by the wrestlers are discussed. All except those of Aspendus represent Heracles, with the Nemean lion or Antaeus." [J. R. Jones, *NIJHS*]

936   ——— *Greek Athletic Sports and Festivals.* London: Macmillan, 1910. Reprint, Dubuque: Brown Reprints, 1970. 533 pp., illus.
A highly regarded history of Greek athletics. Greek coins are occasionally used to illustrate athletic events.

937   **Gardner, Percy.** "Ares as a Sun-God, and Solar Symbols on the Coins of Macedon and Thrace." *Numismatic Chronicle* new ser., 20 (1880):49-61. 1 pl.
Comments on the original sun-god of the Thracians and Macedonians who was known to the Greeks as Ares. Then examines the indications of solar worship on coins of Macedon and Thrace. [Also see E. Thomas "The Indian Swastika" below].

938   ——— "Boat Races among the Greeks." *Journal of Hellenic Studies* 2 (1881): 90-7. Illus.
"Coins of Corcyra of the third century B.C. and of Imperial times seem to refer to a race between galleys, as do those of Nicopolis Epiri. Some literary references to this type of competition are collected, with the addition of inscriptions which provide evidence for boat races at Athens." [J. R. Jones, *NIJHS*]

939   ——— "Floral Patterns on Archaic Greek Coins." *Numismatic Chronicle* 3rd ser., 1 (1881): 1-7. 1 pl.
Gardner comments on the reverse design of the coins of Corcyra, Dyrrhachium, and Apollonia. In his view, the design does not represent the stars of the Dioscuri or the garden of Alcinoüs. He discusses the use of floral types, and concludes that they had a religious meaning. [Also see Kitchell "The Golden Doors," Marotta "Dyrrhachium," Petrányi "On the Reverse Pattern," and Sasianu "Apollonia and Dyrrhachium Drachms" under NORTHERN GREECE—ILLYRIA].

940   ——— "The Gardens of Alcinous." *American Journal of Numismatics* 16, no. 2 (October 1881): 39-40.
An excerpt from Gardner's "Floral Patterns" article (see above) in which he explains the reverse type on coins of Corcyra and Dyrrhachium. Suggests a floral origin for the type.

941   ——— *The Types of Greek Coins: An Archaeological Essay.* Cambridge: University Press, 1883. Reprinted as *Archaeology and the Types of Greek Coins.* Chicago: Argonaut, 1965. 217 pp., 16 pls. [CS 1827, CS 3442, CS 3442a]
Focuses on the artistic development of coinage in relation to other works of art. Includes brief discussions on the origin and function of coinage, minting techniques, inscriptions, monetary alliances, and mother-city/colony relationships. Coin types are then analyzed focusing on their mythological content and artistic style. Includes chapters on the religious character of coin types, symbols, and the use of coins in archaeological studies. The stylistic analysis is divided into time periods and geographical areas. Includes a table which correlates the plates to the section of the text in which each coin is discussed. The reprint includes an introduction by Margaret Thompson. [Reviewed in *Numismatic Chronicle* 3rd ser., 3 (1883): 55-6].

942   ——— "The Gods of Ancient Greece as Represented on the Coins." *Spink Numismatic Circular* 1 (May 1893): 202-6; (June 1893): 235-7; (July 1893): 275-7; (August 1893): 317-20. Illus.
Discusses the representations of gods and goddesses on coins. Includes a list of relevant coin types. Discusses the origins and meanings of the types. [This article consists of a selection from Gardner's *The Types of Greek Coins*].

943   ——— "Copies of Statues on Coins." *Corolla Numismatica: Numismatic Essays in Honour of Barclay V. Head.* Edited by G. F. Hill. London: Oxford University Press, 1906. Pages 104-114. 1 pl. [CS 3443]
Using two examples, the Artemis at Patrae, and the Themistocles at Magnesia, the author attempts to discover how far coins may be trusted in helping in the identification of extant statues. Both of the subject statues are shown on Greek coins of the Roman Imperial period. The statues depicted are Greek statues from an earlier period.

944   **Gemmill, Chalmers L.** "Silphium." *Bulletin of the History of Medicine* 40, no. 4 (July-August 1966): 295-313. [CS 3444]
"The coinage of Cyrene, on which silphium appeared as a coat of arms, provides evidence for identification of the plant, and for determining the period of production and export of silphium from Cyrene. There is a short history of silphium, from the beginning of its usage, in Cyrenaica (ca. 631 B.C.)." [F. Campbell, *NL* 80]. [Also see Riddle et al. "Ever Since Eve" below, Favorito and Baty "The Silphium Connection" under ZEUGITANA, and W. Talbot Ready "The Silphium Plant" under ZEUGITANA].

945   **Gerojannis, Constantin.** "Primitive Shield-Devices and Coin-Types." *Journal International d'Archaéologie Numismatique* (Greece) 9 (1906): 5-41. 1 pl.
"Suggests that the gorgoneion of Greek art evolved from apotropaic animal heads, rather than having any connection with the Gorgon myth, and that gorgoneion and other monstrous types on early coins have no mythical or emblematic character, but are purely apotropaic." [J. R. Jones, *AIJIAN*]

946   **Gerson, Stephen N., and Derek Smith.** "Reflections of a Hymn to Demeter and the Eleusinian Mysteries." *The Celator* 15, no. 9 (September 2001): 16-26. Illus.
Summarizes the Homeric Hymn to Demeter, which tells the story of Demeter and her daughter Persephone. Illustrated by Greek and Roman coins depicting gods, goddesses, and symbols related to the story.

947   **Giacosa, Giorgio.** *Uomo e Cavallo Sulla Moneta Greca.* Milan: Edizioni Arte e Moneta, 1973. 87 pp., 45 pls., maps.
An examination of the depiction of horses on ancient Greek coins. Illustrated by many greatly enlarged photographs of the coins.

948   **Gibson, Carrol.** "The Corinthian Helmet." *SAN—Journal of the Society for Ancient Numismatics* 6, no. 3 (spring 1975): 43.
Discusses variations of the Corinthian helmet, its uses in battle, and its depiction on coins.

949   **Giedroyc, Richard F., and Malcolm W. Heckman, eds.** "Greek Coins Reveal Events and Mythology." *Classical Coin Newsletter* (Maplewood, New Jersey) 3, no. 6 (February 1984): 1-2, 7. Illus.
Describes a few historical events which are alluded to on Greek coins. Also mentions the role of mythology in Greek coin types.

950   "Gods, Goddesses and Personifications: A List of Some of the Principal Deities and Personifications Portrayed on Greek Coin Types." *Seaby Coin and Medal Bulletin* 491 (April 1959): 124-6; 492 (May 1959): 164-7.

Lists fifty-six personifications appearing on Greek coins. Describes their typical appearance and attributes, provides a very brief explanation of the mythology surrounding each, and provides, when appropriate, the Roman name for the deity.

951 **Goldman, Hetty.** "Sandon and Herakles." *Hesperia: Supplement 8: Commemorative Studies in Honor of Theodore Leslie Shear.* American School of Classical Studies at Athens, 1949. Pages 164-74. 1 pl.
Discusses representations of the Sandon monument of Tarsus on coins and on a terracotta plaque. At Tarsus, the local god Sandon's symbol was a club, he carried a bow, and his worship included a fire ritual. Concludes that these features caused the Greeks to identify him as Herakles. [Also see L. McKinney "Tarsus Coinage" under CILICIA].

952 **Goldsborough, Reid.** "Medusa Coins: They'll Transform You." *The Celator* 18, no. 6 (June 2004): 6-22. Illus.
Summarizes the mythology surrounding the Gorgon Medusa. Reviews some theories regarding the origin and meaning of the stories. Then discusses the depiction of Medusa on ancient coins. Concludes with a list of coins from thirty-five Greek cities as well as eleven Roman and Celtic coins depicting Medusa.

953 **Goldstein, Paul.** "Unicorns, Uni-Capricorn and Cornucopia—A Judaic Link." *The Celator* 17, no. 2 (February 2003): 31-3, 35-6. Illus.
Examines the history and development of the unicorn as a coin type. Traces the origin to depictions of two-horned goats, and the Amalthean Goat in particular. Examines the relationship to Capricorn. Explores the origins of the cornucopia, which was a horn removed from the Amalthean goat, thus leaving it as a unicorn. Goldstein then discusses the Jewish symbolism of the double cornucopia with a pomegranate between them.

954 ———— "The Titans: Hebrew Origins and Ancient Coinage." *The Celator* 20, no. 8 (August 2006): 22-6. Illus.
Examines the Titans in Greek mythology—the twelve offspring of Uranus and Gaea. Suggests that the Titans have their origin in the Hebrew Old Testament. Discusses and illustrates images appearing on ancient coins of the gods who were the offspring of the Titans. Shows how rulers would align themselves with the gods who would bestow upon them and their empire the desired attributes. Illustrates coins depicting Helios, Demeter, Zeus, Poseidon, Apollo, Hades, and Mercury on Greek or Roman coins. Also discusses how some Greek cities adopted these gods to promote certain attributes of the cities.

955 **Goodall, John A.** "Civic Devices and Pre-Hellenistic Greek Coin Types: A Survey." *Seaby Coin and Medal Bulletin* 844 (October 1989): 231-5. Illus.; 849 (April 1990): 67-72; 850 (May 1990): 102-7.
Explores the extent to which archaic and classical Greek coin types were actually derived from civic badges or devices.

956 **Gow, A. S. F.** "The Ancient Plough." *Journal of Hellenic Studies* 34 (1914): 249-75. Illus., 4 pls.
"The first plate shows twenty-one coins and gems which illustrate ploughs from the fourth century B.C. to the second century A.D., these being discussed in the text." [J. R. Jones, *NIJHS*]

957 **Gowers, William, and Howard H. Scullard.** "Hannibal's Elephants Again." *Numismatic Chronicle* 6th ser., 10 (1950): 271-83. 2 pls.
"Numismatic evidence shows that Hannibal probably had at least one Indian elephant. The political and economic relations of Carthage and Egypt were such that he might have secured it (or them) from the war-spoil of the Ptolemies. The crucial elephant coins fall into four groups: (1) Barcid silver from Spain depicting African elephants together with the copies in Aes Grave in Central Italy, (2) coins of Capua and Atella with African elephants, (3) a coin depicting the survivor (Surus?) of the few original Indian elephants brought by Hannibal over the Alps, and (4) coins depicting some Indian elephants (perhaps from Raphia via Egypt) among Hannibal's reinforcements of 215 B.C." [Summarized from C. Vermeule, *NL* 36]. [Also see Scullard "Hannibal's Elephants" and Snowden "Hannibal's Mahouts" below].

958 **Grace, Virginia R.** "Stamped Amphora Handles Found in 1931 and 1932." *Hesperia* 3 (1934): 197-310. Illus., 2 pls.
"Describes 290 stamps found during these two years. Stamps of Thasos, Rhodes and Cnidus are the most common, and there are frequent correspondences with the coin types of the cities concerned." [J. R. Jones, *NIAJAH*]. [Also see Grace "The Die" under THE MINTING PROCESS].

959 ———— "Early Thasian Stamped Amphoras." *American Journal of Archaeology* 50 (1946): 31-8. Illus.
"On pp. 33-5 parallels between amphora stamps and coins of the fifth and fourth centuries B.C. are suggested. Coincidences between these and coins of Agrigentum, Leontini, Messana and Aegina, may be explained by anti-Athenian feeling after the downfall of Athens." [J. R. Jones, *NIAJAH*]

960 ———— *Amphoras and the Ancient Wine Trade.* Picture Book No. 6. Princeton: American School of Classical Studies at Athens, 1979. 30 pp., illus.
An overview of the ancient wine trade based on a study of the amphoras found in excavations in the Athenian agora. Includes several examples of amphoras and other wine-related themes illustrated on Greek coins.

961 **Granger, Lewis G.** "Religion in the Ancient Greek Coinage." *The Numismatist* 63, no. 5 (May 1950): 260-2.
A brief note on the religious character of many Greek coin types.

962 **Hart, Gerald D.** "Ancient Coins and Medicine." *The Canadian Medical Association Journal* (Canada) 94 (January 1966): 77-89. Illus.
"Numismatically, the first vestiges of Asclepian worship are found on the coins of Larissa (450-400 B.C.). By employing coin illustrations, the author shows how the cult rose to its peak of popularity during the second and third centuries A.D., how it commenced to decline because of a change in minting policy introduced by Gallienus (A.D. 260-268), and how it came to an ignominious end with the adoption of Christianity by Constantine. The article also includes discussion of pharmacology and ancient coins, the evolution of the caduceus, and diseases shown on coin portraits." [F. Campbell, *NL* 77]. [For several articles discussing diseases shown on coins, see Hart under PORTRAITS].

963 **Head, Barclay V.** "On the Religious Character of Greek Coins." *Numismatic Chronicle* new ser., 10 (1870): 91.
A brief introduction to E. Curtius' article (see Curtius "On the Religious Character" above) which Head translated.

964 **Healy, John F.** "Types and Symbols in Greek Coin Series." *Proceedings of the Classical Association* 62 (1965): 34-5.
"Synopsis of a public lecture, discussing Greek coin types under the headings of artistic expedients (with examples of 'shorthand' types created for small coins), marks of identification, symbols, city badges and *types-parlants*." [J. Jones, *NL* 76]

965 ——— "The Use of Sicilian and Magna Graecian Types in White Gold and Electrum Series of Asia Minor and the Islands." *Congresso Internazionale di Numismatica, Roma 11-16 Settembre 1961. Volume 2.* Rome: Istituto Italiano de Numismatica, 1965. Pages 37-44. 1 pl.
Discusses the types used on early white-gold and electrum coins of Cyzicus, Mytilene, and Lampsacus, noting a similarity in style among these issues. Some types are the same or similar to those used by Greek cities in Italy and Sicily. Healy suggests that the types of the last years of the fifth and first years of the fourth centuries B.C. were not merely copies of western issues, but were due to the arrival of new engravers from the West after the defeat of Athens at Syracuse. Some of these engravers traveled from city to city.

966 **Higgins, R. A., and R. P. Winnington-Ingram**. "Lute-players in Greek Art." *Journal of Hellenic Studies* 85 (1965): 62-71. 2 pls.
Publishes two terracotta representations of lute-players in the British Museum. Lists other known examples of this subject. Comparisons are made to lutes depicted on coins of Lesbos, Methymna, and of the satrap Tissaphernes.

967 **Hill, George F.** "Apollo and St. Michael: Some Analogies." *Journal of Hellenic Studies* 36 (1916): 134-62. Illus.
Draws analogies between Apollo and St. Michael. Illustrates coins of Alexandria Troas of Roman date with types which are related to the story of the foundation of the Temple of Apollo Smintheus. Illustrates coins of Gargara in Troad with a grazing horse, which connects Apollo to the breeding of horses. Discusses the role of cattle in foundation myths. Also illustrates coins of Selinus related to Apollo's role in draining the marshes in the area, and thereby eliminating the plague from the area.

968 **Hoge, Robert W.** "Religion Figures Heavily in Greek Numismatics." *Collecting Ancient Coins: Supplement to Numismatic News* (April 25, 2000); *World Coin News* (May 2000); and *Bank Note Reporter* (May 2000): A4-5. Illus.
A brief overview of the mythological aspects of Greek coin types. Describes some of the characteristics of numerous gods and goddesses.

969 **Houser, Caroline.** *Dionysos and His Circle: Ancient through Modern Times.* Cambridge, Massachusetts: The Fogg Art Museum, Harvard University, 1979. 109 pp., illus.
A catalogue published to accompany an exhibition of art objects related to Dionysos, held at the Fogg Art Museum, December 10 – February 10, 1980. One of the goals of the exhibition was to give an understanding of the historical development of attitudes toward Dionysos. Includes two essays: "Greek and Roman Glimpses of Dionysos" by Albert Henrichs, and "Changing Views of Dionysos" by Caroline Houser. The catalogue includes vase-paintings, coins, and sculptures from ancient through modern times. Greek coins are discussed on pages 45-6 and seventeen Greek coins showing Dionysos or related images are illustrated on pages 47-52.

970 **Hurter, Silvia Mani.** "Das Palladion als Pro-Athenisches Symbol?" *Pour Denyse: Divertissements Numismatiques.* Edited by S. Hurter and C. Arnold-Biucchi. Bern, Switzerland: Privately published, 2000. Pages 87-91. 1 pl.
Examines the use of the Palladion as a pro-Athenian symbol on coins. Illustrates coins of Argos, Samos, and Rhodos.

971 **Imhoof-Blumer, Friedrich W.** "Nymphen und Chariten auf Griechischen Münzen." *Journal International d'Archéologie Numismatique* (Greece) 11 (1908): 1-213. 12 pls. [CS 3454]
"Catalogue of coin types showing nymphs and Graces in Classical, Hellenistic and Roman periods, with index of places and dynasts, names of nymphs and attributes." [J. R. Jones, *AIJIAN*]

972 **Imhoof-Blumer, Friedrich W., and Percy Gardner.** "A Numismatic Commentary on Pausanias." *Journal of Hellenic Studies* 6 (1885): 50-101. 6 pls.; 7 (1886): 57-113. 4 pls.; 8 (1887): 6-49. 5 pls.; supplement on pp. 49-60 and indexes on pp. 60-3. [CS 3456]. Reprinted as *Ancient Coins Illustrating Lost Masterpieces of Greek Art: A Numismatic Commentary on Pausanias.* Chicago: Argonaut, 1964. 176 pp., 36 pls. [CS 1839 and 3457]
The book is a revised version of the series which appeared in the *Journal of Hellenic Studies*. Includes narrative from Pausanias' *Description of Greece*. He toured Greece during the second century A.D. and recorded what he saw. Provides quotations from Pausanias dealing with sculptures, temples, and other works of art. References are provided to plates illustrating numismatic representations of these works. Primarily lists Roman Provincial coins. [Reviewed by John Boardman in *Spink Numismatic Circular* 73, no. 2 (February 1965): 37-8, and by J. F. Healy in *Journal of Hellenic Studies* 88 (1968): 244-5. Also see Lacroix "Les Statues de la Grèce Ancienne" below].

973 **Imhoof-Blumer, Friedrich, and Otto Keller.** *Tier- und Pflanzenbilder auf Münzen und Gemmen des Klassischen Altertumes.* Leipzig: Druck und Verlag von B. G. Teubner, 1889. Reprint, Hildesheim: H. A. Gersetnberg, 1972. Bologna: Forni, 1976. 168 pp., 26 pls. [CS 3458]
Examines the plants and animals which appear on ancient coins and engraved gems. For an English translation, see below.

974 ——— *Animals and Plants on Ancient Coins and Gems.* Chicago: Argonaut, 1969. [CS 3458a]
English reprint of *Tier- und Pflanzenbilder auf Münzen und Gemmen des Klassischen Altertumes* (see above).

975 **Jamgochian, Nicholas.** "The Winged Victory of Samothrace." *SAN—Journal of the Society for Ancient Numismatics* 1, no. 4 (April 1970): 56-7.
This "Letter to the Editor" raises the question—is the famous Winged Victory of Samothrace depicted on the coinage of Demetrius Poliorcetes? Or perhaps on a bronze coin of Rhodes?

976 **Jenkins, G. Kenneth.** "Ancient Coins and Food Production." *Food and Agriculture Organization of the United Nations Bulletin* 3 (1967): 1-4. Illus. [CS 3459]

977 **Johnston, Ann E. M.** "The Earliest Preserved Greek Map: a New Ionian Coin Type." *Journal of Hellenic Studies* 87 (1967): 86-94. 3 pls.
"A hitherto unidentified reverse type of a number of fourth century B.C. coins (*BMC Ionia* 323-4, etc.) with obverse Persian King carrying bow and spear is shown to be a physical relief map of the hinterland of Ephesus. The tetradrachms and small bronze bearing this type are thought to have been struck by Memnon the Rhodian during the defense of the area against Alexander." [A. Johnston, *NL* 80]. [Also see Tameanko "Maps" below, and McMenamin "Cartography" under ZEUGITANA].

978 ———— "Maps on Greek Coins of the 4th Century B.C." *Imago Mundi* 25 (1971): 75-6.

979 **Kagan, Jonathan H.** "Some Archaic Bovine Curiosities." *Museum Notes* 33 (1988): 37-44. 1 pl.
The author examines a group of nine archaic silver coins, including one previously unrecorded variety, with an obverse type of a standing ox or bull, and an incuse punch for the reverse. Although sometimes attributed to Athens, Euboea, Macedonia, Calchedon, or Lycia, Kagan concludes that it is not possible to identify with certainty the mint of any of these coins.

980 **Kahn, Jeff.** "Achelous: A Link Between the Indus and Achaean Civilizations." *The Celator* 25, no. 4 (April 2011): 24. Illus.
Illustrates an electrum stater of Kyzikos depicting the river god Achelous as a man-headed bull. The author traces the origins of the Greek Dionysus to the ancient Indian god Shiva. He also compares the river god Achelous to the Minotaur and the Indian god Nandi, the attendant of Shiva.

981 **Kanitz, L. El.** "The Nike, Winged and Wingless." *SAN—Journal of the Society for Ancient Numismatics* 4, no. 1 (1972-3): 11.
An overview of the mythology and numismatic depictions of Nike.

982 **Klose, Dietrich O. A., and Gerd Stumpf.** *Sport, Spiele, Sieg: Münzen un Gemmen der Antike.* Munich: Staaliche Münzsammlung, 1996. 165 pp., illus.
The catalogue for an exhibition of ancient coins and gems depicting sports, games, and victory.

982a **Knoblauch, Ann-Marie.** "Defining the Satyr in the Archaic and Classical Periods: The Numismatic Evidence." *XII Internationaler Numismatischer Kongress Berlin 1997, Akten-Proceedings-Actes.* Edited by B. Kluge and B. Weisser. Berlin: Staatliche Museen zu Berlin, 2000. Pages 199-202.

983 **Kuritzky, Simcha.** "Feline Coin Motifs Convey the Attributes of the Gods." *The Celator* 11, no. 4 (April 1997): 10-5. Illus.
The author reviews the mythology and motifs related to Kybele, Dionysos, Eros, Apollo, Nemesis, and Sandan. Focuses on the use of lions, leopards, panthers, and other felines as symbols of the deities. Illustrates several Roman and Roman Provincial coins with feline motifs.

984 **Lacroix, Léon.** "Les Statues de la Grèce Ancienne et le Témoignage de Monnaies." *Bulletin de Correspondence Hellénique* (France) 70 (1946): 288-98. [CS 3463]
"Important additions to Imhoof-Blumer's *Commentary on Pausanias*." [E. Clain-Stefanelli]. [See Imhoof-Blumer above].

985 ———— *Les Reproductions des Statues sur les Monnaies Grecques: La Statuaire Archaïque et Classique.* Liege, 1949. 372 pp., illus. [CS 3466]

986 ———— "Réflexions sur les 'Types Parlants' dans la Numismatique Grecque." *Revue Belge de Numismatique* (Belgium) 96 (1950): 5-11. [CS 3467]

987 ———— "Les 'Blazons' des Villes Grecques." *Études d'Archéologie Classique* 1 (1955-56): 91-115. 3 pls. [CS 3471]

988 ———— "A Propos des Représentations de Boucliers sur les Monnaies Grecques." *Centennial Publication of the American Numismatic Society.* Edited by Harald Ingholt. New York: American Numismatic Society, 1958. Pages 401-6. [CS 3472]
Discusses the representation of shields on Greek coins.

989 ———— *Études d'Archéologie Numismatique.* Université de Lyon II: Publications de la Bibliothèque Salomon Reinach, Volume 3. Lyon/Paris: de Boccard, 1974. 148 pp., 36 pls. [CS 1850 and 3476]
"With special reference to Elis, Taras, Delphi, Terina and Marium." [C. Kraay]

990 ———— "À Propos de Quelques Héros de la Légende Troyenne selon le Témoignage des Monnaies Grecques." *Travaux de Numismatique Grecque Offerts à Georges Le Rider.* Edited by M. Amandry and S. Hurter. London: Spink, 1999. Pages 207-14. 1 pl.
Examines the heroes of Troy which appear on Greek coins.

991 **Lange, Kurt.** *Götter Griechenlands: Meisterwerke Antike Münzkunst.* Berlin, 1941. 127 pp., 64 pls. Revised edition, Berlin, 1946. 61 pp., 72 pls. [CS 3478]
"Excellent pictures." [Clain-Stefanelli]

992 **Lattimore, Steven.** "Lysippian Sculpture on Greek Coins." *California Studies in Classical Antiquity* 5 (1972): 147-52. 1 pl. [CS 3479]
The author suggests that coins of Phaistos (Crete), minted ca. 330-325 B.C., depict a sculpture by the artist Lysippos. The coins show Herakles fighting the hydra. Some specimens show the sculpture from the front; others show the sculpture from the back. This depiction of two profiles of a three-dimensional group is a rare feature (perhaps unique) in Greek numismatics. Lattimore presents arguments supporting the attribution of the original sculpture to Lysippos.

993 **Lawton, Carol L.** "Greek Coinage and the Polis." *Bearers of Meaning: The Ottilia Buerger Collection of Ancient and Byzantine Coins at Lawrence University.* Appleton, Wisconsin: Lawrence University Press, 1995. Pages 17-21.
Discusses coin types and symbols as identifiers of the issuing polis and as reflections of a polis' patron deity. Also discusses punning or "canting" types and the introduction of city names (or abbreviations) on coins. Reviews the transition to coin types reflecting the rule of tyrants or dictators, and the introduction of portraits during the Hellenistic period when coin types no longer were symbols of a single polis, but of a larger imperial kingdom stretching across many cities.

994 **Lehman, Phyllis Williams.** *A Numismatic Approach to the Sculpture of South Italy and Sicily in the Classical Period.* New York, 1943. [CS 3480]
A Ph.D. dissertation at New York University.

995 ———— *Statues on Coins of Southern Italy and Sicily in the Classical Period.* New York: H. Bittner & Co., 1946. 72 pp., illus. [CS 3481]
Shows that certain coins exhibit faithful reproductions of contemporary statues, and presents a method whereby sculptures may be attributed to a given region by virtue of a precise relationship to specific coins. Focuses on statues of river-gods, the statue of Apollo at Metapontum, and statues of Herakles. Illustrated throughout by photographs of coins as well as bronze and marble statues. [Reviewed by C. Seltman in *Journal of Hellenic Studies* 66 (1946): 132-3, and by O. Brendel in *American Journal of Archaeology* 53 (1949): 224-7. Also see Van Keuren "A Coin Copy of Lysippus's Heracles" under ITALY—TARAS].

996 **Leschhorn, Wolfgang.** "Ancient Greek Coins and Agones." *Nomismatika Khronika* (Greece) 16 (1997): 87-94. 2 pls.
Describes many coins (mostly Roman Provincial issues) with types related to agones—athletic contests or other competitions.

997 **Levy, G. Rachel.** "The Oriental Origin of Herakles." *Journal of Hellenic Studies* 54 (1934): 40-53. Illus., 1 pl.
Discusses the origin of Herakles and his identification with Sandas. Examines Herakles as a man and as a divinity. Discusses the hydra as the alter-ego of Herakles. Illustrates coins of Tarsus which use the figure of Herakles interchangeably with that of Sandas as tutelary deity of the city.

998 **Lindgren, Henry Clay.** "Imagery on Ancient Coins as Indicators of Changes in Cultural Values: Athena vs. Tyche. Parts 1-2." *The Celator* 8, no. 9 (September 1994): 40-3; no. 10 (October 1994): 40-3. Illus.
Examines coin designs as an indication of the values held by different cultures. Focuses on the minting authorities' decisions to place the images of either Athena or Tyche on their coins. Suggests that societies that favored achieving, self-reliant, and proactive values generally selected Athena as a coin type. People that lacked self-reliance, were passive, and that believed that events in their lives were determined by luck tended to utilize images of Tyche on their coins. Samples of coinage are analyzed by historical periods in order to check the statistical validity of the theory.

999 **Lloyd, W. Watkiss.** "Chorographical Greek Coins." *Numismatic Chronicle* 11 (1849): 105-19.
Examines the significance of the types on the Syracusan decadrachms in relation to the art of the period. Also discusses the interpretation of types at Camarina, Sybaris, and Leontini. Focuses on how the types represent the features of the cities.

1000 **Lorimer, H. L.** "The Country Cart of Ancient Greece." *Journal of Hellenic Studies* 23 (1903): 132-51. Illus.
"On pp. 143-9 coins of Messana, Rhegium, Crannon and the Thraco-Macedonian series are mentioned as examples of representations of ancient carts with cross-bar or four-spoked wheels." [J. R. Jones, *NIJHS*]

1001 **Macdonald, George.** *Coin Types, Their Origin and Development: Being the Rhind Lectures for 1904.* Glasgow: James Maclehose and Sons, 1905. Reprints, Chicago: Argonaut, 1969; Bologna, 1975. 275 pp., illus., 10 pls. [CS 3484]
Presents the text of six lectures which explore the origin and development of the designs on coins from the beginnings of coinage up to the seventeenth century, with the largest part devoted to Greek coinage. The first lecture reviews two theories for the choice of designs—the religious theory and the commercial theory, giving arguments for and against each. Includes an extensive discussion of the theories of Ridgeway (see Ridgeway *The Origin of Metallic Currency* under METROLOGY) with which the author disagrees. The second lecture suggests that coin types have their origins in signets and seals and argues that types are simply the badges of the issuing cities. Also discusses the relationship of coin types to engraved gems, and the use of designs imitative of those of other cities. The third lecture discusses canting types, those alluding to local sites or characteristics, agonistic types, and other commemorative types. Religious types and the use of inscriptions are also examined. The fourth lecture focuses on the use of heads of deities, the religious nature of coinage, and the transition to the use of royal portraits. It continues with a discussion of the types found on Greek Imperial coinage. The fifth lecture deals with Roman coinage, and the sixth focuses on Byzantine and medieval coinage.

1002 **Macdonald, Janet M.** *The Uses of Symbolism in Greek Art.* Chicago: Bryn Mawr University, 1922. 55 pages.
This Ph.D. dissertation notes the various types of symbols found in Greek art and discusses the uses to which these symbols were put: to indicate occupations, time, place, mint, monetary value, landscape, to suggest a narrative, to express abstract ideas and emotions, allusions to historical events, and protection from evil. Examines the relationship between the medium to the types of symbols used, and suggests possible relationships between the Greek treatment of symbolism and that of other nations. Uses vases, coins, gems, and other art forms as examples.

1003 **Magie, David.** "Egyptian Deities in Asia Minor in Inscriptions and on Coins." *American Journal of Archaeology* 57, no. 3 (July 1953): 163-87.
Examines the spread of the worship of Egyptian deities (including Ammon, Sarapis, Isis, Harpocrates, and Anubis) to Asia Minor and the adjacent islands. Uses epigraphical evidence and, most importantly, coins showing Egyptian deities. Describes cult practices and the reasons underlying their popularity with the Greeks.

1004 **Maris, Edward.** "Lists of Types Most Commonly Found on Greek Autonomous Coins." Parts 1-3. *Mason's Coin and Stamp Collectors' Magazine* 5, no. 4 (April 1871): 5-6; no. 5 (May 1871): 5-6; no. 6 (1871): 2-3.

1005 **Marotta, Michael.** "Ancient Coins Show They Knew It Was Round." *The Celator* 12, no. 2 (February 1998): 18-20. Illus.
Marotta shows that the Greeks and Romans knew that the earth was round. In addition to the literary evidence cited, he mentions various astronomical symbols used on coins.

1006 **Matsson, G. O.** *The Gods, Goddesses and Heroes on the Ancient Coins of Bible Lands.* Stockholm: Numismatiska Bokförlaget, 1969. 267 pp., 8 pls.
Describes the divinities, demi-gods, and heroes that are portrayed on the ancient coins of Palestine and Phoenicia, and the mythology connected with them. Draws comparisons with Greek and Roman deities and heroes. Presents the subjects in alphabetical order and reviews the legends and myths related to each. Keyed to plates illustrating the subjects on coins.

1007 **McCartney, E. S.** "Canting Puns on Ancient Monuments." *American Journal of Archaeology* 23 (1919): 59-64.
"Short lists are included of 'canting types' on Greek and on Roman Republican coins." [J. R. Jones, *NIAJAH*]

1008 **McIvor, Robert S.** "A Supernova on Ancient Coins, Part 1." *The Celator* 25, no. 2 (February 2011): 6-22. Illus. "Part 2." *The Celator* 25, no. 3 (March 2011): 6-18. Illus. "Part 3." *The Celator* 25, no. 12 (December 2011): 6-20. Illus. "Part 4." *The Celator* 26, no. 1 (January 2012): 16-33, 36-7, 44. Illus.
A supernova is a star that suddenly explodes in a blaze of brilliance and for a few weeks may dominate the night sky. The author explores whether credible evidence exists that a supernova was observed in the Milky Way galaxy prior to the earliest recorded observation in A.D. 1006. In Part 1, McIvor explores the depiction of stars and related astronomical symbols appearing on ancient coins, including a star and eagle appearing on Parthian drachms of Phraates IV. In Part 2, the author explores the early history of Christians in Rome including the actions of Nero and Domitian, and the Catacombs. He explains a theory that some wall paintings in the catacombs include an ancient star map. In Part 3, McIvor examines the star described by Ignatius in A.D. 108. In Part 4, various explanations for the origin of the *chi rho* monogram are explored, including the theory that it represented a star group related to Christ's birth.

1009 **Mercieri, Dennis J.** "Numismatic Views of Alexander the Great and the Seven Wonders." *The Numismatist* 112, no. 1 (January 1999): 43-8, 73-4. Illus.
The author traces Alexander the Great's campaigns and takes a look at the Seven Wonders of the Ancient World along the way. Ancient coins (and one modern medal) are used to illustrate the monuments (or some aspect of them).

1010 **Middleton, J. H.** "The Temple of Apollo at Delphi." *Journal of Hellenic Studies* 9 (1888): 282-322. Illus.
"On p. 294 the Omphalos is compared to the cone shown in temples on coins of Paphus and Byblus; on p. 299 coins of the Amphictyonic Council, of Cyzicus and of other cities showing the omphalos, are noted. On p. 305 it is pointed out that the tripod as a coin type was much used by cities which, like Croton, had been colonised in obedience to the oracle. Coins of Philippi show the tripod decorated with fillets." [J. R. Jones, *NIJHS*]

1011 **Milavic, Anthony F.** "The Hoplite Race in Armor Served as a Vehicle to Train for War." *The Celator* 5, no. 8 (August 1991): 6-10.
Discusses the hoplite race in armor which was a popular athletic contest. Describes the rules of the event. Shows examples of how this event was depicted on vases and coins. Lists fourteen coins from Cyzicus which depict an armored hoplite in position to start the race.

1012 ——— "Ancient Olympia: The Place, The Games." *The Celator* 6, no. 7 (July 1992): 6-16. Illus.
A detailed history of the ancient Olympic games. Describes the festival sites, the athletic events, and some of the victors. Illustrates five coins related to the games as well as Olympic scenes on vases and bronze sculpture.

1013 ——— "Research and Analysis Reveal the First Greek Wrestler-type Coin." *The Celator* 7, no. 2 (February 1993): 6-12. Illus.
The author believes a previously unknown .095 gram silver coin with wrestlers on the obverse and an incuse square on the reverse was struck in the Thraco-Macedonian region, ca. 530-510 B.C. The attribution is based upon comparisons of the design with archaic period vase paintings and the similarity of the coin's weight to a Thraco-Macedonian standard.

1014 ——— "Pankration and Greek Coins." *The Celator* 13, no. 12 (December 1999): 6-16. Illus.
Describes the ancient combat sport of Pankration—a combination of boxing and wrestling. Milavic suggests that the standing "youthful figure" which appears as a symbol on the reverse of a series of Alexander tetradrachms is a pankratiast. This conclusion supports S. Noe's attribution of the series to the mint of Sicyon—the home of Sostratos, one of the most famous pankriasts in ancient Greece. Martin Price had suggested Aegeae as the mint city for these coins, identifying the figure (without merit in Milavic's opinion) as an orator, actor, boxer, or an athlete jumping.

1015 ——— "Coins of the Greek Pentathlon." *The Celator* 20, no. 7 (July 2006): 6-20. Illus.
Discusses Greek athletic contests and illustrates all the known Greek and Roman Provincial coin types (eleven) bearing designs related to the Greek pentathlon. Includes Greek coins from Kos, Abdera, and Akragas, and Roman Provincial coins from Philippopolis and Bizya in Thrace. The events in the pentathlon were foot race, long jump, javelin, discus, and wrestling. The author also suggests a broader symbolic function for Hermes' kerykeion (caduceus) than that implied by "herald's staff." Hermes is also depicted with the staff when he is in his role as the judge or decider of contests. The kerykeion therefore is also a symbol of a decision maker.

1016 **Milne, Joseph G.** "The History of the Greek Medallion." *Studies Presented to David Moore Robinson on His Seventieth Birthday.* Volume 2. Edited by George E. Mylonas and Doris Raymond. St. Louis: Washington University, 1953. Pages 224-32.
Describes the development from the stages of simple coin types to more elaborate types, to the "medallions"—large pieces, similar to coins, but without any specific connection to the standard coinage system. Describes the "Demareteion" and other so-called decadrachms of Syracuse, Athens, Akragas, and Ptolemaic Egypt. Points out that the decadrachm was an unknown denomination among the Greeks, and these can only have been commemorative medallions.

1017 **Mixter, John R.** "Gorgon Heads Played an Important Role as One of the Most Powerful Symbols in Ancient Greek Art." *The Celator* 4, no. 11 (November 1990): 28-9.
Recounts the mythology of Perseus and Medusa. Presents theories to explain why the gorgon head in Greek art developed from a monstrous head into a beautiful human head. [Also see Daehn "Mythological Themes" above].

1018 **Monney, Pierre R.** "The Bull-Myth and Symbol on Ancient Coins." *The Celator* 21, no. 10 (October 2007): 30, 34, 36. Illus.
Summarizes some of the Greek myths in which a bull plays a key role. Illustrates bulls and man-headed bulls on Greek and Roman coins.

1019 **Murray, Hugh A.** "Coins and Commodities in Ancient Greece." *New Zealand Numismatic Journal* (New Zealand) 8, no. 2 (January-April 1955): 41-9.
Murray discusses the use of commodities as coin types. He attempts to distinguish between commodities that were depicted on coins due to the value of the commodity itself, and those commodities that were depicted due to their association with deities, myths, etc.

1020 ——— "An Ancient Dolphin Story: Oppo and Hippo." *New Zealand Numismatic Journal* (New Zealand) 9, no. 1 (January-August 1956): 1-7. Illus.
Murray relates a story from Pliny the Younger regarding the appearance of a dolphin in the sea near Hippo in North Africa. The dolphin allowed a boy to ride it. This unusual sight attracted many visitors to the city. Murray discusses the tradition of dolphin stories and mentions the use of dolphins as Greek coin types.

1021 **Museum of Fine Arts (Boston).** *Greek Gods and Heroes.* 5th rev. ed. Boston: Museum of Fine Arts, 1962. 105 pp., illus. [CS 3422]
An overview of the history of Greek art from 3000 B.C. to A.D. 200, including vases, figurines, and reliefs. Presents the major gods, goddesses, and heroes and describes the related mythology incorporating quotes from ancient sources and illustrations of coins and other objects from the Boston Museum of Fine Arts.

1022 **Mylonas, George E.** "The Bronze Statue from Artemision." *American Journal of Archaeology* 48 (1944): 143-60. Illus.
"The statue is identified as Zeus, rather than Poseidon or an athlete; the right hand probably held a thunderbolt. Coins showing Zeus or Poseidon hurling a weapon are listed and studied." [J. R. Jones, *NIAJAH*]

1023 **Negishi Equine Museum.** *An Exhibition of Coins and Medals from the British Museum Depicting Horses.* Yokohama: Negishi Equine Museum, 1990. 120 pp. illus.
An exhibition catalogue published for the British Museum by the Negishi Equine Museum in celebration of the Year of the Horse. The exhibition featured coins and medals depicting horses. Many of the items are Greek, Roman, or medieval. Some modern coins are included. Text in English and Japanese.

1024 **Newton, Charles T.** "Statuette of Athenè Parthenos." *Journal of Hellenic Studies* 2 (1881): Illus.
"On pp. 4-5 it is noted that coins of Athens and Amisus show the helmet of Athena ornamented with a row of projecting horses' heads, which are not shown on the statuette from Varvakeion; the coins are more likely to be right, particularly since we have no evidence for later additions to the design of Pheidias." [J. R. Jones, *NIJHS*]

1024a **Nivaille, J.** "Le Type de l'Abeille dans le Monnayage Grec." Three parts. *Bulletin du Cercle d'Études Numismatiques* (Belgium) 15, no. 4 (October-December 1978); 16, no. 1 (January-March 1979); 16, no. 2 (April-June 1979).
Explores Greek coins bearing a bee as the type.

1025 **Nock, A. D.** "Notes on Ruler-Cult I-IV." *Journal of Hellenic Studies* 48 (1928): 21-43. Illus., 1 pl.
"On pp. 29-30 it is noted that Alexander's successors in Bactria showed Dionysus on their coinage very rarely, while Rhodian coins of 43 B.C. and later give his ivy-wreath to Helios; the identification of Alexander with Dionysus seems to be late, and a result of that god's increasing popularity. Similarly, coins of Mithradates showing Ammon are not good evidence for an attempt by the former to put himself forward as an Alexander. On p. 32 it is decided that coin portraits suggest a comparison of Mausolus and Artemis with Heracles and Demeter, rather than a full identification. On pp. 40-41 the writer considers that coin legends make it most unlikely that Antiochus IV bore the title 'Epiphanes' before his reign, and an appendix on p. 43, accompanied by illustrations, suggests a provisional sequence for his issues." [J. R. Jones, *NIJHS*]

1026 **Numismatic Museum, Athens.** *Coinage and Religion: Ancient World—Byzantine World. Proceedings of a One-Day Colloquium.* Obolos 2. Athens: Numismatic Museum, 1997. 187 pp.

1027 **Ober, William B., and Ralph N. Wharton.** "On the Phrygian Cap." *The New England Journal of Medicine* no. 255 (September 20, 1956): 571-2. Illus.
"In medical terminology objects of antique or historical association are occasionally selected to describe normal or pathological configurations or observations. The Phrygian cap, a symbol of liberty, has been so honored by medical men. It refers to a persistent notch in the gall bladder, a configuration in which the fundus is bent down to the breaking point. The authors discovered that the origins of the Phrygian cap are shrouded in mystery. Its use on coins is traced. Mentioned specifically are a silver stater of the fourth century B.C. from Cilicia which shows on the reverse a bearded Persian satrap wearing such a cap, a silver tetradrachm from Sardis struck by Alexander the Great, dated 330-323 B.C., which shows a head wearing a conical cap with the peak bent forward in the left lower quadrant of the reverse, and the silver denarius of the Roman Republic (44-40 B.C.) which shows the bust of Marcus Brutus on the obverse, and on the reverse the *pilleus* flanked by the daggers with the inscription EID MAR below." [*NL* 41]

1028 **Oikonomides, Al N.** "Numismatic Representations of Statues by Alkamenes. Part 1: The Cult Statue of Hephaistos in the Hephaisteion at Athens." *Voice of the Turtle* 5, no. 3 (March 1966): 83-5.
Discusses the statue of Hephaistos in the Athenian Agora created by the Greek sculptor Alkamenes. Suggests that the statue is represented on the reverse of an Athenian New Style tetradrachm, and that this evidence verifies that a copy of the famous statue in the British Museum has been correctly identified.

1029 **O'Neill, J.** "The Cista Mystica." *Spink Numismatic Circular* 23 (March-April 1915): 177-9.
This selection, reprinted from the author's "The Night of the Gods" (1893) discusses the origin, history, and use of the cista mystica.

1030 **Penn, R. G.** *Medicine on Ancient Greek and Roman Coins.* Aspects of Ancient Classical Coins. London: Seaby—B. T. Batsford, 1994. 186 pages, illus.
Discusses ancient coins which are of medical interest, including any coin where the circumstances of its issue, or the features on it, relate to the practice of medicine or history of medicine in general terms either directly or indirectly. Begins with a summary of Greek and Roman medicine. Continues with a discussion of the cult of Aesculapius. Examines coins bearing some relationship to the cult of Aesculapius, various other mythological associations to medicine and healing, medicinal plants on coins, diseases portrayed on coins, Roman emperors and their health, and the water supply at Rome. Illustrates 127 Greek and Roman coins. [Reviewed by Thomas Curtis in *Minerva* 8, no. 2 (March/April 1997): 54-5].

1031 **Perala, Adrew.** "The Rise of the Warrior King: Roots of Kneeling-King Image Run Deep." *Worldwide Coins* (April/May 2009): 48, 50. Illus.
A brief review of coinage from its origins through the coinage of Darius I of Persia. Perala emphasizes the depiction of kings and mythical heroes in a kneeling position on coins, particularly some electrum coins of Kyzikos.

1032 **Phillips, Henry, Jr.** *Head-Dresses Exhibited on Ancient Coins.* Philadelphia: Henry Phillips, Jr., 1881. 8 pp.
This booklet briefly describes the hair-styles, caps, crowns, and diadems seen on Greek and Roman coins. Discusses their symbolism. No illustrations. Two-hundred copies of this booklet were printed. [Also see Sayles "Greek Hairstyles" below].

1033 **Plant, Richard J.** *Greek Coin Types and Their Identification.* London: Seaby, 1979. Reprint, London: Spink, 2004. 344 pp., illus. [CS 1859 and 3492]
A guide to identifying Greek coins. Begins with a brief overview of the Greek alphabet, coin inscriptions, ethnics, and coin denominations. Presents a catalogue of types, illustrated by line drawings, grouped into categories: human figures, animals, and inanimate objects. Includes lists of gods, goddesses, and heroes, and an index to coin-issuing cities. [Reviewed in *Seaby Coin and Medal Bulletin* No. 738 (February 1980): 55-6. For a biographical sketch and interview with Richard Plant, see Mark Fox "Meet the Reverend of Numismatics: Conversations with Richard Plant," *The Celator* 24, no. 3 (March 2010): 20 ff)].

1034 ——— "The Olympic Games: A Delightful Look at the Origins of the Olympics." *World Coin News* (February 16, 1988): 15-9.
Reviews the legendary and historical origins of the Olympic games. Describes some of the events, some famous victors, and Olympic-related themes which appear on ancient coins.

1035 ——— "A Numismatic Lexicon." *The Celator* 22, no. 1 (January 2008): 28-9. Illus.
Reveals the origins and meanings of the following terms: Mithridatize, parchment, phalanx (phalanges), saunter, and Sybarite. Describes the numismatic connections of each term.

1036 **Porada, Edith.** "Greek Coin Impressions from Ur." *Iraq* 22 (1960): 228-34.
Grave goods found at the city of Ur exhibit copies of Greek coin types used as seal designs.

1037 **Porter, Gerald S.** *Elephants in Numismatics and Exonumia from Ancient to Modern Times.* Pittsburgh: Gerald S. Porter, 1993. 244 pp., illus.
A catalogue listing over 2100 types of numismatic and exonumia items depicting elephants. Includes Greek, Ancient Eastern, Islamic, Roman, and modern coins, as well as medals, tokens, political items, and world currency. Includes illustrations of African and Asiatic elephants, pointing out their distinguishing characteristics.

1038 **Price, Martin J.** "Images of the Gods." *Numogram* (Bulletin of the Society for International Numismatics) 57 (1978-79). 4 pp., illus.
Publishes a new type of tetradrachm of Samos which was discovered in 1977 with *obv.*, Zeus; *rev.*, cult statue from the sanctuary of Hera on Samos. The coins was struck ca. 170 B.C. The statue on the reverse is very similar to depictions of Artemis of Ephesus. Price discusses the use of cult images as coin types in western Asia Minor.

1038a **Psoma, Selene.** "Les 'Boucs' de la Grèce du Nord: Problèmes d'Attribution." *Revue Numismatique* (France) 159 (2003): 227-42. 1 pl.
Discusses archaic silver coins with a goat motif struck in Northern Greece. The silver coins with the same type on the obverse previously attributed to the Macedonian capital, Aigeai, are also discussed. Their minting authority was in Eastern Macedonia, as Picard has already pointed out when he identified fractions in the excavation material of Thasos and Amphipolis. The "Thraco-Macedonian" standard of the "goats of Aigai" as well as their system of denominations and control of issues argue for attribution to a city under the influence of Thasos. Fourth century bronze coins of Galepsos, a colony of Thasos, with the "goat of Aigai" on the reverse would suggest that the whole series came from the city of Galepsos, whose phoros to the Athenians was much greater than that paid by Neapolis. The letters ΛΛ and ΑΛ on the obverse of the last issue of these coins, written in the Parian alphabet, could thus be interpreted as the initials (ΓΑ and ΑΓ) of the ethnicum. [From the author's summary]

1039 ——— "*Panegyris* Coinages." *American Journal of Numismatics* 2nd ser., 20 (2008): 227-55. 3 pls.
Presents a survey of panegyris coinages and their functions from those of classical Delphi and Elis to the Hellenistic issues of Asia Minor. A panegyris is a religious gathering. The coinages in question are those issued in the name of a god. The issuing authorities and purposes for such coinages have been unclear. Psoma presents an almost complete list of the silver and bronze coinages issued in the name of a god in pre-Roman times. She also gathered all the numismatic, epigraphic, and literary evidence to understand the connection of these coins with religious festivals. Discusses the reasons the coins were minted and the functions they served. Includes coins struck at Athens for the Eleusinian festival, and coinages in the name of gods: Athena Alea (at Tegea), Zeus Eleutherios (Syracuse and Macedonia), Apollo (Cassandrea), Apollo Iatros (Apollonia Ponica), Artemis Leukophryene (Magnesia on the Meander), Zeus Larasios and Zeus Eumenes (Tralleis), The Great Mother (Pessinous), the Festmünzen of Pergamum, Athena Nikephoros (Pergamum), Artemis Pergaia (Perge, Aspendos, Phaselis, and Sillyon), and The Dionysiac Artists (Teos). Also examines the festival coinages at Elis and Delphi, the Amphictionic Coinage, and the bronze coinages of the Mouseia of Thespiae and the Charitesia of Orchomenos.

1040 **Rakicic, Mark.** "Coinage Reveals the Evolution of the Caduceus from a Simple Staff to a Respected Symbol." *The Celator* 5, no. 11 (November 1991): 28-35.
Discusses the caduceus, the staff of Hermes. The caduceus originated in Greek mythology and became a symbol of immunity and divinity. Mentions some of the Greek and Roman coins on which the caduceus appeared. Also discusses the use of the caduceus as a countermark.

1041 ——— "Depictions of the Lyre and Kithera Indicate the Importance of Music in Ancient Greece." *The Celator* 6, no. 5 (May 1992): 22-4. Illus.
Describes two stringed musical instruments, the lyre and the kithera, which were popular among the Greeks and were depicted on coins. Suggests the popularity of musical instruments as coin types was due to the cities' desire to demonstrate their cultural awareness.

1042 ——— "The Dove on the Coinage of Sicyon is Connected to the Worship of Aphrodite." *The Celator* 6, no. 8 (August 1992): 26-7. Illus.
Discusses the dove found on the coins of Sicyon and other cities. Shows that, to the ancient Greeks, the dove was a symbol of the goddess Aphrodite rather than a symbol of peace as it may be interpreted today.

1043 **Riddle, John M., J. Worth Estes, and Josiah C. Russell.** "Ever Since Eve: Birth Control in the Ancient World." *Archaeology* (March/April 1994): 29-35. Illus.
An examination of birth control methods used by women in ancient times. Focuses on plants used to prevent pregnancy or induce abortion. Discusses the uses of the silphium plant and illustrates an ancient coin of Cyrene bearing the silphium plant and a woman. The coin type implies the use of the plant for the purpose of birth control. [Also see Gemmill "Silphium" above, Favorito and Baty "The Silphium Connection" under ZEUGITANA, and W. Talbot Ready "The Silphium Plant" under ZEUGITANA].

1044 **Robert, Louis.** "Les Boules dans les Types Monétaires Agonistiques." *Hellenica* 8 (1949): 93-104. 3 pls. [CS 3495]

1045 **Robinson, C. A., Jr.** "The Zeus Ithomatas of Ageladas." *American Journal of Archaeology* 49, no. 2 (April-June 1945): 121-7.
Discusses the statue of Zeus Ithomatas by Ageladas of Argos. Argues "that the people of Zankle-Messene in Sicily, rejoicing in the newly-won freedom of their brothers at Naupaktos, struck a coin soon after 450 B.C. which shows the Zeus Ithomatas," and that the Messenians also struck coins showing the statue. Robinson further argues that the statue found in the water off Cape Artemisium in Euboea is probably this statue.

1046 **Robinson, David M.** "Mosaics from Olynthus." *American Journal of Archaeology* 36 (1932): 16-24. 4 pls.
"On p. 18 a mosaic showing Bellerophon slaying the Chimaera is compared to representations of huntsmen and riders on a number of coins." [J. R. Jones, *NIAJAH*]

1047 **Rodger, William.** "Birds, Beasts and Bugs—Coin Creatures from the Ancients." *Numismatic News* (May 23, 1972): 24-5. Illus.
Illustrates and describes a variety of animals depicted on ancient Greek coins.

1048 ——— "Personalities on Ancient Coins: Demeter." *Coins* 20, no. 10 (October 1973): 36. Illus.
This installment of the author's monthly column focuses on the goddess Demeter.

1049 **Rouse, W. H. D.** "The Double Axe and the Labyrinth." *Journal of Hellenic Studies* 21 (1901): 268-74.
"Denies the assumption made by Evans (see Evans "Mycenaean Tree and Pillar Cult" above) that the double axe, which appears on coins of Pherae as well as on those cited in the earlier article, was a symbol of Zeus." [J. R. Jones, *NIJHS*]

1050 **Sayles, Wayne G.** "Antioch's Statue of Fortune Became the Model for City Goddesses." *The Celator* 8, no. 7 (July 1994): 18-20. Illus.
Examines the origin and widespread use of the image of Tyche, the personification of Chance or Fortune. The image began with a sculpture by Eutychides of Sikyon, ca. 296 B.C., and first fully appeared on coinage during the reign of Tigranes II of Armenia, 83-69 B.C. The author lists other coins bearing this representation during the Roman Imperial and Byzantine periods.

1051 ——— "Greek Hairstyles Add Another Level of Interest for Collectors." *The Celator* 11, no. 3 (March 1997): 16. Illus.
A brief review of some of the hairstyles and headdresses commonly seen on Greek coins. Illustrates and describes the ampyx, sakkos, korymbos, and sphendone. [Also see Phillips *Head-Dresses* above].

1052 ——— "Personifications are an Important Aspect of Numismatic Iconography." *The Celator* 11, no. 4 (April 1997): 16. Illus.
A brief description of how the Greeks and Romans used human and animal forms on coins to embody abstract concepts.

1053 ——— "Tools of War were a Recurrent Device on Coinage of the Ancients." *The Celator* 11, no. 5 (May 1997): 12. Illus.
Describes some of the arms and armor that appear on coins.

1054 ——— "Who were Athena and Minerva?" *The Celator* 11, no. 11 (November 1997): 21. Illus.
Reviews the mythology surrounding the goddesses Athena and Minerva. Emphasizes that they were two separate deities, rather than simply the Greek and Roman names for the same deity.

1055 ——— "Coin Motifs and Civic Pride." *The Celator* 11, no. 12 (December 1997): 22-3. Illus.
Discusses how civic pride was reflected through symbols and images on coins, pottery, and other items.

1056 ——— "Images & Meaning III." *The Celator* 12, no. 8 (August 1998): 29. Illus.
Discusses the origin and meaning of the motif of Herakles wearing a lion's scalp. The image was widely used by Alexander the Great and others to associate themselves with the hero Herakles.

1057 ——— "Images That Get Around." *The Celator* 13, no. 7 (July 1999): 37. Illus.
Discusses the symbolism of the "lion-staters" struck by the Persian satrap Mazaios. The Baaltars/lion types were continued by Alexander the Great and later by Seleukos I.

1058 ——— "Herakles: Personification of Virtue." *The Celator* 14, no. 4 (April 2000): 45. Illus.
Discusses the mythology and numismatic iconography of Herakles.

1059 ——— "Aesculapius and Tradition." *The Celator* 14, no. 7 (July 2000): 45. Illus.
Discusses the origin and iconography of the healing deity Aesculapius and his depiction on Greek and Roman coins.

1060 ——— "A Circuitous Route." *The Celator* 15, no. 5 (May 2001): 45. Illus.
Discusses the origin and iconography of the meander pattern (Greek key) which appears on Greek coins. It originally referred to the Meander River in Phrygia.

1061 ——— "Double Your Luck." *The Celator* 15, no. 7 (July 2001): 45. Illus.
Discusses the double cornuacopiae, which is depicted on several Greek and Roman coins. The type symbolizes abundance or prosperity.

1062 ——— "Local Myths and Their Representations." *The Celator* 16, no. 7 (July 2002): 45. Illus.
Discusses city foundation myths and how they were represented on coinage. Illustrated by coinage examples from Mallos.

1063 ——— "Transmigration and Syncretism." *The Celator* 17, no. 8 (August 2003): 47. Illus.

Examines the use of similar coin types at different cities. Demonstrates that different deities can be depicted in a similar way, and that their true identity can be hard to determine.

1064 ——— "A Bird in the Hand." *The Celator* 17, no. 11 (November 2003): 47. Illus.
Examines the common depiction of a seated god with a bird on his outstretched hand, such as the seated Zeus or Baal holding an eagle. Sayles illustrates a similar scene on a stater of Mallos. However, the bird appears to be a dove, rather than an eagle. This suggests that the god may be Aphrodite rather than Baal. The dove was sacred to Aphrodite.

1065 ——— "A Feathered Enigma." *The Celator* 18, no. 2 (February 2004): 47. Illus.
Discusses the iconography of an eagle perched on the back of a lion—sometimes seen on coins of Mallus, Amathus, and Salamis (Cyrpus). G. F. Hill believed the symbolism to be solar. Sayles doubts this association and suggests the design may be a narrative image intended to recall a regional myth or folk legend.

1066 ——— "Cornucopiae." *The Celator* 19, no. 1 (January 2005): 43. Illus.
Sayles explores the origin of the cornucopiae and describes how it is related to the depiction of horned gods on Greek coins.

1067 ——— "Wings and Things." *The Celator* 19, no. 2 (February 2005): 43. Illus.
Examines the mute swan depicted on staters of Mallos in Cilicia. Sayles points out that the swan, which is depicted with its neck curved back and wings half raised, is displaying a threatening posture. Other staters show the swan in a more relaxed posture. Suggests the threatening posture may have been depicted on Mallos' coinage when the city wished to demonstrate defiance or strength to its foes.

1068 ——— "The Plant World." *The Celator* 21, no. 9 (September 2007): 45. Illus.
A brief discussion of plants depicted on Greek coins including barley, silphium, grapes, the fan palm, the date palm, and parsley.

1069 ——— "Wine and Coins." *The Celator* 23, no. 10 (October 2009): 49. Illus.
Discusses ancient Greek coins that illustrate aspects of the production or use of wine.

1070 **Schwabacher, Willy.** "The Olympian Zeus Before Phidias." *Archaeology* 14, no. 2 (summer 1961): 104-9. Illus. [CS 3501]
Discusses the dating of Phidias' statue of Zeus at Olympia, suggesting it was created ca. 430 B.C. Illustrates some small bronze statuettes which provide clues to the appearance of the great statue. Illustrates a rare early stater of Elis which depicts a striding Zeus, which the author dates to ca. 490 B.C. This and later Elean coins provide evidence for the early preeminence of the theme of the striding Zeus with thunderbolt and eagle. Suggests that a very large statue of the striding Zeus may have been planned for the Temple of Zeus before the enthroned Zeus statue was created by Phidias.

1071 **Scullard, Howard H.** "Hannibal's Elephants." *Numismatic Chronicle* 6th ser., 8 (1948): 158-68. Illus.
Draws attention to the numismatic evidence for Hannibal's use of war-elephants. Discusses the use of elephants in war. Illustrates coins depicting elephants including coins of Carthage issued by the Barcids, a small bronze coin from Etruria, Roman *aes grave* issues, and others. [Also see Gowers and Scullard "Hannibal's Elephants Again" above].

1072 ——— *The Elephant in the Greek and Roman World.* London: Thames and Hudson, 1974. 288 pp., illus. [CS 3503]
Examines in depth the knowledge and use of the elephant in the classical world. Includes several plates of Greek coins depicting elephants.

1073 **Sekulich, Lawrence.** "Arethusa, Peerless Nymph." *The Celator* 17, no. 11 (November 2003): 22-30. Illus.
A discussion of the goddess Arethusa, focusing on her appearance in the writings of Virgil, Pindar, Theocritis, Moschus, Bion, and Milton. Illustrated by Syracusan coins which depict the goddess from the author's collection.

1074 **Seltman, Charles T.** "Two Athenian Marble Thrones." *Journal of Hellenic Studies* 67 (1947): 20-30. Illus., 4 pls.
A study of two marble thrones from Athens, now in collections in Scotland. The throne from the collection of the Earl of Elgin bears sketches most likely depicting Achilles and Penthesileia. The figure of Achilles is compared to a figure of Poseidon on a tetradrachm of Demetrius Poliorcetes, ca. 290 B.C. The throne's shape is compared to the throne on a coin of Thebes of 287 B.C. The other throne, belonging to Colonel J. P. Nisbet Hamilton Grant, bears several carvings including the depiction of a table. The table is compared to a similar Agonistic table on Athenian bronze coins of the Roman Imperial period.

1075 ——— "The Wardrobe of Artemis." *Numismatic Chronicle* 6th ser., 12 (1952): 33-51. 2 pls.
The cult statue of Artemis at Ephesus was frequently depicted on coins. Seltman reviews the literature which provides descriptions of the famous statue. Comments on the identity of what are often described as "breasts" on the statue. Seltman rejects this identification and suggests they are clusters of dates. Comments on Artemis' wardrobe. On pages 48-50, "A Note on Bees and Date-Palms" explores their relationship to the cult of Artemis. [For other opinions related to the "breasts," see Mørkholm "Some Pergamene Coins" under MYSIA—PERGAMENE KINGDOM, and Rakicic "The Bees of Ephesos" under IONIA]

1076 ——— *The Twelve Olympians.* London: Pan Books Ltd., 1952. Second edition, *The Twelve Olympians and Their Guests*. London: Max Parrish & Co., 1956. 208 pp., 16 pls. [CS 3505]
Explores the religious beliefs of the Greeks. Describes the attributes, legends, and cults of each of the Olympian gods and goddesses, illustrated by their depictions in art and on coins. The second edition also discusses Herakles and Alexander the Great. [A brief review of the second edition by G. K. Jenkins appears in *Numismatic Chronicle* 6th ser., 17 (1957): 295].

1077 ——— "Coin Types of Wine States in the Aegean Regions." *Spink Numismatic Circular* 64, no. 1 (January 1956): 11-2.
Discusses the propaganda value of coins in the ancient world. The wine-trade was one activity that was frequently advertised on coinage. Presents a list of thirty-one cities in the Aegean region which had coin types related to wine production (grapes, a wine-cup, or an amphora).

1078 **Smith, A. H.** "On the Hermes of Praxiteles." *Journal of Hellenic Studies* 3 (1882): 81-95. Illus.
"A list of thirty-four representations of Hermes carrying a child is given, including coins of Pheneus, Sagalassus and Philadelpheia Lydiae." [J. R. Jones, *NIJHS*]

1078a **Smith, Amy.** "The Transition to Tyche on Southern Black Sea Coins." *XII Internationaler Numismatischer Kongress Berlin 1997, Akten-Proceedings-Actes.* Edited by B. Kluge and B. Weisser. Berlin: Staatliche Museen zu Berlin, 2000. Pages 212-6.

1079 **Smith, Cecil.** "Nike Sacrificing a Bull." *Journal of Hellenic Studies* 7 (1886): 275-85. Illus.
"In the course of a general discussion of representations of this scene, it is noted that it appears on coins of Abydus and of Lampsacus and frequently in the Roman period; it is also common on gems." [J. R. Jones, *NIJHS*]

1080 ———— "Harpies in Greek Art." *Journal of Hellenic Studies* 13 (1892-3): 103-14. Illus.
"On p. 107 the main and subsidiary types of the coinage of the Cyrenaican silphium towns are quoted as an example of the greater interest in nature shown by Greek artists working under Egyptian influence; on p. 113 the type of a vulture at Cyrene (also common as an Egyptian hieroglyphic symbol) is noted as an example of this bird in Greek art." [J. R. Jones, *NIJHS*]

1081 **Snible, Ed.** "Depictions of the Hero Perseus on Greek Coinage." *The Celator* 18, no. 6 (June 2004): 23-6. Illus.
Examines coins depicting Perseus, the hero who killed the Gorgon Medusa. Includes coins from Cyzicus, Seriphos, Astypalaia, Philip V and Perseus of Macedon, Tyana, and Daldis. Discusses the mythology surrounding the hero.

1082 **Snowden, Frank M., Jr.** "A Note on Hannibal's Mahouts." *Numismatic Chronicle* 6th ser., 14 (1954): 197-8.
"Literary evidence is adduced in support of the suggestion of Gowers and Scullard that Hannibal may have used some Negro drivers for both African and Indian elephants. The Negro depicted on bronze coinage generally associated with Hannibal's Italian campaign was probably one of Hannibal's black mahouts who survived the Alpine crossing." [C. Vermeule, *NL* 34]. [Also see Gowers and Scullard "Hannibal's Elephants" and Scullard "Hannibal's Elephants" above].

1083 "Some Classical Myths Represented on Greek Coins." *Spink Numismatic Circular* 23 (March-April 1915): 173-7; (July-August 1915): 404-8; (September-October 1915): 551-6.
Discusses the depictions of Hero and Lysander, Phrixos and Helle, Ino and Melicertes, Callisto and Arcas, Paris, Sterope and Athene, Perseus and Gorgons, Patroclus, Myrrhs, Alexander, Pelops and Hippodameia, Leto, Artemis and Apollo, Androclus, and Aesculapius.

1084 **Sotheby Parke Bernet A.G.** "The Heckett Collection of Classical Coins Depicting Cows or Bulls." *Catalogue of Ancient Coins, Renaissance Medals, and Continental Coins.* Zurich: Sotheby Parke Bernet A.G., 1977. Lots 1-115.
This catalogue for a June 10, 1977 sale of ancient and other coins includes the collection of Mrs. Greta S. Heckett of Pittsburgh, Pennsylvania, featuring ancient coins depicting cows and bulls. Ninety-four of the 115 coins are Greek. [Also see listing 846 in J. Spring, *Ancient Coin Auction Catalogues 1880-1980* (see Spring under Collecting Guides)].

1085 **Stanton, Earle K.** "Gorgons I Have Met." *The Numismatist* 61, no. 8 (August 1948): 523-25. Illus.
A discussion of the gorgon type on Greek coins with illustrations of gorgons on coins of Neapolis (Macedonia) and Camarina (Sicily). Recounts the mythology surrounding gorgons.

1086 **Starck, Jeff.** "Mythological Creatures: Beast-like Animals from All Cultures Appear on Coins." *Coin World* (September 20, 2004): 16. Illus.
A brief description of some of the mythological creatures which have appeared on coins, both ancient and modern.

1087 ———— "A Whale of a Story: Build a Collection of Dolphins, Other Cetaceans on Coins." *Coin World* (November 29, 2004): 16, 20. Illus.
Describes several types of dolphins and whales. Lists numerous ancient and modern coins on which they appear.

1088 **Starr, Chester G.** "The Awakening of the Greek Historical Spirit and Early Greek Coinage." *Numismatic Chronicle* 7th ser., 6 (1966): 1-13. [CS 1873]
Starr offers some preliminary observations on the manifestations of the historical spirit in Greek coinage down to ca. 450 B.C. (i.e., unmistakable commemoration of a specific event, placed on a coin in order that the event be remembered or appreciated). Examples include the wreath of olive leaves on the head of Athena on Athenian coins, the mule cart on coins of Messana, the lion in the exergue of the Syracusan Demareteion. The relatively few examples indicate that in the fifth century B.C., men were just beginning to be historically minded. With respect to the coinage of Greece in the sixth and fifth centuries, in interpreting any specific types, it is safer to think first in a religious or patriotic idiom, and only with the best evidence, seek to advance an historical interpretation of coin types.

1089 **Stevens, M. K.** "Athena, Roma and Britannia." *New Zealand Numismatic Journal* (New Zealand) 8, no. 1 (May-December 1954): 3-9. 1 pl.
Stevens traces the evolution from the depiction of Athena on the coins of Lysimachus, to the depiction of Roma on Roman Imperial coins, to the figure of Britannia on British coins.

1090 **Stoliar, Steven.** "Numismatic Representations of Ancient Sculpture and their Value to the Art Historian." *Journal of Numismatic Fine Arts* 5, no. 2 (summer 1976): 25-30. Illus.
Discusses the depiction of statues on coins including: the Apollo of Delos which appeared on New Style coins of Athens; the Hera of Samos on Samian coins; the figures of Harmodius and Aristogeiton on an electrum stater of Cyzicus; the seated Hera at Argos depicted on coins of Argos and Elis; statues of Athena on coins of Side; and several others, including coins from the Roman Imperial period. Comments on the reliability of these depictions as reflections of the original art works.

1091 **Sullivan, Richard D.** "Royal Coins and Rome." *Ancient Coins of the Graeco-Roman World: The Nickle Numismatic Papers.* Edited by Waldemar Heckel and Richard Sullivan. Waterloo, Ontario: Wilfrid Laurier Press, 1984. Pages 143-58.

Discusses the later coinages of Commagene, Atropatene, Armenia, Parthia, the Seleucids, the Ptolemies, Cappadocia, Pontos, Bosporus, Cilicia, and Thrace to show that coinages of native dynasts after 100 B.C. sometimes reflected the increasing involvement of the Romans, but more often the rulers chose not to reflect that involvement.

1092 **Sunde, C. H.** "A Coin of Kallipolis, Plato's Beautiful City." *The Celator* 21, no. 6 (June 2007): 28-31, 34-5, 37. Illus.
In his *Republic*, Plato laid out a blueprint for the ideal city—Kallipolis. Sunde shows and describes his own vision for the ideal coin design for this ideal city—a city that never existed. Sunde explains his chosen design elements.

1093 **Svoronos, Jean N.** "Sur la Signification des Types Monétaires des Anciens." *Bulletin de Correspondence Hellénique* (France). Reprints, Athens, 1894; Chicago: Obol International, 1980. [CS 3508]
Many animals found on coins can be associated with constellations, stars, or signs of the Zodiac. Therefore, Svoronos suggests astronomical explanations for a large number of Greek coin types. [See next item for an English translation].

1094 ———. "On the Significance of Certain Ancient Monetary Types." *American Journal of Numismatics* 29, no. 3 (January 1895): 76-83; no. 4 (April 1895): 115-20; 30, no. 1 (July 1895): 1-4.
An English translation of a the above.

1095 **Tameanko, Marvin.** "Coins Depict the Use of the Double Axe as a Symbolic Implement of Power." *The Celator* 6, no. 10 (October 1992): 32-9. Illus.
Examines the origins, history, and symbolism of the double-axe which is depicted on the coinage of many cities. It originated during the bronze age, developed into a symbol of royal power, and gained religious significance as the symbol of Zeus and Dionysus. The myths related to the use of the double-axe at Tenedos, Pherai, the Kingdom of Thrace, Thyatira, Mylasa, Plarasa, and Aphrodisias are recounted.

1096 ———. "The Development of 'Rams' Used on Ancient Warships." *The Celator* 7, no. 10 (October 1993): 10-9. Illus.
Discusses the development and use of the bronze prows used as rams on ancient warships from Mycenaean times to the period of the Roman Empire. Describes naval battle tactics as well as the use of these prows in commemorative monuments. Illustrated by drawings of ancient coins which use prows as the type.

1097 ———. "The So-Called 'Butting Bull' on Ancient Coinage." *The Celator* 9, no. 1 (January 1995): 6-11. Illus.
Many Greek and Roman coins depict what is usually described as a "butting" bull. The author suggests these coins actually depict a bull kneeling at the altar of Zeus as part of a Greek religious ceremony.

1098 ———. "Maps on Ancient Coinage." *The Celator* 9, no. 7 (July 1995): 16-24. Illus.
Discusses the earliest known maps from Sumer as well as Greek and Roman maps. Illustrates an Ionian coin of ca. 334 B.C. whose reverse, some believe, contains a relief map of the area around Ephesos. Also discusses coins of Zancle, Knossos, and Rome which depict local sites (the harbors at Zancle and Ostia, and the labyrinth at Knossos). [Also see A. E. M. Johnston "The Earliest Preserved Greek Map" above, and McMenamin "Cartography" under ZEUGITANA].

1099 ———. Goddesses of Medicine: Women Healers on Ancient Coinage." *The Celator* 10, no. 7 (July 1996): 30-4. Illus.
The author discusses the roles of, and attitudes toward, doctors and healers among the Greeks and Romans. Describes the gods and goddesses of healing, and the representations of Asclepius, Hygieia, and Epione (or Panaciea) on Greek, Roman, and Roman Provincial coins.

1100 ———. *Monumental Coins: Buildings and Structures on Ancient Coinage.* Iola: Krause Publications, 1999. 242 pp., illus.
An examination of architectural structures as depicted on ancient coins, including harbors, aqueducts, temples, arches, bridges, altars, and monuments. Includes discussions of cultural and political forces which impacted the architecture and the coins, line drawings of structures and building plans, and drawings and photographs of related coins. Primarily focused on Roman Imperial coinage, although coins of Knossos are used to depict the Labyrinth, and a coin of Himera is used to illustrate the concept of "one point perspective."

1101 ———. "Furniture on Ancient Coins." *Journal of the Classical and Medieval Numismatic Society* (Canada) 2nd ser., 1, no. 3 (December 1, 2000): 5-18. Illus. Also appeared in *Numismatist* 116, no. 4 (April 2003): 50-3. Illus.
Illustrates and describes various forms of furniture which are depicted on Greek and Roman coins including chairs, footstools, thrones, couches, tripods, tables, cabinets, baskets, and chests. Shows how the throne developed from a rock, to a chair, to a chair with a footstool, to a throne. Illustrated by line drawings of coins.

1102 ———. "The Ancient Art of Healing." *Numismatist* 117, no. 11 (November 2004): 55-60. Illus.
Tameanko reviews the Greek gods and goddesses that are related to medicine and the art of healing. Illustrates, through line drawings, a variety of ancient Greek and Roman coins which depict these mythological figures.

1103 **Thallon, Ida C.** "The Cave at Vari, III: Marble Reliefs." *American Journal of Archaeology* 7 (1903): 301-19. 7 pls.
The author examines the findings at a cave in Attica. "Various representations of Pan are discussed with references to coin types. The young reclining Pan shown in one of the reliefs from the cave is placed in a transitional stage between the 'Theseus' of the parthenon and the coins of Messana, the Arcadian League, Megalopolis, Delphi, Panticapaeum and Magna Graecia." [J. R. Jones, *NIAJAH*]. [Also see Brett "The Cave at Vari, V: Coins" under ATTICA—GENERAL WORKS].

1104 **Thomas, Edward.** "The Indian Swastika and its Western Counterparts." *Numismatic Chronicle* new ser., 29 (1880): 18-48. 3 pls.
An examination of the origins and use of the swastika symbol. Thomas concludes the symbol, in all its forms, represents a primitive conception of solar motion—the sun moving through the heavens. Illustrates the symbol in many forms, and includes photographs of coins from Syracuse, Knossos, Lycia, and Aspendus which bear the swastika. [Also see Brett "Symbolism" and Gardner "Ares as a Sun-God" above].

1105 **Touratsoglou, Ioannis.** "Aphrodite and Eros in Kyzikos." *Nomismatika Khronika* (Greece) 26 (2007): 21-7. Illus.

Examines a rare electrum stater of Kyzikos in the Cabinet des Médailles of the Bibliothèque Nationale in Paris, struck ca. 410-330 B.C. The obverse shows the standing goddess Aphrodite, who bends slightly and perhaps leans on some support. To her left is a childish, naked figure of Eros. The composition has a sculptural nature and is identified as the famous Urania Aphrodite. In Greek and English.

1106 **Tsangari, Dimitra.** *Portraying Mythology: The Image of Myth on Ancient Coins.* Athens: Alpha Bank, 2008. 25 pp., illus.
An exhibition catalogue depicting coins from the Alpha Bank collection. The exhibition, held at Nafplion, examined the twelve Olympian gods, minor deities, heroes, mythological stories, the myths of Crete, and mythical creatures and objects.

1107 **Tsangari, Dimitra, Panagiotis Tselekas, Desponia Evgenidou, and S. Makrypodi.** *Myth and Coinage: Representations, Symbolisms and Interpretations from the Greek Mythology.* Athens: Alpha Bank, 2011. 267 pp., illus.
Catalogue for an exhibition held at the National Archaeological Museum (Athens) and the Numismatic Museum of Athens (April to November 2011), featuring coins from the Alpha Bank collection.

1108 **Tselekas, Panagiotis.** *Ancient Olympic Games and Coinage.* Nicosia: Bank of Cyprus Cultural Foundation, 2005.

1109 **Tzamalis, Anastasios P.** *The Olympic Games and Athletics on Coins.* Monographs of the Hellenic Numismatic Society 5. Athens: Hellenic Numismatic Society, 2004. 71 pp., illus.
A general discussion of the coins struck at Olympia as well as the coins struck by various Greek cities to immortalize the Olympic victories of their athletes. Also describes the medals of the Olympic Games of 1896 and 1906 held in Athens. In addition to many black-and-white photographs of coins, the book includes some enlarged color photographs of significant pieces.

1110 **Vagi, David L.** "Predator-Prey Motifs were Frequently Used on Greek Coinage." *The Celator* 11, no. 1 (January 1997): 22-3. Illus.
The author examines the "predator-prey" motif in ancient Greek coinage, the most common theme being an animal attacking another animal. Describes the varieties in type and stylistic treatment on coins of Akanthos, Tarsos, Byblos, Lydia, Velia, Olympia, Locri, and Akragas.

1111 ——— "The Pyre of Sandon on Coins." *The Celator* 11, no. 4 (April 1997): 18-20. Illus.
Discusses the god Sandon and his depiction on coins. Describes the typical "pyre of Sandon" on coins of Tarsos and the Seleucid kings.

1112 ——— "Wreath-Bearers of the Greeks." *Numismatist* 119, no. 12 (December 2006): 77-9. Illus.
Traces the origin and spread of the *stephenophorus* or "wreath-bearing" coin types. The trend started with the New Style Athenian coinage, ca. 132 B.C. The use of a wreath to enclose the reverse design became a common feature on coinage during the Hellenistic age, and was seen at Cyme, Myrina, Smyrna, Lebedus, Heraclea, and other cities and kingdoms.

1113 ——— "Bounty of the Sea." *The Numismatist* 121, no. 6 (June 2008): 68-9. Illus.
Describes the use of the dolphin as a coin type among the Greek cities, including Thera, Zankle, Venusia, Taras, Syracuse, and others.

1114 ——— "Taking It at Face Value." *The Numismatist* 122, no. 10 (October 2009): 59-60. Illus.
Discusses how different denominations were distinguished from each other by the use of design elements or markings.

1115 ——— "Mythological Creatures: Imaginary Beings Frequently on Coins of the Ancients." *Coin World* (June 7, 2010): 110-2. Illus.
In this installment of his "Ancients Today" column, Vagi discusses some of the mythological creatures which appear on Greek and Roman coins.

1116 ——— "Animals Important Part of Life to Ancients: Creatures Agelessly Attractive, from Lion to Murex." *Coin World* (July 5, 2010): 102-5. Illus.
In this installment of his "Ancients Today" column, Vagi discusses the depiction of animals on ancient coins.

1117 ——— "Greek Goddesses." *The Numismatist* 124, no. 4 (April 2011): 55-7. Illus.
Highlights some of the goddesses depicted on Greek coins including Aphrodite, Artemis, Hera, Athena, Demeter, Persephone, Tyche, and Nike.

1118 ——— "Greek Monarchs Claim Ancestry from Gods: Rulers Proclaim Divinity through Images on Coins." *Coin World* (May 9, 2011): 162, 166, 168. Illus.
In this installment of his "Ancients Today" column, Vagi provides a few examples of Hellenistic kings who claimed to be descended from gods, and he shows how this was depicted on their coins.

1119 **Valassiadis, Chrysantyphos.** *Coins and Games.* Athens: Helicon Interactive, 2002. 38 pp., illus.
Provides ten quotes from ancient sources referring to athletic events in the Greek world, illustrated with complimentary coins. In both Greek and English (English translation by Stephen Stafford).

1120 **van Alfen, Peter G.** *A Simple Souvenir: Coins and Medals of the Olympic Games.* New York: American Numismatic Society, 2004. 160 pp., illus.
A catalogue for the American Numismatic Society's exhibition "Full Circle: The Olympic Heritage in Coins and Medals" shown at the Federal Reserve Bank of New York. Illustrates over 120 ancient and modern coins, medals and related Olympic badges, posters, and ephemera. Includes a study of the social and political function of the numismatic heritage of the Olympic Games. Traces the history of the Olympics from its ancient Greek origins to the modern Olympic revival movements, encompassing not only the well-known IOC Olympics, but also the lesser-known Olympics held in Athens before 1896 and in Much Wenlock, England, as well as the Socialist Olympics movements of the 1920s and 1930s.

1121 ——— "Greek Acquisitions: The Mighty Octopus?" *American Numismatic Society Magazine* 3, no. 2 (summer 2004): 46-7. Illus.
Focuses on a fifth century double shekel from Cyprus with *obv.*, lion's head, and *rev.*, octopus, recently donated to the ANS. Discusses the symbolism of the octopus type. Illustrates three other Greek coins depicting the octopus. Discusses prototypes for the type.

1122 **van Buchem, H. J. H.** "Family Coat-of-Arms in Greece." *Classical Review* 40, no. 6 (December 1926): 181.
The author questions Seltman's beliefs about the general use of family badges in Greece (Seltman, in *Athens: Its History and Coinage before the Persian Invasion*, suggested that the types found on Athenian Wappenmünzen signify prominent Athenian families. See Seltman under ATTICA—GENERAL WORKS). Van Buchem rejects all the specimens of family badges discussed, and says there are no texts or monuments which prove the use of family badges in Greece.

1123 **Vermeule, Cornelius C.** "Chariot Groups in Fifth Century Greek Sculpture." *Journal of Hellenic Studies* 75 (1955): 104-13.
"Marble reliefs, gems, vases, and coins of the period 480-380 B.C. are utilized to determine the Attic origins of the chariot compositions on coins of Southern Italy and Sicily, especially Syracuse." [C. Vermeule]

1124 ———. "Herakles Crowning Himself: New Greek Statuary Types and Their Place in Hellenistic and Roman Art." *Journal of Hellenic Studies* 77 (1957): 283-99. 4 pls. [CS 3513]
"The prototype for the Herakles Crowning Himself found on many Roman Imperial medallions was a statue on the balustrade of the steps which led up to the podium of the *aedes Concordiae Augustae*, restored by Tiberius in A.D. 10. A similar type appears on the coins of Demetrius I and Agothokles, kings of Bactria (ca. 190-166 and 175-165 B.C.) and on those of Herakleia in Lucania (281-272 B.C.) and the prototype for these is thought to have been a statue which stood in Corinth. It is further concluded that there were two statue types, from fourth and third century originals respectively. Part 2 of the article concerns the use of paintings and reliefs made by Antonine die-cutters and the originality of composition found in their work." [I. Merker, *NL* 48]

1125 ———. "Protesilaos: First to Fall at Troy and Hero in Northern Greece and Beyond." *Florilegium Numismaticum: Studia in Honorem U. Westermark Edita*. Edited by Harald Nilsson. Stockholm: Svenska Numismatiska Föreningen, 1992. Pages 341-6. Illus.
Protesilaos, a hero from Homer's *Iliad*, was the leader of the men from Phylake in Thessaly. He offered his life in order that others might succeed. The images and cult of Protesilaos were commemorated on the coins of a number of Greek and Roman Provincial cities (including Scione in Macedonia). Vermeule discusses the popularity of the hero as a cult figure and the relationship of his images on coins to those in known bronze sculptures.

1126 **Wace, Alan J. B.** "Apollo Seated on the Omphalos: A Statue at Alexandria." *The Annual of the British School at Athens* 9 (1902-3): 211-42. 1 pl.
Discusses the only known statue of Apollo seated on the omphalos, now in the Museum at Alexandria. Investigates the origin of the type and its occurrence in Egypt using similar types on reliefs, painted vases, and coins. Assigns the statue to the third century B.C. after a discussion of style, including an analysis of the evidence provided by dated coinage. The prototype for the image was probably a cult statue in Antioch.

1127 **Waggoner, Nancy M.** "Seal Impressions in the Manner of the Seleucids." *Studies in Honour of Leo Mildenberg: Numismatics, Art History, Archaeology*. Edited by A. Houghton et al. Wetteren: Editions NR, 1984. Pages 259-68. 1 pl.
The author examines ten Greek clay sealings which at one time had been pressed around a section of thread or cord. They are most likely from Asia Minor or Syria and date from the Seleucid period. The seals bear the portrait of a Seleucid ruler, an unidentified male head, the head of Apollo and other gods, and Herakles strangling a lion. Some of these depictions are compared to coin types.

1128 **Waites, M. C.** "The Deities of the Sacred Axe." *American Journal of Archaeology* 27 (1923): 25-56. Illus.
"It is suggested that the double axe, originally a symbol of the Great Mother, eventually became attached to the male Father of the Gods. Several coins on which this axe appears as a whole or as a part of the type are described and explained. The thunderbolt borne by or combined with Athena on many coins (and with Aphrodite or Artemis in a few cases) is another version of this axe." [J. R. Jones, *NIAJAH*]

1129 **Walker, Raymond J.** "Dioscuri on Ancient Coins." *The Numismatist* 71, no. 5 (May 1958): 519-22. Illus.
"The Dioscuri are well known to students of astrology as the Gemini or twins of the Zodiac. As Castor and Pollux, the sons of Zeus, they held a status similar to that of patron saints in early Christian times and are often found on the coins of Rome, Tarentum and Rhegium. In time, coins bearing the Dioscuri came to be looked upon as charm pieces and were carried by sailors as protection against St. Elmo's Fire; also were often buried as payment of the deceased's toll across the river Styx." [J. Francis, *NL* 48]. [Also see "Curious Ancient Gold Coin" and A. W. Hands "Notes on Charon's Fee" under GENERAL WORKS—GREEK].

1130 **Walston, Charles.** *Notes on Greek Sculpture*. Cambridge: University Press, 1927. 23 pp., 4 pls.
Includes two essays: (1) The Constantinople Pentathlete and Early Athlete Statues, and (2) A Marble Draped Female Figure in Burlington House. The first essay discusses a marble relief depicting a pentathlete, focusing on the sculptor's dilemma in choosing an image to commemorate the victory of a pentathlete. The diskoboli coins of Kos are discussed and illustrated as well as the athlete depicted on coins of Selinus. The second essay examines the art of a marble torso.

1131 **Weber, Charles E.** "Inspiration of the Ancients." *The Numismatist* 115, no. 8 (August 2002): 901-8. Illus.
Illustrates and describes an assortment of modern world coins which bear designs reminiscent of ancient Greek types.

1132 **Wihnyk, Joseph.** "Medusa the Centauress on Greek Coins." *The Celator* 19, no. 6 (June 2005): 18-21. Illus.
A female centaur graces the helmet of Athena on some didrachms of Velia engraved by Kleudoros. Wihnyk argues that the centauress is Medusa of classical mythology. The helmet is identified as Hades' winged Phrygian helmet which renders the wearer invisible. Illustrates an amphora which clearly depicts Medusa as a centaur (half human, half horse). The winged Phrygian helmet and centauress decoration disappears from Velian coinage after 330 B.C.

1133 **Wilkenson, Richard H.** "The Origin and Development of a Greco-Persian Numismatic Motif." *The Numismatist* 102, no. 6 (June 1989): 887-889, 969-70. Illus.
Examines the way in which the symbolic use of the bow influenced the development of a sequence of Greco-Persian coinage. Suggests that the depiction of the bow positioned with the strings held away from the dominant subject is symbolic of divine or royal dominance. Illustrates a gold stater of the Persian satrap Datames of Tarsos which shows the turned bow. Wilkenson contrasts this with the normally unturned bow often depicted on Greek coinage. Suggests the use of the turned bow on Seleucid and Parthian coinage forms a conscious continuity of the motif. Suggests the turned bow may have played a part in the court protocol of the Parthian kings.

1134 **Wilson, L. M.** "Contributions of Greek Art to the Medusa Myth." *American Journal of Archaeology* 24 (1920): 232-40. Illus.

"Wappenmünzen of Athens (here ascribed to Central Greece) and a later coin of Lesbos are used among many other examples to show the progress in representations of Medusa, from an undifferentiated 'Phobos' type to the final form with snakes as locks of hair." [J. R. Jones, *NIAJAH*]

1135 **Wilson, Thomas.** *The Swastika.* Washington, D.C., n.d. (1900).
The use of the swastika on ancient coins is covered on pages 763-1030.

1136 **Wray, David M.** "Crescent and Star and Related Images—A Historical Perspective." *The Celator* 18, no. 2 (February 2004): 6-11. Illus.
An examination of the star and crescent symbol, sometimes seen on coins. Discusses how the symbol came to represent lunar goddesses. Shows how it came to symbolize the deification of Roman aristocrats. Discusses the adoption of the symbol by Christians and Moslims.

1137 **Wroth, Warwick W.** "Hygieia." *Journal of Hellenic Studies* 5 (1884): 82-101. Illus.
"A detailed investigation of representations of this goddess and of their significance, with many references to appropriate coin types." [J. R. Jones, *NIJHS*]

1138 **Zeuner, F. E.** "Dolphins on Coins of the Classical Period." *Bulletin of the Institute of Classical Studies of the University of London* 10 (1963): 97-103.

1139 ——— "Fish on Ancient Coins." *Spink Numismatic Circular* 71, nos. 7-8 (July-August 1963): 142-3. Illus. [CS 3516]
"Describes some of the common, unusual and rare species of fish which appear on ancient coins of the Mediterranean area, including the tunny, mullet, thorn-back ray and the seldom seen orphos mentioned by Aristotle. Coins depicting each species are illustrated." [*NL 66*]

1140 **Zimmerman, Jeremiah.** "Religious Character of Ancient Coins." *Spink Numismatic Circular* 16 (October 1908): 10912-9. Illus.
A survey of the religious nature of Greek and Roman coins.

Also see: Anderson "Stymphalian and Other Birds" under PELOPONNESOS—ARKADIA; Bérend "Histoire de Poulpes" (octopuses) under SICILY—SYRACUSE; Blanchet "Eretrian Coin-Type" under EUBOIA; Blomberg *On Corinthian Iconography* under CORINTHIA; Borba-Florenzano "Coins and Religion" under SICILY—GENERAL WORKS; Borba-Florenzano "A Note on the *Triskeles*" under SICILY—GENERAL WORKS; Brett "Philip of Macedon's Race Horse" under MACEDONIAN KINGDOM—GENERAL WORKS; Clain-Stefanelli "Late Silver Issues" (Janus Head) under ITALY—RHEGION; Coe "Disease" under PORTRAITS; Cohen "Euclid's Proposition" under AEGINA; Esdaile "Homeric Coin Types" under PORTRAITS; Evans "Natural Selection" under CELTIC COINAGE OF BRITAIN; Gabrici "La Nike Funebre delle Monete di Elis" under PELOPONNESOS—ELIS; Gale *The Sacred Tripod* under ITALY—KROTON; Goldsborough "Changing World…Attributing Ancient Greek-Era Coins" under COLLECTING GUIDES; Hadley "Royal Propaganda" under SYRIA—SELEUCID KINGDOM; Hammond "The Lettering and the Iconography" under MACEDONIAN KINGDOM—GENERAL WORKS; Hansen "Pursuing Arethsua" under SICILY—SYRACUSE; Hart "The Diagnosis of Disease" (two items) under PORTRAITS; Havelock "The Archaistic Athena Promachos" under ART; Heurgon "Les Types Monétaires Étrusques" under ITALY—ETRURIA; Heyman "Homer" under IONIA; Hill "Persian Lion-Gryphon" under MACEDONIAN KINGDOM—GENERAL WORKS; Hind "Istrian Faces" under THRACE—ISTROS; Hixenbaugh "Helmets of Perdikkas II" under MACEDONIAN KINGDOM—GENERAL WORKS; Hoge "The Ancient Olympic Games" under PELOPONNESOS—ELIS; Holloway "Choice of Coin Types" under MACEDONIAN KINGDOM—GENERAL WORKS; Hooker "Celtic Coin Iconography" under CELTIC COINAGE—GENERAL WORKS; Hurter "Crickets" under SICILY—GENERAL WORKS.

Jaunzems "Silenus and Nymph" under THRACE—LETE; Kampmann "Herakles the Snake-Strangler" under MYSIA—AUTONOMOUS CITIES; Kardara "Dyeing" (beehive vessel) under THRACE—GENERAL WORKS; Karlsson "The Symbols of Freedom and Democracy" under SICILY—SYRACUSE; Karweise "Heracles the Snake Strangler" under CARIA; Klimowsky "Religious Symbols" under PALESTINE—JUDEA; Klimowsky "Symbols" under PALESTINE—JUDEA; Koerper and Kolls "The Silphium Motif" under CYRENAICA; Kritt, Hoover, and Houghton "Three Seleucid Notes" (Seleucid anchor symbol) under SYRIA—SELEUCID KINGDOM; Kurke *Coins, Bodies, and Gold* under GENERAL WORKS—GREEK; Lacroix "La Typologie du Bronze" under SICILY—GENERAL WORKS; Lagos "Chian Coins and Amphorae" under IONIAN ISLANDS—CHIOS; Lehmann "The Striding God" under SICILY—ZANKLE/MESSANA; Liebert "Palm Trees" under PALESTINE—JUDEA; Liebert "The Pomegranate" under PALESTINE—JUDEA; McIvor "Astronomical" under CELTIC COINAGE—GENERAL WORKS; McMenamin "Cartography" under ZEUGITANA; Meyers "An Amphora Stand" under ITALY—ETRURIA; Mixter "Unrecorded Cilician Type" under CILICIA; Molnar "Mithradates Used Comets" under BOSPOROS; Mørkholm and Zahle "The Coinage of Kuprlli" under LYCIA.

Naster "La Technique des Revers Partiellement Incus" under PHOENICIA; Oikonomides "Coins Fill Historical Blanks" (Macedonian shields) under MACEDONIAN KINGDOM—GENERAL WORKS; Paléothodoros "Le 'Satyre et la Ménade' Thasiens" under THRACE—THASOS; Pudill "Great God of Odessos" under THRACE—GENERAL WORKS; Rakicic "Bucephalus" under SYRIA—SELEUCID KINGDOM; Rakicic "The Lagobolon of Pan" under MACEDONIAN KINGDOM—GENERAL WORKS; Reinach "Achilles" under NORTHERN GREECE—THESSALY; Riddle "Coins and Contraceptives" under CYRENAICA; Robert *Monnaies Grecques* under GENERAL WORKS—GREEK; D. Robinson "Heracles Relief" under ITALY—HERAKLEA; Saatsoglu-Paliadeli "Aspects of Macedonian Costume" under MACEDONIAN KINGDOM—GENERAL WORKS; Sayles "The Locrian Ajax" under CENTRAL GREECE—LOKRIS; Sayles "The Technical Obverse" under THE MINTING PROCESS; C. T. Seltman "Peisistratus" under ATTICA—GENERAL WORKS; E. J. Seltman "Nummi Serrati and Astral Coin Types" under THE MINTING PROCESS; J. Singh "Religious Study" under BACTRIA; M. Singh "Menander I and the Buddhist Iconography" under BACTRIA; Smith "Aphrodite" under CORINTHIA; Stefanakis "Kydon" under CRETE; Stieglitz "The Solar Cult" under MALTA.

Tameanko "The Silphium Plant" under CYRENAICA; Tatman "Silphium, Silver and Strife" under CYRENAICA; Trell "Coins of the Phoenician World" under PHOENICIA; Vagi "Ancient Coins Illuminate the History of Troy" under TROAS; Vagi "Colts of Corinth" under CORINTHIA; Vagi "Imitations" under ART; Vagi "Pegasus Motif" under CORINTHIA; Vermeule "A Fighting Warrior" under ART; Walker "Front Side, Back Side" under MINTING TECHNIQUES; Warren "The Trihemidrachms" under CORINTHIA; Weil "Der Zeus des Phidias" under PELOPONNESOS—ELIS; Westermark "Apollo in Macedonia" under MACEDONIAN KINGDOM—GENERAL WORKS; Westermark "Skylla" under SICILY—AKRAGAS; Wihnyk "Eryx, Aphrodite, and the Myrrh Tree" under SICILY—ERYX; Wihnyk "Tortoise of Aphrodite" under AEGINA; Wirgin "Anchor of Alexander" under MACEDONIAN KINGDOM—GENERAL WORKS; Wirgin "Anchor of Seleucus" under SYRIA—SELEUCID KINGDOM; Wray "Gods, Monsters, Heroes" under SICILY—GENERAL WORKS; Wright *Coins from Asia Minor and the East* under ASIA MINOR—GENERAL WORKS; Wright "Silphium Rediscovered" under CYRENAICA; Zahle "Persian Satraps and Lycian Dynasts" under PERSIA; Zahle "Religious Motifs" under SYRIA—SELEUCID KINGDOM; Zolotnikova "A Female Divinity" under SYRIA—SELEUCID KINGDOM.

Art, Engravers, and Stylistic Trends

Many flourishing artistic traditions could exist simultaneously; and each of these could be absorbed and reproduced well and badly—by the good and the inferior artist working literally side by side, as the coins show them often to have done.

—C. H. V. Sutherland, 1955

1141 **Arnold-Biucchi, Carmen.** "Reflections of Polykleitos's Work on Ancient Coins." *Polykleitos, the Doryphoros and Tradition.* Edited by Warren G. Moon. Madison: University of Wisconsin Press, 1995. Pages 218-28. Illus.
The author examines ancient coins to find possible depictions of the work of the sculptor Polykleitos, including the Hera of Argos and the Doryphoros. Discusses the Hera of Argos and the heads of Hera on coins of Argos, Elis, and other cities. Discusses the statue of Hera on Roman Provincial coins of Argos. Examines the head of the Doryphoros and other depictions of the statue on coins. Concludes that the few examples seen on coins reflect more the style of their time than the style of Polykleitos.

1142 **Ashmole, Bernard.** "The Relation Between Coins and Sculpture." *Transactions of the International Numismatic Congress Organized and Held in London by the Royal Numismatic Society, June 30-July 3, 1936.* Edited by J. Allan, H. Mattingly, and E. S. G. Robinson. London: B. Quaritch, 1938. Pages 17-22. 3 pls. [CS 16462]
The author discusses the relationship between coins and sculpture and suggests much can be gained by an integrated chronological study of coins, sculpture, and vases. Primarily, comparisons can aid in dating, or in determining the origin and geographical distribution of certain artistic styles.

1143 **Barclay, Kent B.** "Stylistic Evolution in Graeco-Roman Coinage." *Classical Coin Newsletter* (Maplewood, New Jersey) 6, no. 3 (fall 1986): 2, 31. Illus.
Examines four of the most familiar ancient coin images which illustrate the continuity of certain archetypes throughout Greek and Roman coinage: (1) the armed horseman which originated with the coinage of King Patraos of Paeonia, (2) the representation of Poseidon with foot on prow, (3) the goddess Nike as a symbol of victory, and (4) the radiate head which originated with Apollo on the coinage of Rhodes.

1144 **Bauslaugh, Robert A.** "Coins." *Echoes from Olympus: Reflections of Divinity in Small-scale Classical Art.* Edited by Darrell A. Amyx. Berkeley: University of California Art Museum. Pages 125-38. Illus.
This booklet is intended for a program in museum training for art history graduate students. Bauslaugh's chapter on Greek and Roman coins illustrates and describes numerous Greek coins.

1145 **Berk, Harlan J.** "Kimon's Lady Arethusa Shows Celators the Way." *World Coin News* (March 16, 1992): 62-3.
This installment of Berk's column "What's Old" discusses Kimon's facing head of Arethusa and the imitations which it inspired such as Eukleida's Athena from Syracuse, Heracleida's Apollo from Catana, and the Athena by Kleudoros of Velia. Nine coin types are illustrated.

1146 **Bertman, Stephen.** "The Challenge of Coinage." *SAN—Journal of the Society for Ancient Numismatics* 10, no. 1 (winter 1979): 15-6.
General commentary on the artistic development of coinage.

1147 **Bieber, Margarete.** *The Sculpture of the Hellenistic Age.* New York: Columbia University, 1955. Revised edition, 1961. Reprint, Hacker Art Books, 1981. 259 pages, 818 photographs.
A comprehensive survey of Hellenistic sculpture. Coins are often used as evidence for the identity of royal portraits and for the reconstruction of statue groups.

1148 **Brauer, George C.** "Non-Celtic Barbarous Imitations of Certain Greek Coins." *SAN—Journal of the Society for Ancient Numismatics* 7, no. 1 (fall 1975): 3-5.
An overview of the imitative coinages of non-Celtic peoples. In contrast to the Celtic coins, these coins were intended to be close copies of the Greek originals. The lack of artistic abilities resulted in barbarous designs. Coins imitative of those of Chalcis, Aspendus, Sinope, and Athens are shown.

1149 **Cahn, Herbert A.** "Lokale Elemente im Stil Archaischer Griechischer Münzen." *Transactions of the International Numismatic Congress Organized and Held in London by the Royal Numismatic Society, June 30-July 3, 1936.* Edited by J. Allan, H. Mattingly, and E. S. G. Robinson. London: B. Quaritch, 1938. Pages 33-9. [CS 3548]

1150 ———— *Monnaies Grecques Archaiques.* Basel, 1947. 31 pp., pls. [CS 3549]. Also a German edition, *Griechische Münzen Archaischer Zeit.* Basel: Amerbach Verlag, 1947. 32 pp., 36 pls. [CS 3550]

1151 ——— *Frühellenistische Münzkunst.* Basel, 1948. 29 pp., 8 pls. [CS 3551]
"Studies the relation between art and coinage." [E. Clain-Stefanelli]

1152 ——— "Sculpture and Coins in Greek Art." *Israel Numismatic Bulletin* (Israel) 3-4 (August-December 1962): 66-8. [CS 3552]
"After studying the three principal periods of Greek art in combination with the related coins, Cahn concludes as follows: In the Archaic Period, individual sculptures were not copied onto coins, but a dominant, conventional type was used; in the Classical Period, original sculptures served as a source of inspiration that left its mark on the coinage designs; in the Hellenistic Period, sculpture was authentically copied on coins, but only in accordance with spatial limitations." [*NL* 66]

1153 **Carpenter, Rhys.** "The Clue of the Missing Feet." *Expedition* 2, no. 1 (fall 1959): 34-7. Illus., pl.
In discussing the problems connected with the restoration of a Greek statue in the Classical Gallery known as the Pitcairn Nike, the author states that its only possible source is the life-size gold-and-ivory Victory alighting on the outstretched hand of the colossal gold-and-ivory statue of Athena made by Pheidias and housed in the Parthenon. A coin of Aphrodisias from the collection of E. T. Newell reproduces an almost contemporary version of this famous statue, judged to be a faithful replica erected in the fourth century B.C. [Summarized from *NL* 52]

1154 **Cheek, Kevin R.** "Artistic Choice: Archaic Style Lived On." *The Celator* 2, no. 12 (December 1988): 1, 24. Illus.
The artistic style of a fifth century B.C. silver drachm of Larissa is discussed. Suggests the style was intentionally archaic even though the coin was minted after the introduction of classical style coinage. [Also see the "Letter to the Editor" written by Greg Franck-Weiby in *The Celator* 3, no. 2 (February 1989): 2, in which an archaic method of coin inscriptions known as "Boustrophedon" is discussed. Alternate lines of text were written in opposite directions, left-to-right and then right-to-left. Letters in the right-to-left inscriptions were written as mirror-images].

1155 **Chittenden, Jacqueline, and Charles T. Seltman.** *Greek Art: A Commemorative Catalogue of an Exhibition held in 1946 at the Royal Academy, Burlington House, London.* London: Faber and Faber, Ltd., 1946. 72 pp., 128 pls.
The catalogue for an exhibition of Greek art works in various media, including coins, from ancient through modern times. Includes *Prefaces* by Seltman and Chittenden. Ninety-five ancient Greek coins are listed on pages 39-42, and several are illustrated on three plates. The coins are from the collections of Chittenden, Seltman, and R. Cyril Lockett.

1156 **Clayton, Peter A.** "Greek Coins and the Ancient Wine Trade." *Coins* (England) 9, no. 2 (February 1972): 14-6. Illus.
"Greek coins with types referring to the various cities concerned with wine and the wine trade are discussed. The similarity between the impressed marks found on the handles of wine amphorae made on Thasos, Chios and Rhodes and the coin types of those islands is noted." [P. Clayton, *NL* 88]

1157 **Congdon, Lenore O. Keene.** "The Mantua Apollo of the Fogg Art Museum." *American Journal of Archaeology* 67, no. 1 (January 1963): 7-13. 4 pls.
"A small, cast head which was acquired by the above museum in 1931 is identified as a second century A.D. copy taken from an early fifth century B.C. statue of Apollo. This Apollo appears on tetradrachms of Leontini from the first half of the fifth century and on various other coins down to the third century A.D." [I. Merker, *NL* 65]

1158 **Cunnally, John.** *The Role of Greek and Roman Coins in the Art of the Italian Renaissance.* Ann Arbor: University Microfilms International, 1987. 460 pp., illus.

1159 **de Callataÿ, François.** "On the Style of the Aitna Master from Eastern Sicily." *Israel Museum Studies in Archaeology* 3 (2004): 43-52. Illus.
"A discussion of stylistic issues and the light they shed on the makers of ancient coins with particular emphasis on the unique tetradrachm of Aetna in the Belgian Coin Cabinet. The article includes tables of dies used in Sicily during the fifth century B.C." [Arnold Spaer, *NL* 149]

1160 **Forrer, Leonard S.** *Biographical Dictionary of Medallists, Coin, Gem, and Seal-Engravers, 500 B.C.-A.D. 1900.* Eight volumes. London, 1902-30. Reprints, London: Spink & Son, 1965; New York: B. Franklin, 1970. New revised edition, London: Baldwin & Sons, 1980. [CS 14115]
Originally published in monthly installments in *Spink's Numismatic Circular* and later published as a book. Provides biographical information on engravers, with the focus on medals. However, the listings include all the known engravers of ancient Greek coins and gems, including those known only by the first letter of their names. Some of the coin types are illustrated. Brief bibliographic references are given. [An *Index*, written by Joan S. Martin (London: Royal Numismatic Society, 1987) provides a subject listing for the medals listed in Forrer's work].

1161 ——— *Notes sur le Signatures de Graveurs sur les Monnaies Grecques.* Brussels: J. Goemaere, 1906. 381 pp., 4 pls. [CS 3580]

1162 **Franke, Peter R., and Max Hirmer.** *Die Griechische Münze als Kunstwerk.* Munich: 1963. 96 pp., 19 pls. [CS 3555]

1163 **Furtwängler, Adolf.** *Masterpieces of Greek Sculpture: A Series of Essays on the History of Art.* Edited by E. Sellers. London, 1895. Reprint, edited by A. N. Oikonomides, Chicago: Argonaut, 1964. 439 pages, illus.
The English translation of *Meisterwerke Der Griechischen Plastik* (Leipzig-Berlin, 1893). A renowned reference book on the works of the great masters of Greek sculpture including Pheidias, Kresilas, Myron, Polykleitos, Praxiteles, Skopas, and Euphranor. Also discusses the Venus of Milo. Extensively illustrated (the reprint uses improved photographs). Numerous Greek coins are illustrated and discussed in relation to other art works.

1164 **Gardner, Percy.** "Coins in Relation to History." *The Principles of Greek Art.* By Percy Gardner. New York: The Macmillan Company, 1914. Reprint, 1926. Pages 324-34. Illus.
General comments on the usefulness of coins in the science of archaeology.

1165 **Gilliland, Cora Lee.** "Coins: Mirrors of Art and History." *The Numismatist* 94, no. 12 (December 1981): 3283-306. Illus.

Explores coins from all periods of history as reflections of art. Compares coins with other art forms (architecture, sculpture, painting) and shows how their style, subject, and focus reveal the period in history from which they came.

1166 **Havelock, Christine Mitchell.** "The Archaic as Survival versus the Archaistic as a New Style." *American Journal of Archaeology* 69, no. 4 (October 1965): 331-40. 2 pls.
"Havelock explores the archaic survivals of the fifth and fourth centuries B.C. (Athenian coins, the Panathenaic amphorae, and idols in sculpture and vase painting) in contrast to the archaistic style which appears in the third and second centuries. The 'archaic' in Athenian tetradrachms, which continued to 322, is described as an unchanged device supporting their value as an accredited series, but is viewed as a type rather than a style. This is compared with 'archaic' statues reproduced on coins, notably the Artemis of Abdera, 400-390. The change to an archaistic style, first noted in the coinage of Amphipolis, 326-5 and Ptolemy I, ca. 315-311, becomes more common during the third and second centuries in the coinage of the mainland, Macedonia, Syria, Sicily and India." [J. Balcer, *NL* 76]

1167 ——— "The Archaistic Athena Promachos in Early Hellenistic Coinages." *American Journal of Archaeology* 84, no. 1 (January 1980): 41-50. 2 pls. [CS 3487]
Havelock notes that the archaizing Athena Promachos used on the reverse of tetradrachms of Ptolemy I was borrowed from Panathenaic amphorai, and this choice reveals an awareness of the propaganda value of an old familiar symbol and is "symptomatic of the strong historicism developing among the Greeks in the later fourth century." Suggests Ptolemy was a promoter of this new "archaistic" artistic style, and the use of this Athena Promachus by other monarchs was directly inspired by Ptolemy. [This archaizing movement in Greek art is explored further in Havelock's "Archaistic Reliefs of the Hellenistic Period," *American Journal of Archaeology* 68, no. 1 (January 1964): 43-58].

1168 **Hill, George F.** *Select Greek Coins: A Series of Enlargements Illustrated and Described.* Paris and Brussels: G. Vanoest, 1927. Reprint, Chicago: Ares Publishers, 1974. 61 pp., 64 pls. [CS 3557]
Reviews the artistic elements of Greek coins. Over 250 of the finest Greek coins are described and shown in enlarged photographs. The coins are arranged according to subject: male heads, female heads, single figures, figures grouped with animals, chariot-groups, animals, monstrous beings, plants, and inanimate objects. The plates in the original edition were printed by Léon Marotte of Paris from photographs by Donald Macbeth of London. Most of the coins are from the British Museum, although some are from the Gulbenkian, Jameson, Lloyd, and Woodward collections. [Reviewed by E. S. G. Robinson in *Numismatic Chronicle* 5th ser., 6 (1926): 483-5, and by J. D. Beazley in *Journal of Hellenic Studies* 48 (1928): 105-6].

1169 ——— *L'Art dans les Monnaies Grecques: Pièces Choisies Reproduites en Grandissement et Décrites.* Paris/Brussels, 1927. 68 pp., 64 pls. [CS 3558]
The French edition of Hill's *Select Greek Coins: A Series of Enlargements* (see above).

1170 **Hoberman, Gerald.** *The Art of Coins and Their Photography: An Illustrated Photographic Treatise with an Introduction to Numismatics.* London: Spink & Son, Ltd. in association with Harry N. Abrams, Inc., 1982. 268 pp., illus.
The introductory chapters briefly discuss the origins of coinage, techniques of striking coins, coin types, counterfeits and debasement. The author then illustrates and describes many coins, from ancient Greek through modern U.S. coins, utilizing superb enlarged color photographs, with accompanying text with line drawings of each coin. The Greek coins are a gold stater of Croesus, a silver diobol of Cyzicus, an electrum stater of Cyzicus, a silver drachma of Naxos, a tetradrachm of Athens, a tetradrachm of Catana, a decadrachm of Syracuse, a gold litra of Syracuse, a tetradrachm of Cyrene, a gold stater of Philip II, a silver obol of Selge, gold staters of Alexander, Ptolemy I, and Lysimachus, a posthumous tetradrachm of Alexander from Clazomenae, and a tetradrachm of Tenedos. Concludes with a guide to numismatic photography. Discusses equipment, lenses, lighting, films, filters, processing and printing. [A critical review by Simon Bendall appears in *Numismatic Chronicle* 145 (1985): 284-5. Bendall points out numerous numismatic errors in the text. Also reviewed in *Seaby Coin and Medal Bulletin* No. 766 (June 1982): 185].

1171 ——— *Exposing Stamps of Another Coin: A Bridge between Contemporary Society and the Culture of the Ancient World, through Numismatic Philately and Photography.* Cape Town: The South African Numismatic Society, 1993. 34 pp., illus.
A booklet from an lecture presented to the South African Numismatic Society illustrating ancient coins which appear on postage stamps. Hoberman points out that both coins and stamps have a common origin in seals. Seals were used as a symbol of authority or as a mark of ownership. Hoberman compares photographs of ancient coins with similar coins depicted on postage stamps and discusses noteworthy aspects of their depiction. Uses mainly ancient Greek coins as examples.

1172 **Keary, Charles F.** "The Morphology of Coins." Parts 1 and 2. *Numismatic Chronicle* 3rd ser., 5 (1885): 165-98; 6 (1886): 41-95. Reprinted as a book, Chicago: Argonaut, 1970. 89 pp., illus., 6 pls. [CS 272]
Discusses the evolution in form and style of ancient and medieval coin types brought about by the special functions which coins are designed to fulfill. Likens coin types to species of animals and focuses on the connecting links between the different species. The first half of the book examines the principal "species" of coin types directly descended from the original Greek class. Shows the influence of Greek coinage on the coinage of the Parthians, Sasanians, Muslims, and Indo-Greeks. The second half of the book discusses coin types derived from the Roman class.

1173 **Lanckoronski, Leo, and Maria Lanckoronski.** *Schönes Geld der alten Welt: Meisterstücke Griechischer Münzkunst.* Munich, 1935. 98 pp., illus. [CS 3561]

1174 **Liegle, Josef.** *Euainetos, eine Werkfolge nach Originalen der Staatlichen Münzsammlung zu Berlin.* Berlin, 1941. 64 pp., 14 pls. [CS 3583]

1175 **Mildenberg, Leo.** "Great Art in Small Greek Coins." *Israel Numismatic Bulletin* (Israel) 2 (April-June 1962): 35-8. 1 pl.
"Mildenberg discusses the highly artistic qualities which are to be found in the smaller Greek coins (i.e., those of drachm size or less)." [I. Merker, *NL* 65]

1176 ——— "The Work of the Die Engraver Kimon of Syracuse and Its Influence." *Nomismatika Khronika* (Greece) 5-6 (1978): 24-6. Illus.
In Greek on pp. 24-5, with an English summary on page 26. States that evidence drawn from the Naro Hoard of 1925 reveals: (1) the Syracusan decadrachms are in fact coins rather than medallions; (2) the Euainetos decadrachms are later in date than the Kimon decadrachms; (3) the signed Kimon coins are earlier than the unsigned "Kimon" pieces; (4) the Akragas decadrachms are much older than the Syracusan decadrachms; and (5) all the Syracusan

decadrachms were struck during the reign of Dionysios I—they were not victory issues minted soon after 413 B.C. Mildenberg also states that all dies signed by Kimon were in fact engraved by him; the unsigned dies in the style of Kimon were not.

1177 ——— "Von der Kunst der Griechischen Kleinmünzen." *Festschift für Dr. Erich Madsack zum 75. Geburtstag am 25 September 1964.* Hannover: Verlag A. Madsack, 1964. Pages 95-106. Illus. [CS 3563]. Reprinted in *Leo Mildenberg. Vestigia Leonis: Studien zur Antiken Numismatik Israels, Palästinas und der Östlichen Mittelmeerweit.* Novum Testamentum et Orbis Antiquus 36. Edited by U. Hübner and E. Knauf. Freiburg: Universitätsverlag, and Göttingen: Vandenhoeck & Ruprecht, 1998. Pages 101-4. 2 pls.
[Also see Hübner and Knauf *Vestigia Leonis* under GENERAL WORKS—GREEK].

1178 **Molinari, Nicholas.** "The Philosopher and the Celator: Complimentary Agents in the Early Greeks' Attempt at Grasping Nature." *The Celator* 22, no. 8 (August 2008): 14-28. Illus.
Molinari gives an account of the emergence of philosophy and coinage in ancient Greece in order to show that the philosopher and the die engraver are complimentary agents in the early Greeks' attempt at understanding and controlling nature. [Also see the "Letter to the Editor" by Alan Walker in *The Celator* 23, no. 1 (January 2009): 4. Walker points out that the die engravers had little influence over the types chosen for coinage, thereby negating some of Molinari's conclusions. Also see Molinari's response to his critics in *The Celator* 23, no. 2 (February 2009): 4].

1179 **Neuburger, Albert.** *Die Technik des Altertums.* Leipzig, 1919. Reprint, Leipzig: Zentralantiquariat der DDR, 1977. 570 pp., illus. [CS 3584]

1180 **Norton, Charles E.** "Greek Coins for Studying the Fine Arts." *American Journal of Numismatics* 16, no. 2 (October 1881): 29.
An extract from an article published in the *Harvard Register* pointing out that Greek coins illustrate the principles and history of Greek art.

1181 "Obscure Artist 'King' of Hellenistic Coinage." *Coin World* (April 21, 1976): 81, 87. Illus.
This brief article highlights the dies engraved by the "Delta" engraver and the influence his coin types had on later coinages. The work of this engraver, who signed his dies with a Δ, first appeared on the tetradrachms of Ptolemy I of Egypt with the portrait of Alexander the Great. He later engraved dies for the portrait coins of Ptolemy I. Elements of his designs were later incorporated into coins of Thessaly, Pyrrhus of Epirus, Antigonus Gonatas, and others. [Also see "Ptolemaic Notes: I. Delta" under EGYPT—PTOLEMAIC KINGDOM].

1182 **Oleson, John.** *Greek Numismatic Art: Coins of the Arthur Stone Dewing Collection.* Cambridge: Fogg Art Museum, Harvard University, 1975. Unpaged, illus., map. [CS 1908]
A discussion of Greek art illustrated through coins. Includes enlarged photographs of sixty-four coins from the Dewing collection. [Also see Mildenberg *The Arthur S. Dewing Collection* under PRIVATE COLLECTIONS].

1183 **Pennington, Paul.** "The Rise and Fall of Classical Art as Shown by Greek and Roman Coins." *Spink Numismatic Circular* 45 (January 1937): 1-8. Illus.
Discusses the artistic development of the Greeks and Romans as displayed in their coinage from the archaic period to the seventh century A.D.

1184 **Poole, Reginald S.** "On Greek Coins as Illustrating Greek Art." *Numismatic Chronicle* new ser., 4 (1864): 236-47. 1 pl. (line drawings). [CS 3564]
Poole makes general comments on Greek coins as works of art. He identifies four geographical "schools" of art: Ionian, Sicily and Italy, Crete, and Asiatic. He discusses the distinctive characteristics of each school.

1185 ——— "Athenian Coin-Engravers in Italy." *Numismatic Chronicle* 3rd ser., 3 (1883): 269-77. 2 pls. [CS 3585]
Examines the coins of Terina as examples of the art of Greece, as opposed to the art of the West typically found on Italian coins. Discusses the artistic style of the dies and the engravers' names. Poole finds that the coins of Terina bear an artistic style distinctive to the Athenian school.

1186 **Ravel, Oscar E.** "The Classification of Greek Coins by Style." *Numismatic Chronicle* 6th ser., 5 (1945): 117-24. 2 pls. [CS 3565]
Using Corinthian staters, Ravel illustrates reverse dies with very different styles, skill of engraving, symbols, etc.—all die-linked to the same obverse die. Concludes that style, symbols, and lettering cannot be of any use for the classification of Corinthian coins. Provides similar examples with coins of other cities. Ravel warns that, unlike statues which are always made by real artists, coins are objects of necessity and are not always made by artists. Urges that the classification of Greek coins through the system of die-sequences is the most useful way to establish a scientific chronology of the emissions.

1187 **Regling, Kurt L.** *Die Antike Münzen als Kunstwerk.* Berlin, 1924. 148 pp., 45 pls. [CS 3567]
Examines ancient coins as works of art. "Includes many otherwise unpublished coins from the Berlin collection." [C. Kraay]. "A classic work." [E. Clain-Stefanelli]

1188 **Richter, Gisela M. A.** *The Sculpture and Sculptors of the Greeks.* New Haven: Yale University Press, 1929. 242 pp., 2 maps, illus. Revised edition, 1950. 625 pp.
Concentrates on sculpture and the sculptors who produced it. Includes illustrations and discussions of numerous Greek coins, many from the collection of E. T. Newell. Only 500 copies of the original edition of this book were printed. In the revised edition, special mention is made of Hellenistic portrait coins and to fine animal representations found on coins. In her discussion of individual sculptors, coin types are used to identify lost works of art.

1189 ——— "A Greek Silver Phiale in the Metropolitan Museum." *American Journal of Archaeology* 45 (1941): 363-89. Illus.
"On pp. 373-5 and figs. 11-15 coins of Syracuse, Catana and Camarina are used to show that the relief decoration of the bowl is of late fifth century B.C. style. On pp. 375-6 it is suggested that the bowl (which shows some double striking) must have been hammered out over a die, a process similar to, but not identical with, the striking of coins." [J. R. Jones, *NIAJAH*]

1190 ——— "Coins." *A Handbook of Greek Art.* New York: Phaidon, 1959. Pages 243-50. Illus.
Briefly describes the stylistic characteristics of coins in the archaic, classical, and Hellenistic periods, often with reference to similar styles found in sculptures, gems, or vases.

1191 **Rizzo, Giulio Emanuele.** "Eukleidas." *Bollettino d'Arte* (1938): 329-53.

1192 **Rodee, H. David.** "Art History on Persian and Phoenician Coinage." *The Numismatist* 69, no. 11 (November 1956): 1219-27. Illus. Reprinted in *Selections from The Numismatist: Ancient and Medieval Coins*. Racine: Whitman Publishing Co., 1960. Pages 163-71. Illus.
"At Sardis, Darius at first copied the old Lydian bimetal standard, adding copper to gold for hardness. These gold pieces became the world's first international gold coinage. Mr. Rodee describes these and also the coins of Sidon, Tyre, Aradus, and Byblus in Phoenicia which were issued before the conquest of Alexander. He includes interesting details of the dies, and a brief history of the period." [J. Francis, *NL* 41]

1193 **Sayles, Wayne G.** "Master Images Reflected in Coins from Antiquity, Part 1: The Kneeling Archer." *The Celator* 1, no. 1 (February/March 1987): 8-9; "Part 2: Chariots Wheeling." 1, no. 2 (April/May 1987): 8, 12; "Part 3: Herakles and the Lion." 1, no. 3 (June/July 1987): 8, 12; "Part 4: The Hero/Warrior." 2, no. 1 (January 1988): 24-5.
A series of articles discussing artistic images from ancient coins which have become the undisputed representation of a particular subject. Part 1 discusses the kneeling archer design such as the Great King on Persian darics and sigloi, and the Herakles figure on coins of Thasos. The development in the style of this image on coins and other works of art is reviewed. Concludes that this image represented power and prestige across a wide geographical base. Part 2 follows the stylistic development of the quadriga on vases and coins. Part 3 discusses artists' portrayals of Herakles and the Nemean Lion. An overview of the related mythology is followed by a discussion of the horizontal, vertical, and circular depictions of this image. Part 4 discusses the hero and warrior figure, usually depicted in a lunging position carrying a shield and spear or sword. This image represented security and virtue.

1194 ———. "Painting Inspires Coins: Death of Locrian Ajax Depicted." *The Celator* 1, no. 2 (April/May 1987): 1, 14. Illus.
Reviews the mythology surrounding Ajax, son of King Oileus of the Locri Opuntii. The author suggests the depiction of Ajax on a second century B.C. bronze coin of Aradus may represent the fall of Ajax as painted by the great artist Apollodorus.

1195 ———. "Original Art on a Budget: Ancient Coins Offer Exquisite Sculpture in Miniature." *The Celator* 2, no. 1 (January 1988): 4, 28-9.
Discusses coins as an art form, suggesting a few coins with artistic appeal which can be acquired at modest cost. Suggests some books which focus on numismatic art.

1196 ———. "The Celator's Point of View." *The Celator* 2, no. 4 (April 1988): 2.
This editorial focuses on the stylistic evolution of the Satyr and Nymph motif on the coins of Thasos and Himera. The influence of private art on the public art of coinage is mentioned.

1197 ———. "New Interpretation: Historical Event Inspired Turkoman Coin Type." *The Celator* 3, no. 5 (May 1989): 1, 24, 26. Illus.
Traces the history of Pheidias' famous statue of Athena Promachus which stood near the Parthenon at Athens. Suggests this statue was the inspiration for the design of a thirteenth century Turkoman coin.

1198 ———. "Classical Coinage Qualifies as a Major Art Form." *The Celator* 3, no. 12 (December 1989): 14-5, 17, 29. Illus.
Discusses the attributes of major arts and minor arts. Shows that the design of coins was a major artistic endeavor and that many products of ancient engravers have been recognized throughout history as major art. Provides evidence that coin collecting has been popular for thousands of years. Mentions famous engravers of Greek coin dies. Discusses transformations in style.

1199 ———. "Aesthetic Judgments Should be Based on Celator's Skill, Not on Overall Style." *The Celator* 4, no. 10 (October 1990): 24-6.
Emphasizes that style is a manner of representation and must not be characterized as good or bad. Differentiates between style and execution.

1200 ———. "Greek Coins Illustrate the Evolution of Emotion in Style." *The Celator* 4, no. 11 (November 1990): 36-7.
Describes the characteristics of the archaic, classical, and Hellenistic styles of coinage. Discusses the archaizing phenomenon and the contributions of the artist Lysippus to the classical style.

1201 ———. "How are Coins Dated by Style?" *The Celator* 13, no. 1 (January 1999): 37. Illus.
Discusses the portrayal of drapery as an element of style which may help in the chronological arrangement of art works, including coins. Illustrates two nice examples of flowing drapery on a Carian stater ca. 420 B.C. and on a tetradrachm of Katana ca. 460 B.C.

1202 ———. "Corinth and Classicism." *The Celator* 13, no. 9 (September 1999): 45. Illus.
Discusses some stylistic features of archaic and classical coins. Stylistic changes during these periods are clearly illustrated on some Corinthian staters.

1203 ———. "Getting a Rein on Things." *The Celator* 11, no. 11 (November 2001): 45. Illus.
This installment of Sayles' "Through the Looking Glass" column focuses on changes in artistic styles that are evident when comparing archaic, classical, and Hellenistic period coins. Illustrated by similar chariot scenes on coins of Syracuse, Gela, and Himera.

1204 ———. "Dating by Artistic Convention." *The Celator* 17, no. 1 (January 2003): 47. Illus.
Discusses the stylistic development of common coin motifs. Points out that there was much sharing of coin types among cities, and each city applied its own artistic interpretation to the type. Illustrates two different depictions of Tyche on coins from Cilicia.

1205 ———. "The Changing Face of Medusa." *The Celator* 17, no. 5 (May 2003): 47. Illus.
Discusses the depiction of the gorgon Medusa in art and coinage. Early depictions show her as a horrible creature. Later depictions showed a beautiful young woman. Sayles discusses the reasons for this metamorphosis.

1206 **Schefold, Karl.** *Meisterwerke Griechischer Kunst*. Basel and Stuttgart, 1960. 327 pp., illus. [CS 3569]

1207 **Schwabacher, Willy.** *Griechische Münzkunst. Kurze Kunstgeschichte an Beispielen aus der Sammlung S. M. Gustaf VI. Adolf, König von Schweden*. Edited by H. A. Cahn. Mainz: Philipp von Zabern, 1974. 180 pp., illus. [CS 3570]

1208   **Seltman, Charles T.** *Approach to Greek Art.* London and New York: The Studio Publications, 1948. 132 pp., 111 pls.
Examines Greek art within the framework of prose and poetry. Seltman defines "prose art" as descriptive and analytic, "poetry art" as organic and concrete. Begins with the Egyptian influence on Greek art and discusses various phases and styles of Greek art. Gives much emphasis to the arts of die-cutting and gem-engraving which the author classes with the fine arts rather than minor arts as is often done. Discusses celature, painting, and sculpture in stone and marble. Coins are frequently shown and discussed as examples of art. [Reviewed by T. B. L. Webster in *Journal of Hellenic Studies* 68 (1948): 157-8, and by G. K. Jenkins in *Numismatic Chronicle* 6th ser., 9 (1949): 126-7].

1209   ——— "Greek Sculpture and Some Festival Coins." *Hesperia* 17, no. 2 (April-June 1948): 71-85. 4 pls. [CS 3504]
Discusses the reflection of the art of the Master of Olympia on the coins of Elis. Also examines the influences of Pheidias, Praxiteles, and Antonianos by tracing the artistic influences evident in the coins of Elis.

1210   ——— *Masterpieces of Greek Coinage.* Oxford: Bruno Cassirer, 1949. Reprint, Chicago: Obol International, 1980. 128 pp., illus. [CS 3573]
Focuses on some of the masterpieces of Greek numismatic art and the men who engraved the dies for these coins: Theodoros, Mnesarchos, the Aetna Master, Phrygillos, Euainetos, Kimon, the Helios Master, Theodotos, and others. Provides historical and personal backgrounds, then presents fifty-four of the finest Greek coins. The artistic aspects of each are discussed and each is illustrated with enlarged photographs. [Reviewed by G. K. Jenkins in *Numismatic Chronicle* 6th ser., 9 (1949): 127, by J. G. Milne in *The Classical Review* 64, no. 3-4 (December 1950): 149-51, and by C. H. V. Sutherland in *Journal of Hellenic Studies* 70 (1950): 84-5].

1211   ——— "The Ring of Polycrates." *Centennial Publication of the American Numismatic Society.* Edited by Harald Ingholt. New York: American Numismatic Society, 1958. Pages 595-601. Illus.
Polycrates was the tyrant of Samos in the sixth century B.C., and he controlled many islands of the Aegean surrounding Samos. Herodotus tells a story involving Polycrates' signet ring: Theodorus, a gem engraver, made a carved-emerald ring for Polycrates. On the advise of Amasis of Egypt, Polycrates threw the ring into the sea. The ring was returned to him when it was found in the belly of a fish. Clement of Alexandria (A.D. 150-216) said the ring bore a musical lyre. Seltman illustrates a sixth century B.C. coin of Calymna (an island south of Samos controlled by Polycrates) bearing an incuse lyre on the reverse. Also illustrated is an ancient carved gemstone with a lyre—perhaps similar to the gem in Polycrates' ring. The author calls for more comparisons to be made between coins and ancient carved gems.

1212   **Sigler, Phares O.** "Art and Coinage in Ancient Greece." *The Numismatist* 84, no. 2 (February 1971): 189-208. Illus.
Provides an overview of the religion, athletics, economics, government, social life, and accomplishments of the Greeks as a background to a discussion of Greek art. Reviews the major arts of sculpture and painting, then discusses gem and seal engraving. Attempts to uncover the reasons for Greek superiority in the art of coinage, concluding that the die engravers' intelligence was the primary reason for the excellence of Greek coinage. Includes a bibliography for Greek art and coinage.

1213   **Slabaugh, Arlie R.** "An Appraisal of Ancient Greece." *Numismatic Scrapbook Magazine* 25, no. 6 (June 1959): 1381-3. Illus.
"Debunking the belief that each and every Greek devoted his full time to the arts, the writer points out that the highly artistic achievements for which Greece is famous were largely the work of an aristocratic minority. They include the coinage, struck in immense quantities from hand-made dies, which is considered to be amongst the finest ever produced." [G. North, *NL* 50]

1214   **Stein, Harry J.** "An Essay on the Appreciation of Greek Coins." *The Numismatist* 53, no. 8 (August 1940): 557-60. Illus.
This brief essay on the aesthetics of Greek coinage discusses rhythm and symmetry in coin designs.

1215   **Stillman, William J.** "The Coinage of the Greeks." *The Century Illustrated Monthly Magazine* 33 (March 1897). Reprint, Chicago: Obol International, 1975. 16 pp., illus.
A discussion of Greek coinage focusing on the artistic influences on Greek coinage and the artistic trends displayed in the coinage. Concludes with a brief discussion of the problems of counterfeits.

1216   **Sutherland, Carol H. V.** "What is Meant by 'Style' in Coinage?" *Museum Notes* 4 (1950): 1-12. [CS 16471]
The classification of coins by style became popular after B. V. Head relied on style in his study of Syracusan coins in 1874. Sutherland lauds the advantages of more modern methods of classification based on weight standard, metallic composition, and die-linkages. He clarifies that it is incorrect to relate styles to periods of time—styles belong to particular individuals. Works of a true artist may be contemporary with the works of a non-artist craftsman. Discusses the effects of copying an original work and clarifies the difference between stylistic treatment and an original work. The author also discusses the attributes which differentiate images of gods, goddesses, and heroes from true human portraits.

1217   ——— *Art in Coinage: The Aesthetics of Money from Greece to the Present Day.* London: Batsford Ltd., 1955. 223 pp. including the 47 pls. [CS 16472]
Provides background information on history, artistic technique, and the artists themselves to give the reader a fuller appreciation of coins as works of art. Two chapters focus on Greek coinage, discussing the problems involved in good coin design, the influences on the artists, and advances in technical skill. Follows the development in the depiction of deities on coins and the use of symbols as aids to their identification. Continues with the development of human portraiture. Illustrates thirty-two Greek coins in enlarged photographs. Subsequent chapters are titled Roman Portraiture, Medieval and Byzantine Formalism, Return of Naturalism, Machinery and the Baroque, Machinery and the Modern Formula. An additional 115 coins are photographed. [Reviewed by C. C. Vermeule in *Numismatic Chronicle* 6th ser., 15 (1955): 259-61, and *Spink Numismatic Circular* 65, no. 3 (March 57): 112-3, by R. A. G. Carson in *Times Literary Supplement* (June 24, 1955): 346, and by J. V. Noble in *American Journal of Archaeology* 60 (1956): 459-60].

1218   **Szego, Paul S.** "Styles of Art in the Greek Coinage." *Coin Collector's Journal* new ser., 8 (August 1941): 114-17, 124. Illus.
In this discussion of the artistic aspects of Greek coinage, Szego says that a real artist takes impressions from nature and expresses them in his own style. The author then describes the attributes of numismatic art from various stylistic periods: the archaic age, the age of rigid style, the parthenonic age, the period of Praxiteles and Skopas, the period of Philip and Alexander, and the Hellenistic age. He warns that there were both skilled artists and less talented craftsmen in every age.

1219 **Tameanko, Marvin.** "Three Dimensional Graphics on Ancient Coinage." *SAN—Journal of the Society for Ancient Numismatics* 18, no. 1 (July 1990): 8-15.
Examines the history of the three-dimensional perspective as applied to the art of ancient coins. Shows how various types of perspective drawing were used, primarily using Roman coins as examples.

1220 **Theodorou, Jerry.** "Pieces of Antiquity: The Art and History of Ancient Greek Coins, I." *The Greek American* (November 4, 1989): 12-3. Illus.
General comments on Greek coins as works of art, illustrated by eleven fine specimens. [Although titled as Part 1, no sequel was published].

1221 ——— "An Appreciation of Ancient Greek Coins." *Journal of the Hellenic Diaspora* 15, nos. 3-4 (1998): 101-26. 8 pls.
Presents various viewpoints regarding the merits of Greek coins as works of art. Argues that Greek coins are legitimate examples of ancient fine art and, unlike the "major" arts of sculpture and painting, coins do not suffer from a scarcity of fine originals, a plethora of later copies, or poor states of preservation. Theodorou continues with a discussion of eight Greek coins which exhibit fine artistic qualities.

1222 **Tompkins, Janice Firth, ed.** *Wealth of the Ancient World: The Nelson Bunker Hunt and William Herbert Hunt Collections.* Fort Worth and Beverly Hills: Kimbell Art Museum, 1983. 329 pp., illus., maps.
The catalogue for the traveling exhibition of the Hunt brothers' ancient art collection. Consists of 16 vases, and 38 bronzes, and 112 ancient Greek, Roman, and Byzantine coins. Includes 395 black and white, and 16 color photographs by Andrew Daneman. Includes essays by six noted authorities, maps, indices, and a bibliography. The essay "Coins of the Ancient World" was written by Arthur Houghton (pp. 145-54). The catalogue of the coins was written by Catharine Lorber. Of the coins, sixty-two are Greek. Each coin is fully described, photographed, and accompanied by a brief essay on its artistic aspects. [Reviewed by M. J. Price in *Spink Numismatic Circular* (March 1984): 46, and by L. Burn in *Journal of Hellenic Studies* 106 (1986): 257. Also see Hunt under PRIVATE COLLECTIONS for the auction sale catalogues of the Hunt collections].

1223 **Tsangari, Dimitra, and Irene Orati.** *Ancient Coins in the Alpha Bank Collection: Contemporary Inspiration for the Sculpture of Giorgos Lappas.* Athens: Alpha Bank, 2008. 26 pp., illus.
The catalogue for an exhibition at the Alpha Bank in Athens covering the history of coins. Special emphasis is given to the iconography of ancient coins and to the engravers' sources of inspiration. It also presents nine works of the contemporary artist Giorgos Lappas which were inspired by coins from the bank's collection.

1224 **Vagi, David L.** "Artist's Signatures on Greek Coins." *The Celator* 10, no. 1 (January 1996): 22-3. Illus.
Discusses the use of engravers' signatures on coins. Describes the variety of signature locations on coins and points out the difficulties often encountered in identifying abbreviated signatures.

1225 ——— "Developing Art Forms Evident on Greek Coinage." *The Celator* 10, no. 7 (July 1996): 24-5. Illus.
This installment of the author's *Through the Looking Glass* column provides an overview of the periods of Greek art as illustrated by archaic, classical, and Hellenistic coinage.

1226 ——— "Imitation a Standard Practice on Greek Coins." *The Celator* 11, no. 5 (May 1997): 26-7. Illus.
Reviews how some coin designs were derived from others. For example, the Siculo-Punic tetradrachms with the head of Herakles were adapted from Alexander's coinage. Vagi also describes some of the imitations derived from the coins of the great Syracusan engravers Kimon, Euainetos, and Eucleidas.

1227 **Vermeule, Cornelius C.** "A Fighting Warrior of the Greek Fifth Century." *Spink Numismatic Circular* 61, no. 2 (February 1952): 53-7.
"Staters of Tarsus and Cyzicus of the middle of the fifth century B.C. show the stylistic unity in Greek design in the generations after Marathon. The scenes of crouching warriors are paralleled on a skyphos by the Pan Painter and derive from compositions such as the so-called Marathon stele in Copenhagen. Later staters of Corinth and Syracuse with the helmeted head of Athena explain the type of helmet worn by a warrior on a chalcedony intaglio gem contemporary with the coins of Tarsus and Cyzicus." [*NL 33*]

1228 ——— "Greek Numismatic Art 400 B.C.-300 A.D.: Some General Remarks." *Greek and Byzantine Studies* 1, no. 2 (October 1958): 97-117. 4 pls. [CS 3576]
The author relates the aesthetics of numismatics to the development of Greek art in other media, focusing on coinage reverse types, 400-27 B.C. Refers throughout to the plates in Head's *A Guide to the Principal Coins of the Greeks* (see B. V. Head under GENERAL WORKS—GREEK) and comments on the art of Head's periods III, IV, V, VI, VII, and the Greek Imperial period.

1229 **Vesely, Zdenek.** "Few Early Greek Coiners use Signatures." *Coin World* (July 31, 1985): 30. Illus.
Describes the coin types engraved by Kimon, Eucleidas, Heracleidas, Eumenes, Euaenetos, and Theodotus.

1230 **Waldstein, Charles.** "Pythagoras of Rhegion and the Early Athlete Statues." *Journal of Hellenic Studies* 1 (1880): 168-201. 3 pls.
"On pp. 173-4 it is argued that hair arranged in two braids wound round the head and fastened on the top is the sign of an athlete rather than of Apollo. Coins of Aenus showing the head of Hermes present one of the only two apparent exceptions to this rule." [J. R. Jones, *NIJHS*]

1231 ——— "Pythagoras of Rhegion and the Early Athlete Statues." *Journal of Hellenic Studies* 2 (1881): 332-51. Illus.
"On p. 348, coins of Metapontum, Pandosia and Selinus, showing river-gods or athletic figures, are compared. Similarity of style suggests a common model, or a local school of sculpture." [J. R. Jones, *NIJHS*]

1232 ——— "The Argive Hera of Polycleitus." *Journal of Hellenic Studies* 21 (1901): 30-44. 2 pls.
Examines a marble head in the British Museum formerly identified as Apollo or Bacchus. Waldstein argues that it is a reproduction of the famous Hera by Polycleitus. Compares the head with heads of Hera shown on coins of Elis, Himera, and Knossos.

1233 **Walston, Charles.** "The Establishment of the Classical Type in Greek Art." *Journal of Hellenic Studies* 44 (1924): 223-53. Illus.

"On pp. 232-3, coins of Poseidonia, Caulonia, Thrace, Elis and Syracuse are used to illustrate survival of the so-called 'Minoan' type in Greek art until ca. 450 B.C. On p. 242 a coin of Catana showing a head of Silenus is taken by contrast as an example of a naturalistic rendering." [J. R. Jones, *NIJHS*]

1234 **Walters, Henry B.** "Greek Coins." *Greek Art*. New York: Dodge, 1906. Pages 222-42. Pls.

1235 **Webster, T. B. L.** "Tondo Composition in Archaic and Classical Greek Art." *Journal of Hellenic Studies* 59 (1939): 103-23. Illus., 2 pls.
"This survey is based for the most part on the decorations of vases and mirrors; but it also includes references to a number of coin types." [J. R. Jones, *NIJHS*]

1236 **Weil, Rudolf.** *Die Künstlerinschriften der Sicilischen Münzen.* Berlin: Vierundvierzigstes Programm zum Winckelmannsfeste der Archaeologischen Gesellschaft zu Berlin, 1884. 32 pp., 3 pls. [CS 3589]
Artists' signatures on Sicilian coins.

Also see: Alfoldi "Eukleidas—Ein Goldschmied?" under SICILY—SYRACUSE; American Numismatic Association *Selections* under GENERAL WORKS—GREEK; Cahn "Artiste ou Magistrat?" under ITALY; Davisson "Collecting Greek Coins as an Art Form" under COLLECTING GUIDES; de Callataÿ "Un Tétradrachme de Lysimaque Signé au Droit" under GENERAL WORKS—HELLENISTIC; de Ciccio *Cimone e Eveneto* under SICILY—SYRACUSE; Du Chastel *Syracuse* under SICILY—SYRACUSE; Evans "Some New Artists' Signatures" under SICILY—GENERAL WORKS; Evans "Syracusan Medallions" under SICILY—SYRACUSE; Evans "The Artistic Engravers of Terina" under ITALY—TARAS; Favorito "The Signed Bronzes" under SICILY—SYRACUSE; Fischer-Bossert "A Lead Test-Piece" under SICILY—SYRACUSE; Forrer "Artist's Signature" under NORTHERN GREECE—AKARNANIA; Gardner *The Types of Greek Coins* under TYPES; Grose "Primitiae Heraclienses" under ITALY—HERAKLEA; Hazzard "Ptolemaic Notes: I. Delta" under EGYPT—PTOLEMAIC KINGDOM; Holloway *Art and Coinage* under ITALY—GENERAL WORKS; Hoover "Illiterate Die Engravers" under SYRIA—SELEUCID KINGDOM.

Imhoof-Blumer "A Numismatic Commentary" under TYPES; Jenkins *Ancient Greek Coins* under GENERAL WORKS—GREEK; Jenkins *Coins of Greek Sicily* under SICILY—GENERAL WORKS; Jenkins "Recent Acquisitions" (1957) under PUBLIC COLLECTIONS—GREAT BRITAIN (LONDON); Jongkees "Le Graveur Cimon à Messana" under SICILY—ZANKLE/MESSANA; Lengyel et al. *Collection: Maitres et Oeuvres* under GENERAL WORKS—GREEK; Mahler "Concerning an Euboian Tetradrachme" under CENTRAL GREECE—EUBOIA; Mildenberg "Kimon" under SICILY—SYRACUSE; Mixter "Gorgon Heads" under TYPES; Moysey "Observations" under PERSIA; Mukherjee *A Plea for Study of Art* under NORTHWEST INDIA; Oeconomides *Archaia Nomismata* under GREEK COINAGE—GENERAL WORKS; Reinach "Un Monument Delphien" under NORTHERN GREECE—AITOLIA; Rizzo *Saggi Preliminari su L'Arte* under SICILY—GENERAL WORKS; Roach "Issues of Style" under ATTICA—GENERAL WORKS; Rudd "Itinerant Engravers?" under CELTIC COINAGE OF BRITAIN; Rutter "Dating the Period of the 'Signing Artists' of Sicilian Coinage" under SICILY—SYRACUSE.

Sayles *Ancient Coin Collecting 2* under COLLECTING GUIDES; Sayles "The Locrian Ajax" under CENTRAL GREECE—LOKRIS; Scaros "In Defense of Magic" under COLLECTING GUIDES; Sear "The Master Engravers" (two items) under SICILY—GENERAL WORKS; C. T. Seltman "The Engravers" under SICILY—AKRAGAS; C. T. Seltman "On the 'Style' of Early Athenian Coins" under ATTICA—GENERAL WORKS; E. J. Seltman "On Some Names, Symbols, and Letters on Coins" under ITALY—THURII; H. Smith "Sculptural Style" under EGYPT—PTOLEMAIC KINGDOM; Tameanko "Syracusan Dekadrachm" under SICILY—SYRACUSE; Tudeer "Die Tetradrachmenprägung von Syrakus" under SICILY—SYRACUSE; Vagi "The Art of Sicilian Naxos" under SICILY—NAXOS; Weil "Der Zeus des Phidias" under PELOPONNESOS—ELIS; Wiesinger "Anmerkung zu Einem Kimonischen Tetradrachmon" under SICILY—SYRACUSE; Wihnyk "Mirror-Image Kleudoros" under ITALY—NEAPOLIS; Zervos "Near Eastern Elements" under MACEDONIAN KINGDOM—GENERAL WORKS.

PORTRAITS

Portraits have been always very interesting to mankind; and there seems to be little doubt but the love of them gave rise, not only to painting, but to sculpture. No where are they to be found so ancient, so numerous, so well preserved as in medals.

—John Pinkerton, 1808

1237 **Babelon, Ernest.** "Portraiture and its Origins in Greek Monetary Types." *American Journal of Numismatics* 44, no. 2 (April 1910): 37-48; 44, no. 3 (July 1910): 105-22. Illus., 1 pl.
A history of the development of portraiture on coins. Begins with the use of likenesses of gods and goddesses as coin types. Then describes the use of human figures and then the use of generic royal figures. Examines the heads on some Persian darics and finds varieties in facial features on coins attributed to different kings. The darics and shekels *with portraits* were struck in the mint attached to the royal residences in the great cities like Susa, Babylon, and Persepolis. Discusses the coin portraits of Lycian dynasts, particularly the satraps Tissaphernes and Pharnabazus. Babelon also sees a portrait on some electrum staters of Cyzicus. He then discusses coins of European Greece. Here he finds no examples of portraiture before the time of Alexander the Great.

1238 **Babelon, Jean.** *Le Portrait dans l'Antiquité d'Après les Monnaies.* Paris: Payot, 1942. Second edition. Paris, 1950. 202 pp., 32 pls. [CS 3517]

1239 ——— "The Human Face on Greek Coins." Chapter 1 in Babelon's *Great Coins and Medals.* Translated by Stuart Hood. London: Viking Press, 1959. Pages 9-14. 34 pls.
A brief history of portraiture on Greek coins from the first gods depicted through the Hellenistic royal portraits. Discusses their stylistic development.

1240 **Balmuth, Miriam S.** "Portraits and Coins." *The Connoisseur* 143, no. 575 (February 1959): 58-61. Illus. [CS 3519]
This brief introduction to ancient coins emphasizes the portraits found on Greek, Roman, and Byzantine coins. Twenty-one coins are illustrated.

1241 **Bieber, Margarete.** "The Portraits of Alexander the Great." *American Philosophical Society Proceedings* 93, no. 5 (1949): 373-427. Illus. [CS 3521]
A life of Alexander accompanied by sculptures and portraits on coins, medallions, cameos, etc. Discusses the history, personality, and appearance of Alexander in connection with portraits based on originals made during his lifetime, and those based on portraits made after his death. Discusses Alexander's earliest coin-portrait on the first issue of Ptolemy I's tetradrachms where he is shown wearing the elephant's scalp. Also reviews the portrait on the coins of Lysimachus.

1242 ——— *Alexander the Great in Greek and Roman Art.* Chicago: Argonaut, 1964. 98 pp., 63 pls.
Begins with an historical outline of Alexander's life and conquests, then presents a thorough study of the surviving ancient portraits of Alexander the Great. Includes statues, coins, medals, mosaics, and paintings. The author shows how the depiction of Alexander differs during various historical periods. [Reviewed by C. M. Kraay in *Spink Numismatic Circular* 73, nos. 7-8 (July-August 1965): 158].

1243 **Brown, Blanche R.** "Styles in the Alexander Portraits on the Coins of Lysimachus." *Coins, Culture, and History in the Ancient World: Numismatic and Other Essays in Honor of Bluma L. Trell.* Edited by Lionel Casson and Martin J. Price. Detroit: Wayne State University Press, 1981. Pages 17-27. Illus.
Discusses the portrait issues minted by Lysimachus from ca. 297 B.C. Briefly reviews the coinage of Lysimachus, then focuses on the similarities and variances in style of the Alexander portraits at various mints. Compares these portrait coins with those minted by the Ptolemies and Seleucids. Illustrated by twelve photographs of portrait coins and marble busts.

1244 ——— "Art History in Coins: Portrait Issues of Ptolemy I." *Alessandria e il Mondo Ellenistico-Romano. Studi in Onore di Achille Adriani. Volume 2.* Rome: di Bretschneider, 1984. Pages 405-17. 2 pls.
Traces the evolution of the portraits on the coinage of Ptolemy I from the standard Alexander type with Herakles/Zeus, to the Alexander head in elephant skin, to the Athena reverse type, to the Ptolemy portrait obverse. Discusses the symbolism of the elephant skin, the Alexander portrait motif, the Athena, and the styles of the Alexander and Ptolemy portraits from an art-historical perspective.

1245 ——— *Royal Portraits in Sculpture and Coins: Pyrrhos and the Successors of Alexander the Great.* Hermeneutics of Art, Volume 5. New York: Peter Lang, 1995. 121 pp., 48 pls.

A study of the head identified as Pyrrhos in the Ny Carlsberg Glyptotek in Copenhagen and the style of royal portraits of the era immediately following the death of Alexander. [Reviewed by J. DeRose Evans in *American Journal of Numismatics* 2nd ser., 9 (1997): 139-43].

1246 **Carradice, Ian A.** *Ancient Greek Portrait Coins.* London: British Museum Publications, 1978. 16 pp., illus., map. [CS 3524]
An excellent summary of the history of coin portraiture from its earliest times through the Hellenistic period, illustrated by sixty-four black and white photographs of portrait coins.

1247 **Cheek, Kevin R.** "Military Victory Inspired Elephant-Skin Headdress." *The Celator* 3, no. 3 (March 1989): 10.
Reviews the use of elephants in war during the Hellenistic period. Suggests the elephant-skin headdress used by some Hellenistic kings on their coin portraits was an attempt to reinforce links to Alexander the Great who defeated the Indian king Porus, and also to convey a sense of strength.

1248 **Coe, John I.** "Disease as Portrayed on Ancient Coins." *SAN—Journal of the Society for Ancient Numismatics* 17, no. 2 (June 1987): 36-8.
Discusses some of the medical abnormalities which apparently afflicted some men portrayed on Hellenistic Greek, Parthian, and Roman Imperial coins. [Also see Hart "The Diagnosis of Disease" below].

1249 "Coin Portrait of Alexander the Great." *American Journal of Numismatics* 19, no. 1 (July 1884): 19.
Describes a process used by Francis Galton whereby he combined photographs of Alexander the Great's coins to create a composite portrait of Alexander which he believes gives a true picture of the man.

1250 **Dickens, Guy.** "Some Hellenistic Portraits." *Journal of Hellenic Studies* 34 (1914): 293-311. Illus.
Discusses portrait busts and coins of: (1) Ptolemy Soter, (2) Ptolemy Philadelphus, (3) Ptolemy Euergetes, (4) Ptolemy IV Philopator, (5) Attalus I of Pergamum, (6) Eumenes II of Pergamum, (7) Antiochus II of Syria, (8) Agathocles of Bactria, and (9) a portrait bust of Aristotle. Lists other known portrait busts of each.

1251 **Esdaile, K. A.** "Essay Towards the Classification of Homeric Coin Types." *Journal of Hellenic Studies* 32 (1912): 298-325. 1 pl.
"After pointing out that ancient artists were likely to have created more than one type of ideal portrait, when representing persons whom they could never have seen, the writer collects and discusses the various 'portraits' of Homer which appear on Greek coins. Contorniates are dismissed as 'draughtsmen' and considered of small value in this context." [J. R. Jones, *NIJHS*]

1252 **Fleischer, Robert.** "Hellenistic Royal Iconography on Coins." *Aspects of Hellenistic Kingship.* Studies in Hellenistic Civilization VII. Edited by Per Bilde, T. Engberg-Pedersen, L. Hannestad, and J. Zahle. Oakville, Conn.: Aarhus University Press, 1996. Pages 28-40. Illus.
Examines Hellenistic royal portraits, comparing the kings' features and discussing how each was depicted.

1253 **Forrer, Leonard S.** "Portraits of Royal Ladies on Greek Coins." *Spink Numismatic Circular* 45-46 (1937-8) [see below for details]. Reprint, Chicago: Argonaut, 1969. 72 pp., illus. [CS 3525]
Lists Greek coins (including Hellenistic, Bactrian, Parthian, Greek Imperial, etc.) portraying royal women. Brief biographical information is provided for each woman along with descriptions and photographs of coins on which she appeared. Originally appeared in installments in *Spink Numismatic Circular* as follows:

Adobogiona—Arsinoë II	45 (February 1937): 51-5.
Arsinoë II—Bernice IV	45 (March 1937): 90-5.
Calliope—Cleopatra Thea	45 (August-September 1937): 289-94.
Cleopatra I, Cleopatra II	45 (October 1937): 337-41.
Cleopatra III—Cleopatra VI	45 (November 1937): 377-80.
Cleopatra VII	45 (December 1937): 419-26.
Cleopatra Selene	46 (January 1938): 1-4.
Dynamis—Jotape	46 (February 1938): 41-7.
Laodice	46 (May 1938): 169-73.
Musa—Philistis	46 (July 1938): 249-53.
Pythodoris—Tryhpaena	46 (November 1938): 387-90.
Zenobia, Anzaze, Azarmidukht, Boran	46 (December 1938): 427-8.

1254 **Gardner, Percy.** "The Apoxyomenos of Lysimachus." *Journal of Hellenic Studies* 25 (1905): 234-59. Illus.
"On pp. 252-3 it is suggested that coins of Lysimachus give one of the best versions of the traditional 'Lysippic' portrait of Alexander the Great." [J. R. Jones, *NIJHS*]

1255 **Hart, Gerald D.** "The Diagnosis of Disease from Ancient Coins." *American Journal of Archaeology* 73 (1969): 236.
A one-paragraph summary of a paper presented at a conference. Hart mentions that the study of coin portraits may reveal the presence of disease.

1256 ——— "The Diagnosis of Disease from Ancient Coins." *Archaeology* 26, no. 2 (1973): 123-7. Also appeared in *The Numismatist* 92, no. 5 (May 1979): 949-55. Illus. [CS 16352]
Discusses evidence of diseases which can be observed on portraits on ancient coins including lesions on the faces of Parthian kings; the prominent voice box and sternomastoid muscle of Seleucus I; goiters on various gods, goddesses, and Hellenistic kings; acromegaly evident on portraits of Ptolemy I; and nasal deformity of the Roman emperor Maximianus Heraclius. [Also see Coe "Disease" above, Hart "Disease" below, and Hart "Trichoepithelioma" and "An Additional Note" under PARTHIA].

1257 ——— "Disease in the Ancient World: the Numismatic Evidence." *Cornucopiæ* (publication of The Ancient Coin Society, Canada) 1, no. 4 (1973): 51-66. Illus. [CS 16353]
Hart reviews the numismatic evidence for several medical abnormalities in the ancient world. He identifies the tumors on the portraits of some Parthian kings as evidence of trichoepithelioma, and he traces this hereditary disease through six generations of kings. He discusses the acromegaly evident on portraits of Ptolemy Soter. He points out that coin portraits of Philetaerus of Pergamum indicate that he was a eunuch. He points to the obesity of Ptolemy VIII. The prominent sternomastoid muscle in the necks of several ancient rulers is an indication of their athleticism. Hart also points out the fat folds on the

necks of several women's portraits, including those of goddesses. He shows that goiter (enlarged thyroid gland) was common in some areas of the Greek world and is quite common on Greek portrait coins. [Also see G. Hart "Ancient Coins and Medicine" under TYPES, and Hart "Trichoepithelioma" and "An Additional Note" under PARTHIA].

1258 **Hinks, Roger P.** "A Portrait of a Ptolemaic Queen." *Journal of Hellenic Studies* 48 (1928): 239-42. Illus., 1 pl.
A miniature portrait head of an Egyptian queen is tentatively identified as Arsinoe II based upon a similarity with her coin portraits.

1259 ——— "A Portrait of Ptolemy III Euergetes." *Journal of Hellenic Studies* 53 (1933): 300. Illus.
Discusses a small, glazed earthenware portrait head found in England. A comparison with coins indicates Ptolemy III Euergetes as the most probable subject.

1260 **Holt, Walter C.** "Portraits of Cleopatra." *The Celator* 22, no. 5 (May 2008): 6-22. Illus.
Illustrates and describes about thirty coin portraits of Cleopatra VII, including those on Roman Provincial issues. Holt compares the portraits and concludes that most were accurate depictions of her, and that she was not classically beautiful.

1261 **Howe, Laurence L.** "The Beginnings of Coin Portraiture." *The Numismatist* 61, no. 3 (March 1948): 152-64. Illus. Reprinted in *Selections from The Numismatist: Ancient and Medieval Coins*. Racine: Whitman Publishing Co., 1960. Pages 221-33. Illus.
Traces the beginnings of portraiture from depictions of gods through the introduction of the portrait coins of Cleopatra VII.

1262 ——— "Hellenistic and Early Roman Coin Portraiture." *The Numismatist* 61, no. 6 (June 1948): 382-96. Reprinted in *Selections from The Numismatist: Ancient and Medieval Coins*. Racine: Whitman Publishing Co., 1960. Pages 234-48. Illus.
A general history of coin portraiture during the Hellenistic and Roman periods.

1263 **Imhoof-Blumer, Friedrich W.** *Porträtköpfe auf Antiken Münzen: Hellenistischer und Hellenisierter Völker, mit Zeittafeln der Dynastien des Alterthums, nach ihren Münzen*. Leipzig: Teubner, 1885. 95 pp., 8 pls. [CS 3528]
Includes portraits of all the kings and the dynasts of the Hellenic or Hellenized world who have struck coins. Also includes the portraits of poets or philosophers which are sometimes found on coins (such as Herodotus, Sappho, and Hippokrates). Includes the names, dates of reign, and a description of the coins, without any commentary. See below for an English edition.

1264 ——— *Hellenistic Portraits on Ancient Coins*. Chicago: Argonaut, 1969. 95 pp., 8 pls. [CS 3529]
English edition of *Porträtköpfe auf Antiken Münzen, Hellenistischer und Hellenisierter Völker* (see above).

1265 **Jentoft-Nilsen, Marit.** *Ancient Portraiture: The Sculptor's Art in Coins and Marble*. Richmond: Virginia Museum, 1980. 63 pp., illus.
A catalogue for a 1980 exhibition at the Virginia Museum containing fifty-two Greek and Roman coins and twelve marble sculptures.

1266 **Jidejian, Nina.** *Lebanon and the Greek World, 333 to 64 B.C.: Portraits of Alexander the Great, the Ptolemies, the Seleucid and Armenian Kings, Illustrated by Coins in the Michael Eddé Collection*. Beirut: Dar el-Machreq sarl, 1988. 144 pp., illus.
An examination of Hellenistic portraiture including Alexander, the successors of Alexander, the Ptolemies, the Seleucids, and the kings of Armenia, illustrated by finely engraved portraits and photographs of coins. Includes historical and biographical commentary for each person.

1267 **Kvist, Kjetil.** "Tetradrachms of Antimachos Exhibit the High Quality of Greek Art." *The Celator* 11, no. 3 (March 1997): 18-20. Illus.
The author comments on the artistic aspects of the portrait tetradrachms of Antimachos I, king of Bactria ca. 190-180 B.C.

1268 **Lange, Kurt.** *Herrscherköpfe des Atlertums im Münzbild iher Zeit*. Berlin and Zürich, 1938. 161 pp., illus. [CS 3533]
Portraits of rulers.

1269 ——— *Charakterköpfe der Weltgeschichte, Münzbildnisse aus zwei Jahrtausenden*. Munich, 1949. 52 pp., 88 pls. [CS 3534]
"Portraits from 400 B.C. to A.D. 1500." [E. Clain-Stefanelli]

1270 **Lawton, Carol L.** "Hellenistic Coin Portraits." *Bearers of Meaning: The Ottilia Buerger Collection of Ancient and Byzantine Coins at Lawrence University*. Appleton, Wisconsin: Lawrence University Press, 1995. Pages 23-7.
A good overview of the development of royal portraits on coins during the Hellenistic period. Points out the variations in portrait style, from the idealized to the realistic.

1271 **Lehmann-Hartleben, Karl.** "Some Ancient Portraits." *American Journal of Archaeology* 46, no. 2 (April-June 1942): 198-216. 2 pls.
Aided by the evidence of coin portraits, a terracotta head is identified as a portrait of Philetairos of Pergamum. Discusses the development of the coin portraits of Philetairos. Speculates on the origin and preservation of the portrait bust. Also discusses a portrait statue of an early Roman poet.

1272 **Macdonald, George.** "Early Seleucid Portraits." Parts 1 and 2. *Journal of Hellenic Studies* 23 (1903): 92-116. 2 pls.; 27 (1907): 145-59. 2 pls.
Examines the Seleucid portrait tetradrachms bearing the inscription ANTIOXOY, but no other distinctive title. Macdonald focuses on tetradrachms on which the diadem worn by the king is furnished with wings, and he attempts to attribute the coins to specific kings. Thirty-four coins are arranged chronologically based on style and die links. Discusses the sequence of issues and the historical background of the period. Assigns to Antiochus II some coins that previously had been given to Antiochus Hierax. In Part 2, the author focuses on the tetradrachms which have a figure of Herakles resting. [Also see Wace "Hellenistic Royal Portraits" below].

1273 **MacFadden, George H.** "The Portrait of Ptolemy I Soter." *Studies Presented to David Moore Robinson on His Seventieth Birthday*. Volume 1. Edited by George E. Mylonas and Doris Raymond. St. Louis: Washington University, 1951. Pages 713-9. 4 pls.
Examines some bronze and marble portraits of Ptolemy I in order to form a judgment whether these were true portraits of the king. Compares them to the known portraits of Ptolemy on coins. Discusses the attributes of the coin portraits.

1274 **Marinescu, Constantin A.** "Statues Compared to Coin Portraiture." *Coin World* (December 29, 1997): 65. Illus.
A summary of a paper presented at a conference in which the author compared coin portraits of Alexander the Great to contemporary statues. [Also see the correction to the picture's caption in *Coin World* (January 5, 1998): 74].

1275 **Marotta, Michael E., and Ann M. Zakelj.** "Portraits and Representations of Alexander the Great." *The Celator* 16, no. 7 (July 2002): 6-20. Illus.
The authors argue that the image on the coinage of Alexander the Great, usually referred to as Herakles, is in fact a portrait of Alexander. Reviews the tradition of royal portraiture. Examines the notion of "Greekness" among the Macedonians. Reviews the symbolism of Alexander as a god. [Also see the strong rebuttal by Reid Goldsborough in a "Letter to the Editor" in *The Celator* 16, no. 9 (September 2002): 4, 37-8. Goldsborough points out numerous perceived flaws in the authors' arguments. Marotta responded to Goldsborough in a "Letter to the Editor" in *The Celator* 16, no. 12 (December 2002): 4].

1276 **Martin, Erik.** "Who's on First? No Easy Answer to 'First Person on Coin.'" *Coin Values,* supplement to *Coin World* (February 6, 2006): 28-30. Illus.
Ponders the question of who was the first human to be portrayed on a coin. After briefly discussing the early development of coinage, Martin offers possible candidates including Darius the Great (shown as the king on gold darics and silver sigloi) and Amyntas III of Macedonia. Concludes that Ptolemy I is the first verifiable historical monarch to be portrayed on a coin in his lifetime.

1277 **Montero, Joaquin.** "The Coinage of Alexander the Great and Alexander's Image on Currency." *ANA Journal: Advanced Studies in Numismatics* 1, no. 3 (fall 2006): 8-23.
Examines the use of Alexander's portrait on Macedonian coinage and the coinage of the Ptolemies and the Seleucids. Continues with a discussion of his image on Roman coins, especially those struck at Alexandria and Macedonia. Concludes with a brief look at Alexander's image on modern coins and currency.

1278 **Mørkholm, Otto.** "Sculpture on Coins: the Portrait of Alexander Balas of Syria." *Quaderni Ticinesi. Numismatica e Antichità Classiche* (Switzerland) 10 (1981): 235-45.

1279 **Museum of Fine Arts (Boston).** *Greek and Roman Portraits 470 B.C.—A.D. 500.* Boston: Museum of Fine Arts, 1959. 73 pp., illus. [CS 1633]
A brief history of the art of portraiture during Greek and Roman times is accompanied by seventy-three photographs of ancient works of art—primarily sculptures, but including twenty-one coins.

1280 **Newell, Edward T.** *Royal Greek Portrait Coins.* New York: Wayte Raymond, 1937. Reprints, Racine: Whitman Publishing, n.d. (1961); New York: Sanford J. Durst, 2000. 128 pp., illus., map. [CS 3542]
An introduction to the portrait coinage of the Hellenistic monarchies, beginning with the coinage of Philip II of Macedon and ending in the mid-first century A.D. Provides an overview of the history and coinage of each of the main Hellenistic rulers illustrated by several portrait coins of each. Concludes with an index of 185 kings, giving reign dates for each.

1281 **Oikonomides, Al N.** "Mithradates Herakles." *Voice of the Turtle* 4, no. 3 (March 1965): 11-4. [CS 2655]
Discusses portraits of Mithradates VI Eupator, king of Pontos, in the guise of Herakles. Compares coin portraits and marble sculptures. Demonstrates the usefulness of coins in identifying portrait sculptures. Includes photographs of coins and marble busts.

1282 ——— "Amyntas Earliest to Appear on Coin?" *Coin World* (August 26, 1981): 44, 46. Illus.
It was previously thought that Philip V (221-179 B.C.) was the first Macedonian king to use his portrait on coinage. But an ivory portrait head found in the royal tombs at Vergina in 1977, which the author believes is a portrait of Amyntas, bears a close resemblance to the portrait of a bearded Herakles on the staters of Amyntas III. The author states that Amyntas was the first Greek king to introduce portrait coinage. Amyntas (king of Macedonia 393-370 B.C.) was the father of Philip II and the grandfather of Alexander the Great.

1283 ——— "Search for Alexander Reveals Philip II." *Coin World* (September 9, 1981): 97, 102. Illus.
Describes a marble bust in the Field Museum of Natural History, Chicago, which the author identifies as a portrait of Philip II of Macedon. Provides descriptive accounts from ancient authors describing Philip's appearance after the loss of his right eye in battle. The marble bust depicts the empty eye socket.

1284 ——— "Nike Confirms Pyrrhos." *Coin World* (April 28, 1982): 33, 38. Illus.
Re-examines the portrait on the "Tarsos Medallion," a gold medallion struck probably ca. 230 A.D., and found near Tarsos in Cilicia about 1858. Originally identified as a portrait of Philip II by Adrien de Longperier in 1869, this portrait became the basis for identifying several other works as portraits of Philip. The author identifies the portrait as king Pyrrhos of Epirus (319-272 B.C.) based on the heraldic symbols appearing on the cuirass of the figure. The symbols include Nike carrying a trophy, and the Epirot thunderbolt. This new identification requires that other works of art be re-identified.

1285 ——— "The Portrait of Pyrrhos King of Epirus in Hellenistic and Roman Art." *The Ancient World* 8, no. 1-2 (October/November 1983): 67-72. Illus.
Reviews the evidence for the statues of Pyrrhos that once existed. The identification of Pyrrhos on the Tarsos medallion (see Oikonomides "Nike Confirms Pyrrhos" above) provided a new basis for looking for his *bearded* portrait on coins of his Italian and Sicilian allies. Concludes that Pyrrhos is portrayed on the bronze coinage of Bruttium (helmeted head to left). The six-rayed fulmen of the Zeus of Dodona appears below the shoulder—this is the national badge of Epirus and confirms the identification. The author also discusses the features used to identify the portrait on the Tarsos medallion as Pyrrhos.

1286 ——— "New Evidence on the Coin-Portrait of Philip II of Macedon." *Perspectives in Numismatics.* Edited by Saul B. Needleman. Chicago: Ares Publishers, 1986. Pages 3-11. Illus.
Argues that the portrait on the tetradrachms of Philip II of Macedon is that of Philip himself rather than Zeus as is often claimed. Calls attention to a portrait-statue of Philip which was taken by Mummius from the city of Thespiae in Boeotia and which had been misattributed as a statue of Zeus

according to Dio Chrysostom. Also describes a portrait-statue of Philip in the Field Museum of Natural History in Chicago which shows Philip with only one eye. The other had been knocked-out during a battle in 355 B.C. Explains that the erroneous identification of the portrait on Philip's coins as Zeus originated in the "pseudo-scholarship" of Adrien de Longpérier in 1868. Contains photographs of the Chicago statue and a Philip tetradrachm.

1287 ——— "The Portrait of King Philip II of Macedonia." *The Ancient World* 20, nos. 1-2 (fall 1989): 5-16. Illus.
Reviews how the portrait on the Tarsos medallion (see Oikonomides "Nike Confirms Pyrrhos" above), an ivory portrait found at Vergina, and a portrait in the Ny Carlsberg Glyptothek came to be identified as Philip II. Oikonomides rejects these identifications. Explains his reasons for identifying the head on Philip II's coins as Philip rather than Zeus. Provides excerpts from ancient writings describing the appearance of Philip. Identifies a marble bust in the Field Museum of Natural History (Chicago) as a portrait of Philip.

1288 **Richter, Gisela M. A.** *Greek Portraits: A Study of their Development.* Collection Latomus, Volume 20. Brussels, 1955. 50 pp., 10 pls.
Examines the portrayal of individuals from the fifth through the first century B.C. Includes an index to portraits and artists.

1289 ——— *Greek Portraits II: To What Extent Were They Faithful Likenesses?* Collection Latomus, Volume 36. Brussels, 1959. 47 pp., 16 pls. [CS 3543]
Discusses statues, herms, busts, coins, engraved gems, bowls, reliefs, statuettes, paintings, and mosaics.

1290 ——— *Greek Portraits III: How Were Likenesses Transmitted in Ancient Times?* Collection Latomus, Volume 48. Brussels, 1960. 59 pp., 50 pls.
Concludes that the majority of surviving portraits represent true likenesses.

1291 ——— "Late Hellenistic Portraiture." *Archaeology* 16, no. 1 (March 1963): 25-8. Illus.
"By presenting realistic coin portraits of Hellenistic rulers—preceding and contemporary with Roman Republican portraiture—the author attempts to disprove the theory that the idea originated with the Romans. Arranged chronologically, the portraits of Nicomedes I of Bythnia, Demetrius I of Bactria, Philoxenus of India, Heliocles of India, Kammeskires I of Elymais, Timarchus of Syria, Ariobarzanes I of Cappadocia, Ariobarzanes II of Cappadocia and Nicias of Cos show a continuing progression of realism." [I. Merker, *NL* 65]

1292 ——— *The Portraits of the Greeks.* London: The Phaidon Press, 1965. 337 pp., illus. (three volumes). Reprinted in one volume, Ithaca, 1984. Abridged and revised by R. R. R. Smith. Oxford: Phaidon, 1984. [CS 3544]
"All reliably and plausibly identified portraits of Greek poets, philosophers, orators, statesmen, generals and artists, and references to such portraits in ancient literature and inscriptions are here collected. Coin portraits are sometimes used to help establish the identity of sculptured portraits. Coins often bear the only known representations of Hellenistic rulers. Portraits engraved on gems are also included." [*NL* 81]

1293 ——— *Greek Portraits IV: Iconographical Studies: A Few Suggestions.* Collection Latomus, Volume 54. Brussels, 1967. 50 pp., 26 pls.
Examines portraits of Perikles, Pythagoras, Archilochos, the three tragedians, Aristotle, Demosthenes, Aischines, Epikouros, Hermarchos, and Hesiod.

1294 **Robinson, David M.** "A Graeco-Parthian Head of Mithradates I." *American Journal of Archaeology* 31 (1927): 338-44. Illus.
"Coins are used to establish the resemblance of this head, carved in serpentine, to Mithradates I of Parthia." [J. R. Jones, *NIAJAH*]

1295 **Ropel, Harold.** "A Coin Portrait of Mithradates VI Dionysus." *Voice of the Turtle* 4, no. 8 (August 1965): 167-8.
Illustrates a coin minted in Amisus which bears a portrait of Mithradates VI as Dionysos. Due to the similarity in style with other coins of Amisus, the author suggests a school of art may have been located there.

1296 **Sayles, Wayne G.** "Divinity." *The Celator* 21, no. 5 (May 2007): 45. Illus.
Illustrates Lysimachus tetradrachms from Kios, Pergamon, and Lampsakos. Comments on the subtle stylistic differences between them. Of particular importance is the alignment of Alexander's eyes toward the sky on the coins from Kios—a sign that he is a god.

1297 **Sheedy, Kenneth A.** "Magically Back to Life: Some Thoughts on Ancient Coins and the Study of Hellenistic Royal Portraits." *Alexander and the Hellenistic Kingdoms: Coins, Image and the Creation of Identity. The Westmoreland Collection.* Ancient Coins in Australian Collections 1. Edited by K. A. Sheedy. Sydney: Australian Centre for Ancient Numismatic Studies, Macquarie University, 2007. Pages 11-16.
Begins with a review of the viewpoint of R. R. R. Smith regarding royal portraits. Sheedy notes there is a more compelling drive to realize something of the individual in coin portraits than is visibly present in the surviving royal portraits in any other medium. This seems to be linked to the fact that they are portraits put out by the state. Few people would have come in contact with major statues of rulers. For most, the image of the ruler—and the compressed message of values and ideas—was largely obtained through coins. The key target of this message was the army. Sheedy points out the persuasive role of coin portraits in promoting an acceptance of continuity between successive rulers. [Also see Sheedy *Alexander and the Hellenistic Kingdoms* under PRIVATE COLLECTIONS].

1298 **Sjöqvist, Erik.** "A Portrait Head from Morgantina." *American Journal of Archaeology* 66, no. 3 (July 1962): 319-22. 1 pl.
A small terracotta head is identified as that of Agathocles of Syracuse. Coins helped provide evidence for its identification.

1299 **Smith, R. R. R.** *Hellenistic Royal Portraits.* Oxford Monographs on Classical Archaeology. Oxford: Clarendon Press, 1988. 196 pp., 80 pls., map.
Presents the major extant Hellenistic portraits and uses documentary evidence to look at their context, meaning, and history. Examines the function of the royal image, provides photographs of the surviving portraits (paintings, vases, sculptures) and, using coins, shows how the various and changing styles of royal image were designed for different political needs. Catalogues 130 portraits and discusses each. [Reviewed by I. Carradice in *Numismatic Chronicle* 150 (1990): 243-4, by A. M. Devine in *The Ancient World* 22, no. 1 (spring 1991): 67-70, and by L. A. Touchette in *Journal of Roman Studies* 82 (1992): 243-5].

1300 **Stefanakis, Manolis I.** "A Posthumous 'Alexander' of A.D. 1990." *Nomismatika Khronika* (Greece) 16 (1997): 101-4. Illus., 1 pl.

Discusses the appearance of Alexander's portrait on Greek coins and variations in his depiction at various cities. Mentions the portrait of Alexander which appears on the 100 drachma coin of modern Greece.

1301 **Tameanko, Marvin.** "The Importance of Homer's Writing Led to His Representation on the Coinage of Greek City States." *The Celator* 5, no. 5 (May 1991): 16-22.
Mentions famous poets and scholars who were depicted on ancient Greek coins. Focuses on Homer. Describes his life and contribution to Greek culture. Presents a list of Greek coins which portray Homer including coins from Ios, Colophon, Smyrna, Amastris, Chios, Nicaea, Cyme, and Temnus. Fully describes each coin and includes several drawings of coins with Homer's portrait.

1302 **Thompson, Dororthy Burr.** "A Portrait of Arsinoe Philadelphos." *American Journal of Archaeology* 59, no. 3 (July 1955): 199-206. 2 pls.
A small stone portrait head, which includes a ram's horn, is identified as that of the Ptolemaic queen Arsinoe Philadelphos through a comparison with her coin portraits.

1303 **Vagi, David L.** "The Foundations of European Coin Portraiture." *The Celator* 7, no. 12 (December 1993): 22.
This installment of the author's "Through the Looking Glass" column presents an overview of the history of Greek coin portraiture.

1304 ——— "Hellenistic *Heavenly Gaze* Resurrected by Constantine." *The Celator* 8, no. 11 (November 1994): 24. Illus.
Examines the "heavenly gaze" portraits found on Greek Hellenistic coins and Constantinian-era Roman coins. Vagi suggests this style of portrait conveys a message of piety and humility before heavenly forces, and it contrasts sharply with other portrait types which might express attributes such as strength, beauty, or pride.

1305 ——— "A Dozen Gems of Greek Portraiture." Parts 1-2. *The Celator* 10, no. 8 (August 1996): 32-3; no. 9 (September 1996): 22-3. Illus.
Illustrates and describes twelve of the best portraits appearing on Greek coins, selected for their accurate portrayals of human beings, rather than for beauty—thus excluding many fine, but idealized, portraits. The portraits are of Tissaphernes (Persian satrap), Seleucus I of Syria, Philip V of Macedon, Mithradates III of Pontos, Pharnaces I of Pontos, Arsinoe II of Egypt, Alexander the Great (on an early tetradrachm of Ptolemy I), Nabis of Sparta, Philetaerus of Pergamum (on a tetradrachm of Eumenes I), Orophernes of Cappadocia, Bagadates of Persis, and Antimachus of Bactria.

1306 ——— "Coins offer the Best Ancient Portrait Gallery: Earliest Portraits are Persian from about 460 B.C." *Coin World* (April 5, 2010): 94-7. Illus.
A brief introduction to portraiture on Greek and Roman coins.

1307 **Wace, A. J. B.** "Hellenistic Royal Portraits." *Journal of Hellenic Studies* 25 (1905): 86-104. 3 pls.
"Comparisons with coins show the unsatisfactory nature of many identifications proposed for bronze and marble portrait heads of the Hellenistic period. Appendix I (pp. 98-101) gives further reasons to support the attribution (made by the same writer in *Journal International d' Archéologie Numismatique* 1903, p. 140) of a Pergamene tetradrachm to Attalus I rather than to Philetaerus. Appendix II (pp. 101-4) suggests that coins attributed to Seleucus son of Antiochus I (see Macdonald "Early Seleucid Portraits" above) belong in fact to Antiochus III." [J. R. Jones, *NIJHS*]

1308 **Wetterstrom, Kerry K.** "Lycian Portraiture." *Classical Numismatic Review* 19, no. 1 (first quarter 1994): 5.
A brief article describing the first coin portraiture, which is found on the coins of a Lycian dynast, Kharai, ca. 425 B.C. Also mentions the development of portraiture on the coinage of later dynasts.

1309 **Winzer, Axel.** *Antike Porträtmünzen der Perser und Griechen aus vor-Hellenistischer Zeit (Zeitraum ca. 510-322 v.Chr): von Dareios I. bis Alexander III.* Kronberg: Axel Winzer, 2005. 70 pp., 6 pls.
A catalogue of about 160 Persian and pre-Hellenistic Greek portrait coins from a private collection. Includes coins of the Achaemenid kings of Persia, Persian satraps and local dynasts, Lycian dynasts, kings of Sidon, kings of Odrysian Thrace, the Macedonian kings Philip II and Alexander III, and Chares of Mytilene. All the coins are photographed.

1310 **Worland, David.** "An 1805 Treatise on the Coin Portraits of Alexander the Great." *The Celator* 11, no. 7 (July 1997): 6-11. Illus.
Discusses Edward Daniel Clarke's book *The Tomb of Alexander: A Dissertation on the Sarcophagus brought from Alexandria*, published in 1805. The book discusses a basalt sarcophagus once believed to belong to Alexander the Great. Worland focuses on Clarke's discussion of the portraits of Alexander on the coins of Lysimachus, especially the use of the horn of Ammon as an indication that Alexander was regarded as a god by the Egyptians and others.

1311 **Zograph, Alexander N.** "Some Greek Coins of the Fifth and Fourth Centuries with Portrait Types." *The Ancient Portrait*. Leningrad, 1929. Pages 14-20.

Also see: American Numismatic Association *Selections* under GENERAL WORKS—GREEK; Arnold-Biucchi *Alexander's Coins and Alexander's Image* under MACEDONIAN KINGDOM—GENERAL WORKS; Baynham "Continuity and Ambition: The Posthumous Philip II Gold Staters from Colophon/Magnesia" under GENERAL WORKS—HELLENISTIC; Bopearachchi and Flandrin under *Le Portrait d'Alexandre* under HOARDS; Breckenridge "Hannibal" under SPAIN; Brett "Cleopatra" under EGYPT—PTOLEMAIC KINGDOM; Brindley "Siglos Lot with Unusual Portraits" under PERSIA; Burns *Money and Monetary Policy* under GENERAL WORKS—GREEK; Cahn and Gerin "Themistocles" under IONIA; Dahmen *Legend of Alexander* under MACEDONIAN KINGDOM—GENERAL WORKS; Davis and Kraay *The Hellenistic Kingdoms* under GENERAL WORKS—HELLENISTIC; Emerson "Portraiture of Alexander" (two items) under MACEDONIAN KINGDOM—GENERAL WORKS; Fischer "A Coin Portrait" under SYRIA—SELEUCID KINGDOM; Flower "Alexander the Great as a Pyrrhus Coin Type" under SICILY—SYRACUSE; Hadley "Seleucus, Dionysus, or Alexander?" under SYRIA—SELEUCID KINGDOM; Hazzard "Portrait Coins of the Ptolemies" under EGYPT—PTOLEMAIC KINGDOM; Hill "A Portrait of Perseus" under MACEDONIAN KINGDOM—GENERAL WORKS; Hill *Select Greek Coins* under ART.

Hoge "Three Mithradatic Alexanders" under PONTOS; Houghton "The Portrait of Antiochus IX" under SYRIA—SELEUCID KINGDOM; Houghton "A Colossal Head" under SYRIA—SELEUCID KINGDOM; Houghton "Equestrian Portrait of Alexander" under SYRIA—SELEUCID KINGDOM; Jakobsson "A Possible New Indo-Greek King Zoilos III" under BACTRIA AND NORTHWEST INDIA; Jenkins "Pyrrhus" under NORTHERN GREECE—EPIRUS; Kiang "An Unpublished Coin Portrait" under EGYPT—PTOLEMAIC KINGDOM; Kleiner "Philipps und Alexanders" under MACEDONIAN KINGDOM—GENERAL WORKS; Kyrieleis "Die Porträtmünzen Ptolemaios' V" under EGYPT—PTOLEMAIC KINGDOM; Lemburg-Ruppelt "Zur Ikonographie" under BACTRIA; Le Rider "Les Tétradrachmes Attalides au Portrait de Philétaire" under MYSIA—

Pergamene Kingdom; Mattingly "Portrait Coin of Eumenes II" under Mysia—Pergamene Kingdom; Mazard "Portraits Monétaires des Princes" under Mauretania; Meischner "Ein Porträt Antiochus VI" under Syria—Seleucid Kingdom; Mørkholm "The Alleged Portrait of Antiochus" under Syria—Seleucid Kingdom; Mørkholm "The Municipal Coinages" under Syria—Seleucid Kingdom; Mørkholm "The Portrait Coinage of Ptolemy V" under Egypt—Ptolemaic Kingdom; Moysey "Observations" under Persia; Newton "Tetradrachm of Orophernes II" under Cappadocia; Nicolau Kormikiari "Numidian Royal Portrait" under Numidia; Nock "Notes on Ruler-Cult" under Types.

Pieper "Greek Influenced Portrait Coins" under Asia—General Works; Queyrel "Le Portrait Monétaire d'Eumène II" under Mysia—Pergamene Kingdom; Queyrel "Les Portraits des Attalides" under Mysia—Pergamene Kingdom; Robinson "Greek Coins Acquired" (1948) under Public Collections—Great Britain (London); Salvesen "Tetradrachm of Orophernes" under Cappadocia; Schachter "Thespian Museia" under Central Greece—Boeotia; Schwabacher "Lycian Portraits" under Lycia; Shore "Parthian Tetradrachms" under Parthia; Sjöquist "Alexander–Heracles" under Macedonian Kingdom—General Works; H. Smith "Sculptural Style" under Egypt—Ptolemaic Kingdom; Spaer "The Royal Male Head and Cleopatra at Ascalon" under Palestine—Philistia; Sutherland *Art in Coinage* under Art; Tameanko "The Poetess Sappho" under Lesbos; Taylor "The Coin Portraits of Ariobarzanes I" under Cappadocia; Tiratsian "Armenian Portrait Art" under Armenia; M. B. Wallace "Black Gods?" under Central Greece—Phokis; Westermark "The Portrait Coin of Eumenes II" under Mysia—Pergamene Kingdom; Wright *Coins from Asia Minor and the East* under Asia Minor—General Works; Zahle "Persian Satraps and Lycian Dynasts" under Persia.

EPIGRAPHY

In any case, without the study of Numismatic epigraphy it is almost impossible to study the stylistic evolution of the Greek or Roman alphabets or the dating of some important changes in letter forms which can only be pin-pointed by the study of ancient coin inscriptions.

—*John E. Hartmann, 1969*

1312 **Clarke, Hyde.** *The Early History of the Mediterranean Populations, &c., in their Migrations and Settlements. Illustrated from Autonomous Coins, Gems, Inscriptions, &c.* London: Trübner & Co., 1882.
Presents an extensive list of Greek cities paired with the emblems used on their coins. Clarke maintains "that in hundreds of cases the records of extinct languages are preserved on coins, to which a totally different significance has been assigned." He suggests that cities with similar sounding names often utilized the same symbol or emblem on their coins, and the name of the emblem is closely related to the name of the city. His arguments are hard to follow and his conclusions are hard to accept.

1313 **Cohen, Edward E.** "Greek Numbers on Coins, Part I: The First Dated Coins and Alphabetic Numbers." *The Celator* 23, no. 2 (February 2009): 22-9. Illus.
Discusses the first dated coins—those which used an alphabetic sequence for numbers to indicate a date (a different single letter was used to denote a year). The Samian settlers who overthrew the city of Zankle added a Greek letter A to their stater to denote Year 1 in 494/3 B.C., and the sequence lasted five years. In 454/3, the Samians of Zankle returned to Samos and struck coins with annual dates A (1) through Ξ (15). Cohen mentions other cities that used Greek letters as numbers on their coins, sometimes denoting months or years, others indicating die sequences (as on the decadrachms of Ptolemy II). Cohen emphasizes that the values of Greek letters varied by the issuing town. Some cities used the letter digamma for the numeral six while others did not, thus causing confusion. [Also see Cohen *Dated Coins of Antiquity* under GENERAL WORKS—GREEK].

1314 ——— "Greek Numbers on Coins, Part II: Re-Dating the Tetradrachms of Ptolemy II." *The Celator* 23, no. 3 (March 2009): 6-18. Illus.
Discusses the introduction of Greek additive numbers (multiple letters which are added together to designate a regnal year). Explains regnal dating systems which restart in the first year of each ruler's reign. In 265/4 B.C., Tyre and other Phoenician and Palestinian cities began using regnal dates in the form of monograms. Later, the use of monograms ceased and the letters were written separately. Cohen demonstrates that in the period when dates appeared as monograms, KI and KH had the respective values of 26 and 27. However, when these cities changed to writing dates as separate letters, KI and KH had the values 27 and 28. The author uses the tetradrachms of Ptolemy II from Phoenicia and Palestine, and presents a table of revised dating for these coins. [Also see Cohen *Dated Coins of Antiquity* under GENERAL WORKS—GREEK].

1315 **Florance, A.** *Grecque: Tableaux Synoptiques des Ethniques des Villes et Peuples Grecs.* Paris: Serrure, 1903. 2 volumes, 105 pp. and 193 pp.
For an English translation, see next item. [Reviewed by A. Dieudonnè in *Revue Numismatique* (France) (1904): 283-4].

1316 ——— *A Geographic Lexicon of Greek Coin Inscriptions.* Paris, 1903. Reprint, Chicago: Argonaut, 1966. 100 pp., 4 maps (reprint only). [CS 1821]
A reprint of *Numismatique Grecque: Tableaux Synoptiques des Ethniques des Villes et Peuples Grecs.* An alphabetical list of ethnics (inscriptions giving the identification of the city) appearing on Greek coins. Indicates the name of the city which used the ethnic and the region in which the city was located. Indicates if the ethnic was used during the autonomous period, or on the federal coinages, Roman colonial coinages, or Roman Imperial coinages. Four maps and a list of Roman provinces were added to the reprint edition.

1317 **Fraser, Peter M., and Elaine Matthews, eds.** *A Lexicon of Greek Personal Names.* Oxford: British Academy, 1987+.
A listing of all names known from the Greek world, from all sources. Arranged as an alphabetical list of names with dates. The city to which the person is attributed is that to which the person is believed to have belonged.

- Vol. I *The Aegean Islands, Cyprus, Cyrenaica.* Edited by Peter M. Fraser and E. Matthews. Oxford: Clarendon Press, 1987. 489 pp. [Reviewed by Martin J. Price in *Numismatic Chronicle* 148 (1988): 224-5].
- Vol. II *Attica.* Edited by M. J. Osborne and S. G. Byrne. Oxford: University Press, 1994. 510 pp. [Reviewed by H. B. Mattingly in *Numismatic Chronicle* 157 (1997): 258-60].
- Vol. IIIA *The Peloponnese, Western Greece, Sicily and Magna Graecia.* Edited by Peter M. Fraser and E. Matthews. Oxford: Clarendon Press, 1997. 519 pp. [Reviewed by A. R. Meadows in *Numismatic Chronicle* 161 (2001): 361].
- Vol. IIIB *Central Greece from the Megarid to Thessaly.* Edited by Peter M. Fraser and E. Matthews. Oxford: Clarendon Press, 2000. 478 pp. [Reviewed by A. R. Meadows in *Numismatic Chronicle* 161 (2001): 361].

Vol. IV   *Macedonia, Thrace, Northern Regions of the Black Sea.* Edited by Peter M. Fraser and E. Matthews. Oxford: Clarendon Press, 2005. 489 pp. [Reviewed by Richard Ashton in *Numismatic Chronicle* 166 (2006): 476].

Vol. VA   *Coastal Asia Minor: Pontos to Ionia.* Edited by T. Corsten. Oxford: Clarendon Press, 2010.

1318   **Gardner, Percy.** "Votive Coins in Delian Inscriptions." *Journal of Hellenic Studies* 4 (1883): 243-7.
Discusses coins mentioned in lists of votive offerings. Explains that at any city the term 'stater' refers to the ordinary staple of currency, whether in gold or silver. Also describes a rare gold "drachm" (stater) of Carystus, as well as various tetradrachms, drachms, and bronze coins, which are mentioned in the votive lists. Mentions some specific coins which are known to have been dedicated in temples due to the inscriptions scratched onto their surfaces. [Also see Jones "Gold Drachma of Carystus" under CENTRAL GREECE—EUBOIA].

1319   **Giedroyc, Richard F., and Malcolm W. Heckman, eds.** "It's Greek to Me." *Classical Coin Newsletter* (Maplewood, New Jersey) 2, no. 6 (February 1983): 1-2, 7.
An introduction to the Greek alphabet and pronunciation.

1320   **Goldstein, Elliott S.** "The Origin and Evolution of Our Alphabet." *The Celator* 16, no. 9 (2002): 20-7. Illus.
Examines the history of the alphabet that developed into the English, Latin, Greek, and Hebrew alphabets. Includes a table showing the Phoenician letters and the Greek, Etruscan, and Latin equivalents. Includes a table showing a cuneiform alphabet, and shows an example of the Hebrew alphabet as used on ancient coins.

1321   **Hartmann, John E.** "Greek Numismatic Epigraphy." Parts 1-4. *Voice of the Turtle* 4, no. 7 (July 1965): 133-7; no. 8 (August 1965): 169-72; no. 9 (September 1965): 201-4; 5, no. 1 (January 1966): 9-12.
Explains the Greek alphabet and numeral systems. Displays various Greek alphabets and includes guidelines for pronunciation. Examines several common coin inscriptions, translates them, and explains how each was used. Discusses inscriptions on Roman Provincial coinage.

1322   ——— "The Contributions of Greek Numismatic Epigraphy to Other Fields of Knowledge." *North American Journal of Numismatics* 8, no. 3 (March 1969): 43-4.
A brief statement on how the study of coin inscriptions has aided historians.

1323   ——— "Publication Symbols and Transcription Methods of Greek Coin Inscriptions." *North American Journal of Numismatics* 8, no. 3 (March 1969): 45-6.
Provides recommendations on how coin inscriptions should be presented in numismatic publications.

1324   **Hartmann, John E., and George Macdonald.** *Greek Numismatic Epigraphy.* Chicago: Argonaut, 1966 and 1969. 92 pp., illus. [CS 1853]
Reprints of Hartmann's articles from *The Voice of the Turtle* (see Hartmann "Greek Numismatic Epigraphy" above) to which are added some papers by Macdonald originally published in the *Numismatic Chronicle,* including his discussion of the numeral letters on Syrian coins and his analysis of the letters inscribed on the amphoras on the reverse of the New Style Athenian tetradrachms.

1325   **Hopkins, Chris.** "Numismatica OldGreek Computer Font Enters Test Phase." *The Celator* 14, no. 10 (October 2000): 38-9, 53-4.
Announces the availability of a computer font for displaying Greek letters, including numerous archaic variants. Discusses the development of the font which is being distributed over the internet.

1326   **Icard, Severin.** *Identification des Monnaies par la Nouvelle Méthode des Lettres-Jalons et des Légendes Fragmentées: Application de la Méthode aux Monnaies Grecques et aux Monnaies Gauloises.* Paris, n.d. (1929). 563 pp, 2 pls. [CS 1835]
Reprinted as *A Dictionary of Greek Coin Inscriptions* (see below).

1327   ——— *Dictionary of Greek Coin Inscriptions.* Chicago: Argonaut, 1968; Chicago: Obol International, 1979; New York: Sanford J. Durst, 1979. 567 pages. [CS 1836]
These are modified reprints of Icard's *Identification des Monnaies par la Nouvelle Méthode des Lettres-Jalons et des Légendes Fragmentées* (see above)—a dictionary of every abbreviated ethnic and every Greek word used in an inscription on a Greek autonomous or Greek Imperial coin. Arranged such that any inscription or any portion of an inscription still visible on a coin can be located in the book, and the full description deciphered. The name of the cities using that inscription are then given. The reprint editions give instructions for use in both English and French. Includes tables of alphabets. [For a complete description of the various editions of this book, see A. Kleeb's review in *SAN—Journal of the Society for Ancient Numismatics* 10, no. 3 (fall 1979): 41, 52].

1328   **Jones, John R. Melville.** "Some Numismatic Problems in the Delian Inscriptions." *Museum Notes* 17 (1971): 127-36.
Discusses some of the references to coins which appear in the records of the treasures held in the sanctuary of Apollo on Delos. Jones raises some new questions and suggests identifications of some of the coins. Examines the references to: Aeginetan and Cretan staters, a drachm of Apollonia, Arbulic obols, a Carian drachm, Chian drachms, coinage of Histiaea, coins of Orchomenus, a coin of Pergamum, a Persic tetradrachm and drachm, Ptolemaic "grasshoppers," "Alliances" coins, and Syrian drachmas. [Also see Jones' follow-up, "Further Notes" below].

1329   ——— "Epigraphical Notes on Hellenistic Bronze Coinage." *Numismatic Chronicle* 7th ser., 12 (1972): 39-43. [CS 1844]
"From the third century B.C. onward some denominations previously struck in silver were issued in bronze. It should be noted that when the word *bronze* is used in earlier inventories to describe coins of large denominations, it is likely that the reference is to counterfeits, imitations or plated coins." [J. Melville Jones, *NL* 89]

1330   ——— "Further Notes on the Delian Inscriptions." *Museum Notes* 19 (1974): 1.
A brief follow-up to Jones' 1971 paper (see "Some Numismatic Problems" above). States that the word tetarton refers to a gold hemidrachm rather than a didrachm as he previously suggested. Also points out that the "Cretan staters" referred to in the Delian inventories were the Pseudaiginetica.

1331 ——— "Greek Coin Names in -phoros." *Bulletin of the Institute of Classical Studies* (London University) 21 (1974): 55-74.
"Terms such as *kistophoros* and *stephanephoros* appear in various documents of the second century B.C. It is clear that these names were given to coins as a means of describing them as briefly as possible, and this convention probably began on Delos." [J. Melville Jones, *NL* 95]

1332 ——— "Darics at Delphi." *Revue Belge de Numismatique et de Sigillographie* (Belgium) 125 (1979): 25-36.
"In two Delphic inscriptions of 327/6 and 324/3 the 'darics' mentioned should be interpreted as Greek gold staters of Attic weight, most probably the new gold coins of Philip II of Macedon; the word 'daric' was used as a general term describing any gold coin." [P. Naster, *NL* 105]

1333 ——— "'Symmachic' Coins in Greek Inscriptions." *Proceedings of the 9th International Congress of Numismatics. Berne, September 1979. Volume 1.* Edited by T. Hackens and R. Weiller. Luxembourg: International Association of Professional Numismatists, 1982. Page 129.
Briefly describes three groups of ancient inscriptions which mention "symmachic" coins. The coins of the first group are identified as the ΣYN coins of Asia Minor. The coins of the second group are identified as a coinage issued by allies of Antigonus Monophthalmus. Those of the third group are identified as coins of the Achaean League. [For further discussion of the ΣYN coins, see Cook "Cnidian Peraea and Spartan Coins" under Peloponnesos—Lakonia, and M. Wallace "After Athens" under Asia Minor—General Works].

1334 ——— *Testimonia Numaria. Greek and Latin Texts Concerning Ancient Greek Coinage. Volume 1: Texts and Translations.* London: Spink and Son, 1993. 552 pages.
Presents 927 passages taken from ancient writings relating to coins, mints, moneyers, forgeries, hoards, denominations, predecessors of coinage, and changing money. The selected documents comprise most of the ancient Greek and Latin texts which might be considered relevant to the study of ancient Greek coinage. The original texts are presented at the left of each page, with the translation into English to the right. The text is divided into sixteen sections, each with an introduction. The sections are: Statements on the nature of ancient Greek coinage, Predecessors of ancient Greek coinage, Documents relating to the coinage of Athens, Inventories from Athens and Attica, Inscriptions from Delphi and Phocis, Extracts from the inventories of the Delian Temples, Coinage of various Greek mints, Regal issues, Minting and mint workers, Forgeries and expedients, Hoards and treasures, Money changers and testers, Various weights and coin denominations, Selections from the *Onomasticon* of Julius Pollux, Selections from the Lexicographers, The coinage of Persia, and Varia and addenda. For commentary on each text, see Volume 2 below. [Reviewed by Martin J. Price in *Spink Numismatic Circular* 101, no. 7 (September 1993): 243, and by T. S. N. Moorhead in *Numismatic Chronicle* 154 (1994): 297-300].

1335 ——— *Testimonia Numaria. Greek and Latin Texts Concerning Ancient Greek Coinage. Volume 2: Addenda and Commentary.* London: Spink, 2007. 362 pp., plus 52 page index compiled by Kate de Costa.
Provides forty-nine additional texts with commentary, and commentary on all the texts appearing in Volume 1. These are grouped under headings corresponding to the chapter titles in the first volume and include cross-references to the texts. Jones provides explanations and insights into the meaning and importance of each text. Includes a select bibliography. The index includes all significant terms found in the texts.

1336 **Leschhorn, Wolfgang, and Peter Robert Franke.** *Lexikon der Aufschriften auf Griechischen Münzen, Band I. Lexicon of Greek Coin Inscriptions, Volume 1: Geographical Terms, Personalities, Gods, Heroes, Mythical Figures, Personifications, Titles and Epithets, Dates, Eras and Other Terms.* Vienna: Verlag der Österreichischen Akademie der Wissenschaften, 2002. 426 pp.
A dictionary of Greek coin inscriptions. Includes geographical terms, gods and heroes, mythical figures, personalities, titles and epithets, agonistic terms, formulae expressing legal status and the authority to strike coins, and notable words. Terms are arranged in alphabetical order and translated into English and German. Mints, dates, references, and comments on the Greek and Latin coin inscriptions are given. [Reviewed by M. Spoerri Butcher in *Revue Suisse de Numismatique* 82 (2003): 183-6].

1337 **Macdonald, George.** "The Original Significance of the Inscription on Ancient Coins." *Mémoirs du Congrès International de Numismatique, 1910.* Pages 281-8.

1338 **Marotta, Michael E.** "The Voice of Classical Greek." *The Celator* 10, no. 1 (January 1996): 13-4.
Provides some basic guidelines for the pronunciation of classical Greek.

1338a **Masson, O.** "Quelques Noms de Magistrats Monétaires Grecs." *Suisse de Numismatique* (Switzerland) (1982).

1339 ——— "Quelques Légends Monétaires Grecques." *Revue Suisse de Numismatique* (Switzerland) 74 (1995): 5-11.

1340 **Miller, M. C. J., ed.** *Supplementum Inscriptionum Atticarum VII.* Chicago: Ares Publishers.
This volume is dedicated to Attic numismatic epigraphy.

1341 **Münsterberg, Rudolf.** "Die Beamtennamen auf Griechischen Münzen: Geographisch und Alphabetisch Geordnet." *Numismatische Zeitschrift* (Austria) 44 (1911): 69-132; 45 (1912): 1-111; 47 (1914): 1-98. *Supplement*, 60 (1927): 42-105. Reprints, Hildesheim and New York: Georg Olms Verlag, 1973, 1985. 337 pp. [CS 4422]
"This important work lists the names of the magistrates that appear on Greek and Roman Provincial coins and cross-references you to the cities that issued them." [D. Kroh, *ACRR*]

1342 **Nicolet-Pierre, Hélène.** "Epigraphie et Numismatique: Quelques Remarques sur les Noms de Monnaies dans des Inscriptions Grecques Archaïques." *Numismatic Archaeology/Archaeological Numismatics: Proceedings of an International Conference held to Honour Dr. Mando Oeconomides in Athens 1995.* Oxbow Monographs 75. Edited by K. Sheedy and C. Papageorgiadou-Banis. Oxford: Oxbow Books and The Australian Archaeological Institute at Athens, 1997. Pages 70-6.

1343 **Pennington, Paul.** *How to Read Greek Coins: An Adventure in Epigraphy for Those Who Know No Greek.* Chicago: Hewitt Brothers, 1946. 22 pp., 2 pls. Reprint, Chicago: Hewitt Brothers (no date).

An off-print from *Numismatic Scrapbook Magazine*, 1945. Provides instructions on how to read the inscriptions on ancient Greek coins. Includes tables of alphabets and guides to pronunciation. Explains the meanings of various word-endings. Lists city names, personal names, and titles commonly found on coins.

1344 **Plant, Richard J.** "The North Semitic Alphabets and Greek Coins." *Seaby Coin and Medal Bulletin* 674 (October 1974): 311-3; 675 (November 1974): 343-7. Illus.
Briefly examines the north Semitic alphabets often found on "Greek" coins. A table presents the English equivalents of the standard twenty-two Semitic letters and shows their variants in Hebrew and ancient Hebrew scripts, as well as scripts from Sicily, Tarsus, Phoenicia, and Parthia. Provides examples of Semitic coin inscriptions and their translations, illustrated by line drawings.

1345 ——— *Greek, Semitic, Asiatic Coins and How to Read Them.* Amherst: Scorpion Publishers, 1979. 257 pp., illus. [CS 324]
The book is divided into four sections: European alphabets such as Greek, Armenian, and Georgian; Semitic alphabets such as Phoenician, Sasanian, and Manchu; Indian alphabets, including Burma and Thailand; and Chinese, including Japan, Korea, and Annam. Includes exercises to assist with learning. Illustrated by 1193 line drawings.

1346 ——— "The Most Ancient Forms of Writing." *Numismatic Fine Arts, Inc. Journal, Publication* 30 (summer 1985): 2-3. Illus.
Discusses early forms of writing which appear on coins, including hieroglyphics and Cypriot script.

1347 **Psoma, Selene.** "The Millenium- and Globe-Spanned Hellas: Coinage as Mirror of the Greek Language." Translated by Yannis Stoyas. *Greek: Always a Modern Language.* Edited by Catharine Mikou-Karachaliou. Athens: Hellenic Ministry of Culture, 1999. Pages 56-71. Illus.
Discusses the use of the Greek language on Greek coins, including the various forms of city names, the use of engravers' signatures, indications of denominations, the identity of deities and nymphs, mint magistrates' names, reign dates, royal titles, and boastful claims made by cities. Illustrated by numerous Greek coins. Text in English and Greek.

1348 **Robert, Louis.** "Monnaies dans les Inscriptions Grecques." *Revue Numismatique* (France) 6, no. 4 (1962): 7-24.

1349 **Robinson, Edward S. G.** "Index of Ethnics Appearing on Greek Coins. *Numismatic Chronicle* 4th ser., 14 (1914): 236-48. [CS 1862]
An alphabetical list of ethnics (a letter or letters signifying the name of the mint city) appearing on Greek coins. All are in the genitive plural case.

1350 **Sosin, Joshua D.** "*Agio* at Delphi." *Numismatic Chronicle* 160 (2000): 67-80.
"P. Marchetti has argued that in the fourth-century temple accounts from Delphi, the Greek word *epikatallage* denoted not agio, a charge for changing currency, but a revaluation of the exchange-rate between Aeginetan and Attic silver in 335 B.C. This paper argues that Marchetti's theory must be abandoned, and that the word indicated simply agio." [J. Sosin, *NL* 145]. Sosin argues that the economics of Marchetti's proposal are implausible.

1351 **Tod, Marcus N.** "Three Greek Numeral Systems." *Journal of Hellenic Studies* 33 (1913): 27-34. Illus.
"Inscriptions of the third and second centuries B.C. from Chalcedon, Nesus and Thespiae are used as evidence for varying numeral systems; on p. 28 it is shown that the obol at Chalcedon contained twelve *chalkoi*." [J. R. Jones, *NIJHS*]

1352 ——— "Epigraphical Notes on Greek Coinage." Parts 1-5. *Numismatic Chronicle* 6th ser., 5 (1945): 108-16; 6 (1946): 47-62; 7 (1947): 1-27; 15 (1955): 125-30; 20 (1960): 1-24. Reprinted as a book, *Epigraphical Notes on Greek Coinage*. Chicago, 1979. 116 pp. [CS 3352]
Parts 1 & 2: The author writes detailed notes on two monetary denominations, the ΚΟΛΛΥΒΟΣ and the ΞΑΛΚΟΥΣ. For κολλυβοσ and its derivative forms the literary evidence is first examined, then the epigraphical. It is maintained that the negative evidence of the Athenian inscriptions shows that no unit called κολλυβοσ was recognized at Athens, at least not after the Peloponnesian War; there is, however, epigraphical evidence for the κολλυβοσ as a denomination in Messenia (probably equal to ½ of a chalkous) and also, now, at Delphi (where the value is uncertain). For χαλκυσ, the author reviews the epigraphical evidence for the word and for its derivatives, and gives a list of numerical signs used at different places to represent a χαλκυσ. He concludes by discussing the number of χαλκυι in an obol: eight at Athens and in Egypt, twelve at Epidauros, Messene, Andania, Tegea, Oropos, Delphi, in Boeotia, and probably at Delos, Chalkedon and Priene as well. [Summarized from W. Wallace's summary in *NL* 3]

Part 3: Discusses the word οβολοσ (obol) and its derivatives, some of which have three senses: a coin, a weight, or a value. Discusses the symbols used in inscriptions to indicate obols, their multiples, and their fractions. [Summarized from W. Wallace's summary in *NL* 8]

Part 4: "Epigraphical notes on the kollybos, the chalkous, and the obolos are supplemented by further comment on inscriptions from Sparta, Attica (including a vase from the Athenian Agora), Epidaurus, Boeotia, and Delos and other islands. Most inscriptions and the comment deal with the manner in which numismatic terms were used in official decrees and temple inventories." [C. Vermeule, *NL* 37]

Part 5: "A discussion of the drachma—which can signify a weight, a silver coin worth six obols, or a sum or value consisting of either a single coin or several small denominations—continues the record of the contribution made by epigraphy to numismatic studies. Qualifying adjectives or other descriptive phrases used in connection with drachmae include: (a) number, (b) metal, (c) state or issuing authority, (d) ruler or dynasty, (e) epithets relating to emblems stamped upon the reverses. Signs and common abbreviations used for the drachma, accompanied by numbers in words, acrophonic or alphabetical numerals, are illustrated in detail, and multiples of the drachma are listed with special reference to epigraphical evidence." [J. Healy, *NL* 60]

1353 **Vagi, David.** "Inscriptions Valuable Tool for Coinage ID: Many Languages on Ancients Offer Collecting Challenge." *Coin World* (January 3, 2011): 202-6. Illus.
A brief discussion of the various languages that appear on ancient coins.

1354 **Volk, T. R.** "From Phanes to Pisanello: 2000 Years of Numismatic Greek." *Greek Script: An Illustrated Introduction.* Edited by P. Easterling and C. Handley. London: Society for the Promotion of Hellenic Studies, 2001.

1355 **Woodward, Arthur M.** "Three New Fragments of Attic Treasure-records." *Journal of Hellenic Studies* 29 (1909): 168-91.
"On p. 174, Phocaean *hektai* are restored in a new fragment of *IG* II², 1408, and other epigraphic occurrences of these coins are noted. On pp. 176-7 the same inscription is recorded as listing *characteres* and *akmoniskoi* for striking coins, which were kept in the Parthenon." [J. R. Jones, *NIJHS*]

Also see: Cheek "Artistic Choice" under ART; Cohen *Dated Coins of Antiquity* under GENERAL WORKS—GREEK; Elayi and Elayi "Abbreviations and Numbers" under PHOENICIA; Galst "Cuneiform in Nummis" under PALESTINE—JUDEA; Goldstein "Concerning the Meaning of Control Marks and Symbols of Power" under PHOENICIA; Hammond "The Lettering and the Iconography" under MACEDONIAN KINGDOM—GENERAL WORKS; Hendin "Coins of the Bible—Epigraphy on Hasmonean Coins" under PALESTINE—JUDEA; Holzer "Secret Inscriptions" under SYRIA—SELEUCID KINGDOM; Imhoof-Blumer "Les Inscription 'TPIH'" under MACEDONIA—CITIES AND TRIBES; Johnston "Horse Sense?" under CORINTHIA; Kadman "The Hebrew Coin Script" under PALESTINE—JUDEA; Knapp "The First Coin of Inner Africa?" under NORTH AFRICA—GENERAL WORKS.

Lassen "Points in the History of the Greek and Indo-Scythian Kings" under BACTRIA; Macdonald "The 'Abiel' Coins of Eastern Arabia" under ARABIA; Maraqten "Notes on the Aramaic Script" under ARABIA; Mildenberg "Les Inscriptions" under ZEUGITANTA; Oikonomides "Soter the Great" under NORTHWEST INDIA; Olson "Greek Letterforms" under PARTHIA; Plant "Sabaean Script" under ARABIA; Psoma "Des Monnaies aux Initiales TPIH" under MACEDONIA—CITIES AND TRIBES; Ramsay "On Some Pamphylian Inscriptions" under PAMPHYLIA; Robinson "Coin-Legends in the Carian Script" under CARIA; Stein "The Monetary Terminology" under ARABIA; Tekin *Ancient History* under GENERAL WORKS—GREEK; Walker "A Mysterious South Arabian Coin-Legend" under ARABIA; Xella "A Propos de Sys dans les Légendes Monétaires Puniques en Sicilie" under SICILY—SICULO-PUNIC COINAGE.

TECHNICAL ASPECTS OF GREEK COINAGE

THE MINTING PROCESS

In antiquity the practice of fixing, or otherwise regulating, the position of the dies varied greatly at different times and places. The analysis of the material, although it has hardly been begun, has already yielded useful results in various ways; if we know, for instance, that the practice was normally in use in one part of the world, or at one period, we shall hesitate to attribute to that district or period a coin which ignores the practice.

—*George F. Hill, 1922*

1356　**Amiran, R., and A. Eitan.** "Excavations in the Courtyard of the Citadel, Jerusalem 1968-1969." *Israel Exploration Journal* (Israel) 20 (1970): 9-17.
Includes a report on the discovery of a fragment of a stone mould used for casting coin flans at the mint in Jerusalem. The fragment was the bottom half of a two-part mould, used for casting flans by the double-mould technique. The authors date the mould to the reign of Antigonus II Mattathias, 40-37 B.C.

1357　"An Ancient Greek Die." *American Journal of Numismatics* 42, no. 3 (1907): 68.
Mentions a die with Athenian types which was found in Egypt. [Also see Svoronos below].

1357a　**Ariel, Donald T.** "A First Century CE Mint South of Jerusalem? Numismatic Evidence." *New Studies in the Archaeology of Jerusalem and its Region. Collected Papers Volume V.* Edited by D. Amit, G. Stiebel, and O. Peleg-Barkat. Jerusalem: Israel Antiquities Authority, 2011. Pages 16-23. Illus.
Discusses some limestone covered molds used for casting coin flans, a number of which have been found in excavations. Describes these molds in detail and discusses how they were used. For a mold found south of Jerusalem, the author poses the question: Is this a forger's mold, or evidence that flans were produced in a separate official facility outside of the city, or evidence of a full mint outside of Jerusalem?

1358　**Balog, Paul.** "Notes on Ancient and Medieval Minting Technique." *Numismatic Chronicle* 6th ser., 15 (1955): 195-202. 1 pl.
Discusses how dies have been manufactured and how the coin-legends and types have been placed on the surface of the dies.

1359　**Beer, Leslie.** "Results of Coin Striking to Simulate the Mint of Aegina." *Proceedings of the 9th International Congress of Numismatics. Berne, September 1979. Volume 1.* Edited by T. Hackens and R. Weiller. Luxembourg: International Association of Professional Numismatists, 1982. Pages 47-51. 2 pls.
The author created dies similar to those used to strike the early staters of Aegina, in an attempt to learn about the wear and subsequent breakdown of incuse punch dies. Describes how the author created the dies and flans, and did the striking. Discusses the varying strike characteristics. Concludes that the quality of strike varied in antiquity—the rows of dots on the turtle's back may not always have been well struck originally, making the coins appear worn.

1360　**Berk, Harlan J.** "Die Pairs Seem Random among Coins in Group." *World Coin News* (August 5, 1991): 57.
Describes a group of bronze coins of Panticapaeum with a Pan head on the obverse and a bull's head on the reverse. Points out that obverse dies were often paired with reverse dies of far different style. Suggests that for this issue of coinage, dies were used in random order rather than one die being used until it wore out, and that die cutters of greatly varied ability worked together.

1361　**Bogaert, Raymond.** "L'Essai des Monnaies dans l'Antiquité." *Revue Belge de Numismatique* (Belgium) 122 (1976): 5-34. [CS 3356]

1362　**Buttrey, S. E., and Theodore V. Buttrey.** "Calculating Ancient Coin Production, Again." *American Journal of Numismatics* 2nd ser., 9 (1997): 113-35.
A critical review of two articles: F. de Callataÿ, G. Depeyrot, L. Villaronga, *L'Argent monnayé d'Alexandre le grand à Auguste* (1993), and F. de Callataÿ, "Calculating Ancient Coin Production: Seeking a Balance" (*Numismatic Chronicle* 1995). The objective of the first monograph is to calculate the number of dies originally used per issue and to determine the coinage total. T. Buttrey and S. Buttrey conclude that the results claimed are without foundation. Questionable statistical techniques were employed. They claim there is no way to calculate output for any issue even when the number of dies is known. Buttrey and Buttrey present a detailed discussion of the methods and conclusions of the articles under review and explain the errors in each.

1363 **Buttrey, Theodore V.** "Calculating Ancient Coin Production II: Why It Cannot Be Done." *Numismatic Chronicle* 154 (1994): 341-52.
Discusses the calculation of the number of dies used to strike an issue and the calculation of the number of coins struck by those dies. Concludes that it is not possible to calculate ancient coin production.

1364 ——— "Calculating Ancient Coin Production: Facts and Fantasies." *Numismatic Chronicle* 153 (1995): 335-52.
Examines the practice of extracting conclusions of historical significance from die counts and coin production figures. Discusses (a) the extrapolation of die numbers, (b) the number of coins struck per die, and (c) the rate of attrition of coins. Roman coins are generally used as examples but the comments may be applicable to other series. Buttrey questions the validity of conclusions previously drawn by others. [For a reply to Buttrey, see de Callataÿ "Calculating" below].

1365 **Campbell, William.** *Greek and Roman Plated Coins.* Numismatic Notes and Monographs, No. 57. New York: American Numismatic Society, 1933. 174 pp., 51 pls. [CS 3357]
Presents the findings of an examination of silver plated coins (fourrées) through the use of a metallographic microscope. Describes the methods used in examining the coins and presents conclusions regarding the method of manufacture for each. Three common methods were: (1) attaching silver foil to the copper core by means of silver solder; (2) attaching the silver to the copper core by heating; (3) using a powder and a flux and heating until the silver melted and formed a regular coating. Greatly enlarged photographs are used to illustrate cross-sections of plated coins.

1366 **Cancio, Leopoldo.** "Repaired Ancient Coin Dies." *Spink Numismatic Circular* 106, no. 7 (September 1998): 313. Illus.
Illustrates two coins struck from repaired dies: (1) the reverse die for a hemidrachm of Tricca, Thessaly (480-344 B.C.); (2) a tetradrachm of Vespasian from Asia Minor. The Triccan coin proves that even in the early Greek centuries, engravers were willing to try their hand at repairing dies.

1367 **Carter, Giles F.** "A Simplified Method for Calculating the Original Number of Dies from Die Link Statistics." *Museum Notes* 28 (1983): 195-206.
Presents an equation for calculating the original number of dies for issues of ancient coins. Uses an improved mathematically defined distribution for die lifetimes rather than assuming equal coin production from all dies as some previous models have done. Presents a table showing the assumed distribution of die lifetimes by percent. Compares the results with the die link data for a certain issue of Roman denarii. Summarizes the keystrokes needed to solve the equation on a hand-held calculator.

1368 **Carter, Giles F., and John W. Moore.** "Calculation of the Approximate Number of Dies and Die-Combinations of Ancient Coins from Die-Link Statistics." *Seaby Coin and Medal Bulletin* 742 (June 1980): 172-7; 743 (July 1980): 212-4; 744 (August 1980): 241-6. [CS 16971]
Presents a method for calculating the probable number of obverse dies for any issue of coins provided ample specimens are known and at least several die links have been determined. This then allows an estimation of the quantity of coins produced from a die and the probable number of anvils used in production of a given issue. This information helps to answer many questions about the operation of ancient mints. Describes the use of random numbers and a computer program in the analysis of die statistics. Presents formulas which assume equal die lives, and variable die lives. The total number of die-combinations and the average number of reverse dies per obverse die may be calculated if there are at least several double-die-links in a sample of coins. An equation is given for calculating the approximate standard deviation for the number of calculated dies.

1369 **Carter, Giles F., and R. S. Nord.** "Calculation of the Average Die Lifetimes and the Number of Anvils for Coinage in Antiquity." *American Journal of Numismatics* 2nd ser., 3-4 (1991-2): 147-64.
Using statistical methods, the authors study 1865 Roman Republican denarii of Crepusius with the goal of calculating the approximate die lifetimes for ancient coinages, the approximate number of anvils used, and the approximate number of dies in the reverse die box. Concludes the average die lifetime was 9-12 hours. Suggests much of the methodology developed in this study should apply to other series of ancient and medieval coins.

1370 **Casson, Stanley.** "Early Greek Inscriptions on Metal: Some Notes." *American Journal of Archaeology* 39 (1935): 510-7. Illus.
"On pp. 512-3, coins of Tanagra are cited as providing early evidence for the use of the ring-punch to produce circles or circular letters." [J. R. Jones, *NIAJAH*]

1371 ——— "The Technique of Greek Coin Dies." *Transactions of the International Numismatic Congress Organized and Held in London by the Royal Numismatic Society, June 30-July 3, 1936.* Edited by J. Allan, H. Mattingly, and E. S. G. Robinson. London: B. Quaritch, 1938. Pages 40-52. [CS 3358]
Discusses the making of dies. Begins with pre-coinage anvil and punch dies used in metal-working. Describes the relationship between metal die engraving and gem-cutting. Describes the instruments used in die production including the graver's wheel, burin, three types of drills, and the compass. Discusses the use of the drill for making lines and the compass for making circles on coin dies. Mentions two lesser-used tools: the ring-punch used at Thebes, and the claw-punch used at Metapontum and Sybaris.

1372 **Conophagos, C., H. Badecca, and C. Tsaîmou.** "La Technique Athenienne de la Frappe de Monnaies a l'Epoque Classique." *Nomismatika Khronika* (Greece) 4 (1976): 4-33. Illus.
Describes how coins were manufactured in classical Athens, with excellent illustrations of the minting process, coin dies, and the striking process. Continues with a discussion of the refinement of silver, the production of the flans, and engraving of the dies. Concludes with some examples of the metallic composition of some early and classical Athenian coins and a few other coins.

1373 **Crawford, Michael H.** "Hubs and Dies in Classical Antiquity." *Numismatic Chronicle* 141 (1981): 176-7.
A brief review of the arguments of Hill, Le Rider, Milne, Schwabacher, Westermark, May, Ravel, Seltman, and others for and against the theory that hubs were used in the production of dies during classical times. Crawford doubts their use.

1374 **de Callataÿ, François.** "Calculating Ancient Coin Production: Seeking a Balance." *Numismatic Chronicle* 155 (1995): 289-312.
"This article is a reply to Buttrey's articles published in 1993 and 1994 in the *Numismatic Chronicle*. Instead of his theoretical 'we should do nothing,' this study assembles facts in order to determine what level of confidence we can have about such problems as extrapolations from hoards, original number of obverse dies, number of coins struck per die (the most controversial issue), attrition rate or simply average. A last development concerns the fortunes of

Crawford's *Roman Republican Coinage*." [F. de Callataÿ, *NL* 140]. [Also see T. V. Buttrey "Calculating Ancient Coin Production" above. For a critical review, see S. Buttrey and T. Buttrey above].

1375 ——— *Les Monnaies Grecques et l'Orientation des Axes.* Mailand, 1996. 120 pp., 3 pls.

1376 ——— "Le Volume des Emissions Monétaires dans l'Antiquité." *Metodi Statistici e Analisi Quantitative della Produzione di Monete nel Mondo Antico. Tendenze e Prospettive della Ricerca.* Annali, Istituto Italiano di Numismatica 44 (1997): 53-62.
"The author comments on the state of research devoted to determining the size of issues in antiquity and presents syntheses of two recent investigations of the problem regarding Hellenistic coinage." [A. Carignani, *NL* 143]

1377 ——— *Recueil Quantitatif des Émissions Monétaires Hellénistiques.* Wetteren, Belgium, 1997. 341 pp., illus.

1378 ——— *Recueil Quantitatif des Émissions Monétaires Archaiques et Classiques.* Wetteren, Belgium, 2003. 265 pp., illus.

1379 ——— *Quantifications et Numismatique Antique: Choix d'Articles (1984-2004).* Moneta 52. Wetteren, Belgium: Moneta, 2006. 260 pp.

1380 ——— "Quantifying Monetary Supplies in Greco-Roman Times: A General Frame." *Quantifying Monetary Supplies in Greco-Roman Times. Third Academia Belgica—Francqui Foundation Conference, Rome, September 29-30, 2008.* Rome: Edipuglia, 2011.
The aim of this paper is to summarize what has been achieved in the attempt to quantify monetary issues struck throughout ancient history. This paper aims at putting this issue into broader historical and intellectual perspectives. It deals with how our knowledge about the quantities of coins produced may modify more general ideas and concepts about finances and societies overall. The manner in which recent numismatic developments may find their place in modern trends in ancient history is also addressed.

1381 **Delamare, François, and Françoise Michaux-Van der Mersch.** "Etude Mécanique de la Frappe des Monnaies. Une Méthode: La Simulation sur Pâte à Modeler et son Application à la Frappe du Statère Éginétique." *Revue d' Archéométrie* (France) 12 (1988): 81-92.

1382 **Denzler, J.-M., Ph. Gauthier, and Tony Hackens, eds.** *Numismatique Antique: Problèmes et Méthodes.* Études d'Archéologie Classique 4. Nancy/Louvain: Peeters, 1975. 245 pp., 12 pls. [CS 16868]

1383 **De Villenoisy, F., and C. Fremont.** "Le Carré Creux des Monnaies Grecques: Evolution des Procédés de Fabrication." *Revue Numismatique* (France) 13 (1909): 449-57. 3 pls.

1384 **Dillon, John B.** "Lenses and Ancient Engraving." *SAN—Journal of the Society for Ancient Numismatics* 2, no. 2 (fall 1970): 24-5.
The author comments on the possible use of magnifying lenses in ancient times. An instrument believed to be a lens holder from ca. A.D. 100 is shown. [Also see articles by Seibert, Sines, and Tameanko below].

1385 **Dinsmoor, W. B.** "The Burning of the Opisthodomos at Athens." *American Journal of Archaeology* 36 (1932): 143-72. Illus.
"On pp. 168-9 a list appears of the inscriptions which mention the presence of dies, hammers and anvils among the sacred treasures of Athens." [J. R. Jones, *NIAJAH*]

1386 **Esty, Warren W.** "Estimation of the Number of Dies used in a Coinage when the Sample Has Few Duplicates." *Spink Numismatic Circular* 86, no. 6 (June 1978): 302.
An estimator and a confidence interval for the true number of dies used in a coinage are given for samples in which relatively few dies are duplicated.

1387 ——— "Estimating the Size of a Coinage." *Numismatic Chronicle* 144 (1984): 180-3.
"Much of the statistical theory for estimating the size of a coinage from die variety analysis has been developed by assuming that the number of coins struck from a die has some particular distribution. For instance, it is supposed that the dies struck equal amounts of coins or that the total from one die is approximately gamma distributed. In this article, a method for estimating the size of a coinage, valid regardless of the actual die output distribution, is explained, and a corresponding method for calculating confidence intervals is presented. The latter are fully justified mathematically and are not wider than restrictive hypotheses. Furthermore, the calculations are easy. This method does not estimate the number of dies from which the coinage was struck; that would require some assumption about the die output distribution." [W. Esty, *NL* 114]

1388 ——— "Estimation of the Size of a Coinage: A Survey and Comparison of Methods." *Numismatic Chronicle* 146 (1986): 185-215.
"Estimators of the size of an ancient coinage and the number of dies used to produce it are compared by evaluating their accuracy when applied to computer-simulated hoards that represent both random and non-random samples from issues with various types of die-outputs. Summary statistics of the results of the computer simulations are presented, and the best estimator is selected by inspection of the summaries of the cases deemed of greatest interest. In the Appendices the formulae are given and the estimators are discussed theoretically. Some are eliminated from further consideration for theoretical reasons, and some because other computer simulations demonstrate that they have undesirable properties." [Esty, *Numismatic Chronicle*]

1389 ——— "The Theory of Linkage." *Numismatic Chronicle* 150 (1990): 205-21.
Determination of die linkage is necessary in arranging dies in chronological order, but assumptions must be made about how a mint operated in order to reach valid conclusions about chronology based on die links. The author discusses those assumptions and their effects on conclusions. Die linkage patterns include continuous usage, die-box, and parallel sequences. Esty emphasizes that the proper sequence of die-usage may be difficult or impossible to establish. Describes a computer program which draws die-link diagrams. Illustrates a rectangular diagram for recording die pair data which more clearly illustrates complex linkage than the traditional "crossed-lines" diagram. Points out the effects of errors in die identification. Discusses methods for calculating reverse-to-obverse die ratios.

1390 **Esty, Warren W., and Giles F. Carter.** "The Distribution of the Number of Coins Struck by Dies." *American Journal of Numismatics* 2nd ser., 3-4 (1991-2): 165-86.

Modern direct evidence from mint records and die-count data from issues of ancient coins are analyzed in an attempt to determine the type of probability distribution for the number of coins struck before a die becomes unusable, and the variability of the distribution.

1391 **Gabrici, Ettore.** *Tecnica e Cronologia delle Monete Greche dal VII al V Secolo* A.C. Collana di Studi Numismatici 2. Rome, 1951. 80 pp., 5 pls. [CS 3360]
"A comprehensive but controversial work." [E. Clain-Stefanelli]

1392 **Gainor, John R.** "Die States and Linkages." *The Anvil* (Canada) 4, no. 2 (March 1, 1994): 13-4, 17. Illus.
A basic explanation of die links and die wear.

1393 **Gerin, Dominique.** "Techniques of Die-Engraving: Some Reflections on Obols of the Arcadian League in the Third Century B.C." *Metallurgy in Numismatics, Volume 3.* Edited by M. M. Archibald and M. R. Cowell. Special Publication No. 24. London: Royal Numismatic Society, 1993. Pages 20-5. 2 pls.
Enlarged photographs of obols of the Arcadian League show that some of the heads appear identical except for some of the fine details of the hair and eyebrow. Although this may suggest that hubs were used for the main type, with details added by hand-engraving each die individually, Gerin suggests that in most cases where hubbing has been suspected, it is no more than a case of a re-cut die (different stages of recutting of the same die). However, the pattern of striking of the Arcadian obols appears to rule out the possibility that recutting was the sole explanation. He suggests hubs may have been used in die production, probably mainly limited to fractional denominations.

1394 **Goddard, J. P.** "The Representation and Measurement of Die-Axes." *Spink Numismatic Circular* (1963): 217-31.

1395 **Gorelick, Leonard, and John A. Gwinnet.** "Close Work Without Magnifying Lenses? A Hypothetical Explanation for the Ability of Ancient Craftsmen to Effect Minute Detail." *Expedition* (University of Pennsylvania) 23, no. 2 (winter 1981): 27-34. Illus.
"The author presents his hypothesis, based on the disciplines of ophthalmology and population genetics, that work involving minute detail was accomplished in ancient times by myopic craftsmen." [*NL* 108]

1396 **Grace, Virginia R.** "The Die Used for Amphora Stamps." *Hesperia* 4 (1935): 421-9. Illus.
"Detailed study of a number of impressions suggests that they were most probably made with baked clay stamps. Similar effects which are visible on some coins lead the writer to conclude that Greek coin dies were occasionally cast." [J. R. Jones, *NIAJAH*]. [Also see Grace "Stamped Amphora Handles" under TYPES].

1397 **Grose, Sidney W.** "A Dekadrachm by Kimon, and a Note on Greek Coin Dies." *Numismatic Chronicle* 4th ser., 16 (1916): 113-32. 1 pl.
Discusses a Syracusan decadrachm struck from a cracked obverse die. The die is at an earlier stage of deterioration than any other known specimen. Discusses the production of dies, their useful life, and the material for making dies. Concludes the dies were made of a hard metal (rather than a soft metal as some have suggested) and that they broke easily.

1398 **Hackens, Tony.** "Le Rythme de la Production Monétaire dans l'Antiquité." *Numismatique Antique: Problèmes et Méthodes.* Nancy and Louvain: Peeters, 1975. Pages 189-96. [CS 3361]

1399 ———. "Terminologie et Techniques de Fabrication." *Numismatique Antique: Problèmes et Méthodes.* Nancy and Louvain: Peeters, 1975. Pages 3-15. [CS 3362]

1400 **Hackens, Tony, Françoise Michaux-Van der Mersch, and François Delamare.** "Facts, Forces, and Chronology." *Metallurgy in Numismatics, Volume 3.* Edited by M. M. Archibald and M. R. Cowell. Special Publication No. 24. London: Royal Numismatic Society, 1993. Pages 1-6.
A brief discussion of the differences in shape and fabric seen on coins struck with a punch and a die, compared to those struck with two dies. Suggests these observations can be applied at Aegina and other island mints to aid in assembling chronological sequences.

1401 **Healy, John F.** "Mint Practice at Mytilene: Evidence for the Use of Hubs." *Metallurgy in Numismatics, Volume 3.* Edited by M. M. Archibald and M. R. Cowell. Special Publication No. 24. London: Royal Numismatic Society, 1993. Pages 7-18. 1 pl.
Presents the metallic composition of Mytilenean and Phokaian hektai, ca. 600-326 B.C., and suggests they were cold struck from cast blanks of electrum. Reviews the opinions of Schwabacher, Hill, and Sellwood regarding the use of hubs. Illustrates coins of Mytilene which may show evidence for the use of hubs.

1402 **Hendin, David.** "How Ancient Coins Were Made." *The Celator* 11, no. 2 (February 1997): 30-1. Illus.
A brief overview of minting methods, focusing on Judean coins. Illustrates an unstruck bronze flan, two unstruck flans which are still connected, and a brockage coin.

1403 ———. "Die Varieties, Die Combinations, and New Types." *The Celator* 21, no. 2 (February 2007): 42-3, 46. Illus.
Explains the difference between die varieties and types. Explains sequences of die combinations using ancient Judean coins as examples.

1404 **Hill, George F.** "Ancient Methods of Coining." *Numismatic Chronicle* 5th ser., 2 (1922): 1-42. 1 pl. Reprint, New York: Attic Books, 1977; New York: Sanford J. Durst, 1998. 42 pp., illus., 1 pl. [CS 3363]
The author provides a detailed description of ancient minting methods including casting and striking. Describes various methods of producing blanks and dies. Suggests that blanks were made as globes rather than flat disks because they would retain heat longer. Suggests the large tetradrachms with hammered edges were overstruck on older coins. Mentions theories explaining the central hole seen on Ptolemaic bronzes. Doubts that drills were used in engraving dies; instead, punches were used. States that die hubs were used. Discusses die cracks and re-engraving. Mentions the causes of some minting errors.

1405 **Hoover, Oliver D.** "Two Seleucid Bronzes Countermarked with Hinged Dies at Panticapaeum." *Journal of the Classical and Medieval Numismatic Society* (Canada) 2nd ser., 3, no. 3 (September 2002): 120-4. Illus.
Publishes two Seleucid bronze coins of Antiochus II, produced by the mint of Sardis, which were apparently countermarked at Panticapaeum using a hinged countermarking device. The obverse countermark is an eight-pointed star; the reverse countermark is a laurel wreath in an incuse circle. The probable design of the hinged countermarking die is shown in a drawing. Illustrates several other countermarked coins.

1406 **Horr, William D.** "Ancient Plated Coins—An Enigma." *SAN—Journal of the Society for Ancient Numismatics* 4, no. 3 (1972-3): 40-2, 53. [CS 16267]
Discusses theories explaining why fourrées were made. Several Greek fourrées are pictured.

1407 **Hu, Di.** "Why Experimental Archaeology Is Important to Numismatics." *The Celator* 20, no. 12 (December 2006): 18-27. Illus.
Summarizes the experiments in ancient minting techniques conducted by Sellwood, Beer, Kleeb, and others.

1408 **Jongkees, Jan Hendrik.** "Athenian Coin Dies from Egypt." *Numismatic Chronicle* 6th ser., 10 (1950): 298-301. Illus.
"The pair of dies under discussion, now in the Allard Pierson Museum of the University of Amsterdam, came from Alexandria. Inasmuch as they are lead, they cannot have been used for striking coins, yet they are close imitations of true coin dies. The author suggests that they were intended for the grave of someone connected with a mint and hence can be considered as proof that there was a mint in Egypt in the fourth century B.C. producing Athenian tetradrachms." [M. Thompson, *NL* 22]

1409 **Kalligas, Peter G.** "A Bronze Die from Sounion." *Numismatic Archaeology/Archaeological Numismatics: Proceedings of an International Conference held to Honour Dr. Mando Oeconomides in Athens 1995.* Oxbow Monographs 75. Edited by K. Sheedy and C. Papageorgiadou-Banis. Oxford: Oxbow Books and The Australian Archaeological Institute at Athens, 1997. Pages 141-7. 1 pl.
A bronze reverse punch die was found in the shrine of Poseidon at Sounion. The die was used to strike the early Athenian wappenmünzen, probably drachmas. Both ends of the punch were similarly cut. This suggests that a wooden cap was placed over one end, absorbing the hammer blows when the other end struck the flans. When one end became worn, the wooden cap would be moved and the other end could then be used for striking. A wooden handle passed through the center of the tool, allowing the punch to be securely held in position with both hands by the minter, while an assistant delivered the necessary blows. Discusses possible reasons for the depositing of the tool in the shrine at Sounion. Suggests that the Wappenmünzen may have been struck in the Laurion mining region.

1410 **Kleeb, Alvin A.** "Ancient Minting Practices." *SAN—Journal of the Society for Ancient Numismatics* 13, no. 3 (fall 1982): 44-7, 54.
A preliminary report on experiments in minting techniques conducted by Harold F. Donald, Gerald N. Kleeb, and the author. They made their own dies and hand struck "coins" under a variety of conditions. Concludes that ancient coins were usually struck when the planchets were only slightly below their melting temperatures. Also discusses causes for double-struck coins, methods of flan production, and other ancient minting procedures. Suggests that four to six men were needed for an efficient minting operation. [Also see Kleeb's follow-up comments in *SAN* 13, no. 4 (winter 1982-3): 76-7].

1411 ——— "Ancient Minting Practices." *SAN—Journal of the Society for Ancient Numismatics* 15, no. 2 (summer 1984): 33-4.
Reports on the progress of the author's investigation into ancient minting practices (see Kleeb "Ancient Minting Practices" above). Discusses the making of molds for casting coinage flans. Suggests that flans cast as a ball may have been used to produce high relief coins. Kleeb advances the theory that most Greek coins were struck with just one hammer blow. The author believes that large edge cracks were likely to occur when impurities existed in the silver which lowered its melting temperature.

1412 **Kutcher, Robert R.** "Fourrées Illuminate Mint and Counterfeiting Practices." *The Celator* 2, no. 6 (June 1988): 10, 12-3.
A general discussion of various types of plated coins. States that both solid silver and plated coins are known from the same pair of dies.

1413 **Laing, Lloyd R.** "Coin Production in the Ancient World." *Seaby Coin and Medal Bulletin* 535 (December 1962): 463-6. Illus.
"After observing that few innovations were made in coin production methods between the striking of the earliest coins and Bramante's invention of the coining press early in the sixteenth century, the writer discusses the following aspects of ancient coin production: The Origin of Coinage, Two Methods of Striking, The Shape of the Flan, The Manufacture of Flans, The Punches, Dies, Eccentricities of Form, Silver Plated Coins, Forgery and Casting." [*NL* 66]

1414 **Larson, Charles.** "Experiments in Coin-Making." *The Numismatist* 115, no. 5 (May 2002): 511-4, 579-2. Illus.
The author engraved dies by hand and struck "coins" in an attempt to better understand the ancient minting process. His dies imitate Persian sigloi and Athenian tetradrachms. Describes his techniques of flan preparation, die engraving, and striking. Discusses the hardening of flans and dies. Larson found that many strikes were required to fully impress each coin. Discusses the difficulties involved in striking. [Also see follow-up "Letters to the Editor": G. P. Franck-Weiby and C. Wood "Adventures in Ancient Minting," *The Numismatist* 115, no. 7 (July 2002): 744; S. Dubow "More on Coin-Making Experiment," *The Numismatist* 115, no. 8 (August 2002): 872; G. Fischer "Ant Noses, Magnifiers," *The Numismatist* 115, no. 9 (September 2002): 992-3; W. Daehn "Ant Noses, Magnifiers," *The Numismatist* 115, no. 9 (September 2002): 993].

1415 **Lemaire, V.** "How Did the Ancients Strike their Coins?" *American Journal of Numismatics* 26, no. 4 (April 1892): 73-7; 27, no. 1 (July 1892): 1-6.
A translation of excerpts from an article published in *Revue Belge de Numismatique* in 1892. Describes the process of die engraving and coin striking. [More recent researchers would disagree with some of Lemaire's conclusions].

1416 **Le Rider, Georges.** "Sur la Fabrication des Coins Monétaires dans l'Antiqué Grecque." *Schweizer Münzblätter* (Switzerland) 8, no. 9 (1958): 1-5. Illus. [CS 3367]

1417 ——— "Contremarques et Surfrappes dans l'Antiquité Grecque." *Numismatique Antique: Problèmes et Methods.* Annales de l'Est Mémoire 44. Etudes d'Archéologie Classique IV. Edited by J. Dentzer, P. Gauthier and T. Hackens. Louvain, 1975. Pages 27-56.

1418 **Lewis, Bart.** "Did Ancient Celators Use Magnifying Lenses?" *The Celator* 11, no. 11 (November 1997): 40-1. Illus.

Summarizes the history of magnifying lenses. Points out that many lenses are known from the ancient world, although some of them have simply been identified as ornaments or gems. The author suggests that lenses may sometimes have been used to aid ancient die engravers, but it would be difficult to prove it.

1419 **MacDonald, David.** *Overstruck Greek Coins: Studies in Greek Chronology and Monetary Theory.* Racine: Whitman, 2009. 271 pp., illus.
Explains how, when, and why Greek coins were overstruck (recoined by striking them with new and different dies, without first having the original design completely removed). Covers the regions of Gaul, Italy, Sicily, Bosporus, Macedonia, Thrace, Greece, Anatolia, Syria, Judea, North Africa, and the Indo-Greek kingdoms. Overstriking was done for various reasons, including to certify the coins' quality, to encourage their circulation, to restrict their export, to validate them for mercenary soldiers' pay, to raise revenue, to avoid recoining fees, or to make a political or patriotic statement. Includes more than 300 photographs and line drawings, an appendix on previously published Mesambrian overstrikes, and an extensive bibliography. Foreword by Harlan Berk. [Reviewed by D. Vagi in *The Celator* 24, no. 9 (September 2010): 38, 40].

1420 **Macdonald, George.** "Fixed and Loose Dies in Ancient Coinage." *Corolla Numismatica: Numismatic Essays in Honour of Barclay V. Head.* Edited by G. F. Hill. London: Oxford University Press, 1906. Pages 178-88. [CS 3368]
Discusses the use of obverse and reverse dies which were in fixed relation to one another—perhaps hinged. States that once fixed dies were adopted at a mint, that mint generally did not return to the use of loose dies in subsequent years. Thus, die alignment is an aid to establishing chronology. Suggests the use of fixed dies originated in southwest Asia Minor. Due to variations in alignment at various mints, alignment may also help to determine the minting location of a coin. Fixed alignments may be seen in three variations: 0°, 45°, and 180°. Macdonald shows the die alignments of some early Bactrian coins, and calls for greater use of die alignments when cataloging collections for publication. Discusses both Greek and Roman coins.

1421 **Malkmus, William.** "Note on a General Solution to the Missing Die Problem." *SAN—Journal of the Society for Ancient Numismatics* 17, no. 1 (December 1986): 15-6, 18.
A mathematical formula is presented for calculating the probable degree of completeness of a catalogue of known dies for a particular issue.

1422 ——— "Addenda to Vermeule's Catalog of Ancient Coin Dies." Parts 1-5. *SAN—Journal of the Society for Ancient Numismatics* 17, no. 4 (September 1989): 80-5; 18, no. 1 (July 1990): 16-22; no. 2 (May 1991): 40-9; no. 3 (June 1992): 72-7; no. 4 (April 1993): 96-105. Illus.
Based on Cornelius Vermeule's catalogue "Some Notes on Ancient Dies and Coining Methods" published in 1954 (see Vermeule below), this paper provides an updated list of known ancient coin dies, an updated list of literature references, a numbering system for the dies, and an annotated bibliography. Part 4 presents a table listing the dies on the basis of their find locations, and a cross-reference to their present locations. Discusses major finds, mostly of Roman dies. Part 5 provides catalogue entries for fourteen additional dies and discusses authenticity and die links to known coins.

1423 **Marotta, Michael.** "Foiled by Fourrees?" *The Celator* 15, no. 12 (December 2001): 20-7. Illus.
Discusses ancient plated coins. Provides opinions from a number of numismatists regarding whether these are the product of official mints, counterfeits, or emergency issues sanctioned by mint officials. Examines issues from both the Greek and Roman periods.

1424 **McGovern, Wayne E.** "Missing Die Probabilities, Expected Die Production and the Index Figure." *Museum Notes* 25 (1980): 209-23.
Presents a statistical method which can be used to find the probability that in a sample of a given size, taken from a universe of a number of coins produced from a known number of dies, coins representing one or more full-life dies will be missing. This index figure can yield significant insights into the structure of a coin series.

1425 **McKenna, Thomas P.** "What Do You Expect from Slave Labor?" *The Celator* 9, no. 4 (April 1995): 18-20. Illus.
Presents a variety of minting errors found on ancient coins and describes their causes. Although the article focuses on Roman coinage, most of the comments would also apply to Greek coins.

1425a **Meadows, Andrew.** "Athenian Coin Dies from Egypt: The New Discovery at Herakleion." *Revue Belge de Numismatique* (Belgium) 157 (2011). 18 pp., 4 pls.
Publishes a set of obverse coin dies discovered in excavations at Herakleion in Egypt. The three dies are engraved on a single block of bronze and thus resemble another set of dies, long known but never published, of which electrotype copies survive in the British Museum. All these dies are for the production of imitations of Athenian tetradrachms. Other evidence for dies from Egypt, and the hoard record for Athenian imitations of possible Egyptian provenance, are surveyed.

1426 **Meshorer, Ya'akov.** *The Production of Coins in the Ancient World.* Catalogue No. 70. Jerusalem: Israel Museum, 1970. 40 pp., illus. [CS 16798]
Describes the production of flans through casting or hammering, the use of dies, and the process of casting coins. Describes striking flaws and ancient forgeries. Discusses some unstruck flans, moulds, and dies which were found in excavations in the Middle East. Illustrated by coins and coin-making tools. Text in both Hebrew and English.

1427 ——— "The Production of Coins in the Ancient World." *The Shekel* 4, no. 3 (fall 1971): 5-11. Illus.
A reproduction of six pages from Meshorer's booklet on coin production (see above). Describes the production of flans through casting or hammering, the use of dies, and the process of casting coins. Describes striking flaws and ancient forgeries. Discusses some unstruck flans, moulds, and dies which were found in excavations in the Middle East.

1428 **Mildenberg, Leo.** "Those Ridiculous Arrows: On the Meaning of the Die Position." *Nomismatika Khronika* (Greece) 8 (1989): 23-9. Illus. Reprinted in *Leo Mildenberg. Vestigia Leonis: Studien zur Antiken Numismatik Israels, Palästinas und der Östlichen Mittelmeerweit. Novum Testamentum et Orbis Antiquus 36.* Edited by U. Hübner and E. Knauf. Freiburg: Universitätsverlag, and Göttingen: Vandenhoeck & Ruprecht, 1998. Pages 263-4.
Discusses the importance of noting the die rotation (obverse die position in relation to the reverse die position) when cataloging coins. Using Siculo-Punic coins as an example, Mildenberg explains how die positions can help reveal the location of minting (Sicily vs. Carthage). He also points out examples in which erroneous die rotations have revealed some coins to be counterfeits. In English on pages 23-4. In Greek on pages 28-9. [Also see Hübner and Knauf *Vestigia Leonis* under GENERAL WORKS—GREEK].

1429 **Milne, Joseph G.** "Two Notes on Greek Dies." *Numismatic Chronicle* 5th ser., 2 (1922): 43-8. [CS 3369]
(1) Discusses the re-cutting of dies. Describes several instances of re-cut dies, primarily using Roman Provincial issues as examples. Discusses the reasons for re-cutting. (2) Discusses variations in die alignment among Roman Provincial coins.

1430 ——— "On Dies in North-West Greece." *Numismatic Chronicle* 5th ser., 16 (1936): 254-5.
Publishes a stater of Thyrrheium (Corinthian type) which is a restruck brockage—the obverse type appears, incuse, on the reverse, partly obliterated by the later impression of the reverse type in the normal form. Describes the minting process which led to this error. The die alignments differed for the first and second strikes, thus showing that the dies were loose—not fixed or hinged, and that the upper die was round in section.

1431 ——— "Ancient Tooling of Coins." *Numismatic Chronicle* 6th ser., 1 (1941): 91-2. Illus.
Illustrates a drachm of Corinth struck from a collapsed die—leaving a lump of metal covering part of the head of Aphrodite. The lump was carefully tooled to produce the appearance of hair. The tooling was done in ancient times and Milne suggests that the coin's owner thought the looks of the coin would affect its acceptance in circulation.

1432 **Mørkholm, Otto.** "The 'Behaviour' of Dies in the Hellenistic Period." *Proceedings of the 9th International Congress of Numismatics. Berne, September 1979. Volume 1.* Edited by T. Hackens and R. Weiller. Luxembourg: International Association of Professional Numismatists, 1982. Pages 209-14. 2 pls.
Imhoof-Blumer demonstrated that when two or more coins have one die in common, this generally proves that the coins in question were approximately contemporary strikings from one and the same minting place. In some cases, there was movement of dies from one place to another, however. Mørkholm examines the question of the minting place of some large mintages of the Hellenistic period. He emphasizes that although the dies may have been produced at one mint, the coins may have been struck at another mint location. He concludes that in the large territorial kingdoms of the Hellenistic period, die linkages can be explained as the result of either a transfer of dies and/or personnel from one place to another, or as the result of the operation of a traveling mint. No compelling reasons point to centralized coin production as some scholars have suggested.

1433 ——— "The Life of Obverse Dies in the Hellenistic Period." *Studies in Numismatic Method Presented to Philip Grierson.* Edited by C. N. L. Brooke et al. Cambridge: University Press, 1983. Pages 11-21.
In the study of die sequences, it is assumed that if two coins are the product of the same die, they were struck at about the same time. This essay attempts to define what is meant by "the same time." Examines the life of some obverse dies from Athenian and Cypriot mints during the Hellenistic period. Concludes that at large and important mints such as Athens, coin production was continuous and usually involved the simultaneous use of several pairs of dies, and the life of an obverse die was perhaps three to five months, with nine months of use being the longest known. At smaller, less active mints, the coining requirements of some years could be met from a single pair of dies, and an obverse die might be used for as long as five years in a row.

1434 **Naster, Paul.** "La Technique des Monnaies Incuses de Grande-Grèce." *Revue Belge de Numismatique* (Belgium) 93 (1947): 5-17. [CS 3371]

1435 **Nicolaou, K.** "Archaeological News from Cyprus." *American Journal of Archaeology* 74 (1970): 71-8. 6 pls.
"On pp. 74-5 the discovery is reported of a Hellenistic workshop at Nea Paphos where flans for coins had been cast *en chapelet*. A mould and two flans are illustrated in pl. 22." [J. R. Jones, *NIAJAH*]. [Also see K. Nicolaou "Discovery" under EGYPT—PTOLEMAIC KINGDOM].

1436 **Noe, Sydney P.** "Countermarked and Overstruck Greek Coins at the American Numismatic Society." *Museum Notes* 6 (1954): 85-93. 1 pl. [CS 3374]
Noe publishes several rare or unusual countermarked coins, including issues of Alexander the Great counterstamped at Sardes, Pergamum, Adramyteum, and Cyzicus, among others. He also discusses some overstruck coins including a Cypriote coin struck over a stater of Aegina. Also a Boeotian stater struck over a coin of Pharsalus which is rare in that the new coin is *higher* in weight than the original undertype coin. Generally, coins have been overstruck after the local weight standard has been *reduced*.

1437 **Nouyon, Bernard, Georges Depeyrot, and Jean-Luc Desnier.** *Systèmes et Technologie des Monnaies de Bronze (4es. Avant J.-C.—3es. Après J.-C.).* Collection Moneta 19. Wetteren: Moneta, 2000. 208 pp., 4 pls.
Examines the processes and technologies involved in the production of bronze coinage from the fourth century B.C. to the third century A.D. Discusses the techniques, alloys, and technologies of producing Ptolemaic bronze coins. Then examines the coinage of Gaul, Italy, Sicily, Sardinia, Thrace, Crete, Asia, Syria, Egypt and central Africa, Armenia, and Parthia.

1438 **Paasch, Kasper M.** "The History of Optics: From Ancient Times to the Middle Ages." *DOPS-NYT: Udgivet af Dansk Optisk Selskab* (Denmark) 1 (1999): 5-8. Illus.
Gives an overview of the possible use of lenses from antiquity up to the invention of eyeglasses in A.D. 1286. Some recent ideas concerning the use of magnifying lenses for gem engraving and for cutting coin dies are discussed. Reviews the literary, archaeological, and indirect (gems, coins) evidence. Concludes there is no direct evidence for the use of magnifying lenses in antiquity, and the sources are contradictory. However, the use of such lenses is highly plausible.

1439 **Palmer, Hazel, and Cornelius C. Vermeule.** "Ancient Gold and Silver in the Museum of Fine Arts, Boston." *Archaeology* 12, no. 1 (spring 1959): 2-7. Illus.
Illustrates and describes twelve objects covering various phases of ancient metalwork from archaic Greek to late Roman. They were acquired by the Museum of Fine Arts in 1958. The objects include a gold bull's head pendant, heads of goddesses, a silver pitcher, a votive chain, a silver vase, silver plaques, and three coins: (1) a silver stater of Perikles, king of Lycia (380-362 B.C.), (2) a silver cistophoric tetradrachm of the young Nero struck at Ephesos, probably in A.D. 51, and (3) a silver octadrachm of Ptolemy I, king of Egypt (304-285 B.C.).

1440 **Prieto Martinez, J. J.** "The Number of Dies Used to Strike the Coinage: A Statistical Problem in Ancient Numismatics." *Gaceta Numismática* (Spain) 144 (2002): 17-20.

1441 **Raubitschek, A. E.** "The Mechanical Engraving of Circular Letters." *American Journal of Archaeology* 55 (1951): 343-4. 3 pls.
"Discusses several inscriptions of the sixth and fifth centuries B.C. which show that a cutting compass or tubular drill was used to cut some letters." [J. R. Jones, *NIAJAH*]

1442 **Richter, Gisela M. A.** "Calenian Pottery and Classical Greek Metalware." *American Journal of Archaeology* 63, no. 3 (July 1959): 241-9. 10 pls.
Examines pottery produced in southern Italy during Hellenistic times which was decorated with reliefs made from moulds of fifth and fourth century Greek metalware, one example showing that Syracusan decadrachms were used for the purpose. Many other examples bear similarity to Greek coins, especially those of southern Italy and Sicily, which suggests the probability that Greek die-cutters also worked on metalware and produced reliefs similar to those on their coins. [Summarized from I. Merker, *NL* 50]

1443 **Rohner, John R.** "Ancient Coin Dies: Engraved or Cast?" *The Numismatist* 96, no. 5 (May 1983): 929-31. Illus.
Suggests that ancient Greek and Roman coin dies may have been produced by pouring molten bronze over a clay model.

1444 **Rottinghaus, Scott, George Cuhaj, and Joe Paonessa.** "New Evidence for Cold Striking of Ancient Coins." *The Celator* 25, no. 8 (August 2011): 6-12. Illus.
The authors created steel dies and hand-struck numerous imitation Corinthian staters on silver planchets. Some of the planchets were cold, while others were heated prior to striking. The results were compared. Acceptable strike quality was achieved with both the cold and hot strikes. However, the hot-struck flans tended to spread slightly, thus enabling more of the die design to be transferred to the flan. The hot-struck pieces tended to have a dark color due to fire scale. The authors concluded that cold striking was a more efficient way to create ancient coins and there is reason to question the long-held view that hot striking was the prevalent method in the ancient mints. [There was an error in the plate of photographs of the hand-struck pieces. A corrected version appeared in *The Celator* 25, no. 11 (November 2011): 4]. But also see Greg Franck-Weiby's Letter to the Editor, "Cold Struck Case Closed? Nowhere Near It!" in *The Celator* 25, no. 12 (December 2011): 4, 20. Franck-Weiby points out flaws in the striking experiment, explains the cause of the fire scale, and discusses the efficiency of hot striking].

1445 **Rowe, Clement E.** "Ancient Plated Coins, an Hypothesis." *Spink Numismatic Circular* 84, no. 4 (April 1976): 150-1. [CS 3379]
"It is hypothesized that ancient plated coins, known as fourrées, might have been produced by slave labor working in the mints." [C. Rowe, *NL* 97]

1446 **Sayles, Wayne G.** "Die Links Help to Determine the Chronology and Sequence of an Issue." *The Celator* 11, no. 1 (January 1997): 12. Illus.
A brief explanation of how die links can be used to determine the sequence of a coin issue.

1447 ——— "The Technical Obverse: Another Archaic Convention." *The Celator* 14, no. 11 (November 2000): 45. Illus.
A brief discussion of the use and meaning of the term "obverse" in numismatics. The obverse of a coin is technically and traditionally regarded as the side of the coin which was struck by the anvil die (with the reverse being struck by the punch die). Sayles argues that the side of the coin which is more *artistically* important should be considered the obverse, thus dispensing with the archaic conventional definition. The staters of Corinth provide a good example. Although the Pegasus side of the coin was struck by the anvil die, Sayles argues that the Athena head should be regarded as the obverse because Athena was more important than Pegasus in Greek religion. [Alan S. Walker disagreed with Sayles' arguments. See his "Letter to the Editor" in *The Celator* 15, no. 1 (January 2001): 4, 15-6. Also see Walker's follow-up article, "Front Side, Back Side" below].

1448 ——— "East is East and West is West (A Rebuttal)." *The Celator* 15, no. 7 (July 2001): 25-8, 36. Illus.
A follow-up to Sayles' previous article (see above) and a rebuttal to Walker's response (see Walker "Front Side" below). Sayles emphasizes that the side of the coin which is more important (artistically, religiously, politically) *is* the obverse, regardless of whether it was created by the anvil die or the punch die. Responds to Walker's criticisms.

1449 ——— "Dating by Fabric." *The Celator* 16, no. 10 (October 2002): 47. Illus.
Discusses the fabric of Greek coins—the physical characteristics of the metal, such as thickness and shape. Sayles provides examples from Soli and Mallos where the comparison of a coin's fabric can provide clues to chronology.

1450 ——— "Hot or Cold?" *The Celator* 20, no. 11 (November 2006): 45.
Reviews the on-going controversy over whether ancient coins were struck while the flans were still hot, or if the flans were struck when cold.

1451 **Schwabacher, Willy.** "Zur Technik der Stempelherstellung in Griechischen Münzstätten Klassischer Zeit." *Actes, Congrès International de Numismatique, Paris, 1953. Volume 2.* Paris, 1957. Pages 521-8. [CS 3380]

1452 ——— "The Production of Hubs Reconsidered." *Numismatic Chronicle* 7th ser., 6 (1966): 41-5. [CS 3383]
The author comments on Sellwood's minting experiments (see Sellwood "Some Experiments" below) and concurs that hubs may have been used in the production of ancient coin dies. Mentions two coins of Poseidonia struck from dies which he had previously thought to have been made by the same hub. He now doubts this attribution. Suggests that hubs may have been created from master dies: the die production sequence being master die, to hub, to working die. Includes a postscript by David Sellwood: He believes that more than twenty dies could be made from the same hub. If used at all, hubs were used to provide the main design, with other details being added to the die after hubbing.

1453 **Seibert, Robert.** "Literary Sources and Historical Records Indicate Optical Aid." *The Celator* 4, no. 4 (April 1990): 11.
Reviews the literary, archaeological, and art historical evidence for the use of magnifying lenses in engraving coin dies in antiquity. Supports the theory that lenses were used. [Also see articles by Dillon, Sines, and Tameanko].

1454 **Sellwood, David G.** "Some Experiments in Greek Minting Technique." *Numismatic Chronicle* 7th ser., 3 (1963): 217-31. Illus. [CS 3384]
The author produced dies similar to ancient dies and struck "coins" with them. He discusses the making of flans, the process of striking, and die life. Discusses hot vs. cold striking of flans. Shows that the use of positive hubs in the process of die production was one of the possible methods of manufacturing ancient coin dies.

1455 ——— "Minting." *Roman Crafts*. Edited by D. Strong and D. Brown. London: Gerald Duckworth, 1976. Pages 62-73. Illus.
    Although this overview of the minting process focuses on Roman coins, most of the material is also relevant to the minting of Greek coins. Discusses the production of flans, the production of dies, and the process of striking coins.

1456 ——— "The Interaction between the Early Minting Technologies of East and West." *Numismatics and Archaeology: The 2nd International Colloquium*. Edited by Parmeshwari Lal Gupta and Amal Kumar Jha. Maharashtra: Indian Institute of Research in Numismatic Studies, 1987. Pages 125-6.
    Comments on how the minting technologies of India and Asia Minor may have influenced each other. Compares the process used to manufacture coin blanks in Persia and India and finds them to be very different. The Indian methods may have had some influence on Western methods in later centuries.

1457 **Seltman, E. J.** "Nummi Serrati and Astral Coin Types." *Numismatic Chronicle* 3rd ser., 19 (1899): 322-43. Illus.
    Examines the reasons for the serrated edges found on certain Greek, Roman, and Carthaginian coins. Examines the use of astronomical objects and symbols as coin types. Svoronos suggested the shape of the serrated coins was meant to symbolize astral bodies. Seltman doubts this in most cases. Suggests in some cases the edges may be intended to distinguish local issues from royal issues. However, in most cases he believes the edges are merely ornamental.

1458 **Sines, George, and Yanni S. Sakellarakis.** "Lenses in Antiquity." *American Journal of Archaeology* 91, no. 2 (April 1987): 191-6. Illus.
    Evidence indicates that the use of lenses was widespread throughout the Middle East and the Mediterranean. States that the quality of some of these lenses was sufficient to permit their use as magnifying glasses. Discusses the probability that magnifying lenses were used by gem carvers and seal engravers. Also presents methods of producing optical quality lenses. Mentions lenses found in the houses of a gem engraver at Pompeii and a Roman artist at Tanis.

1459 **Smith, Douglas.** "Fourrées Appeal to Technically Oriented Collectors." *The Celator* 3, no. 8 (August 1989): 26.
    Mentions methods of producing fourrées. States that the most common Greek fourrées are South Italian coins, drachms of Alexander the Great, and tetradrachms of Athens. Fourrées of Kalchedon, Neapolis, and Parthia are shown along with a few Roman pieces.

1460 **Sutherland, C. H. V.** "Overstrikes and Hoards: The Movement of Greek Coinage Down to 400 B.C." *Numismatic Chronicle* 6th ser., 2 (1942): 1-18.
    Lists overstruck silver coins of the sixth and fifth centuries B.C. arranged according to the mint at which the original striking was done, then by the mint where the overstriking was performed. Discusses the reasons for overstriking coins and suggests that overstrikes may be interpreted as indications of close relationships (commercial and political) between the "overstruck" state and the overstriking state. Includes an excellent summary of the significance of hoard evidence of overstriking and the light it sheds on trade patterns in various areas of the Greek world.

1461 **Svoronos, Joannes N.** "ΣΦΡΑΓΙΣ ΑΘΗΝΑΙΚΟΥ ΤΕΤΡΑΔΡΑΧΜΟΥ." *Corolla Numismatica: Numismatic Essays in Honour of Barclay V. Head*. G. F. Hill. London: Oxford University Press, 1906. Pages 285-95. Illus.
    Examines a reverse die for an Athenian tetradrachm. In Greek (but see next item for an English translation).

1462 ——— "A Die of an Athenian Tetradrachm." *North American Journal of Numismatics: The Turtle* 6, no. 4 (April 1967): 115-22. Illus.
    An English translation of the essay which originally appeared in *Corolla Numismatica* (see previous entry). Suggests that, by law, the ancient Greeks immediately destroyed retired coin dies, accounting for the rarity of surviving dies. Describes in detail the only known genuine Greek coin die (for an Athenian tetradrachm), discovered in Egypt in 1904. The die is pictured. A metallurgical analysis reveals the bronze die to be 75% copper, 25% tin. The author believes the die was used in Athens ca. 322 B.C., and suggests the die was subsequently stolen, taken to Egypt, and used to strike counterfeit tetradrachms. Suggests Egypt was a haven for counterfeiters at this time.

1463 **Talfourd, Ely.** "The Process of Coining as Seen in a Wall-Painting at Pompeii." *Numismatic Chronicle* 3rd ser., 16 (1896): 53-8. 1 pl.
    Illustrates and describes a wall-painting which depicts a coining scene including the processes of melting metal, creating planchets, weighing, and striking with a hammer while holding the planchet with tongs.

1464 **Tameanko, Marvin.** "Literature Points Out Knowledge of Magnifiers." *The Celator* 3, no. 6 (June 1989): 1, 26. Illus.
    Explores the controversial issue of whether ancient die engravers made use of magnifying lenses. Mentions the references to magnifying devices found in the writings of Aristophanes, Seneca, and Pliny. Concludes that ancient celators may have used lenses, but no definite conclusion has been reached. [Also see articles by Dillon, Sines, and Seibert].

1465 ——— "Dimples on Coins." *The Celator* 6, no. 10 (October 1992): 4. Illus.
    In this "Letter to the Editor," Tameanko suggests the indentations found on many Ptolemaic and Seleucid bronze coins may have been created by pincer tongs used to test the temperature and softness of the coinage flans before striking.

1466 ——— "Numismatically Related Artifacts from the Mint in the Athenian Agora." *Journal of the Classical and Medieval Numismatic Society* (Canada) 2nd ser., 2, no. 2 (June 2001): 84-90. Illus.
    Describes some of the objects found during excavations in the Athenian agora, the site of the ancient mint. In addition to the manufacturing of coins, the mint acted as a general foundry for the city. Among the objects found which were probably manufactured at the mint are bronze weights, bronze tokens used in the distribution of armour to the army, and bronze ballots used in the law courts.

1467 **Tobey, Leslie Beer, and A. G. Tobey.** "Experiments to Simulate Ancient Greek Coins." *Metallurgy in Numismatics, Volume 3*. Edited M. M. Archibald and M. R. Cowell. Special Publication No. 24. London: Royal Numismatic Society, 1993. Pages 28-33. 2 pls.
    The authors struck "coins" using ancient methods over a period of years, using flans of 99% silver and dies of 80% copper, 20% tin. They also used reverse punches of iron as well as bronze. They struck coins of the Aeginetan sea-turtle type using two obverse dies. The first die was created with a hub; the second was hand engraved. After striking 1500 coins with each die, only a few hairline cracks resulted on the first die. The second, hand-engraved, die proved less durable—it became more flattened and pitted. The results of these experiments present a strong case for hubbing in antiquity and also suggest that coins were struck in a heated condition. The authors also conducted experiments in over-striking coins. They could not completely obliterate the under-type. During striking, silver never remained trapped in any portion of the dies.

1468 **Vagi, David.** "Ancient Overstrikes: Circulating Coins that were Recycled as Planchets for New Issues Hold Valuable Data for Researchers." *The Numismatist* 121, no. 12 (December 2008): 81-3. Illus.
   A general discussion of overstrikes evident on Greek and Roman coins.

1469 **van Alfen, Peter G.** "Hatching Owls: The Regulation of Coin Production in Later Fifth Century Athens." *Quantifying Monetary Supplies in Greco-Roman Times. Third Academia Belgica—Francqui Foundation Conference, Rome, September 29-30, 2008.* Rome: Edipuglia, 2011. Pages 1-47.

1470 **Van der Dussen, J. W.** "Countermarks on Popular Ancient Silver Coins. Part I." *The Celator* 16, no. 12 (December 2002): 6-12. Illus. "Part II." *The Celator* 17, no. 1 (January 2003): 26-30. Illus.
   Discusses the minting of the first coins in Lydia, and the introduction of the staters of Aegina. Mentions that, because these were among the most popular coins in trade at the time, they were frequently counterfeited or debased. This led to the practice of countermarking. In Part 2, the author examines coins of Athens, Alexander III, and Republican denarii which were frequently countermarked. Suggests some reasons for countermarking, and discusses who may have done the countermarking.

1471 **Vermeule, Cornelius C.** "Some Notes on Ancient Dies and Coining Methods." *Spink Numismatic Circular* 61 (October 1953): 397-402; 61 (November 1953): 447-52; 61 (December 1953): 499-504; 62 (January 1954): 1-5; 62 (February 1954): 53-8; 62 (March 1954): 101-3. Reprinted, *Some Notes on Ancient Dies and Coining Methods.* London: Spink & Son, 1954. 51 pp., illus., map. [CS 15797]
   Lists and describes sixty-two known ancient dies and provides the provenance, present location, and other comments for each. Only twelve of the dies are Greek or Gallic; the rest are Roman. Also lists sculptures, reliefs, etc., which show coining implements or minting scenes. Reviews the evidence that dies contribute to our knowledge of ancient coining methods. Comments on the importance of separating genuine official dies from forgers' dies. Comments on patterns of die usage during the Roman period. Concludes with comments on the artists and die cutters of the early Roman Imperial mints. [Reviewed by Michael Grant in *Numismatic Chronicle* 6th ser., 14 (1954): 228-30, and by C. M. Kraay in *Journal of Roman Studies* 45 (1955): 241. Also see Malkmus "Addenda" above. A bronze die for a tetradrachm of the Bactrian king Demetrios I appeared in Classical Numismatic Group's *Triton XV* sale (January 4, 2012), lot 1344].

1472 ——— "Minting Greek and Roman Coins." *Archaeology* 10, no. 2 (summer 1957): 100-7. Illus. [CS 3388]
   A brief and general description of the minting process in Greek and Roman times. Illustrates some ancient coin dies. Includes a map of find-spots of ancient dies.

1473 **Walker, Alan S.** "Some Plated Coins from the Agora at Athens." *Proceedings of the 9th International Congress of Numismatics. Berne, September 1979. Volume 1.* Edited by T. Hackens and R. Weiller. Luxembourg: International Association of Professional Numismatists, 1982. Pages 131-6. 1 pl.
   Discusses a find of fourteen plated Athenian tetradrachms which had been buried in the fourth century B.C. in the floor of a temple in the Athenian Agora. All were from the same pair of dies. Suggests that their low weight and light plating indicate they were an official emergency issue. These coins apparently had not been used in circulation, and may have been minted during the panic after the battle of Chaeroneia.

1474 ——— "Front Side, Back Side, Which Side?" *The Celator* 15, no. 6 (June 2001): 6-17. Illus.
   A response to Wayne Sayles' article (see "The Technical Obverse" above) in which Sayles suggested that numismatists should disregard the traditional technical definitions of *obverse* and *reverse*. Walker uses coins of Corinth and Elis to point out the flaws in Sayles' arguments. Walker shows that while the coin types varied, Pegasus remained on the technical obverse of the coins, thus proving that the ancient Corinthians thought of the Pegasus as the more important side of the coin. Other examples are given.

1475 **Wells, H. Bartlett.** "Ancient Inventions for Tooling the Surfaces of Objects in Softer Metals." *Expedition* 19, no. 4 (summer 1977): 21-6. Illus. [CS 3389]
   Discusses the central conical cavities sometimes found on Greek bronze coins, especially in the Ptolemaic series. Reviews the theories of G. Dattari. These pits were produced when scraping the flans to remove imperfections in the surfaces and edges, but this was not done to achieve the proper weight as Dattari suggested. Describes the process the author believes to have been used to scrape the flans. The central cavity was created by a pin which held the flan in place as it was turned to be chiseled. Also mentions the tooling of later Greek and Roman Provincial coins.

1476 ——— "Ancient Gold-Plated Coins." *SAN—Journal of the Society for Ancient Numismatics* 9, no. 3 (summer 1978): 39-40, 52. [CS 16269]
   Coins with a refined gold plating attached to a less valuable metal (usually silver) core are discussed. Suggests these may have been made to be used as temple offerings, because the weight difference with pure gold would have led to easy detection in circulation. These pieces are rare, in contrast to silver-plated coins. Gold-plated Alexander staters are known. [Also see Wells "New Material" below, and his several articles on gold-plated coins under MACEDONIAN KINGDOM—GENERAL WORKS].

1477 ——— "New Material on Ancient Gold-Plated Coins." *SAN—Journal of the Society for Ancient Numismatics* 10, no. 2 (summer 1979): 22.
   Some additional comments on gold-plated silver coins. [See Wells "Ancient Gold-Plated Coins" above and his several articles on gold-plated coins under MACEDONIAN KINGDOM—GENERAL WORKS].

1478 ——— "A Note on Coin-Plating with Electrum." *SAN—Journal of the Society for Ancient Numismatics* 13, no. 1 (spring 1982): 18-9.
   Reviews the work of Friedrich Bodenstedt on the electrum coinage of Phocaea and Mytilene, concentrating on his findings of debased electrum and electrum-plated coins. Speculates on the reasons for their manufacture. Discusses weights and metallurgy.

1479 **Wickens, Jere M.** "The Production of Ancient Coins." *Bearers of Meaning: The Ottilia Buerger Collection of Ancient and Byzantine Coins at Lawrence University.* Appleton, Wisconsin: Lawrence University Press, 1995. Pages 7-14. Illus.
   Describes coinage metals, sources of metals, the refining process, the production of flans and dies, and the striking of coins. Briefly comments on countermarks and circulation patterns.

Also see: Bernard et al. "Experimental Study" under METALLURGY; Camp "The Mint" under ATTICA—GENERAL WORKS; Classical Numismatic Group "Countermarks" under AEGINA; Emmons "Overstruck Coinage" under EGYPT—PTOLEMAIC KINGDOM; Fischer-Bossert "A Lead Test-Piece" under SICILY—SYRACUSE; Flament *Contribution à l'Étude des Ateliers* under GENERAL WORKS—GREEK; Fontanille & Baumheckel "Errors on Biblical Coins" under PALESTINE—JUDEA; Garraffo "La Monnetazione dell'età Dionigiana: Contromarche e Riconiazioni" under SICILY—SYRACUSE; Gebhard et al. "Melting and Alloying" under CELTIC COINAGE OF EUROPE; Hall "A Note on the Fabric" under EGYPT—PTOLEMAIC KINGDOM; Healy "Die-Sequences" under METALLURGY; Hendin "Creating Flan Molds" under PALESTINE—JUDEA; Hendin "Striking Methods" under PALESTINE—JUDEA; Houghton "Some Seleucid Test Pieces" under SYRIA—SELEUCID KINGDOM; Holt "Mimesis in Metal" under BACTRIA; Kushnir-Stein "Bevelled Edge" under JUDEA; Koutsoukos "Mass Production" under EGYPT—PTOLEMAIC KINGDOM; Lang *The Athenian Citizen* under ATTICA—GENERAL WORKS.

MacDonald "Movement of Silver" under CRETE; Madsen "Concerning Lines" (two items) and "Concerning Edge Cracks" under METALLURGY; Mattingly "The Second Century B.C. Seleucid Countermarks" under SYRIA—SELEUCID KINGDOM; Miller "Athenian Coinage" under ATTICA—GENERAL WORKS; Milne "Some Greek Coins in Oxford" under PUBLIC COLLECTIONS—GREAT BRITAIN (OXFORD); Milne "Countermarked Coins" under ASIA MINOR—GENERAL WORKS; Milne "The Persian Standard" (discusses overstriking) under IONIA; Milne "The Mint of Kyme" under AEOLIS; Meyer "A Lead Test-Piece" under THRACE; Mørkholm "Production and Use" under GENERAL WORKS—GREEK; Naster "Remarques Charactéroscopiques et Technologiques" under LYDIA; Naster "La Technique des Revers Partiellement Incus" under PHOENICIA; Naster "Un Cas de Tréflage dans la Frappe des Créseides" under LYDIA; Noe "Group of Die-Sequences" under ITALY—POSEIDONIA; Noe "Overstrikes" under ITALY—GENERAL WORKS; Raven "Problems of the Earliest Owls" under ATTICA—GENERAL WORKS; Robbins and Bayley *Coin Pellet Mould* under CELTIC COINAGE OF BRITAIN; Rudd "Coin Moulds Found" under CELTIC COINAGE OF BRITAIN.

Saryan "An Unusual Cut Bronze Coin" under ARMENIA; Sellwood "A Novel Solution" under PARTHIA; Sellwood "Parthian Mint Operations" under PARTHIA; E. J. Seltman "On Some Names, Symbols, and Letters on Coins" under ITALY—THURII; Sutherland "A Corinthian Stater Overstruck" under ITALY—METAPONTUM; Sutherland "The Incuse Coinages" under ITALY—GENERAL WORKS; M. Thompson "Workshops or Mines?" under ATTICA—NEW STYLE COINAGE; M. Thompson "Hoards and Overstrikes" under HOARDS; Thompson and Nasir "The Manufacture of Celtic Coins" under CELTIC COINAGE—GENERAL WORKS; Tylecote "The Method of Use" under CELTIC COINAGE—GENERAL WORKS; van Alfen "Two Unpublished Hoards and Other 'Owls' from Egypt" under ATTICA—GENERAL WORKS; Van Arsdell "Clashed Dies" under CELTIC COINAGE OF BRITAIN; Van Arsdell "Die-Cutting Expertise" under CELTIC COINAGE OF BRITAIN; Van Arsdell "Bad Day at Flat Rock" under CELTIC COINAGE OF BRITAIN; Visonà "An Unusual Ptolemaic Overstrike" under EGYPT—PTOLEMAIC KINGDOM; Warden "Etruscan" under ITALY—ETRURIA; Wells' several articles on plated coins under MACEDONIAN KINGDOM—GENERAL WORKS; Wells "Some Further Remarks on Turtles" under AEGINA; Woodward "Three New Fragments" under EPIGRAPHY; Work "A City's Coinage" under SICILY—KAMARINA.

METALLURGY

Chemical analyses of Greek bronze coins may be useful in arranging such coins in series, in establishing closer limits of dating, and in the solution of other numismatic problems concerning these coins. The numismatic evidence must still remain the primary basis for the solution of such problems, the kind of evidence obtainable through chemical investigations being mainly useful for supplementing the other evidence. However, the conjunction of the chemical and numismatic evidence often leads to conclusions or suggestions that could not be reached from either sort of evidence alone.

—Earle Radcliffe Caley, 1939

1480 **Avaldi, L., L. Confalonieri, M. Milazzo, E. Paltrinieri, R. Testi, and E. Winsemann-Falghera.** "Quantitative Results of XRF Analysis of Ancient Coins by Monochromatic X-Ray Excitation." *Archaeometry* 26, pt. 1 (February 1984): 82-95.
The metallic content of fifty-two Greek gold coins of the seventh and sixth centuries B.C. and four gold coins of the late Roman Empire were examined by X-ray fluorescence. Describes the theory and process of the analytical technique. Results are presented in tables.

1481 **Beer, Leslie.** "Analysis of Coins from the Asyut Hoard: An Introduction." *Metallurgy in Numismatics, Volume 1.* Edited by D. M. Metcalf and W. A. Oddy. Special Publication No. 13. London: Royal Numismatic Society, 1980. Pages 1-2.
An introduction to some of the other papers in this volume. Describes the Asyut hoard of about 900 archaic silver coins found in Egypt in 1969. Because many of these coins had been defaced by test cuts in antiquity, many of them were made available for metallurgical analysis. The other papers present the results of such analysis.

1482 **Beer-Tobey, Leslie, Noel H. Gale, Henry S. Kim, and Zofia A. Stos-Gale.** "Lead Isotope Analysis of Four Archaic Silver Ingots from the Selinus Hoard." *Metallurgy in Numismatics, Volume 4.* Special Publication No. 30. London: Royal Numismatic Society, 1998. Pages 385-92.
An investigation of the sources of silver in the ingots contained in the Selinus Hoard (see Arnold-Biucchi, Beer-Tobey, and Waggoner "A Greek Archaic Silver Hoard from Selinus" under HOARDS) using the technique of lead isotope analysis. Concludes the four ingots came together via trade or accumulation and were not produced from the same source. Silver from Laurion was found in one of the ingots, possibly the earliest evidence for Athenian silver in western Greece. One of the ingots contains silver which cannot be attributed to the Aegean or Anatolia, thus suggesting the western Mediterranean as a possible source. The ingots lend support to the theory that square or rectangular ingots are confined to the western Mediterranean while round ingots are typical of Egypt and the near East.

1483 **Bernard, Dominique, Alain Roux, Jean Barralis, Katherine Gruel, and Francois Wideman.** "Experimental Study of Tin Distribution in Coriosolite Coins." *Scientific Studies in Numismatics.* Edited by W. A. Oddy. London: British Museum, 1980. Pages 44-52.
An examination of some Coriosolite coins of the Treby Hoard. The copper-silver alloy coins show an unusually high concentration of tin near the surfaces. The team struck coins made from alloys containing various percentages of tin. They concluded that the high tin concentration was due to hot striking which brought tin to the surface of the coins.

1484 **Bluyssen, H., and P. B. Smith.** "Determination of the Silver Content of Greek Coins by Neutron Activation." *Archaeometry* 5 (1962): 113-8.
The genuineness of a number of Greek coins of the sixth to fourth centuries B.C. have been investigated non-destructively by means of neutron activation, together with the determination of the specific gravity of the coins. Describes the methods used.

1485 **Bodenstedt, Friedrich, and P. Reimers.** "Zerstorungsfreie Bestimmung der Legierungsbestandteile Gold, Silber, und Kupfer von Elektronmünzen aus Phokaia und Mytilene." *Jahrbuch für Numismatik und Geldgeschichte* 25 (1975): 17-32.

1486 **Buckley, J. A.** "An Analysis of Thirty-one Coins from the Hellenistic Period." *Archaeometry* 27, pt. 1 (February 1985): 102-7.
Thirty-one Hellenistic silver coins were examined by the particle induced X-ray emission technique to determine their elemental composition. Includes Seleucid, Ptolemaic, and Bactrian/Indo-Greek coins. The results are discussed and summarized in a table.

1487 **Burnett, Andrew M., Paul T. Craddock, and K. Preston.** "New Light on the Origins of Orichalcum." *Proceedings of the 9th International Congress of Numismatics. Berne, September 1979. Volume 1.* Edited by T. Hackens and R. Weiller. Luxembourg: International Association of Professional Numismatists, 1982. Pages 263-8.

"Orichalcum was introduced as early as Mithradates V of Pontus. By 50 B.C. it was in use at several mints in Asia Minor. The attractiveness of the metal and the need to avoid large, cumbersome, and non-malleable bronze coins were governing factors in Augustus' decision to incorporate this new material in his reform of ca. 23 B.C." [W. Metcalf, *NL* 111/112]

1488 **Cabral, J. M. Peixoto.** "The Specific Gravity of Fifty-two Electrum Staters of Kyzikos." *A Catalogue of the Calouste Gulbenkian Collection of Greek Coins, Part 2: Greece to East.* Volume 1. By G. Kenneth Jenkins and M. Castro Hipólito. Lisbon: Fundação Calouste Gulbenkian, 1989. Page 200.
The author analyzed fifty-two electrum staters of Kyzikos from the Gulbenkian collection. The weight, specific gravity, and percentage of gold content (minimum and maximum) of each coin are listed in a table.

1489 **Caley, Earle R.** *The Composition of Ancient Greek Bronze Coins.* Memoirs of the American Philosophical Society, Volume 11. Philadelphia: American Philosophical Society, 1939. 203 pp., 4 pls. [CS 3392]
The author describes his experimental procedures and presents the results of his analyses. Reveals the percentage of various metals contained in the bronze coins of various localities including Macedon, Athens, Sicyon, Corinth, Sicily, Olbia, Asia Minor, Syria, and Egypt. Examines the trends over time. Attempts to explain the chronological variations in the metallic content of bronze coins. Analyzes the amount of impurities in the coins. Discusses the microstructure of bronze coins and applications for the knowledge gained through metallurgical analyses. Also examines some Roman coins. Summarizes the major findings: coins of a given type issued within a brief period are very similar in composition; those issued over a long period differ; the Greek coinage composition differs from Roman coinage; the impurities which occur most frequently are iron, nickel, cobalt, zinc, gold, arsenic, sulfur, and oxygen; three types of microstructure exist; the analyses have implications for the proper cleaning of excavation finds. Includes photomicrographs showing the structure of coins. [Reviewed by Harold Mattingly in *Numismatic Chronicle* 5th ser., 19 (1939): 293, and by A. R. Bellinger in *American Journal of Archaeology* 47 (1943): 358-60].

1490 ———— "The Earliest Use of Nickel Alloys in Coinage." *Numismatic Review* 1, no. 1 (June 1943): 17-9.
An analysis of the coins of Euthydemus and other rulers of Bactria revealed a 20% nickel composition (77% copper). Caley suggests that ancient nickel was probably produced by the smelting of naturally combined copper and nickel ores. The author found no other instances, outside of Bactria, of nickel usage in Greek coins. He concludes it is probable that these nickel bronze coins were never intended to pass as silver coins but rather as minor coins either equivalent to the ordinary bronze or copper coins, or at least of lesser value than the silver coins. Suggests that all the coins struck from nickel represent an uninterrupted series and that all rulers who issued the coins should probably be grouped closely together in time.

1491 ———— "The Specific Gravity and Fineness of Persian Darics." *Numismatic Review* (July 1944): 21-3. [CS 15884]
Herodotus stated that "Darius had refined gold to the highest degree of purity in order to have coins struck of it." Caley set out to check the accuracy of this statement. Ten gold darics were subjected to specific gravity analysis. The results are presented in a table. The average specific gravity was 18.98, indicating 98% fineness. An analysis of the variations in weight, gold content, and fineness of these coins appears in another table.

1492 ———— "Methods of Distinguishing Cast from Struck Coins." *Numismatic Review* 2, no. 4 (April-June 1945): 21-4. [CS 15885]
The author briefly describes various methods of determining whether a coin was cast or struck. The methods include microscopic examination of the crystal structure of the metal, examination by X-rays, visual observation of the edges and surfaces, weight and specific gravity measurements, and the measurement of the hardness of the surface of the coin with the aid of a scleroscope.

1493 ———— *Analysis of Ancient Metals.* International Series of Monographs on Analytical Chemistry, No. 19. Oxford, London, Edinburg, and New York: Macmillan, 1964. 176 pp. [CS 15803 and 15889]
"In emphasizing the need for qualitative—but preferably quantitative—analyses of ancient metals the author stresses their importance to the archaeologist in determining date accuracy, and to the museologist in establishing authenticity. Such analyses can be used by the numismatist to illustrate the relationship between coinage and economic conditions, when progressive stages of debasement are observed, and may also be of great help in the detection of forgeries. The work includes tables compiled from completed analyses of a wide variety of ancient metals and alloys, including numerous examples of early coinage." [F. Campbell, *NL* 70]

1494 **Caley, Earle R., and Wallace H. Deebel.** "Chemical Dating of Bronze Blanks from the Athenian Agora." *The Ohio Journal of Science* 55, no. 1 (January 1955): 44-6. [CS 15890]
"Chemical analysis of a coin blank found at the Agora in Athens during 1953 disclosed that the bronze was undoubtedly ancient. A study of the presence and quantities of copper, silver, gold, tin, nickel, lead, iron, and zinc further supported this conclusion. A comparison of the chemical composition of this blank with that of Athenian bronze coins especially in regard to the ratio of lead to tin placed the date of the metal at the latter part of the first century B.C. The author suggests that by this method it may be possible to date ancient coins rendered illegible through wear or corrosion." [B. Wasson, *NL* 35]

1495 **Carter, Giles F.** "Preparation of Ancient Coins for Accurate X-Ray Fluorescence Analysis." *Archaeometry* 7 (1964): 106-13. [CS 15892]
"In the use of X-ray fluorescence analysis, the rays themselves penetrate less than one thousandth of an inch. Thus, in the analysis of a coin specimen, all surface oxides must first be removed or only the surface of the coin will have been accurately analyzed. The article includes a report on the analysis of seven Roman coins." [*NL* 76]

1496 **Cary, M.** "The Sources of Silver for the Greek World." *Mélanges Gustave Glotz.* Paris: Presses Universitaires de France, 1932. Pages 133-42.

1497 **Chamberlain, V. E., and Noel H. Gale.** "The Isotopic Composition of Lead in Greek Coins and in Galena from Greece and Turkey." *Proceedings of the Sixteenth International Symposium on Archaeometry and Archaeological Prospection, Edinburgh 1976.* Edinburgh: National Museum of Antiquities of Scotland, 1980. Pages 139-55. Illus.
"A brief description is given of the application of lead isotope studies to tracing the provenance of the silver used in archaic Greek silver coins. The techniques used are described, and the attainable accuracy of measurement of the lead isotope composition is discussed. Preliminary lead isotope measurements are given for archaic Greek silver coins from Aegina, Athens, Thasos, Acanthus, Mallus, Lydia, Lycia and the tribe of the Orrescioi, as well as for galena samples from Greece and Turkey. Some implications of the analysis are outlined." [V. Chamberlain and N. Gale, *NL* 108]

1498 **Cheng, C. F., and C. M. Schwitter.** "Nickel in Ancient Bronzes." *American Journal of Archaeology* 61, no. 4 (October 1957): 351-63. 2 pls.
The authors present a metallurgical analysis of ancient bronze alloys which shows that nickel is generally present only in trace amounts, if at all. However, a much higher nickel content is found in Bactrian coins minted ca. 170 B.C. The authors conclude this bronze was derived from the Hweili deposits of Sikang Province, China. [Also see Cammann "The Bactrian Nickel Theory" and Schwitter and Cheng "Bactrian Nickel" under BACTRIA].

1499 **Craddock, Paul T.** "Historical Survey of Gold Refining: 1. Surface Treatments and Refining Worldwide and in Europe Prior to A.D. 1500." *King Croesus' Gold: Excavation at Sardis and the History of Gold Refining*. Edited by A. Ramage and P. Craddock. Cambridge: Harvard University Press, 2000. Page 27-53.
Craddock examines the historical evidence for the refining of gold by cementation prior to the Renaissance. The complete separation of silver from gold was probably not practiced in antiquity prior to the Lydian period. [Also see Ramage and Craddock below].

1500 **Craddock, Paul T., Andrew M. Burnett, and K. Preston.** "Hellenistic Copper-base Coinage and the Origins of Brass." *Scientific Studies in Numismatics*. Edited by W. A. Oddy. British Museum Occasional Paper, No. 18. London: British Museum, 1979. Pages 53-64.

1501 **Cunningham, C. J. K.** "The Silver of Laurion." *Greece and Rome* 2nd ser., 14, no. 2 (October 1967): 145-56. 5 pls. [CS 3395]
Describes the mining area and tells the story of mining at Laurion, the famous silver mine of the Athenians. Describes the geology of the area, the tools of the miners, and the process of mining and refining the ore. [Also see Hopper "The Mines and Miners" below].

1502 **Das, H. A.** "Determination of the Gold Content of Electrum Coins via the Specific Gravity Method." *Jaarboek voor Munt-en Penningkunde* 49 (1962): 65-8. [CS 15918]

1503 **Das, H. A., and J. Zonderhuis.** "The Analysis of Electrum Coins." *Archaeometry* 7 (1964): 90-7. [CS 15919]
Discusses the application of the specific gravity method, X-ray fluorescence and X-ray diffraction, and non-destructive activation analysis for determining the composition of electrum coins. Describes the pros and cons of each technique.

1504 **Elam, C. F.** "An Investigation of the Microstructure of Fifteen Silver Greek Coins and Some Forgeries." *Journal of the Institute of Metals* 45 (1931): 57-69. 4 pls.
The text of a paper delivered at the Annual General Meeting of the Institute of Metals. The microstructure of fourteen genuine ancient Greek silver coins is described, together with that of four forgeries. The structure varied considerably, although coins from the same mint and period resembled each other. All the genuine coins showed evidence of striking between dies as opposed to the forgeries which, with one exception, were made by casting only. Analysis indicated that the coins were sometimes made from nearly pure silver, and sometimes copper was added. The forgeries contained copper and, in two cases, zinc. Illustrated by photomicrographs. Pages 66-9 consist of the text of the discussion which took place after Mr. Elam's presentation.

1505 **Evans, John.** "The Lydian Touchstone and Electrum Coins." *American Journal of Numismatics* 30, no. 4 (April 1896): 106.
Evans disputes William Ridgeway's theory that the ancient Greeks could determine the composition of a gold coin with great precision through the use of a touchstone. [Also see Ridgeway "How Far" below].

1506 **Gale, Noel H.** "Lead Isotopes and Archaic Greek Silver Coins." *Proceedings of the 18th International Symposium on Archaeometry and Archaeological Prospection, Bonn, 1978*. Archaeo-Physika 10. 1979. Pages 194-208.

1507 **Gale, Noel H., W. Gentner, and G. A. Wagner.** "Mineralogical and Geographical Silver Sources of Archaic Greek Coinage." *Metallurgy in Numismatics, Volume 1*. Edited by D. M. Metcalf and W. A. Oddy. Special Publication No. 13. London: Royal Numismatic Society, 1980. Pages 3-49. 1 pl.
An analysis of some of the Asyut hoard coins in an attempt to determine the mines which produced the silver for the various mints, and to gain knowledge about the technical methods then in use to produce pure silver for coinage. Examines ores from various regions and compares them with the metal from coins. Describes scientific methods used in the analysis. Presents tables of the percentage of metals found in the coins of various mints. Presents the conclusions for each mint studied including Athens, Aegina, Corinth, the tribe of the Orrescii, Thasos, Acanthus, Samos, Lesbos, Salamis, Lycia, and Mallus. The two chief sources of silver in the archaic period seem to have been Laurion and Siphnos. A third source may have been in Macedonia or Lydia. Few of the coins show evidence of silver from Spain. [Also see Price "The Uses of Metal Analysis" below].

1508 **Gentner, W., Otto Müller, G. A. Wagner, and Noel H. Gale.** "Silver Sources of Archaic Greek Coinage." *Die Naturwissenschaften* (Germany) 65 (May 1978): 273-84. Illus.
The authors report new chemical and lead isotopic results and interpretations of archaic Greek silver coins from the Asyut hoard which was buried ca. 475 B.C. Some of the silver sources in Greece were traced by the combination of analytical methods, and questions of provenance were solved. In addition, processes of silver smelting and refining were studied. The silver for all the Athenian coins analyzed, three of the Corinthian coins, and six of the Aeginetan coins was derived from Laurion. Several silver sources were used for Aeginetan coins. Besides Laurion, Ayso Sostis and other mines were indicated. Spanish silver was not used for any of the one-hundred coins tested. Despite claims that Spanish silver was important for Greek coins, there is no evidence for that statement.

1509 **Gilkes, Paul.** "Researchers Study First Gold Refinery: Clues Point to How Lydian King Croesus became Wealthy." *Coin World* (November 27, 2000): 74. Illus.
Reports that the Harvard-Cornell Sardis Expedition has unearthed evidence suggesting the world's first gold refinery and clues pointing to how Lydian King Croesus became prosperous with the production of the first pure gold and silver coins. The time of the refinery is placed between 561 and 547 B.C. Gilkes briefly describes the refining process that was used. [Also see Ramage and Craddock *King Croesus' Gold* below].

1510 **Gitler, Haim, Matthew J. Ponting, and Oren Tal.** "Metallurgical Analysis of Southern Palestinian Coins of the Persian Period." *Israel Numismatic Research* (Israel) 3 (2008): 13-27.
By means of inductively coupled plasma atomic emission spectrometry (ICP-AES), metallurgical analyses of southern Palestinian coins of the Persian period were performed. The main group of analyzed coins consists of dome-shaped quarter sheqels ("drachms"), which were struck from worn, recut and

repolished obverse dies that based on their circulation were defined as Edomite. In addition, several Philistian coins were analyzed as a reference group. The results suggest that much of the silver bullion used for striking the Edomite and Philistian coins originated in the Greek world, most probably from Athenian "owls" and that Edomite coinage was probably produced by a central Philistian minting authority based on identical silver content.

1511 **Glass, James C.** "Activation Analysis of Ancient Coins: A Review." *SAN—Journal of the Society for Ancient Numismatics* 12, no. 2 (summer 1981): 33-8.
Methods of non-destructive metallurgical analysis are described. Examples of the application of these techniques are discussed such as the determination of the source of metal for ancient mints. The author calls for further use of these techniques in numismatics.

1512 **Hall, E. T., and David M. Metcalf, eds.** *Methods of Chemical and Metallurgical Investigation of Ancient Coinage.* London: Royal Numismatic Society, 1972. 462 pp., 19 pls. [CS 15940 and 15966]
A collection of twenty-seven papers presented at a symposium held by the Royal Numismatic Society at Burlington House, London, in 1970. All are scientific in nature and focus on Roman and medieval coinage. Each deals with methods of analyzing the metal content of coins and the interpretation of the results. Also addresses the sources of metal supply and the detection of fakes. [Reviewed by David Sellwood in *Spink Numismatic Circular* 80, no. 12 (December 1972): 461-2, and by Harold Barker in *Numismatic Chronicle* 7th ser., 14 (1974): 224-6].

1513 **Head, Barclay V.** "Electrum Coins and Their Specific Gravity." *Numismatic Chronicle* 3rd ser., 7 (1887): 277-308. [CS 15943]
Presents tables of weights (minimum, maximum, and normal) for various electrum coins. Comments on mint attributions. Also includes tables showing the composition of the coins (percentages of gold, electrum, and bronze). [For a correction, see Head "Notanda Et Corrigenda" under ATTICA—NEW STYLE COINAGE. Also see Head "Metrological Notes" under METROLOGY and Head "On a Recent Find" under MYSIA—AUTONOMOUS CITIES].

1514 **Healy, John F.** "The Establishment of Die-sequences in Greek 'White Gold' and Electrum Coin Series." *Numismatic Chronicle* 7th ser., 11 (1971): 31-6.
"Relatively few die links are found in Greek 'white gold' and electrum series, which makes the establishment of sequences difficult. Specific gravity measurements may characterize groups of coins belonging to the same original ingot or melt, and make practical the comparative study of issues of Cyzicus with quadripartite incuse reverses. Illustrations of this new technique are drawn from the mint at Mytilene." [J. Healy, *NL* 87]

1515 ——— "Greek Refining Techniques and the Composition of Gold-Silver Alloys." *Revue Belge de Numismatique et de Sigillographie* (Belgium) 120 (1974): 19-33. [CS 3399]
"Present knowledge about the technology of the refining of gold and silver is discussed. Electrum is considered and results of metallic analysis are given." [P. Naster, *NL* 93]

1516 ——— *Mining and Metallurgy in the Greek and Roman World.* London: Thames & Hudson, 1978. 316 pp., illus., 2 maps. [CS 3400]
"A survey of mining and metallurgy in the context of economic geology and petrology is presented. The evidence is derived from literary and epigraphical sources, mining sites and associated archaeological remains, and from the scientific analysis of the extant metal objects themselves. Analytical data relating to the composition, physical properties and production of Greek and Roman coins are included in chapters on the manufacture of alloys and quality control (7), characterization of metals and alloys (8), and the effects of mechanical and thermal treatment (9). Examples of coins struck in the main metals and alloys available are illustrated in Chapter Ten." [J. Healy, *NL* 100]

1517 ——— "Greek White Gold and Electrum Coin Series." *Metallurgy in Numismatics, Volume 1.* Edited by D. M. Metcalf and W. A. Oddy. Special Publication No. 13. London: Royal Numismatic Society, 1980. Pages 194-215.
Defines white gold (natural and unrefined) and electrum (artificially produced alloy). Discusses the exact composition of coins struck in white gold and electrum, and the degree to which the Greeks could control the quality of their gold alloys. Describes analytical techniques. Presents a metallurgical analysis of electrum coins from various mints.

1518 **Hopper, R. J.** "The Mines and Miners of Ancient Athens." *Greece and Rome* 2nd ser., 8, no. 2 (October 1961): 138-51.
An account of the historical and economic background of the Laurion mining district of Greece. Describes the landscape. Discusses the history of the region, the administration of the mines, and working conditions in the mines. [Also see Cunningham "The Silver of Laurion" above].

1519 **Hunkin, J. W.** "Addendum on the Specific Gravity of Darics and Croesus Coins." *Numismatic Chronicle* 4th ser., 16 (1916): 257-9.
Lists the specific gravities of gold staters of Lydia and gold darics of Persia, as well as two Lydian silver coins.

1520 **Jones, John E.** "The Laurion Silver Mines: A Review of Recent Researches and Results." *Greece and Rome* 29, no. 2 (October 1982): 169-83. Illus.
A review of research on the Laurion mines published since 1962.

1521 **Keyser, Paul T.** "Greco-Roman Alchemy and Coins of Imitation Silver." *American Journal of Numismatics* 2nd ser., 7-8 (1995-6): 209-34. 5 pls.
An analysis of over 500 silver coins from the fifth century B.C. to the fourth century A.D. identified numerous coins of imitation silver. This evidence indicates that from Hellenistic times (at the very beginning of alchemy), the use of imitation silver was widespread and continued down to late antiquity. Keyser discusses the ancient methods of creating imitation silver. Lists the composition of seventeen imitation silver coins.

1522 **Keyser, Paul T., and David D. Cook.** "Analyzing and Interpreting the Metallurgy of Early Electrum Coins." *Hacksilber to Coinage: New Insights into the Monetary History of the Near East and Greece.* Numismatic Studies 24. New York: American Numismatic Society, 2001. Pages 105-26. Illus.
The authors explain the levels of other metals that are found in naturally occurring electrum to provide guidelines for determining whether a given sample of electrum has been refined or augmented with other metals. The metal content of numerous ancient objects and electrum coins are given in tables. The authors suggest that Lydian moneyers produced coins of electrum that they diluted with silver and hardened with copper. Any excess value was guaranteed by the state. They suggest that war caused states to over-value electrum by striking coins, because at its true market value, electrum's supply was insufficient to meet the states' demand for labor or other commodities, likely at a time of war. This hypothesis also explains

why the early Lydian electrum coins failed to enter foreign trade—their value was guaranteed only in a *politically isolated* state. It also explains why the coins were large denominations—war materiel would have been purchased wholesale, not retail.

1523 **Kneusel, Ronald T.** "EDXRF: Fun with Ancient Coins." *The Celator* 10, no. 7 (July 1996): 38-40. Illus.
Energy dispersive X-ray fluorescence is a non-destructive method for determining the elemental composition of a sample. The author explains the technique in easy-to-understand language, and describes its usefulness in numismatics. The X-ray spectra for six ancient coins, including a tetradrachm of Alexander the Great, are illustrated in graphs.

1524 **Kraay, Colin M.** "The Composition of Electrum Coinage." *Archaeometry* 1 (spring 1958): 21-3.
Presents the results of the analysis of fifty-six electrum coins to determine their gold, silver, and copper content. Includes coins of Ionia-uncertain, Lydia, Phocaea, Lesbos, and Cyzicus.

1525 ——— "Gold and Copper Traces in Early Greek Silver." Parts 1-2. *Archaeometry* 1 (spring 1958): 1-5; 2 (spring 1959): 1-16. [CS 3401]
The quantities of gold and copper present in groups of silver coins from a number of important Greek mints have been measured by the neutron activation method to discover whether significant differences in composition could be detected. Presents the findings for coins of Athens, Corinth, Akragas, Carthage, Gela, and Croton. The analytical methods used are described by Vera Emeleus on pages 6-15 of the 1958 issue. Part 2 presents the results of the analysis of many more coins including those of Athens, Aegina, Thasos, Macedonia, Thurium, Caulonia, Croton, Akragas, Gela, and Syracuse.

1526 **Kraay, Colin M., and Vera M. Emeleus.** *The Composition of Greek Silver Coins: Analysis by Neutron Activation.* Oxford: Ashmoleon Museum, 1962. 38 pp., 12 diagr. [CS 15952]
The authors analyzed 420 coins from thirteen mints to determine their copper and gold content. Silver from Laurium was traced in the fifth century coinage of Athens. And the silver used in the sixth century turtle coins of Aegina contains more gold than that from Laurium and probably came from Siphnos. [Reviewed by F. C. Thompson in *Spink Numismatic Circular* 71, no. 2 (February 1963): 29, and in *Numismatic Chronicle* 7th ser., 3 (1963): 281-3. Also reviewed by J. F. Healy in *Journal of Hellenic Studies* 84 (1964): 237-8].

1527 **LaNiece, Susan.** "Technology of Silver-Plated Coin Forgeries." *Metallurgy in Numismatics, Volume 3.* Edited by M. M. Archibald and M. R. Cowell. Special Publication No. 24. London: Royal Numismatic Society, 1993. Pages 227-36. 3 pls.
Discusses the main methods of silver plating a base metal to produce a false coinage for contemporary circulation.

1528 **Lewis, David M.** "New Evidence for the Gold-Silver Ratio." *Essays in Greek Coinage Presented to Stanley Robinson.* Edited by C. M. Kraay and G. K. Jenkins. Oxford: Clarendon Press, 1968. Pages 105-10. [CS 3340]
The author examines epigraphical evidence for the gold-to-silver ratio at Athens in the fifth and fourth centuries B.C. Cites evidence for a 14:1 ratio before the Peloponnesian War and a ratio of 11:1 in 402 B.C. The ratio increased in the 370's and was 12:1 at the beginning of the 360's. Philip of Macedon's use of a 10:1 ratio had not yet affected the price of gold at Athens in 354 B.C.

1529 **Madsen, Eardley.** "Concerning 'Lines' on Some Ancient Coins, Part 1." *SAN—Journal of the Society for Ancient Numismatics* 11, no. 3 (fall 1980): 44-5.
Examines the causes of fine lines found on coins, usually called flow-lines. Disputes the traditional explanation that these lines are caused by die wear. Suggests they are formed by a slight surface cooling on the planchets prior to striking, whereby tiny crystals of the metal have already started to form and are then lined-up in a radiating fashion as the metal is spread as it is forced into the die. [Also see "Part 2" below].

1530 ——— "Concerning 'Lines' on Some Ancient Coins, Part 2—A Technical Inquiry" *SAN—Journal of the Society for Ancient Numismatics* 11, no. 4 (winter 1980-1): 64-7.
A scientific analysis of the theory presented in "Part 1" (see above). Concludes that coin planchets cooled slightly when they came in contact with the dies, accounting for the lines on the coins. Suggests these lines formed when the planchets were struck at a temperature of 155-175° C. [Also see *SAN* 11, no. 4 (winter 1980-1): 74-5, for a critical response by Dean M. Ryder. Ryder disputes Madsen's theory that the lines are related to the temperature of the planchet. Argues that the lines are indeed "flow-lines" caused by the flow of metal outward as the coin is struck. In the same issue of *SAN* (pp. 75-6), Madsen responds, claiming his temperature related lines and Ryder's flow lines are two different things].

1531 ——— "Concerning Edge Cracks and Notches on Ancient Coins." *SAN—Journal of the Society for Ancient Numismatics* 12, no. 3 (fall 1981): 56-7.
The authors discuss the minting conditions which led to large V-shaped edge cracks on ancient coins. Specifies temperature ranges for cold-worked, warm-worked, and hot-worked silver. Suggests that large edge cracks resulted when impurities existed in the metal and coins were struck at very high temperatures.

1532 **Marotta, Michael E.** "Electrum." *The Celator* 17, no. 8 (August 2003): 25-31. Illus.
Discusses the metallurgical context and content of electrum. Describes the first electrum coins and the value relationship between electrum, gold, and silver. Briefly describes the electrum coins of Kyzikos, Mytilene, Phokaia, Lampsakos, Chios, Syracuse, and Carthage. Discusses the use of debased gold by the Celts, the Bosporus kings, and the Byzantine Empire. Also mentions the use of electrum in modern coinage.

1533 **Martin, J. P.** "Conducting Your Own Specific Gravity Tests." *The Numismatist* 105, no. 9 (September 1992): 1322-4. Illus.
Describes how to construct an apparatus for performing specific gravity tests using a simple scale. Provides the mathematical formula for calculating specific gravity from the observed dry and wet weights. Provides a table of specific gravities for various alloys commonly used in coinage.

1534 **Mellink, M. J.** "Archaeology in Asia Minor." *American Journal of Archaeology* 74 (1970): 157-78. 8 pls.
"On p. 172 it is noted that the Pactolus North area of the Sardis site shows evidence of gold refining as early as 580 B.C." [J. R. Jones, *NIAJAH*]

1535 **Milne, Joseph G.** "Comments on Corrosion of Ancient Coins." *Numismatic Review* 3, no. 3 (1946): 95. [CS 16100]
Discusses various forms of corrosion commonly occurring on coins which had been buried. Milne warns against placing too much reliance on the weights of such coins. The coin's weight may have changed due to internal corrosion which is not visible on the surface.

1536   **Moesta, Hasso, and Peter Robert Franke.** *Antike Metallurgie und Münzprägung: Ein Beitrag zur Technikgeschichte.* Basel: Birkhäuser Verlag, 1995. 184 pp., illus.
Ancient Metallurgy and Coinage: A Contribution to the History of Technology.

1537   **Mommsen, H., and T. Schmittinger.** "Test Analysis of Ancient Au and Ag Coins Using High Energy PIXE." *Archaeometry* 23, pt. 1 (1981): 71-6.
"The applicability of the high-energy PIXE method for nondestructive quantitative analysis without the use of standards is shown in a comparative analysis of three gold coins and two silver coins. The gold coins are of various provenance; the silver coins are from Athens and belong to the Asyut hoard. The aim of this test is to show that the PIXE method can give satisfactory results in a short time, even if applied in a very simple and straightforward way." [Mommsen and Schmittinger, *NL* 106]

1538   **Oddy, W. A., and Michael R. Cowell.** "The Technology of Gilded Coin Forgeries." *Metallurgy in Numismatics, Volume 3.* Edited by M. M. Archibald and M. R. Cowell. Special Publication No. 24. London: Royal Numismatic Society, 1993. Pages 199-221. 5 pls.
Describes various methods which may have been used to produce contemporary forgeries of gold coins by gilding base metal. Several of the methods may have been used in antiquity.

1539   **Oikonomides, Al N.** "Greek Geologists Rediscover Gold, Silver Mines of Ancient Macedonia." *Coin World* (May 31, 1967): 28. Illus., map.
The National Institute of Geology and Prospecting in Athens released some of the results from their searches for mineral ores in northern Greece. The most important site is at Angistron, near the Bulgarian border. In Angistron, geologists rediscovered one of the gold and silver mines of the ancient Macedonian kings. The discovery verifies the opinions of some late nineteenth century numismatists who believed that the great output of gold and silver coins by Philip II was due to his systematic prospecting to increase the output of base and precious metals in his territories. The reign of Philippus Andriscus (149 B.C.) marks the last period of strong activity for the Macedonian mines and mints. The author discusses the various periods that the mines were in use from the time of Philip II (359 B.C.) through the thirteenth century A.D.—the last period in which the reactivation of the mines in Macedonia can be assumed.

1540   **Pászthory, Emmerich.** "Investigations of the Early Electrum Coins of the Alyattes Type." *Metallurgy in Numismatics, Volume 1.* Edited by D. M. Metcalf and W. A. Oddy. Special Publication No. 13. London: Royal Numismatic Society, 1980. Pages 151-6. 6 pls.
An investigation of the electrum coinage of Lydia with a lion's head on the obverse and an incuse punch on the reverse. Shows that metallurgical analysis can provide information on the method of production and the dating of these coins. The flans were cast and were struck cold without any annealing. They were struck from a natural alloy. Pászthory also examines a plated coin and determines the technology used in its plating.

1541   **Price, M. Jessop.** "The Uses of Metal Analysis in the Study of Archaic Greek Coinage: Some Comments." *Metallurgy in Numismatics, Volume 1.* Edited by D. M. Metcalf and W. A. Oddy. Special Publication No. 13. London: Royal Numismatic Society, 1980. Pages 50-4.
A follow-up to Gale, Gentner and Wagner (see above). The author comments on the mixing of silver from various sources and intentional debasement. Calls for greater metallurgical analysis of museum collections.

1542   **Ramage, Andrew.** "Gold Refining in the Time of the Lydian Kings at Sardis." *Proceedings of the 10th International Congress of Classical Archaeology, Ankara-Izmir 23-30/IX/1973.* Edited by E. Akurgal. Ankara, 1978.

1543   **Ramage, Andrew, and Paul T. Craddock, eds.** *King Croesus' Gold: Excavation at Sardis and the History of Gold Refining.* Cambridge: Harvard University Press, 2000. 264 pp., illus.
The Harvard-Cornell Sardis Expedition has unearthed a gold refinery from the time of King Croesus (the sixth-century B.C.) where impure gold from the Pactolus River was treated to produce pure gold and silver. This volume illuminates the industry and technology that produced the riches and offers an authoritative survey of early gold refining and assaying techniques from around the world. The authors fully describe the excavation of the only known ancient refinery and the scientific study at the British Museum to reconstruct the refining process. The unique evidence from Sardis and accounts from historical sources shed light on ancient metallurgy. [Reviewed by Kenneth Sheedy in *Numismatic Chronicle* 162 (2002): 424-8. Also see Gilkes "Researchers Study First Gold Refinery" above, Craddock "Historical Survey" above, Cowell and Hyne "Scientific Examination" under LYDIA, and Ramage "Golden Sardis" under LYDIA].

1544   ——— "The Significance of the Sardis Refinery in the Classical World." *King Croesus' Gold: Excavation at Sardis and the History of Gold Refining.* Edited by A. Ramage and P. Craddock. Cambridge: Harvard University Press, 2000. Page 212-4.
The authors believe that the Sardis refinery may be the very first gold refinery in the world. The smiths lacked the technology to raise the gold content of the metal found in the Pactolos river. Thus, they were forced to reduce it to a constant composition for use in coinage. But within a short time, the chemistry of surface enrichment was applied to the total removal of the silver throughout the gold. The salt cementation process remained the usual method of gold refining for the next two millennia. [Also see Ramage and Craddock above, and Ramage "Golden Sardis" under LYDIA].

1545   **Ridgeway, William.** "How Far Could the Greeks Determine the Fineness of Gold and Silver Coins? *Numismatic Chronicle* 3rd ser., 15 (1895): 104-9.
Ridgeway quotes a passage from Theophrastus on the use of touchstones for testing gold and silver. Comments on Greek weights and the fineness of coins. Suggests the Greeks were capable of great precision in refining. He contends that the fluctuation in the silver and electrum standards were caused not only by the fluctuation in the values of the precious metals, but also by the quality of the metal put into the coins. [Also see Evans "The Lydian Touchstone" above].

1546   **Schubiger, P. A., and Otto Müller.** "Trace Elements in Ancient Silver Coins by Neutron Activation and Solvent Extraction with Bismuth Diethyldithiocarbamate." *Radiochemical and Radioanalytical Letters* (Lausanne, Budapest) 24, nos. 5-6 (1976): 353-62. Illus.
"A method was developed for the determination of trace elements in ancient Greek silver coins. Shavings from a coin are irradiated with thermal neutrons and then dissolved in acid. Treatment with bismuth diethyldithiocarbamate in chloroform solution results in the extraction of the strong silver, copper and gold radioactivity into the organic phase, thus allowing the determination of the weak activities due to sodium, manganese, cobalt, nickel, arsenic, tin, antimony and iridium, which remain in the aqueous phase." [R. McDowell, *NL* 100]

1547 **Schubiger, P. A., Otto Müller, and W. Gentner.** "Neutron Activation Analysis on Ancient Greek Silver Coins and Related Materials." *Journal of Radioanalytical Chemistry* (Lausanne, Budapest) 39, nos. 1-2 (1977): 99-112. Illus. [CS 15985]
"An analytical scheme is developed using neutron activation for copper and gold, atomic absorption spectroscopy for lead and bismuth, and solvent extraction for other trace elements. Sixty-six silver coins from the Asyut hoard, buried ca. 475 B.C. are analyzed. Gold is homogeneously distributed in the coins, but copper varies widely, even on the scale of an electron microprobe. The significance of the trace elements in understanding the technology of ancient silver smelting is discussed, and cluster analysis is used to identify groups of coins that originate from different parent ores." [R. McDowell, *NL* 100]

1548 ———. "Chemical Studies of Greek Silver Coins from the Asyut Hoard." *Proceedings of the Sixteenth International Symposium on Archaeometry and Archaeological Prospection, Edinburgh 1976.* Edinburgh: National Museum of Antiquities of Scotland, 1980. Pages 164-76. Illus.
"Archaic Greek silver coins from the Asyut hoard, buried about 475 B.C., have been analyzed for their minor and trace-element contents. To analyze the trace elements it was necessary to apply a radiochemical separation procedure, namely an application of solvent extraction technique with bismuth diethyldithiocarbamate. Results and statistical interpretations for coins from Aegina, Acanthus, Athens, Mallos, Messina, Orreskioi, Samos, Sikloi, and Thasos are given." [Schubiger, Müller, and Gentner, *NL* 108]

1549 **Smekalova, Tatyana N., and Jurij L. Djukov.** "The Composition of the Alloy of Cyzicene Electrum Coins." *Revue Belge de Numismatique* (Belgium) 145 (1999): 21-36.

1550 **Stos-Gale, Zofia.** "The Impact of the Natural Sciences on Studies of *Hacksilber* and Early Silver Coinage." *Hacksilber to Coinage: New Insights into the Monetary History of the Near East and Greece.* Numismatic Studies 24. New York: American Numismatic Society, 2001. Pages 53-76.
The author discusses a database of diagnostic lead isotope "fingerprints" of metal-bearing ores from different mineral deposits, which can be compared with those of ancient metals ("lead isotope provenance technique"). Provides an overview of the methodology. Provides an analysis of silver pieces from Tel Miqne-Ekron and the Shechem Hoard (found north of Jerusalem) and coins from the Selinus Hoard (found in Sicily). The analysis shows that the silver came from three regions: the Aegean, Spain, and Iran.

1551 **Thompson, F. C.** "Sources of Metal Used for Ancient Coins." *Cunobelin* (England) 14 (1968): 27-32. Illus. [CS 15815]

1552 **Thompson, F. C., and A. K. Chatterjee.** "Ancient Greek Plated Coins." *Nature* 168 (1951): 158. Illus.
An examination of a plated didrachm of Neapolis (ca. 300 B.C.) provides proof of the use of silver solder in the production of plated coins at this early date.

1553 **Thompson, Margaret.** "Gold and Copper Traces in Late Athenian Silver." *Archaeometry* 3 (1960): 10-5. [CS 3404]
Eighty-six New Style Athenian tetradrachms were analyzed by the neutron activation method to determine the amounts of gold and copper present. The objectives were: (1) to see if variations in content had any chronological significance, (2) to authenticate some suspect coins, (3) to explore the possible relationship between metallic composition and the series of control marks found on the coins, and (4) to compare the composition of these late period coins to earlier Athenian coins previously examined by Kraay (see Kraay "Gold and Copper Traces" above). Concludes there is no clear pattern of consistent changes in gold or copper content in line with the chronological evolution of the coinage. There is also no evidence for a correlation between metallic composition and the control mark combinations found on the coins. Suggests that beginning ca. 130 B.C., Athens' silver supply was being supplemented from sources other than Laurium.

1554 **Varoufakis, George J.** "Quality Control of Silver Coins in Antiquity." *Metallurgy in Numismatics, Volume 4.* Special Publication No. 30. London: Royal Numismatic Society, 1998. Pages 208-22. Illus.
An Athenian law inscribed on a marble stele, dating to the beginning of the fourth century B.C., refers to the quality control of Athenian silver coins. This paper describes the empirical methods that could have been applied at that time for testing silver coins, and emphasizes that standardization, testing, and certification for many products (e.g., metals, alloys, wine, olive oil, wheat, barley, and other agricultural products) was extensively applied in antiquity.

1555 **Weber, Charles E.** "Gravimetric Characteristics of Greek Silver Coins: A Survey." *The Numismatist* 92, no. 5 (May 1979): 971-7.
An overview of the importance of specific gravity measurements in the study of ancient coinage. Specific gravity measurements are essential for determining the fineness or metal content of a coin. Presents a table of specific gravities for 143 Greek silver coins. Includes cross-references to pages in Head's *Historia Numorum*.

1556 ———. "Questions Pertaining to Greek Silver Coins with Low Specific Gravities." *The Celator* 12, no. 12 (December 1998): 36-42. Illus.
Discusses the importance of specific gravity measurements in ancient numismatics. Provides specific gravity measurements for twenty-two Greek coins from the author's collection. Comments on the reasons for the low specific gravities observed. Many of the coins are plated or have suffered surface corrosion. Also includes a table listing fifteen Greek coins with unusually high specific gravities.

1557 **Yao, T. C., and F. H. Stross.** "The Use of Analysis by X-ray Fluorescence in the Study of Coins." *American Journal of Archaeology* 69 (1965): 154-6.
"Three New Style Attic tetradrachms are analysed for silver, copper and lead." [J. R. Jones, *NIAJAH*]

Also see: Allin and Wallace "Impurities in Euboean Monetary Silver" under CENTRAL GREECE—EUBOIA; Aoki "An Analysis" under EGYPT—PTOLEMAIC KINGDOM; Attas "Tarentine Didrachmas" under ITALY—TARAS; Balmuth *Hacksilber to Coinage* under ORIGINS OF COINAGE; Beaumont "Greek Influence" under NORTHERN GREECE—ILLYRIA; Burnett and Hook "The Fineness of Silver Coins" under ITALY—GENERAL WORKS; Caley "Abnormally Low Weight" under METROLOGY; Caley *Chemical Composition* under PARTHIA; Calliari and Vismara "Archaic Coinage of Lycia" under LYCIA; Cammann "The Bactrian Nickel Theory" under BACTRIA; Campbell *Plated Coins* under THE MINTING PROCESS; Carradice and LaNiece "The Libyan War" under ZEUGITANA; Case "Nickel-Containing Coins" under BACTRIA; Clain-Stefanelli "An Application of Physics" under COUNTERFEITS; Conn "Prevalence and Profitability: Re-Examining" under COUNTERFEITS; Conophagos, Badecca, and Tsaimou "La Technique Athenienne" under THE MINTING PROCESS; Cowell and Hyne "Scientific Examination" under LYDIA; Cowell et al. "Analyses" under LYDIA; Cowell and Hyne "Scientific Examination" under LYDIA; Craddock and Burnett "Composition of Etruscan" under ITALY—ETRURIA.

Elayi, Barrandon, and Elayi "The Devaluation of Sidonian Silver" under Phoenicia; Elayi, Barrandon, and Elayi "The Change of Standard of Tyrian Silver" under Phoenicia; Flament, Lateano, and Demortier *Quantitative Analysis of Athenian Coinage* under Attica; Flegler's entries on the Black Sea Hoard under Hoards; Flight "On the Chemical Composition" under Bactria; Gebhard et al. "Melting and Alloying" under Celtic Coinage of Europe; Giedroyc's entries on the Black Sea Hoard under Hoards; Gordus "Non-Destructive Analysis" under Parthia; Grave and Potts "A Trial PIXE/PIGME Analysis" under Arabia; Hardwick et al. "Lead Isotope Analysis" under Ionia; Hazzard "The Composition" under Egypt—Ptolemaic Kingdom; Hazzard and Brown "Silver Standard" under Egypt—Ptolemaic Kingdom; Healy "The Composition" under Lesbos; Hill *A Handbook* under General Works—Greek; Hoge "Original Nickel" under Bactria; International Nickel Company "Nickel" under Bactria; Kallithrakas-Kontos et al. "Composition and Provenance" under Macedonian Kingdom—General Works; Keall "Osroes" and "Parthian Nippur" under Parthia; Krupp "Metallurgical Examination" under Palestine—Judea; Lewis "Analysis" under Zeugitana; Lykiardopoulou-Petrou and Economou "The Debased Silver Coins" under Macedonian Kingdom—General Works.

Milne "An Elymaic Hoard" under Elymais; Moss "Nickel Alloy" under Bactria; Müller and Gentner "Composition and Silver Sources" under Aegina; Nadooshan et al. "Impact" under Parthia; Ponting, Gitler and Tal "Who Minted Those Owls?" under Attica; Prakash and Singh *Coinage in Ancient India* under Northwest India; Ramage "Golden Sardis" under Lydia; Rives "Parthian Drachm Coin Measurements" under Parthia; Saryan "Recent Chemical Studies" under Armenia; Schmitt-Korte and Cowell "The Silver Content" (two articles) under Arabia; Schwitter and Cheng "Bactrian Nickel" under Bactria; Steffgen et al. "Platinum Group" under Celtic Coinage—General Works; Svoronos "A Die of an Athenian Tetradrachm" under The Minting Process; van Alfen "Early Electrum Project" under Origins of Coinage; R. W. Wallace "Remarks on the Value and Standards" under Metrology; Warren "The Silver Coins of Sikyon" under Peloponnesos—Sikyon; Weier-Krystallis et al. "X-Ray Analysis" (two items) under Northern Greece—Thessaly; Wells' articles on plated coins under The Minting Process and under Macedonian Kingdom—General Works.

METROLOGY

This, taken in connection with the fact that in Homer, although silver is known, the weighing of metals is confined to gold, leads us irresistibly to conclude that gold was the first of all substances to be weighed, or, to put it in a different way, the art of weighing was invented for gold.

—William Ridgeway, 1892

1558   **Arbuthnot, Charles.** *Tables of Ancient Coins, Weights and Measures, Explain'd and Exemplify'd in Several Dissertations.* London, 1705. Second edition, London: J. Tonson, 1727. 327 pp., 34 tables. New edition, London, 1854.
Begins with a review of theories regarding who invented money. Discusses the metals used for money. Then reviews the Roman, Greek, and Jewish coin denominations. Discusses the gold-to-silver value ratio in ancient times; Roman, Greek, and Arabic weights; and measures of length and capacity. Includes an extensive examination of the prices of Roman goods and rates of pay in Roman times. Lists the doses of medicines given by ancient physicians. Discusses the history of navigation and trade. The author then lists the types found on coins of the major Greek cities. He then compares the wealth of the Romans to the wealth of the Greeks. Comments on the charging of interest in ancient times. This is followed by numerous tables of weights, measures, and coin denominations.

1559   **Brandis, Johannes.** *Das Nünz-, Mass- und Gewichtswesen in Vorderasien bis auf Alexander den Grossen.* Berlin, 1866. 622 pp. Reprint, Amsterdam: Adolf Mittakkert, 1966. 624 pp. [CS 3325]

1560   **Caley, Earle R.** "On the Occurrence of Abnormally Low Weight and Specific Gravity in Ancient Coins." *Numismatic Review* 3, no. 2 (April 1946): 51-3. [CS 15886]
The author examines coins which are of normal size, but are significantly low in weight and specific gravity. The authenticity of the coins is not in question. He concludes that the coins were originally of full weight and proper specific gravity, that they became extensively corroded internally in the course of long burial in the ground, and that on being cleaned thoroughly by some chemical or electrolytic method the intergranular corrosion products were largely dissolved out, thus leaving behind coins composed of spongy metal abnormally low in weight and specific gravity. Caley warns that the weights of cleaned ancient silver coins of low fineness, which were originally much corroded, should be used with caution in any studies of the ranges in weight of such coins.

1561   ——— *Metrological Tables.* Numismatic Notes and Monographs, No. 54. New York: American Numismatic Society, 1965. 119 pp., 2 pls. [CS 296]
A series of conversion tables which permit the user to convert from one weight or measurement system to another. Weights include grains, grams, and scruples. Diameters include inches, millimeters, and Mionnet's scale.

1562   **Cope, Stephen N.** "The Statistical Analysis of Coin Weights by Computer and a Rationalized Method for Producing Histograms." *Numismatic Chronicle* 140 (1980): 178-84. [CS 15916 and 16972]
Provides statistical formulas for standard deviation, coefficient of variance, and other measures used in analyzing coin weights. Discusses the use of histograms and the advantages of using computers in preparing them. [Corrections to some of the formulas on pages 178-9 appear in *Numismatic Chronicle* 141 (1981): 175].

1563   "Cow-Money and Staters." *American Journal of Numismatics* 30, no. 2 (October 1895): 63-6.
Comments on some of the statements made by Prentiss Cummings (see Cummings "Homer and Astronomic Coin-Types" under TYPES), primarily the assertion that the "unit of value of the ancient world was the cow and the ox." [Also see Ridgeway "The Homeric Talent" below].

1564   **Daehn, William E.** "Contradictory Theories: Making Sense of Greek Coin Weight Standards." *The Celator* 5, no. 8 (August 1991): 28-33.
The theories of Head, Ridgeway, and Gardner for the origin of weight standards for ancient Greek coins are presented. Frequency tables are then used to demonstrate how standard weights can be determined, and factors which contribute to variations in observed weights are discussed.

1565   **Déchelette, Joseph.** "Les Origines de la Drachme et de l'Obole." *Revue Numismatique* (France) (1911). Reprint, Paris, 1911. [CS 3328]
[Also see next item].

1566   ——— "The Origins of the Drachm and Obolus." *American Journal of Numismatics* 46, no. 1 (January 1912): 27-32; no. 2 (April 1912): 50-6.
A condensed translation of the work published in *Revue Numismatique* (Paris, 1911). The author discusses the origin of the drachm—a group of six iron roasting spits. Discusses the history of the use of spits as money and the related chronology. In Part 2, Déchelette examines the "Charon's obol" and the

related funeral rite in which a coin was placed into the mouth of the deceased. [Also see "Curious Ancient Gold Coin" under General Works—Greek and Kroll "Observations on Monetary Instruments" under Origins of Coinage].

1567 **Doyen, Charles.** "Triobole Éginétique Réduit ou Drachme Symmachique?" *Revue Belge de Numismatique et de Sigillographie* (Belgium) 151 (2005): 39-48.

1568 **Elsen, Jean.** "Le Grain d'Orge et le Système Pondéral et Monétaire Attique." *Jean Elsen Liste* 218 (October-November 2001): 1-34.
It is known that Mesopotamian weight systems were based on the weight of barley grains. Elsen discusses whether the Greek weight systems were based on the mass of barley grains, primarily through an examination of the Attic monetary weight system. Begins with a discussion of the cultivation and diffusion of barley in the Aegean world. Concludes that the Attic system was based on the weight of the most coarse barley grain.

1569 **Evans, Arthur J.** "Minoan Weights and Mediums of Currency from Crete, Mycene and Cyprus." *Corolla Numismatica: Numismatic Essays in Honour of Barclay V. Head.* Edited by G. F. Hill. London: Oxford University Press, 1906. Pages 336-67. Illus. [CS 1478]
(1) Mentions the Minoan origins of certain aspects of Greek culture. Mentions gold rings from Mycenae which suggest a Mycenaean weight standard. Evans suggests an Egyptian origin for the standard. (2) Discusses the early weight systems of Egypt. (3) Discusses weights of Minoan Crete and Cyprus. Illustrates a variety of stone and bronze weights found at Knossos and other sites in Crete. Suggests what their original weights were. (4) Evans states that, in addition to the actual weights, there is evidence of several classes of metallic units used as mediums of exchange—suggesting the beginning of a true currency. These units fall into four classes: rings and bars of gold, gold ox-heads, bronze ingots, and dumps of precious metal. The precious metal "dumps," the immediate antecedent stage to coined money, can be dated no later than the twelfth century b.c.

1570 **Giesecke, Walther.** *Antike Geldwesen.* Leipzig: K. W. Hiersemann, 1938. 255 pp., 6 pls. [CS 3330]

1571 **Grierson, Philip.** "Coin Wear and the Frequency Table." *Numismatic Chronicle* 7th ser., 3 (1963): 1-16. [CS 16975]
Problems encountered in determining the original, theoretical weights of worn coins are dealt with, and an explanation is given of the statistical methods used to determine such weights. A review of previous studies on coin wear brings to light a number of other factors (apart from abrasion and corrosion) which must be taken into account. They include the metal or alloy of which the coin is composed, and its denomination (lower denominations, for example, usually show more wear than higher ones). The author warns against over-zealous attempts at statistical preciseness, pointing out that final conclusions must necessarily be adjusted in accordance with the above variables and the object sought. Concludes with a brief discussion of the weight corrections or adjustments to be made in practice, and the justification for "rounding off" the results obtained. [Summarized from F. Campbell, *NL* 75]

1572 **Head, Barclay V.** "Metrological Notes on the Ancient Electrum Coins Struck between the Lelantian Wars and the Accession of Darius." *Numismatic Chronicle* new ser., 15 (1875): 245-97. 4 pls.
Discusses the origin and development of the Greek weight systems. Discusses the derivation of the Greek standards from the Babylonian mina. Includes a detailed discussion of electrum coinage, listing and describing coins struck on each standard. [Also see Head "Electrum Coins" under Metallurgy and "On a Recent Find of Staters of Cyzicus" under Mysia—Autonomous Cities].

1573 ——— "Origin and Transmission of Some of the Principal Ancient Systems of Weight as Applied to Money, from the Earliest Times down to the Age of Alexander the Great." *Journal of the Institute of Bankers* 1 (1879-80): 167-200.
The text of a paper read before the Banker's Institute on November 28, 1879. Head provides a history of systems of weights and measures. Discusses the Babylonian talents, minae, and sixtieth parts, the use of precious metals, the first use of coined money at Lydia, the weight standard at Lydia, the use of gold, electrum, and silver and their relationships to each other, the transmission of weight standards to other cities, and the introduction of bimetallism. Various weight standards and the weights of various coin denominations are summarized in a table. Pages 189-200, "Discussion on Mr. Barclay Head's Paper," consists of comments and questions from the listeners, along with Head's responses. Many of the questions focus on the issue of bimetallism vs. mono-metallism, a topic of great interest at the time.

1574 **Hemmy, A. S.** "The Weight-Standards of Ancient Greece and Persia." *Iraq* 5, pt. 1 (spring 1938): 65-81.
Endeavors to draw conclusions from observed data as to the average loss of weight of worn coins so that statistical methods can be applied. A formula is then obtained connecting the original standard weight of a given series of coins with the mode derived from a statistical investigation. Examines gold and silver coins of the period from Croesus through Alexander III. Attempts to determine standard weights for coins of Lydia, Persia, Aegina, Athens, and Macedonia.

1575 **Hendin, David.** "Israelite Shekel Weights." *The Celator* 15, no. 5 (May 2001): 46-7. Illus.
Discusses the origin of the shekel weight and describes how stone weights were used.

1576 ——— "Ancient Currency and Ancient Scale Weights." *The Celator* 20, no. 2 (February 2006): 42-3. Illus.
A brief discussion of the use of scale weights in the ancient Holy Land.

1577 ——— *Ancient Scale Weights and Pre-Coinage Currency of the Near East.* New York: Amphora Books, 2007. 237 pp., illus.
A fully illustrated catalogue of 460 weights and items of pre-coinage currency made of stone, metal, or glass, and primarily from Hendin's collection. The weights date from the fourteenth century b.c. to the twelfth century a.d. Most were acquired in the Holy Land. Includes an introduction to the use of scales and weights in the Near East, the nature of a barter economy, and prices and goods. The weight systems discussed include those of the Egyptian, Ugaritic, Hittite, Babylonian, Judean, Greek, Roman, Byzantine, and Islamic civilizations. Includes numerous weight tables. Foreword by Shraga Qedar. [Reviewed by Oliver Hoover in *ANS Magazine* 6, no. 2 (summer 2007): 62-5, and by David Vagi in *The Celator* 21, no. 7 (July 2007): 38-9].

1578 ——— "The Beginning of Weighing in Commerce." *The Celator* 21, no. 5 (May 2007): 42-3. Illus.
Summarizes the early history of weighing to facilitate commerce.

1579 **Hildebrandt, Han Joachim.** "Standard Weight of Ancient Coins—The Exact Calculation." *Jahrbuch für Numismatik und Geldgeschichte* (Germany) 47 (1997): 7-12.

"The method of calculating the standard weights of coins struck *al marco* and *al pezzo* is explained, using as examples the silver coinage of Syracuse and the bronze coinage of Rome." [G. Stumpf, *NL* 142]

1580 **Hill, George F.** *Grains and Grammes: A Table of Equivalents for the Use of Numismatists.* London: British Museum, 1920. 35 pp.
These tables provide gram equivalents of weights from 1/10 grain to 350 grains by 1/10 grain increments, and then to 400 grains by one grain increments, and from 400 to 500 by 10 grain increments.

1581 ——— "The Frequency-Table." *Numismatic Chronicle* 5th ser., 4 (1924): 76-85. [CS 3331]
Describes a method of determining the standard weight of a coinage issue by plotting the weights of individual specimens on a chart, showing the frequency of occurrence of each weight. The most commonly occurring weight is assumed to be the standard weight. Explains the advantages of this method over the calculation of a simple average weight, including the identification of the use of multiple weight standards.

1582 **Hultsch, Friedrich Otto.** *Griechische und Römische Metrologie.* Second edition. Berlin, 1882. Reprint, Graz, 1971. 762 pp. [CS 3334]

1583 ——— *Die Gewichte des Altertums nach ihrem Zusammenhang Dargestellt.* Leipzig, 1898. 205 pp. [CS 3335]

1584 **Hussey, Robert.** *An Essay on the Ancient Weights and Money, and the Roman and Greek Liquid Measures, with an Appendix on the Roman and Greek Foot.* Oxford: S. Collingwood, 1836. 254 pp.
A brief history of the study of weights and measures of Greece and Rome and the scholars who have studied the subject. Discusses the origin of Greek weight standards, describes the various coin weight standards of the Greek cities. Discusses weights and standards of the Romans. Also describes liquid measures. An appendix covers the Greek and Roman foot with a table of length measurements compared to yards, feet, and inches.

1585 **Jones, John R. Melville.** "The Value of Gold at Athens in 329/8 B.C." *American Journal of Ancient History* (Cambridge, Mass.) 3 (1978): 184-7.
"An inscription from Eleusis listing coins offered at the sanctuary provides an equation which shows that at this date the value of gold had dropped to 9 ½:1 in terms of silver." [J. Melville Jones, *NL* 106]

1586 ——— "The Value of Electrum in Greece and Asia." *Studies in Greek Numismatics in Memory of Martin Jessop Price.* Edited by Richard Ashton and Silvia Hurter. London: Spink, 1998. Pages 259-68.
The author explores the value of electrum coins in relation to gold and silver coins. Two possibilities exist: either the relationship was one which allowed of easy exchange between coins in the three metals, or the silver coins could not be simply exchanged for gold or electrum, but formed to some extent a separate currency. The author suggests that a relationship between gold and electrum of 12:9, and between electrum and silver of 9:1 is the only one which fits the weights of the coins and allows for the possibility that although the supply of silver had increased, it was still more valuable than it became a few years later. Discusses Herodotus' use of a 13:1 conversion ratio of silver to gold. Discusses the electrum staters of Lampsacus and determines they were valued at one-half a gold stater. Discusses the relative value of the electrum and gold coins of Lydia. Electrum may have been considerably less valuable in Greece than in Asia. Discusses the value of the electrum Cyzicene stater in relationship to the Persian gold daric. Continues with a review of the coinages of the Black Sea area. Concludes that electrum coinage which was produced at certain mints in Asia from the sixth century onwards was given an artificially high value in relation to pure gold and pure silver in areas over which the minting authorities had control, or where such a valuation was acceptable for traditional reasons. In Greece, electrum coins were given a lower value. This might also happen in Asia, if a city wished to benefit from issuing its own coinage.

1587 ——— "Coins as Weights in the Temple Records of Didyma." *Numismatic Archaeology/Archaeological Numismatics: Proceedings of an International Conference held to Honour Dr. Mando Oeconomides in Athens 1995.* Oxbow Monographs 75. Edited by K. Sheedy and C. Papageorgiadou-Banis. Oxford: Oxbow Books and The Australian Archaeological Institute at Athens, 1997. Pages 57-69.
The inscriptions which list some of the objects of value that were stored in the temple of Apollo at Didyma in the third and second centuries B.C. do not mention individual coins. But the weights of other valuable objects were expressed in terms of coinage, often in terms of drachmas and obols of Alexander coinage. The weights of gold objects were expressed in *chrysoi* or gold coins. The author discusses the weight standards employed in the inventories and discusses the dates of the inscriptions which mention coins. In the inventories from Didyma, the Attic/Alexander weight standard is one of the most frequently employed standards. Three others are used: the Milesian, two kinds of Rhodian, and the "symmachic" standard. The term "symmachic" implies that the coins were connected with a symmachy, or military alliance. The author concludes that the symmachic coins were minted at Miletos, Samos, and Carystos, and the minting was connected to Ptolemaeus' campaign in Greece in 313/2 B.C. Also discusses the chronology of the Rhodian plinthophoroi.

1588 **Kraay, Colin M.** "On the Weights of Ancient Coins." *Spink Numismatic Circular* 71, no. 6 (June 1963): 116. [CS 16040]
Twenty-one tetradrachms of Alexander the Great from three successive issues of the mint of Alexandria, all in mint condition and uncorroded, were weighed. Over 60% of the coins clustered around 17.21-17.22 grams, and the rest were not far off. This indicates a very accurate weighing of the flans. Not all Greek mints attained or maintained such a degree of accuracy, although they were technically capable of doing so if required. [Summarized from *NL* 67]

1589 **Kritt, Brian.** "Authenticating Ancients." *Numismatist* 117, no. 11 (November 2004): 105-6. Illus.
Points out that knowledge of weight standards can be important in determining the authenticity of ancient coins. Describes a few of the main Greek weight standards. Standards are summarized in a table.

1590 **Kroll, John H.** "Three Inscribed Greek Bronze Weights." *Studies Presented to George M. A. Hanfmann.* Fogg Art Museum Monographs in Art and Archaeology, No. 2. Cambridge: Fogg Art Museum, 1971. Pages 87-93. 1 pl.
Examines two bronze weights made for use in Athens in the fourth century B.C. One is a ¼ mina weight, bearing a symbol of a half-tortoise and the inscription ΔHMO indicating it is a public weight. Another inscription gives the weight of the object in silver coin. A counterstamp reproduces the reverse type of the Athenian triobol coins. Concludes bronze was the material used for the official standard weights against which all other weights in the city were checked. Also discusses the dating of a third weight, with a facing bull and an inscription, probably from Phokis.

1591 **Lang, Mabel.** "Five Hellenistic Lead Weights." *Museum Notes* 14 (1968): 1-3. 2 pls. [CS 16041]

Describes five lead weights ranging from 180 grains to 1057 grains bearing various designs including Herakles, Apollo, a lion, an anchor, and an elephant. These are identified as mna or half-mna weights on various standards. Compares them to coin types of Cos, Caria, Smyrna, and Syria. The weights may date from the first to the fourth centuries B.C.

1592 **Lang, Mabel, and Margaret Crosby.** *The Athenian Agora, Volume 10: Weights, Measures and Tokens.* Princeton: The American School of Classical Studies at Athens, 1964. 146 pp., 36 pls. [CS 16042]
Presents the metrological material found during the excavations conducted by the American School of Classical Studies at Athens. Part 1, "Weights and Measures" written by Lang, describes bronze, lead, and stone weights. General discussions of each are followed by a catalogue of the objects. Discusses weight standards and changes in standards. Part 2, "Lead and Clay Tokens" written by Crosby, suggests the tokens were used as entrance tickets to festivals, or as evidence of attendance at the assembly or law courts, or were used during the occasional free distribution of wheat. Concludes with a catalogue of the objects.

1593 **Leake, William Martin.** "Weights of Greek Coins." *Numismatic Chronicle* 17 (1855): 201-14.
Explores theories for the origin of Greek weight standards and the motives behind Solon's change in the weight of the drachma.

1594 **Long, A. L.** "A Small Collection of Babylonian Weights." *American Journal of Archaeology* 5 (1889): 44-6.
"Describes eleven objects of stone or metal, preserved at Istanbul and believed to represent units of weight in the Babylonian system." [J. R. Jones, *NIAJAH*]

1595 **Lueke, Jorg.** "Metrology—Getting to Know Your Coins." *The Celator* 20, no. 2 (February 2006): 24-31. Illus.
Describes the usefulness of various measurements including size, weight, die axis, and specific gravity—specifically their use in detecting counterfeit coins and in revealing information about the economy and politics at the time of minting. Describes various spectroscopic techniques for determining the metallic content of coins. Provides examples of specific gravity measurements and metallic content of some Sasanian coins.

1596 **Mattingly, Harold.** "The 'Little' Talents of Sicily and the West." *Numismatic Chronicle* 6th ser., 3 (1943): 14-20.
Normally, the talent was a Greek weight containing sixty minae and 6000 drachma. However, a number of "little" talents were in use in Italy and Sicily with an entirely different system of subdivisions and values. Mattingly argues that the system of subdivisions for these little talents is 1 talent = 12 nomoi = 120 litrae. Also argues that *nomos* and *litra*, at the same time and place, always have the same values. Discusses each of the little talent standards.

1597 **McClean, John R.** "Metrological Note on the Coinage of Populonia." *Numismatic Chronicle* 4th ser., 10 (1910): 209-22. Illus.
Discusses the origin of the central Italian weight standard used for the coinage of Populonia. Concludes the standard is probably based upon the full weight of the Sardinian copper ingot of 360 units, totaling 34,382.25 grams. Discusses its equivalent in gold and silver. Discusses the flaws of Haeberlin's calculations of these standard weights [*Zeitschrift für Numismatik* (Germany) (1909)]. In a postscript, McClean discusses the pitfalls of using averages as a basis for determining standard weights.

1598 ——— "The Origin of Weight." *Numismatic Chronicle* 4th ser., 12 (1912): 333-51. Reprint, Chicago: Obol International, 1979. 61 pages. [CS 16059]
Discusses the original purpose of weights and weighing. Weight was first used as a measure of the *value* of precious metals. Cities evidence from ancient texts. Concludes that weighing and valuing were synonymous in the earliest days. The change from this idea of a measure of quality to one of quantity would come gradually from the use of seals.

1599 **Milne, Joseph G.** "A Note on Festus 359A: Silver and Bronze Coinage of the Hellenistic Period." *Studies in Roman Economic and Social History in Honor of Allan Chester Johnson.* Edited by R. R. Coleman-Norton. Princeton, 1951. Pages 27-35.
"The passage from Festus gives the value of a talent in terms of denarii in the Attic, Rhodian, Cistophoric, Alexandrian, Neopolitan, Syracusan, and Rhegian standards. Since bronze and silver standards existed side by side in these places, the different values of the talent can be explained. Various coins furnish the evidence of these standards which differed from place to place. The relationships of these standards are explained in the article." [H. Adelson, *NL 21*]

1600 **Mommsen, Theodor.** "Note on Greek Weights." *Numismatic Chronicle* new ser., 8 (1868): 74.
Brief follow-up notes to A. S. Murray's article on Greek weights. [See Murray "Greek Weights" below].

1601 **Mørkholm, Otto.** "The Attic Coin Standard in the Levant during the Hellenistic Period." *Studia Paulo Naster Oblata. Volume 1: Numismatica Antiqua.* Edited by S. Scheers. Orientalia Lovaniensia Analecta 12. Louvain: Departement Oriëntalistiek, 1982. Pages 139-49.
An examination of the Attic weight standard in the Levant during the Hellenistic period based on a study of frequency tables of coins issued in the late fourth through first centuries B.C. The author discusses the use of frequency tables, warning of problems and providing suggestions. Then traces the slight reduction in the standard weights of the coins 323-31 B.C.

1602 **Murray, A. S.** "Greek Weights in the British Museum." *Numismatic Chronicle* new ser., 8 (1868): 57-73.
Murray lists the 147 lead weights in the British Museum. The weights follow the same denominations and divisions as Greek coins. He discusses the various systems of weight used by the Greeks and examines the changes in weight standards and the relationship between lead weights and the weights of coins. [Also see Mommsen "Note" above for some brief follow-up notes].

1603 **Naster, Paul.** "Méthode de Métrologie Monétaire Appliquée aux Monnaies d'Athènes." *Revue Belge de Numismatique* (Belgium) 70 (1974): 5-17. [CS 2511]

1604 ——— "La Méthode en Métrologie Numismatique." *Numismatique Antique: Problèmes et Methodes.* Nancy and Louvain: Peeters, 1975. Pages 65-74. [CS 3342]

1605 **Nicolet-Pierre, Hélène.** "Metrologie des Monnaies Grecques: La Grèce Centrale et l'Egée aux Èpoque Archaique et Classique (VIe—IV^{e}s)." *Annali del Istituto Italiano di Numismatica* (Italy) 47 (2000): 11-76.

1606   **Pernice, Erich.** *Griechische Gewichte.* Berlin, 1894. 215 pp., 1 pl. [CS 3345]
Greek weights.

1607   **Reifler, E.** "The Metrological Reasons for the Difference in Aristotle's and Androtion's Statements about Solon's Change in the Weight of the Mina." *American Journal of Archaeology* 68 (1964): 202.
A summary of a paper presented at a conference. "The difference between the two ratios is said to be that whereas Androtion compared either two secular or two sacred standards, Aristotle compared the Pheidonian commercial with the Solonian temple mina." [J. R. Jones, *NIAJAH*]

1608   **Ridgeway, William.** "The Homeric Talent, its Origins, Value and Affinities." *Journal of Hellenic Studies* 8 (1887): 133-58.
"Suggests that the basic primitive unit of currency was the ox, the value of which is represented in the standard units of precious metals common to a number of civilisations." [J. R. Jones, *NIJHS*]. [Also see "Cow-Money and Staters" above].

1609   ———— "Metrological Notes II." *Journal of Hellenic Studies* 9 (1888): 18-30.
"On pp. 26 ff. (as a sequel to the above) it is suggested that the Roman system of money was based on the unit of an ox, valued at one hundred libral *asses*." [J. R. Jones, *NIJHS*]

1610   ———— "Metrological Notes III and IV." *Journal of Hellenic Studies* 10 (1889): 90-7.
"The first of these notes suggests that gold ornaments found at Mycenae provide evidence for a unit of 132-137 grains. The second advances the theory that weight standards for precious metals were first fixed by using seeds or grain of common plants." [J. R. Jones, *NIJHS*]

1611   ———— *The Origin of Metallic Currency and Weight Standards.* Cambridge: University Press, 1892. Reprints, Graz, 1971; New York: Attic Books, 1976. 417 pp., illus. [CS 1495]
Ridgeway presents a detailed and logically organized inquiry into the origins of metallic currency and weight standards. Begins with the writings of Homer. Shows how the value of an ox was related to a talent of gold. Next, he describes numerous primitive (pre-coinage) systems of currency from various areas of the world, explaining the value relationship between barter units. He then puts forth his controversial theory for the origin of weight standards. In his view, the ox had become a standard of value throughout a wide geographical area. Gold was evenly distributed throughout these regions and, furthermore, these lands were connected by heavily traveled trade routes.

The use of scales and weights to facilitate trade is discussed next. He deduces that "gold was the first of all substances to be weighed." He believes that gold was universally weighed by the same standard, and this standard was in all cases the equivalent of the ox. He believes all coin weights were derived from this one original value—the amount of gold that was equivalent to the value of an ox. Describes the weight systems of China and eastern Asia, and then shows that all weight systems were based on units of grain such as barley and wheat. Devotes a chapter to criticism of the theories of other scholars, especially those who suggest that weight standards originated in a scientifically derived value established by a highly civilized people. Specifically addresses Barclay Head's account of the origin of weight standards.

Ridgeway then describes how the weight systems of Egypt, Babylon, Palestine, Persia, Greece, Lydia, and Italy developed from the one original source—the ox, and describes how the bimetallic system of gold and silver coinage was responsible for fluctuating coin weight standards. [Also see Head's review of this book in *Numismatic Chronicle* 3rd ser., 12 (1892): 247-50. Head does not accept Ridgeway's theories. Also see G. Macdonald *Coin Types* under TYPES].

1612   **Sellwood, David G.** "A Basic Program for Histograms." *Numismatic Chronicle* 140 (1980): 201-4. [CS 16981]
Lists the code for a BASIC program which, after entering data, will produce a histogram of coin weights and some related statistics.

1613   **Soutzo, Prince Michel C.** "Systèmes Monétaires Primitifs de l'Asie Mineure et de la Grèce." *Revue Roumaine d'Archéologie, d'Histoire et de Philologie* (Romania) (1883). Reprint, Bucharest, 1884. 63 pp., illus. [CS 3349]

1614   **Thompson, Wesley E.** "Gold and Silver Ratios at Athens during the Fifth Century." *Numismatic Chronicle* 7th ser., 4 (1964): 103-23. [CS 2530 and 3351]
"On the basis of evidence furnished by inscriptions, specifically those which list weights of gold and their equivalent values in silver, Thompson re-examines both the ratios between gold and silver at Athens during the second half of the fifth century and the reasons for their fluctuation." [J. Balcer, *NL* 78]. [Also see J. Melville Jones "The Value of Gold" above].

1615   **Tietz, Werner.** "Der Westlykische Münzstandard Zwischen Athen und Persien." *Brückenland Anatolien? Ursachen, Extensität und Modi des Kulturaustausches Zwischen Anatolien und Seinen Nachbarn.* Edited by H. Blum, B. Faist, P. Pfälzner, and A. Wittke. Tübingen, 2002. Pages 59-67. Illus.
"The west Lycian coin standard is discussed as a link between the Attic drachm (and its multiples/fractions) and the Persian siglos." [H. R. Baldus, *NL* 146]

1616   **Tye, Robert.** *Early World Coins and Early Weight Standards.* York, 2009. 183 pp.
A review of world coins prior to the introduction of machine-struck coinage. Includes a catalogue of over 1200 common or influential ancient and modern coin types from Europe, Persia, India, and China. The development and spread of coinage is illustrated in a series of maps. About 170 coin types and denominations are discusses. Ancient and medieval denomination sets are described. Also provides an overview of pre-modern weight systems and their influence on coin weights. [Reviewed by Michael Mitchiner in *Numismatic Chronicle* 170 (2010): 514-6].

1617   **Vagel, Jürgen.** "How to Determine the Exact Specific Weight of Coins." *Seaby Coin and Medal Bulletin* 783 (March 1967): 110-2.
Describes how to determine the specific gravity of coins using a balance scale. Presents the mathematical formula and a table allowing one to determine the percentage of silver or copper in various alloys based upon the observed specific gravity.

1618   **Vagi, David L.** "Weight Standards Important to Monetary Systems." *The Celator* 8, no. 10 (October 1995): 27. Illus.
A brief overview of the various weight-standards used in coinage. Compares coins of different standards to emphasize the complexities of the ancient monetary systems.

1618a **Van Driessche, Véronique.** *Des Étalons Pré-Monétaires au Monnayage en Bronze.* Études de Métrologie Grecque I. Études Numismatiques 2. Louvain-la-Neuve: Association Professeur Marcel Hoc, 2009. 170 pp.
The author seeks to explain the entwined developments, over the course of 1000 years, of a unified Greek metrological system, encompassing all forms of measurement—volumetric, linear, and mass—and an equally generalized system of values focused in succession on bronze, iron, and finally silver, all of which culminates in the out-of-synch monetary systems of the Aeginetans and Athenians in the classical period, harmonized in the end by the small denomination bronze chalkous. [From the review by Peter van Alfen in *ANS Magazine* 11, no. 1 (2012): 58-9].

1619 **Viedebantt, Oskar.** *Forschungen zur Metrologie des Altertums.* Leipzig, 1917. Reprint, Hildesheim, 1974. 184 pp. [CS 3353]

1620 ——— *Antike Gewichtsnormen und Münzfüsse.* Berlin, 1923. 166 pp. [CS 3354]

1621 **Villaronga, Leandre.** "Méthode de l'Intervalle de Confiance pour l'Étude Comparative des Poids des Émissions Monétaires." *Liber Amicorum Tony Hackens.* Numismatica Lovaniensia 20. Edited by G. Moucharte, M. B. Borba Florenzano, F. de Callataÿ, P. Marchetti, L. Smolderen, and P. Yannopoulos. Louvain-la-Neuve: Université Catholique de Louvain, 2007. Pages 107 ff.

1622 **Wade-Gery, H. T.** "The Ratio of Silver to Gold during the Peloponnesian War: *I.G.I.*^{2}, 301." *Numismatic Chronicle* 5th ser., 10 (1930): 16-38.
Examines a fifth century B.C. Attic document (*I.G.I.*^{2}, 301) which contains statements regarding the gold-to-silver ratio. The document records payments made by the Treasurers of Athens to the Imperial Treasurers for war expenses. [Also see the correction on pages 333-4].

1623 **Wallace, Malcolm B.** "The Reduced Euboio-Attic Coin Weight Standard." *Ancient Coins of the Graeco-Roman World: The Nickle Numismatic Papers.* Edited by Waldemar Heckel and Richard Sullivan. Waterloo, Ontario: Wilfrid Laurier University Press, 1984. Pages 19-37.
A study of the reduced Euboio-Attic weight standard used by the Euboian League, Chalkis, and Carystos, ca. 350-250 B.C. Wallace suggests the League drachms had two intended weights. He tentatively concludes that Carystos adopted the Chian standard before 370 B.C., that Chalkis adopted the Macedonian standard by 340 B.C., and that a unification of standards occurred by ca. 300 B.C.

1624 ——— "Texts, Amphoras, Coins, Standards and Trade." *The Ancient World* 10, nos. 1-2 (November 1984): 11-3.
Discusses standard weights and measures and their interrelationships in ancient Greece. Discusses coin weight standards and the reasons for adopting or changing standards. Examines the evidence of amphora capacities in connection with the Athenian Standards Decree.

1625 **Wallace, Robert W.** "The Date of Solon's Reforms." *American Journal of Ancient History* 8, no. 1 (1983): 81-95.
Many scholars now date Solon's constitutional reforms to the decade 580-570 B.C. Wallace argues that there is insufficient reason to reject the traditional date of 594/3, the year of Solon's archonship. He concludes this date is supported by other evidence, no other date is given by any ancient source, and none of the arguments for the later date is cogent.

1626 ——— "Remarks on the Value and Standards of Early Electrum Coins." *Hacksilber to Coinage: New Insights into the Monetary History of the Near East and Greece.* Numismatic Studies 24. Edited by Miriam S. Balmuth. New York: American Numismatic Society, 2001. Pages 127-34.
Natural electrum was commonly diluted with silver before being struck as coins. Wallace suggests that electrum bullion may *not* have had a fixed intrinsic value in the marketplace, and that its market value may have been *below* its intrinsic value. He questions the idea that 14.2 gm electrum coins were equivalent in value to 10.7 gm gold coins (this standard values the electrum coins as being 75% gold). In fact, the electrum coins were often less than 55% gold, so this one-to one exchange ratio is unlikely. Wallace believes the weight of Croesus' gold and silver staters were not calculated to facilitate the exchange of electrum coins for gold coins. Rather, the 10.7-10.9 gm weight was a traditional standard of the region. The question therefore shifts: Why was a weight of 14.0-14.2 gm chosen for the early electrum issues? He suggests the fifth century B.C. Phoenicians struck on a silver coin standard which was then current in the Greek Aegean—a standard borrowed from an archaic Greek standard for coinage. Or, electrum coins *were* pegged as 75% gold to stabilize the value of electrum at this very high, but natural, level. He also questions the supposed progression from striated electrum coins to electrum with pictures. Both may have been minted at the same time in different places.

1627 **Weber, Charles E.** "Gravimetric Data in General Works on Greek Coins." *The Celator* 15, no. 12 (December 2000): 28-9. Illus.
Decries the lack of metrological data in many numismatic books and catalogues. Points out the importance of noting a coin's weight and specific gravity.

1628 **Wood, H. G.** "Hebrew Influence on Ancient Coinage." *American Journal of Numismatics* 42, no. 2 (1907): 47-51.
Discusses the Eastern influence on the ancient systems of weights and measures.

Note: Articles related to Solon's reform of the weights at Athens are found under ATTICA—GENERAL WORKS. See M. Chambers "Aristotle," Crawford "Solon's Alleged Reform," Johnston "Solon's Reforms," Kraay "An Interpretation," Milne "Monetary Reform," "Chronology," and "Economic Policy," Rhodes "Solon" and "A Commentary."

Also see: Balmuth *Hacksilber to Coinage* under ORIGINS OF COINAGE; Balmuth "The Monetary Forerunners" under ORIGINS OF COINAGE; Bellinger "Bronze Standards" under SYRIA—SELEUCID KINGDOM; Bivar "Achaemenid Coins, Weights, and Measures" under PERSIA; Courbin "Dans la Grèce Archaïque" under ORIGINS OF COINAGE; Dayton "Money in the Near East" under ORIGINS OF COINAGE; Elsen "La Stabilité du Système Pondéral et Monétaire Attique" under ATTICA—GENERAL WORKS; Gardner "Pollux' Account" under GENERAL WORKS—GREEK; Guépin "Persian Bimetallism" under GENERAL WORKS—GREEK; Hackens "Les Equivalences des Metaux Moneaires Argent et Bronze en Sicile" under SICILY—GENERAL WORKS; Hackens "Le Métrologie des Monnaies Étrusques" under ITALY—ETRURIA; Head *The Coinage of Lydia and Persia* under LYDIA; Hendin "The Metrology of Judaean Small Bronze" under PALESTINE—JUDEA; Hill "Chapter 5: Coinage" under ORIGINS OF COINAGE; Hourmouziadas and Weisser "A Metrological Study" under BOSPOROS; Klimowsky *On Ancient Palestinian* under PALESTINE—JUDEA; Kroll "Observations on Monetary Instruments" under ORIGINS OF COINAGE.

Lahiri "The Indo-Greek Standard" under NORTHWEST INDIA; Lahiri "Metrology" under NORTHWEST INDIA; Macdonald "The Silver Coinage" under CRETE; Marchetti "La Métrologie des Monnaies Étrusques avec Marques de Valeur" under ITALY—ETRURIA; Meshorer *Ancient Means of Exchange* under PALESTINE—JUDEA; Milne

"Comments on Corrosion" under METALLURGY; Milne "Medallion" under TYPES; Milne "The Persian Standard" under IONIA; Mukhejee "Some Observations of the Metrology" under BACTRIA; Naster "The Weight-System" under LYDIA; Parise "Il Sistema della Litra Nella Sicilia Antica" under SICILY—GENERAL WORKS; Picard "Weight Standard…Chalcidice" under MACEDONIAN CITIES AND TRIBES; Ridgeway "How Far" under METALLURGY; Rives "Parthian Drachm Coin Measurements" under PARTHIA; Robinson "The Coin Standards" under EGYPT—PTOLEMAIC KINGDOM; Ronen "The Weight Standards" under PALESTINE—JUDEA; Rynearson "Partitioned Coins" under HOARDS.

Schell "Observations on the Metrology" under MACEDONIAN KINGDOM—GENERAL WORKS; Schlösser "Denominations and Weights" under SYRIA—SELEUCID KINGDOM; C. Seltman *The Temple Coins of Olympia* under PELOPONNESOS—ELIS; Sparkes "Gold Coins" under SICILY—SYRACUSE; Stern "The Silver Hoard from Tel Dor" under ORIGINS OF COINAGE; Tal "Coin Denominations and Weight Standards" under PALESTINE—JUDEA; Vagi "Pentekaidekadrachm" under EGYPT—PTOLEMAIC KINGDOM; R. Wallace "Production and Exchange of Early Anatolian Electrum" under ASIA MINOR AND BLACK SEA—GENERAL WORKS; Warden "Etruscan Numismatics and Metrology" under ITALY—ETRURIA; Wedig "Denominations" under GENERAL WORKS—GREEK; Wilkinson "Athenian Silver Coin Fractions" under ATTICA—GENERAL WORKS.

COUNTERFEITS

But when it ceased to be the money of common circulation, and was purchased for the cabinets of the curious; when it became an article of costly luxury, and all legal penalties were at an end respecting it; the inducement to fabricate it was increased an enormous degree.

—Edward Cardwell, 1832

1629   **Acar, Özgen.** "Master Counterfeiter Discloses his Secrets: Cemil of Odemis Practices Craft in Turkey for More than Twenty-five Years." *Coin World.* Parts 1-3. (October 17, 1990): 1, 34, 42; (October 24, 1990): 1, 32, 84; (October 31, 1990): 1, 94. Illus.
The subject is Cemil Kalayci, known as "Cemil of Odemis," a counterfeiter of ancient coins living in western Turkey. The author describes the casting and striking methods Cemil uses to make his coins. Describes how the coins are sold to unsuspecting tourists. Suggests that dealers, collectors, and museums have been fooled by Cemil's creations. Describes the common pastime of searching for genuine coin hoards in Turkey and mentions several famous hoards found in the area in recent years. Points out the importance of noticing the style of a coin when attempting to detect counterfeits. [Also see Arnold R. Saslow's editorial, "Researcher Questions Claims Made by Master Counterfeiter" in *Coin World* (January 9, 1991): 4. Saslow points out that all respected dealers that have seen Cemil's coins have pronounced them to be poor quality, amateurish fakes which would not fool a knowledgeable dealer or collector. Suggests the author had political motives for writing the series of articles].

1630   **Adams, Lawrence A.** "A Few More Slavei Fakes." *SAN—Journal of the Society for Ancient Numismatics* 21 (2002): 45. Illus.
Illustrates seven counterfeit Greek coins produced by the Bulgarian engraver Slavei. Includes coins of Ainos, Mesembria, Larissa, Leontinoi, Istrus, Syracuse, and Apollonia Pontica.

1631   "Ancient Coin Forgeries Selling as Genuine, Journal States Coins Made from Electrotype Copies." *Coin World* (April 13, 1992): 3 ff.
Reports on an announcement in the *Bulletin on Counterfeits* (published by the International Bureau for the Suppression of Counterfeit Coins) that exposes counterfeit ancient coins reproduced from electrotype copies once sold by the British Museum. The coins, mostly copies of very rare types, were distributed in the marketplace until 1990. Lists seven characteristics which may help in identifying these "extremely dangerous" fakes. A companion article on the same page, "Researchers Identify Ancient Counterfeits," lists some of the coins involved.

1632   **Arnold, T. J.** "Becker's Forgeries." *Numismatic Chronicle* new ser., 3 (1863): 246-8. Also appeared in *Spink Numismatic Circular* 2, no. 21 (August 1894): 795-8.
A brief account of Becker's life and the coin forgeries he created.

1633   **Brace, Bruce R.** "Deceptions, Part 1." *Journal of the Classical and Medieval Numismatic Society* (Canada) 2nd ser., 1, no. 3 (December 2000): 40-1. "Part 2." 2, no. 1 (March 2001): 40-1. "Part 3." 2, no. 2 (June 2001): 100-2. "Part 4." 2, no. 4 (December 2001): 187-8. "Part 5." 3, no. 1 (March 2002): 44-7. "Part 6." 3, no. 2 (June 2002): 95-7. "Part 7." 3, no. 4 (December 2002): 204-6. "Part 8." 4, no. 2 (June 2003): 111. "Part 9." 4, no. 3 (September 2003): 142-3. "Part 9 B." 4, no. 4 (December 2003): 188-91. "Part 10." 5, no. 1 (March 2004): 45-6. Illus.
Parts 1 and 2 present brief comments of the dangers of counterfeit coins and how the collector can avoid them. Part 3 discusses electrotypes, illustrates how they are made, and describes how to detect them. Part 4 examines die struck forgeries. Part 5 focuses on cast copies. Part 6 discusses altered (tooled) coins. Part 7 covers plated coins. Part 8 examines patinas and the creation of fake patinas. Part 9 covers Renaissance forgeries and imitations, including the "Paduans" and Cavinos. Part 10 discusses tooling the surfaces of coins.

1634   **Clain-Stefanelli, Vladimir.** "An Application of Physics in Ancient Numismatics: Detection of Certain Counterfeit Aegina Staters through X-ray Diffraction Analysis." *American Journal of Archaeology* 70 (1966): 185.
A summary of a paper presented at a conference. "The principles of this form of analysis are briefly stated." [J. R. Jones, *NIAJAH*]

1635   **Conn, Robert.** *Prevalence and Profitability: The Counterfeit Coins of Archaic and Classical Greece.* Masters thesis, Florida State University College of Arts and Sciences, 2007. 91 pp., illus.
Conn delves into the writings of ancient authors to understand their references to counterfeits and counterfeiters and attitudes toward them. Reviews ancient laws and regulations related to counterfeiting. Examines the role of the Dokimastes in detecting and confiscating counterfeit coins. Reviews epigraphic evidence of the level of awareness of counterfeiting as a problem. Discusses the use of countermarks to validate coins. Conn attempts to gauge the profitability of counterfeiting. He concludes that counterfeiting was a common practice in the archaic and classical periods, that government officials and average citizens were aware of the problem, and there was significant profit to be made by counterfeiting.

1636 ———— "Prevalence and Profitability: Re-Examining the Silver-Plated Counterfeit Coins of Aegina." *The Celator* 23, no. 6 (June 2009): 6-18. Illus.
Examines the frequency of counterfeiting and the profitability to the counterfeiter. Briefly describes the manufacturing of plated coins and the use of test cuts or countermarks by merchants to identify counterfeit coins. Attempts to understand the amount of silver typically used on a plated coin to estimate the possible profit to be gained.

1637 "Copies of Museum Coins Being Sold by English Firm." *Coin World* (April 3, 1995): 41. Illus. Also: "Private Firm Offers Copies of Coinage." *Coin World* (October 2, 1995): 91. Illus.
Reports that copies of coins, including ancient coins, in the Barber Institute of Fine Arts, University of Birmingham, and other institutions are being manufactured and marketed. The copies are composed of either non-precious metal or resin and are molded rather than struck.

1638 **Demetriadi, Basil C.** "Slavey: The Truth behind the Legend." *The Celator* 13, no. 1 (January 1999): 20-5. Illus.
The author and a friend traveled to Bulgaria to meet the well-known counterfeiter Slavey ("Slavei"). They saw his workshop and viewed some of his "coins." Includes photographs (both obverse and reverse) of forty-four of his Greek and forty-two of his Roman coins. [Also see Puetz "The Slavey Interview" below].

1639 **Dimitrov, Dimitar, Ilya Prokopov, and Boyko Kolev.** *Modern Forgeries of Greek and Roman Coins.* Sofia: K&K Publishers, 1997. 72 pp., illus.
"In this small format (22.5 x 12 cm) catalogue is published a large group of contemporary forgeries of ancient Greek and Roman coins from Bulgaria. Over 200 coins in gold, silver and bronze are catalogued and illustrated with black and white photos in chronological order. Of the coins, 66 are Greek (4 in gold, the remainder in silver) and 138 Roman (4 Republican denarii, 27 in gold, 65 in silver, 42 in bronze, including 5 medallions). The series will include a second issue with more than 109 additional forgeries." [Dimitrov, Prokopov, and Kolev, *NL* 142]. [Reviewed by C. A. Marinescu in *Minerva* 9, no. 5 (September-October 1998): 46-8].

1640 **Dodson, Oscar H.** "Counterfeits I Have Known." *Coinage* 3, no. 4 (April 1967): 20 ff. Illus.
"A record is given of the counterfeiter of ancient Greek coins John Garyphallakis and the Greek court order which restored to him the confiscated dies of Constantine Christodoulos and of the relatively unknown forger, Manuel Boufetis of Saloniki." [O. Dodson, *NL* 92]

1641 **Duncan, Jim.** "Robert Ready—Electrotypist." *Classical Numismatic Review* 17, no. 3 (third quarter 1992): 4-5. Illus.
A brief look at the career of Robert Ready (b. 1811; d. 1901), who produced electrotype copies of coins for the British Museum, 1859-97. The copies are marked RR, R, or MB on the edge. In 1882, the British Museum was offering for sale a "full set of Greek coins" consisting of 800 of Ready's electrotypes for £125.

1642 **Emory, Marc.** "Participant Provides Background about 'Black Sea' Diobol Hoard." *Coin World* (April 25, 1990): 4, 12, 14.
An editorial which describes how the Black Sea Hoard coins of Mesembria and Apollonia Pontica came onto the coin market. Presents arguments supporting the authenticity of the coins.

1643 ———— "Black Sea Hoard Genuine." *Coin World* (October 18, 1993): 24, 36.
In response to F. Kovacs' article in *The Celator* (see Kovacs "Sofia Museum" below) this editorial re-states Emory's view that the Black Sea Hoard diobols of Mesembria and Apollonia Pontica are genuine. Also see the rebuttal by A. Saslow (see Saslow "Black Sea Hoard" below).

1644 **Fischer, Thomas.** "Some Further Early Nineteenth-Century Forgeries of Greek Coins." *Numismatic Chronicle* 7th ser., 8 (1968): 267-8. Illus. [CS 3590]
"Examples, genuine and false, of the tetradrachm of Antiochus IX (Newell, *Late Seleucid Mints* No. 41) are published. There is another forgery of Antiochus, the reverse connected with a type of Calymna (*BMC Caria* p. 188 Nos. 3 ff.)." [T. Fischer, *NL* 82]

1645 **Fischer-Bossert, Wolfgang.** "Zwei Sizilische Bleimünzen in Münster." *Boreas* (Germany) 23/24 (2001/2002): 195-205. Illus.
"Publication of two lead coins, donated to the Archaeological Museum of the Münster University in 1999 (pl. 16). (1) A modern fake, combining a frontal bust of Helios (Roman?) with an imitation of the famous fifth century B.C. satyr (seated frontally, drinking) from coins of Naxos, Sicily. (2) An ancient, struck lead version of a bronze hemilitron of Akragas. There follows a detailed presentation and discussion of the meanings of this and other lead versions of coins in antiquity." [H. Baldus, *NL* 145]

1646 **Flegler, Stanley L.** "Evidence Presented: Hoard Coinage Tested Under Electron Microscope." *The Celator* 3, no. 9 (September 1989): 17, 20.
Text of a letter from Stanley Flegler of Michigan State University to Sylvia Hurter of Bank Leu explaining scientific tests conducted by Flegler on the "Black Sea Hoard" coins to determine their authenticity. A test of the amount of radioactive lead 210 present in the hoard coins indicates that the lead in the silver alloy of the coins is at least 100 years old. Scanning electron microscope images suggest the deposits on the coin surfaces have not been produced through artificial methods. A comparison of elements in the center of the coins to elements on the surface suggests that natural corrosion has acted upon the surface of the coins. An X-ray micro-analysis detected trace elements which are normal for ancient coins and which indicate different batches of ore were used. The presence of aluminum and silicon oxides indicate long-term burial in soil. The weight of the hoard coins corresponds to that expected of a 30% silver debased specimen. No traces of casting or of an under-type were detected. Flegler concludes these coins are a genuine ancient debased issue. [Also see related articles by Emory above, and by Giedroyc, Sayles, and Wetterstrom below].

1647 ———— "Letter to the Editor." *The Celator* 3, no. 11 (November 1989): 34; 5, no. 11 (November 1991): 38-9.
The first is a follow-up to Flegler's article in *The Celator*, September 1989 (see above). Mentions that his findings were presented to an international meeting of archaeologists and scientists and the response has been "overwhelmingly positive." The second is a letter discussing newly discovered die-links and rebutting recent criticisms of his theories.

1648 ———— "Black Sea Hoard: Possible Ancient Debased Coin Issue." *World Coin News* (May 28, 1990): 21, 22, 26, 28, 30, 32, 34. Illus.

Presents a detailed review of the results of a scientific analysis of the Black Sea Hoard coins to determine their authenticity. Discusses style, die links, corrosion, soil elements, lead 210 dating, hardness measurements, surface silvering, weights, and alloys, accompanied by photographs of scanning electron micrographs of the hoard coins. Concludes that these coins are most likely an ancient debased issue.

1649 ——— "Scientist Rebuts Stylistic Grounds as Basis for Condemnation." *The Celator* 4, no. 6 (June 1990): 20.
A rebuttal to Sayles' article (see Sayles "Art Historical Perspective" below) regarding the stylistic arguments for concluding that the "Black Sea Hoard" coins are counterfeits. Points out discrepancies in Sayles' arguments. Says that the Corinthian helmet depicted on the coins had not been in use since ca. 500 B.C. and it is unlikely the die engraver had ever seen one. Mentions that an actual helmet with a tapered nose-plate and a rolled lip around the eye cutouts was found in Bulgaria. Mentions evidence for interaction between the cities of Mesembria and Apollonia Pontica. Concludes that the hoard is a newly discovered debased issue.

1650 ——— "Counterfeiter or Artist? Bulgarian's Work Renowned." *World Coin News* (April 11, 1994): 30-3.
Discusses the work of Slavey Petrov.

1651 **Friedlaender, Julius.** *Ein Verzeichnis von Griechischen Falschen Münzen welche aus Modernen Stempeln Geprägt Sind.* Berlin, 1883. 53 pp. [CS 3591]

1652 **Frossard, Edward.** "Becker's Forgeries." *Numisma* 5, no. 2 (March 1881): 3.
A very brief account of the career of Carl W. Becker, the famous counterfeiter.

1653 ——— "The Becker Forgeries." *American Journal of Numismatics* 16, no. 1 (July 1881): 12-5.
A brief account of the life and career of Carl W. Becker, the famous counterfeiter. Includes a list of "coins" which he produced (without any description of the types) arranged by city, emperor, etc.

1654 **Gaebler, Hugo.** *Fälschungen Makedonischer Münzen.* Eight parts. Berlin, 1931-42. Reprinted from *Sitzungsberichte der Preussischen Akademie der Wissenschaften* (1931, 1935-38), and from *Abhandlungen der Preussischen Akademie der Wissenschaften* (1939-41). [CS 3592]

1655 **Gainor, John R.** "Case Study: Decadrachm of Syracuse, by Kimon, 405-380 B.C." *The Anvil* (Canada) 2, no. 5 (September 1, 1992): 4. Illus.
Provides a detailed description and enlarged photographs of a forgery of a decadrachm of Syracuse struck from cast dies.

1656 ——— "Detection of Altered and Counterfeit Ancient Coins Requires Basic Understanding." *The Celator* 6, no. 9 (September 1992): 6-27. Illus.
An overview on detecting altered and counterfeit ancient coins. Discusses different types of patinas and the chemicals which form them; tests for metallic composition including neutron activation; specific gravity and weight. Describes methods of forgery including various types of casting. Discusses methods of manufacturing dies including hand-cut dies, mechanically-cut dies, and punched dies. Discusses plated, tooled, and repaired coins. Briefly describes the careers and products of the famous counterfeiters Cavino, Becker, Zindel, Caprara, Christodoulos, and Rosa. Includes a short bibliography.

1657 **Gainor, John R., and William H. McDonald.** "The Ancient Coin Copies of Peter Rosa." *The Anvil* (Canada) 5, no. 3 (May 1, 1995): 25-8, 31. Illus.
Describes the methods used by Peter Rosa (1926-90) to create copies of ancient Greek and other coins. Rosa created cast dies with which he struck or pressed large quantities of "coins." He stamped "BECKER" on the edges of some of the copies. Others were unmarked. An appendix lists the number of Rosa's coins, dies, and molds which are now in the possession of Rosa's brother. [Also see McDonald "A Peter Rosa Coin" and Gilkes "Firm Continues" below].

1658 **Gerin, Dominique.** "Un Faux Statère de Stymphale Entré au Cabinet du Roi Avant 1685." *Schweizer Münzblätter* (Germany) 220 (March 2006): 3-8. Illus.
"The author discusses a seventeenth century cast forgery of a stater of Stymphalus that can be linked to the mould that produced it." [Oliver D. Hoover, *NL* 149]

1659 **Giedroyc, Richard.** "Dealers Offer Ancient Coins for Examination: Researcher Concentrates Study on Non-Black Sea Hoard Coins." *Coin World* (June 13, 1990): 92.
States that Stanley Flegler is conducting scientific tests on non-hoard coins similar to those found in the "Black Sea Hoard." Discusses the style of the coins and argues that the coins are genuine. [Also see Flegler "Evidence Presented" above].

1660 ——— "New Tests Support Authenticity of Hoard." *Coin World* (August 1, 1990): 84.
Announces results from metallurgical tests undertaken by Stanley Flegler on some of the "Black Sea Hoard" coins, as well as similar non-hoard coins. A statistical analysis of data from neutron activation tests indicates that there is a 99.5% probability that the hoard and non-hoard coin alloys are identical. Flegler states, "It is inconceivable that any modern counterfeiter would by chance be able to find a source of metal with gold traces that happen to match the non-hoard coins."

1661 ——— "Dealer Claims He Purchased Copies of Ancient Black Sea Hoard Coins. Bulgarian Museum Denies Receipt Dealer Says it Issued." *Coin World* (September 27, 1993): 58-9.
A follow-up to Kovacs' article in *The Celator* (see Kovacs "Sofia Museum" below). States that officials of the National Historical Museum in Bulgaria deny the claim that these coins are being sold as copies at the museum's gift shop. States that the receipt given to Kovacs is not a genuine museum gift shop receipt.

1662 ——— "IBSCC Concludes Black Sea Hoard Silver Diobols 'Modern Forgeries.'" *Coin World* (October 18, 1993): 3, 8.

Announces that the International Bureau for the Suppression of Counterfeit Coins has agreed that the controversial "Black Sea Hoard" coins are modern forgeries. Reviews the history of the controversy. [Also see "Experts Say" under HOARDS for an earlier opinion by the IBSCC].

1663 ——— "Ancient Coin Replicas by Slavei Sell at Show." *Coin World* (January 2, 1995): 62. Illus.
Reports that coin replicas by the well-known counterfeiter Slavei were being sold as replicas at the recent New York International Numismatic Convention by the nephew of the counterfeiter.

1664 **Gilkes, Paul.** "Firm Continues Family Legacy: Rosa Nephew Makes Replica Coins." *Coin World* (November 22, 2010): 10, 66. Illus.
Announces that Charles Doyle, a nephew of Peter Rosa, a well-known former maker of coin replicas, has begun making coin replicas using the business name Coin Replicas, Inc. All copies will bear the "copy" markings required by the Hobby Protection Act. Most of the ancient coin replicas will be fabricated using Rosa's original molds. A replica of an Athenian decadrachm is illustrated.

1665 **Goldsborough, Reid.** "Apollonia Pontika Drachms and the 'New York Hoard' of Counterfeits." *The Celator* 18, no. 6 (June 2004): 14-5. Illus.
Discusses a group of counterfeit drachms of Apollonia Pontika which was being disbursed at the 1999 New York International Numismatic Convention. Describes the characteristics of the pieces. Suggests that a high percentage of these drachms are fakes. [Some photo captions are reversed. See note in *The Celator* 18, no. 7 (July 2004): 46].

1666 ——— "Archaic Parion Hemidrachms." *The Celator* 18, no. 6 (June 2004): 20-1. Illus.
Illustrates a group of counterfeit archaic hemidrachms of Parion with a Gorgon/incuse pattern. Describes their characteristics.

1667 **Golenko, Konstantin V.** "The Method of Counterfeiting Ancient Coins of the Bosporus by M. Sazonov as Told by Himself." *Museum Notes* 20 (1975): 25-8. [CS 3594]
In this 1876 confession, a counterfeiter briefly describes his methods of producing fake gold and silver ancient coins.

1668 **Hansen, Peter.** "The Galvano Forgeries (Previously Called the British Museum Forgeries)." *Trident* (Australia) 9 (October 1993): 14-5.
"The author discusses and expands part of an article in the *Bulletin on Counterfeits* of the IBSCC (vol. 17, nos. 1 and 2) concerning recent forgeries of Greek and Roman coins, some of which have been sold at auction." [J. Melville Jones, *NL* 133]

1669 **Hendin, David.** "Biblical Coins Susceptible: Collector Education Aids Counterfeit Detection." *The Celator* 2, no. 3 (March 1988): 12.
Presents basic guidelines for detecting counterfeit and altered coins.

1670 **Hill, George F.** *Becker the Counterfeiter.* Part 1, London: Spink & Son, 1924. 72 pp., 8 pls. Part 2, London: Spink & Son, 1925. 39 pp., 11 pls. Reprinted in one volume, London: Spink, 1955; Amherst: Scorpion Publishers, 1976; Chicago: Obol International, 1979. 111 pp., 19 pls. [CS 3595 and CS 16243]
A brief biography of famed counterfeiter Carl Wilhelm Becker (b. 1772; d. 1830) along with a catalogue of his Greek, Roman, and medieval "coins." He was an active maker of counterfeits by the year 1806 and he openly sold these to friends, acquaintances, and museums. Some people question whether he had intentions to defraud. He engraved his dies by hand and struck the coins with a sledge hammer. He aged them by enclosing them with iron filings in a box attached to the axle of his carriage. One-hundred thirty-four of his Greek coins and 227 of his Roman and medieval coins are listed, described, and photographed. In the original edition, the Greek coins appear in Part 1; the Roman, medieval, and later coins appear in Part 2. [Reviewed by J. G. Milne in *Numismatic Chronicle* 5th ser., 5 (1925): 414].

1671 **Hurter, Silvia M.** "The 'Black Sea Hoard'—The 'Cache' of an Ancient Counterfeit Mint." *Bulletin on Counterfeits* 15, no. 1 (1990): 2-4.

1672 ——— "The Black Sea Hoard, Yet Again." *Bulletin on Counterfeits* 18 (fall 1993).

1673 ——— "More Caprara Forgeries: A Chalcidic League Problem Solved." *Numismatic Chronicle* 159 (1999): 290-2. 1 pl.
Hurter identifies as a Caprara forgery an Olynthus tetradrachm in the Burton Y. Berry collection which had raised questions regarding the chronology of the series. A few other Caprara forgeries are noted.

1674 **International Bureau for the Suppression of Counterfeit Coins.** *Bulletin on Counterfeits.* London, 1976 +. [CS 438]
A periodical sponsored by the International Association of Professional Numismatists. Illustrates and discusses the diagnostic points of recently discovered counterfeit coins. The bulletin was issued four times per year 1976 through 1979. Since 1980, it has been published once or twice per year. Beginning in 2001, the bulletin began to be published by the American Numismatic Association in conjunction with the IAPN and was renamed *Counterfeit Coin Bulletin.*

1675 **Jones, Mark, ed.** *Fake? The Art of Deception.* London: British Museum, 1990. Berkeley and Los Angeles: University of California Press, 1990. 312 pp., illus.
The catalogue for an exhibition at the British Museum exploring fakes and forgeries of artworks, including paintings, sculptures, coins, documents, gems, jewelry, scientific instruments, animal species, and other items. Examines the objects, the history of faking, methods of faking, and the scientific detection of fakes. Illustrated by 335 objects. [Also see Price "Forgeries of Ancient Coins" below].

1676 **Kern, Jonathan K.** "Kern Warns Collectors about Unmarked Copies." *Collecting Ancient Coins: Special Supplement to Numismatic News, World Coin News, & Bank Note Reporter* (1998): A7. Illus.
Illustrates twelve counterfeit Greek coins. [Another ten counterfeits were illustrated in *Numismatic News* (March 17, 1998)].

1677 **Kinns, Philip.** *The Caprara Forgeries.* Royal Numismatic Society Special Publication No. 16; International Association of Professional Numismatists Special Publication No. 10. London and Basle, 1984. 59 pp., 8 pls.
Catalogues the counterfeit Greek coins created by Caprara in the 1820's. He was based in Smyrna and, later, the island of Syros. Reviews the prior publications of Caprara's and Becker's forgeries. Discusses the general artistic traits of Caprara's work and briefly describes his methods. Includes his

seventy-six known pieces plus two forgeries of Velia and Thebes which may have been Caprara's work and thirteen hybrid pieces, coupling unrelated obverse and reverse dies, which may also be his work. Each die is described and commentary is provided on the history of each piece. All are photographed. [Reviewed by R. Hepworth in *Numismatic Chronicle* 146 (1986): 263-4. Hepworth adds three specimens to the catalogue].

1678 ——— "Myrina and Related Forgeries." *Museum Notes* 30 (1985): 45-68. 7 pls.
Describes and illustrates counterfeit coins of Myrina and coins of other cities which emanated from the same workshops including two old forgeries, four twentieth century forgeries, fifteen of the "Baghdad" forgeries (a group produced in Persia or Mesopotamia, ca. 1890-1913), and twenty-one other pieces—mainly Seleucid and Parthian. Describes the characteristics of each piece.

1679 **Kleeb, Alvin A.** "Recent Forgeries of Ancient Coins." Parts 1-2. *SAN—Journal of the Society for Ancient Numismatics* 1, no. 2 (October 1969): 26-8; no. 3 (January 1970): 48-9.
Provides descriptions and enlarged photographs of counterfeits purchased by the author in Athens in 1968. Part 1 includes a stater of Aegina, a tetradrachm of Athens, a stater of Argos, and a fractional silver coin of Metapontum. Part 2 includes a coin of Euboea and a Byzantine silver coin.

1680 ——— "Recent Counterfeits of Ancient Coins." *SAN—Journal of the Society for Ancient Numismatics* 2, no. 2 (fall 1970): 30-1, 38-9. Illus.
Illustrates counterfeit coins of Metapontum and Demetrius Poliorcetes.

1681 ——— "More Counterfeits." *SAN—Journal of the Society for Ancient Numismatics* 5, no. 1 (1973-4): 15.
A counterfeit tetradrachm of Antiochus V is shown which the author purchased in Beirut.

1682 **Kovacs, Frank L.** "Sofia Museum Sells Mesembria and Apollonia Diobols as Modern Copies." *The Celator* 7, no. 8 (August 1993): 6-7. Illus.
Reports that the coins of the so-called "Black Sea Hoard" are being sold as modern copies in the gift shop of the National Historical Museum in Sofia, Bulgaria. The author purchased specimens which are die-linked to other Black Sea Hoard pieces. The proprietor of the gift shop claims to know the manufacturer of the copies. [Also see Giedroyc "Dealer Claims" above].

1683 ——— "New Christodoulou Dies Surface." *The Celator* 8, no. 8 (August 1994): 32-3. Illus.
Announces that seventy-six previously unrecorded dies by the notorious counterfeiter Constantin Christodoulou will soon be published. Twenty-four of the dies are illustrated.

1684 **Kraft, Konrad.** "Zu Einigen Fälschungen Griechischer Gold- und Silbermünzen." *Jahrbuch für Numismatik und Geldgeschichte* (Germany) 8 (1957): 51-6. [CS 3597]

1685 **Kroh, Dennis.** "Knowledge and Experience are Cited as the Best Combatants against Fakes and Forgeries." *The Celator* 4, no. 11 (November 1990): 24-9.
Presents guidelines for detecting counterfeit ancient coins. Differentiates between those intended to fool tourists and those intended to defraud collectors. Describes various types of forgeries including casts, centrifugal castings, electrotypes, struck copies, and altered coins. Tells what to look for: weight, edges, sharpness, die axis, patina, and style. Discusses the use of die studies and reference books. Lists authentication services and a bibliography of references on counterfeit ancient coins.

1686 **Larson, Charles M.** *Numismatic Forgery.* Irvine: Zyrus Press, 2004. 197 pp., illus.
A unique, step-by-step description of how modern forgers create excellent-quality forgeries of ancient and modern coins. Describes methods of altering genuine coins. Describes processes for creating dies, including casting, hand engraving, and explosive impact copying. Explains how to manufacture collars, striking machines, and other coin-making equipment. Discusses striking techniques and techniques for aging and patinating forgeries. Explains methods for hardening and softening metals. An important reference for any collector wishing to better understand the methods used by the best modern forgers.

1687 **Lhotka, John F.** "Falsifications of Ancient Coins." *The Numismatist* 71, no. 2 (February 1958): 131-40. Illus. Reprinted in *Selections from The Numismatist: Ancient and Medieval Coins.* Racine: Whitman Publishing Co., 1960. Pages 190-9. Illus.
The author mentions some of the famous counterfeiters (Becker, Christodoulos, etc.). Discusses various types of counterfeits and lists some basic steps for detection.

1688 **Martin, J. P.** "Authenticating Ancient Coins." *The Numismatist* 105, no. 6 (June 1992): 845-6. Illus.
Emphasizes the stylistic differences between genuine coins and hand-engraved counterfeits. Recommends verifying the weight of suspect coins. Illustrates die erosion marks on a genuine coin, and states that the presence of these crisp, fine die erosion lines are a good indication of authenticity.

1689 ——— "Master Forger Created Convincing Greek Silver." *The Numismatist* 106, no. 3 (March 1993): 406. Illus.
Brief mention of the famed counterfeiter Caprara. Illustrates the diagnostic points of one of his staters of Argos.

1690 ——— "The Challenge of Authenticating Ancients." *The Numismatist* 114, no. 11 (November 2001): 1361-2. Illus.
General comments on the problems associated with authenticating ancient coins. Illustrates a counterfeit Macedonian octadrachm.

1691 **McDonald, William H.** "A Peter Rosa Coin." *The Anvil* (Canada) (July 1, 1995): 43. Illus.
Illustrates and describes the diagnostics of a fake gold octodrachm of Ptolemy IV Philopater created by the well-known copyist Peter Rosa. [Also see Gainor and McDonald "Ancient Coin Copies" and Gilkes "Firm Continues" above].

1692 **McKenna, Thomas P.** "How Can You Tell They Are Real? Some Observations on Fake Ancient Coins." *The Celator* 9, no. 8 (August 1995): 32-40. Illus.

Describes various methods that have been used to produce counterfeit ancient coins. Points out the characteristic flaws of pieces created by these methods. Advises collectors to purchase coins only from knowledgeable dealers who specialize in ancient coins. Both Greek and Roman counterfeits are illustrated and described.

1693 **Moulakis, Christophoros M.** "Christodoulou the Forger—More Dies." *Nomismatika Khronika* (Greece) 13 (1994): 43-54. Illus.
In 1991, seventy-eight dies turned up in a wooden box in Athens. The dies were engraved by Christodoulos, the famous forger. Moulakis describes the provenance of the box of dies. Each die is listed and described, and impressions from each are shown. [In Greek on pp. 43-4; in English on pp. 45-8; plates on pp. 44 and 49-54].

1694 ——— "Christodoulou the Forger: Twenty More Fakes?" *Nomismatika Khronika* (Greece) 14 (1995): 73-5. Illus.
Adds another twenty "coins" to Svoronos' publication of the known counterfeits by Christodoulos. The coins are all illustrated.

1695 ——— "Christodoulou Yet Again." *Μνημη Martin Jessop Price*. Edited by A. P. Tzamalis and M. J. A. Tzamali. Bibliotheca 5. Athens: The Hellenic Numismatic Society, 1996. Pages 157-60. Illus.
Numerous dies created by the famed counterfeiter Christodoulou appeared on the market in Athens in 1995. Here, the author publishes photographs of the dies and of plasticine impressions from the dies. Includes thirteen dies of Macedonian kings Alexander II and Demetrius Poliorketes, Larissa, Pharsalos, Delphi, Chalkis, Karystos, Athens, Aigina, Corinth, and Ptolemy I Soter. [Also see "Previously Unknown Fake Dies" below].

1696 ——— "Inexhaustible Christodoulou." *Nomismatika Khronika* (Greece) 19 (2000): 131-4. Illus.
Publishes seventeen dies and die impressions, all by Christodoulos, found in Athens in 1999. In Greek and English.

1697 **Pinder, Moritz Eduard.** *Die Beckerschen Falschen Münzen Beschrieben von M. Pinder*. Berlin: Nicolaische Buchhandlung, 1843. 73 pp., 2 pls. French edition, Paris, 1853. 92 pp., 2 pls. [CS 10255]
Discusses the forgeries of Carl Wilhelm Becker. Lists 331 pieces.

1698 "Previously Unknown Fake Dies by Counterfeiter Christodoulou Appear." *Coin World* (August 28, 1995): 52. Illus.
Announces that seventy-eight dies, produced by Constantine Christodoulou for striking counterfeit Greek coins, were recently found in an Athens antique shop. [Also see Moulakis "Christodoulou Yet Again" above].

1699 **Price, Martin J.** "Forgeries of Ancient Coins by Becker and Caprara." *Fake? The Art of Deception*. Edited by Mark Jones. London: British Museum, 1990. Berkeley and Los Angeles: University of California Press, 1990. Pages 144-5. Illus.
A brief discussion of the forgers Carl Becker and Caprara.

1700 **Prokopov, Ilya.** *Coin Forgeries and Replicas 2006*. Coin Collections and Coin Hoards from Bulgaria. Sofia, 2007. 80 pp., illus.
Lists 201 counterfeit coins, as well as whole pseudo hoards. Includes forgeries from the Mandev studio and a large group of counterfeit Histiaea tetrobols.

1701 **Prokopov, Ilya, Kostadin Kissyov, and Eugeni Paunov.** *Modern Counterfeits and Replicas of Ancient Greek and Roman Coins from Bulgaria*. Coin Collections and Coin Hoards from Bulgaria No. 1. Sofia, 2003. 78 pp., illus.
Publishes 192 modern forgeries of ancient gold, silver, copper, and bronze coins coming from Bulgaria (112 Greek, 78 Roman, 2 Byzantine). A special section is devoted to a group of 77 fakes of Thasian type Celtic/Thracian imitation tetradrachms. Eight sets of modern steel dies for striking Roman Republican and Imperial coins are illustrated and described. Includes a five-page introduction to modern coin forgery in Bulgaria. Discusses the known workshops and technology.

1702 **Prokopov, Ilya, and R. Manov.** *Counterfeit Studios and Their Coins*. Sofia, 2005. 88 pp., 11 pls.
Describes the work of specific, named Bulgarian forgery studios with photographic illustrations of their work. Illustrates many forgeries of Greek and Roman coins with detailed information on how to detect them. [Also see R. Goldsborough's comments on this book in his "Letter to the Editor" in *The Celator* 19, no. 8 (August 2005): 56].

1703 **Prokopov, Ilya, and Eugeni Paunov.** *Cast Forgeries of Classical Coins from Bulgaria*. Coin Collections and Coin Hoards from Bulgaria No. 3. Sofia, 2004. 88 pp., illus.
A large group of modern and ancient forgeries of Greek and Roman coins coming from Bulgaria is published. Includes 112 gold, silver, and bronze coins. Includes a section devoted to a modern rubber or plastic negative matrix for making imprints of cast models of Roman Imperial denarii.

1704 **Puetz, Bill.** "The Slavey Interview." Two Parts. *The Celator* 14, no. 4 (April 2000): 18-25; no. 5 (May 2000): 31-3. Illus.
An interview with Slavey Petrov, a Bulgarian counterfeiter of ancient coins. Slavey describes how he got started in the business of creating copies of ancient coins and describes his production methods. Includes photographs of Slavey and his workshop. [Also see Demetriadi "Slavey" above].

1705 **Ravel, Oscar E.** *Numismatique Grecque: Falsifications, Moyens pour les Reconnaître*. London: Spink, 1946. 103 pp., 10 pls. Reprint, Chicago: Obol International, 1980. 105 pp. [CS 3598]
A revised and expanded version of an article published in *Revue Numismatique* in 1933.

1706 **Robinson, Edward S. G.** "Some Early Nineteenth Century Forgeries of Greek Coins." *Numismatic Chronicle* 6th ser., 16 (1956): 15-8. 1 pl. [CS 3599]
"A group of extremely skillful forgeries fall into two groups, but a common hand seems to be at work in both. Coins of a number of different places and periods are linked together by dies, since all the forgeries are struck, not cast. Group I (described in detail) comprises tetradrachms of Samos and one of Antiochus IX, with a common reverse die (Herakles and snakes). Group II includes Samos, Samos-Chios (Archaic lion scalp facing/Sphinx l.) and Chios (Sphinx and incuse). There is also a coin seemingly of Athens (Owl on rock/incuse) in the Berlin collection. The first group is far more dangerous, containing pieces which, if genuine, would be of historical importance. For instance, use of no. 3, probably overstruck on a coin of Athens, as evidence for especially close relations between Samos and Athens at the moment of Konon's victory must now be abandoned." [C. Vermeule, *NL* 43]

1707 **Saryon, Leon A.** "Fake Ancient Coins Abound on eBay." *The Centinel* (Journal of the Central States Numismatic Society) 57, no. 4 (winter 2009-2010): 12, 14. Illus.
Warns of the abundance of counterfeit ancient coins offered as genuine on eBay. In particular, the author describes a fake silver coin of Tigranes the Great of Armenia. No genuine coin is known with this obverse/reverse combination.

1708 **Saslow, Arnold R.** "Black Sea Hoard: Saslow Calls Controversial Ancient Coins Fake." *World Coin News* (May 28, 1990): 20.
Recounts the controversy over the authenticity of the Black Sea Hoard coins. Argues that the coins are counterfeit. Criticizes the analysis done by Stanley Flegler. [Also see Flegler, Sayles].

1709 ——— "Coins Modern Counterfeits." *Coin World* (October 18, 1993): 24, 36.
In response to F. Kovacs' article in *The Celator* (see Kovacs "Sofia Museum" above), this editorial re-states Saslow's view that the "Black Sea Hoard" diobols of Mesembria and Apollonia Pontica are counterfeit. [Also see M. Emory's rebuttal "Black Sea Hoard Genuine" above].

1710 **Sayles, Wayne G.** "IBSCC Condemns Fakes of Istros and Black Sea." *The Celator* 4, no. 1 (January 1990): 12, 19.
Mentions comments of the International Bureau for the Suppression of Counterfeit Coins suggesting the diobols of Mesembria and Apollonia Pontica from the recent "Black Sea hoard" are modern counterfeits. Says these pieces resemble in style some newly discovered counterfeit coins of Istros. Author believes the Istros coin dies were engraved by the same person who engraved the Apollonia Pontica dies. [Also see Flegler, Wetterstrom].

1711 ——— "Art Historical Perspective: Hoard Coinage Deviates from Traditional Style." *The Celator* 4, no. 5 (May 1990): 16. Illus.
Reviews the controversy over the "Black Sea Hoard" coins of Mesembria and Apollonia Pontica. Suggests the style of the helmet depicted on the Mesembrian hoard coins differs from that on known genuine coins. Examines the style of the horse-hair tail, the eye-opening, the nose plate, and the cheek protectors of the helmet and concludes that on genuine coins these elements have an unemotional and geometric appearance. The overall appearance of the helmet on the hoard coins is that of a stylized human face, complete with emotions. The face on the Apollonia hoard coins is poorly executed when compared to pre-hoard coins. Concludes that the hoard coins are not genuine ancient coins. [Also see Flegler's rebuttal "Scientist Rebuts" above].

1712 ——— "The Celator's Point of View." *The Celator* 5, no. 4 (April 1991): 2; 5, no. 11 (November 1991): 2.
An editorial on the continuing debate over the authenticity of the "Black Sea Hoard" coins. The first part mentions a *Chicago Tribune* report that the coins have been proven genuine. Sayles maintains the coins are modern counterfeits. The second part is a reaction to a *Coin World* story (see Vagi "Expert Says" below) suggesting the coins are genuine. [Also see other articles by Sayles above].

1713 ——— "Examination of Die-Engraving Technique Exposes 'Black Sea Hoard' Coins as Modern." *The Celator* 6, no. 9 (September 1992): 34-6. Illus.
Reviews the controversy over the "Black Sea Hoard" coins. The die links found through an examination of photographs of hoard coins reveal an unusual pattern of links suggestive of counterfeit coins. States that coins of this type from a Bulgarian museum are die-linked to the hoard coins and suggests the museum coins are also counterfeit. An examination of the die engravings reveals unusual striations which the author concludes are the result of the use of a modern rotary dentist's drill. Presents a table of die-links and enlarged photographs illustrating traces of rotary die engraving.

1714 ——— *Classical Deception: Counterfeits, Forgeries, and Reproductions of Ancient Coins.* Iola: Krause Publications, 2001. 196 pp., illus.
An excellent review of the world of counterfeit ancient coins—essential reading for all collectors. Begins with a discussion of the methods of producing counterfeit ancient coins (casting, stamping, striking from engraved dies, plating, etc.). Reviews the history of some of the most famous counterfeits and their creators, including the Paduans and the forgeries of Becker, Caprara, Cigoi, and Sazonov. Continues with a review of the major twentieth century fakes including the Baghdad forgeries, the Geneva forgeries, the work of Christodoulos, the Utmanzai, Orphanides, Bulgarian School, and other forgeries. Sayles then discusses replicas and reproductions. Next, he reviews various methods of detection and analysis. Continues with reviews of the Hobby Protection Act and the actions of the authentication services and trade and collector associations. Concludes with a catalogue of the works of Peter Rosa, with illustrations of 404 of his copies. [Reviewed by Bruce R. Brace in *Journal of the Classical and Medieval Numismatic Society* 2nd ser., 2, no. 2 (June 2001): 97-100, by Lou Balesteri in *The Celator* 15, no. 8 (August 2001): 34-5, and by O. D. Hoover in *American Numismatic Society Magazine* 2, no. 3 (winter 2003): 62-5].

1715 ——— "The Black Sea Hoard Revisited." *The Celator* 20, no. 3 (March 2006): 49. Illus.
Announces the discovery of two examples of a mule of the counterfeit "Black Sea Hoard" coins. The new pieces combine the reverse of the Mesembria coin with the reverse of the Apollonia coin. The Mesembria die matches a die from one of the normal Mesembria "hoard" specimens, confirming that both the Mesembria and Apollonia pieces were likely made at the same time by the same forger.

1716 **Scyphers, John.** "Letter to the Editor." *The Celator* 2, no. 8 (August 1988): 18.
A counterfeit tetradrachm of Lysimachus is shown. The coin weighs 16.51 gm, has a specific gravity of 10.5 and resembles *Sear* 6816.

1717 **Seeger, John A.** "Forgeries of Greek and Roman Coins." *SAN—Journal of the Society for Ancient Numismatics* 1, no. 1 (July 1969): 11.
Various methods of producing counterfeit coins are mentioned. Several counterfeit coins are pictured.

1718 **Sestini, Domenico.** *Sopra i Moderni Falsificatori di Medaglie Greche Antiche ne tre Metalli e Desrizione di Tutte Quelle Prodotte dai Medesimi Nello Spazio di Pochi Anni.* Firenze: Attilio Tofani, 1826.
Sestini criticizes Carl Becker for his forgeries and publishes a list of them here.

1719 **Steinbüchel von Rheinwald, Anton.** *Die Beckerschen Falschen Münzstämpel in aus Führlichen Verzeichnissen. Für Sammler und Freunde der Münzwissenschaft. Mit einer Einleitung Münzkunde überhaupt.* Vienna: Friedrich Volke's Buchhandlung, 1836. 40 pp., 2 pls. [CS 16259]
Discusses the Becker forgeries.

1720 **Svoronos, Joannes N.** "C. Christodoulos et les Faussaires d'Athènes." *Journal International d'Archéologie Numismatique* (Greece) 20 (1922): 97-107. 9 pls.; 21 (1927): 141-6. 8 pls. Also published as *Synopsis de Mille Coins Faux du Faussaire C. Christodoulos*. Athens, 1922. Reprint, Basel and Amsterdam, 1963. 16 pp., 17 pls. [CS 3600]
"Describes the career of Christodoulos as a forger of ancient coins, with photographs of his work, to Scyros in Vol. 20 and from Attica onward in Vol. 21." [J. R. Jones, *AIJIAN*]. [For an English translation, see *Christodoulos the Counterfeiter* below].

1721 ——— *Christodoulos the Counterfeiter*. 1922. Reprint, Chicago: Ares Publishers, 1974. 38 pp., 17 pls. [CS 3600a]
An English translation, by Al N. Oikonimides, of *Synopsis de Mille Coins Faux du Faussaire C. Christodoulos* (Athens, 1922), with some editorial notes. Discusses the counterfeit Greek coins produced by Constantine Christodoulos in the early twentieth century. Christodoulos engraved his own dies. The introduction describes the confiscation of his dies by authorities and their subsequent dispersal. Presents very brief identifications of over 500 of his counterfeits, all of which are shown in the plates. [Also see Kovacs "New Christodoulou Dies," Moulakis (three items), and "Previously Unknown Fake Dies" above].

1722 **Taylor, George.** "The Gentle Art of Forgery." *Saudi Aramco World* 23, no. 5 (September/October 1972): 2-3.
A brief discussion of the history of ancient coin forgery, from ancient times, through the era of Cavino and Becker, to the present. Discusses the common fakes which are often sold to tourists in the Middle East.

1723 **Tazedakis, Panos.** "The Medals of Christodoulou, Original Works of a Great Counterfeiter." *Nomismatika Khronika* (Greece) (1991): 91-7 (in Greek); 98-102 (in English). Illus.
The author provides biographical information on Konstantinos Christodoulou, the famous counterfeiter. Describes his activities and his adversarial relationship with Ioannis Svoronos, the director of the National Numismatic Collection in Athens. Tazedakis also reveals the existence of seven small silver medals bearing the portrait of the Greek statesman Eleftherios Venizelos (1864-1936), signed by Christodoulou. The medals were previously unknown and were created with the characteristics of ancient coins. The medals are illustrated.

1724 "Unknown Forgers of Ancient Coins: Part 1: George Antoniou & Company in Crete." *North American Journal of Numismatics: The Turtle* 6, no. 4 (April 1967): 109-10.
An excerpt from Leonard Wooley's book *As I Seem to Remember* (New York, 1962) describes the story of an associate of Arthur Evans at Knossos who produced struck forgeries of Greek coins.

1725 **Vagi, David L.** "Expert Says Ancient Hoard Coins Genuine; Study of Die Links Key to Authenticity." *Coin World* (October 9, 1991): 1, 40, 42. Illus.
Suggests that die-links have been established between some of the "Black Sea Hoard" coins and coins from an archaeological excavation in Bulgaria. The "Black Sea Hoard" coins were found in Bulgaria in 1986 and this article recounts the finding of the coins, analysis of the coins, and the resulting controversy over their authenticity. Focuses on Stanley Flegler's trip to Bulgaria to meet local museum officials. Illustrates the die-links. Discusses the style of the coins. [Also see Dennis Kroh's editorial in *Coin World* (November 6, 1991): 4, in which Kroh expresses doubts regarding the die-links, and questions other aspects of the analysis of the hoard coins. Also see responses arguing the authenticity of the coins by Marc Emory in *Coin World* (November 20, 1992): 5, and by Thomas D. Walker in *Coin World* (December 4, 1991): 4. Also see articles by Emory, Flegler, Giedroyc, Saslow, and Sayles above].

1726 ——— "Ancient Coins' Authenticity American Scientist's Hobby: Study Unravels Mystery of Hoard." *Coin World* (October 9, 1991): 34. Illus.
Recounts Stanley Flegler's trip to Bulgaria to research the "Black Sea Hoard" coins, his meeting with Bulgarian museum officials, and his experiences in Bulgaria.

1727 ——— "Slavei Replicas of Roman and Greek Gold." *SAN—Journal of the Society for Ancient Numismatics* 20, no. 1 (1997): 39. Illus.
Presents obverse and reverse photographs of four Roman and four Greek gold counterfeit coins produced by the forger Slavei. The Greek coins are an electrum stater of Cyzicus, and gold staters of Lysimachus, Olynthus, and Lampsakos.

1728 **van Alfen, Peter.** "Ancient Imitative and Counterfeit Coinage in Context." *Making, Moving and Managing: The New World of Ancient Economies, 323-331 B.C.* Edited by Z. H. Archibald, J. Davies, and V. Gabrielsen. London: Oxbow Books, 2005. Pages 322-54.

1729 **Walker, Alan S.** "Why Are You So Sure It's a Fake?" *The Celator* 11, no. 5 (May 1997): 6-11. Illus.
Walker presents steps for determining whether an ancient coin is genuine or counterfeit. He emphasizes the importance of style, and provides an example using gold staters of Panticapaeum. Five staters of the same general type are illustrated, but each is from a different period and exhibits a different style. Walker points out how the details of the design of one of the coins differ from all the others. The coin is determined to be fake.

1730 **Wells, H. Bartlett.** "Counterfeit Ancient Copper Coins." *SAN—Journal of the Society for Ancient Numismatics* 10, no. 3 (fall 1979): 38-40.
A few counterfeit copper coins are described including one which appeared to be a fourth century B.C. coin of the Lycian king Perikles, bearing the Lycian triskeles on the reverse.

1731 ——— "The Macedon, Aesillas, Drachma." *SAN—Journal of the Society for Ancient Numismatics* 9, no. 4 (fall 1981): 71.
A counterfeit drachma of Aesillas is shown and described.

1732 **Wetterstrom, Kerry K.** "Cooperation Noted: Recent Black Sea Hoard Discovered to be Fake." *The Celator* 3, no. 3 (March 1989): 12.
Provides background on a coin hoard supposedly found in Bulgaria and its subsequent dispersal. Author suggests the coins are counterfeit. The hoard consisted of silver diobols of Mesembria and Apollonia Pontica in Thrace. The coins seem to have been struck from newly cut dies, sandblasted to hide traces of tooling, acid-treated, and artificially patinated. British Museum officials declared the coins to be counterfeit. [Also see Flegler above].

1733 **Wilson, Lyn.** "Turkish Adventure: Collector Relates Search for the Ultimate Forgery." *The Celator* 4, no. 1 (January 1990): 27.

Recounts a trip to Turkey during which the author purchased a coin which appeared to be a counterfeit bronze coin with Justinian on the obverse and an Athenian owl on the reverse. After cleaning, it turned out to be a counterfeit silver Athenian tetradrachm—the portrait of Justinian and all traces of bronze had disappeared.

1734 **Wilson, William.** "Ancient Counterfeits and the Odyssey of a Novice." *SAN—Journal of the Society for Ancient Numismatics* 8, no. 1 (fall 1976): 2-3.
Counterfeit ancient coins which the author purchased in Spain are mentioned. Counterfeit coins of Thasos and Athens are pictured.

1735 **Wolenik, Robert.** "The Master Counterfeiter: Carl Wilhelm Becker Flooded the World with His Coin Copies." *Coinage* 14, no. 5 (May 1978): 16-8. Illus.
A brief account of the life and works of Becker the counterfeiter.

Also see: "Another Forgery" under SICILY—AKRAGAS; Ashton "Some Forgeries of Rhodian Didrachms" under CARIAN ISLANDS—RHODES; Ashton "Some Early Rhodian Forgeries" under CARIAN ISLANDS—RHODES; Balcer "The Archaic Coinage of Skyros" (Christodoulos) under NORTHERN GREECE—THESSALY; Bedoukian "Gold Forgeries of Tigranes" under ARMENIA; Caley "Distinguishing Cast from Struck" under METALLURGY; Demetriadi "Larissa 'Facing Head' Forgeries" under NORTHERN GREECE—THESSALY; Demetriadi and Hepworth "Forgeries of Boeotian Autonomous Staters" under CENTRAL GREECE—BOEOTIA; Elam "Microstructure" under METALLURGY; Gonnella "A Previously Unknown Tetradrachm" under PARTHIA.

Handa "Counterfeit Copper Coins" under BACTRIA; Hardwick "A New Variety of Chian Forgery" under IONIAN ISLANDS—CHIOS; Hardwick "Three Groups of Chian Forgeries" under IONIAN ISLANDS—CHIOS; Hendin "Ancient Forgeries" (Coins of the Bible series) under PALESTINE—JUDEA; Hendin *Guide to Biblical Coins* under PALESTINE—JUDEA; Hendin "Coins of the Bible—Request for Information" under PALESTINE—JUDEA; Hendin *Not Kosher* under PALESTINE—JUDEA; Hodder "Carthaginian" under ZEUGITANA; Hurter "New Greek Coin Hoard Questioned" under HOARDS; Ireland "Another Example" under CARIAN ISLANDS—RHODES; Jenkins "A Group of Bactrian Forgeries" under BACTRIA; Jenkins "Numismatic Forgeries of Pyrrhus" under NORTHERN GREECE—EPIRUS; Kinns "Amphictionic" under CENTRAL GREECE—PHOKIS; Kraay "Melos Hoard" under CYCLADES ISLANDS; Kritt "Authenticating Ancients" under METROLOGY; Kutcher "Fourrées" under THE MINTING PROCESS.

LaNiece "Silver-Plated" under METALLURGY; Larson "Experiments in Coin-Making" under THE MINTING PROCESS; Marotta "Copper Owls" under ATTICA—GENERAL WORKS; Marotta "Foiled by Fourrees?" under THE MINTING PROCESS; Mildenberg "False Staters" under LYCIA; Nercessian "A Counterfeit Hemidrachm of Tigranes II" under ARMENIA; Nercessian "More on Counterfeits" under ARMENIA; Nercessian "Tigranes II Counterfeit Tetradrachm" under ARMENIA; Nercessian "Tigranes II Counterfeit Tetradrachm with Imperial Countenance Portrait" under ARMENIA; Nercessian "Tigranes II Gold Coins Discovered in Europe" under ARMENIA; Oddy and Cowell "Gilded" under METALLURGY; Peters *Counterfeit Coins of Celtic Britain* under CELTIC COINAGE OF BRITAIN; Pink "Gold Medallions of Lysimachus" under THRACE—COINAGE OF LYSIMACHOS.

Rudd "17 Celtic Fakes" under CELTIC COINAGE—GENERAL WORKS; Saryan "Counterfeit Ancient Armenian Coins" under ARMENIA; Sheedy and Gore "Asyut 422" under ATTICA—GENERAL WORKS; Shortt "Utmanzai" under BACTRIA; Smith "Fourrées" under THE MINTING PROCESS; Starck "Auction Firms Withdraw Highlight Coin" under ATTICA—GENERAL WORKS; Stefanaki "Les Fausses Monnaies d'Hiérapytna" under CRETE; "Suspicions" under CELTIC COINAGE; Symons "Some New Forgeries" under CELTIC COINAGE OF BRITAIN; Tameanko "Syracusan Dekadrachm" under SICILY—SYRACUSE; Taylor "A Halved Tetradrachm" under CYRENAICA; "Unique Gold Coin" under MACEDONIAN KINGDOM—GENERAL WORKS; Van Arsdell "Haslemere Hoard" (several items) under CELTIC COINAGE OF BRITAIN; Visonà "A Carthaginian Gold Issue" under CYRENAICA; Walker "Forgeries and Inventions of Parthian Coins" under PARTHIA; Wells "Plated Gold Staters" (several items) under MACEDONIAN KINGDOM—GENERAL WORKS.

Important Collections

Public Collections

Although the science of numismatics was one of the earliest branches of archaeology to attract students, it has never yet succeeded in gaining the favour of the general public...They are therefore only too readily disposed to regard numismatists as people afflicted with the collector's mania, and their pretended science as a mere hobby to be placed in the same category with the collecting of autographs, postcards, or military buttons. I do not propose to undertake here the defence of numismatists...But I should like to protest against the unjust contempt of which Numismatics is the object, and to begin by showing in a few words that it is a true science, and one of the most precious aids to historical research.

—Theodore Reinach, 1903

AUSTRALIA

CANBERRA

1736 **Rawson, Beryl.** "Coins." *Antiquities: A Description of the Classics Department Museum in The Australian National University, Canberra.* By J. R. Green. Canberra: The Australian National University, 1981. Pages 128-72. Illus.
A catalogue of the Greek and Roman coins in the museum's collection. The Greek coins (pages 130-7) are neither numerous nor spectacular.

SYDNEY

1737 **Nixon, C. E. V.** *Catalogue of the Coins in the Macquarie University Museum of Ancient Cultures.* Sydney: Macquarie University, 1996. 160 pp., illus.
A catalogue of the Greek, Roman, Roman Provincial, Byzantine, and Islamic coins in the museum's collection. Includes 111 Greek coins. Also includes a few counterfeit pieces. Most of the coins are common types in worn condition.

1738 **Sheedy, Kenneth A.** "Greek Coins in the Museum of Applied Arts and Sciences, Sydney." *Mediterranean Archaeology* (Australia) 5/6 (1992-93): 143-60. 9 pls.
A catalogue of 138 Greek coins, all illustrated.

Also see: Sheedy *Alexander and the Hellenistic Kingdoms* under PRIVATE COLLECTIONS.

BELGIUM

BRUSSELS

1739 **de Callataÿ, François, and Johan van Heesch.** *Greek and Roman Coins from The Du Chastel Collection: Coin Cabinet of the Royal Library of Belgium.* London: Spink, 1999. 162 pp., 41 pls.
A catalogue of 821 Greek, Roman, and Byzantine gold, silver, and bronze coins (306 are Greek). Includes a biographical essay on Count Albéric Du Chastel de la Howardries (b. 1842; d. 1919) and the history of the collection, written by de Callataÿ, and a discussion of the collection by van Heesch. Belgium purchased the collection from du Chastel in1898. The Greek coins were catalogued by de Callataÿ. Includes many gold coins, numerous rarities, and many coins of outstanding artistic merit. The coins are uniformly of excellent quality. [Reviewed by W. G. Sayles in *The Celator* 14, no. 4 (April 2000): 34-5. A group of coins (646 lots) from Du Chastel's collection were sold in 1889 by Rollin & Feuardent. See listing 569 in J. Spring, *Ancient Coin Auction Catalogues 1880-1980* (see Spring under COLLECTING GUIDES)].

1740 **Naster, Paul.** *La Collection Lucien de Hirsch: Catalogue de Monnaies Grecques.* Two volumes. Brussels: Bibliothèque Royale de Belgique, 1959. 353 pp., 104 pls. [CS 1880]
A catalogue of 1877 coins in the Bibliothèque Royale de Belgique.

Brazil

Also see: Nicolau Kormikiari under ZEUGITANA.

Bulgaria

STARA ZAGOA

1741 **Prokopov, Ilja, and Mariana Minkova.** "Die Münzen des 2-1 Jhs v. Chr. in der Sammlung des Historischen Museums von Stara Zagora." *Stephanos Nomismatikos: Edith Schönert-Geiss zum 65. Geburtstag.* Edited by Ulrike Peter. Berlin: Akademie Verlag, 1998. Pages 563-84.

Canada

GENERAL

1742 **Brace, Dorte.** "Some Information on Museum Collections in North America." *The Anvil* (Canada) 4, no. 4 (July 1, 1994): 39-40.
Lists and briefly describes public collections of ancient coins and related libraries in Canada and the United States.

OTTAWA

1743 **Kiernan, Philip.** "The Petrie Bequest to Canada's National Currency Collection." *The Celator* 16, no. 4 (April 2002): 14-22. Illus.
Briefly describes and illustrates seventeen Chinese, Greek, Roman, Byzantine, Sasanian, Islamic, and Artuqid coins bequeathed to Canada's National Currency Collection, in the Bank of Canada in Ottawa, by Alfred Edward Hathaway Petrie (died 2000). Petrie's collection included about 2000 coins in addition to a library of related books.

MONTREAL

1744 **Denis, Paul, and Derek Grout.** *Greek and Roman Coins: The Montreal Museum of Fine Arts Collection.* Montreal, 1981. 64 pp., illus.
A booklet published to accompany the traveling exhibition "Ancient Coins: Greek and Roman Art in Miniature." In English and French.

1745 **Shlosser, Franziska E.** *Ancient Greek Gold and Silver Coins in the McGill University College.* Montreal, 1970.
"A thesis held at McGill University." [M. Tooth and G. Kumpikevicius, *A Bibliography of Classical Numismatics in Canada*]

1746 ——— *The McGill University Collection of Greek and Roman Coins. Volume 2: Greek Gold and Silver Coins in the McGill University Collection.* Edited by Michael Woloch. Amsterdam: B. R. Grüner Publishing, 1975. 72 pp., 25 pls. [CS 1881]
A catalogue of 316 silver, four gold, and four electrum coins. Two-hundred thirteen of the coins are from Tarentum. Each coin is illustrated. Descriptions are brief.

1747 ——— *The McGill University Collection of Greek and Roman Coins. Volume 3: Ancient Bronze Coins in the McGill University Collection.* Edited by Michael Woloch. Amsterdam: B. R. Grüner Publishing, 1984. 149 pp., 18 pls.
About 600 Greek and Roman Provincial bronze coins are catalogued, and a representative selection are photographed. Descriptions are brief.

1748 **Virr, Richard, Barbara Lawson, G. Michael Woloch, and Franziska E. Shlosser.** "The McGill University Collection of Greek and Roman Coins: New Evidence for its History." *Fontanus: From the Collections of McGill University* (Canada) 4 (1991): 109-24.
McGill University, Montreal, has a collection of about 2100 classical, ancient, and oriental coins. The major part of the collection was found in 1966 in a box when the University's McCord Museum of Canadian History was being relocated. This article reconstructs the history of the collection, and sheds light on the connection between a coin collection belonging to Margaret Murray (d. 1927) and the collection of the University's Principal, William Peterson.

1749 **Woloch, G. Michael.** "On Cataloguing the McGill University Collection of Greek and Roman Coins: A Progress Report." *Ancient Coins of the Graeco-Roman World: The Nickle Numismatic Papers.* Edited by Waldemar Heckel and Richard Sullivan. Waterloo, Ontario: Wilfrid Laurier University Press, 1984. Pages 296-7.
A brief history of the McGill University collection and a report on the status of the cataloguing of the collection.

TORONTO

1750 **Easson, Alison Harle.** *Money Alone Sets All the World in Motion: A Brief Introduction to the Exhibit of Greek Coinage in the ROM.* Toronto: Royal Ontario Museum, 1973. 8 pp., illus.
Catalogue for an exhibition of Greek coins at the Royal Ontario Museum. Lists about twenty coins. Reprinted from *Rotunda* (Summer 1973), the museum's official magazine. Provides a very brief introduction to Greek coinage.

1751 ——— "Ancient Coins in the Royal Ontario Museum." *The Picus* (Canada) (1992): 9-27. Illus.
Illustrates forty-five ancient coins in the collection of the Royal Ontario Museum, including twenty Greek coins. A brief explanation of the history surrounding each coin is provided.

1752 **Royal Ontario Museum.** *Greek Coins in the Royal Ontario Museum of Archaeology.* Toronto: Royal Ontario Museum, 1951.
"An introductory pamphlet to the museum's collection." [M. Tooth and G. Kumpikevicius, *A Bibliography of Classical Numismatics in Canada*]

CROATIA

SPLIT

1753 **Bonačić Mandinić, Maja.** *Greek Coins Displayed in the Archaeological Museum Split.* Split: Arheološki Muzej, 2006. 113 pp., illus.
"A catalogue of 214 silver and bronze coins, primarily of the Greek cities of Illyria displayed in the Split Museum (Museum of Croatian Archaeological Monuments). Especially notable is the inclusion of the contents of the Vrbanj hoard of Pharian bronze coins." [Oliver D. Hoover, *NL* 149]

ZAGREB

1754 **Dukat, Zdenka, and Ivan Mirnik.** *The Zagreb Archaeological Museum Numismatic Collection Guide.* Zagreb, 2008. 157 pp.
A brief guide to the museum's collection, including ancient coins.

CYPRUS

Also see: Iacovou *Cypriote Coinage* under CYPRUS; Zapiti and Michaelidou *Coins of Cyprus* under CYPRUS.

EGYPT

Also see: Breccia "Museum of Alexandria" under EGYPT—PTOLEMAIC KINGDOM.

FRANCE

PARIS

1755 **Babelon, Ernest C.** *Catalogue des Monnaies Grecques de la Bibliothèque Nationale.* Two volumes. Paris, 1890-93.

1756 **Babelon, Jean.** *Catalogue de la Collection de Luynes: Monnaies Grecques.* Four volumes of text, four volumes of plates. Paris: Bibliothèque Nationale, 1924-36. Reprint, Bologna: Forni, 1967. [CS 1883]
A collection in the Cabinet des Médailles at the Bibliothèque Nationale.
  1. *Italie et Sicily.* 1924. 292 pp., 56 pls.
  2. *Gréce Continentale et Iles.* 1925. 171 pp., 33 pls.
  3. *Asie Mineure et Phénicie.* 1930. 175 pp., 28 pls.
  4. *Syria, Egypt, Libya, Carthage, Mauretania, Zeugitana, Numidia, and Cyrenaica.* 1936. 168 pp., 37 pls.

1757 **Le Rider, Georges.** "Monnaies Grecques Récemment Acquises par le Cabinet des Médailles." *Revue Numismatique* (France) 6th ser., 3 (1961): 7-26. 3 pls.
Twenty-three recently acquired coins are examined.

1758 **Walcher de Molthein, Leopold.** *Catalogue de la Collection Des Medailles Grecques.* Paris: Rollins & Feuardent, 1895. 294 pp., 30 pls.
Catalogue of a private collection. Includes a preface by Victor de Renner.

Also see: Bhattacharyya *Indian Coins in the Musée Guimet* under BACTRIA; Mainjonet "Monnaies Celtiques" under CELTIC COINAGE—GENERAL WORKS; Touratsoglou "Aphrodite and Eros in Kyzikos" under TYPES.

GERMANY

BERLIN

1759 **Schultz, Han-Dietrich.** *Antike Münzen. Bildheft zur Ausstellung des Münzkabinetts in der Antikesammlung im Pergamonmuseum.* Berlin, 1997. 111 pp.
An illustrated guidebook to the exhibition.

1760 **Schultz, Sabine.** *Griechische Münzen der Klassichen Zeit.* Leipzig: Insel Verlag, 1972. 15 pp., 48 pls. [CS 1885]

1761 **Von Sallet, Alfred.** *Beschreibung der Antiken Münzen.* Three volumes. Berlin: W. Spemann. [CS 1884]
A partial catalogue of the collection of the Königliche Museen zu Berlin, covering only parts of northern Greece and Italy.
  1. *Taurische Chersonesus, Sarmatien, Dacien, Pannonien, Moesien, Thracian, Thracische Könige.* 1888. 357 pp., 8 pls.
  2. *Paeonien, Macedonien, die Macedonischen Könige bis Perdiccas III.* 1889. 207 pp., 8 pls.
  3. *Italien (Aes Rude, Aes Signatum, Aes Grave, die Geprägten Münzen von Etrurien bis Calabrien).* 1894. 315 pp., 14 pls.

HAMBURG

1762 **Postel, R.** *Katalog der Antiken Münzen im der Hamburger Kunsthalle.* Two volumes. Hamburg, 1976. 347 pp., 130 pls.

HANNOVER

1763 **Berger, F.** *Die Antiken Goldmünzen im Kestner-Museum Hannover.* Hannover, 1991. 68 pp.

1764 **Grunauer-von Hoerschelmann, Susanne.** *Griechische Münzen.* Hannover: Kestner Museum, 1988. 90 pp., illus., maps.

A catalogue of 262 Greek coins in the museum's collection. Begins with a brief history of the collection and an introduction to Greek coinage.

1765 **Schlüter, M.** *Griechische Münzen: Katalog der Münzsammlung des Kestner Museums Hannover, Part 1.* Hannover, 1958. 72 pp., 16 pls. [CS 1886]

NÜRNBERG

1766 **Zwicker, Ulrich.** *Griechische Münzen (Griechenland, Ägäis, Pontus, Paphlagonia und Bithynien): Sammlung Zwicker, Teil 2.* Katalog der Münzen in der Universitätsbibliothek Erlanden-Nürnberg 4. Erlangen, 1996.
"An illustrated catalogue of about 1120 coins with commentary on metal content and structure." [H. Baldus, *NL* 145]

1767 ———— *Antike Münzen aus Kleinasien (Mysien bis Pisidien): Sammlung Zwicker, Teil 3.* Katalog der Münzen in der Universitätsbibliothek Erlanden-Nürnberg 5. Erlangen, 1996.
"An illustrated catalogue of about 1810 coins with commentary on metal content and structure. No. Z1811 is actually a coin of Laodicea ad Mare in Syria, not of Laodicea in Phrygia." [H. Baldus, *NL* 145]

Also see: Olshausen *Bronzemünzen* under PONTOS.

GREAT BRITAIN

CAMBRIDGE

1768 **Cloke, Christian.** "Coin Collecting at Cambridge: The Fitzwilliam Museum Department of Coins and Medals." *ANS* 7, no. 3 (winter 2008): 46-50. Illus.
A history of the coin collection in the Fitzwilliam Museum. The museum was founded in 1816, but the Greek coin collection was very small and unimportant until the 1864 purchase of the W. M. Leake collection. It was greatly expanded in 1912 when the J. R. McClean collection of 10,078 mostly Greek coins was bequeathed to the museum. It grew further when the University's colleges combined their collections into the Fitzwilliam Museum, including the Samuel S. Lewis collection from Corpus Christi College. [Also see Grose *McClean Collection* below, and SNG—BRITISH SERIES, Volumes 4 and 6 under SYLLOGE NUMORUM GRAECORUM SERIES].

1769 **Errington, Elizabeth, Joe Cribb, and Maggie Claringbull, eds.** *The Crossroads of Asia: Transformation in Image and Symbol in the Art of Ancient Afghanistan and Pakistan.* Cambridge: The Ancient India and Iran Trust, 1992. 306 pp., illus.
The catalogue of an exhibition at the Fitzwilliam Museum, October 6 – December 13, 1992. The purpose of the exhibition was to chart the eastward, then southerly, transmission of motifs and techniques from the Greek world through Afghanistan to Pakistan and northwest India, and to explore changes in both form and meaning. The primary focus is on small metalwork objects, including ninety-three coins. The objects were drawn from a number of public and private collections.

1770 **Grose, Sidney W.** *Catalogue of the McClean Collection of Greek Coins.* Three volumes. Cambridge: University Press, 1923, 1926, 1929. Reprint, Chicago: Obol International, 1979. 1450 pp., 380 pls. [CS 1887]

1. *Western Europe, Magna Graecia, Sicily.* 380 pp., 111 pls.
2. *The Greek Mainland, The Aegean Islands, Crete.* 563 pp., 137 pls.
3. *Asia Minor, Farther Asia, Egypt, Africa.* 507 pp., 132 pls.

A catalogue of the collection of 10,078 Greek coins (including some Roman Provincial issues) formed by John Robinson McClean. McClean bequeathed the collection to the Fitzwilliam Museum, Cambridge, in 1912. Grose was Keeper of Coins and Medals at the museum. This is one of the great Greek collections, expertly catalogued. The catalogue lists metal, die axis, weight (grains and grams), size (inches and millimeters), descriptions, references to other collections, dates of issue, and some brief historical notes. Most coins are photographed on the good-quality plates (even in the reprint). Also includes some very useful indices, including a geographical index and indices to types, inscriptions, monograms, symbols, and persons. These indices, along with the vast scope of the collection, make this one of the most useful catalogues for scholars, collectors, and dealers in Greek coins. [Volume 1 was reviewed by E. S. G. Robinson in *Numismatic Chronicle* 5th ser., 4 (1924): 113-4. Volume 2 was reviewed by G. F. Hill in *Numismatic Chronicle* 5th ser., 6 (1926): 476, and by E. T. Newell in *American Journal of Archaeology* 31 (1927): 521. Volume 3 was reviewed by Newell in *American Journal of Archaeology* 34 (1930): 524-5. Newell suggests different attributions for a few coins].

1771 **Heichelheim, Fritz M.** "Numismatic Comments: (3) The Sales Policy of a Great English Collector of Antiquities." *Hesperia* 16 (1947): 272-8.
"Sales catalogues which had belonged to W. M. Leake show the provenance of many of his coins in the Fitzwilliam Museum; they include many specimens from famous earlier collections." [J. R. Jones, *NIAJAH*]

1772 **Kumpikevicius, Gordon C.** "Fritz Moritz Heichelheim and the Fitzwilliam Coin Cabinet." *Hekte* (Canada) 2 (July 1996): 14-35.
Discusses the role of Heichelheim in the publication of *SNG Volume IV* and the coin collection of the Fitzwilliam museum.

Also see: Babington *Catalogue* and Leake *Numismata Hellenica* under PRIVATE COLLECTIONS (Leake's collection was later purchased by the Fitzwilliam Museum).

LONDON

1773 **Allan, John, ed.** *A Guide to the Department of Coins and Medals in the British Museum.* Fourth edition. London: Trustees of the British Museum, 1934. 99 pp., illus., 8 pls.
An introduction to the coins displayed at the British Museum. A short history of the collection is followed by introductions to the major eras and types of coinage. The collection of Greek coins was founded upon the collections donated by or purchased from Richard P. Knight, H. P. Borrell, James Woodhouse, Edward Wigan, the Bank of England, Edward Bunbury, Hyman Montagu, and Hermann Weber. Descriptions are provided for the coins then on exhibit at the museum. The Greek coins are described on pages 13-34 and plate 1.

1774 **Ashton, Richard J., Andrew Meadows, Kenneth A. Sheedy, and Ute Wartenberg.** "Some Greek Coins in the British Museum." *Numismatic Chronicle* 158 (1998): 37-51. 3 pls.
Discusses coins acquired by the British Museum including issues of Philip II, Abdera, Seriphos, Parion, Keramos, Aradus, and an eastern imitation of an Athenian tetradrachm.

1775 **Burgon, Thomas.** "On Certain Rare Greek Coins Recently Acquired by the British Museum." *Numismatic Chronicle* 19 (1857): 229-36. 1 pl.
Discusses (1) a Roman Provincial bronze coin from Corinth (Lais of Corinth head right/representation of her tomb), (2) another provincial bronze of Corinth with the obverse type representing the Isthmus, (3) a silver coin of Corinth with Pegasus/head of Medusa. (4) a silver coin of Leucas, (5) an Achaean League bronze coin of Gortys, and (6) a bronze coin of Orchomenus with Boeotian shield/OPX. This coin causes Burgon to speculate on the existence of a Boeotian League or Confederation.

1776 *Catalogue of Greek Coins in the British Museum.* Twenty-nine volumes. London: British Museum, 1873-1927. Reprint, Bologna: Forni, 1963-5. [CS 1888]
These volumes contain full descriptions of the dies, and the collection usually contains multiple specimens for many of the types. Many Greek Imperial coins are included. Most volumes include an introductory section giving extensive historical and numismatic background. Relatively few coins are pictured in the plates. Each volume is described more fully under the appropriate heading in this book (except for Volume 15 which deals exclusively with the Roman Provincial coinage of Egypt). Reference numbers are given below.

  1. *Italy*, by R. S. Poole, 1873. [See 2690].
  2. *Sicily*, by R. S. Poole, B. V. Head, and P. Gardner, 1876. [See 2968].
  3. *Thrace*, by B. V. Head and P. Gardner, 1877. [See 3601].
  4. *Seleucid Kings of Syria*, by P. Gardner, 1878. [See 5273].
  5. *Macedonia*, by B. V. Head, 1879. [See 3254].
  6. *Thessaly to Aetolia*, by P. Gardner, 1883. [See 3853].
  7. *The Ptolemies, Kings of Egypt*, by R. S. Poole, 1883. [See 6666].
  8. *Central Greece*, by B. V. Head, 1884. [See 3955].
  9. *Crete and the Aegean Islands*, by W. Wroth, 1886. [See 4442].
  10. *Peloponnesus*, by P. Gardner, 1887. [See 4292].
  11. *Attica, Megaris, Aegina*, by B. V. Head, 1888. [See 4027].
  12. *Corinth, etc.*, by B. V. Head, 1889. [See 4261].
  13. *Pontus, Paphlagonia, Bithynia, Bosporus*, by W. Wroth, 1889. [See 4602].
  14. *Mysia*, by W. Wroth, 1892. [See 4665].
  15. *Alexandria and the Nomes*, by R. S. Poole, 1892.
  16. *Ionia*, by B. V. Head, 1892. [See 4763].
  17. *Troas, Aeolis, and Lesbos*, by W. Wroth, 1894. [See 4712].
  18. *Caria, Cos, Rhodes, etc.*, by B. V. Head, 1897. [See 4875].
  19. *Lycia, Pamphylia, and Pisidia*, by G. F. Hill, 1897. [See 5023].
  20. *Galatia, Cappadocia, and Syria*, by W. Wroth, 1899. [See 5131].
  21. *Lycaonia, Isauria, and Cilicia*, by G. F. Hill, 1900. [See 5092].
  22. *Lydia*, by B. V. Head, 1901. [See 4989].
  23. *Parthia*, by W. Wroth, 1903. [See 6155].
  24. *Cyprus*, by G. F. Hill, 1904. [See 5178].
  25. *Phrygia*, by B. V. Head, 1906. [See 5010].
  26. *Phoenicia*, by G. F. Hill, 1910. [See 5601]. [Also see R. Kool "The Rediscovery of G. F. Hill's Original Plates" under PALESTINE—JUDEA].
  27. *Palestine*, by G. F. Hill, 1914. [See 5719]. [Also see R. Kool "The Rediscovery of G. F. Hill's Original Plates" under PALESTINE—JUDEA].
  28. *Arabia, Mesopotamia, Persia, etc.*, by G. F. Hill, 1922. [See 5936].
  29. *Cyrenaica*, by E. S. G. Robinson, 1927. [See 6760].

1776a **Combe, Taylor.** *Veterum Populorum et Regum Numi qui in Museo Britannico Adversantur.* London, 1814.
The Coins of Ancient Peoples and Kings Preserved in the British Museum—the first catalogue produced of the British Museum's coin and medal collection.

1777 **Frey, Imre.** "Index to the Catalogue of Greek Coins in the British Museum." *Spink Numismatic Circular* 42 (January 1934): 7-16.
An alphabetical list of Greek cities indicating which volume and pages the city is found on in the *Catalogue of Greek Coins in the British Museum*.

1778 **Gardner, Percy.** "On Some Interesting Greek Coins—Athens, Achaia, Sicyon, Susiana." *Numismatic Chronicle* new ser., 13 (1873): 177-86. 1 pl.
Examines some previously unpublished coins in the British Museum, including an archaic tetradrachm of Athens (with gorgon head), hemidrachms of the Achaean League, a didrachm of Sicyon, and a copper coin of Characene.

1779 ——— "Greek Coins Acquired by the British Museum in 1885." *Numismatic Chronicle* 3rd ser., 6 (1886): 249-64. 1 pl.
Describes a variety of Greek coins recently added to the museum's collection.

1780 **Head, Barclay V.** "On Some Rare Greek Coins Recently Acquired by the British Museum." *Numismatic Chronicle* new ser., 11 (1871): 166-8. 1 pl.
Lists four coins from Aurunca in Campania, Trapezos in Pontus, Mithradates III of Pontus, and Lycia. Discusses the significance of each.

1781 ——— *Synopsis of the Contents of the British Museum. Department of Coins and Medals. Select Greek Coins Exhibited in Electrotype.* London: Trustees of the British Museum, 1872. 48 pp.
Includes detailed descriptions of 209 Greek coins from the museum's collection which were exhibited at the museum. Revised in 1880 (see below).

1782 ———— *Synopsis of the Contents of the British Museum. Department of Coins and Medals. A Guide to the Select Greek and Roman Coins Exhibited in Electrotype. New Edition.* London: Trustees of the British Museum, 1880. 128 pp., 7 pls.
Includes detailed descriptions the most significant pieces in the British Museum's collection of ancient Greek coins. Preface by R. S. Poole. Table of weights. [This guide was revised and expanded, with many plates added, in 1881. See Head *Coins of the Ancients* under GENERAL WORKS—GREEK].

1783 ———— "The Greek Autonomous Coins from the Cabinet of the Late Mr. Edwards Wigan, Now in the British Museum." *Numismatic Chronicle* new ser., 13 (1873): 89-124; 309-34. 6 engraved plates.
Discusses the process of the acquisition of select coins from Wigan's collection by the British Museum. Lists and describes 154 coins from all areas of the Greek world, and discusses the importance of each piece. Many are of outstanding artistic merit.

1784 **Hill, George F.** "Notes on Additions to the Greek Coins in the British Museum, 1887-1896." *Journal of Hellenic Studies* 17 (1897): 78-91. 1 pl.
Publishes nineteen of the most significant coins acquired by the museum in recent years. Includes coins of Philip II, Chalcidice, Euboea, Aegium, Pheneus, Sybrita, Bithynia, Lampsacus, Mytilene, Ephesus, Phocaea, Cnidus, Lycia, and Seleucia ad Calycadnum. Discusses each. [Also see Wroth "Peparethus" under NORTHERN GREECE—THESSALY for a different attribution of the coins Hill assigned to Chalcidice].

1785 ———— "Greek Coins Acquired by the British Museum, 1905-1910." *Numismatic Chronicle* 4th ser., 12 (1912): 134-48. 2 pls.
Includes descriptions of thirty-one Greek coins.

1786 ———— "Greek Coins Acquired by the British Museum, 1911-1912." *Numismatic Chronicle* 4th ser., 13 (1913): 257-75. 2 pls.
Describes Greek coins recently acquired by the museum.

1787 ———— "Greek Coins Acquired by the British Museum in 1913." *Numismatic Chronicle* 4th ser., 14 (1914): 97-109. 2 pls.
Describes Greek coins recently acquired by the museum.

1788 ———— "Greek Coins Acquired by the British Museum, 1914-1916." *Numismatic Chronicle* 4th ser., 17 (1917): 1-30. 3 pls.
Describes Greek coins recently acquired by the museum.

1789 ———— "Greek Coins Acquired by the British Museum in 1917 and 1918." *Numismatic Chronicle* 4th ser., 19 (1919): 1-16. 2 pls.
Describes Greek coins recently acquired by the museum. [Also see the "Erratum" on page 256 for a correction regarding one of the plates].

1790 ———— "Greek Coins Acquired by the British Museum in 1919." *Numismatic Chronicle* 4th ser., 20 (1920): 97-116. 2 pls.
Describes Greek coins recently acquired by the museum. [Also see pages 277-8 for comments on these coins by M. P. Vlasto].

1791 ———— "Greek Coins Acquired by the British Museum in 1920." *Numismatic Chronicle* 5th ser., 1 (1921): 161-78. 2 pls.
Describes some of the most significant coins among the 2970 Greek coins acquired by the museum in 1920.

1792 ———— "Greek Coins Acquired by the British Museum in 1921." *Numismatic Chronicle* 5th ser., 2 (1922): 149-75. 2 pls.
Describes some of the most significant of the Greek coins acquired by the museum in 1921.

1793 ———— "Greek Coins Acquired by the British Museum in 1922." *Numismatic Chronicle* 5th ser., 3 (1923): 211-42. 2 pls.
Describes some of the most significant of the Greek coins acquired by the museum in 1922.

1794 ———— "Greek Coins Acquired by the British Museum in 1923." *Numismatic Chronicle* 5th ser., 4 (1924): 1-18. 2 pls.
Describes some of the most significant of the Greek coins acquired by the museum in 1923.

1795 ———— "Greek Coins Acquired by the British Museum in 1924." *Numismatic Chronicle* 5th ser., 5 (1925): 1-21. 2 pls.
Describes some of the most significant of the Greek coins acquired by the museum in 1924.

1796 ———— "Greek Coins Acquired by the British Museum in 1925." *Numismatic Chronicle* 5th ser., 6 (1926): 117-36. 2 pls.
Describes some of the most significant of the Greek coins acquired by the museum in 1925.

1797 ———— "Greek Coins Acquired by the British Museum in 1926." *Numismatic Chronicle* 5th ser., 7 (1927): 193-208. 3pls.
Describes some of the most significant of the Greek coins acquired by the museum in 1926.

1798 ———— "Greek Coins Acquired by the British Museum in 1927." *Numismatic Chronicle* 5th ser., 8 (1928): 1-15. 2pls.
Describes some of the most significant of the Greek coins acquired by the museum in 1927.

1799 ———— "Greek Coins Acquired by the British Museum in 1928." *Numismatic Chronicle* 5th ser., 9 (1929): 181-90. 1pl.
Describes some of the most significant of the Greek coins acquired by the museum in 1928.

1800 ———— "Greek Coins Acquired by the British Museum in 1929." *Numismatic Chronicle* 5th ser., 10 (1930): 285-99. 3 pls.
Catalogues and discusses thirty-six coins.

1801 **Jenkins, G. Kenneth.** "Greek Coins Recently Acquired by the British Museum." *Numismatic Chronicle* 6th ser., 15 (1955): 131-56. 2 pls.
Lists coins acquired by gift or purchase during the past two years. Includes identifications, references, and discussions of significant information revealed by the coins.

1802 ———— "Recent Acquisitions of Greek Coins." *British Museum Quarterly* 21, no. 2 (July 1957): 38-41. 1 pl.

"Among the Greek coins recently acquired by the British Museum is a coin of exceptional importance and of an entirely new type, namely, a silver tetradrachm of Cyrene which Jenkins labels 'the most impressive acquisition made in the field of Greek coinage since the museum obtained the piece bearing the portrait of Tissaphernes in 1947.' The obverse shows the head of Zeus, upon which rests Zeus-Ammon's great ram's horn. The writer states that 'the placing of this splendid head on the obverse, instead of the reverse of the coin, is a noteworthy feature—it has no precedent at Cyrene…The engraver responsible for this head is clearly one of the masters of his time: his Zeus-Ammon is perhaps the finest surviving image of the god, of unrivaled grandeur and force.' The reverse is also interesting. It shows the head of a bridled horse looking at a silphium plant…Among the other Greek coins acquired may be mentioned a didrachm of Hyria, a didrachm of Tarentum, a very rare didrachm of Thurium, a small but important coin of Rhegium, a didrachm of Gela and a silver tetradrachm struck in Punic Sicily. These specimens are described in some detail and illustrated on the plate." [Summarized from *NL* 44]

1803 ——— "Greek and Graeco-Indian Coins from the Haughton Collection." *British Museum Quarterly* 21 (1958): 70-3. 1 pl.
Coins from the H. L. Haughton collection recently acquired by the British Museum include a rare gold stater of Seleucus I, a unique gold stater of Antiochus II, and a stater of the Kushan emperor Huvishka. Also discusses one bronze and several silver coins from a variety of mints.

1804 ——— "Recent Acquisitions of Greek Coins by the British Museum." *Numismatic Chronicle* 6th ser., 19 (1959): 23-45. 2 pls.
Includes coins of Akragas, Kamarina, Anchialus, Thasos, Potidaia, Amphaxitis, Alexander the Great, Colchis, various Lycian cities, Byblos, and various Seleucid issues.

1805 ——— "Some Newly Acquired Greek Coins." *British Museum Quarterly* 22, nos. 3-4 (April 1960): 71-4. 1 pl.
Lists eleven coins including a previously unknown stater of Tarsus and some new coins of Lycia, including two issued by the dynast Mithrapata.

1806 ——— "Recent Acquisitions of Greek Coins." *British Museum Quarterly* 27, nos. 1-2 (Autumn 1963): 23-7. 1 pl.
Ten coins are described and illustrated including a gold coin of Metapontum, tetradrachms of Catana and Sinope, coins of Phaselis and some Roman Provincial pieces.

1807 ——— "Recent Acquisitions of Greek Coins." *British Museum Quarterly* 29 (1965): 89-93. 1 pl.
Publishes coins of Katana, Panormos, Populonia, Athens, Akanthos, Kyzikos, Lycia, Teos, Alexander the Great, and the Indo-Greek king Theophilos.

1808 **Price, Martin J.** "Recent Acquisitions of Greek Coins by the British Museum." *Archaeological Reports for 1973-4*. London: Society for the Promotion of Hellenic Studies and the British School at Athens, 1974. Pages 66-71.

1809 ——— "Greek Series." *Department of Coins and Medals, New Acquisitions No. 1 (1976-77)*. Occasional Paper No. 25. London: British Museum, 1981. Pages 7-23, including 2 plates.
A full catalogue of the Greek coins (including Roman Provincial issues) acquired by the British Museum during 1976-77. Includes 226 archaic, classical, and Hellenistic coins. Selected specimens are illustrated.

1810 **Robinson, Edward S. G.** "Greek Coins Acquired by the British Museum in 1930-31." *Numismatic Chronicle* 5th ser., 12 (1932): 199-214. 1 pl.
Examines twelve coins recently added to the museum's collection.

1811 ——— "British Museum Acquisitions for the Years 1933-1934." *Numismatic Chronicle* 5th ser., 16 (1936): 169-201. 2 pls.
Discusses fifty-two Greek coins.

1812 ——— "British Museum Acquisitions 1935-1936." *Numismatic Chronicle* 5th ser., 17 (1937): 233-59. 2 pls.
Discusses forty Greek coins.

1813 ——— "Greek Coins Acquired by the British Museum, 1938-1948." *Numismatic Chronicle* 6th ser., 8 (1948): 43-65. 1 pl. [CS 3070]
Reports on three major acquisitions: the Lloyd collection of coins of Italy and Sicily, the Cameron collection of Cretan coins, and a group of coins from the Oman collection. Discusses some important pieces from Cyprus and Asia Minor (Tarsus, Lapethus, Golgi, Issos, Soli) and a unique portrait tetradrachm of the Persian satrap Tissaphernes.

1814 **Vaux, W. S. W.** "On Some Remarkable Greek Coins Lately Acquired by the British Museum." *Numismatic Chronicle* new ser., 1 (1861): 104-8. 1 engraved plate.
Describes the rare Macedonian dodecadrachm with the ox-chariot/helmet obverse, a tetradrachm of Philip V of Macedonia, a stater of Abdera bearing the name ΜΕΛΑΝΙΠΠΟΣ, a rare archaic stater of Elis, and a stater of the Amphictyonic Council of Delphi.

1815 **Wroth, Warwick W.** "Greek Coins Acquired by the British Museum in 1887." *Numismatic Chronicle* 3rd ser., 8 (1888): 1-21. 1 pl.
A catalogue and description of numerous coins recently added to the museum's collection.

1816 ——— "Greek Coins Acquired by the British Museum in 1888." *Numismatic Chronicle* 3rd ser., 9 (1889): 249-67.
A catalogue and description of numerous coins recently added to the museum's collection.

1817 ——— "Greek Coins Acquired by the British Museum in 1889." *Numismatic Chronicle* 3rd ser., 10 (1890): 311-29. 1 pl.
Describes several of the noteworthy pieces among the 347 Greek coins acquired by the British Museum in 1889. Includes a unique stater of Mytilene. [Also see *Numismatic Chronicle* 3rd ser., 11 (1891): 116, for corrections by Wroth of some of the attributions given here. Also see Healy "A New Light on the Unique Stater" under LESBOS].

1818 ——— "Greek Coins Acquired by the British Museum in 1890." *Numismatic Chronicle* 3rd ser., 11 (1891): 118-34. 1 pl.
Describes several of the noteworthy pieces among the 177 Greek coins acquired by the British Museum in 1890.

1819 ——— "Greek Coins Acquired by the British Museum in 1891." *Numismatic Chronicle* 3rd ser., 12 (1892): 1-21. Illus., 1 pl.

Describes several of the noteworthy pieces among the 369 Greek coins acquired by the British Museum in 1891.

1820 ——— "Greek Coins Acquired by the British Museum in 1892." *Numismatic Chronicle* 3rd ser., 13 (1893): 1-20. 1 pl.
Describes several of the noteworthy pieces among the 457 Greek coins acquired by the British Museum in 1892.

1821 ——— "Greek Coins Acquired by the British Museum in 1893." *Numismatic Chronicle* 3rd ser., 14 (1894): 1-17. 1 pl.
Describes several of the noteworthy pieces among the 403 Greek coins acquired by the British Museum in 1893.

1822 ——— "Greek Coins Acquired by the British Museum in 1894." *Numismatic Chronicle* 3rd ser., 15 (1895): 89-103. 1 pl.
Describes several of the noteworthy pieces among the 648 Greek coins acquired by the British Museum in 1894.

1823 ——— "Greek Coins Acquired by the British Museum in 1895." *Numismatic Chronicle* 3rd ser., 16 (1896): 85-100. 1 pl.
Describes several of the noteworthy pieces among the 677 Greek coins acquired by the British Museum in 1895.

1824 ——— "Greek Coins Acquired by the British Museum in 1896." *Numismatic Chronicle* 3rd ser., 17 (1897): 93-117. 4 pls.
Describes several of the noteworthy pieces among the Greek coins acquired by the British Museum in 1896.

1825 ——— "Greek Coins Acquired by the British Museum in 1897." *Numismatic Chronicle* 3rd ser., 18 (1898): 97-123. 3 pls.
Describes several of the noteworthy pieces among the Greek coins acquired by the British Museum in 1897.

1826 ——— "Greek Coins Acquired by the British Museum in 1898." *Numismatic Chronicle* 3rd ser., 19 (1899): 85-111. 3 pls.
Describes several of the noteworthy pieces among the 924 Greek coins acquired by the British Museum in 1898.

1827 ——— "Greek Coins Acquired by the British Museum in 1899." *Numismatic Chronicle* 3rd ser., 20 (1900): 1-26. 2 pls.
Describes several of the noteworthy pieces among the 485 Greek coins acquired by the British Museum in 1899.

1828 ——— "Greek Coins Acquired by the British Museum in 1900." *Numismatic Chronicle* 3rd ser., 20 (1900): 273-96. 2 pls.
Describes several of the noteworthy pieces among the 915 Greek coins acquired by the British Museum in 1900.

1829 ——— "Greek Coins Acquired by the British Museum in 1901." *Numismatic Chronicle* 4th ser., 2 (1902): 313-44. 3 pls.
Describes several of the noteworthy pieces among the 1069 Greek coins acquired by the British Museum in 1901.

1830 ——— "Greek Coins Acquired by the British Museum in 1902." *Numismatic Chronicle* 4th ser., 3 (1903): 317-46. 3 pls.
Describes several of the noteworthy pieces among the 543 Greek coins acquired by the British Museum in 1902.

1831 ——— "Greek Coins Acquired by the British Museum in 1903." *Numismatic Chronicle* 4th ser., 4 (1904): 289-310. 2 pls.
Describes several of the noteworthy pieces among the 551 Greek coins acquired by the British Museum in 1903.

1832 ——— "Select Greek Coins in the British Museum." *Numismatic Chronicle* 4th ser., 5 (1905): 324-41. 2 pls.
Rather than publishing a selection of coins acquired by the museum in the last year, Wroth here publishes a selection of noteworthy Greek coins from the collection regardless of the date of acquisition. In this installment, he describes coins of Scione, Aenus, Apollonia Pontica, Thessalia, Larissa, Elis, Atarneus, and Clazomenae.

Also see: Allen *Catalogue of the Celtic Coins* under CELTIC COINAGE—GENERAL WORKS; Arena "New Acquisitions" under MACEDONIAN KINGDOM—GENERAL WORKS; Sperber "Jewish Museum" under PALESTINE—JUDEA.

OXFORD

1833 **Ashmolean Museum.** *Heberden Coin Room: Guide to the Greek, Roman, English and Chinese Coins.* Oxford, 1948. 51 pp., 10 pls. [CS 16571]
A general guide to an exhibition which opened in 1947. A brief history of the University's collections precedes a description of the contents of the exhibit cases. [Reviewed by G. K. Jenkins in *The Classical Review* 73 (1949): 144].

1834 **Grose, Sidney W.** "The Balliol College Collection." *Numismatic Chronicle* 4th ser., 20 (1920): 117-21. 1 pl.
A general description of the coin collection of Balliol College, Oxford. Publishes six of the Greek coins.

1835 **Kraay, Colin M.** "Greek Coins Recently Acquired by the Ashmolean Museum, Oxford." *Numismatic Chronicle* 6th ser., 14 (1954): 9-17. 1 pl.
Six coins acquired with funds bequeathed by Dr. J. G. Milne and supplemented from another source are described, discussed and illustrated. Includes two exceptionally rare bronzes of Teate in Apulia, a tetradrachm of Terone, a silver coin of Abdera, an imitation of an Athenian tetradrachm, a silver variety of Hierapytna in Crete, and two coins of Lycia. [Summarized from C. Vermeule, *NL* 34]

1836 ——— *Report of the Visitors [of the] Ashmolean Museum.* Oxford, 1968. Pages 43-4.
Mentions an important Lydia electrum coin. [Also see R. W. Wallace "KUKALIM, WALWET, and the Artemision Deposit" under LYDIA].

1837 **Milne, Joseph G.** "Some Greek Coins in Oxford." *Numismatic Chronicle* 6th ser., 7 (1947): 52-61. Illus. [CS 1891]
Ten coins among the recent acquisitions of Oxford University, selected as possible starting points for research by students, are described by the author with notes on suggested lines of investigation. Includes a stater of Tarentum with a trace of another type on reverse (evidence of hubbing?), a lead copy of a gold coin found in Egypt, a small bronze coin of Autocane with head of Dionysos, an overstruck didrachm of Calymna, an inverted double-struck bronze of Philip I of Antioch, and others.

1838 ——— "Unpublished Greek Coins in the Oxford Collection." *Numismatic Chronicle* 6th ser., 13 (1953): 21-6. 1 pl.
Describes twelve coins including some Roman Provincial issues.

Also see: Milne "The Evans Collection" under CRETE.

WARWICK

1839 **Seaby, Wilfred, and Stanley Ireland.** *A Catalogue of Ancient Coins in the Cabinet of Sir Roger Newdigate of Arbury Hall, Warwickshire: A Grand Tour Collection in the Warwickshire Museum.* Special Publication No. 41. London: Royal Numismatic Society, 2005. 116 pp., 68 pls.

GREECE

ATHENS

1840 **Alpha Bank.** *Archaea Nomismata (Ancient Greek Coins at the Collection of Alpha Bank).* Athens: Alpha Bank, 2008. 32 pp., illus.
An exhibition catalogue.

1841 **Ammons, C. Kevin.** "The Numismatic Museum of Athens." *The Celator* 19, no. 5 (May 2005): 22-5. Illus.
Summarizes the history of the museum, founded in 1829.

1842 **Bakes, James R.** "The Numismatic Museum of Athens." *The Journal of the Classical and Medieval Numismatic Society* (Canada) 2nd ser., 6, no. 5 (September 2005): 44-7. Illus.
Discusses the history of the museum and describes its current exhibits. The author had recently visited the museum.

1843 **Galani-Krikou, Mina, Mando Oeconomides, Vasso Penna, Ioannis Touratsoglou, and Eos Tsourti.** *Coins and Numismatics.* Athens: Hellenic Ministry of Culture—Numismatic Museum, 1996. 215 pp., illus.
A history of the Numismatic Museum, Athens. Discusses the collection and donors to the collection, and the role of Heinrich Schliemann. Continues with numerous essays on the invention, evolution, and functions of coinage with an emphasis on ancient Greek coins. Numerous coins are depicted and briefly identified, but no further data is given on them.

1844 **Kroll, John H.** "Athens' Coin Palace." *Archaeology* 53, no. 3 (May/June 2000): 64. Illus.
Announces that the Athens Numismatic Museum is now open to the public after recently relocating from the National Archaeological Museum. Briefly describes the galleries in the new museum, housed in the Heinrich Schliemann mansion.

1845 **Ministry of Culture.** *The First Century of the Numismatic Museum, 1829-1922.* Athens: Gennadius Library of the American School of Classical Studies, 1988. 197 pp., illus.
This book was published in conjunction with an exhibition celebrating the first century of the National Numismatic Museum, Athens, from its foundation by Capodistra in 1829 to the death of Svoronos in 1922. Includes essays on the history of the collection, the coins and books in the collection, and some of the persons who played important roles in the museum's history. The exhibition included archive material of the museum, selected books from its library, and a few coins from its collection. Twenty-six Greek coins are illustrated in color enlargements.

1846 **Oeconomides, Mando Caramessini.** "Some Important Accessions of the Athens Cabinet (I. Greek Coins)." *Nomismatika Khronika* (Greece) 4 (1976): 34-40. 4 pls.
A brief summary of some of the most important Greek coins (including hoards) among the 3000 Greek coins added to the Numismatic Collection of Athens during the period 1964-71. The additions included significant donations from the collections of Ioannis Kindynis and Basil Papavlassopoulos. Forty-five coins are illustrated.

1847 ——— *The Numismatic Museum.* Athens: Ministry of Culture, Archaeological Receipts Fund, 1989. 31 pp., illus.
A guide to the rooms of the Athens numismatic collection when it was housed in the National Archaeological Museum. The museum possesses ancient Greek, Roman, Byzantine, Medieval, and modern coins, Byzantine lead seals, Greek, Roman, and Byzantine weights, gems, tessarae, and plaster casts of coins from a number of foreign museums. Mentions and illustrates some significant items, with an emphasis on ancient Greek coins.

1848 **Postolakos, Achilles.** *Synopsis Nummorum Veterum qui in Museo Numismatico Athenarum Publico.* Athens, 1878. 204 pp. [CS 1892]

1849 **Rakicic, Mark.** "Coin Quest: Exploring the Museums of Greece and Turkey." *The Celator* 9, no. 10 (October 1995): 20-5. Illus.
While vacationing in Greece and Turkey, the author sought out coin exhibits in public museums. He comments on the numismatic content of eight Greek and six Turkish museums and also comments on the collection of the Alpha Credit Bank in Athens.

1850 **Tsagari, Dimitra I.** "Some Important Acquisitions of the Alpha Credit Bank during 1998." Translated by M. J. A. Tzamali. *Nomismatika Khronika* (Greece) 17 (1998): 32-42. Illus., 3 pls.
Lists and illustrates thirty-three coins. Some of the important pieces include an incuse stater of Siris and Pyxus, a cupro-nickel dichalk of Pantaleon of Bactria, a commemorative tetradrachm of Antimachus of Bactria, a rare drachm of Demetrios III of Bactria, a tetradrachm issued by Memnon (?) in Ionia with a reverse which may depict a map of Ionia.

1851 ——— "Some Important Acquisitions of the Alpha Bank Collection during 1999." Translated by Marion J. A. Tzamali. *Nomismatika Khronika* (Greece) 18 (1999): 38-47. 4 pls.
A catalogue of thirty-seven coins, each with commentary, added to the collection of Alpha Bank.

1852 ——— "Some of the Most Important Acquisitions of the Alpha Bank Collection during 2004." Translated by Marion J. A. Tzamali. *Nomismatika Khronika* (Greece) 23 (2004): 24-7. 1 pl. Also in Greek on pp. 21-3.
Lists a beautiful tetradrachm of Kamarina (quadriga/Herakles) by the engraver Exakestidas; a tetradrachm of Katane (charioteer with biga/Apollo) attributed to the "Master of the Leaf;" a tetradrachm of Audoleon, king of Paeonia (Herakles/Zeus enthroned) imitating the types of Alexander the Great; a stater of Alexander, king of the Molassians (Zeus/thunderbolt); three staters of Elis; and a stater of Oinoanda (Zeus/eagle).

1853 ——— "Some of the More Important Acquisitions of the Alpha Bank Collection during 2005." Translated by Marion J. A. Tzamali. *Nomismatika Khronika* (Greece) 24 (2005): 14-5. Illus.
Discusses a tetradrachm of Kleomenis III of Sparta and a dekadrachm of Athens, both acquired by the bank in 2005. Provides a brief historical background for each coin.

1854 ——— "Some of the More Important Acquisitions of the Alpha Bank Collection during 2006." Translated by Marion J. A. Tzamali. *Nomismatika Khronika* (Greece) 25 (2006): 13-5. Photographs on pp. 9-11.
Publishes eight Peloponnesian coins (Aigai, Thouria, Argos, Troizen, Alea, Thelpousa, Mantineia, and Tegea) recently acquired from the BCD collection. Provides a brief historical background for each coin.

1855 ——— *Hellenic Coinage: The Alpha Bank Collection.* Athens, 2007. 212 pp., illus.
Illustrates 206 Greek coins from the collection of Alpha Bank. Prepared for an exhibition, the catalogue provides an overview of ancient Greek coinage from barter to Hellenistic times. Includes quality enlargements of 206 coins. [Also see Tsangari *Coins of Macedonia in the Alpha Bank Collection* below].

1856 ——— "Some of the More Important Acquisitions of the Alpha Bank Collection during 2007." Translated by Marion J. A. Tzamali. *Nomismatika Khronika* (Greece) 26 (2007): 11-19. Illus.
Publishes nine coins: a drachm of Herakleia, stater of Thyrrheion, stater of the Akarnanian Confederacy, tetrobol of Pale (Kephallenia), didrachm of Andros, tetrobol of Gargara, stater of Mytilene, tetradrachm of Hekatomnos, and a tetradrachm of Carthage. Provides a brief historical background for each coin. In Greek and English.

1857 ——— "Some of the More Important Acquisitions of the Alpha Bank Collection during 2008." Translated by Marion J. A. Tzamali. *Nomismatika Khronika* (Greece) 27 (2008-2009): 9-13. Illus.
Publishes seven coins from Katane, Karystos (2), Sikyon (3), and Itanos.

1858 ——— *Coins of Macedonia in the Alpha Bank Collection.* Athens, 2009. 151 pp., illus.
An overview and catalogue illustrating 171 coins, published in conjunction with an exhibition of coins from the Alpha Bank collection exhibited at the Archaeological Museum of Thessaloniki in 2009. Includes Thraco-Macedonian issues, royal and civic issues, and local coinages which used Macedonian coins as prototypes.

1859 ——— "Some of the More Important Acquisitions of the Alpha Bank Collection during 2010." *Nomismatika Khronika* (Greece) 28 (2010): 135-8. Illus.
Describes five coins acquired for the exhibition "Myth and Coinage." The coins are an obol of Stymphalos, a hemidrachm of Argos, a drachm of the Boiotian League, an obol of the Arkadian League, and a stater of Kydonia. [In Greek and English. Also see Tsangari, Tselekas, Evgenidou, and Makrypodi *Myth and Coinage* under TYPES].

1860 **Tzamalis, Anastasios P.** "Some of the Acquisitions of the Alpha Bank during 2000." *Nomismatika Khronika* (Greece) 19 (2000): 13-37. Illus.
Catalogue of forty-five coins with commentary. Includes a wonderful stater of the Arkadian League—the most valuable piece in the bank's collection (at that time). In Greek on pp. 13-23, with an English translation by M. J. A. Tzamali on pp. 28-37; plates on pp. 24-7.

1861 ——— "Some of the More Important Acquisitions of the Alpha Credit Bank Collection during 2002." *Nomismatika Khronika* (Greece) 21 (2002): 47-54. Map, 2 pls.
Describes twenty-eight coins.

1862 **Walker, Alan Stuart.** *Ancient Greek Coins: The Credit Bank Numismatic Collection.* Athens: Hellenic Numismatic Society, 1978. 86 pp., illus. [CS 1893]
"A descriptive catalogue of the 1,165 ancient Greek, Roman, and Byzantine coins, and of Graeco-Roman lead tesserae and seals purchased by the Credit Bank of Greece is presented. The coins came from two private collections: The Andreopoulos collection is interesting because most of its coins are in excellent condition and many Greek mints are represented; the portion from the Meletopoulos collection is ca. 800 coins with a distinct emphasis on mainland Greece and Athens. The Meletopoulos collection as a whole was amassed in the second half of the nineteenth century." [M. Oeconomides, *NL* 103]

Also see: *Alpha Bank Numismatic Collection* under SYLLOGE NUMORUM GRAECORUM—GREECE; Evgenidou "Coins from Samos in the Athens Numismatic Museum" under IONIAN ISLANDS—SAMOS; Evgenidou "Found underneath a Tree Root…" under HOARDS; Mullaly "A New Museum" under CYPRUS; Oeconomides "Athens Collection" under GENERAL WORKS—GREEK; Oeconomides "Les Series de Monnaies Puniques du Musee Numismatique d'Athenes" under PHOENICIA; Papaefthymiou "The Coin Collection of the Foundation of the Hellenic World" under PRIVATE COLLECTIONS; Touratsoglou and Tsourti "The Demetrios Artemis Collection of Cycladic Coins" under CYCLADES ISLANDS.

HUNGARY

BUDAPEST

1863 **Sey, Katalin B., and István Gedai.** *Coins and Medals: The Treasures of the Hungarian National Museum.* Budapest, 1973. 46 pp., illus.
Describes eighty-two items in the Museum's collection, including a few Greek coins.

INDIA

Also see: V. Smith *Coins of Ancient India* under NORTHWEST INDIA.

ISRAEL

JERUSALEM

Also see: Barkay "Rare and Unpublished" under PALESTINE—JUDEA; Kindler *Coins of the Land of Israel* under PALESTINE—JUDEA.

ITALY

BIASSONO

1864 **Arslan Ermanno A.** *Museo Civico "Carlo Verri" Biassono. Catalogo delle Collezioni Numismatiche. Le Monete Greche. Parte I. Hispania-Sicilia.* Commune di Biassono, 2002. 100 pp., illus.
Catalogue of the 405 Greek coins of Sicily and the Iberian peninsula in the collection of the Civic Museum of Biassono. The collection was recently formed and has been built up through donations and small acquisitions.

MILAN

Also see: Arslan *La Moneta* under SICILY—GENERAL WORKS.

CHIETI

Also see: Manfredi *Raccolte Italiane di Monete Punica* under ZEUGITANA.

NAPLES

1865 **Fiorelli, Giuseppe.** *Catalogo del Museo Nazionale di Napoli.* Five volumes. Naples, 1866-72. [CS 1894]

1866 **Gàbrici, Ettore.** "Monete Inedite o Rare del Museo Nazionale di Napoli." *Corolla Numismatica: Numismatic Essays in Honour of Barclay V. Head.* Edited by G. F. Hill. London: Oxford University Press, 1906. Pages 98-103. 1 pl.
Examines ten coins of Cumae, Cora, Campania, Campania or Samnium, Teate, Selinus, Pharsalus, and Patras.

PALERMO

1867 **Cutroni, Aldina.** "Il Medagliere del Museo Nazionale di Palermo." *Annali: Istituto Italiano di Numismatica* (1956): 205-12. [CS 1895]

REGGIO EMILIA

1868 **Bellocchi, Lisa.** *Le Monete Greche.* Reggio Emilia: The Commune, 1974. 91 pp., illus. [CS 1896]
"The Greek collection of the Civic Museum in Reggio Emilia." [Clain-Stefanelli]

TURIN

1869 **Fabretti, A., F. Rossi, and R. V. Lanzone.** *Regio Museo di Torino: Ordinato e Descritto. Monete Greche.* Turin, 1883. 644 pp., 2 pls. Reprints, Bologna: Forni, 1967 and 1978. [CS 16607]
Catalogue of 9266 Greek coins in the collection of the Regional Museum of Torino.

UDINE

1870 **Garraffo, Salvatore.** *Collezione de Brandis del Gabinetto Numismatico dei Civici Musei di Udine. Monete della Sicilia Antica.* Udine: Villa Manin-Passarano, 1998.
A catalogue of 526 coins (49 silver and 477 bronze) from the collection of Augusto de Brandis, in the city museum at Udine. Includes many Sicilian issues.

Also see: Acquaro—several items under ZEUGITANA.

JAPAN

OKAYAMA

1871 **Fallani, Carlo Maria.** "Greek, Etruscan and Roman Coins." *The Kurashiki Ninagawa Museum: Greek, Etruscan and Roman Antiquities.* Edited by Erika Simon. Mainz on Rhine: Verlag Philipp Von Zabern, 1982. Pages 278-91. Illus.
A catalogue of the Greek, Etruscan, and Roman coins the collection of the museum. Includes thirty-nine Greek and Etruscan coins, all of which are illustrated.

JORDAN

AMMAN

1872 **Arif, Aida S.** *A Treasury of Classical and Islamic Coins: The Collection of the Amman Museum.* London: Arthur Probsthain, 1986. 147 pp., 162 pls.

A catalogue of Greek, Roman, Nabataean, Byzantine, and Islamic coins. Many of the coins are common coins in worn condition which were found locally. The catalogue is poorly arranged and the plates are not of high quality.

LEBANON

BEIRUT

1873 **Baramki, Dimitri C.** *The Coin Collection of the American University of Beirut Museum: Palestine and Phoenicia.* Beirut: American University, 1974. 339 pp., 32 pls. [CS 2895]
A catalogue of the coins of Palestine and Phoenicia (excluding the Alexandrine, Seleucid, and Ptolemaic coinages) in the collection of the American University of Beirut Museum. Includes mostly Greek Imperial issues.

THE NETHERLANDS

THE HAGUE

1874 **Royal Coin Cabinet.** *Antieke Munten (Ancient Coins): Koninklijk Penning Kabinet (Royal Coin Cabinet).* Bussum: C. A. J. Van Dishoeck, 1953. 8 pp., 20 pls.
"Descriptive catalogue in Dutch and English together with twenty excellent plates of outstanding specimens of Greek and Roman coins selected from the collection of the Royal Coin Cabinet, The Hague, Netherlands. The publication was issued with the help of the Royal Netherlands Numismatic Society and the Netherlands Classical Association." [R. Breaden, *NL* 33]. Includes ten Greek coins.

NEW ZEALAND

DUNEDIN

1875 **Ehrhardt, Christopher T. H. R., ed.** *Greek Coins in the Otago Museum.* Six parts. Dunedin: University of Otago, 1974-6. Reprinted in one volume, *Greek Coins in the Otago Museum: A Catalogue.* Dunedin: University of Otago, 1981. 318 pp. [CS 1897]
A catalogue of the 1100 Greek coins in the Otago Museum. Includes numerous indices. Most of the collection was formed by Willi Fels (1858-1945). [A review of Part 1, *Gaul and Italy*, by M. J. Price appears in *Numismatic Chronicle* 136 (1976): 275. A brief review of the entire reprinted volume appears in *New Zealand Numismatic Journal* 16, no. 2 (July 1982): 21].

1876 ——— "Some Collections of Greek and Roman Coins in New Zealand." *New Zealand Numismatic Journal* (New Zealand) 14, no. 3 (October 1977): 8-14.
A very brief description of the holdings of Greek and Roman coins in three New Zealand museums: Southland Museum and Art Gallery, Invercargill; Canterbury Museum, Christchurch; and the Classics Department, University of Auckland.

1877 ——— "Some Collections of Greek and Roman Coins in New Zealand, 2: The Greek Coins in the Southland Museum, Invercargill." *New Zealand Numismatic Journal* (New Zealand) 15, no. 1 (June 1979): 7-22.
A brief catalogue, without illustrations, of sixty-seven Greek and Roman Provincial coins from a New Zealand museum.

1878 ——— "Some Collections of Greek and Roman Coins in New Zealand, 3: Ancient Coins in the Wanganui Regional Museum." *New Zealand Numismatic Journal* (New Zealand) 16, no. 2 (July 1982): 15-7.
A very brief listing of the ancient coins (mostly Roman) in the museum's collection. No illustrations.

1879 ——— "Some Collections of Greek and Roman Coins in New Zealand, 4: Coins in Gisborne and Otago." *New Zealand Numismatic Journal* (New Zealand) 16, no. 4 (April 1984): 85-9.
A catalogue of the twelve ancient coins in the Gisborne Museum and Art Gallery, and the twenty-one coins given to the Otago Museum by J. M. Samson. No illustrations.

1880 ——— "Some Collections of Greek and Roman Coins in New Zealand, 5: A Numismatic Tour of Northland." *New Zealand Numismatic Journal* (New Zealand) 69 (December 1991): 16-20.

1881 ——— "Greek and Roman Coins in New Zealand Collections." *Proceedings of the 11th International Numismatic Congress, September 8-13, 1991. Volume 1.* Edited by T. Hackens et al. Louvain-la-Neuve, Belgium: International Association of Professional Numismatists, 1993. Pages 13-22. Map.
Lists the museums in New Zealand which contain ancient coins, and provides brief notes regarding the contents of the collections. Includes a bibliography of ancient coins in New Zealand.

1882 **Murray, Hugh A.** "Ancient Coins: The Gilbertson Cabinet of Electrotypes." Parts 1 & 2. *New Zealand Numismatic Journal* (New Zealand) 4, no. 1 (June-August 1947): 36-47. 1 pl.; no. 2 (September-December 1947): 66-75.
A collection of 800 electrotype copies of ancient coins from the British Museum collection were donated by Charles Gilbertson to the Alexander Turnbull Library in Wellington, New Zealand. This article is a guide to the collection and forms a brief survey of ancient coinage in general. Murray also comments on a number of specific specimens in the collection.

1883 **Turnbull, M. I.** "Some Greek Coins from the Fels Collection in the Otago Museum." *New Zealand Numismatic Journal* (New Zealand) 6, no. 2 (September 1950-August 1951): 48-54. 1 pl.
Discusses sixteen coins selected from the collection of Greek coins presented to the Otago Museum by Willi Fels.

Also see: Hind "Silver and Bronze Coins" under SICILY—SICULO-PUNIC COINAGE; Hind "Greek Coins from the Black Sea Area" under ASIA MINOR AND THE BLACK SEA REGION—GENERAL WORKS.

PORTUGAL

LISBON

1884 **Hipólito, Mário Castro.** *Moedas Gregas Antigas Ouro.* Lisbon: Fundação Calouste Gulbenkian, 1996. 165 pp., illus.
A catalogue of the 143 gold coins in the Calouste Gulbenkian collection with an extensive discussion of the coins. Includes enlarged photographs of each coin. The coins are cross-referenced to the catalogues of the entire collection where they also appeared (see Jenkins and Hipólito below, and Robinson and Hipólito below). Text in Portuguese.

1885 ———— *Ancient Greek Coins: Gold.* Lisbon: The Calouste Gulbenkian Museum, 1998. 165 pp., illus.
The English translation of *Moedas Gregas Antigas Ouro* (see above).

1886 **Jenkins, G. Kenneth, and Mário Castro Hipólito.** *A Catalogue of the Calouste Gulbenkian Collection of Greek Coins, Part 2: Greece to East.* Two volumes. Lisbon: Fundação Calouste Gulbenkian, 1989. 200 pp., 57 pls.
A catalogue of 696 gold, electrum, and silver coins from the collection of Calouste Gulbenkian. The collection now resides in a Lisbon museum. Gulbenkian valued art more than rarity, and collected only coins of "the finest preservation and remarkable beauty" as is evident on the superb plates photographed by Reinaldo S. Viegas. Many of the coins were selected from the Jameson collection and other important collections. The coins are divided into two sections: *The Archaic-Classical Period* and *The Hellenistic Period*. The catalogue includes descriptions of the coins and brief commentary on their art and chronology. Includes the following indices: geographical, rulers, personal names (not rulers), legends, collections, hoards, types. Includes a bibliography and a concordance of each coin's catalogue number to the original museum collection number (covers the coins in both Parts 1 and 2). Foreword by Maria Teresa Gomes Ferreira, Director of the Calouste Gulbenkian Museum. The unbound plates are on card-stock and are housed in a slipcase. Includes an index to the plates. On page 200, there is a note by J. M. Peixoto Cabral, "The Specific Gravity of Fifty-two Electrum Staters of Kyzikos" (see Cabral under METALLURGY). [Reviewed by Philip Kinns in *Spink Numismatic Circular* 98, no. 7 (September 1990): 237, and by Ute Wartenberg in *Numismatic Chronicle* 153 (1993): 271-2. Also see Robinson and Hipólito *Gulbenkian Collection—Part 1* below].

1887 *Museu Eng. António de Almeida: A Catalogue of the Numismatic Collection, Volume 1.* Fundacào Eng. António de Almeida, 1994. 419 pp., illus., maps.
A catalogue of the coins in the museum established in the will of António de Almeida who died in 1968. Includes 966 Greek, Roman, Byzantine, French, and Portuguese coins with an introduction to each section. Most of the coins are gold. The fifty-four Greek coins are catalogued on pages 33-57. Text in Portuguese and English.

1888 **Perdigão, José De Azeredo.** *Calouste Gulbenkian: Collector.* Lisbon, 1979. 237 pp., illus.
A biography of the famed collector of superb Greek coins, written by the Chairman of the Calouste Gulbenkian Foundation. Includes a chapter relating to his collection of Greek coins. Discusses his acquisition of coins from the Jameson collection.

1889 **Robinson, Edward S. G., and Mário Castro Hipólito.** *A Catalogue of the Calouste Gulbenkian Collection of Greek Coins, Part 1: Italy, Sicily, Carthage.* Two volumes. Lisbon: Fundação Calouste Gulbenkian, 1971. 136 pp., 42 pls., map. [CS 1898]
A catalogue of 389 superb Greek coins of Italy, Sicily, and Carthage from the collection of Calouste Gulbenkian. The collection now resides in a Lisbon museum. Gulbenkian valued art more than rarity, and collected only coins of "the finest preservation and remarkable beauty" as is evident on the superb plates photographed by Mário de Oliveira. Many of the coins were selected from the Jameson collection and other important collections. The catalogue includes historical notes, thorough descriptions of the coins, and discussions of their art and historical background. Includes a biography of Gulbenkian by E. S. G. Robinson. Includes indices of mints, personal names other than moneyers, kings and rulers named on their coins, and engravers named on coins. Forewords by José De Azeredo Perdiagão (Chairman of the Calouste Gulbenkian Foundation) and E. S. G. Robinson (Robinson assisted in the formation of Gulbenkian's collection). The unbound plates are on card-stock and are housed in a slipcase. Includes an index to the plates. [Also see Jenkins and Hipólito *Gulbenkian Collection—Part 2* above].

RHODESIA (ZIMBABWE)

SALISBURY

1890 **Kraay, Colin M.** "Notes on the Courtauld Collection of Greek Coins at the University of Zimbabwe." *Proceedings of the African Classical Associations* (1980): 59-61.
[Also see Pollard below].

1891 **Pollard, Graham.** *A Catalogue of the Greek Coins in the Collection of Sir Stephen Courtauld at the University College of Rhodesia.* Salisbury, Southern Rhodesia: University College of Rhodesia, 1970. 92 pp., 15 pls., map. [CS 1899]
Courtauld's collection, formed between 1925-55, contains 116 coins encompassing all areas of the Greek world. The coins are of exceptional quality. The collection is catalogued with full descriptions, provenances, cross references, and brief historical notes. Most types are cross-referenced to the McClean collection and to the types shown in Kraay and Hirmer's *Greek Coins*. Relevant bibliographical listings appear throughout. Includes indices of rulers, types, symbols, and legends. A splendid collection, nicely catalogued. [Reviewed in *Spink Numismatic Circular* 79 (November 1971): 411, by R. T. Williams in *Numismatic Chronicle* 7th ser., 12 (1972): 317-8, by J. G. F. Hind in *New Zealand Numismatic Journal* 13, no. 2 (May 1972): 81-2, and by M. B. Wallace in *Cornucopiæ* 2, no. 1 (1974): 15-6].

ROMANIA

BUCHAREST

1892 **Petac, Emanuel.** *La Collection M. C. Sutzu, Bibliothèque de l'Académie Roumaine, Bucarest, Volume 1: Istros, Kallatis, Tomis.* Moneta 43. Wetteren, Belgium: Moneta, 2005. 120 pp., 24 pls.
A catalogue of the collection formed by Mihail Constantin Sutzu (1841-1933), the founder of the Cabinet of Medals of the Library of the Romanian Academy. This volume includes 49 coins of Istros, 62 coins of Kallatis, and 611 coins of Tomis.

1893 ——— *La Collection M. C. Sutzu, Bibliothèque de l'Académie Roumaine, Bucarest, Volume 2: Cités Grecques du Nord de la Mer Noire, d'Asie Mineure et d'Afrique. Collection Grand-duc A. Mikhailovitch.* Moneta 89. Wetteren, Belgium: Moneta, 2009. 184 pp., illus.

1894 **Preda, Constantin, and Emanuel Petac.** *Les Monnaies d'or de la Bibliothèque de l'Académie Roumaine, I: Monnaies Grecques et Romaines.* Moneta 56. Wetteren, Belgium: Moneta, 2006. 168 pp., 23 pls.

1895 **Vilcu, A., T. Isvoranu, and E. Nicolae.** *Les Monnaies d'Or de l'Institut d'Archéologie de Bucarest.* Moneta 57. Wetteren, Belgium: Moneta 2006. 240 pp. Illus.
A catalogue of the gold coins.

SCOTLAND

EDINBURGH

1896 **Goring, Elizabeth.** "Recent Acquisitions by the Royal Scottish Museum, Edinburgh." *Museum Supplement.* Edinburgh: Royal Scottish Museum, 1985. 2 pp., 3 pls.
Lists the principal classical acquisitions made by the Department of Art and Archaeology since 1982. Includes pottery, terracottas, bronze, jewelry, and eleven Greek coins (Hyria, Neapolis, Selinus, Abdera, Larissa, Knossos, Phaistos, Rhaukos, two Siculo-Punic, and Philip II).

1897 **Rutter, Nicholas K.** *A Catalogue of the Ancient Greek Coins in the Collections of the Royal Scottish Museum, Edinburgh.* The Royal Scottish Museum Information Series, Art and Archaeology 1. Edinburgh: Royal Scottish Museum, 1979. 23 pp., 3 pls. [CS 1900]
The catalogue is prefaced by a ten page introduction to Greek coinage and a brief history of the museum's collection. Catalogues 213 coins, of which fifty are illustrated. Includes the major coin types from all areas of the Greek world. [Reviewed in *Spink Numismatic Circular* 88, no. 10 (October 1980): 355].

GLASGOW

1898 **Macdonald, George.** "Notes on Combe's Catalogue of the Hunter Cabinet." *Numismatic Chronicle* 3rd ser., 16 (1896): 144-54.
The author makes corrections and additional attributions of coins in the Hunterian Collection as catalogued in 1782 by Taylor Combe.

1899 ——— *Catalogue of Greek Coins in the Hunterian Collection, University of Glasgow.* Three volumes. Glasgow: James Maclehose & Sons, 1899-1905. Reprint, Bologna: Forni, 1975. 2040 pp., 102 pls. [CS 1901]
The collection was primarily formed by Dr. William Hunter from 1770 to 1783. Publishes over 12,000 Greek coins. Volume 1 covers Italy, Sicily, Thrace and Thessaly (495 pp., 30 pls.). Volume 2 includes northwestern, central and southern Greece and Asia Minor (648 pp., 32 pls.). Volume 3 includes further Asia, northern Africa and western Europe (799 pp., 35 pls.). Includes various indices. [A review of *Volume 1* by B. V. Head, including notes on the origin of the collection, appears in *Numismatic Chronicle* 3rd ser., 19 (1899): 177-80. A review of *Volume 2* by H. A. Grueber appears in *Numismatic Chronicle* 4th ser., 2 (1902): 188-9].

SOUTH AFRICA

GRAHAMSTOWN

1900 **Salisbury, F. S.** *Guide to the Greek and Roman Coins in the Albany Museum, Grahamstown.* Grahamstown, South Africa: Albany Museum, 1915. 45 pp., 2 pls.
A catalogue of the Greek, Roman, and Byzantine coins with brief commentary. Accompanied by line drawings of some of the coins.

SUDAN

KHARTOUM

1901 **Tsakos, Alexander.** "Ancient Coins in the National Museum of Khartoum." *Nomismatika Khronika* (Greece) 24 (2005): 44-50. 5 pls., 4 maps (pp. 33-41).
The National Archaeological Museum of Khartoum is the only museum in Sudan which has ancient coins. Tsakos lists fifteen coins, including six Ptolemaic coins. The provenance of the coins is largely unknown. Whether the coins were found in the Sudan is uncertain. Also discusses other numismatic finds of Graeco-Roman times in the Sudan. Summarizes some finds from the eastern desert which may suggest the identification of the city of Deraheib as the ancient Berenike Panchrysos. Also mentions the hoard found in Mirgissa containing imitations of Ptolemaic coins (see Le Rider "Monnaies Trouvées" under HOARDS). From all the findings it emerges that it is possible that a moneyed economy developed in Lower Nubia in the early Ptolemaic period. Recounts the historical events in the region during Ptolemaic times.

SWITZERLAND

GENERAL WORKS

1902 **Lederer, Philipp.** "Neue Beiträge zur Antiken Münzkunde aus Schweizerischen Öffentlichen und Privaten Sammlungen." *Revue Suisse de Numismatique* 30 (1943): 1-103; 32 (1946): 5-20; 34 (1948-49): 5-18. [CS 1902]

BERN

1903 **Kapossy, Balász.** "Mittelasiatische Münzen im Berischen Historischen Museum." *Jahrbuch des Bernerischen Museums* (Germany) 47-48 (1967-68): 61-94. [CS 1903]

FRIBOURG

1904 **Grigorova, Valentina.** *Catalogue of the Greek and Roman Coins of the Josef Vital Kopp Collection, University of Fribourg, Switzerland.* Novum Testamentum et Orbis Antiquus 2. University Press, Fribourg: Vanderhoeck and Ruprecht, 2000. 123 pp., pls.
A catalogue of the collection of Josef Vital Kopp, a Swiss writer, theologian, humanist, and collector, bequeathed to the University of Fribourg in 1966. The collection includes 117 Greek and 92 Roman coins. All are photographed.

WINTERTHUR

1905 **Bloesch, Hansjörg.** *Griechische Münzen in Winterthur.*
1. *Spanien, Gallien, Italien, Siziilien, Moesien, Dakien, Sarmatien, Thrakien, Makedonien, Hellas, Inseln.* Two volumes. Winterthur, 1987. 234 pp., 102 pls. 2321 coins.
2. *Kimmerischer, Bosporus, Pontus, Armenia Minor, Paphlagonien, Bithynien, Mysien, Toras, Aeolis, Lesbos, Ionien, Karien, Lydien, Phrygien, Lykien.* Two volumes. Winterthur, 1977. 216 pp., 88 pls. [Reviewed by Wolfgang Fischer-Bossert in *Revue Suisse de Numismatique* 82 (2003): 129-31].

TASMANIA

1906 **Waters, K. H.** *Greek Coins in the University of Tasmania.* Tasmania: University of Tasmania, 1981. 102 pp.
A catalogue of the 173 Greek coins in the John Elliott Classics Museum at the University of Tasmania. Each coin is fully described and is accompanied by brief commentary. [Reviewed by K. A. Sheedy in *Numismatic Chronicle* 144 (1984): 249].

Also see: Hardwick "A New Variety of Chian Forgery" under IONIAN ISLANDS—CHIOS.

TURKEY

AMASYA

1907 **Ireland, Stanley.** *Greek, Roman and Byzantine Coins in the Museum at Amasya (Ancient Amaseia), Turkey.* British Institute of Archaeology at Ankara Monograph 27. Special Publications No. 33. London: Royal Numismatic Society, 2000. 132 pp, map, 61 pls.
A catalogue of over 4500 coins held in the museum, ranging in date from the fifth century B.C. to the eleventh century A.D. Most are finds from the surrounding region. Includes many coins from the mints of Amaseia, Amisus, Sinope, and Cappadocian Caesarea. Also includes coins from more than fifty other mints in Asia Minor and other areas. [Reviewed in *Antiquity* 75 (2001). Also reviewed by C. S. Lightfoot in *Numismatic Chronicle* 161 (2001): 370-4, and by O. D. Hoover in *American Numismatic Society Magazine* 2, no. 1 (spring 2003): 47-9].

ISTANBUL

1908 **Tekin, Oguz.** *Greek and Roman Coins: The Yapi Kredi Collection.* Yapi Kredi Para Koleksiyonian 2. Istanbul: Yapi Kredi Bankasi, 1994. 261 pp., 77 pls.
A catalogue of the ancient Greek and Roman coins in the Vedat Nedim Tör Museum of the Yapi Kredi Cultural Centre. Includes 515 Greek coins and 478 Roman coins. Includes an introduction to ancient numismatics and a catalogue of the collection. Text in Turkish and English.

1909 ——— *Catalogue of the Ancient Coins in the Sadberk Hanim Museum.* Istanbul, 2003. 95 pp., 24 pls.
Catalogue of 2750 coins, including 770 Pontic and Paphlagonian bronzes. Most are from a collection formed by Hüseyin Kocabas between the 1950s to 1970s. Includes 462 Greek and Roman provincial issues. Most are from Asia Minor. In Turkish and English. [Reviewed by R. Ashton in *Numismatic Chronicle* 164 (2004): 338-9].

SINOPE

1910 **Casey, John.** *A Catalogue of the Greek, Roman and Byzantine Coins in the Sinop Museum and Related Historical and Numismatic Studies.* Special Publication No. 44. London: Royal Numismatic Society, 2010.

Also see: Ashton "Coins of Macedonian Kings, Lysimachos and Eupolemos in the Museums of Fethiye and Afyon" under MACEDONIAN KINGDOM—GENERAL WORKS; Rakicic "Coin Quest" under PUBLIC COLLECTIONS—GREECE (ATHENS).

UNITED STATES OF AMERICA

ANN ARBOR, MICHIGAN

1911 **Markham, D.** "The University of Michigan Coin Collections." *The Michigan Alumnus Quarterly Review* 56 (14) (1950): 165-71.

APPLETON, WISCONSIN

1912 **Lawton, Carol L.** *Bearers of Meaning: The Ottilia Buerger Collection of Ancient and Byzantine Coins at Lawrence University.* Appleton: Lawrence University Press, 1995. 213 pp., illus.
Catalogue for an exhibition at the Wriston Art Center Galleries at Lawrence University, April-May, 1995. Describes and illustrates with enlarged photographs fifty-nine Greek, seventy Roman, and eighteen Byzantine coins. An explanation of the historical and artistic significance of each coin is provided. Also includes five essays: "The Production of Ancient Coins" by J. M. Wickens [1479], "Greek Coinage and the Polis" [993] and "Hellenistic Coin Portraits" [1270] by C. L. Lawton, "Roman Coins and History" by D. J. Taylor, and "The Development of the Byzantine Solidus" by M. T. Orr. [Also see the review by A. Walker in *The Celator* 9, no. 12 (December 1995): 45-7].

Athens, Georgia

1913 **Gantz, Timothy, and Frances Van Keuren.** *The Richard E. Paulson Collection of Ancient Coins.* Georgia Museum of Art Bulletin, 1981. Athens, Georgia: Georgia Museum of Art, 1981. 53 pp., illus., 2 maps.
A catalogue of fifty-seven coins donated to the museum by Richard E. Paulson. Each coin is illustrated. Historical commentary is provided for each coin. Includes four Greek, two Parthian, and eleven Bactrian coins. The balance of the collection is focused on Sasanian, Indian, Mongol, and other coins. The coins are rather unspectacular.

Baltimore, Maryland

1914 **Freeman, Sarah Elizabeth.** "Coins: Treasure Trove of History." *Johns Hopkins Magazine* (December 1975): 14-8. Illus.
General comments on the importance of coins to the historian, and the history of ancient Greek and Roman coinage. Illustrated by ten coins, principally Greek, from the collection of Johns Hopkins University.

Bloomington, Indiana

1915 **Hohlfelder, Robert L.** *Ancient Coins at Indiana University: A Catalogue of Three Collections.* Dissertation, Indiana University, Bloomington, 1966. 288 pp. (on microfilm). [CS 16666]
"A corpus of the coins found at Cenchreae (near Corinth) in 1964, principally Pegasus-Trident small bronzes. It is suggested that while they were struck at Corinth in the Hellenistic period they circulated well into Roman Imperial times. Catalogues of the Berry Collection (miscellaneous Greek; the body of the collection is at the ANS) and the Indiana Department of Classics collection (chiefly Greek Imperial and Roman types) are given." [R. Hohlfelder, *NL 81*]

1916 ——— *Ancient Greek Coins from the Collection of Burton Y. Berry.* Bloomington: Indiana University Art Museum, 1972. 78 pp., illus. [CS 1923]
A catalogue of 104 Greek coins presented to Indiana University by Burton Y. Berry in 1961. All coins are photographed and briefly described. Includes approximate dates of issue.

Boston, Massachusetts

1917 **Brett, Agnes Baldwin.** *Catalogue of Greek Coins.* Boston: Museum of Fine Arts, 1955. Reprint, New York: Attic Books, 1974. 340 pp., 115 pls. [CS 1904]
A catalogue of the Greek coins in the Boston Museum of Fine Arts. The bulk of the collection was acquired from Edward P. Warren, with many additions donated by Theodora Wilbour. Lists and describes 2348 coins. Appendices list weight standards and their areas of use, and specific gravities of electrum coins in the collection. The collection is highly regarded for its fine, artistic specimens and broad scope. Also notable is the large group of Cyzicene electrum coins. The original edition has high-quality photographically printed plates. Selections from the collection were sold on June 6, 1980 in Numismatic Fine Arts *Auction 8*. [Reviewed by G. K. Jenkins in *Numismatic Chronicle* 6th ser., 16 (1956): 361-3, by E. S. G. Robinson in *American Journal of Archaeology* (July 1956): 298-9, by W. Schwabacher in *Gnomon* (Germany) 28 (1956): 527-31, and by J. M. F. May in *Journal of Hellenic Studies* 77, pt. 2 (1957): 354. Also see Comstock and Vermeule below for the museum's later acquisitions].

1918 **Caskey, Lacey D.** "Recent Acquisitions of the Museum of Fine Arts, Boston." *American Journal of Archaeology* 40 (1936): 306-13. Illus.
"On pp. 311-2 a 'Demareteion' acquired by the Museum is illustrated, with brief comments." [J. R. Jones, *NIAJAH*]

1919 **Comstock, Mary B., and Cornelius Vermeule.** *Greek Coins, 1950 to 1963.* Boston: Museum of Fine Arts, 1964. 78 pages including the 30 pls. [CS 1905]
A catalogue of 328 coins added to the collection of the Boston Museum of Fine Arts between 1950 and 1963 (see Brett above for the main catalogue). Provides complete descriptions of each coin including dates and provenances. Each coin is photographed. [Reviewed by W. Schwabacher in *Gnomon* (Germany) 37 (1965): 596-9].

1920 **Museum of Fine Arts, Boston.** *Guide to the Catherine Page Perkins Collection of Greek and Roman Coins, Museum of Fine Arts.* Boston and New York, 1902. 111 pp., 5 pls.
A survey of the 609 coins (570 Greek) purchased for the Boston Museum of Fine Arts by Edward P. Warren using funds donated by Catherine Page Perkins. The illustrated coins are of high artistic merit.

Bryn Athyn, Pennsylvania

1921 **Romano, David Gilman, and Irene Bald Romano.** *Catalogue of the Classical Collections of the Glencairn Museum.* Bryn Athyn, Pennsylvania: Glencairn Museum, 1999. 254 pp., illus.
A catalogue of over 500 objects of Greek, Roman, Cypriot, and Etruscan origin from the classical collections of the Glencairn Museum. Includes some Greek, Punic, and Roman coins in addition to Greek and Roman jewelry, stone sculptures, bronze figurines, ceramic vessels, terracotta lamps, and other objects.

Bryn Mawr, Pennsylvania

1922 **Christie's.** *The Elisabeth Washburn King Collection of Ancient Greek Coins, the Property of Bryn Mawr College.* New York: Christie's, 1992. Illus.
Auction catalogue for the December 11, 1992 sale of 141 Greek coins, primarily of the archaic and classical periods. Begins with a brief essay focusing on the artistic aspects of the collection. Each lot is described, and historical comments are provided for many of the coins. Provenances are given for most coins. Each is illustrated by black and white photographs, some enlarged. Includes eight color plates. [Also see Lamb "Elisabeth Washburn King Collection" below].

1923 **Lamb, James.** "Elisabeth Washburn King Collection Exemplifies the Art and History of Classical Greece." *The Celator* 6, no. 12 (December 1992): 40-1. Illus.

A brief discussion of the King collection (see *King* above) which was sold at auction in 1992.

1924 **Vermeule, Cornelius C.** "Greek Coins in the Elisabeth Washburn King Collection at Bryn Mawr College." *Numismatic Chronicle* 6th ser., 16 (1956): 19-41. 5 pls. [CS 1906]
"In 1951 Mrs. King presented to Bryn Mawr College a collection of 141 Greek coins of exceptional importance. Many of these coins come from famous collections and a number are the best known specimens of their type. These coins are now exhibited in the Ella Riegel Memorial Museum of the Department of Classical Archaeology at Bryn Mawr. Each coin is described in detail and illustrated by direct photographs of obverse and reverse." [*NL* 43]

CAMBRIDGE, MASSACHUSETTS

1925 **Hanfmann, George, and Miriam S. Balmuth.** *Ancient Coins: The Fogg Art Museum of Harvard University.* Cambridge, 1956. 40 pp. [CS 16667]
A brief introduction to the history of coinage is followed by a selection of coins from the Harvard collection, forming a survey of coinage from the early Greek through the Byzantine periods. Forty-eight coins are shown, usually one side only. The coins chosen to illustrate this introduction to coinage are of average quality rather than superb specimens.

1926 **Holloway, R. Ross.** "Ancient Coins." *The Frederick M. Watkins Collection. Fogg Art Museum, Harvard University.* Cambridge: Harvard College, 1973. Pages 101-53. Illus. [CS 1907]
A catalogue of the coins donated to the Fogg Art Museum by Frederick M. Watkins. The coins are of excellent artistic quality and are in an exceptional state of preservation. Includes 148 Greek coins, twenty-two Roman coins, and two Byzantine coins. The catalogue also includes thirty-four renaissance to modern coins and medals, and forty-three other ancient works of art (bronzes, vases, etc.).

Also see: Houser *Dionysos* under TYPES; Oleson *Greek Numismatic Art* under ART; Ramage "South Italian and Sicilian Coins" under ITALY—GENERAL WORKS.

COLUMBIA, MISSOURI

1927 "Coins Major Gallery Feature at New U. of Missouri Museum." *Coin World* (November 10, 1976): 1, 3, 6. Illus.
Announces the opening of the new galleries at the Museum of Art and Archaeology at the University of Missouri, Columbia. The museum possesses a significant collection of ancient Greek and Roman coins. Several coins are illustrated.

DENVER, COLORADO

1928 **D'Arms, Edward F., and William P. Wallace.** "Supplement to the Catalogue of Greek and Roman Coins at the University of Colorado." *University of Colorado Studies* (May 1941): 159-63. 1 pl.

1929 **Wallace, William P., and Mary Wallace.** *Catalog of Greek and Roman Coins at the University of Colorado.* University of Colorado Studies, No. 25. Denver: University of Colorado, 1938.

DETROIT, MICHIGAN

1930 "National Bank of Detroit Presents the Money Museum." *Coins and Medals* (March 1974): 18-23. Illus.
A brief article describing the Money Museum of the National Bank of Detroit. The collection was formed by Nate S. Shapero, and contains over 11,000 items. A few Greek coins are illustrated in this article.

Also see: Detroit Institute of Arts *Coins of the Ancient World* under PRIVATE COLLECTIONS; Dodson *Money Tells the Story* under GENERAL WORKS—GREEK.

HANOVER, NEW HAMPSHIRE

1931 *Loan Exhibition: Beulah H. Emmet Collection of Greek Coins. Dartmouth College Museum, April 1 – April 21, 1966.* Hanover: Dartmouth College, 1966. 8 pp., illus.
This guide to the exhibition begins with very brief introductions by Matthew I. Wiencke and Doran A. Jones. Illustrates eleven high-quality Greek coins (Sybaris, Leontini, Syracuse, Amphipolis, Demetrius Poliorcetes, Thasos, Larissa, Thebes, Athens, Olympia, and Cnidus).

MUNCIE, INDIANA

1932 **Sayles, Wayne G.** *The Ned H. and Gloria A. Griner Greek and Roman Coin Collection.* Muncie, Indiana: Ball State University Museum of Art, 2002. 207 pp., illus.
Catalogue of a collection of 109 Greek coins and 44 Roman coins donated to Ball State University in 2000 by the Griners for use in teaching the classics. The coins are of uniformly high quality. Although most are familiar types, each is well preserved and of high artistic merit. The extensive commentary by Sayles makes this catalogue a worthwhile reference. The catalogue is written such that a non-numismatist can understand and appreciate the collection and gain an appreciation for collecting ancient coins. This makes the book an excellent introduction for numismatists as well. In addition to the well-summarized historical narratives, Sayles has provided insightful comments on the artistic features of each coin and the stylistic trends exhibited throughout the collection. Well done and recommended for all. Each coin is illustrated by enlarged black and white photographs.

NEW HAVEN, CONNECTICUT

1933 **Bellinger, Alfred R.** "Greek Coins from the Yale Numismatic Collection." *Yale Classical Studies* 11 (1950): 307-16; 12 (1951): 253-64; 13 (1952): 161-9. [CS 1909]
Volume 11 is a discussion of a half stater of Anaphe, a signed stater of Aspendus, a tetradrachm of Demetrius, a quadruple of Mithradates I struck in Bactria, and a tetradrachm of Trajan struck at Alexandria. Volume 12 is a discussion of coinage of the Achaean League. Volume 13 is a discussion of a hoard of bronze coins of Cyzicus.

1934 **Edwards, Jonathan.** *Catalogue of the Greek and Roman Coins in the Numismatic Collection of Yale College.* New Haven: Tuttle, Morehouse, & Taylor, 1880. 236 pp., illus. [CS 16670]
The reissuance of a book originally published anonymously as *Catalogue of Coins in the Yale Collection* in 1863. A brief history of the collection is followed by the catalogue of Greek and Roman coins. Only six coins are illustrated (by line drawings). The majority of coins are Roman or Roman Provincial.

1935 "Yale Gets Greek, Roman Coins: 4,100 Specimens from European Collection." *Coin World* (June 7, 2004): 86. Illus.
Announces the acquisition of ancient coins by the Yale University Art Gallery. The collection was formed by Peter R. Franke, formerly professor of ancient history and numismatics and head of the Institute for Ancient History at the University of Saarbrücken, Germany. The principal focus of the collection is on Greek coins of the Roman period.

Also see: Thompson and Bellinger "Greek Coins in the Yale Collection" under MACEDONIAN KINGDOM—GENERAL WORKS.

NEW YORK, NEW YORK

1936 **Andrew, John.** "NY Metropolitan Museum of Art's Greek Coins Appear after 32 Years." *Coin World* (August 8, 2005): 76. Illus.
Announces that a group of thirty-eight Greek coins from the John Ward collection, formerly in the New York Museum of Art, were sold at a Morton & Eden auction held in London in May 2005. Briefly recounts the history of the collection and its dispersal in 1973.

1937 **Arnold-Biucchi, Carmen.** "Acquisitions for 1999 in the American Numismatic Society Collection." *American Journal of Numismatics* 2nd ser., 12 (2000): 261-5. 2 pls.
A brief description of a few significant coins among the 277 Greek coins donated to the ANS in 1999.

1938 **Bates, Michael L., Sebastian Heath, Robert W. Hoge, Elena Stolyarik, and Peter G. van Alfen.** "Acquisitions for 2003 and 2004 in the American Numismatic Society Collection." *American Journal of Numismatics* 16-17 (2004-2005): 269-303. 12 pls.
Additions included 141 Greek coins, including many Celtic and Lycian pieces. van Alfen catalogues 21 of the Greek coins on pp. 269-73.

1939 **Heath, Sebastian, Andrew Meadows, and Peter G. van Alfen.** "Acquisitions for 2006 in the American Numismatic Society Collection." *American Journal of Numismatics* 19 (2007): 183-90. 4 pls.
Greek additions included numerous coins of the Peloponnese acquired from the sale of the BCD collection. Includes a catalogue and some discussion of the coins. [See LHS Numismatics *Coins of the Peloponnesos* under PELOPONNESOS—GENERAL WORKS].

1940 **Metropolitan Museum of Art.** *Greek Coins from the John Ward Collection.* New York: Numislides, 1974.
A series of 300 color slides of the finest coins from the Ward collection, which was sold by Sotheby-Parke Bernet in 1973 [see 1945]. Includes a printed description of each coin and a key to the sale catalogue.

1941 **Mosser, Sawyer McArthur.** *The Endicott Gift of Greek and Roman Coins, including the "Catacombs" Hoard.* Numismatic Notes and Monographs, No. 97. New York: American Numismatic Society, 1941. 53 pp., 9 pls. [CS 1911]
Describes the most important of the 427 Greek and 714 Roman coins in the F. Munroe Endicott collection which was given to the ANS in 1935. One hundred Greek coins are catalogued, along with sixty-nine Roman coins. One outstanding Greek coin is an Alexander-style tetradrachm bearing the name of Nikokles of Paphos. Includes a group of Roman denarii and antoniniani from the "Catacombs Hoard." Some are illustrated. [Reviewed by W. Wallace in *American Journal of Archaeology* 48 (1944): 113-4].

1942 **Newell, Edward T.** "Some Rare or Unpublished Greek Coins." *American Journal of Numismatics* 48 (1914): 62-72. 2 pls.
Examines thirty-seven previously unpublished Greek coins in the collection of the American Numismatic Society.

1943 **Noe, Sydney P.** "Greek Coins Acquired during 1945." *Museum Notes* 1 (1945): 5-15. 5 pls.
Describes some of the noteworthy coins added to the American Numismatic Society collection in 1945, including coins of Abydus, Ilium, Abdera, Argos, Siculo-Punic issues (bearing a combination of Greek and Punic letters), Tyre, Sidon, Polyrhenium, Salamis, Bactria, and Alexander coins from Sicyon, Miletus, and Knidus. Noe comments on the combinations of magistrates' names and symbols on the reverses of the coins of Abydus.

1944 ———. "Greek Coins Acquired by the American Numismatic Society in 1947." *Museum Notes* 3 (1948): 1-14. 3 pls.
Discusses some coins added to the American Numismatic Society collection, from the collection of Sir Ronald Storrs. Lists and describes seven Alexander tetradrachms, a rare tetradrachm of Melos, two electrum coins of Ionia, a tetradrachm of Knidus, a drachm of Rhoda Hispaniae, and a rare didrachm of Alexander the Great from the Amphipolis mint.

1945 **Sotheby & Co.** *The Collection of Ancient and Later Coins: The Property of the Metropolitan Museum of Art. Part 2: Greek Coins from the John Ward Collection.* Zurich: Sotheby & Co., April 4-5, 1973. 132 pp., 31 pls. [CS 1910]
An auction catalogue containing 773 lots of Greek coins from the collection of John Ward. Includes a brief history of the coin collection of the Metropolitan Museum of Art and the reasons for its disposal. Also contains a brief biography of John Ward. The coins were donated to the Metropolitan Museum of Art by J. P. Morgan in 1905. Includes maps and some color photographs. Some of these coins previously appeared in the catalogue prepared by G. F. Hill (see Hill *Descriptive Catalogue* under PRIVATE COLLECTIONS, and Ward and Hill *Greek Coins* under PRIVATE COLLECTIONS). Includes illustrations of some coins not appearing in Hill's plates. Also, several coins have now been reattributed in the light of more recent research. [Also see listing 838 in J. Spring, *Ancient Coin Auction Catalogues 1880-1980* (see Spring under COLLECTING GUIDES)].

1946 **Stolyarik, Elena.** "From the Collection Manager: Recent Acquisitions." *ANS* 7, no. 3 (winter 2008): 38-43. Illus.
A report on additions to the American Numismatic Society museum's collection including numerous Greek bronzes from the collection of Christopher Morcom, some Akarnanian coins from the BCD collection, and a group of eighty-seven archaic coins from the Asyut Hoard (*IGCH* 1644) that was found in Egypt in 1969.

1947 ———. "From the Collections Manager: New Acquisitions." *ANS* 9, no. 1 (spring 2010): 24-31. Illus.

Among new acquisitions by the ANS museum was a fourth century B.C. gold stater of Pergamon in Mysia.

1948 **Thompson, Margaret.** "Some Noteworthy Greek Accessions." *Museum Notes* 12 (1966): 1-18. 2 pls.
Discusses twenty-three coins in the American Numismatic Society collection which are rare or of artistic merit: An electrum hecte of Lydia with a new, but not fully readable, legend which is one of the first inscribed issues of Lydia (also discusses the *valvel* issues); five uncertain electrum and silver coins of Asia Minor; a didrachm of Akragas with the reverse inscription "Exakesios;" a previously unknown stater of Mallus with a noteworthy depiction of a pantheress; a gold drachm of Alexander the Great; a rare Ptolemaic gold drachm of Cyrene; a gold didrachm of Ptolemy II; a silver drachm of Antiochus I with a new monogram; a tetradrachm of Antiochus III; a tetradrachm of Alexander Balas issued at Susa; a silver drachm of Demetrius II struck at Tarsus during his first reign; and also some rare pieces from Macedonia, Capsa, Side, Caria, Tarsus, Myriandrus, and Mylasa. [Also see R. W. Wallace "KUKALIM, WALWET, and the Artemision Deposit" under LYDIA].

1949 **van Alfen, Peter.** "Greek Acquisitions." *American Numismatic Society Magazine* 1, no. 1 (spring 2002): 35. Illus.
A brief description of recent additions to the A.N.S. collection including a group of Lycian staters, a stater from Locris Opuntii, Alexander III drachms (some from the Colophon mint), and some Alexander III tetradrachms from a third century hoard.

1950 **van Alfen, Peter, Elena Stolyarik, Sebastian Heath, Michael Bates, and Robert W. Hoge.** "Acquisitions for 2002 in the American Numismatic Society Collection." *American Journal of Numismatics* 2nd ser., 14 (2002): 179-222. 14 pls.
The Greek accessions comprised 465 coins, including many Macedonian issues. Among some Alexander-type imitations are two sets of previously unknown hybrid imitations combining the horned Alexander obverse type of Lysimachos with the Alexandrine enthroned Zeus on the reverse.

1951 **Waggoner, Nancy M.** "New Collection at the American Numismatic Society." *Archaeology* 30, no. 3 (May 1977): 194-5. Illus.
Describes the formation of the Robert F. Kelley collection of 1200 Greek and Byzantine coins, which was donated to the A.N.S. in 1976. Includes some general comments on Greek and Byzantine coinage. Illustrated by two Greek coins and one Byzantine coin. [Also see Troxell and Waggoner "Kelley Bequest" under ASIA MINOR—GENERAL WORKS].

1952 **Wartenberg, Ute, Peter van Alfen, Elena Stolyarik, Sebastian Heath, Michael Bates, and Robert W. Hoge.** "Acquisitions for 2000 and 2001 in the American Numismatic Society Collection." *American Journal of Numismatics* 13 (2001): 151-212. 12 pls.
Additions included 51 Greek coins, catalogued on pp. 151-67.

Also see: Hoge, Meadows, and Wartenberg Kagan "Truth and Plain Dealing" under SPAIN; Troxell and Waggoner "Kelley Bequest" under ASIA MINOR—GENERAL WORKS; van Alfen "Greek Acquisitions" under TYPES.

NORTHAMPTON, MASSACHUSETTS

1953 **Smith College Museum of Art.** *An Exhibition of Greek and Roman Antique Coins Accompanied by Some Renaissance Illustrated Books.* Northampton, 1962. 56 pp., 16 pls.
An exhibition catalogue including two essays: "Greek and Roman Numismatic Art" by Cornelius Vermeule and "Some Comments on Roman Republican Coins" by Reziya Ahmad. Lists forty-two Greek coins and sixty-seven Roman coins. Numerous enlarged photographs.

PHILADELPHIA, PENNSYLVANIA

1954 **Snowden, James Ross.** *A Description of Ancient and Modern Coins in the Cabinet Collection at the Mint of the United States.* Philadelphia: J. B. Lippincott, 1860. 412 pp., illus. [CS 12543]
A description of the United States Mint collection in Philadelphia (subsequently transferred to the Smithsonian Institution in Washington, DC). Contains an overview of Greek coins (pages 3-33) briefly listing about 350 specimens with minimal description or commentary. None of the coins are illustrated.

PRINCETON, NEW JERSEY

Also see: "Princeton Adds Armenian Coin Collection" and "Ancient and Medieval Armenian Coins Acquired" under ARMENIA.

PROVIDENCE, RHODE ISLAND

1955 **Holloway, R. Ross.** *Catalogue of the Classical Collection, Museum of Art, Rhode Island School of Art and Design: Ancient Greek Coins.* Publications d'Histoire de l'Art et d'Archéologie de l'Université Catholique de Louvain XCVI. Archaeologia Transatlantica 15. Providence/Louvain-La-Neuve: Collège Erasme, 1998. Also: Center for Old World Art and Archaeology, Brown University, 1998. 98 pp., illus.
A catalogue of 469 Greek coins, intended to illustrate the development of Greek art. The largest part of the Museum's holdings came from the collection of Henry Augustus Greene. The catalogue is preceded by a lengthy essay on Greek art and Greek coinage. [A very critical review by Alan Walker appears in *Revue Suisse de Numismatique* (Switzerland) 79 (1998): 175-8].

RALEIGH, NORTH CAROLINA

1956 **Brauer, George C., Jr.** "Ancient Coinage." *Classical Art from Carolina Collections: An Exhibition of Greek, Etruscan, and Roman Art from Public and Private Collections in North and South Carolina.* By Charles Randall Mack. Columbia and Raleigh: Columbia Museum of Art, and North Carolina Museum of Art, 1974. Pages 49 ff. 2 pls.
This exhibition of ancient art drawn from twenty-one public and private collections included sixteen Greek coins. The coins are catalogued and illustrated. The brief introduction mentions the origins of coinage and methods of minting.

ST. LOUIS, MISSOURI

1957 **Herbert, Kevin.** *The John Max Wulfing Collection in Washington University.* Ancient Coins in North American Collections, No. 2. New York: American Numismatic Society, 1979. 30 pp., 22 pls.

A catalogue of 437 Greek coins donated to the University by John Max Wulfing in 1928.

1958 **Washington University.** *Ancient Collections in Washington University.* St. Louis: Washington University, 1973. 52 pp., illus. [CS 16676]

WHEATON, ILLINOIS

1959 **Bishop, J. David, and R. Ross Holloway.** *Wheaton College Collection of Greek and Roman Coins.* Ancient Coins in North American Collections, No. 3. New York: American Numismatic Society, 1981. 32 pp., 32 pls. [CS 16681a]
The basis of the collection was a group of coins given to the college by the ANS in 1931. Among other donations was the estate of Adra Marshall Newell, widow of E. T. Newell. The text for the Greek section was written by Holloway and lists 305 Greek coins. Also lists 145 Roman coins.

YUGOSLAVIA

BELGRADE

1960 **Gaj-Popovic, Dobrila.** *Splendor of Coinage: Coins from the Collection of the National Museum of Belgrade.* Belgrade: National Museum, 1979. 66 pp., 53 pls.
Includes a history of the collection and a description of its contents. Fifteen Greek coins are catalogued and illustrated.

THE SYLLOGE NUMMORUM GRAECORUM SERIES

The Sylloge Nummorum Graecorum series publishes only ancient Greek coins, and was begun in 1931 by the British Academy. It is a novel and very useful system that was originally intended to assist with die-studies of precious metal coins, and every single coin in most of the collections is pictured. This is accomplished by utilizing extremely scanty descriptions on the left pages, with the photographic illustrations (usually of excellent quality) on the right pages. Historical information and indices are (with few exceptions) always lacking, as it is assumed that the student has access to this information elsewhere.

—Dennis Kroh, 1991

AMERICAN SERIES

1961   **1:** *Collection of Burton Y. Berry.* New York: American Numismatic Society. [CS 1916]
Includes 1506 coins.

1. *Macedonia to Attica,* by Margaret Thompson and R. Ross Holloway, 1961. 28 pls. [Reviewed by G. K. Jenkins in *Numismatic Chronicle* 7th ser., 1 (1961): 239-40, and by A. R. Bellinger in *American Journal of Archaeology* 66 (1962): 108-9].
2. *Megaris to Egypt,* by Margaret Thompson and Irwin L. Merker, 1962. 30 pls. [Reviewed by C. M. Kraay in *Spink Numismatic Circular* 71, no. 1 (January 1963): 4, and by G. K. Jenkins in *Numismatic Chronicle* 7th ser., 3 (1963): 252-3].

1962   **2:** *American Numismatic Society Collection.* New York: American Numismatic Society. [CS 1917]

1. *Etruria—Calabria,* by Joan E. Fisher, 1969. 39 pls. [Reviewed by M. J. Price in *Numismatic Chronicle* 7th ser., 11 (1971): 347-9].
2. *Lucania,* by Hyla A. Troxell, 1972. 38 pls. [Reviewed by N. K. Rutter in *Numismatic Chronicle* 7th ser., 13 (1973): 229, and by M. B. Wallace in *Cornucopiæ* (Canada) 1, no. 3 (February 1973): 43-8].
3. *Bruttium—Sicily I: Abacaenum—Eryx,* by Hyla A. Troxell, 1975. 38 pls. [Reviewed by G. K. Jenkins in *Journal of Hellenic Studies* 97 (1977): 230].
4. *Sicily II: Galaria—Styella,* by Ava C. Jaunzems, 1977. 25 pls. [Reviewed by R. T. Williams in *Journal of Hellenic Studies* 100 (1980): 289].
5. *Sicily III: Syracuse—Siceliotes,* by Denyse Bérend, 1988. 45 pls. [Reviewed by John Morcom in *Numismatic Chronicle* 150 (1990): 244-6].
6. *Palestine—South Arabia,* by Ya'akov Meshorer, 1981. 54 pls.
7. *Macedonia I: Cities, Thraco-Macedonian Tribes, Paeonian Kings,* by Nancy Waggoner, 1987. 39 pls.
8. *Macedonia II: Alexander I—Philip II,* by Hyla A. Troxell, 1994. 34 pls. [Reviewed by M. J. Price in *Numismatic Chronicle* 149 (1989): 233].
9. *Graeco-Bactrian and Indo-Greek Coins,* by Osmund Bopearachchi. 1998. 76 pls.

AUSTRALIAN SERIES

1963   **1:** *Australian Centre for Ancient Numismatic Studies: The Gale Collection of South Italian Coins,* by Kenneth Sheedy. Sydney: Australian Center for Ancient Numismatic Studies, Macquarie University, 2008. 160 pp., 57 pls.
Catalogue of the 1267 coins representing the mints of South Italy in the W. L. Gale collection, donated to the Australian Centre for Ancient Numismatic Studies in 2007. [Reviewed by Andrew Burnett in *Numismatic Chronicle* 169 (2009): 437].

AUSTRIAN SERIES

1964   **1:** *Sammlung Dreer, Klagenfurt im Landesmuseum für Kärnten.* Klagenfurt: Geschichtsverein für Kärnten, 1967-90. [CS 1918]

1. *Italien-Sizilien,* by Gotbert Moro. 1967. 15 pls. 612 coins.
2. *Spanien-Gallien-Keltenländer,* by Leopoldine Springschnitz. 1984. 9 pl. 220 coins.
3. *Thraien-Macedonien, Päonien,* by Leopoldine Springschnitz. 1990. 27 pls. 676 coins.

1965   **2:** *Sammlung Franz Leypold, Oesterreichische Nationalbank.* Vienna: Kleinasiatische Münzen der Kaiserzeit, 2000+.

1. *Pontus—Lydien,* by W. Szaivert and C. Daburon. Vienna, 2000. 203 pp., 1343 coins. [Reviewed by K. Ehling in *Revue Suisse de Numismatique* 80 (2001): 229-31, and by Ann Johnston in *Numismatic Chronicle* 162 (2002): 445-9].
2. *Phrygien—Kommagene, mit Nachträgen, Korrekturen und Indices zu beiden Bänden.* Vienna, 2004. 304 pp., 125 pls. 1503 coins.

BELGIAN SERIES

1966 **1:** *Bibliothèque Royale de Belgique. La Collection de Bronzes Grecs de Marc Bar,* by Marc Bar. Brussels: Bibliothèque Royale de Belgique, 2007. 277 pp. incl. 97 pls.
Catalogue of 1373 bronze coins struck in the ancient world between the 5th century B.C. and the 3rd century A.D. The catalogue is followed by thirty-six pages of notes on selected coins. Bar donated his collection to the museum in 2002. [Reviewed by A. S. Walker in *The Celator* 22, no. 8 (August 2008): 35 ff].

BRAZILIAN SERIES

1967 **1:** *Museu Histórico Nacional: Moedas Gregas e Provinciais Romanas,* by Marici Martins Magalhaes. Rio de Janeiro: Museu Histórico Nacional, 2011.
Text in English and Portuguese.

BRITISH SERIES

1968 **1:** *Collection of Capt. E. G. Spencer-Churchill of Northwick Park, Salting and Aberdeen Collections.* [Part of CS 1913]
1. *The Salting Collection in the Victoria and Albert Museum,* 1931. 8 pls. Describes 246 coins.
2. *The Newnham Davis Coins in the Wilson College of Classical and Eastern Antiquities Marshall College Aberdeen,* 1936. 14 pls. Describes 490 coins.

[Parts 1 and 2 reviewed by S. Noe in *American Journal of Archaeology* 38 (1934): 496].

1969 **2:** *Lloyd Collection.* [Part of CS 1913]
Describes 1687 precious metal issues of Italy and Sicily. Reprinted in one volume, Chicago: Obol International, 1979.

1. & 2. *Etruria to Thurium,* by Edward S. G. Robinson, 1933. 16 pls. [Reviewed by S. Noe in *American Journal of Archaeology* 38 (1934): 496].
3. & 4. *Velia to Eryx,* 1934. 16 pls.
5. & 6. *Galaria to Selinus,* 1935. 12 pls.
7. & 8. *Syracuse to Lipara,* 1937. 14 pls.

1970 **3:** *Lockett Collection.* [Part of CS 1913]
Includes 3542 coins from the collection of Richard Cyril Lockett. All volumes were reprinted in 1957.

1. *Spain—Italy (gold and silver),* 1938. 12 pls. [Reviewed by E. T. Newell in *American Journal of Archaeology* 43 (1939): 720].
2. *Sicily—Thrace (gold and silver),* 1939. 12 pls.
3. *Macedonia—Aegina (gold and silver),* 1942. 12 pls.
4. *Peloponnese—Aeolis (gold and silver),* 1945. 11 pls.
5. *Lesbos—Cyrenaica: Addenda (gold and silver),* 1949. 16 pls. [Reviewed by G. K. Jenkins in *Numismatic Chronicle* 6th ser., 9 (1949): 127-8; also reviewed by A. B. Brett in *American Journal of Archaeology* 57 (1953): 297].

[Also see Glendining & Co. *Lockett Collection* under PRIVATE COLLECTIONS. Also see J. S. Wilkinson "Notes on the Lockett Collection" in *Canadian Numismatic Journal* 4, no. 8 (1959): 255, where brief comparisons are made between the sales catalogues of the Pozzi and Lockett collections].

1971 **4:** *Fitzwilliam Museum: Leake and General Collections.* [Part of CS 1913]
Includes 6125 coins. Reprinted in 1972.

1. *Spain (Emporiae, Rhoda)—Italy,* 1940. Reprint, London, 1972. 14 pls.
2. *Sicily—Thrace,* 1947. 19 pls. [Reviewed by A. B. Brett in *American Journal of Archaeology* 55 (1951): 431-2].
3. *Macedonia—Acarnania,* 1951. 16 pls. [Reviewed by G. K. Jenkins in *Numismatic Chronicle* 6th ser., 12 (1952): 139].
4. *Acarnania—Phliasia,* 1956. 14 pls.
5. *Sicyon—Thera,* 1958. 8 pls.
6. *Asia Minor: Phrygia,* by Edward S. G. Robinson and F. Heichelheim, 1965. [Reviewed by J. P. Barron in *Numismatic Chronicle* 7th ser., 6 (1966): 345-7].
7. *Asia Minor: Lycia—Cappadocia,* 1967. 15 pls. [Reviewed by Anne E. Jackson in *Numismatic Chronicle* 7th ser., 9 (1969): 333-4].
8. *Syria—Nabathaea,* 1971. 20 pls. [Reviewed by R. T. Williams in *Journal of Hellenic Studies* 95 (1975): 299-300].

The Fitzwilliam Museum purchased the collection of William Martin Leake in 1864. [Also see Heichelheim "Numismatic Comments" and Kumpikevicius "Fritz Moritz Heichelheim and the Fitzwilliam Coin Cabinet" under PUBLIC COLLECTIONS—GREAT BRITAIN (CAMBRIDGE). Also see Babington *Catalogue* and Leake *Numismata Hellenica* under PRIVATE COLLECTIONS].

1972 **5:** *Ashmolean Museum, Oxford.* [Part of CS 1913]
1. *Evans Collection (Italy and Sicily),* by J. G. Milne, 1951. 8 pls. Catalogues 369 coins from the collection of Sir Arthur Evans. [Reviewed by G. K. Jenkins in *Journal of Hellenic Studies* (1952): 157-8].
1A. *Italy: Etruria—Lucania (Thurium),* 1962. 16 pls.
2. *Italy: Lucania (Thurium)—Bruttium, Sicily, Carthage,* by Colin M. Kraay, 1969. 24 pls. [Reviewed by N. K. Rutter in *Numismatic Chronicle* 7th ser., 11 (1971): 349-51].
3. *Macedonia,* by Colin M. Kraay, 1976. 28 pls. [Reviewed by R. T. Williams in *Journal of Hellenic Studies* 97 (1977): 230, and by Martin J. Price in *Numismatic Chronicle* 137 (1977): 237].
4. *Paeonia—Thessaly,* by Cathy E. King and Colin M. Kraay, 1981. 14 pls.
9. *Bosporus—Aeolis,* by Richard Ashton and Stanley Ireland. Oxford University Press and Spink, 2007. 59 pls.

1973 **6:** *The Lewis Collection in Corpus Christi College, Cambridge.* [Part of CS 1913]

1. *The Greek and Hellenistic Coins (with Britain and Parthia),* by Martin J. Price, 1972. 24 pls. Includes 1212 coins. [Reviewed by R. T. Williams in *Journal of Hellenic Studies* 95 (1975): 299-300].
2. *The Greek Imperial Coins,* by Martin J. Price, 1992. 24 pls. Includes 892 coins.

The collection formed by Samuel Savage Lewis, now residing in the Fitzwilliam Museum.

1974 **7:** *The Raby and Güterbock Collections in Manchester University Museum,* by John F. Healy. London: British Academy, Oxford University Press, 1986. 135 pp., 57 pls.
Includes 1472 coins. Includes the coins donated to the museum in 1916 by Alfred Güterbock, as well as coins donated later by Harold Raby. Includes gold, silver, and bronze coins. [Reviewed by P. Kinns in *Numismatic Chronicle* 148 (1988): 223-4].

1975 **8:** *The Hart Collection, Blackburn Museum,* by Keith F. Sugden. London: British Academy, 1989. 132 pp., 56 pls.
Includes 1316 coins bequeathed to the Blackburn Museum, Lancashire, by Edward Hart. [Reviewed by J. F. Healy in *Numismatic Chronicle* 150 (1990): 248-50].

1976 **9:** *The British Museum.*
1. *The Black Sea,* by Martin J. Price. London, 1993. 136 pages, 59 pls., map. Includes 1642 Greek coins.
2. *Spain,* by Peter Bagwell Purefoy and A. Meadows. London: British Museum Press, 2002. 215 pp., 80 pls. [Reviewed by M. H. Crawford in *Numismatic Chronicle* 163 (2003): 410-1, and by F. C. Tristán in *Revue Suisse de Numismatique* 84 (2005): 213-7].

1977 **10:** *The John Morcom Collection of Western Greek Bronze Coins,* by John Morcom. Oxford: University Press, 1995. 96 pp., 38 pls.
This illustrated catalogue of John Morcom's collection of over 900 bronze coins provides an excellent guide to the ancient Greek coinage issued by peoples of Italy and further west. Also includes some Roman coins. [John Morcom's grandfather was Col. R. K. Morcom (1877-1961), who formed an extraordinary collection of Greek coins in the 1920s and 1930s, including coins from many famous collections. Christopher Morcom (John's brother) acquired many of R. K. Morcom's coins, and eventually sold his collection in Classical Numismatic Group's *Sale 76* (September 12, 2007)].

1978 **11:** *The William Stancomb Collection of Coins of the Black Sea Region.* Oxford and London: Spink, 2000. 53 pls.
Catalogues the collection of William M. Stancomb, consisting of 1092 Greek and Roman Provincial bronze coins from the cities ringing the Black Sea. Includes indexes of cities, royal names, Greek magistrates, monograms and symbols, countermarks, and overstrikes. [Reviewed by Mariusz Mielczarek in *Numismatic Chronicle* 161 (2001): 363-4, and by Dimitar Draganov in *Numismatica Bulgarica* 2, no.1 (2004): 81-3].

1979 **12:** *The Hunterian Museum, University of Glasgow.*
1. *Roman Provincial Coins: Spain – Kingdoms of Asia Minor.* By John Goddard. Oxford, 2004. 440 pp., 173 pls. 2428 coins. [Reviewed by Alan Walker in *Spink Numismatic Circular* 113, no. 1 (February 2005): 17-8].
2. *Roman Provincial Coins: Cyprus – Egypt.* By John Goddard. Oxford, 2007. 2581 coins. 157 pls.

1980 **13:** *The Collection of the Society of Antiquaries, Newcastle upon Tyne.* London, 2005. 48 pls.
Catalogues 1036 coins.

Bulgarian Series

1981 **1:** *Bobokov Brothers Collection, Thrace and Moesia Inferior.*
1. *Deultum,* by Dimitar Draganov. Ruse (Bulgaria), 2005. 303 pp., 134 pl. Includes 2010 Roman Provincial coins from the Roman colony of Deultum in Thrace from the reign of Trajan to Philip I. The coins are from the collection of Plamen and Atanas Bobokov. [Reviewed by R. Witschonke in *ANS Magazine* 6, no. 2 (summer 2007): 69, and by Kevin Butcher in *Spink Numismatic Circular* 116, no. 6 (December 2008): 301].

Danish Series

1982 **1:** *The Royal Collection of Coins and Medals, Danish National Museum.* 43 parts. Copenhagen: Danish National Museum, 1942-77. Reprinted in eight volumes, West Milford, New Jersey: Sunrise Publications, 1981-92. [CS 1912]
Describes 22,012 coins. Part 1 includes an essay on the origins and formation of the collection.
1. *Italy, part 1: Etruria—Campania,* 1941. 14 pls.
2. *Italy, part 2: Apulia—Lucania; Metapontum,* 1942.
3. *Italy, part 3: Lucania: Poseidonia—Bruttium,* 1942. 11 pls.
4. *Sicily, part 1: Abacaenum—Petra,* 1942. 12 pls.
5. *Sicily, part 2: Segesta—Sardinia,* 1942. 10 pls.
6. *Thrace, part 1: The Tauric Chersonese—Thrace: Mesembria,* 1942. 12 pls.
7. *Thrace, part 2: Odessus—Sestus, Islands; Kings and Dynasts,* 1943. 11 pls.
8. *Macedonia, part 1: Acanthus—Uranopolis; Dynasts,* 1943. 11 pls.
9. *Macedonia, part 2: Alexander I—Alexander III,* 1943. 15 pls.
10. *Macedonia, part 3: Philip III—Philip VI. Macedonia under the Romans. Kings of Paeonia,* 1943. 8 pls.
11. *Thessaly—Illyricum,* 1943. 11 pls.
12. *Epirus—Acarnania,* 1943. 9 pls.
13. *Aetolia—Euboea,* 1944. 11 pls.
14. *Attica—Aegina,* 1944. 13 pls.
15. *Corinth,* 1944. 8 pls.
16. *Phliasia—Laconia,* 1944. 12 pls.
17. *Argolis—Aegean Islands,* 1944. 16 pls.
18. *Bosporus—Bithynia,* 1944. 16 pls.

19. *Mysia*, 1945. 14 pls.
20. *Troas*, 1945. 11 pls.
21. *Aeolis—Lesbos*, 1945. 9 pls.
22. *Ionia, part 1: Clazomenae—Ephesus*, 1946. 13 pls.
23. *Ionia, part 2: Erythrae—Priene*, 1946. 11 pls.
24. *Ionia, part 3: Smyrna—Teos, Islands*, 1946. 16 pls.
25. *Caria, part 1: Alabanda—Orthosia*, 1947. 10 pls.
26. *Caria, part 2: Sebastopolis—Trapezopolis. Satraps, Islands*, 1947. 11 pls.
27. *Lydia, part 1: Acrasus—Saïta*, 1947. 12 pls.
28. *Lydia, part 2: Sala—Tripolis*, 1947. 10 pls.
29. *Phrygia, part 1: Abbaitis—Eumeneia*, 1948. 11 pls.
30. *Phrygia, part 2: Grimenothyrae—Trajanopolis*, 1948. 12 pls.
31. *Lycia—Pamphylia*, 1955. 13 pls. [Parts 31-33 were reviewed by G. K. Jenkins in *Numismatic Chronicle* 6th ser., 17 (1957): 261-4].
32. *Pisidia*, 1956. 12 pls. [Reviewed by Jenkins; see Part 31].
33. *Lycaonia—Cilicia*, 1956. 15 pls. [Reviewed by Jenkins; see Part 31].
34. *Cyprus—Cappadocia, Uncertain coins. Imperial cistophori*, 1956. 12 pls. [Parts 34-39 were reviewed by G. K. Jenkins in *Numismatic Chronicle* 7th ser., 10 (1970): 321-3].
35. *Syria, Seleucid kings*, 1959. 12 pls. [Reviewed by Jenkins; see Part 34].
36. *Syria, Cities*, 1959. 12 pls. [Reviewed by Jenkins; see Part 34].
37. *Phoenicia*, 1961. 10 pls. [Reviewed by Jenkins; see Part 34].
38. *Palestine—Characene*, 1961. 10 pls. [Reviewed by Jenkins; see Part 34].
39. *Parthia, Bactria, India*, 1965. 11 pls. [Reviewed by Jenkins; see Part 34].
40. *Egypt: the Ptolemies*, 1977. 22 pls.
41. *Alexandria—Cyrenaica*, 1974. 31 pls.
42. *North Africa: Syrtica—Mauretania*, by G. K. Jenkins, 1969. 28 pls.
43. *Spain*, by G. K. Jenkins and Anne Kromann, 1977. 39 pls.

The reprint volumes are arranged as follows:

1. *Italy and Sicily*. 92 pp., 60 pls.
2. *Thrace and Macedonia*. 68 pp., 60 pls.
3. *Thessaly to Aegean Islands*. 96 pp., 80 pls.
4. *Bosporus to Lesbos*. 62 pp., 50 pls.
5. *Ionia, Caria, and Lydia*. 93 pp., 83 pls.
6. *Phrygia to Cilicia*. 73 pp., 63 pls.
7. *Cyprus to India*. 81 pp., 67 pls.
8. *Spain—Gaul, North Africa, Syrtica—Mauretania, Alexandria—Cyrenaica, Egypt—The Ptolemies*. 138 pp., 120 pls.

1983 **1 Supplement:** *The Royal Collection of Coins and Medals, Danish National Museum: Supplement—Acquisitions 1942-1996.* Edited by Sabine Schultz and Jan Zahle. Copenhagen: Danish National Museum, 2002. 60 pp., 54 pls.
A catalogue of all the Greek coins added to the museum's collection between 1942-1966. [Reviewed by O. D. Hoover in *American Numismatic Society Magzine* 2, no. 2 (summer 2003): 59-61, by A. Walker in *Revue Suisse de Numismatique* 82 (2003): 132-6, and by R. Ashton in *Numismatic Chronicle* 164 (2004): 333-5].

1984 **2:** *Aarhus University Denmark.* Edited by Hans Erik Mathiesen. Copenhagen: Aarhus University, 1986. 44 pls.
The nucleus of this collection was formed by Herman Ernst Freund (1786-1840). A comprehensive collection of 1111 coins including many Greek Imperial issues.

1985 **3:** *Knud Fabricius Collection Aarhus University Denmark, and the Royal Collection of Coins and Medals Danish National Museum Copenhagen.* Edited by Hans Erik Mathiesen. Copenhagen: Aarhus University, 1987. 52 pages, including the 21 pls.
Upon his death, the collection of archaic, classical, and Hellenistic coinage formed by Knud Fabricius (1875-1967) was divided between the National Museum (110 coins) and the Aarhus University Collection (396 coins). The collection is focused on coins of Southern Italy and Sicily. All of the coins are catalogued here. [Reviewed by P. Kinns in *Numismatic Chronicle* 149 (1989): 234, and by M. Amandry in *Revue Numismatique* (France) 32 (1990): 294-5].

FINISH SERIES

1986 **1:** *The Erkki Keckman Collection in the Skopbank, Helsinki.*

1. *Karia*, by Ulla Westermark and Richard Ashton. Helsinki, 1994. 37 pp., 32 pls. Catalogues over 900 coins. [Reviewed by K. Butcher in *Spink Numismatic Circular* 103, no. 5 (June 1995): 187, and by Koray Konuk in *Numismatic Chronicle* 155 (1995): 372-3].
2. *Asia Minor except Karia*. Helsinki, 1999. 69 pp., 32 pls.

FRENCH SERIES

1987 **1:** *Bibliothèque Nationale: Cabinet des Médailles.*

1. *Collection Jean et Marie Delepierre*, by Hélène Nicolet. Paris, 1983. 117 pp., 88 pls. 3030 coins.
2. *Cilicie*, by Eduardo Levante. Paris/Zurich, 1993. 137 pp., 137 pls. 2436 coins.
3. *Pamphylie, Pisidie, Lycaonie, Galatie*, by Eduardo Levante. Zurich, 1994. 146 pp., 146 pls.
4. *Alexandrie, 1: Auguste à Trajan*, by Soheir Bakoum. Zurich: Bibliothèque Nationale de France and Numismatica Ars Classica, 1998. 105 pp., 105 pls. [Reviewed by G. M. Staffieri in *Revue Suisse de Numismatique* 78 (1999): 211-5, by Erik Christiansen in *Numismatic Chronicle* 160 (2000): 386-90, and by William Metcalf in *American Journal of Numismatics* 2nd ser., 12 (2000): 247-9].
5. *Mysie*. Paris/Zurich, 2001. 136 pls. 2500+ coins. [Reviewed by S. Ireland in *Numismatic Chronicle* 164 (2004): 335-7].

6. *Italie I: Étrurie to Calabre*, by Anna Rita Parente. Paris, 2003. 141 pls. 2286 coins. [Reviewed by A. Walker in *The Celator* 18, no. 5 (May 2004): 49, 59].

GERMAN SERIES

1988 **1:** *Sammlung v. Aulock.* Berlin: Deutsches Archäologisches Institut, 1957-81. Reprinted in four volumes, West Milford, New Jersey: Sunrise Publications, 1987. 304 pls. [CS 1914]
The collection of Hans von Aulock. Covers the mints in Asia Minor only. Catalogues 8739 coins.

  1–3. *Pontus-Paphlagoni-Bythnia*, by G. Kleiner. 1957. 32 pls.
  4. *Mysien*, by K. Kraft. 1957. Second edition, 1966. 12 pls.
  5. *Troas-Aeolis-Lesbos*, by K. Kraft. 1959. Second edition, 1969. 10 pls.
  6. *Ionien*, by K. Kraft and H. Küthmann. 1960.
  7. *Karien*, by K. Kraft and D. Kienast. 1962. Second edition, 1969. 19 pls.
  8. *Lydien*, by H. von Aulock. 1963.
  9. *Phrygien*, by H. von Aulock. 1964.
  10. *Lykien*, by O. Mørkholm. 1964. Second edition, 1971. 12 pls.
  11. *Pamphylien*, by O. Mørkholm. 1964. 14 pls.
  12. *Pisidien, Lykaonien, Isaurien*, by H. von Aulock. 1964. 21 pls.
  13. *Kilikien*, by H. von Aulock. 1966. 29 pls.
  14. *Galatien, Kappadokien, Kaiserzeitliche Kistophoren, Posthume Lysimachus und Alexander Tetradrachmen, Incerti*, by H. von Aulock. 1967. 19 pls.
  15. *Nachträge I: Pontus, Paphlagonien, Bithynien*, by H. von Aulock. 1967. 19 pls.
  16. *Nachträge II: Mysien, Troas, Aeolis, Lesbos*, by H. von Aulock. 1967. 20 pls.
  17. *Nachträge III: Ionien, Karien, Lydien*, by H. von Aulock. 1968. 18 pls.
  18. *Nachträge IV: Phrygien, Lykien, Pamphylien, Lykaonien, Isaurien, Kilikien, Galatien, Kappadokien, Kaiserzeitliche Kistophoren, Incerti*, by H. von Aulock. 1968. 18 pls.
  19. *Index*, by Peter Robert Franke, Wolfgang Leschhorn, and Armin U. Stylow. 1981. 268 pp., 12 tables.

The four volume reprint is arranged as follows: Volume 1 includes the original volumes 1-6; Volume 2 includes the original volumes 7-11; Volume 3 includes the original volumes 12-14; Volume 4 includes the original volumes 15-18.

1989 **2:** *Staatliche Münzsammlung München.* Berlin: Verlag Gebr. Mann, 1968+. [CS 1915]
The collection owned by the city of Munich.

  1. *Hispania – Gallia Narbonensis*, by P. R. Franke and H. Küthmann, 1968. 17 pls. 432 coins.
  2. *Etruria, Umbria, Picenum, Latium, Samnium, Frentani, Campania, Apulia*, by P. R. Franke and H. Küthmann, 1970. 20 pls. 551 coins.
  3. *Kalabria – Lukanien*, by P. R. Franke and H. Küthmann, 1973. 21 pls. 686 coins.
  4. *Bruttium; Karthager in Italien*, by P. R. Franke and H. Küthmann, 1974. 15 pls. 529 coins.
  5. *Sikelia*, by P. R. Franke and S. Grunauer, 1977. 26 pls. 872 coins.
  6. *Sikelia, Punier in Sizilien, Lipara, Sardinia, Punier in Sardinien, Nachträge.* 1980. 27 pls. 902 coins.
  7. *Taurische Chersones – Moesia Inferior.* 1985. 20 pls. 512 coins.
  10/11. *Makedonian Kingdom*, by Katerini Liampi, 2001. 107 pp., 52 pls. 1228 coins.
  12. *Thessalien, Illyrien, Epirus, Korkyra.* 2007. 701 coins.
  14. *Attika, Megaris, Aegina*, by John H. Kroll. Munich, 2002. 601 coins. [Reviewed by A. Walker in *Revue Suisse de Numismatique* 82 (2003): 132-6].
  19. *Troas – Lesbos*, by Hans Roland. 1991. 29 pls. 813 coins.
  20. *Ionien.* 1995. 29 pls. 882 coins.
  23. *Lydien.* 1997. 35 pls. 507 coins.
  24. *Phrygien.* 1989. 21 pls. 507 coins.
  28. *Syrien: Nicht-Königliche Prägungen.* 46 pl.

1990 **3:** *Münzsammlung der Universität Tübingen.* Six volumes. Berlin: Gebr. Mann Verlag, 1981-97. [CS 1915a]
The collection of Tübingen University.

  1. *Hispania – Sikilia*, by D. Mannsperger. Berlin, 1981. 64 pp. 730 coins.
  2. *Taurische Chersones – Korkyra*, by D. Mannsperger. Berlin, 1982. 58 pp. 812 coins.
  3. *Akarnanien – Bithynien*, by D. Mannsperger and G. Fischer-Heetfeld. Berlin, 1985. 54 pp. 631 coins.
  4. *Mysien – Ionien*, by D. Mannsperger. Munich, 1989. 31 pl. 1133 coins.
  5. *Karien – Lydien*, by D. Mannsperger. Munich, 1994. 20 pl. 580 coins.
  6. *Phrygien – Kappadokien, Römische Provinzielprägung in Kleinasien*, by Michael Matzke and Dietrich Mannsperger. Munich, 1998. 35 pl. [Reviewed by Ann Johnston in *Numismatic Chronicle* 160 (2000): 385].

1991 **4:** *Pfälzer Privatsammlung.* Munich: Hirmer Verlag.
The collection of Karl Eduard Reinhard Donat (see Papaefthymiou "The Coin Collection of the Foundation of the Hellenic World" under PRIVATE COLLECTIONS).

  1-3. Forthcoming.
  4. *Pamphylien.* 1993. 106 pp., 50 pls. 960 coins.
  5. *Pisidien und Lykaonien*, by Johannes Nollé. Munich: Hirmer Verlag, 1999. 36 pls. 586 coins. [Reviewed by Ann Johnston in *Numismatic Chronicle* 161 (2001): 368-70, and by Marguerite Spoerri Butcher in *Revue Suisse de Numismatique* 84 (2005): 221-2].
  6. *Isaurien und Kilikien.* 2001. Munich: Hirmer Verlag, 2001. 1486 coins. [Reviewed by Kevin Butcher in *Revue Suisse de Numismatique* 84 (2005): 223-4].

1992 **5:** *Sammlung der Universitätbibliothek Leipzig.*
The collection of the University of Leipzig.

1. *Autonome Griechische Münzen,* by Sabine Schultz. Munich: Hirmer Verlag, 1993. 90 pp., 76 pls. [Reviewed by M. Oeconomides-Caramessini in *Nomismatika Khronika* (Greece) 13 (1994): 137-8].
2. *Römische Provinzialprägungen, Addenda und Corrigenda zum 1 Band.* 2008.

1993   **6:** *Herzog Anton Ulrich-Museum Braunschweig. Kunstmuseum des Landes Niedersachsen: Katalog der Griechischen Münzen,* by Wolfgang Leschhorn. Brunswick, 1998.
Catalogue of over 1800 Greek and Roman Provincial coins in the Herzog Anton Ulrich Museum in Brunswick. Includes an introduction to the history of the collection.

GREEK SERIES

1994   **1:** *Collection Réna H. Evelpidis, Athènes.* Louvain: Commission International de Numismatique, 1970, 1975. [CS 1919]

1. *Italy, Sicily, Thrace,* by Tony Hackens and R. H. Evelpidis. Louvain, 1970. 35 pp., 31 pls. 1125 coins.
2. *Macédoine, Thessalie, Illyrie, Epire, Corcyre,* by Tony Hackens and R. H. Evelpidis. Louvain, 1975. 26 pp., 22 pls. 919 coins.

1995   **2:** *The Alpha Bank Collection.* Athens: Alpha Bank. 2000+.

1. *Macedonia I: Alexander I – Perseus,* by Sophia Kremydi-Sicilianou. 89 pp., 53 pls. Includes 1148 coins. [Reviewed by A. Walker in *The Celator* 15, no. 3 (March 2001): 34-5, and by R. Ashton in *Numismatic Chronicle* 161 (2001): 362-3].

1996   **3:** *Musee Numismatique d'Athenes: Collection Antoine Christomanos.* Athens: Academy of Athens, 2004+.

1. *Italie—Eubee,* by Mando Oeconomides. Athens: Académie d'Athènes, 2004. 120 pp., 44 pls. Includes 898 coins. [Reviewed by S. Hurter in *Schweizer Münzblätter* (Switzerland) 218 (June 2005): 58].

1997   **4:** *The Numismatic Museum, Athens: The Petros Z. Saroglos Collection.*

1. *Macedonia,* by Selene Psoma and Ioannis Touratsoglou. Athens: Numismatic Museum, 2005. 145 pp., 52 pls. 988 coins. [Reviewed in *Numismatic Chronicle* 166 (2006): 477ff].

1998   **5:** *The Numismatic Museum, Athens: The A.G. Soutzos Collection,* by Eos Tsourti and Maria Daniela Trifiró. Athens: Academy of Athens, 2007.

1998a   **6:** *The Alpha Bank Numismatic Collection: From Thessaly to Euboea.* Athens: Academy of Athens, 2011.

HUNGARIAN SERIES

1999   **1:** *Magyar Nemzeti Múseum, Budapest (Hungarian National Museum).*

1. *Hispania—Sicilia. Part 1: Hispania—Apulia.* Edited by M. Torbágyi. Milan, 1991. 128 pp., 47 pls.
Part 2: Calabria—Bruttium. Edited by M. Torbágyi. Milan, 1992. 134 pp., 48 pls. 647 coins.
Part 3: Sicilia. Edited by M. Torbágyi. Milan, 1993. 142 pp., 48 pls.
2. *Dacia—Moesia Superior.* Edited by Miklos Bakos. Milan, 1994. 138 pp., 51 pls. [Reviewed by K. E. T. Butcher in *Spink Numismatic Circular* 103, no. 5 (June 1995): 186].
3. *Moesia Inferior: Callatis—Dionysopolis—Istrus—Marcianopolis—Nicopolis ad Istrum—Odessus—Tomis.* 2000. 125 pp., 53 pls.

ISRAELI SERIES

2000   **1:** *The Arnold Spaer Collection of Seleucid Coins,* by Arthur Houghton and Arnold Spaer, with assistance from Catherine C. Lorber. London: Italo Vecchi, 1998. 201 pp., 189 pls.
Presents 2919 Seleucid coins acquired by Arnold Spaer since 1940. Lists and illustrates gold, silver, and bronze coins arranged by ruler and mint. Includes a *Foreword* by Spaer, an *Introduction* by Houghton, and a *Préface* (in French) by Georges Le Rider. [Reviewed by Alan Walker in *The Celator* 12, no. 8 (August 1998): 33-4, by W. Leschhorn in *Revue Suisse de Numismatique* 78 (1999): 191-5, and by O. Hoover in *Hekte* 4 (1999): 187-8].

ITALIAN SERIES

2001   **1:** *Milano, Civiche Raccolte Numismatiche.* Milan: Settore Cultura, 1988+.

1. *Hispania – Gallia Anellencia,* by Rodolfo Martini, B. Fischer, and Novella Vismara. 1988. 102 pp., 52 pls.
2. *Gallia Ellenica-Guerra Sociale: Catalogo a Cura di Novella Vismara.* 1990. 122 pp., 41 pls.
3. *Campania – Calabria: Catalogo a Cura di Novella Vismara.* 1989. 89 pp., 53 pls.
4. *Part 1: Lucania.* 1997. 133 pp. incl. 46 pls.
Part 2: Bruttium. 1997. 127 pp. incl. 44 pls.
5. *Sicily. [Forthcoming]*
6. *Part 1: Macedonia Greca, Paeonia, Emissioni di Area Celtica.* 1999. 177 pp., incl. 70 pls.
Part 3: Chersonesus Tauricus, Sarmatia, Thracia, Chersonesus Thracie, Isole della Thracia. 2000. 166 pp., incl. 65 pls.
12. *Syria – Bactria et India, Part 1. Seleucides (Reges) – Chalcidice: A Cura di Novella Vismara.* 1992. 185 pp., incl. 67 pls.
Part 4. Iudae-Bactria et India: A Cura di Novella Vismara. 1991. 191 pp. incl. 71 pls.
13. *Aegyptus, Part 1: Ptolemaei—Catalogo a Cura di Rodolfo Martini.* 1989. 141 pp., 54 pls.
Aegyptus, Part 2. Octavianus – Lucius Verus: Catalogo a Cura di Rodolfo Martini. 1991. 204 pp., 90 pls.
Aegyptus, Part 3. Commodus – Galerius Caesar: Catalogo a Cura di Rodolfo Martini. 1992. 228 pp., 77 pls.

    14. *Cyrenaica – Mauretania: Catalogo a Cura di Rodolfo Martini.* 1989. 117 pp., 79 pls.

2002   **2:** *Sassari, Museo Archeologico "G. A. Sanna."* Milan: Edizioni Ennerre, 1994+.

    1. *Sicilia – Numidia.* Edited by Francesco Guido. 1994. 169 pp., 60 pls.

2002a   **3:** *Firenze, Museo Archeologico Nazionale.*

    1. [Forthcoming].
    2. *Etruria.* Edited by Fiorenzo Catalli. 2009. 196 pp., illus. 1173 coins.

Polish Series

2003   **1:** *The Archaeological and Ethnographical Museum in Lódz.* Krakow: The Polish Academy of Arts and Sciences.

    1-3. [Forthcoming].
    4. *Galatia—Zeugitana,* by Mariusz Mielczarek. Krakow, 1998. 33 pp., 25 pls. Includes 313 coins from a wide geographical area. [Reviewed by M. Oeconomides in *Nomismatika Khronika* (Greece) 18 (1999): 153, and by Andrew Burnett in *Numismatic Chronicle* 160 (2000): 384].

2004   **3:** *The National Museum in Cracow.* Krakow: The Polish Academy of Arts and Sciences.

    1-3. [Forthcoming].
    4. *Sarmatia—Bosporus,* by Jaroslaw Bodzek. Krakow, 2006.

Slovenian Series

2005   **1:** *Ljubljana, Naradni Muzej.* Milan: Edizioni Ennerre, 1996.

    1-2. [Forthcoming].
    3. *Moesia Superior, Collection Kecskés. Part 1: Viminacium,* by Peter Kos and Andre Semrov. Mailand, 1996. 120 pls. 2381 coins.

Spanish Series

2006   **1:** *Museo Arqueológico Nacional Madrid: Hispania, Ciudades Feno-Púnicas.* Madrid: Ministerio de Educacion Cultura y Deporte, Dirección de Bellas artes y Bienes Culturales.

    1. *Gadir y Ebusus,* by C. Alfaro. Madrid, 1994. 163 pp., 40 pls.
    2. *Acuñaciones Cartaginesas en Iberia y Emisiones Ciudadanas (Continuación),* by Carmen Alfaro Asins. 2004. 184 pp, 51 pls.

2007   **2:** *Hispania, Ciudades del Área Meridonal. Acuñaciones con Escriture Indigena.* Madrid, 2005. 246 pp., 92 pls.

Swedish Series

2008   **1:** *Kungliga Myntkabinettet.* Stockholm: International Numismatic Commission. [CS 1921]

    1. *The Collection of His Late Majesty King Gustaf VI Adolf;* and *The Fred Forbat Collection,* by Ulla Westermark. 1974. Part 1 contains 104 silver coins on four plates. Part 2 contains 534 silver and bronze coins on fifteen plates. [Reviewed by G. K. Jenkins in *Numismatic Chronicle* 138 (1978): 198-200].
    2. *Sammlung Eric von Post,* by Eric von Post, 1995. 45 pp., 33 pls. Catalogues 672 coins from Macedonia through Egypt.

2009   **2:** *The Collection of the Royal Coin Cabinet, National Museum of Monetary History, Stockholm.* Stockholm: The Royal Academy of Letters. [CS 1920]

    1. *Gallia—Sicily,* by Ulla Westermark and Harald Nilsson, 1976. 26 pp., 19 pls. [Reviewed by G. K. Jenkins in *Numismatic Chronicle* 138 (1978): 198-200].
    2. *Thrace—Euboia,* by Ulla Westermark and Harald Nilsson. 1980. 27 pp., 20 pls.
    3. *Attica—Lesbos,* by Ulla Westermark and Harald Nilsson. 1991. 67 pp., 72 pls.
    6. *The G. D. Lorichs Collection,* by Pere Pau Ripollès. 2003. 236 pp., 113 pls. 2073 coins from Spain. [Reviewed by M. Amandry in *Revue Numismatique* (France) 160 (2004): 375-6, and by A. R. Meadows in *Numismatic Chronicle* 164 (2004): 337-8].

Swiss Series

2010   **1:** *Levante—Cilicia,* by Edoardo Levante. Edited by Italo Vecchi. Berne: Credit Suisse, 1986. 125 pp., 125 pls.
Catalogues 1861 Greek and Greek Imperial coins from Cilicia in Asia Minor. Includes indices of types, symbols, inscriptions, magistrates' names, and countermarks. [Reviewed by Ian Carradice in *Spink Numismatic Circular* 95, no. 3 (April 1987): 77, and by Ann Johnston in *Numismatic Chronicle* 148 (1988): 243-4. Also reviewed in *Spink Numismatic Circular* 102, no. 1 (February 1994): 8].

2011   **1 Supplement:** *Levante—Cilicia, Supplement 1,* by Edoardo Levante. Edited by Italo Vecchi. Zurich, 1993. 50 pp., 35 pls.
Catalogues 435 coins of the Persian, Greek, and Roman periods acquired by Levante since the publication of the main volume in 1986. Includes cross-references and historical notes.

2012 **2:** *Münzen der Antike: Katalog der Sammlung Jean-Pierre Righetti im Bernischen Historischen Museum,* by B. Kapossy and S. von Hoerschelmann. Berne, 1993. 460 pp., 188 pl.
Publishes 3084 coins, with an emphasis on Roman Provincial mints.

TURKISH SERIES

2013 **1:** *The Muharrem Kayhan Collection,* by Koray Konuk. Istanbul: Turkish Institute of Archaeology, 2002. 102 pp., 45 pls.
Catalogues 1076 coins from a private collection in Söke (near Izmir), covering the mints in western Asia Minor. Rich in coins of Ionia and Caria, including some previously unpublished types. [Reviewed by A. Meadows in *Numismatic Chronicle* 163 (2003): 405-6, and by A. Walker in *Revue Suisse de Numismatique* 82 (2003): 132-6. Also see Konuk *From Kroisos to Karia* under PRIVATE COLLECTIONS].

2014 **2:** *Anamur Museum, Volume 1: Roman Provincial Coins,* by Oguz Tekin and Sencan Altinoluk. Istanbul: Turkish Institute of Archaeology, 2007. 100 pp. incl. 40 pl.
Catalogues 469 coins. [Reviewed by Andrew Meadows in *Numismatic Chronicle* 167 (2007): 323-4].

2015 **3:** *Çanakkale Museum, Volume 1: Roman Provincial Coins of Mysia, Troas, etc.,* by Oguz Tekin, Sencan Altinoluk, and Funda Korpe. Istanbul: Turkish Institute of Archaeology, 2009. 102 pp., 42 pls.
Catalogues 667 Roman Provincial coins.

2016 **5:** *Tire Museum, Volume 1: Roman Provincial Coins from Ionia, Phrygia, and etc.,* by Oguz Tekin, Sencan Altinoluk, and Enver Sagir. Istanbul: Turkish Institute of Archaeology, 2011.

2016a **6:** *Burdur Museum, Volume 1: Pisidia. Part 1: Adada—Prostanna,* by Hüseyin Köker. Istanbul: Turkish Institute of Archaeology, 2011. 93 pp., illus.

PRIVATE COLLECTIONS

A collector of these pieces can have in the drawers of his cabinet, within reach of his hand as he sits by the fire, original pictures of Greek life, created by Greek artists, struck by Greek hands over two thousand years ago. There they lie before him, the same as they were then, after all these centuries of intervening history. They are as modern, many of them, as though they had been struck to-day. They lie, genuine, unaltered examples of the most splendid art the world has known.

—Godfrey Locker Lampson, 1923

Note: Listings are arranged by author or, in the case of auction catalogues, by auction house. Refer to the INDEX OF COLLECTORS AND COLLECTIONS to find collections by collector or museum name.

2017 **Alföldi, Maria R.** *Ancient Gold Coins, from the Deutsche Bundesbank Collection.* Frankfurt am Main, 1983. Illus.
A collection of significant gold coins from the ancient world. Begins with a basic discussion of ancient coinage. Includes a catalogue of 197 coins, including Greek. Seventy-two color plates of enlargements.

2018 **Babelon, Ernst.** "La Collection Waddington au Cabinet des Médailles. Inventaire Sommaire." *Revue Numismatique* (France) 4th ser., 2 (1898). Illus.
The collection of William H. Waddington.

2019 ——— *Inventaire Sommaire de la Collection Waddington Acquises par l'État en 1897.* Paris: Bibliothèque Nationale, 1898.
A catalogue of coins from the Waddington collection which were acquired by the Bibliothèque Nationale in 1897.

2020 **Babington, Churchill.** *Catalogue of a Selection from Colonel Leake's Greek Coins, Exhibited in the Fitzwilliam Museum.* Cambridge: University Press, 1867. 51 pp.
Fifty-one of William Martin Leake's Greek coins were exhibited at the museum, and this guide provides the brief descriptive notes written by Leake which appeared on the identifying tickets accompanying the coins. Supplementary information is provided here by Babington. Because it was intended as a guide to the exhibit's viewers, no illustrations are provided in this catalogue. [For a more extensive catalogue of Leake's collection, see Leake *Numismata Hellenica* below. Leake's collection was later purchased by the Fitzwilliam Museum and was incorporated into the museum's catalogue. See SYLLOGE NUMORUM GRAECORUM SERIES—BRITISH SERIES, Part 4].

2021 **Baker, F. Brayne.** "Some Rare or Unpublished Greek Coins." *Numismatic Chronicle* 3rd ser., 13 (1893): 21-5.
Describes coins acquired during travel in Arcadia. Includes coins of Larissa and Paroreia, and Roman pieces of Parium, Megalopolis, Pagae, Delphi, and Corinth.

2022 **Baldwin's, Dmitry Markov, and M&M Numismatics Ltd.** *The New York Sale Auction XXVII: The Prospero Collection, Spectacular Ancient Greek Coins, Wednesday, January 4, 2012.* London: Baldwin's, 2011. Unpaged, illus.
Catalogue, written by Paul Hill of Baldwin's, for the sale of 642 coins of the archaic, classical, and Hellenistic periods, including some of the rarest and most historically important Greek coins. Billed as "the most important and comprehensive collection since the Bunker Hunt sale of 1990-1991." Many of the coins bear old pedigrees. The hardbound catalogue includes commentary on key coins and stands as an excellent reference on ancient Greek numismatic art. Each coin is illustrated in both full-size and enlarged photographs. Concludes with various indices and a bibliography. [A 16-page brochure was produced to promote the auction which includes commentary on the collection and enlarged color photographs of thirty-one key coins in the sale].

2023 **Bank Leu & Co.** *Collection of Dr. J. H. Judd, Greek Coins: Illustrated List of the Stolen Coins.* Zurich: Bank Leu & Co., 1966. 32 pp., 6 pls.
An illustrated catalogue of Greek coins from the collection of J. Hewitt Judd of Omaha, Nebraska. The collection was stolen in 1965. This list was circulated in an attempt to identify and recover the coins.

2024 ——— *Auktionen 6: Griechische Bronzemünzen Unteritalians und Siziliens aus Sammlung Tom Virzi.* Zurich: Bank Leu AG, 1973. 31 pp., 1 color pl. and 15 black and white pls. [CS 2299]
Catalogue for the May 8, 1973 sale of 300 coins from the outstanding Tom Virzi collection of Greek bronze coins of Southern Italy and Sicily. This sale included only Virzi's higher grade coins. Some of Virzi's coins were previously sold by Jacob Hirsch in 1907, but most of the collection remained intact

until this Bank Leu sale in 1973. The remainder of the collection was sold by American dealer Alex G. Malloy in 1980 (see Malloy below). [Also see listing 416 in J. Spring, *Ancient Coin Auction Catalogues 1880-1980* (see Spring under COLLECTING GUIDES)].

2025 **Bank Leu & Co., and Münzen und Medaillen AG.** *Sammlung Walter Niggeler, 1 Teil: Griechische Münzen.* Zürich and Basel: Bank Leu and Münzen und Medaillen AG, 1965. 67 pp., 32 pls. [CS 1981]
The catalogue for the December 3 & 4, 1965 sale featuring 554 high-quality Greek coins. Includes an introduction by Herbert A. Cahn. [Also see listing 412 in J. Spring, *Ancient Coin Auction Catalogues 1880-1980* (see Spring under COLLECTING GUIDES)].

2026 ——— *Griechische Münzen: Aus der Sammlung Eines Kunstfreundes.* Zurich & Basel: Bank Leu and Münzen und Medaillen, 1974. 372 pp., illus. [CS 1993]
Sale catalogue for the collection of "a friend of the arts," held May 28, 1974. The catalogue includes 253 coins, all illustrated in actual size and enlarged. The coins are superb and each is thoroughly described. The coins were formerly in the collection of Charles Gillet, and were selected from the 1217 Greek coins from Gillet's collection that had been inherited by Marion Schuster. [For more on Gillet and his collection, see Walker "Catalogues and Their Collectors" below. Also see listing 418 in J. Spring, *Ancient Coin Auction Catalogues 1880-1980* (see Spring under COLLECTING GUIDES)].

2027 **Bank Leu & Co., and Numismatic Fine Arts, Inc.** *The Garrett Collection, Part 2. Public Auction of Ancient and Foreign Coins, by Order of Johns Hopkins University. Ancient and Medieval Coins, European Coins from the Fifteenth Century to the Twentieth Century.* Zurich: Bank Leu AG and Numismatic Fine Arts, Inc., 1984. 344 pages, 145 pls.
The catalogue for Part 2 of the sale of the famous John Work Garrett collection, held October 16-18, 1984. The section on Celtic coins is written in German and includes ninety-two lots. The Greek section includes 242 lots and was catalogued (in English) by Silvia Hurter. The catalogue also contains Roman, Byzantine, and European coinage. The Celtic and Greek coins are illustrated on twenty-one plates. [Catharine Lorber's history of the collection, "The Garretts of Baltimore: Collectors and Patrons," appeared in the catalogue for Part 1 of the sale, held May 16-18, 1984].

2028 ——— *The Garrett Collection, Part 3. Mail Bid Auction of Ancient and Foreign Coins and Medals, by Order of Johns Hopkins University. Ancient, Medieval and Modern Coins, Commemorative Medals, Orders and Decorations.* Beverly Hills: Numismatic Fine Arts, Inc. and Bank Leu AG, 1985.
The catalogue for Part 3 of the sale of the Garrett collection, held March 29, 1985. The Greek section includes 172 lots, illustrated on seven plates.

2029 **Bateson, Donal, Ian Campbell, and Paolo Visonà.** "The Early Nineteenth-Century Jackson Collection of Coins from Carthage." *Numismatic Chronicle* 150 (1990): 145-77. 2 pls.
A catalogue of the collection of coins gathered at the ruins of Carthage by Rear Admiral Samuel Jackson (1775-1845) and Sir Thomas Read. The collection includes 66 Greek, 314 Roman, 2 Vandal, 69 Byzantine, 24 Islamic, 3 European, and 5 unidentified coins. Most of the Greek pieces are Punic issues minted at Carthage and in its overseas territories.

2030 **Berry, Burton Y.** *A Numismatic Biography.* Lucerne: Burton Y. Berry, 1971. 90 pp., illus. [CS 17093]
Berry spent a career as a foreign service officer and ambassador (1930s to mid-1950s), which provided great opportunities to acquire Greek coins. Written as a personal reflection on his collection, Berry provides an introduction to ancient Greek coinage and historical commentary on groups of coins in his collection. Brief descriptions of the coins are interspersed with interesting personal reminiscences on collecting and how he acquired certain coins. Berry donated most of his collection to the American Numismatic Society (see *American Series 1: Collection of Burton Y. Berry* under THE SYLLOGE NUMMORUM GRAECORUM SERIES) and he gave some coins to Indiana University [see Hohlfelder *Ancient Coins* under PUBLIC COLLECTIONS—UNITED STATES (BLOOMINGTON)]. Although this is not a true catalogue of the collection, this volume includes illustrations of both sides of 527 of his finest Greek coins.

2031 **Boutin, Serge.** *Catalogue des Monnaies Grecques Antiques de l'Ancienne Collection Pozzi: Monnaies Frappées en Europe.* Two volumes. Wetteren, Belgium: van der Dussen, 1979. 294 pp., 202 pls. Reprint, Monaco, 1992. [CS 1932]
A catalogue of the European portion of the Samuel-Jean Pozzi collection (see Naville & Co. *Ars Classica I* below). Includes 4630 coins. Includes the 2085 European coins that were included in the Naville sale catalogue, plus more than 2500 additional coins that were not included in the sale. Pozzi was murdered in 1918. He had been planning to publish his entire collection. Dieudonné (from the Paris cabinet) had composed all the plates and wrote descriptions for the European section before Pozzi's death ended the project. Boutin acquired a copy of the plates and descriptions and published them with some updating and additional information. Preface by Georges Le Rider. [For more information about Pozzi and his collection, see Walker "Catalogues and Their Collectors" below].

2032 **Boyne, William.** *Catalogue of the Greek Coins in the Collection of William Boyne.* n.p. (1885).
A manuscript held at the University of Toronto in the Thomas Fisher Rare Book Library (catalogue of the manuscript collection, William Boyne, No. 12).

2033 **Classical Numismatic Group.** *A Public and Mail Bid Auction of Classical Coins, Featuring the George and Robert Stevenson Collection of Greek Gold and Electrum and the Property of Other Consignors.* Quarryville: Classical Numismatic Group, 1993. 120 pp., illus.
The catalogue for Classical Numismatic Group's *Auction XXVI*, including 815 lots, primarily Greek, Roman, and Byzantine coins. The sale was held June 11, 1993 and featured the Stevenson collection of Greek gold and electrum coins (lots 1-161). Each lot is fully described and often includes historical and artistic commentary.

2034 ——— *Triton V, Session 1: The David Freedman Collection of Greek Bronze Coins.* Lancaster: Classical Numismatic Group, 2001. 96 pp., illus.
The catalogue for the January 15, 2002 auction sale of 600 Greek bronze coins of outstanding quality. All are illustrated. Includes introductory comments by David Freedman, and a brief introduction to Greek bronze coinage.

2035 ——— "The David Freedman Collection of Greek Bronze Coins, Part II." *Classical Numismatic Group, Inc. Mail Bid Sale 61, September 25, 2002.* Pages 9-27. Illus.
The catalogue for Part 2 of the sale of the Freedman collection of Greek bronze coins, comprising lots 1-331.

2036 **Coin Galleries.** *The Golden Gate Collection: Ancient Greek Coins in Gold, Electrum and Silver.* New York: Coin Galleries, April 14, 1993. Illus.
An auction catalogue listing 389 Greek coins, most of which are photographed. Highlighted by eighty-four electrum and gold coins.

2037 **Comparette, Thomas L.** *A Descriptive Catalogue of Greek Coins, Selected from the Cabinet of Clarence S. Bement, Esq, Philadelphia.* New York: American Numismatic Society, 1921. 106 pp., 25 pls. [CS 1922]
A catalogue of 370 coins fully described, and including extensive notes on the coins and their cities. These coins, selected from Bement's much larger collection, represent pieces that are scarce or rare, and therefore are not readily found in other published collections (at that time). The coins are uniformly in excellent condition. Includes an index of kings and dynasts. Bement was also a collector of books, prints, minerals, and Roman coins. Bement's collection of Greek coins was sold by Naville & Co., Geneva, in 1924 (see Naville & Co. *Ars Classica VI & VII* below). [For more information about Bement and his collection, see Walker "Catalogues and Their Collectors" below].

2038 **de Koehne, Baron B.** *Description du Musée de Feu Le Prince Basile Kotschoubev D'Après Son Catalogue Manuscrit et Recherches Sur L'Histoire et la Numismatique des Colonies Grecques en Russie Ainsi Que des Royaumes du Pont et du Bosphore Cimmérian. Imprimerie des Papiers de la Couronne.* Two volumes. St. Petersburg, 1857. 452 pp., 7 pls; 419 pp., 13 pls.
The collection of Prince Basile Kotschoubev, including many rarities and coins minted in ancient Russia, principally around the Black Sea region (modern Ukraine, Crimea, and the Kuban region) and examples of the gold staters of Pantikapaion. One hundred copies printed.

2039 **Detroit Institute of Arts.** *Coins of the Ancient World, Illustrated from the Collection of Dr. and Mrs. Irving Frederick Burton.* Detroit: The Detroit Institute of Arts, 1964. 32 pp., illus. [CS 1637]
Pages 5-11 comprise a brief introduction to Greek, Roman, and Byzantine coins. This is followed by photographs of fifty-nine representative ancient coins from the Burton collection. The coins are generally common and unspectacular.

2040 **Dumersan, Théophile Marion.** *Description des Médailles Antiques du Cabinet de Feu M. Allier de Hauteroche.* Paris, 1829. 140 pp., 16 engraved plates.
Catalogue listing of the collection of M. Louis Allier de Hauteroche, published after his death.

2041 **Florange, Jules, and Louis Ciani.** *Collection de Monnaies Grecques, H. de Nanteuil.* Two volumes. Paris: Jules Florange and Louis Ciani, 1925. 343 pp., 60 pls. Plate volume reprinted, Crestline, California: George F. Kolbe, 1993. [CS 1931]
Catalogues over 1000 coins, covering Spain to the Aegean Islands.

2042 **Forrer, Leonard S.** *Descriptive Catalogue of the Collection of Greek Coins formed by Sir Hermann Weber M.D., 1823-1918.* London: Spink & Son, 1922-9. Reprint, New York: Attic Books, 1975. 1976 pp., 317 pls. [CS 2001]
> Vol. 1: *Auriol Find Class—Hispania—Gallia, Britannia; Italy and Sicily.* 1922. 69 pls.
> Vol. 2: *Macedon, Thrace, Thessaly, North Western, Central and Southern Greece.* 1924. 101 pls.
> Vol. 3, Part 1: *Asia: Bosporus—Lydia.* 1926.
> Vol. 3, Part 2: *Asia: Phrygia—Bactria, Africa.* 1929. 146 pls.

Each of the three volumes is accompanied by a separate volume of plates. The entire collection was purchased by Spink and Son, Ltd. and was dispersed in the 1920's. [*Volume 1* was reviewed by G. F. Hill in *Numismatic Chronicle* 5th ser., 2 (1922): 251. Also see several articles by Weber below].

2043 **Fox, Charles R.** *Engravings of Unedited or Rare Greek Coins with Descriptions. Part 1: Europe.* London: Bell and Daldy, 1856. 28 pp., 10 pl. *Part 2: Asia and Africa.* London: Bell and Daldy, 1862. 32 pp., 8 pls.
A monograph publishing 281 selected rare Greek coins from the author's collection, beginning with Massalia in France and extending to the Island of Siphnos. Accompanied by engraved plates illustrating the coins.

2044 **Fox, H. B. Earle.** "Greek Coins in the Collection of Mr. Earle-Fox." *Numismatic Chronicle* 3rd ser., 18 (1898): 286-93. 1 pl.
Twenty-two Greek and Roman Provincial coins from the author's collection are published.

2045 **Feuardent Bros.** *Collection R. Jameson: Monnaies Grecques Antiques et Impériales Romaines.* Four volumes. Paris: Chez Feuardent Frères, 1913-32. Revised reprint, Chicago: Obol International, 1980. 908 pp., 164 pls. [CS 1927]
The catalogue of Robert Jameson's collection of Greek and Roman coins. "The most striking thing about this collection is the superb quality and style of the 3152 coins (of which 2620 are Greek). It remains to this day one of the finest collections ever formed by an individual and all the coins are illustrated on 164 plates." [D. Kroh, *ACRR*]. The original volumes were prepared for publication by Jameson himself. Volume 1 was devoted to Greek coins and Volume 2 was devoted to Roman coins. Volumes 3 and 4 were issued as addenda to the Greek and Roman volumes. In the reprint, the Roman addendum was incorporated into Volume 2. Volumes 1, 3, and 4 are Greek. Jameson died in 1942 and his collection was disbursed into museums, private collections, and the market. Many coins went into the Gulbenkian collection (see Jenkins and Hipólito, and Robinson and Hipólito under PUBLIC COLLECTIONS—PORTUGAL). [For more information about Jameson and his collection, see Walker "Catalogues and Their Collectors" below. A group of duplicates from Jameson's collection, 583 lots from Italy and Sicily, were sold in 1906 by Rollin & Feuardent. See listing 579 in J. Spring, *Ancient Coin Auction Catalogues 1880-1980* (see Spring under COLLECTING GUIDES)].

2046 **Gerojannis, Constantin.** "Greek Coins." *Journal International d'Archéologie Numismatique* (Greece) 8 (1905): 177-94. Illus.
Publishes several coins from the author's collection which were previously unpublished or are of special significance. Includes a tetradrachm of Lindos with *obv.*, lion's head; *rev.*, incuse punch; a tetradrachm of Rhodes with *obv.*, Athena head; *rev.*, prow of ship; a hemidrachm of the Lycian League (Apollo/lyre) probably struck at Aulae; and a bronze coin of Seleucia ad Calycadnum (Cilicia) with *obv.*, Athena head; *rev.*, Nike advancing. Includes extensive discussion of the coins' attributions. The coins are illustrated by line drawings.

2047 **Glendining & Co.** *Catalogue of the Celebrated Collection of Coins Formed by the Late Richard Cyril Lockett, Esq.: Greek (four parts).* London: Glendining & Co., 1955-61. [CS 1971 and 2296]
The sale catalogues for the more than 3000 Greek coins in this famous collection. The four parts are:

Part 1: *Spain, Gaul, Italy, Sicily and Siculo-Punic Issues.* London, October 25-28, 1955. 130 pp, 38 pls. Includes 987 lots.
Part 2: *Black Sea District, Thrace, Macedon, Thessaly, Illyricum, Epirus, Corcyra, Acarnania and Aetolia.* London, February 12-13, 1958. 83 pp., 23 pls. Includes 555 lots.
Part 3: *Locris, Phocis, Boeotia, Athens, Aegina, Corinth, Peloponnesus, Crete, Aegaean Islands.* London, May 27-28, 1959. 67 pp., 15 pls. Includes 566 lots.
Part 4: *Asia Minor, Asia and Africa.* London, February 21-23, 1961. 118 pp., 35 pls. Includes 1007 lots.

[Also see *Lockett Collection* under SYLLOGE NUMMORUM GRAECORUM (BRITISH SERIES) Volume 3. Also see listings 232, 233, 234, and 235 in J. Spring, *Ancient Coin Auction Catalogues 1880-1980* (see Spring under COLLECTING GUIDES)].

2048 ——— *Coins of Ancient Greece: The Collection of Olga H. Knoepke of New Town, Connecticut.* London, 1986. 59 pp., 28 pls.
Catalogue for the December 10, 1986 sale of the Olga H. Knoepke collection, including 377 lots of Greek coins, formed between 1957 and 1970. The coins are of high quality and many have important provenances.

2049 **Gordon, Thomas.** *Description of Ancient Coins from the Cabinet of Thomas Gordon, Fellow of the Antiquarian Society of Scotland.* n.p., n.d. 14 pp., 14 engraved pls.
An illustrated catalogue with brief descriptions.

2050 **Greenwell, William (Canon).** "On Some Rare Greek Coins." *Numismatic Chronicle* new ser., 20 (1880): 1-14. 1 pl.
Catalogues some significant coins from the author's collection. Includes coins of Rhegium, Eryx, Abdera, Thasos, Amphipolis, Philip II, Elis, Cyzicus, Lampsacus, and Cyrene. Discusses each.

2051 ——— "On Some Rare Greek Coins." *Numismatic Chronicle* 3rd ser., 5 (1885): 1-14. 1 pl.
The author publishes some significant or previously unpublished coins from various collections. Includes coins of Poseidonia, Camarina, Ichnae, Larissa, Sinope, Cnidus, Cyrene, and Evesperis.

2052 ——— "On Some Rare Greek Coins." *Numismatic Chronicle* 3rd ser., 10 (1890): 20-32. 1 pl.
A continuation of the series started in 1880, describing some of the coins recently added to the author's collection. The coins are principally electrum issues of Cyzicus, supplementing the author's previous listings from that city (see Greenwell "The Electrum Coinage of Cyzicus" under MYSIA—AUTONOMOUS CITIES). Also illustrates and describes coins of Abdera, Dikaia, Chalcis, and Calymna.

2053 ——— "Rare Greek Coins." *Numismatic Chronicle* 3rd ser., 13 (1893): 81-92. 1 pl.
A continuation of the author's series of articles describing coins in his collection. Includes several new electrum staters of Cyzicus, gold staters of Lampsacus, two electrum hekte, and silver coins of Abdera, Iulis, Colchis, Tenedos, Methymna, and Cyrene.

2054 ——— "On Some Rare Greek Coins." *Numismatic Chronicle* 3rd ser., 17 (1897): 253-83. 4 pls.
Publishes more coins from the author's collection including many electrum coins.

2055 **Harvard University.** *Ancient Art in American Private Collections: A Loan Exhibition at the Fogg Art Museum of Harvard University, December 28, 1954 – February 15, 1955. Arranged in Honor of the Seventy-fifth Anniversary of the Archaeological Institute of America.* Cambridge, Massachusetts: Harvard University, 1954. 43 pp., 100 pls.
The exhibit included sculptures, bronzes, jewelry, terracottas, vases, paintings, glass, and coins. Sixteen Greek coins are listed and illustrated in the catalogue.

2056 **Hill, George F.** *Descriptive Catalogue of Ancient Greek Coins Belonging to John Ward, F.S.A.* San Diego: Pegasus Publishing, 1967. 164 pp., illus., 22 pls., maps. [CS 1934]
This is a reprint of the catalogue portion of Ward and Hill *Greek Coins and Their Parent Cities* (see below), consisting of 952 high-quality Greek coins. Includes complete descriptions of the dies, size, weight, dates of issue, references to die matches, and provenance. Most coins are illustrated. Includes a table of monograms. Indexed by cities, personal names, and epithets. [Also see *Metropolitan Museum of Art—Ward Collection* under PUBLIC COLLECTIONS—UNITED STATES (NEW YORK)].

2057 **Hirsch, Jacob.** *Auctions-Catalog XIII: Einer Hochbeteutenden Sammlung Griechischer Münzen aus dem Nachlasse eines Bekannten Archäologen.* Münich. May 15, 1905. 292 pp., 58 pls. [CS 1941 and 1979]
Catalogue for the sale of the collection of Athanasios Rhousopoulos, a Greek archaeologist and philologist (b. 1823; d. 1898). A fantastic collection, encompassing 4627 lots. [For more information on Rhousopoulos and his collection, see Walker "Catalogues and Their Collectors" below. Walker notes this catalogue was "by far the largest and best illustrated auction catalogue of ancient coins to have appeared up to that time." Also see listing 371 in J. Spring, *Ancient Coin Auction Catalogues 1880-1980* (see Spring under COLLECTING GUIDES)].

2058 ——— *Sale XXI: Sammlung Consul Eduard Friedrich Weber, Hamburg. Erste Abteilung: Griechischen Münzen.* Munich: Dr. phil. Jacob Hirsch. November 16, 1908. 340 pp., 61 pls. Reprint, Bologna: Forni, 1970. [CS 2000]
Catalogue for the sale of the collection of Consul E. F. Weber, comprised of 4747 ancient Greek coins. An exceptional and important collection with many rarities, including an Athenian dekadrachm. [Also see listing 378 in J. Spring, *Ancient Coin Auction Catalogues 1880-1980* (see Spring under COLLECTING GUIDES)].

2059 **Hoffmann, Henri.** *Collection Potiadès Pacha: Monnaies Grecques.* Paris. May 19-22, 1890. 1530 lots, 8 pls. [CS 1987]
Auction catalogue for the sale of the ancient Greek coins of Ioannis Photiades Pasha. The collection contained coins from Thessaly through the Cyclades, from Crete, from the cities of Byzantium, and Calchedon. According to Alan Walker, "The importance of this auction was in its specialized nature: no sale had ever before presented such a rich selection of the coins of the Greek Mainland." The catalogue was written by Wilhelm Froehner with the help of Friedrich Imhoof-Blumer. [See Walker "Catalogues and Their Collectors" below. Also see listing 395 in J. Spring, *Ancient Coin Auction Catalogues 1880-1980*. See Spring under COLLECTING GUIDES)].

2060   **Holzer, Hans.** *The Thomas Ollive Mabbott Collection, Part 1: Coins of the Greek World.* New York: Hans M. F. Schulman Gallery, 1969. Two volumes: (1) 148 pp., (2) 81 pls. [CS 1973]
The catalogue for the June 6-11, 1969 sale of the Greek portion of Thomas Ollive Mabbott's collection featuring 3860 lots of coins plus a few seals and weights. Most of the coins are Roman Provincial issues, many of which do not appear in the *British Museum Catalogue.* Includes a portrait drawing of the collector and brief biography written by Holzer and Mabbott. [Also see listing 712 in J. Spring, *Ancient Coin Auction Catalogues 1880-1980* (see Spring under COLLECTING GUIDES. Mabbott's Roman Imperial and later coins are included in the Schulman catalogue for his October 27-29, 1969 sale, which included 1477 lots].

2061   "Hunt Moves Back Into Silver—Ancients." *Coin World* (November 19, 1980): 3. Illus.
Announces that Nelson Bunker Hunt has acquired a nine-piece collection of decadrachms. Eight were acquired as part of a collection acquired for $30 million. The ninth was acquired in a later transaction for $1 million (see "Million Dollar Coin" under SICILY—AKRAGAS). Includes decadrachms from Akragas, Athens, Alexander the Great, Syracuse, Carthage, and the Derrones.

2062   **Imhoof-Blumer, Friedrich W.** *Choix de Monnaies Grecques du la Collection de F. Imhoof-Blumer.* Paris/Leipzig: Rollin et Feuardent and Koehler's Antiquarium, 1883. 6 pp., 9 pls. [CS 1926]
A supplement to Imhoof-Blumer's *Monnaies Grecques* (see Imhoof-Blumer under GENERAL WORKS—GREEK), publishing coins from his own collection, with nine photographic plates.

2063   **Klein, Dieter.** *Sammlung von Griechischen Kleinsilbermünzen und Bronzen.* Nomismata: Historisch-Numismatische Forschungen 3. Milano: Edizioni Ennerre, 1999. 109 pp., 26 pls.
An important catalogue of 820 minor silver and small bronze coins from the author's collection. Most areas of the Greek world are represented. Each coin is described and illustrated. Well indexed. Introduction by Johannes Nollé.

2064   **Knobloch, Frederick S.** "Some Rare or Inedited Greek Coins." *Numismatic Review* 4, no. 1 (January 1947): 11-4. 2 pls.
A catalogue of thirty-one previously unpublished coins. Fourteen are Greek and seventeen are Roman Provincial. The Greek pieces include coins of Caura, Syracuse, Thessala, Corinth, Achaean League, Arcadia, Paros, Ephesus, Chios, Cappadocia, Mauritania, and the Ptolemaic Kingdom.

2065   **Konuk, Koray.** *From Kroisos to Karia: Early Anatolian Coins from the Muharrem Kayhan Collection.* Istanbul, 2003. 204 pp., illus., 2 maps.
An exhibition catalogue including 150 coins of Asia Minor from a private collection. Includes an overview of ancient Anatolian coinage and essays by Konuk on the beginnings of coinage. Each section of the catalogue contains commentary on the historical and technological context of the coins. Includes a section on plated coins. Each coin is illustrated by enlarged photographs and is fully described. All coins appear in actual size photographs at the back of the book. An excellent overview of early electrum and silver coinage. Text in Turkish and English. [Also see *Turkish Series, Vol. 1* under SYLLOGE NUMMORUM GRAECORUM SERIES].

2066   **Kraay, Colin M.** "Kunstwerke der Antike: Sammlung Robert Käppeli Basel." *Schweizer Münzblätter* (Switzerland) 55 (1964): 135-6. Illus. [CS 1928]

2067   **Laffaille, Maurice.** *Choix de Monnaies Grecques en Bronze.* Genève, 1982. 243 pp., 200 pl.
Includes 200 enlarged photographs of Greek bronze coins, some in color. [Also see Straus *Collection Maurice Laffaille* below. Also see Münzen und Medaillen *Auktion 76* below].

2068   **Leake, William Martin.** *Numismata Hellenica: A Catalogue of Greek Coins, Collected by William Martin Leake.* London: J. Murray, 1856. 719 pp., map; also *Appendix to Numismata Hellenica.* London: J. Murray, 1856. 40 pp.; and *A Supplement to Numismata Hellenica.* London: J. Murray, 1859. 189 pp.
The first published catalogue of the collection of Greek coins formed by Colonel Leake (1777-1860) who traveled extensively in Greece and wrote descriptions of its land and monuments. His collection, which contained about 12,000 Greek coins, was purchased by Cambridge University in 1864 and became the foundation for the present collection at the Fitzwilliam Museum (see SYLLOGE NUMORUM GRAECORUM SERIES—BRITISH SERIES, Volume 4). [For the catalogue of an exhibition of Leake's coins held at the museum, see Babington *Catalogue* above].

2069   **Leu Numismatics.** *Greek Coins: An Exceptional Private Collection. Auction 76. 27 October 1999.* Zurich: Leu Numismatics, Ltd., 1999. 109 pp., illus.
The catalogue for the sale of an outstanding collection of Greek coins. Includes 228 coins from all areas of the Greek world. Many of the coins are artistically superb. All are illustrated. The catalogue, by Silvia Hurter, includes full descriptions, provenance, and historical background for each coin. [A report on the sale results by A. Peter Weiss appears in *The Celator* 13, no. 12 (December 1999): 39. Illus.].

2070   ——— *Greek Coins: Auction Leu 81.* Zurich, 2001. 135 pp., illus.
Catalogue for the May 16, 2001 sale of a highly important collection of 355 Greek coins. The collection was formed between 1961 and 1991 by a Portuguese collector, and contains coins of high artistic merit in superb condition, many with important provenances. The catalogue includes extensive notes regarding the history of the coins, their artistic importance, and their provenances. [For a summary of the auction results, see A. Peter Weiss, "Leu Numismatics Auction 81 Reports Strong Results for Important Greek Coinage Collection" in *The Celator* 15, no. 7 (July 2001): 32-3, 37. Illus.].

2071   **Lindgren, Henry Clay.** *Ancient Greek Bronze Coins of European Mints, from the Lindgren Collection.* San Mateo: Chrysopylon Publishers, 1989. 111 pp., 89 pls.
Lists 1840 Greek and Roman Provincial bronze coins from 500 mints from Hispania to the Aegean Islands, including some previously unpublished types. Includes a geographical index, an index of Roman Emperors, Family Members and Officials, an index of Kings and Tyrants, and a general index. A thirteen page listing of estimated values for the coin-types was published separately. [Reviewed by J. Morcom and J. Warren in *Numismatic Chronicle* 151 (1991): 230-2. Also see *Lindgren III* below, and Lindgren and Kovacs *Ancient Bronze Coins* below].

2072 ——— *Lindgren III: Ancient Greek Bronze Coins from the Lindgren Collection.* San Mateo: Chrysopylon Publishers, 1993. 122 pp., 102 pls.

Catalogues and illustrates over 2000 coins that have been acquired by Dr. Lindgren since the publication of the two previous catalogues of his collection (see Lindgren above, and Lindgren and Kovacs below). Includes a section devoted to North Africa and is strong in issues of Cilicia, the Seleucid Empire, Phoenicia, and Syria. Includes a geographical index, an index of Roman Emperors, Family Members and Officials, an index of Kings and Tyrants, and a general index. Also includes a list of corrections to the previous catalogues.

2073 **Lindgren, Henry Clay, and Frank Kovacs.** *Ancient Bronze Coins of Asia Minor and the Levant, from the Lindgren Collection.* San Mateo: Chrysopylon Publishers, 1985. 230 pp., 135 pls.

Lists 3289 Greek and Roman Provincial bronze coins of Asia Minor and the Levant from Lindgren's collection, organized geographically. Includes many previously unpublished types. Includes indices by subject, emperor, and city. [Reviewed by A. Burnett in *Numismatic Chronicle* 147 (1987): 191-2. Also see Lindgren *Ancient Bronze Coins* above, and Lindgren *Lindgren III* above].

2074 **Lorber, Catherine C.** *Treasures of Ancient Coinage from the Private Collections of American Numismatic Society Members.* Lancaster, Pennsylvania: Chrysopylon, 1996. 124 pp., illus.

This catalogue of an exhibition, held in conjunction with the 1996 New York International Numismatic Convention, illustrates 113 Greek and Roman coins, each of which is fully catalogued. Brief historical notes are provided for each coin. Every coin is show in actual size black and white photographs of obverse and reverse, and enlargements are provided for one side of most pieces. The catalogue presents a wide range of coin types, reflecting the interests of the participating A.N.S. members.

2075 **Malloy, Alex G.** *Auction XVII: The Virzi Collection of Greek Bronze.* South Salem, New York: Alex G. Malloy, 1980. 588 lots, 18 pls.

A selection of Greek bronze coins from the collection of Tom Virzi. [Also see Bank Leu *Auktionen 6* above for an earlier sale of Virzi's bronze coins. Also see listing 429 in J. Spring, *Ancient Coin Auction Catalogues 1880-1980* (see Spring under COLLECTING GUIDES)].

2076 **Malter, Joel & Co.** *The Dr. J. S. Wilkinson Collection of Ancient Greek Coins. Auction 49.* Encino: Joel L. Malter & Co., 1992. Illus.

The catalogue for the sale of John S. Wilkinson's collection of over 1000 Greek coins, almost all silver. All coins are photographed. Includes many fractional denominations, scarce types, and pedigreed coins. The sale was held on November 15, 1992. Includes a brief biography of Dr. Wilkinson.

2077 **Mavrogordato, J. A.** "Some Unpublished Greek Coins." *Numismatic Chronicle* 4th ser., 11 (1911): 85-100. 1 pl.

Publishes and discusses nine coins from the author's collection. The coins are from Chios, Chios and Erythrae, Athens, Aegina, Locri Opuntii, and Syracuse.

2078 **Mildenberg, Leo, and Silvia Hurter.** *The Arthur S. Dewing Collection of Greek Coins.* Ancient Coins in North American Collections, No. 6. Volume 1, 194 pages of text. Volume 2, 142 plates. New York: American Numismatic Society, 1985.

Catalogue of the 2797 coins of the Arthur S. Dewing collection. Includes fractional denominations, but no bronze coins. The collection is noted for its fifty-eight Syracusan decadrachms including a specimen of the Demareteion (Dewing purchased Albert Gallatin's Syracusan decadrachms). Begins with three short biographical essays devoted to Dewing (b. 1880; d. 1971). Thirteen prominent numismatists contributed to cataloguing the collection, and the catalogue is well-regarded for its up-to-date scholarship. Includes indices of cities, leagues, tribes, areas, kings, satraps, dynasts, obverse and reverse types, and hoards. The Dewing Collection is now on loan to the Fogg Museum at Harvard University. [Reviewed by D. Kroh in *Classical Coin Newsletter* 5, no. 1 (May 1985): 2-3. Also see Oleson *Greek Numismatic Art* under ART and Gallatin *Syracusan Dekadrachms* under SICILY—SYRACUSE].

2079 **Millingen, James.** *Ancient Coins of Greek Cities and Kings. From Various Collections, Principally in Great Britain. Illustrated and Explained.* London, 1831. 82 pp., 5 engraved pls.

In the preface, the author discusses the importance of accurately representing antiquities in engravings and the importance of preserving antiquities. Also details who in Great Britain has done a notable job of preservation and collection and who has studied and written about antiquities in the late eighteenth and early nineteenth centuries. The book contains descriptions of and histories of the coins illustrated in the plates, discloses whose collection each coin came from, and describes each coin's condition. Includes coins of Italy, Sicily, Greek cities and kings, Macedonia, Thessaly, and Asia.

2080 ——— *Sylloge of Ancient Unedited Coins of Greek Cities and Kings from Various Collections, Principally in Great Britain.* London: privately printed, 1837. 87 pp., 3 line drawing plates.

Recounts the author's previous publications and discusses a few of them. Publishes sixty-eight coins, mostly from the author's collection. [An extensive review article by Vincent Nolte appears in *Numismatic Journal* 2 (1838): 81-94].

2081 **Montagu, Hyman.** "On Some Unpublished and Rare Greek Coins in My Collection." *Numismatic Chronicle* 3rd ser., 12 (1892): 22-39. 2 pls.

The author publishes coins of Tarentum, Croton, Naxos, Zaelii (or Lete), Olynthus, Amphipolis, Philip II of Macedonia, Alexander III of Macedonia, Alexander IV, Abdera, Melitaea, Elis, Arcadia, Gortyna, Praesus, Carystus, Cyzicus, Lesbos, Methymna, Knidus, Cilicia, Celenderis, Alexander II of Syria, Eukratides of Bactria, Persia, and Cyrene. [Montagu's collection was later sold. See Sotheby & Co. below].

2082 **Münzen und Medaillen A.G.** *Monnaies Grecques en Bronze: Collection Maurice Laffaille. Auktion 76.* Basel, 1991. 174 pp., 93 pls.

Catalogue for the September 19-20, 1991 sale of the Maurice Laffaille collection of Greek bronze coins. Includes 1523 lots.

2083 **Münzen und Medaillen Gmbh.** *Auktion 21: Sammlung James H. Joy: The Isles of Greece Collection.* May 24 & 25, 2007. Weil am Rhein: Münzen und Medaillen, 2007. 125 pp., illus.

Includes 1035 lots, featuring the James H. Joy collection of bronze coins, primarily of the Greek islands. A short introduction by James Joy appears on page 10. Lots 1-794 are Greek bronze coins featuring many from island city-states. Lots 795-844 are Greek silver coins. Remaining items are group lots and literature. All coins illustrated in black & white. Includes four color plates of enlargements.

2084 **Naville & Co.** *Ars Classica I: Catalogue de Monnaies Grecques Antiques Provenant de la Collection de feu le Prof. S. Pozzi.* Lucerne: Naville & Co., 1921. Reprints, Zurich/Amsterdam: Bank Leu and Jacques Schulman, 1966 and 1974; Deluxe reprint, Monaco, 1992. 194 pp., 101 pls. [CS 1988]
 The sale catalogue for the superb collection of Samuel-Jean Pozzi which was sold in Geneva in April 1921. Includes 3334 coins, all illustrated. The catalogue includes full die descriptions, weights, and sizes, and has become a popular reference. The 1966 reprint of the catalogue by Bank Leu and Jacques Schulman includes the prices realized bound at the back. The deluxe reprint has higher quality plates. [Another catalogue of a portion of the collection was published in 1979. See Boutin above. For more information about Pozzi and his collection, see Walker "Catalogues and Their Collectors" below. Also see listing 471 in J. Spring, *Ancient Coin Auction Catalogues 1880-1980* (see Spring under COLLECTING GUIDES)].

2085 ———— *Ars Classica IV: Monnaies Grecques Antiques Provenant des Collections de S. A. I. le Grand-Duc Alexandre Michaïlovitch, de Sir Arthur J. Evans, et d'Autres Amateurs.* Lucerne, June 17 & 19, 1922. 1035 lots, 36 pls. [CS 1977]
 The collection of Grand Duke Alexander Michailovitch (b. 1866; d. 1933), the uncle once removed of the last Tsar of Russia, Nicholas II. [Also see listing 474 in J. Spring, *Ancient Coin Auction Catalogues 1880-1980* (see Spring under COLLECTING GUIDES)].

2086 ———— *Ars Classica VI & VII: Catalogue de Monnaies Grecque Antiques en Or en Argent Composant la Collection de feu Clarence S. Bement de Philadelphie (U.S.A.). Première Partie: Ibérie à Eubée Incl.* 1082 lots, 90 pp., 37 pls. *Seconde Partie: Attique à Mauritanie Incl.* 827 lots, 84 pp., 31 pls. Lucerne: Naville & Co., 1924. [CS 1942]
 Catalogues for the January 28, 1924 (part 1) and June 23-24, 1924 (part 2) sales of the Bement collection, consisting of 1909 lots of Greek coins. [Also see Comparette *A Descriptive Catalogue* above. For more information about Bement and his collection, see Walker "Catalogues and Their Collectors" below. Also see listings 476 and 477 in J. Spring, *Ancient Coin Auction Catalogues 1880-1980* (see Spring under COLLECTING GUIDES)].

2087 **Nordbø, Jan H.** "Greek Silver Coins in a Norwegian Private Collection." *Nordisk Numismatisk Årsskrift* (Sweden) (1975-6): 5-22, including 5 pls.
 Publishes the seventy-nine Greek silver and billon coins in the Hunt Christiansen collection in Oslo.

2088 **Papaefthymiou, Eleni G.** "The Coin Collection of the Foundation of the Hellenic World (FHW) and its Unpublished Coin from Kyzikos." *Nomismatika Khronika* (Greece) 28 (2010): 142-4.
 The story of the formation, preservation, and cataloguing of the collection of German collector Karl Eduard Reinhard Donat, and its 2007 acquisition by the Foundation of the Hellenic World. A previously unpublished hemiobol of Kyzikos (two tunny fish heads/incuse square) is also illustrated and described.

2089 **Parke-Bernet Galleries, Inc.** *Important Collection of Coins of Greece and Rome and a Series of Early Italian Coins, from the Collection of the Late Edward T. Newell of New York (Sold by Order of the Heir).* New York: Parke-Bernet Galleries, Inc., 1968. [CS 1980]
 Catalogue for the October 16-17, 1968 sale of a portion of E. T. Newell's collection. Most of his collection was bequeathed to the American Numismatic Society and other institutions, but 412 lots are presented here. Includes, among other coins, nice groups of Alexander III tetradrachms and Seleucid coinage. [Also see listing 502 in J. Spring, *Ancient Coin Auction Catalogues 1880-1980* (see Spring under COLLECTING GUIDES)].

2090 **Ramage, Andrew, ed.** *Emblems of Authority: Greek and Roman Coins from Two Alumni Collections.* Ithaca, New York: Cornell University, 1994. 23 pp., 11 pls.
 The catalogue of an exhibition of two collections, held at the Cornell University's Johnson Museum of Art in 1994. The Jerry Theodorou collection includes eighty-six coins which emphasize Hellenistic portraiture. The collection of David Simpson includes forty-four coins, emphasizing Roman Provincial coinage portraying the Labors of Herakles, especially coins of Alexandria, Egypt.

2091 **Ratto, Rodolfo.** *Monnaies Grecques. Importante Collection de Toutes Régions de l'Epoque Grecque.* Lugano, 1927. 220 pp., 72 pls.
 A collection of 2996 coins.

2092 **Raymond, Wayte.** "The J. Pierpont Morgan Collection." *The Coin Collector's Journal* 16, nos. 5 & 6 (1949); 17, nos. 1-4, 6 (1950).
 This series of installments publishes Morgan's collection of Greek and Roman coins. Later reprinted in book form (see below).

2093 ———— *The J. Pierpont Morgan Collection: Catalogue of the Greek and Roman Coins, Abukir Medallions, Roman Gold Bar.* New York: Wayte Raymond Inc., 1953. 59 pp., illus. [CS 1930]
 Begins with an introduction by Sydney P. Noe. The collection formed by Morgan was loaned to the American Numismatic Society in 1917. Many of the pieces were acquired by Morgan from the M. C. Strozzi collection in 1907. In 1949, the collection was purchased by Raymond, who published this book prior to the collection's dispersal. Some of the coins were reacquired by the ANS. Catalogues forty-four gold and 151 silver Greek coins. All are illustrated. Also discusses the gold medallions found at Abukir, eight of which resided in Morgan's collection. These medallions were probably prizes for winners at the Olympic games in the third century A.D. They bear Greek designs in a Hellenistic style. All are illustrated. Also lists about 200 Roman gold, silver, and bronze coins, Roman gold and bronze medallions, and a Roman gold bar.

2094 **Regling, Kurt L.** *Die Griechische Münzen der Sammlung Warren.* Two volumes. Berlin: Druck und Verlag von Georg Reimer, 1906. 264 pp., 37 pls. [CS 1935]
 A catalogue of the collection of Edward P. Warren, a well-known English connoisseur of Greek art, comprised of 1769 ancient Greek coins of the highest artistic merit. The Boston Museum of Fine Arts later acquired 1419 of these coins which were re-published in Brett's catalogue in 1955. [See Brett under PUBLIC COLLECTIONS—UNITED STATES (BOSTON)].

2095 **Robinson, Edward S. G.** *Catalogue of Ancient Greek Coins Collected by Godfrey Locker Lampson.* London: Arthur L. Humphreys, 1923. 126 pp., 26 pls. [CS 1929]
 Begins with an inspiring *Foreword* by Lampson describing the beauty of Greek coins. Many of his coins were formerly in the collection of Sir Hermann Weber. The catalogue presents 350 coins from throughout the Greek world, of uniformly superb condition and artistic merit. Most are illustrated. Pedigrees are given for the coins when significant.

2096 ———— *Ancient Greek Coins in the Possession of William Harrison Woodward: A Catalogue.* Oxford, 1928. 70 pp., 12 pls. [CS 2004a]

The collection was sold in Numismatica Ars Classica *Auction 15* on February 2, 1930.

2097 **Rosen, Jonathan.** *Archaic Coins: An Exhibition at the J. Paul Getty Museum from the Collection of Jonathan Rosen.* Malibu: The J. Paul Getty Museum, 1983. 43 pp., map, illus.
A companion catalogue to an exhibition of Rosen's collection of archaic Greek coins at the Getty Museum. A brief introduction to the archaic-period coinage of the seventh, sixth, and fifth centuries B.C. is followed by a catalogue describing fifty coins, each of which is illustrated by enlarged photographs. [Also see Waggoner *Early Greek Coins from the Collection of Jonathan P. Rosen* below].

2098 **Schwabacher, Willy.** *Grekiska Mynt ur Konung Gustof VI Adolfs Samling.* Malmö, 1962. 33 pp., illus. [CS 1925]
The collection of King Gustaf VI of Sweden.

2099 **Schwarz, Dietrich, and Leo Mildenberg.** *Aus Einer Sammlung Griechischer Münzen.* Zurich: Verlag Berichthaus, 1961. 65 pp., (including 30 pls. of enlargements), 2 pls.
Catalogue of twenty-five coins selected from the collection of Hans Römer. Includes an introduction by D. Schwarz and catalogue by L. Mildenberg. Includes thirty plates of enlargements (of one side of each coin) of especially artistic coins, and two plates illustrating all the coins (both sides) in actual size.

2100 **Sheedy, Kenneth A.** *Alexander and the Hellenistic Kingdoms: Coins, Image and the Creation of Identity. The Westmoreland Collection.* Ancient Coins in Australian Collections 1. Sydney: Australian Centre for Ancient Numismatic Studies, Macquarie University, 2007. 172 pp., illus.
A catalogue prepared for an exhibition of eighty-seven coins from a private collection—one of the finest collections of Hellenistic coins in Australia. The coins are primarily of Philip II, Alexander III, and portrait issues of the successors. The exhibition was held at Macquarie University in 2007-2008. Begins with five essays: "Magically Back to Life: Some Thoughts on Ancient Coins and the Study of Hellenistic Royal Portraits" by K. A. Sheedy [1297], "Rider in the Chariot: Ptolemy, Alexander and the Elephants" by A. B. Bosworth [884], "Continuity and Ambition: The Posthumous Philip II Gold Staters from Colophon/Magnesia" by E. J. Baynham [267], and "The Coinage of Alexander and his Successors: A Common Hellenic Coinage?" by J. R. Melville Jones [280]. Then each coin is catalogued and its historic and/or artistic background is examined. Each coin is illustrated both by enlarged and actual size photographs. Bibliography, maps.

2101 **Sim, George.** *Catalogue of the Collection of Greek and Roman Coins formed by George Sim.* Edinburgh: Privately printed, 1879. 184 pp.
A catalogue of a private collection consisting of 12,947 coins, including 553 electrotypes. The majority are bronze coins. Descriptions are very brief. No illustrations. One hundred copies of the catalogue were privately printed.

2102 "Some Ancient Coins." *American Journal of Numismatics* 15, no. 3 (January 1881): 49-50. 1 pl.
Illustrates and describes thirty-seven Greek, Roman, and Byzantine coins on a plate from the sale catalogue of the William J. Jenks collection published by W. E. Woodward (this was Woodward's *Sale 34* held in 1881).

2103 **Sotheby & Co.** *Catalogue of the Unique Collection of Greek and Roman Coins of the Honourable Imperial Court Counsellor C. G. Huber of Vienna.* London: Sotheby & Co., 1862. 138 pp.
The catalogue for the sale of the C. G. Huber collection, sold by Sotheby's, June 4-12, 1862. Includes 1444 lots.

2104 ——— *The Montagu Collection of Coins: Catalogue of the Greek Series.* London: Sotheby, Wilkinson, & Hodge, March 23-28, 1896. *Second and Final Portion, Together with a Small Series of Roman Silver and Bronze Coins and Medallions.* March 15-19, 1897. Two volumes. 209 pp., 15 pls. [CS 4980]
The sale catalogue listing 1580 coins from Hyman Montagu's famous collection. Montagu (b. 1844; d. 1895) was a lawyer in London. He began collecting coins in the 1870s, and turned to ancient coins in 1889. He formed one of the finest collections ever sold at auction. [Also see listings 765 and 766 in J. Spring, *Ancient Coin Auction Catalogues 1880-1980* (see Spring under COLLECTING GUIDES)].

2105 ——— *Catalogue of the Bunbury Collection of Greek Coins. First Portion: Italy, Sicily, European Greece, Crete, &C. Second and Final Portion: Asia Minor, Africa &C.* London: Sotheby, Wilkinson & Hodge, 1896. Two parts: 160 pp., 8 pls.; 108 pp., 7 pls. [CS 1950]
The catalogues for the sale of Sir Edward Herbert Bunbury's collection which was sold by Sotheby's in two sessions, June 15-22 and December 7-12, 1896. Includes 2068 lots. Wonderful coins. [Also see listings 767 and 768 in J. Spring, *Ancient Coin Auction Catalogues 1880-1980* (see Spring under COLLECTING GUIDES)].

2106 ——— *Catalogue of the Valuable Collection of Greek Coins Formed by the Late Frank Sherman Benson, Esq. of Brooklyn, New York, Comprising Choice and Interesting Examples of the Ancient Coinages of Italy and Sicily, Greece and the Islands, Asia Minor, &C., Syria, Egypt, Zeugitana, &C.* London: Sotheby, Wilkinson & Hodge, 1909. 110 pp., 26 pls. [CS 1943]
The catalogue for the February 3-11, 1909 sale of Benson's collection which was regarded as one of the most important collections of Greek coins in private hands in the United States. Includes 808 lots. The collection is particularly rich in coins of Italy and Sicily. [Some of Benson's coins were previously published. See Benson "Ancient Greek Coins" under ITALY—GENERAL WORKS. Also see listing 797 in J. Spring, *Ancient Coin Auction Catalogues 1880-1980* (see Spring under COLLECTING GUIDES)].

2107 ——— *Catalogue of a Valuable Collection of Coins: Chiefly of Alexander the Great, his Successors in North-West India, and of the Seleucid Kings of Syria, Formed by the Late Major-General H. L. Haughton, C.B., C.I.E., C.B.E.* London: Sotheby & Co., 1958. 26 pls. [CS 2892]
The sale catalogue for the 618 lot auction of H. L. Haughton's collection which took place on April 30 and May 1, 1958. Haughton (b. 1883; d. 1955) served in India and formed most of his collection there. [Also see listing 831 in J. Spring, *Ancient Coin Auction Catalogues 1880-1980* (see Spring under COLLECTING GUIDES)].

2108 ——— *The Nelson Bunker Hunt Collection: Important Greek and Roman Coins.* Four volumes. New York: Sotheby's, 1990 and 1991. Illus.

Sale catalogues for one of the finest collections of ancient coins ever assembled. The catalogue for the first session (June 19, 1990) contains sixty-two high quality Greek coins. Each coin is shown in actual size black and white photographs as well as enlarged color photographs. Each coin is fully described and cross-referenced to other published collections. Pedigrees are given and historical commentary is included. The second session (June 21, 1990) includes 481 Greek coins. Each is shown in actual size black and white photographs, with a few color enlargements. Descriptions are less extensive than in the first volume. The third session (December 4, 1990) included sixty-four high quality Greek coins. The catalogue is presented in the same format as the initial volume. The final session (June 19 and 20, 1991) contained 644 lots of Greek coins, mostly single coins but including some multiple-coin lots. The catalogue format is the same as for the second session. Volume 1 contains an introduction to the collection by David Sellwood. Volume 2 includes an introduction to collecting ancient art by Margaret Ellen Mayo. Volume 3 includes an introduction by E. E. Clain-Stefanelli. Companion sale catalogues were published for the Hunt collections of Greek vases and Greek, Roman and Byzantine bronzes (one volume) and Byzantine coins (two volumes). [Also see J. Tompkins *Wealth of the Ancient World* under ART for the catalogue of the 1983-4 traveling exhibition of the Hunts' art collection].

2109 ——— *Two Hundred Highly Important Greek and Roman Coins.* London, 1995. 167 pp., illus.
The catalogue for the July 5, 1995 auction of ancient coins featuring eighty-eight Greek and 112 Roman coins. The coins are of the highest quality and many are quite rare. Each coin is fully described. Provenances are given for most coins as well as historical and artistic commentary. Each coin is photographed and there are many enlarged color photographs.

2110 **Straus, Pierre.** *Collection Maurice Laffaille: Monnaies Grecques en Bronze.* Basel, 1990. 168 pp., illus.
Catalogue of the Maurice Laffaille collection of Greek bronze coins. Includes 663 coins, all illustrated in actual size black and white photographs. Introduction by Michel Amandry. [Also see Laffaille above, and Münzen und Medaillen *Auktion 76* above].

2111 **Symons, David, and K. Sugden.** "Greek Silver Coins from the Finney Collection." *Spink Numismatic Circular* 103, no. 10 (December 1995): 377-80. Illus.
A catalogue of forty-seven Greek fractional silver coins from the collection of Ian Finney. Each coin is shown in actual size and twice actual size.

2112 **Tanabe, Katsumi.** *Silk Road Coins: The Hirayama Collection.* Kamakura, Japan: The Institute of Silk Road Studies, 1993. 116 pp., illus., map.
The catalogue for an exhibition at the British Museum in 1993. Illustrates coins with minimal descriptions. Includes Greek, Indo-Greek, Sasanian, Kushan, and other coins. Discusses the art and design of the coins. Text in English and Japanese.

2113 **Troxell, Hyla A.** *The Norman Davis Collection.* Ancient Coins in North American Collections, No. 1. New York: American Numismatic Society, 1969. 53 pp., 28 pls. [CS 1924]
A general collection of 345 Greek coins, all illustrated. Includes brief die descriptions, weights, die axis, and some dates. Includes many Seleucid and Indo-Greek coins. Many of Davis' coins were sold by Numismatic Fine Arts in *Auction 11* (December 8, 1982). Additional coins from the collection were sold in Gemini Numismatic Auctions *Auction VII* (January 9, 2011). [Reviewed by H. Nicolet in *Revue Archéologique* (Paris) 2 (1971): 361, and by N. K. Rutter in *Numismatic Chronicle* 7th ser., 12 (1972): 318].

2114 **Vinchon, Jean.** *Exceptionnelle Collection de Monnaies Grecques Antiques.* Paris: Jean Vinchon, 1985. Illus.
Catalogue for an April 1985 auction of 441 Greek coins of exceptional quality, held in Monaco. Includes commentary and many color plates.

2115 ——— *Numismatique: Collection James et Sneja D. Velkov; Collection Daniel Feret; Major Sale of Greek Electrum.* Paris: Jean Vinchon, 1994. Illus.
Catalogue for a November 1994 sale of 525 lots (all illustrated) including 478 ancients. Includes 173 Greek gold and electrum coins and a nice group of Sicilian bronze coins. French text.

2116 **Waggoner, Nancy M.** *Early Greek Coins from the Collection of Jonathan P. Rosen.* Ancient Coins in North American Collections, No. 5. New York: American Numismatic Society, 1983. 55 pp., 28 pls.
The collection contains 770 Greek coins, focusing on the coinage of the archaic period, especially the fractional denominations. Includes some dates and bibliographic citings. All coins are illustrated. [J. Spier's review in *Numismatic Chronicle* 148 (1988): 220-2, contains many important comments and corrections. Also see the review by A. Johnston in *Journal of Hellenic Studies* 106 (1986): 258. Also see Lorber "Origins of Coinage" under ORIGINS OF COINAGE, and Rosen *Archaic Coins: An Exhibition* above. The collection has been disbursed. The first portion was sold in Münzen und Medaillen *Auction 72* (October 6, 1987). Additional pieces were sold in Numismatic Fine Arts *Winter Mail Bid Sale* (December 18, 1987)].

2117 **Walker, Alan S.** "Catalogues and Their Collectors." *American Journal of Numismatics* 20 (2008): 597-615.
The author presents biographies of seven famous collectors of Greek coins and discusses the publications of their collections. Includes Ioannes Photiades Pasha, Athanasios Rhousopoulos, Arthur John Evans, Robert Jameson, Samuel-Jean Pozzi, Clarence Sweet Bement, and Charles Gillet. Includes an annotated bibliography of the published catalogues featuring their collections, including auction appearances of portions of their collections.

2118 **Ward, John, and George F. Hill.** *Greek Coins and Their Parent Cities.* London: John Murray, 1902. 464 pp., 22 pls., maps. [CS 1933]
Begins with an introductory chapter *The Old Greeks as Pioneers of Trade: Their Artistic and Literary Taste, Survival of Hellenic Types,* which provides a general discussion of Greek history, art, and numismatics. Followed by a catalogue of 952 of Ward's coins, fully described by Hill. The third part, *Imaginary Rambles in Hellenic Lands,* is a narrative tour of Greek lands discussing monuments, ruins, architecture and art. [Reviewed by B. V. Head in *Numismatic Chronicle* 4th ser., 2 (1902): 191-2. Also see Hill *Descriptive Catalogue* above].

2119 **Weber, Hermann.** "On Some Unpublished or Rare Greek Coins." *Numismatic Chronicle* 3rd ser., 12 (1892): 185-208. 2 pls.
The author lists and discusses coins from Velia, Himera, Aenus, Thracic Chersonesus, Euboea, Elis, Gortyna, the alliance of Hyrtacus and Lissus, Phaestus, uncertain Crete, Delos, Assus, the alliance of Smyrna and Troas, Cos, Tarsus, and the alliance of Ococlea and Bruzus (Phrygia). [Also see the author's corrections on page 331].

2120 ——— "On Some Unpublished or Rare Greek Coins." *Numismatic Chronicle* 3rd ser., 16 (1896): 1-33. 3 pls.
The author lists numerous coins from his collection which he acquired in the last four years.

2121 ——— "Rare or Unpublished Coins in My Collection." *Corolla Numismatica: Numismatic Essays in Honour of Barclay V. Head.* Edited by G. F. Hill. London: Oxford University Press, 1906. Pages 296-300. 1 pl.
    Publishes coins of Macedon (uncertain), Pherae (in Thessaly), Acarnania, Atarneus (in Mysia), Smyrna, Trapezopolis (in Caria), Lindus (on Rhodes), and Mopsus (in Cilicia). Some of the coins are from the Roman Imperial period. [Also see Forrer *Descriptive Catalogue* above].

2122 **Wilkinson, John S.** "Unpublished Ancient Greek Coins." *Cornucopiæ* (publication of The Ancient Coin Society, Canada) 4 (1979): 2-5. Illus.
    Describes and illustrates twelve coins not previously published. Includes varieties from the Arcadian League, Abdera, Seleucid Kingdom, Athens (New Style), and Pergamum (Philetaerus).

Note: Catalogues which focus on the coinage of specific cities are listed under the sections appropriate for those cities. Also see the INDEX OF COLLECTORS AND COLLECTIONS for other private collections.

Also see: Brunk "A Tentative Index" under COLLECTING GUIDES; Classical Numismatic Group *Triton IX (BCD Boiotia)* under CENTRAL GREECE—BOEOTIA; Classical Numismatic Group "Todd A. Ballen Collection" under PARTHIA; Hoge, Meadows, and Wartenberg Kagan "Truth and Plain Dealing" under SPAIN; Houghton *Coins of the Seleucid Empire* under SYRIA—SELEUCID KINGDOM; Huth *Coinage of the Caravan Kingdoms* under ARABIA; Jenkins "Haughton Collection" under PUBLIC COLLECTIONS—GREAT BRITAIN (LONDON); Jidejian *Lebanon and the Greek World...Eddé Collection* under PORTRAITS; Kampmann "Record Results (BCD Collection)" under PELOPONNESOS—GENERAL WORKS; Leu Numismatics *Coins of Olympia (BCD Collection)* under PELOPONNESOS—ELIS.

Meadows and Kan *History Re-Stored (Zhuyuetang Collection)* under GENERAL WORKS—GREEK; Meshorer *Coins from the Holy Land* under PALESTINE—JUDEA; Nelson *Numismatic Art of Persia—The Sunrise Collection* under PERSIA; Noehden *A Selection* and *Specimens of Ancient Coins* under ITALY—GENERAL WORKS; Numismatik Lanz München *Auktion 111* (BCD Collection) under CENTRAL GREECE—EUBOIA; Numismatik Lanz München *Auktion 105* (BCD collection) under CORINTHIA; Ravel *Descriptive Catalogue* under ITALY—TARAS; Strauss *Collection C.C.* under ITALY—GENERAL WORKS; Superior Galleries *Abraham Bromberg Collection* under PALESTINE—JUDEA; Waggoner "Wallace Collection" under CENTRAL GREECE—EUBOIA; Wright *Coins from Asia Minor and the East* under ASIA MINOR—GENERAL WORKS.

Western and Central Europe

Spain

It may be laid down as a general rule that the Iberian inscriptions on the reverses of the coins furnish the names of the tribes for whom, or by whom, the coins were issued. These names are in many cases identical with those of the chief towns of the district, but this is by no means always the case; and it is remarkable that on the money of the most important towns the name of the tribe takes the place of that of the city.

—Barclay V. Head, 1911

2123 **Anderson, Paul K., and John F. Lhotka.** "The Chrysaor Head." *The Numismatist* 68, no. 11 (November 1955): 1182-4. Illus.
"The authors restate an old mystery related to the coinage of Emporion without attempting a solution. On the reverse of drachms of Emporion the head of Pegasus has been replaced by a little figure which is identified as Chrysaor, the brother of Pegasus. Why this figure appears and why it has several forms remains a problem." [H. Adelson, *NL* 41]

2124 **Beltran Martinez, Antonio.** *Las Antiguas Monedas Oscenses.* Huesca, 1950. 27 pp., illus. [CS 5047]
"On the Celtiberian and Roman coinage of Osca." [E. Clain-Stefanelli]

2125 ——— *Numismática Antigua, Clasica y de España.* Volume 1 of *Curso di Numismatica.* Second edition. Cartagena, 1950. 459 pp., illus. [CS 5048]

2126 ——— *Las Monedas Hispánicas Antiguas.* Zaragoza, 1954. 44 pp., illus., 8 pls. [CS 5049]

2126a ——— "Notas Sobre los Tipos Monetarios de las Monedas 'Ibericas.'" *Quaderni Ticinesi: Numismatica e Antichità Classiche* (Switzerland) 11 (1982): 161-76.

2127 **Breckenridge, James D.** "Coins Verify Hannibal Identification." *Coin World* (January 27, 1982): 29-30. Illus.
A bronze statue in the Museo Nazionale delle Terme, Rome, which was previously identified only as "The Hellenistic Ruler" has been identified as Hannibal by comparison with coins from the Barcid mint in Spain.

2128 **Burgos, Fernando Alvarez.** *La Moneda Hispánica: Desde sus Origenes Hasta el Siglo V.* Catalogo General de Las Monedas Españolas, Volume 1. Madrid, 1979. 248 pp., illus. New edition, Madrid, 2008. 397 pp., illus. [CS 2016]

2129 **Calicó, Xavier, and Ferran X. Calicó.** *Catálogo de Monedas Antiquas de Hispania.* Barcelona, 1979. 177 pp., illus.
A catalogue for the June 1979 sale of 1277 coins.

2129a **Caltabiano, Maria Caccamo.** "Sulla Cronologia e la Metrologia delle Serie Hispanorum." *Quaderni Ticinesi: Numismatica e Antichità Classiche* (Switzerland) 14 (1985): 159-70.

2130 **Chaves Tristan, Francisca.** "Origen, Uso y Función de la Moneda en la Sociedad Hispana: Siglos IV-I a.C." *Liber Amicorum Tony Hackens.* Numismatica Lovaniensia 20. Edited by G. Moucharte, M. B. Borba Florenzano, F. de Callataÿ, P. Marchetti, L. Smolderen, and P. Yannopoulos. Louvain-la-Neuve: Université Catholique de Louvain, 2007. Pages 213 ff.

2131 **Classical Numismatic Group, Inc.** "A European Collection of Ancient Spanish Coins." *CNG Auction 87* (May 18, 2011). Lancaster, PA: Classical Numismatic Group, 2011. Pages 6-24. Illus.
Lots 1-105 in this auction consist of choice ancient coins of Iberia, primarily bronze, from a European collection.

2132 **Dembski, Günther, ed.** *Kunsthistorisches Museum Wien. Münzkabinett—Katalogu der Antiken Münzen, A. Griechen. I. Hispanien und die Römischen Provinzen Galliens.* Vienna: Kunsthistorisches Museum, 1979. 60 pp., 19 pls., map.
Includes twenty pages of introductory material, including tables of Iberian inscriptions and monograms. Catalogues 541 coins from the museum's collection of coins from Hispania and the Roman Province of Gallia. Most of the material is Roman.

2133 **deSaulcy, Louis Félicien J. C.** *Essai de Classification des Monnaies Autonomes de l'Espagne.* Metz: S. Lamort, 1840. Reprint, Bologna: Forni, 1974. 219 pp., illus. 8 pls. [CS 5074]

2134 **Fernández Gomez, Jorge H.** "La Circulación Monetaria Ibérica en Ebusus." *Numisma* (Spain) 26, nos. 138-143 (1976): 49-57. 1 pl. [CS 5055]

2135 **Garcia y Bellido, María Paz.** "Las Series más Antiguas de Cástulo." *Numisma* (Spain) 26, nos. 138-143 (1976): 97-110. 1 pl. [CS 5056]

2136 ——— "Coinage and Ethnicity in Celtic Spain." *Zeitschrift für Celtische Philologie* 49-50 (1997): 219-42.

2137 **Gil Farrès, Octavio.** *La Moneda Hispanica en la edad Antigua.* Madrid, 1966. 584 pp., 75 pls. [CS 2020]

2138 **Gilliland, Herbert.** "Ebusus: An Old Mystery Revived." *SAN—Journal of the Society for Ancient Numismatics* 12, no. 1 (spring 1981): 4-5. Illus.
A small bronze coin showing Artemis and Bes is presented. The author suggests this is a coin described by Aloïss Heiss in his book on ancient Spanish coins, which Heiss had not actually seen and the existence of which he questioned. Heiss attributed the coin to Minorca. The author tentatively attributes it to Ebusus, and suggests it was struck ca. 214-150 B.C.

2139 **Guadan, Antonio Manuel de.** *La Moneda Ibérico: Catálogo de Numismatica Ibérica e Ibero-Romana.* Cuadernos de Numismatica. Madrid, 1980. 358 pp., illus., 8 pls. [CS 2023]

2140 **Head, Barclay V.** "The Coins of Ancient Spain." *Numismatic Chronicle* 3rd ser., 2 (1882): 183-94.
Summarizes the coinage of Spain in the four centuries prior to the establishment of the Roman Empire. Includes may re-attributions of the coinage previously attributed by other writers.

2141 **Heiss, Aloïss.** *Description Générale des Monnaies Antiques de l'Espagne.* Paris, 1870. Reprint, Amsterdam: A. M. Hakkert, 1966; Bologna: Forni, 1966, 1975; Chicago: Argonaut, 1967. 548 pp., 68 pls. [CS 2024]

2142 ——— *Atlas of the Ancient Coins of Spain.* Chicago: Ares Publishers, 1976. 88 pp., 68 pls. [CS 2025]
A reprint of the plates (line drawings) from Heiss' *Description Générale des Monnaies Antiques de l'Espagne* (see above). The plates illustrate several hundred coins struck in Spain including coins of the Celtic tribes and Roman Provincial issues.

2143 **Hill, George F.** *Notes on the Ancient Coins of Hispania Citerior.* Numismatic Notes and Monographs, No. 50. New York: American Numismatic Society, 1931. 196 pp., 36 pls.
Discusses the ancient coinage of Spain city-by-city, comparing styles, inscriptions and weights, and discussing chronology.

2144 **Hoge, Robert, Andrew Meadows, and Ute Wartenberg Kagan.** "Truth and Plain Dealing: The Fate of the Archer Huntington Collection of Spanish Coinage." *ANS* 7, no. 3 (winter 2008): 22-30. Illus.
A short history and description of the Archer Huntington collection of the coinage of the Iberian Peninsula, the largest and finest collection of this material. Huntington formed the collection and donated it to the Hispanic Society of America, then lent the collection to the American Numismatic Society under a long-term loan arrangement. The Hispanic Society now wants to sell the collection, in contravention of the donor's intent.

2145 **Jenkins, G. Kenneth.** "A Celtiberian Hoard from Granada." *Numario Hispánico* 7, no. 14 (1958): 135-46.

2146 ——— "Notes on Iberian Denarii from the Cordova Hoard." *Museum Notes* 8 (1958): 57-70. 6 pls.
Jenkins presents a catalogue of the Cordova hoard, the earliest silver hoard in which Iberian and Roman denarii appear together, although the hoard provides no significant new information for the dating of the first Roman issues. Jenkins discusses the coins, mint-by-mint. The hoard shows that the Iberian denarii were still being issued at the end of the second century B.C. [A summary of this hoard, together with the 235 Roman Republican denarii which were part of the hoard, was published by H. Mattingly in *Numismatic Chronicle* 5th ser., 5 (1925): 395-6].

2147 ——— "Literaturüberblick der Griechischen Numismatik: Spain." *Jahrbuch für Numismatik und Geldsseschichte* (Germany) 11 (1961): 79-155. [CS 2008]
A bibliography.

2148 ——— "Problems of the Celtiberian Coinage." *Congresso Internazionale di Numismatica, Roma 11-16 Settembre 1961. Volume 2.* Rome: Istituto Italiano de Numismatica, 1965. Pages 219-24. 1 pl. [CS 5044]
Includes general comments on chronology, types, metrology, and mints followed by a consideration of some specific points affecting the issues of Secaisa and Contrebia.

2149 ——— "Spain." *Survey of Numismatic Research, 1960-1965. Volume 1: Ancient Numismatics.* Copenhagen: International Numismatic Commission, 1967. Pages 96-105. [CS 2009]
A narrative bibliography discussing recently published works in the field of Greek numismatics related to Spain.

2150 ——— "The Iberian Peninsula." *Survey of Numismatic Research, 1966-1971. Volume 1: Ancient Numismatics.* New York: International Numismatic Commission, 1973. Pages 206-20. [CS 2010]
A narrative bibliography discussing recently published works in the field of Greek numismatics related to Iberian coinage.

2151 **Kirkby, Todd.** "The Importance of Ulia and its Abstract Iberian Coinage." *The Celator* 11, no. 1 (January 1997): 14-9. Illus.
The author describes how he became interested in the coinage of the ancient city of Ulia, then provides a summary of the city's history during the civil war between Julius Caesar and Pompey. He then discusses the city's coinage which was minted ca. 155-50 B.C. and is quite scarce today.

2152 ——— "Ursone—The City of Bears." *The Celator* 13, no. 6 (June 1999): 25-6. Illus.
A brief discussion of the city of Ursone and its coinage. This city began minting coinage ca. 190-170 B.C. Ursone was a popular bear hunting region in ancient times and bears were commonly depicted on the city's coinage.

2153 **Knapp, Robert C.** "The Date and Purpose of the Iberian Denarii." *Numismatic Chronicle* 137 (1977): 1-18. Illus., map. [CS 5064]
Reviews the controversy over the date of the denarii minted in Iberia. Discusses the origin of the types. Then investigates why these coins were minted and how they were used. Concludes that their origin was in the need for coins for governmental, not private, transactions.

2154 **Kollgaard, Ron.** "Dating and Purpose of Iberian Coinage Provide Challenges for Numismatic Research." *The Celator* 5, no. 12 (December 1991): 18-29.
Discusses ancient Iberian coinage. The first such coins were minted in the city of Emporiai, ca. 350 B.C., and exhibited a Greek-inspired style. Briefly describes Iberian and Celtiberian cultures and presents an outline of the military history of Iberia through the Roman Republican period. Describes the common head/horseman coinage, suggests reasons for the choice of types and reasons for their minting. Suggests these coins may have been minted to facilitate the slave trade or to pay Roman soldiers. Discusses theories for the date of the first Iberian-style coinage and suggests ca. 180 B.C. as the most likely date.

2155 ——— "The History and Coinage of Iberia. Part 1: Spain before the Romans." *The Celator* 7, no. 6 (June 1993): 6-11. "Part 2: The Roman Conquest of Spain." *The Celator* 7, no. 7 (July 1993): 18-23. "Part 3: Spain in the Late Republic and Early Empire." *The Celator* 7, no. 8 (August 1993): 10-5. Illus.
Discusses the colonization of Iberia by Celts, Iberians, Phoenicians, and others. Reviews the coins which made their way into Iberia through trade. Describes the coins of Massalia and coins of Celtiberian tribes. Discusses the appearance of local coins, beginning ca. 350 B.C., at Emporiai, Rhoda, Gades, Ebusus, and Carthago Nova. Part 2 covers the history and coinage during the second Punic War. Part 3 covers the period from the Roman acquisition of Iberian lands from Carthage after the second Punic War, to the end of local issues during the early Roman Empire.

2156 **Martin Valls, Ricardo.** *La Circulacion Monetaria Iberica.* Vallodolid: Universidad de Valladolid, 1967. 183 pp. [CS 5069]

2157 **Ortega Galindo, Julio.** *La España Primitiva a Través de las Monedas Ibéricas.* Bilbao, 1947. 120 pp., 30 pls. [CS 5070]

2158 **Rivero, Casto Maria del.** *La Colección de Monedas Ibéricas del Museo Arqueológico Nacional: Primera Parte, Monedas de la Ulterior.* Madrid, 1923. 115 pp., 31 pls. [CS 5072]

2159 **Robinson, Edward S. G.** "Punic Coins of Spain and Their Bearing on the Roman Republican Series." *Essays in Roman Coinage Presented to Harold Mattingly.* Edited by R. A. G. Carson and C. H. V. Sutherland. Oxford: University Press, 1956. Pages 34-53. 4 pls. [CS 2028]
Robinson examines the coins struck by the Barcids in Spain. Certain of the coin types were used both by the Barcids and by the Romans, and a study of this coinage helps illustrate the political, economic, and cultural background of the period. The author identifies eight series of coinage, and places them in chronological order. He discusses the Punic types and shows parallels on Roman Republican coinage. [Also see Jenkins "Varia Punica" under ZEUGITANA].

2160 **Stannard, Clive.** "Numismatic Evidence for Relations between Spain and Central Italy at the Turn of the Second and First Centuries B.C." *Revue Suisse de Numismatique* (Switzerland) 84 (2005): 47-80. Illus.
"The author discusses the historical implications of shared iconography between minor local coinages of Baetica and central Italy, the large numbers of Ebusan bronze coins found in central Italy and the rarity of other Spanish coinages, and the massive copying in central Italy of Ebusan bronze." [Oliver D. Hoover, *NL* 149]

2161 **van Alfen, Peter G., Martín Almagro-Gorbea, and Pere Pau Ripollès.** "A New Celtiberian Hacksilber Hoard, c. 200 BCE." *American Journal of Numismatics* 2nd ser., 20 (2008): 265-93. 4 pls.
This study presents a Hacksilber hoard recently acquired by the American Numismatic Society and argues for a significant role for Hacksilber in the monetization of Iberia in the third century B.C. The hoard contained 136 silver objects (including eight coins), was found in the eastern zone of southern Celtiberia, and dates to the end of the third or beginning of the second century B.C. The tiny size of the objects is noteworthy (most weigh less than 2 grams), and the authors argue that these fragments served a parallel and complementary function as small change alongside, and at times in lieu of, circulating coinage. Individual noteworthy pieces are discussed, and a full catalogue is included in an Appendix. The authors examine the metrology and chronology of the items.

2162 **Villaronga, Garriga Leandre.** *Las Monedas Hispano-Cartaginesas.* Barcelona, 1973. 189 pp., 21 pls. [CS 2030]

2163 ——— *Numismática Antigua de Hispania: Iniciación a su Estudio.* Barcelona: Cymys, 1979. 350 pp., illus. [CS 2032]

2164 ——— *Corpus Nummum Hispaniae Ante Augusti Aetatem.* Madrid: José A. Herrero, 1994. 518 pp., illus.
The coinage before the reign of Augustus.

2165 **Vives y Escudero, Antonio.** *La Moneda Hispánica.* Madrid: Real Academia de Historia, 1924-6. Reprint, Madrid, 1980. 4 volumes of text and one volume of plates. 557 pp., 173 pls. [CS 5095]

Covers the Celtic coinage of Spain.

1. *Pre-Roman.* 74 pp.
2. *Ibero-Roman.* 200 pp.
3. *Ibero-Roman.* 135 pp.
4. *Imperial.* 148 pp.

2166 **Zobel de Zangroniz, J.** *Estudio Histórico de la Moneda Antigua Española.* Madrid, 1878-1880.

Also see: Akerman *Ancient Coins* under Celtic Coinage—General Works; Jenkins "Carthage, N. Africa, the Iberian Peninsula, Gaul" under North Africa—General Works; Stannard and Frey-Kupper "'Pseudomints' and Small Change in Italy and Sicily" under Italy—General Works; Villaronga "Petit Trésor de la Deuxième Guerre Punique avec une Drachme des Bruttiens" under Hoards.

CELTIC COINAGE

It is interesting that so long as the coinage of a prestigious external community was freely available as reward for mercenary service, few Celtic tribal authorities actually struck much coinage of their own. But when this contact was severed, as happened everywhere when Rome conquered mercenary-using communities, then free Celtic communities sometimes began to strike independent coinages, adapting types familiar from successful relationships in the past.

—Daphne Nash, 1987

GENERAL WORKS

2167 **Akerman, John Yonge.** *Ancient Coins of Cities and Princes, Geographically Arranged and Described Containing the Coins of Hispania, Gallia and Britannia.* London: John Russell Smith, 1846. 203 pp., 24 engraved pls.
This was the first volume in what the author hoped would be a series of books covering the realm of ancient coinage. This volume covers the coinage of Spain, Gaul, and Britain during the Greek and early Roman periods. Presents a catalogue of coin types, a discussion of the coins, and tables of alphabets.

2168 **Allen, Derek F.** "Celtic Coins in the Royal Coin Cabinet, Stockholm." *Nordisk Numismatisk Årsskrift* (Sweden) (1972): 5-26. Illus.
A catalogue of the museum's collection of 132 Celtic coins. Each coin is photographed. Allen discusses a few of the most important pieces.

2169 ——— "Wealth, Money and Coinage in a Celtic Society." *To Illustrate the Monuments: Essays on Archaeology Presented to Stuart Piggott.* Edited by J. V. S. Megaw. London, 1976. Pages 199-208. Illus.
Explores the nature and function of coins in Celtic society. Discusses the purpose of money, uses of money, trade, and the question of who issued the coins.

2170 ——— *An Introduction to Celtic Coins.* London: British Museum Publications, 1978. 80 pp., illus., 3 maps. [CS 5189]
Begins with a brief account of the origins, functions, and development of Celtic coinage. Allen then illustrates examples of coins grouped as follows: Danubian Basin, Po Valley, South-west France, Central and Western France, the Rhône Valley, the quinarius coinage of Gaul, the gold coinage of the East and West, the bronze coinage, the coinage of Britain, and British dynasties. Commentary is provided for each of the coins illustrated, emphasizing their artistic development, Hellenistic prototypes, Celtic type content, and legends. Illustrated by 123 coins from the British Museum collection. [Reviewed by D. Nash in *Numismatic Chronicle* 139 (1979): 255].

2171 ——— *The Coins of the Ancient Celts.* Edited by Daphne Nash. Edinburgh: University Press, 1980. 265 pp., 41 pls., 18 maps. [CS 5012]
An introduction to the Celtic coinages of Europe, their origin and development, and areas of use. Describes the stylistic characteristics of the coins of various tribes. Discusses metrology and metallurgy, denominations, types, and legends. Includes a bibliography. Illustrates 581 coins. [Reviewed by P. A. Clayton in *Seaby Coin and Medal Bulletin* 744 (August 1980): 248-9, by George C. Boon in *Spink Numismatic Circular* 88, no. 11 (November 1980): 403, and by H. Rauch in *SAN* 11, no. 4 (winter 1980-1): 77-8].

2172 ——— *Catalogue of the Celtic Coins in the British Museum with Supplementary Material from Other British Collections.* Five volumes. London: British Museum, 1987+.

1. *Silver Coins of the East Celts and Balkan Peoples.* Edited by John Kent and Melinda Mays. 1987. 80 pp., 31 pls. [Reviewed by B. Overbeck in *Numismatic Chronicle* 149 (1989): 234-5].
2. *Silver Coins of North Italy, South and Central France, Switzerland, and South Germany.* Edited by John Kent and Melinda Mays. 1990. 72 pp., 29 pls. [Reviewed by Jeffrey May in *Spink Numismatic Circular* 99, no. 7 (September 1991): 228, and by A. Chadburn in *Numismatic Chronicle* 152 (1992): 200-1].
3. *Bronze Coins of Gaul.* Edited by Melinda Mays. 1995. 106 pp., 3 maps, 38 pls. [Reviewed by D. Nash Briggs in *Numismatic Chronicle* 157 (1997): 263-4].
4. [See R. Hobbs under CELTIC COINAGE OF BRITAIN].
5. [Forthcoming].

2173 **Arslan, Ermanno A.** "Monete Celtiche nella Collezione Numismatica dell'Istituto di Archeologia dell'Università di Pavia." *Rivista Italiana di Numismatica* 70 (1968): 77-92. 2 pls. [CS 5013]

2174 **Bean, Simon C.** "Two Unpublished Types of Celtic Coin." *Celtic Coin Bulletin* (Bulletin of the Celtic Coin Study Group, University of Nottingham) 1 (1991): 7-8. Illus.

Presents line drawings of two struck Celtic coins and discusses their attribution.

2175 **Behrens, Gustav.** *Keltische Goldmünzen.* Mainz, 1955. [CS 5014]

2176 **Brauer, George C.** "Celtic Imitations of Certain Greek Coins." *SAN—Journal of the Society for Ancient Numismatics* 6, no. 4 (summer 1975): 64-6.
Celtic imitations of Greek coins, especially those of Philip II and Alexander III, are discussed and pictured. Argues that the artistic style of Celtic coins should be considered abstract rather than barbaric. Suggests reasons for the choice of designs and includes comments on chronology.

2177 **Burkhardt, A.** *Quantitative Methoden zur Keltischen Numismatik am Beispiel der Münzfunde aus Latènezeitlichen Siedlungen der Oberrheinregion.* Bern, 1998. 108 pp.

2178 **Christ, Karl.** "Ergebnisse und Probleme der Keltischen Numismatik und Geldgeschichte." *Historia* (Germany) 6, no. 2 (1957): 215-53. [CS 5015]

2179 **Colbert de Beaulieu, Jean-Baptists.** *Traité de Numismatique Celtique, Volume 1: Méthodologie des Ensembles.* Centre de Recherches d'Histoire Ancienne 5, Serie Numismatique. Paris, 1973. 354 pp., 8 pls. [CS 5016 and 5126]
[For *Volume 2*, see Scheers under CELTIC COINAGE OF EUROPE. Also see Nash "The Chronology of Celtic Coinage in Gaul" under CELTIC COINAGE OF EUROPE].

2180 ——— "La Numismatique Celtique: État de la Question." *Études Celtiques* 13 (1973): 445-64. [CS 5017]

2181 **Colbert de Beaulieu, Jean-Baptists, and Brigitte Fischer.** *Recueil des Inscriptions Gauloises, Volume IV: Les Légendes Monétaires.* Supplement XLV à Gallia. Paris: CNRS Editions, 1998. 564 pp.
A detailed study of the corpus of Gaulish inscriptions found on coins. [Reviewed by D. Ellis Evans in *Numismatic Chronicle* 159 (1999): 367-72].

2182 **DeJersey, Philip, ed.** *Celtic Coinage: New Discoveries, New Discussion.* Archaeopress, 2006. 260 pp.
The fourteen papers collected in this volume were, with a couple of exceptions, presented at a conference on Celtic coinage held at the Ashmolean Museum and the Institute of Archaeology, Oxford, in December 2001. The papers are "Early Potin Coinage in Britain: An Update" by Colin Haselgrove; "Metaphors, Meaning and Money: Contextualizing Some Symbols on Iron Age Coins" by Miranda Aldhouse-Green; "Coinage and Wine in Gaul" by Brigitte Fischer; "Shamanic Practices and Trance Imagery in the Iron Age" by Mike Williams and John Creighton; "Distribution and Ritual Deposition of Iron Age Coins in the South Midlands" by Mark Curteis; "The Role of Iron Age Coinage in Archaeological Contexts" by Imogen Wellington; "The Impact of the Roman Conquest on Indigenous Coinages in Belgic Gaul and Southern Britain" by Colin Haselgrove; "Belgic Coins in Britain" by Philip de Jersey; "The Belgae in Hampshire" by Robert Van Arsdell; "The Belgae and Regini" by Chris Rudd; "The Silver Coinage of Tasciovanos" by Rainer Kretz; "The Iceni Early Face/Horse Series" by John Talbot; "An Iron Age Coin Weight from Rotherwick, Hampshire" by Jeffrey May; and "The Silsden Hoard: Discovery, Investigation and New Interpretations" by Gavin Edwards and Megan Dennis.

2183 **Fitzpatrick, A., and Vincent Megaw.** "Further Finds from LeCatillon Hoard." *Proceedings of the Prehistoric Society* 53 (1987).

2184 **Gans, Edward.** "A Vindication of the 'Barbarians.'" *The Numismatist* 64, no 6 (June 1951): 612-6. Illus.
Emphasizes that it is incorrect to describe all Celtic issues as barbaric imitations. The Celtic die-cutters derived their types from Greek coins, but they adapted these designs, producing a distinctive coinage.

2185 **Gilkes, Paul.** "Bureau Details Fake Staters: Purported Ancient Gold Pieces Deceptive." *Coin World* (July 11, 2005): 84. Illus.
Summarizes a report from the International Bureau for the Suppression of Counterfeit Coins. The report condemns a group of counterfeit gold staters known as the Cheriton or Cheriton Smiler. The genuine pieces were struck by the Belgae of the Solent hinterland circa 55 to 45 B.C. (Van Arsdell 1215). About forty of the fake pieces have been on the market since about 1991.

2186 **Green, Miranda.** "The Iconography of Celtic Coins." *Celtic Coinage: Britain and Beyond. The Eleventh Oxford Symposium on Coinage and Monetary History.* Edited by Melinda Mays. British Archaeological Reports, No. 222. Oxford, 1992.

2187 **Gruel, Katherine, and Eric Morin.** *Les Monnaies Celtes du Musée de Bretagne.* Paris: Musée de Bretagne, 1999. 206 pp., 58 pls.
An introduction to Celtic coinage and a catalogue of 1600 coins.

2188 **Hooker, John.** "Notes on Part of the LeCatillon Hoard Purchased by the Societé Jersiase in 1989." *Societ Jersiase Annual Bulletin.* 1993.

2189 ——— "Celtic Coin Iconography." *Hekte* (Canada) 4 (2000): 3-13. Illus.
Begins with a discussion of coins finds in Britain, contrasting the coin types found in various regions. Then discusses the changes and evolutions in Celtic coin types and symbols and examines their significance.

2190 **Hunter, Virginia Joyce.** "A Third Century Hoard from Serbia and Its Significance for Celtic History." *Museum Notes* 13 (1967) 17-40. 8 pls. [CS 5019]
Examines a hoard, buried ca. 220 B.C. and found in Serbia in 1924, which is significant for its combination of Greek and Celtic coins. Includes Macedonian and Seleucid coins of various mints as well as Celtic imitations. Forces some revisions to the dating of Celtic coins proposed by Karl Pink.

2191 **Koenig, Marie E. P.** "Celtic Coins: A New Interpretation." *Archaeology* 19, no. 1 (January 1966): 24-30. Illus. [CS 5021]
Attempts to explain the symbolism inherent in the designs of Celtic coins. Illustrates the similarities between Celtic and Greek coin types, but emphasizes the celestial aspects of Celtic art and the use of ideograms of numerical significance in Celtic coin designs. Suggests the coins reflect not merely stylizations of the Greek originals, but newly created types which grew out of Celtic culture.

2192 ——— *L'Enigme des Monnaies Celtiques.* Saarbrücken, 1976-1977. 83 pp., 17 pls. [CS 5024]

2193 **La Baume, Peter.** *Keltische Münzen: Ein Brevier.* Braunschweig, 1960. 52 pp., 20 pls. [CS 5025]

2194 **Laing, Lloyd R.** "Greeks and Barbarians: The Numismatic Evidence for Greek Contact with Barbarian Europe." Parts 1-4. *Voice of the Turtle* 5, no. 1 (January 1966): 5-8; no. 3 (March 1966): 93-4; no. 4 (April 1966): 101-7; no. 5 (May 1966): 133-7. Illus.
Discusses the Auriol hoard, found near Marseille in 1867, containing about 2130 coins. Suggests these coins belong to a period when Massalia was conducting a vigorous trade with the native inhabitants of Gaul and Britain. Discusses Greek trade with Celtic tribes and Britain, and discusses finds of Greek coins in the British Isles. Examines the influence of Greek coin types on the origin of Celtic coinage.

2195 **Leu Numismatics.** "The Celts in Central Europe and the Balkans." *Ancient Coins: Auction Leu 83.* Zurich, 2002. Pages 124-45. Illus.
This catalogue for a May 6-7, 2002 auction contains a significant group of European Celtic coins (lots 468-592). The coins are from a wide area of central Europe, from the Rhineland in Germany to the Danube basin and the south of present-day Bulgaria.

2196 **Mainjonet, Monique.** "Monnaies Celtiques Acquises par le Cabinet des Médailles en 1960." *Revue Numismatique* (France) 6th ser., 3 (1961): 27-31. 1 pl.
Describes coins added to the collection of the Bibliothèque Nationale.

2197 **McIvor, Robert S.** "Astronomical Celtic Coins." *The Numismatist* 112, no. 2 (February 1999): 161-3. Illus.
Plutarch reported that a comet appeared in the sky after Julius Caesar's assassination in 44 B.C. The comet was also recorded in China and Korea. McIvor illustrates a group of Celtic "Yarmouth type" staters of the mid-first century B.C. which he believes illustrate a recognizable comet with a distinctive tail. He suggests these coins document contemporary Celtic observations of the comet of 44 B.C., including its distinctive appearance and sky location.

2198 **Nash, Daphne.** "The Celts." *Coins: An Illustrated Survey 650 B.C. to the Present Day.* Edited by M. J. Price. New York: Methuen, 1980. Pages 75-85. Illus.
An overview of Celtic coinage from its start in the third century B.C. to its end in the mid-first century A.D. Describes the six main regional divisions of Celtic coinage, each based on a different Greek prototype. Discusses the coinage of neighboring non-Celtic communities, the expansion of Celtic coinage in the first century B.C., the introduction of fractional coinage and bronze coinage. Describes the effects of the wars with Rome, including the drastic decrease in precious metal coinage. Reviews the introduction of Celtic coinage into Britain.

2199 ——— *Coinage in the Celtic World.* London: Seaby, 1987. Reprint, London: Spink, 2004. 153 pp., maps, 24 pls.
Thorough coverage of the origins and development of Celtic coinage which flourished between the late fourth century B.C. and the mid-first century A.D. Begins with a discussion of Celtic culture, focusing on the factors which led to the development of Celtic coinage. Stresses that these coins were modeled after those of employers of Celtic mercenaries, such as the coinage of Philip II of Macedon. Roman domination led to increased use of native Celtic imitative coinage. Describes the coinage of Rome's Gallic provinces and the coinage in the free Celtic world, giving extensive historical and cultural background information. Subsequent chapters discuss the Celts and their coinage in and outside of Gaul, and the book concludes with a chapter on Celtic Britain. Illustrates 239 coins on twenty-four plates. [Reviewed by A. Burnett in *Numismatic Chronicle* 148 (1988): 245-6].

2200 **Neupert, Paul E.** "Celtic Coins." *The Anvil* (Canada) 5, no. 6 (November 1, 1995): 65.
Brief introductory comments on Celtic coinage.

2201 **Nick, Michael.** "Economic and Social Patterns in Celtic Coins Use." *Coins in Context I: New Perspectives for the Interpretation of Coin Finds.* Edited by Hans-Markus Kaenel and Maria R.-Alföldi. Studien zu Fundmünzen der Antike, Band 23. Mainz: Philipp von Zabern, 2009. Pages 187 ff.

2202 **Rauch, Hans.** "The Celts and Their Coinage." Parts 1-8. *SAN—Journal of the Society for Ancient Numismatics* 1, no. 1 (July 1969): 6-9; no. 2 (October 1969): 22-3; no. 3 (January 1970): 44-5, 52; no. 4 (April 1970): 64-7; 2, no. 2 (fall 1970): 36-7; no. 3/4 (spring 1971): 56-7, 62; 3, no. 1 (1971-2): 7-8, 16; no. 2 (1971-2): 30-1, 34. Illus.
A detailed history of Celtic civilization and the coinage of Celtic tribes. Includes maps and photographs of coins. Common coin types are described and shown. Part 3 focuses on Iberia, Part 4 on Gaul, Part 5 on the central group, Part 6 on the central and eastern groups, and Part 7 continues the discussion of the eastern group.

2203 ——— "Celtic Imitations of Coins of Philip II and Alexander III." *SAN—Journal of the Society for Ancient Numismatics* 16, no 4 (May 1986): inside covers.
A brief discussion of Celtic art and imitations of the coins of Philip and Alexander.

2204 **Rudd, Chris.** "Growing Demand for Celtic." *The Celator* 15, no. 9 (September 2001): 40, 54. Illus.
Discusses the dramatic increase in demand for Celtic coins in recent years.

2205 ——— "Ring Money Makes Big Money." *The Celator* 18, no. 4 (April 2004): 37-8. Illus.
Discusses examples of Celtic Ring Money which were recently sold at auction. Describes the origin and uses of these unusual pieces.

2206 ——— "What is So Special about Celtic Coins?" *The Celator* 20, no. 11 (November 2006): 33, 39, 56. Illus.
Cites the growing popularity of collecting Celtic coins and reviews some of the reasons collectors are attracted to the series.

2207 ——— "17 Celtic Fakes Found?" *The Celator* 20, no. 5 (May 2006): 34-5. Illus.
Illustrates seventeen counterfeit Celtic coins recently found in an old collection.

2208 **Sellwood, Lyn.** "The Mount Batten Celtic Coins." *Oxford Journal of Archaeology* 2, no. 2 (1983): 199-211.

2209 **Steffgen, U., R. Gebhard, G. Lehrberger, and G. Morteani.** "Platinum Group Metal Inclusions in Celtic Gold Coins." *Metallurgy in Numismatics, Volume 4.* Special Publication No. 30. London: Royal Numismatic Society, 1998. Pages 202-7. Illus.
A study of the presence of natural alloys of platinum group elements in Celtic gold coins. The inclusion of platinum group elements coincides with the sudden increase in the amount of gold in Celtic Europe during the second century B.C. The increase was due to a growth of gold imports rather than an extended exploitation of local deposits.

2210 **Thompson, F. C., and M. J. Nasir.** "The Manufacture of Celtic Coins from the La Marquanderie Hoard." *Numismatic Chronicle* 7th ser., 12 (1972): 61-73. Illus. [CS 5177]
"The evidence produced by normal metallurgical techniques is that the hoard coins were first cast in the form of rondels, then reheated, struck and fairly rapidly cooled. The coins later underwent considerable age hardening." [Thompson and Nasir, *NL* 89]

2211 **Tylecote, R. F.** "The Method of Use of Early Iron-Age Coin Moulds." *Numismatic Chronicle* 7th ser., 2 (1962): 101-9. Illus.
Describes experiments conducted to determine the conditions under which pre-Roman clay moulds were used and the method of producing spherical globules.

2212 **Van Arsdell, Robert D.** "Ancient Forgeries Demonstrate Celts Used Coins as Money." *Spink Numismatic Circular* 94, no. 4 (May 1986): 111-2. Illus.
Debate exists over whether the Celts used coins as money (or merely as gifts and temple donations) and whether forgeries of gold and silver coins are the work of counterfeiters or are products of the official mints. Two forgeries in the author's collection provide evidence that coins were used as money and that counterfeiters made coins for fraudulent use.

2213 ——— "Take Out the Gold, but Keep the Colour." *Spink Numismatic Circular* 96, no. 3 (April 1988): 82-3. Illus.
Discusses the metallurgical changes in Celtic coinage. The Celts removed half the gold from their staters, bit-by-bit, over a one-hundred year period. They concealed this fact by adjusting the other metals in the alloy to keep the color consistent.

2214 ——— "Semiotics of Celtic Coinage." *Spink Numismatic Circular.* 2007+.
A series of papers dealing with the creation of coded messages and their transmission to a knowing audience. The author attempts to understand and interpret the images on Celtic coins.

1. "Ruding's Challenge." 115 (2007): 206. Illus.
2. Uncertain title. 115 (2007): unknown page.
3. "Amalgamation Switchers." 116, no. 1 (February 2008): 4-5. Illus.
4. "Extensions into the Continuum." 116, no. 3 (June 2008): 124-6. Illus.
5. "It's Not Art." 116, no. 4 (August 2008): 194-6. Illus.
6. "Cunobeline's Ship." 117, no. 1 (March 2009): 11-3. Illus.
7. "The Search for Codes." 117, no. 2 (July 2009): 103-5. Illus.
8. "Seeing Past the Die-Cutters." 118, no. 1 (March 2010): 13-5. Illus.

2215 **Van Heesch, Johan, and Inge Heeren, eds.** *Coinage in the Iron Age: Essays in Honour of Simone Scheers.* London: Spink, 2009. 442 pp., illus.
A festschrift containing twenty-eight papers on the coinage of Iron Age Europe. Deals with all aspects of Celtic coinage and covers the Danubian area, Italy, Gaul, and Britain. The papers cover coin production and coining methods, the early gold series, Gallic bronze coins, iconography, circulation of coins, and more. Papers are in English, French, and German. [Reviewed by Chris Rudd in *The Celator* 23, no. 11 (November 2009): 40-2].

2216 **Ziegaus, Bernward.** *Kelten Geld: Sammlung Flesche.* Munich: Staatliche Münzsammlung München, 2010. 311 pp., illus.
An exhibition catalogue featuring Celtic gold coins from the collection of Christian Flesche.

Also see: Cunliffe *Coinage and Society* under CELTIC COINAGE OF BRITAIN; Rudd "Orchid Grower" under MACEDONIAN CITIES AND TRIBES.

CELTIC COINAGE OF BRITAIN

2217 **Akerman, John Yonge.** "Observations on the Coinage of the Ancient Britons." *Numismatic Journal* 1 (1837): 91-5. Illus.
General comments on early coinage in Briton. Akerman criticizes some outlandish theories proposed by earlier writers, and he comments on some coins of Cunobelinus.

2218 ——— "Further Observations on the Coinage of the Ancient Britons." *Numismatic Chronicle* 1 (1839): 73-90. 1 pl.
Addresses whether the early coins found in Britain were minted there or imported from Gaul. Then explores the origins of some of the objects depicted on ancient British coins including the wheel, helmet, sun, moon, and pentagon.

2219 ——— "Ancient British Coins." *American Journal of Numismatics* 9, no. 3 (January 1875): 55-7.
Akerman comments on the origin of coinage in Britain.

2220 **Allan, John.** "Ancient British Coins from Lincolnshire." *Numismatic Chronicle* 6th ser., 7 (1947): 65-8. Illus.
Describes six uninscribed ancient British coins found in 1851. The coins are attributed by Evans numbers (see Evans *The Coins of the Ancient Britons* below). Discusses their types and attributions.

2221 **Allen, Dave.** "Dobunnic Gold Coinage (35 B.C. to 43 A.D.)." *Dean Archaeology* 8 (1995): 34-5. Illus.

2222 ——— "Striking Celtic Coins: Dobunnic Dabblings or Anted Antics." *Dean Archaeology* 9 (1996): 26-7.
"The author discusses experimental production of dies to strike silver, lead, pewter and aluminum copies of Celtic coins." [M. Allen, *NL* 140]

2223 **Allen, Derek F.** "British Tin Coinage of the Iron Age." *Transactions of the International Numismatic Congress Organized and Held in London by the Royal Numismatic Society, June 30-July 3, 1936.* Edited by J. Allan, H. Mattingly, and E. S. G. Robinson. London: B. Quaritch, 1938. Pages 351-7.
Allen discusses the British coinage made of an alloy of tin and copper, modeled on Gallic coins of the first century B.C. He examines the question of the dating of the British coins. Concludes the coins belong to the first quarter of the first century B.C. and are the first coinage ever made in Britain.

2224 ——— "The Belgic Dynasties of Britain and Their Coins." *Archaeologia* 90 (1944): 1-46. 4 pls. [CS 5185]
A catalogue of the coinage of the Belgic tribes in Britain during the period ca. 60 B.C. to A.D. 70. Includes coinage of the following tribes: Artebates and Regni, Catuvellaum, Trinovantes, Cantii, tribes on the border of the Catuvellaum, Durotriges, Dobuni, Iceni, and Brigantes. Illustrates 164 coin-types.

2225 ——— "Three Ancient British Coins." *British Numismatic Journal* 27 (1952-4): 249-55. 1 pl.
Publishes a quinarius with the name Vosenos, a quinarius with the name Epaticcus, and an uninscribed bronze coin. Discusses the attribution of each coin.

2226 ——— "A Fine Ancient British Coin from Colchester." *British Numismatic Journal* 28 (1955-7): 400-3. 1 pl.
Publishes a well-preserved coin which clearly shows the inscription CΛΛL—a monogram of Camulodunum.

2227 ——— "A Contemporary Forgery of a Dobunni Coin from Wiltshire." *British Numismatic Journal* 28 (1955-7): 404.
Announces the finding of a forgery of *Evans* I9.

2228 ——— "A Remarkable Celtic Coin from Canterbury." *British Numismatic Journal* 28 (1955-7): 443-8. Illus.
"A gold coin recently found at Canterbury and acquired by the Canterbury Museum illustrates exceptionally well the perverse processes of early Celtic art. This quarter stater differs only slightly from *Mack* 38. Its obverse, with parallel indentations, is identical; on the reverse of the new coin the engraver has sought, without departing from the spirit of his model, to make sense of it. The writer illustrates and discusses the development of design, making comparison with the trophies of arms on Roman coins." [J. Martin, *NL* 48]

2229 ——— "Belgic Coins as Illustrations of Life in the Late Pre-Roman Iron Age of Britain." *Proceedings of the Prehistoric Society* 24 (1958): 43-63. 10 pls. [CS 5186]
"In endeavoring to show the extent to which these coins provide a visual illustration of life and customs in Britain immediately prior to the Roman conquest, the author employs enlarged reproductions of eighty-three coins to illustrate an intensive study of the following Belgic types: horsemen with carnyx, horsemen with short-sword, horsemen with long-spear, horsemen with javelin, parade horsemen, other horsemen, horse trappings, fighters on foot, helmeted heads, masculine costume, feminine costume, smiths, bowls, musicians, seated figures, and priestly forms. In conclusion, some attention is given to the system of warfare employed in Britain and to the physical appearance of its inhabitants during the period under discussion." [*NL* 50]

2230 ——— "New Light on the Date of Early British Coins: Notes on the LeCatillon, Jersey, Hoard of Armorican Coins." *Spink Numismatic Circular* 66, no. 4 (April 1958): 85-7. Illus.
Discusses a hoard of over 700 coins, mostly Armorican base silver coins

2231 ——— "Some Ancient British Notes: 1. Two Ancient British Coins in Paris; 2. A New Coin of Verulamium; 3. A Rare Coin from Hampshire; 4. A Rare Coin from Peterborough." *British Numismatic Journal* 29 (1958-9): 1-4. 1 pl.
Note 1 presents a previously unpublished bronze of Dubnovellaunus and a specimen of *Mack* 296. Note 2 discusses a new variety of a coin of Verulamium. Note 3 presents a specimen of *Mack* 33, a local variant of the Chute type. Note 4 publishes an uninscribed gold stater, type *Mack* 49.

2232 ——— "The Origins of Coinage in Britain: A Re-appraisal." *Problems of the Iron Age in Southern Britain.* The 11th Occasional Paper of the Institute of Archaeology. Edited by S. S. Frere. London, 1961. Pages 97-308. 14 pls. [CS 5187]
A new assessment of the origin and early progress of ancient Celtic coinage in Britain, prompted by the discovery of the Le Catillon hoard in 1957 and the excavations conducted at Bagendon. Primarily deals with the uninscribed coins. Contains lists and analyses of all known Celtic coin hoards found in Britain and a classified corpus of all provenanced Celtic coins found in the British Isles. [Reviewed by H. Shortt in *Numismatic Chronicle* 7th ser., 1 (1961): 245-6. For additions to Allen's hoard list, see C. Haselgrove *Supplementary Gazetteer*, "Celtic Coins found in Britain 1977-1982," and "Celtic Coins found in Britain 1982-1987" below].

2233 ——— "Celtic Coins." *Ordnance Survey Map of Southern Britain in the Iron Age.* Chessington, Surrey, 1962. Pages 19-22.
A summary of the Celtic coinage of Britain. Includes eight maps indicating the distribution of coins, a concordance of the principal types of uninscribed coins referred to in the text, a chronological table, and tables showing (a) the approximate duration, in Britain, of British and Gallo-Belgic uninscribed coins, and (b) the approximate dates of inscribed British coins. [Summarized from *NL* 70]

2234 ——— "The Haslemere Hoard." *British Numismatic Journal* 31 (1962): 1-7. 1 pl.
Discusses a hoard of uninscribed gold staters found in Britain in about 1944. The hoard included thirty-two Gallo-Belgic types and fifty-two British types. The coins exhibit some unique features. Allen suggests all the coins were the product of one smith or smithy, their most notable feature being the presence of a flattened area of flan around the edge which has not been touched in the course of striking. The weights of the coins are listed and discussed. [Also see D. F. Allen "The Haslemere Hoard Again" below. Robert D. Van Arsdell later determined the hoard to be fake. See Van Arsdell "Yet Another Surprise" and "The Hallmark of the Haslemere Forger" below].

2235 ——— *Sylloge of Coins of the British Isles, Volume 3: The Coins of the Coritani.* London: British Academy, 1963. 44 pp., 8 pls. [CS 5188]

Begins with a discussion of the coin types, weights and specific gravities, the distribution of hoards, mint locations, inscriptions, and dates. Followed by a catalogue of coins from the British Museum and other collections. [Reviewed by S. S. Frere in *Spink Numismatic Circular* 71, no. 4 (April 1963): 77, and by R. A. G. Carson in *Times Literary Supplement* (December 26, 1963): 1071].

2236 ——— "Celtic Coins from the Romano-British Temple at Harlow, Essex." Parts 1-3. *British Numismatic Journal* 33 (1964): 1-6. 1 pl.; 36 (1967): 1-7. 2 pls.; 37 (1968): 1-6. 2 pls.
A catalogue and discussion of the Celtic coins found at the site of the temple.

2237 ——— "A Celtic Miscellany." *British Numismatic Journal* 34 (1965): 1-7. 1 pl.
A group of short notes, primarily discussing coins of the Coritani.

2238 ——— "The Haslemere Hoard Again." *British Numismatic Journal* 35 (1966): 189-90. 1 pl.
Publishes several more coins from the Haslemere Hoard which have recently turned-up (see D. F. Allen "The Haslemere Hoard" above). The author still believes all the coins from the hoard are the product of the same mint. [Robert D. Van Arsdell later determined the hoard to be fake. See Van Arsdell "Yet Another Surprise" and "Hallmark of the Haslemere Forger" below].

2239 ——— "Iron Currency Bars in Britain." *Proceedings of the Prehistoric Society* 33 (1967): 307-35.

2240 ——— "Three Ancient British Notes: A New Coin from Cunetio; A New Uninscribed Silver Type; A New Minim of Verica." *British Numismatic Journal* 36 (1967): 8-10. Illus.
Publishes a new coin from Cunetio, an new uninscribed silver type, and a new minim of Verica.

2241 ——— "Three Notes on Ancient British Coins: Silver Minims Again; A British Silver Coin in Copenhagen? A Quarter Stater from Worcester." *British Numismatic Journal* 37 (1968): 7-9.
Note 1 publishes a new type of silver minim of Verica. Note 2 illustrates a coin from the Royal Danish Cabinet exhibited among the *Galli Incerti*. Allen believes it is probably an unpublished British type. Note 3 announces that a quarter stater specimen of *Mack* 68 has been found at a Dobunnic site. Suggests the coin type is Dobunnic.

2242 ——— "The Coins of the Iceni." *Britannia* 1 (1970): 1-33. Illus., maps, 6 pls.
Gives a full account of the coinage of the Iceni in East Anglia. Recounts the history of the tribe, describes the coinage, and discusses hoards. The distribution of coin finds is indicated on maps. The types of the gold and silver coins are illustrated by drawings. Includes interpretations of the types and discussion of chronology. Includes lists of hoards and find-spots, a table of dies, and notes on metrology. Concludes with a catalogue of the coinage.

2243 ——— "Cunobelin's Gold." *Britannia* 6 (1975): 1-19. 7 pls.
A die study based on 159 staters and 36 quarter-staters. The existence of 69 obverse dies and 90 reverse dies for the stater are proven. Twenty-one obverse dies and 27 reverse dies are determined for the quarter-staters. The coins fall into five distinct series.

2244 **Allen, Derek F., and Colin Haselgrove.** "The Gold Coinage of Verica." *Britannia* 10 (1979): 1-17. 4 pls., 2 maps.
A die-study of the gold coins of Verica. There are four types of stater and eight types of quarter-stater which bear the name of Verica. The authors catalogue and illustrate ninety-three stater varieties and fifty-seven quarter stater varieties. Discusses the types, the quantities minted, metrology, and specific gravities. Includes maps of find-spots and tables indicating die links.

2245 **Allen, Roy.** "A Find of an Early British Quarter Stater." *Seaby Coin and Medal Bulletin* 713 (January 1978): 1. Illus.
Illustrates a base gold quarter stater with a horse's head on the obverse and a reverse similar to Mack 41 and 43, found in Dorset in 1977. [Also see John Cutting "An Early British Quarter Stater" below].

2246 **Andrew, John.** "Iron Age Find Largest British Hoard, Kept Secret for Three Years, Contains Hundreds of 2,000-Year-Old Coins." *Coin World* (April 28, 2003): 1, 30. Illus.
Reports the discovery by amateur archaeologists of the largest hoard of Iron Age gold and silver coins ever found in Britain. The hoard was found in east Leicestershire during 2000. It contained over 3000 coins of the Corieltauvi. A silver-gilded Roman helmet was also found.

2247 ——— "Iron Age Gold Coin Hoard Largest in 160 Years." *Coin World* (February 9, 2009): 1, 18. Illus.
A report of a find of 825 gold staters of the Iceni, minted ca. 40 B.C. to A.D. 15., found in southeast Suffolk in 2008. All the coins are uninscribed with various obverse types and a horse as the predominant reverse type. The hoard was likely buried ca. A.D. 15-20. [Also see Rudd "Kings Gold" below].

2248 ——— "British Treasure Finders Dispute Split of Iron Age Gold Staters." *Coin World* (August 10, 2009): 60. Illus.
A report on an ownership dispute related to a hoard of 825 gold staters found in 2008 near Woodbridge, Suffolk. The find represents the largest Iron Age hoard to have been discovered since 1849. Most of the coins are of the uninscribed types produced by the Iceni from 40 BC to AD 15.

2249 "Baby Wolf found in Norfolk." *The Celator* 16, no. 1 (January 2002): 18. Illus.
A report from Chris Rudd that an extremely rare Celtic gold coin was found in Norfolk. It is a Norfolk Wolf type gold quarter stater, struck ca. 65-55 B.C. by the Eceni tribe. It features a stylized wolf on the reverse.

2250 **Baldwin, Agnes.** "An Ancient British Quarter-Stater found at Irstead, Suffolk." *British Numismatic Journal* 27 (1952-4): 88. 1 pl.
Publishes a coin of the Iceni.

2251 **Bean, Simon C.** "The 'Sons of Commius' Reconsidered." *Celtic Coin Bulletin* (Bulletin of the Celtic Coin Study Group, University of Nottingham) 1 (1991): 1-6. Illus.
Examines the coins of the three leaders of the Atrebates and Regni, who shared the abbreviated forms of the patronymic "Commi filius"—sons of Commius.

2252 ——— "British Celtic Coins Added to the Finney Collection, 1991: Some Further Observations." *Spink Numismatic Circular* 100, no. 9 (November 1992): 303.
Some comments on the coins of the Finney collection published by David Symons (see Symons "Finney Collection, 1991" below).

2253 ——— "Early British Celtic Staters: British A (*VA* 200-1, 202-1) and British C (*VA* 1220)." *Spink Numismatic Circular* 101, no. 8 (October 1993): 286-8. Map.
The author comments on some early staters.

2254 ——— "The Earliest Staters from the Area of the Dobunni?" *British Numismatic Journal* 64 (1994): 126-7. Illus.
"During a study of British Qb a small but discrete group of staters became apparent. These coins have a discrete metrology, typology and composition. The provenanced specimens also reveal a distinct distribution which is centered on the territory of the Dobunni. The newly identified type is clearly the typological forerunner of British Ra, which has traditionally been recognized as the earliest stater from the area. The new type would appear to be an earlier issue." [S. Bean, *NL* 136]

2255 ——— "A New Stater of the Iceni?" *Spink Numismatic Circular* 104, no. 8 (October 1996): 367. Illus.
Publishes the core of a plated Celtic stater of a new type. It appears to belong to the Icenian uninscribed series.

2256 ——— "Tincomaros but no Tincommius: Clearing the Atrebatic Waters." *Spink Numismatic Circular* 105, no. 7 (September 1997): 238-9. Illus.
Discusses coins attributed to Tincomaros and Tincommius. Concludes that the name Tincommius can be discarded.

2257 ——— *The Coinage of the Atrebates and Regni.* Studies in Celtic Coinage No. 4. Oxford University School of Archaeology Monograph 50. Oxford, 2000. 303 pp., 15 pls.
A detailed study of the late Iron Age coinage from south of the Thames. Begins with a history of the study of this coinage. Includes a catalogue of coins and an examination of the dies. Provides some historical conclusions based on the study of the coins. [Reviewed by Megan Dennis in *Numismatic Chronicle* 163 (2003): 408-10].

2258 **Bone, Anne, and Andrew M. Burnett.** "The 1986 Selsey Treasure Trove." *British Numismatic Journal* 56 (1986): 178-80.
Catalogues and discusses seventeen gold and silver late Iron Age coins found on the coast of Selsey in 1986. Includes anonymous issues as well as issues of Eppillus, Verica, Epaticcus, and Caratacus.

2259 **Booth, James.** *Sylloge of Coins of the British Isles, Volume 48: Northern Museums: Ancient British, Anglo-Saxon, Norman and Plantagenet Coins to 1279.* London: Oxford University Press, and Spink & Son, 1997. 283 pp., 64 pls.
Plates 1 through 5 illustrate coins minted by Celtic tribes in Britain. [Reviewed by J. C. Moesgaard in *Nordisk Numismatisk Unions Medlemsblad* (Denmark) 2 (1998): 25].

2260 **Briggs, Daphne, Colin Haselgrove, and Cathy E. King.** "Iron Age and Roman Coins from Hayling Island Temple." *British Numismatic Journal* 62 (1992): 1-62. 7 pls.
Discusses a hoard of 151 Iron Age coins and 152 Roman coins found during excavations 1976-82. Includes a catalogue of the coins.

2261 **Briscoe, Lady, R. A. G. Carson, and R. H. M. Dolley.** "An Icenian Coin Hoard from Lakenheath, Suffolk." *British Numismatic Journal* 29 (1958-9): 215-9.
Lists the coins found in the Roman field at Lakenheath. Includes 415 ancient British coins, all but two of which are Icenian.

2262 **Brooke, G. C.** "A Small Hoard of British or Gaulish Coins Found near Rochester." *Numismatic Chronicle* 5th ser., 3 (1923): 156.
Lists eleven gold coins found in England. All are of the type *Evans* plate B, no. 7. They were probably struck in Gaul.

2263 ——— "Two Finds of Ancient British Coins." *Numismatic Chronicle* 5th ser., 7 (1927): 370-7. 2 pls.
Lists and discusses fourteen Celtic gold coins found in England.

2264 ——— "The Philippus in the West and the Belgic Invasions of Britain." *Numismatic Chronicle* 5th ser., 13 (1933): 88-138. 3 pls., 9 maps.
Discusses the introduction of coins of Philip of Macedon into Rome, and the introduction of Gaulish coins into Britain. Then discusses the introduction and use of Belgic coins in Britain.

2265 ——— "The Distribution of Gaulish and British Coins in Britain." *Antiquity* 7 (1933): 268-89.

2266 **Burgon, Thomas.** "On a Mode of Ascertaining the Places to Which Ancient British Coins Belong." *Numismatic Chronicle* 1 (1839): 36-53.
Burgon theorizes that it is likely that one could determine the place of minting of ancient British coins by keeping track of where the coins are found. And because the circulation of the coins tended to be limited and local, the coins likely were minted near where they are found. He suggests this method will be especially useful in identifying the uninscribed coins. He urges the cooperation of all in recording such find data.

2267 **Burnett, Andrew M.** "A New Iron Age Issue from Near Chichester." *Spink Numismatic Circular* 100, no. 10 (December 1992): 340-2. Illus.
A catalogue of some recent finds. The evidence of these coins allows some unpublished issues of bronze coins to be attributed to Iron Age Britain.

2268 ——— "Celtic Coinage in Britain, III: The Waltham St. Lawrence Treasure Trove." *British Numismatic Journal* 60 (1990): 13-28. 6 pls.
Discusses a hoard found in 1977 in Berkshire including the contents, metrology of the coins, and date of deposit (probably ca. A.D. 69). Includes a catalogue of the coins.

2269 ——— "Somerton, Suffolk, Treasure Trove." *British Numismatic Journal* 64 (1994): 127-8. 1 pl.
A catalogue and brief discussion of the thirty-one gold staters of Cunobelin found in 1990 in Suffolk.

2270 **Burnett, Andrew M., and Michael R. Cowell.** "Celtic Coinage in Britain II." *British Numismatic Journal* 58 (1988): 1-10. 9 pls.
Publishes some recently discovered hoards and provides information on the metallic composition of these and similar coins. [Also see Cowell, Oddy, and Burnett "Celtic Coinage in Britain" below].

2271 **Carlyon-Britton, P. W. P.** "Attribution of the Ancient British Coins Inscribed DIAS or DEAS." *British Numismatic Journal* 8 (1911): 1-7. Illus.
The author suggests the full-reading of the subject coins is DEASCIO, and attributes these coins to Tasciovan or Theasciovan, father of Cunobeline.

2272 **Carson, R. A. G.** "Ancient British Silver Coins from Chichester." *British Numismatic Journal* 45 (1975): 92-3. 1 pl.
Publishes nine coins found during excavations at Chichester during 1968-73. The coins are mostly minims of the last decades of ancient British coinage before the Roman conquest in A.D. 43. Includes coins of the Atrebates and Regni, the Cantii, and the Catuvellauni.

2273 **Chadburn, Amanda.** "A Hoard of Iron Age Silver Coins from Fring, Norfolk, and Some Observations on the Icenian Coin Series." *British Numismatic Journal* 60 (1990): 1-12. 6 pls.
Discusses a hoard of 153 coins of the Iceni found in 1990, including the archaeological context, composition of the hoard, and the date of deposit (mid-first century A.D.).

2274 ——— "Some Observations on the Icenian Uninscribed Gold Series." *Celtic Coin Bulletin* (Bulletin of the Celtic Coin Study Group, University of Nottingham) 1 (1991): 9-13.
Brief comments on the Icenian uninscribed gold series. Includes a table illustrating the main distinguishing characteristics of the coins.

2275 ——— "New Links between the Icenian Coins of AESV and SAENV." *Celtic Coin Bulletin* (Bulletin of the Celtic Coin Study Group, University of Nottingham) 1 (1991): 14-8.
Discusses the rare silver issues bearing the inscriptions AESV and SAENV.

2276 "Chris Rudd Pays £7000 for Celtic Gold Stater." *The Celator* 15, no. 3 (March 2001): 49-50. Illus.
Announces that coin dealer Chris Rudd purchased a rare Celtic coin that was struck in Norwich. The coin is a late Iron Age gold stater inscribed ECE which was minted by the Eceni tribe of East Anglia around A.D. 1-43. The obverse features three crescent moons forming a hidden face. The reverse features a Celtic-style horse and the inscription ECE.

2277 **Clarke, R. Rainbird.** "A Hoard of Silver Coins of the Iceni from Honingham, Norfolk." *British Numismatic Journal* 28 (1955-7): 1-10. 1 pl. Map.
A hoard of 340 silver coins of the Iceni were found in Norfolk. The author discusses this hoard and similar finds and their chronology. Lists find-spots of Icenian coins.

2278 "Coin Moulds of Early British Tribe Found." *Spink Numismatic Circular* 72, no. 10 (October 1964): 234.
Reports the finding of coin moulds and crucible fragments at the location of a mint of the Coritani tribe.

2279 "Coin of Dubnovellaunus from Colchester." *Spink Numismatic Circular* 88, no. 5 (May 1980): 172. Illus.
Publishes a bronze coin of Dubnovellaunus (*Mack* 278).

2280 "Coins of Boadicea's Tribe Unearthed." *Spink Numismatic Circular* 62, nos. 8-9 (August-September 1954): 337.
Reports that a hoard of over 300 coins of the Iceni tribe was found in Norfolk.

2281 **Cottam, Elizabeth, Philip de Jersey, Chris Rudd, and John Sills.** *Ancient British Coins.* Norfolk: Chris Rudd, 2010. 256 pp., illus.
A catalogue of 999 iron-age coin types from Britain, including 418 new types not shown in Van Arsdell's *Celtic Coinage of Britain*. Each type is described and dated, and additional references are provided for each. The coin types were compiled from the 45,000 coins recorded in the Celtic Coin Index at the Institute of Archaeology at the University of Oxford. Includes estimates of rarity. Each coin is illustrated twice actual size. Includes 4000 photos, other illustrations, diagrams, tables, and maps. [Reviewed by Mike Markowitz in *The Celator* 25, no. 9 (September 2011): 4].

2282 **Cottam, G. L.** "A Possible Minim Coinage of VEP CORF." *Spink Numismatic Circular* 100, no. 9 (November 1992): 305. Illus.
Publishes a new denomination of the Corieltauvi—a lightweight fractional silver unit.

2283 ——— "*Van Arsdell* Type 355: Commius or Tincommios?" *Spink Numismatic Circular* 100, no. 9 (November 1992): 303. Illus.
Publishes a new variant of the silver unit (*Van Arsdell* 355) on which the "E symbol" is replaced by the letters TIN.

2284 ——— "Further Confirmation of a Kentish Alliance? Light Shed by a New Bronze Unit of Verica." *British Numismatic Journal* 66 (1996): 113-6. Illus.
"Until recently, all recorded British Iron Age coins of Verica were of gold or silver and their provenances suggested that he ruled a region around Hampshire, although the style and provenances of rare coins combining his name with those of Epillus and Tincomarus prompted the hypothesis that the three had formed an alliance in Kent. The recent discovery of a bronze coin bearing the name of Verica and stylistically similar to bronze coins current in Kent provides further evidence of his influence there." [G. Cottam, *NL* 140]

2285 ——— "An Overstruck Silver Unit of Verica." *British Numismatic Journal* 67 (1997): 95-7. Illus.

"The first evidence for inscribed British Celtic coins being overstruck in antiquity has recently been identified on a silver unit of Verica. The order in which two of Verica's coins were struck on this coin confirms the sequence proposed for these issues. The existence of such a coin suggests a greater sophistication in the use of Iron Age coinage than previously suspected." [G. Cottam, *NL* 142]. The undertype is *Van Arsdell* 471-1.

2286 **Cowell, Michael R.** "An Analytical Survey of British Celtic Gold Coinage." *Celtic Coinage: Britain and Beyond. The Eleventh Oxford Symposium on Coinage and Monetary History.* Edited by Melinda Mays. British Archaeological Reports, No. 222. Oxford, 1992. Pages 207-33.

2287 **Cowell, Michael R., W. A. Oddy, and Andrew M. Burnett.** "Celtic Coinage in Britain: New Hoards and Recent Analyses." *British Numismatic Journal* 57 (1987): 1-23. 7 pls.
Publishes information on seven hoards of early British currency found recently (Gallo-Belgic E, British B, and Durotrigan coinage). Also discusses the metal analysis carried out on some of these coins and similar coins. Provides tables showing the metallic content of the coins. [Also see Burnett and Cowell "Celtic Coinage in Britain II" above].

2288 **Creighton, John.** "The Decline and Fall of the Icenian Monetary System." *Celtic Coinage: Britain and Beyond. The Eleventh Oxford Symposium on Coinage and Monetary History.* Edited by Melinda Mays. British Archaeological Reports, No. 222. Oxford, 1992. Pages 83-92.
Creighton explores the Icenian coinage in the decades before the Boudiccan Revolt.

2289 ——— *Coins and Power in Late Iron Age Britain.* Cambridge: University Press, 2000. 266 pp., illus., maps.
Creighton traces the rise to dominance of the Celtic dynasties in southeast Britain. His focus is on the perceptions of individuals in the Iron Age, and the nature of their authority and power. Discusses the nature and interpretation of imagery and how it was used by individuals to shape people's thoughts and deeds. Coinage provides the central material for this discussion. Creighton concludes that many of the changes in Britain were the direct consequence of a series of individuals redefining their power in the light of the development of the Principate. The book contains many new theories regarding the Celtic people and their coinages. Illustrates 246 Celtic coins. [Reviewed by Richard Hobbs in *Numismatic Chronicle* 161 (2001): 364-8, and by P. DeJersey in *American Journal of Archaeology* 109, no. 1 (January 2005): 121-2. Also see the review article by Chris Rudd, "Were Celtic Moneyers on Drugs?" below].

2290 **Cuddeford, Michael J.** "A New Variety of Cunobelin Quarter-Stater." *Spink Numismatic Circular* 102, no. 7 (September 1994): 305. Illus.
Publishes a quarter-stater attributed to Cunobelin. [See next article for another specimen].

2291 ——— "Cunobelin 'AGR' Variety Confirmed." *Spink Numismatic Circular* 103, no. 1 (February 1995): 5. Illus.
Publishes another example of the Cunobelin quarter-stater variety which the author previously discovered (see Cuddeford "A New Variety" above). This specimen confirms that the symbol below the exergual line is indeed a barred "A."

2292 ——— "A Tasciovanus Quarter-Stater." *Spink Numismatic Circular* 106, no. 1 (February 1998): 7. Illus.
Publishes a new specimen of *Van Arsdell* 1688 with a partial legend visible.

2293 **Cunliffe, Barry, ed.** *Coinage and Society in Britain and Gaul: Some Current Problems.* Research Report, No. 38. London: The Council for British Archaeology, 1981. 94 pp., illus. [CS 5190]
A collection of essays focusing on the Celtic coinage of Britain. Includes "Early Greek Coinage and the Influence of the Athenian State" by K. Rutter [4100], "Coinage and State Development in Central Gaul" by D. Nash [2587], "The Origins and Evolution of Coinage in Belgic Gaul" by S. Scheers [2613], "Roman Monetary Impact on the Celtic World—Thoughts and Problems" by Richard Reece, "Money and Society in Pre-Roman Britain" by Barry Cunliffe, "The Origins of Coinage in Britain" by J. P. C. Kent, "Lost and Found: the Archaeology of Find-Spots of Celtic Coins" by Warwick Rodwell, "Coinage Oppida, and the Rise of Belgic Power: A Reply" by John Collis, "Iron Age Coinage: A Counter Reply" by Warwick Rodwell, "A Computer-Based Information Storage and Retrieval Scheme for Iron Age Coin Finds in Britain?" by Colin Haselgrove and John Collis. Also includes thirty-one maps of Celtic coin find-spots in Britain.

2294 **Cunliffe, Barry, and Philip DeJersey.** *Armorica and Britian: Cross-Channel Relationships in the Late First Millennium BC.* Studies in Celtic Coinage No. 3. Oxford: University Press, 1997. 117 pp., illus.
The first section examines maritime intercourse between Armorica and southern Britain in the late Iron Age. The second part presents a discussion of Armorican coins in Britain.

2295 "Cunobelin Gold Stater Fetches £3000 in Rudd Sale." *The Celator* 16, no. 2 (February 2002): 41. Illus.
Announces that an extremely rare Celtic gold stater of King Cunobelin, with the horse facing left instead of right, was recently sold by Chris Rudd for £3000. Only ten other specimens of this type are recorded.

2296 **Curteis, Mark.** "An Analysis of the Circulation Patterns of Iron Age Coins from Northamptonshire." *Britannia* 27 (1996): 17-42.
Lists the Iron Age coins found in Northamptonshire by metal detectorists. Shows the find-spots and discusses circulation patterns.

2297 **Cutting, John.** "An Early British Quarter Stater." *Seaby Coin and Medal Bulletin* 716 (April 1978): 105. Illus.
Refers to Roy Allen's note (see above) on a coin which Cutting believes belongs to Derek Allen's class "British O." Suggests the obverse is derived from the Roman "wolf and twins" didrachm (Sydenham S6) of ca. 250 B.C.

2298 **DeJersey, Philip.** "A New Quarter Stater for British G?" *Spink Numismatic Circular* 101, no. 7 (September 1993): 236-7. Illus.
Publishes eleven coins with types similar to British G.

2299 ——— "Some Modern Corieltauvian Forgeries." *Spink Numismatic Circular* 101, no. 10 (December 1993): 347-8. Illus.
Publishes some new examples of modern forgeries of Corieltauvian gold staters.

2300 ———— "A New Celtic Minim." *Spink Numismatic Circular* 103, no. 3 (April 1995): 89-90. Illus.
Publishes a previously unknown type of Celtic minim with *obv*., wreathed head; *rev*., horse facing right. Discusses the coin's attribution and tentatively assigns it to Eppillus, leader of the Atrebates.

2301 ———— *Celtic Coinage in Britain.* Buckinghamshire: Shire Publications Ltd., 1996. Reprint, 2001. 56 pp., illus.
An introduction to the Celtic coinage struck in Britain. The chapters are: Coinage in Celtic Society, Techniques of Manufacture, The Introduction of Coinage to Britain, The First British Coinages, Coinage South of the Thames, Coinage North of the Thames, The Western Periphery, The Northern Periphery, Further Reading, and Places to Visit.

2302 ———— "The Savernake Stater (British MB) and a New, Associated Quarter Stater." *Spink Numismatic Circular* 104 (1996): 161-3. Illus.
Discusses the savernake stater (Allen's MB) and publishes a newly discovered quarter stater which appears to be related to the stater type.

2303 ———— "Cast Away Riches: Estimating the Volume of Celtic Coinage found in Britain." *Yorkshire Numismatist* 3 (1997): 1-13.

2304 ———— "SA and SAM: One and the Same?" *Spink Numismatic Circular* 105, no. 7 (September 1997): 114-5. Illus., 2 maps.
A bronze coin with the inscription SAM adds another letter to the bronze units previously known with the legend SA. The coins were issued by an unidentified ruler. [Also see Holman "Three Further Coins of SAM" below].

2305 ———— "Abingdon Zoo: A New Celtic Silver Unit from Berkshire." *Spink Numismatic Circular* 106, no. 4 (May 1998): 150-1. Illus.
Publishes four coins, examines their apparent links to a bronze issue from Belgic Gaul, and suggests they may be the product of a previously unidentified coin-issuing authority in Berkshire and South Oxfordshire.

2306 ———— "The Stater of Volisios Cartivellaunos." *Spink Numismatic Circular* 107, no. 7 (September 1999): 208-9. Illus.
Publishes a coin which confirms the reading of the reverse legend of *Van Arsdell* 993-1 as CARTIVELLAVNOS.

2307 ———— "A Hoard of Iron Age Coins from Near Woodbridge, Suffolk." *British Numismatic Journal* 70 (2000): 139-41.

2308 ———— "Biga and Better: Cunobelin's First Gold." *Chris Rudd List* 54 (2000): 2-3.

2309 ———— "Iron Age Currency Bars." *Chris Rudd List 50* (2000): 2-4.

2310 ———— "Cunobelin's Silver." *Britannia* 32 (2001): 1-44. Illus.
Examines Cunobelin's silver coinage to identify possible distinct phases of development of the coinage and any regional traits. Also examines coinage production at Verulamium during Cunobelin's reign. Reviews the various choices of classical prototype for the coinage.

2311 ———— "Two Celtic Oddities." *Spink Numismatic Circular* 110 (2002): 264. Illus.

2312 ———— "Deliberate Defacement of British Iron Age Coinage." *Iron Age Coinage and Ritual Practices.* Edited by Colin Haselgrove and David Wigg-Wolf. Studien zu Fundmünzen der Antike Band 20. Mainz: Akademie der Wissenschaften und der Literatur, 2005.
Argues that cuts on the coins were done for ritualistic purposes.

2313 **DeJersey, Philip, and John Newman.** "Staters of Cunobelin from Shotley, Suffolk." *British Numismatic Journal* 65 (1995): 214-5. 1 pl.
"This paper records the discovery of six coins between 1980 and 1984 which probably represent all or part of a scattered hoard. Staters of Cunobelin occur only rarely in hoards, and this find is further distinguished by the inclusion of examples of Allen's wild, classic and plastic series, which have only once before been discovered in combination." [DeJersey and Newman, *NL* 140]

2314 ———— "Iron Age Coins from Barham, Suffolk." *British Numismatic Journal* 67 (1997): 93-5. 1 pl., map.
Seven silver units of the "Bury" type and a gold stater were found between 1990-96 in Suffolk. The coins are listed and discussed.

2315 **DeJersey, Philip, and N. Wickenden.** "A Hoard of Staters of Cunobelin and Dubnovellaunos from Great Waltham, Essex." *British Numismatic Journal* 74 (2004): 175-8. Illus.

2316 **Dolley, R. H. M.** "The Gold Coinage of the Mythical King Lucius." *British Numismatic Journal* 27 (1952-4): 354-8. Illus.
Discusses a coin once thought to have been struck by King Lucius, a mythical Christian prince who is reputed to have ruled Britain, under Roman suzerainty, in the second century A.D. The coin is identified as a Gallic stater of the Antecavi or Andecavi.

2317 ———— "Grimsby Treasure Trove (1954)." *Numismatic Chronicle* 6th ser., 15 (1955): 242-3. Illus.
Reports the find of four gold "Morinic" coins of ca. 70 B.C.

2318 ———— "A Surface Find of Three Silver Coins of the Dobuni." *British Numismatic Journal* 28 (1955-7): 403. 1 pl.
Illustrates three coins found near Chippenham: a specimen of *Mack* 387 and two specimens of *Mack* 382.

2319 **Dunger, G. T.** "Unrecorded Celtic Quarter Staters from the Winchester Area." *Spink Numismatic Circular* 107, no. 8 (October 1999): 247. Illus.
Publishes three gold quarter staters of a previously unknown variety. Dunger attributes the coins to the Atrebates of the south Thames area, ca. 50-38 B.C.

2320 **Evans, John.** "On a Gold Coin of Epaticcus." *Numismatic Chronicle* 20 (1858): 1-8. Illus.
Illustrates a gold coin, recently found, with the obverse legend TASCI F and the reverse legend EPATICCV. Evans suggests Epaticcus was a British prince.

2321 ——— "On Some Coins of Tasciovanus, with the Legend VER BOD." *Numismatic Chronicle* 20 (1858): 57-65. Illus.
Suggests the legend may be the abbreviated name for a town.

2322 ——— *The Coins of the Ancient Britons.* London: J. Russell Smith, 1864. 427 pp., 26 pls., map. [CS 5191]
A comprehensive guide to the ancient coins struck in Britain. Evans begins with a review of prior scholarship regarding this series of coinage. He then discusses the origin of coinage in Britain, the development of coin types, minting methods, and the relevant terminology. A detailed discussion of the coin types follows. The catalogue begins with the uninscribed coins arranged by metal (gold, silver, copper, and tin). The inscribed coins are then presented, arranged by minting district (Western, South Eastern, Kentish, Central, Eastern, and uncertain) and then by tribe or issuing authority. The plates contain line engravings of coins. [Also see *Supplement* below for additional issues].

2323 ——— "Note on a Hoard of Ancient British Coins found at Santon Downham, Suffolk." *Numismatic Chronicle* new ser., 9 (1869): 319-26.
Discusses a hoard of 109 coins, mostly Celtic.

2324 ——— "The Coinage of the Ancient Britons and Natural Selection." *Proceedings of the Royal Society.* London, 1875. Pages 476-87.
The text of a talk in which Evans suggests "the succession of the types of the coins followed certain laws, to a great extent analogous with those by which the evolution of successive forms of organic life appear to be governed." He states that the reduction of a complicated and artistic design into a symmetrical figure of easy execution was the object of each successive engraver of the dies.

2325 ——— *The Coins of the Ancient Britons—Supplement.* London: B. Quaritch, 1890. Includes pages 417-599. 10 pls. [CS 5191]
Primarily lists new specimens which have come to light since the original 1864 catalogue was published (see above). Continues the pagination and plate numbering of the original volume. Includes a map of Britain showing the find-spots of the inscribed British coins. [Reviewed by B. V. Head in *Numismatic Chronicle* 3rd ser., 10 (1890): 330-2].

2326 ——— "Note on a Gold Coin of Addedomaros." *Numismatic Chronicle* 4th ser., 2 (1902): 11-19. Illus.
Publishes a coin of Addedomaros, a British prince. Discusses the coinage of this ruler and lists the find-spots of his known coins.

2327 "Finds: Treasure Trove." *Spink Numismatic Circular* 9 (January 1901): 4417.
Discusses a hoard of Celtic gold coins found at Leighton Buzzard.

2328 **Fischer, Calista.** "Interpreting Celtic River Findings." *The Celator* 14, no. 11 (November 2000): 27-8, 34-7. Illus.
In response to Chris Rudd's previous article (see Rudd "Celtic Currency Bars found in River" below), Fischer seeks to provide a better understanding of river findings and aspects of Celtic sacrificial practices. She finds no evidence pointing to the sacred nature of rivers. Some river finds represent a sacrifice to a war god. Others are non-religious in nature.

2329 **Gray, P. H. K.** "Ancient British Coins from the Upchurch Marshes, Kent." *British Numismatic Journal* 27 (1952-4): 211.
Lists some ancient British coins found at Burntwick Island and Birdcage Marsh.

2330 **Grierson, Philip.** *Sylloge of Coins of the British Isles, Volume 1: Ancient British and Anglo-Saxon Coins in the Fitzwilliam Museum, Cambridge.* London: Oxford University Press, 1958. 70 pp., 32 pls. [CS 5192]
Catalogues 216 ancient British and 777 Anglo-Saxon coins, including coins of the Bellovaci, Artrebates, and related Gaulish tribes. All coins are illustrated. [Reviewed by D. M. Metcalf in *Spink Numismatic Circular* 67, no. 1 (January 1959): 10].

2331 **Grinsell, L. V.** "A Gold Stater from Gloucestershire." *British Numismatic Journal* 27 (1952-4): 88-9. Illus.
Publishes a gold stater of the Dobunni.

2332 ——— "An Inscribed Gold Stater of the Dobunni from King's Weston, Bristol." *British Numismatic Journal* 28 (1955-7): 175. 1 pl.
Discusses a coin bearing the inscription ANTEDRIG. The type resembles *Mack* 386.

2333 **Grove, L. R. A.** "Ancient British Tin Coin from Canterbury." *British Numismatic Journal* 26 (1949-51): 94.
A coin of type *Evans* H8 was found in Canterbury.

2334 **Gunstone, A. J. H.** *Sylloge of Coins of the British Isles, Volume 17: Ancient British, Anglo-Saxon and Norman Coins in Midland Museums.* London: British Academy, 1971. 66 pp., 30 pls. [CS 5193]
Plates 1 and 2 illustrate coins minted by Celtic tribes in Britain.

2335 ——— *Sylloge of Coins of the British Isles, Volume 24: Ancient British, Anglo-Saxon and Norman Coins in West Country Museums.* London: British Academy, 1977. 99 pp., 35 pls. [CS 5194]
Plates 1 through 8 illustrate coins minted by Celtic tribes in Britain.

2336 **Haselgrove, Colin.** *Supplementary Gazetteer of Find-Spots of Celtic Coins in Britain, 1977.* Occasional Paper, No. 11a. London: Institute of Archaeology, 1978. 136 pp. [CS 5195]
A supplement to Derek Allen's list of Celtic coin hoards (see Allen "Origins of Coinage in Britain: A Re-appraisal" above), bringing the list up-to-date. [Also see Haselgrove's 1977-1982 update below].

2337 ——— "The Find-spot of the Alresford Hoard." *British Numismatic Journal* 50 (1980): 131-2.
In 1880, a hoard of gold coins of Verica was supposedly found near Alresford in Hampshire. Doubts exist over the find-spot. Haselgrove suggests that a hoard was found at Bentworth in 1879 and that this may be the same as the "Alresford" hoard—but the matter must remain open to debate.

2338 —— "Celtic Coins found in Britain 1977-1982." *University of London, Institute of Archaeology Bulletin* 20 (1984): 107-54.
The second supplement to Derek Allen's list of Celtic coin hoards (see Allen "Origins of Coinage in Britain: A Re-appraisal" above), bringing the list up-to-date. [Also see Haselgrove's *Supplementary Gazetteer* above, and his 1982-1987 update below].

2339 —— "Celtic Coins found in Britain 1982-1987." *University of London, Institute of Archaeology Bulletin* 26 (1984): 1-75.
The third supplement to Derek Allen's list of Celtic coin hoards (see Allen "Origins of Coinage in Britain: A Re-appraisal" above), bringing the list up-to-date. [Also see Haselgrove's *Supplementary Gazetteer* and his 1977-1982 update above].

2340 —— *Iron Age Coinage in South-East England.* BAR 174. Oxford: British Archaeological Reports, 1987. 2 vols., 524 pp.
Volume 1 includes chapters on the history of the study of British Iron Age coinage, analytical procedures, chronology, the interpretation of coin losses, and patterns of coin losses. Volume 2 is a listing of hoards and coins from archaeological sites. [Reviewed by A. Burnett in *Numismatic Chronicle* 148 (1988): 245-6].

2341 —— "The Archaeology of British Potin Coinage." *Archaeological Journal* 145 (1988): 99-122. 4 maps.
Reviews the origins, chronology, and changing circulation pattern of the potin coinage of Iron Age Britain. Archaeological evidence suggests that British potins were made in north Kent from the later second century to the late first century B.C. although potins continued in circulation after this. They were the first indigenous coinage, apparently copying cast central Gaulish imitations of the struck bronze coinage of Massalia, and possibly originated in the Medway area. Initially, potins circulated alongside the imported Gallo-Belgic coinages and, like them, were probably used as a form of primitive valuable. But in the mid-to-later first century, their circulation pattern and function changed, becoming closely associated with a network of major sites spanning both sides of the Thames estuary and with the later Iron Age developments which accompanied this, notably the elaboration of the well-known "Aylesford Complex." Appendices list stratified coins and sites with potin finds.

2342 —— "The Development of British Iron-Age Coinage." *Numismatic Chronicle* 153 (1993): 31-63. 2 pls.
Reviews recent research related to the development of coinage in Britain. Also draws attention to new work on coin circulation from a quantitative perspective.

2343 —— "Coinage and Currency in Iron Age Wessex." *The Iron Age in Wessex: Recent Work.* Edited by A. P. Fitzpatrick and E. L. Morris. 1994. Pages 22-5. Illus.

2344 **Haselgrove, Colin, and David Wigg-Wolf, eds.** *Iron Age Coinage and Ritual Practices.* Studien zu Fundmünzen der Antike Band 20. Mainz: Akademie der Wissenschaften und der Literatur, 2005. 418 pp.
A collection of seventeen papers from a conference.

2345 **Hedges, E. S., and D. A. Robins.** "Examination of an Ancient British Bronze Coin." *Numismatic Chronicle* 7th ser., 3 (1963): 233-6. Illus.
Presents the results of a metallurgical analysis of so-called "tin" coins. Concludes these coins were cast from an alloy of about 25% tin and 75% copper.

2346 **Henig, Martin.** "The Origin of Some Ancient British Coin Types." *Britannia* 3 (1972): 209-23.
Henig examines the Celtic coins of Britain in an attempt to find prototypes from the Mediterranean world for their types. Parallels are found in engraved gems.

2347 **Heywood, N., et al.** "Illustrations of the Coinage: Ancient British Coins." *British Numismatic Journal* 1 (1903-4): 355-8. 1 pl.
Illustrates and describes twenty-eight Celtic coins.

2348 **Hill, George F.** "A Find of Ancient British Gold Coins." *Numismatic Chronicle* 4th ser., 19 (1919): 172-8. 1 pl.
Publishes a group of coins of the Bellovaci from the collection of John Evans. Discusses their weights.

2349 **Hingley, R.** "Iron Age 'Currency Bars': The Archaeological and Social Context." *Archaeological Journal* 147 (1990): 91-117.

2350 **Hobbs, Richard.** *British Iron Age Coins in the British Museum.* London: British Museum Press, 1996. 246 pp., 137 pls.
Volume 4 of *Catalogue of Celtic Coins in the British Museum* (see D. F. Allen above). Describes and illustrates 4584 coins. [Reviewed by Philip DeJersey in *Numismatic Chronicle* 157 (1997): 265-8, and by Melinda Mays in *British Numismatic Journal* 67 (1997): 149-50].

2351 **Hodgson, T. V.** "Ancient British Coins Recently Found at Mount Batten, Plymouth." *Numismatic Chronicle* 5th ser., 4 (1924): 320-2.
Lists the nine coins (one gold, four silver, and four bronze) found in 1917. The coins are cross-referenced to the plates in Evans' *The Coins of the Ancient Britons*.

2352 **Holman, David J.** "Three Further Coins of SAM." *Spink Numismatic Circular* 106, no. 5 (June 1998): 204. Illus.
Illustrates three new specimens of the SAM bronze coins discussed by DeJersey. [See DeJersey "SA and SAM" above].

2353 **Holmes, Nicholas.** "Some Iron-Age Coins from Hacheston, Suffolk." *Numismatic Chronicle* 138 (1978): 176-8. 1 pl.
Discusses nineteen coins, mostly Icenian types, found during the 1973-5 excavations.

2354 **Hunter, Fraser.** "Celtic Chicanery Questioned." *Spink Numismatic Circular* 102, no. 6 (July 1999): 259. Illus.
The author disputes Van Arsdell's suggestion that a carnyx (war trumpet) is depicted on a Trinovantian D stater. [See Van Arsdell "Celtic Chicanery IV" below, and Rudd "War Trumpet" below].

2355 **Kent, John P. C.** "The Origin and Development of Celtic Gold Coinage in Britain." *Actes du Colloque International d'Archéologie, Centenaire de l Mort de l'Abbe Cochet, 1975.* Rouen, 1978. Pages 313-24. [CS 5196]

2356 **Kretz, Rainer.** "The Early Gold Staters of Tasciovanus—A Re-appraisal of the First Series." *Spink Numismatic Circular* 106, no. 1 (February 1998): 2-7. Illus.
Tasciovanus ruled somewhere between the middle and end of the first century B.C. This paper attempts to identify the full range of recorded types of his gold staters together with their likely order of evolution. Kretz proposes new classifications for the series.

2357 ———. "The problem of Andoco…." *Spink Numismatic Circular* 110 (2002): 267-71. Illus.
"A discussion of the coinage of 'Andoco' in the context of the coinage of the North Thames region, c. 20 B.C.-A.D. 10." [Martin Allen, *NL* 147]

2358 ———. "The Silver Coinage of Tasciovanos." *Celtic Coinage: New Discoveries, New Discussion.* Edited by Philip DeJersey. Oxford, 2006. Pages 183-212.

2359 ———. "The Coinage of Rues." *British Numismatic Journal* 77 (2007): 1-17.

2360 ———. "A New Biga Stater Variant of Cunobelinus." *Spink Numismatic Circular* 116, no. 2 (February 2008): 55-6. Illus.
Examines the biga stater of Cunobelinus with a cruciform wreath design containing two hidden faces. Discusses variants and chronology.

2361 **Laing, Lloyd R.** "Types and Prototypes in Insular Celtic Coinage." *Celtic Coin Bulletin* (Bulletin of the Celtic Coin Study Group, University of Nottingham) 1 (1991): 19-24.
Discusses the design prototypes for Celtic coins of Britain. Discusses the influence of mythological creatures, gods and cult practices, classical subjects with Celtic relevance, and Gallic prototypes.

2362 **Laver, Henry.** "The Coinage of Prasutagus, King of the Icenians." *British Numismatic Journal* 6 (1909): 1-3.
Suggests that the great wealth of Prasutagus consisted principally of precious metals and of coinage—even though no coins have been discovered with his name on them. Some of the uninscribed Icenian coins undoubtedly belong to this king.

2363 **Linecar, Howard.** "On a Find of Early British Tin Coins at Sunbury-on-Thames." *British Numismatic Journal* 26 (1949-51): 339-40.
A hoard of 317 coins of the types *Evans* plate H was found in 1950. Includes a brief list of the types.

2364 **Lister, Clem W.** "Four Ancient British Coins." *British Numismatic Journal* 29 (1958-9): 5-7. 1 pl.
Discusses a silver coin of the Catuvellauni, an uninscribed silver coin of the Sussex-coast type, an inscribed silver coin of Verica, and an uninscribed silver coin of the Coritani.

2365 ———. "Notes on Two Ancient British Forgeries." *Spink Numismatic Circular* 84, no. 9 (September 1976): 321. Illus.
Publishes some cast fake gold staters similar to *Mack* 149.

2366 **Mack, Richard P.** *The Coinage of Ancient Britain.* London: Spink & Son, 1953. 151 pp., 29 pls., 17 maps. Second edition, 1964. 33 pls., 18 maps. Third edition, 1975. 200 pp., 33 pls., 19 maps. [CS 5197]
Covers the period of the first coins of Britain (potin coinage of ca. 100 B.C.) through ca. A.D. 43. Provides a detailed history of the origin and development of coinage in Britain. Includes maps showing the findspots of ancient British coins or hoards. Catalogues 468 coin types, most of which are illustrated. Includes chapters on the coinage of the Atrebates, Regni, Catuvellauni, Trinovantes, Cantii, Durotriges, Dobunni, Iceni, and the Coritani. Lists seventy-eight hoards with brief listings of their contents. [The first edition was reviewed by R. A. G. Carson in *Times Literary Supplement* (October 16, 1953): 665, by H. de. S. Shortt in *Spink Numismatic Circular* 61, no. 7 (July 1953): 304, by C. Sutherland in *Spink Numismatic Circular* (June 1954), and by C. F. C. Hawkes in *Numismatic Chronicle* 6th ser., 14 (1954): 230-3. Carson's review was reprinted in *Spink Numismatic Circular* 61 (1953): 512].

2367 ———. "Three New Ancient British Coins." *British Numismatic Journal* 34 (1965): 166-7. 1 pl.
Discusses an EISU stater of the Dobunni, a quarter stater of the Morini, and a quarter stater of the Atrebates.

2368 **May, Jeffrey.** "Iron Age Coins from the Site of the Romano-British Temple at Thistleton: An Interim Note." *Celtic Coin Bulletin* (Bulletin of the Celtic Coin Study Group, University of Nottingham) 1 (1991): 25-7.
Discusses seventeen coins found at a Romano-British temple. Fifteen of the coins were of the Corieltauvi.

2369 ———. "A New East Midland Inscription." *Celtic Coin Bulletin* (Bulletin of the Celtic Coin Study Group, University of Nottingham) 1 (1991): 28-30. Illus.
Publishes a Corieltauvian coin.

2370 ———. "The Earliest Gold Coinages of the Corieltauvi." *Celtic Coinage: Britain and Beyond. The Eleventh Oxford Symposium on Coinage and Monetary History.* Edited by Melinda Mays. British Archaeological Reports, No. 222. Oxford, 1992.

2371 ———. "Coinage and the Settlements of the Corieltauvi in East Midland Britain." *British Numismatic Journal* 64 (1994): 1-21. 1 pl., maps.
An extensive discussion of the settlement of East Midland Britain and the Iron Age coin finds in this area. Includes maps of find-spots. Both numismatics and settlement archaeology suggest that the Corieltauvi were a relatively advanced people. Their coinage was as early and as advanced as any in Britain. There is little evidence that the coinage continued after the Roman conquest around A.D. 45.

2372 ———. "Test Cuts on a Corieltauvian Stater." *Spink Numismatic Circular* 102, no. 1 (February 1994): 3. Illus.
Illustrates a stater of the Corieltauvi with a test cut revealing a copper-alloy core. Discusses the use of plated coins during the Iron Age.

2373 **Mays, Melinda.** "Inscriptions on British Celtic Coins." *Numismatic Chronicle* 152 (1992): 57-82.

Presents a list of the full inscriptions appearing on British Celtic coins. This is followed by a section on their interpretation, together with references to the important literature.

2374 **Mays, Melinda, ed.** *Celtic Coinage: Britain and Beyond. The Eleventh Oxford Symposium on Coinage and Monetary History.* British Archaeological Reports, No. 222. Oxford, 1992.
A collection of papers by a variety of authors. [Reviewed by R. Hobbs in *Numismatic Chronicle* 153 (1993): 287-9, and by A. M. Burnett in *British Numismatic Journal* 64 (1994): 164].

2375 **Mitchell, Stephen, and Brian Reeds, eds.** "Celtic Coinage." *Standard Catalogue of British Coins: Coins of England and the United Kingdom.* 22nd edition. London: Seaby, 1986. Pages 1-17. Illus.
This standard collectors' handbook lists 306 Celtic coin types with brief descriptions and market values. The major types are illustrated.

2376 **Montagu, Hyman.** "Find of Ancient British Gold Coins in Suffolk." *Numismatic Chronicle* 3rd ser., 6 (1886): 23-37. 1 pl.
Discusses the coin types included in a hoard of ninety gold coins found in Britain.

2377 **Mossop, Henry R.** "Three New Varieties of Ancient British Coins." *British Numismatic Journal* 37 (1968): 190. 1 pl.
Publishes a new Coritani silver half denomination, an unpublished inscribed silver coin of the Coritani, and a new variety of Addedomaros.

2378 ———. "Five Recently Found Ancient British Coins." *British Numismatic Journal* 38 (1969): 181. 1 pl.
Publishes coins of the Coritani found in 1968-9 at Iron Age sites in Lincolnshire and Rutland.

2379 ———. "More Finds of Coritani Coins in Lincolnshire." *British Numismatic Journal* 39 (1970): 162-63. 1 pl.
Describes some recent finds of coins of the Coritani.

2380 ———. "Further Discoveries of Coritanian Coins in Lincolnshire and Rutland." *British Numismatic Journal* 40 (1971): 171. 1 pl.
Publishes and describes four Coritanian coins.

2381 ———. "More Die Linking in Ancient British Coins." *Spink Numismatic Circular* 84, no. 4 (April 1976): 143. Illus.
Shows die links between *Mack* 135 and 138A.

2382 ———. "Another Coin from Cunobelin's Biga Issue." *Spink Numismatic Circular* 84, no. 5 (May 1976): 190. Illus.
Publishes a Cunobelin gold coin from previously unrecorded dies (type of *Mack* 201).

2383 ———. "Die Links in Ancient British Coins." *Spink Numismatic Circular* 84, no. 6 (June 1976): 234. Illus.
Points out a die link between *Mack* 59A and 141.

2384 ———. "Three Recently Discovered Quarter Staters of the Iceni." *Spink Numismatic Circular* 84, nos. 7-8 (July-August 1976): 275. Illus.
Publishes three quarter staters of the Iceni (*Mack* 404) which were found in Suffolk and Cambridgeshire.

2385 ———. "A Coin of Dubnovelaunus." *Spink Numismatic Circular* 84, no. 11 (November 1976): 415. Illus.
Illustrates a coin attributed to Dubnovelaunus (*Mack* 286), the third known specimen.

2386 ———. "A New Silver Celtic Coin found in the Territory of the Iceni." *Seaby Coin and Medal Bulletin* 715 (March 1978): 74. Illus.
Illustrates two coins of the "Early Face-Horse Type" (Mack 412-413). Mossop suggests these two coins may be too early to place them with other coins of the Iceni.

2387 ———. "A New Variation of the Face/Horse Coins of the Iceni." *Seaby Coin and Medal Bulletin* 717 (May 1978): 139. Illus.
Publishes a coin found in Norfolk with *obv.*, crude bust facing, and *rev.*, maned horse to the right (Mack 413G). The obverse is noted to be "very distinctive."

2388 **Northover, J. P.** "Materials Issues in the Celtic Coinage." *Celtic Coinage: Britain and Beyond. The Eleventh Oxford Symposium on Coinage and Monetary History.* Edited by Melinda Mays. British Archaeological Reports, No. 222. Oxford, 1992.

2389 **O'Bee, Michael.** "The second coin of ATT." *Spink Numismatic Circular* 110 (2002): 62. Illus.
"The author discusses a Celtic silver coin found near Malton in North Yorkshire." [Martin Allen, *NL* 147]

2390 ———. "Volisios Daninvilir." *Spink Numismatic Circular* 114, no. 5 (October 2006): 268-9. Illus.
Lists the three known rulers of the Corieltauvi tribe named Volisios. Illustrates a base gold stater bearing this name along with Daninvilir. The author suggests this is yet another ruler of the Corieltauvi.

2391 ———. "The Wolf Unit." *Spink Numismatic Circular* 116, no. 1 (February 2008): 10-1. Illus.
Publishes three Wolf-type units of the Corieltauvi.

2392 **Pegge, Samuel.** *An Essay on the Coins of Cunobelin.* London: Printed for William Bowyer, 1766. 135 pp., 2 pls.

2393 **Penhallurick, R. D.** *Ancient and Early Medieval Coins from Cornwall & Scilly.* Special Publication No. 45. Edited by P. Guest and N. Wells. London: Royal Numismatic Society, 2009.

Summary listings of nearly 17,000 Iron Age, Roman, and early Medieval coins from 289 individual findspots in the county of Cornwall, including 52 hoards (1 Greek, 1 Iron Age, 46 Roman, and 3 Anglo-Saxon) and 21 other groups. The gazetteers of coins from Cornwall and the Isles of Scilly include descriptions of the circumstances of each find and summaries of the coins recovered. Includes four indices listing entries by parish, find type, and period.

2394 **Peters, Ken.** *Counterfeit Coins of Celtic Britain: The Story, Bibliography and Individual Counterfeits' Record.* Kent: Envoy Publicity, 2010. 50 pp., illus., 2 pls.
Discusses the counterfeiting of British Celtic coins and provides a detailed bibliography. Includes information on hoards, specific gravity testing, counterfeits in museums in the United Kingdom, and discusses copies, replicas, and reproductions.

2395 **Poste, Beale.** *The Coins of Cunobeline and of the Ancient Britons.* London: John Russell Smith, 1853. 300 pp. plus 17 page addendum. Illus.
Begins with a review of earlier literature on the coinage of ancient Briton. Then describes the coins of Cunobeline and examines the coinage of other British rulers including Comius, Boadicea, Caractacus, Segonax, Cassibelan, and Arviragus. Illustrated by line drawings of the coins. Discusses coins bearing names of unknown rulers. Illustrates and comments on coins in the collection of J. A. Wigan. Includes an extensive discussion of an inscription by Augustus at Angora that provides information on British history and Cunobeline's father. Suggests the words TASC, TASCIO, etc., are titular in nature—not names of a person. Examines the coins of the Iceni, describes the legends appearing on the coins, explores some controversies over attributions, discusses the origins of coinage in Britain and Gaul and the origin of coin types. Reviews the chronology of the coins, comments on some uninscribed coin types, lists some of the principal collections, examines the coins of the Brigantes, and discusses Celtic titular names. Parts of the book were previously published in the *Journal of the British Archaeological Association* from October 1845 to April 1852.

2396 ——— *Celtic Inscriptions on Gaulish and British Coins, Intended to Supply Materials for the Early History of Great Britain, with a Glossary of Archaic Celtic Words, and an Atlas of Coins.* London, 1861. 11 pls.

2397 ——— *A Vindication of the Celtic Inscription on Gaulish and British Coins.* London, 1862.

2398 **Robbins, K., and J. Bayley.** *Coin Pellet Mould and Crucible Fragments from Old Sleaford, Lincolnshire.* Ancient Monuments Laboratory Report 69/96. London: English Heritage, 1996.
"Analysis of a sample from over 4000 fragments of late Iron Age coin pellet moulds and 320 crucible fragments, excavated in 1963, support the identification of the site as a mint." [M. Allen, *NL* 140].

2399 **Robinson, Paul H.** "The Savernake Forest Find of Ancient British and Roman Coins (1857)." *British Numismatic Journal* 45 (1975): 1-11.
Summarizes the previously published sources for the Savernake hoard which was found in 1857, and describes several further sources. Confirms that only one discovery was made (rather than two) and reassesses the contents of the hoard. Presents accounts of the hoard's discovery. Presents a list of identifiable coins from the hoard.

2400 ——— "A Local Iron Age Coinage in Silver and Perhaps in Gold in Wiltshire." *British Numismatic Journal* 47 (1977): 5-20. Illus.
Examines the relationship that exists between two ancient British quarter stater types, *Mack* 68 and *Mack* 74. Concludes that there are satisfactory grounds for seeing the Irregular Dobunnic L and M coins and the small group of coins from Bromham and Rushall Down as struck either in central and eastern Wiltshire or very close to that county.

2401 ——— "The Problematical Find of Ancient British and Gaulish Coins from 'Near Portsmouth' in 1830." *British Numismatic Journal* 50 (1980): 1-6.
In 1830, a major find of ancient British and Gaulish coins appears to have been made "near Portsmouth." Doubts exist whether the coins did indeed come from a hoard. Robinson summarizes the coin types said to have been found.

2402 **Roth, Bernard.** "Notes on Three British Gold Coins Recently found near Abingdon." *British Numismatic Journal* 1 (1903-4): 61-4. Illus.
Discusses gold staters of Cunobelinus, Tascio-Ricon, and Addedomaros.

2403 ——— "A Find of Ancient British Coins at South Ferriby, near Barton-on-Humber, Lincolnshire." *British Numismatic Journal* 3 (1906): 1-15. 1 pl. Illus.
Illustrates and discusses twenty-eight Celtic coins.

2404 ——— "A Hoard of Staters and 'Gold Bullets' Recently Discovered in France, with Special Reference to the Ancient British Staters of the Type *Evans*, Plate B, No. 8." *British Numismatic Journal* 4 (1907): 221-8. 1 pl.
A hoard of 400 coins was found in 1905 which included coins of the Morini and globular staters marked with a small cross on one side. Discusses their attribution.

2405 ——— "A Large Hoard of Gold and Silver Ancient British Coins of the Brigantes, found at South Ferriby, Lincolnshire, in 1906." *Numismatic Chronicle* 4th ser., 8 (1908): 17-55. 5 pls.
A hoard of sixty-five gold coins is discussed. Describes and illustrates forty-five of the coins.

2406 ——— "A Unique Ancient British Gold Stater of the Brigantes (? a Pattern)." *Numismatic Chronicle* 4th ser., 9 (1909): 7-9. Illus.
Publishes four more coins from the hoard previously published by the author (see above). One of the coins is a unique piece with a centrally placed large trefoil on the obverse. Roth regards it as a pattern issue.

2407 **Rudd, Chris.** "War Trumpet or Snake." *Spink Numismatic Circular* 102, no. 6 (July 1994): 262. Illus.
The author disputes Van Arsdell's suggestion that a carnyx (war trumpet) is depicted on a Trinovantian D stater. Suggests the design is more likely to be a fish-headed snake. [See F. Hunter "Celtic Chicanery Questioned" above, and Van Arsdell "Celtic Chicanery IV" below].

2408 ——— "Alton Coin Discoveries Rename Celtic King." *The Celator* 10, no. 9 (September 1996): 20, 28. Illus.
A brief report of a hoard of late Iron Age gold staters of the Atrebates tribe, as well as Roman jewelry found in England. Thirteen of the staters carry the name of Timcomarus, an Atrebatic king who was previously thought to have been called Tincommios.

2409 ——— "Coins of King Prasutagus in Celtic Hoard." *The Celator* 12, no. 12 (December 1998): 26, 31. Illus.
A report on a hoard of 200 late Iron Age silver coins of the Eceni tribe, found in England. The coins may have been buried at the time of the Eceanian uprising of A.D. 47.

2410 ——— "Husband of British Queen Changes His Name." *The Celator* 14, no. 3 (March 2000): 38-9. Illus.
Two Celtic silver coins recently found by metal detectorists in southwest Norfolk have cast doubt on the interpretation of a coin type traditionally assigned to Prasutagus, the husband of Queen Boudica of the Eceni. The coins indicate that the legend once read as PRASTO SVBI is actually SVB ESVPRASTO. The coins were probably issued by someone called Esuprastus, not Prasutagus, and he may be associated with the Corieltauvian tribal king who struck gold and silver coins inscribed ESVPRASV.

2411 ——— "Celtic Currency Bars found in River." *The Celator* 14, no. 6 (June 2000): 6-12. Illus.
Discusses a hoard of eight late Iron Age bars of "bay-leaf" type which was found in a river near Cambridge. The bars were cast in iron ca. 200-50 B.C., possibly by a blacksmith of the Eceni tribe. They may have served a monetary function. Discusses the known types of these bars (spit-shaped, sword-shaped, plough-share, and bay-leaf) and their possible functions (currency, religious rituals, agriculture). Explores the practice of depositing iron bars into rivers as part of a ritual. [For another opinion, see C. Fischer "Interpreting Celtic River Findings" above].

2412 ——— "Were Celtic Moneyers on Drugs?" *The Celator* 14, no. 7 (July 2000): 34-5, 38-9, 50. Illus.
A review article covering John Creighton's book, *Coins and Power in Late Iron Age Britain* (see Creighton above). Rudd describes Creighton's book, pointing out some of the new theories advanced and focusing on the theory that Celtic die cutters may have been strongly influenced by imagery from trance experiences. These trances may have been induced by hallucinogenic substances, by fasting, or by trance-dancing to a constant rhythmic beat.

2413 ——— "Hengistbury Hairy." *The Celator* 15, no. 4 (April 2001): 17-21. Illus.
Examines the imagery on a coin of the Durotriges, minted at Hengistbury Head, Dorset. Rudd suggests it is one of the few Celtic coins that features male and female sexual organs. Rudd shows that the coin, which bears a simple geometric design of lines, crescents, and pellets, is actually a depiction of the sexual organs. Compares the coin imagery to similar figures on stone pillars and other coins.

2414 ——— "The Face that Launched 80,000 Deaths." *The Celator* 16, no. 3 (March 2002): 21-4. Illus.
Discusses the destruction of the Romano-British cities of Colchester, Verulanium, and London during Queen Boudica's resistance of the Romans. Discusses the Eceni war-goddess Andraste and her depiction on Celtic coins.

2415 ——— "Huge Druid Hoard from Leicestershire Found." *The Celator* 17, no. 7 (July 2003): 38-41, 50. Illus.
Describes the finding of the Market Harborough hoard of 3000-4000 Celtic coins, the largest Iron Age hoard ever excavated. The majority of coins are inscribed silver coins of the Corieltauvi.

2416 ——— "Discovered: King Sam of Kent." *The Celator* 18, no. 6 (June 2004): 37. Illus.
Illustrates a rare silver coin of an obscure Celtic king, unknown to history. The coin was struck in the early first century A.D. by a ruler of the Cantiaci tribe in northern Kent who called himself Sam (Celtic for "summer").

2417 ——— "Celtic Gold Hoards Lost by Slave Traders?" *The Celator* 18, no. 9 (September 2004): 38, 46. Illus.
Discusses two large hoards of Corieltauvi gold staters.

2418 ——— "Thatcher's Sister Sold for £1000 by Chris Rudd." *The Celator* 19, no. 6 (June 2005): 33, 56. Illus.
A report of the sale of a silver coin of the Catuvellauni tribe, minted ca. 45-40 B.C. The coins is known as "Thatcher's Sister" because the obverse figure (likley Epona, an iron-age horse goddess) is said to bear a resemblance to Margaret Thatcher.

2419 ——— "Itinerant Engravers?" *The Celator* 20, no. 5 (May 2006): 35. Illus.
Illustrates a Catuvellaunian coin and an Ecenian coin for which the author suggests the dies may have been cut by the same engraver.

2420 ——— "New Coin Confirms Old King—or Was He a Queen?" *The Celator* 20, no. 7 (July 2006): 37, 36. Illus.
Announces a 2006 find of a silver coin of the Dobunni bearing the abbreviated name INAMN. The coin helps confirm the inscription on a coin published by Evans in 1864. Rudd suggests some possibilities for the full name—including some female names. Rudd observes a phallic symbol incorporated into the I of the name and suggests it may be a wry comment on the virility of the queen.

2421 ——— "The Buckingham Gold Hoard." *The Celator* 21, no. 6 (June 2007): 38-9, 56. Illus.
Describes the finding of a significant hoard of seventy Iron Age gold staters, mostly minted by the Catuvellauni tribe, found in England in 2006.

2422 ——— "New Doubt Cast of Coins of Queen Boudica's Husband." *The Celator* 21, no. 7 (July 2007): 21, 36. Illus.
Summarizes the results of research by John Talbot on the coins of the Iceni. One conclusion: Talbot does not believe that the Iceni issued any coins after the Claudian invasion of A.D. 43. He believes the silver coin inscribed ESV PRASTO were pre-conquest. They were not struck by the historical Prasutagas—husband of Queen Boudica.

2423 ——— "Big Fish Nets £7700." *The Celator* 21, no. 9 (September 2007): 56, 46, 39. Illus.
Discusses a gold stater of Tincomarus which recently sold for £7700. Recounts how numismatists identified the issuing king as TIN or TINCOM, later as TINCOMIUS, and how a hoard found in 1996 finally revealed the king's true name: TINCOMARUS, meaning "Great Fish" or "Big Fish."

2424 ——— "Tribal Boar Goes to Museum." *The Celator* 22, no. 1 (January 2008): 40, 46. Illus.

Announces that a first century B.C. or A.D. bronze boar figurine has been acquired by a museum in Lincolnshire. The boar was a symbol of courage in war and of military prowess, and a representation of a boar was used on many Celtic coins.

2425 ——— "£35,000 of Celtic Gold for £100." *The Celator* 22, no. 7 (July 2008): 40, 46. Illus.
Discusses a group of gold coins found near Westerham in Kent. All forty-one coins were minted in the first century B.C. by the Cantiaci.

2426 ——— "The Good Grass of Turvey." *The Celator* 22, no. 8 (August 2008): 38-40. Illus.
Examines a first century B.C. gold stater of "Andoco" bearing four vegetal motifs, probably representing four ears of corn, with stylized hidden faces. The coin was found by metal detectorists and is described as a masterpiece of Celtic workmanship.

2427 ——— "King's Gold Hoard from Suffolk." *The Celator* 23, no. 2 (February 2009): 34-5, 38-40. Illus.
A discussion of the hoard of 783 ancient British gold coins discovered in 2008 near Wickham Market in southeast Suffolk, one of the largest iron-age hoards ever found in Britain. Rudd describes the finding of the coins and the site and its excavation. Explores whether the hoard may have been a votive offering (probably not), a war chest (perhaps), or tribute money. [Also see Andrew "Iron Age Gold" above].

2428 ——— "Clover King or Clover Queen?" *The Celator* 23, no. 6 (June 2009): 38-40, 46, 55-6. Illus.
Describes a rare 'trefoil type' gold stater of the Corieltavi.

2429 ——— "Coin Moulds Found in Hertfordshire." *The Celator* 23, no. 7 (July 2009): 38-40, 46. Illus.
Announces a find (discovered in 1999) of over 2000 fragments of fixed-clay moulds that were used to produce globular metal pellets that were then hammered flat to provide coin blanks. The moulds likely were prepared for the Catuvellauni.

2430 ——— "Unique Celtic Gold Coin Found in Kent." *The Celator* 23, no. 7 (July 2009): 35. Illus.
Announces the find of an unpublished gold stater struck by a king of the Cantiaci tribe.

2431 ——— "Celtic Hammer-God Found in Kent." *The Celator* 24, no. 1 (January 2010): 4, 46. Illus.
Announces the find of a rare gold quarter stater, struck ca. 250-225 B.C. in the land of the Ambiani tribe. The coin has *obv*., head of Apollo, and *rev*., a Celtic hammer-god driving his chariot. It is one of only two known specimens.

2432 ——— "Killer's Gold Sold" and "Who Was AGR?" *The Celator* 24, no. 6 (June 2010): 38-40. Illus.
The first section discusses a rare gold stater of Tasciovanos. The second deals with a rare gold stater bearing the letters AGR, struck by a Catuvellanian ruler.

2433 ——— "The Last of 'The Big Four' Dies—Major Clement Wynter Lister Dies on June 6, 2010." *The Celator* 24, no. 8 (August 2010): 35. Illus.
The announcement of the death of Clement Wynter Lister, a well-known author and collector of ancient British coinage.

2434 ——— "Lost Coin Rediscovered 261 Years After It Was Found." *The Celator* 25, no. 3 (March 2011): 30-2. Illus.
Reports that a Westerham North gold stater from the 1749 Carn Brea hoard turned up in the collection of Henry Mossop (1918-88). Its whereabouts had been unknown since its original finding. The coin was recently acquired by the Royal Cornwall Museum (see the related article on page 38).

2435 ——— "New Iron Age King Found in Kent." *The Celator* 25, no. 3 (March 2011): 32, 36, 38. Illus.
A unique gold stater of a previously unknown Cantian king AVAREVITO or ANAREVITO has been unearthed.

2436 ——— "The Eye of God." *The Celator* 25, no. 8 (August 2011): 30-3, 36. Illus.
Discusses a silver unit of the Iceni, ca. 50-30 B.C., which the author believes depicts a man's head with one eye blinded and with another eye (open) in his mouth. Rudd suggests the coin depicts the Norse god Odin who sacrificed one eye in order to gain wisdom and the gift of prophecy.

2437 **Scheers, Simone.** "Celtic Coin Types in Britain and their Mediterranean Origins." *Celtic Coinage: Britain and Beyond. The Eleventh Oxford Symposium on Coinage and Monetary History.* Edited by Melinda Mays. British Archaeological Reports, No. 222. Oxford, 1992.

2438 **Seaby, Peter.** "Celtic Britain." Chapter 1 of *The Story of British Coinage.* London: Seaby, 1985. Revised edition, 1990. Pages 1-11, illus.
A brief history of Celtic coinage in Britain. Discusses the first gold staters and the cast potin coins. Continues with the coins of the Atrebates, Regni, Catulellauni, Trinovantes, Cantii, Dobunni, Durotriges, Iceni, and Corieltauvi.

2439 **Sellwood, Lyn.** "Notes on Nine Ancient British Coins from Bath." *British Numismatic Journal* 50 (1980): 128-31. 1 pl.
Publishes the nine Celtic coins found during excavations below the King's Bath in 1979. Discusses their geographical context and dating, as well as the date of burial.

2440 ——— "A Numismatic Note on the Dobunnic Branched Emblem." *Oxford Journal of Archaeology* 1, no. 1 (1982): 113-4.

2441 **Sellwood, Lyn, and David M. Metcalf.** "A Celtic Silver Coin of Previously Unpublished Type from St. Nicolas at Wade, Thanet: The Prototype for Anglo-Saxon Sceattas of *BMC* Type 37?" *British Numismatic Journal* 56 (1986): 181-2. Illus.
Publishes a previously unknown Celtic silver coin which may have served as the proto-type for the design of the sceatta type *BMC* 37.

2442 **Sellwood, P. H.** "Ancient British Silver Coin found in Berkshire." *British Numismatic Journal* 25 (1945-8): 340-1.
Announces that an uninscribed silver coin of the type *Evans* F6 was found on White Horse Hill in 1948.

2443 **Shortt, Hugh de S.** "A Coin of the Dobuni." *British Numismatic Journal* 26 (1949-51): 213.
Announces the find of a debased silver unit of the Dobuni. The obverse is similar to *Evans* F9; the reverse is similar to *Evans* N6.

2444 ——— "A New Durotrigic Hoard from Godshill, Hampshire." *British Numismatic Journal* 30 (1960-1): 1-5. 1 pl.
Examines a hoard of four Durotrigic coins. Discusses the origin of the types and the chronology of the coins.

2445 ——— "Three Ancient British Coins." *British Numismatic Journal* 34 (1965): 166. 1 pl.
Publishes a Gallo-Belgic E stater and two silver staters of the Durotriges.

2446 **Sills, John.** "Interpreting the Coin Legends of the Corieltauvi." *Celtic Coin Bulletin* (Bulletin of the Celtic Coin Study Group, University of Nottingham) 1 (1991): 31-2.
Presents a new interpretation of the VEP CORF legend.

2447 ——— "The Volisios Legend on Coins of the Corieltauvi." *Spink Numismatic Circular* 103, no. 7 (September 1995): 260.
Discusses the *Volisios* and *Vodisius* legends on Corieltauvian coins.

2448 ——— "The Summer of 54 B.C." *Spink Numismatic Circular* 104, no. 7 (September 1996): 334-5. Illus.
Sills publishes four examples of a previously unknown uninscribed Celtic stater which pre-dates British A1. He suggests that these new staters and British A1 were struck by Cassivellaunus as leader of the British coalition of 54 B.C. to finance resistance to Caesar's second invasion, and that the bulk of A1 was minted in 54 B.C. He concludes that both issues were the output of a single mint. [But see Sills "Coinage of the British Coalition" below for a revised conclusion].

2449 ——— "Coinage of the British Coalition against Caesar." *Spink Numismatic Circular* 105, no. 9 (November 1997): 324-6. Illus., map.
In this follow-up to the author's previous article (see Sills "The Summer of 54 B.C." above), Sills presents a new discovery which shows there were two series of staters, struck in parallel at separate mints.

2450 ——— *Gaulish and Early British Gold Coinage.* London: Spink and Son, 2003. 555 pp., 17 pls., map.
A thorough analysis of this coinage, with an emphasis on the coinage of north-eastern France and southern England. Catalogue of 3000 coins. Illustrates 540 types.

2450a **Simon, Lilly.** *Ancient Celtic Coin Art.* Glastonbury: Wooden Books, 2008. 57 pp., illus.

2451 **Smith, R. A.** "The Ancient British Iron Currency." *Proceedings of the Society of Antiquaries* 2nd ser., 20 (1905): 179-95.

2452 **Sutherland, C. H. V.** "Dobunic Silver Coins from Bredon Hill, Worchs." *Numismatic Chronicle* 6th ser., 15 (1955): 241. Illus.
Publishes four British silver coins of the Dobunic class. The metallic composition of the coins is given.

2453 **Sydenham, Edward A.** "The White Horse and Ancient British Coin-Types." *Numismatic Chronicle* 6th ser., 4 (1944): 65-76. Illus.
Discusses the White Horse chalk-carving on the Berkshire Downs which belongs to the first century B.C. Noting similarities in artistic style between the White Horse and the horse depicted on Celtic coins, Sydenham asks whether the Belgic tribes really were trying to copy the horse from the reverse of the staters of Philip II of Macedon as is generally assumed. Suggests the coin types may have derived from purely native ideas found in local religions. Discusses other coin types and their distribution.

2454 **Symons, David.** "A Silver Unit of Andoco." *Spink Numismatic Circular* 97, no. 9 (November 1989): 289. Illus.
Publishes a silver unit (*Van Arsdell* 1868-1) of Andoco which reveals the inscription to be ANDOCO, not ANDOC. [Also see a correction in *Spink Numismatic Circular* 98, no. 5 (June 1990): 159].

2455 ——— "Celtic Coinage in Britain: Some Amendments and Additions." *Spink Numismatic Circular* 98, no. 2 (March 1990): 48-50. Illus.
Publishes coins from the collection of I. D. Finney which amend or expand the descriptions in Van Arsdell's *Celtic Coinage of Britain.*

2456 ——— "Further Celtic Coins from the Finney Collection." *Spink Numismatic Circular* 98, no. 8 (October 1990): 268-72. Illus.
A catalogue of the coins in the Finney collection that either amend or are additional to those described in Van Arsdell's *Celtic Coinage of Britain.* Also lists all the other British Celtic pieces in the Finney collection.

2457 ——— "Recent Additions to the Finney Collection." *Spink Numismatic Circular* 99, no. 4 (May 1991): 112-3. Illus.
Publishes an additional eleven coins recently added to the I. D. Finney collection.

2458 ——— "Some New Forgeries of Celtic Coins." *Spink Numismatic Circular* 100, no. 5 (June 1992): 149. Illus.
Illustrates four silver coins purported to be of Addedomaros of the Trinovantes (*Van Arsdell* 1611-1). The coins are determined to be counterfeit.

2459 ——— "British Celtic Coins Added to the Finney Collection, 1991." *Spink Numismatic Circular* 100, no. 7 (September 1992): 226-7. Illus.
Publishes sixteen coins added to the collection of I. D. Finney in 1991.

2460 ——— "Metallurgical and Metrological Analysis of Pre-Dynastic Staters in Britain: the Corieltauvi—A Correction." *Spink Numismatic Circular* 100, no. 8 (October 1992): 269.
Provides a correction to the weights of two coins as stated in Van Arsdell's article. [See Van Arsdell "Metallurgical and Metrological Analysis" below].

2461 ——— "The Finney Collection—British Celtic Acquisitions, 1992." *Spink Numismatic Circular* 101, no. 6 (July 1993): 188-9. Illus.
Publishes fifteen new additions to the collection of I. D. Finney.

2462 ——— "When is a Horse Not a Horse?" *Spink Numismatic Circular* 106, no. 6 (July 1998): 260-1. Illus.
Suggests the reverse type of *Van Arsdell* 165-1 is not a horse but a griffin.

2463 ——— "When is a Horse Not a Horse?" *Spink Numismatic Circular* 106 (1998): 260-1. Illus.
"The author discusses the griffin on a silver unit of Dubnovellaunus, sometimes described as a horse." [M. Allen, *NL* 142]

2464 **Tatton-Brown, T.** "Potins and Other Iron-Age Coins from Canterbury." *Kent Archaeological Review* 67 (1982): 161-4.

2465 **Thompson, F. C.** "A Note on the Composition of British Pre-Roman 'Tin Money.'" *Numismatic Chronicle* 7th ser., 2 (1962): 111-2.
Presents the results of an analysis of the metallic content of the so-called 'tin money' coins. Comments on their manufacture and chronology.

2466 **Van Arsdell, Robert D.** "A Note on the Earliest Types of British Potin Coins." *Spink Numismatic Circular* 91, no. 1 (February 1983): 8-9. Illus.
Publishes and discusses two coins (*Allen* Type A) which are among the earliest potin cast coins in England. [Also see the related letter from R. D. Van Arsdell in *Spink Numismatic Circular* 91 (May 1983): 120].

2467 ——— "Dumnoc Tigir Seno: A New Reading of a Silver Unit." *Spink Numismatic Circular* 91, no. 5 (June 1983): 154. Illus.
A new specimen of the Coritanian silver unit (*Mack* 462) reveals an additional letter of the obverse legend. The complete reading now stands as DVMNOC TIGIR SENO.

2468 ——— "The Origin of the British L Stater and 'The Problem of the Catuvellauni.'" *Spink Numismatic Circular* 92, no. 1 (February 1984): 9-11. Illus.
Cunobeline has traditionally been identified as ruler of the Catuvellauni tribe. A reappraisal of the numismatic evidence supports assigning him to the Trinovantes.

2469 ——— "The Missing Coins from the Collection of Sir John Evans." *Spink Numismatic Circular* 92, no. 2 (March 1984): 44-5. Illus.
Publishes a Clacton Type I stater (*Mack* 47) which the author believes was originally in the collection of Sir John Evans and which was de-accessioned by the British Museum. Lists the locations of all the known specimens of this stater and the quarter-stater (*Mack* 35).

2470 ——— "Yet Another Surprise from the Haslemere Hoard." *Spink Numismatic Circular* 92, no. 7 (September 1984): 216-7. Illus.
Suggests that a Gallo-Belgic E stater should be considered part of the puzzling Haslemere Hoard. [Van Arsdell later determined the Haslemere Hoard to be a modern fabrication. See Van Arsdell "Hallmark" below. Also see Derek F. Allen "The Haslemere Hoard" and "The Haslemere Hoard Again" above].

2471 ——— "A Note on the Date of the British Potin Coinage." *Spink Numismatic Circular* 92, no. 8 (October 1984): 257-8. Illus.
The evidence of the Snettisham hoard strongly suggests that the British potin coinage was introduced in the early first century B.C. Van Arsdell publishes a gilt coin which he believes strengthens the evidence in support of this date.

2472 ——— "The Hallmark of the Haslemere Forger." *Spink Numismatic Circular* 93, no. 3 (April 1985): 79-80. Illus.
Declares the Haslemere Hoard to be a modern fabrication. The forger attempted to make new types for collectors. [Also see Van Arsdell "Yet Another Surprise" above].

2473 ——— "The Origin and Date of the Silver Coritanian Coinage." *Spink Numismatic Circular* 93, no. 4 (May 1985): 119. Illus.
Suggests that the inspiration for the obverse of the earliest type of Coritanian silver was drawn from the Roman denarii of C. Hosidius C. F. Geta. This supports the dating of the series to the mid-first century B.C.

2474 ——— "False Coritanian Staters from the Hand of the Haslemere Forger." *Spink Numismatic Circular* 93, no. 8 (October 1985): 259-60. Illus.
Identifies a series of fake Coritanian coins which may be assigned to the Haslemere forger.

2475 ——— "An Industrial Engineer (But No Papyrus) in Celtic Britain." *Oxford Journal of Archaeology* 5, no. 2 (July 1986): 205-21. Illus.
Discusses the coin-making methods used in Iron Age Britain, specifically those used to manufacture the cast bronze coins of Kent. The distinctive markings that appear on the coins reveal a series of mould-making experiments that optimize the casting process. The spirit of experimentation and innovation is somewhat akin to that of modern day industrial engineering, and shows Celtic metal-working technology at its best. The hypothesis that papyrus was used in the mould-making procedures is refuted by an analysis of the striations that occur in the fields of some of these coins.

2476 ——— "The Silver Coinage of Commius." *Spink Numismatic Circular* 94, no. 10 (December 1986): 330. Illus.
Presents evidence for attributing a "South of the Thames" coin to Commius.

2477 ——— "The Silver Coinage of Commius—A New Variety." *Spink Numismatic Circular* 95, no. 2 (March 1987): 42. Illus.
Publishes two specimens of a new variety of the silver coins of Commius.

2478 ——— "The Coinage of Queen Boudicca." *Spink Numismatic Circular* 95, no. 5 (June 1987): 150-1. Illus.
Attributes two silver units to Queen Boudicca of the Iceni. [Also see Van Arsdell "A Boudiccan Coin" below].

2479 ——— "Celtic Chicanery." *Spink Numismatic Circular* 96, no. 3 (April 1988): 78. Illus.
Illustrates a stater of Tasciovanus which has a face hidden in the obverse design. [Also see Van Arsdell "Celtic Chicanery II" below].

2480 ——— "The Quarter Staters of Commius." *Spink Numismatic Circular* 97, no. 4 (May 1989): 115. Illus.
Illustrates a quarter-stater belonging to the coinage of Commius.

2481 ——— "Celtic Chicanery II: The Hidden Face on an Atrebatic Stater." *Spink Numismatic Circular* 97, no. 5 (June 1989): 152. Illus.
Publishes another face hidden on a Celtic stater. This one is on a stater of the Atrebates/Regni. [Also see Van Arsdell "Celtic Chicanery" above].

2482 ——— *Celtic Coinage of Britain.* London: Spink & Son, 1989. 584 pp., maps, illus., 54 pls.
Begins with a history of Celtic coinage in Britain from the second century B.C. through the first century A.D. Discusses denominations, functions of the coins, style of Celtic art, and metallurgy. Presents a catalogue of about 800 types. Photographs of the coins are incorporated into the catalogue. Includes concordances with *Mack* [see 2366] and *Allen* [2171] classes. Eighty maps show where the various coin-types have been found. Includes tables of metallurgical and metrological data and hoards and a brief discussion of forgeries. [Reviewed by J. P. C. Kent in *Numismatic Chronicle* 150 (1990): 266-8, and by Jeffrey May in *Spink Numismatic Circular* 98, no. 1 (February 1990): 10].

2483 ——— "The Silver Minims of Commius." *Spink Numismatic Circular* 97, no. 9 (November 1989): 289. Illus.
Publishes two silver minims of Commius.

2484 ——— "A New (But Illegible) Inscription on a Cantian Stater." *Spink Numismatic Circular* 97, no. 10 (December 1989): 323. Illus.
Publishes a coin which may serve to confirm one of the British rulers mentioned by Caesar in his dispatches to the Roman Senate (Carrilius).

2485 ——— "Celtic Chicanery III." *Spink Numismatic Circular* 98, no. 4 (May 1990): 122. Illus.
Publishes a coin with a head on the obverse. Van Arsdell points out that if the coin is turned one-quarter turn, the head appears to be a bird pecking the ground. If intentional, it is the first example of shape-shifting on a Celtic coin. Celtic mythology is full of people who change into animals and back again.

2486 ——— "Inscription on Cunobeline Ship Type Confirmed." *Spink Numismatic Circular* 100, no. 2 (March 1992): 45. Illus.
Publishes the third known example of a bronze ship-type unit of Cunobeline. The reverse clearly bears the inscription CVN.

2487 ——— "Three New Celtic Staters." *Spink Numismatic Circular* 100, no. 3 (April 1992): 80. Illus.
Describes three important new types of Ancient British staters. The first, an Atrebatic type, represents the transition between the uninscribed coins and the first dynastic issues of Commius. The other two staters are dynastic issues of the Iceni, carrying inscriptions ECEN and ECE. The coins provide further confirmation that the relative order of the Icenian coinage is ANTED, followed by ECEN, followed by ECE.

2488 ——— "A Dobunnic Branched Emblem on a Bronze 'Wheel Money' Object." *Spink Numismatic Circular* 100, no. 4 (May 1992): 112. Illus.
Describes two classes of Celtic bronze wheel money—with and without spokes. The spoked variety may have been used as money. The heavier class, lacking spokes, probably was not used as money. They were more likely decorative pendants. Illustrates a "wheel money" object, lacking spokes, which has stick-figure trees between the protruding bosses, reminiscent of the branched emblem on Dobunnic staters. [Also see follow-up comments by S. Perry in *Spink Numismatic Circular* 100 (September 1992): 225].

2489 ——— "Metallurgical and Metrological Analysis of Pre-Dynastic Staters in Britain I: the Corieltauvi." *Spink Numismatic Circular* 100, no. 5 (June 1992): 151.
An analysis of weights and fineness allows corrections to be made to the standard weights and chronology of the earliest Corieltauvi coins. [Also see Symons "Metallurgical…A Correction" above].

2490 ——— "The Coinage of Queen Boudicca: An Update." *Spink Numismatic Circular* 100, no. 9 (November 1992): 306-7.
In a recent article, John Creighton (see Creighton "The Decline and Fall" above) explored the Icenian coinage in the decades before the Boudiccan Revolt. Creighton concluded that Icenian O should not be attributed to Boudicca because the type was struck prior to A.D. 60. Van Arsdell discusses the specifics of Creighton's arguments.

2491 ——— "Trade Routes in Celtic Britain via Trend Surface Analysis." *Spink Numismatic Circular* 100, no. 10 (December 1992): 346-9.
Find-spots of Celtic coins reveal the trading networks of Iron Age Britain.

2492 ——— "Metallurgical and Metrological Analysis of Pre-Dynastic Staters in Britain II: the Atrebates." *Spink Numismatic Circular* 101, no. 4 (May 1993): 117.
An analysis of uninscribed Atrebatic staters.

2493 ——— "Die-Cutting Expertise in Celtic Britain." *Spink Numismatic Circular* 101, no. 5 (June 1993): 153. Illus.
It is sometimes assumed that changes in the style or quality of engraving seen on the Celtic coinage of Britain should be attributed to the influx of engravers from Europe into Britain. The author disputes this idea, suggesting that the skill of native engravers varied. One genuine and two counterfeit gold staters of Addedomaros illustrate variations in the quality of die engraving.

2494 ——— "Bad Day at Flat Rock." *Spink Numismatic Circular* 101, no. 8 (October 1993): 283. Illus.
Describes the "flat rock" method of producing coin blanks—ladling molten metal onto a flat surface, as well as the "muffin mould" method—using clay tablets with depressions for casting the flans. The muffin mould method was used for most of the Celtic coins of Britain. Illustrates a Durotrigan silver stater with an appendage similar to a casting sprue. The appendage supplies evidence that the flat rock method was used to produce the flan.

2495 ——— "Celtic Chicanery IV—The War Trumpet." *Spink Numismatic Circular* 102, no. 3 (April 1994): 103. Illus.
Suggests that the die cutter of the Trinovantian D stater has mis-interpreted the chariot wheel (a remnant of the staters of Philip II of Macedon) and a ring of pellets on the Gallo-Belgic E stater, and created a carnyx (a Celtic war trumpet). [Also see F. Hunter "Celtic Chicanery Questioned" and Rudd "War Trumpet" above].

2496 ——— "Clashed Dies and the Organization of Verica's Mint." *Spink Numismatic Circular* 102, no. 9 (November 1994): 402-3. Illus.

A Verica stater struck from clashed dies reveals operational procedures at a Celtic mint. It reinforces the idea that large numbers of coins were struck, that minting activity was intense, and that the mint had a high degree of organization and control. However, this control did not include a systematic pairing of dies (a die-box system was in use).

2497 ——— *The Coinage of the Dobunni: Money Supply and Coin Circulation in Dobunnic Territory.* With a Gazetteer of Findspots by Philip de Jersey. Studies in Celtic Coinage, No. 1. Oxford University Committee for Archaeology, Monograph 38. Oxford, 1994. 89 pages, illus.
"The coinage of the Dobunni is examined from a number of viewpoints: through typology, distribution, metallurgy, metrology and an analysis of die-links and die-tallies (for the gold coinage). An attempt is made to reconstruct the economic history of the tribe and to estimate the money supply from the inception of minting to the Claudian invasion. It is suggested that a prosperous late Iron Age economy was twice subjected to rapid but short-lived change due to the import or export of large amounts of gold bullion. Consideration is also given to the use of coinage in mapping tribal boundaries. A gazetteer of findspots lists all the provenances of Dobunnic coinage recorded in the Celtic Coin Index at the Institute of Archaeology, Oxford." [P. de Jersey, *NL* 133]. [Reviewed by D. Briggs in *British Numismatic Journal* 64 (1994): 165].

2498 ——— "Some Recent Discoveries." *Spink Numismatic Circular* 103, no. 1 (February 1995): 3. Illus.
Discusses some die varieties of Cantian quarter staters. Discusses whether the object depicted on another coin is a carnyx, a snake, or an abstract zoomorphic pattern.

2499 ——— "A Boudiccan Coin from the German Limes." *Spink Numismatic Circular* 103, no. 3 (April 1995): 87.
In his 1987 article (see Van Arsdell "The Coinage of Queen Boudicca" above), the author mentioned that no hoard of coins of Queen Boudicca could be dated prior to the Boudiccan Rebellion. Here, the author discusses a single Boudiccan coin which was found in a Roman fort on the German Limes. The coin could have disproved the "late date" hypothesis for Icenian O. However, Van Arsdell determined that the coin was deposited in Flavian times.

2500 ——— "Muddying the Atrebatic Waters." *Spink Numismatic Circular* 104, no. 10 (December 1996): 444. Illus.
"The author discusses the attribution of coins of the Atrebates to Tincomarus or Tincommius." [M. Allen, *NL* 140]

2501 ——— "A Statistical Analysis of Icenian Coin Hoards." *Oxford Journal of Archaeology* 15 (1996): 235-43.

2502 **Walker, C.T.** "Concerning a Silver Unit of Verica Ruler of the Atrebates." *Spink Numismatic Circular* 112 (2004): 295-6. Illus.

2503 **Wellington, Imogen.** "An Addition to the Trinovantian Coinage." *Spink Numismatic Circular* 107, no. 2 (March 1999): 47.
Publishes a new variety of the bronze coinage attributed to the northern region of the Iron Age coin-producing areas of Britain.

2504 **Williams, Jonathan H. C.** "Delete-Undelete: *Mack* 280 and Early British Silver." *Numismatic Chronicle* 158 (1998): 53-61. 1 pl.
Attempts to restore scholarly credibility to a rare type of British silver coinage unnecessarily deleted by Van Arsdell in *Celtic Coinage of Britain*. Also reassesses the metrological and iconographical sources and the dating of early British silver coinage.

2505 ——— "Imitation or Invention? A New Coin of Tasciovanus." *Spink Numismatic Circular* 106, no. 8 (November 1998): 350-1. Illus.
Illustrates a previously unpublished type on a bronze coin of Tasciovanus.

2506 ——— "Coin Inscriptions and the Origins of Writing in Pre-Roman Britain." *British Numismatic Journal* 71 (2001): 1-17. Illus.

2507 ——— "Iron-Age and Roman Coins." *British Numismatic Journal* 73 (2003): 44-57.
"A review of research in Celtic and Romano-British numismatics since 1903." [Martin Allen, *NL* 148]

2508 ——— "Stability and Variety in the Weight-Standards of Cunobelin's Precious Metal Coinage." *Numismatic Chronicle* 165 (2005): 125-8.
Discusses the weight differences between the "biga" and "cornear" staters.

2509 ——— "Vinous Symbolism on British Iron Age Coins." *Iron Age Coinage and Ritual Practices*. Edited by Colin Haselgrove and David Wigg-Wolf. Studien zu Fundmünzen der Antike Band 20. Mainz: Akademie der Wissenschaften und der Literatur, 2005.
Examines motifs on British Iron Age coins that draw their inspiration from viniculture, the cult of Bacchus, or the consumption of wine.

2510 **Wise, Philip J.** "Rare Coin Hoard found in Warwickshire." *Coventry District Archaeological Society Bulletin* 316 (1995): 5. Also appeared in *Minerva* 6 (1995): 2-3.
"The author reports on the discovery of a hoard of gold coins of the Corieltauvi near Bedworth in 1994." [M. Allen, *NL* 140]

2511 ——— "The Bedworth Hoard of Celtic Coins." *British Numismatic Journal* 65 (1995): 215-7. 1 pl.
"A hoard of eleven Corieltauvi staters was found near Bedworth, Warwickshire, in 1994. Such hoards are very rare and only in the Bedworth hoard are found both uninscribed and inscribed staters. This hoard and other finds from Warwickshire indicate the spread of Corieltauvian influence away from the tribal heartland." [P. Wise, *NL* 140]

Also see: Bernard et al. "Experimental Study" under METALLURGY; van Heesch and Heeren *Coinage in the Iron Age* under CELTIC COINAGE—GENERAL WORKS; Stills *Gaulish and Early British Gold Coinage* under CELTIC COINAGE OF EUROPE.

CELTIC COINAGE OF EUROPE

2512 **Allan, John.** "The Carn Brea Hoard of 1749." *Numismatic Chronicle* 6th ser., 8 (1948): 235-6.
Records a hoard of coins of Gaulish origin.

2513   ———— "The Snettisham Find." *Numismatic Chronicle* 6th ser., 8 (1948): 233-5.
Records a hoard of thirteen gold coins, all degraded copies of the staters of Philip II of Macedon. Burial is placed in the first century A.D.

2514   **Allen, Derek F.** "The La Marquanderie Hoard of Armorican Coins." *Numismatic Chronicle* 5th ser., 19 (1939): 180-2. 1 pl.
Discusses a hoard of over 11,000 coins found in 1935 on the Island of Jersey. Includes a brief description of the coins.

2515   ———— "The Paul (Penzance) Hoard of Imitation Massilia Drachms." *Numismatic Chronicle* 7th ser., 1 (1961): 91-106. 2 pls.
"A hoard in the Truro Museum collection, discovered in 1907, contains forty-three anonymous imitations of the silver drachms of Massilia. In general, the find spots of these coins—usually in Cisalpine Gaul—indicate that they were struck by the Celtic tribes of the Cenomani and/or Insubres. The hoard furnishes proof of ancient trade relations between the Mediterranean and Britain, probably in tin, and is believed to have been buried in the mid- or late second century B.C." [I. Merker, *NL* 65]

2516   ———— "A Hoard of Cisalpine Coins from Britain." *Congresso Internazionale di Numismatica, Roma 11-16 Settembre 1961. Volume 2.* Rome: Istituto Italiano de Numismatica, 1965. Pages 195-8. [CS 5204]
Discusses a group of forty-three silver imitation drachms of Massilia found in Britain circa 1907.

2517   ———— "The Sark Hoard of Celtic Coins and Phalerae." *Numismatic Chronicle* 7th ser., 8 (1968): 37-54. Illus., 1 pl. [CS 5102]
Discusses a hoard of coins and phalerae (round ornaments) found on the Island of Sark in 1718.

2518   ———— "Monnaies-à-la-Croix." *Numismatic Chronicle* 7th ser., 9 (1969): 33-78. Illus. [CS 5103]

2519   ———— "The Early Coins of the Treviri." *Germania* (Germany) 49 (1971): 91-110. 6 pls. [CS 5104]

2520   ———— "The Serra Ricco Hoard." *Spink Numismatic Circular* 79, no. 1 (January 1971): 15, 14. Illus.
One-hundred forty-eight coins from the Serra Ricco hoard were examined by the author. Of these coins, 147 had types which derive from the late didrachms of Massalia. The reverses bear a cat-like animal. Twenty-four coins are illustrated.

2521   ———— "Celtic Coins in the Royal Coin Cabinet, Stockholm." *Nordisk Numismatisk Årsskrift* (Sweden) (1972): 5-26. [CS 5105]

2522   ———— "The Philippus in Switzerland and the Rhineland." *Revue Suisse de Numismatique* (Switzerland) 53 (1974): 42-74. Illus., maps.
"There is strong evidence that the Celtic coins of Philip type originated in Switzerland and spread from there, especially toward northern regions. The type debases gradually and splits into many varieties, derivatives and imitations. The date of these coins may lie between the late third and the mid-first centuries B.C." [H. Bloesch, *NL* 99]

2523   ———— "The Celtic Coins in the Royal Netherlands Cabinet at the Hague, Part 1." *Jaarboek voor Munten Penningkunde* (The Netherlands) 62-65 (1975-1977): 5-21. 17 pls. [CS 5106]

2524   ———— "The Coins from the Oppidium of Altenburg and the Bushel Series." *Germania* (Germany) 56 (1978): 190-229. 10 pl.

2525   **Blanchet, J. Adrien.** *Traité des Monnaies Gauloises.* Two volumes. Paris, 1905. Reprint (in one volume), Bologna: Forni, 1971. 650 pp., illus., 3 pls. [CS 5109]

2526   **Boudeau, E.** *Monnaies Gauloises.* New edition. Maastrich: A. G. van Dussen, 1970. 42 pp., illus. [CS 5110]

2527   **Boudet, Richard, and Georges Depeyrot.** *Monnaies Gauloises à la Croix.* Moneta 7. Wetteren, Belgium, 1997. 104 pp, 4 pl.

2528   **Breitsprecher, Marc.** "A Brief Introduction to the Celtic Potin Coinage of Gaul." *The Celator* 16, no. 9 (September 2002): 24-8. Illus.
A brief review of the Celtic potin coinage. Potin is an alloy of bronze containing a high percentage of tin. Discusses the designs found on the coins, the distribution of the coinage, and suggests ways to begin collecting examples of this unusual coinage.

2529   **Brenot, Claude, and J.–P. Callu.** *Monnaies de Fouilles du Sud-est de la Gaule (VIe av. J.-C. – VIe s. ap. J.-C.).* Marseille: Nanterre, 1978. 110 pp., 6 pls. [CS 5111]

2530   **Brenot, Claude, and Simone Scheers.** *Catalogue des Les Monnaies Massaliètes et les Monnaies Celtique du Musée des Beaux-Arts de Lyon.* Peeters, 1996. 128 pp., 44 pls.

2531   **Burns, Craig Alden.** "Celts, Oghams, and Hand Signals." *Journal of Numismatic Fine Arts* 2, no. 3 (autumn 1973): 47-9. Illus.
Compares the types on some silver drachms of the Elusates tribes, to the types on the gold staters of Tasciovanus. Suggests that the head on the obverse of the Elusates coins contains *oghams*. Oghams are a cryptic form of Celtic script in which the names of letters replaced the letters themselves in certain syllables. Suggests that these pictorial symbols may represent pictorial heraldry.

2532   **Castelin, Karel O.** "Zur Chronologie des Keltischen Münzwesens in Mitteleuropa." *Jahrbuch für Numismatik und Geldgeschichte* (Germany) 12 (1962): 199-207. [CS 5209]

2533   ———— *Die Goldpägung der Kelten in den Böhmischen Ländern.* Graz, 1965. 270 pp., 6 pls. [CS 5212]

2534   ———— *Keltische Münzen: Katalog der Sammlung im Schweizerischen Landesmuseum, Zürich.* Volume 1. Stäfa-Zürich: Th. Gut & Co. Verlag, 1978. 154 pp., 80 pls. [CS 5230]. Volume 2: *Kommentar.* Stäfa, 1985. 172 pp., illus.

2535 **Chevillon, Jean-Albert.** "Massalia: Les Têtes Casquées/Roue Avec Légende MATA." *Cahiers Numismatiques* (Société d'Études Numismatiques et Archéologiques, France) 38, no. 148 (2001): 5-7. Illus.

2535a **Chimirri-Russell, Geraldine.** "Changing Artistic Perspectives on Celtic Coins." *XIII Congreso Internacional de Numismática, Madrid – 2003: Actas–Proceedings–Actes I.* Edited by Carmen Alfaro, Carmen Marcos, and Paloma Otero. Madrid: International Numismatic Commisson, 2005. Pages 441-5, incl. 1 pl.
 Examines the design elements seen on the obverse of Celtic coins from the Iron Age, primarily from the region of North Western France, to ascertain whether the designs fulfill a practical artistic purpose that allows an image of the human head to be perceived both in profile and as a three-quarter view. The author also discusses the limitations of current numismatic methodology in describing such design features. The sculptural qualities of some Celtic coins has not been recognized in catalogues. The appearance of human heads can change significantly when viewed from an oblique viewpoint resulting in far more realistic, less abstract, images. The craftsmen were following a cultural tradition of incorporating shape changing features into their metal work.

2536 **Colbert de Beaulieu, Jean-Baptists.** "Notes d'Epigraphie de Monnaies Gauloises." *Études Celtiques* (France) 9 (1960): 106-38. [CS 5117]

2537 ——— *Les Monnaies Gauloises des Parisii.* Paris: Imprimerie Nationale, 1970. 171 pp., 66 pls. [CS 5122]

2538 ——— "Chronologie des Bronze Gaulois et 'British Potin Coins.'" *Revue Belge de Numismatique* (Belgium) 119 (1973): 5-41. 2 pls. [CS 5125]

2539 **Davis, Phillip.** "Dacian and Celtic Imitations of Republican Denarii." *The Celator* 18, no. 4 (April 2004): 6-20. Illus.
 Examines the imitations of Roman Republican denarii which are often described as Celtic or Dacian. These pieces were actually struck in Hungary and the Balkans, usually by Geto-Dacians rather than by Celts. Davis arranges these coins into five classes: Geto-Dacian, Pannonian, Other Balkan, Anomalous, and Ancient Forgeries. He describes and illustrates the charateristics of each class.

2540 **DeJersey, Philip.** *Coinage in Iron Age Armorica.* Studies in Celtic Coinage, No. 2. Oxford University Committee for Archaeology, Monograph 39. Oxford, 1994. 266 pp., illus., 29 maps.
 "This volume places the development of Armorican Celtic coinage in its archaeological and geographical context. Chapters on the definition of the region, the late Iron Age archaeological evidence, and the relationship of this part of northwest France to Rome, are followed by a consideration of the function and role of Celtic coinage. Armorican coinage is then discussed in detail, from the first imitations of the stater of Philip II of Macedon through to the production of huge quantities of billon coinage at the time of the Gallic War. The concluding chapter suggests a possible scheme for the development of coinage in the Armorican region. Appendices list details of 170 hoards known from the area, and provenanced finds are plotted on a series of maps with full bibliographic information." [P. DeJersey, *NL* 133]. [Reviewed by J. H. C. Williams in *British Numismatic Journal* 67 (1997): 148-9].

2541 ——— "Deliberate Defacement of a Continental Celtic Coin." *Spink Numismatic Circular* 103, no. 2 (March 1995): 53. Illus.
 Illustrates a plated silver unit of ΚΑΛΕΤΕΔΟΥ, produced by the Lingones or the Aedui in central eastern Gaul. The coin has been punched roughly in the center of the reverse. The author speculates on the nature of this punchmark. Suggests the coin was deliberately defaced to remove it from circulation.

2542 **de la Tour, Henri.** *Atlas des Monnaies Gauloises, Preparé par la Commission de Topographie des Gaules et Publié sous auspices du Ministère de l'Instruction Publique.* Paris: Bibliothèque Nationale, 1892. Reprints, London: Spink & Sons, 1968; Chicago: Ares Publishers, 1976; Wetteren: van der Dussen, 1991. 12 pp., 55 pls. [CS 5139]
 Hand drawn plates. [Also see Scheers "Un Complement" below].

2543 ——— *La Tour II.* Paris: Comptoir Général Financier, 2001. 184 pp. including 127 pls.
 A modified reprint of La Tour's 1892 classic *Atlas de Monnaies Gauloises*, listing gold, silver, bronze, and potin Celtic coins of Gaul, along with Roman Provincial issues of the area. Includes updated and improved line drawings, a chart listing the coins in numerical order, and updated tribal attributions. Includes 1939 coin drawings by Léon Dardel. Includes 198 British Celtic coins, mostly from the collection of Sir John Evans.

2544 **Delestrée, Louis-Pol, and Marcel Tache.** *Nouvel Atlas des Monnaies Gauloises. Volume I: La Gaule du Nord: de la Seine au Rhin.* Saint-Germain-en-Laye: Editions Commios, 2002. 136 pp., 29 pls, 2 maps.
 A catalogue of 730 Celtic coins of ancient France, Belgium, and Germany. The coins are categorized by geographical location and series. [Reviewed by Marc Breitsprecher in *The Celator* 17, no. 6 (June 2003): 34-5, and by O. D. Hoover in *American Numismatic Society Magazine* 2, no. 2 (summer 2003): 57-9].

2545 ——— *Noevel Atlas des Monnaies Gauloises. Volume II: de la Seine á Loire Moyenne.* Saint-Germain-en-Laye: Editions Commios, 2004. 149 pp.
 Part two of this major catalogue of the Celtic coinage of Gaul. Illustrates 680 coins.

2546 ——— *Noevel Atlas des Monnaies Gauloises. Volume III: La Celtique, du Jura et des Alpes à la Façade Atlantique.* Saint-Germain-en-Laye: Editions Commios, 2006.

2547 ——— *Noevel Atlas des Monnaies Gauloises. Volume IV: Supplement aux Tomes I, II, III.* Saint-Germain-en-Laye: Editions Commios, 2008. 91 pp., 15 pls.
 A supplement including a detailed inventory of the first three volumes and an extensive bibliography.

2548 **Dembski, Günther.** "Beginn und Ende der Münzprägung in Noricum." *Stephanos Nomismatikos: Edith Schönert-Geiss zum 65. Geburtstag.* Edited by Ulrike Peter. Berlin: Akademie Verlag, 1998. Pages 199-206.

2549 **Dengis, Jean-Luc.** *Trouvailles et Trésors Monétaires en Belgique, V: Province du Brabant et les Trouvailles Belges Non-Localizées.* Moneta 111. Wetteren, Belgium: Moneta, 2010. 168 pp., illus.
Includes 162,894 coins found in Brabant and another 3161 coins found in uncertain locations in Belgium.

2550 **Depeyrot, Georges.** *Les Monnaies Hellénistique de Marseille.* Collection Moneta 16. Wetteren, Belgium: Moneta, 1999. 128 pp., 4 pls.
A collection and discussion of the nature and circulation of coinage in and around the Greek colony of Marseille. Depeyrot studies stylistic changes and influences from the fifth to the first century B.C., and in particular the adoption of regular features such as the lion depicted on the reverse. Chronological issues and the differing composition of the metals are discussed. Examples are described and illustrated providing a guide to identification.

2551 ——— *Le Numéraire Celtique I: La Gaule du Sud-Est.* Moneta 27. Wetteren, Belgium: Moneta, 2002. 200 pp., 7 pls.

2552 ——— *Le Numéraire Celtique II: La Gaule des Monnaies à la Croix.* Moneta 28. Wetteren, Belgium: Moneta, 2002. 262 pp., 10 pls.

2553 ——— *Le Numéraire Celtique III: De l'Atlantique aux Arvernes.* Moneta 36. Wetteren, Belgium: Moneta, 2003. 246 pp., 14 pls.
A study and analysis of the coinage of the Gaulish populations of Aquitania and Massif Central. This volume is devoted to the Nitiobroges, Bituriges, Vivisques, Petrocores, Santones, Lemovices, Pictons, and Arvernes.

2554 ——— *Le Numéraire Celtique IV: Bituriges, Eduens, Séquanes, Lingons.* Moneta 41. Wetteren, Belgium: Moneta, 2004. 326 pp., 17 pls.

2555 ——— *Le Numéraire Celtique V: Le Centre Parisien.* Moneta 44. Wetteren, Belgium: Moneta, 2005. 276 pp., 22 pls.

2556 ——— *Le Numéraire Celtique VI: De la Manche au Soissonnais.* Moneta 45. Wetteren, Belgium: Moneta, 2005. 316 pp., 22 pls.

2557 ——— *Le Numéraire Celtique VII: La Gaule Orientale.* Moneta 46. Wetteren, Belgium: Moneta, 2005. 280 pp., 12 pls.

2558 ——— *Le Numéraire Celtique VIII: La Gaule Occidentale.* Moneta 47. Wetteren, Belgium: Moneta, 2005. 380 pp., 24 pls.

2559 **Donop, Baron de.** *Les Medailles Gallo-Galliques.* Hanover, 1838.

2560 **Doyen, Jean-Marc.** *Catalogue des Monnaies Antiques: Monnaies du Monde Celtique et des Cites Grecques.* 1987. 86 pp., 10 pls.

2561 **Fischer, Brigitte.** *Les Monnaies Antiques d'Afrique du Nord Trouvées en Gaule.* Paris, 1978.

2562 **Forrer, Robert.** *Keltische Numismatik der Rhein- und Donaulande.* Strassburg, 1908. 373 pp., 46 pls. Reprinted with a new volume by Karel Castelin. Graz: Akademische Druck – u. Verlagsanstalt, 1968. 373 and 245 pp., 46 and 20 pls. [CS 5243]

2563 ——— *Les Monnaies Gauloises ou Celtiques Trouvées en Alsace.* Mulhouse, France, 1925. 117 pp., 7 pls. [CS 5133]

2564 **Furtwängler, Andreas E.** *Monnaies Grecques en Gaule: Le Trésor d'Auriol et le Monnayage de Massalia 525/520-460 av. J.-C.* Typos III. Fribourg: Office du Livre, 1978. 336 pp., 44 pls. [CS 2039]
A die study of the small silver coins found near Auriol (northeast of Marseille) in 1868. The coins are attributed to Massalia in Gaul. The author analyzes 1350 coins from the hoard, including 36 types—now referred to as "Auriol Find Class." Includes chronological, metallurgical, and metrological data, as well as discussions of iconographical and stylistic features of the coins. The coins date from ca. 530 B.C. to 460 B.C. Text in French, with English and German summaries.

2565 **Gebhard, R., G. Lehrberger, G. Morteani, C. Raub, U. Steffgen, and U. Wagner.** "Melting and Alloying Techniques of Celtic Gold Coins in Central Europe." *Metallurgy in Numismatics, Volume 4.* Special Publication No. 30. London: Royal Numismatic Society, 1998. Pages 518-25.
The authors aim to reconstruct the metallurgical processes used in Celtic times for the manufacture of precious metal coins. The analysis focuses on two points: (1) the analysis of the alloys and the metallography of the coins, and (2) the analysis of the technical ceramics, furnace fragments, and coin moulds involved in the manufacturing process. The analyzed coins are from different sites in Central Europe. The technical ceramics were found in the excavations at the Celtic Opidum of Manching. The technique for producing Celtic gold coins in Southern Germany can be summarized as follows: (1) Metal pieces were weighed and placed into clay moulds. The gold and silver sources were probably often Hellenistic objects, mostly coins, from the Mediterranean region. (2) The loaded moulds were covered with preheated charcoal in a small furnace and air was blown into the furnace with bellows. (3) After about two to five minutes, the melting point of the alloy was reached. The coin mould containing the blanks was allowed to cool down in a reducing atmosphere. (4) The blanks were struck and then reheated if necessary. This reheating must have been carried out in a reducing atmosphere to avoid the formation of copper oxide "scale."

2566 **Göbl, Robert.** *Ostkeltischer Typenatlas: Mit Methodischem Kommentar.* Braunschweig: Klinkhardt & Biermann, 1973. 43 pp., 52 pls. [CS 5244]

2566a ——— *Typologie und Chronologie der Keltischen Münzprägung in Noricum.* Denkschriften 113. Vienna: Österreichische Akademie der Wissenschaften, 1973. 154 pp., 50 pls. [CS 5245]

2567 ——— *Münzprägung und Geldverkehr der Kelten in Österreich.* Vienna, 1992.

2568 **Gruel, Katherine.** *Le Tresor de Trébry (Côte du Nord) 1er Siecle Avant Notre Ere.* Paris, 1981.

2569 **Haselgrave, Colin.** "The Development of Iron Age Coinage in Belgic Gaul." *Numismatic Chronicle* 159 (1999): 111-68. 3 pls.
Examines the chronological stages in the development of coinage in Iron Age Gaul from the third century B.C. to the early first century A.D.

2570 ———. "A New Approach to Analysing the Circulation of Iron Age Coinage." *Numismatic Chronicle* 165 (2005): 129-74.
Examines one way of using newly acquired archaeological evidence to investigate how the role and circulation of Iron Age coinage varied between regions and through time.

2571 **Hill, George F.** *On the Coins of Narbonensis with Iberian Inscriptions.* Numismatic Notes and Monographs, No. 44. New York: American Numismatic Society, 1930. 39 pp., 6 pls. [CS 5136]
Discusses a series of coins minted in the district of Narbonensis ca. 200-71 B.C. Discusses inscriptions and suggests factors which may have influenced the coin designs.

2572 **Hooker, John.** *Celtic Improvisations: An Art Historical Analysis of Coriosolite Coins.* British Archaeological Reports International Series 1092. Oxford: British Archaeological Reports, 2002. 120 pp, illus.
An exhaustive study of the coins of the ancient Celtic Coriosolite tribe, using the development of the art as the major theme. Follows the use and migration of symbols and explores their religious significance. Discusses the historical events which caused the minting of these coins, providing insight into money, trade, and warfare. What emerges is a snapshot of the Coriosolite tribe around the time of Caesar's invasion of Gaul. Includes a catalogue of the ninety-three dies found among the 10,000 coins in Jersey's La Marquanderie hoard.

2573 **Howe, T. P.** "Expressionist Fragments of Pre-Roman Gaul." *American Journal of Archaeology* 64 (1960): 186.
A summary of a paper presented at a conference. "The Gallic artists who re-interpreted the coin types of Philip of Macedon were, like other 'Expressionist' artists, submitting the earlier images to symbolic attack." [J. R. Jones, *NIAJAH*]

2574 **Kolníková, Eva.** "The Finds of Celtic Coins in Slovakia and the Main Problems of the East Celtic Coinage." *Proceedings of the 8th International Congress of Numismatics, New York—Washington, September 1973.* Edited by Herbert A. Cahn and Georges Le Rider. International Association of Professional Numismatists Publication, No. 4. Paris/Basel: International Association of Professional Numismatists, 1976. Pages 181-7. Illus., map.
Describes the main types of Celtic coins found in various parts of Slovakia. Discusses the weight standards, dates, and other problems of the coinage. A uniform monetary system did not exist. Rather, each socio-economic unit issued its own coins. The coinage expressed the interests of the ruling class. The coins were mainly of local value, within the tribe itself. The main types of Celtic coins found in Slovakia are illustrated by line drawings. Also includes a map of relevant coin finds in Slovakia.

2575 ———. "The Contribution of Slovak Finds to the Chronology of East Celtic Coinage." *Proceedings of the 10th International Congress of Numismatics, London, 1986.* International Association of Professional Numismatists Publication, No. 11. Edited by I. A. Carradice. London: International Association of Professional Numismatists, 1986. Pages 95-8.
Briefly discusses the contributions of Slovak hoards to the problems of the beginning and end of east Celtic coinage.

2576 **Kos, Peter.** *Keltski Novci Slovenije: Keltische Münzen Sloweniens.* Ljubljana: Narodni Muzej, 1977. 156 pp., illus.
A catalogue of Celtic coins discovered on the territory of present-day Slovenia up to 1975. Includes 1270 coins from 51 sites.

2577 **Kos, Peter, and Ivan Mirnik.** "The Ribnjacka Hoard (Bjelovar, Croatia)." *Numismatic Chronicle* 159 (1999): 298-306. 6 pls.
Examines a hoard of 112 eastern Celtic tetradrachms found in 1941. Seventy-one of the coins are catalogued here. The authors discuss the inscriptions on the coins.

2578 **Kostial, Michaela.** *Kelten im Osten: Gold und Silber der Kelten in Mittel- und Osteuropa. Sammlung Lanz.* Munich: Verlag der Staatlichen Münzsammlung München, 1997. 192 pp., illus. 2 maps.
A catalogue of 1047 middle and eastern European Celtic coins in the Staatlichen Münzsammlung from the collection of Hermann Lanz. Each coin is illustrated and described. Begins with an overview of the coinage which is followed by the catalogue of gold and silver coins.

2579 **Kretz, Rainer.** "A New 'Wolf-Rider' Quarter Stater from Northern Gaul." *Numismatic Circular* 111 (2003): 189-93. Illus.

2580 **Larozas, Christian.** *Les Monnaies de Potin du Sud-Est de la Gaule.* 2000. 92 pp., illus.
Examines the potin coins struck in southeastern Gaul.

2581 **Lengyel, Lancelot.** *L'Art Gaulois dans les Médailles.* Montrouge/Seine: Éditions Corvina, 1954. 59 pp., 48 pls. [CS 5140]
"Excellent photographs." [E. Clain-Stefanelli]

2582 **Lukanc, Ivo.** *Les Imitations des Monnaies d'Alexandre le Grand et de Thasos.* Wetteren, Belgium, 1996. 126 pp., 174 pl.

2583 **Mackensen, Michael.** "The State of Research on the 'Norican' Silver Coinage." *World Archaeology* 6, no. 3 (February 1975): 249-75. 4 pls., maps.
Discusses the west Norican and east Norican tetradrachm coinage, the small silver coinage, metrology of the coins, denominations, overstruck tetradrachms, areas of distribution and currency, and chronology. Concludes that the older "west" Norican coinage began ca. 65 B.C. The disappearance of the west Norican small silver coinage occurred, at the latest, in early Claudian times. The regnum Noricum now appears as a kind of tribal league of several reguli, as a result of restructuring the output from the mints.

2584 **Muret, Ernest, and Anatole Chabouillet.** *Catalogue des Monnaies Gauloises de la Bibliothèque Nationale.* Paris, 1889. Reprint. 327 pp. [CS 5144]

2585 **Nash, Daphne.** "The Chronology of Celtic Coinage in Gaul: the Arvernian 'Hegemony' Reconsidered." *Numismatic Chronicle* 7th ser., 15 (1975): 204-18. 1 pl. [CS 5145]
A review article examining J.-B. Colbert de Beaulieu's *Traité de Numismatique Celtique I: Methodologie des Ensembles* (Paris, 1973). [See Colbert de Beaulieu under CELTIC COINAGE—GENERAL WORKS].

2586 ——— *Settlement and Coinage in Central Gaul, c. 200-50 B.C.* BAR Supplementary Series 39(i). Two volumes. Oxford: British Archaeological Reports, 1978. 353 pp., 34 pls., maps. [CS 5146]
Examines the material remains of settlements and the coinage of Central Gaul from its origins in the late third century B.C. down to the Roman conquest in 50 B.C. Describes the development and chronology of the coinage, using archaeological evidence whenever possible. [Reviewed by D. Nony in *Revue Numismatique* (Paris) 6th ser., 20 (1978): 182-3].

2587 ——— "Coinage and State Development in Central Gaul." *Coinage and Society in Britain and Gaul: Some Current Problems*. Edited by Barry Cunliffe. London: The Council for British Archaeology, 1981. Pages 10-7.
Discusses the connections between the development of the Celtic coinages of the first century B.C. and that of Central Gaulish political formations. Discusses the development of coin-types at various cities and attempts to explain the changes which took place.

2588 ——— "Celtic Coinage in Western and Central Europe." *A Survey of Numismatic Research, 1978-1984. Volume 1: Ancient, Medieval and Modern Numismatics*. Edited by M. J. Price et al. International Association of Professional Numismatists Special Publication, No. 9. London: International Numismatic Commission, 1986. Pages 61-76.
A narrative overview of newly published works in the field of numismatics. Summarizes the major findings, with bibliographic references cited in the footnotes.

2588a **Nick, Michael.** "75 Kilogrammes of Celtic Small Coin—Recent Research on the 'Potinklumpen' from Zurich." *XIII Congreso Internacional de Numismática, Madrid – 2003: Actas–Proceedings–Actes I*. Edited by Carmen Alfaro, Carmen Marcos, and Paloma Otero. Madrid: International Numismatic Commisson, 2005. Pages 455-8. Illus.
A discussion of the clump of fused potin coins, estimated to contain nearly 18,000 coins, which was found in Zurich in 1890. The author refutes the theory that the coins were fused in a house fire. Rather, he provides evidence that they were smelted in a trough and were then slowly cooled. The smelting took place about 100 B.C. and the clump consisted of coins from the local area. The author raises the question of whether the partially melted coins were intended for use in a religious sacrifice.

2589 **Overbeck, Bernhard H.** "A Celtic Mint Recently Discovered in Kelheim-Mitterfeld." *Proceedings of the 10th International Congress of Numismatics, London, 1986*. International Association of Professional Numismatists Publication, No. 11. Edited by I. A. Carradice. London: International Association of Professional Numismatists, 1986. Pages 107-11.
The remains of a first century B.C. Celtic mint were found in Bavaria. Discusses some of the objects found, including clay molds used for producing coin blanks. The use of the molds is described.

2590 **Pauwels, Ghislaine.** *Les Monnaies de la Gaule Belgique*. Numismatic Pocket, Volume 12. Brussels: J. deMay, 1971. 100 pp., illus. [CS 5148]

2591 **Pink, Karl.** *Die Münzprägung der Ostkelten und ihrer Nachbarn*. Dissertationes Pannonicae 2, no. 15. Budapest/Leipzig, 1939. 159 pp., 30 pls. Second edition (enlarged by Robert Göbl), Brunswick, 1974. 136 pp., 30 pls. [CS 5282]

2592 **Ployart, Brigitte, and Monique Mainjonet.** *Choix de Monnaies Gauloises: Catalogue de Ektachromes du Service Photographique*. Paris: Bibliothèque Nationale Photothèque, 1980. 77 pp., 15 pls.

2593 **Rant, A.** "The Berke Hoard and Its Significance for the Study of Celtic Coinage in the Territory of Slovenia." *Proceedings of the 10th International Congress of Numismatics, London, 1986*. International Association of Professional Numismatists Publication, No. 11. Edited by I. A. Carradice. London: International Association of Professional Numismatists, 1986. Pages 113-6. 1 pl.
Records forty-eight Celtic coins found in 1981. They were probably buried ca. 35 B.C.

2594 **Reding, Lucien.** *Les Monnaies Gauloises tu Tetelbierg*. Luxembourg, 1972. 347 pp., 25 pls. [CS 5149]

2595 **Richard, L.** "Monnaies Coriosolites en Espagne." *Societé d' Emulation des Côtes-du-Nord* 102 (1973).

2596 **Rogers, G. B.** "A Bibliography of the Coinages of Massalia and the Related Gallo-Greek and Greco-Gallic Coinages." *Antipolis* (France) 1, no. 2 (1975): 118-22. [CS 2040]

2597 **Rolland, Henri.** "Monnaies Gallo-Grecques." *Congresso Internazionale di Numismatica, I: Relazioni*. Rome, 1961. Pages 111-9. [CS 2036]

2598 **Roth, Bernard.** "Ancient Gaulish Coins, including Those of the Channel Islands." *British Numismatic Journal* 9 (1912): 1-80. 10 pls. [CS 5158]
A catalogue of 235 coin types, providing a good sample of Gaulish types with much discussion and extensive descriptions.

2599 **Rudd, Chris.** "Unique Celtic Coin Named after Finder." *The Celator* 15, no. 7 (July 2001): 43, 47. Illus.
Describes a new variety of Celtic coin which was found with a metal detector in England in 2000. The coin is a new and unpublished gold half-stater of the Ambiani region, struck in the late third or early second century B.C. The reverse features a rider blowing a Celtic war-trumpet and a "surrendering man" below the horse. The variety has been named "Butt's Trumpet" in honor of the finder, Frank Butt.

2600 ——— "Hoard Found in Brittany." *The Celator* 22, no. 5 (May 2008): 35, 56, 55. Illus.
Announces a hoard of Iron Age Amorican coins found at Laniscat in 2007, containing 545 base-gold and silver coins (58 staters, 487 quarter-staters). All were minted in the early first century B.C. by the Osismii tribe of West Brittany. The hoard included six examples of the extremely rare Carantec Type electrum stater.

2601 ——— "The Celtic Coin That Says It Is Celtic." *The Celator* 24, no. 2 (February 2010): 37-40. Illus.
Discusses a rare bronze *as* from southern Spain (*obv.*, laureate male bust; *rev.*, boar standing on spearhead) of the second or first century B.C. It was struck at Celti (the present-day town of Peñaflor). The word CELT appears on the reverse of the coin.

2602 **Saussaye, L. de la.** *Numismatique de la Gaule Narbonnaise.* Paris, 1842. Reprint, Chicago, 1976. 249 pp., 39 pls. [CS 5160]

2603 **Saves, Georges.** *Le Monnaies Gauloises 'à la Croix' et Assimilées du Sud-Ouest de la Gaule: Examen et Catalogue.* Toulouse, 1976. 239 pp., 30 pls. [CS 5161]

2604 **Scheers, Simone.** "Le Premier Monnayage des Ambiani." *Revue Belge de Numismatique* (Belgium) 114 (1968): 45-73. 6 pls. [CS 5163]

2605 ——— *Les Monnaies de la Gaul Inspirées de Celles de la République Romaine.* Louvain: Université de Louvain, 1969. 270 pp., 12 pls., 57 maps. [CS 5164]

2606 ——— "Un Monnayage Ambien Attribué aux Bellovaci." *Revue Belge de Numismatique* (Belgium) 115 (1969): 5-56. 3 pls. [CS 5165]

2607 ——— "Un Monnayage Gaulois non Attribué de la Côte Maritime Belge." *Revue Belge de Numismatique* (Belgium) 116 (1970): 65-90. 2 pls. [CS 5166]

2608 ——— "Les Monnaies des Peuples Belges Portrait une Tête Humaine de Face." *Revue Numismatique* (France) 6th ser., 13 (1971): 38-75. 2 pls. [CS 5168]

2609 ——— "Coinage and Currency of the Belgic Tribes during the Gallic War." *British Numismatic Journal* 41 (1972): 1-6. 1 pl., maps.
Describes a phase of Belgic coinage of special importance derived from a single prototype, the staters of the Ambiani with types on both sides. This series was formerly but wrongly attributed to the Atrebates, and must have been struck immediately before the Gallic War, waged between Caesar and the Belgae from 58 to 50 B.C.

2610 ——— *Les Monnaies Gauloises de la Collection A. Danicourt à Pérrone (France, Somme).* Travaux du Cercle d'Études Numismatiques 7. Brussels, 1975. 121 pp., 24 pls. [CS 5170]

2611 ——— *Traité de Numismatique Celtique, Volume 2: La Gaule Belgique.* Annales Littéraires de l'Universite de Besançon 195. Paris: Belles Lettres, 1977. 986 pp., 28 pls. Second edition. Louvain, 1983. 986 pp., 28 pl. [CS 5172]
[For *Volume 1*, see Colbert de Beaulieu under CELTIC COINAGE—GENERAL WORKS].

2612 ——— *Monnaies Gauloises de Seine-Maritime.* Rouen: Musée Départmentale des Antiquites, 1978. 255 pp., 47 pls. [CS 5173]

2613 ——— "The Origins and Evolution of Coinage in Belgic Gaul." *Coinage and Society in Britain and Gaul: Some Current Problems.* Edited by Barry Cunliffe. London: The Council for British Archaeology, 1981. Pages 18-23.
Discusses the origins of coinage in Belgic Gaul and its evolution after the Gallic war. Describes the birth of Gaulish coins from Greek prototypes. Discusses the date of the introduction of coinage in Gaul and changes in coin weights.

2614 ——— *La Gaule Belgique. Traité de Numismatique Celtique.* Second edition. Peeters, 1983.

2615 ——— "The Face on the Defaced Die." *Spink Numismatic Circular* 97, no. 6 (July/August 1989): 190. Illus.
Discusses the Defaced Die staters. The original die used to strike Gallo-Belgic A staters carried the head of Apollo.

2616 ——— *Un Complement a l'Atlas de Monnaies Gauloises Henri de la Tour.* 1992. 41 pp.
A supplement to Henri de La Tour's classic 1892 catalogue (see 2542) incorporating new information and correcting attributions.

2617 **Stills, John.** *Gaulish and Early British Gold Coinage.* London, 2003. 555 pp., 17 pls.
An analysis of Celtic gold coinage from the arrival of Philip in Gaul to the start of the Gallic wars. Emphasis is placed on the coinage of northeastern France and southern England. Catalogues 3000 coins. Illustrates 540 types. Includes thirty-nine coin distribution maps.

2618 ——— "Identifying Gallic War Uniface Staters." *Chris Rudd List 83* (2005): 2-6.

2619 ——— "Horse Spurs and the Chronology of Belgic Gold Coinage." *Spink Numismatic Circular* 113, no. 6 (December 2005): 367-9. Illus.
Shows that the proposition that closely related Belgic small flan coinages were struck in different archaeological periods fails on numismatic grounds, and that recent modifications to Scheers' 1972 and 1977 classifications have strengthened rather than weakened the arguments in favor of them being Gallic War issues.

2620 "Suspicions Voiced on Celtic Gold Coins' Authenticity." *The Celator* 16, no. 6 (June 2002): 43.
Illustrates and describes a possible modern forgery of a supposedly new variety of Gallo-Belgic gold quarter stater.

2621 **Thirion, Marcel.** "Le Trésor de Fraire: Monnaies Gauloises en Potin." *Revue Belge de Numismatique* (Belgium) 108 (1962): 67-112. [CS 5176]

2622 **Torbágyi, Melinda.** "Bemerkungen zur Chronologie der Keltischen Münzen vom Kapostaler Typ." *Stephanos Nomismatikos: Edith Schönert-Geiss zum 65. Geburtstag.* Edited by Ulrike Peter. Berlin: Akademie Verlag, 1998. Pages 631-42.

2623 **Tzamalis, Anastasios P.** "Waiting for the Barbarians." *Nomismatika Khronika* (Greece) 26 (2007): 5-10. Illus.
Begins with the poem "Waiting for the Barbarians" by C. P. Cavafy. Then Tzamalis relates the poem to a gold half stater of the Parisii. In Greek and English.

2624 **Villard, François.** "La Production Monétaire de Marseille." *La Céramique Grecque de Marseille.* Bibliothèque des Écoles Française d'Athènes et de Rome, Volume 95. Paris, 1960. [CS 2041]

2624a **Villaronga, Leandre.** "Les Rapports Numismatique entre Massalia et Emporium." *Quaderni Ticinesi: Numismatica e Antichità Classiche* (Switzerland) 20 (1991).

2625 **Wernicke, I.** *Die Kelten in Italian. Die Einwanderung und die frühen Handelsbeziehungen zu den Etruskern.* Stuttgart, 1991.

2626 **Wigg, David G., and Josef Riederer.** "Die Chronologie der Keltischen Münzprägung am Mittelrhein." *Stephanos Nomismatikos: Edith Schönert-Geiss zum 65. Geburtstag.* Edited by Ulrike Peter. Berlin: Akademie Verlag, 1998. Pages 661-74.

2627 **Wightman, Edith M.** "The Celtic Coinage of Pre-Roman Gaul: An Historical Introduction." *Cornucopiæ* (publication of The Ancient Coin Society, Canada) 2, no. 3 (1974): 33-46. Illus. [CS 5178]
A general introduction to the pre-Roman, and especially the Gaulish, coinage. Discusses the date of the first Celtic imitations of Greek coin types and the date of the first imitation of Roman types. Discusses the local stylistic variations of the types. Includes a brief bibliographic note. Illustrated by coins in the Royal Ontario Museum, Toronto.

2628 ———. "Gaulish Boars: Two Gold Coins from the Royal Ontario Museum." *Cornucopiæ* (publication of The Ancient Coin Society, Canada) 4 (1979): 23-8. Illus., map.
Two rare Celtic gold staters are examined. The obverses show a stylized head looking left. Below the neck is an inverted stylized wild boar. The reverses depict a horse with a bird above and a boar below. The coins probably came from the Lens hoard.

2629 **Wüthrich, Gottlieb.** "Celtic Numismatics in Switzerland." *Numismatic Chronicle* 6th ser., 5 (1945): 1-33. 7 pls. [CS 5306]
Begins with a summary of the history of Switzerland since prehistoric times. Discusses gold and silver mining in Switzerland. Comments on the various types of Celtic coins minted in Switzerland. Illustrates 171 varieties.

Also see: Bernard et al. "Experimental Study" under METALLURGY; Cunliffe *Coinage and Society* under CELTIC COINAGE OF BRITAIN; Bellido "Coinage and Ethnicity" under SPAIN; Jenkins "Carthage, N. Africa, the Iberian Peninsula, Gaul" under NORTH AFRICA—GENERAL WORKS; Kos "The Monetary Circulation in the Southeastern Alpine Region" under GENERAL WORKS—GREEK; Müseler "A Coin from the Kingdom of Tylis" under THRACE—GENERAL WORKS; Price *Coins: An Illustrated Survey* under GENERAL WORKS—GREEK; Sills *Gaulish and Early British Gold Coinage* under CELTIC COINAGE OF BRITAIN; Stannard and Frey-Kupper "'Pseudomints' and Small Change in Italy and Sicily" under ITALY—GENERAL WORKS; van Heesch and Heeren *Coinage in the Iron Age* under CELTIC COINAGE—GENERAL WORKS.

ITALY

The coins of Magna Graecia of the classical age are, therefore, singularly important in the history of art. Representing a rich segment of the Greek world which has left us so little major art, they have close connections to the utterly perished painting of Zeuxis and Greek painting's achievements in the portrayal of visual space. In their types, moreover, there is a tension between the traditions of archaic art and the energy of the classical style. And even through the oblique language of mythology, they may be interpreted as historical voices from a region of Greece where history is so often silent.

—R. Ross Holloway, 1978

GENERAL WORKS

2630 **Arnold-Biucchi, Carmen.** "Magna Graecia and Sicily." *A Survey of Numismatic Research 1990-1995.* Edited by C. Morrisson and B. Kluge. Berlin, 1997. Pages 27-37.
A narrative bibliography covering newly published works.

2631 **Attianese, Pasquale.** *Calabria Greca—Greek Coins of Calabria.* Three volumes. Collana: Populorum Numismata Omnia, 1974-1980. [CS 2087]

1. *Brettion, Kaulonia, Cosentia, Kroton, Medma, Noyceria, Pandosia, Skyllation, Temsa, Terina.* 1974. 398 pp., illus.
2. *Aminea, Hipponion, Valentia, Laos, Lokron, Kasarium, Mystia ed Hyporon, Ser..o Mer…, Peripolium, Sybaris, Siris, Thurium.* 1977. 439 pp., illus.
3. *Thurium (cont'd), Copia, Rhegium.* 1980. 548 pp., illus.

2631a ——— *Petelia: La Collezione Luigi E. Romano.* Catanzaro: Rubbettino Editore, 2003. 460 pp., illus.
Preface by Italo Vecchi.

2632 **Attianese, Pasquale, and Santelli Giovanni.** *Le Contromarche del Bruttium.* Nummus et Historia XII. Cassino: Editrice Diana, 2007. 63 pp., illus.
Examines the countermarks which appear on coins of Bruttium.

2633 **Benson, Frank Sherman.** "Ancient Greek Coins." *American Journal of Numismatics* 34-40 (details below). Also privately printed in four volumes, Boston, 1900-04. 14 pls.
This series of articles provides an introduction to Greek coinage and a catalogue of types illustrated by specimens from the author's fabulous collection. Part 16 concludes with the statement "To Be Continued." Unfortunately, Benson died on February 28, 1907, bringing an end to the series. Benson's collection was sold in 1909. [See Sotheby & Co., *Catalogue of the Valuable Collection of Greek Coins Formed by the Late Frank Sherman Benson* under PRIVATE COLLECTIONS].

1. Introduction	34, no. 3 (January 1900): 61-8
2. Magna Graecia	34, no. 4 (April 1900): 93-102. 1 pl., map
2. (Continued)	35, no. 1 (July 1900): 1-10. 1 pl., map
3. Magna Graecia	35, no. 2 (October 1900): 33-42. 1 pl., map
4. Terina (Magna Graecia)	35, no. 3 (January 1901): 65-71. 1 pl.
5. Syracuse, Sicily	35, no. 4 (April 1901): 93-102
6. Syracuse, 2	36, no. 1 (July 1901): 1-10. 2 pls.
7. Syracuse, 3	36, no. 2 (October 1901): 33-40. 1 pl.
7. (Continued)	36, no. 3 (January 1902): 65-71. 1 pl.
8. Syracuse, 4	36, no. 4 (April 1902): 97-103. 1 pl.
9. Syracuse, 5	37, no. 1 (July 1902): 1-6. 1 pl.
10. Syracuse, 6	37, no. 2 (October 1902): 33-9. 1 pl.
11. Sicily, 1	37, no. 4 (April 1903): 97-103. 1 pl., map
12. Sicily, 2	38, no. 2 (October 1903): 33-9. 1 pl.
13. Sicily, 3 (Kamarina, Leontinoi)	39, no. 1 (July 1904): 1-8. 1 pl.
14. Sicily, 4 (Katane)	39, no. 2 (October 1904): 29-35. 1 pl.
15. Sicily, 5 (Zankle-Messana)	39, no. 4 (April 1905): 93-9. 1 pl.
16. Sicily, 6 (Motya, Naxos)	40, no. 2 (October 1905): 29-34. 1 pl.

2634 **Breglia, Laura.** "La Coniazione Incusa di Magna Grecia e la sua Attuale Problematica." *Annali, Istituto Italiano de Numismatica* (Italy) 3 (1956): 23-37. [CS 2062]

2635 ——— *Magna Grecia.* Arte e Moneta 1. Rome: Istituto Italiano di Numismatica, 1958. 4 pp., 16 pls. [CS 2063 and 3547]
"Each plate is devoted to an enlargement (x 3 or 4) of a single coin-type selected from the mints of Ami-, Croton, Heraclea, Locris, Metapontum, Neapolis, Rhegium and Tarentum. The reverse of each plate shows in natural size the complete coin from which the enlargement is taken together with a description, a brief bibliography and a discussion of its significance and of problems connected with it. All the specimens are from the Museo Nazionale, Naples. Further similar folders are in course of preparation." [C. Kraay, *NL* 46]

2636 **Brunetti, Lodovico.** *Zecche della Magna Grecia, Visuali Sistematiche.* Trieste, 1967. 43 pp., illus. [CS 2064]

2637 **Burnett, Andrew M.** "The Coinages of Rome and Magna Graecia in the Late Fourth and Third Centuries B.C." *Revue Suisse de Numismatique* (Switzerland) 56 (1977): 92-121. Illus. [CS 2065]

2638 ——— "The South Italy Hoard (*IGCH* 2009 = *RRCH* 36)." *Coin Hoards* 4 (1978): 25. 1 pl.
Briefly describes a hoard of about 300 coins found in 1949, of which only twenty-six coins have been recorded. Provides evidence for the chronology of the coins of Teate, demonstrating that they were contemporaneous with the Campano-Tarentine staters. Shows that the Roman didrachms with the inscription ROMA were struck after the end of the Neopolitan and Campano-Tarentine coinage.

2639 ——— "Naples and South Italy: Coinage and Prosperity, ca. 300 B.C." *La Monetazione di Neapolis nella Campania Antica. Atti del VII Convegni del Centro Internazionale di Studi Numismatici di Napoli 1980.* Edited by A. Stazio and M. Taliercio Mensitieri. Naples, 1986. Pages 23-43.

2640 **Burnett, Andrew M., and D. R. Hook.** "The Fineness of Silver Coins in Italy and Rome during the Late Fourth and Third Centuries B.C." *Quaderni Ticinesi: Numismatica e Antichità Classiche* (Switzerland) 18 (1989): 151-67.

2641 **Cahn, Herbert A.** "Artiste ou Magistrat?" *Travaux de Numismatique Grecque Offerts à Georges Le Rider.* Edited by M. Amandry and S. Hurter. London: Spink, 1999. Pages 103-7. 2 pls.
Discusses the signed dies of Italy and Sicily.

2642 **Cahn, Herbert A., Leo Mildenberg, Roberto Russo, and Hans Voegtli.** *Antikenmuseum Basel und Sammlung Ludwig: Griechische Münzen aus Grossgriechenland und Sizilien.* Basel: Antikenmuseum Basel und Sammlung Ludwig, 1988. 276 pp., illus., 48 pls.
A catalogue of 571 outstanding coins of Italy and Sicily, including many signed coins. All coins are illustrated throughout the book, and many of the finest coins appear in the forty-eight plates of enlargements. All engravers' signatures are photographed and enlarged. Includes extensive attribution notes for each coin. [Also see Numismatica Ars Classica *Auction 13* below for the catalogue of the auction sale of this collection].

2642a **Caltabiano, Maria Caccamo.** "La Monetazione Annibalica di Petelia." *Quaderni Ticinesi. Numismatica e Antichità Classiche* (Switzerland) 5 (1976): 85-101.

2643 **Cantilena, R.** "Le Frazioni." *La Monetazione di Neapolis nel IV-III sec. a.C. Convegni del Centro Internazionale di Studi Numismatici di Napoli.* Napoli, 1986.

2644 **Cesano, S. L.** "Di due Piccoli Ripostigli di Argenti Cartaginesi e dei Brettii." *Transactions of the International Numismatic Congress Organized and Held in London by the Royal Numismatic Society, June 30-July 3, 1936.* Edited by J. Allan, H. Mattingly, and E. S. G. Robinson. London: B. Quaritch, 1938. Pages 56-67. 1 pl.

2645 **Chittendon, Jacqueline.** "Pythagoras and the Incuse Coinage of Magna Graecia." *Numismatic Review* 6, no. 3 (1965): 118-20. Illus., map.
Chittendon attributes the style of the incuse coinage to Pythagoras and suggests these coins were struck from hinged dies. Her theories have not been well accepted.

2646 **Crawford, Michael H.** "The Mugnano Hoard." *Numismatic Chronicle* 149 (1989): 149.
Mentions a hoard found in Campania which included Campanian bronze coins but not Roman pieces. The hoard also included coins from the last period of activity of the mint of Neapolis. [Also see next entry].

2647 ——— "The Mugnano Hoard." *Coin Hoards, Volume VIII: Greek Hoards.* Edited by U. Wartenberg, M. J. Price, and K. A. McGregor. London: Royal Numismatic Society, 1994. Page 82.
A brief mention of a small hoard (*Coin Hoards VIII*, no. 291) from Mugnano in Campania, which was originally published in 1888. Contained 12 bronzes of Suessa, 9 bronzes of Neapolis, and 4 late bronzes of Neapolis. [Also see previous entry].

2648 ——— "Provenances, Attributions and Chronology of Some Early Italian Coinages." *Coin Hoards, Volume IX: Greek Hoards.* Edited by A. Meadows and Ute Wartenberg. London: Royal Numismatic Society, 2002. Pages 269-74.
A discussion of the attribution and dating of some items in *Historia Numorum* (third edition, 2001; see N. Rutter below): the oval series of aes grave sextons (nos. 51-5) usually attributed to Tudor, may belong to Volsinii. Rome (nos. 251-342); fistlus (nos. 611-19); bronze coins with Oscan *tiiatium* (no. 699); Sidion/Silvium (no. 822); Carthaginian electrum with Janiform head/Jupiter in quadriga (no. 2013); head of Dionysus right/panther bronze (nos. 2667-73). Comments on each.

2649 **Daehn, William E.** "The Incuse Coinage of Southern Italy." *The Celator* 7, no. 4 (April 1993): 30-5. Illus.

Explores the reasons for the invention, usage, and demise of the incuse style of coinage in southern Italy during the archaic period. Among other theories examined, the author considers the role Pythagoras may have played in the development of this unusual coinage.

2650 **de la Houssaye, Noël.** *Les Bronzes Italiotes Archaïques et leur Symbolique: Étude de Numismatique Comparée.* Paris, 1938. 42 pp., 5 pls. [CS 2071]

2651 **Friedlaender, Julius.** *Die Oskischen Münzen.* Leipzig: In Commission bei George Wigand, 1850. 91 pp., 10 engraved plates.
Greek coinage of Italy.

2652 **Gardner, Percy.** "Coins Struck by Hannibal in Italy." *Numismatic Chronicle* 3rd ser., 4 (1884): 220-4. Illus.
Gardner suggests that some coins of Campania bear clear traces of the influence of Hannibal. They are electrum coins placed at the end of the Romano-Campanian series (*obv.*, janiform head; *rev.*, Zeus in quadriga). These were minted at Capua. Gardner discusses the reasons for his attributions.

2653 **Garraffo, Salvatore.** *Le Riconiazioni in Magna Grecia e in Sicilia: Emmissioni Argentee dal VI al IV Secolo a.C.* Studi e Materiali di Archeologia Greca 2. Catania, 1984.
Examines the overstriking of silver coinage in Magna Graecia and Sicily from the sixth through the fourth centuries B.C.

2654 ——— "Riconiazioni e Cronologie in Magna Grecia." *Kraay—Mørkholm Essays: Numismatic Studies in Memory of C. M. Kraay and O. Mørkholm.* Numismatica Lovaniensia 10. Edited by G. Le Rider, G. K. Jenkins, N. Waggoner, and U. Westermark. Louvain-la-Neuve: Université Catholique de Louvain, 1989. Pages 59-67. 1 pl.

2655 **Garrucci, P. Raffaele.** *Le Monete dell'Italia Antica.* Rome, 1885. Reprint in two volumes, Bologna: A. Forni, 1967. [CS 2043]
"An old but still useful collection of material." [E. Clain-Stefanelli]

2656 **Giesecke, Walther.** *Italia Numismatica: Eine Geschichte der Italienischen Geldsysteme bis zur Kaiserzeit.* Leipzig, 1928. 373 pp., 24 pls. [CS 2044]
"Emphasizes metrological problems." [E. Clain-Stefanelli]

2657 **Gorini, Giovanni.** *La Monetazione Incusa della Magna Graecia.* Milan: Edizioni Arte e Moneta, 1975. 233 pp., illus., maps. [CS 2067]
Examines the incuse coinage of Southern Italy including coins of Siris and Pyxos, Sybaris, Metapontum, Croton, Caulonia, Tarentum, Poseidonia, and Zankle. Numerous varieties are catalogued and illustrated. Followed by a full discussion of the coinage, accompanied by many greatly enlarged photographs.

2658 ——— "La Prima Fase della Monetazione Greca di Bronzo in Adriatico." *Revista Italiana di Numismatica* 6th ser., 23 (1976): 7-16. 2 pls. [CS 2050]
Includes English, French, and German summaries.

2659 ——— "Per Uno Studio della Monetazione di Medma." *Numismatica e Antichità Classiche* 14 (1985): 127-40.
A study of the coinage of the city of Medma in Southern Italy. [Also see Gorini "Die Sequence" below].

2660 ——— "The Die Sequence of the Silver Staters of Medma." *American Journal of Numismatics* 2nd ser., 20 (2008): 143-54.
A die study of the coinage of the mint of Medma in Southern Italy, incorporating and extending Gorini's earlier study (see "Per Uno Studio" above). The coinage is arranged in six groups which cover the period from 330 to 317 B.C. in a corpus of about eighty-nine specimens. The die analysis makes a contribution to the understanding of the poorly documented history of this ancient town and the connection with the similar coinage at Locri. Lists the five hoards that contained coins of Medma. [The plates for this paper were inadvertently left out. They appear in *American Journal of Numismatics* 2nd ser., 21 (2009), plates 14 and 15].

2661 **Grose, Sidney W.** "Some Rare Coins of Magna Graecia." *Numismatic Chronicle* 4th ser., 16 (1916): 201-45. 2 pls.
Discusses some interesting coins in the McClean Collection including coins from Cales, Neapolis, Graxa, Tarentum, Croton, Laus and Sybaris, Rhegium, Terina, Catana, Entella, Himera, Leontini, Messana, Morgantina, Syracuse, and Tauromenium.

2662 **Hands, Alfred Watson.** *Coins of Magna Graecia: The Coinage of the Greek Colonies of Southern Italy.* London: Spink, 1909. Reprint, Bologna: Forni, 1984. 337 pp., illus., map. [CS 2068]
A reprint of a series of articles which originally appeared in monthly installments in *Spink Numismatic Circular*, 1906-8. Describes the main coin types of Neapolis, Metapontum, Croton, Sybaris, Thurium, Siris, Heracleia, Laüs, Terina, Locri Epizephyrii, Rhegium, Pandosa, Hipponium, Temesa, Mesma, and other cities of Italy. Includes a discussion of weight standards.

2663 ——— *Italo-Greek Coins of Southern Italy.* London: Spink, 1912. 207 pp., illus.
A reprint of a series of articles which originally appeared in monthly installments in *Spink Numismatic Circular*, 1908-10. A study of the Greek coinage of Italy with the goal of providing insights into how Roman coinage evolved from it. Presents a city-by-city discussion of the coinage, providing history of the people and tribes and lists of coin types. Illustrated by photographs throughout.

2664 **Holloway, R. Ross.** "Alexander the Molossian and the Attic Standard in Magna Graecia." *La Circolazione della Moneta Ateniense in Silicia e in Magna Grecia.* Atti del I Convegno del Centro Internazionale di Studi Numismatici: Napoli 5-8 Aprile 1967. Supplement to *Annali. Istituto Italiano di Numismatica* 12-14. Rome, 1969. Pages 131-40.

2665 ——— *Art and Coinage in Magna Graecia.* Bellinzona: Edizioni Arte E Moneta, 1978. 173 pp. including 89 pls., map. [CS 2069]
A study of the coinage of the Greek cities of Southern Italy in the fifth and fourth centuries B.C. as artistic documents. Explores the historical and mythological influences on the coinage. Comparisons are made between the coins and other art works such as sculptures, vase-paintings, tomb paintings,

and bronze reliefs. An historical introduction to the cities is followed by a discussion of each city's art and coinage. Concludes with a chapter discussing artists' signatures on coins. The eighty-nine plates incorporate enlarged photographs of fifty-six coins, each of them a numismatic masterpiece. Many of them are presented in comparison with other works of art displaying similar themes.

2666 **Imhoof-Blumer, Friedrich.** "Zur Münzkunde Grossgriechenlands, Siciliens, Kretas, etc." *Numismatische Zeitschrift* 18 (1886): 205-86. 3 pls. [CS 2070]

2667 **Johnston, Ann.** "Report of a Discussion on South Italian Chronology, 350-280 B.C." *Coin Hoards* 7 (1985): 45-53.
Re-examines the chronologies proposed for the coinage of Taras, Metapontum, and Neapolis, presenting findings from a 1981 seminar on the subject. Reviews recent hoard evidence and proposes revised dating.

2668 **Kraay, Colin M.** "Two Late Fifth Century B.C. Hoards from South Italy." *Revue Suisse de Numismatique* (Switzerland) 49 (1970): 47-76. 2 pls. [CS 3250]
"The later elements of the Paestum 1858 hoard (S.P. Noe, *A Bibliography of Greek Coin Hoards*, 2nd ed. pp. 204-207, No. 782) are examined in detail in order to determine the date of burial. An account of the so-called Oecist hoard, discovered near Taranto about 1948, is here given for the first time. Both hoards were buried within the last quarter of the fifth century and appear to be separated by no more than a decade. The Oecist hoard is the earlier. An appendix shows that Noe no. 277 (pp. 83-84) and no. 506 (p. 138) are both very probably parts of a single hoard discovered near Croton in 1927 and buried ca. 430 B.C." [C. Kraay, *NL* 87]

2669 ——— "Catanzaro Environs, Bruttium, Italy 1967 (*IGCH* 2019)." *Coin Hoards* 3 (1977): 18-20. 2 pls.
Publishes a hoard of thirty-six silver coins of Neapolis, Taras, Heraclea, the Bretti, Carthage, and Rome buried in the late third century B.C.

2670 ——— "A Mid-Fifth Century Hoard from South Italy." Edited by C. E. King. *Revue Suisse de Numismatique* (Switzerland) 66 (1987): 7-46. Illus.
"A major hoard from the south Italian mints of Caulonia, Croton, Laus, Metapontum, Poseidonia, Sybaris, Taras and Velia, deposited ca. 445 B.C., is here published. Implications for relative chronology and metrology are extensively discussed." [A. Walker, *NL* 121]. Slightly modified dates for some incuse issues are suggested.

2671 **Le Rider, Georges.** "À Propos d'un Passage des *Poroi* de Xénophon: La Question du Change et les Monnaies Incuses d'Italie du Sud." *Kraay—Mørkholm Essays: Numismatic Studies in Memory of C. M. Kraay and O. Mørkholm.* Numismatica Lovaniensia 10. Edited by G. Le Rider, G. K. Jenkins, N. Waggoner, and U. Westermark. Louvain-la-Neuve: Université Catholique de Louvain, 1989. Pages 159-72.
Discusses the incuse coinage of Southern Italy.

2672 **Lloyd, A. H.** "Some Rare or Unpublished Coins of Magna Graecia in My Collection." *Numismatic Chronicle* 5th ser., 4 (1924): 129-40. 2 pls.
Describes and discusses the significance of twenty-one coins of Neapolis, Teanum, Tarentum, Heraclea, Metapontum, Thurium, Caulonia, Croton, Rhegium, and Terina. Each is illustrated.

2673 **Luynes, Duc de.** "Monnaies Incuses de la Grande Grèce." *Annales de l'Institut de Correspondance Archéologique* new ser., 2 (1836): 372-83.

2674 **MacDonald, David.** "Sicilian and South Italian Overstrikes on Pegasoi." *Nomismatika Khronika* (Greece) 21 (2002): 55-64. Illus.
Staters of Corinth and her colonies traveled to Sicily and Southern Italy from their beginnings, well into the fourth century B.C. In Italy, they were clipped down to the weight of the Achaian didrachm and overstruck by Taras, Metapontion, Thourioi, Kroton, and Velia. MacDonald explores the reasons for the movement of Pegasoi to Southern Italy—the reasons are found in contemporary events on mainland Greece. Reviews prior scholarship on this issue. Concludes that Timoleon's role in the importation of Pegasoi has been grossly exaggerated. Rather, a famine in Greece required large imports of grain from the west, resulting in the flow of Corinthian coinage into Italy and Sicily.

2675 **Macdonald, George.** "On a Find Made in the Islands, including an Unpublished Coin of Rhegium." *Numismatic Chronicle* 3rd ser., 16 (1896): 185-90. Illus.
Describes a small hoard of silver coins found in ancient Hiera. Includes sixty-two didrachms of Cales, Neapolis, Tarentum, Campano-Tarentine, Velia, Rhegium, one uncertain coin, plus a previously unpublished two-litra coin of Rhegium. The hoard was buried ca. 260 B.C.

2676 **McClean, John R.** "The True Meaning of Φ on the Coinage of Magna Graecia." *Numismatic Chronicle* 4th ser., 7 (1907): 107-10.
The letter Φ is found on coins of Velia, Thurium, Terina, Pandosia, Tarentum, and Metapontum. McClean doubts that the letter designates an engraver or mintmaster due to its long period of use. He believes this, as well as similar letters found on coins, represents either the number of units which the coin contains, or the number of units in the standard upon which it is based. McClean suggests these are marks of value, conveying the relative and absolute values of different coins in contemporary series.

2677 **Milne, Joseph G.** "An Exchange-Currency of Magna Graecia." *Journal of Roman Studies* 34 (1944): 46-8. 1 pl.
Discusses the so-called "Campano-Tarentine" staters with obv., nymph (similar to the head on coins of Neapolis) instead of the type of "boy on dolphin" typically associated with Tarentum. The coins are struck on the standard of the cities of the west coast of Magna Graecia, rather than on the standard of Tarentum. Arthur Evans suggested they were struck by Tarentum, perhaps after 310 B.C., for circulation alongside the Neapolitan coins in Campania. Milne publishes a coin with an inscription which, along with the weight standard, leads him to believe the coins were intended for circulation in Bruttium. He suggests the series may have been struck as early as 350 B.C. Discusses the economic and monetary situation of the "Bruttio-Tarentine" trade area.

2678 ——— "A Hoard of Brettian Bronze." *Numismatic Chronicle* 6th ser., 4 (1944): 114-5.
Lists some coins of the Bretti probably found in Italy.

2679 **Mitchell, Richard E.** "The Fourth Century Origin of the Roman Didrachm." *Museum Notes* 15 (1969): 41-71. 1 pl.

Re-examines the controversy over the dating of Rome's earliest coins, the Romano-Campanian didrachms, variously dated between 326 and 269 B.C. Argues in favor of an early chronology. Suggests Rome's early coinage was an attempt to win influence among the coin-issuing states of Italy and Sicily, such as Neapolis, Metapontum, Thurii, Carthage, and Syracuse.

2680 **Montenegro, E.** *Monete di Italia Antica e Magna Graecia.* Turin, 1996. 992 pp.

2681 **Morcom, John.** "Some South Italian Questions." *Pour Denyse: Divertissements Numismatiques.* Edited by S. Hurter and C. Arnold-Biucchi. Bern, Switzerland: Privately published, 2000. Pages 159-63. Illus.
(1) Examines two bronze coins with stag's head, K–A/plough, BPEIΓ and man-headed bull, TPAEΣ/barley corn, BPEIΓ. The coins have been variously attributed to Brindis, the Bretti, Metapontum, or Thurium. Discusses find spots of these coins. The identity of the mints remains uncertain. (2) Discusses a small bronze coin, *SNG Morcom* 878, with male head wearing a conical helmet/Skylla. The coin probably belongs to Skylletion/Skylakion. Discusses the attribution.

2682 **Noe, Sydney P.** "Overstrikes in Magna Graecia." *Museum Notes* 7 (1957): 13-42. 10 pls. [CS 2072 and 3375]
Lists all the coins of Magna Graecia overstruck on coins for which the undertypes are identifiable. Explores the evidence for the source of silver for the earliest coins of south Italy. Places the end of the incuse coinage ca. 460 B.C. Shows that incuse coins were struck over other incuse coins prior to the overstriking of foreign double-relief coins. Lists and discusses various groups of overstrikes. Concludes that the theory that silver was exported from Corinth in the form of coins has been given far too much emphasis. The incuse coins do not supply evidence for it until after 510 B.C.

2683 **Noehden, George Henry.** *A Selection of Ancient Coins.* London: Septimus Prowett, 1824. 38 pp., 10 pls.
This examination of selected coins of Italy and Sicily begins with a discussion of the meaning of the term "Magna Graecia." Noehden concludes it refers only to Italy, not to Italy and Sicily. He then examines ten coins of Italy and Sicily, providing a detailed description of each coin focusing on the artistic aspects of each. The coins are all illustrated on finely engraved plates and include two gold coins of the Brutti, and silver coins of Agrigentum, Camarina (three), Egesta, Segesta, and Catana (two). [The second part of this book was published in 1826. See below].

2684 ——— *Specimens of Ancient Coins of Magna Graecia and Sicily, Selected from the Cabinet of the Right Hon. The Lord Northwick: Drawn by Del Frate, A Distinguished Pupil of Antonio Canova, and Engraved by Henry Moses.* London: Septimus Prowett, 1826. 63 pp., 20 pls.
The conclusion of Noehden's *A Selection of Ancient Coins* (see above). Finely engraved plates.

2685 **Numismatica Ars Classica.** *Auction 13: Greek Coins of Magna Graecia and Sicily ex Collection Antikenmuseum Basel und Sammlung Ludwig.* Zurich: Numismatica Ars Classica, 1998. Illus., 32 pls.
The catalogue for an October 8, 1998 sale of 575 gold, silver, and bronze coins of Italy and Sicily—the most impressive collection of such coinage ever to appear at auction. The collection was built between 1940-93 by a Swiss collector and was subsequently exhibited at the Antikenmuseum Basel. Each coin is illustrated in actual size black and white photographs, with full descriptions and commentary. Many of the coins also appear in color enlargements on the thirty-two plates. [For a catalogue from an exhibition of the collection, see Cahn et al. *Antikenmuseum Basel und Sammlung Ludwig* above].

2686 **Panvini Rosati, Franco.** "Monetazione Preromana sulla Costa Adriatica Italiana." *Revista Italiana di Numismatica* 76 (1974): 83-93. [CS 2051]
Includes English, French, and German summaries.

2687 **Papadopoulos, John K.** "Minting Identity: Coinage, Ideology and the Economics of Colonization in Akhaian Magna Graecia." *Cambridge Archaeological Journal* 12, no. 1 (April 2002): 21-55. Illus.
Focuses on the early coinage of the Achaian cities of South Italy (Sybaris, Kroton, Metapontion, Kaulonia, Poseidonia) in the context of colonization. These cities issued coins well before their mother-cities did. The author argues that these cities constructed an identity on coinage in order to create relations of dominance and to produce social orders that had not existed before. The images chosen for the coins recall the world of the heroic Achaians of the Bronze Age. He discusses the emblems used: bulls, grain, tripods, smiting gods. Discusses the origins of coinage and the role of coinage in colonization. Alluding to a prehistoric past through their choice of emblems on their coinage helped these cities to achieve economic dominance in South Italy.

2687a **Parente, Anna Rita.** "Monete Suberate Magnogreche: Le Zecche della Campania." *XIII Congreso Internacional de Numismática, Madrid – 2003: Actas–Proceedings–Actes I.* Edited by Carmen Alfaro, Carmen Marcos, and Paloma Otero. Madrid: International Numismatic Commisson, 2005. Pages 277-83, incl. 1 pl.
Silver coins with a copper core from Neapolis and Hyria are examined and twelve specimens are illustrated.

2688 **Parise, Nicola F.** "Struttura e Funzione della Monetazioni Archaiche di Magna Grecia." *Atti del XII Convegno di Studi sulla Magna Grecia, Taranto 1972.* Naples, 1975. Pages 87-124. [CS 2073]

2689 **Pfeiler, Hasso.** "Die Münzprägung der Brettier." *Jahrbuch für Numismatik und Geldgeschichte* (Germany) 14 (1964): 7-50. 3 pls. [CS 2084]

2690 **Poole, Reginald Stuart.** *Catalogue of Greek Coins of Italy.* London: British Museum, 1873. Reprint, Bologna: Forni, 1963. 432 pp., illus. [CS 2045]
Volume 1 of the *Catalogue of Greek Coins in the British Museum.* Line drawings throughout the catalogue. This volume does not contain any introductory text examining the history of this coinage as do many of the other volumes of *BMC*. [See *Catalogue of Greek Coins in the British Museum* under PUBLIC COLLECTIONS–GREAT BRITAIN (LONDON). Reviewed by C. Newton. See Newton "Greek Numismatics" under GENERAL WORKS–GREEK].

2691 **Pozzi, E.** "Le Monete a Leggande 'AMI.'" *Studi Etruschi* (Italy) (1964): 247 ff. [CS 2074]

2692 **Ramage, Andrew.** "South Italian and Sicilian Coins from the Dewing Collection." *Fogg Art Museum Acquisition Report* (1966-7): 36-42. [CS 16732]

2693 **Robinson, Edward S. G.** "A South Italian Hoard." *Numismatic Chronicle* 6th ser., 5 (1945): 96-107. 1 pl.
Discusses a hoard of sixty-three coins of Tarentum, Tarentino-Campanian, Hyria, Neapolis, Cales, Velia, and Rhegium. The hoard was buried ca. 260 B.C. or shortly thereafter. Includes a brief discussion of the coins and a complete listing of the coins. The appendix, "Normal Weights of Some South Italian Nomoi," presents frequency tables of weights of various coin types.

2694 ——— "Carthaginian and Other South Italian Coinages of the Second Punic War." *Numismatic Chronicle* 7th ser., 4 (1964): 37-64. 3 pls. [CS 2075]
Examines the coinage struck by Carthage and her allies (Croton, Metapontum, Capua, Locri, the Bruttians, and others) that circulated during their occupation of much of Italy in 216-203 B.C.

2695 **Rutter, Nicholas Keith.** *Campanian Coinages, 475-380 B.C.* Edinburgh: Edinburgh University Press, 1979. 196 pp., 34 pls. [CS 2089]
A die-study of the early coinages of Cumae, Neapolis, Hyria, Nola, the Campani, Phistelia, Allifae, and the Fensemi. Includes a chronological table of coinages, and a table of dies used at more than one city. Discusses types, weights, and chronology. Followed by a catalogue of 645 coins with concordances to other published collections. [Reviewed by O. Mørkholm in *Nordisk Numismatisk Unions Medlemsblad* (Copenhagen) 7 (November 1980): 160].

2696 ——— "South Italy and Messana." *Le Origini della Monetazione di Bronzo in Sicilia e in Magna Grecia (Atti del VI Convegno del Centro Internazionale di Studi Numismatici, Napoli Aprile 17-22, 1977).* Supplement to *Annali. Istituto Italiano di Numismatica* (Italy) 25 (1979): 193-223. 4 pls.
Examines the earliest bronze coinages of five south Italian cities (Rhegion, Thurii, Velia, Kaulonia, Kroton) and of Messana. For each, the types are arranged and mintage dates are suggested. Comments on the types and hoard evidence. In the appendix, Rutter lists the weights of the bronze coins of Poseidonia in Grunauer's groups I-VI. (see Grunauer von Hoerschelmann "Die Bronzeprägung" under ITALY—POSEIDONIA). Concludes with questions and responses from the convention participants.

2697 ——— "Italy and Sicily: Archaic and Classical Periods." *A Survey of Numismatic Research, 1978-1984. Volume 1: Ancient, Medieval and Modern Numismatics.* Edited by M. J. Price et al. International Association of Professional Numismatists Special Publication, No. 9. London: International Numismatic Commission, 1986. Pages 1-11.
A narrative overview of newly published works in the field of numismatics. Summarizes the major findings, with bibliographic references cited in the footnotes.

2698 ——— "Athens and the Western Greeks in the Fifth Century B.C.: the Numismatic Evidence." *Kraay—Mørkholm Essays: Numismatic Studies in Memory of C. M. Kraay and O. Mørkholm.* Numismatica Lovaniensia 10. Edited by G. Le Rider, G. K. Jenkins, N. Waggoner, and U. Westermark. Louvain-la-Neuve: Université Catholique de Louvain, 1989. Pages 245-57. 1 pl.
Examines the numismatic evidence for Athenian involvement with the Greeks of Italy and Sicily including finds of Athenian coins in the West, overstrikes on Athenian coins by Rhegium and Messana, and the appearance of Athenian types and motifs in Italian coinage. The author looks for explanations for the Athenian types used on coins of Sybaris, Thurium, Velia, and Neapolis. Examines the supposed trip by Zeno and Parmenides to Athens. Discusses cults of Athena in the West.

2699 ——— *Greek Coinages of Southern Italy and Sicily.* London: Spink & Son, Ltd., 1997. 191 pp., illus., 2 maps.
A thorough re-examination of the Greek coinage in Southern Italy and Sicily. Begins with a brief review of the history of the Greeks in the West. Rutter then examines the coinage of Southern Italy, beginning with the early incuse types and proceeding through the third century B.C., city-by-city. The coinage of Sicily is then described in the same manner. Illustrated throughout by quality photographs of the main coin types. Includes a brief glossary of numismatic terms, a list of weight standards used in the West, and a list of ancient authors. [Reviewed by W. Fischer-Bossert in *Revue Suisse de Numismatique* 76 (1997): 269-70, and by C. Arnold-Biucchi in *American Journal of Numismatics* 2nd ser., 12 (2000): 239-47].

2700 ——— *Historia Numorum, Volume 1: Italy.* London: British Museum, 2001. 223 pp., 42 pls., 1 map.
Volume 1 of the greatly expanded revision of Barclay Head's standard work, *Historia Numorum*, first published in 1887. Examines the coinage of the Greek cities of Italy. Includes introductory text for each city, a bibliography, and a list of coin types. The coins are drawn from many public and private collections. [Reviewed by John Morcom in *Numismatic Chronicle* 162 (2002): 431-4].

2701 **Sambon, Arthur.** *Les Monnaies Antiques de l'Italie, I: Italie. Etrurie – Ombrie – Picenum – Samnium – Campanie (Cumnes et Naples).* Paris, 1903. Reprint, Bologna: Forni, 1967, 1984. 445 pp., 5 pls. [CS 2047]
Lists 1161 coins. "Only volume published covers Etruria, Umbria, Picenum, Samnium and Campania." [C. Kraay]

2702 **Sambon, Luigi.** *Recherches sur les Anciennes Monnaies du l'Italie Méridionale.* Naples, 1863. Reprint, Bologna: Forni, 1967. 244 pp. [CS 2076]

2703 ——— *Recherches sur les Monaies de la Presqu'île Italique depuis leur Origine jusqu'à Bataille d'Actium.* Naples, 1870. Reprint, Bologna: Forni, 1967. 374 pp., 24 pls. [CS 2048]

2704 **Savio, Adriano.** "Considerazioni sugli Incusi della Magna Graecia." *Quaderni Ticinesi. Numismatica e Antichità Classiche* (Switzerland) 4 (1975): 7-16. Illus. [CS 2077]

2705 **Sayles, Wayne G.** "The First Romaion Coin." *The Celator* 21, no. 1 (January 2007): 41. Illus.
Sayles discusses his preference for the term "Romaion" rather than the more common "Byzantine" to describe the late Roman Empire in the East. Illustrates a bronze coin of Campania which bears the legend RωMAIωN, struck at Neapolis ca. 326 B.C.

2706   **Scheu, Frederick.** "The Earliest Coins of the Bruttians." *Numismatic Chronicle* 6th ser., 15 (1955): 101-12. [CS 2085]
The coinage of the Bruttians (called the Brettians by the Greeks) probably covers all or most of the interval between Pyrrhus (281-275 B.C.) and Hannibal (216-203). It is also probably a part of the financial system established in southern Italy by Rome. A chronology for the coins may help in charting the complications of the Italian coinage of the third century. The "Apollo-Biga" bronze coins represent the earliest issue, ca. 280 B.C., and probably represent the coinage of the Campanian mutineers ruling from Rhegium. The Dioscuri "octobol" and the heavy bronze coins with symbols sometimes on the obverse belong to the period of Roman reorganization in southern Italy after the Pyrrhic War. The Bruttian bronze coinage reached its culmination after 263 B.C., when Rome's own coinage was developing. [Summarized from C. Vermeule, *NL* 37]

2707   ——— "Bronze Coins of the Bruttians." *Numismatic Chronicle* 7th ser., 1 (1961): 51-66. 1 pl.
"Five denominations—double, unit, half, quarter and sixth—are generally recognized in the Bruttian bronze coinage. The first group, usually with an ear of wheat as symbol, may have been struck at Locri during the First Punic War; the second, with thunderbolt, was probably issued during the last part of the war (after 250). A third group shows various representations, while a fourth—with lyre symbol—may signify a victory issue of 241 B.C. A final group, usually with plough as symbol, may represent the coinage struck during the Bruttian revolt against Rome at the time of the Second Punic War." [I. Merker, *NL* 65]

2708   ——— "Silver and Gold Coins of the Bruttians." *Numismatic Chronicle* 7th ser., 2 (1962): 43-63. 2 pls. [CS 2086]
Silver coins were issued by the Bruttians on two different systems: (1) an octobol of single type, and (2) a group of four types with common features. The weight standard closely resembles the Corcyrean used in the western parts of the Greek mainland during the second half of the third century B.C.; this suggests a direct trade connection. The silver coins were current at least during the period of Hannibal's invasion of Italy (216-203 B.C.) although issues with variable reverse symbols are probably earlier (229-228 B.C.). The two gold series examined were probably successive emergency issues also struck during the Second Punic War. [Summarized from J. Healy, *NL* 75]

2709   ——— "The Coinage of the Lucanians." *Numismatic Chronicle* 7th ser., 4 (1964): 65-74. 1 pl. [CS 2101]
"The coinage issued in the name of the Lucanians in southern Italy during the third century B.C. presents several features of interest. The bronze issues inscribed LOUKANOM or LUKIANON are closely linked to those of the neighboring Bruttians by their types, weight standard and general style, yet at the same time they show significant differences. After an historical survey of the coinage the author provides a descriptive catalogue, including the major types struck and indications of known specimens and their locations." [J. Balcer, *NL* 78]

2710   **Seltman, Charles T.** "The Influence of Agathocles on the Coinage of Magna Graecia." *Numismatic Chronicle* 4th ser., 12 (1912): 1-13. 1 pl.
Deals with the period of Agathocles, Tyrant of Syracuse, 304-289 B.C. Presents a brief review of his attempted conquests in Italy. Discusses the coins of Hipponium, Terina, Metapontum, and Velia struck under the influence of Agathocles.

2711   ——— "A Philosophy and a Coinage; Coinage and a Philosophy." *American Journal of Archaeology* 34 (1930): 50.
The summary of a paper presented at a conference. "It is suggested that the incuse archaic coinages of South Italy were influenced by Pythagorean philosophy; and conversely, that the downfall of the banker Hikesias of Sinope, charged with the defacement or forgery of coinage, was responsible for the bitter and anti-social policy of his son Diogenes." [J. R. Jones, *NIAJAH*]

2712   ——— "The Problem of the First Italiote Coins." *Numismatic Chronicle* 6th ser., 9 (1949): 1-21. 3 pls. [CS 2078]
Examines the possibility of a connection between Pythagoras and the incuse coinage of the south Italian cities. States that the city of Siris issued no coins and attributes these issues to Pyxus—thus eliminating the problem of incuse coins which would have to pre-date the date of Pythagoras' arrival in Croton. Suggests the incuse coins were expensive to produce due to the slower striking required for accurate die alignment and because the dies could not be used after they cracked—this would cause these thin coins to break. Suggests a genius—knowledgeable in metal working techniques, art, and math—was required to invent this coinage type. Traces Pythagoras' life. Mentions his experience working with silver. The author believes the incuse coinage was the personal invention of Pythagoras. He may have been influenced by somewhat similar coins at Calymna. Suggests Croton was the first city to produce incuse coins ca. 535 B.C. [Also see Wartenberg "Calymna Calumniated" under CARIA. Wartenberg questions the attribution of the incuse Calymna coins].

2713   **Soutzo, Michel C.** *Introduction a l'Ètude des Monnaies de l'Italie Antique.* Two volumes. Paris: Imprimerie Jouaust et Sigaux, 1887. 90 pp., illus. Mâcon: Imprimerie Protat Frères, 1889. 64 pp. Illus.

2714   **Spagnoli, Emanuela, and Marina Taliercio Mensitieri.** *Ripostigli dalla Piana Lamentina.* Rossano and Napoli: Rubbettino, 2004. 249 pp., illus.
The publication of numerous hoards primarily composed of Greek coins of Italy: (1) "Sambiase" 1959, 1961 (*IGCH* 1872 and *CH* II, 8)—containing incuse staters of Sybaris; (2) Curinga 1916 (*IGCH* 1881)—incuse staters of Metapontum, Kaulonia, and Kroton; (3) S. Stefano di Rogliano (Noe 915, *IGCH* 1884)—incuse staters of Metapontum and Kroton; (4) S. Eufemia Lamezia 1949 (*IGCH* 1906)—Tarentum, Metapontum, Thurium, Terina, and Kaulonia; (5) Gizzeria 1914 (*IGCH* 1913)—22 minor bronzes of Kroton, 10 minor bronzes of Rhegion, various other small bronzes of Italian cities, 17 bronzes of Messana; (6) Grimaldi 1933 (*IGCH* 1947)—Taras, Herakleia, Metapontum, Thurium, Velia, Kroton, Terina.

2715   **Stannard, Clive, and Suzanne Frey-Kupper.** "'Pseudomints' and Small Change in Italy and Sicily in the Late Republic." *American Journal of Numismatics* 2nd ser., 20 (2008): 351-404. 3 pls.
Two "pseudomints" of the first century B.C. are described: Pseudo-Ebusus/Massalia (almost certainly at Pompeii) and Pseudo-Panormos/Paestum (probably at Minturnae). The circulation of their coins, and of a plethora of foreign coins, suggests that a relatively monetarized economy in Latium and Campania was pressing all available coin into service, in a context of a penury of small change. Appendix 1 considers the circulation and overstriking in central Italy of Koan bronze coins. Appendix 2compiles finds of foreign coins from Rome, Minturnae, and Pompeii.

2716   **Stazio, Attilio.** "Aspetti e Momenti della Monetazione Tarantina." *Atti del Decimo Convegno di Studi sulla Magna Grecia.* Naples, 1971. Pages 147-81.

2717   ——— "Monetazione dei Lucani." *Archivio Storico per la Calabria e la Lucania* (Italy) 40 (1972): 91-105. Illus. [CS 2102]

2718 ———. "Magna Graecia." *Survey of Numismatic Research, 1966-1971. Volume 1: Ancient Numismatics.* Translated by T. V. Buttrey. Edited by P. Naster, J. Colbert de Beaulieu, and J. M. Fagerlie. New York: International Numismatic Commission, 1973. Pages 36-56. [CS 2060]
A narrative bibliography discussing recently published works in the field of Greek numismatics related to Magna Graecia.

2719 ———. "Monetazione Greca e Indigena nella Magna Grecia." *Forme di Contatto e Processi di Trasformazione nelle Società Antiche. Atti Convegno Cortona 1981.* Pisa-Rome, 1983. Pages 963-78.

2720 **Strauss, Pierre.** *Monnaies Grecques d'Italie: Collection C.C.* Two volumes. Zurich: Verlag für Numismatische Publikationen., 1994. Volume 1: 174 pp., illus. Volume 2: 70 pls.
The magnificent C. Canessa collection of 127 Greek coins of Southern Italy. Volume 1 consists of four essays and a catalogue of the coins. The essays are "La Jie de Collectionner" by C. Canessa; "Gaia te pas 'egelasse" by Stefania Fuscagni; and "Profil Historique de la Grande Grèce et de la Sicile Grecque" by Giovanni Pugliese Carratelli. Volume 2 is a portfolio of seventy unbound plates on card stock, with color enlargements of significant coins.

2721 **Suter, Charles.** "Magna Graecia and Coins." *The Celator* 17, no. 11 (November 2003): 6-12. Illus.
A review of the exhibition *Magna Graecia: Greek Art from Italy and Sicily* which appeared at the Cleveland Museum of Art. The author illustrates some Greek coins which parallel the art found on the exhibition items. Suter also presents some reasons why museums do not often exhibit coins.

2722 **Sutherland, Carol H. V.** "The 'Incuse' Coinages of South Italy." *Museum Notes* 3 (1948): 15-26. 1 pl. [CS 3385]
Examines the incuse coinage of Metapontum, Sybaris, Taras, Poseidona, etc. Reviews theories regarding their method of manufacture. Based upon coin weights, Sutherland rejects the theory that these cities belonged to a monetary confederation. Rejects the view that this unusual fabric was meant for ease of stacking, or that the deep rim was intended to prevent the spread of the flan during striking. Also rejects Pythagoras' involvement in the choice of fabric. Supports the theory that the incuse coinage was intended to discourage the export of silver from Italy. Cites evidence of overstrikes for the import of silver coins of other cities, especially Corinth, into Italy for use as coinage blanks. Suggests this peculiar fabric was used because it allowed for overstriking other coins without having to melt them or roll them out before striking. The incuse-style dies were ideal for overstriking the early Corinthian coins bearing an incuse swastika punch—achieving maximum obliteration of the undertype. The incuse fabric also strengthened the thin coins. Shows that the early Corinthian coins were of similar weight as South Italian coins and could be easily used as blanks. Suggests the change in Corinthian coinage from the incuse punch to an Athena head may have required abandonment of the incuse fabric in Italy. [Also see Seltman "The Problem of the First Italiote Coins" above for an alternate theory].

2723 **Thurlow, Bradbury K., and Italo G. Vecchi.** *Italian Cast Coinage: Italian Aes Grave, Italian Aes Rude, Signatum and the Aes Grave of Sicily.* London: V. C. Vecchi & Sons, and Dix Hills, N.Y.: B. & H. Kreindler, 1979. 50 pp., 82 pls., map.
A descriptive catalogue of the primitive cast bronze money of ancient Rome and her dependencies. Begins with a general introduction and some historical background for the coinage. Then provides comments on the coins, both for those minted at Rome and those minted outside of Rome. Includes a chronological summary of Roman Aes Grave and associated struck coinages, a type index, a concordance with Sydenham's numbering system, and estimated values. The cast coinage of Akragas and Selinus is included here.

2724 **Vagi, David.** "Rome's Earliest Silver Coins Struck in Greek Cities." *The Celator* 8, no. 3 (March 1994): 22. Illus.
A brief discussion of Rome's first silver coinage. Describes the types of didrachms struck ca. 300 to 226 B.C. Suggests some of these coins may have been struck at Neapolis.

2725 ———. "The Early Coinage of Greek Italy." *Numismatist* 120, no. 8 (August 2007): 73-5. Illus.
A brief examination of the earliest phase of Greek coinage in Italy including the incuse coins of Sybaris, Metapontum, Croton, and other cities.

2726 **Visonà, Paolo.** "The Coinage of Skylletion: an Archeological Note." *Schweizer Münzblätter* (Switzerland) 40, no. 160 (1990): 91-3. Illus.
"New evidence from the University of Turin excavations at Locri Epizephyrii supports attribution of the bronze coins with male head wearing *pileus*-Skylla (*SNG Cop Italy* 1992-3) to Skylletion, whose site has been located at Roccelletta di Borgia, ca. 85 km north of Locri." [P. Visonà, *NL* 128]

2727 **Wallace, Malcolm B.** "Reviews and Book Notices." *Cornucopiæ* (publication of The Ancient Coin Society, Canada) 1, no. 3 (February 1973): 43-8.
Wallace's review of *Sylloge Nummorum Graecorum: The Collection of the American Numismatic Society 2: Lucania* contains a brief summary of the theories of various researchers for the use of the incuse style of coinage in Southern Italy during the late sixth and early fifth centuries B.C.

2728 **Welz, Karl.** "Unedierte und Seltene Münzen aus dem Griechischen Westen." *Schweizer Münzblätter* (Switzerland) 7, no. 28 (1957): 77-81. Illus. [CS 2079]
Lists some previously unpublished or rare coins of Laos, Poseidonia, Sybaris, Thurion, Terina, Tyndaris, and Thermai-Himeraiai.

2729 **Westermark, Ulla.** "Italy and Sicily: The Hellenistic Period." *A Survey of Numismatic Research, 1978-1984. Volume 1: Ancient, Medieval and Modern Numismatics.* Edited by M. J. Price et al. International Association of Professional Numismatists Special Publication, No. 9. London: International Numismatic Commission, 1986. Pages 12-28.
A narrative overview of newly published works in the field of numismatics. Summarizes the major findings, with bibliographic references cited in the footnotes.

2730 **White, M.** "The Duration of the Samian Tyranny." *Journal of Hellenic Studies* 73 (1953): 36-43.
"On pp. 42-3 the theory that the incuse coinages of South Italy were designed by Pythagoras meets with some approval." [J. R. Jones, *NIJHS*]

Also see: Barth "Athenian Standard" under SICILY—GENERAL WORKS; Crawford *Coinage and Money* under GENERAL WORKS—HELLENISTIC; Evans "Select Sicilian and Magna-Graecian Coins" under SICILY—GENERAL WORKS; Healy "The Use of Sicilian and Magna Graecian Types" under TYPES; Istituto Italiano di Numismatica *Le Origini della Monetazione* under GENERAL WORKS—GREEK; Kraay "Greek Coinage and War" under GENERAL WORKS—GREEK; Kraay "Hoards and Circulation" under HOARDS; Lacroix *Monnaies et Colonisation* under SICILY—GENERAL WORKS; Lehman *Sculpture* under TYPES; Lehman *Statues* under TYPES; Lewis "Hoard" under HOARDS; Mattingly "Little Talents of Sicily and the West" under METROLOGY; Metcalf *Oxford Handbook of Greek and Roman Coinage* under GENERAL WORKS—GREEK.

Price "The Function of Early Greek Bronze Coinage" under GENERAL WORKS—GREEK; Salmon "Trade and Corinthian Coinage in the West" under CORINTHIA; *SNG Australia I: The Gale Collection of South Italian Coins* under SYLLOGE NUMORUM GRAECORUM—AUSTRALIAN SEREIS; Stannard "Numismatic Evidence" under SPAIN; Tsoukanelis "The Tetradrachms of Pyrrhus" under NORTHERN GREECE—EPIRUS; Vermeule "Chariot Groups" under TYPES; Villaronga "Petit Trésor de la Deuxième Guerre Punique avec une Drachme des Bruttiens" under HOARDS; Westermark "Influences from South Italy" under MACEDONIAN KINGDOM—GENERAL WORKS; Williams and Burnett "Alexander the Great and the Coinages of Western Greece" under MACEDONIAN KINGDOM—GENERAL WORKS.

ALBA

2731 **Poole, Reginald Stuart.** "On a New Coin of Ancient Italy." *Numismatic Chronicle* new ser., 2 (1862): 300-1. Illus.
Describes a small silver coin with Poseidon on the obverse and a bull on the reverse, bearing the obverse inscription AΛBA. Poole attributes the coin to a previously unknown city, Alba, situated north of Poseidonia.

2732 **Stazio, Attilio.** "La Monetazione Argentea di Alba Fucens." *Annali, Istituto Italiano di Numismatica* (Italy) 3 (1956): 43-64. [CS 2080]

CUMAE

2733 **Eidswick, Dick.** "In the Eye of the Beholder." *The Celator* 16, no. 10 (October 2002): 34-7. Illus., map.
The acquisition of a nomos of Cumae leads the author to explore the history of the city and the mythology behind the images on the coin. Discusses the role of the city in Homer's *Odyssey*, and the mythology of Sibyl and Skylla.

ETRURIA

2734 **Catalli, Fiorenzo.** "Sulla Circolazione dell' *Aes Grave* Volterrano." *Studi Etruschi* (Italy) 44 (1976): 97-110.

2735 ——— *Monete Etrusche*. Rome: Istituto Poligrafico e Zecca Dello Stato, 1990. 150 pp., illus.
A good introduction to Etruscan coinage.

2736 ——— "Coins." *The Etruscans*. Edited by Mario Torelli. Milan: Bompiani, 2000. Pages 88-95. Illus.
A good overview of Etruscan coinage illustrated with several plates of color enlargements.

2737 *Contributi Introduttivi allo Studio della Monetazione Etrusca*. Atti del V Convegno de Centro Internazionale di Studi Numismatici, Napoli, Aprile 1975. Supplement to *Annali: Istituto Italiano di Numismatica* 22. Rome, 1976.

2738 **Craddock, Paul T., and Andrew M. Burnett.** "The Composition of Etruscan and Umbrian Copper Alloy Coinage." *Metallurgy in Numismatics, Volume 4*. Special Publication No. 30. London: Royal Numismatic Society, 1998. Pages 262-75.
Presents a quantitative analysis of approximately ninety coins and nine bars representative of the main types of Etruscan and Umbrian currency.

2739 **Davis, Mark.** "The Mystery of Etruscan Coinage." *The Celator* 9, no. 1 (January 1995): 16-7. Illus.
A very brief overview of Etruscan coin types, denominations, and weights.

2740 **Hackens, Tony.** "La Métrologie des Monnaies Étrusques les plus Anciennes." *Contributi Introduttivi allo Studio della Monetazione Etrusca. Atti del V Convegno del Centro Internazionale di Studi Numismatici, Napoli 1975*. Supplement to *Annali, Istituto Italiano di Numismatica* 22 (1976): 221-72. [CS 2053]

2741 **Heurgon, Jacques.** "Les Contramarques sur les Revers des Didrachmes de Populonia." *Congresso Internazionale di Numismatica, Roma 11-16 Settembre 1961. Volume 2*. Rome: Istituto Italiano de Numismatica, 1965. Pages 159-66. [CS 2057]

2742 ——— "Les Types Monetaires Étrusques et le Bestiaire Orientalisant." *Contributi Introduttivi allo Studio della Monetazione Etrusca. Atti del V Convegno del Centro Internazionale di Studi Numismatici, Napoli 1975*. Supplement to *Annali, Istituto Italiano di Numismatica* 22 (1976): 310-18. [CS 2054]

2743 **Hoover, Oliver D.** "The Ties that Bind: Roman Expansionism and the Development of Etruscan Coinage in the Third Century B.C." *Hekte* (Canada) 3 (March 1997): 3-15. Illus., map.
Hoover shows that the adoption and evolution of coinage in Etruria is directly related to the economic demands placed on the Etruscan city-states by the conquering Romans. He suggests that the sudden opening of mints at Vulci and Populonia at the beginning of the third century B.C. was related to the need to pay reparations or tribute to Rome. The Etruscan coins were struck on a weight standard based on the scruple—the same standard used for the contemporary Roman didrachm. This forced adoption of coinage heightened the Etruscan dependence on Rome. Hoover shows that by ca. 217 B.C., Rome had the ability to dictate the value of Etruscan coinage. The fact that many Etruscan coins were struck by worn or broken dies may indicate that they were struck in haste to satisfy the great need for money at Rome. The uniface issues of Populonia may also indicate that there was a need to quickly produce a large volume of coinage. The author discusses the possible Roman and Umbrian influences on Etruscan coin types. Eventually, the Etruscans began to grasp the propaganda value of coinage. Illustrates coin types which may indicate anti-Roman sentiments, including types which may indicate support for Hannibal.

2744 **Kollgaard, Ron.** "Etruscan Culture and Politics Influenced the Development of Early Rome." *The Celator* 4, no. 9 (September 1990): 6-18.

Reviews the history of the Etruscans. Important cities are discussed including Populonia where the first Etruscan coins were minted ca. 450 B.C. It is uncertain whether these coins were struck by a central authority or by individuals. Designs, weights, and denominations of the Populonian coinage are discussed. Coins of Vetulonia are also mentioned. [Also see corrections in "Letters to the Editor," *The Celator* 4, no. 10 (October 1990): 4].

2745 **Marchetti, Patrich.** "La Métrologie des Monnaies Étrusques avec Marques de Valeur." *Contributi Introduttivi allo Studio della Monetazione Etrusca. Atti del V Convegno del Centro Internazionale di Studi Numismatici, Napoli 1975.* Supplement to *Annali, Istituto Italiano di Numismatica* 22 (1976): 273-96. [CS 2055]

2746 **Meyers, Robert J.** "An Amphora Stand on a Coin of Etruria." *North American Journal of Numismatics* 7, no. 6 (June 1968): 177-9. Illus.
Describes a double stater of Etruria which depicts an amphora and what has been described as "two helmets in profile." The author suggests these "helmets" are, in fact, an amphora stand.

2747 **Patrillo Serafin, Patrizia.** "Le Serie Monetarie di Populonia." *Contributi Introduttivi allo Studio della Monetazione Etrusca. Atti del V Convegno del Centro Internazionale di Studi Numismatici, Napoli 1975.* Supplement to *Annali, Istituto Italiano di Numismatica* 22 (1976): 105-39. [CS 2058]

2748 **Pavini Rosati, Franco.** "La Gli Studi e la Problematica Attuale sulla Monetazione Etrusca." *Contributi Introduttivi allo Studio della Monetazione Etrusca. Atti del V Convegno del Centro Internazionale di Studi Numismatici, Napoli 1975.* Supplement to *Annali, Istituto Italiano di Numismatica* 22 (1976): 25-39. [CS 2056]

2749 **Sutton, R. F.** "The Populonian Coinage and the Second Punic War." *Contributi Introduttivi Allo Studio della Monetazione Etrusca, Atti V.* Naples, 1976. Pages 203 ff.

2750 **Tripp, David E.** "Coinage." *Etruscan Life and Afterlife.* Edited by Larissa Bonfante. Detroit: Wayne State University Press, 1986. Pages 202-14. Illus.
An overview of the history of Etruscan coinage. Describes the characteristics and types of the coinage of various cities. Illustrated by twenty coin-types. Bibliography.

2751 **Vecchi, Italo G.** "The Coinage of the Rasna: A Study in Etruscan Numismatics." Parts 1-5. *Revue Suisse de Numismatique* (Switzerland) 67 (1988): 43-73. 5 pls.; 69 (1990): 5-25. 7 pls.; 71 (1992): 91-110. 4 pls.; 72 (1993): 63-73. 6 pls.; 78 (1999) 5-25.
Part 1 presents an overview of Etruscan coinage and catalogues the silver coinages of Populonia and Vetulonia struck on the scruple standard before 217 B.C. Part 2 catalogues the silver ten and twenty asses. Part 3 is a die-study of the smaller silver coinage of Populonia. Part 4 catalogues the bronze coinage. Part 5 includes an exhaustive catalogue of the bronze and silver coins of Vetulonia, and silver and gold coins of an uncertain mint (maybe Vetulonia as well).

2752 ——— "A Reassessment of the Dating and Identification of Etruscan Coinage." *The Celator* 17, no. 5 (May 2003): 6-12. Illus.
A review of Etruscan coin types with comments on their chronology, weight standards, and denominations.

2753 ——— "Etruscan Numismatics: A Notorious Dating and Identification Problem." *Etruscan Studies* 10, issue 1 (2007): 87-91.
A summary of current research in Etruscan numismatics, focusing on problems of dating and mint attribution. Vecchi's comments are cross-referenced to coins listed in K. Rutter's *Historia Numorum, Volume 1: Italy* (see Rutter under ITALY—GENERAL WORKS).

2754 **Visonà, Paolo.** "Foreign Currency in Etruria Circa 400-200 B.C.: Distribution Patterns." *Ancient Coins of the Graeco-Roman World: The Nickle Numismatic Papers.* Edited by Waldemar Heckel and Richard Sullivan. Waterloo, Ontario: Wilfrid Laurier University Press, 1984. Pages 222-40. Maps.
The author reviews the evidence for the circulation of non-Etruscan currency in Etruria from the late fifth century B.C. to the end of the Second Punic War, after which Roman coins became the sole medium for monetary transactions among the Etruscans. Magna Graecia supplied most of the late fourth and third century B.C. Greek-type currency in the area. Punic coins represent another type commonly found. Lists the related coin finds, accompanied by nine maps indicating find-spots of foreign coins. Non-Etruscan currency became increasingly known in Etruria in the third century B.C. and contributed to a very confused monetary situation. The Roman conquest did not suddenly alter this situation.

2755 **Warden, William B., Jr.** "Etruscan Numismatics and Metrology." *Journal of Numismatic Fine Arts* 5, no. 1 (May-June 1976): 1-4.
Warden comments on the weights and weight standards used for coins which can be attributed to specific Etruscan cities. A variety of standards were used. Cities which relied upon trade generally adopted foreign weight standards which facilitated trade with the nearby Greek cities. Cities not dependent on trade relied on their own native standards.

Also see: McClean "Metrological Note" under METROLOGY; *Italian Series 3 Volume 2* under SYLLOGE NUMMORUM GRAECORUM SERIES.

HERAKLEA

2756 **Grose, Sidney W.** "Primitiae Heraclienses." *Numismatic Chronicle* 4th ser., 17 (1917): 169-89.
Examines some coins of Heraclea. Includes a full list of the letters which appear on the coins, and discusses the theory that these represent artists' signatures. He seriously doubts the theory.

2757 **Otto, Brinna.** "Athena und die Kreuzfackel: Zwei Bronzemünzen aus dem Demeter-Heiligtum von Herakleia in Lukanien." *Zurück zum Gegenstand. Festschrift für Andreas E. Furtwängler.* Zentrum für Archälogie und Kulturgeschichte des Schwarzmeerraumes, Band 16. Edited by Ralph Einicke et al. Langenweibach: Beier and Beram, 2009.

2758 **Robinson, David M.** "A New Heracles Relief." *Hesperia* 17 (1948): 137-40. 1 pl.

"On pp. 139-40 a list of other similar renderings of Heracles is given, including that which appears on coins of Heracleia Lucaniae; this must go back to a Lysippan archetype." [J. R. Jones, *NIAJAH*]

2759 **Van Keuren, Frances.** "Mint Study of the Late Staters from Heraclea Lucaniae." *The Age of Pyrrhus: Proceedings of an International Conference Held at Brown University, April 8th-10th, 1988.* Edited by T. Hackens, N. D. Holloway, R. R. Holloway, and G. Moucharte. Louvain-la-Neuve and Providence, Rhode Island, 1992. Pages 237-65. Illus.
"The author lists and illustrates all the die combinations for 383 specimens and assigns the staters to three chronological groups extending from the beginning of the Pyrrhic period in 281 B.C. to the middle of the third century B.C." [F. Van Keuren, *NL* 135]

2760 ——— *The Coinage of Heraclea Lucaniae.* Archaeologica 110. Rome: Giorgio Bretschneider Editore, 1994. 100 pp., 25 pls.
Covers the whole of Heraclea's output of silver and gold coinage from the fifth to the third century B.C., and the bronze coinage from the third to the second or first century B.C. An historical introduction precedes the discussion of the coinage. Presents a descriptive catalogue of all coin varieties, although this is not a full die-study. A specimen of each variety is illustrated. [Reviewed by A. M. Burnett in *American Journal of Numismatics* 2nd ser., 9 (1997): 137-9, and by W. Fischer-Bossert in *Revue Suisse de Numismatique* 76 (1997): 271-6].

2761 **Work, Eunice.** *The Earlier Staters of Heraclea Lucaniae.* Numismatic Notes and Monographs, No. 91. New York: American Numismatic Society, 1940. 40 pp., 8 pls. [CS 2095]
Provides the groundwork for establishing the chronology of the staters of Heraclea Lucaniae to ca. 300 B.C. Examines the history of the city, contemporary coins of neighboring cities, hoards, and the sequence of dies in the coins of Heraclea. Presents a catalogue of ninety-two coins, each of which is illustrated in the plates, and a table of die links.

Also see: Evans "A Recent Find" under ITALY—METAPONTUM.

KAULONIA

2762 **Birch, Samuel.** "Notes on Types of Caulonia." *Numismatic Chronicle* 8 (1846): 163-9.
Birch attempts to explain the types on the archaic incuse coins of Caulonia. Reviews previous theories. Suggests the figures are Apollo pursuing the young Hermes, after the theft committed by the juvenile divinity—the subject of a Homeric hymn to Hermes.

2763 **Kraay, Colin M.** "Caulonia and South Italian Problems." *Numismatic Chronicle* 6th ser., 20 (1960): 53-82. 1 pl. [CS 2090]
"The present article reconsiders the coinage of Caulonia and wider problems connected with the Magna Graecian issues, the latest incuse series being extended and a die link with the double-relief types established. Groups H-J are re-examined in the light of a more detailed study of the ethnic. The author aims at confirming and amplifying Noe's chronology (see Noe *The Coinage of Caulonia* below) and establishes an overall pattern for the period from the end of the incuse fabric issues. The change to medium incuse flans occurred ca. 500 B.C. Dumpy incuse flans began at Caulonia, Croton and Metapontum ca. 480 B.C. Double relief fabric was used at Caulonia from ca. 475 B.C. A tentative chronological scheme down to the year 389/8 B.C. is proposed, metrology and overstrikes are again examined, and finally, a brief account of the development of coinage in south Italy is attempted." [J. Healy, *NL* 60]. [Also see Bicknell "Some Fractions of Kroton" under ITALY—KROTON].

2764 ——— "The Chronology of Caulonia—Once Again." *Annali. Istitutio Italiano di Numismatica* (Italy) 25 (1978): 9-21. Tables.
"The chronology of emissions of Caulonia is established by means of study of legends, letter-forms of legends, die links and common symbols. Using the chronology as a working hypothesis, hoard evidence is adduced to place the coinage between two termini: beginning ca. 475 with the double relief; ending with the destruction of Caulonia in 389/388 B.C." [C. Cassani, *NL* 105]

2765 **Lacroix, Leon.** "L'Apollon de Caulonia." *Revue Belge de Numismatique* (Belgium) 105 (1959): 5-24. [CS 3474]

2766 **Lloyd, William Watkiss.** "On the Types of the Coins of Caulonia." *Numismatic Chronicle* 10 (1848): 1-20. Illus.
Discusses the interpretation of the types on the coins of Caulonia, focusing on the identity of the small running figure. Examines the arguments of Birch and Panofka. Theories include Hermes, Perseus, and wind-gods. Reviews the mythology surrounding the origin of the city. Concludes that the larger figure represents Apollo as sun-god and god of health and purification; the smaller figure being a type or emblem symbolizing Apollo's special influence over the winds—a personified power of the air.

2767 **Noe, Sydney P.** *The Coinage of Caulonia.* Numismatic Studies, No. 9. New York: American Numismatic Society, 1958. 62 pp., 20 pls. [CS 2091]
Establishes a sequence for the coinage of Caulonia including the incuse and double-relief types down to 388 B.C. when coinage stopped with the destruction of the city. Discusses the controversial interpretations of the types and changes in the types and fabric. Over 230 varieties are catalogued including fractional denominations, bronze coins, and plated coins. [Reviewed by R. R. Holloway in *American Journal of Archaeology* 65 (1961): 215].

Also see: Attianese *Calabria Greca* under ITALY—GENERAL WORKS; Rutter "South Italy and Messana" under ITALY—GENERAL WORKS.

KROTON

2768 **Attianese, Pasquale.** *Kroton, ex Nummis Historia: Dalle Monete, la Storie il Culto il Mito de Crotone.* 1993. 224 pp., illus.

2768a ——— *Kroton: Le Monete di Bronzo.* Catanzaro: Rubbettino Editore, 2005. 406 pp., illus.
Preface by Italo Vecchi.

2769 **Bicknell, Peter J.** "An Early Incuse Stater of Croton Overstruck on a Pegasus." *Antichthon* (Australia) 3 (1969): 1-4. Illus.
"This coin, now in Berlin, formerly in the Löbbecke collection, may have been chosen for overstriking because of its low weight. It was probably an early issue from the Croton mint, postdating the coins of similar fabric from Sybaris and Metapontum." [J. Jones, *NL* 85]

2770 ——— "Some Fractions of Kroton." *Schweizer Münzblätter* (Switzerland) 21, no. 81 (February 1971): 1-4. Illus. [CS 2092]
"A study of Croton small pieces which imitate Tarentine types leads to the suggestion that Cahn's dates for the Phalanthos series are about two decades too early. The fractions with Tarentine reverses were designed to facilitate trade, since the Croton stater was lighter than that of Tarentum. As an appended note, four small coins with crab reverses are added to Kraay's list in *Numismatic Chronicle* 6th ser., 20 (1960): 53-82." [D. Raymond, *NL* 89]. [Also see Kraay "Caulonia and South Italian Problems" under ITALY–KAULONIA].

2771 **Cahn, Herbert A.** "Die Storche von Kroton." *Pour Denyse: Divertissements Numismatiques.* Edited by S. Hurter and C. Arnold-Biucchi. Bern, Switzerland: Privately published, 2000. Pages 31-2. Illus.
A discussion of the stork depicted on coins of Kroton.

2772 **Gale, W. L.** *The Sacred Tripod: Kroton and Its Coins.* Mosman (New South Wales, Australia): Ocean Spray Pty. Ltd., 1995. 40 pp. (including plates), map.
A brief history of the city of Kroton with commentary on its major coin types integrated into the historical discussion. This is followed by a listing of seventy-two coins of Kroton from the author's collection, each of which is illustrated in the plates. Includes several plates of greatly enlarged coin photographs. A nice introduction to this important city and its coinage. Brief bibliography.

2773 ——— "Shooting the Python: the Tripod on the Coins of Kroton." *The Celator* 11, no. 4 (April 1997): 34-5. Illus.
Mentions Pythagoras and his teachings (Pythagoras was a citizen of Kroton), and the worship of Apollo by the people of Kroton. Discusses the significance of the tripod in the worship. Illustrates a stater of Kroton, struck ca. 420 B.C., with *obv.*, Herakles seated (as founder of the city), and *rev.*, tripod with Apollo shooting at the python with a bow (to take possession of the shrine at Delphi).

2773a **Garraffo, Salvatore.** "Crotoniensia dall'Incuso al Doppio Rilievo." *Studi per Laura Breglia: Bollettino di Numismatica Supplemento* 4 (1987).

2774 **Grose, Sidney W.** "Croton." *Numismatic Chronicle* 4th ser., 15 (1915): 179-91. 1 pl. [CS 2093]
Examines the staters of Croton minted 330-299 B.C. Lists eight types (and numerous specimens of each). Discusses the weight standards and chronology of the coins. Publishes two fifth-century B.C. staters bearing the letters PA on the reverse. Also publishes staters which may indicate alliances between Laus and Sybaris, and between Sybaris and Croton.

2775 **Hansen, Peter.** "Kroton Faces Syracuse." *Trident* (Australia) 9 (October 1993): 8 ff.
"The facing heads on coins of these and other cities should be interpreted as examples of artistic rivalry rather than copying." [J. Melville Jones, *NL* 132]

2776 **Kraay, Colin M.** "A Propos des Monnaies Divisionnaires de Croton." *Schweizer Münzblätter* (Switzerland) 32 (1958): 99-102. [CS 2094]

2777 **Lloyd, William Watkiss.** "On Coins of Crotona." *Numismatic Chronicle* 11 (1849): 1-18. Illus.
Examines the mythology and traditions which led to the choice of coin types at Croton. Focuses on Apollo and Herakles.

2778 **Wihnyk, Joseph.** "Coins Commemorate Croton's Pythian Prizewinners." *The Celator* 20, no. 6 (June 2006): 34. Illus.
Cites B. V. Head's suggestion that coins of Croton depicting an eagle and a tripod refer to victories in the Olympics, and coins with a filleted branch and a tripod refer to the Pythian games. Also illustrates a tetradrachm of Aeolis depicting Apollo standing, holding a filleted branch—a reference to the Pythian games.

Also see: Attianese *Calabria Greca* under ITALY–GENERAL WORKS; Gardner "A Numismatic Note on the Lelantian War" under CENTRAL GREECE–EUBOIA; Rutter "South Italy and Messana" under ITALY–GENERAL WORKS.

LAOS

2778a **Bugno, Maurizio.** "L'Inizio della Monetazione Arcaica di Laos in Magna Graecia." *Annali: Istituto Italiano di Numismatica* (Italy) 44 (1997): 281-7.
"The author discusses various theories on the beginnings of the coinage of Laos in Magna Graecia (end of the sixth to beginning of the fifth century B.C.). In particular, he discusses the relationship between the first issues and coins of Croton, Sybaris, and Poseidonia." [A. Carignani, *NL* 143]

2778b ——— "La Cronologia dei Primi Incusi di Laos in Magna Grecia." *Il Mondo Enotrio tra VI e I Secolo a.C., Atti dei Seminari Napoletani (1996-1998).* Quaderni di Ostraka 1. Edited by Maurizio Bugno and Concetta Masseria. Napoli, 2001. Pages 145-7

2778c **Giacosa, Giorgio.** "Un Quarto Esemplare di Drachma e un Inedito Triobolo Incuso di Laos." *Revista Italiana di Numismatica* (Italy) 84 (1982): 95-100.

2779 **Sternberg, Heinz-Rainer.** "Die Silberprägung von Laos." *Actes du 8eme Congrès International de Numismatique. New York-Washington, Septembre 1973.* Paris/Basel, 1976. Pages 143-62. 4 pls. [CS 2096]

LOCRI EPIZEPHYRII

2780 **Larizza, Pietro.** *Locri Epizephyrii.* Reggio Calabria, 1942. 232 pp., illus. [CS 2099]

2781   **Paolini, E. Pozzi.** "La Monnetazione." *Locri Epizefirii: Atti del Sedicesimo Convegno di Studi sulla Magna Grecia, Taranto, 3-8 Ottobre 1976.* Napoli, 1977. Pages 217-340.

2782   **Parise, Nicola Franco.** "Sulla Circolazione de Moneta Straniera a Locri fra VI e IV Secolo. La Documentazione dei Ripostigli." *Studi Miscellanei* 22 (Rome, Istituto di Archaeologia dell'Università) (1974-75): 169-76. [CS 2100]

2783   **Rynearson, Paul.** "On Collecting—A Coin of Locri Epizephyrii." *SAN—Journal of the Society for Ancient Numismatics* 1, no. 1 (July 1969): 4. Illus.
Describes a stater of Locri Epizephyrii which was overstruck on a stater of Corinth. A photograph and a drawing are included.

Also see: Mattingly "Zephyritis" under Egypt—Ptolemaic Kingdom.

Luceria

2784   **Gruebner, Herbert A.** "The Coinage of Luceria." *Corolla Numismatica: Numismatic Essays in Honour of Barclay V. Head.* Edited by G. F. Hill. London: Oxford University Press, 1906. Pages 115-34.
The author examines the coinage of the Roman colony of Luceria, which began 314 B.C. When Luceria became a Latin colony, it was allowed to issue an independent bronze coinage based on the libral standard of Rome, but bearing its own types.

Metapontum

2785   **Caltabiano, Maria Caccamo.** "Le Monete di Metaponto e l'Influenza di Agatocle." *Pour Denyse: Divertissements Numismatiques.* Edited by S. Hurter and C. Arnold-Biucchi. Bern, Switzerland: Privately published, 2000. Pages 33-42. 2 pls.

2786   **Eaglen, Robin J.** "Portraits of Greek Coinage 3: Metapontum." *Spink Numismatic Circular* 113, no. 2 (April 2005): 89. Illus.
This installment of the author's on-going series examines the coinage of Metapontum. Reviews the history of the city, its mythology, and the coin types.

2787   **Evans, Arthur J.** "A Recent Find of Magna-Graecian Coins of Metapontum, Tarentum, and Heraclea." *Numismatic Chronicle* 4th ser., 18 (1918): 133-54. 2 pls.
Publishes a group of Italian coins including 66 coins of Metapontum, 3 of Tarentum, and 13 of Heraclea. Presents a catalogue of the coins and a discussion of their chronology.

2788   **Forrer, Leonard S.** "An Unpublished Didrachm of Metapontum Signed by the Artist Aristippos." *Spink Numismatic Circular* 8, no. 87 (February 1900): 3787. Illus.
Presents a photograph of a coin signed ΑΡΙΣΤΙ on the truncton of the head.

2789   **Johnston, Ann.** "The Bronze Coinage of Metapontum." *Kraay—Mørkholm Essays: Numismatic Studies in Memory of C. M. Kraay and O. Mørkholm.* Numismatica Lovaniensia 10. Edited by G. Le Rider, G. K. Jenkins, N. Waggoner, and U. Westermark. Louvain-la-Neuve: Université Catholique de Louvain, 1989. Pages 121-36. 4 pls.
An outline of the bronze coinage of Metapontum including a catalogue of types with a preliminary chronological classification. Commentary on the types, denominations, and dating. Emphasizes the problems encountered when attempting to establish a more firm chronology for this coinage.

2790   ———. *The Coinage of Metapontum, Part 3.* Numismatic Notes and Monographs, No. 164. New York: American Numismatic Society, 1990. 102 pp., 21 pls.
This study of the coinage of Metapontum is a continuation of Noe and Johnston *The Coinage of Metapontum, Parts 1 and 2* below. Begins with a review of Metapontine history, ca. 340-280 B.C. Continues with discussions of hoards containing Metapontine coins, overstrikes, gold coins, fractional coinage, symbols and signatures, fabric, weights, and die positions. Summarizes the chronological implications of this study, and presents a catalogue of 406 die varieties, all of which are photographed. Dies and die combinations are listed and divided into four classes based on relative chronology. The characteristics of each class are described. A concordance to coins catalogued in the *Sylloge Nummorum Graecorum* series is included. Also includes a discussion of forgeries along with descriptions and photographs of forty-five counterfeit coins. [Reviewed by A. M. Burnett in *Numismatic Chronicle* 152 (1992): 185-7, and by K. A. Sheedy in *Journal of Hellenic Studies* 113 (1993): 215].

2791   **Kraay, Colin M.** "Épis de Métaponte—Un Supplement." *Schweizer Münzblätter* (Switzerland) 7, no. 28 (1957): 73-7. Illus. [CS 2103]

2791a **Lazzarini, Lorenzo.** "Su Alcune Spighe Inedite: Nouve Attribuzioni alle Zecche di Metaponto e Thurio." *Review Suisse de Numismatique* (Switzerland) 88 (2009): 73-80.

2792   **Noe, Sydney P.** *The Coinage of Metapontum, Part 1.* Numismatic Notes and Monographs, No. 32. New York: American Numismatic Society, 1927. 134 pp., 23 pls. *Part Two.* Numismatic Notes and Monographs, No. 47. New York: American Numismatic Society, 1931. 134 pp., 43 pls. [CS 2104]
Thorough die studies of the coinage of Metapontum. [*Part 1* was reviewed by S. H. Weber in *American Journal of Archaeology* 33 (1929): 147-8. *Part 2* was reviewed by A. R. Bellinger in *American Journal of Archaeology* 36 (1932): 204, and by E. S. G. Robinson in *Numismatic Chronicle* 5th ser., 11 (1931): 247-8. Also see Noe and Johnston *The Coinage of Metapontum* below for the revised version of these works].

2793   **Noe, Sydney P., and Ann Johnston.** *The Coinage of Metapontum, Parts 1 and 2.* Numismatic Notes and Monographs, Nos. 32 and 47 (Revised). New York: American Numismatic Society, 1984. 120 pp., illus., 23 pls.
A combined and revised reprint of Noe's monographs published as *ANS Numismatic Notes and Monographs No. 32* (1927) and *No. 47* (1931). A thorough die study of the coinage of Metapontum. Begins with a brief history of the city, a discussion of the peculiar incuse fabric of the coinage, and

minting techniques. Suggests that hubs were used to create the reverse dies. Continues with discussions of types, symbols, hoards, and dating. Segregates the coinage into twelve classes. Suggests that Metapontine coinage began ca. 550 B.C. Johnston suggests the incuse fabric may have been intended to limit circulation of these coins to southern Italy, and that the double-relief coinage began ca. 440 B.C. She also adds a discussion of overstrikes and dating. Part 1 concludes with Noe's detailed descriptions of 309 die varieties, to which eight new varieties are added by Johnston. All are photographed in the plates. Part 2 covers the double-relief coinage down to ca. 340 B.C. and includes a discussion of plated coins. Johnston updates Noe's chronology based upon new hoard evidence. Part 2 concludes with the description of 238 die varieties, all of which are photographed. A concordance between Noe's catalogue and the volumes of *Sylloge Nummorum Graecorum* has also been added. [Reviewed by N. K. Rutter in *Numismatic Chronicle* 146 (1986): 262-3. Also see Johnston's *Metapontum Part 3* above for a continuation of this study].

2794 **Pokorney, Ted.** "The Stater of Metapontum 530 B.C." *Numismatic Scrapbook Magazine* 23, no. 10 (October 1957): 1898-1900. Illus.
Describes the incuse coinage of Metapontum and discusses the possible involvement of Pythagoras in its design.

2795 **Schwabacher, Willy.** "Some Coins from Metapontum in the Royal Collection at Copenhagen." *Acta Archaeologica* (Denmark) 10 (1939): 120-31. Illus.
Describes eighteen coins of Metapontum and points out additions and corrections which they provide for Noe's corpus on the early coinage of the city.

2796 **Stazio, Attilio.** "Osservazioni sulla Monetazione di Metaponto." *Atti Magna Grecia Taranto 1973.* Taranto, 1974.

2797 **Sutherland, Carol H. V.** "A Corinthian Stater Overstruck by Metapontum." *Numismatic Chronicle* 6th ser., 12 (1952): 115-6. Illus.
Illustrates a coin of Metapontum which was struck over a stater of Corinth (Pegasos/Athena), probably ca. 490 B.C. Discusses the problems of overstriking. [Also see Sutherland "The Incuse Coinages" above].

Also see: Hurter "Crickets" under SICILY—GENERAL WORKS; Johnston "Report of a Discussion on South Italian Chronology" under ITALY—GENERAL WORKS; Lorber "Notes on West Greek Gold" under SICILY—GENERAL WORKS; McClean "The True Meaning of Φ" under ITALY—GENERAL WORKS.

NEAPOLIS

2798 **Burnett, Andrew M., and Michael H. Crawford.** "Overstrikes at Neapolis and Coinage at Poseidonia-Paestum." *Studies in Greek Numismatics in Memory of Martin Jessop Price.* Edited by Richard Ashton and Silvia Hurter. London: Spink, 1998. Pages 55-7. 1 pl.
Focuses on the bronze coinage of Neapolis with *obv.*, head of Apollo, and *rev.*, man-faced bull being crowned by Nike. The dating of this issue is important for the dating of a number of other issues. The authors publish a new overstrike which confirms the other evidence for a dating in the 250's B.C. This is the only bronze type of Neapolis known to have been overstruck. The authors discuss related hoard evidence. Several of the bronzes of Neapolis in question were found in a hoard along with coins of Aesernia. The Neapolis coins under discussion are overstruck on coins of Aesernia. Other archaeological evidence is considered, and the issue is firmly placed in the mid-third century B.C. The chronological implications for the coinage of Paestum are discussed.

2798a **Talierco Mensitieri, Marina.** "Il Bronzo di Neapolis." *La Monetazione di Neapolis nella Campania Antica: Atti del VII Convegno del Centro Internazionale di Studi Numismatici, Napoli 20-24 Aprile 1980.* Napoli, 1986. Pages 219-373.

2798b ——— "Simboli, Lettere, Sigle sul Bronzo di Neapolis." *Studi per Laura Breglia: Bollettino di Numismatica Supplemento* 4 (1987): 161-78.

2799 **Wihnyk, Joseph.** "Mirror-Image Kleudoros Monogram on Coins of Neapolis." *The Celator* 21, no. 8 (August 2007): 40. Illus.
Illustrates a nomos of Velia bearing the monogram of the engraver Kleudoros on the reverse. Also illustrates a nomos of Neapolis with a mirror-image of this monogram on the obverse. Wihnyk suggests this may be evidence that the engraver created dies for both cities.

2800 ——— "Dionysos Unmasked on Neopolitan Nomoi." *The Celator* 22, no. 11 (November 2008): 6-18. Illus.
The figure on the obverse of the silver nomoi of Neapolis is usually identified as Parthenope. The man-headed bull on the reverse is usually identified as Parthenope's father, the river god Achelous. However, A. W. Hands believed the reverse figure was sometimes a depiction of the god Dionysos Hebon, and the nymph on the obverse is sometimes Persephone (Dia Hebe). Wihnyk presents an image of Dionysos on a Roman marble relief which closely resembles the face of the man-headed bull on a coin of Neapolis. The obverse of the coins usually also bears a symbol behind the nymph's head. Wihnyk discusses these symbols and explains the connection of each to Dionysos.

Also see: Brunetti "Contributo alla Cronologia delle Zecche di Velia e Neapolis" under ITALY—VELIA; Burnett "South Italy Hoard" and "Naples" under ITALY—GENERAL WORKS; Johnston "Report of a Discussion on South Italian Chronology" under ITALY—GENERAL WORKS; Kozik and Carlton "The Man-Headed Bull" under SICILY—GELA; Parente "Monete Suberate" under ITALY—GENERAL WORKS.

PANDOSIA

2801 **Feuardent, G. L.** "A Coin of Pandosia." *American Journal of Numismatics* 19, no. 4 (April 1885): 92-3.
Recounts how a coin of Pandosia helped to determine the location of this city in Bruttium. The coin bears the inscription ΚΡΑΘΙΣ. This confirmed that the city was located on a tributary of the well-known river Crathis. [Also see "Lost Countries Found by Coins" under CYCLADES ISLANDS].

Also see: Chittenden "The Master of Animals" under TYPES; "Lost Countries" under CYCLADES ISLANDS; McClean "The True Meaning of Φ" under ITALY—GENERAL WORKS.

Poseidonia

2802 **Brousseau, Louis.** "Sur l'Étalon Monétaire en Usage à Poseidonia." *Liber Amicorum Tony Hackens*. Numismatica Lovaniensia 20. Edited by G. Moucharte, M. B. Borba Florenzano, F. de Callataÿ, P. Marchetti, L. Smolderen, and P. Yannopoulos. Louvain-la-Neuve: Université Catholique de Louvain, 2007. Pages 47 ff.

2803 **Crawford, Michael H.** "Paestum and Rome: The Form and Function of a Subsidiary Coinage." *La Monetazione di Bronzo di Poseidonia-Paestum. Atti del III Convegno del Centro Internazionale di Studi Numismatici, Napoli, Aprile 1971.* Supplement to *Annali: Istituto Italiano di Numismatica* 18. Rome, 1973. Pages 47-110. [CS 2110]

2804 **Ebner, Pietro.** *La Monetazione di Posidonia-Paestum.* Salerno, 1964. 44 pp., illus. [CS 2111]

2805 **Gale, W. L.** "A Coin from Ancient Poseidonia: Games in Honor of Hera?" *The Celator* 11, no. 11 (November 1997): 34-5. Illus.
Briefly summarizes the history of the city of Poseidonia and its coinage. Publishes a Poseidonian stater bearing the obverse inscription ΣΕΙΛΑ. Barclay Head suggested this inscription may stand for Silaria, and that the coin may have been issued to commemorate games celebrated on the banks of the river Silaros, the northern boundary of Poseidonian territory.

2806 **Grunauer von Hoerschelmann, Susanne.** "Die Bronzeprägung von Poseidonia." *La Monetazione di Bronzo di Poseidonia-Paestum. Atti del III Convegno del Centro Internazionale di Studi Numismatici, Napoli, Aprile 1971.* Supplement to *Annali: Istituto Italiano di Numismatica* 18. Rome, 1973. Pages 25-46. [CS 2112]

2807 **Hoge, Robert W.** "Museum Receives Rare Stater of Poseidonia." *The Numismatist* 111, no. 8 (August 2000): 974. Illus.
Illustrates and briefly discusses an incuse stater of Poseidonia which was recently donated to the museum of the American Numismatic Association.

2808 **Holloway, R. Ross.** "Poseidonia-Paestum: Relazione tra Monetazione d'Argento e Monetazione di Bronzo." *La Monetazione di Bronzo di Poseidonia-Paestum. Atti del III Convegno del Centro Internazionale di Studi Numismatici, Napoli, Aprile 1971.* Supplement to *Annali: Istituto Italiano di Numismatica* 18. Rome, 1973. Pages 135-48. 3 pls. [CS 2113]

2809 **Istituto Italiano di Numismatica.** *La Monetazione di Bronzo di Poseidonia-Paestum. Atti del III Convegno del Centro Internazionale di Studi Numismatici, Napoli, Aprile 1971.* Supplement to *Annali: Istituto Italiano di Numismatica* 18. Rome, 1973. 171 pp., 14 pls. [CS 2115]

2810 **Kraay, Colin M.** "Gli Stateri a Doppio Relievo di Poseidonia." *Atti e Memorie della Società Magna Grecia* 8 (1967): 112-37. [CS 2114]

2811 **Noe, Sydney P.** "Group of Die-Sequences at Poseidonia, ca. 430-410 B.C." *Museum Notes* 5 (1952): 9-19. 2 pls. [CS 2116]
Examines the coins of Poseidonia marked with single letters, dated ca. 430-410 B.C. Suggests these letters, from alpha to iota, indicate a sequence of dies. The use of lettered dies seems to have been interrupted and later resumed. Lists and describes twenty-nine dies, and lists numerous specimens of each in public collections. Suggests the change to double-relief coinage at Poseidonia preceded the change at Metapontum and Croton.

2812 **Sallusto, Federico.** "Monete Inedite di Poseidonia." *Annali Istituto Italiano di Numismatica* (Italy) 16-17 (1969-70): 47-53. Illus. [CS 2117]

2813 ——— *Le Monete di Bronzo di Poseidonia-Paestum nella Collezione Sallusto.* Naples: Museo Civico, 1971. 54 pp., pls. [CS 2118]

2814 **Stazio, Attilio.** "Poseidonia-Paestum: Problemi della Circolazione Monetale." *La Monetazione di Bronzo di Poseidonia-Paestum. Atti del III Convegno del Centro Internazionale di Studi Numismatici, Napoli, Aprile 1971.* Supplement to *Annali: Istituto Italiano di Numismatica* 18. Rome, 1973. Pages 111-34. [CS 2119]

2815 **Tzamalis, Anastasios P.** "The Poseidonians: A Poem by C. P. Cavafy." *Nomismatika Khronika* (Greece) 22 (2003): 8. [Also in Greek on pp. 7, illus.].
A short poem about the city of Poseidonia, illustrated by a stater from the Alpha Bank collection.

2816 **Zancani Montuoro, Paola.** "Dosseno a Poseidonia." *Atti e Memorie della Società Magna Grecia* ser. 2 (1958): 79-94. 3 pls. [CS 2120]

Also see: Burnett "Overstrikes" under ITALY—NEAPOLIS.

Rhegion

2817 **Caltabiano, Maria Caccamo.** "La Monetazione de Rhegion nell'età della Tirannide." *Klearchos* 137-138 (1993-1995): 103-22. Illus.

2817a **Castrizio, Daniele.** "The Final Series of the Rhegion Mint." *Numismatic Chronicle* 171 (2011).

2818 **Clain-Stefanelli, Elvira Eliza.** "Late Silver Issues of Rhegium: A Janus Head Type in Rhegium." *Florilegium Numismaticum: Studia in Honorem U. Westermark Edita.* Edited by Harald Nilsson. Stockholm: Svenska Numismatiska Föreningen, 1992. Pages 119-26. Illus.
The author publishes some late fractional issues of Rhegium, including an obol bearing a janiform head. Discusses the origin and use of janiform heads on Greek and Roman Republican coins. Discusses the reasons for issuing small fractional denominations at Rhegium during this period.

2819 **Garrucci, P. Raffaele.** "Le Monnayage Antique de Rhegium de Calabre." *Annuaire de la Société de Numismatique* (1882): 213-27. 2 pls.

2820 **Herzfelder, Hubert.** "Les Monnaies d'Argent de Rhegion, frappées entre 461 et le Milieu du IVe Siècle av. J.-C." *Revue Numismatique* (France) 17 (1955): 25 ff.; 18 (1956): 7 ff. Reprint, Paris, 1957. 154 pp., 20 pls. [CS 2122]
Examines the silver coins of Rhegion.

2821 **Kraay, Colin M.** "Fifth Century Overstrikes at Rhegium and Messana." *La Circolazione della Moneta Areniese in Sicilia e in Magna Grecia.* Atti del I Convegno de Centro Internazionale di Studi Numismatici 1967. Supplement to *Annali. Istituto Italiano di Numismatica* (Italy) 12-14 (1969): 141-50.

2822 **Larizza, Pietro.** *Rhegion Chalcidense: La Storia e la Numismatica.* Rome, 1905.

2823 **Seltman, E. J.** "The Type Known as 'The Demos' on Coins of Rhegium." *Numismatic Chronicle* 3rd ser., 17 (1897): 173-89. 1 pl.
Discusses the coins bearing a seated male figure. The issuance of these coins supposedly coincided with the establishment of the rule of democracy at the city of Rhegium in 466 B.C. The figure on the coins has been identified as the Demos—the impersonation of the Common Wealth. Seltman examines this theory on archaeological and numismatic grounds and concludes that the figure is meant to represent the deity Aristaeus, the patron of rural life. [Also see next article].

2824 ———. "The Seated Figure on Silver Coins of Rhegium." *Numismatic Chronicle* 3rd ser., 19 (1899): 5-11.
In the previous article (see above), Seltman rejected the identification of the type on the early coins of Rhegium as the "Demos" in favor of Aristaeus, the guardian of the city's culture. J. P. Six suggested that the type is the eponymous oekist (the founder) of the city, similar to the oekist shown on the early coins of Tarentum. Seltman compares the Rhegium and Tarentum types and concludes the figure on the coins of Rhegium is not the oekist and confirms Aristaeus as the identity.

2825 **Vallet, G.** *Rhégion et Zancle: Histoire, Commerce, et Civilisation des Cités Chalcidiennes du Détroit de Messine.* Paris, 1958. 406 pp., 20 pls. [CS 2288]
"A well-documented historical study, an excellent source for numismatics." [E. Clain-Stefanelli]

Also see: Caltabiano *La Monetazione di Messana* under SICILY—ZANKLE/MESSANA; Clain-Stefanelli "Fractional Silver" under SICILY—GENERAL WORKS; Lorimer "The Country Cart" under TYPES; Macdonald "On a Find Made in the Islands" under ITALY—GENERAL WORKS; Robinson "Rhegion, Zankle Messana and the Samians" under SICILY—ZANKLE/MESSANA; Rutter "South Italy and Messana" under ITALY—GENERAL WORKS; Waldstein "Pythagoras of Rhegion" (second article) under ART.

SERDAIOI

2826 **Arnold-Biucchi, Carmen.** "A New Coin of the Serdaioi (?) at the ANS." *Essays in Honour of Robert Carson and Kenneth Jenkins.* Edited by M. J. Price, A. M. Burnett and R. Bland. London: Spink & Son, 1993. Pages 1-3. Illus.
Publishes an obol from the collection of the American Numismatic Society with *obv.*, Dionysos head; *rev.*, MEP in circle of dots. The style of engraving is unusual in that the head is made up of small dots. Eight other coins are known with similar types and inscriptions. The attribution of these coins is uncertain—they have been variously attributed to cities in Italy or Sicily. An inscription on a bronze tablet provides new evidence for attributing the coins. The tablet mentions a treaty between Sybaris and the Serdaioi. Arnold-Biucchi attributes the coins to the Serdaioi, located somewhere between Poseidonia and Sybaris. The author suggests a date around 480 B.C. for the coins.

2827 **Cahn, Herbert A.** "Serdaioi." *Schweizer Münzblätter* (Switzerland) 28, no. 112 (1978): 81-8. Illus. [CS 2127]

2827a **Zacani-Montuoro, Paola.** "Serdaioi?" *Schweizer Münzblätter* (Switzerland) 28, no. 119 (1980).

SIRIS

2828 **Gale, W. L.** "The First Italian Coinage." *The Celator* 10, no. 4 (April 1996): 34. Illus.
Illustrates a stater bearing the same types as those of Sybaris (bull in relief/bull incuse) but with different inscriptions. The coin has been variously attributed to Siris, Pyxus, or Sirinos. The author discusses the implications of the attribution for the dating of the first Italian coins. Suggests that if the coin truly belongs to Siris, the start of Italian coinage may need to be pushed back to the early sixth century B.C. [Also see the author's "Letter to the Editor" below].

2829 ———. "Letter to the Editor: Early Italian Coinage." *The Celator* 12, no. 6 (June 1998): 4.
This brief follow-up to the author's article "The First Italian Coinage" (see above) mentions an exhibition catalogue which makes reference to a drachm of Siris in the collection of the Museo del Archeologica di Napoli. This is the only coin solely from Siris know to the author, and it may confirm his view about the early emergence of coinage in Italy.

SYBARIS

2830 **Bicknell, Peter J.** "A Triobol of Sybaris." *New Zealand Numismatic Journal* (New Zealand) 12, no. 1 (October 1966): 2-5. Illus.
Bicknell examines a triobol (*McClean* 1187) with a bull of Sybaris as an obverse type and the tripod of Croton as the reverse type. Grose attributed the coin to Croton and dated it to ca. 453-447 B.C. Kraay attributed the coin to Sybaris I (before 510 B.C.). Bicknell agrees with Kraay's attribution and suggests that it represents an issue struck on the occasion of the engagement of the daughter of Telys, tyrant of Sybaris, to Philippus of Croton.

2831 ———. "A Stater of Sybaris II?" *New Zealand Numismatic Journal* (New Zealand) 12, no. 4 (June 1969): 148-51. 1 pl.

Bicknell identifies three series of coins belonging to Sybaris II (the refounded city after the destruction of Sybaris by Croton) and dating to the period ca. 500-475 B.C.: obols with bull obverse and acorn incuse reverse, triobols with bull obverse and amphora incuse reverse, and staters with bull obverse and bull incuse reverse. The staters were attributed to Sybaris II by Kraay, and Bicknell concurs with this attribution.

2832 **Breglia, Laura.** "Le Monete delle Quattro Sibari." *Annali. Istituto Italiano de Numismatica* (Italy) 2 (1955): 9-26. 1 pl. [CS 2128]

2833 **Fabricius, Knud.** "Sybaris, Its History and Coinage." *Congrès International de Numismatique, Paris, 6-11 Juillet 1953. Volume 2.* Paris: Commission International de Numismatique, 1957. Pages 65-76. [CS 2130]
Suggests the incuse fabric of the coinage was intended to prevent the coins from leaving Italy, due to a lack of silver mines in the area. Discusses the early history of commerce in Sybaris. Compares the coins with those of other cities and discusses the stylistic development of Sybaris' coinage. Includes evidence from hoards. Speculates there may have been two mints coining simultaneously. Discusses the chronology of the coinage.

2834 **Kraay, Colin M.** "The Coinage of Sybaris After 510 B.C." *Numismatic Chronicle* 6th ser., 18 (1958): 13-37. 2 pls. Reprint, New York: Attic Books, 1977. 27 pp., 2 pls. [CS 2131]
The destruction of the city of Sybaris in 511/510 B.C. brought an end to its famous incuse bull coinage and marks an important point in the chronology of south Italian coinage. Several re-foundings of the city resulted in various phases of coinage after 510 B.C. This paper explores these coins and their relationship to the coinage of Croton, Laus, and Poseidonia. The author attempts to determine which Sybarite coins were issued during each re-founding of the city.

2835 **Plant, Richard J.** "An Obol of Sybaris." *Classical Numismatic Review* 18, no. 4 (fourth quarter 1993): 5. Illus.
Presents a line-drawing of an obol of Sybaris. Plant discusses the inscription VM, the abbreviation for the city name. He explains that early Greek writing was done from right to left. The M is not simply a Greek sigma turned side-ways. It is an early style S used in Western Greek scripts, derived from the Semitic letter Tsade (rather than Sin, the root letter of Sigma). The author also recounts the destruction of the city in 510 BC.

Also see: Attianese *Calabria Greca* under ITALY—GENERAL WORKS; Benton "Cattle Egrets" under TYPES; Gardner "A Numismatic Note on the Lelantian War" under CENTRAL GREECE—EUBOIA; Lloyd "Chorographical" under TYPES.

TARAS

2836 **Attas, Michael.** "The Fineness of Tarentine Didrachmas." ΣΥΝΕΙΣΦΟΡΑ *McGill 1: Papers in Greek Archaeology and History in Memory of Colin D. Gordon.* Edited by John M. Fossey. Amsterdam: J. C. Gieben, 1987. Pages 99-115.
Describes the techniques involved in performing X-ray fluorescence analysis of silver coins. The author used this method to determine the copper content of 135 silver didrachms of Tarentum from the McGill University collection. The results are noted in a table and in histograms. Attas concludes that the proportions of copper in Tarentine coins is not sufficient to support the hypothesis of official devaluations.

2837 **Birch, Samuel.** "Note on Some Types of Tarentum." *Numismatic Chronicle* 7 (1845): 107-9.
The author identifies the boy riding a dolphin on the coins of Tarentum as Phalanthus, the founder of the state, rather than Taras, son of Poseidon, as had been previously claimed. He also identifies the horse-rider on the reverse of the coins as the Equestrian Taras.

2838 **Brauer, George C., Jr.** *Taras: Its History and Coinage.* New Rochelle, New York: Aristide D. Caratzas, 1986. 231 pp., illus., map.
An extensive history of the city of Taras (Tarentum) from the foundation of the city, ca. 700 B.C., to the beginning of the Roman period. Presents political and military events, a description of life in the city, and a discussion of famous men of the city, drawing much information from the ancient authors. A discussion of the coinage is woven throughout the text, with an emphasis on descriptions of the coin types. Illustrated by sixty-one coin photographs throughout. Includes a detached, fold-out map of the ancient Mediterranean area.

2839 **Brunetti, Lodovico.** "To Tarantos Parasemon: Contributo alla Numismatica Tarentina." *Italiana di Numismatica* (Italy) 5 (1948): 8-70. [CS 2132]

2840 ——— "Sulle Frazioni dell'Argento Tarentino." *Numismatica* 15 (1949): 1-33. "Part 2." *Numismatica* 16 (1950): 1-21. [CS 2133]

2841 ——— "Nuovi Orientamenti sulla Zecca di Taranto." *Rivista Italiana di Numismatica* (Italy) 62 (1960): 2-132. [CS 2134]

2842 **Cahn, Herbert A.** "Early Tarentine Chronology." *Essays in Greek Coinage Presented to Stanley Robinson.* Edited by C. M. Kraay and G. K. Jenkins. Oxford: Clarendon Press, 1968. Pages 59-74. 2 pls. [CS 2135]
A re-examination of Ravel's die sequence of the early coins of Tarentum, ca. 520-460 B.C., as listed in his catalogue of the Vlasto collection (see Ravel *Descriptive Catalogue* below). Lists specimens from numerous published collections, points out die-links, and suggests a rearrangement of the die sequence. Ravel's catalogue numbers are shown. Suggests the earliest issues of Tarentum, the incuse coinages with a youth holding a flower, began ca. 520-510 B.C. and the dies were not engraved by a local person. Next came the incuse type of the dolphin-rider, which Cahn believes was engraved in a local style. Suggests the dolphin-rider is Phalanthos and the horseman is Taras. Compares the style of succeeding issues through the hippocamp type, which he dates to 470-460 B.C., and the seated Taras—the so-called 'oecist' coins, the first of which he dates to ca. 480 B.C.

2843 **Evans, Arthur J.** "The 'Horsemen' of Tarentum." *Numismatic Chronicle* 3rd ser., 9 (1889): 1-228. 11 pls. [CS 2136]
A major study of the Tarentine coinage bearing the horse with rider, and dolphin with rider types. Includes historical background and a discussion of the coin types. The detailed catalogue of coins includes much discussion about each chronological period. Appendices list the contents of several hoards containing Tarentine coins.

2844 **Fischer-Bossert, Wolfgang.** *Chronologie der Didrachmenpraegung von Tarent 510-280 v. Chr.* Antike Münzen und Geschnittene Steine 14. Berlin: Walter de Gruyter, 1999. 495 pp., 78 pls., map.
A die study of the didrachms of Tarentum. Illustrates all known varieties. [Reviewed by Carmen Arnold-Biucchi in *Revue Suisse de Numismatique* 80 (2001): 207-20, and by Kenneth Sheedy in *American Journal of Archaeology* 106, no. 2 (April 2002): 338-9].

2845   **Giubba, A.** "Numismatica Tarentina." *Studi di Storia Pugliese in Onore di G. Chiarelli. Volume 1.* Galatina, 1972. Pages 61-86.

2846   **Hands, Alfred Watson.** "Common Greek Coins: Tarentum." *Spink Numismatic Circular* 13 (October 1905): 8625-32; 14, no. 157 (December 1905): 8762-7; no. 158 (January 1906): 8825-38; no. 159 (February 1906): 8889-92. Illus.
Classifies the coinage of Tarentum into chronological periods and discusses each. Lists inscriptions and monograms grouped by period.

2847   **Jenkins, G. Kenneth.** "Note sur Quelques Monnaies d'or de Tarente." *Cercle d'Études Numismatique* 11, no. 1 (1974): 2-7. Illus. [CS 2137]

2848   ———. "A Tarantine Footnote." *Greek Numismatics and Archaeology: Essays in Honor of Margaret Thompson.* Edited by O. Mørkholm and N. M. Waggoner. Wetteren: Numismatique Romaine, 1979. Pages 109-14. 1 pl.
Jenkins examines the well-known gold stater of Tarentum, the reverse of which shows Poseidon seated on a throne, and in front of him, a boy (Taras) raising his hand to his father in supplication or greeting. Evans interpreted the type as a Tarentine appeal for help from Sparta, which occurred in 344 B.C. Jenkins discusses this interpretation and he doubts Evans' conclusion. He presents evidence from hoards and overstrikes for the chronology of the issue. These coins are traditionally regarded as the first gold issues of the Tarentine mint. However, after analysis, Jenkins suggests these belong to the period ca. 320 B.C. and are not among the first gold coins of the mint. No firm new interpretation of the reverse type is offered, but Jenkins suggests the type may signify sea-power at a time when the Tarentine fleet became important, with its readiness to support Naples in 326 and its actual support of Akrotatos in 315.

2849   **Jentoft-Nilsen, Marit.** "A Fourth- and Third-Century B.C. Hoard of Tarentine Silver." *J. P. Getty Museum Journal* 12 (1984): 167-72. Illus.
"Thirty-six coins—twenty-nine staters and six drachms from Tarentum as well as a single stater from Croton—reported to have been found in Tarentum span periods II-IX in Evans' 'horseman' series; the single coin from Croton is at least forty years earlier than the Tarentum pieces. The hoard has two instances of die linkage and one variant reverse." [Jentoft-Nilsen, *NL* 114]. The hoard was buried ca. 235 B.C.

2850   **Lacroix, Léon.** "Hyakinthos et les Monnaies Incuses de Tarente." *Études d'Archéologie Numismatique.* Université de Lyon II: Publications de la Bibliothèque Salomon Reinach, Volume III. Lyon/Paris: de Boccard, 1974.

2851   **Luynes, Duc de.** "Médailles de Tarente Relatives à l'Apollon Hyacinthien." *Annales de l'Institut de Correspondance Archéologique* 2 (1830): 337-42.

2852   **Madsen, Eardley, and Ethel Madsen.** "Tarentum." *SAN—Journal of the Society for Ancient Numismatics* 13, no. 3 (fall 1982): inside covers.
A brief overview of the history and coinage of Tarentum.

2853   **McDaniel, W. B.** "Dischi Sacri." *American Journal of Archaeology* 28 (1924): 24-46. Illus.
"The writer concludes that these terracotta disks from Tarentum are secular and commercial in character, rather than sacred. On pp. 39-43 it is noted that a great number of the emblems which appear on them may also be found on coins of Tarentum." [J. R. Jones, *NIAJAH*]

2854   **Raoul-Rochette, M.** "Essai sur la Numismatique Tarantine." *Mémoires de Numismatique et d'Antiquité (Mémoires de l'Académe des Inscriptions).* Paris, 1840. Pages 167-256.

2855   **Ratto, Rodolfo.** *Collection Claudius Côte, De Lyon: Monnaies de Tarente.* Lugano, 1929. Reprint, New York: Attic Books, Ltd., 1975. 42 pp., 19 pls. [CS 2144]
The auction catalogue for the January 28-29, 1929 sale, comprised of 611 coins of Tarentum from the collection of Claudius Côte. A nice reference collection of this coinage. The plates in the reprint edition are of modest, but usable, quality. Text in French. [Also see listing 546 in J. Spring, *Ancient Coin Auction Catalogues 1880-1980* (see Spring under COLLECTING GUIDES)].

2856   **Ravel, Oscar E.** *Descriptive Catalogue of the Collection of Tarentine Coins Formed by M. P. Vlasto.* London: Spink and Son, 1947. Reprint, Chicago: Obol International, 1977. 197 pp., 53 pls., map. [CS 2140]
The catalogue of Michel P. Vlasto's collection of the coinage of Tarentum, the most complete collection of this coinage ever formed. Lists 1881 coins, mostly of high quality. All are photographed in the plates. A brief biography of Vlasto (b. 1874; d. 1936) is followed by a general description of the collection. The catalogue describes the die varieties, and gives weights and dates for each coin. Includes tables of weight standards and symbols. [Reviewed by G. K. Jenkins in *Numismatic Chronicle* 6th ser., 8 (1948): 106-7. [Also see Cahn "Early Tarentine Chronology" above for suggested revisions to Ravel's die sequences].

2857   **Vagi, David.** "Tarentine Gold Struck During Times of War." *The Celator* 8, no. 2 (February 1994): 18. Illus.
Comments on the beautiful, but scarce, gold staters of Tarentum. Most were struck to meet wartime needs during the periods 344-334 B.C., ca. 315 B.C., 334-330 B.C., and in 280 B.C.

2858   **Van Keuren, Frances.** "A Coin Copy of Lysippus's Heracles at Tarentum." *Ancient Coins of the Graeco-Roman World: The Nickle Numismatic Papers.* Edited by Waldemar Heckel and Richard Sullivan. Waterloo, Ontario: Wilfrid Laurier University Press, 1984. Pages 203-19. 2 pls. (pages 305-6).
Illustrates two gold quarter-staters of Heraclea Lucaniae (*obv.*, Athena in Corinthian helmet; *rev.*, nude Heracles seated), believed to be an emergency issue minted in 280 B.C. to pay Greek troops who fought in Pyrrhus' battle against the Romans at Heraclea. Phyllis Lehman previously suggested the reverse was copied from a statue (see Lehman *Statues on Coins* under TYPES). Van Keuren now proposes that the coin type is based on Lysippus' Heracles at Tarentum. He compares the depiction of the statue on the coin to the known copies of the statue, a list of which appears in the Appendix.

2859 **Vlasto, Michel P.** "Les Monnaies de Bronze de Tarente." *Journal International d'Archéologie Numismatique* (Greece) 2 (1899): 1-8. 1 pl.
"Bronze coinage begins in 281 and continues until 209 B.C. Description of types and legends." [J. R. Jones, *AIJIAN*]

2860 ——— "Les Monnaies d'Or de Tarente." *Journal International d'Archéologie Numismatique* (Greece) 2 (1899): 303-40. 5 pls. *Supplément.* 4 (1901): 93-113. 4 pls.
"Agrees with Babelon's theory that gold coinage signifies regal issues or emergencies, and finds that Tarentine coinage confirms this. Classification and description of gold issues, ca. 340-209 B.C." [J. R. Jones, *AIJIAN*]. Also see the note on page 403 by Babelon and Vlasto concerning a magistrate's name.

2861 ——— "Rare or Unpublished Coins of Taras." *Numismatic Chronicle* 4th ser., 7 (1907): 277-90. 1 pl.
A catalogue of nineteen coins of Tarentum from the author's collection, selected for their great rarity, novelty, or unusually fine condition.

2862 ——— "On a Recent Find of Coins Struck During the Hannibalic Occupation at Tarentum." *Numismatic Chronicle* 4th ser., 9 (1909): 253-63. 1 pl.
The author discusses a hoard of 114 silver coins of Tarentum, buried ca. 210 B.C. The coins were struck ca. 212-209 B.C. Some of the more scarce and interesting varieties are published here.

2863 ——— "A Find of Tarentine Nomoi, Etc., from Italy." *Numismatic Chronicle* 5th ser., 2 (1922): 245-7.
Lists and discusses 42 coins found in Italy including 32 nomoi, 3 drachms, 3 diobols, and 1 litra of Tarentum. Also includes two didrachms of Croton and one didrachm of Thurium.

2864 ——— *ΤΑΡΑΣ ΟΙΚΙΣΤΗΣ: A Contribution to Tarentine Numismatics.* Numismatic Notes and Monographs, No. 15. New York: American Numismatic Society, 1922. 234 pp., 13 pls. [CS 2142]
Vlasto describes and puts into chronological sequence the known die varieties of the nomoi of Tarentum with a seated male figure on the reverse (Taras, the eponymous founder, or "oekist," of the city). The "oekist" coins do not form a single continuous issue but were alternated, and often struck simultaneously with, other early Tarentine nomoi of varying types. The author divides the issues into four periods, 485-400 B.C., and provides detailed descriptions and lists of known specimens. Sixty types are catalogued. The contents of three hoards are listed in the Appendices.

2865 ——— "The Late Mr. E. P. Warren's Hoard of Tarentine Horsemen and Other Contributions to Tarentine Numismatics." *Numismatic Chronicle* 5th ser., 10 (1930): 107-63. 3 pls. [CS 2143]
Discusses a hoard of 425 "horseman" coins of Tarentum. The date and provenance of the hoard remains unknown. Catalogues some of the coins and discusses the coinage of Tarentum.

2866 **Westermark, Ulla.** "Overstrikes of Taras on Didrachms of Acragas." *Greek Numismatics and Archaeology: Essays in Honor of Margaret Thompson.* Edited by O. Mørkholm and N. M. Waggoner. Wetteren: Numismatique Romaine, 1979. Pages 287-93. 1 pl.
Discusses some overstrikes of Taras on didrachms of Acragas which were not included in Noe's study (see Noe "Overstrikes in Magna Graecia" above). Discusses the implications for the chronology of Tarentine coinage.

Also see: Evans "A Recent Find" under ITALY—METAPONTUM; Holloway "Remarks on the Taranto Hoard" under HOARDS; Johnston "Report of a Discussion on South Italian Chronology" under ITALY—GENERAL WORKS; McClean "The True Meaning of Φ" under ITALY—GENERAL WORKS; Shlosser *The McGill University Collection, Volume 2* under PUBLIC COLLECTIONS—CANADA (MONTREAL); Villaronga "The Tangier Hoard" under HOARDS.

TERINA

2867 **Birch, Samuel.** "On the Types of Terina." *Numismatic Chronicle* 7 (1845): 142-5.
Attempts to identify the types on some early coins of Terina.

2868 **Evans, Arthur J.** "The Artistic Engravers of Terina and the Signature of Euaenetos on its Later Didrachm Dies." *Numismatic Chronicle* 4th ser., 12 (1912): 21-62. 3 pls.
A re-examination of the engravers of the coinage of Terina and their artistry. Discusses the works of engravers Φ, Π, and others. Shows that the early signed dies of Terina bear strong evidence of the influence of Athenian models. Publishes a didrachm bearing on the reverse EYA—the signature of the engraver Euaenetos. Discusses the date of this issue and places it ca. 375 B.C.

2869 **Gabrici, Ettore.** "La Figura Femminile Alata Sulle Monete della Magna Graecia." *Problemi di Numismatica Greca della Sicilia e Magna Grecia.* Memorie dell' Accademia di Archeologia Lettere e Belle Arti di Napoli, Volume 4. 1959. Pages 111-120.
Explores the identity of the goddesses represented on the coins of Terina.

2870 **Holloway, R. Ross, and G. Kenneth Jenkins.** *Ex Antiquitate Nummi: Terina.* Bellinzona: Edizioni Arte E Moneta, 1983. 74 pp., 24 pls., map.
A study of Terina's coinage of the fifth and fourth centuries B.C. Includes a brief history of the city. Updates and expands the earlier catalogue by Kurt Regling (*Terina*, Berlin, 1906). Includes staters, fractions, and a few bronze coins. The silver coinage is classified into seven groups; the bronze coins are classified into two series. Includes enlarged photographs of some of the most artistic staters.

2871 **Regling, Kurt L.** "Terina." *Programme zur Winckelmannsfeste* (Germany) 66 (1906). Reprint, Bologna, 1984. 80 pp., 3 pls. [CS 2145]
"The chronology is now considered way off. Effectively superseded by Holloway and Jenkins." [D. Kroh, *ACRR*]. [See Holloway and Jenkins *Terina* above].

2872 **Von Fritze, Hans, and Hugo Gaebler.** "Terina." *Nomisma* (Germany) 1 (1907): 14-28.

Also see: McClean "The True Meaning of Φ" under ITALY—GENERAL WORKS; Poole "Athenian Coin-Engravers in Italy" under ART.

THURII

2873 **Eaglen, Robin J.** "Portraits of Greek Coinage 25: Thurium." *Spink Numismatic Circular* 116, no. 6 (December 2008): 296-7. Illus.
This installment of the author's on-going series examines the coinage of Thurium. Reviews the history of the city and its coin types.

2874 **Ehrenberg, Victor.** "The Foundation of Thurii." *American Journal of Philology* 69 (1948): 149-70.
Ehrenberg uses numismatic evidence argue that Athens took the lead in the foundation of Thurii after the destruction of Sybaris and struck coins bearing *obv.*, Athena; *rev.*, bull looking back. [Also see Kagan "Foundation of Thurii" below for a rebuttal of the use of numismatic evidence in this case].

2875 **Emerson, A.** "An Engraved Bronze Bull at Metaponto." *American Journal of Archaeology* 4 (1888): 28-38. Illus.
"The plaque which the writer describes represents a bull in the same attitude as that shown on coins of Thurium." [J. R. Jones, *NIAJAH*]

2876 **Flower, Michael A.** "Some Reflections on the Coinage of Thurium." *Seaby Coin and Medal Bulletin* 693 (May 1976): 153-4. Illus.
Thurium was a colony sponsored by Athens. The author suggests that the coinage of Thurium, the work of Athenian die-engravers, represents what Athens' coinage would have looked like if it would have been allowed to develop freely. Mentions the influence of this coinage on the coinage designs of other south Italian cities. Describes the changes in the design of Thurium's coins after the Athenian siege of Syracuse.

2877 **Forrer, Leonard S.** "An Unpublished Tetradrachm of Thurium in Signor Cav. Ignazio Virzi's Collection." *Spink Numismatic Circular* 15 (March 1907): 9705. Illus.
Publishes a fourth century B.C. tetradrachm of Thurium. The style of the head of Athena is compared to that on a coin of Adranum. Virzi believes the dies for the two coins were engraved by the same artist.

2878 ———. "Didrachm of Thurium with the Head of Athens to Left." *Spink Numismatic Circular* 31 (March-April 1923): 118-9. Illus.
Publishes a didrachm of Thurium with the Athena head facing to the left. Left-facing heads are scarce in this series.

2879 **Jörgensen, Christian.** "On the Earliest Coins of Thurioi." *Corolla Numismatica: Numismatic Essays in Honour of Barclay V. Head.* Edited by G. F. Hill. London: Oxford University Press, 1906. Pages 166-77. 2 pls.
A brief attempt at arranging the earliest coins of Thurioi (those with the head of Athena adorned with an olive branch) in their proper sequence. The author divides the coins into three series, and sub-divides each series into several groups. He dates these issues to ca. 443-425 B.C.

2880 **Kagan, Donald.** "Appendix F: The Foundation of Thurii." *The Outbreak of the Peloponnesian War.* Ithaca and London: Cornell University Press, 1969. Pages 382-4.
Kagan summarizes the numismatic evidence of Athenian influence in the foundation of Thurii after the destruction of Sybaris. Ehrenberg (see above) argued that Athens took the lead in founding Thurii, based mainly on parallels between the coin types of Thurii, Sybaris, and Athens. Kagan discounts the value of numismatic evidence in explaining these political events. [Also see Ehrenberg "The Foundation of Thurii" above].

2881 **Lederer, Philipp.** "Bemerkungen zu einem Stater von Thourioi." *Revue Suisse de Numismatique* (Switzerland) 27 (1939): 7-15.

2882 **Noe, Sydney P.** *The Thurian Di-Staters.* Numismatic Notes and Monographs, No. 71. New York: American Numismatic Society, 1935. 68 pp., 11 pls. [CS 2146]
A corpus of the distaters of Thurium. Lists 322 specimens representing 111 die combinations. The coins are divided into twelve groups. [Reviewed by A. R. Bellinger in *American Journal of Archaeology* 40 (1936): 563-4].

2883 **Robinson, Edward S. G.** "Coins of Thurium from the Collection of the Marchese Ginori." *Numismatic Chronicle* 5th ser., 7 (1927): 297-303. 1 pl.
Publishes nine staters and one distater of Thurium of unusual interest or rarity.

2884 **Seltman, E. J.** "On Some Names, Symbols, and Letters on Coins." *Journal International d'Archaéologie Numismatique* (Greece) 15 (1913): 3-10. Illus.
Discusses the identity of the small bird, the *fringilla*, on some staters of Thurium and discusses the bird's relationship to the man named ΦΡΥΓΙΛΛΟΣ whose name appears on some Thurian coins. States that it is uncertain whether the man was a city magistrate, a mint official, or a die-engraver. Illustrates a silver ingot bearing a distinctive mark—showing that such stamps were used for control purposes. Discusses the letters appearing on some early staters of Thurium. Seltman suggests that most of the letters which appear on coins are simply alphabetical control marks, but a few represent the initial of a mint official.

2885 **Wihnyk, Joe.** "French Silver Hallmark is Obverse of Thourioi." *The Celator* 25, no. 7 (July 2011): 27, 30. Illus.
Shows that a silver hallmark introduced in France in 1838 is an exact copy of the Athena head with Skylla helmet from an ancient coin of Thourioi.

Also see: Attianese *Calabria Greca* under ITALY—GENERAL WORKS; Benton "Cattle Egrets" under TYPES; Lazzarini "Su Alcune Spighe Inedite" under ITALY—METAPONTUM; McClean "The True Meaning of Φ" under ITALY—GENERAL WORKS; Rutter "South Italy and Messana" under ITALY—GENERAL WORKS.

VELIA

2886 **Bicknell, Peter J.** "Zeno of Elea and the Tyrant Demylus." *New Zealand Numismatic Journal* (New Zealand) 12, no. 3 (January 1968): 113-6. Illus.

The city of Hyele (later known as Elea or Velia) was the home of the philosopher-politician Zeno. It is believed that Zeno was put to death by the tyrant Demylus. Bicknell publishes a silver stater of Hyele which bears the letters ΔH (De) on the reverse. He suggests these letters may signify the name of the tyrant Demylus.

2887 **Breglia, Laura.** "Notizie sulla Monetazione Arcaica di Velia." *La Parola del Passato. Rivista di Studi Antichi* (Italy) 108-110 (1966): 227-38. 2 pls. [CS 2147]

2888 **Brunetti, Lodovico.** "Contributo alla Cronologia delle Zecche di Velia e Neapolis." *Rivista Italiana di Numismatica* (Italy) 5th ser., 3 (1955): 5-34. [CS 2148]

2889 **Burnett, Andrew M.** "The Last Silver Coins of Velia in the Light of Two Unpublished Hoards." *Kraay—Mørkholm Essays: Numismatic Studies in Memory of C. M. Kraay and O. Mørkholm.* Numismatica Lovaniensia 10. Edited by G. Le Rider, G. K. Jenkins, N. Waggoner, and U. Westermark. Louvain-la-Neuve: Université Catholique de Louvain, 1989. Pages 41-57. 11 pls.
Publishes two hoards, from Foggia and Lucania, containing large numbers of Velian coins. Discusses relative and absolute chronologies using the evidence of overstrikes, historical considerations, and other hoards. Provides an estimate of the volume of coinage issued. Concludes that the increase in minting at this time can be related to the period of continuous warfare. The end of this coinage is explained by the end of the need to hire mercenaries.

2890 **Ebner, Pietro.** "Altre Epigrafi e Monete di Velia." *La Parola del Passato* (Italy) 33, no. 178 (1978): 61-73. Illus. [CS 2151]

2891 **Forrer, Leonard S.** "An Unpublished Didrachm of Velia with a New Artist's Signature." *Spink Numismatic Circular* 10, no. 110 (January 1902): 5067-8.
Mentions a coin bearing Φ, the initial letter of the engraver Philistion. Lists seventeen signatures of probable artists known on Velian coins.

2892 **Mangieri, Giuseppe Libero.** *Velia and Its Coinage.* Lugano: Edizioni Arte e Moneta, 1986. 140 pp., 27 pls. Translation, 33 pp.
Contains an historical introduction and a discussion of the coinage of Velia. Examines the archaic coinage, and then the new style coinage broken down into six time periods. Also discusses the bronze coinage. Concludes with a catalogue of 223 coin types, each of which is illustrated. The main book is written in Italian, is hardcover, and contains the plates. A separate paperback English translation is included.

2893 ——— *Velia e la sua Monetazione.* Two volumes. Lugano: Edizioni Arte e Moneta, 1986. 140 pp., 27 pls.
The Italian edition of the above.

2894 **Pontrandolfo, A. G.** "Ripostiglio Monetale da Velia." *Annali. Istituto Italiano di Numismatica* 18-19 (1971-1972): 91-111. 3 pls.
Publishes a first century B.C. hoard containing 333 bronze coins of Velia.

2895 **Williams, Roderick T.** *The Silver Coinage of Velia.* Special Publication No. 25. London: Royal Numismatic Society, 1992. 164 pp., 47 pls., map.
A complete die-study of the silver coinage of the city of Velia, minted ca. 535-275 B.C. The catalogue is divided into ten chronological periods plus a section on obols and diobols. Each section includes introductory text and a catalogue of die varieties. Catalogues 639 die-varieties, under which up to fifty individual pieces are listed. All die combinations are illustrated in the plates. Also includes an index of specimens arranged by their source collections. [An extensive review by Harold B. Mattingly appears in *Spink Numismatic Circular* 102, no. 9 (November 1994): 404-6. Also reviewed by K. Rutter in *Numismatic Chronicle* 154 (1994): 303-4].

Also see: McClean "The True Meaning of Φ" under ITALY—GENERAL WORKS; Rutter "South Italy and Messana" under ITALY—GENERAL WORKS.

SICILY

We shall here be considering some of the particular forms taken by coinage among the Greeks of Sicily; and some of their coins rank without exaggeration among the most notable works of art which we have from classical times, frequently to be found in a fine state of preservation.

—G. K. Jenkins, 1966

GENERAL WORKS

2896 **Appleton, William S.** "Coins of Ancient Sicily." *American Journal of Numismatics* 12, no. 4 (April 1878): 81-3. 1 pl.
Illustrates and describes twelve silver coins of Sicily.

2897 **Arnold-Biucchi, Carmen.** *The Randazzo Hoard 1980 and Sicilian Chronology in the Early Fifth Century B.C.* Numismatic Studies, No. 18. New York: American Numismatic Society, 1990. 77 pp., 20 pls.
Analysis of 539 Sicilian tetradrachms from a hoard discovered near Randazzo, Sicily, in 1980. The author believes this was a savings hoard gathered over many years by an individual or family. The years covered by the hoard coins are ca. 510-450 B.C. Provides an overview of the history of this period along with commentary on the mints involved (Rhegion, Akragas, Gela, Katane, Leontinoi, Messana, Naxos, and Syracuse). The hoard was probably buried about 450 B.C. Discusses the evidence provided by other fifth century hoards. Argues that the Syracusan decadrachm known as the Demareteion was not primarily a commemorative issue but was struck for economic reasons, perhaps ca. 475-470 B.C. Includes a catalogue of the coins with photographs of each. [Reviewed by H. B. Mattingly and J. Morcom in *Numismatic Chronicle* 152 (1992): 187-93].

2898 ———. "Litras en Argent Contremarquées en Sicile et les Fractions de Sélinonte." *Pour Denyse: Divertissements Numismatiques.* Edited by S. Hurter and C. Arnold-Biucchi. Bern, Switzerland: Privately published, 2000. Pages 13-7. 1 pl.
Discusses countermarked silver coins from Akragas, Himera, Syracuse, and Selinus.

2899 **Arslan, Ermanno A.** *La Moneta della Sicilia Antica: Catalogo delle Civiche Raccolte Numismatiche di Milano.* Milan, 1976. 68 pp., 52 pls. [CS 2166]
Illustrates 1419 coins.

2900 **Barth, Henry.** "The Adoption of the Athenian Standard in the Coinage of Some Italian and Sicilian Cities, about Olymp. 75 (B.C. 480), Corroborated and Accounted for by Historical Evidence." *Numismatic Chronicle* 7 (1845): 156-71.
The author reviews the historical connections between Athens and Sicily and concludes that Athenian influence, combined with a desire to oppose Corinthian ascendancy, led to the introduction of the Athenian weight standard in the coinage of the cities of Italy and Sicily.

2901 **Berk, Harlan J., and Simon Bendall.** "Eunus/Antiochus: Slave Revolt in Sicily." *The Celator* 8, no. 2 (February 1994): 6-8. Illus.
Recounts a slave revolt in Sicily, ca. 140 B.C., led by a Syrian slave, Eunus, who was proclaimed king and changed his name to Antiochus. The slave revolt was eventually put down and Eunus was imprisoned. Describes a rare series of bronze and gold coins struck for Eunus. The authors suggest that these coins bear "the only ancient coin portrait of a slave and a usurper against the Roman Republic." [Also see Lorber "Image and Symbol" below and E. S. G. Robinson "Antiochus" below].

2902 **Bertino, Antonio.** "La Prima Monetazione Sicula d'Argento." *Atti.* Volume 2 of *Congresso Internzaionale di Numismatica, Roma 1961.* Rome, 1965. Pages 151-8. [CS 2168]
Discusses coins of Abacaenum, Enna, Galaria, Longane, and Morgantina.

2903 **Boehringer, Christof.** "Die Barbarisierten Münzen von Akragas, Gela, Leontinoi und Syrakus im 5. Jahrhundert v.Chr." *Annali dell'Istituto di Numismatica Volume 20 & Atti del IV Congresso del Centro Internzionale di Studi Numismatici.* Naples, 1973. Reprinted, Naples, 1975. 33 pp., 5 pls. [CS 2169]

2904 ———. "Bemerkungen zur Sizilischen Bronzeprägung im 5. Jahrhundert v. Chr." *Schweizer Münzblätter* (Switzerland) 28, no. 111 (1978): 49-65. 2 pls. [CS 2170]

2905 ———— "Bronze—Silver—Gold. Überlegungen zu den Nominalen Eininger Sizilischer Goldmünzen." *Revue Belge de Numismatique et de Sigillographie* (Belgium) 145 (1999): 49-59.

2906 **Borba-Florenzano, Maria Beatriz.** "Sicily: The Hellenistic Period." *A Survey of Numismatic Research 1985-1990. Volume 1.* International Association of Professional Numismatists Special Publication, No. 12. Edited by T. Hackens, P. Naster, et al. Brussels: International Association of Professional Numismatists, 1991. Pages 48-54.
A narrative overview of newly published works in the field of numismatics during 1985-1990. Summarizes major findings related to the fourth through first centuries B.C., with bibliographic references cited in the footnotes.

2907 ———— "Coins and Religion: Representations of Demeter and of Kore/Persephone on Sicilian Greek Coins." *Revue Belge de Numismatique et de Sigillographie* (Belgium) 151 (2005): 1-28.

2908 ———— "A Note on the *Triskeles* as the Badge of Sicily: Territorial Identity in Ancient Greek Coinage." *Liber Amicorum Tony Hackens.* Numismatica Lovaniensia 20. Edited by G. Moucharte, M. B. Borba Florenzano, F. de Callataÿ, P. Marchetti, L. Smolderen, and P. Yannopoulos. Louvain-la-Neuve: Université Catholique de Louvain, 2007. Pages 153 ff.

2909 **Buttrey, Theodore V., Jr.** "The Morgantina Gold Hoard and the Coinage of Hicetas." *Numismatic Chronicle* 7th ser., 13 (1973): 1-17. 2 pls. [CS 2240]
"The hoard, discovered in 1966 during Princeton's excavations at Morgantina, stretches from Philip to Pyrrhus, but is richest in the gold of Hicetas. Burial occurred ca. 275-270 B.C. The twenty-one examples of Hicetas' hemistaters provoke a reconsideration of his gold coinage and a survey by die pair is provided. Close die linkage shows that the issue was struck only at the end of his rule, 279/278 B.C., probably to finance the unsuccessful Carthaginian campaign. The chronology of Diodorus Siculus' account should be amended to accord with the numismatic evidence. See also *Inventory of Greek Coin Hoards* No. 2204." [T. Buttrey, *NL* 92]

2910 **Calciati, Romolo.** *Corpus Nummorum Siculorum: La Monetazione di Bronzo (The Bronze Coinage).* Three volumes. Mortara: Edizioni G.M. Vol. 1: 1983, 397 pp.; vol. 2: 1986, 460 pp.; vol. 3: 1987, 428 pp. [CS 2172a]
A comprehensive catalogue of the bronze coinage of Sicily. Volume 1 includes over 2500 coins of the autonomous cities and the coinage during the Carthaginian domination. Volume 2 is devoted to the bronze coinage of Syracuse from its beginning through the Roman period. Includes discussion of Roman restrikes over Syracusan coins. More than 1750 coins are listed. Volume 3 covers all other Sicilian mints, Carthaginian issues, minor islands, and uncertain mints. The text is in both Italian and English. [Reviewed by J. Morcom in *Numismatic Chronicle* 148 (1988): 227-9; and 150 (1990): 246-8].

2911 **Castellus, Gabriele Lancillotto.** *Sicilie Populorum et Urbium Regum Quoque et Tyrannorum Verteres Nummi Saracenorum Epocham Antecedents.* Three volumes. Panormii: Typis Regiis, Facta Potestate, 1781, 1789, 1791. 138 pp., 125 pls.
Gabriele Lancilloto Castellus, Prince of Torremuzza, was one of the greatest collectors of the Greek coins of Southern Italy and Sicily. This work was a significant study of these coins and includes finely engraved plates of ancient Greek coins by Melchior de Bella. Many of the illustrated pieces were from Castellus' own collection, which was subsequently purchased en bloc by Lord Northwick. The first volume focuses on Sicilian coinage from ca. 550 to 240 B.C. The second volume lists the coins that Castellus added to his collection since the original publication. The third volume was a further supplement published shortly before his death. [Information digested from G. F. Kolbe's numismatic literature *Auction Sale 108* (January 10, 2009), lot 253. Also see Hurter "Torremuzza's SEGESTANORVM" under SICILY—SEGESTA].

2912 **Castrizio, Daniele.** *La Monetazione Mercenariale in Sicilia: Strategie Economiche e Territoriali fra Dione e Timoleonte.* Antiqua et Nove 5. Catanzaro: Rubbettino Editore, 2000. 126 pp., illus.

2913 **Christ, Karl.** "Historische Probleme der Griechisch-Sizilischen Numismatik." *Historia* (Germany) 3, no. 4 (1954-5): 385-95. [CS 2175]

2914 ———— "Literaturüberblick der Griechischen Numismatik: Sizilien." *Jahrbuch für Numismatik und Geldsseschichte* (Germany) 6 (1954-5): 179-228. [CS 2163]
A bibliography.

2915 **Cirami, Giacomo.** *La Monetazione Greca della Sicilia Antica.* Two volumes. Bologna: Edizioni dello Studio Numismatico Gamberini, 1959. [CS 2176]
A catalogue of Sicilian coin types.
1. *Testo e Descrizione delle Monete.* 108 pp.
2. *Tavole.* 147 pls., maps. The coins are illustrated by line drawings.

2916 **Clain-Stefanelli, Elvira E.** "On Some Fractional Silver Coinage of Sicily and Magna Graecia During the Fifth Century B.C." *Revue Belge de Numismatique et de Sigillographie* (Belgium) 133 (1987): 39-66. Illus.
"A special study is devoted to the fractional coins, which are for the most part neglected: hemilitron, diobol, obol, tetartemorion, hemitetartemorion, pentonkion, hexas, tetras, trias, onkia. The fifth century coinages from Syracuse, Gela, Zancle, Messana and Rhegium are discussed." [P. Naster, *NL* 119]

2917 **Counts, Derek B., and Anthony S. Tuck, eds.** *KOINE: Mediterranean Studies in Honor of R. Ross Holloway.* Joukowsky Institute Publication 1. Oxford/Oakville, CT: Oxbow Books, 2009. 223 pp. illus.
This collection of essays dedicated to R. Ross Holloway is divided into four sections: (1) A View of Classical Art: Iconography in Context, (2) Crossroads of the Mediterranean: Cultural Entanglements Across the Connecting Sea, (3) Coins as Culture: Art and Coinage from Sicily, and (4) Discovery and Discourse: Archaeology and Interpretation. Includes twenty-four papers plus an introductory essay for each of the four sections. The section on coins is comprised of an introduction by Carmen Arnold-Biucchi (pp. 123-4, an overview of Holloway's numismatic writings) and three papers: "Dating the Period of the 'Signing Artists' of Sicilian Coinage" by N. K. Rutter [3197], "New Coin Types in Late Fifth-Century Sicily" by S. Pope [2969], and "Ancient Sicilian Coins in a Brazilian Private Collection" by M. B. Florenzano [2924]. [Reviewed by Catalin Pavel in *Bryn Mawr Classical Review* 2010.06.08].

2918 **Cutroni, A. Tusa.** "La Circolazione della Moneta Bronzea in Sicilia." *Le Origini della Monetazione di Bronzo in Sicilia e in Magna Grecia (Atti del VI Convegno del Centro Internazionale di Studi Numismatici, Napoli Aprile 17-22, 1977).* Supplement to *Annali. Istituto Italiano di Numismatica* 25 (1979): 225-64. Maps.
A study of the circulation patterns of bronze coinage in Sicily. Includes a series of twelve maps showing find spots of coins.

2919 **de Hirsch de Gereuth, L.** "Rare and Inedited Sicilian Coins." *Numismatic Chronicle* 3rd ser., 3 (1883): 165-70. 1 pl.
Publishes coins of Aetna, Gela, Zancle, Nacona, and Sicilian Federal Coinage from the author's collection. [For further comments on some of these coins, see B. V. Head "Remarks" under SICILY—AITNA].

2920 **Evans, Arthur J.** "Some New Artists' Signatures on Sicilian Coins." *Numismatic Chronicle* 3rd ser., 10 (1890): 285-310. 1 pl.
(1) Describes a tetradrachm signed KIMΩN from about 450 B.C.—an earlier date than any other Kimon issue. Discusses the style of the coin. Suggests this Kimon may be the grandfather of the famous Kimon known from Syracusan coins. (2) Publishes a tetradrachm of Himera with *obv.*, Nike holding a tablet bearing the engraver's name MAI. Evans dates the coin to not later than 409 B.C. (3) Publishes a tetradrachm of Messana signed by Kimon (of Syracusan fame). (4) Publishes a tetradrachm of Syracuse signed by Evarchidas. (5) Publishes a Syracusan tetradrachm signed ΠΑΡ which exhibits a new variety of this engraver's signature. (6) Publishes Syracusan hemidrachms by Euanetos, Φ (probably Phrygillos), and EY (which Evans attributes to Evarchidas). (7) Finally, he publishes a tetradrachm of Kamarina signed by Exakestidas. [Also see Evans *Syracusan 'Medallions' and Their Engravers* (1892) under SICILY—SYRACUSE].

2921 ——— "Contributions to Sicilian Numismatics." *Numismatic Chronicle* 3rd ser., 14 (1894): 189-242. 3 pls.
Evans discusses numerous issues related to Greek coinage in Sicily: (1) Discusses a recently discovered "Demareteion" from a new die; (2) Discusses the significance of the Demareteion in Sicilian numismatics; (3) Discusses the Villabate Hoard of 147 archaic and transitional Sicilian coins found near Palermo (includes coins of Syracuse, Gela, Leontini, Himera, Akragas, Messana, Rhegion); (4) Discusses some of the "monetary frauds" of Dionysios' reign (plated coins, weight reductions); (5) Discusses the effects of Dionysios' changes on the silver systems of Etruria and Rome; (6) Discusses the symbolism on the alliance coinage of Herbessus and Morgantina; (7) Discusses the African gold stater struck by Agathokles and the reasons for striking it.

2922 ——— "Contributions to Sicilian Numismatics." *Numismatic Chronicle* 3rd ser., 16 (1896): 101-43. 3 pls.
Evans discusses numerous issues related to Greek coinage in Sicily: (1) A hoard found near Messina which included incuse coins of Zankle; (2) An alliance coin of Messana and Lokri; (3) Numismatic evidence of a temporary restoration of Zankle; (4) Monetary records of the alliance of 425 B.C. between Messana and Syracuse, and a new engraver's signature on a coin of Messana; (5) A fourth century B.C. litra of the Hyblean Megara; (6) An alliance coin of Leontini and Katane; (7) The evolution of the scheme of a butting bull on Sicilian and Italian coin types; (8) An alliance coin of Western Sicily with the alter of the Krimissos.

2923 ——— "Select Sicilian and Magna-Graecian Coins, Some with New Artists' Signatures." *Numismatic Chronicle* 5th ser., 6 (1926): 1-19. 3 pls.
Publishes some significant coins from the author's collection, some of which were previously unpublished. Some of the coins bear engravers' signatures. The coins are from Tarentum, Heraclea, Metapontum, Poseidonia, Mesma, Rhegion, Messana, Akragas, Katane, Syracuse, and Herbessos.

2924 **Florenzano, Maria Beatriz Borba.** "Ancient Sicilian Coins in a Brazilian Private Collection." *KOINE: Mediterranean Studies in Honor of R. Ross Holloway.* Joukowsky Institute Publication 1. Edited by Derek B. Counts and Anthony S. Tuck. Oxford/Oakville, CT: Oxbow Books, 2009. Pages 138-41. Illus.
Publishes two Syracusan tetradrachms, a bronze coin of Syracuse, and a bronze coin of Aetna. The coins are from the collection of Alain J. Costilhes. Includes brief iconographical commentary.

2925 **Gabrici, Ettore.** *La Monetazione del Bronzo nella Sicilia Antica.* Atti R. Accad. Di Palermo 15. Palermo, 1927. Reprint, Bolonga: Forni, 1969, 1985. 214 pp., 10 pls. [CS 2180]

2926 ——— "Notes on Sicilian Numismatics." *Numismatic Chronicle* 5th ser., 11 (1931): 73-90. 2 pls.
Discusses some previously unpublished coins of Agrigentum, Himera, Morgantina, Catana, Eryx, Hipana, Selinus, Panormus, Motya, Siculo-Punic issues, Gela, Imachara, Halaesa, Crimissa, and Libyes.

2927 ——— *Problemi di Numismatica Greca della Sicilia e Magna Grecia.* Naples, 1959. 166 pp., illus. [CS 2182]
"Essays on various themes." [E. Clain-Stefanelli]

2928 **Gardner, Percy.** "Sicilian Studies." *Numismatic Chronicle* new ser., 16 (1876): 1-44. 4 pls.
Gardner attempts to closely date the coins of the various cities of Sicily. He comments on three methods of dating (political references on coins, mythological characters and style of art, and epigraphy) and provides detailed comments on how each method can be applied to Sicilian coins. Discusses the forms of letters and their periods of use.

2929 **Giesecke, Walther.** *Sicilia Numismatica: Die Grundlagen des Griechischen Münzwesens auf Sicilien.* Leipzig: Verlag Karl W. Hiersemann, 1923. Reprint, Bologna: Forni, 1969. 193 pp., 27 pls. [CS 2183]
The original has excellent plates. "Valuable for its metrological studies." [E. Clain-Stefanelli]

2930 **Gorini, Giovanni.** "Un Gruppo di Frazioni di Zecche Siciliane." *Pour Denyse: Divertissements Numismatiques.* Edited by Silvia Hurter and Carmen Arnold-Biucchi. Bern, Switzerland: Privately published, 2000. Pages 59-69. 2 pls.
Examines forty-nine silver fractions from Aitna, Akragas, Camarina, Katane, Entella, Gela, Himera, Leontini, Zancle, Messana, Selinos, Syracuse, Panormos, and Cartagena.

2931 **Hackens, Tony.** "Les Equivalences des Metaux Moneaires Argent et Bronze en Sicile au Ve s. av. J.-C." *Le Origini della Monetazione di Bronzo in Sicilia e in Magna Grecia (Atti del VI Convegno del Centro Internazionale di Studi Numismatici, Napoli Aprile 17-22, 1977).* Supplement to *Annali. Istituto Italiano di Numismatica* (Italy) 25 (1979) 309-50.

A study of the relationship of the weights of the bronze coinage to the silver coinage at the Sicilian cities. Includes a chart of the frequency of observed weights by city.

2932 **Hands, Alfred Watson.** "The Ancient Coins of Sicily." Published in monthly installments in *Spink Numismatic Circular* 18 (August 1910) through 23 (July-August 1915).
Reviews the coinage of Sicily, city-by-city.

2933 **Head, Barclay V.** "Note on a Find of Sicilian Copper Coins Struck about the Year B.C. 344." *Numismatic Chronicle* new ser., 19 (1879): 217-9.
A brief report on a hoard of fifty-two bronze coins. Includes coins of Syracuse, Adranum (?), and two uncertain towns.

2934 **Hill, George F.** *Coins of Ancient Sicily.* Westminster: Archibald Constable & Co., 1903. Reprint, Bologna: Forni, 1976. 256 pp., 16 pls., map. [CS 2185]
Hill begins with a summarized account of Sicilian history from the foundation of Greek colonies down to the beginning of the Roman Imperial period. Then he discusses the coinage of the cities in five chapters: the earliest coinage (before 480 B.C.), and the coinage of the periods 480-413, 413-346, 346-274 B.C., and from the time of Hiero II to that of Tiberius. His focus throughout is the artistic aspects of the coinage. He describes the main coin types of each city during each of these periods and discusses the types, symbols, and artistic styles of each. Reviews the signed coins, the introduction of gold and bronze coins, the Siculo-Punic series, the portrait issues of Hiero II and his family, and the Sicilian coinage under the Roman domination. The coinage of the Maltese Islands and Pantellaria are covered briefly in an appendix. Includes a bibliography, an index of coin subjects, and an index of Greek inscriptions. Most of the coins discussed, which include some of the finest works of Greek numismatic art, are illustrated in the plates; some are illustrated by line drawings. Also includes a select bibliography of relevant works published 1697-1902.

2935 **Hirmer, Max.** *Die Schönsten Griechenmünzen Siziliens.* Insel-Bücherei, No. 559. Leipzig: Im Insel-Verlag, 1940. 66 pp. including the 48 pls. [CS 3559]
A small picture book featuring enlargements of forty-eight beautiful coins of Greek Sicily. Concludes with a brief discussion of the coins.

2936 **Holloway, R. Ross.** "Monetary Circulation in Central Sicily to the Reign of Augustus as Documented by the Morgantina Excavations." *Congresso Internazionale di Numismatica, Roma 11-16 Settembre 1961. Volume 2.* Rome: Istituto Italiano de Numismatica, 1965. Pages 135-50. [CS 2186]
Based on excavations at the site of the ancient city of Morgantina, Holloway sketches a history of monetary circulation at Morgantina from the fifth century B.C. until the reign of Augustus. Summarizes the coins found (by mint city, type, number of specimens) dating from various historical periods. Several Sicilian mints are represented, but Syracusan coins predominate. Third century bronzes of Hieron II remained in use at Morgantina into the second and first centuries B.C.

2937 ——— "Le Monetazioni di Agyrion, Aluntion, Entella, Hispana, Nakone, Stiela." *Le Emissioni dei Centri Siculi Fino All'Epoca di Timoleonte e i Loro Rapporti Con la Monetazione Delle Colonie Greche di Sicilia. Atti del IV Convegno del Centro Internazionale di Studi Numismatici, Napoli, 9-14 Aprile 1973.* Supplement to *Annali. Istituto Italiano di Numismatica* 20. Rome: Istitutio Italiano di Numismatica, 1975. Pages 133-56. [CS 2187]

2938 ——— "Il Problema dei 'Pegasi' in Sicilia." *Numismatica e Antichità Classiche* (1982): 129-36.

2939 ——— "The Coinage Production of the Sicilian Greek Mints of the Sixth and Fifth Centuries B.C." *Rythmes de la Production Monétaire, de l'Antiquité à nos Jours. Actes du Colloque International Organisé à Paris du 10 au 12 Janvier 1986.* Edited by G. Depeyrot, T. Hackens, and G. Mouchart. Louvain-la-Neuve: Séminaire de Numismatique Marcel Hoc, 1987. Pages 11-20.
"The author argues that it was the intention of the Greek cities in Sicily to issue coinage at regular intervals, which can be demonstrated by obverse die statistics." [J. Van Heesch, *NL* 125]

2940 ——— "Coinage." Chapter 4 in *The Archaeology of Ancient Sicily,* by R. R. Holloway. London and New York: Routledge, 1991. Pages 121-40. Illus.
An excellent overview of the coinage of the Greek city-states of Sicily from the mid-sixth century B.C. through 211 B.C., illustrated by thirty-eight coin types. Includes the appendix "Numismatic Evidence and the Timoleontic Recovery of Sicily in the Fourth Century B.C."

2941 ——— "Sicily: Archaic and Classical." *A Survey of Numismatic Research 1985-1990. Volume 1.* International Association of Professional Numismatists Special Publication, No. 12. Edited by T. Hackens, P. Naster, et al. Brussels: International Association of Professional Numismatists, 1991. Pages 45-7.
A narrative overview of newly published works in the field of numismatics during 1985-90. Summarizes major findings, with bibliographic references cited in the footnotes.

2942 **Holm, Adolf.** *Storia della Moneta Siciliana.* Translated by Giuseppe Kirner. Palermo, 1906. Reprint, Bologna: Forni, 1965. 364 pp., 8 pls. [CS 2189]

2943 **Hurter, Silvia M.** "Crickets/Grasshoppers/Locusts: A New View on Some Insect Symbols on Coins of Magna Graecia and Sicily." *Nomismatika Khronika* (Greece) 23 (2004): 11-17. 2 pls. [Also in Greek on pp. 18-20].
Discusses the crickets, grasshoppers, and locusts which often appear on coins (usually as a subsidiary symbol) at Metapontum, Akragas, Syracuse, and Segesta. Points out the confusion over the proper identification of these insects. Hurter suggests that when the creature is a grasshopper, no special significance should be attached to it—it was simply a popular creature as a pet or as food. When it is a locust, a creature which brings devastation, its appearance may have been an invocation to the pests to stay away.

2944 **Istituto Italiano di Numismatica.** *Le Emissioni dei Centri Siculi Fino All'Epoca di Timoleonte e i Loro Rapporti Con la Monetazione Delle Colonie Greche di Sicilia. Atti del IV Convegno del Centro Internazionale di Studi Numismatici, Napoli, 9-14 Aprile 1973.* Supplement to *Annali. Istituto Italiano di Numismatica* 20. Rome: Istitutio Italiano di Numismatica, 1975

2945 **Jenkins, G. Kenneth.** "A Note on Corinthian Coins in the West." *Centennial Publication of the American Numismatic Society.* Edited by Harald Ingholt. New York: American Numismatic Society, 1958. Pages 367-79. [CS 2190]
Suggests the change in Sicilian coinage from flat spread fabric to thick dumpy fabric followed the change from the swastika to the Athena reverse at Corinth in the late sixth century B.C. Examines hoard evidence showing that one-fourth of the fifth century B.C. hoards in Sicily contained coins of Athens. Down to 400, in Sicily there were no imported coins at all except those of Athens; and in Italy, Corinthian coins were not imported in any significant quantity. During the fourth century, Athenian coins remained plentiful in Sicily, but most imported coins were from Corinth. The same patterns are found in Italy, though to a lesser extent. Examines the hoard evidence for pegasi in Sicily. Concludes there is no good reason for dating the arrival of large quantities of Corinthian coins in Sicily before the time of Timoleon.

2946 ——— "Piakos." *Schweizer Münzblätter* (Switzerland) 12, no. 46 (1962): 17-20. Illus. [CS 2251]
A site near Adranon.

2947 ——— *Coins of Greek Sicily.* London: British Museum, 1966. 31 pp., 16 pls, map. Second edition, 1976. Reprint, New York: Sanford J. Durst, 2000. 64 pp., illus., map. [CS 2191]
Discusses the coinage of the Sicilian cities, primarily during the archaic and classical periods. Provides historical background, and focuses on the artistic masterpieces of Sicilian coinage. Discusses the engravers who signed their dies and compares their styles. Illustrated by eighty enlarged black and white photographs of coins.

2948 ——— "The Coinages of Enna, Galaria, Piakos, Imachara, Kephaloidion and Longane." *Le Emissioni dei Centri Siculi Fino All'Epoca di Timoleonte e i Loro Rapporti Con la Monetazione Delle Colonie Greche di Sicilia.* Atti del IV Convegno del Centro Internazionale di Studi Numismatici, Napoli, 9-14 Aprile 1973. Supplement to *Annali. Istituto Italiano di Numismatica* 20. Rome: Istitutio Italiano di Numismatica, 1975. Pages 77-103. [CS 2193]

2949 **Karouzos, C. J.** "An Early Classical Disk Relief from Melos." *Journal of Hellenic Studies* 71 (1951): 96-110. Illus., 1 pl.
"The head on this marble disk, discovered in 1937, is dated to 460-455 B.C. On p. 107 this date is supported by comparison with similar heads on a variety of Sicilian coins." [J. R. Jones, *NIJHS*]

2950 **Lacroix, Léon.** *Monnaies et Colonisation dans l'Occident Grec.* Brussels: Académie Royale de Belgique, 1965. 178 pp., 12 pls. [CS 2194]
"Deals with numerous coin types of South Italy and Sicily." [C. Kraay]

2951 ——— "La Typologie du Bronze par Rapport à Celle de l'Argent." *Le Origini della Monetazione di Bronzo in Sicilia e in Magna Grecia (Atti del VI Convegno del Centro Internazionale di Studi Numismatici, Napoli Aprile 17-22, 1977).* Supplement to *Annali. Istituto Italiano di Numismatica* 25 (1979): 265-92. 4 pls.
A discussion of the types on the bronze coinage in comparison to the silver coinage.

2952 **Langher, S. Consolo.** *Contributo alla Storia della Antica Moneta Bronze in Sicilia.* Milan, 1964. 406 pp., 172 pls. [CS 2178]

2953 **Lazzarini, Lorenzo.** "La Monetazione e il Sito di Halykiai (Alicie) Città della Sicilia Occidentale." *Review Suisse de Numismatique* (Switzerland) 84 (2005): 15-26. Illus.
"This paper attributes for the first time a silver litra and a few bronze coins to the western Sicilian town of Alicie, and localizes its hitherto unknown site at the top of mount Polizzo, close to the present day village of Vita, on the basis of coin finds. The coinage of Halykiai started around 415 B.C. with the emission of tetrantes, apparently a unique obol fraction struck by the town, and continued with a litra and related tetras to be dated immediately before the destruction of Motya by Dionisios of Syracuse in 397 B.C. After the quick reconquest of Western Sicily by the Carthaginians, Alicie struck more abundant tetrantes to be dated around 390-370 B.C. The coin types are connected with the peculiarity of the site, covered by a thick forest and the place of origin of the river Màzaro, the most important in the region: a nymph offering to a dog, Heracles, a boar, a man-headed bull and a dog. The latter is connected with the chthonian cult of the dog attested at Segesta, Eryx and other poleis of western and eastern Sicily." [Lorenzo Lazarini, *NL* 149]

2954 **Lloyd, A. H.** "A Recent Find of Sicilian Coins." *Numismatic Chronicle* 5th ser., 5 (1925): 277-300. 5 pls.
A catalogue of 153 coins (out of the 472 coins found) recently found near Selinus. Includes coins of Akragas, Catana, Gela, Himera, Leontini, Selinus, and Syracuse. Comments on the various mints. Suggests the hoard was buried ca. 454 B.C. during a local war.

2955 ——— "A Recently Discovered Hoard of Greek and Siculo-Punic Coins." *Numismatic Chronicle* 5th ser., 5 (1925): 151-72. 3 pls.
Examines a hoard found in 1924 which included sixty-seven tetradrachms: 17 of Agathocles of Syracuse, 28 Siculo-Punic, 21 barbarous imitations of Syracusan coins, 1 of Alexander the Great. Presents a catalogue of all the dies represented. Discusses the chronology of the coins and Sicilian history during the period the coins were minted. The hoard was buried ca. 300 B.C.

2956 **Lorber, Catharine C.** "Notes on West Greek Gold." *Nomismatika Khronika* (Greece) 11 (1992): 11-26. Illus.
Begins with a discussion of donatives (distributions of bonuses by military commanders, or payments made to the public or to officers of state during landmark occasions in the life of the imperial family) in Roman and Greek history. A major victory may often have entailed the payment of a donative. It may also have been necessary to reinforce the loyalty of troops during a disappointing campaign by the distribution of a donative. Lorber identifies six criteria which may indicate that a coin was minted for donative purposes. She then discusses three gold issues which are suspected donatives: (1) the gold issues of Metapontum, (2) special coinages associated with the Carthaginian invasion of Sicily in 406-405 B.C. (gold issues of Syracuse, Akragas, and Gela), and (3) the electrum coinage of Agathokles. In English with illustrations on pp. 11-19; in Greek on pp. 20-6. Greek translation by A. P. Tzamalis.

2957 ——— "Image and Symbol on Artifacts of the First Sicilian Slave Revolt: A Fresh Look at Eunus-Antiochus." *Harlan J. Berk, Ltd. 83rd Bid or Buy Sale* (October 26, 1994): 1-3. Illus.
    Recounts the story of a slave revolt in Sicily ca. 139 B.C. led by Eunus, who was crowned king, taking the name Antiochus. Discusses the significance of a symbol found on sling bullets related to the revolt. Discusses bronze and gold coins struck in the name of Eunus-Antiochus and examines their types, iconography, and function. [Also see Berk and Bendall "Eunus/Antiochus" above and E. S. G. Robinson "Antiochus" below].

2958 **Manganaro, Giacomo.** "Dai Mikra Kermata di Argento al Chalkokratos Kassiteros in Sicilia nel. V. Sec. A.C." *Jahrbuch für Numismatik und Geldgeschichte* (Germany) 34 (1985): 27 ff. Illus.

2959 ——— "Ancora sui Culti della Sicilia Greca: Zeus Soter e il Fiume Sichas." *Revue Suisse de Numismatique* (Switzerland) 82 (2003): 5-15. Illus.
    "The article publishes a Greek silver ring with two eagles picking at a serpent. Parallel scenes on Sicilian coins are discussed, as is the term ΣΟΤΕΡ in ancient Sicily. Further, a unique silver fraction of the [S]ichaninoi of the early 4th century B.C. is presented; its reverse type was so far only known from Greek vase painting and depicts a sanctuary of the river-god Sichas." [Silvia Hurter, *NL* 149]

2960 ——— "Iscrizioni Greche del V sec. a.C. della Sicilia." *Zeitschrift für Papyrologie und Epigraphik* (Germany) 144 (2003): 147-56. Illus.
    "On pp. 153-156, chapt. 2, the author discusses the localization of the town of Stielana and the gold and silver coins (ca. 405 B.C.) signed ΣΤΙΕΛΑΝΑΙΟΝ (retrograde) or ΣΤΙ / ΣΤΙΑ." [Hans R. Baldus, *NL* 148]

2961 **Mattingly, Harold.** "Methodology and History in Third Century Sicilian Numismatics." *Revue Suisse de Numismatique* (Switzerland) 79 (2000): 35-52.

2962 **Milne, John G.** "The Early Coinages of Sicily." *Numismatic Chronicle* 5th ser., 18 (1938): 36-52. [CS 2196]
    Milne discusses the earliest coins of Zankle, Rhegium, Himera, Selinus, and other Sicilian cities. In an attempt to determine which city was the first in Sicily to strike coins, Milne discusses chronology, the sequence of issues, and the use of the incuse fabric in Italy and Sicily.

2963 **Minì, Adolfo.** *Monete di Bronzo della Sicilia Antica.* Palermo: Cassa Centrale di Risparmio, 1979. 508 pp., 19 pls. [CS 2197]

2964 **Mirone, Salvatore.** "Copies de Statues sur les Monnaies Antiques de la Sicilie." *Revue Numismatique* (France) (1920): 1-45; (1922): 1-23. [CS 3485]

2965 **Orsi, Paolo.** "Monete Siceliote Inedite o Rare Del R. Museo Archeologico di Siracusa." *Atti e Memorie dell'Istituto Italiano di Numismatica* 4 (1921): 5-45. Illus. [CS 2198]

2966 **Orville, Jacob Philipp d'.** *Sicula, Quibus Sicilae Veteris Rudera, Additis Antiquitatum Tabulis, Illustrantur. Editit, et Commentarium ad Numismata Sicula, XX Tabulis Aeneis Incisa, et ad Tres Inscriptiones Majores, Geloam, Tauromenitanam, et Rheginam; Nec non Minorum Inscriptionum Syllogen, Orationem in Auctoris Obitum, et Praefationem Adjecit Petrus Burmannus Secundus. Pars Prima & Pars Secundus.* Amstelaedami: Apud Gerardum Tielenburg, 1764. 276 and 395 pp. Engraved illustrations.
    A rare and classic work on the coinage of Sicily by Jacob Philip Lord d'Orville of Amsterdam (1696-1751), edited by Pieter Burman II and published posthumously. [From G. F. Kolbe's numismatic literature *Auction Sale 108* (January 10, 2009), lot 219].

2967 **Parise, Nicola F.** "Il Sistema della Litra Nella Sicilia Antica tra V e IV Secolo A.C." *Le Origini della Monetazione di Bronzo in Sicilia e in Magna Grecia (Atti del VI Convegno del Centro Internazionale di Studi Numismatici, Napoli Aprile 17-22, 1977).* Supplement to *Annali. Istituto Italiano di Numismatica* 25 (1979): 293-307.

2968 **Poole, Reginald S., Barclay V. Head, and Percy Gardner.** *Catalogue of Greek Coins of Sicily.* Edited by R. S. Poole. London: British Museum, 1876. Reprint, Bologna: Forni, 1963. 292 pp., illus. [CS 2199]
    Volume 2 of the *Catalogue of Greek Coins in the British Museum*. Line drawings are included throughout the catalogue. This volume does not contain any introductory text examining the history of this coinage as do many of the other volumes of the *British Museum Catalogue*. [See *Catalogue of Greek Coins in the British Museum* under PUBLIC COLLECTIONS—GREAT BRITAIN (LONDON). Reviewed by C. Newton. See Newton "Greek Numismatics" under GENERAL WORKS—GREEK].

2969 **Pope, Spencer.** "New Coin Types in Late Fifth-Century Sicily." *KOINE: Mediterranean Studies in Honor of R. Ross Holloway.* Joukowsky Institute Publication 1. Edited by Derek B. Counts and Anthony S. Tuck. Oxford/Oakville, CT: Oxbow Books, 2009. Pages 131-7. Illus.
    Pope examines the new coin types appearing in Sicily as a result of the expansion of Syracusan power in the region, including mints of indigenous cities and mercenary groups in Sicily, towards the end of the fifth century B.C.

2970 **Rizzo, Giulio Emanuele.** *Saggi Preliminari su L'Arte della Moneta nella Sicilia.* Rome: La Libreria dello Stato, 1938. Reprint, Bologna: Forni, 1980. 104 pp., illus.

2971 ——— *Intermezzo: Nuovi Studi Archeologici su le Monete Greche de la Sicilia.* Rome, 1939. Pages 49-71. Illus. [CS 2201]

2972 ——— *Monete Greche della Sicilia.* Two volumes. Rome: La Libreria dello Stato, 1945-6. Reprint, Bologna: Forni, 1968, 1974, 1997. Volume 1: 327 pp.; Volume 2: 75 pls. [CS 2202]
    "Chiefly concerned with the esthetic aspects of the coinage." [E. Clain-Stefanelli]. "Valuable mainly for its series of fine plates." [C. Kraay]. Text in Italian.

2973 **Robinson, Edward S. G.** "Antiochus, King of the Slaves." *Numismatic Chronicle* 4th ser., 20 (1920): 175-6. Illus.

Publishes a bronze coin with *obv.*, Demeter and *rev.*, ear of corn and the inscription BACI ANTIO. The coin had been variously attributed to the city of Morgantina or to a Seleucid king. Robinson concludes it was struck by Eunus, the leader of the slaves in the first Sicilian slave war ca. 135 B.C. Syrian by birth, Eunus adopted the title "Antiochus, King of the Syrians." [Also see Berk and Bendall "Eunus/Antiochus" and C. Lorber "Image and Symbol" above].

2973a **Rossini, Fabrizio.** "Lopadusa: An Elusive Mint." *XIII Congreso Internacional de Numismática, Madrid – 2003: Actas–Proceedings–Actes I.* Edited by Carmen Alfaro, Carmen Marcos, and Paloma Otero. Madrid: International Numismatic Commisson, 2005. Pages 369-75. 1 pl.
The island of Lopadusa lies south of Sicily. It produced a little-known bronze coinage during the fourth century B.C. with just one known type (Zeus/fish). The author reviews the history of the discovery and cataloguing of this rare type. Six specimens are now known and all are listed and illustrated here.

2974 **Salinas, Antonio.** *Le Monete delle Antiche Città di Sicilia.* Palermo, 1867. Reprint, Bologna: Forni, 1971. 79 pp., 34 pls. [CS 2203]

2975 **Sear, David. R.** "The Master Engravers of Fifth Century Sicily." *SAN—Journal of the Society for Ancient Numismatics* 16, no. 3 (fall 1985): 51-2.
An overview of the art of Sicilian coinage and the famous engravers who signed their dies in the fifth century B.C.

2976 ——— "The Master Engravers of 5th Century Sicily." *The Numismatist* 110, no. 9 (September 1997): 1035-6. Illus.
A brief discussion of the signed coins of Sicily. Illustrated by three tetradrachms and two decadrachms.

2977 **Seltman, E. J.** "On Some Rare Sicilian Tetradrachms." *Numismatic Chronicle* 4th ser., 10 (1910): 223-37. Illus.
(1) Discusses some rare tetradrachms of Thermae Himerenses, a city founded after the destruction of Himera. Illustrates four tetradrachms and discusses their style and sequence. (2) Illustrates a tetradrachm of Camarina (*obv.*, bearded Melkarth head in lion skin; *rev.*, female charioteer with fast quadriga) and lists two others from different dies, all signed EXI. Seltman suggests they were struck at the time of the Carthaginian invasion of Camarina in 405 B.C. They may have been struck by the Carthaginian occupiers of the city, thus accounting for their Punic character and scarcity. (3) Publishes a Siculo-Punic tetradrachm with a swimming swan in the exergue below the chariot on the reverse. Suggests the coin may have been struck at Camarina while under Carthaginian occupation.

2978 **Vagi, David L.** "The Early Coinage of Greek Sicily." *Numismatist* 120, no. 10 (October 2007): 69-71. Illus.
A brief discussion of the earliest coins from Sicily, focusing on their artistic development.

2979 ——— "Sicilian Decadrachms and More." *The Numismatist* 122, no. 4 (April 2009): 71-3. Illus.
A brief discussion of Greek decadrachms, particularly the "Demareton," Kimon, and Euainetos issues of Syracuse. Also mentions the decadrachm of Acragas and the five-shekel coin of Carthage.

2980 **Van Buren, A. W.** "News Letter from Rome." *American Journal of Archaeology* 57 (1953): 211-8. 5 pls.
"On. p. 218 the discovery of hoards at Cassibile, Centuripe and Mandanici is noted; some Sicilian tetradrachms from the first hoard with engravers' signatures are illustrated on pl. 65." [J. R. Jones, *NIAJAH*]

2981 **Vaux, W. S. W.** "On a Coin Bearing a Phoenician Legend, and Referring to an Alliance between Motya and Agrigentum, in Sicily." *Numismatic Chronicle* new ser., 6 (1866): 128-33. Illus.
Illustrates a tetradrachm with the standard types of Akragas (eagle/crab), but with a Phoenician inscription referring to Motya on the obverse. Vaux interprets the inscription as evidence of an alliance between Acragas and Motya. Vaux also describes coins which he suggests indicate alliances between Motya and Gela, Motya and Segesta, and Syracuse and Gela.

2982 **Von Matt, Leonard.** *Ancient Sicily.* Explanatory text by Luigi Pareti. Notes on plates by Pietro Griffo. Translated by M. Grindrod. New York: Universe Books, 1960. 234 pp., pls., map.
"Von Matt, a distinguished photographer, has selected 235 photographs in illustration of what he considers to be the most outstanding artistic and architectural remains of ancient Sicily. Chiefly his own work, they include an amazing variety of Greek temples, theatres, Roman mosaics, statues, and coins struck in the ancient Sicilian cities of Syracuse, Kamarina, Naxos, Leontini, Katane, Zankle, Gela, Akragas, Selinus, Herakleia Minoa, Himera, and Egesta." [*NL 56*]

2983 **Walker, Raymond J.** "Coins of the Greek Period in Sicily." *The Numismatist* 69, no. 8 (August 1956): 851-6. Illus. Reprinted in *Selections from The Numismatist: Ancient and Medieval Coins.* Racine: Whitman Publishing Co., 1960. Pages 33-8. Illus.
A good summary of the history of Sicily ca. 735-212 B.C., including a review of the major coin types of the principal cities.

2984 **Wray, David M.** "Gods, Monsters, Heroes and Salvation: A Review of the Mythology of Sicily." *The Celator* 20, no. 6 (June 2006): 6-31, 36-7. Illus.
Reviews the mythology of Sicily. Provides genealogies showing connections between specific gods, monsters, and mortals. Examines (1) creation mythology, (2) native Sicilian gods, (3) other mythologies, and (4) Greek mystery religions. Illustrated by Sicilian coins. Sicilian river gods and nymphs are summarized in a table.

Also see: Arnold-Biucchi "Magna Graecia and Sicily" under ITALY—GENERAL WORKS; Arnold-Biucchi "A New Coin" under ITALY—SERDAIOI; Bank Leu *Auktionen 6: Griechische Bronzemünzen* under PRIVATE COLLECTIONS; Benson "Ancient Greek Coins" under ITALY—GENERAL WORKS; Benton "Cattle Egrets" under TYPES; Cahn "Artiste ou Magistrat?" under ITALY—GENERAL WORKS; Cahn et al. *Antikenmuseum Basel* under ITALY—GENERAL WORKS; Cozzolino "Corinth" under CORINTHIA; Garraffo *Le Riconiazioni in Magna Grecia e in Sicilia* under ITALY—GENERAL WORKS; Grose "Some Rare Coins of Magna Graecia" under ITALY—GENERAL WORKS; Healy "The Use of Sicilian and Magna Graecian Types" under TYPES; Imhoof-Blumer "Zur Münzkunde Grossgriechenlands, Siciliens, Kretas, etc." under ITALY—GENERAL WORKS; Istituto Italiano di Numismatica *Le Origini della Monetazione* under GENERAL WORKS—GREEK; Kraay "Greek Coinage and War" under GENERAL WORKS—GREEK; Lehman *Sculpture* under TYPES; Lehman *Statues* under TYPES; Lewis "Hoard" under HOARDS; MacDonald "Sicilian and South

Italian Overstrikes" under ITALY—GENERAL WORKS; Mattingly "The 'Little' Talents of Sicily and the West" under METROLOGY; Metcalf *Oxford Handbook of Greek and Roman Coinage* under GENERAL WORKS—GREEK.

Noehden *A Selection of Ancient Coins* under ITALY—GENERAL WORKS; Noehden *Specimens of Ancient Coins* under ITALY—GENERAL WORKS; Numismatica Ars Classica *Auction 13* under ITALY—GENERAL WORKS; Price *Greek Bronze Coinage* under GENERAL WORKS—GREEK; Price "Early Greek Bronze Coinage" under GENERAL WORKS—GREEK; Price "The Function of Early Greek Bronze Coinage" under GENERAL WORKS—GREEK; Ramage "South Italian and Sicilian Coins" under ITALY—GENERAL WORKS; Rutter "Early Greek Coinage" under ATTICA—GENERAL WORKS; Rutter *Greek Coinages of Southern Italy and Sicily* under ITALY—GENERAL WORKS; Rutter "Italy and Sicily" under ITALY—GENERAL WORKS; Sallery "Leontini Hoard" under HOARDS; Stannard and Frey-Kupper "'Pseudomints' and Small Change in Italy and Sicily" under ITALY—GENERAL WORKS; Stillwell "Excavations" (three items) under HOARDS; Stillwell and Sjöqvist "Excavations" under HOARDS; Vermeule "Chariot Groups" under TYPES; A. Walker "Some Hoards from Sicily" under HOARDS; Weil *Die Künstinschriften* under ART; Westermark "Italy and Sicily" under ITALY—GENERAL WORKS; Williams and Burnett "Alexander the Great and the Coinages of Western Greece" under MACEDONIAN KINGDOM—GENERAL WORKS.

AITNA

2985 **Boehringer, Christof.** "Hieron's Aitna und das Hieroneion." *Jahrbuch für Numismatik und Geldgeschichte* (Germany) 18 (1968): 67-98. 3 pls. [CS 2210]
"Publishes a second tetradrachm of Aitna with important historical consequenes." [C. Kraay]

2986 **de Callataÿ, François, and Haim Gitler.** *The Coin of Coins (מטבע דיר).* Jerusalem: The Israel Museum, 2004. 48 pp. Illus.
"A discussion of the unique De Hirsch Aetna tetradrachm and related Sicilian coinage on the occasion of its public exhibition at the Israel Museum. Parallel text in English and Hebrew." [Oliver D. Hoover, *NL* 148]. [See de Hirsch "Rare and Inedited" under SICILY—GENERAL WORKS. Also see "The Greek Mona Lisa" and Starck "Israel Museum" below].

2987 "The Greek Mona Lisa." *Numismatist* 117, no. 8 (August 2004): 30. Illus.
Announces the exhibition "The Coin of Coins" at The Israel Museum featuring a fifth century B.C. tetradrachm from Aitna which is attributed to the engraver known as "The Master of Aitna." [Also see de Callataÿ and Gitler *The Coin of Coins* above and Starck "Israel Museum" below].

2988 **Head, Barclay V.** "Remarks on Two Unique Coins of Aetna and Zancle." *Numismatic Chronicle* 3rd ser., 3 (1883): 171-6. [CS 2286]
Head provides further comments on two coins published by de Hirsch (see de Hirsch "Rare and Inedited" under SICILY—GENERAL WORKS) including a marvelous tetradrachm of Aetna (*obv.*, head of Selinus; *rev.*, Zeus seated) and a tetradrachm of Zancle (*obv.*, striding Zeus; *rev.*, dolphin and shell). Discusses the types, artistic style, and dates of the coins. Also makes brief comments on a few other coins published by de Hirsch. [Also see Starck "Israel Museum" below].

2989 **Starck, Jeff.** "Israel Museum Features Celebrated Ancient Coin." *Coin World* (July 5, 2004): 78. Illus.
Announces that the Israel Museum in Jerusalem has mounted "The Coin of Coins" exhibit featuring a unique tetradrachm from Aitna, ca. 476-460 B.C. The coin features Selinos on the obverse and a seated figure of Zeus on the reverse. The dies were engraved by the "Master of Aitna" and promoters are calling the tetradrachm the world's most valuable coin. [Also see de Callataÿ and Gitler *The Coin of Coins* above and "Greek Mona Lisa" above].

2990 ——— "On the Block: Unique Sicilian Coin." *Coin World* (June 6, 2011): 180-1. Illus.
Announces the upcoming sale of a unique silver drachm of Aitna, minted 475-460 B.C. The coin depicts a naked youth on horseback on the obverse and Zeus Aitnaios, the patron god of Mount Etna, on the reverse. The coin appears in a June 9, 2011 Morton and Eden auction.

Also see: Florenzano "Ancient Sicilian Coins" under SICILY—GENERAL WORKS; Holloway "Damarete's Lion" under SICILY—SYRACUSE; Vagi "A Previously Unknown Overstrike" under SICILY—KATANA.

AKRAGAS

2991 "Another Forgery of a Tetradrachm of Akragas." *Spink Numismatic Circular* 83, no. 4 (April 1975): 153. Illus.
Publishes a counterfeit tetradrachm of Akragas. The obverse die was copied from *BMC* 55.

2992 **Bernhart, Max.** "Dekadrachmnen von Agrigent." *Numismatik* (May 1932).
Discusses the coinage of Akragas.

2993 **Brunetti, Lodovico.** "Di Alcuni Valori Inediti di Akragas e Syrakosai." *Rivista Italiana di Numismatica* (Italy) 4th ser., 6 (1949): 23-31. [CS 2211]

2994 **Grueber, Herbert A.** "The 'Medallion' of Agrigentum." *Numismatic Chronicle* 4th ser., 9 (1909): 357-64. 1 pl.
Discusses the decadrachms of Akragas (*obv.*, two eagles tearing at hare; *rev.*, quadriga of horses with charioteer). Sambon has suggested that all these coins are eighteenth century fakes. Grueber reprints a letter from E. J. Seltman which describes the known specimens of Akragantine decadrachms. Seltman and Grueber agree that the specimen in the Munich museum is genuine. [Also see E. J. Seltman "The Authenticity" below].

2995 **Meadows, Andrew.** "The Fairest of Mortal Cities: The History and Coinage of Akragas." *ANS* 8, no. 1 (spring 2009): 20-5. Illus.
A brief history of the city with an overview of its main coin types.

2996 "Million Dollar Coin Finally Makes Arrival." *Coin World* (November 26, 1980): 1 ff. Illus.
Announces that Bruce McNall of Numismatic Fine Arts, Inc. has acquired a decadrachm of Akragas for the Hunt collection for $1 million. Mentions the controversy that once existed over the authenticity of this coin type. Describes the coin and its history. [Also see "Hunt Moves Back Into Silver" and Sotheby & Co. *Nelson Bunker Hunt Collection* under PRIVATE COLLECTIONS].

2997 **Seltman, Charles T.** "The Engravers of the Akragantine Decadrachms." *Numismatic Chronicle* 6th ser., 8 (1948): 1-9. 4 pls. Reprinted as a booklet, London, 1948. 10 pp., 4 pls. [CS 3588]
"Deals with a compact group of Akragas coins showing a quadriga on the obverse and a pair of eagles on the reverse. The thirty-five tetradrachms and six decadrachms on which the study is based are divided into sixteen separate issues and arranged by die combinations and symbols in the probable order of minting. All are assigned to the years 413-406 B.C. The author believes that the twenty-three dies represented came from the hands of four men: 'the Trier,' MYP (Myron?), Polykrates, and Kimon of Syracuse. Only two dies are signed, one MYP and the other ΓΟΛVKP; the attribution of the remainder is on the basis of style. Myron and Polykrates are credited with the engraving of the decadrachms." [M. Thompson, *NL* 11]

2998 **Seltman, E. J.** "The Authenticity of Decadrachms of Agrigentum." *American Journal of Numismatics* 43, no. 4 (1908-1909): 160-3. 1 pl.
In a 1918 article, Sambon condemned all the decadrachms of Akragas as counterfeits. In this response, Seltman argues that the specimen in Munich is genuine, but condemns the Paris specimen as a cast copy. Presents a careful description of the chariot race scene depicted on the coin. [Also see H. A. Grueber "The 'Medallion' of Agrigentum" above].

2999 **Sikora, Michael A.** "An Enigmatic Bronze Coin from Akragas, Sicily." *The Celator* 23, no. 8 (August 2009): 30-1. Illus.
Discusses a previously unpublished bronze coin of Akragas which bears attributes of both onkia and six onkiai denominations. The obverse bears an eagle grasping a fish or hare and has a single pellet; the reverse bears a crab with conch shell below, and six pellets. The author lists several possible explanations for the unusual coin and asks readers for feedback and opinions.

3000 **Westermark, Ulla.** "The Fifth Century Bronze Coinage of Akragas." *Le Origini della Monetazione di Bronzo in Sicilia e in Magna Grecia (Atti del VI Convegno del Centro Internazionale di Studi Numismatici, Napoli Aprile 17-22, 1977).* Supplement to *Annali. Istituto Italiano di Numismatica* 25 (1979): 3-25. 5 pls.
Discusses the cast, cone-shaped bronze pieces which Westermark believes were true coins. Their unusual shape was likely adopted due to the ease of casting. Reviews the denominations, types, and weights. The cast coins seems to have begun ca. 460 B.C. and were replaced ca. 425 B.C by struck bronze. Describes the denominations, weights, types. Comments on the species of fish, eagle, crab, and other animals depicted on the coins. Reviews legends, symbols, and letter forms. Briefly discusses the countermarked types, usually dated to the time of Timoleon. The countermarks were applied after the coins were already well worn. Concludes with the text of "questions and answers" in various languages.

3001 ——— "The Bronze Hemilitra of Akragas." *Quaderni Ticinesi. Numismatica e Antichità Classiche* (Switzerland) 13 (1984): 71-80. Illus.
"A new order for the fifth series of hemilitra of Akragas is proposed: (1) Triton, (2) polyp, (3) leaf, (4) crayfish, (5) sea horse. Their many variations are also considered." [A. Gabucci, *NL* 114]

3002 ——— "An Overstrike of Akragas on Corinth." *Schweizer Münzblatter* (Switzerland) 140 (1985): 85-7.

3003 ——— "Skylla on the Coins of Akragas." *Pour Denyse: Divertissements Numismatiques.* Edited by S. Hurter and C. Arnold-Biucchi. Bern, Switzerland: Privately published, 2000. Pages 215-21. Illus., 1 pl.
Examines the depiction of Skylla on coins of Akragas. Skylla is portrayed as a woman, nude down to the waist where foreparts of two dogs are attached; the lower part of her body is transformed into the long body of a fish. It first appeared on coins of Akragas c. 425 B.C. Describes Skylla on coins of other cities and discusses the mythology of the creature.

3003a ——— "Some Ancient Forgeries of Dekadrachms of Akragas." *Quaderni Ticinesi. Numismatica e Antichità Classiche* (Switzerland) 36 (2007).

3004 **Winter, Jeff.** "Akragas Cast Bronzes May Have Been Among the West's Earliest Fiduciary Coinage." *The Celator* 10, no. 2 (February 1996): 20-2. Illus.
Discusses the odd-shaped cast bronze coins of Akragas in onkia, hexas, tetras, and trias denominations. The author believes these coins were a transitional step between a barter economy and a coin-based economy. He suggests that the odd shapes prevented confusion between this new currency and the more familiar silver coins. The symbols marking the denominations helped to ease acceptance of this fiduciary coinage.

Also see: Arnold-Biucchi "Litras en Argent Contremarquées" under SICILY—GENERAL WORKS; Boehringer "Die Barbarisierten Münzen" under SICILY—GENERAL WORKS; Bunbury "On the Date" under SICILY—HIMERA; Grace "Early Thasian Stamped Amphoras" under TYPES; Jenkins "Himera: The Coins of Akragantine Type" under SICILY—HIMERA; Milne "The History of the Greek Medallion" under TYPES; Thompson "Some Noteworthy Greek Accessions" under PUBLIC COLLECTIONS—UNITED STATES (NEW YORK); Thurlow and Vecchi *Italian Cast Coinage* under ITALY—GENERAL WORKS; Westermark "Himera: The Coins of Akragantine Type" under SICILY—HIMERA; Westermark "Overstrikes" under ITALY—TARAS.

ERYX

3005 **Lee, Ian.** "The Flower of Adonis at Eryx." *Numismatic Chronicle* 159 (1999): 1-31. 8 pls.
Examines a series of west Sicilian fractions with a leaf on obverse and a flower on the reverse from the fifth century B.C. The two varieties are (1) no inscription, and (2) legend ERVKINO. The coins are sometimes assigned to Selinos or Eryx respectively. Includes a catalogue of the coins and a discussion of chronology. Lee discusses Adonis, Aphrodite, and the cult of Adonis in Sicily. Concludes that the flower is the anemone, a flower sacred to Adonis whose shrine at Eryx was well known. Suggests both varieties are hemilitrons and belong to Eryx. They were struck ca. 464-455 B.C.

3006 ——— "Two West Sicilian Misattributions." *Numismatic Chronicle* 159 (1999): 287-90. 1 pl.
"By reattributing, respectively from Egesta to Selinous and from Selinous to Eryx, two silver fractions, the author seeks to dispel the notion that Egesta and Eryx shared a coin type they held in common (a hound) with Selinous." [I. Lee, *NL* 145]

3007 **Robinson, Edward S. G.** "Petra or Eyrx." *Numismatic Chronicle* 6th ser., 8 (1948): 131-3. Illus.
"Refutation, on epigraphical grounds, of deCiccio's rejection of the author's assignment to Petra in Sicily (*BMC Sicily*, p. 63, no. 15 and *SNG Lloyd Coll.* no. 1164) of coins formerly given to Eryx. Pieces in the Lloyd Collection and the British Museum and a former Strozzi piece are reviewed, and the attribution to Petra sustained." [A. Boyce, *NL* 13]

3008 **Wihnyk, Joseph.** "Eryx, Aphrodite, and the Myrrh Tree." *The Celator* 24, no. 10 (October 2010): 30. Illus.
Describes and explains the myrrh tree which appears on coins of Eryx. The symbolism of the tree originated in a story of Aphrodite in Ovid's *Metamorphoses*.

3008a **Zodda, Daniela.** "Contributo alla Storia della Monetazione di Erice nel V Sec. a.C." *Revista Italiana di Numismatica* (Italy) 41 (1989).

Also see: Cutroni "Riflessioni" under SICILY—SEGESTA; Greenwell "On Some Rare Greek Coins" under PRIVATE COLLECTIONS; Gabrici "Notes on Sicilian Numismatics" under SICILY—GENERAL WORKS; Lazzarini "La Monetazione" under SICILY—GENERAL WORKS.

GELA

3009 **Jenkins, G. Kenneth.** "The Coinage of Gela in the Period of the Tyrants." *Congresso Internazionale di Numismatica, Roma 11-16 Settembre 1961. Volume 2.* Rome: Istituto Italiano de Numismatica, 1965. Pages 131-4. 1 pl. [CS 2223]
A brief examination of the coinage of Gela. Concludes that the Gela mint, which had issued a prolific coinage for both Gelon and Hieron, became inactive during the reign of Polyzalos and resumed minting only at the time when the tyranny came to an end.

3010 ———. *The Coinage of Gela.* Two volumes. Deutsches Archäologisches Institut. Antike Münzen und Geschnittene Steine, Volume 2. Berlin: W. de Gruyter, 1970. 312 pp., 56 pls., 3 maps. [CS 2224]
A comprehensive study of the coinage of Gela. Begins with an historical summary of the city. Includes an extensive study of the hoard evidence for the coinage and its interpretation. Recut dies are closely examined for die links. The discussion of weights includes a table of comparative weights for the coins of various cities and frequency tables for the coins of Gela. Provides statistics on die combinations. Discusses river gods in art and mythology, and the development of the man-headed bull coin type. Catalogues 559 varieties. Includes a list of fakes. All varieties are shown in the separate volume of plates. Some of the most impressive coins are shown in enlargements. [Reviewed by R. J. Hopper in *Spink Numismatic Circular* 79, no. 2 (February 1971): 60-1, and by C. M. Kraay in *Numismatic Chronicle* 7th ser., 11 (1971): 332-8].

3011 ———. "The Fifth Century Bronze Coins of Gela and Kamarina." *Le Origini della Monetazione di Bronzo in Sicilia e in Magna Grecia (Atti del VI Convegno del Centro Internazionale di Studi Numismatici, Napoli Aprile 17-22, 1977).* Supplement to *Annali. Istituto Italiano di Numismatica* 25 (1979): 181-92. 7 pls.
Jenkins reviews the types of bronze coins of Gela and arranges them into a chronological sequence, using similarities to the silver coinage as a guide. Suggests the bronze coins began about 420 B.C. and ended with the city's destruction in 405. Next he examines the bronze coins of Kamarina. Describes the stylistic variations of the Gorgon head and discusses the species of the owl on the reverse of some coins. States that the significance of the letters which appear on some coins cannot be determined for certain. The most plausible explanation is that they are the initial of an official or engraver. Suggests the period 420-405 for the bronze coins of Kamarina.

3012 **Kozik, Vic, and Walker Carlton.** "The Man-Headed Bull on the Coins of Gela and Neapolis." *SAN—Journal of the Society for Ancient Numismatics* 17, no. 1 (December 1986): 11-4.
Discusses the history and mythology surrounding the cities of Gela and Neapolis, focusing on the man-headed bulls depicted on the coinage.

3013 **Madsen, Ethel.** "River-Gods and the Civic Badge of Gela." *SAN—Journal of the Society for Ancient Numismatics* 17, no. 1 (December 1986): 9-10.
Discusses the mythological origins for Achelous, the man-headed bull. This river-god became the standard reverse type for the coinage of Gela.

3014 **Rizzo, Giulio E.** "I Cavalieri di Gela." *Numismatica* 4 (1938): 93-8. Illus. [CS 2225]

Also see: Boehringer "Die Barbarisierten Münzen" under SICILY—GENERAL WORKS.

HIMERA

3014a **Arnold-Biucchi, Carmen.** "La Monetazione d'Argento di Himera Classica I Tetradrammi." *Quaderni Ticinesi. Numismatica e Antichità Classiche* (Switzerland) 17 (1988): 85-100.

3014b ———. "Miscellanea Himerensia." *Revue Suisse de Numismatique* (Switzerland) 88 (2009): 47-58.

3015 **Bicknell, Peter.** "An Himera Mystery." *Journal of the Numismatic Association of Australia* 8 (1995): 15-20.
"The author examines the die linkages of the 147 extant specimens of post-476 didrachms in an attempt to reconstruct the Himera production program. His findings suggest a large number of small production runs (each of about 600 coins) and each involving a small number of obverse dies and a larger number of reverse dies. The author questions the rationale of such a minting strategy and the interpretation of the available evidence." [J. Sharples, *NL* 136]

3016 **Boehringer, Christof.** "Himera im IV. Jahrhundert v. Chr." *Kraay—Mørkholm Essays: Numismatic Studies in Memory of C. M. Kraay and O. Mørkholm.* Numismatica Lovaniensia 10. Edited by G. Le Rider, G. K. Jenkins, N. Waggoner, and U. Westermark. Louvain-la-Neuve: Université Catholique de Louvain, 1989. Pages 29-40. 2 pls.
The fourth century B.C. coinage of Himera.

3017 **Breglia, Laura.** "Il Gallo di Himera." *La Monetazione Arcaica di Himera Fino al 472 A.C. Atti del II Convegno del Centro Internazionale di Studi Numismatici, Napoli, 15-19 Aprile 1969.* Supplement to *Annali. Istituto Italiano di Numismatica* 16-17. Naples: Istituto Italiano di Numismatica, 1971. Pages 37-51. 2 pls. [CS 2226]

3018 **Bunbury, Edward H.** "On the Date of Some of the Coins of Himera." *Numismatic Chronicle* 7 (1845): 179-86.
The author discusses the political changes which led to the change in the weight standard in use at Himera, as well as the adoption of the Akragantine type on one side of the coins. Suggests the change took place ca. 475 B.C. after Theron initiated a mass execution of his enemies. The Dorian people who then settled in Himera formed a close alliance with Akragas and adopted changes in their coinage to accommodate commerce between the cities.

3019 **Centro Internazionale di Studi Numismatici.** *La Monetazione Arcaica di Himera Fino al 472 a.C. Atti del II Convegno del Centro Internazionale di Studi Numismatici, Napoli, 15-19 Aprile 1969.* Supplement to *Annali: Istituto Italiano di Numismatica* 16-17 (1971). Naples: Istituto Italiano di Numismatica, 1971. [CS 2227]

3020 **Cutroni, Aldina Tusa.** "La Monetazione di Himera: Aspetti e Problemi." *Studi e Materiali* (Università di Palermo) 1 (1972): 111-22. Illus. [CS 2233]

3021 ——— "Le Monete." *Himera II: Campagne di Scavo 1966-1973.* Rome, 1976. Pages 703-80. [CS 2234]

3022 **Gabrici, Ettore.** *Topografia Numismatica dell'Antica Imera (e di Terme).* Napoli, 1894. Reprint, Bologna: Forni, 1972. 109 pp., 8 pls. [CS 2228]
Examines the coinage of Himera.

3023 **Giedroyc, Richard F., and Malcolm W. Heckman, eds.** "The Coinage of Himera." *Classical Coin Newsletter* (Maplewood, New Jersey) 2, no. 12 (August 1983): 1-2, 7. Illus.
Describes the main coin types of Himera.

3024 **Gutman, Friederike, and Willy Schwabacher.** "Die Tetradrachmenund und Didrachmenprägung von Himera (472-409 v. Chr.)." *Mitteilungen der Bayerischen Numismatischen Gesellschaft* (Germany) 47 (1929): 101-44. 3 pls. [CS 2229]
Examines the tetradrachms and didrachms of Himera. "Twenty varieties of tetradrachms and four of didrachms are classified and the locations of all known specimens (at that time) are documented." [D. Kroh, *ACRR*]

3025 **Hamilton, R.** "*Olympian* 12 and the Coins of Himera." *Phoenix* (Canada) 38, no. 3 (autumn 1984): 261-4.
A disputed passage in Pindar's *Olympian* 12, written in 466 B.C., may be clarified by the tetradrachms of Himera showing a female in the center, pouring a libation over an alter and, to one side, a figure reaching out with one hand into the fountain in which he is bathing.

3026 **Hoge, Robert W.** "Notable Bronze Hemilitron of Himera." *The Numismatist* 104, no. 6 (June 1991): 975. Illus.
In this installment of his "Curator's Corner" column, Hoge describes a hemilitron of Himera recently added to the collection of the American Numismatic Association.

3027 **Jenkins, G. Kenneth.** "Himera: The Coins of Akragantine Type." *La Monetazione Arcaica di Himera Fino al 472 A.C. Atti del II Convegno del Centro Internazionale di Studi Numismatici, Napoli, 15-19 Aprile 1969.* Supplement to *Annali. Istituto Italiano di Numismatica* 16-17. Naples: Istituto Italiano di Numismatica, 1971. Pages 21-36. 3 pls.
Discusses the coinage of Himera during the period the city was dominated by the tyrants of Akragas. Examines types, denominations, the arrangement of dies, hoards, and the estimation of sizes of issues. Presents tables of weights and comments on chronology. Includes an appendix on Punic imitations. [Also see Westermark below].

3028 **Kraay, Colin M.** "The Archaic Coinage of Himera." *La Monetazione Arcaica di Himera Fino al 472 A.C. Atti del II Convegno de Centro Internazionale di Studi Numismatici 1969.* Supplement to *Annali. Istituto Italiano di Numismatica* (Italy) 16-17. Rome: Istituto Italiano di Numismatica, 1971. Pages 3-13. 1 pl. [CS 2230]
A discussion of the coin types, their development, die links, and chronology. A table summarizes the types.

3029 ——— "The Bronze Coinage of Himera and 'Himera.'" *Le Origini della Monetazione di Bronzo in Sicilia e in Magna Grecia.* Atti del VI Convegno del Centro Internazionale di Studi Numismatici, Napoli, Aprile 17-22, 1977. Supplement to *Annali. Istitutio Italiano di Numismatica* 25. Rome: Istitutio Italiano di Numismatica, 1979. Pages 27-52. 1 pl.
Kraay reexamines the attribution and chronology of the early bronze coins usually given to Himera. Discusses the anonymous issues with *obv.*, Gorgoneion, and *rev.*, pellets, which are struck on thick flans with beveled edges. He lists the types and denominations including some very rare varieties. Kraay notes the wide range of weights. Next he examines the issues bearing the ethnic of Himera. Then he discusses the find sites of the coins to see if they support the attributions of these coins to Himera. Mentions the Gorgoneia 4-onkia coin formerly in the Strozzi collection which bears the letters HIMERA. The coin is unique and its present location is unknown. It is possible that the letters were added in modern times. If so, there would be no remaining evidence to support a firm attribution of the anonymous issues to Himera. Kraay rules out Solus and Panormos. Suggests Motya as a possibility. If so, the use of pellets as marks of value would be a distinctively Punic practice (along with Solus and Panormos). Reconstructs the chronology of these coins, including the evidence from overstrikes. Suggests the Carthaginian invasion of Sicily in 410/409 may have occasioned a reduction in the weight standard for the bronze coinage. Proposes that the Gorgoneion series may have begun no earlier than ca. 425/420 B.C. Heavy bronzes may have started at Motya ca. 425 on a standard of 35 gm for the hemilitron, with a fall to about 23 gm before 415. The Himera goat rider series likely began no earlier than 420 and ended ca. 409. The issue with the nymph's head should be attributed to Himera after 409. Kraay summarizes the chronology of these issues in a table. Lists the published specimens. Concludes with 'questions and answers' from the conference participants.

3030 ——— *The Archaic Coinage of Himera.* Bibliotheca 1. Napoli: Centro Internazionale Di Studi Numismatici, 1984. 102 pp., 15 pls.
Examines the coinage of Himera down to 483 B.C. Points out two major phases in the coinage marked by the presence or absence of the hen reverse type. Describes eight distinct groups based on die sequences. The complex die-linking in many groups suggests a succession of brief periods of intense activity rather than a low level of uniform activity over a long period at the Himera mint. Suggests the silver bullion may have been acquired in Spain and that friendly relations existed between Carthage and Himera at this time. Reviews various suggested dates for the start of this coinage. A date between 550-540 seems most appropriate. Discusses legends and the weight of the drachm and its fractions. Describes six hoards which contained coins of

Himera. Presents a catalogue of 307 coins in eight groups, with a discussion of the characteristics of each group. Includes some fractions and three suspect coins. Includes diagrams of die links.

3031 **Longo, Anna Maria.** "La Circolatione della Moneta di Himera." *Annali. Istututo Italiano di Numismatica* 18-19 (1974): 25-57. [CS 2231]

3032 **Macdonald, George.** "The Legend IATON on Coins of Himera." *Numismatic Chronicle* 3rd ser., 18 (1898): 185-92.
Discusses the coins of Himera that supposedly bear the inscription IATON. The author suggests this is an incorrect reading of the inscription. It should be read ΡΕΤΟΣ (retrograde for Soter) based on a re-examination of the relevant coins.

3033 **Molinari, C.** "Considerazioni sulle Emissioni Frazionarie di Imera in età Arcaica." *Rivista Italiana di Numismatica* (Italy) 88 (1986): 21-6.

3034 **Seltman, E. J.** "Supposed Signs of Value on Early Coins of Himera." *Numismatic Chronicle* 3rd ser., 17 (1897): 1-24. Illus.
On certain didrachms of Himera (cock/crab), certain letters or globular marks appear which have been interpreted as marks of value. Seltman explains the theory espoused by others, but disputes that these are marks of value. The author's arguments are based largely on the problems these marks would pose related to the weight standards of the coins. Seltman suggests some of the marks may indicate an alliance of cities. Others may be artists' signatures.

3035 **Westermark, Ulla.** "Himera: The Coins of Akragantine Type. 2. Based on a Catalogue by Kenneth Jenkins." *Travaux de Numismatique Grecque Offerts à Georges Le Rider.* Edited by M. Amandry and S. Hurter. London: Spink, 1999. Pages 409-34. 6 pls.
Presents photographs of didrachms and drachms of Himera which Jenkins studied in his paper "Himera: The Coins of Akragantine Type" (see Jenkins above). The photographs illustrate all obverse dies and the majority of reverse dies for the didrachms, and all the dies for the drachms for the coinage minted during the period of domination by Akragas. Includes a catalogue of 130 varieties, and discussion of chronology and types.

Also see: Arnold-Biucchi "Litras en Argent Contremarquées" under SICILY—GENERAL WORKS; Arnold-Biucchi et al. "A Greek Archaic Silver Hoard" under HOARDS; Sayles "The Celator's Point of View" under ART; E. J. Seltman "On Some Rare Sicilian Tetradrachms" under SICILY—GENERAL WORKS; Waldstein "The Argive Hera" under ART.

KAMARINA

3036 **Jenkins, G. Kenneth.** "Some Camarinean Questions." *Nordisk Numismatisk Unions Medlemsblad* (Denmark) 15, no. 6 (1967): 154-61.
Also appeared in *Numismatiska Studier Tillagnade Willy Schwabacher.* Pages 10-7. [CS 2214]

3037 ——— "Notes on Some New or Rare Coins of Kamarina." *Quaderni Ticinesi. Numismatica e Antichità Classiche* (Switzerland) 11 (1982): 47-58.

3038 **Poole, Reginald S.** "The Use of the Coins of Kamarina in Illustration of the Fourth and Fifth Olympian Odes of Pindar." *Transactions of the Royal Society of Literature* 2nd ser., 10 (1874): 427-49. Illus.
Examines the silver coins of Kamarina, issued ca. 461-405 B.C., which have as the reverse type a quadriga accompanied by a flying Nike about to crown the charioteer or the horses. Seeks to determine whether this reverse type refers to the same event as the Fourth Olympian Ode of Pindar, which records the victory in a chariot race of Psaumis of Kamarina during the same period. Includes a table listing relevant coin types.

3039 **Westermark, Ulla.** "A New Tetradrachm of Kamarina." *Studies in Greek Numismatics in Memory of Martin Jessop Price.* Edited by Richard Ashton and Silvia Hurter. London: Spink, 1998. Pages 373-7. 1 pl.
Examines a tetradrachm of Kamarina (*obv.*, quadriga; *rev.*, head of Herakles three-quarter facing left). The obverse is *Westermark-Jenkins* 135, but the reverse die was previously unrecorded. The head is "tilted slightly back and toward the viewer, thus his gaze is directed upward." Westermark discusses the stylistic treatment of the head. The new head is characterized as an experiment in the direction of a three-quarter view, but the view is not fully attained. Discusses the chronology of the coin and suggests it was minted ca. 420 B.C.

3040 **Westermark, Ulla, and G. Kenneth Jenkins.** *The Coinage of Kamarina.* Special Publication No. 9. London: Royal Numismatic Society, 1980. 283 pp., 40 pls. [CS 2215]
This die study of the coinage of Kamarina begins with a history of the city. The examination of the coinage is broken into chronological periods beginning around 492 B.C. and each section presents an extensive discussion of the coinage during that period. Includes a list of relevant hoards. Points-out erroneous attributions in older catalogues. Presents a catalogue of 218 die varieties. Also lists pseudo-Kamarinean litrai of Panormous, ancient imitations, and modern forgeries.

3040a ——— "Notes on Some New or Rare Coins of Kamarina." *Quaderni Ticinesi. Numismatica e Antichità Classiche* (Switzerland) 11 (1982).

3041 **Work, Eunice.** "A City's Coinage: The Mint of Camarina." *Archaeology* 8, no. 2 (summer 1955): 102-7. Illus. [CS 2216]
Describes, in general terms, the process of die-linking, establishing a chronology for a series of ancient coins, the minting process, and makes a few brief comments on the history of Kamarina.

Also see: Jenkins "The Fifth Century Bronze Coins" under SICILY—GELA; E. J. Seltman "On Some Rare Sicilian Tetradrachms" under SICILY—GENERAL WORKS.

Katana

3042 **Boehringer, Christof.** "Kataneische Probleme: Silberne Kleinstmünzen." *Proceedings of the 9th International Congress of Numismatics. Berne, September 1979.* Edited by T. Hackens and R. Weiller. Luxembourg: International Association of Professional Numismatists, 1982. Pages 71-83.

3043 **Forrer, Leonard S.** "A Variety of the Tetradrachm of Catana with Facing Head of Apollo." *Spink Numismatic Circular* 11 (February 1903): 5813. Illus.
Describes a previously unpublished tetradrachm variety of Katana which was probably the work of Herakleidas.

3044 **Manganaro, Giacomo.** "Catania, dai Mikra Kermata di Argento al Chalkokratos Kassiteros." *Jahrbuch für Numismatik und Geldgeschichte* (Germany) 34 (1984): 11-39. 6 pls.

3045 **Mirone, Salvatore.** "Le Monete dell'Antica Catana." *Revista Italiana di Numismatica* (Italy) (1917): 107-42, 203-36; (1918): 9-76. [CS 2219]

3046 **Schwabacher, Willy.** "Zu den Münzen von Katana." *Mitteilungen des Deutschen Archaeologischen Institutes, Römische Abteilung* (Germany) 48 (1933): 121-6. Pl. [CS 2220]

3047 **Thompson, J. A.** "Catana's Tetradrachm Shows High Artistic Quality Enduring over the Centuries." *World Coin News* 17, no. 20 (October 1, 1990): 34-5. Illus.

3048 **Vagi, David L.** "A Previously Unknown Overstrike of Katane and Naxos." *SAN—Journal of the Society for Ancient Numismatics* 19, no. 1 (1995): 24-6. Illus.
Describes a tetradrachm of Katane, ca. 460-450 B.C., which is attributed to the engraver known as the "Aetna Master," struck over a tetradrachm of Naxos of ca. 460 B.C. Suggests that the famous Naxos coin may have been created by the same engraver. Provides historical background for the issuance of these coin types.

3048a **Weiser, Wolfram.** "Die älteste Bronzemünze von Katana." *Schweizer Münzblätter* (Switzerland) 153 (1989): 1-3.

Also see: Boehringer "Die Frühen Bronzemünzen" under SICILY—LEONTINOI.

Kentoripai

3049 **Malaise, Oscar.** "The Coinage of Centuripae." *Spink Numismatic Circular* 56 (June 1948): 269.
Briefly lists the known bronze coin types from the Sicilian city of Kentoripai.

Leontinoi

3050 **Boehringer, Christof.** "Die Frühen Bronzemünzen von Leontinoi und Katane." *Le Origini della Monetazione di Bronzo in Sicilia e in Magna Grecia (Atti del VI Convegno del Centro Internazionale di Studi Numismatici, Napoli Aprile 17-22, 1977).* Supplement to *Annali. Istituto Italiano di Numismatica* 25 (1979): 145-79. 5 pls.
Includes a catalogue of die varieties.

3051 ——— "Zur Münzgeschichte von Leontinoi in Klassischen Zeit." *Studies in Greek Numismatics in Memory of Martin Jessop Price.* Edited by Richard Ashton and Silvia Hurter. London: Spink, 1998. Pages 43-53. 4 pls.

Also see: Boehringer "Die Barbarisierten Münzen" under SICILY—GENERAL WORKS; Chantraine "Syrakus und Leontinoi" under SICILY—SYRACUSE; Congden "The Mantua Apollo" under ART; Grace "Early Thasian Stamped Amphoras" under TYPES; Holloway "Damarete's Lion" under SICILY—SYRACUSE; Lloyd "Chorographical" under TYPES; Sallery "Leontini Hoard" under HOARDS.

Lipara

3052 **Manganaro, Giacomo.** "Una Vittoria Navale dei Liparaioi sui Tyrrhenoi e l'Inizio della Monetazione Bronzea a Lipara." *Le Origini della Monetazione di Bronzo in Sicilia e in Magna Grecia (Atti del VI Convegno del Centro Internazionale di Studi Numismatici, Napoli Aprile 17-22, 1977).* Supplement to *Annali. Istituto Italiano di Numismatica* 25 (1979): 91-122. 5 pls. Map.

3053 **Zagami, Leopoldo.** *Le Monete di Lipara.* Messina, 1959. 59 pp., 15 pls. [CS 2290]

Morgantina

3054 **Antonaccio, Carla M.** "KUPARA, a Sikel Nymph? *Zeitschrift für Papyrologie und Epigraphik* (Germany) 126 (1999): 177-85. Illus.
"The nymph on tetradrachms of Morgantina copying Syracusan prototypes (figs. 1-2) may be Kypara. The young laureate male head on a bronze hexas (group III) of Morgantina (rev. tripod) seems to be named [A]LABOC, i.e. the river god Alabos-Alabon." [H. Baldus, *NL* 143]

3055 **Bregli, Laura.** "Morgantina: Studi e Problemi." *Annali. Istituto Italiano di Numismatica* 5-6 (1958-59): 336-44. [CS 2239]

3056 **Buttrey, Theodore V., Kenan T. Erim, Thomas G. Groves, and R. Ross Holloway.** *Morgantina Studies, Volume 2: The Coins.* Princeton: University Press, 1989. 245 pp., 49 pls.

Presents the results of the excavations conducted at Morgantina by Princeton University, the University of Illinois, and the University of Virginia during 1955-63, 1966-71, and 1980-81. Begins with a full study of the Morgantina mint based on a corpus of types from major collections. Then presents a catalogue of 777 coins found during the excavations. A total of 9898 identifiable coins were found, mostly Sicilian Greek and Roman bronze coins struck before the end of the first century B.C. Also includes a catalogue, by stratigraphic layer, of other coins found which provide evidence for the dating of the Morgantina coins. [Reviewed by C. Hersh. See Hersh "At Last, Morgantina" below. Also reviewed by M. C. Molinari in *Numismatic Chronicle* 151 (1991): 239-40].

3057 **Erim, Kenan T.** "Morgantina." *American Journal of Archaeology* 62, no. 1 (January 1958): 79-90. [CS 2241]

Examines the bronze coins of Sicily with the Latin legend on the reverse reading "Hispanorum," and those combining a helmeted female head or a male head on the obverse with a galloping horseman on the reverse, which are generally dated to 43-36 B.C. Suggests these coins were struck at Morgantina. Discusses the coins and the history and location of the ancient city.

3058 ——— "La Zecca di Morgantina." *Le Emissioni dei Centri Siculi fino All'Epoca di Timoleonte. Atti del IV Convegno del Centro Internazionale di Studi Numismatici, Napoli 1973.* Naples, 1975. Pages 67-76. [CS 2242]

3059 ——— "The Mint of Morgantina." *Morgantina Studies 2: The Coins.* Edited by T. V. Buttrey, K. T. Erim, T. D. Groves, and R. R. Holloway. Princeton, 1988. Pages 3-66.

3060 **Hersh, Charles A.** "At Last, Morgantina." *American Journal of Numismatics* 2nd ser., 3-4 (1992): 187-94.

A review article examining *Morgantina Studies, Volume 2: The Coins* by Buttrey, Erim, Groves, and Holloway (see above). Provides information on the Enna hoard (see Burnett "The Enna Hoard" under SICILY—SYRACUSE) and the Morgantina A and B hoards, focusing on the early Roman denarius system.

3061 **Sjöqvist, Erik.** "Numismatic Notes from Morgantina: 1, The ΣΙΚΕΛΙΩΤΑΝ Coinage." *Museum Notes* 9 (1960): 53-63. 1 pl. [CS 2244]

Examines the rare Sicilian coins bearing the inscription ΣΙΚΕΛΙΩΤΑΝ (the coinage of the Siceliotes). The inscription seems to suggest a political unity of city-states—an alliance coinage. The author reviews various theories for the chronology of the coins and their place of minting. Examines the monogram found on the series, variously identified as ΗΣ, ΙΣ, or ΤΜ. Reviews the historical background of the period ca. 214 B.C. Concludes the monogram should be read MT (Morgantina). The author suggests these coins were struck at Morgantina—a center of anti-Roman sentiment—ca. 214-213 B.C. [Also see Holloway "Numismatic Notes from Morgantina 2" under SICILY—SYRACUSE].

Also see: Holloway "Monetary Circulation" under SICILY—GENERAL WORKS; Robinson "Antiochus, King of the Slaves" under SICILY—GENERAL WORKS.

NAXOS

3062 **Cahn, Herbert A.** *Die Münzen der Sizilischen Stadt Naxos.* Ein Beitrag zur Kunstgeschichte des Griechischen Westens. Basel: Birkhäuser, 1944. Reprint, Chicago: Obol International, 1978. 168 pp., 12 pls. [CS 2246]

A die study of the coins of Naxos. "Emphasizes economic as well as artistic aspects." [E. Clain-Stefanelli].

3063 **Pafford, Isabelle.** "Sicilian Naxos: The Distinctive Coinage of Sicily's First Greek Colony." *The Celator* 10, no. 4 (April 1996): 6-11. Illus.

The author describes the history of the city of Naxos: its foundation by Greek colonists in the eighth century B.C., the forced abandonment in 476, the reoccupation in 461, the destruction by Dionysius of Syracuse in 403, and the rediscovery by archaeologists in modern times. The author then describes the coinage during the archaic and classical periods, emphasizing its changing styles. Also describes an ancient forgery of a Naxos tetradrachm.

3064 **Starck, Jeff.** "A.D. [sic] 460 Tetradrachm Sets Price Record in Swiss Auction: Greek Coin Realizes Equivalent of $809,779 in Nomos AG's Initial Sale." *Coin World* (June 8, 2009): 28. Illus.

Reports that a tetradrachm of Naxos from ca. 460 B.C. with *obv.*, Dionysos, *rev.*, Silenos, was sold by Nomos AG on May 6, 2009 for 914,500 Swiss francs. Includes comments on the coin by Alan Walker.

3065 **Vagi, David L.** "The Art of Sicilian Naxos: Part 1, The Evolution of Dionysus." *The Celator* 10, no. 10 (October 1996): 40-1. Illus. "Part 2, Masterful Frontal Depictions of Silenus." *The Celator* 10, no. 11 (November 1996): 22-3. Illus.

A brief review of the artistic development displayed on the coinage of Naxos. Part 1 focuses on the evolving style of the heads of Dionysus. Part 2 focuses on the depictions of Selinus which served as the standard reverse type for the coinage. The frontal depictions, as opposed the more common profile views, make this coinage artistically remarkable.

Also see: Holloway "Damarete's Lion" under SICILY—SYRACUSE; Vagi "Previously Unknown Overstrike" under SICILY—KATANE.

SEGESTA

3066 **Bérend, Denyse.** "Le Monnayage de Bronze de Ségeste." *Le Origini della Monetazione di Bronzo in Sicilia e in Magna Grecia (Atti del VI Convegno del Centro Internazionale di Studi Numismatici, Napoli Aprile 17-22, 1977).* Supplement to *Annali. Istituto Italiano di Numismatica* 25 (1979): 53-77. 4 pls.

Bérend places the bronze coinage into five groups. Includes a catalogue of fifty varieties.

3067 **Cutroni, A. Tusa.** "Riflessioni sulla Monetazione di Segesta ed Erice." *ΑΠΑΡΧΑΙ. Nuove Ricerche e Studi sulla Magna Grecia e la Sicilia Antica in Onore de Paola Enrico Arias.* Pisa, 1982. Pages 239-44.

3068 **Hurter, Silvia M.** *Die Didrachmenprägung von Segesta mit einem Anhang der Hybriden, Teilstücke und Tetradrachmen sowie mit einem Überblick über Bronzeprägung.* Schweizer Studien zur Numismatik Band I. Biel, 2008. 236 pp., 29 pls.

A catalogue of the didrachm coinage struck at Segesta, beginning with the first issues of 475/470 B.C. and continuing through the end of the didrachm coinage after 400. Includes a die study of the coins listing each obverse and reverse die as well as a record of the examples in major collections and auction catalogues. Appendices present a die study of the silver fractions and tetradrachms, an overview of the bronze issues of the fifth and fourth centuries, a listing of hybrid issues (dies of Segesta used with dies of other cities), ancient imitations and fourées, and modern fakes. Also includes a detailed introduction to the city and its coinage, a bibliography, and a six-page English summary.

3069 ———. "Segesta, the City of the Dog." *The Celator* 22, no. 11 (November 2008): 38-9. Illus.

A brief discussion of the mythological origins of the city of Segesta and of the dogs that appear on its coins.

3070 ———. "Torremuzza's SEGESTANORVM." *American Journal of Numismatics* 2nd ser., 20 (2008): 113-7. 4 pls.

Among the first books on ancient coins was *Siciliae Populorum et Urbium Regum Quoque et Tyrannorum Veteres Nummi Saracenorum Epocham Antecedents*, by Gabriele L. Castellus (Count Torremuzza), published in Palermo in 1781 (see Castellus under SICILY—GENERAL WORKS). The author attempts to link Segestan coins, especially those with long pedigrees, to the drawings in Torremuzza's book.

3071 **Lederer, Philipp.** *Die Tetradrachmenprägung von Segesta.* Munich: In Kommission von A. Buchholz, 1910. 54 pp., 1 pl. [CS 2252]

Examines the tetradrachms of Segesta.

3072 **Mildenberg, Leo.** "Kimon in the Manner of Segesta." *Proceedings of the 8th International Congress of Numismatics, New York—Washington, September 1973.* Edited by Herbert A. Cahn and Georges Le Rider. International Association of Professional Numismatists Publication, No. 4. Paris/Basel: International Association of Professional Numismatists, 1976. Pages 113-21. 2 pls. Reprinted in *Leo Mildenberg. Vestigia Leonis: Studien zur Antiken Numismatik Israels, Palästinas und der Östlichen Mittelmeerweit.* Novum Testamentum et Orbis Antiquus 36. Edited by U. Hübner and E. Knauf. Freiburg: Universitätsverlag, and Göttingen: Vandenhoeck & Ruprecht, 1998. Pages 110-5. 2 pls.

The Carthaginians destroyed several Greek cities on Sicily during the last decade of the fifth century B.C. The city of Segesta survived. Some have suggested that Segesta lost her independence ca. 409 B.C. However, the author illustrates a newly discovered tetradrachm of Segesta with a design copied from one of Kimon's coins struck at Syracuse ca. 405. If Segesta had lost her independence by 409, the Kimon coin could not have reached the Segesta copyist. Kimon engraved two dies with facing heads—the first of which was imitated at Segesta. Mildenberg discusses the meaning of the popular "hunting youth with hounds" type and connects it with the war between Segesta and Selinus. He then discusses some strange legends found on coins depicting Aigeste, the city's ancestress. He suggests the Segestans and their dialect originated from the west coast of Asia Minor—probably Aeolia, and the legend in question should be read, "I am the goddess Segesta." Mentions other examples of Segestan coins copied from Syracusan types, as well as other Sicilian coins copied from Kimon's types. Mildenberg suggests a revised chronology for the tetradrachms of Segesta: ca. 415-397 B.C. (Lederer had suggested 454-409). [Also see Hübner and Knauf *Vestigia Leonis* under GENERAL WORKS—GREEK].

3072a **Morcom, John.** "Some Thoughts on Early Segestan Bronze Coinage." *Revue Suisse de Numismatique* (Switzerland) 88 (2009): 41-6.

3073 **Rutter, Nicholas K.** "The Mysterious Segestans." *Pour Denyse: Divertissements Numismatiques.* Edited by S. Hurter and C. Arnold-Biucchi. Bern, Switzerland: Privately published, 2000. Pages 177-85. 1 pl.

Reviews the origins of the people and town of Segesta. Discusses the early coin types and their iconography and inscriptions. The dog represents the river Krimissos, and the female head is his consort, the Trojan Segesta. A river god is usually depicted as a bull, so the dog is an original creation of Segesta based on the religious and cultural traditions of the city. The Segesta heads are very similar in style to heads of Arethusa at Syracuse. Rutter suggests this may reveal some type of Syracusan interest or involvement at Segesta. Next, Rutter discusses the practice of using the Greek alphabet to write in the local language (Elymian). He raises questions regarding the scheme of linguistic development and a possible hellenization of the con inscriptions.

3073a ———. "Segesta: Hybrid Issues and the Question of a Central Mint." *Revue Suisse de Numismatique* (Switzerland) 88 (2009): 25-40.

Also see: Chittenden "The Master of Animals" under TYPES.

SELINUS

3074 **Arnold-Biucchi, Carmen.** "The Archaic Coinage of Selinus." *American Journal of Archaeology* 91, no. 2 (April 1987): 312.

An abstract of a paper given at the 88th general meeting of the Archaeological Institute of America in San Antonio, Texas, in December 1986.

3075 ———. "The Beginnings of Coinage in the West: Archaic Selinus." *Florilegium Numismaticum: Studia in Honorem U. Westermark Edita.* Edited by Harald Nilsson. Stockholm: Svenska Numismatiska Föreningen, 1992. Pages 13-9. Illus.

This brief report on the preliminary stages of the author's study of the coinage of Selinus presents a framework for the coinage of didrachms and fractions during the archaic period. All bear the selinon leaf on the obverse, coupled with a reverse bearing (1) a simple incuse or (2) an incuse with a smaller selinon leaf. The author comments on the stylistic development of the obverse and reverse types. Concludes that Selinus was the most important Sicilian mint during the sixth century B.C. and that the archaic coinage was probably struck c. 540-470 B.C.

3076 ———. "Some New Cast Bronze Coins from Selinus at the ANS." *Italiam Fato Profvgi: Numismatic Studies Dedicated to Vladimir and Elvira Eliza Clain-Stefanelli.* Numismatica Lovaniensia 12. Edited by T. Hackens. Louvain-la-Neuve: De L'Université Catholique De Louvain, 1996. Pages 9-19. 1 pl.

Publishes fifteen cast bronze coins of Selinus now in the collection of the American Numismatic Society. The obverse types are gorgoneion, Silenus mask, head of nymph, or head of male. The reverse types are gorgoneion, crater, or Selinon leaf. The coins are in poor condition. The author presents histograms of the weights of the coins and concludes that they were issued on a very irregular standard. She interprets this as simply poor workmanship and inexperience at the very beginnings of bronze coinage. No chronological significance should be attached to the variations in weights. Hoard evidence for these coins is minimal. The author comments on their style. She concludes these represent a short experimental issue of 450-440 B.C.

3077 **Bernhard, O.** "Die Kupfermünzen von Selinunt." *Revue Suisse de Numismatique* (France) 24 (1928): 207-17.

3078 ——— "Eine Bisher Unbekannte Kupfermünze von Selinunt." *Zeitschrift für Numismatik* (Germany) 36 (1962): 73-4.

3079 **Cozzolino, Michael.** "Selinus." *SAN—Journal of the Society for Ancient Numismatics* 18, no. 4 (April 1993): inside covers.
A brief history of the city and coinage of Selinus.

3080 **Lloyd, A. H.** "The Coin Types of Selinus and the Legend of Empedocles." *Numismatic Chronicle* 5th ser., 15 (1935): 73-93. 3 pls. [CS 2253]
Examines the tetradrachms and didrachms of Selinus with obv., biga or quadriga; rev., sacrifice scene. The type is usually associated with a story of the philosopher Empedocles. Empedocles stopped a pestilence in Selinus by purifying a nearby river or marsh by combining two rivers. This scene is often thought to be the one referred to on the coins. Lloyd reviews his reasons for doubting that this actually happened at Selinus. Due to geographical considerations, Lloyd suggests the event may have happened at Acragas, where the topography is more favorable to such an event. The site of the story was then transferred to Selinus through the re-telling of the story over hundreds of years.

3081 **Lloyd, W. Watkiss.** "Observations on Coins of Selinus." *Numismatic Chronicle* 10 (1848): 108-26. Illus.
Examines the types on the coins of Selinus. Focuses on myths and historical events related to the purification of nearby rivers.

3082 **Price, Martin J.** "Selinus." *Le Origini della Monetazione di Bronzo in Sicilia e in Magna Grecia (Atti del VI Convegno del Centro Internazionale di Studi Numismatici, Napoli Aprile 17-22, 1977)*. Supplement to *Annali. Istituto Italiano di Numismatica* (Italy) 25 (1979): 79-90. 1 pl.
Price briefly discusses the early silver coinage of Selinus and then examines the bronze. The cast pieces bearing a selinon leaf date before 415 B.C. and Price identifies five groups among this series. Suggests the cast pieces may not have been produced by the state mint. Rather, these crudely cast pieces may have been privately produced—perhaps by various individuals—to meet the need for small change. These pieces may have given way to the city's struck bronze shortly before 409. He tentatively suggests 435-415 for the cast bronze and 415-409 for the struck bronze. The city was destroyed in 409 B.C. Concludes with questions and answers from the congress participants.

3083 **Schwabacher, Willy.** "Die Tetradrachmenprägung von Selinunt." *Mitteilungen der Bayerischen Numismatischen Gesellschaft* (Germany) 43 (1925): 1-89. 3 pls. [CS 2254]
Examines the tetradrachms of Selinus. "Forty-five types, with fourteen obverse dies and thirty-five reverse dies are published, with the location of all known examples listed." [D. Kroh, *ACRR*]

3084 ——— "Zu den Kupfermünze von Selinunt." *Zeitschrift für Numismatik* (Germany) 37 (1927): 272-3.

3085 **Tameanko, Marvin.** "Selinus—Ancient City of Many Temples and Wild Celery Plants." *Journal of the Classical and Medieval Numismatic Society* 2, no. 4 (December 2001): 165-74. Illus.
A summary of the history and coinage of Selinus. Discusses the Selinon leaf used on the early coinage. Describes the city and its history, until its destruction by the Carthaginians in 409 B.C. Illustrates an early litra and several coins commemorating the draining of the marshes.

Also see: Arnold-Biucchi "Litras en Argent Contremarquées" under SICILY—GENERAL WORKS; Arnold-Biucchi et al. "A Greek Archaic Silver Hoard" under HOARDS; Lee "Flower of Adonis" and "Two West Sicilian Misattributions" under SICILY—ERYX; Thurlow and Vecchi *Italian Cast Coinage* under ITALY—GENERAL WORKS; Waldstein "Pythagoras of Rhegion" (second article) under ART.

SICULO-PUNIC COINAGE

3086 **Burnett, Andrew M.** "The Coinage of Punic Sicily during the Hannibalic War." *La Sicilia tra l'Egitto e Roma. La Monetazione Siracusana Dell'età di Ierone II (Sicily between Egypt and Rome: the Syracusan Coinage in Hiero II's Age)*. Edited by M. Caccamo Caltabiano. Messina, 1995. Pages 383-99. Illus.
"The author comments on Carthaginian issues in Sicily during the Punic Wars, considering the series of issues in silver and bronze with the running horse, the various denominations of this coinage, and the relationship between this Siculo-Punic coinage and that of Rome." [A. Carignani, *NL* 136]

3087 **Buttrey, Theodore V., Jr.** "A Siculo-Punic Bronze Hoard from Cínisi (PA), Sicily." *Quaderni Ticinesi. Numismatica e Antichità Classiche* (Switzerland) 9 (1980): 137-43. Illus.
"A hoard composed almost entirely of Tanit head l./horse before palm r. bronzes is likely of Sicilian striking, probably from a Punic mint at Palermo." [T. Buttrey, *NL* 110]

3088 ——— "A Siculo-Punic Control Mark at Syracuse." *Quaderni Ticinesi. Numismatica e Antichità Classiche* (Switzerland) 12 (1983): 135-9. Illus.
"A bronze with obv., head of Persephone and rev., chariot is usually attributed to Iceta (287-278) but it probably originated during the period between the death of Agathocles and the accession of Iceta." [A. Gabucci, *NL* 111/112]

3089 **Cahn, Herbert A.** "A Litra of Entella." *Numismatic Chronicle* 5th ser., 17 (1937): 107-11. Illus.
Publishes a coin (obv., female head, rev., man-headed bull) which has been variously attributed to Neëton, Entella, or Naxos. Discusses the problems of attribution and assigns the coin to Entella. The coin was struck ca. 460 B.C.

3090 **Cavallaro, Giuseppe.** "Panormos Pre-Romana." *Archivo Storico Siciliano* (1950-51): 7-180. [CS 2247]

3091 **Eaglen, Robin J.** "Portraits of Greek Coinage 23: Siculo-Punic Coinage." *Spink Numismatic Circular* 116, no. 4 (August 2008): 187-8. Illus.
This installment of the author's on-going series examines the Siculo-Punic coinage. Reviews the history and coin types.

3092 **Hardy, David B.** "A Second Look at Some Fourth Century Sicilian Tetradrachms." *North American Journal of Numismatics: The Turtle* 6, no. 2 (February 1967): 39-42. Illus. [CS 2184]
A brief look at Siculo-Punic tetradrachms. Through comparisons with the style of coins of Alexander the Great, the author concludes the Siculo-Punic tetradrachms were copied from coins minted at Side and Ake. He dates the Siculo-Punic issues to ca. 330-310 B.C.

3093 **Healy, Lawrence P.** "Western Punic Mints." *North American Journal of Numismatics: The Turtle* 6, no. 4 (1967): 103-5. Map. [CS 3189]
Discusses the relationship between Carthage and the Punic cities of Sicily. Discusses the translation and meaning of the Punic coin inscription MACHANAT—usually translated as "the camp."

3094 **Hind, John G. F.** "Silver and Bronze Coins of the Siculo-Punic and Carthaginian Series in the Otago Museum." *New Zealand Numismatic Journal* (New Zealand) 12, no. 3 (January 1968): 92-100, including 2 pls. [CS 3190]
Hind begins with a brief history of the Carthaginians in Sicily. He then presents a catalogue of the twenty-two Siculo-Punic and Carthaginian coins in the Otago Museum in New Zealand. Includes both silver and bronze coins, and each is photographed.

3095 **Hurter, Silvia Mani.** "Addenda et Corrigenda zu G. K. Jenkins, *Coins of Punic Sicily Part I*." *Revue Suisse de Numismatique* (Switzerland) 84 (2005): 5-14. Illus.
"This article deals with two issues of Motya didrachms which were omitted from Jenkins' *Coins of Punic Sicily Part I*, one because it was wrongly condemned and another which was classified under Segesta in the Naples cabinet; and with an issue of Panormos that was included in Jenkins' work, but now, 35 years later turns out to be false. It further publishes a reverse die of Segesta of ca. 412 B.C. which was reengraved for use by Panormos." [S. Hurter, *NL* 149]. [See Jenkins below].

3096 **Imhoof-Blumer, Friedrich.** "Sur Quelques Monnaies Grecque de Panormus." *Revue Numismatique* (France) 14 (1869): 361-3. [CS 2248]

3097 **Jenkins, G. Kenneth.** "Coins of Punic Sicily." Parts 1-4. *Revue Suisse de Numismatique* (Switzerland) 50 (1971): 25-78, 24 pls.; 53 (1974): 23-41, 7 pls.; 56 (1977): 5-65, 22 pls.; 57 (1978): 5-68, 24 pls. Reprinted as a book, *Coins of Punic Sicily*. Zurich: Swiss Numismatic Society, 1997. 198 pp., 77 pls. [CS 2192]
In Part 1, the author deals with the coinage of Motya, Panormus, the "RSMLQRT" issues, Thermai, and Solus (uncertain). Discusses the influence of the coinage of other cities on the coin types of these cities. Discusses die links and presents a catalogue of die varieties. Jenkins discusses the possible locations for the RSMLQRT (meaning "Cape of Melqart") coinage but the location cannot be determined at present. Jenkins states that the legend SYS on Punic coinage can best be interpreted as the Punic name for Panormus, and he attributes these coins to this city.

In Part 2, Jenkins examines the first series of the regular issues of Carthage. Jenkins attempts to determine the date at which Carthage first began to mint coins. After considering the evidence of a tetradrachm of Akragas overstruck on a Carthaginian coin, he proposes 410 B.C. as the starting date for the series. These first tetradrachms (*obv.*, forepart of a bridled horse) were struck at Carthage. The later "free horse" types may have been minted at Lilybaeum in Sicily. Presents a catalogue of the die varieties of this coinage.

Part 3 covers the coins of Series 2 (head of goddess/horse with palm-tree) dating from ca. 350 to ca. 315 B.C., Series 3 (head of goddess/horse head with palm-tree) dating from ca. 320 to near the end of the century, and Series 4 (head in Phrygian cap/lion and palm-tree). Series 3 is marked by the appearance of the legend MMHNT (people of the camp). Jenkins discusses the identification of the head on the coins of Series 2 and 3. Also discusses the legends, mints, die links, and die sequences. Concludes with a catalogue of the coin varieties.

In Part 4, Jenkins examines the coins of Series 5 (Melqart head/horse head) which started ca. 300 B.C., and Series 6. Jenkins argues that Series 5 was a parallel production of two separate mints. The date of these issues must be contemporary with Agathocles' coins with Nike erecting a trophy, ca. 300-289 B.C. Discusses the legends (which include MMHNT and MHSBM), the types, and die links. Includes a catalogue of coin varieties. Series 6 includes electrum triple-shekels, and silver 1, 3, 5, and 6 shekel pieces. These are primarily large flat coins with the head of Kore on obverse and a prancing horse, horse head, or winged horse on the reverse. They belong to the early years of the first Punic War, ca. 264 B.C. Includes a catalogue of these coins. Concludes with appendices providing more commentary on the legend SYS, a summary of hoards, and an index of coins. Includes three plates of forgeries. [Also see Hurter "Addenda et Corrigenda" above].

3098 **Kraay, Colin M.** "Zu Einigen Stempelgleichen Tetradrachmen aus Panormus." *Schweizer Münzblätter* (Switzerland) 14, nos. 51-54 (1964): 61-65. Illus. [CS 2249]

3099 **Kutcher, Robert R.** "Siculo-Punic Coinage." *SAN—Journal of the Society for Ancient Numismatics* 17, no. 3 (June 1992): inside covers.
A brief history and description of the various phases of the Siculo-Punic coinage. A tetradrachm is illustrated.

3100 **Lee, Ian.** "The Silver Coinage of the Campanian Mercenaries and the Site of the First Carthaginian Mint 410-409 B.C. *Numismatic Chronicle* 160 (2000): 1-66. 3 pls.
"The author publishes an overstrike of a coin of Entella on a drachm of Athens and argues that the Campanian mercenaries who founded Entella arrived there in 410 B.C., and that the overstriking took place in 410/09 B.C. Circumstantial evidence suggests that Entella had become the Carthaginian military headquarters prior to the invasion of Sicily in 409, and that this was the site of the first Carthaginian (Siculo-Punic) mint." [I. Lee, *NL* 145]. Lee provides a catalogue of overstruck coins, a chronology for the undertypes, and discusses literary and historical evidence for mercenaries in Sicily, 410-396 B.C.

3101 **Lloyd, A. H.** "The Legend ZIZ on Siculo-Punic Coins." *Numismatic Chronicle* 5th ser., 5 (1925): 129-50. [CS 2250]
Examines the Punic inscription, transliterated as ZIZ, which appears on large numbers of Siculo-Punic coins. DeSaulcy concluded that it is the Punic equivalent of the Greek *Panormos*. This conclusion is not universally accepted. Lloyd re-examines the problems involved in the interpretation of this legend.

Reviews the theories of other researchers. Lloyd suggests ZIZ means "shining" and may have been the colloquial Siculo-Punic name for coins in general. Although most of the ZIZ coins may have been struck at Panormos, some were struck at other cities including Akragas, Camarina, Eryx, Gela, and Motya. In a brief note, Lloyd discusses the legend I I B and finds no connection with the legend ZIZ. In a final note, he concludes there is not sufficient ground for connecting the Siculo-Punic coin legend ZIZ with the Jewish coin-name *zuz*. [Also see McEwen "Notes on ZIZ and ZUZ" below].

3102 **Madsen, Eardley, and Ethel Madsen.** "Siculo-Punic Coinage." *SAN—Journal of the Society for Ancient Numismatics* 14, no. 2 (summer 1983): inside covers.
A brief overview of the history and coinage of Carthage.

3102a **Manfredi, Lorenzo-Ilia.** "SYS, A Coin Legend: A Proposal of Interpretation." *Revue Belge de Numismatique et de Sigillographie* (Belgium) 138 (1992): 25-31.

3103 **Marchetti, Patrick.** "Monnayages Puniques en Sicile au Cours de la Deuxieme Guerre Punique." *Numismatique et Histoire Économique Phéniciennes et Puniques. Actes du Colloque tenu à Louvaine-la-Neuve 13-16 Mai 1987.* Studia Phoenicia IX, Numismatica Lovaniensia 58. Edited by Tony Hackens and Ghislane Moucharte. Louvain-la-Neuve, 1992. Pages 107-20.

3104 **McEwen, H. D.** "Notes on ZIZ and ZUZ." *Numismatic Chronicle* 5th ser., 5 (1925): 393-4.
McEwen doubts Lloyd's interpretation that ZIZ (meaning "shiner") denoted a silver coin (see Lloyd "The Legend ZIZ" above). Examines the origin of the word and finds no evidence for assuming it was a monetary term. It may have simply referred to something illustrious or pre-eminent, and may have referred to Panormos as the illustrious port city.

3105 **Mildenberg, Leo.** "Punic Coinage on the Eve of the First War against Rome: A Reconsideration." *Punic Wars.* Edited by H. Devijer and E. Lipinski. Studia Phoenicia 10. Leuven, 1989. Pages 5-14. Reprinted in *Leo Mildenberg. Vestigia Leonis: Studien zur Antiken Numismatik Israels, Palästinas und der Östlichen Mittelmeerweit.* Novum Testamentum et Orbis Antiquus 36. Edited by U. Hübner and E. Knauf. Freiburg: Universitätsverlag, and Göttingen: Vandenhoeck & Ruprecht, 1998. Pages 138-43. 3 pls.
Mildenberg attempts to clarify the structure of Punic coinage in Sicily and Africa from the fifth century B.C. to the First War against Rome. Three categories of coinage emerge: local, provincial, and metropolitan. The author interprets the legend "qrthdst" together with "mhnt" as meaning Carthaginian Military Administration, and concludes that Punic coinage began in Sicily. He summarizes the characteristics which demonstrate where a Punic coin was struck: at Carthage, coins were struck with fixed dies, mintmarks, and no legends; at Sicily, coins were struck with loose dies, flan protuberances, and institutional legends. [Also see Hübner and Knauf *Vestigia Leonis* under GENERAL WORKS—GREEK].

3106 ——— "RSMLQRT." *Essays in Honour of Robert Carson and Kenneth Jenkins.* Edited by M. J. Price, A. M. Burnett, and R. Bland. London: Spink & Son, 1993. Pages 7-8. Illus. Reprinted in *Leo Mildenberg. Vestigia Leonis: Studien zur Antiken Numismatik Israels, Palästinas und der Östlichen Mittelmeerweit.* Novum Testamentum et Orbis Antiquus 36. Edited by U. Hübner and E. Knauf. Freiburg: Universitätsverlag, and Göttingen: Vandenhoeck & Ruprecht, 1998. Pages 147-9.
It has been generally accepted that the inscriptions RSMLQRT and R'SMLQRT are the name of a city in Sicily. Mildenberg disagrees with this interpretation, asserting that the inscription refers instead to a Carthaginian provincial *institution* in Western Sicily. The translation "Melqart's Cape" has to be abandoned and the literal meaning "Melqart's Head" accepted. It might have been the name of an army unit, but it indicates a Carthaginian provincial institution, not a Sicilian city. [Also see Hübner and Knauf *Vestigia Leonis* under GENERAL WORKS—GREEK].

3107 ——— "Sikulo-Punische Münzlegenden." *Revue Suisse de Numismatique* (Switzerland) 72 (1993): 5-21. Reprinted in *Leo Mildenberg. Vestigia Leonis: Studien zur Antiken Numismatik Israels, Palästinas und der Östlichen Mittelmeerweit.* Novum Testamentum et Orbis Antiquus 36. Edited by U. Hübner and E. Knauf. Freiburg: Universitätsverlag, and Göttingen: Vandenhoeck & Ruprecht, 1998. Pages 150-60. 3 pls.

3108 ——— "Zu Einigen Sikulo-Punischen Münzlegenden." *Italiam Fato Profvgi: Numismatic Studies Dedicated to Vladimir and Elvira Eliza Clain-Stefanelli.* Numismatica Lovaniensia 12. Edited by T. Hackens. Louvain-la-Neuve: De L'Université Catholique De Louvain, 1996. Pages 259-72.

3108a **Piras, Enrico.** *Le Monete Sardo-Puniche. Con uno Studio Storico-Bibliographico di Maria Valeria Giberti.* Montenegro: Montenegro SAS Edizioni Numismatiche, 1993.

3109 **Visonà, Paolo.** "Carthaginian Bronze Coinage in Southern Italy and Sicily during the Second Punic War." *Proceedings of the 10th International Congress of Numismatics, London, 1986.* International Association of Professional Numismatists Publication, No. 11. Edited by I. A. Carradice. London: International Association of Professional Numismatists, 1986. Pages 83-8. 1 pl.
A summary of the bronze series issued in Italy and Sicily by the Carthaginians during the second Punic War. The Italian coinage was minted on a small scale, by a single mint, primarily during the period 216-211 B.C. The Sicilian coinage probably belongs to either Akragas or Morgantina, ca. 212-211 B.C.

3110 ——— "Carthaginian Bronze Coinage in Sardinia." *Numismatique et Histoire Économique Phéniciennes et Puniques.* Studia Phoenicia 9. Edited by T. Hackens and G. Moucharte. Louvain: Université Catholique de Louvain, 1992. Pages 121-32. 1 pl.
A study of Carthaginian bronze coins found in Sardinia. The author suggests that a single Punic mint (Sulcis?) was active from the early third century B.C. until 238 B.C. and that local production of bronze coins may have followed the centralized model established by the Carthaginians in north Africa. Most of the hoard coins were buried after the end of the first Punic war, presumably in connection with the Roman conquest. No Roman bronze coins were minted locally until 211 B.C.

3111 ——— "An Overstruck Punic Bronze Coin in Volterra." *Annotazioni Numismatiche* (Italy) 4, no. 16 (1994): 339-40. Illus.
"A small bronze of the Sardinian mint with the head of Kore and a standing horse was restruck with a male head on the obverse. The author proposes Roman reutilization between 214 and 208 B.C." [S. Sorda, *NL* 135]

3112 **Xella, P.** "A Propos de Sys dans les Légendes Monétaires Puniques en Sicilie." *Revue Suisse de Numismatique* (Switzerland) 73 (1994): 13-8.

Also see: Kraay "Greek Coinage and War" under GENERAL WORKS—GREEK; Kraay "The Bronze Coinage of Himera" under SICILY—HIMERA; Lloyd "A Recently Discovered Hoard" under SICILY—GENERAL WORKS; Lorber "Notes on West Greek Gold" under SICILY—GENERAL WORKS; Markoe "Phoenician Coinage" under PHOENICIA; Mildenberg "First Carthaginian Coins" under ZEUGITANA; E. J. Seltman "On Some Rare Sicilian Tetradrachms" under SICILY—GENERAL WORKS; Tameanko "Coins Reveal" under PHOENICIA; Villaronga "Petit Trésor de la Deuxième Guerre Punique avec une Drachme des Bruttiens" under HOARDS; Villaronga "The Tangier Hoard" under HOARDS; A. Walker "Some Hoards from Sicily" under HOARDS.

SYRACUSE

3113 **Alfoldi, Maria R.** "Eukleidas—Ein Goldschmied?" *Florilegium Numismaticum: Studia in Honorem U. Westermark Edita.* Edited by Harald Nilsson. Stockholm: Svenska Numismatiska Föreningen, 1992. Pages 357-63. Illus.

3114 **Arnold-Biucchi, Carmen, and Arnold-Peter C. Weiss.** "The River God Alpheios on the First Tetradrachm Issue of Gelon at Syracuse." *Quaderni Ticinesi: Numismatica e Antichità Classiche* (Switzerland) 36 (2007): 59-74. Illus.
[The outstanding tetradrachm with the facing head of Apheios, illustrated on plate I (1-1a), appeared as lot 1003 in *Masterpieces of Ancient Greek Coinage: Selections from Cabinet W*, the January 4, 2012 sale by Classical Numismatic Group in association with Nomos AG].

3115 **Bérend, Denyse.** "Histoire de Poulpes." *Kraay—Mørkholm Essays: Numismatic Studies in Memory of C. M. Kraay and O. Mørkholm.* Numismatica Lovaniensia 10. Edited by G. Le Rider, G. K. Jenkins, N. Waggoner, and U. Westermark. Louvain-la-Neuve: Université Catholique de Louvain, 1989. Pages 23-8. 1 pl.
An examination of the coins of Syracuse (and one of Adranon) bearing an octopus on the reverse. [Also see Bérend "Le Lièvre et le Poulpe" under TYPES].

3116 ——— "De l'Or d'Agathocle." *Studies in Greek Numismatics in Memory of Martin Jessop Price.* Edited by Richard Ashton and Silvia Hurter. London: Spink, 1998. Pages 37-41. 1 pl.

3117 **Boehringer, Christof.** "Zu Finanzpolitik und Münzprägung des Dionysios von Syrakus." *Greek Numismatics and Archaeology: Essays in Honor of Margaret Thompson.* Edited by O. Mørkholm and N. M. Waggoner. Wetteren, Belgium: Numismatique Romaine, 1979. Pages 9-32. 2 pls.

3118 ——— "Ehrenrettung Einer Syrakusanischen Goldmünze." *Florilegium Numismaticum: Studia in Honorem U. Westermark Edita.* Edited by Harald Nilsson. Stockholm: Svenska Numismatiska Föreningen, 1992. Pages 73-80. 2 pls.

3119 **Boehringer, Christof, and Orazio Pennisi di Floristella.** "Syrakusanischer Münzstempel der Epoche des Agathokles." *Studies in Honour of Leo Mildenberg: Numismatics, Art History, Archaeology.* Edited by Arthur Houghton et al. Wetteren: Editions NR, 1984. Pages 31-42. 3 pls.

3120 **Boehringer, Erich.** *Die Münzen von Syrakus.* Two volumes. Berlin/Leipzig: Verlag von Walter de Gruyter & Co., 1929. Reprint, Bologna: Forni, 1978. 297 pp., 32 pls. [CS 2257]
"A die corpus of the early silver issues from 510 to 415 B.C. Over 733 die couples are listed with 364 obverse and 500 reverse dies illustrated." [D. Kroh, *ACRR*]. "Remains a viable corpus down to c. 425 B.C." [C. Kraay]

3121 **Borba-Florenzano, Maria Beatriz.** "Political Propaganda in Agathocles' Coins." *Proceedings of the 11th International Numismatic Congress, September 8-13, 1991. Volume 1.* Edited by T. Hackens et al. Louvain-la-Neuve, Belgium: International Association of Professional Numismatists, 1993. Pages 71-7. Illus.
Analyzes the coin types which Agathocles (317-289 B.C.) used on his tetradrachms, especially the Kore/Persephone representation. Discusses the origin, development, and symbolism of the types.

3122 **Brett, Agnes Baldwin.** *Victory Issues of Syracuse After 413 B.C.* Numismatic Notes and Monographs, No. 75. New York: American Numismatic Society, 1936. 6 pp., 2 pls.
Discusses the coinage issued by Syracuse shortly after its victory over Athenian forces in 413 B.C. Identifies some of the coin types, including Nike holding the aphlaston, Persephone, Herakles, and Athena heads, as expressions of the homage paid by Syracuse to her principal deities in its exultation over the defeat of the Athenians. Explains the use of Eucleidas' head of Athena, rather than the traditional Arethusa, as honoring Syracuse' own Athena, whose temple stood nearby. Brett examines the nature of other types and symbols that were used to commemorate the victories over Athens. Discusses the use of Herakles as a reverse type on the small gold coins struck ca. 410 B.C., and connects it with a victory gained shortly after the Syracusan priests and generals offered sacrifices at the nearby sanctuary of Herakles.

3123 **Budde, Adelaide M.** "A Syracusan Dekadrachm by Kimon—Fractured Die Type." *Museum Notes* (Museum of Art, Rhode Island School of Design, Providence) 8, no. 4 (May 1951). 3 pp., illus.
"The dekadrachm under discussion, now in the Museum of Art at Providence, is from the collection of the late Henry A. Greene and may have come originally from the hoard found at Santa Maria di Licodia in 1894. After discussing the three stages in the fracture of the reverse die, which possibly represents the last work of Kimon, the author reviews the mythological and historical significance of the coin types and gives a listing of the eleven known specimens of the fractured die group." [M. Thompson, *NL* 17]

3124 **Burnett, Andrew M.** "The Enna Hoard and the Silver Coinage of the Syracusan Democracy." *Revue Suisse de Numismatique* (Switzerland) 62 (1983): 5-26. Illus.
"A hoard of 177 coins (*IGCH* 2232) which was found near Enna contains mostly Syracusan pieces. These date from late in the reign of Hiero II until 212 B.C. Directly following, from 212 to 211, is a series of thirty-nine Punic coins. Their type, male head/prancing horse, may have been minted at Akragas since

they are linked by style, control letters, and weight with a group of fourteen Akragantine half shekels. There are some single coins from various mints as indicated in *IGCH*. Finally, a group of nineteen quadrigati are thought to have been a separate lot in the hands of the owner since 214, who subsequently added them to the rest of the hoard. A corpus of Syracusan coins issued during the democracy of 214-212 is appended." [H. Bloesch, *NL* 111/112]

3125 **Cahn, Herbert A.** "Olynthus and Syracuse." *Greek Numismatics and Archaeology: Essays in Honor of Margaret Thompson*. Edited by O. Mørkholm and N. M. Waggoner. Wetteren: Numismatique Romaine, 1979. Pages 47-52. 1 pl.

Examines a tetradrachm, with a chariot on the obverse, similar to the type usually attributed to Olynthus in the Chalcidice, except that the incuse square on the reverse of the coin is divided by diagonal bars rather than containing a flying eagle. The author doubts the attribution to Olynthus for either coin type. Compares the chariot to that on early coins of Syracuse and suggests the Syracusan type was adapted from the "Olynthus" types. The new Syracusan types were intended to replace the Athenian owls common in circulation. Cahn comments on the chronology of the "Olynthus" and Syracusan issues. Lists the fourteen known specimens of the "Olynthus" tetradrachms.

3126 ——— "Die Bekränzte Arethusa." *Florilegium Numismaticum: Studia in Honorem U. Westermark Edita*. Edited by Harald Nilsson. Stockholm: Svenska Numismatiska Föreningen, 1992. Pages 99-102. 1 pl.

3127 ——— "Arethusa Soteira." *Essays in Honour of Robert Carson and Kenneth Jenkins*. Edited by M. J. Price, A. M. Burnett, and R. Bland. London: Spink & Son, 1993. Pages 5-6. Illus.

Cahn points out the previously unnoticed letters ΣΩ on one of Kimon's dies for a Syracusan tetradrachm with the facing head of Arethusa (*Tudeer* obverse die no. 29). Cahn suggests the inscription stands for Soteira—"the deliverer." Discusses the significance of Arethusa in Syracusan mythology. Suggests the inscription refers to the victory of Syracuse over the invading Athenians in 413 B.C.

3128 **Calciati, Romolo.** *A Hoard of Dionysius Drachms from Gela*. Milan, 1983.

3129 ——— *The Countermarks of the Series Athena-Hippocamp of Syracuse*. Pavia: Società Pavese di Numismatica e Medaglistica, 1985. 22 pp., illus.

A study of the dozen countermarks found on bronze coins with type of Athena head/hippocamp beginning circa 409 B.C. The author suggests a chronological sequence and suggests the purpose for the countermarks and the cities which used them. In English and Italian.

3129a ——— "La Monetazione di Kainon: Problemi, Tipologici, Metrologici e Cronologici." *Ermanno A. Arslan Studia Dictata*. Glaux 7. Edited by R. Martini and N. Vismara. Milan: Edizioni Ennerre, 1991.

[Also see Holloway "The Kainon Coinage" below].

3130 **Caltabiano, Maria Caccamo, B. Carroccio, and E. Oteri.** *Siracusa Ellenistica. Le Monete 'Regali' di Ierone, della sua Famiglia e dei Siracusani*. Pelorias 2. Messina: Collana del Dipartimento di Scienze dell'Antichità di Messina, 1997. 255 pp., 53 pls.

A detailed study of the silver coinage minted at Syracuse towards the end of the reign of Hiero II, in the late third century B.C. Includes commentary and a die catalogue of these issues and some smaller denominations which the author believes are contemporary. The catalogue is based on a large number of specimens from public collections and sale catalogues. [Reviewed by Andrew Burnett in *Numismatic Chronicle* 159 (1999): 364-6].

3131 **Cammarata, Enzo.** *Da Dionisio a Timoleonte: Problemi di Numismatica della Sicilia Antica*. Modica: La Grafica, 1984. 129 pp., 20 pls.

3131a **Carroccio, B.** *Dal Basileus Agatocle a Roma: Le Monetazione Siciliane d'eta Ellenistica*. Pelorias 10. Messina: Collana del Dipartimento di Scienze dell'Antichità di Messina, 2004.

3131b ——— *La Monetazione Aurea e Argentea di Ierone II*. Torino: Circolo Numismatico Torinese, 1994.

The gold and silver coinage of Hieron II.

3132 **Caskey, Lacey D.** "Coins of Syracuse." *The Numismatist* (1962). 8 pp., illus. Reprinted.

A brief overview of the artistic development of Syracusan coinage with some historical background. Illustrated by fine specimens from the Boston Museum of Fine Art.

3133 **Chantraine, Heinrich.** "Syrakus und Leontinoi: Ein Numismatisch-Historischer Beitrag zur Älteren Westgriechischen Tyrannis." *Jahrbuch für Numismatik und Geldgeschichte* (Germany) 8 (1957): 7-29. [CS 2258]

3134 **Christ, Karl.** "Zur Chronologie der Syrakusanischen Münzprägung des 4. Jahrhunderts v. Chr." *Jahrbuch für Numismatik und Geldgeschichte* (Germany) 8 (1957): 21-9. [CS 2259]

The chronology of fourth century B.C. coinage of Syracuse.

3135 **Comparette, Thomas L.** "The Decadrachms of Syracuse." *The Numismatist* 26, no. 2 (February 1913): 57-64. Illus.

Compares the artistic merits of the decadrachms of Kimon and Euainetos. Numerous varieties of each are illustrated.

3136 **de Ciccio, Giuseppe.** *Gli Aurei Siracusani di Cimone e Eveneto*. Collana di Studi Numismatici, No. 4. Naples, 1922. Second edition, Rome, 1957. 54 pp., 3 pls. [CS 2260]

3137 **Du Chastel de la Howardries, Comte Albéric.** *Syracuse: Ses Monnaies d'Argent et d'Or au Point de vue Artistique. La Coiffure et ses Dévelopements Successifs*. London: Spink & Son Ltd., 1898. 34 pp., 13 pls.

3138 **Evans, Arthur J.** "Syracusan 'Medallions' and Their Engravers, in the Light of Recent Finds." *Numismatic Chronicle* 3rd ser., 11 (1891): 205-376. Illus., 7 pls.

Evans comments on the artistry of the Syracusan decadrachms of Kimon and Euanetos. Then he describes a hoard found in Sicily in 1890 which included 67 decadrachms as well as coins of Motya and Messana. One of the decadrachms includes the signature of Euanetos fully spelled-out. Evans discusses the chronology of the hoard coins and suggests a burial date of ca. 380 B.C. He then examines the style of engraving on a decadrachm which he attributes to a "new artist," providing a thorough description of the types in comparison with the works of Kimon and Euanetos. The coin bears the engraver's signature in the form of a monogram, HK or NK. Evans concludes this coin is slightly earlier than the first issues of Euanetos, and suggests Euanetos modeled his Persephone after that of the "new artist."

Next, Evans examines the decadrachms by Kimon. He attempts to place Kimon's work in time by comparison with other coin types. Discusses the influence of Kimon on other engravers in other Sicilian cities. He then traces the career of Euanetos and the influence his decadrachms had on other Greek, Phoenician, and Celtic coins. The author suggests Euanetos was a gem-engraver.

Evans discusses the historical occasions for the issuance of the first decadrachm—the Demareteion—and later decadrachms. Discusses the connection with Demarete, wife of Gelon. Concludes the next decadrachms were struck in 412 B.C. in connection with the New Assinarian Games commemorating the defeat of the Athenians. Discusses the implications for the chronology of other Syracusan coin types of the last decades of the fifth and the first half of the fourth centuries B.C., and suggests many revisions are necessary. By 400 B.C., the tetradrachm issues of Syracuse ended. Small change was provided by the "pegasi" issues of Corinth until Syracuse struck its own "pegasi." Presents a table of suggested dates for the decadrachms of Eumenes, Euanetos, and Kimon, as well as other Syracusan and Carthaginian coins.

In an appendix, Evans lists and provides commentary on sixty-two coins from a hoard recently discovered in Western Sicily. In another appendix, he discusses the Great Naxos hoard of over 2000 Sicilian coins found at Naxos in 1853. The hoard had previously been assigned a burial date of ca. 403 B.C. Evans argues for a date not later than 410 B.C.

3139 ——— *Syracusan 'Medallions' and Their Engravers, in the Light of Recent Finds, and An Essay on Some New Artists' Signatures on Sicilian Coins.* London: Bernard Quaritch, 1892. 215 pp., illus., 10 pls.
Edited versions of two essays originally published in *The Numismatic Chronicle*, supplemented with an index and two additional plates. [See Evans *Numismatic Chronicle* 1891 above and Evans "Some New Artists' Signatures" under SICILY—GENERAL WORKS].

3140 ——— "Supplement 4: Numismatic Lights on the Sicily of Timoleon." In Volume 4 of *The History of Sicily from Earliest Times,* by Edward A. Freeman. Oxford: Clarendon Press, 1894. Pages 349-55. 1 pl.
Examines the alliance coinage of Syracuse and the minor cities of Sicily which gathered under Timoleon around the time of the battle of Crimisus. Discusses the coin types, the historical background, and the historical evidence that can be gathered from the coins.

3141 **Favorito, Emilio N.** *The Bronze Coinage of Ancient Syracuse.* Boston: Society Historia Numorum, 1990. 54 pp., 9 pls.
Prepared by members of Boston's Society Historia Numorum. Lists 104 types of Syracusan bronze coins beginning with types listed in eight major published reference collections, and supplemented by types from the collections of the Society's members and a few other sources. The types are described along with their weights, sizes, and symbols. Each is cross-referenced to other published collections and a rarity-rating is assigned to each type. The catalogue is arranged by reverse type. Includes a chapter covering the historical background of the city of Syracuse and a guide to attributing the coin types. Most of the types are photographed.

3142 ——— "The Signed Bronzes of Syracuse." *The Celator* 10, no. 7 (July 1996): 6-15. Illus.
Examines the little-known bronze coins of Syracuse which are signed by the engravers. Five main types are known. The author reviews each type, illustrating the diagnostic points of dies signed by Euanetos, Phrygillos, Kimon, and Eukleidas. Also discusses coins signed with MI (or IM) and EΞ. The names of these engravers are not known. Provides brief comments on the dating of the coins.

3143 **Fischer-Bossert, Wolfgang.** "Nachahmungen und Umbildungen in der Sizilischen Münzprägung." *Sweizerische Numismatische Rundschau* 77 (1998): 24-39. Illus.
"This article deals with some copies of the works of Euainetos and Kimon and discusses the problems of distinguishing between original and imitation. It is argued that the quadriga on one of the Kimonian tetradrachms is an artistic variant of a Euainetos composition." [M. Peter, *NL* 145]

3144 ——— "A Lead Test-Piece of a Syracusan Tetradrachm by the Engravers *Euth…* and *Eum….*" *Numismatic Chronicle* 162 (2002): 1-9. 3 pls.
An examination of a test strike on a square lead piece from the dies of fifth century B.C. Syracusan tetradrachm (Tudeer 46). The author comments on the dies and alterations made to the obverse die. The lead piece was produced before the obverse die was used to strike coins. The reverse die had already been used. Fischer-Bossert suggests the piece may have been preserved by the engraver as a model for future dies and may later have been left as a votive offering at a temple.

3145 **Flower, Michael.** "Alexander the Great as a Pyrrhus Coin Type." *Seaby Coin and Medal Bulletin* 680 (April 1975): 117-9.
The author suggests that the head of Herakles on Pyrrhus' bronze coins from Syracuse bears the features of Alexander the Great. Discusses the coin portrait's similarity to other coin portraits of Alexander and provides historical background which may support this attribution.

3146 **Franke, Peter R.** "Historisch-Numismatische Probleme der Zeit Heirons II von Syracus." *Jahrbuch für Numismatik und Geldsgeschichte* (Germany) 9 (1958): 57-85. [CS 2261]
"On the chronology of coins struck between 275-215 B.C." [E. Clain-Stefanelli]

3147 **Freeman, Edward Augustus.** "The Assinarian Games and Coinage." In Volume 3 of *The History of Sicily from Earliest Times,* by Edward A. Freeman. Oxford: Clarendon Press, 1892. Pages 719-22.
Discusses the Assinarian Games held at Syracuse on the anniversary of the surrender of Nikias at the Assinaros. Syracusan coins may have been struck with reference to the games and the coins themselves may have been part of the prizes for the victors. The author briefly discusses this coinage.

3148 **Gallatin, Albert.** *Syracusan Dekadrachms of the Euainetos Type.* London: Humphrey Milford, and Cambridge: Harvard University Press, 1930. 53 pp., 12 pls. [CS 2262]

Illustrates all the known varieties of the Syracusan dekadrachms which bear the signature of Euainetos or which have a similar head on the obverse and are similar in design to the coins so inscribed. Includes forty-two obverse dies and twenty-four reverse dies. A list is given of the known specimens from each die. Includes brief discussions of the coin type, chronology, and engravers. [Reviewed by D. M. Robinson in *American Journal of Archaeology* 35 (1931): 359-60, and by E. S. G. Robinson in *Numismatic Chronicle* 5th ser., 11 (1931): 245-6].

3149 **Gans, Edward.** "Dekadrachms of Syracuse and Their Historical and Mythological Background." *The Numismatist* 53, no. 9 (September 1940): 633-7. Illus.
The author presents a history of the Demareteion and the decadrachms engraved by Euainetos and Kimon. He describes the circumstances of their issuance and comments on their artistic styles. Reviews the mythology surrounding Artemis, Arethusa, Persephone, and Demeter.

3150 **Garraffo, Salvatore.** "La Monnetazione dell'età Dionigiana: Contromarche e Riconiazioni." *La Monetazione dell'età Dionigiana: Atti dell'VIII Covegna del Centro Internationale di Studi Numismatici, Napoli, 29 Maggio-1 Guigno 1983*. Rome, 1993. Pages 191-244.
The Coinage of the Age of Dion: Countermarks and Recoinage.

3151 **Gilmore, Starr.** "World's Most Beautiful Coin: Dekadrachms of Syracuse." *Numismatic Scrapbook Magazine* 410 (April 1970): 512-21. Illus.
Presents an outline of Greek history during the period 490-415 B.C. Recounts the Athenian expedition to Syracuse and the recall and escape of Alcibiades. Reviews the events at Syracuse leading up to the Athenian siege of 413 B.C. Then describes the Syracusan dekadrachms, their engravers, and the possible reasons for placing an image of Persephone on the coins.

3152 **Hansen, Peter.** "Pursuing Arethusa." *Trident* (Australia) 7 (December 1992-February 1993): 6 ff. Illus.
An examination of the identity of the female head, usually identified as Arethusa, appearing on many Syracusan coins. Reviews the reasons for this identification, the mythology surrounding Arethusa, her importance to the Syracusans, and other possible identities for the head.

3153 **Head, Barclay V.** "On the Chronological Sequence of the Coins of Syracuse." *Numismatic Chronicle* new ser., 14 (1874): 1-80. 15 pls. [CS 2263]
A history of the coinage of Syracuse with an emphasis on attempting a chronological arrangement of the issues. Head divides the coinage into fifteen historical periods, and incorporates historical commentary with his numismatic analysis. Lists the main coin types in gold, silver, and copper for each period. Presents a table of weights of the principal coins during each period, and a table showing the proportionate value of gold to silver in each period.

3154 **Headlam, Arthur C.** "Some Notes on Sicilian Coins." *Numismatic Chronicle* 4th ser., 8 (1908): 1-16. 1 pl. Reprinted as a booklet, London. 16 pp.
Publishes a previously unrecorded variety of a Syracusan tetradrachm struck on an unusually large flan. Discusses the date of the signed tetradrachms and suggests they began ca. 420 B.C. Discusses the coinage of Gelon and Hieron. Examines an unpublished copper coin of Syracuse.

3155 **Hoge, Robert W.** "A Syracusan Dekadrachm by Euainetos." *The Numismatist* 107, no. 11 (November 1994): 1648. Illus.
Describes a dekadrachm recently added to the collection of the American Numismatic Association museum. Comments on the known dies signed by Euainetos.

3156 **Holloway, R. Ross.** "Numismatic Notes from Morgantina: 2, Half Coins of Hieron II in the Monetary System of Roman Sicily." *Museum Notes* 9 (1960): 65-73. Illus. [CS 2243]
Discusses the half-coins of Hieron II, ruler of Syracuse 274-215 B.C., found during excavations at Morgantina. The bronze coins of Poseidon/trident type were all carefully cut. Discusses their relationship to the Roman bronze coinage and the changes in the Roman weight standards. Holloway concludes that after the decline of the Roman bronze standard to the reduced sextantal level, the Poseidon/trident coins of Hieron were used to produce sextants by overstriking, unciae by halving, and semiunciae by quartering. Discusses the chronology of the coins and related hoards. Concludes the use of the cut coins was adopted between 214-211 B.C. [Also see Sjöqvist "Excavations at Morgantina" under HOARDS, and R. Stillwell "Excavations at Morgantina 1960: Preliminary Report 5" under HOARDS].

3157 ——— "Eagle and Fulmen on the Coins of Syracuse." *Revue Belge de Numismatique* (Belgium) 108 (1962): 5-28.

3158 ——— "Damarete's Lion." *Museum Notes* 11 (1964): 1-11. 2 pls. [CS 2264]
(1) Reviews Diodorus' account of the origins of the Damareteion, a dekadrachm struck by Syracuse. The author states this coin and the related tetradrachms and fractions are a victory coinage, but rejects the traditional theory that Damarete, queen of Syracuse, was awarded a crown by the Carthaginians which enabled the minting of these special coins. Points out that the lion in the exergue of the Damareteion obverse matches the lion in the exergue on tetradrachms of Leontinoi. The lion was the family seal of the Emmenids of Akragas, and Damarete was an Emmenid. Concludes the lion on the coins of Syracuse and Leontinoi was a compliment paid by Gelon, the tyrant of Syracuse, to his father-in-law Theron, the tyrant of Akragas, and to the Emmenid clan. (2) Points out stylistic differences between the head on the Damareteion reverse and the head on a tetradrachm of Aitna (Boehringer suggested they were done by the same engraver). Suggests that the Aitna tetradrachm was engraved by the same artist as the famous Naxos tetradrachm. Suggests the stylistic differences between these two coins existed because the Zeus on the reverse of the Aitna coin was a rendering of an archaic painting, while the Naxos satyr was the engraver's own creation. [Also see Kraay "The Demareteion," Mattingly "The Demareteion Controversy," Rutter "The Myth," Rutter "The Coinage of Syracuse," and Williams "The Demareteion Reconsidered" below].

3159 ——— *The Thirteen-months Coinage of Hieronymos of Syracuse*. Berlin: Walter de Gruyter & Co., 1969. 47 pp., 12 pls. [CS 2265]
Examines the Syracusan coins of 215-214 B.C., the period during which the city changed sides in the war between Rome and Carthage. Presents the history of the brief reign of Hieronymous and a catalogue of 245 gold and silver coin types, indicating die links. A chapter on metrology presents frequency tables of coin weights. Discusses control marks on the coins. [Reviewed by S. A. Jameson in *Numismatic Chronicle* 7th ser., 11 (1971): 344-7].

3160 ——— "The Bronze of the Third Syracusan Democracy (344-316 B.C.)." *Annali. Istituto Italiano di Numismatica* 16-17 (1969-70): 129-42. [CS 2266]
"Syracusan issues are analyzed and the propagandistic function of their typology is discussed." [S. Sorda, *NL* 91]

3161 ——— "La Struttura delle Emissioni di Siracusa nel Periodo del 'Signierende Künstler.'" *Annali. Istituto Italiano di Numismatica* 21-22 (1974-75): 41-8. [CS 2267]

Holloway re-examines Thudeer's 1913 corpus and determines on the basis of the symbols in the exergue of the coins, that the mint of Syracuse was organized into different workshops, which may have been operated by private individuals under state contract, with the major engravers in charge. He suggests that Kimon was in charge of the "ear of grain" workshop and Euainetos was in charge of the "dolphin" workshop.

3162 ——— "The Bronze Coinage of Agathocles." *Greek Numismatics and Archaeology: Essays in Honor of Margaret Thompson.* Edited by O. Mørkholm and N. M. Waggoner. Wetteren: Numismatique Romaine, 1979. Pages 87-95. 1 pl.

The author presents an arrangement of the bronze coinage of Agathokles, king of Syracuse (316-289 B.C.). This coinage exhibits a single pair of dies (*obv.*, Persephone; *rev.*, bull butting) in three different series. Holloway discusses the denominations and weights of the coinage, reviews the chronological evidence provided by hoards and overstrikes, and discusses the iconography of the types.

3163 ——— "L'Inizio della Monetazione in Bronzo Siracusana." *Le Origini della Monetazione di Bronzo in Sicilia e in Magna Grecia (Atti del VI Convegno del Centro Internazionale di Studi Numismatici, Napoli Aprile 17-22, 1977).* Supplement to *Annali. Istituto Italiano di Numismatica* 25 (1979): 123-44. 2 pls.

Includes weight frequency tables.

3163a ——— "Syracusan Coinage between Dion and Timoleon." *Quaderni Ticinesi: Numismatica e Antichità Classiche* (Switzerland) 20 (1991): 57-62.

3164 ——— "Syracusan Bronzes with the Legend ΣΥΡΑΣΩΣΙΑ." *Proceedings of the 11th International Numismatic Congress, September 8-13, 1991. Volume 1.* Edited by T. Hackens et al. Louvain-la-Neuve, Belgium: International Association of Professional Numismatists, 1993. Pages 83-4.

Discusses the Syracusan bronze coins bearing the legend ΣΥΡΑΣΩΣΙΑ. Suggests the coins represent the work of a die cutter seeking to make Syracusan coins, but unfamiliar with how the city's name was written, mistaking ΣΩ for ΚΟ. Suggests these are barbaric imitations of Syracusan coins.

3165 ——— "Further Notes on the Early Bronze Coinage of Syracuse." *Italiam Fato Profvgi: Numismatic Studies Dedicated to Vladimir and Elvira Eliza Clain-Stefanelli.* Numismatica Lovaniensia 12. Edited by T. Hackens. Louvain-la-Neuve: De L'Université Catholique De Louvain, 1996. Pages 217-22. 1 pl.

Holloway reconsiders the chronology of several series of Syracusan bronze coins. The coins bearing a head of Athena in Corinthian helmet on the obverse, with a hippocamp on the reverse, previously assigned to the reign of Timoleon (ca. 344-330 B.C.), are now shown to have begun prior to 405 B.C.

3166 ——— "The Kainon Coinage." *Liber Amicorum Tony Hackens.* Numismatica Lovaniensia 20. Edited by G. Moucharte, M. B. Borba Florenzano, F. de Callataÿ, P. Marchetti, L. Smolderen, and P. Yannopoulos. Louvain-la-Neuve: Université Catholique de Louvain, 2007. Pages 223 ff.

Holloway presents evidence that the so-called "Kainon" coinage (*obv.*, griffin; *rev.*, free horse), often attributed to the city of Alaisa, was actually struck at Syracuse as part of a monetary reform by Dionysius II, ca. 367 B.C. [Reviewed by A. S. Walker in *The Celator* 22, no. 8 (August 2008): 35-7, 40, 56. Also see Calciati "La Monetazione di Kainon" above].

3166a **Ierardi, Michael.** "The Tetradrachms of Agathocles of Syracuse: A Preliminary Study." *American Journal of Numismatics* 2nd ser., 7-8 (1995-6): 1-73. 11 pls.

Agathocles controlled Syracuse from 317 to 289 B.C. This paper provides a preliminary die study of his most substantial silver issues—the "Arethusa/quadriga" tetradrachms and the "Kore/Nike with trophy" tetradrachms (the study does not include all known examples of the coinage). Presents die link diagrams and estimates of the original volume of the coinage and its total value in Attic talents. Discusses chronology and summarizes the views of other researchers including Head and Jenkins. Includes charts which summarize the hoard evidence for this coinage. Discusses the date of the Syracusan electrum coinage. Presents a catalogue of 242 die varieties of the coinage.

3167 **Imhoof-Blumer, Friedrich W.** "Syrakosai—Lysimachos—Derdas." *Corolla Numismatica: Numismatic Essays in Honour of Barclay V. Head.* Edited by G. F. Hill. London: Oxford University Press, 1906. Pages 160-5. Illus.

Examines a coin of Syracuse (Athena/Artemis), several coins of Lysimachos, and a coin of the Elimiote Dynasty bearing the name Derdas.

3167a **Istituto Italiano di Numismatica.** *La Monetazione dell'età Dionigiana: Atti dell'VIII Covegna del Centro Internazionale di Studi Numismatici, Napoli, 29 Maggio-1 Guigno 1983.* Rome, 1993.

3168 **Jenkins, G. Kenneth.** "Dionysios I of Syracuse and His Coinage." *Bulletin of the Institute of Classical Studies* (1961): 86.

A summary of a paper delivered to the London Classical Association on March 1, 1961.

3169 ——— "Electrum Coinage at Syracuse." *Essays in Greek Coinage Presented to Stanley Robinson.* Edited by C. M. Kraay and G. K. Jenkins. Oxford: Clarendon Press, 1968. Pages 145-62. 2 pls. [CS 2268]

A comparison of the chronology of the electrum coinage of Syracuse as proposed by various authorities. Head dated the electrum series to the period between Timoleon and Agathokles. Holm and Reinach assigned the coins to Dion. Seltman suggested Dionysios I. Giesecke and Christ assigned the coins to Dionysios II. Jenkins describes the four types of electrum coins, their symbols, and their gold content. Reviews hoard evidence. Concludes these coins may belong to the reign of Agathokles. Presents a list of specimens showing weights and gold content. Includes a list of suspected forgeries in published collections.

3170 **Jongkees, Jan Hendrik.** *The Kimonian Dekadrachms: A Contribution to Sicilian Numismatics.* Utrecht: Keminken Zoon N.V., 1941. Reprint, Amsterdam A. M. Hakkert, 1967. 151 pp., 2 pls. [CS 2269]

A catalogue of 187 specimens of the decadrachms signed by Kimon, struck ca. 405 B.C. The dies are arranged chronologically to the best of the author's ability. A novel method of measuring the relief of the coins is employed. The author contends that Kimon and Euainetos made only the first set of dies for their decadrachms, and that all subsequent dies were made by other engravers even though they bear Kimon's and Euainetos' signatures. Includes chapters on the identification of the work of other great engravers, on the technique of striking, on metrology, and on hoards.

3171 **Karlsson, Lars.** "The Symbols of Freedom and Democracy on the Bronze Coinage of Timoleon." *Ancient Sicily.* Acta Hyperborea 6. Edited by Tobias Fischer-Hansen. Rome: Museum Tusculanum Press, 1995. Pages 149-69. Illus., 2 maps.
Examines the minting places of the bronze coins generally attributed to "the period of Timoleon" and addresses their chronological relationships. The most important of these issues are the 'Zeus Eleutherios/free horse' issues. Discusses the political message of the Zeus Eleutherios type, regarded as a symbol of democracy and freedom from tyranny. Discusses the political situation at Syracuse during the period of Dion (350's B.C.) and the period of Timoleon (344-316). Based on the political and historical evidence, the author gives these coins to the *symmachia* of Timoleon. He puts the coins into two chronological groups: (1) the early group: Zeus with short hair, and the ΣYMMAXIKON coins, and (2) the late group: long-haired Zeus and the free horse. Discusses the symbolism of the free horse type and concludes that it symbolizes the defeat of the Carthaginians. Timoleon revised the Syracusan monetary system, basing it on the Corinthian stater. The long-haired Zeus/free horse coins formed the new *litra* in Timoleon's monetary reform.

3172 **Knight, Richard Payne.** "On the Large Silver Coins of Syracuse." *Archaeologia* (England) 19 (1821): 369 ff.
One of the earliest essays in which the inscription KIMΩN on Syracusan decadrachms is identified as the signature of the engraver.

3173 **Knoepfler, Denis.** "La Chronologie du Monnayage de Syracuse sous le Deinoménides." *Revue Suisse de Numismatique* (Switzerland) 71 (1991): 1-41. 3 pls.
"A recent and excellent revision of the early issues of Syracuse." [D. Kroh, *ACRR*]

3174 **Kraay, Colin M.** "The Demareteion and Sicilian Chronology." *Greek Coins and History: Some Current Problems.* London: Methuen; and New York: Barnes & Noble, 1969. Pages 19-42. 4 pls.
Quotes Diodorus' account of the origin of the Demareteion coinage at Syracuse. Questions whether the coin referred to by Diodorus was a gold coin. Examines the stylistic development and die volumes and sequences of Syracusan tetradrachms. Reviews hoard evidence for clues to the dating of the early Syracusan coinage. Concludes the coinage with dolphins around Arethusa was issued after 485, and for the first few years was very restricted in volume. The decadrachm cannot be dated 480/479—it must be later and therefore is not the Demareteion. Examines hoard evidence for the chronology of coinage at Himera, Leontini, and Gela. Provides a table with a suggested revised chronology for Syracusan coinage during the fifth century B.C. Suggests the decadrachm was minted ca. 461 and that the Demareteion was actually a small gold coin minted in 479, of which no specimens have survived. [Also see Holloway "Damarete's Lion" above, and Kraay "A Reply," Mattingly "The Demareteion Controversy," Rutter "The Myth," Rutter "The Coinage of Syracuse," and Williams "The Demareteion Reconsidered" below].

3175 ——— "The Demareteion Reconsidered: A Reply." *Numismatic Chronicle* 7th ser., 12 (1972): 13-24. [CS 2270]
"The arguments adduced by R. T. Williams (see Williams "The Demareteion Reconsidered" below) in support of the traditional date of 480-479 B.C. for the Demareteion are countered. The case for a date in the sixties proposed in *Greek Coins and History*, pp. 19-42 is restated with a fresh treatment of the hoard evidence." [C. Kraay, *NL* 89]. [Also see Kraay "The Demareteion and Sicilian Chronology" above].

3176 ——— "Timoleon and Corinthian Coinage in Sicily." *Numismatic Chronicle* 7th ser., 13 (1973): iv-x. [CS 2271]
The Presidential address to the Royal Numismatic Society. Discusses the change to the Corinthian weight standard at Syracuse.

3177 ——— "Timoleon and Corinthian Coinage in Sicily." *Proceedings of the 8th International Congress of Numismatics, New York—Washington, September 1973.* Edited by Herbert A. Cahn and Georges Le Rider. International Association of Professional Numismatists Publication, No. 4. Paris/Basel: International Association of Professional Numismatists, 1976. Pages 99-105. 1 pl.
Kraay observes that near the middle of the fourth century B.C., Sicilian hoards suddenly become dominated by Corinthian pegasi, struck at a number of mints. Pegasi had rarely appeared in Sicilian hoards before this time. He addresses three issues: (1) When did the pegasi become the accepted currency of eastern Sicily? (2) In what circumstances did this come about? (3) Why was the pegasus adopted by a number of mints in northwestern Greece over which Corinth had no political control? Kraay determines that the pegasi came to dominate after the re-foundation of Syracuse in 344 B.C. It is normally assumed that the pegasus, a well-known trade coin, was adopted to take advantage of the new, prosperous trade between Sicily and Greece. However, Kraay argues that the pegasus became established for non-commercial reasons, and only later became the medium for commerce. He concludes that the northwestern Greek cities supplied money for Timoleon's expedition to Sicily, and they took care to advertise their contribution on pegasi specially minted for the occasion to conform with the currency of the major contributor, Corinth.

3178 **Lederer, Philipp.** "A Work on the Small Silver Coins of Syracuse." *Spink Numismatic Circular* 21 (September 1913): 663-5.
Presents an English summary of the classification system for coins of Syracuse used by Lederer in an article published in *Berliner Münzblätter* in 1913.

3179 ——— "Eine Verschollene Bronzemünze von Syrakus." *Transactions of the International Numismatic Congress Organized and Held in London by the Royal Numismatic Society, June 30-July 3, 1936.* Edited by J. Allan, H. Mattingly, and E. S. G. Robinson. London: B. Quaritch, 1938. Pages 80-5. 1 pl.

3180 **Lloyd, A. H.** "A New Bronze of Syracuse." *Numismatic Chronicle* 5th ser., 3 (1923): 150-2. 1 pl.
The previously unpublished coin has *obv.*, veiled female head; *rev.*, piloi of the Dioskuroi. The types are similar to those of Tyndaris. Lloyd suggests the coin may have been minted while the Syracusan army occupied the territory of Tyndaris.

3181 **Manganaro, Giacomo.** "Dall'Obolo alla Litra e il Problema del 'Demareteion.'" *Travaux de Numismatique Grecque Offerts à Georges Le Rider.* Edited by M. Amandry and S. Hurter. London: Spink, 1999. Pages 239-55. 3 pls.
Discusses the date of the Syracusan "Demareteion."

3182 **Mattingly, Harold B.** "The Damareteion Controversy—A New Approach." *Chiron* (Germany) 22 (1992): 1-12 including 1 pl.
Re-examines the dating of the famous Syracusan decadrachm which has been dated to 480 B.C., or 470-461 by various scholars. Examines the coinage of other cities to find coin types which imitate the Demareteion and which can be securely dated. Discusses coins of Kymai and Leontinoi. Reviews hoard evidence for the dating of the Leontinoi issue. An appendix examines the Seltmann hoard of 1890. Suggests the Demareteion may have been issued to

celebrate the end of the tyranny at Syracuse (466 B.C.). [This essay was reprinted in Mattingly's *From Coins to History: Selected Numismatic Studies* (see Mattingly under GENERAL WORKS—GREEK). Also see Holloway "Damarete's Lion" above, Kraay "The Demareteion" above, Rutter "The Myth," Rutter "The Coinage of Syracuse," and Williams "The Demareteion Reconsidered" below].

3183 **Mildenberg, Leo.** "Über Kimon und Euainetos im Funde von Naro." *Kraay—Mørkholm Essays: Numismatic Studies in Memory of C. M. Kraay and O. Mørkholm.* Numismatica Lovaniensia 10. Edited by G. Le Rider, G. K. Jenkins, N. Waggoner, and U. Westermark. Louvain-la-Neuve: Université Catholique de Louvain, 1989. Pages 181-9. 2 pls. Reprinted in *Leo Mildenberg. Vestigia Leonis: Studien zur Antiken Numismatik Israels, Palästinas und der Östlichen Mittelmeerweit.* Novum Testamentum et Orbis Antiquus 36. Edited by U. Hübner and E. Knauf. Freiburg: Universitätsverlag, and Göttingen: Vandenhoeck & Ruprecht, 1998. Pages 116-26. 2 pls.
[Also see Hübner and Knauf *Vestigia Leonis* under GENERAL WORKS—GREEK].

3184 **Minì, Adolfo.** *Monete Antiche di Bronzo della Zecca di Siracusa.* Palermo: Cassa Centrale di Risparmio, 1977. 191 pp., illus. [CS 2275]
Ancient bronze coins from the mint of Syracuse.

3185 **Morcom, John.** "Syracusan Bronze Coinage in the Fifth and Early Fourth Centuries B.C." *Studies in Greek Numismatics in Memory of Martin Jessop Price.* Edited by Richard Ashton and Silvia Hurter. London: Spink, 1998. Pages 287-91. 1 pl.
Explores the chronology of the earliest bronze coinage issued by Syracuse (*obv.*, female head with hair in top-knot). Reviews the evidence provided by the Chalcis Hoard. Describes the types of Syracusan bronze coins from the fifth and early fourth centuries B.C. and puts them in chronological order. Considers types, weights, heads, signatures. Concludes with a brief discussion of the denominations represented by these coins.

3186 **Mudd, Douglas.** "A Masterful Work: A Silver Decadrachm is Just One Example of the Beautiful Coinage Produced in 5th-Century Syracuse, Sicily." *The Numismatist* 124, no. 4 (April 2011): 78-9. Illus.
Highlights a decadrachm by Euainetos in the museum of the American Numismatic Association.

3187 "New Coin Type of Syracuse." *Spink Numismatic Circular* 10 (August 1902): 5456.
Describes a previously unpublished bronze coin of Syracuse with *obv.*, female head, and *rev.*, caps of the Dioscuri.

3188 **Phillips, Wayne C.** "Greek Coppers: Precious Metals Not Only Medium for Ancient Coins." *Coin World* (May 6, 1996): 78. Illus.
A brief description of the bronze coinage of Syracuse.

3189 ———. "Bronzes of Agathokles: Varieties Abound among Greek Rulers' Issues." *Coin World* (June 3, 1996): 40.
In this installment of the author's "Let's Talk Ancients" column, he provides an overview of the coin types of Agathokles and his successors in Sicily.

3190 ———. "Three Score: Hieron II's 60-year Reign Bronze-Filled." *Coin World* (July 1, 1996): 44. Illus.
In this installment of the author's "Let's Talk Ancients" column, he continues the discussion of Syracusan bronze coinage, focusing on the types of Hieron II, Hieronymos, and the Republic.

3191 **Puglisi, Mariangela.** *La Sicilia da Dionisio I a Sesto Pompeo: Circolazione e Funzione della Moneta.* Pelorias 16. Messina: Dipartimento di Scienze dell'Antichità dell'Università degli Studi di Messina (Di.Sc.A.M.), 2009.

3192 **Ravel, Oscar E.** "On a Hoard of Uninscribed Agathoclean 'Pegasi.'" *Numismatic Chronicle* 5th ser., 5 (1925): 22-8. 1 pl.
The author acquired some Syracusan uninscribed silver eight-litrae coins of the Pegasus type. The coins were originally from a hoard discovered in 1921 near the site of ancient Syracuse. Lists all the dies and die combinations of these coins known to the author. Suggests they were struck by Agathokles at the same time as his gold staters, ca. 305-289 B.C.

3193 **Raven, E. J. P.** "The Leucaspis Types at Syracuse." *Congrès International de Numismatique, Paris, 6-11 Juillet 1953. Volume 2.* Paris: Commission International de Numismatique, 1957. Pages 77-81.
The author discusses three groups of drachms from Syracuse minted during the late fifth century B.C. with the figure of the hero Leucaspis. Discusses the chronology of the coins and reasons for the appearance of the type. Describes the legends of Leucaspis and their connection to Sicilian history. Suggests the type was used to inspire loyalty among the Syracusans during times of war.

3194 **Regling, Kurt L.** "Dekadrachmen des Kimon." *Amtliche Berichte aus den Königlichen Kunstsammlungen* (Germany) 36 (1914): 3-11. [CS 2276]

3195 **Rutter, Nicholas K.** "The Myth of the Damareteion." *Chiron* (Germany) 23 (1993): 171-88.
Rutter examines the evidence for a coin said to have been named a "Damareteion" after Damarete, consort of Gelon who was tyrant of Syracuse, 485-478 B.C. Quotes the original Greek sources of the story including Diodorus Siculus, Pollux, Hesychius, Schol. Pindar, and Eustathius. Summarizes these accounts and then examines the numismatic evidence for such a coin. Discusses the origin and practice of bestowing honorary crowns. Rutter concludes this is a Hellenistic practice, not a fifth century B.C. practice. He also discusses examples of a coin being named after the person responsible for striking it. Concludes the story of a crown being presented by the Carthaginians to Damarete in 480 B.C. is "wholly unhistorical." Discusses the practice of women giving jewelry to be melted and coined. Concludes that the existence of the coin is a myth created by the propaganda of a Syracusan tyrant, and perpetuated in the third century B.C. Hellenistic world. [Also see Holloway "Damarete's Lion" above, Kraay "The Demareteion" above, Mattingly "The Demareteion Controversy" above, Rutter "The Coinage of Syracuse," and Williams "The Demareteion Reconsidered" below].

3196 ———. "The Coinage of Syracuse in the Early Fifth Century B.C." *Studies in Greek Numismatics in Memory of Martin Jessop Price.* Edited by Richard Ashton and Silvia Hurter. London: Spink, 1998. Pages 307-15. 1 pl.
A survey of some of the problems of the early coinage of Syracuse. Summarizes Boehringer's arrangement of the types (his Groups I – IV) of the early fifth century B.C. Then discusses their absolute chronology. Rutter believes that ancient literary accounts of the *Demareteion* cannot be used as serious evidence for a 480 B.C. date for this coin; rather, numismatic evidence must be used. Discusses problems with Diodorus' account of the Demareteion. Discusses hoard evidence which sheds light on dating and the spread of early Syracusan coinage. Discusses the change of letters from *qoppa* to *kappa* on the coins and

suggests the change happened between 478-474 B.C. Makes stylistic comparisons with coinage of Aitna, whose dating is known within broad limits. Also explores stylistic comparisons and die links with coins of Leontini. Concludes that the decadrachm is an issue of the closing years of the Deinomenid tyranny—not an issue celebrating its fall. Therefore, the coin was struck prior to 466 B.C.

3197 ——— "Dating the Period of the 'Signing Artists' of Sicilian Coinage." *KOINE: Mediterranean Studies in Honor of R. Ross Holloway*. Joukowsky Institute Publication 1. Edited by Derek B. Counts and Anthony S. Tuck. Oxford/Oakville, CT: Oxbow Books, 2009. Pages 125-30. Illus.
Rutter attempts to determine the beginning and end dates for the period of the "signing artists" (when several engravers produced dies that they signed). Focuses on the Syracusan tetradrachms studied by Tudeer and the decadrachms of Euanetos and Kimon. Shows that the coins signed by Euainetos, Eukleidas and Kimon were produced for just over a decade, 413-400 B.C.

3198 **Sambon, Arthur.** "Incisori Siracusani del V. Seculo e dei Primordi del IV." *Rivista Italiana di Numismatica* (Italy) 27 (1914): 11-44, 147-68. [CS 2277]

3199 **Sambon & Co., Arthur.** *Catalogue d'Une Collection de Monnaies Antiques Grande-Grèce & Sicile*. Paris: Arthur Sambon & Co. and E. Canessa, 1907. 72 pp., 21 pls. [CS 2156]
The sale catalogue of the collection of Giuseppe de Ciccio, listing 527 lots of Greek coins including eleven Syracusan decadrachms.

3200 **Schwabacher, Willy.** "Contributions to Greek Numismatics from Stockholm: 1. Kimonian Dekadrachms in Stockholm; 2. A Stater of Mallus." *Nordisk Numismatisk Årsskrift* (Sweden) (1947): 165-75.
The author publishes a signed decadrachm of Kimon which was recently re-discovered in the Royal Cabinet in Stockholm. The coin was not listed by Jongkees. Two other varieties are noted. Schwabacher discusses the view of Jongkees that some dies were signed by the master engraver himself, while others were signed "Kimon" by other artists. The author also publishes a hitherto unrecorded specimen of an important bilingual silver stater of the Cilician town Mallus, and he assigns it to late in the first quarter of the fourth century B.C.

3201 ——— *Das Demareteion*. Opus Nobile, Meisterwerke der Antiken Kunst, No. 7. Bremen, 1958. 30 pp., 7 pls. [CS 2278]

3202 **Sekulich, Lawrence.** "Arethusa's Enigmatic Headband." *The Celator* 25, no. 9 (September 2011): 30-7. Illus.
The author examines the unusual headband on Arethusa on a scarce variety of a Syracusan didrachm. He speculates on the ovoid pendants attached to the headband which may be myrtle leaves or laurel leaves. The author explores some possible mythological connections of these leaves to Arethusa.

3203 **Sotheby's.** *An Important Syracusan Decadrachm by Cimon Sold to Benefit a Charitable Foundation*. New York: Sotheby's, 1990. 2 pp., illus.
Sale brochure featuring a decadrachm of Syracuse engraved by Kimon. One of the finest known specimens, it brought $407,000 when sold on December 4, 1990. Includes enlarged color photographs.

3204 **Sparkes, G.** "On Some Gold Coins of Syracuse." *Numismatic Chronicle* 17 (1855): 12-8.
A brief inquiry into the weight standard used for early Syracusan gold coins.

3205 **Stein, Jacob K.** "Speculations Upon a Tetradrachm of Syracuse." *Seaby Coin and Medal Bulletin* 610 (June 1969): 188-90. Illus.
Examines a Syracusan tetradrachm from the time of Gelon. The Arethusa die is very similar to *Pozzi* 561, yet some details differ. The author suggests both pieces were struck from the same dies, but the Arethusa die was re-engraved after striking the author's specimen in order to repair damage—thus the slight differences noted on the *Pozzi* coin.

3206 **Talbert, R. J. A.** "Corinthian Silver Coinage and the Sicilian Economy, c. 340 to c. 290 B.C." *Numismatic Chronicle* 7th ser., 11 (1971): 53-66. [CS 2205]
"Evidence for Timolean's revival of the Sicilian economy in the second half of the fourth century is presented. The information provided by hoards of Corinthian pegasi is examined. Contemporary pegasus issues of twenty-four cities in western Greece, south Italy and Sicily are discussed." [R. Talbert, *NL* 87]

3207 **Tameanko, Marvin.** "Syracusan Dekadrachm Serves as Model for Copies." *The Celator* 4, no. 7 (July 1990): 14, 21. Illus.
Discusses the decadrachms of Syracuse. Points out the differences in the dies engraved by Kimon and Euainetos. Because of the renowned beauty of these coins, they have been extensively copied. Describes methods for copying coins. Mentions a decadrachm copy used as a merchant's advertising token. Also see corrections in "Letters to the Editor," *The Celator* 4, no. 9 (August 1990): 2 and 25, stating that the tokens were made in Syracuse, New York, rather than in London as originally stated.

3208 **Tudeer, Lauri O. Th.** "Die Tetradrachmenprägung von Syrakus in der Periode der Signierenden Künstler." *Zeitschrift für Numismatik* (Germany) 30 (1913): 1-292. Reprint, Berlin, 1913; Bologna: Forni; Chicago: Obol International, 1979. 292 pp., 7 pls. [CS 2280]
Examines the signed tetradrachms of Syracuse, struck ca. 415-390 B.C. [Also see Holloway "La Stuttura" above].

3209 **Vagi, David L.** "Searching for a Pedigree: One Coin's Story." *The Celator* 9, no. 11 (November 1995): 25. Illus.
Traces pedigree of a Syracusan decadrachm of Euainetos from its recent purchase back to its first known appearance in an 1878 Sotheby's auction.

3210 ——— "The Syracuse-Alexandria Connection." *The Celator* 11, no. 2 (February 1997): 22-3. Illus.
Discusses the reign of Hieron II (275-215 B.C.) focusing on his relationship with the Ptolemaic kings of Egypt. Illustrates a 16-litrae coin issued by Hieron II depicting his wife Philistris in a style copied from the Ptolemaic coins struck in the names of Arsinoe and Berenice.

3211 ——— "The Last Greek Dynasty of Syracuse." *The Numismatist* 123, no. 12 (December 2010): 65-7. Illus.
Vagi discusses the reign of Hieron II at Syracuse and describes the coins of Hieron II, his wife Philistis, and sons Gelon II and Hieronymus.

3212   **White, Donald.** "The Morris Coin: A Masterpiece by Euaenetus." *Expedition* 28, no. 3 (1986): 13-21. Illus.
Describes and illustrates a Syracusan decadrachm struck from dies signed by Euaenetos. The coin was donated to the Princeton University Museum by J. T. Morris in 1916. White summarizes the political and economic background of Sicily during the period surrounding the coin's issuance. Discusses the practice of placing artists' signatures on dies. Discusses the meaning of the types and the identification of the female head on the coin's reverse. Summarizes the mythology related to Arethusa. The author suggests another possible identification for the head: the water nymph Cyane, or Persephone-Cyane. White briefly outlines the provenance of twenty-three Syracusan decadrachms once owned by the Pennsylvania Academy of Fine Arts. The coins were later in the collection of A. S. Dewing. Discusses the significance of the victory commemorated by the decadrachm's obverse type.

3213   **Wiesinger, H.** "Anmerkung zu Einem Kimonischen Tetradrachmon." *Transactions of the International Numismatic Congress Organized and Held in London by the Royal Numismatic Society, June 30-July 3, 1936.* Edited by J. Allan, H. Mattingly, and E. S. G. Robinson. London: B. Quaritch, 1938. Pages 122-7. Illus.

3214   **Williams, Roderick T.** "The Demareteion Reconsidered." *Numismatic Chronicle* 7th ser., 12 (1972): 1-11. 1 pl. [CS 2282]
"The down-dating of the Demareteion by Kraay (see Kraay "The Demareteion and Sicilian Chronology" above) and Boehringer in *Die Münzen von Syrakus* based on the evidence of hoards and epigraphy is held to be unjustified provided that adjustments are made to fill the coinless gaps left by Boehringer (479-474, 435-425). The new Aetna tetradrachm (ca. 476) could have been influenced by the Demareteion. It is conjectured that *demareteion* is a corruption of *damatreion*." [R. Williams, *NL* 89]. [Also see Holloway "Damarete's Lion," Kraay "The Demareteion," Mattingly "The Demareteion Reconsidered," Rutter "The Myth," and Rutter "The Coinage of Syracuse" above].

Also see: Arnold-Biucchi "Litras en Argent Contremarquées" under Sicily—General Works; Boehringer "Die Barbarisierten Münzen" under Sicily—General Works; Brunetti "Di Alcuni Valori Inediti" under Sicily—Akragas; Caskey "Recent Acquisitions" under Public Collections—United States (Boston); Castrizio "La Monetazione Mercenariale" under Sicily—General Works; de Callataÿ "On the Style of the Aitna Master" under Art; Florenzano "Ancient Sicilian Coins" under Sicily—General Works; Gainor "Case Study: Decadrachm" under Counterfeits; Grose "A Dekadrachm by Kimon" under The Minting Process; Hansen "Kroton Faces Syracuse" under Italy—Kroton; Kraay "Historical Interpretations" under General Works—Greek; Kraay "Greek Coinage and War" under General Works—Greek.

Liegle *Euainetos* under Engravers; Lloyd "Chorographical" under Types; Lorber "Notes on West Greek Gold" under Sicily—General Works; Mildenberg "The Work of the Die Engraver Kimon" under Engravers; Milne "The History of the Greek Medallion" under Types; Rizzo "Eukleidas" under Engravers; Sallery "Leontini Hoard" under Hoards; C. Seltman "The Influence of Agathocles" under Italy—General Works; Sjöqvist "Excavations at Morgantina" under Hoards; Sjöqvist "A Portrait Head" under Portraits; Stillwell and Sjöqvist "Excavations" under Hoards; Vagi "Sicilian Decadrachms" under Sicily—General Works; Vermeule "Chariot Groups" under Types.

Zankle/Messana

3215   **Boehringer, Christof.** "Ein Lot Kleiner Silbermünzen von Zankle-Messana." *Italiam Fato Profvgi: Numismatic Studies Dedicated to Vladimir and Elvira Eliza Clain-Stefanelli.* Numismatica Lovaniensia 12. Edited by T. Hackens. Louvain-la-Neuve: De L'Université Catholique De Louvain, 1996. Pages 51-60.

3216   **Burgon, Thomas.** "On the Coins of Zancle; and on a Very Remarkable Variation in the Types of a Coin of that City, in the British Museum." *Numismatic Chronicle* 3 (1841): 40-8. Illus.
Identifies the semicircular object on the obverse of Zanclean coins as a representation of the fortified pier which formed the harbor of Zancle.

3217   **Caltabiano, Maria Caccamo.** "Le Più Antiche Emissioni Bronzee di Messana." *Quaderni Ticinesi: Numismatica e Antichità Classiche* (Switzerland) 8 (1979): 67-83.

3218   ——— *La Monetazione di Messana: Con le Emissioni di Rhegion dell'età della Tirannide.* Antike Münzen und Geschnittene Steine 13. Berlin and New York, 1993. 383 pp., 94 pls.
The coinage of Messana, with the issues of Rhegion, from the age of the tyranny.

3218a   **Carollo, Salvatore, and Antonio Morello.** *Mamertini: Storia e Monetazione.* Nummus et Historia III. Formia: Circolo Numismatico Mario Rasile, 1999. 169 pp., illus.

3219   **di Floristella, Pennisi.** "A Unique Gold Coin of Messana." *American Journal of Numismatics* 42, no. 4 (1908): 129-30.
Discusses a gold coin of Messana, struck ca. 491 B.C. Translated from Italian by Agnes Baldwin.

3220   **Dodd, C. H.** "The Samians at Zancle-Messana." *Journal of Hellenic Studies* 28 (1908): 56-76. 1 pl.
Examines the numismatic evidence relating to the settlement of Samians at Zancle and the change of the name of the city to Messana. Reviews the literary evidence. Lists the relevant coins of Rhegium and Zancle-Messana. Suggests there is a conflict between the literary and the numismatic evidence. Dodd attempts to reconcile the two. Concludes the Samians went to Rhegium, not to Zancle, where they left their mark on the coinage. The Samians later settled at Zancle and changed its name to Messana. [Also see Robinson "Rhegion, Zankle-Messana" below; Robinson draws different conclusions].

3221   **Eaglen, Robin J.** "Portraits of Greek Coinage 7: Messana." *Spink Numismatic Circular* 113, no. 6 (December 2005): 369. Illus.
This installment of the author's on-going series examines the coinage of Messana. Reviews the history of the city and its coin types.

3222   **Gielow, Hertha Edith.** "Die Silberprägung von Dankle-Messana (ca. 515-396 v. Chr.)." *Mitteilungen der Bayerischen Numismatischen Gesellschaft* (Germany) 148 (1930): 1-54. 7 pls. [CS 2285]
The silver coinage of Zankle-Messana.

3223 **Holloway, R. Ross.** "A Drachm of Zankle with Pellets Indicating Value in the Museum of Art, Rhode Island School of Design." *Travaux de Numismatique Grecque Offerts à Georges Le Rider.* Edited by M. Amandry and S. Hurter. London: Spink, 1999. Pages 167-8. 1 pl.
Publishes a coin with *obv.*, DANKLE below dolphin within sickle-shaped harbor; *rev.*, stylized incuse of nine compartments. The dies do not appear in Gielow's catalogue (see Gielow above). Six pellets appear on the obverse, denoting its value of six units—a litra. Holloway believes this was Sicily's first experiment with marks of value on silver coins.

3224 **Jongkees, Jan H.** "Le Graveur Cimon à Messana." *Revue Belge de Numismatique* (Belgium) 100 (1954): 25-9. [CS 3581]

3225 **Lehmann, Clayton M.** "The Striding God of Zankle-Messana." *Revue Belge de Numismatique et de Sigillographie* (Belgium) 127 (1981): 19-32. Illus.
"The striding god on Messana's unique tetradrachm is identified as Zeus rather than as Poseidon. The coin, bearing the legend DANKLAION (Brussels, *Coll. de Hirsch,* No. 446), should be dated from the inception of the fifth century when Hippokrates, tyrant of Gela, enslaved the Messanians. Confirmation for such a date is obtained by comparison with Greek vase-painting." [P. Naster, *NL* 110]

3226 **Robinson, Edward S. G.** "Rhegion, Zankle-Messana and the Samians." *Journal of Hellenic Studies* 66 (1946): 13-20. 1 pl. [CS 2124]
A response to Dodd's paper (see Dodd "The Samians" above) exploring the evidence for the settlement of the Samians at Zancle and the change of the name of the city to Messana. Contrary to Dodd's conclusions, Robinson suggests the numismatic evidence does not conflict with the literary evidence. Lists the relevant coins of Rhegium and Zankle-Messana. Comments on the weight-standards, mint attributions, and the significance and dates of the mule-car issues. [Also see W. Wallace "Kleomenes" under PELOPONNESOS—ARKADIA].

3227 **Särström, Margit.** *A Study in the Coinage of the Mamertines.* Lund, 1940. 182 pp., 54 pls. [CS 2238]
In this doctoral thesis, Särström examines the bronze coinage struck in Messana while under the occupation of Oscan mercenaries (the Mamertini) from 288 to 278 B.C. The coinage is divided into five groups and twenty-three special series.

3227a **Schwabacher, Willy.** "Zur Münzprägung der Samier in Zankle-Messana." *Wandlungen, Studien zur Antiken und Neueren Kunst.* Edited by E. Hamann-Wedeking. Waldsassen, 1975. Pages 107-11. 1 pl. [CS 2287]

Also see: Grace "Early Thasian Stamped Amphoras" under TYPES; Head "Remarks" under SICILY—AITNA; Kraay "Fifth Century Overstrikes" under ITALY—RHEGION; Lorimer "The Country Cart" under TYPES; Rutter "South Italy and Messana" under ITALY—GENERAL WORKS; Thallon "The Cave at Vari" under TYPES; Vallet "Rhegion et Zancle" under ITALY—RHEGION.

Mainland Greece and the Islands

Macedonia

Through the possession of mines in Macedonia and Thrace, especially the important gold and silver mines of the Pangaean region which according to some sources supplied a yearly income of a thousand talents, Philip had been able to issue coins in larger quantities than his predecessors and far beyond the resources of any Greek city-state except perhaps Athens.

—Otto Mørkholm, pub. 1991

Cities and Tribes

3228   **Adam-Veleni, P.** *Coinage in the Macedonian Region. Proceedings of the 2nd Scientific Meeting.* Obolos 4. Thessaloniki: University Studio Press, 2000. 375 pp.
Twenty-six papers presented at the 2nd Scientific Meeting held in Thessaloniki in May 1998. Those related to ancient Greek coinage are: "La Monnaie de la Macédoine" by O. Picard [3279], "The Weight Standards of the 5th and 4th Century Mints of the Cities of the Chalcidice" by S. Psoma [3281], "A Tetrobol of Goat-Type, Attributed to Alexander I, King of Macedonia" by E. Papaeuthymiou [3462], "The Lion and the Donkey: The Case of an Unidentified Mint" by P. Tselekas, "Macedonia and Acarnania: Coins Struck on Macedonian Bronzes" by S. Kremydi-Sicilianou [3258], "Drachmes d'Argent et Statères d'Or dans les Inscriptions de Macédoine" by M. B. Hatzopoulos [3252], "Two Hellenistic Hoards from Macedonia" by C. Gatzolis [561], "Four Hoards from the Hellenistic City at Petres (Florina – West Macedonia)" by P. Adam-Veleni [478], "Regal Silver Macedonian Coinage (413-360): Metal Analysis and Historical Approach" by M. Lykiardopoulou and S. Psoma [3406], and "Composition and Provenance of the Tetradrachms of Alexander the Great" (in Greek) by N. Kallithrakas-Kontos, A. Katsanos, G. Blamakis, and Y. Touratsoglou [3390].

3229   **Alexander, John A.** "The Coinage of Potidaea." *Studies Presented to David Moore Robinson on His Seventieth Birthday. Volume 2.* Edited by George Mylonas and Doris Raymond. St. Louis: Washington University, 1953. Pages 201-17. 1 pl. [CS 2321]
The author breaks the silver and bronze coinage of Potidaea into three groups based on style and historical considerations, and attempts to establish a chronological arrangement. Describes the characteristics of the silver coinage during each period. Places the bronze coinage in the first half of the fourth century B.C. Coinage at Potidaea ended with Philip's conquest of the city in 356 B.C.

3230   ——— *Potidaea: Its History and Remains.* Athens, Georgia: University of Georgia, 1963. 146 pp., illus.
"Silver coinage of Potidaea to 432 B.C. and bronze issues are discussed." [*NL* 87]

3231   **Babelon, Ernest C.** "La Trouvaille de Mendé." *Revue Numismatique* (France) (1922): 103-20.

3232   **Bellinger, Alfred R.** "Notes on Coins from Olynthus." *Studies Presented to David Moore Robinson on His Seventieth Birthday. Volume 2.* Edited by George E. Mylonas and Doris Raymond. St. Louis: Washington University, 1953. Pages 180-6.
Examines some of the coins of the Macedonian cities and kings found during Robinson's excavations at Olynthus. Suggests that before 348 B.C., Macedonian communities composed a self-sufficient economy into which the royal coinage intruded to only a minor degree.

3233   ——— "Philippi in Macedonia." *Museum Notes* 11 (1964): 29-52. 6 pls. [CS 2319]
A general study of the gold and silver coinage of the mint of Philippi in Macedonia. Begins with two gold staters struck at the new settlement of Krenides (later renamed "Philippi") ca. 360-356 B.C. Then lists and describes twenty coins struck at Philippi 356-345 B.C. Also discusses a hoard of bronze coins (*IGCH* 404) found at Drama in Macedonia consisting of coins of Philippi as well as coins of Philip II and Alexander III. Lists the 145 coins in the hoard. Discusses possible mint attributions for the Philip and Alexander coins. Argues for and against Philippi as the main mint for the royal bronze issues, although no conclusion could be reached based on the present evidence.

3234   **Benner, Steve M.** "History and Coinage of the Chalkidian League." *The Celator* 23, no. 1 (January 2009): 6-22. Illus.
A good overview of the coinage of the Chalkidian League, which had its capital and only known mint at Olynthus. Begins with a brief history of the league, which was founded ca. 432 B.C. in the region of Chalkidike. There is no known list of all the cities that were members of the league. The league ended in 348 when it was defeated by Philip II. Benner discusses the weight standards of the coinage, the types, denominations, chronology, symbols, and legends. In a

table, Benner summarizes the chronological groups of the coinage as defined by Robinson and Clement (see Robinson and Clement *Excavations at Olynthus* below).

3235 **Bloesch, Hansjörg.** "Die Löwen von Skione." *Revue Suisse de Numismatique* (Switzerland) 38 (1957): 5-10. [CS 2322]
The lions on the coins of Skione.

3236 **Bompois, H. Ferdinand.** *Examin Chronologique des Monnaies Frappées par la Communauté de Macèdoniens avant, Pendant et Après la Conquête Romaine.* Paris, 1876. Reprint, Chicago: Obol International, 1980. 102 pp., 10 pls. [CS 2309]

3236a **Bon, Anne-Marie.** "Monnaie Inédite de Galepsos." *Bulletin de Correspondance de Hellénique* (France) 60 (1936): 172-4. 1 pl.
[Also see Demetriadi "Galepsus" below].

3237 **Cahn, Herbert A.** "Ein Tetradrachmon von Stagira." *Antike Kunst* (Switzerland) 1, no. 2 (1958): 37-40. 1 pl.

3237a ——— "Skione, Stagira, Akanthos." *Antike Kunst* (Switzerland) 9 (1973): 7-13. Illus. [CS 2323]

3238 ——— "Stagira in Tel-Aviv." *Studies in Honour of Leo Mildenberg: Numismatics, Art History, Archaeology.* Edited by Arthur Houghton et al. Wetteren: Editions NR, 1984. Pages 43-50. 1 pl.

3239 **Clement, Paul A.** "The Silver Coinage of the Chalcidic Mint at Olynthus." *American Journal of Archaeology* 42 (1938): 124.
The summary of a paper presented at a conference. "A brief survey of this coinage during the later fifth and earlier fourth centuries B.C., giving the results of die analysis, and epitomizing part of section I of *Excavations at Olynthus, IX. The Chalcidic Mint and the Excavation Coins, 1928-1934*, Baltimore 1938." [J. R. Jones, *NIAJAH*]. [Also see Robinson and Clement below].

3240 ——— "The Chalcidic Coinage: Epilogue." *Arcaia Macedonia: First International Symposium.* Thessalonike, 1970. Pages 252-5.

3241 **Demetriadi, Vassili.** "Galepsus in Chalcidice: A Newly Discovered Mint." *Nomismatika Khronika* (Greece) 3 (1974): 32-3. Illus.
Publishes two bronze coins with *obv.*, young male head to left, hair bound with ivy; *rev.*, forepart of goat looking back, inscription ΓΑΛΗΥΙΩΝ. Discusses the location of the city of Galepsus and attributes the coins to the city of Galepsus on the western coast of the Sithonian peninsula in Chalcidice (rather than the city of the same name lying on the east coast of the Strymonian Gulf). The coins were probably issued in the first half of the fourth century B.C. The author states that coinage from this city was previously unknown (but see Bon "Monnaie Inédite de Galepsos" above).

3242 ——— "Dion in Macedonia: A Bronze Coinage of the Classical Period." *Studies in Greek Numismatics in Memory of Martin Jessop Price.* Edited by Richard Ashton and Silvia Hurter. London: Spink, 1998. Pages 115-7. 1 pl.
A catalogue of some rare bronze coins which have in the past been generally classified as uncertain. The author attributes the coins to Dion in Macedonia, a mint which hitherto had no recorded coinage before the foundation of the Roman colony in the first century B.C. Dion was a religious center situated in southern Macedonia on the northern foothills of Mount Olympos. The coin types are *obv.*, head of Zeus, and *rev.*, Demeter. The coins bear the inscriptions Δ or ΔIAΩN. They were probably issued in the early fourth century B.C. The author suggests this was a small and short-lived emission intended for local use in a town that was part of the Macedonian Kingdom and presumably used Macedonian regal coinage for most of its needs.

3243 **Desneux, Jules.** "Les Tetradrachmes d'Akanthos." *Revue Belge de Numismatique* (Belgium) 95 (1949): 5-122. 38 pls. Reprint, Brussels: Société Royale de Numismatique, 1949. 122 pp., 38 pls. [CS 2318]

3244 **Dragonov, Dimitar.** "The Bronze Coinage of Dionysopolis." *Spink Numismatic Circular* 105, no. 10 (December 1997): 371-7. Illus.
Presents a list and description of all the bronze coin types of Dionysopolis (situated on the west coast of the Black Sea) of the Hellenistic age, as well as some unpublished Greek Imperial types. All fifty-two types are illustrated.

3245 **Forrer, Leonard S.** "Coins of Getas, King of the Edoni." *Spink Numismatic Circular* 6 (July 1898): 2862-3.
Announces that the Cabinet des Médailles, Paris, has recently acquired two new varieties of the rare octodrachm of Getas, Kind of the Edoni.

3246 **Franke, Peter R.** "Literaturüberblick der Griechischen Numismatik: Makedonien." *Jahrbuch für Numismatik und Geldsseschichte* (Germany) 7 (1956): 105-38. [CS 2301]
A bibliography.

3247 **Gaebler, Hugo.** *Die Antiken Münzen Nord-Griechenlands, Band III, i-ii: Makedonia und Paionia, Zweite Abteilung.* Two parts. Edited by F. Imhoof-Blumer. Berlin: Prussian Academy of Sciences, 1906, 1935. 196 pp., 5 pls; 234 pp., 40 pls. Reprint, Graz, 1971. [CS 1806 and 2305]

3248 ——— "Die Münzen von Stagira." *Sonderausgabe aus den Sitzungsberichten der Preussischen Akademie der Wissenschaftern, Phil.-Hist. Klasse XIX.* Berlin, 1930. [CS 2324]

3249 **Gerassimov, Theodore.** "A Hoard of Decadrachms of the Derrones from Velitchkovo (Bulgaria)." *Numismatic Chronicle* 5th ser., 18 (1938): 80-4. 2 pls.
A pot containing nine decadrachms of the Derrones (*obv.*, ox-cart; *rev.*, triskeles) was found in 1937. All of the coins were well preserved and are illustrated here. The author catalogues and discusses the coins.

3250 ——— "Une Fausse Monnaie Péonienne." *Bulletin de l'Institut d'Archéologie* (France) 27 (1964): 249-51.
Condemns a stater in the Bulgarian National Museum of History that appears to belong to a Paionian king Teutames. Points out the stylistic irregularities which cause his suspicion. [Also see Kretz "Teutamados," and Lilcic and Josifovski "A Silver Diabol" below].

3251 **Hardwick, Nicholas.** "The Coinage of Terone from the Fifth to the Fourth Centuries B.C." *Studies in Greek Numismatics in Memory of Martin Jessop Price.* Edited by Richard Ashton and Silvia Hurter. London: Spink, 1998. Pages 119-34. 1 pl.
This survey of the mint of Terone outlines the major issues and their chronology. The mint was active from the beginning of the fifth to the middle of the fourth century B.C. Describes the types and the ethnics used on the coins and describes the weight standards employed. Discusses the hoard evidence, including the evidence provided for circulation patterns. Includes a list of relevant hoards.

3252 **Hatzopoulos, M. B.** "Drachmes d'Argent et Statères d'Or dans les Inscriptions de Macédoine." *Coinage in the Macedonian Region. Proceedings of the 2nd Scientific Meeting.* Obolos 4. Edited by P. Adam-Veleni. Thessaloniki: University Studio Press, 2000.
A paper presented at the 2nd Scientific Meeting held in Thessaloniki in May 1998.

3253 **Head, Barclay V.** "On an Unpublished Archaic Tetradrachm of Olynthus." *Numismatic Chronicle* new ser., 18 (1878): 85-9. Illus.
Head examines a tetradrachm with *obv.*, quadriga, and *rev.*, incuse square. The coin bears no inscription and was struck on the Euboic weight standard. He attributes the coin to Olynthus based on the obverse type.

3254 ——— *Catalogue of Greek Coins of Macedonia.* Edited by R. S. Poole. London: British Museum, 1879. Reprint, Bologna: Forni, 1963. lxiii, 200 pp., illus., map. [CS 2306]
Volume 5 of the *Catalogue of Greek Coins in the British Museum.* Covers the Paeonian Kings, cities of Macedonia, Thraco-Macedonian tribes, and the kings of Macedonia prior to Philip II. Sixty-three pages of introductory text precede the 200 page catalogue of coins. Illustrated by line drawings throughout. [Also see *Catalogue of Greek Coins in the British Museum* under PUBLIC COLLECTIONS—GREAT BRITAIN (LONDON)].

3255 ——— "Early Macedonian Coins of the Pangaen District." *American Journal of Numismatics* 27, no. 1 (July 1892): 27-9.
A general description of the coinage of this region.

3256 **Hoge, Robert W.** "Hinterland Hellenism: Lykkeios' Paeonian Stater." *The Numismatist* 113, no. 5 (May 2000): 580. Illus.
Illustrates and describes a stater of King Lykkeios of Paeonia and discusses the history of the Paeonian kingdom.

3257 **Imhoof-Blumer, Freidrich.** "Les Inscription 'TPIH' sur des Monnaies Grecques Antiques." *Numismatic Chronicle* new ser., 13 (1873): 1-18. [CS 3337]
[Also see Psoma "Des Monnaies aux Initiales TPIH" below, and Gardner "On Some Coins with the Inscription 'TPIH'" under CORINTHIA].

3257a **Josifovski, P.** "Coins with ΠΑΙ–ΝΩΝ from the Collection of the National Bank of the Republic of Macedonia." *Macedonian Numismatic Journal* 1 (1994).

3258 **Kremydi-Sicilianou, Sophia.** "Macedonia and Acarnania: Coins Struck on Macedonian Bronzes." *Coinage in the Macedonian Region. Proceedings of the 2nd Scientific Meeting.* Obolos 4. Edited by P. Adam-Veleni. Thessaloniki: University Studio Press, 2000.
A paper presented at the 2nd Scientific Meeting held in Thessaloniki in May 1998.

3259 **Kretz, Rainer.** "Teutamados—A New King of Paionia." *Spink Numismatic Circular* 114, no. 5 (October 2006): 259-64. Illus.
Examines a tetradrachm with Zeus/horseman galloping with fallen enemy beneath. The reverse bears the name ΤΕΥΤΑΜΑΔΟ. If genuine, the coin would add a new king to the Paionian series, and the name may be of Celtic origin. Kretz summarizes the history of the Paionian Kingdom. Cites Gerasimov's condemnation of the coin type as a fake and argues that the coin is genuine (see Gerasimov "Une Fausse Monnaie" above). Points out the probable Celtic origin of the name. Discusses both the obverse and reverse types. The nominative case of the name perhaps places the coin after Patraos and before Audoleon. Kretz suggests Teutamatos betrayed the Greek general Eumenes, leading to Eumenes' death at the hands of Antigonos Monophthalmos. The origin and ethnicity of Teutamatos cannot be determined with certainty. He may have been installed as king by his Macedonian backers ca. 315 B.C., but he kept the throne for only about two years. The author briefly mentions three other possible contenders for the Paionian throne around this time: Bastareos, Eupolemos, and Nicarchos. [Also see Lilcic and Josifovski "A Silver Diabol" below].

3260 **Lambros, Paul.** *Gold Coins of Philippi.* Translated by Betty Gardiakos. 1854. Reprint, Chicago: Obol International, 1970. 19 pp. illus. [CS 2320]
A very brief essay on the gold coinage of the city of Philippi before the time of Philip II. A brief history of the city is included. Lists and describes six coins, each of which is shown in a line drawing. The obverse of each shows Herakles in a lion's skin; the reverse shows a tripod.

3261 **Liampi, Katerini.** "The Mint of Phagres." *Nomismatika Khronika* (Greece) 10 (1991): 25-35. Illus.
The location of the ancient town of Phagres is debatable, but it is likely the modern village of Orphani. The city minted a small issue of bronze coins in the first half of the fourth century B.C. and nine pieces are known (*obv.*, Apollo; *rev.*, lion and ΦΑΓΡ). Liampi discusses the coin types and chronology, and summarizes the history of the town. In Greek with plates on pp. 25-31; in English on pp. 32-5. English translation by M. J. Tzamali.

3262 ——— "Argilos—History and Coinage." *Nomismatika Khronika* (Greece) 13 (1994): 7-36. Illus., map.
The town of Argilos is near the eastern edge of Chalcidice. Liampi describes the history of the city and comments on the site. Argilos struck silver coins at the start of the fifth century B.C. and copper coins ca. 375 B.C. Barclay Head had attributed these coins to Therma. Liampi refutes Head's arguments and lays out her case for Argilos. Discusses the chronology of the coins. Reviews the economic situation leading to the long gap in coinage and its eventual end. In Greek, with illustrations, on pp. 7-20; in English on pp. 21-36.

3263 ——— "The Coinage of King Derdas and the History of the Elimiote Dynasty." *Coins of Macedonia and Rome: Essays in Honour of Charles Hersh.* Edited by Andrew Burnett, Ute Wartenberg, and Richard Witschonke. London: Spink, 1998. Pages 5-11. 2 pls.
Outlines the history of Elimeia, a region encompassing the southern part of Upper Macedonia, and reviews the coinage of the Elimiote dynasty. Bronze coins were struck in the name of Derdas in the fifth and fourth centuries B.C. Derdas I lived during the reign of the Macedonian king Perdiccas II, but there may have been at least two other kings named Derdas. Liampi catalogues thirty-three Elimiote bronze coins, including eighteen different varieties. The coins are arranged in the sequence of striking. The author searches for similarities in types and style among the coins of other kingdoms and cities, and she

concludes the coinage belongs to the period after 390 B.C. to ca. 375 B.C. The mint may have been Aiane. Liampi comments on the political orientation of the Elimiote dynasty as indicated by the numismatic evidence. [Also see Imhoof-Blumer "Syrakosai—Lysimachos—Derdas" under SICILY—SYRACUSE].

3264 ——— *Argilos: A Historical and Numismatic Study.* Kerma 1. Athens: Society for the Study of Numismatics and Economic History, 2005. 377 pp., 27 pls.

A political and economic history of ancient Argilos and Bisaltia, with a detailed examination of the coinage from archaic to classical times. Includes a corpus of coin types. The discussion of the silver coinage is broken into seven phases and the bronze coinage is discussed separately. Includes discussion of the coin types, mythology, style, legends, metrology, and mint techniques. Concludes with a review of hoard evidence and coins from excavations. Includes a Greek summary. [Reviewed by William Bubelis in *Numismatic Chronicle* 167 (2007): 315-21].

3265 **Lilcic, V., and P. Josifovski.** "A Silver Diobol of the Paeonian Ruler TEYTAO(Σ)." *Macedonian Numismatic Journal* (Macedonia) 1 (1994): 27-37.

Discusses a diobol of Teutaos, a Paionian chieftain (ca. 430-400 B.C.), who shares the same name element (Teuta-) with Teutamados, lending support to Teutamados being a historic figure. [Also see Kretz "Teutamados" above].

3266 **Lorber, Catharine C.** *Amphipolis: The Civic Coinage in Silver and Gold.* Los Angeles: Numismatic Fine Arts International, 1990. 196 pp., 31 pls., map.

Based on a study begun by Willy Schwabacher, this book catalogues over 100 tetradrachms and gold coins, and 150 silver fractions of Amphipolis, with all die combinations illustrated in the plates. Discusses production techniques, stylistic developments, and the engravers of the coinage. Classifies the tetradrachm coinage into nine groups and discusses each. Analyzes eight hoards containing coins of Amphipolis. Attempts to present an absolute chronology of the coinage. Then discusses the monetary policies of Philip of Macedon and the chronologies of a number of contemporary northern coinages including those of Abdera, Maroneia, and the Chalcidian League. Publishes the Abdera hoard of 1986 and the Aenus hoard of 1987. Also includes a listing of all known forgeries. [Reviewed by Martin J. Price in *Spink Numismatic Circular* 98, no. 10 (December 1990): 354, by D. Bérend in *American Journal of Numismatics* 2nd ser., 3-4 (1992): 201-7, and by U. Wartenberg in *Numismatic Chronicle* 152 (1992): 193-5].

3267 ——— "The Goats of 'Aigai.'" *Pour Denyse. Divertissements Numismatiques.* Edited by S. M. Hurter and C. Arnold-Biucchi. Bern, Switzerland: Privately published, 2000. Pages 113-133. 1 pl.

"North Greek staters and diobols featuring a semi-kneeling goat, traditionally attributed to Aegae, were identified as a tribal coinage by Olivier Picard, *Bulletin de la Société Française de Numismatique* 50/6 (1995), pp. 1071-1075 (see Picard below). The present article sequences the issues, based on hoard evidence, fabric, style, and links to other tribal coinages. The time frame is c. 490/85—c. 470. Shared letters, monograms, and types indicate an alliance c. 475 among the tribe of the goat staters, the Bisaltae, and Alexander I of Macedon; a second alliance c. 470 between the tribe of the goat staters and the Bisaltae; and a third alliance shortly thereafter between the Bisaltai and Alexander I. These patterns point to the Mygdones or the Crestones as the issuing authority of the 'Aegae' coinage." [C. Lorber, *NL* 146]

3268 **MacDonald, David.** "Macedonian Civic Bronze Overstrikes and Circulation Areas." *Nomismatika Khronika* (Greece) 19 (2000): 115-21. Illus.

Describes three bronze overstrikes not recorded by Touratsoglou (see Touratsoglou "The Coin Circulation in Ancient Macedonia" under HOARDS): (1) Pella over Thessalonica, (2) Thessalonica over Amphipolis, and (3) Thessalonica over Pella. Along with countermarking, overstriking was a method commonly employed to remonetize coins that had previously been demonetized. But the overstriking of the coins of the three principal cities of Macedonia was not massive. The bronze coins of Macedonia circulated in two distinct areas: (1) the city itself and its immediately surrounding territory, and (2) Macedonia in general—where the coins circulated widely but where the supply was insufficient to meet the demand. In this wide area, any bronze coins were acceptable. But when some of these coins re-entered the city, they were required to be remonetized by overstriking. Thus, the overstriking was done in a non-uniform manner with a variety of overstrikes on a variety of undertypes.

3269 **Madsen, Eardley, and Ethel Madsen.** "The Chalcidian League." *SAN—Journal of the Society for Ancient Numismatics* 14, no. 1 (spring 1983): inside covers.

A brief overview of the history and coinage of the Chalcidian League.

3269a **Michaux, Françoise.** "Les Tétroboles de Mendé." *Revue Belge de Numismatique* (Belgium) 127 (1981): 5-18. 1 pl.

3270 **Noe, Sydney P.** *The Mende (Kaliandra) Hoard.* Numismatic Notes and Monographs, No. 27. New York: American Numismatic Society, 1926. 73 pp., 10 pls. [CS 3261]

Noe examines a hoard of about 320 tetradrachms of Mende, found in 1913 at Kaliandra, the site of the ancient city of Mende. The author divides the coins, minted ca. 450-423 B.C., into three groups. Ninety-three of the coins are catalogued here. Noe suggests the hoard was buried ca. 423 B.C. He describes the historical background for the hoard's burial. Discusses the significance of the types and symbols on the coins: Dionysus, the bird, the grapevine. He suggests that two die-cutters were at work at the Mende mint. [Reviewed by G. W. Elderkin in *American Journal of Archaeology* 30 (1926): 470].

3271 **Parke-Bernet Galleries, Inc.** *The Extremely Important Greek Hoard, being Coins in Gold and Silver of Northern Macedonia.* New York: Parke-Bernet Galleries, 1969. 24 pp., 8 pls. [CS 2362]

The catalogue for a December 9, 1969 auction featuring coins from a hoard. Includes 278 lots including gold staters and silver tetradrachms of Philip II, gold staters and distaters of Alexander, two tetradrachms of the Paeonian king Lykkeios, many tetradrachms of the Paeonian king Patraos, and numerous local imitations of Paeonian coinage. [Also see listing 503 in J. Spring, *Ancient Coin Auction Catalogues 1880-1980* (see Spring under COLLECTING GUIDES). Also see Sotheby & Co. *Paeonian Hoard* below for the primary auction of coins from this hoard].

3272 **Pavlovska, Eftimija.** *The Coins of Paeonia. From the Numismatic Collection of the National Bank of the Republic of Macedonia.* Skopje: National Bank of the Republic of Macedonia, 2008.

3273 **Perkins, Jonathan.** "The Art of the Coinage of Mende." *The Celator* 18, no. 8 (August 2004): 6-16. Illus.

An examination of the classical period tetradrachms of Mende from an art historical perspective. Focuses on the series struck ca. 460-423 B.C. featuring Dionysos lying backward on an ass. Describes stylistic variations in the coin types. Compares the coin types with similar types at Abdera and on a painted vase. Also illustrates a marble sculpture of Dionysos on an ass in the Minneapolis Institute of Arts, and points out some likely errors in its restoration based on the coin types.

3273a **Petrova, Eleonora.** "A Derronian Octodrachm from the Collection of the Museum of Macedonia." *Macedonian Numismatic Journal* (Macedonia) 1 (1994): 17-9.

3273b ——— "Coins of King Dropion of Paeonia in the Museum of Macedonia." *Macedonian Numismatic Journal* (Macedonia) 1 (1994): 49-56.

3274 ——— "The Fifth Century B.C. Coins from the Museum of Macedonia." *Macedonian Numismatic Journal* (Macedonia) 2 (1996): 7-12.
"The author examines several coins recently obtained by the Museum of Macedonia in the light of existing treatment of these types by Head, Gaebler, Svoronos, and Hammond. The two types under consideration (obverse: goat kneeling right with head facing left, and obverse: goose and salamander surrounded by circle of dots; both with reverse: incuse square) are dated to the end of the sixth and the first four decades of the fifth century B.C., and attributed to the town of Aegeae, or to the first coinage of Alexander I, or to the Paeoplai and Edones in the region east of the lower Axus River." [C. Smith, Jr., *NL* 139]

3274a ——— "The Coinage of the Paeonian Tribal Organizations and Paeonian Kings (VI to III Centuries B.C.)." *Coins and Mints in Macedonia*. Edited by C. Grozdanov. Skopje: Macedonian Academy of Arts and Sciences, 2001. Pages 13-27.

3275 **Picard, Olivier.** "Le Lion et le Taureau sur les Monnaies d'Acanthe." *Kraay—Mørkholm Essays: Numismatic Studies in Memory of C. M. Kraay and O. Mørkholm*. Numismatica Lovaniensia 10. Edited by G. Le Rider, G. K. Jenkins, N. Waggoner, and U. Westermark. Louvain-la-Neuve: Université Catholique de Louvain, 1989. Pages 225-31. 1 pl.
Discusses the lion staters of Acanthus.

3276 ——— "Le Monnayage Bronze d'Oisymè." *Nomismatika Khronika* (Greece) 12 (1993): 13-9. Illus.
Discusses the bronze coins of the city of Oisyme (near Galepsos and Apollonia). [In French on pp. 13-6; in Greek on pp. 17-9].

3276a ——— "Deux Emissions de Bronzes d'Amphipolis." *Bulletin de Correspondance de Hellénique* (France) 118, no. 1 (1994): 207-14.

3277 ——— "Les Monnaies du Bouc Attribuées à Aigai." *Bulletin de la Société Française de Numismatique* (France) 50, no. 6 (1996): 1071-5.
North Greek staters and diobols featuring a semi-kneeling goat, traditionally attributed to Aigai, are identified as a tribal coinage. [Also see Lorber "The Goats of 'Aigai'" above].

3278 ——— "The Weight Standard of the 5th and 4th Century Mints of the Cities of the Chalcidice." *To Nomisma Sto Makedoniko Choro. Kongres in Thessaloniki vom 15-17, Mai 1998*. Thessaloniki, 2000. Pages 25-36.

3279 ——— "La Monnaie de la Macédoine." *Coinage in the Macedonian Region. Proceedings of the 2nd Scientific Meeting*. Obolos 4. Edited by P. Adam-Veleni. Thessaloniki: University Studio Press, 2000.
A paper presented at the 2nd Scientific Meeting held in Thessaloniki in May 1998.

3279a **Prokopov, Ilya S.** *The Silver Coinage of the Macedonian Regions, $2^{nd} – 1^{st}$ Centuries B.C.* Moneta 131. Wetteren: Editions Moneta, 2012. 322 pages. Illus.

3280 **Psoma, Selene.** "Des Monnaies aux Initiales ΤΡΙΗ." *Μνημη Martin Jessop Price*. Edited by A. P. Tzamalis and M. J. A. Tzamali. Bibliotheca 5. Athens: The Hellenic Numismatic Society, 1996. Pages 104-10, incl. 1 pl.
[Also see Imhoof-Blumer "Les Inscription 'ΤΡΙΗ'" above, and Gardner "On Some Coins with the Inscription 'ΤΡΙΗ'" under CORINTHIA].

3281 ——— "The Weight Standards of the 5th and 4th Century Mints of the Cities of the Chalcidice." *Coinage in the Macedonian Region. Proceedings of the 2nd Scientific Meeting*. Obolos 4. Edited by P. Adam-Veleni. Thessaloniki: University Studio Press, 2000.
A paper presented at the 2nd Scientific Meeting held in Thessaloniki in May 1998.

3282 ——— *Olynthe et les Chalcidies de Thrace: Étude de Numismatique et d'Histoire*. Stuttgart: Franz Steiner, 2001. 311 pp., 22 pls, map.
A study of the 4000 coins found at Olynthus which were deposited in the Numismatic Museum at Athens in 1930. It includes a corpus of bronze and silver coins minted in Chalcidice between the fifth and early fourth centuries B.C. The catalogue is followed by a discussion of the evidence and the circulation of money at Olynthus, set within its historical context.

3283 ——— "Στατερ Μαχον: The 'Sermylia' Group of Coins." *Nomismatika Khronika* (Greece) 20 (2001): 13-44. 1 pl.
Discusses a group of coins attributed to Sermylia, with a focus on a silver coin in the Alpha Bank collection with the obverse inscription ΣΤΑΤΕΡ ΜΑΧΟΝ. The author argues that a quarter stater found at Olynthus, with an obverse type similar to that of Sermylia (horseman) likely belongs to Sermylia. Based on the stylistic variations in the horseman and the incuse on the reverse, seven groups are differentiated. The ΣΤΑΤΕΡ coins are dated ca. 500 B.C. Psoma discusses the fractional coinage, and then extensively examines the inscriptions on the coins, focusing on the use of personal names. This is the only known use of the word "stater" on a coin. Psoma concludes the term was used to indicate the heaviest coins issued by the cities of Chalkidike, which are tetradrachms. The work Machon is likely the name of the obverse figure of the warrior. It is not known whether Machon was a local leader, king, or mint official. The obverse type is described as the oldest known horseman type from Northern Greece. Includes a list of relevant hoards and a list of names starting with MAX.

3284 ——— "Methone, Pieria: A New Numismatic Type." *Nomismatka Khronika* 21 (2002): 78-81. Photographs on pp. 73-7.
Describes a bronze coin of Methone, ca. 365 B.C. Also describes a chalkous and a silver fraction of Methone recently added to the Alpha Bank collection. Examines the historical background for the coins.

3285 **Raymond, Doris.** "Northern Horses on Coins of Olynthus." *Studies Presented to David Moore Robinson on His Seventieth Birthday. Volume 2.* Edited by George E. Mylonas and Doris Raymond. St. Louis: Washington University, 1953. Pages 197-200. 1 pl.
Discusses (1) the tetradrachms of Attic weight having on the obverse a man driving a horse-drawn chariot and on the reverse an eagle flying left within an ornamental border, and (2) the tetrobols of Attic weight having on the obverse a leaping horse and on the reverse an eagle flying right, carrying a snake. Examines letter-forms and the horses and eagles. Assigns the coins to Olynthus or other Chalcidian cities.

3286 **Regling, Kurt L.** "Amphipolis." *Zeitschrift für Numismatik* (Germany) 33 (1921).

3287 ——— "Phygela, Klazomenai, Amphipolis." *Zeitschrift für Numismatik* (Germany) 33 (1922): 46-67.

3288 ——— "Mende." *Zeitschrift für Numismatik* (Germany) 34 (1923): 7-35.

3289 **Robinson, David M., and Paul A. Clement.** *Excavations at Olynthus, Part 9: The Chalcidic Mint and the Excavation Coins Found in 1928-1934.* Studies in Archaeology, No. 26. Baltimore: The Johns Hopkins Press, 1938. 413 pp., 36 pls. [CS 3281]
Examines the gold and silver coinage issued by the Olynthian Chalcidians to establish its chronology. Gives a detailed account of the coins found during the 1934 excavations at Olynthus and at Mecyberna. Presents a corpus of every known specimen of the gold and silver coinage of the Chalcidic mint at Olynthus. [Reviewed by C. T. Seltman in *Journal of Hellenic Studies* 59 (1939): 319-20, and by M. Wallace in *American Journal of Archaeology* 44 (1940): 163-4. Also see Clement "Chronological Notes" under HOARDS, and D. M. Robinson "Excavations at Olynthus, Part 3" and "Part 6" under HOARDS].

3290 **Rudd, Chris.** "Orchid Grower Unearths New King." *The Celator* 20, no. 12 (December 2006): 34. Illus.
Illustrates a tetradrachm of the Paeonian king Teutamados (ca. 315-310 B.C.). Suggests the king may have been of Celtic descent and may have been given the throne as a reward for betraying his Greek general. [Also see R. Kretz "Teutamados" above].

3291 **Schwabacher, Willy.** "Zur Silberprägung der Derronen." *Schweizer Münzblätter* (Switzerland) 3, no. 9 (1952): 1-4. Illus. [CS 2316]

3292 **Seldarov, Nikola, and Kolekcija Seldarov.** *Makedonija i Pajonija (Macedonia and Paeonia. Seldarov Collection).* Skopje: National Bank of the Republic of Macedonia, 2003.

3293 **Sotheby & Co.** *Catalogue of the Extremely Important Paeonian Hoard, Being Coins in Gold and Silver of the Kings of Macedon and Silver of the Independent Kingdom of Paeonia.* London: Sotheby & Co., 1969. 56 pp., map, 9 pls. [CS 2363]
The catalogue for an April 16, 1969 sale composed of 575 lots, featuring tetradrachms of the Kingdom of Paeonia from a recently discovered hoard. Includes numerous tetradrachms of King Lykkeios and hundreds of King Patraos. Also includes several gold staters and silver tetradrachms of Philip II. [Also see listing 833 in J. Spring, *Ancient Coin Auction Catalogues 1880-1980* (see Spring under COLLECTING GUIDES). Also see Parke-Bernet Galleries *The Extremely Important Greek Hoard* above for a later auction of coins from this hoard].

3294 **Svoronos, Joannes N.** "L'Hellénisme Primitif de la Macédoine Prouvé par la Numismatique et l'Or du Pangée." *Journal International d'Archéologie Numismatique* (Greece) 19 (1918-19): 1-262. 20 pls. Reprinted as a monograph, Athens: Eleftheroudakis, and Paris: Leroux, 1919. Reprint, Chicago: Argonaut, 1969; Chicago: Obol International, 1979. 265 pp., map, metrological table, 19 pls. [CS 2317]
"A useful collection of material, but the treatment includes elements of propaganda." [C. Kraay]

3295 **Tameanko, Marvin.** "Dium: A Minor City of Major Consequence." *Journal of the Classical and Medieval Numismatic Society* 2nd ser., 5, no. 3 (June 2004): 59-71. Illus.
Reviews the history and coinage of the city of Dium in Macedonia. The city grew to some prominence in the Roman era. Coins from the Greek period include an Alexander-type bronze coin with the legend ΔΙΑΤΩΝ. An Alexander tetradrachm bearing a bunch of grapes as a symbol on the reverse may have been struck at Dium.

3296 **Tatscheva, Margarita.** "ΓΕΤΑΣ ΗΔΟΝΕΟΝ ΒΑΣΙΛΕΥΣ." *Stephanos Nomismatikos: Edith Schönert-Geiss zum 65. Geburtstag.* Edited by Ulrike Peter. Berlin: Akademie Verlag, 1998. Pages 613-26.
A comprehensive study of the coinage of King Geta of the Edones.

3297 **Tselekas, Panagiotis.** "The Coinage of Pydna." *Numismatic Chronicle* 156 (1996): 11-32. 4 pls.
Reviews the historical background of the city of Pydna, then continues with a discussion of its coinage which began in the first half of the fourth century B.C. Concludes with a catalogue of the coins, segregated into two series.

3298 ——— "Late Archaic Overstruck Staters in the Chalkidike." *Nomismatika Khronika* (Greece) 21 (2002): 26-40. Map, 2 pls.
Discusses the coin output of some of the cities in the Chalkidike peninsula during the first two decades of the fifth century B.C.—a time when the area was under the authority of the Great King of Persia. These issues are probably associated with the payment of taxes to the Persian authority and to overseas trading activities. Local coinage was also needed to fund building projects in preparation for Xerxes' invasion. Numerous overstrikes exist from this period. The majority of the flans are of Akanthos.

3299 **Tzamalis, Anastasios P.** "Uncertain Thraco-Macedonian Coins." *Nomismatika Khronika* (Greece) 16 (1997): 13-20. 3 pls.
The author describes thirty-five anepigraphic coins in the Alpha Credit Bank collection which are classified as Thraco-Macedonian Uncertain.

3300 ——— "Uncertain Thraco-Macedonian Coins, Part 2." *Nomismatika Khronika* (Greece) 17 (1998): 15-22. Illus.
The author describes and comments on forty-three coins. Most are small fractions and come from the collection of Athanasios Ghertsos.

3301 ——— "Uncertain Thraco-Macedonian Coins, Part 3." Translated by Marion J. A. Tzamali. *Nomismatika Khronika* (Greece) 18 (1999): 11-6. Illus.
Publishes twenty-two uncertain Thraco-Macedonian fractions (twenty-one silver and one electrum) mainly from the Ghertsos collection. Most of the coins portray a horse, foreparts of a horse, or the head of a horse.

3302 **Ujes, Dubravka.** "A Tetradrachm-Subaeratus of the Paeonian King Patraos Found at Risan." *Macedonian Numismatic Journal* (Macedonia) 2 (1996): 23-32.
"Described is a silver-plated piece bearing features of the tetradrachm of Patraos but unique both among official issues and known counterfeits. Despite being plated bronze, the author characterizes the piece as closer to official issues than to known barbarian imitations. The piece was found in 1977 near the site of ancient Rhizon/Risinium in modern Montenegro." [C. Smith, Jr., *NL* 139]

3303 **Waggoner, Nancy M.** "Another Alexander Tetradrachm of Audoleon." *Studia Paulo Naster Oblata, Volume 1: Numismatica Antiqua.* Orientalia Lovaniensia Analecta 12. Edited by S. Scheers. Louvain: Departement Oriëntalistiek, 1982. Pages 99-103, including 1 pl.
Waggoner publishes an Alexander-type tetradrachm acquired by the American Numismatic Society in 1981. The coin is of Attic weight and bears the legend ΒΑΣΙΛΕΩΣ ΑΥΔΟΛΕΟΝΤΟΣ. It is the seventh example known and is die-linked to some of the others. Audoleon, king of the Paeonians and son of Patraus, ruled ca. 315-286 B.C. The author suggests his Alexander tetradrachms were struck at the end of 287 to commemorate Audoleon's share in the military ventures that ousted Demetrius from Athens and Macedonia. [Also see Waggoner "Further Reflections" below].

3304 ——— "Further Reflections on Audoleon and His Alexander Mint." *Revue Belge de Numismatique* (Belgium) 129 (1983): 5-21. Illus. Reprint, Bruxelles, 1983. 17 pp. 5 pls.
"This article follows up that appearing in *Studies Naster* (see Waggoner "Another Tetradrachm of Audoleon" above) in assigning a series of Alexander-inscribed tetradrachms to Audoleon, King of Paeonia, ca. 315-286 B.C." [N. Waggoner, *NL* 114]

3305 **Wartenberg, Ute.** "Philotas? A New Coinage from Macedonia." *Coins of Macedonia and Rome: Essays in Honour of Charles Hersh.* Edited by Andrew Burnett, Ute Wartenberg, and Richard Witschonke. London: Spink, 1998. Pages 13-17. 1 pl.
Reconsiders a small issue of bronze coins with *obv.*, beardless Herakles head; *rev.*, eagle on thunderbolt, and legend ΦΙΛΩ. The coins had previously been attributed as uncertain bronzes of Thessaly. Wartenberg notes that the obverse die of the coins was also used with another reverse, possibly of a different mint. Judging from the style of the Herakles heads, she assigns the coins to ca. 400-380 B.C. The inscription is almost certainly a personal name and Wartenberg suggests is it Philotas. Suggests Philotas was a ruler ca. 400 B.C. in the southern part of Upper Macedonia. This may well be the Philotas who was the father of Parmenion, one of Alexander the Great's generals.

3306 **Weber, Hermann.** "A Small Find of Coins of Mende, etc." *Numismatic Chronicle* 3rd ser., 18 (1898): 251-8. 1 pl.
Publishes twenty-three coins found in 1897. Most of the coins are from Mende.

3307 **Westermark, Ulla.** "The Coinage of the Chalcidian League Reconsidered." *Studies in Ancient History and Numismatics Presented to Rudi Thomson.* Edited by Aksel Damsgaard-Madsen, Erik Christiansen, and Erik Hallager. Denmark: Aarhus University, 1988. Pages 91-103. Illus.
A reconsideration of the chronology of the gold and silver coins of the Chalcidian League. Reviews the conclusions of previous scholarship. A table summarizes hoard evidence for the coinage. Concludes that the coinage did not begin before the start of the fourth century B.C.

Also see: Adam-Veleni "Four Hoards from the Hellenistic City" under HOARDS; Cahn "Olynthus" under SICILY—SYRACUSE; Franke "Η Μακεδονια Και Τα Νομισματα Τησ" under MACEDONIAN KINGDOM—GENERAL WORKS; Fried "The Decadrachm Hoard" under HOARDS; Gardner "Ares as Sun-God" under TYPES; Gatzolis "Two Hellenistic Hoards from Macedonia" under HOARDS; Hammond "The Coinage of Tribes, Cities, and Kings" under MACEDONIAN KINGDOM—GENERAL WORKS; Hammond "The Lettering and the Iconography" under MACEDONIAN KINGDOM—GENERAL WORKS; Hurter "More Caprara Forgeries: a Chalcidic League Problem Solved" under COUNTERFEITS; Kraay "Greek Coinage and War" (Potidaea) under GENERAL WORKS—GREEK; Lorimer "The Country Cart" under TYPES.

May *Coinage of Damastion* under NORTHERN GREECE—ILLYRIA; Milavic "Wrestler-type" under TYPES; Price *Coins of the Macedonians* under MACEDONIAN KINGDOM—GENERAL WORKS; Psoma "Les 'Boucs' de la Grèce du Nord" under TYPES; D. Robinson "Olynthus" (various articles) under HOARDS; Schwabacher "Illyro-Paeonian" under NORTHERN GREECE—ILLYRIA; Touratsoglou *The Coin Circulation in Ancient Macedonia* under HOARDS; Tsangari *Coins of Macedonia in the Alpha Bank Collection* under PUBLIC COLLECTIONS—GREECE (ATHENS); Vagi "Slavei Replicas" under COUNTERFEITS; Vaux "On Some Remarkable Greek Coins" under PUBLIC COLLECTIONS—GREAT BRITAIN (LONDON); Vermeule "Protesilaos" (Scione) under TYPES; Youroukova *Coins of the Ancient Thracians* under THRACE—GENERAL WORKS.

MACEDONIAN KINGDOM—GENERAL WORKS

3308 **Andreades, A.** "Les Finances de Guerre d'Alexandre le Grand." *Annales d'Histoire Économique et Sociale* 1 (1929): 321-4. [CS 2332]

3309 **Apostolou, Eva.** "Rhodian(?) Stater with the Types of Alexander the Great." Translated by Marion J. A. Tzamali. *Nomismatika Khronika* (Greece) 18 (1999): 73-6. Illus.
Suggests that an Alexander gold stater, which Price attributed to the Memphis mint, should instead be attributed to the Rhodian mint. The coin in question was found in Rhodes and bears the letter and symbol combination EY, cornucopia, and rose.

3310 **Arena, Valentina.** "New Acquisitions at the British Museum: Additions to Price, *Alexander*, and to the 1870 Larcana Hoard." *Numismatic Chronicle* 163 (2003): 49-57. 6 pls.
"The bequests of the collections formed by Edward Gilbertson (1813-1904) and Charles Hersh (1923-99) have greatly enriched the British Museum's holdings of Macedonian regal coins in the names of Philip II, Alexander III and Philip III. They add 44 new varieties to the issues in the names of Alexander III and Philip III recorded by Martin Price, and 50 staters of Philip II and Alexander III from the Gilbertson collection probably derive from the Larcana hoard (*IGCH* 1472)." [Martin Allen, *NL* 148]

3311 **Arnold-Biucchi, Carmen.** *Alexander's Coins and Alexander's Image.* Cambridge: Harvard University Art Museums, 2006. 84 pp., illus.

A synthesis of the most recent research on the coinage of Alexander and his successors, produced to accompany an exhibit at the Arthur M. Sackler Museum and to serve as an introductory numismatic text for Harvard undergraduate students. The author charts the evolution of Alexander's coinage and discusses the dissemination and imitation of Philip's and Alexander's coin types. Examines the origin and development of Alexander's numismatic image. [Reviewed by Andrew Stewart in *Bryn Mawr Classical Review* 2007.08.58, and by Oliver Hoover in *American Numismatic Society Magazine* 6, no. 3 (winter 2007): 61-5].

3312 **Ashton, Richard.** "The Coins of the Macedonian Kings, Lysimachos, and Eupolemos in the Museums of Fethiye and Afyon." *Coins of Macedonia and Rome: Essays in Honour of Charles Hersh.* Edited by Andrew Burnett, Ute Wartenberg, and Richard Witschonke. London: Spink, 1998. Pages 19-48. 1 pl.

A catalogue of the coins of Macedonian kings, of Lysimachus, and of Eupolemos in two Turkish Museums: Fethiye Archaeological Museum (346 coins) and Afyon Museum (178 coins). The bulk of the coins in the museums were found locally, therefore providing evidence of coin circulation in the areas in ancient times. Ashton comments on the Alexander, Poliorketes, and Eupolemos bronzes in the collections (Eupolemos was one of Kassander's generals). Points out evidence which may be cause for re-attributing some coins, or for confirming previously tentative attributions. Concludes that the 3:00 die-axis position was used on Herakles/bowcase bronzes of Miletos. Comments on the mint for Poliorketes bronzes. Kaunos should be considered as a candidate for the mint of certain issues. Suggests the mint of Eupolemos perhaps was Kaunos as well. [Mylasa was generally thought to be the mint for his coinage. See Wroth "Eupolemus" under CARIA. Also see Ashton "Kaunos, not Miletos or Mylasa" under CARIA].

3313 **Ashton, Richard, Mevlut Uyumez, and Ugur Hosgören.** "Five Alexander Hoards in Afyon Museum." *Numismatic Chronicle* 156 (1996): 259-68. 6 pls.

The Afyon museum in Phrygia possesses five hoards containing coins struck in the names of Alexander the Great, Philip Arrhidaeus, and Lysimachus. Summaries of the hoards' contents are given.

3314 **Babington, Churchill.** "On an Unpublished Tetradrachm of Alexander III, Struck at Rhodes; with Some Observations on the Rhodian Symbol, and Other Matters Connected with Rhodes." *Numismatic Chronicle* new ser., 4 (1864): 1-6.

Discusses an Alexander tetradrachm which bears the rose symbol of Rhodes and a monogram which the author reads as ΑΙΝΤΩΡ. The reading of the monogram is based on the evidence of another coin which bears this name spelled-out.

3315 **Bauslaugh, Robert A.** "The Posthumous Alexander Coinage of Chios." *Museum Notes* 24 (1979): 1-45. 17 pls. [CS 2333]

Re-examines the Alexander-type coinage at Chios based on a study of about 325 drachms, tetradrachms, and staters. Diagrams the sequence of all known dies and indicates links. The coins are grouped into four periods: ca. 280-270 B.C., 270-220 B.C., 202/1-190 B.C., and 190-160 B.C. Each period is discussed. Lists thirty-four hoards which contained Alexander coins of Chios.

3316 **Bellinger, Alfred R.** "An Alexander Hoard from Byblos." *Berytus* (Denmark) 10 (1952-3): 37-49. 1 pl.

Re-examines a hoard of 140 tetradrachms of Alexander the Great and Philip III found at Byblos. Arranges the coins by mint and adds observations on the significance of the hoard which was buried ca. 309 B.C.

3317 ——— "The Drachmae of Alexander the Great." *American Journal of Archaeology* 59, no. 2 (April 1955): 170.

A brief summary of a paper Bellinger presented at a meeting of the American Philological Association in 1954. Hoard evidence shows that in the fourth century B.C., most of the drachmae used throughout Alexander's empire were minted by seven mints in Asia Minor. These mints also struck gold staters but rarely struck tetradrachms. The reasons for this must be economic rather than political.

3318 ——— *Essays on the Coinage of Alexander the Great.* Numismatic Studies, No. 11. New York: American Numismatic Society, 1963. Reprint, New York: Sanford J. Durst, 1979. 132 pp., 3 pls. [CS 2334].

Reviews various theories for the identification and origins of the Athena and Nike on Alexander's gold staters, the Herakles and Zeus on the silver coinage, and the Herakles and bow on the bronze coinage. Recounts the debate over whether the Herakles head was intended to portray Alexander himself. No firm conclusion is reached. Also summarizes the debate over the meaning of the symbols found in the fields of Alexander's coins and concludes that most refer to mint officials, while some are mintmarks. Discusses denominations, weights, and gold-to-silver ratios. Discusses the finances of the Macedonian Kingdom, the currency system, and the expansion of Alexander's mint system. Describes the changes in the coinage after Alexander's death and the distribution of his mints among his successors. Presents a chronology of historical events which are important to the study of the coinage of Alexander and his successors. Includes a bibliography and photographs of the major coin types. [Reviewed by R. A. G. Carson in *Times Literary Supplement* (November 14, 1963): 934, by G. K. Jenkins in *Numismatic Chronicle* 7th ser., 4 (1964): 339-41, and by W. Schwabacher in *Gnomon* (Germany) 37 (1965): 83-7].

3319 **Berk, Harlan J.** "A New Distater of Alexander." *The Celator* 7, no. 5 (May 1993): 6-7. Illus.

Describes a new variety of Alexander's gold distater on which the reverse figure of Nike is shown running with her chiton flowing, rather than standing as is usually found on these coins. The coin is die-linked to a standing Nike type. Suggests the running type was rejected in favor of the standing type.

3320 **Bing, J. Daniel.** "Reattribution of the Myriandrus Alexanders: The Case for Issus." *American Journal of Numismatics* 2nd ser., 1 (1989): 1-32. 2 pls., map.

Examines the Persian staters and obols without mintmarks which Newell attributed to Myriandrus (see Newell "Myriandros—Alexandria Kat'isson" below). Bing attributes these to Issus based on its geographical setting and the evidence of Persian administrative arrangements in Cilicia and Syria.

3321 **Boehringer, Christof.** "Beobachtungen und Überlegungen zu den Ären der Pamphylischen Alexandreier." *Travaux de Numismatique Grecque Offerts à Georges Le Rider.* Edited by M. Amandry and S. Hurter. London: Spink, 1999. Pages 65-75. 3 pls.

Examines the Alexander-type coinage struck at Phaselis, Perge, and Aspendos in Pamphylia.

3322 **Brace, Bruce R.** "An Interesting Variety." *The Anvil* (Canada) 8, no. 2 (June 1998): 30. Illus.

Reports a new variety of an Alexander-type tetradrachm in the McMaster Museum of Art. The reverse of the coin is similar to *Price* 441, although the McMaster coin lacks the cross-strut to the legs of the throne beneath the monogram. [Also see *The Anvil* 8, no. 3 (September 1998): 45, for a correction related to the monogram and inscription on the coin].

3323 **Breitenstein, Niels.** "Studies in the Coinages of the Macedonian Kings." *Acta Archaeologica* (Denmark) 13 (1942): 242-58. Illus.
Examines coins in the Royal Collection at Copenhagen to provide new information on the coinage of Philip II and Alexander the Great. Describes double staters of gold with Philip's types, some Gallic-style gold double staters of Philip, a gold stater (probably of Philip III) with the inscription ΒΑΣΙΛΕΟΣ. Discusses tetradrachms of Alexander attributed to Uranopolis, and tetradrachms attributed to Mesembria, Babylon, and Chios, as well as an obol and triobol from Aradus.

3324 **Brett, Agnes Baldwin.** "Philip of Macedon's Race Horse, Winner at the Olympic Games, 356 B.C." *Numismatic Review* 1 (1943): 5-7. Illus.
Points out that the "jockey on horseback" scene on the tetradrachms of Philip II is the only equestrian type which is known to refer to a particular event. Brett notes that on some early specimens, both the rider and the horse are crowned with the fillet, a symbol of victory. Illustrates a similar scene on a Panathenaic amphora.

3325 **Bunbury, Edward H.** "On Some Unpublished Tetradrachms of Alexander the Great." *Spink Numismatic Circular* 42, no. 4 (1868). Also in *Numismatic Chronicle* new ser., 8 (1868): 309-20.
Publishes a number of broad, spread-flan tetradrachms not listed by Müller or von Prokesch-Osten. Includes coins from the following mints: Kyme, Temnos, Miletus (or Heraclea), Smyrna, Teos, Rhodes, and one uncertain.

3326 ——— "Additional Tetradrachms of Alexander the Great." *Numismatic Chronicle* 3rd ser., 3 (1883): 1-17. 2 pls.
Lists and discusses Alexander tetradrachms not listed by Müller, including coins attributed to Cos, Smyrna, and Sicyon. Also includes photographs of coins discussed in Bunbury's previous article (see "On Some Unpublished Tetradrachms" above).

3327 **Burnett, Andrew M., Ute Wartenberg, and Richard Witschonke, eds.** *Coins of Macedonia and Rome: Essays in Honour of Charles Hersh.* London: Spink, 1998. 229 pp., 34 pls.
A collection of essays on Macedonian and Roman Republican coins written in honor of Charles A. Hersh on the occasion of his seventy-fifth birthday. Includes ten essays on Macedonian numismatics and twelve on Roman Republican numismatics. All are in English. The Macedonian essays are: "The Coinage of King Derdas and the History of the Elimiote Dynasty" by K. Liampi [3263], "Philotas? A New Coinage from Macedonia" by U. Wartenberg [3305], "The Coins of the Macedonian Kings, Lysimachos and Eupolemos in the Museums of Fethiye and Afyon" by R. Ashton [3312], "Alexander in Asia Minor" by G. Le Rider [3399], "The 'Ain Tab Hoard (*IGCH* 1542)" by W. Metcalf [3423], "Ants and Eagles: Some Late Alexander Staters from Amphipolis" by H. Troxell [3520], "Back to the Future. Alexander the Great's Silver and Gold in the Balkans: The Hoard Evidence" by Y. Touratsoglou [3514], "Two Hoards of Minor Silver" by A. Spaer [780], "Lions and Lionesses, Eagles and a Few Heads: A New Uncertain Mint in Caria" by S. Hurter [599], and "The Coins in the Name of Sura" by F. de Callataÿ [3573]. Also includes a bibliography of Hersh's published writings compiled by Francis D. Campbell.

3327a **Burrer, F.** "Die Tetradrachmenprägung Philipps V. von Makedonien Serie II." *Jahrbuch für Numismatik und Geldgeschichte* (Germany) 59 (2009): 1-70.

3328 **Cancio, Leopoldo.** "A Cowrie Shell Symbol on an Alexander Tetradrachm." *Spink Numismatic Circular* 98, no. 3 (April 1990): 85-86. Illus.
Illustrates an Alexander tetradrachm with a cowrie shell symbol in the left field of the reverse—a previously unknown variety. [A correction in the positioning of the illustrations for this article appears in *Spink Numismatic Circular* 98, no. 5 (June 1990): 159].

3329 **Cheek, Kevin R.** "Demetrios Poliorcetes: Theatrical Mentality Defines Coinage." *The Celator* 5, no. 9 (September 1991): 6-7.
Discusses the reign and coinage of the Macedonian king Demetrios Poliorcetes. Suggests that his theatrical mentality was a reflection of the Hellenistic mind-set and helped to equate him with Alexander the Great. Describes how Demetrios used coinage as propaganda to further his political ambition.

3330 **Cordova, Simon.** "Dating the Silver Coinage of Alexander the Great." *SAN—Journal of the Society for Ancient Numismatics* 12, no. 1 (spring 1981): 6-8.
Presents a means of chronological classification for the silver coins of Alexander III. Briefly describes Müller's seven classes. The author then describes his own three broad classes: (1) right leg of Zeus visible in front of left leg, ca. 336-300 B.C.; (2) right leg of Zeus bent back behind left leg, standard size coins in fine style, ca. 323-270 B.C.; (3) right leg bent back behind left leg, poor style, low relief, sometimes on large flans, ca. 250-50 B.C.

3331 ——— "Some Drachms of Alexander the Great." Parts 1-2. *SAN—Journal of the Society for Ancient Numismatics* 14, no. 3 (fall 1983): 57-58; 15, no. 4 (winter 1984-5): 70, 78. Illus.
These articles describe silver drachms of Alexander the Great which are not among the 357 drachms listed by Müller. Photographs are included along with weights, diameters, die orientation, and complete descriptions.

3332 **Dahmen, Karsten.** *The Legend of Alexander the Great on Greek and Roman Coins.* London & New York: Routledge, 2007, 179 pp., illus.
Examines the posthumous appreciation of Alexander's legend by Hellenistic kings, Greek cities, and Roman emperors, combining an introduction to the historical background and basic information on the coins with a comprehensive study of Alexander's numismatic iconography. Items include Poros medallions, Egyptian bronzes from Memphis and Naukratis, Diodochi coins of Ptolemy, Seleukos, and Lysimachos, Aesillas tetradrachms, Koinon of Macedonia bronzes, Aboukir medallions, and Roman contorniates, and others. [Reviewed by R. Goldsborough in *The Celator* 21, no. 12 (December 2007): 38-40, by Stanley Ireland in *Bryn Mawr Classical Review* 2007.07.55, and by Oliver Hoover in *American Numismatic Society Magazine* 6, no. 3 (winter 2007): 61-5].

3333   de Callataÿ, François. "Certains Alexandres de Mésembria et le Problème des Imitations." *Cahiers Numismatiques* (France) 24, no. 91 (1987): 238-42.

3334   ——— "Les Derneirs Alexandres Posthumes frappes a Odessos et Mésembria." *Studies on the Settlement Life of Ancient Thrace. Proceedings of the Third International Symposium "Cabyle," 17-23 May, 1993.* Jambol, 1994. Pages 300-42.

3335   de Callataÿ, François, and I. Prokopov. "A Late Alexander of Mesembria Overstruck over Athens." *Spink Numismatic Circular* 102, no. 4 (April 1994): 207. Illus.
"The authors publish a late tetradrachm of Alexander of Mesembria overstruck on a tetradrachm of Athens. This piece belongs to the Rudnik hoard (near Burgas in Bulgaria). The Athenian tetradrachm dates to ca. 123/2 B.C." [de Calataÿ and Prokopov, *NL* 134]

3336   DeShazo, Alan S. "A New Die for Sidonian Chronology." *The Celator* 20, no. 7 (July 2006): 27, 26. Illus.
Illustrates a tetradrachm of Alexander the Great from the Sidon mint, struck from a newly discovered reverse die. The die, dated Year 10 (325/4 B.C.), depicts Zeus with uncrossed legs. The obverse die of this coin was previously used with reverse dies dated Years 7 and 8. At Sidon, the transition from uncrossed to crossed legs of Zeus happened before Alexander's death in 323 B.C. DeShazo claims that the new die variety confirms that the change took place during Year 10. [Also see the author's "Letter to the Editor" in *The Celator* 20, no. 11 (November 2006): 4, in which he discusses a coin in the American Numismatic Society collection on which the reverse die has been altered from year *heth* to *teth*. His conclusion remains unchanged. Also see the "Letter to the Editor" by Edward Cohen in *The Celator* 21, no. 3 (March 2007): 38, and by DeShazo in *The Celator* 21, no. 5 (May 2007): 4].

3337   DeWaele, F. J. "The Greek Stoa North of the Temple at Corinth." *American Journal of Archaeology* 35 (1931): 394-423. 1 pl.
"On pp. 418-20 a preliminary account is given of a hoard of fifty-one gold coins of Philip and Alexander the Great, and all the coins are illustrated. An attempt is made to assign them to their respective mints." [J. R. Jones, *NIAJAH*]. [Also see Edwards and Thompson "A Hoard" below].

3338   Dimitrov, Kamen. "Notes on Some Alexander Coinages from the Early Hellenistic Period: (Seleucia on the Tigris, Marathus, Laodicea ad Mare, Antioch on the Orontes)." *Proceedings of the 10th International Congress of Numismatics, London, 1986.* International Association of Professional Numismatists Publication, No. 11. Edited by I. A. Carradice. London: International Association of Professional Numismatists, 1986. Pages 17-22. 1 pl.
Examines twelve Alexander-type drachms and tetradrachms from *IGCH* 859, buried ca. 270-265 B.C., bearing the names of Alexander the Great, Philip III, Seleucus I, and Antiochus I. Includes a tetradrachm of Philip III Arridaeus attributed to Seleucia, and a tetradrachm of Antiochus I struck in the name of Alexander.

3339   ——— "Trésor Avec des Monnaies de Bronze de Philippe II, etc." *Archaeologia* (Bulgaria) 28 (1986): 32-40.

3340   ——— "Early Hellenistic Hoards of Alexander-type Silver Coins from the Museum of History and Art in Varna." *Études Balkaniques* (Bulgaria) 3 (1989): 87-110.

3341   Djukov, Y. L., T. N. Smekalova, A. V. Mel'Nikov, and N. M. Vecherukhin. "Studies of Silver Coins of Alexander of Macedon from the Collection of the State Hermitage." *Liber Amicorum Tony Hackens.* Numismatica Lovaniensia 20. Edited by G. Moucharte, M. B. Borba Florenzano, F. de Callataÿ, P. Marchetti, L. Smolderen, and P. Yannopoulos. Louvain-la-Neuve: Université Catholique de Louvain, 2007. Pages 87-94.
Over 600 silver coins in the Hermitage were analyzed to determine the level of copper, gold, and lead they contain. The authors suggest that the alloys used for coins struck in known mints can be compared with those used at uncertain mints and may be able to provide a geographic link. [Reviewed by A. S. Walker in *The Celator* 22, no. 8 (August 2008): 35-7, 40, 56].

3342   Dodson, Oscar H. "The Coins of Alexander." *Coinage* 2, no. 3 (March 1966): 54 ff. Illus. Also in *Coinage* 8, no. 4 (April 1972): 33 ff.
"Alexander's military campaigns, his mints and coinage are described." [O. Dodson, *NL* 82]

3342a   Dorsey, P. F. "The Posthumous Alexander Tetradrachms of Odessos." *Jahrbuch für Numismatik und Geldgeschichte* (Germany) (1991).

3342b   Draganov, Dimitar. *Monetite na Makedonskite Tsare. Ch. 1. Om Aleksandur I do Aleksandut Veliki.* Jambol, 2000.
The Coins of the Macedonian Kings, Part 1: From Alexander I to Alexander the Great.

3343   Duane, Matthew. *Coins of the Kings of Macedonia, from Amyntas I to Alexander the Great.* Engravings by F. Bartolozzi. London, no date (circa 1780).
A catalogue of coins from the author's collection.

3344   Eaglen, Robin J. "Portraits of Greek Coinage 5: Perseus." *Spink Numismatic Circular* 113, no. 4 (August 2005): 248. Illus.
In this installment of the author's on-going series, Eaglen examines the coinage of Perseus. Reviews the history and coin types.

3345   ——— "Portraits of Greek Coinage 8: Philip II of Macedon (359-336 B.C.)." *Spink Numismatic Circular* 114, no. 1 (February 2006): 7-8. Illus.
In this installment of the author's on-going series, Eaglen examines the coinage of Philip II. Reviews the history and coin types.

3346   ——— "Portraits of Greek Coinage 28: Demetrius I Poliorcetes ('The Beseiger')." *Spink Numismatic Circular* 117, no. 3 (July 2009): 101-2. Illus.
In this installment of the author's on-going series, Eaglen examines the history and coinage of Demetrius Poliorcetes.

3347   ——— "Portraits of Greek Coinage 32: Antigonus III Doson ("the Giver") (229-221 B.C.)." *Spink Numismatic Circular* 118, no. 2 (May 2010): 68. Illus.

In this installment of the author's on-going series, Eaglen examines the coinage of Antigonus Doson.

3348 **Edwards, G. Roger, and Margaret Thompson.** "A Hoard of Gold Coins of Philip and Alexander from Corinth." *American Journal of Archaeology* 74, no. 4 (October 1970): 343-50. 4 pls. [CS 2326]
A hoard consisting of fifty-one gold staters of Philip and Alexander and a gold necklace was discovered during excavations in 1930. Edwards reports on the black-glazed saucer which contained the hoard. Thompson presents a catalogue of the coins and a discussion of their chronology. Both concluded that burial took place in the second half of Alexander's reign, perhaps ca. 327 B.C. [Also see DeWaele "The Greek Stoa" above].

3349 **Ehrhardt, Christopher.** "The Coins of Cassander." *Journal of Numismatic Fine Arts* 2, no. 2 (summer 1973): 25-32. Illus. [CS 2355]
Summarizes the historical background of Macedonia from the death of Alexander the Great in 323 B.C., through the reign of Cassander, and until Demetrius the Besieger took the Macedonian throne in 294. Cassander struck bronze coins in his own name, probably beginning in 311 B.C. Discusses the various coin types, their chronology, and mint attributions. Silver coins were also struck during Cassander's reign, but all bear the name and type of Alexander or Philip II. Ehrhardt reviews the hoard evidence in an attempt to assign certain issues to Cassander's reign. Discusses die links among groups of coins.

3350 ———. "A Catalogue of Issues of Tetradrachms from Amphipolis, 318-294 B.C." *Journal of Numismatic Fine Arts* 4, no. 4 (March 1976): 85-9.
A catalogue of Alexander-type tetradrachm issues from the Amphipolis mint struck during the reigns of Cassander and his sons. Lists sixty-nine varieties, arranged into eight stylistic and chronological groups. Discusses die links and the chronology of the groups. Lists fourteen hoards with significant numbers of Amphipolis coins buried before 294 B.C., when Amphipolis ceased producing Alexander types.

3351 **Elayi, Josette.** "Un Trésor de Tétradrachmes aux Types d'Alexandre Trouvé dans la Beqa." *Travaux de Numismatique Grecque Offerts à Georges Le Rider.* Edited by M. Amandry and S. Hurter. London: Spink, 1999. Pages 135-8. 1 pl.
Discusses forty tetradrachms of Alexander the Great found in Lebanon in 1995.

3352 **Elder, Thomas.** *Remarkable Collection of Greek Tetradrachms. Three Hundred Silver Coins of Alexander the Great. Unearthed During the Spring of 1908, at Demanhur, Near Alexandria, Egypt.* New York, undated (ca. 1911). 6 pls.
Well-known dealer Thomas Elder printed these six monochrome plates (16 ½" x 17 ½") illustrating 300 tetradrachms of Alexander the Great from the Demanhur hoard. About 150 different monograms/mint-marks are represented. Look for the one Ptolemaic tetradrachm (not from the Demanhur hoard) hidden among these coins!

3353 **Emerson, A.** "The Portraiture of Alexander the Great: a Terracotta Head in Munich." *American Journal of Archaeology* 2 (1886): 408-13
"An introductory chapter, collecting the literary evidence for portraits of Alexander." [J. R. Jones, *NIAJAH*]

3354 ———. "The Portraiture of Alexander the Great: a Terracotta Head in Munich. 2." *American Journal of Archaeology* 3 (1887): 243-60. 2 pls.
"On pp. 245-6 it is noted that later Greeks believed that Alexander's coins preserved his portrait; but the writer feels that even in the case of the Heracles heads there is only an occasional approximation to his features." [J. R. Jones, *NIAJAH*]

3355 **Erim, Kenan T., and David J. MacDonald.** "A Hoard of Alexander Drachms from Aphrodisias." *Numismatic Chronicle* 7th ser., 14 (1974): 174-6. 1 pl.
A hoard of eleven Alexander drachms was discovered in 1969 on the outskirts of ancient Aphrodisias, ten of which are published here. Six are from the Colophon mint. The others are from Miletus, Sardes, Teos, and Abydus. The coins were buried about the last decade of the fourth century B.C.

3356 **Finn, D. J.** "The Chigi Athena." *Journal of Hellenic Studies* 32 (1912): 43-56. Illus., 1 pl.
"On pp. 50-1 it is noted that the figure of Poseidon which appears as one of the subsidiary decorations is reminiscent of the Poseidon on a coin of Demetrius Poliorcetes; the wide circulation of this coin probably did much to fix the type." [J. R. Jones, *NIJHS*]

3357 **Franke, Peter R.** "Zur Finanzpolitik des Makedonischen Königs Perseus während des Krieges mit Rom, 171-168 v. Chr." *Jahrbuch für Numismatik und Geldgeschichte* (Germany) 8 (1957): 31-50. [CS 2360]

3358 ———. "Η Μακεδονια Και Τα Νομισματα Τησ." *Nomismatika Khronika* (Greece) 1 (1972): 22-36. Illus.
A general survey of the history of ancient Macedonia with a description of its coins issued by the tribes and kings until the time of Roman domination. Franke discusses the use of coins as the personal propaganda of the rulers—helping to safeguard and extend their power. He also calls for the publication of a comprehensive catalogue of Macedonian coins. In Greek, with an English summary on page 36.

3359 **Gaebler, Hugo.** "Zur Münzkunde Makedoniens." *Zeitschrift für Numismatik* (Germany) (1897): 169-92, 289-99; (1902): 141-89; (1904): 245-338; (1906): 1-38; (1925): 193-216; (1926): 183-99; (1927): 223-53; (1929): 255-70. [CS 2311]

3360 **Gardiakos, Soterios, ed.** *The Coinages of Alexander the Great.* Three volumes. Chicago: Obol International, 1981. 1007 pp., 157 pls.
A compilation of papers by leading experts of the nineteenth and early twentieth centuries in their original languages—Greek, English, French, and German. Includes Alfred Bellinger's "Essays on the Coinage of Alexander the Great;" Gerhard Kleiner's "Alexanders Reichsmünzen;" the complete text of C. L. Müller's "Numismatique d'Alexandre le Grand" including his tables of all known mintmarks of Philip II, Alexander III, and Philip III; E. T. Newell's "Reattribution of Certain Tetradrachms of Alexander" which updates some of the attributions of Müller; Newell's "Some Cypriote Alexanders," "The Dated Alexander Coinage of Sidon and Ake," "Tarsos under Alexander," "The Alexandrine Coinage of Sinope," and "Myriandros–Alexandria Kat'Isson." Also includes Heinrich Dressel's "Fuenf Goldmedallions aus dem funde von Abukir" (Five Gold Medallions from the Find of Abukir), J. N. Svoronos' "The Medallions of Aboukir," as well as Sydney P. Noe's "The Alexander Coinage of Sicyon."

3361 **Gibson, Thomas L.** "The Silver and Bronze Mints of Philip II and Alexander the Great in Macedonia." *The Celator* 25, no. 6 (June 2011): 6-22. Illus.

Gibson attempts to attribute groups of silver and bronze coins to particular mints based upon stylistic characteristics, types, and monograms. Numerous coins are described which he attributes to the "main" Macedonian mint (likely Pella) during six time periods, and to an eastern Macedonian mint (likely Amphipolis) during five time periods. Numerous coins are illustrated.

3362 **Goldsborough, Reid.** "Misattribution of Alexander III Tetradrachms." *The Celator* 16, no. 1 (January 2002): 20-4. Illus.
Collectors often assume that all tetradrachms of Alexander the Great which bear an image of Zeus with open legs on the reverse were struck during Alexander's lifetime, and that all issues showing Zeus with crossed legs are posthumous issues. While this is often the case, Goldsborough presents some statistics, based on Price's *Coinage in the Name of Alexander*, to show that this is not always true. The author presents counts and percentages of the exceptions.

3363 **Gomer, John L.** "Apollo, Herakles and Wolf: Macedonian Myths on Coins of Archelaus." *The Celator* 12, no. 3 (March 1998): 14-6. Illus.
Gomer begins with a brief history of the Macedonian Kingdom during the reign of King Archelaus (413-399 B.C.). He then discusses the innovations Archelaus brought to the Macedonian coinage. In an attempt to improve the reputation of Macedonia as a civilized Greek state, Archelaus introduced new coin designs which promoted Macedonian foundation myths. He was the first Macedonian king to use Greek gods on his coins including Apollo and Herakles. He introduced the wolf on coins—previous kings used the horse, lion, or goat. The author discusses the reasons for depicting the wolf. [Also see Westermark "Apollo in Macedonia" below].

3364 **Gottschewski, Gerhard.** *Die Münze als Politisches Werkzeug in der Hand Philipp II und Alexander des Grossen.* Minden: Münzfreunde Minden, 1975. 40 pp., illus. [CS 2327]

3365 **Greenwalt, William S.** "The Iconographical Significance of Amyntas III's Mounted Hunter Stater." *Ancient Macedonia: Fifth International Symposium, Volume 1.* Thessaloniki (Greece): Institute for Balkan Studies, 1993. Pages 509-19. 1 pl.
Focuses on a stater of Amyntas II (the father of Philip II) bearing a full horse and rider on the obverse who is depicted as hunting the lion depicted on the reverse. The author interprets this type as a potent symbol of political legitimacy which linked the Argead notion of kingship to that of other northern peoples. Examines the numismatic reforms of Archelaus (d. 399 B.C.) who introduced a new weight standard and larger denominations. Suggests that Amyntas' rider type established a bond with the memory of Alexander, Perdiccas, and Archelaus while rejecting any connection with the kings between Archelaus and Amyntas. This was intended to link Amyntas' reign to that of successful royal predecessors, since his claim to the Argead throne was weak.

3366 **Hammond, Nicholas G. L.** "The Coinages of Tribes, Cities, and Kings, c. 550-480." *A History of Macedonia, Volume 2: 550-336 B.C.*, by N. G. L. Hammond and G. T. Griffith. Oxford: Clarendon Press, 1979. Pages 69-91. 1 pl.
In this discussion of early Macedonian coinage, the author relates the coins to their historical context, and emphasizes the centers of mineral ores in Macedonia. Hoard evidence is used and much important information is given for the dating of this coinage.

3367 ———— "The Coinage of Alexander and Other Balkan Kings." *A History of Macedonia, Volume 2: 550-336 B.C.*, by N. G. L. Hammond and G. T. Griffith. Oxford: Clarendon Press, 1979. Pages 104-15. 2 pls.
Hammond makes use of hoard evidence and discusses the meaning of the coin types. Special attention is given to the coinage of Alexander I (died 452 B.C.).

3368 ———— "The Lettering and the Iconography of 'Macedonian' Coinage." *Ancient Greek Art and Iconography.* Edited by Warren G. Moon. Madison: University of Wisconsin Press, 1983. Pages 245-58. Illus.
An overview of Macedonian coinage including the 'Lete' coinage, coins of the Bisaltae, and coins of the Macedonian kings. Focuses on the inscriptions on the coins and their iconography. Illustrated by line drawings of coins.

3369 **Hands, Alfred Watson.** "Common Greek Coins: The Coinage of Alexander the Great." *Spink Numismatic Circular* 13 (January 1905): 8057-63.
Discusses the symbolism of the obverse and reverse types of the coinage of Alexander as well as the use of the title ΒΑΣΙΛΕΥΣ.

3370 ———— "Common Greek Coins: The Classification of the Tetradrachms." *Spink Numismatic Circular* 13 (February 1905): 8121-9. Illus.
Classifies the tetradrachms of Alexander into three groups based upon fabric, type, and size, thoroughly describing the characteristics of each group. Arranges Müller's seven classifications into these three groups. Provides dates for each classification. Also briefly discusses the dated coins, weight standards, and some bronze coins.

3371 ———— "Common Greek Coins: The Coinage of Alexander the Great, 336-334 B.C." *Spink Numismatic Circular* 13 (April 1905): 8251-7.
Describes the coinage Alexander, lists the symbols found on the coins and attributes each to a city. Discusses the use of magistrate's names on the coins.

3372 **Hardy, David B.** "An Unpublished Tetradrachm of Alexander the Great." *North American Journal of Numismatics: The Turtle* 6, no. 5 (May 1967): 147-9. Illus.
Describes a previously unpublished tetradrachm which the author attributes to the mint at Side. The reverse contains a Corinthian helmet symbol and the letters ΔΙ.

3373 **Head, Barclay V.** "Coinage of Alexander the Great: An Explanation." *Numismatic Chronicle* 3rd ser., 3 (1883): 18-9.
Head clarifies his opinions regarding the interpretation of symbols and monograms on Macedonian coins. He emphasizes that on the regal issues (down to about 280 B.C.), these symbols and letters refer to magistrates. However, on the later city coinages, they often identify the issuing city.

3374 **Heichelheim, Fritz M.** "Numismatic Evidence of the Battle of Lysimachia." *American Journal of Philology* 64 (1943): 332-3.
Describes a Macedonian coin with *obv.*, Macedonian shield with a monogram for "Antigonus," and *rev.*, Macedonian helmet. It was in doubt whether the coins of this type were struck by Antigonus Gonatas or Antigonas Doson. Here, the author publishes a coin of this type which was struck over a coin with *obv.*, head of Athena, and *rev.*, lion. The overstrike suggests that these coins were struck by Gonatas after he had liberated Macedonia from the Celts by his victory in the battle of Lysimachia. The coins were struck to fulfil demand for his coins in the re-gained territory.

3375 **Heintges, E. R.** "Babylonian (?) Alexander Hoard, 1996." *American Journal of Numismatics* 2nd ser., 22 (2010): 17-23. 4 pls.
Presents a hoard of twenty-one imitative Alexandrine tetradrachms with stylistic and control affinities to known official issues (primarily Babylonian) struck in the period ca. 320-311 B.C.

3376 **Herman, Ira.** "Alexander as Herakles: Silver Tetradrachm Portrays Alexander as Mythic Hero." *Coin World* (December 11, 2000): 92. Illus.
Illustrates and discusses an early lifetime tetradrachm of Alexander the Great, attributed as *Price* 4, struck at Amphipolis in 333 B.C. Briefly discusses Alexander and his coinage.

3377 **Hersh, Charles A.** "An Unpublished Coin of Philip II of Macedonia, from His First Issue of Bronzes." *American Journal of Numismatics* 2nd ser., 1 (1989): 33-6. 1 pl.
Presents a bronze coin of Philip II with types which are exactly those of the last issue of bronzes of his brother and predecessor, Perdiccas III.

3378 ——— "A Fifth-Century Circulation Hoard of Macedonian Tetrobols." *Mnemata: Papers in Memory of Nancy M. Waggoner.* Edited by William E. Metcalf. New York: American Numismatic Society, 1991. Pages 3-19. 8 pls.
Describes a fifth century B.C. hoard of 223 tetrobols found in 1989, probably in eastern Macedonia. A brief review of Macedonian history from 510 to 399 B.C. is followed by a detailed listing of the die combinations of the hoard coins. Concordances are given to Raymond's *Macedonian Regal Coinage* (see Raymond below). The weights of the hoard coins and the coins known to Raymond are summarized in a table. The hoard increased by 150% the number of known coins of this denomination. The coins are of a poor alloy. The plates illustrate 159 of the coins.

3379 ——— "Three Unpublished Macedonian Regal Coins of the Decade of the 360's." *Nomismatika Khronika* (Greece) 15 (1996): 7-12. Illus.
Hersh reviews the coinage of the Macedonian Kingdom during the period 450-367 B.C. He then describes a bronze coin attributed to Alexander II, previously the only coin type (*obv.*, Apollo; *rev.*, horse) known to have been issued by this king. He also publishes another bronze coin of Alexander II, but of a different type. This coin is one-half the denomination of the previous coin. The author reviews the reign of Perdiccas III (368-359 B.C.). Describes the rare issues of this king: silver stater, hemidrachm, diobol, and four copper issues. Publishes two previously unknown silver hemi-obols of Perdiccas III.

3380 ——— "Additions and Corrections to Martin J. Price's 'The Coinage in the Name of Alexander the Great and Philip Arrhidaeus.'" *Studies in Greek Numismatics in Memory of Martin Jessop Price.* Edited by Richard Ashton and Silvia Hurter. London: Spink, 1998. Pages 135-44. 1 pl.
Lists ninety-one additions to Martin Price's *The Coinage in the Name of Alexander the Great* (see Price below). Also includes sixty-three brief corrections to the catalogue.

3381 ——— "The Phoenicia 1997 Hoard of Alexander-Type Tetradrachms." *American Journal of Numismatics* 2nd ser., 10 (1998): 37-40.
Lists some of the coins from a hoard which came onto the market in 1997. The hoard was most likely found in Lebanon. The hoard includes issues bearing the names of Alexander, Demetrius Poliorcetes, and Seleucus I. Many mints are represented including Ake, Tyre, Sidon, Byblos, and Kitium, among others.

3382 ——— "A 1992 Hoard of Bronze Coins of Philip II from Beroia in Thrace." *Travaux de Numismatique Grecque Offerts à Georges Le Rider.* Edited by M. Amandry and S. Hurter. London: Spink, 1999. Pages 161-5. 1 pl.
Describes a hoard of sixty-eight bronze coins—sixty-seven of Philip II and one of Alexander III. The hoard was supposedly found in Beroia in south-central Bulgaria. Hersh briefly mentions other hoards which contained bronze coins of Philip II. Then he lists the coins of the Beroia hoard. The coins are cross-referenced to the Drama Hoard (see Bellinger "Philippi in Macedonia" under MACEDONIAN CITIES AND TRIBES). Emphasizes the need for a systematic study of Philip's bronze coinage.

3383 **Hersh, Charles A., and Hyla A. Troxell.** "A 1993 Hoard of Alexander Drachms from the Near East." *American Journal of Numismatics* 2nd ser., 5/6 (1993-94): 13-42. 4 pls.
A hoard of Alexander the Great drachms, found in the Near East, was disbursed into the market in 1993. The authors present a catalogue of the reconstructed hoard. Most of the coins are from Asia Minor mints (53% from Miletus). They compare the composition of the hoard to other similar hoards, and discuss mints and die links. They suggest a burial date ca. 322 B.C. They discuss the implications of this hoard for the coinage of each mint represented. The hoard included some new varieties of Alexander's coinage. [Also see Le Rider "Alexander in Asia Minor" below].

3384 **Hill, George F.** "A Portrait of Perseus of Macedon." *Numismatic Chronicle* 3rd ser., 16 (1896): 34-9. 1 pl.
Publishes a sculpture of a head found at Hadrian's Villa, now in the British Museum. The head was previously thought to be Philip V of Macedon. Hill identifies the head as Perseus, Philip's eldest son, based on a comparison with coin portraits of Perseus.

3385 ——— "Alexander the Great and Persian Lion-Gryphon." *Journal of Hellenic Studies* 43 (1923): 156-61. Illus.
Hill examines the decoration on the bowl of the helmet of Athena on Alexander's gold coinage to determine whether it is purely decorative or has meaning. Varieties of helmet decoration include: (1) no decoration, (2) serpent, (3) sphinx, (4) gryphon with eagle head and straight wing, (5) gryphon with lion head and curved wing. Hill concludes that the lion-gryphon was conceived by Greeks as the enemy of the Persians. This motif was used by Alexander as a symbol of his claim to the sovereignty of Persia. Discusses the place and time of issue of coins bearing the lion-gryphon. Its use was discontinued shortly after Alexander's death.

3386 **Hixenbaugh, Randall.** "The Helmets of Perdikkas II." *The Celator* 24, no. 6 (June 2010): 6-20, 56. Illus.
An illustrated study of ancient Greek bronze helmets, with a comparison to their illustrations on coins of the early Macedonian kings Alexander I, Perkikkas II, and Archelaus. [Also see M. Marotta's "Letter of the Editor" in *The Celator* 24, no. 8 (August 2010): 4, and Hixenbaugh's response in the same issue, pages 4 and 46].

3387 **Holloway, R. Ross.** "Alexander the Great's Choice of Coin Types." *Annali. Istituto Italiano di Numismatica* (Italy) 27-28 (1980-1): 57-60.

"The author believes Alexander the Great's propaganda program to have been simple and direct. Its central focus was to emphasize the harmony between father and son and consequently that of the central power. Also important are the heroic victories of Platea and Salamis." [A. Gabucci, *NL* 109]

3388 **Houghton, Arthur.** "Aradus, Not Marathus." *Studies in Greek Numismatics in Memory of Martin Jessop Price.* Edited by Richard Ashton and Silvia Hurter. London: Spink, 1998. Pages 145-6. Illus.
Martin Price had noted (in *The Coinage in the Name of Alexander the Great*) a die link indicating that posthumous Alexander coins of Marathus and Aradus may have been struck at a single mint. He concluded that there are problems of chronology and attribution in the early posthumous issues of Aradus and Marathus which are yet to be resolved. Houghton examines a group of such coins and lists a group which he believes belongs to Aradus and another group which belongs to Marathus. Die links are indicated as well as probable dates of issue.

3389 **Hurter, Silvia.** "Alexander the Great—A Numismatic Itinerary." *Nomismatika Khronika* (Greece) 5-6 (1978): 35-40. Illus.
An overview of Alexander's military campaigns, highlighting the coins struck in his name at various mints along the way.

3390 **Kallithrakas-Kontos, N., A. Katsanos, G. Blamakis, and Yannis Touratsoglou.** "Composition and Provenance of the Tetradrachms of Alexander the Great." *Coinage in the Macedonian Region. Proceedings of the 2nd Scientific Meeting.* Obolos 4. Edited by P. Adam-Veleni. Thessaloniki: University Studio Press, 2000.
A paper presented at the 2nd Scientific Meeting held in Thessaloniki in May 1998. Text in Greek.

3391 **Kleiner, Fred S.** "The Alexander Tetradrachms of Pergamum and Rhodes." *Museum Notes* 17 (1971): 95-125. 14 pls. [CS 2336]
A re-examination of the spread-flan posthumous Alexander coinage of Pergamum and Rhodes based on a study of 280 specimens. Includes some changes to the attributions suggested by Imhoof-Blumer. Discusses style, die links, and hoard evidence. Reviews the history of Pergamum and Rhodes during the period ca. 205-172 B.C. Concludes that the issuance of Alexander-types, which began at these cities ca. 202 and ended in 189/8 B.C., seems to have been directly dependent on the existence of a brief Attalid-Rhodian alliance. These coins were contemporary with Rhodian autonomous issues and Pergamene regal types and were earmarked for a specific purpose.

3392 **Kleiner, Gerhard.** "Alexanders Reichsmünzen." *Abhandlungen der Deutschen Akademie der Wissenschaften zu Berlin, Phil.-Hist. Klasse, No. 5. 1947.* Berlin, 1949. 55 pp., 1 pl. [CS 2337]
[Also see Zervos "The Earliest Coins of Alexander the Great" below].

3393 ——— "Philipps und Alexanders Münzbildnisse." *Berliner Numismatische Zeitschrift* (Germany) 1 (1949): 5-12. [CS 3530]

3394 **Kremydi-Sicilianou, Sophia.** "The Financing of Alexander's Asian Campaign." *Nomismatika Khronika* (Greece) 18 (1999): 61-8. 1 pl.
Summarizes Alexander's accumulation of wealth as his campaign to liberate the Greek cities of Asia Minor progressed. He began with very little financial resources. The author describes the taxes Alexander imposed in the various cities along his route in order to pay for the upkeep of his troops. Discusses the monetary reforms of Alexander which began after the Battle of Issos was fought in Cilicia in 333 B.C. He soon entrusted some mints with the striking of his own coins. Soon, Alexander had major mints at Amphipolis and Babylon. He thus created a unified currency for his empire. The author explains Alexander's vast accumulation of wealth after conquering the Persian Empire.

3395 **Lagos, Constantinos.** "Posthumous Alexander Type Tetradrachms of Chios and Associated Civic Drachms of the Early Second Century B.C." *Μνημη Martin Jessop Price.* Edited by A. P. Tzamalis and M. J. A. Tzamali. Bibliotheca 5. Athens: The Hellenic Numismatic Society, 1996. Pages 141-4. Illus.
The author summarizes the chronology suggested by Bauslaugh, Kinns, Price, and Mavrogordato for the posthumous Alexander coins of Chios. Suggests that the Alexander-type tetradrachms bearing full magistrate's names, struck during the first half of the second century B.C., were struck contemporaneously with the civic type coinages, and were perhaps even struck by the same moneyers. [Also see Bauslaugh "The Posthumous Alexander Coinage" above, Kinns *Studies in the Coinage of Ionia* under IONIA, Price *The Coinage in the Name of Alexander the Great* below, and Mavrogordato "A Chronological Arrangement" under IONIAN ISLANDS—CHIOS].

3396 **Lederer, Philipp.** "Ein Goldstater Alexanders des Großen." *Zeitschrift für Numismatik* (Germany) 33 (1922): 185-205.

3397 **Le Rider, Georges.** *Le Monnayage d'Or et d'Argent de Philippe II Frappé en Macédoine de 359 à 294 avant J.-C.* Paris, 1977. 484 pp., 95 pls. [CS 2328]

3398 ——— *Monnayage et Finances de Phillipe II: Un État de la Question.* Meletemata 23. Athens, 1996. 108 pp.
[Reviewed by C. Lorber in *Revue Suisse de Numismatique* 78 (1999): 205-9].

3399 ——— "Alexander in Asia Minor." *Coins of Macedonia and Rome: Essays in Honour of Charles Hersh.* Edited by Andrew Burnett, Ute Wartenberg, and Richard Witschonke. London: Spink, 1998. Pages 49-57.
Summarizes the political situation in Asia Minor after Alexander's victory at the Granicus River in 334 B.C. by drawing on the views of other scholars including Tarn, Bickermann, Badian, and others. Concludes that Alexander's arrival in Asia Minor changed little—he retained much of the Persian administrative system. Le Rider attempts to understand Alexander's monetary policies in Asia Minor by examining the coinage struck under Alexander and shortly after his death. Newell and Thompson have shown that part of Alexander's coinage was produced in western Asia Minor. Summarizes their conclusions, as modified by Price, regarding mint locations and dates of issue. Le Rider then reviews Hersh and Troxell's publication of a hoard of 1412 drachms mostly from Asia Minor (see Hersh and Troxell "A 1993 Hoard of Alexander Drachms" above) and their conclusions regarding the dates various mints were active. Le Rider then concludes that the mints of western Asia Minor only began to issue Alexander coinage toward the end of his reign, in 325 B.C. Le Rider states, "The idea of a unique coin—his own—throughout his territories does not seem to have formed part of the conqueror's intentions." Until 325, Alexander left these cities the prerogatives that they had enjoyed under the Persians. They would still have been able to strike their own coins after 334. In 325/4, the monetary situation in western Asia Minor was modified. "Royal money was from now on struck in several mints in the province, and it is plausible that most of these were located in Greek cities." The reasons for these changes were explained by Thompson (see M. Thompson "Paying the Mercenaries" below).

3400 ———— "Les Tétradrachmes Macédoniens d'Alexandre: Réflexions sur leur Classement, le Nombre des Ateliers et les Lieux de Frappe." *Studies in Greek Numismatics in Memory of Martin Jessop Price*. Edited by Richard Ashton and Silvia Hurter. London: Spink, 1998. Pages 237-45. Map, 1 pl.

3401 ———— *Alexandre le Grande: Monnaie, Finances, et Politique*. 2003. 384 pp., 3 maps, 8 pls.
[Also see the English translation below. Reviewed by Y. Touratsoglou in *Revue Suisse de Numismatique* 83 (2004): 180-92, and by Hadrien Rambach in *Spink Numismatic Circular* 113, no. 1 (February 2005): 18-9].

3402 ———— *Alexander the Great: Coinage, Finances, and Policy*. Translated by W. E. Higgins. Philadelphia: American Philosophical Society, 2007. 272 pp., 3 maps, 8 pls.
An English translation of Le Rider's *Alexandre le Grande: Monnaie, Finances, et Politique* (see above) incorporating corrections and updates. An in-depth treatment of Alexander's coinage and finances. The discussion of coinage focuses on the lifetime silver and gold issues, and includes discussion of the owl imitative issues, the lion staters, and the rare "elephant medallions." LeRider explains how Alexander's campaigns and conquests impacted the finances of his empire and its coinage. He reviews the current research and asks questions that cause one to rethink the accepted theories of other numismatists. [Reviewed by R. Goldsborough in *The Celator* 23, no. 8 (August 2009): 38-40].

3403 **Liampi, Katerini.** "Zur Chronologie der Sogenannten 'Anonymen' Makedonischen Münzen des Späten 4 Jhdts. v. Chr." *Jahrbuch für Numismatik und Geldgeschichte* (Germany) 36 (1986): 41-66. 3 pls.

3404 ———— "A Hoard of Bronze Coins of Alexander the Great." *Studies in Greek Numismatics in Memory of Martin Jessop Price*. Edited by Richard Ashton and Silvia Hurter. London: Spink, 1998. Pages 247-53. 2 pls.
A hoard of forty bronze coins (dichalka) of Alexander was discovered somewhere east of the Strymon. The coins fall into two groups: one inscribed with Alexander's name, the other bearing only the royal title. Presents a catalogue of the hoard coins. Discusses other hoards of similar coins. Discusses the chronology and mint attribution of the coins. [Also see W. J. Winter "A Fourth Century B.C. Hoard" below].

3405 ———— "The Circulation of Bronze Macedonian Royal Coins in Thessaly." *From the Parts to the Whole. Volume 1: Acta of the 13th International Bronze Congress, held at Cambridge, Massachusetts, May 28-June 1, 1996*. Journal of Roman Archaeology Supplementary Series 39. Edited by Carol C. Mattusch, Amy Brauer, and Sandra E. Knudsen. Portsmouth, Rhode Island, 2000. Pages 220-5.
The author examined 10,000 published coins of Thessalian origin to get a picture of the spread of Macedonian bronze coins into Thessaly proportionally by king. The results are summarized in two charts, showing the frequency of coins from Archelaus through Perseus.

3406 **Lykiardopoulou, Marina, and Selene Psoma**. "Regal Silver Macedonian Coinage (413-360): Metal Analysis and Historical Approach." *Coinage in the Macedonian Region. Proceedings of the 2nd Scientific Meeting*. Obolos 4. Edited by P. Adam-Veleni. Thessaloniki: University Studio Press, 2000.
A paper presented at the 2nd Scientific Meeting held in Thessaloniki in May 1998.

3407 **Lykiardopoulou-Petrou, Marina, and George Economou.** "The Debased Silver Coins of Amyntas III." *Metallurgy in Numismatics, Volume 4*. Special Publication No. 30. London: Royal Numismatic Society, 1998. Pages 161-70, including 2 pls.
A metallurgical analysis of the silver coins of Amyntas II, father of Philip II of Macedon, reveals that the triobol and most Type A staters of Amyntas III are silver-plated on a copper core, while the Type B staters are silver.

3408 **Mamroth, Alfred.** "Die Silbermünzen des Königs Perseus von Makedonien." *Zeitschrift für Numismatik* (Germany) 38 (1928): 1-28. [CS 2361]

3409 ———— "Die Silbermünzen des Königs Philippos V von Makedonien." *Zeitschrift für Numismatik* (Germany) 40 (1930): 277-303. [CS 2358]

3410 ———— "Die Bronzemünzen des Königs Philippos V von Makedonien." *Zeitschrift für Numismatik* (Germany) 42 (1935): 219-51. [CS 2359]

3411 ———— "Die Tetradrachmen des König Philippos II von Makedonien." *Berliner Numismatische Zeitschrift* (Germany) 1 (1949): 13-6. [CS 2329]

3412 **Manton, Gavin.** "Coins and History: Alexander the Great 336-323 B.C." *Seaby Coin and Medal Bulletin* 682 (June 1975): 188-91. Illus.
A brief biography of Alexander the Great.

3413 **Mathisen, Ralph W.** "The Shield/Helmet Bronze Coinage of Macedonia: A Preliminary Analysis." *SAN—Journal of the Society for Ancient Numismatics* 10, no. 1 (winter 1979): 2-6.
Over 250 Macedonian bronze coins of the shield and helmet type were analyzed. The coins are classified based upon the monograms and some attributions to Macedonian kings are suggested. The series as a whole is attributed to Macedonia or the northern Aegean coast, ca. 294-270 B.C.

3414 ———— "Antigonus Gonatas and the Silver Coinages of Macedonia circa 280-270 B.C." *Museum Notes* 26 (1981): 79-124. 6 pls.
Examines the Alexander-type Macedonian silver coinage minted after 280 B.C. Organizes these issues into eight groups based on style, symbols, and die links. Describes the characteristics of each group and their relationships to the other groups. Suggests mint attributions and dates for each group based on a study of the coins and the history of the period 288-270 B.C. Discusses the introduction of the Pan head tetradrachms under Antigonus Gonatas, his silver resources and coinage output, and his scarce issue of Alexander-type tetradrachms. Concludes the Pan head coins were issued ca. 271-265 B.C. Includes frequency tables of weights for some of the issues under discussion.

3415 ——— "The Administrative Organization of the Mint of Amphipolis in Early Antigonid Macedonia (c. 280-270 B.C.)." Parts 1-3. *SAN—Journal of the Society for Ancient Numismatics* 14, no. 1 (spring 1983): 10-12, 18; no. 2 (summer 1983): 24-27; no. 3 (fall 1983): 44-6.
A die study of several groups of posthumous Alexander tetradrachms struck at Amphipolis. The methods followed in a die study are mentioned. Various types of control-markings are explained, and then a catalogue of the coins is presented and grouped by their control-markings. Full descriptions are given including weights, monograms, die orientation, and provenance. Various theories for the meaning of the control-markings are mentioned. The author speculates on the names which might be represented by some of the monograms. Concludes that the Macedonian mint system was well organized at this time and that control marks may have been used to identify mint officials and the amounts of metal to be turned into coin.

3416 ——— "Variant Coins Prove Interesting Subject." *Coin World* (September 7, 1983): 112-4. Illus.
"The author investigates the circumstances surrounding the production of certain non-standard issues of Antigonus Gonatas' Pan-Head tetradrachms: those with Athena right on the reverse; those reverses with a Ψ or trident; and a unique specimen with the symbol of the Macedonian helmet on the reverse. These were undoubtedly ceremonial issues struck at Pella concurrently with the very large issue of Pan Heads from Amphipolis. Apparently, two die-cutters worked on them." [R. Mathisen, *NL* 111/112]

3417 ——— "Pan Heads and Poseidon Heads: Two Third Century Macedonian Tetradrachm Types." *SAN—Journal of the Society for Ancient Numismatics* 16, no. 2 (summer 1985): 29-35.
A reassessment of I. L. Merker's attribution (see Merker "The Silver Coinage of Antigonos Gonatas" below) of Macedonian tetradrachms with Pan heads to Antigonus Gonatas and those with Poseidon heads to Antigonus Doson. After considering the evidence of hoards and monogram links, the author concludes that Demetrius II may have struck one or both of these types and that the attribution of the Poseidon heads to Doson is not supported by the evidence.

3418 **Merker, Irwin L.** "The Silver Coinage of Antigonos Gonatas and Antigonos Doson." *Museum Notes* 9 (1960): 39-52. [CS 2357]
Discusses the coinage of Antigonos I Monophthalmos, Antigonos II Gonatas, and Antigonos III Doson in an attempt to determine the proper attributions for their coins. Merker assigns the tetradrachms with *obv.*, Macedonian shield with Pan head, *rev.*, Athena Alkidemos, to Gonatas; the tetradrachms with *obv.*, bearded head of Poseidon, *rev.*, Apollo seated on prow of ship, to Doson; and the drachms with *obv.*, Zeus, *rev.*, Athena Alkidemos, to Gonatas. Merker's conclusions differ from that of previous authors. He reviews hoard evidence for these coins. Then he discusses varieties of the Pan head tetradrachms, noting their monograms and suggesting some mint attributions. Then he discusses the mythological and historical significance of the types appearing on the three coin types in this study. [Also see Mathisen "Pan Heads" above].

3419 ——— "Notes on Abdalonymos and the Dated Alexander Coinage of Sidon and Ake." *Museum Notes* 11 (1964): 13-20. [CS 2338]
Reviews Newell's conclusions regarding the chronology of the dated coinage of Sidon and Ake. (1) Focuses on a coin of Sidon with Ptolemaic types which is important for the chronology of the Alexander coinage. The coin is marked X (the Greek *chi*), indicating the twenty-second year of the era (312 B.C. under Newell's system). Condemns Kleiner's theory that Alexander's coinage was first struck after the fall of Tyre in 332/1 B.C. (2) Newell demonstrated that the coins of Ake are dated from 20-39, followed by those dated 8-11, indicating there was a change in the dating system in year 39. Newell equated the year 20 with 326 B.C.; Kleiner suggested 327. Presents hoard evidence suggesting Ake's year 20 was 328/7 B.C. Suggests the era in use at Sidon is an era of Alexander rather than an era of a local king, Abdalonymos. Comments on the reign of this king and the history of Sidon during this period. [Also see Newell *The Dated Alexander Coinage* below, and G. Kleiner "Alexanders Reichsmünzen" above].

3420 ——— "The Ancient Kingdom of Paionia." *Balkan Studies* (Greece) 6 (1965): 35-54. 1 pl., map.
"In this historical prelude to a future numismatic study of Paionia, Merker utilizes the ancient literary sources, epigraphical materials and numismatic evidence to reconstruct a history of the region—*Iliad B*, through the third century B.C.—with special emphasis upon the fourth to third century Kingdom of Paionia." [J. Balcer, *NL* 76]

3421 ——— "Demetrios Poliorcetes and Tyre." *Ancient Society* (Belgium) 5 (1974): 119-26.
Comments on the evidence from the Galilee Hoard (see Spaer "A Hoard of Alexander Tetradrachms" below) for the dates of Antigonid control of Tyre and Sidon. Suggests this control ended in 296 B.C. Suggests a revision of Newell's dating of three series of Alexander tetradrachms from Tyre based on evidence from the Galilee Hoard. [See Newell *Tyrus Rediviva* under PHOENICIA].

3422 **Metcalf, William E.** "A Late Second Century Hoard of Posthumous Alexanders." *Revue Suisse de Numismatique* (Switzerland) 73 (1994): 19-60. Illus.
"The author records an extensive hoard (since dispersed) of broad-flan Alexander tetradrachms with a special study of the occurring countermarks and comparing the date of deposit with other hoards of the period." [*NL* 133]

3423 ——— "The 'Ain Tab Hoard (*IGCH* 1542)." *Coins of Macedonia and Rome: Essays in Honour of Charles Hersh*. Edited by Andrew Burnett, Ute Wartenberg, and Richard Witschonke. London: Spink, 1998. Pages 59-66.
A catalogue of 105 Alexander tetradrachms from the 'Ain Tab hoard found in 1920 or 1921. The coins are from a variety of mints. Various scholars have proposed dates between 185 and 160 B.C. for burial of the hoard, but Metcalf believes a date as late as the 120's cannot be ruled out.

3424 **Mihailescu, Barliba.** "Eastern Geto-Dacian World and the Macedonian Coins." *The Seventh International Congress of Thracology, May 1996 (Constanta-Tulcea-România). Report and Summaries*. Bucharest, 1996. Page 303.
"The author comments on the circulation of Macedonian coins from Philip II and Alexander the Great in the Geto-Dacian and Celtic world." [C. Preda, *NL* 137]

3425 **Miller, M. C. J.** "The Macedonian Pretender Pausanias and His Coinage." *The Ancient World* 13, nos. 1-2 (March 1986): 23-7. Illus.
Examines the regal Macedonian coinage with the inscription ΠΑΥΣΑΝΙΑ which has been assigned to King Pausanias, the son of Aeropus. There was another Pausanias however—a pretender to the throne in the 360's and possibly a grandson of Archelaus. Miller attributes the coins with the walking horse reverse type to the pretender Pausanias. He states that all the pretenders (Archelaus, Argaeus, and Pausanias) issued their own coinage.

3426 ——— "The Regal Coinage of Kassander." *The Ancient World* 22, no. 2 (fall 1991): 49-55. Illus.
A history of Kassander's rise to power and his reign as king of Macedonia. Describes his coin types and suggests that Kassander used coins to advance his image as king.

3427 **Mirnik, Ivan, and Zdenka Dukat.** "The Hoard of Macedonian Bronze Coins from Dojran." *Numizmaticke Vigesti* (Croatia) (1986): 44 ff.
Discusses *IGCH* 555.

3428 **Montgomery, Hugo.** "The Economic Revolution of Philip II—Myth or Reality?" *Symbolae Osloenses* (Norway) 40 (1985): 37-47.
"A critical re-examination of the so-called economic revolution which Philip II is sometimes supposed to have brought on in Macedonia." [U. Westermark, *Swedish Archaeology*].

3428a **Moore, Nancy J.** *The Early Issues of Alexander the Great from the Mint of Amphipolis.* Master's thesis, Princeton University, 1977.

3429 ——— *The Lifetime and Early Posthumous Coinage of Alexander the Great from Pella.* Doctoral dissertation, Princeton University, 1984.

3430 ——— "The Silver Coinage of Alexander from Pella." *Ancient Coins of the Graeco-Roman World: The Nickle Numismatic Papers.* Edited by Waldemar Heckel and Richard Sullivan. Waterloo, Ontario: Wilfrid Laurier University Press, 1984. Pages 41-56.
Moore presents the results of a die-link study of the silver coinage of Alexander the Great from the mint at Pella. She summarizes G. Le Rider's arguments related to the mintage of Philip II's coinage at Pella. Suggests some of Philip's and Alexander's coins, previously attributed to Sicyon, should be given to Pella. The final series of Alexander coins from Pella were minted 316-314 B.C. during the reign of Cassander.

3431 **Morawiecki, L.** "The Power Conception of Alexander the Great and of Gaius Julius Caesar in the Light of Numismatic Sources." *Eos* (Poland) 63 (1975): 99-127. [CS 2340]

3432 **Mørkholm, Otto.** "The Era of the Pamphylian Alexanders." *Museum Notes* 23 (1978): 69-75. 1 pl. [CS 2339]
Examines the posthumous Alexander tetradrachms struck between 250-150 B.C. at several mints in Pamphylia including Sillyum, Aspendus, Perge, and Phaselis. These coins are dated. Mørkholm attempts to determine the era used for their dating. Reviews and doubts the conclusions of Boehringer. Examines die link evidence. Agrees that the start of the Pamphylian era was 221/0 B.C., as suggested earlier by Seyrig, rather than 219/8 as suggested by Boehringer.

3433 **Müller, C. Ludwig.** *Numismatique d'Alexandre le Grand, suivie d'un Appendice Contenant les Monnaies de Philippe II et III, et Lysimaque.* Copenhagen, 1855. Reprint, Basel/Stuttgart, 1957; Bologna, 1974-75. 401 pp., 29 pls. [CS 2341]
Reprinted in English (see next item).

3434 ——— *The Coinage of Alexander the Great. Followed by a Supplement Containing the Coins of Philip II, III and Lysimachus.* Translated by L. A. Naughton. Copenhagen, 1855 and 1858. Reprinted as *An Atlas: The Coinage of Alexander the Great.* New York: Attic Books, 1976. 49 pp., illus. [CS 2343]
Some of the monograms which Müller interpreted as mint indicators have been determined to be magistrate's marks by Newell, resulting in mint reattributions. [See Newell "The Reattribution" below].

3435 ——— "Tetradrachm of Alexander." *Numismatic Chronicle* 20 (1859): 39-42.
A response to W. H. Scott's previous letter in the 1858 issue of *Numismatic Chronicle* (see Scott "On a Tetradrachm of Alexander" below). Müller states that an example of this coin is in the British Museum and he attributes it to Melitaea in Thessaly. What Scott interpreted as a Phoenician Aleph, Müller believes is the Greek digamma or a monogram.

3436 ——— *Numismatics of Alexander the Great: Mints and Mintmarks.* Chicago: Argonaut, 1969. 16 pp., 32 pls. [CS 2342]
A reprint of the mint-tables and coin plates of Müller's *The Coinage of Alexander the Great* (see above). [Also see Newell "The Reattribution" below for updates and corrections].

3437 **Myers, Robert J.** "An Unpublished Silver Fraction of Philip II of Macedon." *Numismatic Chronicle* 156 (1996): 227. 1 pl.
Publishes an obol of Thraco-Macedonian weight with *obv.*, beardless head of Herakles, and *rev.*, club and bow crossed. The coin is most likely from the mint of Aegea. Myers suggests the coin represents an experiment by Philip of returning to the minting of silver and striking on the Thraco-Macedonian light standard of Perdikkas.

3438 **Newell, Edward T.** "The Reattribution of Certain Tetradrachms of Alexander the Great." *American Journal of Numismatics* 45, no. 1 (January 1911): 1-10. 7 pls.; no. 2 (April 1911): 37-45. 6 pls.; no. 3 (July 1911): 113-25. 2 pls.; no. 4 (October 1911): 194-200; 46, no. 1 (January 1912): 22-4; no. 2 (April 1912): 37-49. 3 pls.; no. 3 (July 1912): 110-6. 12 pls. [CS 2344]
A study of Alexander tetradrachms based on the Demanhur hoard found in 1905, which contained about 8000 Alexander-type coins. A reassessment of Müller's attributions. Newell shows that many issues previously attributed to various cities shared the same obverse dies and thus must have been struck at a single location. Distinguishes eleven groups of issues, each containing different issue marks and sharing obverse dies. An analysis of style, die links, and inscriptions allowed him to assign all the groups to one mint and put them in relative chronological order. [Also see Newell's later and expanded publication of the Demanhur hoard, *Alexander Hoards 2*, below].

3439 ——— "Some Cypriote Alexanders." *Numismatic Chronicle* 4th ser., 15 (1915): 294-322. 4 pls. Reprint, Chicago: Obol International, 1974. 29 pp., 4 pls. Also published in *Numismatic Report* (Cyprus) 8 (1977): 55-83. Illus. [CS 2345]
Describes the gold, silver, and bronze coinage system of Alexander the Great which displaced the Persian and Athenian coinage as a world currency, and mentions the recent attribution of some of Alexander's coinage to the mints of Cyprus. During earlier times, Cypriote mints produced an abundant coinage, but during Alexander's reign, the coinage output seemed to be meager. Newell attempts to identify the coins of Alexander which were struck in Cyprus through an examination of the inscriptions and monograms. Describes the characteristics of and illustrates fifty-four Alexander-type coins minted between 333-306 B.C. at Kition, Salamis, Paphos, and Marion. [Also see Troxell "A New Look at Some Alexander Staters" below. Troxell revises Newell's order of mintage for some issues and questions their attribution to Salamis].

3440 —— *The Dated Alexander Coinage of Sidon and Ake.* Yale Oriental Series, Researches 2. New Haven: Yale University Press, 1916. Reprint, Rockville Center: Sanford J. Durst, 2000. 72 pp., 10 pls. [CS 2346]
These coins of the cities of Sidon and Ake are the only Alexander-type coins struck before the middle of the third century B.C. that are dated. This makes them useful for dating contemporary but undated Alexander issues of neighboring mints. The Ake coins fall into two dated series from distinct eras. Newell catalogues seventy varieties from Sidon and fifty-one from Ake, drawn from numerous public and private collections. Discusses the significance of each group of coins. [The Durst reprint was made from Newell's personal copy of the book and contains a few margin notes, primarily indications of Müller numbers. Reviewed by G. F. Hill in *Numismatic Chronicle* 4th ser., 16 (1916): 407-9. Also see I. Merker's "Notes on Abdalonymos" above].

3441 —— "The Alexandrine Coinage of Sinope." *American Journal of Numismatics* 52 (1918): 117-27. Illus., 2 pls. Reprinted as a booklet: *The Alexandrine Coinage of Sinope.* Rockville Center: Sanford J. Durst, 2008. 11 pp., 2 pls.
A catalogue of coins minted at Sinope under Alexander the Great. Müller had previously attributed many of these coins to Sidon.

3442 —— "Tarsos under Alexander." *American Journal of Numismatics* 52 (1918): 69-115. 8 pls. [CS 2347]
A catalogue of the coinage struck at Tarsos under Alexander the Great beginning ca. 333 B.C. Includes extensive discussion.

3443 —— "Myriandros—Alexandria Kat'Isson." *American Journal of Numismatics* 53, pt. 2 (1919): 1-42. 2 pls.
Re-examines the mint of the Persian staters of Mazaios which bear a prowling lion. All these coins had been previously attributed to Tarsos. Newell begins with a catalogue of the coins which *were* struck by Mazaios at Tarsos. He then presents a catalogue of the lion-staters—which also bear the name Mazaios—which Newell assigns to the mint of Myriandros, including issues struck under Alexander the Great. Continues with an extensive discussion of these issues. [Also see Bing "Reattribution" above].

3444 —— *Alexander Hoards 1: Introduction and Kyparissia Hoard.* Numismatic Notes and Monographs, No. 3. New York: American Numismatic Society, 1921. 21 pp., 2 pls.
This hoard of thirty-five coins represents the oldest burial of all known Alexander hoards. Twenty of the coins are Alexander tetradrachms; the others are coins of Larissa, Locri Opuntii, Thebes, Sicyon, Histiaea, and Philip II. The Alexander coins are attributed to the mints of Amphipolis, Tarsus, and Ake. The hoard was found in the western Peloponnese. Newell discusses the dating of the coins and places their burial around 327 B.C. He comments on the possible circumstances of their burial. Six coins are illustrated.

3445 —— *Alexander Hoards 2: Demanhur, 1905.* Numismatic Notes and Monographs, No. 19. New York: American Numismatic Society, 1923. 162 pp., 8 pls. [CS 2348]
Newell revisits the Demanhur hoard of Alexander tetradrachms, found in Egypt in 1905. Part of the hoard was discussed in his 1911 and 1912 articles (see Newell "The Reattribution" above). Newell revises some previous conclusions and publishes additional specimens. Discusses the finding and dispersal of the hoard. This is the largest and second earliest hoard of Alexander tetradrachms ever found. Provides a listing and classification of 4826 coins from the hoard. The coins are divided into nine geographical divisions in which there were active mints during Alexander's lifetime. These are subdivided into series, each attributable to one mint (although the mint city is not always known). Briefly summarizes the stylistic variations between mints and regions. Lists the number of each variety found and a cross-reference to Müller. A discussion of each mint or region follows, in which Newell describes his reasons for assigning each coin to a particular mint or region. Burial of the hoard is place at 318-317 B.C. The circumstances of the burial are discussed.

3446 —— *Alexander Hoards 3: Andritsaena.* Numismatic Notes and Monographs, No. 21. New York: American Numismatic Society, 1923. 39 pp., 6 pls.
Describes a hoard of tetradrachms of Philip II and Alexander III from various mints, as well as a few coins of Boeotia, Aegina, Sicyon, and Olympia. The hoard was found near Andritsaena in the Peloponnesos. It was buried ca. 315 B.C. Discusses the political and military situation of the time which may have led to the burial of the coins.

3447 —— *The Coinages of Demetrius Poliorcetes.* London, 1927. Reprint, Chicago: Obol International, 1978. 174 pp., 18 pls. [CS 2356]
A detailed study of the coinage of Demetrius the Besieger including chapters on the issues from the mints in Greece, Asia Minor, Cyprus, and the Levant. All known varieties in bronze, silver, and gold are described and illustrated. Sections are devoted to forgeries, imitations, and hoards. [Reviewed by A. Kleeb in *SAN* 9, no. 2 (spring 1978): 27].

3448 —— "The Coinage of Philip of Macedon." *The Coin Collector's Journal* 1, no. 3 (June 1934): 51-3. Illus.
A brief account of the reign and coinage of Philip II.

3449 —— "The Coinage of Alexander the Great." *The Coin Collector's Journal* 1, no. 6 (September 1934): 123-6, 128. Illus.
After brief comments on the conquests of Alexander, Newell presents a survey of the mints which Alexander established and the coinage he inaugurated.

3450 —— "The Coinages of Demetrius Poliorcetes." *The Coin Collector's Journal* 1, no. 8 (November 1934): 169-71, 179. Illus.
A brief account of the reign and coinage of Demetrius Poliorcetes.

3451 **Newton, Charles T.** "On the Coin Attributed by Mr. Borrell to Alexander of Pherae." *Numismatic Chronicle* 7 (1845): 110-3. Illus.
A re-examination of a coin previously attributed to a King Alexander in Thessaly. Suggests the coin may be from Paeonia.

3452 **Noe, Sydney P.** *The Alexander Coinage of Sicyon. Arranged from Notes of Edward T. Newell, with Comments and Additions.* Numismatic Studies, No. 6. New York: American Numismatic Society, 1950. 41 pp., 18 pls. [CS 2349]
A work started by Newell and completed by Noe after Newell's death. A catalogue of seventy varieties of the Alexander-type coinage minted at Sicyon. Includes commentary on chronology, types, and symbols. Indices of symbols and monograms. [Reviewed by G. K. Jenkins in *Numismatic Chronicle* 6th ser., 10 (1950): 320-4].

3453 **Oeconomides, Mando C.** "The 1979 Tricala Hoard of Alexanders." *Studies in Greek Numismatics in Memory of Martin Jessop Price.* Edited by Richard Ashton and Silvia Hurter. London: Spink, 1998. Pages 301-5. 2 pls.
A catalogue of a hoard of 109 silver coins (108 tetradrachms and one drachm) found in Thessaly in 1979. Includes sixty-seven tetradrachms of Alexander, four of Philip III, twenty-four of Athens, and others. The eastern mints of Alexander's coinage are well represented. Suggests a burial ca. 250 B.C. or a little later.

3454 ———— "Le Trésor d'Épidaure 1977." *Travaux de Numismatique Grecque Offerts à Georges Le Rider.* Edited by M. Amandry and S. Hurter. London: Spink, 1999. Pages 307-11. 3 pls.
The hoard consisted primarily of gold staters of Philip II and Alexander III.

3455 **Oikonomides, Al N., ed.** *The Coins of Alexander the Great: An Introductory Guide for the Historian, the Numismatist, and the Collector of Ancient Coins.* Chicago: Ares Publishers, 1981. 177 pp., maps, illus.
Provides a list of 2300 Alexander-type coins by combining the list compiled by Ludwig Müller in 1855 (see Müller *The Coinage of Alexander* above) with the addenda by Baron A. von Prokesch-Osten published in 1869 and 1871. The author comments on the current usefulness of Müller's numbering system, and the impact of the Demanhur hoard (see Newell "The Reattribution" and *Alexander Hoards 2* above) on the study of Alexander's coinage. Reproduces the introductory text from Barclay Head's *Historia Numorum* covering the historical and metrological information related to the coinage of Alexander the Great. Incorporates a new bibliography for Alexander's coinage (current to September 1980).

3456 ———— "Decadrachm Aids in Identification of Alexander." *Coin World* (November 25, 1981): 31-2. Illus.
Discusses the famous Poros decadrachms of Alexander the Great. Points out their usefulness in historical research. Discusses the interpretation of the coin type by numismatists. Describes the helmet and armor of Alexander as displayed on these coins and the battle scene shown on the obverse of the coins.

3457 ———— "Amyntas, Sons Leave Coin Legacy." *Coin World* (June 2, 1982): 67, 73, 77. Illus.
The identification of the bearded Herakles in lion-skin on early Macedonian coins as a portrait of Amyntas III (see Oikonomides "Amyntas" under PORTRAITS) leads to the reattribution of some later Macedonian coins. Reviews what is known of the history of Amyntas' successors Alexander II, Perdiccas, Philip, Archelaos, Arridaeos, Menelaos, and Argaios. Suggests reattributions of some of their coins.

3458 ———— "Coins Fill Historical Blanks." *Coin World* (July 14, 1982): 59, 64, 67. Illus.
Examines the round Macedonian shields shown on Macedonian coins. Compares the shields on coins to the known surviving shields. Discusses the symbolism of the stars and crescents decorating the shields (and making up the border of the coins) and the royal eight-rayed star.

3459 **Oman, C. W. C.** "Half and Quarter Obols of Alexander the Great." *Numismatic Chronicle* 3rd ser., 14 (1894): 186-7.
Publishes a quarter obol of Alexander. This denomination was previously unknown. Also publishes two half obols of a new variety. Suggests a Syrian or Cilician mint for the coins.

3460 **Panagopoulou, Katerina.** "The Antigonids: Patterns of a Royal Economy." *Hellenistic Economies.* Edited by Zofia H. Archibald, John Davies, Vincent Gabrielsen, and G. J. Oliver. London/New York: Routledge, 2001. Pages 313-64.
Focuses on problems of interpretation of the precious metal coinage struck in the name of King Antigonos, especially the tetradrachms bearing the Pan and Posidon types. The author concludes these primarily served the political purpose of celebrating victories in the Chremonidean War. Other coinage, particularly posthumous Alexanders, provided the majority of the coinage for the kingdom. [Reviewed by O. D. Hoover in *American Numismatic Society Magazine* 2, no. 2 (summer 2003): 54-7].

3461 **Papaeuthymiou, Eleni.** "Un Trésor (1995) de 80 Drachmes aux Types d'Alexandre III." *Μνημη Martin Jessop Price.* Edited by A. P. Tzamalis and M. J. A. Tzamali. Bibliotheca 5. Athens: The Hellenic Numismatic Society, 1996. Pages 130-40. Illus.

3462 ———— "A Tetrobol of Goat-Type, Attributed to Alexander I, King of Macedonia." *Coinage in the Macedonian Region. Proceedings of the 2nd Scientific Meeting.* Obolos 4. Edited by P. Adam-Veleni. Thessaloniki: University Studio Press, 2000.
A paper presented at the 2nd Scientific Meeting held in Thessaloniki in May 1998.

3463 **Pegan, Efrem.** "Due Frühesten Tetradrachmen Alexanders des Grossen mit dem Adler, ihre Herkunft und Entstehung." *Jahrbuch für Numismatik und Geldgeschichte* (Germany) 18 (1968): 99-111. Illus. [CS 2350]

3464 **Perlman, S.** "The Coins of Philip II and Alexander the Great and their Pan-Hellenic Propaganda." *Numismatic Chronicle* 7th ser., 5 (1965): 57-67. [CS 2330]
"The coins of the Delphic Amphictyony, whose issue begins in 336 under the sponsorship of Philip II, show certain particularities of size and legend which are intended to convey a sense of the independence of the Amphictyony and the freedom of its constituent states in alliance with the Macedonian king. The appearance of a figure of *Nike* on the first gold coinage of Alexander the Great apparently antedates any actual victory. It is connected iconographically with the city of Athens, and represents an attempt to persuade Athens to bring her naval capacities into alliance with Macedon for the coming attack against Persia." [P. MacKay, *NL* 79]

3465 **Picard, Olivier.** "Un Monnayage Alexandrin Énigmatique le Trésor d'Alexandrie 1996." *Travaux de Numismatique Grecque Offerts à Georges Le Rider.* Edited by M. Amandry and S. Hurter. London: Spink, 1999. Pages 313-21. 1 pl.

3465a ———— "Remarques sur le Monnayage de Bronze Macédonien avant Philippe II." *Bulletin de la Société Française de Numismatique* (France) 58, no. 5 (May 2003): 73-7.

3466 **Portolos, Dimitris.** "Some Early Issues of Philip II." *Μνημη Martin Jessop Price.* Edited by A. P. Tzamalis and M. J. A. Tzamali. Bibliotheca 5. Athens: The Hellenic Numismatic Society, 1996. Pages 111-8. 3 pls.

Based largely on style and similarities between the bronze and silver coinage, Portolos attempts to establish a sequence for the bronze coinage of Philip II and suggests a rearrangement of the silver coinage. He identifies three separate bronze issues and three different denominations. The author believes Philip's early coins were all struck at the same mint.

3467 **Price, Martin J.** *Coins of the Macedonians.* London: Trustees of the British Museum, 1974. Reprints, New York: Sanford J. Durst, 1993, 2000. 47 pp., 16 pls., map. [CS 2315]
An introduction to Macedonian coinage including coinage of the tribes, the kings, and Macedonia under the Romans. The plates illustrate ninety-one coins. [Reviewed by J. Warren in *Numismatic Chronicle* 136 (1976): 275-6].

3468 ——— "The Coinage of Alexander the Great." *British Museum Society Bulletin* 18 (March 1975): 7-9.

3469 ——— "In Search of Alexander the Great." *Nomismatika Khronika* (Greece) 5-6 (1978): 27-34. Illus.
Discusses the process of classifying the 5000+ varieties of Alexander's coinage by mint and by chronological sequence. Classification starts with the symbols found on the coins, but Price points out some flaws in L. Müller's arrangement of the symbols. The next factor is the style of the coins and die links between them. Price also states that the coins of Alexander's successors can sometimes be linked with Alexander's own coinage—the same mints and sometimes the same engravers were used. He points out that Alexander did not necessarily put an end to local coinage in his new territories. Discusses the phenomenon of posthumous issues.

3470 ——— "The Coinage of Philip II." *Numismatic Chronicle* 139 (1979): 230-41. 1 pl.
A review article discussing G. Le Rider's *Le Monnayage d'Argent et d'or de Philippe II, frapp en Macédoine de 359 à 294* (Paris: E. Bourgey, 1977). The book is a die study of the gold and silver coinage of Philip II struck in Macedonia, both lifetime and posthumous, to the late fourth century B.C., a brief sketch of the final phase of the silver coinage at Amphipolis, and a discussion of relevant hoard material. In this article, Price presents a table of the issues showing die links between varieties, and he comments on the chronology of this coinage.

3471 ——— "On Attributing Alexanders—Some Cautionary Tales." *Greek Numismatics and Archaeology: Essays in Honor of Margaret Thompson.* Edited by O. Mørkholm and N. M. Waggoner. Wetteren: Numismatique Romaine, 1979. Pages 241-50.
To demonstrate the need for caution in numismatic studies, Price examines several controversial issues related to the coinage of Alexander the Great. (1) Price summarizes the debate over the mint for certain Alexander coins bearing Phoenician letters and numbers. Newell attributed these to Ake; André Lemaire attributed them to Tyre [*Revue Numismatique* (1976): 11-24]. The numerals on the coins may represent regnal years of a Tyrian king Azemilkos and his co-regent. Price cites historical and numismatic evidence for and against the attribution to Tyre. Discusses possible reasons for the use of the Attic weight standard, and discusses the apparent change in the eras of dating at the end of the Alexander series. (2) Discusses the debate over the location of Alexander's main lifetime mint, generally believed to be Pella, and the location of the main posthumous mint, generally believed to be Amphipolis. (3) Discusses a group of Alexander coinage which Newell attributed to the area of Lycia-Pamphylia. Some have suggested Side as the mint location.

3472 ——— "The Earliest Coins of Alexander the Great: 2. Alexander's Reform of the Macedonian Regal Coinage." *Numismatic Chronicle* 142 (1982): 180-90. 2 pls.
"In the second part of this debate (for Part 1, see O. Zervos "The Earliest Coins of Alexander" below) the chronology and circumstances of Alexander's earliest coinage, issued from the chief Macedonian mint, are reviewed. The design of the Zeus figure attracts much attention: oriental influence, especially that of the Achaemenid currency of Tarsus with its depictions of Baal, is discounted. The evidence substantiates the coinage's having been reformed in 336." [M. Price, *NL* 110]

3473 ——— "In the Wake of Alexander—Coins as Evidence for the Clash of Cultures under the Macedonian Empire." Πρακτικα του XII Διεθνουσ Συνεδριου Κλασσικησ Αρχαιολογιασ, Αθηνα 4–10 Σεπτεμβριου 1983. Athens, 1985. Pages 243-7.

3474 ——— *The Coinage in the Name of Alexander the Great and Philip Arrhidaeus. A British Museum Catalogue.* Two volumes. Zurich and London: The Swiss Numismatic Society in association with the British Museum Press, 1991. 637 pp., 159 pls.
Describes about 4100 varieties of coins struck in the name of Alexander the Great (lifetime and posthumous issues), his half-brother and successor, Philip Arrhidaeus, and those of Lysimachus of the Alexander types. The introductory text discusses designs, titles, portraiture, symbols and monograms, denominations, weights, hoard evidence, circulation patterns, countermarks, counterfeits, and chronology. The catalogue of coin varieties is arranged by mints. References are given to similar specimens in other collections and hoards. The list of varieties is supplemented by more specific listings of coins in the British Museum collection for which weights, die axes, and provenances are given. The plates illustrate coins in the British Museum's collection. Includes tables of concordances to Müller and von Prokesch-Osten, and indices of hoards and issue marks (symbols, Greek and Aramaic letters, monograms). Also includes brief listings of barbarous issues and modern forgeries. This is the most comprehensive study of the Alexander coinage ever published and is the standard reference for the series. [Reviewed by R. Ashton in *Numismatic Chronicle* 153 (1993): 276-80, and by R. Bauslaugh in *American Journal of Numismatics* 2nd ser., 5/6 (1993/4): 221-34. Also see Hersh "Additions and Corrections" above].

3475 ——— "Alexander's Policy on Coinage." *Alexander the Great: Reality and Myth.* Analecta Romana Instituti Danici, Supplement 20. Rome: L'Erma di Bretschneider, 1993. Pages 171-6. Illus.

3476 **Rahmani, Levi Y.** "A Hoard of Alexander Coins from Tel Tsippor." *Schweizer Münzblätter* (Switzerland) 16, no. 64 (1966): 129-45. [CS 3276]

3477 **Rakicic, Mark.** "Alexandrian Trader Relates Story of Demetrios Poliorcetes' Siege of Rhodes." *The Celator* 5, no. 9 (September 1991): 10-2.
A fictional account of the experiences of merchants in Rhodes at the time of Demetrios Poliorcetes' attack on the city, based on the writings of Diodorus Siculus. Describes the siege and the assistance provided to Rhodes by Ptolemy.

3478 ——— "The Forgotten Prince: Philip III Arrhidaeus." *The Celator* 7, no. 10 (October 1993): 36-41. Illus.
A fictional account of the life of Philip III Arrhidaeus as told by his doctor. Suggests Arrhidaeus suffered from epilepsy. Describes his life, brief kingship, and his death at the hands of Olympias.

3479 ———— "The Lagobolon of Pan on the Coinage of Antigonus Gonatas." *The Celator* 10, no. 3 (March 1996): 6-12. Illus.
Discusses the symbolism of the lagobolon—a stick for throwing at hares in order to kill them. The lagobolon is shown behind the head of Pan on the tetradrachms of Antigonus Gonatas, ca. 271 B.C. Discusses the mythology of the god Pan and his role in the military victories of Antigonus Gonatas.

3480 **Raymond, Doris.** *Macedonian Regal Coinage to 413 B.C.* Numismatic Notes and Monographs, No. 126. New York: American Numismatic Society, 1953. 170 pp., 15 pls. [CS 2325]
Presents a corpus of Macedonian regal coins and attempts to place them in the proper die sequence. Includes discussions of the early history of Macedonia, weight standards, and coin types. Includes a catalogue of coin varieties with commentary. [An extensive review by J. M. F. May appears in *Numismatic Chronicle* 6th ser., 13 (1953): 165-70].

3481 **Reinach, A. J.** "La Base aux Trophées de Délos et les Monnaies de Philippe Andriskos." *Journal International d'Archéologie Numismatique* (Greece) 15 (1913): 97-142. 2 pls.
"A trophy base found on Delos, with representations of Macedonian shields, with club and head of Perseus, belongs to a monument erected by Metellus after the defeat of Philip Andriscus, 147 B.C. Coins of Philip V are distinguished from those of Andriscus." [J. R. Jones, *AIJIAN*]

3482 **Rodger, William.** "Philip the Great." *Coins* 22, no. 3 (March 1975): 106. Illus.
This installment of the author's column "Personalities on Ancient Coins" focuses on Philip II.

3483 ———— "Demetrius Poliorcetes." *Coins* 22, no. 10 (October 1975): 98. Illus.
This installment of the author's column "Personalities on Ancient Coins" focuses on Demetrius Poliorcetes.

3484 ———— "Philip V of Macedon." *Coins* 23, no. 4 (April 1976): 88. Illus.
This installment of the author's column "Personalities on Ancient Coins" focuses on Philip V.

3485 **Saatsoglu-Paliadeli, C.** "Aspects of Macedonian Costume." *Journal of Hellenic Studies* 113 (1993): 122-47. 4 pls.
"The main part of this paper is devoted to a discussion of the *kausia*, a form of Macedonian headgear. The author uses the coinage of Philip II, amongst other archaeological and literary evidence, to relate its development and use in Macedonian society." [M. Tooth, *Hekte* 2]

3486 **Salton, M. M.** "The Pegasus on a Gold Stater of Alexander." *Schweizer Münzblätter* (Switzerland) 2 (1951): 42-3.

3487 **Schell, James A.** "Iconography of the Control Marks on the Alexander Issues of Soli, Cyprus." *American Journal of Numismatics* 2nd ser., 10 (1998): 29-35. 1 pl.
Examines the interpretation of the primary control mark, the prow, on a series of gold staters, silver tetradrachms, and bronze hemiobols struck at Soli on Cyprus. The author suggests these control marks announce, both to Alexander and to the world at large, the identity of the individual or entity acknowledging submission to Alexander. Suggests the prow icon was recognized as a control mark of the Amphipolis series at the time the Cypriot mints began the striking of Alexander issues. With the ultimate maritime symbol, the prow, unavailable by virtue of prior use, adoption of the naval ram by Soli conveys a similar meaning while remaining fully distinguishable to the elite of the fourth century B.C.

3488 ———— "Observations on the Metrology of the Precious Metal Coinage of Philip II of Macedon: The 'Thraco-Macedonian' Standard or the Corinthian Standard?" *American Journal of Numismatics* 12 (2000): 1-8.
Le Rider asserts that Philip II adopted the standard of the Chalcician League (14.3 gm) for his silver issues. Schell shows that the so-called Thraco-Macedonian standard of 14.3 gm was actually an adaptation of the Corinthian standard. Philip's stater was a pentadrachm, resulting in a drachm weight of 2.86 gm—matching the weight of a Corinthian drachm. Schell highlights the parallels between the Macedonian/Corinthian standard and the Attic standard—a different denominational system was used, but both were based on a 17.2 gm stater. Schell shows that Alexander III's adoption of the 17.2 gm Attic standard for his tetradrachm can be seen as merely adding a Macedonian/Corinthian hexadrachm to the denominations in circulation. Shows that with a gold-to-silver ratio of 1: 13 1/3, it made sense to strike gold on the Attic standard while striking silver on the Macedonian/Corinthian standard—the gold issues represented integer multiples of the silver pentadrachms (1 gold Attic stater = 8 silver Corinthian tetradrachms). Alexander I also struck coinage on two different standards.

3489 **Schwabacher, Willy.** "An Unrecorded Alexander Hoard from Baalbek." *Nordisk Numismatisk Årsskrift* (Sweden) (1963): 5-12. Illus. [CS 3289]
"Twenty-two Alexander type tetradrachms, here illustrated and described, were among the contents of a hoard of several hundred pieces reportedly discovered in the environs of Baalbek and purchased, in 1885, by the Swedish diplomat, Marquis Claes Lagergren. The fact that seventeen of the twenty-two coins are from Amphipolis (Macedonia) and Babylon clearly indicates the importance of these mints as compared with the minor minting centers closer to Baalbek (represented by only five coins)." [R. Breaden, *NL* 78]

3490 **Scott, William H.** "On a Tetradrachm of Alexander Struck at Aradus." *Numismatic Chronicle* 19 (1858): 221-2.
Mentions what the author thought was a previously unpublished bilingual Alexander tetradrachm bearing the letters A and F (the Phoenician 'aleph') which the author attributed to the mint of Aradus in Phoenicia. [But see Müller "Tetradrachm of Alexander" above in which Müller responds, pointing out Scott's error].

3491 **Sear, David R.** "The Legacy of Alexander the Great." *Numismatist* 116, no. 12 (December 2003): 57-9. Illus.
An overview of the coinage of Alexander, his changes in weight standards, coin types, and the use of Alexander's portrait on the coinage of his successors.

3492 **Seldarov, Nikola.** *Kings of Ancient Macedonia and their Coins found in the Territory of the Republic of Macedonia.* Skopje, 1994.

3493 ———— "Hellenistic Coin Hoard from Isar-Marvinci." *Macedonian Numismatic Journal* (Macedonia) 2 (1996): 41-7. Illus.

"The author describes the preserved part of a hoard discovered before February 1994. Included among twenty bronze coins were eighteen of Philip V of Macedon, one anonymous issue, and one illegible coin. The first eighteen pieces are of four types dated by Touratsoglou to 183-179 B.C., a dating which appears to be confirmed by this hoard. The anonymous issue, a Hercules/horse type inscribed MAKEΔONON, from the Amphipolis mint and usually attributed to Philip V or Perseus, is here dated by the author to 187-179 B.C., during the reign of Philip V." [C. Smith, *NL* 141]

3494 **Seltman, Charles T.** "A Synopsis of the Coins of Antigonus I and Demetrius Poliorcetes." *Numismatic Chronicle* 4th ser., 9 (1909): 264-73. 1 pl.
Publishes a tetradrachm which the author believes was struck by Antigonus within his Asiatic domains before the year 306 B.C. The types are those of the ordinary tetradrachms of Alexander the Great. Also publishes other coins of Antigonus and of Demetrius Poliorcetes.

3495 **Sergueenkova, Valeria.** "The Stylis on the Gold of Alexander the Great." *Numismatica e Antichità Classiche. Quaderni Ticinesi* (Switzerland) 35 (2006).

3496 **Sjöqvist, Erik.** "Alexander—Heracles: A Preliminary Note." *Bulletin of the Museum of Fine Arts, Boston* 51 (1953): 30-3.
Discusses the likeness of Heracles to the features of Alexander the Great in the traditional Heracles iconography on the early tetradrachms struck by Alexander in Sicyon about 330 B.C.

3497 **Spaer, Arnold.** "A Hoard of Alexander Tetradrachms from Galilee." *Israel Numismatic Journal* (Israel) 3 (1965/6; publ. 1970): 1-7. 3 pls.
"A hoard of about forty coins found near Tarshiha in Western Galilee and consisting of issues of Ace, Sidon and Tyre is described. E. T. Newell's view in *Tyrus Rediviva* that the Alexander issues of that city continued until ca. 287 B.C. is discussed; the issues probably terminated simultaneously with those of Ace and Sidon in the last years of the fourth century B.C." [A. Spaer, *NL* 85]. [Also see Merker "Demetrios Poliorcetes" above, and Newell *Tyrus Rediviva* under PHOENICIA].

3498 ——— "A New Type of Alexander the Great." *Israel Numismatic Journal* (Israel) 5 (1981): 1-3. 1 pl.
"A drachm, obol and hemiobol showing a head of Herakles in lionskin on obverse and club and bow-case on the reverse are attributed to the mint of Babylon after 317 B.C." [A. Spaer, *NL* 109]

3499 **Spengler, William F.** "An Echo of Bucephalus and Aornos." *Newsletter of the Boulder Society of the Archaeological Institute of America* 4 (spring 2003): 34-41. Reprinted in *The Celator* 18, no. 7 (July 2004): 34-6. Illus.
A brief summary of Alexander's campaigns in Pakistan and India. Quotes a passage from Lt. Colonel James Abbott, a British soldier, from his article "Aornos" published in the *Journal of the Asiatic Society of Bengal* (1863) in which he reveals that a white rock near Umb on the bank of the Indus river is called "Tchitta Butt Kephale Bous"—meaning "white rock bull's head"—a reference to Alexander's horse Bucephalus. Umb is Ambolina, where Alexander camped to prepare for his assault on Aornos. Illustrates the "Poros" dekadrachm of Alexander.

3500 **Stanton, Earle K.** "Macedonian Numismatics." *The Numismatist* 67, no. 11 (November 1954): 1170-4.
A good overview of the coinage of Philip II and Alexander the Great.

3501 **Stoller, Steve.** "Alexander's Thunderbolt Stater." *SAN—Journal of the Society for Ancient Numismatics* 1, no. 4 (April 1970): 71.
A gold stater of Alexander the Great is published. It has a thunderbolt symbol in the obverse field. The author requests information from others regarding this coin. [Also see *SAN* 2, no. 1 (July 1970) for a response from a reader].

3502 **Tarn, William W.** "The Battles of Andros and Cos." *Journal of Hellenic Studies* 29 (1909): 264-85.
"Andros is placed in 246 B.C. and on pp. 273-4 the writer concludes that coins of Antigonus Gonatas showing Pan before a trophy refer to this battle, while he agrees with Usener that the common type with Pan's head on a shield refers to his victory over the Gauls at Lysimacheia (further discussion of the historical problems involved is to be found in articles by the same writer and by W. S. Ferguson in *Journal of Hellenic Studies* 30 (1910): 189-225)." [J. R. Jones, *NIJHS*]

3503 "Tetradrachm of Alexander the Great." *Numismatic Journal* 2 (1838): 77-8. Illus.
Illustrates a tetradrachm with a reverse symbol described by Mionnet as a cap of the Dioscuri. The author suggests the conical object is a cone-shaped rock. The mint city remains unknown. [No author is listed for this article].

3504 **Thompson, Margaret.** "The Alexandrine Mint of Mylasa." *Quaderni Ticinesi. Numismatica e Antichità Classiche* (Switzerland) 10 (1981): 207-17.

3505 ——— "The Cavalla Hoard (*IGCH* 450)." *Museum Notes* 26 (1981): 33-49. 7 pls.
Describes a hoard of 340 silver coins found at Cavalla in 1951—primarily drachms of Alexander type struck in the names of Alexander, Philip III, or Lysimachus from various mints. Focuses on a few coins of special merit: drachms of Amphipolis, Pella, Side, and Ephesos. The hoard was buried ca. 280 B.C.

3506 ——— "The Coinage of Philip II and Alexander III." *Studies in the History of Art, Volume 10. Symposium Series 1: Macedonia and Greece in Late Classical and Early Hellenistic Times*. Edited by Beryl Barr-Sharrar and Eugene Borza. Washington: National Gallery of Art, 1982. Pages 113-21. Illus., 1 pl.
An overview of the coinage of Philip II and the Alexander-type coinage of Alexander the Great and his successors. Points out the stylistic variations in the coinage at various mints.

3507 ——— "Posthumous Philip II Staters of Asia Minor." *Studia Paulo Naster Oblata, Volume 1: Numismatica Antiqua*. Orientalia Lovaniensia Analecta 12. Edited by S. Scheers. Louvain: Departement Oriëntalistiek, 1982. Pages 57-63, including 2 pls.
Thompson catalogues the posthumous staters of Philip II struck at mints in Asia Minor (Miletus, Colophon, Teos, Sardes, and Lampsacus). Many of the coins exhibit evidence of either a central minting or a sharing of dies between mints. The coins, struck ca. 323-316 B.C., were struck during the joint reign

of Philip Arrhidaeus and Alexander IV. The author suggests the purpose of the coinage by Arrhidaeus was to evoke memories of Philip II to gain political support. The coinage stopped upon Arrhidaeus' death.

3508 ——— *Alexander's Drachm Mints 1: Sardes and Miletus.* Numismatic Studies, No. 16. New York: American Numismatic Society, 1983. 98 pp., 38 pls.
Under Alexander III and his successors down to the end of the fourth century B.C., seven mints in Asia Minor produced the small change of the entire empire—mostly drachms: Lampsacus, Abydus, Sardes, Colophon, Magnesia, Miletus, and probably Teos. This volume presents a catalogue of many of these issues from the Sardes (412 coins) and Miletus (272 coins) mints. Primarily a listing of drachms, but includes some gold staters and silver tetradrachms. Discusses die links and chronology. Provides a listing of relevant hoards with a discussion of the contents of each.

3509 ——— "Paying the Mercenaries." *Studies in Honour of Leo Mildenberg: Numismatics, Art History, Archaeology.* Edited by A. Houghton et al. Wetteren: Editions NR, 1984. Pages 241-7. 2 pls.
In the year or two preceding the death of Alexander the Great, many of his mints substantially increased their output including Miletus, Colophon, Abydus, Lampsacus, Magnesia, Amphipolis, Alexandria, and especially Side. Thompson lists the control marks on the ten known issues from Side. She concludes that Alexander made no significant payments to his troops while campaigning in the East. In the course of his retreat from India, Alexander decided to disband the mercenary forces of the satraps and presumably some of his own followers once he reached Babylon. To get these potential troublemakers out of the region, compensation was withheld until they returned to their homelands. The increased coinage reflects the need to pay these returning mercenaries. The coinage probably began no earlier than February of 324 B.C. Twenty-four coins are illustrated.

3510 ——— *Alexander's Drachm Mints 2: Lampsacus and Abydus.* Numismatic Studies, No. 19. New York: American Numismatic Society, 1991. 77 pp., 34 pls.
Following the format of *Volume 1* above, this volume presents a catalogue of many of the Alexander issues from the Lampsacus and Abydus mints. Primarily a listing of drachms, but includes some gold staters and silver tetradrachms. Discusses die links and chronology. Provides a listing of relevant hoards with a discussion of the contents of each. Lists about 500 coins from Lampsacus and about 400 coins from Abydus. [Reviewed by M. J. Price in *Spink Numismatic Circular* 100, no. 8 (October 1992): 272-3, and in *Numismatic Chronicle* 153 (1993): 280-7].

3511 **Thompson, Margaret, and Alfred R. Bellinger.** "Greek Coins in the Yale Collection 4: A Hoard of Alexander Drachms." *Yale Classical Studies* 14 (1955): 3-45. 8 pls. Reprinted as a book, 45 pp., 8 pls. [CS 3299]
Presents a catalogue of a large hoard of Alexander drachms, chiefly from Asia Minor and adjacent islands. Includes 108 different dies. Discusses the output of each mint.

3512 **Torrey, Charles C.** *Aramaic Graffiti on Coins of the Demanhur Hoard.* Numismatic Notes and Monographs, No. 77. New York: American Numismatic Society, 1937. 13 pp., 2 pls.
A follow-up to Newell's work on the Demanhur hoard (see Newell *Alexander Hoards 2* above). Provides evidence of the use of the Aramaic language by the Jews in Egypt.

3512a **Touratsoglou, Yannis (Ioannis) P.** "Macedonia." *The Coinage of the Roman World in the Late Republic.* Edited by A. M. Burnett and M. H. Crawford. BAR International Series 326. Oxford, 1987.
Examines the bronze coins of Philip V through the Roman period in Macedonia.

3513 **Touratsoglou, Yannis (Ioannis) P.** "Back to the Future. Alexander the Great's Silver and Gold in the Balkans: The Hoard Evidence." *Coins of Macedonia and Rome: Essays in Honour of Charles Hersh.* Edited by Andrew Burnett, Ute Wartenberg, and Richard Witschonke. London: Spink, 1998. Pages 71-101. 4 maps.
Traces the principles of the circulation of the drachms, tetradrachms, and gold staters of Philip II and Alexander III based on the hoard evidence from Greece, the former Yugoslavia, Albania, Bulgaria, Romania, and Moldavia. First deals with the denominations as represented in the hoards and then presents a general interpretation of the hoards based on general historical considerations. Accompanied by maps indicating the find-spots of hoards and tables summarizing the contents of the hoards.

3514 ——— "The Price of Power: Drachms in the Name of Alexander in Greece (On the Occasion of the Thessaly/1993 Confiscation)." *Eulimene* (Mediterranean Archaeological Society, Rethymno, Greece) 1 (2000): 91-118.

3515 ——— *A Contribution to the Economic History of the Kingdom of Ancient Macedonia (6th–3rd cent. BC).* KERMA 2. Athens: Lydia Lithos, Society for the Study of Numismatics and Economic History, 2010. 236 pp., illus.
Provides economic data on the Macedonian Kingdom along with historical events, reconstructing the financial management of the state by the Macedonian kings. Includes an historical, economic, and political review beginning with the reign of Alexander I and continuing through the Hellenistic period. Presents archaeological evidence and an examination of the coin issues from Alexander I through Kassander. [Reviewed by Dimitris Plantzos in *Nomismatika Khronika* 28 (2010): 149-51].

3516 **Troxell, Hyla A.** "The Peloponnesian Alexanders." *Museum Notes* 17 (1971): 41-94. 12 pls. [CS 2353]
Reviews the Alexander-type coins from Peloponnesian mints (Sicyon, Argos, Megalopolis). Catalogues a hoard of nine Alexander tetradrachms, found in the Peloponnese, acquired by the American Numismatic Society in 1962. Re-examines the chronology and attribution of the issues previously assigned to Sicyon, and the chronology of those assigned to Argos and Megalopolis. Suggests other Peloponnesian mints, including Corinth, also briefly struck Alexanders.

3517 ——— "Alexander's Earliest Macedonian Silver." *Mnemata: Papers in Memory of Nancy M. Waggoner.* Edited by William E. Metcalf. New York: American Numismatic Society, 1991. Pages 49-61. 5 pls.
Presents an outline of Newell's analysis of Alexander's coinage (see Newell *Alexander Hoards 2* above). Discusses the dated coinage of Sidon and Ake, commenting on the conclusions of Newell (see Newell "The Dated Alexander Coinage of Sidon and Ake" above). Discusses whether the Zeus of Macedon on Alexander's coinage was derived from the Zeus of Tarsus. Concludes that Alexander's tetradrachms from Tarsus must have made their way

to Macedon before the introduction of the Alexander coinage there. Therefore, the Asian mints struck his coinage prior to the Macedonian mint which, then, started coinage ca. 332 B.C. Suggests these conclusions fit in well with Newell's earlier observations.

3518 ——— *Studies in the Macedonian Coinage of Alexander the Great.* Numismatic Studies, No. 21. New York: American Numismatic Society, 1997. 161 pp., 31 pls.
Part 1 covers the silver coinage issued by Alexander III and Philip II ca. 332-310 B.C. from the major Macedonian mint, usually identified as Amphipolis. Includes the small denominations which accompanied the tetradrachms and the re-issues using Philip II's types, name, and weights made after Alexander's death. Part 2 covers Alexander's lifetime gold coins. For each group of coins, Troxell investigates the issues and groups, die linkage, hoards, and relative and absolute chronology. Includes twenty-four tables, four appendices, and three indices. The plates illustrate the coins and die links, early Macedonian coinage, and previously unpublished hoard material. [Reviewed by G. Le Rider in *Revue Suisse de Numismatique* 77 (1998): 179-90].

3519 ——— "Alexanders from Soli on Cyprus." *Studies in Greek Numismatics in Memory of Martin Jessop Price.* Edited by Richard Ashton and Silvia Hurter. London: Spink, 1998. Pages 339-44. 2 pls.
A re-examination of some Alexander coins with the prow symbol on the reverse (*Price* 3091-99) which were previously attributed to Amathus. Troxell now attributes these coins to Soli in Cyprus. The coins include gold staters, silver tetradrachms, and some bronze issues. Reviews the relevant hoard evidence. Reviews the history of the attribution of these coins.

3520 ——— "Ants and Eagles: Some Late Alexander Staters from Amphipolis." *Coins of Macedonia and Rome: Essays in Honour of Charles Hersh.* Edited by Andrew Burnett, Ute Wartenberg, and Richard Witschonke. London: Spink, 1998. Pages 67-70. 1 pl.
Lists thirteen issues of late posthumous Alexander gold staters. The issues have received a variety of mint attributions in M. J. Price's *The Coinage in the Name of Alexander.* Discusses attributions and chronology.

3521 ——— "A New Look at Some Alexander Staters from 'Salamis.'" *Travaux de Numismatique Grecque Offerts à Georges Le Rider.* Edited by M. Amandry and S. Hurter. London: Spink, 1999. Pages 359-67. 2 pls.
A follow-up to Newell's "Some Cypriote Alexanders" (see Newell above). Newell assigned a group of gold staters of Alexander to the mint of Salamis—those bearing the symbols bow, quiver, eagle, harpa, and spearhead. Troxell shows that Newell's order of mintage must be reversed. This rearrangement leads Troxell to question the attribution of these early gold staters to Salamis, although no satisfactory alternate mint is suggested.

3522 ——— "A Partial Hoard of Royal Macedonian Bronzes." *Pour Denyse: Divertissements Numismatiques.* Edited by Silvia Hurter and Carmen Arnold-Biucchi. Bern, Switzerland: Privately published, 2000. Pages 189-95. 2 pls.
A summary catalogue of a portion of a hoard which may have numbered over 1000 coins. Three hundred are listed here, including 290 bronzes in the name of Philip II and ten of Alexander III. The coins are arranged by obverse and reverse markings, symbols, and letters. Troxell comments on the various groups.

3523 "A Unique Gold Coin of Alexander the Great?" *American Journal of Numismatics* 45, no. 1 (January 1911): 21-3.
Reports the discovery of an Asiatic gold "mohur" of Alexander the Great with the head of Alexander wearing an elephant scalp. The editor suggests the coin is a forgery—perhaps the creation of a forger name Chandur Mal.

3524 **Vagi, David.** "Alexander: The Conqueror and His Coinage." *The Numismatist* 106, no. 12 (December 1993): 1687-95, 1741-4. Illus.
Begins with a brief biographical sketch of Alexander's life. Then describes the creation of an "imperial" coinage for use throughout his empire. Describes the standard designs of Alexander's gold, silver, and bronze coinage. Discusses the establishment of a network of mints and the stylistic variations in the coinage of these mints. Concludes with an overview of the coinage of Alexander's successors.

3525 ——— "Later Alexandrine Coinage is Civic in Nature." *The Celator* 8, no. 1 (January 1994): 12. Illus.
Briefly describes the coinages struck after Alexander's death which retain his types. This was a civic coinage struck throughout the Near East. The fabric of the coins generally differs from the regal Macedonian issues. The author contrasts these with the royal Hellenistic issues which followed.

3526 **Van Driessche, Véronique.** "Arguments pour une Datation (Très) Tardive du Début des Émissions Monétaire en Argent de Philippe II de Macedoine." *Liber Amicorum Tony Hackens.* Edited by G. Moucharte, M. B. Borba Florenzano, F. de Callataÿ, P. Marchetti, L. Smolderen, and P. Yannopoulos. Numismatica Lovaniensia 20. Louvain-la-Neuve: Université Catholique de Louvain, 2007. Pages 11 ff.

3526a **Valassiadis, Chrysanthos.** "A Contribution to Cassander's Bronze Coinage." *XIII Congreso Internacional de Numismática, Madrid – 2003: Actas–Proceedings–Actes I.* Edited by Carmen Alfaro, Carmen Marcos, and Paloma Otero. Madrid: International Numismatic Commisson, 2005. Pages 405-13, incl. 1 pl.
Begins with a general overview of Cassander's bronze coin types and then the attribution of some bronze coins to certain mints is discussed. The author concludes that the Apollo/tripod series was struck parallel to the horseman series at a different mint, and the city of Cassandreia has been proposed as the place of issue. The helmet/spearhead and the Athena/weapons series have been attributed to a mint in Asia Minor. The helmet coins were issued in Caria during the time of Pleistarchos and the weapons coins were produced a bit earlier in Asia Minor, perhaps during Cassander's campaigns of 302-301 B.C.

3527 **Vaux, W. S. W.** "Extract of a Letter from Charles T. Newton, Esq., Her Majesty's Vice Consul at Mytilene, to Mr. Burgon, of the British Museum, Chiefly Relating to a Hoard of Coins of Alexander the Great, Discovered near Patras, in 1850." *Numismatic Chronicle* 16 (1854): 29-37.
Lists coins from a hoard including numerous Alexander tetradrachms and the coins found with them, including Athenian tetradrachms—showing that the Athenian coins continued to circulate at the time of Alexander. Also mentions an Athenian decadrachm owned by a jeweler in Athens.

3528 **Visonà, Paolo.** "Twenty-Two Alexanders in Ann Arbor." *American Journal of Numismatics* 2nd ser., 16-17 (2004-2005): 63-73. 4 pls.
A group of twenty-one Alexander tetradrachms donated in 1909 to the University of Michigan by G. Dattari includes nineteen issues of Macedonia, Side (?), Tarsus, Myriandrus, Aradus, Babylon, Memphis, and Salamis, dated between ca. 333-317 B.C. Dattari's coins are in the collection of the Kelsey Museum of Archaeology in Ann Arbor. Their Egyptian provenance, and the fact that these issues are known to have been among the contents of the Demanhur hoard of 1905, raise the possibility that they came from that assemblage. Dattari himself was one of E. T. Newell's principal sources of information on the

Demanhur hoard. Two other tetradrachms in Dattari's gift consist of an issue of Ake minted in 317/16 B.C. and an issue of uncertain mint in Greece or Macedonia struck under Phillip III, which cannot be linked to Demanhur. The Kelsey Museum's collection also contains an Alexander tetradrachm of Ake minted possibly in 310/09 B.C.

3529 **von Prokesch-Osten, Anton.** "List des Alexandres de ma Collection qui ne se Trouvent pas dans le Catalogue de Mr. L. Müller." *Numismatische Zeitschrift* (Austria) 1 (1869): 31-64.

3530 **Waggoner, Nancy M.** "The Early Alexander Coinage at Seleucia on the Tigris." *Museum Notes* 15 (1969): 21-30. 3 pls. [CS 3012]
Presents evidence indicating Newell's Series I coinage at the Seleucia mint requires re-alignment and re-dating. Discusses the numismatic and political implications which result.

3531 ——— "Cassander in Babylon?" *SAN—Journal of the Society for Ancient Numismatics* 16, no. 4 (May 1986): 68.
Exposes a tetradrachm of Alexander the Great which had been retooled to show the name of Cassander—a name which only appears on his bronze coinage.

3532 **Wartenberg, Ute.** "A Small Group of Tetradrachms of Alexander I of Macedon." *Coin Hoards, Volume IX: Greek Hoards.* Edited by A. Meadows and Ute Wartenberg. London: Royal Numismatic Society, 2002. Pages 85-6. 1 pl.
Seven coins of Alexander I appeared in 1999 and likely came from the same hoard. Additional pieces have since surfaced. The coins have the types mounted horseman/goat's head within incuse square. All belong to Raymond's groups I to III (see Doris Raymond *Macedonian Regal Coinage* above). The new coins provide a die link between Raymond's groups II and III. Wartenberg suggests the tetradrachms of Alexander I were only struck at times when they were needed for a specific purpose.

3533 **Wells, H. Bartlett.** "Another Gold-Plated Alexander Stater." *SAN—Journal of the Society for Ancient Numismatics* 12, no. 2 (summer 1981): 29.
A fifth gold-plated silver stater of Alexander III is described. [Also see Wells "Ancient Gold-Plated Coins" and "New Material" under THE MINTING PROCESS, and "Macedonian Plated Gold" below].

3534 ——— "More Gold-Plated Alexander Staters." *SAN—Journal of the Society for Ancient Numismatics* 12, no. 3 (fall 1981): 54-5.
Three staters of Alexander III are described. These are gold-plated copper coins. Weights are given. [Also see Wells "Ancient Gold-Plated Coins" and "New Material" under THE MINTING PROCESS, and "Macedonian Plated Gold" below].

3535 ——— "Macedonian Plated Gold Staters." *Italiam Fato Profvgi: Numismatic Studies Dedicated to Vladimir and Elvira Eliza Clain-Stefanelli.* Numismatica Lovaniensia 12. Edited by T. Hackens. Louvain-la-Neuve: De L'Université Catholique De Louvain, 1996. Pages 341-8. 1 pl.
Reformulates and amends the series of articles which the author previously published in *SAN* (see above). Discusses the five known examples of Alexander the Great gold staters made by gold-plating a silver core. Four of the pieces are now accepted as genuine ancient coins; one is deemed to be an ancient counterfeit. Wells also discusses three examples of gold-plating on a copper core. These copper-core "staters" may be ancient counterfeits or may have come from official mints in times of emergency. These are the only known cases of ancient Greek coins being produced by gold-plating an inferior metal.

3536 **West, Allen Brown.** "The Early Diplomacy of Philip II of Macedon Illustrated by His Coins." *Numismatic Chronicle* 5th ser., 3 (1923): 169-210. [CS 2331]
Discusses Philip's monetary reforms, the events and conditions that led to them, and the goals he intended to achieve through them. Discusses Philip's selection of a weight standard for his coinage, the dates of issue of various coins, the influences on his selection of coin types, the gold-to-silver value ratio, and the monetary aspects of his foreign policy.

3537 **Westermark, Ulla.** "Notes on Macedonian Bronze Coins." *Studi per Laura Breglia.* Bolletino di Numismatica, Supplement 4. Rome, 1988. Pages 179-87.

3538 ——— "Remarks on the Regal Macedonian Coinage ca. 413-359 B.C." *Kraay—Mørkholm Essays: Numismatic Studies in Memory of C. M. Kraay and O. Mørkholm.* Numismatica Lovaniensia 10. Edited by G. Le Rider, G. K. Jenkins, N. Waggoner, and U. Westermark. Louvain-la-Neuve: Université Catholique de Louvain, 1989. Pages 301-15. 2 pls.
Reviews the history of the period. Examines the coinage of Archelaus (identifies the head on his coinage as that of Apollo), Aeropus, Amyntas II, Pausanias, Amyntas III, Alexander II, and Perdikkas III. Discusses weights standards and coin types. Presents a catalogue of bronze coin types, ca. 413-359 B.C. The plates illustrate fifty coins.

3539 ——— "The Staters of Archelaus: A Die Study." *Essays in Honour of Robert Carson and Kenneth Jenkins.* Edited by M. J. Price, A. M. Burnett, and R. Bland. London: Spink & Son, 1993. Pages 17-30. 6 pls.
Summarizes events in the reign of Archelaus 413-399 B.C. Then presents a die study of his staters based on 246 examples, 146 of which came from the Ptolemais Hoard (*IGCH* 365). Discusses dies, weights, and types. Presents a catalogue of the coins divided into two groups.

3540 ——— "Apollo in Macedonia." *Opus Mixtum: Essays in Ancient Art and Society.* ActaRom 8, no. 21. Stockholm, 1994. Pages 149-54. Illus.
"The representation of Apollo in the regal Macedonian coin series is discussed." [U. Westermark, *NL* 134]. [Also see Gomer "Apollo, Herakles and Wolf" above].

3541 ——— "Influences from South Italy on Early Macedonian Bronze Coins." *Hellas und der Griechische Osten: Festschrift für Peter Robert Franke zum 70. Geburtstag.* Studien zur Geschichte und Numismatik der Griechischen Welt. Edited by W. Leschhorn, A. V. B. Miron, and A. Miron. Saarbrücken: SDV Saarbrücer Druckerei und Verlag, 1996. Pages 291-9. 1 pl.

3542 **Williams, J. H. C., and Andrew M. Burnett.** "Alexander the Great and the Coinages of Western Greece." *Studies in Greek Numismatics in Memory of Martin Jessop Price.* Edited by Richard Ashton and Silvia Hurter. London: Spink, 1998. Pages 379-93. 1 pl.

An investigation of the immediate reaction in Italy and Sicily in the late fourth and early third centuries B.C. to the tremendous events in the East during and after the reign of Alexander. Focuses on three principal themes: (1) the circulation of Macedonian coinage in the West, (2) the extent to which the designs of Alexander's coinage provided an influence on coinage in the West, (3) the increase in coin output and warfare in the West in order to assess the extent to which it was a cultural reflection of the example set by Alexander and his father. The authors' conclusions are: (1) Hoard evidence shows that Macedonian coinage saw very limited use in the West, perhaps due to its weight standard and the preference for Corinthian coinage. (2) Symbolism derived from Macedonian coinage and iconography had some influence on the cultural outlook of Italy and Sicily, but the infrequent incidence on Western coinage suggests that political motivations were minimal. (3) The output of the principal mints of Italy increased significantly. This is perhaps attributable to the increasing use of mercenaries in the West as a result of increased military aggressiveness. But this does not entirely account for the increased coinage. Concludes that perhaps Rome was more influenced by Macedonia than were the Greek cities of Italy and Sicily.

3543 **Wilson, Ladislav.** "The Coins of Alexander the Great." *Ancient: The Bimonthly Magazine of Antiquity* 56 (April 1997).

3544 **Winter, W. Jeffrey.** "A Fourth Century B.C. Hoard of Macedonian AE Coins." *The Celator* 13, no. 9 (September 1999): 40, 42, 43, 50. Illus.

Discusses a hoard of 295 Macedonian bronze coins which came onto the market in 1998. The hoard included ten Philip II units, twelve Alexander III half-units of the Herakles/eagle series, three Alexander III units of the Herakles/bow and club series, and 270 Alexander III half-units of the shield/helmet series. A brief catalogue of the coins is presented. [Also see K. Liampi "A Hoard of Bronze Coins of Alexander the Great" above].

3545 **Wirgin, Wolf.** "The Origin of the Anchor of Alexander the Great." *Spink Numismatic Circular* 74, nos. 7-8 (July-August 1966): 181-2. Illus.

In this follow-up to the author's article on the anchor of Seleucus (see Wirgin "Appian" under SYRIA—SELEUCID KINGDOM), he discusses the anchor symbol found on coins of Marathus and Aradus. At these cities, Wirgin suggests the anchor is not a symbol of Seleucus. Rather, it is an attribute of the deified Alexander. Suggests the anchor evolved into a double symbol: to Seleucus, the anchor was a sign of safety; to the Phoenicians, it stood for continuation of life after death. [Also see follow-up comments by B. Oestreicher in *Spink Numismatic Circular* 74 (October 1966): 243, and by Wirgin in *Spink Numismatic Circular* 75 (January 1967): 5].

3546 **Zachos, Konstantinos, Katerini Liampi, and Dimitra Tsangari.** *Alexander the Great: From Macedonia to the Edge of the World.* Athens: Alpha Bank, 2010. 200 pp., illus.

An exhibition catalogue depicting 218 coins from the Alpha Bank collection. The exhibition, held at the Archaeological Museum of Ioannina, examined the history of Alexander the Great through his coinage and its effect on the ancient world even after his death.

3547 **Zervos, Orestes H.** "Near Eastern Elements in the Tetradrachms of Alexander the Great: The Eastern Mints." *Greek Numismatics and Archaeology: Essays in Honor of Margaret Thompson.* Edited by O. Mørkholm and N. M. Waggoner. Wetteren: Numismatique Romaine, 1979. Pages 295-305. 1 pl.

Explores the influence of the Orient on the style of coinage of Alexander the Great struck at eastern mints—bounded by Cilicia and Cyprus in the Northwest, and by Egypt and Babylon in the Southeast. Identifies and describes some of the elements which came from the east, and by exploring the reasons underlying these eastern borrowings, Zervos lends insight into the history of the coinage. Focuses on the adaptation of the figure of Baaltarz on the coins of Mazaios to the seated figure of Zeus on the coinage of Alexander. Also discusses the adaptation of the throne and crown of Baaltarz to those of Zeus.

3548 ——— "Additions to the Demanhur Hoard of Alexander Tetradrachms." *Numismatic Chronicle* 140 (1980): 185-8. [CS 3309]

Lists thirty varieties of Alexander tetradrachms not previously published by Newell.

3549 ——— "The Earliest Coins of Alexander the Great: 1. Notes on a Book by Gerhard Kleiner." *Numismatic Chronicle* 142 (1982): 166-79. 3 pls.

"The theory has been proposed by Six, Head, Schlumberger, etc., that the coinage of Alexander the Great did not commence at the beginning of his reign (336 B.C.). Its fullest exposition is given in *Alexanders Reichsmünzen* (1949) in which G. Kleiner tries to establish that the coinage actually began after Alexander had invaded Asia, and had taken Tarsus (333). His supporting facts and inferences have been downplayed however, as most scholars have refused to accept Kleiner's thesis. A re-examination of the evidence, shows that Kleiner is probably correct. New and unknown facts are adduced which help to discover some of the 'lost' models of Alexander's coinage, and which also help demonstrate the connection of that coinage with the East, as Kleiner suggests. The argument can thus be made that Alexandrian coinage started following the Battle of Isus (fall of 333) and that its first issues were probably struck at the neighboring mint of Tarsus." [O. Zervos, *NL* 109]. [Also see G. Kleiner "Alexanders Reichsmünzen" and M. J. Price "The Earliest Coins of Alexander" above].

Also see: Adams "The Search for Coson" under THRACE—GENERAL WORKS; Amandry and Le Rider *Tresors* under GENERAL WORKS—GREEK; Arnold-Biucchi "Arabian Alexanders" under ARABIA; Arslan and Özen "Hoard" under EGYPT—PTOLEMAIC KINGDOM; Arslan and Price "A Hoard from the Durmaz Collection" under HOARDS; Ashton "A Series of Pseudo-Rhodian Drachms" under CARIAN ISLANDS—RHODOS; Ashton "Pseudo-Rhodian" under THRACE—SAMOTHRACE; Bauslaugh "Two Unpublished Overstrikes" under ATTICA—NEW STYLE COINAGE; Bellinger "Notes on Coins" under MACEDONIAN CITIES AND TRIBES; Bellinger "The Coins from the Treasure of the Oxus" under HOARDS; Baynham "Continuity and Ambition: The Posthumous Philip II Gold Staters from Colophon/Magnesia" under GENERAL WORKS—HELLENISTIC; Bellinger "Philippi" under MACEDONIAN CITIES AND TRIBES; Bernard "Alexandre, Ménon et les Mines d'Or d'Armenie" under ARMENIA; Bieber "Portraits of Alexander" under PORTRAITS; Bieber "Alexander the Great in Greek and Roman Art" under PORTRAITS; Bivar "The Bactrian Treasure" under BACTRIA; Boon "Toward a Numismatic History" under SYRIA—AUTONOMOUS CITIES; Bopearachchi and Flandrin under *Le Portrait d'Alexandre* under HOARDS; Bosworth "Rider in the Chariot: Ptolemy, Alexander and the Elephants" under TYPES; Brett "Athena ΑΛΚΙΔΕΜΟΣ" under TYPES; "Coin Portrait" under PORTRAITS; Cox "Gordian Hoards III" under HOARDS; Cox *A Tarsus Coin Collection* under CILICIA.

de Callataÿ "Athenian New Style Tetradrachms in Macedonian Hoards" under ATTICA—NEW STYLE COINAGE; Davesne and Le Rider *Gülnar II* under HOARDS; Destrooper-Georgiades "Un Bronze Surfrappé de Ptolémée Ier/Démétrios Poliorcète Dimitrov" under EGYPT—PTOLEMAIC KINGDOM; "A Hoard of Gold Staters" under HOARDS; Dimitrov "The Development of Thrace" under THRACE—GENERAL WORKS; Gaebler *Fälschungen Makedonischer* under COUNTERFEITS; Gardner "The Apoxyomenos" under PORTRAITS; Gardner "Ares as a Sun-God" under TYPES; Gardner "Macedonian" under SYRIA—SELEUCID KINGDOM; Gardner "New Greek Coins of Bactria and India" under BACTRIA; Gardner "Numismatic Reattributions" under GENERAL WORKS—GREEK; Head *Catalogue of Greek Coins* under

MACEDONIAN CITIES AND TRIBES; Head "The Earliest Graeco-Bactrian" under BACTRIA; Healy "Alexander" under LESBOS; Hill "Notes on the Alexandrine Coinage of Phoenicia" under PHOENICIA; "Hoard of Greek Coins" under HOARDS; Houghton "Equestrian Portrait of Alexander" under SYRIA—SELEUCID KINGDOM; Houghton "Some Alexander Coins of Seleucus" under SYRIA—SELEUCID KINGDOM; Hunter "Hoard from Serbia" under CELTIC COINAGE—GENERAL WORKS.

Jamgochian "Winged Victory" under TYPES; Jenkins "An Early Ptolemaic Hoard" under EGYPT—PTOLEMAIC KINGDOM; Jidejian *Eddé Collection* under PORTRAITS; Jones "The Coinage of Alexander and his Successors" under GENERAL WORKS—HELLENISTIC; Kraay "Greek Coinage and War" under GENERAL WORKS—GREEK; Kraay "Historical Interpretations" under GENERAL WORKS—GREEK; Kraay "On the Weights" under METROLOGY; Kraay and Moorey "Two Fifth Century Hoards" under HOARDS; Lang "Treasure-Trove" under HOARDS; Le Rider and de Callataÿ *Les Séleucides et les Ptolémées* under SYRIA—SELEUCID KINGDOM; G. Macdonald "Athenian and Macedonian Coins in India" under NORTHWEST INDIA; Marinescu "Statues" under PORTRAITS; Marotta and Zakelj "Portraits and Representations of Alexander" under PORTRAITS; Martin "Hoard from Thessaly" under HOARDS; May "Alexander Coinage of Nikokles" under CYPRUS; May "Macedonia and Illyria" under NORTHERN GREECE—ILLYRIA; Milavic "Pankration" under TYPES; Mildenberg "A Note on the Coinage of Hierapolis" under PERSIA; Miller "East Arachosia (Quetta) Hoard" under HOARDS; Mitchiner *Indo-Greek and Indo-Scythian, Vol. 1: The Early Greeks* under BACTRIA; Montero "The Coinage of Alexander the Great" under PORTRAITS; Mørkholm "Alexander Coinage of Nicocles" under CYPRUS.

Nash "The Kuft Hoard" under HOARDS; Newell *Alexander Hoards 4* under HOARDS; Newell "Nikokles" under CYPRUS; Newell *Tyrus Rediviva* under PHOENICIA; Noe "The Corinth Hoard" under HOARDS; Oikonomides "Amyntas" under PORTRAITS; Oikonomides "Greek Geologists" under METALLURGY; Oikonomides "New Evidence" under PORTRAITS; Oikonomides "The Portrait of King Philip II" under PORTRAITS; Oikonomides "Search for Alexander Reveals Philip II" under PORTRAITS; Oikonomides "Victory" under NORTHERN GREECE—EPIRUS; Oliver "Politics of Coinage" under ATTICA—GENERAL WORKS; Parke-Bernet Galleries *The Extremely Important Greek Hoard* under MACEDONIAN CITIES AND TRIBES; Petrova "The Fifth Century B.C. Coins" under MACEDONIAN CITIES AND TRIBES; Price "Circulation at Babylon" under MESOPOTAMIA.

D. Robinson "The Alexander Hoard of Megalopolis" under HOARDS; E. S. G. Robinson "Aspeisas" under PERSIA; Russeva "Coin Hoard from Rakitovo" under HOARDS; Sayles "Images & Meaning" under TYPES; C. Seltman "Two Athenian Marble Thrones" under TYPES; Sotheby & Co. *Catalogue...Haughton Collection* under PRIVATE COLLECTIONS; Spaer "Two Hoards of Minor Silver" under HOARDS; Stefanakis "A Posthumous Alexander" under PORTRAITS; Tameanko "Nikokles" under CYPRUS; Taylor "Valuing the Numismatic Legacy" under COLLECTING GUIDES; Thompson "The Armenak Hoard" under HOARDS; Thompson "Byzantium Over Aesillas" under THRACE—COINAGE OF LYSIMACHOS; Touratsoglou "The Adam Zagliveriou/1983 Hoard" under ATTICA—NEW STYLE COINAGE; Touratsoglou *The Coin Circulation in Ancient Macedonia* under HOARDS; Touratsoglou *Disjecta Membra* under HOARDS; Touratsoglou "Statères d'Alexandre et Statères de Cyzique" under HOARDS; "Treasure-Trove" under HOARDS; Tsangari *Coins of Macedonia in the Alpha Bank Collection* under PUBLIC COLLECTIONS—GREECE (ATHENS).

Vagi "Alexander's Legacy" under HELLENISTIC COINAGE—GENERAL WORKS; van Alfen et al. "Acquisitions for 2002" under PUBLIC COLLECTIONS—UNITED STATES (NEW YORK); Vaux "On Some Remarkable Greek Coins" under PUBLIC COLLECTIONS—GREAT BRITAIN (LONDON); Vaux "Select Coins" under ASIA—GENERAL WORKS; Waggoner "Another Alexander" and "Further Reflections" under MACEDONIAN CITIES AND TRIBES; Waggoner "The Alexander Mint" (two items) under BABYLONIA; Waggoner "The Propontis Hoard" (two items) under HOARDS; Waggoner "Tetradrachms" under MESOPOTAMIA; W. P. Wallace "The Meeting-Point of the Histiaian and Macedonian Tetrobols" under CENTRAL GREECE—EUBOIA; Wartenberg "The Alexander-Eagle Hoard" under HOARDS; Wartenberg and Kagan "Some Comments on a New Hoard" under HOARDS; Wells "The Macedon, Aesillas, Drachma" under COUNTERFEITS; Westermark "Notes on the Saida Hoard" under HOARDS; Worland "An 1805 Treatise" under PORTRAITS; Touratsoglou "The Price of Power" under HOARDS; Zervos *The Alexander Mint* under EGYPT—PRE-PTOLEMAIC PERIOD; Zervos "Two Early Ptolemaic Hoards" under EGYPT—PTOLEMAIC KINGDOM; Zervos "Newell's Manuscript" under HOARDS.

ALEXANDER'S PORUS COINS/MEDALLIONS

3550 **Arnold-Biucchi, Carmen.** "I Decadrammi nel Mondo Greco: Monete o Medaglie?" *Rivista Italiana di Numismatica e Scienze Affini* (Italy) 95 (1993): 243-50.
The author suggests the "Porus" coins were struck in Babylon by a local satrap.

3551 **Banerji, J. N.** "The Obverse Device of Some Decadrachms with Alexandrian Association." *Journal of the Numismatic Society of India* (India) 12 (1950): 118-20.
Banerji attempts to match the scene on the Porus decadrachms with Curtius' description of Porus' surrender. Banerji suggested that the brief moment before the collapse of Alexander's horse was the scene captured on the medallions.

3552 **Bernard, Paul.** "Le Monnayage d'Eudamos, Satrape Grec du Panjab et 'Maître des Éléphants.'" *Orientalia Iosephi Tucci Memoriae Dicata*. Edited by G. Gnoli and L. Lanciotti. Rome: Istituto Italiano per il Medio ed Estremo Oriente, 1985. Pages 65-94.
Bernard suggests the elephant medallions were minted in the area of Babylon after Alexander's death. The coinage may have been initiated by Eudamos, one of Alexander's former satraps of the Punjab, to highlight Alexander's achievements.

3553 **Chugg, Andrew M.** "Is the Gold Porus Medallion a Lifetime Portrait of Alexander the Great?" *The Celator* 21, no. 9 (September 2007): 28-31, 34-5. Illus.
The "Porus Medallions" are a small group of silver coins with designs celebrating the victory of Alexander the Great over the Indian Rajah Porus in the Battle of the Hydaspes in 326 B.C. Holt has argued they were minted in India by Alexander himself (see Holt *Alexander the Great* below). Chugg reviews a gold coin of distater or double daric weight with similar types which turned up in 2003. Its authenticity has been questioned. The obverse bears a portrait of Alexander similar to that used by Ptolemy I on his early Egyptian satrapal coinage. Chugg points out stylistic variations which cause suspicion (details of the aegis, Alexander's profile, the elephant trunk in relation to the border, the placement of the monograms, and other considerations). Chugg strongly suggests the piece is a forgery. [Also see G. P. Franck-Weiby's "Letter to the Editor" in *The Celator* 21, no. 11 (November 2007): 4. Franck-Weiby points out further stylistic features and details of the die engraving techniques evident from the gold piece that lend additional weight to the claim of a forgery].

3554 **Dürr, Nicholas.** "Neues aus Babylonien." *Schweizer Münzblätter* 24 (1974): 33-6.
An examination of the "tetradrachms" with elephant/bowman, which were found in the 1973 Iraq Hoard. An English translation by A. Ilsch with updated notes appeared in *Numismatic Digest* (India) 2 (1978): 4-7.

3555 ———. "Ein 'Elephantenstater' für Porus." *Actes du 8ème Congrès International de Numismatique, New York—Washington, Septembre 1973*. Edited by Herbert A. Cahn and Georges Le Rider. Paris: Association Internationale des Numismates Professionnels, 1976. Pages 43 ff.

3556 **Fox, Robin Lane.** "Text and Image: Alexander the Great, Coins and Elephants." *Bulletin of the Institute of Classical Studies* 41 (1996): 87-108.

Comments on some of the theories regarding the Alexander/elephant medallions. Fox examines a theory put forward by Martin Price that the monograms AB and Ξ on the elephant medallions may represent the satrap at Susa, Abulites and the commander Xenophilos. A passage in Plutarch claims that, rather than bringing badly needed provisions, Abulites brought 3000 talents of coinage to Alexander. Alexander angrily threw the coins to his horses. These coins may have been the elephant medallions.

3557 **Hill, George F.** "Decadrachm Commemorating Alexander's Indian Campaign." *British Museum Quarterly* 1 (1926-27): 36-7.

The first publication of the second known "Porus Decadrachm," acquired by the British Museum in 1926. Hill identifies the horseman on the obverse as Alexander.

3558 **Hollstein, Wilhelm.** "Taxiles' Prägung für Alexander den Grossen." *Schweizerische Numismatische Gesellschaft* (Switzerland) 68 (1989): 5-17.

Curtius reported that Alexander receieved eighty talents of coined silver from Taxiles (also known as Omphis). Hollstein suggests this coined silver was the "Porus" coins, and therefore they were struck by Taxiles.

3559 **Holt, Frank L.** *Alexander the Great and the Mystery of the Elephant Medallions.* Berkeley and Los Angeles: University of California Press, 2003. 198 pp., illus.

A thorough examination of the history and significance of the series of medallions or coins known as the Porus or elephant medallions. Holt traces the history of the decadrachm from its supposed find as part of the Oxus Treasure (buried ca. 150 B.C.), located in 1877. It was purchased by Augustus W. Franks, a British Museum official. Franks donated it to the museum in 1887 and it was first mentioned in an anonymous notice in the *American Journal of Numismatics* in 1887 (see "Rare Bactrian Decadrachm" below), identified as a Bactrian decadrachm. Gardner suggested it was struck by Eucratides or Heliocles to celebrate their success over the invading hordes of Yueh-chi in the second century B.C. (see Gardner "New Greek Coins of Bactria" under BACTRIA).

Holt next summarizes Alexander's strategy in battle against the Indian rajah Porus in the Battle of the Hydaspes River (326 B.C.). Head (*NC* 1906) attributed the decadrachms to Alexander's time and suggested the reverse shows a standing Alexander in Persian helmet and records his invasion of the Punjab in 326. Head believed the medal was intended for presentation to Macedonian officials. In the second edition of his *Historia Numorum*, Head changed his interpretation and now suggested the piece illustrated a passage by Arrian: Porus retreats on his elephant after his defeat at the Hydaspes, and is pursued by Prince Taxiles, a vassal of Alexander. Suggests the piece was struck in the name of Alexander, perhaps by Taxiles in commemoration of that episode. Holt reveals Head's misinterpretation of Arrian.

A second specimen of the decadrachm appeared in 1926 and Hill wrote about it, identifying the horseman as Alexander (see Hill above). A third specimen was donated to the American Numismatic Society in 1959 by Burton Y. Berry. Its origin is unknown. Holt summarizes other theories, including those of Pandley and Mitchiner. Discusses the use of elephants in war. Discusses the known forgeries of the decadrachm.

In 1973, the "Iraq Hoard" came to light, consisting of 1800 coins including as many as seven Porus decadrachms and several tetradrachms of elephant/bowman type or elephant/chariot type. These coins are clearly related to the decadrachms. Duerr, who brought the hoard to light, believed these new coins honored Porus. Holt reviews theories put forward by Oikonomides, Hammond, Price, Bernard, Lane Fox, Hollstein, and Bosworth.

Price first suggested in 1982 that the monograms AB and Ξ may represent Abulites and Xenophilos—the satrap and commander of the garrison at Susa. Examines how Alexander has been depicted by various historians over the years. Examines the designs on the decadrachms and concludes with a high level of confidence that the standing figure on the reverse is Alexander. His helmet, sword, and wardrobe closely match items from the Macedonian royal tomb at Vergina and those depicted in the Alexander mosaic from Pompeii. On the obverse, the horseman matches the figure from the reverse and must be Alexander. The elephant driver's large size suggests that he is Porus—who was reported to be very tall. The scene is remarkably similar to that on the Alexander mosaic. Both scenes depict Alexander as the heroic warrior deflecting a brave and worthy opponent.

The identity of the figures on the tetradrachms remain quite uncertain. The figures seem to be Indian, and seem to be in retreat. Not much else can be certain about them. Holt discusses mintage quantities and concludes these were very small issues of commemorative pieces. The weights of neither the large or small coins adhere closely to the decadrachm or tetradrachm weight standard. The erratic weights, uneven and off-center striking, and inconsistent die axis, point to a hurried and poorly supervised minting.

Holt concludes these pieces functioned both as medals and as coins. They were hurriedly minted ca. 326-325 B.C. as special issues for veterans of the Indian campaign to commemorate the victory at the Battle of the Hydaspes River. The minting was authorized by Alexander and produced as best as could be managed in the East (without benefit of a Greek mint). They were intended as valuable rewards for distinguished military service. They were regarded as Macedonian decadrachms and tetradrachms, rather than foreign five and two shekel pieces on a Babylonian standard. The dies were created by Greek die cutters and were struck by Indian workers unfamiliar with striking round, high-relief medallions.

The archers and chariots on the tetradrachms must be Porus' forces. Alexander's victory was partly enabled by the heavy rainstorms on the eve of the battle. The thunderbolt in Alexander's hand on the decadrachms indicates Zeus' assistance in the victory, or the assistance of Alexander as a god. The archers and chariots which appear on the tetradrachms were rendered ineffective by the muddy conditions. The unifying theme on all the medallions is thus the divine intervention which played a key role in the battle. Holt recounts numerous examples in history in which divine intervention in weather has been credited for aiding in the defeat of an enemy. Thus, on the decadrachms Alexander shows himself as an equal of the gods.

In the appendices, Holt lists the known specimens and includes notes on the provenance of each. He also lists known forgeries, and provides information on the 1973 Iraq Hoard. Concludes with an extensive bibliography. [An extensive review by Oliver Hoover appears in *American Numismatic Society Magazine* 3, no. 2 (summer 2004): 58-61. Hoover thinks Holt has overstated the importance of the weather as a factor in the battle and doubts that this can be considered the unifying theme for this coinage series. Also reviewed by M. Markowitz in *The Celator* 18, no. 2 (February 2004): 39-40].

3560 ——— "Stealing Zeus's Thunder." Illustrated by Norman MacDonald. *Saudi Aramco World* 56, no. 3 (May/June 2005): 10-19. Illus.

Recounts the story of the Alexander medallions, summarizing information from Holt's 2003 book, *Alexander the Great and the Mystery of the Elephant Medallions* (see above). [Also see Holt "Ptolemy's Alexandrian Postscript" under EGYPT—PTOLEMAIC KINGDOM].

3561 **Holt, Frank L., and Osmund Bopearachchi.** *The Alexander Medallion: Exploring the Origins of a Unique Artefact.* Lacapelle-Marival, France: Imago Lattara, 2011. 103 pp., illus.
An examination of the gold double daric of Alexander, bringing together several papers on the subject. The authors tackle the problems of the coin's authenticity and conclude that it is genuinely ancient.

3562 **Miller, M. C. J.** "The 'Porus' Decadrachm of Alexander and the Founding of Bucephala." *The Ancient World* 25, no. 1 (1994): 109-20. Illus.
Describes the two decadrachm coin types of Alexander the Great and discusses the symbolism found on the "Porus" decadrachm: Alexander's plumed helmet, his cuirass, his pelte, and the thunderbolt. Discusses the weight standard used for the coins, its date of minting, the reasons for its minting, and the meaning of the single letter and monogram found on the coins. Miller suggests the coin depicts the last charge of Alexander's horse Bucephalus, and was minted to commemorate the death of the horse and the foundation of the city of Bucephala.

3563 **Nicolet-Pierre, Hélène.** "Monnaies 'à l'Elephant.'" *Bulletin de la Société Française de Numismatique* (France) 33 (1978): 401-3.
The author examines the three types of medallions acquired from the 1973 Iraq Hoard by the Bibliothèque Nationale in Paris. She notes the possibility that the decadrachms may have been struck over earlier coins. She also notes the presence of a hooked elephant goad in the elephant driver's left hand. She stresses the stylistic unity of this group of coins, and suggests they are Persian coins of a small local mintage.

3564 "Ninth Specimen of Poros Decadrachm is Finest Yet Known." *The Celator* 4, no. 8 (August 1990): 12.
Announces the discovery of a ninth specimen of Alexander the Great's Poros decadrachm. The design of the coin is fully described. The location of all known specimens is given and the historical background for the coin is presented.

3565 **Pandey, Deena B.** "The Hydaspese-Battle Commemorative Medal of Alexander the Great—A Fresh Approach." *Journal of the Numismatic Society of India* (India) 33 (1971): 1-7.
Pandey argues that the "Porus" medallions must commemorate Alexander's defeat of the Persian King Darius at Gaugamela, not Porus at the Hydaspes River.

3566 **Price, Martin J.** "The 'Porus' Coinage of Alexander the Great: A Symbol of Concord and Community." *Studia Paulo Naster Oblata, Volume 1: Numismatica Antiqua.* Edited by S. Scheers. Orientalia Lovaniensia Analecta 12. Louvain: Departement Oriëntalistiek, 1982. Pages 75-88, including 3 pls.
Re-examines Alexander the Great's famous "Porus" decadrachm and the related tetradrachm issue based on the evidence of some new specimens found in Iraq in 1973. Price states these coins are more properly labeled as 5-shekel and 2-shekel coins. The 2-shekel coins from the 1973 hoard are linked to the 5-shekel coins by a letter on the reverse and a monogram on the obverse. He states that Alexander's normal royal coinage decadrachms were not overstruck to make the "Porus" 5-shekel pieces as is sometimes claimed. The existence of the 2-shekel coins shows that the purpose of these and the 5-shekels was as coinage—not as commemorative medallions. The hoard, buried 323/2 B.C., also shows that these are lifetime issues, and may have been struck prior to Alexander's victory over Porus in 326 B.C. Discusses the types of the 5-shekels and concludes they do not show a battle scene involving Porus. The 5-shekels represents Macedonian forces; the 2-shekels represents Indian forces. Together they suggest an element of Alexander's policy of fusion in his Eastern empire. Discusses Alexander's use of elephants. Comments on possible mints for these issues: suggests Babylon, Susa, Persepolis, or Ecbatana. The mint is unlikely to be Bactra or Taxila.

3567 "A Rare Bactrian Decadrachm." *American Journal of Numismatics* 22, no. 1 (July 1887): 40.
Describes a "Bactrian" decadrachm (the famous Porus decadrachm of Alexander the Great) recently presented to the British Museum by A. W. Franks.

3568 **Stauffer, D. E.** "Die Londoner Dekadrachme von 324 und die Indeenpolitik Alexanders." *Jahrbuch für Numismatik und Gledgeschichte* (Germany) 2 (1950-51): 132.
Stauffer suggests the "Porus" medallions had been minted at Babylon in 324 B.C. and likely bore the designs of Alexander's master gem-engraver, Pyrgoteles.

3568a **Tameanko, Marvin.** "Alexander the Great's Elephant Coins." *Coin News* (August 2011).

Also see: Bopearachchi and Flandrin *Le Portrait d'Alexandre le Grand: Histoire d'une Découverte Pour l'Humanité* under HOARDS; Gardner "New Greek Coins of Bactria and India" under BACTRIA; Head "Earliest Graeco-Bactrian and Graeco-Indian Coins" under BACTRIA; Holt "Ptolemy's Alexandrian Postscript" under EGYPT—PTOLEMAIC KINGDOM; Le Rider *Alexander the Great: Coinage, Finances, and Policy* under MACEDONIAN KINGDOM—GENERAL WORKS; Macdonald "Athenian and Macedonian Coins" under BACTRIA; Oikonomides "Decadrachm Aids in Identification" under MACEDONIAN KINGDOM—GENERAL WORKS; Price "Circulation at Babylon" under MESOPOTAMIA; Spengler "An Echo of Bucephalus" MACEDONIAN KINGDOM—GENERAL WORKS; Whitehead "Eastern Satrap Sophytes" under BACTRIA.

THE ROMAN PROVINCE OF MACEDONIA

3569 **Bauslaugh, Robert A.** "Reconstructing the Circulation of Roman Coinage in First Century B.C. Macedonia." *Numismatic Archaeology/Archaeological Numismatics: Proceedings of an International Conference held to Honour Dr. Mando Oeconomides in Athens 1995.* Oxbow Monograph 75. Edited by K. A. Sheedy and Ch. Papageorgiadou-Banis. Oxford: Oxbow Books, 1997. Pages 118-29. Map, 2 pls.
Early in the first century B.C., the Romans issued an Attic weight coinage in the name of the Macedonians. The author explores the circulation of these Aesillas issues and the role they played in the expansion of Roman power across the Balkan Peninsula. Lists and discusses hoards in which Aesillas tetradrachms have been found, and examines the implications for the chronology and circulation of these coins. Evidence suggests that the Aesillas coinage was intended for payments to Thracian tribes for their assistance to Rome in controlling the regions of Thrace and Macedonia.

3570 ———. *Silver Coinage with the Types of Aesillas the Quaestor.* Numismatic Studies 22. New York: American Numismatic Society, 2000. 119 pp., 15 pls.

A complete examination of the first century B.C. silver coins issued by the Romans in the name of the Macedonians. The reverse of the coins bear the name AESILLAS Q(uaestor) or, on two dies, SVVRA LEG PRO Q, and on the obverse, MAKEΔONΩN with a portrait of Alexander the Great. It is likely that most were minted at Thessalonika, while other were minted at Pella or Bottiaeans, and another uncertain mint. Bauslaugh catalogues all known varieties of the coinage, including about 1000 tetradrachms (102 obverse dies, 378 reverse dies), 8 drachms, 4 overstruck examples, and 14 imitations. The coins are segregated into eight groups arranged chronologically. All known specimens are listed for each variety, from published and unpublished collections, with commentary on die links, style, weights, and chronology. Includes chapters on metrology and production control systems and marks, overstrikes and the implications for chronology, and hoards and circulation patterns. Concludes with a summary of the sequence of issues, stylistic changes over time, and weight changes. Bauslaugh concludes the coins were minted during 90-70 B.C., with production being sporadic. The series was produced to facilitate special payments by the Romans, probably to Thracian tribes. The coins were gradually replaced by the Roman denarii.

3571 **Burnett, Andrew M.** "Aesillas: Two New Hoards." *Coin Hoards* 7 (1985): 54-67, including 6 pls.
Examines the problems surrounding the dating of the coinage of the Roman quaestor Aesillas in Macedonia. Reviews the theories of Thompson, Lewis, Mattingly, and Boehringer. Uses evidence of overstrikes and recent hoards.

3572 **de Callataÿ, François.** "Les Monnaies au Nom d'Aesillas." *Italiam Fato Profvgi: Numismatic Studies Dedicated to Vladimir and Elvira Eliza Clain-Stefanelli.* Numismatica Lovaniensia 12. Edited by T. Hackens. Louvain-la-Neuve: De L'Université Catholique De Louvain, 1996. Pages 113-52.

3573 ———. "The Coins in the Name of Sura." *Coins of Macedonia and Rome: Essays in Honour of Charles Hersh.* Edited by Andrew Burnett, Ute Wartenberg, and Richard Witschonke. London: Spink, 1998. Pages 113-7. 2 pls.
The name of Q. Bruttius Sura, who opposed Mithradates' invasion of Thessaly, appears on some rare varieties of Macedonian tetradrachms with types similar to those struck in the name of Aesillas. Sura's name also appears on some tetradrachms of Thasos. A die-study of the Macedonian tetradrachms reveals that those bearing the name of Aesillas were issued just after those struck in the name of Sura. The author lists the known specimens of the Macedonian and Thasian coins bearing the name Sura and suggests reasons for the issuance of these coins.

3574 **Fisher, Roger S.** "Two Notes on the Aesillas Tetradrachms: Mint Attribution and a Die Control System." *Museum Notes* 30 (1985): 69-88. 2 pls.
Examines the first century B.C. Aesillas tetradrachms of the Roman province of Macedonia. Shows that the nineteenth century mint attributions based solely on obverse die marks must be reconsidered, and that the obverse and reverse die marks are part of a die control system. Reviews various interpretations of the obverse die marks. Examines die links and frequency tables of weights. Concludes the Aesillas issues fall into two distinct groups, and in one of the groups, a combination of letters and pellets as die marks was employed in a die control system. Presents a catalogue of 160 varieties arranged by issue and die control marks.

3575 **Gaebler, Hugo.** "Zur Münzkunde Makedoniens III, Makedonien im Aufstand unter Andriskos. Makedonien als Römische Provinz." *Zeitschrift für Numismatik* (Germany) 23 (1902): 141-89.
[Also see MacKay "Numismatic Evidence" below].

3576 **Kourempanas, Theodoros.** "Attribution of Bronze Coins to Philip VI." *Nomismatika Khronika* (Greece) 28 (2010): 5-14. Illus.
The author attributes some bronze coins to Philip VI Andriskos based on overstrikes, hoard evidence, and excavation finds. The coins had previously been given to Philip V due to the lack of evidence for a coinage by Philip VI. [In Greek on pp. 5-11 (with 2 pls.) and in English on pp. 12-14. Translation by M. Tzamali].

3577 **MacDonald, David J.** "Overstrikes of Macedonian Bronze Coins." *Nomismatika Khronika* (Greece) 17 (1998): 97-107, including 2 pls.
(1) MacDonald discusses the Macedonian "Silenos/Ethnikon" bronze coins struck over an issue of Amphipolis. The entire issue of Silenos/Ethnikon bronze may be overstruck on coins struck in the name of the Roman questors Gaius Publilius and Lucius Fulcinnius. The issues have been variously assigned to ca. 148-141 B.C. or ca. 168-165. The author examines the historical background for the issues and concludes the questors Publilius and Fulcinnius issued coins ca. 168-167, many of which were overstruck with the Silenos/Ethnikon type in 141 as a fiscal rather than an ideological measure.(2) MacDonald examines a group of ancient imitations of Macedonian bronze coins, at least eight of which are struck over recognizable host coins. Eight such coins are described and illustrated. The types are river-god Strymon/trident with dolphins. The purpose of striking the Strymon/trident designs over a variety of Macedonian city issues was to create bronze coins uniform in type and denomination.

3578 ———. "Imitations of Macedonia First Meris Tetradrachms over Myrina." *Nomismatika Khronika* (Greece) 16 (1997): 55-61. 2 pls.
MacDonald publishes three tetradrachms from a recently discovered hoard. All are of the type of Macedonia First Meris and are struck over tetradrachms of Myrina in Aeolis (*obv.*, Apollo; *rev.*, laurel wreath containing Apollo Grynios standing). Discusses the chronology of the Macedonia First Meris coinage (generally accepted as ca. 158-146 B.C.). These coins were copied in Thrace and Dacia. The author concludes that these three specimens are imitations of the Macedonia First Meris type, and were probably struck ca. 150-140 B.C. Hoard evidence suggests that tetradrachms of Myrina moved into Thrace and Dacia in significant numbers, perhaps in response to tribal unrest and hostilities—either as payment for slaves or for the services of mercenary troops.

3579 **MacKay, Pierre A.** "Numismatic Evidence for the Study of the Macedonian Uprising in 149-8 B.C." *American Journal of Archaeology* 67, no. 2 (April 1963): 214.
A summary of a paper presented at the 1962 meeting of the Archaeological Institute of America. The author questions the chronology of the insurrections in Macedonia under Philip VI Andriscus, which had been established through the study of coins. The die-sequence established by Gaebler is reviewed. The analysis of a recent die draws Gaebler's conclusions into question, subjecting this whole coinage series to reinterpretation. [Also see Gaebler above, and Thompson "A Hoard from Northern Greece" under Hoards].

3580 ———. "Bronze Coinage of Macedonia, 168-166 B.C." *Museum Notes* 14 (1968): 5-13. 1 pl. [CS 2313]
The author re-examines some Macedonian bronze coins bearing the names Fulcinnius and Publilius which had previously been dated to the years after the defeat of Philip VI Andriscus in 148 B.C. For these and some other coins bearing both Roman and Macedonian elements, the author suggests dates ca. 167 B.C.

3581 ——— "Macedonian Tetradrachms of 148-147 B.C." *Museum Notes* 14 (1968): 15-40. 5 pls. [CS 2314]
Examines the tetradrachms struck ca. 148 B.C. in Macedonia while under Roman control. Describes twenty-four die varieties and lists numerous specimens of each. Reviews the conclusions regarding this coinage reached by Hugo Gaebler (1902, 1906) and disputes some of Gaebler's findings. Examines the die of the MAKE/ΔONΩN type which Gaebler believed was cut over a die of the LEG type and disputes this conclusion. Also doubts the re-cutting of an Andriscus-type die. Discusses die life and die sequences. Suggests the legend LEG together with the hand holding a branch on some of the reverse dies indicates "the presence in Macedonia of an embassy from Rome to an essentially friendly allied state." Discusses the wreath added to the head of Artemis on later dies and suggests it symbolized the re-establishment of Macedonian independence in 147 B.C. [Reviewed by H. Nicolet in *Revue Archéologique* (Paris) 2 (1971): 358-9. Also see Gaebler above].

3582 ——— "The Coinage of the Macedonian Republics, 168-146 B.C." *Ancient Macedonia: International Symposium, Thessalonica, Aug. 26-29, 1968.* Edited by Vasileios Laourdas. Thessalonica: The Society for Macedonian Studies, Institute for Balkan Studies, 1970. Pages 256-64. 2 pls.
"All the coinages associated with Macedonia during the brief period of independence after the fall of the Antigonid monarchy are reviewed. Special attention is given to the tetradrachms of the First Region and a rough outline of the technical history of this issue is suggested." [P. MacKay, *NL* 85]

3583 **Prokopov, Ilya.** "Sur la Circulation des Tétradrachmes d'Argent du Questeur Aesillas dans les Régions du Sud-Est de la Bulgarie et leur Datation." *Numizmatika* (Bulgaria) 19 (1985): 3-11.
In Bulgarian with a French summary.

3584 **Vagi, David.** "Hoard Evidence Can Often Play Havoc with Conventional Wisdom." *The Celator* 7, no. 11 (November 1993): 22. Illus.
Reviews the controversy over the chronology of the Macedonian "legatio" tetradrachms previously dated to ca. 148 B.C. Discusses a hoard containing these coins along with Aesillas tetradrachms dated to the early first century B.C. Based on this evidence, the legatio coins are now tentatively attributed to the period 100-95 B.C. [Also see Bauslaugh "Two Unpublished Overstrikes" under ATTICA—NEW STYLE COINAGE].

Also see: de Callataÿ "Abydos sur Aesillas" under TROAS; Thompson "Byzantium over Aesillas" under THRACE—COINAGE OF LYSIMACHOS; Tsangari *Coins of Macedonia in the Alpha Bank Collection* under PUBLIC COLLECTIONS—GREECE (ATHENS).

Thrace

A man's character can often be shown by his actions. When generals were allocating portions of Alexander's empire to each other, Justin states that "...the most warlike nations were assigned to Lysimachos as the bravest of them all; so far, by general consent, had he the pre-eminence over the rest in military merit."

—*Mark Rakicic, 1992*

General Works

3585   **Adams, Lawrence A.** "The Search for Coson." *SAN—Journal of the Society for Ancient Numismatics* 15, no. 4 (winter 1984-85): 64-6, 68. Illus.
Discusses a gold stater with the inscription ΚΟΣΩΝ generally attributed to a Thracian king, Coson. The coin has long been assumed to be an imitative issue derived from the Roman denarius of Marcus Junius Brutus. Evidence is provided suggesting that the coin was actually struck by Brutus in Macedonia in 42 B.C. in the name of a Dacian king, Coson.

3586   "Bulgarian Treasures—New York Met Exhibits Thracian Coins." *Coin World* (July 13, 1977): 65, 68. Illus.
A summary of Thracian history written to publicize an exhibition of Thracian gold and silver treasure, including coins, at the Metropolitan Museum of Art in New York.

3587   **de Callatay, François.** "Le Derniers Alexandres Posthumes d'Odessos à Lumière d'Une Trouvaille Récente." *Stephanos Nomismatikos: Edith Schönert-Geiss zum 65. Geburtstag.* Edited by Ulrike Peter. Berlin: Akademie Verlag, 1998. Pages 169-92.

3588   **Dimitrov, Kamen.** "The Coinage of Spartocus and Some Problems in the Political Development of Thrace in the Beginning of the Hellenistic Age." *Études Balkaniques* (Bulgaria) 3 (1981): 98-107. Illus.
"New examples of the bronze coinage of Spartokos, excavated at Scythopolis and at Cabyle, are published. They are rare and date to the beginnings of Cabyle's coinage, toward the first years of the third century B.C." [I. Youroukova, *NL* 114]

3589   ——— "The Development of Thrace in the Early Hellenistic Age (340-270 B.C.) according to Hoards of Coins of Philip II and Alexander the Great Types." *Istor. Pregled.* Pages 20-38.

3590   ——— *Seuthopolis II, Part 1: Ancient Coins from Seuthopolis.* Sofia, 1984.
In Bulgarian, with English summary.

3591   ——— "The Contacts of Thrace during the Early Hellenistic Age Reflected in Some Coin Hoards." *Bulgarian Historical Review* (Bulgaria) 18, no. 4 (1990): 47-65.

3591a   ——— "Le Monnayage et l'Idéologie Royale en Thrace Préhellénistique (Fin de VIe-Première Moitié IVe s. av. J.-C.)." *Proceedings of the 11th International Numismatic Congress, September 8-13, 1991. Volume 1.* Edited by T. Hackens et al. Louvain-la-Neuve, Belgium: International Association of Professional Numismatists, 1993. Pages 151-63.

3592   **Draganov, Dimitar.** "Debut du Monnayage de Bronze d'Odessos." *Numizmatika* (Bulgaria) 24, no. 3 (1990): 19-25.
In Bulgarian, with French summary.

3592a   ——— "The Bronze Coinage of Dionysopolis." *Spink Numismatic Circular* (December 1997). Pages 371-7.

3592b   ——— "Coins of the Unknown Mint of Apros in Thrace." *XIII Congreso Internacional de Numismática, Madrid – 2003: Actas–Proceedings–Actes I.* Edited by Carmen Alfaro, Carmen Marcos, and Paloma Otero. Madrid: International Numismatic Commisson, 2005. Pages 339-43, incl. map and 1 pl.
Examines a rare bronze coin with Apollo/Celtic shield and ΑΠΡΗ—ΝΩΝ. Three specimens are known (all are illustrated here). The author attributes the type to Apros, a city in southeastern Thrace. This is the first coin to be attributed to the city. The coin is dated ca. 250-210 B.C. The shield causes the author

to raise the question of whether the coinage was related to a Celtic presence in the region. But he notes that the Celtic shield was also a popular emblem among Greeks and Thracians.

3593 **Elagin, Vladimir.** "A Very Rare Tetradrachm of Mostis." *Spink Numismatic Circular* 56 (June 1948): 270. Illus.
Illustrates a tetradrachm (*obv.*, king's head right; *rev.*, Athena Nikephoros seated left) found in Asia Minor. Elagin attributes the coin to King Mostis of Thrace.

3593a **Gatzolis, Christos, V. Poulios, and Domna Terzopoulou.** "Coins of Thracian Kings and Rulers from Western Thrace, Eastern and Central Macedonia (5th-3rd c. B.C.)." *Thrace in the Graeco-Roman World: Proceedings of the 10th International Congress of Thracology, Komotini-Alexandroupolis 18-23 October 2005.* Athens: Institute for Greek and Roman Antiquity, 2007. Pages 176-87.

3593b **Gatzolis, Christos, and Selene Psoma.** "More on the Bottiaeans of Thrace." *ΚΕΡΜΑΤΙΑ ΦΙΛΙΑΣ: Volume in Honor of Ioannis Touratsoglou.* Edited by S. Drougou et al. Athens: Alpha Bank, 2009. Pages 135-43.
[Also see Psoma "Les Bottiéens" below].

3594 **Gerassimov, Theodore D.** "Rare Coins of Thrace." *Numismatic Chronicle* 6th ser., 17 (1957): 1-5. 1 pl. [CS 2365]
"Three newly discovered tetradrachms of the Gaulish king Cavarus in Thrace, datable to ca. 218 B.C., are discussed and illustrated. The obverse die—a head of young Herakles right, wearing a lion's skin—is shared with two previously known specimens; it combines with three different dies of a reverse type showing Zeus seated to left, with Artemis in field left facing him and holding two torches. Also recorded is a bronze coin of an otherwise unknown Thracian king—Sroios—who probably ruled over territory situated to the north of the middle and lower course of the river Hebros during the period ca. 336-306 B.C. The head on the obverse and the horseman on reverse both represent the king himself." [J. Healy, *NL* 49]

3595 ——— "Pre-Coinage Forms of Money among the Thracian Tribe of the Asti." *Arkheologiya* (Bulgaria) 1, no. 1-2 (1959): 85-7.
[An English translation is held in the library of the American Numismatic Association]. Mentions numerous hoards of copper arrow-like objects. A mould for casting the objects was found along with one of the hoards. The objects served as a small-change medium throughout the western and northern Black Sea coastal region. The arrow-money is dated to the sixth century B.C. based on the archaeological context of the hoards.

3596 ——— *Antique Coins Struck and in Circulation in the Bulgarian Lands.* Sofia: Septemvri Publishing House, 1977. 93 pp., illus. [CS 2416]
An overview of the coins struck in present day Bulgarian lands. Illustrated by coins of Macedonian tribes and kings, Thracian cities, and cities near the Black Sea struck during the Greek and Roman periods. Enlarged color plates show both the obverse and reverse of thirty-four coins.

3597 **Gibson, Thomas.** "Money for Kings and Peasants: Bronze Coinage of Thrace and the Black Sea Region." *The Celator* 13, no. 1 (January 1999): 30-3. Illus.
The author describes and illustrates numerous bronze coins of Thracian cities and discusses the role of bronze coins in the economy and history of the region.

3598 **Gökyldirim, Turan.** "A Bronze Coin of Perinthus with a Magistrate: ΠΡΟΚΑ." *Annotazioni Numismatiche* (Italy) 5, no. 20 (December 1995): 437-8. Illus.
"A new autonomous bronze coin of Perinthus from the excavations at Canakça (Turkey) is published." [N. Vismara, *NL* 142]

3599 **Gorini, Giovanni.** "Le Monete di Imbros dal Santuario dei Cabiri a Lemno." *Stephanos Nomismatikos: Edith Schönert-Geiss zum 65. Geburtstag.* Edited by Ulrike Peter. Berlin: Akademie Verlag, 1998. Pages 295-300.

3600 **Gramaticu, Steluta, and Virgil Ionita.** "Monnaies de Bronze Inédites de Callatis du 1er Siècle av. J.-C. et du 1er Siècle ap. J.-C." *Numismatic Chronicle* 167 (2007): 33-45. 2 pls.
Publishes some new bronze coins of Callatis.

3601 **Head, Barclay V., and Percy Gardner.** *Catalogue of Greek Coins of Thrace.* Edited by R. S. Poole. London: British Museum, 1877. Reprint, Bologna: Forni, 1963. 274 pp., illus. [CS 2367 and 2420]
Volume 3 of the *Catalogue of Greek Coins in the British Museum.* Covers the Tauric Chersonese, Sarmatia, Dacia, Moesia, and Thrace. This volume does not contain introductory text as do some of the *British Museum Catalogue* volumes. [Also see *Catalogue of Greek Coins in the British Museum* under PUBLIC COLLECTIONS—GREAT BRITAIN (LONDON)].

3602 **Hill, George F.** "Zone ad Serrheum." *Numismatic Chronicle* 5th ser., 2 (1922): 248-50. Illus.
Publishes a bronze coin (*obv.*, Apollo; *rev.*, lyre and ΙΩ ΝΑΙ) which Hill attributes to the city of Zone on the Samothracian Peraea. Discusses the little-known city.

3603 **Jones, H. Stuart.** "The Chest of Kypselos." *Journal of Hellenic Studies* 14 (1894): 30-80. 1 pl.
"On p. 35, coins of Cypsela showing a two-handled jar are mentioned among other evidence which shows that a *kypsele* was originally of this form, and that the 'chest' appears only in later versions of the legend." [J. R. Jones, *NIJHS*]

3604 **Kardara, Chrysoula.** "Dyeing and Weaving Works at Isthmia." *American Journal of Archaeology* 65, no. 3 (July 1961): 262-6. 4 pls.
A two-handled vessel, found among the remains of a textile works dating from ca. 360-240 B.C., is identified as a beehive (honey having been used in ancient textile operations to preserve the color of the purple dye). A similar vessel is shown on coins of Kypsela in Thrace. [Summarized from I. Merker, *NL* 57]

3605 **Koychev, Atanas.** "The Coinage with the Legend ΟΔΡΟΣΩΝ and the Rulers of the Odrysian, Astian, Cenian and Sapeian Dynasties during the 2nd-1st Centuries B.C." *Numismatica Bulgarica* 2, no.1 (2004): 14-68. Illus.

3606 **Kutajsov, V. A.** "Cast Money and Coins of Kerkinitis of the Fifth Century B.C." *Ancient Civilizations from Scythia to Siberia* (Netherlands) 2, no. 1 (1995): 39-59.

3607 **Lazarenki, I.** "The Coinage of Odessos at the End of the 4th c. BC." *Acta Musei Varnaensis* (Bulgaria) 2 (2004): 33-5.

3608 **Lederer, Philipp.** "A Coin of the Danteletai: A New Thracian Mint." *Numismatic Chronicle* 6th ser., 1 (1941): 169-74. Illus.
Publishes a bronze coin with obv., head of Dionysos, and rev., warrior holding a sword and shield. The inscription on the coin is determined to be ΔΑΝΤΗΛΗΤΩΝ—the name of a Thracian tribe (the Danteletai) on the river Strymon. The coin was struck in the fourth or early third century B.C. The Danteletai is therefore the only Thracian tribe known with certainty to have struck coinage. Lederer discusses the coin's types and artistic style.

3609 **May, John M. F.** "The Coinage of Dikaia-by-Abdera, c. 540/35-476/5 B.C." *Numismatic Chronicle* 7th ser., 5 (1965): 1-25. 2 pls. [CS 2385]
"The early silver coinage of Dikaia-by-Abdera, beginning ca. 540/35 B.C., was struck on a light Thraco-Macedonian standard, in relation with the coinage of Thasos, and later (ca. 492) changed to a heavy Thraco-Macedonian standard, in relation with the coinage of Maroneia. Coining ended in 476/5 with Kimon's successful campaign in Eion." [J. Balcer, *NL* 79]

3610 **Medvedeva, L. I.** "Coinage of Kerkinitis." *Numizmatika i Epigrafika* (Russia) 14 (1984): 40-9.
In Russian.

3611 **Monov, Metodi.** "On the Coins with the Legend ΟΔΡΟΣΩΝ." *Numismatica Bulgarica* (Bulgaria) 2, no.1 (2004): 69-75. Illus.
"It is argued that Heracles/bull types naming the Odrysians were struck during the Thracian uprising (184/3 B.C.) against Philip V at Philipopolis led by Cotys. Bulgarian text with English summary." [Oliver D. Hoover, *NL* 149]

3612 **Moushmov, Nikola A.** [*Ancient Coins of the Balkan Peninsula and the Coins of the Bulgarian Tsars*]. Sofia, 1912. 509 pp., 70 pls. [CS 7248]
Published in Old Bulgarian with Latin translations of the headings. Includes a French summary. A comprehensive catalogue of 7460 coins, particularly strong in the Roman Provincial coins of Moesia and Thrace. Includes coins of the ancient Greek cities and the kings of Odrysian Thrace. Arranged alphabetically by city and chronologically by ruler within each city, then by reverse type.

3613 ——— *Les Monnaies des Rois Thraces*. Sofia, 1927. [CS 2399]

3614 **Münzer, Friedrich, and Max L. Strack.** *Die Antiken Münzen Nord-Griechenlands, Band II: Thrakien*. Edited by F. Imhoof-Blumer. Berlin: Prussian Academy of Sciences, 1912. 308 pp., 8 pls. [CS 1806 and 2368]

3615 **Müseler, Wilhelm.** "A Coin from the Kingdom of Tylis." *Nomismatika Khronika* (Greece) 16 (1997): 21-3. Illus. Also appeared in *The Celator* 13, no. 7 (July 1999): 25-6. Illus.
Tylis was the center of Celtic settlements in Thrace during the period of Celtic rule in Thrace, which ended late in the third century B.C. The names of three of the "Galatian" rulers are known from coins: King (ΒΑΣΙΛΕΥΣ) Orsoaltios, King Kersivaulos, and King Kavaros. The first two appear only on tetradrachms of the Alexander type. The third appears on tetradrachms as well as on some small bronze coins. A die link between a tetradrachm of Kavaros and a posthumous Alexander tetradrachm suggests a terminus post quem of 219 B.C. for the dating of the posthumous Alexander tetradrachms from Kabyle. The author suggests that local authorities confiscated the tetradrachms struck in the name of the Celtic rulers after the death of Kavaros and used them as flans for their own civic coinage, thus accounting for the rarity of the silver coins from the Kingdom of Tylis.

3616 "Odd Money Hoard Find." *Coin World* (April 5, 1993): 48 ff. Illus.
Discusses a hoard of more than 100 pieces of bronze arrowhead money which is being offered to collectors.

3617 **Peter, Ulrike.** *Die Münzen der Thrakischen Dynasten (5-3 Jahrhundert v. Chr.): Hintergründe Ihrer Prägung*. Griechisches Münzwerk. Berlin: Akademie Verlag, 1997. 313 pp.
A catalogue of Thracian royal coins from the pre-Roman period, with numismatic and historical background. [Reviewed by W. Fischer-Bossert in *Revue Suisse de Numismatique* 77 (1998): 195-202, and by Zosia Archibald in *Numismatic Chronicle* 159 (1999): 362-4.]

3618 **Picard, Olivier.** "La Diffusion du Classicisme par les Monnaies en Thrace, à la fin du V et au Début du IV Siècle." *Actes du XII Congès International d'Archaeologie Classique, Athènes 1983*. 1985. Pages 180-5.

3619 ——— "Monnayages en Thrace à l'Èpoque Achémenide." *Mécanismes et Innovations Monétaires dans l'Anatolie Achémenide, Numismatique et Histoire, Actes de la Table Ronde Internationale d'Istanbul, 22-23 Mai 1997*. Edited by O. Casabonne. Istanbul: Institut Français d'Etudes Anatoliennes d'Istanbul; Paris: de Boccard, 2000. Pages 239-52.

3620 **Pick, Behrend.** *Die Antiken Münzen Nord-Griechenlands, Band I, i: Dacien und Moesien*. Edited by F. Imhoof-Blumer. Berlin: Prussian Academy of Sciences, 1898. 518 pp., 20 pls. [CS 1806 and 2417]

3621 **Pick, Behrend, and Kurt L. Regling.** *Die Antiken Münzen Nord-Griechenlands, Band I, ii: Dacien und Moesien*. Edited by F. Imhoof-Blumer. Berlin: Prussian Academy of Sciences, 1910. Reprint, Graz, 1971. 402 pp., 1 pl. [CS 1806 and 2418]

3622 **Preda, Constantin.** "Ein Neuer Vorschlag zur Chronologie der Koson-Münzen." *Stephanos Nomismatikos: Edith Schönert-Geiss zum 65. Geburtstag*. Edited by Ulrike Peter. Berlin: Akademie Verlag, 1998. Pages 555-62.

3623 **Prokopov, Illya.** "The Circulation of Bronze Coins in South-Western Thrace from the End of the Third to the End of the First Century B.C." *Proceedings of the 10th International Congress of Numismatics, London, 1986.* International Association of Professional Numismatists Publication, No. 11. Edited by I. A. Carradice. London: International Association of Professional Numismatists, 1986. Pages 89-93. Map.
Examines hoards found in Bulgaria to learn more about coin circulation in Thrace during two periods: (1) the reigns of Philip V and Perseus, and (2) Macedonia under Roman rule and the reign of Augustus.

3624 ———— "Notes about the Character of Some Large-scale Coinages in Thrace during the Second-First Centuries B.C." *Proceedings of the 11th International Numismatic Congress, September 8-13, 1991. Volume 1.* Edited by T. Hackens et al. Louvain-la-Neuve, Belgium: International Association of Professional Numismatists, 1993. Pages 173-85. Illus., maps.
Examines two of the more numerous coin types which flooded Thrace after the fall of Macedonia under the Romans: the Thasos tetradrachms and their imitations, and the tetradrachms of the First Macedonian Region and their imitations. Discusses the classification of the coins, the variety of dies, and the chronology of the issues.

3625 ———— "Imitations of Bronze Coins in Thracia during the First Century B.C." *XXI Internationaler Numismatischer Kongress Berlin 1997, Akten. Volume 1.* Edited by B. Kluge and B. Weisser. Berlin, 2000. Pages 369-77.

3625a **Psoma, Selene.** "Les Bottiéens de Thrace aux Ve et IVe Siècles avant J.-C." *Revue Numismatique* (France) 154 (1999): 41-55.
The silver and bronze coins of the Bottiaeans depicting a head of Demeter on the obverse and a bull on the reverse had been attributed to the Bottiaean cities of North Bottike that had formed a separate federal state from 422 to ca. 370 B.C. The Bottiaean cities of South Bottike and Crousis, Spartolos and Sinos, remained allies of the Chalcideans during the last decades of the fifth century and became members of the Chalcidean League in the fourth century B.C. Their bronze coins with Chalcidean types date from this period. [Psoma]. [Also see Gatzolis and Psoma above].

3626 ———— "Agathokles Son of Lysimachos in Thrace and Asia Minor: The Numismatic Evidence." *Ancient History, Numismatics, and Epigraphy in the Mediterranean World: Studies in Memory of Clemens E. Bosch and Sabahat Atlan and in Honor of Nezahat Baydur.* Edited by Oguz Tekin. Instanbul: Ege, 2009.

3627 **Pudill, Rainer.** "The Great God of Odessos—Darzalas: An Example of Continuity of Worship and Syncretism in Thrace." *The Celator* 15 no. 10 (October 2001): 6-22. Illus., map.
Begins with a general discussion of the Thracian region and its people, tracing developments from earliest times through late Roman times. Pudill then focuses on the city of Odessos, describing its history and mythology, especially the role played by chthonic deities. Discusses the deity Darzalas, who, in his role as principal god of Odessos, was called "Great God of Odessos Darzalas." Pudill reviews the attributes of Darzalas and the parallels with the Egyptian deity Sarapis. Describes and illustrates various depictions of Darzalas on coins of Odessos (from both pre-Roman and Roman Imperial times).

3628 **Regling, Kurt.** "Charaspes." *Corolla Numismatica: Numismatic Essays in Honour of Barclay V. Head.* G. F. Hill. London: Oxford University Press, 1906. Pages 259-65. Illus.
Text in German.

3629 **Robert, Louis.** "Les Monétaires et un Décret Hellénistiques de Sestos." *Revue Numismatique* (France) 6th ser., 15 (1973): 43-53.

3630 **Schönert-Geiss, Edith.** *Die Münzpägung von Perinthos.* Two volumes (text and plates). Berlin: Deutsche Akademie der Wissenschaften zu Berlin, 1965. [CS 2392]
Also see the 1973 supplement below.

3631 ———— "Literaturüberblick der Griechischen Numismatik: Mösien." *Jahrbuch für Numismatik und Geldsseschichte* (Germany) 15 (1965): 75-112. [CS 2411]
A bibliography.

3632 ———— "Literaturüberblick der Griechischen Numismatik: Thrakien." *Jahrbuch für Numismatik und Geldsseschichte* (Germany) 15 (1965): 113-93. [CS 2364]
A bibliography.

3633 ———— "Zur Geschichte Thrakiens anhand von Griechischen Münzbildern aus der Römischen Kaiserzeit." *Klio* (Germany) 49 (1967): 217-64. [CS 2369]

3634 ———— "Supplementum Perinthicum." *Klio* (Germany) 55 (1973): 151-7. [CS 2393]
A supplement to the author's 1965 study *Die Münzprägung von Perinthos.*

3635 ———— *Griechisches Münzwerk: Die Münzprägung von Bisanthe, Dikaia, Selymbria.* Deutsche Akademie der Wissenschaften zu Berlin, Schriften zur Geschichte und Kultur der Antike 13. Berlin: Akademie Verlag, 1975. 62 pp., 8 pls. [CS 2370]

3636 ———— "Die Münzstätte Zone in Thrakien." *Florilegium Numismaticum: Studia in Honorem U. Westermark Edita.* Edited by Harald Nilsson. Stockholm: Svenska Numismatiska Föreningen, 1992. Pages 313-6.
A small number of bronze coins were minted by the town of Zone in Thrace in the third century B.C. George F. Hill (1922) was the first person to describe the coins and only nine coins have been described in the literature. Text in German.

3637 ———— *Bibliographie zur Antiken Numismatik Thrakians und Mösiens.* Berlin: Akademie Verlag, 1999. 1710 pp.

3638   **Severeano, G.** "On the Primitive Coins of the Scythians: Coin Ingots in the Shape of Arrow-Points." *Buletinul Societatii Numismatice Române* (Romania) 57-58 (1926).

3639   **Sofia Press Agency.** "Coins Shed Light on Thracian Tribes." *Coin World* (July 13, 1977): 65, 68. Illus., map.
A brief overview of Thracian coinage.

3640   **Stancomb, William M.** "Arrowheads, Dolphins and Cast Coins in the Black Sea Region." *Classical Numismatic Review* 18, no. 3 (third quarter 1993): 5. Illus.
A review of the cast money pieces from the Black Sea region. The author summarizes that cast bronze arrowheads were made in Apollonia, Istria, and Berezan ca. 550-450 B.C. These cities used the electrum coins of Cyzicus for their international trade but used the arrowhead tokens when bartering with the local people. The arrowheads were replaced by wheel money at Istria and bronze dolphins at Olbia and these lasted until the mid-fourth century B.C.

3641   **Stolba, Wladimir F.** "Ein Münzfund aus Eupatoria von 1917 und der Beginn der Prägung von Kerkinitis." *Hellas und der Griechische Osten: Festschrift für Peter Robert Franke zum 70. Geburtstag. Studien zur Geschichte und Numismatik der Griechischen Welt.* Edited by W. Leschhorn, A. V. B. Miron, and A. Miron. Saarbrücken: SDV Saarbrücer Druckerei und Verlag, 1996. Pages 225-41.
[Also see Stolba "The Numismatics of Chersonesos and Kerkinitis" under BOSPOROS].

3642   **Taceva, Margarita.** "The 'Scythian Kings' and Greek Cities of Thracia Pontica." *The Seventh International Congress of Thracology, May 1996 (Constanta-Tulcea-România). Report and Summaries.* Bucharest, 1996. Page 161-2.
"The author proposes a new chronology and territorial arrangement of the Scythian kings from Doboudja, Kanites, Sariakes, Ailios and Charaspes. The king Ailios probably has a Celtic origin and he is located in the north of the Danube delta. Kanites reigned first in the northern Danube region and later in southern Dobroudja, conquering Charaspes and Tanusa." [C. Preda, *NL* 137]

3643   **Tameanko, Marvin.** "The Coinage of Ataias, King of the Scythians, 339 B.C." *The Picus* (Canada) (1996): 8-21. Illus.
Summarizes the history of the Scythian tribes from the eighth century B.C. to the third century A.D. Ataias was the principal Scythian king who fell in battle against Philip II of Macedon in 339 B.C. The coins attributed to Ataias are silver didrachms, slightly smaller and lighter than the didrachms of Philip. They all show a Scythian horse-archer riding left on the reverse with the inscription ΑΤΑΙΑΣ above. The obverse bears either the head of Herakles or a bust of Artemis. The coins were struck before 339 B.C. and are very rare (perhaps only six known). The coins illustrate the weapons and dress of the Scythian warrior. Tameanko describes Scythian weapons and tactics.

3644   **Tasaklaki, M., and K. Chatziprokopiou.** "Coins of the Aegean Islands in Aegean Thrace." *Coins in the Aegean Islands. Proceedings of the Fifth Scientific Meeting, Mytilene, 16-29 September 2006. Volume 1: Ancient Times.* Obolos 9. Edited by Panagiotis Tselekas. Athens: The Friends of the Numismatic Museum, 2010. Pages 27-44.

3645   **Terzopoulou, Domna.** "Small Silver Fractions from Ancient Stryme." Translated by M. J. A. Tzamali. *Nomismatika Khronika* (Greece) 22 (2003): 9-30. Map, 1 pl., tables.
Stryme was a small Thasian settlement on the Thracian coast. Among the coins found in excavations, twenty-three small silver fractions could not be attributed to a particular mint and no coins of these types have been found at other locations. The coins bear either a bunch of grapes or a kantharos on the reverse. Most are now attributed to Dikaia or Maroneia, although some attributions remain uncertain. In English on pp. 23-30 and in Greek on pp. 9-22.

3646   **Topalov, Stavri.** *Formes Prémonétaires de Moyens d'Echange. Les Fléche-Monnaies Couleés d'Apollonie du Pont VII-V^{e}s. av. ne.* Sofia, 1993. 40 pp., illus.
Examines the bronze arrowhead-shaped money which circulated in the Black Sea area during the seventh to fifth centuries B.C. Twenty-two pieces from private collections are described and illustrated with detailed line drawings and photographs.

3647   ——— *The Odrysian Kingdom from the Late 5th to the Mid-4th C. BC: Contributions to the Study of Its Coinage and History.* Sofia: Nasko, 1994. 174 pp., 6 pls.
A study of the coinage of the Thracian (Odrysian) kings and dynasts. Includes discussion of new types, chronology, and circulation within the historical framework of ancient Thrace.

3648   ——— "Bronzemünzen der Amatokos vom Typ Weintraube/Doppelaxt mit Einem Bisher Unbekannten Symbol, dem Kantharos." *Stephanos Nomismatikos: Edith Schönert-Geiss zum 65. Geburtstag.* Edited by Ulrike Peter. Berlin: Akademie Verlag, 1998. Pages 627-30.

3649   ——— *Tribes and Rulers from the Lands of the Odrysian Kingdom and its Border South-western Territories from the End of the VI Century to the Middle of the IV Century B.C. Contributions to the Study of the Mintage and History of Ancient Thrace.* Sofia, 1998. 360 pp., illus.
Text in Bulgarian.

3650   ——— *Odessos: Contribution to the Study of the Coin Minting of the City 4th-1st Century B.C.* Sofia, 1999. 344 pp., illus.
Text in Bulgarian with 20-page English summary.

3651   ——— *Information about the Unknown Types of Early Thracian Tribal and Ruler's Coins, Minted in the 6th-4th c. B.C., Kept in Private Collections and the Studies Made on their Basis. Appendix: Catalogue of the Odrysian Coins and the Coins of the Odrysian Rulers from the Late 6th to the Mid-4th c. B.C.* Sofia, 2000. 54 pp., illus.
Catalogue of coins with historical background. The appendix presents a description and rarity guide of forty-eight Odrysian coins.

3651a   ——— *Ancient Thrace: Contributions to the Study of the Early Thracian Tribal Coinage and It's Relations to the Coinage of the Odrysians and the Odrysian Kingdom during 6th – 4th c. B.C.* Sofia, 2003. 280 pp., illus.

Text in English.

3651b   ——— *New Contribution to the Study of the Coinage and History of the Early Odrysian Kingdom in the Lands of Ancient Thrace.* Sofia, 2004. 280 pp., illus.
Text in Bulgarian.

3652   **Wells, H. Bartlett.** "The Arrow-Money of Thrace and Southern Russia: A Review and Discussion of Eastern European and Soviet Writing." Parts 1-2. *SAN—Journal of the Society for Ancient Numismatics* 9, no. 1 (winter 1978): 6-9; no. 2 (spring 1978): 24-6, 31. Illus. [CS 1606]
Reviews the literature, gives historical background, and provides a description of bronze arrowhead imitations, 3-4 cm in length, found in the Black Sea region. Perhaps dating to the sixth century B.C., these may have been a form of money. Suggests these were not true arrowheads in an unfinished state of manufacture. Questions remain regarding their metallic content and places of origin. [Also see Wells "A Further Study" below].

3653   ——— "A Further Study of the Arrowhead Money." *SAN—Journal of the Society for Ancient Numismatics* 12, no. 3 (fall 1981): 53-4.
Discusses new evidence for interpreting the arrowhead money, based on the Jurilovca hoard containing about 2000 specimens, found ca. 1918. Confirms earlier theories: these arrowheads were a medium of exchange, cast by Ionian Greeks settled near the Black Sea. Their issuance probably began ca. 530-525 B.C. and ended ca. 450 B.C. Includes a discussion of their weights. [Also see Wells "The Arrow-Money" above and "A Western Archaeologist's Article" below].

3654   ——— "A Western Archaeologist's Article on the Arrowhead-Money." *SAN—Journal of the Society for Ancient Numismatics* 13, no. 3 (fall 1982): 57-8.
A commentary on the writings of Sara Sorda concerning bronze arrowhead money of the Black Sea region. Sorda concluded that these pieces served as a medium of exchange based upon their number, not based upon their weight. She does not agree that they were produced by Greek colonists, but instead by the indigenous peoples. She does not believe these were true arrowheads in a semi-manufactured state. [Also see Wells "The Arrow-Head Money" above].

3655   **West, Allen B.** *Fifth and Fourth Century Gold Coins from the Thracian Coast.* Numismatic Notes and Monographs, No. 40. New York: American Numismatic Society, 1929. 183 pp., 15 pls. [CS 3305]
A study of the political, commercial, and numismatic relations of the cities of the Thracian coast. Examines chronology and weight standards, the influence of Athens and Persia. Lists coin types for Thasos, Maroneia, Aenus, Amphipolis, and Athens. [Reviewed by A. R. Bellinger in *American Journal of Archaeology* 36 (1932): 202-4].

3656   **Yarkin, Ural.** "The Coinage of Alopeconnesus in Thracian Chersonesus." *Numismatic Chronicle* 138 (1978): 1-6. 1 pl.
"A corpus based on eighty coins of Alopeconnesus, which struck only bronze issues ca. 400-200 B.C., is provided. Provenances of the coins obtained or seen at the site or the nearby village confirm that the site of Alopeconnesus was at the promontory of Küçük Kemikli." [U. Yarkin, *NL* 101]

3657   **Youroukova, Yordanka.** *Coins of the Ancient Thracians.* BAR Supplementary Series, No. 4. Translated by V. Athanassov. Oxford: British Archaeological Reports, 1976. 129 pp., 28 pls. [CS 2373]
Examines the coinage of the Thraco-Macedonian tribes in the fifth and fourth centuries B.C., the Thracian rulers of the fifth through second centuries B.C., some rare Thracian coins of the first century B.C. and coins of Rhoemetalces I and his heirs through the 40's A.D. Presents a catalogue of 213 coin types. Includes tables of diameters and weights. Does not cover the coinage of Lysimachus. [Reviewed by W. Stancomb in *Numismatic Chronicle* 138 (1978): 200].

3658   ——— "Le Monnayage du Souverain Thrace Seuthès II." *Kraay—Mørkholm Essays: Numismatic Studies in Memory of C. M. Kraay and O. Mørkholm.* Numismatica Lovaniensia 10. Edited by G. Le Rider, G. K. Jenkins, N. Waggoner, and U. Westermark. Louvain-la-Neuve: Université Catholique de Louvain, 1989. Pages 317-21. 1 pl.

3659   ——— *The Coins of Thracian Rulers and Tribes.* Monetary Treasures from Bulgarian Lands 1. Sofia, 1992.
In Bulgraian.

3660   ——— "The Coinage of the Danteletai." *Macedonian Numismatic Journal* (Macedonia) 3 (1999): 9-15. Illus.
"In addition to the one known bronze coin ascribed to the coinage of the Thracian tribe of Danteletai, according to the inscription ΔΑΝΤΗ / ΛΗΤΩΝ published by Ph. Lederer in 1941 (*Numismatic Chronicle* 6, no. 1, pp. 169-74), two more specimens have been discovered in South Bulgaria, along the upper course of Maritsa river (ancient Hebros). The iconography, metrology (weights: 15.95-16.80-18.55 gm., diam. 23 mm., thickness 4-6 mm) and style of the new coins match contemporary coinages from the middle of the fourth century B.C." [J. Youroukova, *NL* 143]

3661   ——— "Sur le Monnayage des Tribus Thraces." *Travaux de Numismatique Grecque Offerts à Georges Le Rider.* Edited by M. Amandry and S. Hurter. London: Spink, 1999. Pages 435-9. 1 pl.

Also see: Alekseyev *Rare and Unpublished Coins* under ASIA MINOR AND THE BLACK SEA REGION—GENERAL WORKS; Arslan and Özen "A Hoard" under EGYPT—PTOLEMAIC KINGDOM; Berk "Brutus Revisited" under PONTOS; Berk and MacDonald "Gold Staters" under PONTOS; Cawkwell "A Note" under CARIA; Dimitrov "Studies" under HOARDS; Gardner "Ares as a Sun-God" under TYPES; Gardner "The Date of King Mostis" under THRACE—THASOS; Goldsborough "Apollonia Pontika Drachms" under COUNTERFEITS; Kraay "Greek Coinage and War" under GENERAL WORKS—GREEK; LeRider *Deux Trésors* under HOARDS; Lorimer "The Country Cart" under TYPES; Oguz *Talking Coins* under ASIA MINOR—GENERAL WORKS; *SNG British Museum 9, Part 2: Thrace and Lysimachus* under THE SYLLOGE NUMMORUM GRAECORUM SERIES (BRITISH SERIES); Stolba "The Numismatics of Chersonesos and Kerkinitis" under BOSPOROS; Vagi "Previously Unpublished" (Apollonia Pontika) under GENERAL WORKS—GREEK; Winzer *Antike Portraitmünzen* under PORTRAITS.

COINAGE OF LYSIMACHOS

3662 **Arnold-Biucchi, Carmen.** "The Pergamene Mint under Lysimachus." *Studies in Greek Numismatics in Memory of Martin Jessop Price.* Edited by Richard Ashton and Silvia Hurter. London: Spink, 1998. Pages 5-15. 3 pls.
Style creates an unusual problem in the study of the coinage of Lysimachus. Issues with very different reverse markings, usually interpreted as characteristics of separate mints, often share obverse dies. Arnold-Biucchi attempts to examine in detail one issue of Lysimachus' coinage that can be attributed to a specific city with certainty. The coins studied here are all tetradrachms with *obv.*, Alexander with horn of Ammon; *rev.*, Athena Nikephoros enthroned. Lists eighty-one varieties. Segregates the issue into two groups: one with symbols and monograms; the other with symbols and single letters as control marks. Newell had attributed the coins to the mint of Pergamon, and Arnold-Biucchi confirms this attribution. Also confirms the identity of the little cult statue which appears on the reverse as Athena Nikephoros. Discusses chronology and concludes the coins were probably struck 287/6 to 282 B.C.

3663 **Babington, Churchill.** "On an Unpublished Tetradrachm of Lysimachus, Probably Struck at Byzantium, Reading ΛΥΣΙΜΑΧΟ." *Numismatic Chronicle* new ser., 5 (1865): 181-90.
Describes a tetradrachm of Lysimachus which exhibits "the termination of the genitive in O in place of OY." The coin was unlisted by Müller. Babington discusses the significance of the coin. He also publishes four other coins of Lysimachus not listed by Müller.

3664 **Bunbury, Edward H.** "On Some Unpublished Coins of Lysimachus." *Numismatic Chronicle* new ser., 9 (1869): 1-18.
Lists some previously unpublished tetradrachms of Lysimachus, as well as a gold stater. Discusses the difficulty in relying on monograms and symbols to assist in the attribution of coins to particular mint cities. [Also see Müller *Lysimachus* and "Remarks" below].

3665 **Burstein, Stanley M.** "Lysimachus the Gazophylax: A Modern Scholarly Myth?" *Ancient Coins of the Graeco-Roman World: The Nickle Numismatic Papers.* Edited by Waldemar Heckel and Richard Sullivan. Waterloo, Ontario: Wilfrid Laurier University Press, 1984. Pages 57-68.
Lysimachus was known as the "gazophylax" or treasurer, due to his supposed tight-fisted approach to money and his great wealth. Burnstein summarizes Lysimachus' achievements and minting activities as indicators of his fiscal affairs. The author suggests that, prior to 301 B.C., Lysimachus' fiscal austerity was forced upon him. He controlled a limited—and relatively poor—kingdom. But after 301 B.C., his territories expanded. The author cites evidence for Lysimachus' fiscal policies after 301. Suggests his increased coinage output after that date was directly related to the amount of treasure his armies captured during their conquests.

3666 **Fisher-Bossert, Wolfgang.** "Die Lysimacheier des Skostokos." *Revue Belge de Numismatique et de Sigillographie* (Belgium) 151 (2005): 49-74.

3667 **Madsen, Eardley, and Ethel Madsen.** "Lysimachus, King of Thrace." *SAN—Journal of the Society for Ancient Numismatics* 14, no. 3 (fall 1983): inside covers.
An overview of the history and coinage of Lysimachus. A barbaric-style gold stater of Lysimachus is pictured.

3668 **Marinescu, Constantin A.** *Making and Spending Money along the Bosporus: The Lysimachi Coinages Minted by Byzantium and Chalcedon and Their Socio-Cultural Context.* Ph. D. dissertation, Columbia University, New York, 1996.

3668a ——— "The Posthumous Lysimachi Coinage and the Dual Monetary System at Byzantium and Chalcedon in the Third Century B.C." *XII Internationaler Numismatischer Kongress Berlin 1997, Akten-Proceedings-Actes.* Edited by B. Kluge and B. Weisser. Berlin: Staatliche Museen zu Berlin, 2000. Pages 333-7.

3669 ——— "From Byzantium to the Black Sea: Dies, Engravers and the Production of Posthumous Lysimachi Coinage during the 3rd-2nd Century B.C. *Numismatic and Sphragistic Contributions to History of the Western Black Sea Coast: International Conference, Varna, September 12th-15th, 2001.* Acta Musei Varnaensis 2. Varna, Bulgaria, 2001.

3670 **Müller, C. Ludwig.** *Den Thraciske Konge Lysimachus's Mynter.* Kjöbenhavn, 1857. 90 pp., 9 engraved plates.
The first edition of Müller's work, published the following year in German (see below).

3671 ——— *Die Münzen des Thrakischen Königs Lysimachos.* Copenhagen, 1858. Reprint, Bologna: Forni, 1978. 92 pp., 9 pls. [CS 2403]

3672 ——— *Lysimachus, King of Thrace: Mints and Mintmarks.* New York: Frederick S. Knobloch, 1966. 7 pp., 2 pls. [CS 2403a]
This reprint of a segment of Müller's 1858 book, *Die Münzen des Thrakischen Königs Lysimachus,* is comprised of seven tables listing 565 combinations of symbols and monograms arranged by mint city to assist in attributing the coinage of Lysimachus to particular mints. Includes two plates of line drawings. [Also see Bunbury "On Some Unpublished Coins" above].

3673 ——— "Remarks on the Classification of Some Coins of Lysimachus." *Numismatic Chronicle* new ser., 10 (1870): 1-10.
Müller comments on Bunbury's article (see Bunbury "On Some Unpublished Coins" above) and questions some of Bunbury's attributions.

3674 **Newell, Edward T.** "The Coinage of Lysimachus." *The Coin Collector's Journal* 2, no. 2 (May 1935): 33-5. Illus.
A brief account of the reign and coinage of Lysimachus.

3674a **Petac, Emanuel.** "About the Chronology of the Posthumous Lysimachus Type Staters from Western and Northern Black Sea Region." *Bulletin du Cercle d'Études Numismatiques* (Belgium) 43, no. 3 (September-December 2006). 12 pp. incl. 3 pls.
Presents several gold coins, staters of Alexander the Great and Lysimachus type, struck in the Western and Northern Black Sea region, at Istros, Tomis and Tyras. Except the second one, all of them belong to the collection of the Library of the Romanian Academy and they represent one of the most famous, interesting and discussed coins from their category. Both by their rarity and significance they offer important suggestions concerning the monetary history and politics in the Pontic area.

3675 **Pink, Karl.** "Gold Medallions of Lysimachus and Kindred Forgeries." *Numismatic Chronicle* 5th ser., 17 (1937): 73-90. 1 pl.
Presents a catalogue of known fake gold medallions of Lysimachus and discusses their origin and method of production. The pieces are modeled after the silver tetradrachms of Lysimachus, a bronze coin of Nikias (tyrant of Cos), or a dupondius of Julia Titi. The medallions were first produced by Cavino in the sixteenth century.

3676 **Rakicic, Mark.** "Ancient Literary Sources Offer Glimpses into the Character of Lysimachos." *The Celator* 6, no. 4 (April 1992): 6-10.
Explores the character of King Lysimachos of Thrace, citing ancient sources which provide clues to his personality. Concludes that conflicting information causes his true character to remain a mystery.

3677 **Seyrig, Henri.** "Monnaies Hellénistiques de Byzance et de Calcédoine." *Essays in Greek Coinage Presented to Stanley Robinson.* Edited by C. M. Kraay and G. K. Jenkins. Oxford: Clarendon Press, 1968. Pages 183-200. 3 pls. [CS 2382]
Primarily discusses the tetradrachms of Lysimachos struck at Byzantion and Chalcedon.

3678 **Sicurella, Nicholas A.** "Unpublished Stater of Lysimachus." *SAN—Journal of the Society for Ancient Numismatics* 14, no. 2 (summer 1983): 28.
A gold stater of Lysimachus is pictured and described. Unlike typical coins of this type, this coin has the legend ΛΥΣΙΜΑΧΟΥ on the right side of the seated Athena where ΒΑΣΙΛΕΩΣ is usually found. The style suggests it may have been struck at an Asia Minor mint, possibly Ephesos. [Also see the author's follow-up article "Gold Stater of Lysimachus Revisited" below].

3679 ——— "An Unpublished Drachm of Lysimachus." *The Celator* 10, no. 6 (June 1996): 14-6. Illus.
Describes the general coin types of Lysimachus and describes a previously unpublished drachm variety. The new coin is a variation of *Price* L-25 and bears a dolphin over the forepart of a lion in the reverse field. The name ΛΥΣΙΜΑΧΟΥ is on the right, and ΒΑΣΙΛΕΩΣ is in the exergue. The coin shares an obverse die with *Price* L-12.

3680 ——— "Gold Stater of Lysimachus Revisited." *The Celator* 13, no. 1 (January 1999): 34-5. Illus.
This is a follow-up to a previous article by the author (see "Unpublished Stater of Lysimachus" above). The author has now located another specimen of this unusual stater in the British Museum collection. The new specimen confirms that the word ΒΑΣΙΛΕΩΣ appears on the left reading upward. It is the second known specimen.

3681 **Tekin, Oguz.** "A Hellenistic Hoard of Lysimachean Bronze Coins with Tyche and Lion Type." *Ancient History, Numismatics, and Epigraphy in the Mediterranean World: Studies in Memory of Clemens E. Bosch and Sabahat Atlan and in Honor of Nezahat Baydur.* Edited by Oguz Tekin. Instanbul: Ege, 2009.

3682 **Thompson, Margaret.** "The Mints of Lysimachus." *Essays in Greek Coinage Presented to Stanley Robinson.* Edited by C. M. Kraay and G. K. Jenkins. Oxford: Clarendon Press, 1968. Pages 163-82. 7 pls. [CS 2404]
Discusses the mints controlled by Lysimachus and their output during his reign. Uses evidence from the Armenak Hoard. States that Cassander supplied the bulk of Lysimachus' coinage until ca. 300 B.C. Lysimachus began silver and bronze coinage ca. 306 in Lysimachia using the types of Philip II but bearing his own initials. Gold and silver coins with Alexander types followed shortly thereafter. He acquired mints in Asia Minor after the battle of Ipsus. Summarizes the output of each mint. Suggests that some dies were produced in a central location and then distributed to the mints, accounting for the similarity in style among coins from diverse mints. Lists 257 coins grouped by mint. Includes monograms, die links, and suggested chronology.

3683 ——— "Byzantium over Aesillas." *Revue Numismatique* (France) 6th ser., 15 (1973): 54-65. 2 pls. [CS 2383]
"A tetradrachm of Byzantium of Lysimachus type struck over an issue of Aesillas sheds new light on the chronology of the Macedonian coinage. On the evidence of several recently-published hoards, the Byzantine issue belongs to the '80's of the first century B.C. and very probably to the early years of that decade. The overstrike, therefore, serves to confirm the traditional dates of Aesilla's quaestorship, 94-88 B.C." [M. Thompson, *NL* 94]

3684 **Vagi, David.** "The Development of Lysimachus' Coinage." *The Celator* 7, no. 9 (September 1993): 22. Illus.
A brief overview of the coinage of Lysimachus.

3685 **Zograph, Alexander N.** "The Tooapse Hoard, with Some Notes on the Lysimachean Staters Struck at Byzantium." *Numismatic Chronicle* 5th ser., 5 (1925): 28-52.
Discusses a hoard of staters of Lysimachus found in 1908 in the Black Sea district. Fifty-two of the coins are in the Hermitage Museum. All were struck by the same dies at the mint of Byzantium. Describes the coins and discusses their chronology. Lists the weights of the coins. Also, the weights of similar coins in other collections are summarized in tables. Zograph compares these weights to the weights of similar coins from other mints (Callatis and Tomi).

Also see: Ashton "The Coins of the Macedonian Kings, Lysimachos and Eupolemos" under MACEDONIAN KINGDOM—GENERAL WORKS; Brown "Styles in the Alexander Portraits" under PORTRAITS; de Callataÿ "Un Tétradrachme de Lysimaque" under GENERAL WORKS—HELLENISTIC; Gardner "The Apoxyomenos" under PORTRAITS; Hadley "Royal Propaganda" under SYRIA—SELEUCID KINGDOM; Imhoof-Blumer "Syrakosai—Lysimachos—Derdas" under SICILY—SYRACUSE; Le Rider "L'Atelier Séleucide de Lysimachie" under SYRIA—SELEUCID KINGDOM; Müller *The Coinage of Alexander the Great* under MACEDONIAN KINGDOM—GENERAL WORKS; Petac "From the Types of Alexander to Lysimachus" under THRACE—MESAMBRIA; D. Robinson "The Alexander Hoard of Megalopolis" under HOARDS; Sayles "Divinity" under PORTRAITS; Seyrig "Monnaies Hellénistiques" under GENERAL WORKS—HELLENISTIC; *SNG British Museum 9, Part 2: Thrace and Lysimachus* under THE SYLLOGE NUMMORUM GRAECORUM SERIES (BRITISH SERIES); M. Thompson "The Armenak Hoard" under HOARDS; Troxell "Greek Accessions" under ASIA MINOR—GENERAL WORKS; Vagi "Alexander's Legacy" under GENERAL WORKS—HELLENISTIC; Vagi "Slavei Replicas" under COUNTERFEITS; Wartenberg and Kagan "Some Comments on a New Hoard from the Balkan Area" under HOARDS; Worland "An 1805 Treatise" under PORTRAITS.

ABDERA

3686 **Ashton, Richard.** "Hellenistic Bronze Coins of Abdera with a Male Portrait." *Studies in Greek Numismatics in Memory of Martin Jessop Price.* Edited by Richard Ashton and Silvia Hurter. London: Spink, 1998. Pages 17-21. 1 pl.

Discusses a group of five bronze coins of Abdera with *obv.*, beardless male head, in diadem, with small wing, and *rev.*, griffin recumbent. The head is usually identified as that of a Ptolemy. However, Ashton believes the Ptolemaic hypothesis has no firm foundation. He assumes only that the portrait represented an unidentified foreign or local ruler, whose wing was copied from the Seleucid coins struck nearby on the Hellespont, and who perhaps ruled during the second quarter of the third century B.C. Discusses the chronology of the coinage. Discusses the countermark found on the coins. The countermark is similar to that found on some coins of Thasos—possibly a sign of a shared crisis effecting both Abdera and Thasos.

3687   **Chryssanthaki, Katerina.** *L'Histoire Monétaire d'Abdère vu VIe avant J.-C. au IIe Siècle Après J.-C.* Unpublished doctoral thesis, Université Paris IV Sorbonne. Paris, 2000.
[Also see Crysanthaki-Nagle below for a revised, published version].

3688   **Chryssanthaki-Nagle, Katerina.** *L'Histoire Monétaire d'Abdère en Thrace (VIe Siècle avant J.-C. - IIe Siècle Après J.-C.).* ΜΕΛΕΤΗΜΑΤΑ 51. Athens: Kentron Hellenikes kai Romaikes Archaiotertos, 2007. 432 pp., 64 pls.

3689   **Kagan, Jonathan H.** "Small Change and the Beginning of Coinage at Abdera." *Agoranomia: Studies in Money and Exchange Presented to John H. Kroll.* Edited by Peter G. van Alfen. New York: American Numismatic Society, 2006. Pages 49-60. 1 pl.
Examines a sixth century B.C. hoard which appeared in 2000. The hoard contained about thirty-one coins of Abdera, mostly small denominations, and included eighteen hemiobols—a previously unknown denomination for Abdera. Kagan presents a catalogue of the coins, and notes the increasing population of small denomination coins found in hoards in recent years. It is now clear that small denomination coins in Northern Greece appeared along with larger denomination coins, and this may change our thinking regarding the origins of coinage in Northern Greece. Kagan believes the Abderan small denominations were struck by allocating a certain amount of metal to produce a certain number of coins, but the individual weights of the coins could vary significantly. Discusses weight standards and chronology. Suggests that coinage began at Abdera about 530 B.C.

3690   **May, John M. F.** *The Coinage of Abdera, 540-345 B.C.* Special Publication No. 3. Edited by Colin M. Kraay and G. K. Jenkins. London: Royal Numismatic Society, 1966. 298 pp., 24 pls. [CS 2376]
A detailed study of the coinage of Abdera. Presents a historical introduction to the city. Detailed discussion of weight standards in use in Abdera, and discussions of magistrates and symbols on the coinage. Presents a catalogue of coins with explanatory discussions of each period, ca. 540 to 345 B.C. The plates illustrate 553 coins. [Reviewed by R. R. Holloway in *American Journal of Archaeology* 71, no. 3 (July 1967): 320-1, by E. J. P. Raven in *Numismatic Chronicle* 7th ser., 7 (1967): 289-97, and by Peter A. Clayton in *Spink Numismatic Circular* 77, no. 3 (March 1969): 89].

3691   **Price, Martin J.** "Thrace, 1980." *Coin Hoards* 7 (1985): 42-4. 1 pl.
Discusses some staters of Philip II, some tetradrachms and one gold stater of Abdera. Suggests May's chronology for period IX should be revised.

3692   **von Fritze, Hans.** "Die Autonomen Münzen von Abdera: Eine Chronologische Studie." *Nomisma* (Germany) 3 (1909): 1-30. [CS 2375]

Also see: Greenwell "On Some Rare Greek Coins" (1890) under PRIVATE COLLECTIONS; MacDonald "A Teos/Abdera Overstrike" under IONIA; Moustaka and Tselekas "Coins from the Excavations" under IONIA; Wilkinson "Unpublished" (Abdera) under PRIVATE COLLECTIONS; Vaux "On Some Remarkable Greek Coins" under PUBLIC COLLECTIONS—GREAT BRITAIN (LONDON).

AINOS

3693   **Forrer, Leonard S.** "An Apparently Unpublished Tetradrachm of Aenus, Thraciae." *Spink Numismatic Circular* 8, no. 86 (January 1900): 3723-4. Illus.
The reverse of the coin has a goat walking right; in front is a Macedonian helmet and a tree. This is the first published example bearing these symbols. Illustrated by a drawing.

3694   **May, John M. F.** *Ainos: Its History and Coinage, 474-341 B.C.* London: Oxford University Press, 1950. 288 pp., 9 pls., maps. [CS 2378]
A die study of the coins of Ainos. Provides historical background for the city and its mint, and a listing of the main coin types with commentary. Discussion of weight standards and types. Appendices briefly discuss the bronze and gold coinage and barbarous issues. [Reviewed by G. K. Jenkins in *Journal of Hellenic Studies* 72 (1952): 158, and by W. Schwabacher in *Gnomon* (Germany) 23 (1951): 193-200].

3695   **von Fritze, Hans.** "Die Autonomen Münzen von Ainos: Eine Chronologische Studie." *Nomisma* (Germany) 4 (1909): 16-32. [CS 2377]

Also see: Waldstein "Pythagoras" under ART.

BERGE

See LETE below (the coins traditionally attributed to the city of Lete may in fact belong to Berge).

BYZANTION

3696   **Le Rider, Georges.** "Sur le Monnayage de Byzance au IVe Siècle." *Revue Numismatique* (France) 6th ser., 13 (1971): 143-53. [CS 2380]

3697   **Psoma, Selene.** "Numismatic Evidence on the Ptolemaic Involvement in Thrace during the Second Syrian War." *American Journal of Numismatics* 2nd ser., 20 (2008): 257-63.
Presents a numismatic survey of the city of Byzantion. The city was renamed "Ptolemais" for a short period to honor Ptolemy II. It was after the intervention of the Ptolemaic fleet that the siege of Byzantion by Antiochos II came to an end. The author re-examines a hoard (see Arslan and Özen "A Hoard of Unpublished Bronze Coins of Ptolemy Ceraunus" under EGYPT—PTOLEMAIC KINGDOM) which is divided into three distinct groups. Psoma offers further observations concerning the denominations, the issuing authority of Groups II and III, and the dates of all three groups of coins from Eastern Thrace.

3698 **Schönert-Geiss, Edith.** *Die Münzprägung von Byzantion, Part 1: Autonome Zeit.* Berlin: Akademie Verlag, 1970. 174 pp., 62 pl. *Part 2: Kaiserzeit.* Amsterdam: A. Hakkert, 1972. Two parts, four volumes (text and plates). [CS 2381]

Also see: Marinescu "The Posthumous Lysimachi Coinage and the Dual Monetary System at Byzantium and Chalcedon" under THRACE—COINAGE OF LYSIMACHOS; Pollack "A Bithynion Hoard" under HOARDS; Seyrig "Monnaies Hellénistiques" under THRACE—COINAGE OF LYSIMACHOS; Stancomb "Some Countermarked and Overstruck" under BITHYNIA; Thompson "A Countermarked Hoard" under HOARDS; Thompson "Byzantium over Aesillas" under THRACE—COINAGE OF LYSIMACHOS. Also see numerous other items under THRACE—COINAGE OF LYSIMACHOS.

CABYLE

3699 **Draganov, Dimitar.** "The Minting of Silver Coins of Cabyle and of King Cavarus." *Études Balkaniques* (Bulgaria) 4 (1984): 94-109. Illus.
"According to the author, the tetradrachms of Cabyle, those depicting the symbol of the city, Artemis with two long torches, and those with the name of Cavarus, are of four different series. This silver coinage was issued by the Thracian city between 230 and 180 B.C." [I. Youroukova, *NL* 116]

3700 ——— "Chronology of the Autonomous Coinage of Kabyle." *Terra Antiqua Balcanica* (Bulgaria) 5 (1990): 74-84.

3701 ——— "The Countermarks of Cabyle." *Klio* (Germany) 73 (1991): 220-5.

3702 ——— *The Coinage of Cabyle.* Sofia, 1993. 160 pp., 46 pls.
A study of the coinage of the cities of Spartok, Skostok, Kavar, and Kabile. Describes over 9000 coins (illustrates about 400). Text in Bulgarian, with English summary.

3703 **Gerassimov, Theodore D.** "The Alexandrine Tetradrachms of Cabyle in Thrace." *Centennial Publication of the American Numismatic Society.* Edited by Harald Ingholt. New York: American Numismatic Society, 1958. Pages 273-7.
The author re-examines the posthumous Alexander tetradrachms bearing, on the reverse, a small Artemis in long chiton, facing, holding two torches. Müller assigned these coins to the city of Perinthus based on the similarity of the Artemis figure with that on the coins of Perinthus. Gerassimov finds stylistic differences between the Artemis figures, and assigns these coins to the city of Cabyle in Thrace. He dates the issues to ca. 219 B.C. Lists and illustrates fourteen varieties.

DEULTUM

3704 **Draganov, Dimitar.** *The Coinage of Deultum.* Sofia, 2007.

3705 **Youroukova, Yordanka.** *Griechisches Münzwerk: Die Münzen von Deultum.* Schriften zur Kultur der Antike 8. Two volumes (text, plates). Berlin: Akademie Verlag, 1973. 169 pp., 32 pls. [CS 2384]

Also see: *SNG Bulgaria I* under SYLLOGE NUMMORUM GRAECORUM SERIES—BULGARIAN SERIES.

ISTROS

3706 **Butler, J. D.** "A Numismatic Critique—Cracks in John Bull's Crack Geography." *American Journal of Numismatics* 11, no. 2 (October 1876): 38-9.
Points out an error in William Smith's *Dictionary of Classical Geography.* Smith illustrates a coin described as being of "Istrus" in Crete. Butler clarifies that the coin is actually from Istria, the Danubian city.

3707 **Dimitrov, Kamen.** "*CH IV* 28 and Chronology of the Silver Coinage of Histria in the late Fourth Century B.C." *The Seventh International Congress of Thracology, May 1996 (Constanta-Tulcea-România). Report and Summaries.* Bucharest, 1996. Page 140.
"The dating of the latest coins of Histria between 315 and 300 B.C. shows that Lysimachus' policy toward the Greek cities of the Thracian coast was a tolerant one." [C. Preda, *NL* 137].

3708 ——— "*CH IV* 28 et la Chronologie des Monnaies d'Argent d'Histria au 4e Siècle av. J.C." *Stephanos Nomismatikos: Edith Schönert-Geiss zum 65. Geburtstag.* Edited by Ulrike Peter. Berlin: Akademie Verlag, 1998. Pages 215-20.
[For an English version, see previous item].

3709 **Gerassimov, Theodore D.** "A Hoard of Bronze Arrow-Coins." *Izvestiya na Bulgarskiya Arkheologicheski Institut* (Bulgaria) 12 (1938): 424-8. Illus. [An English translation is held in the library of the American Numismatic Association].
A brief report on a hoard of over 1000 bronze arrow-coins found in a clay pot in Bulgaria in 1934. A mould for casting the pieces was also found. Mentions other hoards of arrow-coins. Assigns the pieces to the fourth or third century B.C.

3710 **Hind, John G. F.** "Istrian Faces and the River Danube: The Type of the Silver Coins of Istria." *Numismatic Chronicle* 7th ser., 10 (1970): 7-17. [CS 2433]
Discusses the coins of Istros with two young male heads side-by-side, one of them inverted. The coins were issued during the late fifth and fourth centuries B.C. Discusses die variants and weight standards and the introduction of coinage at Istros in comparison with neighboring cities. Then the discussion focuses on the interpretation of the inverted heads obverse type at Istros. Theories include representations of the Dioskouroi, the winds represented by a facing Janiform head, the rising and setting sun, or a reference to the Istrian slave trade. Hind rejects these interpretations and suggests the type represents the two supposed mouths of the river Ister—one flowing into the Black Sea and the other into the Adriatic Sea. Notes that when

geographical knowledge disproved the existence of a mouth into the Adriatic, the coin type was discontinued. Therefore, the type is the personification of a river god.

3711 ——— "City Heads/Personifications and Omens from Zeus (the Coins of Sinope, Istria and Olbia in the V-IV Centuries B.C.)" *Numismatic Chronicle* 167 (2007): 9-22. 2 pls.
Hind examines the "eagle with dolphin" motif on coins of Sinope, Istria, and Olbia and determines it to be a symbol of Zeus Ourios. The coins are discussed in detail. Next, he discusses the obverse types of these coins—frontal and profile heads, and makes suggestions for the identity of the deities depicted.

3712 **Iliescu, Octavian.** "Drachms of Histria First Rumanian Coins. Coined Fifth Century before Christ." *Coin World* (July 20, 1962): 42. Illus.
"In this discussion of the drachms struck in the middle of the fifth century B.C. at Histria—a Greek colony located on the shores of Lake Sinoe, adjoining the Black Sea—Iliescu includes a brief monetary history of ancient Dacia, much of which lies within the boundaries of present-day Rumania." [*NL* 65]

3713 ——— "Le Système Monétaire et Pondéral à Histria, Callatis et Tomis au Ve-IIe Siècle Avant Notre Ère." *Actes du 8ème Congès International de Numismatique. New York-Washington, Septembre 1973.* Paris and Basel, 1976. Pages 85-98. [CS 2435]

3714 **Meyer, Casper.** "A Lead Test-Piece from Histria in the Ashmolean Museum, Oxford." *Numismatic Chronicle* 166 (2006): 25-6. Illus.
Illustrates a lead test-piece showing the impression of a Histrian obverse coin die. A bronze coin from the same die exists in the William Stancomb collection (acquired after publication of *SNG Stancomb*, and thus not included). Discusses the possible purposes of such pieces.

3715 **Preda, Constantin.** "Über die Silbermünzen der Stadt Istros." *Dacia* (Hungary) 19 (1975): 77-85. [CS 2436]

3716 **Preda, Constantin, and H. Nubar.** *Histria III: Descoperirile Monetare 1914-1970.* Bucharest, 1973.

3717 **Talmatchi, Gabriel.** *Les Monnaies Autonomes d'Istros, Callatis et Tomis: Circulation et Contexte.* Moneta 51. Wetteren, Belgium: Moneta, 2006. 212 pp.

Also see: Petac *La Collection M. C. Sutzu* under PUBLIC COLLECTIONS—ROMANIA (BUCHAREST).

LETE

3718 **Jaunzems, Ava C.** "Silenus and Nymph." *SAN—Journal of the Society for Ancient Numismatics* 7, no. 3 (spring 1976): 38-40, 42. Illus.
The Silenus-nymph series of coinage, traditionally attributed to Lete, is examined. Stylistic evidence suggests this design may have been a standard type chosen by a large number of Thracian tribes.

3719 **Psoma, Selene.** "Le Trésor de Gazôros et les Monnaies aux Légendes ΒΕΡΓ, ΒΕΡΓΑΙ, ΒΕΡΓΑΙΟΥ." *Bulletin de Correspondance Hellénique* (France) 126 (2002): 205-29.
Discusses coins found near Gazoros, Greece in 1994/5 (*Coin Hoards* 9, no. 61).

3720 ——— "The 'Lete' Coinage Reconsidered." *Agoranomia: Studies in Money and Exchange Presented to John H. Kroll.* Edited by Peter G. van Alfen. New York: American Numismatic Society, 2006. Pages 61-86. 2 pls.
An examination of the coins usually attributed to Lete, with *obv.*, dancing maenad and satyr; *rev.*, incuse square. Not all researchers have agreed with this attribution. Psoma discusses the iconography, weight standards, circulation areas, and chronology of the coins. The coins show strong ties with the island of Thasos and the mainland opposite the island—an important mining district. But Psoma says Barclay Head was wrong in attributing the coins to Lete, and Svornos was wrong in attributing them to Sirra. Rather, the 'Lete' coinage should be attributed to a civic mint of the mining district, and Psoma focuses on those cities which appear in the Athenian Tribute Lists. She concludes that the city of Berge, east of the Strymon River, is the most likely mint city.

3721 **Smith, Michael N.** *The Mint of "Lete" and the Development of Coinage in the North Aegean.* Unpublished doctoral dissertation, Brown University, Rhode Island, 1999.

3722 ——— "The Archaic Coinage of 'Lete.'" *XII Internationaler Numismatischer Kongress Berlin 1997, Akten-Proceedings-Actes.* Edited by B. Kluge and B. Weisser. Berlin: Staatliche Museen zu Berlin, 2000. Pages 217-21.

Also see: Hammond "The Lettering" under MACEDONIAN KINGDOM—GENERAL WORKS.

MARONEIA

3723 **Arnold, T. J.** "Blundered Coin of Maroneia." *Numismatic Chronicle* new ser., 7 (1867): 338.
A brief mention of a copper coin of Maroneia with a legend beginning MAT rather than MAP.

3724 **Casagrande, Armonde.** "Attribution of Coin from Maroneia Takes Collector on Numismatic Adventure." *The Celator* 4, no. 10 (October 1990): 28-9.
Recounts the efforts of a collector to attribute and authenticate what appeared to be a previously unknown silver triobol of Maroneia with the same design as coins known to be struck in bronze. It turned out to be the usual bronze type which had a silver color due to arsenic in the alloy.

3724a **de Callataÿ, François.** "Une Tétradrachme de Mithradate Surfappé à Maronée." *Quaderni Ticinesi. Numismatic e Antichità Classiche* (Switzerland) 20 (1991).

3725 **Eaglen, Robin J.** "Portraits of Greek Coinage: Maroneia." *Spink Numismatic Circular* 114, no. 5 (October 2006): 264-5. Illus.

This installment of the author's on-going series examines the a stater of Maroneia (horse/vine) with the reverse inscription ΕΠΙ ΧΟΡΗΓΙΟ (magistrate's name). Discusses the coinage of Maroneia and nearby cities.

3726 **MacDonald, David.** "More Maroneia Overstrikes." *Quaderni Ticinesi. Numismatic e Antichità Classiche* (Switzerland) 23 (1994): 177-82.

3727 **Mattingly, Harold B.** "The Fifth-Century Tetradrachm Coinage of Maroneia." *Numismatic Chronicle* 160 (2000): 261-3. Illus.
Mattingly provides details for a revision of Schönert-Geiss' Period V chronology at Maroneia. "The first phase of Maroneia's tetradrachm coinage copies the winestock reverse type of Mende closely. The recent Skione hoard (*CH VIII*, 63) closes just before the new Mende type and can be dated c. 432 B.C. Maroneia's coinage probably ended with Mende's: both mints closed as a result of the Athenian Standards Decree of 425/4 B.C." [H. Mattingly, *NL* 145]

3728 **May, John M. F.** "The Coinage of Maroneia, c. 520-449/8 B.C." *Numismatic Chronicle* 7th ser., 5 (1965): 27-56. 3 pls. [CS 2386]
"The coinage of Maroneia struck on a light Thraco-Macedonian standard from ca. 520 B.C. changes ca. 510/05 to a heavy Thraco-Macedonian standard. The magisterial names which appear in full ca. 495/490 may be the earliest in Greek coinage. With the promulgation of the Athenian currency decree ca. 449/8, the Maroneian mint was closed." [J. Balcer, *NL* 79]

3729 **Psoma, Selene, Chryssa Karadima, and Domna Terzopoulou.** *The Coins from Maroneia and the Classical City at Molyvoti: A Contribution to the History of Aegean Thrace.* Melethmata 62. Athens: Institute of Greek and Roman Antiquity, 2008, 437 pp., illus.
A publication of the coins found at the site of Zone, on the Aegean coast of Thrace. Includes coins found at two sites: Maroneia and a previously unidentified city site on Cape Molyvoti.

3730 **Schönert-Geiss, Edith.** "Imitations Maroneischer Münzen." *Klio* (Germany) 66 (1984): 85-92.
Discusses the imitations of the coins of Maroneia.

3731 ——— *Griechisches Münzwerk: Die Münzprägung von Maroneia.* Schriften zur Geschichte und Kultur der Antike 26. Two volumes. Berlin, 1987. 254 pp., 94 pls.

3732 **Terzian, Gregory, and Gonda van Steen.** "A Hoard of Bronze Coins of Maroneia." *Numismatic Chronicle* 163 (2003): 344-7. 2 pls.
The hoard contained eighty small bronze coins of Maroneia, and they are catalogued here. Discusses chronology, types, metrology.

Also see: Mirnik "A Thracian Silver Coin Hoard" under HOARDS.

MESAMBRIA

3733 **Dimitrov, Kamen.** "Hoard of Hellenistic Bronze Coins from Mesambria Pontica in the Depository of the National Archaeological Museum in Sofia. (*IGCH* 884)." *Studia in Honorem Alexandri Fo.* Thracia 11. Sofia, 1995. Pages 409-18. Illus.
"A part of the *IGCH* 884 hoard, containing originally over 500 bronze coins of Mesambria Pontica, is published. It consists of twenty-four specimens of two types: "Athena Alcis" and "helmet in profile"—late issues of that city coinage." [I. Prokopov, *NL* 142]

3734 **Hind, John G. F.** "Homer's 'Stout Helmet' on the Coins of Mesambria on the Black Sea." *Numismatic Chronicle* 167 (2007): 23-4. Illus.
Examines the "helmet/rayed wheel" types on Mesambrian coins. The reverse is explained as a symbol of the sun and a visual pun on the city name (Mesambria is interpreted as 'site of noon-day sun'). The obverse helmet, it is suggested, relates to a line in Homer's *Iliad* referring to a frontal, sturdy helmet.

3735 **Karayotov, Ivan.** "The Chronology of Mesembrian Tetradrachms." *Numismatica* (Bulgaria) 18, no. 4 (1984): 5-15.

3736 ——— *The Coinage of Mesambria, Volume 1: Silver and Gold Coins of Mesambria.* Sozopol, Bulgaria: Centre of Underwater Archaeology, 1994. 134 pp., map, 44 pls.
A comprehensive study of the silver and gold coins of Mesambria, including a catalogue of 770 coins, all illustrated. Includes an introduction to the history of the city, a discussion of the coinage, and a critical bibliography. Examines the dies, monograms, and hoards.

3737 **Lazarov, Latchezar.** "An Interesting Autonomous Bronze Coin of Mesambria." *Revue Belge de Numismatique et de Sigillographie* (Belgium) 143 (1997): 17-20.
"A bronze coin from Mesambria Pontica, depicting a head of Dionysos and a bunch of grapes, is published. The coin belongs to the age of Augustus." [J. van Heesch, *NL* 141]

3737a **Petac, Emanuel.** "From the Types of Alexander to Lysimachus: The Chronology of Some Mesembrian and Other West Pontic Staters." *American Journal of Numismatics* 2nd ser., 23 (2011): 7-15. 2 pls.
"The Numismatic Department of the Library of the Romanian Academy recently acquired a unique Lysimachus-type stater from Mesembria, with the controls Helmet/ΛΑ on the reverse left field. Iconographic details, such as the absence of the goddess' spear on the reverse, horse leg of the throne and the chiton of Athena, are noted. There are few die-links between the obverses of the different issues of Mesembrian staters of Lysimachus type, so it is possible to propose their succession. It is proposed that the example with ΛΑ is the first from the known Lysimachus staters. A relative chronology around 253-246 B.C.—no later—is also sustainable. The adoption of Lysimachus type stater is one of the political effects of the growing Ptolemaic influence in the region in the second half of the third century B.C., especially after the Monopoly War (253-250/47 B.C.)." [Petac]

3738 **Schwabacher, Willy.** "Mesembria on the Aegean." *Numismatic Chronicle* 6th ser., 2 (1942): 94-7. Illus.
Discusses some bronze coins which had been attributed by some researchers to an obscure town of Mesembria-on-the-Aegean, on the Thracian coast. Schwabacher presents evidence that the coins belong to the more well-known Mesembria, on the Black Sea between Odessus and Apollonia.

3739 **Topalov, Stavri.** *Messambria Pontica: Contribution to the Study of the Coin Minting of the City 5th-1st Century* B.C. Sofia, 1995. 216 pp., illus.
Text in Bulgarian.

3740 ———— *Contribution to the Study of the Countermarks of the West Pointive Cities of Apollonia, Messambria, and Odessos, III-I Century* B.C. Sofia, 1997. 144 pp., illus.
Text in Bulgarian.

Also see: de Callataÿ "Certain Alexandres de Mésembria" under MACEDONIAN KINGDOM—GENERAL WORKS; de Callataÿ "Les Derniers Alexandres" under MACEDONIAN KINGDOM—GENERAL WORKS; de Callataÿ and Prokopov "A Late Alexander of Mesembria" under MACEDONIAN KINGDOM—GENERAL WORKS.

OLBIA

3741 **Dittrich, K.** *Antike Münzen aus Olbia und Pantikapäum.* Prague, 1959. 175 pp., illus. [CS 2659]
For an English translation, see Dittrich et al. *Ancient Coins from Olbia and Panticapaeum* below.

3742 **Dittrich, K., Milos Hrbas, and Jindrich Marco.** *Ancient Coins from Olbia and Panticapaeum.* Photographs by Hrbas and Marco; text by Dittrich. Translated by I. Havlu. London: Spring Books, 1961. 168 pages, including 115 pls. [CS 2659a and 2661]
A catalogue of the beautiful coinage of Panticapaeum and the unusual coinage of Olbia. An introductory text describes the history of these two important Black Sea coast cities. Lists 121 coins of Olbia and 157 coins of Panticapaeum illustrated by dramatic, greatly enlarged black and white photographs. [Reviewed by R. A. G. Carson in *Spink Numismatic Circular* 67, no. 10 (October 1959): 180].

3743 **Hirst, G. M.** "The Cults of Olbia." *Journal of Hellenic Studies* 22 (1902): 245-67; 23 (1903): 24-53. Illus.
"Numismatic evidence is consistently used in estimating the extent and nature of the cults of Apollo (Prostates, Ietros or Delphinios), Demeter and Cybele (Part I), and Artemis, Athene, Zeus, Hermes, Poseidon, Ares, the Dioscuri, Achilles Pontarches, Heracles and the River Borysthenes (Part II)." [J. R. Jones, *NIJHS*]

3744 **Hoge, Robert W.** "Two Dolphin Coins of Olbia." *The Numismatist* 112, no. 11 (November 1999): 1374. Illus.
Illustrates two bronze dolphin-shaped coins of Olbia which were recently donated to the American Numismatic Association museum. Discusses the mythology surrounding dolphins and their connection to the god Apollo and the town of Delphi.

3745 **Karyshkovski, P. O.** "The Olbian Asses." *Items from the History of the Currency and Monetary Circulation at Olbia 2. Studies of the Metchnikov Odessa State University 149.* Historical Sciences Series 7. 1959. Pages 47-68.
In Ukranian.

3746 ———— "Olbian Coins Found Near Odessa." *Studies of the Metchnikov Odessa State University 149.* Historical Sciences Series 7. 1959. Pages 138-42.
In Ukranian.

3747 ———— "The Coins of the Olbian Council of Seven." *Artistic Culture and Archaeology of the Ancient World.* B. V. Farmakovsky Memorial Volume. Moscow, 1976. Pages 109-17.
In Russian.

3748 **Laum, Bernhard.** *Das Fischgeld von Olbia.* Frankfort, 1918. 12 pp., illus. Reprinted from *Frankfurter Münzeitung.* [CS 2664]

3749 **Lis, Akio.** "The Coinage of Olbia—A Reflection of External Influence." *The Celator* 11, no. 11 (November 1997): 22-3. Illus.
Comments on the prominence of Apollo and dolphins in the mythology related to Olbia. Reviews the development of coinage at Olbia.

3750 **Robinson, Edward S. G.** "Coins of Olbia." *Numismatic Chronicle* 5th ser., 17 (1937): 91-101. 1 pl.
Publishes twenty-six coins of Olbia which were recently added to the British Museum collection. Discusses their types and monograms.

3751 **Wells, H. Bartlett.** "The 'Borysthenes' Coins of Olbia." *SAN—Journal of the Society for Ancient Numismatics* 6, no. 4 (summer 1975): 56-8. [CS 2666]
An "extended abstract" of an article by P. O. Karyshovski published in Kiev in 1968. A series of copper coins from Olbia is discussed, demonstrating how a scholar analyzes a long-lasting series to determine an approximate chronology. Stylistic features of the coins are examined, along with monograms and die links.

3752 **Zograph, Alexander N.** "The Coins of Olbia." *Ancient Coins.* Moscow-Leningrad, 1951. Pages 121 ff. 1 pl.

Also see: Alekseyev *Rare and Unpublished Coins* under ASIA MINOR AND THE BLACK SEA REGION—GENERAL WORKS; Hermitage Museum *Coins from Ancient Towns* under BOSPOROS; Hind "City Heads/Personifications and Omens from Zeus" under THRACE—ISTROS; Stolba "Monetary Crises" under BOSPOROS.

SAMOTHRACE

3753 **Ashton, Richard.** "Pseudo-Rhodian Drachms from Samothrace." *Numismatic Chronicle* 148 (1988): 129-34. 1 pl.
Ashton argues that some rare issues of Pseudo-Rhodian drachms were struck at Samothrace, probably in the late 170's B.C. in support of Perseus' war against the Romans. Catalogues and illustrates all eleven known examples. Comments on weights, dating, and attribution.

3754 **Schönert-Geiss, Edith.** "Zur Münzprägung von Samothrake, ein Überblick." Χαρακτηρ: Αψιερωμα στη Μαντω Οικονομιδου. Athens, 1996.

3755 **Schwabacher, Willy.** "Ein Fund Archaischer Münzen von Samothrake." *Transactions of the International Numismatic Congress Organized and Held in London by the Royal Numismatic Society, June 30-July 3, 1936.* Edited by J. Allan, H. Mattingly, and E. S. G. Robinson. London: B. Quaritch, 1938. Pages 109-20. 1 pl.

3756 ———. "Cabiri on Archaic Coins of Samothrace." *Museum Notes* 5 (1952): 49-51. 1 pl.
Discusses the head on an early diobol of Samothrace from the Jameson collection, now at the American Numismatic Society. The coin originally came from the Kiourpet hoard and was published by Schwabacher in 1936 (see "Ein Fund Archaischer Münzen von Samothrake" above), where he identified the type as a bearded head in Corinthian helmet. A second specimen was in the collection of E. T. Newell. Newell says it is not a helmet, but a cap, and the head is a bearded *Cabirus*. The type on a hemiobol from the hoard is also now identified as a *Cabirus*. The *Cabiri* were non-Hellenic deities who promoted fertility and protected sailors. Samothrace was the center of their worship.

THASOS

3757 **de Callataÿ, François, and C. Mattheeuws.** "À Propos d'Une Série Exceptionnelle de Grands Bronzes Thasiens (fin IVe-Début IIIe Siècle." *Bulletin de Correspondance Hellénique* (France) 117 (1993): 481-90.

3758 **de Callataÿ, François, and I. Prokopov.** "An Overstrike of a Hellenistic Tetradrachm of Thasian Type on Athens in the Popina Hoard (*IGCH* 930)." *Nomismatika Khronika* (Greece) 13 (1994): 37-42. Illus.
The Popina Hoard contained 170+ tetradrachms of Thasian type and was discovered in 1957. The coins were buried ca. 125-100 B.C. One of these tetradrachms shows traces of overstriking—it was struck over an Athenian New Style tetradrachm of the Heracleides-Eukles issue (dated by Thompson to ca. 139-136 B.C., or by others ca. 107-104 B.C.). The authors conclude that Athenian tetradrachms in Thrace and Macedonia were restruck over several decades in the first half of the first century B.C. [In English on pp. 37-9, 42; in Greek on pp. 40-1. Also see Prokopov and Batchvarov "Trésor Monétaire de Popina" below].

3759 **Gale, Noel H., Olivier Picard, and Jean-Noël Barrandon.** "The Archaic Thasian Silver Coinage." *Antike Edel— und Buntmetallgewinnung auf Thasos.* Edited by G. A. Wagner and G. Weisgerber. Bochum: Deutschen Bergbau-Museums, 1988. Pages 212-23.

3760 **Gardner, Percy.** "The Date of King Mostis, and of Certain Later Coins of Thasos." *Numismatic Chronicle* new ser., 16 (1876): 299-306.
Discusses a tetradrachm of a Thracian or Epirote king Mostis, now in the British Museum. The coin is re-struck on a coin of Thasos. Gardner concludes that Mostis' kingdom was in Eastern Thrace (not in Epirus). He discusses the evidence this coin provides for the dating of the coins of Thasos.

3761 **Goldsborough, Reid.** "Barbarism, Art, and Thracian Tetradrachms, Part 1." *The Celator* 18, no. 7 (July 2004): 6-20. "Part 2." *The Celator* 18, no. 8 (August 2004): 18-24. "Part 3." *The Celator* 18, no. 9 (September 2004): 16-28. "Part 4." *The Celator* 18, no. 10 (October 2004): 22-231 Illus.
Examines the barbarous imitations of the tetradrachms of Thasos and related numismatic, historical, and mythological issues. Goldsborough discusses imitative coinage, Thrace, and Dionysos. Reviews the concept of imitations—coins produced by cities/cultures based on a design prototype from another city/culture. Lists the most common examples from the ancient world. The Thracian people were mostly illiterate and were composed of many tribes. The author describes the rituals related to the worship of Dionysos. Describes the second century B.C. tetradrachms of Thasos. Although many of the imitative issues are clearly degraded in style, Goldsborough argues that some are intentional abstractions created by skilled engravers working in an abstract or expressionistic style. Some engravers introduced new design elements. Recommends that collectors refer to these pieces as "Thracian tetradrachms" rather than "imitation Thasos tetradrachms." Rather than "barbarous" or "imitation," he suggests these should be referred to as adaptations. The author explores the nature and perceptions of barbarism. Also discusses the chronology of these issues and provides tips for attribution and classification. Goldsborough examines the origins of these coins, presents guidelines for collecting them, and discusses counterfeit detection. [Also see comments and criticisms in the Letters to the Editor by R. Witschonke in *The Celator* 18, no. 11 (November 2004): 4, 36, and by P. Monney in *The Celator* 18, no. 11 (November 2004): 36-7. Goldsborough responded to these letters in *The Celator* 19, no. 1 (January 2005): 35, 37. Also see Smith "Copies of Thasos" below].

3762 **Grandjean, Yves, and François Salviat.** "Chapter VII. Les Monnaies." *Guide de Thasos.* Paris: Ecole Française d'Athènes, 2000.

3763 **Hind, John G. F.** "Centaurs, Satyrs and Nymphs on the Early Silver Coins of Thasos and the Tribes of Mount Pangaion." *Numismatic Chronicle* 161 (2001): 279-87. 1 pl.
"The earliest coin-types of Thasos and the tribes on the mainland of Thrace are rebuses (visual puns). It is suggested that the 'satyr carrying off nymph' of the Orreskioi is a reference to the 'mountain beasts' (phersin orreskooisi), and that the 'satyr following nymph' refers to the Satrai (Satyriko thiasos). The thiasos of mountain and woodland beasts is the common theme, bearing reference to the cult of Dionysos, centered at the important oracle in the hill-country of the Satrai." [J. G. F. Hind, *NL* 146]

3764 **Katsarova, G.** "New Data about the Dating of Tetradrachms of the Island of Thasos from the Second Coinage Period and of Thracian Tetradrachms from the First Century B.C. *Bulletin de l'Institut Archéologique Bulgare* (Bulgaria) 27 (1964): 131-52.
In Bulgarian with an English summary.

3765 **Le Rider, Georges.** "Les Monnaies Thasiennes." *École Francaise d' Athenes, Guide de Thasos.* Paris: E. de Boccard, 1967. Pages 185-91. 5 pls. [CS 2398]
Le Rider classifies the coinage of Thasos into ten chronological groups, from 525 B.C. to Imperial times, and provides a brief synopsis for each group. Each coin type is illustrated (seventy-three types). LeRider's type classifications have become the standard for this coinage. [Also see Picard "The Coinage of Thasos" below].

3766 **MacDonald, David.** "A Group of Thasian-Type Tetradrachms Overstruck on Athenian New Style Tetradrachms." *Nomismatika Khronika* (Greece) 22 (2003): 31-9, incl. 2 pls. Also in Greek on pp. 40-5.
Publishes four Hellenistic Thasian-type tetradrachms overstruck on Athenian New Style tetradrachms. MacDonald distinguishes between the "mass issue" tetradrachms and "tribal issue" tetradrachms. Suggests the overstrikes were confined to the early first century B.C. Discusses the importation of the New Style coins into Macedonia.

3767 **Meadows, Andrew R.** "'Thasos'/New Style Hoard, 1996 (*CH* 9.265)." *Coin Hoards IX: Greek Hoards*. Special Publication No. 35. London: Royal Numismatic Society, 2002. Pages 256-8. 2 pls.
Twenty-two tetradrachms appeared on the market in 1996. The findspot is unknown but likely was the area of ancient Macedonian Thrace. The coins consisted of eighteen New Style tetradrachms of Athens and four imitations of Thasos. A burial date of ca. 123-100 B.C. seems reasonable. A new obverse die among the Thasian coins represent a hitherto missing link between issues.

3768 **Paléothodoros, Dimitri.** "Le 'Satyre et la Ménade' Thasiens: Étude d'Iconographie Numismatique." *Liber Amicorum Tony Hackens*. Numismatica Lovaniensia 20. Edited by G. Moucharte, M. B. Borba Florenzano, F. de Callataÿ, P. Marchetti, L. Smolderen, and P. Yannopoulos. Louvain-la-Neuve: Université Catholique de Louvain, 2007. Pages 143 ff.

3768a **Picard, Olivier.** "L'Organisation de l'Atelier de Thasos IVe Siècle." *Proceedings of the 9th International Congress of Numismatics. Berne, September 1979. Volume 1.* Edited by T. Hackens and R. Weiller. Luxembourg: International Association of Professional Numismatists, 1982. Pages 123-8.

3769 ——— "Monnayage Thasien du Ve Siècle av. Jésus-Christ." *Comptes Rendus des Séances* (France) 126, no. 3 (1982): 412-24.

3769a ——— "Thasos et la Macédoine au IVe et au IIIe Siècle." *Comptes Rendus des Séances* (France) 129, no. 4 (1985): 760-76.

3769b ——— "L'Administration de l'Atelier Monétaire à Thasos au IVe Siècle." *Revue Numismatique* (France) 29 (1987): 7-14.

3770 ——— "The Coinage of Thasos." *Nomismatika Khronika* (Greece) 9 (1990): 15-31. Illus.
A preliminary summary of Picard's research aimed at refining the classifications of the coinage of Thaos presented by Le Rider in 1967 (see G. Le Rider "Les Monnaies Thasiennes" above). Le Rider proposed ten chronological groups from 525 B.C. to Imperial times. Picard divides the coinage into three main series (each subdivided into groups), some isolated issues, and four Imperial issues. Each group is briefly described and illustrated. [In French, with illustrations, on pp. 15-22; in English on pp. 23-7; in Greek on pp. 28-31].

3771 ——— "Monnaies de Fouilles et Histoire Grecque: L'Exemple de Thasos." *Numismatic Archaeology/Archaeological Numismatics: Proceedings of an International Conference held to Honour Dr. Mando Oeconomides in Athens 1995*. Oxbow Monographs 75. Edited by K. Sheedy and C. Papageorgiadou-Banis. Oxford: Oxbow Books and The Australian Archaeological Institute at Athens, 1997. Pages 29-39.

3772 ——— "Iconographie et Mémoire Monétaire: L'Example de Thasos." *Coins in the Aegean Islands. Proceedings of the Fifth Scientific Meeting, Mytilene, 16-29 September 2006. Volume 1: Ancient Times.* Obolos 9. Edited by Panagiotis Tselekas. Athens: The Friends of the Numismatic Museum, 2010. Pages 45-57.

3773 **Prokopov, Illya.** "Les Tétradrachmes Thraces aux Types de Thasos." *Nomismatika Khronika* (Greece) 21 (2002): 83-90, incl. 1 pl.
"The author discusses the difficulties in interpreting the three different series of Thasian imitations struck in the name of the Thracians in the first century B.C. Text in French with Greek translation by E. Papaeuthumiou and M. J. A. Tzamales on pp. 88-90." [Oliver D. Hoover, *NL* 147]

3774 ——— *Die Silberprägung der Insel Thasos und die Tetradrachmen des "Thasischen Typs" vom 2. bis 1. Jahrhundert v. Chr.* Griechisches Munzwerk. Berlin: Akademie Verlag, 2006.
Catalogue of the silver coins of Thasos and the tetradrachms of Thasian type, from the second to the first century B.C. The Thasos tetradrachms are Greek coins from the North Aegean island of Thasos. The "Thasian-type" tetradrachms are early copies, usually more crude, minted on the Thracian mainland. Provides estimated mintage dates for the coins. [Reviewed by R. Goldsborough in *The Celator* 21, no. 7 (July 2007): 39-40, 46].

3775 **Prokopov, Illya, and I. E. Batchvarov.** "Trésor Monétaire de Popina, Région de Silistra." *Numizmatika* (Bulgaria) 24, no. 1 (1990): 3-22.
An examination of the Popina Hoard which contained 170+ tetradrachms of Thasian type and was discovered in 1957. The coins were buried ca. 125-100 B.C. In Bulgarian. [Also see de Callataÿ and Prokopov "An Overstrike" above].

3776 **Robinson, Edward S. G.** "A Find of Coins of Thasos." *Numismatic Chronicle* 5th ser., 14 (1934): 244-54. 2 pls.
Describes a hoard composed of four coins of Abdera, one of Byzantium, and thirty-six of Thasos. The Thasos coins include some previously unrecorded magistrates and symbols, some of the rare didrachms, as well as drachms and tetradrachms. Robinson believes the hoard was buried in the Thraco-Macedonian region shortly after 360 B.C.

3777 **Sasianu, Alexandru.** "Copies and Imitations of Thasian Tetradrachms." *Proceedings of the 11th International Numismatic Congress, September 8-13, 1991. Volume 1.* Edited by T. Hackens et al. Louvain-la-Neuve, Belgium: International Association of Professional Numismatists, 1993. Pages 123-31. Illus., map.
Catalogues many copies and imitations of the tetradrachms of Thasos. Sasianu distinguishes between copies (good quality copies of the original coins by non-Greek engravers) and imitations (personal creations of a barbarian engraver). Dates these issues to 83-63 B.C. Comments on possible minting locations.

3778 **Smith, David Spencer.** "Copies of Thasos Tetradrachms Revisited." *The Celator* 19, no. 9 (September 2005): 6-28. Illus.

Examines the tetradrachms bearing *obv*., head of Dionysos, *rev*., standing Herakles, which are imitative of the coins of Thasos. Begins with comments on Goldsborough's series of articles (see Goldsborough above). Smith attributes the coins to Celtic tribes rather than Thracians. He reviews the classifications defined by Göbl (see Göbl *Ostkeltischer Typenatlas* under CELTIC COINAGE OF EUROPE) and Lukanc (see Lukanc *Les Imitations des Monnaies d'Alexandre le Grand et de Thasos* under CELTIC COINAGE OF EUROPE). Describes various stages in the degradation of the images of Dionysos and Herakles, illustrated by many interesting examples of the coinage. Concludes with some comments on the metrology of the coins.

3779 **Topalov, Stavri.** *Contribution to the Study of Tetradrachms of Thasos from the Second Period of Mintage, Their Imitation and Coins Related to Them, as Well as Imitative Coins from the Thracian Lands during the II-I Century B.C.* Sofia, 1996. 200 pp., illus.
A study of the tetradrachms of Thasos and its many imitations. Text in Bulgarian.

3780 **Torbágyi, Melinda.** "The Circulation of Thasian Coins in the Carpathian Basin." *Proceedings of the 10th International Congress of Numismatics, London, 1986.* International Association of Professional Numismatists Publication, No. 11. Edited by I. A. Carradice. London: International Association of Professional Numismatists, 1986. Pages 23-5. Map.
Calls attention to the problems of the late Thasos coinage (after 180 B.C.). More study of hoard material will be necessary before definite answers can be found.

Also see: Ashton "Hellenistic Bronze Coins" under THRACE—ABDERA; Ashton, Hardwick, Konuk, and Meadows "Pixodarus Hoard" under HOARDS; de Callataÿ "The Coins in the Name of Sura" under MACEDONIA—ROMAN PROVINCE; de Callataÿ and Prokopov "The Boljarino Hoard" under HOARDS; Grace "Stamped Amphora Handles" under TYPES; Hoover *Handbook of Coins of the Islands* under CYCLADES ISLANDS; Mattingly "Coins and Amphoras" under IONIAN ISLANDS—CHIOS; Mirnik "A Thracian Silver Coin Hoard" under HOARDS; Moushmov *Ancient Coins of the Balkan Peninsula* under THRACE—GENERAL WORKS; Nicorescu "Two Gold Coins of Tyras" under PHOENICIA; Prokopov and de Callataÿ "A Late Hellenistic Hoard" under HOARDS; Sayles "The Celator's Point of View" under ART; M. Thompson "A Hoard from Thessaly" under HOARDS; Wartenberg "After Marathon: Money" under GENERAL WORKS—GREEK.

Northern Greece

The Aetolians, notwithstanding their ancient heroic fame, were in historical times the most turbulent and uncivilized people of Hellas. Before the age of Alexander there is no trace of Aetolian money, nor was it until after the consolidation of the Aetolian League, brought about by the invasions of Aetolia by the Macedonians (B.C. 314-311) and by the Gauls (B.C. 279), that Federal coinage began.

—Barclay V. Head, 1887

Aitolia

3781 **Benner, Steve M.** "History and Coinage of the Aetolian League." *The Celator* 22, no. 3 (March 2008): 6-22. Illus.
Benner summarizes the history of the Aetolian League and describes its coinage. The League rose to power in the third century B.C. and was centered in Aetolia. It adopted a constitution, levied taxes, raised armies, and set up a common currency and weight system. The League challenged Macedonian power in the area and defended Delphi from the invading Gauls in 279. It sided with Rome against Macedon in 197, then sided with Antiochus III against Rome. But in 146, the League ceased to exist and Aetolia was incorporated into the Roman province of Achaea. All the coins of the League bear the legend AITΩΛΩN on the reverse. Benner discusses the dating of the coins—which remains controversial—and provides suggestions from a forthcoming book by Tsangari (see Tsangari *Corpus des Monnaies* below). Describes the denominations, weight standards, types, and variations.

3782 **de Laix, Roger A.** "The Silver Coinage of the Aetolian League." *California Studies in Classical Antiquity, Volume 6.* University of California Press, 1974. Pages 47-75. 1 pl.
The author attempts to establish a basic chronology for the silver coinage of the Aetolian League and relate the coinage to its historical settings. Suggests this coinage belongs to the period ca. 220-135 B.C. Discusses the control markings and moneyers' monograms on the coins and suggests a new theoretical principle, the "heptad" principle, which is useful in corroborating the suggested chronological groupings. Concludes that the monograms probably represent the names of seven annual ταμιαι (officials). Tables summarize the various issues and illustrate die links and control markings. Includes a cross-reference of de Laix's issue numbers to the coins illustrated in Thompson's publication of the Agrinion hoard. [See M. Thompson *The Agrinion Hoard* under Hoards].

3783 **Liampi, Katerini.** "On the Chronology of the Bronze Coinages of the Aetolian League and its Members (Spearhead and Jawbone Types)." *ΑΡΧΑΙΟΓΝΩΣΙΑ* (Greece) 9 (1995-1996): 83 ff.

3784 **Madsen, Eardley, and Ethel Madsen.** "Aetolia." *SAN—Journal of the Society for Ancient Numismatics* 13, no. 4 (winter 1982-3): inside covers.
A brief overview of the history and coinage of Aetolia.

3785 **Reinach, A. J.** "Un Monument Delphien: l'Etolie sur les Trophées Gaulois de Kallion." *Journal International d'Archéologie Numismatique* (Greece) 13 (1911): 177-240. 1 pl.
"Offers a reconstruction of the statue of Aetolia, based on the representations on Aetolian coin types." [J. R. Jones, *AIJIAN*]

3786 **Scheu, Frederick.** "Coinage Systems of Aetolia." *Numismatic Chronicle* 6th ser., 20 (1960): 37-52. 1 pl. [CS 2466]
"Some reflection of the importance of the Aetolian League, which played a large part in the history of the third century B.C., is seen in the coinage. Most Aetolian coins are distinguished by monograms, initials, or letters. These do not, however, refer to strategoi, but changes of standard and type within the coinage help in establishing a chronology somewhat more precise than an overall 279-168 B.C.: the chief issues at least can be given an approximate date. Two groups of Attic tetradrachms—the earliest—are differentiated by style. In addition there occur three denominations (stater, drachm, hemidrachm or triobol) of silver of Corcyrean standard. The gold staters of Attic weight, together with issues of the Acarnanian League, are the only gold coins struck in Greece between 281 and 196-190 B.C. Bronze coins fall into two categories: 'Naturalist' and pro-Roman Aes." [J. Healy, *NL* 60]

3787 **Tsangari, Dimitra I.** *Corpus des Monnaies d'Or, d'Argent et de Bronze de la Confédération Étolienne.* Athens: Helicon, 2007. 508 pp., 99 pls.
This catalogue establishes a new chronology for the Aitolian League coinage. Includes 2658 coins (43 gold, 863 silver, and 1752 bronze).

3788 **Vagi, David L.** "Military Themes Pervade Aetolian League Coinage." *The Celator* 9, no. 5 (May 1995): 24. Illus.
A brief description of the coinage of the Aitolian League. Many of the coin types have a military theme.

Also see: Gardner *Catalogue of Greek Coins of Thessaly to Aetolia* under NORTHERN GREECE—THESSALY; Losada "The Aetolian Indemnity" under HOARDS; Münzen & Medaillen *Auktion 23* under NORTHERN GREECE—AKARNANIA; M. Thompson *The Agrinion Hoard* under HOARDS.

AKARNANIA

3789 **Benner, Steve M.** "History and Coinage of the Akarnanian Confederacy." *The Celator* 25, no. 7 (July 2011): 6-24. Illus.
Benner begins with a brief mythological account of the foundation of Akarnania and he then summarizes its military and political history from the seventh to the second centuries B.C. Next, he provides an overview of the coinage. Weights for each denomination under the various standards in use during the confederacy period (240-167 B.C.) are summarized in a table. Local cities continued to strike their own coins even while a part of the confederacy, including Corinthian-style staters and its fractions. The author examines the Corinthian-style coins, the confederacy coins minted at Stratos and Leukos, and the federal bronze coins.

3790 **Carter, C.** "The Staters of Leucas: A Numismatic and Historical Study." *Convegno del Centro Internazionale de Studi Numismatici. La Monetazione Corinzia in Occidente: Atti del IX Convegno del Centro Internazionale di Studi Numismatici, Napoli, 27-28 Ottobre 1986*. Rome: Istituto Italiano di Numismatica, 1993. Pages 35-41.

3791 **Eaglen, Robin J.** "Portraits of Greek Coinage 2: Anactorium." *Spink Numismatic Circular* 113, no. 1 (February 2005): 14. Illus.
This installment of the author's on-going series examines the coinage of Anactorium. Reviews the history of the city, its mythology, and the Corinthian-style coinage of the city.

3792 **Foraste, D. D.** "The Fourth Century Mint of Anaktorian." *Convegno del Centro Internazionale de Studi Numismatici. La Monetazione Corinzia in Occidente: Atti del IX Convegno del Centro Internazionale di Studi Numismatici, Napoli, 27-28 Ottobre 1986*. Rome: Istituto Italiano di Numismatica, 1993. Pages 43-59.

3793 **Forrer, Leonard S.** "An Unpublished Artist's Signature on a Stater of Leucas." *Spink Numismatic Circular* 11, no. 128 (July 1903): 6085.
Mentions a stater of Leucas bearing the letter N, which is believed to be the initial letter of an engraver. This is quite unusual for the Corinthian series.

3793a **Georgiou, Evangelia.** "Acarnanian Astacus: New Numismatic Evidence." *XIII Congreso Internacional de Numismática, Madrid – 2003: Actas–Proceedings–Actes I*. Edited by Carmen Alfaro, Carmen Marcos, and Paloma Otero. Madrid: International Numismatic Commisson, 2005. Pages 253-8, incl. 1 pl.
Astacus was an important port city in Akarnania which minted a small number of coins in the fourth century B.C. Georgiou discusses the city's silver coins and then presents five previously unpublished bronze coins (all illustrated) that provide new types. Previously, no bronze coins had been attributed to this mint.

3794 **Imhoof-Blumer, Friedrich W.** "Die Münzen Akarnaniens." *Numismatische Zeitschrift* (Austria) (1878). Reprint, Graz, 1971. 186 pp., 3 pls. [CS 2465]

3795 **Münzen & Medaillen Gmbh.** *Auktion 23, Sammlung BCD: Akarnanien und Aetolien*. October 18, 2007. Weil am Rhein, 2007. 176 pp., illus.
Sale catalogue for the "BCD" collection of coins from Akarnanian and Aetolia, including 591 lots. Forward by the collector. An outstanding collection of types and varieties, including many rarities, fully illustrated. Catalogue written by Dr. Hans Voegtli, with occasional notes by the collector highlighting coins of special interest. [For other portions of the collection, see "BCD" in the INDEX OF COLLECTORS AND COLLECTIONS].

3796 **Ralli-Photopoulou, Euterpe.** "Bronze Tetradrachms and Drachms from Palairos, Akarnania (4th Century B.C.)." *Nomismatika Khronika* (Greece) 19 (2000): 39-54. Illus., map.
A catalogue of twenty-two coins (twenty from the Alpha Bank collection), including a recently found bronze coin with the inscription [TETRA]ΔRAXMON. In 1906, Svoronos described a similar piece as a weight—used to check the weight of silver tetradrachms of the Attic standard. The piece shares several characteristics with a group of bronze drachms attributed to Palairos (galloping horse/bearded head). The indication of value, though not common, is seen on coins at several other cities (examples are listed). The weight of the pieces does not match the Attic standard. The author believes the piece in question is a coin. The series of coins were struck from hastily engraved dies on flans of widely varying weights. These may have been emergency issues struck during the poor wheat harvest of 330-326 B.C. In Greek on pp. 39-47 and in English on pp. 50-4; plates on pp. 48-9. [Also see Regling below].

3797 **Regling, Kurt.** "Kupfernes TETRAΔRAXMON." *Journal International d'Archéologie Numismatique* (Greece) 11 (1908): 243-4.
Examines two bronze coins bearing the inscription TETRAΔRAXMON. [Also see Ralli-Photopoulou above].

3798 **Schwabacher, Willy.** "Some Unknown Federal Coins of the Acarnanians." *Studies Presented to David Moore Robinson on His Seventieth Birthday. Volume 2*. Edited by George E. Mylonas and Doris Raymond. St. Louis: Washington University, 1953. Pages 218-23.
Describes two previously unpublished coins of the Akarnanian League: a gold stater and a silver third stater. These coins support the dating of the beginning of the later Federal Series to ca. 250 B.C. and mark the transition to new types, with bearded coins of Achelous struck ca. 192 B.C.

Also see: Bonelou *Numismatic Circulation* under HOARDS; Chittenden "Diaktoros" under PELOPONNESOS—ARGOLIS; Fraser and Rönne *Boeotian and West Greek Tombstones* under TYPES; Gardner *Catalogue of Greek Coins of Thessaly to Aetolia* under NORTHERN GREECE—THESSALY; Kraay "A Hoard of Corinth and Leucas" under CORINTHIA; Milne "On Dies in North-West Greece" (Thyrrheium) under THE MINTING PROCESS.

Corcyra

3799 **Earle-Fox, Harry B.** "The Initial Coinage of Corcyra." *Numismatic Chronicle* 4th ser., 8 (1908): 80.
Suggests that certain early triobols, trihemiobols, and hemiobols ascribed to Phocis in the *British Museum Catalogue* actually belong to Corcyra.

3800 **Fried, Sallie.** *The Autonomous Silver Coinage of Korkyra from the Earliest Strikings through 229 B.C.* Ph.D. dissertation. Boston: Brown University, 1982.

3801 **Hind, John.** "The Coin-Type on the Reverse Side of the Early Silver Coins of Corcyra." *Numismatic Chronicle* 159 (1999): 284-6. 1 pl.
Examines the floral/stellate pattern, the interpretation of which has proven elusive. Hind suggests it represents a stylized representation of the 'temenos and blooming garden of Alcinous' (a distinctive phrase in Homer's Odyssey), an important cult center.

3802 **Kitchell, K. F.** "The Golden Doors of Alcinous as a Coin-Type (Corcyra, Apollonia, Dyrrhachium)." *Antipolis* (France) 1, no. 2 (1975): 123-8. Illus.
[Also see Gardner "Floral Patterns" under Types, Marotta "Dyrrhachium" under Northern Greece—Illyria, Petrányi "On the Reverse Pattern" under Northern Greece—Illyria, and Sasianu "Apollonia and Dyrrhachium Drachms" under Northern Greece—Illyria].

3802a **Nicolet-Pierre, Hélène.** "A Propos du Moyennayage Archaïque de Corcyre." *Revue Suisse de Numismatique* (Switzerland) 88 (2009): 103-16.

3803 **Visonà, Paolo.** "The Coinage of Corcyra Melaina." *Proceedings of the Fourth International Numismatic Congress in Croatia, September 20-25, 2004. Stari Grad (Pharos), the Island of Hvar and M/S Marko Polo, Croatia.* Edited by Julijan Dobrinic. Rijeka: Dobrinic & Dobrinic, 2005.
Analyzes the typology and fabric of four third-century B.C. coins from Corcyra Melaina with the types of Apollo/barley ear and an inscription naming the Corcyreans. Visonà finds a connection between these and some bronzes from Issa. Concludes these were struck by colonists from Issa.

Also see: Gardner "Boat Races" under Types; Kraay "Greek Coinage and War" under General Works—Greek; Petrányi "On the Reverse Pattern" under Northern Greece—Illyria.

Epirus

3804 **Babelon, Jean.** "Le Roi Pyrrhos." *Centennial Publication of the American Numismatic Society.* Edited by Harald Ingholt. New York: American Numismatic Society, 1958. Pages 53-71. 1 pl. [CS 2457]

3805 **de Callataÿ, François.** "Un 'Octobole' de Pyrrhus Surfrappé sur un Statère de Type Corinthien: Réflexions sur les Masses Monnayées par Pyrrhus en Or et en Argent." *Annali, Istituto Italiano di Numismatica* (Italy) 47 (2000): 189-213. 4 pls.

3806 **Franke, Peter R.** *Die Antiken Münzen von Epirus.* Wiesbaden, 1961. 344 pp., 67 pls. [CS 2459]

3807 **Garoufalis, P.** *Pyrrhus, King of Epirus.* London: Stacey International, 1979. 488 pp., illus.
"Chapter 13 (pp. 199-214) discusses coins minted by Pyrrhus." [E. Marles, *NL* 106]

3808 **Jenkins, G. Kenneth.** "Numismatic Forgeries of Pyrrhus." *British Museum Quarterly* 25, nos. 1-2 (1962): 26-9.
"There is no portrait of Pyrrhus on his coinage. The supposed portrait coins (one, listed by Mionnet, was noted as false, and others are in Barcelona and the British Museum) are forgeries." [I. Merker, *NL* 62]

3809 **Kraay, Colin M.** "The Earliest Issue of Ambracia." *Quaderni Ticinesi. Numismatic e Antichità Classiche* (Switzerland) 6 (1977): 35-52. Illus. [CS 2461]
"The die sequence of Corinthian and Ambracian issues is tied to the use of a common reverse die. This phenomenon seems to be verified about 480 B.C., when the die sequence seems to prove that a great quantity of silver was converted into coinage. The previous metal came from booty secured from the Persians after the battle of Platea." [S. Sorda, *NL* 101]

3810 ———. "The Coinage of Ambracia and the Preliminaries of the Peloponnesian War." *Quaderni Ticinesi. Numismatic e Antichità Classiche* (Switzerland) 8 (1979): 37-66. Illus.
"Ambracia began to strike coinage again after an interval of a few decades following 479 B.C. The first emissions of this group are studied by means of stylistic connections with contemporaneous issues of Corinth, Leucas, Corcyra and other minor mints. All these issues seem to have been coined during a brief period when Corinth was preparing an expedition against Corcyra in aid of Epidamnus, ca. 430." [S. Sorda, *NL* 104]. [Also see Kagan "Epidamnus or Ephyre" under Corinthia].

3811 **Oikonomides, Al N.** "Victory Leads to Special Coinage." *Coin World* (February 17, 1982): 73, 76. Illus.
Recounts the victory of the army of Pyrrhos of Epirus over the forces of Antigonus Gonatas of Macedonia. The oval shields of the defeated Galatian rear guard were dedicated as a trophy erected by Pyrrhos in Thessaly. Suggests that the Galatian shield on the trophy carried by Nike on a gold stater of Pyrrhos confirms that these coins were struck either by Pyrrhos' traveling mint or by a Epirot mint in 274/3 B.C. Also suggests these coins were minted from gold captured from Antigonus. These coins had previously been credited to the Syracusan mint, ca. 278 B.C.

3812 **Ravel, Oscar E.** *The "Colts" of Ambracia.* Numismatic Notes and Monographs, No. 37. New York: American Numismatic Society, 1928. 180 pp., 19 pls. [CS 2462]

Examines the Corinthian-type staters of Ambracia in Epirus. Presents a brief history of the city and a study of the Ambracian mint up until its closing ca. 338 B.C. Discusses symbols and chronology. The catalogue of types lists 192 coins. Includes commentary on the types, the sequence of dies, and weight standards. [Reviewed by A. R. Bellinger in *American Journal of Archaeology* 34 (1930): 115. For some additions to this catalogue, see Ravel "Rare and Unpublished Coins" under CORINTHIA].

3813 **Seltman, E. J.** "Un Monnaie Importante de Pyrhus, Roi d'Epire." *Revue Belge de Numismatique* (Belgium) (1912): 5-10.

3814 **Tsoukanelis, Kimon.** "The Tetradrachms of Pyrrhus: A Preliminary Die Study." *The Celator* 24, no. 5 (May 2010): 20-8, 56. Illus.
A catalogue of sixty-one tetradrachms of Pyrrhus, struck in Bruttium, Italy in the early third century B.C. Twenty-two of the coins are photographed here.

3815 **Vlasto, Michel P.** "Alexander, Son of Neoptolemus of Epirus: His Gold, Silver, and Bronze Coinage." *Numismatic Chronicle* 5th ser., 6 (1926): 154-231. 3 pls. [CS 2460]
Presents a tentative chronological classification of all of Alexander of Epirus' rare coinage (342-332 B.C.). Provides a catalogue and descriptions of the coin types followed by discussions of mint attributions and weight standards. Discusses the Carosino 1904 hoard and the Molossian 1925 hoard. Concludes with brief comments on his bronze coinage.

Also see: Brett "Athena ΑΛΚΙΔΕΜΟΣ" under TYPES; Oikonomides "Nike Confirms Pyrrhos" under PORTRAITS; Oikonomides "The Portrait of Pyrrhos" under PORTRAITS; Touratsoglou *The Coin Circulation in Ancient Macedonia* under HOARDS.

ILLYRIA

3816 **Beaumont, R. L.** "Greek Influence in the Adriatic Sea before the Fourth Century B.C." *Journal of Hellenic Studies* 56 (1936): 159-204.
"On pp. 181-4 the questions of the silver mines of Damastium and of the use of Illyrian silver for Corinthian coinage are discussed." [J. R. Jones, *NIJHS*]

3817 **Ceka, Hasan.** *Questions de Monnaie Illyrienne, avec un Catalogue des Monnaies d'Apollonie et de Dyrrhachium.* French translation by Kole Luka. Tirana: Université d'État de Tirana, Institut d'Histoire, 1972. 200 pp., illus. [CS 2452]

3818 **Gjongecaj, Shpresa.** "Archéologie et Numismatique en Albanie: Remarques sur l'Activité Monétaire au IV-II Siècle." *Numismatic Archaeology/Archaeological Numismatics: Proceedings of an International Conference held to Honour Dr. Mando Oeconomides in Athens 1995.* Oxbow Monographs 75. Edited by K. Sheedy and C. Papageorgiadou-Banis. Oxford: Oxbow Books and The Australian Archaeological Institute at Athens, 1997. Pages 130-40. Map.

3819 **Maier, A.** *Die Silbermünzen von Apollonia und Dyrrhachion.* Dissertation, Tübingen, 1906. *Zeitschrift für Numismatik* (Germany) 41 (1908): 1-33.

3820 **Marotta, Michael E.** "Dyrrachium: Rome's Doorway to Greece." *The Celator* 11, no. 4 (April 1997): 6-8. Illus.
A brief history of the city of Dyrrachium (the city's earlier name was Epidamnos) in Illyria. The city was founded by the Korkyans and the Corinthians ca. 625 B.C. Describes the major coin types. Identifies the reverse design on Dyrrachium's staters as the garden of Alcinous. [For another opinion, see Gardner "Floral Patterns" under TYPES. Also see Kitchell "The Golden Doors" above, Petrányi "On the Reverse Pattern" below, and Sasianu "Apollonia and Dyrrhachium Drachms" below].

3821 **May, John M. F.** *The Coinage of Damastion and the Lesser Coinages of the Illyro-Paeonian Region.* London: Oxford University Press, 1939. 207 pp., table, map, 12 pls. Reprint, Darmstadt: Scientia Verlag Aalen, 1979. [CS 2455]
Discusses the location of the ancient cities of Damastion and Pelagia. Provides a historical introduction to the cities. This area was an important mining district and the local mints apparently produced coins as bullion. Lists and discusses the major coin types of Damastion, Daparria, Pelagia, Nicharchus, the Tenestini, Sarnoa, and Dadado. Discusses the Risan hoard of 250-300 coins. [Reviewed by C. Seltman in *Journal of Hellenic Studies* 59 (1939): 320-1. Also see Schwabacher "Illyro-Paeonian Silver Coins" and Søkolovska "The Coinage of Agrianes" below].

3822 ——— "Macedonia and Illyria." *Journal of Roman Studies* 36 (1946): 48-56. 1 pl.
"The author points out that the now accepted dating of Macedonian tetrobols to after 186 B.C. has destroyed the basis of Evans' historical interpretation of the evidence of the hoard from Selci in Albania. He then proceeds to discuss the rare local bronze issues of the Illyrian towns of Scodra and Lissus known from this hoard and from three individual specimens in Scutari, Zagreb, and Copenhagen. He decides that each town first struck an autonomous issue—Scodra using Macedonian types, Lissus the native pirate boat, the *lembus*; that then at Scodra, there was a small issue carrying both the name of the inhabitants and that of King Genthius (this is uncertain—the single specimen is in poor condition); and that then, within a year or so of 170 B.C., Genthius issued bronze in his own name but with the local types both at Scodra and at Lissus. The coins in question are illustrated, and there is a good map of the district." [*NL* 3]

3823 **Mirnik, Ivan.** "A Contribution to the Study of the Circulation of the Drachms of Apollonia and Dyrrhachium in Southern Pannonia Plain." *Annotazioni Numismatiche* (Italy) 6, no. 24 (December 1996): 526-9.
"The author lists some hoards from the former Yugoslavia which contain drachms of Apollonia and Dyrrhachium." [N. Vismara, *NL* 142]

3824 **Petrányi, Gyula.** "Comments on the Chronology of the Final Minting Period of the Apollonian-Dyrrhachion Drachms." *Buletinul Societatii Numismatice Române* (Romania) 86-87 (1992-93): 67-75. Illus.
"The author discusses some chronological and metrological issues with the drachms from Apollonia and Dyrrhachium and proposes new ideas." [C. Preda, *NL* 139]

3825 ——— "Relative Chronology of the Drachms of Apollonia and Dyrrhachium in the Final Period of Minting." *Numizmatikai Közlöny* (Hungary) 94-95 (1995-96): 3-18. Illus.

3826 ——— "On the Reverse Pattern of the Silver Coins from Corcyra, Apollonia and Dyrrhachium." *The Celator* 12, no. 11 (November 1998): 22-4. Illus.

Reviews the controversy over the interpretation of the reverse design on the coins of Corcyra, Apollonia, and Dyrrhachium. Petrányi argues that it is a double stellate pattern rather than a floral pattern. [Also see Gardner "Floral Patterns" under TYPES, Kitchell "The Golden Doors" above, Marotta "Dyrrachium" above, and Sasianu "Apollonia and Dyrrhachium Drachms" below].

3827 ——— "On the Position of the Aibatios/Chairenos Issue in the Sequence of Apollonia Drachms." *Studii si Cercetari de Numismatica* (Romania) 11 (1995): 59-63. Illus.

"The author proposes to put this issue at the end of the series, preceding the Xenokles/Chairenos issue and in general the drachms which belong to the 'drumstick-type' and to the 'petal type.'" [G. P. Bordea, *NL* 141]

3827a ——— "The Greek-Illyrian Drachms of Apollonia and Dyrrhachium—Trade Coins for the North-Eastern Balkan Region in the Early Phase of the 1st Century B.C.?" *Bulletin du Cercle d'Études Numismatiques* (Belgium) 43, no. 3 (September-December 2006).

Numerous hoards found throughout the North and East Balkan Region but not in modern Greece contain the uniform drachms of Apollonia and Dyrrhachium, sometimes in vast quantities, alone or intermixed with the tetradrachms of Thasos and Macedonia Prima. No smaller denominations (half drachms or bronze issues) of the two Illyrian cities accompany them. There are a lot of unresolved questions concerning this coinage: the beginning and the end of minting, the exact date of each individual emission, the meaning of the symbols and monograms on the obverse, and the reasons why they can be found also in far territories. A meticulous study of the hoards enabled the establishment of a relative chronology of the issues in the second half of the series, and also some tentative conclusions. The massive arrival of these coins to territories far away from the producing towns seems to be relatively short, hardly exceeding the last fifteen years of minting. Within this a small gap is also observable. It is the last ten years when the majority of the drachms became exported. The increased demand was met by the blow-up of production and with its usual consequences: less careful die preparation and minting, gradual weight decline, and increased counterfeiting activity throughout the area of their occurrence. It is still unknown what the purpose of these coins was outside of the minting cities, but based on numismatic evidence, they suggest a one-way type of commerce: some goods were bought for them and the coins became hoarded as bullion without entering real coin circulation. [From the Petrányi's summary].

3828 **Sasianu, Alexandru.** "The Apollonia and Dyrrhachium Drachms: Typological Explanation." *Proceedings of the 10th International Congress of Numismatics, London, 1986.* International Association of Professional Numismatists Publication, No. 11. Edited by I. A. Carradice. London: International Association of Professional Numismatists, 1986. Pages 27-33. Illus.

Discusses some hybrid drachms (Dyrrhachium obverse coupled with Apollonia reverse, and vice versa) which typologically constitute a peculiar group. Suggests the minting of the hybrids was not accidental. Discusses a few drachms bearing the names of previously unknown magistrates and Prytaneis. Also presents a brief summary of seven interpretations of the reverse design for the Apollonia and Dyrrhachium drachms: (1) the square represents Alkinoos' garden; (2) it is a simple accidental convergence of lines; (3) it is the plan of the place for animal sacrifice; (4) floral type (floral cult); (5) decorative scheme; (6) stellate type stars of the Dioscuroi; (7) Alkinoos' garden gate. The first is most commonly accepted. The author suggests the twelve "sticks" which make up the design inside the square are stylized forms of sceptres or clubs. It is not a floral design. [Also see Gardner "Floral Patterns" under TYPES, Kitchell "The Golden Doors" under NORTHERN GREECE—CORCYRA, Marotta "Dyrrachium" above, and Petrányi "On the Reverse Pattern" above].

3829 **Schwabacher, Willy.** "Illyro-Paeonian Silver Coins in the Royal Collection." *Acta Archaeologica* (Denmark) 14 (1943): 83-91. Illus.

Discusses May's book on the coinages of the Illyro-Paeonian mining district (see May *The Coinage of Damastion* above) and illustrates numerous coins from the Royal Collection at Copenhagen which supplement May's publication. Some of the coins help to confirm May's theories, while others provide new information.

3830 **Sokolovska, Viktorija.** "The Coinage of Agrianes." *Macedonian Numismatic Journal* (Macedonia) 2 (1996): 13-22.

"The author proposes that the minor coinages of May's *Coinage of Damastion* (Pelagia, Daparria, Sarnoa, Darado, Tenestini, Nicharchus and Simonos) be considered coins of towns and rulers of the Paeonian tribe of the Agrianes struck in the mint of Damastion. The latter mint is identified with epigraphic references to Municipium DD (interpreted as Damastion Dardanorum) near Socanica in northern Kosovo." [C. Smith, Jr., *NL* 139]. [Also see May *The Coinage of Damastion* above].

3831 **Visonà, Paolo.** "Early Greek Bronze Coinage in Dalmatia and the Skudljivac Hoard: A Reappraisal of *IGCH* 418-420." *Proceedings of the 9th International Congress of Numismatics. Berne, September 1979. Volume 1.* Edited by T. Hackens and R. Weiller. Luxembourg: International Association of Professional Numismatists, 1982. Pages 147-55. 1 pl.

A discussion of the characteristics of the earliest Greek minting activity in Northern Illyria, followed by a reassessment of the contents of the Skudlijivac hoard—the largest hoard of bronze coins of Heracleia and Pharos, and the only hoard containing a combination of the earliest Greek Illyrian issues as well as overstrikes. The hoard was buried ca. 330-320 B.C.

3832 ——— "Colonization and Money Supply at Issa in the Fourth Century B.C." *Chiron* (Germany) 25 (1995): 56-62. Illus.

"The archaeological record of the island of Vis (ancient Issa) in Dalmatia does not support recent attempts to date the earliest phase of monetary circulation at Issa to the first half of the fourth century B.C. The presence of Syracusan bronze coins may be linked to the arrival of colonists from the neighboring island of Hvar (ancient Pharos) after 350 B.C. Pharos, rather than Syracuse, provided the impetus for the adoption of coinage by the Issaean settlers." [V. Paolo, *NL* 134]

3833 ——— "The Chronology of Issa's Early Hellenistic Coinage." *1. Medjunaroldni Numizmatici Kongres u Hrvatskoj, 12-15.X.1995, Zbornik Radova.* Opatija, 1996. Pages 149-60.

"The author reviews his 1974 conclusions regarding the dating of the coinage of Issa (modern Vis) on the basis of new coin finds and archaeological research. Positing the foundation of the colony shortly after 344 B.C., he places the earliest civic issues after 330 B.C. Considering the dating and context of overstriking, he argues that it demonstrates sufficient international trade to yield a steady supply of foreign bronze coinage, rather than indicating isolation and a lack of local resources." [C. Smith, Jr., *NL* 139]

3834 ——— "J. M. F. May's Contributions to the Study of Greek-Illyrian Coinage." *Proceedings of the 2nd International Numismatic Congress in Croatia, October 15-17, 1998.* Edited by Dobrinic and Dobrinic. Zagreb, 2000.

"Unpublished papers in J. M. F. May's Archives in Oxford's Ashmolean Museum contain insightful remarks on the coinages of Issa and Pharos in central Dalmatia, and on the chronology of Ballaios' bronze and silver issues. May was the first to argue that the earliest coins of this Illyrian king were minted at Rhizon in the late 190s B.C." [P. Visonà, *NL* 144]

3835 ——— "Greek-Illyrian Coins in Trade, 1904-2005." *Revue Suisse de Numismatique* (Switzerland) 84 (2005): 27-46. Illus.
"For the study of the Greek mint-cities in northern Illyria, dealer catalogues are an important tool. In auction catalogues printed between 1904 and 2005 there were 61 specimens of Herakleaia, Pharos, Issa, and King Ballaios, as well as one example from an unidentified mint." [Paulo Visonà, *NL* 149]

3835a ——— "Greek Coinage in Dalmatia and Trans-Adriatic Relations in the 4th Century B.C." *Chiron* (Germany) 37 (2007): 479-94.

Also see: Bonačić Mandinić *Greek Coins* under PUBLIC COLLECTIONS—CROATIA (SPLIT); Barry and Beasley "Topical Collecting" under COLLECTING GUIDES; Gardner "Floral Patterns" under TYPES; Head *Catalogue of Greek Coins of Thrace* under THRACE—GENERAL WORKS; Kagan "Epidamnus" under CORINTHIA; Kraay "Greek Coinage and War" under GENERAL WORKS—GREEK; Visonà "Bronze Coins of Paros" under CYCLADES ISLANDS.

THESSALY

3836 **Ammons, C. Keven.** "A Brief History of Larissa." *The Celator* 17, no. 7 (July 2003): 26-31, 36-7. Illus.
A review of the history of the city of Larissa from its founding through modern times. Describes some of the archaeological remains of the ancient city and the surrounding area. A didrachm of ca. 350 BC is illustrated.

3837 **Balcer, Jack M.** "Peparethos: The Early Coinage Reconsidered." *Revue Suisse de Numismatique* (Switzerland) 46 (1967): 25-33. 1 pl. [CS 2447]
"In a review of past scholarship concerning a group of early Greek silver tetradrachms, didrachms and tetrobols which bear the obverse type of the grape cluster, the coins are identified as those minted in Peparethos; on the evidence of the Kos (*Noe* 273) and Taranto (*Noe* 1052) hoards and the high coincidence of die linkage the series is dated to ca. 500 B.C." [J. Balcer, *NL* 81]. [For another photograph of one of the tetradrachms of Peparethos illustrated here, which is one of only two known specimens, see coin No. 3 in C. Lorber's *Treasures of Ancient Coinage*. See Lorber under PRIVATE COLLECTIONS].

3838 ——— "Peparethos: Further Notes." *Revue Suisse de Numismatique* (Switzerland) 54 (1975): 33-66. Illus. [CS 2448]
"The mint of Peparethos is to be located on this island; the activity of the mint is dated in the second decade of the fifth century. An overstrike on a didrachm of Methymna is published." [H. Bloesch, *NL* 99]

3839 ——— "The Archaic Coinage of Skyros and the Forgeries of Konstantinos Christodoulos." *Revue Suisse de Numismatique* (Switzerland) 57 (1978): 69-101. 3 pls.
A re-examination of the corpus of forty-five archaic silver coins attributed to the mint of Skyros, the authenticity of which has sometimes been questioned due to the existence of numerous counterfeits produced by Christodoulos. Balcer discusses the reasons for attributing the coins to Skyros and agrees that this attribution is valid. Balcer does a die-by-die comparison of the coins to the forgeries and dies of Christodoulos. The weights of the forgeries are correct for the Attic-Euboeic standard. Concludes that one of the three tetradrachms may be fake, one of the fifteen didrachms is fake, perhaps all eight of the known tetrobols may be fake, two of the nine diobols are fake, and none of the ten hemiobols are fake. Discusses the chronology of the coinage and concludes the mint at Skyros probably operated ca. 485-480 B.C. Balcer also suggests that Christodoulos struck his Skyros forgeries during the period 1911-1913.

3840 **Benner, Steve M.** "An Accidental Collection: Thessalian League Coinage." *The Celator* 20, no. 1 (January 2006): 29-30, 34. Illus., map.
The author describes how he formed a small collection of coins of the Thessalian League. Describes the various coin types.

3841 **Birch, Samuel.** "On the Coins of Thessalian Larissa." *Numismatic Chronicle* 1 (1839): 222-30. 1 pl. of coin drawings.
Identifies the reverse type of a silver coin of Larissa as Jason's sandal. Recounts the related myth.

3842 **Borrell, H. P.** "Restitution to Histiaeolis, in Thessaly, of Several Coins Hitherto Classed to Histiaea in Euboea." *Numismatic Chronicle* 2 (1840): 232-7.
The bronze coin in question bears on the obverse the head of a Bacchante, and on the reverse a female sitting on the prow of a galley.

3843 **Classical Numismatic Group.** *Triton XV: The BCD Collection of the Coinage of Thessaly.* Lancaster: Classical Numismatic Group, January 3, 2012. 413 pp., illus.
The sale catalogue for the final installment of the BCD Collection, including 1000 lots of Thessalian coins (including numerous group lots), incorporating an incredible number of die varieties from each city in outstanding condition. Begins with "A Note from the Collector" and an "Historical Introduction." Each coin is fully described, and many include extensive discussion. Some include brief comments from the collector. All coins are illustrated—most coins by actual size and enlarged photographs. [For other Thessalian coins from the collection, see Nomos AG *Auction 4* below. For the other installments of the BCD collection, see BCD in the INDEX OF COLLECTORS AND COLLECTIONS].

3844 **Colvin, S.** "On Representations of Centaurs in Greek Vase Painting" *Journal of Hellenic Studies* 1 (1880): 107-67. Illus., 3 pls.
"On p. 151, coin types of Thessaly which show pride in horses or bull-fighting are listed. A late issue of the Magnetes is the only one which shows any trace of Centaur mythology, and it is therefore argued that the fable did not owe its origin to the introduction of horse-riding or of cattle-driving." [J. R. Jones, *NIJHS*]

3845 **Demetriadis, Vassili.** "Larissa 'Facing Head' Forgeries." *Nomismatika Khronika* (Greece) 7 (1988): 12-7. Illus.
Lists five counterfeit didrachms and five counterfeit drachms of Larissa which have been published or offered for sale by auction or fixed price list as genuine. Also lists, illustrates, and describes seven didrachm and five drachm forgeries from the author's collection. In Greek on pages 12-14 and in English on pages 15-17.

3846 ———— "Some New Fractions from Central and Southern Greece." *Pour Denyse: Divertissements Numismatiques.* Edited by Silvia Hurter and Carmen Arnold-Biucchi. Bern, Switzerland: Privately published, 2000. Pages 47-55. 1 pl.

The author publishes and discusses seven silver fractions: (1) An obol of Atrax in Thessaly from the mid-fourth century B.C. The silver coins of this city are rare. The obverse features a facing draped female bust—possibly the local nymph Bura. (2) An obol of Philippopolis (formerly known as Gomphi) in Thessaly, minted in the 350's B.C. with the types Hera/Zeus. (3) An obol of Pherai in Thessaly with *obv.*, Artemis Ennodia, and *rev.*, head of a dog. (4) A hemiobol of Skotussa in Thessaly, minted ca. 400 B.C., with *obv.*, facing Herakles, and *rev.*, a bunch of grapes. (5) A tetartemorion of Tanagra in Boeotia with *obv.*, Boeotian shield, and *rev.*, horse's head, struck ca. 458-446 B.C. (6) A tetartemorion of Thespiai with *obv.*, Boeotian shield, and *rev.*, head of Aphrodite Melainis, struck ca. 387-374 B.C. (7) A anepigraphic tetartemorion of Psophis in Arcadia. Each coin is illustrated in actual size and in an enlargement.

3847 **Eaglen, Robin J.** "Portraits of Greek Coinage 4: Larissa." *Spink Numismatic Circular* 113, no. 3 (June 2005): 172-3. Illus.

This installment of the author's on-going series examines the coinage of Larissa. Reviews the history of the city, its mythology, and the coin types.

3848 ———— "Portraits of Greek Coinage: Larissa & Facing Heads." *Spink Insider Magazine* 10 (summer 2011): 62-3. Illus.

A discussion of the facing head on didrachms and drachms of Larissa, emphasizing that the engraver's inspiration was Kimon's facing Arethusa on tetradrachms of Syracuse.

3849 **Franke, Peter R.** "Zur Chronologie der Strategen und der Münzprägung des Koinen der Thessaler." *Schweizer Münzblätter* (Switzerland) 9, no. 35 (1959): 61-7. Illus. [CS 2441]

3850 ———— "ΦΕΘΑΛΟΙ ΦΕΤΑΛΟΙ ΠΕΤΦΑΛΟΙ ΘΕΣΣΑΛΟΙ. Zur Geschichte Thessaliens im 5. Jahrhundert v. Chr." *Archäologischer Anzeiger* (Germany) 1 (1970): 85-93. 1 pl. [CS 2442]

3851 ———— "Αι Αρχαιαι Σψμμαχιαι Το Κοινον των Θεσσαλων" *Nomismatika Khronika* (Greece) 2 (1973): 5-13. Illus.

Numismatic evidence on the existence of a Thessalian confederacy during the 5th century B.C. In Greek.

3851a **Friends of the Numismatic Museum.** *Coins in the Thessalian Region: Mints, Circulation, Iconography, History, Ancient, Byzantine, and Modern: Proceedings of the Third Scientific Meeting.* Obolos 7. Athens: Council of the Friends of the Numismatic Museum, 2004.

3852 **Gardner, Percy.** "Lamia." *Numismatic Chronicle* new ser., 20 (1880): 268.

In an 1868 article (see Gardner "Numismatic Reattributions" under GENERAL WORKS—GREEK), Gardner identified the head on a coin as a portrait of Lamia, the celebrated courtesan. Subsequently, Friedländer attacked this view, reasserting that it is the head of Apollo. Gardner here supports his identification of Lamia based on the diadem (which has ends that hang down) rather than a taenia (which has no ends). The taenia belongs to gods; the diadem to kings and queens. The coin in question shows ends—thus Gardner justifies his attribution.

3853 ———— *Catalogue of Greek Coins of Thessaly to Aetolia.* Edited by R. S. Poole. London: British Museum, 1883. Reprint, Bologna: Forni, 1963. lxiii, 234 pp., 32 pls. [CS 2443]

Volume 6 of the *Catalogue of Greek Coins in the British Museum.* Covers Thessaly, Illyria, Epirus, Corcyra, Acarnania, and Aetolia. Sixty-three pages of introductory text precede the catalogue of coins. [Also see *Catalogue of Greek Coins in the British Museum* under PUBLIC COLLECTIONS—GREAT BRITAIN (LONDON)].

3853a **Helly, Bruno.** "Le Groupe des Monnaies Fédérales Thessaliennes avec Athéna *aux Pompons.*" *Revue Numismatique* (France) 6, no. 8 (1966): 7-32. 2 pls.

3854 **Herrmann, Fritz.** "Die Thessalische Münzunion im Fünften Jahrhundert." *Zeitschrift für Numismatik* (Germany) 33 (1921): 33-43.

3855 ———— "Die Silbermünzen von Larissa in Thessalien." *Zeitschrift für Numismatik* (Germany) 35 (1924): 1-69. 8 pls. [CS 2446]

An overview of the silver coinage of Larissa, classified into eight groups. [Also see Lorber "Thessalian Hoards" and T. Martin "The Chronology" below for refinements to Herrmann's catalogue].

3856 **Heyman, Carlo.** "Les Monnaies de Peuma en Thessalie." *Revue Belge de Numismatique* (Belgium) 113 (1967): 1-9. 2 pls. [CS 2449]

3857 **Kagan, Jonathan.** "The So-Called Persian Weight Coins of Larissa." *Coins in the Thessalian Region: Proceedings of the 3rd Scientific Meeting.* Obolos 7. Athens: Numismatic Museum, 2004. Pages 79-86.

3858 **Klose, Dietrich O.** "Zur Chronologie der Thessalischen Koinongrägung im 2 und 1 Jh. v. Chr.: Ein Weiterer Schatzfund aus Südthessalien." *Stephanos Nomismatikos: Edith Schönert-Geiss zum 65. Geburtstag.* Edited by Ulrike Peter. Berlin: Akademie Verlag, 1998. Pages 333-50.

3859 **Kourebanas, T.** "La Circulation des Monnaies Hellénistiques de Thessalonique aux Iles de la Mer Egée." *Coins in the Aegean Islands. Proceedings of the Fifth Scientific Meeting, Mytilene, 16-29 September 2006. Volume 1: Ancient Times.* Obolos 9. Edited by Panagiotis Tselekas. Athens: The Friends of the Numismatic Museum, 2010. Pages 527-34.

3860 **Lavva, Stella.** *Die Münzpragung von Pharsalos.* Saarbrücker Studien zur Archäologie und Alten Geschichte Band 14. Herstellung: SDV Saarbrücker Druckerei und Verlag GambH, 2001. 254 pp., 29 pls.

A systematic classification of the silver and bronze coin types of Pharsalos in Thessaly. The types are interpreted and historically arranged. Includes illustrations of all 359 types and a complete catalogue. Includes many previously unpublished types, some of which bear artists' signatures. Also publishes twenty-four counterfeit types. [Reviewed by Wolfgang Fischer-Bossert in *Numismatic Chronicle* 163 (2003): 399-405, and by Catharine Lorber in *Revue Suisse de Numismatique* 82 (2003): 147-57].

3861 **Liampi, Katerini.** "Das Corpus der Obolen und Hemiobolen des Thessalischen Bundes und die Politische Geschichte Thessaliens im 2 Viertel des 5 Jahrhunderts v. Chr." *Hellas und der Griechische Osten: Festschrift für Peter Robert Franke zum 70. Geburtstag. Studien zur Geschichte und Numismatik der Griechischen Welt.* Edited by W. Leschhorn, A. V. B. Miron, and A. Miron. Saarbrücken: SDV Saarbrücer Druckerei und Verlag, 1996. Pages 99-126.

3862 ———. "Iolkos and Pagasai: Two New Thessalian Mints." *Numismatic Chronicle* 165 (205): 23-40. 1 pl.
Presents two new issues of bronze coins of the mid-fourth century B.C. from Ioklos and Pagasai, neighboring cities in eastern Thessaly. The cities previously had not been convincingly credited with any coinage.

3863 **Lorber, Catherine C.** "The Early Facing Head Drachms of Thessalian Larissa." *Florilegium Numismaticum: Studia in Honorem U. Westermark Edita.* Edited by Harald Nilsson. Stockholm: Svenska Numismatiska Föreningen, 1992. Pages 259-82. Illus.
This study of the drachms of Larissa, dating from the first decades of the fourth century B.C., is based on a large lot from at least two hoards, supplemented by private and public collections. It expands on the varieties of the drachms listed by Fritz Herrmann ["Die Silbermünzen von Larissa in Thessalien," *Zeitschrift für Numismatik* 35 (1924-25): 1-69], and focuses on the early facing head drachms of Herrmann's *Group 7*. Lists ninety-one dies arranged into seven groups based on die linkage and stylistic affinity. Attempts to form a chronological sequence of the issues. Discusses variations in the obverse and reverse types and the methods used by mint officials to segregate issues. Comments on the signed dies. The signature Simo, earlier interpreted as a magistrate's name, is here identified as the name of an engraver. Metrological data is provided in tables.

3864 ———. "Thessalian Countermarks." *Travaux de Numismatique Grecque Offerts à Georges Le Rider.* Edited by M. Amandry and S. Hurter. London: Spink, 1999. Pages 221-37. 2 pls.
Three recent hoards provided an opportunity to study the small countermarks that are sometimes found on coins of Larissa, Tricca, and Pharsalos. The countermarks appear only infrequently. Lorber describes the various marks and discusses their geographic distribution. The countermarks provide some evidence for the chronology of the coins. She comments on the use of control letters on dies and countermarks on coins. The function of the countermarks is not known with certainty, but they likely played a role in the control or oversight of the coinage supply. Some countermarks may have been applied in the process of hoard formation. As opposed to the private marks frequently applied to archaic-period coins, Lorber tentatively suggests the Thessalian countermarks were employed by bankers or moneychangers acting as agents, contractors, or licensees of the state. She also discusses the possible uses of countermarks as a guarantee of metal content, a guarantee of weight, or a validation of foreign currency. She suggests the Thessalian countermarks were applied by bankers or moneychangers, under some form of state regulation, in order to guarantee the full value of coinage offered in specified payments, by certifying either its weight or its metal content. Concludes with a catalogue of the countermarked coins from the three hoards studied.

3865 ———. "A Hoard of Facing Head Larissa Drachms." *Revue Suisse de Numismatique* (Switzerland) 79 (2000): 7-25. Illus.
"Coin Hoards 9, 87 allows the identification of a middle phase of facing head drachms at Larissa (Herrmann Group 7, Series L and B-H) and a detailed classification of the late facing head drachms into four phases. The third phase, a mass coinage with associated staters, can be dated by the occurrence of specimens in hoards containing coins of Philip of Macedon. It belongs before his death and most likely before c. 348, implying a role in financing the Third Sacred War." [C. Lorber, *NL* 146]

3866 ———. "Thessalian Hoards and the Coinage of Larissa." *American Journal of Numismatics* 2nd ser., 20 (2008): 119-42. 6 pls.
Thessalian coin hoards recorded over the last twenty years clarify the development of the coinage of Larissa. They also help to define the relative chronology of Thessalian monetary *koina* of the fifth century B.C. The paper includes a die study of Larissa's bull wrestler hemidrachms of the mid-fifth century, which revises the catalogue prepared by F. Herrmann (see Herrmann "Die Silbermünzen" above).

3867 **Madsen, Eardley, and Ethel Madsen.** "Thessaly." *SAN—Journal of the Society for Ancient Numismatics* 12, no. 3 (fall 1981): inside covers.
A brief overview of the history and coinage of Thessaly.

3868 **Marchetti, Patrich.** "La Fin des Émissions de Larissa et le Monnayage Amphictionique." *Coins in the Thessalian Region: Proceedings of the 3rd Scientific Meeting.* Obolos 7. Athens: Numismatic Museum, 2004. Pages 87-100.

3869 **Martin, Thomas R.** "The End of Thessalian Civic Coinage in Silver: Macedonian Policy or Economic Reality?" *Proceedings of the 9th International Congress of Numismatics. Berne, September 1979. Volume 1.* Edited by T. Hackens and R. Weiller. Luxembourg: International Association of Professional Numismatists, 1982. Pages 157-64.
Argues against the commonly held view that Thessalian civic coinage was suppressed by the Macedonians in favor of their own coinage. Based on hoard evidence and the historical record, Martin suggests that Thessalian civic coinage ended in the last quarter of the fourth century B.C. as a result of the devastation of the Thessalian economy.

3870 ———. "The Chronology of the Fourth-Century B.C. Facing-Head Silver Coinage of Larissa." *Museum Notes* 28 (1983): 1-34. 1 pl.
Re-examines the coinage of Larissa with *obv.*, female facing head, which Fritz Herrmann believed began ca. 395 and ended in 344/3 B.C. (see Herrmann "Die Silbermünzen" above). Reviews hoard evidence and presents some objections to Herrmann's arrangement. Reconsiders the date of the end of civic coinage at Larissa and suggests the coinage ended not long after 321 B.C. Herrmann's beginning date for the coinage was based on the date of Larissa's victory over Pharsalos in 395. Martin does not suggest a revised date for the beginning of this coinage, but prefers to believe the adoption of the facing head type was merely the response to current trends in numismatic art rather than being related to some event in political or military history.

3871 **Moustaka, Aliki.** *Kulte und Mythien auf Thessalischen Münzen.* Würzburg: Konrad Triltsch Verlag, 1983. 168 pp., 16 pls.
Includes a catalogue of 199 Thessalian coins. Index of cities, types, kings.

3872 ———. "Bendis in Thessalian: Zu Zwei Varianten Eines Münztypus der Stadt Phaloreia." *Zurück zum Gegenstand. Festschrift für Andreas E. Furtwängler.* Zentrum für Archälogie und Kulturgeschichte des Schwarzmeerraumes, Band 16. Edited by Ralph Einicke et al. Langenweibach: Beier and Beram, 2009.

3873　**Nomos, A.G.** *Auction 4: Coins of Thessaly: The BCD Collection.* Zurich: Nomos A.G., May 10, 2011. 167 pp., illus.
Auction catalogue for the sale of the BCD collection of coins of ancient Thessaly—probably the most comprehensive such collection ever formed. The catalogue, by Alan Walker, includes 1437 lots (some with multiple coins) featuring outstanding coins selected from the collection. Begins with an introduction to Thessaly by Walker and a one-page note from the collector. Includes a list of Thessalian cities with brief information on each. Each coin is fully described, and most include extensive discussion. Some include brief comments from the collector. All coins are illustrated—most coins by actual size and enlarged photographs. A superb catalogue of an important collection. [For another portion of BCD's Thessalian collection, see Classical Numismatic Group *Triton XV* above. For the other installments of the BCD collection, see BCD in the Index of Collectors and Collections].

3874　**Papaevangelou, Cleopatra E.** "The Coinage of Phakion." *Revue Suisse de Numismatique* (Switzerland) 75 (1996): 33-45. 3 pls.
The author attempts a brief history of the city of Phakion in northern Thessaly, based on literary and epigraphic evidence. A small and rather insignificant city, its trade seems to have been confined within the borders of Thessaly. However, Phakion was numismatically active during a certain period of its history, probably in the third century B.C., with the production of a limited issue of bronze coins. The author is aware of just forty-two coins of Phakion, only six of which have been previously published. Includes a catalogue of all the known coins. All are small (18-22 mm) bronzes with *obv.*, head of nymph; *rev.*, horseman and inscription ΦΑΚΙΑΣΤΩΝ. Discusses the types, weights, minting sequence, and die linking. Distinguishes two groups of coins, and both are dated to the third century B.C. The city was destroyed by Philip V in 198 B.C.

3875　**Pendleton, Elizabeth J.** "The Enigmatic Crouching Horse of Larissa." *The Celator* 10, no. 2 (February 1996): 14-6. Illus.
The horse on the reverse of the popular facing-head drachms of Larissa is often described as grazing. However, the position of the horse (head down, hind legs bent, left fore-leg pulled back) doesn't seem realistic for a grazing horse. The author suggests the horse is shown at the moment just before the horse rolls on the ground, an activity common to horses. She suggests this position would have been a familiar one in Thessaly—horse country.

3876　**Prentzas, Kostas.** "A New Interpretation of the 'Aleus' Issue." *Proceedings of the Fourth International Numismatic Congress in Croatia, September 20-25, 2004. Stari Grad (Pharos), the Island of Hvar and M/S Marko Polo, Croatia.* Edited by Julijan Dobrinic. Rijeka: Dobrinic & Dobrinic, 2005.
Suggests that the fourth century B.C. Larissa drachms marked ΑΛΕΥ and ΕΛΛΑ were struck by the Aleuadae of Larissa as a means of promoting their claim to the tageia of Thessaly against the competing claims of Alexander of Pherae. Suggests that the eagle on thunderbolt reverse was adopted for this issue in order to advertise the longstanding close relations between the Aleuadae and the Argead kings of Macedonia.

3877　**Reinach, Theodore.** "Achilles on Thessalian Coins." *Corolla Numismatica: Numismatic Essays in Honour of Barclay V. Head.* Edited by G. F. Hill. London: Oxford University Press, 1906. Pages 266-74. 1 pl.
Reinach attributes some rare bronze coins bearing Achilles on the obverse to Thessaly (the coins were struck under Hadrian). Discusses the use of Achilles as a type on Thessalian coins.

3878　**Reinders, H. Reinder.** "The Coinage of Halos" and "Appendix 3: The Coins of the City of Halos." *New Halos: a Hellenistic Town in Thessalia, Greece,* by H. Reinder Reinders. Utrecht: Hes Publishers, 1988. Pages 164-6, illus.; pages 236-51, including six plates.
Briefly describes the types used on the coins of Halos and suggests a chronology for the issues. The appendix presents a catalogue of the coins of this city. The author arranges the coins into four groups and twenty-one series. Lists the coins of Halos in public and private collections and includes weights and die positions. Twenty-nine coins are photographed, including at least one from each of the twenty-one series.

3879　**Robinson, David M.** "The Bronze State Seal of Larissa Kremaste." *American Journal of Archaeology* 38 (1934): 219-22. Illus.
"This object (diameter 0.047 m.) shows on one side Thetis riding a hippocamp, as on fourth century coins of Larissa; Scylla appears on the other side, and may be the personal sign of a magistrate." [J. R. Jones, *NIAJAH*]

3880　**Rogers, Edgar.** "The Copper Coinage of Thessaly." Appeared in nineteen installments in *Spink Numismatic Circular* 36 (January 1928) through 38 (August 1930). Reprinted, *The Copper Coinage of Thessaly.* London: Spink, 1932. 199 pp., illus. [CS 2444]
Begins with a description of the geography and history of Thessaly. Relates the coin types to the local legends, heroes, and gods. Discusses the Thessalian Confederacy. Presents a catalogue of 577 copper coins, including some Roman Provincial issues, arranged by mint city or tribe, or by Roman emperor. Indicates coin sizes but not weights. The main types are photographed throughout. Includes a general index as well as indices of types, magistrates, and emperors.

3881　**Schwabacher, Willy.** "Pelinna: An Early Thessalian Mint." *Numismatic Chronicle* 5th ser., 17 (1937): 102-6. Illus.
Illustrates three previously unpublished small silver coins with *obv.*, bull's head with man's arm hanging over it; *rev.*, indistinct object. The author attributes the coins to Pelinna in Thessaly and dates them to 479-465 B.C.

3882　**Shahar, Charles.** "Factors Influencing Auction Estimates & Final Prices of Larissa Facing Head Drachms." *The Celator* 20, no. 3 (March 2006): 16-26. Illus.
A statistical analysis of the factors which influence the price that Larissa drachms have brought at auction. Considers the impact of grade and defects, artistic style, year of the auction, currency used to settle the auction, and scarcity of the reverse type. Determines which factors most influence the price realized, and the factors that influence the variance between the pre-sale estimate and the price realized.

3883　**Starck, Jeff.** "Silver Stater Sets Record Price: Ancient Coin Realizes $781,546." *Coin World* (May 30, 2011): 10, 44. Illus.
Report on the results of the May 10, 2011 auction of the "BCD Collection" of coins of Thessaly (see Nomos A.G., *Auction 4* above). A silver stater issued under Alexander of Pherai realized 684,400 Swiss Francs ($781,546). The coin is illustrated.

3884　**Svoronos, Joannes N.** "Archaic Coins of Scyros." (In Greek). *Journal International d'Archéologie Numismatique* (Greece) 13 (1911): 127-30.
"Identification and description of types, including coins of the Athenian cleruchs on Scyros, Imbros and Lemnos." [J. R. Jones, *AIJIAN*]

3885　**Wade-Gery, H. T.** "Jason of Pherae and Aleuas the Red." *Journal of Hellenic Studies* 44 (1924): 55-64. Illus.

"On pp. 62-4 it is decided that the coin of Larissa showing a double axe as symbol in the field, and the legends ΑΛΕΥΑΣ and ΕΛΛΑ(Σ), was issued by Jason of Pherae; 'Hellas' stands for Thessaly's leadership against Persia." [J. R. Jones, *NIJHS*]

3886 **Warren, Jennifer A. W.** "Two Notes on Thessalian Coins." *Numismatic Chronicle* 7th ser., 1 (1961): 1-8. 1 pl.
"(1) The Thessalian town of Eurea is known only from its fourth century coins, which should be dated after 352 B.C.; the coins are paralleled by those of Eurymenai and Rhizious. Eurea should be in Magnesia, and is perhaps to be recognized in the Myrai of Ps-Scylax. (2) A rare Thessalian copper coin (*obv.*, Macedonian shield; *rev.*, ΤΗΕΣΣΑΛΟΝ, and an uncertain object) suggests a connection with Macedon and may have been struck as a propaganda issue at Demetrias during the Third Macedonian War (171-168 B.C.). The unidentified object is possibly a *kestrosphendone* (dart-sling), used by Perseus as a secret weapon during the war." [I. Merker, *NL* 65]

3887 **Wartenberg, Ute.** "The History and Coinage of Alexander of Pherae." *Hypereia 2: Proceedings of the Second Symposium 'Pheron-Velestino-Rega,' Velestino 1992.* Pages 151-9.

3888 **Weier-Krystallis, L., M. Pilakouta, and A. Karydas.** "X-Ray Analysis of Ancient Coins from Thessaly. Part 2." *Nomismatika Khronika* (Greece) 14 (1995): 21-6. Illus.
A follow-up to the 1991 study (see Weier-Krystallis et al. below). Presents the results of a metallurgical analysis of a large group of Larissa Persian-standard obols, Larissa Aeginetic-standard obols, Larissa Aeginetic trihemiobols, Pharcadon Aeginetic obols, and Pharsalus Aeginetic hemidrachms. A table lists the percentages of silver, copper, gold, lead, bismuth, bromine, and iron in each coin. Discusses the results.

3889 **Weier-Krystallis, L., M. Pilakouta, A. Karydas, and E. Mantzouka.** "X-Ray Analysis of Ancient Coins from Thessaly." *Nomismatika Khronika* (Greece) 10 (1991): 11-8.
Forty-three Thessalian silver coins of the fifth and fourth centuries B.C. were examined by X-ray fluorescence analysis. Seven groups of coins were tested. The general objective was to determine if any groups and/or mints demonstrated homogeneous traits concerning metal composition which would suggest a common ore source. Describes the analytical methods employed. Results are then summarized and discussed. Ninety percent of the coins contained between 94.5% to 99.5% silver, 0.1% to 4.0% copper, and other elements in smaller amounts. Includes scatter diagrams showing the metallic contents. Generally, this study shows a group of coins with relatively high gold and bismuth contents and low lead content. The high copper content indicates intentional addition of copper. There is no startling indication to suggest a very different silver source for the Persian standard obols or the unknown fractions. The coins which form the most homogeneous group are the Larissa obols. In English on pp. 11-18, and in Greek on pp. 18-24; plates on pp. 20-1. [Also see Weier-Krystallis et al. "Part 2" above].

3890 **Westlake, H. D.** "The Medism of Thessaly." *Journal of Hellenic Studies* 56 (1936): 12-24.
"The earliest coins of Larissa were struck by the Aleuadae on the Persian standard; this, together with other evidence, confirms the opinions concerning their support of Persia which are preserved by Herodotus." [J. R. Jones, *NIJHS*]

3891 **Wetterstrom, Kerry K.** "A Brief Survey of the Coinage of Larissa." *Classical Numismatic Review* 15, no. 1 (first quarter 1990): 3. Illus.
Briefly reviews the mythology related to the city of Larissa. Describes the main coin types and their dates of issue.

3892 **Wroth, Warwick W.** "Peparethus and its Coinage." *Journal of Hellenic Studies* 27 (1907): 90-8. 1 pl.
Wroth examines a series of coins bearing a bunch of grapes on the obverse. Barclay Head attributed these coins to Cyrene (see Head "Archaic Coins" under CYRENAICA). Wroth doubted Head's attribution [see Wroth "Greek Coins Acquired by the British Museum in 1891" under PUBLIC COLLECTIONS—GREAT BRITAIN (LONDON)]. George Hill suggested the coins belong to Chalcidice in Macedonia [see Hill "Notes on Additions" under PUBLIC COLLECTIONS—GREAT BRITAIN (LONDON)]. Wroth here proposes that all these grape-type coins belong to Peparethus (an island off the coast of Thessalian Magnesia). Discusses the attribution and dates of the coins. Presents a brief catalogue of types. [Also see J. G. Milne "A Group of Coins" under CYCLADES ISLANDS. Milne suggests the coins belong to the island of Naxos].

Also see: Cancio "Repaired Ancient Coin Dies" under THE MINTING PROCESS; Cheek "Artistic Choice" under ART; Gardner "Numismatic Reattributions" under GENERAL WORKS—GREEK; Liampi "The Circulation of Bronze" under MACEDONIAN KINGDOM—GENERAL WORKS; Martin "Hoard from Thessaly" under HOARDS; Newton "On the Coin" under MACEDONIAN KINGDOM—GENERAL WORKS; Rouse "The Double Axe" under TYPES; Touratsoglou *The Coin Circulation in Ancient Macedonia* under HOARDS; Touratsoglou *Disjecta Membra* under HOARDS.

CENTRAL GREECE

The most striking characteristic of the money of Boeotia is that it is in great part a Federal currency. The various Boeotian cities were from the first united in an Amphictyonic confederation, as members of which they adopted a common coin-type, which serves to distinguish the Boeotian currency from that of all other Greek states.

—Barclay V. Head, 1887

BOEOTIA

3893 **Akerman, John Yonge,** ed. "Coins of Lebadia and of Zacynthus." *Numismatic Chronicle* 1 (1839): 248-52. Illus.
Describes a bronze coin of Lebadia in Boeotia, a previously unknown town. Also describes a silver coin of Zacynthus with a seated figure of Zacynthus on the reverse. The research on these coins was done by Thomas Burgon.

3894 **Classical Numismatic Group, Inc.** *Triton IX: BCD Boiotia.* Lancaster: Classical Numismatic Group, 2005. 136 pp., illus.
Catalogue for the January 10, 2006 auction of the "BCD" collection of coins of Boiotia. Includes 630 lots, including Boiotian federal coinage, coins of Akraiphion, Haliartos, Kopai, Koroneia, Lebadeia, Mykalessos, Orchomenos, Pharai, Plataiai, Tanagra, Thebes, and Thespiai. Certainly the finest private collection of these coins ever formed. Thoroughly catalogued by the collector himself. Includes an introduction and a short history of Boiotia and the Boiotian League. A standard catalogue for this series of coinage. [Reviewed by Alan Walker in *The Celator* 20, no. 1 (January 2006): 35-7. For other portions of the collection, see "BCD" in the INDEX OF COLLECTORS AND COLLECTIONS].

3895 **Demetriadi, Vassili, and R. G. Hepworth.** "Forgeries of Boeotian Autonomous Staters." *Numismatic Chronicle* 144 (1984): 186-91. 1 pl.
"Forgeries of early fourth-century staters from Tanagra and Orchomenos can be attributed to Caprara, who worked in the early nineteenth century A.D. Counterfeited specimens can be identified by excessive weight, by style, and by the fact that Caprara used the same obverse die in one case for 'issues' of both Boeotian cities. At least four examples of the forgeries have been traded as genuine since 1968, and catalogues of known specimens are included." [Demetriadi and Hepworth, *NL* 114]

3896 **Feyel, M.** "L'Argent Symmachique en Grèce Centrale au Second Siècel Avant Notre Ère." *Revue des Ètudes Grecque* (France) 52 (1939): 11-12.
Discusses the alliance coinages of Central Greece in the second century B.C.

3897 **Fowler, Barbara H.** "Thucydides 1.107-108 and the Tanagran Federal Issues." *The Phoenix* (Canada) 11, no. 4 (1957): 164-70. 1 pl.
Three staters of Tanagra, special issues of disputed date, show on obverse the shield of the Boeotian League, and differ from all other Tanagran issues (as well as from all other Boeotian League coinage) in that they bear both federal and local inscriptions. This, the writer believes, is unmistakable evidence that Tanagra, issuing coinage in the name of all the Boeotians, at the time claimed leadership of the League, and further explains the reason for the presence of the Lacedaemonians in Tanagra in 457 B.C. [Summarized from *NL* 45]

3898 **Hackens, Tony.** "La Circulation Monétaire dans la Béotie Hellénistique: Trésor de Thèbes 1935 et 1965." *Bulletin de Correspondance Hellénistique* (France) 93 (1969): 701-29. [CS 2470]

3899 **Hands, Alfred Watson.** "Common Greek Coins: Coins of the Boeotian League." *Spink Numismatic Circular* 12 (October 1904): 7866-73; (November 1904): 7921-6; 13 (December 1904): 7986-90.
Examines the coinage of Thebes, ca. 600-338 B.C., listing and discussing the main coin varieties.

3900 **Head, Barclay V.** "On the Chronological Sequence of the Coins of Boeotia." *Numismatic Chronicle* 3rd ser., 1 (1881): 177-275. 6 pls. Reprinted (see Roberts and Head below). [CS 2471]
The author arranges the coinage of Boeotia into sixteen historical periods extending from about 600 B.C. down to A.D. 192. He begins with brief descriptions of the coinage of each period. Then he examines the coinage of each period in detail, providing a catalogue of coin types and varieties.

3901 ——— *Coinage of Boeotia.* Chicago: Argonaut, 1969. 104 pp., 6 pls. [CS 2468a]
A reprint of the Boeotian portion of Head's *Catalogue of Greek Coins of Central Greece* (see Head under CENTRAL GREECE—LOKRIS).

3902 **Hepworth, R. G.** "Epaminondas' Coinage." *Proceedings of the 10th International Congress of Numismatics, London, 1986.* International Association of Professional Numismatists Publication, No. 11. Edited by I. A. Carradice. London: International Association of Professional Numismatists, 1986. Pages 35-40. 1 pl.
The author attempts to resolve the disputed attribution of certain coins to the Theban statesman and general Epaminondas, based on a detailed study of the fourth century B.C. coinage of Boeotia. The coins traditionally assigned to Epaminondas have five reverse varieties, including three abbreviated spellings of the magistrate's name. Examines the chronology of the issues. The sequence of issues suggests the normal term of office of the magistrate was annual. If the series began in 379 B.C. as suggested by Head, the ΕΠΠΑ / ΕΠΑΜ and related issues would have to be dated after the death of Epaminondas (362 B.C.). Epigraphical and other evidence may support an earlier start date, however. And the author suggests the use of the rose symbol on some of the ΕΠΠΑ / ΕΠΑΜ issues may be related to Epaminondas' naval expedition which separated Rhodes from the Athenian alliance in 365 B.C.

3903 ———. "The 4th Century B.C. Magistrate Coinage of the Boiotian Confederacy." *Nomismatika Khronika* (Greece) 17 (1998): 61-89. Illus.
Identifies the different types and the relative chronologies of the series of silver magistrate staters issued by the Boiotian Confederacy in the fourth century B.C., including the period when the Theban statesmen Epaminondas and Pelopidas constructed an alliance which overthrew the Spartan hegemony of Greece. Ninety-seven varieties are identified, along with forty-four different magistrate names. The relative rarity of each variety is noted. [Also see Schroll below for a reproduction of Hepworth's table of magistrates].

3904 **Imhoof-Blumer, Friedrich W.** "Zur Münzkunde und Palaeographie Boeotiens." *Numismatische Zeitschrift* (Austria) 3 (1871): 321-87.

3905 ———. "Zur Münzkunde Boeotiens und des Peloponnesischen Argos." *Numismatische Zeitschrift* (Austria) 9 (1877): 1-62. [CS 2472]

3906 **Knoepfler, Denis.** "Des Ateliers de Drachmes Pseudo-Rhodiennes en Béotie? Examen de Quelques Hypothèses Récentes." *Travaux de Numismatique Grecque Offerts à Georges Le Rider.* Edited by M. Amandry and S. Hurter. London: Spink, 1999. Pages 197-206.

3907 **Koumanoudes, Stephanos N.** "The Lion Astias: Coins and Boeotian Archaeology." *Voice of the Turtle* 4, no. 6 (June 1965): 101-2.
Describes a sculpture of a seated lion found near Thebes, bearing the inscription ΓΑΣΤΙΑΣ. Concludes that the sculpture was part of a funeral monument for the Boeotarch Astias whose name appears on Theban coins of 378-338 B.C.

3908 **Kraay, Colin M.** "Mainland Greece and Asia Minor." *Survey of Numismatic Research, 1960-1965. Volume 1: Ancient Numismatics.* Copenhagen: International Numismatic Commission, 1967. Pages 35-53. [CS 2303]
A narrative bibliography discussing recently published works in the field of Greek numismatics.

3909 **Lacroix, Leon.** "Le Bouclier: Emblème des Béotiens." *Revue Belge de Philologie et d' Historie* (Belgium) 36, no. 1 (1958): 5-30. 4 pls. [CS 3473]
Discusses shields on coins of Boeotia.

3910 **Lagos, Constantine.** "Athena Itonia at Koroneia (Boiotia) and in Cilicia." *Numismatic Chronicle* 161 (2001): 1-10. 1 pl.
"This article proposes that two silver fractional issues attributed to Cilicia (*SNG France* 2, Cilicie, 476 and 489a-b) may in fact have been struck at Koroneia in Boiotia during the early Hellenistic period. The Athena bust on these issues is identified as that of Athena Itonia whose sanctuary near Koroneia was an important religious centre for the Boeotians. Finally the article suggests that the cult statue of this deity at Koroneia, made by the fifth-century B.C. artist Agorakritos of Paros, could be identified with a type depicted on an issue of staters from Aphrodisias in Cilicia (*HN*2, p. 718)." [C. Lagos, *NL* 146]. [The coin types are (1) Boiotian shield/bust of Athena ¾ facing, and (2) Boiotian shield/Athena facing right, wearing Attic helmet].

3911 **MacDonald, David.** "The Significance of the 'Boiotian League/Chalkis' Silver Issue." *Jahrbuch für Numismatik und Geldgeschichte* (Germany) 37/38 (1987-1988): 23-9.

3912 **Madsen, Eardley, and Ethel Madsen.** "Thebes." *SAN—Journal of the Society for Ancient Numismatics* 17, no. 2 (summer 1981): inside covers.
A brief overview of the history and coinage of Thebes.

3913 **Martin, Erik.** "Identity of Greek Coin? Expert Should Authenticate." *Coin World* (June 27, 2011): 75. Illus.
A reader submitted a photograph of a rare tetradrachm of Thebes (Zeus/Poseidon seated), seeking more information about the piece. Martin identified the piece but warned that it should be authenticated by an expert.

3914 **Phoungas, A.** *Catalogue des Statères Béotiens au Type de l' "Amphore," Ve–IVe Siècle av. J.-C.* Dissertation. Lyon, 1986.

3915 **Rakicic, Mark.** "Operation Petticoat: The Rescue of Thebes." *The Celator* 8, no. 1 (January 1994): 6-11. Illus.
A narrative account of the plot by Pelopidas and other conspirators to assassinate the Theban Polemarch and his Spartan supporters in 379 B.C. Some of the conspirator's names can be found on Theban staters. The story is based upon Plutarch's *Life of Pelopidas*.

3916 **Roberts, W. Rhys, and Barclay V. Head.** *The Ancient Boeotians and the Coinage of Boeotia.* Chicago: Ares Publishers, 1974. 191 pp., 6 pls., map.
A reprint of Head's "On the Chronological Sequence of the Coins of Boeotia" (see Head above for a summary of his essay) combined with Roberts' *The Ancient Boeotians: Their Character and Culture and Their Reputation* (originally published at Cambridge in 1895). Roberts reviews literary accounts related to Boeotia, focusing on those which describe the character of its people. He then reviews the political history of the region including their internal wars and their relationships with Attica and Persia. The author then discusses well-known Boeotians involved in literature including Hesiod, Pindar, Plutarch, and others. Discusses the arts of lyric poetry, flute-playing, and sculpture. Then he examines the life and military leadership of Epaminondas. Concludes with a comparison of the ancient Boeotians to the people of modern-day Holland. Includes a table summarizing important dates in Boeotian history.

3917 **Schachter, Albert.** "Horse Coins from Tanagra." *Numismatic Chronicle* 6th ser., 18 (1958): 43-6. Illus.
"The fifth century silver staters discussed bear the Boeotian shield as obverse type; three variants of the reverse type—a horse protome—are distinguished. The horse holds grain (or grass) in its mouth, and therefore is not simply an agonistic symbol. Radke's suggestion that the staters are connected with Leukippos and Ephippos is accepted; the reverse type mirrors an early cult relating to horses and agriculture." [J. Healy, *NL* 52]

3918 ———. "A Note on the Reorganization of the Thespian Museia." *Numismatic Chronicle* 7th ser., 1 (1961): 67-70. Illus.
"Thespiae, a small city in Boeotia, minted a series of bronze coins which can be described as follows: *obv.*, female head r., laureate, wearing *polos* or *stephanos*, with veil; the whole encircled by a border of dots; *rev.*, ΘΕΣΠΙΕΟΝ, with lyre in laurel wreath. At the sanctuary of the Muses on Mt. Helicon Thespiae celebrated a music festival known as the Museia, which, after being reorganized at the end of the third century, received the support of the Ptolemies. From a comparison with a gold octadrachm of Arsinoë III (dated 211) the author concludes that the female head on the coins of Thespiae is also that of Arsinoë, depicted as the tenth muse, and is to be dated to 210-208. Coins of Orchomenos which are copied from those of Thespiae and which refer to an Orchomenian festival of the *Charities* may also depict Arsinoë III." [I. Merker, *NL* 65]

3919 **Schroll, Wayne K.** "Boiotian Magistrate Staters." *The Celator* 25, no. 8 (August 2011): 14-8. Illus.
Schroll briefly describes the Boiotian staters with shield and amphora and then reproduces the table of magistrate names appearing on the coins (97 varieties), taken from R. Hepworth's 1998 paper in *Nomismatika Khronika* (see Hepworth above).

3920 **Sosin, Joshua D.** "Boeotian Silver, Theban *Agio* and Bronze Drachmas." *Numismatic Chronicle* 162 (2002): 333-9.
The author proposes a new interpretation of the "Boeotian" drachms mentioned in an account by the Theban hipparch Pompidas in the mid-second century B.C. (*IG* III 2426).

3921 **Vlachogianni, Elena.** "A Hoard of Coins from Thebes: The Problem of the Boiotian Overstrikes." *Nomismatika Khronika* (Greece) 19 (2000): 55-113. Illus.
A hoard of 457 bronze and silver coins, including 449 bronzes of the Boiotian League, was found in 1997 in an excavation at what was likely the agora of ancient Thebes. The coins are catalogued here. The League bronzes (Demeter/Poseidon) are overstruck on Macedonian coins (Herakles/naked rider). Discusses the numismatic evidence for the chronology of the coins. Examines the reason for and date of the overstriking. The author cites examples of bronze coins struck for the purpose of providing financial aid to another city. The coins were likely struck over coins of Antigonos Gonatas. The reason is uncertain (numerous opinions from other researchers are put forward) but it is likely that it took place ca. 225 B.C. The author suggests that concealment of the hoard took place ca. 168-146 B.C.

3922 **Wartenberg, Ute.** "The History and Coinage of Alexander of Pherae." *Hypereia*. Athens, 1994.

Also see: Burgon "On Certain Rare Greek Coins Recently Acquired" under PUBLIC COLLECTIONS—GREAT BRITAIN (LONDON); Casson "Early Greek Inscriptions" (Tanagra) under THE MINTING PROCESS; Gesche "Literaturüberblick" under CENTRAL GREECE—LOKRIS; Head "Catalogue of Greek Coins under CENTRAL GREECE— LOKRIS; Hurter "Teos over Tanagra" under IONIA; Lacroix "A Propos des Représentations de Boucliers" under TYPES; Lacroix "Le Bouclier" under TYPES; Liampi "Graffiti on Sicyonian and Theban Staters" under HOARDS; Mackil and van Alfen "Cooperative Coinage" under GENERAL WORKS—GREEK; Noe "Countermarked and Overstruck" under THE MINTING PROCESS; C. Seltman "Two Athenian Marble Thrones" under TYPES.

EUBOIA

3923 **Allin, E. J., and William P. Wallace.** "Impurities in Euboean Monetary Silver." *Museum Notes* 6 (1954): 35-67. 4 pls. [CS 3391]
Presents the results of a spectrographic examination of about 300 silver drachms of Chalkis and Eretria from the fourth century B.C., as well as about 100 coins of other mints to serve as comparative material. The spectrographic technique is explained, as are the procedures followed in the testing. The results, showing the percentage of copper and the level of other impurities present, are summarized in several tables.

3924 **Ashton, Richard H. J.** "Pseudo-Rhodian Drachms from Eretria (Euboia)." *Revue Numismatique* (France) (1989): 42-9. Illus.
"The author argues that a small group of pseudo-Rhodian drachms with names Biottos, Damasias, Epagetos, Kephisodoros and Kleon was struck by Eretria during the Third Macedonian War, and can be associated with autonomous coinage of Eretria struck in the names of Biottos, Damasias and Kleon." [R. Ashton, *NL* 122]

3925 **Blanchet, J. Adrien.** "Observations Relative au Type des Monnaies d'Erétrie, de Dicaea et de Mende." *Revue Belge de Numismatique* (Belgium) 51 (1895): 165-9.

3926 ———. "A Curious Eretrian Coin-Type." *American Journal of Numismatics* 30, no. 3 (January 1896): 69-71.
Some coins of Eretria in Euboea depict a cow with head turned back, with a bird on the cow's back. Blanchet suggests the type was inspired by the observation of actual occurrences (birds commonly perch upon cattle, rhinoceros', etc., and feed on parasites). Similar natural occurrences may provide better explanations for Greek coin types than some of the mythology-based explanations which are often encountered.

3927 **Carlson, Carl W. A.** "The Broad Flan Tetradrachm of Eretria." *Journal of Numismatic Fine Arts* 4, no. 1 (August 1975): 1. Illus.
Publishes a fifth century B.C. tetradrachm of Eretria (*obv.*, bull standing, scratching nose with rear hoof; *rev.*, octopus) struck on a broad, thin planchet. Most Greek states were striking tetradrachms on smaller, thicker planchets at this time. Provides provenance information on this rare coin.

3928 **Chantraine, Heinrich.** "Zur Münzprägung von Chalkis im 6/5 Jahrhundert." *Jahrbuch für Numismatik und Geldsseschichte* (Germany) 9 (1958): 7-17. [CS 2478]

3929 ——— "Literaturüberblick der Griechischen Numismatik: Euboea." *Jahrbuch für Numismatik und Geldsseschichte* (Germany) 9 (1958): 19-56. [CS 2473]
A bibliography.

3930 **Gardner, Percy.** "A Numismatic Note on the Lelantian War." *Classical Review* 34 (1920): 90-1.

Examines numismatic evidence to provide clues to the nature of the battle between Chalcis and Eretria for the possession of the Lelantian plain. Some have argued that it was a long war involving many cities. Gardner suggests it was a brief battle between the two cities which left no lasting effect. Mentions the coins of the monetary union of Croton and Sybaris to show that these cities did not join the war on opposite sides. Also describes the uniform didrachms issued by Euboea, Athens, and Megara and suggests that Chalcis and Eretria would not have adhered to this uniform coinage if there had been a standing feud between them.

3931 **Head, Barclay V.** "On Coins Recently Attributed to Eretria." *Numismatic Chronicle* 3rd ser., 13 (1893): 158-65.
In this reply to H. Howorth (see Howorth below), Head reaffirms his attribution of certain coins to Eretria rather than Phocis, and of the Wappenmünzen coins to Euboea rather than Athens. [For a further discussion of the Wappenmünzen series, see Howorth "Initial Coinage of Athens" and Head's reply "Initial Coinage of Athens" under ATTICA—WAPPENMÜNZEN].

3932 **Howorth, Henry H.** "On Coins Recently Attributed to Eretria." *Numismatic Chronicle* 3rd ser., 13 (1893): 153-7.
In a letter to Barclay V. Head, the author suggests some coins attributed by Head (in his *Historia Numorum*) to Eretria actually belong to Phocis. Suggests these issues were struck on the Corinthian weight standard rather than the Aeginetic standard as Head believes. Also suggests the coins with the Gorgon head/incuse square (diagonally divided or with lion's head and paws) belong to Athens and were struck before 526 B.C. Head assigned these to Eretria. [Also see the reply by B. V. Head above. For a further discussion of the Wappenmünzen series, see Howorth "Initial Coinage of Athens" and Head's reply "Initial Coinage of Athens" under ATTICA—WAPPENMÜNZEN].

3933 **Imhoof-Blumer, Friedrich W.** "Le Système Monétaire Euboique." *Annuaire de la Société Française de Numismatique et d'Archéologie* (1882): 1-17.

3934 **Jones, John R. Melville.** "The Date of the Gold Drachma of Carystus." *Numismatic Chronicle* 140 (1980): 28-32.
Examines the date of minting of the gold stater of Carystus. This issue was struck before 225 B.C., and may perhaps be connected with the campaigns of Ptolemaeus against Macedon in 313/12 B.C. Lists the seven known specimens of this coin. [Also see Gardner "Votive Coins" under EPIGRAPHY].

3935 **Mahler, Arthur.** "Concerning an Euboian Tetradrachme." *Journal International d'Archéologie Numismatique* (Greece) 3 (1900): 194-6. 1 pl.
Identifies the female head on a tetradrachm of Euboia as being modeled from a sculpture head of Apollo which is now in the Louvre at Paris. Discusses the artistic style of the sculpture. The head is considered a major work of the Polycleitan school.

3936 **Newell, Edward T.** *The Octobols of Histiaea.* Numismatic Notes and Monographs, No. 2. New York: American Numismatic Society, 1921. 25 pp., 2 pls. [CS 2479]
The author publishes the second known specimen of an octobol from Histiaea, stuck on the Attic standard. The only other specimen resides in the Bibliothèque Nationale in Paris. The new specimen is in better condition than the Paris coin, and allows the decipherment of part of the inscription on the cross-bar of the stylis held in the Nymph's hand on the reverse: AΘA(NA). Illustrates a drachm of Histiaea with the cow and vine reverse which has an obverse very close in style to the new octobol. This forces the dating of both coins to the period 369 to 338 B.C. Newell recounts the historical events of this period during which Macedonia and Athens struggled for control of Euboea. Newell concludes the change in type, from the cow and vine to the Nymph on prow, corresponds to the expulsion of the Macedonians from Euboea in 340 B.C., and the inscription on the stylus credits the liberation to the guidance of Athena. Newell also publishes the first known obol of the same type, and dates these obols, octobols, and tetrobols to 340-338 B.C. [Also see Noe "A Tetrobol" below].

3937 **Noe, Sydney P.** "A Tetrobol of Histiaea." *Museum Notes* 8 (1958): 55-6. 1 pl.
A follow-up to Newell's *The Octobols of Histiaea* (see Newell above) and a 1914 article by Svoronos. Noe publishes a drawing from a vase referred to by Svoronos. It clearly shows an inscription on the stylus of a ship. Newell had pointed out such an inscription, AΘA(NA), on an octobol of Histiaea. Noe now publishes a tetrobol which reveals NIK(H) on the stylus. These names signified the divinities presiding over the ships and their crews. Newell suggested the reverse type referred to a victory of the joint forces of Athens and Histiaea. Noe believes the tetrobol bearing NIK confirms this interpretation, and the dating of the series to 340-338 B.C. is upheld.

3938 **Numismatik Lanz München.** *Auktion 111: Münzen von Euboia: Sammlung BCD.* Munich: Numismatik Lanz München, 2002. 116 pp., illus.
The sale catalogue for the BCD collection of the coins of Euboia, comprised of 604 coins, all illustrated. Includes coins of the Euboian League, Chalkis, Eretria, Histiaia, and Karystos. Brief introduction by the collector. Catalogue in German, with introduction and occasional notes in English. [For other portions of the collection, see "BCD" in the INDEX OF COLLECTORS AND COLLECTIONS].

3939 **Picard, Olivier.** *Chalcis et la Confederation Eubéene: Etude de Numismatique et d'Historie (IV-Ier Siècle).* Paris, 1979. 376 pp., 32 pls.
A die study of the mint of Chalcis. [Reviewed by O. Mørkholm in *Gnomon* (Germany) 52 (1980): 451-6].

3940 ——— "Monnaies Contremarquées en Eubée." *Bulletin de la Société Française de Numismatique* (France) 31 (1976): 29-31.

3941 **Robert, Louis.** "La Circulation des Monnaies d'Histiée." *Études de Numismatique Grecque.* Paris, 1951. Pages 179-216.

3942 ——— "Circulation des Monnaies d'Histiée." *Hellenica* 11/12 (1960): 63-9.

3943 **Tsourti, Eos.** *Euboea through the Coins: The Evidence of Hoards.* Obolos 3. Athens: Numismatic Museum, 1999. 29 pp.

3944 **Vanderpool, Eugene, and William P. Wallace.** "The Sixth Century Laws from Eretria." *Hesperia* 33 (1964): 381-91. 3 pls.
"The Inscription *IG* XII, 9, 1273-4 (Eretria, 550-25 B.C.) is restudied. The readings *chremata dokima* and *deka stateras* which are preserved suggest that Eretria was coining by this time, and an early stater with cow on obverse and incuse reverse is suggested (pp. 390-1) as an example of this currency." [J. R. Jones, *NIAJAH*]

3945   **Waggoner, Nancy M.** "Coins from the William P. Wallace Collection." *Museum Notes* 25 (1980): 1-15. 2 pls.
Catalogues and discusses several of the more significant coins of Euboean mints from the collection of W. P. Wallace which were donated to the American Numismatic Society. Includes coins of Carystus, Chalcis, and Eretria. Reviews the controversy over the beginning date for the "stephanephorus" coinage (coins of thin spread fabric with reverse type encircled by a wreath) at various mints.

3946   **Wallace, Malcolm B.** *The History and Coinage of Karystos.* Toronto, 1973.
An unpublished doctoral thesis held at the University of Toronto.

3947   **Wallace, William P.** "Some Eretrian Mint Magistrates." *The Phoenix* (Canada) 4, no. 1 (summer 1950): 21-6.
Discusses the magistrates whose names appear on a series of Eretrian silver coins in the early second century B.C.: Phanias, Damasias, Hagnon, Epiteles, Charidamnos, Kleon, Philippos, and Amphinikos. Suggests "that some of them can be identified with men who appear in contemporary Eretrian inscriptions, and who are shown by various indications to have been men of wealth and consideration."

3948   ———. "The Coinage of the Euboian League." *Archaeology* 8, no. 4 (winter 1955): 264-7. Illus.
Reviews what little is known of the history of the Euboian League and its coinage. Numerous coins are illustrated.

3949   ———. *The Euboian League and Its Coinage.* Numismatic Notes and Monographs, No. 134. New York: American Numismatic Society, 1956. 180 pp., 16 pls., map. [CS 2476]
Examines the coinage of the Euboian League, minted at Eretria. Provides an extensive history of the League founded by Eretria, Chalkis, and Karystos in 411 B.C. Summary of relevant hoards and their chronology. Analysis of dies and weights of the silver issues. Discussion of the bronze issues. Presents a catalogue of 159 varieties. [Reviewed by G. K. Jenkins in *Numismatic Chronicle* 6th ser., 17 (1957): 273-5, and by J. M. F. May in *Journal of Hellenic Studies* 78 (1958): 159-60].

3950   ———. "Loans to Karystos about 370 B.C." *The Phoenix* (Canada) 16, no. 1 (1962): 15-28. 1 pl.
An inscription recording the payment of interest to various creditors of Karystos shows that the city borrowed considerable sums of money ca. 370 B.C. The money was perhaps needed for the construction of a temple. The money could hardly have been used in the miscellaneous form in which it was received from various sources. It is therefore reasonable to suppose that Karystos struck one or more issues of her own coinage about this period. [Summarized from I. Merker, *NL* 64]

3951   ———. "The Meeting-Point of the Histiaian and Macedonian Tetrobols." *Numismatic Chronicle* 7th ser., 2 (1962): 17-22. 2 pls.
"Five tetrobols of Histiaia are examined and compared with the maenad head tetrobols of Perseus with which they are strictly contemporary. The Macedonian tetrobols are of the decade 178-168 B.C. The Histiaian tetrobols belong halfway through the series issued by Histiaia and tentatively confirm Head's overall date (196-146 B.C.) for the series, for which E. Babelon had proposed 313-146 B.C. Wallace further suggests that Macedonian tetrobols may even have been struck at Histiaia." [J. Healy, *NL* 75]

3952   ———. "A Tyrant of Karystos." *Essays in Greek Coinage Presented to Stanley Robinson.* Edited by C. M. Kraay and G. K. Jenkins. Oxford: Clarendon Press, 1968. Pages 201-9. 1 pl. [CS 2477]
Discusses the rare didrachms of Karystos in Euboia with an anonymous head on the obverse and Nike in biga on the reverse. Suggests the issuer was a late third century B.C. tyrant of Karystos who is otherwise unknown to history. Lists forty-eight known specimens of this coinage. Photographs are provided for each known die variety. These coins had previously been attributed to Demetrios Poliorcetes, Antiochus the Great, or Alexander, son of Krateros. Cites hoard evidence to date the coins between 235-200 B.C., thus ruling out the previous attributions. The name of the issuer remains unknown.

Also see: Ashton "More Pseudo-Rhodian Drachms from Central Greece" under CARIAN ISLANDS—RHODOS; Borrell "Restitution to Histiaeolis" under NORTHERN GREECE—THESSALY; Greenwell "On Some Rare Greek Coins" (1890) under PRIVATE COLLECTIONS; Head "Catalogue of Greek Coins under CENTRAL GREECE—LOKRIS; J. Jones "Coins as Weights" under METROLOGY; T. Jones "Athens or Chalcis?" under ATTICA—GENERAL WORKS; Milne "Early Coinages of Athens and Euboea" under ATTICA—WAPPENMÜNZEN; D. M. Robinson *A Hoard of Silver Coins from Carystus* under HOARDS; H. Thompson "The Excavation" (Histiaea) under HOARDS; M. Thompson "The Beginnings of Athenian New-Style" under ATTICA—NEW STYLE COINAGE; M. Wallace "The Reduced Euboio-Attic Weight Standard" under METROLOGY; W. Wallace "The Early Coinages" under ATTICA—WAPPENMÜNZEN.

LOKRIS

3953   **Eaglen, Robin J.** "Portraits of Greek Coinage 21: Locri Opuntii." *Spink Numismatic Circular* 116, no. 2 (February 2008): 58-9. Illus.
This installment of the author's on-going series examines the coinage of Locri Opuntii. Reviews the history of the city and its coin types.

3954   **Gesche, Helga.** "Literaturüberblick der Griechischen Numismatik: Zentralgriechenland: Locris, Phocis, Boeotien." *Jahrbuch für Numismatik und Geldsseschichte* (Germany) 17 (1967): 35-93. [CS 2467]
A bibliography.

3955   **Head, Barclay V.** *Catalogue of Greek Coins of Central Greece.* Edited by R. S. Poole. London: British Museum, 1884. Reprint, Bologna, Forni, 1963. lxix, 158 pp., 24 pls. [CS 2468]
Volume 8 of the *Catalogue of Greek Coins in the British Museum.* Covers Locris, Phocis, Boeotia, and Euboea. Sixty-nine pages of introductory text precede the 158-page catalogue of coins. [Also see *Catalogue of Greek Coins in the British Museum* under PUBLIC COLLECTIONS—GREAT BRITAIN (LONDON)].

3956   **Numismatica Ars Classica NAC AG.** *Auction 55: The BCD Collection: Lokris – Phokis.* Zurich. October 8, 2010. 179 pp., illus.
Sale catalogue for a portion of the "BCD Collection." Includes 475 lots, including numerous group lots. The catalogue was written by the collector and provides extensive commentary on the coinage of Lokris and Phokis. An outstanding catalogue of a comprehensive collection, and a standard reference for this coinage. [For other portions of the collection, see "BCD" in the INDEX OF COLLECTORS AND COLLECTIONS].

3957 **Sayles, Wayne G.** "The Locrian Ajax: Stylistic Change in the Fourth Century B.C." *SAN—Journal of the Society for Ancient Numismatics* 16, no. 2 (summer 1985): 27-8, 35.
Discusses the depiction of the hero Ajax and suggests that a stylistic change which took place in this depiction on coins ca. 360 B.C. may have been influenced by the artist Lysippus.

PHOKIS

3958 **Crawford, Michael H.** "The Treasures of Delphi." *Annali. Istituto Italiano di Numismatica* (Italy) 27-28 (1980-81): 299-300.
"A reopening of the discussion on the use of the Delphic treasures by the Phocaeans between 356 and 346 B.C.: if they really paid the mercenaries with them, as related by the literary sources, did they also strike a new coinage of which nothing has survived? According to the author's interpretation of the verb χαταχδππω in this context, the Phocaeans converted the offerings into cash." [S. Sorda, *NL* 109]

3959 **Kinns, Philip.** "The Amphictionic Coinage Reconsidered." *Numismatic Chronicle* 143 (1983): 1-22. 4 pls.
"This article builds on the study of E. J. P. Raven (see Raven "The Amphictionic Coinage of Delphi" below) and utilizes subsequent research on the Delphic treasurers' accounts. The new catalogue comprises twenty-six staters (struck from seven obverse and twelve reverse dies), three drachms (one obverse, two reverses), and two hemidrachms (two obverses and two reverses). The original number of stater obverses undoubtedly did not exceed nine. Detailed reconsideration of the epigraphical evidence indicates that the total value struck was between 125 and 175 talents, and probably 80% of that was coined as staters. Calculations of survival rate and die output entail the conclusion that, for this issue, the minimum average output of each stater obverse die was 23,333 coins. An appendix lists modern struck and cast forgeries of the staters and drachms." [P. Kinns, *NL* 111/112]

3960 **Lacroix, Leon.** "Delphos et les Monnaies de Delphes." *Etudes d'Archéologie Numismatique* (France) (1974): 37-51. 3 pls. [CS 2558]

3961 **Langton, Neville.** "Note on Some Phocian Obols." *Numismatic Chronicle* 4th ser., 3 (1903): 197-210. 1 pl.
Records fourteen coins of Phocis from a recent find in Central Greece. Langton suggests dates for these coins ranging from 550 to 421 B.C.

3962 **Raven, E. J. P.** "The Amphictionic Coinage of Delphi, 336-334 B.C." *Numismatic Chronicle* 6th ser., 10 (1950): 1-22. [CS 2559]
"A series of treasurers' accounts found at Delphi throws new light on the monetary practices of the Amphictionic council. One inscription devoted to the new coinage gives a listing of various mints with some denomination of the coinage of each followed by three sets of figures: an amount of money in the given denomination, a deficit or *apousia*, and a remainder, representing the difference between the two expressed in 'Amphictionic' money. The most logical explanation of these records is that it was customary for the officials at Delphi to melt down the treasury contributions and reissue the silver in Amphictionic coins, the *apousia* reflecting the inevitable waste of the re-coining process as well as short weight in some of the original pieces due to wear or light striking. On the basis of the same accounts, the author calculates roughly how much of the new silver was issued, and from this, the survival rates of the Amphictionic coins and the average amount struck by each obverse die. The resulting statistics are extremely interesting." [M. Thompson, *NL* 17]. [Also see Kinns "The Amphictionic Coinage Reconsidered" above for updated information. For more information on the term *apousia*, see Woodward below].

3963 **Simpson, A. J.** "History and the Delphic Amphictiony." *New Zealand Numismatic Journal* (New Zealand) 13, no. 1 (January 1971): 33-5.
A brief account of the Amphictionic League (the group of states that operated the shrine at Delphi) and the battles for control of Delphi.

3964 **Svoronos, Joannes N.** ΝΟΜΙΣΜΑΤΙΚΗ ΤΩΝ ΔΕΛΦΩΝ. *Bulletin de Correspondence Hellénique* (France) 20 (1896).
The coins of Delphi.

3965 **Tameanko, Marvin.** "Delphi—City at the Center of the Earth." *The Celator* 15, no. 12 (December 2001): 6-18. Illus.
A good summary of the history of Delphi and its sanctuary of Apollo from earliest times through the Roman period. Includes descriptions of some of the coin types of Delphi and the Amphiktyonic League, which controlled the sanctuary. Describes the sanctuary and some of the mythology surrounding Apollo and the Delphian oracle.

3966 **Wallace, Malcolm B.** "Black Gods on Parnassus?" *Cornucopiæ* (publication of The Ancient Coin Society, Canada) 2, no. 3 (1974): 47-8. Illus.
Wallace re-examines the question of whether certain female heads on silver half drachms of the Phokian League ca. 460 B.C. reflected features of black women. He points to black men portrayed on third century B.C. Etruscan bronze coins and on late archaic silver fractions of Delphi. Based on differences from the depictions of the heads generally accepted as blacks, the author concludes that the heads on the Phokian coins are Greek—not black.

3967 **Williams, Roderick T.** *Silver Coinage of the Phokians.* Special Publication No. 7. London: Royal Numismatic Society, 1972. 138 pp., 16 pls., map. [CS 2732]
An attempt to reconstruct the sequence of the silver issues struck by the Phokians in the sixth and fifth centuries B.C. and the silver struck in the fourth century during the Third Sacred War. Suggests mint locations for some of the coins. The coins are grouped into five periods: (1) 510-478 B.C.; (2) 478-460; (3) 460-446; (4) 445-early fourth century; (5) 356-346 B.C. Each section includes a detailed discussion of the history of the period followed by a description of the coinage. Emphasizes the distinguishing characteristics of the coinage of the period and die linkages. Followed by a catalogue of 416 coins representing all the die varieties known to the author. All are illustrated in the plates. An appendix describes hoards which contained Phokian coins. Includes an index to published collections and sale catalogues which include significant groups of Phokian coins. [Reviewed A. M. de Guadan in *Acta Numismatica* 3 (1973): 345-7, by T. Hackens in *Revue Belge de Numismatique et de Sigillographie* 119 (1973): 200-2, by M. J. Price in *Journal of Hellenic Studies* 94 (1974): 255-6, by N. Waggoner in *American Journal of Archaeology* 78, no. 1 (January 1974): 97-8, by J. Warren in *Numismatic Chronicle* 7th ser., 14 (1974): 210-2, and by D. Mannsperger in *Gnomon* 51, no. 7 (November 1979): 700-2].

3968 **Woodward, Arthur M.** "ΑΠΟΥΣΙΑ." *Numismatic Chronicle* 6th ser., 11 (1951): 109-11.
"With reference to Raven's discussion of the Amphictionic coinage (see Raven above), Woodward agrees that the word *apousia* is to be interpreted as the deficit incurred in re-minting old coins. He then cites two similar terms—*apokausis* and *aphepsesis*—used in Attic inscriptions to indicate the loss in melting gold votive offerings." [M. Thompson, *NL* 26]

Also see: Earle-Fox "The Initial Coinage of Corcyra" under NORTHERN GREECE—CORCYRA; Gesche "Literaturüberblick" under CENTRAL GREECE—LOKRIS; Head "Catalogue of Greek Coins under CENTRAL GREECE—LOKRIS; Numismatica Ars Classica *Auction 55: The BCD Collection: Lokris - Phokis* under CENTRAL GREECE—LOKRIS; Thallon "The Cave at Vari" under TYPES.

Attica

True, there is no branch of ancient numismatics which has occasioned more controversy than the coinage of Athens before the Persian Wars. Theory has been advanced against theory, conjecture has combated conjecture, while the fields of scientific research have lain fallow.

—Charles T. Seltman, 1924

General Works

3969 **Anderson, Lisa, and Peter G. van Alfen.** "A Fourth Century BCE Hoard from the Near East." *American Journal of Numismatics* 2nd ser., 20 (2008): 155-98. 12 pls.
Presents a hoard of 475 coins (residing at the American Numismatic Society), mostly Athenian owls, found in the Near East that was buried between 334 and 330 B.C. The study is divided into four parts: (1) a description of the hoard coins and their dating; (2) an analysis of the cuts, countermarks, and graffiti found on the coins; (3) a study of the weights of *pi*-style owls that encompasses 1063 Athenian tetradrachms from this hoard and from other hoards found in the Aegean and Near East; and (4) general conclusions.

3970 **Babelon, Ernst.** "Une Obole au Nom d'Hippias." *Corolla Numismatica: Numismatic Essays in Honour of Barclay V. Head.* Edited by G. F. Hill. London: Oxford University Press, 1906. Pages 1-9. Illus.
Examines an obols with *obv.*, head of Athena, and *rev.*, owl and the letters ΗΙΠ. [Also see E. J. Seltman "A Tetradrachm with the Name of Hippias" below].

3971 **Babelon, Jean.** "Athéna à Chouette." *Revue Numismatique* (France) 5th ser., 11 (1949): 1-7. [CS 3408]
Examines the owl on Athenian coinage.

3972 **Badian, Ernst.** "Rome, Athens, and Mithradates." *American Journal of Ancient History* 1, no. 2 (May 1976): 105-28. [CS 2481]
Reviews the history of Athens at the beginning of the first century B.C., the period of the Mithradatic War. Reviews literary evidence and the evidence provided by coins and inscriptions. Discusses the chronology of the New Style Athenian coinage.

3973 **Balmuth, Miriam S.** "Athens or Phlius?" *Schweizer Münzblätter* (Switzerland) 61 (1966): 1-4. [CS 2482]
Includes a French summary.

3974 **Beckman, Martin.** "Athenian Coinage in a Worldwide Perspective." *The Anvil* (Canada) 8, no. 1 (March 1998): 11-6.
The author outlines the role that Athenian coinage played not only in Athens, but in the West and East. Presents hoard evidence to show how the use of Athenian coinage in the West, as well as in the Persian Empire, fluctuated over time. When Athens began producing plated coins, many imitations of Athenian coins were produced in Asia Minor, the Levant, and Egypt.

3975 **Bellinger, Alfred R.** *Two Hoards of Attic Bronze Coins.* Numismatic Notes and Monographs, No. 42. New York: American Numismatic Society, 1930. 14 pp. 2 pls. [CS 3210]
Discusses two hoards of Athenian bronze coinage. The first contained 244 coins. Includes a discussion of their chronology. The second hoard contained forty-five coins. Provides a list of the types and a discussion of symbols on the coins and their relationship to the silver coinage of Athens.

3976 **Beulé, Charles Ernest.** *Les Monnaies d'Athènes.* Paris: Chez Rollin, 1858. Reprint, Bologna: Forni, 1967. 420 pp., illus. [CS 2485]
Engraved coin illustrations in the text. Only 300 originals printed. [Also see Bunbury "Some Unpublished Coins" below].

3977 **Bicknell, Peter J.** "The Dates of the Archaic Owls of Athens Belonging to Seltman's Groups H and L." *L'Antiquité Classique* (Belgium) 38 (1969): 175-80.
"Using evidence of fractions, not previously mentioned in the work of C. M. Kraay and by W. P. Wallace, it is concluded that at least some of the earliest owls of class H were issued by Hippias and that at least some of the second group of class L were issued after the tyranny fell in 511/510." [P. Naster, *NL* 84]

3978 ——— "The Comet of 480 B.C. and the Owls of Athens." *New Zealand Numismatic Journal* (New Zealand) 14, no. 3 (October 1977): 18-21.

Kraay and Starr both hold the view that the crescent on the reverse of Athenian tetradrachms is a moon, and is a purely decorative element associated with the owl. Bicknell finds the crescent to be not at all decorative, and instead suggests that the crescent is associated with the crucial naval victory of the Athenians over the Persians at Salamis in 480 B.C. Bicknell cites a passage from Pliny the Elder describing various forms of comets. Bicknell believes the crescent on the tetradrachms is not a moon at all. Rather, it is a type of comet known to Pliny as the κερατιασ, a bi-horned comet visible from Greece at the time of the Salamis campaign and interpreted by the Athenians as an omen of victory. [Also see next item, and Brown "A Reverse in Attic Key," and Hammond "The Campaign" below].

3979 ——— "Again the Comet of 480 and the Owl of Athens." *New Zealand Numismatic Journal* (New Zealand) 15, no. 2 (June 1980): 62-3.
In a follow-up to the author's previous article (see above), a passage from L. Apuleius mentions the crescent-shaped comet that appeared at the time of the battle of Salamis, lending support to the passage from Pliny cited earlier by the author. [Also see Brown "A Reverse in Attic Key" and Hammond "The Campaign" below].

3980 **Blankley, Jack.** "A Further Croak from Aristophanes' Frogs." *Trident* 8 (March-May 1993): 7-8.
"An Athenian tetradrachm showing signs of being plated is probably one of those issued by the mint during the Peloponnesian War." [J. Melville Jones, *NL* 132]

3981 **Boeckh, August.** *The Public Economy of Athens; to Which is Added, A Dissertation on the Silver Mines of Laurion.* Second edition. London, 1842. 688 pp., 1 pl.
"A translation by George Cornewall Lewis, based on the 1828 German edition of this substantial work, first published in 1817. Written from an economic perspective, there is, nonetheless, much of numismatic interest in the text." [G. F. Kolbe]

3982 **Brake, Cindy.** "Athenian Owls: Silver Coins Known for Purity Circulate Widely." *Coin World* (October 15, 2007): 76-7. Illus.
A synthesis of basic information on the Athenian owl coinage drawn from various authors including Starr, Goldsborough, Jenkins, Hobson, and Vagi.

3983 **Brett, Agnes Baldwin.** "The Cave at Vari, V: Coins." *American Journal of Archaeology* 7 (1903): 335-7.
Thirteen coins were found in a cave in Attica, including one bronze coin of Athens (ca. 220-86 B.C.) and twelve Roman Imperial coins. A simple catalogue of the coins is presented. [Also see Thallon "The Cave at Vari, III: Marble Reliefs" under TYPES].

3984 **Brown, Brian A.** "A Reverse in Attic Key: The Crescent Moon and the Battle of Salamis." *The Celator* 5, no. 11 (November 1991): 36.
Argues that the crescent moon was added to the reverse field on Athenian coins to commemorate the battle of Salamis rather than the battle of Marathon as is often supposed. Suggests the crescent moon represents the letter Σ, the first letter of Salamis. Discusses the battle's importance to the Athenians. Suggests that the moon symbolism can be better explained in relation to the Eleusinian Mysteries which were being celebrated at the time of the battle of Salamis, rather than in relation to the battle of Marathon which was fought when the moon was full. [Also see Bicknell "The Comet of 480 B.C." (two items) above and Hammond "The Campaign" below].

3985 **Buchanan, James J.** *Theorika: A Study of Monetary Distributions to the Athenian Citizenry During the Fifth and Fourth Centuries B.C.* Locust Valley, New York: J. J. Augustin, 1962. 95 pp.
The author's Ph.D. dissertation at Princeton University, 1954. "In his introduction the author deals with early monetary distribution down to the early years of the pentacontaetia, but unfortunately neglects one important problem: namely, whether or not the citizen donatives from the profits of Laurium were made with the now famous Athenian tetradrachms. The greater part of the book is devoted to civil misthophora such as the *dikastikon* (payment for jury duty), *bouleutikon* (payment for council service), *ekklesiastikon* (payment for attendance at the assembly) and the *theorikon* (payment for participation in state religious functions, especially the theatre)." [I. Merker, *NL* 62]

3986 **Bunbury, Edward H.** "On Some Unpublished Coins of Athens and One of Eleusis." *Numismatic Chronicle* 3rd ser., 1 (1881): 73-90.
Publishes some new varieties of Athenian coins not listed by Beule (*Les Monnaies d'Athènes*, Paris 1858). Includes two archaic owl tetradrachms and two New Style tetradrachms. Also publishes a bronze coin of Eleusis (Demeter/vase).

3987 **Buttrey, Theodore V.** "The Athenian Currency Law of 375/4 B.C." *Greek Numismatics and Archaeology: Essays in Honor of Margaret Thompson.* Edited by O. Mørkholm and N. M. Waggoner. Wetteren: Numismatique Romaine, 1979. Pages 33-45.
Examines the law regarding Athenian and foreign currency at Athens focusing on those parts of the law which bear on the coins and their handling. Comments on the translation of the Greek texts by Stroud and recommends modifications in the reading. Buttrey argues that non-Attic coins bearing the Attic types did not enjoy forced circulation even if of good metal. The money tester (dokimastes) would not validate such coins, thereby discouraging their circulation. Suggests the point of the law was not to force merchants to accept Athenian coins. [Also see Giovannini "Athenian Currency" below].

3988 ——— "More on the Athenian Coinage Law of 375/4 B.C." *Quaderni Ticinesi. Numismatica e Antichità Classiche* (Switzerland) 10 (1981): 71-94.

3989 ——— "Seldom What They Seem: The Case of the Athenian Tetradrachm." *Ancient Coins of the Graeco-Roman World: The Nickle Numismatic Papers.* Edited by Waldemar Heckel and Richard Sullivan. Waterloo, Ontario: Wilfrid Laurier University Press, 1984. Pages 292-4.
In this abstract of his presentation, the author discusses a circulation hoard of 350 Athenian tetradrachms found in Egypt in 1934. Most of the coins have the frontal eye. Buttrey suggests that the frontal vs. profile eye is not a reliable criterion for dating Athenian tetradrachms, and consequently many of them have been dated too early. He suggests this hoard was buried in the fourth century B.C. The hoard also contained twelve Athenian imitation tetradrachms, some of which are die-linked. The author concludes that many of the imitation Athenian tetradrachms were an official issue struck in Egypt, and that they circulated locally. Many of what were thought to be late fifth century B.C. Athenian tetradrachms may, in fact, be fourth century Egyptian imitations.

3990 **Buxton, Richard Fernando.** "The Northern Syria 2007 Hoard of Athenian Owls: Behavioral Aspects." *American Journal of Numismatics* 2nd ser., 21 (2009): 1-27. 3 pls.
Buxton discusses a sample of 2626 coins from an immense hoard of Athenian tetradrachms (primarily 5th century types) deposited ca. 400 B.C. in northern Syria. A vast majority of the coins exhibit multiple types of surface markings including countermarks, cut countermark-like designs, graffiti, punch marks, cut edges and chisel cuts especially. Such markings are typical of smaller, contemporary hoards containing Athenian coinage found throughout the Near

East. However, the large sample size offered by this hoard further demonstrates that all of the different systems of surface marking conform to consistent patterns in placement and execution. There is nevertheless no similar consistency in the relationship between different marking systems appearing on the same coin. This suggests that each type of surface marking functioned independently but not exclusively as a regularized system of signification and circulation control within the Near East.

3991 **Cahn, Herbert A.** "Zur Frühattischen Münzprägung." *Museum Heveticum* (Switzerland) 3 (1946): 133-43. [CS 2488]

3992 ——— "Dating the Early Coinage of Athens." *Kleine Schriften zur Münzkunde und Archäologie.* Edited by H. A. Cahn. Basel: Archäologischer Verlag, 1975. Pages 81-97. [CS 2489]
Text of a lecture given at the American Numismatic Society in 1971.

3993 **Camp, John M.** "The Mint and Athenian Coinage." *The Athenian Agora: Excavations in the Heart of Classical Athens.* London: Thames and Hudson, 1986. Pages 128-35. Illus.
A brief description of the mint building found during excavations of the Agora in Athens. Furnaces for bronze-working were found on the site, along with dozens of unstruck bronze coin flans. This is believed to be the mint where Athenian bronze coins were struck in the third and second centuries B.C. Briefly discusses the use of coins at Athens and the law of 375/4 B.C. regulating the quality of coins circulating in the Agora.

3994 **Cancio, Leopoldo.** "Athenian Miscellanea 2." *Spink Numismatic Circular* 102, no. 7 (September 1994): 303-5. Illus.
Comments on the relatively low number of die links among the archaic coins of Athens, primarily due to low survival rates. Comments on the Athenian decadrachms in the famous "Decadrachm Hoard" but suggests that the Lycian staters in the hoard are probably more worthy of study. Comments on the relative ugliness of the Athena head on Athenian coins. Publishes a new Athenian imitation from Babylon, as well as a coin of "uncertain fabric"—possibly counterfeit. Publishes a new variety of an Athenian imitation of Sabakes, the Persian satrap of Egypt. Publishes a coin possibly minted at Gaza. Publishes a cast copy of an Athenian tetradrachm, produced by the Metropolitan Museum of Art. Publishes an Athenian counterfeit made from a very soft metal.

3995 ——— "Athenian Miscellanea." *Italiam Fato Profvgi: Numismatic Studies Dedicated to Vladimir and Elvira Eliza Clain-Stefanelli.* Numismatica Lovaniensia 12. Edited by T. Hackens. Louvain-la-Neuve: De L'Université Catholique De Louvain, 1996. Pages 81-6. 1 pl.
Cancio briefly addresses five topics: (1) Publishes an Athenian Wappenmünzen didrachm with a beetle on the obverse, the second known specimen. He mentions another specimen discussed by Hopper (see Hopper "Observations on the Wappenmünzen" below), but it is uncertain whether this is the same coin. If not, a third specimen exists. (2) Discusses the relative lack of die links known among the archaic tetradrachms of Athens. Illustrates one such die-linked pair, as well as a linked pair of third century B.C. tetradrachms. (3) Mentions the Decadrachm Hoard and notes that the well-known hoard contained about one thousand Lycian staters, a series about which relatively little is known. (4) Comments on the relative ugliness of the Athenian tetradrachm's obverse type in comparison with other classical period coins. The degradation in style from the classical to the Hellenistic periods is the opposite of what is generally observed at other cities. (5) Examines several imitations and counterfeits of Athenian tetradrachms including: (a) a coin on which the owl faces left; (b) a tetradrachm with an unusual arrangement of the olive leaves on Athena's helmet—the coin may be counterfeit; (c) an Athenian imitation tetradrachm of Sabakes, the Persian satrap of Egypt, bearing an unusual symbol in the reverse field. This new reverse variety was formerly in the Garrett collection; (d) publishes two counterfeit tetradrachms.

3996 ——— "Athenian Miscellanea 4." *Spink Numismatic Circular* 105, no. 1 (February 1997): 3-4.
A count of Athenian Wappenmünzen, gold fractions, and New Style pieces in various collections. Notes that Athenian coins were not attractive to dealers or collectors prior to the 1920's.

3997 **Carlson, Carl W. A.** "Rarities 5—The Missing Athenian Dekadrachm." *SAN—Journal of the Society for Ancient Numismatics* 5, no. 1 (1973-4): 8.
Carlson, then the Curator of Numismatics at Johns Hopkins University, describes a decadrachm of Athens in the University's collection. The pedigree of the coin includes a 1907 Sotheby's sale, the Delbeke collection, Schulman, and John Garrett. Includes a photograph and the size and weight of the coin.

3998 **Carradice, Ian, ed.** *Coinage and Administration in the Athenian and Persian Empires: The Ninth Oxford Symposium on Coinage and Monetary History.* British Archaeological Reports International Series, No. 343. Oxford, 1987. 167 pp., 15 pls.
The text of eight papers presented at a 1986 symposium which brought together numismatists and archaeologists to focus on "The Impact of Empire on Fifth Century Coinage," and to consider new evidence from the recently discovered "Decadrachm" hoard. Papers included (individually abstracted elsewhere; see index numbers below) are: "The Decadrachm Hoard: An Introduction" by S. Fried [559], "The Decadrachm Hoard: Chronology and Consequences" by J. Kagan [609], "Lycian Coins in the Decadrachm Hoard" by J. Spier [5041], "The Coinage of the Northern Aegean" by M. J. Price [187], "The Athenian Coinage Decree" by D. M. Lewis [4202], "The Athenian Coinage Decree and the Assertion of Empire" by H. Mattingly [4207], "The 'Regal' Coinage of the Persian Empire" by I. Carradice [6188], and "The Administration of the Achaemenid Empire" by C. Tuplin [6144]. [Reviewed by Andrew Burnett in *Spink Numismatic Circular* 95, no. 8 (October 1987): 259, and by N. K. Rutter in *Numismatic Chronicle* 148 (1988): 226-7].

3999 **Chambers, James T.** "Athenian Imperial Bronze: Its Historical Significance and Chronology." *The Numismatist* 91, no. 5 (May 1978): 921-7.
Discusses the bronze coinage struck at Athens during the Roman period. Athenian officials oversaw the minting process, and these coins are free of the imperial propaganda which dominates most other coinages of the Roman Empire. Describes the types and presents various theories for their chronological arrangement. Discusses Josephine Shear's dating of the coinage to 31 B.C.-A.D. 268. Discusses more recent evidence from excavations in the Athenian Agora, dating the coins to A.D. 117-267.

4000 **Chambers, Mortimer.** "Aristotle on Solon's Reforms of Coinage and Weights." *California Studies in Classical Antiquity, Volume 6.* University of California Press, 1974. Pages 1-16.
Re-examines the controversies involved in the interpretation of Chapter 10 of Aristotle's *Athenaion Politeia*. Comments on Pheidonian measures, the increase in the weight of the mina, the increase in the size of the standard coin, the increase in other weights, and the evidence provided by the writings of Androtion. Discusses the views of Kraay and Kraft on each issue. Discusses the rise in commercial weights. Concludes that Solon abolished the Pheidonian measures and revised the weight-mina upward so that it weighed 100 weight-drachmae. But Solon did not increase the standard coin from a

didrachm to a tetradrachm, and did not institute new weights in relation to the currency. [Also see related articles by Crawford, Freeman, Gomme, Hill, Johnston, Kraay, Milne, and Rhodes].

4001 **Clark, Cathy L.** "History in Your Hands: A Gold Athenian Stater that Goes on the Block this Month Tells an Epic Story of War and Desperation." *Numismatist* 116, no. 5 (May 2003): 29. Illus.
Illustrates an Athenian gold stater, struck in 407/406 B.C. which appeared in a Leu Numismatics auction. One of four known specimens, the coin was struck while Athens was struggling for survival at the end of the Peloponnesian War. Provides a brief historical background of the period.

4002 **Crawford, Michael H.** "Solon's Alleged Reform of Weights and Measures." *Eirene* (Czechoslovakia) 10 (1972): 5-8. [CS 3327]
"Aristotle's ambiguous account of Solon's reforms relating to weights, measures, and coinage is based on an anachronistic fourth century interpretation of an earlier tradition. Since it is now generally accepted that coins of Athens did not exist in Solon's day, and given the absence of archaic Attic weights, no reliance should be placed on an ancient text associating Solon with a currency reform." [N. Waggoner, *NL 95*]. [Also see related articles by M. Chambers, Freeman, Gomme, Hill, Johnston, Kraay, Milne, and Rhodes].

4003 **Davis, Gil, and Kenneth Sheedy.** "Seltman, The *Wappenmünzen*, and the Early Owls: A New Research Project in Athenian Coinage." *ANS* 8, no. 3 (winter 2009): 46-50. Illus.
Discusses Charles Seltman and his early research in Athenian coinage, which culminated in his book *Athens, Its History and Coinage before the Persian Invasions* (1924). Points out some of the flaws in Seltman's conclusions, often the result of the limited number of coins he was able to examine. Announces a new research effort by G. Davis, K. Sheedy, and P. Tselekas which is underway. The Early Attic Coinage project is designed to be a complete reexamination of all aspects of the archaic coinage of Athens and will incorporate a new die study of the coinage. The study is based at the Australian Centre for Ancient Numismatic Studies at Macquarie University, Sydney.

4004 "Decadrachm Sells, Brings $600,000 in Private Sale." *Coin World* (November 25, 1987): 1 ff. Illus.
Reports that an Athenian decadrachm from the famous "Decadrachm Hoard" has been sold for $600,000. [See Acar "Hoard of the Century" under HOARDS].

4005 **Diebolt, Jean, and Hélène Nicolet-Pierre.** "Recherches sur le Métal de Tétradrachmes à Types Athéniens." *Revue Suise de Numismatique* (Switzerland) 56 (1977): 79-91. 4 pls. [CS 2490]

4006 **Dinsmoor, W. B.** "The Repair of the Athena Parthenos." *American Journal of Archaeology* 38 (1934): 93-106. Illus.
"On pp. 96-7 the story of the removal of the gold from the statue by Lachares ca. 300 B.C. is accepted, and it is noted that it would have provided 132,000 staters. On pp. 103-5 reproductions of the statue on coins and in other media are listed." [J. R. Jones, *NIAJAH*]

4007 **Douglas, E. M.** "The Owl of Athena." *Journal of Hellenic Studies* 32 (1912): 174-8. Illus.
"A black-figure amphora at Uppsala, showing a sacrifice before an altar on which an owl stands, is used to prove that in some cases at least an animal form may serve as the direct equivalent of a deity." [J. R. Jones, *NIJHS*]

4008 **Earle-Fox, Harry B.** "Some Athenian Problems." *Numismatic Chronicle* 4th ser., 5 (1905): 1-9. 1 pl.
Fox examines the bronze coins of Athens which B. V. Head believed were a necessity issue equivalent to the silver coins bearing similar types. Fox disagrees, suggesting they were not a necessity issue—they were coined simultaneously with the silver issues. Fox suggests changes in the chronology of other Athenian coins of the fourth century B.C. He rejects the theory that Athenian coinage came to an end about 322 and began again with the New Style coins in 220. Instead, he suggests the coinage continued well into the third century B.C.

4009 **Elayi, Josette, and Alain G. Elayi.** "Un Nouveau Trésor de Tétradrachmes Athéniens et Pseudo-Athéniens." *Revue Numismatique* (France) 6th ser., 36 (1994): 26-33. 3 pls.
Discusses a hoard found in the Near East in 1992 which included thirty-six silver tetradrachms. Certain stylistic and technical details as well as symbols indicate that at least some of the coins are pseudo-Athenian. The most remarkable feature is their deliberate marking: 28 had been tested, 9 countermarked, and 2 bear graffiti. The hoard was probably buried in the last third of the fourth century B.C.

4010 **Elsen, Jean.** "La Stabilité du Système Pondèral et Monétaire Attique (VIe-IIe s. avant Notre Ére)." *Revue Belge de Numismatique et de Sigillographie* (Belgium) 148 (2002): 1-32.

4011 **Figueira, Thomas J.** *The Power of Money: Coinage and Politics in the Athenian Empire.* Philadelphia: University of Pennsylvania Press, 1998. 627 pp.
The author makes a comprehensive re-appraisal of the Athenian Coinage Decree after examining the literary, epigraphical, archaeological, and numismatic source materials relating to the political history of money in the fifth century B.C. Reviews the historical and economic context of Athenian monetary policy. Discusses the numismatic evidence for monetary policy, including hoard evidence and metrological evidence. Examines the minting activity of Athens and her allies during the fifth century B.C. Discusses the evidence found in the writings of Aristophanes. Discusses the Athenian tribute system. Figueira reconstructs the Coinage Decree from existing fragments. Reviews monetary legislation, including the Coinage Law of 375/4. Reviews various arguments for the chronology of the decree. Discusses the electrum, gold, and bronze coinage of the fifth century. Discusses imitations of Athenian coins. Concludes that the Decree likely was first passed in the 440's B.C. and served to codify existing practices. His conclusions do not substantiate that there were vast confiscations, demonetizations, or replacements of allied coinages. [Reviewed by Alan Johnston in *Numismatic Chronicle* 159 (1999): 359-62, by M. Crawford in *Journal of Hellenic Studies* 121 (2001): 199-201, by H. B. Mattingly in *American Journal of Archaeology* 103 (1999): 712-3, and by D. Foraboschi in *Revista Italiana di Numismatica e Scienze Affini* 103 (2002): 482-4].

4012 **Fischer-Bossert, Wolfgang.** *The Athenian Decadrachm.* Numismatic Notes and Monographs No. 168. New York: American Numismatic Society, 2008. 95 pp., 41 pls.
A comprehensive examination of the Athenian decadrachm and its social, political, and economic background. Begins with a discussion of the types, fabric, and die sequences. Reviews hoards containing Athenian decadrachms and discusses the provenance of each known specimen. Continues with a catalogue of the dies and all forty known specimens in public and private collections, as well as some lead trial pieces. Then Fischer-Bossert lists and discusses more than

ninety modern forgeries. In the appendix, he discusses the British Museum's attempted acquisition of the Prokesch-Osten specimen. Most of the decadrachms, both genuine and false, are illustrated.

4012a ——— "More Athenian Decadrachms." *Revue Suisse de Numismatique* (Switzerland) 88 (2009): 117-26.

4013 **Flament, Christophe.** "À Propos des Styles d'Imitations Athéniennes Définis par T. V. Buttrey." *Revue Belge de Numismatique et de Sigillographie* (Belgium) 147 (2001): 39-50.

4014 ——— "Imitations Athéniennes Authentiques? Nouvelles Considérations sur Quelques Chouettes Athéniennes Habituellement Identifiées Comme Imitations." *Revue Belge de Numismatique et de Sigillographie* (Belgium) 149 (2003): 1-10.

4015 ——— "Un Trésor de Tétradrachmes Athéniens Dispersés suivi de Considérations Relatives au Classement, à la Frappe et à l'Attribution des Chouettes à des Ateliers Étrangers." *Belge de Numismatique et de Sigillographie* (Belgium) 151 (2005): 29-38.

4016 ——— "L'Atelier Athénien: Réflexions sur la 'Politique Monétaire' d'Athènes à l'Époque Classique." *Liber Amicorum Tony Hackens*. Edited by G. Moucharte, M. B. Borba Florenzano, F. de Callataÿ, P. Marchetti, L. Smolderen, and P. Yannopoulos. Numismatica Lovaniensia 20. Louvain-la-Neuve: Université Catholique de Louvain, 2007. Pages 1 ff.

4017 ——— *Le Monnayage en Argent d'Athènes: De l'Époque Archaïque à l'Époche Hellénistique (c. 550 to c. 40 av. J.-C.)*. Études Numismatiques I. Louvain-la-Neuve, 2007. 310 pp., 39 pls.
[Reviewed by Peter van Alfen in *Journal of Hellenic Studies* 129 (2009): 190-1].

4017a ——— "Quelques Considerations sur les Monnaies Athéniennes Émises au IVe S." *Quaderni Ticinesi. Numismatica e Antichità Classiche* (Switzerland) 36 (2007): 91-110.

4017b ——— "Monnayage en Argent d'Athènes au IIIe Siècle avant Notre Ère." *Revue Belge de Numismatique et de Sigillographie* (Belgium) 156 (2010). 32 pp., 5 pls.
Flament reviews the evidence for the Athenian coinage of the third century B.C. which takes advantage of a preliminary die-study. After chronological adjustments concerning the pi- and QD-styles, the author distributes the tetradrachms, drachms, pentobols and tetrobols with symbols among two main issues which, through stylistic comparisons with bronze coinage, can be dated, respectively, from the beginning and from the last quarter of the third century. The last section of this study is devoted to the signification of the symbols characteristic of those issues— those marks are actually not magistrates' signets, but control combinations.

4017c ——— "A Note on the Laurion Stratigraphy and the Early Coins of Athens: The Work of D. Morin and A. Photiades and its Impact on the Study of Athenian Coinage." American Journal of Numismatics 2nd ser., 23 (2011): 1-6.
"Based on the underappreciated work of D. Morin and A. Photiades, it is argued that the use of Laureotic silver cannot be used as a reliable criterion for establishing the relative chronology of Athenian *Wappenmünzen*. However, because it can be shown that the early Athenian owls were struck from first-hand Laureotic silver, their inception and the Laurium mining leases should be connected with the financial apparatus established to support the new Cleisthenic democracy in 508 B.C." [Flament]

4018 **Flament, Christophe, O. Lateano, and Guy Demortier.** *Quantitative Analysis of Athenian Coinage by PIXE*. BAR International Series. 2008. Pages 445-450.
An examination by proton-induced x-ray emission.

4019 **Forrer, Leonard S.** "A Peculiar Type of Athenian Tetradrachm." *Spink Numismatic Circular* 8, no. 90 (May 1900): 3947. Illus.
Mentions a rare tetradrachm bearing a facing owl on the reverse. Includes a drawing of the coin.

4020 **Foster, C. W.** "Democracy and the Owls." *Numismatic Scrapbook Magazine* 28, no. 4 (April 1962): 998-9. Illus.
"An envisioned day in the life of a tetradrachm, beginning with its payment as salary to a jurist and ending with its purchase of wine from Chios." [B. Shonnard, *NL* 61]

4021 **Freeman, Kathleen.** "Solon's Work on the Attic Coinage." *The Work and Life of Solon. With a Translation of his Poems*. Cardiff: University of Wales Press Board. London: Milford, 1926. Pages 90-111.
A restatement of various theories by numismatic researchers regarding possible reforms of the Athenian weights and coinage by Solon. Attempts to reconcile the statements found in Androtion and Aristotle with the archaeological evidence. [A brief review by G. F. Hill appears in *Numismatic Chronicle* 5th ser., 6 (1926): 304. Also see related articles by M. Chambers, Crawford, Gomme, Hill, Johnston, Kraay, Milne, and Rhodes].

4022 **Giovannini, Adalberto.** "Athenian Currency in the Late Fifth and Early Fourth Century B.C." *Greek, Roman and Byzantine Studies* 16, no. 2 (summer 1975): 185-95. [CS 2494]
Argues against the commonly held view that Athens issued plated coins at the end of the Peloponnesian war. Follows-up on Stroud's discussion of the Athenian law of 375/4 B.C. (see Stroud "An Athenian Law" under ATTICA—ATHENIAN COINAGE DECREE). Stroud found no satisfactory explanation for the fact that the Athenians refused to accept their own coinage and needed this law to force acceptance. Suggests a different interpretation of one of the clauses, which helps explain the circumstances which led to this critical situation. (1) Argues that the bronze coins referred to in Aristophanes' *Frogs* were not plated drachma but rather, ordinary plain bronze coins—those bearing the inscription AΘH. Suggests Athens never issued plated coins. The plated coins were made by counterfeiters. Suggests the bronze coins were issued in 406 in exchange for silver coins which Athens needed to finance the war (in effect, a loan from the people to the state), to be exchanged at the end of the war when the bronze coins were to be demonetized. (2) The document published by Stroud shows that the Athenians were reluctant to accept their own coins. But why? Stroud suggested the Athenians feared counterfeits (due to a shortage of silver, counterfeits became common in circulation). Stroud concluded the law required acceptance of the counterfeits of good silver.

Giovannini suggests an alternate interpretation: counterfeit coins of good silver were to be returned to their owner by the tester—but they were not to be accepted in the marketplace. [Also see Buttrey "The Athenian Currency Law" above, and Kroll "Aristophanes" below].

4023 **Gitler, Haim, Matthew J. Ponting, and Oren Tal.** "Athenian Tetradrachms from Tel Mikhal (Israel): A Metallurgical Perspective." *American Journal of Numismatics* 2nd ser., 21 (2009): 29-49. 1 pl.
The authors use the analytical results from inductively-coupled plasma atomic emission spectrometry (ICP-AES) and lead isotope analysis (Q-ICP-MS) of a group of Athenian-style tetradrachms found in the excavations of Tel Mikhal to investigate their origins. The majority of these coins were thought to be Eastern imitations based on style, but the analysis suggests that these coins may actually be authentic Athenian issues—they were clearly produced from bullion that came from the silver mines of Laurion. Given their stylistic variability, the authors assume they are representative of the 'owls' that were circulated in Achaemenid Palestine. Therefore, although it would be premature to argue that the term Eastern imitation is an erroneous scholarly convention, this paper demonstrates that it is a clear possibility.

4024 **Gomme, A. W.** "Two Notes on the Constitution of Athens." *Journal of Hellenic Studies* 46 (1926): 171-8.
"On pp. 171-3 the writer supports a textual emendation (*meiosin*) which would make it clear that Solon reduced the weight of the Attic drachma." [J. R. Jones, *NIJHS*]. [Also see related articles by M. Chambers, Crawford, Freeman, Hill, Johnston, Milne, and Rhodes].

4025 **Grandjean, Catherine.** "Athens and Bronze Coinage." *Agoranomia: Studies in Money and Exchange Presented to John H. Kroll.* Edited by Peter G. van Alfen. New York: American Numismatic Society, 2006. Pages 99-108.
Explores the reasons why Athens did not strike bronze coinage until long after bronze coins had become common at other cities. Reviews the financial struggles the city faced in the late fifth and early fourth centuries B.C. and the consequences for Athens' coinage. After a brief period of producing plated silver coins, the city demonetized the plated coins (ca. 394/3 B.C.) and returned to striking pure silver coins. By this time, bronze coinage was associated in the Athenian mind with financial crises. It was this negative perception of bronze that prevented it from being readily adopted for coinage.

4026 **Hammond, N. G. L.** "The Campaign and the Battle of Marathon." *Journal of Hellenic Studies* 88 (1968): 13-57. Maps.
A re-analysis of the campaign and battle of Marathon, supported by topographical and literary evidence. On pages 40-1, Hammond suggests that the waning moon on coins of Athens is not a reference to the date of the battle. Rather, he suggests it is more likely that the moon-goddess Hecate/Artemis played an important role in the victory, and this fact was commemorated on the coinage. [Also see Bicknell "The Comet of 480 B.C." (two items) and Brown "A Reverse in Attic Key" above].

4027 **Head, Barclay V.** *Catalogue of Greek Coins of Attica, Megaris, and Aegina.* Edited by R. S. Poole. London: British Museum, 1888. Reprint, Bologna: Forni, 1963. lxix, 174 pp., 26 pls. [CS 2495]
Volume 11 of the *Catalogue of Greek Coins in the British Museum*. Sixty-nine pages of introductory text precede the 174 page catalogue of coins. [Also see *Catalogue of Greek Coins in the British Museum* under PUBLIC COLLECTIONS—GREAT BRITAIN (LONDON)].

4028 **Herrmann, John J., Jr.** *In the Shadow of the Acropolis: Popular and Private Art in Fourth Century Athens.* Brockton, Massachusetts: Brockton Art Museum, 1984. 89 pp., illus.
This catalogue for an exhibition of fourth century B.C. art includes three sections dealing with coinage. "Athenian Coinage" (pages 61-4) includes a short essay on Athenian coinage of the fourth century illustrated by nine Athenian coins ranging from a gold stater to a silver one-fourth obol. "Coins of Attica" (page 64) illustrates and describes two bronze coins of Eleusis and one bronze coin of Salamis. "Foreign Coins at Athens" (pages 64-71) discusses the use of coinage in Athens during the fourth century, and lists twenty-eight non-Athenian coins (most illustrated) found in the Agora.

4029 **Hill, B. H., and Benjamin D. Merritt.** "An Early Athenian Decree Concerning Tribute." *Hesperia* 13 (1944): 1-15. Illus.
"On p. 11 an interpretation is offered of lines 14-16 of this fifth century inscription. Cities sending tribute to Athens were to write the amount of this upon a tablet, stamp this with their seal (rather than seal the containers in which the money was sent), and deliver the sealed tablet as a guarantee that the proper sum had been sent." [J. R. Jones, *NIAJAH*]

4030 **Hill, George F.** "Solon's Reform of the Attic Standard." *Numismatic Chronicle* 3rd ser., 17 (1897): 284-92.
An attempt to interpret the changes implemented by Solon in regard to weights and coinage as described in *Athenaion Politeia*.

4030a **Holloway, R. Ross.** "The Early Owls of Athens and the Persians." *Revue Belge de Numismatique* (Belgium) 145 (1999): 5-15.

4031 **Hopper, R. J.** "The Attic Silver Mines in the Fourth Century B.C." *Annual of the British School at Athens* 48 (1953): 200-54. [CS 2496]
A re-examination of the administration and importance of the mines in the Laurion region. Considers the property rights involved, presents an account of their administration, lease lists, location and boundaries, tenure and system of payment, and theories of other scholars. Assesses the economic importance of the mines through a study of the individuals involved as mine operators or property owners.

4032 **Johnston, Joseph.** "Solon's Reforms of Weights and Measures." *Journal of Hellenic Studies* 54 (1934): 180-4.
In Johnston's opinion, general economic considerations led to the conclusion that Solon reduced the weight of the standard coin of Athens. Other considerations suggest that he made a similar reduction in the unit of weight for commercial purposes, and also in the units of capacity. The plain interpretation of the evidence of *Athenaion Politeia* 10 is that he did reduce the weight standard, except that he left it five percent heavier than the corresponding coin standard. The theory that Solon *increased* the unit of capacity is ultimately based on an identification of the Pheidonian with the Aeginetan system of weights and measures, which ignores part of the evidence, and on a literal interpretation of a sentence in the *Athenaion Politeia* which is a mistake either of the author or of a copyist. [Also see related articles by M. Chambers, Crawford, Freeman, Gomme, Hill, Kraay, Milne, and Rhodes].

4033 **Jones, John R.** "The Coinage Reform of Hippias." *Spink Numismatic Circular* 72, nos. 7-8 (July-August 1964): 169.
Suggests the Athena/owl coinage of Athens must be placed much later in the sixth century than earlier scholars would have been ready to admit. The earliest owls cannot be taken back even as far as the last years of Pisistratus, and in the most recent discussions of the subject, 525 and 510 B.C. are suggested as upper and lower limits for the new types. In support of this determination, Jones quotes a passage from Pseudo-Aristotle. [Summarized from *NL* 71]. [Also see J. Melville Jones "Revised Datings" under ORIGINS OF COINAGE].

4034 **Jones, T.** "Athens or Chalcis?" *Numismatic Chronicle* 3rd ser., 6 (1886): 19-22.

Examines the rare didrachm commonly assigned to Athens (B. V. Head, *A Guide to the Principal Gold and Silver Coins of the Ancients*, pl. 6, no. 26) with *obv.*, owl to left; *rev.*, incuse square, diagonally divided. Suggests the coin may belong to Chalcis. Jones believes the obverse type is a *type parlant* of Chalcis (χαλκισ = owl). He suggests the design of the later coins with reverse type of a wheel were derived from this early incuse reverse—the diagonal of this type being derived from the four spokes of a wheel.

4035 **Jongkees, Jan Hendrik.** "Notes on the Coinage of Athens." *Mnemosyne* (The Netherlands) 3rd ser., 12 (1944): 81-117. 2 pls.
Miscellaneous notes on topics in Athenian numismatics: (1) Pre-Solonian coinage and Solon's reforms: comments on Seltman's conclusions regarding the Wappenmünzen series and Solon's monetary laws. (2) Athenian electrum coinage: comments on Seltman's theories regarding electrum coinage which Seltman says were struck by the Alcmeonids. Examines some of the electrum coin types and presents a table of weights. (3) The chronology of sixth century coinage: discusses the transition from the Wappenmünzen, to gorgoneion type, to the owl tetradrachms. (4) The monetary reform of Hippias: comments on Six's theories regarding the re-coinage and reforms under Hippias. (5) The decadrachm series: explores the question—were Athenian decadrachms commemorative issues, or merely an expedient way to quickly coin a vast amount of silver? Suggests a large quantity of silver made these coins possible, but did not cause them to be struck (based on the high quality and the high relief of the art). Comments on the date of the decadrachms, placing them at 480 B.C. (6) Athenian coins and art: asks why Athenian coins maintained an archaic and rather poor artistic style. Other cities with popular international trade coins (Corinth, Tarentum) changed types and kept a high standard of art. Why not Athens? No conclusion is reached.

4036 ——— "Notes on the Coinage of Athens. Part 8: The Owl of Athens; Part 9: Again the Chronology of the Sixth Century Coinage." *Mnemosyne* (The Netherlands) 4th ser., 5 (1952): 28-56. 2 pls.
(8) "The emergence of the owl as the attribute of Athena, and the change of Athena from an unarmed into an armed war-goddess occurred about 560 B.C., about the time of the institution of the Panathenaic festival and the coming to power of Pisistratus. This is revealed by the study of vase-paintings, sculpture and coins. Two previous coin types, the owl and the head of Athena, were combined fortuitously in the new coinage of Pisistratus. The owl as the badge of Athens became well known through the spread of the coinage, and the comic interpretation of the owl contributed to its popularity and influence." (9) "Corroborative evidence for the author's earlier published notes on the arrangement and chronology of sixth century coinage of Athens is presented. Topics considered are pre-Solonian coinage, interpretation of the monetary law of Solon, the use of family and public badges on coins, electrum coins found in Athens, and the coinage of Pisistratus' time. Stylistic comparisons between coins and other works of art do not yield dependable results, and should not be used to date or arrange coins." [R. Laurer, *NL* 35]

4037 **Jungfleisch, Marcel.** "Remarques sur une Trouvaille de Tétradrachmes Athéniens Faite au Voisinage de Pithom." *Revue Numismatique* (France) 11 (1949): 27-34.

4038 **Kleiner, Fred S.** *Greek and Roman Coins in the Athenian Agora.* Excavations of the Athenian Agora, Picture Book 15. Princeton: American School of Classical Studies at Athens, 1975. 32 pp., 37 illus. [CS 3233 and 16165]
Begins with a brief introduction to the minting process and various aspects of Athenian coinage. Briefly discusses the earliest coins, the silver coinage of Athens, counterfeit "owls," the New Style coinage, Athenian bronze coins, foreign coins used at Athens, and the coinage of Roman Athens. Then discusses Roman Provincial and Imperial coins. Illustrated exclusively by coins found during excavations in the Athenian Agora. [Reviewed by A. G. McKay in *Cornucopiæ* 4 (1979): 66-7].

4039 ——— "Some Unpublished Athenian Bronze Coins." *Museum Notes* 20 (1975): 1-5. 1 pl.
Presents some previously unpublished Hellenistic Athenian fractions (*obv.*, Athena head r., wearing Corinthian helmet; *rev.*, owl r., on thunderbolt) found during excavations in the Athenian Agora. Discusses the evidence for the dating of the coins. Concludes they belong to the third century B.C.

4040 ——— "The Agora Excavations and Athenian Bronze Coinage, 200-86 B.C." *Hesperia* 45, no. 1 (January-March 1976): 1-40. 4 pls. [CS 2500]
Attempts to establish a reasonably precise relative and absolute chronology for the Athenian bronzes struck between 200 and 86 B.C. Lists sixteen major types. Discusses denominations, weights, and countermarks. Discusses the evidence provided by hoards found in the Athenian Agora. Lists hundreds of such coins and concludes with a list of coin types grouped by decade of issue.

4041 **Knapp, Jamie.** "In Owl We Trust." *The Celator* 17, no. 10 (October 2003): 6-16. Illus.
Knapp explores the coins struck throughout the Greek world whose types were imitative of or derived from the Athenian tetradrachm. Discusses and illustrates coins struck in Italy, Sicily, Asia Minor, Syria, Phoenicia, Palestine, Judea, Egypt, Arabia, Bactria, and others.

4042 **Köhler, U.** "Über die Attische Goldprägung." *Zeitschrift für Numismatik* (Germany) 21 (1898): 5-16.
Examines the gold coinage of Athens.

4043 **Kraay, Colin M.** "The Archaic Owls of Athens: Classification and Chronology." *Numismatic Chronicle* 6th ser., 16 (1956): 43-68. 1 pl. [CS 2502]
Suggests revisions to Seltman's classification of the archaic owls. Using the evidence of technique, design and epigraphy, the evidence of hoards, the evidence of the helmets, and the evidence of the barbarous issues, a classification can be drawn up for the early owls. The earliest owls are in Seltman's Group H, and Seltman's Groups C, E, F, and G are to be placed late in the series of archaic owls and are to be dated after 500 B.C. The Wappenmünzen didrachms led into the tetradrachms; the earliest owls derived their technique from these coins, but they soon developed a standard design, after some uncertainty over the details of the reverse type. Various reasons can be adduced for dating the change from Wappenmünzen to owls about 525 and the termination of the early owl series about 479. The Wappenmünzen series may be said to begin about 575 or after. Solon's reforms, like those of Pheidon of Argos, could not have involved coins but only names for weights which were later given to coins. [Summarized from C. Vermeule, *NL* 43]. [Also see Kraay "An Interpretation" and C. Seltman *Athens* below].

4044 ——— "The Early Coinage of Athens: A Reply." *Numismatic Chronicle* 7th ser., 2 (1962): 417-23. [CS 2503]
"This is a reply to Wallace's proposed new chronology for the early coinages of Athens. Kraay argues that hoard evidence is against Wallace's 490 B.C. for the end of the series of archaic owls and suggests that the wreathed type began near 480 B.C. Wallace fails to prove the existence of wreathed owls before that date. Whichever chronology is chosen there emerges a somewhat lower date for the appearance of the Athena heads at Corinth than has of late been generally accepted." [J. Healy, *NL* 75]

4045 ——— *Coins of Ancient Athens.* Minerva Numismatic Handbooks, No. 2. Newcastle upon Tyne: Corbitt & Hunter, 1968. 39 pp. including the 8 pls. [CS 2504]

An overview of the coinage of Athens beginning with the Wappenmünzen issues, continuing with the archaic owls, the coinage of the fifth, fourth, and third centuries B.C., the New Style coinage, and concluding with the late bronze coinage.

4046 ——— "An Interpretation of *Ath. Pol.* Ch. 10." *Essays in Greek Coinage Presented to Stanley Robinson.* Edited by C. M. Kraay and G. K. Jenkins. Oxford: Clarendon Press, 1968. Pages 1-9. [CS 2505]

Reconsiders chapter 10 of the *Athenaion Politeia* describing the changes made by Solon in the system of weights, measures, and coinage. Kraay asks that this paper replace the "inadequate" treatment of his 1956 paper (see Kraay "The Archaic Owls" above). Compares the text written by Aristotle with that of Androtion—Kraay prefers the text by Aristotle. Presents a section of the original texts in Greek. Refutes the theory of K. Kraft that the pre-Solonian mina of 70 drachmae was divided into 100 lighter drachmae. Argues instead that: the measures of Pheidon were replaced by the larger Attic measures; the mina was increased from a weight of 70 to that of 100 Attic drachmae; the Attic didrachm was replaced by the tetradrachm as the standard denomination. States that the mint used special weights which were five percent below normal, and that the mint was permitted by law to strike coins at a weight five percent below face value. Also suggests that Solon's reform of weights was separated in time from his reform of debts. [Also see related articles by M. Chambers, Crawford, Freeman, Gomme, Hill, Johnston, Milne, and Rhodes].

4047 ——— "Archaic Owls of Athens: New Evidence for Chronology." *Thorikos and the Laurion in Archaic and Classical Times.* Miscellanea Graeca 1. Edited by H. Mussche. Ghent: Belgian Archaeological Mission in Greece, 1975. Pages 145-60.

4048 **Kraft, Konrad.** "Zur Solonischen Gewichts- und Münzreform." *Jahrbuch für Numismatik und Geldgeschichte* (Germany) 19 (1969): 7-24. [CS 2501]

Solon's reform of weights and coinage.

4049 **Kroll, John H.** "Two Hoards of First-Century B.C. Athenian Bronze Coins." *Archaiologikon Deltion* (Greece) 27 (1972): 86-120. 7 pls.

Discusses two hoards containing late Hellenistic Athenian bronze coins: the Chaidari hoard (*IGCH* 230) which included 483 coins, and the Agia Varvara hoard (*IGCH* 473) which included 230 coins. These two cities are neighboring Athenian suburbs. The coins belong to the period following the Sullan invasion of 86 B.C. Kroll divides the issues into three groups: heavy owl-on-amphora issues, issues with changing reverse types, and cleruchy issues (signed jointly by Athens, Lemnos, Imbros, and Skyros). Discusses the types and their chronology. Presents a catalogue of the coins.

4050 ——— "Aristophanes' Πονερα Χηαλκια: A Reply." *Greek, Roman, and Byzantine Studies* 17, no. 4 (winter 1976): 329-41.

Discusses the "wicked little bronzes" (ponera chalkia)—silver plated bronze coins—produced in Athens in 405 B.C. and mentioned by Aristophanes in *The Frogs*. Giovannini challenged the widely held view that these coins, issued in the closing years of the Peloponnesian War, were silver plated. Giovannini suggested the coins were undisguised bronze with a distinctive type: Athena head in Corinthian helmet/owl left or right, with AΘH. Kroll supports the view that the coins were indeed plated, and shows that Giovannini's chronology is wrong regarding the AΘH inscriptions and that Giovannini ignored issues of style and the evidence of the dies. [See Giovannini above].

4051 ——— "A Chronology of Early Athenian Bronze Coinage ca. 350-250 B.C." *Greek Numismatics and Archaeology: Essays in Honor of Margaret Thompson.* Edited by O. Mørkholm and N. M. Waggoner. Wetteren: Numismatique Romaine, 1979. Pages 139-54. 2 pls.

Kroll examines four hoards found in Athens and proposes a revision of the previously accepted dating of Athenian bronze coinage ca. 350-250 B.C. Includes a catalogue of 104 coins from a hoard found in the Agora (*IGCH* 157). [Also see J. P. Shear "Analytical Table" under HOARDS].

4052 ——— "Evidence for Identifying the Denominations of Hellenistic Athenian Bronze Coinage." *American Journal of Archaeology* 86 (1982): 273.

An abstract of a paper delivered at a 1981 conference. Recent work at the Athenian Agora has made it possible to deduce the probable values of the bronze coins in the Athenian monetary system. Kroll describes the chalkous, triobol, and obol coins.

4053 ——— "Athenian Bronze Coinage and the Propagation of the Eleusinian Mysteries." *American Journal of Archaeology* 96, no. 2 (April 1992): 355-6.

A summary of a paper presented at the 93rd Annual Meeting of the Archaeological Institute of America (1991). Margaret Thompson proved that fourth and third century B.C. bronze coins with Triptolemos/piglet types and the legend EΛEΥΣI were struck by Athens, and the legend does not relate to the deme of Eleusis as minting authority (see Thompson "Coins for the Eleusinia" below). Rather, the legend refers to the Eleusinia—the agonistic festival at Eleusis. It was the first base metal coinage at Athens and was introduced to benefit the many foreign visitors attending the festival. Occasional strikings of Eleusinian bronze issues throughout the Hellenistic period represent later revivals of the festival coinage tradition—struck when the festival was celebrated with special prominence.

4054 ——— *The Athenian Agora, Results of Excavations Conducted by the American School of Classical Studies at Athens, Volume 26: The Greek Coins.* Princeton: The American School of Classical Studies at Athens, 1993. 376 pp., 36 pls.

A catalogue of the 16,577 identifiable coins found during excavations in Athens, 1931-1990. Most of the coins are Athenian bronzes from the fourth century B.C. through the third century A.D. Begins with a general discussion of the finds. Continues with discussions of Athenian silver and bronze coins, and concludes with a discussion of the non-Athenian coins found. Each section incorporates a catalogue of the coins, including a catalogue of the Athenian imperial bronze coinage by Alan Walker. Also catalogues hundreds of non-Athenian coins that were lost in the Agora in ancient times. [Reviewed by Ian Carradice in *Numismatic Chronicle* 155 (1995): 376-7, and by Edith Schönert-Geiss in *Gnomon* (Germany) 69 (1997): 561-2].

4055 ——— "The Bronze Coinage of Salamis: A Synopsis." *Classical Numismatic Group Auction 38.* Lancaster, Pennsylvania: Classical Numismatic Group, 1996. Pages 38-41. Illus., 2 maps.

A brief account of the bronze coinage of the island of Salamis. Kroll suggests this coinage is unusual because it was not the coinage of a sovereign state—Salamis was an Athenian possession. He suggests this coinage may have been struck to fill the need for small change at a time when Athens was minting exclusively in silver. The coinage may have been minted by the people of Athens in the name of Salamis. It was discontinued in the third quarter of the fourth century B.C. Sixteen coins of Salamis are illustrated in this catalogue for a June 6-7, 1996 auction.

4056 ——— "The Piraeus 1902 Hoard of Plated Drachms and Tetradrachms (*IGCH* 64)." *ΞΑΡΑΚΤΗΡ: Αφιερωμα στη Μαντω Οικονομιδου (Character: Offerings to Mando Oeconomides)*. Publications of Archaeological Deltion, No. 57. Athens: Treasury of Archaeological Resources and Expropriations, 1996. Pages 139-46. 1 pl.
   The Piraeus Hoard of 1902 (actually *IGCH* 46, not 64 as the title indicates) contained fourré Athenian drachms and tetradrachms. It originally contained thousands of pieces, but only about a hundred have survived. Kroll discusses the known coins and comments on their chronology. Includes a catalogue of 100 coins from the hoard. [Also see M. Oeconomides-Caramessini "Note on the Piraeus Hoard" below].

4057 ——— "Silver in Solon's Laws." *Studies in Greek Numismatics in Memory of Martin Jessop Price*. Edited by Richard Ashton and Silvia Hurter. London: Spink, 1998. Pages 225-32.
   Reviews the surviving fragments of Solon's laws to see what they tell us about the state of currency in Attica in the early sixth century B.C. Lists laws that prescribe fines, mention public revenues and expenditures, prices, payments, and usury. Shows that Athenians in Solon's time were accustomed to dealing in silver currency, even though they had no coins.

4057a ——— "The Evidence of Athenian Coins." *The Macedonians in Athens, 322-229 B.C.: Proceedings of an International Conference held at the University of Athens, May 24-26, 2001*. Editd by O. Palagia and S. V. Tracy. Oxford: Oxbow Books, 2003. Pages 206-12.

4058 ——— "The Reminting of Athenian Silver Coinage, 353 B.C." *Hesperia* 80, no. 2 (April-June 2011): 229-59. Illus.
   Combining evidence from Athenian silver coins, an unpublished Agora inscription, and several accounts concerning historical figures, Kroll reconstructs the Athenian program of 353 B.C. whereby all of the larger-denomination silver coinage in the city was demonetized and called in for restriking as a means of raising revenue during the fiscal crisis in the aftermath of the Social War. The folded-flan technique and erratic, substandard appearance of the resulting "pi-style" coins, attestations of their hurried production in that year, were retained in all subsequent Athenian silver coinage down into the third century as recognized attributes of good Athenian money. Includes Appendices "Dating the Pi-Style Gold" and "Coin Hoards Cited." Extensive bibliography.

4058a ——— "Athenian Tetradrachm Coinage of the First Half of the Fourth Century B.C." *Revue Belge de Numismatique* (Belgium) 157 (2011): 3-26, incl. 5 pls.
   Because all earlier fourth century tetradrachms in Attica were called in and restruck in the year 354/3 B.C., hardly any of that coinage has survived except for specimens that had been exported before the restriking and were buried abroad, especially in Egyptian and Sicilian hoards. The Athenian components of several of these hoards together with other published and unpublished tetradrachms make it clear that this coinage of ca. 400/390 to 353 was not only substantial, but was one of the most prolific Greek coinages of the period. Discussed also is the literary evidence pertaining to the start of the coinage and the origin of the owl tetradrachms belonging to Buttrey's style x. [From Kroll's abstract].

4059 **Kroll, John H., and Nancy M. Waggoner.** "Dating the Earliest Coins of Athens, Corinth and Aegina." *American Journal of Archaeology* 88, no. 3 (1984): 325-40.
   A response to Kagan's essay attributing the first coinage to Lydia, ca. 700 B.C. (see Kagan "The Dates of the Earliest Coins" under ORIGINS OF COINAGE). Kroll and Waggoner review the literary, stylistic, and numismatic evidence for the chronology of archaic Aeginetan, Corinthian, and Athenian coinage. They conclude that, regardless of the date of the first coinage in western Asia Minor, coinage was not introduced at Aegina, Corinth, or Athens until the sixth century B.C. Explains the arguments supporting both the traditional "high" chronology and the more recently accepted "low" chronology for the introduction of coinage. Discusses the controversy over Solon's reforms at Athens and the traditions surrounding Pheidon of Argos. Dates the first coins of Corinth to ca. 575 B.C.; of Athens to ca. 550 B.C.; Aeginetan coinage began early in the sixth century B.C. Tables summarize hoards significant for the chronology of the archaic coinage of these cities.

4060 **Lacroix, Leon.** "La Chouette et le Croissant sur les Monnaies d'Athènes." *L'Antiquité Classique* (Belgium) 34 (1965): 130-43. 2 pls. [CS 2506]
   Examines the owl and crescent moon on coins of Athens.

4061 **Lang, Mabel.** *The Athenian Citizen*. Excavations of the Athenian Agora, Picture Book 4. Princeton: American School of Classical Studies at Athens, 1960. 32 pp., illus.
   "The compiler uses evidence derived from the excavations in making sundry observations concerning Athenian currency and its use by the local citizenry. Discovered in the neighborhood of a building now identified as the mint (at the southeastern corner of the Agora) was a bronze rod and several blanks which had been cut from it—providing evidence of one of the early stages in coin manufacture. Both rod and blanks are illustrated, together with three silver tetradrachms, issued in the fifth, fourth and second centuries B.C. respectively." [*NL* 57]. [Also see H. A. Thompson "Activities in the Athenian Agora: 1959" below].

4062 **Lewis, David M.** "The Public Seal of Athens." *Phoenix* (Canada) 9 (1955): 32-4.
   "Mr. Lewis shows (correcting W. P. Wallace's note) that Athens had a public seal at least as early as 397 B.C., and probably earlier. He discusses the meaning and use of symbolism." [W. Wallace, *NL* 39]. [See Wallace "The Public Seal" below].

4063 **Lönnqvist, Kenneth.** "Studies on the Hellenistic Coinage of Athens: The Impact of Macedonia on the Athenian Money Market in the Third Century B.C." *Early Hellenistic Athens: Symptoms of a Change*. Papers and Monographs of the Finnish Institute at Athens 6. Edited by Jaakko Frösén. Helsinki: Suomen Ateenan-Instituutin Säätiö, 1997. Pages 119-45. Illus.
   "The paper discusses the impact of Macedonia on the monetary policy of Hellenistic Athens in the third century B.C. in the light of Macedonian coins (mainly bronze) discovered in the Athenian excavations, and to some extent in Attic territory generally. A detailed statistical investigation of the coin finds is presented. The paucity of royal silver in Attica and Athens shows that the target area of the Macedonian coinage was somewhere else: none of the Antigonid silver suggested to have been minted in Athens during the occupation of the city before 262/1 B.C. can, in fact, have been minted there. There is also direct evidence that the Macedonian authorities would have restricted local coinage in any case. Existing evidence shows rather that the diminishing Athenian coin volume minted in the third century was more the outcome of the poor economic situation. Numismatic and historical evidence implies that the enormous bulk of Macedonian coinage that was circulated inside Athens ended up in the city indirectly as a result of the impact of the Macedonian garrison stationed in the area or in the form of an otherwise unrecorded donation of coins to the city by Antigonos Gonatas following the restoration of the liberty to Athens in 255 B.C." [K. Lönnqvist, *NL* 144]

4064 **Marotta, Michael E.** "Copper Owls: The Emergency Coinage of Athens 406 B.C." *The Celator* 19, no. 10 (October 2005): 6-16. Illus.

Examines the silver-plated copper coins of Athens which have been described as official emergency issues of 406 B.C. Thousands of such coins were discovered in 1902 in the Peiraeus near Athens (reported by Svoronos). This hoard is No. 46 in Thompson's *Inventory of Greek Coin Hoards*. The coins were struck during the period of the Thirty Tyrants. Whether they were the work of the democratic opposition to the oligarchy, or the work of a forger is unknown. The coins share a characteristic with the rare gold stater of Athens: Athena's upper and lower eyelids do not touch. Marotta summarizes T. V. Buttrey's opinion that many silver owls, commonly attributed to Athens, were likely minted in Egypt. The comedies of Aristophanes are sometimes provided as evidence that official silver-coated copper coins were issued. However, these references are clearly to "copper" coins—not plated coins. Marotta argues that the Athenians would have differentiated plated coins from silver coins by some differences in design. He tentatively concludes that the plated coins of the Peiraeus Hoard were simply fakes—not an official emergency issue. Any official emergency issues were likely pure copper.

4065 **Martin, Thomas R.** "Silver Coins and Public Slaves in the Athenian Law of 375/4 B.C." *Mnemata: Papers in Memory of Nancy M. Waggoner*. Edited by William E. Metcalf. New York: American Numismatic Society, 1991. Pages 21-47. 1 pl.
An inscription found in the Athenian agora in 1970 states that Athenian coinage that has been shown to be of silver and to carry the public type must be accepted in financial transactions. A public slave worked as the official certifier of the coinage, and was responsible for confiscating any counterfeit coins and certifying genuine coins. Non-Athenian coins imitative of Athenian types (such as those minted in Egypt) were to be returned to their owner. Describes the monetary situation in Athens in the fourth century B.C., including the minting of plated coins as well as the introduction of imitative types and the abundance of counterfeits. The conditions made the job of the official certifier very important. Describes the role of public slaves in Athens, including their use in responsible administrative positions. Emphasizes that the certifier of coinage had unusual powers for a slave—he could decide which coins to certify and his decisions were not subject to the scrutiny that was standard in Athenian public administration.

4066 **Mattingly, Harold B.** "Athens and the Western Greeks: c. 500-413 B.C." *La Circolazione della Moneta Ateniese in Sicilia e in Magna Grecia. Atti del I Convegno del Centro Internazionale di Studi Numismatici: Napoli 5-8 Aprile 1967.* Annali. Istituto Italiano di Numismatica Supplement 12-14. Rome, 1969. Pages 201-22.
"The epigraphic and literary sources which form the basis for dating political events determining and accompanying the Athenian penetration of the West are discussed and correlated with numismatic evidence. Only after the foundation of Thurium (443 B.C.) are Athenian political interest and diplomatic activity in the West visible." [S. Sorda, *NL* 85]

4067 **Merritt, Benjamin D.** "Greek Inscriptions." *Hesperia* 32 (1963): 1-56. 21 pls.
"On pp. 31-2 an inscription is described which appears to list overseers of the mint of Athens at a date in the first half of the fourth century B.C." [J. R. Jones, *NIAJAH*]

4068 ——— "Perikles, the Athenian Mint, and the Hephaisteion." *Proceedings of the American Philosophical Society* 119 (1975): 267-74.
Provides the text of the Athenian Coinage Decree. Summarizes some of the arguments over its date and interpretation. Restores some lines in the decree which the author believes authorized the building of the Hephaisteion in Athens in 449 B.C.

4069 **Miller, Richard P.** "Athenian Coinage: Progress and Problems." *The Celator* 11, no. 5 (May 1995): 14-25. Illus.
Miller reviews the progress which has been made in the study of Athenian coinage and outlines some remaining problems. Summarizes the latest research on the chronology of the Wappenmünzen, the gorgoneion issues, the introduction of the owl tetradrachms, the New Style coinage, and the decadrachms. He reviews the controversy over Solon's reforms and the Athenian Coinage Decree. Miller also discusses the melting of the gold Nike statues for the minting of gold staters and fractions, and the issuance of silver-plated bronze tetradrachms. Discusses the introduction of bronze coinage at Athens.

4070 **Milne, Joseph G.** "The Monetary Reform of Solon." *Journal of Hellenic Studies* 50 (1930): 179-85.
A consideration of the changes introduced by Solon into the currency system of Athens. Milne reviews the economic conditions and the monetary system in Athens prior to the reforms. The reforms of Solon meant the stabilization of the Attic drachma and its embodiment in a national coinage, whereby he secured the Attic farmers against the money lenders who exploited foreign exchange values, and gave the Athenian traders a definite basis for prices in a currency guaranteed by the State. [Also see related articles by M. Chambers, Crawford, Freeman, Gomme, Hill, Johnston, Kraay, and Rhodes. Also see Milne "The Chronology" and "The Economic Policy" below].

4071 ——— "The Origin of Certain Copies of Athenian Tetradrachms." *Iraq* 4 (1937): 54-8. Illus.
A reconsideration of two base silver coins and one bronze coin mentioned by Hill in the *British Museum Catalogue of Greek Coins*. Hill tentatively attributed these as early examples of Arabian imitations of Athenian types circulating in the northern part of the Arabian peninsula. Milne concludes they were likely struck in northern Syria in the last quarter of the fifth century B.C.

4072 ——— "Athenian Coins Found in Egypt." In Michael I. Rostovtzeff's *The Social and Economic History of the Hellenistic World, Volume 3*. Oxford: Clarendon Press, 1941. Page 1632.
An extract from a letter written by Milne giving his opinion that very few Athenian tetradrachms were imported into Egypt after about 350 B.C. He also suggests that Chabrias brought some old Athenian dies with him to Egypt to strike "owls" for paying the Greeks who served under him. Local artists later made barbarous dies and struck inferior coins.

4073 ——— "The Chronology of Solon's Reforms." *Classical Review* 57, no. 1 (March 1943): 1-3. [CS 2510]
Discusses the increase in measures, weights, and coinage referred to by Aristotle (*Ath. Pol.* 10). Argues that νομισμα does not mean coin or coinage. Rather, it should be interpreted as "unit"—any form of currency. Argues that Solon increased the unit of currency by substituting the tetradrachm for the didrachm. Discusses Solon's trip to Egypt and his decision to establish an export trade with Athenian silver. [Also see related articles by M. Chambers, Crawford, Freeman, Gomme, Hill, Johnston, Kraay, and Rhodes. Also see Milne "The Monetary Reform" above and "The Economic Policy" below].

4074 ——— "The Economic Policy of Solon." *Hesperia* 14 (1945): 230-45.
Reviews the economic conditions at Athens at the end of the seventh century B.C. Discusses trade patterns, the development of coinage, and the reforms of Pheidon. Explores the problems which Solon sought to correct. Describes Solon's coinage reform and its effects on the economy, as well as his trip to Egypt and the initiation of a trade coinage upon his return. [Also see related articles by M. Chambers, Crawford, Freeman, Gomme, Hill, Johnston, Kraay, and Rhodes. Also see Milne "The Monetary Reform" and "The Chronology" above].

4075 **Moledor, Victoria Stone.** "Coins of Athens: First Coins Depict Images from Owls to Stags." *Coin World* (July 24, 2000): 88. Illus.

A rudimentary and brief survey of Athenian coinage.

4076 **Moon, George Washington.** "A Unique Coin of Athens." *Spink Numismatic Circular* 1 (June 1893): 247.
An Athenian pentadrachm is described in correspondence from a reader.

4077 ——— "Crescents on the Obverse of Athenian Coins." *Spink Numismatic Circular* 1 (July 1893): 280-1.
In this "Letter to the Editor," the author asks for guidance on where he can find written reference to crescents on the obverse of Athenian coins. He knows of no such reference.

4078 **Naster, Paul.** "Un Trésor de Tétradrachmes Athéniens Trouvés à Tell el Maskhouta (Égypte)." *Revue Belge de Numismatique* (Belgium) 94 (1948): 5-14.
Examines the Tell El-Mashkuta Hoard of Athenian tetradrachms. [Also see E. S. G. Robinson "The Tell El-Mashkuta Hoard" below].

4079 **Nicolet-Pierre, Hélène.** "Autour du Décadrachme Athenien Conservé à Paris." *Studies in Greek Numismatics in Memory of Martin Jessop Price*. Edited by Richard Ashton and Silvia Hurter. London: Spink, 1998. Pages 293-9. 2 pls.

4080 ——— "Tétradrachmes Athéniens en Transeuphratène." *Transeuphratène* (France) 20 (2000): 107-19.

4081 **Nicolet-Pierre, Hélène, and Carmen Arnold-Biucchi.** "Le Trésor de Lentini (Sicile) 1957 (*IGCH* 2117)." *Pour Denyse: Divertissements Numismatiques*. Edited by S. Hurter and C. Arnold-Biucchi. Bern, Switzerland: Privately published, 2000. Pages 165-71. 2 pls.
Discusses some Athenian-type tetradrachms from three hoards: Lentini 1957, Delos 1910, and Tell el Athrib 1904.

4082 **Nicolet-Pierre, Hélène, and John H. Kroll.** "Athenian Tetradrachm Coinage of the Third Century B.C." *American Journal of Numismatics* 2nd ser., 2 (1990): 1-35. 6 pls.
A survey of the Athenian coins in twenty-four hoards of the third century B.C. General discussion of the style and chronology of the issues, followed by a listing and brief description of the hoards under examination. The coins were also analyzed for copper and gold impurities.

4083 "Numismatics Extraordinary!" *Spink Numismatic Circular* 12 (May 1904): 7578.
Discusses a triobol of Athens.

4084 **Oeconomides-Caramessini, Mando.** "The 1973 Peiraeus Hoard of Athenian Bronze Coins." *Archaiologika Analechta et Athenon* (Greece) 9 (1976): 220-3.

4085 ——— "Note on the Piraeus Hoard of 1902 of Athenian Plated Coins." *Coin Hoards* 7 (1985): 40-1.
Comments on a hoard of thousands of Athenian fourrée drachms. Other coins originally part of the hoard have been located. [Also see Kroll "The Piraeus 1902 Hoard" above].

4086 ——— "Contribution à l'Étude du Monnayage Athénien à l'Époque Classique: Le Trésor Trouvé au Pirée en 1977." *Revue Belge de Numismatique* (Belgium) 145 (1999): 17-20.

4087 **Oliver, Graham.** "The Politics of Coinage: Athens and Antigonus Gonatas." *Money and Its Uses in the Ancient Greek World*. Edited by A. Meadows and K. Shipton. Oxford: University Press, 2001. Pages 35-52. 1 pl.
Oliver analyzes the relationship between Athens and Antigonus Gonatas, King of the Macedonians. The role of coinage in this relationship is re-assessed along with the meaning of "freedom" when studying the Greek polis in the Hellenistic age. Gonatas defeated Athens, Sparta, and their allies in the Chremonidean War (ended 262 B.C.). Then, according to Eusebius, Gonatas returned freedom to Athens in 256. What did this mean? Oliver looks for evidence of Antigonus' influence over politics at Athens to determine whether a city can issue coins but not be free. Reviews the archaeological evidence from mining regions as a clue to continued silver production and coining activity at Athens during Antigonus' rule. Concludes that it appears Athens continued to produce coins between the late 260's and 229, and that Antigonus did little to disrupt the ways in which the Athenians organized their political structures. The return to freedom claimed by Eusebius likely refers to the removal of a military garrison from the Mouseion Hill in Athens.

4088 **Papaefthymiou, Eleni.** "A Study of One of the 'Exceptional' Decadrachms of Athens." *The Celator* 21, no. 4 (April 2007): 33, 38-9. Illus.
Discusses theories for the date of the Athenian decadrachms and points out slight stylistic variations in the known examples. Suggests all were struck between 465-404 B.C. Illustrates a specimen to be offered by Baldwins Auctions in April 2007.

4089 **Pászthory, Emmerich.** "Zwei Kleinmünzen aus Athen (1. Eine Plattierte Wappen-Kleinmünze; 2. Unediertes Kleinsilber aus Athen)." *Schweizer Münzblätter* (Switzerland) 113 (Febraury 1979). 7 pp., illus.

4090 **Picard, Olivier.** "Hippias et les Premières Chouettes Athéniennes." *Revue Numismatique* (France) 6th ser., 16 (1974): 151-4. [CS 2513]
Hippias and the first owls of Athens.

4090a **Ponting, Matthew, Haim Gitler, and Oren Tal.** "Who Minted Those Owls? Metallurgical Analysis of Athenian-Styled Tetradrachms found in Israel." *Revue Belge de Numismatique* (Belgium) 157 (2011): 117-34, incl. 2 pls.
The authors use the analytical results from inductively-coupled plasma atomic emission spectrometry (ICP-AES) and lead isotope analysis (Q-ICP-MS) of Athenian-style tetradrachms found in excavations in Israel, in order to investigate their origins. Some of these coins have been classified as Eastern imitations based on style, but the analysis suggests that many of these coins may actually be authentic Athenian issues. This is because they were in all probability produced from bullion that came from the silver mines of Laurion in Attica. Given the stylistic variability of the Athenian-style tetradrachms found in Israel, we can assume that they are representative of the "owls" circulating in the East in Achaemenid times.

4091 **Raven, E. J. P.** "Problems of the Earliest Owls of Athens." *Essays in Greek Coinage Presented to Stanley Robinson.* Edited by C. M. Kraay and G. K. Jenkins. Oxford: Clarendon Press, 1968. Pages 40-58. [CS 2515]
A review and assessment of recent studies of the early owl coinage, especially the works of Kraay ("The Archaic Owls of Athens" and "The Early Coinage of Athens") and Wallace ("The Early Coinages of Athens and Euboia"). Supports a date of 480/479 B.C. for the addition of the olive wreath to Athena's helmet (Wallace suggests 490 B.C.). Examines the problems involved in dating the early owls: the coinage is so uniform that there are few links with contemporary historical events; the low survival rate of the early owls results in difficulty in establishing die links and sequences. Discusses a statistical method for estimating the number of unrecorded dies based on the number of coins known from known dies, and shows how a low survival rate hampers the search for links. One reason for low survival is that these coins were frequently exported to the East, where they were often regarded as mere bullion and were melted. Many eastern hoards have been melted in modern times as well. Raven disputes the notion that changes in coin types generally coincide with political changes at a city. Discusses some problems encountered in interpreting hoard evidence and concludes that, so far, hoards have not provided a secure foundation for an exact dating of these coins. Discusses Athens' sources of silver and suggests the coinage of owls must have begun at a time when Athens had a secure and plentiful source of silver. Concludes that, for now, the first owls can only be dated to sometime between 520 and 512 B.C. [See W. McGovern "Missing Die Probabilities" under THE MINTING PROCESS for more information on the statistical method used here].

4092 **Rhodes, P. J.** "Solon and the Numismatists." *Numismatic Chronicle* 7th ser., 15 (1975): 1-11.
"*Ath. Pol.* 10 is correctly interpreted by Kraay, and should not be forced into agreement with Androtion. The quotation from a 'Solonian' law in *Ath. Pol.* 8.iii may be an embarrassment to the view that the earliest Athenian coinage is post-Solonian; that there were Solonian measures and weights should not be doubted, but Solon need not have changed Athens' standards." [P. Rhodes, *NL* 96]. [Also see related articles by M. Chambers, Crawford, Freeman, Gomme, Hill, Johnston, Kraay, and Milne. Also see Rhodes "A Commentary" below].

4093 ——— "Solon and the Numismatists: Postscript." *Numismatic Chronicle* 137 (1977): 152.
A correction to the author's previous comments on weight standards (see above).

4094 ——— *A Commentary on the Aristotelian Athenaion Politeia.* Oxford: Clarendon Press; New York: Oxford University Press, 1981.
[Also see related articles by M. Chambers, Crawford, Freeman, Gomme, Hill, Johnston, Kraay, and Milne. Also see Rhodes "Solon" above].

4095 **Roach, Steven R.** "Issues of Style in the Decadrachm of Athens." *The Centinel* (Journal of the Central States Numismatic Society) 49, no. 4 (winter 2001-2002): 15-22. Illus.
Examines the artistic style of the Athena head on the Athenian decadrachms. The usual explanation for the continued use of the archaic style on Athenian coinage is the need to maintain consistency of style in order to ensure the continued acceptance of Athenian coinage in foreign trade. Roach questions this explanation in regard to the decadrachms. After some stylistic comparisons with vase paintings and sculptures, he concludes that the archaic style of the decadrachm's Athena was intended to maintain the idealized image of Athena and to reinforce the unaging constancy of the gods themselves.

4096 **Robinson, David M.** "A New Attic Onos or Epinetron." *American Journal of Archaeology* 49, no. 4 (October-December 1945): 480-90. Illus.
Examines an onos (a ceramic covering placed over the knee to protect a woman's clothing while preparing wool for spinning) in the author's collection. The onos is decorated with a female head. The head is compared to similar heads on Athenian coins and, based on the similarity in styles, the author dates the onos to ca. 490-480 B.C. and attributes it to the Diosphos Painter.

4097 **Robinson, Edward S. G.** "The Tell El-Mashkuta Hoard of Athenian Tetradrachms." *Numismatic Chronicle* 6th ser., 7 (1947): 115-21. 1 pl.
A hoard of more than 6000 Athenian tetradrachms was found in Egypt, of which the author examined 262 coins. Discusses the style and chronology of the pieces.

4098 ——— "Some Problems in the Late Fifth Century Coinage of Athens." *Museum Notes* 9 (1960): 1-15. 2 pls. [CS 2517]
Robinson criticizes the monotony of the early fifth century coinage of Athens and discounts the theory that the unchanging types were intended to avoid hurting the coinage's role in international trade. Discusses the effects of the Athenian Currency Decree on the coinage of her allies (the near cessation of silver coinage), but states that Athens was unable to fill the void with her own coins. Reviews the political situation in the late fifth century B.C., and describes the changes in Athenian coinage after Athens' defeat at Syracuse in 415 B.C. Describes the small bronze *kollybos*, which some have identified as tessarae but the author believes was a coin which was needed in these difficult economic times (Athens suffered from a lack of dues from her allies, and the conflicts with Sparta led to decreased output from the Laurion mines). Silver-plated bronze coins appeared at Athens, along with silver drachms and gold staters with slightly varied types. Silver fractional issues then appeared, also with varied reverse types. Robinson discusses the relative values of gold, silver, and bronze. Shows that the debased coins circulated while the good coins were hoarded. Bronze obols and silver diobols with marks of value and the unusual inscription AΘH appeared. The author quotes passages from Aristophanes to support his identification of the denominations of the small marked bronzes and the identification of the kollybos as a coin. Pure silver coinage soon resumed.

4099 **Robinson, Edward S. G., and M. Jessop Price.** "An Emergency Coinage of Timotheos." *Numismatic Chronicle* 7th ser., 7 (1967): 1-6. Illus. [CS 2518]
"An issue of bronze coins previously believed to be the emergency issue of Athens at the end of the Peloponnesian War is re-attributed to the Athenian general Timotheos; it was struck during his siege of Olynthus in 363-359 B.C." [Robinson and Price, *NL* 82]

4100 **Rutter, N. Keith.** "Early Greek Coinage and the Influence of the Athenian State." *Coinage and Society in Britain and Gaul: Some Current Problems.* Edited by Barry Cunliffe. London: The Council for British Archaeology, 1981. Pages 1-9.
Discusses the Wappenmünzen coinage of Athens and the role it played in the economy of the sixth century B.C., and the change to the owl tetradrachms. Suggests the reasons for the appearance of these coins is related to internal Athenian politics, rather than the needs of external trade. Discusses hoards of Athenian coins found in south Italy and Sicily and attempts to find a reason for the circulation of Athenian coins abroad. Presents examples of state payments which required coinage. Briefly discusses the introduction of bronze coinage in Magna Graecia.

4101 **Salveson, Harald.** "Didrachms of Athens: Among the Most Sought after of Greek Coins." *The Celator* 10, no. 2 (February 1996): 6-7. Illus., tables.

Chester Starr listed thirty-five Athenian didrachms in his *Athenian Coinage 480-449 B.C.* and he knew of one other. Since then, six more didrachms have appeared. Salveson lists all forty-two coins in tables indicating their present locations (when known), Starr groups/numbers, and sales catalogue appearances.

4102 **Schönert-Geiss, Edith.** "Die Geldzirkulation Attikas." *Klio* (Germany) 56 (1974): 377-414. [CS 2520]

The circulation of Athenian gold coinage.

4103 **Seltman, Charles T.** *Athens: Its History and Coinage before the Persian Invasion.* Cambridge: University Press, 1924. Reprints, Bologna: Forni, 1967; Chicago: Ares Publishers, 1974. 228 pp., 24 pls., map. [CS 2521]

Covers the history and coinage of Athens until 480 B.C. Begins with the pre-coinage era and progresses through the introduction of coinage at Athens and the reforms of Solon, and continues through the period of the Persian invasion. Includes chapters on denominations and weights, and mines and trade. This is followed by a catalogue of 490 Athenian coins, fully described and illustrated. Die links are noted. [An extensive review by E. S. G. Robinson appears in *Numismatic Chronicle* 5th ser., 4 (1924): 329-41. Also see Kraay "The Archaic Owls" above, and van Buchem "Family Coat-of-Arms" under TYPES].

4104 ———— "On the 'Style' of Early Athenian Coins." *Numismatic Chronicle* 6th ser., 6 (1946): 97-110. 3 pls. [CS 3572]

"To demonstrate the continuous and growing artistic activity in Athens, Seltman gives an interesting decade-by-decade summary of the best-known productions with an outline of contemporary historical events during the late seventh and sixth centuries. The great majority of the artists worthy of the name in sixth century Athens, as well as later, must have been and obviously were employed in the fields of major art. Except for a few special issues, no efforts were wasted on a fine coinage and the few superb dies were, for the most part, happy accidents. For this reason, just any coin cannot be contrasted with other forms of art as a means of comparative dating. The style of the best coins is clearly related to contemporary sculpture and painting, but the many pieces which in the author's opinion were struck from dies produced by 'blacksmiths' and 'plumbers,' cannot be dated with any accuracy by the comparative method. Many Athenian coins which have been claimed to be 'crudely early' are 'just simply bad.'" [*NL* 5]

4105 ———— "Peisistratus of Athens." *History Today* 5, no. 7 (July 1955): 438-45. Illus.

"Using archaeological and numismatic material to illuminate his article, Mr. Seltman has studied and re-evaluated the two most significant events in the early career of Peisistratus. In the first place the author has shown that the recovery of Salamis by the Athenians in 570 B.C. was due primarily to the strategy and tactics of Peisistratus, rather than of Solon. His evidence that Herodotus' story which ascribes the victory to Solon is the result of skillful propaganda on the part of the Alcmaeonidae, and therefore false, is derived primarily from a drinking-cup (ca. 490 B.C.) which commemorates the event. The obvious hero of the battle has on his armor the emblem of the clan of Peisistratus, the forepart of a horse. And secondly, even more important for the numismatist, Mr. Seltman has shown that it was Peisistratus who issued the first coins in the history of the world to have types on both sides and to bear several letters of the city's name. They were issued in 566 B.C., at the time of the first Greater Panathenaia which he instituted. And Mr. Seltman also claims that Peisistratus was the first man in history to realize, and to utilize, the propaganda value of coinage." [J. Nadell, *NL* 34]

4106 **Seltman, E. J.** "A Tetradrachm with the Name of Hippias." *Numismatic Chronicle* 4th ser., 8 (1908): 278-80. Illus.

Illustrates a tetradrachm of Athens in the McClean Collection. On the obverse of the coin, the letters Π I appear in front of Athena's head. The letters may have been added after the dies had been in use for some time. Seltman suggests the letters refer to Hippias. He suggests Hippias had his name engraved on the die while he was besieged on the Acropolis immediately before his banishment. [Also see E. Babelon "Une Obolos au Nom d'Hippias" above].

4107 **Shapiro, H. A.** "From Athena's Owl to the Owl of Athens." *Nomodeiktes: Greek Studies in Honor of Martin Ostwald.* Edited by Ralph M. Rosen and Joseph Farrell. Ann Arbor: University of Michigan Press, 1993. Pages 213-24.

Examines the relationship of Athena and her owl, based on an owl and inscription on an amphora in Munich. Compares the owl to the owl on early Athenian tetradrachms. Comments on chronology and the standardization of the owl as a symbol of Athens.

4108 **Shear, Josephine P.** "Excavations in the Athenian Agora: The Coins of Athens." *Hesperia* 2 (1933): 231-78. 1 pl.

"Describes the processes used to clean and preserve the coins, 4350 of which were found during the first season's excavations. The account which follows is not a straightforward catalogue, but a survey of the development of Athenian coinage, based on material from the neighborhood of the Royal Stoa. Seltman and Sundwall provide a framework for the period of Greek independence. Later coinage is arranged from the time of Hadrian onwards, but with some misgivings. Appendixes list the statues, ancient monuments, mythological subjects, historical events and symbolical representations shown on the coins discussed." [J. R. Jones, *NIAJAH*].

4109 **Shear, Theodore L.** "The Campaign of 1936." *Hesperia* 6 (1937): 333-81. 9 pls., illus.

Discusses the excavations of the Athenian Agora. "On pp. 357-8 some coins of unusual interest are noted: a very early 'amphora' coin of Athens, a bronze Imperial issue with types of Athena head and tripod, the legend showing that it was struck by Megara, and a bronze with agonistic table as type, struck for the festival of the Eleusinia." [J. R. Jones, *NIAJAH*]

4109a **Sheedy, Kenneth A., and Damian B. Gore.** "Asyut 422, Seltman Group P, and Imitation of Attic Coins." *Revue Belge de Numismatique et de Sigillographie* (Belgium) 157 (2011): 37-54.

The Attic tetradrachm, Asyut 422, was identified by Price and Waggoner as a contemporary imitation. Seltman placed a die-linked example in his group P. His arguments for the attribution of this group to a mint set up by an Athenian colony at Chalcis on Euboea are challenged. Compositional analyses using X-ray fluorescence spectrometry are presented, which indicate that Asyut 422 was not made of silver from Laurion.

4110 **Six, Jean Pieter.** "Some Undescribed Greek Coins." *American Journal of Numismatics* 30, no. 3 (January 1896): 72-5.

A translation (from the original French) of a portion of a paper which Six contributed to the *Numismatic Chronicle.* Describes coins attributed to the alliances of Athens with Lampsacus, and Athens with the Arcadians. Discusses their chronology.

4111 **Smyth, Melissa D.** "Athena and the Parthenon: The Spread of Greek Culture and Power through Coins." *The Centinel* (Journal of the Central States Numismatic Society) 54, no. 3 (fall 2006): 20-25. Illus.

Describes the statue of Athena Parthenos that stood in the Parthenon at Athens. Describes how the symbols of Greek culture were spread throughout the Hellenistic world through the image of Athena and the depiction of her statue on coins.

4112 **Spiegel, Sam.** "The Athenian Emergency Issue of the Peloponnesian War." *The Celator* 22, no. 12 (December 2008): 22-30, 40. Illus.
The author summarizes the events of the Peloponnesian War, fought 431-404 B.C. The war had a devastating impact on the Athenian navy, and the city had to take extraordinary measures to raise the funds necessary to rebuild its fleet. It was around this time that the plated "fourree" tetradrachms appeared at Athens. Spiegel believes the coins were created for use by merchants within the city and were produced in an effort to stimulate the local economy at a time of monetary shortage. Discusses the possible methods of manufacture of the fourrees.

4113 **Starck, Jeff.** "Athens Decadrachm Sets Record: $575,000 Represents Highest Price for Ancient Greek Coin." *Coin World* (February 5, 2007): 103, 105. Illus.
Report on an Athenian dekadrachm which was sold by Classical Numismatic Group in their *Triton X* auction held on January 9, 2007. Summarizes the bidding and summarizes some theories for the date and occasion for the dekadrachm's issuance based on notes from the auction catalogue. [Also see Wetterstrom "CNG Sets Record" below].

4114 ——— "Auction Firms Withdraw Highlight Coin: Athenian Decadrachm Deemed Deceptive Forgery." *Coin World* (May 9, 2011): 1, 20. Illus.
Reports that an Athenian decadrachm was withdrawn from the April 14, 2011 auction conducted by Gemini Numismatics and Heritage Auction Galleries. The piece was determined to be a forgery. It had been promoted as the finest-known specimen and had a pre-auction estimate of $875,000. [This specimen was not listed in Fischer-Bossert's book *The Athenian Decadrachm*].

4115 **Starr, Chester G.** *Athenian Coinage 480-449 B.C.* Oxford: Clarendon Press, 1970. Reprint, New York: Sanford J. Durst, 1980. 96 pp., 26 pls. [CS 2522]
Presents a new chronological arrangement of the coinage of Athens between 480-449 B.C., revising the chronologies proposed by Svoronos and Seltman. Rejects the long-held view that the stagnant design on Athenian coins was intended to ensure continued acceptability in the marketplace. Presents a list of 217 die varieties classified chronologically and stylistically into five groups. For each group, Starr presents a stylistic analysis followed by a listing of varieties including weight, die axis, and a description of dies and concluding with an assessment of the factors contributing to his dating. Includes a chapter describing Athenian history and coinage after 449 B.C. Concludes with comments on Athenian mint operations, coin weights, and history. Points out that coinage was not as plentiful during the period under study as it was in the preceding and subsequent periods, a fact he attributes to financial problems at Athens. Hoard evidence supports his conclusions. Includes a brief description of hoards cited in the text, and some notes on a spectrographic analysis of the coinage metals. [Reviewed by T. Hackens in *Revue Belge de Numismatique et de Sigillographie* (Belgium) 117 (1971): 312-4, by C. M. Kraay in *Numismatic Chronicle* 7th ser., 12 (1972): 313-7, and by S. Eddy in *American Journal of Philology* 94, no. 3 (fall 1973): 308-10. Also see Starr "New Specimens" below].

4116 ——— "Athenian Coinage Before and After 449 B.C." *Journal of Numismatic Fine Arts* 1, no. 4 (May-June 1971): 72-3. Illus.
Fifth century Athenian coins are generally dated to the broad period 480-404 B.C. Starr provides some simple guidelines for segregating this vast coinage into two groups: those struck before 449 B.C. and those struck after 449. Discusses why the post-449 mintages were so much higher than the pre-449 mintages. Describes some of the variations in style commonly seen on the post-449 issues.

4117 ——— "A Sixth Century Athenian Tetradrachm Used to Seal a Clay Tablet from Persepolis." *Numismatic Chronicle* 136 (1976): 219-22. Illus.
"A sealing on a clay tablet found at Persepolis which is dated to the period 509-494 B.C. was made from an Athenian coin of C. T. Seltman, *Athens: Its History and Coinage*, group H. This group must accordingly be placed at or before 500 B.C." [C. Starr, *NL* 97]. [Also see Root "Evidence from Persepolis" under PERSIA].

4118 ——— "New Specimens of Athenian Coinage, 480-449 B.C." *Numismatic Chronicle* 142 (1982): 129-34. 3 pls.
"Thirty-six examples of Athenian coinage from 480-449 B.C., having appeared since the publication of the author's last book on the subject, are catalogued. The view that Athens' mint increased its activity during and after the 450's is reinforced." [C. Starr, *NL* 110]

4119 **Stevens, Gorham P.** "A Silver Three-Obol Piece from Athens." *Archaeology* 4, no. 2 (June 1951): 104-5. Illus.
"An Athenian triobol, dating probably from the time of Clisthenes, was recently found in Aegina: it bears the helmeted head of Athena on the obverse and the head of Athena Ergane, unhelmeted, on the reverse. Svoronos has published the type in *Les Monnaies d'Athènes*; to the author's knowledge, no examples of it have been discovered since. Enlarged photographs show that the obverse and reverse dies, both finely executed, are the work of two different die-cutters." [B. Emmons, *NL* 18]

4120 **St. Pasteur, Julian.** "The Old Style Drachm of Athens: The Politics behind It." *Ancient* 25 (July/August 1991): 12-3. Illus.
A brief discussion of the introduction of the Athenian "owls" and the historical forces that precipitated the coinage.

4121 **Svoronos, Joannes N.** "Laurion." *Journal International d'Archéologie Numismatique* (Greece) 17 (1915): 53-70. 1 pl.
"(1) The Athenian mint was at Laurium rather than in the city and was under the protection of Apollo Stephanephorus (a relief of a victor from the Acropolis is claimed as a representation of this Apollo). Description of remains of shrine at Laurium in which silver may have been stored. (2) Literary sources are given for the revolts of the mine-workers in 133 and 104-2 B.C. Some New Style tetradrachms have monograms which can be read as ΛΑΥΠΙΑΜΕΤΑΛΛΑ, and are assigned to the revolt, while those with ΑΘΕ Ο ΔΗΜΟΣ are given to the period immediately after its final suppression." [J. R. Jones, *AIJIAN*]

4122 ——— *Trésor de la Numismatique Grecque Ancienne: Les Monnaies d'Athènes.* Three parts. Munich: S^{té} A^{me} F. Bruckmann Éditeurs, 1923-26. Reprint, Bologna: Forni, 1967. 19 pp., 114 pls. [CS 2524]
Begun by Svoronos and completed by Pick. "The most useful reference on Athenian coins ever published as it included illustrations of every coin that was in all known public or private collections at the time, from 'owls' through the Imperial period." [D. Kroh, *ACRR*]. [Also see Svoronos *Corpus of the Ancient Coins of Athens* below].

4123 ——— "La Monnaie d'Or Attique." *Journal International d'Archéologie Numismatique* (Greece) 21 (1927): 147-70.

"Electrum coins are attributed to Peisistratus, and gold issues to 407 B.C., 297-5 B.C. (Lachares) and 86 B.C. (Aristion)." [J. R. Jones, *AIJIAN*]

4124 ———— *Corpus of the Ancient Coins of Athens.* Chicago: Argonaut, 1975. 264 pp., 229 pls. [CS 2524a]
A revised reprint of *Les Monnaies d'Athènes*, published 1923-6. Covers the Athenian coinage from the Wappenmünzen to Roman Imperial bronzes, and including tesserae, Eleusianian issues, coins of Delos, countermarked Athenian tetradrachms, eastern imitations, Athenian-style coins from Crete, and forgeries. Minimal descriptions and commentary. Plate captions and indices are in English. Illustrates over 4500 coins. [Also see J. H. Kroll "A Chronology of Early Athenian Bronze Coinage" above. Based on new evidence, Kroll criticizes Svoronos' dating of Athenian bronze coinage as "arbitrary and unreliable"].

4125 **Tebben, Gerald.** "Athenian Tetradrachms Workhorses of International Coinage before Rome." *Coin World* (June 19, 1995): 44. Illus.
A commentary on the use and value of the Athenian tetradrachm. Includes numerous references to prices of everyday items in Greek lands in ancient times.

4126 ———— "Solving a Mystery: Theories Abound for Issue of Greek Decadrachm." *Coin World* (March 19, 2001): 68. Illus.
In this installment of his "Coin Lore" column, Tebben focuses on the Athenian decadrachm. He suggests the coin may have been issued to celebrate Athens' victory at the Battle of Marathon. Briefly discusses the sale of the Nelson Bunker Hunt specimen and the finding of the "Decadrachm Hoard."

4127 **Theodorou, Jerry.** "Athenian Silver Coins: 6th–3rd Centuries B.C., The Current Interpretation." *Μνημη Martin Jessop Price.* Edited by A. P. Tzamalis and M. J. A. Tzamali. Bibliotheca 5. Athens: The Hellenic Numismatic Society, 1996. Pages 51-81. Illus.
A guide to identifying and dating Athenian silver coins of the sixth century B.C. down to the early third century B.C. The author summarizes the latest thinking on Athenian coinage and describes the historical context of the issues. Reviews prior scholarship related to the coin types and their chronology. Then provides detailed descriptions of variations in types, denominations, and weights. Illustrated by sixty-nine coin types. Includes a brief bibliography.

4128 **Thompson, Dorothy Burr.** "The Golden Nikai Reconsidered." *Hesperia* 13 (1944): 173-209. Illus.
An examination of the golden statues of Nike placed on the Athenian acropolis in celebration of Athenian military victories in the fifth and fourth centuries B.C. The statues were later melted down to make coins. Illustrates Athenian gold coins as well as staters of Alexander bearing Nike on the reverse. Reviews the evidence for how the statues were constructed and the amount of gold used in their construction. Discusses the artistic style of the statues. [Also see Wesley Thompson "The Golden Nikai" below].

4129 **Thompson, Homer A.** "Excavations in the Athenian Agora: 1953." *Hesperia* 23, no. 1 (January-March 1954): 31-67. 6 pls.
"One of the early buildings along the south side of the Agora square has been tentatively identified as the mint of Athens. The rectangular structure, apparently dating from the second half of the fifth century B.C., is divided into rooms of various sizes, within which were found remains of two furnaces and at least two water basins. A small mass of bronze was discovered during the excavation of this building. Upon cleaning, it was found to consist of eight complete discs, all showing chisel marks, two fragmentary discs and the tail end of a rod from which discs had been cut. Such discs have long been recognized as coin flans. Analysis of one of the broken pieces from the Agora shows a composition similar to that found in Athenian bronze coinage of the late Hellenistic and early Imperial periods." [M. Thompson, *NL* 33]

4130 ———— "Activities in the Athenian Agora: 1954." *Hesperia* 24 (1955): 50-71. 8 pls., illus.
"On p. 55 it is reported that further excavations have shown that the mint was larger than had been supposed. On pp. 69-70 a pair of bronze measures of kotyle size is discussed. The fact that they were discovered near the mint suggests the possibility that official weights and measures were made there." [J. R. Jones, *NIAJAH*]

4131 ———— "Activities in the Athenian Agora: 1955." *Hesperia* 25 (1956): 46-68. 16 pls., illus.
"On p. 53 it is reported that the mint was even larger than had been supposed after the two previous excavations." [J. R. Jones, *NIAJAH*]

4132 ———— "Activities in the Athenian Agora: 1959." *Hesperia* 29, no. 4 (October-December 1960): 327-68. Illus., 8 pls.
Discusses the Southeast Temple which was constructed on a site once occupied by a building tentatively identified as the mint. The excavations in 1959 yielded eight blanks for the making of bronze coins, all imbedded in the ancient floor in one of the rooms of the southwest block. [Summarized from *NL* 57]. [Also see M. Lang *The Athenian Citizen* above].

4133 **Thompson, Margaret.** "Some Athenian 'Cleruchy' Money." *Hesperia* 10, no. 3 (July-September 1941): 199-236. 2 pls.
Examines the bronze coins which Svoronos attributed to Peparethus and Skiatos, as well as the Eleusis issues with Demeter and a kerchnos on the reverse. All bear the letters AΘE. Svoronos suggested they were issued by Athenian dependencies during the period 255-229 B.C. Thompson re-considers this attribution. Reviews the history of the period. Discusses these coins in relation to the New Style series of coins at Athens. Attributes the coins to Athens. Includes a table showing the metallic content of the coins and a listing of such coins found in hoards.

4134 ———— "Coins for the Eleusinia." *Hesperia* 11 (1942): 213-29. 1 pl.
Examines the large group of bronze coins bearing Eleusinian divinities and inscribed ΕΛΕΥΣΙ or AΘE. Some scholars have attributed the coins to Eleusis, but it is highly unusual that an Attic deme would have issued autonomous money. Thompson suggests these were a festival coinage, and suggests they were struck by the Athens mint for the periodic observance of the Greater Eleusinia. She examines the types and symbols in comparison with other Athenian coins. Discusses chronology and assigns the coins to five groups: (1) c. 325-295 B.C., (2) 294-288 B.C., (3) 287-263 B.C., (4) 262-230 B.C., and (5) 229-30 B.C. [Also see Kroll "Athenian Bronze Coinage and the Propagation of the Eleusinian Mysteries" above].

4135 ———— "The 'Owls' of Athens." *Archaeology* 3, no. 3 (autumn 1950): 151-4. Illus. [CS 2525]
"A popular paper dealing with the consistent use of the Athena head and owl types on Athenian tetradrachms from the early sixth century B.C. to the time of Augustus." [*NL* 16]

4136 ———— "A Hoard of Athenian Fractions." *Museum Notes* 7 (1957): 1-11. 4 pls. [CS 3295]

Thompson discusses a hoard consisting of eighty-nine fractions found in Piraeus in 1956. The coins include drachms, triobols, diobols, obols, tritartemoria, and hemiobols. Discusses the Athenian gold staters and fractions of ca. 295 B.C. as stylistic comparative material from the Hellenistic period. Suggests ca. 330-290 B.C. for the burial, and based on the stylistic similarity with the gold coins, perhaps 315-295 B.C. would be justified.

4137 ——— "The Grain-Ear Drachms of Athens." *Centennial Publication of the American Numismatic Society.* Edited by Harald Ingholt. New York: American Numismatic Society, 1958. Pages 651-71. 3 pls. [CS 2528]

The author studies the New Style drachms marked on the reverse with an ear of grain next to the owl. An unusual feature of these drachms is the lack of monograms or names of magistrates. Also, they are stylistically different from the grain-ear tetradrachms. Thompson presents a table of Athenian drachm issues, including three groups of grain-ear pieces. She also presents a catalogue of grain-ear drachms, along with a discussion of sequence, chronology, and weights. She assigns the coins to 180-165 B.C. The drachms are compared to the tetradrachm issues of this period. The author concludes that the coinage was something apart from the routine responsibility of the annual mint magistrates and was connected in some way with grain. Perhaps the coins are evidence of three distributions of grain to the Athenian people. She suggests that gifts of grain may have been received from Antiochus IV, Timarchus, and Nikagoras, and that the grain was sold and the drachms were distributed to the people. The citizens were free to redeem their drachms for grain, or to spend the money on other goods.

4138 **Thompson, Wesley E.** *The Athenian Gold and Bronze Coinages of the Dekeleian War.* Ph.D. dissertation, Princeton University, 1963. 171 pp.

4139 ——— "The Date of the Athenian Gold Coinage." *American Journal of Philology* 86, no. 2 (April 1965): 159-74.

Hellanicus said that Athens minted gold coinage during the archonship of Antigenes (407/6). However, Ferguson (*The Treasures of Athena*, Cambridge, 1932) argued that the gold coinage took place in 406/5 during the archonship of Kallias. Through an analysis of ancient inscriptions, Thompson attempts to show that the inscription upon which Ferguson mainly relied cannot be used to disprove Hellanicus' statement.

4140 ——— "The Functions of the Emergency Coinages of the Peloponnesian War." *Mnemosyne: Bibliotheca Classica Batava* (Germany) 4th ser., 19, no. 4 (1966): 337-43.

Near the end of the Peloponnesian War, Athens began to mint both gold and bronze coins because the city's reserves of silver had been almost exhausted. Thompson shows that gold continued to be minted and employed by the magistrates of Athens even after the introduction of bronze, and that the two issues had distinct functions: the gold served as foreign exchange, the bronze as a token coinage for domestic use. The author relies primarily on the evidence of inscriptions.

4141 ——— "The Golden Nikai and the Coinage of Athens." *Numismatic Chronicle* 7th ser., 10 (1970): 1-6. Illus. [CS 2531]

"A review of epigraphic evidence indicates that the golden statues of Nike provided fourteen talents for the Athenian gold coinage of the Decelean War. It is impossible to determine how much gold was coined from other sources." [W. Thompson, *NL* 85]. [Also see D. B. Thompson "The Golden Nikai" above].

4142 **Touratsoglou, Ioannis.** "Who Brought the Owl to Athens? (Aristophanes, *The Birds*, 301)." Translated by Marion J. A. Tzamali. *Nomismatika Khronika* (Greece) 18 (1999): 20-2. Illus.

A brief discussion of the Athenian dekadrachms, examining their dates of issue, stylistic variations, number of specimens known, the "Dekadrachm Hoard," and the acquisition of a specimen for the Numismatic Museum of Athens.

4143 **Trevett, Jeremy.** "Coinage and Democracy at Athens." *Money and Its Uses in the Ancient Greek World.* Edited by Andrew Meadows and Kristy Shipton. Oxford: University Press, 2001. Pages 23-34.

Explores the relationship between coinage and democracy in late archaic and classical Athens. Trevett contends that certain features of Athens' coins can best be understood in the light of Athens' democratic ideologies and practices. Suggests that policies of payment for serving in public offices led to an increase in minting activity. Argues that a democracy cannot function without the use of money. Suggests that the change from Wappenmünzen to "owls" may be tied to the introduction of the democracy. Trevett suggests that the lack of magistrates' names from the classical period owls can be attributed to Athens' democratic ideals. The unchanging types also point toward democracy—rather than commercial reasons—as a sign of stability and continuity. Suggests that alteration of coinage was linked with tyranny in the Greek mind. Explores reasons for Athens' relatively unattractive coins which were carelessly engraved in comparison to coins of some other cities. Suggests that in a democracy, there was no incentive to produce beautiful coins.

4144 **Tzamalis, Anastasios P.** "Carrying Owls from Athens: An Old Story that Speaks for Itself." *Nomismatika Khronika* (Greece) 17 (1998): 127-33. Illus.

Discusses three documents concerning an Athenian decadrachm. Reproduces a letter from George Finlay (an Englishman living at Athens) to the British Museum offering to secure an Athenian decadrachm in the possession of a jeweler. Also reproduces the response from Edwin Hawkins of the British Museum expressing interest, but only at less that the asking price. The coin was eventually purchased by von Prokesch-Osten and now resides in the Berlin State Museum.

4145 **Vagi, David.** "The Owls of Athens." *Numismatist* 119, no. 4 (April 2006): 78-80. Illus.

A short discussion of the coinage of Athens, from the Wappenmünzen to the New Style series.

4146 **van Alfen, Peter G.** "Two Unpublished Hoards and Other 'Owls' from Egypt." *American Journal of Numismatics* 2nd ser., 14 (2002): 59-71. 5 pls.

Publishes parts of two reassembled hoards, encompassing twenty-four Athenian tetradrachms, in the American Numismatic Society collection. Both hoards are believed to have been found in Egypt in the 1920's and are referred to here as Nahman's hoard (nine owls, none of which bear cuts or countermarks) and Endicott's hoard (fifteen owls, all heavily countermarked). The coins were likely buried ca. 350 B.C. van Alfen also publishes nine owls from the Tell El-Maskhouta hoard (*IGCH* 1649) and twenty-five miscellaneous owls likely with an Egyptian provenance. Discusses the use and purpose of countermarks. Suggests that the quatrefoil countermark found on some of the coins may have served an administrative purpose, perhaps for internal accounting by an organization like the state treasury.

4146a ——— "Mechanisms for the Imitation of Athenian Coinage: Dekeleia and Mercenaries Reconsidered." *Revue Belge de Numismatique* (Belgium) 157 (2011): 55-93.

4147 **Visonà, Paolo.** "A Hoard of 4th Century Athenian Tetradrachms from Nablus." *Quaderni Ticinesi. Numismatica e Antichità Classiche* (Switzerland) 27 (1998): 141-9. Illus.
"The hoard of seventeen tetradrachms was uncovered between 1890 and 1891 at Nablus in Samaria and is now at the Kelsey Museum of Archaeology at the University of Michigan. The author proposes a burial date of 333-330 B.C." [A. Carignani, NL 142]

4148 **Wade-Gery, H. T.** "The Question of Tribute in 449/8." *Hesperia* 14 (1945): 212-29.
Through an examination of epigraphical and historical evidence, the author explores the theory that no tribute was collected by Athens in 449/8 B.C. The author analyzes various decrees related to the collection of tribute.

4149 **Wallace, William P.** "The Public Seal of Athens." *The Phoenix* (Canada) 3, no. 2 (autumn 1949): 70-3.
Discusses the public seal which Aristotle says was in the possession of the president of the Athenian Boule. The author suggests that Athens did not have a public seal until just before the middle of the fourth century B.C. Says there is no evidence that other Greek cities had official seals at an earlier date. Mentions state badges used on coins. [See D. M. Lewis "The Public Seal" above for another opinion. Also see Wallace's response, "Note" in *The Phoenix* 9 (1955): 34].

4150 **Wetterstrom, Kerry K., ed.** "CNG Sets Record Price for a Greek Coin: $575,000." *The Celator* 21, no. 3 (March 2007): 35. Illus.
Announces the sale at auction of an Athenian dekadrachm for $575,000. Provides historical background for the coin. [Also see Starck "Athens Decadrachm Sets Record" above].

4151 **Wilkinson, John S.** "Athenian Silver Coin Fractions, 520 B.C.-290 B.C." *Canadian Numismatic Journal* (Canada) 14, no. 6 (June 1969): 187-90, 196. Illus. Reprinted in *Cornucopiæ* (publication of The Ancient Coin Society, Canada) 1, no. 2 (November 1972): 18-25. Illus. [CS 2534]
Wilkinson examines the weights of Athenian fractional coins and suggests that the unusual number of fractional denominations of the Athenian standard coin was intended to facilitate exchange with other currencies on different standards and more specifically, that half of the Athenian denominations were equivalent to Corinthian and half to Aeginetan denominations. This equivalence was precise for the Corinthian issues, but only approximate for the Aeginetan coins. [The version of this article which was published in *Cornucopiæ* includes footnotes].

4152 **Williams, Roderick T.** "The 'Owls' and Hippias." *Numismatic Chronicle* 7th ser., 6 (1966): 9-13. [CS 2535]
"The theory that the first Athenian 'owls' were struck by Hippias is supported by the evidence of sculpture and vase-painting. Before ca. 525 the crest on Athena's helmet was always of the split type which stands away from the bowl; after this date the ridge crest was introduced and tended to displace the stilt type. On the 'owls' with the exception of one example (Seltman's Group H, which on Kraay's reconstruction was the earliest) the ridge crest is uniform. The conclusion is that the earliest 'owls' should not antedate ca. 525." [R. Williams, NL 80]

4153 **Woodward, Arthur M.** "A Note on the First Issue of Gold Coins at Athens." *Numismatic Chronicle* 4th ser., 11 (1911): 351-6.
Discusses an incomplete inscription dating to the period 385-375 B.C., which is a fragment of a record of the sacred objects preserved in the Parthenon. Woodward attempts to restore the missing parts of the inscription, and concludes that it confirms the commonly accepted date of Athens' first gold coins (407-406 B.C.). Furthermore, Woodward suggests that this first issue of gold coins, and perhaps the second issue as well, was actually struck within the walls of the Parthenon.

Also see: Babelon "Les Origines de la Monnaie à Athènes" under ATTICA—WAPPENMÜNZEN; Barry and Beasley "The Most Popular Coin" under COLLECTING GUIDES; Beazley "Bakchos-Rings" under TYPES; Beckman "An Athenian Coin from Persian Palestine" under PALESTINE—PHILISTIA; Bingen "Le Trésor Monétaire Thorikos" under HOARDS; Buttrey "Pharaonic Imitations" under EGYPT—PRE-PTOLEMAIC PERIOD; Caley and Deebel "Bronze Blanks" under METALLURGY; Calhoun *Business Life of Ancient Athens* under GENERAL WORKS—GREEK; Cohen "Elasticity of the Money Supply at Athens" under GENERAL WORKS—GREEK; Conophagos, Badecca, and Tsaimou "La Technique Athenienne" under THE MINTING PROCESS; Dattari "Comments on a Hoard of Athenian Tetradrachms" under HOARDS; Davidson and Thompson "Small Objects" under HOARDS; Dinsmoor "The Burning" under THE MINTING PROCESS; Earle-Fox "The Early Coinages" under ORIGINS OF COINAGE; Eddy "The Value of the Cyzicene Stater" under MYSIA—AUTONOMOUS CITIES; Elsen "Le Grain d'Orge" under METROLOGY; Gardner "On Some Coins of Syria and Bactria" under BACTRIA; Gardner "The Earliest Coins" under ORIGINS OF COINAGE; Gitler "A Hacksilber and Cut Athenian Tetradrachm Hoard from the Environs of Samaria" under HOARDS; Havelock "The Archaic" under ART; Head "On Himyarite" under ARABIA; Hopper "The Mines" under METALLURGY; Huber "Essay" under HOARDS.

Johnston "An International Managed Currency" under MYSIA—AUTONOMOUS CITIES; Jones "The Value of Gold" under METROLOGY; Jones "The Laurion Silver Mines" under METALLURGY; Jongkees "Athenian Coin Dies from Egypt" under THE MINTING PROCESS; Kleiner "The 1926 Piraeus Hoard" under HOARDS; Kosmetatou "Commentary of the Inventory Lists" under HOARDS; Kourouniotes and Thompson "The Pynx" under HOARDS; Kraay "Greek Coinage and War" under GENERAL WORKS—GREEK; Kraay "Hoards, Small Change" under ORIGINS OF COINAGE; Kraay and Emeleus *The Composition* under METALLURGY; Kroll "Bronze Weights" under METROLOGY; Kroll "Observations on Monetary Instruments" under ORIGINS OF COINAGE; Lang "On Coins Discovered" under HOARDS; Losada "The Aetolian Indemnity" under HOARDS.

G. Macdonald "Athenian and Macedonian Coins" under NORTHWEST INDIA; Martin "A Third-Century B.C. Hoard" under HOARDS; Meadows "Athenian Coin Dies from Egypt" under THE MINTING PROCESS; Metcalf *Oxford Handbook of Greek and Roman Coinage* under GENERAL WORKS—GREEK; Miller *Supplementum Inscriptionum Atticarum* under EPIGRAPHY; Milne "The Beni Hasan Coin-Hoard" under HOARDS; Milne "A Hoard of Coins from Egypt" under HOARDS; Milne "Medallion" under TYPES; Mørkholm "Some Reflections" under GENERAL WORKS—GREEK; Naster "Méthode de Métrologie" under METROLOGY; Nicolet-Pierre and Amandry "Un Nouveau Trésor…Pseudo-Atheniennes" under BACTRIA; Noe "The Corinth Hoard" under HOARDS; Pokras "A New Iconography" under MYSIA—AUTONOMOUS CITIES; Poole "Athenian Coin-Engravers in Italy" under ART; Price "More from Memphis" under HOARDS; Price "New Owls" under EGYPT—PRE-PTOLEMAIC PERIOD; E. S. G. Robinson "A Hoard from Sidon" under HOARDS; Root "Evidence from Persepolis" under PERSIA; Rutter "Athens" under ITALY—GENERAL WORKS.

C. Seltman "Two Athenian Marble Thrones" under TYPES; Seltman "Survival of Ancient Coins" under HOARDS; Shear "Analytical Table" under HOARDS; Sheedy "Early Classical Coinage of Siphnos" under CYCLADES ISLANDS; Shipton "Money and the Élite" under GENERAL WORKS—GREEK; Svoronos "ΣΦΡΑΓΙΣ ΑΘΗΝΑΙΚΟΥ ΤΕΤΡΑΔΡΑΧΜΟΥ" under THE MINTING PROCESS; Svoronos "A Die of an Athenian Tetradrachm" under THE MINTING PROCESS; Tameanko "Numismatically Related Artifacts from the Mint" under THE MINTING PROCESS; W. Thompson "Gold and Silver Ratios" under METROLOGY; W. Thompson "The Value" under MYSIA—AUTONOMOUS CITIES; Tsagari "Some of the More Important Acquisitions…2005" under PUBLIC COLLECTIONS—GREECE (ATHENS); van Alfen "A New Athenian Owl and Bullion Hoard" under HOARDS; van Alfen "Hatching Owls: The Regulation of Coin Production in Later Fifth

Century Athens" under THE MINTING PROCESS; van Alfen "The 'Owls' from the 1989 Syria Hoard" under EGYPT—PRE-PTOLEMAIC PERIOD; van Alfen "The 'Owls' from the 1973 Iraq Hoard" under HOARDS; Varoufakis "Quality Control" under METALLURGY; Vaux "Extract of a Letter" under MACEDONIAN KINGDOM—GENERAL WORKS; Vickers "Early Greek" under ORIGINS OF COINAGE; Waddington "Fifth Century Athens" under GENERAL WORKS—GREEK; Walker "Some Plated Coins" under THE MINTING PROCESS; Wartenberg "After Marathon" (two items) under GENERAL WORKS—GREEK.

WAPPENMÜNZEN

4154 **Babelon, Ernest C.** "Les Origines de la Monnaie à Athènes." *Journal International d'Archéologie Numismatique* (Greece) 7 (1904): 209-54; 8 (1905): 7-52. Reprint, Chicago: Obol International, 1979. 92 pp., illus. [CS 2480]
"Consideration of literary evidence and historical probabilities leading to a dating system for Wappenmünzen and 'owls.'" [J. R. Jones, *AIJIAN*]

4155 **Cancio, Leopoldo.** "The Wappenmünzen—An Athenian Beetle." *Spink Numismatic Circular* 102, no. 1 (February 1994): 6. Illus.
Publishes a rare didrachm of the Athenian Wappenmünzen series which depicts a beetle on the obverse. The coin is one of only two or three known, one being in the British Museum.

4156 **Haymes, Christopher.** "The First Coinage of Athens." *SAN—Journal of the Society for Ancient Numismatics* 17, no. 2 (May 1991): 28-36.
Traces the debate over the attribution and dating of the Wappenmünzen series using the arguments of Head, Jones, Gardner, Seltman, Robinson, Kraay, Kroll, Waggoner, and others. Discusses theories for the significance of the types, suggesting they are probably moneyers' signatures or mint marks. Discusses possible dates for the introduction of the Athena/owl series. Suggests the first Athenian coins may have been struck ca. 545 B.C. with the owls being introduced ca. 515 B.C.

4157 **Head, Barclay V.** "The Initial Coinage of Athens." *Numismatic Chronicle* 3rd ser., 13 (1893): 247-54.
In this reply to H. H. Howorth's letter (see Howorth "The Initial Coinage" below), Head examines the contention that Hippias changed the Athenian coinage and he disputes Howorth's interpretation of a passage in Pseudo-Aristotle's *Oeconomica*. Head stands firm in attributing the Wappenmünzen series to Eretria. [Also see Howorth "Eretria" and Head "Eretria" under CENTRAL GREECE—EUBOIA, and Hill "Neapolis" below].

4158 **Hill, George F.** "Neapolis Datenon." *Numismatic Chronicle* 3rd ser., 13 (1893): 255-8.
Henry Howorth found a connection between the coins of Neapolis and those of Athens (see Howorth "The Initial Coinage" below). He suggested that the type of the earliest coins of Athens was the Gorgoneion and that the Gorgoneion on coins of Neapolis was borrowed from the early coins of Athens. Hill disputes this and agrees with Head's attribution of the Gorgoneion issues to Euboia (see Head "The Initial Coinage" above).

4159 **Hopper, R. J.** "Observations on the Wappenmünzen." *Essays in Greek Coinage Presented to Stanley Robinson.* Edited by C. M. Kraay and G. K. Jenkins. Oxford: Clarendon Press, 1968. Pages 16-39. 4 pls. [CS 2497]
A reconsideration of Seltman's arrangement of the Wappenmünzen coinage of Athens (see C. Seltman *Athens: Its History and Coinage before the Persian Invasion* below). Discusses the unity of the Wappenmünzen series. Discusses die links and re-examines Seltman's identification of links. An appendix lists coins overlooked by Seltman or found after 1924. Provides comments on coin weights and illustrates some examples using histograms. Hopper agrees the series belongs to Athens, but questions Seltman's belief that these are family or clan issues. Rather, he suggests the types are religious or may be related to a festival. [Also see Cancio "Athenian Miscellanea" (1996) above].

4160 **Howorth, Henry H.** "The Initial Coinage of Athens." *Numismatic Chronicle* 3rd ser., 13 (1893): 241-6.
In this letter to Barclay V. Head, Howorth suggests that the Pisistratidae substantially changed the coin types of Athens—supporting his contention that the Wappenmünzen series belongs to Athens. Artistic considerations confirm that the Athena/owl coins are later than the gorgon-head coins and related issues. [Also see Head "The Initial Coinage" above for a reply to this letter. Also see Howorth "Eretria" and Head "Eretria" under CENTRAL GREECE—EUBOIA, and Hill "Neapolis" above].

4161 **Kroll, John H.** "From Wappenmünzen to Gorgoneia to Owls." *Museum Notes* 26 (1981): 1-32. 2 pls.
A re-examination of Athens' Wappenmünzen coinage and the transition to the owl coinage. Discusses the changing types of the Wappenmünzen. Reviews the theories of Seltman (the types were hereditary family badges), which he rejects, and Kraay. Points out the use of changing coin types at Samos, Abdera, and other Ionian cities and suggests these are the pictorial signatures of moneyers—personal rather than national in character. Speculates on the motives which influenced the selection of types at Athens. Then discusses the gorgoneion types which he argues are a special transitional stage in the evolution to the owl coinage. Suggests the gorgoneion tetradrachms, which retained the same obverse type through two issues, were the first public or national types. The gorgoneion didrachms were the first Athenian coins to have been struck without a magistrate's badge. Comments on the metallurgy of the gorgoneion types. The introduction of the owl coinage was due to Athens' desire to create a coin easily recognizable and readily acceptable in international trade. Discusses the transition to the owl types. Reviews the implications of his conclusions for the chronology of sixth century Athenian coinage. Concludes that the Wappenmünzen started between 546-535 B.C., the gorgoneion tetradrachms were struck 520-518, the owl tetradrachms began 517-515, and the owl fractions began 510-509.

4162 **Mielczarek, Mariusz.** "The Szubin Hoard Reconsidered." *Wiadomosci Numizmatyczne* (Poland) 29 (1985): 1-14. Illus.
"The author discusses a hoard of thirty-six Athenian Wappenmünzen (ca. 545-530 B.C.) reputedly found in Szubin, Great Poland, in 1824. He rejects the possibility of these coins being unearthed in Poland." [A. Mikolajczyk, *NL* 118]. Includes a Polish summary.

4163 **Milne, Joseph G.** "The Early Coinages of Athens and Euboea." *Numismatic Chronicle* 6th ser., 1 (1941): 8-16. [CS 2509]
Reconsiders the date of the Wappenmünzen series and the location of striking. Suggests they were struck at Chalcis for use in Euboea and Athens. The bull's head type was used on coins intended for Euboea and the gorgon type was intended for Athens. Milne comments on the monetary reforms of Solon at Athens. Discusses the first issue of owl tetradrachms at Athens and comments on their crude artistic style.

4164 **Wallace, William P.** "The Early Coinages of Athens and Euboia." *Numismatic Chronicle* 7th ser., 2 (1962): 23-42. [CS 2533]
"Athens, Eretria, Chalkis and, perhaps, Thebes began to issue coins near the commencement of the third quarter of the sixth century B.C. The coins carry an obverse type, with an incuse punch as reverse. Wappenmünzen at Athens and coins of Chalkis have similar punches and the types are surrounded by a linear circle. The series ends with similar tetradrachms. The Eretrian issues follow and, finally, ca. 510 B.C. or soon after, all four cities (including Karystos) strike

two-type coins. All of these first appear in early fifth century B.C. hoards in fresh condition." [J. Healy, *NL* 75]. [Also see W. Wallace "Note on the New Anatolian Hoard" under HOARDS].

Also see: Cancio "Athenian Miscellanea" under ATTICA—GENERAL WORKS; Cancio "Athenian Miscellanea 4" under ATTICA—GENERAL WORKS; Davis and Sheedy "Seltman, The Wappenmünzen, and the Early Owls" under ATTICA—GENERAL WORKS; Earle-Fox "The Early Coinages" under ORIGINS OF COINAGE; Flament "A Note on Laurium Stratigraphy" under ATTICA—GENERAL WORKS; Head "On Coins Recently Attributed to Eretria" under CENTRAL GREECE—EUBOIA; Howorth "On Coins Recently Attributed to Eretria" under CENTRAL GREECE—EUBOIA; Kalligas "A Bronze Die from Sounion" under THE MINTING PROCESS; Kraay "Hoards, Small Change" under ORIGINS OF COINAGE; Miller "Athenian Coinage" under ATTICA—GENERAL WORKS; van Buchem "Family Coat-of-Arms" under TYPES; Vickers "Early Greek" under ORIGINS OF COINAGE; L. Wilson "Contributions of Greek Art" under TYPES.

NEW STYLE COINAGE

4165 **Apostolou, Eva.** "Three Hoards of the Athenian New Style Coins from Delos." *Coins in the Aegean Islands. Proceedings of the Fifth Scientific Meeting, Mytilene, 16-29 September 2006. Volume 1: Ancient Times.* Obolos 9. Edited by Panagiotis Tselekas. Athens: The Friends of the Numismatic Museum, 2010. Pages 379-411.

4166 **Augé, C., Alain Davesne, and R. Ergeç.** "Le Début des Tétradrachmes d'Athènes du 'Noveau Style': Un Trésor Trouvé de Gaziantep en 1994." *Anatolia Antiqua* (France) 5 (1997): 44-82.

4167 **Bauslaugh, Robert A.** "Two Unpublished Overstrikes: New Style Athens and Aesillas the Questor." *Museum Notes* 32 (1987): 11-21. 2 pls.
Presents an Athenian New Style tetradrachm struck over a tetradrachm of Prusias II or Nicomedes II of Bithynia. Discusses the implications for the chronology of the New Style coinage. If the undertype is indeed Nikomedes II, this would rule out Thompson's high chronology of ca. 176 B.C. for the early period coinage. Also examines a tetradrachm of the Roman questor Aesillas struck over an Athenian New Style tetradrachm. Concludes that the coin offers evidence in support of the traditional dating of 94-88 B.C. for the introduction of the Aesillas type. Fourteen coins are illustrated. [Also see Vagi "Hoard Evidence" under MACEDONIAN KINGDOM].

4168 **Bellinger, Alfred R.** "The Chronology of the Attic New Style Tetradrachms." *Hesperia, Supplement 8: Commemorative Studies in Honor of Theodore Leslie Shear.* American School of Classical Studies at Athens, 1949. Pages 6-30. 1 pl. [CS 2484]
Reviews previous scholarship on the subject. Presents a table showing magistrates' names and the date assigned to the coins of each. Discusses the date of the introduction of the New Style coinage. Re-examines the accepted sequence of issues and discusses the problems raised by the proposed dating of each.

4169 **Berk, Harlan J.** "Thompson 0.1: The First Wreath Bearer." *The Celator* 8, no. 5 (May 1994): 30. Illus.
Describes the first die of the New Style Athens tetradrachm, which was previously unpublished. Three specimens are recorded. Thompson wrongly published it as an imitation (No. 1350). The coin is described as the missing link between the old and New Style types: it bears nearly the same obverse of the last old-style die, and the wreath and amphora reverse of the New Style.

4170 **Cancio, Leopoldo.** "Athenian Miscellanea 3." *Spink Numismatic Circular* 103, no. 7 (September 1995): 264. Illus.
Publishes a New Style tetradrachm belonging to Thompson's *Nike* issue. Both dies were unknown to Thompson.

4171 **de Callataÿ, François.** "Athenian New Style Tetradrachms in Macedonian Hoards." *American Journal of Numismatics* 2nd ser., 3-4 (1991-2): 11-20.
Examines the implications about the circulation of silver coinage in Macedonia which follow from the appearance of Athenian New Style tetradrachms in Macedonian hoards. Did the entry of Athenian coinage into Macedonia coincide with the invasion of Macedonia by the Scordisces and Thracian tribes ca. 139-92 B.C.? Presents tables analyzing the hoards and suggests a massive import of Athenian currency into Macedonia took place ca. 126-120 B.C.

4172 **Dreyer, Boris.** "Roms Ostpolitik, Athen und der Beginn der Neustil-Silberprägung." *Zeitschrift für Papyrologie und Epigraphik* (Germany) 129 (2000): 77-83.
"The beginning of the Athenian New Style coinage around 190 B.C is directly connected with Roman treaties (with Aetolia 189, Apamea 188) in which sums were demanded in good/best Attic silver." [H. Baldus, *NL* 144]

4173 **Habicht, C.** "Zu den Münzmagistraten der Silberprägung des Neuen Stils." *Chiron* (Germany) 21 (1991): 1-23.
Discusses the magistrate names appearing on the Athenian New Style coins.

4174 **Head, Barclay V.** "Notanda Et Corrigenda." *Numismatic Chronicle* 3rd ser., 9 (1889): 229-41.
A response to an article by T. Reinach suggesting there were thirteen Prytanies at Athens in the later part of the third century B.C. Reinach's conclusion has implications for the chronology of the New Style tetradrachms of Athens. Reinach suggested that in every instance where the numeral N (= 13) appears on the amphora, the series to which it belongs must be assigned to the period during which Athens had thirteen tribes (255-200 B.C.). Previously, it has been assumed that in such cases, the N is merely an engraver's blunder for M, and Head is still convinced of this. Head also addresses some issues related to Roman coinage. He concludes with a brief note (page 241) correcting an earlier work (see Head "Electrum Coins" under METALLURGY). A new test confirms that the specific gravity of a gold stater of Croesus shows the coin to be pure gold. The earlier article reported the specific gravity to be higher than pure gold. [Also see Macdonald "The Amphora Letters" below].

4175 **Jongkees, Jan Hendrik.** "Notes on the Coinage of Athens, Part 7." *Mnemosyne* (The Netherlands) 3rd ser., 13 (1947): 145-60. Illus.
Deals with a New Style tetradrachm bearing the reverse inscription AΘE / O / ΔEMO / Σ. There are four known specimens of this variety. The types are executed in a barbarous style, and the usual magistrates' names are absent. The coin is unusually low in weight. Jongkees suggests it was struck by Athenian fugitives in Sulla's camp in 87/6 B.C. Also discusses the symbol on the reverse, which the author identifies as a statue of Harmodias.

4176 **Kambanis, M. L.** *Notes sur le Classement Chronologique des Monnaies d'Athènes. Series avec Noms de Magistrats.* Paris, 1928. Reprint, Chicago: Obol International, 1980. 15 pp., 2 pls. [CS 2498]
Deals with the chronology of the New Style coinage.

4177 **Kleiner, Fred S.** "The Earliest Athenian New Style Bronze Coins: Some Evidence from the Athenian Agora." *Hesperia* 44 (1975): 302-30. 2 pls. [CS 2499]
Examines the coins found in the construction fills of the three Hellenistic stoas in the Athenian Agora to assist in dating of the New Style bronze coins with *obv.* Athena; *rev.* fulminating Zeus. Lists hundreds of coins found and summarizes the numismatic evidence. Concludes that 180 B.C. is the earliest possible date for the first New Style bronze issues, and that the *obv.* Cicada; *rev.* Amphora fractional bronzes were struck for use in Athens as well as in Delos, and must have been issued before 180 B.C.

4178 **Lewis, David M.** "The Chronology of the Athenian New Style Coinage." *Numismatic Chronicle* 7th ser., 2 (1962): 275-300. Also appeared in Lewis' *Selected Papers in Greek and Near Eastern History.* Edited by P. J. Rhodes. Cambridge: University Press, 1997. Pages 294-320. [CS 2507]
Criticizes Thompson's annual dating of the New Style coinage (see M. Thompson *The New Style Silver Coinage* below). Suggests that the coinage started ca. 164 and ended ca. 50 B.C. Also proposes a post-Sullan date for the tetradrachm overstruck by Aesillas. [Also see M. Thompson "Athens Again" for her response. Also see M. Thompson "Ptolemy Philometor" below, and Mørkholm "Chronology" below].

4179 **MacDonald, David.** "A New Athenian Intercalary Tetradrachm." *Schweizer Münzblätter* (Switzerland) 48, no. 192 (1998): 85-90. Illus.

4180 **Macdonald, George.** "The Amphora Letters on Coins of Athens." *Numismatic Chronicle* 3rd ser., 19 (1899): 288-321.
Attempts to determine the significance of the letters on the amphora of Athens' New Style coinage, especially the letter N which is generally attributed to carelessness on the part of the die-engraver. The sixteen known coins which undoubtedly bear the N are listed in a table. Macdonald rules out the engraver's error theory and confirms that thirteen different letters do exist. Therefore, the letters cannot refer to the number of the prytany during which they were issued. He then examines the theory that the numerals indicate calendar months (the Attic year had thirteen months at recurring intervals). He accepts this theory and suggests that a system of double dating the coins was introduced, the second system being based on a solar calendar. [Also see Head "Notanda Et Corrigenda" above].

4181 **Mattingly, Harold B.** "Some Third Magistrates in the Athenian New Style Silver Coinage." *Journal of Hellenic Studies* 91 (1971): 85-93.
"This paper examines the silver coinage of Athens, specifically the New Style series which began to be produced c. 140 B.C. Particular emphasis is placed on the 'magistrates' who, to some extent, subsidized its production. The author also suggests a new chronology for the minting of certain issues." [M. Tooth, *Hekte* 2]. [This essay was reprinted in Mattingly's *From Coins to History: Selected Numismatic Studies.* See Mattingly under GENERAL WORKS—GREEK].

4182 ——— "The Beginning of Athenian New Style Silver Coinage." *Numismatic Chronicle* 150 (1990): 67-78.
"Against Mørkholm's argument that Athenian New Style coinage began intermittently in the 180s and became annual and continuous only with Issue 20 in 145 B.C., the evidence of a number of Near Eastern hoards appears conclusive. Whereas Mørkholm claimed that Issue 8 was struck ca. 170 B.C. on the evidence of the Bakërr Hoard (Albania), in the East Issue 8 is not found until the Babylon hoard (ca. 155 B.C.) and Issue 13 not until Trabzon (ca. 152 B.C.). The Bakërr hoard contains the latest Epirot League silver (down to 167 B.C.), but this coin continued circulating after the League's debacle. Coin evidence from Dodona suggests that troubles later than the 167 B.C. crisis caused coin loss and hoard burial. From Polybius we can deduce a plausible historical context for the Bakërr hoard in 157/6 B.C., which is the likely date for the appearance of Issue 8." [H. Mattingly, *NL* 126]. [This essay was reprinted in Mattingly's *From Coins to History: Selected Numismatic Studies.* See Mattingly under GENERAL WORKS—GREEK].

4183 **Mitrea, Bucur.** "Un Tétradrachme Athénien du Nouveau Style Découvert en Dacie." *Greek Numismatics and Archaeology: Essays in Honor of Margaret Thompson.* Edited by O. Mørkholm and N. M. Waggoner. Wetteren: Numismatique Romaine, 1979. Pages 197-201. 1 pl.
Examines a New Style Athenian tetradrachm discovered in Dacia.

4184 **Mørkholm, Otto.** "The Chronology of the New Style Coinage of Athens." *Museum Notes* 29 (1984): 29-42.
Mørkholm suggests a solution to the controversy surrounding the chronology of the new style coinage as put forward by Margaret Thompson and D. M. Lewis (see M. Thompson *The New Style Silver Coinage* below, and D. M. Lewis "Chronology" above). Suggests the first nineteen issues appeared with gaps from the 180's to circa 145 B.C., and then issues were struck without interruption from 145-78 B.C. Reviews the controversy over the chronology of these issues. Discusses overstrikes, hoard evidence, and historical evidence. Thompson has agreed with Mørkholm's suggestions.

4185 **Nicolet-Pierre, Hélène.** "De l'Ancien au Nouveau Style Athénien: Une Continuité?" *Studia Paulo Naster Oblata I: Numismatica Antiqua.* Edited by S. Scheers. Louvain, 1982. Pages 104-14. 2 pls.
"Concerning the very rare Athenian silver issues of the late owl type that bear symbols in the reverse field. These coins form the link between the old and new style Athenian tetradrachms and can now be dated to the first quarter of the second century B.C." [D. Kroh, *ACRR*]

4186 **Özbek, Osman.** "The Herakleia Hoard." *Recent Turkish Coin Hoards and Numismatic Studies.* British Institute of Archaeology at Ankara Monograph, No. 12. Edited by C. S. Lightfoot. Oxford: Oxbow Books, 1991. Pages 275-312 including 25 pls.
Catalogues a hoard of 505 New Style Athenian tetradrachms, 165-136 B.C. Lists magistrate names, symbols, and weights. Includes references to Thompson's *The New Style Silver Coinage.* Two-hundred ninety-eight of the coins are photographed.

4187 **Picard, Olivier.** "Le Contre Exemple du Monnayage Stéphanéphore d'Athenes." *Revue Numismatique* (France) 156 (2000): 79-86.

4188 **Price, Martin J.** "The New-Style Coinage of Athens: Some Evidence from the Bronze Issues." *Numismatic Chronicle* 7th ser., 4 (1964): 27-36. [CS 2514]

"Evidence of hoards and datable deposits from the excavations of the Agora at Athens is used to attempt to show that the Athenian New Style issue in the name of King Mithradates, with symbol star between crescents, must have been issued at the time of Mithradates VI's occupation of Athens." [M. Price, *NL* 80]

4189 **Price, Martin J., and P. Aydemir.** "The Candarli Hoard of New Style Athenian Silver." *Studies in Ancient Coinage from Turkey.* Edited by R. Ashton. Special Publication No. 29. British Institute at Ankara Monograph, No. 17. London, 1996. Pages 3-4.

4190 **Sear, David R.** "A Case of Mistaken Identity." *Numismatist* 117, no. 4 (April 2004): 61-3. Illus.
Discusses the chronology of the New Style coinage of Athens. Explains how the tetradrachms bearing the names Mithradates and Artistion led to the clarification of the chronology. Discusses the struggles of Mithradates VI, Philip V, and Antiochus III against the Roman Republic.

4191 **Thompson, Margaret.** "The Beginnings of Athenian New-Style Coinage." *Museum Notes* 5 (1952): 25-33. 3 pls. [CS 2526]
The author attempts to reconstruct a hoard of Euboean and Athenian silver coins which was found near Anthedon on the Boeotian coast in 1935. The four New Style Athenian tetradrachms in the hoard are the first four of the entire New Style coinage. The rare Eretrian tetradrachms in the hoard may constitute four annual issues, and may closely coincide with the issuance of the four Athenian coins. Thompson suggests ca. 196 B.C. for the start of the New Style series, and ca. 192 B.C. for the burial of the hoard.

4192 ——— "Workshops or Mines?" *Museum Notes* 5 (1952): 35-48. 1 pl. [CS 2527]
The author examines the letters placed below the amphora (or occasionally in the left field) on the New Style coinage. These are the initial letters of words, and stand either for the workshops of the Athenian mint or for the mines from which the silver came. Thompson rejects the workshop theory and spells out her reasoning in detail. She does, however, find a correlation between the letters on the dies and the names of mines at Laurium. Furthermore, she suggests the purpose of marking the dies may have involved both the purity of the metal and an over-all accounting system on the part of the state. Thompson explains how such a system could be used to monitor the flow of silver from mine, to mint, to coinage.

4193 ——— "A Monetary Liturgy in Hellenistic Athens." *American Journal of Archaeology* 64 (1961): 192.
A summary of a paper presented at a conference. "Study of the names of magistrates on Athenian New Style coinage shows that the best explanation for their selection and rotation is that of a monetary liturgy performed by wealthy citizens." [J. R. Jones, *NIAJAH*]

4194 ——— *The New Style Silver Coinage of Athens.* Numismatic Studies, No. 10. New York: American Numismatic Society, 1961. Vol. 1: 747 pp.; vol. 2: 202 pls. [CS 2529]
Begins with a review of previous research, an extensive bibliography, and a list of monograms according to the issue sequence. Presents a catalogue of 1272 varieties with commentary divided into the Early Period (196/5-169/8 B.C.), the Middle Period (168/7-132/1 B.C.), and the Late Period (131/0-88/7 B.C.). Within each division, the catalogue and commentary is followed by a discussion of the group as a whole and the evidence upon which its chronological order is based. Includes discussions of the Sullan issues (86-84 B.C.), imitations of the New Style coinage, hoards, magistrates, symbols, and a statistical survey of Amphora letters and control combinations. Also includes discussions of the metallurgical analysis of the silver and bronze issues, weights, die-positions, and annual distributions of the coinage. Concludes that the letters on the overturned amphorae indicate annual groups. Includes an accordion plate with coinage arranged according to magistrates in chronological order. [Reviewed by J. F. Healy in *Numismatic Chronicle* 7th ser., 2 (1962): 429-31; by R. J. Hopper in *Spink Numismatic Circular* 70 (May 1962): 109-11, (June 1962): 139-41, and (July-August 1962): 163-5; by R. R. Holloway in *American Journal of Archaeology* 67 (1963): 92-3; and by G. K. Jenkins in *Journal of Hellenic Studies* 83 (1963): 215-6. A review by David M. Lewis appears in Lewis' *Selected Papers in Greek and Near Eastern History.* Edited by P. J. Rhodes. Cambridge: University Press, 1997. Pages 321-4. Also see D. M. Lewis "Chronology" above, and O. Mørkholm "Chronology" above].

4195 ——— "Athens Again." *Numismatic Chronicle* 7th ser., 2 (1962): 301-33.
"Miss Thompson reviews the objections raised by D. M. Lewis (see Lewis "The Chronology" above) to her absolute chronology for the Athenian New Style silver coinage, noting that historical and prosopographical arguments provide only circumstantial evidence which can obviously be interpreted in different ways. The strength of any argument for the low dating lies in the hoard evidence. New material, however, available from the Abruzzi and Agrinion hoards, confirms 196 B.C. as the commencement date for the series, this being in accord with the implications of the Anthedon hoard and the Delian inventories. The author again surveys the problem of Aesillas and re-affirms that he clearly belongs to the 90's. All this evidence, together with the conflict of intercalary years and the wear of coins in the hoards, proves decisively that there are no grounds for accepting Lewis' alternative chronology." [J. Healy, *NL* 75]

4196 ——— "Ptolemy Philometor and Athens." *Museum Notes* 11 (1964): 119-29. 3 pls. [CS 3174]
Describes the beautification of Athens during the second century B.C. resulting from the donations of the Attalids of Pergamon, Antiochus IV of Syria, and Ptolemy VI Philometor of Egypt. Illustrates an Athenian New Style tetradrachm of the magistrate Aphrodisios bearing as a reverse symbol a double cornucopia with fillet, almost identical with the reverse type of the coins of Ptolemy II and his successors. Concludes that the appearance of this symbol is connected with the Ptolemaia—the ritual observances of the Ptolemaic cult at Athens. The use of this symbol would make sense before 126 or after 102 B.C., when the cult was popular at Athens. However, D. Lewis (see Lewis "The Chronology" above) dates this coin issue ca. 119/118 B.C.—a time when the Ptolemaia was no longer celebrated. Thompson suggests this issue could be dated 152/1 when the cult was at its apogee and a statue of Ptolemy VI was erected on the Acropolis.

4197 **Tod, Marcus N.** "Greek Inscriptions at Cairness House." *Journal of Hellenic Studies* 54 (1934): 140-62. 1 pl.
"On p. 155 the term δραχμαι στεφανηφοροι which appears in a decree of the Poseidoniasts of Berytus from Delos, is interpreted as a reference to New Style Athenian coinage." [J. R. Jones, *NIJHS*]

4198 **Touratsoglou, Ioannis.** "The Adam Zagliveriou/1983 Hoard in the Museum of Thessaloniki (Athenian 'New Style' Tetradrachms in Macedonia)." *Nomismatika Khronika* (Greece) 8 (1989): 7-20. Illus.
This hoard of New Style tetradrachms of Athens may provide information relevant to the on-going debate over the starting date of the New Style series. Margaret Thompson argued for 196/5 B.C. (see M. Thompson, *The New Style Silver Coinage of Athens* above). David Lewis has argued for 164/3 B.C. (see D. Lewis, "The Chronology of the Athenian New Style Coinage" above). The author lists the researchers who have supported Lewis' dating. Summarizes the chronological conclusions of Mørkholm and Nicolet. Outlines the political situation in Macedonia in the second and first centuries B.C. Hoard evidence from Macedonia seems to provide support for Mørkholm's suggested chronology (see O. Mørkholm, "The Chronology of the New Style Coinage of Athens" above). Mørkholm believed the New Style coinage flowed into Macedonia during periods of upheaval and threat from abroad. The hoard evidence also

suggests that revisions need to be made to the chronology of the LEG ΜΑΚΕΔΟΝΩΝ, ΜΑΚΕΔΟΝΩΝ, and AESILLAS issues. Thirty-eight New Style tetradrachms from the hoard are illustrated. A table provides a cross-reference to the Thompson varieties and the suggested dating in accordance with Thompson, Lewis, and Mørkholm. In Greek on pages 7-11. In English on pages 17-20. Plates on pages 12-15 and table on page 16.

Also see: Apostolou "A Review on the New Style Silver Coinage of Athens: The Role of Delos" under CYCLADES ISLANDS; Badian "Rome, Athens, and Mithradates" under ATTICA—GENERAL WORKS; Bunbury "On Some Unpublished Coins" under ATTICA—GENERAL WORKS; Cancio "Athenian Miscellanea 4" under ATTICA—GENERAL WORKS; de Callataÿ and Prokopov "Boljarino Hoard" under HOARDS; de Callataÿ and Prokopov "An Overstrike" under THRACE—THASOS; Hartmann and Macdonald *Greek Numismatic Epigraphy* under EPIGRAPHY; Hoover and MacDonald "Syrian Imitations of New Style Tetradrachms Struck over Myrina" under SYRIA—SELEUCID KINGDOM; Kraay "Greek Coinage and War" under GENERAL WORKS—GREEK; Kraay "Historical Interpretations" under GENERAL WORKS—GREEK; Le Rider "Un Groupe de Monnaies Crétoises à Types Athéniens" under CRETE; Lorber "Commerce ('Demetrius I' Hoard) 2003" under HOARDS.

D. MacDonald "A Group of Thasian-type Tetradrachms Overstruck on Athenian New Style" under THRACE—THASOS; Meadows and Houghton "The Gaziantep Hoard" under HOARDS; Miller "Athenian Coinage" under ATTICA—GENERAL WORKS; Newton "Statuette of Athenè Parthenos" under TYPES; Oeconomides and Kleiner "The Hierapytna Hoard" under HOARDS; Oikonomides "Numismatic Representations" under TYPES; Prokopov and de Callataÿ "A Late Hellenistic Hoard" under HOARDS; M. Thompson "Gold and Copper Traces" under METALLURGY; Wilkinson "Unpublished" under PRIVATE COLLECTIONS; Yao and Stross "The Use of Analysis" under METALLURGY.

ATHENIAN COINAGE DECREE

4199 **Gardner, Percy.** "Coinage of the Athenian Empire." *Journal of Hellenic Studies* 33 (1913): 147 88. 2 pls.
Discusses the Athenian Currency Decree and its effects on the coinage of the members of the Delian League during the period 480-400 B.C. Examines the coinage of these areas separately: (1) Cyzicus, Lampsacus, and Phocaea, (2) the Aegean Islands, (3) Ionia and Caria, (4) Pontus and Propontis, (5) Thrace and Macedonia, and (6) Italy and Sicily. Also discusses the introduction of gold and bronze coinage at Athens. [Also see Woodward "Notes and Queries" below].

4200 **Georgiades, A., and W. Kendrick Pritchett.** "The Koan Fragment of the Monetary Decree." *Bulletin de Correspondance Hellénique* (France) 89 (1965): 400-40.
Part 1, by Georgiades, is written in French and presents an analysis of the marble on which the Athenian Coinage Decree was written. In Part 2, Pritchett comments on the provenance of the marble, the date of the disappearance of the three-barred sigma at Athens, the geographical groupings of the tribute districts, and the epigraphy on the Koan fragment.

4200a **Hadji, Athena, and Zoë Kontes.** "The Athenian Coinage Decree: Inscriptions, Coins and Athenian Politics." *XIII Congreso Internacional de Numismática, Madrid – 2003: Actas–Proceedings–Actes I.* Edited by Carmen Alfaro, Carmen Marcos, and Paloma Otero. Madrid: International Numismatic Commisson, 2005. Pages 263-7.
The authors provide a good summary of the controversy surrounding the interpretation of the Athenian Coinage Decree. Then they focus on a fragment of the decree discovered near Aphytis in 1969. This fragment preserves the end of the decree which refers to the punishment of those who fail to comply with the mandates of the decree. It also resolves the ambiguity regarding the officials who are to oversee the enforcement of the decree. They were Athenian archons placed in allied city-states, rather than local magistrates. The authors conclude the decree is best interpreted as an attempt by the Athenian state to reassert control over its allies at a time when that control was weakening.

4201 **Henry, Alan.** "The Sigma Enigma." *Zeitschrift für Papyrologie und Epigraphik* (Germany) 120 (1998): 45-8.
"In the discussion of the disappearance of the three-barred sigma in fourth century B.C. Greek epigraphy, the date of the Athenian Coinage Decree is important. Anomalous payments by some poleis of Asia Minor in non-Attic currency, known down to the twenties (pp. 47 ff.), do 'not require us to draw the inference that, at the time of such payments, the Decree was not yet in force.'" [H. Baldus, *NL* 141]

4202 **Lewis, David M.** "The Athenian Coinage Decree." *Coinage and Administration in the Athenian and Persian Empires.* Edited by Ian Carradice. Oxford: British Archaeological Reports, 1987. Pages 53-63. Also appeared in Lewis' *Selected Papers in Greek and Near Eastern History.* Edited by P. J. Rhodes. Cambridge: University Press, 1997. Pages 116-30.
Presents the history of the interpretation of the Athenian coinage decree which attempted to impose Athenian coins, weights, and measures upon the members of the Athenian confederacy. Reviews the discovery of fragments of the decree, the attempts at determining the date of the decree, and the evidence of the epigraphy used in the decree. Provides a summary of the known text of the decree by piecing together the surviving fragments. Reassesses the conclusions of other researchers. Discusses two theories for the motivation which drove Athens to issue the decree: stimulating economic activity through the creation of a free-trade zone, and profiting from the resulting re-coinage of numerous currencies. Examines the controversy over the dating of the decree.

4203 **Mattingly, Harold B.** "The Athenian Coinage Decree." *Historia* (Germany) 10, no. 2 (April 1961): 148-88. [CS 2508]
Through an extensive examination of epigraphical evidence, Mattingly suggests there are strong reasons for dating the Athenian Coinage Decree (which imposed Athenian currency on the Empire) to ca. 420 B.C. rather than ca. 450 B.C. as is often argued. Discusses the Coinage Decree and the Decree of Kleinias, the first Decree for Athena Nike, the Eleusinian επισταται, the Hermione Treaty, and the Miletus Decree. [Also see Merritt and Wade-Gery "The Dating of Documents" below].

4204 ——— "The Protected Fund in the Athenian Coinage Decree (*ATL* D, par. 7f)." *American Journal of Philology* 95, no. 3 (fall 1974): 280-5.
"The orthodox dating of the Athenian coinage decree to ca. 445 B.C., based on the assumption that the three-barred sigmas in the Kos copy are inconceivable after that date, is challenged. Stylistic analysis of the Hephaisteia decree, archon-dated 421-420, suggests that it cannot be fully a quarter-century later than the coinage decree; the Sigeion decree is reassigned to 418-417, thus providing evidence for the use of three-barred sigmas at so late a date. The coinage decree itself is placed ca. 425-424." [W. Metcalf, *NL* 94]

4205 ——— "The Mysterious 3000 Talents of the First Kallias Decree." *Greek, Roman, and Byzantine Studies* 16, no. 1 (spring 1975): 15-22.
"The conventional dating of 434/3 B.C. for the Kallias Decrees associated with the Parthenon inventories of Athena's treasures is challenged. A date of 422/1 for Kallias is proposed, which would place the decrees at the close of the Peloponnesian War. The lower dating presents a problem in explaining the deposit

of 3000 talents with Athena shortly before Kallias proposed his decrees—an inordinately large sum for Athens to have been able to render after an exhausting war. The solution is found mainly in the transfer of annual contributions in the form of foreign indemnities and revenues from the public treasury to the Acropolis under Athena's protection, once peace was made in 422/1." [N. Waggoner, *NL* 95]

4206 ——— "The Second Athenian Coinage Decree." *Klio* (Germany) 1, no. 59 (1977): 83-100.
Examines the decree banning allied minting and the use of non-Athenian silver currency. Presents a detailed examination of the arguments for the dating of the first Coinage Decree. Concludes the second decree is neither a major measure in itself nor a reactivation of the first decree. Rather, it is a mere supplementary decree passed in the same year, designed to ensure prompt and effective execution of the tough new policy.

4207 ——— "The Athenian Coinage Decree and the Assertion of Empire." *Coinage and Administration in the Athenian and Persian Empires.* BAR International Series 343. Edited by Ian Carradice. Oxford: British Archaeological Reports, 1987. Pages 65-71.
Reviews theories for the dating and purpose of the Athenian coinage decree. Reassesses the epigraphic evidence, especially the use of the three-bar sigma.

4208 ——— "New Light on the Athenian Standards Decree (*ATL* II, D14)." *Klio* (Germany) 75 (1993): 99-102.
"In the second half of the fifth century B.C. the Athenians imposed uniformity of coinage, weights and measures on their tributary allies and required each to put up a copy of the measure. Since the discovery of the Attic copy from Kos with three-barred sigma the decree has been put back by almost all scholars to the early 440s. Elmar Schwertheim has recently published what he saw as an Athenian decree for Hamaxitos in the Troad. It is in fact a seventh copy of the Standards Decree, stoichedon and in Attic script. Now Hamaxitos came under Athenian control only in 427 B.C. after the collapse of the Mytilenean revolt. Either then each new member of the Empire had to put up a copy on entry or the decree itself was not passed till 425/4 B.C. Some strong evidence, numismatic, literary and archaeological, virtually proves that the late date for the measure is correct." [H. B. Mattingly, *Klio*]. [This essay was reprinted in Mattingly's *From Coins to History: Selected Numismatic Studies*. See Mattingly under GENERAL WORKS—GREEK].

4209 **Meiggs, Russell.** "The Dating of Fifth-Century Attic Inscriptions." *Journal of Hellenic Studies* 86 (1966): 86-98.
"Further reasons are cautiously advanced for supporting an early dating for the Athenian Coinage Decree." [J. R. Jones, *NIJHS*]

4210 ——— *The Athenian Empire.* Oxford: University Press, 1972. 620 pp.
"On pp. 167-172 and 599-601 an early date for the Athenian coinage decree is supported. On pp. 441-443 evidence is presented for attributing the coinage of the Ionian Revolt to separate cities rather than to a central mint, and for the valuation of the Cyzicene stater at 27 drachms at Athens." [J. Melville Jones, *NL* 90]

4211 **Merritt, Benjamin D., and H. T. Wade-Gery.** "The Dating of Documents to the Mid-Fifth Century. Part 1." *Journal of Hellenic Studies* 82 (1962): 67-74.
"Written in answer to the article by H. B. Mattingly (see Mattingly "The Athenian Coinage Decree" above), the present paper is not concerned with numismatic questions, but looks for epigraphic arguments to support the authors' dating of the decree of Clearchus to 448-7 B.C. Part 2 of this study, which appeared in vol. 83 (1963): 100-17, continues the discussion of epigraphic problems presented by other documents which appear to be contemporary." [J. R. Jones, *NIJHS*]

4212 **Robinson, David M.** "A New Fragment of the Athenian Decree on Coinage." *American Journal of Philology* 56 (1935): 149-54. 1 pl.
Illustrates a limestone fragment of the Athenian Coinage Decree now in the Archaeological Museum in Salonica. Presents the text of this new fragment with commentary.

4213 **Robinson, Edward S. G.** "The Athenian Currency Decree and the Coinage of the Allies." *Hesperia, Supplement 8: Commemorative Studies in Honor of Theodore Leslie Shear.* American School of Classical Studies at Athens, 1949. Pages 324-40. [CS 2516]
A new fragment of the coinage decree, found in Cos, leads to a re-examination of this decree which was intended to prevent the striking of silver coins in Athens' allied cities and to prevent the use of currency, weights, and measures other than Athenian. Robinson takes issue with some of Segre's readings of the new inscription. By examining the volume of issues at allied mints in the fifth century B.C., Robinson attempts to determine if the mints were in fact closed, and if the Athenian currency was in fact substituted for the various local currencies. Concludes that from the 440's onward, the ban on coinage was not absolute. Athens was not successful in forcing the exclusive use of either her standards or her coins on the allies. The owls supplemented, rather than replaced, the silver coinage of the cities, perhaps because much Athenian silver coinage was exported from the area.

4214 **Schönhammer, Maria.** "Some Thoughts on the Athenian Coinage Decree." *Proceedings of the 11th International Numismatic Congress, September 8-13, 1991. Volume 1.* Edited by T. Hackens et al. Louvain-la-Neuve, Belgium: International Association of Professional Numismatists, 1993. Pages 187-91. Charts.
Examines whether recent numismatic research has provided any support to the thesis that in the middle of the fifth century B.C., Athens monopolized the right to coin money. Re-examines the hoard evidence, the sequence of local issues, and the epigraphical evidence. Suggests that the decree may have dictated that local mints must utilize the Attic standard when minting coins. The decree did not order the closing of local mints.

4215 **Sokolowski, F.** "The Athenian Law Concerning Silver Currency (375/4) B.C." *Bulletin de Correspondance Hellénique* (France) 100 (1976): 511-5.
Comments on Stroud's reading of the text (see Stroud "An Athenian Law" below) and suggests a new reading. Discusses the history and purpose of the Athenian currency law.

4216 **Stroud, Ronald S.** "An Athenian Law on Silver Coinage." *Hesperia* 43, no. 2 (April-June 1974): 157-88. 3 pls. [CS 2523]
Discusses a complete marble stele from ca. 375 B.C. which preserves a law related to the circulation of coins at Athens and Peiraieus and information on the function of the Dokimastes—the tester of coins—and mentions ten different public officials. Publishes the Greek text of the stele with an English translation. Comments on the epigraphy and its interpretation. Discusses the duties of the Dokimastes, the disposition of coins found to be counterfeit, and the penalties imposed on the Dokimastes for failure to carry out his duties. The author suggests reasons for the abundance of counterfeit coins in the Athenian marketplace. [For an alternate interpretation of one of the clauses of the law, see Giovannini "Athenian Currency" under ATTICA—GENERAL WORKS].

4217 **Vickers, Michael.** "Fifth Century Chronology and the Coinage Decree." *Journal of Hellenic Studies* 116 (1996): 171-4.

Discusses the controversy over the dating of the Athenian Coinage Decree which forced Athenian standards on the tributary allies. Some have dated the decree to 449 B.C. while others argue for a date in the 420's. Vickers discusses the forms of payment referred to in tribute lists and shows that payment may have been made in currencies struck on a variety of weight standards. Persian coins may have been used for tribute payments, thus leading to the need for the decree.

4218 **Woodward, Arthur M.** "Notes and Queries on Athenian Coinage and Finance." *Journal of Hellenic Studies* 34 (1914): 276-92.
A follow-up to Gardner's article on the effects of the Athenian Currency Decree on the coinage of Athens and members of its empire (see Gardner "Coinage of the Athenian Empire" above). Woodward applies the evidence of inscriptions to reveal information on the circulation of coins in the various cities under Athens' influence.

Also see: Austin and Vidal-Naquet *Economic and Social History* under GENERAL WORKS—GREEK; Barron "The Fifth Century Diskoboloi" under CARIAN ISLANDS—KOS; Figueira *The Power of Money* under ATTICA—GENERAL WORKS; Mattingly "A New Light…Teos" under IONIA; Merritt "Perikles" under ATTICA—GENERAL WORKS; Miller "Athenian Coinage" under ATTICA—GENERAL WORKS; Mørkholm "Some Reflections" under GENERAL WORKS—GREEK; Van der Dussen "Fifth Century Greek Wars" under GENERAL WORKS—GREEK.

AEGINA

The assertion that Pheidon issued coins at Aegina is a statement which we cannot accept. In the first place, no coins of Greece proper seem to be so early as the eighth century; and in the second place, Pheidon never had any authority in Aegina. Probably the Aeginetans were the first people of Greece to strike money; and their money was on the Pheidonian standard: hence a natural confusion. It was the weight, not the coinage of Greece, which were due to Pheidon.

—Percy Gardner, 1911

4219 **Ashton, N. G.** "What Does the Turtle Say?" *Numismatic Chronicle* 147 (1987): 1-7. 1 pl.
"An ancient Greek silver stater, minted on the island of Aegina in the late sixth century B.C., has been uniquely super-inscribed on the obverse with the lengthiest known coin graffito from antiquity. The inscription, which is a mixture of retrograde and orthograde script produced by more than one 'hand,' is datable to the early decades of the fifth century B.C. It is probable that the stater was one of a number placed as a dedication to a local Aeginetan deity, as a tithe from the moneys received for the ransoming of captives." [N. Ashton, *NL* 120]. [Also see P. Bicknell "Turtle Tattle" below. Bicknell's conclusions contradict those of Ashton].

4220 **Beer, Leslie.** *The Coinage of Aegina: A Chronological Reappraisal Based on Hoards and Technical Studies.* Dissertation, Oxford University, 1980.

4221 **Bicknell, Peter.** "Turtle Tattle." *Numismatic Chronicle* 150 (1990): 223-4.
"A new reading is proposed of the long graffito inscribed on an early Aeginetan stater. If the reading is correct, the coin was part of a payment to an Aeginetan shrine for some kind of religious service rather than a ransom money as suggested by N. G. Ashton." [P. Bicknell, *NL* 126]. [See Ashton "What Does the Turtle Say?" above].

4222 **Brown, W. Llewellyn.** "Pheidon's Alleged Aeginetan Coinage." *Numismatic Chronicle* 6th ser., 10 (1950): 177-204. 1 pl. [CS 2536]
Brown examines the role of Pheidon in the development of Aegina's coinage. He doubts Pheidon's control of Aegina at the time coinage began. Also doubts that the dedication of the iron spits at the Argive Heraeum had anything to do with the introduction of coinage. Suggests the literary source attesting to Pheidon's involvement with the introduction of coinage, Ephorus, is unreliable. Suggests a chronology for Aeginetan staters based on the development of the incuse reverses. [See Kagan's rebuttal, "Pheidon's Aeginetan Coinage" below. Also see Holloway "An Archaic Hoard" below for suggested revisions to Brown's classes and chronology. Also see Price and Waggoner *Archaic Greek Coinage: The Asyut Hoard* under HOARDS (pages 69-76) for suggested revisions to Brown's chronology].

4223 **Classical Numismatic Group, Inc.** "Countermarks on Coins of Aegina: Being of Full Weight and Good Metal." *Mail Bid Sale 46.* Lancaster: Classical Numismatic Group, 1998. Pages 38-43. Illus.
This auction sale catalogue includes fifty-nine countermarked Aeginetan staters (lots 304-362). Each is photographed, including enlarged photographs of the countermarks. Includes a brief essay on the purpose of countermarks and the history of the island of Aegina.

4224 **Cohen, Edward E.** "Euclid's Proposition on Ancient Turtles and Tortoises." *The Celator* 14, no. 8 (August 2000): 12-5. Illus.
The famous mathematician Euclid lived ca. 300 B.C. One of his books dealt with the geometry of rectangles. Cohen describes the reverse punch used on the staters of Aegina (a hollow rectangle divided into four smaller rectangles by a cross; a skew line at the intersection of the cross further divides one rectangle into two triangles). Citing mathematician Benno Artmann, Cohen suggests that the fundamental geometry of Euclid's binomial equation $[(a + b)^2 = a^2 + b^2 + 2ab]$ is reflected in the layout of the reverse design on the Aeginetan coins. [Also see the Eike Druckrey's "Letter to the Editor" in *The Celator* 14, no. 11 (November 2000): 16. Druckrey doubts Cohen's theory and believes there was no mathematical significance to the Aeginetan coins' reverse type].

4225 **Eaglen, Robin J.** "Portraits of Greek Coinage 22: Aegina." *Spink Numismatic Circular* 116, no. 3 (June 2008): 116-7. Illus.
This installment of the author's on-going series examines the coinage of Aegina. Reviews the history of the island and its coin types.

4226 **Gresham, Carling.** "Aegina Countermark Torturous Enigma." *World Coins* (Sidney, Ohio) 96 (December 1971): 1586-90. Illus.
"A bronze of Aegina with a turtle and countermarks is described." [*NL* 88]

4227 **Grunauer von Hoerschelmann, Susanne.** "Zwei Schatzfunde Archaischer Satere von Aigina." *Chiron* (Germany) 5 (1975): 13-20. 6 pls. [CS 2537]

4228 **Hands, Alfred Watson.** "Common Greek Coins: Aegina, Pheidon, The Aeginetic Standard." *Spink Numismatic Circular* 12 (August 1904): 7745-9.
Reviews the history of the city of Aegina and examines the "turtles." Attributes the coinage to Pheidon and discusses the Aeginetic weight standard.

4229 ———. "Common Greek Coins: Aegina, The Tortoise Type." *Spink Numismatic Circular* 12 (September 1904): 7801-7.
An introduction to the various periods of coinage in Aegina. Extensive discussion of the tortoise type and its significance.

4230 **Holloway, R. Ross.** *The Elder Turtles of Aegina.* Ph.D. dissertation in History and Archaeology. Princeton University, 1960.

4231 ———. "An Archaic Hoard from Crete and the Early Aeginetan Coinage." *Museum Notes* 17 (1971): 1-21. 8 pls.
Examines the Dunbabin hoard of sixty-eight Aeginetan staters found in Crete in 1943. An analysis of the coins provides the basis for refining the conclusions of W. L. Brown (see "Pheidon's Alleged Aeginetan Coinage" above) regarding the foundation and early development of the Aeginetan mint. Reviews Brown's chronology and the reasoning behind it. Discusses the "Cyclades" hoard of staters. Summarizes the suggested revisions to Brown's classes and chronology. In an appendix, the author re-considers the proto-tortoise group which E. S. G. Robinson attributed to Cydonia, a colony of Aegina in Crete. Holloway suggests these coins belong to Aegina. [See Robinson "Pseudaeginetica" under CRETE].

4232 **Jones, Francis Follin.** "Fifteen Turtles and Tortoises." *Greek Numismatics and Archaeology: Essays in Honor of Margaret Thompson.* Edited by O. Mørkholm and N. M. Waggoner. Wetteren: Numismatique Romaine, 1979. Pages 115-8. 1 pl.
Jones publishes the twelve "turtle" and three "tortoise" coins of Aegina given to Princeton University in 1973 by the bequest of J. Penrose Harland. Each coin is attributed to Holloway's catalogue (see Holloway *The Elder Turtles* above).

4233 **Kagan, Donald.** "Pheidon's Aeginetan Coinage." *Transactions and Proceedings of the American Philological Association* 91 (1960): 121-36. [CS 2538]
Kagan re-examines the evidence for and against Pheidon of Argos as the originator of coinage, presenting a rebuttal to the arguments of Brown who challenged the traditional attribution of Aegina's first coinage to Pheidon. Reviews Brown's main arguments. Reviews theories of the first coins: Lydia vs. Aegina. Reviews evidence for the date of Pheidon's life and suggests he ruled ca. 675-625 B.C. Discusses the iron spits dedicated at the Argive Heraeum and their role in the development of coinage. Suggests there was a gradual replacement of iron spits by coins. Concludes the Peloponnesian measures were invented by Pheidon, he dedicated the spits, and introduced silver coinage. [See Brown "Pheidon's Alleged Aeginetan Coinage" above and Kroll "Observations on Monetary Instruments" under ORIGINS OF COINAGE].

4234 **Kollgaard, Ron.** "Coins of Aigina Indicate Historical Political Change." *The Celator* 3, no. 5 (May 1989): 1, 22-3. Illus.
An overview of the history and coinage of Aegina. Speculates on the species of turtle depicted on the coinage. Mentions a unique type with triskeles on the reverse which may have been minted during the Athenian siege of 456 B.C.

4235 **Lis, L. J.** "History of Aegina is Reflected in Coinage Designs." *The Celator* 11, no. 6 (June 1997): 40-1. Illus.
A brief, but good, general review of the history and coinage of Aegina.

4236 **Mabbott, Thomas O.** "The Reverse-Type at Aegina by Olybrius." *Numismatic Review* 4, nos. 2-4 (April-October 1947): 67. Illus.
"A brief discussion of the reverse design of early Aeginetic staters. The novel theory advanced concerning these rude punch markings is accompanied by a sketch outlining the mint letters, as seen by the author." [F. Knobloch, *NL* 9]

4237 **Mathisen, Ralph W.** "The Early Development of Aeginetan Coinage." *SAN—Journal of the Society for Ancient Numismatics* 6, no. 1 (fall 1974): 3-5.
Discusses the weight standard of Aeginetan coinage and presents a chart showing the "typological development" of Aegina's stater, which compares the chronologies suggested by Head, Milbank, and Brown for the various stages of the coinage. [Also see follow-up comments by Wells, "Some Further Remarks" below].

4238 **Milbank, Samuel R.** *The Coinage of Aegina.* Numismatic Notes and Monographs, No. 24. New York: American Numismatic Society, 1924. 66 pp., 5 pls. [CS 2539]
Begins with an examination of the role of Pheidon in Aegina's history and his role in the change in the island's standards of weights and measures. Describes the relationship of silver to bronze and provides the weights of various coin denominations under the Aeginetan standard. Briefly discusses coin striking methods and the use of counterstamps. Then provides a history of the island and the variations in its coinage, segregated into nine time periods covering 650 B.C. to A.D. 221. Discusses the possibility of Aeginetan coins struck at Thyreatis (where the Aeginetans were temporarily settled after their expulsion from the island in 431 B.C.) and the possibility of coins struck by the Athenian cleruchs who resettled the island upon the expulsion of the Aeginetans. The plates illustrate seventy-nine coin types. [Much of Milbank's chronology is no longer accepted. See W. L. Brown "Pheidon's Alleged Aeginetan Coinage" above for a more recent chronology. Also see Price and Waggoner *Archaic Greek Coinage: The Asyut Hoard* under HOARDS (pages 69-76) for suggested revisions to Brown's chronology].

4239 **Müller, Otto, and W. Gentner.** "On the Composition and Silver Sources of Aeginetan Coins from the Asyut Hoard." *Proceedings of the 18th International Symposium on Archaeometry and Archaeological Prospection, Bonn, 1978.* Archaeo-Physika 10. 1979.

4240 **Nicolet-Pierre, Hélène.** "Remarques sur le Monnayage d'Egine au VIe et Ve Siecle d'Apres la Trouvaille de Mégalopolis de 1936." *Frappe et Ateliers Monétaires dans l'Antiquité et au Moyen Age.* Belgrade, 1976. Pages 5-12.

4241 **Nicolet-Pierre, Hélène, and S. Gjongecaj.** "Le Monnayage d'Argent d'Égine et le Trésor de Hollm (Albanie) 1991." *Bulletin de Correspondance Hellénistique* (France) 119 (1995): 283-332.

4242 **Oeconmides, Mando Caramessini.** "The 1970 Myrina Hoard of Aeginetan Staters." *Greek Numismatics and Archaeology: Essays in Honor of Margaret Thompson.* Edited by O. Mørkholm and N. M. Waggoner. Wetteren: Numismatique Romaine, 1979. Pages 231-9. 2 pls.

The catalogue of a hoard composed exclusively of 149 Aeginetan staters, found in Myrina in Thessaly in 1970. The specimens include sea-turtle, land-tortoise, and "pseudoaeginetan" varieties. Most are countermarked and some have graffiti. The author compares the contents of this hoard to the Koumares 1936 hoard (*IGCH* 21) and the Chavara 1933 hoard (*IGCH* 28). She comments on the chronology of the coins and suggests ca. 440 B.C. as the burial date for the hoard.

4243 ——— "Deux Trésors de Statères Éginètes du Cabinet des Médailles d'Athènes." *Revue Suisse de Numismatique* (Switzerland) 120 (1980): 81-90.

4244 ——— "The *IGCH* 101 Hoard and the Circulation of the Tortoise in the Peloponnesus." *Florilegium Numismaticum: Studia in Honorem U. Westermark Edita*. Edited by Harald Nilsson. Stockholm: Svenska Numismatiska Föreningen, 1992. Pages 307-12. Illus.
The author examines a fourth century B.C. circulation hoard of thirty-five tortoise coins of Aegina found in the Peloponnesus. The coins included five staters, twenty-seven drachms, and three triobols. Oeconomides proposes a burial date ca. 325 B.C. This and similar hoards show that the Aeginetan coins were still much used in the Peloponnesus in the fourth century B.C. Only three of the coins were of the "inscribed" variety; several coins bear two pellets on the reverse. A catalogue of the coins is presented with cross-references to Milbank (see Milbank above).

4245 **Stingl, Timo.** "Äginetische Elektronprägungen? Zwei Schildkröten auf Münzen aus dem Tresor des Münzkabinetts der Staatlichen Museen zu Berlin." *Zurück zum Gegenstand. Festschrift für Andreas E. Furtwängler*. Zentrum für Archälogie und Kulturgeschichte des Schwarzmeerraumes, Band 16. Edited by Ralph Einicke et al. Langenweibach: Beier and Beram, 2009.

4246 **Wallace, Malcolm B.** "The First Coins of Greece Proper." *Cornucopiæ* (publication of The Ancient Coin Society, Canada) 3, no. 4 (1975): 49-56. Illus., map. [CS 2308]
Discusses the introduction of coinage in east central Greece. Suggests that Aegina was most likely the first state in Greece proper to use silver as a coinage metal, perhaps ca. 580 B.C. Wallace questions why electrum was not chosen as the preferred metal. He believes Aegina avoided electrum due to the variability of its gold content. He comments on the prevalence of coins with no legends and non-anthropomorphic types during this early period of coinage. Includes a table of comparative volumes of some early silver coinages.

4247 **Wells, H. Bartlett.** "Species Indeterminacy in the 'Elder Turtle' Coins of Aegina." Parts 1-2. *SAN—Journal of the Society for Ancient Numismatics* 1, no. 4 (April 1970): 60-1, 72; 2, no. 1 (July 1970): 8-10. Illus.
Describes various species of marine turtles in an attempt to determine the specific species depicted on the early silver coinage of Aegina. Concludes that the species cannot be specifically identified. [Also see erratum, *SAN* 2, no. 1 (July 1970): 2, and follow-up comments in *SAN* 2, no. 2 (fall 1970): 22-3. Also see "Some Further Remarks" below].

4248 ——— "Some Further Remarks on Turtles, Texts, and Techniques." *SAN—Journal of the Society for Ancient Numismatics* 6, no. 2 (winter 1974-5): 22-3, 25.
Follow-up comments related to Mathisen's paper (see "The Early Development" above) on Aeginetan coinage and Wells' article on the turtle coinage (see "Species" above). Cites other references that pertain to Aeginetan iron spit money and turtle coinage. Also contains a discussion of methods of manufacturing coin planchets, and cites several useful references.

4249 **Wihnyk, Joe.** "The Tortoise of Aphrodite on Coins of Aigina." *The Celator* 20, no. 12 (December 2006): 30-3. Illus.
Suggests that the tortoise on coins of Aegina is a symbol of the goddess Aphrodite. Cites Pausanias' account of a statue of Aphrodite at Olympia in which the goddess stands with one foot atop a turtle. Later copies of the statue survive. The author also notes the existence of a temple of Aphrodite near the harbor at Aegina. Reviews the history of the island and its importance in regional trade. Aphrodite was a goddess of commerce and she protected sailors and navigators. [Also see the "Letter to the Editor" by Mark Gredler in *The Celator* 21, no. 3 (March 2007): 38].

Also see: Beer "Analysis of Coins" under METALLURGY; Beer "Results of Coin Striking" under THE MINTING PROCESS; Clain-Stefanelli "An Application of Physics" under COUNTERFEITS; Conn "Prevalence and Profitability: Re-Examining" under COUNTERFEITS; Delamare and Van der Mersch "Etude Mécanique" under THE MINTING PROCESS; Earle-Fox "Early Coinages" under ORIGINS OF COINAGE; Gardner "Earliest Coins" under ORIGINS OF COINAGE; Grace "Early Thasian Stamped Amphoras" under TYPES; Hackens et al. "Facts" under THE MINTING PROCESS; Head *Catalogue of Greek Coins* under ATTICA—GENERAL WORKS; Hoover *Handbook of Coins of the Islands* under CYCLADES ISLANDS; Johnston "Horse Sense?" under CORINTHIA; Kraay and Emeleus *The Composition* under METALLURGY; Kroll "Observations on Monetary Instruments" under ORIGINS OF COINAGE; Kroll and Waggoner "Dating the Earliest Coins" under ATTICA—GENERAL WORKS; Metcalf *Oxford Handbook of Greek and Roman Coinage* under GENERAL WORKS—GREEK; Milne "The Perachora Drachma" under PELOPONNESOS—ARGOLIS; Oeconomides "À Propos du Trésor de Lappa" under HOARDS; Price and Waggoner *Archaic Greek Coinage: The Asyut Hoard* under HOARDS; Robinson "Pseudaeginetica" under CRETE; M. Wilkinson "Athenian Silver Coin Fractions" under ATTICA—GENERAL WORKS.

MEGARIS

Megara, in ancient times the flourishing capital of the territory between Attica and the isthmus of Corinth, commanded the trade routes between Peloponnesus and Central Greece.

—Barclay V. Head, 1911

4249a **Pafford, Isabelle.** "Megara: The Denominational System and Chronology of the Hellenistic Coinage." *XII Internationaler Numismatischer Kongress, Berlin 1997: Akten.* Berlin: Staatliche Musen zu Berlin, 2000. Pages 347-50.

Also see: Dreni "The Hoard *IGCH* 137 (Megara 1904)" under HOARDS; Gardner "A Numismatic Note on the Lelantian War" under CENTRAL GREECE—EUBOIA; Head *Catalogue of Greek Coins of Attica, Megaris, and Aegina* under ATTICA; Shear "The Campaign of 1936" under ATTICA; Waage *Greek Bronze Coins from a Well at Megara* under HOARDS.

CORINTHIA

Great care was devoted to the details of the designs and the thousands of devices that served as mint-marks. Very probably, the moneyers were changed each year and, therefore, the newly appointed officials had to use symbols to indicate that they were responsible for the products of the mint. Animals, birds, musical instruments, parts of ships, flowers, pieces of armor, fabulous beasts and even gods and goddesses were used. Unfortunately, we cannot link these beautifully-produced 'signatures' with historical figures, because we have no detailed history of the internal politics of Corinth.

—John Anthony, 1983

4250 **Bellinger, Alfred R.** "Corinthian Fractional Currency." *Yale Classical Studies* 2 (1931): 187-98. 2 pls. [CS 2540]
Catalogues seventy-four fractional silver coins of Corinth and her colonies, mostly from a hoard, now in the collection of Yale University. Thirty-two of the coins are illustrated.

4251 **Blomberg, Peter E.** *On Corinthian Iconography: the Bridled Winged Horse and the Helmeted Female Head in the Sixth Century B.C.* Acta Universitatis Upsaliensis BOREAS. Uppsala Studies in Ancient Mediterranean and Near Eastern Civilizations 25. Uppsala, Sweden, 1996. 109 pp., illus.
A study of two motifs in the sixth century B.C.: the bridled winged horse, and the helmeted female head. These are the obverse and reverse types of the Corinthian stater. The style and chronology of Pegasus on vases and coins is compared, and it is argued that the motif was used as a symbol for the fall of the tyrants. The helmeted head motif is commonly thought to be Athena Chalinitis. This identification is rejected by Blomberg. He suggests the head on the coins is Aphrodite, the main goddess of Corinth. He concludes the reverse motif on Corinthian coins represents Aphrodite Ourania in her two aspects: protectress of the city and goddess of love and beauty. [Also see Derek Smith "New Evidence" and "Aphrodite" below. Smith validates Blomberg's conclusions].

4252 **Brown, W. Llewellyn.** "Note Chronologique sur les Monnaies de Corinth." *Schweizer Münzblätter* (Switzerland) 4 (1953): 49-51. [CS 2541]
"Dating of the earliest Corinthian coins." [E. Clain-Stefanelli].

4253 **Calciati, Romolo.** *Pegasi.* Two volumes. Mortara: Edizioni I. P., 1990. 732 pp. Illus., maps.
A corpus of the silver coinage of Corinth, her colonies in Greece, Italy, and Sicily, and the independent cities which issued coins of Corinthian type. The catalogue is arranged by city and then by coin type. Includes a brief historical and economic framework for each city. Catalogues 13,650 coins and includes 2855 illustrations. Includes a table of all the symbols which appear on the coins. The five appendices are: (1) a fully illustrated catalogue of the East Sicily Hoard of 1983 comprised of 783 Corinthian-type staters, (2) an examination of overstrikes, (3) an examination of graffiti found on the coins, (4) technique in coinage, and (5) hoards and distribution. Extensive bibliography. The text is in both English and Italian.

4254 **Cammann, Jean B.** *The Symbols on Staters of Corinthian Type: A Catalogue.* Numismatic Notes and Monographs, No. 53. New York: American Numismatic Society, 1932. 130 pp., 14 pls., map. [CS 2543]
A catalogue of the symbols which appear on the staters of Corinth and her colonies. The symbols are listed in alphabetical order and are numbered. At least one illustration is given of each symbol and the illustrations are numbered to correspond with the alphabetical listing. References are given for specimens in published collections. Includes an index of symbols arranged by mint city. Includes a map of Corinth and her colonies—the locations where these staters were issued or used.

4255 **Cozzolino, Michael.** "Corinth." *SAN—Journal of the Society for Ancient Numismatics* 18, no. 2 (May 1991): inside covers.
An early Corinthian coin provides evidence that Corinthian coinage influenced coin development in Sicily.

4256 **Forrer, Leonard S.** "A Rare Corinthian Stater." *Spink Numismatic Circular* 56 (June 1948): 271-2.
Briefly describes a Corinthian stater of the period 400-350 B.C. bearing the magistrate name ΕΥΘΥΜΕΝΟΣ.

4257 **Gardner, Percy.** "On Some Coins with the Inscription 'TPIH.'" *Numismatic Chronicle* new ser., 11 (1871): 162-5.
Discusses coins with *obv.*, Medusa facing, and TPIH in an incuse square; *rev.*, Pegasus with curled wing. The coins had previously been attributed to Tirida in Thrace, Trieres in Thrace, Trieres in Lycia, or Teria in Troas. Gardner attributes the coins to Corinth. [Also see Imhoof-Blumer "Les Inscription 'TPIH'" and Psoma "Des Monnaies aux Initiales TPIH" under MACEDONIA—CITIES AND TRIBES].

4258 **Grubb, Steven W.** "Pegasus and the Colts of Corinth." *The Numismatist* 110, no. 12 (December 1997): 1390-2. Illus.
This article appears in the *First Strike* section of the magazine, which is devoted to young and beginning collectors. The author discusses the staters of Corinth, focusing on the mythology surrounding Pegasus and Bellerophon.

4259 **Hands, Alfred Watson.** "Common Greek Coins: The Coins of Ancient Corinth." *Spink Numismatic Circular* 12 (June 1904): 7625-31; (July 1904): 7681-4.
Examines the swastika pattern found on the reverse of early Corinthian coins. Presents theories for its origin and symbolism. The author concludes the type began with the early incuse die punch-marks and developed into a standard type which was probably a solar symbol.

4260 **Harris, Josephine M.** "Numismatic Reflections on the History of Corinth." *American Journal of Archaeology* 44, no. 1 (January-March 1940): 112.
The summary of a paper presented to a meeting of the Archaeological Institute of America in 1939. Harris notes that the numerical distribution of coins found at Corinth is in direct proportion to the prominence and commercial activity of the city during the period the coins were issued. The largest number of coins are found at excavation levels representing periods during which the city thrived.

4261 **Head, Barclay V.** *Catalogue of Greek Coins of Corinth.* Edited by R. S. Poole. London: British Museum, 1889. Reprint, Bologna: Forni, 1963. lxviii, 174 pp., 39 pls. [CS 2544]
Volume 12 of the *Catalogue of Greek Coins in the British Museum*. Covers the coinage of Corinth and other cities which assimilated Corinthian coinage. Sixty-eight pages of introductory text precede the 174-page catalogue of coins. [Also see *Catalogue of Greek Coins in the British Museum* under PUBLIC COLLECTIONS—GREAT BRITAIN (LONDON)].

4262 **Jenkins, G. Kenneth.** "Notes on the Mint of Corinth." *La Monetazione Corinzia in Occidente. Atti del IX Convegno CISN 1986.* Rome, 1993. Pages 21-7.

4263 **Johnston, Alan.** "Horse Sense?" *Numismatic Chronicle* 159 (1999): 277-80. Illus., 1 pl.
The author illustrates and discusses a Corinthian stater with graffiti on it, and attempts to read and interpret the inscription.

4264 **Kagan, Jonathan H.** "Epidamnus or Ephyre (Elea): A Note on the Coinage of Corinth and her Colonies at the Outbreak of the Peloponnesian War." *Studies in Greek Numismatics in Memory of Martin Jessop Price.* Edited by Richard Ashton and Silvia Hurter. London: Spink, 1998. Pages 163-73. 2 pls.
Kagan states that two of the crucial conflicts leading up to the Peloponnesian War, the Corcyra and Potidaea episodes, have left their mark on the coinage. Thus, this coin evidence may help illuminate historical events. In his *Archaic and Classical Greek Coins*, Colin Kraay attributed a Corinthian-style stater with the letter *epsilon* beneath the winged horse to the mint of Epidamnus, ca. 435 B.C. In a 1979 article (see Kraay "The Coinage of Ambracia" under NORTHERN GREECE—EPIRUS), Kraay suggested Ephyre or Elea, and a slightly earlier date. Kagan believes that Kraay's initial attribution to Epidamnus was correct. He suggests the coin may have been minted on behalf of Epidamnus (or at least financed by it or its Corinthian sponsors) rather than by the Epidamnians themselves. This series can be connected with Corinthian military expenditures in the period 436-432 B.C.

4265 **Keppel, Derek H. E.** "A Small Collection of Corinthian Copper Coins." *Spink Numismatic Circular* 38 (April 1930): 151-2.
A brief description of the autonomous and Imperial copper coins of Corinth.

4266 **Kollgaard, Ron.** "Symbols Important: Pegasos Was Corinth's Logo." *The Celator* 3, no. 10 (October 1989): 1, 24-5.
Traces the history and coinage of Corinth.

4267 **Kraay, Colin M.** "A Hoard of Corinth and Leucas from N.W. Greece." *Coin Hoards* 5 (1979): 19-33 including 7 pls.
Discusses a hoard of staters from Corinth and Leucas found circa 1964. Confirms Ravel's classification of the early fifth century issues of Corinth.

4268 **Madsen, Eardley, and Ethel Madsen.** "Corinth." *SAN—Journal of the Society for Ancient Numismatics* 12, no. 4 (winter 1981-2): inside covers.
A brief overview of the history and coinage of Corinth.

4269 **Numismatik Lanz München.** *Auktion 105: Münzen von Korinth: Sammlung BCD.* Munich: Numismatik Lanz München, 2001. 147 pp., illus.
The sale catalogue for BCD's unsurpassed collection of the coins of Corinth, comprised of 981 coins, all illustrated. Includes autonomous and Roman coins minted at Corinth. Brief introduction by the collector. [Reviewed by Alan Walker in *The Celator* 16, no. 2 (February 2002): 26-7, 34-5. For other portions of the collection, see "BCD" in the INDEX OF COLLECTORS AND COLLECTIONS].

4270 **Oman, Charles W. C.** "The Chronological Sequence of the Coins of Corinth, B.C. 450-390." *Corolla Numismatica: Numismatic Essays in Honour of Barclay V. Head.* Edited by G. F. Hill. London: Oxford University Press, 1906. Pages 208-16. 1 pl.
Oman attempts a general arrangement of the staters of Corinth, excluding the earliest archaic issues. He divides the series into seven classes and discusses the characteristics of each. [See next item for additions to this catalogue].

4271 ——— "The Fifth-Century Coins of Corinth." *Numismatic Chronicle* 4th ser., 9 (1909): 333-56. 4 pls.
Oman publishes some additions to the catalogue of Corinthian coins which he compiled for the *Corolla Numismatica* volume (see above). Adds several subdivisions to the previous classifications. Includes extensive discussion of the chronology of the coins.

4272 ——— "Some Problems of the Later Coinage of Corinth." *Numismatic Chronicle* 5th ser., 6 (1926): 20-35. 1 pl.
Explores the coinage of Corinth during the period 338-223 B.C. Discusses mint magistrates and the history of the city during this period.

4273 **Phillips, Wayne C.** "Corinth Once a Thriving Commercial Metropolis; Coinage Begins Early in City." *Coin World* (April 6, 1992): 48.
This installment of Phillips' feature column "Let's Talk Ancients" reviews the history and coinage of Corinth during the Greek and Roman periods.

4273a   **Puglisi, Mariangela.** "Monetazione Corinzia: Le Frazioni Argentee." *XII Internationaler Numismatischer Kongress, Berlin 1997: Akten.* Berlin: Staatliche Musen zu Berlin, 2000. Pages 203-11.

4274   **Ravel, Oscar E.** "Notes on Some Rare or Unpublished 'Pegasi' of My Collection." *Numismatic Chronicle* 5th ser., 6 (1926): 305-21. 2 pls.
Discusses twenty-nine "Pegasus" staters of various mints. Describes the unique features of each die.

4275   ——— "Numismatique Corinthienne." *Aréthuse: Revue Trimestrielle d'Art et d'Archéologie* (France) (1929). Also in *Revue Numismatique* (France) (1932).

4276   ——— *Corinthian Hoards (Corinth and Arta).* Numismatic Notes and Monographs, No. 52. New York: American Numismatic Society, 1932. 27 pp., 3 pls. [CS 3277]
Ravel examines two small hoards of Corinthian-style coins. The first contained thirty-five coins and was found near Corinth in 1928. All of these coins were Corinthian except for three coins traditionally attributed to Tegea. The author concludes these are trihemiobols of Corinth. Illustrates the evolution of the incuse reverses of the archaic issues. Suggests the hoard was buried ca. 470-460 B.C. The second hoard was found near Arta in Ambracia about 1929. It was comprised of late issues of Corinthian pegasi. Ravel rejects the theory that the olive wreath on Athena's helmet signifies a military victory. [Also see Ravel "Corinthian Hoard from Chiliomodi" under HOARDS].

4277   ——— "Rare and Unpublished Coins of Corinthian Types." *Numismatic Chronicle* 5th ser., 15 (1935): 1-15. 2 pls.
Illustrates and discusses some gold trihemiobols of Corinth. Concludes they are worth a silver stater and were issued about 406 B.C. Publishes several new additions to the author's catalogue *The "Colts" of Ambracia* (see Ravel under NORTHERN GREECE—EPIRUS). Also publishes two coins of Locri overstruck on coins of Corinth, and a pegasi coin (of uncertain mint) struck over a coin probably from Segesta, Motya, Eryx, or Panormus.

4278   ——— *Les "Poulains" de Corinthe: Monographie des Statéres Corinthiens.* Volume 1: Basel, 1936. Volume 2: London, 1948. Reprint (in one volume), Chicago: Obol International, 1979. 444 pp., 78 pls. [CS 2545]

4279   **Salmon, J.** "Trade and Corinthian Coins in the West." *La Monetazione Corinzia in Occidente: Atti del IX Convegno del Centro Internazionale de Studi Numismatici: Napoli 27-28 Ottobre 1986.* Rome: Istituto Italiano di Numismatica, 1993. Pages 3-17.

4280   **Schwabacher, Willy.** "Corinthian Contributions from Copenhagen." *Acta Archaeologica* (Denmark) 12, nos. 1-2 (1941): 53-65. Illus.
Discusses some rare early coins of Corinth in the Royal Collection including a trihemiobol previously attributed to Tegea. Compares the Athena heads on some Corinthian coins with sculptures. Discusses a bronze coin previously attributed to Aegina, and some gold coins.

4281   **Smith, Charles F.** "Corinthians Honored Poseidon through Their Games, Myths, and Coinage." *The Celator* 8, no. 9 (September 1994): 16-20. Illus.
Discusses the stories of Poseidon and their influence on Corinth, and the use of Poseidon-related motifs on Corinthian coinage.

4282   **Smith, Derek R.** "New Evidence for the Identification of Aphrodite on Staters of Corinth." *Numismatic Chronicle* 165 (2005): 41-3. 1 pl.
A bronze coin of Corinth struck under Hadrian offers evidence that the helmeted female deity on the reverse of Corinthian staters of the archaic and classical periods was Aphrodite rather than Athena. [Also see Blomberg *On Corinthian Iconography* above].

4283   ——— "Aphrodite: Classical Greek Goddess of War." *The Celator* 20, no. 1 (January 2006): 6-18. Illus.
Argues that the deity portrayed on Corinthian staters is Aphrodite, not Athena as is commonly claimed. Reviews the origins of Aphrodite and shows that she was the principal deity in Corinth, and in some early depictions, she is armed. Illustrates a bronze coin of Hadrian, minted at Corinth, which clearly shows the temple of Aphrodite on the Acrocorinth. Aphrodite wears a Corinthian-style helmet. The demise of Aphrodite's role as a war goddess may have come about through Alexander's use of ambiguous iconography—the deity on Alexander's gold staters could be interpreted as either Athena or Aphrodite, depending on the home polis of the viewer. This may have served as a way of uniting the Greek cities of Alexander's empire. [Also see Smith's "Letter to the Editor" in *The Celator* 20, no. 7 (July 2006): 4, 21, in which he summarizes the evidence for and against Aphrodite or Athena on the Corinthian staters. Also see Blomberg *On Corinthian Iconography* above].

4284   **Vagi, David.** "Pegasus Motif Revives the Story of Bellerophon." *The Celator* 7, no. 8 (August 1993): 24. Illus.
Relates the story of Bellerophon slaying the Chimera and makes brief comments on the Pegasus coin types employed by Corinth and her colonies.

4285   ——— "The 'Colts' of Corinth." *Numismatist* 119, no. 8 (August 2006): 65-7. Illus.
A brief discussion of the Corinthian-type staters and how the type spread to the colonies of Corinth.

4286   **Warren, Jennifer.** "The Trihemidrachms of Corinth." *Essays in Greek Coinage Presented to Stanley Robinson.* Edited by C. M. Kraay and G. K. Jenkins. Oxford: Clarendon Press, 1968. Pages 125-44. 1 pl. [CS 2548]
Examines the Corinthian coins showing Bellerophon riding Pegasus on the obverse and the chimera on the reverse. Provides a detailed list of such specimens in public collections. Reviews the mythological stories related to Bellerophon. Discusses the stylistic variations of the coins and compares the representations of Bellerophon and the chimera to similar figures on vases and sculptures as well as on the coins of Sicyon and Leukas. The author attempts to form a chronological sequence for the issues.

4287   **Will, Édouard.** "Note sur les Origines du Pégase Monétaire Corinthien." *Revue Numismatique* (France) 5th ser., 14 (1952): 239-44. [CS 2549]
"An attempt to establish the earliest issues." [E. Clain-Stefanelli].

4288 **Zograph, Alexander.** "Pegasos Staters from a Sicilian Hoard Found in the Past Century." *Numismatic Chronicle* 5th ser., 8 (1928): 115-30. 1 pl.

A catalogue of a hoard of pegasus-type staters found in Sicily, probably in 1837. Includes 90 staters of Corinth, 2 of Syracuse, 3 of Dyrrhachium, 5 of Ambracia, 1 of Alyzia, 4 of Anactorium, 25 of Leucas, and 1 of an uncertain mint.

Also see: Beaumont "Greek Influence" under NORTHERN GREECE–ILLYRIA; Broneer "The Isthmian Victory Crown" under TYPES; Burgon "On Certain Rare Greek Coins Recently Acquired" under PUBLIC COLLECTIONS–GREAT BRITAIN (LONDON); Edwards *Corinth: Results of Excavations* under HOARDS; Edwards "Report on the Coins" under HOARDS; Fisher "Corinth" and "Acrocorinth" (six items) under HOARDS; Earle-Fox "The Early Coinages" under ORIGINS OF COINAGE; Gardner "The Earliest Coins" under ORIGINS OF COINAGE; Harris "Coins Found at Corinth" under HOARDS; Hohlfelder *Ancient Coins* under PUBLIC COLLECTIONS–UNITED STATES (BLOOMINGTON); Jenkins "A Note on Corinthian Coins" under SICILY–GENERAL WORKS; Knaap, MacIsaac, and Miller *Excavations at Nemea III* under HOARDS; Kraay "Ambracia" (two items) under NORTHERN GREECE–EPIRUS; Kraay "The Earliest Coinage of Athens: A Reply" under ATTICA–GENERAL WORKS; Kraay "Timoleon and Corinthian Coinage" under SICILY–SYRACUSE; Kraay "Greek Coinage and War" under GENERAL WORKS–GREEK; Kroll "Observations on Monetary Instruments" under ORIGINS OF COINAGE; Kroll and Waggoner "Dating the Earliest Coins" under ATTICA–GENERAL WORKS.

MacDonald "Sicilian and Southern Italian Overstrikes on Pegasoi" under ITALY–GENERAL WORKS; MacIssac "Corinth" under HOARDS; Milne "Ancient Tooling" under THE MINTING PROCESS; Milne "The Perachora Drachma" under PELOPONNESOS–ARGOLIS; Pemberton "Ten Hellenistic Graves" under HOARDS; Price *Greek Bronze Coinage* under GENERAL WORKS–GREEK; Price "Coins from Some Deposits" under HOARDS; Ravel "The Classification" under ART; Ravel *The Colts* under NORTHERN GREECE–EPIRUS; Ravel "Corinthian Hoard from Chiliomodi" under HOARDS; H. S. Robinson "Excavations" under HOARDS; Rynearson "Locri-Epizephyrii" under ITALY–LOCRI-EPIZEPHYRII; Sayles "The Technical Obverse" under THE MINTING PROCESS; Stroud "Acrocorinth" (two items) under HOARDS; Sutherland "A Corinthian Stater Overstruck" under ITALY–METAPONTUM; Talbert "Corinthian Silver" under SICILY–SYRACUSE; Westermark "An Overstrike" under SICILY–AKRAGAS; Wilkinson "Athenian Silver Coin Fractions" under ATTICA–GENERAL WORKS; Zervos' series on the excavations at Corinth under HOARDS.

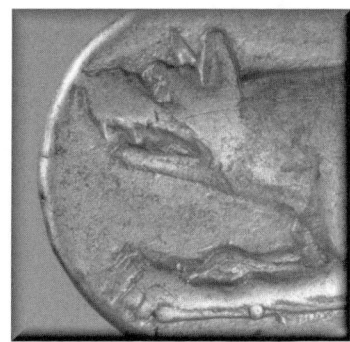

Peloponnesos

And at Olympia, the religious, the artistic centre of Hellas, the priests issued, what many will agree with the writer in calling, the most uniformly beautiful coinage of the Greeks.

—*Charles T. Seltman, 1921*

General Works

4289　**Alpha Bank.** *Ancient Coins of the Peloponnese.* Athens: Alpha Bank, 2006. 25 pp., illus.
Catalogue from an exhibition of coins from the Alpha Bank collection, held at Nafplio in 2006.

4290　**Chantraine, Heinrich.** "Literaturüberblick der Griechischen Numismatik: Peloponnes." *Jahrbuch für Numismatik und Geldsseschichte* (Germany) 8 (1957): 57-120. [CS 2551]
A bibliography.

4291　**Classical Numismatic Group, Inc.** *The BCD Collection of Coins of the Peloponnesos, Part II.* Mail Bid Sale 81/2 (May 20, 2009). Lancaster: Classical Numismatic Group, Inc., 2009. 128 pp., illus.
The remaining coins from the famed BCD collection of coins of the Peloponnesos, including 921 lots. Includes many bronze coins and many die varieties that were not included in the first sale (see LHS Numismatics Ltd. below). [For other portions of the collection, see "BCD" in the Index of Collectors and Collections].

4292　**Gardner, Percy.** *Catalogue of Greek Coins of Peloponnesus (excluding Corinth).* Edited by R. S. Poole. London: British Museum, 1887. Reprint, Bologna: Forni, 1963. liv, 230 pp., 37 pls. [CS 2552]
Volume 10 of the *Catalogue of Greek Coins in the British Museum.* Fifty-four pages of introductory text precede the 230-page catalogue of coins. [Reviewed by W. Wroth in *Journal of Hellenic Studies* 8 (1887): 538-40. Also see *Catalogue of Greek Coins in the British Museum* under Public Collections—Great Britain (London)].

4293　**Grandjean, Catherine.** "Les Dernières Monnaies d'Argent du Péloponnèse." *Travaux de Numismatique Grecque Offerts à Georges Le Rider.* Edited by M. Amandry and S. Hurter. London: Spink, 1999. Pages 37-64.
Examines the late silver coinage of Elis, Sparta, Messene, Argos, Megalopolis, Dyme, Aigion, and Patras.

4293a　**Hackens, Tony.** "A Propos de la Circulation Monétiare dans le Péloponnèse au IIIe s. av. J.-C." *Studia Hellenistica* 16 (1968): 69-95.

4294　**Hoover, Oliver D.** *Handbook of Coins of the Peloponnesos: Achaia, Phleiasia, Sikyonia, Elis, Triphylia, Messenia, Lakonia, Argolis, and Arkadia, Sixth to First Centuries BC.* The Handbook of Greek Coinage Series, Volume 5. Lancaster: Classical Numismatic Group, 2011. lxxiv + 293 pp., illus.
A comprehensive guide to the coin types, heavily illustrated, with extensive background information and estimates of rarity. Lists 1092 coin types. Includes a *Foreword* by Alan Walker, a *Preface* by D. Scott VanHorn and Bradley R. Nelson which provides an overview of the history of Greek coinage, minting methods, denominations, types, epigraphy, and basic information for collectors regarding grading, and good summaries of the coinage of each region by Hoover. [For a general description of the format of these catalogues and a list of all the volumes in this series, see Hoover *The Handbook of Greek Coinage* under Collecting Guides].

4295　**Kampmann, Ursula.** "Record Results at LHS Numismatics Auctions 96 and 97 in Zurich—BCD Collection of Peloponnesos." *The Celator* 20, no. 7 (July 2006): 33-5. Illus.
A report on the results from (1) the auction of the collection of Peloponnesian coins formed by "BCD," the most complete collection of coins of the Peloponnesos ever to appear at auction, and (2) a sale of Roman and Byzantine coins. [See LHS Numismatics below].

4296　**LHS Numismatics Ltd.** *Coins of the Peloponnesos: The BCD Collection. Auction LHS 96, 8-9 May 2006.* Zurich: LHS Numismatics Ltd., 2006. 423 pp., illus.
An important sale catalogue featuring 1775 lots of coins of the Peloponnesos from the collection of "BCD." The collection is the largest and most extensive collection of the coins of the Peloponnesos ever formed. The catalogue, by Alan Walker, is extraordinary. Coin descriptions are complete, and many include extensive notes. BCD collected by die variety, so this hardcover catalogue is a detailed reference work of permanent importance. [Also see Classical

Numismatic Group above for Part 2 of the BCD collection of coins of the Peloponnesos. For other portions of the collection, see "BCD" in the INDEX OF COLLECTORS AND COLLECTIONS].

4297 **Warren, Jennifer A. W.** "After the Boehringer Revolution: The 'New Landscape' in the Coinage of the Peloponnese." *Topoi Orient-Occident* (France) 7, no. 1 (1997): 109-14.

4298 ——— "More on the 'New Landscape' in the Late Hellenistic Coinage of the Peloponnese." *Travaux de Numismatique Grecque Offerts à Georges Le Rider.* Edited by M. Amandry and S. Hurter. London: Spink, 1999. Pages 375-93. 1 pl.
A re-examination of the coinage of the Peloponnese in the second and first centuries B.C. Boehringer proposed to downdate the Final period emissions of the Achaian League coinage and associated autonomous silver, from c. 150-146 B.C. into the late second century and on through 31 B.C. This results in a reconsideration of how the cities of the Peloponnese reacted to the increasing Roman power during this period. The author concludes that there appears to be an almost complete cessation of coin production in the Peloponnese in the second half of the second century B.C. Substantial coinages resumed early in the first century B.C.

4299 ——— "From Macedonia and Epirus to the Peloponnese, with the Sporades, Cyclades, and Crete." *A Survey of Numismatic Research, 1978-1984. Volume 1: Ancient, Medieval and Modern Numismatics.* Edited by M. J. Price et al. International Association of Professional Numismatists Special Publication, No. 9. London: International Numismatic Commission, 1986. Pages 117-35.
A narrative overview of newly published works in the field of numismatics. Summarizes the major findings, with bibliographic references cited in the footnotes.

4299a ——— "Financing the Peloponnesian War: The Peloponnesian Perspective." *XIII Congreso Internacional de Numismática, Madrid – 2003: Actas–Proceedings–Actes I.* Edited by Carmen Alfaro, Carmen Marcos, and Paloma Otero. Madrid: International Numismatic Commisson, 2005. Pages 317-20.
Warren explores the question of what coinage the Peloponnesians used during the Peloponnesian War. She cites the lack of coinage by Sparta and the limited coinage of other allies at the time. The coinage of Sikyon may have been the major coinage used.

Also see: Kolitsida-Makri "O Thesauros Gytheiou" under HOARDS; MacDonald "Mercenaries" under CRETE; Oeconomides "The IGCH 101 Hoard" under AEGINA; Oeconomides et al "Le Trésor de Zougra et la Circulation Monétaire dans le Péloponnèse" under HOARDS; M. Thompson *The Agrinion Hoard* under HOARDS; Troxell "The Peloponnesian Alexanders" under MACEDONIAN KINGDOM—GENERAL WORKS; M. Thompson "A Hoard of Greek Federal Silver" under HOARDS; Warren "The 1980 Kato" under HOARDS.

ACHAIA

4300 **Benner, Steve M.** "Achaean League Hemidrachms." *Numismatist* 118, no. 5 (May 2005): 54-8. Illus.
A brief introduction to the coinage of the Achean League. Summarizes some of the letters and monograms appearing on the hemidrachms and the cities to which each is attributed. [Also see two "Letters to the Editor" in *Numismatist* 118, no. 7 (July 2005): 15-6, explaining the Greek letter digamma].

4301 ——— *Achaian League Coinage of the 3rd Through 1st Centuries B.C.E.* Classical Numismatic Studies No. 7. Lancaster and London: Classical Numismatic Group, 2008. 188 pp., illus.
A systematic overview of the coinages of the Achaian League. The book is divided into four parts. Part 1 provides a brief historical overview of the Achaian League from its earliest incarnation to its reconstitution in the third century B.C. down to its end in 146 B.C. Part 2 introduces the Achaian League coinage, discussing issuing cities, the chronology of issues, as well as brief discussions of types and metrology. This section concludes with tables of issuing magistrates' names and monograms. Parts 3 and 4 comprise the catalogue of issues. Each entry provides information in a tabular format and is cross-referenced to Clerk, Warren, and *BCD Peloponnesos* (see LHS Numismatics under PELOPONNESOS—GENERAL WORKS). Appendices provide a quick reference for attribution of both the silver and bronze coins, as well as concordances to the major references. Includes a bibliography and a list of abbreviations. [A scathing review by Alan Walker appears in *The Celator* 23, no. 9 (September 2009): 36-40, 44, 50. Walker comments on the book's many errors, omissions, poor organization, and other problems. Also see Benner's reply in *The Celator* 23, no. 11 (November 2009): 4, 44, 48. Benner points out that the book was intended to be a guide for collectors, not a work of scholarly research. Also see Wayne Sayles' "Through the Looking Glass" column in the same issue, pages 49-50, in which Sayles defends Benner's work as a valuable contribution by an amateur numismatist].

4302 **Boehringer, Christof.** "Zu Chronologie und Interpretation der Münzpägung der Achaischen Liga nach 146 v. Chr." *Topoi Orient-Occident* (France) 7, no. 1 (1997): 103-8.

4303 ——— "Zur Geschichte der Achaischen Liga im 2. und 1. Jh. v. Chr. im Lichte des Münzfundes von Poggio Picenze (Abruzzen)." *Achaia und Elis in der Antike: Akten des 1. Internationalen Symposiums, Athens, 19-21, Mai 1989.* Edited by A. D. Rizakes. Paris: De Boccard, 1991. Pages 163-70.
A recently uncovered coin hoard sheds light on the history of the Achaean League in the second and first centuries B.C.

4304 **Borrell, H. P.** "Some Observations on the Coins of Pellene, in Achaia; Which Have Been Erroneously Classed by Numismatic Writers to Pella, in Macedonia, Pelinna, in Thessaly, and to the Island of Peparathus." *Numismatic Chronicle* 2 (1840): 237-42. Illus.
A reattribution of four coins.

4305 **Chantraine, Heinrich.** "Der Beginn der Jüngeren Achäischen Bundesprägung." *Chiron* (Germany) 2 (1972): 175-90. [CS 2553]
Examines the Achaean League coinage.

4306 **Clerk, Malcolm G.** *Catalogue of the Coins of the Achaean League.* London: B. Quaritch, 1895. 35 pp., 13 pls.
A complete catalogue of all the known varieities of coins of the Achaean League. Lists 443 coins, 311 of which are illustrated. Clerk listed all combinations of letters, monograms, and symbols found on the coins in order to attribute them to specific mints. For the bronze coins, which bear the mint names, Clerk collected all the known variants. He dated the League coinage to the period 280-146 B.C. There is no discussion of the league's history. [A

brief review by G. F. Hill appears in *Numismatic Chronicle* 3rd ser., 17 (1897): 246. Also see M. Thompson *The Agrinion Hoard* under HOARDS, Crosby *An Achaean League Hoard* below, and J. Warren *The Bronze Coinage* below].

4307 **Crosby, Margaret, and Emily Grace.** *An Achaean League Hoard.* Numismatic Notes and Monographs, No. 74. New York: American Numismatic Society, 1936. 44 pp., 4 pls.
A catalogue and analysis of a hoard comprised chiefly of Achaean League triobols. After considering the numismatic and historical evidence, the authors conclude the hoard was buried ca. 185-182 B.C. Concludes that Elis coined annual issues of Achaean League coins between the years 191 and 146 B.C. Some issues assigned to Messene by Clerk (see M. Clerk above) are here assigned to Megalopolis. Crosby and Grace further examine the Arcadian League coins included in this hoard, but they are unable to assign the coins to a specific mint. However, they show that Arcadian League coinage continued to be minted in the second century B.C. They also examine the Achaean League coins with the trident symbol. Gardner (*Catalogue of Greek Coins of Peloponnesus*) had assigned these to Troezen; Clerk assigned them to Mantinea. The authors suggest these coins were minted by Mantinea between 195-190 B.C., although this conclusion is tentative. Although the Achaean League coinage in general has been dated "after 280 B.C.," the authors suggest there may not have been a significant federal coinage before 222 B.C. A catalogue of the 231 coins of the hoard is presented, followed by two Appendices. Appendix 1 examines the Achaean League coins of Elis. The authors correct some of Clerk's readings and divide the coinage into three groups: (a) those with one monogram, (b) those with two monograms, and (c) those with two monograms plus a name in full. In Appendix 2, the Achaean League coins of Antigoneia-Mantinea are divided into four types, to which a chronological sequence is given. [Also see M. Thompson *The Agrinion Hoard* under HOARDS and Jennifer Warren *The Bronze Coinage of the Achaian Koinon* below].

4308 **Finlay, George.** "Thoughts about the Coinage of the Achaian League." *Numismatic Chronicle* new ser., 6 (1866): 21-35.
Finlay examines five questions related to the coinage of the Achaean League: (1) What weight standard was used? (2) Why didn't the League strike larger denomination coins (e.g., drachms, didrachms, tetradrachms)? (3) What was the purpose of the monograms and symbols found on the coins? (4) Was the copper coin a chalcus? (5) Why did the federation make each city put its own name on its coins? Also includes a supplement to Warren's catalogue of copper coins (see John Warren "The Copper Coinage" below) and an index to the names on Achaean League coins.

4309 **Friedlaender, Julius.** "A Coin of Helike." *Numismatic Chronicle* new ser., 1 (1861): 216-7. Illus.
Illustrates a coin of Helike in Achaia bearing the head of Poseidon. [Also see Jucker "Helike" and Oikonomides "Helike" below].

4310 **Grandjean, Catherine.** "Guerres et Monnaie en Grèce Ancienne: Le Cas du *Koinon* Achaien." *Économie Antique. La Guerre dans les Économies Antiques, Entretiens d'Archéologie et d'Histoire.* Edited by J. Andreau, P. Briant, and R. Descat. Saint-Bernard-de-Comminges: Musée Archéologique Départmental, 2000. Pages 315-36.

4311 **Hands, Alfred Watson.** "Silver Coins of the Achaean League." *Spink Numismatic Circular* 13 (May 1905): 8322-8; (June 1905): 8377-82; (July 1905): 8449-55; (August 1905): 8513-8. Illus.
Presents the history of the Achaean League, discusses the coin types, weight standards, and magistrates' names. Provides a city-by-city review of the coinage.

4312 **Hill, George F.** "Dryops at Asine." *Corolla Numismatica: Numismatic Essays in Honour of Barclay V. Head.* Edited by G. F. Hill. London: Oxford University Press, 1906. Pages 156-59. Illus.
Asine was a city in the Peloponnese founded by the Dryopians from northern Greece. The city issued bronze coins of the Achaean League. The author publishes a coin which has been in the British Museum since 1816, which he now attributes to Asine. The coin bears Apollo on the obverse. The reverse bears a seated figure of Dryops derived from a monument seen by Pausanias, and paralleled in a terra-cotta hero-relief.

4313 **Jucker, Hans.** "Helike." *Schweizer Münzblätter* (Switzerland) 66 (May 1967): 63-5. Illus.
"Description of a coin of Helike now at Winterthur, thought to have been one of the last struck in the city before its submerging in 373 B.C." [D. Raymond, *NL* 81]. [Also see Friedlaender "Helike" above and Oikonomides "Helike" below].

4314 **Lindsay, John.** "On the Coins of the Achaian League." *Numismatic Journal* 2 (1838): 38-44.
Lists cities which belonged to the Achaean League and the city names which appear on the league's bronze coinage. Discusses the symbols and monograms appearing on the principal silver coins. He attempts to attribute the silver coins to their mint cities.

4315 **Oikonomides, Al N.** "Helike: The Lost Greek City Known from Only One Coin-Type." *North American Journal of Numismatics* 7, no. 2 (February 1968): 37-9. Illus.
Illustrates and describes the only known coin type of the city of Helike, for which only two specimens are known. The city now lies at the bottom of the Gulf of Corinth as a result of an earthquake in 373 B.C. [Also see Friedlaender "Helike" and Jucker "Helike" above].

4316 **Touratsoglou, John, and Eos Tsourti.** "Contribution to the Circulation of the Achaean League Triobols in Mainland Greece and the Peloponnese: the Evidence of the Hoards." *Proceedings of the 1st International Congress on Achaver and Elis.* Heletimata L3. Athens, 1991. Pages 121-8.
"This is a thorough discussion of various coin hoards and their distribution through Mainland Greece, the Peloponnese, Crete, the Cyrenaica and the Italian peninsula. There is a discussion of hoards found outside the Mainland Greece and Peloponnese and how these hoards arrived at the locations where they were discovered." [M. Oeconomides, *NL* 129]

4317 **Warren, Jennifer A. W.** "The Bronze Coinage of the Achaian League: The Mints of Achaia and Elis." *Achaia und Elis in der Antike: Akten des 1. Internationalen Symposiums, Athens, 19-21, Mai 1989.* Edited by A. D. Rizakes. Paris: De Boccard, 1991. Pages 151-4.

4318 ——— "Towards a Resolution of the Achaian League Silver Coinage Controversy: Some Observations on Methodology." *Essays in Honour of Robert Carson and Kenneth Jenkins.* Edited by M. J. Price, A. M. Burnett, and R. Bland. London: Spink & Son, 1993. Pages 87-99. 1 pl.
Warren examines the controversy over the date of minting of the final group of Achaean League triobols and the civic triobols contemporary with them. The traditional view, supported by M. Price, M. Thompson, and J. Touratsoglou, holds that this coinage ceased upon the dissolution of the League in 146 B.C.

Christof Beohringer challenged this view, arguing that the Achaean League coinage continued into the first century B.C. Warren examines the evidence: she discusses the persons named on the coins, the letter forms used in coin inscriptions, the weight loss evident in hoard coins, other hoard evidence, stylistic comparisons with other Peloponnesian coinage during the period 146-31 B.C., and the historical context of the issues. She concludes that the weight of the evidence favors Boehringer's lower dating.

4319 ——— "The Achaian League, Sparta, Lucullus: Some Late Hellenistic Coinages." *ΞΑΡΑΚΤΗΡ: Αφιερωμα στη Μαντω Οικονομιδου (Character: Offerings to Mando Oeconomides)*. Publications of Archaeological Deltion, No. 57. Athens: Treasury of Archaeological Resources and Expropriations, 1996. Pages 297-308.

4320 ——— "The Achaian League Silver Coinage Controversy Resolved: A Summary." *Numismatic Chronicle* 159 (1999): 99-109. 1 pl.
Summarizes the literature and arguments regarding Boehringer's proposed dating of a large body of Peloponnesian triobols to the first century B.C. (rather than ca. 150-146).

4321 ——— *The Bronze Coinage of the Achaian* Koinon: *The Currency of a Federal Ideal*. Special Publication No. 42. London: Royal Numismatic Society, 2007. 212 pp., 39 pls.
A detailed study of the bronze coinage of the Achaean League, including a catalogue of the 929 legible examples of the coinage from about 45 mints. Every known coin is listed. Includes a good bibliography. Although the original mintage was immense, Warren believes the coins were actively withdrawn from circulation after 146 B.C. [Extensive review and commentary by Alan Walker in *ANS* 7, no. 3 (winter 2008): 53-8. Also reviewed by W. Fischer-Bossert in *Numismatic Chronicle* 168 (2008): 475-8. Also see M. Thompson *The Agrinion Hoard* under HOARDS, Clerk *Catalogue* above, and Crosby *An Achaean League Hoard* above].

4322 ——— "The Peloponnesian Officials Responsible for the Second-Century B.C. Bronze Coinage of the Achaian Koinon." *Onomatologos: Studies in Greek Personal Names Presented to Elaine Matthews*. Edited by R. W. V. Catling, F. Marchand, and M. Sasanow. Oxford: Oxbow Books, 2010.
The bronze coinage of the Achaian League in the first half of the second century B.C., with its forty-five (or forty-six) members, provides sixty-five complete or completed names. Warren explores these names and the responsibilities these men held.

4323 **Warren, John L.** "The Copper Coinage of the Achaean League." *Numismatic Chronicle* new ser., 4 (1864): 77-95. 3 pls.
Illustrates a single federal copper coin from each of thirty-two Achaean cities. Discusses the inscriptions and magistrates' names on each. Also illustrates silver coins of five Achaean cities for which no copper coinage is known. [For a supplement to this listing, see George Finlay's "Thoughts" above].

4324 **Weil, Rudolph.** "Das Münzwesen des Achäischen Bundes." *Zeitschrift für Numismatik* (Germany) 9 (1882): 199-272. [CS 2554]
The coinage of the Achaean League.

Also see: Jones "Symmachic Coins" under EPIGRAPHY; LHS Numismatics *Coins of the Peloponnesos* under PELOPONNESOS—GENERAL WORKS; Mackil and van Alfen "Cooperative Coinage" under GENERAL WORKS—GREEK; M. Thompson *The Agrinion Hoard* under HOARDS; M. Thompson "A Hoard of Greek Federal Silver" under HOARDS; Warren "After the Boehringer Revolution" under PELOPONNESOS—GENERAL WORKS; Warren "More on the New Landscape" under PELOPONNESOS—GENERAL WORKS.

ARGOLIS

4325 **Borrell, H. P.** "On Some Coins of Argos in Argolis, and Particularly on an Early Coin Struck for Phidon, King of the Argives." *Numismatic Chronicle* 6 (1844): 42-52.
The author examines six coins, some of which he attributes to the city of Argos during the reign of Pheidon.

4326 **Chittenden, Jacqueline.** "Diaktoros Argeiphontes." *American Journal of Archaeology* 52 (1948): 24-33. 1 pl.
"The second of these epithets used in poetry to describe Hermes is explained as meaning 'dog-slayer'. On p. 28 and pl. 2, coins of Peloponnesian and Acarnanian Argos with type or symbol of a dog are quoted as evidence to support this interpretation." [J. R. Jones, *NIAJAH*]

4327 **Forrer, Leonard S.** "A Very Rare Drachm of Epidauris Argolidis." *Spink Numismatic Circular* 12, no. 134 (January 1904): 7305-6. Illus.
The coin is the third known specimen. The obverse has the head of Asklepios. The reverse shows Asklepios seated to left on a throne with a dog at his feet. Includes a photograph of the coin.

4328 **Gill, D.** "The Coinage of Methana." *A Rough and Rocky Place: The Landscape and Settlement History of the Methana Peninsula*. Edited by C. Mee and H. Forbes. Liverpool, 1997. Pages 278-81.

4329 **Grandjean, Catherine.** "Le Monnayage d'Argent et de Bronze d'Hermionè, Argolide." *Revue Numismatique* (France) 6th ser., 32 (1990): 28-55. 4 pls.
A few bronze issues, attributed in the past to Eresos (on the island of Lesbos), are plausibly reattributed to Hermione.

4330 **Hackens, Tony.** "À Propos du Monnayage d'Argos." *Proceedings of the 8th International Congress of Numismatics, New York—Washington, September 1973*. International Association of Professional Numismatists Publication, No. 4. Edited by Herbert A. Cahn and Georges Le Rider. Paris/Basel: International Association of Professional Numismatists, 1976. Pages 83-4.
Provides an updated chronology of the coinage of Argos.

4331 **Holloway, R. Ross.** "A Group of Argive Coins at Brown University." *Pour Denyse: Divertissements Numismatiques*. Edited by S. Hurter and C. Arnold-Biucchi. Bern, Switzerland: Privately published, 2000. Pages 75-82. 2 pls.

Argos has the longest-lived coin type in Greek coinage. The forepart of the wolf on the Argive hemidrachms was struck from late archaic times until well into the second century B.C. Holloway catalogues fifty-four coins of Argos in the collection of Brown University (Providence, R.I.). Includes forty-two hemidrachms, one trihemiobol, one hemiobol, and ten bronzes.

4332 **Milavec, Anthony F.** "A Numismatic Conundrum." *The Celator* 19, no. 3 (March 2005): 6-12. Illus.
Presents an unusual bronze coin which the author attributes to the city of Argos. Another numismatist (Alan Walker) argues that the coin belongs to the Thracian-Macedonian region (the 10 mm coin was found in Bulgaria) because bronze coins rarely traveled far from their place of minting. Milavec and Walker present differing interpretations of the reverse monogram.

4333 **Milne, Joseph G.** "The Perachora Drachma Inscription." *The Classical Review* 58 (1944): 18-9.
Milne discusses an inscription dated ca. 650 B.C. referring to a drachma deposited in the Temple of Hera. It has been suggested that the "drachma" referred to was one of the bundles of iron spits which were accepted as currency in Argos. Milne argues that it was actually an Aeginetan half-stater which was exhibited in the temple to assure citizens that the new currency was acceptable to Hera and was thus safe to accept as money in Corinthia.

4334 **Mitsos, M. T.** Αργολικη Προσωπογραφια. Βιβλιοθηκη της εν Αθηναις Αρχαιολογικης Εταιρειας 36. Athens, 1952.
Lists the magistrates whose names appear on the coins of Argos.

4335 **Oraiopoulos, Zacharias L.** "Hermione." Translated by M. J. A. Tzamali. *Nomismatika Khronika* (Greece) 23 (2004): 33-5. [Also in Greek with illustrations, pp. 29-32].
Recounts the mythology related to the region around Hermione, a city on the southeast coast of Argolis. Summarizes the three periods of the city's coinage: (1) ca. 370-229 B.C. saw the minting of silver coins with Demeter, (2) 229-146 B.C. (after joining the Achaian League, to the Roman conquest) when only bronze coins were minted, and (3) a short period after A.D. 195. Thirteen coins are listed.

4336 **Palmer, Thomas A.** "A Coin of Tiryns." *The Celator* 13, no. 11 (November 1999): 6-12. Illus., map.
Summarizes the history of the city of Tiryns in the Mycenean period. In the fifth century B.C., most of the inhabitants were driven out of Tiryns and forced to resettle in Argos. A few inhabitants escaped and went to live in Halice. These exiles struck coins in the name of Tiryns in about 350 B.C. Describes the coins and the author's attempt to acquire one. They are quite scarce in the market.

4337 **Requier, P.** "Le Monnayage d'Epidaure à la Lumière d'Un Nouveau Trésor." *Revue Suisse de Numismatique* (Switzerland) 72 (1993): 29-46.
The coinage of Epidaurus in the light of a new hoard.

4338 **Welch, F. B.** "An Argive Hoard." *Numismatic Chronicle* 5th ser., 4 (1924): 318-20.
Lists the contents of a hoard of 215 copper coins of Argos. The coins are dated to 228-146 B.C.

Also see: Arnold-Biucchi "Reflections of Polykleitos's Work" under ART; Hill "Dryops" under PELOPONNESOS—ACHAIA; Hurter "Das Palladion" under TYPES; Imhoof-Blumer "Zur Münzkunde Boeotiens und Peloponnesischen Argos" under CENTRAL GREECE—BOEOTIA; Tandy "Spits" under ORIGINS OF COINAGE; Waldstein "The Argive Hera" under ART; Westermark "Coins from the Swedish Excavations" under HOARDS.

ARKADIA

4339 **Anderson, J. K.** "Stymphalian and Other Birds." *Journal of Hellenic Studies* 97 (1977): 146.
"Observation upon the site produces agreement with S. Benton that the bird on certain coins of Stymphalus is the Great Crested Grebe." [J. Melville Jones, *NL* 97]. [See Benton below].

4340 **Benner, Steve M.** "History and Coinage of the Arkadian League of 370 BCE." *The Celator* 24, no. 2 (February 2010): 6-22. Illus., map.
An overview of the history of the Arkadian League and a summary of its silver and bronze coinage. Discusses weights, chronology, federal silver and bronze issues from Megalopolis, coinage of other league members, and comments on the non-federal "civic" coinage of league members.

4341 **Benton, Sylvia.** "Note on Sea-birds." *Journal of Hellenic Studies* 92 (1972): 172-3.
A follow-up to an article by J. K. Anderson [*Journal of Hellenic Studies* 92 (1972): 171-2] on the Greek names of sea-birds. Benton identifies the bird on coins of Stymphalos as the Great Crested Grebe. [Anderson agreed with this identification. See Anderson "Stymphalian" above].

4342 **Dengate, James A.** "The Triobols of Megalopolis." *Museum Notes* 13 (1967): 57-110. 9 pls. [CS 2569]
Begins with an overview of the history of the city of Megalopolis which was founded as the capital of the Arcadian League and later was an important member of the Achaean League. Presents a catalogue of the triobols struck at Megalopolis, 195-146 B.C., including Arcadian League types, Achaean League types, and Arcadian types with the inscription ΜΕΓ. Each group is discussed. Includes charts of die combinations and frequency tables of weights. Also summarizes seven hoards containing coins of Megalopolis and discusses the chronology of the issues. [Some of Dengate's conclusions are questioned by Jennifer Warren. See Warren "The Earliest Triobols" below].

4343 "Further Notes on Mantinean Coins." *American Journal of Numismatics* 30, no. 4 (April 1896): 101-5. Illus.
A follow-up to Svoronos' discussion (see Svoronos "Ulysses" below) of the type on an unusual coin of Mantinea. Svoronos believes the coin represents Ulysses planting his oar in the ground after a long journey. This paper provides passages from Homer which confirm Svoronos' theory.

4344 **Gerin, Dominique.** "Les Statères de la Ligue Arcadienne." *Revue Suisse de Numismatique* (Switzerland) 65 (1986): 13-31.
The author examines the staters of the Arkadian League.

4345 **Hill, George F.** "Eua in Arcadia." *Numismatic Chronicle* 4th ser., 17 (1917): 319.
Publishes a bronze coin of the Achaean League with the inscription [ΑΧΑΙΩ]Ν ΕΥΑΕΩΝ—the name of the city of Eua. This coin and a silver half-drachm of the League (also bearing this inscription) are the first known coins of this city.

4346 **Milne, Joseph G.** "The Currency of Arcadia." *Numismatic Chronicle* 6th ser., 9 (1949): 83-92.
Discusses a group of coins gathered near Megalopolis and considered to be representative of the coins circulating in the area at various periods. The coins, both bronze and silver, date from the fifth century B.C. to the nineteenth century A.D. Of the Greek issues, 265 come from Peloponnesian mints including Corinth and forty-two from outside, with Sicyon and Arcadia contributing most heavily to the total. Appendices tabulate coins by mint, and analyze six large Peloponnesian hoards for comparison. [Summarized from M. Thompson, *NL* 14]

4347 **Nielsen, Thomas Heine.** "Was There an Arkadian Confederacy in the Fifth Century B.C.? *More Studies on the Ancient Greek Polis*. Papers from the Copenhagen Polis Centre 3. Edited by M. H. Hansen and K. Raaflaub. *Historia* (Germany) 108 (1996): 39-61.
"The fifth century coins (*obv.*, Zeus Lykaios with eagle; *rev.*, Despoina/Artemis APKAΔIKON, or different abbreviations thereof) are often claimed to have been struck by a fifth-century Arkadian Confederacy and are used to reconstruct the political history of contemporary Arkadia and the Peloponnese. This article reconsiders and rejects this approach by examining the serious methodological problems involved and by reviewing the internal affairs of fifth-century Arkadia. Instead, the author proposes that the coinage may more reasonably be thought of as struck by an Arkadian Amphictiony centered on the cult of Zeus on Mt. Lykaion. Alternatively, it may be conceived of as the civic coinage of the powerful Arkadian city-state Tegea, a city which demonstrably entertained ambitions of pan-Arkadian hegemony." [T. Nielson, *NL* 137]

4348 **Schultz, Sabine.** "Die Staterprägung von Pheneos." *Revue Suisse de Numismatique* (Switzerland) 71 (1992): 47-74. 8 pls.
"A corpus and die study of the very rare and beautiful silver staters of Phenos in Arcadia." [D. Kroh, *ACRR*]

4349 **Svoronos, Jean N.** "Ulysses on a Coin of Mantinea." *American Journal of Numismatics* 30, no. 2 (October 1895): 33-7.
Argues that certain types on coins of Mantinea can be explained in relationship to Arcadian myths. Identifies the hero on these coins as Ulysses. [Also see "Further Notes" above].

4350 **Wallace, William P.** "Kleomenes, Marathon, the Helots, and Arkadia." *Journal of Hellenic Studies* 74 (1954): 32-5.
"E. S. G. Robinson's numismatic date of 489/8 B.C. for the seizure of Zankle by Anaxilas and the Messenians (see Robinson "Rhegion, Zankle-Messana" under SICILY—ZANKLE/MESSANA) fits with Miss Jeffrey's epigraphical argument for a helot revolt in 490 B.C. (*Journal of Hellenic Studies* 1949); this revolt was perhaps arranged by King Kleomenes of Sparta who was in exile in Arkadia at the time. In any case he organized an anti-Spartan Arkadian League to which the earliest Arkadian coins (often called 'festival coins') should be attributed." [*NL* 39]

4351 **Warren, Jennifer A. W.** "The Earliest Triobols of Megalopolis." *Museum Notes* 15 (1969): 31-40. 1 pl. [CS 2570]
The author questions some of the conclusions of J. Dengate (see Dengate "The Triobols" above) who suggested the triobols of Megalopolis with no eagle on the reverse were struck ca. 195-182 B.C. Warren believes these were struck before the city entered the Achaean League in 235 B.C. and are therefore Arcadian League coins.

4352 ——— "Thisoa by Mount Lykaion: Further Light on an Arkadian Problem." *Numismatic Archaeology/Archaeological Numismatics: Proceedings of an International Conference held to Honour Dr. Mando Oeconomides in Athens 1995*. Oxbow Monographs 75. Edited by K. Sheedy and C. Papageorgiadou-Banis. Oxford: Oxbow Books and The Australian Archaeological Institute at Athens, 1997. Pages 96-104. Map, 1 pl.
There are two cities named Thisoa in Arkadia. Warren suggests the Achaian League bronze coinage of Thisoa was struck by the southwestern Thisoa, on the slopes of Mount Lykaion. Describes the characteristics of these coins. States that all the Peloponnesian towns that struck the Achaian League bronze coins were acting autonomously.

4353 **Williams, Roderick T.** *The Confederate Coinage of the Arcadians in the Fifth Century B.C.* Numismatic Notes and Monographs, No. 155. New York: American Numismatic Society, 1965. 141 pp., 14 pls. [CS 2556]
Discusses the half-drachmas, obols, and the rare half-obols with Zeus seated and the inscription APKAΔIKON on the reverse. Through a study of all available dies and the establishment of their sequence, Williams attempts to determine the site of the mint, character of the coinage (religious or political), date of the beginning of the series, identity of the deities represented on the coins, and an interpretation of the inscription APKAΔIKON. Presents a catalogue of 320 coins, almost all of which are illustrated. Frequency tables illustrate coin weights. Includes die-linkage charts. [Reviewed by M. J. Price in *Numismatic Chronicle* 7th ser., 6 (1966): 342-5, by J. A. W. Warren in *Journal of Hellenic Studies* 88 (1968): 245-6, and by W. Schwabacher in *Gnomon* (Germany) 40 (1968): 92-4].

4354 ——— "The Archaic Coinage of Arcadian Heraea." *Museum Notes* 16 (1970): 1-12. 1 pl. [CS 2566]
Examines the hemidrachms and obols struck at Heraea ca. 510-470 B.C. Divides the coinage into five chronological periods and catalogues fifteen coin types. Discusses the forms of letters in the ethnics as a method of establishing the chronology of the series.

Also see: Gerin "Arcadian League" under THE MINTING PROCESS; Gerin "Un Faux Statère de Stymphale" under COUNTERFEITS; D. Robinson "The Alexander Hoard of Megalopolis" under HOARDS; Six "Some Undescribed Greek Coins" under ATTICA—GENERAL WORKS; Thallon "The Cave at Vari" under TYPES; M. Thompson *The Agrinion Hoard* under HOARDS; Weir "The Stymphalos Hoard" under HOARDS; Wilkinson "Unpublished" under PRIVATE COLLECTIONS.

ELIS

4355 **Berg, Joseph.** "Coinage of the Ancient Olympic Games." *Numismatic Scrapbook Magazine* 30, no. 11 (November 1964): 2980-2.
"Three coins of ancient Greece, each issued on the occasion of an Olympiad, mirror strikingly the stages in transition from the late Archaic to the early Classical style in Greek art: (1) Eagle/Thunderbolt type; (2) a recently discovered unpublished stater of Elis, preserved in the Royal Coin Cabinet, Stockholm; it depicts a striding Zeus, encircled by the legend OΛYMΠIKON; (3) majestic eagle, shown with outstretched wings (*obv.*); on the reverse, a running Nike." [B. Shonnard, *NL* 71]

4356 **Franke, Peter R.** "Olympia und Seine Münzen." *Antike Welt* (Germany) 15, no. 2 (1984).

4357   **Gabrici, Ettore.** "La Nike Funebre delle Monete di Elis." *Centennial Publication of the American Numismatic Society.* Edited by Harald Ingholt. New York: American Numismatic Society, 1958. Pages 201-8. Illus.
Discusses the depiction of Nike seated, with her head facing down, resting on her hand, which appears on the coins of Elis. A comparison is made to similar depictions of Europa on coins of Gortyn, Crete.

4358   **Gardner, Percy.** "The Coins of Elis." *Numismatic Chronicle* new ser., 19 (1879): 221-73. 6 pls.
Gardner discusses the history of Elis, divided into fifteen periods (before 471 B.C. to A.D. 217), and incorporates a discussion of the major coin types of each period. He attempts to establish a chronology and die sequence for the coinage based on the theory that only one mint existed. [Also see Seltman *The Temple Coins of Olympia* below. Seltman believes two mints were in operation at Olympia].

4359   ———. "Zacynthus." *Numismatic Chronicle* 3rd ser., 5 (1885): 81-107. 3 pls.
Gardner begins with a review of the history of the island of Zacynthus, and then discusses its coinage. Includes a catalogue of coin types from the earliest issues through the Roman Imperial period.

4360   **Hoge, Robert W.** "The Ancient Olympic Games: A Celebration in Coinage." *SAN—Journal of the Society for Ancient Numismatics* 19, no. 2 (1995): 39-43. Illus.
Presents a general discussion of the coinage of Olympia, other coinage with types related to the Olympic games, and coins with types related to other athletic festivals. Discusses the weight standard of the coins of Olympia. The Aeginetan standard was initially used, and some of the coins were overstruck on coins of Aegina. Summarizes the conclusions of Seltman (see C. Seltman, *The Temple Coins of Olympia* below). The dies were used for an unusually long time, thus many worn and cracked dies are encountered among the series. Weak strikes and off-center strikes are common. The series is extensively die-linked. Briefly describes the issues inscribed ΟΛΥΜΠΙΑ, struck in 364 B.C. Mentions the reduction in the weight standard ca. 191 B.C. when Elis joined the Achaean League. Discusses the league coinage of Elis. Hoge then mentions some coins of other cities which exhibit Olympic themes including the mule-cart types of Messana, the chariot types common in Sicily, and the coin types of Philip II. Briefly mentions coins with themes related to other athletic festivals.

4361   **Jongkees, Jan Hendrik.** "Zur Chronologie der Münzen von Olympia." *Jahrbüch des Deutschen Archäologischen Instituts* (Germany) 54 (1939): 219-229.
The chronology of the coinage of Olympia.

4362   ———. "Notes on Coin Types of Olympia." *Revue Numismatique* (France) 6th ser., 10 (1968): 51-63. Illus. [CS 2560]
"Criticizing the dating of the coins of Olympia, a probable date of deposition of the Katoche hoard of 399 B.C. is proposed. Seltman's reading of Πολυκα(ων) is refuted; ΠΟ is the remainder of the signature of Polycleitus the younger; the other marks are uncertain. A coin representing Nike crowning a fountain inspires a study of coins commemorating baths (at Himera, Terina, Pherae and probably at Larissa), and is connected with the bath at Olympia found just before World War II and dated ca. 450 B.C. There are comparable representations on Attic hydriae found at Vulci. The seated Nike which appears on Olympian coins a little before 432 B.C. is not in mourning but is agitated. The motif has parallels in sculpture and vase painting, and is thought to allude to the Peloponnesian War. The engraver may be one of Phidia's assistants." [J. Jongkees, *NL* 83]

4363   **Kampmann, Ursula.** "Olympia and Its Coins." Translated by Alan Walker. *The Celator* 18, no. 5 (May 2004): 40-2, 50. Illus.
A brief history of the coinage of Olympia, illustrated by specimens from the BCD Collection (see Leu Numismatics below).

4364   **Leu Numismatics.** *Coins of Olympia: The BCD Collection.* Auction Leu 90 (May 10, 2004). 100 pp., illus.
Catalogue for the sale of the coins of Elis/Olympia from the collection of "BCD." Contains 345 lots thoroughly catalogued by Alan Walker. Includes a preface by the collector, an historical description of the ancient Olympic games with a description of the site of Olympia, and an essay on the coinage of Olympia. An outstanding collection, with each lot illustrated. [For other portions of the collection, see "BCD" in the INDEX OF COLLECTORS AND COLLECTIONS].

4365   **Madsen, Eardley.** "Olympia." *SAN—Journal of the Society for Ancient Numismatics* 15, no. 1 (spring 1984): inside covers.
An overview of the history and coinage of Olympia and Elis, including comments on the Olympic Games. A stater of Olympia with the engraver's initial A on the obverse die is pictured.

4366   **Milne, Joseph G.** "The Coinage of the Eleians." *Numismatic Chronicle* 5th ser., 11 (1931): 171-80. [CS 2562]
Discusses the ratio of obverse dies to reverse dies at various mints. Milne finds the ratio of Eleian dies to be similar to that in Sicily. Notes that in Elis, unlike at Syracuse, one die may be associated with others of different groups and varying styles. Therefore, the changing of dies at Elis cannot be related to reasons of die wear, and a reason is sought in the economic purposes of the coinage. The author notes the frequency of changing types, the relative lack of small denominations, and the inexact weights of Eleian coins. The common occurrence of countermarks on these coins indicates that the coins did not circulate in other cities except as bullion. Together, these facts indicate that Elis did not produce coins for the purpose of facilitating trade. Milne suggests the coins were produced as commemorative medals or souvenirs to be sold to visitors of the Olympic games. The fact that the best artists were employed to create a wide variety of coin types strengthens Milne's arguments.

4367   **Moon, Warren G.** "A Note on a Zacynthian Obol." *Museum Notes* 18 (1972): 1-3. Illus.
Attempts to more clearly identify and explain the reverse type on a rare obol of Zacynthus previously identified as an altar with a conical cover. Moon concludes that the triangular figure is not a cover. It is a gable-shaped barrier or fender meant to reduce disturbances of the consecrated ashes by the wind.

4368   **Nicolet-Pierre, Hélène.** "Remarques sur la Chronologie Relative des Plus Anciennes Séries de Statères Éléens." *Revue Numismatique* (France) 6th ser., 17 (1975): 7-18. Illus. [CS 2563]

4369   ———. "A Propos de Monnaies d'Elis Portent des Contremarques." *Bulletin de la Société Française de Numismatique* (France) (April 1992).

4370 —— "Monnaies de Bronze dans le Péloponnèse, Époques Classique et Hellénistique: Quelques Remarques sur le Monnayage de Bronze d'Elis et de Tégée." *Revue Numismatique* (France) 153 (1998): 41-4.

4370a **Oeconomides, Mando, and Héléne Nicolet-Pierre.** "Recherches sur le Monnayage d'Élis-Olympie à l'Époque Hellénistique." *Proceedings of the 11th International Numismatic Congress, September 8-13, 1991. Volume 1.* Edited by T. Hackens et al. Louvain-la-Neuve, Belgium: International Association of Professional Numismatists, 1993. Pages 193-203.

4371 **Schwabacher, Willy.** "A Hoard of Drachms of Elis." *Numismatic Chronicle* 5th ser., 19 (1939): 239-65. 1 pl. [CS 3288]
A catalogue of 222 drachms of Elis of the Hellenistic period, one fourth-century coin of Elis, and two late Boeotian drachms. The author divides the coins of Elis into four groups according to the varieties of type and the die links. Discusses each group including metrology, techniques of striking, and dates of issue.

4372 **Sear, David R.** "Coinage of Olympic Proportions." *Numismatist* 117, no. 8 (August 2004): 67-9. Illus.
A good overview of the coinage of Olympia and the history of the ancient Olympic games.

4373 **Seltman, Charles T.** *The Temple Coins of Olympia.* Cambridge, 1921. Reprints, Bologna: Forni, 1967; New York: Attic Books, 1975. 117 pp., 12 pls. [CS 2565]
A detailed examination of the coinage which had traditionally been attributed to the city of Elis. Seltman concludes that this coinage was minted at Olympia. Two separate mints were in operation: one in the precinct of the temple of Zeus which began operations ca. 510 B.C., and one in the precinct of the temple of Hera, which operated ca. 420-323 B.C. Seltman establishes a die sequence for each mint and proposes a new chronology for these issues. Presents a listing of all die varieties of the staters with historical and numismatic commentary on each grouping. Presents a table of countermarks. Discusses the development and symbolism of the thunderbolt of Zeus. By relying on the average weight of a sample of the heaviest coins, Seltman concludes that this coinage used an Olympian weight standard of 12.44 gm rather than the Aeginetan standard. Briefly mentions a hoard of Olympian coins found in Greece in 1920. [George F. Hill's review of this book, which originally appeared in *Numismatic Chronicle* 5th ser., 3 (1923): 359-61, is included in the Attic Books reprint edition. Hill doubts that there was a separate mint at the temple of Hera. He also questions Seltman's calculation of the Olympian weight standard. Hill recommends the use of a frequency table, which results in a lower standard weight. Another review of Seltman's book appears in *Journal of Hellenic Studies* 42 (1922): 124-6.]

4374 —— "The 'Katoché' Hoard of Elean Coins." *Numismatic Chronicle* 6th ser., 11 (1951): 40-55. 4 pls.
"This hoard found during the Occupation (from which it derives its name) is reported to have come from the Achaia-Elis district, possibly from the vicinity of Olympia. It consists of twenty-three didrachms and one drachm from the Olympian Zeus mint and twelve didrachms from the Hera mint. One of the coins is struck over a Boeotian didrachm, and many pieces are countermarked. There are two superb specimens with engraver's signatures: one marked ΔΑ and the other ΓΟΛΥΚΑ, the latter form not hitherto recorded. The earliest hoard coin dates from before ca. 471 B.C. and the latest ca. 380 B.C. Dr. Seltman would divide the lot into three savings groups: one put away by 416 B.C., the second by 396 B.C., and the last by ca. 380 when the hoard as a whole was buried." [M. Thompson, *NL* 27]

4375 **Vagi, David L.** "Coins of the Ancient Olympics Break Typical Model." *The Celator* 8, no. 8 (August 1994): 12. Illus.
Summarizes Seltman's conclusions regarding the coinage of Elis: the coins were struck at Olympia at two different mints, one at the temple of Zeus and one at the temple of Hera. Suggests the coins were struck quickly and in large quantities just prior to the Olympic festivals.

4376 **Walker, Alan S.** "Sanctuary: Elean Coins of Olympia." *Minerva* 15, no. 4 (July/August 2004).

4377 **Warren, Jennifer A. W.** "A Neglected Hoard of Elean Coins." *Numismatic Chronicle* 7th ser., 2 (1962): 413-5.
"The author lists and describes nine coins from an Elean hoard, noting the total absence of Hera head staters when comparison is made with other hoards of the period. In view of the melted condition of the coins—for which a terminal date of 400 B.C. is proposed—it is suggested that they were probably subjected to fire during the Spartan invasion of Elis ca. 400-399 B.C. A table showing the output of the Hera mint in the fourth century is included." [F. Campbell, *NL* 70]

4378 **Weil, Rudolf.** "Der Zeus des Phidias auf Elischen Münzen der Kaiserzeit." *Zeitschrift für Numismatik* (Germany) 29 (1912).

Also see: Akerman "Coins of Labadia and Zacynthus" under CENTRAL GREECE—BOEOTIA; Arnold-Biucchi "Reflections of Polykleitos's Work" under ART; Milavic "Ancient Olympia" under TYPES; Newell *Alexander Hoards 4: Olympia* under HOARDS; Oeconomides "À Propos du Trésor de Lappa" under HOARDS; Schwabacher "The Olympian Zeus" under TYPES; Seltman "Greek Sculpture" under ART; Tzamalis *The Olympic Games* under TYPES; van Alfen *A Simple Souvenir* under TYPES; J. Warren "The Bronze Coinage" under PELOPONNESOS—ACHAIA.

ITHAKA

4379 **Cavafy, C. P.** "Ithaca: A Poem by C. P. Cavafy." *Nomismatika Khronika* (Greece) 27 (2008-2009): 5-7.
A poem by the Greek poet Cavafy, with commentary by A. P. Tzamalis. Illustrated by a bronze coin of Ithaca.

LAKONIA

4380 **Chambers, James T.** "Coinage of Ancient Sparta." *The Numismatist* 94, no. 4 (April 1981): 882-9. Illus.
A review of Spartan coinage from its beginning through the Roman Imperial period. Re-examines the belief that gold and silver coinage was outlawed in Sparta by Lycurgus, and that an iron money was used. Discusses the rare third century B.C. Alexander-type tetradrachms of the Spartan king Areus, the portrait coins of Cleomenes III, and later Spartan coins including those struck during the Roman period, the last of which were minted during the reign of Gallienus (A.D. 253-268).

4381 **Cook, J. M.** "Cnidian Peraea and Spartan Coins." *Journal of Hellenic Studies* 81 (1961): 56-72. Map.

(1) Cook disputes the belief that Chersonese was controlled by Rhodes in early times. Coins are used to support his arguments. (2) Cook discusses coins bearing the letters ΣYN. Many scholars date these coins to immediately after the Battle of Cnidus in 394 B.C., and believe that they testify to an anti-Spartan alliance between the victors of that battle and the minting states. Cook proposes the theory that the alliance was pro-Spartan, and that the minting cities were within Sparta's area of influence. The coins may have been minted for the convenience of army and navy paymasters, and to announce the liberation from Persian oppression. [For further discussion of the ΣYN coins, see Jones "Symmachic Coins" under EPIGRAPHY, and M. Wallace "After Athens" under ASIA MINOR—GENERAL WORKS].

4382 **Dawkins, R. M.** "Artemis Orthia: Some Additions and a Correction." *Journal of Hellenic Studies* 50 (1930): 298-9.
"On p. 299 a correction is made concerning the dating of iron spits found during excavations at Sparta. Although it is still true that the bulk of them were associated with pottery of the seventh century, others appeared with pottery of styles up to Laconian IV, so that some of the dedications may have been made as late as the first half of the third century B.C." [J. R. Jones, *NIJHS*]

4383 **Gansiniec, Zofia.** "The Iron Money of the Spartans and the Obolos Currency." *Archaologia* 8 (1956): 367-413. [CS 2572]
[Also see Dawkins "Artemis Orthia" above].

4384 **Grunauer von Hoerschelmann, Susanne.** "Lacedaemonian Tetradrachms in Peloponnesian Coin Hoards: A Redating of Noe 997 (*Inventory* 179) and 1004 (*Inventory* 181)." *Actes du 8ème Congrès International de Numismatique. New York—Washington, Septembre 1973*. Edited by S. Grunauer von Hoerschelmann. Paris/Basel: International Association of Professional Numismatists, 1976. Pages 78-81. Illus.
"The tetradrachms with Athena head and seated Heracles can be firmly attributed to Nabis based on a corpus of Lacedaemonian coins. The specimens from S. P. Noe, *A Bibliography of Greek Coin Hoards*, 2nd ed., nos. 997 and 1004 (*IGCH* 179, 181) represent the later series, followed by the portrait specimen in London, and can therefore be attributed to the beginning of the second century B.C. The time of burial for these coins cannot be dated before 197 B.C." [S. Grunauer von Hoerschelmann, *NL* 98]. [Nabis was a Spartan king. He was assassinated in 192 B.C.].

4385 ——— *Die Münzprägung der Lakedaimonier*. Deutsches Archäologisches Institut, Antike Münzen und Geschnittene Steine 7. Berlin: De Gruyter, 1978. 207 pp., 32 pls., 14 color pls. [CS 2567]
Examines the coinage of Sparta.

4386 **Michell, Humfrey.** "The Iron Money of Sparta." *The Phoenix* (Canada) 1, supplement (spring 1947): 42-4. [CS 2573]
The author reviews the evidence for the use of iron ("spits" and "sickles") as money in Sparta. Fails to find reliable evidence, but suggests that iron may have been used in trade and that the legend arose that this iron was money. [Also see Kroll "Observations on Monetary Instruments" under ORIGINS OF COINAGE].

4387 **Seltman, E. J.** "Lacedaemon *Versus* Allaria." *Numismatic Chronicle* 4th ser., 9 (1909): 1-6. Illus.
Seltman re-considers a tetradrachm which has variously been attributed to Lacedaemon, or to Allaria in Crete. The obverse of the coin is generally thought to depict Pallas Athena. Reviews the types used on Lacedaemonian tetradrachms. Seltman gives the subject coin to Lacedaemon and suggests the peculiar-style head on the obverse may be the king Nabis disguised as Apollo. [Also see C. Newton "Proposed Attribution" under CRETE].

Also see: Cook "Spartan Coins" under CARIA; Newton "Proposed Attribution" under CRETE; Tsagari "Some of the More Important Acquisitions" under PUBLIC COLLECTIONS—GREECE (ATHENS).

MESSENIA

4388 **Grandjean, Catherine.** *Les Messéniens de 370/369 au 1er Siècle de Notre Ère: Monnayages et Histoire*. Bulletin de Correspondance Hellénique Supplément 44. Athens: École Française d'Athenes, 2003. 332 pp., 28 pls.
Dies studies and commentary on the silver and bronze coins struck at Messene from the city's foundation in 370 B.C. to the first century B.C. A chapter is also devoted to the bronze coinage of the Messenian city of Thouria. The coins are also discussed in the historical and economic context of the decline of the Achaean League. Appendices list (1) the excavated coins from the site of Mavromati (ancient Messene), (2) modern forgeries of Messenian silver coins, and (3) comparative metallurgical data on Peloponnesian silver coinages of the fourth and third centuries B.C. [Reviewed by Oliver Hoover in *American Numismatic Society Magazine* 4, no. 3 (winter 2005)].

4388a ——— "Coinage and History of Messenia (Peloponnesus) until the End of the Hellenistic Period." *XIII Congreso Internacional de Numismática, Madrid – 2003: Actas–Proceedings–Actes I*. Edited by Carmen Alfaro, Carmen Marcos, and Paloma Otero. Madrid: International Numismatic Commisson, 2005. Pages 259-62, incl. 1 pl.
A brief overview of Messenian coinage, which is here divided into three periods. Fifteen coin types are illustrated.

PHLIASIA

4389 **MacIsaac, John D.** "Phliasian Bronze Coinage." *Museum Notes* 33 (1988): 45-54.
Discusses the bronze coinage of the city of Phlius. More than seventy such coins have been found in recent excavations, allowing further study of these issues. MacIsaac examines the types and attempts to establish a chronology. Mentions the rare iron coins of Phlius.

Also see: Balmuth "Athens or Phlius?" under ATTICA—GENERAL WORKS.

SIKYONIA

4390 **Hill, George F.** "A Dedication to Artemis." *Journal of Hellenic Studies* 18 (1898): 302-5. Illus.
"A fourth-century stater of Sicyon has an inscription pricked into it which appears to be a dedication to Artemis, either, as has been suggested, with the title 'Helketas' or, as the writer believes, 'The Artemis in Lacedaemon.'" [J. R. Jones, *NIJHS*]

4391 **Lacroix, Léon.** "Quelques Aspects de la Numismatique Sicyonienne." *Revue Belge de Numismatique* (Belgium) 110 (1964): 5-52. 4 pls. [CS 2571]

4392 **Phillips, Henry.** "Remarks upon a Coin of Sicyon in Achaia." *American Journal of Numismatics* 16, no. 2 (October 1881): 61-4. Reprinted as "A Coin of Sicyon." *Numismatics International* 11, no. 2 (February 1977): 45 ff.
An in-depth discussion of the origin and meaning of the obverse and reverse types (chimaera/dove) of a hemidrachm of Sicyon, ca. 250 B.C.

4393 **Seltman, E. J.** "An Unpublished Gold Stater of Sikyon." *Journal International d'Archaéologie Numismatique* (Greece) 14 (1912): 177-80. Illus.
Publishes a gold stater with *obv.*, young male head, and *rev.*, fast biga with a dove below, with the legend ΦΙΛΙΠΠΟΥΣΙΚ. Suggests the coin was minted at Sikyon and that the male on the obverse may be the young son of Alexander the Great and Roxana, in the guise of Apollino.

4394 **Warren, Jennifer A. W.** "The Autonomous Bronze Coinage of Sicyon." *Numismatic Chronicle* 143 (1983): 23-56; 4 pls.; 144 (1984): 1-24; 3 pls.; 145 (1985): 45-66.
The author aims to date the bronze coins of Sicyon. Arranges the coins into twelve groups, ca. 420-146 B.C. and presents a catalogue of the coin varieties taken from numerous major collections. Die links have been noted only for certain groups. Part 3 includes appendices listing relevant hoards, deposits, and excavation coins along with a brief discussion of each. [Also see Warren "Updating" below].

4395 ———. "Updating (and Downdating) the Autonomous Bronze Coinage of Sikyon." *Studies in Greek Numismatics in Memory of Martin Jessop Price.* Edited by Richard Ashton and Silvia Hurter. London: Spink, 1998. Pages 347-61. 2 pls.
A supplement to the author's previous article "The Autonomous Bronze Coinage of Sikyon" (see above). Reviews the scholarship related to early bronze coinage. Then discusses the dates of the bronze coins of Sikyon. Lists new varieties and comments on chronology. Includes a catalogue of the "Group 5 Hoard" of bronze coins of Sikyon. Discusses the volume and circulation of the coinage based on hoard evidence.

4396 ———. "The Silver Coins of Sikyon in Leiden: Analyses and Some Comments on the Coinage." *Pour Denyse: Divertissements Numismatiques.* Edited by S. Hurter and C. Arnold-Biucchi. Bern, Switzerland: Privately published, 2000. Pages 201-10. 2 pls.
Presents the results of metallurgical analysis on thirty-six silver coins of Sikyon from the Koninklijk Penningkabinet (now in the collection of Leiden University). Warren dates the earliest drachms and hemiobols to the opening decades of the fifth century B.C. Discusses stylistic variations, metallic content, hoard evidence, and historical evidence which provide clues to the chronology of the coinage. The analysis reveals the metal used over five centuries. Consistent and deliberate adulteration with copper is notable in the Hellenistic period, but is also practiced intermittently earlier.

4397 ———. "Sikyon: A Case-Study in the Adoption of Coinage by a Polis in the Fifth Century B.C." *Numismatic Chronicle* 169 (2009): 1-13. 1 pl.
Examines the arrival of coinage into the economic and cultural life of a middle-sized Peloponnesian polis, Sikyon. Discusses the date of the start of coinage at the city, the introduction of various types, and the introduction of bronze coinage.

Also see: Lacroix "Quelques" under TYPES; Liampi "Graffiti on Sicyonian and Theban Staters" under HOARDS; Milavic "Pankration" under TYPES; Noe *The Alexander Coinage of Sicyon* under MACEDONIAN KINGDOM—GENERAL WORKS; Rakicic "The Dove" under TYPES; F. Waage *Greek Bronze Coins* under HOARDS; Yorke "Excavations" under HOARDS.

Crete

Unskilled engravers were employed in the Cretan mints far more freely than in the mints of any other part of the Hellenic world. Consequently, in applying the criterion of style, it is not always possible to distinguish between degeneration, strictly so called, and mere clumsiness in the copying of first-rate models.

—George Macdonald, 1920

4398 **Arnold, T. J.** "On the Coin of *Knosos* with the Legend ΠΟΛΧΟΣ." *Numismatic Chronicle* new ser., 10 (1870): 11-3.
Arnold suggests that the word ΠΟΛΧΟΣ, found on the obverse of a coin of Knossos, is a magistrate's name rather than an epithet of a deity.

4399 **Ashton, Richard H. J.** "Rhodian-type Silver Coinages from Crete." *Schweizer Münzblätter* (Switzerland) 146 (May 1987): 29-39.
"The author lists nine Rhodian-type silver issues, and argues that they were struck ca. 200 B.C. by Rhodian commanders on Crete in order to pay Cretan mercenaries. A tenth silver issue with Rhodian types is attributed to a local Cretan authority." [R. Ashton, *NL* 123]

4400 **Birch, Samuel.** "Notes Upon a Type of Phaestus, in Crete." *Numismatic Chronicle* 3 (1841): 69-82.
Examines the types on coins of Phaestus to determine their significance. Recounts the related myths.

4401 **Cameron, J. S., and George F. Hill.** "Some Cretan Coins." *Numismatic Chronicle* 4th ser., 13 (1913): 381-8. 1 pl.
Publishes twenty-six coins from Cameron's collection, mostly from Crete. Includes a new type of stater from Gortyna.

4402 **Chapman, Anne E.** "Some First Century B.C. Bronze Coins of Knossos." *Numismatic Chronicle* 7th ser., 8 (1968): 13-26. 3 pls. [CS 2583]
"The Cnossian bronzes, of Zeus head/eagle type (Svoronos, *Numismatique de la Crète Ancienne*, pl. 7, Nos. 19-23) are compared with certain bronzes of Roman Cyrenaica (*BMC Cyrenaica* p. 113, Nos. 1-26). It is shown from this comparison how the two series should be linked and how they illuminate events in Crete in 67-31 B.C." [A. Chapman, *NL* 82]

4403 **Clayton, Peter A.** "The Coinage of Knossos, the Minotaur Legend and the Archaeological Evidence." *Seaby Coin and Medal Bulletin* 830 (May 1988): 107-8; 831 (June 1988): 131-3; 832 (July 1988). Illus.
Recounts the minotaur legend. Discusses various periods of Cretan coinage. Then discusses the coins of Knossos, focusing on how their types relate to the minotaur legend.

4404 **Freeman & Sear.** *Mail Bid Sale 13, Featuring the F. Martin Post Collection.* August 25, 2006. Los Angeles: Freeman & Sear, 2006. 156 pp., illus.
This auction catalogue, featuring 907 lots of ancient coins, includes a good collection of the silver coins of Crete (lots 1-41).

4405 **Hackens, Tony.** "L'Influence Rhodienne en Crète aux IIIe et IIe s. av. J.-C. et le Trésor de Gortyne, 1966." *Revue Belge de Numismatique* (Belgium) 116 (1970): 37-58. 1 pl. [CS 2575]

4406 **Halbherr, Federico.** "Epigraphical Researches in Gortyna." *American Journal of Archaeology* 1 (1897): 159-238. 2 pls.
"On pp. 191-7 an inscription, which the writer dates to the early fourth century B.C., is described and illustrated; it records a decree enforcing the use of bronze coinage (now *SIG*^{3}, 525, and more probably of the mid-third century)." [J. R. Jones, *NIAJAH*]

4407 ——— "An Important Inscription for the History of Coinage in Crete." *Journal International d'Archéologie Numismatique* (Greece) 1 (1898): 165-72.
Publishes an inscription, found on the corner block of an archaic building, which orders that bronze money shall be used and that silver obols and payments in kind are not to be accepted. The author dates the inscription to the early fourth century B.C. The intent was probably to establish the newly introduced bronze coinage as an acceptable medium of exchange among the people. Discusses letter forms and meanings of the text. [On pages 173-80, J. N. Svoronos disputes the fourth century date of the inscription, suggesting that it belongs to the period 220-215 B.C. Svoronos' article is in Greek].

4408 **Hill, George F.** "The Seager Bequest of Coins." *British Museum Quarterly* 1, no. 1 (May 1926): 22-3. 1 pl.
Publishes eight of the most important Cretan coins bequeathed to the British Museum by R. B. Seager. Includes coins of Sybrita, Arcadia, Phaestus, Cydonia, and other cities.

4409 ——— "Cretan Coins from the Seager Collection." *Essays in Aegean Archaeology Presented to Sir Arthur Evans in Honour of His 75th Birthday.* Oxford: Clarendon Press, 1927. Pages 43-54. 1 pl.
Discusses twelve Cretan coins from the collection of Richard B. Seager which was bequeathed to the British Museum. Describes each coin and discusses its significance.

4410 **Hogg, John.** "On Some Coins of Cnossus in Crete." *Transactions of the Royal Society of Literature* (England) 2nd ser., 9 (1870): 15-24. Illus.
Examines four coins of Knossos, commenting on their types and inscriptions.

4411 **Jackson, Anne E.** "The Bronze Coinage of Gortyn." *Numismatic Chronicle* 7th ser., 11 (1971): 37-51. 3 pls.
"An attempt is made to sort Gortynian bronze coinage into its constituent issues and to arrange these issues in chronological order of striking. The decree (M. Garducci, ed., *Inscriptiones Creticae* 4, no. 162) enjoining the use of bronze coinage at Gortyna is examined; an attempt is made to ascertain which bronze issue is referred to. Denominations and countermarking are discussed." [A. Jackson, *NL* 87]

4412 ——— "The Chronology of the Bronze Coins of Knossos." *The Annual of the British School at Athens* 66 (1971): 283-95. 2 pls.
Attempts to arrange the bronze coinage of the autonomous city of Knossos into chronological order. Summarizes the types and their probable dates covering the period ca. 320 to 67 B.C. Summarizes the weights and sizes of the various denominations. Forty-one coins are illustrated.

4413 **Jenkins, G. Kenneth.** "The Cameron Collection of Cretan Coins." *Numismatic Chronicle* 6th ser., 9 (1949): 36-56. 3 pls. [CS 2576]
Catalogues eighty-six coins from the collection of 2700 Cretan coins bequeathed to the British Museum in 1947. Those published here are variations or previously unpublished specimens. Many are overstruck or countermarked. Includes an appendix showing the quantity and distribution of the bronze coins in the collection.

4414 **Lambros, J. P.** "On a Coin of Hierapynta, in Crete, Hitherto Wrongly Attributed." *Numismatic Chronicle* 3rd ser., 17 (1897): 31-4. Illus.
A bronze coin with the inscription Π – A was attributed to Pannona in Crete by Svoronos. Lambros reads the inscription as I – A and attributes the coin to Hierapynta.

4415 **Le Rider, Georges.** *Monnaies Crétoises du Ve au Ier Siècle avant J.-C.* Études Crétoises 15. Paris: École Française d'Athènes, 1966. 345 pp., 48 pls. [CS 2577]
"A fundamental study based largely on the evidence of overstrikes." [C. Kraay]

4416 ——— "Les Arsinoéens de Crète." *Essays in Greek Coinage Presented to Stanley Robinson.* Edited by C. M. Kraay and G. K. Jenkins. Oxford: Clarendon Press, 1968. Pages 229-40. 1 pl. [CS 2578]

4416a ——— "Un Groupe de Monnaies Crétoises à Types Athéniens." *Humanisme Actif: Mélanges d'Art et Littérature Offerts à Julien Cain.* Paris: Hermann, 1968. Pages 313-35. Illus.
Discusses a group of Cretan coins with types imitating those of the New Style Athenian tetradrachms.

4417 **Levi, Doro.** "Gleanings from Crete." *American Journal of Archaeology* 49, no. 3 (July-September 1945): 270-329.
Examines the motifs used in art objects of the Near East to gauge their contribution to Minoan art. Mentions coins of Axos.

4418 **MacDonald, David J.** "Mercenaries and the Movement of Silver to Crete in the Late Fourth Century B.C." *Nomismatika Khronika* (Greece) 15 (1996): 41-7. 1 pl.
Many silver coins from North Africa were imported to Crete and were overstruck at local mints there in the fourth century B.C. Also, many silver coins from Central Greece and the northern Peloponnesos were imported to Crete and were overstruck. MacDonald reviews the history of the conflicts in Crete and Kyrenaica and the heavy use of mercenaries in the late fourth and early third centuries B.C. He compares the two groups of overstruck coins and confirms that Cretan mercenaries brought the coins to Crete where they were overstruck.

4419 **Macdonald, George.** "The Silver Coinage of Crete: A Metrological Note." *Proceedings of the British Academy* 9 (1920): 289-318. 1 pl. Reprint, Chicago: Obol International, 1974. 29 pp., 1 pl. [CS 2579]
The author's discovery of a silver stater of Itanus which had a weight considerably higher than the norm set the stage for this examination of the metrology of Cretan coinage. Begins with the use of the Aeginetic weight standard and compares the weights of staters at different Cretan cities. Concludes that some cities used a lower-weight Aeginetan stater which bore a slightly modified design and circulated simultaneously with the heavier coins. Also discusses the more limited use of the Attic and Rhodian standards, and suggests some reasons for the introduction of different standards. Concludes with a discussion of Cretan coinage during the Roman period.

4420 **Marshall, F. H.** "Some Recent Acquisitions of the British Museum." *Journal of Hellenic Studies* 29 (1909): 151-67. Illus.
"On pp. 156-7 a small Boeotian bronze statuette showing Apollo holding a pair of goat's horns is compared to fourth century B.C. coins of Tylissa, both being explained as portrayals of the god as a hunter." [J. R. Jones, *NIJHS*]

4421 **Milne, Joseph G.** "The Evans Collection at Oxford: The Cretan Coins." *Numismatic Chronicle* 6th ser., 3 (1943): 77-91. 2 pls.
Discusses the diversity of weights evident in Cretan coins, as well as the use of plated coins and the sharing of dies between cities. Publishes 266 coins formerly in the collection of Arthur Evans. Lists the weights, diameters, and die-axes. Each coin is attributed to Svoronos' *Numismatique de la Crète Ancienne*.

4422 **Myres, John C.** "On Some Bronze Coins from Crete." *Numismatic Chronicle* 3rd ser., 14 (1894): 89-100.
Describes several coins recently found in Crete.

4423   **Newton, Charles T.** "Proposed Attribution to Allaria in Crete, of a Coin at Present Ascribed to Lacedaemon." *Numismatic Chronicle* 7 (1845): 114-5.
   The subject coin is a silver tetradrachm in the British Museum bearing the head of Pallas on the obverse and a seated Herakles on the reverse. Newton suggests the coin was minted at Lacedaemon. [Also see E. J. Seltman "Lacedaemon *Versus* Allaria" under PELOPONNESOS—LAKONIA. Seltman maintains that the coin belongs to Lacedaemon and suggests a different identity for the head depicted on the coin].

4424   **Poole, Reginald Stuart.** "On Two Cretan Coins in the British Museum." *Numismatic Chronicle* new ser., 1 (1861): 168-74. 1 engraved plate.
   Discusses the coinage of Crete, emphasizing its artistic aspects. Shows three tetradrachms, identical to Athenian New Style tetradrachms, struck at Gortyna, Polyrhenium, and Prianus and bearing the badges of these cities in the reverse fields of the coins.

4425   **Price, Martin J.** "A Hoard from Gortyn." *Revue Numismatique* (France) 6th ser., 8 (1966): 128-43. 3 pls.
   "The hoard containing 285 drachms of Gortyna and forty-four local imitations of Rhodes is described. The issues at Gortyna are dated in an annual sequence, and on the evidence of internal chronology a date of ca. 85 B.C. is suggested for the deposit of the hoard." [M. Price, *NL 83*]

4426   **Robinson, Edward S. G.** "Pseudaeginetica." *Numismatic Chronicle* 5th ser., 8 (1928): 172-98. 2 pls.
   Certain coins currently attributed to Aegina, principally hemidrachms both of sea-turtle and land-tortoise types, stand out from the general series by peculiarities of style and fabric, most of them being marked by the crescent symbol. Similar peculiarities mark the coins of Crete, and many of these coins are found in Crete. The crescent symbol is frequently used in Crete as a symbol of Artemis-Dictynna. Robinson concludes that the earliest coins of this group are the early coinage of Cydonia, a colony of Aegina in Crete. Most of the later coins are also from Cydonia, but some may have been struck at other cities of western Crete. [Also see Holloway "An Archaic Hoard" under AEGINA. Holloway suggests these coins belong to Aegina].

4427   **Seager, Richard B.** *A Cretan Coin Hoard.* Numismatic Notes and Monographs, No. 23. New York: American Numismatic Society, 1924. 55 pp., 13 pls.
   This hoard of 1003 coins contained silver minors of Cydonia, Tanos, and Itanos, as well as a number of non-Cretan mints.

4428   **Sippel, Donald V.** "The Cretan 'Labyrinth' on the Coinage of Knossos." *SAN—Journal of the Society for Ancient Numismatics* 17, no. 2 (June 1987): 32-5.
   Recounts the myth of Theseus and the Minotaur and concludes that the pseudo-labyrinth portrayed on Knossian coinage was not intended to be an accurate depiction of the palace of Minos, but was merely intended to associate the classical city with its legendary past.

4429   **Spratt, T.** "Note on Three Gold Coins from Crete." *Numismatic Chronicle* 3rd ser., 7 (1887): 309-11. Illus.
   Publishes three gold coins found near Polyrhenium, Crete. The obverse of each shows a bird in flight; the reverses show an oenochoe, a bee, and a star or incuse, respectively. Spratt suggests the first two coins belong to Lyttus because of the flying bird type. The third coin, which is of cruder style, may belong to Polyrhenium.

4430   **Stefanaki, Vasiliki E.** "Sur Deux Monnaies de Bronze Inédites d'Hiérapytna. Monnayage Hiérapytnien et Timbres Amphoriques à l'Époque Hellénistique." *Eulimene* 2 (Mediterranean Archaeological Society, Rethymno, Greece) (2001): 121-8.
   "The silver coins of Hierapytna (tetradrachms, didrachms and drachms) bearing the head of Tyche on the obverse were minted between 110 and 80 B.C. and probably reflect the prosperity of the city during this period. This prosperity was the result not only of the Hierapytnian control over the rich territory of Praisos, but also of the increase in wine production in Hierapytna. The last suggestion is based on the finds of sealed Hierapytnian amphorae in Alexandria in Egypt, Kallatis in the Black Sea area and at the Trypitos promontory in the area of Siteia, where excavation has revealed part of an important Hellenistic site. The bee emblem that has been used to seal an amphora, as the official badge of Hierapytna, is also depicted on the reverse of two Hierapytnian bronze coins in the collection of the Ashmolean Museum in Oxford. It is possible that the selection of the bee as a symbol was related to the conquest of Praisos by Hierapytna, since the type is typical for the Praisian coinage. The inscription engraved on the amphora sealing and on the two bronze coins is an abbreviation of the Hierapytnian ethnic: IE. On other seals on Hierapytnian amphoras the ethnic is inscribed in whole (IE(A)P?ΠYTNI[ON]) and names of officials (ΣΟΣΟΣ, ΠΑΣΙΟΝ) are inscribed too. Something similar is evident on the silver coinage of Hierapytna bearing the head of Tyche, minted from 110 B.C. onwards. The ethnic does not appear in full on any coin before 110 B.C. and names of the officials start appearing on coins in the second half of the second century B.C. It is probably the period during which Hierapytna starts organizing its coinage in order to ease economic and administrative control of her expanded territory. The same control was probably applied during this period on commerce. It is therefore suggested that Hierapytnian amphorae and coins depicting a bee should be dated after 145 B.C. and rather towards the end of the second century B.C. [Manolis I. Stefanakis, *NL 147*]

4431   ——— "Les Fausses Monnaies d'Hiérapytna: Monnaies Fourrées et Imitations Modernes." *Nomismatika Khronika* (Greece) 26 (2007): 29-50, including 2 pls. and 1 map.
   Discusses counterfeit coins of Hierapytna, including fourrees and other imitations. Twenty-four pieces are catalogued and illustrated. In French and Greek.

4431a   ——— "Le Monnayage de Bronze de Viannos et de Malla en Crète Orientale." *ΚΕΡΜΑΤΙΑ ΦΙΛΙΑΣ: Volume in Honor of Ioannis Touratsoglou.* Edited by S. Drougou et al. Athens: Alpha Bank, 2009.
   The coins of Biannos and Malla.

4432   **Stephanakis, Manolis I.** "Polichne." *Μνήμη Martin Jessop Price.* Edited by A. P. Tzamalis and M. J. A. Tzamali. Bibliotheca 5. Athens: The Hellenic Numismatic Society, 1996. Pages 152-6. 1 pl.
   The author examines the copper fractions struck by Polichne, a small town in Western Crete. Lists the six specimens known to the author. The coins have the head of Diktyna on the obverse, and a hound running right within a wreath on the reverse. Also illustrates two larger fractions which Svoronos had attributed to Polichne—the author rejects this attribution. Discusses the history of the city. Stephanakis suggests that Polichne struck these coins, which closely resemble the types of Kydonia, in the first quarter of the second century B.C. to enable trade with their neighboring allies, the Kydonians.

4432a   ——— *Studies in the Coinages of Crete with Particular Reference to Kydonia.* Ph.D. dissertation, University of London, 1997.

4433 ——— "The Introduction of Monetary Economy and the Beginning of Local Minting in Crete." *From Minoan Farmers to Roman Traders: Sidelights on the Economy of Ancient Crete.* Edited by Angelos Chaniotis. Stuttgart: Steiner, 1999. Pages 247-68.

4434 ——— "Kydon the Oikist or Zeus Cretagenes Kynotraphes? The Problem of Interpreting Cretan Coin Type." *Eulimene* (Mediterranean Archaeological Society, Rethymno, Greece) 1 (2000): 79-90.
"Interpreting coin types is often a difficult task and the difficulty becomes even greater when it comes to Cretan coinage. Among the many narrative or non-narrative types of Cretan numismatic iconography, for example, the dog that suckles an infant on the silver staters, drachms, tetrobols and tetradrachms of Kydonia is of particular interest, since different interpretations have been offered over the years. Similar is the case of the silver staters of Gortyn of the second half of the fourth and first half of the third century B.C., where a female figure is depicted seated on the branch of a tree. The problem of interpreting types such as these and many more narrative scenes and figures on Cretan coins is caused partly [by] the proliferation of myth in the late Classical and Hellenistic periods and partly [by our] lack [of] local sources for Cretan mythology. Surviving sources are based on myths and variations of myth from mainland Greece, [and are] often misleading as far as Cretan iconography is concerned. In addition, artistic influences from mainland Greece or the execution of dies by traveling non-Cretan engravers make things even mistier since the individuality of Cretan tradition is 'contaminated' with foreign elements, thereby making the proper interpretation of numismatic types virtually impossible." [M. I. Stefanakis, *NL* 147]

4434a ——— "The 'Chania 1922' Hoard (*IGCH* 254 & *CH* VII 104): A Reassessment." *Cretan Studies* 7 (2002): 231-44.

4434b **Stefanakis, Manolis I., and Burkhard Traeger.** "Counter-stamping Coins in Hellenistic Crete: A First Approach." *XIII Congreso Internacional de Numismática, Madrid – 2003: Actas–Proceedings–Actes I.* Edited by Carmen Alfaro, Carmen Marcos, and Paloma Otero. Madrid: International Numismatic Commisson, 2005. Pages 383-94, incl. 1 pl.
This paper is a first approach of a wider project to gather, classify and present chronologically the types of Cretan counterstamps from the early third century B.C. down to the Roman era. The aim is to compile an updated catalogue of countermarked Cretan coins. Gold and silver Hellenistic coinages have been surveyed and some preliminary results are presented here. Typology and iconography are used as a tool to identify the mints to which counterstamps may belong. In some cases, counterstamping was a means of converting foreign coins into domestic currency by towns that had a shortage of coinage. Sometimes the counterstamp is the result of an alliance. Suggested attributions are provided for some counterstamps. A systematic pattern for counterstamping cannot be recognized for all groups of coins.

4435 **Suter, Charles.** "Coins of Knossos and the Minataur." *The Celator* 19, no. 7 (July 2005): 34-7, 46. Illus.
Recounts the mythology of the Minotaur and describes the Mycenaean civilization and a few coins of Knossos.

4436 **Svoronos, Jean N.** "The Inscription SORVMST (ΤΙΣΥΡΟΙ) on Coins of Gortyna." *Numismatic Chronicle* 3rd ser., 7 (1887): 126-31.
Examines a didrachm of Gortyna (Europa/bull). The coin's unusual inscription has been a subject of interest for several researchers. Svoronos summarizes their conclusions. He then suggests the inscription may be a name (Τισυροι) referring to the people of Gortyna.

4437 ——— *Numismatique de la Crète Ancienne.* Macon, 1890. Reprints, Bologna: Forni, 1967; Bonn, 1972. 367 pp., 35 pls. [CS 2581]

4438 ——— "Britomartis, the So-called Europa on the Plane Tree of Gortyna." *American Journal of Numismatics* 29, no. 1 (July 1894): 1-9; no. 2 (October 1894): 33-41. Also see the editorial in *American Journal of Numismatics* 29, no. 2 (October 1894): 65.
A English translation of a work published in *Revue Belge de Numismatique*. Explores the mythology of the "Europa" upon a plane-tree, the type of the didrachm of Gortyna, Crete. Svoronos rejects the identity of Europa and instead suggests Britomartis. Also claims the tree is an oak. The editorial contains critical commentary by B. V. Head and others.

4439 **Tameanko, Marvin.** "Phalasarna, an Ancient Pirate City in Crete." *Journal of the Classical and Medieval Numismatic Society* (Canada) 2nd ser., 5, no. 4 (December 2004): 177-87. Illus., 2 maps.
Explores the early history of Crete, especially the harbor city of Phalasarna in western Crete. The island was a refuge for pirates. Discusses the city's geography, its relationship with Rome, and its history as an independent city. Examples of the city's coinage are illustrated.

4440 **Vagi, David L.** "The Ancient Coinage of Crete." Parts 1-3. *The Celator* 10, no. 4 (April 1996): 26-7; no. 5 (May 1996): 22-3; no. 6 (June 1996): 22-3. Illus.
The author describes the coinage of Crete. The main silver supply was Aeginetan staters which were restruck with Cretan dies. In Part 1, the author points out that the design of Cretan coinage varies from superb artistry to "barbaric atrocities." In Part 2, the author discusses the coinage from other Greek cities which influenced the design of Cretan coins. In Part 3, he describes the coinage of Crete during the early Roman period. Some of the Roman designs were closely modeled on those of earlier Greek coins.

4441 **Wroth, Warwick W.** "Cretan Coins." *Numismatic Chronicle* 3rd ser., 4 (1884): 1-58. 3 pls.
A description of several unpublished coins of Crete and some remarks on types and attributions. Begins with a summary of Cretan history, then continues with general comments on the coinage. Lists and discusses coins of Apollonia, Aptera, Ptolemaic issues, Axus, Cnossus, Chersonesus, Cydonia, Eleutherna, Elyrus, Erythraea, Gortyna, Itanus, Latus, Lyttus, Olus, Phaestus, Phalasarna, Polyrhenium, Praesus, Priansus, Thalassa, and some Roman Imperial coins bearing the names of Cretan cities.

4442 ——— *Catalogue of Greek Coins of Crete and the Aegean Islands.* Edited by R. S. Poole. London: British Museum, 1886. Reprint, Bologna: Forni, 1963. lxix, 152 pp., 29 pls. [CS 2582]
Volume 9 of the *Catalogue of Greek Coins in the British Museum*. Sixty-nine pages of introductory text precede the 152-page catalogue of coins. [Also see *Catalogue of Greek Coins in the British Museum* under PUBLIC COLLECTIONS—GREAT BRITAIN (LONDON)].

4443 ——— Review of J. N. Svoronos' "Cretan Coin-Types Relating to the Nurture of the Infant Zeus." *Numismatic Chronicle* 3rd ser., 13 (1893): 237-9.
A review of Svoronos' paper which was published in *Ephemeris Archaiologike* in 1893. The paper examines Cretan coin types which Svoronos interpreted as relating to the nurture of the infant Zeus in Crete. Wroth summarizes the paper and voices his disagreement with some aspects of it.

Also see: Ashton "Knossos Royal Road" under HOARDS; Forrer "Le Labyrinthe de Knossos" under TYPES; Gabrici "La Nike Funebre delle Monete di Elis" under PELOPONNESOS—ELIS; Imhoof-Blumer "Zur Münzkunde Grossgriechenlands, Siciliens, Kretas, etc." under ITALY—GENERAL WORKS; Lattimore "Lysippian Sculpture" under TYPES; Raven "The Hierapytna Hoard" under HOARDS; Touratsoglou *Disjecta Membra* under HOARDS; Waldstein "The Argive Hera" under ART.

CYCLADES ISLANDS

Within the context of mainland Greece and the Aegean during the sixth century B.C. there clearly was a significant early interest in local coinage in the Cyclades and the issues, though limited in size, are remarkable for their diversity. The islanders were enthusiastic minters.

—Kenneth Sheedy, 2006

4444 **Apostolou, Eva.** "A Review on the New Style Silver Coinage of Athens: The Role of Delos." *Nomismatika Khronika* (Greece) 28 (2010): 15-23.
Examines the role of the Athenian New Style tetradrachms in the commercial markets at Delos and the role of the Roman Republic in Delos. Includes a list of hoards found at Delos with a summary of their contents. [In Greek on pp. 15-19 and in English on pp. 20-23].

4445 **Arnold, T. J.** "On a Type on Some Coins of Aigiale." *Numismatic Chronicle* new ser., 13 (1873): 125-9. Illus.
Arnold examines the type occurring on the reverse of a coin of Aigialê, one of the cities on the island of Amorgos. The type resembles "a vase without handles, reversed, a ring instead of a foot, as if it were intended to be suspended." The object is identified as a Σικυα (*cucurbita* in Latin)—a cupping instrument used by physicians. The figure on the obverse of the coin is identified as Asklepios.

4446 **Artemis-Gyselen, L.** "Les Monnaies Archaïques de Ténos." *Revue Belge de Numismatique* (Belgium) 123 (1977): 5-15.

4446a **Boutin, Serge.** "Essai de Classement de Monnaies Archaiques de la Mer Égee au Type des Deux Dauphins." *Numismatics—Witness to History*. Publication 8. Edited by R. Margolis and H. Voegtli. London: International Association of Professional Numismatics, 1986.

4447 **Dreni, Stella.** "The Bronze Coins of Andros (4th – 1st c. B.C.)." *Coins in the Aegean Islands. Proceedings of the Fifth Scientific Meeting, Mytilene, 16-29 September 2006. Volume 1: Ancient Times*. Obolos 9. Edited by Panagiotis Tselekas. Athens: The Friends of the Numismatic Museum, 2010. Pages 301-19.

4448 **Étienne, Roland.** *Ténos II: Ténos et les Cyclades du Milieu du IVe Siècle av J.-C. au Milieu du IIIe Siècle ap. J.-C.* Athens-Paris, 1990. Pages 225-52.

4449 **Forrer, Leonard S.** "Drachm of Syros (Cyclades)." *Spink Numismatic Circular* 8, no. 88 (March 1900): 3843.
Mentions the finding of "the only silver coin hitherto known of the early coinage of Syros."

4450 **Fox, Charles R.** "On a Coin of Glauconnesus." *Numismatic Chronicle* new ser., 9 (1869): 25-7. Illus.
Publishes a coin with *obv*., Zeus; *rev*., bee with inscription ΓΛΑΥ (Glau). Suggests it may belong to the island of Glauconnesus in the Cyclades.

4451 **Hackens, Tony.** "Le Monnayage de l'Atelier de Délos à l'Époque Archaïque." *Bulletin de Correspondance Hellénique. Supplement 1: Études Déliennes* (France) (1973): 209-26. [CS 2584]

4452 **Holloway, R. Ross.** "The Crown of Naxos and the Coinage of the Persians." *American Journal of Archaeology* 64 (1960): 186.
A brief summary of a paper presented at a conference. This paper was later published in *Museum Notes* (see below).

4453 ——— "The Crown of Naxos." *Museum Notes* 10 (1962): 1-8. 1 pl. [CS 2585]
There are three obverse varieties of the archaic staters of Naxos: plain kantharos, plain kantharos with a bunch of grapes, and kantharos with an ivy-wreath and a bunch of grapes. The author believes the addition of the ivy-wreath was a policy decision by the Naxian government rather than a mere decision by the engraver, and he explores the reason for its addition. He suggests the wreath was added as a symbol celebrating the victory of the Naxians over the Persian invaders in 500 B.C. He calls this "the first known commemorative coinage." Holloway summarizes the hoard evidence for the wreathed issues and presents a catalogue of thirty-four specimens.

4454 **Hoover, Oliver D.** *The Handbook of Coins of the Islands: Adriatic, Ionian, Thracian, Aegean, and Carpathian Seas (Excluding Crete and Cyprus), Sixth to First Centuries BC*. The Handbook of Greek Coinage Series, Volume 6. Lancaster: Classical Numismatic Group, 2010. lxxxii + 358 pp., illus.

A comprehensive guide to the coin types, heavily illustrated, with extensive background information and estimates of rarity. Lists 1482 coin types. Includes a *Foreword* by Richard Ashton, a *Preface* by D. Scott VanHorn and Bradley R. Nelson which provides an overview of the history of Greek coinage, minting methods, denominations, types, epigraphy, and basic information for collectors regarding grading, and good summaries of the coinage of each island by Hoover. [For a general description of the format of these catalogues and a list of all the volumes in this series, see Hoover *The Handbook of Greek Coinage* under COLLECTING GUIDES].

4455 **Jameson, Robert.** "Une Trouvaille de Statères de Melos." *Revue Numismatique* (France) 4th series, 12 (1908): 301-10. 1 pl.

4456 **Kagan, Jonathan H.** "Paros, Melos, and Naxos: Archaic and Early Classical Coinages of the Cyclades." *American Journal of Numismatics* 2nd ser., 20 (2008): 105-11.
In this extended review of Sheedy's book *The Archaic and Early Classical Coinages of the Cyclades* (see Sheedy below), Kagan proposes additional theories about the island coinages, including the possibility that Parian drachms were minted in the region around Thasos and shipped to Paros.

4457 **Kraay, Colin M.** "The Melos Hoard of 1907 Re-examined." *Numismatic Chronicle* 7th ser., 4 (1964): 1-20. 3 pls. [CS 3249]
"This is an attempt to establish the contents of the hoard discovered on Melos in 1907 (*Noe* 672), which contained many hitherto unknown Melian types, and to examine the incidence of die links between different types. A by-product of this study is the unmasking of a number of forgeries which were put on the market in the years following the discovery of the hoard. The historical context of the hoard in relation to the views of J. G. Milne (see Milne *The Melos Hoard* below) is discussed, and it is concluded that the hoard was buried at the time of the Athenian attack in 416 B.C. and contains for the most part issues of the preceding decade." [C. Kraay, *NL* 80]. [Also see Kraay "Greek Coinage and War" under GENERAL WORKS—GREEK].

4458 **Kyrou, Adonis K., and Dimitris N. Artemis.** "The Silver Coinage of Kythnos in the Early Fifth Century B.C." *Studies in Greek Numismatics in Memory of Martin Jessop Price*. Edited by Richard Ashton and Silvia Hurter. London: Spink, 1998. Pages 233-6. 2 pls.
A hoard of coins found on Kythnos in 1976 included thirty-one silver third-staters struck on the Aeginetan standard. Twenty-nine of the coins had the head of a wild boar on the obverse, while two had a gorgoneion. The reverses had a quadripartite square incuse. Presents a catalogue of these and ten related coins. The authors attribute the coins to the mint of Kythnos.

4459 ——— "The Boar of Kythnos: The Silver Coins of a Cycladic Island." *Nomismatika Khronika* (Greece) 17 (1998): 43-60. Illus., 3 pls., map.
Despite the abundance of coins attributed to various Cycladic Islands, no silver coins had been attributed to Kythnos. A hoard of thirty-one coins, which was found on Kythnos, appeared on the market in 1976. Twenty-nine of the coins had a boar's head on the reverse. A list of the coins which can now be attributed to Kythnos appears here in Greek. The list was published in English in the authors' essay "The Silver Coinage of Kythnos" (see above). The conclusions of the authors regarding the attribution of various coins are summarized here. This English summary was translated by M. J. A. Tzamali.

4460 "Lost Countries Found by Coins." *American Journal of Numismatics* 14, no. 4 (April 1880): 94-5.
Explains how coins of Glauconesus (an island in the Aegean Sea) and Pandosia (a city in Bruttium, Italy) helped researchers to determine the locations of these previously lost cities. [Also see G. Feuardent "A Coin of Pandosia" under ITALY—PANDOSIA for a more in-depth explanation of the Pandosia coin].

4461 **Liampi, Katerini.** "The Coinage of Amorgos: Aigiale, Arkesine, Minoa and the Koinon of the Amorgians." *Revue Numismatique* (France) 6, no. 160 (2004): 63-113. 5 pls.
The coins minted by the cities and the Koinon of the Amorgians comprise a source of information of great interest for the economic and social conditions of the island. A small number of silver coins were produced solely by the mint of Aigiale at the beginning of the second century B.C. Whereas, in Hellenistic times, short-lived issues of bronzes were produced by Aigiale as well as Arkesine and Minoa at the end of the third/beginning of the second century B.C. During the Imperial period, only Aigiale and Minoa minted coins. Through the iconography of the coins, the author makes interesting conclusions regarding political connections of the Amorgian cities with great centers such as Athens, Samos, Miletos, Rhodes, and the Ptolemaic and Macedonian monarchies. The numismatic activity of the cities was contemporary and their production of coins probably coincided with the Rhodian domination of the Cyclades islands. [Paraphrased from the author's summary].

4462 **Milne, Joseph G.** *The Melos Hoard of 1907*. Numismatic Notes and Monographs, No. 62. New York: American Numismatic Society, 1934. 19 pp., illus.
Examines a hoard of seventy-nine coins, including thirty-one distinct types, found on the island of Melos in 1907. Most of the types were previously unknown. Extensive discussion of Melian coinage. [Also see Kraay "The Melos Hoard of 1907 Re-Examined" above, and Kraay "Greek Coinage and War" under GENERAL WORKS—GREEK].

4463 ——— "A Group of Coins Attributable to the Revolt of Naxos in 467." *Numismatic Chronicle* 5th ser., 20 (1940): 76-88.
Milne re-examines a group of staters of four types which Wroth attributed to Peparethos (see Wroth "Peparethus" under NORTHERN GREECE—THESSALY). For some of the types, Milne argues that the revolt of Naxos seems to offer the most probable explanation for their issuance. These coins cannot be connected by their types with any other series known among Greek city coinages.

4464 **Nicolet-Pierre, Hélène.** "Types Monétaires des Îles." *Mer Égée Grèce des Îles. Exposition 26 Avril—3 Septembre 1979. Musée du Louvre*. Paris, 1979. Pages 232-45.

4465 ——— "Remarques sur le Monnayage de Naxos (Cyclades) à l'Époque Classique." *Proceedings of the 12th International Conference on Classical Archaeology, 1983*. Athens, 1988. Pages 159-62.

4465a ——— "Naxos (Cyclades) Archaique: Monnaie et Histoire. La Frappe des Canthares de la fin du IVe Siècle." *Quaderni Ticinesi: Numismatica e Antichità Classiche* (Switzerland) 26 (1997): 63-121.

4466 ——— "Les Cratérophores de Naxos (Cyclades): Emissions Monétaires d'Argent á l'Époque Hellénistique." *Revue Numismatique* (France) 150 (1999): 95-119.
Coins of Naxos with a reverse type of a krater.

4466a ——— "Naxos (Cyclades): Les Émissions de Monnaies de Bronze du IVᵉ au Ier Siècle av. J.-C." *Revue Numismatique* (France) 161 (2005): 17-46.

4467 ——— "Naxos (Cyclades) et son Monnayage: Essai de Chronologie." *Coins in the Aegean Islands. Proceedings of the Fifth Scientific Meeting, Mytilene, 16-29 September 2006. Volume 1: Ancient Times.* Obolos 9. Edited by Panagiotis Tselekas. Athens: The Friends of the Numismatic Museum, 2010. Pages 321-33.

4468 **Nicolet-Pierre, Hélène, and Michel Amandry.** "Les Monnaies d'Argent de Syros." *Florilegium Numismaticum: Studia in Honorem U. Westermark Edita.* Edited by Harald Nilsson. Stockholm: Svenska Numismatiska Föreningen, 1992. Pages 295-306. Illus.
  The authors discuss some coins from the island of Syros. Includes a catalogue with commentary, and some related counterfeits by Caprara and others.

4469 **Oraiopoulos, Zacharias L.** "The Cuttlefish of Kea." *Nomismatika Khronika* (Greece) 27 (2008-2009): 21-3. Illus.
  Illustrates and briefly describes a coin depicting a cuttlefish. The coin was struck at Korresia on the island of Keos (Kea). In Greek and English.

4470 **Papageorgiadou-Banis, Charikleia.** "Koinon of the Keians? The Numismatic Evidence." *Revue Belge de Numismatique et de Sigillographie* (Belgium) 139 (1993): 9-16.

4471 ——— *The Coinage of Kea.* ΜΕΛΕΤΗΜΑΤΑ Vol. 24. Athens: Research Center for Greek and Roman Antiquity, National Hellenic Research Foundation, 1997. 108 pp., 21 pls.
  A comprehensive study of the poleis and federation mints of the island of Keos. [An extensive review by Kenneth Sheedy appears in *Numismatic Chronicle* 158 (1998): 249-57. See Sheedy "Keian Federations" below].

4472 **Seltman, Charles T.** "Aegean Mints." *Numismatic Chronicle* 5ᵗʰ ser., 6 (1926): 137-53. 2 pls. [CS 2580]
  Seltman attempts a new arrangement of the coins with an incuse square on the reverse, minted during the seventh and sixth centuries B.C. on the islands and shores of the Aegean Sea. He divides the coins into three groups: (1) The Aeginetan Group, including Aegina, Athens, Siphnos, Seriphos, Ceos (Carthaea, Coresia, and Iulis), and Corinth; Aegina provided the prototypes for the coinage of these cities. (2) The Delian Group, including Delos, Naxos, Tenos, and Paros. (3) The Coan Group, including Cos, Cnidus, Thera, and Caunos. Discusses the development of coinage within these groups and the influence the cities had on the coinage of the other groups. [Also see Sheedy "The Dolphins" below].

4473 **Sheedy, Kenneth A.** "Changes in Personnel at the Archaic Mint of Paros." *ΞΑΡΑΚΤΗΡ: Αφιερωμα στη Μαντω Οικονομιδου (Character: Offerings to Mando Oeconomides).* Publications of Archaeological Deltion, No. 57. Athens: Treasury of Archaeological Resources and Expropriations, 1996. Pages 277-82.

4474 ——— "The Origins of the Second Nesiotic League and the Defense of Kythnos." *Historia* (Germany) 45 (1996): 423-49.
  On pages 438-41, "the author discusses the coinage of Tenos and Kythnos after 197 B.C., when these Cycladic islands were members of the Second Nesiotic League dominated by Rhodes. He emphasizes the meaning of the rose emblem on coins of Kythnos." [J. Nollé, *NL* 138]

4475 ——— "The Dolphins, the Crab, the Sphinx, and 'Aphrodite.'" *Studies in Greek Numismatics in Memory of Martin Jessop Price.* Edited by Richard Ashton and Silvia Hurter. London: Spink, 1998. Pages 320-5. 1 pl.
  A reconsideration of some Aegean coins of the archaic period for which Seltman proposed attributions to Thera, Cos, Caunus, and Cnidus (see Seltman "Aegean Mints" above). Kraay later attributed them as "possibly Caria" in his *Archaic and Classical Greek Coins.* The coin types in question are: (1) two dolphins leaping in the same direction, (2) crab, (3) sphinx, and (4) head of a woman (Aphrodite?). The reverses are all incuse. Presents a catalogue of all known specimens. Notes a previously unseen die link between the dolphin and sphinx issues, and suggests all but the "head of a woman" issues belong to the same mint. Sheedy makes a case for a Lycian origin for the coins. Concludes that "in seeking to locate this mint we should be focusing on the maritime route which linked the states along the coast of south west Asia Minor rather than on the broader and more diverse territories of Caria or Lycia as a whole."

4476 ——— "Keian Federations and Keian Coinage." *Numismatic Chronicle* 158 (1998): 249-57.
  An extensive review of Charikleia Papageorgiadou-Banis' book *The Coinage of Kea* (see Papageorgiadou-Banis above). Sheedy suggests some revisions to the author's chronological arrangement of the coinage.

4477 ——— "Archaic Parian Coinage and Parian Marble." *ΠΑΡΙΑ ΛΙΘΟΣ/PARIA LITHOS. Parian Quarries, Marble and Workshops of Sculpture. Proceedings of the First International Conference on the Archaeology of Paros and the Cyclades. Paros, 2-5 October 1997.* Edited by D. U. Schilardi and D. Katsonopoulou. Athens, 2000. Pages 117-121.

4478 ——— "The Early Classical Coinage of Siphnos: Some Thoughts on the Influence of Athens." *XIII Congreso Internacional de Numismática, Madrid – 2003: Actas–Proceedings–Actes I.* Edited by Carmen Alfaro, Carmen Marcos, and Paloma Otero. Madrid: International Numismatic Commisson, 2005. Pages 303-6, incl. 1 pl.
  Sheedy discusses the earliest coinage of Siphnos and finds close stylistic similarities with the early coins of Athens. He suggests that Athenian die engravers were employed at the mint of Siphnos.

4479 ——— *The Archaic and Early Classical Coinages of the Cyclades.* Special Publication No. 40. London: Royal Numismatic Society, 2006. 261 pp., 20 pls., map.
  A comprehensive study of the early coinage of the Cyclades Islands including Keos, Karathaia, Ioulis, Korressos, Kythnos, Seriphos, Siphnos, Melos, Thera, Anaphe, Tenos, Delos, Naxos, and Paros. Sheedy defines the "Cyclades" and discusses the islands and their history. He then presents an island-by-island examination of the coinage, its chronology, hoard evidence, weights, and die varieties. Includes a catalogue of all the known coins struck ca. 540 to 440 B.C. generally grouped by reverse die. Extensive bibliography and list of provenances. A major contribution to our understanding of this coinage. [Also see Kagan "Paros, Melos, and Naxos" above].

4480 ——— "The Early Hellenistic Coinage of Tenos." *Coins in the Aegean Islands. Proceedings of the Fifth Scientific Meeting, Mytilene, 16-29 September 2006. Volume 1: Ancient Times.* Obolos 9. Edited by Panagiotis Tselekas. Athens: The Friends of the Numismatic Museum, 2010. Pages 335-46.

4481 **Sheedy, Kenneth A., and Charikleia Papageorgiadou.** *The Coinage of Kythnos: History and Archaeology, Proceedings of the International Symposium, Kea-Kythnos, 22-25 June 1994.* ΜΕΛΕΤΗΜΑΤΑ 27. Athens: Research Center for Greek and Roman Antiquity, National Hellenic Research Foundation, 1998. Pages 649-55.
"The authors present the unique mint activity of Kythnos, from the second century B.C. to the first century B.C. and perhaps even to the first century A.D. They also strengthen the hypothesis of the Rhodian domination of the island, based on the numismatic iconography." [M. Oeconomides, *NL* 142]

4482 **Touratsoglou, Ioannis, and Eos Tsourti.** "The Demetrios Artemis Collection of Cycladic Coins: A New Acquisition of the Athens Numismatic Museum." *Coins in the Aegean Islands. Proceedings of the Fifth Scientific Meeting, Mytilene, 16-29 September 2006. Volume 1: Ancient Times.* Obolos 9. Edited by Panagiotis Tselekas. Athens: The Friends of the Numismatic Museum, 2010. Pages 355-77.

4483 **Tsangari, Dimitra.** *Journey to the Islands: The Numismatic Evidence.* Athens: Alpha Bank, 2009. 25 pp., illus., maps.
An exhibition catalogue depicting thirty-four coins from the Alpha Bank collection. The exhibition, held at the Cultural Centre in Nafplio, presented the history and coinage of the Greek islands.

4484 **Tselekas, Panagiotis, ed.** *Coins in the Aegean Islands. Proceedings of the Fifth Scientific Meeting, Mytilene, 16-29 September 2006. Volume 1: Ancient Times.* Obolos 9. Athens: The Friends of the Numismatic Museum, 2010. 534 pp., illus.
Papers presented at a conference held at the Archaeological Museum of Mytilene. Includes "Iconographie et Mémoire Monétaire: L'Example de Thasos" by O. Picard [3772], "Coins of the Aegean Islands in Aegean Thrace" by M. Tasaklaki and K. Chatziprokopiou [3644], "A Contribution to the Study of the Archaic Billon Coinage of Lesbos" by L. Lazzarini [4729], "The Koinon of the Lesbians through the Coin Evidence" by G. Vavliakis and F. Lyrou [4738], "Countermarks on the Hellenistic Coinages of Lesbos" by P. Tselekas [4737], "The Coinage of Chios 600-300 B.C.: New Research Developments 1991-2008" by N. Hardwick [4831], "Coinage of Chios during the Hellenistic and Roman Periods" by K. Lagos [4837], "The Bronze Coins of Andros ($4^{th}-1^{st}$ c. B.C.)" by S. Dreni [4447], "Naxos (Cyclades) et son Monnayage: Essai de Chronologie" by H. Nicolet-Pierre [4467], "The Early Hellenistic Coinage of Tenos" by K. Sheedy [4480], "Le Monnayage des Isles Égéennes à l'Époque Classique Tardive et Hellénistique: L'Influence Rhodienne" by V. Stefanaki [4975], "The Hellenistic Silver Coinage of Kalymnos" by K. Höghammar [4916], "Ein 'Hortfund' Bronze und Silber Münzen aus dem Grundstück, P. Vousvounis im Gebiet Perama auf Lesbos" by K. Rougou [4734], "Mytilene: The Hoard of Krene Street" by E. Ralli and M. Kombou [4732], "A Hoard of Ptolemaic Silver Coins from Chios" by G. Grigorakis [6589], "The Gymnasium of Ancient Samos/2001 Hoard: The Excavation Data" by M. Biglaki-Sophianou [4846], "The Gymnasium of Ancient Samos/2001 Hoard" by I. Touratsoglou [4853], "Three Hoards of the Athenian New Style Coins from Delos" by E. Apostolou [4165], "A Hoard of Bronze Coins of the Hellenistic Period from Kos: Monetary System and Fractions of the Bronze Coins of Kos" by A. Giannikouri and V. Stefanaki [4924], "Numismatic Evidence from the City of Hephaistia, Lemnos: New Coin Finds from the Theatre Excavations" by L. Souchleris [776], "Coins from the Ancient Harbour Installations in the Northern Port of Mytilene" by I. Kourtzellis [627], "The Messon Sanctuary of Lesbos through the Coin Evidence" by L. Acheilara [477], "Coin Finds and Sanctuaries: A Case Study from the Island of Kos" by H. Ingvaldsen [602], "La Circulation des Monnaies Hellénistiques de Thessalonique aux Iles de la Mer Egée" by T. Kourebanas [3859], "The Demetrios Artemis Collection of Cycladic Coins: A New Acquisition of the Athens Numismatic Museum" by I. Touratsoglou and E. Tsourti [4482], "Coins from Samos in the Athens Numismatic Museum" by D. Evgenidou [4847]. Each paper includes a summary in Greek, English, French, or German. *Volume 2* (257 pages) contains conference papers dealing with coins of the the middle ages through modern times. [Reviewed by E. G. Papaefthymiou in *Nomismatika Khronika* 28 (2010): 162-4. An extensive review article by Andrew Meadows appears in *American Journal of Numismatics* 2nd ser., 23 (2011): 265-84].

4485 **Tsourti, Eos.** *The Aegean of the Coins.* Athens: Ministry of Culture, Archaeological Receipts Fund, 2001. 128 pp., illus., map.
A catalogue for a traveling exhibition on the coins of the Aegean islands. Includes general comments on the coinage of each island along with enlarged photographs of many fine coins. Includes coins of Thasos, Samothrace, Tenedos, Imbros, Lemnos, Lesbos, Mytilene, Methymna, Samos, Chios, Ikaria, Peparethos, Skiathos, Skyros, Eretria, Karystos, Aigina, Andros, Kea, Syros, Tenos, Delos, Naxos, Seriphos, Siphnos, Melos, Thera, Paros, Amorgos, Kos, Rhodos, Kamiros, Ialysos, Karpathos, Kalymnos, Nisyros, Knossos, Phaistos, Gortyna, Kydonia, Elyros, Lyttos, and Itanos. Text in Greek and English.

4486 **Visonà, Paolo.** "Bronze Coins of Paros from the Island of Hvar." *Vjesnik za Arheologiju I Historiju Dalmatinsku* (Croatia) 86 (1994): 253-60. Illus.
"The author describes and illustrates a group of twelve small bronze coins found at Stari Grad on Hvar in 1901 or before, including a coin of Paros which, with one possible exception, is the first found in Dalmatia and possibly the model for the Pharos issues. The coins, now in the Archaeological Museum in Zagreb, were from the collection of L. Berualdi Lucic of Stari Grad. Also described are an additional five coins of unknown provenance and in poor condition, one of Paros and four of Pharos. All bear on the obverse a head right of Demeter (for Pharos the identification is more uncertain) and on the reverse a goat standing (Paros) or walking (Pharos) right." [C. Smith, Jr., *NL* 142]

Also see: Apostolou "Three Hoards of the Athenian New Style Coins from Delos" under ATTICA—NEW STYLE COINAGE; Greenwell "On a Find of Archaic Greek Coins, Principally of the Islands" under HOARDS; Kraay "Greek Coinage and War" under GENERAL WORKS—GREEK; Sheedy "Late Archaic Hoards in the Cyclades" under HOARDS; Wroth *Catalogue of Greek Coins of Crete and the Aegean Islands* under CRETE.

Asia Minor and the Black Sea Region

General Works

Under the kings of the Pergamene dynasty the so-called Cistophori made their first appearance as the chief medium of circulation for Western Asia Minor. The Cistophorus was so named from its type, the Sacred Bacchic Chest or Cista.

—Barclay V. Head, 1887

4487 **Alekseyev, Vladimir P.** *Rare and Unpublished Coins of Northern Black Sea Area Region Ancient Cities.* Translated by Oksana A. Dovgopolova. Odessa: Polis Press, 1996. 32 pp., 30 pls.
Publishes coins from the Black Sea region residing in private collections in Russia. Includes illustrations and extensive discussions of twenty-six coins from Tyra, Olbia, Chersonesus, and Panticapaeum. An additional twelve coins are listed in an Appendix. All are illustrated by enlarged photographs or drawings.

4488 **Anokhin, Vladilen Afanas'evich.** *Coins of the Ancient Cities of the North-West Black Sea Coast.* Kiev, 1989.
In Russian.

4489 **Ashton, R. H. J., and Philip Kinns.** "Opuscula Anatolica." *Numismatic Chronicle* 162 (2002): 11-31. 3 pls.
Six brief notes: (1) A Rhodian-type Coinage for Memnon and Mentor, (2) Portrait Bronzes of Demetrius Poliorcetes at Erythrae, (3) The Hellenistic Silver and Bronze Coinage of Phocaea, (4) A Sinope-Kos or Kos-Sinope Overstrike, (5) A Civic Bronze of Xanthos with Lykian Legend, and (6) Damnatio Memoriae in Second-Century Karia or Lykia?

4490 ——— "Opuscula Anatolica II." *Numismatic Chronicle* 163 (2003): 1-47. 8 pls.
Eight short papers: (1) A Didrachm of Rhodes Countermarked at Byzantion (Ashton), (2) Milesian Notes (Kinns), (3) A Teos on Ephesus Overstrike (Kinns), (4) A Rhodes on Chios Overstrike (Ashton), (5) Lepsynos at Euromos (Ashton), (6) Kaunian Notes (Ashton), (7) Macedonian Months on Cistophoric Coins of Tralles (Ashton), and (8) The First Bronze Coinage of Apameia in Phrygia (Ashton).

4491 ——— "Opuscula Anatolica III." *Numismatic Chronicle* 164 (2004): 70-107. 6 pls.
Four notes on the ancient Greek coinages of Anatolia: (1) A Hoard of Third Century Hemichalka from Magnesia (Kinns), (2) The Pre-Imperial Coinage of Metropolis in Ionia (Kinns), (3) Re-Dating the Earliest Alexander Tetradrachms of Rhodes (Ashton), and (4) Dated Cistophori of Apameia (Ashton).

4492 **Brace, Bruce R.** "Some Notes on Asia Minor, Part 1." *Journal of the Classical and Medieval Numismatic Society* (Canada) 2nd ser., 5, no. 1 (March 2004): 21-8. Illus, 2 maps. "Part 2." 5, no. 2 (June 2004): 91-3. Illus. "Part 3." 5, no. 3 (September 2004): 152-3. Illus.
The author provides a geographical description of the regions of Asia Minor, pointing out the main features of each during the Greek and Roman periods. Part 1 covers Troas, Mysia, Aeolis, Ionia, and Caria. Part 2 includes Lycia, Pamphylia, and Cilicia. Part 3 covers Bithynia, Paphlagonia, Pontos, and Lesser Armenia.

4493 **Bunbury, Edward H.** "Unpublished Cistophori." *Numismatic Chronicle* 3rd ser., 3 (1883): 181-201. 1 pl.
Lists forty-six previously unpublished cistophoric tetradrachms, both dated and undated issues. Discusses the coins.

4494 **Caskey, Lacey D.** "Greek Electrum Coins." *The Numismatist* 26, no. 1 (January 1913): 18-22. Illus.
A general description of Greek electrum coinage, illustrated by coins of Cyzicus, Lydia, Lesbos, and Phocaea from the collection of the Boston Museum of Fine Arts.

4495 **Droysen, H.** "Due Münzen der Persischen Satrapen in Kleinasien." *Zeitschrift für Numismatik* (Germany) 2 (1875): 309-19.

4496 **Dumersan, Théophile Marion.** "On the Coins Called 'Cistophori.'" *Numismatic Chronicle* 9 (1847): 1-16, 66-79.
A brief discussion of the cistophoric coinage in Asia, followed by a catalogue of such coins in the Cabinet of France. A translation from the original French text.

4497 **Göktürk, M. Tevfik.** "The Polatli Hoard." *Recent Turkish Coin Hoards and Numismatic Studies.* British Institute of Archaeology at Ankara Monograph, No. 12. Edited by C. S. Lightfoot. Oxford: Oxbow Books, 1991. Pages 205-12 including 3 pls.
A catalogue of a hoard of thirty-seven cistophoric tetradrachms from five mints, ca. 166-128 B.C. The mints represented are Apameia, Pergamum, Ephesus, Tralles, and Sardis. The hoard was discovered in 1985 in the province of Ankara, Turkey. Each coin is photographed.

4498 **Hebert, Raymond J.** "Ten Greek Tidbits." *SAN—Journal of the Society for Ancient Numismatics* 17, no. 3 (June 1988): 57-9.
Pictures and describes ten small Greek silver coins including six from Selge with gorgon heads, two from Cilicia, and one each from Lycia and an uncertain Persian satrap.

4499 **Hill, George F.** "A Find of Cistophori." *Numismatic Chronicle* 5th ser., 9 (1929): 73-6.
Publishes a hoard of sixty-three cistophoric tetradrachms, buried soon after 129 B.C. The place of burial is unknown. The coin are of Pergamum, Ephesus, Sardes, Tralles, Apamea, and two uncertain mints.

4500 **Hind, John G. F.** "Greek Coins from the Black Sea Area in the Otago Museum." *New Zealand Numismatic Journal* (New Zealand) 13, no. 1 (January 1971): 1-20. 4 pls., map.
Presents a catalogue of the forty-five coins minted in the Black Sea Area, now housed in the Otago Museum in New Zealand. The majority are of struck or cast bronze. The coins are of Olbia, Pantikapaion, Sinope, Amisos, Pharnakeia, Herakleia Pontica, and Mesembria.

4501 **Hoover, Oliver D.** *Handbook of Coins of Northern and Central Anatolia: Pontus, Paphlagonia, Bithynia, Phrygia, Galatia, Lykaonia and Kappadokia (with Kolchis and the Kimmerian Bosporos), Fifth to First Centuries BC.* The Handbook of Greek Coinage Series, Volume 7. Lancaster: Classical Numismatic Group, 2012. lxxxii + 352 pp., illus.
A comprehensive guide to the coin types, heavily illustrated, with extensive background information and estimates of rarity. Lists 878 coin types. Includes a *Foreword* by François de Callataÿ, a *Preface* by D. Scott VanHorn and Bradley R. Nelson which provides an overview of the history of Greek coinage, minting methods, denominations, types, epigraphy, and basic information for collectors regarding grading, and good summaries of the coinage of each region by Hoover. [For a general description of the format of these catalogues and a list of all the volumes in this series, see Hoover *The Handbook of Greek Coinage* under COLLECTING GUIDES].

4502 **Imhoof-Blumer, Friedrich W.** *Kleinasiatische Münzen.* Two volumes. Vienna, 1901-02. Reprints, Graz, 1970-71; Hildesheim, 1974. 378 pp., 20 pls. [CS 2593]

4503 ——— "Zur Griechischen und Römischen Münzkunde." *Revue Suisse de Numismatique* (Switzerland) 1905, 1908. Reprints, Geneva, 1908; Hildesheim, New York: Olins, 1977. 323 pp., 10 pls. [CS 2594]
"Contains excellent index of coin types. Cistophores, Bythinia, Lykia, Greek city coins." [E. Clain-Stefanelli]

4504 **Isik, E.** *Frühe Silberprägung in Städten Westkleinasiens.* Saarbrücken, 2003. 198 pp., 18 pls.

4505 **Jenkins, G. Kenneth.** "Two Coins from Asia Minor." *British Museum Quarterly* 36, nos. 3-4 (1973): 97-100.
Describes a silver coin from Caria (*obv.*, Persian king slaying a griffin; *rev.*, a star) and a silver coin of Tarsus (*obv.*, a mounted horseman; *rev.*, the god Nergal on the back of a recumbent lion).

4506 **Kakhidze, Amiran, I. Iashvili, and Michael Vickers.** "Silver Coins of Black Sea Coastal Cities from the Fifth Century B.C. Necropolis at Pichvnari." *Numismatic Chronicle* 161 (2001): 282-7. 1 pl.
Discusses coins found in burial contexts which provide material for the study of the contacts with cities on both the southern and northern shores of the Black Sea during the fifth century B.C. Discusses coins of Sinope, Panticapaeum, and Theodosia.

4507 **Kienast, Dietmar.** "Literaturüberblick der Griechischen Numismatik: Cistophoren." *Jahrbuch für Numismatik und Geldsseschichte* (Germany) 11 (1961): 157-88. [CS 2602]
A bibliography.

4508 **Kinns, Philip.** "Asia Minor and Cyprus." *A Survey of Numismatic Research, 1978-1984. Volume 1: Ancient, Medieval and Modern Numismatics.* Edited by M. J. Price et al. International Association of Professional Numismatists Special Publication, No. 9. London: International Numismatic Commission, 1986. Pages 150-79.
A narrative overview of newly published works in the field of numismatics. Summarizes the major findings, with bibliographic references cited in the footnotes.

4509 **Kleiner, Fred S.** "The Cistophoric Coinage of Asia Minor." *Year Book. American Philosophical Society* (Philadelphia) (1972): 633-4.
"Die linkage between cities proves that the earliest cistophori are not a federal currency, as has been traditionally thought, but a regnal coinage struck by and for the king of Pergamum from bullion provided by the Attalid treasury." [F. Kleiner, *NL* 91]

4510 ——— "Further Reflections on the Early Cistophoric Coinage." *Museum Notes* 25 (1980): 45-52. 1 pl.
Reviews Mørkholm's arguments (see Mørkholm "Some Reflections" below) regarding: (1) The dating of the first cistophoric coinage. Mørkholm argues for 175 B.C. while Kleiner continues to support a date of 166 B.C. (2) The identification of the mint using the AΠ monogram. Mørkholm argues for Parium or Apollonia while Kleiner continues to support an attribution to Apameia. Also publishes a new cistophorus from a private collection.

4511 **Kleiner, Fred S., and Sydney P. Noe.** *The Early Cistophoric Coinage.* Numismatic Studies, No. 14. New York: American Numismatic Society, 1977. 129 pp., 38 pls. [CS 2606]
Reviews prior research on the cistophori, the chief currency of Asia Minor for over 300 years. Suggests the cistophoric coinage began in 166 B.C. Presents a corpus of the tetradrachms, didrachms, and drachms of the cistophoric type minted at Pergamum, Ephesos, Tralles, Sardes, Synnada, Apameia, Laodiceia, Thyatira, Apollonis, and Stratoniceia. Includes commentary on each mint. Also discusses one coin with the ethnic KOP, and one of uncertain origin. Includes a listing of hoards containing cistophori and discussions of the royal mint at Pergamum, the circulation of the cistophori, and the nature of the coinage. Concludes that these coins were "the king's money" subject to supervision by the Pergamene king for purposes of creating a closed economy. Includes tables of die links and weights. [Reviewed in *Spink Numismatic Circular* 85, no. 10 (October 1977): 431. Also reviewed by U. Westermark in *Schweizer Münzblätter* (Switzerland) 29, no. 113 (February 1979): 15-6. See Mørkholm "Some Reflections" below for several suggested revisions].

4512 **Marinescu, Constantin A.** "A First-Century B.C. Hoard of Late Cistophori." *Numismatic Chronicle* 155 (1995): 325-30. 4 pls.
A catalogue of a hoard of 177+ cistophori of Laodice (140), Apameia (24), and Tralles (8), buried in Phrygia ca. 70 B.C.

4512a **Mielczarek, Mariusz.** "Coinage of Nikonion: Greek Bronze Cast Coins between Istrus and Olbia." *XIII Congreso Internacional de Numismática, Madrid – 2003: Actas–Proceedings–Actes I.* Edited by Carmen Alfaro, Carmen Marcos, and Paloma Otero. Madrid: International Numismatic Commisson, 2005. Pages 273-6. Illus.
Some cast bronze coins bearing the name of the Scythian king Scyles can be attributed to the city of Nikonion. They had previously been given to Olbia. About seventy coins of Scyles are known, in three denominations. The coins bear an owl, wheel, and/or the letters ΣΚ, ΣΚΥ, ΣΚΥΛ, or ΣΚΥΛΕ. The coins are dated to ca. 475-450 B.C. This is the third city in the northwestern Black Sea region, along with Olbia and Istros, in which cast bronze coins were produced and which formed the basis of the local economy.

4513 **Milne, Joseph G.** "Countermarked Coins of Asia Minor." *Numismatic Chronicle* 4th ser., 13 (1913): 388-98.
Describes a hoard of copper coins of Kyme, some of which bear countermarks. The countermarked coins all belong to one series. Discusses why the coins were countermarked. Also publishes a hoard of copper coins of Alexander the Great found at Ephesos. Some of these coins are countermarked, and Milne suggests the countermarking was done by Lysimachus during his short occupation of Ephesos in 302 B.C., or during the period of his control of the town, 295-280 B.C.

4514 ———. "The Early Gold Coins of Asia Minor." *Numismatic Chronicle* 6th ser., 6 (1946): 1-6. [CS 2596]
States that the early "electrum" coins of Asia Minor were known in antiquity as "white gold" while the later, artificially alloyed coins of Carthage were designated "electrum" by Roman writers. Milne suggests the types appearing on the early electrum coins of Asia Minor are personal signets, and that these coins were produced chiefly at Cyzicus, Mytilene and Phocaea. The types may have been selected to suit the export markets for which they were intended. [Briefly reviewed by A. Baldwin in *ANS Numismatic Literature* 2 (1948): 8].

4515 **Mørkholm, Otto.** "Some Reflections on the Early Cistophoric Coinage." *Museum Notes* 24 (1979): 47-61. 2 pls., map.
A follow-up to Kleiner and Noe's *The Early Cistophoric Coinage* (see Kleiner and Noe above) suggesting some revisions to their chronology and attributions. (1) Re-examines evidence for the date of the introduction of the cistophoric coinage and suggests a date between 179-172 B.C. (2) Discusses the rare cistophoric issues of Synnada which Kleiner and Noe suggested were struck at Pergamum (from a common pool of dies) for use at Synnada. Mørkholm believes some of these coins were struck at Pergamum, but later, a mint was established at Synnada where striking continued. (3) Discusses the issues with the AΠ monogram which Kleiner and Noe attributed to Apameia in Phrygia. Mørkholm suggests Parium or Apollonia rather than Apameia. (4) Kleiner and Noe suggested the issues of Laodiceia were minted at Tralles. Mørkholm suggests that these coins were struck at Laodiceia from dies prepared by die cutters from Tralles. Reviews historical events during the periods in question.

4516 **Naster, Paul.** "Asie Mineure, Mésopotamie, Iran et Inde." *Survey of Numismatic Research, 1966 to 1971. Volume 1: Ancient Numismatics.* New York: International Numismatic Commission, 1973. Pages 135-76. [CS 2586]
A narrative bibliography discussing recently published works in the field of Greek numismatics.

4517 **Noe, Sydney P.** "Beginning of the Cistophoric Coinage." *Museum Notes* 4 (1950): 29-41. 1 pl. [CS 2609]
The author summarizes Livy's accounts of the treasures, including many cistophori, acquired by the Romans following military victories in 190-189 B.C. Reviews the evidence and theories for the dating of the cistophoric series. Reviews the debate over the location of the origin of the cistophori: Pergamum, Ephesos, Sardes, or Apameia. Also adds a new mint, Hieropolis in Phrygia, to those which struck this coinage.

4518 **Nollé, Johannes.** "Münzen als Zeugnisse für die Geschichte der Hellenisierung Kleinasiens." *Stephanos Nomismatikos: Edith Schönert-Geiss zum 65. Geburtstag.* Edited by Ulrike Peter. Berlin: Akademie Verlag, 1998. Pages 503-22.

4518a **Oguz, Tekin.** *Talking Coins: Anatolian Cities and Their Coins through History (Konusan Paralar: Tarih Boyunca Anadolu Kentleri ve Sikkelleri).* Istanbul: Türkiye Is Bankasi Kultur Yayinlari, 2012. 263 pp., illus.
Presents a selection of coins minted in the cities of Anatolia and Turkish Thrace from the invention of coinage through the founding of the modern Republic of Turkey. Examines the coins as a reflection of the cultural history of the cities. Text in English and Turkish.

4519 **Rigsby, Kent J.** "The Era of the Province of Asia." *Phoenix* (Canada) 33, no. 1 (1979): 39-47.
"Late cistophori of Ephesus bear dates ranging from 1 to 86. The last years are securely tied to dateable Roman proconsuls and the first year of this era has long been recognized as 134/3 B.C. The exclusive use of this era at Ephesus shows that it was an Ephesian, not a provincial, era; it is argued that it reflects Attalus III's bequest of liberty to the city, which was subsequently confirmed by the Romans after the organization of Asia as a province." [W. Metcalf, *NL* 103]

4520 **Robinson, Edward S. G.** "Some Electrum and Gold Greek Coins." *Centennial Publication of the American Numismatic Society.* Edited by H. Ingholt. New York: American Numismatic Society, 1958. Pages 585-94. [CS 2763]
Attempts to assign attributions to fourteen previously unidentified early electrum and gold coins. Includes issues assigned to Lydia (electrum stater of Croesus), Miletus, Ephesos (electrum trite bearing the name Phanes), Cyzicus, Phokaia, Samos, Caria, and Abydos. Includes several pieces struck in lead which may be trial strikes, or may be pieces that had been (or were going to be) gold-plated.

4521 **Stancomb, William M.** "Agathopolis: A Mint on the Black Sea Coast." *Studies in Greek Numismatics in Memory of Martin Jessop Price.* Edited by Richard Ashton and Silvia Hurter. London: Spink, 1998. Pages 335-8. 1 pl.
Presents evidence for locating the city of Agathopolis on the western coast of the Black Sea. It had previously been thought to lie in the Thracian Chersonese or Mysia. Some third century B.C. coins are attributed to this city. Also identifies some coins which were countermarked at this city.

4522 **Tameanko, Marvin.** "Xenophon's 'Anabasis', 401-399 B.C." *The Celator* 12, no. 5 (May 1998): 6-22. Illus., map.
In 401 B.C., Cyrus II, satrap of Asia Minor, set-out to overthrow Artaxerxes II, king of Persia. Tameanko traces the route of Xenophon and the Greek mercenary army during "The Anabasis of Cyrus." Cyrus was killed in battle and his troops agreed to withdraw from Persian territory. Summarizes the journey and describes some of the coins issued by cities along the route of the army. Illustrated by line drawings of coins.

4523 **Trokay, Madeleine.** "Oiseaux et Poissons dans l'Art du Proche-Orient Ancien et sur les Monnaies Grecques de la Propontide et du Pont-Euxin." *Numismatique et Histoire Économique Phéniciennes et Puniques. Actes du Colloque tenu à Louvaine-la-Neuve 13-16 Mai 1987.* Studia Phoenicia IX, Numismatica Lovaniensia 58. Edited by Tony Hackens and Ghislane Moucharte. Louvain-la-Neuve, 1992. Pages 77-85.

4524 **Troxell, Hyla A.** "Greek Accessions: Asia Minor to India." *Museum Notes* 22 (1977): 9-27. 2 pls.
Describes fifteen accessions to the American Numismatic Society museum: a bronze test strike for a Lysimachus tetradrachm; a silver didrachm of Priene; a hemidrachm of Cheronessus which is a new type and denomination for that mint; a new issue of an uncertain Lycian dynast; two coins here attributed to Cetis; three early coins of Mithradates I Callinicus of Commagene; two Seleucid coins now attributed to Phocaea; and three previously unknown Bactrian issues of Diodotus and Agathocles.

4525 **Troxell, Hyla A., and Nancy M. Waggoner.** "The Robert F. Kelley Bequest." *Museum Notes* 23 (1978): 1-41. 6 pls.
Discusses fifty-three coins donated to the American Numismatic Society by Robert F. Kelley, focusing on coins of Asia Minor. Includes several early electrum coins, gold coins of Rhodes, and coins of Sinope, Heraclea Pontica, Bithynian Kings, Cyzicus, Magnesia, Cnidus, Iasus, Tabae, Thyatira, Lycian Dynasts, Side, Selge, Issus, the satrap Pharnabazus, Cyprus, and Seleucid Kings.

4526 **Vagi, David L.** "Coins of the 'Hospitable Sea': Ancient Greek Merchants Encountered a Variety of Cultures and Coinages in the Black Sea Trade." *The Numismatist* 123, no. 6 (June 2010): 61-3. Illus.
A brief review of the coinage of the Greek cities surrounding the Black Sea.

4527 ——— "A Tale of Two Seas: The Hellespont and the Propontis Were Important Waterways Traversed by Ancient Merchants and Armies." *The Numismatist* 123, no. 8 (August 2010): 65-7. Illus.
An overview of the coinage of the cities adjoining the Hellespont and the Propontis—the waterways which join the Aegean Sea to the Black Sea.

4528 ——— "Bronzes of Asia Minor Offer Opportunity." *Coin World* (September 5, 2011): 148-51. Illus.
Vagi discusses some ways to collect bronze coins of Asia Minor.

4529 **Waddington, William H., Ernest C. Babelon, and Theodore Reinach.** *Recueil Général des Monnaise Grecques d'Asie Mineure.* Four volumes. Paris, 1904-12. Reprints, Bologna: Forni, 1967; Hildesheim, 1974 (in one volume). 640 pp., 125 pls. [CS 2600]
1. *Pont et Paphlagonie.* 1904. Second edition, Paris, 1925.
2. *Bithynie jusqu'à Juliopolis.* 1908.
3. *Nicée et Nicomedie.* 1910.
4. *Prusa, Prusias, Tius.* 1912.

4530 **Waggoner, Nancy M.** "Three Recent Greek Accessions." *Museum Notes* 21 (1976): 1-9. 1 pl.
Examines three coins: (1) A stater of Side, previously unpublished, with an unwreathed Athena head on the reverse, dated to ca. 480 B.C. (2) A stater of Issus, ca. 380 B.C., overstruck on a stater of the Cypriote king, Euagoras I. The coin helps to clarify the significance of the wreath symbol and ankh sign on the Issus coin. (3) A previously unknown "uncertain" stater of Caria. The type resembles a bronze plaque from Samos whose design is thought to represent an Aeolic capital. Waggoner tentatively attributes the coin to Samos, ca. 530-510 B.C.

4531 **Wallace, Malcolm B.** "After Athens: Some Notes on Greek Coinage, 413-386 B.C.E." *The Picus* (Canada) 2 (1993): 37-43.
Begins with a general discussion of the trends in Greek coinage after the end of the Peloponnesian War. Then focuses on the coins from various eastern Aegean cities which bear common types and the inscription ΣYM (for ΣYMMAXIKON?). Suggests this inscription signifies a possible alliance hostile to Sparta. The cities which issued these coins are Rhodes, Byzantium, Cyzicus, Ephesos, Samos, Cnidus, and Iasos. The coinage began shortly after the Athenian navy's defeat at Syracuse in 413 B.C. [For further discussion of the ΣYM coins, see Jones "Symmachic Coins" under EPIGRAPHY, and Cook "Cnidian Peraea and Spartan Coins" under PELOPONNESOS—LAKONIA].

4532 **Wallace, Robert W.** "On the Production and Exchange of Early Anatolian Electrum Coinages." *Revue des Études Anciennes* (France) 91, no. 1-2 (1989): 87-95.
"This paper examines the weights of 165 early electrum coins. I show that the weight standards used by some mints differed slightly from those used by others; that mints did not issue smaller denominations that were proportionally lighter than larger denominations; and that larger denominations were more variable in weight than smaller denominations. This last phenomenon is explained by the use of larger denominations within the economy." [R. Wallace, *Revue des Études Anciennes*]

4532a **Wright, Nicholas L., ed.** *Coins from Asia Minor and the East: Selections from the Colin E. Pitchfork Collection.* Ancient Coins in Australian Collections 2. Adelaide, Australia: Australian Centre for Ancient Numismatic Studies/Numismatic Association of Australia, 2011. 192 pp., illus.

A catalogue prepared in conjunction with an exhibition at the Macquarie University Museum of Ancient Cultures. Begins with essays: "Understanding the Earliest Coinages" by Gil Davis, "The Island of Hippokrates, Silver Coins and a Portrait Myth" by Håkon Ingvaldsen, "The Heroic Image and the Portrait Coinages of Lykian Dynasts" by Kenneth Sheedy, "The Dating on Coins: A Phoenician Invention" by Josette Elayi, "The Problem of the Autonomous Wreathed Coinage of Asia Minor" by Lauren Horne, "The Iconography of Succession under the Late Seleucids" by Nicholas Wright, and "The Emergence of the Greco-Baktrian and Indo-Greek Kingdoms" by Osmund Bopearachchi. Concludes with "Selections from the Colin E. Pitchfork Collection" by Nicholas Wright, which is illustrated by enlarged photographs of the coins. The catalogue is organized as follows: (a) Cities and Dynasts of Asia Minor, (b) Pergamon and the Autonomous Wreathed Tetradrachms of Asia Minor, (c) Cities and Dynasts of Southern Anatolia, (d) Phoenicia, (e) Imitative Attic Issues of Palestine and Babylonia, (f) Seleukid Kings, (g) Parthian Kings, and (h) Greco-Baktrian Kings.

4533 **Zograph, Alexander N.** *Coinage of Tyra.* Moscow, 1957.
In Russian.

See more items related to cistophoric coinage under PERGAMENE KINGDOM and IONIA.

Also see: Adams "Aristonikos" under CAPPADOCIA; Apostolou et al. *Coins in the Dodecanese and its Asia Minor Peraia* under CARIAN ISLANDS—RHODOS; Ashton *Studies in Ancient Coinage from Turkey* under GENERAL WORKS—GREEK; Ashton "Excavation Coins from Phanagoreia" under HOARDS; Broughton "A Significant Break" under IONIA; de Koehne *Description du Musée de Feu Le Prince Basile Kotschoubev* under PRIVATE COLLECTIONS; Gibson "Money for Kings" under THRACE—GENERAL WORKS; Kiyonaga "The Date of the Beginning of Coinage" under ORIGINS OF COINAGE; Konuk *From Kroisos to Karia* under PRIVATE COLLECTIONS; Kraay "Mainland Greece and Asia Minor" under BOEOTIA; Kraay and Moorey "A Black Sea Hoard" under HOARDS; Le Rider "Alexander in Asia Minor" under MACEDONIAN KINGDOM—GENERAL WORKS; Lindgren and Kovacs *Ancient Bronze Coins* under PRIVATE COLLECTIONS.

Marinescu "From Byzantium to the Black Sea" under THRACE—COINAGE OF LYSIMACHOS; Meadows "The Chian Revolution: Changing Patterns of Hoarding" under HOARDS; Metcalf *Oxford Handbook of Greek and Roman Coinage* under GENERAL WORKS—GREEK; "Odd Money" under THRACE—GENERAL WORKS; Robinson "A Find of Archaic Coins from South-West Asia Minor" under HOARDS; Smith "The Transition to Tyche on Southern Black Sea Coins" under TYPES; Stingl "Barren oder Münzen?" under ORIGINS OF COINAGE; Stolba "The Numismatics of Chersonesos and Kerkinitis" under BOSPOROS; Tameanko "The Coinage of Ataias" under THRACE—GENERAL WORKS; M. Thompson "Posthumous Philip II Staters" under MACEDONIAN KINGDOM—GENERAL WORKS; Weidauer *Probleme* under ORIGINS OF COINAGE; Wells (three items on arrowhead money) under THRACE—GENERAL WORKS; Zograph *Anitchnye Money* under GENERAL WORKS—GREEK; Zograph *Ancient Coinage* under GENERAL WORKS—GREEK.

BOSPOROS

There is an important development of a purely Greek style of coinage in several of the lesser kingdoms of Asia—Pontus, Bithynia, Kappadokia—which though not Greek by origin were deeply infused with Greek culture and art; and some of the portrait coins produced for these kingdoms are among the finest of the Hellenistic age. In Pontus, for example, where the royal line was of partly Persian descent, we have a head of Mithradates III (246-190 B.C.) which is an example of the most brilliantly conceived realistic portraiture coupled with an insight into character, and which can only be due to a Greek artist of the highest calibre.

—G. K. Jenkins, 1972

4534 **Abramzon, Mikhail G., and Nina A. Frolova.** "A Hoard of Silver Coins of the 6th-4th Centuries B.C. from the Taman Peninsula." *Revue Numismatique* (France) 6, no. 160 (2004): 27-48. 4 pls.
The Taman hoard of 1948 included fifty-four archaic silver coins and two lead ingots. It is of great interest for the study of the early Bosporan monetary system (types, denominations, standards). It provides information regarding the political and economic relations between the Kimmerian Bosporos and some of the other cities of the Greek world. [Paraphrased from the author's summary].

4535 **Anokhin, Vladilen Afanas'evich.** *Monetoe delo Khersonesa.* Kiev: Nauk Dumka, 1977. 175 pp., 16 pls. [CS 2641]

4536 ——— *The Coinage of Chersonesus IV Century B.C.-XII Century A.D.* BAR Supplementary Series, No. 69. Translated by H. Bartlett Wells. Oxford: British Archaeological Reports, 1980. 182 pp., 32 pls. [CS 2642]
An introduction to the coinage of the area arranged by periods, discussing the chronology of the coinage, inscriptions, types, and metrology. Includes historical background information. Covers the autonomous period (ca. 390 to 110 B.C.), the period of Bosporan influence (ca. 110 B.C. to A.D. 138) and later periods. The catalogue of types lists about 200 coins for the period ca. 390 B.C. to 1 B.C. plus an additional 280 coins from later periods. [A review article by R. N. Bridge, "The Coinage of Chersonesus," appears in *Numismatic Chronicle* 141 (1981): 183-7].

4537 ——— *Monetoe delo Bospora.* Kiev, 1986.
In Russian.

4538 **Bridge, R. N.** "The Coinage of the Ancient Crimea." *Seaby Coin and Medal Bulletin* 723 (November 1978): 338-42; 724 (December 1978): 372-7. Illus. [CS 2621]
"The history of the Crimean mints from the early fifth century B.C. to the close of the tenth century A.D. is traced. Greek issues of Panticapaeum and the Bosporus, and the issues of Chersonesus during the Greek, Roman and Byzantine periods are described. Particular attention is paid to Russian sources." [R. Bridge, *NL* 102]

4539 **D'Alexeieff, G.** *Dissertation sur une Monnaies Inédite d'un Roi Ínconnu du Bosphore Cimmérien.* Paris: Laroux, 1876.

4540 **Forrer, Leonard S.** "Copper Coins of Panticapaeum (Tauric Chersonese)." *Spink Numismatic Circular* 8 (January 1900): 3724.
A brief description of three recently found coins of Panticapaeum.

4541 **Frolova, Nina A.** "On the Monetary Circulation of the Bospsus in the IIIrd Century B.C." *Sovetskaia Arkheologiia* (U.S.S.R.) (1970): 33-40.
In Russian.

4542 ——— *The Coinage of the Kingdom of Bosporus, A.D. 69-238.* Translated from Russian by H. Bartlett Wells. British Archaeological Report, Supplement 56. Oxford, 1979. 249 pp., 63 pls. [CS 2631]

4543 ——— "Toward a History of Bosphoran Coinage (First Century B.C.)." *Ancient Civilization from Scythia to Siberia* (The Netherlands) 3, nos. 2-3 (December 1996): 151-68.

4544 ——— *Die Frühe Münzpragung von Kimmerischen Bosporos (Mitte 6. Bis Anfang 4. Jh. v. Chr.): Die Münzen der Städte Pantikapaion, Theodosia, Nymphaion und Phanagoria sowie der Sinder.* Berlin: Academie Verlag, 2004.

A catalogue of coins from the Kingdom of Bosporos, covering the very beginnings of Bosporan coinage. [Reviewed by Stanley Ireland in *Numismatic Chronicle* 165 (2005): 385-8].

4545 ——— "Über die Darstellungen von Schild und Schwert auf einem Münztyp des Bosporanischen Königs Leukon II (Zweite Hälfte des 2 Jhs. V. Chr.)." *Stephanos Nomismatikos: Edith Schönert-Geiss zum 65. Geburtstag.* Edited by Ulrike Peter. Berlin: Akademie Verlag, 1998. Pages 251-70.

4546 **Frolova, Nina A., and Stanley Ireland.** "A Hoard of Bosporan Coins in the Period Third Century B.C. to A.D. 238 from Ancient Gorgippia (Anapa) 1987." *Numismatic Chronicle* 155 (1995): 21-42. 11 pls.

4546a ——— *The Coinage of the Bosporan Kingdom from the First Century B.C. to the Middle of the First Century A.D.* BAR International Series 1102. Oxford, 2002. 94 pp., 62 pls.
A die study. Much of the material is from Russian museums. [Reviewed by W. M. Stancomb in *Numismatic Chronicle* 164 (2004): 339-40].

4547 **Golenko, Konstantin V.** "Nördliches Schwarzmeergebiet (Sarmatia Europea, Chersonesus Taurica, Bosporus Cimmerius)." *Chiron* (Germany) 5 (1975): 497-642. [CS 2619]
A bibliography.

4548 **Golenko, Konstantin V., and P. O. Karyszkowski.** "The Gold Coinage of King Pharnaces of Bosporus." *Numismatic Chronicle* 7th ser., 12 (1972): 25-38. 2 pls.
"These very rare staters were minted from 55/4 to 51/0 B.C. in Panticapaeum with the title 'Great King of Kings,' which was assumed by the Bosporan ruler after the death of Tigranes II of Armenia; the strengthening of the power of Orodes II in Parthia forced Pharnaces to give up his claims for the sake of the common struggle against Rome." [K. Golenko, *NL* 89]

4549 **Hermitage Museum.** *Coins from Ancient Towns of the Black Sea Coast.* Leningrad: Aurora Art Publishers, n.d.
This is a group of fifteen postcard-size color plates (unbound) within a folded card cover. The plates illustrate ancient Greek coins from cities on the Black Sea coast. Brief descriptions of the coins, in both English and Russian, appear on the back of each card. Includes coins of Olbia, Panticapaeum, the Bosporan Kingdom, Chersonesus, and Pontus.

4550 **Hind, John G. F.** "Two Notes on Early Coin Types of Pantikapaion and Phanagoreia." *Numismatic Chronicle* 168 (2008): 1-8. 1 pl.
The author discusses the reverse type on early coins of Pantikapaion and argues that it was not a mere adaptation of the previous punch impression nor inspired simply by floral ornamentation. Rather, it was a deliberate reference to the geographical location of the Greeks on the Bosporos and to a religious cult of the Milesian Greeks. Also examines the obverse type (Kabeiros head) on Phanagoreian coins of the early fourth century B.C.

4551 **Hourmouziadas, J., and B. Weisser.** "A Metrological Study of Bosporan Coins, 437-375 B.C." *Numismatic Chronicle* 167 (2007): 1-8. Illus.
An examination of the weights of coins of Panticapaeum, Phanagoria, and the Sindi.

4552 **Kovalenko, Sergei A.** "Struck Lead Pieces from Tauric Chersonesos: Coins or Tesserae?" *Numismatic Chronicle* 162 (2002): 33-58. 4 pls.
Examines some struck lead pieces from Tauric Chersonesos which some researchers have labeled coins and others tokens. Discusses the use of lead in ancient Greek coinage. The pieces were made in the late third or early second century B.C. The author argues they may have been tickets for participation in public festivals, sacrifices, and games, and the related distributions of meat and other products. Includes a catalogue of the pieces.

4553 **Kovalenko, Sergei A., and Arcady A. Molchanov.** "The Coinage of Theodosia in the 5th – 4th Centuries B.C." *Numismatic Chronicle* 165 (2005): 15-22. 1 pl.
A catalogue and die study of forty-one early bronze coins of Theodosia based on some recently found coins.

4554 **Kutcher, Robert R.** "History and Coinage of Panticapaion." *SAN—Journal of the Society for Ancient Numismatics* 17, no. 4 (September 1989): inside covers.
A brief survey of the history and coinage of Panticapaion.

4555 **Lagos, Constantine.** "Two Second Century B.C. Bronze Hoards from the Black Sea." *Numismatic Chronicle* 160 (2000): 268-74.
A catalogue of sixty-two coins of Panticapaeum and Phanagoria. The coins may have been found in Russia, east of the Cimmerican Bosporos, near Phanagoria.

4556 **MacDonald, David.** *An Introduction to the History and Coinage of the Kingdom of the Bosporus.* Classical Numismatic Studies, No. 5. Quarryville, Pennsylvania: Classical Numismatic Group, 2005. 144 pages. Illus.
Drawing from Ukrainian and Russian sources, MacDonald presents a systematic, chronological overview of the region's major coin-types of the Bosporan rulers, arranged by regnal and Bosporan Era years. Begins with the Archaeanactid Kings at Panticapaeum (480s B.C.) and includes the Spartocid Kings, the Pontic Kings, and the Roman client-kings Asander to Rhescuporis V. Covers the coinage of Panticapaeum (with Apollonia and Myrmecium), Phanagoria, Gorgippia, Sindicus Limen or the Sindoi, Nymphaeum, Theodosia, and the Kings of the Cimmerican Bosporus. Includes regional maps and figures of specific reverse types for the early silver issues, and important regnal monograms, as well as an appendix covering re-engraved bronze coins. Includes a concordance to the major references and a select bibliography. [Reviewed by Oliver Hoover in *American Numismatic Society Magazine* 4, no. 2 (summer 2005)].

4557 **Madsen, Eardley.** "History and Coinage of Chersonesus." *SAN—Journal of the Society for Ancient Numismatics* 17, no. 1 (December 1986): inside covers.
A brief survey of the history and coinage of Chersonesus.

4558 **Nawotka, Krzysztof.** "Asander of the Bosporus." *American Journal of Numismatics* 2nd ser., 3-4 (1991-1992): 21-48. 2 pls.
King Asander, who reigned in the Bosporos in the second half of the first century B.C., minted gold and bronze coins. His staters are dated with regnal years. The author draws conclusions regarding his coinage output. Most of Asander's bronze coins were struck early in his reign and were struck over previous city issues. Discusses problems surrounding the chronology of his reign, and discusses the historical background of his reign and death. Presents a catalogue of his coins (twenty-nine gold and thirty-four bronze specimens).

4559 **Shelov, Dimitrii B.** *Monetnoe delo Bospora VI-II vv. do n.e.* Moscow: Akademiya Nauk SSSR, 1956. 220 pp., 9 pls. [CS 2639]
For an English translation, see below.

4560 ——— *Coinage of the Bosporus VI-II Centuries B.C.* BAR International Series (Supplementary) 46. Translated by H. Bartlett Wells. Oxford: British Archaeological Reports, 1978. 227 pp., 6 pls. [CS 2639]
Discusses the coins of the Bosporos, their weight standards and monetary circulation, during the sixth and fifth centuries B.C., the coinage of Panticapaeum in the fourth and third centuries, and the currency of the Bosporos during the period of the late Spartocid dynasty. Illustrates and describes 115 coins.

4561 **Stolba, Wladimir F.** "ΣΑΜΜΑΣ. Zur Prägung eines Bosporanischen Tyrannen." *Stephanos Nomismatikos: Edith Schönert-Geiss zum 65. Geburtstag.* Edited by Ulrike Peter. Berlin: Akademie Verlag, 1998. Pages 601-12.

4561a ——— "Monetary Crises in the Early Hellenistic Poleis of Olbia, Chersonesos and Pantikapaion: A Re-Assessment." *XIII Congreso Internacional de Numismática, Madrid – 2003: Actas–Proceedings–Actes I.* Edited by Carmen Alfaro, Carmen Marcos, and Paloma Otero. Madrid: International Numismatic Commisson, 2005. Pages 395-403, incl. map and 1 pl.
The beginning of the third century B.C. was a period of economic decline in the Black Sea region, apparently caused by a monetary crisis. This is reflected in the region's coinage by an increasing lead content in the bronze coins and the use of countermarking. The attacks of nomads may have devastated the rural areas, thus undermining the basis of their economies. Whether these were Sarmatians, Celts, or Scythians is uncertain. Climate change may also have resulted in poorer agricultural yields and the resulting economic distress.

4562 ——— "The Numismatics of Chersonesos and Kerkinitis as Evidence of Greek and Barbarian Interrelations in Western Tauris." *Une Koinè Pontique: Cités Grecques, Sociétés Indigènes et Empires Mondiaux sur le Littoral Nord de la Mer Noire (VIIe s. a.C. – IIIe s. p.C.).* Edited by A. Bresson, A. Ivantchik, and J.-L. Ferrary. Ausonius Éditions, Mémoires 18. Paris: DeBoccard, 2007. Pages 85-97. Illus.
Stolba examines the impact of barbarian relations and incursions on the production and circulation of the coins of Chersonesos and Kerkinitis in the fourth to second centuries B.C. Archaeological evidence shows that Chersonesos suffered from barbarian sieges, but barbarian themes were not reflected on its coinage. The author compares the reverse on a bronze coin of Kerkinitis to the Scythian horseman on a silver coin of Kallatis. Concludes that the constant presence of Scythian themes on the coins of Kerkinitis indicates close connections between the city and the neighboring nomadic tribes or the Scythian kingdom as a whole. Nonetheless, there does not seem to have been any acculturation between these Greek cities and their Scythian neighbors.

4563 **Stolyarik, Elena.** "The Reign and Chronology of the Archon Hygiaenon." *American Journal of Numismatics* 2nd ser., 10 (1998): 61-70. 1 pl.
The archon Hygiaenon is represented by a unique gold stater and two silver drachms. Some scholars attribute a small copper coin to Hygiaenon as well. The coins of Hygiaenon are related by type to the gold issues of the Spartocids, the ruling dynasty of the Bosporan kingdom. Most scholars have considered Hygiaenon to be a contemporary of Mithradates VI. Discusses the chronological evidence for the issues and concludes the coins belong to the first quarter of the second century B.C. Suggests that Hygiaenon was an eminent member of the Bosporan aristocracy, although not a member of the royal house. He supported Queen Camasarye before her marriage to Paerisades III.

4564 ——— "The Gold Coinage of the Bosporan Kingdom under the Late Spartocids." *XII Internationaler Numismatischer Kongress, Berlin 1997: Akten.* Berlin: Staatliche Musen zu Berlin, 2000. Pages 378-83.

4565 ——— "Silver Coinage of the Bosporan King Spartocus: The Problem of Attribution." *American Journal of Numismatics* 2nd ser., 16-17 (2004-2005): 75-85. 2 pls.
Two didrachms are known with an obverse portrait of Spartocus and a bowcase on the reverse. The date and attribution of this Bosporan issue entails definite difficulties. Spartocus silver coins should not be treated in isolation. Analysis of the reverse type shows a close association with the Panticapaeum silver and bronze issues of the Apollo/bowcase type. In addition, the image of the trident and two dolphins beneath the bowcase on the reverse demonstrates the intimate relationship with the posthumous Lysimachus coinage from Byzantium, which itself was imitated by the royal issues of the Bosporan kings during the second century B.C. The new classification of the Lysimachus and Paerisades issues, and analysis of the silver and bronze issues from Panticapaeum, make it possible to attribute the Spartocus silver coins to a specific period of Bosporan history. They must have been minted by an otherwise unknown Spartocus VI, sometime around 140 B.C.

4566 "Third Known Specimen: Rare Panticapaeum Issue to be Auctioned." *The Celator* 2, no. 4 (April 1988): 5. Illus.
The third known specimen of a silver stater of Panticapaeum is shown. The ca. 475 B.C. coin has a lion's head on the obverse and a swastika reverse design with the first three letters of the city name in the squares.

4567 **von Sallet, Alfred.** *Numismatik der Könige des Bosporus und Pontus.* Berlin, 1866.

4568 **Wells, H. Bartlett.** "In Quest of an Identification." *SAN—Journal of the Society for Ancient Numismatics* 10, no. 1 (winter 1979): 7-9.
Presents a silver coin weighing 6.85 gm with the forehead and muzzle of a lion on the obverse, and a reverse containing two incuse impressions. Opinions from several experts were sought. Although the type resembles that of Panticapaeum, the author rejects this attribution. Lindos is also suggested but doubted by the author. The attribution remains uncertain.

4569 **Widawski, Maciej.** "The Exchange of Coins in the Bosporan State in the Third Century B.C." *Wiadomosci Numizmatyczne* (Poland) 34, no. 3-4 (1990): 101-12. Illus.

"The author studies the purpose of overstriking and countermarking Bosporan coins in the third century B.C. Prevailing theories on this subject are presented and examined in light of the results of recent research. General reflections on the problem are presented in the conclusion." [M. Mielczarek, *NL* 127]. Includes a summary in Polish.

Also see: Alekseyev *Rare and Unpublished Coins* under ASIA MINOR AND THE BLACK SEA REGION—GENERAL WORKS; Dittrich et al. *Ancient Coins from Olbia and Panticapaeum* under THRACE—OLBIA; Draganov "An Unknown Hybrid" under MYSIA—AUTONOMOUS CITIES; de Koehne *Description du Musée de Feu Le Prince Basile Kotschoubev* under PRIVATE COLLECTIONS; Golenko "The Method" under COUNTERFEITS; Hoover *Handbook of Coins of Northern and Central Anatolia* under ASIA MINOR—GENERAL WORKS; Hoover "Two Seleucid Bronzes Countermarked" under THE MINTING PROCESS; Marinescu *Making and Spending Money along the Bosporus* under THRACE—COINAGE OF LYSIMACHOS; Thallon "The Cave at Vari" under TYPES; Walker "Why Are You So Sure?" under COUNTERFEITS; Wartenberg and Kagan "Some Comments on a New Hoard from the Balkan Area" under HOARDS; Wroth *Catalogue of Greek Coins* under PONTOS.

KOLCHIS

Colchis, or western Georgia, was renowned from mythical times as a source of precious metals, a fact illustrated by the legend of the Golden Fleece.

—David Lang, 1955

4570 **de Koehne, Baron B.** "Drachms of Aristarchos, Dynast of Colchis." *Numismatic Chronicle* new ser., 17 (1877): 1-10. Illus.
Publishes the second known specimen of a drachm of king Aristarchos. Discusses the history of Kolchis and its coinage.

4571 **Dundua, G. F., and G. A. Lordkipanidze.** "Hellenistic Coins from the Site of Vani, in Colchis (Western Georgia)." *Numismatic Chronicle* 139 (1979): 1-5. 1 pl.
"Hellenistic coins revealed by archaeological excavation (1947-75) in ancient Vani, one of the most important political and administrative centers of the kingdom of Colchis, are discussed. The coins not only help to establish the chronological stratigraphy of the site, but also answer some political and economic questions relating to the history of the kingdom of Colchis, situated in Western Georgia." [Dundua and Lordkipanidze, *NL* 104]

4572 **Golenko, Konstantin V.** "Kolchis (Literaturüberblick der Griechischen Numismatik)." *Chiron* (Germany) 2 (1972): 565-610. [CS 2617]
A bibliography.

4573 **Hind, J. G. F.** "The Types on the Phasian Silver Coins of the Fifth-Fourth Centuries B.C. (The 'Kolkhidki' of Western Georgia)." *Numismatic Chronicle* 165 (2005): 1-14. 1 pl.
Argues that the coin types struck in the area of Kolchis were inspired by local geography and cults or regional legends. Examines eight coin types: (1) lion head with open jaws/forepart of winged horse, (2) lion with head turned back/kneeling figure with bovine head, (3) lion's head/protome of lioness, (4) lion's scalp/bovine head, (5) youthful head/two small human heads facing each other, (6) youthful head/two small bovine heads, (7) youthful head in archaic style/head of bovine creature, and (8) youthful head/bird.

4574 **Lang, David M.** *Studies in the Numismatic History of Georgia in Transcaucasia, based on the Collection of the American Numismatic Society.* Numismatic Notes and Monographs, No. 130. New York: American Numismatic Society, 1955. 138 pp., 15 pls., maps. [CS 9031]
An examination of the coinage struck in the region of Georgia over a 2000 year period. The bulk of the book covers the Sasanian and later periods but pages 6-11 cover the coinage of the classical period. Includes the coins of Kolchis (hemidrachm, drachm, didrachm, and tetradrachm), two distorted imitations of Alexander staters, and two bronze coins from the Greek colony of Dioscurias.

4575 **Vickers, Michael, Amiran Kakhidze, and Irine Varshalomidze.** "Kolkhidki: A Footnote." *Numismatic Chronicle* 170 (2010): 1-2. 1 pl.
Discusses the triobols with the archaizing head/bull's head. A ring found in an aristocrat's grave bears an image of a bull's head in a circle, very similar to that on the reverse of the coins.

Also see: Hoover *Handbook of Coins of Northern and Central Anatolia* under ASIA MINOR—GENERAL WORKS.

Pontos

On these coins the supposed Persian descent of Mithradates is emphasized by the types relating to Perseus. Dionysiac types are frequent at Amisus, and the head of the god is often assimilated to that of Mithradates himself.

—Barclay V. Head, 1911

4576 **Baldwin, Agnes.** "Les Monnaies de Bronze dites Incertaines de Pont ou du Royaume de Mithridate Eupator." *Revue Numismatique* (France) (1913): 284 ff. 2 pls.
[Also see Kolb below].

4577 **Berk, Harlan J.** "Brutus Revisited." *The Celator* 14, no. 1 (January 2000): 22-4. Illus.
A point-by point reply to Murphy's rebuttal of Berk and MacDonald's assertion that some gold staters, which are usually described as issues of Mithradates VI of Pontus, are in fact issues of Brutus, struck 44-42 B.C. Berk continues to support the attribution to Brutus. [See Berk and MacDonald "Gold Staters of Brutus" and B. Murphy "Mithradates VI" below].

4578 **Berk, Harlan J., and David J. MacDonald.** "Gold Staters of Brutus." *The Celator* 13, no. 9 (September 1999): 39. Illus.
Discusses a group of Lysimachus-style gold staters which has recently come onto the market. The coins have been described as issues of Mithradates VI of Pontus. The authors argue that these are in fact issues of Brutus, struck 44-42 B.C. to pay Thracian mercenaries fighting against the forces of Mark Antony and Octavian. [Also see the rebuttal by Barry P. Murphy below].

4579 **de Callataÿ, François.** *L'Histoire des Guerres Mithridatiques vue par les Monnaies.* Publications d'Historie d'Art et d'Archéologie de l'Université Catholique de Louvain 98. Numismatica Lovanensia 18. Louvain-la-Neuve, 1997. 480 pp., 54 pls.
[Reviewed by R. Bauslaugh in *Revue Suisse de Numismatique* 77 (1998): 191-4, and by W. Leschhorn in *Gnomon* (Germany) 74, no. 4 (2002): 371-2].

4580 ———. "Guerres et Monnayages à l'Époque Hellénistique. Essai de Mise en Perspective suivi d'une Annexe sur le Monnayage de Mithridate VI Eupator." *Économie Antique. La Guerre dans les Économies Antiques, Entretiens d'Archéologie et d'Histoire.* Edited by J. Andreau, P. Briant, and R. Descat. Saint-Bernard-de-Comminges: Musée Archéologique Départemental, 2000.

4580a ———. "The First Royal Coinages of Pontos (from Mithradates III to Mithradates V)." *Mithradates VI and the Pontic Kingdom.* Black Sea Studies 9. Edited by Jakob Munk Højte. The Danish National Research Foundation's Centre for Black Sea Studies. Aarhus University Press, 2009. Pages 63-94. Illus.

4581 **Golenko, Konstantin V.** *Pontic Anonymous Copper (Chronology, Classification, Nature of Coinage).* Privately produced. 67 pp., 2 pls.
This is an unpublished English translation of an article which appeared in *Vestnik Drevnei Istorii* (Moscow, 1969), pages 130-54. It resides in the library of the American Numismatic Association. Golenko examines the series of copper coins which always bear an eight-pointed star on the reverse, and usually bear a head wearing a leather helmet on the obverse. No city or ruler name appears on the coins. They are believed to have been struck in the Black Sea area in the late Hellenistic period. The coins have previously been attributed to Mithradates III, IV, or VI. The author discusses the time of issuance, weights, metal, countermarks, hoard evidence, and examines the question of the mint. He concludes the anonymous copper coins were issued in the kingdom of Pontus in the period which preceded the reign of Mithradates VI there. Comments on the economic basis for the coinage, the peculiarities of the coinage in Cappadocia, and examines the coin types and their symbolism. Concludes with an extensive discussion of the sequence of issues and a description of the coins. Twenty-nine coins are illustrated.

4582 ———. "Pontus und Paphlagaonien (Veröffentlichungen in Russland und der Sowietunion)." *Chiron* (Germany) 3 (1973): 467-99. [CS 2618]
A bibliography.

4583 ———. "Pontic Currency of the Period of Mithradates VI on the Bosporus." *Spink Numismatic Circular* 111 (2003): 64-9.

4584 **Hoge, Robert W.** "Three Mithradatic Alexanders from Odessus." *The Numismatist* 111, no. 2 (February 1998): 228-9. Illus.
The author publishes three tetradrachms issued by Mithradates VI of Pontus, minted at Odessus ca. 83 B.C. The coins, which reside in the museum of the American Numismatic Association, show a progression in the features of Herakles on their obverses, from a likeness similar to that found on the original

Macedonian tetradrachms of Alexander, to one that apparently is an actual portrait of Mithradates himself. Hoge summarizes the history of Mithradates' kingdom and its struggles against the Romans.

4585 **Imhoof-Blumer, Friedrich W.** "Die Kupfergrägung des Mithridatischen Reiches und andere Münzen de Pontos und Paphlagoniens." *Zeitschrift für Numismatik* (Germany) new ser., 5 (1912): 169-92. [CS 2651]

4586 **Ireland, Stanley, and Peter Cook.** "A New Mint for Mithradates VI of Pontus?" *Numismatic Chronicle* 168 (2008): 135-9. 1 pl.
The authors publish a bronze coin with Athena Parthenos/Perseus standing, holding Medusa's head. The coin was minted at Sarbinissa—a new mint for this issue. It may have been struck over a coin of Amisos. The chronology of the coin is examined.

4587 **Kleiner, Gerhard.** "Bildnis und Gestalt des Mithradates VI." *Jahrbuch des Deutschen Archäologischen Institut* (Germany) 68 (1953): 73-95. [CS 2653]

4588 ——— "Pontische Reichsmünzen." *Deutsche Archäologisches Institut: Abteilung Istanbul* (Germany) 6 (1955): 1-22. [CS 2654]

4589 **Kolb, P.** "Monnaies de Bronze Incertaines du Pont. Remarqués sur l'Article de m-lle Baldwin a Propos de la Decouverte d'une Monnaie Nouvelle." *Revue Numismatique* (France) (1926): 23 ff. Illus.
[Also see Baldwin above].

4590 **Malloy, Alex G.** *The Coinage of Amisus.* South Salem: Alex G. Malloy, 1970. 31 pp., including 11 pls. [CS 2650]
Lists all the major types of the coins of Amisus drawn from major published works. Includes a brief history of the city and its coinage. Lists of symbols and types. Includes 248 coin types from the Greek and Roman periods. Most are illustrated. Concludes with a list of the approximate market values for each coin type.

4591 **Mattingly, Harold B.** "The Coinage of Mithradates III, Pharnakes and Mithradates IV of Pontos." *Studies in Greek Numismatics in Memory of Martin Jessop Price.* Edited by Richard Ashton and Silvia Hurter. London: Spink, 1998. Pages 255-8. 1 pl.
A discussion of the reigns of Mithradates III, Pharnakes, and Mithradates IV of Pontos, using their respective coinages for clues to their chronology. [This essay was reprinted in Mattingly's *From Coins to History: Selected Numismatic Studies*. See Mattingly under GENERAL WORKS—GREEK].

4592 **Molnar, Michael R.** "Mithradates used Comets on Coins as Propaganda Device." *The Celator* 11, no. 6 (June 1997): 6-8. Illus.
The author begins with a few examples of how comets were sometimes interpreted as portents of things to come during the period of the Roman Empire. Illustrates a bronze coin showing on *obv.*, a horse's head with a star at the neck, and on *rev.*, a star with a tail. The coin is attributed to Bosporus and Pontus. Molnar quotes an account by Justinus giving a description of "hippeus" comets that appeared during the life of Mithradates the Great of Pontus (c. 134-63 B.C.). The author concludes that Mithradates was propagandizing the comets that appeared at his birth and coronation as portents of his removing the Romans from the East.

4593 **Monney, Pierre R.** "A Hole through 'The Looking Glass.'" *The Celator* 15, no. 4 (April 2001): 37, 39. Illus.
The author discusses a worn and holed tetradrachm of Mithradates VI which he purchased in an auction. Monney showed the coin to François de Callataÿ at the Belgian Royal Library, who identified it as a coin which was published in the *Naville* V auction catalogue in 1923. The provenance of the coin could be traced to a Russian Grand Duke and to the well-known collector Bertier de Lagarde.

4594 **Murphy, Barry P.** "Mithradates VI or M. Junius Brutus?" *The Celator* 13, no. 11 (November 1999): 13-4. Illus.
A rebuttal of the assertion by Berk and MacDonald that a group of gold staters, generally believed to have been struck in 88-86 B.C. by Mithradates VI, were issued by Brutus between 44-42 B.C. to pay his mercenaries fighting against the forces of Antony and Octavian (see Berk and MacDonald "Gold Staters of Brutus" above). Murphy reviews the evidence and supports the traditional attribution to Mithradates VI of Pontus. [This essay also appeared on pages 95-6 of the catalogue for the *Triton III* sale, held November 30-December 1, 1999 by Classical Numismatic Group, Freeman & Sear, and Numismatica Ars Classica. Berk replied to Murphy's rebuttal. See Berk "Brutus Revisited" above].

4595 **Olshausen, Eckart.** *Bronzemünzen aus der Zeit Mithradates' VI im Museum von Samsun.* Stuttgart: Franz Steiner Verlag, 2009. 205 pp.
A catalogue of 5981 bronze coins from the time of Mithradates VI.

4596 **Price, M. Jessop.** "Mithradates VI Eupator, Dionysus, and the Coinages of the Black Sea." *Numismatic Chronicle* 7th ser., 8 (1968): 1-12. 4 pls. [CS 2657]
"Mithradates' regal coinage is briefly described, and a chronological framework is given to the late posthumous tetradrachms in the name of Alexander the Great at Odessus and Mesembria, and of Lysimachus at Byzantium. The final issues at Byzantium might have been struck by Mithradates himself in preparation for an invasion of Rome at the time of his death." [M. Price, *NL* 82]

4597 **Reinach, Theodore.** *Mithradates Eupator, Roi de Pont.* Paris, 1890. 494 pp., 3 maps, 4 pls. [CS 2658]
A German translation appeared in 1895.

4598 **Stolyarik, Elena.** "Scythians in the West Pontic Area: New Numismatic Evidence." *American Journal of Numismatics* 2nd ser., 13 (2001): 21-34. 2 pls.
The author discusses two groups of Scythian coins: (1) nine silver coins struck in the name of King Ateas (360-339 B.C.) which contribute to our understanding of the Scythian strategic position just prior to the rise of Macedonian power, and (2) some anonymous bronzes probably struck by a Greek polis in the Dobrudja (the West Pontic region around the delta at the mouth of the Danube) which show that the Scythians remained an important political factor in the region. Coins of the first group have types Herakles/horseman or Herakles/horse galloping. Coins of the second group bear the types Dionysos/galloping horseman.

4599 **Tekin, Oguz.** *Sivas Definesi: VI. Mithradates Donemi Pontos ve Paphlagonia Kentlerinin Bronz Sikkeleri (The Sivas Hoard: Bronze Coins of Pontos and Paphlagonia from the Reign of Mithradates VI).* Istanbul, 1999. 111 pp., 69 pls.

4600 **Wells, H. Bartlett.** "Connection and Continuity in Mithradatic Pontus Coins." *SAN—Journal of the Society for Ancient Numismatics* 13, no. 2 (summer 1982): 35-7.
Presents evidence linking the latest Pontic anonymous coins with the first of the Mithradatic civic copper coins. Discusses prior published references to anonymous coins of Pontos. Then shows a badly worn and corroded coin which has a standard Pontic anonymous reverse type but an obverse type which may have been used early in the reign of Mithradates VI for coinage at Amisus and Sinope. [However, upon further study the author retracted this theory. See Wells "A Pontic Reappraisal" in *SAN* 13, no. 4 (winter 1982-3): 78. Due to the poor state of preservation, the obverse type was difficult to see clearly, but the author now believes it to be the usual anonymous Pontic type].

4601 **Williams, Daniela.** "The Coins of Pontus, Paphlagonia and Bithynia in the Collection of the Archaeological Museum in Florence." *Numismatic Chronicle* 169 (2009): 105-36. 11 pls.
A catalogue of 130 coins with a discussion of their history from the 16th to 18th centuries. Includes ten coins from the ancient Greek period.

4602 **Wroth, Warwick.** *Catalogue of Greek Coins of Pontus, Paphlagonia, Bithynia, and the Kingdom of Bosporus.* Edited by R. S. Poole. London: British Museum, 1889. Reprint, Bologna: Forni, 1964. xliv, 252 pp., 39 pls. [CS 2627]
Volume 13 of the *Catalogue of Greek Coins in the British Museum*. Forty-four pages of introductory text precede the 252-page catalogue of coins. [Also see *Catalogue of Greek Coins in the British Museum* under PUBLIC COLLECTIONS—GREAT BRITAIN (LONDON)].

Also see: Burnett et al. "Origins of Orichalcum" under METALLURGY; Hoover *Handbook of Coins of Northern and Central Anatolia* under ASIA MINOR—GENERAL WORKS; Kleiner "The Giresun Hoard" under HOARDS; Kleiner "The 1926 Piraeus Hoard" under HOARDS; Newton "Statuette of Athenè Parthenos" under TYPES; Nock "Notes on Ruler-Cult" under TYPES; Oguz *Catalogue of Ancient Coins* under PUBLIC COLLECTIONS—TURKEY (ISTANBUL); Oikonomides "Mithradates Herakles" under PORTRAITS; Pollak "The Bithynian Hoard" under HOARDS; Ropel "A Coin Portrait of Mithradates VI" under PORTRAITS; von Sallet *Numismatik der Könige des Bosporus und Pontus* under BOSPOROS; Waddington et al *Recueil Général* under ASIA MINOR—GENERAL WORKS.

Paphlagonia

The earliest coins of Sinope were crude issues bearing the head of an eagle on the obverse, and a decorated incuse square on the reverse. The eagle's head ranges from a bold, artistic depiction to an abstract shape which scarcely resembles its subject.

—David Vagi, 1994

4603 **Hind, John G. F.** "The Eagle-Head Coins of Sinope." *Numismatic Chronicle* 136 (1976): 1-6. Illus. [CS 2670]
"The earliest series of coins of Sinope are silver issues with *obv.*, eagle-head type dating to ca. 480-440 B.C. It is suggested that the hitherto unexplained type puns on the city name, Sinope, the two elements of which mean, in Greek, 'ravaging face.'" [J. Hind, *NL* 97]

4604 **Ireland, Stanley.** "An Addition to Amastrian Coin-Types." *Numismatic Chronicle* 164 (2004): 219-21. 1 pl.
Publishes a newly discovered bronze coin type of Amastris (Zeus/thunderbolt). Discusses the dates of minting.

4605 **Marotta, Michael E.** "The Crime of Diogenes." *The Celator* 13, no. 5 (May 1999): 20-1. Illus.
Diogenes of Sinope was exiled to Athens (ca. 400 B.C.) along with his father because either he or his father was accused of altering, debasing, or counterfeiting the coinage of Sinope in some way. Marotta summarizes various accounts of the crime. Illustrates a drachm of Sinope which bears the letters ΔIO, contains a test cut, and has a low specific gravity indicating a debased silver alloy. Marotta suggests this coin may be evidence of the crime of Diogenes or his father. [Also see Seltman "Diogenes" below].

4606 **Mixter, John.** "Paphlagonian History: Tyche is Identified as Goddess on Coins of Kromna." *The Celator* 4, no. 4 (April 1990): 1, 26-7. Illus.
Reviews the history and coinage of the city of Kromna. Discusses the common Zeus/Tyche coin types. Explores theories on whether the reverse design on the coinage of Kromna represents Hera or the city goddess Tyche. Concludes that Tyche is depicted. [Also see "Letter to the Editor," *The Celator* 4, no. 6 (June 1990): 2].

4607 **Nordbö, Jan H.** "An Imitation of a Drachm of Sinope Paphlagoniae." *Proceedings of the International Numismatic Symposium (1976)*. Edited by I. Gedai and K. Biró-Sey. Budapest: Akadémiai Kiadó, 1980. Pages 37-40. Charts, 1 pl.
Examines a drachm in the Oslo University collection bearing the magistrate name ΚΑΡΓ-. Coins with this magistrate are dated after Alexander the Great's conquest of Asia Minor and into the early third century B.C. These coins were heavily imitated in the area. Nordbö studies the weights of the Sinopean drachms and their imitations.

4608 **Robinson, Edward S. G.** "A Find of Coins of Sinope." *Numismatic Chronicle* 4th ser., 20 (1920): 1-16. 1 pl. [CS 2671]
A catalogue of thirty-six drachms of Sinope, most found in the Crimea. Discusses their chronology.

4609 ——— "Sinope." *Numismatic Chronicle* 5th ser., 10 (1930): 1-15. 2 pls. [CS 2672]
Records a portion of a hoard of coins chiefly of Sinope. Includes some new magistrates. Lists and discusses twenty-seven coins. The magistrates which are linked by obverse die-couplings are indicated in a table.

4610 **Sayles, Wayne G.** "The Road to Paphlagonia." *The Celator* 18, no. 1 (January 2004): 47. Illus.
Examines the importance of the road between Cilicia and Paphlagonia—an important trade route. Coins struck by various cities along this route show similarities in iconography during the fourth century B.C.

4611 **Seltman, Charles T.** "Diogenes of Sinope, Son of the Banker Hikesias." *Transactions of the International Numismatic Congress Organized and Held in London by the Royal Numismatic Society, June 30-July 3, 1936*. Edited by J. Allan, H. Mattingly, and E. S. G. Robinson. London: B. Quaritch, 1938. Page 121.
A brief summary of the paper presented at the Congress. Hikesias, father of Diogenes, was imprisoned for the defacement of the coinage. Hikesias' name appears on good quality coins of Sinope issued ca. 362-310 B.C. Other coins, with Sinopean types but Aramaic legends, were poor quality imitations and are frequently found defaced with chisel cuts which were intended to put them out of circulation. These may be the coins defaced by Hikesias. [The full text of the paper was published in *Proceedings of the Cambridge Philological Society* 142-144 (page 7). Also see Marotta "The Crime of Diogenes" above].

4612 **Six, Jean P.** "Sinope." *Numismatic Chronicle* 3rd ser., 5 (1885): 15-65. 1 pl.
Includes a catalogue of 197 coin types of Sinope with commentary. In French.

4613 **Vagi, David.** "Fourth Century Drachms of Sinope." Parts 1-2. *The Celator* 8, no. 6 (June 1994): 12; no. 7 (July 1994): 22-3. Illus.

Part 1 describes the main types of Sinope's coinage and focuses on the fourth century issues struck after the city was captured by the Persian satrap Datames. Datames replaced the city ethnic with his own name during his revolt from the Persian king. Part 2 examines the drachms bearing Aramaic inscriptions, most of which appear to be names of satraps, dynasts, and local rulers. Although generally thought to have been struck in Sinope while the city was under control of the persons named on the coins, the author concurs with Newell's conclusions based on style and fabric, that these issues were imitations struck elsewhere.

Also see: Hind "City Heads/Personifications and Omens from Zeus" under THRACE—ISTROS; Hoover *Handbook of Coins of Northern and Central Anatolia* under ASIA MINOR—GENERAL WORKS; Imhoof-Blumer "Die Kupfergrägung" under PONTOS; Kraay and Moorey "A Black Sea Hoard" under HOARDS; Newell "The Alexandrine Coinage of Sinope" under MACEDONIAN KINGDOM—GENERAL WORKS; Newell *The Küchük Köhne Hoard* under HOARDS; Oguz *Catalogue of Ancient Coins* under PUBLIC COLLECTIONS—TURKEY (ISTANBUL); Williams "The Coins of Pontus, Paphlagonia and Bithynia" under PONTOS.

BITHYNIA

In the sixth century B.C., Cyrus the Great incorporated Bithynia into the Persian Empire, but allowed the native tribes some autonomy. One of the earliest tribal chieftains to rule the area was Doidalses, about 435 B.C. The Bithynians took advantage of the warring factions among the successors of Alexander the Great to secure freedom from the Seleucids in 297 B.C. At this time the leader, Zipoetes, took the title of King and established a dynasty which lasted until the death of Nicomedes IV in 74 B.C.

—Ethel and Eardley Madsen, 1985

4614　**Brett, Agnes Baldwin.** "A Bronze Coin of Bithynia: The Lyre, ΧΕΛΥΣ." *Journal International d'Archaéologie Numismatique* (Greece) 4 (1901): 67-76. 1 pl.
Illustrates a bronze coin of Bithynia (Prusias II) with a tortoise-lyre as the reverse type. It is "the best if not the only example of this primitive form of the lyre." Discusses the symbolism and mythology of the tortoise and the lyre and their relationship to Hermes. The coin provides information on the construction of these early lyres.

4614a　**de Callataÿ, François.** "Les Derniers Rois de Bithynie: Problèms de Chronologie." *Revue Belge de Numismatique et de Sigillopraphie* (Belgium) 132 (1986): 5-30. 5 pls.

4615　**Forrer, Leonard S.** "Tetradrachms of Prusias I of Bithynia." *Spink Numismatic Circular* 6 (March 1898): 2638-9.
Publishes a tetradrachm of Prusias I. Summarizes the history of his reign as king of Bithynia.

4616　**Glew, Dennis G.** "The Cappadocian Expedition of Nicomodes III Euergetes, King of Bithynia." *Museum Notes* 32 (1987): 23-55. 3 pls.
Examines the numismatic evidence for the dating of the Bithynian and Pontic invasions of Cappadocia. Concludes that Nicomedes III entered Cappadocia in the summer of 105 B.C., and the Pontic counterattack probably occurred in October or November of 105 B.C. Presents a catalogue of the tetradrachms of Nicomedes III.

4617　**Madsen, Eardley, and Ethel Madsen.** "Bithynia." *SAN—Journal of the Society for Ancient Numismatics* 16, no. 1 (spring 1985): inside covers.
A brief overview of the history and coinage of Bithynia.

4618　**Stancomb, William M.** "A Group of Staters of Timotheus and/or Dionysius, Tyrants of Heraclea Pontica." *Numismatic Chronicle* 160 (2000): 263-8. 2 pls.
"The twenty-four staters in this hoard are all of the same type: an apparently unique coin in the sole name of Timotheus, fifteen in joint names, and eight in the sole name of Dionysius. The author suggests that the coinage in the sole name of Dionysius was short-lived, as Alexander the Great would have been hostile to its implications." [W. Stancomb, *NL* 145]. The coins are cataloged and discussed.

4619　——— "Some Countermarked and Overstruck Hellenistic Coins from the Region of the Thracian Bosporus." *Numismatic Chronicle* 167 (2007): 25-32. 2 pls.
The author records some coins from Thrace and Bithynia, most of which were countermarked by the cities of Byzantium or Chalchedon, ca. 275-175 B.C.

4620　——— "The Autonomous Bronze Coinage of Heraclea Pontica." *Numismatic Chronicle* 169 (2009): 15-28. 4 pls.
The author groups the coins into eleven general types, beginning ca. 364 B.C. and discusses each group.

Also see: Hoover *Handbook of Coins of Northern and Central Anatolia* under ASIA MINOR—GENERAL WORKS; Kleiner "The Giresun Hoard" under HOARDS; LeRider *Deux Trésors* under HOARDS; Marinescu "The Posthumous Lysimachi Coinage and the Dual Monetary System at Byzantium and Chalcedon" under THRACE—COINAGE OF LYSIMACHOS; Pollak "A Bithynian Hoard" under HOARDS; Richter "Late Hellenistic Portraiture" under PORTRAITS; Seyrig "Monnaies Hellénistiques" under THRACE—COINAGE OF LYSIMACHOS; Tod "Three Greek Numeral Systems" under EPIGRAPHY; Wroth *Catalogue of Greek Coins* under PONTOS; Williams "The Coins of Pontus, Paphlagonia and Bithynia" under PONTOS.

Mysia

These coins of Cyzicus, together with the Persian darics, constituted the staple of the gold currency of the whole ancient world until such time as they were both superseded by the gold staters of Philip and Alexander the Great.

—Barclay V. Head, 1887

Autonomous Cities

4621 **Brett, Agnes Baldwin.** "The Gold Coinage of Lampsacus." *Journal International d'Archaéologie Numismatique* (Greece) 5 (1902): 5-26. 3 pls.
Examines the gold staters of the fourth century B.C. Describes each type and notes each known example. Also includes an analysis of each type from an artistic and mythological standpoint and a brief history of Lampsacus.

4622 ——— *The Electrum Coinage of Lampsakos.* New York: American Numismatic Society, 1914. 34 pp., 2 pls. [CS 2694]
Examines the electrum staters of Lampsakos. This coinage is unusual in that no fractional denominations were struck. Previous authors have placed the entire coinage in a single period of issue, although this period was variously dated. Brett suggests there were two separate issues: one struck ca. 525-500 B.C., the other struck ca. 450 B.C. Presents a catalogue of the issues of both periods (thirteen varieties of Period I, one variety of Period II). Reviews the evidence supporting the attribution of these coins to Lampsakos. Comments on the evolution of their style. Discusses at length the evidence for the dating of the coins.

4623 ——— "Lampsakos: The Gold Staters, Silver and Bronze Coinages." *American Journal of Numismatics* 53, pt. 3 (1924): 1-77. Illus., 10 pls. [CS 2695]
A detailed study of the gold coinage of Lampsakos. Includes a catalogue of types, discussion of dies and die sequences, chronology, and comments on the types. Concludes with brief comments on the silver and bronze coinage, the coinage under Alexander and Lysimachus, and Roman Provincial issues.

4624 **Bulatovich, S. A.** "A Hoard of Cyzicenes from Orlovka." *Vestnik Drevnei Istorii* (U.S.S.R.) 2 (1970): 73-86. 4 pls. [An English translation is held in the library of the American Numismatic Association].
A catalogue of part of a hoard of over 200 electrum staters of Cyzicus found in 1967. Seventy-one pieces entered the Odessa Archaeological Museum. Among these, forty-four types are represented, including two previously unpublished types. The coins are divided into three groups based on the chronology established by von Fritze (see von Fritze "Die Elektronprägung von Kyzikos" below). The coins are dated to 500-330 B.C. The catalogue of coins includes commentary on the coins and a discussion of their weights and gold content. [Also see Kravchenko below].

4625 **Cairns, D. and T. P. Hutchinson.** "Did the Gold Content of Cyzicene Electrum Coins Decline Over Time? A Study using Elaboration as a Statistical Strategy." *Revue Belge de Numismatique et de Sigillopraphie* (Belgium) 147 (2001): 51-6.

4626 **Clark, Hyde.** "Apollo Smintheus at Pergamon." *Numismatic Chronicle* 3rd ser., 2 (1882): 352.
Comments on Wroth's article on the significance of the depiction of the rat and mouse on coins of Pergamon. Wroth suggested it indicated an assimilation of the cults of Asklepios and Apollo Smintheus. Clark suggests it is merely a reflection of the occasional influx of these creatures into the city. [See Wroth "Asklepios" below].

4627 **Draganov, Dimitar.** "An Unknown Hybrid Hemidrachm of Parium and Thracian Chersonesus." *Proceedings of the 11th International Numismatic Congress, September 8-13, 1991. Volume 1.* Edited by T. Hackens et al. Louvain-la-Neuve, Belgium: International Association of Professional Numismatists, 1993. Pages 169-72. Illus.
Examines a coin from the Gorno Novo Selo hoard of 1961 (*IGCH* 751), wrongly attributed to Parium. The obverse of the coin bears the legend ΠΑ/ΡΙ with a cow standing, looking back. The reverse has a quadripartite incuse. It is a hybrid hemidrachm bearing an obverse from Parium and a reverse from Thracian Chersonesus. It is the earliest Greek hybrid coin known and dates from the second half of the fourth century B.C. The coin proves the collaboration between Parium and Thracian Chersonesus in the field of coinage during the second half of the fourth century. Discusses the circumstances of its minting.

4628 **Eddy, Samuel K.** "The Value of the Cyzicene Stater at Athens in the Fifth Century." *Museum Notes* 16 (1970): 13-22. [CS 3314]
The author attempts to determine the official value placed upon the Cyzicene electrum staters at Athens. Examines the metrological, metallurgical, and epigraphical evidence. Suggests the stater was valued at twenty-four drachms in Athens. [Also see W. Thompson "The Value" below].

4629 **Gaebler, Hugo.** "Die Silberprägung von Lampsakos." *Nomisma* (Germany) 13 (1923): 1-33. [CS 2696]

4630 **Gardner, Percy.** "The Exchange-Value of Cyzicene Staters." *Numismatic Chronicle* 3rd ser., 7 (1887): 185-90.
Examines the exchange-value of the electrum staters of Cyzicus. Presents evidence from ancient writers. Includes a table of weights, specific gravities, and approximate proportions of gold and silver for various types of Cyzicene staters. Gardner concludes the staters were equivalent in value to the Persian darics and, at Athens, were equal to twenty-eight Attic drachms. At Cyzicus, they would pass for seven and one-half silver staters. [Also see Greenwell "The Electrum Coinage" below].

4631 **Gerasimov, Theodore D.** "Finds of Electrum Coins of the City of Cyzicus in Bulgaria." *Annual of the National Museum* (Bulgaria) 7 (1943).

4632 **Greenwell, William.** "The Electrum Coinage of Cyzicus." *Numismatic Chronicle* 3rd ser., 7 (1887): 1-125. 6 pls. Also released as an offprint, London: Rollin & Feuardent, 1887. 132 pp., 6 pls. [CS 2689]
Presents the historical background of Cyzicus and its coinage, its religious origin, monetary standards, supply of metals, types, styles, various issues and denominations. Catalogues 172 varieties of the Cyzicene electrum coins. Over 160 varieties are illustrated. [For some additional coins, see Greenwell "On Some Rare Greek Coins" (1890) under PRIVATE COLLECTIONS. Also see Gardner "The Exchange-Value" above].

4633 **Hasluck, F. W.** "Notes on Coin-Collecting in Mysia." *Numismatic Chronicle* 4th ser., 6 (1906): 26-36.
The author summarizes the results of four seasons of collecting in the neighborhood of Cyzicus. Describes several unpublished coins and corrects or establishes attributions for others. Includes autonomous issues as well as Roman Provincial issues.

4634 **Head, Barclay V.** "On a Recent Find of Staters of Cyzicus, etc." *Numismatic Chronicle* new ser., 16 (1876): 277-98.
Discusses the group of fifty-six electrum staters (of twenty-seven different types) and at least one gold daric found in Smyrna. Assigns the electrum coins to the period 478-387 B.C. [Also see Head "Additional Notes" below and "Metrological Notes" under METROLOGY].

4635 ——— "Additional Notes on the Recent Find of Staters of Cyzicus and Lampsacus." *Numismatic Chronicle* new ser., 17 (1877): 169-76. 1 pl.
Publishes thirty more examples of electrum staters from a hoard which recently came to light (see Head "On a Recent Find" above). Also publishes a letter from J. P. Six (in French) commenting on Head's previous paper.

4636 **Healy, John F.** "The Gold Staters of Lampsakos: A Preliminary Investigation." *Proceedings of the 10th International Congress of Numismatics, London, 1986.* International Association of Professional Numismatists Publication, No. 11. Edited by I. A. Carradice. London: International Association of Professional Numismatists, 1986. Pages 45-50.
A brief report of research in-progress aimed at establishing a definitive sequence for the gold staters of Lampsakos in the light of new evidence. Discusses an attempt to determine the source of gold based on a metallurgical analysis of the coins. Summarizes hoard evidence and the development of the coin types. Suggests these coins were issued soon after 387 B.C. and were phased out after 334 B.C.

4637 "Hoard of Electrum Staters of Cyzicus Found in Odessa Field (Orlovka) in USSR." *North American Journal of Numismatics* 7, no. 6 (June 1968): 199-200.
Reports a hoard of sixty Cyzicene staters, the only group of these coins ever found in the USSR (the story is excerpted from *Soviet News*).

4638 **Hurter, Silvia M., and Hans-Joachim Liewald.** "Neue Münztypen der Kyzikener Elektronprägung." *Revue Suisse de Numismatique* (Switzerland) 81 (2002): 21-39. Illus.

4639 **Johnston, Joseph.** "An International Managed Currency in the Fifth Century." *Hermathena* (Ireland) 47 (1932): 132-57.
The Ionian Revolt of 499 B.C. was associated with a currency revolution in which the Ionian cities reverted to an electrum currency—the earliest example of the deliberate mixing of silver and gold so as to produce an artificial electrum suitable for coinage. This was continued in the well-known electrum coinages of Cyzicus, Lampsacus, Mytilene, and Phocea. Johnston explores the relationship between the Cyzicene electrum and Athenian and other mono-metallic currencies. Argues that the Cyzicene stater was equivalent to twenty-four Athenian drachms. Explores the on-going relationship between the Cyzicene and the Athenian currencies.

4640 **Kampmann, Ursula.** "Herakles the Snake-Strangler." *The Celator* 19, no. 9 (September 2005): 39-56. Illus.
Recounts the story of the infant Herakles strangling a snake. Illustrates a rare electrum stater of Kyzikos depicting this scene. [Also see Karwiese "Lysander as Herakliskos Drakonopnigon" under CARIA].

4641 **Kiechle, Franz.** "Literaturüberblick der Griechischen Numismatik: Mysien, Troas, Aeolis, Lesbos." *Jahrbuch für Numismatik und Geldsseschichte* (Germany) 10 (1959-60): 91-164. [CS 2677]
A bibliography.

4642 **Kravchenko, A. A.** "A Hoard of Cyzicus Staters from the Odesskaya Oblast." *Sovietskaya Arkheologiya* (Russia) 1 (1969): 274-7.
Discusses a hoard of over 200 electrum staters of Cyzicus found in 1967. [Also see Bulatovich above].

4643 **Laloux, Monique.** "La Circulation des Monnaies d'Electrum de Cyzique." *Revue Belge de Numismatique* (Belgium) 67 (1971): 31-69. 3 maps. [CS 2690]

4644 ——— "Quelques Paralleles Stylistiques Entre les Types Monetaires Cyziceniens et l'Art du VIe au IVe s. avant J.-C." *Actes du 8e Congrès International de Numismatique. New York-Washington, Septembre 1973.* Paris/Basel, 1976. Pages 107-109.

4645 **Maffre, Frédéric.** "Le Monnayage de Pharnabaze Frappé dans l'Atelier de Cyzique." *Numismatic Chronicle* 164 (2004): 1-32. 2 pls.

A study of the hemidrachms, drachms, and tetradrachms of Pharnabazos from Cyzicus.

4646 **Marchetti, Patrich.** "Le Cours du Cyzicène au IVe Siècle." *Revue Belge de Numismatique* (Belgium) 122 (1976): 35-58. [CS 2691]

4647 **Mildenberg, Leo.** "The Cyzicenes: A Reappraisal." *American Journal of Numismatics* 2nd ser., 5/6 (1993-94): 1-12 (plus two-page insert accidentally omitted from original publication). 2 pls. Reprinted in *Leo Mildenberg. Vestigia Leonis: Studien zur Antiken Numismatik Israels, Palästinas und der Östlichen Mittelmeerweit. Novum Testamentum et Orbis Antiquus 36.* Edited by U. Hübner and E. Knauf. Freiburg: Universitätsverlag, and Göttingen: Vandenhoeck & Ruprecht, 1998. Pages 127-35. 2 pls.
Examines the electrum staters and hekte issued by Cyzicus ca. 550-330 B.C. The coins display a variety of constantly changing obverse types (with no inscription) combined with simple incuse reverses. These were widely accepted as trade coins throughout the Greek world—unusual for coins of a small city with little access to precious metals. The trade value of the coins was fixed, even though their gold content varied. Mildenberg explores the reasons this became a popular trade coinage, and why the types were changed so often. He concludes the changing types were not annual issues, and did not signify changing magistrates. Apparently, the public had a preference for changing types, and it was Persian policy to permit local control over coinage production. Twenty-eight coins are illustrated, including original types, imitative types, and types not listed in H. v. Fritze's *Die Elektronprägung von Kyzikos* (1912). [Also see Hübner and Knauf *Vestigia Leonis* under GENERAL WORKS—GREEK].

4648 **Pokras, Yuri.** "A New Iconography for the Electrum Coins of Kyzikos." *The Celator* 14, no. 11 (November 2000): 18-26. Illus.
Unlike most popular trade coins, the electrum staters of Kyzikos exhibited hundreds of different designs over several centuries of use, the only constant being a tunny fish always being present as a minor element. Pokras suggests the varying designs of the Kyzikenes correspond to the typical designs of the coins of the members of the Delian League. The treasury of the Athenian league needed to mark the contributions of each member, and this was achieved by converting the member's contributions into Kyzikenes of the design specific to that contributor. Proposes some corrections to the arrangement and chronology of the issues established by H. von Fritze in "Die Elektronprägung von Kyzikos" (see von Fritze below).

4649 **Sandstrom, Faith Ford.** "The Fourth Century B.C. Silver ΣΩΤΕΙΡΑ Coinage of Cyzicus: The Question of the Fractions." *Proceedings of the 11th International Numismatic Congress, September 8-13, 1991. Volume 1.* Edited by T. Hackens et al. Louvain-la-Neuve, Belgium: International Association of Professional Numismatists, 1993. Pages 243-7. Illus.
A study of the silver tetradrachms and fractions of Rhodian weight, with Kore on the obverse along with the legend ΣΩΤΕΙΡΑ. Discusses weights, symbols, and monograms to draw conclusions regarding the chronology of this coinage.

4650 **Seyrig, Henri.** "Parion au 3e Siècle avant Notre Ère." *Centennial Publication of the American Numismatic Society.* Edited by Harald Ingholt. New York: American Numismatic Society, 1958. Pages 603-25. 3 pls. Maps. [CS 2697]
Examines the large flan tetradrachms bearing the types of Lysimachos.

4651 **Thompson, Margaret.** "The Coinage of Proconnesus." *Revue Numismatique* (France) 6th ser., 7 (1965): 30-5. 1 pl. [CS 2700]
"A unique tetradrachm of Proconnesus, recently acquired by the American Numismatic Society, prompts a reconsideration of the sequence and chronology of the coinage of that mint. Like other cities in the area, Proconnesus began striking on the Persic standard, first hemiobols and then hemidrachms, issues which seem to have appeared sporadically between 450 and 387 B.C. At the time of the Peace of Antalcidas the Rhodian standard was adopted by a group of Propontic cities and its use persisted until ca. 340 B.C. when it was replaced by the old Persic system. The new tetradrachm of Rhodian weight, together with associated fractions and bronzes, may be dated ca. 360-340; later issues of Persic fractions and small bronzes probably belong to the next decade." [M. Thompson, *NL* 79]

4652 **Thompson, Wesley E.** "The Value of the Kyzikene Stater." *Numismatic Chronicle* 7th ser., 3 (1963): 1-4. [CS 2693]
"On the basis of epigraphical evidence, Kyzikene staters of the fifth century B.C. are shown to be worth more than twenty-four Attic drachmae." [A. Bellinger, *NL* 74]. [Also see S. Eddy "The Value" above, and W. Thompson's follow-up article below].

4653 ——— "The Official Tariff of the Kyzikene Stater at Athens." *L'Antiquité Classique* (Belgium) 40 (1971): 574-88.
"The opinions of S. K. Eddy are discussed on the basis of a re-examination of Attic inscriptions." [P. Naster, *NL* 89]. [See Eddy "The Value" above].

4654 **Troxell, Hyla A.** "Orontes, Satrap of Mysia." *Revue Suisse de Numismatique* (Switzerland) 60 (1981): 27-37. Illus.
"A history of Orontes, satrap of Mysia, who is known to have been active between 401 and 348, is traced. The silver and copper coins minted in his name were issued not at Lampsacus and Clazomenae but in Mysia, the silver in the late 350's. The Lampsacene gold coins with satrapal heads are not his." [H. Bloesch, *NL* 109]

4655 **Vagi, David.** "One Humble Bronze, and a Mystery Solved." *The Celator* 9, no. 3 (March 1995): 22-3. Illus.
Describes how a seemingly insignificant bronze coin became the link which allowed certain coins, previously attributed to Clazomenae and Lampsacus, to be attributed to Orontes, the Persian satrap of Mysia.

4656 "A Very Rare Coin." *Spink Numismatic Circular* 65, no. 10 (October 1957): 420. Illus.
Illustrates a rare coin of Cyzicus with *rev.*, Apollo on omphalos holding a lyre. The coin was minted ca. 100 B.C. or later.

4657 **von Fritze, Hans.** "Zur Chronologie der Autonomen Prägung von Pergamon." *Corolla Numismatica: Numismatic Essays in Honour of Barclay V. Head.* Edited by G. F. Hill. London: Oxford University Press, 1906. Pages 47-62. [CS 2698]

4658 ——— "Die Münzen von Pergamon." *Abhandlungen der Akademie der Wissenschaften, Philosophisch-Historische Classe Anhang* (Germany) 1 (1910): 1-108. 9 pls. Reprint, Berlin: Verlag der Königl, 1910. [CS 2699]

4659 ——— "Die Elektronprägung von Kyzikos: Eine Chronologische Studie." *Nomisma* (Germany) 7 (1912): 1-38. 6 pls. [CS 2686]
Describes and illustrates 223 electrum coin types from Kyzikos.

4660 ———— *Die Antiken Münzen Mysiens, Part 1: Adramytion-Kisthene.* An unnumbered volume of *Die Antiken Münzen Nord-Griechenlands.* Edited by F. Imhoof-Blumer. Berlin, 1913. 223 pp., 10 pls. [CS 2678]

4661 ———— "Die Silberprägung von Kyzikos: Eine Chronologische Studie." *Nomisma* (Germany) 9 (1914): 34-56. [CS 2687]

4662 ———— "Die Autonome Kupferprägung von Kyzikos." *Nomisma* (Germany) 10 (1917): 1-32. [CS 2688]

4663 **Wace, Alan J. B.** "An Unpublished Pergamene Tetradrachm." *Journal International d'Archéologie Numismatique* (Greece) 6 (1903): 140-8. 1 pl.
Describes some tetradrachms from a hoard including issues of Antiochus I, Antiochus III, Eumenes I, Attalus I, Eumenes II, and an unknown king. The coin of the unknown king has not previously been published. Wace concludes the hoard was buried ca. 187 B.C. He also concludes the coin bears the portrait of Attalus I.

4664 **Wroth, Warwick W.** "Asklepios and the Coins of Pergamon." *Numismatic Chronicle* 3rd ser., 2 (1882): 1-51. 3 pls.
Examines the mythology surrounding Asklepios. Wroth then discusses Asklepios' appearance on Pergamene coins from 400 B.C. through the Roman Imperial period. [Also see Clark "Apollo" above].

4665 ———— *Catalogue of Greek Coins of Mysia.* Edited by R. S. Poole. London: British Museum, 1892. Reprint, Bologna: Forni, 1964. xxxv, 217 pp., 35 pls., map. [CS 2680]
Volume 14 of the *Catalogue of Greek Coins in the British Museum.* Thirty-four pages of introductory text precede the 217-page catalogue of coins. [Also see *Catalogue of Greek Coins in the British Museum* under PUBLIC COLLECTIONS—GREAT BRITAIN (LONDON)].

4666 **Zograph, Alexander N.** "Cyzicenes of the Collection of S. G. Stroganov." *Symposium of the State Hermitage* (Leningrad) 3 (1926): 60 ff.

Also see: Arnold-Biucchi "Pergamene Mint under Lysimachus" under THRACE—COINAGE OF LYSIMACHOS; Ashton, Hardwick, Konuk, and Meadows "Pixodarus Hoard" under HOARDS; Bellinger "Greek Coins from the Yale Numismatic Collection" under PUBLIC COLLECTIONS—UNITED STATES (NEW HAVEN); Cabral "Specific Gravity of Fifty-two Electrum Staters of Kyzikos" under METALLURGY; Caskey "Greek Electrum Coins" under ASIA MINOR—GENERAL WORKS; Cawkwell "Heracles Coinage Alliance" under CARIA; Cook "Spartan Coins" under CARIA; Goldsborough "Archaic Parion Hemidrachms" under COUNTERFEITS; Greenwell "Rare Greek Coins" (1893) under PRIVATE COLLECTIONS; Healy "The Establishment of Die-Sequences" under METALLURGY; Healy "The Use of Sicilian and Magna Graecian Types" under TYPES.

Köker "The Greek Coins" under HOARDS; Meiggs *The Athenian Empire* under ATTICA—ATHENIAN COINAGE DECREE (discusses value of Cyzicene stater); Moysey "Observations…Satrapal Revolt" under PERSIA; Papaefthymiou "The Coin Collection of the Foundation of the Hellenic World" under PRIVATE COLLECTIONS; Robinson "Some Electrum and Gold" under ASIA MINOR—GENERAL WORKS; Six "Some Undescribed Greek Coins" under ATTICA—GENERAL WORKS; Smekalova and Djukov "The Composition of the Alloy of Cyzicene Electrum Coins" under METALLURGY; M. Thompson *Alexander's Drachm Mints 2: Lampsacus and Abydos* under MACEDONIAN KINGDOM—GENERAL WORKS; Touratsoglou "Statères d'Alexandre et Statères de Cyzique" under HOARDS; Touratsoglou "Aphrodite and Eros in Kyzikos" under TYPES; Vagi "Slavei Replicas" under COUNTERFEITS.

PERGAMENE KINGDOM

4667 **Ashton, Richard.** "The Attalid Poll-Tax." *Spink Numismatic Circular* 102, no. 4 (May 1994): 159-60.
A letter from Eumenes II of Pergamum to Artemidoros, the Attalid governor of Telmessos, reveals that the Attalid poll-tax was normally levied at an annual rate of four Rhodian drachms and one obol per adult. Ashton suggests the drachms referred to were the plinthophoric rather than the earlier drachms. Ashton attempts to find the reason for the odd amount of the tax. An examination of the weights of these drachms reveals that the silver weight of the tax would equal the weight of the early cistophoric tetradrachm. The tax may have been collected in Rhodian, rather than cistophoric, coins because the cistophoric coins rarely circulated outside Attalid territory. If Ashton's interpretations are accurate, they indicate that the cistophoroi were in circulation by 181 B.C.

4668 **Bauslaugh, Robert A.** "The Unique Portrait Tetradrachm of Eumenes II." *Museum Notes* 27 (1982): 39-51. 2 pls.
The author examines an Attic-weight tetradrachm with *obv.*, portrait of Eumenes II (197-159 B.C.) and *rev.*, two male figures standing within wreath, which is the only Attalid coin to portray a king other than the dynasty's founder Philetaerus. Reviews the numismatic and iconographical evidence for the identity of the reverse figures, comparing them to figures on coins of Syros and Bactria. Considers a dedicatory inscription. Concludes the coin may have been struck in 172 B.C. by Attalus II, the temporary successor to Eumenes II when it was thought he was dead. Identifies the figures as Eumenes II and Attalus II. Two specimens are now known. [Also see H. Mattingly "The Portrait Coin" below. Mattingly dates the coin to 166 B.C.].

4669 ———— "Cistophoric Countermarks and the Monetary System of Eumenes II." *Numismatic Chronicle* 150 (1990): 39-65. 3 pls.
"Countermarks of a bowcase and letters identifying eleven authorities (ten of which are cities within the territory of the post-Apamean Pergamene Kingdom) were placed on the obverses of autonomous tetradrachms of Side and posthumous Alexander tetradrachms of Phaselis, Aspendus and Perge. Based on a catalogue of more than 150 examples and the examination of the hoard record for countermarked varieties, the countermarking activity can be dated to the years immediately after the Peace of Apamea (188-183 B.C.) and connected with the indemnity paid by Antiochus III to Eumenes II. The countermarks therefore appear to have been used as a device to legalize circulation of a special group of foreign, Attic-weight coins, during the years immediately before the introduction of the reduced weight cistophoric coinage. All of this suggests close supervision of the Pergamene monetary system by the Attalids." [R. Bauslaugh, *NL* 126]

4670 **Doyen, Charles.** "Remarques Numismatiques à Propos d'Un Traité Entre Attale Ier de Pergame et la Cité de Malla (Crète)." *Liber Amicorum Tony Hackens.* Numismatica Lovaniensia 20. Edited by G. Moucharte, M. B. Borba Florenzano, F. de Callataÿ, P. Marchetti, L. Smolderen, and P. Yannopoulos. Louvain-la-Neuve: Université Catholique de Louvain, 2007. Pages 95 ff.

4671 **Harl, K.** "Livy and the Date of the Introduction of the Cistophoric Tetradrachm." *Classical Antiquity* 10 (1991): 268-97.

4672   **Harlick, Robert M.** "Cistophoric Tetradrachms: An Overview." *The Celator* 19, no. 4 (April 2005): 12-20. Illus.
Reviews the history of the cistophoric tetradrachms, first struck in the Pergamene kingdom in the early second century B.C. The series was continued by the Romans until around A.D. 200.

4673   **Imhoof-Blumer, Friedrich W.** "Die Münzen der Dynastie von Pergamon." *Abhandlungen* (Germany) (1884): 1-40. 4 pls. [CS 2679]

4674   **Ingvaldsen, Håkon.** "Philetaerus in Norway." *Florilegium Numismaticum: Studia in Honorem U. Westermark Edita.* Edited by Harald Nilsson. Stockholm: Svenska Numismatiska Föreningen, 1992. Pages 175-81. Illus.
The author publishes a new die variety of a tetradrachm bearing the portrait of Seleucus I struck in Pergamon when Philetaerus was governor (ca. 275-263 B.C.). Reviews the history of Pergamum during the period after Lysimachus' death (281 B.C.) to the introduction of the first coins bearing Philetaerus' name (ca. 275/4). Lists forty-one specimens of the coins of this series, including six new reverse dies, and comments on their sequence. The author suggests that further study may turn-up other new varieties.

4675   **Ireland, Stanley.** "A New Specimen of the KOP Cistophorus." *Numismatic Chronicle* 164 (2004): 221-3. 1 pl.
Discusses a second known example of a cistophoric tetradrachm with the letters KOP and AP and Γ. Suggests Γ represents a date, AP represents the name of a magistrate, and KOP is probably *not* the name of a known city—which suggests there is an unknown city to which the coin belongs.

4676   **Kampmann, Ursula.** *Die Homonoia-Verbindungen Der Stadt Pergamon.* Saarbrücker Studien zur Archäologie und Alten Geschichte, Bank 9. Saarbrücker: Druckeres und Verlag, 1996. 134 pp., 11 pls.
Catalogues 160 alliance coins of Pergamum.

4677   **Kleiner, Fred S.** "Hoard Evidence and the Late Cistophori of Pergamum." *Museum Notes* 23 (1978): 77-105. 8 pls. [CS 2605]
The author uses hoard evidence in an attempt to establish a chronology for the cistophoric tetradrachms of Pergamum struck between ca. 123 B.C. and 67 B.C. He divides the series into three groups. Lists all the Group 2 and 3 issues known, including fifty-one tetradrachms, one didrachm, and three drachm varieties. Lists nine important hoards of cistophori and provides a detailed discussion of seven of them. Presents an arrangement of the coins in a suggested chronological order.

4678   **Kosmetatou, Elizabeth.** "Cistophori and Cista Mystica: A New Interpretation of the Early Cistophoric Types." *Revue Belge de Numismatique* (Belgium) 144 (1998): 11-20.

4678a   **Le Rider, Georges.** "La Politique Monetaire du Royaume de Pergame après 188." *Journal des Savants* (France) 3, nos. 3-4 (July-September 1989): 163-90, incl. 1 pl.

4679   ——— "Les Tétradrachmes Attalides au Portrait de Philétaire." *Florilegium Numismaticum: Studia in Honorem U. Westermark Edita.* Edited by Harald Nilsson. Stockholm: Svenska Numismatiska Föreningen, 1992. Pages 233-45. 1 pl.

4680   **Mattingly, Harold B.** "The Portrait Coin of Eumenes II of Pergamon." *Proceedings of the 11th International Numismatic Congress, September 8-13, 1991. Volume 1.* Edited by T. Hackens et al. Louvain-la-Neuve, Belgium: International Association of Professional Numismatists, 1993. Pages 281-2.
The author discusses the chronology for the portrait tetradrachm of Eumenes (see Bauslaugh "The Unique Portrait Tetradrachm" above). A second specimen of the coin is now known. Bauslaugh dated the coin to 172 B.C. Mattingly suggests 166 B.C., and discusses the historical circumstances surrounding its minting.

4681   **Mørkholm, Otto.** "Some Pergamene Coins in Copenhagen." *Studies in Honour of Leo Mildenberg: Numismatics, Art History, Archaeology.* Edited by A. Houghton et al. Wetteren: Editions NR, 1984. Pages 181-92. 2 pls.
Publishes and discusses nine coins of Pergamum added to the Royal Collection since the publication of Volume 19, *Mysia*, of the *SNG Copenhagen* in 1945. Includes a third siglos (or diobol), an Alexander-type tetradrachm struck at Pergamum ca. 282-280 B.C., coins of Philetaerus bearing the portrait of Seleucus, coins of Eumenes bearing the portrait of Philetaerus, a coin of Attalus I, and a rare tetradrachm with *obv.*, Medusa head with wings; *rev.*, Athena Nikephoros. On this coin, the statue resembles the famous statue of Artemis at Ephesus. The Oriental elements of the goddess are predominant over the Greek elements. This merging of the "bearer of victory" with the "bringer of fertility" reveals the syncretistic religious policy of the Attalids. Mørkholm discusses the so-called breasts on the statue of Artemis at Ephesus and notes the lack of nipples on the "breasts." Gérard Seiterle ["Artemis–Die Grosse Götten von Ephesos," *Antike Welt* 10, no. 3 (1979): 2-16] has proposed that these are not breasts, but are the scrota of bulls sacrificed to the goddess. Mørkholm finds Seiterle's arguments convincing. [For other opinions related to the "breasts," see Rakicic "The Bees of Ephesos" under IONIA, and Seltman "The Wardrobe of Artemis" under TYPES]

4682   **Newell, Edward T.** "Philetaerus." *The Coin Collector's Journal* 1, no. 1 (April 1934): 8-9. Illus.
A brief account of the reign of Philetaerus and the coinage depicting him.

4683   ——— *The Pergamene Mint under Philetaerus.* Numismatic Notes and Monographs, No. 76. New York: American Numismatic Society, 1936. 34 pp., 10 pls. [CS 2701]
Newell recounts the history of the period, ca. 284-282 B.C., leading up to Seleucus Nicator's control over Pergamum, and the issuance of coins by the Pergamene mint while under the control of Philetaerus beginning ca. 280 B.C. He examines the coins in the context of the history of the period. The coins bear the name of Alexander, Seleucus, or Philetaerus. Philetaerus began coinage bearing his own name (and the bust of Seleucus) ca. 274 B.C. Fifteen coin types are listed.

4684   **Nicolet-Pierre, Hélène.** "Monnaies de Pergame." *Kraay—Mørkholm Essays: Numismatic Studies in Memory of C. M. Kraay and O. Mørkholm.* Numismatica Lovaniensia 10. Edited by G. Le Rider, G. K. Jenkins, N. Waggoner, and U. Westermark. Louvain-la-Neuve: Université Catholique de Louvain, 1989. Pages 203-16. 3 pls.

4685 **Queyrel, François.** "Le Portrait Monétaire d'Eumène II: Problèmes d'Interpretation et de Datation." *Travaux de Numismatique Grecque Offerts à Georges Le Rider*. Edited by M. Amandry and S. Hurter. London: Spink, 1999. Pages 323-36. 1 pl.

4686 ———. *Les Portraits des Attalides: Fonction et Représentation*. Bibliothèque des Écoles Françaises d'Athènes et de Rome 308. Paris: de Boccard, 2003. 371 pp., 75 pls.
An examination of Attalid royal portraiture. The first part addresses issues of function and representation, including dynastic image, problems of physiognomy, as well as the function and types of portraits, their dimensions, and reception. It also includes the presentation of a number of portraits. The second and largest part handles iconographical issues related to the Pergamene royal family. It is divided into nine chapters, describing the six Attalid rulers, the two queens (Apollonis and Stratonike), and unidentified members of the Pergamene royal family. Four appendices follow. The first contains an epigraphic dossier featuring texts and their French translation on honors that Eumenes II received from Miletos, including portrait statues. The second appendix offers information on the setting up of colossal Attalid portraits on pillars in Athens. In appendix 3, Queyrel discusses the so-called "Terrace of Attalos I" in Delphi. Finally, Appendix 4 expands on the case Queyrel makes in the core of the book suggesting that the development of the type of Apollo Delphinios was influenced by images of Eumenes II. [Excerpted from the review by Elizabeth Kosmetatou in *Bryn Mawr Classical Review* 2006.10.37].

4687 **Regling, Kurt L.** "Der Griechische Goldschatz von Prinkipo." *Zeitschrift für Numismatik* (Germany) 41 (1931): 1-46. 4 pls. [CS 3278]

4688 **Reinach, Theodore.** "A Stele from Abonuteichos." *Numismatic Chronicle* 4th ser., 5 (1905): 113-9.
The inscription on a stele found in Paphlagonia throws light on some disputed points of Pontic numismatics. Reinach presents a translation of the inscription on the stele. It helps to confirm that the Zeus-types on a unique coin of Abonuteichos refer to a local cult of Zeus. The inscription also confirms that Euergetes and Philopater Philadelphos were two separate kings.

4689 **Robinson, Edward S. G.** "Cistophori in the Name of King Eumenes." *Numismatic Chronicle* 6th ser., 14 (1954): 1-8. 1 pl.
"The unartistic cistophorus appears to have developed out of the light Rhodian tetradrachm and in its later stages was important in the Graeco-Roman economy built up in the province of Asia under the Republic. The chronological arrangement of the series is still open to much debate, but study of the extremely rare group of coins from the mints of Thyateira, Apollonis, and Stratonikeia with the abbreviation for King Eumenes leads to a firmer chronological core for at least a fraction of the series. This group of coins cannot have been struck under Eumenes II because any probable dates are too early for the Attalid foundation or acquisition of the towns. Chronological difficulties seem resolved if the coins are attributed to Aristonikos, the bastard son of Eumenes II, who raised the standard of revolt when Attalos III died in 133 B.C. and bequeathed the Attalid inheritance to the Roman people. Before being starved into surrender at Stratonikeia in the fourth year of his revolt, Aristonikos would seem to have used the cistophorus to make his claim to royalty under the name of his father, Eumenes. A full list of varieties of cistophori with the name of Eumenes III is provided." [C. Vermeule, *NL* 34]. [Also see Kraay "Historical Interpretations" under GENERAL WORKS—GREEK].

4690 **Sear, David R.** "Pergamum—The Kingdom That Was Given Away." *SAN—Journal of the Society for Ancient Numismatics* 15, no. 4 (winter 1984-5): 67-8.
A brief account of the history and coinage of the Pergamene Kingdom.

4691 **Seltman, E. J.** "Unpublished Gold Staters Issued by an Attalid King." *Journal International d'Archaéologie Numismatique* (Greece) 15 (1913): 81-4.
"Describes coins with types of Philip of Macedon (one with portrait of Philetaerus), probably issued from Sinope by Eumenes II." [J. R. Jones, *AIJIAN*]

4692 **Thonemann, Peter.** "Cistophoric Geography: Toriaion and Kormasa." *Numismatic Chronicle* 168 (2008): 43-60. 2 pls.
Examines some new evidence for the location of the town of Toriaion which was settled by Eumenes II of Pergamon, and discusses its status within the Attalid kingdom after 188 B.C. Also discusses the city of Kormasa. Thonemann suggests this may be the mint of the cistophori bearing the letters KOP.

4693 **Vagi, David.** "A Coin of Four Kings and the Story of Philetaerus." *The Celator* 7, no. 2 (July 1993): 24. Illus.
Presents an Alexander-type tetradrachm bearing the name of Seleucus which was struck at Pergamum by Philetaerus. Discusses the historical background for the coin.

4694 ———. "Pergamum: The Kingdom That Was Given Away." *The Numismatist* 109, no. 1 (January 1996): 70-2. Illus.
An outline of the history and coinage of the city and kingdom of Pergamum. Begins with Lysimachus' deposit of the royal treasure at the city and traces the city's relationship with Seleucus, the kingdom established by Philetaerus, the rise of the kingdom under Philetaerus' successors, and its end when Attalus III bequeathed the kingdom to Rome. Briefly describes the major coin types issued during this period.

4695 **Westermark, Ulla.** *Das Bildnis des Philetairos von Pergamon: Corpus der Münzprägung*. Stockholm, 1961. 84 pp., 24 pls. [CS 2702]
A die study of the Philetairos tetradrachms struck by the Pergamene Kingdom.

4696 ———. "The Portrait Coin of Eumenes II of Pergamon." *Lagom: Festschrift für Peter Berghaus zum 60. Geburtstag*. Edited by Thomas Fischer and Peter Ilisch. Münster, 1981. Pages 19-23.
Discusses the unique portrait coin of Eumenes II with the full-length figures of the Dioscuri on the reverse. The coin is in the British Museum. Reviews the previous scholarship regarding the chronology and interpretation of the type. Suggests this coin was a special festive issue without any close relationship with the standard coinage of the period.

4697 ———. "Bronze Coins of Pergamon." *Quaderni Ticinesi: Numismatica e Antichità Classiche* (Switzerland) 20 (1991): 147-59.

4698 ———. "On the Pergamene Bronze Coins in the Name of Athena Nikephoros." *Studii si Cercetari de Numismatica* (Romania) 11 (1995): 29-35. Illus.
"The author defines five typological series with two nominal values and discusses the chronology, function and metrology in relation to the monetary reform of Eumenes II and the cistophoric system." [G. P. Bordea, *NL* 141]

Also see: Various works on cistophoric coinage under ASIA MINOR—GENERAL WORKS; Arnold-Biucchi "The Pergamene Mint under Lysimachus" under THRACE—COINAGE OF LYSIMACHOS; Hill "A Find of Cistophori" under ASIA MINOR—GENERAL WORKS; Kleiner "Cistophoric Coinage of Asia Minor" under ASIA MINOR—GENERAL WORKS; Kleiner "The Dated Cistophori" under IONIA; Noe "Beginning of the Cistophoric Coinage" under ASIA MINOR—GENERAL WORKS; F. Kleiner "Pergamum and Rhodes" under MACEDONIAN KINGDOM—GENERAL WORKS; Kraay "Historical Interpretations" under GENERAL WORKS—GREEK; Lehmann-Hartleben "Some Ancient Portraits" under PORTRAITS; Rostovtzeff "Some Remarks" under GENERAL WORKS—HELLENISTIC; Waggoner "The Propontis Hoard" (two items) under HOARDS; Wilkinson "Unpublished" under PRIVATE COLLECTIONS; Wroth *Catalogue of Greek Coins of Mysia* under MYSIA—AUTONOMOUS CITIES.

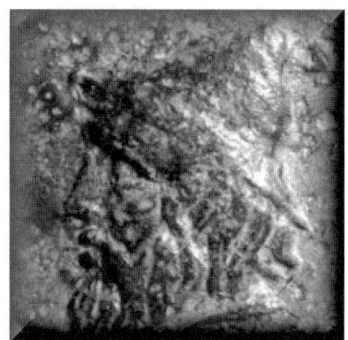

Troas

The tetradrachms of Ilium bearing her own types, and the name of Athena must obviously have been produced with the acquiescence of the dominant power in Asia Minor and we may be sure not only on grounds of general probability, but on the important analogy of the dated tetradrachms of Alexandria Troas that this power was Pergamum.

—*Alfred Bellinger, 1958*

4699 **Bellinger, Alfred R.** "The Earliest Coins of Ilium." *Museum Notes* 7 (1957): 43-9. 1 pl.
The author reviews the conflicting opinions regarding the role of Lysimachus in Ilium's renewal, and the time of its first coinage. He concludes that the city's first coinage belongs to the period of Lysimachus' control, 300-281 B.C. Seven coins are illustrated.

4700 ——— "The First Civic Tetradrachms of Ilium." *Museum Notes* 8 (1958): 11-24. 2 pls.
The first civic tetradrachms of Ilium are generally dated ca. 188 B.C. The twenty-one known varieties are listed here in sequence. Bellinger discusses the purpose for the mint magistrates' monograms on the coins and concludes, "So far as the Greek series are concerned we may reject the conventional theory that names are used as a check on the issuing authorities." He suggests that having one's name on a coin was a distinction of honor, and this was simply why they were used. Discusses the function of the tetradrachms and drachms of Ilium in the monetary pattern of the district. Suggests the city struck these coins simply to display its independence, not because coinage was needed for local commerce. Discusses the reasons some cities struck coins specifically to be exported, but suggests this does not apply to Ilium.

4701 ——— *Troy: The Coins.* Supplementary Monograph 2. Princeton University Press, 1961. 220 pp., 27 pls. Reprint, New York: Sanford Durst, 1979. [CS 3212]
Presents a catalogue of the coins found during the excavations conducted by the Archaeological Expedition of the University of Cincinnati, 1932-1938. Discusses the historical background and coinage of the mints of Ilium and Alexandria Troas from the earliest coinage in the fourth century B.C. through the Roman period. Catalogues the 575 identified coins including Greek, Seleucid, and Roman Provincial issues, as well as a hoard of 218 Roman antoniniani found during excavations. Includes some coins from minor mints in the region. Also presents a discussion of the currency of the Troad during the Hellenistic and Roman periods. Includes indices to mints, rulers, and types, and a table of monograms. [Reviewed by G. K. Jenkins in *Numismatic Chronicle* 7th ser., 3 (1963): 249-50].

4702 **Burnett, Andrew.** "The Earliest Coins of Alexandria Troas." *Stephanos Nomismatikos: Edith Schönert-Geiss zum 65. Geburtstag.* Edited by Ulrike Peter. Berlin: Akademie Verlag, 1998. Pages 165-8.

4702a **de Callataÿ, François.** "Abydos sur Aesillas." ΞΑΡΑΚΤΗΡ: Αφιερωμα στη Μαντω Οικονομιδου *(Character: Offerings to Mando Oeconomides).* Publications of Archaeological Deltion, No. 57. Athens: Treasury of Archaeological Resources and Expropriations, 1996.

4703 ——— "Les Monnaies Hellénistiques en Argent de Ténédos." *Studies in Greek Numismatics in Memory of Martin Jessop Price.* Edited by Richard Ashton and Silvia Hurter. London: Spink, 1998. Pages 99-114. 5 pls.

4704 **Gilliland, Herbert.** "Denomination and Design in the Minor Coinage of Ilium Under Antiochus Hierax." *SAN—Journal of the Society for Ancient Numismatics* 9, no. 1 (winter 1978): 17.
A half-unit bronze coin of Ilium under Antiochus Hierax (241-228 B.C.) is published, filling the gap between the units and quarter-units published by Bellinger. Concludes that denominations were indicated by alternating the designs—Athena is shown wearing a Corinthian helmet on the double and half unit, and an Attic helmet on the unit and quarter-unit.

4705 **Hoge, Robert W.** "Some Ancient Greek Fractional Silver." *The Numismatist* 109, no. 8 (August 1996): 1026. Illus.
The author publishes a hemiobol and a diobol of Kebren in Troas. He also publishes a 1/96 stater, probably from Miletos. All three coins are archaic-period pieces.

4706 **Kagan, Jonathan H.** "Hellenistic Coinage at Scepsis after its Refoundation in the Third Century B.C." *Museum Notes* 29 (1984): 11-24. 1 pl.
The inhabitants of Scepsis in the Troad were relocated in 310 B.C., and it has been believed that autonomous coinage at Scepsis ceased at that time. The people were allowed to return to their homes at a later date. The author attempts to determine whether autonomous coinage was struck at the city after 310 B.C. A tetradrachm of Seleucus Hierax (246-228/7 B.C.) bears, as a subsidiary symbol, a rhyton in the shape of the forepart of a winged horse, and the author suggests the coin was struck at Scepsis. This causes the author to suggest that bronze coins bearing this symbol (and traditionally dated before 310)

may have been struck at Scepsis after the refoundation of the city. The author suggests some silver coins of Scepsis with a reel-and-bead border may belong to the period 197-188 B.C. along with these bronze coins.

4706a **Lazzarini, Lorenzo.** "Note sulle Monete Bronze di Kebren nella Troade." *Revista Italiana di Numismatica* (Italy) 88 (1986).

4707 **Meadows, Andrew.** "The Earliest Coinage of Alexandria Troas." *Numismatic Chronicle* 164 (2004): 47-70. 1 pl.
The appearance of a new silver coin (Apollo/horse) in commerce in 2003 leads to a re-assessment of the earliest coins that can be attributed to the city of Alexandria Troas. Meadows discusses the early coinage of the city and then provides an overview of the revised order of the early issues of the mint. The Appendix is a catalogue of the silver, gold, and bronze issues in the name of Lysimachos attributed to the Alexandria Troas mint.

4708 **Robert, Louis.** *Monnaies Antiques en Troade.* Hautes Ètudes Numismatiques 1. Geneva and Paris, 1966. 141 pp., 4 pls. [CS 2703]

4709 **Robinson, Edward S. G.** "Greek Coins from the Dardanelles." *Numismatic Chronicle* 5th ser., 1 (1921): 1-25. 1 pl.
Publishes coins acquired by the British Museum from a collection formed during residence in the Dardanelles. The coins are mostly Roman Provincial issues but include a few Greek autonomous issues of Abydus, Assus, and Ilium.

4710 **Tameanko, Marvin.** "Alexandria Troas, City of the 'Mouse God.'" *Journal of the Classical and Medieval Numismatic Society* (Canada) 2nd ser., 3, no. 3 (September 2002): 125-39. Illus.
Discusses the city of Alexandria in Troas. Apollo Smintheus (the Mouse God) was worshipped at the city. Examines the legends related to the city's religion. Discusses the history of the city. Coins were issued at Alexandria which bear a grazing horse as a symbol or type, including a tetradrachm of Alexander the Great type, struck 189-180 B.C. Tameanko traces the coinage of the city through the Roman period.

4711 **Vagi, David L.** "Ancient Coins Illuminate the History of Troy." *The Celator* 8, no. 12 (December 1994): 20. Illus.
A brief description of the small and sporadic coinage of Troy, as well as coins with themes revolving around Homer's stories.

4712 **Wroth, Warwick.** *Catalogue of Greek Coins of Troas, Aeolis, and Lesbos.* London: British Museum, 1894. Reprint, Bologna: Forni, 1964. lxxxiii, 260 pp., 43 pls., map. [CS 2704]
Volume 17 of the *Catalogue of Greek Coins in the British Museum*. Eighty-three pages of introductory text precede the 260-page catalogue of coins. [Also see *Catalogue of Greek Coins in the British Museum* under PUBLIC COLLECTIONS—GREAT BRITAIN (LONDON)].

Also see: Kiechle "Literaturüberblick" under MYSIA—AUTONOMOUS CITIES; Noe "Greek Coins Acquired during 1945" (discusses Abydus) under PUBLIC COLLECTIONS—UNITED STATES (NEW YORK); Robinson "Some Electrum and Gold" under ASIA MINOR—GENERAL WORKS; M. Thompson *Alexander's Drachm Mints 2: Lampsacus and Abydus* under MACEDONIAN KINGDOM—GENERAL WORKS; Vagi "Previously Unpublished" (Dardanos, Troas) under GENERAL WORKS—GREEK.

AEOLIS

Kyme was the principal city of Aeolis and had a steady history of coinage from 350 B.C. until 133 B.C. when Asia Minor became a Roman Province.

—John Oakley, 1982

4713 **Hoge, Robert W.** "A Beautiful Tetradrachm of Myrina in Aeolis." *The Numismatist* 108, no. 11 (November 1995): 1451. Illus.
Describes and illustrates a tetradrachm of Myrina which was donated to the museum of the American Numismatic Association. The coin's reverse die was previously unrecorded.

4714 **Milne, Joseph G.** "A Hoard of Coins of Temnos." *Numismatic Chronicle* 4th ser., 14 (1914): 260-1.
Discusses a hoard of ninety copper coins of Temnos of four varieties. Lists dies, weights.

4715 ——— "The Mint of Kyme in the Third Century B.C." *Numismatic Chronicle* 5th ser., 20 (1940): 129-37.
Milne examines the coinage of Kyme to learn about the organization of Greek city mints and the position of the authorities responsible for the issuance of coins. Lists sixty-four magistrates' names and thirty-one monograms. States that minting was a spasmodic activity at all but the largest commercial centers. Discusses the dates of issue and the denominations used at Kyme.

4716 **Oakley, John H.** "The Autonomous Wreathed Tetradrachms of Kyme, Aeolis." *Museum Notes* 27 (1982): 1-37. 14 pls.
Examines the wreathed tetradrachms of Kyme, many of which were found along with coins of Magnesia and Myrina in a Cilician hoard in 1972. A die-study revealed seventy-nine obverse dies and twelve magistrate's names on the Kymaean coins. The author arranges these magistrates in a suggested chronological order based on die links and style. A table shows the coins' weight distribution by magistrate. Lists thirteen hoards which contained this coin type and reviews the historical background of the period these coins circulated in order to establish dates of issue. Suggests the earliest date for these is 165 B.C. and the latest date is before 140 B.C. Reviews the conclusions of other researchers regarding the issue dates for wreathed coinages at various cities. Catalogues seventy-nine die varieties and lists numerous specimens of each.

4717 **Sacks, K. S.** "The Wreathed Coins of Aeolian Myrina." *Museum Notes* 30 (1985): 1-43. 22 pls.
Reviews the history of the city of Myrina and suggests the city remained autonomous into the second century B.C. Describes three stylistic variations in the portrait on the wreathed tetradrachms, and together with metrological data and the monograms on the coins, suggests an order of emission. The three series are extensively die-linked. Based upon hoard evidence, Sacks suggests the coins were minted for about ten years beginning perhaps as early as the mid-150's B.C. Discusses coins-per-die ratios in comparison with those of Magnesia and Kyme. Agrees with Mørkholm that the wreathed coinage at Myrina merely reflects the current artistic style rather than being a political symbol. Concludes that Myrina was an extremely prosperous city in the second century B.C. Presents a catalogue of over 100 coins.

Also see: Kiechle "Literaturüberblick" under MYSIA—AUTONOMOUS CITIES; Hoover and MacDonald "Syrian Imitations of New Style Tetradrachms Struck over Myrina" under SYRIA—SELEUCID KINGDOM; Houghton "The Seleucid Mint of Aegae in Aeolis" under SYRIA—SELEUCID KINGDOM; Kinns "Myrina" under COUNTERFEITS; Lorber "Commerce ('Demetrius I' Hoard) 2003" under HOARDS; Lorber and Hoover "An Unpublished Tetradrachm" under IONIA; MacDonald "Imitations of Macedonia First Meris over Myrina" under MACEDONIAN KINGDOM—GENERAL WORKS; Meadows and Houghton "The Gaziantep Hoard" under HOARDS; Milne "Countermarked Coins" under ASIA MINOR—GENERAL WORKS; Wroth *Catalogue of Greek Coins* under TROAS.

Lesbos

In the later archaic period important centres of electrum coinage certainly existed at Phokaia, and at Mytilene on the island of Lesbos. Around 500 B.C. both these mints began a series of small hektai (= sixths of the stater) which maintain the characteristic Ionian tradition of a coin series with constantly changing types, and continued it down to the time of Alexander the Great.

—G. K. Jenkins, 1972

4718 **Bodenstedt, Friedrich.** "Observations on Some Early Electrum Types of Mytilene and Phocaea." *Museum Notes* 22 (1977): 1-7. 2 pls. [CS 2708]
Examines a previously unpublished hekte of Mytilene, ca. 460 B.C., with a bull on the obverse and an incuse lion head on the reverse. Compares the style with an earlier piece of similar type. Clarifies the design types on other hektes of Mytilene and Phocaea. Suggests certain misunderstood details in the prototype dies were altered on the later dies which were re-cut by other hands. [Also see Bodenstedt and Reimers "Zerstorungsfreie Bestimmung der Legierungsbestandteile" under METALLURGY].

4719 **Borrell, Maximilian.** "Coins of Lesbos—Lesbi, Considered as a City Distinct from that of Mytilene." *Numismatic Chronicle* new ser., 5 (1865): 337-41.
Discusses ten coins which Leake attributed to Mytilene. Leake believed there was no city of Lesbos distinct from Mytilene. Mytilene was called "Lesbus" in the time of Homer. Borrell suggests a separate city may have existed on a small island opposite Mytilene.

4720 **Burelli, Laura.** "L'Accordo Monetale tra Focea e Mitilene (I.G. XII, 2, 1)." *Numismatica e Antichità Classiche* 7 (Switzerland) (1978): 43-51.

4721 **Franke, Peter R.** "Zur Münzprägung von Methymna." *Methymna*. Edited by H. G. Bucholz. Mainz, 1975. Pages 163-76.

4722 **Gardner, Percy.** "A Female Figure in the Early Style of Pheidias." *Journal of Hellenic Studies* 38 (1918): 1-26. Illus., 3 pls.
"On p. 10 it is suggested that a head which appears on bronze coins of Mytilene ca. 300 B.C. is that of Sappho." [J. R. Jones, *NIJHS*]

4723 **Giacchero, Marta.** "I Motivi Finanziari e Commerciali della Unione Monetaria fra Mitilene e Focea." *Rivista Italiana di Numismatica* (Italy) 82 (1980): 1-10.

4724 **Healy, John F.** "The Composition of Mytilenean Electrum." *Congrès International de Numismatique, 5th, Paris, 1953. Volume 2.* Paris, 1957. Pages 529-36. [CS 3398]
The series of hektai struck by Mytilene from ca. 488-330 B.C., with interruption after an unsuccessful attempt at secession from the Athenian empire in 427 B.C., provides the only evidence for a mint known to have issued coinage with an electrum alloy of controlled quality as its base. An inscription relating to a monetary union with Phokaia in the early fourth century B.C. indicates that the alloy was artificial. Analysis brings out the qualitative variance of these coins. [Summarized from C. Vermeule, *NL* 43]

4725 ——— "Notes on the Monetary Union between Mytilene and Phokaia." *Journal of Hellenic Studies* 77 (1957): 267-8. [CS 2709]
The author re-examines the meaning of a phrase in an ancient inscription recording the terms of a monetary union between Mytilene and Phokaia whereby each agreed to issue, in alternate years, an electrum coinage for circulation in both cities. The passage in question deals with the alloy of the metal for coinage and the responsibility of the official alloying the gold. [Also see Marotta "Electrum Sixths" below].

4726 ——— "A New Light on the Unique Stater of Mytilene." *Museum Notes* 8 (1958): 1-9. 1 pl. [CS 2710]
Briefly reviews the history of the city of Mytilene from its founding to the Ionian revolt of 499 B.C. Mytilene began issuing electrum coinage ca. 485 B.C. Unlike Cyzicus which regularly issued both staters and hektai, Mytilene normally struck only hektai. However, a unique stater of Mytilene was discovered in 1889 [see Wroth "Greek Coins Acquired by the British Museum in 1889" under PUBLIC COLLECTIONS—GREAT BRITAIN (LONDON)]. This essay discusses the significance of the stater and its relationship to the hektai series. Healy compares the style of the Apollo head on the stater with similar heads on the hektai and on other coins. The alloy of the coin is of poor quality, suggesting a scarcity of gold at Mytilene when the coin was struck, perhaps during the siege of the city by Athens in 427 B.C. The obverse inscription MYTI leads Healy to suggest it may have been struck to signal the city's secession from the Delian League. [C. Kraay has a different opinion regarding the reason for the issuance of the stater. See Kraay "Greek Coinage and War" under GENERAL WORKS—GREEK. Also see McDowall "Two Heads" below for a stylistic comparison of the Apollo head].

4727 ——— "Alexander the Great and the Last Issue of Electrum Hektai at Mytilene." *Numismatic Chronicle* 7th ser., 2 (1962): 65-71. Illus. [CS 2711]
"Newly acquired evidence now permits the attribution of the obverse of the type in question (youthful male head r., wearing a close-fitting helmet with ram's horn attached in imitation of Zeus Ammon) to be reconsidered in its historical context. In disagreeing with the earlier attributions of Wroth and Imhoof-Blumer (to Zeus Ammon and Apollo Karneios, respectively) Healy suggests that the type may be more properly interpreted from a close study of the contemporary political situation. After the complete success achieved by Alexander in Asia Minor, an alliance was concluded with Mytilene and Tenedos. Mytilene's record of vacillation towards Alexander made the city especially grateful for this recognition, and the issue depicting a beardless male head wearing a helmet and ram's horn was probably struck as a compliment to Alexander." [*NL 68*]

4728 **Hurter, Silvia M.** "Die Nike von Mytilene: Eine Anonyme Siegesprägung." *Schweitzer Münzblätter* (Switzerland) 51 (2001): 21-2. Illus.

4729 **Lazzarini, Lorenzo.** "A Contribution to the Study of the Archaic Billon Coinage of Lesbos." *Coins in the Aegean Islands. Proceedings of the Fifth Scientific Meeting, Mytilene, 16-29 September 2006. Volume 1: Ancient Times.* Obolos 9. Edited by Panagiotis Tselekas. Athens: The Friends of the Numismatic Museum, 2010. Pages 83-111.

4730 **Marotta, Michael.** "Electrum Sixths and the Treaty of Mytilene." *Classical Numismatic Review* (Lancaster, Pennsylvania) 20-2 (summer 1995): 7-8. Illus.
Discusses a treaty between Phokaia and Mytilene, ca. 400 B.C., in which the two cities agreed on a common coinage. Discusses terms of the treaty and the composition of the resulting electrum hektai. [Also see Healy "Notes on the Monetary Union" above].

4731 **McDowall, Katharine A.** "Two Heads Related to the Choiseul-Gouffier Type." *Journal of Hellenic Studies* 24 (1904): 203-7. Illus.
McDowall finds a stylistic parallel between the Apollo head on the unique stater of Mytilene and a sculptured head in the British Museum—the Choiseul-Gouffier Apollo. [J. F. Healy disagrees. See *Note 17* of Healy's essay "A New Light on the Unique Stater of Mytilene" (see above)].

4732 **Ralli, Euterpe, and M. Kombou.** "Mytilene: The Hoard of Krene Street." *Coins in the Aegean Islands. Proceedings of the Fifth Scientific Meeting, Mytilene, 16-29 September 2006. Volume 1: Ancient Times.* Obolos 9. Edited by Panagiotis Tselekas. Athens: The Friends of the Numismatic Museum, 2010. Pages 171-83.

4733 **Ralli-Photopoulou, Euterpe, and Constantinos Lagos.** "The Coinage of Eresos (4th c. B.C. – 3rd c. A.D.)." *Nomismatika Khronika* (Greece) 20 (2001): 45-70. Illus.
Eresos, located on the western part of the island of Lesbos, began coinage in the fourth century B.C. and continued until the mid-third century A.D. (Roman Imperial issues). Most likely, the city only struck bronze coinage. The authors describe and catalogue the coin types, and comment on chronology.

4734 **Rougou, K.** "Ein 'Hortfund' Bronze und Silber Münzen aus dem Grundstück, P. Vousvounis im Gebiet Perama auf Lesbos." *Coins in the Aegean Islands. Proceedings of the Fifth Scientific Meeting, Mytilene, 16-29 September 2006. Volume 1: Ancient Times.* Obolos 9. Edited by Panagiotis Tselekas. Athens: The Friends of the Numismatic Museum, 2010. Pages 155-69.

4735 **Rynearson, Paul.** "The Electrum Coinage of Lesbos: A Brief Introduction." *SAN—Journal of the Society for Ancient Numismatics* 1, no. 2 (October 1969): 24.
Describes three classes of early electrum coins of Lesbos.

4736 **Tameanko, Marvin.** "The Poetess Sappho on Ancient Coinage." *The Anvil* (Canada) 3, no. 2 (March 1, 1993): 11-12, 14. Illus.
A biography of Sappho, the famous female poet from the island of Lesbos. Illustrates a coin of Mytilene with a portrait of Aphrodite that some say is Sappho. Also illustrates several Roman coins depicting the poetess.

4737 **Tselekas, Panagiotis.** "Countermarks on the Hellenistic Coinages of Lesbos." *Coins in the Aegean Islands. Proceedings of the Fifth Scientific Meeting, Mytilene, 16-29 September 2006. Volume 1: Ancient Times.* Obolos 9. Edited by Panagiotis Tselekas. Athens: The Friends of the Numismatic Museum, 2010. Pages 127-53.

4738 **Vavliakis, G., and F. Lyrou.** "The Koinon of the Lesbians through the Coin Evidence." *Coins in the Aegean Islands. Proceedings of the Fifth Scientific Meeting, Mytilene, 16-29 September 2006. Volume 1: Ancient Times.* Obolos 9. Edited by Panagiotis Tselekas. Athens: The Friends of the Numismatic Museum, 2010. Pages 113-25.

Also see: Acheilara "The Messon Sanctuary of Lesbos through the Coin Evidence" under HOARDS; Balcer "Peparethos: Further Notes" under NORTHERN GREECE—THESSALY; Bodenstedt *Die Elektronprägung* under IONIA; Bodenstedt and Reimers "Zerstorungsfreie Bestimmung der Legierungsbestandteile" under METALLURGY; Caskey "Greek Electrum Coins" under ASIA MINOR—GENERAL WORKS; Kiechle "Literaturüberblick" under MYSIA—AUTONOMOUS CITIES; Healy "The Establishment of Die-Sequences" under METALLURGY; Healy "Mint Practice at Mytilene" under THE MINTING PROCESS; Healy "The Use of Sicilian and Magna Graecian Types" under TYPES; Kourtzellis "Coins from the Ancient Harbour Installations in the Northern Port of Mytilene" under HOARDS; Mackil and van Alfen "Cooperative Coinage" under GENERAL WORKS—GREEK; Wells "A Note on Coin-Plating with Electrum" under THE MINTING PROCESS; Wroth *Catalogue of Greek Coins* under TROAS; Wroth "Greek Coins Acquired by the British Museum in 1889" under PUBLIC COLLECTIONS—GREAT BRITAIN (LONDON).

IONIA

If the coinage of a city is to be taken as in any way proportionate to its commercial prosperity, we shall be inclined to assign to Ephesus by no means the first place among the trading cities of the coast of Asia Minor during this period. On the other hand it is probable that the chief of her trade continued to be carried on with the interior of Asia Minor in uncoined metal, and that the circulation of the municipal currency did not extend beyond the territory of the city and the markets of the neighbouring Ionian towns.

—Barclay V. Head, 1880

4739   **Amandry, Michel.** "Les Tétradrachmes à la Couronne de Feuillage Frappés à Lébedos (Ionie)." *Kraay—Mørkholm Essays: Numismatic Studies in Memory of C. M. Kraay and O. Mørkholm.* Numismatica Lovaniensia 10. Edited by G. Le Rider, G. K. Jenkins, N. Waggoner, and U. Westermark. Louvain-la-Neuve: Université Catholique de Louvain, 1989. Pages 1-7. 1 pl.
Catalogues 32 tetradrachms of Lebedos, with analysis and commentary.

4740   ——— "Une Monnaie de la Cité Ionienne D'Airai." *Pour Denyse: Divertissements Numismatiques.* Edited by S. Hurter and C. Arnold-Biucchi. Bern, Switzerland: Privately published, 2000. Pages 11-2. Illus., map.
Examines a bronze coin of Airai with Apollo/eagle.

4741   **Balcer, Jack M.** "The Early Silver Coinage of Teos." *Revue Suisse de Numismatique* (Switzerland) 47 (1968): 5-51. 9 pls. [CS 2736]
"Based mainly on a stylistic analysis of the 130 known staters, this study demonstrates that the early silver coins of Teos struck on the Aeginetan standard are to be classified in three periods, 540-478, 478-449, and 412-407 B.C. The opinion that the Athenian currency decree of ca. 449 was not applied to Teos is rejected." [H. Isler, *NL* 84]

4742   ——— "Phokaia and Teos: A Monetary Alliance." *Revue Suisse de Numismatique* (Switzerland) 49 (1970): 25-46. Illus. [CS 2724]
"In the early spring of 412 B.C., following the Ionian Revolt against Athens, Phocaea and Teos concluded a monetary alliance similar to the alliance which Phocaea later contracted with Mytilene, ca. 394 B.C. The measures were to prevent a serious economic inflation and crisis at a time when the Athenian international silver tetradrachm had failed. Upon Teos' brief series of silver staters, the Teian minters struck Teian "griffins" with Phocaean "seals" which denote the alliance and the long mythological and sociological relations between the two states. The alliance, however, did not last more than five years. With the further economic decline of the Attic standard, many Ionian states, including Teos, abandoned their former monetary standards and adopted the Chian standard and new types in an attempt to seek that economic stability once offered by the Athenian *moneta franca*." [J. Balcer, *NL* 87]

4743   **Betancourt, Philip P.** "A Hoard of Bronze Coins from Erythrae." *Museum Notes* 17 (1971): 23-39.
Catalogues a hoard of forty-two Erythraean bronzes, divided into nine types. The evidence provided, including epigraphical evidence, sheds light on a portion of the Erythraean minor currency.

4744   **Bodenstedt, Friedrich.** "Studien zur Elektronprägung von Phokaia und Mytilene." *Revue Suisse de Numismatique* (Switzerland) 52 (1973): 17-51. 10 pls. [CS 2725]
A study of the electrum coinage of Phocaea and Mytilene.

4745   ——— *Phokäisches Elekton-Geld von 600-326 v. Chr.* Studien zur Bedeutung und zu den Wandlungen einer Antiken Goldwährung. Mainz: Philip von Zabern, 1976. 170 pp., illus. [CS 2726]

4746   ——— "Satrapen und Dynasten auf Phokäischen Hekten." *Schweizer Münzblätter* (Switzerland) 26, no. 104 (1976): 69-75. Illus. [CS 2727]

4747   ——— *Die Elektronmünzen von Phokaia und Mytilene.* Tübingen: Verlag Ernst Wasmuth, 1981. 390 pp., 63 pls. [CS 2730]
A full die study of the electrum coinages of Phocaea and Mytilene. The standard reference for these coins. Includes extensive discussion of the coinage, the city sites, and a complete catalogue of coin varieties. Numerous maps, plates of enlargements, and plates illustrating all varieties.

4748   **Borrell, H. P.** "Restitution to the City of Ephesus (when Called Arsinoe) of the Coins Hitherto Attributed to Arsinoe, in Cyrenaica, and to Arsinoe, in Cilicia." *Numismatic Chronicle* 2 (1840): 171-6.

Argues that the city of Ephesus was known as "Arsinoe" during the latter period of the reign of Lysimachus. Attributes several coins to this city which were previously assigned to the cities of Arsinoe in Cyrenaica and Cilicia.

4749 **Broughton, T. R. S.** "A Significant Break in the Cistophoric Coinage of Asia." *American Journal of Archaeology* 41 (1937): 248-9.
Suggests an explanation for the cessation of cistophoric coinage at Ephesus between 67-58 B.C. Presents evidence that the Roman government was conserving the supply of precious metals for its own purposes.

4750 **Cahn, Herbert A.** "Ionische Damen." *Studies in Greek Numismatics in Memory of Martin Jessop Price.* Edited by Richard Ashton and Silvia Hurter. London: Spink, 1998. Pages 59-63. 2 pls.

4751 **Cahn, Herbert A., and Dominique Gerin.** "Themistocles at Magnesia." *Numismatic Chronicle* 148 (1988): 13-20. 2 pls.
Examines the coins struck by Themistocles at Magnesia (ca. 460 B.C.) after his banishment from Athens. Examines weights and types. Suggests some of the coins bear his portrait—the first to appear on coins. [Also see Cahn and Mannsperger "Themistocles" below, Smith "From Themistokles" below, and Nollé "Münzen" below].

4752 **Cahn, Herbert A., and Dietrich Mannsperger.** "Themistocles Again." *Numismatic Chronicle* 151 (1991): 199-202. 1 pl.
"The note publishes two additions to the article by H. A. Cahn and D. Gerin "Themistocles at Magnesia" (see Cahn and Gerin above). D. Mannsperger describes in detail an Attic tetartemorion, already published (*SNG* Tübingen 4, Munich 1989, no. 1922) which shows a bearded head (*obv.*) and a flying eagle set diagonally in an incuse square (*rev.*). H. A. Cahn returns to a coin which appeared in Hess-Leu Sales 24, Lucerne 1964, no. 210, perhaps an Attic diobol (1.16 g: *obv.* bearded head, *rev.* eagle head in an incuse square, legend A - M), which had been tentatively attributed to Methymna. Both coins belong to the coinage issued by Themistocles at Magnesia in Ionia. This coinage shows a great variety of types in the small denominations. It is suggested that both coins show the portrait of the statesman as on the Oxford and Munich coins published previously." [Cahn and Mannsperger, *NL* 129]

4753 **Dengate, James A.** *The Coinage of Klazomenai: A Dissertation in Classical Archaeology, Presented to the University of Pennsylvania, 1967.* University Microfilms International, 1988. 270 pages, 6 pls.

4754 ——— "A Mint for the Coinage of the Ionian Revolt." *American Journal of Archaeology* 72, no. 2 (April 1968): 164.
The summary of a paper presented at a meeting of the Archaeological Institute of America in 1967. A study of the electrum staters thought to have been minted by the Ionian cities which revolted against Persia in 499 B.C. suggests that Klazomenai may have been the mint of these coins. Despite the diversity of types, all may have come from one mint.

4755 **Deppert-Lippitz, B.** *Die Münzprägung Milets vom Vierten bis Ersten Jahrhundert v. Chr.* Typos 5. Aarau/Frankfurt/Salzburg, 1984. 233 pp., 36 pls.
A study of the coinage of Miletus.

4756 **Eaglen, Robin J.** "Portraits of Greek Coinage 31: Clazomenae." *Spink Numismatic Circular* 118, no. 1 (March 2010): 12-3. Illus.
In this installment of his on-going series, the author examines the history and coinage of Clazomenae.

4757 **Gardner, Percy.** "The Coinage of the Ionian Revolt." *Journal of Hellenic Studies* 31 (1911): 151-60. 1 pl.; 33 (1913): 105. Also appeared in *Numismatic Report* (Cyprus) 22-25 (1991-94): 85-96. Illus. [CS 2591a]
"The author puts forward the theory that when the revolt of the cities of the Ionian coast and the Ionian islands took place against the Persian King, all participants agreed to an electrum coinage of a uniform standard. As Cyprus had participated in the revolt, the author suggests that certain coins of Salamis, struck by the successors of Evelthon, are in fact coins struck when the Cypriots had united with the Ionians in the revolt against Persia." [M. Santamas, *NL* 135]

4758 **Georges, Pericles B.** "Persian Ionia under Darius: The Revolt Reconsidered." *Historia* (Germany) 1, no. 49 (2000): 1-39.
"In the first chapter, the wealth of Persian Ionia, Greek silver coinages and their circulation around 500 B.C. are sketched." [H. Baldus, *NL* 144]

4759 **Gillespie, J.** "ΚΟΙΝΟΝ ΙΓ ΠΟΛΕΩΝ: A Study of the Coinage of the 'Ionian League.'" *Revue Belge de Numismatique et de Sigillographie* (Belgium) 102 (1956): 31-53.

4760 **Head, Barclay V.** "Ephesus and its Coinage." *Canadian Antiquarian and Numismatic Journal* (Canada) 9, no. 1 (July 1880): 8-10. Also appeared in *American Journal of Numismatics* 15, no. 2 (October 1880): 26-7.
This brief article, which was originally published in *Saturday Review*, discusses the types of the coins of Ephesus and the use of magistrates' names on the coins. Head suggests that the magistrates held an annual office.

4761 ——— "On the Chronological Sequence of the Coins of Ephesus." *Numismatic Chronicle* new ser., 20 (1880): 85-173. Also an offprint, London: Rollin & Feuardent, 1880. Reprinted as *History of the Coinage of Ephesus.* Chicago: Obol International, 1979. 89 pp., 5 pls. [CS 2719]
Discusses the chronology of the coins of Ephesus from their beginning down to the time of Augustus. Segregates the study into historical periods. Begins with a review of the history of the city during the period under examination, then describes the coinage of the period. Through an analysis of the magistrates' names which appear on the coins, Head attempts to determine the duration of each coin-issue and assign each to a particular historical period. Summarizes Ephesian coinage in a table split into ten time periods and indicates the number of known mint magistrates for each period. Concludes that the magistrate whose name appears regularly on the coinage is an annual magistrate and that this magistrate was the first Prytanis, who at Ephesus was the President of the Committee of Prytaneis. Includes an alphabetized list of the Prytaneis showing their dates of office. [Also see Head "Addenda Et Corrigenda" below].

4762 ——— "Coinage of Ephesus—Addenda Et Corrigenda." *Numismatic Chronicle* 3rd ser., 1 (1881): 13-23.
A follow-up to Head's paper on the coinage of Ephesus (see Head "On the Chronological Sequence" above). Adds seventy-seven new names to the list of magistrates and corrects a few erroneous readings. Modifies the conclusions reached previously. The new names partially invalidate his conclusion that

the magistrate whose name appears on coins was an annual magistrate. There are now too many names for the number of years in some periods of coinage. Lists the new names and provides commentary on the effects on the groupings given earlier.

4763 ——— *Catalogue of Greek Coins of Ionia.* Edited by R. S. Poole. London: British Museum, 1892. Reprint, Bologna: Forni, 1964. lvii, 453 pp., 39 pls. [CS 2714]
Volume 16 of the *Catalogue of Greek Coins in the British Museum.* Fifty-seven pages of introductory text precede the 453-page catalogue of coins. [Also see *Catalogue of Greek Coins in the British Museum* under PUBLIC COLLECTIONS—GREAT BRITAIN (LONDON)].

4764 **Heyman, Carlo.** "Homer on Coins from Smyrna." *Studia Paulo Naster Oblata, 1. Numismatica Antiqua.* Edited by S. Scheers. Louvain: Department Oriëntalistiek, 1982. Pages 161-74, including 1 pl.
Smyrna claimed to be the home of Homer and he appears on their coins beginning ca. 190 B.C. Discusses the bronze coins minted 190-30 B.C. showing Homer. Discusses the source of the type and concludes that a model was used. Discusses its style. Other coins of Smyrna showing Homer are discussed: a silver drachm minted 190-170 B.C., a coin issued under Nero (A.D. 54-68), and a coin of the second century A.D. Discusses the source of the Homer image used on each coin.

4764a **Horne, Lauren.** "The Problem of the Autonomous Wreathed Coinage of Asia Minor." *Coins from Asia Minor and the East: Selections from the Colin E. Pitchfork Collection.* Ancient Coins in Australian Collections 2. Adelaide, Australia: Australian Centre for Ancient Numismatic Studies/Numismatic Association of Australia, 2011. Pages 35-40.

4765 **Hurter, Silvia.** "42 Tetradrachmen von Klazomeai: Ein Fundbericht." *Revue Suisse de Numismatique* (Switzerland) 45 (1966): 26-35. 7 pls. [CS 2716]

4766 ——— "Teos over Tanagra." *Florilegium Numismaticum: Studia in Honorem U. Westermark Edita.* Edited by Harald Nilsson. Stockholm: Svenska Numismatiska Föreningen, 1992. Pages 171-3. Illus.
Publishes a silver stater of Teos which was struck over a coin of Tanagra. The Tanagra coin bore the Boeotian shield on the obverse and was struck ca. 456-446 B.C. Hurter comments on the implications for the chronology of the coins of Teos and suggests that the commonly accepted terminal date of 449 for the coinage of Teos can no longer be accepted.

4767 **Isik, E.** *Elektronstatere aus Klazomenei: Der Schatzfund von 1989.* Saarbrücken Studien zur Archäologie und alten Geschichte 5. Saarbrücken, 1992. 59 pp., 8 pls.

4768 **Jenkins, G. Kenneth.** "Hellenistic Gold Coins of Ephesos." *Festschrift Akurgal.* Anadolu 21 (1978-80). Ankara, 1987. Pages 183-8.

4769 **Jones, Nicholas F.** "The Autonomous Wreathed Tetradrachms of Magnesia On-Maeander." *Museum Notes* 24 (1979): 63-109. 7 pls.
Examines the wreathed tetradrachms struck by the autonomous city of Magnesia, based on a study of 243 coins—many from the Kirikhan hoard. Discusses the chronology of the issues, which are divided into eight groups based on the signatures found on the reverses. Provides diagrams of die links. Reviews hoard evidence and suggests the series was minted ca. 155-140 B.C. Suggests the names on the reverse dies may be those of men selected by the state to contribute toward the production of this new silver coinage. Presents the text of a contemporary decree suggesting the existence of such liturgies. Discusses the historical background for this coinage and presents a catalogue of the coins.

4770 **Karwiese, Stefan.** "The Artemisium Coin Hoard and the First Electrum Coins of Ephesus." *Revue Belge de Numismatique et de Sigillographie* (Belgium) 137 (1991): 1-28.

4771 ——— *Die Münzprägung von Ephesos. I. Die Anfänge: Due ältesten Prägungen und der Beginn der Münzprägung Überhaupt.* Wien: Böhlau Verlag, 1995. 207 pp., 8 pls.
A study of the first coins of Ephesos struck in electrum and silver, presented within their historical framework. Examines the metrology of the coins and includes a catalogue of types. [Reviewed by Ute Wartenberg in *Revue Suisse de Numismatique* (Switzerland) 76 (1997): 263-7].

4772 **Kienast, Dietmar.** "Literaturüberblick der Griechischen Numismatik: Ionien." *Jahrbuch für Numismatik und Geldsseschichte* (Germany) 12 (1962): 113-98. [CS 2712]
A bibliography.

4773 ——— "Bemerkungen zum Jonischen Aufstand und zur Rolle des Artaphernes." *Historia* (Germany) 51, no. 1 (2002): 1-31.
"On pp. 14-16 the author describes the electrum coinage of the Ionian confederation during the Revolt of 499 B.C." [H. Baldus, *NL* 145]

4774 **Kinns, Philip.** *Studies in the Coinage of Ionia: Erythrae, Teos, Lebedus, Colophon, c. 400-30 B.C.* Ph.D. dissertation. University of Cambridge, 1980.

4775 ——— "The Coinage of Miletus." *Numismatic Chronicle* 146 (1986): 233-60.
"An extended review of B. Deppert-Lippitz, *Die Münzprägung Milets vom vierten bis ersten Jahrhundert v. Chr.*, Typos 5, Aarau-Franfurt am Main-Salzburg, 1984, presents substantial additions and corrections. Deppert-Lippitz's approach to the organization and interpretation of her material comes under scrutiny, and it is argued that the second century gold staters (e.g., *BMC* 112-114), which she has condemned as false, must in fact be authentic. Significant changes to the relative and absolute chronology of this coinage are proposed." [P. Kinns, *NL* 118]. [Also see Kinns "*CH* 8, 474" below].

4776 ——— "Ionia: The Pattern of Coinage during the Last Century of the Persian Empire." *Revue des Études Anciennes* (France) 91, no. 1-2 (1989): 183-93.

"This article discusses the coinages issued by the cities of mainland Ionia between c. 404 and c. 332, and attempts to assess their significance and relative importance. Whereas many of these coinages were clearly intended for local use only, the electrum sixths of Phocaea and the silver tetradrachms of Ephesus stand out as series struck on a large scale and enjoying wide circulation." [*Revue des Études Anciennes*]

4777 ——— "Two Studies in the Silver Coinage of Magnesia on the Maeander." *Kraay—Mørkholm Essays: Numismatic Studies in Memory of C. M. Kraay and O. Mørkholm.* Numismatica Lovaniensia 10. Edited by G. Le Rider, G. K. Jenkins, N. Waggoner, and U. Westermark. Louvain-la-Neuve: Université Catholique de Louvain, 1989. Pages 137-48. 2 pls.

Examines: (1) The "Persic" didrachms (horseman/butting bull types) which the author dates to ca. 210-200 B.C. Fourteen such specimens are listed. (2) A series of three silver denominations which represent the last appearance at Magnesia of the standard horseman/butting bull in maeander-circle types. These bear alphabetical marks of value and were issued ca. 155-145 B.C. The corpus of twelve specimens is listed. The author suggests this value-marked coinage was influenced by Seleucid coinage.

4778 ——— "A Group of Coins from Colophon." *Coin Hoards, Volume VIII: Greek Hoards.* Edited by U. Wartenberg, M. J. Price, and K. A. McGregor. London: Royal Numismatic Society, 1994. Pages 90-2.

Brief list of thirty-six coins of Colophon and two coins of Miletus from a hoard (*Coin Hoards VIII*, no. 599) that appeared on the market in 1983. The group also included twelve coins of Colophon that were possible intrusions in the hoard, plus a few other coins.

4779 ——— "CH 8, 474: Milesian Silver Coinage in the Second Century B.C." *Studies in Greek Numismatics in Memory of Martin Jessop Price.* Edited by Richard Ashton and Silvia Hurter. London: Spink, 1998. Pages 175-95. 9 pls.

Examines a hoard containing one didrachm, 215 drachms, and 289 hemidrachms of Miletus. The coins belong to Deppert-Lippitz's period V (ca. 225-195 B.C.) (see Deppert-Lippitz, *Die Münzprägung Milets* above). The hoard contained many types not listed by Deppert-Lippitz. Includes a catalogue of the hoard and an extensive discussion of the coins. [Also see Kinns "The Coinage of Miletus" above].

4780 ——— "The Attic Weight Drachms of Ephesos: A Preliminary Study in the Light of Recent Hoards." *Numismatic Chronicle* 159 (1999): 47-97. 6 pls.

A re-examination of the series, based on a study of 590 coins. Discusses the contents of eight hoards.

4781 ——— "A New Didrachm of Magnesia on the Meander." *Numismatic Chronicle* 166 (2006): 41-7. 1 pl.

A previously unknown didrachm of Magnesia on the Meander appeared on the market in 2003. The types are draped bust of Artemis/grazing stag and magistrate name ΜΑΙΑΝΔΡΙΟΣ ΑΡΤΕΜΙΔ[ΩΡΟ]Υ. The author attempts to offer an interpretation of this coin. He suggests the coin provides evidence that the city sided with Mithradates and that the coin was struck ca. 88-85 B.C.

4782 ——— "The Coinage of Leukai." *Onomatologos: Studies in Greek Personal Names Presented to Elaine Matthews.* Edited by R. W. V. Catling, F. Marchand, and M. Sasanow. Oxford: Oxbow Books, 2010. 3 pls.

The coinage of the small city of Leukai, founded ca. 383 B.C., preserves an archives of twenty-eight personal names but has not been the subject of any previous study. This article presents a corpus of over 300 coins (mostly bronze) and discusses their chronology and significance in relation to the history and coinage of neighboring Klazomenai. Evidence suggests that the coinage ceased before the arrival of Alexander.

4783 **Kleiner, Fred S.** "The Dated Cistophori of Ephesus." *Museum Notes* 18 (1972): 17-32. 5 pls. [CS 2604]

Examines the dated cistophori of Ephesus. It was previously thought that these coins were not dated until after the formation of the Roman Province of Asia in 134/133 B.C. Presents a corpus of the known specimens of years A, B, K, and AK (1, 2, 20, and 21). Concludes that the coins marked K and AK were minted in the twentieth and twenty-first years of the reign of Attalus II (140/139 and 139/138 B.C.); those marked A and B were minted in the first two years of the reign of Attalus III (139/138 and 138/137 B.C.). These date markings demonstrate the political influence of Pergamum over the coinage of its possessions in Asia Minor. Also lists all issues of dated Ephesus cistophori after 134 B.C., representing most years from 133 to 67 B.C. This suggests these were a continuous series of annual emissions. Discusses the symbols and monograms, which Kleiner believes are the personal marks of mint magistrates. Also discusses some cistophoric coins struck over other coins. Suggests that the overstriking was done because foreign coins were not legal tender in Attalid territory.

4784 **Kraay, Colin M.** "Monnaies Provenant du Site de Colophon." *Revue Suisse de Numismatique* (Switzerland) 42 (1962-1963): 5-13. 1 pl. [CS 2717]

4785 **Lawson, A. J.** "Unpublished Coins of Ephesus." *Numismatic Chronicle* 3rd ser., 2 (1882): 351.

Lists seven varieties of bronze coins of Ephesus not listed by Head. [See Head "On the Chronological Sequence" above].

4786 **Lorber, Catharine C., and Oliver D. Hoover.** "An Unpublished Tetradrachm Issued by the Artists of Dionysos." *Numismatic Chronicle* 163 (2003): 59-68. 3 pls.

Publishes a tetradrachm issued not by a polis, but by a professional guild—an association of Dionysiac artists. Associations of this type were formed primarily to protect the artists as they crossed political boundaries to participate in dramatic and music festivals. The coin appeared on the market in 2001. It was likely struck at Teos, ca. 155-145 B.C. It bears strong stylistic similarities to the wreathed tetradrachms of Myrina.

4787 **MacDonald, David J.** "A Teos/Abdera Overstrike." *Schweizer Münzblätter* (Switzerland) 44, no. 174 (1994): 37-40.

4788 ——— "A Note on *CH VIII*, no. 47: Ionia 1983." *Numismatic Chronicle* 155 (1995): 321-3. 1 pl.

Examines a hoard of staters of Teos discovered in Anatolia in 1983. The hoard was quickly dispersed. It may have contained 100-300 staters, beginning with the earliest issues, ca. 460 B.C. It included at least five overstruck staters. MacDonald discusses chronological issues and suggests a burial date of ca. 445-435 B.C.

4789 **Madsen, Eardley.** "Miletus." *SAN—Journal of the Society for Ancient Numismatics* 15, no. 3 (fall 1984): inside covers.

A brief history of the city of Miletus, illustrated by a silver diobol.

4790 **Marotta, Michael E.** "Two Unpublished Archaic Coins of Miletos." *The Anvil* (Canada) 6, no. 1 (January 1, 1996): 1. Illus.
Describes and illustrates two electrum sixth-staters of Miletos with *obv.*, recumbent lion and *rev.*, complex pattern of punches. The reverse punch marks on these coins are unlike those on archaic coins of Miletos published in reference books. The author seeks further information on these coins.

4791 ——— "Kolophon: A Quiet Place to Raise a Family." *The Celator* 11, no. 8 (August 1997): 32-5. Illus.
Begins with a summary of the history of the city of Kolophon. Highlights the famous people who lived in the city during ancient times. Then the author briefly describes the coins of Kolophon, their types, denominations, and weight standards.

4792 ——— "Archaic Greek Gold Coin, One of Three Known, Sets Record." *Coin World* (May 22, 2000): 1, 93. Illus.
Reports that an electrum stater struck by Phanes was recently sold at auction for 480,000 Swiss Francs. It bears the legend "I am of Phanes." Discusses the significance of the coin and describes how it differs from the other two known similar specimens. [Also see Newton "On an Electrum Stater" below and "Record Price" below].

4793 **Mattingly, Harold B.** "A New Light on the Early Silver Coinage of Teos." *Revue Suisse de Numismatique* (Switzerland) 66 (1987): 79-85. Illus.
"Based on a stater of Teos overstruck on a datable Boeotian coin, the author strongly advocates that Teian coinage did not come to an end in ca. 449 B.C. but continued for another decade or so, thus furnishing an additional argument in favor of the 'low' dating of the Athenian Coinage Decree." [*NL* 133]. [This essay was reprinted in Mattingly's *From Coins to History: Selected Numismatic Studies*. See Mattingly under GENERAL WORKS—GREEK].

4794 **Matzke, M.** "Die frühe Münzpraegung von Teos in Ionien: Chronologische und Metrologische Untersuchungen um die Frühzeit der Silbermünzpraegung." *Jahrbuch für Numismatik und Geldgeschichte* (Germany) 50 (2000): 21-53.

4795 **McFadden, Eric J.** "A Hoard of Early Multi-Denominational Electrum Coins." *SAN—Journal of the Society for Ancient Numismatics* 21 (2002): 17-9. Illus.
Discusses a hoard of thirty-nine electrum coins which entered the numismatic trade in 1997. The hoard was composed of "geometric" types including trites, hectes, hemihectes, and obols. The coins likely were struck in Ionia in the late seventh to mid-sixth century B.C. Lists the quantities and weights of the coins. Presents a brief metrological analysis showing the coins contain about 40% gold on average. Also mentions that a 1/48 stater and a stater that later appeared on the market. These pieces were likely from the same hoard. Although this series of coins was previously published, some of the denominations had not been previously known.

4796 **Meadows, Andrew R.** "The Hellenistic Silver Coinage of Clazomenae." *Ancient History, Numismatics, and Epigraphy in the Mediterranean World: Studies in Memory of Clemens E. Bosch and Sabahat Atlan and in Honor of Nezahat Baydur.* Edited by Oguz Tekin. Instanbul: Ege, 2009. Pages 247-62.

4797 **Milne, Joseph G.** "The Silver Coinage of Smyrna." *Numismatic Chronicle* 4th ser., 14 (1914): 273-98. 3 pls. [CS 2734]
Discusses the tetradrachms and drachms struck at Smyrna in the second and first centuries B.C. Milne attempts to identify the magistrates whose names appear on the coins, and to put them into chronological order.

4798 ——— "A Hoard of Bronze Coins of Smyrna." *Numismatic Chronicle* 4th ser., 16 (1916): 246-50.
Discusses a hoard of seventy-four bronze coins acquired by the British Museum. All of the coins are from Smyrna. Discusses the magistrates' names and monograms found on the coins.

4799 ——— "Silver Drachma of Smyrna." *Numismatic Chronicle* 5th ser., 1 (1921): 143-4. 1 pl.
Discusses a previously unpublished drachm of Smyrna (Apollo/Homer) and assigns it to ca. 180 B.C.

4800 ——— "The Autonomous Coinage of Smyrna." Parts 1-3. *Numismatic Chronicle* 5th ser., 3 (1923): 1-30. 2 pls.; 7 (1927): 1-107. 5 pls.; 8 (1928): 131-71. 2 pls. [CS 2735]
This discussion of the coinage of Smyrna begins in 304 B.C. Milne divides the coinage into seven periods. Lists the types and discusses the magistrates and their chronology. Part 3 includes an index of magistrates' names.

4801 ——— "The Persian Standard in Ionia, ca. 320-280 B.C." *Numismatic Chronicle* 5th ser., 4 (1924): 19-30.
Milne examines the change from the Rhodian weight standard to the Ionian standard which took place in the coins of several Ionian cities in the period 320-280 B.C. He suggests that these cities began to use Persian sigloi as their coin blanks without any adjustment in weight.

4802 ——— "The Use of *Cognomina* at Smyrna." *Numismatic Chronicle* 5th ser., 4 (1924): 316-8.
Lists the magistrates' names on coins of Smyrna which may be taken as *cognomina*. Milne points out that this is the only city in the Greek world at which *cognomina* occur on coins.

4803 ——— *Kolophon and its Coinage: A Study*. Numismatic Notes and Monographs, No. 96. New York: American Numismatic Society, 1941. 113 pp., 19 pls. [CS 2718]
A detailed discussion of the coins of Kolophon from their beginning ca. 525 B.C. through the Roman period. The development of types, denominations, and chronology are reviewed. Lists 276 coin types. Includes a table of minting officials during both the autonomous and Imperial periods. [Reviewed by W. Wallace in *American Journal of Archaeology* 48 (1944): 112-3].

4804 **Moustaka, Aliki, and Panagiotis Tselekas.** "Coins from the Excavations of G. Oikonomos at Klazomenai in 1921." *Klazomenai, Teos and Abdera: Metropoleis and Colony. Proceedings of the International Symposium Held at the Archaeological Museum of Abdera, 20-21 October 2001.* Thessaloniki 2004. Edited by A. Moustaka, E. Skarlatidou, M.-C. Tzannes and Y. E. Ersoy. Pages 161-8.

4804a **Müller, Jörg W.** "The Chronology of Ephesos Revisited." *Revue Suisse de Numismatique* (Switzerland) 77 (1998): 73-80. Illus.

4805 **Newton, Charles T.** "On an Electrum Stater, Possibly of Ephesus." *Numismatic Chronicle* new ser., 10 (1870): 237-9. Illus.
Illustrates a stater with *obv.*, stag and legend ΦΑΕΝΟΡΕΜΙΣΕΜΑ; *rev.*, incuse punch. Mionnet had attributed the coin to Erythrae in Ionia. The author reads the inscription (EMI ΣHMA) as "I am the coin." He suggests that ΦΑΕΝΟΡ is probably not the name of a place. He suggests the coin was minted at Ephesus. [The inscription on this now-famous coin is currently interpreted as "I am the badge of Phanes." Also see Gardner's comments on the coin, "Numismatic Reattributions" under GENERAL WORKS—GREEK. Also see Fort "Badge of Phanes" under ORIGINS OF COINAGE, and "Record Price" below].

4806 **Nollé, Johannes.** "Münzen und Alte Geschichte: Neues von Themistokles!" *Antike Welt* (Germany) 34, no. 2 (2003): 189-98. Illus.
"The history and coinage of Themistokles as lord of Ionian Magnesia-ad-Maeandrum and of his son and successor, Archepolis, is illustrated by, among other things, coins of Magnesia and a hitherto unpublished bronze coin of Ionian Myus/Myes (*obv.*, Laureate head of Apollo r.; *rev.*, MY-H; fish r., all within Maeander circle)." [H. R. Baldus, *NL* 147]. [Also see Nollé and Wenninger "Themistokles" below, and Smith "From Themistokles" below].

4807 **Nollé, Johannes, and A. Wenninger.** "Themistokles und Archepolis." *Jahrbuch für Numismatik und Geldgeschichte* (Germany) 48 (1998).
[Also see Nollé "Münzen" above].

4808 **Oman, Charles W. C.** "Unpublished or Rare Coins of Smyrna in the Bodleian Cabinet." *Numismatic Chronicle* 3rd ser., 20 (1900): 203-8.
Publishes twenty-five coins of Smyrna from the collection of the Bodleian Library. Some of the types were previously unpublished. Others are new varieties of known types. Includes sixteen Greek and nine Roman Provincial issues.

4809 **Pfeiler, Bärbel.** "Die Silberprägung von Milet im 6. Jahrhundert v. Chr." *Revue Suisse de Numismatique* (Switzerland) 45 (1966): 5-25. 1 pl. [CS 2721]

4810 **Rakicic, Mark.** "The Bees of Ephesos." *The Celator* 8, no. 12 (December 1994): 6-12. Illus.
Explores the symbolism of the bee found on the coins of Ephesus and the importance of bees and honey in the ancient world. Also discusses the multi-breasted cult idol which was popular at Ephesus, presenting alternate theories to explain the "breasts" (eggs, date-palms, etc.). [For further information on the significance of the bees, see Franck-Weiby's "Letter to the Editor" in *The Celator* 9, no. 1 (January 1995): 4, 40. For other opinions related to the "breasts," see Mørkholm "Some Pergamene Coins" under MYSIA—PERGAMENE KINGDOM, and Seltman "The Wardrobe of Artemis" under TYPES].

4811 "Record Price Set for an Archaic Greek Coin." *The Celator* 14, no. 5 (May 2000): 41, 50. Illus.
Reports that an electrum stater struck by Phanes, the first coin ever to bear a legend, was recently sold at auction for 480,000 Swiss Francs (approximately $290,000). The coin is thought to have been minted at Ephesus or Halicarnassus in the last quarter of the seventh century B.C. and is the third known example of the type. It bears the legend "I am of Phanes." Discusses the significance of the coin and the possible identity of Phanes. [Also see Newton "On an Electrum Stater" above and Marotta "Archaic Greek Gold Coin" above].

4812 **Regling, Kurt L.** "Phygela, Klazomenai, Amphipolis." *Zeitschrift für Numismatik* (Germany) 33 (1921): 46-67. [CS 2715]

4813 ——— *Die Münzen von Priene.* Berlin, 1927. 218 pp., 5 pls. [CS 2733]

4814 **Roebuck, Carl.** *Ionian Trade and Colonization.* New York: Archaeological Institute of America, 1959. 148 pp., maps.
A history of the economic development of the Ionians beginning with their appearance in the eleventh century B.C. Discusses population growth, colonization, mercenary service, and the development of a system of trade covering the Mediterranean basin. Examines the use of coinage which began in the Lydian-Ionian area, from where it spread to the rest of the ancient world. [Summarized from I. Merker, *NL* 57]

4815 **Smith, Derek R.** "From Themistokles, *Metroxenos*, to Perikles." *The Celator* 23, no. 2 (February 2009): 6-18. Illus.
Themistokles was a metroxenos—a son of an Athenian father and a foreign mother. Smith traces the life and travels of Themistokles, highlighted by contemporary coins minted at cities where Themistokles lived or played a role. Also discusses Themistokles' direct impact on the coinage, including the coins he minted in Magnesia-on-the-Meander before ca. 460 B.C. [These issues are explored further in Nollé and Wenninger "Themistokles und Archepolis" above].

4816 **Starck, Jeff.** "Tiny Coin's Origin Mystery for 2,000+ Years: Fourth Known Phanes Stater May Be from Ephesus." *Coin World* (March 8, 2010): 114-5. Illus.
Illustrates and discusses an electrum stater attributed to Phanes. It is said to be the fourth known specimen of the stater, and it will be sold in an upcoming Gorny & Mosch sale (March 2010). Provides some background information on the coin and other coins bearing inscriptions related to Phanes.

4817 **Sugden, Keith.** "Miniature Ionians and Carians." *Spink Numismatic Circular* 101, no. 6 (July 1993): 190-2. Illus.
Publishes a catalogue of fifty-one fractions from various Ionian and Carian cities. Each is illustrated. The coins may be from a recent hoard or hoards found in Turkey. The author comments on some of the coins.

4818 **Tameanko, Marvin.** "Priene: The Epitome of Hellenistic Cities." *The Journal of the Classical and Medieval Numismatic Society* (Canada) 2nd ser., 6, no. 5 (September 2005): 5-15. Illus.
Traces the history of the prosperous Ionian city of Priene from its founding through the Roman period. Describes the coins which circulated in the city throughout its history, including its own coinage.

4819 **Vagi, David L.** "A Rare Electrum Half Stater of Ephesus." *SAN—Journal of the Society for Ancient Numismatics* 19, no. 1 (1995): 13-4. Illus.
The author examines a previously unpublished electrum half-stater of Ephesus, dated to ca. 600-550 B.C. Points out stylistic variations from known Ephesian coins.

4820 **Weil, Rudolf.** "Themistokles als Herr von Magnesia." *Corolla Numismatica: Numismatic Essays in Honour of Barclay V. Head.* G. F. Hill. London: Oxford University Press, 1906. Pages 301-9. Illus.

4821 **Welz, Karl.** "Kleinmünzen aus Milets." *Schweizer Münzblätter* (Switzerland) 10, no. 40 (1961): 99-101. Illus. [CS 2722]

Also see: Adams "Aristonikos" under CAPPADOCIA; Ashton "Kaunos, not Miletos or Mylasa" under CARIA; Ashton, Hardwick, Konuk, and Meadows "Pixodarus Hoard" under HOARDS; Ashton and Kinns "Opuscula Anatolica II" and "Opuscula Anatonlica III" under ASIA MINOR—GENERAL WORKS; Ashton, Kinns, Konuk, and Meadows "Hecatomnus Hoard" under HOARDS; Baynham "Continuity and Ambition: The Posthumous Philip II Gold Staters from Colophon/Magnesia" under GENERAL WORKS—HELLENISTIC; Becker "Ein Fund von 75 Milesischen Obelen" under HOARDS; Bodenstedt "Observations" under LESBOS; Bodenstedt and Reimers "Zerstorungsfreie Bestimmung der Legierungsbestandteile" under METALLURGY; Cancio "A New Satrapal Coin" under PERSIA; Caskey "Greek Electrum Coins" under ASIA MINOR—GENERAL WORKS; Cawkwell "Heracles Coinage Alliance" under CARIA; Cook "Cnidian Peraea and Spartan Coins" under CARIA; Cowell et al. "Analyses" under LYDIA; Fort "The Badge of Phanes" under ORIGINS OF COINAGE.

Gardner "Numismatic Reattributions" under GENERAL WORKS—GREEK; Greenwell "On Some Rare Greek Coins" (1890) under PRIVATE COLLECTIONS; Head "Archaic Coins" (Clazomenae) under CYRENAICA; Healy "The Composition" under LESBOS; Healy "Mint Practice at Mytilene" under THE MINTING PROCESS; Healy "Notes on the Monetary Union" under LESBOS; Hoge "Some Ancient Greek Fractional Silver" under TROAS; Johnston "The Earliest Preserved Greek Map" under TYPES; Jones "Coins as Weights" under METROLOGY; Kern "Origins of Coinage" under ORIGINS OF COINAGE; Kim and Kroll "A Hoard of Archaic Coins of Colophon" under HOARDS; Konuk *From Kroisos to Karia* under PRIVATE COLLECTIONS; Linzalone *Electrum and the Invention of Coinage* under ORIGINS OF COINAGE; Mackil and van Alfen "Cooperative Coinage" under GENERAL WORKS—GREEK; Marotta "Electrum Sixths" under LESBOS; Meadows and Houghton "The Gaziantep Hoard" under HOARDS; Meiggs *The Athenian Empire* (discusses Ionian Revolt coinage) under ATTICA—ATHENIAN COINAGE DECREE; Milne "Countermarked Coins" under ASIA MINOR—GENERAL WORKS; Mørkholm "Some Pergamene Coins" under MYSIA—PERGAMENE KINGDOM.

Nivaille "Le Type de l'Abeille" under TYPES; Noe "Beginning of the Cistophoric Coinage" under ASIA MINOR—GENERAL WORKS; Rigsby "The Era" under ASIA MINOR—GENERAL WORKS; Robinson "The Coins from the Ephesian Artemision" under ORIGINS OF COINAGE; Robinson "Some Electrum and Gold Coins" under ASIA MINOR—GENERAL WORKS; Robinson "Rhegion, Zankle-Messana" under SICILY—ZANKLE/MESSANA; Seltman "The Wardrobe of Artemis" under TYPES; Tameanko "The Importance of Homer's Writing" under PORTRAITS; M. Thompson *Alexander's Drachm Mints 1: Sardes and Miletus* under MACEDONIAN KINGDOM—GENERAL WORKS; Vagi "Previously Unpublished" (Miletos) under GENERAL WORKS—GREEK; Wells "A Note on Coin-Plating with Electrum" under THE MINTING PROCESS; Wells "Observations" under PERSIA; Woodward "Three New Fragments of Attic Treasure-records" under EPIGRAPHY.

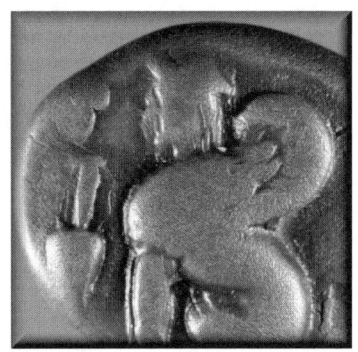

Ionian Islands

The city of Chios boasted the finest harbour of the eastern seaboard. She was a centre of art and literature, one of the many cities of Ionia which claimed to be the birthplace of Homer.

—Norman Davis, 1967

Chios

4822 **Benson, I.** "The Silver Coinage of Chios." *Numismatic Review* 4, no. 1 (January 1947): 26.
The silver coins of Chios, until the first century B.C., did not bear inscriptions indicating the mint city. The reverse of the early issues had an incuse with four squares sunk in the metal, separated by two intersecting ridges which form a cross. Later, the incuse was abandoned, but the slightly raised cross remained. The author suggests that the Greeks came to read the cross as the letter "chi" and associated the coins with Chios. This would explain why Chios did not inscribe the city name on its silver coins as most other states did.

4823 **Brett, Agnes Baldwin.** "The Electrum and Silver Coins of Chios, Issued during the Sixth, Fifth, and Fourth Centuries B.C.: A Chronological Study." *American Journal of Numismatics* 48, no. 1 (1914): 1-60. Illus., 7 pls. Reprint, Chicago: Obol International, 1979. [CS 2737]
Presents a concise overview of the numismatic history of Chios. Illustrates all the coin types. The list of magistrates aids the placement of the coins into chronological order. Includes a list and illustrations of counterfeits. Also illustrates and describes coins issued at Lampsakos which are similar to those of Chios.

4824 **Classical Numismatic Group.** "An Unique Chios Fraction." *The Classical Numismatic Review* 22, no. 2 (spring/summer 1997): 12. Illus.
This price list includes a previously unpublished electrum hekte of Chios (lot 9). No fractional electrum coins were previously known from Chios.

4825 **Gardner, Percy.** "The Financial History of Ancient Chios." *Journal of Hellenic Studies* 40 (1920): 160-73.
"The financial history of the city and the island are traced, primarily from coins, from the sixth century to the period after 190 B.C., when the Romans had broken the power of Antiochus III." [C. Vermeule]. "Particular attention is paid to the significance of the weight of the silver coinage during the archaic and the later fifth century B.C." [J. R. Jones, *NIJHS*]

4826 **Hardwick, Nicholas.** *The Coinage of Chios from the Sixth to the Fourth Century B.C.* D. Phil. thesis. University of Oxford, 1991.

4827 ———. "The Coinage of Chios from the Sixth to the Fourth Century B.C." *Proceedings of the 11th International Numismatic Congress, September 8-13, 1991. Volume 1.* Edited by T. Hackens et al. Louvain-la-Neuve, Belgium: International Association of Professional Numismatists, 1993. Pages 211-22. Illus., maps.
A study of the coinage of Chios in the archaic and classical periods. Based on hoard evidence, Hardwick establishes a chronology for the issues. Shows that there are changes in the nature of the coinage which coincide with the major upheavals of the Ionian revolt and the end of the Peloponnesian War.

4828 ———. "The Solution to Thukydides VIII 101.1: the 'Chian Fortieths.'" *Quaderni Ticinesi. Numismatica e Antichità Classiche* (Switzerland) 25 (1996): 56-69. Illus.
"The author discusses a passage of Thucydides in which are mentioned the 'tessarakostai' struck by the mint of Chios in the second half of the fifth century B.C. to pay the sailors of the fleet. According to the author, this was a silver fraction of 2.6 grams whose value represented 1/40 of the value of the Persian gold daric (8.35 grams)." [A. Carignani, *NL* 138]

4829 ———. "Three Groups of Chian Forgeries." *Numismatic Chronicle* 164 (2004): 224-6. 1 pl.
Publishes two groups of forgeries which may have been from the same forger as those published earlier by Ireland (see Ireland "Another Example" under CARIAN ISLANDS—RHODOS) and Ashton (see Ashton "Some Early Forgeries of Rhodian Coins" under CARIAN ISLANDS—RHODOS).

4830 ———. "A New Variety of Chian Forgery in Hobart." *Numismatic Chronicle* 168 (2008): 9-13. 1 pl.
A bronze coin in the Tasmanian Museum and Art Gallery in Hobart seems to be a new variety of Chian forgery by the same forger as those described earlier by Hardwick (see "Three Groups of Chian Forgeries" above).

4831 ——— "The Coinage of Chios 600-300 B.C.: New Research Developments 1991-2008." *Coins in the Aegean Islands. Proceedings of the Fifth Scientific Meeting, Mytilene, 16-29 September 2006. Volume 1: Ancient Times.* Obolos 9. Edited by Panagiotis Tselekas. Athens: The Friends of the Numismatic Museum, 2010. Pages 217-45.

4832 **Hardwick, Nicholas, Zofia Stos-Gale, and Michael R. Cowell.** "Lead Isotope Analysis of Greek Silver Coins of Chios from the Sixth to the Fourth Century B.C." *Metallurgy in Numismatics, Volume 4.* Special Publication No. 30. London: Royal Numismatic Society, 1998. Pages 367-84. Illus.
An extensive metallurgical analysis has identified the likely sources of the silver for coins of Chios and Maroneia. Twenty coins were tested: eighteen from Chios and two from Maroneia in Thrace, Chios' only colony. The Maroneian coins were chosen to test the hypothesis that silver for the Chian mint may have been derived from north Greece by trade through its colony. The silver sources identified include Sardinia, Spain, Rhodope, Thrace, and Laurion. The sources are consistent with what is known about the history and trade contacts of Chios during the period 525-330 B.C.

4833 **Kinns, Philip.** "A New Third Century B.C. Didrachm of Chios in Ionia." *Numismatic Chronicle* 166 (2006): 31-9. 1 pl.
Kinns publishes a previously unknown didrachm of Chios with sphinx/amphora and magistrate name ΑΓΓΕΛΙΣΚΟΣ. A date of 260-240 B.C. is suggested for the coin. The types correspond with those on an Attic-weight drachm of the same magistrate. The new coin represents a unique usage after the fourth century B.C. of the sphinx type of Chios for a local silver coin above the weight of an Attic drachm.

4834 **Kollgaard, Ron.** "Chios Served as Major Trade Center in Ancient Aegean." *The Celator* 4, no. 7 (July 1990): 1, 26-9. Illus.
A detailed political, military, and economic history of Chios beginning in Mycenaean times, focusing on the classical period, and ending with the Roman domination. Discusses weight standards, denominations, and coin types.

4835 **Lagos, Constantinos.** *A Study of the Coinage of Chios during the Hellenistic and Roman Periods.* D. Phil. dissertation. Durham University, U.K., 1998.

4836 ——— "Chian Coins and Amphorae during the Hellenistic and Roman Periods." *Nomismatika Khronika* (Greece) 18 (1999): 61-8. 1 pl.
Many coins of Chios feature a wine amphora, probably because the wine trade was an important source of the island's wealth. Amphorae appeared as a type or symbol on Chian coins from the archaic period through the Roman period. Lagos examines the close similarities between the amphorae depicted on coins and real jars from the same period. Describes changes in the amphorae over time and discusses the chronological issues. Concludes that clear stylistic changes are evident in successive coin types, reflecting developments occurring on real jars contemporary with the coinage.

4837 ——— "Coinage of Chios during the Hellenistic and Roman Periods." *Coins in the Aegean Islands. Proceedings of the Fifth Scientific Meeting, Mytilene, 16-29 September 2006. Volume 1: Ancient Times.* Obolos 9. Edited by Panagiotis Tselekas. Athens: The Friends of the Numismatic Museum, 2010. Pages 247-62.

4838 **Mattingly, Harold B.** "Coins and Amphoras—Chios, Samos and Thasos in the Fifth Century B.C." *Journal of Hellenic Studies* 101 (1981): 78-86.
"A large number of fragments of Punic and Chian amphorae were found during excavations in the Forum at Corinth. Using the evidence from these fragments, the author investigates Thasian amphora capacity utilizing coin hoard data. He also presents arguments about the chronology of Chian and Samian coinage." [M. Tooth, *Hekte* 2]

4839 **Mavrogordato, J. A.** "Some Uncertain Coins Associated with Chios." *Numismatic Chronicle* 4th ser., 13 (1913): 427-8.
Discusses some coins bearing the sphinx. They may belong to Chios but their attribution remains uncertain.

4840 ——— "A Chronological Arrangement of the Coins of Chios." Parts 1-4. *Numismatic Chronicle* 4th ser., 15 (1915): 1-52, 361-432. 4 pls.; 16 (1916): 281-355. 2 pls.; 17 (1917): 207-56. 1 pl.; 18 (1918): 1-79. 2 pls. All parts reprinted, Oxford: University Press, 1918. 331 pp., 8 pls. [CS 2738]
A detailed discussion of the coinage of Chios, from its origins through the Roman Provincial period. Discusses the weight standards. Lists the coin types by chronological period. Includes lists of magistrates' names and indicates on which denominations they appear.

4841 ——— "Some Further Notes on the Coins of Chios." *Numismatic Chronicle* 4th ser., 19 (1919): 217-20.
Discusses the magistrates' names on coins of Chios from the Hermann Weber collection and the collection of Talbot Ready.

4842 **Thompson, Wesley E.** "The Chian Coinage in Thucydides and Xenophon." *Numismatic Chronicle* 7th ser., 11 (1971): 323-4.
"A comparison of the financial resources of Miletus and other cities supports the theory that when Miletus supplied a Chian pentadrachm to each sailor in the Peloponnesian fleet in 406, the total amounted to some sixteen talents." [W. Thompson, *NL* 87]

Also see: Ashton, Hardwick, Konuk and Meadows "The Pixodarus Hoard" under HOARDS; Bauslaugh "The Posthumous Alexander Coinage of Chios" under MACEDONIAN KINGDOM—GENERAL WORKS; Grigorakis "A Hoard of Ptolemaic Silver Coins from Chios" under EGYPT—PTOLEMAIC KINGDOM; Hoover *Handbook of Coins of the Islands* under CYCLADES ISLANDS; Lagos "Posthumous Alexander Type Tetradrachms of Chios" under MACEDONIAN KINGDOM—GENERAL WORKS; LeRider *Deux Trésors* under HOARDS; Linzalone *Electrum and the Invention of Coinage* under ORIGINS OF COINAGE; Meadows "The Chian Revolution: Changing Patterns of Hoarding" under HOARDS; Münzen und Medaillen *Auktion 21: Joy Collection* under PRIVATE COLLECTIONS; Vagi "Previously Unpublished" under GENERAL WORKS—GREEK.

SAMOS

4843 **Barron, John Penrose.** *The Silver Coins of Samos.* London: The Athlone Press, 1966. 244 pp., 32 pls. [CS 2739]
A study of the coinage of Samos from its inception ca. 600 B.C. to its end ca. 200 B.C. focusing on the history of the city. Presents a corpus of the tetradrachms minted before 365 B.C., and a great majority of the known varieties of other denominations and later issues. Grouped into die-linked series.

Establishes a relative chronology. Discusses the meaning of the types, weight standards, and sources of silver. Presents frequency tables of coin weights. [Reviewed by C. M. Kraay in *Journal of Hellenic Studies* 87 (1967): 196-7, and by R. J. Hopper in *Spink Numismatic Circular* 79, no. 2 (February 1971): 61].

4844 ——— "The Silver Coins of Samos Come of Age." *Kraay—Mørkholm Essays: Numismatic Studies in Memory of C. M. Kraay and O. Mørkholm.* Numismatica Lovaniensia 10. Edited by G. Le Rider, G. K. Jenkins, N. Waggoner, and U. Westermark. Louvain-la-Neuve: Université Catholique de Louvain, 1989. Pages 9-22. 4 pls.
Examines the Samian coins in the Asyut hoard and the Decadrachm hoard. Presents frequency tables of the weights of the tetradrachms from the hoards. Discusses the chronology of Samian coinage at Zancle. Concludes the Samian mint was closed in 439 B.C. Presents a catalogue of tetradrachms and identifies die links.

4845 ——— "Two Goddesses in Samos." *Studies in Greek Numismatics in Memory of Martin Jessop Price.* Edited by Richard Ashton and Silvia Hurter. London: Spink, 1998. Pages 23-36. 2 pls.
(Part 1) Barron publishes a unique tetradrachm of Samos with *obv.*, lion's mask, and *rev.*, Athena Promachos; an owl stands at her heel and a sprig of olive appears in the upper field—an unmistakable allusion to Athens. The coin was apparently struck at a time of particularly close relations between Samos and Athens. But when? The years 405/4 and 394 B.C. have been suggested on historical grounds. However, the artistic style of the Athena Promachos on the coin suggests a date in the Hellenistic period. But the Samians were thought to have been expelled from the island in 366 B.C. Barron suggests the coin was minted between 360-340 B.C. by a native Samian population which remained on the island during the period of the Athenian cleruchy. (Part 2) Discusses a Samian tetradrachm with *obv.*, head of Zeus, and *rev.*, statue of Hera. The Hera statue alludes to the sacred marriage of Zeus and Hera, of which Samos was the site. Barron comments on the artistic style of the Hera statue. Concludes with an *Appendix* listing depictions of Athena Promachos on dated Panathenaic amphoras.

4846 **Biglaki-Sophianou, M.** "The Gymnasium of Ancient Samos/2001 Hoard: The Excavation Data." *Coins in the Aegean Islands. Proceedings of the Fifth Scientific Meeting, Mytilene, 16-29 September 2006. Volume 1: Ancient Times.* Obolos 9. Edited by Panagiotis Tselekas. Athens: The Friends of the Numismatic Museum, 2010. Pages 283-6.

4847 **Evgenidou, Desponia.** "Coins from Samos in the Athens Numismatic Museum." *Coins in the Aegean Islands. Proceedings of the Fifth Scientific Meeting, Mytilene, 16-29 September 2006. Volume 1: Ancient Times.* Obolos 9. Edited by Panagiotis Tselekas. Athens: The Friends of the Numismatic Museum, 2010. Pages 119-34.

4848 **Gardner, Percy.** "Samos and Samian Coins." *Numismatic Chronicle* 3rd ser., 2 (1882): 201-90. 6 pls. Reprinted as a book, London: Macmillan, 1882. 90 pp., 6 pls. [CS 2740]
An extensive discussion of the history of Samos followed by a review of the principal coin types. Discusses the meaning of the types and comments on attributions. Also describes the coin types of the colonies of Samos including Samothrace, Anaea, Nagidus, Celenderis, Perinthus, and others. Covers the coinage from the earliest period (before 494 B.C.) through the Roman Imperial period.

4849 **Grace, Virginia R.** "Samian Amphoras." *Hesperia* 40, no. 1 (January-March 1971): 52-95. Illus.
"Among the types on a group of stamped handles probably of the last quarter of the 4th century B.C. found on Samos in 1902-1904 are the principal coin devices of Samos, sometimes accompanied by the ethnic ΣΑ; a cult statue which may be that of the Samian Hera; and twenty-four impressions of engraved rings or gems. The association of local legend and ritual with the stamps is investigated. Amphora shapes represented on fifth-century Samian trihemiobols are compared with actual jars, and an adjustment is proposed for J. P. Barron's dating of the trihemiobols in *The Silver Coins of Samos*, pp. 71, 92. Samian measures and standards are discussed." [V. Grace, *NL* 87]

4850 **Konuk, Koray.** "The Electrum Coinage of Samos in the Light of a Recent Hoard." *Neue Forschungen zu Ionien: Fahri Işık zum 60. Geburtstag Gewidmet.* Edited by Elmar Schwertheim and Engelbert Winter. Asia Minor Studien, Band 54. Bonn, 2005.
Examines the early electrum coinage of Samos, which began ca. 600 B.C. The Samian coinage used the Euboic-Samian weight standard, whereas the Milesian standard prevailed in Lydia and most of Ionia. A 1998 hoard (*RNS Coin Hoards IX*, no. 341) provided numerous new examples of this rare coinage. Konuk lists forty-four specimens from the hoard, along with a metallurgical analysis of twelve of the coins. Konuk concludes that the Samians took great care over the weights of their coins, but the alloy used to strike them was quite variable. It appears that copper was added when necessary to ensure that coins with low gold content looked the same as those with high gold content. This lends credence to Robert Wallace's theory (see Wallace "The Origin of Electrum" under ORIGINS OF COINAGE) that coinage was invented because of the varying value of electrum, which could not circulate without a guarantee. By putting a device on a carefully weighed lump of electrum, the issuing authority fixed the face value of electrum.

4851 **Nicolet-Pierre, Hélène, and Jean-Noël Barrandon.** "Monnaies d'Électrum Archaïques. Le Trésor de Samos de 1894 (*IGCH* 1158) Conservé à Paris." *Revue Numismatique* (France) 152 (1997): 121-35.

4852 **Oeconomides, Mando.** "Les Monnaies de Samos de la Collection Grégoire Empédoclès." *Zurück zum Gegenstand. Festschrift für Andreas E. Furtwängler.* Zentrum für Archälogie und Kulturgeschichte des Schwarzmeerraumes, Band 16. Edited by Ralph Einicke et al. Langenweibach: Beier and Beram, 2009.

4853 **Touratsoglou, Ioannis.** "The Gymnasium of Ancient Samos/2001 Hoard." *Coins in the Aegean Islands. Proceedings of the Fifth Scientific Meeting, Mytilene, 16-29 September 2006. Volume 1: Ancient Times.* Obolos 9. Edited by Panagiotis Tselekas. Athens: The Friends of the Numismatic Museum, 2010. Pages 287-300.

Also see: Ashton, Hardwick, Konuk and Meadows "The Pixodarus Hoard" under HOARDS; Ashton, Kinns, Konuk, and Meadows "Hecatomnus Hoard" under HOARDS; Cohen "Greek Numbers on Coins" under EPIGRAPHY; Hoover *Handbook of Coins of the Islands* under CYCLADES ISLANDS; Hurter "Das Palladion" under TYPES; Kyrou "The Coin and History" under GENERAL WORKS—GREEK; Linzalone *Electrum and the Invention of Coinage* under ORIGINS OF COINAGE; Mattingly "Coins and Amphoras" under IONIAN ISLANDS—CHIOS; Münzen und Medaillen *Auktion 21: Joy Collection* under PRIVATE COLLECTIONS; Waggoner "Three Recent Greek Accessions" under ASIA MINOR—GENERAL WORKS.

CARIA

By the time of Strabo, Carian had become a dead language, studied by antiquaries.
—Michael Grant, 1986

4854 **Akarca, Askidill.** *Les Monnaies Grecques de Mylasa.* Bibliothèque Archéologique et Historique de l'Institut Français d'Archéologique d'Istanbul 1. Paris, 1959. 106 pp., 20 pls. [CS 2747]
Examines the Hellenistic and Roman Provincial issues of Mylasa.

4855 **Ashton, Richard H. J.** "A Pseudo-Rhodian Drachm from Kaunos." *Schweizer Münzblätter* (Switzerland) 151 (May 1988): 67-70.
"The author attributes to Kaunos a unique pseudo-Rhodian drachm with magistrate's name Megistos, and dates it to not long before Kaunos' liberation from Rhodian suzerainty in 166. The very rare name Megistos also occurs on some post-167 Athena/sheathed sword hemidrachms of Kaunos." [R. Ashton, *NL* 120]

4856 ——— "A New Silver Issue from Mylasa." *Numismatic Chronicle* 150 (1990): 224-5. 1 pl.
"The author publishes an apparently unique, anepigraphic silver drachm with types rose/human male head r., associates it with the unique Mylasan drachm *J. Hirsch 25*, 2364 (now Berlin), and suggests that the portraits on their reverses are those of Hybreas, the leading politician of Mylasa from the 40s B.C. onward." [R. Ashton, *NL* 126]

4857 ——— "The Pseudo-Rhodian Drachms of Mylasa." *Numismatic Chronicle* 152 (1992): 1-39. 10 pls.
"The author provides a die-study of over 600 pseudo-Rhodian drachms of Mylasa (distinguished by an eagle on the cheek of Helios); establishes that two of the letters on the issues with four or more letters-monograms on the reverse are the initials of months; arranges the series into annual issues; and argues that it lasted for about 30-35 years around the middle of the second century B.C." [R. Ashton, *NL* 130]. [Also see Ashton and Reger "Pseudo-Rhodian" below].

4858 ——— "The Hellenistic Hemidrachms of Kaunos." *Revue Belge de Numismatique et de Sigillographie* (Belgium) 145 (Hackens Memorial Volume) (1999): 141-54.

4859 ——— "The Late Classical/Early Hellenistic Drachms of Knidos." *Revue Numismatique* (France) 154 (1999): 63-95.

4860 ——— "Kaunos, not Miletos or Mylasa." *Numismatic Chronicle* 164 (2004): 33-46. 1 pl.
Ashton argues that some bronze issues in the names of Alexander III and Philip II, previously assigned to Miletos or Mylasa, actually belong to Kaunos. [Also see Ashton "The Coins of the Macedonian Kings" under MACEDONIAN KINGDOM—GENERAL WORKS].

4861 ——— "The Beginning of Bronze Coinage in Karia and Lykia." *Numismatic Chronicle* 166 (2006): 1-14. 5 pls.
Examines the early bronze coinage of Kamiros, Rhodes, Idyma, Kaunos, Keramos, Halikarnassos, Iasos, Mylasa, Karydanda, Kranaos, Pitane, and the Lykian dynasts.

4862 ——— "The Pre-Imperial Coinage of Iasos." *Numismatic Chronicle* 167 (2007): 47-78. 9 pls.
An update to Wolfram Weiser's survey of the coinage of Iasos, providing new material. [See Weiser below].

4863 **Ashton, Richard H. J., and Gary Reger.** "The Pseudo-Rhodian Drachms of Mylasa Revisited." *Agoranomia: Studies in Money and Exchange Presented to John H. Kroll.* Edited by Peter G. van Alfen. New York: American Numismatic Society, 2006. Pages 125-50. 2 pls.
The pseudo-Rhodian drachms of Mylasa are distinguished by an eagle on the cheek of Helios on the obverse. In Part 1, Reger examines some well-known Mylasian inscriptions related to land transactions. He argues that these lease inscriptions should be re-dated to before ca. 185 B.C. Reger and Ashton also suggest the beginning of the eagle-on-cheek drachms, previously placed in the 170's or early 160's, should perhaps be placed a decade or two earlier to coincide with the inscriptions. In Part 2, Ashton publishes and comments on some new coins from a hoard of Mylasian pseudo-Rhodian drachms (*Coin Hoards* 9, no. 525) which appeared in 1999. All fifty-three drachms from the hoard are illustrated. A further 146 drachms came to light later and are also listed here. These coins supplement those in Ashton's 1992 publication (see Ashton "The Pseudo-Rhodian Drachms of Mylasa" above).

4864 **Bean, G. E., and J. M. Cook.** "The Carian Coast III." *Annual of the British School of Archaeology at Athens* 52 (1957): 58-146.

"The main purpose of this article is to describe the remains still visible on the ground and to discuss questions of topography, but some numismatic material is included. A discovery of twenty archaic coins was recorded at Alâkilise in 1954, with obverse showing the head of a griffin and reverse an incuse square containing a diamond-shaped lattice frame. Attributions to Phocaea or Lycia have been proposed, but the find points rather to a Carian mint; the authors suggest one of the dynasts of Syangela. The apparent contravention of the fifth century monetary decree by the issue of tetradrachms at Cos is also discussed. This may have been due to the setting up of an Athenian administrative center on the island, which would also explain the unusual fact that the copy of the monetary decree found on Cos is of Athenian origin. References to site-finds of coins are made on pp. 67, 69, 75 and 136." [C. Kraay, *NL* 49]. [Also see Kagan and Kritt "The Coinage of Kindya" below].

4865 **Boehringer, Christof.** "Ein Lot Silberner Kleinstmünzen aus Karien." *Pour Denyse: Divertissements Numismatiques.* Edited by S. Hurter and C. Arnold-Biucchi. Bern, Switzerland: Privately published, 2000. Pages 21-6. 2 pls.
An examination of seventeen small silver coins from Caria. The mint cities are uncertain.

4866 **Cahn, Herbert A.** "A New Carian Mint." *Numismatic Chronicle* 6th ser., 2 (1942): 92-4. Illus.
Publishes a drachm (*obv.*, Helios; *rev.* E – Y, rose) of the light Rhodian standard. Similar types, but bearing M – E, and N – I, have been attributed to Megiste and Nisyrus respectively—both islands were under Rhodian influence. The new drachm is attributed to Euthenai, a small town on the Carian mainland. Also mentions a similar coin with Γ – Λ / ? – Y and a rose. This coin is attributed to Syme, an island under Rhodian influence.

4867 ——— *Knidos: Die Münzen des Sechsten und des Fünften Jahrhunderts v. Chr.* Antike Münzen und Geschnittene Steine 4. Berlin: Walter De Gruyter & Co., 1970. 245 pp., 20 pls. [CS 2745]

4868 **Cawkwell, G. L.** "A Note of the Heracles Coinage Alliance of 394 B.C." *Numismatic Chronicle* 6th ser., 16 (1956): 69-75.
A small group of coins bear on the reverse the emblems and ethnics of various cities and on the obverse the symbolic type of the young Herakles strangling two snakes, together with the legend ΣΥΝ. The cities are Rhodes, Cnidus, Iasus, Ephesus, Samos, Byzantium, Cyzicus, and perhaps Lampsacus. An alliance of these cities is unrecorded, and opinions on the circumstances have varied. The alliance was likely formed and flourished in the months after the battle of Cnidus, ca. 394 B.C. Rhodes may have been the hegemon of the alliance. [Summarized from C. Vermeule, *NL* 43]. [Also see R. Cook "Cnidian Peraea and Spartan Coins" and S. Karweise "Lysander as Herakliskos Drakonopnigon" below, Kraay "Greek Coinage and War" under GENERAL WORKS—GREEK, and Ashton, Kinns, Konuk, and Meadows "Hecatomnus Hoard" under HOARDS].

4869 ——— "The ΣΥΝ Coins Again." *Journal of Hellenic Studies* 83 (1963): 151-4.
"A reply to the suggestion made by J. M. Cook (see below) that these coins represent a pro-Spartan alliance." [J. R. Jones, *NIJHS*]

4870 **Cook, J. M.** "Cnidian Peraea and Spartan Coins." *Journal of Hellenic Studies* 81 (1961): 56-72. Maps.
"In the first two sections, entitled *Cnidian Chersonese and Rhodian Peraea*, the author shows that it was Cnidus and not Rhodes which dominated the Loryma peninsula before the end of the fifth century. In the second section it is suggested that the alliance coinage inscribed ΣΥΝ (with obverse depicting the infant Herakles strangling two serpents) was struck by Rhodes, Cnidus, Iasus, Samos, Ephesus, Byzantium, Cyzicus and Lampsacus in 391/90. It was issued under the influence of Thibron and represents a pro-Spartan rather than an anti-Spartan alliance." [I. Merker, *NL* 65]. [Also see G. Cawkwell "A Note of the Heracles Coinage Alliance" above, S. Karweise "Lysander as Herakliskos Drakonopnigon" below, Kraay "Greek Coinage and War" under GENERAL WORKS—GREEK, and Ashton, Kinns, Konuk, and Meadows "Hecatomnus Hoard" under HOARDS].

4871 **Delrieux, Fabrice.** "Les Monnaies de Mylasa aux Types de Zeus *Osogôa* et Zeus *Labraundeus*." *Numismatic Chronicle* 159 (1999): 33-45. 2 pls.

4872 ——— *Les Monnaies des Cités Grecques de la Basse Vallée de l'Harpasos en Carie (IIe s. a.C. – IIIe s. p.C.).* Ausonius Editions. Numismatic Anatolica 3. 2008. Bordeaux, 2008. 311 pp.
Explores the coinage of the four cities which developed in the valley of the Harpasos river in Caria: Bargasa, Harpasa, Neapolis, and Orthosia. Coinage began in these cities in the second or first century BC, with the majority struck in the third century AD.

4873 **Estrada, Rudolph I.** "Satraps of Caria." *Journal of Numismatic Fine Arts* 6, no. 1 (spring 1977): 1-2. Illus.
Briefly describes the satrapal system of political organization in southwestern Asia Minor. Briefly describes the coinage issued by the three sons of Hecatomnus: Mausolus (377-353 B.C.), Hidriaeus (351-344 B.C.), and Pixodarus (340-334 B.C.).

4874 **Glass, James C.** "Rarities of Cidramus and Idyma." *SAN—Journal of the Society for Ancient Numismatics* 12, no. 1 (spring 1981): 17-8. Illus.
The history of Caria is outlined and two rare coins are discussed. One is a first century A.D. bronze from Cidramus and one is a fourth century B.C. bronze from Idyma. [Due to a printing error, the photograph of the Idyma coin was omitted, but does appear in *SAN* 12, no. 2 (summer 1981): 38].

4875 **Head, Barclay V.** *Catalogue of Greek Coins of Caria, Cos, Rhodes, etc.* London: British Museum, 1897. Reprint, Bologna: Forni, 1964. cxiii, 325 pp., 45 pls. [CS 2742]
Volume 18 of the *Catalogue of Greek Coins in the British Museum.* The 325-page catalogue of coins is preceded by 113 pages of introductory text. [Also see *Catalogue of Greek Coins in the British Museum* under PUBLIC COLLECTIONS—GREAT BRITAIN (LONDON)].

4876 **Hill, George F.** "Some Coins of Caria and Lycia." *Numismatic Chronicle* 4th ser., 3 (1903): 399-402. Illus.
Lists a new silver half drachm tentatively attributed to Lydae in Caria. Also lists a Roman-period coin of Caria and two of Lycia.

4877 **Imhoof-Blumer, Friedrich.** "Karische Münzen." *Numismatische Zeitschrift* (Austria) (1912): 193-208. [CS 2743]

4878 **Jenkins, G. Kenneth.** "The Carian Coast III." *Annual of the British School of Archaeology at Athens* 52 (1957): 95-6. Illus.
Publishes a hoard of twenty silver tetrobols with *obv.*, head of sea monster (ketos). The type has been previously published, but has not been assigned to a particular mint. The coins were found at the ancient site of Alâkilise, and Jenkins assigns the issue to an uncertain mint in Caria. The coins may have been struck by the Syangelan dynast Pigres or by his predecessor. Examples of the coins are illustrated on plate 23. [These coins have recently

been attributed to the Carian mint of Kindya. Also see Bean and Cook "The Carian Coast III" above, and Kagan and Kritt "The Coinage of Kindya" below].

4879 **Johnston, Ann.** "Aphrodisias Reconsidered." *Numismatic Chronicle* 155 (1995): 43-100. 2 pls.
"On the basis of David MacDonald's recent corpus (see MacDonald *The Coinage of Aphrodisias* below), the author re-examines the Hellenistic and Roman Provincial bronze coins, correcting some misattributions and refining the chronology. The author discusses production, circulation, types, and legends." [M. Allen, NL 140]

4880 **Kagan, Jonathan H., and Brian Kritt.** "The Coinage of Kindya." *Numismatic Chronicle* 155 (1995): 261-5. 1 pl.
"The authors reattribute to the Carian city of Kindya certain ca. 2 gram coins formerly assigned to Syangela by Bean and Cook. The obverse type is recognized as a head of a sea monster (ketos), not a griffin's head. The fractions are associated with two ANS coins that depict ketea, one of which is inscribed KI." [Kagan and Kritt, *NL* 140]. [Also see Bean and Cook "The Carian Coast III" above].

4881 **Karwiese, Stefan.** "Lysander as Herakliskos Drakonopnigon ('Heracles the Snake-Strangler')." *Numismatic Chronicle* 140 (1980): 1-27. 2 pls.
"Which, of all the allegedly possible moments, could have been the sole cause for the alliance coinage represented by the ΣYN coins from Byzantium, Cyzicus, Lampsacus, Ephesus, Samos, Iasus, Cnidus, and Rhodes is investigated. An account of the involved cities during 479-386 B.C. is given in order to discover when and in which way these cities could have been able to unite and subsequently use for a symbol of their union the particular type of young Heracles strangling two snakes. It is concluded that only during the last years of the Peloponnesian War when the Attic maritime union broke and most of its members revolted against Athens was there the opportunity and, above all, a good reason for those cities to unite." [S. Karwiese, *NL* 106]. [Also see G. Cawkwell "A Note of the Heracles Coinage Alliance" above, J. Cook "Cnidian Peraea and Spartan Coins" above, Kraay "Greek Coinage and War" under GENERAL WORKS—GREEK, and Kampmann "Herakles the Snake-Strangler" under MYSIA—AUTONOMOUS CITIES].

4881a **Konuk, Koray.** "Quelques Réflexions sur le Monnayage des Satrapes Hécatomnides de Carie." *Proceedings of the 11th International Numismatic Congress, September 8-13, 1991. Volume 1.* Edited by T. Hackens et al. Louvain-la-Neuve, Belgium: International Association of Professional Numismatists, 1993. Pages 237-42. Illus.

4882 ——— "The Early Coinage of Kaunos." *Studies in Greek Numismatics in Memory of Martin Jessop Price.* Edited by Richard Ashton and Silvia Hurter. London: Spink, 1998. Pages 197-223. 4 pls.
A group of early Carian coins, nicknamed "winged Carians" by Troxell (see H. Troxell "Winged Carians" below) because the obverse depicts a winged deity, have puzzled numismatists for many years. They are the product of at least two distinct mints. Konuk discusses the issues of Mint A which he identifies as Kaunos. Presents a catalogue intended to be a corpus of the coinage. Includes 560 staters, drachms, hemidrachms, tritartemoria, trihemitartemoria, trihemiobols, and bronze issues. Also catalogues a few forgeries. Discusses chronology, attribution, weight standards, denominations, and types.

4883 ——— "Coin Evidence for the Carian Name of Keramos." *Kadmos* (Germany) 39 (2000): 159-64. 1 pl.
A series of bronze coins bearing Carian letters on their reverse throws light on the original Carian name of the city whose Greek name was Keramos (now Ören, Turkey). The coins are securely attributed to Keramos. Konuk provides a die study of all specimens known to him, and all are illustrated. The coins are copper chalkoi with *obv.*, foreport of bull, *rev.*, dolphin with legend ΔΛΟ. The letters are transcribed as *k-b-o*. The author concludes that *k-b-o* are the first three letters of the city's name.

4884 ——— "Influences et Éléments Achéménides dans le Monnayage de la Carie." *Mécanismes et Innovations Monétaires dans l'Anatolie Achéménide. Numismatique et Histoire. Actes de la Table Ronde Internationale d'Istanbul, 22-23 Mai 1997.* Varia Anatolica XII. Edited by O. Casabonne. Istanbul: Institut Français d'Etudes Anatoliennes d'Istanbul; Paris: de Boccard, 2000. Pages 171-83.

4884a ——— "The Coinage of Latmos." *Feldforschungen im Latmos: Die Karische Stadt Latmos.* Milet Volume 3, no. 6. Berlin and New York: Walter de Gruyter, 2005. Pages 55-8. 1 pl.

4885 ——— "The Coinage of Hyssaldornos, Dynast of Mylasa." *Zurück zum Gegenstand. Festschrift für Andreas E. Furtwängler.* Zentrum für Archälogie und Kulturgeschichte des Schwarzmeerraumes, Band 16. Edited by Ralph Einicke et al. Langenweibach: Beier and Beram, 2009. Pages 357-63.

4885a ——— "Kasolaba, a New Mint in Karia?" *KEPMATIA ΦΙΛΙΑΣ: Volume in Honor of Ioannis Touratsoglou.* Edited by S. Drougou et al. Athens: Alpha Bank, 2009. Pages 177-83. Illus.
A tentative attribution to a new mint in Karia is presented here for a prolific series of classical silver fractions. Their legend in the Karian script and some recorded provenances would indicate Kasolaba, a city which is mentioned in the Athenian Tribute Lists but whose precise location is uncertain.

4886 **Lampinen, Peter.** "Two Greek Notes." *The Celator* 18, no. 8 (August 2004): 35, 37. Illus.
Publishes a variety of a silver drachm of Stratonikeia not listed by Meadows (see Meadows "Stratonikeia in Caria" below). Also examines a bronze coin bearing the letters AP which has long been attributed as a Roman Provincial issue of Termessos in Galatia. Lampinen concludes that this coin (and others) actually is an issue of Arycanda in Lycia.

4887 **Le Rider, Georges.** "Un Tétradrachme Hellénistique de Cnide." *Greek Numismatics and Archaeology: Essays in Honor of Margaret Thompson.* Edited by O. Mørkholm and N. M. Waggoner. Wetteren: Numismatique Romaine, 1979. Pages 155-7. 1 pl.
Examines a Hellenistic-period tetradrachm of Cnidus.

4888 **MacDonald, David J.** *Greek and Roman Coins from Aphrodisias.* BAR Supplementary Series 9. Oxford: British Archaeological Reports, 1976. 50 pp., 3 pls. [CS 2744]

A brief outline of the history of the city of Aphrodisias in Caria, followed by a listing of the 816 pre-A.D. 305 coins excavated by New York University between 1961 and 1973. Dies are cross-referenced to other published collections. Includes commentary on the history of the mints at the city.

4889 ——— *The Coinage of Aphrodisias.* Special Publication No. 23. London: Royal Numismatic Society, 1992. 184 pp., 32 pls.
A complete catalogue and die study of the coinage of Aphrodisias, focusing on the Roman Provincial coinage in bronze. Includes the series of silver drachms of the first century B.C. Lists 240 types. Illustrates 300 obverse and 591 reverse dies. The introduction includes discussions of die-sharing among Asian cities, the die-cutters, the evidence for the circulation of coins, denominations, designs, and magistrates. [Reviewed by Kevin Butcher in *Spink Numismatic Circular* 101, no. 3 (April 1993): 81-2, and in *Journal of Roman Studies* 84 (1994): 256-8. Also reviewed by Ann Johnston in *Numismatic Chronicle* 154 (1994): 306-10. Also see Johnston "Aphrodisias Reconsidered" above].

4890 **Meadows, Andrew R.** "Stratonikeia in Caria: the Hellenistic City and its Coinage." *Numismatic Chronicle* 162 (2002): 79-133. 12 pls.
Publishes the Mugla 1965 Hoard (*IGCH* 1357), providing details of the coins of Stratonikeia and Rhodes from that hoard. Also examines the history of the Hellenistic city of Stratonikeia and its coinage. [Also see Lampinen "Two Greek Notes" above].

4891 ——— *Alabanda in Caria: The Hellenistic City and its Coinage.* Ph.D. thesis. Oxford, 2008.

4892 **Milne, Joseph G.** "Hoard of Silver Coins of Knidos." *Numismatic Chronicle* 4th ser., 11 (1911): 197-8.
Publishes eighteen silver coins minted at Knidos in the third century B.C. Most of the magistrates' names on the coins were previously unpublished.

4893 ——— "The Dadia Hoard of Coins of Knidos." *Numismatic Chronicle* 4th series, 14 (1914): 378-81.
Publishes what is known of a hoard of hemidrachms and tetrobols of Knidos. Lists the magistrates present. Indicates dies and weights.

4894 **Nordbø, Jan H. A.** "A Note on the Early Bronze Coinage of Cnidus Cariae." *Spink Numismatic Circular* 85, no. 4 (April 1977): 147. Illus.
Publishes a tiny bronze coin which the author believes was minted in Cnidus in the fourth century B.C. (*obv.*, Aphrodite). Kraay (in his *Archaic and Classical Greek Coins*) stated that no fourth century B.C. bronze coinage of Cnidus has been identified.

4895 ——— "The Coinage of Cnidus after 394 B.C." *Proceedings of the 10th International Congress of Numismatics, London, 1986.* International Association of Professional Numismatists Publication, No. 11. Edited by I. A. Carradice. London: International Association of Professional Numismatists, 1986. Pages 51-6. 2 pls.
A summary of the author's Master of Arts thesis. Provides an overview of the denominations, types, and chronology of the coinage of Cnidus during the period 394 B.C.-A.D. 210.

4896 **Numismatik Lanz München.** *Auktion 131: Münzen von Karien. Sammlung Karl.* November 27, 2006. 120 pp., illus.
Auction catalogue for the collection of Erich Karl, encompassing 837 ancient coins from Caria. Each coin is illustrated by an actual size color photograph.

4897 **Paton, W. R.** "Find of Coins near Halicarnassus." *Numismatic Chronicle* 3rd ser., 10 (1890): 279-81.
Lists coins found in 1880 near Halicarnassus, including coins of Halicarnassus and Myndus. Also lists some previously unpublished coins of Myndus from the author's collection.

4898 **Poetto, Massimo.** "Nuove Monete Carie." *Kadmos: Zeitschrift für Vor- und Frühgriechische Epigraphik* (Germany) 23, no. 1 (1984): 74-5. 1 pl.
Publishes two coins found near Aphrodisias that bear a cone-like object on the reverse, with letters which Poetto believes are Carian. [Also see the follow-up paper by John Ray below. These coins have more recently been attributed to the Carian city of Kaunos].

4899 **Price, Martin J.** "Histiaeus, Son of Tymnes, Tyrant of Termera, Caria." *Norwegian Numismatic Journal* (Norway) (September 1979): 4-12.
Publishes a stater and siglos attributed to Histiaeus of Termera, Caria. The coins are inscribed with his name on the reverse and were issued ca. 490-480 B.C.

4900 **Rakicic, Mark.** "Pixodarus-Alexander Affair Furnishes Intrigue for a Blockbuster Movie." *The Celator* 6, no. 11 (November 1992): 10-1. Illus.
Short narrative, in mock movie script format, describing the relationships between Alexander III, his half-brother Arrhidaeus, and their father's (Philip II) dealings with Pixodarus of Caria.

4901 **Ray, John D.** "The Carian Coins from Aphrodisias." *Kadmos: Zeitschrift für Vor- und Frühgriechische Epigraphik* (Germany) 24, no. 2 (1985): 86-8.
Ray re-examines the two coins found near Aphrodisias that were discussed in 1984 by M. Poetto (see Poetto above). The reverse of the coins bears a cone-like object with letters which Poetto took to be the Carian letters *p* and *l*. Rays accepts that the letters may be Carian, and discusses the meaning of the letters. He suggests the letters may represent *k* and *b*, but this is uncertain. The mint city remains uncertain. [These coins have more recently been attributed to the Carian city of Kaunos].

4902 **Robinson, Edward S. G.** "Coin-Legends in the Carian Script." *Anatolian Studies Presented to William Hepburn Buckler.* Edited by W. M. Calder and J. Keil. Manchester: University Press, 1939. Pages 269-75.
The author examines some rare coins bearing inscriptions in Carian script. The specific cities are uncertain. Discusses the form and meaning of the legends.

4903 **Tameanko, Marvin.** "The Coinage of the 'Herculean Alliance,' 394-387 B.C." *Journal of the Classical and Medieval Numismatic Society* (Canada) 2nd ser., 1 (June 1, 2000): 53-64. Illus.
A review of the controversy surrounding the coins struck by Ephesos, Kyzikos, Samos, Knidos, Iasos, Rhodos, and Byzantion—all bearing the same reverse design (Hercules strangling two serpents) and the inscription ΣΥΝ (an abbreviation for ΣΥΝΜΑΧΙΚΟΝ, meaning "alliance"). Presumably,

these cities were part of a political confederation. These extremely rare silver coins are classified as tridrachms or double-sigloi. Some scholars believe the "Herculean" alliance was a Persian-sponsored alliance opposed to Sparta, and that the coins were struck 394-387 B.C. Others suggest the confederation was formed in 390-390 in support of Sparta against Athens. Other theories exist as well. Tameanko outlines the confusing history of this period. No firm conclusion is likely to be reached regarding the true nature or chronology of this coinage until further evidence comes to light. [Also see these related articles above: Cawkwell "A Note," Cook "Cnidian Peraea," and Karweise "Lysander." Also see Kraay "Greek Coinage and War" under GENERAL WORKS—GREEK].

4904 **Troxell, Hyla A.** "Winged Carians." *Greek Numismatics and Archaeology: Essays in Honor of Margaret Thompson*. Edited by O. Mørkholm and N. M. Waggoner. Wetteren: Numismatique Romaine, 1979. Pages 257-68. 1 pl.
The author examines two groups of archaic staters portraying winged deities. The coins of Mint A portray female deities; those of Mint B portray male deities. E. S. G. Robinson (see Robinson "A Find of Archaic Coins from South-West Asia Minor" under HOARDS) assigned both series to southern Caria, but the specific mint cities remain uncertain. Troxell summarizes the output of these two mints through several successive periods. Describes the coins attributed to each mint. Discusses the possible identities of the mints. Likely candidates are Caunus, Calynda, Crya, and Telandria. No conclusion is likely until the Carian script on the coins can be deciphered and the original Carian city names become known. [Also see Konuk "The Early Coinage of Kaunos" above].

4905 ——— "Carians in Miniature." *Studies in Honour of Leo Mildenberg: Numismatics, Art History, Archaeology*. Edited by Arthur Houghton et al. Wetteren: Editions NR, 1984. Pages 249-57. Illus.
Troxell examines twelve issues or series of tiny Carian coins, some previously unpublished. Most of those which were previously known had been misattributed, and others had only been described as belonging somewhere in Asia Minor. All bear animal heads or foreparts on the obverse. Some bear inscriptions in the Carian script. The Carian legends and new find-spots lead to Carian attributions for all, although specific mints cannot always be suggested. All are from the late fifth or early fourth century B.C.

4906 **Tzamalis, Anastasios P.** "Nothing New Under the Sun." *Nomismatika Khronika* (Greece) 21 (2002): 145-6. Illus.
A brief discussion of the alliance coinage minted by Byzantion, Kyzikos, Lampsacus, Samos, Ephesos, Knidos, and Rhodes bearing the syllable ΣΥΝ. Presents a count of known specimens of each denomination from each city.

4907 **van Alfen, Peter.** "Greek Acquisitions: A Mausolus Tetradrachm." *American Numismatic Society Magazine* 1, no. 2 (summer 2002): 11. Illus.
Illustrates a facing-head tetradrachm of Mausolus recently donated to the ANS. Briefly discusses the coinage of Mausolus, Hidreus, Pixodarus, Ornotobates, and Hecatomnus.

4908 **Waggoner, Nancy.** "A New Wrinkle in the Hellenistic Coinage of Antioch/Alabanda." *Kraay—Mørkholm Essays: Numismatic Studies in Memory of C. M. Kraay and O. Mørkholm*. Numismatica Lovaniensia 10. Edited by G. Le Rider, G. K. Jenkins, N. Waggoner, and U. Westermark. Louvain-la-Neuve: Université Catholique de Louvain, 1989. Pages 283-90. 2 pls.
Reviews the coinage of the Alabanda (Antioch of the Chrysaorians) mint in Caria, ca. 197-142 B.C. Reviews Seyrig's arrangement of the five identifiable series of coins and proposes a re-arrangement. Focuses on the coinage of the later series. Discusses chronology, monograms, hoards, and weights. Describes a tetradrachm recently added to the American Numismatic Society collection and suggests this new coin served as an experimental transition from the Attic weight coinage to one of a lighter weight. [Seyrig's review of this coinage appeared in *Trésors du Levant Anciens et Nouveaux*. See Seyrig *Trésors Monétaires Séleucides* under SYRIA—SELEUCID KINGDOM].

4909 **Walker, Alan S.** "Kranaos, a New Mint in Caria." *Schweizer Münzblätter* (Switzerland) 28, no. 112 (November 1978): 86-8. Illus. [CS 2746]
"The mint issuing small bronze coins hitherto located at either Cranaë or Crannon is the Carian town of Cranaus, as types (head of Helios) and the provenance of two newcomers, from near Halicarnassus, prove." [H. Bloesch, *NL* 103]

4910 **Weiser, Wolfram.** "Zur Münzprägung von Iasos und Bargylia." *Die Inschriften von Iasos, Teil II*. Edited by W. Blümel. Bonn, 1985. Pages 170-85.
[Also see Ashton "The Pre-Imperial Coinage of Iasos" above].

4911 **Wroth, Warwick W.** "Eupolemus." *Numismatic Chronicle* 3rd ser., 11 (1891): 135-9.
Discusses a bronze coin with *obv.*, three Macedonian shields; *rev.*, sword with strap and the inscription ΕΥΠΟΛΕΜΟΥ. Wroth attributes the coin to Eupolemus, the general of King Cassander of Macedonia. Discusses the type, inscription, and monogram. Suggests these coins were minted at Mylasa in Caria. Eupolemus campaigned in Caria ca. 314 B.C. [Also see Ashton "Coins of the Macedonian Kings, Lysimachos and Eupolemos" under MACEDONIAN KINGDOM—GENERAL WORKS. Ashton suggests Kaunos for the mint of Eupolemos' coinage].

4912 **Yarkin, Ural.** "The Coinage of Syangela in Caria." *Numismatic Chronicle* 7th ser., 15 (1975): 12-8. 1 pl. [CS 2749]
"Coins dated between ca. 390 and 275 B.C. bearing the inscription ΣΥ are attributed to the Carian town of Syangela, ca. 12 miles east of Halicarnassus, and not to Syros or Syme. The eight known coins are catalogued." [U. Yarkin, *NL* 96]. [Also see the author's follow-up article below].

4913 ——— "More Coins of Syangela from Theangela." *Numismatic Chronicle* 137 (1977): 152-3.
Five more coins of Syangela have come to light since the author's previous article (see above) and are listed here.

4914 **Zabel, B, and Andrew R. Meadows.** "The 'Myndos' 1996 Hoard (*CH* 9.522)." *Coin Hoards, Volume IX: Greek Hoards*. Edited by A. Meadows and Ute Wartenberg. London: Royal Numismatic Society, 2002. Pages 244-52. 3 pls.
Discussion of a hoard that contained about 300 drachms of Myndos, 10-20 drachms of Halicarnassos, and 60+ fractions of unspecified mints. The findspot is unknown. One hundred thirty-eight of the drachms of Myndos and six of Halicarnassos are catalogued here. Comments on chronology and the pattern of mintage. Burial likely was in the mid-second century B.C.

Also see: Ashton and Kinns "Opuscula Anatolica II" under ASIA MINOR—GENERAL WORKS; Ashton, Hardwick, Konuk, and Meadows "Pixodarus Hoard" under HOARDS; Ashton, Kinns, Konuk, and Meadows "Hecatomnus Hoard" under HOARDS; Cancio "A New Satrapal Coin" under PERSIA; Gardner "Numismatic Reattributions" under GENERAL WORKS—GREEK; Gargali "Coins from a Hellenistic Cemetery" under CARIAN ISLANDS—KALYMNOS; Grace "Stamped Amphora Handles" (Cnidus) under TYPES; Hurter "Lions and Lionesses, Eagles" under HOARDS; Hurter "The Pixodaros Hoard" under HOARDS; Jamgochian "The Winged Victory of Samothrace" under TYPES; Jenkins "Two Coins" under ASIA MINOR—GENERAL WORKS; Jones "Coins as Weights" under METROLOGY; Konuk *From Kroisos to Karia* under PRIVATE COLLECTIONS; Le Rider "Antiochos II à Mylasa" (two items) under SYRIA—SELEUCID KINGDOM.

Meadows and Houghton "The Gaziantep Hoard" under HOARDS; Moysey "Observations…Satrapal Revolt" under PERSIA; Münzen und Medaillen *Auktion 21: Joy Collection* under PRIVATE COLLECTIONS; "Record Price Set" under IONIA; E. S. G. Robinson "A Find of Archaic Coins from South-West Asia Minor" under HOARDS; Robinson "Some Electrum and Gold" under ASIA MINOR—GENERAL WORKS; Sugden "Miniature Ionians and Carians" under IONIA; Thompson "The Alexandrine Mint of Mylasa" under MACEDONIAN KINGDOM—GENERAL WORKS; Troxell and Kagan "Cilicians and Neighbors" under CILICIA; Waggoner "Three Recent Greek Accessions" under ASIA MINOR—GENERAL WORKS; Wells "Observations" under PERSIA.

CARIAN ISLANDS

About the same time an important new coinage came into being in the eastern Aegean, that of Rhodes; in 408 B.C. the cities of the island were amalgamated into one, and one of the first signs of the existence of the new Rhodes is to be seen in the issue of remarkable tetradrachms displaying the head of Helios. The first of these heads is extraordinarily vivid and the flame-like hair suggests the radiating power of the god.

—G. K. Jenkins, 1972

KALYMNOS

4915 **Gargali, Nomiki.** "Coins from a Hellenistic Cemetery on Kalymna, and New Light on the Coinage of Kos in the Second Century B.C." *Numismatic Chronicle* 169 (2009): 29-37. 1 pl.
Catalogues twelve coins from Carian mints found during excavations, including coins of Kaunos, Knidos, Kalymna, Kos, and Rhodes. Discusses the use of coins for Charon's fee. The coins found were deposited in the graves to serve as Charon's fee for transportation across the River Styx.

4916 **Höghammar, Kerstin.** "The Hellenistic Silver Coinage of Kalymnos." *Coins in the Aegean Islands. Proceedings of the Fifth Scientific Meeting, Mytilene, 16-29 September 2006. Volume 1: Ancient Times.* Obolos 9. Edited by Panagiotis Tselekas. Athens: The Friends of the Numismatic Museum, 2010. Pages 495-526.

4917 **Wartenberg, Ute.** "Calymna Calumniated—A Nineteenth Century Misattribution?" *Studies in Greek Numismatics in Memory of Martin Jessop Price.* Edited by Richard Ashton and Silvia Hurter. London: Spink, 1998. Pages 363-71. 2 pls.
Wartenberg examines a small series of staters (*obv.*, head of a warrior in a crested Corinthian helmet; *rev.*, lyre in incuse) which is usually attributed to the Carian island of Calymna and dated to ca. 530-520 B.C. Only three specimens of this coinage are known. Some researchers have questioned the authenticity of the coins. The author summarizes previous scholarship regarding the attribution and chronology of the coins. She suggests other possible attributions. The three specimens are all struck from the same dies, although some show repair and alteration to the dies. One is struck on a different weight standard than the other two. Discusses areas which may have used both of these weight standards. Points to stylistic similarities to coins of some northern Greek mints. Much of the evidence points to a northern Greek mint as the origin of these coins. Concludes with a discussion of known forgeries of these coins.

Also see: Seltman "The Ring of Polycrates" under ART.

KARPATHOS

4918 **Cahn, Herbert A.** "Poseidion on Karpathos?" *Numismatic Chronicle* 6th ser., 17 (1957): 11-2. 1 pl.
"This article re-examines the evidence for the attribution of archaic silver staters with obverse type of three dolphins (two large, one smaller) within a dotted square, and reverse showing an incuse square divided into rectangles. The evidence is not strong enough to support Imhoof-Blumer's original assignment to Poseidion on Karpathos." [J. Healy, *NL* 49]

KOS

4919 **Ashton, Richard H. J.** "A Hoard of Koan Coins." *Numismatic Chronicle* 156 (1996): 278-9. 1 pl.
Describes a hoard of seven bronze coins of Kos.

4920 ——— "The Pseudo-Rhodian Drachms of Kos." *Numismatic Chronicle* 158 (1998): 223-8. 1 pl.
Ashton argues that certain pseudo-Rhodian drachms were struck on Kos in the late 170's B.C. All die combinations are illustrated here.

4921 **Barkay, Rachel.** "An Archaic Coin from the 'Shoulder of Hinnom' Excavations in Jerusalem." *Israel Numismatic Journal* (Israel) 8 (1984-85): 1-5. Illus.
"An archaic hemidrachm or diobol (1.76 g) of Cos, dated to the end of the sixth century, was found in a seventh to early fifth century tomb discovered in Jerusalem. A list of similar coins is given in a Table of Archaic Coins also found in Israel." [A. Spaer, *NL* 117]

4922 **Barron, John P.** "The Fifth-Century Diskoboloi of Kos." *Essays in Greek Coinage Presented to Stanley Robinson.* Edited by C. M. Kraay and G. K. Jenkins. Oxford: Clarendon Press, 1968. Pages 75-89. 3 pls. [CS 2750]
Examines the coinage of Kos depicting a discus-thrower on the obverse and a crab on the reverse, struck during the fifth century B.C. Attempts to closely date the coinage to determine whether Kos defied the Athenian currency decree of ca. 448 B.C. which prohibited the striking of silver coinage by Athens's subject states. Some authorities have dated the coinage to post-448 B.C., thus signaling defiance of the decree. Barron demonstrates that the weight standard is not Attic. Suggests these coins are triple sigloi on the Persian standard. Comments on the style of the engraving and the epigraphy, and finds these elements to be consistent with the styles of the second quarter of the fifth century—therefore, the coins pre-date the decree. Cites evidence of Kos' resistance to Athenian control. Suggests that the coins were still being struck in 448, but that Athens closed the mint shortly thereafter. Coinage may have resumed 446-442 B.C. while Kos was in revolt.

4923 **Gardiner, Edward N.** "Throwing the Diskos." *Journal of Hellenic Studies* 27 (1907): 1-36. Illus., 3 pls.
"On pp. 29-31 coins of Cos with a discobolus as type are illustrated; it is decided that the athlete is represented in approximately the same pose as that of Myron's discobolus, allowances having been made for the limitations of the artist and the shape of the space on the coin." [J. R. Jones, *NIJHS*]

4924 **Giannikouri, A., and Vasiliki E. Stefanaki.** "A Hoard of Bronze Coins of the Hellenistic Period from Kos: Monetary System and Fractions of the Bronze Coins of Kos." *Coins in the Aegean Islands. Proceedings of the Fifth Scientific Meeting, Mytilene, 16-29 September 2006. Volume 1: Ancient Times.* Obolos 9. Edited by Panagiotis Tselekas. Athens: The Friends of the Numismatic Museum, 2010. Pages 447-80.

4925 **Höghammar, Kerstin.** "A Group of Koan Issues from c. 200 BC." *Numismatic Chronicle* 167 (2007): 79-92. 2 pls.
The author presents four Hellenistic silver issues of Kos, focusing on their dates and examining their historical context.

4926 **Ingvaldsen, Håkon.** *Utmyntningen på Kos 366-190 f. Kr.* Ph.D. dissertation. Uppsala University, 1994.

4927 **Kroll, John H.** "The Late Hellenistic Tetrobols of Kos." *Museum Notes* 11 (1964): 81-117. 7 pls. [CS 2751]
Examines the tetrobols of Kos bearing the head of Asklepios/coiled snake, customarily dated to the period 166-88 B.C., based on two previously unpublished hoards. Discusses the historical background of this period. Suggests these coins were struck in the second half of the second century B.C. and may have continued into the opening decades of the first century. Discusses the Koan-Rhodian weight standard and its relationship to the Attic standard. Presents a table of the thirty-four issues of three kinds: (1) those bearing two magistrates' names, (2) those with one magistrate's name, and (3) those with one name with an abbreviation for an official body. Presents an extensive discussion of the inscriptions in an attempt to identify the men named on the reverses, concluding that they were financially responsible for the coinage issues. Explains the sequence of issues and presents a catalogue of the coins.

4928 **Milne, Joseph G.** "Two Hoards of Coins of Kos." *Numismatic Chronicle* 4th ser., 12 (1912): 14-20. 1pl.
Discusses a hoard of twenty-one drachms of Kos. The coins are from the third century B.C. Lists the magistrate, weight, size, and die axis for each coin. Discusses the dies and the magistrates. Also examines a hoard of third century B.C. copper coins of Kos. Lists magistrate, size, weight, and die axis for each, but there is no further discussion of the coins.

4929 **Requier, P.** "Les Premiers Tétradrachmes Hellénistiques de Cos." *Revue Suisse de Numismatique* (Switzerland) 75 (1996): 53-64.

Also see: Ashton, Kinns, Konuk, and Meadows "Hecatomnus Hoard" under HOARDS; Gargali "Coins from a Hellenistic Cemetery" under CARIAN ISLANDS—KALYMNOS; Ingvaldsen "Coin Finds and Sanctuaries: A Case Study from the Island of Kos" under HOARDS; Richter "Late Hellenistic Portraiture" under PORTRAITS; Stannard and Frey-Kupper "'Pseudomints' and Small Change in Italy and Sicily" under ITALY—GENERAL WORKS.

NISYROS

4930 **Ashton, Richard H.** "The Coinage of Nisyros." *Travaux de Numismatique Grecque Offerts à Georges Le Rider.* Edited by M. Amandry and S. Hurter. London: Spink, 1999. Pages 15-24. 1 pl.
Discusses some coins previously attributed to the Carian city of Nisyros, which the author believes belong to other cities (including *BMC Nisyros* 1, 2, 3; *SNG Copenhagen,* Caria 709; and *SNG Von Aulock* 2770). Ashton then lists and discusses the autonomous coinages which can reasonably be attributed to Nisyros, including four bronze issues and two silver issues. Examines the dating of the coins. The polis was independent during most of the fourth and third centuries B.C.

Also see: Cahn "A New Carian Mint" under CARIA.

RHODOS

4931 **Apostolou, Eva.** "Les Drachmes Rhodiennes et Pseudo-Rhodiennes de la Fin du IIIe et du Début du IIe Siècle av. J.-C." *Revue Numismatique* (France) 150 (1955): 7-19.

4932 ——— "Rhodes Hellénestique: Les Trésors et la Circulation Monétaire." *Eulimene* (Mediterranean Archaeological Society, Rethymno, Greece) 3 (2002): 117-82.
"The study of hoards containing issues of the Rhodian state from its foundation in 408 B.C. until the beginning of the first century B.C., leads to the following conclusions: (1) The circulation of Rhodian coinage during the above mentioned period was restricted mainly within the borders of the Rhodian state. (2) The systematic control of coin circulation within Rhodian territory was achieved through the gradual decrease and withdrawal of the pre-existing local coinage (or part of it) and its simultaneous replacement by new issues. (3) The 'closed' character of the Rhodian economy supported the commercial and political activities of the Rhodians and was an important factor in their prosperity during this period." [M. I. Stefanakis, *NL* 147]

4933 ——— *Hellenistic Rhodes: Its Economic History Deduced from the Study of the Coinage.* Obolos 6. Athens: Numismatic Museum, 2003. 30 pp.

4934 **Apostolou, Eva et al., ed.** *Coins in the Dodecanese and its Asia Minor Peraia: Proceedings of the 4th Scientific Meeting.* Obolos 6. Athens: Numismatic Museum, 2006. 439 pp.

4935 **Arslan, Melih.** "The Kargi Hoard of Rhodian Plinthophoroi." *Recent Turkish Coin Hoards and Numismatic Studies.* British Institute of Archaeology at Ankara Monograph, No. 12. Edited by C. S. Lightfoot. Oxford: Oxbow Books, 1991. Pages 59-69 including 6 pls. and 2 maps.
A catalogue of sixty-one early plinthophoric drachms of Rhodes found in Kargi, western Lycia, in 1974. The coins were likely buried ca. 170-165 B.C. Each coin is photographed.

4936 **Ashton, Richard H. J.** "Rhodian Bronze Coinage and the Earthquake of 229-226 B.C." *Numismatic Chronicle* 146 (1986): 1-18. 4 pls.
"The author connects three groups of Rhodian bronze coinage (types *BMC* 219-222, 226-227, and 228, respectively) with the help given by Ptolemy III to Rhodes after the earthquake of 229-226 B.C., and identifies the obverse type of *BMC* 226-227 and 228 as Berenike II. Rhodian tetradrachms with magistrates Ameinias, Aristokritos, Eukrates and Tharsytas (*BMC* 120-127) are connected with the needs of reconstruction after the earthquake." [R. Ashton, *NL* 118]

4937 ——— "Rhodian Coinage and the Colossus." *Revue Numismatique* (France) 6, no. 30 (1988): 75-90. 4 pls.
"No account of the outward appearance of the Colossus of Rhodes survives from antiquity, and more recent attempts to identify it in extant pieces of ancient art are unconvincing. The author suggests that the head of the Colossus is depicted on a short-lived special series of Rhodian didrachms (*BMC* 41) struck in parallel with the mint's regular output in the early third century B.C. The author provides a chronology of Rhodian coinage (principally didrachms) between ca. 333-ca. 230 B.C." [R. Ashton, *NL* 121]

4938 ——— "A Series of Pseudo-Rhodian Drachms from Mainland Greece." *Numismatic Chronicle* 148 (1988): 21-32. 3 pls.
A catalogue of ninety-five drachms with Helios/rose, representing all die combinations known to the author. The reverse bears a magistrate's name but no ethnic. Presents a table of weights. Concludes these were struck on the mainland and are merely imitations of Rhodian types. Reviews hoards containing similar coins. Dates these coins to ca. 180's to early 160's B.C. (most likely 171 or 170). Suggests these were struck to pay Cretan mercenaries in Perseus' army. May have been struck by an official Macedonian mint or by Larissa.

4939 ——— "A Series of Rhodian Didrachms from the Mid-Third Century B.C." *Numismatic Chronicle* 149 (1989): 1-13. 5 pls.
"The author discusses a series of Rhodian didrachms which have on the reverse the letter-symbol combinations ΔI and star, ΔI and star on pileus, and EY and harpa (*BMC* 49-55). Principally on the basis of the hoard evidence, he concludes that either they belong to a short gap between the unrayed and the rayed didrachms with magistrates' names in full (*BMC* 43-48 and 129-152, respectively), or they are contemporary with the first issues of the latter. They are dated to ca. 250 B.C." [R. Ashton, *NL* 122]

4940 ——— "The Solar Disk Drachms of Caria." *Numismatic Chronicle* 150 (1990): 27-38. 3 pls.
"The author provides a corpus of the Carian drachms with profile head of Helios on a radiate solar disk on the obverse and rose flanked by E Y, M E, or N I, together with associated bronzes. He argues that they date to ca. 360-340 B.C., and that the traditional attributions to Euthana, Megista and Nisyros are mistaken. He very tentatively suggests that they may have been struck by the Hekatomnids." [R. Ashton, *NL* 126]

4941 ——— "A Hoard of Late Rhodian Plinthophoric Hemidrachms (*CH* 4, 72)." *Numismatic Chronicle* 151 (1991): 202-4. 5 pls.
"The author publishes a hoard of fifty Rhodian plinthophoric hemidrachms of *Jenkins* groups D/D and E, including some issues not in *Jenkins*, together with eleven further Rhodian coins which might have belonged to it. The hoard was probably buried some time after 84 B.C." [R. Ashton, *NL* 129]

4942 ——— "Rhodian Coinage in the Early Imperial Period." *Recent Turkish Coin Hoards and Numismatic Studies.* British Institute of Archaeology at Ankara Monograph, No. 12. Edited by C. S. Lightfoot. Oxford: Oxbow Books, 1991. Pages 71-90 including 6 pls.
A catalogue of seventy Rhodian bronze obols and drachms from a hoard discovered ca. 1976. Each coin is photographed. The coins include issues with a full-blown rose on reverse, as well as issues with a profile rose. Ashton attempts to organize the coins into a chronological sequence. Compares the types with those on silver drachms of Rhodes.

4943 ——— "Some Forgeries of Rhodian Didrachms of the Mid Third Century B.C." *Florilegium Numismaticum: Studia in Honorem U. Westermark Edita.* Edited by Harald Nilsson. Stockholm: Svenska Numismatiska Föreningen, 1992. Pages 29-32. Illus.
Ashton publishes two groups of forgeries of Rhodian didrachms, each group struck from a single pair of dies. The first group of forgeries bears the magistrate's name ΦΙΛΩΝΙΔΑΣ and a "lamp" symbol. This type belongs to the period 265-250 B.C. These pieces are cast. Lists the corpus of genuine coins of this variety. The second group are struck copies and bear the name ΑΓΗΣΙΔΑΜΟΣ. The author discusses the diagnostics of both groups.

4944 ——— "A Third Century B.C. Hoard of Coins of Western Asia Minor." *Classical Numismatic Review* 17, no. 3 (third quarter 1992): 3-4. Illus.
Describes a hoard containing 449 Rhodian didrachms from 340-250 B.C., an Alexander-type drachm of Lysimachus of a type sometimes attributed to Kolophon, and a Rhodian plinthophoric drachm. Mentions other coins which probably were part of the original hoard. Describes each of the major types of Rhodian didrachms present, giving approximate dates of issue, and illustrating several types. No rayed-head Helios types are included.

4945 ——— "A Revised Arrangement for the Earliest Coinage of Rhodes." *Essays in Honour of Robert Carson and Kenneth Jenkins.* Edited by M. Price, A. Burnett, and R. Bland. London: Spink & Son, 1993. Pages 9-15. 2 pls.
Denyse Bérend and others contend that the first federal emissions of Rhodes were the so-called Attic weight tetradrachms (see Bérend "Les Tétradrachmes de Rhodes" below). Ashton contends the first coins were the Chian weight tetradrachms with symbol and no control letter in the reverse field, struck shortly after 408/7 B.C. These may be regarded as triple-sigloi on the Persian standard. Ashton outlines a new sequence of issues, describes the stylistic development of the early Rhodian coinage, and suggests a new chronology. Ashton lists the known varieties of the Alliance tridrachms/double sigloi, the early hemidrachms, and the early obols of Rhodes.

4946 ——— "Pseudo-Rhodian Drachms from Central Greece." *Numismatic Chronicle* 155 (1995): 1-20. 5 pls.

"The author dates six issues of pseudo-Rhodian drachms to the early years of the Third Macedonian War. He assigns one issue to Haliartos and the others to a second mint, possibly Larymna." [R. Ashton, *NL* 140]. [Also see "More Pseudo-Rhodian Drachms" below].

4947 ——— "More Pseudo-Rhodian Drachms from Mainland Greece." *Numismatic Chronicle* 157 (1997): 188-91. 1 pl.
"The author produces new evidence to corroborate the attribution to Haliartos of certain pseudo-Rhodian drachms (and more archaic coinage) made in *Numismatic Chronicle* 155 (1995). He suggests that two further issues of pseudo-Rhodian drachms signed by Sokrates and Phaon may be connected with the well-known Hermias drachms of the 1968 Larissa hoard." [R. Ashton, *NL* 140]. [See Ashton "Pseudo-Rhodian Drachms from Central Greece" above].

4948 ——— "Some Early Forgeries of Rhodian Coins." *Numismatic Chronicle* 159 (1999): 293-4. 1 pl.
"The author argues that four Rhodian drachms are cast forgeries made in the eighteenth century from moulds taken from a genuine Rhodian didrachm now in the Hunterian Museum, Glasgow." [R. H. J. Ashton, *NL* 145]. [Also see Ireland "Another Example" below].

4949 ——— "More Pseudo-Rhodian Drachms from Central Greece: Haliartos (Again), Chalkis, and Euboia Uncertain(?)." *Numismatic Chronicle* 160 (2000): 93-116. 5 pls.
Argues that (1) a recent attempt to deprive Haliartos of pseudo-Rhodian drachms should be resisted, (2) that certain rare issues of pseudo-Rhodian drachms were struck at Chalkis during the Third Macedonian War, and (3) that some other pseudo-Rhodian drachms may belong to a Euboian mint in the same period, possibly Histiaia. The Appendices examine two mixed hoards of the same period (Third Macedonian War), and discuss new variants of the "grapes" pseudo-Rhodian drachms and a die-linked series of pseudo-Rhodian issues of unknown attribution.

4950 ——— "The Coinage of Rhodes 408 - c. 190 B.C." *Money and Its Uses in the Ancient Greek World.* Edited by A. Meadows and K. Shipton. Oxford: University Press, 2001. Pages 79-115. 12 pls.
Ashton examines the coinage of Rhodes from the time the three cities (Kamiros, Ialysos, and Lindos) combined to form Rhodos in 408 B.C. Rhodos adopted the Chian weight standards (15.3 gm tetradrachm) and began issuing tetradrachms bearing the rose reverse type. Includes an extensive review of the coin types, symbols, control marks, magistrate names, weights, and hoard evidence to determine the sequence and chronology of the coinage. Discusses the reduced weight standard of a 6.8 gm didrachm which was adopted in the 340s. Reviews the introduction of the plinthophoric system which replaced the Rhodian standard and drove the older, heavier coins out of circulation. These entered circulation by the mid-180s. Ashton also addresses the bronze coinage. The first federal Rhodian bronze appeared shortly after the federal mint opened, with greatly increased quantities minted in the second half of the fourth century B.C. The author continues with an examination of the volume, pattern, and historical associations of the coinage. Comments on the circulation of the coins and the function of the coinage. Ashton suggests the coinage was primarily struck to facilitate state expenditures (maintenance of the fleet and payments to mercenaries, military and civic officials). Makes comparisons with the output of other mints. The plates present all significant coin types.

4951 ——— "Rhodian Bronze Coinage and the Siege of Mithradates VI." *Numismatic Chronicle* 161 (2001): 53-66. 16 pls.
"The author provides a die-study of the large Rhodian bronzes of type *BMC* 312-323, associates them with the last issues of silver plinthophoroi, and argues that they were struck at the time of the siege of Rhodes by Mithradates VI in 88 B.C. Some of their symbols may reflect the miraculous aid given by Isis to the besieged city." [R. H. J. Ashton, *NL* 145]

4952 ——— "Clubs, Thunderbolts, Torches, Stars and Caducei: More Pseudo-Rhodian Drachms from Mainland Greece and the Islands." *Numismatic Chronicle* 162 (2002): 59-78. 8 pls.
A catalogue of several issues of pseudo-Rhodian drachms from mainland Greece with symbols club and thunderbolt. It is unknown where they were struck. Also, the author suggests that two large issues of pseudo-Rhodian drachms with the name Gorgos and symbols torch (or torch and star) and caduceus may belong to Samothrace.

4953 ——— "Recent Epigraphic Evidence for the Start of the Rhodian and Lykian League Plinthophoroi." *Numismatic Chronicle* 165 (2005): 85-9.
Discusses a treaty, ca. 166 B.C., settling a border dispute between the Termessians at Oinoanda and Tlos. The text refers to "new Rhodian plinthophoric money." Discusses the meaning of "new."

4954 ——— "The Only Recorded Name on Rhodian Plinthophoric Chalkoi." *Numismatic Chronicle* 169 (2009): 39-43. 1 pl.
The name Mousais, accompanied by one of two monograms, can be detected on a dozen plinthophoric Rhodian chalkoi of the second century B.C., the only coins among the many hundreds of the series extant to bear the name of an official.

4955 **Ashton, Richard H., and Arnold-Peter C. Weiss.** "The Post-Plinthophoric Silver Drachms of Rhodes." *Numismatic Chronicle* 157 (1997): 1-40. 16 pls.
"The authors discuss a corpus of Attic weight drachms of Rhodes (*BMC* 334-341) struck from 120 obverse dies, unsigned and signed by forty-three names. A relative chronology is proposed. The authors argue that the series ended in the reign of Augustus, and that its starting-date is somewhat later than the conventional 88 or 84 B.C. Also discussed are twenty-one later drachms of similar types (ch. 2, p. 33, fig. 13) which differ in style and are of cistophoric weight." [R. Ashton and A.-P. Weiss, *NL* 140]

4956 **Ashton, Richard H. J., Melih Arslan, and Ali Dervisagaoglu.** "The Köycegiz Hoard of Late Rhodian Plinthophoric Drachms." *Coin Hoards, Volume VIII: Greek Hoards.* Edited by U. Wartenberg, M. J. Price, and K. A. McGregor. London: Royal Numismatic Society, 1994. Pages 84-7. 2 pls.
Brief discussion of a hoard (*Coin Hoards VIII*, no. 524) of sixty-six late Rhodian plinthophoric drachms found in 1989 near ancient Kaunos. The coins are now in the Fethiye Museum.

4957 **Bérend, Denyse.** "Les Tétradrachmes de Rhodes de la Première Période. 1ère Partie." *Revue Suisse de Numismatique* (Switzerland) 51 (1972): 5-39. 10 pls. [CS 2752]
[Also see Ashton "A Revised Arrangement" above].

4958 ——— "Rhodes, Encore." *Revue Numismatique* (France) 150 (1995): 251-5.

4959 **Boehringer, Christof.** "A 1971 Group of Rhodian Coins (from Karia?)." *Numismatic Chronicle* 157 (1997): 214-7. 3 pls.
Discusses a hoard of forty-seven silver coins of Rhodes, found in Turkey. The coins were buried after 84 B.C. Includes a catalogue of the coins with commentary.

4960 **Bresson, A.** "La Circulation Monétaire Rhodienne Jusqu'en 166." *Dialogues d'Histoire Ancienne* (France) 19 (1993): 119-69.

4961 ——— "Drachmes Rhodiennes et Imitations: Une Politique Économique de Rhodes?" *Revue des Études Anciennes* (France) 98 (1996): 65-77.

4962 ——— "Rhodes, Cnide et les Lyciens au Début du IIe Siècle av. J.-C." *Revue des Études Anciennes* (France) 100 (1996): 65-88.

4963 **Cahn, Herbert A.** "Die Archaischen Silberstatere von Lindos." *Charites: Studien zur Altertumswissenschaft—Festschrift Ernst Langlotz*. Edited by K. Schauenburg. Bonn: Athenaum-Verlag, 1957. Pages 17-26. [CS 2753]

4964 **Delrieux, Fabrice.** "Les Monnaies de Mylasa au Types de Zeus Osogôa et Zeus Labraundeis." *Numismatic Chronicle* 159 (1999): 33-45.

4965 **Grace, Virginia R.** "The Eponyms Named on Rhodian Amphora Stamps." *Hesperia* 22 (1953): 116-28. 3 pls.
"On pp. 127-8 it is noted that an amphora stamp consisting of a bunch of grapes with the letter *epsilon* is also used as a subsidiary type on Rhodian coins of the fourth century B.C. (cf. *BMC Caria* pl. 36, nos. 5 and 8-10)." [J. R. Jones, *NIAJAH*]. [Also see Grace "Stamped Amphora Handles" under TYPES].

4966 **Grierson, Philip.** "The Thirty Pieces of Silver and Coins of Rhodes." *Spink Numismatic Circular* 63, no. 10 (October 1955): 422. [CS 16414]
"Evidence of travelers to Rhodes in the fifteenth century indicates that between A.D. 1413 and 1479 the coins shown (and occasionally presented) to pilgrims as the Thirty Pieces of Silver for which Christ was betrayed changed from Rhodian fourth century B.C. drachms or didrachms to Rhodian tetradrachms. Since the Spanish voyager Pero Tafur saw a number of coins in 1436 when he visited the church of St. John, while earlier travelers saw single small coins, it seems that a small hoard of tetradrachms discovered between 1413 and 1436 allowed the Knights to exhibit and make gifts of the larger coins as those of the Betrayal. Writers of the end of the fifteenth century clearly identify the relic as a tetradrachm by comparing it with contemporary coins of known weight and size." [C. Vermeule, *NL* 36]

4967 **Ireland, Stanley.** "Another Example of a Rhodian Forgery." *Numismatic Chronicle* 164 (2004): 223-4. 1 pl.
Publishes a cast forgery of a drachm of Rhodes. This is another example of the forgeries published by Ashton in 1999 (see Ashton "Some Early Forgeries of Rhodian Coins" above). The new specimen sheds light on the date these were made—likely ca. 1738-40.

4968 **Jenkins, G. Kenneth.** "Rhodian Plinthophoroi: A Sketch." *Kraay—Mørkholm Essays: Numismatic Studies in Memory of C. M. Kraay and O. Mørkholm*. Numismatica Lovaniensia 10. Edited by G. Le Rider, G. K. Jenkins, N. Waggoner, and U. Westermark. Louvain-la-Neuve: Université Catholique de Louvain, 1989. Pages 101-19. 6 pls.
Jenkins examines the coins with an incuse square (plinthos) reverse, summarizing the results drawn from a study of the Marmaris hoard and other hoards. This coinage began ca. 177-173 B.C. and ended early in the first century B.C. Examines the use of magistrates' names and symbols, but the author is unable to draw firm conclusions as to their significance (perhaps distinguishing terms of office). Doubts the existence of any hiatus in the sequence of plinthophoric issues as suggested by Troxell. Lists coins and denotes die links. Includes charts of names, symbols, and weights.

4969 **Kollgaard, Ron.** "Commercial Importance: Rhodos Coins Reflect Trade." *The Celator* 3, no. 2 (February 1989): 1, 23. Illus.
Traces the history of the city of Rhodes from its origins in Greek colonialism to the period of Roman dominance. Mentions the changes in the design and weight of the Rhodian coinage which resulted from various economic circumstances.

4970 **Leschhorn, Wolfgang.** "Zu den Rhodischen Didrachmen des 4. und 3. Jh. v. Chr. Der Schatzfund von Usak (*Coin Hoards* 11.68)." *Jahrbuch für Numismatik und Geldgeschichte* (Germany) 35 (1985): 7-20.

4971 **Madsen, Eardley, and Ethel Madsen.** "Rhodes." *SAN—Journal of the Society for Ancient Numismatics* 13, no. 2 (summer 1982): inside covers.
A brief overview of the history and coinage of Rhodes.

4972 **Melville-Jones, John R.** "Les Premières Monnaies Plinthophores de Rhodes." *Revue Belge de Numismatique et de Sigillographie* (Belgium) 125 (1979): 53-4.

4973 **Sheridan, Walter W.** "A Hoard of Rhodian-Type Drachms." *Museum Notes* 18 (1972): 5-15. 10 pls.
Presents a catalogue of 203 Rhodian type light-weight silver drachms with eagle partially covering the right cheek of Helios, from a recent hoard. Suggests the coins were minted at Caunus starting in 189 B.C., and that the eagle represents a Ptolemaic influence at the city.

4974 **Sippel, Donald V.** "The Purposes of Rhodian Alexander-Type Tetradrachms." *The Ancient World* 10, nos. 1-2 (November 1984): 61-7.
Sippel searches for the motivation which led to the minting of the series of posthumous Alexander-type tetradrachms at Rhodes. Sippel suggests that Rhodes began this coinage in 200 B.C.—the time that Rhodes became the acknowledged hegemon of the Nesiotic League. The motivation was essentially propagandistic—announcing Rhodes' arrival as a major Hellenistic power.

4975 **Stefanaki, Vasiliki E.** "Le Monnayage des Isles Égéennes à l'Époque Classique Tardive et Hellénistique: L'Influence Rhodienne." *Coins in the Aegean Islands. Proceedings of the Fifth Scientific Meeting, Mytilene, 16-29 September 2006. Volume 1: Ancient Times*. Obolos 9. Edited by Panagiotis Tselekas. Athens: The Friends of the Numismatic Museum, 2010. Pages 413-46.

4976 **Weiss, Arnold-Peter C., and Silvia Hurter.** "The Silver Staters of Ialysos." *Sweizerische Numismatische Rundschau* (Switzerland) 77 (1998): 5-23. Illus.
"The authors present a detailed study of the rare silver coins from Ialysos (Rhodes). The staters and fractions were struck ca. 510-480 B.C. in an unusual weight standard." [M. Peter, *NL* 145]

4977 **Wells, H. Bartlett.** "A First Coinage of Lindos?" *Schweizer Münzblätter* (Switzerland) 31, no. 122 (May 1981): 29-34. Illus.
"A coin with lion's head facing is cautiously attributed to the mint of Lindos. The two impressions on the reverse are made in the peculiar technique that was used for striking the earlier specimens of the known Lindos series. The punch bears the figure of a Greek lambda." [H. Bloesch, *NL* 109]

4978 **Zacharas, Andreas A.** "Helios, Canting Type." *Nomismatika Khronika* (Greece) 24 (2005): 23-4. Illus.
Discusses a silver coin of Rhodes bearing a counterstamp on the obverse. The coin bears the head of Medusa, rather than the more common Helios. The reverse bears the name of the archon ΓΟΡΓΟΣ (Gorgos). The counterstamp is identified as Nike. A similar coin in a recent auction was described as a mercenary wage drachm struck in Crete. The author suggests the archon Gorgos directed the mint to produce a coin with the standard head of Helios modified with wings and snakes to become the gorgon Medusa. Suggests this was an intentional canting type playing off the archon's name.

Also see: Apostolou "Rhodian Stater" under MACEDONIAN KINGDOM—GENERAL WORKS; Ashton "The Attalid Poll-Tax" under MYSIA—PERGAMENE KINGDOM; Ashton "The Pseudo-Rhodian Drachms of Mylasa" under CARIA; Ashton "Pseudo-Rhodian Drachms from Eretria" under CENTRAL GREECE—EUBOIA; Ashton "A Pseudo-Rhodian Drachm from Kaunos" under CARIA; Ashton "Rhodian-type Silver" under CRETE; Ashton "Pseudo-Rhodian" under THRACE—SAMOTHRACE; Ashton "Pseudo-Rhodian Drachms and the Beginning of the Lycian League Coinage" under LYCIA; Ashton and Kinns "Opuscula Anatolica II" and "Opuscula Anatonlica III" under ASIA MINOR—GENERAL WORKS; Ashton, Kinns, Konuk, and Meadows "Hecatomnus Hoard" under HOARDS; Ashton and Meadows "The Letoon Deposit" under HOARDS; Ashton and Warren "A Hoard of Western Greek and Pseudo-Rhodian Silver" under HOARDS; Babington "On an Unpublished Tetradrachm" under MACEDONIAN KINGDOM—GENERAL WORKS; Gargali "Coins from a Hellenistic Cemetery" under CARIAN ISLANDS—KALYMNOS; Gerojannis "Greek Coins" under PRIVATE COLLECTIONS; Grace "Stamped Amphora Handles" under TYPES; Hurter "Das Palladion" under TYPES; Kleiner "The Alexander Tetradrachms of Pergamum and Rhodes" under MACEDONIAN KINGDOM—GENERAL WORKS; Nock "Notes on Ruler-Cult" under TYPES; Wells "In Quest of an Identification" (Lindos) under BOSPOROS.

TELOS

4979 **Stefanaki, Vasiliki E.** "The Early Coinage of Telos in the Late Classical and Early Hellenistic Periods." *Numismatic Chronicle* 168 (2008): 21-32. 4 pls.
A study of twenty-two bronze coins of Telos. Includes a catalogue and discussion.

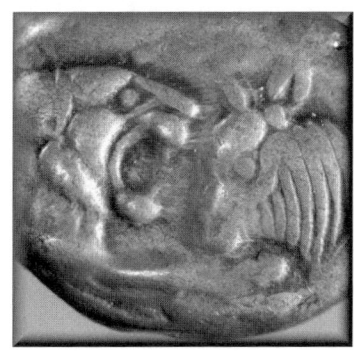

Lydia

So far as we have any knowledge, the Lydians were the first nation to introduce the use of gold and silver coin.

—Herodotus, circa 450 B.C.

4980 **Berk, Harlan J.** "The Coinage of Croesus: New Types Support Traditional Theories." *The Celator* 4, no. 10 (October 1990): 6-9.
The author discusses the evolution of the lion and bull coinage traditionally attributed to King Croesus of Lydia. Describes the heavy gold stater which served as the prototype for the series. Theorizes that master engravers created the first dies which were then copied by less skilled engravers leading to deviations from the intended design. The prototype shows the lion leaping, but subsequent dies show the lion standing. Suggests that a stater and half stater from the same dies served as the prototype for the silver coinage. Concludes that Croesus was indeed responsible for this coinage series. Contains photographs of gold and silver staters and fractions from various periods. [Also see Price "Croesus or Pseudo-Croesus?" below].

4981 ——— "The Coinage of Croesus: Another Look." *SAN—Journal of the Society for Ancient Numismatics* 20, no. 1 (1997): 14-5. Illus.
Berk discusses the evolution in the style and weight of Croesus' gold and silver coinage. He identifies the prototype coins from which the later issues were copied. Illustrates prototype gold and silver staters and a silver siglos. Also illustrates regular issues in gold and silver, struck on both a heavy and a light standard, in denominations ranging from the stater to the 1/24 stater.

4982 **Borrell, H. P.** "An Inquiry into the Early Lydian Money, and an Attempt to Fix the Classification of Certain Coins to Croesus." *Numismatic Chronicle* 2 (1840): 216-23.
Borrell argues that the early gold and silver lion and bull types belong to King Croesus of Lydia. [Also see Price "Croesus or Pseudo-Croesus?" below].

4983 **Breglia, Laura.** "Interrogativi sulle 'Creseidi.'" *Annali della Scuola Normale Superiore di Pisa* (Italy) (1974): 659-85.

4984 **Buckler, W. H.** "A Lydian Text on an Electrum Coin." *Journal of Hellenic Studies* 46 (1926): 36-41. Illus.
Publishes an early electrum coin of the lion-type on which the Lydian inscription is complete. Lists known specimens of electrum coins with Lydian inscriptions. Reads the inscription as "walwesh." Based on this reading, the former attribution of these coins to Alyattes is rejected. Explores a possible meaning for the word. Suggests it may be the name of the river Alês—the coins proclaiming that the port on the Alês river now belongs to the Lydian kingdom. But the author admits this theory is purely speculative. [Also see Wallace "WALWE" below].

4985 **Carruba, O.** "VALVL e RKALIL: Monetazione Arcaica della Lidia: Problemi e Considerazioni Linguistiche." *Ermanno A. Arslan Studia Dictata.* Glaux 7. Edited by R. Martini and N. Vismara. Milan: Edizioni Ennerre, 1991. Pages 13-23.

4986 **Cowell, Michael R., and K. Hyne.** "Scientific Examination of the Lydian Precious Metal Coinage." *King Croesus' Gold: Excavations at Sardis and the History of Gold Refining.* Edited by A. Ramage and P. Craddock. Cambridge: Harvard University Press, 2000. Pages 169-74.
Reviews recent and earlier work on the metallic content of Lydian coinage. Summarizes the findings of Kraay, Gordus, Meyers, Pászthory, Avaldi, Vismara, and Cowell. Results are presented in tables showing the percentages of gold, silver, copper, lead, and other metals for the various Lydian electrum coins examined. Cowell concludes that Lydian gold and silver coins typically show 98% or more of the principal metal—very high purity. The coins were likely produced from an artificial alloy—probably by adding silver to the natural gold alloy.

4987 **Cowell, Michael R., K. Hyne, N. D. Meeks, and Paul T. Craddock.** "Analyses of the Lydian Electrum, Gold, and Silver Coins." *Metallurgy in Numismatics, Volume 4.* Special Publication No. 30. London: Royal Numismatic Society, 1998. Pages 526-38. Illus.
A selection of coins of Lydia and Ionia were examined. Some plated forgeries were also examined. The results of previous analyses of Lydian coins by Paszthory and Vismara are shown for comparison. The Lydian electrum royal coinage is shown to be of very consistent composition. It is likely that this coinage was produced from an artificial alloy, perhaps with the intention of producing a coinage alloy of consistent value. It was previously assumed that these coins were manufactured directly and solely from unrefined gold from the Pactolus and Hermus rivers.

4988 **Head, Barclay V.** *The Coinage of Lydia and Persia.* London, 1877. Reprint, San Diego: Pegasus Publishing, 1967. 52 pp., 3 pls. [CS 2754a]
Begins with an explanation of the weight-systems used for gold and silver prior to coinage, and shows how the coin-weight systems of Asia Minor were derived. Discusses the history of the Lydian kingdom and its coinage. Describes the major coin types giving emphasis to the weight-standards employed. Describes the royal coinage of the Persian empire and the Persian provincial coinage with royal types. [Also see Head and Hill under PERSIA for another reprint of this work].

4989 ——— *Catalogue of Greek Coins of Lydia.* London: British Museum, 1901. Reprint, Bologna: Forni, 1964. cl, 440 pp., 45 pls., map. [CS 2754]
Volume 22 of the *Catalogue of Greek Coins in the British Museum*. The 440-page catalogue of coins is preceded by 150 pages of introductory text. [Also see *Catalogue of Greek Coins in the British Museum* under PUBLIC COLLECTIONS—GREAT BRITAIN (LONDON)].

4990 **Imhoof-Blumer, Friedrich W.** *Lydische Stadtmünzen.* Genf/Leipzig, 1897. Reprint, Graz, 1971. 213 pp., 7 pls. [CS 2755]
An examination of the coinage of the cities in Lydia, including the Roman Provincial coinage. [Reviewed by Leonard Forrer in *Spink Numismatic Circular* 6, no. 61 (December 1897): 2494-5].

4991 **Jongkees, Jan Hendrik.** "Kroiseios en Dareikos." *Jaarbericht van het Vooraziatisch-Egyptisch Gezelschap ex Oriente Lux* (The Netherlands) 9 (1944): 163-8.

4992 **Meaghar, John.** "The Lydian One Third Stater." *The Anvil* (Canada) 2, no. 5 (September 1, 1992): 7. Illus.
The author speculates that the head of an eagle can be seen in the incuse reverse punch of an electrum third stater of Lydia.

4993 **Naster, Paul.** "Remarques Charactéroscopiques et Technologiques au Sujet des Créséides." *Congresso Internazionale de Numismatica, Rome, 1961; Volume 2: Atti.* Rome, 1965. Pages 25-36. [CS 2757]

4994 ——— "The Weight-System of the Coinage of Croesus." *Proceedings of the 8th International Congress of Numismatics, New York—Washington, September 1973.* International Association of Professional Numismatists Publication, No. 4. Edited by Herbert A. Cahn and Georges Le Rider. Paris/Basel: International Association of Professional Numismatists, 1976. Pages 125-33. [CS 2758]. Reprinted in *Scripta Nummaria: Contributions à la Méthodologie Numismatic.* Edited by Paul Naster. Louvain-la-Neuve: Société Royale de Numismatique de Belgique, 1983. Pages 68-75.
Naster investigates the exact value of the earliest gold and silver coins of the bimetallic system of Croesus, king of Lydia (561-546 B.C.). There were two gold systems (heavy and light) and one silver system corresponding to the heavy gold. The author uses frequency tables to determine the most frequently occurring weights for the heavy and light gold staters, and the silver stater and hemistater. Presents the results in a table along with the standard weights determined by Regling, Giesecke, and Hemmy. Naster's results are: heavy gold stater = 10.71 gm; silver stater = 10.7 gm; light gold stater = 8.055 gm; and silver stater = 5.35 gm. He also determines that the gold-to-silver value ratio was 1:13 1/3.

4995 ——— "Un Cas de Tréflage dans la Frappe des Créseides." *Revue Belge de Numismatique et de Sigillographie* (Belgium) 145 (1999): 1-4.

4996 "New Hoard Increases Supply of Earliest Coins." *Coin World* (January 2, 1995): 65. Illus.
A brief report on a talk given by Harlan Berk on "Ancient Coinage of Lydia from before Croesus to after." Focuses on the stylistic development of the lion-and-bull staters.

4997 **Nimchuk, Cindy L.** "The Lion-and-Bull Coinage of Croesus." *Journal of the Classical and Medieval Numismatic Society* (Canada) 2nd ser., 1 (June 1, 2000): 5-44. Illus.
A study of the gold and silver coins with the confronted lion and bull on obverse, generally attributed to King Croesus of Lydia (ca. 560-547 B.C.). The author examined 205 coins from various sources. Lists the range of denominations struck and defines six categories of style seen among the coins. Describes the distribution of coins among the various denominations, weights, and styles. Most scholars have assumed that coins of the heavy and light standards were issued sequentially; Nimchuck suggests they were issued concurrently and that they represent different denominations. The coins were struck using an obverse die and two reverse punches. In the group of 205 coins examined, the author identified 152 obverse dies and 167 reverse punches—80 left punches and 81 right punches (the five fractions use only one reverse punch and one coin used the same punch for both left and right). Explores die/punch linking between denominations, metals, styles, and weight standards. Discusses hoards and findspots. Summarizes the conclusions: The progression of style moved from "natural" to "stylized." Suggests a mid-sixth century date for the beginning of both the silver and gold staters; however, the silver coinage comes to an end earlier than the gold (ca. 525 and ca. 500 B.C. respectively). Silver half-staters began ca. 525 and continued to ca. 490. Silver fractions began ca. 525. The production of the lion-and-bull coinage continued under the Achaemenids until the introduction of the Persian "archers."

4998 **Nollé, M. K., and Johannes Nollé.** "Gamerses: Überlegungen zur Identität eines Lokalen Münzherrn im Achämenidenreich." *Hellas und der Griechische Osten: Festschrift für Peter Robert Franke zum 70. Geburtstag.* Studien zur Geschichte und Numismatik der Griechischen Welt. Edited by W. Leschhorn, A. V. B. Miron, and A. Miron. Saarbrücken: SDV Saarbrücer Druckerei und Verlag, 1996.

4999 **Price, Martin J.** "Croesus or Pseudo-Croesus? Hoard or Hoax? Problems Concerning the Sigloi and Double-Sigloi of the Croeseid Type." *Studies in Honour of Leo Mildenberg: Numismatics, Art History, Archaeology.* Edited by A. Houghton et al. Wetteren: Editions NR, 1984. Pages 211-21. Illus.
Discusses the origin of the attribution of the lion-and-bull coinage to King Croesus of Lydia (see Borrell "An Inquiry into the Early Lydian Money" above). After considering the evidence of changes in weight standards, Price suggests the entire lion-and-bull series was struck at Sardis during the Persian period, rather than in Lydia during the reign of Croesus. Mentions a hoard of silver staters and half-staters which passed through London in 1981. The coins were said to have been found at Ödemis, not far from Sardis. The style of the coins raised questions of authenticity. Die links were sought and a metallurgical analysis was performed on the hoard coins. Their weights and compositions were compared to other hoard coins and coins from the British Museum. Although some doubt remains, Price believes the hoard coins are genuine. Lists the coins in the hoard, which includes some previously unpublished types. [Also see Berk "The Coinage of Croesus" above. Also see Cahill and Kroll "New Archaic Coin Finds at Sardis" under HOARDS for new information which may firmly place the lion-and-bull coinage into the reign of Croesus].

5000 **Ramage, Andrew.** "Golden Sardis." *King Croesus' Gold: Excavation at Sardis and the History of Gold Refining.* Edited by A. Ramage and P. Craddock. Cambridge: Harvard University Press, 2000. Page 14-26. Illus.

The Harvard-Cornell excavations at Sardis have uncovered a series of installations that would have enabled the Lydians to separate the major components of mixed metals to produce refined gold and silver. Ramage discusses the beginnings of coinage and the change from electrum to gold and silver coins, which has been attributed to the reign of King Croesus (561-547 B.C.). The finds at Sardis are consistent with this theory. Ramage discusses the sources for Lydian gold, and the value and quantity of gold produced. The Pactolus North refinery is likely to have been capable of processing several hundred kilograms of gold each year. Examines the storage and use of the gold that was produced. Reviews the history of digging at the site. The current excavations began in 1958. Discusses the layout of the site. [Also see Ramage and Craddock *King Croesus' Gold* under METALLURGY].

5001 **Robinson, Edward S. G.** "The Electrum Coinage of Lydia and Ionia." *Numismatic Gazette* (England) 2, no. 2 (1963): 22-5. [CS 2764]

5002 **Shear, Theodore Leslie.** "Sixth Preliminary Report on the American Excavations at Sardis in Asia Minor." *American Journal of Archaeology* 26 (1922): 389-409. Illus.
A report on the results of excavations at Sardis in 1922. The most important discovery was a pot, hidden in a burial tomb, containing thirty gold staters of Croesus, of which six are illustrated.

5003 **Spier, Jeffrey.** "Notes on Early Electrum Coinage and a Die-linked Issue from Lydia." *Studies in Greek Numismatics in Memory of Martin Jessop Price*. Edited by Richard Ashton and Silvia Hurter. London: Spink, 1998. Pages 327-34. 2 pls.
In 1984, Martin Price presented a paper (unpublished) titled "Coins from the Artemision: the Evidence of Context" in which he examined the electrum coins found in the excavations at Ephesos (see B. Head "Chapter V: The Coins" under HOARDS). Spier draws on the content of Price's paper and adds new discoveries, including a group of die-linked Lydian coins and additional commentary. Publishes some relevant hoards containing electrum coins: Colophon 1940s, Ephesos 1970, and Priene *IGCH* 1157.

5004 **Walburg, R.** "Lydisch oder Persisch? Ein Goldobjekt aus der Frühzeit der Münzprägung." *Revue Suisse de Numismatique* (Switzerland) 70 (1991): 5-17.

5005 **Wallace, Robert W.** "WALWE. and .KALI." *Journal of Hellenic Studies* 108 (1988): 203-7.
Wallace summarizes the theories of Weidauer, J. P. Six, J. H. Jongkees, Hanfmann, and others regarding the meaning of the inscriptions WALWE and KALI which appear on early electrum coins of Asia Minor. Studies published by F. Steiner and H. Oten in 1968 and 1969 show that the Luwain word *walwe* means "lion." Discusses locations where the Luwain language was used (western Anatolia including Lydia. Concludes these inscriptions cannot be names of kings or mint-masters. WALWE simply means "lion." Wallace claims there is certainly a letter preceding K on the KALI coins. Suggests the inscription may be read "I am of *kas*," indicating the person who supplied the bullion for the coinage. The WALWE inscription may suggest the phrase "I am of the lion." The identity of the "lion" is unclear, but it may refer to the Lydian king. Wallace suggests the king allowed an important subordinate (KALI) to put his name on coins which were issued roughly simultaneously with the WALWE issues upon which the king put his identification in order to distinguish the issues. When the KALI coinage was complete, there was no longer a need to mark the royal coinage.

5006 ——— "KUKALIM, WALWET, and the Artemision Deposit: Problems in Early Anatolian Electrum Coinage." *Agoranomia: Studies in Money and Exchange Presented to John H. Kroll*. Edited by Peter G. van Alfen. New York: American Numismatic Society, 2006. Pages 37-48. 1 pl.
Thompson and Kraay each published an electrum sixth of the Lydia lion-head type inscribed with the letters KALI. Other specimens were later published, with various opinions regarding the inscriptions on the coins, including KUKALIM—perhaps to be identified as Gyges, king of Lydia. Also mentions the coins inscribed WALWAT. Examines the names, chronology of the coins, and the punches used for the reverses. Wallace recommends numerous revisions to Weidauer's sequence of dies. Wallace suggests most of the die-linked Lydian coins in the Artemesion temple deposit were struck at Sardis and constitute a single dedication by Alyattes or, more likely, by Croesus. He believes Croesus was king by ca. 580 B.C. Wallace suggests the WALWET and KUKALIM coins reflect an experiment of perhaps two mints during one brief period. The WALWET coins were struck first.

Some of Wallace's conclusions: (1) WALWET is king Alyattes; (2) KUKALIM was a royal person of Alyattes' period; (3) the coins marked -LATE- may not be royal issues and may not have been struck at Sardis; (4) some of the WALWET coins were struck at Sardis, others may have been struck at a branch mint; (5) the die-linked Lydian coins in the Artemesion deposit may have been a dedication by Alyattes or Croesus. Wallace also discusses the reverse punches and suggests that two sizes of punches were used to show that the coins were not plated and may reproduce the customary practice of multiple test punchings. [Also see Thompson "Some Noteworthy Greek Accessions" under PUBLIC COLLECTIONS—UNITED STATES (NEW YORK), Kraay *Report of the Visitors of the Ashmolean Museum* under PUBLIC COLLECTIONS—GREAT BRITIAN (OXFORD), and Weidauer *Probleme der frühen Elektronprägung* under ORIGINS OF COINAGE. An electrum trite bearing the KUKALIM inscription appeared as lot 1241 in Classical Numismatic Group's *Triton XV* sale (January 4, 2102). The lot description included a good review of the debate surrounding these early inscribed coins].

5007 **Young, Rodney S.** "The 1963 Campaign at Gordion." *American Journal of Archaeology* 68 (1964): 279-92. 8 pls.
"On p. 283 the discovery of a hoard of Lydian electrum coins is described, a selection of them being illustrated on pl. 86." [J. R. Jones, *NIAJAH*]. [Also see R. S. Young "Operation Gordion" under HOARDS].

Also see: Ashton and Kinns "Opuscula Anatolica II" under ASIA MINOR—GENERAL WORKS; Balmuth "Remarks on the Appearance of the Earliest Coins" under ORIGINS OF COINAGE; Bellinger "Electrum Coins from Gordion" (two items) under HOARDS; Carradice "Two Achaemenid Hoards" under PERSIA; Cahill and Kroll "New Archaic Coin Finds at Sardis" under HOARDS; Caskey "Greek Electrum Coins" under ASIA MINOR—GENERAL WORKS; Cahill and Kroll "New Archaic Coin Finds" under HOARDS; Gardner "Numismatic Reattributions" (Phanes) under GENERAL WORKS—GREEK; Gilkes "Researchers Study First Gold Refinery" under METALLURGY; Hunkin "Addendum" under METALLURGY; Konuk *From Kroisos to Karia* under PRIVATE COLLECTIONS; Linzalone *Electrum and the Invention of Coinage* under ORIGINS OF COINAGE; Marotta "Electrum" under METALLURGY; Moysey "Observations…Satrapal Revolt" under PERSIA; Pásztory "Investigations of the Early Electrum Coins" under METALLURGY.

Ramage and Craddock *King Croesus' Gold* under METALLURGY; Richardson "Coins of Lydia" under ORIGINS OF COINAGE; E. Robinson "Coins from the Ephesian Artemision" under ORIGINS OF COINAGE; E. Robinson "The Date of the Earliest Coins" under ORIGINS OF COINAGE; E. Robinson "Some Electrum and Gold" under ASIA MINOR—GENERAL WORKS; Rodee "Art History" under ART; Thompson *Alexander's Drachm Mints 1: Sardes and Miletus* under MACEDONIAN KINGDOM—GENERAL WORKS; Thompson "Some Noteworthy Greek Accessions" under PUBLIC COLLECTIONS—UNITED STATES (NEW YORK); van Alfen "Early Electrum Project" under ORIGINS OF COINAGE.

PHRYGIA

A Bronze Age center, Gordium became the capital of Phrygia in the ninth or eighth century, attaining a high and grandiose degree of civilization under King Midas (c. 738-695), named after a mythical forerunner whose relations with the gods formed the subject of many well-known Greek stories.

—*Michael Grant, 1986*

5008 **Balty, Jean Charles.** "À la Recherche de l'Apamée Hellénistique: Les Témoignages Archéologiques." *TOΠOI Supplement 4* (2003): 223-52. Illus.
"The author describes excavation finds from the Syrian city of Apamea, including a quasi-municipal coin of Alexander I Balas. The author also provides a brief history of the Seleucid mint at Apamea." [Oliver D. Hoover, *NL* 148]

5009 **Fulco, William J.** "The Rare Coinage of Sanaus in Phrygia." *SAN—Journal of the Society for Ancient Numismatics* 5, no. 4 (1973-74): 65.
One of the three known coins from the Hellenistic town of Sanaus in Phrygia is published. The 19 mm bronze coin with Apollo on the obverse and a tripod on the reverse resides in the numismatic collection of the Jesuit School of Theology at Berkeley. The other two coins are in the Pergamon Museum in Berlin. The coins are dated to ca. 200 B.C. [See also *SAN* 6, no. 1 (fall 1979): 7, for the correction of a typographical error].

5010 **Head, Barclay V.** *Catalogue of Greek Coins of Phrygia.* London: British Museum, 1906. Reprint, Bologna: Forni, 1964. cvi, 491 pp., 53 pls., map. [CS 2767]
Volume 25 of the *Catalogue of Greek Coins in the British Museum.* The 491-page catalogue of coins is preceded by 106 pages of introductory text. [Also see *Catalogue of Greek Coins in the British Museum* under PUBLIC COLLECTIONS—GREAT BRITAIN (LONDON)].

5011 **Kleiner, Fred S.** "The Late Cistophori of Apameia." *Greek Numismatics and Archaeology: Essays in Honor of Margaret Thompson.* Edited by O. Mørkholm and N. M. Waggoner. Wetteren: Numismatique Romaine, 1979. Pages 119-30. 3 pls.
Kleiner examines the late cistophoric coinage of Apameia. The ethnic appears as AΠA on the reverse of these coins, rather than an AΠ monogram as on the earlier issues. Also, the magistrate's name is usually spelled-out in full. The author presents a catalogue of this coinage, arranged by magistrate. The minting sequence could not be reliably determined due to the lack of die links.

Also see: Ashton and Kinns "Opuscula Anatolica II" and "Opuscula Anatonlica III" under ASIA MINOR—GENERAL WORKS; Crowfoot "The Lions of Kybele" under CILICIA; Hill "A Find of Cistophori" under ASIA MINOR—GENERAL WORKS; Hoover *Handbook of Coins of Northern and Central Anatolia* under ASIA MINOR—GENERAL WORKS; Hoover "Quasi-Municipal Coinage in Seleucid Apamea" under SYRIA—SELEUCID KINGDOM; Moysey "Observations...Satrapal Revolt" under PERSIA; Noe "Beginning of the Cistophoric Coinage" under ASIA MINOR—GENERAL WORKS.

LYCIA

Even under the Persian Empire, whose strength they could not resist, the Lycians retained some degree of autonomy, for local dynasts coined in their own names throughout the fifth and fourth centuries. During this time, although inevitably influenced by the Greek and Achaemenid worlds, a vigorous and original culture flourished in Lycia, whose architecture, sculpture, and coins all evoke admiration today.

—Hyla Troxell, 1982

5012 **Arslan, Melih.** "A Hoard of Lycian Staters in Fethiye Museum." *Belleten* (Turkey) 63, no. 236 (April 1999): 1-3. 2 pls.

5013 **Arslan, Melih, Chris Lightfoot, and Cihan Tibet.** "A Group of Unknown Coins in Antalya Museum." *Spink Numismatic Circular* 106, no. 1 (February 1998): 7-8. 1 pl. Also appeared in *Belleten* 62, no. 235 (December 1998): 727-34. 2 pls.
Publishes five bronze coins attributed to Kitannaura. This is the first numismatic evidence for the existence of this city, situated between Trebenna and Termessos in Lycia. The coins are from the late Hellenistic period.

5014 **Ashton, Richard H. J.** "Pseudo-Rhodian Drachms and the Beginning of the Lycian League Coinage." *Numismatic Chronicle* 147 (1987): 8-25. 2 pls.
"The article argues that two series of Rhodian-type drachms (*BMC* 179-80 and 203, with names, respectively, Mousaios and Iason) were struck on the mainland of Asia Minor, in Caria and/or Lycia, probably in the late 180's or 170's. It argues that some countermarks on these and certain other Rhodian or pseudo-Rhodian drachms were applied in Lycia, and foreshadowed or reflected the types of the earliest Lycian League coinage. The beginning of Lycian League silver coinage is put at 167 B.C. or not long afterwards. The article also discusses apparent links between Crete and Lycia in the earlier second century B.C." [R. Ashton, *NL* 120]

5015 ——— "The Coinage of Oinoanda." *Numismatic Chronicle* 165 (2005): 65-84. 5 pls.
A catalogue of some of the coins of Oinoanda from a recent hoard of one hundred didrachms which came to the market in 2002. Includes a table of weights, notes on the bronze coins of Termessos Minor and Termessos Major, and an appendix "A Note on the Tauric Sword and Shield Symbol" by Nicholas V. Sekunda.

5016 **Cahn, Herbert A.** "Dynast oder Satrap?" *Schweizer Münzblätter* (Switzerland) 25, no. 100 (1975): 84-91. Illus. [CS 2769]

5017 **Calliari, Irene, and Novella Vismara.** "Archaic Coinage of Lycia: Remarks Based on X-ray Fluorescence Analyses." *Metallurgy in Numismatics, Volume 4.* Special Publication No. 30. London: Royal Numismatic Society, 1998. Pages 483-90.
An analysis of 116 Persian sigloi and 239 Lycian coins by energy dispersive X-ray spectrometry (EDXRF). Concludes that Lycian coinage is not uniform—the silver content ranged from 84-99%. In contrast, the Persian sigloi adhere more closely to a standard, with silver ranging between 92 and 98% for 93% of the specimens. The sigloi contained more lead than the Lycian coins.

5018 **de Callataÿ, François.** "Le Monnayage en Argent d'Oinoanda: Après Apamée (188 av. J.-C.) ou Après Mithradate (85-82 av. J.-C.)?" *Liber Amicorum Tony Hackens*. Numismatica Lovaniensia 20. Edited by G. Moucharte, M. B. Borba Florenzano, F. de Callataÿ, P. Marchetti, L. Smolderen, and P. Yannopoulos. Louvain-la-Neuve: Université Catholique de Louvain, 2007. Pages 203 ff.

5019 **Elazin, W.** "Two Variants of Coins of Lycia." *Spink Numismatic Circular* 70, no. 1 (January 1962): 5. Illus.
"Two staters are described and illustrated. The first shows the forepart of a lion on the obverse, and on the reverse a large triskeles with legend ΜΙΤΗΡΑΠΑΤΑ. Similar reverses are generally accompanied by a lion's mask on the obverse. The reverse field of the second coin depicts a fighting Ajax flanked by the legend ΠΕΡΕΚΛΑ; on the obverse, a lion's mask is shown instead of the usual head of Zeus." [*NL* 61]

5020 **Fellows, Charles.** *Coins of Ancient Lycia before the Reign of Alexander with an Essay on the Relative Dates of the Lycian Monuments in the British Museum.* London: J. Murray, 1852. Reprint, Chicago: Obol International, 1976. 20 pp., 19 pls., map. [CS 2770]
An examination of the early Lycian coins (pre-333 B.C.) with a goal of establishing their order or date. Comparisons with figures and inscriptions on monuments found in Lycia are used to shed light on the chronology and attribution of the coins. Fellows describes the area inhabited by the Caunians, the Troes, and the Tramelae (the area known to later Greeks as Lycia) and assigns some of the coins to each of these tribes.

5021   **Heipp-Tamer, C.** *Die Münzprägung der Lykischen Stadt Phaselis in Griechischer Zeit.* Saarbrücker Studien zur Archaelogie und Alten Geschichte Band 6. Saarbrücken, 1994. 182 pp., 32 pls.

5022   **Hill, George F.** "Coinage of Lycia, to the Time of Alexander the Great." *Numismatic Chronicle* 3rd ser., 15 (1895): 1-44. 2 pls.
Hill attempts a chronological rearrangement of the early coinage of Lycia. Lists the types and includes cross-references to the lists prepared by J. P. Six and C. Fellows. Discusses the attributions.

5023   ——— *Catalogue of Greek Coins of Lycia, Pamphylia, and Pisidia.* London: British Museum, 1897. Reprint, Bologna: Forni, 1964. cxxii, 353 pp., 44 pls., map. [CS 2773]
Volume 19 of the *Catalogue of Greek Coins in the British Museum*. The 353-page catalogue of coins is preceded by 122 pages of introductory text. [Also see *Catalogue of Greek Coins in the British Museum* under PUBLIC COLLECTIONS—GREAT BRITAIN (LONDON)].

5024   ——— "Oinoanda: A New Greek Mint." *Numismatic Chronicle* 3rd ser., 17 (1897): 25-30. 1 pl.
Publishes a didrachm struck in the late third or early second century B.C. at Oinoanda, a town on the northern border of Lycia. The coin is the only known coin of that city. The types are *obv.*, Zeus; *rev.*, eagle with OINOANΔEON. The types are similar to those on some bronze coins of Termessos. The attribution of this coin suggests the need to reattribute certain coins of Termessos to a new town, "Little Termessos," near Oinoanda.

5025   **Hurter, Silvia M.** "Kuprlli und Idâ: Ein Neuer Lykischer Stater." *Kraay—Mørkholm Essays: Numismatic Studies in Memory of C. M. Kraay and O. Mørkholm.* Numismatica Lovaniensia 10. Edited by G. Le Rider, G. K. Jenkins, N. Waggoner, and U. Westermark. Louvain-la-Neuve: Université Catholique de Louvain, 1989. Pages 99-100. 1 pl.

5026   ——— "A New Lycian Coin Type: Kherei, Not Kuperlis." *Israel Numismatic Journal* (Israel) 14 (2001-2002): 15-18. Illus.

5027   **Kolb, Frank, and Werner Tietz.** "Zagaba: Münzprägung und Politische Geographie in Zentrallykien." *Chiron* (Germany) 31 (2001): 347-416. Illus.
"Zagaba, known from coins of the fifth and fourth centuries B.C., now seems to be the name of an important Central Lycian town, rather than of a Lycian dynast. The ruins of Zagaba have recently been discovered. The discovery has several consequences for the understanding of Lycian coinages. The Central Lycian issues of the fifth century B.C. are the main focus of this important study, illustrated by some sixty numismatic objects." [H. Baldus, *NL* 145]

5028   **Kosmetatou, Elizabeth.** "The Coinage of Lycian Termesson pros Oinoandois." *Quaderni Ticinesi. Numismatica e Antichità Classiche* (Switzerland) 27 (1998): 161-83. Illus.
"Based on 135 bronze coins, the author identifies fifteen series between the first century B.C. and the Tiberian epoch." [A. Carignani, *NL* 142]

5029   **Marotta, Michael E.** "Lycian League Issued Interesting Series of Coinage." *The Celator* 9, no. 11 (November 1995): 6-12. Illus., map.
Begins with a brief history of civilization in the area of Lycia. Describes the Lycian language and the entrance of the Greeks into Lycia. Discusses the early history of the Lycian League. Then discusses the coinage of Lycian cities and dynasts, including the League coinage. Seven coins are illustrated.

5030   **McIntyre, Andrew P.** "The Alexander Tetradrachms of Termessos Major." *Numismatic Chronicle* 166 (2006): 27-30. 2 pls.
Demonstrates that the whole issue of posthumous Alexanders from Termessos were struck from a single die. The previous reading of dates on the coins is shown to be a simple mis-reading of successive changes in the die. McIntyre presents a corpus of the coins (nine specimens).

5031   **Mildenberg, Leo.** "False Staters of Mithrapata and Pericles." *Spink Numismatic Circular* 70 (February 1962): 29.
Briefly mentions the existence of counterfeit staters of Mithrapata and Pericles.

5032   ——— "Mithrapata und Perikles." *Atti: Congresso Internazionale di Numismatica, Roma 1961, Volume 2.* Rome, 1965. Pages 45-55. [CS 2774]. Reprinted in *Leo Mildenberg. Vestigia Leonis: Studien zur Antiken Numismatik Israels, Palästinas und der Östlichen Mittelmeerweit.* Novum Testamentum et Orbis Antiquus 36. Edited by U. Hübner and E. Knauf. Freiburg: Universitätsverlag, and Göttingen: Vandenhoeck & Ruprecht, 1998. Pages 105-9. 3 pls.

5033   **Mørkholm, Otto.** "The Classification of Lycian Coins before Alexander the Great." *Jahrbuch für Numismatik und Geldsseschichte* (Germany) 14 (1964): 65-76. 1 pl. [CS 2775]
Mørkholm shows that three different weight standards were used in Lycia, which he refers to as heavy, intermediate, and light. These have not yet been identified with standards in use outside Lycia.

5034   **Mørkholm, Otto, and Günter Neumann.** *Die Lykischen Münzlegenden.* Machrichten der Akademie der Wissenschaften in Göttingen I. Philologisch-Historische Klasse, No. 1. Göttingen, 1977. 38 pp., 4 pls. [CS 2776]

5035   **Mørkholm, Otto, and Jan Zahle.** "The Coinage of Kuprlli: A Numismatic and Archaeological Study." *Acta Archaeologica* (Denmark) 43 (1972): 57-113. 5 pls. Illus. [CS 2777]
Presents the coinage of the dynast Kuprlli (485-440 B.C.) at Lycia, comparing the coins with contemporary artifacts from the same area to improve our understanding of the art and culture of Lycia in the fifth century B.C. Presents a catalogue of 193 coin types, each of which is illustrated. Discusses weights, geographical distribution, and chronology. Comments on the history and symbolism of various coin designs including the triskeles, boar, lion, griffin, eagle, winged-bull, sphinx, and warrior. Discusses epigraphical and other evidence for the identity of Kuprlli. Comments on the political organization of Lycia.

5036   ——— "The Coinages of the Lycian Dynasts Kheriga, Kherêi and Erbbina: A Numismatic and Archaeological Study." *Acta Archaeologica* (Denmark) 47 (1976): 47-90. Illus. [CS 2778]
A continuation of the earlier study of Kuprlli (see above). Examines the coins of Kheriga, Kherêi and Erbbina—the most important dynasts of the two generations following Kuprlli in Lycia. Presents a catalogue of seventy-five coin types. Comments on the coin weights, denominations, chronology, and

distribution. Provides an analysis of the types, including the portraits. Summarizes the historical conclusions for the genealogy of Lycian dynasts and the social and political institutions of Lycia.

5037 **Noe, Sydney P.** "A Lycian Hoard." *Centennial Publication of the American Numismatic Society.* Edited by Harald Ingholt. New York: American Numismatic Society, 1958. Pages 543-51. 2 pls.
The author examines a hoard of sixty-seven silver staters of Persic weight, found in Anatolia in 1954. The coins have Pegasus on the obverse, and the reverse bears either an irregular incuse punch, a bull's head, a lion's mask, or a square frame. The coins are all struck from very worn dies. Noe identifies the coins as fifth century B.C. issues of Lycia, from a single isolated mint with an inexperienced staff. The coins cannot be further identified based on the current evidence.

5038 **Robert, Louis.** "Villes et Monnaies de Lycie." *Hellenica* (France) 10 (1955): 188-222. [CS 2779]

5039 **Robinson, Edward S. G.** "Coins from Lycia and Pamphylia." *Journal of Hellenic Studies* 34 (1914): 36-46. 1 pl.
Robinson lists coins which he acquired on a journey to Lycia and Pamphylia, and suggests these may represent the coins which circulated in the area during ancient times. Most of the coins are Roman Provincial types, including some previously unpublished varieties. Includes coins of Thrace, Lesbos, Caria, Lydia, Phrygia, Lycia, Pamphylia, Pisidia, Cilicia, Galatia, Cappadocia, Syria, Phoenicia, and Alexandria.

5040 **Schwabacher, Willy.** "Lycian Coin Portraits." *Essays in Greek Coinage Presented to Stanley Robinson.* Edited by C. M. Kraay and G. K. Jenkins. Oxford: Clarendon Press, 1968. Pages 111-24. 2 pls. [CS 2780]
A discussion of the portrait coins of Lycia from an art-historical perspective. Illustrates a coin thought to be of the Lycian dynast Khäräi, which Barclay Head states is the first portrait to appear on a coin, ca. 400 B.C. (see Head *Coins of the Ancients 700 B.C.-A.D. 1*, period II, plate 11, no. 38; and *BMC Lycia* no. 102). Discusses the development in portrait styles. Illustrates several extraordinary coins showing the satraps Mithrapata and Päriklä.

5041 **Spier, Jeffrey.** "Lycian Coins in the Decadrachm Hoard." *Coinage and Administration in the Athenian and Persian Empires.* BAR International Series 343. Edited by Ian Carradice. Oxford: British Archaeological Reports, 1987. Pages 29-37. 2 pls.
The majority (about 1000) of the coins in the Decadrachm hoard were Lycian. These coins included previously unknown types, inscriptions, and dynast's names. Many die links existed. The author reviews the existing literature on Lycian coinage. Examines types, inscriptions, weight standards, die links, overstrikes, and relationships to other hoards. The Lycian coins suggest a closing date of 470-450 B.C. for the hoard.

5042 **Spier, Jeffrey, Melih Arslan, and Ali Dervisagaoglou.** "The Demirler, Lycia (c. 1972) Hoard. (*CH* 1.6, 8.40, 9.351)." *Coin Hoards, Volume IX: Greek Hoards.* Edited by A. Meadows and Ute Wartenberg. London: Royal Numismatic Society, 2002. Pages 87-93. 4 pls.
The authors examine a hoard of 107 coins, now in the Fethiye Museum, found near the village of Demirler. All (69 staters, 38 third staters) are likely from mints in the Xanthos River valley in western Lycia. Most have a boar or boar protome as the obverse type. The hoard's burial date is likely ca. 475 B.C. The authors comment on the weight standards. Three coins with a panther seated/winged horse are tentatively attributed to Tlos.

5043 **Troxell, Hyla A.** *The Coinage of the Lycian League.* Numismatic Notes and Monographs, No. 162. New York: American Numismatic Society, 1982. 255 pp., 44 pls., map.
Examines the federal coinage of the post-Alexander league, ca. 200 B.C. to A.D. 43. Presents an overview of the geography and history of Lycia. About twenty cities struck the coinage. Examines the bronze and silver issues broken into five time periods. Presents a catalogue of dies with commentary using evidence of hoards, many frequency tables of weights, and a discussion of chronology. Discusses the actual places of minting. Coins in other collections misattributed to the League as well as known forgeries of League coins are listed in Appendices. [An extensive review by Ralph Mathisen appears in *American Journal of Archaeology* 88 (1984): 616-8. Also reviewed by J. Zahle in *Journal of Hellenic Studies* 105 (1985): 242, and by J. Warren in *Numismatic Chronicle* 150 (1990): 251-3].

5044 **Vismara, Novella.** *Monetazione Arcaica della Lycia II: La Collection Winsemann Falghera.* Glaux 3. Milan, 1989.
[Also see Vismara *Monetazione Arcaica* under ORIGINS OF COINAGE].

5045 ———. "Proposte per un Nuovo Ordinamento della Monetazione Arcaica della Lycia." *Akten des II. International Lykien-Symposios.* Edited by J. Borchardt and G. Dobesch. Vienna, 1993. Pages 191-201.

5046 ———. "Considerazioni sulle Emissioni Della Lycia Arcaica a Nome de Xinaxa." *Travaux de Numismatique Grecque Offerts à Georges Le Rider.* Edited by M. Amandry and S. Hurter. London: Spink, 1999. Pages 369-74. 1 pl.

5047 **Visonà, Paolo.** "A Diobol of Uvug in the Correr Museum Coin Collection." *Spink Numismatic Circular* 88, no. 9 (September 1980): 308. Illus.
"The coin in question is an unpublished variety of the Lycian dynast Uvug which can be assigned to the third quarter of the fifth century B.C." [P. Visonà, *NL* 105]

5048 **Warren, John B. DeTabley.** "On Some Coins of Lycia under the Rhodian Domination and of the Lycian League." *Numismatic Chronicle* new ser., 3 (1863): 40-5. 1 pl.
Describes ten coins (illustrated by line drawings) struck in Lycia after 188 B.C. including coins of Patara and Arendae in alliance, Pinara and Myra in alliance, Patara and Arycanda in alliance, Xanthus and Patara in alliance, Phaselis, and a coin of Massicytes with the head of Augustus.

5049 **Zahle, Jan.** "Politics and Economy in Lycia during the Persian Period." *Revue des Études Anciennes* (France) 91, no. 1-2 (1989): 169-82. Illus.
"A survey of coin circulation in Lycia and the circulation of Lycian coins outside Lycia illuminates important aspects of Lycian civilization. The strategically situated area appears at the same time very wealthy, relatively isolated and autonomous. The Lycian dynasts had strong common interests with the Persians in keeping their territory outside the sphere of Greek political influence. The origin of the Lycian silver is not known. It is argued that a considerable part may derive from the Persians, who thereby underpinned the loyal dynasts. Tissaphernes minted in Xanthos himself, in local weight standard and with inscriptions in Lycian. He most probably spent his own silver in order to pay for military services in Lycia itself. He and other satraps may

on other occasions have delivered bullion to be minted and distributed by their allies. The Decadrachm and Podalia hoards exemplify huge fortunes that probably were formed for military purposes." [*Revue des Études Anciennes*]

Also see: Ashton "Beginning of Bronze Coinage" under CARIA; Ashton "Recent Epigraphic Evidence for the Start of the Rhodian and Lykian League Plinthophoroi" under CARIAN ISLANDS—RHODOS; Ashton and Meadows "The Letoon Deposit" under HOARDS; Bivar "A Satrap of Cyrus" under PERSIA; Bresson "Rhodes, Cnide et les Lyciens" under CARIAN ISLANDS—RHODOS; Cancio "Athenian Miscellanea" under ATTICA—GENERAL WORKS; Fried "The Decadrachm Hoard" under HOARDS; Gerojannis "Greek Coins" under PRIVATE COLLECTIONS; Hoover "Commerce ('Pamphylia or Cilicia' Hoard), 2000" under HOARDS; Lampinen "Two Greek Notes" (Arycanda) under CARIA; Olçay and Mørkholm "The Coin Hoard from Podalia" under HOARDS; Palmer and Vermeule "Ancient Gold and Silver" under THE MINTING PROCESS; Sheedy "The Dolphins" under CYCLADES ISLANDS; Tietz "Der Westlykische Münzstandard Zwischen Athen und Persien" under METROLOGY; Troxell "Greek Accessions" under ASIA MINOR—GENERAL WORKS; Wetterstrom "Lycian Portraiture" under PORTRAITS; Winzer *Antike Portraitmünzen* under PORTRAITS; Wright *Coins from Asia Minor and the East* under ASIA MINOR—GENERAL WORKS; Zahle "Persian Satraps and Lycian Dynasts" under PERSIA.

PAMPHYLIA

The astonishing abundance of the silver money of Aspendus is a proof of the commercial importance of the town; and the number of countermarks and barbarous imitations shows that it circulated largely in the country.

—Barclay V. Head, 1911

5050 **Atlan, Sabahat.** *Untersuchungen über die Sidetischen Münzen des V. und IV. Jahrhunderts v. Chr.* Ankara, 1967. 181 pp., 12 pls. [CS 2783]
Examines the coinage of Side in Pamphylia. "Text in German and Turkish, except coin catalogue in Turkish only." [C. Kraay]. [Also see Kraay "Notes on the Mint of Side" below].

5051 ——— "Side'de Basilan Amyntas Sikkeleri." *Belleten* (Turkey) 39 (1975): 575-611. [CS 2784]
A die study of the silver coins with the types of Side but bearing the name of the Galatian king Amyntas. Text in Turkish.

5051a **Baydur, Nezahat.** "Die Münzen von Attaleia in Pamphylia." *Jahrbuch für Numismatik und Geldsseschichte* (Germany) 25 (1975): 33-72.

5052 **Colin, H. J.** *Die Münzen von Perge in Pamphylien aus Hellenistischer Zeit.* Köln: Kölner Münzkabinett, 1996. 101 pp., 50 pls.

5053 **Destrooper-Georgiades, Anne.** "An Unusual Coin from Side." *Nomismatika Khronika* (Greece) 14 (1995): 13-7. Illus.
Publishes a unique stater of Side in the collection of Alpha Credit Bank in Athens, with *obv.*, pomegranate, and *rev.*, raven. The reverse bears a previously unpublished inscription in a local Sidetic script, believed to be the name of the king of Side who struck the coin. The name of the city appears on the obverse in an archaic Greek script. The coin is tentatively dated ca. 450 B.C. [Also see the next item].

5054 ——— "Addition to the Alphabet of Side." *Nomismatika Khronika* (Greece) 16 (1997): 109-10. Illus.
This follow-up to the author's previous article (see above) provides supplementary information about the alphabet used in the inscription of a stater of Side. Six of the letters used are those of the normal Sidean alphabet. The seventh letter used has kept a form closer to the original Phoenician letter.

5055 **Eaglen, Robin J.** "Portraits of Greek Coinage 27: Aspendus." *Spink Numismatic Circular* 117, no. 2 (May 2009): 53. Illus.
This installment of the author's on-going series examines the coinage of Aspendus. Reviews the history of the city and its coin types.

5056 **Kraay, Colin M.** "Notes on the Mint of Side in the Fifth Century B.C." *Numismatic Chronicle* 7th ser., 19 (1969): 15-20. 1 pl. [CS 2785]
"Comments are given on S. Atlan's *Untersuchungen über die Sidetischen Münzen des V. und IV. Jahrhunderts v. Chr.* Several coins not known to Atlan are published, and some corrections of die identifications are made; consequential changes in the sequence of issues are noted. A chronology lower than that of Atlan is proposed, with the earliest issues of Side dated not before 460 B.C." [C. Kraay, *NL* 84].

5057 **Le Rider, Georges.** "Les Tétradrachmes Pamphyliens de la Fin du IIIe Siècle et du Début du IIe Siècle avant Notre Ère." *Revue Numismatique* (France) 6th ser., 14 (1972): 253-9. [CS 2781]

5058 **Madsen, Eardley, and Ethel Madsen.** "Celenderis." *SAN—Journal of the Society for Ancient Numismatics* 14, no. 4 (winter 1983-84): inside covers.
A silver stater of Celenderis is pictured. The reverse shows a horse-rider holding a whip, in the midst of dismounting from a galloping horse prior to mounting a second horse. This activity appears to be different from the Kalpe event of the Olympics as discussed by Brauer. [See Brauer "Kalpe" under TYPES].

5059 **McIntyre, Andrew P.** "The Eras of the Alexanders of Aspendos and Perge." *Numismatic Chronicle* 167 (2007): 92-8. 3 pls.
Examines the dated posthumous Alexander tetradrachms of Aspendos and Perge to answer the question—do the numerals on these coins represent one era or several eras? The author concludes that the coins do not share the same era—the same conclusion reached by Boehringer.

5060 **Meadows, Andrew R.** "Amyntas, Side, and the Pamphylian Plain." *Agoranomia: Studies in Money and Exchange Presented to John H. Kroll.* Edited by Peter G. van Alfen. New York: American Numismatic Society, 2006. Pages 151-76. 6 pls.
It has been thought that the coast was the only part of Pamphylia that did not belong to King Amyntas (based on a 1934 article by Donald Syme). But this ignores a silver coinage of King Amyntas copying the types of Side (Athena/Nike) but bearing ΒΑΣΙΛΕΩΣ ΑΜΥΝΤΟΥ. These coins may indicate that

Amyntas controlled Side, but this possibility requires close scrutiny. Meadows analyzes the hoard evidence for the coinage of Side and summarizes the data in tables including burial dates and magistrate names. Meadows then discusses the coins bearing the magistrate name KΛE, KΛEY, or KΛEYX, usually taken to mean the magistrate Kleuchares. Atlan's die study of the coinage of Amyntas (see Atlan, "Side'de Basilan Amyntas Sikkeleri" above) revealed a die-link with a coin of Kleuchares Meadows differentiates four stylistic groups of Kleuchares coins and assigns dates beginning ca. 183 B.C. and extending to the mid-first century B.C. The Amyntas coins are placed ca. 39-25 B.C. The same Kleuchares cannot have been the magistrate responsible for all four groups struck over a span of 150 years. Meadows concludes that the last two groups, produced in the mid-first century, must be imitations of the earlier issues of Kleuchares, and may not have been struck at Side. Due to the die-links, he suggests that the Kleuchares groups III and IV were struck at the royal mint of Amyntas—which may or may not have been at Side. Whether Amyntas controlled the Pamphylian coast remains uncertain.

5061 ———. "The Eras of Pamphylia and the Seleucid Invasion of Asia Minor." *American Journal of Numismatics* 2nd ser., 21 (2009): 51-88. 3 pls.
The author attempts to identify eras by which the Pamphylian cities dated their posthumous Alexander coinage of the late third and early second century. The following start dates are suggested: Perge – ca. 223/2 B.C.; Aspendus – ca. 213/2; Phaselis – ca. 213/2. Meadows argues that the beginning of the issues of Perge and Aspendus, as well as of their eras, is connected with Seleucid military activity in Pamphylia. The same reason is suggested for the over-representation in hoards of certain issues of the mints of Perge and Aspendus. A connection between the arrival of Antiochus III in Asia Minor in 203 is further proposed as the possible context for the beginning of the coinage of Side with autonomous types. The posthumous Alexander coinage of Phaselis is suggested, on the basis of its pattern of hoarding, to be a different phenomenon, to be regarded as more truly civic in nature. The Seleucid coinages of Seleucus III and Antiochus III previously given to Seleucia ad Calycadnum (*SC* 916 and 1016) are attributed to Termessos.

5062 **Mossop, J. C.** "An Autonomous Coin of Magydus in Pamphylia." *Numismatic Chronicle* 7th ser., 10 (1970): 319-20. Illus.
"A new coin attributed to the second-to-first centuries B.C. moves the date of Magydus as a city-state back by 150-200 years." [J. Mossop, *NL* 85]

5063 **Mowat, Robert.** "Trois Contremarques Inédites sur des Tétradrachmes de Sidé: Extension de l'Union Monétaire Cistophorique." *Corolla Numismatica: Numismatic Essays in Honour of Barclay V. Head*. Edited by G. F. Hill. London: Oxford University Press, 1906. Pages 189-207. 1 pl.

5064 **Ramsay, W. M.** "On Some Pamphylian Inscriptions." *Journal of Hellenic Studies* 1 (1880): 242-57. With a note by A. H. Sayce on pp. 257-8.
"The first part of this article discusses the spelling of the ethnic on coins of Sillyum of the third century B.C. It is claimed that one of the letters represents a parasitic 'w' or digamma, and this argument is supported by reference to inscriptions. In the second part (pp. 246 ff), the spelling in local script of the reverse legend of coins of Perga is similarly discussed." [J. R. Jones, *NIJHS*]

5065 **Schubert, Helmut.** "Ein Unbekannter Gegenstempel auf einer Tetradrachme von Side." *Stephanos Nomismatikos: Edith Schönert-Geiss zum 65. Geburtstag*. Edited by Ulrike Peter. Berlin: Akademie Verlag, 1998. Pages 591-600.

5066 **Tekin, Oguz.** "A Note on BA: FE and BAΛYΣ on the Aspendian Staters." *Annotazioni Numismatiche* (Italy) 4, no. 15 (1994): 315.
"The author presents a new proposal for the reading of the legend BA—ΛYΣ which appears on some staters of Aspendos." [S. Sorda, *NL* 135]

5067 ———. "Aspendian 'Wrestlers': An Iconographic Approach." *Mecanismes et Innovations Monétaires dans l'Anatolie Achéménide: Numismatique et Histoire. Actes de la Table Ronde International d'Istanbul, 22-23 Mai 1997*. Varia Anatolica XII. Edited by O. Casabonne. Istanbul: Institut Français d'Etudes Anatoliennes d'Istanbul; Paris: de Boccard, 2000. Pages 159-69.

5068 **Troxell, Hyla A., and Jonathan H. Kagan.** "Cilicians and Neighbors in Miniature." *Kraay—Mørkholm Essays: Numismatic Studies in Memory of C. M. Kraay and O. Mørkholm*. Numismatica Lovaniensia 10. Edited by G. Le Rider, G. K. Jenkins, N. Waggoner, and U. Westermark. Louvain-la-Neuve: Université Catholique de Louvain, 1989. Pages 275-81. 25 pls.
A catalogue of twenty-seven minute silver coins—hemiobols and tetartemoria—apparently from a hoard of eighty-one coins. Very little can be said with certainty about their date or attribution, but many are Cilician from the satrapal times of the first half of the fourth century B.C. Some are Carian. The authors comment on similarities with known coin types. The coins are illustrated actual size and in 3x enlargements.

5069 "A Very Rare Coin." *Spink Numismatic Circular* 62, no. 5 (May 1954): 192. Illus.
Illustrates a previously unpublished fractional gold coin (Herakles/lion) struck by the Persian satrap Mazaeus during the campaign of Alexander the Great in the eastern provinces of Asia Minor.

Also see: Boehringer "Beobachtungen und Überlegungen zu den Ären der Pamphylischen Alexandreier" under MACEDONIAN KINGDOM—GENERAL WORKS; Hill *Catalogue of Greek Coins of Lycia, Pamphylia, and Pisidia* under LYCIA; Hoover "Commerce ('Pamphylia or Cilicia' Hoard), 2000" under HOARDS; Kraay "The Isparta Hoard" (Aspendus) under HOARDS; Mørkholm "The Era of the Pamphylian Alexanders" under MACEDONIAN KINGDOM—GENERAL WORKS; Olçay and Mørkholm "The Coin Hoard from Podalia" under HOARDS; Robinson "Coins from Lycia and Pamphylia" under LYCIA; Seltman *A Hoard from Side* under HOARDS; Waggoner "Three Recent Greek Accessions" under ASIA MINOR—GENERAL WORKS.

Pisidia and Lykaonia

Termessos, an international commercial center, had used the coins of other Greek city-states, received as tolls or in trade, as its circulating money but it only began to strike its own, autonomous coins in 71 B.C.

—*Marvin Tameanko, 1998*

5070 **Kosmetatou, Elizabeth.** "The Hero Solymos on the Coinage of Termessos Major." *Revue Suisse de Numismatique* (Switzerland) 76 (1997): 41-56. Illus.

5071 **Lewis, Peter E.** "From Iconium to the Home of Saint Luke: A Numismatic Odyssey." *The Celator* 24, no. 11 (November 2010): 6-12. Illus.
The spelling of the city's name on a second century B.C. coin of Eikonion may provide evidence for determining which of the extant manuscripts of the *Book of Acts* is the most accurate version. One of the manuscripts perhaps provides evidence that Saint Luke was originally from Cyrene.

5072 **Tameanko, Marvin.** "The Coinage of Termessos: A Mountain Fortress City." *The Celator* 12, no. 2 (February 1998): 6-12. Illus.
Tameanko begins with a brief history of the city of Termessos in Pisidia. He then summarizes the main trends in the city's coinage during the Greek and Roman periods.

5073 **Troxell, Hyla A.** "A Coin of Coropassus in Lycaonia." *Schweizer Münzblätter* (Switzerland) 37, no. 147 (August 1987): 56-8. Illus.
"The first known coin of Coropassus in Lycaonia is published: it is distinguished from issues of the quasi-homonymic city of Coropissus in Cilicia." [A. Walker, *NL* 121]

Also see: Hill *Catalogue of Greek Coins of Lycaonia, Isauria, and Cilicia* under CILICIA; Hoover *Handbook of Coins of Northern and Central Anatolia* under ASIA MINOR—GENERAL WORKS.

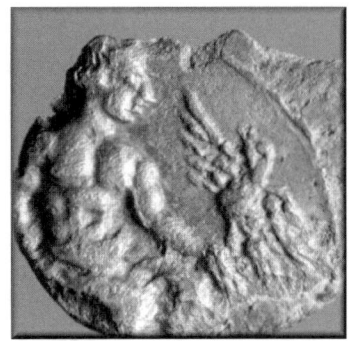

CILICIA

The coin legends, as might be expected in a country with a mixed population like Cilicia, are frequently bilingual, the Greek language prevailing in the western, and the Aramaic in the eastern half of the country.

—Barclay V. Head, 1911

5074 **Arnold-Biucchi, Carmen.** "Un Trésor de Tétradrachmes Hellénistiques d'Aigeai en Cilicie." *Travaux de Numismatique Grecque Offerts à Georges Le Rider.* Edited by M. Amandry and S. Hurter. London: Spink, 1999. Pages 1-13. 2 pls.

5075 **Bing, J. Daniel.** "Datames and Mazaeus: The Iconography of Revolt and Restoration in Cilicia." *Historia* (Germany) 47, no. 1 (1998): 41-76. Illus.
"Datames was governor of Cilicia—not Cappadocia—when he revolted against Artxerxes II around 370 B.C. and started to strike coins in several Cilician mints, mainly at Tarsus. A few Tarsian specimens of his successor, Mazaeus, are illustrated (all enlarged ca. 2:1 or more)." [H. Baldus, *NL* 140]

5076 **Bloesch, Hansjörg.** "Tetradrachms of Aegeae (Cilicia)." *Greek Numismatics and Archaeology: Essays in Honor of Margaret Thompson.* Edited by O. Mørkholm and N. M. Waggoner. Wetteren: Numismatique Romaine, 1979. Pages 1-7. 1 pl.
The author compares the style of the four known tetradrachms of Aegeae with tetradrachms of Seleucia and copper coins of Aegeae bearing a similar obverse type in an attempt to establish a chronological framework. [Also see Mørkholm "The Date of the Autonomous Tetradrachms" below].

5077 ——— "Hellenistic Coins of Aegaea (Cilicia)." *Museum Notes* 27 (1982): 53-96. 6 pls.
Presents a catalogue of 280 autonomous coins of Aegeae beginning in the late third/early second century B.C. and continuing to ca. 27 B.C. Includes bronze units, two-thirds units, and third units segregated into six chronological periods plus a group of special issues. Includes a table of die links and die axes. Discusses dated coins, hoards, coin legends, lettering, monograms, die links, and shapes of flans to develop a chronological framework for the bronze coinage. Briefly reviews the evidence provided by the silver tetradrachms (see Bloesch "Tetradrachms" above). Reviews the types used (gods, heroes, mortals, animals), countermarks, denominations, and weights.

5078 **Brindley, James C.** "Early Coinages Attributable to Issus." *Numismatic Chronicle* 153 (1993): 1-10. 1 pl.
"Six issues, starting at the end of the fifth century B.C., are shown to precede the 'walking lion' staters of Mazaeus (ca. 361 B.C.) which have recently been reattributed to the Issus mint. On the first three of these an abbreviated Aramaic inscription probably represents the name of a local ruler; it is replaced by a second, comparable, inscription within group 3. The well-known Baal/Ahuramazda staters of Tiribazus (group 4) substitute the Greek ethnic of Issus for the Aramaic letters, and their obverse type is that of group 3. Continuity of fabric, style and types shows this to be a regular series and further supports the Issus reattribution of the 'walking lion' staters." [J. Brindley, *NL* 134]. [Also see Sayles "Images That Get Around" under TYPES].

5079 ——— "A Note on the Amazon Coins of Soli in Cilicia." *Spink Numismatic Circular* 102, no. 6 (July 1994): 264-5. Illus.
The archer figure on early coins of Soli has been identified as an Amazon. Brindley publishes two earlier issues of this type. Discusses the development of the types from ca. 480-386 B.C. [The footnotes for this article were omitted in error. They appear in the next issue, no. 7 (September 1994): 307].

5080 ——— "Some Silver Fractions of Tarsus." *Spink Numismatic Circular* 102, no. 9 (November 1994): 400-1. Illus.
Publishes and discusses several fractional issues of Tarsus: (1) A third-stater and a 1/32 stater with hippocamp and hippocamp protome, respectively, emphasize the strong influence of the Nergal cult in the coinage of Tarsus. These coins belong to the period 420-400 B.C. (2) A 1/32 stater with horse walking with seated rider. The rider may be the Cilician ruler of the Syennesis dynasty. These coins belong to the period 410-400 B.C. (3) A 1/16 stater with Dionysos-in-tree/cow standing. This coin, along with three related staters with Dionysos-in-tree/ploughing scene, emphasize fertility. These coins belong to the period 400-386 B.C. Overall, these fractional issues illustrate the dominance of Eastern themes at this stage in the numismatic history of Tarsus.

5081 ——— "Baetyls and the Early Coinage of Mallus." *Spink Numismatic Circular* 104, no. 7 (September 1996): 331-2. Illus.
Some coins featuring a baetyl (a cult object in the form of a conical stone which was worshipped as the abode of the gods) have been attributed to Carian mints (see Troxell "Winged Carians" under CARIA). However, some recently discovered coins seem to re-establish the baetyl as a feature of the early coinage of Mallus in Cilicia.

5082 ——— "The Fourth Century Wolf Protome Coins from South-East Asia Minor." *Spink Numismatic Circular* 107, no. 4 (May 1999): 115-9. Illus.
Examines the fractional silver coins with a wolf protome reverse, which have been variously attributed to fourth century B.C. Tarsus, Mazaeus in Cilicia, or uncertain Cilicia.

5083 **Callander, T.** "The Tarsian Orations of Dio Chrysostom." *Journal of Hellenic Studies* 24 (1904): 58-69.
"On pp. 63-4 the theory of Imhoof-Blumer, that the Herakles-Sandan who appears on coins of Tarsus in Seleucid times is an Asiatic god of much greater antiquity, is accepted." [J. R. Jones, *NIJHS*]

5083a **Casabonne, O.** "Conquete Perse de Phenomene Monetaire: L'Exemple Cilicien." *Mécanismes et Innovations Monétaires dans l'Anatolie Achéménide. Numismatique et Histoire. Actes de la Table Ronde Internationale d'Istanbul, 22-23 Mai 1997.* Varia Anatolica XII. Edited by O. Casabonne. Istanbul: Institut Français d'Etudes Anatoliennes d'Istanbul; Paris: de Boccard, 2000. Pages 21-91.

5084 **Cox, Dorothy H.** *A Tarsus Coin Collection in the Adana Museum.* Numismatic Notes and Monographs, No. 92. New York: American Numismatic Society, 1941. 67 pp., 12 pl. [CS 2805]
A catalogue of part of the collection of 815 coins donated to the Adana Museum by Hetty Goldman in 1935. The collection consists of Armenian, Macedonian, Seleucid, Ptolemaic, Cappadocian, Ionian, Phrygian, Cilicican, and Roman coins. One-hundred thirty are from Tarsus. Describes 246 of the coins, many of which have not been previously published. Among the Greek coins are 56 coins of the Macedonian kings, 75 Seleucid coins, and 15 Ptolemaic coins.

5085 **Crowfoot, J. W.** "The Lions of Kybele." *Journal of Hellenic Studies* 20 (1900): 118-27.
"On pp. 120-1 coins of Tarsus and Hierapolis in Phrygia are noted as examples of 'bull-slaying' scenes; it is not, however, to be taken as certain that these are connected with the worship of Cybele." [J. R. Jones, *NIJHS*]

5086 **de Callataÿ, François.** "Les Monnayages Ciliciens du Premier Quart du IVe s. av. J.-C." *Mecanismes et Innovations Monnetaires dans l'Anatolie Achemenide: Numismatique et Histoire: Actes de la Table Ronde Internationale d'Istanbul, 22-23 Mai 1997.* Edited by O. Casabonne. Istanbul: Institut Français d'Etudes Anatoliennes d'Istanbul; Paris: de Boccard, 2000. Pages 93-127.

5087 **Eaglen, Robin J.** "Portraits of Greek Coinage 6: Celenderis." *Spink Numismatic Circular* 113, no. 5 (October 2005): 307. Illus.
In this installment of the on-going series, Eaglen examines the coinage of Celenderis. Reviews the history of the city and its coin types.

5088 ——— "Portraits of Greek Coinage 26: Balacrus (Balakros)." *Spink Numismatic Circular* 117, no. 1 (March 2009): 8. Illus.
In this installment of the on-going series, Eaglen examines the coinage of Balakros, a satrap under Alexander the Great. Reviews the history and coinage.

5088a **Göktürk, T.** "Small Coins from Cilicia and Surroundings." *Mécanismes et Innovations Monétaires dans l'Anatolie Achéménide. Numismatique et Histoire. Actes de la Table Ronde Internationale d'Istanbul, 22-23 Mai 1997.* Varia Anatolica XII. Edited by O. Casabonne. Istanbul: Institut Français d'Etudes Anatoliennes d'Istanbul; Paris: de Boccard, 2000. Pages 143-51.

5089 **Hebert, Raymond J.** "Ba'al of Tarsus and the Wolf." *SAN—Journal of the Society for Ancient Numismatics* 18, no. 3 (June 1992): 68-71 including 1 plate.
Examines eleven silver anonymous Greek minors in the Smithsonian collection, possibly struck in the fourth century B.C. at Tarsus in Cilicia. The obverse shows Baal seated; the reverse shows the forepart of a wolf and a crescent moon. The coins each weigh approximately 0.6 grams. Presents tables showing weights, diameters, die axis, and the position of the crescent in the reverse field. Discusses the denomination represented by the coins. Concludes these are 1/6 staters, or Persic obols.

5090 **Hendin, David.** "Are Jerusalem's Walls Seen on a Cilician Coin?" *The Celator* 6, no. 10 (October 1992): 44-5. Illus.
Examines the reverse type on a coin of Tarsus which depicts a lion attacking a bull and two lines of turreted city walls. The author suggests these are the walls of Jerusalem described and built by Nehemiah and Ezra in Biblical accounts.

5091 ——— "Jerusalem's Walls on a Coin of Mazaeus?" *The Celator* 12, no. 6 (June 1998): 24. Illus.
A fourth century B.C. coin of Tarsus bears the biblical phrase "Beyond the River" written in Aramaic. The author suggests that the city walls depicted on the coin's reverse may be intended to represent the walls of Jerusalem.

5092 **Hill, George F.** *Catalogue of Greek Coins of Lycaonia, Isauria, and Cilicia.* London: British Museum, 1900. Reprint, Bologna: Forni, 1964. cxxxii, 296 pp., 40 pls., map. [CS 2793]
Volume 21 of the *Catalogue of Greek Coins in the British Museum*. The 296-page catalogue of coins is preceded by 132 pages of introductory text. [Also see *Catalogue of Greek Coins in the British Museum* under PUBLIC COLLECTIONS—GREAT BRITAIN (LONDON)].

5093 **Houghton, Arthur, and Simon Bendall.** "A Hoard of Aegean Tetradrachms and the Autonomous Tetradrachms of Elaeusa Sebaste." *Museum Notes* 33 (1988): 71-89. 1 pl.
A follow-up to Mørkholm's paper on the coins of Aegeae (see Mørkholm "The Date of the Autonomous Tetradrachms" below). Mentions new hoard evidence supporting Mørkholm's dating. Reviews the various weight standards in use during the period in question. Discusses dies, coin production rates, and circulation in the region of northern Syria and Cilicia. Suggests dates for Aegeae's autonomy. Discusses chronology, metrology, types, symbols, and monograms on the tetradrachms of Elaeusa Sebaste.

5094 **Howorth, Henry H.** "A Note on Some Coins Generally Attributed to Mazaios, the Satrap of Cilicia and Syria." *Numismatic Chronicle* 4th ser., 2 (1902): 81-7.
The author disagrees with Babelon, Hill, and Six on the attribution of some coins which they had assigned to Mazaios of Cilicia. The coins in question do not bear Mazaios' name and are inscribed in Greek rather than Aramaic letters. Howorth suggests they were struck by the Greek governors of Cilicia appointed by Alexander the Great and his successors.

5095 **Imhoof-Blumer, Friedrich W.** *Mallos, Megaros, Antioche du Pyramos. Étude Géographique, Historique et Numismatique.* Paris, 1883. Reprint, Chicago: Obol International, 1980. 39 pp., 4 pls. [CS 2801]

5096 ——— "Coin Types of Some Kilikian Cities." *Journal of Hellenic Studies* 18 (1898): 161-81. 2 pls. [CS 2796]
"Fifty-six coin types are discussed and illustrated, many being previously unpublished, although they appear again in the same author's *Kleinasiatische Münzen.*" [J. R. Jones, *NIJHS*]. [Also see Imhoof-Blumer *Kleinasiatische Münzen* under Asia Minor and the Black Sea—General Works].

5097 **Jenkins, G. Kenneth.** "Two New Tarsos Coins." *Revue Numismatique* (France) 6th ser., 15 (1973): 30-4. 1 pl.
"Two recently discovered coins of Tarsus, both displaying images of the god Negal, are described. The cult of this ancient Babylonian deity is attested at various dates and places in the Near East, and notably at Palmyra, where the god was identified with the Graeco-Roman Heracles." [G. K. Jenkins, *NL* 94]

5098 **Karo, G.** "Notes on Amasis and Black-figured Pottery." *Journal of Hellenic Studies* 19 (1899): 135-64. Illus., 2 pls.
"On p. 164 a note by G. F. Hill points out the similarities between a vase by this painter and coins of Nagidus in Cilicia, showing Aphrodite seated smelling a flower." [J. R. Jones, *NIJHS*]

5099 **Lederer, Philip.** "Die Staterprägung der Stadt Nagidos." *Zeitschrift für Numismatik* (Germany) 41 (1931): 153-267. Reprinted, Berlin, 1932. 134 pp., 8 pls. [CS 2803]
A study of the coinage of Nagidos in Cilicia.

5099a **Le Rider, Georges.** "Le Monnayage Perse en Cilicie au IVe Siècle." *Quaderni Ticinesi: Numismatica e Antichità Classiche* (Switzerland) 26 (1997): 151-69.

5100 **Levante, Edoardo.** "The Coinage of Alexandria Katisson in Cilicia." *Numismatic Chronicle* 7th ser., 11 (1971): 93-102. 3 pls.
"Of the 97 coins listed, 58 belong to Hellenistic and 39 to Imperial times. Trajan, Plotina, Hadrian, Commodus, Severus, Caracalla, Severus Alexander, Julia Mammaea and Gordian III are represented. Monograms, symbols and specimens from the same dies are noted. There is an unusually high number of countermarks on the Hellenistic issues." [H. von Aulock, *NL* 87]

5101 ——— "The Coinage of Adana in Cilicia." *Numismatic Chronicle* 144 (1984): 81-94. 8 pls.
"The known coinage of Adana begins during the reign of Antiochus IV of Syria and ends with the emperor Gallienus, notably excluding Severus Alexander. The latter, however, issued an extensive coinage in the neighboring cities of Tarsus, Anazarbus and Aegeae. The specimens from Adana's mint number 283 and include interesting types of the local hero Adanos, city-goddess within the Zodiac signs, and Dionysos with satyr seated on wineskin." [E. Levante, *NL* 114]. A catalogue of the coins is presented here.

5102 ——— "The Coinage of Zephyrion in Cilicia." *Numismatic Chronicle* 148 (1988): 134-41. 4 pls.
A catalogue of 96 coins of Zephyrion: 46 autonomous, 15 pseudo-autonomous, and 36 with Roman Imperial portraits. Table of monograms.

5103 **McKinney, Larry E.** "Tarsus Coinage Commemorated the Great Sandon." *The Celator* 3, no. 12 (December 1989): 1, 25. Illus.
Discusses the mountain, fire, and storm god Sandon who was worshipped in Cilicia. Illustrates a monument built to honor the god. Discusses the relationship between Sandon and Herakles, and the coinage showing the Sandon monument minted in Tarsus during the Seleucid dynasty. [Also see H. Goldman "Sandon" under Types].

5104 **Mixter, John R.** "An Unrecorded Cilician Type Combination and Iconography." *The Celator* 17, no. 1 (January 2003): 37, 36. Illus.
Describes a silver obol with a bust of Athena, three-quarter facing on the obverse. The reverse bears a female head facing front with a circular device or medallion on top of her headdress. The coin bears no inscriptions. Mixter discusses the iconography of the deities and suggests the circular device is a sun-disk. Concludes that the coin was struck in Cilicia, most likely at Tarsos.

5105 **Mørkholm, Otto.** "The Date of the Autonomous Tetradrachms of Aegeae in Cilicia." *Museum Notes* 32 (1987): 57-60.
Raises objections to Bloesch's dating of the autonomous tetradrachms of the city of Aegeae in Cilicia to 105-83 B.C., based upon coin inscriptions and weights (see Bloesch "Tetradrachms of Aegeae" above). Mørkholm dates the coins to the second half of the first century B.C. [Also see Houghton and Bendall "A Hoard of Aegean Tetradrachms" above].

5106 **Moysey, Robert A.** "The Silver Stater Issues of Pharnabazos and Datames from the Mint of Tarsus in Cilicia." *Museum Notes* 31 (1986): 7-61. 5 pls.
The author examines six silver stater issues of the Persian satraps Pharnabazos and Datames, issued ca. 379-372 B.C. Presents a die study of these coins with the goal of establishing their relative chronology, and examines their weights and iconography. Suggests the two satraps minted separately—not concurrently, and that Pharnabazos' lady/Ares staters precede those of Datames. Explores the historical significance of the coins. Lists several hundred of these coins from various collections.

5107 **Naster, Paul.** "Les Statères Ciliciens de Pharnabaze et de Datame à Types Communs." *Kraay—Mørkholm Essays: Numismatic Studies in Memory of C. M. Kraay and O. Mørkholm.* Numismatica Lovaniensia 10. Edited by G. Le Rider, G. K. Jenkins, N. Waggoner, and U. Westermark. Louvain-la-Neuve: Université Catholique de Louvain, 1989. Pages 191-201. 1 pl.

5108 **Poole, Reginald Stuart.** "On a Coin of Mallus in Cilicia." *Numismatic Chronicle* new ser., 1 (1861): 87-90. Illus.
Poole examines the deities depicted on a silver coin of Mallus.

5109 **Robinson, Edward S. G.** "A Stater of Issos." *Numismatic Chronicle* 6th ser., 9 (1949): 114. Illus.
Publishes a stater of Issos with two countermarks on the reverse: (1) a dolphin and an eagle with upright trident behind, and (2) a stamp found on other Cilician issues, which may be the mark of Mylasa or of a mint farther east.

5110 **Sayles, Wayne G.** "Zarbos and the Cult of Zeus." *Nomismatika Khronika* (Greece) 19 (2000): 123-30. Illus.

A discussion of the coinage of Anazarbos in Cilicia. Reviews the origins of the city's name. The worship of Zeus at Anazarbos is emphasized repeatedly on the city's coinage. The earliest coins of the city are bronzes struck under the Tarkondimotid kings before 31 B.C. Publishes a new specimen on which the legends make clear that 'Anazarbos' is a reference to the city on or near the holy mountain of Zarbos. The entrance to a cave lying just outside the city walls is shown on a coin of the Roman period. Zeus and the cave played an important part in the local population's religious beliefs. In Greek and English.

5111 ——— "Coins as Geographical Evidence." *The Celator* 18, no. 3 (March 2004): 43. Illus.
Describes the river gods which appear on coins of Cilician cities: Chydnus at Tarsus, Sarus at Adana, and Pyramus at Mallus. Illustrates a coin of Mallus (from the time of Augustus) depicting two river gods swimming in opposite directions—evidence that the river changed its course.

5112 ——— "Some Thoughts on the Chronology of Cilician Staters." *The Celator* 20, no. 9 (September 2006): 46. Illus.
Discusses the "lion and bull" staters struck at Tarsos ca. 333 B.C. Some coins bear a letter B on the reverse. Some contain a trace of an erased B and some contain no B. Sayles suggests the governor Balakros continued to issue the lion and bull staters with Zeus obverse for a short time after Mazaios, then introduced the Athena Head staters with the B. When Balakros died in 328 B.C., the B was erased. Eventually, the dies were replaced with new dies without the B. A similar arrangement can be seen in the coinage of Mazaios.

5113 ——— "An Interesting Coin of Mallos." *The Celator* 22, no. 1 (January 2008): 45. Illus.
Again examines some "lion and bull" staters, with and without the letter B (see Sayles "Some Thoughts" above). Some issues bear a letter M under the throne of Baal. Theses coins may have been minted at Mallos. The author discusses some questions surrounding the mint locations.

5114 ——— "A New Coin of Mallos." *The Celator* 22, no. 3 (March 2008): 45. Illus.
Sayles finds parallels between coin types used in Sicily and Italy and the types used on some Cilician coins. Also illustrates an unpublished bronze coin of Mallos depicting an eagle standing on the head of a boar.

5115 ——— "Athena at Mallos." *The Celator* 25, no. 1 (January 2011): 45. Illus.
Sayles examines the image of Athena on the coinage of Mallos. He comments on H. C. Lindgren's view that images of Athena and Tyche on ancient coins serve as a reflection of comtemporary cultural values, with Athena reflecting the values of a self-reliant society, and Tyche representing the values of a passive society lacking in self-reliance.

5116 ——— "Tyche at Mallos." *The Celator* 25, no. 3 (March 2011): 45. Illus.
A continuation of Sayles' previous article.

5117 ——— "Early Dated Anazarbus Coins." *The Celator* 25, no. 5 (May 2011): 45. Illus.
Examines some coins of the Tarkondimotid Dynasty of Cilicia (client kings under Roman hegemony), 70 B.C. to A.D. 17. At least three different coin types issued under these kings bear dates related to that epoch. Four coins are illustrated.

5118 ——— "A Tarkondimotid Clue." *The Celator* 25, no. 6 (June 2011): 45. Illus.
Examines the monograms on some bronze coins of the Tarkondimotid Dynasty of Cilicia and discusses some possible identities for the initials.

5119 **Sear, David R.** "Mazaeus: Satrap Extraordinaire." *Coin and Medal News* (England) 19, no. 4 (March 1982): 31. Illus. Also appeared in *The Numismatist* 110, no. 3 (March 1997): 289-90. Illus.
A brief description of the life of Mazaeus who was appointed satrap of Cilicia, a province of the Persian Empire, in 361 B.C. His reign lasted twenty-seven years, during which the mint at Tarsus issued silver staters of three main types. In 331, Mazaeus was appointed satrap of Babylonia under Alexander the Great.

5120 **Shore, Fred B.** "A New Greek Fraction." *The Celator* 19, no. 5 (May 2005): 39. Illus.
Publishes three silver fractions with three-quarter facing head of Athena. Two of the coins bear the legend ΠΟΣΙΔ. Shore concludes the coins are the first coins attributable to Posidium in Cilicia, and were struck ca. 333 B.C.

5121 **Six, Jean P.** "Le Satrape Mazaïos." *Numismatic Chronicle* 3rd ser., 4 (1884): 97-159. 2 pls. [CS 2797]

5122 ——— "Some Archaic Gorgons in the British Museum." *Journal of Hellenic Studies* 6 (1885): 275-86. Illus., 2 pls.
"On p. 285 it is suggested that silver coins with obverse type of a gorgon and reverse of a harpy are to be attributed to Mallus." [J. R. Jones, *NIJHS*]

5123 **Tahberer, Bekircan.** "Apollo Lykeios in Ancient Tarsus Numismatics." *The Celator* 18, no. 1 (January 2004): 30-1, 34-8. Illus.
Begins with a brief review of the history of the city of Tarsus from its founding (ca. 5500 B.C.) through the Roman period. Discusses the god Apollo, worshiped at Tarsus as Lykeios. Discusses possible meanings of the term Lykeios: (1) wolf slayer, (2) god of light, or (3) god of Lykia. Discusses the relationship between Apollo and the wolf, and the wolf-cult at Tarsus.

5124 **van Alfen, Peter G.** "The Later Fourth Century BCE Coinage of Issos." *American Journal of Numismatics* 2nd ser., 20 (2008): 199-208. 1 pl.
The author argues that a unique coin from a late fourth century Near Eastern hoard (now at the American Numismatic Society) is from one of the last series of coins produced in Issos before the Macedonian take-over in 222 B.C. The coin has *obv.*, Baal of Tarsus seated on throne, B'LDGN in Aramaic, and *rev.*, lion walking, MZDY in Aramaic. Discusses the place of minting, the etymology of the inscriptions, the identity of the deity represented, and the denomination of the coin (didrachm or shekel).

5125 **Von Aulock, Hans.** "Die Prägung des Balakros in Kilikien." *Jahrbuch für Numismatik und Geldsseschichte* (Germany) 14 (1964): 79-82.

5126 **Ziegler, Ruprecht.** "Münzen Kilikiens als Zeugnis Kaiserlicher Getreidespenden." *Jahrbuch für Numismatik und Geldgeschichte* (Germany) 27 (1977): 29-67. 4 pls. [CS 2798]

5127 ——— *Kaise, Heer und Städtisches Geld, Untersuchungen zur Münzprägung von Anazarbos und Anderer Ostkilikischer Städte.* Vienna, 1993.

Also see: Amandry and Le Rider *Tresors* under General Works—Greek ; Borrell "Restitution" under Ionia; Destroopers-Georgiades "Two Cilician Hoards" under Hoards; Gerojannis "Greek Coins" under Private Collections; Herbert "Ten Greek Tidbits" under Asia Minor—General Works; Houghton "The Second Reign of Demetrius II of Syria at Tarsus" under Syria—Seleucid Kingdom; Houghton "The Royal Seleucid Mint of Soli" under Syria—Seleucid Kingdom; Houghton "The Seleucid Mint of Mallus" under Syria—Seleucid Kingdom; Jenkins "Two Coins" under Asia Minor—General Works; Kraay "The Celenderis Hoard" under Hoards; Kraay "Greek Coinage and War" under General Works—Greek; Lagos "Athena Itonia" under Central Greece—Boeotia; Levy "The Oriental Origin of Herakles" under Types; Lorber and Kovacs "A Ptolemaic Mint at Soli" under Egypt—Ptolemaic Kingdom.

Mildenberg "Notes on the Coin Issues of Mazday" under Persia; Mørkholm "Seleucid Coins from Cilicia" under Syria—Seleucid Kingdom; Moysey "Observations…Satrapal Revolt" under Persia; Newell "A Cilician Find" under Hoards; Newell "Myriandros—Alexandria Kat'Isson" under Macedonian Kingdom—General Works; Newell "Tarsos under Alexander" under Macedonian Kingdom—General Works; E. S. G. Robinson "Coins from the Excavations at Al-Mina" under Hoards; Sayles "Feathered Enigma" under Types; Sayles "Local Myths" under Types; Sayles "Wings" under Types; Schwabacher "Contributions" (Mallus) under Sicily—Syracuse; *Levante—Cilicia* under The Sylloge Nummorum Graecorum Series (Swiss Series); Vagi "The Pyre of Sandon" under Types; Vagi "Fourth Century Drachms of Sinope" under Paphlagonia; Waggoner "Three Recent Greek Accessions" under Asia Minor—General Works; Wilkenson "The Origin and Development" under Types.

GALATIA

After they had sided with the Seleucid king Antiochus III the Great against the Romans, their general Cnaeus Manlius Vulso overran their territory, carrying off a huge quantity of loot; and after Rome's first war against Mithradates VI of Pontus, Galatia became its protectorate.

—M. Grant, 1986

5128 **Babington, Churchill.** "On an Autonomous Coin of Pessinus in Galatia, Together with Some Remarks on the Origin of the Name of the City." *Numismatic Chronicle* new ser., 2 (1862): 136-9. Illus.
The author examines the inscription on a bronze coin of Pessinus. [Further comments on the inscription appear in *Numismatic Chronicle* new ser., 16 (1876): 79].

5129 **Burgon, Thomas.** "On Two Newly Discovered Silver Tetradrachms of Amyntas, King of Galatia: with Some Remarks on the Diminution in Weight of the Attic Drachma." *Numismatic Chronicle* 8 (1846): 69-96. Illus.
Examines two tetradrachms with Athena facing right on the obverse, and Nike advancing left on the reverse (similar to the types of Side in Pamphylia). One of the coins is dated. The reverses bear the inscription ΒΑΣΙΛΕΩΣ ΑΜΥΝΤΟΥ. No silver coins of this king have been previously published. Reviews the history of the king's reign. Discusses the weight of the Attic drachma in comparison with the Roman denarius. The author concludes these coins and the silver coins of Side were minted in the same city at about the same time.

5130 **Luynes, Duc de.** "Médailles Inédites d'Amyntas." *Revue Numismatique* (France) 10 (1845): 253-65.

5131 **Wroth, Warwick.** *Catalogue of Greek Coins of Galatia, Cappadocia, and Syria.* London: British Museum, 1899. Reprint, Bologna: Forni, 1964. xci, 341 pp., 38 pls., map. [CS 2812]
Volume 20 of the *Catalogue of Greek Coins in the British Museum.* The 341-page catalogue of coins is preceded by ninety-one pages of introductory text. [Also see *Catalogue of Greek Coins in the British Museum* under PUBLIC COLLECTIONS—GREAT BRITAIN (LONDON)].

Also see: Atlan "Side'de Basilan Amyntas Sikkeleri" under PAMPHYLIA; Hoover *Handbook of Coins of Northern and Central Anatolia* under ASIA MINOR—GENERAL WORKS; Meadows "Amyntas, Side, and the Pamphylian Plain" under PAMPHYLIA.

CAPPADOCIA

The publication of a catalogue containing the coins issued by the kings of Cappadocia is justified by the interest attached to those coins, both from an artistic point of view—for some are certainly among the most beautiful pieces of Greek coinage in the Middle East—and from an historical one, for nearly all the coins give the regnal year of the king, supplying us with fundamental information about the different reigns.

—B. Simonetta, 1977

5132 **Adams, John Paul.** "Aristonikos and the Cistophoroi." *Historia* (Germany) 29, no. 3 (1980): 302-14.
"Two cistophoroi survive with the reverse legend ΒΑ ΣΥ ΑΡ. Attribution to King Ariarathes V of Cappadocia and the mint of Synnada by D. Kienast [*Historia* 26 (1977)] is rejected on geographical and political grounds, and likewise attribution by Kleiner and Noe (see Kleiner and Noe *The Early Cistophoric Coinage* under ASIA MINOR—GENERAL WORKS) to the mint of Pergamum in the 160/150s on the grounds of obverse die links is rejected. The surviving specimens show retooling and anomalies: there is an unusual disposition of the legends, there are peculiarities in the use of 'symbols,' and the name of the minting city is unligatured (a late practice). The reverse dies were reworked in the first years of Aristonikos (133 B.C.) by his supporters in order to issue emergency coinage to finance the revolt of the pretender. From his second year (133/2) Aristonikos was styled Basileus Eumenes. The date Year 1 at Ephesos (133 B.C.) is deliberately ambiguous. Its natural and traditional interpretation was an Attalid regnal year (thus Aristonikos, Year 1), but Ephesos early joined the side of Aristonikos' enemies, and thus Year 1 is a year in an era of *eleutheria*. It is not, in any case, a Roman provincial era." [J. Adams, *NL* 108]

5132a **Arslan, Melih.** "A Unique Tetradrachm of Ariarathes, King of Cappadocia, from a Hoard found at Kotyora (Ordu)." *XII Internationaler Numismatischer Kongress Berlin 1997, Akten-Proceedings-Actes.* Edited by B. Kluge and B. Weisser. Berlin: Staatliche Museen zu Berlin, 2000.

5133 ——— "The Cappadocian King Ariarathes VI and the Star on the Tiara—An Unique Drachm of the Cappadocian King Ariarathes VI." *The Celator* 17, no. 3 (March 2003): 24-8. Illus.
Publishes a unique Cappadocian drachm with a draped bust of a young king facing right and wearing an ornate tiara with diadem. At the center of the upper part of the diadem is a prominently displayed star. Arslan reviews the controversy over the attribution of Cappadocian coins, especially issues which have variously been assigned to Ariarathes IV and Ariarathes VI. Provides evidence from other coins and engraved gems. Points out that no star is seen on any other tiara portrait coins before Ariarathes VI, and it is to this king that Arslan assigns the new drachm.

5134 **Bendall, Simon.** "A Coin of Year One of Ariobarzanes I of Cappadocia." *Spink Numismatic Circular* 76, no. 11 (November 1968): 337. Illus.
Illustrates a silver drachm of Ariobarzanes which the author believes was struck in the first year of the king's reign, 96/5 B.C. The portrait is "a younger and more vigorous representation" of the king in comparison to the portraits on coins of years 2 and 3.

5135 **Borrell, Maximilian.** "Coins of the Kings of Cappadocia." *Numismatic Chronicle* new ser., 2 (1862): 1-19.
Borrell reviews the history of the Cappadocian kingdom and describes some of its coins.

5136 **Cavafy, Constantine P.** "Orophernes." Translated by M. J. A. Tzamali. *Nomismatika Khronika* (Greece) 21 (2002): 7.
A short poem based on the life of Orophernes, king of Cappadocia. Written in 1915. [Also see Salvesen "Cavafy Poem" below].

5137 **Mørkholm, Otto.** "Some Cappadocian Problems." *Numismatic Chronicle* 7th ser., 2 (1962): 407-11. 1 pl. [CS 2814]
"Mørkholm questions Reinach's interpretation of the series of numerals found in the reverse exergues of Cappadocian drachms and tetradrachms as referring to their dates in regnal years. Since Reinach's theory does not hold true in all cases the author suggests the possibility of a new approach to the arrangement of the series, confining his remarks to the coinage of the Ariarathids in the second and early first centuries B.C. The resultant rearrangement produces several changes in attribution." [F. Campbell, *NL* 70]. [Also see Mørkholm "The Coinages of Ariarathes VIII and Ariarathes IX" below for a more detailed follow-up to the discussion of the coinage of Ariarathes IX].

5138 ——— "Some Cappadocian Die-Links." *Numismatic Chronicle* 7th ser., 4 (1964): 21-5. 1 pl. [CS 2815]
"In reply to the article of Simonetta (see Simonetta "Remarks" below) the theory is advanced that the letters on Cappadocian coins are sometimes but not always to be interpreted as dates. The use of identical obverse dies connects issues that would be widely separated if the value as date is maintained. The author is now preparing a corpus of the Cappadocian coinage." [A. Bellinger, *NL* 79]. [Also see B. Simonetta "Some Additional Remarks" below].

5139 ——— "The Coinages of Ariarathes VIII and Ariarathes IX of Cappadocia." *Essays in Greek Coinage Presented to Stanley Robinson.* Edited by C. M. Kraay and G. K. Jenkins. Oxford: Clarendon Press, 1968. Pages 241-58. 4 pls. [CS 2816]
This follow-up to Mørkholm's 1962 paper in *The Numismatic Chronicle* explores the coinage of the Cappadocian king Ariarathes IX and assigns a series of coins to the little known king Ariarathes VIII. Lists coins attributed to Ariarathes IX, divided into two series. Mørkholm's series II coins had been previously attributed to Ariarathes IV or V. Suggests two mints operated simultaneously in Cappadocia and these may have been located at Mazaca and Tyana. Also assigns two groups of coins to the obscure king Ariarathes VIII. Summarizes the history and coinage of this period. Briefly describes the "Cappadocian Hoard" of 170 Cappadocian drachms from which much of his evidence was gathered. [Also see Mørkholm "A Further Comment" below].

5140 ——— "The Classification of Cappadocian Coins." *Numismatic Chronicle* 7th ser., 9 (1969): 21-31. 1 pl. [CS 2817]
"In a reply to Simonetta's paper (see Simonetta "Some Additional Remarks" below), the attributions of Cappadocian coins down to ca. 100 B.C. are defended, and earlier conclusions are supported by a new arrangement of the royal Cappadocian bronze coinage from the third and second centuries B.C." [O. Mørkholm, *NL* 84]

5141 ——— "A Further Comment on the Coinages of Ariarathes VIII and Ariarathes IX." *Quaderni Ticinesi: Numismatica e Antichità Classiche* (Switzerland) 4 (1975): 109-38. Illus. [CS 2818]
"In a reply to criticism of attribution by B. Simonetta, the findings regarding Ariarathes VIII and IX are reaffirmed. The letter appearing in the exergue is confirmed as indication of regnal year and the known issues, now more numerous than previously noted, are divided into three groups originating in three different mints." [S. Sorda, *NL* 98]. Text in Italian and English. [See Mørkholm "The Coinages of Ariarathes VIII and Ariarathes IX" above. Simonetta's comments appeared in *Rivista Italiana di Numismatica e Scienze Affini* (Italy) in 1970 and *Quaderni Ticinesi: Numismatica e Antichità Classiche* (Switzerland) in 1974].

5142 ——— "The Coinages of Ariarathes VI and Ariarathes VII of Cappadocia." *Revue Suisse de Numismatique* (Switzerland) 57 (1978): 144-63. Illus. [CS 2819]
"Coins of both kings are divided into four groups corresponding to four mints working contemporaneously. The supposition that the letters found in the exergue represent dates is rejected. Die links, common use of monograms, and stylistic criteria help to build up groups and sequences. Frequency tables and metallic analyses are added, and a discussion of the historical background is included." [H. Bloesch, *NL* 104]

5143 ——— "The Cappadocians Again." *Numismatic Chronicle* 139 (1979): 242-6.
A review article discussing Simonetta's *The Coins of the Cappadocian Kings* (see below). Mørkholm continues to disagree with Simonetta on the attribution of various issues to the different Cappadocian kings of the name Ariarathes. Here, Mørkholm focuses on Simonetta's re-dating of Orophernes' usurpation of the Cappadocian throne which Simonetta moved from 158-157 B.C. to 161-159 B.C. Mørkholm strongly disagrees with this shift.

5144 **Newton, Charles T.** "On an Inedited Tetradrachm of Orophernes II, King of Cappadocia." *Numismatic Chronicle* new ser., 11 (1871): 19-27. Illus.
Six coins (of the same type) were discovered under the pedestal of a statue in April 1870, on the site of the Temple of Athene Polias at Priene. The coins were portrait tetradrachms of Orophernes II. Describes the probable circumstances surrounding the burial of the coins. [Also see H. Salvesen "Tetradrachm" below].

5145 **Phillips, Wayne C.** "Cappadocian Coinage Greek, Roman Issues." *Coin World* (February 1, 1993): 56. Illus.
This installment of Phillips' "Let's Talk Ancients" column provides an overview of the history and coinage of the Cappadocian Kingdom.

5146 **Salvesen, Harald.** "Tetradrachm of Orophernes is Regarded by Some as the Ultimate Hellenistic Portrait Coin." *The Celator* 5, no. 4 (April 1991): 6-8.
Discusses a tetradrachm of King Orophernes of Cappadocia, 160-156 B.C. Recounts the history of his reign, and describes how the coin was found in Turkey in 1870. Nine specimens of the coin are known. The known coins are listed in a table along with their present location, weight, die variety, and pedigree. [Also see C. Newton "On an Inedited Tetradrachm of Orophernes II" above, for the original publication of the finding of these coins].

5147 ——— "Cavafy Poem Was Inspired by Tetradrachm of Orophernes." *The Celator* 9, no. 6 (June 1995): 26-7. Illus.
Presents a poem by the Greek poet Constantine P. Cavafy (1863-1933) which focuses on the portrait tetradrachm of Orophernes. Also illustrates two newly discovered counterfeits of this important coin. [Also see Cavafy above].

5148 ——— "The Tetradrachm of Orophernes." *Nomismatika Khronika* (Greece) 21 (2002): 8-11. Illus.
A slightly modified reprint of Salvesen's earlier article from *The Celator* (see above).

5148a **Simonetta, Alberto M.** "The Coinage of the Cappadocian Kings: A Revision and a Catalogue of the Simonetta Collection." *Parthica* 9 (2007/2008): 9-124. Illus.
[Also see B. Simonetta *The Coins of the Cappadocian Kings* below].

5149 **Simonetta, Bono.** "Notes on the Coinage of the Cappadocian Kings." *Numismatic Chronicle* 7th ser., 1 (1961): 9-50. 3 pls. [CS 2820]
"By way of an introduction the writer presents an historical survey of the kings of Cappadocia and their coinage, from Ariarathes I to Archelaos; he also discusses weights, forgeries, and the various monograms found on the coins. The numerous types and varieties issued, presented in catalogue form, include specimens from the following collections: The Cabinet des Mèdailles (219), British Museum (150) American Numismatic Society (136), Simonetta Collection (123), Copenhagen Museum (37) and the Lockett Collection (8)." [I. Merker, *NL* 65]

5150 ——— "Remarks on Some Cappadocian Problems." *Numismatic Chronicle* 7th ser., 4 (1964): 83-92. Illus. [CS 2821]
"Defense of the theory that the letters in the exergue of Cappadocian coins are always regnal years against the suggestion of Mørkholm (see Mørkholm "Some Cappadocian Die-Links" above) that collection of a corpus of them will show that there are cases where they must have another meaning. Simonetta's arguments are based on general historical probability, Mørkholm's on study of the dies." [A. Bellinger, *NL* 79]

5151 ——— "Some Additional Remarks on the Royal Cappadocian Coinage." *Numismatic Chronicle* 7th ser., 7 (1967): 7-12.

"The author disagrees with the re-attribution of certain series of royal Cappadocian coins by Mørkholm in *NC* 1964 (see Mørkholm "Some Cappadocian Die-Links" above) and elsewhere, and restates his evidence and arguments." [B. Simonetta, *NL* 82]

5152 ———— "Ariarathes IV o Ariarathes VI?" *Quaderni Ticinesi* (Switzerland) (1973): 37-42. [CS 2822]

5153 ———— "Problemi di Numismatica dei re di Cappadocia: l'Ipotetica Monetazione di Ariarathes VIII." *Quaderni Ticinesi* (Switzerland) (1973): 49-62. [CS 2824]

5154 ———— "Osservazioni su Talune Emissioni Barbariche dei re di Cappadocia." *Rivista Italiana di Numismatica* (Italy) 76 (1974): 95-105. Illus. [CS 2823]
Italian text with English, French, and German summaries.

5155 ———— "Sulla Prima Monetazione di Ariarathes VI di Cappadocia." *Schweizer Münzblätter* (Switzerland) 25, no. 97 (1975): 4-7. Illus. [CS 2825]

5156 ———— "Raffronto tra Alcuni Sateri di Mazaeus a Tarsus e le Dramme di Ariarathes I di Cappadocia." *Schweizer Münzblätter* (Switzerland) 25, no. 100 (1975): 91-5. Illus. [CS 2826]

5157 ———— *The Coins of the Cappadocian Kings.* Typos, Band 2. Monographien Zur Antiken Münzkunde. Fribourg: Office du Livre, 1977. 54 pp., 7 pls. [CS 2827]
A catalogue with biographical sketches covering the coinage of Ariarathes I through Archelaus, 333 B.C. to A.D. 17, with a brief section on unattributed bronzes. [Also see Otto Mørkholm's review "The Cappadocians Again" above, in which Mørkholm disagrees with some of Simonetta's attributions. Also see A. M. Simonetta "The Coinage of the Cappadocian Kings: A Revision" above].

5158 ———— "Monete Inedite dei re di Cappadocia." *Schweizer Münzblätter* (Switzerland) no. 97 (1979): 55-8. Illus. [CS 2828]

5159 **Taylor, George.** "The Coin Portraits of Ariobarzanes I." *Spink Numismatic Circular* 76, no. 12 (December 1968): 372-3. Illus.
Illustrates seven portrait drachms of the Cappadocian king Ariobarzanes I, each from a different regnal year. Taylor comments on the realistic portraiture and how the aging of the king is reflected. Points out that the obverse portraits were consistently well engraved, while the reverse types were often crudely executed.

5160 ———— "A Countermarked Coin of Ariarathes VII?" *Numismatic Chronicle* 7th ser., 8 (1968): 269-70. Illus.
"A countermarked coin of Ariarathes VII purchased in Beirut in 1964 has inconsistencies in weight, inscription, portrait and position of monogram, suggesting that it is false. A second countermarked coin of the same king has now appeared in Aleppo and this too seems to be a forgery." [G. Taylor, *NL* 82]

5161 ———— "A Find of Cappadocian Silver." *Berytus* (Denmark) 20 (1971): 43-5. Illus.
Lists 208 drachms of Ariobarzanes I recently found in Turkey, sorted by regnal years and monograms.

5162 **Yarkin, Ural.** "An Unpublished Coin of Ariarathes III for Cybistra in Cappadocia." *Numismatic Chronicle* 141 (1981): 144-5. Illus.
"An unpublished bronze coin of Ariarathes III (ca. 240?-220 B.C.), an extremely rare issue of the mint of Cybistra in Cappadocia, confirms the existence of the city ca. third century B.C." [U. Yarkin, *NL* 108]

5163 **Yarkon, Barry J.** "Kings of Cappadocia Struck Independent Coinage." *The Celator* 3, no. 8 (August 1989): 1, 22-3. Illus.
The author describes the history of Cappadocian dynasties and their coinage from the fourth century B.C. until their absorption into the Roman empire in A.D. 17. The coinage followed the Hellenistic pattern of royal portraits, and tended to decrease in weight and deteriorate in style during this period. The names and reign dates of the Cappadocian kings are presented in a table. Six coins are illustrated.

Also see: Glew "The Cappadocian Expedition" under BITHYNIA; Hoover *Handbook of Coins of Northern and Central Anatolia* under ASIA MINOR—GENERAL WORKS; Krengel and Lorber "Early Cappadocian Tetradrachms" under SYRIA—SELEUCID KINGDOM; Lorber "Commerce ('Demetrius I' Hoard) 2003" under HOARDS; Lorber and Houghton "Cappadocian Tetradrachms" under SYRIA—SELEUCID KINGDOM; Richter "Late Hellenistic Portraiture" under PORTRAITS; Wroth *Catalogue of Greek Coins of Galatia, Cappadocia, and Syria* under GALATIA.

Cyprus

Cyprus in the sixth century contained several small kingdoms ruling over a mixed population of Greek or Phoenician origin. Production of silver coinage seems to have begun late in the sixth century and the wide variety of early-style issues, represented in large numbers in hoards from Cyprus and Egypt, indicates that many separate mints were probably operating on the island by the early fifth century.

—I. Carradice and M. Price, 1988

5164   **Amandry, Michel.** "Le Monnayage d'Amathonte." *Amathonte 1, Testimonia 1, Auteurs Anciens—Monnayage—Voyageurs—Fouilles—Origines—Geographie.* Edited by P. Aupert and M.-C. Hellmann. Paris: École Française d'Athènes, 1984. Pages 57-76.
Examines the coinage of Amanthus in Cyprus.

5164a   **Barag, Dan.** "Ptolemaic Silver Currency of Cyprus in Seleucid Phoenicia and Coele-Syria." *Israel Numismatic Journal* (Israel) 16 (2007-8): 38-48.

5165   **Bubelis, William S.** "An Overstruck Stater of the Cypriot Kingdom of Salamis." *American Journal of Numismatics* 2nd ser., 16-17 (2004-2005): 1-5. 1 pl.
An overstruck silver stater in the American Numismatic Society collection provides evidence for a previously unknown king of Salamis, Cyprus, of the mid-fifth century B.C. The distinctive traces of the host coin suggest that it was originally issued by King Euanthes of Salamis earlier in the fifth century, and then restruck with standard Salaminian types by a King Sophysas. Despite the difficulties posed by the syllabic legend, the name Sophysas remains the most plausible interpretation, and would be linguistically and culturally appropriate for a Cypriot ruler of this period.

5166   **Destrooper-Georgiades, Anne.** *The Spread of Cypriot Archaic and Classical Coins inside Cyprus and Abroad: Its Significance for the National and International Relations of the Island.* Ph.D. thesis in the Department of History, Catholic University of Louvain, Belgium.

5167   ——— "Bibliographical Survey of Cypriot Archaic and Classical Numismatics 1970-1981." *Numismatic Report* (Cyprus) 12 (1981): 55-77.
"Eighty-five titles with short abstracts are entered." [M. Santamas, *NL* 110]

5168   ——— "The Cypriot Coin with Solar Disk of the Adana Hoard." *Numismatic Report* (Cyprus) 15-21 (1984-90): 295-8. Illus.
"A stater depicting the heads of a boar and a lion on the obverse and a winged sun on the reverse is discussed. The author considers previous theories put forward about this coin and argues for its attribution to Paphos in the fifth century B.C." [M. Santamas, *NL* 135]

5169   ——— "The Hoard of Soloi." *Nomismatika Khronika* (Greece) 10 (1991): 37-42. Illus.
A brief description of a hoard of about sixty-one bronze coins found in 1928 by the Swedish Cyprus Expedition in Soloi (although only 15 coins could be separated from the mass). The coin types are *obv.*, female head to left with hair tied in chignon, and *rev.*, an ankh in a laurel wreath. The coins are probably from the mint of Soloi (or possibly Marion), and date to the late fourth century B.C. The hoard was likely deposited ca. 330-310 B.C. In English, with illustrations, on pp. 37-40; in Greek on pp. 41-2.

5170   ——— "Presentation of New Material and Work in Progress on Cypriote Classical Numismatics." *Acta Cypria 2* (Acts of an International Congress on Cypriote Archaeology held in Göteborg on 22-24 August 1991). Studies in Mediterranean Archaeology and Literature, Pocket-book 117. Edited by Paul Astrom. 1992. Pages 54-66. Illus.
"The author considers Cypriote coins in general but also looks at old coin hoards and discusses the context in which numismatists have previously examined them with a view to their attribution. Mention is made for the first time of the discovery of four didrachms of Pumiathon of Kition (361-312 B.C.) who until now was believed to have struck only gold coins." [M. Santamas, *NL* 135]

5171   ——— "Les Bronze Chypriotes Représentant une Tête Féminine et une Croix Ansée dans une Couronne Laurée." *Florilegium Numismaticum: Studia in Honorem U. Westermark Edita.* Edited by Harald Nilsson. Stockholm: Svenska Numismatiska Föreningen, 1992. Pages 365-76. 2 pls.

5171a   —— "Le Monnayage de Paphos au IVe s., Nouvelles Perspectives." *XIII Congreso Internacional de Numismática, Madrid – 2003: Actas–Proceedings–Actes I.* Edited by Carmen Alfaro, Carmen Marcos, and Paloma Otero. Madrid: International Numismatic Commisson, 2005. Pages 245-52.

5171b   —— "The Cypriote Coinage during the 4th Century B.C.: Unified or Chaotic Evolution in the Hellenistic Period?" *Proceedings of the International Conference from Evagoras I to the Ptolemies: The Transition from the Classical to the Hellenistic Period in Cyprus, Nicosia 29-30 November 2002.* Nicosia: Department of Antiquities, 2007. Pages 265-82.

5172   —— "Les Débuts du Monnayage en Bronze à Chypre." *Numismatic Chronicle* 168 (2008): 33-41. 1 pl.
Examines the introduction of bronze coinage at Cyprus.

5173   **Dikaios, P.** "A Hoard of Silver Cypriote Staters from Larnaca." *Numismatic Chronicle* 5th ser., 15 (1935): 165-79. 4 pls. Reprinted in *Numismatic Report* (Cyprus) 7 (1976): 31-45. Illus. [CS 2807]
Discusses a hoard found in 1933 which contained silver staters of the sixth and fifth centuries B.C. from the mints of Citium, Idalium, Lapethus, Paphos, Salamis, as well as several coins of uncertain origin. Includes a catalogue of 564 coins with brief discussion. [Also see E. S. G. Robinson "Notes" below].

5174   —— "A Silver Stater of Idalium." *Numismatic Chronicle* 5th ser., 15 (1935): 282-3. Illus.
Publishes a stater of Idalium (Cyprus) with *obv.*, sphinx; *rev.*, lotus flower. Proposes a new reading of the king's name on the coin: ΑΡΓΑΛΟΣ. A note by E. S. G. Robinson is appended in which Robinson welcomes the new reading as a plausible name. [However, see G. F. Hill "The Supposed Idalian Stater" below, in which Hill argues that this is not a correct reading of the name].

5175   **Fitikides, T. J.** "The Coinage of the Ancient Kingdoms of Cyprus." *World Coins* 12, no. 2 (February 1975): 4 ff. Illus., map.
"Greek coinage on Cyprus is discussed." [*NL* 94]

5176   **Gesche, Helga.** "Literaturüberblick der Griechischen Numismatik: Cypern." *Jahrbuch für Numismatik und Geldsseschichte* (Germany) 20 (1970): 161-216. [CS 2806]
A bibliography for the coinage of Cyprus.

5177   **Gjerstad, Einar.** "Four Kings." *Opuscula Archaeologica* (Sweden) 4 (1946): 21-4.
Discusses four staters belonging to a previously uncertain archaic Cypriote series. The coins were recently attributed to Marion by E. S. G. Robinson. On the evidence of the obverse inscription, the author recognizes the sequence of Persian and Greek dynasties in Marion, each consisting of two kings: Doxandros and Sasmai, and Stasioikos and Timocharis.

5178   **Hill, George F.** *Catalogue of Greek Coins of Cyprus.* London: British Museum, 1904. Reprint, Bologna: Forni, 1964. cxliv, 119 pp., 26 pls., map. [CS 2808]
Volume 24 of the *Catalogue of Greek Coins in the British Museum.* The 119-page catalogue of coins is preceded by 144 pages of introductory text. [Also see *Catalogue of Greek Coins in the British Museum* under PUBLIC COLLECTIONS—GREAT BRITAIN (LONDON)].

5179   —— "The Supposed Idalian Stater of Argalos." *Numismatic Chronicle* 5th ser., 16 (1936): 88.
Hill disputes Dikaios' reading of *Argalos* on a stater of Idalium. Based on a knowledge of Cypriote syllabary, Hill states that this reading is not possible. Dikaios mis-read the sign for *ra* as *ar*. [See Dikaios "A Silver Stater of Idalium" above].

5180   —— "Some Notes on the Coinage of Cyprus." *Anatolian Studies Presented to William Hepburn Buckler.* Edited by W. M. Calder and J. Keil. Manchester: University Press, 1939. Pages 89-97. Reprinted in *Numismatic Report* (Cyprus) 15-21 (1984-90): 162-70.
Discusses the coins of Cyprus struck at Marion, Soli, and Idalion utilizing archaeological evidence. Also mentions a Ptolemaic coin of Paphos struck under Philometer.

5181   **Iacovou, Maria.** *Cypriote Coinage, from Evelthon to Marc Antonio Bragadino.* Nicosia: Bank of Cyprus Cultural Foundation, 1991. 57 pp.
A catalogue of 222 Cypriote coins from the collection of the Bank of Cyprus Cultural Foundation, published in conjunction with an exhibition. The coins span the ancient Greek, Roman, Byzantine, Frankish and Venetian periods. Includes brief historical notes and a catalogue of the coins. Text in English and Greek. Text by Maria Iacovou; coin catalogue by Andreas Pitsillides and Maria Iacovou; editing by Lana der Parthogh; coin photographs by Alekos Metaxas and Chris Economides.

5182   **Karageorghis, Jacqueline, and Vassos Karageorghis.** "The Menico Hoard of Silver Coins." *Numismatic Report* (Cyprus) 15-20 (1984-90): 35-65. Illus.
"The authors present a detailed study of this important hoard of 394 small denomination silver coins uncovered accidentally in 1952. Five cities of Cyprus are represented in the hoard at different periods between the end of the fifth century and the middle of the fourth century B.C." [M. Santamas, *NL* 135]

5183   **Kraay, Colin M.** "Archaic and Classical Greek Coins: Cyprus." *Numismatic Report* (Cyprus) 15-21 (1984-90): 13-27. Illus.
A reprint of the portion of Kraay's text focusing on Cyprus (see Kraay *Archaic and Classical Greek Coins* under GENERAL WORKS—GREEK). "The difficulty pertaining to the attribution of Cypriot coins, be it to rulers or mints, is discussed. The author considers the great Larnaca Hoard (1933), believed to have been buried ca. 480, and which included most of the Cypriot coins which had been struck by the various city kingdoms of Cyprus to that date. Other hoards found either locally or abroad also are considered." [M. Santamas, *NL* 135]

5184   **Lang, R. Hamilton.** "The Coinage of Cyprus." *American Journal of Numismatics* 13, no. 3 (January 1879): 50.
A brief mention of some Cypriote coins discovered at the temple of Idalium.

5184a **Markou, Evangéline.** "Les Monnaies Chypriotes d'Or du IVe s. avant J.-C." *XIII Congreso Internacional de Numismática, Madrid – 2003: Actas–Proceedings–Actes I*. Edited by Carmen Alfaro, Carmen Marcos, and Paloma Otero. Madrid: International Numismatic Commisson, 2005. Pages 269-72. Illus.
 The gold coinage of Cyprus in the fourth century B.C.

5184b ——— *L'Or des Rois de Chypre: Numismatique et Histoire à Époque Classique*. ΜΕΛΕΤΗΜΑΤΑ 64. Centre de Recherches de l'Antiquite Grecque et Romaine. Fondation Nationale de la Recherche Scientifique, 2011.

5185 **May, John M. F.** "The Alexander Coinage of Nikokles of Paphos with a Note on Some Recently Identified Tetradrachms from the Demanhur Find." *Numismatic Chronicle* 6th ser., 12 (1952): 1-18. 1 pl.
 May examines a tetradrachm which was struck by Nikokles of Paphos, probably not later than 320 B.C. The coin bears the normal types of Alexander tetradrachms, but has the inscription ΝΙΚΟΚΛΕΥΣ added in minute letters on the first row of locks on the lion's mane on the obverse. Includes a catalogue of known specimens. The coins were perhaps minted beginning shortly after the death of Alexander and ending in or shortly after 320. Discusses the style of the coins. Also presents a catalogue of sixty-nine tetradrachms from the Demanhur hoard. [Also see Mørkholm "The Alexander Coinage of Nicocles" below and Tameanko "Nikokles" below].

5186 **McGregor, Kaelyn Ann.** *The Coinage of Salamis, Cyprus, from the Sixth to the Fourth Centuries B.C.* Ph.D. dissertation. University College, London, 1999.

5187 **Michaelidou-Nicolaou, Ino.** "Coins of Timarchos from Nea Paphos." *Kraay—Mørkholm Essays: Numismatic Studies in Memory of C. M. Kraay and O. Mørkholm.* Numismatica Lovaniensia 10. Edited by G. Le Rider, G. K. Jenkins, N. Waggoner, and U. Westermark. Louvain-la-Neuve: Université Catholique de Louvain, 1989. Pages 179-80. 1 pl.
 The author describes five coins of Timarchus (ca. 350-325 B.C.), father of Nicocles, found at the House of Dionysos at Nea Paphos. It was believed Nicocles was the founder of the city but the new find casts doubt on this theory.

5188 ——— "Cyprus: Archaic to Roman Times." *A Survey of Numismatic Research 1985-1990. Volume 1.* International Association of Professional Numismatists Special Publication, No. 12. Edited by T. Hackens, P. Naster, et al. Brussels: International Association of Professional Numismatists, 1991. Pages 91-5.
 A narrative overview of newly published works in the field of numismatics during 1985-90. Summarizes major findings, with bibliographic references cited in the footnotes.

5189 **Milne, Joseph G.** "Overstruck Cypriote Staters." *Numismatic Chronicle* 6th ser., 5 (1945): 78-9. Illus. Reprinted in *Numismatic Report* (Cyprus) 5 (1974): 58-9.
 Publishes three staters of Azbaal, king of Citium. All are overstruck. Unlike most overstruck coins from Cyprus which are struck over other Cypriote coins, these are not. At least one, and probably a second, are overstruck on Aeginetan staters, while the third is overstruck on an Athenian coin. Discusses their weights and the process of striking.

5190 **Mørkholm, Otto.** "The Alexander Coinage of Nicocles of Paphos." *Chiron* (Germany) 8 (1978): 135-47. 1 pl.
 The author addresses some of the conclusions reached in a paper by H. Gesche. Gesche contends that some Alexander issues of Paphos which carry the name of Nicocles (hidden in the lion's mane of the Herakles head) should be dated ca. 310/309 B.C. Mørkholm's rebuttal examines the general principles for dating the Alexander coinage of the late fourth century. Reviews Newell's dating of the issues of Sidon and Ake and discusses the coinage of Cyprus ca. 323-ca. 310 in its historical setting. [Also see May "The Alexander Coinage of Nikokles" above and Tameanko "Nikokles" below].

5191 **Mullaly, Terence.** "A New Museum of Cypriot Coinage." *Minerva* 7, no. 2 (March/April 1996): 44-5. Illus.
 Describes the Bank of Cyprus' Museum of the Coinage of Cyprus which recently opened in Nicosia. Several ancient coins struck on Cyprus are illustrated.

5192 **Newell, Edward T.** "Nikokles, King of Paphos." *Numismatic Chronicle* 4th ser., 19 (1919): 64-5. Reprinted in *Numismatic Report* (Cyprus) 15-21 (1984-90): 177-8. Illus.
 Publishes an Alexander-type tetradrachm struck at Paphos on which the name ΝΙΚΟΚΛΕΟΥΣ appears in tiny letters hidden among the hairs of the lion's mane covering Herakles' head. The name is the first instance of any ruler, except Alexander himself or his immediate successor Philip III, placing his own name in full upon the coinage of the Alexander type. [Also see Mosser *The Endicott Gift* under PUBLIC COLLECTIONS—UNITED STATES (NEW YORK) for a specimen of this coin].

5193 **Pierides, D.** "Inedited Copper Coin of Evagoras." *Numismatic Chronicle* new ser., 5 (1865): 165. Reprinted in *Numismatic Report* (Cyprus) 5 (1974): 41.
 Describes a coin of Evagoras I, King of Salamis. The coin bears a helmeted head of Athena on the obverse, and a lion walking on the reverse.

5194 ——— "On the Coins of Nicocreon, One of the Kings of Cyprus." *Numismatic Chronicle* new ser., 9 (1869): 19-24.
 Discusses a stater (previously attributed to Nicocles) bearing the monogram NI, and another bearing NK. The author attributes both coins to Nicocreon. Discusses the history of Cyprus during the period ca. 350-300 B.C.

5195 **Robinson, Edward S. G.** "Notes on the Larnaca Hoard." *Numismatic Chronicle* 5th ser., 15 (1935): 180-90. Reprinted in *Numismatic Report* (Cyprus) 7 (1976): 45-56. [CS 2809]
 Comments on the coins from the Larnaca hoard published by Dikaios (see Dikaios "A Hoard of Silver Cypriote Staters" above). Robinson suggests the hoard was buried ca. 480 B.C.

5196 **Schwabacher, Willy.** "The Coins of the Vouni Treasures: Contributions to Cypriote Numismatics." *Opuscula Archaeologica* (Sweden) 4 (1946): 25-46.

The author examines a pot hoard of c. 380 B.C. which included four gold Persian darics, and 248 silver coins, primarily of Marion, Citium, and Paphos. The coins help to clarify the sequence of kings at Marion and Paphos.

5196a ——— "The Coins of the Vouni Treasure Reconsidered." *Nordisk Numismatisk Årsskrift* (Sweden) (1946): 67-104.

5197 ——— "Bibliographical Notes on Cypriote Numismatics." In Einar Gjerstad's *The Swedish Cyprus Expedition, Volume 4, Part 2*. Stockholm, 1948. Pages 508-9.
Lists books, papers, and articles published after 1904 dealing with Cypriote coinage before the Hellenistic age.

5198 **Seltman, A. J.** "Some Cypriot Coins." *Numismatic Chronicle* 7th ser., 4 (1964): 75-82. Illus. [CS 2810]
A re-examination of several attribution problems of Cypriot coins in the light of recent hoard evidence. Some attributions of coins to Paphos and Idalium are suspect on epigraphical grounds. Attributions to Curium, Soli, Amathus, and Golgi are also problematical.

5199 **Sheedy, Kenneth A.** "The Idalion Stater found in a Tomb at Marion in 1886." *Numismatic Chronicle* 159 (1999): 281-4. 2 pls.
Publishes a stater of Idalion (sphinx/incuse square) found at Marion, which was mentioned by Hill in *BMC Cyprus*.

5200 **Spyridakis, C.** "Evagoras I, King of Salamis." *Numismatic Report* (Cyprus) 10 (1979): 11-42. Illus.
"The numismatic section of a study of Evagoras I of Salamis is published. Seventy-five coins are considered which provide information about Evagoras' rule. Reprinted from *Kypriakai Epoudai* (1945)." [M. Santamas, *NL* 105]

5201 **Stein, Louise, and Harry J. Stein**. "A Coin from Paphos." *Numismatic Review* 3, no. 3 (July 1946): 114. 1 pl.
"A reattribution of an obol on the Persic standard to the city of Paphos. The coin, except for the presence of a Cypriote character, is the same as that assigned by Babelon to the satrap Orontas in Asia Minor. The Cypriote character on the coin discussed stands for either the syllable "Bo" or "Po" and is the initial of the river-god Bokarus who personifies the river on which the city of Paphos was situated. The authors therefore concluded the coin to be an issue of Paphos." [*NL* 2]

5202 **Stieglitz, Robert R.** "Egypto-Phoenician Motifs on Early Cypriot Coins." *Second International Congress of Cypriot Studies (Nicosia, 20-25 April 1982)*. Nicosia, 1985. Pages 273-7. Illus. Reprinted in *Numismatic Report* (Cyprus) 15-21 (1984-90): 28-34. Illus.
"Discusses symbols of Egypto-Phoenician origin found on Cypriot coins struck at Greek as well as Phoenician cities on the island of Cyprus." [M. Santamas, *NL* 115]

5203 **Tameanko, Marvin.** "Nikokles, A Micro-Monarch of Cyprus, 325-310 B.C." *The Celator* 21, no. 12 (December 2007): 28-30, 34-6. Illus.
Traces the career of Nikokles, including his years as ruler at Paphos. Examines the rare tetradrachms from the Demanhur Hoard which contain tiny letters spelling out Nikokles name hidden in the lion's mane. Suggests some possible reasons for the appearance of these unusual letters. [Also see May "Alexander Coinage of Nikokles" above, and Mørkholm "Alexander Coinage of Nicocles" above].

5204 **Travis, Gar.** *Cypriot Coins*. Jacksonville: Takey Crist and the Cyprus Museum, 2006. 60 pp.
Examines the history and coinage of Cyprus from the sixth century B.C. through modern times. Includes ancient, Byzantine, Kings of Cyprus, Venetian period, Ottoman Period, British coins, and the Republic of Cyprus. Based on the collection of the Cyprus Museum in Jacksonville, North Carolina.

5205 **Tziambazis, Elias.** *A Catalogue of the Coins of Cyprus (from 560 B.C. to 1571 A.D.)*. Larnaca, 2002. 89 pp., illus.
A catalogue describing 398 Cypriot coins from the archaic, classical, hellenistic, Roman, Byzantine, Frankish, and Venetian periods. Coins of the Greek period are arranged by city and ruler, and are illustrated by photographs. Some of the later coins are illustrated by line drawings.

5206 **Vermeule, Cornelius C.** *Greek and Roman Cyprus*. Boston, 1976. 134 pp., 120 pls. [CS 2811]

5206a **Zapiti, Eleni, and Lefki Michaelidou.** *Coins of Cyprus from the Collection of the Bank of Cyprus Cultural Foundation*. Nicosia: Bank of Cyprus Cultural Foundation, 2008. 329 pp., illus.
Includes ancient through modern coinage.

Also see: Destrooper "Coins from the New York University Excavations" under EGYPT–PTOLEMAIC KINGDOM; Destroopers-Georgiades "Two Cilician Hoards" under HOARDS; Falkland "Notes on Coins Found in Cyprus" under HOARDS; Gitler and Kushnir-Stein "The Chronology of a Late Ptolemaic Bronze" under EGYPT–PTOLEMAIC KINGDOM; Hazzard "Cyprus Hoard" under HOARDS; "Israeli Shipwreck" under HOARDS; Kagan "Archaic Greek Coin Hoard" under HOARDS; Kraay and Moorey "Two Fifth Century Hoards" under HOARDS; Kreuzer *The Coinage System of Cleopatra VII and Augustus in Cyprus* under EGYPT–PTOLEMAIC KINGDOM; Lang "On Coins Discovered" under HOARDS; Lorber "A Gold Mnaieion of Ptolemaic Cyprus" under EGYPT–PTOLEMAIC KINGDOM; Lorber and Kovacs "A Ptolemaic Mint at Soli" under EGYPT–PTOLEMAIC KINGDOM; Mørkholm "Cyprus Hoard" under EGYPT–PTOLEMAIC KINGDOM; Mørkholm "The Last Ptolemaic Silver" under EGYPT–PTOLEMAIC KINGDOM; Mørkholm "Two Cypriot Coins" under SYRIA–SELEUCID KINGDOM; Mørkholm and Kromann "The Ptolemaic Silver Coinage on Cyprus" under EGYPT–PTOLEMAIC KINGDOM.

Newell "Some Cypriote Alexanders" under MACEDONIAN KINGDOM–GENERAL WORKS; Newell *Some Unpublished Coins of Eastern Dynasts* under ASIA–GENERAL WORKS; Nicolaou *Paphos 2* under HOARDS; Plant "Most Ancient Forms of Writing" under EPIGRAPHY; Robinson "Greek Coins Acquired by the British Museum, 1938-1948" under PUBLIC COLLECTIONS–GREAT BRITAIN (LONDON); Sayles "Feathered Enigma" under TYPES; Schell "Iconography" under MACEDONIAN KINGDOM–GENERAL WORKS; Troxell "Alexanders from Soli" under MACEDONIAN KINGDOM–GENERAL WORKS; Troxell "A New Look at Some Alexander Staters" under MACEDONIAN KINGDOM–GENERAL WORKS; Waggoner "Three Recent Greek Accessions" under ASIA MINOR–GENERAL WORKS.

Asia

General Works

The period B.C. 371-335 is a peculiarly interesting one for Asiatic coins. Many of the Persian satraps were then allowed by the central power to issue money of their own, whether for currency in their districts, or as some rather think, on the occasion of military expeditions. And several cities, Cyzicus and Lampsacus especially, struck an abundance of coin. And this coin is the more valuable because it represents the highest limits attained by Graeco-Asiatic art. In the next age the art of Asia is flooded and destroyed by that of Athens and Sicyon, so as almost to lose its individual character, except when it returns in copies of the semi-barbarous statues of oriental antiquity.

—Percy Gardner, 1883

5207 **Allan, John.** "A Brief Survey of the Coinages of Asia from the Earliest Times (700 B.C.) to the Present Day." *A Literary and Historical Atlas of Asia.* By John G. Bartholomew. London: J. M. Dent; New York: E. P. Dutton & Co., 1914. Pages 99-128 including 10 pls.
This general overview of Asian coinage includes a section on "Ancient Coins of Western and Central Asia" (pp. 99-104). Briefly describes the origin of coinage in Lydia, coins of Persia, Phoenicia, imitations of Athenian coins, and coins of Alexander, the Seleucid kings, Bactria, Judea, Parthia, and the Sassanian Empire.

5208 **Gardner, Percy.** "The Gold Coinage of Asia before Alexander the Great." *Proceedings of the British Academy, Volume 3 (1907-1908).* London: British Academy, 1908. Pages 107-38. 2 pls. Also published as an offprint, 32 pp., 2 pls.
A brief account of the gold issues in Asia down to the time of Alexander. Includes a chronological survey of the relations between the Persian state and the subject cities as they are reflected in the issues of gold and electrum coins. Examines whether the issue of gold coins was truly the exclusive privilege of the Great King. Twenty-nine coins are illustrated.

5209 **Guépin, J. P.** "East Greek Numismatics: Syria to India." *Survey of Numismatic Research, 1960-1965. Volume 1: Ancient Numismatics.* Copenhagen: International Numismatic Commission, 1967. Pages 54-84. [CS 2831]
A narrative bibliography discussing recently published works in the field of Greek numismatics related to Eastern coinages.

5210 **Hoover, Oliver D.** *Handbook of Coins of the Southern Levant: Phoenicia, Southern Koile Syria (including Judaea), and Arabia, Fifth to First Centuries BC.* The Handbook of Greek Coinage Series, Volume 10. Lancaster: Classical Numismatic Group, 2010. lxxix + 201 pp., illus.
A comprehensive guide to the coin types, heavily illustrated, with extensive background information and estimates of rarity. Lists 744 coin types. Includes a *Foreword* by David Hendin, a *Preface* by D. Scott VanHorn and Bradley R. Nelson which provides an overview of the history of Greek coinage, minting methods, denominations, types, epigraphy, and basic information for collectors regarding grading, and good summaries of the coinage of each region by Hoover. [For a general description of the format of these catalogues and a list of all the volumes in this series, see Hoover *The Handbook of Greek Coinage* under Collecting Guides].

5211 **Houghton, Arthur.** "Syria and the East." *A Survey of Numismatic Research, 1978-1984. Volume 1: Ancient, Medieval and Modern Numismatics.* Edited by M. J. Price et al. International Association of Professional Numismatists Special Publication, No. 9. London: International Numismatic Commission, 1986. Pages 180-200.
A narrative overview of newly published works in the field of numismatics. Summarizes the major findings, with bibliographic references cited in the footnotes.

5212 **Mitchiner, Michael B.** *The Early Coinage of Central Asia.* London: Hawkins Publications, 1973. 77 pp., 14 pls., maps. [CS 2832]
Includes the coinage of Dahae, the Sogdian kingdom, Bactria, Kushan Yueh Chi, Choresmian kingdom, Greco-Saka states, and the Kushan coinage in the Kabul valley, in North Pakistan and Bactria. Covers the period from the fourth century B.C. to the second century A.D.

5213 ——— *Oriental Coins and Their Values, Volume 2: The Ancient and Classical World, 600 B.C. to A.D. 600.* London, 1978. 760 pp., illus. [CS 5858]

The history and coinage of the lands east of the Mediterranean are dealt with in chronological order until the Western part of this region was embraced by Islam during the seventh century A.D. Lists over 5500 coins, all of which are illustrated. Includes an historical discussion of more than 350 dynasties. Begins with the origins of Western coinage in Asia Minor. Proceeds through the coinage of the Persian Empire, the Phoenicians, Alexander the Great and the Hellenistic Kingdoms, the Celts and Scythians, the Arabian Peninsula, Parthia, the Sasanian Empire, Indo-Greeks and Indo-Scythians, India, Southeast Asia, China, and other areas. Coin weights, sources of the coins catalogued, and values are dealt with in the Appendices. Includes an extensive bibliography.

5214 **Newell, Edward T.** *Some Unpublished Coins of Eastern Dynasts.* Numismatic Notes and Monographs, No. 30. New York: American Numismatic Society, 1926. 21 pp., 2 pls.
Newell publishes some previously unknown varieties and proposes their attributions. Includes coins of Melekiathon minted at Citium in Cyprus; Nicocles, minted at Salamis in Cyprus; Soli in Cyprus (uncertain city); Kings of Byblus in Phoenicia; Tigranes II of Armenia; and Ariarathes II of Cappadocia. The author discusses the reasons for his attributions. Ten coins are illustrated.

5215 ——— *Miscellanea Numismatica: Cyrene to India.* Numismatic Notes and Monographs, No. 82. New York: American Numismatic Society, 1938. 101 pp., 6 pls.
Newell presents some previously unpublished varieties from the south and east of the Mediterranean Sea chosen from his collection. Includes coins from various mints in Cyrenaica, Cyprus, Syria, Armenia, Commagene, Phoenicia, Palestine, Arabia, and Greek India. The significance of each is discussed.

5216 **Pieper, Wilfried.** "Greek Influenced Portrait Coins in Central Asia and India." *The Celator* 10, no. 5 (May 1996): 30-5. Illus.
The author discusses the influence of Alexander the Great and his successors on the coin designs of Parthia and the Indo-Parthian and Indo-Greek kingdoms, focusing on the development of coin portraits.

5217 **Sellwood, David G.** "The Ancient Near East." *Coins: An Illustrated Survey 650 B.C. to the Present Day.* Edited by M. J. Price. New York: Methuen, 1980. Pages 250-7. Illus.
A very brief overview of the ancient coinages of Parthia, Persis, the Sassanians, Elymais, Characene, Nabatea, the Sabeans, the Himyarites, and the kingdom of Axum. Heavily illustrated by photographs of the main coin types.

5218 **Tufnell, R. H. C.** "Oriental Coins." *American Journal of Numismatics* 20, no. 4 (April 1886): 82-6. Illus.
A brief introduction to the coins of Parthia, Armenia, Bactria, and India. Reprinted from the *London Antiquary*.

5219 **Tzamali, Marion J. A.** "They Should Have Taken the Trouble: A Poem by K. P. Cavafy." *Nomismatika Khronika* (Greece) 17 (1998): 7-14. Illus.
An analysis of a poem by Konstantine P. Cavafy, the subject of which is the thoughts of a mercenary offering his services to four different leaders who are causing unrest in the area of Syria. The author identifies various persons alluded to in the poem: "the malefactor" (Ptolemy VIII), "Zavinas" (Alexander II), "Grypos" (Antiochus VIII), and "Hyrkanus" (John Hyrcanus, King of the Jews).

5220 **Vaux, W. S. W.** "Select Coins from the Cabinet of Major Rawlinson, C.B." *Numismatic Chronicle* 13 (1851): 70-85. Illus.
Vaux describes some coins acquired in Persia including a previously unknown decadrachm of Alexander (he suggests it was struck on the occasion of Alexander's wedding to Darius' daughter), tetradrachms of Antimachus of Bactria, a portrait tetradrachm and obol of Seleucus I, drachms of Diodotus of Bactria and Demetrius I Soter of Syria, a tetradrachm of Demetrius and Laodice overstruck on a tetradrachm of Timarchus of Babylon, and several Parthian and Mohommedan coins.

5221 ——— "On Some Coins, Chiefly Greek, Which Have Been Lately Brought from the East." *Numismatic Chronicle* 18 (1856): 137-52.
Vaux describes a gold coin of Seleucus I Nicator, silver coins of Apodacus of Characene, and other Eastern coins.

5222 **Waddington, William H.** "Mémoires et Dissertations: Études de Numismatique Asiatique." *Revue Numismatique* (France) new ser., 5 (1860).

5223 **Westermark, Ulla.** "Syria, Phoenicia, and Palestine." *Survey of Numismatic Research, 1966-1971. Volume 1: Ancient Numismatics.* New York: International Numismatic Commission, 1973. Pages 177-98. [CS 2840]
A narrative bibliography discussing recently published works in the field of Greek numismatics related to Syria, Phoenicia, and Palestine.

Also see: Whitehead "The Eastern Satrap Sophytes" under BACTRIA; Zervos "Near Eastern Elements" under MACEDONIAN KINGDOM—GENERAL WORKS.

Syria

In some cases, usurpers assumed control of one or more cities and were themselves defeated and replaced by a legitimate ruler. In others, a king may have been expelled from one city but maintained his authority at another. Some rulers exercised power over vast territory but never ruled at the Seleucid capital, Antioch. As a result, a simple list of Seleucid kings tends to be misleading about the breadth of an individual ruler's authority; and an arrangement of kings at a single selected city, such as Antioch, would give only a fragmentary picture about the extent of each ruler's control.

—Arthur Houghton, 1983

AUTONOMOUS CITIES

5224 **Alischan, S. M.** "Posidium in Coele-Syria." *Numismatic Chronicle* 3rd ser., 18 (1898): 124-5. Illus.
Describes a silver coin with *obv.,* Baal seated; *rev.,* head of Odysseus, which the author attributes to Posidium in Cassiotis (south of the mouth of the Orontes). [Also see Hill "Posidium" below].

5225 **Boon, George C.** "Toward a Numismatic History of the Kingdom of Serendip" *Seaby Coin and Medal Bulletin* 839 (April 1989): 73-4.
"A reference to the use of copper coins of Alexander the Great as amulets in ancient Antioch is discussed." [E. Besly, *NL* 123]

5226 **Hill, George F.** "Posidium in Syria." *Numismatic Chronicle* 3rd ser., 18 (1898): 246-50. Illus.
A follow-up to S. M. Alischan's publication of a coin of Posidium (see Alischan "Posidium" above). Hill presents further evidence confirming the attribution of the coin to Posidium in Syria. However, Hill states that the head on the reverse is probably not Odysseus as Alischan believes. [Also see E. S. G. Robinson "Coins from the Excavations at Al-Mina" under HOARDS].

5227 **Mørkholm, Otto.** "The Autonomous Tetradrachms of Laodicea ad Mare." *Museum Notes* 28 (1983): 89-107. 7 pls.
Examines the autonomous tetradrachm coinage of Laodicea, an important seaport on the Syrian coast, which began ca. 81 B.C. Discusses the types, inscriptions, control marks, dates, weights, die position, dies, and circulation patterns as shown by hoard evidence. Forty-nine coins are illustrated.

5228 **Plant, Richard J.** "Hadad on a Coin of Rhosus." *Seaby Coin and Medal Bulletin* 703 (March 1977): 98-9. Illus.
Illustrates (by a drawing) a bronze coin of Rhosus in northern Syria. The obverse bears a head of Tyche with an aphlaston countermark. The reverse bears a statue of the Aramaean god Hadad. Discusses the symbolism of the reverse type.

5229 **Waddingham, Gary.** "Numismatic Evidence of a Benevolent Biblical Goddess." *The Celator* 12, no. 1 (January 1998): 6-9. Illus.
The author examines a series of coins produced in Bambyce of the district of Cyrrhestica in Syria. The coins portray the goddess Ateh, also known as Atargatis. Discusses the aspects and cult of this goddess.

Also see: Bopearachchi "Sophytes" under BACTRIA; de Morgan *Manual de Numismatique Orientale* under GENERAL WORKS—GREEK; Gardner "On Some Coins of Syria and Bactria" under BACTRIA; Harrison "Hellenization in Syria-Palestine" under PALESTINE—JUDEA; Hoover *Handbook of Syrian Coins* under SYRIA—SELEUCID KINGDOM; Hoover *Handbook of Coins of the Southern Levant* under ASIA—GENERAL WORKS; McAlee "The Livia Hoard of Pseudo-Philip Tetradrachms" under SYRIA—SELEUCID KINGDOM; Mildenberg "A Note on the Coinage of Hierapolis" under PERSIA; Milne "Origin of Certain Copies" under ATTICA—GENERAL WORKS; Newell "The Pre-Imperial Coinage of Roman Antioch" under SYRIA—SELEUCID KINGDOM; E. Robinson "Coins from the Excavations at Al-Mina" under HOARDS; Spaer "Ascalon: From Royal Mint to Autonomy" under SYRIA—SELEUCID KINGDOM; Wroth *Catalogue of Greek Coins of Galatia, Cappadocia, and Syria* under GALATIA.

SELEUCID KINGDOM

5230 **Andersen, Morten.** "A New Tetradrachm from the Reign of Seleucus II, 246-225 B.C." *The Celator* 25, no. 5 (May 2011): 24-6. Illus.
Publishes and discusses a tetradrachm issued by Seleucus II at "Uncertain mint 37" (Lorber and Hoover, *Seleucid Coins*). The mint likely was located in Mesopotamia.

5231 **Aperghin, Makis.** "Population—Production—Taxation—Coinage: A Model for the Seleukid Economy." *Hellenistic Economies.* Edited by Zofia H. Archibald, John Davies, Vincent Gabrielsen, and G. J. Oliver. London/New York: Routledge, 2001. Pages 69-102.
The author attempts to understand the relationships between population, production, taxation, and coinage in the Seleukid economy. [Reviewed by O. D. Hoover in *American Numismatic Society Magazine* 2, no. 2 (summer 2003): 54-7].

5232 **Aperghis, G. G.** "Chapter 11: Coinage." *The Seleukid Royal Economy: The Finances and Financial Administration of the Seleukid Empire.* Cambridge: University Press, 2004. Pages 213-246.
Discusses mints, coinage issues and categories, circulation, peacetime and wartime coinages, and special issues.

5233 **Arslan, Melih.** "A Hoard of Bronze Coins of Lysimachia." *Stephanos Nomismatikos: Edith Schönert-Geiss zum 65. Geburtstag.* Edited by Ulrike Peter. Berlin: Akademie Verlag, 1998. Pages 77-82.

5233a **Augé, C., and Frédérique Duryat, eds.** *Les Monnayages Syriens: Quel Apport pour l'Histoire du Proche-Orient Hellénistique et Romain?* Acts du la Table Ronde de Damas, 10-12 Novembre 1999. Bibliothèque Archéologique et Historique 162. Beirut: Institut Français du Proche-Orient, 2002.

5234 **Babelon, Ernest C.** *Catalogue des Monnaies Grecques de la Bibliothèque Nationale: Les Rois de Syrie, d'Arménie et de Commagène.* Two volumes. Paris: Chez C. Rollin & Feuardent, 1890. Reprint, Bologna: Forni, 1971. 268 pp., 32 pls. [CS 2850]

5235 **Baldus, Hans Roland.** "Zu den Phönizischen Bronzemünzen des Tryphon aus Askalon." *Schwizer Münzblätter* (Switzerland) 13/14, no. 56 (1964): 145-7. [CS 2851]

5236 ——— "Der Helm de Tryphon und die Seleukidische Chronologie der Jahre 146-138 v. Chr." *Jahrbuch für Numismatik und Geldgeschichte* (Germany) 20 (1970): 217-39. Illus. [CS 2852]

5237 **Barag, Dan P.** "The Mint of Antiochus IV in Jerusalem: Numismatic Evidence on the Prelude to the Maccabean Revolt." *Israel Numismatic Journal* (Israel) 14 (2001-02): 59-77. Illus.

5238 **Barkay, Rachel.** "The Marisa Hoard of Seleucid Tetradrachms Minted in Ascalon." *Israel Numismatic Journal* (Israel) 12 (1992/3): 21-6. Illus.
"A pot hoard of twenty-five Seleucid tetradrachms of Phoenician standard struck at the mint of Ascalon was found during excavations at Marisa. They cover the period from 191 A.S. (122/1 B.C.) to 200 A.S. (113/2 B.C.). They probably were buried about the time of the destruction of Marisa by John Hyrcanus I, ca. 111 B.C." [A. Spaer, *NL* 134]

5239 **Bellinger, Alfred R.** "The Bronze Standards of Antiochus III, Seleucus IV, and Antiochus IV." *Numismatic Review* 2 (October 1944): 5-6.
Discusses the weights of the bronze coins of Antiochus III, Seleucus IV, and Antiochus IV and attempts to determine the denominations represented. Discusses the coin types and their relationship to denominations, and discusses changes in bronze weight standards.

5240 ——— "Crassus and Cassius at Antioch." *Numismatic Chronicle* 6th ser., 4 (1944): 59-61. 1 pl.
Publishes a tetradrachm bearing the types and inscriptions of Philip Philadelphus (89-83 B.C.) but which Bellinger believes was minted by the Romans, probably in 53 B.C. The monograms on the reverse may be those of Crassus and Cassius.

5241 ——— "The Bronze Coins of Timarchus, 162-0 B.C." *Museum Notes* 1 (1945): 37-44. 2 pls.
Publishes an octuple of Timarchus, the satrap of Babylon and Media who refused to recognize Demetrius I as king of Syria, and in 162 B.C. took the royal title himself. Summarizes what is known of the rare issues of this monarch, including bronze octuples, quadruples, doubles, and units; gold staters; silver tetradrachms, and drachms. Discusses various opinions regarding the mint for the bronze coins and concludes it was Ecbatana.

5242 ——— "King Antiochus in 151/0 B.C." *Hesperia* 14 (1945): 58-9.
"Suggests that the coin of an Antiochus discussed by Heichelheim (see Heichelheim "Numismatic Comments 2" below) may have been struck for Antiochus VIII at Side or elsewhere in Asia Minor." [J. R. Jones, *NIAJAH*]

5243 ——— "A Seleucid Mint at Elaeusa Sebaste." *Museum Notes* 3 (1948): 27-30. 1 pl.
Bellinger lists the known varieties of a rare tetradrachm of Antiochus VIII and a common one of Seleucus VI which have Pallas Nicephorus as a reverse type, and a little plant with four branches or leaves outside the inscription to the left. The coins bear a variety of monograms. Imhoof-Blumer attributed these coins to the mint of Seleucia-ad-Calycadnum. Bellinger argues for Elaeusa-Sebaste as the place of minting and he concludes it was the chief mint for Seleucus VI.

5244 ——— "The End of the Seleucids." *Transactions of the Connecticut Academy of Arts and Sciences* 38 (June 1949): 51-102. [CS 2853]
This discussion of the history of the late Seleucids, from Antiochus VII on, utilizes numismatic evidence to supplement and correct the surviving written records of this troubled age. Among the issues discussed, the author suggests that the mint for the joint tetradrachm of Antiochus XI and Philip I must have lain in the coastal region of North Syria and Cilicia and proposes to assign Philip's son, Philip II, certain coins not in the usual style of the father's issues. [Summarized from F. Waage, *NL* 10]. [Reviewed by W. Wallace in *American Journal of Archaeology* 56 (1952): 103-4].

5245 ——— "Notes on Some Coins from Antioch in Syria." *Museum Notes* 5 (1952): 53-63. 3 pls. [CS 2884]
Bellinger publishes a bronze coin of Cleopatra Selene and Antiochus XIII, probably struck at Antioch in 92 B.C. Also publishes some Roman Provincial coins from Antioch.

5246 **Bellinger, Alfred R., and Edward T. Newell.** "A Seleucid Mint at Dura-Europos." *Syria* (France) 21 (1940): 77-81. 1 pl.
Examines three series of Seleucid bronze coins found in excavations at Dura-Europos belonging to the reign of Antiochus I (280-261 B.C.). Each series consists of units and double units, all of which seem to have been struck in the town itself. Twenty coins are illustrated.

5247 **Ben-Dor, Stella.** "Some New Seleucid Coins." *Palestine Exploration Quarterly* (England) 12 (1946): 43-8. 1 pl.
"Notes on three new Seleucid coins: a tetradrachm of Antiochus VI of 144/3 B.C. from a hoard of eight tetradrachms appearing in Jerusalem in 1942, and another dated 142/1, both issued at Ptolemais-Ake; and a bronze piece of Demetrius II struck at Gaza in 142/1. The first coin shows that Antiochus VI held Ptolemais at least as early as 144/3, while the second proves that Antiochus was killed by Tryphon in the Seleucid year 171, or 142/1 B.C., not 170 as generally thought. The bronze coin indicates that Gaza was again under Demetrius II's rule after having been briefly under the Maccabees." [*NL* 2]

5248 **Bevan, E. R.** "A Note on Antiochus Epiphanes." *Journal of Hellenic Studies* 20 (1900): 26-30.
"On pp. 28-9 it is argued that the Nike which appears as an attribute of Zeus on the later issues of Seleucus I is an indication that this monarch, like Antiochus IV, identified himself with Zeus. The title 'Nicephorus' is explained by the figure of Victory which he holds." [J. R. Jones, *NIJHS*]

5249 ——— "Antiochus III and his Title 'Great-King.'" *Journal of Hellenic Studies* 22 (1902): 241-4.
"The evidence of coins and inscriptions suggests that the title *Basileus Megas* indicated that the holder was an Oriental, not a Hellenic monarch." [J. R. Jones, *NIJHS*]

5250 **Bijovsky, G.** "A Coin of Demetrius I from Akko-Ptolemais." *Israel Numismatic Journal* (Israel) 13 (1994-99): 39-45.

5251 **Birch, Samuel.** "Unedited Coin of Demetrius the Second." *Numismatic Chronicle* 4 (1842): 11-5. Illus.
The author describes a previously unpublished type and discusses its historical background.

5252 **Boehringer, Christof.** "Antiochos Hierax am Hellespont." *Essays in Honour of Robert Carson and Kenneth Jenkins*. Edited by M. J. Price, A. M. Burnett and R. Bland. London: Spink & Son, 1993. Pages 37-47. 3 pls., maps.

5253 **Bopearachchi, Osmund.** "Les Monnaies Seleucides de l'Asie Centrale et l'Atelier de Bactres." *Travaux de Numismatique Grecque Offerts à Georges Le Rider*. Edited by Michel Amandry and Silvia Hurter. London: Spink, 1999. Pages 77-93. 2 maps.

5254 **Borrell, Maximilian.** "Regal Syrian Tetradrachms Found at Tarsus." *Numismatic Chronicle* 15 (1853): 40-57. Illus.
The author describes 139 coins of the Seleucid kings found near Tarsus in 1848. Includes twelve types and numerous varieties, including some unique coins.

5255 **Brett, Agnes Baldwin.** "Seleucid Coins of Ake-Ptolemais in Phoenicia: Seleucis IV to Tryphon." *Museum Notes* 1 (1945): 17-35. 6 pls. [CS 2854]
Presents a catalogue of the Seleucid coins minted at Ake-Ptolemais from the reign of Seleucus IV through the reign of Tryphon, as well as the bronze coins of Antiochus IV and Demetrius I. Discusses the types appearing on the coins. Also discusses the Phoenician issues of Alexander.

5256 ——— "The Mint of Ascalon under the Seleucids." *Museum Notes* 4 (1950): 43-54. 2 pls. [CS 2855]
The dove was a symbol of Derceto, a goddess worshipped at Ascalon. The dove, along with the inscription AΣ, was used as a mintmark on Seleucid coins struck at Ascalon. Presents a catalogue of twenty-two coin types from the Ascalon mint. Includes coins of ten rulers. [Also see Spaer "Ascalon" below].

5257 **Bunbury, Edward H.** "Rare and Unpublished Coins of the Seleucidan Kings of Syria." *Numismatic Chronicle* 3rd ser., 3 (1883): 65-107. 2 pls.
Bunbury publishes and discusses coins from his collection which were previously unpublished and which do not appear in the British Museum collection. [Also see P. Gardner's comments on Bunbury's attributions on pages 261-3].

5258 **Burgess, Michael.** "The Moon is a Harsh Mistress—The Rise and Fall of Cleopatra II Selene, Seleukid Queen of Syria." *The Celator* 18, no. 3 (March 2004): 18-25. Illus.
Reviews the turmoil of the late period in the history of the Seleukid Empire, Ptolemaic interference in Syria ca. 150 B.C., and the reign of Queen Cleopatra II Selene. The name Selene refers to the moon and to the moon goddess. There are just three known coins from this queen. These bronze coins, depicting the queen and one of her sons, Antiochus XIII, were likely issued as propaganda pieces, both to emphasize her son's claims on the throne, and also to solidify her own rule. Burgess presents a suggested chronology of events during the period 103-16 B.C.

5259 **Carlton, Walker.** "Demetrius I of Syria." *SAN—Journal of the Society for Ancient Numismatics* 17, no. 2 (June 1987): inside covers.
A summary of the history and coinage of Demetrius I.

5260 **Carmey, A.** *Plates of the Coins of the Kings of Syria*. London, 1761.

5261 **Cavafy, C. P.** "The Displeasure of Demetrios." *Nomismatika Khronika* (Greece) 25 (2006): 7-8. Illus.
A poem by Cavafy, translated by M. J. A. Tzamali, with commentary by A. P. Tzamalis. Summarizes the reign of Demetrios.

5262 **Davesne, Alain.** "La Deuxième Guerre de Syrie (ca. 261-255 avant J.-C.) et les Témoignages Numismatiques." *Travaux de Numismatique Grecque Offerts à Georges Le Rider*. Edited by M. Amandry and S. Hurter. London: Spink, 1999. Pages 123-34. 1 pl.

5263 **Doyen, Jean-Marc.** *Les Monnaies Antiques du Tell Abou Danne et d'Oumm el-Marra (Campagnes 1976-1985). Aspects de la Circulation Monetaire en Syrie du Nord sous les Seleucides*. Bruxelles, 1987. 177 pp., 14 pls.

5264 **Draganov, Dimitar.** "A New Bronze Issue of Antiochus II of Sardes." *American Journal of Numismatics* 2nd ser., 5/6 (1993-94): 43-6. 1 pl.
Examines two previously unpublished bronze coins found in Bulgaria with *obv.*, Apollo, and *rev.*, anchor. The author finds the coins to be stylistically similar to issues of Alexander III. Based on other coins found in the area, the author suggests these coins were minted at Sardes.

5265 **Draganov, Dimitar, Arthur Houghton, and Wayne Moore.** "Four Seleucid Notes." *American Journal of Numismatics* 2nd ser., 5/6 (1993-94): 43-68. 2 pls.
Includes "A New Bronze Issue of Antiochus II of Sardes" by Draganov (see Draganov above), "The Chronology of the Later Coinage of Demetrius I at Ecbatana" by Houghton (see Houghton below), "The ΕΥΠΑΤΡΕΩΝ Coinage of Alexander I Balas" by Moore (see Moore below), and "Countermarks of Tryphon: Comments on the Circulation of Currency in Northern Syria ca. 150-140 B.C." by Houghton (see Houghton below).

5266 **Eaglen, Robin J.** "Portraits of Greek Coinage 24: Seleucus I (312-280 B.C.)." *Spink Numismatic Circular* 116, no. 5 (October 2008): 256-7. Illus.
This installment of the author's on-going series examines the coinage of Seleucus I.

5267 ——— "Portraits of Greek Coinage 30: Antiochus VIII Grypus ('Hook-nose') (125-96 B.C.)." *Spink Numismatic Circular* 117, no. 5 (December 2009): 197-8. Illus.
This installment of the author's on-going series examines the history and coinage of Antiochus VIII.

5268 **Elayi, Josette, and Alain G. Elayi.** "Un Nouveau Trésor de Tétradrachmes d'Alexandre II Zebina." *Annotazioni Numismatiche* (Italy) 43 (2001): 999-1004.

5269 **Fischer, Thomas.** "A Coin Portrait of King Antiochus, the Son and Co-Regent of King Antiochus the Great?" *Numismatic Chronicle* 7th ser., 13 (1973): 220-1. Illus.
"The tetradrachm E. T. Newell, *Western Seleucid Mints* No. 381 is tentatively attributed to the son and co-regent of Antiochus III the Great. It was issued at Tyre between 202/200 and 193/192 B.C." [T. Fischer, *NL* 92]

5269a ——— *Molon und Seine Münzen (222-220 v. Chr.)*. Studienverlag Dr. Norbert Brockmeyer. Bochum, 1988. 31 pp.

5270 **Fontana, Alan F., and Jeffrey M. Fontana.** "Unholy Triangle: Seleukos II, Antiochus Hierax and Laodike." *The Celator* 8, no. 12 (December 1994): 14-8. Illus.
The coinage of Seleukos II deviated from Seleucid monarchical tradition in three ways: the depiction of Apollo standing (rather than seated on the omphalos), the presentation of the king's face as bearded (rather than clean-shaven), and the use of a draped-bust (rather than undraped). The authors review the political and military struggles between the Seleucids and the Ptolemies over the control of Asia Minor and Syria. Suggests that Seleukos II's break from coinage traditions reveals his independence from his controlling mother and adds valuable information to our interpretation of the political history of the period.

5271 **Forrer, Leonard S.** "Stater of Seleucus II Callinicus, B.C. 246-226, with an Unpublished Monogram." *Spink Numismatic Circular* 7 (March 1899): 3243.
Describes a recently discovered gold stater of Seleucus II.

5272 **Froelich, E.** *Annales Compendiarii Regum, & Rerum Syriae, Numis Veteribus Illustrati, Deducti ab obitu Alexandri Magni, ad Cn. Pompeji in Syriam Adventum, cum amplis Prolegomenis.* Wien: Leopold Johann Kaliwoda, 1750/1754. 158 pp., illus.

5273 **Gardner, Percy.** *Catalogue of Greek Coins, the Seleucid Kings of Syria.* Edited by R. S. Poole. London: British Museum, 1878. Reprints, Bologna: Forni, 1963; New York: Sanford Durst, 1983. xxxix, 126 pp., 28 pls. [CS 2861]
Volume 4 of the *Catalogue of Greek Coins in the British Museum*. The 126-page catalogue of coins is preceded by thirty-nine pages of introductory text. [Also see *Catalogue of Greek Coins in the British Museum* under PUBLIC COLLECTIONS—GREAT BRITAIN (LONDON)].

5274 ——— "Macedonian and Greek Coins of the Seleucidae." *Numismatic Chronicle* new ser., 18 (1878): 90-102. 1 pl.
Gardner publishes seven copper coins of Antiochus I minted at the time he was aspiring to the Macedonian throne, coins minted during the European campaign of Antiochus bearing the name of Aetolia and Carystus, and others.

5275 ——— "Coins from Central Asia." *Numismatic Chronicle* 3rd ser., 1 (1881): 8-12. 1 pl.
(1) Publishes a silver tetradrachm with *obv.*, head of a City wearing a turreted crown, and *rev.*, ΑΝΔΡΑΓΟΡΟΥ (Andragoras). The identity of Andragoras and the mint city are unknown to Gardner. He speculates that Andragoras may have been a satrap of Parthia under Alexander the Great. [Today, the coin is catalogued as Sear *Greek Coins and Their Values* No. 6167. Andragoras may have been governor of Media in the period immediately preceding the first Seleucid issues from Ecbatana]. (2) Publishes nine Seleucid coins (including six gold staters) from the collection of Alexander Grant. The coins are probably from the Oxus Treasure found in 1877.

5276 **Garlaschelli, M.** "L'Iconographia Monetale dei Seleucidi." *Quaderni Ticinesi* (Switzerland) (1972): 61-77. [CS 2862]

5277 **Gera, D.** "Tryphon's Sling Bullet from Dor." *Israel Exploration Journal* (Israel) 35 (1985): 153-63. Illus.
"The inscription on a leaden sling bullet found at Dor is read as a fifth year in the reign of this Seleucid usurper. The coins issued by him up to Year 4 are discussed and, in the author's opinion, do not negate a fifth year." [A. Spaer, *NL* 117]

5278 **Golenko, Konstantin V.** "Notes on the Coinage and Currency of the Early Seleucid State." Parts 1-2. *Mesopotamia* 28 (1993): 71-167; 30 (1995): 51-215.

5279 **Gough, R.** *Coins of the Seleucidae, Kings of Syria from Seleucus Nicator to Antiochus Asiaticus with Historical Memoirs of each Reign, Illustrated with Coins from the Cabinet of Matthew Duane.* Plates by Bartolozzi. London, 1803. 212 pp., 24 engraved pls.

5280 **Hadley, Robert A.** "Royal Propaganda of Seleucus I and Lysimachus." *Journal of Hellenic Studies* 94 (1974): 50-65. Illus. [CS 2863]
"Investigation of the coinages of Seleucus I and Lysimachus indicates that the coin types were chosen to serve as propaganda to enhance the royal image and lend an aura of personal charisma, thereby fostering among subjects loyalty to each dynasty as a whole. It is argued, with the support of ancient literary texts, that the types and symbols are specific visual references to good omens, prophecies and dreams, the fulfillment of which was marked by individual victories and achievements. The role of Alexander the Great as a patron and protecting deity is stressed, and consideration is given to the audiences for which the various propaganda types would have been intended." [N. Waggoner, *NL* 94]

5281 ——— "Seleucus, Dionysus, or Alexander?" *Numismatic Chronicle* 7th ser., 14 (1974): 9-13. 1 pl. [CS 2864]
"Attempts are made to resolve the controversy over the identity of the portrait on the obverse of coins minted by Seleucus I after 400 B.C., the reverses of which carry a motif celebrating his victory at Ipsus in 301. The history of the controversy is reviewed; evidence related to the development of Hellenistic ruler worship is used to suggest that the portrait could not be that of Seleucus himself, but must be of Alexander the Great." [R. Hadley, *NL* 94]. [Also see Hoover *Kingmaker* below. Hoover disagrees with Hadley's conclusion].

5282 **Heichelheim, Fritz M.** "Numismatic Comments: (1) Cebren, Not Sigeum; (2) A Seleucid Pretender Antiochus in 151/0 B.C." *Hesperia* 13 (1944): 361-4. 1 pl.
"(1) A bronze coin of Antiocheia-Cebren with owl as countermark suggests that this, rather than Sigeum, was the mint at which some Seleucid coins with reverse type of owl were struck. (2) Explanations are suggested for the existence of this dated coin issued by an Antiochus, in a year when the only Seleucid rulers were Demetrius I and Alexander I Bala." [J. R. Jones, *NIAJAH*]. [Also see Bellinger "King Antiochus" above].

5283 **Hendin, David.** "Seleucids and the God Made Manifest." *The Celator* 14, no. 9 (September 2000): 42-3. Illus.
Discusses the reign of Antiochus III, focusing on his treatment of the Jews. Illustrated by two Seleucid coins.

5284 **Holzer, Hans.** "Secret Inscriptions on Syrian Silver Coins of the Second and First Centuries B.C." *Numismatic Review* 2, no. 4 (April-June 1945): 33-4. 1 pl.
Illustrates a tetradrachm of Demetrius II Nicator from the Tyre mint, struck in 127 B.C. The coin shows a circle of Phoenician letters around the king's head. The letters are integral parts of the portrait, forming parts of the head and face. Some letters had to be deformed to make them look more like hairs, lips, and ears. Although he transliterates most of the letters into English, the author makes no attempt to translate the inscription.

5285 **Hoover, Oliver D.** "Illiterate Die Engravers in the Seleucid Empire?" *The Celator* 10, no. 8 (August 1996): 34-7. Illus.
Illustrates a drachm of Demetrius I Soter from the Antioch mint, on which the reverse inscription ΒΑΣΙΛΕΩΣ is backward. The author believes this die was the work of an illiterate engraver. He also discusses the form of the monogram and the lack of a Seleucid date as further evidence of the engraver's illiteracy.

5286 ——— *Kingmaker: A Study in Seleukid Political Imagery.* Hamilton, Ontario: Oliver D. Hoover, 1996. 147 pp., illus.
A revised version of Hoover's Masters thesis at McMaster University. Discusses various aspects of the iconography employed by Seleucid kings from Seleukos I Nikator to Antiochos XII Dionysos. Seleukos I invented and developed a series of symbols designed to promote himself to his subjects as a powerful and self-sufficient ruler. These visual emblems which were supported by propaganda myths include Apollo, bulls, elephants, horned horse's heads, and anchors. Antiochus I took up the personal symbols of his father and tried to reinvent them so that they had a new meaning for himself. This change resulted in the creation of an official Seleucid dynastic image which was recognized and respected by later generations of Seleucid kings and their subjects. Coin types are frequently used as examples of Seleucid iconography. In the appendix, Hoover rejects Hadley's claim that the victory coinage of Seleucus I depicts Alexander. Rather, Hoover argues the coin depicts "a standard Greek hero"—neither Alexander nor Seleucus (see Hadley "Seleucus, Dionysus, or Alexander?" above). Includes an extensive bibliography. The obverse of one coin is illustrated. [A descriptive review by Bruce Brace appears in *The Anvil* (Canada) 6, no. 5 (September 1996): 51].

5287 ——— "A Dedication to Aphrodite Epekoos for Demetrius I Soter and his Family." *Zeitschrift für Papyrologie und Epigraphik* (Germany) 131 (2000): 106-110.
"A new cult inscription dedicated on behalf of Demetrius I and his family securely proves that the woman depicted with the king on certain silver and bronze issues is Laodice V. She was probably also the sister of Demetrius." [O. Hoover, *NL* 144]

5288 ——— "Quasi-Municipal Coinage in Seleucid Apamea: Countermarks and Counterrevolution." *Revue Suisse de Numismatique* (Switzerland) 80 (2001): 21-34. 2 pls.
"The deity depicted on Apamean quasi-municipal coins under Alexander I Balas should be identified as Zeus rather than Poseidon. This series, which only bears the date 163 SE (=150/49 B.C.), should be seen as a type of Seleucid adventus coinage referring to Alexander's arrival at the city during a general tour of Syria Seleucis beginning in 150 B.C. The quasi-municipal coins of other cities in the region, dated to the period 151/0-149/8 B.C., are all related to the same royal tour. Unlike the other quasi-municipal coinages under Alexander, the Apamean series was frequently countermarked with a stamp depicting a palm branch. Because it often appears over the city ethnic, it may have been applied by the partisans of Demetrius II Nikator after the fall of Alexander I, as part of Demetrius' repressive political and military policies toward the city." [O. Hoover, *NL* 145]

5289 ——— "The Identity of the Helmeted Head on the 'Victory' Coinage of Susa." *Revue Suisse de Numismatique* (Switzerland) 81 (2002): 51-9. Illus.

5290 ——— "Laodice IV on the Bronze Coinages of Seleucus IV and Antiochus IV." *American Journal of Numismatics* 2nd ser., 14 (2002): 81-7. 2 pls.
Discusses a series of bronze coins issued by Seleucus IV and continued by Antiochus IV. The coins bear a veiled female bust on the obverse and an elephant's head on the reverse. The female has been described as either an unknown member of the royal family or perhaps Demeter. Hoover argues that it is Laodice IV—the wife of each of these kings in succession.

5291 ——— "Anomalous Tetradrachms of Philip I Philadelphus Struck by Autonomous Antioch (64-58 B.C.)." *Schweizer Münzblätter* (Switzerland) 214 (June 2004): 31-5. Illus.

"The author suggests that certain tetradrachms in the name of Philip I Philadelphus of unusual style and bearing monograms apparently naming autonomous Antioch were struck by the city in the period between Pompey's deposition of Antiochus XIII in 64 and the arrival of Aulus Gabinius in 58 B.C." [Oliver D. Hoover, *NL* 148]

5292 ——— "Dethroning Seleucus VII Philometor (Cybiosactes): Epigraphical Arguments Against a Late Seleucid Monarch." *Zeitschrift für Papyrologie und Epigraphik* (Germany) 151 (2005): 95-9. Illus.

"The coin type, thought by Kritt to depict Cleopatra Selene and Seleucus Philometor—and to have been struck at Ake-Ptolemais—de facto is a Damascene bronze issue of that queen together with her son Antiochus XIII, minted between 84/3 and 72/1 B.C." [Hans R. Baldus, *NL* 149]

5293 ——— "A Second Look at the Aradian Bronze Coinage Attributed to Seleucus I (*SC* 72-73)." *American Journal of Numismatics* 2nd ser., 18 (2006): 43-50. 2 pls.

Hoover reattributes a series of Aradian bronze coins with Heracles/prow types from the early reign of Seleucus I to the late reign of Seleucus II based on the similarities of the obverse type to issues of Carne produced in 226/5 – 225/4 B.C. Traditionally, such dates would place the coins in the reign of Seleucus III, but the evidence of cuneiform documents now shows that Seleucus II did not die in 226 B.C., but rather lived into the early months of 225/4.

5294 ——— *Coins of the Seleucid Empire in the Collection of Arthur Houghton, Part II*. Ancient Coins in North American Collections. New York: American Numismatic Society, 2007. 247 pp., illus.

Publishes 900 coins and related objects in Houghton's New Series collection, primarily consisting of new types, control variants, and historical-economic interpretations that have been discovered in the years since *Part I* was published (see Houghton *Coins of the Seleucid Empire* below). Follows the organizational principles from Houghton and Lorber's *Seleucid Coins*, and includes brief historical introductions for each ruler, commentary on remarkable coins, and new attributions. Includes type, ruler, and mint indices.

5295 ——— "A Seleucid Coinage of Demetrias by the Sea." *Israel Numismatic Research* (Israel) 2 (2007): 77 ff.

Hoover defends the controversial identification of Demetrias by the Sea as a Seleucid re-foundation of Strato's Tower in southern Phoenicia. He further suggests that a dated series of drachms of the Seleucid king Demetrius II from an unknown Phoenician mint and marked with a particular monogram should be attributed to Demetrias-Strato's Tower. The dates link the coinage to the crisis that ensued in Phoenicia and Coele Syria after the murders of Jonathan Apphus and Antiochus VI. The later civic coinage of Demetrias may have drawn its cornucopia type from the drachms of Demetrius II.

5296 ——— *The Handbook of Syrian Coins: Royal and Civic Issues, Fourth to First Centuries BC*. The Handbook of Greek Coinage Series, Volume 9. Lancaster: Classical Numismatic Group, 2009. lxviii + 332 pp., illus.

A catalogue of all known types of Seleucid coins and civic issues of Syria. Includes historical background for each king and city. Includes 1465 coin types. Each coin is cross-referenced to Houghton and Lorber's *Seleucid Coins: A Comprehensive Catalogue* or other major references. Includes a *Preface* by D. Scott VanHorn and Bradley R. Nelson which provides an overview of the history of Greek coinage, minting methods, denominations, types, epigraphy, and basic information for collectors regarding grading. [For a general description of the format of these catalogues and a list of all the volumes in this series, see Hoover *The Handbook of Greek Coinage* under COLLECTING GUIDES].

5297 **Hoover, Oliver D., Arthur Houghton, and Petr Veselý.** "The Silver Mint of Damascus under Demetrius III and Antiochus XII (97/6 BC-83/2 BC." *American Journal of Numismatics* 2nd ser., 20 (2008): 305-36. 10 pls.

The authors present a die study with historical, iconographic, numismatic, and statistical analysis for the silver coinages struck at Damascus under the Seleucid kings Demetrius III and Antiochos XII. Based on the evidence of a production gap in 93/2 B.C. and die links between issues of 94/3 and 92/1 B.C., it is suggested that Demetrius may have briefly lost the city in 93/2, thereby explaining conflicting evidence for the king's arrival at Damascus. A new coin of Antiochus XII extends his reign into 83/2 B.C.—a year later than previously known.

5298 **Hoover, Oliver D., and Panagiotis P. Iossif.** "A Lead Tetradrachm of Tyre from the Second Reign of Demetrius II." *Numismatic Chronicle* 169 (2009): 45-50. 1 pl.

A coin that appeared on the market in 2009 is the first recorded Seleucid lead piece bearing types from the mint of Tyre, and it shares its obverse die with a regular Tyrian silver emission of Demetrius II's second reign. The piece is probably either a mint die trial or is a form of token currency struck during a period of emergency.

5299 **Hoover, Oliver D., and David MacDonald.** "Syrian Imitations of New Style Tetradrachms Struck over Myrina." *Berytus* 44 (1999-2000): 109-117. Illus.

"The authors discuss four imitation Athenian New Style tetradrachms overstruck on tetradrachms of Myrina from a recent Syrian hoard. It is suggested that the Attic weight issues of Myrina came to Syria largely as Attalid financial support for Alexander I Balas' invasion of Syria in 153/2 B.C. The overstriking of these coins with imitation Athenian types occurred in the 140s-130s when New Style issues began to flood the Near East." [O. Hoover, *NL* 144]

5300 **Houghton, Arthur.** "The Seleucid Mint at Lampsacus." *Museum Notes* 23 (1978): 59-68. 1 pl. [CS 2865]

The author re-examines two coin series struck at the time of Antiochus II and Antiochus Hierax which Newell attributed to Lampsacus and Abydus. Houghton presents evidence to assign both series to a single mint, Lampsacus. Proposes a rearrangement of the issues of Antiochus Hierax struck at Lampsacus. Houghton suggests this mint struck coins with distinctive symbols for use at Abydus.

5301 ——— "The Second Reign of Demetrius II of Syria at Tarsus." *Museum Notes* 24 (1979): 111-6. 3 pls.

A catalogue of the silver issues of Demetrius II's second reign at Tarsus demonstrates die links between coins with the seated Zeus reverse type and those with the pyre of Sandon reverse type. Several issues previously attributed to Antioch are now attributed to Tarsus based on this evidence. Houghton suggests the coins were struck ca. 128 B.C.

5302 ——— "Notes on the Early Seleucid Victory Coinage of 'Persepolis.'" *Revue Suisse de Numismatique* (Switzerland) 59 (1980): 5-14. Illus.

"On the basis of new evidence and the analysis of monograms and symbols on victory-type coins of Seleucus I attributed to Persepolis, the author concludes that all such issues were struck instead at Susa, probably ca. 305-301 B.C. A drachm issue of the same type is published, and a coherent series of small silver imitations of the Susian victory coinage is attributed to an unknown mint in Baluchistan operating briefly after the accession of Antiochus I in 280 B.C." [A. Houghton, *NL* 106]

5303 —— "Tarik Darreh (Kangavar) Hoard." *Museum Notes* 25 (1980): 31-44. 2 pls.
A hoard of sixty gold coins of the fourth and third centuries B.C. was found in Iran in 1974. The coins included twenty-five Alexandrine staters, a stater of Cyrene, a stater of Carthage, an octodrachm of Ptolemy III, and at least thirty-four Seleucid staters. The hoard was buried ca. 226/5 B.C. Houghton catalogues the thirty-four Seleucid coins (of Antiochus I and II, and Seleucus I and II) from a variety of Eastern mints. He comments on new varieties and the numismatic questions they raise. Discusses the Eastern mints involved.

5304 —— "A Tetradrachm of Seleucia Pieria at the Getty Museum: An Archaizing Zeus and the Accession of Alexander Balas in Northern Syria." *J. P. Getty Museum Journal* 10 (1982): 153-8. Illus.
"The tetradrachm is not part of a regular series issued by Alexander, but is one of ten recorded examples of a royal silver issue struck for essentially local purposes. All were issued at Seleucia Pieria in 146 B.C. The significance of this coin lies in the understanding it provides of stylistic processes current in Hellenistic Syria in the second century B.C. and its implications for a reconstruction of Alexander's occupation of northern Syria." [C. Carter, *NL* 117]

5305 —— *Coins of the Seleucid Empire from the Collection of Arthur Houghton.* Ancient Coins in North American Collections, No. 4. New York: American Numismatic Society, 1983. 122 pp., 77 pls.
A catalogue of one of the most important Seleucid collections ever formed. Contains 1323 coins catalogued according to mints, then chronologically by ruler. Presents chronological charts of selected mints illustrating reign dates for rulers. [Reviewed by Catharine C. Lorber in *Numismatic Fine Arts Quarterly Journal, Publication 29* (March 1985): 6, and by L. Cancio in *Spink Numismatic Circular* 95, no. 9 (November 1987): 298-9. Also see C. Lorber "Coins of the Seleucid Kings" below for the auction catalogue of part of Houghton's collection. Also see Oliver Hoover *Coins of the Seleucid Empire, Part II* above].

5306 —— "The Portrait of Antiochus IX." *Antike Kunst* (Switzerland) 27 (1984): 123-8. Illus.
"A sculptured head discovered at Esen Tepe, Iskenderum, Turkey, in the spring of 1972, can be identified on the basis of the coins of Antiochus IX as a portrait of this king, likely executed during his first period of rule in the Syrian north shortly after 113 B.C. The coin portraits of the king are reviewed." [A. Houghton, *NL* 117]. [Also see Houghton "A Colossal Head" below for a companion sculpture].

5307 —— "The Seleucid Mint of Mallus and the Cult of Athena Magarsia." *Studies in Honour of Leo Mildenberg: Numismatics, Art History, Archaeology.* Edited by A. Houghton et al. Wetteren: Editions NR, 1984. Pages 91-110. 2 pls.
Examines the city of Mallus and the nearby cult center at Magarsia. Hellenistic coins of Mallus preserve the image of the cult statue of Athena Magarsia. A full record of the coins of Mallus during this period reveals new information about her form and about the city's mint. Houghton catalogues the Seleucid coins of Mallus from Demetrius I (162-150 B.C.) through Antiochus IX (113-95 B.C.). Twenty-six coins are listed. Summarizes the activity of the mint of Mallus during the second and early first centuries B.C. Discusses the cult statue, pointing out variations in how it is depicted on the coins. Comments on the iconography of the statue. The author suggests the goddess' origins are rooted in the Mesopotamian cult of Inanna/Ishtar/Astarte, and she was assimilated into the image of the Greek goddess Athena.

5308 —— "A Colossal Head in Antakya and the Portraits of Seleucus I." *Antike Kunst* (Switzerland) 29 (1986): 52-62. Illus.
"At Esen Tepe, Iskenderun, Turkey, in 1972, was discovered a sculptured head, of colossal size, with bases for horns on either side, and carved in a baroque style fundamentally different from that of its companion (see Houghton "The Portrait of Antiochus IX" above). The author suggests it is a posthumous representation of Seleucus. Other representations which have occasionally been identified as portraits of Seleucus are discussed." [A. Houghton, *NL* 117]

5309 —— "The Elephants of Nisibis." *Museum Notes* 31 (1986): 107-24. 3 pls.
The author examines the gold, silver, and bronze issues struck by Antiochus III bearing the reverse type of a standing or striding elephant. Lists 113 coins of this type. Attributes the series to Nisibis, rather than Ecbatana as Newell suggested. Discusses the chronology of the series.

5310 —— "A Victory Coin and the Parthian Wars of Antiochus VII." *Proceedings of the 10th International Congress of Numismatics, London, 1986.* International Association of Professional Numismatists Publication, No. 11. Edited by I. A. Carradice. London: International Association of Professional Numismatists, 1986. Page 65. 1 pl.
Historical sources record that Antiochus VII (138-129 B.C.) embarked on a campaign against the Parthians which ended with his death. Antiochus is not recorded as having undertaken any other military activity, yet a recently found gold stater indicates that the king campaigned in the East at some point shortly before 134/3 B.C. when the coin is dated. Suggests either the written records have reversed the order of events, or that he undertook an earlier and unrecorded expedition against the Parthians which the coin commemorates.

5311 —— "The Double Portrait Coins of Antiochus XI and Philip I: A Seleucid Mint at Beroea?" *Revue Suisse de Numismatique* (Switzerland) 66 (1987): 79-85. Illus.
"Soon after the death of Seleucus VI in 94 B.C., Seleucus' younger brothers, Antiochus and Philip, struck rare tetradrachms with the portrait of both kings and the reverse type of Zeus Nikephoros. The author classifies the seven known coins of the series into two groups, one of which he suggests may have been issued at Beroea (Aleppo), the other at an unknown Cilician mint. He concludes that the portraits are not likenesses, but idealizing representations of the two brothers, twinned in the same manner as the images of the Dioscuri on the contemporaneous tetradrachms of Tripolis, which likely served as their model." [A. Houghton, *NL* 119]

5312 —— "The Double Portrait Coins of Alexander I Balas and Cleopatra Thea." *Revue Suisse de Numismatique* (Switzerland) 67 (1988): 85-95. Illus.
"A survey of all known coins bearing the joint portraits of Alexander Balas and his wife Cleopatra Thea is coupled with a discussion of their probable places of minting and of their historic and iconographic importance." [A. Walker, *NL* 121]

5313 —— "A Didrachm Issue of Antiochus VI of Byblus." *Israel Numismatic Journal* (Israel) 9 (1988-89): 22 ff.

5314 ——— "The Royal Seleucid Mint of Seleucia on the Calycadnus." *Kraay—Mørkholm Essays: Numismatic Studies in Memory of C. M. Kraay and O. Mørkholm.* Numismatica Lovaniensia 10. Edited by G. Le Rider, G. K. Jenkins, N. Waggoner, and U. Westermark. Louvain-la-Neuve: Université Catholique de Louvain, 1989. Pages 77-98. 6 pls.

The author examines the Seleucid tetradrachms with Athena Nikephoros on the reverse and the symbol of a little plant in the field. Attributes these coins to a Cilician mint: Seleucia on the Calycadnus. Discusses the plant type. Identifies the Athena figure as a cult statue. Catalogues and discusses 146 coins struck at the mint, 197-94 B.C. Discusses the mint's production under Seleucus VI and the implications for the dates of this reign.

5315 ——— "The Royal Seleucid Mint of Soli." *Numismatic Chronicle* 149 (1989): 15-32. 5 pls.

"The article reviews the known Seleucid coinage produced at the mint of Soli in Cilicia, which began as an important operation during the later reign of Antiochus III (at Soli, 197-187 B.C.). The mint's production thereafter did however become increasingly intermittent until the mint closed under Antiochus VII (138-129 B.C.). Issues of Antiochus III, Seleucus IV, Antiochus IV, Demetrius I and Demetrius II (first reign) are added to the Solian coins already identified by Mørkholm, Le Rider and the author." [A. Houghton, *NL* 124]

5316 ——— "Two Late Seleucid Lead Issues from the Levant." *Israel Numismatic Journal* (Israel) 11 (1990-91): 26 ff.

5317 ——— "The Antioch Project." *Mnemata: Papers in Memory of Nancy M. Waggoner.* Edited by William E. Metcalf. New York: American Numismatic Society, 1991. Pages 73-97.

A brief review of scholarship related to the Seleucid coinage at Antioch since the publication of Newell's study of Western Seleucid mints (see E. Newell *The Coinage of the Western Seleucid Mints* below) in 1941. Suggests there is a need for a study that updates the coinage of Antioch, incorporating die, metrological, and metallurgical data. Presents a survey of Antioch's silver coinage of selected rulers of the third and second centuries B.C. Presents eight tables of data on this coinage. Suggests that the Antioch mint may have produced less than 1200 tetradrachm obverse dies over the course of its history.

5318 ——— "Some Alexander Coinages of Seleucus I with Anchors." *Mediterranean Archaeology* (Australia) 4 (1991): 99-117. 3 pls.

In his catalogue of the coins of the western Seleucid mints, Newell attributed certain coins bearing the name of Alexander and with an anchor in the left field of their reverses to the neighboring mints of Aradus and Marathus during the years preceding the assumption of power by Seleucus I. In recent years, doubt has been expressed about the mint and chronology of these issues. Houghton here tries to answer the outstanding questions related to these coins. The coins, including staters, tetradrachms, drachms, and fractions, are divided into four groups. Houghton presents a catalogue of the coins and discusses their chronology. Lists the recorded hoards which contained these coins. Presents conclusions regarding the mints and chronology.

5319 ——— "The Coinage of Demetrius I at Ake-Ptolemais." *Florilegium Numismaticum: Studia in Honorem U. Westermark Edita.* Edited by Harald Nilsson. Stockholm: Svenska Numismatiska Föreningen, 1992. Pages 163-9. Illus.

Lists the coins struck at Ake-Ptolemais during the reign of Demetrius I and provides extensive commentary on this coinage. Discusses the symbols and control marks used on the coins to designate the mint city. Discusses the sequence, chronology, and metrology of the issues. Houghton concludes that the Seleucid court had dies engraved at Antioch in accordance with a canonical standard of portraiture, and that these dies were sent to Ake to be used for Demetrius' first issue at that city.

5320 ——— "The Revolt of Tryphon and the Accession of Antiochus VI at Apamea." *Revue Suisse de Numismatique* (Switzerland) 71 (1992): 119-48. Illus.

"In an expanded version of a paper given at the Brussels Congress, September 1991, the author publishes a corpus of tetradrachms, drachms, and hemidrachms of Antiochus VI of the mints of Apamea and Antioch." [S. Hurter, *NL* 130]

5321 ——— "The Royal Seleucid Mint of Aegae in Aeolis." *Revue Numismatique* (France) 6th ser., 34 (1992): 229-32. Illus.

"The article discusses the limited coinage of Antiochus II (261-246 B.C.) that can be securely attributed to Aegae in Aeolis. The two principal series of Aegae's Seleucid include twenty-two coins that can be divided into nine issues. *WSM* 1510, a tetradrachm seated on a rock that E. T. Newell gave to Aegae, is here reassigned to Temnos. The known coins of Aegae now indicate that this city was not acquired by Pergamum until some years after the peace of 252 B.C. that brought an end to the Second Syrian War." [A. Houghton, *NL* 133]

5322 ——— "The Accession of Antiochus VI at Apamea: the Numismatic Evidence." *Proceedings of the 11th International Numismatic Congress, September 8-13, 1991. Volume 1.* Edited by T. Hackens et al. Louvain-la-Neuve, Belgium: International Association of Professional Numismatists, 1993. Pages 277-9. Illus.

A review of numismatic evidence shows that Antioch did not strike coinage for Antiochus until year 169 of the Seleucid era, and the city remained in Demetrius' hands until that date. Instead, Apamea became Antiochus' first mint.

5323 ——— "The Reigns of Antiochus VIII and Antiochus IX at Antioch and Tarsus." *Revue Suisse de Numismatique* (Switzerland) 72 (1993): 87-106. 3 pls.

During the period 114-95 B.C., Antiochus VIII Grypus and his half-brother Antiochus IX Cyzicenus fought each other across Syria, Cilicia, and Phoenicia in a struggle for power that encompassed the entire Seleucid kingdom and led to the collapse of the Seleucid monarchy. The numismatic evidence is the principal means to clarify the history of this period. Houghton examines the coins struck at Antioch, presenting a catalogue of the dated bronze coins struck between 121/0 and 108/7 B.C.—the year of Antioch's last recorded dated coinage. Also examines the coinage of the Tarsus mint.

5324 ——— "The Chronology of the Later Coinage of Demetrius I at Ecbatana." *American Journal of Numismatics* 2nd ser., 5/6 (1993-94): 46-53. 1 pl.

Publishes a number of coins that help clarify the production of the Ecbatana mint during the later reign of Demetrius I (162-150 B.C.). These include a gold stater, tetradrachms, and drachms carrying both a star and the letter K on their obverses, and a tetradrachm with the partial magistrate's names ΦΙΛΙΠ and ΔΙΟΝ on the reverse. All have the epithet ΣΩΤΗΡΟΣ that was added to the king's name and title at Antioch about 158 B.C. The author discusses the sequence of issues and the relative and absolute chronologies.

5325 ——— "Countermarks of Tryphon: Comments on the Circulation of Currency in Northern Syria ca. 150-140 B.C." *American Journal of Numismatics* 2nd ser., 5/6 (1993-94): 59-68. 1 pl.

The author presents a catalogue of fourteen coins of Heraklea, Kyme, Syros, and Lebedos bearing a counterstamp consisting of a Macedonian helmet adorned with an ibex horn. Houghton discusses the purpose and specific date of the counterstamps. They appear only on tetradrachms of Western Asia Minor mints—none are known on Seleucid or Alexander-type coins. Includes a table of hoards summarizing finds in north Syria dating from the period in question (ca. 150 B.C.).

5326 ——— "Some Seleucid Test Pieces." *American Journal of Numismatics* 2nd ser., 9 (1997): 1-5. 1 pl.
Houghton describes and discusses the five known Seleucid test pieces. These pieces were struck in lead and were employed by mints to determine the viability of coin dies and designs. The five pieces are identified as being struck during the reigns of Antiochus II, III, VI, and VIII.

5327 ——— "The Struggle for the Seleucid Succession, 94-92 B.C." *Revue Suisse de Numismatique* (Switzerland) 77 (1998): 65-71. Illus.
"The new tetradrachm of Antiochus XI and Philip I of Antioch helps to explain the complicated situation in the Seleucid kingdom in the years 94/92 B.C. For a very brief time in 93 the two brothers ruled jointly in Antioch before the city fell back to Antiochus X Eusebus." [M. Peter, *NL* 145]

5328 ——— "The Early Seleucid Mint of Laodicea ad Mare (c. 300-246 B.C.)." *Travaux de Numismatique Grecque Offerts à Georges Le Rider*. Edited by M. Amandry and S. Hurter. London: Spink, 1999. Pages 169-84. 3 pls.
A catalogue of the Seleucid coinage of Laodice—the most important Seleucid mint operating in Syria during the first half of the third century B.C. The coins are of the Alexander type. Houghton segregates the coins into three major series and thirty-five groups. Discusses chronology and refines Newell's dating with assistance of evidence from the Armenak and Meydancikkale hoards. Concludes the city's coinage began early in the reign of Seleucus I (ca. 300 B.C.) and continued sporadically until 246 B.C. (under Antiochos II). Comments on types, symbols, denominations, metrology, and die alignments.

5329 ——— "A Seleucid Mint at Samaria-Sebaste?" *The Celator* 14, no. 7 (July 2000): 22-5. Illus.
Examines a set of silver coins (hemidrachms and obols of Attic weight) with *obv.*, portrait of Antiochus IX Cyzicenus, and *rev.*, Athena standing left holding Nike. The coins bear no dates, symbols, or control marks—their mint city was unknown. All specimens of known provenance were acquired in or near Sebaste—ancient Samaria, and thus Sebaste is suggested as the likely minting place. Houghton summarizes the history of the city, and examines the question: Why did the Seleucids confer Samaria the right to coin silver, particularly just hemidrachms and obols? Houghton suggests the mint was established by Cyzicenus shortly after his arrival in Coele-Syria in or about 112 B.C. The mint was intended to confirm his intention to support the threatened city during his battle with Hyrcanus I. [Also see an updated and expanded version of this paper in Kritt, Hoover, and Houghton, "Three Seleucid Notes" below].

5330 ——— "The Production of Money by Mints of the Seleucid Core." *Les Monnayages Syriens. Quel Apport Pour l'Historie du Proche-Orient Hellénistique et Romaint? Actes de la Table Ronde de Damas, 10-12 November 1999*. Bibliothèque Archéologique et Historique 162. Edited by Chr. Augé and Frédérique Duyrat. Beyrouth: Institut Française du Proche-Orient, 2002. Pages 5-19.

5330a ——— "New Light on Coin Production under Seleucus II in Northern Syria, Commagene, and Mesopotamia." *American Journal of Numismatics* 2nd ser., 23 (2011): 17-34. 4 pls.
"The author relocates Uncertain Mint 42 from Mesopotamia to, probably, northern Syria; reattributes tetradrachms and related drachms previously given to Seleucus III to Seleucus II at a new mint that probably operated west of the Euphrates River; separates Mints 40A and 40, which were previously considered as a single facility; and attributes two tetradrachms to the so-called NO (monogram) Mint which probably operated in the general region of Commagene or Mesopotamia. The picture that the new material makes raises fundamental questions about the purpose of Seleucus' mints in the upper Euphrates area." [Houghton]

5331 **Houghton, Arthur A., and Catharine C. Lorber.** "The *Great Seleucid Catalogue*: A Work in Progress, A Request." *The Celator* 8, no. 2 (February 1994): 10-3.
The authors describe a new comprehensive catalogue of Seleucid coinage which they are in the process of writing (see *Seleucid Coins* below). They request information on previously unlisted varieties.

5332 ——— "Antiochus III in Coele-Syria and Palestine." *Israel Numismatic Journal* (Israel) 14 (2001-02): 44-58. Illus.
"The authors identify coinages issued by Antiochus III in Coele-Syria during and after the Fifth Syrian War, based on provenance information and suggestions from Donald Tzvi Ariel and Danny Syon of the Israel Antiquities Authority. All of the coinages were known previously, but were attributed to mints within the pre-war boundaries of the Seleucid kingdom and, in a few cases, to earlier kings. Certain Apollo/elephant bronzes exhibit such irregular technical features that they appear to be products of a temporary military mint. They are interpreted as sitarchia, provision money paid to individual soldiers, and the frequency of countermarks suggests the need for guarantees of the invader's fiduciary coinage in a shifting war zone. Most of the other coinages are also bronzes with military types, probably minted to support garrisons and military colonies after the Seleucid annexation. Regular Seleucid silver coinage was not introduced, however, and it appears that Antiochus maintained the closed currency market established by the Ptolemies, allowing the continued circulation of older Ptolemaic silver." [C. Lorber, *NL* 146]

5333 ——— *Seleucid Coins: A Comprehensive Catalogue. Part I: Seleucus I through Antiochus III*. Two volumes. New York: American Numismatic Society, and Lancaster, PA: Classical Numismatic Group, 2002.
A comprehensive treatment of Seleucid coinage, expanding on Newell's catalogues with hundreds of new varieties. Organized in historical and geographical order, first by reign, then by mint, then by metal, denomination, and issue. A representative sample of each type is illustrated. Includes extensive historical information. [Reviewed in *The Celator* 17, no. 2 (February 2003): 34, and in *American Numismatic Society Magazine* 2, no. 1 (spring 2003): 33. Also see Houghton, Lorber, and Hoover, *Seleucid Coins Part II* below].

5334 **Houghton, Arthur A., Catharine C. Lorber, and Oliver D. Hoover.** *Seleucid Coins: A Comprehensive Catalogue. Part II: Seleucus IV through Antiochus XIII*. Two volumes. New York: American Numismatic Society, and Lancaster, PA: Classical Numismatic Group, 2008. 748 pp.; 536 pp. and 119 pls.
A comprehensive treatment of Seleucid coinage, continued from Houghton and Lorber, *Seleucid Coins Part I* (see above). Includes many new mint attributions and a new chronology for the later Seleucid kings. Includes additions and corrections to *Part I*. Volume 2 includes plates, maps, appendices, concordances, and indices. An up-to-date listing of coin hoards containing relevant coins is included as an appendix, along with a supplement to the hoard list that appeared in *Part I*. Other appendices cover metrology, flan production, countermarks, overstrikes, imitations, and fourees.

5335 **Houghton, Arthur, and Wayne Moore.** "Some Early Far Northeastern Seleucid Mints." *Museum Notes* 29 (1984): 1-9. 2 pls.
The authors examine the output of two unknown mints operating in the far northeastern part of the Seleucid empire: (1) "Mint X" struck Alexander-type tetradrachms, drachms, and hemidrachms in the name of Antiochus. All contain a distinctive monogram and have cupped flans. Suggests possible locations for this mint. (2) "Mint Y" issued Alexander-type drachms in the name of Antiochus. These do not bear a common monogram, but are unified by the configuration of their inscriptions.

5336 ——— "Five Seleucid Notes." *Museum Notes* 33 (1988): 55-69. 2 pls.
Five topics are given brief treatment: (1) new issues of Seleucus I and Antiochus I, (2) some drachms from the first reign of Demetrius II, (3) units of the divine couple series of Demetrius II, (4) an unknown mint of Antiochus VII in Cilicia, and (5) Seleucus VI at Elaeusa Sebaste.

5336a **Houghton, Arthur, and Wilhelm Müseler.** "The Reigns of Antiochus VIII and Antiochus IX at Damascus." *Schweizer Münzblätter* (Switzerland) 159 (August 1990).

5337 **Houghton, Arthur, and Arnold Spaer.** "New Silver Coins of Demetrius III and Antiochus XII at Damascus." *Schweizer Münzblätter* (Switzerland) 157 (February 1990): 1-5. Illus.
"The authors add a drachm and hemidrachm issues to the coinage of Demetrius III struck at Damascus, and suggest that the reverse diadem motif of the latter may have been the prototype of the reverse of certain coins of the Hasmonaean king, Alexander Jannaeus. Four tetradrachms of Antiochus XII are added to the three cited by Newell in *Late Seleucid Mints*." [A. Houghton, *NL* 124]

5338 **Houghton, Arthur, and Andrew Stewart.** "The Equestrian Portrait of Alexander the Great on a New Tetradrachm of Seleucus I." *Schweizerische Numismatische Rundschau* (Switzerland) 78 (1999): 27-35.

5339 **Howorth, Henry H.** "The Eastern Capital of the Seleucidae." *Numismatic Chronicle* 3rd ser., 8 (1888): 293-9.
A response to Percy Gardner regarding the attribution of some coins from the Oxus Treasure.

5340 **Janis, Edward.** "Antiochus V: A Hapless Boy-King." *The Shekel* 21, no. 6 (November-December 1988): 8-10. Illus. Also appeared in *The Celator* 10, no. 9 (September 1996): 32-4. Illus.
Describes the uprisings in Judea during the brief reign of Antiochus V.

5341 **Jenkins, G. Kenneth.** "Notes on Seleucid Coins." *Numismatic Chronicle* 6th ser., 11 (1951): 1-21. 2 pls.
"Although no gold or silver of Demetrius I has as yet been attributed to the mint of Seleucia-on-the-Tigris, the bronze coins found in the excavations there provide evidence for the assignment of an important section of Demetrius' coinage to that mint. The issues in question are gold staters and tetradrachms with jugate heads of Demetrius and Laodice, an obverse type which appears on the bronze, and a second group of tetradrachms with the head of Demetrius alone, which are linked with the preceding issues by symbol and monogram. Demetrius also used the Ecbatana mint for tetradrachms, drachms and five denominations of bronze. The tetradrachms have the horse's head symbol which was a mint mark at Ecbatana from the time of Seleucus II on; the drachms are of eastern style and fabric and their provenances indicate an Iranian origin. This extensive coinage at Ecbatana under Demetrius I makes it clear that Media was not conquered by Mithradates I ca. 160 B.C. but was held by Demetrius, perhaps until the end of his reign. Two final notes discuss an unpublished bronze striking of Demetrius II at Seleucia, another bronze issue of the same king which may belong to Ecbatana, and an apparently unique tetradrachm of Antiochus IX Cyzicenus which has as a symbol the same kind of fire-alter as that which appears on autonomous coins of Mopsus and is, therefore, probably to be attributed to that mint." [M. Thompson, *NL* 27]

5342 **Klose, Dietrich O. A.** "Zwei Beiträge zur Seleukidischen Münzprägung des. 2 Jahrhunderts v. Chr." *Travaux de Numismatique Grecque Offerts à Georges Le Rider*. Edited by M. Amandry and S. Hurter. London: Spink, 1999. Pages 185-95. 2 pls.

5343 **Klose, Dietrich O. A., and Wilhelm Müseler.** *Statthalter Rebellen Könige: Die Münzen aus Persepolis von Alexander dem Großen zu den Sasaniden*. Munich: Staatliche Münzsammlung München, 2008. 90 pp., illus.

5344 **Krengel, Elke, and Catharine C. Lorber.** "Early Cappadocian Tetradrachms in the Name of Antiochus VII." *Numismatic Chronicle* 169 (2009): 51-104. 10 pls.
The authors examine other Cappadocian tetradrachms in the name of Antiochus VII that are earlier than those discussed by Lorber and Houghton (see Lorber and Houghton "Cappadocian Tetradrachms" below) and are not obviously related to the royal Cappadocian coinage.

5345 **Kritt, Brian.** *Seleucid Coins of Bactria*. Classical Numismatic Studies, No. 1 Lancaster, Pennsylvania: Classical Numismatic Group, 1996. 80 pp., 5 pls.
A detailed study of the series of Seleucid coins struck in Bactria during a half-century of Seleucid occupation beginning ca. 290 B.C. Begins with a study of a series of Seleucid coins previously attributed to the southern Persian city of Susa, and concludes these coins belong to a mint in Bactria. A central theme is the importance of the mint of the recently discovered Seleucid colony at Ai Khanoum in Afghanistan. Kritt reattributes the former Bactra series to the mint of Ai Khanoum. The analysis of a number of other coinages reveals a complex pattern of Seleucid minting operations in Bactria, and provides insight into the history and administration of Seleucid Bactria. Includes a "Foreword" by Arthur Houghton.

5346 ——— *The Early Seleucid Mint of Susa*. Classical Numismatic Studies, No. 2. Lancaster, Pennsylvania: Classical Numismatic Group, 1997. 202 pp. including the 34 pls.
The author examines the beginnings of Seleucid coinage at Susa and studies the series to the end of the reign of Seleucus I. The book contains die studies of the tetradrachm issues and rearranges the previously known issues, while incorporating the "Persepolis" series recently reattributed to Susa by Houghton, as well as a large number of new Susa varieties recently discovered. Besides establishing a new chronology for these coins, the author presents hoard evidence supporting the new arrangement, including an important new and unpublished hoard of coins from southern Persia. A number of the historical consequences deriving from the new chronology of Susa are presented. In addition, a new picture is presented for the transition of minting operations from Babylon to Seleucia-on-the-Tigris, and the roles of the fourth century Seleucid mints are explored as related to the history and coinages of the beginning of the Seleucid Empire. A chapter is devoted to establishing the origin of the mysterious Susa Alexander bronzes, and describing their relation to the other contemporary coinages of the period of the creation of the Seleucid mythology. Aramaic inscriptions appearing as graffiti or in the dies of Susa trophy-coins are examined

5347 ——— "Numismatic Evidence for a New Seleucid King: Seleucus (VII) Philometor." *The Celator* 16, no. 4 (April 2002): 25-8, 36. Illus.
Describes a new coin which includes an inscription bearing a Seleucid king's name which had previously been unknown to history. The coin sheds light on the incomplete record of the fall of the Seleucid dynasty in the first century B.C., and complements information published long ago by Bellinger. The coin bears the names of Cleopatra Selene and Seleucus Philometor. The coin belongs to the period 92-69 B.C. or 83-69 B.C., and was struck at an uncertain mint in Syria or Cilicia.

5348 **Kritt, Brian, Oliver D. Hoover, and Arthur Houghton.** "Three Seleucid Notes." *American Journal of Numismatics* 2nd ser., 12 (2000): 93-112. 3 pls.
Three brief papers: (1) Kritt, "Coinage of Antiochus III in Bactria." The Seleucid coinage in Bactria has been considered to have ended with the coins of Antiochus II struck at Ai Khanoum. However, Kritt here publishes two new discoveries which he believes were struck at Ai Khanoum by Antiochus III, ca. 208-206 B.C. Discusses the historical significance of this discovery. (2) Hoover, "A Unique Tetradrachm of Demetrius II Nikator at Seleucia-in-Pieria." Examines a previously unpublished tetradrachm struck in the name of Demetrius II Nikator. The coin is related to a series of drachms and two series of bronze coins attributed to an uncertain North Syrian mint. Hoover suggests these coins were minted at Seleucia-in-Pieria. Discusses the origin of the inverted anchor symbol and its connection to the Seleucids. (3) Houghton, "A Mint of Antiochus IX at Samaria-Sebaste?" A group of previously unassigned silver hemidrachms and obols with the portrait and reverse types of Antiochus IX Cyzicenus is assigned by Houghton to the mint at Samaria-Sebaste. Nearly all the known specimens are reported to have been found in or near this location. Houghton describes the historical context of the city during the late second century B.C. Suggests the mint here was opened ca. 112 and closed ca. 108 B.C. [This is an updated version of Houghton's paper published in *The Celator* in July 2000 (see above)].

5349 **Lamb, William Eliot.** "A Description of Four Syrian Coins Shown to the Boston Numismatic Society." *American Journal of Numismatics* 6, no. 2 (October 1871): 25-9.
Describes coins of Antiochus III, Antiochus Epiphanes, Demetrius Soter, and Alexander I. Comments on the reigns of these kings and provides some historical background for each coin.

5350 **Lederer, Philipp.** "Einige Seleukidenmünzen." *Zeitschrift für Numismatik* (Germany) 35 (1925): 222-9.

5351 **Le Rider Georges.** *Suse sous les Séleucides et les Parthes: les Trouvailles Monétaires et l'Historie de la Ville.* Memoirs de la Mission Archéologique en Iran 38: Mission de Susiane. Paris: Libraire Orientaliste Paul Geuthner, 1965. 491 pp., 74 pl.

5352 ——— "Un Atelier Monétaire Séleucide dans la Province de la Mer Érythrée?" *Revue Numismatique* (France) 6th ser., 7 (1965): 36-43. [CS 2866]
Explores the possibility of a Seleucid mint in the district of the Erythrean Sea. [Also see Mørkholm "The Seleucid Mint at Antiochia on the Persian Gulf" below].

5353 ——— "Un Trésor de Monnaies Séleucides Trouvé dans le Hauran en 1979 ou 1980: Antiochos VI à Ptolemaïs." *Studies in Honour of Leo Mildenberg: Numismatics, Art History, Archaeology.* Edited by Arthur Houghton et al. Wetteren: Editions NR, 1984. Pages 165-9. 1 pl.

5353a ——— "L'Enfant-Roi Antiochos et la Reine Laodice." *Bulletin de Correspondence Hellénique* (France) 110 (1986): 409-17. Illus.

5354 ——— "Les Alexandres d'Argent en Asie Mineure et dans l'Orient Séleucide au IIIe s. av. J.C. (ca. 275-225)." *Journal des Savants* (France) 1-3 (1986): 3-57.

5354a ——— "L'Atelier Séleucide de Lysimachie (*WSM* 1610-1621)." *Quaderni Ticinesi. Numismatica e Antichità Classiche* (Switzerland) 17 (1988): 195-205.

5354b ——— "Antiochos II à Mylasa." *Bulletin de Correspondance Hellénique* (France) 114 (1990): 543-51. 1 pl.
[Also see Le Rider's "Note Additionalle" (1996) below].

5355 ——— "Les Ressources Financières de Séleucos IV (187-175) et le Paiement de l'Indemnité aux Romains." *Essays in Honour of Robert Carson and Kenneth Jenkins.* Edited by M. J. Price, A. M. Burnett and R. Bland. London: Spink & Son, 1993. Pages 49-67. 3 pls.

5355a ——— "Antiochos IV (175-164) et la Monnayage de Bronze Sileucide." *Bulletin de Correspondance Hellénique* (France) 118 (1994): 17-34.

5356 ——— "La Politique Monétaire des Séleucides en Coelé Syrie et en Phénicie après 200." *Bulletin de Correspondance Hellénique* (France) 119 (1995): 391-404.

5356a ——— "Antiochos II à Mylasa (*BCH* 114 [1990], p. 543-551): Note Additionalle." *Bulletin de Correspondance Hellénique* (France) 120 (1996): 773-5.
Additions to Le Rider's 1990 paper (see above).

5357 ——— *Séleucie du Tigre. Les Monnaies Séleucides et Parthes.* Monographie de Mesopotamia 6. Florenz: Casa Editrice Le Lettre, 1998. 384 pp., 15pls.

5358 ——— *Antioche de Syrie sous les Séleucides: Corpus de Monnaies d'Or et d'Argent I: de Séleucos I à Antiochos V, c. 300-161.* Paris: Institut de France, Academie des Inscriptions et Belle Lettres, 1999. 260 pp., 27 pls.
An extensive die study of the silver and gold coinage of the mint of Antioch from its beginnings as a pre-Seleucid mint at Antigonea or Seleucia Pieria through the reign of Antiochus V. Extensively amends E. T. Newell's *Seleucid Mint of Antioch* and his *Western Seleucid Mints*. [Part 2 of this catalogue was to be prepared by Arthur Houghton, covering the reigns of Demetrius I through Antiochus XIII].

5359 ——— "Apamée de Syrie: Un Chapitre Contestable de E. T. Newell dans WSM." *Pour Denyse: Divertissements Numismatiques.* Edited by S. Hurter and C. Arnold-Biucchi. Bern, Switzerland: Privately published, 2000. Pages 95-108. 2 pls.

5360 **Le Rider, Georges, and François de Callataÿ.** *Les Séleucides et les Ptolémées: L'Héritage Monétaire et Financier d'Alexandre le Grand.* Monaco: Rocher, 2006.

5361 **Lorber, Catharine C.** "Coins of the Seleucid Kings." *An Auction of Ancient Greek Coins and Coins of the Seleucid Kings.* Los Angeles: Numismatic Fine Arts, Inc., 1987. Unpaged, map.
A catalogue for a March 31, 1987 auction featuring, among other coins, 129 high quality coins of the Seleucid Kingdom from the collection of Arthur Houghton. The catalogue contains an extensive essay by Cathy Lorber providing historical and numismatic information for each of the coins and the rulers portrayed on them. All coins are photographed, many with enlargements. Each coin is fully described. Includes a genealogical table of the Seleucid dynasty.

5362 ——— "Antiochus III the Great." *SAN—Journal of the Society for Ancient Numismatics* 19, no. 2 (1995): 30, 50. Illus.
Provides a brief history of the reign of Antiochus III. Illustrates a gold octodrachm of Antiochus III from Seleucia on the Tigris, the only known octodrachm of Antiochus III which can be attributed to a mint other than Antioch. Suggests that the rarity of Seleucid gold is a result of the Treaty of Apamea—Antiochus was probably obliged to send most of the Seleucid gold coins to Rome where they were melted.

5363 ——— "The Tyre, 1987 Hoard of Seleucid Silver (*CH* 9.533)." *Coin Hoards IX: Greek Hoards.* Special Publication No. 35. London: Royal Numismatic Society, 2002. Pages 253-5. 6 pls.
A hoard of 108 tetradrachms and one drachm of the Tyre mint appeared on the market in 1987, said to have been found in Tyre. The latest issues date to 129/8 B.C. The coins are catalogued here without further comment. Consists of issues of Antiochus VII and Demetrius II (second reign).

5364 ——— "Commerce ('Seleucia on the Calycadnus' Hoard), 2002 (*CH* 10.340)." *Coin Hoards, Volume X: Greek Hoards.* Edited by Oliver Hoover, Andrew Meadows, and Ute Wartenberg Kagan. New York: Royal Numismatic Society and The American Numismatic Society, 2010. Pages 243-4.
Catalogue of a hoard of ten Seleucid tetradrachms minted at Seleucia on the Calycadnus in Cilicia. Most were varieties not listed in Houghton's "The Royal Seleucid Mint of Seleucia on the Calycadnus" (1998).

5365 **Lorber, Catharine C., and Arthur Houghton.** "Cappadocian Tetradrachms in the Name of Antiochus VII." *Numismatic Chronicle* 166 (2006): 49-97. 12 pls.
A remarkable coin appeared on the market in 2002—a tetradrachm issued in the name of Ariarathes VII but bearing the portrait of the Seleucid king Antiochus VII Euergetes. Other die-linked coins establish that these apparent Seleucid tetradrachms were in fact posthumous issues reviving the types of Antiochus VII, struck in Cappadocia by as many as four different kings. The authors provide a full examination of these issues. [Also see Krengel and Lorber "Early Cappadocian" above].

5366 ——— "Antiochus III Hoard." *American Journal of Numismatics* 2nd ser., 21 (2009): 89-104. 6 pls.
A Hellenistic hoard containing twenty-seven tetradrachms, recorded from commerce in 2005, has brought to light a new Antigonid variety as well as a tetradrachm of Antiochus III that raises questions about the treatment of Uncertain Mint 68 (part of Newell's Nisibis) in *Seleucid Coins, Part 1* (see Houghton and Lorber above). The hoard was deposited ca. 196 B.C. or shortly after.

5367 **MacDonald, George.** "Seltene und Unedierte Seleukidenmünzen." *Zeitschrift für Numismatik* (Germany) 29 (1912): 89-106.

5368 **Maharian, E.** "Shaqed (West)." *Hadashot Archaeologioth* (Israel) 112 (2000): 43-4, 52-4.
"Three Seleucid and five late Roman coins were found at this site midway between Caesarea and Beth Shean." [A. Spaer, *NL* 144]

5369 **Mattingly, Harold B.** "The Second Century B.C. Seleucid Countermarks: Anchor and Facing Helios Head." *Quaderni Ticinesi. Numismatica e Antichità Classiche* (Switzerland) 27 (1998): 237-43. Illus.
"The author advances a new hypothesis about these countermarks on some coins of Side, Perge, and Aspendos from the second century B.C. He considers them symbols of the authority and power of Demetrius I at the moment at which, coming from Lycia, he arrived at Tripolis in Syria (162 B.C.) with a mercenary army and looking for new recruits." [A. Carignani, *NL* 142]. [This essay was reprinted in Mattingly's *From Coins to History: Selected Numismatic Studies*. See Mattingly under GENERAL WORKS—GREEK].

5370 **McAlee, Richard G.** "The Livia Hoard of Pseudo-Philip Tetradrachms." *American Journal of Numismatics* 2nd ser., 11 (1999): 1-12. 3 pls.
An examination of a hoard of 677 "pseudo-Philip" tetradrachms. These coins were believed to have been issued by the Seleucid king Philip Philadelphus until Newell identified them as an issue struck under Roman rule (see Newell "The Pre-Imperial Coinage of Roman Antioch" below). The hoard included coins of one previously unknown date (year 23) and confirmed the previously reported terminal date of the series (year 36). McAlee discusses die varieties, weights, and chronology. Suggests that the absence from the hoard of coins with the monogram of Aulus Gabinus may indicate that Gabinus' coins, which may have been struck on a higher silver standard, were systematically removed from circulation by the mint authorities for re-coinage as pseudo-Philip tetradrachms at the lower silver standard.

5371 **McDowell, Robert H.** "Models of Seleucid Coins." *Stamped and Inscribed Objects from Seleucia on the Tigris.* Edited by R. H. McDowell. Ann Arbor: University of Michigan Press, 1935. Pages 241-50. 1 pl.

Among the objects found during excavations at Seleucia-on-the-Tigris 1927-32, were nineteen disks of unbaked clay, both faces of which bear designs similar to Seleucid coin types (tetradrachms). Discusses the possible uses of these disks. They may have been used as admission tokens to public events. Presents a catalogue of the tokens, eleven of which are illustrated on plate 6. [For further discussion of these tokens, see Edward Newell's *The Coinage of the Eastern Seleucid Mints,* page 98].

5372 **McKinney, Larry E.** "Anchors, Elephants and More: Seleucid Coin Symbols Reveal History of an Epoch." *The Celator* 3, no 7 (July 1989): 1, 20-1, 26. Illus.
The author explores three symbolic motifs used on Seleucid coinage: the anchor, the elephant, and Apollo seated on the omphalos. Seleucus' adoption of the anchor symbol may have originated when he was given command of Ptolemy's fleet or may have come from the story of Seleucus finding an anchor-shaped stone. Mentions coins on which the anchor appears as a subsidiary symbol or as the main type. The elephant type originated when the Indian king Chandragupta gave Seleucus I a gift of hundreds of elephants. Traces the use of elephants in warfare and the development of the elephant as a coin type. The worship of Apollo led to the use of his seated and standing figures on coins. The significance of the tripod and the omphalos rock is discussed.

5373 **Meischner, Jutta.** "Ein Porträt Antiochos' VI Epiphanes Dionysos in Mersin." *Mitteilungen des Deutschen Archäologischen Instituts, Istanbuler Abteilung* (Germany) 51 (2001): 273-8. Illus.
"A small marble head of the Seleucid king (Arch. Mus. of Mersin/Turkey) is compared with his Attic-weight portrait tetradrachms and with those of his successor, Tryphon (fig. 2 a-b)." [H. R. Baldus, *NL* 146]

5374 **Miller, Richard P.** "A Galatian Tetradrachm of Seleucid Type." *Schweizer Münzblätter* (Switzerland) 211 (September 2003): 51-3. Illus.
"The author presents a barbarous imitation of a tetradrachm of Antiochus III and suggests that it may have been struck by the Galatians of central Asia Minor after 223-222 B.C." [Oliver D. Hoover, *NL* 148]

5375 **Miller, Richard P., and Oliver D. Hoover.** "The Sardes Mint under Seleucus I Nicator." *American Journal of Numismatics* 2nd ser., 22 (2010): 25-34. 8 pls.
A die study of the early Seleucid silver mint of Sardes that expands on and corrects the study originally done by E. T. Newell (*The Coinage of the Western Seleucid Mints*). A new chronological arrangement for the Sardian series is suggested on the basis of die sequence and hoard evidence. Stylistic affinities between the first die of Sardes and the last of Seleucia in Pieria raise the possibility that the equipment and personnel of the latter may have been moved to Sardes to serve as a supplemental military mint. This suggests that the opening of the Lydian mint was connected to the closure of the mint at Seleucia in Pieria.

5376 **Mittag, Peter Franz.** "Beim Barte des Demetrios: Überlegungen zur Parthischen Gefangenschaft Demetrios' II." *Klio* (Germany) 84, no. 2 (2002): 373-99. Illus.
"In chap. VI (pp. 389-398) the bearded coin portraits of the Seleucid king Demetrius II (second reign) are interpreted: According to Mittag, the bearded king is not imitating Parthian hair-style but is taking over the beard of a senior Greek god—presumably Zeus." [H. R. Baldus, *NL* 146]

5377 **Moore, Wayne.** "An Antiochus III Octuple from Ecbatana." *SAN—Journal of the Society for Ancient Numismatics* 16, no. 4 (May 1986): 67.
A photograph and description of a possible octuple bronze coin. Newell, in his *The Coinage of the Eastern Seleucid Mints* (see E. T. Newell below) speculated on its existence and provided number 599 for it in his book, but had never seen such a coin.

5378 ——— "The Divine Couple of Demetrius II, Nicator, and his Coinage at Nisibis." *Museum Notes* 31 (1986): 125-43. 2 pls.
Examines the "divine couple" bronze coinage of Demetrius II, who had two reigns. Some have placed the series with the inscription "Philadelhou" during the first reign and those without the inscription during the second reign. Lists thirty specimens. Discusses die links, moneyers, and the iconography of the reverse type. Analyzes the portraits and suggests the lightly bearded portrait coins belong to the first reign. Attributes the divine couple bronzes to the mint at Nisibis.

5379 ——— "A Serrated Bronze Issue of Demetrius I from Seleucia on the Tigris." *Revue Numismatique* (France) 6th ser., 29 (1987): 21-4. 1 pl.
"A rare bronze issue of the Seleucid king Demetrius I, carrying his portrait and employing serrated flans, is proposed to have been produced at the mint of Seleucia on the Tigris. In support of this attribution, evidence involving consideration of typological characteristics, metrology and provenance is presented. These factors are compared, in a contrasting manner, with characteristics of the contemporary royal bronze coinage issued at Antioch on the Orontes." [W. Moore]

5380 ——— "A Bronze Half-Unit of Cleopatra Thea and Antiochus VIII from Akko-Ptolemais." *Israel Numismatic Journal* (Israel) 9 (1988-89): 27 ff.

5381 ——— "The ΕΥΠΑΤΡΕΩΝ Coinage of Alexander I Balas." *American Journal of Numismatics* 2nd ser., 5/6 (1993-94): 54-9. 2 pls.
The author examines a rare series of bronze coins that carry dates in close accordance with the three-year period of Ptolemaic occupation of Phoenicia, 148-145 B.C. The coins bear the portrait of Alexander I Balas. The reverse inscription includes ΕΥΠΑΤΡΕΩΝ, indicating these are a quasi-municipal issue for local circulation. The reverse type, the configuration of the inscription, and the use of "L" as a prefix for the Seleucid-era date, all indicate Ptolemaic influence. The coins probably were minted in a Ptolemaic community serving Balas in north Phoenicia, perhaps at Orthosia.

5382 **Mørkholm, Otto.** "Two Seleucid Notes." *Numismatic Chronicle* 6th ser., 17 (1957): 6-10. 1 pl.
"Three Seleucid coins from the Royal Collection in Copenhagen are examined and commented upon in detail: (1) A tetradrachm of Antiochus IV (Nikephoros) period 166-164 B.C., assigned to Ake-Ptolemais. Syrian expeditions against the rebellious Jews under Judas Maccabaeus make this military center the natural base for the armies operating in Palestine; (2) An unpublished tetradrachm of Antiochus VII, with reverse type a cult statue of Athena Magarsia. This and a drachm (*Naville* X, 1307) are the only extant coins of this emperor (138-129 B.C.) from Mallos in Cilicia; (3) A further tetradrachm of Antiochus VII with reverse type of Athena left and customary attributes; in the field is a plant with five leaves, and in the exergue ΙΣΙ and AN. The coin is attributed to Seleukeia." [J. Healy, *NL* 49]

5383 ——— "A Posthumous Issue of Antiochus IV of Syria." *Numismatic Chronicle* 6th ser., 20 (1960): 25-30. 1 pl.
"Tetradrachms belonging to the period 146-145 B.C. carry on the obverse the diademed head of Antiochus IV (r.); *rev.*, Zeus seated on throne (l.) with the legend reading ΒΑΣΙΛΕΟΣ ΑΝΤΙΟΧΗΟΥ ΕΠΙΠΗΑΝΟΥΣ. A number of drachms and bronzes also belong to the same issue although they bear no date. These coins, recorded by Mørkholm, originate from the central mint of Antioch and are a posthumous issue of Antiochus IV of Syria." [J. Healy, *NL* 60]

5384 ——— *Studies in the Coinage of Antiochus IV of Syria.* Copenhagen: E. Munksgaard, 1963. 75 pp., 15 pls. [CS 2867]
A die study of the silver and gold coinage of Antiochus IV struck at Antioch-on-the-Orontes and Ake-Ptolemais. Revises the previously established chronology. Provides historical commentary and a catalogue of the coins of both mints. Illustrates seventy-six coins of Antioch and twenty-eight coins of Ptolemais. [Reviewed by U. Westermark in *Hamburger Beiträge zur Numismatik* 6, no. 18/19 (1964-5): 223-6].

5385 ——— "The Accession of Antiochus IV of Syria: A Numismatic Comment." *Museum Notes* 11 (1964): 63-76. 3 pls. [CS 2868]
Publishes a corpus of the silver coins of the boy-king Antiochus from the mint of Antioch together with the first series of silver issued at the same mint by Antiochus IV, in order to extract all available numismatic evidence to positively identify the boy whose portrait appears on the coins. It has been suggested that this boy was a son of Seleukos IV or a son of Antiochus IV. Mørkholm concludes that the boy was a son of Seleukos IV, proclaimed king by Heliodoros after his father's death and later, at the accession of Antiochus IV (the boy's uncle), adopted by his uncle. The boy was murdered in 170 B.C.

5386 ——— "Seleucid Coins from Cilicia, ca. 220-150 B.C." *Museum Notes* 11 (1964): 53-62. 2 pls. [CS 2869]
The author examines the apparent lack of Seleucid coinage from ca. 220-150 B.C. which can be attributed to the district of Cilicia. Discusses the evolution of the coin portrait of Antiochus III at other mints, as well as the symbols used on his coinage. Ascribes to Tarsus the silver coins formerly given to Tyre. Establishes that there was a continuous issue of silver coinage at Tarsus down to the reign of Demetrius I (162-150 B.C.). Also attributes to a mint in Soli the coins of Seleucus IV, Antiochus IV, Demetrius I, and Demetrius II which bear either the head of Athena or an owl as reverse symbols.

5387 ——— "A Greek Coin Hoard from Susiana." *Acta Archaeologica* (Denmark) 36 (1965): 127-56 including 6 pls. Map. [CS 3051 and 3258]
Discusses a hoard of about 200 tetradrachms of Seleucid kings found near Susa in Iran around 1958-1959, about sixty percent of which are published here. The coins were probably buried ca. 139 B.C. Includes coins of kings from Seleucus IV to Alexander Balas. Discusses the operations of the mint of Susa and the chronology of the coins. Strongly suggests that the coins previously attributed to an uncertain eastern mint belong to Antiochia at the Erythrean Sea. [Also see Mørkholm "The Seleucid Mint at Antiochia" below].

5388 ——— "Le Monnayage de Séleucus IV à Nisibe." *Revue Numismatique* (France) 6th ser., 7 (1965): 44-50. 2 pls. [CS 2870]

5389 ——— "The Municipal Coinages with Portrait of Antiochus IV of Syria." *Congresso Internazionale di Numismatica, Roma 11-16 Settembre 1961. Volume 2.* Rome: Istituto Italiano de Numismatica, 1965. Pages 63-7. 1 pl. [CS 2871]
Discusses the bronze coins with a portrait of the king on the obverse and the name of a city on the reverse. These coins were produced at nineteen mints. Discusses types, legends, and denominations. Suggests the minting of these coins originated with a central administration and may reflect a weakening of royal authority.

5390 ——— "Some Western Seleucid Mints." *Israel Numismatic Journal* (Israel) 3 (1965-6): 8-14. 1 pl.
"Several Seleucid issues are described with mint attribution and proposed dating. These include issues of Seleucus IV attributed to Ake-Ptolemais, Antiochus IV to Seleucia Pieria, Demetrius II, first reign, to Seleucia Pieria or Laodicea ad Mare, and Antiochus VIII to Damascus." [A. Spaer, *NL* 85]

5391 ——— "The Monetary System of the Seleucid Kings until 129 B.C." *The Patterns of Monetary Development in Phoenicia and Palestine in Antiquity: International Numismatic Convention, Jerusalem, 27-31 December 1963.* Edited by A. Kindler. Tel-Aviv and Jerusalem: Schocken Publishing House, 1967. Pages 75-87. 2 pls. [CS 2874]
The author examines the Seleucid issues of Aradus and Marathus after 259 B.C. Emphasizes the economic ties between Phoenicia and the Seleucid Kingdom. Suggests some Seleucid issues before Alexander Balas, generally attributed to Tyre, were actually struck at Tarsus in Cilicia. Some other issues which had been previously identified as "unknown Coele-Syria" he believes were minted at Soli. Suggests the Phoenician coins of Antiochus V were minted posthumously. The introduction of the Phoenician weight standard loosened the economic ties between Phoenicia and the rest of the Seleucid Kingdom. Cites hoard evidence to support this claim. Mørkholm then discusses the bronze coinage including the royal, semi-autonomous, and autonomous issues. States that the semi-autonomous issues were started at several mints at the same time—indicating the project was initiated by a central authority.

5392 ——— "Some Seleucid Coins from the Mint of Sardes." *Nordisk Numismatisk Årsskrift* (Sweden) (1969): 5-20. Illus.
Discusses the Seleucid mint at Sardes from ca. 239 to 189 B.C. Suggests new attributions for some coins previously catalogued by Newell in his *The Coinage of the Western Seleucid Mints*.

5393 ——— "The Seleucid Mint at Antiochia on the Persian Gulf." *Museum Notes* 16 (1970): 31-44. 4 pls. [CS 2875]
Republishes the coins from Mørkholm's earlier paper (see "A Greek Coin Hoard from Susiana" above) in which he suggested the existence of a Seleucid mint in the district of the Erythrean Sea. Includes some new material and arguments. Through a discussion of style, die alignment, and moneyers' marks, Mørkholm argues that these coins are Eastern in origin and form a distinctive series from ca. 170-141 B.C. He suggests they were minted at Antiochia. [Also see Le Rider "Un Atelier Monétaire Seleucide dans la Province de la Mer Érythrée?" above].

5394 ——— "Two Cypriot Coins of Antiochus IV of Syria." *Numismatic Report* (Cyprus) 12 (1981): 51-3. Illus.
"Two coins struck by Antiochus IV at Cyprus in 168 B.C. during the brief Seleucid occupation of the island are examined." [M. Santamas, *NL* 110]

5395 ——— "A Posthumous Issue of Antiochus IV of Syria." *Numismatic Chronicle* 143 (1983): 57-63. 1 pl.
"A Seleucid bronze coin (*SNG Fitzwilliam* no. 5681), dated 151/0 B.C., has been the subject of controversy since 1719. Its various attributions are most frequently to Antiochus VII. The recent appearance of a couple of parallel undated pieces indicates that the issues were struck by Alexander Balas at Apamea in Syria with the portrait and name of his alleged father, Antiochus IV." [O. Mørkholm, *NL* 111/112]

5396 ——— "The Alleged Portrait of Antiochus, Son and Co-Regent of Antiochus the Great." *Numismatic Chronicle* 144 (1984): 184-6. 1 pl.

"The suggestion that 'a Seleucid tetradrachm in Dr. Thomas Fischer's possession represents the young Antiochus, son and co-regent of Antiochus III from 210/209 to 192, rather than Antiochus III himself at the beginning of his reign, as assumed by Newell and others' is rejected." [A. Thygesen, *NL* 114]

5397 ——— "The Monetary System in the Seleucid Empire after 187 B.C." *Ancient Coins of the Graeco-Roman World: The Nickle Numismatic Papers.* Edited by Waldemar Heckel and Richard Sullivan. Waterloo, Ontario: Wilfrid Laurier University Press, 1984. Pages 93-113.

The author summarizes the mints operating in the Seleucid empire and the output of each after 187 B.C. He then discusses the denominations issued and the inscriptions and types utilized. Discusses the use of municipal and civic coinages in the empire. Describes the circulation patterns of both Seleucid coins and the foreign coins imported into Syria. Comments on the use of countermarks on the foreign coins. Mørkholm concludes with an examination of the monetary policy of Antiochus IV during the period ca. 173-171 B.C. to illustrate the kind of detailed historical information that an examination of the numismatic evidence can provide.

5397a **Naster, Paul.** "Les Monnaies Séleucides Atibutées à l'Atelier d'Elaeusa Sebasté." *Revue Belge de Numismatique et de Sigillographie (Belgium)* (1950).

5398 ——— "Empreintes de Sceaux Hellénistiques de Warka et Monnaies Séleucides." *Greek Numismatics and Archaeology: Essays in Honor of Margaret Thompson.* Edited by O. Mørkholm and N. M. Waggoner. Wetteren: Numismatique Romaine, 1979. Pages 215-9. 1 pl.

Compares a seal impression to coin images.

5399 **Newell, Adra M.** "A Note on *Western Seleucid Mints* No. 1310: Antiochus II at Tarsus." *Museum Notes* 2 (1947): 13.

A well-centered specimen of E. T. Newell's *The Coinage of the Western Seleucid Mints* No. 1310 has been located. The second monogram on the reverse is clearly AI. Based on the off-center specimen available to E. T. Newell at the time of his publication, he was uncertain of the correct reading of the monogram.

5400 **Newell, Edward T.** "The Seleucid Mint of Antioch." *American Journal of Numismatics* 51 (1917): 1-151. 13 pls. Reprint, Chicago: Obol International, 1978. [CS 2876]

A study of the Seleucid coinage minted at Antioch, beginning with Seleucus II, 246-226 B.C. Describes 461 coins arranged by ruler and discusses their inscriptions, symbols, monograms, and control marks. Provides historical background. States that monograms on the coins of Antioch are all personal names and cannot be translated into city names. Concludes with a summary of the dies and monograms, types, and denominations. The major types appear in the plates.

5401 ——— "The Pre-Imperial Coinage of Roman Antioch." *Numismatic Chronicle* 4th ser., 19 (1919): 69-113. 2 pls. Reprints, Chicago: Argonaut, 1971; Chicago: Obol International, 1980. 45 pp., 2 pls. [CS 2885]

Newell examines a series of tetradrachms which bear the name and types of the Seleucid king Philip Philadelphus, but which stands out because of the distinctiveness of its fabric and style, and because the coins always display the monogram ATX. Newell concludes that this series was not struck by Philip. Rather, the coins were struck at Antioch between 64 and 7 B.C. These are a municipal reissue of the Philip tetradrachms, but they now bear the monogram of the city and, in the exergue, dates reckoned according to the Caesarian era. [Also see McAlee "The Livia Hoard" above.]

5402 ——— *The First Seleucid Coinage of Tyre.* Numismatic Notes and Monographs, No. 10. New York: American Numismatic Society, 1921. 40 pp., 8 pls. [CS 2877]

It was previously thought that the first coinage minted at Tyre under the Seleucid dynasty was in 150 B.C. during the reign of Alexander I Balas. This meant that no Seleucid coinage was struck at this important city from the inception of Seleucid control under Antiochus III (201 B.C.) until 150 B.C. Newell here identifies an earlier series of Seleucid coins (tetradrachms, drachms, and bronze coins) which he attributes to Tyre. Presents a catalogue of fifty-five coin types and discusses the reasons for attributing these to Tyre. Newell shows that all Seleucid monarchs struck coins at Tyre beginning in 201 B.C. [Also see Edgar Rogers *The Second and Third Seleucid Coinage of Tyre* below].

5403 ——— "The Coinages of Seleucus I." *The Coin Collector's Journal* 1, no. 10 (January 1935): 217-20. Illus.

A brief account of the reign and coinage of Seleucus I.

5404 ——— *Seleucid Coinages of Tyre: A Supplement.* Numismatic Notes and Monographs, No. 73. New York: American Numismatic Society, 1936. 34 pp., 5 pls. [CS 2878]

An update to Newell's *The First Seleucid Coinage of Tyre* above and Rogers' *The Second and Third Seleucid Coinage of Tyre* below. Lists additions and corrections.

5405 ——— *The Coinage of the Eastern Seleucid Mints, from Seleucus I to Antiochus III.* Numismatic Studies, No. 1. New York: American Numismatic Society, 1938. 307 pp., 56 pls., map. Revised edition, New York: American Numismatic Society, 1978. [CS 2880]

A catalogue of 765 coin types of the first six Seleucid kings minted at Seleucia-on-the-Tigris, Babylon, Susa, Persepolis-Istakhr, Ecbatana, Bactra, Hecatompylus (or Artacoana), and uncertain Eastern mints. Presents a discussion of the coinage for each city. Includes a short chapter on the bronze coinage. The revised edition includes a summary of recent scholarship, and additions and corrections by Otto Mørkholm. [Reviewed by A. R. Bellinger in *American Journal of Archaeology* 43 (1939): 533-4].

5406 ——— *Late Seleucid Mints in Ake-Ptolemais and Damascus.* Numismatic Notes and Monographs, No. 84. New York: American Numismatic Society, 1939. 107 pp., 17 pls. [CS 2879]

A study of the coins struck at the mints of Ake-Ptolemais and Damascus during the Seleucid period. Describes fifty-one coins of Ake-Ptolemais struck between 129 B.C. and 106 B.C. Then describes 101 coins minted at Damascus ca. 138-70 B.C. Includes much discussion of reign dates and chronology for the coins.

5407 ——— *The Coinage of the Western Seleucid Mints, from Seleucus I to Antiochus III.* Numismatic Studies, No. 4. New York: American Numismatic Society, 1941. 450 pp., 85 pls. Revised edition, New York: American Numismatic Society, 1977. [CS 2881]

Begins with an addenda to Newell's *The Coinage of the Eastern Seleucid Mints* describing a number of new varieties of Seleucid coinage from Eastern mints. Presents a catalogue of 1701 coin types of the first six Seleucid kings minted at at Carrhae, Edessa, Nisibis, Dura-Europus, Antigonea on the Orontes, Seleucia Pieria, Antioch-on-the-Orontes, Apamea, Laodicea ad Mare, Marathus, Tyre, Ascalon, Damascus, Tarsus, Seleucia-on-the-Calycadnus, Cappadocia and Northern Syria, Sardes, Magnesia ad Sipylum, Magnesia-on-the-Maeander, Ephesos, Smyrna, Phocea, Aegae, Cyme, Myrian, Pergamum, Lampsacus, Abydus, Ilium, Alexandria Troas, Scepsis, Sigeum, Lysimachia in Thrace, and various uncertain mints. Concludes with a summary of the coinage of the Seleucid kings, 312-187 B.C. The revised edition includes a summary of recent scholarship and additions and corrections by Otto Mørkholm. [Reviewed by A. R. Bellinger in *American Journal of Archaeology* 46 (1942): 452-4. Also see a clarification by Adra Newell above. Also see Miller and Hoover "The Sardes Mint" above].

5408 **Noe, Sydney P.** "Coinage at Alexandria Troas under Antiochus Hierax." *Museum Notes* 5 (1952): 21-3. 1 pl. [CS 2882]
A posthumous tetradrachm of Alexander bearing a feeding horse in exergue is mentioned. This horse was used as the mintmark of Alexandria Troas on later Seleucid coinage. A tetradrachm of Antiochus Hierax, from the Alexandria Troas mint, is published. The coin bears the same monogram as the Alexander coin of that mint. Another Alexander tetradrachm shares the same monogram, but the horse stands on a fulmen. Noe dates the coins to ca. 230 B.C.

5409 **Oman, Charles W. C.** "The Chronology of the Coinage of Antiochus VIII of Syria." *Numismatic Chronicle* 4th ser., 17 (1917): 190-206. 1 pl.
Antiochus Grypus ("the hook nosed") was king of the Seleucid Empire 125-96 B.C. Oman discusses the history of his reign and the chronology of his coinage. Traces the evolution of his coin portraits.

5410 ——— "The Chronology of the Coinage of Antiochus IX of Syria." *Numismatic Chronicle* 4th ser., 19 (1919): 201-16. 2 pls.
Examines the coinage of Antiochus IX Philopator (also known as Antiochus Cyzicenus). Includes a brief history of his reign and a discussion of his coinage.

5411 **Phillips, Wayne C.** "Seleucid Kingdom Coins Abundant for Collectors." *Coin World* (March 1, 1993): 32.
This segment of Phillip's "Let's Talk Ancients" column provides a brief overview of the history and coinage of the Seleucid Kingdom.

5412 **Plant, Richard J.** "King Antiochus Epiphanes." *Numismatic Fine Arts Quarterly Journal, Publication* 26 (October 1983): unpaged (2 pages).
Briefly describes the coinage of the Seleucid ruler Antiochus IV Epiphanes. He renamed numerous cities Antioch, used a radiate portrait on his coins, and issued a varied bronze coinage.

5413 **Plantzos, Dimitris.** "A Royal Seal of Antiochus IV of Syria and Some Contemporary Minima Ptolemaica." *Revue Belge de Numismatique et de Sigillographie* (Belgium) 148 (2002): 33-40.

5414 **Poole, Reginald Stuart.** "On a Copper Coin of the Class Struck after the Death of Alexander the Great, by his Generals, before They Assumed Regal Titles." *Numismatic Chronicle* new ser., 1 (1861): 137-9. Illus.
Poole examines a bronze coin with male head in elephant skin, with an anchor reverse, struck between 323-306 B.C., which he attributes to Seleucus I.

5415 **Rakicic, Mark.** "Rakicic's Reverie Resumes." *The Celator* 7, no. 3 (March 1993): 34-6. Illus.
A fictional account of time travel in which the author is on the trail of a drachm of Seleucus I Nikator.

5416 ——— "Bucephalus or Not? The Horned Horse Head on Coins of Seleucus I." *The Celator* 7, no. 9 (September 1993): 30-7. Illus.
Examines the horned horse's head which appears as the type or a symbol on some coins of Seleucus I and Antiochus I. Possible explanations for the horned horse are: represents Seleucus' favorite battle horse; symbolizes the role of the cavalry in the battle of Corupedium; or, as the author believes, represents Bucephalus, the horse of Alexander the Great. Recounts stories involving the horse and Alexander's attachment to it. Discusses the use of horns as a divine attribute, the meaning of Bucephalus in Greek (bull headed), and the benefit to Seleucus of maintaining a link with Alexander.

5417 **Regling, Kurt L.** "Hellenistischer Münzschata aus Babylon." *Zeitschrift für Numismatik* (Germany) 38 (1928): 92-132.

5418 **Retsinas, G. A.** "A Select Bibliography of Seleucid Numismatic and Historical Works." *Hekte* (Canada) 1 (February 1996): 3-8. Map.
A brief listing of some of the important books and articles available for the study of Seleucid coinage and history.

5419 **Rodger, William.** "Seleucus I." *Coins* 21, no. 7 (July 1974): 71. Illus.
In this installment of the "Personalities on Ancient Coins" column, the author focuses on Seleucus I.

5420 **Rogers, Edgar.** "Rare and Unpublished Coins of the Seleucid Kings of Syria." *Numismatic Chronicle* 4th ser., 12 (1912): 237-64. 3 pls.
Describes thirty-two Seleucid coins from the author's collection. The coins range from Seleucus I to Antiochus XI.

5421 ——— "Three Rare Seleucid Coins and Their Problems." *Numismatic Chronicle* 4th ser., 19 (1919): 17-34. 1 pl.
Examines three coins: (1) discusses the date of a Phoenician-weight tetradrachm of Alexander Balas; (2) discusses the interpretation of the monogram on a previously unpublished tetradrachm of Antiochus VIII; (3) Publishes a tetradrachm of Philip Philadelphus from Antioch with a previously unrecorded date.

5422 ——— "Some New Seleucid Copper Types." *Numismatic Chronicle* 5th ser., 1 (1921): 26-36. 1 pl.
Discusses some previously unpublished Seleucid coin types including coins of Seleucus I, Antiochus II, Antiochus III, Seleucus IV, Demetrius I, Antiochus VII, Alexander Zabinas, and Antiochus VIII.

5423 ——— *The Second and Third Seleucid Coinage of Tyre.* Numismatic Notes and Monographs, No. 34. New York: American Numismatic Society, 1927. 33 pp., 4 pls. [CS 2890 and 2906]
Rogers takes up where Newell left off (see Newell *The First Seleucid Coinage of Tyre* above). Rogers examines the Seleucid coinage minted at Tyre beginning with the reign of Alexander I Balas (151 B.C.) and ending with the coinage of Antiochus VII (138-129 B.C.). Catalogues 131 coins.

5424 **Sawaya, Ziad.** "Le Monnayage Municipal Séleucide de Bérytos (169/8-114/3? av. J.-C.)." *Numismatic Chronicle* 164 (2004): 109-46. 9 pls.
A study of the Seleucid coinage of Berytos, including a discussion and catalogue.

5425 ——— "Les Tétradrachmes Séleucides à l'Aigle de Bérytos." *Numismatic Chronicle* 165 (2005): 99-124. 6 pls.

5426 **Sayles, Wayne G.** "Through the Looking Glass: Getting Around." *The Celator* 15, no. 1 (January 2001): 45. Illus.
Sayles mentions and illustrates a tetradrachm of Antiochus I bearing control marks which identify its place of origin as the city of Seleucia on the Tigris. The coin also bears a countermark from the city of Byzantium. The countermark was applied sometime between 235-225 B.C.

5427 **Schlösser, Eckart.** "Denominations and Weights of Bronze Coins of Antiochus IV of Syria and Their Relation to the Silver Coinage." *Schweizer Münzblätter* (Switzerland) 35 (1985): 33-6. Illus.
"The series of bronze coins of Antiochus IV with marks of value from Seleucia and Tigris was used to determine the standard weights of his bronze coins. Based on a tetradrachm weight of 16.80 g and a regression analysis (r equals 0.9822) of available bronze coins, the following denomination-weight relation became apparent: the corresponding denominations—tetrachalkon (tetradrachm), dichalkon (didrachm), chalkos (drachm), hemichalkon (hemidrachm)—had the same standard weights of 16.80 g, 8.40 g, 4.20 g, and 2.10 g, respectively." [E. Schlösser, *NL* 117]

5428 ——— "Multiples and Fractions of the Seleucid Chalkous of Attic Standard." *Proceedings of the 10th International Congress of Numismatics, London, 1986.* International Association of Professional Numismatists Publication, No. 11. Edited by I. A. Carradice. London: International Association of Professional Numismatists, 1986. Pages 66-73.
The author examines the relationship between coin weights and denominations for Seleucid bronze coinage issued at the mint of Antioch on the Orontes. He attempts to determine the standard weights of bronze coins and their relationship to the silver coins.

5429 ——— "Egyptian Bronze Coins of Antiochus IV of Syria." *Schweizer Münzblätter* (Switzerland) 37 (1987): 54-6. Illus.
"Two bronze coins are identified as having been issued by Antiochus IV during his conquest of Egypt in 170/169 B.C." [A. Walker, *NL* 121]

5430 **Schönert, Edith.** "Die Wirtschaftliche Auswertung Seleukidischer und Ptolemäischer Münzfunde." *Neue Beiträge zur Geschichte der Alten Welt.* Vol. 1. Berlin: Akademie-Verlag, 1964. Pages 355-62.

5431 **Seeger, John A.** "An Unpublished Drachm of Antiochus VI." *Numismatic Chronicle* 7th ser., 12 (1972): 305. Illus.
Publishes a new drachm from the mint of Tarsus with *obv.*, diademed head of Antiochus VI, and *rev.*, Sandan standing on an animal, holding a double-headed axe. The author suggests that the coin provides proof that the usurpers Tryphon and Antiochus IV controlled Tarsus, at least for a short time.

5432 ——— "The Stratagem of Tryphon." *Spink Numismatic Circular* 94, no. 8 (October 1986): 262. Illus.
Recounts Tryphon's career. Suggests that the group of coins of Tryphon found in 1938 north of Tripolis, Lebanon, may have been some of the money that Tryphon used as a stratagem to slow the pursuit of Antiochus VII.

5433 **Seltman, E. J.** "Re-attribution of a Seleucid Tetradrachm." *American Journal of Numismatics* 47 (1913): 121-9. Illus., 1 pl.
Some previously unpublished Seleucid coins are examined and attributed to Antiochus III.

5434 **Seltman, John.** "A Find of Tetradrachms of Seleucus I." *Numismatic Chronicle* 6th ser., 6 (1946): 67-9. Illus.
Records a hoard of nine tetradrachms of Seleucus I of three varieties. All of the dies are previously unpublished. All are of the type with *obv.*, Zeus; *rev.*, Athena in chariot drawn by four horned elephants. The coins were found in south Iraq. The three varieties are illustrated.

5435 **Seyrig, Henri.** *Notes on Syrian Coins.* Numismatic Notes and Monographs, No. 119. New York: American Numismatic Society, 1950. 35 pp., 2 pls. [CS 2842]
Includes two articles: (1) The Khan el-abade Find and the Coinage of Tryphon; (2) Some Abbreviations on Syrian Coins. Part 1 lists 118 coins from the find including Attic tetradrachms, tetradrachms of Tryphon, and tetradrachms of the Ptolemies. Provides a summary of the coinage of Tryphon in which the author suggests the helmet reverse-type is a symbol of Zeus rather than a personal badge of Tryphon. The author concludes that Tryphon reigned 142/1-139/8 B.C. Part 2 discusses mint marks on coins of Aradus, letters used on coins of Tyre and Sidon, and the method of indicating a date on Syrian coins. [Reviewed by G. K. Jenkins in *Numismatic Chronicle* 6th ser., 10 (1950): 325-6].

5436 ——— "Antiquités Syriennes. 67. Monnaies Contremarquées en Syrie." *Syria* (France) 35, no. 3-4 (1958): 187-97. [CS 2843]

5437 ——— *Trésors Monétaires Séleucides.* Two volumes. Paris, 1965, 1973. [CS 3291]
1. *Le Trésor de Mektepini en Phrygie,* by N. Olçay and H. Seyrig. Bibliothèque Archéologique et Historique de l'Institut Français de Beyrouth, Volume 82. Paris, 1965. 32 pp., 33 pls. [Also see Olçay and Seyrig *Le Trésor* under HOARDS].
2. *Trésors du Levant Anciens et Nouveaux,* by H. Seyrig. Bibliothèque Archéologique et Historique de l'Institut Français de Beyrouth, Volume 94. Paris, 1973. 126 pp., 37 pls.

5438 ——— "Monnaies Hellénistiques 18. Séleucos III et Simyra." *Revue Numismatique* (France) 6th ser., 13 (1971): 7-11. [CS 2883]

5439 **Spaer, Arnold.** "Antiochus IV at Ake-Ptolemais." *Proceedings of the 8th International Congress of Numismatics, New York—Washington, September 1973.* Edited by Herbert A. Cahn and Georges Le Rider. International Association of Professional Numismatists Publication, No. 4. Paris/Basel: International Association of Professional Numismatists, 1976. Pages 139-41. 1 pl.
Spaer attempts to build a series out of certain issues of Antiochus IV Epiphanes. The coins include the quadruple, double, unit, and half-unit. After comparisons with other coins of known mints, the series in question is assigned to the mint of Ake-Ptolemais as a royal issue struck either parallel with the municipal series or, possibly, preceding it, on the assumption that the autonomous coinage started in ca. 169/8 B.C. only.

5440 ———— "Ascalon: From Royal Mint to Autonomy." *Studies in Honour of Leo Mildenberg: Numismatics, Art History, Archaeology.* Edited by A. Houghton et al. Wetteren: Editions NR, 1984. Pages 229-39. 3 pls.

Ascalon gained its autonomy in 103 B.C. There was no gap between the royal issues of Ascalon at the end of Seleucid rule and the beginning of the autonomous tetradrachm series. Spaer publishes a hoard of fifty-two tetradrachms and didrachms which illustrate the transition from royal to autonomous coinage. The hoard was found in 1968 south of Ascalon and contained forty-nine royal issues and three autonomous issues covering the period 126-71 B.C. The author also lists fourteen other coins (not from the hoard) which are relevant to this period. Discusses the portraits on the coins. The coins may portray Ptolemaic rulers. [See Spaer's follow-up to this paper, "The Royal Male Head" under PALESTINE—PHILISTIA. Also see Brett "The Mint of Ascalon" above, and Brett "A New Cleopatra Tetradrachm" under EGYPT—PTOLEMAIC KINGDOM].

5441 ———— "More on the 'Ptolemaic' Coins of Aradus." *Kraay—Mørkholm Essays: Numismatic Studies in Memory of C. M. Kraay and O. Mørkholm.* Numismatica Lovaniensia 10. Edited by G. Le Rider, G. K. Jenkins, N. Waggoner, and U. Westermark. Louvain-la-Neuve: Université Catholique de Louvain, 1989. Pages 267-73. 5 pls.

Spaer examines the didrachms struck at Aradus beginning 151 B.C., using the Ptolemaic weight standard and types. Publishes two hoards, Dura and Yatta, which confirm the conclusions reached by Mørkholm in "The Ptolemaic Coins of an Uncertain Era" (see Mørkholm under EGYPT—PTOLEMAIC KINGDOM). Concludes these coins were intended to serve the needs of a Seleucid area which was still integrated with the Ptolemaic economic system.

5442 ———— "The Seleucid Mint of Simyra." *Schweizer Münzblätter* (Switzerland) 212 (December 2003): 75-6. Illus.

"The author presents a new tetradrachm of Seleucus III struck at the mint of Simyra in the Aradian paralia." [Oliver D. Hoover, *NL* 148]

5443 **Sydenham, Edward A.** "A Tetradrachm of Antiochus Epiphanes Reissued by Antiochus VI." *Numismatic Chronicle* 5th ser., 17 (1937): 147-8. Illus.

Illustrates a coin issued in 145 B.C. during the first reign of Antiochus VI. The portrait on the coin is of Antiochus IV Epiphanes. The author suggests the young king, at the very beginning of his reign, adopted the policy of issuing tetradrachms with the portrait and types of Epiphanes in order to emphasize his (fictitious) claim to the Seleucid throne.

5444 "Tetradrachm of Sardanapalus." *American Journal of Numismatics* 24, no. 2 (October 1889): 33-4.

Describes a tetradrachm of Antiochus VIII Epiphanes bearing on the reverse a structure identified as a monument to Sardanapalus, the builder of the city of Anchiale.

5445 **Thompson, Margaret.** "A Pot Hoard from Gordion." *American Journal of Archaeology* 68 (1964): 201.

A brief summary of a paper presented at a conference. "Two of the five gold coins in this deposit, struck for Seleucus III and Antiochus I, were from the same dies as silver coins of these rulers; this circumstance casts doubt on the attribution of some issues to the mint of Apameia." [J. R. Jones, *NIAJAH*]

5446 **Vagi, David L.** "The Coinage of Seleucus Consists of Four Main Types." *The Celator* 8, no. 5 (May 1994): 42-3. Illus.

Vagi reviews the main coin types of Seleucus: the Alexandrine type, the victory type, the elephant chariot type, and the lion staters of Babylon.

5447 **Vaillant, J. Foy.** *Seleudidarum Imperium, Sive Historia Regum Syriae, ad Fidem Numismatum Accommodata, per J. Foy-Vaillant, Bellov.D.Med. & Regis Antiq.* Editio Secunda, Nitidior et Emendatior. Hagea-Comitum: Apud P. Gosse & J. Neaulme, 1732. 274 pp.

"The revised and best edition of the first book devoted solely to the ancient coins of Syria." [G. F. Kolbe]

5448 **Vaux, W. S. W.** "On a Small Silver Coin of Seleucus I—Nicator." *Numismatic Chronicle* new ser., 10 (1870): 133-8. Illus.

The author publishes a unique coin with *obv.*, helmeted portrait of Seleucus I, and *rev.*, Nike crowning a trophy. Comments on the types. The denomination of the coin is uncertain.

5449 **Volkmann, Hans.** "Zur Münzprägung des Demetrius I und Alexander I von Syria." *Zeitschrift für Numismatik* (Germany) 34 (1923): 51-66.

5450 **Voulgaridis, Georges.** "Some Thoughts on Mints, Monograms and Monetary Magistrates. Two Case Studies: The Mints of 'Akko-Ptolemais and of Ascalon under the Seleucids." *Israel Numismatic Research* 3 (2008): 65-80.

Based on his experience in studying two important Seleucid mints in Palestine, 'Akko-Ptolemais and Ascalon, the author poses several questions about the monograms and the symbols on Seleucid coins: Who is behind them? Why do they appear on the dies? What information about the mints do they provide? No firm answers are given, but a discussion is begun.

5451 **Wells, H. Bartlett.** "An Antiochus Lepton of the Tyre Mint." *Schweizer Münzblätter* (Switzerland) 35 (1985): 62-3. Illus.

"A bronze coin of Tyre is tentatively attributed to Antiochus III." [S. Grunauer, *NL* 117]

5452 **Wirgin, Wolf.** "Appian and the Origin of the Anchor of Seleucus." *Spink Numismatic Circular* 69, no. 2 (February 1961): 34-5. Illus.

"Concerning the origin of the anchor of Seleucus I Nicator, Wirgin cites and discusses a passage from Appian (*Syriaca* 56) which is seen to contain authentic information as to why this Seleucid king adopted the anchor as an heraldic figure. From his study of the above passage, combined with an authoritative history of the anchor and the available archaeological evidence, he concludes thus: There should be no doubt that when the nautical anchor was given the shape of the symbolic anchor, the ancients transferred the inherent power of the symbol to the implement in its new form. If we realize that two different anchors existed in antiquity—the simple stone anchor, and the later Admiralty anchor with its shape reminiscent of holy symbols—then Appian's narrative is no longer incomprehensible and, at the same time, gives us the clues to understand why this symbol was used by Seleucus I and his dynasty." [*NL* 57]. [Also see Wirgin "The Origin of the Anchor of Alexander" under MACEDONIAN KINGDOM].

5453 **Wright, Nicholas L.** "A Late Seleukid Bronze Hoard, c. 1988 (*CH* 10.349)." *Coin Hoards, Volume X: Greek Hoards.* Edited by Oliver Hoover, Andrew Meadows, and Ute Wartenberg Kagan. New York: Royal Numismatic Society and The American Numismatic Society, 2010. Pages 245-64. 2 pls.

Examines a hoard of 244 bronze coins of the third-to-first centuries B.C. and one coin stamped on a lead flan. Included 200 Seleucid royal issues, predominantly from Damascus. The coins were probably buried in Coele Syria ca. 72/1 B.C. Includes a catalogue of the coins and discussion of the Seleucid issues. The hoard contained no coins of illegitimate Seleucid rulers.

5454 **Zahle, Jan.** "Religious Motifs on Seleucid Coins." *Religion and Religious Practice in the Seleucid Kingdom.* Studies in Hellenistic Civilization 1. Edited by Per Bilde. Aarhus: Aarhus University Press, 1990. Pages 125-39. 2 pls.

A general inquiry into the development of the religious motifs used by Seleucid kings in their coinage. Focuses on the gradual reappearance of local, non-dynastic deities that took place concurrently with the decline of Seleucid power after the peace of Apamea in 187 B.C. The function of religion as an official expression of self-awareness, identity, and political independence is illustrated. Zahle points out that Alexander's types conformed with his ideas of a fusion between East and West, and developed earlier features of religious syncretism. However, Zahle concludes that the Seleucids rejected this inter-ethnic notion and aimed their coin type propaganda at their Greek subjects, disregarding Oriental sensibilities.

5455 **Zolotnikova, Olga.** "A Female Divinity in the Religious Policy of Antiochus IV through the Greek Religious Iconography." *Quaderni Ticinesi: Numismatica e Antichità Classiche* (Switzerland) 26 (1997): 255-76. Illus.

"The author studies the theme of the female on a throne, a type which runs throughout the reign of Antiochus IV. The figure of the seated goddess, deriving perhaps from the prototype of Hera or Athena, is also found on coins issued by the mint of Seleucis of the Tigris." [A. Carignani, *NL* 140]

Also see: Ariel "Coins from Khirbet Zemel" under HOARDS; Balty "À la Recherche de l'Apamée" under PHRYGIA; Bellinger "The Coins" (*Final Report VI of the Excavation at Dura-Europas*) under HOARDS; Bosworth "Rider in the Chariot: Ptolemy, Alexander and the Elephants" under TYPES; Clarke et al. *Jebel Khalid* under HOARDS; Cox "Gordian Hoards III" under HOARDS; Cox *A Tarsus Coin Collection* under CILICIA; Dimitrov "Notes on Some Alexander Coinages" under MACEDONIAN KINGDOM—GENERAL WORKS; Fischer "Another Hellenizing Coin" under PALESTINE—JUDEA; Fischer "Nineteenth-Century Forgeries" under COUNTERFEITS; Frenkel "The Sanctuary" under HOARDS; Fulco and Zayadine "Coins from Samaria-Sebaste" under HOARDS; Gardner "On Some Coins of Syria and Bactria" under BACTRIA.

Hartman and Macdonald *Greek Numismatic Epigraphy* under EPIGRAPHY; Hoover "Commerce ('Pamphylia or Cilicia' Hoard), 2000" under HOARDS; Hoover "Northern Israel Hoard" under HOARDS; Hoover "Notes on Some Imitation Drachms of Demetrius" under ARMENIA; Hoover "Ptolemaic Lead Coinage in Coele Syria" under EGYPT—PTOLEMAIC KINGDOM; Hoover "The Seleucid Coinage of John Hyrcanus I" under PALESTINE—JUDEA; Hoover "Two Seleucid Bronzes Countermarked" under THE MINTING PROCESS; Hoover *Handbook of Coins of the Southern Levant* under ASIA—GENERAL WORKS; Houghton "Timarchus" under BABYLONIA; Houghton and Hendin "Defining Rarity" under COLLECTING GUIDES; Huth and Potts "Antiochus in Arabia" under ARABIA; Series 1: *The Arnold Spaer Collection* under THE SYLLOGE NUMMORUM GRAECORUM SERIES (ISRAELI SERIES); Jenkins "A Hellenistic Hoard" under HOARDS; Jidejian *Lebanon and the Greek World...Eddé Collection* under PORTRAITS; Kagan "Hellenistic Coinage of Scepsis" under TROAS; Kindler *Beer Sheba I* under HOARDS; Kritt *Dynastic Transitions* under BACTRIA; Kushnir-Stein "Late Hellenistic Silver Coinage" under GENERAL WORKS—HELLENISTIC.

Lorber "Commerce ('Demetrius I' Hoard), 2003" under HOARDS; Lorber "Ptolemaic Bronzes of Antiochus IV" under EGYPT—PTOLEMAIC KINGDOM; Macdonald "Early Seleucid Portraits" under PORTRAITS; Magen "Mt. Gerazim" under HOARDS; Mattingly "Ma'Aret En-Nu'man Hoard" under HOARDS; McDowell *Coins from Seleucia* under HOARDS; Meadows "Beth Ummar, Israel" under HOARDS; Meadows "The Era of Pamphylia" under PAMPHYLIA; Meadows and Houghton "The Gaziantep Hoard" under HOARDS; Meadows and Lorber "Commerce ('Achaeus' Hoard), 2002" under HOARDS; Metcalf *Oxford Handbook of Greek and Roman Coinage* under GENERAL WORKS—GREEK; Miller "East Arachosia (Quetta) Hoard" under HOARDS; Mørkholm "Sculpture on Coins" under PORTRAITS; Nelson "Commerce ('Seleucus I') Hoard" under HOARDS; Nock "Notes on Ruler-Cult" under TYPES; Olçay and Seyrig *Le Trésor de Mektepini en Phrygie* under HOARDS.

Rappaport "Ascalon and the Coinage of Judaea" under PALESTINE—JUDEA; Richter "Late Hellenistic Portraiture" under PORTRAITS; Ronde "Contribution au Monnayage Pré-Alexandrin en Égypte" under EGYPT—PRE-PTOLEMAIC PERIOD; Rostovtzeff "Some Remarks" under GENERAL WORKS—HELLENISTIC; Sotheby & Co. *Catalogue...Haughton Collection* under PRIVATE COLLECTIONS; Spaer "A Hoard of Seleucid Silver" under HOARDS; Spaer "A Hoard from Jericho" under HOARDS; Syon "Coins from the Excavations at Khirbet esh-Shuhara" under HOARDS; Tameanko "Dimples" under THE MINTING PROCESS; Troxell "Greek Accessions" under ASIA MINOR—GENERAL WORKS; Troxell *The Norman Davis Collection* under PRIVATE COLLECTIONS; Vagi "A Coin of Four Kings" under MYSIA—PERGAMENE KINGDOM; Vagi "The Pyre of Sandon" under TYPES; Waggoner "Seal Impressions" under TYPES; Waggoner "A New Wrinkle in the Hellenistic Coinage of Antioch/Alabanda" under CARIA; Wartenberg and Kagan "Some Comments on a New Hoard" under HOARDS; Wilkinson "Unpublished" under PRIVATE COLLECTIONS; Wirgin "On the Right of Asylum" under PALESTINE—JUDEA; Wright *Coins from Asia Minor and the East* under ASIA MINOR—GENERAL WORKS; Wroth *Catalogue of Greek Coins of Galatia, Cappadocia, and Syria* under GALATIA.

Armenia

This was another mountainous area that proved difficult for the Persians to rule. It was situated in the southern Caucasus, the extreme east of Asia Minor and, depending on the fortunes of war, extended at times as far as the headwaters of the Tigris and Euphrates. We have a few bronze coins minted by earlier kings, but the only Armenian ruler likely to appeal to modern collectors is Tigranes II, "the Great."

—John Anthony, 1983

5456 **Abgarians, Mesrop.** "Four Rare Artaxiad Copper Coins." *Armenian Numismatic Journal* 1st ser., 16, no. 3 (1990): 23-7.
A copper coin is attributed to Artavasdes III. The coin had been attributed by Donabedian to Artaxias I. [See Donabedian "A Copper Coin of Artaxias I" below].

5457 **Allotte de la Füye, F. M.** "Une Monnaie Incertaine au Nom d'Artavasde." *Revue Numismatique* (France) 4th ser., 18 (1914): 153-69.
A bronze coin is discussed and attributed to Artavasde III. The history of the period is reviewed, along with a chronology of the Armenian kings. The author attributes the coins with a quadriga and a Nike reverse to Artavasdes I, and the coins with Artavasdes-Augustus to Artavasdes II.

5458 "Ancient and Medieval Armenian Coins Acquired by Princeton Numismatic Collection." *The Celator* 24, no. 5 (May 2010): 35-6.
Announces that Princeton University has recently acquired a collection of Armenian coins. The collection consists of ancient and medieval coins, and includes two tetradrachms and nineteen bronze coins of Tigranes the Great as well as coins of his successors. Also includes coins of the Byzantine Empire and coins of Cilician Armenia. [Also see "Princeton Adds Armenian Coin Collection" below].

5459 **Bedoukian, Paul Z.** "Gold Forgeries of Tigranes the Great of Armenia." *Museum Notes* 11 (1964): 303-6. 1 pl. Reprinted in *Selected Numismatic Studies of Paul Z. Bedoukian*. Special Publication No. 1. By Paul Z. Bedoukian. Los Angeles: Armenian Numismatic Society, 1981. Pages 72-6, incl. 1 pl. [CS 2833]
Describes and illustrates six gold forgeries of coins of Tigranes the Great, both cast and struck. No genuine gold coins are known to have been struck by the rulers of the Artaxiad dynasty.

5460 ——— "A Classification of the Coins of the Artaxiad Dynasty of Armenia." *Museum Notes* 14 (1968): 41-66. 3 pls. Reprinted in *Selected Numismatic Studies of Paul Z. Bedoukian*. Special Publication No. 1. By Paul Z. Bedoukian. Los Angeles: Armenian Numismatic Society, 1981. Pages 113-41 incl. 3 pls. [CS 2834]
Presents a concise history of the kingdom of Armenia during the reign of the Artaxiads, 189 B.C.-A.D. 6. Discusses their relationships with the Parthians and Romans. Describes the characteristics of the coinage of each Artaxiad king. Attributes to Tigranes I the copper coins with "head left" which Seyrig attributed to Tigranes II (the Great). Presents a catalogue of forty coin types. Includes a genealogical chart of the Artaxiad dynasty.

5461 ——— "Five Hoards Containing Coins of the Artaxiads of Armenia." *Revue des Études Arméniennes* (France) new ser., 5 (1968): 421-33. Reprinted in *Selected Numismatic Studies of Paul Z. Bedoukian*. Special Publication No. 1. By Paul Z. Bedoukian. Los Angeles: Armenian Numismatic Society, 1981. Pages 142-54.
Discusses five hoards found in Turkish Armenia during 1966-67. Focuses on the coins struck by the Artaxiad kings. Concludes that Armenian coins circulated along with Seleucid and other coins following the conquest of Tigranes.

5462 ——— "A Coin of Tigranes the Great of Armenia, Struck in Commagene." *Numismatic Chronicle* 7th ser., 10 (1970): 19-22. Reprinted in *Selected Numismatic Studies of Paul Z. Bedoukian*. Special Publication No. 1. By Paul Z. Bedoukian. Los Angeles: Armenian Numismatic Society, 1981. Pages 182-5. Illus. [CS 2838]
"A copper coin having *obv.*, image of Tigranes of Armenia, and *rev.*, the legend ΒΑΣΙΛΕΟΣ ΑΝΤΙΟΧΟΥ with a lion walking, is attributed to Tigranes who controlled Commagene prior to his conquests of Syria and Palestine. The coin was probably struck before 69 B.C. when Tigranes was defeated by Pompey, and Antiochus became a vassal of Rome." [P. Bedoukian, *NL* 85]

5463 ——— "Coinage of the Later Artaxiads." *Museum Notes* 17 (1971): 137-9. 1 pl. Reprinted in *Selected Numismatic Studies of Paul Z. Bedoukian*. Special Publication No. 1. By Paul Z. Bedoukian. Los Angeles: Armenian Numismatic Society, 1981. Pages 186-9 incl. 1 pl. [CS 2837]
A supplement to the author's 1968 paper (see "A Classification" above) publishing eight additional coins. Confirms the joint rule of Tigranes IV and Erato and supports the author's earlier attribution of the bearded coin types to Tigranes IV. Several copper coins provide evidence that Artavasdes III succeeded Tigranes IV. Reattributes three coins to Tigranes V.

5464 ——— "Some Unpublished Coins of the Artaxiads of Armenia." *Near Eastern Numismatics, Iconography, and History: Studies in Honor of George C. Miles.* Edited by Dickran K. Kouymjian. Beirut: American University, 1974. Pages 27-35. 1 pl. Reprinted in *Selected Numismatic Studies of Paul Z. Bedoukian, II.* Special Publication No. 1. By Paul Z. Bedoukian. Los Angeles: Armenian Numismatic Society, 2003. Pages 70-7. 1 pl.

Begins with an overview of Artaxiad rule in Armenia and then presents a catalogue of seventeen coins of Tigranes II, III, and IV, fourteen of which were previously unpublished. The three previously known coins are the first to provide full legends for these issues.

5465 ——— *Coinage of the Artaxiads of Armenia.* Special Publication No. 10. London: Royal Numismatic Society, 1978. 81 pp., 8 pls. [CS 2836]

A survey of the coinage of the Artaxiad period, ca. 190 B.C. to A.D. 34. Begins with a family tree of the Artaxiad dynasty and very brief comments on the dynasty's history. Then the coinage is examined, with comments made about the coinage of each ruler including Zariadres, Artaxias I, Artavasdes I, Tigranes I, Tigranes II the Great, Artavasdes II, Alexander, Artaxias II, Tigranes III, Tigranes IV, Artavasdes III, Tigranes IV and Erato, Artavasdes IV, Tigranes V, Vonones, and Artaxias. Lists and illustrates 168 coin types. Includes biographical sketches of the rulers, a list of legends, and a discussion of weight standards. [Reviewed by N. Jamgochian in *SAN* 10, no 2 (summer 1979): 23]

5466 ——— *Selected Numismatic Studies of Paul Z. Bedoukian.* Special Publication No. 1. Los Angeles: Armenian Numismatic Society, 1981. 570 pp., 72 pls.

A collection of forty-seven of Bedoukian's articles dealing with the coinage of ancient and medieval Armenia, reprinted from various periodicals. Includes 206 pages in Armenian with English summaries; the rest is in English. Articles related to the Artaxiad period are: Gold Forgeries of Tigranes the Great of Armenia, A Classification of the Coins of the Artaxiad Dynasty of Armenia, Five Hoards Containing Coins of the Artaxiads of Armenia, A Coin of Tigranes the Great of Armenia Struck in Commagene, and Coinage of the Later Artaxiads. Each of these is described separately above. [Also see the second volume of *Selected Numismatic Studies* (2003) below].

5467 ——— "Coinage of the Armenian Kingdoms of Sophene and Commagene." *Museum Notes* 28 (1983): 71-88. 2 pls.

A chronological classification of the coinage of Sophene and Commagene. Presents a chronology of the rulers of these two kingdoms beginning ca. 260 B.C. (Sophene) and ca. 163 B.C. (Commagene). Presents a catalogue of nineteen coin types of Sophene and eight types of Commagene. [Reprinted as a booklet in 1985. See below].

5468 ——— *Coinage of the Armenian Kingdoms of Sophene and Commagene.* Special Publication No. 4. Los Angeles: Armenian Numismatic Society, 1985. 37 pp., 2 pls. Reprinted in *Selected Numismatic Studies of Paul Z. Bedoukian, II.* Special Publication No. 10. By Paul Z. Bedoukian. Los Angeles: Armenian Numismatic Society, 2003. Pages 39-69. 2 pls.

A reprint of the article from *Museum Notes* 28 (see above) supplemented by an Armenian translation.

5469 ——— *Armenian Coin Hoards.* Special Publication No. 5. Los Angeles: Armenian Numismatic Society, 1987. 64 pp., 6 pls.

A description of fifty-one hoards containing Armenian coins, some from the Artaxiad Dynasty and many from the Roupenian Dynasty. Most of the hoards contain varieties of the coins of a single king. Text in English and Armenian.

5470 ——— "An Unpublished Coin of Tigranes III (20-8 B.C.)." *Armenian Numismatic Journal* 13, no. 2 (1987): 11-3. 1 pl. Reprinted in *Selected Numismatic Studies of Paul Z. Bedoukian, II.* Special Publication No. 10. By Paul Z. Bedoukian. Los Angeles: Armenian Numismatic Society, 2003. Pages 78-80. 1 pl.

Publishes a previously unknown 4 chalci copper coin of Tigranes III with *obv.*, youthful king wearing a tall tiara with a ten-pointed star, and *rev.*, horse turned left with foreleg raised. Provides historical background for the king. The coin bears similarities to Parthian types and likely is a transitional piece issued at a time when Armenia and Parthia shared a mutual interest in resisting Rome.

5471 ——— *A Hoard of Copper Coins of Tigranes the Great, and a Hoard of Artaxiad Coins.* Special Publication No. 7. Los Angeles: Armenian Numismatic Society, 1991. 30 pp., 2 pls., map.

Lists ten coin hoards from the Artaxiad period of Armenian history. Describes a hoard of 133 copper Armenian coins, giving weight, die axis, and a brief description of each coin. Also describes a hoard of thirty-three early Armenian coins. Text is in English and Armenian.

5472 ——— *Selected Numismatic Studies of Paul Z. Bedoukian, II.* Special Publication No. 10. Los Angeles: Armenian Numismatic Society, 2003. 376 pp., 61 pls.

A collection of forty articles dealing with the coinage of ancient and medieval Armenia reprinted from various periodicals. Includes papers related to the Armenian Kingdoms of Sophene and Commagene, the Artaxiads of Armenia, Cilician Armenia, and Crusader States. Also includes papers on minting, metal, art, ringstones, tokens, medals, antiquities, early printed books, and book reviews. Begins with an autobiography of Bedoukian. The articles dealing with the ancient period are: Coinage of the Armenian Kingdoms of Sophene and Commagene, Some Unpublished Coins of the Artaxiads of Armenia, and An Unpublished Coin of Tigranes III (20-8 B.C.). Each of these is described separately above. [Also see the first volume of *Selected Numismatic Studies* (1981) above].

5473 **Bernard, Paul.** "Alexandre, Ménon et les Mines d'Or d'Armenie." *Travaux de Numismatique Grecque Offerts à Georges Le Rider.* Edited by M. Amandry and S. Hurter. London: Spink, 1999. Pages 37-64.

5474 **Classical Numismatic Group.** "The Araratian Collection, Part 1." *Auction 36* (December 5 & 6, 1995): lots 529-918. "Part 2." *Mail Bid Sale 46* (June 24, 1998): lots 657-797. "Part 3." *Mail Bid Sale 51* (September 15, 1999): lots 750-804. Illus.

These auction sale catalogues include the "Araratian Collection" of Armenian coins. Includes Armenian-related coins struck from the fourth century B.C. to the nineteenth century A.D. Also includes coins of other cultures with Armenian-related subjects. Most of the coins are illustrated. [See Saryan "An Analysis" below for follow-up comments on Part 1 of the sale. Also see Saryan "Analyzing" below for comments on Part 2 of the sale].

5475 ——— "Armenian Coins from the J. S. Wagner Collection." *Mail Bid Sale 82* (September 16, 2009): lots 678-706. Illus.

Sale catalogue for a nice group of Armenian bronze coins, including several coins issued by the kings of Sophene, Commagene, and Media-Atropatene.

5476 ——— "The R. A. Collection of Armenian and Related Coinage." *Auction 85* (September 15, 2010): lots 1-132. Illus.
Sale catalogue for a private collection of Armenian coins including coins of the Artaxiad dynasty, coins issued by the kings of Sophene, Commagene, and Media-Atropatene, Armenian civic issues, Roman and Byzantine coinage related to Aremenia, and medieval coinage of Armenia. Includes gold, silver, and bronze coins. Includes several group lots. All coins are illustrated.

5477 **de Callataÿ, François.** *L'Historie des Guerres Mithradatiques vue par les Monnaies.* Lovain-la-Neuve, 1997. 480 pp., 5 maps, 54 pls.
"A doctoral dissertation dedicated to the Mithradatic Wars. The book includes two chapters and three plates on the silver coins of Tigranes II. It is the first and a thorough die study. The catalogue of 49 obverse and 192 reverse tetradrachm dies of Tigranes include: a description of the types of a characteristic example, number of coins per obverse and reverse dies, reference to the original source, metrological data (weight and diameter), die axis orientation, reference to the plates if the dies are illustrated, counterfeits, and estimation of original coins from the dies." [Y. Nercessian, "Silver Coins of Tigranes II of Armenia"]

5478 **Donabedian, Asbed H.** "Money, Numismatics, and the Coinage of Tigranes the Great." *Shirak* (Armenia) 11, no. 7 (July 1967): 346-55.
In Armenian.

5479 ——— "A Copper Coin of Artaxias I: The Founder of the Artaxiad Dynasty." *Haigazian Armenological Review* (Lebanon) 2 (1971): 135-43.
Publishes a coin which the author attributes to Artaxias I. In Armenian with an English summary. [Also see Abgarians "Four Rare Artaxiad Copper Coins" above].

5480 ——— "Unique and Unpublished Coins of Tigranes II and Tigranes III." *Haigazian Armenological Review* (Lebanon) 7 (1979): 131-40.
In Armenian.

5481 **Ebeyan, A.** *The Coins of the Armenian Kings of Cilicia.* Beirut, 1973. 127 pp., illus. [CS 2839]
Text in Armenian and English.

5482 **Foss, Clive.** "Tigranes the Younger." *SAN—Journal of the Society for Ancient Numismatics* 16, no. 4 (May 1986): 64-6. Illus.
An overview of the history of the Armenian Kingdom during the reign of Tigranes the Great with an emphasis on his disputes with his son Tigranes the Younger. The author suggests bronze coins with young heads portray Tigranes the Younger. Foss speculates that a coin with head facing left may have been struck by Tigranes the Younger when he was in revolt against his father.

5483 ——— "The Coinage of Tigranes the Great: Problems, Suggestions and a New Find." *Numismatic Chronicle* 146 (1986): 19-66. 3 pls.
"The detailed presentation of a find of over 100 bronzes of Tigranes the Great provides the point of departure for a general study of his coinage. It provides a classification for the tetradrachms and makes suggestions for their mints and chronology. The bronze coinage is treated similarly, with special attention to overstrikes, new and old attributions, metrology and possible mints. All are set in a historical and geographical context." [C. Foss, *NL* 118]

5484 **Gardner, Percy.** "On an Unpublished Coin of Artavasdes II, King of Armenia." *Numismatic Chronicle* new ser., 12 (1872): 9-15.
Summarizes the history of Armenia after the death of Tigranes. Only Tacitus mentions an Artavasdes as holding the throne. Gardner publishes a coin bearing the name Artavasdes, struck between 10 B.C. and A.D. 14. He suggests the Roman generals in Asia Minor set up a prince name Artavasdes, coined money in his name at some town in Syria, to pay the troops with which they supported his pretensions to the throne of Armenia. These troops were defeated, and the prince disappeared from history.

5485 **Hoover, Oliver D.** "Notes on Some Imitation Drachms of Demetrius I Soter from Commagene." *American Journal of Numismatics* 2nd ser., 10 (1998): 71-94. 3 pls.
In addition to the official silver drachms of Demetrius Soter I (162-150 B.C.) issued at Antioch-on-the-Orontes, a series of barbarous imitations also circulated in the Hellenistic Near East. New examples of these imitations have recently been found in the areas of ancient Cappadocia and Commagene. Hoover explores the nature of these coins. Suggests they were struck from at least 125 different dies, and perhaps as many as 250 dies. An unusual feature of these coins is the use of cursive letter forms on some of the dies and the use of an angular sigma. These letter forms suggest a late date (first century B.C. or later) and an origin in Commagene. The legends are frequently blundered, suggesting the use engravers not familiar with Greek letter forms. Hoover discusses the control marks and the names and titles appearing on the coins. He concludes that the imitation drachms were probably issued by the royal house of Orontes, which ruled in Commagene since the second century B.C. Early in Demetrius' reign, Ptolemy, the Seleucid satrap and member of the Orontid house, declared his independence and established the kingdom of Commagene. The first of the imitation drachms were probably struck by Ptolemy and the series was continued by his successors. Includes a catalogue of the known varieties.

5486 **Jamgochian, Nicholas.** "The Orontids of Armenia." *SAN—Journal of the Society for Ancient Numismatics* 7, no. 4 (summer 1976): 68-9. Illus.
The history of the Orontid dynasty in Armenia is reviewed. This hereditary dynasty of satraps and kings ruled between the times of the Uratian and Artaxiad kingdoms. Ten rulers are named, approximate dates are assigned, and several bronze coins are pictured.

5486a **Khurshudian, E.** "A Coin of Mitridat, King of Tosp." *Oriental Numismatic Society Newsletter* 157 (1998): 8.

5487 **Kouymijian, Dickran, and Y. T. Nercessian, eds.** *Essays in Armenian Numismatics in Memory of Father Clement Sibilian on the Centennial of his Death. Armenian Numismatic Journal* 1st ser., 4 (1978). 167 pp., 21 pls.
A collection of twenty-one essays on Armenian numismatics written in honor of Father Clement Sibilian, considered to be the father of Armenian numismatics. Some of the essays are related to the ancient period. Sixty-seven pages are in Armenian with English summaries; the remainder are in English.

5488 **Kovacs, Frank L.** "Additions and Corrections to *Armenian Coins and Their Values.*" *Armenian Numismatic Journal* 30 (2004): 83-6.
Suggests revisions to Nercessian's book.

5489 ——— "Tiridates I of Armenia." *Jahrbuch für Numismatik und Geldgeschichte* (Germany) 55/56 (2005-2006): 105-10.

5490 ——— "Tigranes IV, V, and VI: New Attributions." *American Journal of Numismatics* 2nd ser., 20 (2008): 337-50. 2 pls.
The author considers a number of coins traditionally attributed to Tigranes the Great, Tigranes III, Tigranes IV, and Tigranes V with respect to their legends and the detail of their portraits, and reassigns them to the reigns of Tigranes IV, Tigranes IV with Erato, Tigranes V (Herodian Tigranes I), and Tigranes VI (Herodian Tigranes II). New examples of previously known coins also permit new readings and interpretations of designs. Among other conclusions, Kovacs argues that all coins previously attributed to Tigranes and Erato belong to Tigranes IV, and the coins with bearded portraits generally attributed to Tigranes IV should be divided between Tigranes V and VI.

5491 **Langlois, Victor.** *Numismatique de l'Armenie dans l'Antiquité.* Paris: Bibliothèque Historique Arménienne, 1859. Reprint, Bologna: Forni, 1979. 87 pp., 6 pls.
"Langlois was the first to publish a major and comprehensive study on ancient Armenian coins. In this work he included not only the coins of the Orontid and Artaxiad dynasties of Armenia, but also the Armenian satraps, Arsacids, Roman coins relating to Armenia, and the coins of Edessa. His book contained numerous inaccuracies." [Y. Nercessian, "Silver Coins of Tigranes II of Armenia"]. Illustrated by line drawings of the coins.

5492 **Macdonald, George.** "Coinage of Tigranes I." *Numismatic Chronicle* 4th ser., 2 (1902): 193-201. Reprinted in *Armenian Numismatic Journal* 5 (1979): 13-22 (with Armenian summary).
"MacDonald proposed to divide the coinage of Tigranes into three periods: undated tetradrachms with 'King of Kings' title, dated coins with 'King of Kings Tigranes' inscription, and coins with 'King Tigranes' title but of inferior style." [Y. Nercessian, "Silver Coins of Tigranes II of Armenia"]

5493 **Maksudian, William.** "Coins Overstruck by Tigranes the Great." *Armenian Numismatic Journal* 15 (1989): 51-8.

5494 **Matiossian, V.** "The Coinage of Sophene and Commagene: Nothing New Under the Sun." *Armenian Numismatic Journal* 26, no. 1 (2000): 17-20.

5495 **Mousheghian, Anahit, and Georges Depeyrot.** *Hellenistic and Roman Armenian Coinage (1st Century B.C. – 1st Century A.D.).* Moneta 15. Wetteren: Editions Moneta, 1999. 256 pp., 8 pls.
Written in both Armenian and English. "During the first century B.C. and the beginning of the first century A.D., the Armenian kingdom struck silver and bronze coinage. The bulk of this was issues of Tigranes II. He began to strike after his invasion of the Seleucid kingdom and continued producing coins during and after the war against Lucullus and Pompey. His successors continued to strike coins, but the quantities of coins decreased. The last Armenian issues were Roman denarii of the C L CAESARES type. This book presents a new corpus of the Armenian issues of the Hellenistic and Roman periods. More than 2500 coins are catalogued. A new chronology and organization of coinage are presented. The coins are attributed to several mints of Syria and Armenia. The work is preceded by a general survey of the context of the issues and a study of the metrology." [Mousheghian and Depeyrot, *NL* 141]. [In his article "Silver Coins of Tigranes II of Armenia," Y. T. Nercessian states, "Despite some of the effort consumed on this book, its impressive appearance, format, and promising objective, it disregards the research of several previous scholars, including Ernest A. Babelon, George MacDonald, Paul Z. Bedoukian, and Khatchadour A. Mousheghian. The book is full of contradictions, improper attributions, and suffers considerably from typographical errors and the lack of proof reading."].

5496 **Mousheghian, Khachadour A.** "Numismatics Witness." *Armenia Today* 2, no. 14 (February 1971): 37-9. Illus.
"Coins found in excavations in historical Armenia from the Achaemenid period to the end of the Artaxiad dynasty are surveyed; monetary circulation in Armenia during the period is discussed." [D. Kouymjian, *NL* 88]

5497 ——— *The Coin Hoards of Armenia.* Erevan, 1973. 184 pp., 70 pls.
In Armenian with summaries in English and Russian.

5498 ——— "The Origin and Development of the Monetary Circulation in Armenia, V Century B.C. – XIV Century A.D." *Armenian Numismatic Journal,* 1st ser., vol. II, no. 1 (March 1976): 4-5; no. 2 (June 1976): 14-15; no. 3-4 (December 1976): 34-7; vol. III, no. 1 (March 1977): 4-5.
Discusses the coins that circulated in Armenia over many centuries.

5499 ——— "The Armenian Hoard of Artaxata." *Armenian Numismatic Journal* 4 (1978): 105-37. 3 pls.
In Armenian with an English summary.

5500 ——— *Dramakan Shrjanarut'yune Hayastanum (Monetary Circulation in Armenia).* Numismatics in the History of Armenia. Erevan: Armenian Academy of Sciences, 1983. 351 pp., 54 pls.
In Armenian with summaries in English and Russian. Discusses the circulation of money in Armenia from the fifth century B.C. to the fourteenth century A.D. The first chapter covers Achaemenid and Hellenistic coins, the coinage of the Armenian kings of Sophene, and the coins of the Artaxiads of Armenia. [Reviewed by Paul Bedoukian in *Selected Numismatic Stuides of Paul Z. Bedoukian, II* (2003): 343-5. See Bedoukian above].

5501 ——— *The Numismatics of Armenian History.* Yerevan: ANAHIT Publishers, 1997. 166 pp., illus., 3 maps.
Presents an overview of Armenia's coinage from its origins until the Middle Ages, based on coins now preserved in the collection of the State Historical Museum. Includes the earliest coins discovered on Armenian territory, satrapal coinage of Tiribazus and Orontas, the circulation of coinage of Alexander the Great and his Hellenistic successors in the Transcaucasus, coinage of the Armenian kings of Sophene Commagene and the Artaxiad dynasty, coinage of Rome pertaining to Armenia, coinage of Sassanian Iran struck in Armenia, Arabic coinage struck at Armenian mints, and Byzantine coinage including coins struck by emperors of Armenian origin. The coinage of Cilician Armenia (struck between A.D. 1080-1375) is not included. The full text is in English, Armenian, and Russian.

5502 **Mousheghian, Khachadour A., Anahit Mousheghian, and Georges Depeyrot.** *History and Coin Finds in Armenia, Antiquity.* Moneta 17. Wetteren: Editions Moneta, 2000. 184 pp., 23 pls.

Presents catalogues of the following hoards containing Armenian coins: Artashat (70 B.C. and 59 B.C.), Armenia (55 B.C.), Artik (45 B.C.), Parakar (38 B.C.), Sarnakounk (25 B.C.), Tovuz (25 B.C.), Aparan (2 B.C.), Gurmi and Artashat (first century B.C.), Echmiadzin (A.D. 175), Garni (A.D. 192), Oshakan (third century A.D.), and Yerevan (fifth century A.D.). Includes a list of site finds in Armenia (for coins from the fourth century B.C. to the fifth century A.D.) and a list of coin finds out of the actual Republic of Armenia. Concludes with two studies of coin circulation, the first dealing with the first century B.C. and the second devoted to second century denarii hoards in the Roman Empire.

5503 **Mousheghian, Khachadour A., Anahit Mousheghian, C. Bresc, Georges Depeyrot, and F. Gurnet.** *History and Coins Finds in Armenia: Coins from Garni (4th Century B.C. to 19th Century A.D.).* Moneta 20. Wetteren: Editions Moneta, 2000. 120 pp., 8 pls.
A catalogue of about 1000 coins found during excavations at Garni, an ancient city in Armenia.

5504 ———— *History and Coins Finds in Armenia: Coins from Ani, Capital of Armenia (4th Century B.C. to 19th Century A.D.).* Moneta 21. Wetteren: Editions Moneta, 2000. 160 pp., 16 pls.
A catalogue of coins found during excavations at Ani, an ancient city in Armenia. Nearly 2000 coins and twelve hoards were found in Ani, the most important being Byzantine bronze coins.

5505 **Nercessian, Yeghia T.** *Outline and Rarity: Coinage of Artaxiad Dynasty of Armenia.* Los Angeles: Armenian Numismatic Society, 1974. 1 p.
An outline of the published coin types and chronology of all rulers of the Artaxiad dynasty of Armenia. The rarity of each coin type is assessed on a scale of 1 to 10.

5506 ———— "In Search of an Armenian Monogram." *Armenian Numismatic Journal* 3, no. 3 (September 1977): 29-31. Illus. Reprinted in *Armenian Numismatic Studies.* Special Publication No. 8. By Yeghia T. Nercessian. Los Angeles: Armenian Numismatic Society, 2000. Pages 110-3. Illus.
Publishes a bronze coin of Tigranes II with a reverse bearing a standing figure of Herakles, who is identified with the Armenian hero Vahagn. The reverse bears a monogram—possibly a retrograde Greek N. The author provides several possibilities for its meaning but can reach no conclusion.

5507 ———— "Comments on 'Tigran's Crown in Commagene.'" *SAN—Journal of the Society for Ancient Numismatics* 8, no. 2 (winter 1977): 34.
In this letter, the author comments on Haji Toro's paper "Tigran's Crown in Commagene" (see below). He suggests the crown on coins should not be compared to the crown on a stone sculpture.

5508 ———— *Armenian Numismatic Bibliography and Literature.* Special Publication No. 3. Los Angeles: Armenian Numismatic Society, 1984. 729 pp.
A bibliography listing 1349 works published through 1980, covering all phases and eras of Armenian numismatics. Includes abstracts in both English and Armenian, pointing out what information a work provides for Armenian numismatics. Appendices provide a chronology of Armenian dynasties and legends on Artaxiad and Cilician Armenian coins. [Reviewed by N. V. Jamgochian in *SAN* 16, no. 2 (summer 1985): 36, and by P. Bedoukian in *Numismatic Chronicle* 145 (1985): 284. Bedoukian's review was reprinted in *Selected Numismatic Stuides of Paul Z. Bedoukian, II* (2003): 346-50. See Bedoukian above].

5509 ———— "The Evolution of the Armenian Tiara." *Armenian Numismatic Journal* 11, no. 1 (March 1985): 2-12. 2 pls. Reprinted in *Armenian Numismatic Studies.* Special Publication No. 8. By Yeghia T. Nercessian. Los Angeles: Armenian Numismatic Society, 2000. Pages 138-48. 3 pls.
Describes varieties of the Armenian tiara, from its predecessors on Persian satrapal coins through its peak on the coins of Tigranes II. Traces its origins to the headdress of common Armenian folk. Discusses the symbolism of the peaks of the tiara, the diadem, neck and ear flaps, eagles, and the eight-rayed star.

5510 ———— "An Unpublished Coin of Tigranes I." *Armenian Numismatic Journal* 17, no. 2 (1991): 13-21. Reprinted in *Armenian Numismatic Studies.* Special Publication No. 8. By Yeghia T. Nercessian. Los Angeles: Armenian Numismatic Society, 2000. Pages 1-9. 1 pl., map.
Begins with an overview of the history of the Artaxiad Dynasty and its early kings. Discusses the controversy over the existence of Tigranes I and whether he struck coins. Lists five con types now attributed to Tigranes I. A new specimen of copper coin is published here. In English and Armenian.

5511 ———— "A Hoard of Silver Coins of Tigranes II." *Armenian Numismatic Journal* 20, no. 1 (1994): 3-12. 4 pls. Reprinted in *Armenian Numismatic Studies.* Special Publication No. 8. By Yeghia T. Nercessian. Los Angeles: Armenian Numismatic Society, 2000. Pages 12-26. 12 pls.
Provides some background on Tigranes II and his coinage. Publishes a hoard of Tigranes II tetradrachms which reached the market in 1990, including 78 tetradrachms and 9 drachms. Discusses metrology, dies, chronology, and monograms. Catalogue of the coins, including several dies not listed by Bedoukian in *Coinage of the Artaxiads of Armenia.* In English and Armenian.

5512 ———— *Armenian Coins and Their Values.* Special Publication No. 8. Armenian Numismatic Society, 1995. 254 pages, 48 pls.
Catalogues 515 coin types from the Artaxiads, the Armenian Kingdom of Commagene, and the coinage of Cilician Armenia. Provides rarity information and approximate values in three grades. Includes historical background on the rulers and discussions of counterfeits and grading. [Reviewed by J. Garner in *SAN* 19, no. 2 (1995): 51].

5513 ———— "A Hoard of Copper Coins of Tigranes II." *Armenian Numismatic Journal* 21, no. 1 (1995): 3-14. 1 pl. Reprinted in *Armenian Numismatic Studies.* Special Publication No. 8. By Yeghia T. Nercessian. Los Angeles: Armenian Numismatic Society, 2000. Pages 55-72. 2 pls.

Begins with a brief history of the reign of Tigranes II. Then discusses a hoard of seventy-five copper coins of Tigranes II. The coins are classified into seven groups based on reverse types. Also includes a group of overstruck coins. Examines metrology, denominations, dies, chronology, and mints. In English and Armenian.

5514 ——— "A Hoard of 50 Coppers of Tigranes II." *Armenian Numismatic Journal* 21, no. 1 (1995): 15-6. Reprinted in *Armenian Numismatic Studies*. Special Publication No. 8. By Yeghia T. Nercessian. Los Angeles: Armenian Numismatic Society, 2000. Pages 92-4.
A listing of fifty copper coins of Tigranes II from a recent hoard. Diameters, weights, die alignments, types, die numbers, and catalogue numbers in Bedoukian's *Coinage of the Artaxiads of Armenia* are tabulated without further commentary.

5515 ——— "Tigranes the Great of Armenia and the Mint of Damascus." *Armenian Numismatic Journal* 22, no. 1 (March 1996): 3-12. 1 pl., map. Reprinted in *Armenian Numismatic Studies*. Special Publication No. 8. By Yeghia T. Nercessian. Los Angeles: Armenian Numismatic Society, 2000. Pages 95-107. 2 pls., map.
Begins with an overview of the history of ancient Armenia. Then presents a catalogue of the silver and bronze coins struck by Tigranes II at the mint of Damascus. The coins are different in style from those issued at Antioch and other mints. All of the silver coins are tetradrachms, and just five are known. The bronze coins are more abundant. Also lists some coins with a "young-looking" head of the king. Nercessian suggests these were struck at a remote mint, possibly in Seleucia. Includes a brief summary in Armenian.

5516 ——— "Overstruck and Countermarked Coins of the Artaxiad Dynasty of Armenia." *Armenian Numismatic Journal* 22, nos. 2 & 3 (1996): 23-62. 6 pls. Reprinted in *Armenian Numismatic Studies*. Special Publication No. 8. By Yeghia T. Nercessian. Los Angeles: Armenian Numismatic Society, 2000. Pages 150-204. 10 pls., map.
Begins with a brief history of the Armenian Empire by L. A. Saryan. This is followed by a catalogue of 143 examples of Armenian coins overstruck on other coins—generally Phoenician or Seleucid issues. Also lists 42 countermarked coins. The number of overstruck coins and their distribution by ruler are presented in charts. The majority of the undertypes are coins of Arados. Discusses the metrology of the coins, their chronology, and mints. Lists possible reasons for countermarking.

5517 ——— "A Silver Coin of Artaxias II (30-20 B.C.)." *Armenian Numismatic Journal* 24, no. 3 (1998): 29-31. Reprinted in *Armenian Numismatic Studies*. Special Publication No. 8. By Yeghia T. Nercessian. Los Angeles: Armenian Numismatic Society, 2000. Pages 133-6. 1 pl.
Discusses a coin (*obv.*, bust of Artaxias; *rev.*, helmeted Athena) that has been variously attributed. The author assigns the coin to Artaxias II.

5518 ——— "Tigranes the Great Copper Coins with Horse Design." *Armenian Numismatic Journal* 24, no. 3 (1998): 28. Reprinted in *Armenian Numismatic Studies*. Special Publication No. 8. By Yeghia T. Nercessian. Los Angeles: Armenian Numismatic Society, 2000. Pages 115-6. 1 pl.
Describes a new type of copper coin of Tigranes II with *obv.*, head of Tigranes II, the ray of one of the stars in his tiara appearing as a comet; *rev.*, horse grazing.

5519 ——— "A Classification of the Tetradrachms of Tigranes the Great of Armenia." *Armenian Numismatic Journal* 25, no. 1 (1999): 3-12. 2 pls. Reprinted in *Armenian Numismatic Studies*. Special Publication No. 8. By Yeghia T. Nercessian. Los Angeles: Armenian Numismatic Society, 2000. Pages 117-31. 6 pls.
The author attempts to link the obverse tiara and portrait to the reverse monograms appearing on the rock and in the fields on tetradrachms of Tigranes II.

5520 ——— *Armenian Numismatic Studies*. Special Publication No. 8. Los Angeles: Armenian Numismatic Society, 2000. 678 pp., 96 pls.
A collection of fifty-five articles by Nercessian dealing with ancient and medieval Armenian coinage, banknotes, and medals. Most are reprinted from various periodicals. Those related to the ancient period are: An Unpublished Coins of Tigranes I, A Hoard of Silver Coins of Tigranes II, A Hoard of Copper Coins of Tigranes II, A Hoard of 50 Copppers of Tigranes II, Tigranes the Great of Armenia and the Mint of Damascus, In Search of an Armenian Monogram, Tigranes the Great Copper Coins with Horse Design, A Classification of the Tetradrachms of Tigranes the Great of Armenia, A Silver Coin of Artaxias II (30-20 B.C.), The Evolution of the Armenian Tiara, and Overstruck and Counterstamped Coins of the Artaxiad Dynasty of Armenia. Some are written in both English and Armenian. Each of these is described separately above. [Reviewed by Leon A. Saryan in *The Centinel* 48, no. 4 (winter 2000): 33-4].

5521 ——— "A Newly Discovered Coin of Tigranes I." *Armenian Numismatic Journal* 26, no. 2 (2000): 25-30. 1 pl. Reprinted in *Armenian Numismatic Studies II*. Special Publication No. 8. By Y. T. Nercessian. Los Angeles: Armenian Numismatic Society, 2009. Pages 1-10. 2 pls.
Lists the main types of copper coins attributed to Tigranes I. Tigranes I struck coins with the head of the king to left and a tiara with four points. On a newly discovered coin the tiara is five-pointed. This is evidence that during the reign of Tigranes I the design of Armenian coinage was in a formative state. In English and Armenian.

5522 ——— "Silver Coins of Tigranes II of Armenia." *Armenian Numismatic Journal* 26, nos. 3-4 (December 2000): 43-108. 10 pls.
Begins with a brief history of ancient Armenia, followed by a summary of the most important literature related to ancient Armenian numismatics. Continues with a list and discussion of hoards of Armenian coins. Then presents a catalogue of the silver coins of Tigranes II, listing all of the coins accessible to the author either as a photograph, digital image, or copy of a photograph. The coins are classified based on the king's portrait, tiara, star and eagles on the tiara, ear and neck flaps and their curvature, reverse legends, field letters, monograms, and other characteristics. Metrological data is provided. The coins are grouped by mint. Includes discussions of the portraits, tiara, monograms, style, and metrology. Also discusses chronology and counterfeits.

5523 ———— "The Myth of Tigranes the Younger Coins." *Armenian Numismatic Journal* 27, no. 4 (2001): 95-8. 1 pl. Reprinted in *Armenian Numismatic Studies II*. Special Publication No. 8. By Y. T. Nercessian. Los Angeles: Armenian Numismatic Society, 2009. Pages 90-5. 1 pl.
Publishes a new copper coin. States that the series of coppers previously assumed to belong to Tigranes the Younger actually are variants of the coins of Tigranes II. The coins were probably struck at a satellite mint of Damascus. In English and Armenian.

5524 ———— "Silver Coins of Tigranes II of Armenia: A Summary." *The Celator* 15, no. 2 (February 2001): 34-5.
A summary of an article appearing in *Armenian Numismatic Journal* 26 (see above). Summarizes the known population the coins of Tigranes II, providing die counts for various denominations and mints, as well as average weights and diameters. Coins of Tigranes struck in Antioch represent almost 98% of all his silver tetradrachms and 80% of all his silver coins.

5525 ———— "Two Unpublished Coins of Tigranes III of Armenia." *Armenian Numismatic Journal* 26 (2001): 39-9. 1 pl. Reprinted in *Armenian Numismatic Studies II*. Special Publication No. 8. By Y. T. Nercessian. Los Angeles: Armenian Numismatic Society, 2009. Pages 124-35. 1 pl.
Describes two previously unpublished coins. Lists the forms of legends used on the coins of Tigranes I, Tigranes II, Artavasdes II, Tigranes III, Tigranes IV, and Artavasdes III. Comments on the subject coins and assigns them to Tigranes III based on their characteristics. In English with Armenian summary.

5526 ———— "A Small Hoard of Tigranes II the Great Tetradrachms." *Armenian Numismatic Journal* 28, no. 4 (2002): 91-6. 1 pl. Reprinted in *Armenian Numismatic Studies II*. Special Publication No. 8. By Y. T. Nercessian. Los Angeles: Armenian Numismatic Society, 2009. Pages 11-20. 3 pls.
A catalogue of a hoard of twenty-one tetradrachms of Tigranes II, discovered in 2001 probably in the Middle East. The "Freeman and Sear" hoard was scattered to various collections. The coins are here arranged in eight groups, and metrological and other data is provided. The hoard included ten new die reverse varieties. In English and Armenian.

5527 ———— "The Armenian Coin Auctions of Gerhard Hirsch 161, 163, 166." *Armenian Numismatic Journal* 28, no. 2 (June 2002): 33-40.

5528 ———— "The Armenian Coin Auctions of Classical Numismatic Group, Inc. 58, Triton V (2001, 2002)." *Armenian Numismatic Journal* 28, no. 3 (September 2002): 63-82.

5529 ———— "A Counterfeit Hemidrachm of Tigranes II." *Armenian Numismatic Journal* 29, no. 3 (2003): 79-80. 1 pl. Reprinted in *Armenian Numismatic Studies II*. Special Publication No. 8. By Y. T. Nercessian. Los Angeles: Armenian Numismatic Society, 2009. Pages 533-6. 1 pl.
Provides diagnostics for a counterfeit hemidrachm of Tigranes II which bears designs copied from a copper coin. Also publishes a counterfeit copper coin and a genuine half chalcus. In English with Armenian summary.

5530 ———— "Some Unpublished Coins of Tigranes the Great of Armenia." *Armenian Numismatic Journal* 29, no. 3 (2003): 61-4. 1 pl. Reprinted in *Armenian Numismatic Studies II*. Special Publication No. 8. By Y. T. Nercessian. Los Angeles: Armenian Numismatic Society, 2009. Pages 24-40. 2 pls.
Describes several previously unpublished varieties of coins of Tigranes II. Includes tetradrachms, drachms, 4 chalci, and 2 chalci denominations. In English and Armenian.

5531 ———— "More on Counterfeits." *Armenian Numismatic Journal* 30, no. 1 (2004): 1. Reprinted in *Armenian Numismatic Studies II*. Special Publication No. 8. By Y. T. Nercessian. Los Angeles: Armenian Numismatic Society, 2009. Page 532. 1 pl.
Describes a counterfeit drachm of Tigranes II. It was likely made from a known medal originally hanging from a key chain.

5532 ———— "Tigranes II Gold Coins Discovered in Europe." *Armenian Numismatic Journal* 2nd ser., 1, no. 3 (2005): 69-70. 1 pl. Reprinted in *Armenian Numismatic Studies II*. Special Publication No. 8. By Y. T. Nercessian. Los Angeles: Armenian Numismatic Society, 2009. Pages 523-9. 1 pl.
Describes two gold coins of Tigranes II struck from the same dies, but on flans of different diameters. List the diagnostics of the pieces. Bedoukian considered them to be forgeries. Nercessian reaches no conclusion, but has doubts about them. In English and Armenian.

5533 ———— "A Newly Discovered Copper Coin of Tigranes II Struck in Damascus." *Armenian Numismatic Journal* 2nd ser., 2, no. 4 (2006): 71. 1 pl. Reprinted in *Armenian Numismatic Studies II*. Special Publication No. 8. By Y. T. Nercessian. Los Angeles: Armenian Numismatic Society, 2009. Pages 56-7. 1 pl.
Publishes a copper coin of Tigranes II struck at Damascus on a very large flan (25 mm). Nercessian makes observations on the coin. In English and Armenian.

5534 ———— *Silver Coinage of the Artaxiad Dynasty of Armenia*. Special Publication No. 11. Los Angeles: Armenian Numismatic Society, 2006. 212 pp., 96 pls.
A catalogue of more than 1000 silver coins of the Armenian kings, 189 BC to AD 34. A significant percentage of all known Armenian coins were submitted to the author for this die study. Chapters include: Historical Background, Survey of Major Numismatic Works, Survey of Hoards, Catalogue, Analysis, and Auction Catalogue Publishers. Also includes a summary in Armenian and an extensive bibliography. [Reviewed by Jirair Christianian in *The Celator* 21, no. 8 (August 2007): 38, and by Oliver D. Hoover in *American Numismatic Society Magazine* 7, no. 1 (spring 2008): 67-72].

5535 ———— "Tigranes II Counterfeit Tetradrachm with Imperial Countenance Portrait." *Armenian Numismatic Journal* 2nd ser., 2, no. 4 (2006): 72. Reprinted in *Armenian Numismatic Studies II*. Special Publication No. 8. By Y. T. Nercessian. Los Angeles: Armenian Numismatic Society, 2009. Pages 530-1. 1 pl.
Publishes a tetradrachm of Tigranes II purchased in 2006. Lists the diagnostics of the piece and concludes it is counterfeit.

5536 ——— "Two Drachms of Tigranes II with Unrecorded Field Letters." *Armenian Numismatic Journal* 2nd ser., 3, no. 4 (2007): 79-80. Reprinted in *Armenian Numismatic Studies II*. Special Publication No. 8. By Y. T. Nercessian. Los Angeles: Armenian Numismatic Society, 2009. Pages 21-3. 1 pl.

Publishes two drachms of Tigranes II bearing letters in the field that were previously unrecorded. The coins provide evidence that the letters do not represent the month of issue. They likely are indicators of a minting sequence. In English with Armenian summary.

5537 ——— *Catalogue of Armenian Coins Collected by Y. T. Nercessian*. Special Publication No. 14. Los Angeles: Armenian Numismatic Society, 2008. 387 pp., 128 pls.

The collection was formed over forty years (1968-2008). Includes the author's biography and a catalogue of the coins of the Armenian kingdom of Sophene (6 coins, 260 to 70 B.C.), the Artaxiad dynasty of Armenia (264 coins, 189 B.C. to A.D. 34), the Armenian kingdom of Commagene (51 coins, 163 B.C. to A.D. 72), Tosp (1 coin) and the Roupenian dynasty of Cilician Armenia (1499 coins, A.D. 1080 to 1375). Also includes counterfeit and fantasy pieces (19 coins). Illustrates 1397 coins. [A review appears in *The Celator* 22, no. 6 (June 2008): 56].

5538 ——— "Tigranes II Mint Where Coppers of Wheat Design were Struck." *Armenian Numismatic Journal* 2nd ser., 4, no. 3 (2008): 53-5. Reprinted in *Armenian Numismatic Studies II*. Special Publication No. 8. By Y. T. Nercessian. Los Angeles: Armenian Numismatic Society, 2009. Pages 96-100. 1 pl.

There are Armenian copper coins which display wheat, cornucopia, a cypress tree, palm-branch, and a horse on their reverses. Nercessian proposes that each of these designs designate a mint location. He focuses on the coins with the wheat design and suggests they may have been struck at the Armenian city of Nisibis. In English with Armenian summary.

5539 ——— "Tigranes II the Great of Armenia and the Mint of Damascus." *Armenian Numismatic Studies II*. Special Publication No. 8. By Y. T. Nercessian. Los Angeles: Armenian Numismatic Society, 2009. Pages 41-55. 2 pls.

Describes the characteristics of the coins of Tigranes II struck at Damascus. Those coins exhibit stylistic differences from coins struck at other mints. A new type of copper coin with a "young-looking" Tigranes provides a missing link to other "young looking" Tigranes coins not previously attributed to any mint. Concludes there may have been more than one mint operating in or near Damascus. In Armenian with a two-page summary in English.

5540 ——— "Tigranes the Great and the Myth of Tigranes the Younger Coins." *Armenian Numismatic Studies II*. Special Publication No. 8. By Y. T. Nercessian. Los Angeles: Armenian Numismatic Society, 2009. Pages 58-89. 3 pls.

A newly discovered copper coin portrays Tigranes with boyish features. The author argues that Tigranes II was deified on his coins and was represented much younger than his age. He suggests that all coins with the boyish portrait can be attributed not to Tigranes the Younger but to Tigranes II. In Armenian with a two-page summary in English.

5541 ——— "Coinage of Artaxias II of Armenia." *Armenian Numismatic Studies II*. Special Publication No. 8. By Y. T. Nercessian. Los Angeles: Armenian Numismatic Society, 2009. Pages 101-23. 2 pl.

A newly discovered silver drachm has been variously attributed to Artaxias II or Artavasdes III. The author argues that the coin belongs to Artaxias II. In Armenian with a two-page summary in English.

5542 ——— *Armenian Numismatic Studies II*. Special Publication No. 15. Los Angeles: Armenian Numismatic Society, 2009. 580 pp., 60 pls.

A collection of nearly forty articles by Nercessian dealing with the coinage and antiquities of ancient and medieval Armenia reprinted from various periodicals. The articles are grouped into three major periods: ancient, medieval, modern. A fourth section deals with medals, antiquity, counterfeit coins, and fantasy pieces. Those related to the ancient period are: A Newly Discovered Coin of Tigranes I, A Small Hoard of Tigranes II the Great Tetradrachms, Two Drachms of Tigranes II with Unrecorded Field Letters, Some Unpublished Coins of Tigranes the Great of Armenia, Tigranes II the Great of Armenia and the Mint of Damascus, A Newly Discovered Copper Coin of Tigranes II Struck in Damascus, Tigranes the Great and the Myth of Tigranes the Younger Coins, Tigranes II Mint where Coppers of Wheat Design were Struck, Two Unpublished Coins of Tigranes III of Armenia, Tigranes II Gold Coins Discovered in Europe, Tigranes II Counterfeit Tetradrachm with Imperial Countenance Portrait, More on Counterfeits, and A Counterfeit Hemidrachm of Tigranes II. Each of these is described separately above.

5542a ——— "Coinage of the Armenian Kingdom of Sophene (ca. 260-70 B.C.)." *Armenian Numismatic Journal* 37.3 (September 2011).

5543 **Nercessian, Yeghia T., and Leon A. Saryan.** "Overstruck and Countermarked Coins of the Artaxiad Dynasty of Armenia." *Armenian Numismatic Journal* 22, nos. 2 & 3 (June 1996): 23-62. 6 pls. Offprint, 40 pp., 6 pls.

Begins with a summary of the history of the Artaxiad dynasty in Armenia (189 B.C. to A.D. 34). Provides general comments on the prevalence of Armenian coins struck over other coins (the majority are copper coins of Tigranes the Great struck over Phoenician or Seleucid coins). Provides statistics on the overstruck coins and their undertypes, and statistics on coin weights. Concludes that perhaps twenty percent of Tigranes' coins were overstrikes. Discusses the chronology of the coins and their undertypes. Suggests possible mints which performed the overstriking—most likely Artaxata or a mint which traveled with the army. Briefly comments on counterstamped coins. Presents a catalogue of about 200 overstruck or counterstamped Armenian coins.

5544 **Nurpetlian, Jack.** "The Dating of the Civic Coins of Artaxata." *Numismatic Chronicle* 170 (2010): 9-16. 1 pl.

Discusses the dating of the civic bronze coins of Artaxata, the capital of ancient Armenia. Proposes the dates 34-30 B.C. for the coins.

5545 "Princeton Adds Armenian Coin Collection to its Holdings." *Coin World* (March 29, 2010): 92. Illus.

Announces that Princeton University has recently acquired 112 Armenian coins. The collection consists of ancient and medieval coins, and includes two tetradrachms and nineteen bronze coins of Tigranes the Great as well as coins of his successors. Also includes coins of the Byzantine Empire and coins of Cilician Armenia. [For the announcement in *The Celator*, see "Ancient and Medieval Armenian Coins Acquired" above].

5546 **Saryan, Leon A.** "An Ancient Bronze Depicting an Armenian Tiara." *Spink Numismatic Circular* 99, no. 4 (May 1991): 112. Illus.

Publishes a drawing of a coin with *obv.*, a tiara, and *rev.*, a horse. The tiara is similar to that found on coins of Tigranes II. The author is seeking further information on this unattributed coin.

5547 ———— "Three Unreported Tetradrachms of Tigranes the Great." *Armenian Numismatic Journal* 18, no. 2 (June 1992): 37-8.

5548 ———— "Overstruck Bronze Coins of Tigranes the Great." *The Celator* 7, no. 10 (October 1993): 32-4.
Presents a census of the known overstruck bronze coins of Tigranes II. Discusses the reasons for overstriking and identifies some of the common undertypes.

5549 ———— "Some Ancient Copper Hoards of Tigranes II of Armenia." *The Centinel* (Journal of the Central States Numismatic Society) 42, no. 1 (spring 1994): 19-25. Illus., map.
Describes ten reverse types found on coins of Tigranes II. Catalogues forty-nine copper coins in the author's collection (forty-seven of Tigranes II, one of Artavasdes II, and one for which the ruler is unknown).

5550 ———— "Recent Chemical Studies on Ancient and Medieval Armenian Coins Using SEM-EDS." *The Centinel* (Journal of the Central States Numismatic Society) 43, no. 3 (fall 1995): 12-20. Illus.
The author discusses the value of scanning electron microscopy with energy dispersive X-ray spectrometry in determining the composition of coins. Focuses on medieval Armenian coins, but does provide the composition of a bronze coin of Tigranes II. Suggests such analysis may assist in attributing coins to specific mints.

5551 ———— "An Analysis of the Araratian Coin Auction." *The Celator* 10, no. 2 (February 1996): 30-2. Illus.
A review of the results from the sale of the Araratian collection of Armenian coins sold by Classical Numismatic Group in December 1995 (see Classical Numismatic Group "The Araratian Collection" above). The collection included coins struck in the area of Armenia from ca. 380 B.C. through the middle ages. The author highlights the prices realized for some of the most significant pieces. [Also see Saryan's "Analyzing" below, in which he discusses Part 2 of the sale].

5552 ———— "An Unpublished Silver Drachm Attributed to Artaxias III (A.D. 18-34) of Armenia." *American Journal of Numismatics* 2nd ser., 9 (1997): 7-16. Illus.
Saryan discusses an apparently unique silver coin bearing a portrait of the king wearing an Armenian tiara, and bearing an inscription referring to an unknown king, Artaxerxes. The design of the tiara differs from that on coins of Tigranes. The reverse bears the APT monogram of the mint city Artaxata. The coin was subjected to metallurgical tests and was deemed genuine. Saryan tentatively attributes the coin to King Artaxias III (Zeno), who ruled Armenia from A.D. 18-34. The coin was possibly struck in A.D. 32.

5553 ———— "Analyzing Armenian Coin Values." *The Celator* 12, no. 10 (October 1998): 37-9.
A review of the results from Part 2 of the sale of the Araratian collection of Armenian coins sold in June 1998 (see Classical Numismatic Group "The Araratian Collection" above). This part of the collection included 140 coins struck in the area of Armenia from ca. 380 B.C. through the middle ages. The author highlights the prices realized for some of the most significant pieces and suggests estimated values for several popular Armenian coin types and denominations. [Also see Saryan "An Analysis" above].

5554 ———— "An Unusual Cut Bronze Coin of Tigranes the Great of Armenia." *The Centinel* (Journal of the Central States Numismatic Society) 48, no. 1 (spring 2000): 15-9. Illus.
Discusses the practice of cutting coins in ancient times as a means of making change for transactions. Illustrates and describes a bronze coin of Tigranes II which has had a one-fourth portion cut off. Saryan suggests such cut Armenian coins are extremely rare.

5555 ———— "Armenian Coins from Bedoukian Collection on Display." *The Centinel* (Journal of the Central States Numismatic Society) 48, no. 4 (winter 2000): 21-3. Illus.
Reports that the collection of Armenian Coins and antiquities formed by Paul Z. Bedoukian is on display at the Armenian Library and Museum of America in Watertown, Massachusetts. Provides some biographical information on Bedoukian and discusses the formation of his collection.

5556 ———— "Counterfeit Ancient Armenian Coins in Internet Auctions." *The Celator* 21, no. 1 (January 2007): 24, 26-7, 32. Illus.
Saryan discusses his experience buying Armenian coins via the internet. Most experiences were positive, but he describes incidents in which he encountered a counterfeit Tigranes II tetradrachm and a counterfeit Tigranes II copper coin, both on eBay.

5557 **Seyrig, Henri.** "Un Tétradrachme d'Artavazde I." *Revue Numismatique* (France) 6th ser., 6 (1964): 139-40. Illus.

5558 **Sullivan, Richard D.** "Diadochic Coinage in Commagene after Tigranes the Great." *Numismatic Chronicle* 7th ser., 13 (1973): 18-39. 1 pl. [CS 2886]
"The series showing Antiochus I of Commagene wearing a tiara similar to that on coins of Armenia in the first century B.C. was diadochic and formed a part of his general program of dynastic monuments, sculpture, and inscriptions. These proclaimed that the succession of Antiochus to the throne of his father Mithradates had been correct, preserving both the Iranian and the Seleucid lines of descent in Commagene, and entailing recognition by Romans, Armenians, Parthians, and Greeks. This precise coinage reflects concern with the dynastic succession and political independence that continued for over a century after Antiochus." [R. Sullivan, *NL* 92]

5559 **Tekin, Oguz.** "The Coins from Üçtepe with a Problematic Emission of Tigranes the Younger." *Epigraphica Anatolica* (Germany) 20 (1992): 43-54.
Twenty-three coins were found during excavations at Üçtepe mound in modern Armenia. The earliest are assigned to Tigranes the Younger. Describes these five Armenian coins, which are countermarked APK. Tekin finds no firm evidence that Tigranes I reigned as king of Armenia.

5560 **Thomas, Edward.** "Early Armenian Coins." *Numismatic Chronicle* new ser., 7 (1867): 141-56, 216-44; 8 (1868): 214-22, 284-304; 11 (1871): 202-26. Illus.

Discusses the early history of Armenia. Includes a list of early kings and a discussion of the Armenian alphabet. Examines a few important early coins. Discusses the inscriptions on the coins and the symbolism of the types.

5561 **Tiratsian, G. A.** "Armenian Portrait Art in the Coins of Tigranes II and Artavasdes II." *Armenian Numismatic Journal* 19, no. 2 (June 1993): 29-42.

5562 **Toros, Haji (Paul Carnig).** "Tigran's Crown." *SAN—Journal of the Society for Ancient Numismatics* 1, no. 1 (July 1969): 13-4.
The author compares the crown worn by the Hittite goddess Kubaba on a ca. 800 B.C. architectural relief slab to the crown worn by the Armenian king Tigranes the Great on his coins. Discusses the possible symbolic meaning of the crown's design. Suggests the resemblance was intentional and announced Tigranes' adoption of Anahit-Kubaba as his patron deity. [For a rebuttal to these theories and follow-up comments by the author, see *SAN* 1 no. 2 (October 1969): 16, 32-3, and "Letters to the Editor" in *SAN* 1, no. 3 (January 1970): 36].

5563 ———— "Tigran's Hoax." *SAN—Journal of the Society for Ancient Numismatics* 1, no. 2 (October 1969): 29-31.
Describes how the Tyche statue of Antioch was adopted by Tigranes of Armenia as a device on his coinage. Discusses the differences between Tyche and the goddess Cybel. Suggests that Tigranes intentionally blurred the distinction between Tyche and Cybel on his coinage in order to appeal to both his Greek and Armenian subjects.

5564 ———— "Tigran's Fantasy." *SAN—Journal of the Society for Ancient Numismatics* 1, no. 4 (April 1970): 68-9, 73. Illus.
A previously unknown variety of a tetradrachm of Tigranes is published and the author suggests an interpretation of the reverse type which shows a nude male (Tigranes?) seated in place of the usual Tyche, and a beheaded female figure swimming in place of the usual male representation of the river Orontes. The author suggests that Tigranes may have symbolized his taking control of Antioch through violent means. He is not sure of the authenticity of the coin.

5565 ———— "Tigran's Tetradrachms." *SAN—Journal of the Society for Ancient Numismatics* 2, no. 1 (July 1970): 17-8.
One hundred tetradrachms of Tigranes are examined and classified according to the symbols found on their reverses. They are grouped into nine classes and the author suggests mint identifications for some of the classes.

5566 ———— "Tigran's Crown in Commagene." *SAN—Journal of the Society for Ancient Numismatics* 7, no. 4 (summer 1976): 65-6.
The symbolism of the crown of Tigranes the Great is discussed. Coins of Marc Antony and Augustus with the crown as a symbol or type are pictured, demonstrating that this crown had become representative of Armenia. The sun symbolism of the crown is related to Mithraism, and a combined civil and religious authority is suggested. [Also see Nercessian "Comments" above for related comments].

5567 ———— "Tigran's Fantasy Enhanced." *Essays on Armenian Numismatics in Memory of Father Clement Sibilian on the Centennial of His Death.* Edited by Dickran Kouymjian and Y. T. Nercessian. *Armenian Numismatic Journal* 1st ser., 4 (1978): 125-8. Illus.
Discusses a recently discovered gold coin of Tigranes II on which the reverse depicts Tyche seated on a rock, holding the decapitated head of Orontes. The author speculates that this gold issue was the last that Tigranes struck while ruling both Syria and Armenia combined, and that this piece commemorated the death of Cleopatra Selene in the city of Seleucia, where the coin was minted. [From Y. T. Nercessian, *Armenian Numismatic Bibliography and Literature*]

5568 **Vardanyan, Ruben E.** "A Dated Copper Coin of Artaxias II: Evidence on the Use of the Pompeyan Era in Artaxata." *Armenian Numismatic Journal* 27, no. 4 (December 2001): 89-94. 1 pl.

Also see: Babelon *Catalogue des Monnaies* under SYRIA—SELEUCID KINGDOM; Howorth "Early Parthian and Armenian Coins" under PARTHIA; Howorth "Some Notes" under PARTHIA; Jidejian *Eddé Collection* under PORTRAITS; Klimowsky *On Ancient Palestinian* under PALESTINE—JUDEA; Newell *Some Unpublished Coins* under ASIA—GENERAL WORKS; "Positive ID" under PERSIA; Saryon "Fake Ancient Coins" under COUNTERFEITS; Saryan "Sarnakounk Hoard" under HOARDS; Sayles "Antioch's Statue of Fortune" under TYPES; Seyrig "Trésor Monétaires de Nisibe" under HOARDS; Sullivan "Royal Coins" under TYPES; von Petrowicz *Arsaciden-Münzen* under PARTHIA.

PHOENICIA

The Phoenician coins of greatest appeal to collectors were issued in the fifth and fourth centuries B.C., when the cities paid allegiance to the Persian Empire. They are thick silver pieces with a pronounced oriental look about them. Nearly all feature a galley, a warship, to remind everyone of Phoenician sea-power.

—John Anthony, 1983

5569   **Basch, Lucien.** "Phoenician Oared Ships." Parts 1-2. *Mariner's Mirror* 55, no. 2 (1969): 139-82; no. 3 (1969): 227-32. Illus.
"The coins of the Phoenician cities are used as evidence; they are compared with archaeological material, such as boat models, and with Assyrian and Greek iconography." [P. Naster, *NL* 84]

5570   **Betlyon, John W.** "A New Chronology for the Pre-Alexandrine Coinage of Sidon." *Museum Notes* 21 (1976): 11-35. 3 pls. [CS 2904]
Recently discovered inscriptions naming four previously unknown Sidonian kings provide information leading the author to propose a revised chronology for the pre-Alexander coinage of Sidon. He traces the development of Sidonian coin types.

5571   ——— *The Coinage and Mints of Phoenicia: the Pre-Alexandrine Period.* Harvard Semitic Monographs 26. Chico, California: Scholars Press, 1980. 172 pp. including 10 pls. [CS 2895a]
A revised version of a doctoral dissertation, Harvard University, 1978. Examines the early coinage of Sidon, Tyre, Aradus, and Byblos up to ca. 332 B.C. Arranges the coins in chronological order by mint. Types are described and interpreted. The author discusses the historical background and the inscriptions on each type. Includes a bibliography. [Reviewed by M. J. Price in *Israel Numismatic Journal* 9 (1987): 92-3].

5572   **Boneschi, Paulo.** "Three Coins of Judaea and Phoenicia." *Journal of the American Oriental Society* 62 (1942): 262-6. Illus.
Publishes three coins: (1) A shekel of Judea which the author attributes to Simon Maccabaeus (142-134 B.C.). Discusses the reasons for this attribution. (2) A small bronze of the Roman Procurators of Judea (A.D. 6-59). (3) A silver drachm of Aradus bearing on the obverse a bee, with NP to left and BC to right (reverse, stag). Suggests the Greek letters on the obverse produce a date of issue according to the two eras of Aradus and of the Seleucidae. The letters NP indicate the year 150 of the Aradus era which began in 259 B.C., giving a date of 109 B.C. The letters BC indicate the year 202 of the Seleucid era which began 312/1 B.C., giving a date of 110/109 B.C.

5573   **de Callataÿ, François.** "Les Tétradrachmes Hellénistiques de Tripolis." *Quaderni Ticinesi: Numismatica e Antichità Classiche* (Switzerland) 22 (1993): 111-26.

5574   **de Luynes, LeDuc.** *Essai sur la Numismatique des Satrapies de la Phénicie.* Paris: Didot Frères, 1846. 100 pp.

5575   ——— "Coins of Abdemon, Pharnabazus, Syphax, and of Alexander Bala." *Numismatic Chronicle* 14 (1852): 8-20.
Describes numerous scarce coins of Phoenician kings.

5576   **Duyrat, Frédérique.** "Les Ateliers Monétaires de Phénicie du Nord à l'Époque Hellénistique." *Les Monnayages Syriens. Quel Apport Pour l'Historie du Proche-Orient Hellénistique et Romaint? Actes de la Table Ronde de Damas, 10-12 November 1999.* Bibliothèque Archéologique et Historique 162. Edited by Chr. Augé and Frédérique Duyrat. Beyrouth: Institut Française du Proche-Orient, 2002.

5577   ——— "La Politique Monétaire d'Arados: les Alexandres (IVe-IIe Siècles avant Notre Ère)." *ΤΟΠΟΙ* Supplement 4 (2003): 25-48.
"A study of the tetradrachms struck by Aradus with the types of Alexander the Great. Their production is linked to the needs of international trade and periods of war." [Oliver D. Hoover, *NL* 148]

5578   ——— *Arados Hellénistique: Etude Historique et Monétaire.* Bibliothèque Archéologique et Historique 173. Beirut: Institut Français du Proche-Orient, 2005. 442 pp., 50 pls.
[An extensive review article by Ziad Sawaya appears in *Numismatic Chronicle* 166 (2006): 439-71. In French].

5579   **Elayi, Alain G., Jean-Noël Barrandon, and Josette Elayi.** "The Devaluation of Sidonian Silver Coinage in 365 B.C.E. and the First Bronze Issues." *American Journal of Numismatics* 2nd ser., 19 (2007): 1-8. 3 pls.
The authors utilized Fast Neutron Activation Analysis to determining the metallic composition of Sidonian coinage. Their goal was to study the devaluation of the silver coinage ordered by king 'Abd'astart I of Sidon in 365 B.C. and to determine if the composition of the coinage changed during the period of

Persian domination. They relate the changes in composition to the political and military events surrounding the city. The results of the metallurgical analysis are summarized in tables.

5580 ———. "The Change of Standard of Tyrian Silver Coinage in about 357 B.C. as Determined by Fast Neutron Activation Analysis." *Numismatic Chronicle* 168 (2008): 15-20. 3 pls.

An examination of the metallic composition of Tyrian silver coins. Tyre changed its weight standard in about 357 B.C. The authors investigate the reasons for this change by determining the composition of Tyrian coins and its evolution during the Persian domination of the city. Thirty-nine coins were examined.

5580a Elayi, Josette. "Le Monnayage de Byblos avant Alexandre: Probémes et Perspectives." *Transeuphratène* (France) 1 (1989): 9-20.

5581 ———. "Le Phenomene Monetaire dans les Cites Pheniciennes e l'Epoque Perse." *Numismatique et Histoire Économique Phéniciennes et Puniques. Actes du Colloque tenu à Louvaine-la-Neuve 13-16 Mai 1987.* Studia Phoenicia IX, Numismatica Lovaniensia 58. Edited by Tony Hackens and Ghislane Moucharte. Louvain-la-Neuve, 1992. Pages 21-31.

5581a ———. "Les Sicles de Tyr au Dauphin." *Ticinesi: Numismatica e Antichità Classiche* (Switzerland) 21 (1992): 37-49.

5582 ———. "Gerashtart, King of the Phoenician City of Arwad in the 4th Cent. B.C." *Numismatic Chronicle* 167 (2007): 99-104. 1 pl.

Arwad was one of the five Phoenician cities known in the Persian period. Two kings of Arwad are known. The author investigates what is known about the reign of the king Gerashtart. His coins and a few passages in classical writings are the only sources of information on this king. Elayi concludes the king ascended the throne in 339 B.C. and reigned for at least seven years.

5582a ———. "An Updated Chronology of the Reigns of Phoenician Kings during the Persian Period (539-333 B.C.)." *Transeuphratene* (France) 34 (2007): 11-43.

5583 Elayi, Josette, and Alain G. Elayi. "The Aradian Pataecus." *Museum Notes* 31 (1986): 1-5. Illus.

Examines the figurehead depicted standing on the prow of the war galley on the pre-Alexandrine silver coinage of Aradus. Numismatists have disagreed over its identification, but some have identified the figure as that of the Pataecus, described by Herodotus as being similar to the Greek Hephaestus. These were depicted as dwarfs and were carried on the prows of Phoenician ships. The authors suggest the figure depicted on the coins is a mythical animal rather than a man or dwarf, but conclude that the figure is a Pataecus. The appearance of Pataeci differed at various Phoenician cities.

5584 ———. "Abbreviations and Numbers on Phoenician Pre-Alexandrine Coinage: the Sidonian Example." *Quaderni Ticinesi: Numismatica e Antichità Classiche* (Switzerland) 17 (1988): 27-36.

5584a ———. "Systems of Abbreviations Used by Byblos, Tyre and Arwad in their Pre-Alexandrine Coinages." *Jahrbuch für Numismatik und Geldsseschichte* (Germany) 37-38 (1987-88): 11-22. 2 pls.

5585 ———. "The First Coinage of Sidon with a Galley Bearing the So-Called Triangular Sail." *American Journal of Numismatics* 2nd ser., 3-4 (1991-92): 1-9. 2 pls.

Examines the small silver denominations of Sidon without inscriptions, bearing a war galley with what had been identified as a triangular sail. The authors suggest these were the first Sidonian coins, beginning ca. 440 B.C. Presents a complete catalogue of this series. After comparison with Assyrian reliefs, they conclude this is not a triangular sail. Rather, the triangular lines represent brails, fastened to the mast in several places. Emphasizes the types selected for Sidon's first coins were all military symbols expressing the power of the city.

5586 ———. *Trésors de Monnaies Pheniciennes et Circulation Monetaire V^e – IVe Siècles avant J.-C.* Supplement No. 1 À Transeuphraténe. Paris: Gabalda, 1993. 445 pp., 37 pls.

Discusses seventy-five hoards of Phoenician coins.

5586a ———. "Une Série de Petits Bronzes d'Alexandre frappes Tyr." *Revue Numismatique* (France) 153 (1998): 107-17. 2 pls.

The authors present a new series of small bronze coins of Alexander and propose to attribute them to the mint of Tyre. These coins (average weight 0.62 gm) have the types *obv.*, head of Herakles, and *rev.*, bow in bow-case. This series is dated to Alexander's lifetime, after Tyre's surrender (ca. 333-323).

5587 ———. "La Divinité Marine des Monnaies Préalexandrines d'Arwad." *Transeuphratène* (France) 21 (2001): 133-48.

Explores the identity of the marine deity on the pre-Alexander coinage of Arados.

5588 ———. *Le Monnayage de la Cité Phénicienne de Sidon à l'Epoque Perse (V^e-IVe s. av. J.-C.).* Supplément No. 11 à Transeuphratène. Paris: Gabalda, 2004. 2 volumes. 855 pp., 77 pls.

A catalogue of 2608 coins from the Persian period (fifth and fourth centuries B.C.). Examines the epigraphic, iconographic, technical, metrological, and historical aspects of the coinage. [Reviewed by Oliver Hoover in *American Numismatic Society Magazine* 5, no. 1 (spring 2006): 78-82].

5589 ———. "Le Monnayage Sidonien de Mazday." *Transeuphratène* (France) 27 (2004): 155-62.

The Sidonian coinage of the Persian satrap Mazday.

5590 ———. *The Coinage of the Phoenician City of Tyre in the Persian Period (5th to 4th Century BCE).* Orientalia Lovaniensia Analecta 188. Studia Phoenicia 20. Leuven: Peeters Publishers, 2009. 518 pp., 51 pls.

A corpus of Tyrian coinage in the Persian period (fifth to fourth centuries B.C.), containing a chronological catalogue of 1814 silver and bronze coins. Includes discussion of monetary production, volume of emissions, manufacturing techniques and processes, monetary inscriptions, and iconography. The authors use their own statistical method to process the data, reaching many interesting metrological conclusions. The Tyrian workshop was innovative— around 388 B.C. it inaugurated a yearly dating system. Also incorporates important historical information on Tyre and the Persians' western policy, based on the results of numismatic analysis, combined with all the other sources. In particular, the city's significant difficulties in the first part of the fourth century and its prosperity during the reign of King Ozmilk (347-333/2), in stark contrast to the decay of Sidon at that time.

5591 ——— "A Series of Coins from Byblos with the Names of the City (4th Cent. B.C.)." *Numismatic Chronicle* 170 (2010): 3-8. Illus.
A catalogue of fifteen specimens of a series of small silver coins of Byblos featuring the name of the city. The authors suggest the coins were struck ca. 336-333 B.C.

5592 **Elayi, Josette, Alain G. Elayi, and R. Bour.** "A New Variety of an Aradian Series and the Representation of Turtles on Aradian Coins." *Transeuphratène* (France) 33 (2007): 11-22.

5592a **Gitler, Haim, and Alla Kushnir-Stein.** "A Late Hellenistic Anonymous (?) Coin from Southern Phoenicia." *Revue Suisse de Numismatique* (Switzerland) 88 (2009): 169-72.

5593 **Goldstein, Paul.** "Concerning the Meaning of Control Marks and Symbols of Power on the Shekels of Tyre." *The Celator* 24, no. 1 (January 2010): 16-30, 35. Illus.
Begins with a comparison the Proto-Canaanite, Phoenician, Greek, and Hebrew alphabets. Then Goldstein describes the symbols or Phoenician/Hebrew letters found on the reverse of the shekels of Tyre (below the eagle's legs). Describes the meaning of those letters in Phoenician culture. Also lists the Greek letters or symbols which appear. It remains controversial which letters were used on the coins—some researchers believe some characters are merely variations of a limited number of letters. Explores the possible meanings of the letters or symbols.

5594 **Gubel, Eric.** "La Glyptique et la Genese de l'Iconographie Monetaire Phenicienne." *Numismatique et Histoire Économique Phéniciennes et Puniques. Actes du Colloque tenu à Louvaine-la-Neuve 13-16 Mai 1987.* Studia Phoenicia IX, Numismatica Lovaniensia 58. Edited by Tony Hackens and Ghislane Moucharte. Louvain-la-Neuve, 1992. Pages 1-11.

5595 **Hackens, Tony, and Ghislane Moucharte, eds.** *Numismatique et Histoire Économique Phéniciennes et Puniques. Actes du Colloque tenu à Louvaine-la-Neuve 13-16 Mai 1987.* Studia Phoenicia IX, Numismatica Lovaniensia 58. Louvain-la-Neuve, 1992. 341 pp., 43 pls.
Includes fifteen essays on monetary history and eleven on economic history. Those related to ancient Greek coinage are: "Contributions la Definition des Domaines Monetaires Numides et Mauretaniens" by J. Alexandropoulos [6770], "Le Phenomene Monetaire dans les Cites Pheniciennes e l'Epoque Perse" by J. Elayi [5581], "La Glyptique et la Genese de l'Iconographie Monetaire Phenicienne" by E. Gubel [5594], "Graffiti Monetaires Ouest-Semitiques" by A. Lemaire and J. Elayi [5612], "Per la Cronologia delle Emissioni a Leggenda Libyen" by G. Manganaro [6751], "Monnayages Puniques en Sicile au Cours de la Deuxieme Guerre Punique" by P. Marchetti [3103], "The Philisto-Arabian Coins—A Preview. Preliminary Studies of the Local Coinage in the Fifth Persian Satrapy (Part 3)" by L. Mildenberg [5892], "Tresors de Monnaies de Byblos du IVe s. av. J.-C. Trouves e Byblos" by P. Naster [5625], "Les Series de Monnaies Puniques du Musee Numismatique d'Athenes" by M. Oeconomides [5628], "Oiseaux et Poissons dans l'Art du Proche-Orient Ancien et sur les Monnaies Grecques de la Propontide et du Pont-Euxin" by M. Trokay [4523], "Les Monnaies Hispano-Carthaginoises du Systeme Attique" by L. Villaronga [6733], and "Carthaginian Bronze Coinage in Sardinia" by P. Visonà [3110].

5596 **Hendin, David.** "Ituraean Kings of the North." *The Celator* 20, no. 1 (January 2006): 42-3. Illus.
The Ituraeans were a nomadic tribe from the Arabian Peninsula, and they played a small role in the history of Lebanon. Hendin discusses and illustrates a scarce series of coins struck by Ituraean rulers between 73 and 25 BC.

5597 ——— "More on the Tyre Shekels." *The Celator* 19, no. 9 (September 2005): 40-1. Illus.
Discusses the shekels of Tyre which were minted to pay the Jewish temple tax. Reviews the controversy whether those bearing the letters KAP or KP were minted at Jerusalem.

5598 **Herman, Daniel.** "The Coins of the Itureans." *Israel Numismatic Journal* (Israel) 1 (2006): 51-71.
The Itureans, who formed a tetrarchy in Lebanon during the first century B.C.E., minted coins during the reign of Ptolemy Son of Mennaios (85–40 B.C.E.), Lysanias (40–36 B.C.E.), and Zenodorus (30–20 B.C.E.). Many Iturean coins have come to light in recent years, mostly from auctions and private collections. This article presents and analyzes all the known Iturean coin types and their variants, and excludes a number of erroneous ascriptions. [Herman's abstract. Also see Kindler "On the Coins of the Itureans" below].

5599 **Hersh, Charles.** "*Tyrus Rediviva* Reconsidered." *American Journal of Numismatics* 2nd ser., 10 (1998): 41-59. 4 pls.
Mentions some of the errors made by Newell in his *Tyrus Rediviva* (see Newell below). Mentions the recently discovered "Phoenicia Hoard" (see Hersh "The Phoenicia 1997 Hoard" under MACEDONIAN KINGDOM) which contained some significant Tyrian tetradrachms. Presents revisions and a re-ordering of the issues of the mint of Tyre under Demetrius Poliorcetes. New issue numbers have been assigned to more closely indicate the sequence of emission. Discusses the arrangement of the issues and the chronology of the Tyre mint under Demetrius Poliorcetes.

5600 **Hill, George F.** "Notes on the Alexandrine Coinage of Phoenicia." *Nomisma* 4 (1909): 1-15.

5601 ——— *Catalogue of Greek Coins of Phoenicia.* London: British Museum, 1910. Reprint, Bologna: Forni, 1965. clii, 361 pp., 45 pls., map. [CS 2896]
Volume 26 of the *Catalogue of Greek Coins in the British Museum.* The 361-page catalogue of coins is preceded by 152 pages of introductory text. [Also see *Catalogue of Greek Coins in the British Museum* under PUBLIC COLLECTIONS—GREAT BRITAIN (LONDON). Also see Kool "Rediscovery" under PALESTINE—JUDEA].

5602 ——— "Some Graeco-Phoenician Shrines." *Journal of Hellenic Studies* 31 (1911): 56-64. 2 pls.
"Discusses a variety of Phoenician coins representing Greek or local deities, their shrines and their symbols." [J. R. Jones, *NIJHS*]

5603 ——— "The Anonymous Shekels of Tyre." *Numismatic Chronicle* 5th ser., 17 (1937): 143-4.
A correction to the author's recent paper in the *Quarterly of the Department of Antiquities of Palestine* in which he stated the autonomous shekel-series of Tyre came to an end in A.D. 65/6. He now states that the series ended in 69/70.

5604 **Horvitz, Peter S.** "A Jewish Isolde in Chalcis." *The Celator* 10, no. 8 (August 1996): 38-9. Illus. Previously appeared in *The Shekel*.
Briefly discusses the bronze coinage issued by Ptolemy, son of Mennaeus (85-40 B.C.) and his son Lysanias in the kingdom of Chalcis (in present-day Lebanon). Ptolemy's wife, Queen Alexandra, was a Maccabee and a sister of Mattathias Antigonus. The author relates the queen's life to that of the Arthurian story of Tristam and Isolde. Three coins are illustrated.

5605 **Janis, Edward.** "The Numismatics of Akko." *The Shekel* 23, no. 6 (November-December 1990): 29-34. Illus.
A summary of coins minted in or related to the city of Akko (Ake, Ptolemais) from the ancient through the modern period.

5606 **Kindler, Arie.** "The Mint at Tyre as the Major Source of Silver in Ancient Palestine." *Eretz Israel* (Israel) 8 (1967): 318-24. Illus.

5607 ——— "On the Coins of the Itureans." *Proceedings of the 11th International Numismatic Congress, September 8-13, 1991. Volume 1.* Edited by T. Hackens et al. Louvain-la-Neuve, Belgium: International Association of Professional Numismatists, 1993. Pages 283-8. Illus.
The Itureans were a nomadic tribe. Kindler lists the Iturean coins in the Kadman Numismatic Museum, Tel-Aviv, and discusses this complex coinage. [Also see Herman "The Coins of the Itureans" above].

5608 **Kindler, Arie, ed.** *The Patterns of Monetary Development in Phoenicia and Palestine in Antiquity: International Numismatic Convention, Jerusalem, 27-31 December 1963.* Tel-Aviv and Jerusalem: Schocken Publishing House, 1967. 326 pp., 22 pls.
Contains the text of the papers (twenty in English, one in French) presented at the convention of the International Numismatic Commission. The papers dealing with pre-Roman period coinage are: "Le Developpement des Monnayages Phéniciens avant Alexandre d'Après les Trésors" by P. Naster [5624], "The Monetary Forerunners of Coinage in Phoenicia and Palestine" by M. Balmuth [372], "The Monetary Systems in the Early Hellenistic Time, with Special Regard to the Economic Policy of the Ptolemaic Kings" by G. K. Jenkins [278], "The Monetary System of the Seleucid Kings until 129 B.C." by O. Mørkholm [5391], "The Monetary Pattern and Function of the Jewish Coins" by A. Kindler [5747], "Denominations in Jewish Coinage" by B. Oestreicher [5815], "The Monetary Development of Palestine in the Light of Coin Hoards" by L. Kadman [5734]. Also includes "Eulogy at the Halting of the Cortege before the Kadman Numismatic Museum" by E. W. Klimowsky (Leo Kadman died during the convention).

5609 **Krishnamurthy, R.** "Coins from Phoenicia Found at Karur, Tamilnadu." *Studies on South Indian Coins* (India) 4 (1994): 19-27. Illus.
"The author publishes four copper coins of four city-states of Phoenicia, which were recovered from the Amaravathi river at Karur in Tiruchirapalli district of Tamilnadu. The coins belong to the second and first centuries B.C." [A. Jha, *NL* 136]

5610 **Kromann, Anne.** "Greek and Phoenician Letters on Aradian Tetradrachms." *Studies in Ancient History and Numismatics Presented to Rudi Thomson.* Edited by Aksel Damsgaard-Madsen, Erik Christiansen, and Erik Hallager. Denmark: Aarhus University, 1988. Pages 104-13. Illus.
The authors examine the significance of the Phoenician and Greek letters appearing on tetradrachms of Aradus, 138-43 B.C. These may be officinae marks, months, abbreviated names, a dating system, or serial numbers. Presents a catalogue of seventy-seven coins and a table summarizing the letters used on the coins. Draws no conclusion as to their meaning.

5611 **Lambert, C.** "A Hoard of Phoenician Coins." *Quarterly of the Department of Antiquities in Palestine* 1, no. 1 (1931): 10-20. 1 pl.
A hoard of 109 Phoenician coins was found at Tall Abu Hawwam, near Haifa in 1930. All the coins have the same types and belong to a series attributed to Tyre: *obv.*, winged sea-horse over waves; *rev.*, eagle-owl with crook and flail. Lambert suggests some of the coins were minted at Tyre and some may have been minted at Acre. Concludes with a catalogue of the coins.

5612 **Lemaire, André, and Josette Elayi.** "Graffiti Monetaires Ouest-Semitiques." *Numismatique et Histoire Économiques Phéniciennes et Puniques. Actes du Colloque tenu à Louvaine-la-Neuve 13-16 Mai 1987.* Studia Phoenicia IX, Numismatica Lovaniensia 58. Edited by Tony Hackens and Ghislane Moucharte. Louvain-la-Neuve, 1992. Pages 59-76.

5613 **Levy, Brooks.** "Tyrian Shekels and the First Jewish War." *Proceedings of the 11th International Numismatic Congress, September 8-13, 1991. Volume 1.* Edited by T. Hackens et al. Louvain-la-Neuve, Belgium: International Association of Professional Numismatists, 1993. Pages 267-74. Illus.
Examines the evidence for and against Meshorer's proposal (in his *Ancient Jewish Coinage, Volume 2*) that the minting of Tyrian shekels was transferred in 18/17 B.C. to Jerusalem, where it continued until it was replaced by the shekel of Israel in A.D. 66 at the start of the Jewish War. Levy casts doubt on Meshorer's proposal and he believes it remains unproven.

5614 ——— "Tyrian Shekels: the Myth of the Jerusalem Mint." *SAN—Journal of the Society for Ancient Numismatics* 19, no. 2 (1995): 33-5. Illus.
The author examines the shekels and half-shekels of Tyre bearing the monogram KP which have been attributed to the mint of Jerusalem. Describes the importance of these high-purity silver coins for paying Temple dues in Jerusalem. Mentions Meshorer's theory that the Tyrian coins continued to be minted specifically for use at the Temple at a time when most other local coinage had been debased. However, Meshorer also suggested that the shekels were actually struck at Jerusalem beginning in 18/17 B.C. Levy reviews Meshorer's arguments, but suggests they are flawed. Levy argues against a Jerusalem mint, and attributes the coins to Tyre. He does suggest that some imitations of the Tyrian shekels, made of good silver, were unofficially produced in Jerusalem to supplement the reduced supply of pure coins coming out of Tyre after the Romans reduced Tyre's silver supply.

5615 ——— "The Autonomous Silver of Sidon (107/106 B.C.–A.D. 43/44)." *XII Internationaler Numismatischer Kongress Berlin 1997. Akten I.* Edited by B. Kluge and B. Weisser. Berlin, 2000. Pages 324-32.

5616 **Magness, J.** "Two Notes on the Archaeology of Qumran." *Bulletin of the American Schools of Oriental Research* 312 (November 1998): 41-4.
"This is an attempt to connect Tyrian coins from the second century B.C. to the first century A.D. found in Qumran (only partially published to date) with the Temple Tax due from every adult male Jew." [A. Spaer, *NL* 143]

5617 **Markoe, Glenn E.** "Phoenician Coinage." *Peoples of the Past: Phoenicians.* Berkeley and Los Angeles: University of California Press, 2000. Pages 98-101, 105-7. 2 pls.
An overview of Phoenician coinage. Discusses the adoption of coinage ca. 450 B.C. by the cities on the Phoenician coast, partly as an expression of their autonomy. Examines their choices of coin types and discusses the economic role of coinage in the region. Discusses the development of coinage in the western Phoenician cities—at Carthage and in Sicily. Describes the coin types and denominations.

5618 **Meir, Cecilia.** "Tyrian Sheqels and Half Sheqels with Unpublished Dates from the 'Isifya Hoard in the Kadman Numismatic Pavillion." *Israel Numismatic Research* (Israel) 3 (2008): 117-24.
The history of the 'Isfiya hoard consisting primarily of sheqels and half-sheqels of the autonomous coinage of Tyre is summarized. Ten unrecorded dates deriving from the Kadman Numismatic Pavilion holdings of the hoard are presented.

5619 **Meshorer, Ya'akov.** "One Hundred Ninety Years of Tyrian Shekels." *Studies in Honour of Leo Mildenberg: Numismatics, Art History, Archaeology.* Edited by A. Houghton et al. Wetteren: Editions NR, 1984. Pages 171-9. Illus.
The "shekels of Tyre" replaced the Seleucid coinage at Tyre beginning in 126 B.C. Meshorer begins with a discussion of other silver coins which circulated contemporaneously with the Tyrian shekels. Reviews the reign of King Herod at Jerusalem and notes the apparent lack of a silver or gold coinage during his reign despite Jerusalem's great economic power. This leads to a re-consideration of the mint of the Tyrian shekels. Discusses the stylistic differences between the earlier issues (large concave flans, well engraved dies) and the later issues (small flat flans, poorly engraved dies). Divides the coinage into two groups: those without the letters KP (struck 126-19 B.C.) and those with the letters or monogram (struck 18 B.C. - A.D. 66).

Reviews the issues of the nearby cities Antioch, Sidon, Aradus, Ascalon, and Caesarea in Cappadocia, and shows that these cities stopped striking autonomous silver coins no later than the reign of Augustus. Roman Provincial issues followed. Why, then, did Tyre apparently continue striking an autonomous coinage? Religious laws required every male to pay an annual tribute of a half-shekel to the Temple at Jerusalem, and the payment was to be made in pure silver. The author proposes that the late "Tyrian" shekels (after A.D. 54) were struck by the Temple authorities in Jerusalem to facilitate the tribute payments (the Roman Provincial coinage that was available in the area at that time was debased). Summarizes the hoard evidence. Publishes a Seleucid didrachm of Antiochus VII bearing a countermark—probably indicating the approval of Temple authorities to use it as if it were a Tyrian shekel.

5620 ——— "The Coins of the Mint of Dora." *Excavations at Dor, Final Report Volume 1A Qedem Reports.* Jerusalem, 1995. Pages 355-65. 3 pls.
An illustrated catalogue of the coins of Dora from the Hellenistic and Roman periods. It was reprinted with minor changes and additions from *Israel Numismatic Journal* 9 (1986-87): 59-72. Dora is on the coast about 30 km south of Haifa.

5621 **Mildenberg, Leo.** "Baana: Preliminary Studies of the Local Coinage in the Fifth Persian Satrapy, Part 2." *Eretz-Israel* (M. Avi-Yonah Memorial Volume) 19 (1987): 28-35. Reprinted in *Leo Mildenberg. Vestigia Leonis: Studien zur Antiken Numismatik Israels, Palästinas und der Östlichen Mittelmeerweit.* Novum Testamentum et Orbis Antiquus 36. Edited by U. Hübner and E. Knauf. Freiburg: Universitätsverlag, and Göttingen: Vandenhoeck & Ruprecht, 1998. Pages 35-42.
Discusses coinage policy in the fifth satrapy (the provinces west of the Euphrates river). Examines the b 'n' (Baana) series, an enigmatic group of silver staters with *obv.*, Melqart struggling with a lion; *rev.*, cow. Mildenberg states that Baana is the name of a person, and the coins likely date to the late fifth century B.C. Discusses the "Eshmun" inscription which names Baana as king of the Sidonians. Mildenberg accepts that the coins were minted by this king and thus the inscription establishes a new Sidonian dynasty. He suggests the coins were struck for a special purpose, apart from the Sidonian city coinage. [Also see Hübner and Knauf *Vestigia Leonis* under GENERAL WORKS—GREEK].

5622 **Milne, John G.** "The Coinage of Aradus in the Hellenistic Period." *Iraq* (England) 5, pt. 1 (spring 1938): 12-21.
Milne examines the letters on the reverses of the silver coins struck at Aradus in the last two centuries B.C. in an attempt to learn more about the organization of this and neighboring mints. Suggests possible interpretations for these control marks.

5623 **Naster, Paul.** "La Technique des Revers Partiellement Incus de Monnaies Phéniciennes." *Centennial Publication of the American Numismatic Society.* Edited by Harald Ingholt. New York: American Numismatic Society, 1958. Pages 503-11. 1 pl. [CS 3373]
Examines the incuse design on the reverse of the coins of Arados, Byblos, Sidon, and Tyre.

5624 ——— "Le Developpement des Monnayages Phéniciens avant Alexandre d'Après les Trésors." *The Patterns of Monetary Development in Phoenicia and Palestine in Antiquity: International Numismatic Convention, Jerusalem, 27-31 December 1963.* Edited by A. Kindler. Tel-Aviv and Jerusalem, 1967. Pages 3-24. [CS 2897]
In French with an English summary. Discusses the coinage circulating in Phoenicia prior to the time of Alexander the Great. At least four cities were issuing coins: Byblos, Aradus, Tyre, and Sidon. Naster summarizes the hoard evidence related to the coin circulation in the area.

5625 ——— "Tresors de Monnaies de Byblos du IVe s. av. J.-C. Trouves e Byblos." *Numismatique et Histoire Économique Phéniciennes et Puniques. Actes du Colloque tenu à Louvaine-la-Neuve 13-16 Mai 1987.* Studia Phoenicia IX, Numismatica Lovaniensia 58. Edited by Tony Hackens and Ghislane Moucharte. Louvain-la-Neuve, 1992. Pages 41-9.

5626 **Newell, Edward T.** *Tyrus Rediviva.* New York: American Numismatic Society, 1923. Reprinted, Rockville Center: Sanford J. Durst, 2008. 23 pp., 3 pls.
Presents a catalogue of the coinage struck at the mint of Tyre, beginning with the Alexandrine coinage under Antigonus and Demetrius (ca. 306 B.C.) through the first issues of Tyre under Ptolemaic rule (after ca. 186 B.C.). Includes thirty-three varieties of staters, tetradrachms, and drachms arranged in die sequences. Newell discusses the coins, related hoard evidence, and chronology. [Also see Hersh "*Tyrus Rediviva* Reconsidered" above, Merker "Demetrios Poliorcetes and Tyre" under MACEDONIAN KINGDOM, and Spaer "A Hoard of Alexander Tetradrachms from Galilee" under MACEDONIAN KINGDOM].

5627 **Nicorescu, Paul.** "Two Gold Coins of Tyras." *Transactions of the International Numismatic Congress Organized and Held in London by the Royal Numismatic Society, June 30-July 3, 1936.* Edited by J. Allan, H. Mattingly, and E. S. G. Robinson. London: B. Quaritch, 1938. Pages 96-7. Illus.

Publishes two gold staters of Lysimachus bearing *obv.*, head of Alexander the Great, and *rev.*, Nike seated on a throne. Both coins are illustrated. One is in the British Museum and the other is in the collection of the Roumanian Academy. Both coins bear the TY mintmark, but exhibit different magistrates' monograms.

5628 **Oeconomides, Mando.** "Les Series de Monnaies Puniques du Musee Numismatique d'Athenes." *Numismatique et Histoire Économique Phéniciennes et Puniques. Actes du Colloque tenu à Louvaine-la-Neuve 13-16 Mai 1987.* Studia Phoenicia IX, Numismatica Lovaniensia 58. Edited by Tony Hackens and Ghislane Moucharte. Louvain-la-Neuve, 1992. Pages 88-92.

5629 **Plant, Richard.** "The Coins of Tyre and the Bible." *Numismatic Fine Arts Quarterly Journal, Publication* 28 (spring 1984): unpaged (2 pp.). Illus.
A brief discussion of the coinage of Tyre and the depiction of Melqart on Tyrian coinage.

5630 **Potts, Dan T.** "Pre-Alexandrine Phoenician Staters from Northeastern Arabia." *Arabian Archaeology and Epigraphy* (Denmark) 2, no. 1 (February 1991): 24-30.
Five Phoenician staters from northeastern Saudi Arabia, four of them previously unpublished, are presented and discussed (*obv.*, male head; *rev.*, war galley). The potential significance of Phoenician material in this region is briefly explored.

5631 **Rouvier, Jules.** "Numismatique des Villes de Phénicie." *Journal International d'Archéologie Numismatique* (Greece) 3 (1900): 125-68, 237-312; 4 (1901): 35-66, 125-52, 193-232; 5 (1902): 99-134, 229-84; 6 (1903): 17-46, 269-332; 7 (1904): 65-108. 33 pls. [CS 2899]
Examines the coinage of Aradus, Botrys, Gebal-Byblus, Carne, Dora, Marathus, Orthosia, Ptolemais-Ace, Sidon, Tripolis, and Tyre.

5632 **Sawaya, Ziad.** "Les Monnaies Civiques Non Datées de Berytos: Reflet d'un Passage Discret de'Hegémonie Séleucidae à l'Autonomie (102/1-82/1 av. J.-C.)." *Numismatic Chronicle* 168 (2008): 61-109. 8 pls.

5633 ——— *Historie de Berytos et d'Heliopolis d'Apres leurs Monnaies 1er Siecle av. J.-C. – IIIe Siècle apr. J.-C.* Bibliotheque Archeologique et Historique, Tome 185. Beyrouth, 2009.

5634 **Seyrig, Henri.** "Le Monnayage de Ptolémais en Phénicie." *Revue Numismatique* (France) 6th ser., 4 (1962): 25-50. Illus. [CS 2903]

5635 **Six, Jean Pieter.** "Observations sur les Monnaies Phéniciennes." *Numismatic Chronicle* new ser., 17 (1877): 177-239.

5636 **Stern, Ephraim.** "The Dating of Stratum II at Tell Abu Hawan." *Israel Exploration Journal* (Israel) 18, no. 4 (1968): 213-9.
"On pp. 215-217, the dating of Tyrian didrachms of Attic standard (type of *BMC Phoenicia* Nos. 25-42) found in the Tell Abu Hawan hoard, and published by Lambert in *QDAP* Vol. 1 (1932) pp. 10-20, is discussed. On archaeological grounds, Cross' view [*BiblArch* 26 (1936) pp. 110-121] that these coins are not post-Alexander but date to the period 360-332 B.C. is supported." [A. Spaer, *NL* 84]

5637 **Syon, Danny.** *Tyre and Gamla. A Study in the Monetary Influence of Southern Phoenicia on Galilee and the Golan in the Hellenistic and Roman Periods.* Ph.D. dissertation. Jerusalem: Hebrew University, 2004.

5638 ——— "The Bronze Coinage of Tyre: The First Years of Autonomy." *American Journal of Numismatics* 2nd ser., 20 (2008): 295-304. 2 pls.
A study of the bronze coinage of Tyre, based on the coins found during excavations at Gamla, minted in the decades following the city's autonomy in 125 B.C. Coins of four different types are dated "year 1," and another type showing Melqart and a palm tree is dated from year 3 to 28. A checklist is provided for identifying and differentiating the coins of this civic type from similar Seleucid coins. Most of the bronze coins presented here are previously unpublished.

5639 **Tameanko, Marvin.** "Coins Reveal the Extensive Explorations of the Ancient Phoenicians." *The Celator* 6, no. 8 (August 1992): 34-40. Illus.
Reviews the history of the Phoenicians, including the cities of Sidon, Tyre, Carthage, and others, from very early times through the end of the Punic wars with Rome. Includes brief descriptions of Tyrian, Siculo-Punic, and Carthaginian coinage. Mentions a hoard of Carthaginian coins found in the Azores in 1778.

5640 **Thompson, H. O.** "A Tyrian Coin in Jordan." *Biblical Archaeologist* 50, no. 2 (June 1987): 101-4. Illus.
"The author discusses a Tyrian stater of type *BMC* 19-21, found during excavations at Khirbet al-Hijjar, southwest of Amman in Jordan." [A. Spaer, *NL* 199]

5641 **Trell, Bluma.** "The Coins of the Phoenician World—East and West." *Ancient Coins of the Graeco-Roman World: The Nickle Numismatic Papers.* Edited by Waldemar Heckel and Richard Sullivan. Waterloo, Ontario: Wilfrid Laurier University Press, 1984. Pages 117-39. 1 pl. (page 302).
The author compares Eastern and Western Phoenician/Punic coinages in order to identify, date, define, and explain the sacred symbols, conventions, and deities represented on them, and to show how coins can supplement other archaeological evidence. A comparison of coins shows a correspondence between Near Eastern and Western art, architecture, and religion, and the dependence of the West on the East. Among the many coin symbols cited are architectural elements, the winged sun-disk, thymaiaterion, the Caduceus, and the Tanit symbol.

5642 **Wacks, Mel.** "Dating the Shekel of Tyre." *Augur* (United States) 21 (1979): 81-2. Illus.
"How to transform dates from the Tyrian era (starting in 126 B.C.) to the Christian era." [M. Wacks, *NL* 106]

5643 ——— "One of the Most Important (But Often Overlooked) Ancient Biblical Coins." *The Shekel* 22, no. 5 (September-October 1989): 8-9. Illus.
Describes a double shekel of Byblos. Includes a brief history of the city.

5644 **Weil, Rudolf.** "The Phoenician Drachma with the Jahve-Inscription." *Spink Numismatic Circular* 18 (November 1910): 12385-8. Illus.
In this article translated from *Zeitschrift für Numismatik*, Weil discusses the early influence of the Greeks in Palestine and describes a Phoenician drachm bearing the inscription *Jahve* (Jehovah). [Also see A. W. Hands "Notes on a Phoenician Drachm" under PALESTINE—PHILISTIA].

5645 **Wheatley, Pat V.** "The Year 22 Tetradrachms of Sidon and the Date of the Battle of Gaza." *Zeitschrift für Papyrologie und Epigraphik* (Germany) 144 (2003): 268-76.
"The paper is based on an up-to-date catalogue of the year 22 (= 312/11 B.C.) silver from the Phoenician mint (Alexander type or Ptolemaic 'Satrapal' type: Alexander/Athena); Alexander type tetradrachms of years 21 and 23 are also catalogued." [Hans R. Baldus, *NL* 148]

5646 **Yarkon, Barry J.** "Fathers Day Gift: Shekel Inspires Research." *The Celator* 2, no. 10 (October 1988): 1, 21-2. Illus.
Reviews the history of the city of Tyre and discusses the silver shekels minted there. Suggests that the shekels produced after 19 B.C. may have been minted in Jerusalem.

Also see: American Numismatic Association *Selections* under GENERAL WORKS—GREEK; Babelon *Les Perses Achéménides* under PERSIA; Balmuth "Epigraphical Intimations of Early Coinage" and "Monetary Forerunners" under ORIGINS OF COINAGE; D. Baramki *The Coin Collection* under PUBLIC COLLECTIONS—LEBANON; Berrol "Hellenistic Influences" under PALESTINE—JUDEA; Brett "Seleucid Coins of Ake-Ptolemais" under SYRIA—SELEUCID KINGDOM; Butcher *Small Change in Ancient Beirut* under HOARDS; de Morgan *Manual de Numismatique Orientale* under GENERAL WORKS—GREEK; DeShazo "A New Die for Sidonian Chronology" under MACEDONIAN KINGDOM—GENERAL WORKS; Falkland "Notes on Coins Found in Cyprus" under HOARDS; Frenkel "The Sanctuary" under HOARDS; Giedroyc "Ancient Coins Associated with Dead Sea Scrolls" under HOARDS; Hendin "Coins of the Bible—Tyre Coins" under PALESTINE—JUDEA; Hoover *Handbook of Coins of the Southern Levant* under ASIA—GENERAL WORKS; Hoover "A Second Look at the Aradian Bronze Coinage" under SYRIA—SELEUCID KINGDOM; Hoover and Iossif "A Lead Tetradrachm of Tyre" under SYRIA—SELEUCID KINGDOM; Houghton "Aradus, not Marathus" under MACEDONIAN KINGDOM—GENERAL WORKS; Houghton and Lorber "Antiochus III" under SYRIA—SELEUCID KINGDOM; Jenkins "The Monetary Systems" under GENERAL WORKS—HELLENISTIC; Jidejian *Lebanon and the Greek World* under PORTRAITS; Kindler "Greco-Phoenician Coins" under PALESTINE—JUDEA; Klimowsky *On Ancient Palestinian* under PALESTINE—JUDEA; Kraay and Moorey "Two Fifth Century Hoards" under HOARDS; Kool "Rediscovery" under PUBLIC COLLECTIONS—GREAT BRITAIN (LONDON).

Lambert "Egypto-Arabian" under HOARDS; Lang "On Coins Discovered" under HOARDS; LeRider "La Politique Monétaire des Séleucides en Coelé Syrie et en Phénicie" under SYRIA—SELEUCID KINGDOM; Lorber "Commerce ('Demetrius I' Hoard) 2003" under HOARDS; Lorber "The Last Ptolemaic Bronze Emission of Tyre" under EGYPT—PTOLEMAIC KINGDOM; Lorber "Ptolemaic Bronze Coinage of Tyre" under EGYPT—PTOLEMAIC KINGDOM; Lorber and Vagi "Ptolemaic Mint of Tyre" under EGYPT—PTOLEMAIC KINGDOM; Meadows "Beth Ummar, Israel" under HOARDS; Merker "Notes on Abdalanymos" under MACEDONIAN KINGDOM—GENERAL WORKS; Meshorer "Coins from Areas A and C" under HOARDS; Mildenberg "Notes on the Coin Issues of Mazday" under PERSIA; Mildenberg "Philisto-Arabian Coins" under PALESTINE—PHILISTIA; Moore "Bronze…from Akko-Ptolemais" under SYRIA—SELEUCID KINGDOM; Moore "The ΕΥΠΑΤΡΕΩΝ Coinage of Alexander I Balas" under SYRIA—SELEUCID KINGDOM; Mørkholm "The Attic Coin Standard" under METROLOGY; Mørkholm "Didrachm Issue of Antiochus VI of Byblus" under SYRIA—SELEUCID KINGDOM; Mørkholm "A Group of Ptolemaic Coins from Phoenician" under EGYPT—PTOLEMAIC KINGDOM; Mørkholm "The Monetary System of the Seleucid Kings" under SYRIA—SELEUCID KINGDOM; Mørkholm "The Ptolemaic Coinage in Phoenicia" under EGYPT—PTOLEMAIC KINGDOM; Mørkholm "The Ptolemaic Coins of an Uncertain Era" under EGYPT—PTOLEMAIC KINGDOM; Moysey "Observations" under PERSIA.

Newell *Some Unpublished Coins* under ASIA—GENERAL WORKS; Newell *The Dated Alexander Coinage of Sidon and Ake* under MACEDONIAN KINGDOM—GENERAL WORKS; Price "On Attributing Alexanders" under MACEDONIAN KINGDOM—GENERAL WORKS; E. S. G. Robinson "Coins from the Excavations at Al-Mina" under HOARDS; Rodee "Art History" under ART; Rogers *The Second and Third Seleucid Coinage of Tyre* under SYRIA—SELEUCID KINGDOM; Sawaya "Le Monnayage" under SYRIA—SELEUCID KINGDOM; Sayles "Painting Inspires Coins" under ART; Scott "On a Tetradrachm" under MACEDONIAN KINGDOM—GENERAL WORKS; Seyrig *Notes on Syrian Coins* under SYRIA—SELEUCID KINGDOM; Seyrig "Monnayage de Ptolémaïs en Phénicie" under EGYPT—PTOLEMAIC KINGDOM; Sheridan "From Cyzicus to Tyre" under HOARDS; Spaer "Ascalon" under SYRIA—SELEUCID KINGDOM; Spaer "A Hoard from Jericho" under HOARDS; Spaer "More on the Ptolemaic Coins of Aradus" under SYRIA—SELEUCID KINGDOM; Syon "Coins from the Excavations at Khirbet esh-Shuhara" under HOARDS; Vagi "Previously Unpublished" (Sidon) under GENERAL WORKS—GREEK; Weinberg "Tel Anafa" under HOARDS; Wells "An Antiochus Lepton of the Tyre Mint" under SYRIA—SELEUCID KINGDOM; Wright *Coins from Asia Minor and the East* under ASIA MINOR—GENERAL WORKS.

PALESTINE

In Jewish numismatics we must look neither for masterpieces nor for portraits. The engravers of Jewish coins were very indifferent artists, and the principal resource of their art, the reproduction of the human figure or of animal form, was denied them by the strict observance of the command in the Decalogue, "Thou shalt not make to thyself any graven image, nor the likeness of anything that is in the heaven above, or in the earth beneath, or in the waters under the earth."

—Theodore Reinach, 1903

JUDEA AND "COINS OF THE BIBLE"

5647   *Ancient Coins and Artifacts of the Bible.* 47 pp., illus. (Editor, publisher, and date unknown).
A reprint of three articles, probably from the late nineteenth century. Includes A. L. Rawson's "Historical Illustrations of Bible Texts" (see Rawson below), F. W. Madden's "Coins, Money, and Weights of the Bible" (see Madden below), and "Biblical Illustrations Showing the Manners and Customs of the Ancients, Comprising a Gallery of Jewish and Egyptian Antiquities" (author unknown).

5648   **Ariel, Donald T.** "Hasmonean Coins found in the Cave of the Warrior." *The Cave of the Warrior: A 4th Millenium Burial in the Judean Desert*, by T. Schick. IAA Reports 5. Jerusalem, 1998. Pages 131-7. Illus.
"Nine coins of Antigonus Mattathias, 40-37 B.C., were found in this cave, pointing to its use about 2000 years after the burial which is the main subject of the book. Four coins are of the type of *BMC* 2 et. seq. And five of the half denomination *BMC* 35 et seq." [A. Spaer, *NL* 142]

5649   **Attwood, T. W.** "Jewish Coins and Money of the Bible." Parts 1 & 2. *New Zealand Numismatic Journal* (New Zealand) 5, no. 4 (November 1949 - February 1950): 119-23; 6, no. 2 (September 1950 - August 1951): 39-43.
A brief review of the coinage used in Judea during Biblical times.

5650   **Banks, Florence Aiken.** *Coins of Bible Days.* New York: Macmillan, 1955. Reprint, New York: Sanford J. Durst. 178 pp., 28 pls. [CS 16412]
Begins with a general description of Greek coinage through the period of the Hellenistic monarchies. Briefly mentions the autonomous Jewish coinage, and then discusses the Roman and other coinages which circulated in the Holy Land at the time of Jesus, and relates them to the stories found in the Bible. [Reviewed in *Spink Numismatic Circular* 64, no. 1 (January 1956): 13-4. Also reviewed by A. Kleeb in *SAN* 16, no. 2 (summer 1985): 36].

5651   **Barag, Dan P.** "Some Examples of Lead Currency from the Hellenistic Period." *Studies in Honour of Leo Mildenberg: Numismatics, Art History, Archaeology.* Edited by A. Houghton et al. Wetteren: Editions NR, 1984. Pages 1-5. Illus.
Barag discusses the lead coins of Alexander Jannaeus. In 1948, Kindler interpreted them as currency issued at a time of economic emergency. Kirschner argued that they were merely trial strikes and were not issued for circulation. Meshorer agreed with Kirschner in 1967. Recent finds have significantly increased the number of known lead pieces, and Barag concludes they were indeed coins struck for circulation during the last period of Alexander Jannaeus' reign (79/8 B.C.), after the striking of the copper Year 25 series in 79 B.C. An acute shortage of copper forced Jannaeus to strike coins in lead. The author lists other lead coins, showing that lead coins were not an exceptional phenomenon in the Hellenistic period. The other pieces are from Ascalon and the Ptolemaic, Nabataean, and Seleucid Kingdoms.

5652   ——— "Some Notes on a Silver Coin of Johanan the High Priest." *Biblical Archaeologist* (September 1985): 166-8.
Reviews the controversy over the Judean coins with the "Yehud" inscription. Mentions the conclusions of Sukenik and Rahmani. Describes a coin with an inscription "Johanan, Priest." Examines historical evidence in an attempt to identify this Johanan.

5653   ——— "A Silver Coin of Yohanan the High Priest and the Coinage of Judea in the Fourth Century B.C." *Israel Numismatic Journal* (Israel) 9 (1988-89): 4 ff.

5654   ——— "Jewish Coins in Hellenistic and Roman Times." *A Survey of Numismatic Research 1985-1990. Volume 1.* International Association of Professional Numismatists Special Publication, No. 12. Edited by T. Hackens, P. Naster et al. Brussels: International Association of Professional Numismatists, 1991. Pages 106-8.
A narrative overview of newly published works in the field of numismatics during 1985-90. Summarizes major findings, with bibliographic references cited in the footnotes.

5655 ——— "New Evidence on the Foreign Policy of John Hyrcanus I." *Israel Numismatic Journal* (Israel) 12 (1992-93): 1-12.
"The author shows by analyzing the coins found in excavations at Marisa, Tel Beer-Sheva, Mt. Gerizim, Shechem, and Samaria that the destruction and conquest of these sites by John Hyrcanus I took place between 112 and 110 B.C. and not as hitherto assumed in or immediately after the second reign of Demetrius II (130-125 B.C.)." [A. Spaer, *NL* 134]

5656 ——— "Bagoas and the Coinage of Judea." *Proceedings of the 11th International Numismatic Congress, September 8-13, 1991. Volume 1.* Edited by T. Hackens et al. Louvain-la-Neuve, Belgium: International Association of Professional Numismatists, 1993. Pages 261-5. Illus.
The author examines a unique silver drachm (in the British Museum) with *obv.*, head right, in Corinthian helmet; *rev.*, winged divinity seated on wheel, and legend "Yehud." Barag reviews prior theories regarding this coin. Concludes the coin bears the portrait of Bagoas, the strategos of Artaxerxes III (obverse), and a representation of the God of Yehud (reverse). The coin was perhaps struck in Gaza, ca. 345-343 B.C.

5657 ——— "The Coinage of Yehud and the Ptolemies." *Studies in Honor of Arie Kindler. Israel Numismatic Journal* (Israel) 13 (1994-99): 27-38.

5658 **Barag, Dan P., and Shraga Qedar.** "The Beginning of Hasmonean Coinage." *Israel Numismatic Journal* (Israel) 4 (1980): 8-21.
[Also see Meshorer's comments in "Again on the Beginning of Hasmonean Coinage" below].

5659 ——— "A Reply to Dr. Meshorer." *Qadmoniot* (Israel) 15, nos. 2-3 (1982): 92. Illus.
"A rejoinder to Meshorer's argument with the authors maintaining that Jewish coinage began under John Hyrcanus I." [A. Spaer, *NL* 109]. [Also see Meshorer's response "On D. Barag and S. Qedar" below].

5660 **Barkay, Rachel.** "A New Variant of a Coin of Alexander II Zebinas." *Israel Numismatic Journal* (Israel) 9 (1988-89): 26 ff.

5661 ——— "Rare and Unpublished Coins from the Bank of Israel Numismatic Collection." *Israel Numismatic Journal* (Israel) 14 (2001-2002): 185-8. Illus.
[Also see Kindler *Coins of the Land of Israel* below].

5662 **Barr Sage, Shirley.** *Biblical Numismatics: Thirty Pieces of Silver.* Phoenix: Heritage Publishers, 2001. 486 pp., illus., 23 pls.
A well illustrated overview of Biblical numismatics. Includes scripture passages, historical background. [Reviewed by P. Goldstein in *The Celator* 16, no. 9 (September 2002): 34].

5663 **Barton, John L.** "Judaean History is Traced with Coins." *The Celator* 2, no. 2 (February 1988): 1, 13-5. Illus. Also appeared in *The Shekel* 21, no. 5 (September-October 1988): 32-7. Illus.
Reviews the historical background of the Jewish people from ca. 600 B.C. through Roman times. Presents an overview of the coinage during each period in Jewish history. The principal coin types are illustrated.

5664 **Ben-David, Arye.** "When Did the Maccabees Begin to Strike Their First Coins?" *Palestine Exploration Quarterly* (England) 104 (July-December 1972): 93-103. [CS 2913]
Refutes Wirgin's assertion that the thick shekels were struck by Simon Maccabaeus (143-135 B.C.). Shows these to have been struck during the first revolt against Rome (A.D. 66-70). Comments on Meshorer's hypothesis that the Maccabees' first bronze coins were struck by Alexander Jannaeus (103-76 B.C.). Contrary to Meshorer's theory, the author suggests Simon's successors were compelled to establish a mint of their own to strike bronze coins. Also questions Meshorer's assertion that Simon bequeathed to his successors no right of coinage. Argues that no such right was required for bronze coins. Shows that the supply of bronze coins had dwindled "almost to vanishing point" after the time of Demetrius II Nicator (125 B.C.) creating a need for a new coinage of small change. The author states that Hyrcanus I struck the first Jewish coins.

5665 **Berrol, Ronn.** "Coinage for Redeeming the Firstborn: An Ancient and Modern Jewish Ritual." *The Celator* 16, no. 12 (December 2002): 14-22.
The Pidyon Ha-Ben is a religious ceremony that allows the father of a firstborn son to buy back his child from service to the Priesthood of god. Berrol discusses the practice in ancient and modern times. He then discusses the coins that may have been used for the purpose in ancient times. Candidates include the Athenian tetradrachm, coins of Alexander the Great, Seleucid coins, shekels of Tyre, and Judean coins.

5666 ——— "Hellenistic Influences on Hasmonean Attitudes Toward Graven Images and Shekels of Tyre." *The Celator* 18, no. 2 (February 2004): 23-30. Illus.
Discusses the use of "graven" images on Judean coins and the Shekels of Tyre.

5667 ——— "Notes on a Jerusalem Mintage Vespasian Tetradrachm." *The Celator* 20, no. 4 (April 2006): 22-8, 36. Illus.
Summarizes the three periods during which the Jews minted silver coins at Jerusalem: (1) the Yehud period (c. 350-270 B.C.), (2) the first Jewish revolt (A.D. 65-70), and (3) the period of Roman provincial tetradrachms minted at Jerusalem (Aelia Capitolina) (ca. A.D. 215-218). Reviews Meshorer's theory that the Tyre shekels with the monogram KP were minted at Jerusalem, while debased coins were produced in other Roman Eastern Provinces. Examines McAlee's theory that certain Vespasian tetradrachms previously attributed to Tyre should be assigned to a Judea Capta mint.

5668 **Brenner, Sandy.** "'Firsts' in Ancient Judaean Coins." *The Celator* 16, no. 6 (June 2002): 29-30, 34-6. Illus.
Discusses the first coin minted in Jerusalem, the first ruler of Judea to issue coins, the first coin minted in Jerusalem during the reign of a Jewish ruler, the first genuinely Jewish coin, the first coin to be officially accepted as payment for the annual Temple Tax in Jerusalem, the first bilingual Jewish coin, the first Jewish ruler to depict himself on a coin, the first silver Jewish coin, the first Roman coin to include Judea in the legend, the first Jewish coin to depict the Temple in Jerusalem, and the first sovereign Jewish coin with Modern Hebrew legends. [Also see the "Letter to the Editor" by Ronn Berrol suggesting some other "firsts" in Judean coinage: *The Celator* 16, no. 8 (August 2002): 18].

5669 ——— "The Burden of the Temple Tax: 'the rich shall not pay more and the poor shall not pay less.'" *The Celator* 22, no. 2 (February 2008): 6-24. Illus.
Examines the annual Jewish temple tax, the people's attitudes toward it, and the use of the donated funds. Attempts to determine the tax's modern equivalent in dollars and concludes the ancient half shekel tax was roughly equal to about $100 today. The tax was voluntarily paid by free Jewish males over twenty years old. The tax, as traditionally observed, was ended by Vespasian in A.D. 70 and replaced with an equivalent tax payable to Rome. The tax was expanded by Domitian, and ended in 362 by Julian the Apostate.

5670 **Bressett, Kenneth.** *Money of the Bible.* Racine: Whitman Publishing, 2005. 114 pp., illus. Second edition, 2007. 120 pp., illus.
A beautifully illustrated, large format book, with wonderful photography. Expands on Bible texts. Examines how the Bible was written, discusses commerce before coins, coins of Old Testament times, coins mentioned in the New Testament, first century money and trade, coins mentioned in Jesus' parables and lessons, coins with Biblical themes, and how to collect Biblical coins. Illustrated with enlarged color photographs of pertinent coins.

5671 **Brimelow, William.** "Jewish Money." *Numismatic Scrapbook Magazine* 10 (January 1944): 46-50.
Brimelow reviews Bible passages which refer to money and coins. He searches for clues to the identity of the coins mentioned.

5672 **Brin, Howard B.** "The Mystery of the Inscription on Hasmonean Coins." *SAN—Journal of the Society for Ancient Numismatics* 11, no. 1 (spring 1980): 9-13, 17. Illus.
Examines the usage of the phrase "Hever ha Yehudim" on Jewish coinage. Reviews the debate over the interpretation of the phrase. Discusses the history of the Hasmonean period and the development of the use of titles on coins and concludes that the phrase is part of the king's title and that Hasmonean rulers were copying the style of those rulers around them who showed their names, inherited titles, and laudatory appellations on their coins. [Also see Brin's continuation below, and the critical response by Rappaport. See Rappaport "Letter to the Editor" below].

5673 ——— "The Mystery Solved: A New Definition of HVR ha YEHUDIM." *SAN—Journal of the Society for Ancient Numismatics* 11, no. 2 (summer 1980): 29-31.
Discusses the translation of "Haver ha Yehudim" on Jewish coins. Examines the development of coin inscriptions and concludes the title on the coins in question is "High Priest and Friend of the Jews." [Also see Brin "Rosh Hvr Ha Yehudim" below and Rappaport "Letter to the Editor" below].

5674 ——— "Rosh Hvr Ha Yedudim." *SAN—Journal of the Society for Ancient Numismatics* 11, no. 4 (winter 1980-81): 72-3.
Brin suggests that the inscription "Rosh" on Hasmonean coins was used by Hyrcanus on the occasion of Caesar naming him ethnarch in 47 B.C.

5675 **Brindley, James C.** "Enigmatic Fourth Century B.C. Coin Issues from the Levant." *Spink Numismatic Circular* 105, no. 3 (April 1997): 78-9. Illus.
Some eastern Mediterranean issues dating to the early part of the fourth century B.C. remain unattributed. Brindley suggests these coins represent limited joint issues by some of the major Levantine mints in the middle of the 390's B.C. to assist Evagora's and Conon's naval activities in the eastern Mediterranean in association with the king of Persia.

5676 **Conder, Francis R.** "Measures, Weights, and Coins of the Bible." *Bible Educator, Volume 3.* Edited by E. H. Plumptre. London, 1874. Pages 69-71, 96-100, 175-80, 222-4.

5677 **Cumberland, Richard.** *An Essay toward the Recovery of the Jewish Measures and Weights, Comprehending Their Monies.* Second edition. London, 1686. 140 pp., 1 pl.

5678 **Dale, L. J.** "Biblical Numismatics." *The Numismatist* 62, no. 9 (September 1949): 519-28. Illus.
Discusses the prices of goods, in terms of metals and other goods, in Biblical times with cross-references to Biblical passages. Also illustrates coins known to have circulated in Palestine, with references to Bible passages. Reviews the teachings of Jesus related to money.

5678a **deSaulcy, Félicien.** "Observation sur la Numismatique Judïque." *Revue Numismatique* (France) new ser., 2 (1857): 280-98.
[Also see Madden "Remarks" and "Jewish Coins" below for some comments on deSaulcy's attributions].

5679 **Deutsch, R.** "Six Unrecorded 'Yehud' Silver Coins." *Israel Numismatic Journal* (Israel) 11 (1990-91): 4-6.
Among other coins, Deutsch publishes a drachm bearing the Hebrew letter *yod* on the reverse. This was only the second such drachm to be published. The first is in the British Museum (see G. F. Hill, *Catalogue of the Greek Coins of Palestine* below). Since this publication, a third has surfaced (see D. Hendin "Three New Types" below).

5680 ——— "Five Unrecorded 'Yehud' Silver Coins." *Israel Numismatic Journal* (Israel) 13 (1994-99): 25-6.

5681 **Dow, Joseph A.** *Ancient Coins through the Bible.* Mustang, Oklahoma: Tate Publishing, 2011. 352 pp., illus., maps.
Following the course of time from Abraham to the Crusaders, the author chronicles the history of various locations mentioned throughout the Bible and presents photographs of ancient coins minted in these cities, thus allowing the reader to experience the Biblical stories visually through the coins depicted.

5682 **Dunning, Mark.** "Biblical Ancient Coinage Checklists." *The Celator* 9, no. 3 (March 1995): 30-2.
Presents checklists of mint cities, persons, deities, and coins mentioned in the Bible. Includes cross-references to the Bible verses where they are mentioned.

5683 **Evans, Jane DeRose.** *The Joint Expedition to Caesarea Maritima Excavation Reports, Volume VI: The Coins and the Hellenistic, Roman, and Byzantine Economy of Palestine.* Boston: The American Schools of Oriental Research, 2006. 240 pp., 8 pls.
The sixth volume chronicling the finds from the exploration of the city of Caesarea Maritima conducted from 1971 to 1987. Examines the city's place within the larger context of coin circulation in the ancient Near East. Catalogues the 2734 coins from the fourth century B.C. to the sixth century A.D. found during the excavations. [Reviewed in *Israel Numismatic Research* 2 (2007): 179 ff, and reviewed by Oliver D. Hoover in *American Numismatic Society Magazine* 7, no. 1 (spring 2008): 59-63].

5684 **Fischer, Thomas.** "Another Hellenizing Coin of Alexander Jannaeus?" *Israel Exploration Journal* (Israel) 34, no. 1 (1984): 47-8. Illus.
Fischer comments on a coin published by Meshorer (see Meshorer "The Beginning of the Hasmonaean Coinage" below) with *obv.*, radiate head, and *rev.*, lily with BA LK. Meshorer attributed the coin to Antiochus VII (102 B.C.) and to the mint of Jerusalem. Fischer is unconvinced and suggests the coin may belong to Alexander Jannaeus (103-76 B.C.).

5685 **Fontanille, Jean-Philippe.** "Treasures of the Temple." *Numismatist* 119, no. 9 (September 2006): 45-8. Illus.
Discusses the religious objects of the Temple in Jerusalem which were portrayed on just five Judean coins. The objects are the menorah and showbread table, the golden vine, the tripod table, the golden eagle, and the arc and scrolls.

5686 ——— "Two Unrecorded Hasmonean Coins." *Israel Numismatic Research* (Israel) 2 (2007): 89 ff.
Examines two new Hasmonean coins which appeared in the market in 2005 and in 2006. One is a Hyrcanus I variant with star symbol and the other is a new lead type of Alexander Jannaeus.

5687 ——— "Extreme Deterioration and Damage on Yehud Coin Dies." *Israel Numismatic Research* (Israel) 3 (2008): 29-44.
A significant proportion of Yehud coins was struck from dies that had been damaged one way or another. The damage could have been caused by excessive wear, breaks or errors during the striking process (clashed dies). The paper presents illustrations of all three phenomena and discusses their implications.

5688 **Fontanille, Jean-Philippe, and Ken Baumheckel.** "Cultic Images or Ship's Prow? A New Look at Pilate's Coinage." *The Celator* 17, no. 5 (May 2003): 34-5, 38-9. Illus.
A reconsideration of the identity of some symbols depicted on coins of Pontius Pilate. The author's question the "simpulum" and suggest it may actually be a ship's prow. Stylistic variations from an actual simpulum are noted. The "bound grain ears" on a coin of Pilate may actually be a modius (a grain measure). The lituus (wooden staff) may actually be a galley's prow stempost or a portion of the Eye of Horus. The authors encourage comments on their observations.

5689 ——— "Errors on Biblical Coins." *The Celator* 19, no. 2 (February 2005): 6-17. Illus.
Describes and illustrates numerous minting errors which can be found on Biblical coins including varieties in main devices, varieties in inscriptions, countermarks, and striking varieties.

5690 **Fontanille, Jean-Philippe, and Sheldon Lee Gosline.** *The Coins of Pontius Pilate.* Marco Polo Monographs 4. Warren Center, Pennsylvania: Shangri-La Publications, 2001. 176 pp., illus.
Includes a description of Judea in Pilate's time and a review of Jewish money before Pilate. Then examines Pontius Pilate and his coinage. Discusses Pilate's coins and their possible connection with the Shroud of Turin. Includes a Preface by David Hendin. Text in English and French. [Reviewed by E. Caine in *The Celator* 16, no. 1 (January 2002): 34-5, by Bruce Brace in *Journal of the Classical and Medieval Numismatic Society* 2nd ser., 2, no. 4 (December 2001): 175-7, by Oliver Hoover in *American Numismatic Society Magazine* 1, no. 1 (spring 2002): 40-2, and by D. F. Fanning in *The Asylum: The Quarterly Journal of the Numismatic Bibliomania Society* 20, no. 3 (summer 2002): 92-3].

5691 **Fontanille, Jean-Philippe, and Catharine Lorber.** "Silver Yehud Coins with Greek or Pseudo-Greek Inscriptions." *Israel Numismatic Research* (Israel) 3 (2008): 45-50.
The authors report the discovery of a new class of Yehud coins that share the facing head/owl types of Meshorer *A Treasury of Jewish Coins*: 199, Nos. 20–23, but are inscribed with Greek characters instead of paleo-Hebrew or Aramaic.

5692 **Friedberg, Arthur L.** *Coins of the Bible.* Racine: Whitman Publishing, 2004. 112 pp., illus.
An introduction to coinage struck in Biblical lands. Includes replica coins (some books were packaged with six replica coins; others were packaged with just two replica coins).

5693 **Gitler, Haim, Oren Tal, and Peter van Alfen.** "Silver Dome-Shaped Coins from Persian-Period Southern Palestine." *Israel Numismatic Research* (Israel) 2 (2007): 47-62.
The authors discuss a previously unknown group of Athenian-styled Palestinian coins. This group, which includes mainly drachms but some obols as well, was struck from worn obverse dies which were then recut and repolished. As a result, the coins' obverse in many cases is simply dome-shaped, with no traces of Athena's head or helmet being recognizable. The coins' distribution suggests that they circulated in the boundaries of Edom in the later part of the Persian period and might well have been the silver money mentioned in several of the Edomite ostraca.

5694 **Gerson, Stephen N.** "The Lily as a Symbol of Ancient Israel." *The Celator* 23, no. 6 (June 2009): 20-30. Illus.
Discusses the lily (shoshanah) as a symbol of Israel and illustrates its use on early Yehud and later coins and other objects.

5695 **Geva, H.** "Jewish Quarter Excavations in the Old City of Jerusalem Conducted by Nachman Avigad in 1969-1982." *Vol. III. Azen E. and Other Studies. Final Report.* Jerusalem, 2006. 480 pp., illus.
"On pp. 192-217 and pl. 1, D. T. Ariel catalogues and analyzes the 933 bronze and one lead coin found in the excavations. Twenty coins are pre-Hasmonaean (Ptolemaic and Seleucid), 716 are of Alexander Jannaeus, or probably so, 51 are Herodian, 22 post Herodian, and 145 unidentified." [Arnold Spaer, *NL* 149]

5696 **Goldstein, Isadore, and Jean-Philippe Fontanille.** "Ten Great Rarities of Judaean Coinage." *The Celator* 23, no. 8 (August 2009): 6-19. Illus.
Illustrates and discusses ten rarities: (1) Yehud drachm with deity, (2) Yehud obol with "Shofar," (3) Yehud obol depicting Ptolemy–Berenike/Ptolemy II–Arsinoe, (4) Herod–Vine branch lepton, (5) Herod Antipas with grain and palm tree, (6) Monobazus I, (7) First Revolt year one shekel prototype, (8) First Revolt year one quarter-shekel, (9) First Revolt year five quarter-shekel, and (10) First Revolt year five half-shekel.

5697 **Goldstein, Paul.** "Jewish Names of Kings on Biblical Coins Reflect the Name of G-d." *The Celator* 15, no. 9 (September 2001): 28, 34-5. Illus.
The Jewish kings used Hebrew names on their coinage, since they wanted to honor themselves and show that their power was derived through their special connection with God. These names frequently incorporate letters from God's name (YHVH). Goldstein discusses the Jewish king names which appear on coins and the meanings and symbolism incorporated into the names.

5698 **Grossman, Lee.** "The Widow's Mite—What Was It?" *Numismatics International* 18, no. 1 (January 1984): 15-8. Illus.
"A discussion of various theories about what the denomination which the Bible calls the widow's mite could have been as well as its relative buying power in modern commerce." [J. Uphoff, *NL* 115]

5699 **Harrison, R.** "Hellenization in Syria-Palestine: The Case of Judea in the Third Century B.C.E." *Biblical Archaeology* 57, no. 2 (June 1994): 98-108. Illus.
"On pages 100-102 some Yehud and Philisto-Arabian coins are illustrated and discussed in the context of Ptolemaic monetary policy and economic development in Judea." [A. Spaer, *NL* 133]

5700 **Heltzer, M.** "The Provincial Taxation in the Achaemenian Empire and 'Forty Shekels of Silver' (Neh. 5, 15)." *Michmanim* (Hecht Museum, Haifa University, Israel) 6 (October 1992): 15-25.
"The author discusses the taxation by the Persian governors of Judaea, Samaria, etc.: how it was calculated and how it was paid by produce or in silver and in what coin." [A. Spaer, *NL* 137]

5701 **Hendin, David.** *Guide to Ancient Jewish Coins.* New York: Attic Books Ltd., 1976. 134 pp., 9 pls., map. [CS 2918]
Lists 283 Jewish coin types beginning with the Persian period and continuing through the reign of Hadrian. Includes city coins and Roman Provincial coins. Each chronological period includes an historical introduction. The catalogue describes the coins including their types, weights, and diameters, and is cross-referenced to other collections, and illustrated by line drawings throughout. One photographic plate. Appendices include a conversion table from Meshorer to Reifenberg numbers, a map of mints, and tables of mint cities and alphabets. Includes approximate values by Herbert Kreindler. [Superseded by Hendin's *Guide to Biblical Coins* below].

5702 ——— *Guide to Biblical Coins.* Dix Hills, New York: Amphora Books, 1987. 204 pp., 16 pls. Third edition, 1996. 315 pp., 32 pls. Fourth edition, 2001. 472 pp., 38 pls. Fifth edition, 2010. 648 pp., 55 pls.
A revised and enlarged version of the author's *Guide to Ancient Jewish Coins* (see above). Includes sections on hoards, denominations, minting, cleaning, and counterfeit detection. Includes market values by Herbert Kreindler. Discusses weight systems, and Persian, Macedonian, Ptolemaic, and Seleucid coins used in Palestine. Then discusses the Hasmonean and Herodian coins, and coins of the prefects and procurators. Continues with coins of the Jewish War, the Bar Kochba War, the Judea Capta and related issues, city coins of Israel and Transjordan, New Testament coins, and some related issues. Each chronological period includes an historical introduction. Includes a map of mints and tables of alphabets. The photographic plates are supplemented by line drawings throughout. The second edition lists 308 major coin types. The third edition lists 525 coin types, has improved plates, contains some revised attributions, and incorporates new scholarship. The numbering system begins with 401, to distinguish the numbers from those of the second edition. The fourth edition lists 938 coin types, but maintains the number system from the third edition. It again incorporates new scholarship and some new sections have been added. Cross-referenced to Meshorer, *British Museum Catalogue*, and Sear. The fifth edition includes an illustrated catalogue of the Judaea Capta series, with a concordance to other major references. It also includes extensive new research on the metrology of the Judean bronze coins. [The third edition was reviewed by David Vagi in *SAN* 20, no. 1 (1997): 32-3, and by Philip Kiernan in *The Anvil* (Canada) 8, no. 4 (December 1998): 61-2. The fourth edition was reviewed by David Vagi in *The Celator* 15, no. 7 (July 2001): 34-5. The fifth edition was reviewed by Harlan Berk in *The Celator* 24, no. 10 (October 2010): 38, 56].

5703 ——— "Coins of the Bible." Regular feature in *The Celator*.
Hendin's column focuses on Judean coins of the Biblical period. Those discussing coins prior to the Roman Imperial period are listed here. A few of the most significant articles (as noted) are also summarized separately below.

Shekel of Tyre	3, no. 1 (January 1989): 24
Lepton of Mattathias Antigonus	3, no. 2 (February 1989): 22
Widow's Mite	3, no. 3 (March 1989): 26
Shekel of Tyre	3, no. 10 (October 1989): 26
Quadrans, Lepton, Prutot, and Prutah	4, no. 5 (May 1990): 29
Inscriptions Related to Zionism	4, no. 6 (June 1990): 25
Annual Temple Tribute	4, no. 8 (August 1990): 27
Coins of the Second Temple Period	4, no. 9 (September 1990): 36-7
(Corrections regarding illustrations for above)	4, no. 10 (October 1990): 2
Forgeries of Menorah Coins of Mattathias	5, no. 7 (July 1991): 32-3
What are "Coins of the Bible?"	6, no. 4 (April 1992): 34-5
Hasmonean Chronology/Dead Sea Scrolls	6, no. 6 (June 1992): 40-1
Jerusalem's Walls on a Cilician Coin?	6, no. 10 (October 1992): 44-5
Shekel of Tyre/Bronze Shekel	6, no. 11 (November 1992): 36-7
The Cornucopia Served as a Jewish Symbol	7, no. 1 (January 1993): 38-9
More Information about the Tyre Shekels	7, no. 3 (March 1993): 38-9
Bar Kochba Bronze Struck over Ptolemaic Coin	7, no. 9 (September 1993): 16
Early Southern Mints in Ancient Israel	8, no. 6 (June 1994): 44-5
The Symbolism of Lilies, Anchors, and Stars	8, no. 7 (July 1994): 44-5
Prices and Denominations of Coins	8, no. 8 (August 1994): 44-5
The First John Hyrcanus: the Man and His Reign	8, no. 9 (September 1994): 48-9
The Reign of Judah Aristobulus	8, no. 9 (October 1994): 32
Marisa: A New Mint City Described	9, no. 2 (February 1995): 44-5
Poor Widow's Mite Revisited	9, no. 3 (March 1995): 42-3
No Coins in the Old Testament	9, no 11 (November 1995): 42-3
Early Coins of Ancient Israel	9, no. 12 (December 1995): 24-5

Pre-Maccabean Era as Portrayed on Coins	10, no. 2 (February 1996): 25
Five Groups of Jewish Coinage	10, no. 3 (March 1996): 32-3
Error Coins Serve as Learning Tool	10, no. 4 (April 1996): 35
How Did They Date Ancient Jewish Coins?	10, no. 6 (June 1996): 24
What are Barbaric Coins?	10, no. 7 (July 1996): 42
Coins at the Time of Jesus: Part 1	10, no. 12 (December 1996): 22-3
Part 2: The Tribute Penny	11, no. 1 (January 1997): 38-9
How Ancient Coins Were Made	11, no. 2 (February 1997): 30-1
Coins of Alexander Were Struck in Israel	11, no. 3 (March 1997): 32-3
Prices of Goods and the Value of Coins	11, no. 6 (June 1997): 20-1
Cut Coins Indicate Small Change Shortages	11, no. 7 (July 1997): 22-3
Roman and Biblical Coin Denominations	11, no. 8 (August 1997): 36
The Thirty Pieces of Silver	11, no. 10 (October 1997): 18-22
Collecting Biblical Coins	11, no. 11 (November 1997): 24-5
A Time before Coins	12, no. 2 (February 1998): 24-5
The Yehud Coins	12, no. 3 (March 1998): 22-3
Jerusalem's Walls on a Coin of Mazaeus?	12, no. 6 (June 1998): 24
Herod Archelaus, 4 B.C.E. to 6 C.E.	12, no. 8 (August 1998): 30
John Hyrcanus II (Yonatan), 67 and 63-40 B.C.E.	12, no. 9 (September 1998): 34-5
The Samarian Coins	13, no. 3 (March 1999): 46-7
Prutahs, Leptons and Mites	14, no. 4 (April 2000): 46-7, 50. [Summarized below]
Symbolism of the Feast of Tabernacles	15, no. 1 (January 2001): 46-7, 50. Illus.
Pentatuchal Code Regarding Graven Images	15, no. 7 (July 2001): 46. Illus.
The Coin in the Fish's Mouth (Shekel of Tyre)	15, no. 12 (December 2001): 46. Illus.
Writing the Book on It.	16, no. 1 (January 2002): 46-7. Illus.
Tyre Coins and Graven Images	16, no. 2 (February 2002): 46-7.
Surcharge of the Money Changers	16, no. 3 (March 2002): 46-7.
Request for Information on Fakes and Forgeries	16, no. 7 (July 2002): 46. Illus.
How Ancient Coins are Dated	16, no. 9 (September 2002): 46. Illus.
What are Biblical Coins?	17, no. 1 (January 2003): 44. Illus.
Creating Flan Molds in Ancient Judaea	17, no. 10 (October 2003): 44. Illus.
Surcharge of the Money Changers—Revised	18, no. 2 (February 2004): 44-5, 50.
Ancient Forgeries Are Discussed	18, no. 4 (April 2004): 44-5. Illus.
Unusual Views of Rare Biblical/Judaean Coins	18, no. 11 (November 2004): 40-1. Illus.
Differential Diagnostics of Forgeries	19, no. 1 (January 2005): 40-1, 45. Illus.
Chronology of Hasmonean Coins	19, no. 6 (June 2005): 40-1, 46. Illus. [Summarized below]
Historical Notes on the Jerusalem Temple Tax	19, no. 8 (August 2005): 40-1. Illus.
More on the Tyre Shekels	19, no. 9 (September 2005): 40-1. Illus. [Summarized under PHOENICIA]
Ancient Currency and Ancient Scale Weights	20, no. 2 (February 2006): 42-3. Illus.
New Book on Earliest Ancient Israel Coins	20, no. 9 (September 2006): 42-3, 46. Illus.
New Tales of Miracles, Fantasies, and Forgeries	20, no. 10 (October 2006): 42-3. Illus.
When the Mite Became a Mite	20, no. 11 (November 2006): 42-3. Illus.
Jesus and Numismatics: Re-considering Jesus and His World	21, no. 6 (June 2007): 42-3. Illus.
The Chronology of Jannaeus Coinage	21, no. 7 (July 2007): 42-3. Illus.
New Observations on Tiny YEHUD Coins	21, no. 8 (August 2007): 42-3, 46. Illus. [Also see Oct '07 revision]
Further Discussions on an Interesting Yehud Type	21, no. 10 (October 2007): 42-3, 40. Illus. [Revision of Aug '07 article]
Who Were the Wise Men of the East?	21, no. 12 (December 2007): 42. Illus.
The First Dated Jewish Coin	22, no. 1 (January 2008): 42. Illus.
Old Testament Mountain on Coins	22, no. 5 (May 2008): 42-3. Illus.
Yehud Coinage, on Further Consideration	22, no. 9 (September 2008): 42-3, 46. Illus. [Summarized below]
Coin Denominations in 4th Century B.C.E. Palestine	22, no. 10 (October 2008): 46-7, 50. Illus.
If It Looks Like a Duck…	22, no. 12 (December 2008): 46-7, 50. Illus. [Summarized below]
Epigraphy on Hasmonean Coins	23, no. 2 (February 2009): 46-7. Illus.
Much More on the Jannaeus Coin Chronology	23, no. 3 (March 2009): 46-7, 50. Illus. [Summarized below]
Re-examining the Prutah and Lepton	23, no. 4 (April 2009): 46-7, 50. Illus. [Summarized below]
Dan Barag Dies in Jerusalem—Giant of Biblical Numismatics	24, no. 1 (January 2010): 42-3, 46. Illus.
Metrology of the Jewish Bronze Coins	24, no. 5 (May 2010): 42-3, 46. Illus.
Lessons from the Poor Widow's Mite	24, no. 12 (December 2010): 42-3, 46. Illus.
A Collective Mint in Philistia?	25, no. 1 (January 2011): 42-3. Illus. [Summarized under PHILISTIA]
Sofaer Collection at Federal Reserve Bank of New York	25, no. 5 (May 2011): 42-3, 46. Illus.
Museum Exhibit: It Takes a Village	25, no. 6 (June 2011): 42-3. Illus.

5704 ——— "New Data Sheds Light on Hasmonean Coin Theories." *The Celator* 5, no. 6 (June 1991): 6-8.
Discoveries of coins near Nabulus in Samaria have led to agreement between scholars that John Hyrcanus I (135-104 B.C.) was the first Jewish ruler to issue coins in his own name. Suggests all coins of Yehohanan belong to Hyrcanus I. Reviews various theories related to this long-controversial subject

5705 ——— "Three New Types of Yehud Drachms." *SAN—Journal of the Society for Ancient Numismatics* 19, no. 2 (1995): 44-5. Illus.
Publishes three new types of drachms from the Yehud series. Each bears the Hebrew letter *yod* on the reverse (the first letter in the Hebrew word *Yhud*, the Persian name for the province of Judea). Two of the coins are Athenian imitation types; the third is a new type for the Yehud coinage. The author briefly discusses the use of one letter to designate the minting authority on coins of Judea, Gaza, and Samaria.

5706 ——— "Prutahs, Leptons and Mites." *The Celator* 14, no. 4 (April 2000): 46-7, 50. Illus.
Discusses the difference between prutahs, leptons, and mites. Lepton is a Greek word and prutah is a Hebrew word. The lepton is equivalent to one-half of a prutah. The weight standards used for these coins varied. It is uncertain whether the widow's mite of the Bible was a lepton or a prutah.

5707 ——— "In Memoriam, Prof. Ya'akov Meshorer 1935-2004." *The Celator* 18, no. 8 (August 2004): 40-1, 45-6. Illus.
Hendin describes the career of Ya'akov Meshorer, the well-known expert on Judean coinage. Hendin also provides some personal reminiscences of his friendship with Meshorer who died of cancer in 2004.

5708 ——— *Not Kosher: Forgeries of Ancient Jewish and Biblical Coins.* Nyack, NY: Amphora, 2005. 224 pp., illus.
Describes types of forgeries, methods of forgers, and diagnostics of forgeries. Catalogues and photographs more than 550 forgeries of more than 125 Jewish and Biblical coin types from collections around the world. [An extensive review by Oliver Hoover appears in *American Numismatic Society Magazine* 4, no. 1 (spring 2005): 69-71. Also reviewed by Wayne Sayles in *The Celator* 19, no. 5 (May 2005): 38].

5709 ——— "Chronology of Hasmonean Coins." *The Celator* 19, no. 6 (June 2005): 40-1, 46. Illus. "More and More." *The Celator* 19, no. 11 (November 2005): 40-1, 56.
Hendin criticizes an article by Ilan Shachar (see Shachar below) regarding the chronology of the YEHONATAN and YONTAN coins. [Also see Hendin's "Letter to the Editor" in *The Celator* 19, no. 11 (November 2005): 4, 37, in which he responds to Shachar's letter. Also see Hendin "Much More on the Jannaeus Coin Chronology" below, in which Hendin now accepts Shachar's attributions].

5710 ——— "Striking Methods and Striking Errors in Ancient Judaea." *The Celator* 20, no. 4 (April 2006): 46-7. Illus.
Illustrates and describes ten examples of striking errors or unusually cut Judean coins and comments on the minting techniques that led to the errors.

5711 ——— "Yehud Coinage, on Further Consideration." *The Celator* 22, no. 9 (September 2008): 42-3, 46. Illus.
A discussion of the earliest coins struck in Judea—the tiny Persian-period coins with the inscription YHD. Hendin points out that two different weight standards were in use and that these coins were used to pay the temple tax. He states that the Yehud series is the only contemporary series of the region where fouree coins do not exist.

5712 ——— "If It Looks Like a Duck…" *The Celator* 22, no. 12 (December 2008): 46-7, 50. Illus.
Examines a fourth century B.C. Yehud coin (Meshorer, *A Treasury of Jewish Coins* 27; Hendin 440), for which the obverse type is often described as a horse's head, and the reverse type has been identified as an eagle's head. Hendin believes the obverse type is actually the head of a chimera. He also provides convincing evidence that the reverse type is a duck. Various stages in the deterioration of the obverse die are also shown, in which the type is reduced to a small, egg-like object.

5713 ——— "The Metrology of Judaean Small Bronze Coins." *American Journal of Numismatics* 2nd ser., 21 (2009): 105-21. Illus.
Based on the weights of more than 10,000 bronze coins dating from 134 B.C. to A.D. 70, this study offers a comprehensive analysis of the weight standards for each series, and of the role of fiduciary coinage in ancient Judea. [Also see Hendin's summary of this paper in his column in *The Celator* 24, no. 5 (May 2010): 42-3, 46].

5714 ——— "Much More on the Jannaeus Coin Chronology." *The Celator* 23, no. 3 (March 2009): 46-7, 50. Illus.
Publishes a double overstruck coin: a Yehonatan coin was struck upon a Yonatan coin that was struck upon a Yehonatan coin. It establishes that these are all coins of the same ruler—Alexander Jannaeus. [Also see Shachar "The Historical and Numismatic Significance" below].

5715 ——— "Re-Examining the *Prutah* and *Lepton*." *The Celator* 23, no. 4 (April 2009): 46-7, 50. Illus.
It has often been thought that a denomination smaller than the prutah existed in ancient Judea. This was the half-prutah which is also often referred to as a lepton. Hendin argues that these were actually the same denomination, with the smaller coins merely being degraded versions of the prutah.

5716 ——— *Cultural Change: Jewish, Christian and Islamic Coins of the Holy Land.* New York: American Numismatic Society, 2011. 128 pp., illus.
A catalogue of all the coins in an American Numismatic Society exhibit at the Federal Reserve Bank of New York, comprised of coins from the Abraham and Marian Sofaer collection. Provides a brief history of the Holy Land region from the fourth century B.C. to Crusader times, illustrated by the Hellenistic, Roman, Byzantine, Islamic, and Crusader coinage that was produced there. Includes explanatory text, illustrations of related material, maps, and family trees. Many of the coins are the finest of their kind. [Reviewed by Andrew Meadows in *ANS* 10, no. 3 (2011): 53].

5717 **Hendin, David, and Ilan Shachar.** "The Identity of YNTN on Hasmonean Overstruck Coins and the Chronology of the Alexander Jannaeus Types." *Israel Numismatic Research* (Israel) 3 (2009): 87-94.
A previously unpublished Hasmonean coin, which was overstruck twice, proves beyond doubt that at least one group of coins bearing the name *yntn* must be attributed to Alexander Jannaeus. This coin also contributes to establishing a definitive chronology for the striking of the various Jannaeus types.

5717a **Hendin, David, and Nathan Bower.** "Irregular Coins of Judaea, First Century BCE—First Century CE: New Insights from Comparisons of Stylistic, Physical, and Chemical Analyses." *American Journal of Numismatics* 2nd ser., 23 (2011): 35-54. 2 pls.
"A minimum of five ancient Judaean coins from each of eleven different paired (irregular versus standard) types of coins (117 in total) spanning the period from 130 BCE (Hyrcanus I) to 70 CE (the first Jewish revolt against the Romans) were selected for a non-destructive elemental analysis by x-ray fluorescence that was used to calculate compositional diversity. The results are coupled with stylistic, metrological and die orientation analyses in order to shed light on the nature and origins of the many irregular coins struck during this period in Judaea. The results strongly suggest that the majority of the irregular coins were imitative issues produced at non-official mints, probably to fulfill the need for additional coins during periods or in regions with shortages." [Hendin and Bower]

5717b **Heritage Auctions.** *The Shoshana Collection of Ancient Judaean Coins.* March 8-9, 2012. Dallas: Heritage Auctions, 2012. 186 pp., illus.
Sale catalogue for what was described as "the greatest-known private collection of ancient Jewish coins." The auction was held in New York on March 8-9, 2012. The collection of over 1800 coins was built over forty years by a Los Angeles collector. Nearly half of the collection is offered here (875 coins offered in 712 lots) and includes a large group of Philistian and Yehud coins, bronzes of the Hasmonean and Herodian dynasties, coins of the Jewish War (including a Year 5 shekel formerly in the Hunt collection), coins of the Bar Kochba uprising, 164 silver and bronze coins from Roman Jerusalem (including 80 coins from Meshorer's book *The Coinage of Aelia Capitolina*), and many city coins struck under Imperial rule in Judaea, Samaria, and Phoenicia. The catalogue

was written by David Hendin and Herb Kreindler. Each coin is fully described and the catalogue includes many historical notes. [Part 2 of the collection will be sold at a later date].

5718 **Herbst, Jonathan A.** "Hasmonean Judea: A Vassal State." *The Shekel* 26, no. 5 (September-October 1993): 25-31. Illus.
An overview of ancient Jewish coinage.

5719 **Hill, George F.** *Catalogue of the Greek Coins of Palestine (Galilee, Samaria, and Judaea).* London: British Museum, 1914. Reprint, Bologna: Forni, 1965. cxiv, 363 pp., 42 pls., map. [CS 2919]
Volume 27 of the *Catalogue of Greek Coins in the British Museum.* The 363-page catalogue of coins is preceded by 114 pages of introductory text. [Also see *Catalogue of Greek Coins in the British Museum* under PUBLIC COLLECTIONS—GREAT BRITAIN (LONDON). Also see Kool "Rediscovery" below].

5720 **Hirsch, Herbert.** "A New Hypothesis about the Chronology of Hasmonaean Coinage." *SAN—Journal of the Society for Ancient Numismatics* 3, no. 3 (1971-2): 43-6, 50. Illus.
Argues that all Yehohanan coins were struck by Hyrcanus I, contradicting Meshorer's attribution to Hyrcanus II. Also discusses theories of Kindler.

5721 ——— "Chronology of Hasmonaean Coinage." *World Coins* (United States) 12, no. 2 (February 1975): 34 ff. Illus.

5722 **Hirschfeld, Y., and Donald T. Ariel.** "A Coin Assemblage from the Reign of Alexander Jannaeus Found on the Shore of the Dead Sea." *Israel Exploration Journal* (Israel) 55 (2005): 166-89.

5723 **Hooper, Joseph.** "The Coins of the Jews." *The Numismatist* 8, no. 1 (January 1895): 1-4; no. 2 (February 1895): 29-32; no. 3 (March 1895): 58-61; no. 4 (April 1895): 79-82. Illus.
Reviews the history of Jewish coinage from its beginnings through the period of Roman domination. Discusses the coin types and inscriptions. Of course, the chronology suggested here is no longer accepted.

5724 **Hoover, Oliver.** "Striking a Pose: Seleucid Types and *Machpolitik* on the Coins of John Hyrcanus I." *The Picus* (Canada) (1994): 41-57. Illus.
Examines the symbolism on the coins of John Hyrcanus (134-104 B.C.). Discusses the anchor symbol as a Seleucid emblem of the king, and the lily as an emblem of the High Priest. Reviews Hyrcanus' use of symbols in his later coins, their link to Seleucid coinage, and his use of Seleucid symbols on his coins to empower himself and engage in politics with foreigners.

5725 ——— "The Seleucid Coinage of John Hyrcanus I: The Transformation of a Dynastic Symbol in Hellenistic Judaea." *American Journal of Numismatics* 2nd ser., 15 (2003): 29-39. 1 pl.
In ca. 133 B.C. a Seleucid bronze mint opened in Jerusalem after the fall of the city to Aniochos VII. The bronze coinage with the types of a lily (representing the Hasmonaeans) and anchor (symbolizing the Seleucid kings) struck at Jerusalem in the name of Antiochos VII should be reinterpreted as a sign of the Hasmonaean state's relative autonomy. This coinage ended with the death of Antiochos VII in 129 B.C., but the anchor and the lily reappeared on the coinage of Hyrcanus' son, Alexander Jannaeus, to illustrate the continuity of his reign with his father's. The anchor symbolism continued to be potent in Judea after the fall of the Hasmonaeans, reappearing on several series of bronze coins struck at Jerusalem under Herod the Great. Even after Herod's death in 4 B.C., the anchor emblem lived on, apparently now as a Herodian symbol. Again, the purpose seems to have been to express continuity and legitimacy.

5726 ——— "The Authorized Version: Money and Meaning in the King James Bible." *American Numismatic Society Magazine* 6, no. 2 (summer 2006): 13-18. Illus.
The King James version of the Bible is of interest to numismatists due to its tendency to reinterpret the ancient coin denominations of the Greek, Latin, and Hebrew scriptural sources in terms of contemporary sixteenth- and seventeenth-century English money. Thus, the King James Bible serves as a document for the circulating coinage of early modern Great Britain. Hoover explores the coins mentioned in the Bible to gain insight into the identity of the original coins.

5727 **Israel Numismatic Society.** *Studies in Honor of Arie Kindler. Israel Numismatic Journal* 13 (2000). 200 pp. including 20 pls.
A collection of twenty essays on ancient numismatics related to Israel, compiled in honor of the eightieth birthday of Dr. Arie Kindler, first director of the Kadman Numismatic Museum in Tel Aviv. Includes "The Coinage of Yehud and the Ptolemies" by Dan Barag, and "The Chronology of a Late Ptolemaic Bronze Coin-Type from Cyprus" by Haim Gitler and Alla Kushnir-Stein. Also includes a bibliography of 178 articles, monographs, and books by Kindler.

5728 **Jeselsohn, D.** "A New Coin Type with Hebrew Inscription." *Israel Exploration Journal* (Israel) 24, no. 2 (1974): 77-8. Illus.
Describes three Jewish coins discussed by Kindler (see Kindler "Silver Coins Bearing the Name of Judaea" below). Jeselsohn says the identification of the coin portrait as Ptolemy I is beyond doubt. This is the first coin type of the Yehud class which bears the head of an identifiable historic figure. The author suggests a date of 301-284 B.C. for the coins.

5729 ——— "Hever Yehudim—A New Jewish Coin." *Palestine Exploration Quarterly* (England) 112 (January-June 1980): 11-7. 1 pl.
"Some coins of Hasmonean *prutah* type bear the inscription *Hever Yehudim* without the name and title of the high priest. They are attributed to the opponents of Alexander Jannaeus during the war against him in 88 B.C." [A. Spaer, *NL* 106]

5730 ——— "Hever Ha-Yehudim—A Rejoinder." *SAN—Journal of the Society for Ancient Numismatics* 11, no. 3 (fall 1980): 47.
A critical response to Brin (see Brin "The Mystery Solved" above) concluding that the phrase in question refers to a sovereign entity of considerable authority.

5731 **Kadman, Leo.** "The Hebrew Coin Script: A Study in the Epigraphy of Ancient Jewish Coins." *Israel Exploration Journal* (Israel) 4, nos. 3 & 4 (1954): 151-68. 1 pl. [CS 2920]
"This article treats in detail the early Hebrew script of the autonomous and sovereign Jewish coinage of the three periods: (1) the coins of the Maccabean dynasty (135-37 B.C.), (2) the coins of the First War against Rome (A.D. 66-70), and (3) the coins of the War of Bar-Kokhba (A.D. 132-135). These

conclusions are reached: The theory that the characters on ancient Jewish coins were only an artificial revival of the ancient Hebrew alphabet can no longer be held. These letters are now considered as a direct offshoot of the ancient Hebrew alphabet with their own peculiar development during the 270 years of their use in the three periods of sovereign Jewish coinage. During this development many of the letters changed without altering the basic forms of the alphabet. The development of the Hebrew letters upon the coinage is governed by the trend to bring the shape of the letters into harmony with the symbols and the general character of the coins themselves. Because of this development the appearance of the Hebrew letters upon the ancient coinage gradually becomes quite similar to the contemporary Hebrew square letters." [R. Breaden, *NL* 33]

5732 ——— "The Development of Jewish Coinage." *The Dating and Meaning of Ancient Jewish Coins and Symbols: Six Essays in Jewish Numismatics.* Numismatic Studies and Research, Volume 2. Edited by Leo Kadman et al. Jerusalem and Tel Aviv: Israel Numismatic Society, 1958. Pages 98-103. 1 pl.
A summary of Jewish coinage from 135 B.C. to A.D. 66, briefly describing the major coin types of the period. Twenty coins are illustrated.

5733 ——— "Temple Dues and Currency in Ancient Palestine in the Light of Recent Discovered Coin-Hoards." *Israel Numismatic Bulletin* 1 (January-March 1962): 9-11. 1 pl. Also in *Congresso Internazionale di Numismatica, Roma 11-16 Settembre 1961. Volume 2.* Rome: Istituto Italiano de Numismatica, 1965. Pages 69-76.
Describes a hoard discovered on Mount Carmel in 1960 containing 3400 Tyrian shekels and 1000 half-shekels among other coins. The shekels and half-shekels dated from 40 B.C. to A.D. 54. Such coins did not constitute regular currency in Palestine at the time of concealment (after A.D. 53). Kadman concludes the hoard represents a transport of temple dues destined for the Temple of Jerusalem. Tyrian shekels were prescribed exclusively for the payment of Temple Dues (yearly contributions made to the Temple by male Jews).

5734 ——— "The Monetary Development of Palestine in the Light of Coin Hoards." *The Patterns of Monetary Development in Phoenicia and Palestine in Antiquity: International Numismatic Convention, Jerusalem, 27-31 December 1963.* Edited by A. Kindler. Tel-Aviv and Jerusalem: Schocken Publishing House, 1967. Pages 311-22. [CS 2924]
Discusses the nature of coin hoards and the problems encountered in the historical interpretation of hoards. Focuses on hoards found in Palestine.

5735 **Kadman, Leo et al., eds.** *Recent Studies and Discoveries on Ancient Jewish and Syrian Coins.* Publications of the Israel Numismatic Society, Volume 1. Jerusalem: Israel Numismatic Society, 1954. 100 pp., 9 pls.

5736 **Kadman, Leo, Arie Kindler, Ernst W. Klimovsky, Joseph Meyshan, Leo Mildenberg, G. Cohn, eds.** *The Dating and Meaning of Ancient Jewish Coins and Symbols: Six Essays in Jewish Numismatics.* Numismatic Studies and Research, Volume 2. Jerusalem and Tel Aviv: Israel Numismatic Society, 1958. 116 pp., 1 pl. [CS 2916]
A collection of six essays: "The Coinage of the Hasmonaean Dynasty" by Arie Kindler [5744], "The Coins of the Herodian Dynasty" by Josef Meyshan, "The Coins of the Jewish-Roman War" by Leo Kadman, "The Coinage of the Bar-Kokhba War" by Arie Kindler, "Symbols on Ancient Jewish Coins" by E. W. Klimowsky [5754], and "The Development of Jewish Coinage" by Leo Kadman [5732].

5737 **Kanael, Baruch.** "The Beginning of Maccabean Coinage." *Israel Exploration Journal* (Israel) 1, no. 3 (1950-1): 170-5. [CS 2925]
"Discussing first the permission to issue coins granted by Antiochus VII to Simon Maccabeus, the author believes that Simon did not avail himself of this privilege at the time since it would have involved open rebellion against Tryphon, the actual ruler of Syria. Shortly thereafter when Antiochus became sure of his kingdom, he revoked the permit. The first Maccabean coins were struck by John Hyrcanus, probably about 110 B.C. after the defeat of the Syrian army and the capture of Samaria and Scythopolis." [M. Thompson, *NL* 20]

5738 ——— "Ancient Jewish Coins and Their Historical Importance." *Biblical Archaeologist* 26, no. 2 (May 1963): 38-62. Illus. [CS 2926]
Discusses the use of ancient coins as sources of information for Jewish history from the late Persian period until the time of the Bar Kochba revolt. Fifty-seven coins are illustrated.

5739 ——— "The Transition from Priestly Predominance to Lay Predominance in the Light of Ancient Jewish Coinage." *Congresso Internazionale di Numismatica, Roma 11-16 Settembre 1961. Volume 2.* Rome: Istituto Italiano de Numismatica, 1965. Pages 87-92. 1 pl.
Describes the transition from the priestly coin types of the Maccabean rulers to types stressing the importance of laymen in the Temple in later years.

5740 ——— "Literaturüberblick der Griechischen Numismatik: Altjüdische Münzen." *Jahrbuch für Numismatik und Geldsseschichte* (Germany) 17 (1967): 159-298. [CS 2909]
A bibliography.

5741 **Kaufman, J. Chaim.** *Unrecorded Hasmonean Coins from the J. Ch. Kaufman Collection.* Publications of the Israel Numismatic Society. Numismatic Studies and Researches 8. Jerusalem: Israel Numismatic Society, 1995. 80 pp., 68 pls.
A catalogue of about 500 coins in the author's collection which are new variants not listed in Meshorer's *Ancient Jewish Coinage I* and *Addendum I*. Most of the coins are perutah (dileptons) issued in the names of the Hasmonean rulers from John Hyrcanus I to Mattathias Antigonus (135-37 B.C.). Includes an alphabetic classification of the coin inscriptions (in Hebrew).

5742 ——— *Unrecorded Hasmonean Coins from the J. Ch. Kaufman Collection, Part II.* Publications of the Israel Numismatic Society. Numismatic Studies and Researches 10. Jerusalem: Israel Numismatic Society, 2004. 206 pp, illus.
Covers the entire range of Hasmonean coinage from ca. 125 to 37 B.C. All the coins are illustrated in actual size and enlarged 3:1.

5743 **Kindler, Arie.** "The Jaffa Hoard of Alexander Jannaeus." *Israel Exploration Journal* (Israel) 4, nos. 3/4 (1954): 170-85. 2 pls. Reprinted in *Recent Studies and Discoveries on Ancient Jewish and Syrian Coins.* Publications of the Israel Numismatic Society, Volume 1. Edited by Kadman, Leo et al. Jerusalem: Israel Numismatic Society, 1954. Pages 34-49.
A hoard of 851 coins and some fragments of King Alexander Jannaeus was found in 1949. All coins but one were of the same type—the Star and Anchor type. Includes an inventory of the hoard together with a detailed discussion of the type and the imitated Jewish legends. The coins were probably struck at Jaffa, ca. 90-85 B.C. [Summarized from R. Breaden, *NL* 33]. [Also see Wirgin "Letter to the Editor" below].

5744 ——— "The Coinage of the Hasmonaean Dynasty." *The Dating and Meaning of Ancient Jewish Coins and Symbols: Six Essays in Jewish Numismatics*. Numismatic Studies and Research, Volume 2. Edited by Leo Kadman et al. Jerusalem and Tel Aviv: Israel Numismatic Society, 1958. Pages 10-28.
A brief history of the Maccabaean and Hasmonaean dynasties. An introduction to the coinage describes the types, legends used by each ruler, denominations, minting authority, and dating. Primarily discusses the numerous errors and misattributions found in Wirgin and Mandel's *The History of Coins and Symbols in Ancient Israel* (see below).

5745 ——— *Thesaurus of Judaean Coins, from the Fourth Century B.C. to the Third Century A.D.* Jerusalem, 1958. 90 pp., 67 pls. [CS 2931]
In Hebrew.

5746 ——— "The Mint of Tyre—The Major Source of Silver Coins in Ancient Palestine." *Eretz-Israel: Archaeological, Historical and Geographical Studies* (Israel) 8 (1967): 318-24.
This article is in Hebrew, but a brief English summary appears on page 79. A hoard of twenty-five coins (owl/hippocamp type), minted at Tyre or Acco, was found at the site of ancient Acco. These types have been dated to the post-Alexandrine period. Kindler suggests a pre-Alexandrine date for these coins (ca. 364-346 B.C.). He also discusses the activity of the Tyre mint during later periods.

5747 ——— "The Monetary Pattern and Function of the Jewish Coins." *The Patterns of Monetary Development in Phoenicia and Palestine in Antiquity: International Numismatic Convention, Jerusalem, 27-31 December 1963*. Edited by A. Kindler. Tel-Aviv and Jerusalem: Schocken Publishing House, 1967. Pages 180-205. 4 pls. [CS 2934]
Examines the place of Jewish coins in the economic situation prevailing in Palestine from 110 B.C. to A.D. 135. Begins with a discussion of Hellenistic coinage and its reflection in the Hasmonean issues. Discusses the denominations used (chalkous, hemichalkous, delepton, and lepton) and examines the relative values of each denomination. Compares coin sizes and weights. Discusses the use within Palestine of silver coins from other mints. Continues with a discussion of the issues of the Roman procurators, the coinage of the Jewish Wars, and the Bar-Kokhba coinage. [Also see Kindler and Klimowsky *The Function and Pattern* below].

5748 ——— "Addendum to the Dated Coins of Alexander Jannaeus." *Israel Exploration Journal* (Israel) 18 (1968): 188-91. 1 pl. [CS 2935]
"In reference to J. Naveh's 'Dated Coins of Alexander Jannaeus' (see Naveh below) proposing a reading and dating of the Hebrew inscription on the small bronze coins of Alexander Jannaeus of the type *BMC Palestine* pp. 210-211, Nos. 1-18, the view is advanced that corresponding regnal years in Greek numerals appear on the anchor side of these coins." [A. Spaer, *NL* 82]

5749 ——— *Coins of the Land of Israel: Collection of the Bank of Israel—A Catalogue*. Translated by R. Grafman. Jerusalem: Keter Publishing House, 1974. 138 pp., illus. [CS 16584]
A catalogue of the Jewish coins in the collection of the Bank of Israel, containing descriptions of each coin along with extensive discussions of historical background. Covers the Persian period, Hasmonean period, Herodian dynasty, period of Roman rule, and the city coin issues. Describes and illustrates 207 coins. [Also see R. Barkay "Rare and Unpublished Coins" above].

5750 ——— "Silver Coins Bearing the Name of Judaea from the Early Hellenistic Period." *Israel Exploration Journal* (Israel) 24, no. 2 (1974): 73-6. 1 pl.
Describes several previously unknown quarter-obol silver coins with a diademed head (probably Ptolemy I) on the obverse and an eagle on the reverse. The coins bears a Paleo-Hebrew inscription "Yhdh." The coins appeared on the market in Jerusalem. Lists the main types of Yehud coins. Discusses their historical background and the new coins' place in the Yehud series. Concludes the coins were struck in Jerusalem in 301 B.C. or later. [Also see Jeselsohn "A New Coin Type" above].

5750a ——— "The Hellenistic Influence on the Hasmonean Coins." *XII Internationaler Numismatischer Kongress Berlin 1997, Akten-Proceedings-Actes*. Edited by B. Kluge and B. Weisser. Berlin: Staatliche Museen zu Berlin, 2000.

5751 **Kindler, Arie, and Alla Stein.** *A Bibliography of the City Coinage of Palestine from the 2nd Century B.C. to the 3rd Century A.D.* BAR International Series 374. Oxford: British Archaeological Reports, 1987. 261 pp.
Lists about 2700 books and articles, dating from 1671 to 1984, dealing with the coinage of thirty-seven Palestinian cities. Includes items dealing with numismatics as well as history, mythology, archaeology, and economics when linked to the coins. The listings are presented in city-name order.

5752 **Kindler, Arie, and Ernst W. Klimowsky.** *The Function and Pattern of the Jewish Coins and the City Coins of Palestine and Phoenicia.* Publication of the Israel Numismatic Society, No. 5. Jerusalem: Schocken Publishing House, 1968. 79 pp., 4 pls. [CS 2937]
Contains two papers: "The Monetary Pattern and Function of the Jewish Coins" by Kindler (see Kindler above) and "The Monetary Function of City Coins" by Klimowsky which discusses the autonomous city coinage during the Roman Imperial period.

5753 **Kleeb, Alvin A.** "Letter from James Pollack Regarding Biblical Coins." *SAN—Journal of the Society for Ancient Numismatics* 16, no. 3 (fall 1985): 44, 52.
The transcript of an 1870 letter written by the director of the U.S. Mint discussing Biblical coins in the Mint's collection, with correcting and updating comments by Kleeb.

5754 **Klimowsky, Ernst W.** "Symbols on Ancient Jewish Coins." *The Dating and Meaning of Ancient Jewish Coins and Symbols: Six Essays in Jewish Numismatics*. Numismatic Studies and Research, Volume 2. Edited by Leo Kadman et al. Jerusalem and Tel Aviv: Israel Numismatic Society, 1958. Pages 81-97.
Examines the meaning of the lulab and ethrog, the chalice, the palm branch, the seven-branched candlestick, pomegranates and ears of barley, the umbrella, the cross, the Temple and its utensils, and the palm tree.

5755 ——— "Religious Symbols on Ancient Jewish Coins." *Israel Numismatic Bulletin* (Israel) 3-4 (August-December 1962): 81-8. 1 pl. [CS 2938]

This article is an attempt to introduce an appropriate evaluation of symbols into numismatic studies. The subject falls into three parts: the first concerned with symbols, to be distinguished from any other sort of signs; the second devoted especially to religious symbols; and the third and main part dealing with religious symbols represented on ancient Jewish coins.

5756 ——— "Danka and *Prutah*: The *Prutah*." *Israel Numismatic Journal* (Israel) 1, no. 4 (1963): 68-9.

5757 ——— *On Ancient Palestinian and Other Coins: Their Symbolism and Metrology.* Numismatic Studies and Researches, Volume 7. Tel-Aviv: Israel Numismatic Society, 1974. 179 pp., 15 pls. [CS 2942]
"There are four parts to this collection of numismatic papers published between 1954 and 1973. In the first, the importance of symbols depicted on Greek, Roman, Jewish and Indian coins is shown and specific symbols, such as the umbrella, chalice and amphora are interpreted. In the second part, the title of Herod Agrippa I as ΒΑΣΙΛΕΥΣ ΜΕΓΑΣ and the coinage of the Herodian kings of Armenia are discussed. The third part is dedicated to the relation between the metrology of Phoenician and Palestinian city coins and to the migration of denominations. The fourth part calls for the systematic study of Greek Imperials." [E. Klimowsky, *NL* 93]

5758 **Kogan, Howard.** "Faiths Intertwined: Jewish Bronze Coins Help Clarify Biblical History." *The Celator* 2, no. 10 (October 1988): 1, 20-2. Illus.
A general review of the bronze coins mentioned in the Old and New Testaments.

5759 ——— *Ancient Kings of Israel and Their Coins. A New Guide for Investors and Collectors of the Bronze Perutah: Its Origins and Historical Background.* Israel: H. Kogan, 1987. 55 pp., illus., map.
Reviews the historical background of the bronze coins used in Israel during the period of Persian and Seleucid rule. Then examines the Jewish perutah. Lists and illustrates the various types, provides estimated market values and brief historical comments on each issue through A.D. 70. Includes brief comments on the minting process and mint errors. Includes a list of mint cities with a map and commentary on each. Brief discussion of the valuation and grading of the coins.

5760 ——— "Widow's Mites Thought to be Alexander Yannai Issues." *The Celator* 4, no. 4 (April 1990): 14, 31. Illus.
The author discusses Jewish temple taxes and argues that the prutah of Alexander Yannai should be considered the "widow's mite" of the Bible. Illustrates prutah of Alexander Yannai and Herod I.

5761 **Kokkinos, N.** "A Coin of Herod the Great Commemorating the City of Sebaste." *Liber Annuus* (Israel) 35 (1985): 303-6. Illus.
"The author reattributes to Herod the Great, 22 B.C., a coin attributed by Meshorer in *Ancient Jewish Coinage* (No. 21, Vol. II, p. 253) to Agrippa II, A.D. 79/80." [A. Spaer, *NL* 117]

5762 **Kool, Robert.** "The Rediscovery of G. F. Hill's Original Plates of *BMC Palestine* and *Phoenicia* in Jerusalem." *Israel Numismatic Journal* 14 (2001-2002): 260-2. Illus.

5763 **Krupp, Michael.** "Some Remarks on the Palm-Branch/Lily Half-Prutah of Alexander Jannaeus." *Israel Numismatic Journal* (Israel) 4 (1980): 22 ff.

5764 ——— "A Metallurgical Examination of Hasmonean Coins." *Israel Numismatic Journal* (Israel) 16 (2007-2008): 57-75.

5765 **Kushnir-Stein, Alla.** "Some Observations on Palestinian Coins with a Bevelled Edge." *Israel Numismatic Journal* (Israel) 14 (2001-02): 78-83.

5766 **Lambert, C.** "A Hoard of Bronze Coins from Ophel." *Quarterly Statement of the Palestine Exploration Fund* (England) (1927): 184-8.
Reports on a hoard of 319 coins, almost all of Alexander Jannaeus, found during excavations on Mount Ophel. All the Alexander Jannaeus coins are of the anchor/wheel variety. Suggests a burial date ca. 95 B.C. for the hoard. Concludes that the anchor/wheel coins were the first type to be struck by Alexander Jannaeus. Attempts to arrange the coin types of Jannaeus in the order in which they were struck.

5767 **Lemaire, André.** "MBGY/Menbigi, Monétaire de Transeuphratène avant Alexandre?" *Travaux de Numismatique Grecque Offerts à Georges Le Rider.* Edited by M. Amandry and S. Hurter. London: Spink, 1999. Pages 215-19. 1 pl.
The pre-Alexander coinage of Gaza, Ascalon, Ashdod, Judea, and Samaria.

5768 **Lewis, Peter E., and Ron Bolden.** *The Pocket Guide to Saint Paul: Coins Encountered by the Apostle on His Travels.* Kent Town, South Australia: Wakefield Press, 2002. 202 pp., illus.
Traces St. Paul's journey through Asia Minor, the Middle East, and Greece to Rome. Discusses the circulating coinage that Paul likely used. Offers a theory that the Antioch tetradrachm is the "tribute penny" of the Bible. Includes commentary on Biblical references and sites depicted on the coinage. [Reviewed in *The Numismatist* 115, no. 10 (October 2002): 1207, by O. D. Hoover in *American Numismatic Society Magazine* 2, no. 1 (spring 2003): 52-4, and by Peter Dunstan in *The Celator* 17, no. 6 (June 2003): 35, 50].

5769 **Liebert, David.** "Palm Trees Served as Symbol of Judaean Prosperity." *The Celator* 4, no. 5 (May 1990): 8. Illus.
The palm was one of the central symbols of Jewish iconography representing the abundance of the land. Discusses the use of the palm in religious ritual and its appearance as a coin type.

5770 ——— "The Pomegranate in the Art of the Ancient Holy Land." *The Celator* 10, no. 9 (September 1996): 48. Illus.
Discusses the pomegranate as a symbol in art and coinage.

5771 **Lovette, James. B.** *Biblical Related Coins, Including Both the Old and New Testaments.* Little Rock, Arkansas: James B. Lovette, 1996. 207 pp., illus., 2 maps.

Provides a list of actual places, persons, and things that either issued coins or were mentioned directly or indirectly in the Bible. Includes 236 coin entries and 567 illustrations. Each entry includes a brief history, Scripture reference, and market price range.

5772 **Madden, Frederick W.** "Coins, Money, and Weights of the Bible." *Ancient Coins and Artifacts of the Bible.* Pages 16-9. (Editor, publisher, and date unknown).
A reprint of an article from an unknown source, probably of the late nineteenth century. Reviews Biblical references to money and coins. Lists the denominations and monetary terms mentioned in the Bible and discusses their origins and meanings. Reviews the weights mentioned in the Bible. Summarizes the accounts of mining and metallurgy in the Bible.

5773 ——— *History of Jewish Coinage and of Money in the Old and New Testament.* London: Bernard Quaritch, 1864. Reprints, New York: Ktav Publishing House; and San Diego: Pegasus Publishing Co., 1967. 350 pp., illus. [CS 2943a]
Includes an introduction to the origin of coinage and the pre-coinage forms of money employed by the Jews. Discusses the first Judean coinage and continues through the Roman period. Includes discussions of Roman coins commemorating the capture of Jerusalem and Roman Imperial colonial coins struck at Jerusalem. Includes chapters on money in the New Testament and coin inscriptions. Includes an extensive discussion of weights. Concludes with an appendix on counterfeits. Two hundred fifty-four woodcut illustrations are incorporated into the text. Although Madden published a revised edition of this work (see *Coins of the Jews* below), the reprint is of the 1864 edition. The reprint includes an introduction pointing out the places where the conclusions of more recent research differ from Madden's writings. Also, Reifenberg numbers have been added to each illustration when possible. [Reviewed by A. Negev in *Israel Exploration Journal* 21, nos. 2-3 (1971): 184. Also see Madden's supplement "Jewish Numismatics" below].

5774 ——— "Remarks in Reply to the New Observations on 'Jewish Numismatics' by M. F. DeSaulcy." *Numismatic Chronicle* new ser., 5 (1865): 191-216. "Additional Observations." Pages 342-6.
Criticism of Félicien deSaulcy's attributions of Jewish coins (see deSaulcy above) with arguments for alternate attributions.

5775 ——— "Jewish Coins." *Numismatic Chronicle* new ser., 12 (1872): 1-8.
Further comments on deSaulcy's attributions of Jewish coins (see previous item).

5776 ——— "Jewish Numismatics: Being a Supplement to the 'History of Jewish Coinage and Money of the Old and New Testaments,' Published in 1864." Parts 1-3. *Numismatic Chronicle* new ser., 14 (1874): 281-316; 15 (1875): 41-80, 101-39, 169-95, 298-333; 16 (1876): 45-70, 81-132, 177-234. 1 pl.
This supplement to the author's *History of Jewish Coinage* (see above) presents the latest opinions and examines questions that have arisen since its publication. Part 1 focuses on silver shekels, half shekels, and copper coins usually attributed to Simon Maccabaeus, and coins of the Hasmonaean family. Part 2 examines coins of the Herodian family, coins struck by the Procurators, and coins of the two revolts of the Jews. Part 3 examines coins struck in Palestine commemorating the capture of Jerusalem, Imperial colonial coins struck at Jerusalem, Arab coins, and money in the Old and New Testaments.

5777 ——— *Coins of the Jews.* London: Trübner & Co., 1881 and 1903. 329 pp., illus. [CS 2943]
In effect, the second edition of Madden's *History of Jewish Coinage* above. Illustrated by 279 woodcuts. Includes a table of alphabets.

5778 ——— "Money and Coins of the Jews." *Spink Numismatic Circular* 5, no. 54 (May 1897): cols. 2203-15. Illus.
Reviews the money of the Jews from the early mentions of gold in the Bible, to the use of coined money. Discusses coin-related terms used in the Bible, as well as money-changers and weights mentioned in the Bible. Illustrates a family tree of the Herodian family.

5779 **Maltiel-Gerstenfeld, Jacob.** *260 Years of Ancient Jewish Coins: A Catalogue.* Tel Aviv: Kol Printing Services, 1982. 317 pp., illus., maps.
A catalogue with illustrations, a discussion of historical background, new finds, changes and discoveries, the forgery of coins by the State, and countermarks. The relative values of different denominations is compared. Includes genealogical tables, maps of the Jewish state at various time periods, and comparative tables of scripts. [Reviewed by D. Jeselsohn in *SAN* 15, no. 1 (spring 1984): 12-3].

5780 ——— *New Catalogue of Ancient Jewish Coins.* Tel Aviv: Minerva, 1987. 155 pp., 33 pls.
A revised version of the catalogue above, correcting many of its errors. [Reviewed by A. Burnett in *Numismatic Chronicle* 148 (1988): 233].

5781 **Marmorstein, Arthur.** "The Coins of Alexander Jannaeus." *Quarterly Statement of the Palestine Exploration Fund* (England) (1928): 48-50.
Discusses the reason behind the use of two different spellings of the ruler's name on coins of Alexander Jannaeus. The author discusses this change and its possible connection to a reluctance to pronounce God's name.

5782 **Mayer, Leo Ary.** *A Bibliography of Jewish Numismatics.* Edited by Michael Avi-Yonah. Jerusalem: The Magnes Press, Hebrew University, 1966. 78 pp. [CS 2910]
A bibliography of works in all languages dealing with coins struck by a Jewish authority in the land of Israel in ancient times. Lists 822 works arranged by author. Includes a subject index. [Numerous additions and corrections are provided in the review by Daniel Sperber in *Numismatic Chronicle* 7th ser., 7 (1967): 301-2].

5783 **McLean, Mark D.** "The Initial Coinage of Alexander Jannaeus." *Museum Notes* 26 (1981): 153-61. 1 pl.
Concurs with Meshorer's attribution of the first Hasmonaean coins to Alexander Jannaeus. Reorders the coinage of Jannaeus into a relative chronology, ca. 100-79 B.C. Discusses the shift from the use of *yhwntn* to *yntn*.

5784 **Mendelssohn, Edwin.** "Development of the Monetary System in Ancient Palestine." *The Numismatist* 88, no. 10 (October 1975): 2163-9. Illus.
The author traces the development of money in Palestine from the barter stage to the use of pre-weighed precious metals. Quotes various Bible passages which refer to the use of money. Reviews the development of the Babylonian weight standard.

5785 **Meshorer, Ya'akov.** "An Archaic Coin from Jerusalem." *Journal of the Israel Department of Antiquities* (Israel) 3 (1961): 185. 1 pl. [CS 2944]

5786 ———— "A New Coin of Yehud." *Israel Numismatic Journal* (Israel) 2, nos. 3-4 (1964): 3. [CS 2945]

5787 ———— "Maritime Symbols on Ancient Jewish Coins." *Israel Numismatic Journal* (Israel) 2, nos. 1-2 (1964): 8-10. Illus. [CS 2946]
"Describes and illustrates ten ancient Jewish coins bearing maritime symbols. The period covered begins with the Hasmonaean dynasty and ends with the reign of Agrippa II." [*NL* 73]

5788 ———— "New Denominations in Ancient Jewish Coins." *Israel Numismatic Journal* (Israel) 2, nos. 3-4 (1964): 4-7. [CS 2947]

5789 ———— "A New Type of YHD Coin." *Israel Exploration Journal* (Israel) 16, no. 4 (1966): 217-19. 1 pl. [CS 2950]
"This recently discovered silver coin has *obv.*, a bird with outspread wings, believed to be a falcon, and inscription YHD in ancient Hebrew characters, and *rev.*, a lily. The coin is attributed to Judaea, fifth-to-fourth century B.C." [W. Wirgin, *NL* 79]

5790 ———— *Jewish Coins of the Second Temple Period.* Translated by I. H. Levine. Tel Aviv: Am Hassefer, 1967. 184 pp., 32 pls.
Provides an historical overview of Jewish history from the Persian period through the Ptolemaic domination, the Seleucid domination, the Hasmonaean Revolt, the period of Roman domination, the Herodian dynasty, Roman Procurators, War against Rome, and the Bar Kochba War. Includes a discussion of the coinage of each period. Presents a catalogue of eighty coin types.

5791 ———— "The Beginning of the Hasmonaean Coinage." *Israel Exploration Journal* (Israel) 24, no. 1 (1974): 59-61. Illus. Also appeared in *The Shekel* 8, no. 4 (winter 1975): 23-5. Illus. [CS 2953]
"In support of the view that Hasmonean coinage commenced under Alexander Jannaeus (103-76 B.C.), an unpublished Seleucid copper coin showing *obv.*, royal portrait and *rev.*, lily with letters BA and LK is described. Attribution to year twenty of Antiochus VIII's reign and the mint of Jerusalem is proposed, confirming that until that date (102 B.C.) Jerusalem was still a Seleucid mint." [A. Spaer, *NL* 94]. [Also see Fischer "Another Hellenizing Coin" above].

5792 ———— "Again on the Beginning of Hasmonean Coinage." *Israel Numismatic Journal* (Israel) 5 (1981): 11-6. Illus.
"Another installment in the ongoing discussion as to whether Hasmonean coinage began under John Hyrcanus I, as claimed by Barag and Qedar in their note in *Israel Numismatic Journal* 4 (1980): 8-21 (see above), or under Alexander Jannaeus as propounded by the author." [Y. Meshorer, *NL* 109]

5793 ———— "New Types of Judaean Silver Coins." *Israel Numismatic Journal* (Israel) 5 (1981): 4. Illus.
"Two hemidrachms with inscription YHDH (Judaea), one of them also showing the letters BA and assigned to Ptolemy II, are published. So far only hemiobols of this type have been published." [A. Spaer, *NL* 109]

5794 ———— "On D. Barag and S. Qedar: When Did the Hasmonaeans Begin Minting Coins." *Qadmoniot* (Israel) 15, no. 2-3 (1982): 92. Illus.
"A reply to Barag and Qedar's article (see "The Beginning of Hasmonean Coinage" above). The author argues for the beginning of Jewish coinage only under Alexander Jannaeus." [A. Spaer, *NL* 109]

5795 ———— *Ancient Jewish Coinage, Volume 1: Persian Period through Hasmonaeans.* 184 pp., 56 pls. *Volume 2: Herod the Great through Bar Cochba.* 295 pp., 36 pls. Dix Hills, New York: Amphora Books, 1982-1983.
The standard reference on Jewish coinage, replacing Madden's *Coins of the Jews.* Includes extensive discussions of Jewish history, the interpretation of Jewish symbols, and Jewish epigraphy. Presents a catalogue of all coin types, and many variants, making use of all the important collections of Jewish coins in the world. The plates are of high quality, and many of the small coins have been enlarged. Volume 1 covers the YHD coins and coins of the Hasmonaeans, as well as coins struck by foreign rulers for use in Israel. [Also see *Addendum 1* below. These volumes were replaced in 2001 by Meshorer's *A Treasury of Jewish Coins* (see below)].

5796 ———— "Judaea, Samaria, and Galilee." *A Survey of Numismatic Research, 1978-1984. Volume 1: Ancient, Medieval and Modern Numismatics.* Edited by M. J. Price et al. International Association of Professional Numismatists Special Publication, No. 9. London: International Numismatic Commission, 1986. Pages 201-3.
A narrative overview of newly published works in the field of numismatics. Summarizes the major findings, with bibliographic references cited in the footnotes.

5797 ———— "Ancient Jewish Coinage. Addendum 1." *Israel Numismatic Journal* (Israel) 11 (1990-91): 104 ff. Illus. Reprinted as a booklet, 1991. 25 pp., 16 pls.
Corrects and supplements Meshorer's *Ancient Jewish Coinage* (see above). Lists 175 new coin types and varieties. The text is divided into sections paralleling the arrangement of *Ancient Jewish Coinage.*

5798 ———— *Ancient Means of Exchange: Weights and Coins.* Haifa: University of Haifa, 1998. 199 pp., illus.
"This is the first volume of a catalogue of the collections in the Reuben and Edith Hecht Museum at the University of Haifa. It covers 761 coins (mainly Jewish or connected with the Levant), fifty ancient weights and four metal objects used for exchange before the appearance of coinage. All coins are described and illustrated and the chapters include reference to the historical background." [A. Spaer, *NL* 140]. [In English and Hebrew].

5799 ———— *TestiMoney.* Jerusalem: The Israel Museum, 2000. 63 pp., illus.
The coins described in this book highlight points in history and culture with an emphasis on the Holy Land, from the Persian period to the Crusader period. The coins represent the three monotheistic religions, Judaism, Christianity, and Islam, as well as pagan civilizations. Beautifully illustrated by coins from the collection of the Israel Museum. Chapters are: Caiaphas and Pontius Pilate, the seven species of the land of Israel, Hebrew script, historical buildings and monuments in Jerusalem, Helena and the holy places, the names of Jerusalem, the Samaritans, the binding of Issac, the utensils of the Jerusalem Temple, the lily, hot springs, money in the Old and New Testament, the tenth Roman legion "Fretensis," and the Zodiac.

5800 ——— *A Treasury of Jewish Coins, from the Persian Period to Bar Kochba.* Jerusalem: Yad Ben-Zvi Press, and Nyack, N.Y.: Amphora Books, 2001. 356 pp. incl. 80 pls.
The standard reference on Jewish coinage, this volume is a complete revision of Meshorer's *Ancient Jewish Coins* volumes 1 and 2 (1982-3) and *Addendum* 1 (1993). Discusses the period of Persian and Ptolemaic rule, catalogues the coinage of the Hasmoneans, the Herodian Dynasty, the coins of the Jewish war against Rome, and the coins of the Bar Kochba War. Supplements cover the coins of the Roman procurators of Judea, the coins of Agrippa II, the Jewish kings of Chalcis and Lesser Armenia, the minimas of Caesarea, the Judea Capta coins minted in Caesarea, and the Roman Administration coinage under Domitian. [Reviewed by Edward Caine in *The Celator* 16, no. 4 (April 2002): 34-5, and by Oliver Hoover in *American Numismatic Society Magazine* 1, no. 1 (spring 2002): 36-9].

5801 ——— *Coins of the Holy Land: The Abraham D. Sofaer Collection at the American Numismatic Society.* Ancient Coins in North American Collections. New York: American Numismatic Society, 2012. 2 volumes, 154 pls.
A comprehensive catalogue of approximately 5000 coins from the late Persian period to the Crusaders in the Middle Ages. Includes city coins from Israel, Palestine, and adjoining countries, as well as coins issued by Jewish, Samaritan, Nabataean, and other rulers.

5802 **Meyshan, Joseph.** "What is a Prutah?" *Eretz-Israel: Archaeological, Historical and Geographical Studies* (Israel) 8 (1967): 325-6.
This article is in Hebrew, but a brief English summary appears on page 79. The term *prutah*—a small Jewish coin similar to the small Greek lepton—is used to signify most of the coins of the Hasmoneans, the Roman procurators of Judea, the Herodian dynasty, and the First Revolt. Meyshan discusses the origin of the term. Suggests that all Jewish copper coins of less than four grams should be call *prutot*.

5803 ——— *Essays in Jewish Numismatics.* Numismatic Studies and Researches, No. 6. Jerusalem: Israel Numismatic Society, 1968. 165 pp., 6 pls. [CS 2957]
Contains a collection of twenty-three essays (twenty-one in English) previously published by the author, mainly on the coins of the Herodian dynasty. [Reviewed by Daniel Sperber in *Spink Numismatic Circular* 76, no. 11 (November 1968): 341, and by G. K. Jenkins in *Numismatic Chronicle* 7th ser., 10 (1970): 331-2].

5804 **Mildenberg, Leo.** "Yehud: A Preliminary Study of the Provincial Coinage of Judaea." *Greek Numismatics and Archaeology: Essays in Honor of Margaret Thompson.* Edited by O. Mørkholm and N. M. Waggoner. Wetteren: Numismatique Romaine, 1979. Pages 183-96. 2 pls. Reprinted in *Leo Mildenberg. Vestigia Leonis: Studien zur Antiken Numismatik Israels, Palästinas und der Östlichen Mittelmeerwelt.* Novum Testamentum et Orbis Antiquus 36. Edited by U. Hübner and E. Knauf. Freiburg: Universitätsverlag, and Göttingen: Vandenhoeck & Ruprecht, 1998. Pages 67-76.
Mildenberg examines a drachm in the British Museum which bears the inscription *yhd* ("Judea" in Aramaic). The obverse has a bearded man in Corinthian helmet; the reverse has a bearded deity seated on a winged wheel. The author discusses the mint, minting authority, weight standard, and date of the coin. He assigns it to ca. 380-360 B.C. He also discusses the series of minute Yehud silver coins issued under Persian rule, those issued during the Macedonian occupation, and those issued in the period of the Ptolemaic Kingdom. He concludes all were issued in Judea by order of the local governor on behalf of the foreign overlords. Mildenberg dates the coins issued under Persian rule to 360-331 B.C., those issued under Macedonian rule to 330-312, and those issued under Ptolemaic rule to 300-282. Concludes with a catalogue of the twenty-eight coins discussed. [Also see Hübner and Knauf *Vestigia Leonis* under GENERAL WORKS—GREEK].

5805 ——— "On the Money Circulation in Palestine from Artaxerxes II till Ptolemy I: Preliminary Studies of the Local Coinage in the Fifth Persian Satrapy, Part 5. *Transeuphratène* (France) 7 (1994): 63-71. Reprinted in *Leo Mildenberg. Vestigia Leonis: Studien zur Antiken Numismatik Israels, Palästinas und der Östlichen Mittelmeerwelt.* Novum Testamentum et Orbis Antiquus 36. Edited by U. Hübner and E. Knauf. Freiburg: Universitätsverlag, and Göttingen: Vandenhoeck & Ruprecht, 1998. Pages 59-66.
Briefly reviews the hoard evidence for Greek coins found in Palestine, noting that few coins of the sixth and fifth centuries B.C. have been found. Discusses the Yehud coinage and Samarian coinage, noting that the Persian administration of these two provinces produced their own coins for circulation in their territories during the fourth century B.C. before the arrival of Alexander the Great. But the bulk of the money supply came from local mints. Summarizes the local coinage struck at Gaza, Ashdod, and Ascalon. [Also see Hübner and Knauf *Vestigia Leonis* under GENERAL WORKS—GREEK].

5806 ——— "*yehud* und *smryn*: Über das Geld der Persischen Provinzen Juda und Samaria im 4 Jahrhundert." *Geschichte-Tradition-Reflexion: Festschrift für Martin Hengel zum 70. Geburtstag. Band I: Judentum.* Edited by H. Canik, H. Lichtenberger, and P. Schäfer. Tübingen, 1996. Pages 119-46.

5807 **Minc, Henryk.** "The Inscription 'Hever Hayehudim' on Hasmonaean Coins." *SAN—Journal of the Society for Ancient Numismatics* 6, no. 2 (winter 1974-5): 32-3.
Discusses alternate interpretations of the inscription "hever hayehudim" which appears on the obverse of Hasmonaean coins. The author disputes the interpretation as "The Jewish People" and argues that the inscription refers to a specific organization such as the Senate or Sanhedrin.

5808 ——— "Yehohanan, The High Priest." *SAN—Journal of the Society for Ancient Numismatics* 8, no. 2 (winter 1977): 30-3.
Minc reconsiders the attribution of Hasmonaean coinage with the Yehohanan inscription. Commonly attributed to Hyrcanus I, it has recently been suggested these coins belong to Hyrcanus II. The author reviews the arguments of various researchers and concludes that the attribution to Hyrcanus II is very speculative, and prefers the attribution to Hyrcanus I.

5809 ——— "Some Rare and Unusual Jewish Coins." *SAN—Journal of the Society for Ancient Numismatics* 10, no. 1 (winter 1979): 10-4. Illus.
Ten coins from the author's collection are pictured and described. Each is a rare variant of a common Jewish coin.

5810 ——— "Coins of Alexander Yannai." Parts 1-2. *SAN—Journal of the Society for Ancient Numismatics* 12, no. 3 (fall 1981): 49-52, 55, 57; no. 4 (winter 1981-2): 64-7. Illus.
Discusses the chronological problems surrounding the coinage of Alexander Yannai (103-76 B.C.). A general classification scheme is given, followed by a critical examination of the chronologies proposed by Lambert, Narkiss, Reifenberg, Kanael, Meshorer, and Kindler. Examines the evidence supplied by Yannai's overstruck coins, and proposes a chronological order for the coins.

5811 ——— "Hasmonaean Coinage." *SAN—Journal of the Society for Ancient Numismatics* 15, no. 2 (summer 1984): 26-32.
An overview of the history of the Hasmonaean dynasty and a discussion of the coinage. Includes enlarged photographs of the major types of bronze coinage. Discusses the interpretation of inscriptions and gives guidelines for the attribution of the coins.

5812 **Naveh, J.** "Dated Coins of Alexander Janneus." *Israel Exploration Journal* (Israel) 18 (1968): 20-6. 2 pls.
"The 'barbarous Hebrew' script appearing on the minor bronze coins of Alexander Janneus, 103-76 B.C. (*BMC Palestine* pp. 210-211, Nos. 1-18), hitherto considered unintelligible, is here shown to be Aramaic. It reads 'Malka Alexandros' together with a regnal year. So far the only dates noted are year 20 and 25 (83/82 B.C. and 78/77 B.C.)." [A. Spaer, *NL* 82]. [Also see A. Kindler "Addendum" above].

5813 **Nussbaum, Harold J.** "The Seventh Coin Type of Herod Archelaus." *The Numismatist* 84, no. 8 (August 1971): 1295-6. Illus.
Publishes the fourth known specimen of a rare bronze coin of Herod Archelaus. The obverse inscription is EΘNAPXOY.

5814 **Oestreicher, Bruno.** "The Denominations of Ancient Jewish Coins." *Israel Numismatic Journal* (Israel) 1 (April 1963): 7-12. 1 pl. [CS 2964]
Previous writers generally listed coins only by size and weight. The author identifies numerous denominations and describes their types. For Alexander Jannaeus, he identifies prutah and half-prutah; for Herod I, double prutah and half-prutah.

5815 ——— "Denominations in Jewish Coinage." *The Patterns of Monetary Development in Phoenicia and Palestine in Antiquity: Proceedings, International Numismatic Convention, Jerusalem, 27-31 December 1963.* Edited by A. Kindler. Tel-Aviv and Jerusalem: Schocken Publishing House, 1967. Pages 212-9. 2 pls. [CS 2963]
Discusses the value of the prutah and half-prutah coins when they were in circulation. Discusses variations in coin sizes and weights, and the significance of the sizes, weights, and types.

5816 **Ostermann, Siegfried.** *Die Münzen der Hasmonäer: Ein Kritischer Bericht zur Systematik und Chronologie.* Novum Testamentum et Orbis Antiquus 55. Fribourg: Academic Press; Göttingen: Vandenhoeck and Ruprecht, 2005. 89 pp., illus.
An introduction to Hasmonaean coinage. Provides a summary of the chronological theories put forward by Meshorer, Rappaport, and Barag, Qedar, and others for the Hasmonaean coinage. Includes a concordance of all the systems of numbering the coins. Includes drawings of the coins in the Fribourg University collection. [Reviewed by W. Fischer-Bossert in *American Numismatic Society Magazine* 5, no. 1 (spring 2006):82-3].

5817 **Pick, Behrend.** "Contributions to Palestinian Numismatics." Translated by Hans Holzer. Introduction by Thomas Ollive Mabbott. *Numismatic Review* 2, no. 4 (April-June 1945): 5-11.
In this brief article, the author contends that Simon Maccabee struck no coins. He discusses the "thick shekels" and the related bronze coinage, other bronze coins, and coins of the second revolt. Examines the types and inscriptions and the problems of their interpretation. [Also see H. Stein "Some Additional Remarks" below].

5818 **Plant, Richard J.** "The Coinage of the Jews." *Coins, Incorporating Coins and Medals* (England) 17, no. 6 (June 1980): 12-6. Illus.
"A summary of Jewish coinage from 350-332 B.C. to Roman times." [E. Marles, *NL* 105]

5819 ——— *A Numismatic Journey through the Bible.* London: Rotographic Press, 2007. 206 pp., illus.
An attempt to link Biblical stories to coins. The chapters are written in Biblical order. Also covers reading inscriptions and provides price data for the nearly 600 biblical-related coins featured in the book. Indexed by person and place name. Foreword by David Hendin. Line illustrations throughout.

5820 **Price, Martin.** *Coins and the Bible.* London: V. C. Vecchi & Sons, 1975. 37 pp., illus. [CS 16422]
Reviews and illustrates fifty ancient coins which illustrate Biblical scenes, are mentioned in Biblical passages, or were used in the Holy Land or in areas where the apostles traveled. Also includes a list of Biblical passages which mention money.

5821 **Prime, William C.** *Money of the Bible.* Philadelphia: The Sunday School Times Company, 1906. Reprint, New York: Elder Numismatic Press, n.d. 22 pp., illus.
Discusses money as mentioned in the Bible. Discusses coinage before the Christian era, focusing on Judea. Describes the money of the New Testament.

5822 **Rahmani, Levi Y.** "Silver Coins of the Fourth Century B.C. from Tel Gamma." *Israel Exploration Journal* (Israel) 21, nos. 2-3 (1971): 158-60. Illus.
Examines a small hoard of silver coins from Tel Gamma, southeast of Gaza. Includes two coins with the inscription "Yehezqiyah ha-peha" (Yehezqiyah the governor), which casts doubt on identifying him with the high priest Hezekiah as has been believed.

5823 **Rappaport, Uriel.** "Ascalon and the Coinage of Judaea." *Studies in the History of the Jewish People and the Land of Israel. Volume 4.* Haifa: University of Haifa, 1978. Pages 77-88.
In Hebrew with an English abstract. "The author holds that there was no Seleucid mint at Jerusalem and that the issues attributed to Jerusalem were struck at Ascalon which was the main mint supplying Judea with coinage in the second half of the second century B.C. The symbols of the Hasmonean coinage were also inspired by Seleucid issues of Ascalon. Finally, the first series of coins of Herod the Great, dated Year 3, was also a product of the mint of Ascalon." [A. Spaer, *NL* 123]

5824 ——— "The Coins of Judaea at the End of the Persian Rule and the Beginning of the Hellenistic Period." *Jerusalem in the Second Temple Period: Abraham Schalit Memorial Volume.* Edited by A. Oppenheimer et al. Jerusalem: Yad Ben Zvi, 1980. Pages 8-21.
In Hebrew with an English abstract. "The author discusses the small silver issues of the Yehud and Hezeqio types with an attempt at fixing their sequence during the late Persian, Alexandrine and early Ptolemaic periods." [A. Spaer, *NL* 119]

5825 ——— "Letter to the Editor Regarding the Inscription 'Hever ha Yehudim' on Hasmonaean Coins." *SAN—Journal of the Society for Ancient Numismatics* 11, no. 4 (winter 1980-1): 73-4.
A response to Brin's article (see Brin "The Mystery Solved" above) disputing Brin's conclusions regarding the meaning of the inscription "Hever ha Yehudim."

5826 ——— "The First Judean Coinage." *Journal of Jewish Studies* (England) 32, no. 1 (spring 1981): 1-17.
A good summary of the Yehud coins of ca. 350-283 B.C. Discusses the location of the mint which struck them, the minting authority, denomination, and chronology. Explores whether these were an imperial or a provincial coinage.

5827 **Rawson, A. L.** "Historical Illustrations of Bible Texts, Derived from Ancient Coins and Gems of the Period of Time from Alexander the Great to the Destruction of Jerusalem, 336 B.C. to 138 A.D." *Ancient Coins and Artifacts of the Bible.* Pages 4-15. Illus. (Editor, publisher, and date unknown).
A reprint of an article from an unknown source, probably of the late nineteenth century. Includes drawings of Greek and Roman coins from the Biblical period along with historical commentary.

5828 **Raynor, Joyce T., Ya'akov Meshorer, and Richard S. Hansen.** *The Coins of Ancient Meiron.* Meiron Excavation Project Series 4. American Schools of Oriental Research and Scholars Press, 1988. 140 pp. incl. 18 pls.
Catalogue of 1017 coins found during five seasons of excavations at Meiron, presented by chronologically by period and reign. Includes a numismatic profile of Meiron by mint, city coins found at Meiron, and a list of Roman Imperial coins by mint. This volume is intended as a supplement to the final excavation report on ancient Meiron. [Reviewed by A. Kindler in *The Jewish Quarterly Review* 84, no. 1 (July 1993): 104].

5829 *Recent Studies and Discoveries on Ancient Jewish and Syrian Coins.* Tel-Aviv and Jerusalem, 1954+. Issued by Israel Numismatic Society. [CS 2966]

5830 **Reichardt, Henry C.** "Remarks on Some Jewish Coins, and on Some Inedited Coins of Phoenicia, Judaea, Etc." *Numismatic Chronicle* new ser., 4 (1864): 174-89. Illus.
Lists and discusses several Judean coins, as well as three Ptolemaic coins.

5831 ——— "Unpublished Coin of John Hyrcanus." *Numismatic Chronicle* 3rd ser., 2 (1882): 306-7.
Describes a new variety of a bronze coin not listed by Madden (*Coins of the Jews*, 1881).

5832 **Reifenberg, Abraham.** "Ancient Jewish Coins." *Journal of the Palestine Oriental Society* (Jerusalem) 19 (1939-40). Reprinted as a booklet, *Ancient Jewish Coins.* Jerusalem: Rubin Mass, 1940. 51 pp., 15 pls. Second edition, 1947. 66 pp., 16 pls. Third edition, 1963. Fourth edition, 1965. Fifth edition, 1969. Revised edition, 1974. 66 pp., 16 pls. [CS 2968]
An introduction to Jewish numismatics from the earliest period through the Roman period, including Roman coins struck in Palestine. Followed by a catalogue of 207 coin types. [Reviewed by F. O. Waage in *American Journal of Archaeology* 47 (1943): 508-9].

5833 **Reifenberg, Adolph.** "On the Chronology of Maccabaean Coins." *Quarterly Statement of the Palestine Exploration Fund* (England) (1927): 47-50.

5834 ——— "A Hebrew Shekel of the Fifth Century B.C." *Quarterly Statement of the Palestine Exploration Fund* (England) (1943): 100-4. 1 pl.
Describes a coin of archaic style found near Hebron (*obv.*, male head; *rev.*, female head and Hebrew inscription). Discusses the types, inscription, and denomination. The author concludes that the coin was minted in Palestine in the mid-fifth century B.C. and was equivalent to an Attic drachm. Suggests it may have been struck under the authority of Nehemiah.

5835 ——— *Israel's History in Coins.* London, 1953. 43 pp., illus.

5836 **Reinach, Théodore.** *Les Monnaies Juives.* Paris: Ernest Leroux, 1887. 74 pp., illus. [CS 2970]
This work was translated into English. See below.

5837 ——— *Jewish Coins.* Translated by Mary Hill. London, 1903. Reprint, Chicago: Argonaut, 1966. 92 pp., 12 pls. [CS 2970a]
An revised English translation of Reinach's *Les Monnaies Juives* (Paris, 1887). The original text was revised by Reinach, then translated by Hill. A narrative history of Jewish coinage from its beginning through the Roman Imperial period. Includes a tables of alphabets and Hebrew inscriptions. Also includes an appendix discussing counterfeit shekels which was extracted from an article in *The Reliquary and Illustrated Archaeologist* (October 1902). This appendix did not appear in the original French edition.

5838 **Rogers, Edgar.** "A Simple Guide to Jewish Coins." Published in twelve monthly installments in *Spink Numismatic Circular* 21, pt. 1 (January 1913) through pt. 12 (December 1913). Reprinted in book form, *A Handy Guide to Jewish Coins.* London: Spink & Son, 1914. Reprints, New York: Sanford J. Durst, 1977, 2001. 108 pp., 9 pls. [CS 2971]
An introduction to Jewish coinage. Translates the legends on the coins. Lists the main types. Includes a catalogue of 115 coins. The original articles were revised for the book. Recently found specimens were added along with a table of cross-references, a table of alphabets, and nine plates. [Reviewed by G. F. Hill in *Numismatic Chronicle* 4th ser., 14 (1914): 95-6, and by A. Kleeb in *SAN* 8, no. 4 (fall 1977): 59, 61].

5839 **Romanoff, Paul.** "Jewish Symbols on Ancient Jewish Coins." *Jewish Quarterly Review* 33 (1942-43): 1-15, 435-44; 34 (1943-44): 161-77, 299-312, 425-40. Reprint, *Jewish Symbols on Ancient Jewish Coins.* Philadelphia: The Dropsie College for Hebrew and Cognate Learning, 1944. Reprint, New York: American Israel Numismatic Association, 1971. 79 pp., 7 pls. [CS 2972]

Discusses the historical and social significance of the symbols found on ancient Jewish coins. Coin types are grouped around several themes: agricultural, the Temple building, astronomical subjects, and various utensils connected with the Temple service. The Jewish meaning of the types are interpreted. Seventy-two coins are shown in the plates, grouped by type. [Reviewed by Harold Mattingly in *Numismatic Chronicle* 6th ser., 5 (1945): 79-80].

5840 **Ronen, Yigal.** "The First Hasmonean Coins." *Biblical Archaeologist* 50, no. 2 (June 1987): 105-7. Illus.
Ronen suggests the first Hasmonean coins were struck by Yehuda Aristobulus I in the year 104/103 B.C., rather than Alexander Jannaeus as Meshorer suggests. Concludes "that the Hebrew name of Aristobulus II was Yonathan, and that he was the one who overstruck his name on his father's coins, and also minted his own."

5841 ——— "The Weight Standards of the Judean Coinage in the Late Persian and Early Ptolemaic Period." *Near Eastern Archaeology* 61, no. 2 (June 1998): 122-6. Illus.
The author maintains that the early *YHD* coins of the Persian period are based on the weight of the shekel of the First Temple period. Many of these coins are 1/24 shekel in weight and are thus termed "gerah." The *YHD* coins in the Ptolemaic period were struck on the Athenian standard.

5842 **Samuels, Claudia Wallack, Paul Rynearson, and Ya'akov Meshorer.** *The Numismatic Legacy of the Jews as Depicted by a Distinguished American Collection.* New York: Stack's Publications/Numismatic Review, 2000. 212 pages, 11 pls.
An interweaving of Jewish history and religious traditions, illustrated by selected coins from the Alan I. Casden collection of ancient Jewish Coins. Casden's collection is one of the most outstanding collections of ancient Jewish coinage. Includes a detailed catalogue of 228 coins of the Persian and Ptolemaic periods, the bronze issues of the Jewish rulers and Roman governors, the silver issues of the two Revolts, the city coins, and the Roman issues relating to Judea. All 228 coins are photographed in the plates, and enlarged photos of selected coins appear throughout the text. [Reviewed by David Hendin in *The Celator* 15, no. 3 (March 2001): 46].

5843 **Sarfatti, Gad B.** "Notes on the Inscription on Some Jewish Coins and Seals." *Israel Exploration Journal* (Israel) 27, no. 4 (1977): 204-6. 1 pl.
The legend on the bulla of the Hasmonean king Alexander Jannaeus raises a serious linguistic problem. The legend presents a proper name followed by an apposition without the definite article, in contrast to established Hebrew usage. Inscriptions on coins of Alexander Jannaeus are used as examples. Sarfatti explains the omission of the article as due to Greek influence.

5844 **Shachar, Ilan.** "The Historical and Numismatic Significance of Alexander Jannaeus's Later Coinage as Found in Archaeological Excavations." *Palestine Exploration Quarterly* (England) 136, no. 1 (2004): 5-33.
Shachar tries to establish the occupation of various cities during Hasmonean periods. Suggests that both the YEHONATAN and the YONTAN coins should be attributed to Alexander Jannaeus. Discusses the evidence of overstruck coins. [Also see Hendin "Chronology of Hasmonean Coins" above for critical comments on Shachar's article. Shachar responded to Hendin's criticisms in a "Letter to the Editor" in *The Celator* 19, no. 11 (November 2005): 4. Also see Hendin "Much More on the Jannaeus Coin Chronology" above, in which Hendin now accepts Shachar's attributions].

5845 **Sievers, Joseph.** "Jonathan Aristobolus III and Hasmonean Names." *Israel Numismatic Journal* 8 (1984-85): 7 ff.

5846 **Smyser, Donald S.** "The Widow's Mite." *The Numismatist* 71, no. 3 (March 1958): 263-6. Illus.
The author recounts the Biblical story of the widow's mite. Reviews the many copper coins of Judea and comments on which are possible candidates to be called the widow's mite.

5847 **Snowden, James Ross.** *The Coin of the Bible and its Money Terms.* Philadelphia, 1864. 72 pp., illus. [CS 16427]

5848 **Spaer, Arnold.** "Some More 'Yehud' Coins." *Israel Exploration Journal* (Israel) 27, no. 4 (1977): 200-3. 1 pl.
Publishes some additional new types of Yehud coins (see Jeselsohn "A New Coin Type" and Kindler "Silver Coins" above). The types include Athena/owl, lily/owl, head/animal (with the inscription "Yehezqiyo/ah"), head/Ptolemaic eagle, and head of Ptolemy I/head of Berenice I. The dates of the coins extend well into the third century B.C. No mint attribution is proposed for the coins, and there seems to be no solid basis for claiming Jerusalem as the mint city.

5849 ——— "A Coin of Jeroboam?" *Israel Exploration Journal* (Israel) 29, nos. 3-4 (1979): 219. 1 pl.
Discusses some minor silver coins of the Persian period with male head left and the inscription "Jeroboam." The reverses are unclear. The identity of Jeroboam remains in question. The coins are likely from the fourth century B.C. and, judging from the script, may belong to Samaria.

5850 ——— "More about Jeroboam" *Israel Numismatic Journal* (Israel) 4 (1980): 2-3. 1 pl.
"Two more pre-Alexander III oboli, one with the inscription 'Jeroboa,' are described and tentatively attributed to Samaria and the Samaritans." [A. Spaer, *NL* 105]

5851 **Sperber, Daniel.** "Catalogue of Coins in the Jewish Museum (London)." *Palestine Exploration Quarterly* (England) 49 (July-December 1967): 106-13.
A catalogue of thirty-six coins, 120 B.C. to A.D. 70, fully described.

5852 **Stein, Harry J.** "Hitherto Unexplained Symbols on the Coins of John Hyrcanus." *Numismatic Review* 1, no. 2 (September 1943): 19-21. 1 pl.
The author discusses the meaning of the Greek letter A which appears on the Class II coins of John Hyrcanus. Publishes three new varieties showing Greek letters M, and Π. Concludes that the letters do not denote a date or a mintmark. Rather, they are the initials of mint magistrates.

5853 ——— "Some Additional Remarks on Jewish Coins." *Numismatic Review* 3, no. 4 (October 1946): 133-4.
Presents brief follow-up notes to B. Pick's article. [See Pick "Contributions" above].

5854 **Sukenik, Eleazar L.** "Paralipomena Palaestinensia: I. The Oldest Coins of Judaea." *Journal of the Palestine Oriental Society* (Jerusalem) 14, no. 3 (1934): 178-82. 2 pls.

Examines three Philisto-Arabian or Egypto-Arabian coins bearing an inscription previously read as "Yahu." The author suggests the proper reading is "Yehud," the Aramaic name of the province of Judea. These coins, probably from the fourth century B.C., are the earliest preserved specimens of a coinage in Judea. A companion essay (pages 182-4) examines similar inscriptions on jar-handles.

5855 ——— "More about the Oldest Coins of Judaea." *Journal of the Palestine Oriental Society* (Jerusalem) 15, nos. 3-4 (1935): 341-3.
A follow-up to the above, presents further evidence of a pre-Hasmonean coinage in Palestine. Presents a coin with a clear inscription which the author reads as "Yehud." Points out a few passages in Talmudic literature which seem to refer to these types of coins.

5856 **Superior Galleries, Inc.** *The Abraham Bromberg Collection of Jewish Coins. Part 1.* Beverly Hills: Superior Galleries, Inc., December 5, 1991. 154 pp., illus. *Part 2.* Beverly Hills: Superior Galleries, Inc., December 10, 1992. 147 pp., illus.
Auction catalogues for the sale of the Bromberg collection, one of the most complete collections of Jewish coinage ever formed. Includes an introduction and biographical information by Bromberg and an overview of Jewish coinage by Leo Mildenberg. Part 1 includes 315 coins (Yehud, Hasmonaeans, Herodians, Procurators). Part 2 includes 311 coins (general, Judea under the Romans, Judea Capta issues). Cataloguing by Paul Rynearson, who calls this "the finest private collection of Jewish coins ever yet formed." All coins are photographed.

5857 **Tal, Oren.** "Coin Denominations and Weights Standards in Fourth Century B.C.E. Palestine." *Israel Numismatic Research* (Israel) 2 (2007): 17 ff.
Epigraphic material of the fourth century B.C.E. and other written sources are surveyed in order to identify the weight denominations and standards of contemporaneous Palestinian coins. It was found that there were probably local denominational systems and weight standards in the region, and that these were apparently based on the shekel and its fractions. The Greek (Attic) denominational system and weight standard formerly associated with the coins were probably not known in Palestine. [Also see David Hendin's discussion and summary of Tal's paper in his "Coins of the Bible" column in *The Celator* 22, no. 10 (October 2008): 46-7, 50].

5858 **Tameanko, Marvin.** "Joseph and his Brothers, and the First Hebrew Coinage." *The Shekel* 35, no. 2 (March-April 2002): 16 ff.
In the Biblical story of Joseph, the son of Jacob, Joseph helped his brothers to fill their grain and money-bags when they arrived in Egypt in search of relief from a famine. Just what kind of money may have filled these bags has long intrigued numismatists, because coins did not exist at that time. The answer may lie in archaeological evidence found at the site of Phoenician harbor warehouses at Dor. Linen bags were found, containing standard size and weight silver ingots. The bags were sealed with a stamp of the owner to confirm the purity and weight of the contents. Tameanko suggests these bags may qualify as being early coins of biblical days. [A summary of this article appeared in *Coin World* (May 13, 2002): 69].

5859 **Underhill, Randall M.** "Thoughts on the Widow's Mite." *Journal of the Classical and Medieval Numismatic Society* 2nd ser., 5, no. 3 (June 2004): 94. Illus.
Briefly reviews the candidates for the Biblical widow's mite.

5860 **Wacks, Mel.** *The Handbook of Biblical Numismatics from Abraham to the Crusaders.* Houston: Israel Numismatic Service, 1976. 38 pp., illus. [CS 16429]
A narrative review of the coins used in Biblical lands from the Persian period through the Crusader period, intended as a guide to forming a collection of Biblical-related coins. Recommends appropriate coin types for a collection. Illustrated by 122 coins and medals. Includes a concordance table of Wacks, Reifenberg, Meshorer, and Cohen catalogue numbers. Another table provides transcriptions and translations of Hebrew coin legends.

5861 ——— "Ashkelon." *Augur* (United States) 1, no. 11 (December 1977): 42-3. Illus.
The city's coinage from before 104 B.C. to the Arab period is surveyed." [M. Wacks, *NL* 101]

5862 **Williamson, George C.** *The Money of the Bible.* London: The Religious Tract Society, 1894. New York, 1895. 96 pp., illus.
Intended as a guide for Bible students, this book describes the uncoined money of Old Testament times, coined money of Old and New Testaments times, coins actually mentioned in the Bible, and coins which are illustrative of Bible stories. Also lists scriptural references to coins and money.

5863 **Wirgin, Wolf.** "Some Notes on Coins Attributed to King Alexander Jannaeus." *Seaby Coin and Medal Bulletin* 372 (1949): 220-2; 373 (1949): 268-71. Illus.
Focuses on the small Jewish bronze coins bearing the legend "King Alexander's." Describes the types: sun-wheel type, star type, and flower type. Discusses the inscriptions and the origins of the types.

5864 ——— "The Widow's Mite Story." *The Numismatist* 58, no. 4 (April 1955): 354-60. 2 pls.
"Rogers, in his *Handy Guide to Jewish Coins* (1914) defines the Biblical widow's mite as a coin of the Hasmonaean king Alexander Janneus. Halliday follows the same path in *Money Talks About the Bible* (1948) but also quotes a theory which attributes it to the infamous Pontius Pilate. In opposing these views, Wirgin prefers to identify it as a Jewish lepton, equal in value to half a Roman quadrans and struck in Jerusalem in the traditional pattern of Alexander the Great. Substantial reasons are given in support of this conclusion, augmented by illustrations of coins from the author's own collection." [G. North, *NL* 43]

5865 ——— "On the Right of Asylum in Hellenistic Syria." *Congrès International de Numismatique, Paris, 6-11 Juillet 1953. Volume 2.* Paris: Commission International de Numismatique, 1957. Pages 137-48.
Wirgin examines the development of the privilege of asylum and the extent to which communities, in particular the temple and city of Jerusalem, possessed the right of asylum or an independence equivalent to it. Relates this to the dating of the shekels with the inscription "Jerusalem the Holy." The author cannot reach a conclusion for the date of their issuance.

5866 ——— "Letter to the Editor Regarding 'The Jaffa Hoard of Alexander Jannaeus.'" *Israel Exploration Journal* (Israel) 8 (1958): 288.
A follow-up to Kindler's "The Jaffa Hoard of Alexander Jannaeus" (see above) in which Wirgin disputes Kindler's claim that the coins in question were not minted in Jerusalem. Wirgin claims that many such coins have been found in the area of Jerusalem. (Kindler has a short reply urging acceptance of his theory until authentic archaeological finds of these coins are made in the Jerusalem area).

5867 ——— "Maccabaean History from Coins." *Palestine Exploration Quarterly* (England) 104 (July-December 1972): 104-10. [CS 2983]

Discusses the question of whether the thick shekels were minted by Simon Maccabaeus. Draws no definite conclusion, but presents evidence to generally support Simon as the minter of the shekels. Interprets the floral design on the shekel as the Biblical *sneh* or thornbush—the burning bush from which the Angel spoke to Moses.

5868 ——— "On the Nature of Some Hasmonaean Coin Finds." *Palestine Exploration Quarterly* (England) 105 (July-December 1973): 141-9. 4 pls. [CS 2984]
Discusses the coins of Alexander Jannaeus. Notes their prevalence in hoards. Discusses the names of the Hasmonaean high priests. Discusses the anchor symbol on coins—which the author claims signifies the deification of Alexander the Great.

5869 **Wirgin, Wolf, and Siegfried Mandel.** *The History of Coins and Symbols in Ancient Israel.* New York: Exposition Press, 1958. 264 pp., 32 pls. [CS 2985]
Begins with the story of ancient Jewish coinage. Discusses the first Jewish coins, the Hasmonaeans, the widow's mite, Herod and his successors, and Bar Kochba coins. Includes appendices on genealogy, alphabets, hoards, and symbols. Discusses the views of other authors. Discusses fertility symbols in ancient Near Eastern civilizations. This volume is not well regarded by numismatists. Many of the arguments and conclusions have been discredited by other researchers. [See Kindler "The Coinage of the Hasmonaean Dynasty" above for a discussion of errors and misattributions. Dennis Kroh, in his *Ancient Coin Reference Reviews*, suggested avoiding this book and stated, "If you have it already, throw it away!"].

5870 **Wood, Bryant G.** "Notes and News—Excavations and Surveys—Khirbet Nisya, 1994." *Israel Exploration Journal* (Israel) 45, nos. 2-3 (1995): 197-200. Illus.
A coin of Antiochus IV Epiphanes (195-164 B.C.) and a coin of Alexander Jannaeus (ca. 103-76 B.C.) were found in an ash pit near pottery kilns discovered at Khirbet Nisya, thus dating the kilns to the late second or first century B.C.

5871 **Yeoman, Richard S.** *Moneys of the Bible.* Racine: Whitman Publishing Co., 1961. Reprint, New York: Sanford J. Durst, 1982. 61 pp., illus. [CS 16431]
A beginners' guide to coins related to the Old and New Testaments. Describes and pictures about seventy-five coins, quoting Biblical passages to demonstrate their relationship to Biblical times. Includes Greek, Hellenistic, Judean, and Roman coinage.

5872 **Zerman, Percy.** "The Coinage of Judea." *The Numismatist* 92, no. 5 (May 1979): 957-69. Map, illus.
A good blend of history and numismatics, covering Judean coinage through the period of Roman dominance. Describes the coinage of the Hasmoneans, the First Revolt, and the Second Revolt periods. Includes comments on chronology, metallurgy, metrology, types, and inscriptions.

5873 **Zlotnik, Yehoshua.** "The Beginning of Hasmonean Minting." *The Celator* 25, no. 3 (March 2011): 20-8. Illus.
Begins with a review of the coinage minted for Judea under the Persians, Ptolemies, and Seleucids. Continues with the historical background of the first Hasmonean coinage, discusses the authority granted to Simon to mint coins, and the minting of the bronze coins with the lily and anchor.

Also see: Amiran and Eitan "Excavations" under THE MINTING PROCESS; Ariel "A First Century CE Mint South of Jerusalem?" under THE MINTING PROCESS; Balmuth "Monetary Forerunners" under ORIGINS OF COINAGE; Barag "Lead Currency" under GENERAL WORKS—HELLENISTIC; Barag "Mint of Antiochus IV" under SYRIA—SELEUCID KINGDOM; D. Baramki *The Coin Collection* under PUBLIC COLLECTIONS—LEBANON; Ben-Eli *Ships* under TYPES; Boneschi "Three Coins" under PHOENICIA; Brett "A New Cleopatra Tetradrachm of Ascalon" under EGYPT—PTOLEMAIC KINGDOM; Brett "The Mint of Ascalon under the Seleucids" under SYRIA—SELEUCID KINGDOM; Gerson "Ptolemaic Coin of Yehud" under EGYPT—PTOLEMAIC KINGDOM; Gitler "A Comparative Study" under HOARDS; Gitler and Lorber "A New Chronology for the Ptolemaic Coins of Judah" under EGYPT—PTOLEMAIC KINGDOM; Gitler and Lorber "Small Silver Coins" under EGYPT—PTOLEMAIC KINGDOM; Gitler, Ponting, and Tal "Metallurgical Analysis of Southern Palestinian Coins" under METALLURGY; Goldstein "Unicorn" under TYPES; Grierson "The Thirty Pieces of Silver" under CARIA; Hendin *Ancient Scale Weights* under METROLOGY; Hendin "Israelite Shekel Weights" under METROLOGY; Hendin "Die Varieties" under THE MINTING PROCESS; Hendin "How Ancient Coins Were Made" under THE MINTING PROCESS; Hendin "Jerusalem's Walls" (two items) under CILICIA.

Hoover *Handbook of Coins of the Southern Levant* under ASIA—GENERAL WORKS; Horvitz "A Jewish Isolde" under PHOENICIA; Houghton and Hendin "Defining Rarity" under COLLECTING GUIDES; Hübner and Knauf *Leo Mildenberg: Vestigia Leonis* under GENERAL WORKS—GREEK; Huth "Beyond Gaza: Two South Arabian Problems" under ARABIA; Janis "Antiochus V" under SYRIA—SELEUCID KINGDOM; Jenkins "The Monetary Systems" under GENERAL WORKS—HELLENISTIC; Kindler "The Mint at Tyre" under PHOENICIA; Kindler *The Patterns of Monetary Development in Phoenicia and Palestine* under PHOENICIA; Levy "Tyrian Shekels" (two items) under PHOENICIA; Lewis "From Iconium to the Home of Saint Luke" under LYKAONIA; Lönnqvist and Lönnqvist "The Numismatic Chronology of Qumran" under HOARDS; Magen "Mt. Gerazim" under HOARDS; Magness "Two Notes on the Archaeology of Qumran" under PHOENICIA; Matsson *The Gods, Goddesses and Heroes* under TYPES; Meshorer "Tyrian Shekels" under PHOENICIA; Metcalf *Oxford Handbook of Greek and Roman Coinage* under GENERAL WORKS—GREEK; Mørkholm "Some Coins of Ptolemy V from Palestine" under EGYPT—PTOLEMAIC KINGDOM; Moysey "Observations" under PERSIA; Plant "Coins of Tyre and the Bible" under PHOENICIA; Sayles "Who Were the Magi?" under ELYMAIS; Sheedy et al. *Pella in Jordan* under HOARDS; Spaer "Ascalon" under SYRIA—SELEUCID KINGDOM; Sutherland "The Pattern of Monetary Development" under PHOENICIA; Syon "The Coins from Gamala" under HOARDS; Syon "Coins from the Excavations at Khirbet esh-Shuhara" under HOARDS; Waddingham "Numismatic Evidence" under SYRIA—SELEUCID KINGDOM; Yarkon "Fathers Day Gift" under PHOENICIA.

PHILISTIA

5874 **Beckman, Martin.** "Fraternizing with the Enemy: An Athenian Coin from Persian Palestine." *The Picus* (Canada) (1994): 28-38. Illus.
An Athenian tetradrachm (ca. 450 B.C.) was found in Jordan at a site which, it was believed, had not been occupied since the eighth century B.C. Summarizes the history of Palestine in the first millennium B.C. and discusses the coins of Athens which have been found in and around Palestine. Briefly discusses Persian imitations of Athenian coins which have been found in Palestine. Notes the scarcity of finds of genuine Athenian coins in Palestine. Suggests that Athenian coins were in frequent use in Palestine—the scarcity of such finds may merely be due to the lack of documentation of coin finds.

5875 **Eph'al, I.** "Changes in Palestine during the Persian Period in Light of Epigraphic Sources." *Israel Exploration Journal* (Israel) 48, nos. 1-2 (1998): 106-18.
"This survey of the history of Palestine during the two centuries prior to the arrival of Alexander the Great is based on the epigraphic material now available and makes considerable use of coins and the names appearing on them, including issues from Samaria, Judea and the coastal cities of southern Palestine." [A. Spaer, *NL* 141]

5876 **Eshel, Hanan.** "A Philisto-Arabian Coin from Sha'albim." *Israel Numismatic Journal* (Israel) 11 (1990-91): 7 ff.

5877 **Fischer-Bossert, Wolfgang.** "Notes on the Coinages of the Philistian Cities." *Coinage of the Caravan Kingdoms: Studies in the Monetization of Ancient Arabia.* Numismatic Studies No. 25. Edited by Martin Huth and Peter G. van Alfen. New York: American Numismatic Society, 2010. 602 pp., 42 pls. Pages 133-96. Illus.
Describes the popularity of Athenian-imitation coinage in Arabia, Phoenicia, and Philistia. Discusses the problems and general state of research in Philistian coinage. The author then explores some problems: the relative chronology of the Athenian-styled and Philistian-styled issues, an overstrike of a Philistian coin over a Samarian coins and two new hoards, and the great variety of types. He then examines the metrology of the issues. Presents a listing of weights of numerous Athenian-styled coins, Philistian-styled coins, and Edomite and Samarian coins of various denominations, as well as early and late Athenian-type tetradrachms. Finally, Fischer-Bossert examines the fabric of the coinage. Two appendices provide (1) metrological data, and (2) a listing and description of hoards with alleged Philistian coins. Includes an extensive bibliography.

5878 **Gitler, Haim.** "New Fourth-Century B.C. Coins from Ascalon." *Numismatic Chronicle* 156 (1996): 1-9. 7 pls.
Discusses the "Philisto-Arabian" coins struck in Palestine during the Persian period (ca. 400-333 B.C.). Describes a hoard of thirty-one obols of Athena/owl type found at Ascalon in 1989, as well as some rare and unpublished coins of Ascalon from the fourth century B.C.

5879 ——— "Achaemenid Motives in the Coinage of Ashdod, Ascalon and Gaza from the Fourth Century B.C." *Transeuphratène* (France) 20 (2000): 73-87.

5880 **Gitler, Haim, and Oren Tal.** *The Coinage of Philistia of the Fifth and Fourth Centuries BC: A Study of the Earliest Coins of Palestine.* Collezioni Numismatiche 6. Milano: Edizioni Ennerre, and New York: Amphora Books and B. & H. Kreindler, 2006. 411 pp., 123 pls.
A study of the earliest coins minted in Palestine, during Achaemenid rule. These "Philisto-Arabian" coins were issued by three coastal cities of Philistia (south-western Palestine): Ashdod, Ashkelon, and Gaza. The catalogue includes 311 Philistian coin types (684 coins) from public and private collections, 192 of which were previously unpublished. The authors differentiate between the Athenian-style coinage (imitating the type of Athens) and the Philistian-style coinage. Includes much discussion of iconography, motifs, weights, forgeries, and historical background. Extensive discussion of the early use of weighed metal as money—a pre-coinage stage. Lists the sixth and fifth century B.C. coins that have been found in Palestine. Includes photographs of 814 coins, 750 enlargements, and drawings of 151 coins. Extensive bibliography. The standard work on these issues. [Summarized and reviewed by D. Hendin in *The Celator* 20, no. 9 (September 2006): 42-3, 46. Also reviewed by W. Fischer-Bossert in *ANS Magazine* 6, no. 2 (summer 2007): 73-6.]

5881 **Hands, Alfred W.** "Notes on a Phoenician Drachm Bearing the Name IAHVE." *Numismatic Chronicle* 4th ser., 9 (1909): 121-31. Illus.
A drachm or quarter-shekel struck on the Phoenician standard with *obv.*, bearded head, helmeted; *rev.*, divinity in Eastern dress, seated in a car with a winged wheel. The coin was probably issued at Gaza between 405-380 B.C. The inscription is interpreted as "Jehovah." The author discusses the inscription and the obverse and reverse types. [Also see R. Weil "The Phoenician Drachma with the Jahve-Inscription" under PHOENICIA].

5882 **Hendin, David.** "Important New Work Outlines Previously Unpublished Coinage of Ancient Samaria." *The Celator* 5, no. 11 (November 1991): 6-8.
Discusses the silver coins of Samaria minted in the fourth century B.C. Suggests these are the first issue of Jewish coins. Describes the contents of a new book on Samarian coinage (see *The Coinage of Samaria in the Fourth Century B.C.E.* by Ya'akov Meshorer and Shaga Qedar below). These coins imitate the coins of Sidon and Cilicia. Provides an overview of Samarian history.

5883 ——— "Early Southern Mints in Ancient Israel." *The Celator* 8, no. 6 (June 1994): 44-5. Illus.
Briefly examines the early coins of Gaza which resemble those of Athens, and other Philisto-Arabian coinages.

5884 ——— "A Collective Mint in Philistia?" *The Celator* 25, no. 1 (January 2011): 42-3. Illus.
Hendin explains a theory put forward by Gitler and Tal that the mint of Philistia may have been a collective mint which struck coins in the names of the cities of Gaza, Ascalon, and Ashdod, as well as generic coins of Philistia without a specific city name. Metallurgical evidence is cited and die links are discussed.

5885 **Janis, Edward.** "The Periods of Gaza Coinage." *The Shekel* 21, no. 3 (May-June 1988): 19-21. Illus. Also appeared in *The Celator* 10, no. 11 (November 1996): 42-3. Illus.
A summary of the periods of coinage, the types of coins, the minting authority, the common devices and legends, and periods of issue of coins struck in the ancient city of Gaza.

5886 **Kindler, Arie.** "The Greco-Phoenician Coins Struck in Palestine in the Time of the Persian Empire." Parts 1-2. *Israel Numismatic Journal* (Israel) 1 (April 1963): 2-6; 2 (June 1963): 25-7. [CS 2933]
Part 1 includes a descriptive catalogue of fifty-six coins of the Greco-Phoenician series. Part 2 deals with the influence of Greek and Phoenician art on the die-cutters of the period.

5887 ——— "Four Silver Drachms and One Bronze Obol of the City of Ashdod, Israel, form the Persian Period." *Annotazioni Numismatiche* (Italy) 5, no. 19 (September 1995): 411-5. Illus.
"The author presents five rare or unpublished Ashdod coin types. Four are from the Kadman Numismatic Museum and one at the American Numismatic Society." [N. Vismara, *NL* 142]

5888 **Kogan, Howard.** "Philistine Coins Reveal History of Ancient Gaza." *The Celator* 3, no. 8 (August 1989): 8.
A brief description of the coinage of Gaza which often copied Greek denominations and types, and included Hebrew script to identify the mints. Flans are often crude and irregular.

5889 **Kushnir-Stein, Alla.** "Gaza Coinage Dated LIC—A Reappraisal." *Revue Suisse de Numismatique* (Switzerland) 74 (1995): 49-57.

"The author shows that the date on a coin of Gaza, *BMC Palestine* 144.6-7, was misread. She reads instead LIC LI Γ and connects this date with a new era of Gaza. This era was started with the conferring of autonomy to Gaza by the Seleucid kings. The date of a second coin, M. Rosenberger, City-Coins 52, Nr. 37, has to be read LI Θ instead of LIC, and refers also to the new era." [U. Kampmann, *NL* 135]

5890 ——— "Late Hellenistic Coins of Gaza and the Date of the Hasmonean Conquest of the City." *Schweizer Münzblätter* (Switzerland) 198 (2000): 22-4.

5891 **Meshorer, Ya'akov.** "Three Gaza Coins from the Persian Period." *Israel Museum News* (Israel) 12 (1977): 78-9.

5892 **Mildenberg, Leo.** "The Philisto-Arabian Coins—A Preview. Preliminary Studies of the Local Coinage in the Fifth Persian Satrapy, Part 3." *Studia Phoenicia, Volume 9. Numismatique et Histoire Économique Phéniciennes et Puniques.* Edited by T. Hackens and G. Moucharte. Louvain: Université Catholique De Louvain, 1992. Pages 33-40. 3 pls. Reprinted in *Leo Mildenberg. Vestigia Leonis: Studien zur Antiken Numismatik Israels, Palästinas und der Östlichen Mittelmeerweit.* Novum Testamentum et Orbis Antiquus 36. Edited by U. Hübner and E. Knauf. Freiburg: Universitätsverlag, and Göttingen: Vandenhoeck & Ruprecht, 1998. Pages 88-94.
Discusses the coinage policy of the Persian Empire and the circulation of money in the fifth satrapy (west of the Euphrates, encompassing Syria, Phoenicia, Palestine, and Cyprus). This satrapy did not issue its own coinage as many others did (e.g., Tissaphernes, Datames, Mazaios, Hekatomnos), probably because there was enough coinage available from other cities which circulated in the area, as shown by hoards. The author also discusses issues struck in the Persian Empire's Southern Provinces (beginning near southern Judea and Ashdod)—the so-called Philisto-Arabian issues which likely began ca. 430 B.C. Briefly comments on possible mint locations for these issues (probably Gaza) and the interpretation of the coin types. [Also see Hübner and Knauf *Vestigia Leonis* under GENERAL WORKS—GREEK].

5893 ——— "Gaza Mint Authorities in Persian Times. Preliminary Studies of the Local Coinages in the Fifth Persian Satrapy. Part 4." *Transeuphratène* (France) 2 (1990): 137-146. Illus. Reprinted in *Leo Mildenberg. Vestigia Leonis: Studien zur Antiken Numismatik Israels, Palästinas und der Östlichen Mittelmeerweit.* Novum Testamentum et Orbis Antiquus 36. Edited by U. Hübner and E. Knauf. Freiburg: Universitätsverlag, and Göttingen: Vandenhoeck & Ruprecht, 1998. Pages 79-87. 4 pls.
Reviews the city of Gaza's place in the Persian Empire geographically, legally, and monetarily. Mildenberg emphasizes that the city had a prolific and organized coinage of its own. Its coins should not be viewed in simply as "Philisto-Arabian" and are distinct from other coins from the vast territories around Gaza. The municipal coinage likely began around 420-410 B.C. The minting authority was the city—not a provincial governor or the Persian central administration. However, Arab authorities also had coins struck at Gaza—either at the Gaza city mint or at another workshop in the area—to facilitate the development of their desert trade. [Also see Hübner and Knauf *Vestigia Leonis* under GENERAL WORKS—GREEK].

5894 ——— "Bes on Philisto-Arabian Coins." *Transeuphratène* (France) 9 (1995): 63-5. Reprinted in *Leo Mildenberg. Vestigia Leonis: Studien zur Antiken Numismatik Israels, Palästinas und der Östlichen Mittelmeerweit.* Novum Testamentum et Orbis Antiquus 36. Edited by U. Hübner and E. Knauf. Freiburg: Universitätsverlag, and Göttingen: Vandenhoeck & Ruprecht, 1998. Pages 95-98.
Mildenberg explains and defends G. F. Hill's use of the term "Philisto-Arabian" as the best description for the coinages from the southern cities on the shore of the Mediterranean and the borders of the desert. Mildenberg then briefly discusses the coins bearing the guardian-genius Bes, which Hill labeled "Egypto-Arabian." Mildenberg rejects that term. There was no direct Egyptian influence in these coinages. Bes was popular in the Levant, and the Bes coins form an indivisible part of the Philisto-Arabian coinage. [Also see Hübner and Knauf *Vestigia Leonis* under GENERAL WORKS—GREEK].

5895 ——— "On the Imagery of the Philisto-Arabian Coinage—A Preview." *Transeuphratène* (France) 13 (1997): 9-17.

5896 ——— "On Fractional Silver Issues in Palestine." *Transeuphratène* 20 (France) 16 (2000): 89-100.

5897 **Rappaport, Uriel.** "Gaza and Ascalon in the Persian and Hellenistic Periods in Relation to their Coins." *Israel Exploration Journal* (Israel) 20, nos. 1-2 (1970): 75-80.
"Gaza's importance during the Persian and Ptolemaic periods far exceeded that of its neighbor Ascalon; the reason was that it served as the main outlet for Arabian trade. This position changed only after the Seleucid conquest in 200 B.C. Gaza enjoyed a short revival at the end of the second century B.C. when the Nabataean Arabs again used it as their trade outlet after the Seleucid power had weakened. However the city was destroyed by Alexander Jannaeus in 96 and from then Gaza had no real revival during the rest of the first century B.C. These developments seem to be borne out by the quantity of coin types struck in Gaza and Ascalon respectively." [A. Spaer, *NL* 86]

5898 **Spaer, Arnold.** "The Royal Male Head and Cleopatra at Ascalon." *Travaux de Numismatique Grecque Offerts à Georges Le Rider.* Edited by M. Amandry and S. Hurter. London: Spink, 1999. Pages 347-50. 1 pl.
A follow-up to Spaer's "Ascalon: from Royal Mint to Autonomy" (see Spaer under SYRIA—SELEUCID KINGDOM) where the author argued that the royal heads on the autonomous tetradrachms of Ascalon do not depict any Ptolemaic kings. Here, Spaer shows that in the historical context, there is no basis for identifying any of the male heads with a Ptolemy. He also shows that there are issues in this series which do bear the portrait of Cleopatra VII. He lists all dated issues known to him down to the end of Cleopatra's reign (30 B.C.). Spaer suggests that by putting Cleopatra's portrait on its coins of 38/37 B.C., Ascalon intended to flatter the new overlord of the area. [Also see Brett "The Mint of Ascalon" under SYRIA—SELEUCID KINGDOM, and Brett "A New Cleopatra Tetradrachm" under EGYPT—PTOLEMAIC KINGDOM].

5899 *[Listing removed]*

Also see: Barkay "Marissa Hoard…Minted in Ascalon" under SYRIA—SELEUCID KINGDOM; Gitin and Golani "Tel Miqne-Ekon Silver Hoard" under HOARDS; Gitler "A Unique 'Philisto-Arabian' Coin" under ARABIA; Gitler, Ponting, and Tal "Metallurgical Analysis of Southern Palestinian Coins" under METALLURGY; Harrison "Hellenization" under PALESTINE—JUDEA; Heritage Auctions *The Shoshana Collection* under PALESTINE—JUDEA; Hoover *Handbook of Coins of the Southern Levant* under ASIA—GENERAL WORKS; Hübner and Knauf *Leo Mildenberg: Vestigia Leonis* under GENERAL WORKS—GREEK; Lemaire "Monétaire de Transeuphratène avant Alexandre?" under PALESTINE—JUDEA; Mildenberg "On the Money Circulation in Palestine from Artaxerxes II till Ptolemy I" under PALESTINE—JUDEA.

SAMARIA

5900 **Berrol, Ronn.** "A New Variant of a 'Provisional' Samarian Coin." *The Celator* 22, no. 5 (May 2008): 24-7. Illus.
Publishes a new variant of *Meshorer & Qedar* IC-5—a coin listed as provisionally being from Samaria. In addition to the "eagle on thunderbolt" on the reverse of IC-5, the new coin has a club in the field to the right of the eagle. Berrol suggests the club may reflect the influence of the coinage of Alexander the Great. Illustrates other coins that may have influenced the design of the Samarian coin, including a fraction from Olympia. The author suggests the new coin and IC-5 are Samarian and that the new coin is an obol from the same series (IC-5 is a hemiobol).

5901 **Bodzek, Jaroslaw.** "Remarks on the Iconography of Samarian Coinage: Hunting in *Paradeisos*?" *Israel Numismatic Research* (Israel) 2 (2007): 35 ff.
This study examines a hunting scene on the reverse of a Samarian coin (Meshorer and Qedar, *Samarian Coinage*, p. 106, no. 123). Depicted is a mounted hunter, wearing an Iranian cavalryman's costume and galloping over the body of a fallen animal (probably a lion or a boar). The general prototype of the scene should be sought in the repertoire of Greco-Persian art, and probably refers to a hunt in the garden precinct called *paradeisos*.

5902 ——— "A Note on a Samarian Coin-Type." *Israel Numismatic Research* (Israel) 3 (2008): 3-12.
"Focuses on a Samarian issue showing on the obverse a head in a tiara (kyrbasia) and the forepart of a horse on the reverse (Meshorer and Qedar 1999: 97, Nos. 75–76). The forerunner for the types under discussion must be sought among issues produced by different Achemenid officials in northwestern Asia Minor (Mysia, Troas), where coins of the same or similar types were relatively widespread in the fourth century B.C.E. It is probable that the Samarian issuing authority consciously chose iconographic types recalling the Achemenid aristocratic ethos with which the local community was presumably familiar." [Abstract in *INR*]

5903 **Chaya, Gil.** "The Samarian Greek Gorgoneion Coin Series." *Israel Numismatic Journal* (Israel) 14 (2001-02): 19-25, Illus.

5904 **Galst, Jay M.** "Cuneiform in Nummis." *The Celator* 11, no. 7 (July 1997): 36-7. Illus.
Illustrates and discusses two fourth century B.C. coins of Samaria (a drachm and an obol) which bear cuneiform inscriptions of the Neo-Assyrian or Neo-Babylonian period. The meaning of the inscriptions is unclear.

5905 **Hendin, David.** "The Samarian Coins." *The Celator* 13, no. 3 (March 1999): 46-7. Illus.
A brief introduction to the coinage of Samaria. Compares the coins to the Judean "Yehud" coins. Discusses the types and their rarity.

5906 **Leith, M. J. W.** "Seals and Coins in Persian Period Samaria." *The Dead Sea Scrolls Fifty Years after their Discovery: Proceedings of the Jerusalem Congress, July 20-25, 1997*. Edited by L. H. Schiffmann and J. C. Vanderkam. 2000. Pages 691-707. Illus.
"A comparison of seals found in Wadi Daliyeh and coming from Samaria with coins struck in Samaria indicates that the depictions on the seals are under Western influence as are the coins. However, the imperial Persian style seems to be stronger on the latter." [A. Spaer, *NL* 144]

5907 **Meshorer, Ya'akov.** "The Coins of Samaria in the Persian Period." *Michmanim* (Hecht Museum, Haifa University, Israel) 6 (October 1992): 7-13. Illus.
"This is a brief summary of the recently discovered fourth century B.C. coinage of Samaria with an historical outline and discussion of some of the names appearing on the coins." [A. Spaer, *NL* 137]

5908 **Meshorer, Ya'akov, and Shraga Qedar.** *The Coinage of Samaria in the Fourth Century B.C.E.* Jerusalem: Numismatic Fine Arts International, 1991. 84 pp., 52 pls.
The first part of this book is a study of all the coins attributed to the mint of Samaria. The Samarian coinage is concentrated in the period 375-332 B.C. The authors begin with historical commentary on the region of Samaria. They discuss the inscriptions found on the coins. An extensive review of the prototypes for Samarian coin types follows. The prototypes were primarily coins of Sidon, Tyre, Cilicia, and Athens. Includes a catalogue of 106 coin types, each of which is illustrated by line drawings. The second part of the book is a catalogue of the "Samaria Hoard" which included 334 coins: 182 from the mint of Samaria, 43 coins of Sidon, 32 of Tyre, 11 of Aradus, and 66 imitations of Athenian prototypes. The non-Samarian coins are important to the understanding of the chronology of Samarian coinage. Discusses the chronology of the coins, the minting techniques used, the quantities of coins struck, and the denominations. The plates include photographs of the obverse and reverse of each of the 106 Samarian coin types and each of the 334 hoard coins. Each coin is shown actual size as well as in 3:1 enlargements. [Reviewed by M. J. Price in *Numismatic Chronicle* 154 (1994): 312-5. For a revised edition, see below].

5909 ——— *Samarian Coinage*. Publications of the Israel Numismatic Society, Numismatic Studies and Researches, Volume 9. Jerusalem: Graphit Press Ltd., 1999. 160 pp., 31 pls.
A major revision of the authors' *The Coinage of Samaria in the Fourth Century B.C.E.* The catalogue of types now lists 224 coins. Does not includes the catalogue of the Samaria Hoard, which made up Part 2 of the original edition. [Reviewed by Stephen N. Gerson in *The Celator* 13, no. 11 (November 1999): 34-5].

5910 **Ronen, Yigal.** "Twenty Unrecorded Samarian Coins." *Israel Numismatic Research* (Israel) 2 (2007): 29 ff.
Twenty unrecorded Samarian coins are presented, of which ten are different denominations of previously recorded coins. The attribution of the other ten coins to Samaria is based on the motifs on the coins, as well as on their provenance. These additional Samarian coins add to the great variety of types of Samarian coins. The fact that so many types of coins were minted in such a short period is an interesting enigma.

5911 **Vagi, David L.** "Samarian Coinage Offers Fanciful Designs." *The Celator* 10, no. 2 (February 1996): 23-4. Illus.
A brief introduction to the ancient coinage of Samaria which borrows many designs from other cities and kingdoms. Designs borrowed from Persia, Athens, and Sidon, although modified and bearing local inscriptions, are frequently encountered on Samarian coinage. Most of this coinage was struck ca. 350-333 B.C.

5912 **van Alfen, Peter.** "Greek Acquisitions: Three Samarian Obols." *American Numismatic Society Magazine* 1, no. 3 (winter 2002): 14. Illus.

Discusses three obols of Samaria which were presented to the American Numismatic Society museum. The coins came from a hoard. They are small, crudely produced imitations of the Athenian owls and were minted in the fourth century B.C. The author comments on the economic and artistic significance of the coins.

Also see: Fulco and Zayadine "Coins from Samaria-Sebaste" under HOARDS; Gitler "A Hacksilber and Cut Athenian Tetradrachm Hoard from the Environs of Samaria" under HOARDS; Heltzer "The Provincial Taxation" under PALESTINE—JUDEA; Heritage Auctions *The Shoshana Collection* under PALESTINE—JUDEA; Hoover *Handbook of Coins of the Southern Levant* under ASIA—GENERAL WORKS; Houghton "A Seleucid Mint at Samaria-Sebaste?" under SYRIA—SELEUCID KINGDOM; Lemaire "Monétaire de Transeuphratène avant Alexandre?" under PALESTINE—JUDEA; Meshorer *Coins of the Holy Land* under PALESTINE—JUDEA; Mildenberg "Notes on the Coin Issues of Mazday" under PERSIA; Mildenberg "On the Money Circulation in Palestine from Artaxerxes II till Ptolemy I" under PALESTINE—JUDEA; Mildenberg "*yehud* und *smryn*" under PALESTINE—JUDEA.

ARABIA

The ancient coinage of Southern Arabia is one of the most obscure branches of numismatics. In origin, it is Greek; but in development it is Semitic. For the proper study of it a numismatist who is equally equipped on the Greek and Semitic sides is required; and such a scholar has yet to be discovered.

—George F. Hill, 1915

5913 **'Abdullah, Yusuf M., Abbu O. Ghaleb, and Alexander V. Sedov.** "Early Qatabanian Coinage: the as-Surayrah Coin Hoard." *Arabian Archaeology and Epigraphy* (Denmark) 8, no. 2 (November 1997): 203-29.
In 1994, a hoard of more than 300 silver coins was found near the village of as-Surayrah, in the area of Ta'izz. Typologically, it consists of three groups: (1) 'old style' Athenian imitations with the head of Athena on the obverse and an owl on the reverse (further divided into the tetradrachm, didrachm, and hemidrachm (triobol) denominations according to the pseudo-Attic standard), (2) imitations of owls with the head of the local king on the obverse, and (3) coins with the head of the local king on the obverse and a 'hellenistic' head on the reverse. This hoard is attributed to the early period of Qatabanian coinage due to the region where the coin hoard was found and the presence of the legend on the third group of coins as *Yd'b* on the obverse and *mlk Qibn* or *mlk Qtbn s'ym* on the reverse, written in the South Arabian script.

5914 **Arnold-Biucchi, Carmen.** "Arabian Alexanders." *Mnemata: Papers in Memory of Nancy M. Waggoner.* Edited by William E. Metcalf. New York: American Numismatic Society, 1991. Pages 99-115. 4 pls., map.
Discusses the coinage which is related to the lifetime issues of Alexander III by their types and weight standards, but which were presumably minted in Arabia. The author describes the major types and discusses their chronology and mint attributions. Divides the coinage into two groups: third century B.C. silver issues, and the later debased silver and bronze issues. Symbolism and inscriptions are discussed. Hoard evidence is reviewed for its chronological implications. This coinage is generally dated to ca. 240-200 B.C.

5915 **Barkay, Rachel.** "Undated Coins from Hellenistic Marisa." *Israel Numismatic Journal* (Israel) 15 (2003-2006): 54-5.

5916 ——— "Seven New Silver Coins of Malichus I and Obodas III." *Numismatic Chronicle* 166 (2006): 99-103. Illus.
Four previously unpublished silver coins of the Nabataean kings Malichus I and Obodas III and four other new Nabataean coins are described.

5917 ——— "New Nabataean Coins." *Israel Numismatic Journal* (Israel) 16 (2007-2008): 92-9.

5918 **Boneschi, Paulo.** "L'Inscription Lihyānite d'Anciennes Monnaies Tenues pour Sabéennes." *Rivista degli Studi Orientali* (Italy) 26 (1951): 1-15.

5919 **Bowsher, J. M. C.** "Early Nabataean Coinage." *ARAM Periodical, First International Conference—The Nabataeans.* Oxford, 1990. Pages 221-8.

5920 ——— "Monetary Exchange in Nabataean Petra." *The World of the Nabataeans: International Conference on the World of the Herods and the Nabataeans held at the British Museum, 17-19 April 2001, Volume 2.* Oriens et Occidens 15. Stuttgart, 2007. Pages 337-43.

5921 **Breton, J.–F., and Stuart Munro-Hay.** "New Himyaritic Coins from Axum." *Arabian Archaeology and Epigraphy* (Denmark) 13, no. 2 (2002): 255-8.

5922 **Callot, Olivier.** "Les Monnaies dites 'Arabes' dans le Nord du Golfe Arabo-Persique à la Fin du IIIème Siècle avant Notre Ère." *Failaka: Fouilles Française, 1986-1988.* Edited by Y. Calvet and J. Gachet. Lyon: Maison de l'Orient, 1990. Pages 221-40.

5923 ——— "A New Chronology for the Arabian Alexanders." *Coinage of the Caravan Kingdoms: Studies in the Monetization of Ancient Arabia.* Numismatic Studies No. 25. Edited by Martin Huth and Peter G. van Alfen. New York: American Numismatic Society, 2010. 602 pp., 42 pls. Pages 383-402. Illus.
Describes the Arabian coins which imitate the types of Alexander the Great, sometimes based on Seleucid prototypes. Summarizes the history of coinage in northeast Arabia, emphasizing the chronology of the issues including those bearing the name Shams (*s'ms'*). Callot then describes the coins from the Oman Peninsula including those naming a certain Abi'el, focusing on evidence for their chronology. The author then examines (1) the small number of coins that bear the name of Harithat, king of Hagar, which imitated the coins of Abiel and were minted in the mid-second century

B.C., and (2) the imitations inspired by the posthumous Alexanders minted in the third and second centuries B.C. at Miletus in Asia Minor. Ends with a chronological synopsis of the Arabian Alexander coinage and a table laying out the main varieties and comparing the dating proposed by Mørkholm, Robin, Callot (1990), Arnold-Biucchi, Huth & Potts, Callot (2004), and Callot (2010).

5924 **Davidde, B.** "Three Unpublished Collections of South Arabian Coins." *Arabian Archaeology and Epigraphy* (Denmark) 13, no. 1 (2003): 63-70.

5925 **de Luynes, LeDuc.** "Monnaies de Nabatéens." *Revue Numismatique* (France) 3 (1858): 292-316.

5926 **Dembski, Günther.** "The Coins of Arabia Felix." *Yemen: 3000 Years of Art and Civilization in Arabia Felix.* Edited by W. Daum. Innsbruck/Frankfurt, 1987. Pages 125-8.

5927 **De Vogüé, M.** "Monnaies de Rois de Nabatène." *Revue Numismatique* (France) 13 (1868): 153-68.

5928 **Dussaud, R.** "Monnaies de Nabatéennes." *Revue Numismatique* (France) 9 (1905): 170-6.

5929 **Gitler, Haim.** "A Unique 'Philisto-Arabian' Coin of Ashod from the Fourth Century B.C.E." *The Israel Museum Journal* (Israel) 17 (1999): 62-3.
"The article contains a description of a drachm bearing the inscription "Ashod." The obverse depicts hybrid heads of a male and an animal. On the reverse are two bull protomes. The author believes the depictions point to strong Achaemenid influence." [A. Spaer, *NL* 143]

5930 **Grave, Peter, Roger Bird, and Dan T. Potts.** "A Trial PIXE/PIGME Analysis of Pre-Islamic Arabian Coinage." *Arabian Archaeology and Epigraphy* (Denmark) 7, no. 1 (May 1996): 75-81.
Eight previously unpublished pre-Islamic coins minted in Arabia were subjected to non-destructive ion beam analysis by Proton Induced X-Ray (PIXE) and Gamma-Ray Emission (PIGME). The results were interpreted using Principal Components Analysis (PCA). The relative X-ray intensities of fifteen elements, supplemented with additional L alpha lines for two of the elements, were extracted for this analysis. PCA was first carried out on the whole dataset where the distinctive high iron and nickel composition of two coins resulted in their position as outliers. A second analysis of the subset of silver coins showed the compositional similarity between four coins and distinguished two separate outliers. One of these has a high lead and tin content while the other has a greater proportion of elements present as impurities including iron and nickel. The two outliers and the relatively homogenous compositions of the group of four coins suggest that three compositional types of silver coinage are represented in the dataset: (1) a relatively silver-rich group of four coins, (2) silver coins debased with lead, and (3) silver coins debased with iron and nickel.

5931 **Haerinck, E.** "More Pre-Islamic Coins from Southeastern Arabia." *Arabian Archaeology and Epigraphy* (Denmark) 9, no. 2 (November 1998): 278-301.
In recent years, several coin collections amassed by several expatriates in the United Arab Emirates have appeared on the market. Here 193 coins collected at ed-Dur and Mleiha are presented. Three of the coins represent previously unknown types. The purpose of the article is to document as many coins as possible and to thereby contribute to the avoidance of a distorted image of coin circulation in this little-known area. The classification elaborated by D. T. Potts has been followed.

5932 ——— "South and (South) East Arabian Silver Athenian Owl Imitations from Mleiha." *Arabian Archaeology and Epigraphy* (Denmark) 9, no. 1 (May 1998): 137-9.
Several collections of coins found at Mleiha (United Arab Emirates) have appeared on the market. The author presents six Arabian imitations of Athenian coins including a folded-flan specimen, a specimen with the Arabian letter Z on the reverse, and three coins which the author suggests may be the first local issues to have been minted in southeastern Arabia.

5933 **Head, Barclay V.** "On Himyarite and Other Arabian Imitations of Coins of Athens." *Numismatic Chronicle* new ser., 18 (1878): 273-84.
Discusses the origin and use of the Himyarite coins which imitate the types of Athens. Lists and describes nine coins.

5934 ——— "On a Himyaritic Tetradrachm and the Trésor De San'â." *Numismatic Chronicle* new ser., 20 (1880): 303-10. 1 pl.
Describes a Himyarite tetradrachm modeled after a tetradrachm of Alexander struck ca. 200 B.C. Comments on the chronology of other Himyarite coins.

5935 **Hettger, Joel.** "Land of the Queen of Sheba, Frankincense and Myrrh: Sabaean and Himyaritic Coins Revisited." *The Celator* 6, no. 2 (February 1992): 28-33.
Reviews the history and numismatic literature related to the coinage of the Sabaean and Himyarite rulers of Southern Arabia. The discussion focuses on the translation of coin legends and inscriptions.

5936 **Hill, George F.** *Catalogue of Greek Coins of Arabia, Mesopotamia, and Persia.* London: British Museum, 1922. Reprint, Bologna: Forni, 1965. ccxix, 359 pp., 55 pls., map. [CS 3001]
Volume 28 of the *Catalogue of Greek Coins in the British Museum.* Also includes Babylonia, Nabatea, Assyria, Persis, Elymais, and Characene. The 359-page catalogue of coins is preceded by 219 pages of introductory text. [Reviewed by E. T. Newell in *Numismatic Chronicle* 5th ser., 3 (1923): 159-64. Also see *Catalogue of Greek Coins in the British Museum* under PUBLIC COLLECTIONS—GREAT BRITAIN (LONDON)].

5937 ——— "The Ancient Coinage of Southern Arabia." *Proceedings of the British Academy, Volume 7.* London, 1915. Pages 57-84. 1 pl. Reprint, Chicago: Argonaut, 1969. 28 pp., 1 pl. [CS 3002]
Examines the coinage of the Minaeans, Sabaeans, Katabanians, and Himyarites in Southern Arabia. Describes the types and inscriptions of each class of coinage: imitations of the older Attic types, imitations of the later Attic types, and coins with and without a king's name. Discusses the weight standards and denominations employed.

5938 **Hoover, Oliver D.** "A Reassessment of Nabataean Lead Coinage in Light of New Discoveries." *Numismatic Chronicle* 166 (2006): 105-19. 4 pls.

Numerous new specimens of Nabataean lead coins have recently appeared (there previously were only two known). Hoover discusses their chronology, portraits, types, and inscriptions. The known lead coins are catalogued. He suggests the coins belong to the second half of the first century B.C. and later. Discusses whether they should be considered coins or tokens. He suggests they were tokens or tesserae distributed by the king on important occasions.

5939 ——— "Petra on the Hudson: The Nabataeans and their Coins at the American Numismatic Society." *ANS Magazine* 10, no. 1 (2011): 20-7. Illus.
A good overview of the history and coinage of the Nabataean kingdom, illustrated by coins in the ANS collection from the collections of David Hendin and Abraham Sofaer.

5940 **Hoover, Oliver D., and Rachel Barkay.** "Important Additions to the Corpus of Nabataean Coins since 1990." *Coinage of the Caravan Kingdoms: Studies in the Monetization of Ancient Arabia.* Numismatic Studies No. 25. Edited by Martin Huth and Peter G. van Alfen. New York: American Numismatic Society, 2010. 602 pp., 42 pls. Pages 197-212. 2 pls.
This paper presents a catalogue of 130 new Nabataean coins, augmenting the listings of Meshorer (see *Nabataean Coins* below) and Schmitt-Korte (see "Nabataean Coinage, Part 2" below). Includes some new types, varieties, and dates. Seven hoards with Nabataean content are listed and briefly described in the appendix.

5941 **Howgego, Christopher J., and Dan T. Potts.** "Greek and Roman Coins from Eastern Arabia." *Arabian Archaeology and Epigraphy* (Denmark) 3, no. 3 (October 1992): 183-9.
The authors record several Greek and Roman coins found in eastern Arabia, including an Athenian imitation tetradrachm.

5942 **Huth, Martin.** "The 'Folded Flan' Coinage of Eastern Arabia: Some Preliminary Comments." *Arabian Archaeology and Epigraphy* (Denmark) 9, no. 2 (November 1998): 273-7.
In recent years, a small number of peculiar coins has emerged from the southern shores of the Persian/Arabian Gulf imitating Athenian tetradrachms of the old style and sharing the oddity of being struck on a flan that has been folded before striking. The author provides an overview of the pieces known so far and attempts to present some preliminary conclusions.

5943 ——— "An Important Hoard of Early South Arabian Coins from the Kingdom of Qataban." *Revue Suisse de Numismatique* (Switzerland) 78 (1999): 37-51. Illus.
"A hoard from As-Surayrah (Yemen) with 190 recorded silver coins throws new light on the coinage of the kingdom of Qataban. The bulk of the hoard consists of tetradrachms, didrachms and drachms which imitate old style Athenian coins and many of which bear the 'royal' Qatabanian monogram. The obverse of three owl coins shows a male head with an inscribed diadem. The hoard also contains several hemidrachms with male heads on both sides and inscriptions relating to the king of Qataban." [M. Peter, *NL* 145]

5944 ——— "Beyond Gaza: Two South Arabian Problems." *Israel Numismatic Journal* (Israel) 14 (2001-02): 26-33. Illus.

5945 ——— "Imitations of Athenian Coins from the Kingdom of Qataban." *Oriental Numismatic Society Newsletter* 169 (autumn 2001): 2-3. Illus.

5946 ——— "A Coin in the Name of Hawfi'amm Yuhan'im and the Sequence of Qatabanian Coinages." *Arabian Archaeology and Epigraphy* (Denmark) 15, no. 1 (2004): 89-92.

5947 ——— *Coinage of the Caravan Kingdoms: Ancient Arabian Coins from the Collection of Martin Huth.* Ancient Coins in North American Collections 10. New York: Amercian Numismatic Society, 2010. 162 pp., illus.
A catalogue of Martin Huth's collection of pre-Islamic coins of the Arabian Peninsula—a companion volume to Huth and van Alfen's *Coinage of the Caravan Kingdoms: Studies in the Monetization of Ancient Arabia* (see below) where many of the coins are discussed in detail. Includes 478 coins fully described and illustrated. The collection covers Gaza, the Idumaea or Kingdom of Lihyan, Nabataean coinage, coinage of the western Arabian Gulf, the Kingdom of Hagar, coinage of the Oman peninsula, Minaean coinage, Sabaean coinage, Qatabanian coinage, Himyarite coinage, coinage of Hadramawt, and a number of uncertain issues. Indices of monograms and inscriptions.

5948 ——— "Gods and Kings: On the Imagery of Arabian Coinage." *Coinage of the Caravan Kingdoms: Studies in the Monetization of Ancient Arabia.* Numismatic Studies No. 25. Edited by Martin Huth and Peter G. van Alfen. New York: American Numismatic Society, 2010. 602 pp., 42 pls. Pages 107-23. 4 pls.
Examines the religious imagery on early Arabian coins. (1) Huth suggests that the continued use of Athena's head for several centuries as the sole coin-type in Northwest and South Arabia may have been because it was interpreted as a local deity—Shams, al-Lat, al-'Uzza, or Manat. The seated Zeus figure on Arabian Alexanders may have been interpreted locally as Shams. (2) Huth discusses the names and representations of Arabian deities on non-imitative coins, including a unique coin of Obodas II which may depict the god Dushara. (3) Discusses the use of the human head in Arabian coinage. And (4) examines religious symbols, objects, animals, and monograms.

5949 ——— "The Gold Coins." *Coinage of the Caravan Kingdoms: Studies in the Monetization of Ancient Arabia.* Numismatic Studies No. 25. Edited by Martin Huth and Peter G. van Alfen. New York: American Numismatic Society, 2010. 602 pp., 42 pls. Pages 125-32. 1 pl.
Early Arabian coinage was almost exclusively silver. The few gold coins appear to be experimental in nature. Huth provides some possible reasons for the lack of a gold coinage before the late Roman period, and describes the few gold examples known.

5950 ——— "Monetary Circulation in South West Arabia between the Fourth and Second Centuries BCE: The al-Jawf Hoards of 2001 and 2002." *Coinage of the Caravan Kingdoms: Studies in the Monetization of Ancient Arabia.* Numismatic Studies No. 25. Edited by Martin Huth and Peter G. van Alfen. New York: American Numismatic Society, 2010. 602 pp., 42 pls. Pages 83-105. 8 pls.
Examines two hoards found in the area of the Minaean Kingdom: the al-Jawf Hoard of 2001 and the al-Jawf Hoard of 2002. The 2001 hoard was comprised of twenty tetradrachms of fifth and fourth century style—both Athenian and Egyptian or Levantine imitations. The coins were likely buried ca. 300 B.C. The 2002 hoard contained 247 coins of Ma'in, the Kingdom of Saba (units, quarter-units, and eighth-units), Kingdom of Qataban (three coins), and Himyarite and other uncertain Arabian coins as well as coins of several Greek states. The hoard was likely buried ca. 100 B.C. The Ma'in coins consisted of folded-flan

silver coins struck with stylized Athenian types. Huth illustrates how the folded-flan coins were fabricated by folding one or two coins, then overstriking them. Alexander-type tetradrachms provided the flans for the folded owls. The coins were probably minted ca. 200-100 B.C. Both hoards show that there was an uninterrupted influx of foreign coins into South Arabia from the fourth to the second centuries B.C., and show that in some areas, Alexanders were the dominant currency while in other areas, Athenian owls were dominant. Concludes with an appendix listing twenty-three South Arabian coin hoards.

5951 ——— "Some Nabataean Questions Reconsidered." *Coinage of the Caravan Kingdoms: Studies in the Monetization of Ancient Arabia.* Numismatic Studies No. 25. Edited by Martin Huth and Peter G. van Alfen. New York: American Numismatic Society, 2010. 602 pp., 42 pls. Pages 213-26. Illus.
Provides a table of reign dates for Nabataean rulers as well as dates of their silver and bronze coinage. Publishes some new coin varieties and explores some questions related to Nabataean coinage: (1) Examines the attribution of some coins to Obodas II and suggests all coins bearing the name of Obodas belong to the same ruler—the king known as Obodas III—who should now be known as Obodas II. (2) Discusses the purpose of the first coinage of Malichus I. (3) Discusses the portraits of Nabataean queens on coins and illustrates a newly discovered coin bearing the name of Obodas II's queen Hagaru. (4) Discusses the dating of the coins attributed to the usurper Syllaeus—were the coins already minted during the reign of Obodas II, do they fall into the reign of the successor Aretas IV, or did the usurper himself issue an independent coinage? Huth confirms that a series of coins was a joint issue of Syllaeus and Aretas bearing a portrait of Obodas II. Also confirms the sign F stands for Syllaeus' initial *shin*. (5) Presents a revised table of the reign dates of the Nabataean rulers and the dates of their regnal-dated silver and bronze coinage based on a coin bearing the name of Aretas' daughter Phasael. (6) Discusses a possible 'emergency issue' of bronze coins of Aretas IV. No silver coins are known from the 7th to 12th years of his reign, but a series of bronze coins was struck in years 10 and 11 with inscriptions that may indicate their values in terms of silver. Meshorer suggested this was an emergency issue. Huth explores the nature of this coinage and rejects the notion that it was an emergency replacement for the silver coinage. He suggests that it could have been a necessary coinage to support exceptional state expenditures. Alternately, it may have been simply an attempt to introduce a fractional bronze coinage. He shows that the inscription in question may not refer to silver, but merely to money in a more general sense.

5952 ——— "Athenian Imitations from Arabia." *Coinage of the Caravan Kingdoms: Studies in the Monetization of Ancient Arabia.* Numismatic Studies No. 25. Edited by Martin Huth and Peter G. van Alfen. New York: American Numismatic Society, 2010. 602 pp., 42 pls. Pages 227-56. Illus.
Discusses the minting and use of imitation Athenian coins in Egypt in the fourth century B.C. including those bearing the name of the Persian king Artaxerxes III, those struck after the Persians re-gained control of Egypt in 343 B.C., those bearing symbols or letters, and unmarked crude copies. The coins were generally struck at a time when trade was becoming increasingly monetized and the inflow of Athenian coins into Egypt had decreased significantly. Some issues combine Athenian and non-Athenian types. Huth then describes coins based on Athenian types that circulated in North Arabia, some of them of local origin, from the end of the fourth century B.C. to the first century B.C. (this coinage may have ended concurrently with the start of Nabataean coinage). He then describes a unique Sabaean tetradrachm from the al-Jawf hoard (2002) bearing the so-called Totschläger (curved symbol) in front of the owl, and the series of Athenian imitations bearing denomination marks on Athena's cheek. A table presents an overview of the letters, monograms, and symbols that appear on Sabaean coins of the third to second centuries B.C. Also presents an illustrated chart of the development of South Arabian coinage of the kingdoms of Saba, Qataban, and Ma'in. Huth suggests that South Arabia had a largely monetized economy supported by a highly organized monetary system. Concludes with a summary of the factors which led to the Arabian imitation coinage. An Appendix is a table listing all known epigraphic variants of Sabaean coinage, with enlarged photographs of the letters, symbols, and monograms.

5953 **Huth, Martin, and Dan T. Potts.** "Antiochus in Arabia." *American Journal of Numismatics* 2nd ser., 14 (2002): 73-81. 1 pl.
Publishes three imitations of tetradrachms of Antiochus III. The coins are unusual in style and bear an Arabian letter in the exergue. They likely were minted in Arabia ca. 200-187 B.C. and may be related to Antiochus III's campaigns in Arabia.

5954 **Huth, Martin, and Shraga Qedar.** "A Coin from North Arabia with an Aramaic Inscription and Related Coins of the Incense Road." *Numismatic Chronicle* 159 (1999): 295-8. 2 pls.
"This paper identifies five interrelated groups of Athenian imitations minted in the Arabian peninsula from the fourth century B.C., and which appear to have provided an international coinage along the incense road connecting Gaza with South Arabia and the Persian Gulf." [M. Huth and S. Qedar, *NL* 145]

5955 **Huth, Martin, and Peter Stein.** "The So-Called Cursive Legend Reconsidered." *Coinage of the Caravan Kingdoms: Studies in the Monetization of Ancient Arabia.* Numismatic Studies No. 25. Edited by Martin Huth and Peter G. van Alfen. New York: American Numismatic Society, 2010. 602 pp., 42 pls. Pages 345-56. Illus.
A legend occurring on two groups of Arabian coins, both Old and New Style Athenian imitations, is written in an unknown cursive script. The legend is different from that found on all other Arabian coins and has been subject to various interpretations since its discovery in 1872. The authors summarize the earlier interpretations. After comparison with inscriptions on wooden sticks, they read the cursive legend as *s'mh'ly*, a well-known personal name in ancient South Arabia. It refers to a Sabaean ruler of the fourth or early third century B.C., and is written in ancient South Arabian minuscule script. This ruler bears the cognomen YNF. This cursive legend may have been considered an individual signature of the issuing authority, the Sabaean king.

5956 **Huth, Martin, and Peter G. van Alfen, eds.** *Coinage of the Caravan Kingdoms: Studies in the Monetization of Ancient Arabia.* Numismatic Studies No. 25. New York: American Numismatic Society, 2010. 602 pp., 42 pls.
A comprehensive examination of the ancient coinages of the Arabian peninsula. Includes discussion of Philistian, Nabataean, Minaen, Qatabanian, Sabaen, Himyarite, Gerrhean, and other coinages. The numerous essays include die studies of the Athenian owl imitations and Alexander imitations struck in Arabia. The essays explore the coinage within their political, social, and economic contexts. In addition to the overview of Arabian coinage by Huth and van Alfen, the papers are: "The Arabian Peninsula, 600 BCE to 600 CE" by D. Potts [5988], "The Circulation of Foreign Coins within Arabia and of Arabian Coins outside the Peninsula in the Pre-Islamic Period" by D. Potts [5989], "Monetary Circulation in South West Arabia between the Fourth and Second Centuries BCE: The al-Jawf Hoards of 2001 and 2002" by M. Huth [5950], "Gods and Kings: On the Imagery of Arabian Coinage" by M. Huth [5948], "The Gold Coins" by M. Huth [5949], "Notes on the Coinages of the Philistian Cities" by W. Fischer-Bossert [5877], "Important Additions to the Corpus of Nabataean Coins since 1990" by O. Hoover and R. Barkay [5940], "Some Nabataean Questions Reconsidered" by M. Huth [5951], "Athenian Imitations from Arabia" by M. Huth [5952], "Die Studies of the Earliest Qatabanian and Sabaean Coinages" by P. van Alfen [6010], "The Monetary Terminology of Ancient South Arabia in Light of New Epigraphic Evidence" by P. Stein [6007], "The So-Called Cursive Legend Reconsidered" by M. Huth and P. Stein [5955], "Himyarite Kings on Coins" by C. Robin [5992], "A New Chronology for the Arabian Alexanders" by O. Callot [5923], "The 'Abiel' Coins of Eastern Arabia: A Study of the Aramaic Legends" by M. MacDonald [5964], and "A Die Study of the 'Abiel' Coinage of Eastern Arabia" by P. van Alfen [6011]. The plates and script tables that accompany MacDonald's paper appear on a CD-ROM that is attached at the back of the book. [Also see M. Huth *Coinage of the Caravan Kingdoms* above for the companion catalogue of Huth's Arabian coins].

5957   **Irvine, A. K.** "Some Notes on Old South Arabian Monetary Terminology." *Journal of the Royal Asiatic Society* (1964): 18-36.

5958   **Khairy, N. I.** "Silver Nabataean Coins in Jordan." *Dirasat* (Jordan) 12, no. 8 (1985): 73-90.

5959   **Kropp, M., and W. Hahn.** "Letters on the Cheek of Athena: The Denominations of the Sabaean Sigloi and their Numerical Signs." *Proceeding of the Seminar for Arabian Studies* 27 (1997): 159-64.

5960   **Kubitschek, J. W., and D. H. Müller.** "Münzen (Himyarite and Other South Arabian Coins)." *Südarabische Alterthümer im Kunsthistorischen Hofmuseum.* Edited by D. H. Miller. Vienna, 1899. Pages 65-79. 2 pls.

5961   **Kushnir-Stein, Alla, and Haim Gitler.** "Numismatic Evidence from Tel Beer-Sheva and the Beginning of Nabatean Coinage." *Israel Numismatic Journal* (Israel) 12 (1992-3): 13-26. Illus.
"The coins excavated at this site end with issues dated to 112/111 B.C. after which a gap of about a century occurs in the dates of coins found. A substantial part of the coins found among those dated before 112/111 B.C. are copper coins of the type published by E. S. G. Robinson in *Numismatic Chronicle* 16 (1936): 290-1 and identified by him as the earliest Nabatean issues. This attribution is confirmed by the excavation coins which also prove that their issue began before 112/111 B.C." [A. Spaer, *NL* 134]. [See E. S. G. Robinson "Coins of Petra" under HOARDS].

5962   ——— "A New Date on Coins of Marisa in Idumaea and its Historical Implications." *Revue Suisse de Numismatique* (Switzerland) 83 (2004): 87-94.

5963   **Langlois, Victor.** *Numismatique des Arabes avant l'Islame.* Paris: Rollin, 1859.

5964   **Macdonald, Michael C. A.** "The 'Abiel' Coins of Eastern Arabia: A Study of the Aramaic Legends." *Coinage of the Caravan Kingdoms: Studies in the Monetization of Ancient Arabia.* Numismatic Studies No. 25. Edited by Martin Huth and Peter G. van Alfen. New York: American Numismatic Society, 2010. 602 pp., 42 pls. Pages 403-547.
An epigraphical study of the inscriptions on a number of the Arabian Alexander imitations which bear the name Abiel (*'b(y)'l*) in the Aramaic script. Discusses their interpretation and the resulting implications. Concludes that the Abiels named were queens, not kings. Macdonald examined 376 relevant coins. Extensive bibliography. The plates and script tables that accompany this paper are included on a CD-ROM that is attached at the back of the book. [Also see van Alfen "A Die Study of the 'Abiel' Coinage" below].

5965   **Maraqten, Mohammed.** "Notes on the Aramaic Script of Some Coins from East Arabia." *Arabian Archaeology and Epigraphy* (Denmark) 7, no. 2 (November 1996): 304-15.
The author provides some preliminary remarks on the Aramaic scripts on coins from eastern Arabia. After giving a presentation of the palaeography of some coins from Mleiha, he offers suggestions for the reading of the Aramaic legends and the origin of the Aramaic script on them.

5966   **Meshorer, Ya'akov.** *Nabataean Coins.* Qedem: Monographs of the Institute of Archaeology, the Hebrew University of Jerusalem, No. 3. Edited by Y. Yadin, N. Avigad, J. Aviram, D. Barag, and A. Ben-Tor. Translated from Hebrew by I. H. Levine. Jerusalem: Hebrew University of Jerusalem, 1975. 112 pp., 8 pls. [CS 3003]
The standard catalogue for the coinage of the Nabataeans from its beginning in 62 B.C. to its end in A.D. 106 when the Nabataean Kingdom was absorbed into the Roman Province of Arabia. Includes historical background for the kingdom and its coinage. Examines the coinage of each of the kings (Obodas II, Malichus I, Obodas III, Syllaeus, Aretas IV, Malichus II, and Rabbel II). Discusses inscriptions, chronology, and metallurgy. Presents a catalogue of 164 coin types. [Reviewed by M. J. Price in *Israel Exploration Journal* 27 (1977): 59-61. Also see Schmitt-Korte "Nabataean Coinage, Part 2" below, and Hoover and Barkay above for additional coin types].

5967   **Milik, J. T., and Henri Seyrig.** "Trésor Monétaire de Murabba'àt." *Revue Numismatique* (France) 6th ser., 18 (1958): 11-26.

5968   **Mitchiner, Michael B.** "Unusual Early South Arabian Coins of the Himyarite-Katabanian Series." *Coin Hoards* 7 (1985): 74-6. Illus.
Discusses four rare Himyarite coins bearing the mint name Raidan. The coins are from a recent hoard.

5969   **Mordtmann, J. H.** "New Himyaritic Money." *Numismatische Zeitschrift* (Austria) (1880): 307-16.

5970   **Munro-Hay, Stuart C.** "The Coinage of Shabwa (Hadhramawt), and Other Ancient South Arabian Coinage in the National Museum, Aden." *Syria* 68 (1991): 393-418.

5971   ——— "Coins of Ancient South Arabia." *Numismatic Chronicle* 154 (1994): 191-203. 6 pls.
A catalogue of a collection of 317 South Arabian coins, including some previously unpublished types.

5972   ——— "Coins of Ancient South Arabia, II." *Numismatic Chronicle* 156 (1996): 33-47. 3 pls.
In this supplement to the author's previous article (see above) some new types are added and the previously established chronology is revised.

5973   ——— "South Arabian Coins in a Private Collection (PC 1996)." *Arabian Archaeology and Epigraphy* (Denmark) 8, no. 2 (November 1997): 230-40.
A private collection of 106 South Arabian coins is documented, including several new types, some coins from the al-Surayrah hoard, and a copper coin of King 'Amdan Bayin.

5974   ——— "South Arabian Coins in a Private Collection 2 (PC 1998). *Arabian Archaeology and Epigraphy* (Denmark) 13, no. 1 (2003): 71-80.

5975 ——— *Coinage of Arabia Felix: The Pre-Islamic Coinage of the Yemen.* Nomismata 5. Milan: Edizioni Ennerre, 2003. 221 pp., 61 pls.
Examines the imitation Athenian series, the bucranium series, the royal series, and copper and bronze coins of Hadramawt. The author links the coinage to known historical and archaeological developments in the Yemen in terms of religious, political, and cultural factors. Includes an overview of the history of the study of Arabian coinage and a history and chronology of the kingdoms of Southern Arabia. Catalogue of the coins of the Qataban, Hadhramawt, Saba', and Himyar kingdoms (no coins were struck by the Ma'in kingdom). [Reviewed by Oliver Hoover in *American Numismatic Society Magazine* 3, no. 2 (summer 2004): 63-7, and by Andrew Oddy in *Numismatic Chronicle* 165 (2005): 395-7].

5976 **Naster, Paul.** "Remarques au Sujet des Imitations des Monnaies d'Athènes dans la Presqu'ile Arabique." *Proceedings of the International Numismatic Symposium.* Edited by I. Gedai and K. Biró-Sey. Budapest, 1980. Pages 31-6.

5977 **Negev, Avraham.** "Numismatics and Nabataean Chronology." *Palestine Exploration Quarterly* (England) 114, pt. 2 (July-December 1982): 119-28.
The author charts the fluctuation in the silver content of Nabataean coins from 60 B.C. to A.D. 100. The coinage shows a gradual debasement during this period. He comments on the implications of this debasement for the study of Nabataean history.

5978 **Nordbø, Jan H. A.** "A Hoard of Silver Coins from Arabia Felix." *Meddelelser fra Norsk Numismatisk Forening* (Norway) 1 (1985): 8-16.
"One hundred three Himyaritic coins, all of the same type (male head r./bucranium) from a pot hoard found in 1983, are published. The catalogue includes photo, weight, die-axis, obverse and reverse symbols of all coins. The author concludes from the large number of dies that the output was plentiful and proposes a new dating for the series: A.D. 1-40/50." [H. Nilsson, *NL* 116]

5979 ——— "The First Arabic Coinage." *Araby* 1 (1987): 21-2

5980 **Oddy, Andrew.** "Two Putative Coin Hoards from South Arabia." *Arabian Archaeology and Epigraphy* (Denmark) 9, no. 1 (May 1998): 131-6.
Bonham's sale catalogue no. 26247 listed a South Arabian striated alabaster pyxis, with lid and pierced lug side handles, and a five-character inscription incised below the thick neck on both sides, from the 1st-3rd centuries A.D. Inside the pyxis, but not mentioned in the catalogue, was a polythene bag containing a small hoard of coins and some metal casting waste. The hoard and pyxis are illustrated.

5981 **Oikonomides, Al N.** "Hellenistic Numismatics and 'The Philhellene' of C. P. Cavafy." *The Ancient World* 13, nos. 1-2 (March 1986): 47-51. Illus., map.
Attempts to identify the Hellenistic king whom Constantine P. Cavafy (1863-1933) had in mind when he was writing his famous poem "The Philhellene." Using historical hints in the poem, Oikonomides identifies the king as Aretas III of Nabataea. Discusses the coin portraits and representations of this king.

5982 **Plant, Richard J.** "The Nabateans: an Introduction to Their Coins." *Numismatics in Israel* 4 (1977): 39-41. Illus., map. [CS 3004]

5983 ——— "The Sabaean Script on the Coins of South Arabia." *Seaby Coin and Medal Bulletin* 710 (October 1977): 350-2. Illus. [CS 3005]
The Sabaeans were a great power in South Arabia during ca. 650-115 B.C. Their coins often imitated the types of Athens. Plant illustrates the Sabaean script with its English and Hebrew equivalents. Translates some words and phrases which appear on Sabaean coins. Sabaean was also used on Himyarite and Axumite coins. Includes line drawings of typical Sabaean and Himyarite coins. Lists the five Himyarite kings.

5984 ——— "The Coinage of the Nabataeans." *Seaby Coin and Medal Bulletin* 727 (March 1979): 81-4. Illus. [CS 3006]
A brief introduction to Nabataean coins. Includes a table of the Nabataean alphabet and numerals with their English and Hebrew equivalents. Lists the names of the kings (62 B.C. to A.D. 106) in both English and Nabataean script, as well as several other words found on the coins. Illustrated by line drawings of typical Nabataean coins.

5985 **Potts, Dan T.** *The Pre-Islamic Coinage of Eastern Arabia.* The Carsten Niebuhr Institute of Ancient Near Eastern Studies. Copenhagen: Museum Tusculanum, 1991.
A presentation of the coin issues that circulated in Eastern Arabia during the pre-Islamic era as attested in five private collections studied by the author. Includes 529 coins selected from those collections. The coins came from two distinct regions which today comprise the Eastern Province of the Kingdom of Saudi Arabia and the Emirate of Umm al-Qaiwain in the United Arab Emirates. Foreign issues were rare in these areas, although a handful of Sasanian, Roman, Seleucid, Greek, Phoenician, Nabataean, Elymaean, Parthian and Sabaean coins are found in the collections. [Also see Potts *Supplement* below].

5986 ——— "Nabataean Finds from Thaj and Qatif." *Arabian Archaeology and Epigraphy* (Denmark) 2, no. 2 (June 1991): 138-44.
Ties between the Nabataean area of northwestern Arabia and southern Palestine and the northeastern portion of the Arabian peninsula have been discussed for some years. The material evidence of such ties is meager, but nonetheless important. Two Nabataean coins from Thaj and one from Qatif are presented here, along with a painted Nabataean sherd from Thaj. Their implications are briefly explored.

5987 ——— *Supplement to the Pre-Islamic Coinage of Eastern Arabia.* CNI Publications 16. Copenhagen, 1994.
A supplement to Potts' 1991 catalogue (see above).

5988 ——— "The Arabian Peninsula, 600 BCE to 600 CE." *Coinage of the Caravan Kingdoms: Studies in the Monetization of Ancient Arabia.* Numismatic Studies No. 25. Edited by Martin Huth and Peter G. van Alfen. New York: American Numismatic Society, 2010. Pages 27-64.
Potts divides the Arabian Peninsula into five geographic regions: southeast, northeast, southwest, northwest, and central Arabia. For each region, he provides an overview of the political and military history, kingship, administrative and power structures, external relations, religion, and social and economic structure. Includes an extensive bibliography.

5989 ——— "The Circulation of Foreign Coins within Arabia and of Arabian Coins outside the Peninsula in the Pre-Islamic Period." *Coinage of the Caravan Kingdoms: Studies in the Monetization of Ancient Arabia*. Numismatic Studies No. 25. Edited by Martin Huth and Peter G. van Alfen. New York: American Numismatic Society, 2010. 602 pp., 42 pls. Pages 65-82. 3 pls.
A discussion of (1) foreign coins circulating in Arabia, based on finds, and segregated by region, and (2) Arabian coins circulating outside of Arabia. Lists the documented hoards found in the region. The finds are relatively few and small.

5990 **Rizack, Martin A.** "A Coin with the Aramaic Legend SHRW, a King-Governor of Lihyân." *Museum Notes* 29 (1984): 25-8. Illus.
Illustrates a small silver coin bearing the Aramaic inscription SHRW in addition to AΘE. The reverse design imitates the owl coinage of Athens. The author identifies the inscription as the name of a ruler in Northern Arabia, ca. 400-350 B.C. States "an Aramaic inscription of the name of a local ruler on fractional coinage is consistent with the practice of the Persian Empire."

5991 **Robin, Christian.** "Monnaies Provenant de l'Arabie du Nord-Est." *Semitica* 24 (1974): 83-127.

5992 ——— "Himyarite Kings on Coins." *Coinage of the Caravan Kingdoms: Studies in the Monetization of Ancient Arabia*. Numismatic Studies No. 25. Edited by Martin Huth and Peter G. van Alfen. New York: American Numismatic Society, 2010. 602 pp., 42 pls. Pages 357-81. Illus.
The names of the six Himyarite rulers that appear on coins are listed in relative order. Robin provides epigraphic arguments for the proposed identifications and reconsiders their validity in the light of the numismatic evidence. Provides a history of Himyar until AD 375 and discusses the date of the beginning of the kingdom. He then discusses each king, the forms of their names, and the dates of their reigns.

5993 **Robinson, Edward S. G.** "Himyarite Coins." *Numismatic Chronicle* 5th ser., 3 (1923): 356-8.
Publishes several Himyarite coins probably from the San'â Hoard.

5994 **Schlumberger, Gustave Leon.** *Le Trésor de San'â: Monnaies Himyaritiques*. Paris: E. Leroux, 1880. 65 pp., 3 pls. of line drawings.
Examines a hoard of Himyarite coins.

5995 ——— "Monnaies Inédites des Ethiopiens et des Homérites." *Revue Numismatique* (France) 16 (1886): 356-71.

5996 **Schmitt-Korte, Karl.** "Nabataean Coinage, Part 2: New Coin Types and Variants." *Numismatic Chronicle* 150 (1990): 105-33. 6 pls.
A catalogue of eighty-eight coins, including the sixty coins examined in Part 1 (see Schmitt-Korte and Cowell below) along with a discussion of each coin. Intended as a continuation of Meshorer's book *Nabataean Coins* (see Meshorer above). Comments on chronology. [Also see Schmitt-Korte and Price below for "Part 3", and Hoover and Barkay "Important Additions" above].

5997 **Schmitt-Korte, Karl, and Michael R. Cowell.** "The Silver Content of Nabataean Coins." *Proceedings of the 10th International Congress of Numismatics, London, 1986*. International Association of Professional Numismatists Publication, No. 11. Edited by I. A. Carradice. London: International Association of Professional Numismatists, 1986. Pages 75-82.
Presents the results of X-ray fluorescence analysis of Nabataean coins, 87 B.C.-A.D. 106. Identifies three phases in the minting during which the silver content decreased from 90% to 50%. These results are more accurate than those published by Meshorer (*Nabataean Coins*, 1975) based on specific gravities. Meshorer calculated the silver content to be as low as 20% in some coins.

5998 ——— "Nabataean Coinage—Part 1. The Silver Content Measured by X-Ray Fluorescence Analysis." *Numismatic Chronicle* 149 (1989): 33-58. 7 pls.
Presents the results of the analysis of the silver content of Nabataean coins using X-ray fluorescence and scanning electron microscopy. Includes a comparison of the results from different studies, and the destructive analysis of a coin. Discusses chronology. Summarizes the general trends observed. [Also see Schmitt-Korte above for "Part 2," and Schmitt-Korte and Price below for "Part 3"].

5999 **Schmitt-Korte, Karl, and Martin Price.** "Nabataean Coinage, Part 3: The Nabataean Monetary System." *Numismatic Chronicle* 154 (1994): 67-131. 3 pls.
Deals with the Nabatean coinage of ancient Arabia which was struck by kings of Petra during the first centuries B.C./A.D. A total of 300 silver and 400 bronze coins from published sources have been used to compile the metrology and devise a system of nine or ten types each for the silver and bronze pieces. Their equivalents in the contemporary Hellenistic, Greek, and Jewish systems are now established. [Summarized from Schmitt-Korte and Price, *NL* 134]. [Also see and Schmitt-Korte and Cowell above for "Part 1," and Schmitt-Korte above for "Part 2"].

6000 **Schwentzel, C.-G.** "Les Thèmes du Monnayage Royal Nabatéen et le Modèle Monarchique Hellenistique." *Syria* 82 (2005): 149-66.

6001 **Sedov, Alexander V.** "Two South Arabian Coins from Mleiha." *Arabian Archaeology and Epigraphy* (Denmark) 6, no. 1 (February 1995): 61-4.
Two coins found at Mleiha (United Arab Emirates) of south Arabian origin are examined: an Athena/owl imitation, and a coin with male head/eagle with open wings.

6002 ——— "Hadramawt Coinage: Its Sequence and Chronology." *Archäologische Berichte aus dem Jemen* (Germany) 10 (2005): 161-73.

6003 ——— "On the Beginning of Coin Circulation in South Arabia." *Sabaean Studies. Festschrift A. de Maigret*. Edited by Y. Abdullah et al. Naples/Sanaa, 2005. Pages 423-41.

6004 **Sedov, Alexander V., and U. Aydarus.** "The Coinage of Ancient Hadramawt: the Pre-Islamic Coins in the al-Mukalla Museum." *Arabian Archaeology and Epigraphy* (Denmark) 6, no. 1 (February 1995): 15-60.
The pre-Islamic coins of the al-Mukalla Museum come principally from Shabwa, the capital of the kingdom of Hadramawt. The collection consists of seventy-six coins, three of which could not be identified because of their poor condition. Sixty-seven silver and bronze Hadrami coins, five silver and bronze

Himyarite and Sabaean coins, and one gold Roman coin comprise the collection. This material provides a general overview of the coinage of the ancient Hadramawt, permitting the authors to distinguish the issues of certain individual Hadrami rulers.

6005   **Sedov, Alexander V., and M. Omar Aydrus.** "Rare Himyaritic Coins from Hadramawt." *Arabian Archaeology and Epigraphy* (Denmark) 3, no. 3 (October 1992): 177-82.
Three rare Himyarite coins found in the territory of the ancient Hadramawt kingdom are published for the first time. Two of the coins bear the name of the king 'Amdan Bayyin, while the third has the name Tha'ran Ya'ub.

6005a   **Senior, Robert C.** *Coinage and Trade in Eastern Arabia c. 100 B.C. – 100 A.D.* Somerset: R. Senior, 1994.

6006   **Seyrig, Henri.** "Une Question de Numismatique Gréco-Arabe. *Scripta Numismatica.* Edited by Georges LeRider. Paris: Librairie Orientalist Paul Geuthner, 1986. Pages 7-10.

6007   **Stein, Peter.** "The Monetary Terminology of Ancient South Arabia in Light of New Epigraphic Evidence." *Coinage of the Caravan Kingdoms: Studies in the Monetization of Ancient Arabia.* Numismatic Studies No. 25. Edited by Martin Huth and Peter G. van Alfen. New York: American Numismatic Society, 2010. 602 pp., 42 pls. Pages 303-43. Illus.
Stein briefly reviews the current state of research into epigraphic sources related to the coinage of ancient South Arabia. The author then introduces new material found among 350 examined inscriptions. Discusses the identification of terminology and coins, the value of the currency units, and the dating of the epigraphic material. All relevant terms of ancient South Arabian monetary terminology are collected, discussed, and alphabetically arranged in the form of a lexicon. A systematic and historical overview of all the material is presented in tables. The letters appearing on the cheek of Athena, or in the obverse or reverse fields, are identified as abbreviations for the denominations.

6008   **Tameanko, Marvin.** "The Incense Road: Background to the Coinage of Ancient Southern Arabia." *The Celator* 8, no. 5 (May 1994): 6-16. Illus.
Describes the incense trade in ancient Arabia: the involvement of local kingdoms including Qataban, Ma'in, the Sabaeans, and Himyarites, their contacts with the Roman world, the influences of the Jews and Christians, and the resulting battles for control of the incense trade. Reviews the coinage used in Southern Arabia including imitations of Athenian tetradrachms, coins of the Minaean kingdom, and imitations of Roman coinage. Traces the development of the distinctive Himyarite coinage.

6009   **van Alfen, Peter.** "Coinage of the Caravan Kingdoms: A New ANS Publication." *ANS Magazine* 9, no. 1 (spring 2010): 12-8. Illus.
Announces a forthcoming publication devoted to the early coinage of the Arabian peninsula (see Huth and van Alfen *Coinage of the Caravan Kingdoms* above). Provides a brief overview of the coinages covered in the new book.

6010   ———— "Die Studies of the Earliest Qatabanian and Sabaean Coinages." *Coinage of the Caravan Kingdoms: Studies in the Monetization of Ancient Arabia.* Numismatic Studies No. 25. Edited by Martin Huth and Peter G. van Alfen. New York: American Numismatic Society, 2010. 602 pp., 42 pls. Pages 257-302. 10 pls.
The author provides a corpus of published specimens of Qatabanian and Sabaean imitations of Athenian coins, notes any observed die links, notes the die axes, and comments on style, dating, and metrology. Includes frequency tables of weights and extensive commentary.

6011   ———— "A Die Study of the 'Abiel' Coinage of Eastern Arabia." *Coinage of the Caravan Kingdoms: Studies in the Monetization of Ancient Arabia.* Numismatic Studies No. 25. Edited by Martin Huth and Peter G. van Alfen. New York: American Numismatic Society, 2010. 602 pp., 42 pls. Pages 549-94. 14 pls.
A die study of the eastern Arabian imitations of Alexander's coinage bearing the name Abiel in Aramaic. The author explores the economic factors of this coinage through an examination of die statistics and weight standards. [Also see M. Macdonald "The 'Abiel' Coins" above for an epigraphical study of these inscriptions on these coins].

6012   **Walker, John.** "A New Type of South Arabian Coinage." *Numismatic Chronicle* 5th ser., 17 (1937): 260-79. 1 pl.
An examination of twelve bronze coins bearing Sabaean inscriptions recently acquired by the British Museum. Walker discusses their types and inscriptions in detail. Suggests the coins were struck no earlier than the second century A.D.

6013   ———— "A Mysterious South Arabian Coin-Legend." *Numismatic Chronicle* 6th ser., 8 (1948): 39-42. Illus.
Illustrates Southern Arabian coins bearing a cursive script alongside letters of ordinary Sabaean type. The author translates the script as the name of the king Sahar Hilal. The coin may have been intended for commercial dealings with neighboring tribes who used this particular script.

6014   ———— "The Moon-God on Coins of the Hadramawt." *Bulletin of the School of Oriental and African Studies* 14, no. 3 (1952): 623-6.

6015   ———— "The Lihyanite Inscription of South Arabian Coins." *Rivista degli Studi Orientali* (Italy) 34 (1959): 77-81.

6016   ———— "A New Katabanian Coin from South Arabia." *Eretz Israel* (Israel) 7 (1963): 127.

6017   **Yousef, F. A. A.** "Coinage of the Nabataeans." *Adumatu* (Saudi Arabia) 10 (2004): 51-70.

Many items on Philisto-Arabian coins appear under PALESTINE–PHILISTIA. Also see: de Morgan *Manual de Numismatique Orientale* under GENERAL WORKS—GREEK; Gardner "On Some Coins of Syria and Bactria" under BACTRIA; Hendin "Ituraean Kings" under PHOENICIA; Hoover *Handbook of Coins of the Southern Levant* under ASIA—GENERAL WORKS; Kindler *Beer Sheba I* under HOARDS; Kindler "On the Coins of the Itureans" under PHOENICIA; Lambert "Egypto-Arabian" under HOARDS; Meshorer *Coins from the Holy Land* under PALESTINE—JUDEA; Mildenberg "The Philisto-Arabian Coins" under PHOENICIA; Milne "Origin of Certain Copies" under ATTICA—GENERAL WORKS; Potts "Pre-Alexandrine Phoenician Staters from Northeastern Arabia" under PHOENICIA; E. Robinson "Coins of Petra" under HOARDS; Sellwood "The Ancient Near East" under ASIA—GENERAL WORKS.

Mesopotamia, Babylonia, and Assyria

In B.C. 331 the Persian satrap Mazaeus surrendered Babylon to Alexander the Great. Reappointed governor, he ruled until his death in 328. To him and to his successors have been assigned several groups of coins, mostly of thick fabric with a characteristic edge. The attribution to the Babylonian mint has been disputed, and is of course somewhat conjectural, but none better has been suggested in its place.

—Barclay V. Head, 1911

6018 **Butcher, Kevin.** "Natounia on the Kapros: Coinage of a Lost Assyrian City." *Spink Numismatic Circular* 99, no. 1 (February 1991): 4. Illus.
Publishes a newly discovered coin denomination of the lost Assyrian city of Natounia. The coin is a new denomination and a new type for the city, and it links another group of anonymous coins in the Nisibis hoard to the same city.

6019 **Houghton, Arthur.** "Timarchus as King in Babylonia." *Revue Numismatique* (France) 6th ser., 21 (1979): 213-7. Illus. [CS 3014]
"A recently discovered tetradrachm of Timarchus struck at Seleucia-on-the-Tigris indicates that this usurper of Syrian rule held Babylonia as well as Media for a few months in 161 B.C. Timarchus' bronze coins also suggest that his control extended even beyond these areas." [A. Houghton, *NL* 106]

6020 **Howorth, Henry H.** "Some Coins Attributed to Babylon by Dr. Imhoof-Blumer." *Numismatic Chronicle* 4th ser., 4 (1904): 1-38. 3 pls.
Reviews the reign of Mazaios who was satrap of Cilicia ca. 330 B.C. After being named satrap of Babylon by Alexander the Great, he issued a series of coins bearing his name in Aramaic characters. The author questions Imhoof-Blumer's attribution of these coins to Babylon (*Numismatik Zeitschrift*, 1895). Howorth suggests the coins were struck earlier, while Mazaios was satrap in Cilicia, and were struck expressly to pay mercenaries. The author also discusses coins attributed by Imhoof-Blumer to other satraps of Babylon. Howorth rejects Babylon as the mint for many of these and suggests instead, a mint on the southern sea-board of Asia Minor or in Syria. [Also see Imhoof-Blumer's reply below].

6021 **Imhoof-Blumer, Friedrich.** "The Mint at Babylon: A Rejoinder." *Numismatic Chronicle* 4th ser., 6 (1906): 17-25.
In this reply to H. Howorth (see Howorth "Some Coins Attributed to Babylon" above), Imhoof-Blumer strongly refutes Howorth's claims. Imhoof-Blumer re-affirms his contention that the group of coins in question were struck in inland Asia after Alexander's conquest of Babylon. The series begins with the signed tetradrachms of Mazaios and the famous double-darics, and concludes with the rare elephant tetradrachms of Seleucus and the double-darics with the head of Alexander.

6022 **Iossif, Panagiotis, and Catharine Lorber.** "Marduk and the Lion: A Hoard of Babylonian Lion Staters." *Liber Amicorum Tony Hackens.* Edited by G. Moucharte, M. B. Borba Florenzano, F. de Callataÿ, P. Marchetti, L. Smolderen, and P. Yannopoulos. Numismatica Lovaniensia 20. Louvain-la-Neuve: Université Catholique de Louvain, 2007. Pages 345 ff.
The authors discuss a recent hoard of lion staters that was buried ca. 301 B.C.

6023 **Le Rider, Georges.** "Tetradrachmes 'au Lion' et Imitations d'Athènes en Babylonie." *Schweizer Münzblätter* (Switzerland) 22, no. 85 (1972): 1-7. Illus. [CS 3015]

6024 **Nicolet-Pierre, Hélène.** "Argent et Or Frappés en Babylonie entre 331 et 311 ou de Mazdai à Séleucos." *Travaux de Numismatique Grecque Offerts à Georges Le Rider.* Edited by M. Amandry and S. Hurter. London: Spink, 1999. Pages 285-305. 3 pls.
Examines the 'lion staters' and other issues.

6025 **Price, Martin J.** "Circulation at Babylon in 323 B.C." *Mnemata: Papers in Memory of Nancy M. Waggoner.* Edited by William E. Metcalf. New York: American Numismatic Society, 1991. Pages 63-72. 3 pls.
Describes a hoard found at Babylon in 1973 which was probably buried in 323/2 B.C. The hoard included decadrachms (including a specimen of the Poros decadrachm), 5-shekel and 2-shekel coins (now considered part of Alexander's Porus coinage; see MACEDONIAN KINGDOM—ALEXANDER'S PORUS COINS/MEDALLIONS). Some of the smaller coins show an Indian, demonstrating the blending of Greek and Eastern cultures. The hoard also included some of the so-called lion staters (shekels on the local standard) and imitations of Athenian tetradrachms which were struck by at least two Mesopotamian mints. Discusses Alexander the Great's coinage at Babylon shortly before his death. Price concludes that the hoard provides evidence that Alexander "blended his imperial coinage with others that were more fitted to the traditions of the area over which he held sway." Includes a partial list of the hoard coins.

6026 **Waggoner, Nancy M.** *The Alexander Mint at Babylon.* Dissertation, Columbia University. New York, 1968. 257 pp., 41 pls., 8 charts. [CS 2354]
"A total of eleven lifetime and posthumous issues in gold and silver with Alexander's well known types, represented here by 2143 specimens, comprises the body of known coinage from the mint at Babylon. The study is based on foundations laid by E. T. Newell; it includes a catalogue and commentary, barbaric imitations and appendices which, for comparative purposes, contain tentative lists describing silver lion staters and gold double darics. The combined evidence of die linkage, stylistic development and the contents of hoards determines the relative and absolute chronology which suggests that: (1) the mint at Babylon operated continuously from its inception in 331/30 B.C. until its activity terminated ca. 305 B.C.; (2) that the Alexander coinage was Western oriented. Findings lead to the re-dating of Newell's series I at Seleucia-on-the-Tigris." [N. Waggoner, *NL* 81]

6027 ——— "The Alexander Mint at Babylon." *Year Book 1970. American Philosophical Society.* Philadelphia: American Philosophical Society, 1971. Pages 710-1.
A description of the research conducted by Waggoner during a trip to Turkey, funded by a grant from the Society. The purpose of the trip was to obtain a record of the lifetime and posthumous Alexander coins from the mint of Babylon now in the collection of the Archaeological Museum at Istanbul.

6028 ——— "Tetradrachms from Babylon." *Greek Numismatics and Archaeology: Essays in Honor of Margaret Thompson.* Edited by O. Mørkholm and N. M. Waggoner. Wetteren: Numismatique Romaine, 1979. Pages 269-80. 2 pls.
The author attempts to establish the die-linkage and sequence of striking of Alexander's second lifetime issue of tetradrachms struck at Babylon. Babylon was Alexander the Great's easternmost mint. Lists the subsidiary symbols and monograms which distinguish this issue. Waggoner identifies six annual series within the issue. Waggoner records each obverse die and then under each one, she records all other obverses to which it is joined by at least one reverse die.

Also see: Bellinger "The Bronze Coins of Timarchus" under SYRIA—SELEUCID KINGDOM; Brindley "Early Coinages Attributable to Issus" under CILICIA; Hill *Catalogue of Greek Coins of Arabia, Mesopotamia, and Persia* under ARABIA; McDowell *Coins from Seleucia on the Tigris* under HOARDS; Mildenberg "Notes on the Coin Issues of Mazday" under PERSIA; Sayles "Images That Get Around" under TYPES; Sear "Mazaeus" under CILICIA; Spaer "A New Type" under MACEDONIAN KINGDOM—GENERAL WORKS; van Alfen "Owls" under HOARDS; Waggoner "Cassander in Babylon?" under MACEDONIAN KINGDOM—GENERAL WORKS; Waggoner "Early Alexander Coinage at Seleucia on the Tigris" under MACEDONIAN KINGDOM—GENERAL WORKS.

PARTHIA

As was natural for an empire under autocratic control, the obverses of Arsacid coins habitually depict the royal portrait always diademed and often with some further headgear such as a bashhik or a tiara. The former was the felt cap of the nomads which had been introduced into satrapal iconography by the Achaemenids, while the latter was an original creation like a tea-cozy in shape and embroidered with pearls.

—David Sellwood, 1980

6029 **Abgarians, Mesrop T., and David G. Sellwood.** "A Hoard of Early Parthian Drachms." *Numismatic Chronicle* 7th ser., 11 (1971): 103-19. 4 pls.
"According to current scholarly opinion, the earliest Arsacid coinage was struck for Mithradates I. The hoard published here contains many hitherto unpublished varieties differing considerably from those already known; these are attributed to the period before the eastern anabasis of Antiochus III which began in 209 B.C." [Abgarians and Sellwood, *NL* 87]

6030 **Allotte de la Füye, F. M.** "Monnaies Arsacides de la Collection Petrowicz." *Revue Numismatique* (France) (1905). 43 pp., 1 pl.
[Also see Naville & Co. *Auction XII* below].

6031 **Ashton, Richard H. J., David G. Sellwood, and Mevlut Üyümez.** "A Hoard of Parthian Coins in Afyon Museum (*CH* 9.585)." *Coin Hoards IX: Greek Hoards.* Edited by A. Meadows and U. Wartenberg. Special Publication No. 35. London: Royal Numismatic Society, 2002. Page 291. 1 pl.
Ten coins were acquired in 1977, likely from a hoard which may have been found in north central Turkey. The coins include issues of Gotarzes I, Phraates III, and Orodes II. Brief listing of the coins. No discussion or commentary.

6032 **Assar, Gholamreza R. F.** "Some New Coins of Vologases V." *Spink Numismatic Circular* 98, no. 10 (December 1990): 348. Illus.
Lists thirty profile-bust drachms of Vologases V from a hoard. All are from the same die pair. Lists the weight and die axis of each coin.

6033 ——— "Some Remarks Concerning the Parthian Gold Coins: The Parthian Calendars." *Proceedings of the 11th International Numismatic Congress, September 8-13, 1991. Volume 1.* Edited by T. Hackens et al. Louvain-la-Neuve, Belgium: International Association of Professional Numismatists, 1993. Pages 289-94.
Discusses the Parthian calendar systems. Numismatic evidence suggests the Arsacids had three different but compatible calendrical systems.

6034 ——— "Recent Studies in Parthian History: Part 1." *The Celator* 14, no. 12 (December 2000): 6-22. Illus. "Part 2." *The Celator* 15, no. 1 (January 2001): 17-27, 41. Illus. "Part 3." *The Celator* 15, no. 2 (February 2001): 17-22. Illus.
Discusses the various calendars used by the Parthians for dating their documents and coins. Much of the evidence comes from a study of cuneiform documents. In Part 1, Assar examines the identity of Parthian kings in the period 91-54 B.C. In Part 2, Assar examines the kings of the period 148-123 B.C. In Part 3, Assar examines a tetradrachm of Bagasis overstruck on a tetradrachm of Hyspaosines from Seleucia-on-the-Tigris. The coin helps to confirm that although Hyspaosines controlled Seleucia in Phraates' absence, he was eventually supplanted and his coinage suppressed by an Arsacid ruler.

6034a ——— "Genealogy and Coinage of the Early Parthian Rulers – 1." *Parthica: Incontri di Culture nel Mondo Antico* 6. Pisa/Rome: Istituto Editoriali e Poligrafici Internazionali, 2005.

6034b ——— "Genealogy and Coinage of the Early Parthian Rulers – 2." *Parthica: Incontri di Culture nel Mondo Antico* 7. Pisa/Rome: Istituto Editoriali e Poligrafici Internazionali, 2005

6035 ——— "The Genealogy of the Parthian King Sinatruces (93/2-69/8 B.C.). *Journal of the Classical and Medieval Numismatic Society* (Canada) 2nd ser., 6, no. 2 (June 2005): 16-33. Illus.
Presents new evidence for the genealogy of some of the Parthian kings. Describes their ancestry and illustrates their coins.

6036 ——— "A Revised Parthian Chronology of the Period 91-55 B.C." *Parthica: Incontri di Culture nel Mondo Antico.* Pisa/Rome: Istituto Editoriali e Poligrafici Internazionali, 2006. Pages 25-36.

6036a ——— "A New Date on the Tetradrachms of Vardanes II." *Journal of the Oriental Numismatic Society* 194 (2008): 5-7.

6036b ——— "Some Remarks on the Chronology and Coinage of the 'Parthian Dark Age.'" *Electrum* 15 (2009): 195-234.
[Also see B. Simonetta "The Coinage of the So-Called Parthian 'Dark Age'" below].

6037 **Assar, Gholamreza R. F., and Morteza Ghassem Bagloo.** "An Early Parthian 'Victory' Coin." *Parthica: Incontri di Culture nel Mondo Antico* 8. Pisa/Rome: Istituto Editoriali e Poligrafici Internazionali, 2006. Pages 25-36.

6038 **Barker, A. L.** "Identification Tables for Parthian Drachms and Tetradrachms." *Spink Numismatic Circular* 26 (July-August 1918): 324-6.
Provides brief descriptions of the coin types and inscriptions used on Parthian coins and indicates which king issued each type. Also indicates reign dates of the kings.

6039 **Bartlett, R. G.** "Arsakes: Theos and Dikaios." *Numismatic Chronicle* 7th ser., 3 (1963): 37-45. 1 pl. [CS 3018]
Describes Parthian coins bearing the names Theos and Dikaios. Who these persons were is uncertain.

6040 **Bellinger, Alfred.** "Parthian Drachmae of Orodes II and Phraates IV." *Numismatic Chronicle* 6th ser., 4 (1944): 62-4. 1 pl. [CS 3019]
Discusses the drachms of Orodes II and Phraates IV found during excavations at Dura Europas. Orodes is represented by thirteen drachmae on which nine different mint-marks are found.

6041 **Brindley, James C.** "The Organisation of the Parthian Bronze Coinage." *Proceedings of the 8th International Congress of Numismatics, New York—Washington, September 1973.* Edited by Herbert A. Cahn and Georges Le Rider. International Association of Professional Numismatists Publication, No. 4. Paris/Basel: International Association of Professional Numismatists, 1976. Pages 31-8. [CS 3020]
Brindley begins by summarizing the work of McDowell (see McDowell *Coins from Seleucia on the Tigris* under HOARDS) and Le Rider (see Le Rider *Suse Sous les Séleucides et les Parthes* under SYRIA—SELEUCID KINGDOM) regarding the Parthian bronze coinage. He then discusses the Parthian bronzes, their mints, monograms, types, and chronology. Includes a table of sizes and weights of the copper denominations during the period Mithradates II to Orodes II.

6042 **Caley, Earle R.** *Chemical Composition of Parthian Coins.* Numismatic Notes and Monographs, No. 129. New York: American Numismatic Society, 1955. 104 pp., 3 pls. [CS 3393]
Summarizes the author's laboratory analyses on Parthian coins. Describes the methods used. Tables show percentages of various metals contained in Parthian drachms. Silver content ranged from 41% to 94%, and comparisons are made of the silver content of the coins of various rulers and to other Greek and Roman coins. Also includes analyses of gold and bronze coins. Caley studies the debasement of the coins of Orodes I. Analyzes the relationship between fineness and specific gravity of Parthian silver coins. Recommends a procedure to be followed for estimating the fineness of ancient silver coins by means of specific gravity measurements. [Reviewed by F. C. Thompson in *Numismatic Chronicle* 6th ser., 15 (1955): 271-2, and in *Spink Numismatic Circular* 63, no. 12 (December 1955): 534].

6043 **Classical Numismatic Group.** *Auction 36.* Lancaster: Classical Numismatic Group, 1995. 240 pp., illus.
The catalogue for an auction of ancient and medieval coins (2542 lots), including the Fred B. Shore collection of Parthian coins (lots 1-528), one of the finest collections of Parthian coins ever formed. Includes notes on the Parthian coins taken from Shore's book (see Shore *Parthian Coins and History* below). Most of the coins are illustrated.

6044 ——— "The Todd A. Ballen Collection of Parthian and Related Coinage." *Triton XIII, Sessions 1 and 2 (January 5, 2010).* Lancaster: Classical Numismatic Group, 2009. Pages 161-228. Illus.
The catalogue for the auction of the Todd A. Ballen collection of Parthian coins (lots 501-852). All of the coins are illustrated. The collection contains a broad range of silver and bronze coinage representing most of the Parthian kings from Arsakes I to Arabanos V. Includes many denominations and varieties from numerous mints. Also includes a selection of coins of the Kings of Elymais, Persis, and the Indo-Parthians. A comprehensive and quality collection, thoroughly catalogued.

6045 **Curtis, Vesta Sarkosh.** "The Parthian Costume and Headdress." *Das Partherreich und seine Zeugnisse.* Historia Einzelschriften 122. Edited by J. Wiesehöfer. Stuttgart: Steiner, 1998. Pages 61-73. Illus.
"A series of obverses and reverses of Parthian coins illustrates the paper." [H. Baldus, *NL* 142]

6046 **Dabrowa, Edward.** "The Conquests of Mithradates I and the Numismatic Evidence." *Parthica: Incontri di Culture nel Mondo Antico* 8. Pisa/Rome: Istituto Editoriali e Poligrafici Internazionali, 2006. Pages 37-40.

6047 **Dayet, Maurice.** "Un Tétradrachme Arsacide Inédit." *Aréthuse: Revue Trimestrielle d'Art et d'Archéologie* (France) 2 (1925): 63-7.

6048 ——— "Une Trouvaille de Monnaies Séleucides et Arsacides." *Aréthuse: Revue Trimestrielle d'Art et d'Archéologie* (France) 2 (1925): 131-9.

6049 **de Callataÿ, François.** *Les Tétradrachmes d'Orodès II et de Phraates IV: Étude du Rythme de leur Production Monétaire à la Lumière d'Une Grande Trouvaille.* Studia Iranica Cahier 14. Paris: Association Pour l'Avancement des Études Iraniennes, 1994. 96 pp., 20 pls.

6050 ——— *L'Histoire des Guerres Mithridatiques vue par les Monnaies.* Numismatica Lovaniensa 18. Louvain-La-Neuve, 1997. 480 pp., 54 pls.

6051 **Dilmaghani, J.** "Parthian Coins from Mithradates II to Orodes II." *Numismatic Chronicle* 146 (1986): 216-24. 1 pl.
"This note deals with the attribution of the coins from Mithradates II to Orodes II. A brief review of progress achieved so far concludes that the sequence of coins derived by Mørkholm (*Numismatic Chronicle* 1980) is satisfactory. By considering the coins of other dynasties contemporary with the Parthians,

the cuneiform tablets from Babylonia and the Parthian drachms, conclusions regarding the attributions and duration of each king's reign are reached." [J. Dilmaghani, *NL* 118]. [See Mørkholm "The Parthian Coinage of Seleucia on the Tigris" below].

6052 **Dobbins, K. Walton.** "Mithradates II and His Successors: A Study of the Parthian Crisis 90-70 B.C." *Antichthon* (Australia) 8 (1974): 63-79. [CS 3021]
Dobbins summarizes recent improvements in the knowledge of early Parthian history and presents a reconstruction of events in Parthia and her non-involvement in West Asian affairs between 90-70 B.C. Numismatic evidence is cited throughout.

6053 ———. "The Successors of Mithradates II of Parthia." *Numismatic Chronicle* 7th ser., 15 (1975): 19-45. 2 pls. [CS 3022]
"Parthian kings mentioned in inscriptions and literary sources are correlated with the various classes of coins from Mithradates II to Phraates III. The evidence is discussed under the headings of epigraphic and literary sources, tetradrachms, drachms, hoards, countermarked drachms and evidence from Susa, including overstruck bronze coins." [K. Dobbins, *NL* 96]

6054 **Dressel, Heinrich A.** "Ein Tetradrachm des Arsakiden Mithradates III." *Zeitschrift für Numismatik* (Germany) 33 (1922): 156-77.

6055 **Eiland, Murray L.** "The Parthian 'Dark Age': History from Coins." *The Celator* 13, no. 3 (March 1999): 38-42. Illus.
Focuses on Parthian history during the period 87-57 B.C. (the period between the death of Mithradates II and the ascension of Orodes II), a chaotic period of dynastic succession. Numismatic evidence for dynastic succession of utilized. Reviews the evidence of facial lesions on Parthian kings. [Also see Hart "Trichoepithelioma" below].

6056 **Faizkhah, Said, Tahereh Azizipoure, Farhang Khademi Nadooshan, and Sabir Hassan Niah.** "The Socio-Political Condition of Azerbaijan in the Parthian Period." *Journal of the Classical and Medieval Numismatic Society* (Canada) 2nd ser., 6, no. 3 (September 2005): 5-11. Illus.
Discusses the circulation of Parthian coins in northern and southern Media and the use of northern Media to expand Parthian power in the northwest. Illustrated by twenty-one Parthian coins from the Tabriz Museum, one of Iran's oldest museums, located in the Azarbaijan province of northwestern Iran.

6057 **Frölich, Christine.** *Monnaies Indo-Scythes et Indo-Parthes: Catalogue Raisonné.* Paris: Bibliothèque Nationale de France, 2008. 192 pp. incl. 29 pls.
A catalogue of the Scythian and Parthian coins in the collection of the Bibliothèque Nationale, Paris. Includes 499 coins.

6058 **Gardner, Percy.** *The Parthian Coinage.* International Numismata Orientalia, Volume 5. London, 1877. 68 pp., 7 pls. [CS 3023]
Gardner begins with an overview of Parthian history and a discussion of the coinage. Then he presents a catalogue of coin types with commentary. Includes a table of titles adopted by Parthian kings. [Also see Gardner and Malter *The Coinage of Parthia*, and Wroth "On the Rearrangement" below].

6059 **Gardner, Percy, and Joel Malter.** *The Coinage of Parthia, with an Introduction and Supplementary Catalog of a Recent Hoard.* Chicago: Argonaut, 1967; San Diego: Malter & Westerfield, 1968. Reprint, New York: Sanford J. Durst, 2000. 68 pp., 11 pls. [CS 3023a]
A reprint of Gardner's *The Parthian Coinage* (see Gardner above) preceded by a brief recap of the literature on Parthian numismatics. Concludes with added material by Joel Malter describing "A Recent Hoard of Parthian Drachms" found in Iran in 1968. The hoard contained about 200 early Parthian drachms and 600 drachms of Alexander the Great. Twenty-two of the Parthian drachms are illustrated on three plates. Also includes one plate illustrating a helmet and a rock sculpture.

6060 **Ghirshman, Roman.** "Trois Monnaies Parthes Inédites." *Centennial Publication of the American Numismatic Society.* Edited by Harald Ingholt. New York: American Numismatic Society, 1958. Pages 279-84. 1 pl.
Examines two drachms of Mithradates II and a drachm of Artavasdes.

6061 ———. *Persian Art: The Parthian and Sassanian Dynasties, 249 B.C. – A.D. 651.* Translated by Stuart Gilbert and James Emmons. New York: Golden Press, 1962. 401 pp., illus.
A survey of Parthian and Sassanian art. Includes discussion and photographs of Parthian coins.

6061a **Gonnella, Robert.** "Eine Bisher Unbekannte Kupferdrachme von Artaban II (10-38 n.Chr.)." *Schweizer Münzblätter* (Switzerland) (May 1993).

6061b ——— "Ein Überprägtes Tetradrachmon des Vonones I (8 bis 12 n.Chr.)." *Schweizer Münzblätter* (Switzerland) (August 1995).

6062 ——— "New Evidence for Dating the Reign of Vonones I." *Numismatic Chronicle* 161 (2001): 67-73. 2 pls.
"The date of the reign of Vonones I, king of Parthia is mostly attested by coins, mainly tetradrachms. The author follows the majority of historians in believing that the Macedonian calendar was used on them, and describes two new tetradrachms which show that the reign of Vonones I, hitherto assumed to date from about A.D. 8 to 12, must be extended to September A.D. 15 at least." [R. Gonnella, *NL* 145]

6063 ——— "Neue Überlegungen zur Parthischen Münzstätte Artemita." *Jahrbuch für Numismatik und Geldgeschichte* (Germany) 51/52 (2001/2002): 1-16.
"The author reviews the numismatic material, the literature, and the geographical situation of the city of Artemita. He concludes that this city never had a Parthian mint, contradicting the positions of Sellwood and Shore. Artemita was of no importance in relation to trade routes and its coinage needs would have been met by the mints of Seleucia-on-the-Tigris and Ecbatana." [G. Stumpf and B. Overbeck, *NL* 148]

6064 ——— "A Previously Unknown Tetradrachm of Phraates IV (38 to 2 BC): An Ancient Counterfeit?" *The Celator* 24, no. 8 (August 2010): 31, 36-40. Illus.
The author discusses a Parthian copper tetradrachm of Phraates IV that is, in his opinion, an ancient counterfeit which had been covered with a silver wash that has worn away. He thoroughly explains his reasoning and eliminates the possibility that the piece is a test strike or an example of an emergency coinage.

6064a **Gordus, A. A.** "Non-Destructive Analysis of Parthian, Sasanian, and Umayyad Silver Coins." *Near Eastern Numismatics, Iconography, Epigraphy and History: Studies in Honor of George C. Miles.* Edited by D. K. Kouymajian. Beirut: American University of Beirut, 1974. Pages 141-62.

6065 **Hart, Gerald D.** "Trichoepithelioma and the Kings of Parthia." *Canadian Medical Association Journal* (Canada) 94 (1966).
Hart diagnoses that the Parthian kings were afflicted with Brook's tumor (Trichoepithelioma).

6066 ——— "An Additional Note on Trichoepithelioma." *Cornucopiæ* (publication of The Ancient Coin Society, Canada) 3, no. 1 (1975): 10.
In addition to those rulers mentioned in a previous article (Orodes II, Phraates IV, Phraataces, Vardanes I, Vardanes II, and a certain Vologases) (see Hart "Disease in the Ancient World" under PORTRAITS), Hart now identifies two additional Arsacids as having the condition trichoepithelioma: Artabanus IV and Mithradates IV. [For a different theory, see Eiland "The Parthian Dark Age" above].

6067 **Hazelton, James R.** "New Finds..." *The Celator* 3, no. 11 (November 1989): 30.
Reports a previously unpublished Parthian drachm of Mithradates I (*Sellwood* type 10) with an unusual inscription. Suggests the inscription was not a casual error as is frequently found on Parthian coins, but was a deliberate attempt to render the Parthian Aramaic language into transliterated Greek.

6068 **Howorth, Henry H.** "The Initial Coinage of Parthia." *Numismatic Chronicle* 3rd ser., 10 (1890): 33-41.
Discusses two coins listed by Gardner in *The Coins of the Greek and Scythic Kings of Bactria and India in the British Museum*, which Howorth believes are not Bactrian or Indian. Discusses the coins' provenance (Oxus Hoard, 1878). The coins bear the inscription "Andragoras." The author discusses the coin types of Andragoras and examines passages from Justin referring to him. Howorth identifies Andragoras as a Persian who was appointed satrap of Parthia by Alexander the Great.

6069 ——— "Some Notes on Coins Attributed to Parthia." Parts 1-2. *Numismatic Chronicle* 4th ser., 5 (1905): 209-46; 7 (1907): 125-44. 1 pl.
Suggests the gold staters and silver tetradrachms of Andragoras are fakes. Reviews the history of the period and suggests that Andragoras did not exist. Also discusses the "beardless" coin types and assigns these to Armenia. [Also see Wroth "The Earliest Parthian Coins" below. Wroth assigns these to Parthia]. In Part 2, Howorth focuses on the bearded issues, commenting on their attribution and chronology.

6070 ——— "Early Parthian and Armenian Coins." *Numismatic Chronicle* 4th ser., 6 (1906): 221-31.
A follow-up to Wroth's comments (see Wroth "The Earliest Parthian Coins: A Reply" below) in which Wroth attributed the 'beardless' coins as the earliest issues of Parthia. Howorth again argues for attributing these coins to Armenia.

6071 **Keall, E. J.** "Osroes: Rebel King or Royal Delegate?" *Cornucopiæ* (publication of The Ancient Coin Society, Canada) 3, no. 2 (1975): 17-32. Illus.
It has been generally accepted that Osroes acted in concert with Trajan during his invasion of Parthia in A.D. 116, and was a contender for the throne of Parthia. Coins recovered from excavations by the Oriental Institute of Chicago at the ancient site of Nippur in Southern Iraq shed additional light on this issue. Keall discusses the history of Parthia in the period A.D. 50-116. The author concludes that Osroes (A.D. 109-128) may have been rewarded with the control of Babylonia (in which Nippur lies) as a petty kingdom in return for his opposition to the invasion of Trajan. Presents a table summarizing the Seleucid and Parthian coins found at Nippur. Includes a chart showing the relative silver content of Parthian drachms vs. tetradrachms. Also includes a table outlining the chronology of the Parthian kings A.D. 50-147 based on the numismatic evidence.

6072 ——— "Parthian Nippur and Volagases' Southern Strategy: An Hypothesis." *Journal of the American Oriental Society* 95, no. 4 (October-December 1975): 620-32.
"A discussion of the history of Nippur in the Parthian era includes remarks on the silver fineness of Parthian drachms and tetradrachms, with two figures showing changes over the years." [M. Bates, *NL* 96]

6073 **Koch, Heidemarie.** *A Hoard of Coins from Eastern Parthia.* Numismatic Notes and Monographs, No. 165. New York: American Numismatic Society, and Malibu: J. Paul Getty Museum, 1990. 64 pp., 12 pls., map.
A study of 266 copper coins in the J. Paul Getty Museum from a hoard found in Iran. Most of the coins are from the northeastern part of the Parthian kingdom, and some are from Elymais. The Parthian coins are of the common type with the king's profile and a seated archer. All are described and photographed. The coins are classified into groups, each of which is analyzed and mint attributions are attempted. The coins date from ca. 38 B.C. to ca. A.D. 200. The hoard provides important information on the relative order of some Elymaean kings and rulers in the area of Khorasan. The lack of silver coins in the hoard indicates that an unfavorable economic situation characterized this period. [Reviewed by D. Sellwood in *Numismatic Chronicle* 153 (1993): 311-2].

6074 **Lindsay, John.** *A View of the History and Coinage of the Parthians, with Descriptive Catalogues and Tables.* Cork: John Crowe, 1852. 251 pp., 12 pls.
The first 163 pages are devoted to an extensive history of the Parthian Empire, discussing each king separately, and including some comments on the coins. Descriptive listings of the coins follow, divided into three sections, each with its own discussion of the coinage: drachms and smaller silver coins (127 coins), tetradrachms (152 coins), and bronze coinage (147 coins). Includes a chronological table of kings, a table of titles, a table of unusual letter forms, and a table showing the succession of the kings. The plates show 111 colored engravings of the coins.

6074a **Loginov, S. D., and A. B. Nikitin.** "Parthian Coins from Margiana: Numismatics and History." *Bulletin of the Asia Institute* 10 (1996): 39-51.
[Also see Nikitin below].

6075 **Malter, Joel.** "The 'Unknown King': Some Additional Hoard Data." *Journal of Numismatic Fine Arts* 1, no. 2 (February-March 1971): 22-7, including map and 2 pls.

Discusses a hoard of Parthian drachms found in western Iran about 1970. The coins are either issues of the "Unknown King," Darius, or Phraates III. Forty-seven coins are listed along with their weights and die axes. All are illustrated. Two previously unpublished monograms are found on the hoard coins. Also includes a concordance of attributions by Sellwood, Gardner, *British Museum Catalogue*, and Petrowicz.

6075a **Markov, A. de.** *Les Monnaies des Rois Parthes: Supplément a l'Ouvrage de M. le Comte Prokesch-Osten.* Paris: C. van Peteghem, 1877.
[Also see von Prokesch-Osten *Les Monnaies des Rois Parthes* below].

6076 **Minns, E. H.** "Parchments of the Parthian Period from Avroman." *Journal of Hellenic Studies* 35 (1915): 22-65. 3 pls.
"On pp. 38-9 the titulature employed in documents by Parthian kings during the first century B.C. is compared with the shorter formulae used on coins." [J. R. Jones, *NIJHS*]

6077 **Mørkholm, Otto.** "The Parthian Coinage of Seleucia on the Tigris, c. 90-55 B.C." *Numismatic Chronicle* 140 (1980): 33-47. 3 pls.
"The tetradrachm coinage of Seleucia on the Tigris is arranged in a chronological sequence by purely numismatic criteria. It is argued that the evidence derived from coins is more important than the sparse written evidence for reconstructing the so-called Parthian 'Dark Age,' the period between the death of Mithradates II and the firm establishment of Orodes II as king of the Parthian Empire. The attribution to different rulers is still a matter of speculation." [O. Mørkholm, *NL* 106]

6078 **Nadooshan, Farhang Khademi, Faezeh Arkan, Ali Reze Arkan, and Mohammad Saffari.** "Scythian in Eastern Border of Parthia: A Numismatic Evidence." *Parthica: Incontri di Culture nel Mondo Antico* 8. Pisa/Rome: Istituto Editoriali e Poligrafici Internazionali, 2006. Pages 195 ff.

6079 **Nadooshan, Farhang Khademi, Tahereh Azizipoure, and Batul Qanbari.** "Parthian Forgeries: The Numismatic Evidence." *The Celator* 20, no. 4 (April 2006): 34-6. Illus.
The authors discuss two main types of Parthian counterfeits, illustrated by three coins: a fouree drachm of Orodes I in the Museum of Meshkinshar, a reduced-weight drachm from an eastern Iranian mint, and a modern silver-plated forgery of a drachm of Darius.

6080 **Nadooshan, Farhang Khademi, Hussain Sadeghi, and Sadrondin Moosavi.** "The Impact of Political-Economic Conditions of the Parthian Period on Composition of Silver Coins." *Journal of the Classical and Medieval Numismatic Society* 2nd ser., 5, no. 3 (September 2004): 131-6. Illus.
The authors used spectrographic investigations to determine the content of Parthian coins from the Ecbatana, Seleucia, and Ragha mints. They then studied how political and economic conditions influenced the metallic content of the coinage. The authors conclude the Parthians used lead silver mines as a metal source, and that copper was added to the coins when the government was in financial trouble.

6081 **Naville & Co.** *Auction XII: Catalogue des Monnaies Grecques et Romaines...de a Série Parthe de feu Alexandre de Petrowicz, et al.* Lucerne: Naville & Co., 1926. 3172 lots, 89 pls. [CS 3047]
The sale catalogue for Alexander von Petrowicz' collection of Parthian coins, including over 500 lots, most of which are illustrated. Also includes coins from E. Bissen, J. Wertheim, A. J. Evans, and others. The sale was held October 18, 1926. [Also see Allotte de la Füye "Monnaies Arsacides" above, and von Petrowicz below. Also see listing 481 in J. Spring, *Ancient Coin Auction Catalogues 1880-1980* (see Spring under COLLECTING GUIDES)].

6082 **Newell, Edward T.** "A Parthian Hoard." *Numismatic Chronicle* 5th ser., 4 (1924): 141-80. 6 pls.
Discusses a hoard of 304 coins found in eastern Iraq. Presents a catalogue of the coins, most of which are Parthian.

6083 ——— *Mithradates of Parthia and Hyspaosines of Characene: A Numismatic Palimpsest.* Numismatic Notes and Monographs, No. 26. New York: American Numismatic Society, 1925. 18 pp., 2 pls.
Describes six copper coins, previously unknown, attributed by De la Füye to Mithradates I. Suggests that the reign date on the coins corresponds to the Seleucid system, and that the coins are of Mithradates II, 122-121 B.C. All are overstruck on an unknown bronze issue of the first king of Characene, Hyspaosines son of Sagdodonakos. Newell suggests reasons for the overstriking.

6084 ——— "The Coinage of the Parthians." *A Survey of Persian Art from Prehistoric Times to the Present, Volume 1: Text, Pre-Achaemenid, Achaemenid, Parthian and Sasanian Periods.* Edited by Arthur Upham Pope. London and New York: Oxford University Press, 1938. Pages 475-92. 5 pls. (The plates appear as plates 140-4 in *Volume 4: Plates 1-510*). [CS 3027]
A summary of the history of Parthian coinage. Comments on the chronology of the kings, changes in the inscriptions, and the artistic styles of the coin types.

6084a **Nikitin, A. B.** "Early Parthian Coins from Margiana." *The Art and Archaeology of Ancient Persia.* Edited by V. S. Curtis et al. London and New York, 1998.
[Also see Loginov and Nikitin above].

6085 **Olson, Richard A.** *Studies in the Coinage of the Arsacid Rulers of Parthia from Mithradates I to Artavasdes.* Ph.D. dissertation, University of Minnesota, 1968. 196 pp.
A major study of Parthian coinage, 171 B.C. to A.D. 229, which addresses some of the problems of attribution and chronology. Presents a catalogue of 230 Parthian coins based on the private collection of Maurice Quam, consisting of 2 tetradrachms, 206 drachms, and 22 bronzes catalogued by reign with full descriptions. Olson attempts to accurately reproduce the inscriptions on the coins and he notes the significance of certain variations and inconsistencies which appear. Comments on the chronology proposed by other researchers. The catalogue is followed by a discussion of the reign and coinage of each king. Includes three appendices: (1) a list of the Arsacid rulers of Parthia with reign dates, (2) a table of the Babylonian months and their Macedonian counterparts, (3) and a discussion of Parthian Pahlevi and how it appears on the drachms. Includes footnotes and an extensive bibliography for Parthian history, art, and numismatics.

6086 ——— "Greek Letterforms on the Parthian Drachms." *Visible Language* 7, no. 1 (winter 1973): 19-40. Illus.

The Parthians were a non-Greek people who used Greek as their first official language of state and as the predominant language on their coins. The letterforms underwent a significant transformation throughout the 450 years of Parthian coinage. Olson examines this transformation in letterforms. Discusses the arrangement of the coin inscriptions and the degradation in letterforms over time.

6087 ——— "The Maurice Quam Collection of Parthian Coins." *Journal of Numismatic Fine Arts* 2, no. 4 (winter-spring 1974): 69-77. Illus.
An overview of Parthian coinage, written as an introduction to a catalogue of the Maurice Quam collection. Discusses the kings and their coins—legends, denominations, chronology, and mints. [Also see Olson *Studies* above].

6088 **Paruck, Furdoonjee D. J.** "Novelties in Parthian Coins." *Journal of the Asiatic Society of Bengal* (India) 14 (1918): 372-8. Illus.
After a brief summary of the standard works on Parthian coinage, the author describes a previously unpublished drachm attributed to Phraates IV and discusses its attribution. Also publishes an unusual drachm of Mithradates IV.

6089 ——— "Parthian Numismatics." *Sanj Vartaman 'Parsi* (India) (September 11, 1919). Reprinted in *North American Journal of Numismatics: The Turtle* 6, no. 6 (June 1967): 165-77, 188-90. [CS 3028]
This article begins with a summary of previously published works on Parthian coinage. Continues with reviews of Parthian history, royal titles, royal dress, and religion. Then describes the coinage including denominations, weights, and types.

6090 **Quinnell, A.** "Persian Coins." *The Numismatist* 52, no. 2 (February 1939): 94 ff. Reprinted in *Selections from The Numismatist: Ancient and Medieval Coins*. Racine: Whitman Publishing Co., 1960. Pages 181-4.
General comments regarding the history and coinage of Persia, primarily discussing Parthian coins and coins of the Sasanian period.

6091 ——— "Parthians and their Coins." Parts 1 & 2. *New Zealand Numismatic Journal* (New Zealand) 5, no. 1 (October-December 1948): 11-16. 1 pl.; no. 2 (January-June 1949): 52-5.
A brief history of the Parthian Kingdom with a few comments on the coinage.

6092 **Rapson, Edward J.** "Markoff's Unpublished Coins of the Arsacidae." *Numismatic Chronicle* 3rd ser., 13 (1893): 203-19. 1 pl.
Publishes a list of the Parthian coins previously published in Russian by M. Alexis de Markoff in the *Journal of the Russian Oriental Society*. Comments on his attributions and chronology.

6093 **Rives, Robert G.** "Parthian Drachm Coin Measurements and Conclusions." *The Celator* 18, no. 11 (November 2004): 30-1, 34-5. Illus.
The author made weight and specific gravity measurements of more than one hundred Parthian drachms (particularly those of Orodes II) in order to understand the extent to which the coins may have been debased over the course of Parthian history. Shows that the coins prior to the reign of Orodes II have a slightly higher average weight and silver content than those struck during or after the reign of Orodes II.

6094 **Sawaya, Ziad.** "The Akura Hoard of Parthian Coins, 1994 (*CH* 9.591)." *Coin Hoards IX: Greek Hoards*. Edited by A. Meadows and U. Wartenberg. Special Publication No. 35. London: Royal Numismatic Society, 2002. Page 292.
A hoard of Parthian tetradrachms was found in 1994 at Akura (Lebanon). Twenty-nine of the coins are listed here, including issues of Artabanos II, Vardanes I, Gotarzes II, and Volagases I.

6095 **Scott, William H.** "On Parthian Coins." *Numismatic Chronicle* 17 (1855): 131-73. Illus.
Discusses the date of the founding of the Parthian kingdom, supporting a date of 250 B.C. Provides extensive discussions of numerous Parthian coins, many previously unpublished.

6096 **Sellwood, David G.** "The Parthian Coins of Gotarzes I, Orodes I, and Sinatruces." *Numismatic Chronicle* 7th ser., 2 (1962): 73-89. 2 pls. [CS 3031]
"In presenting a revised listing of the kings of the Arsacid kingdom, Sellwood replaces Artabanus II with Gotarzes I and Orodes I. Wroth's series of Artabanus II coins (*BMC Parthia*) are given to Gotarzes, and his Sinatruces coins to Orodes. To Sinatruces are assigned the issues which Wroth placed tentatively under the name of Phraates III." [F. Campbell, *NL* 70]

6097 ——— "Wroth's Unknown Parthian King." *Numismatic Chronicle* 7th ser., 5 (1965): 113-35. 2 pls. [CS 3032]
"In *BMC Parthia*, Wroth postulated an Unknown King reigning before 57 B.C. Drachm monograms and other evidence are used to vindicate Wroth's theories and a tentative identification is made with Darius of Media Atropatene, an opponent of Pompey. The relevance of data from Susa is also considered." [D. Sellwood, *NL* 80]

6098 ——— "A Die-Engraver Sequence for Later Parthian Drachms." *Numismatic Chronicle* 7th ser., 7 (1967): 13-28. 2 pls. [CS 3033]
"The probable chronological sequence of the main engravers of the reverse dies of Parthian drachms from A.D. 12-150 is established. From this follow certain re-attributions of the associated obverse types; thus most of the drachms given by Wroth to Gotarzes II are placed earlier. Reference is also made to new readings of the later Pahlevi legends." [D. Sellwood, *NL* 82]

6099 ——— "The Parthian 'Dark Age' in the Light of 'Susa.'" *Spink Numismatic Circular* 75, no. 11 (November 1967): 293-4.
Sellwood considers how the bronze coins from the Susa mint confirm or conflict with his hypotheses concerning Parthian history between 100-50 B.C. as advanced in his articles in *The Numismatic Chronicle* in 1962 and 1965 (see above). He suggests changes to Wroth's attributions of coins (see Wroth *Catalogue of Greek Coins of Parthia* below) and the sequence of Parthian kings.

6100 ——— "The Parthian New Year." *Spink Numismatic Circular* 76, no. 5 (May 1968): 155-6.
The Macedonian calendar was aligned with the Seleucid Era. Sellwood presents a table showing how the official Parthian year relates to the Macedonian/Seleucid year and the Babylonian year. He discusses how date indicators were used on Parthian coins. He concludes that ca. A.D. 80, the official year of the Parthian mint of Seleucia commenced in the autumn.

6101 ———— "A Currently Emerging Parthian Hoard." *Spink Numismatic Circular* 76, no. 12 (December 1968): 371. Illus.
Sellwood mentions that a hoard containing perhaps hundreds of early Parthian drachms recently appeared on the market and has been dispersed. The coins included many rare or previously unknown types.

6102 ———— "A Small Hoard of Parthian Drachms of the First Century B.C." *Seaby Coin and Medal Bulletin* 611 (July 1969): 227-32. Illus. [CS 3034]
Sellwood publishes a hoard of nineteen Parthian drachms of seven different types. He discusses each type, and suggests the hoard was buried ca. 70 B.C. in eastern Iran.

6103 ———— "Deux Notes sur les Drachmes Arsacides." *Revue Numismatique* (France) 13 (1971): 154-9.

6104 ———— *An Introduction to the Coinage of Parthia.* London: Spink & Son, 1971. 315 pp., 8 pls. Second edition, 1980. 322 pp., 10 pls., map, illus. [CS 3035]
A catalogue of the coinage of the Parthian Kingdom. An introductory chapter describes the basic features of Parthian coinage and presents a table of monograms and a guide to dating. The catalogue is arranged by king and brief historical notes are given for each. The major coin types are described and at least one coin of each major type is photographed in the plates. The distinguishing marks of each type are also illustrated by line drawings. Ninety-two major types, each with several variations, are listed. An appendix gives value estimates for each type in U.S. dollars. A bibliography lists 105 sources of information. Sellwood hand-wrote this book in his unique style of calligraphy. [The first edition was reviewed by James C. Brindley in *Numismatic Chronicle* 7th ser., 12 (1972): 319-21, and in *Spink Numismatic Circular* 81, no. 2 (February 1973): 52-3. The second edition was reviewed by Otto Mørkholm in *Numismatic Chronicle* 142 (1982): 214-6.]

6105 ———— "A Novel Solution to a Parthian Mint Dilemma." *SAN—Journal of the Society for Ancient Numismatics* 2, no. 3/4 (spring 1971): 46-7.
Some late Parthian drachms are presented, including two on which the king's beard had been altered after striking, apparently by mint workers. Sellwood suggests this was done after the accession of a new king, to make the old portraits appear to be the new king before new dies could be produced.

6106 ———— "Some Politic Alterations in the Parthian Series." *Mints, Dies and Currency: Essays Dedicated to the Memory of Albert Baldwin.* Edited by R. A. G. Carson. London: Methuen, 1971. Pages 33-7. 1 pl.
Discusses Parthian coins for which either the dies or the coins themselves had been altered by the mint, possibly in reaction to changing political situations.

6107 ———— "A Parthian Overstrike." *Journal of Numismatic Fine Arts* 1, no. 7 (spring 1972): 128-9. Illus. [CS 3036]
"A coin of Gotarzes II struck over an issue of Artabanus II is discussed." [*NL* 89]

6108 ———— "Parthian Mints." *Journal of Numismatic Fine Arts* 4, no. 3 (November 1975): 57-60.
Sellwood attempts to establish the identity of the Parthian mints, relying on coin hoard evidence and inferences from style, monograms, and die links. He identifies several monograms as mint names.

6109 ———— "The Drachms of the Parthian 'Dark Age.'" *Journal of the Royal Asiatic Society of Great Britain and Ireland* (1976, no. 1): 2-25. 4 pls.
The author examines the coinage from the death of Mithradates II in about 88 B.C. to the accession of Orodes II in 57 B.C. Examines the style of the coins to establish a sequence of die engravers and attempts to attribute the coins to specific rulers. Discusses hoard evidence. Identifies seventeen different engravers and attempts to assign each engraver to a particular mint. One hundred-eight coins are illustrated.

6110 ———— "The Mint-Towns of Parthia." *The Memorial Volume of the VIth International Congress of Iranian Art and Archaeology, Oxford, September 11-16, 1972.* Tehran, 1976. Pages 293-8.

6111 ———— "Parthian Coins." Chapter 8(a) in *The Cambridge History of Iran, Volume 3, Part 1: The Seleucid, Parthian and Sasanian Periods.* Edited by Ehsan Yarshater. Cambridge: University Press, 1983. Reprinted, 1993. Pages 279-98. 9 pls., map.
A detailed review of the history of Parthian coinage with much commentary on the chronology of the kings. An index to the plates appears on pages 318-20. A table of monograms and scripts appears on page 316.

6112 ———— "New Parthian Coin Types." *Numismatic Chronicle* 149 (1989): 162-9. 1 pl.
Examines coins from a 1984 hoard which contained mostly diobols of the kings of Persis. However, the hoard also included a small group of Parthian coins, all of them previously unpublished types (includes one drachm; the others are fractions). Sellwood discusses their chronological order and attributions.

6113 ———— "The End of the Parthian Dynasty." *Spink Numismatic Circular* 98, no. 5 (June 1990): 157. Illus.
Publishes some coins which show that the last king of the house of Arsaces was Tiridates.

6114 ———— "Trade Routes through Parthia." *Coinage, Trade, and Economy: The 3rd International Colloquium, January 8th-11th, 1991.* Edited by Amal Kumar Jha. Maharashtra: Indian Institute of Research in Numismatic Studies, 1991. Pages 23-7. 1 pl., map.
Examines the Parthian coinage for information about the probable routes by which Indian produce could be exported to the Mediterranean world. Discusses mint locations, metals employed for coinage, denominations, weights, shapes, types, and inscriptions. Describes some of the difficulties of exchange that might have faced the traders. Also suggests dates when the trade routes were in use.

6115 ———— "Parthian Gold Coins." *Proceedings of the 11th International Numismatic Congress, September 8-13, 1991. Volume 1.* Edited by T. Hackens et al. Louvain-la-Neuve, Belgium: International Association of Professional Numismatists, 1993. Pages 295-8. Illus.
Sellwood presents an analysis of gold coins from a hoard (316 coins) bearing Parthian types and inscriptions. The Arsacids were generally believed to have struck no gold coins. Sellwood's examination leads him to conclude the coins are genuine.

6116 ———. "Parthian Mint Operations." *Essays in Honour of Robert Carson and Kenneth Jenkins.* Edited by M. J. Price, A. M. Burnett, and R. Bland. London: Spink & Son, 1993. Pages 101-5. 2 pls.
Sellwood examines some aspects of the minting process in the Parthian Kingdom. Describes the process of engraving dies and illustrates some coins which reveal engraving errors or re-cut dies. Also discusses variations in flan production and striking, including the practices of countermarking and overstriking.

6117 ———. "The 'Victory' Drachms of Phraates IV." *American Journal of Numismatics* 2nd ser., 7-8 (1995-6): 75-81. 1 pl.
Phraates IV took the Parthian throne in 38 B.C. Sellwood examines the series of drachms issued by Phraates. The coins bear no dates, but do contain monograms which are presumed to indicate the mints at which the coins were struck. After assigning the coins to mints, the coins are then compared to the larger silver issues in an attempt at establishing a chronological arrangement.

6118 ———. "A Die Count for a Group of Parthian Drachms." *Studies in Greek Numismatics in Memory of Martin Jessop Price.* Edited by Richard Ashton and Silvia Hurter. London: Spink, 1998. Pages 317-20. 1 pl.
The author selected a sample of one hundred Parthian drachms of Vologases III (*Sellwood* type 78) from a large hoard unearthed in 1995. He performed a statistical analysis to determine the quantity of dies involved in the striking of these coins. Suggests at least 160 obverse dies were used for this issue. Also suggests that the pairing of obverse and reverse dies during this period was not wholly indiscriminate. Also discusses the alterations of obverse dies by re-engraving and suggests a possible reason for this practice.

6119 ———. "Parthians and Scythians." *Ex Moneta: Essays on Numismatics, History and Archeology in Honour of Dr. David W. MacDowall, Volume 1.* Edited by Amal Kumar Jha and Sanjay Garg. New Delhi: Harman Publishing House, 1998. Pages 97-102. Illus.
Considers fresh numismatic evidence concerning the relationships between Parthians and Scythians in about 130 B.C.

6120 ———. "A Remarkable Offering of Early Parthian Tetradrachms." *Triton V: Sessions 2, 3, and 4. January 15-16, 2002.* Lancaster: Classical Numismatic Group, 2002. Page 118.
Introductory comments preceding lots 1559 to 1666, an unusually large group of Parthian tetradrachms, which are the contents of a hoard. Includes many tetradrachms of Phraates II, Bagasis, Artabanos I, and Mithradates II.

6121 **Sellwood, David G., and Alberto Simonetta.** "Notes on the Coinage and History of the Arsacids from the Advent of Orodes II to the End of the Reign of Phraates IV." *Quaderni Ticinesi: Numismatica e Antichità Classiche* (Switzerland) 35 (2006): 283-315.

6122 **Senior, Robert C.** "Arsacid Prince Resurfaces Again after 2000 Years." *The Celator* 5, no. 10 (October 1991): 18. Illus.
Discusses a coin of uncertain legend and type, apparently issued by a satrap of Arsaces which Newell thought to be unique. Newell read the issuer as Cheires. Announces that two new specimens have surfaced. Drawings of the coins are presented with partially reconstructed legends.

6123 **Sherozia, Medea, and Jean-Marc Doyen.** *Les Monnaies Parthes de Musée de Tbilissi (Géorgie).* Collection Moneta 62. Wetteren: Moneta, 2007. 206 pp., 21 pls.
A catalogue of 547 Parthian coins of local provenance.

6124 **Shore, Fred B.** "A Symbol on a Parthian Drachm of Phraataces." *SAN—Journal of the Society for Ancient Numismatics* 14, no. 3 (fall 1983): 50, 58. Illus.
Discusses a symbol found on a Parthian drachm from the Nisa mint. Sellwood identified the symbol as a fire-alter. Shore searches for similar symbols on other coins in an attempt to discover the possible origin for the symbol and decides it may have been derived from a Seleucid symbol. The symbol is also similar to one used by the Indo-Greek king Soter Megas. Shore suggests that the personal symbol of Soter Megas may have been derived from the Parthian symbol.

6125 ———. "Parthian Tetradrachms Rival Hellenistic Portraiture." *The Celator* 4, no. 7 (July 1990): 30.
Discusses the tetradrachms of the Parthian kingdom during the mid-second century B.C. to the mid-first century B.C. During this period, the tetradrachms bore realistic portraits rivaling the best work of the Hellenistic Greek engravers. Seven tetradrachms of Mithradates I, Mithradates II, Orodes I, Darius, and an unknown king are illustrated.

6126 ———. *Parthian Coins and History: Ten Dragons Against Rome.* Quarryville, Pennsylvania: Classical Numismatic Group, 1993. 188 pages. Illus.
The first eighty-seven pages are an introduction to the history of the Parthian Empire, ca. 238 B.C. to A.D. 224. Discusses the culture of the Parthians and their interactions with the Roman Empire. This is followed by a catalogue of 645 coin types from the author's collection. Each of the silver types is illustrated. The types are cross-referenced to Sellwood's catalogue. Includes tables of monograms, mints, legends, and dates. Concludes with a chronological list of Parthian kings and a brief bibliography for Parthian history. Shore's collection of Parthian coins was sold in 1995 (see Classical Numismatic Group, *Auction 36* above).

6127 ———. *Parthian Coins and History: Rarity and Value Guide.* Quarryville, Pennsylvania: Classical Numismatic Group, 1993. 8 pages.
This supplement to the main catalogue (see Shore *Parthian Coins and History* above) provides estimates of rarity and market prices for drachms, tetradrachms, fractional silver, and bronze types of each ruler. The rarity scale used is C = common, S = scarce, and ratings R-1 through R-5. The market values are given in U.S. dollars for three grades: fine, very fine, and extremely fine.

6128 **Simonetta, Alberto M.** "The Drachms of Volagases I and Artabanus IV." *Numismatic Chronicle* 6th ser., 9 (1949): 237-9. Illus.
"Drachms which Wroth (*BMC—Parthia*, Pl. 29, 6) regards as late issues of Volagases I are reattributed to Artabanus IV on the evidence of style and letter-forms." [M. Thompson, *NL* 15]

6129 ———. "Notes on the Parthian and Indo-Parthian Issues of the First Century B.C." *Congrès International de Numismatique, Paris, 6-11 Juillet 1953, Volume 2.* Paris: Commission International de Numismatique, 1957. Pages 111-21.
Briefly examines some dated coins of Orthagnes and of Abdagases. Reviews the history of Parthia during the period 91-55 B.C. Describes the characteristics of the coins minted during this period. Discusses some coins for which the attribution has been uncertain and suggests some attributions.

6130 ———— "Some Remarks on the Arsacid Coinage of the Period 90-57 B.C." *Numismatic Chronicle* 7th ser., 6 (1966): 15-40. 2 pls. [CS 3037]
"The evidence available for the arrangement and attribution of the Arsacid coins issued between 90 and 57 B.C. is revised by a reappraisal of the historical sources and especially of a new translation of some cuneiform documents. Two hoards of Parthian drachms and Syrian and Cappadocian coins are also briefly described. A new arrangement of the chronology, including the suggestion that a ruler of unknown name ruled Parthia after Gotarzes I and Orodes I and previous to Sinatruces, is proposed. While most traditional attributions appear to be warranted, part of the coins traditionally attributed to Phraates III as well as those formerly attributed by Wroth to 'Artabanus II' and to the 'Unknown King' require new attributions." [A. Simonetta, *NL* 80]

6131 ———— "Overstrikes, Mules, Modified Dies and Retouched Coins in the Arsacid Coinage: A Discussion of Their Significance." *Parthica: Incontri di Culture nel Mondo Antico* 8. Pisa/Rome: Istituto Editoriali e Poligrafici Internazionali, 2006. Pages 41-54.

6132 **Simonetta, Alberto, and David G. Sellwood.** "Again on the Parthian Coinage from Mithradates II to Orodes II." *Quaderni Ticinesi: Numismatica e Antichità Classiche* (Switzerland) 7 (1978): 95-119. Illus. [CS 3040]
"A new chronology for the Parthian coinage at Susa is proposed." [S. Sorda, *NL* 103]

6133 **Simonetta, Alberto, and Bono Simonetta.** "The Vicissitudes of Phraates IV, King of Parthia, Reconstructed by the Aid of the Tetradrachms Minted by Him." Parts 1 & 2. Translated by H. A. Murray. *New Zealand Numismatic Journal* (New Zealand) 7, no. 2 (May-August 1953): 54-8. 1 pl.; no. 3 (September-December 1953): 79-87. Table.
Summarizes what is known of the reign and personality of King Phraates IV based on ancient sources. Illustrates ten coins of Phraates IV and Phraataces. Discusses the dating of Parthian coins. Then examines the series of tetradrachms minted during the reign of Phraates IV.

6134 **Simonetta, Bono.** "Observations on the Coins Minted by the First Parthian Kings." Translated by H. A. Murray. *New Zealand Numismatic Journal* (New Zealand) 7, no. 1 (January-April 1953): 12-28. 1 pl.
Examines the coinage of Arsaces I (250 B.C.) to Mithradates II (123 B.C.). Simonetta discusses the views of numerous scholars regarding the attribution of these coins, focusing on the differences between the bearded and beardless portrait coins. He concludes both series belong to Parthia. Presents different opinions regarding the identification of the obverse and reverse figures on the coins. Simonetta concludes the earliest portraits probably represent Arsaces I. Thirteen coins are illustrated. [Also see Simonetta's "Concerning Arsacid Coins" below for further discussion of early Parthian issues].

6135 ———— "Concerning Arsacid Coins with the Satraps Cap." Translated by H. A. Murray. *New Zealand Numismatic Journal* (New Zealand) 8, no. 4 (September-December 1955): 115-20. 1 pl.
Continuing the discussion of the attribution of early Parthian coins (see Simonetta "Observations" above), the author disputes DeMorgan's claim that the early beardless issues bearing the satrap's cap represent priestly issues attributable to Arsacid princes between 128-88 B.C. Simonetta places these coins prior to 138 B.C. and claims these are the first Arsacid coinage.

6136 ———— "A Note on Vologeses V, Artabanus V and Artavasdes." *Numismatic Chronicle* 6th ser., 16 (1956): 77-82. Illus.
"The uncertainties in the royal chronology of Parthia are as great as ever in the years of that kingdom's decline and fall. Identification of a misattributed tetradrachm of Vologeses V, A.D. 228-229, in the Cabinet des Médailles (Paris), however, leads to the following regal dates: Vologeses V: A.D. 208-209 to 228-229; Artabanus V: A.D. 213-214 to 226-227; and Artavasdes: A.D. 226-227 to an uncertain date, perhaps as late as A.D. 260. The Artavasdes, king of Armenia in the period of the humiliation of Valerian, was more probably a cousin, the son of Artabanus' brother, rather than the king listed above." [C. Vermeule, *NL* 43]

6137 ———— "Notes on Parthian Numismatics." Translated by H. A. Murray. *New Zealand Numismatic Journal* (New Zealand) 9, no. 2 (September 1956-March 1957): 65-9. Illus.
This essay focuses on the final phase of Parthian coinage, the period of Vologases V, Artabanus V, and Artavasdes (ca. A.D. 208-27). Simonetta discusses the history of the period and the problems surrounding the attribution and dating of the coinage of the last Parthian kings.

6137a ———— "Un Interessante Tesoretto di Tetradrammi di Vologeses III." *Revista Italiana di Numismatica* (Italy) (1971).

6137b ———— "Problemi di Numismatica Partica: Tetradramma di Mitridate II o di Re Ignoto? Osservazioni sulle Monete Coniate fra il 90 ed il 70 A.C." *Revista Italiana di Numismatica* (Italy) 76 (1974): 115-38.

6137c ———— "Problemi di Numismatica Partica: Osservazioni sulle Attribuzioni delle Monete Partiche Coniate fra il 70 ed il 57 A.C." *Revue Suisse de Numismatique* (Switzerland) 54 (1975): 65-78.

6137d ———— "Un Tetradramma Inedito di Artabanus I di Parthia." *Quaderni Ticinesi: Numismatica e Antichità Classiche* (Switzerland) 4 (1975): 151-6.

6137e ———— "Sui Probabile Significato di un Monogramma su Alcune Dramme Partiche." *Quaderni Ticinesi: Numismatica e Antichità Classiche* (Switzerland) 5 (1976): 103-6.

6137f ———— "Sulla Monetazione di Fraate IV e di Tiridates II di Parthia." *Revista Italiana di Numismatica* (Italy) 6, no. 23 (1976): 19-34.

6138 ———— "On Some Tetradrachms of Orodes II and the Probable Issues of Pacorus I." *Numismatic Chronicle* 138 (1978): 7-13. 1 pl. [CS 3044]
"Imperfectly known tetradrachms of Orodes II described were coined to commemorate the conquest of Gaza by his son Pacorus I in 40 B.C. It is now possible to ascribe to Pacorus some rare tetradrachms with ΚΤΙΣΤΗΣ (until now generally thought to belong to the first coins of Orodes) issued probably in 40 B.C. when Pacorus won his first war in Syria and Palestine." [B. Simonetta, *NL* 101]

6138a ——— "Note di Numismatica Partica: La Monetazione di Tiridates (c. 30-26 a.C.)." *Revue Suisse de Numismatique* (Switzerland) (1987).

6138b ——— "Sui *Chalkoi* di Arsaces II." *Schweizer Münzblätter* (Switzerland) (February 1988).

6138c ——— "The Coinage of the So-Called Parthian 'Dark Age' Revisited." *Electrum* 11 (2009).
[Also see Assar "Some Remarks" above].

6139 **Stein, Jacob K.** "An Unpublished Drachm of Phraataces with Musa." *Spink Numismatic Circular* 80, no. 4 (April 1972): 137. Illus.
Illustrates a previously unpublished variety of a Parthian drachm similar to *Sellwood* 58.9. The unique feature is the absence of a symbol or mint mark beneath Musa's chin. Based on style, the author suggests the coin belongs to the Ecbatana mint. The absence of the symbol was likely an oversight by the die engraver.

6140 **Swift, R. H.** "Notes on the Drachms of Parthia." *The Numismatist* 44, no. 2 (February 1931): 81-6. Illus. Reprinted in *Selections from The Numismatist: Ancient and Medieval Coins*. Racine: Whitman Publishing Co., 1960. Pages 176-81. Illus.
The author illustrates both sides of thirty-two Parthian drachms of different kings, and presents a brief review of Parthian history and a description of the coinage.

6141 **Swinton, John.** *A Dissertation on a Parthian Coin.* London, 1757.

6142 **Thomas, Edward.** "On the Oriental Legends on Certain Imperial Arsacid and Partho-Persian Coins." *Numismatic Chronicle* 12 (1850): 68-77, 91-114. Illus.
Thomas discusses the decipherment of Parthian coin legends. He correlates the Pahlevi characters to those of other languages (Hebrew, Sasanian, Persian). Deciphers the legends on numerous Parthian coin types.

6143 ——— "Indo-Parthian Coins." *Journal of the Royal Asiatic Society of Great Britain and Ireland,* new ser., 4 (1870): 503-21. Illus. Also appeared in *Numismatic Chronicle* new ser., 10 (1870): 139-63. Illus.
Examines a few recently found coins (four silver and one bronze) and determines them to be Parthian.

6144 ——— "Parthian and Indo-Sassanian Coins." *Journal of the Royal Asiatic Society of Great Britain and Ireland* new ser., 15 (1883): 73-99. Illus.
Examines three Indo-Parthian coins and a number of Sassanian coins.

6145 **Tzamali, Marion J. A.** "Philhellene: A Poem by C. P. Cavafy." *Nomismatika Khronika* (Greece) 19 (2000): 7-12. Illus.
Begins with a poem about a king giving instructions to his coin engraver to put "Philhellene" in the inscription. Some of the Parthian kings used this word on their coins—Mithradates I was the first to do so. The author briefly comments on the reigns of Mithradates I, Orodes II, Phraatakes and Musa, and Volagasses VI. In Greek on pp. 7-9, and in English on pp. 10-12.

6146 **Vardanjan, Ruben.** "Zur Deutung des Königsprofils auf Parthischen Münzen." *Arch Mitt aus Iran und Turan* 32 (2000): 253-9. Illus.
"Explains the meaning of left and right on Parthian and related coin portraits." [H. Baldus, *NL* 144]

6147 ——— "Some Remarks on the Arrangement of the Parthian 'Dark Age' Coin Series." *Parthica: Incontri di Culture nel Mondo Antico* 8. Pisa/Rome: Istituto Editoriali e Poligrafici Internazionali, 2006. Pages 105-30.

6148 **Visonà, Paolo.** "The Two Nehavend Hoards Reconsidered." *Coin Hoards* 7 (1985): 68-73. Map.
Re-examines two hoards of Parthian bronze coins (*Noe* 736 and 737) found in Iran in 1935. New evidence suggests many of the coins in the first hoard were silver—not bronze, and some of the coins in the second hoard are counterfeits. Visonà also suggests some mint attributions for coins in the first hoard.

6149 **von Petrowicz, Alexander Ritter.** *Arsaciden-Münzen: Sammlung Petrowicz.* Vienna, 1904. 206 pp., 25 pls. Reprint, Graz: Akademische Druck, 1968. 206 pp., 25 pls. [CS 3029]
A catalogue of the author's collection of Parthian coins. Also includes several coins of Armenia and Elymais. Index of inscriptions. Well illustrated. [Also see Allotte de la Füye "Monnaies Arsacides" above and Naville & Co. above].

6149a **von Prokesch-Osten, Baron Anton.** *Les Monnaies des Rois Parthes de la Collection de M. le Comte Prokesch-Osten.* Paris: Société Francaise de Numismatique et d'Archéologie, 1874-1875.
[Also see Markov *Les Monnaies des Rois Parthes* above].

6150 **Waggoner, Nancy M.** "The Coinage of Phraates III of Parthia: Addenda." *Near Eastern Numismatics, Iconography, and History: Studies in Honor of George C. Miles.* Edited by D. K. Kouymjian. Beirut: American University, 1974. Pages 15-26. Illus. [CS 3045]
Examines three Parthian coins (one drachm and two tetradrachms) recently acquired by the American Numismatic Society. Discusses the drachms which include "theueupatoros" in the inscription which have previously been attributed to various kings. Waggoner assigns these to Mithradates III. Also places the series of coins identified by the fleur-de-lis and anchor symbols, previously given to Phraates III (ca. 70-57 B.C.), into the reign of an earlier ruler—possibly Orodes I (ca. 80-77 B.C.).

6150a **Walker, Alan S.** "Forgeries and Inventions of Parthian Coins." *IAPN Bulletin on Counterfeits* (Switzerland) 19, no. 2 (1994/1995).

6151 **Weiskopf, Michael.** "The Kuh Dasht Hoard and the Parthian Dark Age." *Museum Notes* 26 (1981): 125-52. 3 pls.

Examines 131 Parthian drachms of the first century B.C. from a hoard of about 700 coins found in Iran in 1971. Discusses the hoard's original composition. Catalogues the 131 documented coins and analyzes each type. The coins are cross-referenced to Sellwood's types. Comments on the political situation at the time of the hoard's burial, which the author suggests was ca. 56-55 B.C.

6152 **Winkelmann, Sylvia.** "Waffen und Waffenträger auf Parthischen Münzen." *Parthica: Incontri di Culture nel Mondo Antico* 8. Pisa/Rome: Istituto Editoriali e Poligrafici Internazionali, 2006. Pages 131-52.

6153 **Wroth, Warwick W.** "On the Rearrangement of Parthian Coinage." *Numismatic Chronicle* 3rd ser., 20 (1900): 181-202. 3 pls.
Wroth suggests a rearrangement of the Parthian coins before Phraates IV as catalogued by Gardner. [See Gardner *The Parthian Coinage* above].

6154 ——— "Otanes, and Phraates IV." *Numismatic Chronicle* 3rd ser., 20 (1900): 89-95.
Publishes four Parthian coins not listed by Gardner (see Gardner *The Parthian Coinage* above). The first two coins bear the inscription OTANNHC (Otanes) and are of the class attributed by Gardner to Mithradates II. Wroth discusses the identity of Otanes. The third coin bears a date ΓΟΣ (year 273 of the Seleucid era: 40-39 B.C.). The inscription names Phraates, identified here as Phraates IV. Wroth places coins three and four into the closing years of the reign of Orodes (40-37 B.C.) while Orodes was under the influence of Phraates. The author suggests some other coins assigned by Gardner to Mithradates III may belong to Orodes.

6155 ——— *Catalogue of Greek Coins of Parthia.* London: British Museum, 1903. Reprint, Bologna: Forni, 1964. lxxxviii, 289 pp., 37 pls., map. [CS 3046]
Volume 23 of the *Catalogue of Greek Coins in the British Museum.* The 289-page catalogue of coins is preceded by eighty-eight pages of introductory text. [Also see *Catalogue of Greek Coins in the British Museum* under PUBLIC COLLECTIONS—GREAT BRITAIN (LONDON)].

6156 ——— "The Earliest Parthian Coins: A Reply to Sir Henry Howorth." *Numismatic Chronicle* 4th ser., 5 (1905): 317-23.
In this reply to Howorth's article (see Howorth "Some Notes" above), Wroth disputes Howorth's attribution of the "beardless" coin types to Armenia. Wroth re-affirms the commonly accepted attribution to Parthia. [For Howorth's reply to this essay, see Howorth "Early Parthian and Armenian Coins" above].

Also see: American Numismatic Association *Selections* under GENERAL WORKS—GREEK; Bellinger "The Coins" *Final Report VI* under HOARDS; Bopearachchi "Indo-Parthians" under BACTRIA; de Morgan *Manual de Numismatique Orientale* under GENERAL WORKS—GREEK; Gardner "Coins from Central Asia" under SYRIA—SELEUCID KINGDOM; Hill "A Hoard of Coins from Nineveh" under HOARDS; Le Rider *Suse sous les Séleucides et les Parthes* under SYRIA—SELEUCID KINGDOM; McDowell *Coins from Seleucia on the Tigris* under HOARDS; McIvor "A Supernova" under TYPES; Metcalf *Oxford Handbook of Greek and Roman Coinage* under GENERAL WORKS—GREEK; Mittag "Beim Barte des Demetrios" under SYRIA—SELEUCID KINGDOM; Pieper "Greek Influenced" under ASIA—GENERAL WORKS; H. Prinsep *Note on the Historical Results* under BACTRIA; D. Robinson "A Graeco-Parthian Head of Mithradates I" under PORTRAITS; Rogers *Graeco-Bactrian...Parthian* under BACTRIA; Sayles "Who Were the Magi?" under ELYMAIS; Sear *Greek Imperial Coins and Their Values* under COLLECTING GUIDES; Sellwood "The Ancient Near East" under ASIA—GENERAL WORKS; Simonetta "An Essay" and "A New Essay" under BACTRIA; Tod "An Account" under BACTRIA; Wilkenson "The Origin and Development" under TYPES.

CHARACENE

For over three centuries, the kingdom of Characene, located at the head of the Persian Gulf near the mouth of the Tigris River, served as a trading center for goods enroute between the Far East and the Roman Empire. Because few contemporary accounts of the area have survived, historical reconstruction of the kingdom has relied largely upon numismatic evidence.

—*Ed Dobbins, 1995*

6157 **Babelon, Ernest C.** "Sur la Numismatique et la Chronologie des Dynastes de la Characène." *Journal International d'Archéologie Numismatique* (Greece) 1 (1898): 381-401. 2 pls.
"Gives a list of kings of Characene, and their coins, from 124 B.C. to ca. A.D. 118." [J. R. Jones, *AIJIAN*]

6158 **Bellinger, Alfred R.** "Hyspaosines of Charax." *Yale Classical Studies* 8 (1942): 53-67. 1 pl. [CS 3053]
This historical examination reviews what is known of Hyspaosines of Charax, a descendant of Antiochus II. Six coins are illustrated.

6159 ——— "A Tetradrachm of Hyspaosines." *Numismatic Chronicle* 6th ser., 4 (1944): 58-9. 1 pl.
Publishes a unique tetradrachm of Hyspaosines of Charax, dated to 121-120 B.C. Bellinger suggests that the earliest possible date for Hyspaosines' birth is 206 B.C. He may have been a satrap of Antiochus IV, not Antiochus III as previously thought.

6160 **Dobbins, Ed.** "Inscribed Statue of 'Weary Hercules' Solves Numismatic Mystery in Characene." *The Celator* 7, no. 1 (January 1993): 32-5. Illus.
The inscription on a recently discovered bronze statue of Hercules provides the information needed to attribute a Characene tetradrachm to Miradates, son of Pacorus. The coin had been previously attributed to "Meheredates, son of Phobus" although there was no known Parthian or Characene ruler named Phobus.

6160a ——— "Two New Dates on Characene Coins." *Oriental Numismatic Society Newsletter* 137 (Summer 1993).

6161 ——— "Countermarked Characene Tetradrachms of Attambelos IV." *American Journal of Numismatics* 2nd ser., 7-8 (1995-96): 83-112. 2 pls.
The coinage series of the Characene kings contains a number of controversial attributions and there are long periods for which coinage is unknown. A list of kings and their estimated reign dates is presented. A large group of issues in the Characene coin series occurs in the second half of the first century A.D. This paper analyzes a hoard of 272 bronze Characene tetradrachms which date between A.D. 53 and 112. Of these, 267 may be attributed to Attambelos IV and dated between A.D. 53-64. All these have one to four countermarks on their obverses. Dobbins discusses the symbols found on the reverses. Presents tables showing coin monograms which he correlates to years of the Seleucid era. Also discusses the obverse symbols and countermarks. He concludes that "the history of the coins and, by extension, the Characene kingdom in this era, may be separated into three periods: (1) 53 to 64, when the coins were minted; (2) 64 to 103, when few tetradrachms were struck but countermarking occurred on three occasions; and (3) 103-112 to 143, when no tetradrachms were issued and a fourth instance of countermarking took place." Dobbins examines the history and coinage of each of these periods.

6162 **Hill, George F.** *Attambelos I of Characene.* Numismatic Notes and Monographs, No. 14. New York: American Numismatic Society, 1922. 12 pp., 3 pls.
A catalogue of all fifty-two coins of Attambelos known to the author. The coins are arranged into three groups, and their chronology is discussed.

6163 **Le Rider, Georges.** "Monnaies de Characène." *Syria* (France) 36 (1959): 229-53. 4 pls. Reprint, Paris: Extrait de la Revue *Syria*, 1959. 25 pp., 4 pls. [CS 3056]

6164 **Mørkholm, Otto.** "A Hoard of Coins from Characene." *Coin Hoards* 4 (1978): 25-7. 1 pl.
Briefly describes a hoard of tetradrachms of Attambelos I (sixty coins) and Thionesius I (thirteen coins) of the second half of the first century B.C., found in Southern Iraq in 1976. Provides evidence supporting the dating of the end of Attambelos' reign to 25/4 B.C. and that Thionesius succeeded him directly.

6165 **Morris, Robert.** "Some Coins of Characene." *American Journal of Numismatics* 22, no. 1 (July 1887): 11-2. Illus.
Describes some copper coins of Attambelos of Characene found in Bactria.

6166 **Nodelman, S. A.** "A Preliminary History of Characene." *Berytus* (Denmark) 13, fasc. 2 (1960): 83-121. 2 pls.

A brief history of Characene which was founded as a city by Alexander the Great, was later a part of the Seleucid kingdom, and then became an independent kingdom under Hyspaosines. Because of the lack of other evidence, coins struck by the Characene rulers furnish important evidence for the study of Characene history. [Digested from I. Merker, *NL* 57]. Includes a good survey of the coinage.

Also see: Nelson *Numismatic Art of Persia* under Persia; Newell *Mithradates of Parthia and Hyspaosines of Characene* under Parthia; Sellwood "Minor States" under Persis.

Elymais

Just as the history of Elymais reflected the great political events of Asia—the struggle between the Seleucids of Syria and the Romans against the Arsacid sovereigns of Persia—in the same manner, the numismatics of this principality is composed of diverse periods and answers to two political divisions of life: the first dynasty, probably indigenous, and the second undoubtedly Arsacid.

—Jacques de Morgan, 1930

6167 **Allotte de la Füye, F. M.** *Monnaies de l'Élymaïde.* Extract from *Mission de Morgan.* Chartres, 1905. 67 pp., 5 pls. [CS 3049]

6168 ——— "Les Monnaies de l'Élymaïde: Modifications au Classement Proposé en 1907." *Revue Numismatique* (France) (1919). Reprint, Paris, 1919. 42 pp., 2 pls. [CS 3050]

6168a **Assar, Gholamreza R. F.** "History and Coinage of Elymais during 150/149-122/121 B.C." *Name-ye Iran-e Bastan: The International Journal of Ancient Iranian Studies* (Iran) 4, no. 2 (2004/2005): 27-91.

6169 **Bell, Benjamin R.** "New Inscription Alters Elymais Type Chronology." *The Celator* 16, no. 4 (April 2002): 38-9, 50. Illus.
The coins of Elymais were struck under five different kings, each known by the name Kamnaskires. Bell illustrates a billon tetradrachm traditionally attributed to Kamnaskires V and his successors. The portrait features a bunch of hair at the back of the bust, and there is a symbol in the field before the bust. This symbol proved to be an Aramaic inscription giving the king's name [W]RWD, "Orodes." Bell concludes that the inscription suggests Arsakid influence in Elymais during this time period. [Also see the write-up on this tetradrachm in *Classical Numismatic Group Mail Bid Sale* 60 (May 22, 2002): 116 (lot 1041)].

6170 ——— "A New Model for Elymaean Royal Chronology." *The Celator* 16, no. 5 (May 2002): 34-9, 50, 59.
Presents arguments for a revision to the previously accepted chronology of the kings of Elymais, based upon a new analysis of numismatic evidence. The traditional chronology incorporates some unexplained gaps. Bell proposes an explanation for the gap after 35 B.C. traditionally assigned to "unknown successors of Kamnaskires V."

6171 **DeMorgan, Jacques.** *Ancient Persian Numismatics: Elymais.* Translated by Dominique G. Churchill. 1930. Reprint, New York: Attic Books, 1975. 45 pp., 5 pls. [CS 3052 and 3052a]
Examines the coinage of the principality of Elymais. Attempts to establish a chronology for the rulers and their coinage. Includes discussions of coin types, symbols, and epigraphy. Presents a table of proposed reign dates. Concludes with full descriptions of fifty-six coin types, 163 B.C. to A.D. 224.

6172 **Dobbins, Ed.** "Hoard Evidence Aids Attribution and Chronology of Arsacid Bronze Drachms of Elymais." *The Celator* 6, no. 8 (August 1992): 42-5. Illus.
Describes the bronze coins of the sub-Parthian kingdom of Elymais which were issued ca. 82 B.C. to ca. A.D. 200. Presents the chronologies suggested by various authors for this controversial series.

6173 **Hansman, John.** "Coins and Mints of Ancient Elymais." *Iran* (England) 28 (1990): 1-11. 2 pls.
Discusses the coins of the ancient kingdom of Elymais which show features not attested on previously published specimens. The use of symbols as mint indicators on Elymaean coins is also considered.

6173a **LeRider, Georges.** "Duex Nouveaux Tétradrachmes frappés a Suse." *Revue Numismatique* (France) 6, no. 20 (1978): 33-7. Illus.

6174 **Milne, Joseph G.** "An Elymaic Hoard." *Numismatic Chronicle* 6th ser., 1 (1941): 92-4.
Publishes a hoard of bronze coins (Seleucid, Parthian, and Elymaic) as well as twenty-four tetradrachms attributed to Elymais. The types are imitative of those of Kamnaskires III. Includes a brief appendix by H. J. Plenderleith of the British Museum laboratory which summarizes his metallurgical analysis of the tetradrachms.

6175 **Sayles, Wayne G.** "Who Were the Magi?" *The Celator* 13, no. 10 (October 1999): 45. Illus.
A brief discussion of the magi (the "three wise men") of the Bible. Suggests they may have been priests or astrologers from the kingdoms of Parthia, Elymais, or Characene. Three royal portrait coins are shown.

6176 **Van't Haaff, P. A.** *Catalogue of Elymaean Coinage, ca. 147 B.C.—A.D. 228.* Lancaster and London: Classical Numismatic Group, 2007. 167 pp., illus.

A comprehensive catalogue of the Elymaean series, incorporating the extensive evidence that has surfaced since the publication of DeMorgan's book. Begins with an overview of the history of Elymais and its coinage, and examines the three dynasties that ruled the kingdom: the Early Kamnaskirids, the Later Kamnaskirids, and the Arsacids. Summarizes recent numismatic research and examines the coinage system, mints, iconography, and metrology. The catalogue of coins is arranged by ruler, type, and subtype. Some of the photographs of the coins are supplemented by line drawings to clarify details of worn specimens. [Reviewed by Oliver D. Hoover in *American Numismatic Society Magazine* 7, no. 2 (summer 2008): 50-5, by Andrew Oddy in *Numismatic Chronicle* 168 (2008): 487-8, and by A. S. Walker in *The Celator* 22, no. 8 (August 2008): 35 ff].

Also see: Hill "Coinage of the Ancient Persians" under PERSIA; Koch *A Hoard of Coins from Eastern Parthia* under PARTHIA; Nelson *Numismatic Art of Persia* under PERSIA; Sellwood "Minor States" under PERSIS; von Petrowicz *Arsaciden-Münzen* under PARTHIA.

Persia

The famous Persian Darics, "the archers," so frequently alluded to in the history of Greece and of which the influence was often so detrimental to the mortality of the Hellenes, form the connecting link between the coinage of the Empire of Croesus on the one hand and that of Alexander the Great on the other.

—Barclay V. Head, 1877

6177 **Alram, Michael Von.** *Nomina Propria Iranica in Nummis: Materialgründlagen zu den Iranischen Personennamen auf Antiken Münzen.* Iranisches Personennemenbuch Herausgegeben von M. Mayrhofer und R. Schmitt. Vienna: Austrian Academy of Wissenschaften University Press, 1986. 348 pp., 47 pls.
Lists Persian names appearing on coins.

6178 ——— "Dareikos und Siglos: Ein Neuer Schatzfund Achaimenidischer Sigloi aus Kleinasien." *Circulation des Monnaies, des Marchandises et des Biens.* Res Orientales 5. Edited by Rika Gyselen. Bures-sur-Yvette, France, 1993. Pages 23-53.

6179 "Ancient Persian Coins." *American Journal of Numismatic* 4, no. 11 (March 1870): 81.
Describes some Persian coins including the daric. Never having seen a daric, the author (unknown) states "we have not one, and we know not of any man who has one."

6180 **Babelon, Ernest C.** "Les Monnaies des Satrapes dans l'Empire des Persees Achéménides." *Revue Numismatique* (France) 3rd ser., 10 (1892).

6181 ——— *Catalogue des Monnaies Grecques de la Bibliothèque Nationale: Les Perses Achéménides, Les Satrapes et les Dynastes Tributaires de leur Empire Chypre et Phénicie.* Paris, 1893. Reprint, Bologna: Forni, 1974. 412 pp., 39 pls. [CS 3059]
A catalogue of the Persian coins in the collection of the Bibliothèque Nationale.

6182 **Bivar, A. D. H.** "A Satrap of Cyrus the Younger." *Numismatic Chronicle* 7th ser., 1 (1961): 119-27. Illus.
"A cylinder-seal in electrotype recently acquired by the British Museum, a bilingual (Aramaic and Greek) inscription from Limyra in Lycia, a passage in Xenophon's *Anabasis* and a copper coin (*obv.*, Persian archer; *rev.*, ibex and Aramaic inscription) all show the name Artimas and are associated with the history of a family influential in the Achaemenian province of Lycia during the fifth and fourth centuries B.C." [I. Merker, *NL* 65]

6183 ——— "Achaemenid Coins, Weights and Measures." *The Cambridge History of Iran, Volume 2: The Median and Achaemenian Periods.* Edited by Ilya Gershevitch. Cambridge: University Press, 1985. Pages 610-39.
In the Achaemenid Empire, two separate currency systems were used in different geographic regions, one based on gold, the other on silver. Silver was used as currency irrespective of its shape or form—it need not be coined. Silver was used in trade based strictly on its weight. The Babylonian weight standard was used. Bivar discusses the forms in which bulk silver is found. Also discusses the relationship of the Achaemenid system to the Athenian weight standard. In Western Anatolia, gold was the standard currency. Discusses the gold darics of Croesus and the later Persian issues. Examines the relationship between gold and silver, and the chronology of the coin types. Also includes discussions of the standards of weight, and the units of measure and distance. Presents several tables of weights and measures.

6184 **Brindley, James C.** "A Siglos Lot with Unusual Portraits." *Spink Numismatic Circular* 109 (2001): 90-2. Illus.

6185 **Broneer, Oscar.** "Excavations at Isthmia 1959-1961." *Hesperia* 31, no. 1 (January-March 1962): 1-25. 12 pls.
"In the course of excavations carried out at Isthmia between 1959 and 1961, three oblong Persian darics of varying size were discovered in the floor of the entrance court of the Northeast Cave. The weight and measurement of each specimen are given." [*NL* 62]

6186 **Butcher, Kevin.** "A Hoard of Sigloi." *Coin Hoards, Volume VIII: Greek Hoards.* Edited by U. Wartenberg, M. J. Price, and K. A. McGregor. London: Royal Numismatic Society, 1994. Pages 73-4. 2 pls.
This report on a hoard (*Coin Hoards VIII*, no. 94) lists thirty-five Persian sigloi, twenty-five of which are now in the Fitzwilliam Museum. Most are counterstamped or punched.

6187 **Cancio, Leopoldo.** "A New Satrapal Coin of the KIM – EKA Series." *Swiss Numismatic Gazette* 39, no. 156 (1989): 83. Illus.

Publishes a silver hemidrachm of an uncertain Persian satrap of Ionia or Caria. The coin bears an M on the reverse, which Cancio believes stands for the issuing authority. The coin should be placed before the issues with similar types and with the names KIM and EKA, perhaps in the decade 390-380 B.C. [Also see Wells "Observations on the Signature KIM" below].

6188 **Carradice, Ian A.** "The 'Regal' Coinage of the Persian Empire." *Coinage and Administration in the Athenian and Persian Empires.* BAR International Series 343. Edited by Ian Carradice. Oxford: British Archaeological Reports, 1987. Pages 73-95. 6 pls.
Examines the gold darics and silver sigloi of the Persian kings, as well as the gold and silver Croesids of Lydia. Reviews the controversy over the dating of the lion-and-bull series which some authors attribute to Croesus and some attribute to the Persian period of rule in Lydia. Discusses the use of the terms "croesid" and "daric" in ancient times. The difference between the terms is ambiguous. Describes the four major varieties of the royal archer obverse type and the chronologies assigned to them by Babelon, Hill, and Kraay. The contents of numerous hoards are summarized and the evidence they provide for the chronology and circulation pattern of the coinage is discussed. The plates illustrate the major stylistic developments of the dies. Concludes that the early croesids were probably contemporary with Athenian Wappenmünzen and the first Aeginetan issues. Later croesids and the earliest sigloi were probably issued under Darius I. Later types of sigloi were likely produced by different mints in the fifth and fourth centuries B.C.

6189 ———. "The Dinar Hoard of Persian Sigloi." *Studies in Greek Numismatics in Memory of Martin Jessop Price.* Edited by Richard Ashton and Silvia Hurter. London: Spink, 1998. Pages 65-81. 4 pls.
A catalogue of Persian sigloi in two Turkish museums (Fethiye and Afyon): 145 of the coins are of *Carradice* type IIIb, and 279 are of type IV (see Carradice *The 'Regal' Coinage* above). All the coins may have originated from the same hoard. The coins are listed by reverse die. Discusses the chronology of the two types.

6190 ———. "Two Achaemenid Hoards." *Numismatic Chronicle* 158 (1998): 1-23. 12 pls.
A discussion of 303 coins from two hoards. The first hoard described here contained 170 coins—most were Croesids or early Persian archers. The second hoard contained 133 Persian sigloi. The chief interest of theses hoards is that they include types covering all the early phases of Achaemenid coinage: the lion-and-bull types and Persian "archer" sigloi of Types I, II, and IIIa. The author presents a die study and discussion of the coins. The results confirm the commonly accepted sequence of issues.

6191 **Casabonne, O., ed.** *Mécanismes et Innovations Monétaires dans l'Anatolie Achéménide. Numismatique et Histoire. Actes de la Table Ronde Internationale d'Istanbul, 22-23 Mai 1997.* Varia Anatolica XII. Istanbul: Institut Français d'Etudes Anatoliennes d'Istanbul; Paris: de Boccard, 2000. 284 pp., 39 pls.
A collection of essays including "Conquete Perse et Phenomene Monetaire: L'Exemple Cilicien" by O. Casabonne [5083a], "Small Coins from Cilicia and Surroundings" by T. Göktürk [5088a], and "On the So-Called Satrapal Coinage" by L. Mildenberg [6218].

6192 **Cunningham, Alexander.** "Relics from Ancient Persia in Gold, Silver, and Copper." *Journal of the Royal Asiatic Society of Bengal* (India) (1881): 151-86.
A description of some of the coins from the Oxus Treasure appears on pages 169-82.

6193 ———. "Relics from Ancient Persia in Gold, Silver, and Copper." *Journal of the Royal Asiatic Society of Bengal* (India) (1883): 64-7.
Lists fourteen gold and seventy-six silver coins from the Oxus Treasure located since the author's 1881 publication (see above).

6194 **Curiel, Raoul, and Daniel Schlumberger.** *Trésors Monétaires d'Afghanistan.* Mémoires de la Délégation Archéologique Française en Afghanistan 14. Paris, 1953. 130 pp., 16 pls. [CS 3224]
Contains "L'Argent Grec dans l'Empire Achéménide" by Schlumberger (see below), "Le Trésor de Mir Zakah Près de Gardez" by Curiel and Schlumberger (see Curiel and Schlumberger under HOARDS), and a paper focusing on Sassanian coinage.

6195 **Daehn, William E.** "Half-Figure of the King: Unraveling the Mysteries of the Earliest Sigloi of Darius I." *The Celator* 26, no. 2 (February 2012): 6-26. Illus.
Begins with a brief history of the Persian Empire, focusing on the reign of Darius I. The author then reviews the various types of the siglos coinage and traces the theories and hoard evidence related to the chronology of the four main types of Persian siglos. Daehn focuses on the sigloi showing a half-figure of the king and he explains various theories regarding its chronology and unusual iconography, including those of Carradice, Price, Vargyas, and Zournatzi. He then discusses the number of known specimens and reviews the market appearances of these scarce coins over the last three decades. Discusses their die varieties. In a supplement to this article, made available online to readers of *The Celator*, the author published a full catalogue of the known specimens of the half-figure siglos. [See next item].

6196 ———. *Half-Figure of the King: Unraveling the Mysteries of the Earliest Sigloi of Darius I. Including a Catalogue of All Known Specimens.* Printable document made available online by the author, 2012. 61 pp., illus.
This booklet, made available online as a PDF document, incorporates the author's paper from *The Celator* (see above) and appends additional information on die and punch varieties and a fully illustrated catalogue of all known specimens of the Type I half-figure siglos in public and private collections. Ninety-seven specimens are listed, plus one possible counterfeit. Each known appearance of each specimen is noted. The reverse punches are analyzed, and various stages of punch deterioration are illustrated. Four distinct reverse punches are identified, and specimen counts are provided for each.

6197 **Descat, Raymond.** "Notes sur l'Historie du Monnayage Achéménide sous le Règne Darius Ier." *Revue des Études Anciennes* (France) 91, no. 1-2 (1989): 15-31.
A study of the chronology and function of the Achaemenid coinage during the reign of Darius I. Suggests the light Croesids began ca. 513 B.C. and the gold darics ca. 493 B.C.

6198 **Figulla, H. H.** "A 'Coin' of Cyrus." *Numismatic Chronicle* 6th ser., 14 (1954): 173.
"The square fragment of silver bearing an inscription of two cuneiform characters which D. Schlumberger published in a hoard found at Kabul, Afghanistan, can be dated approximately 500 B.C., for the inscription can be interpreted as the name of the Persian Cyrus, written in late Neo-Babylonian forms. It is uncertain whether the object was for monetary purposes." [C. Vermeule, *NL* 34]. [Also see P. Hulin "Kabul Silver" below for another opinion].

6199 **Forrer, Leonard S.** "The Persian Daric and Siglos." *Spink Numismatic Circular* 68 (July 1898): 2860-2. Illus.
Discusses the history of the daric and siglos including the origin of the word *daric*, places of minting, and chronology.

6200 **Harrison, C. M.** *Coins of the Persian Satraps.* Ph.D. dissertation, University of Pennsylvania, 1982.

6201 ——— "Persian Names on Coins of Northern Anatolia." *Journal of Near Eastern Studies* 41 (1982): 181-94.

6202 **Head, Barclay V., and George F. Hill.** *The Coinage of Lydia and Persia, and Notes on the Imperial Persian Coinage.* New York: Sanford J. Durst, 2000. 80 pp., 4 pls.
A combined reprint of Head's *The Coinage of Lydia and Persia* (see Head under LYDIA) and Hill's "Notes on the Imperial Persian Coinage" (see Hill below).

6203 **Henkelman, Wouter.** "The Royal Achaemenid Crown." *Archaeologische Mitteilungen aus Iran* (Germany) 28 (1995-96): 275-93. Illus.
"The Achaemenid crowns have a dynastic rather than a personal character. Chapter 6 deals with their representations on coins." [H. Baldus, *NL* 139]

6204 **Herzfeld, E.** "Notes on the Achaemenid Coinage and Some Sasanian Mint-Names." *Transactions of the International Numismatic Congress Organized and Held in London by the Royal Numismatic Society, June 30-July 3, 1936.* Edited by J. Allan, H. Mattingly, and E. S. G. Robinson. London: B. Quaritch, 1938. Pages 413-26. Illus.
Coins were found under the foundation of the apadana (public part of the royal palace) of Darius at Persepolis in 1934. These included gold coins of Croesus (lion and bull type) of the lighter series, and silver coins of various Greek cities. The foundation is dated to ca. 516 B.C. Either the Persians used the Croesus coinage until 516, or the light series was coined somewhere in the Persian Empire before the introduction of the "archers." Herzfeld comments on the origin of the word δαρεικοι (daric) and concludes the similarity between the name of the king (Darius) and the coin is merely accidental. He also discusses some city names found on Sasanian seal impressions, and the information the seals provide regarding the names of Sasanian mint cities.

6205 **Hill, George F.** "Notes on the Imperial Persian Coinage." *Journal of Hellenic Studies* (1919): 116-29. 1 pl. Reprinted as *Imperial Persian Coinage.* Chicago: Obol International, 1969 and 1977. 17 pp., 1 pl. [CS 3063]
Lists the rulers of Persia, 521-330 B.C., and provides reign dates. Briefly summarizes denominations and weights. Classifies four major variants of the type and presents Babelon's further breakdown into four series. Attempts to sequentially arrange the varieties of the series taking into account their fabric, style, and hoard evidence. Discusses the punch-marks (bankers/merchant's countermarks) frequently found on these coins and comments on their possible sources. Presents a table of 187 different marks. The plate illustrates fourteen coin types in enlarged photographs. [Also see Head and Hill above for another reprint of this title].

6206 ——— "The Coinage of the Ancient Persians." *A Survey of Persian Art from Prehistoric Times to the Present, Volume 1: Text, Pre-Achaemenid, Achaemenid, Parthian and Sasanian Periods.* Edited by Arthur Upham Pope. London and New York: Oxford University Press, 1938. Pages 397-405. 3 pls. (The plates appear as plates 125-7 in *Volume 4: Plates 1-510*).
Discusses the Persian Imperial issues of Darius I and other coinages of Persia including coins of northeast Persia bearing the name Andragoras, coins of Persis, and coins of Susiana or Elymais. Emphasizes artistic styles and changes in type.

6207 **Howorth, Henry H.** "The History and Coinage of Artaxerxes III, his Satraps and Dependents." *Numismatic Chronicle* 4th ser., 3 (1903): 1-46.
A history of the Persian Empire 358-334 B.C., with discussion of the relevant coin types throughout.

6208 **Hulin, P.** "The Signs on the Kabul Silver Piece." *Numismatic Chronicle* 6th ser., 14 (1954): 174-6. Illus.
"The author points out that Figulla's date of 500 B.C. for a coin from a hoard from Kabul seems difficult for an object showing little or no wear in a hoard of 380 B.C. A connection with Cyrus the Younger rather than Cyrus the Great would be chronologically less improbable, but Figulla's reading cannot command acceptance. Comparison with Achaemenid Elamite documents from Persepolis leads to the conclusion that the signs on the Kabul piece are to be taken as in the Elamite script and to be read as originally taken by Labat, whom Schlumberger consulted. Since the only Achaemenid treasury documents discovered at Persepolis are written in the Elamite script and language, this should not cause surprise." [C. Vermeule, *NL* 34]. [See Figulla "A 'Coin' of Cyrus" above].

6209 **Hurter, Silvia.** "Der Tissaphernes-Fund." *Greek Numismatics and Archaeology: Essays in Honor of Margaret Thompson.* Edited by O. Mørkholm and N. M. Waggoner. Wetteren: Numismatique Romaine, 1979. Pages 97-108. 2 pls.
Catalogue of a hoard.

6210 **Lewis, David M.** "Persian Gold in Greek International Relations." *Revue des Études Anciennes* (France) 91, no. 1-2 (1989): 227-35. Reprinted in Lewis' *Selected Papers in Greek and Near Eastern History.* Edited by P. J. Rhodes. Cambridge: University Press, 1997. Pages 369-79.
"Persian attitudes to gifts and the divergent Greek attitudes to bribes are discussed, together with a selective analysis of occasions on which Persian financial support was used to maintain Greek armies or bribe Greek politicians. The possible effect of such expenditures on the Greek money-supply is considered." [*Revue des Études Anciennes*]

6211 **Macdonald, George.** "Ancient Persian Coins in India." *The Cambridge History of India, Volume 1: Ancient India.* Edited by E. J. Rapson. New York: Macmillan, 1922. Pages 342-4. 1 pl.
Macdonald discusses the use of Persian gold darics in India. Because the gold-to-silver ratio in India was 1:8 (vs. 1:13 $^1/_3$ in the Persian Empire), gold tended to flow out of India quickly. This ratio accounts for the relative scarcity of Persian gold coins in India, and the abundance of Persian silver sigloi. The author briefly discusses the use of countermarks on the sigloi.

6212 **MacDowall, David W.** "Numismatics, Early Period, Achaemenids and Greeks." *The Archaeology of Afghanistan from Earliest Times to the Timurid Period.* Edited by F. R. Allchin and Norman Hammond. London/New York/San Francisco: Academic Press, 1978. Pages 201-14. Illus.

"The coinage and currency of pre-Islamic Afghanistan is reviewed and the principal hoards and site finds on which the reconstruction is based are discussed." [D. MacDowall, *NL* 102]

6213 **Mildenberg, Leo.** "Notes on the Coin Issues of Mazday." *Israel Numismatic Journal* 11 (1990-1991): 9-23. 2 pls. Reprinted in *Leo Mildenberg. Vestigia Leonis: Studien zur Antiken Numismatik Israels, Palästinas und der Östlichen Mittelmeerweit.* Novum Testamentum et Orbis Antiquus 36. Edited by U. Hübner and E. Knauf. Freiburg: Universitätsverlag, and Göttingen: Vandenhoeck & Ruprecht, 1998. Pages 43-53. 2 pls.
The Persian satrap Mazday (Mazaios) was appointed as satrap of Cilicia ca. 361 B.C. by Artazerxes II. He later fought and almost defeated Alexander the Great at Gaugamela. After Darius III's defeat, Mazday withdrew to Babylon where he surrendered the city to Alexander, and was soon appointed satrap of Babylonia. His coins bear his name "mzdy" on the reverse. Mildenberg discusses his coins minted at Tarsos, Myriandrus, Issos, Sidon, Samaria, and Babylon, including the "lion" tetradrachms. Illustrates the legends appearing on the coins. Mildenberg finds it extraordinary that after fighting Alexander, Mazday was allowed to strike his own coins, displaying his own name and types, at a time when Alexander was striking his new international currency. And the coins were inscribed only in Semitic script—another noteworthy achievement of Mazday. [Also see Hübner and Knauf *Vestigia Leonis* under GENERAL WORKS—GREEK].

6214 ——— "Über das Münzwesen im Reich der Achämeniden." *Archaeologische Mitteilungen au Iran* 26 (1993): 55-79. Reprinted in *Leo Mildenberg. Vestigia Leonis: Studien zur Antiken Numismatik Israels, Palästinas und der Östlichen Mittelmeerweit.* Novum Testamentum et Orbis Antiquus 36. Edited by U. Hübner and E. Knauf. Freiburg: Universitätsverlag, and Göttingen: Vandenhoeck & Ruprecht, 1998. Pages 3-30. 14 pls.
[Also see Hübner and Knauf *Vestigia Leonis* under GENERAL WORKS—GREEK].

6215 ——— "Money Supply under Artaxerxes III Ochus." *Studies in Greek Numismatics in Memory of Martin Jessop Price.* Edited by Richard Ashton and Silvia Hurter. London: Spink, 1998. Pages 277-86. 4 pls.
Discusses the monetary production and circulation within the Achaemenid Empire, especially during the reign of Artaxerxes III Ochus, 359/8 to 338 B.C. Ochus restored the imperial money production and provided Egypt with its own coinage. Mildenberg summarizes Ochus' political and military achievements. Shows that the monetary supply and circulation within the sphere of influence of this king were extraordinary. The coinage was quite diverse in weight standards, languages, scripts, types, and denominations—evidence of a strong economy fostered by a powerful king. Suggests the tetradrachms with the shooting archer/rider, usually described as satrapal issues, were a new imperial coinage instituted by Ochus. Discusses the owl tetradrachms he struck for Egypt, bearing an inscription proclaiming his title as Egyptian Pharaoh.

6216 ——— "Artaxerxes III Ochus (358-338 B.C.): A Note on the Maligned King." *Zeitschrift des Deutschen Palästina-Vereins* (Germany) 115, no. 2 (1999): 201-227.
"This fascinating new view of the Achaemenid Great King contains, *inter alia*, a chapter '4.5. Coinage': pp. 214-216." [H. Baldus, *NL* 144]

6217 ——— "A Note on the Coinage of Hierapolis-Bambyce." *Travaux de Numismatique Grecque Offerts à Georges Le Rider.* Edited by M. Amandry and S. Hurter. London: Spink, 1999. Pages 277-84. 2 pls.
Mildenberg examines the coinage of this city in Syria. Begins with a discussion of chronology. Seyrig attributed these didrachms to the early period of Macedonian rule. Mildenberg shows that some issues belong to the Persian period and others to the Macedonian period. Discusses the iconography of the coinage including the imitations of Kimon's Arethusa head which appear here as the goddess Atargatis. Discusses the reason for the coinage at this remote city. Concludes with a catalogue of the coins, which the author attributes to Abyaty, an unknown ruler, Ab…, Abdahad, Mazday, and another unknown ruler.

6218 ——— "On the So-Called Satrapal Coinage." *Mécanismes et Innovations Monétaires dans l'Anatolie Achéménide. Numismatique et Histoire. Actes de la Table Ronde Internationale d'Istanbul, 22-23 Mai 1997.* Varia Anatolica XII. Edited by O. Casabonne. Istanbul: Institut Français d'Etudes Anatoliennes d'Istanbul; Paris: de Boccard, 2000. Pages 9-20.

6219 ——— "Über das Kleingeld des 4. Jahhunderts im Perserreich" *Pour Denyse: Divertissements Numismatiques.* Edited by S. Hurter and C. Arnold-Biucchi. Bern, Switzerland: Privately published, 2000. Pages 137-51. 3 pls.
Discusses and catalogues sixty-three small coins struck by satraps of the Persian Empire in the fourth century B.C. from Aiolis, Karia, Lycia, Cilicia, Phoenicia, and Palestine.

6220 **Milne, Joseph G.** "A Hoard of Persian Sigloi." *Numismatic Chronicle* 4th ser., 16 (1916): 1-12. 1 pl. [CS 3256]
Milne discusses a hoard of fifty-five coins, all Persian sigloi, found in Ionia. Many of the coins are countermarked. He describes the fifty-two coins he was able to acquire from the hoard, focusing on the appearance of the countermarks and the shape of the reverse punch die. Discusses the countermarks, the possible cities where they were marked, and the possible reasons for countermarking the coins.

6221 **Mørkholm, Otto.** "A Coin of Artaxerxes III." *Numismatic Chronicle* 7th ser., 14 (1974): 1-4. 1 pl. [CS 3066]
"A tetradrachm of Athenian types with an inscription in demotic Egyptian, reading 'Artaxerxes Pharaoh,' is published. The king is identified as Artaxerxes III of Persia, who reconquered Egypt in 343 B.C., mainly because the coin came from a hoard from Mesopotamia buried in the last [quarter of the] fourth century B.C." [O. Mørkholm, *NL* 94]. [Also see Shore "The Demotic Inscription" below].

6222 **Moysey, Robert A.** "Observations on the Numismatic Evidence Relating to the Great Satrapal Revolt of 362/1 B.C." *Revue des Études Anciennes* (France) 91, nos. 1-2 (1989): 107-39.
"This paper presents a synthesis of recent scholarship concerning the numismatic evidence for the history of the general satrapal revolt of 362/1 B.C. Coinage associated with five Persian satraps (Datames of Cilicia, Orontes of Mysia, Ariobarzanes of Hellespontine Phrygia, Autophradates of Lydia and Mausolos of Caria), Tachos of Egypt, Strato of Sidon, and the Lycian dynasts Mithrapata, Artumpara and Perikles are studied for possible relevance to the satrapal revolt. In addition, evidence for the relationship between the satraps and Greek civic mints such as Sinope and Lampsakos, the alleged satrapal coin portraits, the possible association of the engravers who cut the dies used to mint these coins with the engravers of seals which bear similar motifs, and the possible relevance of the 'Yehud' coins minted in Judea are considered. The conclusions reached may be summarized as follows: of the satrapal coins only two series of Datames are likely to have been minted specifically to pay troops during the course of that satrap's rebellion. Coins of Tachos and Strato minted

during the period of the revolt can also be identified and provide useful chronological information. Some Lycian issues as well as some 'Yehud' coins may have been minted during this period, but those assertions cannot be proved." [*Revue des Études Anciennes*]

6223 **Naster, Paul.** "Les Sicles Persiques à la Demi-Figure dans leur Contexte Numismatique et Archéologique." *Bulletin de la Société Française de Numismatique* (France) 17, no. 6 (1962): 70-1. [CS 3068]

6224 ——— "Were the Laborers of Persepolis Paid by Means of Coined Money?" *Ancient Society* (Belgium) 1 (1970): 129-34. 1 pl.
Addresses the question of whether the laborers at Persepolis ca. 490-459 B.C. were paid partly with coins. Naster concludes that no coins were used, unless eventually as plain silver lumps, for the payments to the workers.

6225 **Nelson, Bradley R., ed.** *Numismatic Art of Persia. The Sunrise Collection, Part 1: Ancient—650 B.C. to A.D. 650.* Lancaster: Classical Numismatic Group, 2011. 430 pp., illus.
Catalogue of a collection of 1044 coins from ancient Persia—one of the finest private collections ever formed. Coins of Parthia, Persis, and the Sasanian Empire form the core of the collection. Also includes coins of the Achaemenids, Alexander the Great, Seleukos Nikator, the kingdoms of Characene and Elymais, the Kushan Empire, the Indo-Parthians, the Indo-Scythians, Khwarazmia, and the Iranian Huns. Includes essays by G. R. F. Assar, Oliver D. Hoover, Wilhelm Müseler, Khodadad Rhezakhani, and R. C. Senior, providing introductions to the history and coinage of each culture. Includes lists of the original Aramaic and Pahlavi coin legends, transliterated and translated. Many enlarged photographs of significant coins.

6226 **Nimchuk, Cindy L.** "The 'Archers' of Darius: Coinage or Tokens of Royal Esteem?" *Ars Orientalis* 32 (2002): 55-79. Illus.
Nimchuk reconsiders the traditional view that the Achaemenid imperial coinage bearing emblems of the Royal Archer (gold darics and silver sigloi) was instituted by Darius I primarily to serve economic needs as a mode of payment for mercenaries in the west. The author emphasizes the communicative and ideological aspects of the coins over their economic function. She suggests that, unlike the Croesids, these coins were not initially intended to facilitate monetary exchange. Iconographical analysis of the Type I and II archers designed in the reign of Darius I shows the force of the messages these items conveyed as tokens of wealth, power, obligation, identity, and protection. The primary intended recipients of these messages were Persian elites in Asia Minor, with non-Persian elites as a secondary audience. The archers can thus be considered a part of the system of royal gifting from the king to his nobles that reinforced symbolic relationships by offering tokens of value well beyond the mere guaranteed weight and content of the metal.

6227 **Noe, Sydney P.** *Two Hoards of Persian Sigloi.* Numismatic Notes and Monographs, No. 136. New York: American Numismatic Society, 1956. 44 pp., 15 pls. [CS 3263]
A discussion of two hoards. The first contained 255 coins, all Persian sigloi except for one half-stater of Croesus, which appeared on the market in 1950. The coins are described and separated into eight groups. Discusses die links, stylistic variations, and reasons for the variations in size and shape of the flans. Describes the steps in the minting process to suggest reasons for these variations. Discusses the countermarks which appear on forty of the coins. Presents the results of a metallurgical analysis of the coins. The second hoard was found near Smyrna circa 1952. It contained 652 coins, some of which are catalogued here. Discusses minting techniques and suggests that two obverse dies were cut into an anvil. Presents a frequency table analyzing the weights and discusses the dating of the hoards. [Reviewed by G. K. Jenkins in *Numismatic Chronicle* 6th ser., 17 (1957): 276-8, and by D. H. Cox in *American Journal of Archaeology* 63 (1959): 94. Also see Robinson "The Beginnings of Achaemenid Coinage" below].

6228 **Petrie, Alfred E. H.** "The Iranians and Early Persian Coinage." *Canadian Numismatic Journal* (Canada) 3, no. 2 (February 1958): 37-46. Illus.
A brief history of Persia with commentary on the coinage. Covers the Achaemenian Empire, Alexander and the Seleucids, the Parthians, the Sassanian Empire, and Persia under early Islam.

6229 **Plant, Richard J.** "The Persian Story." *Coins, Incorporating Coins and Medals* (England) 17, no. 4 (April 1980): 17-21. Illus.
"A brief account of Persian coinage from earliest times up to the present day." [E. Marles, *NL* 105]

6230 "Positive ID Provided for Unknown Hellenistic King." *The Celator* 2, no. 11 (November 1988): 8. Illus.
A coin of Asinnalus of Media, a previously unknown Hellenistic monarch of the first century B.C., has been identified and offered for sale. The king wears an Armenian-style crown.

6231 **Price, Martin J.** "Darius I and the Daric." *Revue des Études Anciennes* (France) 91, no. 1-2 (1989): 9-14.
"The author describes the place of the daric in the development of the coinage of Sardes, and links its weight with that of the Babylonian shekel of Darius I. He explores the question of exchange between the earlier electrum and the gold and silver issues struck at Sardes under the Persians, suggesting that there was a significant fall in the value of silver over the second half of the sixth century B.C." [*Revue des Études Anciennes*]. [Also see Vargyas "Darius I and the Daric Reconsidered" below].

6232 **Qedar, Shraga.** "Tissaphernes at Dor?" *Israel Numismatic Journal* (Israel) 14 (2001-02): 9-14. Illus.

6233 "A Rare Coin: Acquisition by the British Museum." *Spink Numismatic Circular* 21 (December 1913): 870.
Discusses a silver coin of the rebel satrap Timarchus.

6234 **Robinson, Edward S. G.** "Aspeisas, Satrap of Susiana." *Numismatic Chronicle* 5th ser., 1 (1921): 37-8. 1 pl.
Examines an Alexander-type tetradrachm with the inscription ΑΣΠΕΙΣΟΥ on the reverse. Robinson concludes the coin names a Persian satrap, Aspeisas. Suggests it was minted at Susa ca. 316-312 B.C.

6235 ——— "A Hoard of Persian Sigloi." *Numismatic Chronicle* 6th ser., 7 (1947): 173-4. Illus. [CS 3283]
Based on an examination of 198 Persian sigloi from a hoard supposedly containing about 300 coins, the author divides the series into three types: (1) half-length figure of the king, (2) king shooting with bow, (3) king running with bow and spear. One specimen of each type is illustrated. Robinson comments on the wear on the coins which seems to indicate that Types I and II are earlier than Type III. He speculates on the reigns to which they may be assigned, but the evidence is inconclusive.

6236 ——— "The Beginnings of Achaemenid Coinage." *Numismatic Chronicle* 6th ser., 18 (1958): 187-93. 1 pl. [CS 3071]
A follow-up to Noe's *Two Hoards of Persian Sigloi* (see Noe above). Discusses evidence from the Smyrna hoard which suggests the type of sigloi with king running was introduced ca. 490 B.C. This and evidence from the Tchai hoard suggests the following sequence of types: (1) king in half-length, (2) king shooting, (3) king running. This sequence is also supported by metrological evidence. Discusses reasons for the unusually high ratio of obverse dies to reverse dies in the Lydian and Persian types. Deteriorated punch dies could continue in use despite their condition. Points out that the patterns formed by deteriorated punch dies can sometimes resemble a design, but must not be interpreted as such.

6237 **Root, Margaret Cool.** "Evidence from Persepolis for the Dating of Persian and Archaic Greek Coinage." *Numismatic Chronicle* 148 (1988): 1-12. 1 pl.
A response to Michael Vickers' 1985 paper—in particular, his comments on the evidence of the Persepolis hoard material and its implications for the chronology of early coinage (see Vickers "Early Greek Coinage" under ORIGINS OF COINAGE). Focuses on three points: (1) The content and dating of the Persepolis Apadana foundation deposits. Root discusses the coins and the inscribed tablet, and rejects Vickers' down-dating. (2) The identity and chronology of Croesids and Darics. Root disputes Vickers' assertion that the lion/bull coins traditionally given to Croesus were in fact coins of Darius. Root primarily uses iconographic evidence to support the traditional attributions. (3) The date of the owl tetradrachms. Disputes Vickers's down-dating of the introduction of the owls to after 480 B.C. Discusses the impression of an early Athenian tetradrachm used as a seal on a clay tablet at Persepolis which Root attributes to the reign of Darius, thereby supporting an earlier date for the owls. Cites evidence from other tablets to show that the Persian archer coins were in use by 500 B.C. [Also see Starr "A Sixth Century Athenian Tetradrachm" under ATTICA—GENERAL WORKS which focuses on the Athenian tetradrachm used as a seal].

6238 ——— "The Persian Archer at Persepolis: Aspects of Chronology, Style and Symbolism." *Revue des Études Anciennes* (France) 91, no. 1-2 (1989): 33-50. Illus.
"The purpose of this paper is to discuss selected aspects of the Persian Archer coinage within the context of Persepolis. First I shall discuss the Apadana foundation deposits at the site, since they play such a significant role in scholarship on the chronology of early Persian and archaic Greek coinage. The thrust of this section will be to shed new light both on the absence of Archer coins in this deposit and on the emphatic presence of gold 'Croeseids.' Then I shall proceed to a discussion of the rhetorical nature of the Apadana deposits. The aim here is to penetrate in a deeper way the imperial ideology which is reflected in the Apadana palace very literally from the foundations upward. This discussion attempts to see the foundation deposits (with their exclusion of Archer coins) as part of a rhetorical program of the building which is also articulated (albeit in different terms) on the façade of its great stairways. Finally, in Section III, I shall take initial steps toward analysing the artistic properties of the Persian Archer series within the broad context of the Achaemenid imperial program as we know it best: from Persepolis." [M. Root, *Revue des Études Anciennes*]

6239 **Schlumberger, Daniel.** "L'Argent Grec dans l'Empire Achéménide." *Trésors Monétaires d'Afghanistan*. Mémoires de la Délégation Archéologique Française en Afghanistan 14. Paris, 1953. Pages 3-64. [CS 3072]
"A survey based on the incidence of hoards." [C. Kraay]

6240 **Sear, David R.** "Orient and Occident: Historic Coinage Reflects the Age-Old Struggle between People of Different Cultures." *Numismatist* 118, no. 10 (October 2005): 49-51. Illus.
A review of coinage which illustrates the clash of Western and Eastern cultures.

6241 **Seyrig, Henri.** "Le Roi de Perse? *Syria* 36 (1959): 52-6.

6242 **Shore, A. F.** "The Demotic Inscription on a Coin of Artaxerxes." *Numismatic Chronicle* 7th ser., 14 (1974): 5-8. Illus.
"An Egyptian legend reading 'Artaxerxes King' on a coin recently acquired by the Nationalmuseet, Copenhagen, and assigned to Artaxerxes III is discussed. The inscription completes the text and provides the correct reading of a coin of the same issue in the British Museum. The presence of the demotic script shows that the issue can have nothing to do with the need to provide a stamped coinage to pay Greek or other mercenaries, but was intended to be used in Egypt by Egyptians." [A. Shore, *NL* 94]. [Also see Mørkholm "A Coin of Artaxerxes III" above].

6243 **Stronach, David B.** "Early Achaemenid Coinage: Perspectives from the Homeland." *Mélanges Pierre Amiet, Volume 2*. Iranica Antiqua 24. Leuven: E. Peeters, 1989. Pages 255-83.

6244 **Tuplin, Christopher.** "The Administration of the Achaemenid Empire." *Coinage and Administration in the Athenian and Persian Empires*. BAR International Series 343. Edited by Ian Carradice. Oxford: British Archaeological Reports, 1987. Pages 109-58.
Describes some geographically defined administrative units of the Achaemenid Empire and the Persian tribute system. It was a multilingual empire with which the central authority communicated in writing. The Persians built upon existing administrative structures and did not have a uniform legal code. The military was closely connected with the king. Describes the roles of satraps and scribes, geographical subdivisions of the satrapy, treasuries, and personal estates. Discusses the paying of tribute in silver and in kind, and the system of collecting tribute including land taxes, temple taxes, and taxes assessed against individuals. Cites many previous researchers. Includes a bibliography.

6245 ——— "The Coinage of Aryandes." *L'Or Perse et l'Histoire Grecque. Table Ronde CNRS. Bordeaux, 20-22 Mars 1989. Revue des Études Anciennes* (France) 91, no. 1-2 (1989): 61-83.
"The author examines Herodotus' account of Aryandes' silver coinage, rejects various attempts to replace it by a different story (which Herodotus is supposed to have misunderstood) and concludes that the best course is to accept its veracity." [*Revue des Études Anciennes*]

6246 **Vargyas, Péter.** "*Kaspu Ginnu* and the Monetary Reform of Darius I." *Zeitschrift für Assyriologie und Vorderasiatische Archäologie* (Germany) 89 (1999): 247-68.
Many sixth century B.C. tablets include the words *kaspu ginnu*. Yargyas determines this to mean "legal money" and it specifically refers to the Persian sigloi introduced by Darius I. The texts provide strong evidence that the siglos was introduced by Darius, and that the lion-and-bull coinage did not continue after the Lydian conquest. Furthermore, Vargyas concludes the Persian siglos coinage began in for before 521, and was begun for military and propaganda purposes—to help legitimize Darius as the new king. Contrary to what some other researchers have proposed, Vargyas believes the "archers" were indeed a coinage struck for use throughout the Persian Empire, rather than being struck to facilitate transactions only in Asia Minor and the west.

6247 ——— "Darius I and the Daric Reconsidered." *Iranica Antiqua* (Belgium) 35 (2000): 33-46.

It has been suggested that the coinage of Darius I was oriented toward the Greek west to compete with the Attic tetradrachm. The author disputes this premise and suggests the daric was intended to increase the prestige of the Persian king. He then examines the dating of the introduction of the daric, which he places in the period 519-512 B.C. Vargyas concludes the siglos was introduced before the end of 521 for military and propagandistic reasons, and the daric was introduced before 512 for purposes of prestige. It was seldom used in the economic life of the Achaemenid Empire. [Also see Price "Darius I and the Daric" above].

6248   **Vickers, Michael.** "Persian Gold in Parthenon Inventories." *Revue des Études Anciennes* (France) 91, no. 1-2 (1989): 249-57.
"The study of the Parthenon inventories reveals some weights might be explained by regarding them as having been made to a Persian standard (daric and siglos). The Achaemenid weight standards were accepted because of Persia's economic power." [*Revue des Études Anciennes*]

6249   **Wells, H. Bartlett.** "Observations on the Signature KIM." *Schweizer Münzblätter* (Switzerland) 34, no. 135 (August 1984).
Examines some coins of uncertain Persian satraps in Ionia or Caria which bear the signature KIM. [Also see Cancio "A New Satrapal Coin of the KIM – EKA Series" above].

6250   **Zahle, Jan.** "Persian Satraps and Lycian Dynasts: The Evidence of the Diadems." *Proceedings of the 9th International Congress of Numismatics. Berne, September 1979. Volume 1.* Edited by T. Hackens and R. Weiller. Luxembourg: International Association of Professional Numismatists, 1982. Pages 101-12. 2 pls.
Discusses the fillet which commonly circles the tiara on portrait coins from Asia Minor during the classical period. The fillet is rarely omitted. It is usually placed or tied around the tiaras in four different ways. The author argues that the fillets are distinct types of Persian diadems and are symbols of rank. Both satraps and indigenous rulers are depicted on the coins. Diadems are rarely shown on portraits of local dynasts. Tiaras of satraps are often tied below the chin, whereas this is never seen on coins of local dynasts. [For contrary opinions, see H. A. Cahn "Dynast oder Satrap?" under LYCIA, and F. Bodenstedt "Satrapen und Dynasten auf Phokäischen Hekten" under IONIA].

Also see: American Numismatic Association *Selections* under GENERAL WORKS—GREEK; Bellinger "The Coins from the Treasure of the Oxus" under HOARDS; Bellinger "The Bronze Coins of Timarchus" under SYRIA—SELEUCID KINGDOM; Caley "The Specific Gravity and Fineness of Persian Darics" under METALLURGY; Carradice *Coinage and Administration* under ATTICA—GENERAL WORKS; Casabonne "Conquete Perse de Phenomene Monetaire" under CILICIA; de Morgan *Manual de Numismatique Orientale* under GENERAL WORKS—GREEK; Droysen "Die Münzen der Persischen Satrapen" under ASIA MINOR—GENERAL WORKS; Georges "Persian Ionia" under IONIA; Guépin "Greek Coinage and Persian Bimetallism" under GENERAL WORKS—GREEK.

Head *The Coinage of Lydia and Persia* under LYDIA; Hill *Catalogue of Greek Coins of Arabia, Mesopotamia, and Persia* under ARABIA; Holloway "The Early Owls of Athens and the Persians" under ATTICA—GENERAL WORKS; Hunkin "Addendum" under METALLURGY; Jongkees "Kroiseios en Dareikos" under LYDIA; Koch *A Hoard* under PARTHIA; Konuk "Influences et Éléments Achéménides" under CARIA; Kraay "The Isparta Hoard" under HOARDS; Kroll "Who Minted the First 'Croeseids'?" under LYDIA; Le Rider "Le Monnayage Perse en Cilicie" under CILICIA; Meadows "The Apadana Foundation Deposit" under HOARDS; Metcalf *Oxford Handbook of Greek and Roman Coinage* under GENERAL WORKS—GREEK; Mildenberg "Gaza Mint Authorities in Persian Times" under PALESTINE—PHILISTIA; Mildenberg "The Philisto-Arabian Coins" under PHOENICIA; Milne "An Elymaic Hoard" under ELYMAIS; Mørkholm "Some Seleucid Coins from the Mint of Sardes" under SYRIA—SELEUCID KINGDOM; Newell *Mithradates of Parthia and Hyaosines of Characene* under PARTHIA; Nimchuk "The Lion-and-Bull Coinage of Croesus" under LYDIA.

Picard "Monnayages en Thrace à l'Èpoque Achémenide" under THRACE; Reade "Hoard…From Achaemenid Babylon" under HOARDS; Richter "Late Hellenistic Portraiture" under PORTRAITS; Rizack "A Coin with the Aramaic Legend SHRW" under ARABIA; Robinson "Greek Coins Acquired by British Museum, 1938-1948" under PUBLIC COLLECTIONS—GREAT BRITAIN (LONDON); Rodee "Art History" under ART; Sear *Greek Imperial Coins and Their Values* under COLLECTING GUIDES; Sellwood "The Ancient Near East" under ASIA—GENERAL WORKS; Sellwood "New Parthian Coin Types" under PARTHIA; Vickers "Early Greek Coinage" under ORIGINS OF COINAGE; von Petrowicz *Arsaciden-Münzen* under PARTHIA; Walburg "Lydisch oder Persisch?" under LYDIA; Wilkenson "The Origin and Development of a Greco-Persian Numismatic Motif" under TYPES; Winzer *Antike Portraitmünzen* under PORTRAITS; Zournatzi "Apadana Coin Hoards" under HOARDS.

Persis

After the conquest by Alexander the Great, Persis seems to have enjoyed a quasi-independence, having, at any rate, its own line of kings who were more or less subject to the Seleucid and the Parthian monarchs.

—Barclay V. Head, 1911

6251 **Allotte de la Füye, F. M.** "Étude sur la Numismatique de la Perside." *Corolla Numismatica: Numismatic Essays in Honour of Barclay V. Head.* G. F. Hill. London: Oxford University Press, 1906. Pages 63-97. 1 pl., table of legends. [CS 3058]
Extensive discussion of the coinage of the Kingdom of Persis with a description of the coin types, table of legends, one excellent plate, and a bibliography. Text in French.

6251a **Alram, Michael.** "Eine Neue Drachme des Vahbarz (Oborzos) aus der Persis?" *Litterae Numismaticae Vindobonenses* (Austria) 3 (1987): 147-56.

6251b **Classical Numismatic Group.** "An American Collection of the Kings of Persis." *CNG Auction 90: An Internet and Mail Bid Sale, May 23, 2012.* Pages 162-73. Illus.
Lots 787-862 in this sale catalogue represent an excellent collection of coins of Persis. Begins with a brief introduction to the kingdom and its coinage.

6251c **Naster, Paul.** "Note d'Épigraphic Monétaire de Perside: Fratakara, Frataraka, ou Fratadara?" *Iranica Antiqua* 8 (Netherlands) (1968): 74-80.

6252 ———. "Fire-Alter or Fire Tower on the Coins of Persis?" *Orientalia Lovaniensia Periodica* 1. Louvain, 1970. Pages 125-9. Reprinted in *Scripta Nummaria: Contributions à la Méthodologie Numismatic.* Edited by Paul Naster. Louvain-la-Neuve: Société Royale de Numismatique de Belgique, 1983. Pages 135-8. 1 pl.
Discusses coins of Persis with reverses showing a figure, the dynast, standing in the attitude of worship before a fire-alter. Concludes that these coins give evidence that the dynasts of Persis were a link between the Great Kings of Persia and the Sassanian kings.

6252a **Potts, Dan T.** "Foundation Houses, Fire Altars and the Frataraka: Interpreting the Iconography of Some Post-Achaemenid Persian Coins." *Iranica Antiqua* (Netherlands) 42 (2007): 271-300.
The iconography on Persid coins of the Frataraka dynasty has been discussed by many scholars. Interpretations have considered whether the building shown on the reverse of these coins was (a) a fire temple, (b) an *atāshgah*, i.e. a repository of holy fire, (c) a tomb, (d) a coronation tower, (e) a 'foundation house' or repository for Zoroastrian paraphernalia, (f) a tower altar/fire altar. These putative functions, and the building's relationship to the similarly shaped Zendan-e Sulaiman at Pasargadae and Ka'ba-e Zardosht at Naqsh-e Rustam, are evaluated. [Potts]

6252a **Rezakhani, Khodadad.** "The 'Unbekannter König IV' and the Coinage of Hellenistic and Arsacid Persis." *Name-ye Iran-e Bastan: The International Journal of Ancient Iranian Studies* (Iran) 15 (2010).

6253 **Sellwood, David G.** "Minor States in Southern Iran." Chapter 8(b) in *The Cambridge History of Iran, Volume 3, Part 1: The Seleucid, Parthian and Sasanian Periods.* Edited by Ehsan Yarshater. Cambridge: University Press, 1983. Pages 299-321. 7 pls., map.
Reviews the history of coinage in Persis, Elymais, and Characene. Includes a chronological table of kings and a table of monograms and scripts.

6254 **Tyler-Smith, S.** "A Parcel of Persis Drachms, Half Drachms and Obols." *Numismatic Chronicle* 164 (2004): 253-71. Illus.
"This parcel, probably part of a much larger hoard, contained 231 coins—drachms (5), half drachms (91) and obols (135)—dating from 'Unknown king' (second half of second century B.C.) to Artaxerxes IV (end of second century A.D.). They have been catalogued according to Alram's classification with the legends transliterated when readable but with all varieties in the details of the bust, symbol etc. not noted by Alram listed." [S. Tyler-Smith, *NL* 149]. [See Alram *Nomina Propria Iranica in Nummis* under Persis].

6254a **Van't Haaff, P. Anne, and Scott VanHorn.** *Catalogue of the Coins of Persis, circa 280 B.C.–A.D. 224.* Lancaster and London: Classical Numismatic Group (forthcoming).

Also see: Classical Numismatic Group "The Todd A. Ballen Collection" under PARTHIA; Hill *Catalogue of Greek Coins of Arabia, Mesopotamia, and Persia* under ARABIA; Klose and Müseler *Statthalter Rebellen Könige* under SYRIA—SELEUCID KINGDOM; Nelson *Numismatic Art of Persia* under PERSIA; Sellwood "New Parthian Coin Types" under PARTHIA.

Bactria and Northwest India

Apart from one or two casual references in classical authors, coins are the only material we possess for the reconstruction of the history of Alexander's successors south of the Indian Caucasus.

—R. B. Whitehead, 1940

6255 **Agrawal, R. C.** "A Note on an Interesting Greek Coin in the Sardar Museum." *Oriental Numismatic Studies* 1 (1996): 9-10.
"A tiny silver coin, preserved in the Sardar Museum at Jodhpur, is described. It bears a bust of the king, r., on one side and a crab with twelve appendages and a Greek inscription on the other. The author reads the inscription as *Demetriou* and attributes it to the Greek ruler Demetrius. Earlier, B. M. Reu, who had acquired the coin from a dealer from Rawalpindi, had discussed and illustrated this coin (*JNSI* 7, pt. 2, pp. 114-5) and tentatively attributed it to Alexander." [Amiteshwar Jha, *NL* 143]

6256 **Allan, John.** "The Beginnings of Coinage in India." *Transactions of the International Numismatic Congress Organized and Held in London by the Royal Numismatic Society, June 30-July 3, 1936.* Edited by J. Allan, H. Mattingly, and E. S. G. Robinson. London: B. Quaritch, 1938. Pages 387-92. Illus.
Allan examines the evidence available for dating the earliest Indian coins (the punch-marked silver coins) and to ascertain what chronological and other deductions it is possible to make regarding them. Concludes the idea of coinage came to India through Persia in the late fourth century B.C. and was inspired by the siglos. The original weight of the Indian coins was 2/3 siglos (1/3 stater). They remained in circulation for some time along with coins of Greek type.

6257 **Allouche-LePage, Th.** *L'Art Monétaire des Royaumes Bactriens: Essai d'Interprétation de la Symbolique Religieuse Gréco-Orientale du IIIe au Ier s. av. J.C.* Paris, 1956. 246 pp., 14 pls. [CS 3074 and 3546]

6258 **Altekar, Anant S.** "A New Didrachm of Nikias." *Journal of the Numismatic Society of India* (India) 9, pt. 1 (June 1947): 24-5.
The author publishes a didrachm of the Indo-Greek ruler Nikias which differs from other known specimens in that Nikias is shown wearing a helmet.

6259 ———. "Some New Hermaios-Kujula Kadphises Coins." *Journal of the Numismatic Society of India* (India) 9, pt. 1 (June 1947): 6-10. 1 pl.
Describes five coins found in the fields near Taxila. The coins, which differ from other published specimens, are assigned to a period of time after the death of Hermaios.

6260 ———. "Some Rare and Interesting Indo-Bactrian Coins." *Journal of the Numismatic Society of India* (India) 9, pt. 1 (June 1947): 16-23.
Publishes some rare coins of Epander, Plato, Archebios, Strato I, Euthydemus II, and Philoxenos.

6261 ———. "A Knotty Problem Connected with the Coinage of Azes." *Centennial Publication of the American Numismatic Society.* Edited by Harald Ingholt. New York: American Numismatic Society, 1958. Pages 45-51. Illus.
Altekar examines the coins bearing the inscription AZOY or AZIΛIΣOY on the obverse and Ayilishasa or Ayasa on the reverse. Some researchers believe these rare coins indicate a joint reign involving some combination of Azes I, Azes II, Azilises I, and Azilises II. The author summarizes the theories of Rapson and Whitehead regarding the relationship and chronology of these rulers. He concludes that the coins in question are not evidence of a joint rule. Rather, they are the result of a mint error in the use of the obverse or reverse of the previous reign of Azes with the reverse or obverse of the subsequent reign of Azilises. There was no Azes II or Azilises II.

6262 **Andrew, John.** "Tetradrachms Lead Baldwin's Sale." *Coin World* (December 8, 2003): 74. Illus.
A summary of the results of a Baldwin's auction held in London in October 2003. The highlight of the sale was a tetradrachm of the Bactrian king Theophilus, one of four known specimens. The coin was struck ca. 90 BC. It sold for £33,350 (including commission).

6263 **Audouin, Rémy, and Paul Bernard.** "Trésor de Monnaies Indiennes et Indogrecques d'Ai Khanoum (Afghanistan)." *Revue Numismatique* (France) 6th ser., 15 (1973): 238-89. 2 pls. [CS 3209]

6264 **Basu, S. P.** *The Second Supplementary Catalogue of Coins.* Calcutta: Indian Museum, 1977. 84 pp., 16 pls.
A supplement to V. A. Smith's catalogue of the Indian Museum Collection (see V. Smith *Coins of Ancient India* below). Catalogues 463 new acquisitions including many Indo-Greek issues. Also see the first supplement by Bidyabinode (see below).

6265 **Berk, Harlan J.** "The Two Eucratides *and* His Old Self." *The Celator* 8, no. 1 (January 1994): 22. Illus.

The author points out that there were two kings named Eucratides: Eucratides I ruled 171-155 B.C.; Eucratides II ruled 155-135 B.C. Illustrates tetradrachms of both men. Those coins now identified as coins of Eucratides II were previously believed to be poor-style coins of Eucratides I. [Also see the follow-up comments by Alan Walker, Wilfried Piper, and Berk in *The Celator* (March 1994): 42-5. Walker and Piper dispute Berk's findings].

6266 **Bernard, Paul.** "An Ancient Greek City in Central Asia." *Scientific American* 246, no. 1 (January 1982): 148-59. Illus.
A French archaeological group has unearthed Ai Khanum in Afghanistan, which may have been one of the capitals. Discusses the history of the city. Describes the layout of the city and some of its architectural structures. Some bronze blanks for coins were found during the excavations. These may shows that Ai Khanum had its own mint.

6267 ——— *Fouilles d'Aï Khanoum IV: Les Monnaies hors Trésors; Questions d'Histoire Gréco-Bactrienne*. Mémoires de la Délégation Archéologique Française en Afghanistan 28. Paris: Diffusion de Boccard, 1985.

6268 ——— "Monnaies d'Argent Pré-Seleucides." *Fouilles d'Aï Khanoum IV: Les Monnaies hors Trésors; Questions d'Histoire Gréco-Bactrienne*. Mémoires de la Délégation Archéologique Française en Afghanistan 28. By P. Bernard. Paris: Diffusion de Boccard, 1985. Pages 19-28.

6268a **Bernard, Paul, and Olivier Guillaume.** "Monnaies Inédites de la Bactriane Grecque a Aï Khanoum (Afghanistan)." *Revue Numismatique* (France) 6th ser., 22 (1980): 9-32.

6269 **Besom, Tom.** "An Introduction to Bactrian Coinage." *The Numismatist* 98, no. 5 (May 1985): 906-11. Illus., map.
An overview of Bactrian history, followed by an introduction to the coins. Points out things that can be learned about Bactrian history from the study of the coinage, such as the names of kings and the chronological arrangement of their reigns. Includes a genealogical table of Indo-Greek kings.

6270 **Bhattacharyya, Asoke K.** *Indian Coins in the Musée Guimet.* Calcutta: Firma K. L. Mukhopadhyay, 1971. 49 pp., 6 pls.
A catalogue of the Indian coins in the Musée Guimet in Paris. A short introduction is followed by a catalogue of 55 coins of the Greek kings of Bactria and India, 52 Indo-Parthian coins, 52 Indo-Scythian coins, and 37 Kushan and later coins.

6271 **Bidyabinude, B. B.** *Supplementary Catalogue of Coins in the Indian Museum of Calcutta.* Calcutta: Indian Museum, 1932.
A supplement to V. A. Smith's catalogue of the Indian Museum Collection (see V. Smith *Coins of Ancient India* below). Also see the second supplement by Basu (see Basu above).

6272 **Bivar, A. D. H.** "The Bactra Coinage of Euthydemus and Demetrius." *Numismatic Chronicle* 6th ser., 11 (1951): 22-39. 2 pls., illus. [CS 3076]
"In this study the gold and silver issues of Euthydemus and Demetrius from the mint of Bactra are arranged chronologically. Five groups are listed for each ruler, the sequence based primarily on style and die alignment. The author considers the last two groups of Euthydemus contemporary with the first two of Demetrius and suggests that after Antiochus III retired from the siege of Bactra, Euthydemus designated his son as sub-king, permitting him to strike coinage in his own name. Two appendices are provided: (1) coins of the two rulers minted elsewhere than in Bactra, and (2) bronze issues from Bactra which cannot be related closely to the gold and silver strikings of Euthydemus and Demetrius." [M. Thompson, *NL* 27]

6273 ——— "Indo-Greek Victory Medallions." *Spink Numismatic Circular* 61, no. 5 (May 1953): 201-2. Illus.
"The Museum at Kabul (Afghanistan) recently acquired five Indo-Greek silver twenty-drachm (Attic weight) pieces of Amyntas Nikator, who must have ruled in Gandhara about 150 B.C. The medallions are unquestionably genuine and must have been struck to commemorate a major victory at the outset of this ruler's ephemeral reign. The pieces are modeled generally on the gold twenty-stater piece of Eucratides, in the Bibliothéque Nationale." [C. Vermeule, *NL* 33]

6274 ——— "The Chaman Huzuri Hoard: Countermarked Greek Flans as the Prototypes of the Indian Punch-Marked Coinage." *Numismatic Chronicle* 6th ser., 14 (1954): 163-72. 1 pl.
"In the important hoard of Greek and Oriental coins discovered in 1933 on the parade ground of Kabul, twenty-nine coins fall into no previously recognized category. The flans of these 'countermarked coins' appear to be of Greek origin, although attempts to attribute these flans to their exact cities of origin on the evidence of the undertypes is inconclusive. The countermarks bear some determined relationship to the weight-standard of the undertypes. Stylistic analysis of the countermarks leads to attribution of the whole group to the same area as the wheel-marked coins, amongst the earliest currencies of ancient India. Historical conclusions on the origins of the punch-marked coinage are: (1) the flans of the countermarked coins are re-used flans of ancient Greek coins current within the Achaemenian Empire before 380 B.C., (2) the countermarks correspond to specific examples of a number of Greek weight-standards, and (3) the countermarks circulated within the most eastern territories of the Achaemenian Empire. A further plausible suggestion is that the Maurya Emperors invented the punch-marked coinage after the Macedonian interlude to replace the exhausted supply of countermarked Greek silver flans of the Achaemenids." [C. Vermeule, *NL* 34]

6275 ——— "The Qunduz Treasure." *Spink Numismatic Circular* 62, no. 5 (May 1954): 187-91. Illus.
"A find made in Northern Afghanistan and now possibly in the Kabul Museum contains 610 recorded coins. Fourteen types or varieties previously unpublished include Bactrian (Attic weight) tetradrachms of Lysis, Theophilus, Archebius, Philoxenus and Hermaeus. Greek rule in Bactria probably carried on for many years after it was believed to have ended, and a Greek enclave at Qunduz may have survived until 90 B.C., the true date of Hermaeus." [C. Vermeule, *NL* 33]. The Qunduz hoard revealed that kings later than Antialkidas struck tetradrachms of Attic weight bearing Greek legends alone.

6276 ——— "The Bactrian Treasure of Qunduz." *Journal of the Numismatic Society of India* (India) 17, pt. 1 (1955): 37-52. 8 pls.
"Six-hundred ten coins from Afghanistan displayed by the Kabul Museum in 1952-53 are discussed and fifty-four representative or unusual examples are illustrated. It is believed that 90% of the hoard is at Kabul, and that it consists almost entirely of Greco-Bactrian tetradrachms. Two new reverse types of the sun-god, apparently Mithra, are illustrated, and the find also includes Attic-weight coins of later rulers previously known only for their lighter bilingual issues, but identical reverses. This reinforces the belief that each ruler clung to one reverse type through his lifetime, and that we may regard any other variety as an emergency issue. A double decadrachm of Amyntas, weighing eighty-four grams is illustrated and presented as the largest Greek silver coin recorded to date. It was issued both with Zeus and with Tyche upon its reverse. Greco-Bactrian, rather than lighter weight Indo-Bactrian, tetradrachms of late date indicate a revised chronology for the early first century B.C., which the author believes to be the terminal date of burial of the hoard. Among others,

6277 ——— "Indo-Bactrian Problems." *Numismatic Chronicle* 7th ser., 5 (1965): 69-108. Map, 3 pls. [CS 3077]
(1) Describes and illustrates a recently discovered hoard of Indo-Bactrian coins from the northwest frontier. The coins relate to the reign of Menander and his immediate successors. (2) Presents a theoretical analysis of the coinage of Strato and Archebius, together with some associated rulers. The aim is to demonstrate the strict succession of rulers at each mint and the interlocking pattern of characteristics (monograms, legends, types) which help to connect each issue with its successor.

6278 ——— "The Sequence of Menander's Drachmae." *Journal of the Royal Asiatic Society of Great Britain and Ireland* (1970): 123-36. 6 pls. [CS 3078]
Establishes a sequence for the drachms of Menander. Attempts to determine whether the issues with continuous legends are of earlier dates while those with divided legends are later dates. Attempts to attribute the monograms to rulers.

6279 **Bopearachchi, Osmund.** "Monnaies Indo-Grecques Surfrappées." *Revue Numismatique* (France) 6, no. 31 (1989): 49-79.
An examination of overstruck Indo-Greek coins.

6279a ——— "Un Roi Indo-Grec: Télèphe: Observations sur l'Iconographie de son Monnayage et la Date de son Règne." *Schweizer Münzblätter* (Switzerland) 39, no. 156 (1989): 88-94.

6280 ——— "Graeco-Bactrian Issues of Later Indo-Greek Kings." *Numismatic Chronicle* 150 (1990): 79-103. 3 pls.
"The aim of this study is (1) to give a complete inventory of all published and some hitherto unknown Graeco-Bactrian coins minted by Menander and his successors south of the Hindu Kush mountains and (2) to reexamine the various hypotheses put forward by scholars after the discovery of the Qunduz hoard. The inventory comprises forty-seven pieces, of which twelve are unpublished. The author shows (1) that once completely overpowered by the Yüeh-chi around 130 B.C., the Greeks had no further control whatsoever over the provinces north of the Hindu Kush, and (2) that all the Graeco-Bactrian coin issues by Indo-Greek kings were struck in the mints situated in their territories south of the Hindu Kush. Three possibilities are examined to account for the existence of the Graeco-Bactrian coins issued in the name of kings who normally should have minted only the bilingual coinages: (1) these coins were prestige issues; (2) they were the currency for commercial exchanges with Bactria; (3) they constituted the tribute paid to menacing neighbors used to the Attic standard. The author excludes the first proposition and presents the remaining two as possible hypotheses." [O. Bopearachchi, *NL* 126]

6281 ——— *Monnaies Gréco-Bactriennes et Indo-Grecques: Catalogue Raisonné.* Paris: Bibliothèque Nationale, 1991. 458 pp., 69 pls.
"This is the finest and most up-to-date reference for the Bactrian and Indo-Greek coinage. Besides being a catalogue of the 1227 coins in the Cabinet des Médailles of the Bibliothèque Nationale in Paris, it also records all other types not present in that collection but published elsewhere including those in private collections known to the author and the contents of published hoards. Excellent historical summaries of each reign are included in the introduction, and the catalogue itself contains full cross-references to all standard works and many sale catalogues." [D. Kroh, *ACRR*]

6282 ——— *Indo-Greek, Indo-Scythian and Indo-Parthian Coins in the Smithsonian Institution.* New Delhi: Manohar Publishers, 1993. Also: Washington, D.C.: Smithsonian Institution, 1993. 142 pp., map, 41 pls.
Catalogues the 275 Graeco-Bactrian and Indo-Scythian coins in the Smithsonian's collection, as well as 257 Indo-Parthian and Indo-Parthian coins from the "Malakand" hoard. The hoard includes coins of Azes II, Azes with Aspavarma, Gondophares, and Abdagases. The author reviews the historical background of the subject coinage, explains his attributions and chronology, and provides some answers to problems regarding the order and dating of the kings. Also includes metrological information on the hoard coins, a table and index of monograms, and a select bibliography.

6283 ——— "Sophytes, the Enigmatic Ruler of Central Asia." *Nomismatika Khronika* (Greece) 15 (1996): 19-32. 1 pl.
The author publishes two coins of Sophytes representing two previously unreported denominations: a tetradrachm of the Attic standard and a didrachm of the local standard. Reviews the opinions of other scholars regarding the identity and reign dates of Sophytes as well as the location of his kingdom. Three series of coins are identified as being associated with this king: (1) coins which bear the name Sophytes, (2) imitations of Athenian coins, and (3) coins bearing Athena on the obverse and an eagle on the reverse. The author believes these coins were struck towards the very end of the fourth century B.C. and were the pre-cursors of the Bactrian issues of the Seleucids. [Also see articles by Cunningham, Kirkpatrick, G. Macdonald, and Whitehead below].

6284 ——— "The Posthumous Coinage of Hermaios and the Conquest of Gandhara by the Kushans." *Gandharian Art in Context. East-West Exchanges at the Crossroads of Asia.* Edited by R. Allchin, B. Allchin, N. Kreitman, and E. Errington. Cambridge: The Ancient India and Iran Trust, 1997. Pages 189-213.

6285 ——— "Indo-Parthians." *Das Partherreich und seine Zeugnisse.* Edited by J. Wiesehöfer. Historia Einzelschriften 122. Stuttgart: Steiner, 1998. Pages 389-406. Illus.
The author surveys the coins of those Parthians who reigned over India." [H. Baldus, *NL* 142]

6286 ——— "Two Unreported Coins from the Second Mir Zakah Deposit." *Oriental Numismatic Society Newsletter* 165 (autumn 2000): 15-6. Illus.
"Two Graeco-Bactrian gold staters are described." [M. Allen, *NL* 145]

6287 ——— "Some Interesting Coins from the Pandayale Hoard: 1. Coin of Heliocles II Overstruck on a Coin of Hermaios." *Oriental Numismatic Society Newsletter* 169 (autumn 2001): 19-20. Illus.

6288 ——— "Two More Unique Coins from the Second Mir Zakah Deposit." *Oriental Numismatic Society Newsletter* 169 (autumn 2001): 21-2. Illus.
"A gold Graeco-Bactrian coin and a lead coin from Mir Zakah in Pakistan are described." [M. Allen, *NL* 145]

6289 ——— "Diomedes Overstruck by Agathocleia." *Oriental Numismatic Society Newsletter* 172 (summer 2002): 13-4. Illus.

6289a   ———— "Three Interesting Indo-Greek Coins." *Oriental Numismatic Society Newsletter* 172 (summer 2002): 15-6.

6290   ———— "Was Indo-Greek Artemidoros the Son of Indo-Scythian Maues? Amluk Dara Hoard Revisited." *Nomismatika Khronika* (Greece) 27 (2008-2009): 25-46. Illus.
A re-examination of a hoard published by R. C. Senior in 2006 (*Indo-Scythian Coins and History, Volume IV*). The hoard contained seventeen bronze coins, including eight coins of Artemidoros. Bopearachchi concludes that the translation of the reverse legend in Gandhari proposed by Senior making Artemidoros the son of Indo-Scythian Maues is not absolutely certain. Includes a catalogue of the coins. In English and Greek.

6291   **Bopearachchi, Osmund, and Klaus Grigo.** "Thundering Zeus Revisited." *Oriental Numismatic Society Newsletter* 169 (autumn 2001): 22-4. Illus.
"A hoard of Graeco-Bactrian gold staters from Vaisili." [M. Allen, *NL* 145]

6292   ———— "To Err is Human." *Oriental Numismatic Society Newsletter* 172 (summer 2002): 14-15. Illus.
"The authors discuss a die-engraving error on an Indo-Greek coin of King Lysias." [Martin Allen, *NL* 147]

6293   **Bopearachchi, Osmund, and Wilfried Pieper.** *Ancient Indian Coins.* Turnhout, Belgium: Brepols Publishers, 1998. 289 pp., 59 pls.
In Part 1, Pieper develops a historical commentary about the earliest coinages of India, the imperial period of late Magadha and Maurya rule (ca. late fourth to early second centuries B.C.), Ujjain and Eran, the Satavahanas (ca. first century B.C. to early second century A.D.), and tribal republics and kingdoms in post-Mauryan northern India (ca. 200 B.C. to ca. A.D. 300). This commentary is followed by a detailed catalogue with precise drawings of more than 600 coins. In Part 2, Bopearachchi begins with historical commentary about foreign powers in ancient northern India, from Bactrian Greeks until the time of the early Kushans. This is followed by a catalogue of more than 300 Greek, Graeco-Bactrian, Indo-Greek, Indo-Scythian, Indo-Parthian, and early Kushan coins. The catalogue is based on a private collection of Indian coins.

6294   ———— "Over-Struck and Double-Struck." *Oriental Numismatic Society Newsletter* 178 (winter 2004): 20. Illus.
"Discussion of a Graeco-Bactrian tetradrachm of Euthydemos I." [Martin Allen, *NL* 149]

6295   **Bopearachchi, Osmund, and Aman Ur Rahman.** *Pre-Kushana Coins in Pakistan.* Karachi: Iftikhar Rasul IRM Associates Ltd., 1995. 237 pp., illus.
Publishes 1090 coins with a detailed account of the history of the rulers who issued the coins. Covers the earliest coins found in Central Asia (imported and local issues of the Achaemenid kings of Iran during the fifth century B.C.) down to the issues of the local Indo-Parthian kings of the first century A.D. The catalogue is composed of all the Greek, Bactrian, Indo-Greek, Indo-Scythian, and Indo-Parthian coins and of selected Achaemenid and early Indian coins in the private collection of Aman Ur Rahman, supplemented by some rare and unique coins in the Peshawar Museum and in the private collection of Khurshid Ahmad Khan. Includes historical and technical commentary and discussions of metallurgy and coin cleaning. Concludes with the catalogue of coins with color plates facing the descriptions. [Reviewed by Martha L. Carter in *American Journal of Numismatics* 2nd ser., 10 (1998): 149-51].

6296   **Brett, Agnes Baldwin.** "Indo-Bactrian Coins Acquired by the American Numismatic Society in 1947." *Museum Notes* 3 (1948): 31-43. 1 pl.
Describes and discusses four rare Indo-Bactrian tetradrachms and a one drachm from the 1947 Shaikhano Dheri Hoard (or the Lal Dheri Hoard). The coins are tetradrachms of Zoilos I Dikaios, Antialkidas, Artemidoros, and Hermaios with Kalliope, and a drachm of Agathokleia.

6297   **Browne, Gerald M.** "Bayer's Coin of Eucratides." *Zeitschrift für Papyrologie und Epigraphik* (Germany) 145 (2003): 212. Illus.
"The coin illustrated in G. S. Bayer's *Historia Regni Graecorum Bactriani* (1738), which has been thought to be a tetradrachm, is reinterpreted as a drachm based on its weight." [Hans R. Baldus, *NL* 148]

6298   **Cammann, Schuyler V. R.** "The Bactrian Nickel Theory." *American Journal of Archaeology* 62, no. 4 (October 1958): 409-14. [CS 15846]
"The theory that the copper-nickel alloy used by several Graeco-Bactrian kings for their minor coinage came from Southwest China is vigorously refuted by the author who outlines the arguments advanced by proponents of the theory and indicates what he considers the fallacies involved. In summary, he points out that we have no evidence for the mining of nickel-copper in Southwest China in the early second century B.C. and that even if one assumes the availability of such ore, its transportation to Bactria would have been an extremely difficult and expensive procedure." [M. Thompson, *NL* 48]. [Also see Schwitter and Cheng "Bactrian Nickel" below, and Cheng and Schwitter "Nickel in Ancient Bronzes" under METALLURGY].

6299   ———— "On the Renewed Attempt to Revive the Bactrian Nickel Theory." *American Journal of Archaeology* 66, no. 1 (January 1962): 92-4.
"The writer refutes the theory which named China as the source of the ore used in the cupro-nickel coinage of Bactria [see *American Journal of Archaeology* (1957): 351 ff]. The primitive means of land transport available at the time, he suggests, would have made it economically unfeasible to carry large quantities of ore over the mountain route between Southern China and Bactria." [I. Merker, *NL* 62]. [Also see Cammann above, and Schwitter and Cheng "Bactrian Nickel" below].

6300   **Case, Ralph E.** "Nickel-Containing Coins of Bactria, 235-170 B.C." *The Coin Collector's Journal* new ser., 1 (August 1934): 102-3, 117. Illus.
Some of the coins of the Bactrian kings Euthydemos II, Pantaleon, and Agathocles contain nickel. These coins were the last coins to contain nickel until the coinage of modern Switzerland in 1850. The author describes the metallurgical method by which the nickel content was determined. Suggests the nickel was mined and smelted in the Chinese provinces of Yunan and Szechwan and the ingots transported to Bactria.

6301   **Cavafy, K. P.** "Coins." Translated by Marion J. A. Tzamali. *Nomismatika Khronika* (Greece) 18 (1999): 9-10. Illus.
A short poem by Greek poet Konstantine P. Cavafy mentions the Indo-Greek kings Hermaios, Eukratides, Strato, and Menander. Provides brief commentary on each king.

6302 **Chabouillet, Anatole.** "L'Eucratidion." *Revue Numismatique* (France) (1867): 382-415.
Discusses the large gold coin of Eucratides weighing 169 gm, found in Bukhara. It is the largest coin ever minted in the ancient world.

6303 **Chaudhary, K.** "Dionysos on Indo-Greek Coins—A Study." *Journal of the Numismatic Society of India* (India) 45 (1983): 119-33.
"The depiction of Dionysos on certain coins of the Indo-Greek kings Pantaleon and Agathocles is discussed in detail, and the deity is identified with Balarama, the Indian god. Diodorus Siculus reported that Megasthenes mentions three Dionysos, who lived in different ages; of them, the most ancient one was Indos (Indian). The identity of Dionysos with Balarama is suggested and certain similarities in the legends surrounding the two are noticed." [P. Gupta, *NL* 113]

6304 **Classical Numismatic Group.** "Baktrian Coinage featuring the K.-D. Walkhoff-Jordan Collection." *Triton II Auction Catalogue.* Lancaster, Pennsylvania, 1998. Pages 101-10. Illus.
An important collection of Bactrian coins is offered in lots 577 through 615 in the Triton II auction conducted jointly by Classical Numismatic Group, Freeman & Sear, and Numismatica Ars Classica on December 1-2, 1998. Described as one of the most important Bactrian collections to ever appear at auction, the collection includes many great rarities including seven of the nine dynastic or "pedigree" tetradrachm issues. Each coin is illustrated.

6305 "Coin of Eucratides." *American Journal of Numismatics* 14, no. 1 (July 1879): 18-20.
An interesting account of the finding of an immense (2 ½ inches diameter) gold coin of Eucratides of Bactria, its sale to a "French gentleman" and its placement in the Bibliotheque Nationale. Reprinted from the *London Athenaeum* from March 1868. [Also see A. Narain "The Twenty Stater Gold Piece" and S. Narain "The Twenty-Stater Gold Piece" below].

6306 **Cribb, Joe.** "The Earliest Ganesa: A Case of Mistaken Identity." *Numismatic Digest* (India) 6 (1982): 30-3. Illus.
"In answer to A. K. Narain (see Narain "Ganesa" below), the author suggests that Ganesa on Hermaeus' coin is actually Zeus-Mithra. However, photographs of the piece appear to support both Narain's and the author's view simultaneously." [P. Gupta, *NL* 113]

6307 ———. "The End of Greek Coinage in Bactria and India and Its Evidence for the Kushan Coinage System." *Studies in Greek Numismatics in Memory of Martin Jessop Price.* Edited by Richard Ashton and Silvia Hurter. London: Spink, 1998. Pages 83-98. 3 pls.
An inscription, written using Greek script but in the Bactrian language, was discovered in 1993 which throws light on the end of the use of Greek language and the continued use of Greek script in Bactria and India. The document has also provided new evidence for dating the end of Greek coinage at its most easterly extent to the first year of the Kushan king Kanishka I, about A.D. 108-120. This paper discusses the end of the use of Greek inscriptions on coins in this region in light of the new inscription. Discusses the Greek coinage tradition in Bactria and India, the monetary reforms in the early Kushan period, and the role of gods on Kanishka's coins. New insights are also gained regarding the organization of Kushan gold coinage.

6308 **Cubelli, Vincenzo.** "Moneta e Ideologia Monarchica: Il Caso di Eucratide." *Rivista Italiana di Numismatica e Scienze Affini* (Italy) 95 (1993): 251-59.
Discusses the large gold coin of Eucratides weighing 169 gm, found in the 1870's in Bukhara. It is the largest coin ever minted in the ancient world.

6309 **Cunningham, Alexander.** "Descriptions and Deductions from a Consideration of Some New Bactrian Coins." *Journal of the Asiatic Society of Bengal* 9 (India) (1840): 867-89. 1 pl. of engravings.
Describes ten Bactrian coins and attempts to attribute them to the issuing rulers.

6310 ———. "Second Notice of Some New Bactrian Coins." *Journal of the Asiatic Society of Bengal* 11 (India) (1842): 130-7.
Describes some Bactrian coins containing eight new names. Also publishes a copper coin of Demetrius and a new drachm of Azas.

6311 ———. "An Attempt to Explain Some of the Monograms Found Upon the Grecian Coins of Ariana and India." *Numismatic Chronicle* 8 (1846): 175-97.
Examines the monograms appearing on Indo-Greek coins. Presents a table of monograms on Bactrian coins assigning each to a king's reign, and a chronological and geographical table of Alexander's successors in the East. Discusses the significance of the monograms and the historical results which can be deduced from them.

6312 ———. "Coin of the Indian Prince Sophytes, a Contemporary of Alexander the Great." *Numismatic Chronicle* new ser., 6 (1866): 220-31.
The author publishes a rare coin with obv., aged head of Sophytes; rev., cock standing, and inscription ΣΟΦΥΤΟΥ. Cunningham identifies Sophytes as the Indian prince Sophites, a contemporary of Alexander the Great. He concludes the coin was struck ca. 312-306 B.C. Discusses the possible location of Sophytes' kingdom and attempts to interpret the coin types and symbols. [Also see articles by Bopearachichi above, and Kirkpatrick, G. Macdonald, and Whitehead below].

6313 ———. *Coins of Alexander's Successors in the East (Bactria, Ariana and India).* 1884. Reprint, Chicago: Argonaut, 1969. 337 pp., 14 pls. (line drawings). [CS 3079, 3079a]
First published in the *Numismatic Chronicle* in eleven parts in 1868, 1870, 1872, and 1873. Reviews the history of Alexander's conquests in the east and the division of his empire after his death. Focuses on the eastern provinces of Bactriana, Ariana, and India. Describes the major cities in the region. Reviews the Arian alphabet and translates the common coin inscriptions. Lists and explains 150 monograms. A history of each ruler's reign includes a detailed listing of the major coin types. Finally, a general description of the eastern monetary system is presented.

6314 **Curiel, Raoul, and Gérard Fussman.** *Le Trésor Monétaire de Qunduz.* Mémoires de la Délégation Archéologique Française en Afghanistan 20. Paris: Librairie C. Klincksieck, 1965. 93 pp., 60 pls. [CS 3223]
An analysis of a hoard of 627 Bactrian coins, mostly tetradrachms. The hoard included 12 tetradrachms of Euthydemos, 50 of Demetrius II, 144 of Eucratides I, 130 of Eucratides II, and 204 of Heliocles. Includes a full catalogue of the coins and a discussion of the hoard and its implications.

6315 **Dani, A. H.** "Greek Monograms." *Indian Numismatics, History, Art, and Culture: Essays in the Honour of Dr. P. L. Gupta, Volume 1.* Edited by D. W. MacDowall, Savita Sharma, and Sanjay Garg. Agam Indological Series, No. 14. Delhi: Agam Kala Prakashan, 1992. Pages 99-114.

An analysis of the monograms appearing on the coins of the Greek kings who ruled Bactria, Afghanistan, and Pakistan from the middle of the third century B.C. to the middle of the first century B.C. Dani classifies the monograms by the principal Greek letter in the monogram, and then summarizes the occurrences of these principal letters under each of the Indo-Greek kings. They are most probably the initials of the names of persons, families, or workshops. Dani believes they cannot be the names of mint towns because the number of monograms is too large. [Also see MacDowall "The Geographical Distribution of Monograms" below].

6316 **Dawdy, David R.** "Puzzle Remains: Control Marks Offer Clues to Indo-Greek Mints." *The Celator* 3, no. 8 (August 1989): 14.
Mentions the views of Mitchiner, Gardner, and Cunningham regarding the interpretation of the control marks which appear on Bactrian and Indo-Greek coinage. Examines the marks found on 107 drachms of Menander from a recent hoard. No conclusion is drawn regarding the validity of Mitchiner's attributions. [Also see Dawdy "Further Research" below].

6317 ——— "Further Research Changes Control Mark Percentages." *The Celator* 4, no 3 (March 1990): 30.
A continuation of "Puzzle Remains" above. The author examined eighty-one more drachms of Menander and presents an updated table of control mark frequencies.

6318 **De, Gaurisankar.** "A Copper Coin of Antimachus II." *Journal of the Numismatic Society of India* (India) 55 (1993): 27-30. Illus.
"The author publishes a copper coin of Antimachus II with winged victory/king on horseback." [Amiteshwar Jha, *NL* 143]

6319 **Deyell, John S.** "Indo-Greek and Ksaharata Coins from the Gujarat Seacoast." *Numismatic Chronicle* 144 (1984): 115-27. 3 pls.
Discusses a hoard discovered prior to 1973 near the ancient port of Gogha in India. The hoard consisted exclusively of the silver coins of the Indo-Greek kings Apollodotus II and Dionysius, and the Ksaharata ruler Nahapana. The hoard probably contained over 5000 coins. Includes a catalogue of a small group of the coins. Deyell comments on the significance of the hoard.

6320 **Dobbins, K. Walton.** "The Question of the Imitation Hermaios Coinage." *East and West* (Italy) 20, no. 3 (September 1970): 307-26. Illus.
"The problems of the transition between genuine Indo-Greek coins of the ruler Hermaeus and suspected imitation silver issues, their place of mintage, and their position in the chronology of coinage in the Peropamisadae, Arachosia and Gandhara are discussed. The relation of this problem to other controversies concerning Indo-Greek coins, notably other imitation issues of coins, and the question of one or two kings named Apollodotus is noted." [P. Hogan, *NL* 88]

6321 ——— "Sanabares and the Gondophares Dynasty." *Numismatic Chronicle* 7th ser., 11 (1971): 135-42. Illus.
Dobbins examines the coinage of King Sanabares and concludes that it belongs to the early first century A.D.

6322 ——— "The Sequence of Bactrian Coins." *Numismatic Digest* (India) 2, pt. 2 (December 1978): 1-13.
"A sequence is adduced from type analysis. The Euthydeman and Eucratidean groups came to terms and for a while the Greeks in Bactria and India were united under the rule of Eucratides. A son of Demetrius was associate king with Eucratides and captured and killed him." [P. Gupta, *NL* 103]

6323 ——— *A Schema of Indo-Baktrian Coinage.* Numismatic Notes and Monographs, No. 18. Varanasi: The Numismatic Society of India/Banaras Hindu University, 1980. 82 pp.
Arranges the Indo-Bactrian coinage into thirty-three periods or typological phases. Attempts to more firmly establish the proper chronological sequence of the issues. Examines monograms.

6324 **Flight, Walter.** "On the Chemical Composition of a Bactrian Coin." *Numismatic Chronicle* new ser., 8 (1868): 305-8.
A Bactrian coin was examined to determine its metallic composition. The coin contained copper, nickel, iron, and other metals in small amounts. Flight comments on the use of nickel in coinage, and the techniques the ancients may have used to obtain nickel.

6324a **Francfort, Henri-Paul.** "Deux Nouveaux Tétradrachmes Commémoratifs d'Agathocle." *Revue Numismatique* (France) 6th ser., 17 (1975): 19-22.

6325 **Gardner, Percy.** "New Coins from Bactria." *Numismatic Chronicle* new ser., 19 (1879): 1-12. 1 pl.
Publishes six coins and mentions others, all from the Oxus Treasure found in Bokhara, India in 1877. Includes gold coins of Andragoras, two gold coins of a Persepolitan king (attribution uncertain), and silver coins of Antiochus I and II. Discusses the significance of each.

6326 ——— "On Some Coins of Syria and Bactria." *Numismatic Chronicle* new ser., 20 (1880): 181-91. 1 pl.
Discusses the coins of Agathocles with the types of Alexander, as well as coins of Eucratides, Antimachus, and coins of the early Seleucid kings. Also discusses an imitation of the coins of Athens.

6327 ——— *The Coins of the Greek and Scythic Kings of Bactria and India in the British Museum.* London: British Museum, 1886. Reprint, Chicago: Argonaut, 1966. 193 pp., 32 pls. [CS 3080]
Volume 1 of *A Catalogue of Indian Coins in the British Museum.* Although it is now out-of-date, when first published, this was the most complete corpus of nearly all the known types issued by the Hellenistic and Hellenized kings and rulers of Bactria and India. Includes an historical introduction beginning ca. 320 B.C. Discusses inscriptions, monograms, types, and weights. Includes tables of alphabets. Followed by a catalogue of several hundred coins.

6328 ——— "New Greek Coins of Bactria and India." *Numismatic Chronicle* 3rd ser., 7 (1887): 177-84. Illus., 1 pl.
Publishes some Bactrian coins recently added to the British Museum collection. (1) Publishes the now famous "Porus" decadrachm. Gardner believes the coin was minted in Bactria, not in India. He identifies the standing figure on the reverse as Alexander the Great. He does not believe the coin depicts the Indian king Porus on the elephant on the obverse. Rather, he suggests the riders are Scythic kings. The coin was issued on the occasion of some notable victory won by a Greek king of Bactria over the invading hordes of Yueh-chi in the second century B.C. Gardner suggests the issuer was Eucratides or Heliocles. (2) Lists numerous didrachms of Greek kings Diomedes, Strato I, Strato and Agathocleia, Philoxenus, and Hermaeus. [For a more recent opinion on the Porus decadrachm, see Miller "The 'Porus' Decadrachm" under MACEDONIAN KINGDOM—ALEXANDER'S PORUS COINS/MEDALLIONS].

6329 **Gauba, K.** "Coins of the Graeco-Bactrian Kings." *Spink Numismatic Circular* 25 (March-April 1917): 139-40.
A brief account of the reign of the Bactrian kings from Sophytes through Hermaeus. Briefly mentions some of the coin types.

6330 **Giedroyc, Richard.** "Specialists Voice Concerns over Appearance of Some Bactrian Coins." *Coin World* (August 12, 1996): 106. Illus.
Voices concern over the appearance on the market of many Bactrian coins soon after the looting of the National Museum of Afghanistan. Calls for the return of any coins which are suspected of coming from the museum.

6331 **Goyal, Shankar.** *Ancient Indian Numismatics: A Historiographical Study.* India: Kusumanjali Book World, 1998. 226 pp.
Goyal critically examines important works and research articles on Indian numismatics published during the last two hundred years. Covers the origin of coinage in India, the punch-marked coins, the tribal and local coins, the Indo-Greek coinage, the imperial Scytho-Parthian and Western Kshatrapa coinage, the coinage of the Kushanas, the Satavahana coinage, the coinage of the Gupta Empire, the coinage of the Vakatakas, and the coins of the North Indian dynasties of the post-Gupta period (A.D. 550-750).

6332 **Guillaume, Olivier.** *Analysis of Reasonings in Archaeology: The Case of Graeco-Bactrian and Indo-Greek Numismatics.* French Studies in South Asian Culture and Society 4. Translated by Osmund Bopearachchi. Delhi: Oxford University Press, 1990. 134 pp.
A study of Graeco-Bactrian numismatics from the methodological viewpoint. Examines how numismatists describe the coins in their catalogues and how historians use the catalogues to establish historical reconstructions. Looks at the definition of the Graeco-Bactrian and Indo-Greek group of coins, its division into sub-sets, and the process of sifting through coins to be catalogued. Discusses how coins are described, the methods of notation, and the classification of coins. The author then studies several historical reconstructions based upon numismatic evidence. [Reviewed by J. Cribb in *Numismatic Chronicle* 153 (1993): 314-6].

6333 **Guillaume, Olivier, ed.** *Graeco-Bactrian and Indian Coins from Afghanistan.* Translated by Osmund Bopearachchi. French Studies in South Asian Culture and Society 5. Delhi: Oxford University Press, 1991. 199 pages, 14 pls.
An English translation of several works that previously existed only in French. Includes Curiel and Schlumberger's account of the Mir Zakah hoard, Curiel and Fussman's account of the Qunduz hoard, and several articles on the Aï Khanoum hoards. [Reviewed by J. Cribb in *Numismatic Chronicle* 153 (1993): 314-6].

6334 **Gupta, Parmeshwari L.** "Three Commemorative Tetradrachms of Agathocles." *Journal of the Numismatic Society of India* (India) 38, pt. 2 (1976): 92-4. 1 pl.
Describes three coins of Agathocles which are extremely rare and historically important. The coins commemorate Diodotus, Euthydemus, and Pantaleon.

6335 **Handa, D.** "Counterfeit Copper Coins of Hippostratos and Azes I." *Spink Numismatic Circular* 104, no. 9 (November 1996): 403-4. Illus.
"Two modern cast forgeries of Bactrian coins are published." [M. Allen, *NL* 140]

6336 **Haughton, Henry L.** "The Shaikhano Dheri Hoard, March 1940." *Numismatic Chronicle* 5th ser., 20 (1940): 123-6.
A brief record of a hoard of Indo-Greek coins found near Utmanzai. About 130 coins were found, mostly of Menander, Hermaios, and Philoxenos. [This paper was reprinted in R. Whitehead's *Indo-Greek Numismatics*. See Whitehead "Notes on Indo-Greek Numismatics" below].

6337 ——— "Some Rare Indo-Greek Hemidrachms from the North Western Frontier." *Journal of the Numismatic Society of India* (India) 4 (1942): 146-7. 1 pl.
Publishes six rare coin types of Menander, Epander, Agathokleia and Strato, Apollophanes, Polyxenos, and Philoxenos.

6338 ——— "A Note on the Distribution of Indo-Greek Coins." *Numismatic Chronicle* 6th ser., 3 (1943): 50-9. Map.
A record of find-spots and observations on the distribution of Indo-Greek coins. Lists are arranged by find-spot (the nearest village) and ruler (with find-spots indicated).

6339 ——— "Notes on Greek and Kushan Coins from North-West India: (a) The Bajaur Hoard of 1942; (b) Some Rare Copper Coins from the North-West Frontier of India; (c) Two Unrecorded (?) Coins of Huvishka." *Numismatic Chronicle* 6th ser., 6 (1946): 141-5. Illus.
In Note A, Haughton describes a hoard of 800-1000 Indo-Greek coins found in 1942. All are hemidrachms of Menander, Antimachos, Apollodotos, and Zoilos. Presents the results of the author's examination of 120 of the coins, showing the distribution among rulers and the monograms found on the coins of each ruler. The coins are cross-referenced to Whitehead's *Catalogue of Coins in the Panjab Museum*. In Note B, the author publishes eight Indo-Greek coins. In Note C, two copper coins of Huvishka are published.

6340 ——— "The Silver Coinage of Strato and of Strato and Agathocleia." *Numismatic Chronicle* 6th ser., 8 (1948): 134-41. 2 pls.
A supplement to Rapson's article in *Corolla Numismatica* (see Rapson "Coins of the Graeco-Indian Sovereigns" below). Includes a list of Rapson's conclusions on the identity and reigns of these rulers, and the deterioration of the coinage of Strato I. The author then treats the coinage chronologically, analyzing portraits and legends, particularly those of Strato I because of the many variations in the inscriptions. Presents a catalogue of twenty-two varieties of the silver coinage of Strato I, arranged primarily by obverse types. [Summarized from A. Boyce, *NL* 13]

6341 ——— "Some Coins of Eukratides and Apollodotos from Afghanistan, c. 1840." *Numismatic Chronicle* 6th ser., 8 (1948): 103.
"The collection of the late General A. C. Haughton contained thirteen copper coins of Eukratides and eighteen of Apollodotos which it is assumed were obtained by him near Charikar. Because of their uniform appearance they are considered to have formed one small hoard, or possibly two found in similar conditions of soil." [*NL* 11]

6342 **Head, Barclay V.** "The Earliest Graeco-Bactrian and Graeco-Indian Coins." *Numismatic Chronicle* 4th ser., 6 (1906): 1-16. Reprints, London, 1916; Chicago: Argonaut, 1969. 16 pp., 2 pls. [CS 3081]
Head discusses a tetradrachm (*obv.*, head of Zeus; *rev.*, eagle) which Imhoof-Blumer believed to be the first issue of Alexander the Great struck in Macedon. Head attributes the coin to the northwestern corner of India after Alexander the Great's invasion of that region in 326 B.C. Also discusses some other coins in the British Museum collection that may have been struck in India or Bactria, including various gold double-darics, silver coins with the same obverse type, and some copies of Athenian coins. In discussing the famous "Porus" medallions, Head suggests these may have been intended as medals for presentation to

Macedonian officers rather than for use as coinage. [For more on the "Porus" medallions, see MACEDONIAN KINGDOM—ALEXANDER'S PORUS COINS/MEDALLIONS].

6343 **Hebert, Raymond J.** "A Unique Greek Coin from Afghanistan." *Indian Numismatics, History, Art, and Culture: Essays in the Honour of Dr. P. L. Gupta, Volume 1.* Agam Indological Series, No. 14. Edited by D. W. MacDowall, Savita Sharma, and Sanjay Garg. Dehli: Agam Kala Prakashan, 1992. Pages 115-7. Illus.
Publishes an apparently unique late fourth century B.C. Greek coin believed to have come from Afghanistan. It is a silver coin with *obv.*, cista; *rev.*, two owls opposed, with a common head.

6344 **Hoge, Robert W.** "Indo-Greek Errors: Two Misengraved Drachms of Menander." *The Numismatist* 108, no. 4 (April 1995): 495. Illus.
Describes two bilingual drachms of Menander attributed to the Pushkalavati mint, each featuring a different engraver's error in its Greek obverse legend. This suggests the engravers were less familiar with the Greek language than with the native language.

6345 ———. "An Original 'Nickel.'" *The Numismatist* 114, no. 5 (May 2001): 594. Illus.
Publishes a copper-nickel dichalkon of Agathokles, minted ca. 190-180 B.C. The coin represents one of the earliest uses of nickel in coinage. The Bactrian kings Euthydemos and Pantaleon also minted copper-nickel coins. The coin is an example of Bopearachchi Series 5C, nos. 8-9.

6346 **Holt, Frank L.** "The Euthydemid Coinage of Bactria: Further Hoard Evidence from Ai Khanoum." *Revue Numismatique* (France) 6th ser., 23 (1981): 7-44. 12 pls.
"A hoard from Ai Khanoum, the site of a recently excavated Hellenistic city in northeastern Afghanistan, is published. Part 1 of the article presents the details of the treasure's discovery and deposition, followed by a catalogue of 139 of the 141 Bactrian coins. In Part 2, the author examines the group's historical significance in light of recent evidence for the Euthydemid period of Bactrian history." [F. Holt, *NL* 113]

6347 ———. "Discovering the Lost History of Ancient Afghanistan: Hellenistic Bactria in Light of Recent Archaeological and Historical Research." *The Ancient World* 9, nos. 1-2 (May 1984): 2-11. Illus.
A survey of recent research in Bactrian history including archaeological discoveries, numismatic discoveries, epigraphical research (including coin inscriptions), and anthropological research.

6348 ———. "The So-Called 'Pedigree Coins' of the Bactrian Greeks." *Ancient Coins of the Graeco-Roman World: The Nickle Numismatic Papers.* Edited by Waldemar Heckel and Richard Sullivan. Waterloo, Ontario: Wilfrid Laurier University Press, 1984. Pages 69-91.
A re-examination of the "pedigree" tetradrachm series issued by Bactrian kings Antimachus and Agathocles. These coins have on the obverse the portrait of some other king whose name, in the genitive case, and epithet appear in the right and left fields, respectively. The reverses carries the type of the king being commemorated, but the legends read ΒΑΣΙΛΕΤΟΝΤΟΣ ΑΝΤΙΜΑΞΟΤ ΘΕΟΤ for the one issuing authority, and ΒΑΣΙΛΕΤΟΝΤΟΣ ΑΓΑΘΟΚΛΕΟΤΣ ΔΙΚΑΙΟΤ for the other. Holt summarizes previous research on these issues, especially the views and theories of Tarn and Narain. He mentions important new coin discoveries at Ai Khanoum and the discoveries of new commemorative types issued by Agathocles. Holt concludes that the "pedigree" coin types were a political and religious proclamation of legitimacy, not a personal pedigree. An appendix provides a catalogue of the commemorative coins issued by Antimachus (two types) and Agathocles (seven types).

6349 ———. "A History in Silver and Gold." *Saudi Aramco World* 45, no. 3 (May/June 1994): 2-13. Illus.
Discusses the lack of written sources concerning Bactrian history after the departure of Alexander the Great. Then provides an excellent review of the knowledge of Bactrian history that has been gathered from the study of coins. Also recounts the story of the discovery of the 20-stater gold coin of Eukratides, the excavation of Ai Khanoum, and the discovery of hoards, including the Oxus and Kunduz hoards.

6350 ———. "Eukratides of Bactria." *The Ancient World* 27, no. 1 (1996): 72-6. Illus.
Describes the rare gold coinage of Eukratides and urges the publication of all known specimens.

6351 ———. "The Autobiography of a Coin." *Saudi Aramco World* 48, no. 5 (September/October 1997): 10-15. Illus.
A narrative told from the point of view of a coin. A gold stater of Eukratides tells the story of its minting, being made into a ring, being lost and buried, being re-discovered in the nineteenth century, being removed from the ring and sold at auction. The coin was purchased by Col. Strutt, later purchased by Montagu, sold again by Sotheby's in 1896, purchased by Charles Seltman in 1908, purchased by E. T. Newell in 1921, and bequeathed to the American Numismatic Society in 1941.

6352 ———. "Mimesis in Metal: The Fate of Greek Culture on Bactrian Coins." *The Eye Expanded: Life and the Arts in Greco-Roman Antiquity.* Edited by F. B. Titchener and R. F. Moorton, Jr. Berkeley: University of California Press, 1999. Pages 93-104.
Comments on the challenges of engraving coin inscriptions.

6353 ———. *Thundering Zeus: The Making of Hellenistic Bactria.* Hellenistic Culture and Society 32. Berkeley and Los Angeles: University of California Press, 1999. 221 pp., map, 8 pls.
Examines the story of Diodotus I and II, Bactria's first independent Greek rulers after the death of Alexander. Intended to be a history of Bactria during the Diodotid dynasty, an introduction to Hellenistic civilization, and a numismatic handbook. Begins with the Hellenistic background of Bactria, the role of the Seleucids in Central Asia, and the spread of coinage in the East during Alexander's reign. Continues with the emerging independence of Diodotus I from the Seleucid empire. Reviews the evolutionary process that the study of Bactrian coinage underwent, beginning with the studies of Bayer in 1738. Holt explains how he put together the numismatic evidence to form his conclusions. Discusses the scarcity of Diodotid bronze coins and the use of bronze coins as historical evidence. Explains the role of bronze coins in the monetization of the East. Reviews the transition from purely Greek coin types to types representing local culture. Holt continues the historical survey with the tribal invasions of Bactria and the eventual domination by Rome. Includes four appendices: (1) a catalogue of Diodotid coinage in silver and Gold, (2) a catalogue of Diodotid coinage in bronze, (3) a listing of some Diodotid gold forgeries, and (4) English translations of the main ancient texts related to Bactrian history. Concludes with a bibliography.

6354 ———. "Did King Euthydemus II Really Exist? *Numismatic Chronicle* 160 (2000): 81-91. 1 pl.

"The author addresses the renewed controversy in Bactrian studies regarding the possible existence of a second Euthydemus. A close examination of coin-types, portraiture, monograms, die-axes, metrology, and hoards verifies the reign of Euthydemus as a successor of Euthydemus I and Demetrius I, and a near-contemporary of Pantaleon and Agathokles." [F. Holt, *NL* 145]

6355 **International Nickel Company.** "Nickel in the Numismatic Arts." *The Numismatist* 124, no. 2 (February 2011): 57-9. Illus.
A survey of the use of nickel in coinage throughout history. Includes mention of copper-nickel coins minted in the Kingdom of Bactria, perhaps as early as 253 B.C. and certainly during the reigns of the Bactrian kings Euthydemus II, Pantaleon, and Agathokles.

6356 **Jakobsson, Jens.** "Relations between the Indo-Greek Kings after Menander, Part 1." *Journal of the Oriental Numismatic Society* 191 (2007): 25-7.

6357 ———— "The Greeks of Afghanistan Revisited." *Nomismatika Khronika* (Greece) 26 (2007): 51-88. Illus.
A review of the kings of Bactria and their coinage. Jakobsson attempts to unravel the confusing sequence of kings and their chronology, and suggests new possible reconstructions. He argues that royal epithets and deities were often inherited. In English on pp. 51-70 and in Greek on pp. 71-88.

6358 ———— "Antiochus Nicator, the Third King of Bactria?" *Numismatic Chronicle* 170 (2010): 17-33. Illus.
The kingdom of Bactria became independent from the Seleucid Empire in ca. 250 B.C. Its first kings were Diodotus I and II. The coins traditionally attributed to these two kings bear the legend "of king Diodotus" or "of king Antiochus." The latter have generally been interpreted as the first issues of Diodotus I, before he made himself entirely independent. An alternative would be that a third member of the dynasty, by the name of Antiochus, struck these coins. This king would be identical with the "Antiochus Nicator" commemorated by the later Bactrian king Agathocles. The author criticizes the established interpretation, and tentatively attempts to show that the numismatic analysis of F. L. Holt can be rearranged to accommodate the existence of a king Antiochus Nicator.

6359 ———— "A Possible New Indo-Greek King Zoilos III, and an Analysis of Realism on Indo-Greek Royal Portraits." *Numismatic Chronicle* 170 (2010): 35-51. Illus.
The author argues that the coins attributed to the Indo-Greek king Zoilos II Soter may belong to two separate kings, proposes some changes in the chronology of the period, and tentatively places the last Indo-Greek kings in a dynastic framework. This thesis is to some extent based on differences between coin portraits, and the interpretation of royal portraits is discussed in Appendix I. Appendix II contains a general analysis of when Indo-Greek coinage issued under one name should be attributed to more than one king; hitherto the preference has been to keep the number of kings to a minimum.

6360 **Jenkins, G. Kenneth.** "Azes and Taxila." *Congrès International de Numismatique, Paris, 6-11 Juillet 1953, Volume 2.* Paris: Commission International de Numismatique, 1957. Pages 123-30. [CS 3082]
Discusses the classification of the coins of the Saka kings of Northwest India, especially those struck in the name of Azes. Discusses evidence from coin finds at Taxila and points out distinguishing characteristics between the coins of Azes I and Azes II.

6361 ———— "The Apollodotus Question: Another View." *Journal of the Numismatic Society of India* (India) 21, pt. 1 (1959): 20-33.
"A reply to the view expressed by Narain (see Narain "Apollodotus" below) that there was only one king named Apollodotus and probably three named Eucratides. Jenkins finds the evidence used by Narain in identifying some of the monograms on the coins of Apollodotus I with Hermaeus and Antalciades is not acceptable. Furthermore, finds of copper coins of Apollodotus I from Afghanistan, Begram, Mir Zakah and Charikar include chiefly the types given to this ruler, while those from Spinawarai, Taxila and Sialkot contain mostly the types assigned to Apollodotus II. The majority of the coins of Apollodotus I thus derive from Afghanistan, those of Apollodotus II from the territory east of the Indus. From these indications, Apollodotus I would appear to be contemporary with Menander, while Apollodotus II, on the other hand, should probably be assigned to the first century B.C." [I. Merker, *NL* 50]

6362 ———— "A Group of Bactrian Forgeries." *Revue Numismatique* (France) 6th ser., 7 (1965): 51-7. 1 pl. [CS 3083 and CS 3596]
"A group of Bactrian coins linked by identical dies are described. Certain of them have been accepted as authentic; isolated, some of them give a good impression. But the completely die-linked group also contains many specimens which cannot in any case be authentic. It is therefore concluded that the group as a whole is forged. A whole series of coins of Antiochus I, Antiochus II and Diodotus are thereby condemned." [G. Le Rider, *NL* 81]. [Also see Noble "Three Bactrian Forgeries" below for related forgeries].

6363 ———— "Indo-Greek Tetradrachms." *British Museum Quarterly* 32 (1967-68): 108-12. 1 pl.
Describes some purely Greek-style and Greek-inscribed later Bactrian coins recently acquired by the British Museum. Includes tetradrachms of Menander, Antialkidas, Archebios, and Theophilos. Discusses some questions regarding the historical interpretation of the coins.

6364 ———— "Some Recent Indo-Greek Accessions of the British Museum." *Journal of the Numismatic Society of India* (India) 30 (1968): 23-7. 1 pl.
"Some recent accessions of Indo-Greek tetradrachms of the British Museum are described and the problems related to them discussed. The coins were issued by Menander, Lysias, Theophilus and Archebius." [A. Narain, *NL* 83]

6365 ———— "Some Indo-Greek Tetradrachms." *Journal of the Numismatic Society of India* (India) 35 (1973): 78-81. Illus.
"Three Indo-Greek tetradrachms recently acquired by the British Museum are described. One relates to Philoxenus and is the only specimen of its kind published. It is suggested on the basis of this coin that Philoxenus ruled in Alexandria ad Caucasum. The other two coins are issues of Archebius and are overstrikes. A close study of these coins shows that Peucolaus was the predecessor of Archebius." [P. Gupta, *NL* 94]

6366 **Jha, Amiteshwar.** "Coins of Menander in the Collections of the Patna Museum and Asiatic Society of Bombay: A Die Study." *Ex Moneta: Essays on Numismatics, History and Archaeology in Honour of Dr. David W. MacDowall, Volume 1.* Edited by Amal Kumar Jha and Sanjay Garg. New Delhi: Harman Publishing House, 1998. Pages 81-92. Illus.
A die-link analysis and die-count analysis of the coins of Menander from two collections.

6367 **Kala, Satish Chandra.** "A Rude Imitation Coin of Heliokles." *Journal of the Numismatic Society of India* (India) 9 (1947): 26-7. 1 pl.
"The coin described is in the collection of the Museum at Pauri, Garhwal district, and was found during the excavation of Dharmarajika Stupa at Taxila. The piece is a Scythian imitation." [*NL* 6]

6368 **Kirkpatrick, C.** "Three Rare Indo-Greek Coins." *Journal of the Numismatic Society of India* (India) 34 (1972): 65-7.
"A hitherto unknown small bronze of Euthydemus I, a rare coin of Heliocles, and one of Amyntas are described." [P. Gupta, *NL* 91]

6369 ——— "A New Coin Type of Eucratides I." *Spink Numismatic Circular* 81, no. 1 (January 1973): 6. Illus.
The author publishes two new obols which present novel features. The obverse shows a bust of Eucratides facing right wearing a medusa helmet. The reverse depicts Herakles standing facing, crowning himself with his right hand and holding a club and lion skin in his left. Kirkpatrick tentatively assigns the coins to Eucratides I rather than Eucratides II.

6370 ——— "Some New Coins of Sophytes." *Spink Numismatic Circular* 81, no. 10 (October 1973): 372-3. Illus.
Publishes four fractional coins of Sophytes (*obv.*, king's head r., or Athena's head r.; *rev.*, cock standing r.). The author suggests Sophytes was a Bactrian king, not an Indian ruler. Lists the twenty known coins of this king. [Also see articles by Bopearachichi, Cunningham, G. Macdonald, and Whitehead].

6371 ——— "Some New Barbarous Coins of Eucratides I of *Lahiri* Type 21." *Spink Numismatic Circular* 81, no. 11 (November 1973): 423. Illus.
Illustrates three bronze coins similar to *Lahiri* No. 21 (see Lahiri *Corpus of Indo-Greek Coins* below). Lahiri's listing suggests he regarded the coin as an official issue. Kirkpatrick suggests these are not official issues but, rather, imitations made either during or shortly after Eucratides' reign. The "palm behind head" in Lahiri's description is identified by Kirkpatrick as a barbarous rendering of the plume on the king's helmet.

6372 ——— "Heliocles II, Fact or Fiction?" *Spink Numismatic Circular* 83, no. 3 (March 1975): 98-9. Illus.
Summarizes the views of other scholars on whether a second king named Heliocles existed. Discusses the evidence provided by coins of Heliocles overstruck on coins of Strato and suggests this as evidence of a second Heliocles. Illustrates a bilingual bronze coin of Heliocles overstruck on a coin of Antialcidas. Suggests a later date than is commonly assumed for the reign of Antialcidas. Kirkpatrick tentatively concludes that the monolingual coins were struck by Heliocles I in Bactria, and the bilingual coins were struck by Heliocles II in India.

6373 **Kozolubski, Julius.** "Bactrian and Indo-Greek Coinage." *Seaby Coin and Medal Bulletin* 415 (December 1952): 502-3; "Chapter 22." 428 (January 1954): 2-5; "Chapter 22 (cont'd)." 429 (February 1954): 45-9; "Chapter 27." 443 (April 1955): 137-40.
Examines the Bactrian and Indo-Greek coinage, ruler-by-ruler, providing a catalogue of types and extensive historical and numismatic commentary.

6374 **Kraay, Colin M.** "Demetrius in Bactria and India." *Quaderni Ticinesi: Numismatica e Antichità Classiche* (Switzerland) (1981): 219-33. Reprinted in *Numismatic Digest* (India) 9 (1985): 12-30. Illus.
"Indo-Greek coins bearing the name of Demetrius are examined exhaustively. The author concludes that the tetradrachm and drachm that bear the epithet Anaketoy for King Demetrius, hitherto attributed by the scholars to either Demetrius I or II, were issued by a third Demetrius. This Demetrius was a ruler in India who had nothing to do with Bactria." [P. Gupta, *NL* 116]

6375 **Kritt, Brian.** *Dynastic Transitions in the Coinage of Bactria: Antiochus—Diodotus—Euthydemus.* Classical Numismatic Studies, No. 4. Lancaster: Classical Numismatic Group, 2001. 207 pp., illus.
Presents attributions for the bronze coinages struck in Bactria to the end of the third century B.C., and a discussion of the attribution of the coinages, into the reign of Euthydemus. Utilizes new archaeological evidence to study the circulation and diffusion patterns of bronze coins from Bactrian mints of the third century, providing important new information for mint identification. Includes new attributions and chronologies for most of the third century coinages of post-Seleucid Bactria. The locations and function of the bronze mints have been established. Explores the transitions between the three Bactrian dynasties of the third century. Presents a newly discovered coinage of Antiochus III in Bactria. [Reviewed in *The Celator* 15, no. 6 (June 2001): 37].

6376 **Lahiri, Amarendra Nash.** "Coins of Queen Agathocleia and the Attribution of the Legendless Indo-Greek Staters." *Journal of the Numismatic Society of India* (India) 16, pt. 2 (1954): 189-96. 1 pl.
Recounts the career of Agathocleia, wife of Menander, who ruled as queen after her husband's death. She ruled on behalf of her minor son Strato until he was old enough to rule on his own. Some of her coins depict Agathocleia in the guise of Athena. Includes a list of her coins.

6377 ——— "The Diodotus Coins." *Indian Historical Quarterly* (India) 33, no. 3 (September 1957): 222-8.
A survey of the coinage attributed to Diodotus I and II. Attempts to determine which king struck the coins. Lahiri is critical of Narain's treatment of the Diodotid coins. Concludes that all coins bearing the legend *Basileos Diodotou* were the issues of one and the same king—Diodotus I.

6378 ——— "The Case for a Second Menander." *Journal of the Numismatic Society of India* (India) 20, pt. 1 (1958): 71-3. Illus.
"It has generally been held that coins with the epithet ΔΙΚΑΙΟΣ were struck by Menander Soter in his last years, at which time his interests inclined toward Buddhism. The author, nevertheless, gives various reasons for believing that they were issued by a second Menander, who might or might not have been the missing son of Strato I or the father of Strato II." [*NL* 48]. [Also see H. Prasad "No Two Menanders" below for another opinion].

6379 ——— *Corpus of Indo-Greek Coins.* Calcutta: Poddar Publications, 1965. 287 pp., 34 pls. [CS 3119]
A corpus of almost all the coin types of the Greek rulers of Bactria and India. The introduction covers the history of the study of Greek coins in Bactria and India, the importance of the coins, artistic merits of the coins, weights, metals, methods of striking, types, special issues, language, scripts, legends, monograms, and forgeries. Includes a summary of the views of various scholars on the meanings of the monograms found on the coins. Appendices list coin types, monograms, kings, titles and epithets of Indo-Greek rulers, and the problems of the attributions of coins bearing royal names. [Comments from C. Panish, *NL* 78: "A number of weaknesses are evident: e.g., coin sizes and weights are seldom given, the Karoshthi legends have been Romanized, there is a complete absence of chronology, and no attempt has been made to show either genealogic or geographic relations. Moreover, no reference is made to the Indo-Scythians or Indo-Parthians, although their coins logically form part of the Indo-Greek series." Reviewed by H. De S. Shortt in *Numismatic Chronicle* 7th ser., 6 (1966): 350-1].

6380 ——— "Metrology of the Indo-Greek Silver Coins." *Journal of Ancient Indian History* (India) 1 (1967-8): 52-64. [CS 3120]
Summarizes the views of other researchers regarding the weight-standard used by the Indo-Greek kings. Suggests a new standard was developed, based on the Indian weight-systems. Discusses the use of this standard by various rulers and its area and period of use.

6381 ——— "The Indo-Greek Standard and Its Impact on Successive Indian Coins." *Journal of the Numismatic Society of India* (India) 31, pt. 2 (1969): 113-21.
"The bilingual silver coins of the Indo-Greeks were struck on an indigenous standard for the drachm, equal to 20 rattis or 2.33 gm., which differed from the Persian and Attic standards which preceded it. This new drachm standard also largely superseded the earlier Indian standard for the punch-marked karshapana, which weighed 32 rattis or 3.73 gm. The 20-ratti standard, starting about 160 B.C., prevailed in northern India for nearly 1000 years thereafter." [C. Panish, *NL* 87]

6382 ——— "The So-called Joint Coins of the Indo-Greeks." *Journal of the Numismatic Society of India* (India) 39 (1977): 69-76.
"The Indo-Greek issues of Strato-Agathocleia, Hermaeus-Calliope, and two Stratos are discussed. Strato was the husband of Agathocleia, not her son. Calliope was the daughter of the reigning sovereign and his marriage with Hermaeus had political significance; the coins commemorate the marriage. The third issue is attributed to Strato II and III, not Strato I and II." [P. Gupta, *NL* 103]

6383 **Lassen, Christian.** "Points in the History of the Greek, and Indo-Scythian Kings of Bactria, Cabul and India, as Illustrated by Deciphering the Ancient Legends on Their Coins." *Journal and Proceedings of the Asiatic Society of Bengal* (India) (1840): 251 ff. Translated by T. H. E. Röer. Reprinted as *Greek and Indo-Scythian Kings and Their Coins*. Delhi: Indological House, 1972. 185 pp. [CS 3085]
A translated reprint of the treatise originally published in Bonn in 1838. Seeks to decipher the alphabet used in coin legends, and to define the language of the native words on the coins.

6384 **Lemburg-Ruppelt, Edith.** "Zur Ikonographie eines Münzportraits des Eukratides I von Baktrien." *Proceedings of the Fourth International Numismatic Congress in Croatia, September 20-25, 2004. Stari Grad (Pharos), the Island of Hvar and M/S Marko Polo, Croatia.* Edited by Julijan Dobrinic. Rijeka: Dobrinic & Dobrinic, 2005.
Examines the transmission of Bactrian heroic iconography from the Bactrian coinage of Eukratides I and Archebius to Macedonia and Roman cameos of the second and first centuries B.C./A.D.

6385 **MacDonald, David J.** "A Problematic Indo-Greek Overstrike." *Oriental Numismatic Society Newsletter* 150 (1996): 11.
In the catalogue for Classical Numismatic Group's *Auction 38* (June 1996), lot 528 is catalogued as a bronze hemiobol of Heliokles II struck over a coin of Polyxenos. MacDonald has determined it was actually struck over a coin of Agathokleia with Strato I.

6386 ——— "The First and Second Heliocles II/Hermaios Overstrikes." *Oriental Numismatic Society Newsletter* 163 (spring 2000): 22-1.

6387 **MacDonald, David J., and Robert C. Senior.** "The Rectangular Copper/Bronzes of Antimachos." *Numismatic Studies* (India) 5. Edited by M. Kumar. New Delhi, 1997.

6388 **Macdonald, George.** "Athenian and Macedonian Coins in India." *The Cambridge History of India. Volume 1: Ancient India.* Edited by E. J. Rapson. New York: Macmillan, 1922. Pages 386-90. 1 pl.
Macdonald discusses the use of Athenian owl imitations in India. Mentions the coins inscribed ΣΟΦΥΤΟΥ, attributed to Sophytes, and the famous "Porus" decadrachm of Alexander the Great. Also discusses the finds of gold double darics, probably minted at Babylon. [For more on the Sophytes coins, see articles by Bopearachichi and Cunningham above, and Kirkpatrick and Whitehead below].

6389 **MacDowall, David W.** "The Dynasty of the Later Indo-Parthians." *Numismatic Chronicle* 7th ser., 5 (1965): 137-48. 1 pl. [CS 3024]
An analysis of the later Indo-Parthian coinage in Arachosia and Seistan provides clear evidence of the sequence of most of the kings, and provides information on the chronology of their reigns.

6390 ——— "The Copper Denominations of Menander." *Acta Iranica* 5 (Monumentum Nyberg II) (The Netherlands) (1975): 39-52.

6391 ——— "Ancient India." *Coins: An Illustrated Survey 650 B.C. to the Present Day.* Edited by M. J. Price. New York: Methuen, 1980. Pages 278-85. Illus.
An overview of the ancient coinage of India including the earliest native Indian coinage, the coinage of the Indo-Greek kings, the Indo-Scythians, the Indo-Parthians, the Kushans, and the Guptas. Heavily illustrated by photographs of the main coin types.

6392 ——— "Indo-Greek and Kushana Coins in the Magyar Nemzeti Múzeum, Budapest." *Numizmatikai Közlöny* (Hungary) 84-85 (1985-86): 3-11.

6393 ——— "The Impact of Alexander the Great on the Coinages of Afghanistan and NW India." *Numismatic Digest* (India) 11 (December 1987): 5-12. Illus.
Discusses the currency of the eastern Achaemenid satrapies which was primarily silver in various forms which was accepted as bullion. MacDowall then examines the monetary changes made by Alexander the Great—the institution of a universal coinage and the choice of a weight standard. Follows the impact of his innovations on later Graeco-Bactrian and Indo-Greek coinages.

6394 ——— "Experimentations in the Coinage of Apollodotus I." *Ratna Chandrika, Panorama of Oriental Studies.* Shri R. C. Agrawala Festschrift. Edited by D. Handa and A. Agrawal. New Delhi: Harmon Publishing House, 1989. Pages 47-55.
Examines the coins of Apollodotus I including their monograms, mints, and metrology. The coinage shows an interesting range of experimentation to ensure the acceptability of his new coinage in territories that had previously used punch-marked silver.

6395 ——— "The Hazrajat Hoard of Indo-Greek Silver Drachms." *Pakistan Archaeology* (Pakistan) 26 (1991): 188-98.
A study based on 120 silver drachms of Menander (*IGCH* 1842). The hoard was found in Afghanistan (not Pakistan) in or before 1831. Discusses the sequence of Menander's drachms and the monograms appearing on the coins. Includes a catalogue of the hoard coins.

6396 ———— "The Geographical Distribution of Monograms on the Coinage of Menander and Antimachus Nikephorus." *Indian Numismatics, History, Art, and Culture: Essays in the Honour of Dr. P. L. Gupta, Volume 1*. Agam Indological Series, No. 14. Edited by D. W. MacDowall, Savita Sharma, and Sanjay Garg. Dehli: Agam Kala Prakashan, 1992. Pages 119-29.
Attempts to establish the geographical distribution in hoards and site finds of the monograms appearing on coins of Antimachus Nikephorus and Menander. Suggests that one of the monograms represents the name of the city of Charsadda—the principal mint for Menander's silver drachms and copper denominations. Suggests that the use of monograms changes over time—sometimes they represent mint-masters or city magistrates, other times they become fossilized and misunderstood. One explanation may not be valid for all coin series. [Also see Dani "Greek Monograms" above].

6396a ———— "The Weight of the Graeco-Bactrian Chalkous." *XIII Congreso Internacional de Numismática, Madrid – 2003: Actas–Proceedings–Actes I*. Edited by Carmen Alfaro, Carmen Marcos, and Paloma Otero. Madrid: International Numismatic Commisson, 2005. Pages 345-8.
Discusses the weights and denominations of Graeco-Bactrian bronze coins, some of which bear marks of value. While the term 'chalkous' came to denote any copper or bronze coin in general, by the time of Antiochus IV it refered to a particular Seleucid denomination—the bronze coin that normally weighed about 4 grams.

6396b ———— "The Sequence of Menander's Copper Coinages." *Journal of Inner Asian Art and Archaeology* 1, no. 1 (2006): 60-4.

6397 **Mackenzie, Kenneth M.** "Letter Provides a Glimpse of the Past." *The Celator* 9, no. 5 (May 1995): 32. Illus.
The author found a letter from Alexander Cunningham inside a book. The text of the letter is presented, in which Cunningham identifies a Bactrian coin for a friend. [Also see comments in M. Cole's "Letter to the Editor" in *The Celator* (June 1995): 42].

6398 **Martin, M. F. C.** "A Find of Indo-Greek Hemidrachms in Bajaur." *Journal of the Asiatic Society of Bengal, Numismatic Supplement* 40 (1926-7): 18-25. [Supplement to *Journal of the Asiatic Society of Bengal* (India) new ser., 23 (1927)].
Discusses a find of approximately 1200 hemidrachms in 1926, primarily of Apollodotus, Antimachos Nikephorus, and Menander. Includes a brief discussion, a list of varieties, and some comments on the monograms found on the coins.

6399 **Masson, Charles.** "Memoir on the Ancient Coins Found at Beghrám, in the Kohistán of Kabul." *Journal of the Asiatic Society of Bengal* (India) 3 (1834): 153-75. 6 pls.
Lists and describes coins found by the author in India in 1833. Illustrated by engraved plates.

6400 ———— "Second Memoir on the Ancient Coins Found at Beghrám, in the Kohistân of Kábul." *Journal of the Asiatic Society of Bengal* (India) 5 (1836): 1-28. 3 pls.
Lists and describes coins found by the author in India. Illustrated by engraved plates.

6401 ———— "Third Memoir on the Ancient Coins Discovered at the Site Called Beghrám in the Kohistán of Kabul." *Journal of the Asiatic Society of Bengal* (India) 5 (1836): 537-47.
Lists and describes coins found by the author in 1833-35. [For illustrations, see J. Prinsep "New Varieties of Bactrian Coins" below].

6402 **Mielczarek, Mariusz.** "Some Remarks about the Coinage of Euthydemus I and Demetrius, Kings of Bactria." *Proceedings of the 11th International Numismatic Congress, September 8-13, 1991, Volume 1*. Edited by T. Hackens et al. Louvain-la-Neuve, Belgium: International Association of Professional Numismatists, 1993. Pages 299-303. Illus.
The author examines the monograms and control marks on Bactrian coins to find out what conclusions can be drawn about the early Bactrian kings. Focuses on coins bearing the names of Euthydemus I and Demetrius.

6403 **Mitchiner, Michael B.** *Indo-Greek and Indo-Scythian Coinage*. 9 volumes. London: Hawkins Publications, 1975-76. [CS 3124]
Covers the coinage of Afghanistan and Pakistan between the introduction of Greek culture by Alexander the Great in 330 B.C. and the foundation of the Sasanian empire in A.D. 226. Includes over 10,000 coins in nine volumes:

1. *The Early Indo-Greeks and Their Antecedents. Alexander the Great; the Satraps of Egypt, Babylon, Ecbatana, Bactra and Kapisa; the Seleucids: ca. 330-150 B.C.* 1975. 133 pp.
2. *The Apogee of the Indo-Greeks; ca. 160 to 120 B.C.* 1975. 99 pp.
3. *The Decline of the Indo-Greeks: circa 130 to 0 B.C.* 1975. 99 pp.
4. *Contemporaries of the Indo-Greeks: Mints, Coins, Denominations and Forgeries.* 1975. 108 pp.
5. *Establishment of the Scythians in Afghanistan and Pakistan.* 1976. 90 pp.
6. *The Dynasty of Azes, circa 60 to 1 B.C.* 1976. 115 pp.
7. *The Decline of the Indo-Scythians. The Contemporaries of the Indo-Scythians.* 1976. 92 pp.
8. *The Indo-Parthians: Their Kushan Neighbors.* 1976. 108 pp.
9. *Greeks, Sakas and Their Contemporaries in Central and Southern India.* 1976. 139 pp.

6404 **Mohan, Mehta Vasishtha Dev.** *The Indo-Greek Coins*. Ludhiana: Indological Research Institute, 1967. 196 pp., 7 pls. [CS 3125]
Reviews the work of previous scholars. Presents a broad introduction to Indo-Greek numismatics. Discusses denominations, shapes, metals, legends, and portraits. Includes chapters on divinities, monograms, the determination of dates, family affiliations and joint issues, and the propaganda or "pedigree" series. Concludes with an appendix on divinities, alphabetically arranged, describing the attributes of each. [Reviewed by A. D. H. Bivar in *Numismatic Chronicle* 7th ser., 9 (1969): 354-5].

6405 **Moss, A. A.** "The Origin of the Nickel Alloy Used for Bactrian Coins (c. 200 B.C.)." *Numismatic Chronicle* 6th ser., 10 (1950): 317-8. [CS 3403]
Moss disputes Rapson's assertion that some Bactrian coins were struck in an alloy with a high proportion of nickel. He also disputes Khan's assertion that the nickel used in Bactrian coins came from a meteorite. Rather, it came from copper-nickel ore which was known to exist in China and Persia.

6406 **Mukherjee, Bratindra Nath.** "The Location of a Mint of the Azes Dynasty." *Numismatic Chronicle* 7th ser., 5 (1965): 109-12. 1 pl.
"On the basis of the Kharoshthi inscriptions on a gold half-stater or medal now in the British Museum, it is concluded that the Azes group of Indo-Scythian rulers of northwest India operated a mint at the city of Pushkalavati (near Charsadda in West Pakistan)." [C. Panish, *NL* 84]

6407 ——— "Some Observations of the Metrology of the Indo-Greek and Scytho-Parthian Coins." *Journal of the Numismatic Society of India* (India) 32, pt. 2 (1970): 144-9. [CS 3127]
A brief discussion of the weight standards used by the Greek kings in India. It appears that the Indo-Greeks introduced a sort of Hellenic-Persian standard in Northwestern India.

6408 ——— "The Location of the Mint of Some Indo-Parthian Coins." *Journal of the Numismatic Society of India* (India) 33 (1971): 110-1.
"Seistan is identified as the mint of some of the copper and billon coins of Gondophares, which bear a Greek legend only and show *obv.*, seated figure, and *rev.*, winged Nike." [P. Gupta, *NL* 94]

6409 ——— *A Plea for Study of Art in Coinage.* Numismatic Notes and Monographs, No. 19. Varanasi: The Numismatic Society of India, 1983. 53 pp., 9 pls.
Examines the stylistic features of coinage struck by non-Indian rulers for circulation in the Indian subcontinent and/or its borderlands during the centuries immediately before and after the beginning of the Christian era.

6410 **Narain, Awadk K.** "The Coin-Types of the Indo-Greek Kings." *Journal of the Numismatic Society of India* (India) 16, pt. 2 (1954): 293-331.
Lists the coin types of the Indo-Greek kings of Afghanistan and India, with short descriptions. [This article was reprinted as a monograph in 1955. See *The Coins of the Indo-Greeks* below].

6411 ——— "Some New Attic Tetradrachms of the Indo-Greeks." *Journal of the Numismatic Society of India* (India) 16, pt. 2 (1954): 183-8. 2 pls.
Describes fourteen newly discovered Attic-weight tetradrachms of the Indo-Greeks found in the Qunduz Treasure and elsewhere. The coins are attributed to Agathocles, Plato, Lysias, Theophilus, Antialcidas, Archebius, Philoxenus, and Hermaeus.

6412 ——— *The Coins of the Indo-Greek Kings.* Numismatic Notes and Monographs, No. 1. Bombay: Numismatic Society of India, 1955. Reprinted as *The Coin Types of the Indo-Greek Kings, 256-54 B.C.* Chicago: Argonaut, 1968. 37 pp. [CS 3129]
Lists the main coin types of the Indo-Greek kings of Afghanistan and India with short descriptions. Reign dates and inscriptions are listed. No illustrations are included. [Originally published in *Journal of the Numismatic Society of India* in 1954. See above].

6413 ——— "The Twenty Stater Gold Piece of Eucratides I." *Journal of the Numismatic Society of India* (India) 18, pt. 2 (1956): 217-8. 1 pl.
"The coin is described, and the story of its acquisition by the French briefly sketched with reference to an article in the *American Journal of Numismatics* 14, no. 1 (July 1879): 18-20)." [*NL* 45]. [See "Coin of Eucratides" above. Also see S. Narain "The Twenty-Stater Gold Piece" below].

6414 ——— "Apollodotus and His Coins." *Journal of the Numismatic Society of India* (India) 19, pt. 2 (1957): 121-34. 1 pl. [CS 3086]
Narain re-examines the coinage of Apollodotus. He concludes there are no grounds for the existence of two kings named Apollodotus as suggested by Gardner and Tarn. Examines the evidence for the reign of Apollodotus and suggests there was no Apollodotus I before the reign of Eucratides I.

6415 ——— *The Indo-Greeks.* Oxford: Clarendon Press, 1957. 201 pp., 6 pls. 4 maps. [CS 3130]
Narain's Ph.D. thesis is a highly regarded reconstruction of the political history of the Indo-Greeks, making frequent use of numismatic evidence, but also strengthened by an analysis of the literary sources. Lists the rulers and their coin types, monograms, and legends. Several coins are illustrated. [Reviewed by G. K. Jenkins in *Numismatic Chronicle* 6th ser., 17 (1957): 266-9].

6416 ——— "The Two Hindu Divinities on the Coins of Agathocles from Aï Khanoum." *Journal of the Numismatic Society of India* (India) 35 (1973): 73-7. 1 pl.
Discusses six rectangular bronze coins issued by the Indo-Greek king Agathokles, who reigned ca. 180-165 B.C. The obverse of the coins bears two masculine personages standing to front, identically dressed in an Indian *pagne* and *chale*. P. Bernard has identified these as the Indian divinities Vishnu and Siva. If this is correct, these are the earliest anthropomorphic representations of these divinities, and perhaps the first example of syncretism in art and religion arising out of the encounter of India with the Yavanas. However, Narain suggests some other possibilities for the identification of the figures. He suggests Vasudeva (Krishna) or the Buddha, and Balarama.

6417 ——— "Ganesa on Hermaeus' Coin." *Numismatic Digest* (India) 6 (1982): 26-9. Illus.
"On a coin of the Indo-Greek ruler Hermaeus, housed in the British Museum, the author noticed a male deity with an elephant's head. He identifies him as the Hindu deity Ganesa and comments on his origin. This paper was originally published in *Senart Paranivitana Commemoration Volume* (Leiden 1978)." [P. Gupta, *NL* 113]. [Also see J. Cribb "The Earliest Ganesa" above].

6418 ——— "The Greek Monogram ΔO and Ai-Khanum—The Bactrian Greek City." *Numismatic Digest* (India) 10 (1986): 4-15. Illus.
"Certain inscribed bricks found during the excavations at Ai-Khanum depict a monogram of a circle within which is a triangle on whose base is a semicircle. In connection with this symbol, certain monograms on Greek coins are discussed. The author suggests that the coins were minted at Ai-Khanum, known then as Dionysopolis or Diodoleica, founded ca. 300-275 B.C." [P. Gupta, *NL* 118]

6419 ——— "Iconographic Origins of Ganesa and the Evidence of the Indo-Greek Coinage." *Orientalia Iosephi Tucci Memoriae Dicata.* ISMEO, Serie Orientale Roma, LVI, 3. Edited by G. Gnoli and L. Lanciotti. Rome, 1988. Pages 1007-19.

6420 **Narain, Sudha.** "The Twenty-Stater Gold Piece of Eucratides I." *Journal of the Numismatic Society of India* (India) 18, pt. 2 (1956): 217-8. 1 pl.

A photograph of the unique coin in the Bibliothèque Nationale, Paris. Provides a brief account of the coin's discovery. [Also see A. Narain "The Twenty Stater Gold Piece" above].

6421 **Nicolet-Pierre, Hélène, and Michel Amandry.** "Un Nouveau Trésor de Monnaies d'Argent Pseudo-Atheniennes venu d'Afghanistan (1990)." *Revue Numismatique* (France) 6th ser., 36 (1994): 34-54. 4 pls.
A lot comprising sixty-five pseudo-Athenian silver coins came onto the market from Afghanistan in 1990 and a selection was acquired by the Cabinet des Médailles (Paris). They extend our knowledge of the irregular issues of coinage in central Asia prior to the major royal coinages of Hellenistic Bactria.

6422 **Noble, W. J.** "Three Bactrian Forgeries." *Report of the Australian Numismatic Society* (Australia) (April 1972): 164-7, 171. Illus.
"Three nineteenth century forgeries of gold staters of Antiochus II, Diodotus and Euthydemus I are closely linked to those described by G. K. Jenkins in *Revue Numismatique* (France) 6th ser., 7 (1965)." [C. Pitchfork, *NL* 89]. [See Jenkins "A Group of Bactrian Forgeries" above].

6423 **Oikonomides, Al N.** "The Gold Coinage of the Indo-Greek King Eucratides I (171-155 B.C.)." *North American Journal of Numismatics* 7, no. 6 (1968): 180-3. Illus. [CS 3087]
Briefly re-examines the rare gold issues of Eucratides I. Lists all the known types the present locations of the few known specimens.

6424 ——— "Soter the Great, the Last of the Indo-Greek Kings." *North American Journal of Numismatics* 8, no. 1 (January 1969): 7-13. Also appeared in *Journal of the Numismatic Society of India* (India) 35 (1973): 82-9.
Deals with the epigraphy of the coinage of Soter Megas. Examines the inscriptions ΗΕΡΜΑΙΟΣ and ΣΤΗΡΟΣΣΥ on Indo-Greek coins. Discusses the problems of translation.

6425 ——— "Eukratides Wears Helmet of Boetians." *Coin World* (October 27, 1982): 31, 34, 47. Illus.
Identifies the helmet worn by Eukratides in his coin portraits as the helmet of the Thessalian units of Alexander's cavalry. Discusses the symbolism of the horn and horse's ear trim on the helmet, identifying it as a reference to Bucephalus, the famed horse of Alexander the Great. Summarizes what is known of the reign of Eukratides and discusses his little-known gold coins.

6426 ——— "Eukratides the Great and Hellenistic Bactria." *The Ancient World* 9, nos. 1-2 (May 1984): 29-34. Illus.
Points out the knowledge that can be gained from an examination of the symbolism of various elements of Eukratides' portrait coins: the Boeotian helmet, his diadem, and the frontlet with his special badge (a horse's ear and a short horn) attached to the helmet The ear may refer to Alexander's horse Bucephalus. Discusses the gold coins of Eukratides and mentions the existence of a 30 mm gold coin listed in a 1953 auction catalogue. Discusses the dates of Eukratides' reign.

6427 ——— "A Little Known Poem by C. P. Cavafy: Coins with Indian Inscriptions." *The Ancient World* 9, nos. 1-2 (May 1984): 35-7. Illus.
A translation of the poem "Coins with Indian Inscriptions" by the modern Greek poet Constantine P. Cavafy (1863-1933). Includes line drawings of appropriate Indo-Greek coins and commentary on the poet's meanings and intentions.

6428 ——— "Mercenary Armies and Commanders in the Graeco-Bactrian Empire." *The Ancient World* 15, nos. 1-2 (winter 1987): 17-9. Illus.
Illustrates a silver drachm of Demetrius I with the king's portrait defaced by the countermark of the mercenary general *Phar[...]*. Illustrates an obol of Pabes, a mercenary general who may have been in the service of Eukratides. Discusses coins of other mercenary commanders in Bactria including Sapadivizes and Agesiles.

6429 **Pandey, Deena Bandhu.** "Notes on Indo-Greek Coins." *Journal of the Numismatic Society of India* (India) 28 (1966): 198-200.
"In the first note, coins of two Diodoti, with the name of Antiochus II, which were not issued by independent rulers are discussed. In the second note, coins with reverse legend 'Hiranasame' and obverse legend 'agathukreyasa' are discussed." [P. Gupta, *NL* 87]

6430 **Pieper, Wilfried.** "The Beauty of the 'Tribal' Coinages of Ancient India." *The Celator* 9, no. 4 (April 1995): 30-3. Illus., map.
A review of the native coinages of India.

6431 ——— "Euthydemus I, King of Bactria: A Portrait Raises Questions." *The Celator* 12, no. 6 (June 1998): 36-8. Illus.
Illustrates a tetradrachm of Euthydemus I, King of Bactria 230-200 B.C. Presents a brief history of Bactria and of the reign of Euthydemus. Describes the coin. Bopearachchi dates the coin to late in the reign of the king (*Monnais Gréco-Bactriennes et Indo-Grecques*, Paris, 1991). However, Pieper points out that the portrait is of a young man, suggesting that the coin belongs to the early part of the king's reign. This may indicate that a parallel die-axis was used earlier than previously thought.

6432 **Prakash, Satya, and Rajendra U. Singh.** *Coinage in Ancient India: A Numismatic, Archaeochemical and Metallurgical Study of Ancient Indian Coins.* Foreword by Earle R. Caley. New Delhi: Research Institute of Ancient Scientific Studies, 1968. 546 pp., 14 pls.
"The findings of previous authors on the early Indian coinages, from Vedic times (ca. 1000 B.C.) to about A.D. 1000, are summarized. Chapters are provided on the punch-marked coins, and on the coins of the Indo-Greeks, the Sakas, Pahlavas and Western Satraps, the Kushans, the Guptas and the Hunas (Hephthalites). Reference is made both to the coins and to the ancient literary sources. Numerous chemical analyses of ancient coins are given. Sample micro-photos appear in the plates, and conclusions drawn from them are given in the text. The conclusion is drawn that the Indo-Greek coins were cast rather than struck, and that they were subject to non-uniform heat treatment." [C. Panish, *NL* 82]

6433 **Prasad, Hari Kishore.** "Indo-Greek Coins of the Patna Museum." *Indian Numismatic Chronicle* (India) 2, pt. 2 (1961): 236, 275.
"One hundred thirteen Indo-Greek coins from the Cabinet of the Patna Museum are listed with obverse and reverse descriptions and museum accession numbers." [P. Gupta, *NL* 86]

6434 ——— "No Two Menanders." *Israel Numismatic Journal* (Israel) 5, pt. 2 (1966): 54-8.
"The coins of Menander bear two distinct titles, *Soteros* and *Dikaioy*, which has led to the belief that there were two Menanders. The arguments of Lahiri are examined and it is concluded that there is no valid reason to suggest two Menanders." [P. Gupta, *NL* 86]. [Also see A. N. Lahiri "The Case for a Second Menander" above].

6435 **Prinsep, Henry T.** *Note on the Historical Results Deducible from Recent Discoveries in Afghanistan, Based on the Note Books and the Coin-Cabinet of James Prinsep.* London: W. H. Allen and Co., 1844. Reprinted as *Historical Results from Bactrian Coins and Other Discoveries in Afghanistan.* Chicago: Ares Publishers, 1974. 125 pp., 15 engraved plates. [CS 3088]
The author recounts Alexander's eastern conquests. Then presents brief discussions of the coinage of Parthia, Bactria, Aria, and Ariana with many comments on the inscriptions found on the coins.

6436 **Prinsep, James.** "Further Notes and Drawings of Bactrian and Indo-Scythic Coins." *Journal of the Asiatic Society of Bengal* (India) 4 (1835): 327-48. 8 pls.
Discusses and illustrates (engravings) a group of Bactrian and Indo-Scythic coins with an extensive discussion of the Pahlevi inscriptions found on them.

6437 ——— "New Types of Bactrian and Indo-Scythic Coins Engraved as Plate XLIX." *Journal of the Asiatic Society of Bengal* (India) 5 (1836): 720-4. 1 pl.
Engraved illustrations of some newly found Bactrian coins (which actually appear on plate 46, not plate 49 as indicated in the title).

6438 ——— "New Varieties of Bactrian Coins, Engraved as Plate XXXV from Mr. Masson's Drawings and Other Sources." *Journal of the Asiatic Society of Bengal* (India) 5 (1836): 548-54. 1 pl.
Presents engravings of some of the coins described by Charles Masson (see Masson "Third Memoir" above).

6439 **Rapson, Edward J.** "Coins of the Graeco-Indian Sovereigns Agathocleia, Strato I Soter, and Strato II Philopater." *Corolla Numismatica: Numismatic Essays in Honour of Barclay V. Head.* G. F. Hill. London: Oxford University Press, 1906. Pages 245-58. 1 pl.
An examination of the coins of Strato I and II, and a discussion of the relationship between the two rulers. Rapson confirms that Heliocles re-struck coins of Strato, but Strato did not re-strike coins of Heliocles as has been suggested. He also examines the relationship of Agathocleia to Strato. [Also see H. L. Haughton's supplement "The Silver Coinage of Strato" above].

6440 ——— *Sources of Indian History: Coins.* Reprinted as *The Coinage of Ancient and Medieval India.* San Diego: Malter-Westerfield Publishing Co., no date. 56 pp., 5 pls.
A history of coinage in India from the earliest times until the fourteenth century. Includes a summary of: (1) the earliest native coinage, (2) early foreign coins used in India, (3) Graeco-Indian coins, (4) coins of the Scythic invaders of India, (5) coins of the Indian native states, (6) Indo-Parthian coins, (7) Kusana coins, (8) the coinage of dynasties contemporary with the Kusanas, (9) the coinage of the Guptas and their contemporaries, (10) later coins of north, east, central, and western India, and (11) coinages in southern India. Ninety-eight coins are illustrated.

6441 **Rogers, Charles J.** *Graeco-Bactrian and Indo-Scythian, Parthian, Sassanian and Miscellaneous Coins.* Calcutta, 1896. 288 pp., 6 pls. [CS 3089]
A volume of the *Catalogue of Coins of the Indian Museum*.

6442 ——— "Two New Coins from the Panjab." *Numismatic Chronicle* 3rd ser., 16 (1896): 268-70. Illus.
Illustrates and describes two Indo-Greek coins not listed by Cunningham in his *Coins of Alexander's Successors*. The attributions of these coins are uncertain.

6443 **Schwitter, C. M., and C. F. Cheng.** "Bactrian Nickel and Chinese Bamboo." *American Journal of Archaeology* 66, no. 1 (January 1962): 87-92.
"The use of a cupro-nickel alloy in coins issued by the Bactrian kings Euthydemus II, Agathocles and Pantaleon ca. 170 B.C. is believed to be the only known instance of an alloy of this type having been used for coinage before comparatively modern times. On the basis of results obtained from metallurgical analyses the writers attempt to show that ores for this alloy were obtained from China (probably Sikang province, or possibly Szechwan or Yunnan). The views expressed are basically a restatement of the theory previously published in the *American Journal of Archaeology* 61 (1957): 361-5, 409-14." [*NL* 62]. [See Cheng and Schwitter "Nickel in Ancient Bronzes" under METALLURGY. Also see S. Cammann "The Bactrian Nickel Theory" above].

6444 **Sear, David R.** "The Eastern Greeks." *SAN—Journal of the Society for Ancient Numismatics* 16, no. 1 (spring 1985): 4-5. Also appeared in *The Numismatist* 109, no. 3 (March 1996): 309-11.
A brief discussion of the history and coinage of Bactria and the Indo-Greek kingdoms.

6445 ——— "Then and Now: Kunduz in the News." *The Numismatist* 115, no. 1 (January 2002): 63-5. Illus.
A brief discussion of the hoard of 627 Bactrian silver coins discovered in August 1946 at Khisht Tépé on the river Oxus near Kunduz (Qunduz) in Afghanistan. Among the coins, which were mostly tetradrachms, were five double decadrachms of Amyntas (ca. 95-90 B.C.). The author recounts Alexander's conquest of the area.

6446 **Senior, Robert C.** "The Coinage of the Indo-Scythians and the Indo-Parthians." *Oriental Numismatic Society Informational Sheet* (England) 7 (1973). 19 pp., illus. [CS 3139]

6447 ——— "An Important New Coin of Apollodotos II." *Oriental Numismatic Society Newsletter* (England) 106 (1987).

6448 ——— "Indo-Scythic and Indo-Parthian Coin Hoards." *Oriental Numismatic Society Newsletter* (England) 107 (1987). "Part 2." *Oriental Numismatic Society Newsletter* 115 (1988).

6449 ——— "Victorious Indo-Parthians." *Spink Numismatic Circular* 96, no. 10 (December 1988): 312-3. Illus.
Publishes a Parthian-style silver drachm of Gondophares, the founder of the Indo-Parthian Empire. The coin includes the word NIKE in addition to the usual epithet. Senior suggests the coin is the first of the series issued on Gondophares' declaration of independence.

6450 ——— "The Gondopharid Countermark." *Spink Numismatic Circular* 97, no. 1 (February 1989): 3. Illus.
Discusses the coins bearing the countermark (a planetary symbol) of the Indo-Parthian ruler Gondophares.

6451 ——— "Two Indo-Scythic Hoards." *Spink Numismatic Circular* 97, no. 2 (March 1989): 44-5. Illus.
Comments on the areas of circulation of various Indo-Scythic coins, based on the coins from two recent hoards.

6452 ——— "Indo-Parthian Problems." *Spink Numismatic Circular* 97, no. 7 (September 1989): 220-2. Illus.
Publishes some coins which provide evidence related to the reign of Gondophares.

6453 ——— "Zeus and Pallas on Coins of Azes I." *Oriental Numismatic Society Newsletter* (England) 117 (1989).

6454 ——— "The Initial Pallas Coinages of Azes II." *Oriental Numismatic Society Newsletter* (England) 119 (1989).

6455 ——— "New Chronology Established for the Coinage of Gondophares, Who Met St. Thomas in India." *The Celator* 5, no. 9 (September 1991): 16-8.
Discusses the coinage of various kings named Gondophares. Suggests that the king Gondophares Sarpedanes was the king who met St. Thomas in India in the first century A.D. Includes photographs of the coins of the kings named Gondophares.

6456 ——— "The Indo-Greek/Scythian Succession and Coin Types." *Spink Numismatic Circular* 99, no. 8 (October 1991): 261-2. Illus.
Discusses the transition from Indo-Greek to Indo-Scythian (Saka) coin types in the first century B.C. Publishes a group of five tetradrachms which help illustrate this transition. Includes coins of Apollodotos II, Hippostratos, Artemidoros, and Maues.

6457 ——— "More Gondophares, Less Azes and Just Who Met St. Thomas." *Oriental Numismatic Society Occasional Paper* (England) 25 (1991). 12 pp., 3 pls.
Examines issues of chronology in the first century B.C. Concludes there was one king called Azes, and he was succeeded by Gondophares. Gondophares I's Seistan coinage was inspired by those of contemporary Parthian kings. Several kings used the name Gondophares, and it was one of the later ones that met St. Thomas.

6458 ——— "The Coinage of Strato III, Last of the Indo-Greeks Identified." *Oriental Numismatic Society Newsletter* (England) 128 (1991).

6459 ——— "A New Mint Monogram on a Rare Eukratides Drachm." *Oriental Numismatic Society Newsletter* (England) 128 (1991).

6460 ——— "An Indo-Greek Hoard from Akhnoor." *Spink Numismatic Circular* 100, no. 9 (November 1992): 299. Illus.
Summarizes an unpublished hoard of 215 drachms found at Akhnoor. Confirms "that the older portrait coins bearing the names of Strato alone and joint Strato with his grandson Strato portray Strato II while the young portrait coins bearing the name Strato are of the grandson alone. Strato III is therefore the last Indo-Greek king."

6461 ——— "A New Look at Some Indo-Parthian Coins." *Spink Numismatic Circular* 101, no. 10 (December 1993): 351-4. Illus.
Examines the scarce coinage of the provinces south of Arachosia. The earliest coins bear the swastika on the reverse. Compares the coinage of various Indo-Parthian satraps.

6462 ——— "The Posthumous Hermaeus Coinage." *Numismatic Digest* (India) 19 (1995): 43-72.

6463 ——— "Some Rare Indo-Greek Coins." *Oriental Numismatic Society Newsletter* (England) 143 (1995).

6464 ——— "A New Type for Azes (Seated Deity Drachm)." *Oriental Numismatic Society Newsletter* (England) 148 (1996).

6465 ——— "Menander Versus Zoilos: Another Overstrike." *Oriental Numismatic Society Newsletter* (England) 150 (autumn 1996): 12.

6466 ——— "An Indo-Greek Overstrike." *Oriental Numismatic Society Newsletter* (England) 151 (winter 1997): 10.

6467 ——— "The Last Greek Kings in India." *Nomismatika Khronika* (Greece) 16 (1997): 67-77. Map, 1 pl.
Senior reviews the Greek kings and their reigns in the eastern part of India in the first century B.C. He attempts to unravel the events and rulers of the final years of Greek rule. The author claims that Strato III was the last Greek king in India. Explains his opinion of the sequence of kings and their relationship to each other. Contrasts his opinions with those of Bopearachchi. Suggests which of the four mints in operation were used by each king. Discusses hoards which contained coins of these kings.

6468 ——— "An Enigmatic Indo-Greek Gold Coin." *Oriental Numismatic Society Newsletter* (England) 158 (1998).

6468a ——— "Indo-Greek and Indo-Scythic Ramblings and Novelties." *Oriental Numismatic Society Newsletter* (England) 161 (autumn 1999).

6469 ——— *The Coinage of Hermaios and its Imitations Struck by the Scythians.* Classical Numismatic Studies, No. 3. Lancaster: Classical Numismatic Group, 2000. 86 pp., 23 pls., maps.
A detailed examination of the coins bearing the legend ΒΑΣΙΛΕΩΣ ΣΩΤΗΡΟΣ ΕΡΜΑΙΟΥ (Savior King Hermaios) in Greek and Kharosthi (Hermaios was an Indo-Greek king who ruled ca. 95-80 B.C.). The majority of these coins are actually posthumous or imitative issues. Senior provides guidelines for distinguishing the imitative issues and shows that it was the Scythians and Indo-Parthians who struck these coins. Catalogues the lifetime issues of Hermaios and the imitative issues. Includes tables of monograms and a good bibliography. Extensively illustrated by line drawings.

6470 ——— *Indo-Scythian Coins and History.* Four volumes. Lancaster: Classical Numismatic Group, 2001, 2006.

1. *An Analysis of the Coinage.* 2001. 226 pp., illus.
2. *The Illustrated Catalogue of Indo-Scythian and Indo-Parthian Coins.* 2001. 244 pp., illus.
3. *The 'Easy Finder' Catalogue of Types, Monograms and Letters Appearing on Indo-Scythian and Indo-Parthian Coins.* 2001. 76 pp., illus.
4. *Supplement—Additional Coins and Hoards; The Sequence of Indo-Greek and Indo-Scythian Kings.* 2006. 152 pp., illus.

The Scythians were a federation of nomadic tribes who sporadically migrated west and southwest into Hindu Kush from central Asia. They were famous for their archery and horsemanship. During the third and second centuries B.C., they migrated south to India, carving out kingdoms, and absorbing the cultures and religions of Greece, Persia, and India into their own. Their coinage provides important historical evidence of their chronology, geography, and events. The first volume is an account of the history of the Indo-Scythians, analyzing their bilingual coinage (Greek and Karosthi) struck in the style of Bactrian coinage. The second volume compiles the coins into a comprehensive catalogue. The third volume provides a summary of this catalogue incorporating clear line drawings of the coins with tables listing every known variety. Volume four examines hoards and the sequence of kings.

6471 ——— "Some Unpublished Ancient Coins, Part 2." *Oriental Numismatic Society Newsletter* (England) 171 (spring 2002): 11-14. Illus.
"The author presents sixteen new types or varieties of Bactrian, Indo-Greek and Indo-Scythian coins." [Martin Allen, *NL* 147]

6472 ——— "Some More Rare Indo-Greek and Indo-Scythic Coins." *Oriental Numismatic Society Newsletter* (England) 172 (summer 2002): 16-17. Illus.

6473 ——— "More Unpublished Indo-Greek Coins." *Oriental Numismatic Society Newsletter* (England) 175 (spring 2003): 9-11. Illus.

6474 ——— "A Few More Rare Indian Ancient Coins." *Oriental Numismatic Society Newsletter* (England) 179 (spring 2004): 25-6.

6475 ——— "The Indo-Greek and Indo-Scythian King Sequences in the Second and First Centuries B.C." *Journal of the Oriental Numismatic Society* (England) 179 (2004), supplement.

6476 **Senior, Robert C., and Arthur Houghton.** "Two Remarkable Bactrian Coins." *Oriental Numismatic Society Newsletter* (England) 159 (1999).

6477 **Senior, Robert C., and David J. MacDonald.** *The Decline of the Indo-Greeks: A Reappraisal of the Chronology from the Time of Menander to that of Azes.* Monographs of the Hellenic Numismatic Society, No. 2. Athens: Hellenic Numismatic Society, 1998. 126 pp., 3 pls., map.
The authors attempt to re-order the succession of the various Indo-Greek kings after Menander. They also examine the evidence showing the transition of power from the Indo-Greeks to their successors, the Indo-Scythians. The study begins with a bronze coin of Hermaios struck over an issue of Heliokles II. The authors are convinced of the existence of two rulers named Heliokles. Discusses the evidence of hoards, monogram progression, type similarities, and overstrikes for the sequence of the Indo-Greek kings. Continues with a list of Menander's successors with arguments supporting their proposed order in the succession. Also publishes a bronze coin of Artemidoros which states that he is the son of Maues. This remarkable coin proves that there was a definite link between the Indo-Greeks and one group of Indo-Scythians. Written in both English and Greek.

6478 **Senior, Robert C., and S. Mirza.** "An Indo-Greek Overstrike." *Oriental Numismatic Society Newsletter* (England) 149 (summer 1996): 5.
Discusses a coin of Amyntas struck over a coin of Heliocles II.

6479 **Shortt, Hugh de S**. "Utmanzai Coins." *Numismatic Chronicle* 7th ser., 3 (1963): 11-36. 4 pls. [CS 3090]
Discusses a group of well-made forgeries of Indo-Greek and Bactrian coins. The coins were purported to be from a hoard found near the village of Utmanzai in the Northwest Frontier of India. Shortt discusses his analysis of the coins and exposes them as forgeries.

6480 **Simonetta, Alberto M.** "An Essay on the So-called 'Indo-Greek' Coinage." *East and West* (Italy) 8, no. 1 (April 1957): 44-66. Illus.
"Coinage of the Greek, Saka, and Parthian rulers of East Iran and Northwest India in the period ca. 165 B.C. continues to throw light on the dynasties and events of the area. The same holds true for the period down to the end of the Roman Republic. Tables show chronologies of Indo-Parthian kings and contemporary kings of other dynasties, 315 monograms and symbols of kings from Eucradites I through Azes II, and a synopsis of the Greek and Bactrian rulers of Bactria, Northwest India and adjoining regions, the last table arranged to show dynastic and/or family relationships. The mints or mint areas of Bactria, the Kabul Valley, Arachosia, Taxila, and Bucephala are classified in relation to groups of monograms and resulting groups of kings." [C. Vermeule, *NL* 43]

6481 ——— "A New Essay on the Indo-Greeks: The Sakas and the Pahlavas." *East and West* (Italy) 9, no. 3 (September 1958): 154-83. Illus.
"This forms a sequel to the author's earlier paper (see above). It is based on additional evidence and incorporates the results of more recent scholarship. Written for the "unspecialized" reader, it [covers] the Bactrian kingdom, the Indo-Greeks, Yüeh-Chi, the Sakas, the Parthian kingdom, and the Pahlavas from 247 B.C. to A.D. 242. Tables list the Greek monograms found on Indo-Greek, Saka and Pahlava coins, the kings and cities which used these monograms, and the tentative chronology and relationships of the dynasts discussed. A bibliography consisting chiefly of post-war material is included." [I. Merker, *NL* 49]

6482 ——— "Indo-Parthian Dynasty—New Consideration and Hypothesis." *Journal of Ancient Indian History* (India) 1 (1967-68): 150-73. 1 pl. [CS 3038]
Attempts to establish the succession order of Indo-Parthian kings, ca. 52 B.C. to A.D. 66, through the evidence of dated coins.

6483 **Singh, Jai P.** "A Religious Study of the Indo-Greek Coins." *Journal of the Numismatic Society of India* (India) 33, no. 2 (1971): 8-24. [CS 3142]
Lists and discusses the Greek gods and goddesses that are found on the coins of the Indo-Greeks. Also briefly discusses representations of animals and Indian deities on these coins. Discusses the Greek interest in Buddhism and the Hindu view of the Greeks. Concludes that the Greek kings only tried to maintain their own religion, but local conditions forced them to allow some indigenous cultural elements in order to increase the local support for their kingships. Certain Greeks were either attracted toward Indian religions or took to them for political reasons.

6484 **Singh, Milan.** "Menander I and the Buddhist Iconography on Indo-Greek Coins." *The Celator* 25, no. 7 (July 2011): 25-6. Illus.
Menander reigned ca. 160-145 B.C. and is considered to be one of the greatest of the Indo-Greek kings. The author describes a square bronze coin of Menander depicting the Dharmachakra (or Dharma wheel)—one of the main symbols of Buddhism. Also describes other Indo-Greek coins bearing Buddhist symbols including the lion and thunderbolt.

6485 **Singh, Rajendra U.** "Some Rare Indo-Greek Coins." *Journal of the Numismatic Society of India* (India) 44 (1982): 39-41. Illus.
"Three tetradrachms, one each of Strato I, Philoxenos, and Hippostratus, and nine drachms, one of Apollodotus I, two of Apollodotus II, three of Menander, two of Antialkidas, and one of Antimachus Nikephoros, are described." [P. Gupta, *NL* 114]

6486 **Smith, David Spencer.** "Early Central Asian Imitations I: The Coinage of Eukratides I." *The Celator* 14, no. 7 (July 2000): 6-20. Illus.
Traces the history of the Greek Bactrian rulers and focuses on the "barbarous" or "caricature" coinage issues of these rulers. Part 1 deals with the coins of Eukratides I. Smith describes how this king was portrayed on the official coins of the finest style, and then contrasts this portrayal with that on the imitation or barbarous issues. Also contrasts Eukratides' depiction on the garlanded-head issues with that on the helmeted-head issues. The degradations in artistic quality and the corruption of the inscriptions are noted. Suggests the imitation issues began ca. 130 B.C., and were probably produced by Scythians. Discusses the tetradrachms, drachms, and the rectangular bronze issues.

6487 ——— "Early Central Asian Imitations II: Athenian Owls and After." *The Celator* 15, no. 6 (June 2001): 18-24. Illus.
Discusses the imitations of Athenian tetradrachms which were struck in Palestine, Babylonia, and Egypt. Then Smith discusses the imitations of coins of the Bactrian kings Euthydemos and Demetrius. Comments on the changes in artistic style, degradation in the inscriptions, and possible minting locations for the imitation coinages.

6488 ——— "Early Central Asian Imitations III: Coinage of Heliokles I and the Kushan Connection." *The Celator* 15, no. 11 (November 2001): 6-16. Illus.
Examines central Asian coins whose designs were based on the coinage of the Greek Bactrian ruler Heliokles (the reign of Heliokles began ca. 135 B.C.). Includes Scythian and Kushan issues.

6489 **Smith, R. Morton.** "The First Bactrian Coinage: An Introduction." *Cornucopiæ* (publication of The Ancient Coin Society, Canada) 4 (1979): 6-13. Map.
Focuses on the coinage of Diodotus I, Diodotus II, Antiochus Hierax, Seleucus II and Euthydemus I of Magnesia. Includes a table of mint marks.

6490 ——— *Kings and Coins in India: Greek and Saka Self-Advertisement.* New Delhi: Harman Publishing House, 1997. 154 pp.
Seeks to establish a chronology that makes historical sense paying attention to the Indian information of the period of the Indo-Greeks and Indo-Scythian kings down to the establishment of the Kushan dynasty.

6491 **Smith, Vincent A.** *Coins of Ancient India: Catalogue of the Coins in the Indian Museum, Calcutta. Including the Cabinet of the Asiatic Society of Bengal. Volume 1.* Oxford, 1906. Reprint, Dehli: Indological Book House, 1972. 346 pp., 31 pls.
A short introduction is followed by a catalogue of several hundred coins, including many Bactrian and Indo-Greek coins. [Also see the supplements by Bidyabinude, and Basu above. Reviewed by E. J. Rapson in *Numismatic Chronicle* 4th ser., 7 (1907): 273-6].

6492 **Sohoni, S. V.** "God-like Queen Agathocleia." *Indian Numismatic Chronicle* (India) 5, pt. 2 (1966): 51-3. 1 pl.
"The occurrence of a portrait of Athena with the features of Agathocleia on coins of Menander suggests the king found it necessary to claim divinity for his wife, Agathocleia, as part of his psychological warfare with Antiochus IV, who had announced he was married to Atargatis, the northern Syrian goddess. After Menander's death the queen described herself as god-like on the coins of her son Strato I." [P. Gupta, *NL* 86]

6493 **Srivastava, A. K.** *Catalogue of Indo-Greek Coins in the State Museum, Lucknow.* Catalogue Series, No. 2. Lucknow: State Museum, 1969. xxxii, 47 pp., 7 pls.
The introduction discusses the fundamental features of the Indo-Greek coinage including types, shapes, metals, legends, and monograms. Catalogue of 245 coins (1 gold, 158 silver, 86 copper) of twenty-five kings. Includes appendices of coin types of kings not represented in the collection. Also includes a glossary of Greek titles, Prakrit epithets and their English renderings, and tables of alphabets and monograms.

6494 **Srivastava, Prashant.** "On the Identification of the 'Female between Vines' on the Poseidon Type of Coins." *Journal of the Numismatic Society of India* (India) 55 (1993): 112-3.
"The female figure shown standing facing between two vines on some coins of Maues and Azes is identified as Amphitrite, wife of Poseidon. The legend of Amphitrite is briefly recounted." [Amiteshwar Jha, *NL* 143]

6495 **Starck, Jeff.** "On the Block: Ancient Coins Dominate European Sales; Unique Gold Stater of Sophytes Tops London Auction." *Coin World* (October 3, 2011): 160. Illus.
Announces that a unique gold stater of Sophytes (315-305 B.C.) will appear in an October 2, 2011 auction held by Roma Numismatics. Briefly discusses the coin, about which little is known. The coin bears a portrait, thought to be Seleukos I, on the obverse and a caduceus and the name Sophytes on the reverse.

6496 **Swiney, J.** "On the Explanation of the Indo-Scythic Legends of the Bactrian Coins, through the Medium of the Celtic." *Journal of the Asiatic Society of Bengal* (India) 6 (1837): 98-101.
Attempts to explain some coin legends through comparison to Celtic script.

6497 **Tarn, William W.** "Notes on Hellenism in Bactria and India." *Journal of Hellenic Studies* 22 (1902): 268-93. Illus.
"On pp. 274-7 the relationship between coinage of Taxila and that of Pantaleon and Agathocles is discussed. On pp. 288-92 coins are used as part of the evidence for trade connections between the Greek world and India." [J. R. Jones, *NIJHS*]

6498 ———. *The Greeks in Bactria and India.* Cambridge: University Press, 1938. 539 pages, 1 pl., 3 maps. Second edition, 1951. Reprinted, 1966. 561 pp., 1 pl. of coin portraits, 3 maps. [CS 3091]
A history of Eastern Iran and Northern India under Greek rule to the end of the Hellenistic period, focusing on the period 206-145 B.C. Examines the rule of Euthydemus, Demetrius, Antiochos IV, Eukratides, Menander, and others. Tarn makes extensive use of the coinage as historical evidence and frequently comments on coin types. Includes three appendices with numismatic topics: "Appendix 1: Monograms and Find-Spots," "Appendix 3: Agathocles' Pedigree Coins," and "Appendix 17: The Hermaeus-Kujula Kadphises Coins" (see all three below). [Reviewed by A. R. Bellinger in *American Journal of Archaeology* 45 (1941): 646-8].

6499 ———. "Agathocles' Pedigree Coins." *The Greeks in Bactria and India,* by W. W. Tarn. Cambridge: University Press, 1938. Second edition, 1951. Reprinted, 1966. Page 446-51.
Tarn examines the fictitious pedigree of the Seleucid house which derived the descent of the dynasty from Alexander. A series of tetradrachms of Agathocles, which bear on the obverse the head of a former king with his name, give the Euthydemid pedigree back to where it branches off from the Seleucid pedigree, followed by the fictitious Seleucid pedigree from that point back to Alexander. Tarn suggests the Euthydemid kings did not believe in this descent, but used this fictitious pedigree as propaganda by Agathocles and Antimachos to influence the common people.

6500 ———. "The Hermaeus-Kujula Kadphises Coins." *The Greeks in Bactria and India,* by W. W. Tarn. Cambridge: University Press, 1938. Second edition, 1951. Reprinted, 1966. Page 503-7.
Tarn discusses the coins of Kadphises which used the name and portrait of a Greek king and gave him extravagant titles which he never bore. Tarn concludes these are pedigree coins—the Kushan Kadphises was trying to announce his blood relationship to Hermaeus in order to make himself more acceptable to the Greeks in that country. Suggests the Kushan Miaos was a prince of the Yueh-chi and was a contemporary of Hermaeus and an ancestor of Kadphises I. Tarn concludes that Miaos' coins were struck in Kapisa.

6501 ———. "Monograms and Find-Spots." *The Greeks in Bactria and India,* by W. W. Tarn. Cambridge: University Press, 1938. Second edition, 1951. Reprinted, 1966. Page 437-41.
Tarn reviews the question of whether monograms on Bactrian coins represent the names of mint cities or the names of mint masters or city magistrates. Tarn rejects the "mint city" theory. Also comments on the find spots of coins—suggesting that few conclusions can be drawn regarding this as evidence of a ruler's rule in an area.

6502 **Thomas, Edward.** "Catalogue of Bactrian Coins." *Numismatic Chronicle* 19 (1858): 13-45, 49-63. Illus.
A catalogue of Bactrian coin types with brief descriptions and occasional commentary. Accompanied by a table of monograms.

6503 ———. "Bactrian Coins." *Numismatic Chronicle* new ser., 2 (1862): 178-88, 259-67. 1 engraved plate.
A follow-up to his earlier paper (see "Catalogue" above) providing additional commentary and illustrations and describing some new specimens. Provides comments on the historical conclusions which can be drawn from the coins.

6504 ———. "Bactrian Coins and Indian Dates." *Journal of the Royal Asiatic Society of Great Britain and Ireland* new ser., 9 (1877): 1-21. Illus.
Discusses the dating systems used on some Bactrian and Scythian coins.

6505 **Tod, James.** "An Account of Greek, Parthian, and Hindu Medals Found in India." *Transactions of the Royal Asiatic Society of Great Britain and Ireland, Volume 1.* London: Royal Asiatic Society, 1827. Pages 313-42. 1 pl.
Discusses some coins of Apollodotus, Menander, and some Parthian coins found in India. Reviews the history and geography of the Bactrian and Parthian kingdoms. Presents an engraved plate of coins.

6506 **Tzamali, Marion J. A. (transl.).** "A Tax Receipt from Hellenistic Baktria." *Nomismatika Khronika* (Greece): 16 (1997): 47-8.
This is an English summary of related articles in Greek by John Rea, Robert C. Senior, and A. S. Hollis which appear on pages 25-46 (with bibliography and plates on pages 49-54). Mr. Senior acquired a parchment bearing the name of King Theos Antimachos and other names. The parchment was determined by Dr. John Rea to be a tax receipt written on skin. Dr. Hollis provided the numismatic and historical background of the tax receipt. It gives the first reference outside of coins to King Theos Antimachos. It also mentions a junior colleague Eumenes, not previously known from coins. The third legible name is Antimachos, providing evidence that there were two kings of that name whose reigns overlapped. A possible chronology for these kings is provided.

6507 **Vassiliou, John.** "The Greek Kings on the Square Coins of Bactria." *Nomismatika Khronika* (Greece) 3 (1974): 34-8. Illus.
Examines some square coins of Bactria donated by the author to the Numismatic Collection of the National Archaeological Museum in Athens. Sixteen of the coins are illustrated. In Greek, with a brief English summary on page 38.

6508 **Vaux, W. S. W.** "Remarks on Four Rare Coins of Afghanistan, Lately Acquired by the British Museum." *Numismatic Chronicle* 13 (1851): 7-13.
Describes four coins of Bactrian kings including two silver coins of Strato, one of Demetrius, and a gold coin of Eukratides.

6509 ———. "On Some Rare Bactrian Coins." *Numismatic Chronicle* 16 (1854): 108-13. Illus.
Describes six rare coins of the Bactrian kings Lysias, Amyntas, Archebius, Apollodotus, Hippostratus, and Dionysius.

6510 ———. "On an Unique Coin of Platon, a King of Bactriana." *Numismatic Chronicle* new ser., 15 (1875): 1-19. Illus.
Examines a tetradrachm (*obv.*, bust of the king; *rev.*, the king as Helios, driving a quadriga). This king was previously unknown. Discusses his role in Bactrian history and comments on other Bactrian kings. [Also see follow-up comments in *Numismatic Chronicle* new ser., 16 (1876): 79-80].

6511 **Walker, Ralph.** "The Meaning of the Greek Legend on the Coins of Soter Megas." *SAN—Journal of the Society for Ancient Numismatics* 3, no. 4 (1971-72): 60-2; and "Supplementary Notes." *SAN—Journal of the Society for Ancient Numismatics* 4, no. 2 (1972-73): 26.
Discusses various interpretations of the legend on the coins of Soter Megas, the "nameless" Indo-Greek king. Disputes previous researchers' beliefs that the legend was a blundered attempt at "King of Kings." Suggests instead that it should be translated as "Ruling King," meaning Soter Megas was a

sub-king, a vassal king, or a viceroy. Discredits the theory that Soter Megas and Wima Kadphises are the same person. In Walker's continuation, "Supplementary Notes," he mentions the findings of other researchers whose conclusions agree with his own.

6512 ——— "Soter Megas' Coins: His Sole Legacy." *World Coins* 98 (February 1972): 140-68. Illus.
Begins with a brief review of Alexander's conquest of the East and the establishment of Indo-Greek kingdoms in Bactria, the establishment of the Indo-Scythian (Saka) kingdoms, the encroachment of the Parthians, and the coming of the Kushans. At some time between the reigns of the Greek king Hermaios and the Kushan king Kanishka, a king ruled for many years over much of the Bactrian territory. This unknown king struck coins bearing the epithet "Soter Megas," the Great Savior. Describes the various coin types of this king. Summarizes the theories of various scholars regarding the identity and dates of rule of this unnamed king.

6513 **Whitehead, Richard B.** "Some Rare Indo-Greek and Scythian Coins." *Journal of the Asiatic Society of Bengal, Numismatic Supplement* 14 (1910): 557-65. 2 pls. Supplement to *Journal of the Asiatic Society of Bengal* (India) 6 (1910).
Discusses some coins recently acquired by the author.

6514 ——— *Catalogue of Coins in the Panjab Museum, Lahore, Volume 1: Indo-Greek Coins.* Oxford, 1914. Reprint, Chicago: Argonaut, 1969. 218 pp., 20 pls. [CS 10071]
Describes the collection of Indo-Greek coins in the Lahore Museum, Panjab, India. Made up of the government collection and the collection of C. J Rogers. The catalogue is in three parts: (1) Greek kings of Bactria and India (698 coins); (2) Indo-Scythians (400 coins) and Indo-Parthians (141 coins); and (3) Kushans (241 coins). Each section is preceded by a brief introduction. Includes a table of monograms. The major coin types are illustrated in the plates. [Reviewed by "J. A." in *Numismatic Chronicle* 4th ser., 14 (1914): 383-7].

6515 ——— *The Pre-Mohammedan Coinage of Northwestern India.* Numismatic Notes and Monographs, No. 13. New York: American Numismatic Society, 1922. 56 pp., 14 pls., map.
A review of the coinage of the early foreign invaders of India—Greeks, Scythians, Parthians, Kushans, and Ephthalites (White Huns)—and of the indigenous coins which are found in Northwestern India from the earliest times down to the Mohammedan invasion. Begins with a summary of Alexander's conquests, the rule of Seleukos, the establishment of an independent Bactrian kingdom under Diodotus, the expansion into India under Demetrios II, and the end of Greek rule after the invasion of the Scythians. Summarizes events during the reigns of the Bactrian kings and mentions some of the characteristics of their coinage. Provides general descriptions of the common coin types. Briefly summarizes the history of the Saka-Scythians, Kushans, and subsequent foreign rulers. The typical coin types are described. Continues with a brief discussion of the coinage of the indigenous rulers of India. Concludes with an account of the incursions of the White Huns.

6516 ——— "Notes on Indo-Greek Numismatics." *Numismatic Chronicle* 5th ser., 3 (1923): 294-343. 4 pls. [CS 3148], and "Notes on the Indo-Greeks." *Numismatic Chronicle* 5th ser., 20 (1940): 89-128. 1 pl.; 6th ser., 7 (1947): 28-51. 2 pls.; 10 (1950): 205-32. 1 pl. [CS 3149], Reprinted as a book, *Indo-Greek Numismatics.* Chicago: Argonaut, 1970. 144 pp., 8 pls., illus. [CS 3149a]
Part 1 (1923) discusses the origins and scope of Indo-Greek numismatics, metals, weights, historical background, and monograms. Whitehead describes seventy rare coin types which were unknown when his *Catalogue of Coins in the Panjab Museum* (see above) was published. Part 2 discusses epigraphy, overstrikes, portraits, and monograms. Much discussion of coin types and their interpretation. Discusses some of the conclusions of Tarn and Cunningham. The reprinted book also presents H. L. Haughton's "Shaikhano Dheri Hoard, March 1940" which was originally published in *The Numismatic Chronicle* in 1940, providing a brief description of a hoard of Indo-Greek coins (see Haughton above).

6517 ——— "The Eastern Satrap Sophytes." *Numismatic Chronicle* 6th ser., 3 (1943): 60-72. 1 pl.
Reviews the evidence for the coins attributed to Sophytes—the first Indian king whose name appears on a coin. This Sophytes has been identified as the Sopeithes, a contemporary of Alexander the Great, mentioned by Arrian and Strabo. Whitehead reviews the opinions of various scholars and concludes: (1) the Sopeithes of Arrian is not the Sophytes of the coins; (2) Sophytes and his coins belong to the Oxus region and are probably earlier than 320 B.C.; (3) Sophytes was probably a local satrap who asserted his independence upon the fall of the Persian Empire. [Also see articles by Bopearachichi, Cunningham, Kirkpatrick, and G. Macdonald above]. Whitehead also discusses the findspot of the second known "Porus Decadrachm" of Alexander, found in 1926. [See additional articles under MACEDONIAN KINGDOM—ALEXANDER'S PORUS COINS/MEDALLIONS].

6518 ——— "Coins and Indian History." *Centennial Publication of the American Numismatic Society.* Edited by Harald Ingholt. New York: American Numismatic Society, 1958. Pages 697-712. 1 pl. [CS 3150]
A revised version of the author's "The Place of Coins in Indian History" (*Journal of the Panjab Historical Society,* 1913). The author provides numerous examples of how coin inscriptions have provided information on Indian history which was not available from other historical writings. Begins with the early punch-marked coins of the sixth century B.C. Then discusses the coinage of the Greek invaders of India. Kings mentioned in historical texts whose existence was confirmed by discoveries of their coins include Eukratides, Euthydemos, Antimachus Theos, and Demetrios. Coins also provided the names of some previously unknown princes including Agathokles, Archebios, Pantaleon, and Hermaios, Peukolaos, and Polyxenos. Coins also furnished the clues necessary to the decipherment of the Kharoshthi script. The existence of King Gandophares, who is said to have met the Apostle Thomas, was confirmed by coins. Other examples are given for the Kushan, Saka, and Mughal periods. Twenty coins are illustrated.

6518a **Widemann, François.** "Contremarques du Monnayage Indo-Grec." *Quaderni Ticinesi* (Switzerland) 6 (1977).

6519 ——— "Une Confirmation Numismatique de l'Ère Yavana de 186/185. Une Hypothèse sur les Causes et les Conséquences de l'Assassinat d'Eucratide." *Nomismatika Khronika* (Greece) 23 (2004): 37-45. Illus. [Also in Greek on pp. 46-53].
"The author looks at the dated coinages of the Indo-Greek rulers Heliocles and Platon and argues that the dates are calculated according to a Yavana Era beginning in 186/5 B.C. Text in French and Greek." [Oliver D. Hoover, *NL* 149]

6520 ——— *Les Successeurs d'Alexandre en Asie Centrale et Leur Héritage Culturel: Essai.* Paris: Riveneuve, 2009. 527 pp., pls., illus., maps.
An extensive examination of the successors of Alexander in Central Asia, beginning with the Greeks in Central Asia and India under the Achaemenids, then focusing on the coins minted by Greek, Bactrian, and Indo-Greek kings, the Scythians, Indo-Parthians, Shakas, Yuezhi, and early Kushans. Includes an overview of the cultural heritage of the Greeks on Central and South Asia. [Reviewed by Jeffrey D. Lerner in *ANS Magazine* 9, no. 2 (summer 2010): 71-2].

6521 **Wilson, L. M.** "Two Coinage Types of Eukratides II and the Murderer of Eukratides I." *Oriental Numismatic Society Newsletter* (England) 179 (spring 2004): 26-8. Illus.

6522 ——— "Demetrios II of Bactria and Hoards from Ai Khanoum." *Oriental Numismatic Society Newsletter* 180 (summer 2004): 12-13.

6523 ——— "Demetrios I of Bactria and the 'Greek Era.'" *Oriental Numismatic Society Newsletter* 178 (winter 2004): 48.

6524 **Wilson, L. M., and G. R. F. Assar.** "Re-Dating Eukratides I Relative to Mithradates I." *Journal of the Oriental Numismatic Society* 191 (2007): 24-5.

6525 **Wilson, Horace Hayman.** *Ariana Antiqua: A Descriptive Account of the Antiquities and Coins of Afghanistan, with a Memoir on the Buildings Called Topes, by C. Mason, Esq.* London: East India Company, 1861. 452 pp., 22 engraved plates.
An account of discoveries in Bactria. Includes "Account of the Progress of Bactro-Indian Numismatics and Antiquarian Discovery, and Observations on the Edifaces, Called 'Topes.'"

6526 **Wilson, Professor.** "Graeco-Bactrian Coins." *Numismatic Journal* 2 (1838): 144-81. 3 pls. of coin drawings.
Begins with a brief history of the study of Bactrian coinage. Wilson then describes some of the most important coin types. Thirty-five coins are illustrated.

6527 **Zograph, Alexander N.** *The Coins of Heraüs.* Tashkent: Publishing House of the Sciences Committee of the Uzbek Socialist Soviet Republic, 1937. [An English translation (61 pages) resides in the library of the American Numismatic Association].
A new analysis of the coins of the ruler Heraüs, supported by five tetradrachms and two obols housed in museums in the Uzbek Socialist Soviet Republic. Zograph reviews the opinions of other scholars for the attribution and dating of the coins of this little-known ruler. These opinions show a great diversity in dates and geography. He then provides his own analysis, and concludes the coins of Heraüs belong to a northern Bactrian mint and were produced in the middle of the first century B.C.

6528 **Zygman, Edmund.** "A Tetradrachm of Azes II Struck at Sangala-Euthydemia." *Museum Notes* 7 (1957): 51-6. 1 pl.
The author publishes a tetradrachm of Azes II (A.D. 5-19) bearing an unpublished Kharosthi monogram (read as Sangala) and a faulty inscription. He reviews the debate over the meaning of the monograms found on Bactrian and Indian coins. Cunningham suggested they refer to mint cities; others have suggested they refer to magistrates. Zygman draws no firm conclusion on the matter.

Also see: Barnett "Treasure of the Oxus" under HOARDS; Bellinger "Treasure of the Oxus" under HOARDS; Bopearachchi "Les Monnaies Seleucides" under SYRIA—SELEUCID KINGDOM; Bopearachchi *SNG ANS—Graeco-Bactrian and Indo-Greek Coins* under THE SYLLOGE NUMMORUM GRAECORUM SERIES (AMERICAN SERIES); Caley "The Earliest Use of Nickel Alloys" under METALLURGY; Chugg "Gold Porus Medallion" under MACEDONIAN KINGDOM—ALEXANDER'S PORUS COINS; de Morgan *Manual de Numismatique Orientale* under GENERAL WORKS—GREEK; Errington et al. *The Crossroads of Asia* under PUBLIC COLLECTIONS—GREAT BRITAIN (CAMBRIDGE); Jenkins "Greek and Graeco-Indian Coins from the Haughton Collection" under PUBLIC COLLECTIONS—GREAT BRITAIN (LONDON); Kritt *Seleucid Coins of Bactria* under SYRIA—SELEUCID KINGDOM; Kvist "Tetradrachms of Antimachos" under PORTRAITS; Macdonald "Ancient Persian Coins in India" under PERSIA; Mitchiner *Oriental Coins and Their Values* under ASIA—GENERAL WORKS.

Nicolet-Pierre "Monnaies Grecques Trouvées" under HOARDS; Nock "Notes on Ruler-Cult" under TYPES; Petitot-Biehler and Bernard "Trésor de Monnaies Grecques" under HOARDS; Pieper "Greek Influenced Portrait Coins" under ASIA—GENERAL WORKS; Price *Coins: An Illustrated Survey* under GENERAL WORKS—GREEK; "Rare Bactrian Decadrachm" under MACEDONIAN KINGDOM—ALEXANDER'S PORUS COINS; Richter "Late Hellenistic Portraiture" under PORTRAITS; Shore "A Symbol on Parthian Drachm" under PARTHIA; A. Simonetta "Notes on the Parthian and Indo-Parthian Issues" under PARTHIA; Sotheby & Co. *Catalogue...Haughton Collection* under PRIVATE COLLECTIONS; Troxell "Greek Accessions" under ASIA MINOR—GENERAL WORKS; Troxell *The Norman Davis Collection* under PRIVATE COLLECTIONS; Troxell and Spengler "A Hoard of Early Greek Coins from Afghanistan" under HOARDS; Wright *Coins from Asia Minor and the East* under ASIA MINOR—GENERAL WORKS.

North Africa

General Works

Africa's earliest coins were produced in Cyrenaica in the late sixth century B.C. When these first coins were issued, Cyrenaica was part of the Persian Empire but was governed by the kings of Cyrene of the Battid dynasty, who remained in power until about 435 B.C.

—J. Cribb, B. Cook, and I. Carradice, 1990

6529 **Alexandropoulos, Jacques.** *Les Monnaies de l'Afrique Antique 400 av. J.-C. – 40 ap. J.-C.* Toulouse: Presses Universitaires du Mirail, 2000. 507 pp., 17 pls. Second edition, 2007. 507 pp., 20 pls.
Begins with a 357-page historical overview. The catalogue of the coins is divided into three parts: all the coins struck under the authority of Carthage until 146 B.C. (109 coin types), the coinage minted by the Kings of Numidia and Mauretania (364 types), and the coins issued by various North African cities from Tripolitania to western Mauretania between the second Punic War and the reign of Tiberius (188 types). Does not cover the coinage of Cyrenaica. Includes an appendix on the stylistic development of the female head on the obverse of Punic coins, a select bibliography, a map of North African mints, and a table of Punic and Neo-Punic alphabets and symbols. In addition to the photographs, the author has included line drawings of coins borrowed from Müller's *Numismatique de l'Ancienne Afrique* and from Mazard's *Corpus Nummorum Numidiae Mauretaniaeque*. [First edition reviewed by Paolo Visonà in *Numismatic Chronicle* 163 (2003): 406-7].

6530 **Jahn, J.** "Karthago und Westliches Nordafrika (Literaturüberblick der Griechischen Numismatik)." *Chiron* (Germany) 7 (1977): 411-85. [CS 3180]
A bibliography.

6531 **Jenkins, G. Kenneth.** "Africa." *Survey of Numismatic Research, 1960-1965. Volume 1: Ancient Numismatics.* Copenhagen: International Numismatic Commission, 1967. Pages 85-95. [CS 3152]
A narrative bibliography discussing recently published works in the field of Greek numismatics related to North Africa.

6532 ——— "Egypt and North Africa." *Survey of Numismatic Research, 1966-1971. Volume 1: Ancient Numismatics.* New York: International Numismatic Commission, 1973. Pages 199-205. [CS 3153]
A narrative bibliography discussing recently published works in the field of Greek numismatics related to North Africa.

6533 ——— "Carthage, N. Africa, the Iberian Peninsula, Gaul." *A Survey of Numismatic Research 1972-1977.* International Association of Professional Numismatists Publication, No. 5. Berne: International Numismatic Commission, 1979. Pages 106-17.
A narrative overview of newly published works in the field of ancient numismatics.

6534 **Knapp, Jamie.** "The First Coin of Inner Africa?" *The Celator* 23, no. 1 (January 2009): 33-4. Illus.
Discusses a tetradrachm, with types imitating those of Athens, previously believed to be an Egyptian issue. The coin was discovered in 1858 but was an enigma because of its indecipherable script on the reverse. The coin is now revealed to likely be of black African origin—from the Kingdom of Kush (Nubia) located in modern day Sudan. The script is an early form of Meroitic and can be translated as "Candace of Irem." It is among the very first coins ever produced by an African black culture.

6535 **Müller, Ludwig.** *Numismatique de l'Ancienne Afrique.* Copenhagen, 1860-62. *Supplément*, 1874. Four volumes. Reprints, Basel/Stuttgart, 1957; Bologna: Forni, 1964 (in one volume); Chicago: Obol International, 1977 (in two volumes); New York: Sanford J. Durst (no date; 1977 Obol reprint bound in Durst cover; in two volumes). [CS 3154]
Originally written by C. F. Falbe and J. C. Lindberg in the 1840's, and expanded and published by Müller. Covers Cyrenaica (including the Ptolemaic coinage of Cyrenaica), Zeugitana, Numidia, and Mauretania. The original volumes are:

1. *Les Monnaies de la Cyrénaïque.* 1860. 174 pp.
2. *Les Monnaies de la Syrtique, de la Byzacène et de la Zeugitane.* 1862. 188 pp.
3. *Les Monnaies de la Numidie et de la Mauretanie.* 1862. 194 pp.
4. *Supplément.* 1874. 96 pp.

6536 **Tameanko, Marvin.** "Meroe: a Fabulous Ancient Kingdom without a Coinage." *The Celator* 9, no. 10 (October 1995): 44-51. Illus., map.

A short history of the kingdom of Meroe in Africa, south of Egypt. Describes the kingdom's interaction with the Egyptians, Greeks, Romans, Axumites, and Himyarites. Meroe had no coinage of its own and the author discusses what this lack of coinage reveals about the social, political, and economic status of these people.

EGYPT

The long series of the coins of the Ptolemies is generally admitted to be the most difficult to classify in the whole range of Greek numismatics. In spite of the enormous number of issues, the types present comparatively little variety. The inscriptions are mostly conventional and, although dates are frequent, the era of reckoning is not always certain.

—Barclay V. Head, 1887

Pre-Ptolemaic Period

6537   **Bogaert, Raymond.** "De Muntcirculatie in Egypte voor de Macedonische Overheersing." *La Vie Numismatique* (France) 30, no. 1 (1980): 19-27.
Coin circulation in Egypt prior to Macedonian domination.

6538   **Bolshakov, A. O.** "The Earliest Known Gold Pharaonic Coin." *Revue d'Égyptologie* 43 (1992): 3-9.

6539   **Buttrey, Theodore V.** "Pharaonic Imitations of Athenian Tetradrachms." *Proceedings of the 9th International Congress of Numismatics. Berne, September 1979. Volume 1.* Edited by T. Hackens and R. Weiller. Luxembourg: International Association of Professional Numismatists, 1982. Pages 137-40. 1 pl.
Describes a hoard of Egyptian imitations of Athenian tetradrachms found in Egypt in 1934-1935. Suggests such issues were very large. Indicates that the frontal eye was used in Egypt as late as ca. 340 B.C. Many of these coins were exported from Egypt and have been found in Phoenicia, Syria, Anatolia, and Sicily. Warns that numismatists must distinguish between Athenian coins and Egyptian imitations when studying the distribution of Athenian coinage.

6540   **Chauveau, M.** "La Première Mention du Statère d'Argent en Égypte." *Transeuphratène* (France) 20 (2000): 137-43.

6541   **Curtis, James W.** "Media of Exhange in Ancient Egypt." *The Numismatist* (1951): 482-91. Reprinted in *Selections from The Numismatist: Ancient and Medieval Coins.* Racine: Whitman Publishing Co., 1960. Pages 153-62. Illus.
Curtis examines the reasons the Egyptians didn't develop a coinage system before the rule of the Ptolemies. Begins with a survey of early Egyptian history starting with the Old Kingdom (3200 B.C.). Discusses the transition from the use of agricultural goods in barter to the use of gold, silver, and copper items, then to the use of gold and copper rings as money. Discusses the introduction of Greek coins into Egypt, including the rare gold coin of Nectanebo II. Curtis believes this coin was a pattern coin struck in a limited quantity as part of a coinage plan that failed to develop.

6542   ——— "The Coinage of Pharaonic Egypt." *Journal of Egyptian Archaeology* 43 (1957): 71-6. 1 pl. Reprint, Chicago: Ares Publishers, n.d. 6 pp., 1 pl.
Begins with a review of the reasons for the lack of coinage in early Egypt, previously set forth by Jenkins (lack of private enterprise, geographic isolation, the royal monopoly on trade). In the Twenty-Ninth Dynasty, King Acoris established a quasi-permanent corps of Greek mercenaries which staved-off Persian invasions during the reigns of Nectanebo I and II. These mercenaries would not accept payment in kind, but insisted upon monetary recompense. Curtis examines the gold stater issued by Nectanebo II. Acoris formed an alliance with Athens, and Athens furnished coin dies to Egypt. The resulting Egyptian silver tetradrachms were indistinguishable from Athenian issues. Recognizable Egyptian coins, in silver and gold, apparently began during the Thirtieth Dynasty during the reigns of Nectanebo I, Teos, and Nectanebo II (early fourth century B.C.). The coins contain hieroglyphs.

6543   **Dattari, Giovanni.** "The Gold Exagium with Hieroglyphs." *Journal International d'Archeologie Numismatique* (Greece) 5 (1902): 165-6.
In 1901, Svoronos published a gold piece discovered in Egypt bearing hieroglyphs as types. Svoronos believed the piece to be genuine, but suggested it is not a coin. Rather, it is a piece which was struck for Egyptians when currency first came to Egypt. George Hill doubted the authenticity of the piece (see Hill "The Supposed Gold Coin" below). Here, Dattari supports the conclusions of Svoronos.

6544   **Daumas, F.** "Monnaies Égyptiennes Antérieures au Règne des Ptolémées." *Bulletin de la Socièté Française de Numismatique* (France) 29 (1974): 571-5.

6545   ——— "Le Problème de la Monnaie dans l'Égypt Antique avant Alexandre." *Mélanges de l'École Française de Rome Antiquité* (France) 89, no. 2 (1977): 425-41.

6546 **Hill, George F.** "The Supposed Gold Coin with Hieroglyphs." *Journal International d'Archeologie Numismatique* (Greece) 5 (1902): 25-6.
In 1901, Svoronos published a gold piece discovered in Egypt bearing hieroglyphs as types. Svoronos believed the piece to be genuine, but suggested it is not a coin. Rather, it is a piece which was struck for Egyptians when currency first came to Egypt. Here, George Hill casts doubt on the authenticity of the piece. [Also see Dattari "The Gold Exagium" above].

6547 **Jenkins, G. Kenneth.** "An Egyptian Gold Stater." *British Museum Quarterly* 20, no. 1 (March 1955): 10-1. Illus.
"There is documentary evidence for the existence of a kind of currency in ancient Egypt, but the earliest coins known before the conquest of Alexander the Great comprise gold and silver pieces issued by Tachos (361-359 B.C.) in the period of Egyptian independence from Persian domination. The Museum has acquired a specimen of a rare gold coinage of Graeco-Egyptian character, probably struck by the last of the native kings, 'Nectanebo II' (359-343 B.C.), who reigned until Artaxerxes Ochus once more brought Egypt into the Persian Empire." [C. Vermeule, *NL* 35]

6548 **Lipinski, Edouard.** "Egyptian Aramaic Coins from the Fifth and Fourth Centuries B.C." *Studia Paulo Naster Oblata, Volume 1: Numismatica Antiqua.* Edited by S. Scheers. Louvain: Departement Oriëntalistiek, 1982. Pages 23-33, including 1 pl.
The author examines the fourth century B.C. imitations of Athenian tetradrachms which circulated in Egypt. They bear four Aramaic letters, *swyn*, which the author believes represented the name of the important Aramaic colony of Syene. Imitations of coins of other cities exist which also bear the inscription *swyn*. Lipinski also discusses Egyptian imitative issues inscribed *mnpt* and *n*. Although some numismatists have attributed these as Palestinian or Philisto-Arabian, the author suggests these were minted at Heliopolis.

6549 **Mavrogordato, J. A.** "Was There a Pre-Macedonian Mint in Egypt?" *Numismatic Chronicle* 4th ser., 8 (1908): 197-207. Illus.
Describes two small silver coins: (1) obv., Athena in helmet; rev., ΑΘΕ, owl standing right; (2) obv., lion's head; rev., owl standing right. Both coins bear Egyptian symbols and were probably struck between 390-350 B.C. The author suggests the coins may have been minted in Egypt.

6550 **Nicolet-Pierre, Hélène.** "Les Monnaies des Deux Derniers Satrapes d'Egypte avant la Conquête d'Alexandre." *Greek Numismatics and Archaeology: Essays in Honor of Margaret Thompson.* Edited by O. Mørkholm and N. M. Waggoner. Wetteren: Numismatique Romaine, 1979. Pages 221-30. 2 pls.
Discusses the Artaxerxes and satrapal coinage struck in Egypt with Athenian types.

6551 ——— "Les Imitations Égyptiennes des Tétradrachmes Athéniens d'Époque Classique (V^e-VIe s. av. J.-C.)." *Arkhaiologike Ephemeris* (Greece) 142 (2003): 139-54.

6552 **Price, Martin Jessop.** "New Owls for the Pharaoh." *Minerva* 1 (1990): 39-40.

6552a **Ronde, André.** "Contribution au Monnayage Pré-Alexandrin en Égypte (Une Émission de Petits Bronzes sous Nectanebo II?)." *Bulletin de la Société Française de Numismatique* 60, no. 1 (January 2005): 2-3.
[The bronze coin attributed here to Nectanebo has been reattributed by Butcher to a mint in Syria].

6553 **Tameanko, Marvin.** "Naucratis—A Greek Emporium City in Ancient Egypt, circa 500 B.C." *The Celator* 16, no. 8 (August 2002): 6-18. Illus.
Presents the history of the city of Naucratis. The city was an important Greek trading outpost in Egypt. Mentions the many Greek coins that have been found in the city—evidence of the city's importance as trading center.

6554 **van Alfen, Peter G.** "The 'Owls' from the 1989 Syria Hoard, with a Review of Pre-Macedonian Coinage in Egypt." *American Journal of Numismatics* 2nd ser., 14 (2002): 1-57. Illus.
Begins with an examination of the 1989 Syria Hoard (*Coin Hoards* 8, no. 158) consisting of 164 coins (142 Athenian owls and 22 coins of Sinope, Cyzicus, Ephesos, Tarsos, Hierapolis-Bambyce, and Tyre). The hoard was likely buried ca. 330 B.C. Some of the owls are imitative and some are likely of Attic origin (all are fourth century "pi-style"). The owls provide important evidence for the Artaxerxes and Sabakes series of Athenian imitations from Egypt and are studied here. The imitative issues are divided into five stylistic groups. Many bear cuts or counterstamps which, van Alfen suggests, were not done to test the metal. Rather, they served as a marking system. He also reviews evidence for the production of coins in Egypt during the Persian period (sixth to fourth centuries B.C.). Provides an introduction to the different series of pre-Macedonian Egyptian coins and a list of most published examples as well as some unpublished pieces from the American Numismatic Society collection: (1) Buttrey's types, (2) marked and unmarked fractions, (3) Takhos, (4) Nektanebo II, (5) Artaxerxes, (6) Sabakes, (7) Mazakes series. Presents a general discussion of the phenomenon of imitative issues and why they remained popular in Egypt for so long. Imitations of Athens' owl began in the fifth century, and by the beginning of the fourth century were produced extensively in Egypt and the Levant. By the end of the fourth century, they had spread to Babylonia, Bactria, and South Arabia. Discusses weights of the imitative tetradrachms. Suggests the design, legends, and production of the Sabakes and Mazakes coins remained under Persian control. Discusses the unique gold coin of Takhos, who briefly ruled as pharaoh of Egypt. Suggests that Takhos could have been responsible for some of the silver Athenian tetradrachm imitations. He was the first indigenous pharaoh for whom there is evidence of programmatic minting. [Also see van Alfen "A New Athenian Owl and Bullion Hoard" under HOARDS, and van Alfen "The 'Owls' from the 1973 Iraq Hoard" under HOARDS].

6555 ——— "Herodotus' 'Aryandic' Silver and Bullion Use in Persian-Period Egypt." *American Journal of Numismatics* 2nd ser., 16-17 (2004-2005): 7-46. 4 pls.
Examines a mid-fifth century B.C. Egyptian hoard containing three large silver ingots and nineteen coins and coin fragments. van Alfen reviews the hoard and textual evidence for bullion use in Persian-period Egypt (ca. 525-330 B.C.). He concludes that silver bullion in the form of Hacksilber and ingots was used for a large range of monetary transactions, and that within these transactions the Egyptians recognized at least three grades of silver, the most pure of which was the "Aryandic silver" mentioned by Herodotus (4.166). He argues that ingots were sometimes produced by private parties to pay specific debts.

6556 **Wetterstrom, Kerry.** "Hieroglyphs Reflect Egypt on Enigmatic Gold Stater." *Coin World* (November 6, 2006): 36.

A report on Wetterstrom's presentation at the American Numismatic Association convention, which focused on the unique gold stater of the pharoah Takhos. Also discusses the gold coinage of the pharaoh Nektanebo II which bears a hieroglyph inscription. Mentions a series of bronze coins which may also belong to Nektanebo II.

6557 **Zervos, Orestes H.** *The Alexander Mint of Egypt.* Ph.D. dissertation at New York University, 1974.

Also see: Buttrey "Seldom What They Seem" under ATTICA—GENERAL WORKS; Dattari "Comments on a Hoard of Athenian Tetradrachms" under HOARDS; Huth "Athenian Imitations from Arabia" under ARABIA; Jongkees "Athenian Coin Dies" under THE MINTING PROCESS; Kroll "A Small Find" under HOARDS; Milne "Athenian Coins found in Egypt" under ATTICA—GENERAL WORKS; Moysey "Observations" under PERSIA; Newell "Egyptian Coin Hoards" under HOARDS; Plant "Most Ancient Forms of Writing" under EPIGRAPHY; Price "More from Memphis" under HOARDS; Reid "The Coins of Alexandria" under EGYPT—PTOLEMAIC KINGDOM; E. Robinson "Greek Coins from the Pyramids" under HOARDS; Tuplin "The Coinage of Aryandes" under PERSIA; Vagi "Egyptian Gold" under EGYPT—PTOLEMAIC KINGDOM; van Alfen "Two Unpublished Hoards and Other 'Owls' from Egypt" under ATTICA—GENERAL WORKS; Von Reden *Money in Ptolemaic Egypt* under EGYPT—PTOLEMAIC KINGDOM; Zervos "A Ptolemaic Hoard of 'Athena' Tetradrachms" under EGYPT—PTOLEMAIC KINGDOM.

PTOLEMAIC KINGDOM

6558 **Aoki, Paul N.** "An Analysis of Eight Ptolemaic Staters." *The Picus* (Canada) 2 (1993): 45-57.
As a follow-up to Hazzard's study (see Hazzard "The Composition" below), Aoki analyzed eight Ptolemaic staters by X-ray fluorescence. Explains the method and his procedure. Then presents the results of the analysis which support Hazzard's conclusions. Refutes a conclusion of a previous study (D. Walker and C. King, *Metrology of the Roman Silver Coinage*) regarding the level of debasement of the Ptolemaic tetradrachms after 53/2 B.C. Walker and King concluded these tetradrachms are about 46% silver. Aoki supports Hazzard's findings (33% silver).

6559 **Arslan, Melih, and Ayça Özen.** "A Hoard of Unpublished Bronze Coins of Ptolemy Ceraunus." *American Journal of Numismatics* 2nd ser., 12 (2000): 59-66. 3 pls.
A hoard found in Thrace in 1997 was comprised of 61+ previously unknown bronze coins bearing a variation of the inscription ΒΑΣΙΛΕΩΣ ΠΤΟΛΕΜΑΙΟΥ. The authors conclude the named king is Ptolemy Ceraunus, the oldest son of Ptolemy I Soter, who briefly ruled Macedon and Thrace in 281-279 B.C. The coins range in weight between 0.67 and 3.69 gm. They may have been struck at Byzantium. These coins also may be related to a hitherto unexplained bronze coin in the British Museum that has been attributed to an otherwise unattested Thracian dynast Ptolemaeus. Includes a catalogue of sixty-one coins from the hoard. [Also see S. Psoma "Numismatic Evidence" under THRACE—BYZANTION].

6560 **Ashton, Richard H. J.** "The Ptolemaic Coins in Fethiye Museum." *Numismatic Circular* 110 (2002): 7-12. Illus.

6561 **Ashton, Richard H. J., Melih Arslan, and Ali Dervisagaoglu.** "A Ptolemaic Hoard in Fethiye Museum (*CH* VIII, 246)." *Numismatic Chronicle* 156 (1996): 269-72. 2 pls.
A catalogue of a hoard of eighteen tetradrachms of Ptolemy I and II, deposited in the mid-third century B.C.

6562 **Bagnall, Roger S.** *The Administration of the Ptolemaic Possessions outside Egypt.* Leiden: E. J. Brill, 1976. 28 pp., maps.
"Chapter Eight (pp. 176-212) on coinage and circulation argues that the assumption that, whenever possible, Greek cities in the Ptolemaic empire were prevented from using their own currency is an oversimplification of a complex situation." [J. Melville Jones, *NL* 98]

6563 **Biddle, M.** "Ptolemaic Coins from Winchester." *Antiquity* (England) 49, no. 194 (June 1975): 213-5. Map.
A follow-up to Collis (see Collis "The Coin of Ptolemy V" below). Lists numerous Ptolemaic coins found in Britain. Suggests the coins are legitimate ancient losses, not a joke played on the archaeologists as suggested by Collis.

6564 **Breccia, Ev.** "The Numismatic Cabinet of the Museum of Alexandria in Egypt." *The Voice of the Turtle* 5, no. 9 (September 1966): 261-6. Illus.
This reprint of a portion of the author's *Alexandrea ad Aegyptum* (1922) is an overview of Egyptian coinage of the Ptolemaic period arranged as a guide to the museum's exhibit.

6565 **Brett, Agnes Baldwin.** "A New Cleopatra Tetradrachm of Ascalon." *American Journal of Archaeology* 41 (1937): 452-63. Illus.
Presents a Cleopatra tetradrachm with the date "year 66"—effectively disposing of Svoronos' hypothetical era of 84 B.C. which would indicate this coin was struck ten years after her death. Suggests revised dates for tetradrachms of Ascalon with Ptolemaic portraits. Discusses the style of Cleopatra portraits and the history of the city. [Also see Spaer "Ascalon" under SYRIA—SELEUCID KINGDOM, and Spaer "The Royal Male Head" under PALESTINE—PHILISTIA].

6566 ——— "Dated Coins of Ptolemy V, 204-180 B.C." *Museum Notes* 2 (1947): 1-11. 2 pls. [CS 3156]
Discusses the dates of Ptolemy V's reign and the application of these dates to his regnally dated coinage. Places his accession in 204 B.C. Presents a catalogue of the dated coinage bearing the magistrate mark NI from the mint of Alexandria.

6567 ——— "The Benha Hoard of Ptolemaic Gold Coins." *Museum Notes* 5 (1952): 1-8. 4 pls. [CS 3217]
A hoard of Ptolemaic gold coins, mostly octadrachms, was found in 1936 near Benha in Egypt. It was buried ca. 220 B.C. The author publishes and discusses twenty-nine coins from the hoard, including coins of Ptolemy II, III, and IV.

6568 **Broughton, T. Robert S.** "Cleopatra and the 'Treasure of the Ptolemies.'" *American Journal of Philology* 63 (1942): 328-32.
Broughton re-examines W. W. Tarn's rejection (*Cambridge Ancient History*, Volume 10) of the story that after the Battle of Actium, Cleopatra despoiled the temples of Egypt to provide funds for further resistance to Rome. Broughton argues that the Egyptian finances had in fact been depleted and there was no "Treasure of the Ptolemies" remaining. He states "the increased importance of the copper coinage during the second century B.C. can possibly be explained as a reversion to the native system, but the silver coinage was after 170 B.C. continuously debased until an Egyptian tetradrachm became about equal in value to a Roman denarius." He maintains that Cleopatra did in fact raid the temples for treasure.

6569 **Cheshire, Wendy A.** *The Bronzes of Ptolemy II Philadelphus.* Aegypten und Altes Testament, Band 77. Wiesbaden: Harrassowitz Verlag, 2009.

6570 **Clarysse, W., and E. Lanciers.** "Currency and the Dating of Demotic and Greek Papyri from the Ptolemaic Period." *Ancient Society* (Belgium) 20 (1989): 117-32.
The authors examine the Ptolemaic copper inflation ca. 210 B.C. as described by Reekmans (see below) and the subsequent doubling of the prices of common products. The date of this event provides evidence for dating Greek papyri and ostraca.

6571 **Collis, John.** "The Coin of Ptolemy V from Winchester." *Antiquity* (England) 49, no. 193 (March 1975): 47-8.
Suggests that an Egyptian coin found in Britain was a modern stray rather than a coin used in Britain and lost in antiquity. [But see Biddle "Ptolemaic Coins from Winchester" above for a different opinion].

6572 **Davesne, Alain, and André Lemaire.** "Trésors Hellénistiques du Proche-Oriente: 4e lot: Trésors de 252 Monnaies de Bronze Ptolémaïques." *Revue Numismatique* (France) 151 (1996): 67-76.

6573 **Denkler, Kirk.** "The Attribution of Later Ptolemaic Tetradrachms." *SAN—Journal of the Society for Ancient Numismatics* 13, no. 1 (spring 1982): 11-7.
Presents an overview of the history and an accurate chronology for the Ptolemaic dynasty of Egypt. Presents guidelines for attributing the Ptolemaic tetradrachms of the first century B.C. based on a combination of regnal dates and stylistic features. Includes a conversion table for the regnal dates of Ptolemy IX (116 B.C.) through Cleopatra VII (30 B.C.).

6574 **Destrooper, Anne.** "Coins from the New York University Excavations on Geronisos (Cyprus), 1990-1997." *Numismatic Chronicle* 164 (2004): 329-31.
A report on thirteen Ptolemaic coins found during the excavations.

6575 **Destrooper-Georgiades, Anne.** "Un Bronze Surfrappé de Ptolémée Ier/Demétrios Poliorcète Trouvé dans les Fouilles de l'Université d'Arizona à Dali (Chypre)." *Stephanos Nomismatikos: Edith Schönert-Geiss zum 65. Geburtstag.* Edited by Ulrike Peter. Berlin: Akademie Verlag, 1998. Pages 207-14.

6576 **Duyrat, Frédérique.** "Le Trésor de Damanhour (*IGCH* 1664) et l'Évolution de la Circulation Monétaire en Egypte Hellénistique." *L'Exception Egyptienne? Production et Échanges Monétaires en Egypte Hellénistique et Romaine. Actes du Colloque d'Alexandrie, 13-15 Avril 2002.* Edited by F. Duyrat and O. Picard. Cairo, 2005. Pages 17-51.
A re-examination of the Demanhur hoard and the evidence it provides for the circulation of Alexander coinage in Egypt.

6577 **Duyrat, Frédérique, and Olivier Picard, eds.** *L'Exception Egyptienne? Production et Échanges Monétaires en Egypte Hellénistique et Romaine. Actes du Colloque d'Alexandrie, 13-15 Avril 2002.* Cairo, 2005.

6578 **Edgar, C. C.** "A Statue of a Hellenistic King." *Journal of Hellenic Studies* 33 (1913): 50-2. 1 pl.
"Comparison with coin types aids the identification of this statue as a portrait of Ptolemy II." [J. R. Jones, *NIJHS*].

6579 "Egyptian Silver Coin Depicts Berenice, but Which One? Does Coin Show Ptolemy III's Wife, or his Sister? *Coin World* (July 1, 1996): 80. Illus.
A brief discussion of the controversy over the identity of the woman portrayed on the Ptolemaic dodecadrachms, based on information in R. Hazzard's book, *Ptolemaic Coins*. Hazzard argues the woman is Berenice, the sister of Ptolemy III. Mørkholm has argued that the woman is Berenice II, the wife of Ptolemy III. [The weight standard and denomination of the coin are also open to dispute. See R. Giedroyc "Ancient Weight Standard" below].

6580 **Emmons, Brooks.** "The Overstruck Coinage of Ptolemy I." *Museum Notes* 6 (1954): 69-84. 2 pls. [CS 3157]
Emmons slightly revises the dating of Ptolemy I's coinage as put forth by Svoronos in his 1904 corpus. The author studies overstrikes in the series of gold staters and silver tetradrachms of the period 305-285 B.C., in order to shed light on the dating of earlier coin series and on the financial policy of Ptolemy I. He attempts to demonstrate that a shortage of silver caused Ptolemy to reduce the weight of the coinage and restrike the old coins. He also connects changes in type to Ptolemy's territorial gains rather than with the deaths of Ptolemy's superiors as has been assumed. Discusses the gold-to-silver ratio in Egypt, the supply of silver, and economic policies during the reign of Ptolemy I.

6581 **Faucher, Thomas, and Catharine Lorber.** "Bronze Coinage of Ptolemaic Egypt in the Second Century B.C." *American Journal of Numismatics* 2nd ser., 22 (2010): 35-80. 5 pls.
Drawing primarily on hoards, but also on metrological and metallurgical analyses, the authors propose a relative chronology and classification for Egyptian bronze coinage of the second century B.C. This coinage is characterized by diverse obverse types that served as consistent denomination markers, even as weights of the several denominations were reduced in piecemeal fashion. A debasement of the alloy introduced a metrologically stable currency that remained in circulation from before mid-century to 115 B.C. The subtlety of the early weight reductions and the long period of stability raise doubt whether changes to the currency could have caused the much-studied price inflation of the second century.

6582 **Feuardent, Felix B.** *Collections Giovanni di Demetrio. Numismatique Egypte Ancienne.* Two parts. Paris: Rollin et Feuardent.
1. *Premeiere Partie: Monnaies de Rois.* Paris, 1869. 159 pp., 12 engraved plates.
2. *Dieuxieme Partie: Domination Romaine.* Paris, 1871. 342 pp., 24 engraved plates.

6583 **Gerson, Stephan N.** "A Newly Discovered Ptolemaic Coin of Yehud." *Israel Numismatic Journal* (Israel) 14 (2001-02): 43. Illus.

6584 **Giedroyc, Richard.** "Ancient Weight Standard Determines Denomination." *Coin World* (December 7, 1998): 90. Illus.

Giedroyc discusses the large Ptolemaic silver coins depicting Berenice. The identity of Berenice has been the subject of dispute (see "Egyptian Silver Coin" above). In this brief article, the author reviews the controversy over the weight standard and denomination of the coin. Some argue it is a dodekadrachm (12-drachma) coin struck on the Attic standard. Others argue it is a pentekaidekadrachm (15-drachma) coin struck on the Ptolemaic or Phoenician standard. [Also see D. Vagi "The Ptolemaic Pentekaidekadrachm" below].

6585 **Giesecke, Walther.** *Das Ptolemäergeld: Eine Entwicklungsgeschichte des Ägyptischen Münzwesens unter Berücksichtigung der Verhältnisse in Kyrene.* Leipzig, 1930. 98 pp., 4 pls. [CS 3159]

6586 **Gitler, Haim, and Alla Kushnir-Stein.** "The Chronology of a Late Ptolemaic Bronze Coin-Type from Cyprus." *Studies in Honor of Arie Kindler. Israel Numismatic Journal* (Israel) 13 (1994-99): 46 ff.

6587 **Gitler, Haim, and Catharine C. Lorber.** "Small Silver Coins of Ptolemy I." *Israel Numismatic Journal* (Israel) 14 (2001-02): 34-42. Illus.
"Ptolemy issued very little fractional silver smaller than a drachm. Two varieties are published here for the first time. The first is an obol issue of the Alexander/Athena type from a Palestinian mint, probably issued c. 312 B.C. The second is a diobol of Ptolemy's later Alexandrian portrait coinage, known in two specimens acquired in Damascus and Jerusalem, respectively. A silver diobol seems superfluous in Egypt, which was now furnished with five bronze denominations. The provenances suggest the possibility that a single emission of diobols was struck for disbursement in the Ptolemaic province of Syria and Phoenicia, where the circulating medium consisted largely of small silver coins." [C. Lorber, *NL* 146]

6588 ——— "A New Chronology for the Ptolemaic Coins of Judah." *American Journal of Numismatics* 2nd ser., 18 (2006): 1-41. 2 pls.
The authors present a new classification and chronology for the Ptolemaic coins of Judah. They sought to understand to which reign the Ptolemaic coins of Judah belong, the date of the coins depicting Berenice I, and the attribution of the coins that do not completely replicate the Ptolemaic types. They begin with a summary of prior research. Then they review the numismatic evidence provided by metrology, types, legends, die axes, dies studies, and hoards. They present a catalogue of over 200 specimens of the coinage of Judah that are clearly Ptolemaic, as well as a few others that might be Ptolemaic. The coins are classified into eight groups, and each group is discussed. The results of analysis by X-ray fluorescence are shown in tables, and the analysis indicates that these coins were made from the purest silver bullion available at the time.

6588a **Gitler, Haim, and Daniel M. Master.** "Cleopatra at Ascalon: Recent Finds from the Leon Levy Expedition." *Israel Numismatic Research* (Israel) 5 (2010): 111-42.
"All known specimens of the autonomous tetradrachms of Ascalon minted during the first century B.C.E. are presented. Included are the specimens depicting royal male portraits (type immobilis of Antiochus VIII) minted between 99/8 and 50/49 B.C.E., at which point there was a radical break with the appearance of portraits of Cleopatra VII on the city's silver. These tetradrachms are very rare and so far only four issues of year 55 (50/49 B.C.E.) and one of year 66 (39/8 B.C.E.) were known. Three recently identified specimens of an unpublished year (65=40/39 B.C.E.) have also been recorded." [Abstract in *INR*]

6589 **Grigorakis, G.** "A Hoard of Ptolemaic Silver Coins from Chios." *Coins in the Aegean Islands. Proceedings of the Fifth Scientific Meeting, Mytilene, 16-29 September 2006. Volume 1: Ancient Times.* Obolos 9. Edited by Panagiotis Tselekas. Athens: The Friends of the Numismatic Museum, 2010. Pages 263-82.

6590 **Hall, H. P.** "A Note on the Fabric of Ptolemaic Bronze." *Numismatic Chronicle* 5th ser., 6 (1926): 301-2. Illus.
Suggests the central depression found on many Ptolemaic bronze coins was made by a punch and was intended as the central support for a tool used to scrape off the surface irregularities from the cast blanks before striking.

6591 **Hazzard, Michael.** "Cleopatra Coinage." *Journal of the Society for International Numismatics.* Reprint, California: May Company (no date). 10 pp., illus.
The reprint was put out by May Department Stores when they offered ancient coinage.

6592 **Hazzard, Richard A.** "Cleopatra: Career, Coinage and Legend." *Cornucopiæ* (publication of The Ancient Coin Society, Canada) 1, no. 1 (August 1972): 3-13. Illus.
A well written summary of Cleopatra's career, with brief mentions of a few of the related coins. Begins with Cleopatra's assumption of the throne upon the death of her father, Auletes, in 51 B.C. She kept the Egyptian kingdom independent of Rome for another twenty years. She reformed the currency, reducing its silver content and re-valuing it, and increased its supply. Hazzard traces Cleopatra's relationships with Julius Caesar, Mark Antony, and Octavius, and recounts their military exploits and the death of Cleopatra.

6593 ——— "The Regnal Years of Ptolemy II Philadelphos." *The Phoenix* (Canada) 41, no. 2 (summer 1987): 140-58.
Ptolemy II first reckoned his reign from Soter's death in 282 B.C. and he later renumbered his regnal years from some point in 285, when, he alleged, he got the reins of power from his parent. This essay reviews the diverse kinds of evidence for regnal years and submits two dates for Ptolemy II's reform: 282 for the Macedonian calendar and 267 for the Egyptian calendar. Dated coins are cited as evidence.

6594 ——— "The Composition of Ptolemaic Silver." *Journal of the Society for the Study of Egyptian Antiquities* (Canada) 20 (1990): 89-107.
The author used a combination of metallurgical methods to perform an analysis on 141 Ptolemaic silver coins. Concludes that Ptolemaic silver remained nearly 100% pure until 149/8 B.C., about 98% pure from 149/8 to 137/6 B.C., about 90% pure from 137/6 to 53/2 B.C., and about 33% pure from 53/2 to 30 B.C. [Also see P. Aoki "An Analysis" above for a confirmation of Hazzard's results].

6595 ——— "The Regulation of the Ptolemaieia: a Hypothesis Explored." *Journal of the Royal Astronomical Society of Canada* (Canada) 85 (1991): 6-23. Illus.
"The author assigns a series of Ptolemaic tetradrachms and didrachms to the city of Pelusium and an era commencing in 262. Ptolemy II introduced the era because he wanted to fix the Ptolemaieia, the memorial games and sacrifices to his father, to the winter of every quadrennial year in and after 262. Since Ptolemy II had originally dated these rites to every fourth year on his Macedonian calendar of 369 days, the date of the festival had moved forward with respect to the seasonal cycle from winter of 282, when Ptolemy I had died, to spring of 266, when his son had held the last festival on the Macedonian

calendar. Support for this hypothesis comes from numismatic and textual evidence and from the appearance of Venus as a morning star close to the acronychal rising of Canopus about the 25th of January in 262." [J. Petko, *NL* 135]

6596 ——— "Did Ptolemy I Get His Surname from the Rhodians in 304?" *Zeitschrift für Papyrologie und Epigraphik* (Germany) 93 (1992): 52-6.
"The author questions whether the Rhodians attached an epiklesis to Ptolemy I when they deified the king in 304. Rhodian inscriptions did not use the surname if they referred to him; Ptolemaic inscriptions referred to Ptolemy I and Berenice I as the Theoi Soteres from 282, but referred to Ptolemy I *individually* as Ptolemy or as King Ptolemy. The same terminology appeared on Ptolemaic coins until the 23rd regnal year of Ptolemy II or 263/2, when they started to employ the phrase Ptolemaios Soter." [J. Petko, *NL* 135]

6597 ——— "Portrait Coins of the Ptolemies." *The Picus* (Canada) 2 (1993): 8-35. Illus.
Provides historical and biographical information on the Ptolemaic kings and queens, and illustrates twenty-six portrait coins. Also illustrates two portrait heads of Arsinoe III and Ptolemy V for which positive identifications were made by comparisons with coin portraits.

6598 ——— "Ptolemaic Notes: I. Delta, the Greatest Engraver of the Ptolemies." *The Anvil* (Canada) 4, no. 3 (May 1, 1994): 25-7. Illus.
Briefly describes the tetradrachms, octadrachms, staters, and triobols struck during the reign of Ptolemy I from dies engraved by an artist who signed his dies with a small Δ. [Also see "Obscure Artist" under ART].

6599 ——— "Ptolemaic Notes: II. The Debasement of the Silver." *The Anvil* (Canada) 4, no. 5 (September 1, 1994): 49-50.
Outlines the historical and political events leading to the gradual debasement of the Ptolemaic silver coinage which began as almost 100% silver under Ptolemy I, but ended up as a base metal coin by the end of the Ptolemaic dynasty.

6600 ——— "Two Hoards of Ptolemaic Silver: IGCH 1713 and 1722." *Numismatic Chronicle* 154 (1994): 53-66.
"The Sharnûb hoard (*IGCH* 1713) consisted of fifty-six tetradrachms chosen from the available stock of unworn silver in order to avoid a progressive discount on worn tetradrachms. Since the last dated coin was struck in the 24th regnal year of Ptolemy X Alexander (91/90), the hoarder might have hidden his cash during the crisis of 89/88, when Alexander fled into exile. The second hoard (*IGCH* 1722) consisted of 169 tetradrachms; 162 of them were of fine silver (about 100% to 90% pure), while seven were of base silver (about 33% pure). After the great debasement of 53/52, the Ptolemies priced both fine and debased tetradrachms at 2000 copper drachms per coin, and the hoarder apparently saved the old coins of fine silver until the supply became exhausted during the very early years of Cleopatra VII (51-30 B.C.)." [R. Hazzard, *NL* 134]

6601 ——— *Ptolemaic Coins: An Introduction for Collectors.* Toronto: Kirk & Bentley, 1995. 132 pp., illus., map.
A thorough introduction to the coinage of the Ptolemaic Kingdom. Begins with a discussion of the portrait coins, providing biographical information on the Ptolemy family, from the issues of Ptolemy I (304 B.C.) through Cleopatra Selene (ca. 25 B.C.). Then Hazzard discusses the coins designed by the engraver who signed his dies with Δ. The standard silver tetradrachm series is then reviewed in a reign-by-reign analysis, describing the types and regnal dates used by each ruler. The author discusses the debasement of the coinage. Then he examines the bronze coinage, discussing various methods of dating the coins, methods of manufacture, and theories regarding the denominations represented by the coins. Discusses the uses of coinage within the kingdom, and coinage reforms. Provides a list of ancient authors mentioned in the text. Concludes with a catalogue of 156 coin types chosen for their historical importance or their availability to collectors. The book is heavily illustrated by coin photographs and includes extensive footnotes for each chapter. [Reviewed by C. Lorber in *American Journal of Numismatics* 2nd ser., 7-8 (1995-6): 256-76, by C. Schulze in *The Celator* 10, no. 1 (January 1996): 40-1, by T. M. James in *Journal of the Society for the Study of Egyptian Antiquities* 23 (1993, publ. 1996): 75-7, by G. Kumpikevicius in *Hekte* 1 (February 1996): 11-9, and by E. B. Banning in *The Celator* 11, no. 6 (June 1997): 28-9. Also see Cathy Lorber's extensive descriptive review in *SAN* 20, no. 1 (1997): 33-8].

6602 ——— "Ptolemaic Notes: III. A Problem of Chronology." *The Anvil* (Canada) 5, no. 1 (January 1, 1995): 1-2. Illus.
Explains the two calendar systems used by Ptolemy II—the Egyptian and the Macedonian. The study of the use of date-letters on Ptolemy's coinage reveals some errors previously made by scholars in interpreting these dating systems.

6603 ——— "Ptolemaic Notes: IV. The Soter Era." *The Anvil* (Canada) 5, no. 4 (July 1, 1995): 37, 44.
Describes the numismatic, epigraphical, and literary evidence for the Soter era—a new calendar system which the author suggests was introduced in 262 B.C. by Ptolemy II.

6604 ——— "Ptolemaic Notes: V. The Early Bronze Coinage." *The Anvil* (Canada) 5, no. 5 (September 1, 1995): 49-53. Illus.
Describes the denominations, types, and weight standards used for the bronze coinage of Ptolemy I, II, III, and IV (323-210 B.C.).

6605 ——— "Theos Epiphanes: Crisis and Response." *Harvard Theological Review* 88, no. 4 (October 1995): 415-36.
"The loss of Coele-Syria about 199 lowered the prestige of the Ptolemaic monarchy. That it also faced revolts in Upper and Lower Egypt forced Aristomenes, regent for Ptolemy V, to make a stupendous effort to restore the child's prestige. The regent proclaimed the child a God Manifest at Alexandria in 199/8, because a comet had appeared in the year of his birth (210) and another in the year of his accession to the throne (204). Zeus, the regent declared, had sent these comets to augur the future greatness of the king. Silver tetradrachms rendered the message in symbols (*Svoronos* 1249). The obverse of these tetradrachms showed the draped and diademed bust of Ptolemy V, while the reverse bore the legend ΠΤΟΛΕΜΑΙΟΥ ΕΠΙΦΑΝΟΥΣ and a comet on either side of a winged thunderbolt, symbol of Zeus, lord of the heavens and protector of the Ptolemies." [J. Petko, *NL* 135]

6606 ——— Ptolemaic Notes: VI. The Crisis of 199/8." *The Anvil* (Canada) 6, no. 2 (May 1, 1996): 25-6, 28. Illus.
Ptolemy V timed his celebration of the Ptolemaieia to coincide with a comet. He used this event as propaganda to elevate his status as he proclaimed himself Theos Epiphanes in 198 B.C. [For a more extensive discussion of this topic, see Hazzard's "Theos Epiphanes" above].

6607 ——— "A Review of the Cyprus Hoard, 1982." *Numismatic Chronicle* 158 (1998): 25-36. 2 pls.
The hoard contained at least twenty-seven Ptolemaic silver coins—sixteen tetradrachms and eleven smaller denominations. Hazzard corrects errors in Mørkholm's catalogue and commentary and suggests termini for the coins bearing a portrait of Dionysos. [See Mørkholm "Cyprus Hoard, 1982" below].

6608 ——— "The Use of the Macedonian Calendar under Ptolemies V and VI." *Travaux de Numismatique Grecque Offerts à Georges Le Rider*. Edited by M. Amandry and S. Hurter. London: Spink, 1999. Pages 145-59.

The author examines the calendars used in Egypt: the Egyptian, the Macedonian, and an assimilated calendar. Hazzard re-dates some tetradrachms bearing the regnal years of Ptolemy V (204-180 B.C.) or VI (180-145 B.C.) on the Macedonian calendar and places the commencement of Ptolemy VI's reign in his *second* Macedonian year (180/179 B.C.). In an appendix, Hazzard lists the gold and silver coins bearing a date between 193/2 and 146/5 B.C.

6609 **Hazzard, Richard A., and I. D. Brown**. "The Silver Standard of the Ptolemaic Coinage." *Revue Numismatique* (France) 26 (1984): 231-9.
"The authors present the results of the analysis of seventy-six silver coins of Lagides, performed by different researchers and according to different methods, chemical and nuclear. They were thus able to examine the authenticity of certain decadrachms and to perceive a slight decline in the standard (about 10%), which only happens around 135 and the fall to one third is placed at the reform of Cleopatra VII in 51." [Hazzard and Brown, *NL* 116]

6610 **Hill, D. K.** "Material on the Cult of Serapis." *Hesperia* 15 (1946): 60-72. Illus.
"On pp. 68-9 it is decided that the original statue of Serapis cannot be earlier than the time of Ptolemy II. The earliest dated representation appears on a coin of Ptolemy IV, and coins of Hadrian and Antoninus Pius show that the story of its transport from Sinope continued to be believed." [J. R. Jones, *NIAJAH*]

6610a **Hollstein, Wilhelm**. "Münzen des Ptolemaios Keraunos." *Revue Suisse de Numismatique* (Switzerland) 74 (1995): 13-25.

6611 **Holt, Frank L.** "Ptolemy's Alexandrian Postscript." *Saudi Aramco World* 57, no. 6 (November/December 2006): 4-9. Illus.
Recounts the battle between Ptolemy and Perdiccas in 320 B.C. Describes Ptolemy's new coinage bearing the likeness of Alexander in elephant headdress. Holt finds the prototype for this bold new portrait in a newly discovered gold coin, supposedly from the Mir Zakah hoard found in Afghanistan. [Also see Bopearachchi and Flandrin *Le Portrait d'Alexandre le Grand* under HOARDS. Bopearachchi and Flandrin publish coins from the hoard. But Fischer-Bossert condemns the subject gold coin as a forgery].

6612 **Hoover, Oliver D.** "Ptolemaic Lead Coinage in Coele Syria (103-101 BCE)." *Israel Numismatic Journal* (Israel) 3 (2008): 81-5.
Two lead series frequently found in the Transjordan and bearing the types of Zeus-Ammon/eagle and Zeus/eagle are catalogued and discussed. On the basis of typology and the inscription B–A it is argued that the lead issues imitate and evolved from a Ptolemaic bronze coinage probably produced under Cleopatra III and Ptolemy X. On the basis of the connection to the Ptolemaic bronze series, it is suggested that the lead series were struck as a form of emergency money during the "War of Scepters" (103–101 B.C.), which involved Ptolemaic troop movements in Transjordan and elsewhere in Coele Syria.

6613 **Hultsch, Friedrich**. *Die Ptolemaischen Münz-Und Rechnungs-Werte*. Leipzig, 1903. Reprints, Amsterdam: A. M. Hakkert, 1967; Chicago: Obol International, 1980. 60 pp. [CS 3336]

6614 **Huston, Stephen M., and Catharine C. Lorber**. "A Hoard of Ptolemaic Coins in Commerce, October 1992 (*CH* 8, 413): Part 1. Bronze Coins of Ptolemy IV and V. Part 2: Currency Reform under Ptolemy IV and V." *Numismatic Chronicle* 161 (2001): 10-40. 13 pls.
In Part 1, the authors document numerous coins from a hoard published as *Coin Hoards* 8, no. 413, including many that were not examined and recorded by Martin Price at the British Museum. The coins are predominantly large denomination bronzes of Ptolemy II, Ptolemy III, and one of Ptolemy IV. Includes a catalogue of the coins and commentary. The coins may present evidence of a reform of the bronze currency. Examines the date of the reform and the metrology of the coins. In Part 2 (written by Lorber), the hoard evidence is used to show that the Ptolemaic bronze currency underwent an official reform late in the reign of Ptolemy Philopater. The reform involved demonetization, use of countermarks, and the introduction of new coinage with redesigned types, struck on a lighter standard.

6615 **Hutt, Cecelia**. "Ptolemaic Queens." *CalCoin News* 13, no. 2 (March 1959): 29-32. Illus.
"Concisely written biographical and historical notes on the Berenices, Arsinoes and Cleopatras, queens of the royal line of ancient Egypt which began shortly after the death of Alexander in 323 B.C. and ended with Cleopatra Selene, daughter of Mark Antony and Cleopatra VII. Illustrations of a silver denarius of Antony and a Ptolemaic bronze both show portraits of Cleopatra VII, the first with diademed bust, draped, f.r., the second with fairly young face, in profile, f.l." [G. North, *NL* 49]

6616 **Jenkins, G. Kenneth**. "An Early Ptolemaic Hoard from Phacous." *Museum Notes* 9 (1960): 17-37. 3 pls. [CS 3162]
Examines a hoard discovered near Phacous in the Nile delta in 1956. The hoard included tetradrachms of Alexander the Great, and tetradrachms and octodrachms of Ptolemy Soter, from a variety of mints. Catalogues a sample from the hoard. Summarizes the coins by mint, in comparison to the Kuft hoard. Calls attention to the lack of coins of Amphipolis after 318 B.C. and the greatly reduced presence of coins of Asia Minor mints after that date. Notes the relative lack of "Alexander in elephant skin" types of Ptolemy, which were minted on a reduced standard, and suggests this type began prior to 305 B.C. Rearranges the sequence of the reduced-weight coinage as published by Svoronos, and suggests it began ca. 312-310 rather than 305 as has been suggested by Svoronos and Brooks Emmons. Discusses the relationship of the heavy and reduced-standard coins in circulation, as well as their relationship to the gold coins. [See Mørkholm "Cyrene and Ptolemy I" under CYRENAICA for a suggested revision to Jenkins' chronology. Also see Nash "Kuft Hoard" under HOARDS for a confirmation of some of Jenkins' conclusions].

6617 **Jenkins, Michael R.** "A Hoard from Elephantine Island." *Numismatic Chronicle* 160 (2000): 274-6. 2 pls.
A brief examination of a hoard of thirteen Ptolemaic bronze coins found in Egypt.

6618 **Jungfleisch, Marcel**. "Réflexions de 'Practicien' sur les Monnaies Ptolémïques en Bronze." *Bulletin de l'Institut d'Egypte* (Egypt) 30 (1947-48): 47-60. [CS 3164]
"Minting procedures used in determining certain attributions." [E. Clain-Stefanelli]

6619 **Kiang, Dawson**. "An Unpublished Coin Portrait of Ptolemy VI Philometer." *Museum Notes* 10 (1962): 69-76. 1 pl.
Examines a Ptolemaic coin from the Burton Berry collection, now in the American Numismatic Society. The coin has *obv*., portrait and six-pointed star; *rev*., eagle and six-pointed star. The coin is possibly unique. The author compares the portrait on the coin to those on Ptolemaic finger-rings and seal impressions. He reviews prior attempts to identify the king portrayed on these items. He identifies the king as Ptolemy VI Philometor.

6620 **Kindler, Arie**. "A Ptolemaic Coin Hoard from Tel Mikhal." *Tel Aviv* (Israel) 5, nos. 3-4 (1978): 159-69. Illus.

"A hoard of forty-seven tetradrachms of Ptolemy I-III includes issues of Alexandria and the Phoenician and Palestinian mints, two pieces dated 47 and 48 and attributed to Aradus (apparently the latest coins in the hoard), and two coins assigned to Ephesos under Ptolemy III." [A. Spaer, *NL* 103]. [Also see Mørkholm "A Group of Ptolemaic Coins" below. Mørkholm disputes the attribution of some coins and suggests a different burial date for the hoard].

6621 **Koch, W.** "Die Ersten Ptolemäerinnen nach ihren Münzen." *Zeitschrift für Numismatik* (Germany) 34 (1923): 67-106.

6622 **Koutsoukos, Eduardo A. M.** "The Mass Production of Bronze Blank Castings for Coining in Ptolemaic Egypt." *Spink Numismatic Circular* 92, no. 4 (May 1984): 115-6. Illus.
Discusses the method of manufacture of blanks for Ptolemaic bronze coins. Describes the process of casting blanks in rows. Describes the process of using a lathe to trim the edges of the blanks after striking. Includes some good enlarged photographs of a casting sprue, edges, and central holes. Interestingly, Koutsoukos claims that a whole row of coins was struck at one time—the flans being separated after striking.

6623 **Kreuzer, Matthew.** *The Coinage System of Cleopatra VII and Augustus in Cyprus.* Springfield, Massachusetts: published by the author, 2004. 131 pp., illus.
Examines the coins struck in Cyprus between ca. 55 BC and AD 14. Many coins previously attributed to other mints are reattributed to Cypriot mints based on flan characteristics, style, mintmarks, mint finds, and archaeological finds. Kreuzer suggests the Ptolemaic coins with the ΠΑ mintmark were in fact struck at Paphos on Cyprus. Most researchers attribute these coins to Alexandria. The author also suggests that some coin portraits, previously identified as Ptolemy I, are in fact portraits of Cleopatra VII. Provides an extensive list of suggested attribution changes for the coinage of this period. Includes extensive metrological data. [An extremely critical review by Oliver Hoover appears in *American Numismatic Society Magazine* 4, no. 3 (winter 2005): 68-71. Hoover derides Kreuzer's "incoherent reattributions" and "extensive use of fallacious arguments" combined with "the low standard of presentation." He concludes with the hope that this book "will soon disappear" and be forgotten before it can cause too much damage].

6624 **Kuschel, B.** "Das Neue Münzbilder des Ptolemaios Soter." *Jahrbuch für Numismatik und Geldgeschichte* (Germany) 11 (1961): 9-18.

6625 **Kyrieleis, H.** "Die Porträtmünzen Ptolemaios' V, und seiner Eltern. Zur Datierung und Historischen Interpretation." *Jahrbuch des Deutschen Archäologischen Institutes* (Germany) 88 (1973): 213-46. Illus. [CS 3166]

6626 **Lorber, Catherine C.** "Large Ptolemaic Bronzes in Third-Century Egyptian Hoards." *American Journal of Numismatics* 2nd ser., 12 (2000): 67-92. 6 pls.
A re-assessment of the chronology of Ptolemaic bronze coins in the third century B.C. and of the denominations of that currency, based on numerous hoards found in Egypt. Defines seven denominations by grouping the coins by weight and diameter. Discusses control marks and their emission sequences. Several of the hoards examined here were closed at the same point in the reign of Ptolemy IV. Lorber supports the theory that a monetary reform happened around this time. Describes papyrological evidence for a monetary reform. Evidence points to a demonetization of circulating bronze currency during the reign of Ptolemy IV.

6627 ——— "Development of Ptolemaic Bronze Coinage in Egypt." *L'Exception Egyptienne? Production et Échanges Monétaires en Egypte Hellénistique et Romaine. Actes du Colloque d'Alexandrie, 13-15 Avril 2002.* Edited by F. Duyrat and O. Picard. Cairo, 2005. Pages 135-57.

6628 ——— "A Revised Chronology of the Coins of Ptolemy I." *Numismatic Chronicle* 165 (2005): 45-64.
Lorber reviews the currently accepted chronology of the early Ptolemaic coinage. She then proposes a down-dating of most of the Ptolemaic-weight coins of the Alexander/Athena type to the early reign of Ptolemy I as king. These were previously thought of as late satrapal issues of Ptolemy I.

6628a ——— "The Last Ptolemaic Bronze Emission of Tyre." *Israel Numismatic Journal* (Israel) 1 (2006): 15-20.
"A bronze coin of Ptolemy V, struck at Tyre, bears his epithet Epiphanes and a spearhead symbol. These features associate the bronze with a few precious metal coins (Svoronos 1904: 206, Nos. 1247–1249), confirming Otto Mørkholm's attribution of the "Monogram and Spearhead Series" to Syro-Phoenicia. Ptolemy V assumed the demotic form of his epiklesis before December 11, 199/January 9, 198. Our bronze and the tetradrachm Svoronos 1904: 206, No. 1249 are apparently the earliest documents with the Greek form of the epiklesis. The numismatic evidence indicates that Tyre passed from Ptolemaic to Seleucid control in the Egyptian/Macedonian year 199/8." [Lorber's abstract].

6629 ——— "Ptolemaic Bronzes of Antiochus IV." *Revue Belge de Numismatic et de Sigillographie* (Belgium) 153 (2007): 31-44.

6630 ——— "The Ptolemaic Era Coinage Revisited." *Numismatic Chronicle* 167 (2007): 105-17. Illus.
Lorber examines a series of coins with dates in the reverse field referring to an unidentified era. A newly discovered coin bearing numerals 115 adds evidence—it is the only tetradrachm recorded for the years 100-117 when the coinage otherwise consisted solely of didrachms. The era remains uncertain, but the coins may have been minted at Arsinoe near Salamis, and may be related to the ship building activity in that area.

6631 ——— "The Ptolemaic Mint of Ras Ibn Hani." *Israel Numismatic Research* (Israel) 2 (2007): 63-76.
Bronze coins with a diademed female portrait and the obverse legend ΒΕΡΕΝΙΚΗΣ ΒΑΣΙΛΙΣΣΗΣ are reattributed from Tyre, Sidon, and Ioppe or Gaza to Ras Ibn Hani, a Ptolemaic stronghold on the Syrian coast near Lattaqiyah (ancient Laodicea ad Mare). The portrait iconography is ambiguous and the fabric of the coins anomalous. But the assemblage of Ptolemaic coin-finds at Ras Ibn Hani supports the attribution of the Berenice bronzes to the reign of Ptolemy III, even as it suggests that the Lagid occupation of the site may have begun earlier.

6631a ——— "Ptolemaic Bronze Coinage of Tyre." *Israel Numismatic Journal* (Israel) 16 (2007-8).

6631b ——— "A Gold Mnaieion of Ptolemaic Cyprus at Tel Kadesh: Background and Context." *Israel Numismatic Research* (Israel) 5 (2010): 59-77.
"A gold coin from Ptolemaic Cyprus, dated 191/0 B.C.E., was found during excavation of a Seleucid administrative building at Tel Kedesh. A review of pertinent hoards suggests that money did not flow from Cyprus to Coele Syria and Phoenicia in the first decades of the second century B.C.E. Most likely this

high-value coin reached Kedesh through some contact between the Ptolemaic and Seleucid elites." [Abstract from *INJ*. Also see E. Martin "Gold Coin Find in Israel" below].

6632 **Lorber, Catherine C., and Frank L. Kovacs.** "A Ptolemaic Mint at Soli: A Tale of Two Magistrates." *Schweizer Münzblätter* (Switzerland) 47, no. 187 (1997): 92-9. Illus.
"Soli functioned briefly as a mint for Ptolemy V, issuing tetradrachms with the Serapis-Isis obverse type. The attribution rests on the owl mintmark and control links to Soli's coinage for the Seleucid king Antiochus III." [C. Lorber, *NL* 146]

6633 **Lorber, Catherine C., and David L. Vagi.** "The Inaugural Issue of the Ptolemaic Mint of Tyre." *SAN—Journal of the Society for Ancient Numismatics* 19, no. 1 (1995): 6-7. Illus.
Examines a tetradrachm of Ptolemy I which the authors identify as the first issue of the Tyre mint after Phoenicia fell under the control of Ptolemy in 287 B.C. Discusses the stylistic similarities, including the use of a dolphin symbol, between this coin and the last issue of Demetrius Poliorcetes, who previously controlled the Tyre mint. It is suggested that this coin was a special issue struck to reward the troops whose defection had delivered Phoenicia into Ptolemy's hands.

6634 **Mamroth, Alfred.** "Die Münzbildnisse der Königin Kleopatra VII Philopater." *Berliner Numismatische Zeitschrift* (Germany) 6 (1951) 161-5. [CS 3537]

6635 **Manning, J. G.** "Coinage as 'Code' in Ptolemaic Egypt." *The Monetary Systems of the Greeks and Romans*. Edited by W. V. Harris. Oxford: University Press, 2008. Pages 84-111.
Discusses the use of money in Ptolemaic Egypt in relationship to the development of the state. Begins with a short history of money in Egypt and then discusses the Ptolemaic economy. Discusses the reforms of the tax system by Ptolemy II and shows how coinage represented the authority of the king. The codification of coinage by the state was an important institutional shift in the economic history of Egypt. Coinage was a public symbol of political sovereignty.

6636 **Martin, Erik.** "Gold Coin Find in Israel Excites Specialists: Heaviest, Most Valuable Ancient Gold Coin Find There." *Coin World* (August 30, 2010): 4, 40. Illus.
A report of the discovery of a gold octodrachm of Arsinoë II at Tel Kedesh, Israel. The coin is referred to as a "mnaieion" and is reported to be the heaviest gold coin (27.71 gm) ever found in an excavation in Israel. [Also see Lorber "A Gold Mnaieion" above].

6637 **Mattingly, Harold.** "Zephyritis." *American Journal of Archaeology* 54, no. 2 (April 1950): 126-8.
Reviews the commercial relations between Rome and Ptolemaic Egypt in Southern Italy. Discusses a series of Roman silver coins that parallels—stylistically, epigraphically, and chronologically—a Ptolemaic series probably minted in the same general area. The author suggests that Arsinoe II's connection with Locri Epizephyrii, where she was worshipped after her death, makes that South Italian city a likely mint for the Ptolemaic series. [Summarized from J. Breckenridge, *NL* 13]

6638 **Meadows, Andrew.** "La Monetazione di Cleopatra VII." *Cleopatra, Regina d'Egitto: Catalogo della Mostra a Cura di Susan Walker e Peter Higgs. Roma 12 Ottobre 2000—25 Febgraio 2001*. Edited by Susan Walker and Peter Higgs. 2000. Page 128-9. Illus.

6639 ——— "Ptolemy VI, VIII, Cleopatra II, Cyprus and Argos: an Enigmatic Monetary Transaction of the 2nd Century B.C." *Numismatic Chronicle* 165 (2005): 91-7.
Publishes and discusses an inscription found at Argos in 1981 which includes references to coins.

6640 **Metcalf, David M.** "Ptolemaic and Roman Coins found in Nubia." *Kush* (publication of the National Corporation for Antiquities and Museums of the Sudan) 14 (1966): 334-5.
Catalogues three Ptolemaic coins found in the region of Kalabsha.

6641 **Milne, Joseph G.** "The Copper Coinage of the Ptolemies." *Annals of Archaeology and Anthropology* 1. Liverpool: University Press, 1908. Pages 30-40.
Milne discusses the silver-to-copper value ratio in the third century B.C. in Egypt. Explores what means were adopted to enable the public to distinguish the denominations of the copper coins—they bear no marks of value and the types are similar. Discusses the weights and diameters of the coins, and the tendency of the weight of a particular denomination to fall over time.

6642 ——— "Ptolemaic Coinage in Egypt." *Journal of Egyptian Archaeology* (England) 15 (1929): 150-3.
Examines the gold-to-silver ratio in Egypt. Emphasizes the relative scarcity of silver in Egypt. Discusses the adoption of a monetary standard based on copper. Reviews the changes in the weight standard for silver coins.

6643 ——— "The Currency of Egypt under the Ptolemies." *Journal of Egyptian Archaeology* (England) 24 (1938): 200-7.
A good summary of the history of coinage in Egypt before Roman times. Discusses the near total lack of coinage in Egypt before Alexander the Great, the use of imported Greek coins as bullion, the introduction of coinage under Alexander, weight standards, the introduction of bronze coins under Ptolemy, the establishment of bronze as a true monetary standard metal, and fluctuations in the gold-to-silver ratio.

6644 **Mørkholm, Otto.** "Ptolemaic Coins and Chronology: the Dated Silver Coinage of Alexandria." *Museum Notes* 20 (1975): 7-24. 5 pls. [CS 3168]
Presents a survey of the dated silver coinage of Alexandria to further our knowledge of Ptolemaic chronology in the second and first centuries B.C. Explains the Egyptian use of the regnal year. Explains regnal years used on the coinage of each ruler from Ptolemy VI Philomor (155/4 B.C.) through Caesarion (31/30 B.C.). Includes a tabular summary of reign dates.

6645 ——— "The Ptolemaic 'Coins of an Uncertain Era.'" *Nordisk Numismatisk Årsskrift* (Sweden) (1975-76): 23-58, including 8 pls. Map. [CS 3169]

Examines a series of Ptolemaic silver coins which are distinguished by being dated according to an era. Surveys the earlier opinions of other researchers, including Huber, Six, and the *British Museum Catalogue,* regarding the identification of this era. Presents a catalogue of the coins in question (370 coins). Includes a frequency table of weights. Discusses hoard evidence to determine the circulation area of the coins—this points to the Phoenicia-Palestine region. Comments on chronology. Suggests the coins are attributable to Aradus and are dated according to the Aradian era of 259/8 B.C. These are a pseudo-Ptolemaic issue of Aradus. This was considered a municipal coinage designed to meet the commercial needs of an independent city. [Mørkholm's conclusions are supported by A. Spaer. See Spaer "More on the 'Ptolemaic' Coins of Aradus" under SYRIA—SELEUCID KINGDOM].

6646 ——— "The Portrait Coinage of Ptolemy V: The Main Series." *Greek Numismatics and Archaeology: Essays in Honor of Margaret Thompson.* Edited by O. Mørkholm and N. M. Waggoner. Wetteren: Numismatique Romaine, 1979. Pages 203-14. 2 pls.

The portrait coins of Ptolemy V, silver tetradrachms and gold octodrachms, have usually been attributed to the mint at Alexandria (those known to have been minted at Phoenicia are not addressed in this article). There are two series of these coins: (1) those with a single letter or monogram on the reverse, and (2) those with a single letter, plus the Greek letters NI between the legs of the eagle. The letters denote magistrates—not annual dates. Mørkholm examines ninety-five specimens (including nine gold). He divides the coins into seventeen different issues and shows the interrelationships of dies and issues. Based on die links and hoard evidence, Mørkholm suggests these coins were all minted in or near Phoenicia, rather than Alexandria, before 199 B.C.

6647 ——— "A Group of Ptolemaic Coins from Phoenicia and Palestine." *Israel Numismatic Journal* (Israel) 4 (1980): 4-7. 2 pls.

"A group of tetradrachms struck in Phoenicia and Palestine is reassigned to Ptolemy III instead of Ptolemy II, affecting the burial date of the Tel Mickal hoard published by A. Kindler (see Kindler "A Ptolemaic Coin Hoard" above) and reinforcing the author's conclusions that certain Ptolemaic silver issues are dated by the Aradian era." [A. Spaer, *NL* 105]

6648 ——— "Some Coins of Ptolemy V from Palestine." *Israel Numismatic Journal* (Israel) 5 (1981): 5-10. Illus.

"Certain silver tetradrachms of Ptolemy V with his or Ptolemy I's portrait are assigned to the mints of Joppe and Dora. A stylistically linked group, including gold octodrachms, is tentatively assigned to a traveling mint in Palestine during the Fifth Syrian War of 202-199 B.C." [A. Spaer, *NL* 109]

6649 ——— "The Last Ptolemaic Silver Coinage in Cyprus." *Chiron* (Germany) 13 (1983): 69-79. 4 pls.

Discusses the criteria for separating the Cypriot coinage of Ptolemy IX and Ptolemy X, and supplements the publication of the Paphos hoard (see Nicolaou and Mørkholm *Paphos* below) with a list of the Cypriot emissions in silver later than 110/109 B.C.

6650 ——— "The Ptolemaic Coinage in Phoenicia and the Fifth War with Syria." *Egypt and the Hellenistic World: Proceedings of the International Colloquium, Leuven 24-26 May 1982.* Studia Hellenistica, Volume 27. Louvain, 1983. Pages 241-51. 4 pls.

Discusses Ptolemaic coinage in Phoenicia during the reign of Ptolemy V. During this period, Ptolemaic coins were issued at Joppa, Dora, Tyre, Sidon, Berytus, Byblus, Tripolis, and another mint, probably Damascus. Another large coinage, which Mørkholm dubs the "Main Series," is explained as the production of a traveling mint which followed the Ptolemaic army during the Fifth Syrian War. Mørkholm states that this coinage demonstrates the Egyptian government's efforts to maintain dominance over Phoenicia. Reviews the literary evidence for Egyptian policy in Phoenicia.

6651 ——— "Cyprus Hoard, 1982." *Numismatic Chronicle* 147 (1987): 156-8. 2 pls. Reprinted in *Numismatic Report* (Cyprus) 15-21 (1984-90): 179-82. Illus.

A hoard of twenty-seven Ptolemaic silver coins minted in Alexandria, Phoenicia, and Cyprus appeared in 1982 and was acquired by The Department of Coins and Medals, Copenhagen. It included coins of Ptolemy I/II, IV/V, V and VI. Mørkholm dates the burial to ca. 170-168 B.C. The deposit may have had some connection with the invasion of Cyprus by Antiochus IV of Syria in 168 B.C. [Also see Hazzard "A Review of the Cyprus Hoard" above for comments and corrections].

6652 **Mørkholm, Otto, and Anne Kromann.** "The Ptolemaic Silver Coinage on Cyprus, 192/1 - 164/3 B.C." *Chiron* (Germany) 14 (1984): 149-73 including 8 pls.

Presents a listing of the Ptolemaic silver coinage of Cyprus from its inception on a regular basis during the reign of Ptolemy V (204-181 B.C.). Presents a table of coin weights for the three main mints (Salamis, Citium, and Paphos). Briefly mentions hoards containing coins from this series. Lists 75 coins of Salamis, 54 of Citium, 3 of Amanthus, and 67 of Paphos.

6653 **Newell, Edward T.** *Two Recent Egyptian Hoards.* Numismatic Notes and Monographs, No. 33. New York: American Numismatic Society, 1927. 34 pp., 3 pls.

Describes two hoards found in Egypt in 1923-24. The "Delta Hoard" contained twenty-one Ptolemaic coins and was probably buried in the first quarter of Philopater's reign (ca. 220 B.C.). The "Keneh Hoard" contained forty-five gold and over 200 silver Ptolemaic coins, all in excellent condition. This hoard was possibly buried ca. 144 B.C. A few of the coins are shown. Possible circumstances surrounding the burial of the hoard are discussed.

6654 ——— "The Coinages of Ptolemy I." *The Coin Collector's Journal* 1, no. 12 (March 1935): 261-4. Illus.

A good summary of the reign and coinage of Ptolemy I. Discusses his rise to power as king of Egypt, his battles against Perdiccas, Antigonus, and Demetrius Poliorcetes, and his conquests of Palestine and Cyprus. Correlates these historical events with changes in his coinage including the evolution of types from those of Alexander to those bearing Ptolemy's portrait and name, and the change from the Attic to the Rhodian, and then to the Phoenician, weight standard.

6655 ——— "Standard Ptolemaic Silver." *The Coin Collector's Journal* (October 1939): 83-98. Also published as a booklet, *Standard Ptolemaic Silver.* The Coin Collector Series, No. 7. New York: Wayte Raymond, Inc., 1941. Reprint, Racine: Western Publishing, 1969. 16 pp. including the 7 pls. Revised reprint, New York: Sanford Durst, 1981. 17 pp. including the 7 pls. [CS 3170]

Provides clear and concise guidelines for attributing the standard-type Ptolemaic silver tetradrachms to the reign of a particular king or queen. Discusses the features of each ruler's coinage. Attribution aids include legends, magistrates' letters and monograms, mintmarks, and artistic style. Illustrates and identifies seventy varieties. Includes a table of Greek letters and numerals. Also presents a list of corrections to Svoronos's attributions. The 1981 reprint includes a page giving reclassifications of the coinage of certain rulers and estimated market values for the tetradrachms of each ruler in Very Fine condition.

6656 **Nicolaou, Ino.** "The Paphos Hoard of Ptolemaic Tetradrachms." *Numismatic Report* (Cyprus) 4 (1973): 30.

"The hoard of 2484 tetradrachms of the period Ptolemy V to Ptolemy X found during excavations in 1964 contained issues of Alexandreia, Paphos, Citium and Salamis and was buried ca. 95 B.C. See *Inventory of Greek Coin Hoards* No. 1477." [N. du Quesne-Bird, *NL* 92]

6657 ——— "The Contribution of the Numismatic Evidence to the Dating of the Seal Impressions from the 'Archives' of the City of Ancient Paphos." *Numismatic Archaeology/Archaeological Numismatics: Proceedings of an International Conference held to Honour Dr. Mando Oeconomides in Athens 1995.* Oxbow Monographs 75. Edited by K. Sheedy and C. Papageorgiadou-Banis. Oxford: Oxbow Books and The Australian Archaeological Institute at Athens, 1997. Pages 47-53. Illus.
Excavations at the House of Dionysos in Paphos brought to light a hoard of 2484 silver Ptolemaic tetradrachms, a workshop for casting bronze Ptolemaic coins, and more than 11,000 clay seal impressions which are believed to have belonged to the Archives of the city of Paphos. Some coins were found along with the seal impressions and these coins provide evidence for the dating of the seal impressions.

6658 **Nicolaou, Ino, and Otto Mørkholm.** *Paphos, Volume 1: A Ptolemaic Coin Hoard.* Nicosia: Department of Antiquities, Cyprus, 1976. 115 pp., 22 pls., map. [CS 3260]
A study of a hoard of 2484 Ptolemaic silver tetradrachms found in Cyprus during excavations at the "House of Dionysos" in 1964 at Nea Paphos, the capital of ancient Cyprus during late Hellenistic times. The hoard, concealed in an amphora, was buried in the foundation of an earlier house during the first century B.C. The coins were struck at Salamis, Kition, Paphos, and Alexandria. The Alexandrian coins bear the mintmark of Paphos. Some bronze coin flans and a casting mould were also found. Presents an historical survey of Cyprus and its coinage. Includes a table of regnal years for the Ptolemaic kings. The coins are listed, giving regnal years, weights, and die numbers. Lists 496 coins of the Salamis mint, 466 of Kition, 271 of Paphos, and 1251 of Alexandria. Provides commentary on the mints and frequency tables of weights. The appendices include a reconsideration of Svoronos's attributions, and a discussion of the dated coinage of Cyprus. Many of the coins are illustrated. [Also see Mørkholm "The Last Ptolemaic Silver Coinage" above for a supplement of coins later than 110/109 B.C. Also see Nicolaou *Paphos 2* under HOARDS].

6659 **Nicolaou, K.** "Discovery of a Ptolemaic Mint at Nea Paphos." *Numismatic Report* (Cyprus) 5 (1974): 53-7.
"In 1964 a Hellenistic workshop where metal was cast into planchets was discovered." [M. Santamas, *NL* 94]. [Also see K. Nicolaou "Archaeological News" under THE MINTING PROCESS].

6660 **Noeske, Hans-Christoph.** "Ein Frühptolemäischer Bronzeschatz in Deutschem Privatbesitz." *Stephanos Nomismatikos: Edith Schönert-Geiss zum 65. Geburtstag.* Edited by Ulrike Peter. Berlin: Akademie Verlag, 1998. Pages 491-502.

6661 ——— *Die Münzen der Ptolemäer.* Frankfurt am Main: Historisches Museum, 2000. 189 pp., 73 pls.
A catalogue of the Ptolemaic coin collection formed by Eduard Rüppell in the nineteenth century, now held in the Historisches Museum. Begins with an essay by Wolfgang Klausewitz presenting an overview of Rüpell's life. Continues with an essay by Klaus Bringmann providing a brief history of the Ptolemaic dynasty. Then Hans-Christoph Noeske presents an introduction to the Ptolemaic monetary system. A catalogue of the collection follows, in standard sylloge format. Includes 406 coins. [Reviewed by Oliver Hoover in *American Numismatic Society Magazine* 1, no. 1 (spring 2002): 39-40].

6662 **Phillips, Wayne C.** "Coins of Ptolemaic Egypt Retain Designs Indefinitely." *Coin World* (April 4, 1994): 61.
This installment of the author's "Money Talks" column presents a brief description of Ptolemaic coinage, emphasizing the similarity of the coin designs through the years.

6663 **Pincock, Richard.** "A Possibly Unique Isis Head Bronze Coin of Cleopatra I (180-176 B.C.)." *Numismatic Chronicle* 170 (2010): 53-62. Illus.
The Isis bronze coins of Ptolemaic Egypt show a female head with corkscrew locks and a wreath of barley. Both features indicate the Egyptian-Greek goddess Isis-Demeter. A recently discovered example of an Isis coin with the obverse legend ΒΑΣΙΛΙΣΣΗΣ ΚΛΕΟΠΑΤΡΑΣ belongs to a group of coins, all with a particular monogram and obverse legend for 'Queen Cleopatra,' which were produced during the joint reign of Cleopatra I with her co-regent son Ptolemy VI, although this coin may have been produced in the reign of Cleopatra II with Ptolemy VI. Various published views of the portraiture of Cleopatra I are reviewed but some uncertainty remains. However, the bronze Ptolemaic Isis coins of Alexandria represent Queen Cleopatra as Isis.

6664 **Pitchfork, Colin E.** *The Jon Hosking Collection of Ptolemaic Coins.* Sydney: Nicholson Museum, University of Sydney, 2000. 72 pp., illus.
A catalogue of the collection of Ptolemaic coins formed by Jon Martin Hosking and now in the possession of the Nicholson Museum at the University of Sydney. Begins with a description of Hosking's career and the formation of his collection. Continues with a brief introduction to Ptolemaic coinage. The catalogue includes 178 coins (including three modern copies). Includes forty-seven coins of Cleopatra VII. Each is illustrated and described.

6665 **Poole, Reginald Stuart.** "The Coins of the Ptolemies." *Numismatic Chronicle* new ser., 4 (1864): 7-16, 159-73, 231-5. 4 pls. of line drawings; 5 (1865): 126-60, 321-36. 3 pls.; 6 (1866): 1-20. Illus.; 7 (1867): 161-202.
An early attempt to organize the Ptolemaic coinage into chronological order and to differentiate the coins of various kings. Poole notes the lack of attention the series has received and the general disarray of the Ptolemaic coins in museum collections. Listings of coins are accompanied by comments on history and explanations for the author's arrangement and conclusions. Discusses the eras used in dating Ptolemaic coinage.

6666 ——— *Catalogue of Greek Coins: The Ptolemies, Kings of Egypt.* London: British Museum, 1883. Reprint, Bologna: Forni, 1963. ciii, 136 pp., 32 pls. [CS 3171]
Volume 7 of the *Catalogue of Greek Coins in the British Museum.* The 136-page catalogue of coins is preceded by 103 pages of introductory text. [Also see *Catalogue of Greek Coins in the British Museum* under PUBLIC COLLECTIONS—GREAT BRITAIN (LONDON)].

6667 **Price, Martin Jessop.** "The Coins." *The Sacred Animal Necropolis at North Saqqâra: The Southern Dependencies of the Main Temple Complex.* By Geoffrey Thorndike Martin. London: Egypt Exploration Society, 1981. Pages 156-65. 3 pls.

Coin hoards found during excavations at Saqqâra provide evidence for the circulation of coinage at Saqqâra during the Hellenistic period and for the chronological sequence of the bronze issues of Ptolemy V. Lists hoards and deposits found during excavations. Over 1500 Ptolemaic tetradrachms and numerous Hellenistic bronze coins were found.

6668 ——— "The Coins." Chapter 11 in *The Anubieion at Saqqâra I: The Settlement and the Temple Precinct.* By D. G. Jeffreys and H. S. Smith. London: Egypt Exploration Society, 1988. Pages 66-76. 4 pls.
A hoard of large Ptolemaic bronze coins helps to clarify the chronological sequence of the issues of Ptolemy II and Ptolemy III. Includes a catalogue of coins, a discussion of chronology, weights, and denominations. Includes 633 Ptolemaic bronze coins and other Hellenistic and later issues.

6669 **Reekmans, Tony.** "Monetary History and the Dating of Ptolemaic Papyri." *Studia Hellenistica* 5. Louvain: Universite Catholique, 1948. Pages 15-43.
Compiles financial data (about wages, prices, taxes, etc.) found in datable Ptolemaic papyri to assist in the dating of other papyri which are not otherwise datable. Discusses inflation during the Ptolemaic period and changes in exchange ratios between gold, silver, and copper. Includes tables of ratios by date.

6670 ——— "Economic and Social Repercussions of the Ptolemaic Copper Inflation." *Chronique d'Egypte* (Belgium) 24 (1949): 324-42.
From ca. 220 B.C. onwards, the supply of silver in circulation in Egypt was seriously reduced (silver coins had to be saved for foreign trade) and the backing of the copper currency was severely affected. Convertibility at 1:60 no longer existed and copper became a token currency. Reekmans discusses the monetary experiments which took place 217-170 B.C. Copper was cut loose from silver and became an official inland currency. In 174 B.C., the link between copper and silver was re-established at 1:480. Discusses the effects of this inflation on wages, prices, taxes, trade, agricultural production, and social unrest. [Also see Clarysse and Lanciers "Currency" above, and Segrè "The Ptolemaic Copper Inflation" below].

6671 ——— "The Ptolemaic Copper Inflation." *Studia Hellenistica 7: Ptolemaica.* Edited by E. van 'T Dack and T. Reekmans. Louvain: Universitaires de Louvain, 1951. Pages 61-118.

6672 **Reid, Matthew S.** "The Coins of Alexandria: Four Regimes of Closed Currencies." *The Celator* 19, no. 5 (May 2005): 6-20. Illus.
Examines the coinage which circulated within the closed economy of Egypt beginning during the Persian period (fifth century B.C.) when Athenian owls were used in Egypt, followed by imitation owls. The Ptolemaic period brought Alexander-style coinage, soon to be replaced by Ptolemy's distinctive issues, struck on a reduced weight standard. This reduced standard kept the coins from circulating outside of Egypt. Discusses possible reasons for Egypt's closed economy. Most likely, the goal was to retain silver within Egypt where silver was scarce. In the Roman era, the isolation was likely due to political and economic reasons—Rome desired to fully control the currency as a means of exerting control on Egypt and preventing any outside influences. The fineness and fabric of Egypt's coins during the imperial period continue to be distinguished from other coins. Even during the Byzantine period, denominations struck in Egypt differed from those issued elsewhere.

6673 **Rigsby, Kent J.** "An Edict of Ptolemy I." *Zeitschrift für Papyrologie und Epigraphik* (Germany) 72 (1988): 273-4.
"The fine prescribed in a recently published Ptolemaic papyrus of 305/4 B.C. was not expressed in drachmas 'sacred to Alexander' but in Alexander drachmas, which were 'sacred' because they were forfeited to the state. The papyrus therefore supports the proposition that Alexanders were still a regular currency in 304 B.C. in Egypt." [J. Melville Jones, *NL* 123]

6674 **Robinson, David M.** "Queen Mary's Necklace of Greek Gold Coins of Arsinoe II." *Classical Bulletin* 32, no. 3 (January 1956): 25-9. Illus.
Reviews the life of Queen Arsinoe II of Egypt. Illustrated by a necklace made of twelve gold octadrachms of Arsinoe II, accompanied by another octadrachm.

6675 **Robinson, Edward S. G.** "The Coin Standards of Ptolemy I." *The Social and Economic History of the Hellenistic World, Volume 3.* Edited by Michael I. Rostovtzeff. Oxford: Clarendon Press, 1941. Pages 1635-9.
Summarizes the changes in the coin weight standards in Ptolemaic Egypt. Reviews the chronology of changes in standards. States that the changes are related to changes in the ratio of the value of gold to silver. Summarizes the changes in the gold-to-silver ratio.

6676 **Rodger, William.** "Ptolemy I." *Coins* 19, no. 7 (July 1972): 63. Illus.
In this installment of "Personalities on Ancient Coins," the author focuses on Ptolemy I.

6677 ——— "Ptolemy III." *Coins* 21, no. 6 (June 1974): 100. Illus.
In this installment of "Personalities on Ancient Coins," the author focuses on Ptolemy III.

6678 ——— "Ptolemy II." *Coins* 22, no. 5 (May 1975): 96. Illus.
In this installment of "Personalities on Ancient Coins," the author focuses on Ptolemy II.

6679 **Samuel, D. H.** "The 'Kappa' Octodrachms of Arsinoe II: A Partial Die Study." *Cornucopiæ* (publication of The Ancient Coin Society, Canada) 4 (1979): 14-22, including 2 pls.
After the death of Arsinoe II in 268 B.C., her husband/brother Ptolemy II issued silver tetradrachms and gold octadrachms which bore her portrait. The octodrachms were discontinued under Ptolemy III or IV, but were reissued from the reign of Ptolemy V (204-180 B.C.) until perhaps 70 B.C. Those minted at Alexandria have a K in the lower left field of the obverse. This paper re-examines the possible significance of the letter K. Svoronos believed the portrait on these coins was Kleopatra. His theory that these were special coins struck on the tenth wedding anniversaries of various Kleopatras is rejected. Samuel discusses various other theories, but draws no definite conclusion. The author lists numerous specimens of this coinage and illustrates die links among the coins.

6680 **Schulze, W.** "Exclusively from Cyprus? New Ptolemaic Countermarks 'Trident' from Israel and Jordan." *Spink's Numismatic Circular* 112 (2004): 5-6. Illus.

6681 **Sear, David R.** "The Greek Pharaohs." *The Numismatist* 111, no. 3 (March 1998): 307-9. Illus.

A summary of the history of Egypt under the Ptolemies with a brief mention of the coinage.

6682 **Segrè, Angelo.** "The Ptolemaic Copper Inflation, ca. 230-140 B.C." *American Journal of Philology* 63 (1942): 174-92.
The author presents tables illustrating the prices of commodities and the rates of exchange of silver drachma with copper drachma during the inflationary period 230-140 B.C. in Ptolemaic Egypt. Discusses the political events of the period and their effects on the inflation. [Also see related articles by Reekmans above].

6683 **Seyrig, Henri.** "Le Monnayage de Ptolémaïs en Phénicie." *Revue Numismatique* (France) 6th ser., 4 (1962): 25-50. 1 pl.

6684 **Shahin, M.** "A Ptolemaic Bronze and Silver Hoard from Kom Trouga." *L'Exception Egyptienne? Production et Échanges Monétaires en Egypte Hellénistique et Romaine. Actes du Colloque d'Alexandrie, 13-15 Avril 2002.* Edited by F. Duyrat and O. Picard. Cairo, 2005. Pages 91-116.
Publication of coins from the Kom Trouga I hoard, found in Egypt in 1934. The hoard included fifty-nine Ptolemaic silver coins and was buried ca. 39 B.C.

6685 **Shaw, Carol.** "Early Ptolemaic Coinage Associated with the Ruler Cult." *Journal of the Classical and Medieval Numismatic Society*, 2nd ser., 6, no. 1 (March 2005): 5-16. Illus.
Examines the coinage of the Ptolemys, focusing on how the rulers were depicted on the coins. Their coin portraits were carefully crafted to connect the current ruler with his or her ancestors and to connect the Ptolemaic dynasty to Alexander the Great. Examines the ruler cults that sprang up in Egypt.

6686 **Smith, Helen Wade.** "Sculptural Style on Ptolemaic Portrait Coins." *Berytus* (Denmark) 10 (1952-53): 21-36. 3 pls. [CS 3574]
Seeks to identify and examine the successive stylistic phases of art exhibited on Greek coins struck by the Ptolemies. Reviews prior studies of portrait style. Reviews the coinage of the Ptolemies from the third century B.C. to the end of the dynasty. Concludes the Egyptian die-cutters produced portraits very different from those struck in the provinces.

6687 **Stein, Harry J.** "The Career and Egyptian Coinage of Ptolemy Soter." *The Numismatist* 51, no. 12 (December 1938): 1029 ff. Illus. Reprinted in *Selections from The Numismatist: Ancient and Medieval Coins.* Racine: Whitman Publishing Co., 1960. Pages 171-6. Illus.
A review of the history of Ptolemy I's rise to power and his reign as King of Egypt. Includes a brief overview of his coinage.

6688 **Svoronos, Joannes N.** *Ta Nomismata tou Kratous ton Ptolemaion.* Four volumes. Athens, 1904-08. 68 pls. [CS 3173]
The standard die study of the Ptolemaic series. Lists 1919 coin varieties. Volumes 1-3 are in Greek. Volume 4 is in German.

6689 **Thompson, Dorothy Burr.** "A Numismatic Commentary on the Ptolemaic Cult Oinochoai." *Greek Numismatics and Archaeology: Essays in Honor of Margaret Thompson.* Edited by O. Mørkholm and N. M. Waggoner. Wetteren: Numismatique Romaine, 1979. Pages 251-5. 2 pls.
Thompson discusses the relief scenes on oinochoai (faience jugs used for pouring libations before the alter of the dynastic cult) which represent the reigning queen pouring a libation. Examines oinochoai bearing references to Philopater. A comparison of the depictions of the queen on the jugs with coin portraits provides clues to the date of the oinochoai and provides information on the Ptolemaic dynastic cult.

6690 **Thompson, Margaret.** "A Ptolemaic Bronze Hoard from Corinth." *Hesperia* 20, no. 4 (October-December 1951): 355-67. 1 pl. [CS 3294]
Discusses the thirty-four bronze coins of the Ptolemaic period found during excavations at Corinth in 1948, buried ca. 146 B.C. Provides evidence that the coins with the inscription ΚΛΕΟΠΑΤΡΑΣ were minted by Cleopatra I and the Isis head coins by either the same queen or by her husband Ptolemy V. Presents an overview of Egyptian history ca. 204-145 B.C. Suggests the coins belonged to a mercenary in the service of the Ptolemaic army. Discusses the value of the coins in terms of the contemporary silver coinage.

6691 **Troxell, Hyla A.** "Arsinoe's Non-Era." *Museum Notes* 28 (1983): 35-70. 9 pls.
Examines the early posthumous portrait coins of Arsinoe II struck under Ptolemy II and Ptolemy III (silver tetradrachms and decadrachms, and gold octadrachms) which bear unusual alphabetic issue-marks on the obverse. Offers a rebuttal to Svoronos' belief that these marks denoted an "Era of Arsinoe" beginning with her death in 270 B.C. Mørkholm suggested these letters are die numbers. Troxell points out die links between the octadrachms and tetradrachms of the series. Segregates these coins into four groups based on style and differences in details of the dies. By demonstrating that there is no correlation between the octadrachms' obverse letters and those on the tetradrachms, Troxell shows that these letters cannot denote years of an era. Assigns approximate dates to each of the groups. Comments on a number of other Ptolemaic series whose interpretation or chronology must be revised based on Troxell's conclusions about the Arsinoe coins. Sixty-two coins are illustrated.

6692 **Vagi, David L.** "The Ptolemaic Pentekaidekadrachm." *SAN—Journal of the Society for Ancient Numismatics* 20, no. 1 (1997): 5-10. Illus. Also appeared in *The Celator* 13, no. 10 (October 1999): 6-18. Illus.
Vagi examines the coin long considered to be a dodekadrachm (12 drachms) struck on the Attic standard by Ptolemy III ca. 246-221 B.C. Based on a study of the weights of known specimens, the author concludes this is a pentekaidekadrachm (15 drachms) struck on the Ptolemaic (or Phoenician) standard. Summarizes the historical background of the period. Discusses the Ptolemaic and Phoenician weight standards and concludes they are the same. Discusses the identity of the woman on the obverse of the coin who has been identified as either Ptolemy II's sister Berenike Syra, or his wife Berenike II. Based on the iconography of the portrait, Vagi concludes it is Berenike II. [Also see R. Giedroyc "Ancient Weight Standard" above].

6693 ——— "Egyptian Gold." *The Numismatist* 123, no. 2 (February 2010): 70-2. Illus.
A general overview of the gold coinage of Egypt, from the rare issues of Takhos and Nectanebo II, through issues of the Ptolemies.

6694 **Vermeule, Cornelius C.** "A Ptolemaic Contribution Box in Boston." *Museum Notes* 10 (1962): 77-80. 2 pls.
The author describes a bronze moneybox containing ten bronze coins, now in the Boston Museum of Fine Arts. One of the coins is Ptolemaic; the others are too corroded to be positively identified, but are probably Ptolemaic. The box is inscribed ΥΓΙΑΙΝΕ ("Be of Good Health"), suggesting that contributors could hope for favors from Asklepios or Hygeia. The box seems to be of Egyptian origin.

6695 **Visonà, Paolo.** "A Hoard of Ptolemaic Bronze Coins in the J. Paul Getty Museum." *J. Paul Getty Museum Journal* 6/7 (1978-79): 153-62. Illus.
Catalogues and briefly discusses 137 bronze coins which made up perhaps two-thirds of a hoard. The composition of the entire hoard is rather homogenous, and only a few, very common types of the Ptolemaic kings Philadelphus, Euergetes, and Philopater are represented.

6696 ——— "An Unusual Ptolemaic Overstrike in Ann Arbor." *Spink Numismatic Circular* 89, no. 6 (June 1981): 199. Illus.
"A Ptolemaic bronze specimen from G. Dattari's coin collection in the Kelsey Museum of Archaeology at the University of Michigan is illustrated. The coin is a rarely overstruck denomination; its second types may belong to Ptolemy VIII." [P. Visonà, *NL* 107]

6697 ——— "A Tetradrachm of Cleopatra VII from Este." *Spink Numismatic Circular* 91, no. 2 (March 1983): 47. Illus.
"The author describes a base silver issue of Cleopatra VII dated to 32/31 or 31/30 B.C. and reviews the finds of Greek coins from Este's environs as well as Ptolemaic silver currency from the Adriatic." [P. Visonà, *NL* 110]

6698 **Von Reden, Sitta.** "Money and Coinage in Ptolemaic Egypt: Some Preliminary Remarks." *Akten des XXI Internationalen Papyrologenkongresses, Berlin 1995.* Archiv für Papyrusforschung, Beiheft 3. Berlin, 1997. Pages 1003-8.

6699 ——— "The Politics of Monetization in Third-Century B.C. Egypt." *Money and Its Uses in the Ancient Greek World.* Edited by A. Meadows and K. Shipton. Oxford: University Press, 2001. Pages 65-76.
The author argues that the dynamics of monetization in the first generations of Ptolemaic Egypt rested not only on the enforcement of monetization through taxation, and a prior Greek familiarity with coinage, but also on the importance of coinage in the Ptolemaic imagery of power coupled with the king's commitment to monetary exchange. Examines the place of coinage in the imagery of Ptolemy II Philadelphus, whose reign is associated with a rapid increase in monetary circulation. Discusses some papyrological material which suggests a high degree of monetization of the public economy despite a notable scarcity of coinage in circulation. Contrasts aspects of the Ptolemaic monetary economy with classical Athens.

6700 ——— *Money in Ptolemaic Egypt: From the Macedonian Conquest to the End of the Third Century B.C.* Cambridge: University Press, 2008. 378 pp., illus.
Explores the impact of Alexander the Great's introduction of coined money on the economy and society of Egypt and its political implications for the formation of the Ptolemaic state. Von Reden argues that the introduction of coinage happened slowly, spreading gradually from Alexandria into the immediately surrounding area. Under Ptolemy II, however, Egypt was aggressively monetized. Using numismatic and papyrological evidence, the workings of a rural monetary economy are reconstructed where coinage was in high demand but short supply. She argues that, once monetized, the degree of monetization was sustained only by an extensive credit economy as well as the commutation of monetary payments into kind.

6701 **Waddingham, Gary.** "Library a Marvel: Ptolemaic Dynasty Fostered Scholarly Research." *The Celator* 3, no. 2 (March 1989): 1, 22. Illus.
Focuses on the Ptolemaic dynasty's dedication to scholarship and the formation of a great library. Discusses the Greek translation of the Hebrew Bible.

6702 **Weiser, Wolfram.** *Katalog Ptolemäischer Bronzemünzen der Sammlung de Instituts für Altertumskunde der Universität zu Köln.* Sonderreiche Papyrologica Coloniesia 23. Opladen: Westdeutscher Verlag, 1995. 127 pp., 45 pls.
A catalogue of the Ptolemaic bronze coins in the collection of the Institute for Ancient Studies of the University of Cologne.

6702a **Wolf, Daniel, and Catharine C. Lorber.** "The 'Galatian Shield without (monogram)' Series of Ptolemaic Bronze Coins." *Numismatic Chronicle* 171 (2011): 7-53. 3 pls.
An important series of coins, minted at Alexandria under Ptolemy II, features a monogram above an oval shield in the reverse left field. The authors investigate a special class of these coins with an oval shield to the left of the eagle, without the monogram above it. They propose that the stylistic influence for the coins flowed from Sicily to Alexandria. The coins also may help to date Ptolemy Philadelphus' reform of the bronze coinage. Includes a die study and statistical analysis of the coins.

6703 **Yarbrough, Bill.** "The Alexander Tetradrachms of Ptolemy I." *Journal of Numismatic Fine Arts* 1, no. 3 (March-April 1971): 46-9. Illus.
Provides diagnostic points for the various types and issues of the Alexander-type tetradrachms of Ptolemy I, ca. 324-315 B.C. Seven types are illustrated.

6704 **Zervos, Orestes H.** "The Early Tetradrachms of Ptolemy I." *Museum Notes* 13 (1967): 1-16. 4 pls. [CS 3175]
Attempts to arrange the early tetradrachms of Ptolemy I (most of these coins were struck in the name of Alexander the Great) in a chronological sequence on the evidence of die-linkage, style, and hoards. Revises some of the order proposed by Svoronos, Newell, and Emmons. The coins are arranged in four series. Twenty-six coins are illustrated.

6705 ——— "The Delta Hoard of Ptolemaic Alexanders." *Museum Notes* 21 (1976): 37-58. 4 pls.
A re-examination of some of the coins from a hoard found in Egypt in 1896. These Ptolemaic Palladion tetradrachms were all of the reduced weight standard. Presents a table listing the characteristics of 148 coins from the reconstructed hoard. Discusses the control marks on the coins and the circumstances surrounding the hoard's burial, ca. 305 B.C.

6706 ——— "A Ptolemaic Hoard of 'Athena' Tetradrachms at ANS." *Museum Notes* 23 (1978): 43-58. 1 pl.
Discusses a hoard of thirty-four tetradrachms of the Athena type found in Egypt, now residing in the American Numismatic Society museum. Attempts to identify the hoard from which these coins came. They were probably found in the region of the Nile Delta. The author segregates the coins into two groups: regular issues and special issues. Examines the weight standards in use. The hoard coins are all debased-weight coins. Concludes the hoard was formed 305-301 B.C. Suggests the disappearance of Attic-weight silver in Egypt was a feature of Ptolemy's radical policy.

6707 ——— "An Unpublished Ptolemaic Find at ANS." *Coin Hoards* 5 (1979): 35-7.
Lists ninety-three early Ptolemaic tetradrachms purchased by E. T. Newell now in the American Numismatic Society collection.

6708 —— "Two Early Ptolemaic Hoards from Egypt." *Schwiezer Münzblätter* (Switzerland) 30, no. 120 (November 1980): 90-4.
"An Egyptian hoard found in 1856 (*IGCH* 1684) was reported as consisting of silver tetradrachms of Alexander III, Philip III, Ptolemy I (satrapal and regal) and Arsinoe II, queen of the second Ptolemy. A find of such a composition is without parallel, but as it turns out the Arsinoe II coin belongs to an entirely different deposit (not in *IGCH*), one mainly comprising tetradrachms of Ptolemy II. Neither hoard is unusual and each can be matched with other known examples." [O. Zervos, *NL* 108]

Also see: Barag "The Coinage of Yehud and the Ptolemies" under PALESTINE—JUDEA; Barag "Ptolemaic Silver Currency of Cyprus" under CYPRUS; Berkhout "Cleopatra VIII Selene" under MAURETANIA; Bopearachchi and Flandrin under *Le Portrait d'Alexandre* under HOARDS; Bosworth "Rider in the Chariot: Ptolemy, Alexander and the Elephants" under TYPES; Brett "Athena ΑΛΚΙΔΕΜΟΣ" under TYPES; Brown "Art History in Coins" under PORTRAITS; Burgess "The Moon is a Harsh Mistress" under SYRIA—SELEUCID KINGDOM; Cheek "Elephant-Skin Headdress" under PORTRAITS; Cohen "Greek Numbers on Coins, Part II: Re-Dating the Tetradrachms of Ptolemy II" under EPIGRAPHY; Cox *A Tarsus Coin Collection* under CILICIA; Davis and Kraay *The Hellenistic Kingdoms* under GENERAL WORKS—HELLENISTIC; Davesne "La Deuxième Guerre de Syrie" under SELEUCID EMPIRE; Dickens "Some Hellenistic Portraits" under PORTRAITS; Dodson and Wallace "The Kozani Hoard" under HOARDS; Fulco and Zayadine "Coins from Samaria-Sebaste" under HOARDS; Haatvedt and Peterson *Coins from Karanis* under HOARDS; Havelock "The Archaistic Athena" under ART; Hazzard "Tyre Hoard" under HOARDS; Head "Coins Discovered" under HOARDS; Hendin "Coins of the Bible—Bar Kochba Bronze Struck over Ptolemaic Coin" under PALESTINE—JUDEA; Hinks "A Portrait of a Ptolemaic Queen" under PORTRAITS; Hinks "A Portrait of Ptolemy III" under PORTRAITS; "Hoard of Greek Coins Found" under HOARDS; Holt "Portraits of Cleopatra" under PORTRAITS; Hoover "Northern Israel Hoard" under HOARDS; Houghton and Lorber "Antiochus III in Coele-Syria" under SYRIA—SELEUCID KINGDOM; Huber "Essay" under HOARDS; "Israeli Shipwreck" under HOARDS.

Jenkins "The Monetary Systems" under GENERAL WORKS—HELLENISTIC; Jidejian *Lebanon and the Greek World* under PORTRAITS; Jongkees "Athenian Coin Dies from Egypt" under THE MINTING PROCESS; Kindler *Beer Sheba I* under HOARDS; Kindler "Silver Coins bearing the Name of Judaea" under PALESTINE—JUDEA; Lambert "Egypto-Arabian" under HOARDS; Le Rider and de Callataÿ *Les Séleucides et les Ptolémées* under SYRIA—SELEUCID KINGDOM; MacFadden "The Portrait of Ptolemy I" under PORTRAITS; Meadows "Athenian Coin Dies from Egypt" under THE MINTING PROCESS; Merker "Notes on Abdalonymos" under MACEDONIAN KINGDOM—GENERAL WORKS; Meshorer "New Types of Judaean Silver Coins" under PALESTINE—JUDEA; Metcalf *Oxford Handbook of Greek and Roman Coinage* under GENERAL WORKS—GREEK; Michaelidou-Nicolaou "Four Ptolemaic/Roman Hoards" under HOARDS; Milne "The History of the Greek Medallion" under TYPES; Moore "The ΕΥΠΑΤΡΕΩΝ Coinage of Alexander I Balas" under SYRIA—SELEUCID KINGDOM; Mørkholm "Cyrene and Ptolemy I" under CYRENAICA; Müller *Numismatique de l'Ancienne Afrique* under NORTH AFRICA—GENERAL WORKS; Nash "The Kuft Hoard" under HOARDS; Newell *Five Greek Bronze Coin Hoards* under HOARDS; Newell "Nikokles" under CYPRUS; Newell *Tyrus Rediviva* under PHOENICIA; Nicolaou *Paphos 2* under HOARDS; Nouyon et al. *Systèmes et Technologie* under THE MINTING PROCESS.

"Obscure Artist" under ART; Palmer and Vermeule "Ancient Gold and Silver" under THE MINTING PROCESS; Plantzos "A Royal Seal of Antiochus IV of Syria and Some Contemporary Minima Ptolemaica" under SYRIA—SELEUCID KINGDOM; Rahmani "Descriptions" (1964) under HOARDS; Ravel "Corinthian Hoard from Chiliomodi" under HOARDS; Reichardt "Remarks" under PALESTINE—JUDEA; D. Robinson "The Alexander Hoard of Megalopolis" under HOARDS; Rowlandson "Money Use among the Peasantry" under GENERAL WORKS—HELLENISTIC; Schachter "A Note on the Reorganization of the Thespian Museia" under CENTRAL GREECE—BOEOTIA; Schlösser "Egyptian Bronze Coins of Antiochus IV" under SYRIA—SELEUCID KINGDOM; Schönert "Die Wirtschaftliche Auswertung Seleukidischer und Ptolemäischer Münzfunde" under SYRIA—SELEUCID KINGDOM; Spaer "More on the 'Ptolemaic' Coins of Aradus" under SYRIA—SELEUCID KINGDOM; Spaer "The Royal Male Head" under PALESTINE—PHILISTIA; Tameanko "Dimples on Coins" under THE MINTING PROCESS; D. Thompson "A Portrait of Arsinoe Philadelphos" under PORTRAITS; M. Thompson "Ptolemy Philometor" under ATTICA—NEW STYLE COINAGE; Torrey *Aramaic Graffiti* under MACEDONIAN KINGDOM—GENERAL WORKS; Tsakos "Ancient Coins" under PUBLIC COLLECTIONS—SUDAN (KARTOUM); Vagi "The Syracuse-Alexandria Connection" under SICILY—SYRACUSE; Vanderpool et al. "Koroni: A Ptolemaic Camp" under HOARDS; Wells "Ancient Inventions" under THE MINTING PROCESS; Zervos "Newell's Manuscript of the Kuft Hoard" under HOARDS.

ZEUGITANA

It is noteworthy that this wealthy commercial state (Carthago), with its population of some 700,000 inhabitants, made no use whatever of coined money until the great invasion of Sicily, B.C. 410, brought her armies for the second time into contact with the Greeks.

—Barclay V. Head, 1887

6709 **Acquaro, Enrico.** *Le Monete Puniche del Museo Nazionale di Cagliari: Catalogo.* Collezione di Studi Fenici 4. Rome: Consiglio Nazionale delle Ricerche, 1974. 96 pp., 28 pls. [CS 3182]
Catalogue of the Punic coins in the National Museum of Cagliari. "One of the best sources for Carthaginian bronze issues with 1682 coins listed and illustrated." [D. Kroh, *ACRR*].

6710 ——— "Problematica e Prospettiva degli Studi di Numismatica Punica." *Quaderni Ticinesi* (Switzerland) 4 (1975): 97-108. Illus. [CS 3183]

6711 ——— *La Monetazione Punica: Catalogo delle Civiche Raccolte Numismatiche di Milano.* Milan: Commune di Milano, 1979. 35 pp. illus. [CS 3184]

6712 ——— *Monete Puniche nelle Collezione Italiane, Parte III: Napoli, Museo Archeologica Nazionale.* BullNum Monografia 6.3. 2002. 154 pp., illus., 30 pls.
A catalogue of the Punic coins in the museum's collection. [Reviewed by P. Visonà in *Numismatic Chronicle* 166 (2006): 473-6].

6713 **Alexandropoulos, Jacques, ed.** *Numismatique et Histoire de la Monnaie en Tunisie. Tome I: L'Antiquité.* Banque Centrale de Tunisie Collections Monetaires. Tunis, 2006. 335 pp.
Includes 1083 Punic and 361 Numidian coins as well as many later issues. Includes introductory essays on the coinage. [Reviewed by Paolo Visoná in *Numismatic Chronicle* 169 (2009): 439-42].

6714 **Cancio, Leopoldo.** "The Carthaginian Silver Five-Shekel and the Electrum Three-Shekel Coins." *The Celator* 13, no. 8 (August 1999): 33-4. Illus.
Cancio discusses the weight and fineness of the silver five-shekel and electrum three-shekel coins of Carthage. He determines that one electrum three-shekel coin was equivalent to three silver five-shekel coins. He also suggests that the five-shekel coin was roughly equivalent to ten Roman denarii, and that the three-shekel coin was roughly equivalent to thirty denarii.

6715 **Carradice, Ian A., and Susan LaNiece.** "The Libyan War and Coinage: a New Hoard and the Evidence of Metal Analysis." *Numismatic Chronicle* 148 (1988): 33-52. 6 pls.
Examines a hoard of 167 Libyan and Carthaginian coins, mostly bronze. Provides new information on the coinage of the Libyan War of 241-238 B.C. Presents a catalogue of the coins. Compares contents to other hoards. A table shows the metallurgical analysis of the coins, including coins of arsenical copper. Discusses the links between the coinage and events of the war.

6716 **Guido, Francesco.** *Le Monete Puniche della Collezione Lorenzo Forteleoni.* Sassari: Soprintendenza ai Beni Arqueologici, 1977. 121 pp., illus. [CS 3188]

6717 **Hodder, Michael.** "Carthaginian Sailor Theory Coin is Fake." *Coin World* (August 21, 1983): 96. Illus.
A Siculo-Punic coin found in the western United States had been presented as evidence of a Carthaginian presence in America in the fourth century B.C. However, the coin, illustrated here, is exposed as a fake.

6718 **Jenkins, G. Kenneth.** "A Carthaginian Copper Hoard from the South of France." *Numismatic Chronicle* 6th ser., 17 (1957): 13-4.
"Records a hoard of fifty Carthaginian copper coins found inland, not far from Marseilles (cf. *Noe* 702, a similar, smaller hoard) and recently acquired by a private collector. The coins are all of one type combination—head of Tanit f.l. and horse's head f.r. They are probably of Sicilian origin, although some may have been minted in Sardinia." [J. Healy, *NL* 49]

6719 ——— "The Mqabba (Malta) Hoard of Punic Bronze Coins." *Studi di Numismatica Punica. Supplemento al Rivista di Studi Fenici* (Italy) 11 (1983): 19-36.

6720 ——— "Varia Punica." *Studies in Honour of Leo Mildenberg: Numismatics, Art History, Archaeology.* Edited by A. Houghton et al. Wetteren: Editions NR, 1984. Pages 127-36. 2 pls.

Jenkins addresses four issues related to Carthaginian coinage: (1) He examines a group of Carthaginian coins showing numeral marks equivalent to twenty-five. Suggests these are one-and-a-quarter shekels. Discusses precedents for one-and-a-quarter shekel weights. Discusses the bronze-to-silver value ratio at the time these coins were struck. (2) Jenkins disputes Villaronga's theory that the Punic letter *kaph* followed by two upright strokes on a series of Punic coins represent the number twenty-two. Villaronga thought this was intended to express the number of such coins which would total the weight of a Roman pound. Jenkins tentatively suggests the letter stands for "silver" or "money" and the strokes mean "two," indicating that these coins may have been struck in billon at an earlier time. Also briefly discusses the numerals which appear on some coins of Ebusus. (3) Publishes a base silver shekel (Athena head/plough) overstruck on a Punic shekel with Demeter/horse standing. The undertype is a regular Carthaginian shekel and not a "Libyan" imitation (see Robinson's three articles related to Libyan coinage below). Jenkins suggests the coin was struck in Africa. (4) The coins of the "El Djem" types were dated by Robinson (see Robinson "Punic Coins of Spain" under SPAIN) to the beginning of the period after the first Punic War, based on an overstruck coin in the American Numismatic Society collection. Jenkins believes the coin in question was struck over another Spanish type. He places the series in the last phase of the Second Punic War (ca. 209/8 B.C.).

6720a ——— "Some Coins of Hannibal's Time." *Studi per Laura Breglia: Bollettino di Numismatica Supplemento* (Italy) 4 (1987).

6721 **Jenkins, G. Kenneth, and R. B. Lewis.** *Carthaginian Gold and Electrum Coins.* Special Publication No. 2. London: Royal Numismatic Society, 1963. 140 pp., 38 pls. [CS 3191]

Catalogues 506 major varieties of the gold and electrum coinage of Carthage from the British Museum and various other major collections. Also includes Sicilian coinage, coinage of the military revolt, coins issued by the Barcids in Spain, Hannibal's campaign coinage, and Sardinian coinage. Includes much discussion of the metallic content of the coins as well as their types and metrology. The historical and numismatic backgrounds are provided for each group of coins. Lists the relevant hoards. Includes tables of weights and specific gravities. All coins are illustrated and die links are noted. [Reviewed by C. M. Kraay in *Spink Numismatic Circular* 71, no. 10 (October 1963): 207, 202. An extensive review by E. S. G. Robinson appears in *Numismatic Chronicle* 7th ser., 3 (1963): 285-92. Also reviewed by M. Thompson in *American Journal of Archaeology* 68 (1964): 316, by J. P. Guépin in *Journal of Hellenic Studies* 85 (1965): 248-9, by Margaret Thompson in *Spink Numismatic Circular* 73, no. 2 (February 1965): 38, by J. P. Barron in *Classical Review* new ser. 15, no. 1 (March 1965): 102-4, by P. Whitting in *Spink Numismatic Circular* 73, no. 10 (October 1965): 213, and by R. A. G. Carson in *Times Literary Supplement* (January 2, 1964): 14-5. Carson's review was reprinted in *Spink Numismatic Circular* 72 (1964): 30].

6722 **Lewis, R. B.** "Analysis of a Carthaginian Stater." *Numismatic Chronicle* 6th ser., 17 (1957): 15.

"This short note records a complete analysis of a Carthaginian electrum stater (a variant of *Luynes* 3738): it contained 60.8 Au, 36.3 Ar, 2.3 Cu and 0.1 Fe. The results, which showed the inaccuracy of colorimetric analysis, were, however, gratifyingly close to the estimate deduced from specific gravity measurements (14.4), assuming the alloy to have been binary." [J. Healy, *NL* 49]

6723 **Lorber, Catharine C.** "A Hoard of Punic 'Horse and Palm' Billon Tetradrachms (*CH* 9.690)." *Coin Hoards IX: Greek Hoards.* Edited by A. Meadows and U. Wartenberg. Special Publication No. 35. London: Royal Numismatic Society, 2002. Pages 275-90. 13 pls.

The hoard, found in 1995, contained Carthaginian billon coins, 255 of which were made available for study. Burial is placed ca. 210-205 B.C. This is the first reported hoard of these billion coins. Both the "Tanit head" and "young head" types were present. Lorber reviews the past scholarship on these issues, focusing on various suggested chronologies. Lorber groups the coins into four broad classifications based on types, fabric, and control marks. She notes that pellets are a recurrent feature and must have had a control function. Discusses stylistic differences between the "young" and "Tanit" head issues. Comments on weights. All are 1½ shekels (tridrachm) on the Phoenician standard of a 7.6 gm shekel/didrachm. Establishes a relative chronology and discusses the military function of the coinage and its historical context. Concludes the young head issue was likely introduced in late 216 or early 215 B.C. when Hannibal's glory was at its zenith. The production of the young head series was entirely separate from the Tanit head series, but the relative chronology cannot yet be determined. The transition from these coins with horse/palm reverse to those with a collared horse reverse may have taken place ca. 210-205. A few bronzes were also included in the hoard. The bronze coins provide overstrike evidence that allows the production of the coins to be placed during the Second Punic War, beginning no later than 215 B.C. Includes a catalogue of the hoard coins.

6723a **Manfredi, Lorenzo-Ilia.** *Raccolte Italiane di Monete Puniche.* Rivista di Studi Fenici, Supplement 33. Pisa: Fabrizio Serra Editore, 2007. 130 pp., illus.

A catalogue of Punic coins in Italian collections including the Archaeological Museum of Chieti and the private collections of Salvatore Camedda, Giuseppe Lulliri, and Mauro Viola.

6724 **McMenamin, Mark.** *Carthaginian Cartography: A Stylized Exergue Map.* South Hadley, Massachusetts: Meanma Press, 1996. 26 pp., illus.

An examination of the markings which appear in the reverse exergue on certain staters minted at Carthage. The author interprets the markings as a map of the Mediterranean. [Also see "Cartography" below. A related article by the author, "The Phoenician World Map," appeared in *Mercator's World* 2, no. 3 (1997): 46-51].

6725 ——— "Cartography on Carthaginian Gold Staters." *The Numismatist* 109, no. 11 (November 1996): 1315-7. Illus.

Examines the markings which appear in the reverse exergue on certain staters minted at Carthage, 350-320 B.C. (*Jenkins and Lewis* Group IIIa). The author believes the markings represent a map of the Mediterranean area, including the southern coast of Europe, North Africa, Sardinia, Britain, and Ireland. A mark to the right represents India and a mark to the left may indicate part of America, perhaps the coast of Brazil. [Also see R. Ponder's "Letter to the Editor" in *The Numismatist* 110, no. 2 (February 1997): 127. Ponder suggests the mark which McMenamin interpreted to be America is more likely to be the Cape Verde Islands or the Canary Islands. Also see the "Letter to the Editor" by D. Temple and C. Cunningham in *The Numismatist* 110, no. 3 (March 1997): 239, in which they do not accept the theory that these markings represent a map at all. Also see A. E. M. Johnston "The Earliest Preserved Greek Map" and M. Tameanko "Maps on Ancient Coinage" under TYPES. Also see McMenamin's later opinion "What's in a Name?" below].

6726 ——— "What's in a Name? Decipherment of a Carthaginian Exergue Inscription." *The Celator* 13, no. 12 (December 1999): 17-24. Illus.

An examination of the controversial characters found in the exergue on some Carthaginian gold staters. The author had previously interpreted the figures as a map of the Mediterranean area (see McMenamin "Cartography" above). He now interprets the figures as a Punic inscription *qrthdsht*, meaning "New City" or "Carthage." However, the author suggests these letters may have been stylized to represent a map of the world—thus he is not completely negating his previous theory. An illustration shows the progressive stylization of the inscription.

6727 **Mildenberg, Leo.** "Les Inscriptions des Monnaies Carthaginoises." *Commission Internationale de Numismatique, Paris 6-11 Juillet 1953. Tome II: Actes.* Paris: Commission Internationale de Numismatique/Société Française de Numismatique/Bibliotèque Nationale, 1957. Pages 149-51. Reprinted in *Leo Mildenberg. Vestigia Leonis: Studien zur Antiken Numismatik Israels, Palästinas und der Östlichen Mittelmeerweit.* Novum Testamentum et Orbis Antiquus 36. Edited by U. Hübner and E. Knauf. Freiburg: Universitätsverlag, and Göttingen: Vandenhoeck & Ruprecht, 1998. Pages 136-7.

6728 ———— "The Mint of the First Carthaginian Coins." *Florilegium Numismaticum: Studia in Honorem U. Westermark Edita.* Edited by Harald Nilsson. Stockholm: Svenska Numismatiska Föreningen, 1992. Pages 289-93. Illus. Reprinted in *Leo Mildenberg. Vestigia Leonis: Studien zur Antiken Numismatik Israels, Palästinas und der Östlichen Mittelmeerweit.* Novum Testamentum et Orbis Antiquus 36. Edited by U. Hübner and E. Knauf. Freiburg: Universitätsverlag, and Göttingen: Vandenhoeck & Ruprecht, 1998. Pages 144-6. 2 pls.
Jenkins had concluded (see Jenkins "Coins of Punic Sicily" under SICILY—SICULO-PUNIC COINAGE) that Carthaginian tetradrachms began to be struck in Western Sicily after 397 B.C. Mildenberg illustrates a tetradrachm of Akragas, struck before 406 B.C., which was struck over a Siculo-Punic tetradrachm, thus proving that the Siculo-Punic issues must have begun earlier, perhaps ca. 410 B.C. Jenkins had later accepted this fact. Jenkins maintained, however, that the first tetradrachm series was minted at Carthage itself. Mildenberg here demonstrates that the mint was in fact Sicilian, based partly on hoard evidence (no Siculo-Punic tetradrachms have ever been found in Africa). Also, protuberances are visible on the edges of coins struck in Sicily but not on coins struck in Carthage (he states that these flans were made in a row of molds, but see G. F. Hill, "Ancient Methods of Coining" under THE MINTING PROCESS for a more likely explanation). Also, the die axis of Sicilian coins shows that loose dies were used, whereas the axis for Carthaginian coins shows that fixed dies were used. Also, the exclusive use of the tetradrachm denomination in the Siculo-Punic series shows Carthage's effort to put forward a strong and lasting currency in Sicily. Together, these facts demonstrate that the first Siculo-Punic coins, and in fact the first Carthaginian coins, were struck in Sicily. [Also see Hübner and Knauf *Vestigia Leonis* under GENERAL WORKS—GREEK].

6729 **Nicolau Kormikiari, Maria Cristina.** "Punic Coins in Brazilian Public Collections." *Proceedings of the 11th International Numismatic Congress, September 8-13, 1991, Volume 1.* Edited by T. Hackens et al. Louvain-la-Neuve, Belgium: International Association of Professional Numismatists, 1993. Pages 45-8. Illus.
A brief catalogue of the ninety-eight Punic coins found in public collections in Brazil.

6730 **Phillips, Wayne C.** "Coins of Carthage Present Several Areas of Collecting." *Coin World* (March 7, 1994): 48.
In this installment of Phillips' "Money Talks" column, he provides an overview of Carthaginian coinage in Africa, Sicily, and Spain.

6731 **Tatman, John.** "'Horse/Palm Tree' Tetradrachms: The First Carthaginian Coins." *The Celator* 18, no. 1 (January 2004): 6-16. Illus.
Carthaginian troops came to Sicily to aid Segesta in 410 BC. A large amount of money was needed to pay for the services of this large mercenary army, resulting in the first minting of Carthaginian coins (tetradrachms with obv., horse, or horse crowned by Nike; rev., palm tree. The design was likely inspired by contemporary Sicilian tetradrachms. Tatman describes changes in design over the years. The location of the mint of the early coins (Carthage or Sicily?) is uncertain. The horse/palm series probably ended ca. 392 B.C. after a truce limited Carthaginian influence to the western end of Sicily. Tatman discusses the series with forepart of horse facing left, and a rare gold shekel with a galloping free horse/palm tree.

6732 **Vaux, W. S. W.** "On the Coins Reasonably Presumed to be Those of Carthage." *Numismatic Chronicle* new ser., 3 (1863): 73-102.
The author argues in favor of the attribution to Carthage of a large number of coins in gold, electrum, silver, and copper which have been usually classed with the Sicilian coins of Panormous. Provides a list of the different types in the collection of the British Museum.

6733 **Villaronga, Leandre.** "Les Monnaies Hispano-Carthaginoises du Systeme Attique." *Numismatique et Histoire Économique Phéniciennes et Puniques. Actes du Colloque tenu à Louvaine-la-Neuve 13-16 Mai 1987.* Studia Phoenicia IX, Numismatica Lovaniensia 58. Edited by Tony Hackens and Ghislane Moucharte. Louvain-la-Neuve, 1992. Pages 149-52.

6734 **Visonà, Paolo.** "Punic and Greek Bronze Coins from Carthage." *American Journal of Archaeology* 89, no. 4 (October 1985): 671-5. 1 pl.
Visonà draws preliminary conclusions from the Punic coins found during recent excavations at Carthage. Some of the earliest Punic coins circulated at Carthage. The numbers of Punic bronze coins found at Carthage 1974-82, are listed in a table (by *SNG Copenhagen* number), and another table summarizes the finds of Greek and non-Carthaginian Punic bronze coins found at Carthage. Discusses the chronology of the coins.

6735 ———— "Carthage: A Numismatic Bibliography." *Studi di Egittologia e di Antichità Puniche* (Italy) 13 (1994). Edited by E. Acquaro and S. Perignotti.
"This bibliography lists over 466 titles with commentary by the author, covering coins found at Carthage from earliest excavations to the most recent." [K. Ben Romdhane, *NL* 139]

6736 ———— "Carthaginian Coinage in Perspective." *American Journal of Numismatics* 2nd ser., 10 (1998): 1-27. 4 pls.
Hoard evidence and studies of die sequences over the last few decades have provided evidence for mint attributions of Carthaginian coinages. As a result, Punic coinage may now be viewed as the product of distinctive North African, Sicilian, Sardinian, Spanish, and South Italian coinage systems. This essay reconstructs the development of the coinage minted under the direct authority of Carthage in the central Mediterranean from the late fifth to the mid-second centuries B.C., and discusses the characteristics of each Carthaginian issue.

6737 ———— "A Carthaginian Gold Issue that Never Was." *Annotazioni Numismatiche* (Italy) 9, no. 36 (December 1999): 834-5. Illus.
"The forgery in question combines the reverse of an early fourth-century Carthaginian tetradrachm with an obverse derived from that of electrum issues minted at Carthage between ca. 251-241 B.C. It was probably made in Greece in the 1980s." [P. Visonà, *NL* 144]

6738 ———— "The Punic Coins in the Collection of Florence's Museo Archeologico: Nonulla Notanda." *Rivista di Studi Fenici* (Italy) 2 (1999): 147-9.
"The author calls attention to several misidentified, rare, and noteworthy specimens among the Punic issues in Florence's Archaeological Museum's collection." [P. Visonà, *NL* 144]

6739 ———— "A New Wrinkle in the Mid-Carthaginian Silver Series." *Numismatic Chronicle* 166 (2006): 15-23. 2 pls.
Visonà shows that there are significant differences between some sub-groups of Carthaginian coins which have a direct bearing on their chronology and help illuminate the development of Carthaginian coinage during the last years of the first Punic War.

6740 ———— "Prolegomena to a Corpus of Carthaginian Bronze Coins." *Numismatica e Antichità Classiche. Quaderni Ticinesi* (Switzerland) 35 (2006).

6740a ———— "Tradition and Innovation in Carthaginian Coinage during the Second Punic War." *Revue Suisse de Numismatique* (Switzerland) 88 (2009): 173-84.

6741 **Volk, T.** "The 'Mazarrón' Hoard (*IGCH* 2325) Revisited." *Numisma* (Spain) 250 (2006): 205-28.
A re-examination of a hoard of Carthaginian silver coins found at Mazarrón, Spain, in 1861.

Note: Most items related to Siculo-Punic coinage are listed under SICILY—SICULO-PUNIC COINAGE. See: Healy "Western Punic Mints," Hill *Coins of Ancient Sicily*, Hind "Silver and Bronze Coins," Jenkins "Himera" (Punic imitations), Jenkins "Coins of Punic Sicily," Kutcher "Siculo-Punic Coinage," Lee "Silver Coinage of the Campanian Mercenaries," Lloyd "The Legend ZIZ on Siculo-Punic Coins," Lloyd "A Recently Discovered Hoard of Greek and Siculo-Punic Coins," Madsen "Siculo-Punic Coinage," Mildenberg "Punic Coinage," Mildenberg "RSMLQRT," E. Robinson "Carthaginian," Visonà "Carthaginian Bronze Coinage," and Visonà "An Overstruck Punic Bronze Coin."

Also see: Alexandropoulos *Les Monnaies* under NORTH AFRICA—GENERAL WORKS; Borrell "Restitution" under IONIA; Breckenridge "Coins Verify Hannibal" under SPAIN; Cesano "Di due Piccoli Ripostigli di Argenti Cartaginesi" under ITALY—GENERAL WORKS; Gemmill "Silphium" under TYPES; Gowers and Scullard "Hannibal's Elephants Again" under TYPES; Jahn "Karthago und Westliches Nordafrika" under NORTH AFRICA—GENERAL WORKS; Jenkins "Recent Acquisitions (1957)" under PUBLIC COLLECTIONS—GREAT BRITAIN (LONDON); MacDonald "Mercenaries and the Movement of Silver" under CRETE; Markoe "Phoenician Coinage" under PHOENICIA; Müller *Numismatique de l'Ancienne Afrique* under NORTH AFRICA—GENERAL WORKS; Riddle et al. "Ever Since Eve: Birth Control" under TYPES; E. Robinson "Greek Coins Found in the Cyrenaica" under HOARDS; E. Robinson "Punic Coins of Spain" under SPAIN; Scullard "Hannibal's Elephants" under TYPES; C. Smith "Harpies" under TYPES; Snowden "A Note on Hannibal's Mahouts" under TYPES; Vagi "Sicilian Decadrachms and More" under SICILY—GENERAL WORKS; Walker "Some Hoards from Sicily" under HOARDS.

CYRENAICA

The archaic coinage of Cyrene is remarkably varied and abundant. The richness of the country, and the trade in wool and silphium which Cyrene carried on with Greece and with Egypt, will fully account for this.

—*Percy Gardner, 1918*

6742   "Cyrenaic Coins and Antiquities." *American Journal of Numismatics* 14, no. 4 (April 1880): 49-50, 56.
Brief descriptions of some Cyrenaic coins and antiquities which were brought from Cyrenaica by Liet. Commander Henry H. Gorringe.

6743   **Estrada, Rudolph I.** "Cyrene and Cyrenaica." *SAN—Journal of the Society for Ancient Numismatics* 7, no. 3 (spring 1976): 41-2.
A general overview of the history and coinage of Cyrenaica.

6744   **Favorito, Emilio N., and Kurt Baty.** "The Silphium Connection." *The Celator* 9, no. 2 (February 1995): 6-8. Illus.
Describes the ancient uses of the now-extinct silphium plant and lists examples of its depiction on coins and other art objects. Suggests the "heart-shaped" seed of the plant may be the origin of the familiar heart shape which is used as the modern symbol of love. [Also see Gemmill "Silphium" and Riddle et al. "Ever Since Eve" under TYPES].

6745   **Forrer, Leonard S.** "The Silphium Plant on Coins of Cyrenaica." *Spink Numismatic Circular* 20 (July 1912): 13721-2. Illus.
Discusses the silphium plant and its uses in antiquity. [Also see Favorito and Baty "The Silphium Connection" above, W. Talbot Ready "The Silphium Plant" below, Gemmill "Silphium" under TYPES, and Riddle et al. "Ever Since Eve" under TYPES].

6746   **Head, Barclay V.** "Archaic Coins Probably of Cyrene." *Numismatic Chronicle* 3rd ser., 11 (1891): 1-11. Illus., 1 pl.
Coins from a recent find of archaic coins on the island of Cos are described. The author discusses how he came to attribute the coins to Cyrene. He also gives to Cyrene a coin (*obv.*, lion devouring prey; *rev.*, forepart of a winged lion) previously attributed by him to Clazomenae in Ionia (and so listed in his *Historia Numorum*). [Also see Wroth "Peparethus" under NORTHERN GREECE—THESSALY for a re-attribution of some of the coins Head assigned to Cyrene].

6747   **Hill, George F.** "A Hoard of Cyrenaic Bronze Coins." *Numismatic Chronicle* 3rd ser., 19 (1899): 175-6. Illus.
Discusses a hoard of coins which was apparently buried in a bowl. Most of the coins are encrusted together in a lump. The coins are all from Cyrenaica and are of the type Apollo/KYPA with kithara.

6748   **Jenkins, G. Kenneth.** "Some Ancient Coins of Libya." *Society of Libyan Studies, Fifth Annual Report* (1973-74): 29-35.

6749   **Koerper, Henry C., and A. L. Kolls.** "The Silphium Motif Adorning Ancient Libyan Coinage: Marketing a Medical Plant." *Economic Botany* 53, no. 2 (April-June 1999): 133-43. Illus., map.
Ancient texts provide an extensive list of purported medicinal benefits for Cyrenaic silphium, but omit reference to its use as an aphrodisiac. However, the plant may have been so regarded as evidenced by the ithyphallic and testicular imagery in the stylized representations of the plant on coins of ancient Cyrenaica. Discusses silphium's place in the economy and lists it known uses. Numismatic depictions of the plant are highly stylized to convey an ithyphallic metaphor. Includes illustrations of several coins.

6750   **Laronde, André.** "Le Silphium sur les Monnaies de Cyrène." *Scritti di Antchità in Memoria di Sandro Stucchi, Vol. 1.* Studi Miscellanei 29. Edited by L. Bacchielli and M. Bonanno Aravantinos. Rome, 1996. Pages 157-68. Illus.

6751   **Manganaro, Giacomo.** "Per la Cronologia delle Emissioni a Leggenda Libyen." *Numismatique et Histoire Économique Phéniciennes et Puniques. Actes du Colloque tenu à Louvaine-la-Neuve 13-16 Mai 1987*. Studia Phoenicia IX, Numismatica Lovaniensia 58. Edited by Tony Hackens and Ghislane Moucharte. Louvain-la-Neuve, 1992. Pages 93-105.

6752   **Marotta, Michael E.** "The Purse of Eratosthenes: The Coinage and Commerce of Cyrene." *The Celator* 8, no. 1 (January 1994): 18-20. Illus.
An overview of the history and coinage of Cyrene. [Also see S. Hurter's follow-up comments in a "Letter to the Editor" in *The Celator* 8, no. 2 (February 1994): 4].

6753   **Mørkholm, Otto.** "Cyrene and Ptolemy I: Some Numismatic Comments." *Chiron* (Germany) 10 (1980): 145-59. 2 pls.

Examines the chronology of the coinage of Cyrene ca. 315-280 B.C. taking into consideration the new chronology suggested by F. Chamoux and E. Will. Suggests a slight down-dating of the chronology established by Jenkins (see Jenkins "An Early Ptolemaic Hoard from Phacous" under EGYPT—PTOLEMAIC KINGDOM). Summarizes the chronology of the coinage of Cyrene and Alexandria during the period ca. 322-280 B.C. The proposed chronology has implications for the date of the introduction of silver portrait coins of Ptolemy I.

6754 **Naville, Lucien.** *Les Monnaies d'Or de la Cyrénaïque de 450 à 250 avant J.C.: Contribution à l'Etude des Monnaies Grecques Antiques.* Geneva, 1951. 124 pp., 8 pls. [CS 3176]
Examines the gold coinage of Cyrenaica.

6755 **Poole, Reginald Stuart.** "On a Coin from the Cyrenaïca, Presented to the British Museum by the Late F. H. Crowe, Esq., H. M. Consul at Cairo." *Numismatic Chronicle* new ser., 1 (1861): 201-3. Illus.
Examines a tetradrachm with the silphium plant on obverse and a gazelle on reverse, with KK in the fields of the reverse, struck ca. 450 B.C. Poole interprets KK as KYPANAION KOINON, meaning "the community of the Cyrenaïca." Suggests this helps to determine the date of the establishment of the republic.

6756 **Ready, W. Talbot.** "The Silphium Plant on Coins of Cyrenaica." *Spink Numismatic Circular* 21 (September 1913): 709.
In this follow-up to Leonard S. Forrer's "The Silphium Plant" (see Forrer above), Ready mentions that "the plant was identified and shown to be still growing on the N. African littoral by Admiral Smyth, the well-known writer on Roman coins."

6757 **Reis, Bob.** "City of Kyrene Issued First Libyan Coins." *World Coin News* (September 1996): 54, 56. Illus.
A good numismatic history of Cyrene from the sixth century B.C. through modern times. Describes the coinage of the independent city as well as the coinage during the periods of Ptolemaic, Carthaginian, and Roman domination.

6758 **Riddle, John M.** "Coins and Contraceptives: The Plant that Made Kyrene Famous." *The Celator* 17, no. 12 (December 2003): 34-5. Illus.
Discusses the history of the silphium plant, once found in abundance near the city of Kyrene. The plant had many uses, including as a contraceptive. The popularity of the plant resulted in its depiction on the coins of Kyrene.

6759 **Robinson, Edward S. G.** "Quaestiones Cyrenaicae." *Numismatic Chronicle* 4th ser., 15 (1915): 53-104, 137-78, 249-93. 4 pls.
Discusses the coinage of Cyrene from ca. 570 B.C. through Ptolemaic times. Includes detailed discussions of types, styles, magistrates' names, gold coinage, chronology, weights, and bronze coinage. Includes a list of coin types.

6760 ——— *Catalogue of Greek Coins of Cyrenaica.* London: British Museum, 1927. Reprint, Bologna: Forni, 1965. cclxxv, 154 pp., 47 pls. [CS 3177]
Volume 29 of the *Catalogue of Greek Coins in the British Museum.* The 154-page catalogue of coins is preceded by 275 pages of introductory text. [Reviewed by J. G. Milne in *Journal of Hellenic Studies* 48 (1928): 108. Also see *Catalogue of Greek Coins in the British Museum* under PUBLIC COLLECTIONS—GREAT BRITAIN (LONDON)].

6761 ——— "Coinage of the Libyans and Kindred Sardinian Issues." *Numismatic Chronicle* 6th ser., 3 (1943): 1-13. 2 pls. [CS 3178]
An analysis of a hoard of base-metal coins with a catalogue of types. Many of these coins are overstruck on Carthaginian issues. Includes historical commentary on the circumstances of issue.

6762 ——— "A Hoard of Coins of the Libyans." *Numismatic Chronicle* 6th ser., 13 (1953): 27-32. 2 pls. [CS 3284]
"A hoard found recently near Tunis is said to have consisted of 117 coins (5 electrum, 41 base silver pieces with Carthaginian types, and 71 base silver pieces of the Libyans, including 15 double shekels). Twenty-eight coins, representing all the types in the hoard, are described in detail. The hoard confirms the attribution of the coins with the name of the Libyans to the War of the Mercenaries, 241-238 B.C. and suggests that the first rebel issue was of Carthaginian types, including small, if not large, gold pieces as well as silver. The debasement of the coins of both metals demonstrates the reduced straits of Carthaginian finances at the end of the First Punic War." [C. Vermeule, *NL* 30]

6763 ——— "The Libyan Hoard (1952): Addenda, and the Libyan Coinage in General." *Numismatic Chronicle* 6th ser., 16 (1956): 9-14. 1 pl. [CS 3285]
The examination of an additional fifty or more coins in the collection of R. B. Lewis from the Libyan Hoard provides more information on the hoard (see Robinson "A Hoard of Coins of the Libyans" above). These and other recent finds indicate that this rebel coinage implies a more important and stable political organization than the military account given by Polybius. The historical significance of the evidence provided demands a summary of the whole coinage, beginning with a detailed list of addenda to the recent hoard. Examines the significance of the Punic inscription *mem*, suggesting it is a magistrate's name. [Summarized from C. Vermeule, *NL* 43]

6764 **Tameanko, Marvin.** "The Silphium Plant: Wonder Drug of the Ancient World Depicted on Coins." *The Celator* 6, no. 4 (April 1992): 26-8.
Discusses Asklepios, the legendary god of healing, Hippokrates the physician, and other important medical people in the ancient world. Describes the silphium plant which had many medicinal uses, and was depicted as the reverse type on the coinage of Cyrene. The plant was used for food, medicine, and perfume. Lists its many medicinal uses.

6765 ——— "Lepcis Magna: Ancient Emporium City in North Africa." *Journal of the Classical and Medieval Numismatic Society* (Canada) 2nd ser., 6, no. 2 (June 2005): 5-15. Illus.
Tameanko presents a history of this city in Cyrenaica, from its founding by Phoenicians around 600 B.C., to the present day. Illustrates typical coins used in the city over the centuries.

6766 **Tatman, John.** "Silphium, Silver and Strife: The History of Kyrenaika and its Coinage." *The Celator* 14, no. 10 (October 2000): 6-24, 36. Illus.

Describes the foundation of the city of Kyrene, its political history, and the popularity of its chief agricultural product—silphium. Silphium had a variety of food and medicinal uses. Tatman describes the coinage of Kyrenaika and variations in the depiction of the silphium plant on the coins. Discusses coin denominations, weight standards, and changes in the coinage at the various cities in Kyrenaika. Reviews the political history of the region, through the period of Roman rule, until the city was abandoned.

6767 **Taylor, George.** "A Halved Tetradrachm from Cyrene." *Berytus* (Denmark) 22 (1973): 23-4. Illus.
"The coin has *obv.*, silphium plant and KYP[A], and *rev.*, head of Zeus Ammon right. It was probably a counterfeit, halved to prevent circulation." [*NL* 94]

6768 **Ward, John.** "The Riches of Cyrenaica." *Spink Numismatic Circular* 20 (December 1911): 13251-2.
Mentions the agricultural riches that once were found in Cyrenaica, including the silphium plant which is found on the reverse of Cyrenaican coins. Bemoans the neglect of the land by the current Islamic government, and the restrictions placed on coin hunters.

6769 **Wright, William S.** "Silphium Rediscovered." *The Celator* 15, no 2 (February 2001): 23-4. Illus.
Reports that the silphium plant, long believed to be extinct, has been found to be still growing in Libya. The plant was commonly depicted on the coinage of the cities of Cyrenaica. When Professor Susan Kane of Oberlin College conducted excavations at Cyrene in the early 1980s, specimens of the plant were found growing nearby. Includes photographs of the plant and its heart-shaped seeds. Suggests that the plant continued to grow in remote areas away from the settled areas. Suggests that the plant may also still grow in Sicily and Sardinia. [The bibliography for this article was inadvertently omitted. It appears in *The Celator* 15, no. 4 (April 2001): 27].

Also see: Feuardent "Réflexions Relatives au Silphium" under TYPES; Müller *Numismatique de l'Ancienne Afrique* under NORTH AFRICA—GENERAL WORKS.

Numidia, Mauretania, and Malta

Only the northern, coastal regions of Algeria were touched by ancient civilization. Cities were founded on the coast by Phoenician traders and two major kingdoms were established: Numidia in the east and Mauretania in the west. Numidia became part of the Roman province of Africa in 46 B.C., while Mauretania became a Roman province in A.D. 40.

—J. Cribb, B. Cook, and I. Carradice, 1990

6770 **Alexandropoulos, Jacques.** "Contributions la Definition des Domaines Monetaires Numides et Mauretaniens." *Numismatique et Histoire Économique Phéniciennes et Puniques. Actes du Colloque tenu à Louvaine-la-Neuve 13-16 Mai 1987.* Studia Phoenicia IX, Numismatica Lovaniensia 58. Edited by Tony Hackens and Ghislane Moucharte. Louvain-la-Neuve, 1992. Pages 133-47.

6771 **Barry, Kevin, and Zachary Beasley.** "North Africa—It's More Than Just Egypt!" *The Celator* 25, no. 6 (June 2011): 44, 46, 56. Illus.
A brief summary of the coinage of Mauretania, Numidia, and Axum.

6772 **Berkhout, Nina H.** "Cleopatra VIII Selene: Last of the Ptolemaic Queens." *Journal of the Classical and Medieval Numismatic Society* (Canada) 2nd ser., 1, no. 2 (September 1, 2000): 29-39. Illus.
Cleopatra VIII Selene was one of three children of Cleopatra VII and Mark Antony. Selene was married to Juba II of Mauretania in 19 B.C. Berkhout examines the coins bearing only Juba's title, the coins bearing the titles of both Juba and Selene, and the coins bearing only Selene's title. Some of the coin types exhibit Egyptian elements and clearly demonstrate Selene's attempt to preserve her line and ancestral customs.

6773 **Charrier, L.** *Description des Monnaies de la Numidie et de la Maurétanie et leu Prix Basé sur le Degré de Rareté.* Macon, 1912. 163 pp., illus., 22 pls. [CS 3194]

6774 **Mazard, Jean.** "Les Monnayage d'Or des Rois de Numidie et de la Maurétanie." *Revue Numismatique* (France) 5th ser., 14 (1952): 1-20. [CS 3196]
Examines the gold coins of Numidia and Mauretania.

6775 ——— "Portraits Monétaires des Princes de la Dernière Dynastie Mauretanienne." *Nomisma* (Italy) 4, no. 13 (1954): 73-84. [CS 3539]
Discusses the portrait coinage of the Mauretanian kings.

6776 ——— "Essai de Relcassification Méthodique des Monnaies de Numidie ed de Mauritanie." *Actes, Congrès International de Numismatique, Paris, 1953.* Volume 2. Paris, 1957. Pages 153-64. [CS 3197]

6777 ——— *Corpus Nummorum Numidiae Mauretaniaeque.* Paris: Arts et Métiers Graphiques, 1955. 264 pp. incl. 28 pls. *Supplement.* 1958. [CS 3198]
A corpus of the coins of Numidia and Mauretania including royal and autonomous city issues. The standard reference for these coins. Describes 691 types. The coins are illustrated by engravings throughout the catalogue and by photographic plates at the back of the book. Indices of names, Punic legends, Latin legends, regnal dates, and countermarks. Preface by Jean Babelon. Text in French.

6778 ——— "Troisème Supplément au *Corpus Nummorum Numidiae Mauretaniaeque.*" *Libyca* (Algeria) 4 (1956): 57 ff. *Libyca* 5 (1957): 51 ff. *Libyca* 8 (1960): 133-45. Illus. [CS 3199]
Supplements to the author's 1955 publication.

6779 **Nicolau Kormikiari, Maria Cristina.** "Numidian Royal Portrait." *XIII Congreso Internacional de Numismática, Madrid – 2003: Actas–Proceedings–Actes I.* Edited by Carmen Alfaro, Carmen Marcos, and Paloma Otero. Madrid: International Numismatic Commisson, 2005. Pages 349-56, incl. 3 pls.
The author addresses the Berber tribe called the Massyli—a group that came to be known as the Numidians. Discusses the inscriptions MLK, HMMLK, or HT and their meanings. They may not refer to a 'king' in the Greek or Roman sense of the term. Discusses the nature of the Numidian leadership and how it was depicted on coins. Concludes that the Numidian leaders were described as supreme chiefs both of the magistrates in the towns and of the other tribes' chiefs in the countryside. Use of the horse on the reverse of Numidian coins is seen not as a copy of Carthaginian coins, but as a way of emphasizing the Berbers' ferocity of a horse and the importance of the cavalry.

6780 **Rostovtzeff, Michael I.** "Numidian Horsemen on Canosa Vases." *American Journal of Archaeology* 50, no. 2 (June 1946): 263-7. 2 pls.
The author uses Numidian coins to identify the horsemen represented in two South Italian terracotta statuettes as Numidian based upon the hairstyles and horses. The coins are illustrated.

6781 **Scott, William H.** "African Regal Coins." *Numismatic Chronicle* 15 (1853): 82-92. Illus.
Describes ten coin types which the author attributes to the kings of Numidia.

6782 **Seltman, Charles T.** "The Ancient Coinage of Malta." *Numismatic Chronicle* 6th ser., 6 (1946): 81-90. 2 pls. [CS 3207]
Describes the early coins of Malta focusing on the coin types and their origins. The coinage began ca. 220 B.C. The types show the influence of Cyrene, Egypt, and Philistia.

6783 **Solé, J. M. Solá.** "Los Rótulos Monetarios Púnicos de Numidia y Mauretania." *Numisma* (Spain) 8, no. 35 (1958): 9-23.

6784 **Stieglitz, Robert R.** "The Solar Cult on the Coins of Ancient Malta." *Proceedings of the 9th International Congress of Numismatics. Berne, September 1979. Volume 1.* Edited by T. Hackens and R. Weiller. Luxembourg: International Association of Professional Numismatists, 1982. Pages 203-8. 2 pls.
The symbolism on the local coinage of the Maltese islands is concerned with the Maltese religion, which was dominated by a solar cult whose origins can be traced back to Phoenicia and Egypt. Stieglitz examines the iconography of Maltese coins, beginning with the earliest coins of Roman Malta, ca. 211 B.C.

6785 **Tameanko, Marvin.** "Masinissa, King of Numidia: A Forgotten Monarch from Ancient History." *The Celator* 15, no. 1 (January 2001): 6-15. Illus.
Masinissa was king of Numidia, 202-148 B.C. Tameanko discusses the king's role in the battles between Rome and Carthage. Masinissa led the Numidian infantry and cavalry against the Carthaginians at the battle of Zama to end the second Punic War. After gaining full power over his North African kingdom, he struck a large series of bronze coins. The article is illustrated by line drawings of seven coins relevant to the history of the kingdom.

6786 ——— "Ancient Tipasa—A Probable Mint City in North Africa." *The Celator* 21, no. 3 (March 2007): 6-21, 34. Illus.
Tameanko presents a history of this city in Mauretania, from its archaic origins as a Carthaginian trade station through the Byzantine period. Tipasa may have become a mint city under King Masinissa (ca. 200 B.C.) and may have continued minting through the reign of Juba II and the reign of his son Ptolemy (ca. A.D. 40).

6787 **Thomas, Georges.** "Sur Une Trouvaille de Monnaies Numides." *Revue Numismatique* (France) (1949).

6788 **Visonà, Paolo.** "Finds of Numidian Coins (c. 204-148 B.C.) in North Africa." *Trésors Monétaires* (France) 11 (1989): 18 ff.

6789 **Walsh, P. G.** "Massinissa." *The Journal of Roman Studies* 55 (1965) 149-60. [CS 3200]
Discusses (1) the history of Massinissa (King of Numidia, 210-148 B.C.) as a Roman military ally, and (2) the rise of Numidia in the second century B.C. as shown by archaeological evidence. Suggests that Carthage, not Numidia, was the main Roman fear, and that Massinissa's diplomatic pressure at Rome played an important part in influencing the Roman decision. Mentions the role of coins in the economy.

Also see: Alexandropoulos *Les Monnaies de l'Afrique* under NORTH AFRICA—GENERAL WORKS; Alexandropoulos *Numismatique et Histoire de la Monnaies* under ZEUGITANA; Müller *Numismatique de l'Ancienne Afrique* under NORTH AFRICA—GENERAL WORKS.

CONCORDANCE: CLAIN-STEFANELLI TO DAEHN

CS	DAEHN	CS	DAEHN	CS	DAEHN	CS	DAEHN
53	41	1817	97	1889	91	1993	2026
100	137	1818	55	1890	88	2000	2058
107	149	1819	274	1891	1837	2001	2042
122	189	1820	128	1892	1848	2004a	2096
127	196	1821	1316	1893	1862	2008	2147
127a	196	1822	64	1894	1865	2009	2149
174	60	1823	65	1895	1867	2010	2150
272	1172	1824	66	1896	1868	2016	2128
296	1561	1825	70	1897	1875	2020	2137
324	1345	1826	72	1898	1889	2023	2139
438	1674	1827	941	1899	1891	2024	2141
1000	33	1828	169	1900	1897	2025	2142
1051	16	1831	84	1901	1899	2028	2159
1061	160	1832	90	1902	1902	2030	2162
1463	374	1833	98	1903	1903	2032	2163
1464	369	1835	1326	1904	1917	2036	2597
1465	373	1836	1327	1905	1920	2039	2564
1473	385	1837	106	1906	1924	2040	2596
1474	386	1838	107	1907	1926	2041	2624
1478	1569	1839	972	1908	1182	2043	2655
1481	400	1840	109	1909	1933	2044	2656
1493	441	1841	110	1910	1945	2045	2690
1495	1611	1842	111	1911	1941	2046	184
1497	452	1843	410	1912	1982	2047	2701
1501	474	1844	1329	1913	1968-1973	2048	2703
1502	475	1846	326	1914	1988	2050	2658
1570	170	1847	122	1915	1989	2051	2686
1580	443	1848	124	1915a	1990	2053	2740
1606	3652	1849	127	1916	1961	2054	2742
1622	112	1850	989	1917	1962	2055	2745
1624	239	1851	143	1918	1964	2056	2748
1626	1	1853	1324	1919	1994	2057	2741
1627	2	1854	162	1920	2009	2058	2747
1630	22	1855	165	1921	2008	2060	2718
1633	1279	1856	288	1922	2037	2062	2634
1635	31	1859	1033	1923	1916	2063	2635
1637	2039	1860	201	1924	2113	2064	2636
1638	42	1861	202	1925	2098	2065	2637
1643	62	1862	1349	1926	2062	2067	2657
1646	75	1866	345	1927	2045	2068	2662
1648	321	1867	346	1928	2066	2069	2665
1650	95	1868	347	1929	2095	2070	2666
1655	136	1869	217	1930	2093	2071	2650
1656	138	1870	216	1931	2041	2072	2682
1661	151	1871	298	1932	2031	2073	2688
1664	164	1872	299	1933	2118	2074	2691
1668	198	1873	1088	1934	2056	2075	2694
1671	208	1874	224	1935	2094	2076	2702
1672	209	1875	226	1941	2057	2077	2704
1676	352	1876	353	1942	2086	2078	2712
1677	366	1877	246	1943	2106	2079	2728
1679	265	1878	247	1950	2105	2080	2732
1680	266	1880	1740	1971	2047	2084	2689
1800	150	1881	1746	1973	2060	2085	2706
1804	254	1883	1756	1977	2085	2086	2708
1806	3247, 3612	1884	1761	1979	2057	2087	2631
"	3620-21	1885	1760	1980	2089	2089	2695
1807	305	1886	1765	1981	2025	2090	2763
1809	19	1887	1770	1987	2059	2091	2767
1810	20	1888	1776	1988	2084	2092	2770

Concordance: Clain-Stefanelli to Daehn

CS	Daehn	CS	Daehn	CS	Daehn	CS	Daehn
2093	2774	2191	2947	2270	3175	2354	6026
2094	2776	2192	3097	2271	3176	2355	3349
2095	2761	2193	2948	2275	3184	2356	3447
2096	2779	2194	2950	2276	3194	2357	3418
2099	2780	2196	2962	2277	3198	2358	3409
2100	2782	2197	2963	2278	3201	2359	3410
2101	2709	2198	2965	2280	3208	2360	3357
2102	2717	2199	2968	2282	3214	2361	3408
2103	2791	2201	2971	2285	3222	2362	3271
2104	2792	2202	2972	2286	2988	2363	3293
2110	2803	2203	2974	2287	3227a	2364	3632
2111	2804	2204	783	2288	2825	2365	3594
2112	2806	2204	783	2290	3053	2367	3601
2113	2808	2205	3206	2296	2047	2368	3612
2114	2810	2210	2985	2299	2024	2369	3633
2115	2809	2211	2993	2301	3246	2370	3635
2116	2811	2214	3036	2303	3908	2373	3657
2117	2812	2215	3040	2304	269	2375	3692
2118	2813	2216	3041	2305	3247	2376	3690
2119	2814	2219	3045	2306	3254	2377	3695
2120	2816	2220	3046	2308	4246	2378	3694
2122	2820	2223	3009	2309	3236	2380	3696
2124	3226	2224	3010	2311	3359	2381	3698
2127	2827	2225	3014	2313	3580	2382	3677
2128	2832	2226	3017	2314	3581	2383	3683
2130	2833	2227	3019	2315	3467	2384	3705
2131	2834	2228	3022	2316	3291	2385	3609
2132	2839	2229	3024	2317	3294	2386	3728
2133	2840	2230	3028	2318	3243	2392	3630
2134	2841	2231	3031	2319	3233	2393	3634
2135	2842	2233	3033	2320	3260	2398	3763
2136	2843	2234	3034	2321	3229	2399	3615
2137	2847	2238	3227	2322	3235	2403	3671
2140	2856	2239	3055	2323	3237a	2403a	3672
2142	2864	2240	2909	2324	3248	2404	3682
2143	2865	2241	3057	2325	3480	2411	3631
2144	2855	2242	3058	2326	3348	2416	3596
2145	2871	2243	3156	2327	3364	2417	3620
2146	2882	2244	3061	2328	3397	2418	3621
2147	2887	2246	3062	2329	3411	2420	3601
2148	2888	2247	3090	2330	3464	2433	3710
2151	2890	2248	3096	2331	3536	2435	3713
2156	3199	2249	3098	2332	3308	2436	3715
2163	2914	2250	3101	2333	3315	2441	3849
2166	2899	2251	2946	2334	3318	2442	3850
2168	2902	2252	3071	2336	3391	2443	3853
2169	2903	2253	3080	2337	3392	2444	3880
2170	2904	2254	3083	2338	3419	2447	3837
2172a	2910	2257	3120	2339	3432	2448	3838
2175	2913	2258	3133	2340	3431	2449	3856
2176	2915	2259	3134	2341	3433	2452	3817
2178	2952	2260	3136	2342	3436	2455	3821
2180	2925	2261	3146	2343	3434	2457	3804
2182	2927	2262	3148	2344	3438	2459	3806
2183	2929	2263	3153	2345	3439	2460	3815
2184	3092	2264	3158	2346	3440	2461	3809
2185	2934	2265	3159	2347	3442	2462	3812
2186	2936	2266	3160	2348	3445	2465	3794
2187	2937	2267	3161	2349	3452	2466	3786
2189	2942	2268	3169	2350	3463	2467	3954
2190	2945	2269	3170	2353	3516	2468	3955

Concordance: Clain-Stefanelli to Daehn

CS	Daehn	CS	Daehn	CS	Daehn	CS	Daehn
2468a	3901	2539	4238	2653	4587	2739	4843
2470	3898	2540	4250	2654	4588	2740	4848
2471	3900	2541	4252	2655	1281	2742	4875
2472	3905	2543	4253	2657	4596	2743	4877
2473	3929	2544	4261	2658	4597	2744	4888
2476	3949	2545	4278	2659	3741	2745	4867
2477	3952	2548	4286	2659a	3742	2746	4909
2478	3928	2549	4287	2661	3748	2747	4854
2479	3936	2551	4290	2664	3748	2749	4912
2480	4154	2552	4292	2666	3751	2750	4922
2481	3972	2553	4305	2670	4603	2751	4927
2482	3973	2554	4324	2671	4608	2752	4957
2484	4168	2556	4353	2672	4609	2753	4963
2485	3976	2558	3960	2677	4641	2754	4989
2488	3991	2559	3962	2678	4660	2754a	4988
2489	3992	2560	4362	2679	4673	2755	4990
2490	4005	2562	4366	2680	4665	2757	4993
2494	4022	2563	4368	2686	4659	2758	4994
2495	4027	2565	4373	2687	4661	2761	447
2496	4031	2566	4354	2688	4662	2762	448
2497	4159	2567	4385	2689	4632	2763	4520
2498	4176	2569	4342	2690	4643	2764	5001
2499	4177	2570	4351	2691	4646	2767	5010
2500	4040	2571	4391	2693	4652	2769	5016
2501	4048	2572	4383	2694	4622	2770	5020
2502	4043	2573	4386	2695	4623	2773	5023
2503	4044	2575	4405	2696	4629	2774	5032
2504	4045	2576	4413	2697	4650	2775	5033
2505	4046	2577	4415	2698	4657	2776	5034
2506	4060	2578	4416	2699	4658	2777	5035
2507	4178	2579	4419	2700	4651	2778	5036
2508	4203	2580	4472	2701	4683	2779	5038
2509	4163	2581	4437	2702	4695	2780	5040
2510	4073	2582	4442	2703	4708	2781	5057
2511	1603	2583	4402	2704	4712	2783	5050
2513	4090	2584	4451	2708	4718	2784	5051
2514	4188	2585	4453	2709	4725	2785	5056
2515	4091	2586	4516	2710	4726	2793	5092
2516	4213	2591a	4757	2711	4727	2796	5096
2517	4098	2593	4502	2712	4772	2797	5121
2518	4099	2594	4503	2714	4763	2798	5126
2520	4102	2596	4514	2715	4812	2801	5095
2521	4103	2600	4529	2716	4765	2803	5099
2522	4115	2601	472	2717	4784	2805	5084
2523	4216	2602	4507	2718	4803	2806	5176
2524	4122	2604	4783	2719	4761	2807	5173
2524a	4124	2605	4677	2721	4809	2808	5178
2525	4135	2606	4511	2722	4821	2809	5195
2526	4191	2609	4517	2724	4742	2810	5198
2527	4192	2618	4582	2725	4744	2811	5206
2528	4137	2619	4547	2726	4745	2812	5131
2529	4194	2621	4538	2727	4746	2814	5137
2530	1614	2625	296	2730	4747	2815	5138
2531	4141	2627	4602	2732	3967	2816	5139
2533	4164	2631	4542	2733	4813	2817	5140
2534	4151	2639	4559, 4560	2734	4797	2818	5141
2535	4152	2641	4535	2735	4800	2819	5142
2536	4222	2642	4536	2736	4741	2820	5149
2537	4227	2650	4590	2737	4823	2821	5150
2538	4233	2651	4585	2738	4840	2822	5152

CONCORDANCE: CLAIN-STEFANELLI TO DAEHN

CS	Daehn	CS	Daehn	CS	Daehn	CS	Daehn
2823	5154	2914	874	3035	6104	3162	6616
2824	5153	2916	5736	3036	6107	3163	278
2825	5155	2918	5701	3037	6130	3164	6618
2826	5156	2919	5719	3038	6482	3166	6625
2827	5157	2920	5731	3040	6132	3168	6644
2828	5158	2924	5734	3044	6138	3169	6645
2831	5209	2925	5737	3045	6150	3170	6655
2832	5212	2926	5738	3046	6155	3171	6666
2833	5459	2931	5745	3047	6081	3173	6688
2834	5460	2933	5886	3049	6167	3174	4196
2836	5465	2934	5747	3050	6168	3175	6704
2837	5463	2935	5748	3051	5387	3176	6754
2838	5462	2937	5752	3052	6171	3177	6760
2839	5481	2938	5755	3052a	6171	3178	6761
2840	5223	2942	5757	3053	6158	3180	6530
2842	5435	2943	5777	3056	6163	3182	6709
2843	5436	2943a	5773	3058	6251	3183	6710
2850	5234	2944	5785	3059	6181	3184	6711
2851	5235	2945	5786	3062	81	3188	6716
2852	5236	2946	5787	3063	6205	3189	3093
2853	5244	2947	5788	3066	6221	3190	3094
2854	5255	2950	5789	3068	6223	3191	6721
2855	5256	2953	5791	3070	1813	3194	6773
2861	5273	2957	5803	3071	6236	3196	6774
2862	5276	2963	5815	3072	6239	3197	6776
2863	5280	2964	5814	3074	6257	3198	6777
2864	5281	2966	5829	3076	6272	3199	6778
2865	5300	2968	5832	3077	6277	3200	6789
2866	5352	2970	5836	3078	6278	3207	6782
2867	5384	2970a	5837	3079	6313	3208	700
2868	5385	2971	5838	3079a	6313	3209	6263
2869	5386	2972	5839	3080	6327	3210	3975
2870	5388	2983	5867	3081	6342	3211	500
2871	5389	2984	5868	3082	6360	3212	4701
2874	5391	2985	5869	3083	6362	3213	381
2875	5393	3001	5936	3085	6383	3217	6567
2876	5400	3002	5937	3086	6414	3218	516
2877	5402	3003	5966	3087	6423	3219	519
2878	5404	3004	5982	3088	6435	3220	521
2879	5406	3005	5983	3089	6441	3221	522
2880	5405	3006	5984	3090	6479	3222	523
2881	5407	3011	659	3091	6498	3223	6314
2882	5408	3012	3530	3119	6379	3224	6194
2883	5438	3014	6019	3120	6380	3225	541
2884	5245	3015	6023	3124	6403	3233	4038
2885	5401	3018	6039	3125	6404	3234	577
2886	5558	3019	6040	3127	6407	3235	578
2890	5423	3020	6041	3129	6412	3239	590
2892	2107	3021	6052	3130	6415	3241	595
2894	372	3022	6053	3139	6446	3243	605
2895	1873	3023	6058	3142	6483	3244	606
2895a	5571	3023a	6059	3148	6516	3247	628
2896	5601	3024	6389	3149	6516	3248	418
2897	5624	3026	58	3149a	6516	3249	4457
2899	5631	3027	6084	3150	6518	3250	2668
2903	5634	3028	6089	3152	6531	3251	631
2904	5570	3029	6149	3153	6532	3252	635
2906	5423	3031	6096	3154	6535	3253	643
2909	5740	3032	6097	3156	6566	3255	676
2910	5782	3033	6098	3157	6580	3256	6220
2913	5664	3034	6102	3159	6585	3258	5387

Concordance: Clain-Stefanelli to Daehn

CS	Daehn	CS	Daehn	CS	Daehn	CS	Daehn
3259	681	3358	1371	3472	988	3583	1174
3260	6658	3360	1391	3473	3909	3584	1179
3261	3270	3361	1398	3474	2765	3585	1185
3262	701	3362	1399	3476	989	3588	2997
3263	6227	3363	1404	3479	992	3589	1236
3264	702	3367	1416	3480	994	3590	1644
3265	708	3368	1420	3481	995	3591	1651
3267	710	3369	1429	3484	1001	3592	1654
3270	712	3371	1434	3485	2964	3594	1667
3272	721	3373	5623	3487	1167	3595	1670
3274	725	3374	1436	3492	1033	3596	6362
3275	726	3375	2682	3495	1044	3597	1684
3276	3476	3379	1445	3501	1070	3598	1705
3277	4276	3380	1451	3503	1072	3599	1706
3278	4687	3383	1452	3504	1209	3600	1720
3279	737	3384	1454	3505	1076	3600a	1721
3280	741	3385	2722	3508	1093	4422	1341
3281	3289	3388	1472	3513	1124	4980	2104
3282	742	3389	1475	3516	1139	5012	2171
3283	6235	3391	3923	3517	1238	5013	2173
3284	6762	3392	1489	3519	1240	5014	2175
3285	6763	3393	6042	3521	1241	5015	2178
3286	752	3395	1501	3524	1246	5016	2179
3288	4371	3398	4724	3525	1253	5017	2180
3289	3489	3399	1515	3528	1263	5019	2190
3290	768	3400	1516	3529	1264	5021	2191
3291	5437	3401	1525	3530	3393	5024	2192
3292	775	3403	6405	3533	1268	5025	2193
3293	784	3404	1553	3534	1269	5044	2148
3294	6690	3406	860	3537	6634	5047	2124
3295	4136	3408	3971	3539	6775	5048	2125
3296	795	3410	873	3542	1280	5049	2126
3297	796	3411	874	3543	1289	5055	2134
3298	797	3418	878	3544	1292	5056	2135
3299	3511	3420	879	3546	6257	5064	2153
3300	800	3422	1021	3547	2635	5069	2156
3301	809	3424	889	3548	1149	5070	2157
3305	3655	3425	888	3549	1150	5072	2158
3308	848	3426	898	3550	1150	5074	2133
3309	3548	3427	899	3551	1151	5095	2165
3314	4628	3430	916	3552	1152	5102	2517
3325	1559	3432	923	3555	1162	5103	2518
3327	4002	3436	926	3556	65	5104	2519
3328	1565	3437	929	3557	1168	5105	2521
3330	1570	3438	931	3558	1169	5106	2523
3331	1581	3441	932	3559	2935	5109	2525
3334	1582	3442	941	3561	1173	5110	2526
3335	1583	3442a	941	3562	140	5111	2529
3336	6613	3443	943	3563	1177	5117	2536
3337	3257	3444	944	3564	1184	5122	2537
3340	1528	3454	971	3565	1186	5125	2538
3342	1604	3456	972	3567	1187	5126	2179
3345	1606	3457	972	3569	1206	5133	2563
3349	1613	3458	973	3570	1207	5136	2571
3351	1614	3458a	974	3572	4104	5139	5542
3352	1352	3459	976	3573	1210	5140	2581
3353	1619	3463	984	3574	6686	5144	2584
3354	1620	3466	985	3576	1228	5145	2585
3356	1361	3467	986	3580	1161	5146	2586
3357	1365	3471	987	3581	3224	5148	2590

Concordance: Clain-Stefanelli to Daehn

CS	Daehn	CS	Daehn	CS	Daehn	CS	Daehn
5149	2594	15985	1547				
5158	2598	16040	1588				
5160	2602	16041	1591				
5161	2603	16042	1592				
5163	2604	16059	1598				
5164	2605	16100	1535				
5165	2606	16126	756				
5166	2607	16137	556				
5168	2608	16165	4038				
5170	2610	16243	1670				
5172	2611	16259	1719				
5173	2612	16267	1406				
5176	2621	16269	1476				
5177	2210	16352	1256				
5178	2627	16353	1257				
5185	2224	16412	5650				
5186	2229	16414	4966				
5187	2232	16422	5820				
5188	2235	16427	5847				
5189	2170	16429	5860				
5190	2293	16431	5871				
5191	2322, 2325	16462	1142				
5192	2330	16471	1216				
5193	2334	16472	1217				
5194	2335	16571	1833				
5195	2336	16584	5749				
5196	2355	16607	1869				
5197	2366	16666	1915				
5204	2516	16667	1925				
5209	2532	16670	1934				
5212	2533	16676	1958				
5230	2534	16681a	1959				
5243	2562	16732	2692				
5244	2566	16798	1426				
5245	2566a	16868	1382				
5282	2591	16874	4				
5306	2629	16925	46				
5858	5213	16971	1368				
7248	3614	16972	1562				
9031	4574	16975	1571				
10255	1697	16981	1612				
10071	6514	17093	2030				
12543	1954	17445	97				
14115	1160	17998	128				
15797	1471						
15803	1493						
15815	1551						
15846	6298						
15884	1491						
15885	1492						
15886	1560						
15889	1493						
15890	1494						
15892	1495						
15916	1562						
15918	1502						
15919	1503						
15940	1512						
15943	1513						
15952	1526						
15966	1512						

Index of Cities, Districts, Kingdoms, and Tribes

City, etc.	Appears Under
A	
Abdera	Thrace—Abdera
Abonuteichos	Paphlagonia
Abydos	Troas (also Seleucid Kingdom)
Acanthus	Macedonian Cities and Tribes
Achaia	Peloponnesos—Achaia
Achaean League	Peloponnesos—Achaia
Adana	Cilicia
Aedui	Celtic Coinage of Europe
Aegae	Aeolis (also Seleucid Kingdom)
Aegeae	Cilicia (also Seleucid Kingdom)
Aegina (Aigina)	Aegina
Aenus (Ainos)	Thrace
Aeolis	Aeolis
Aetna	Sicily—Aitna
Aetolia	Northern Greece—Aetolia
Aetolian League	Northern Greece—Aetolia
Africa	North Africa
Agathopolis	Black Sea Region—General
Agrigentum (Akragas)	Sicily—Akragas
Aiane	Macedonian Cities and Tribes
Ai Khanum	Bactria and Northwest India
Aigai	Macedonian Cities and Tribes
Aigeai	Cilicia
Aigiale	Cyclades Islands
Aigina	Aegina
Ainos	Thrace—Ainos
Airai	Ionia
Aitna	Sicily—Aitna
Akarnania	Northern Greece—Akarnania
Akarnanian League	Northern Greece—Akarnania
Ake	Phoenicia (also Seleucid Kingdom)
Akko	Phoenicia
Akragas	Sicily—Akragas
Akraiphion	Central Greece—Boeotia
Alabanda	Caria (also Seleucid Kingdom)
Alba	Italy—Alba
Alexandria	Egypt
Alexandria Kat'Isson	Cilicia
Alexandria Troas	Troas (also Seleucid Kingdom)
Alicie	Sicily—General Works
Allaria	Crete
Allifae	Italy—General Works
Alopeconnesus	Thrace
Amastris	Paphlagonia
Amathos	Cyprus
Ambiani	Celtic Coinage of Europe
Ambracia	Northern Greece—Epirus
Amisos	Pontos
Amorgos	Cyclades Islands
Amphipolis	Macedonian Cities and Tribes
Anaktorion	Northern Greece—Akarnania
Anaphe	Cyclades Islands
Anazarbos	Cilicia
Andros	Cyclades Islands
Antigonea-on-the-Orontes	Seleucid Kingdom
Antioch-on-the-Orontes	Seleucid Kingdom
Antiochia	Seleucid Kingdom
Apameia	Phrygia (also Seleucid Kingdom)
Aphrodisias	Caria
Apollonia	Northern Greece—Illyria
Apollonia Pontika	Thrace
Apollonis	Lydia
Apros	Thrace
Arabia	Arabia
Arachosia	Bactria and Northwest India
Arados	Phoenicia (also Seleucid Kingdom)
Arcades	Crete
Argilos	Macedonian Cities and Tribes
Argos	Peloponnesos—Argolis
Ariana	Bactria and Northwest India
Arkadia	Peloponnesos—Arkadia
Arkadian League	Peloponnesos—Arkadia
Arkesine (Amorgos)	Cyclades Islands
Armenia	Armenia
Armorica	Celtic Coinage of Europe
Arsinoe (Ephesos)	Ionia
Artemita	Parthia
Arycanda	Lycia
Ascalon	Palestine—Philistia (also Seleucid Kingdom)
Ashdod	Palestine—Philistia
Ashkelon	Palestine—Philistia
Asine	Peloponnesos—Argolis
Aspendos	Pamphylia
Assos	Troas
Assyria	Assyria
Astacus	Northern Greece—Akarnania
Asti	Thrace
Athens	Attica
Atrax	Northern Greece—Thessaly
Atrebates	Celtic Coinage of Britain
Attica	Attica
Axos	Crete
B	
Babylon	Babylonia (also Seleucid Kingdom)
Babylonia	Babylonia
Bactra	Bactria (also Seleucid Kingdom)
Bactria	Bactria
Bactriana	Bactria and Northwest India
Baetica	Spain
Bargasa	Caria
Belgae	Celtic Coinage of Europe
Bellovacci	Celtic Coinage of Britain
Berge	Thrace—Berge
Beroea	Seleucid Kingdom
Berytos	Phoenicia
Biannos	Crete
Bisaltai	Macedonian Cities and Tribes
Bithynia	Bithynia
Boeotia	Central Greece—Boeotia

Index of Cities, Districts, Kingdoms, and Tribes

City, etc.	Appears Under
Boeotian League	Central Greece—Boeotia
Bosporos	Bosporos
Bretti	Italy—General Works
Brigantes	Celtic Coinage of Britain
Britain	Celtic Coinage of Britain
Bucephala	Bactria and Northwest India
Byblos	Phoenicia
Byzantium	Thrace—Byzantion

C

City, etc.	Appears Under
Cabyle	Thrace—Cabyle
Callatis	Thrace
Calymna	Carian Islands—Kalymnos
Camarina	Sicily—Kamarina
Campani	Italy—General Works
Campania	Italy—General Works
Cantiaci	Celtic Coinage of Britain
Cantii	Celtic Coinage of Britain
Cappadocia	Cappadocia
Capua	Italy—General Works
Caria	Caria
Carian Islands	Carian Islands
Carrhae	Seleucid Kingdom
Carthage	Zeugitana
Carthago Nova	Spain
Carystus	Central Greece—Euboia
Catana	Sicily—Katana
Catuvellauni	Celtic Coinage of Britain
Caulonia	Italy—Kaulonia
Caunos	Caria
Celenderis	Cilicia
Celtic Tribes	Celtic Coinage—General Works
Cenomani	Spain
Centuripae	Sicily—Kenturipai
Chalchedon	Bithynia
Chalcidian League	Macedonian Cities and Tribes
Chalcidice	Macedonian Cities and Tribes
Chalkis	Central Greece—Euboia
Characene	Characene
Charax	Characene
Chersonesos	Bosporos
Chios	Ionian Islands—Chios
Cidramus	Caria
Cilicia	Cilicia
Citium	Cyprus
Clazomenae	Ionia
Cnidian Peraea	Caria
Cnidus	Caria
Colchis	Kolchis
Colophon	Ionia
Commagene	Armenia
Contrebia	Spain
Corcyra	Northern Greece—Corcyra
Corieltauvi	Celtic Coinage of Britain
Corinth	Corinthia
Corinthia	Corinthia

City, etc.	Appears Under
Coriosolites	Celtic Coinage of Europe
Coritani	Celtic Coinage of Britain
Coropassus	Lycaonia
Coropissus	Cilicia
Cos	Carian Islands—Kos
Crestones	Macedonian Cities and Tribes
Crete	Crete
Crimea	Bosporos
Croton	Italy—Kroton
Cumae	Italy—Cumae
Curium	Cyprus
Cybistra	Cappadocia
Cyclades Islands	Cyclades Islands
Cydonia	Crete
Cyme	Aeolis (also Seleucid Kingdom)
Cyprus	Cyprus
Cyrenaica	Cyrenaica
Cyrene	Cyrenaica
Cyzicus	Mysia

D

City, etc.	Appears Under
Dacia	Thrace
Dadado	Northern Greece—Illyria
Dahae	Asia—General Works
Dalmatia	Northern Greece—Illyria
Damascus	Seleucid Kingdom
Damastion	Northern Greece—Illyria
Danteletai	Thrace
Daparria	Northern Greece—Illyria
Delos	Cyclades Islands
Delphi	Central Greece—Phokis
Derrones	Macedonian Cities and Tribes
Deultum	Thrace—Deultum
Dikaia	Thrace
Dionysopolis	Thrace
Dium	Macedonian Cities and Tribes
Dobunni	Celtic Coinage of Britain
Dora	Phoenicia
Dura-Europas	Seleucid Kingdom
Durotriges	Celtic Coinage of Britain
Dyrrhachium	Northern Greece—Illyria

E

City, etc.	Appears Under
Ebusus	Spain
Ecbatana	Parthia (also Seleucid Kingdom)
Edessa	Seleucid Kingdom
Edones	Macedonian Cities and Tribes
Egesta	Sicily—Segesta
Egypt	Egypt
Eikonion	Lykaonia
Elaeusa-Sebaste	Seleucid Kingdom
Eleusis	Attica
Elimeia	Macedonian Cities and Tribes
Elimiote	Macedonian Cities and Tribes
Elis	Peloponnesos—Elis
Elusates	Celtic Coinage of Europe

Index of Cities, Districts, Kingdoms, and Tribes

City, etc.	Appears Under
Elymais	Elymais
Emporion	Spain
Enna	Sicily—General Works
Entella	Sicily—Siculo-Punic Coinage
Ephesos	Ionia (also Seleucid Kingdom)
Epidamnos	Northern Greece—Illyria
Epidauris	Peloponnesos—Argolis
Epirus	Northern Greece—Epirus
Eresos	Lesbos
Eretria	Central Greece—Euboia
Erythrae	Ionia
Eryx	Sicily—Eryx
Etruria	Italy—Etruria
Eua	Peloponnesos—Arkadia
Euboia	Central Greece—Euboia
Euboian League	Central Greece—Euboia
Eubusus	Spain
Eurea	Thessaly
Euthenai	Caria

F

City, etc.	Appears Under
Fensemi	Italy—General Works

G

City, etc.	Appears Under
Gades	Spain
Galaria	Sicily—General Works
Galatia	Galatia
Galepsus	Macedonian Cities and Tribes
Galilee	Palestine
Garni	Armenia
Gaul	Celtic Coinage of Europe
Gaza	Palestine—Philistia
Gela	Sicily—Gela
Glauconnesus	Cyclades Islands
Golgi	Cyprus
Gortyna	Crete

H

City, etc.	Appears Under
Hadramawt	Arabia
Haliartos	Central Greece—Boeotia
Halicarnassos	Caria
Halos	Thessaly
Halykiai	Sicily—General Works
Harpasa	Caria
Hecatompylus	Seleucid Kingdom
Helike	Peloponnesos—Achaia
Heraea	Peloponnesos—Arkadia
Heraklea	Italy—Heraklea
Herakleia Minoa	Sicily—General Works
Heraklea, Pharos	Northern Greece—Illyria
Heraklea Pontica	Bithynia
Herbessos	Sicily—General Works
Hermione	Peloponnesos—Argolis
Hierapytna	Crete
Hierapolis	Phrygia
Hierapolis	Syria—Autonomous Cities
Hierapolis (Bambyce)	Persia
Himera	Sicily—Himera
Himyarites	Arabia
Hipponium	Italy—General Works
Histiaea	Central Greece—Euboea
Histiaeolis	Northern Greece—Thessaly
Histria (Istros)	Thrace
Hyria	Italy—General Works

I

City, etc.	Appears Under
Ialysos	Carian Islands—Rhodos
Iassus	Caria
Iberia	Spain
Iceni	Celtic Coinage of Britain
Iconium	Lykaonia
Idalium	Cyprus
Idumaea	Arabia
Idyma	Caria
Ilion (Ilium)	Troas (also Seleucid Kingdom)
Illyria	Northern Greece—Illyria
Illyro-Paeonian Region	Northern Greece—Illyria
Imbros	Thrace
India	Bactria and Northwest India
Indo-Greeks	Bactria and Northwest India
Indo-Parthians	Bactria and Northwest India
Indo-Scythians	Bactria and Northwest India
Insubres	Spain
Iolkos	Thessaly
Ionia	Ionia
Ionian Islands	Ionian Islands
Ioulis	Cyclades Islands
Isauria	Cilicia
Issa	Northern Greece—Illyria
Issos	Cilicia
Istros	Thrace—Istros
Italy	Italy
Ithaka	Peloponnesos—Ithaka
Itureans	Phoenicia

J

City, etc.	Appears Under
Jerusalem	Palestine—Judea
Judaea	Palestine—Judea

K

City, etc.	Appears Under
Kalchedon	Bithynia
Kalymnos	Carian Islands—Kalymnos
Kamiros	Carian Islands—Rhodos
Karpathos	Carian Islands—Karpathos
Karthaia	Cyclades Islands
Karystos	Central Greece—Euboia
Katabanians	Arabia
Katana	Sicily—Katana
Kaulonia	Italy—Kaulonia
Kaunos	Caria

Index of Cities, Districts, Kingdoms, and Tribes

City, etc.	Appears Under
Kebren	Troas
Kea (Keos)	Cyclades Islands
Kentoripai	Sicily—Kentoripai
Keos (Kea)	Cyclades Islands
Kephaloidion	Sicily—General Works
Keramos	Caria
Kerkinitis	Thrace
Kindya	Caria
Kitannaura	Lycia
Kition	Cyprus (also Egypt)
Knidos	Caria
Knossos	Crete
Kolchis	Kolchis
Kopai	Central Greece—Boeotia
Korakesion	Cilicia
Koressos	Cyclades Islands
Kormasa	Mysia—Pergamene Kingdom
Koroneia	Central Greece—Boeotia
Kos	Carian Islands—Kos
Kranaos	Caria
Krannon	Northern Greece—Thessaly
Krenides	Macedonian Cities and Tribes
Kromna	Paphlagonia
Kroton	Italy—Kroton
Kush (Kingdom)	Africa—General Works
Kymai	Italy—Cumae
Kyme	Aeolis (also Seleucid Kingdom)
Kypsela	Thrace
Kyrenaica	Cyrenaica
Kythnos	Cyclades Islands
Kyzikos	Mysia

L

City, etc.	Appears Under
Lacedaemon	Peloponnesos—Lakonia
Lamia	Northern Greece—Thessaly
Lampsacus	Mysia (also Seleucid Kingdom)
Lamus	Cilicia
Laodice-ad-Mare	Seleucid Kingdom
Laodiceia	Phrygia
Laos	Italy—Laos
Larissa	Northern Greece—Thessaly
Larissa Kremaste	Northern Greece—Thessaly
Latmos	Caria
Laus	Italy—Laos
Lebadia	Central Greece—Boeotia
Lebanon	Phoenicia
Lebedos	Ionia
Leontinoi	Sicily—Leontinoi
Lepcis Magna	Cyrenaica
Lesbos	Lesbos
Lete	Thrace—Lete
Leukai	Ionia
Leukas	Northern Greece—Akarnania
Libya	Cyrenaica
Lihyân	Arabia
Lilybaeum	Sicily—Siculo-Punic Coinage
Lindos	Carian Islands—Rhodos
Lingones	Celtic Coinage of Europe
Lipara	Sicily—Lipara
Lissus	Northern Greece—Illyria
Locri-Epizephyrii	Italy—Locri Epizephyrii
Lokris	Italy—Locri Epizephyrii
Lokris (Opuntia)	Central Greece—Lokris
Longane	Sicily—General Works
Lopadusa	Sicily—General Works
Lucania	Italy
Lykaonia	Lykaonia
Lycia	Lycia
Lycian Dynasts	Lycia
Lycian League	Lycia
Lydia	Lydia
Lysimachia	Seleucid Kingdom

M

City, etc.	Appears Under
Ma'in	Arabia
Macedonia (Roman Province)	Macedonian Kingdom
Macedonian Kingdom	Macedonian Kingdom
Magnesia	Ionia
Magnesia-ad-Sipylum	Seleucid Kingdom
Magnesia-on-the-Meander	Ionia (also Seleucid Kingdom)
Magydus	Pamphylia
Malla	Crete
Mallos	Cilicia (also Seleucid Kingdom)
Malta	Malta
Mamertini	Sicily—Zankle/Messana
Mantinea	Peloponnesos—Arkadia
Marathus	Phoenicia (also Seleucid Kingdom)
Marion	Cyprus
Marisa	Arabia
Maroneia	Thrace—Maroneia
Massalia	Celtic Coinage of Europe
Mauretania	Mauretania
Media	Persia
Medma	Italy
Megalopolis	Peloponnesos—Arkadia
Megara	Megaris
Megara Hyblaea	Sicily
Megaris	Megaris
Megiste	Caria
Meiron	Palestine—Judea
Melaina	Northern Greece—Corcyra
Melos	Cyclades Islands
Mende	Macedonian Cities and Tribes
Meroe	North Africa—General Works
Mesambria (Mesembria)	Thrace—Mesambria
Mesma	Italy—General Works
Mesopotamia	Mesopotamia
Messana	Sicily—Zankle/Messana
Messenia	Peloponneos—Messenia
Metapontum	Italy—Metapontum
Methana	Peloponnesos—Argolis
Methone	Macedonian Cities and Tribes

INDEX OF CITIES, DISTRICTS, KINGDOMS, AND TRIBES

City, etc.	Appears Under
Methymna	LESBOS
Miletus	IONIA
Minaeans	ARABIA
Minoa (Amorgos)	CYCLADES ISLANDS
Minorca	SPAIN
Mleiha	ARABIA
Moesia	THRACE
Mopsus	CILICIA (also SELEUCID KINGDOM)
Morgantina	SICILY—MORGANTINA
Morini	CELTIC COINAGE OF BRITAIN
Motya	SICILY—SICULO-PUNIC COINAGE
Myndos	CARIA
Mygdones	MACEDONIAN CITIES AND TRIBES
Mykalessos	CENTRAL GREECE—BOEOTIA
Mylasa	CARIA
Myndus	CARIA
Myrina	AEOLIS (also SELEUCID KINGDOM)
Mysia	MYSIA
Mytilene	LESBOS

N

City, etc.	Appears Under
Nabatea	ARABIA
Nabis	PELOPONNESOS—LAKONIA
Nagidus	CILICIA
Narbonensis	CELTIC COINAGE OF EUROPE
Natounia	ASSYRIA
Naxos (City)	SICILY—NAXOS
Naxos (Island)	CYCLADES ISLANDS
Neapolis	CARIA
Neapolis	ITALY—NEAPOLIS
Nicharchus	NORTHERN GREECE—ILLYRIA
Nikonion	BLACK SEA REGION—GENERAL WORKS
Nisibis	SELEUCID KINGDOM
Nisyros	CARIAN ISLANDS—NISYROS
Nola	ITALY—GENERAL WORKS
Noricum	CELTIC COINAGE OF EUROPE
Numidia	NUMIDIA

O

City, etc.	Appears Under
Odessos	THRACE
Odrysian Kingdom	THRACE
Oinoanda	LYCIA
Oisyme	MACEDONIAN CITIES AND TRIBES
Olbia	THRACE—OLBIA
Olympia	PELOPONNESOS—ELIS
Olynthos	MACEDONIAN CITIES AND TRIBES
Orchomenos	CENTRAL GREECE—BOEOTIA
Orthosia	CARIA
Osismii	CELTIC COINAGE OF EUROPE

P

City, etc.	Appears Under
Paeonia	MACEDONIAN CITIES AND TRIBES
Pagasai	THESSALY
Palairos	NORTHERN GREECE—AKARNANIA
Palestine	PALESTINE
Pamphylia	PAMPHYLIA
Pandosia	ITALY—PANDOSIA
Pangaean District	MACEDONIAN CITIES AND TRIBES
Panormos	SICILY—SICULO-PUNIC COINAGE
Panticapaeum	BOSPOROS
Paphlagonia	PAPHLAGONIA
Paphos	CYPRUS (also EGYPT)
Parion (Parium)	MYSIA
Parisii	CELTIC COINAGE OF EUROPE
Paros	CYCLADES ISLANDS
Parrhasia	PELOPONNESOS—ARKADIA
Parthia	PARTHIA
Parthian Kingdom	PARTHIA
Pelagia	NORTHERN GREECE—ILLYRIA
Pelinna	NORTHERN GREECE—THESSALY
Pella	MACEDONIAN KINGDOM
Pellene	PELOPONNESOS—ACHAIA
Peloponnesos	PELOPONNESOS
Pelusion	EGYPT
Peparethos	NORTHERN GREECE—THESSALY
Peraea	CARIA
Pergamene Kingdom	MYSIA
Pergamon	MYSIA (also SELEUCID KINGDOM)
Perge	PAMPHYLIA
Perinthus	THRACE
Persepolis	SELEUCID KINGDOM
Persia	PERSIA
Persis	PERSIS
Pessinos	GALATIA
Petra	SICILY and ARABIA
Phaestos	CRETE
Phagres	MACEDONIAN CITIES AND TRIBES
Phakion	NORTHERN GREECE—THESSALY
Phalasarna	CRETE
Phanagoria	BOSPOROS
Pharai	CENTRAL GREECE—BOEOTIA
Pharos	NORTHERN GREECE—ILLYRIA
Pharsalos	NORTHERN GREECE—THESSALY
Phaselis	PAMPHYLIA
Pheneos	PELOPONNESOS—ARKADIA
Pherae	NORTHERN GREECE—THESSALY
Philippi	MACEDONIAN CITIES AND TRIBES
Philippopolis	NORTHERN GREECE—THESSALY
Philisto-Arabian	PALESTINE—PHILISTIA
Philistia	PALESTINE—PHILISTIA
Phistelia	ITALY—GENERAL WORKS
Phlius	PELOPONNESOS—PHLIASIA
Phocaea	IONIA (also SELEUCID KINGDOM)
Phoenicia	PHOENICIA
Phokis	CENTRAL GREECE—PHOKIS
Phrygia	PHRYGIA
Piakos	SICILY—GENERAL WORKS
Pisidia	PISIDIA
Plataiai	CENTRAL GREECE—BOEOTIA
Polichne	CRETE
Polyrhenium	CRETE
Pontos	PONTOS

Index of Cities, Districts, Kingdoms, and Tribes

City, etc.	Appears Under
Populonia	Italy—Etruria
Poseidion	Carian Islands—Karpathos
Poseidonia	Italy—Poseidonia
Posidium	Cilicia
Posidium	Syria
Potidea	Macedonian Cities and Tribes
Prianus	Crete
Priene	Ionia
Proconnesus	Mysia
Psophis	Peloponnesos—Arkadia
Ptolemaic Kingdom	Egypt
Ptolemais (Byzantion)	Thrace
Pydna	Macedonian Cities and Tribes
Pyxus	Italy—General Works

Q

Qataban	Arabia

R

Raidan	Arabia
Rasna	Italy—General Works
Regni	Celtic Coinage of Britain
Rhegion	Italy—Rhegion
Rhoda	Spain
Rhodos (Rhodes)	Carian Islands—Rhodos
Rhosus	Syria

S

Sabaeans	Arabia
Saka	Bactria and Northwest India
Salamis	Attica
Salamis	Cyprus (also Egypt)
Sangala-Euthydemia	Bactria and Northwest India
Samaria	Palestine—Samaria
Samos	Ionian Islands—Samos
Samothrace	Thrace—Samothrace
Sanaus	Phrygia
Sardes	Lydia (also Seleucid Kingdom)
Sardinia	Sicily—Siculo-Punic Coinage
Sarmatia	Thrace
Sarnoa	Northern Greece—Illyria
Scepsis	Troas
Scione	Macedonian Cities and Tribes
Scodra	Northern Greece—Illyria
Scythians	Thrace (also Bactria)
Secaisa	Spain
Segesta	Sicily—Segesta
Seleucia Pieria	Seleucid Kingdom
Seleucia-ad-Calycadnum	Seleucid Kingdom
Seleucia-on-the-Tigris	Seleucid Kingdom
Seleucid Kingdom	Syria
Selge	Pisidia
Selinus	Sicily—Selinus
Serdaioi	Italy—Serdaioi
Seriphos	Cyclades Islands

City, etc.	Appears Under
Sermylia	Macedonian Cities and Tribes
Seuthopolis	Thrace
Sicily	Sicily
Siculo-Punic	Sicily—Siculo-Punic Coinage
Side	Pamphylia
Sidon	Phoenicia
Sigeum	Seleucid Kingdom
Sikyon	Peloponnesos—Sikyonia
Sillyum	Pamphylia
Sindi	Bosporos
Sinope	Paphlagonia
Siphnos	Cyclades Islands
Siris	Italy—Siris
Skotussa	Northern Greece—Thessaly
Skylletion	Italy—General Works
Skyros	Northern Greece—Thessaly
Smyrna	Ionia (also Seleucid Kingdom)
Sogdian Kingdom	Asia—General Works
Soli	Cilicia (also Seleucid Kingdom)
Soli	Cyprus
Solus	Sicily—Siculo-Punic Coinage
Sophene	Armenia
Spain	Spain
Sparta	Peloponnesos—Lakonia
Spartocids	Bosporos
Stagira	Macedonian Cities
Stielana	Sicily—General Works
Stratoniceia	Lydia
Stryme	Thrace
Stymphalus	Peloponnesos—Arkadia
Susa	Seleucid Kingdom
Susiana	Persia
Syangela	Caria
Sybaris	Italy—Sybaris
Sybrita	Crete
Syme	Caria
Synnada	Phrygia
Syracuse	Sicily—Syracuse
Syros	Cyclades Islands

T

Tabae	Caria
Tanagra	Central Greece—Boeotia
Taras	Italy—Taras
Tarentum	Italy—Taras
Tarsos	Cilicia (also Seleucid Kingdom)
Taxila	Bactria and Northwest India
Teanum	Italy—General Works
Tegea	Arkadia (Peloponnesos)
Telos	Carian Islands—Telos
Temesa	Italy—General Works
Temnos	Northern Greece—Aeolis
Tenedos	Troas
Tenestini	Northern Greece—Illyria
Tenos	Cyclades Islands
Teos	Ionia
Terina	Italy—Terina

Index of Cities, Districts, Kingdoms, and Tribes

City, etc.	Appears Under
Termera	Caria
Termessos	Pisidia
Termessos Minor	Lycia
Terone	Macedonian Cities and Tribes
Thasos	Thrace—Thasos
Thebes	Central Greece—Boeotia
Thera	Cyclades Islands
Thermae	Sicily—General Works
Thermae Himerenses	Sicily—General Works
Thespiae	Central Greece—Boeotia
Thessaly	Northern Greece—Thessaly
Thisoa	Peloponnesos—Arkadia
Thurii	Italy—Thurii
Thurion (Thurium)	Italy—Thurii
Thyatira	Lydia
Thyrrheium	Akarnania
Tipasa	Mauretania
Tiryns	Peloponnesos—Argolis
Titiopolis	Cilicia
Tomis	Thrace
Toriaion	Mysia—Pergamene Kingdom
Tralles	Lydia
Treviri	Celtic Coinage of Europe
Trinovantes	Celtic Coinage of Britain
Tripolis	Phoenicia
Troas	Troas
Troy	Troas
Tylis	Thrace
Tylissos	Crete
Tyndaris	Sicily
Tyra	Black Sea Region
Tyre	Phoencia (also Seleucid Kingdom)

U

City, etc.	Appears Under
Ulia	Spain
Uranopolis	Macedonian Kingdom
Ursone	Spain

V

City, etc.	Appears Under
Vani	Kolchis
Velia	Italy—Velia
Vetulonia	Italy—Etruria

Y

City, etc.	Appears Under
Yemen	Arabia

Z

City, etc.	Appears Under
Zacynthus	Peloponnesos—Elis
Zagaba	Lycia
Zankle	Sicily—Zankle/Messana
Zephyrion	Cilicia
Zeugitana	Zeugitana
Zone	Thrace

Index of Authors

A

'Abdullah, Yusuf M. 5913
Abgarians, Mesrop T. 5456, 6029
Abramzon, Mikhail G. 4534
Acar, Özgen 476, 1629
Acheilara, L. 477
Acquaro, Enrico 6709-12
Adams, John Paul 5132
Adams, Lawrence A. 1630, 3585
Adam-Veleni, P. 478, 3228
Agrawal, R. C. 6255
Akarca, Askidill 4854
Akerman, John Yonge 302-3, 2167, 2217-9, 3893
Alekseyev, Vladimir P. 4487
Alexander, David T. 479
Alexander, John A. 3229-30
Alexandropoulos, Jacques 6529, 6713, 6770
Alfaro, Carmen 1, 2006
Alföldi-Radnoti, Marie 1a-3, 608, 2017, 3113
Alischan, S. M. 5224
Allan, John 4, 1773, 2220, 2512-3, 5207, 6256
Allen, Dave 2221-2
Allen, Derek Fortrose 2168-72, 2223-44, 2514-24
Allen, Roy 2245
Allin, E. J. 3923
Allotte de la Füye, F. M. 480, 5457, 6030, 6167-8, 6251
Allouche-LePage, Th. 6257
Almagro-Gorbea, Martín 2161
Alpha Bank 5, 858, 1107, 1840, 2815, 3283-4, 3796, 4289, 4483
Alram, Michael Von 159a, 6177-8, 6251a
Altekar, Anant Sadashiv 6258-61
Altinoluk, Sencan 2014-6
Amandry, Michel 6-7, 2110, 4468, 4739-40, 5164, 6421
Ambrosoli, Solone 8
American Numismatic Association 9
American Numismatic Society 10
Amiran, R. 1356
Ammons, C. Keven 1841, 3836
Andersen, Morten 5230
Anderson, J. K. 4339
Anderson, Lisa 3969
Anderson, Paul Kenneth 2123
Andreades, A. 3308
Andrew, John 1936, 2246-8, 6262
Andrews, Alfred C. 859
Anohin, V. A. (see Anokhin, V. A.)
Anokhin, Vladilen Afanas'evich 4488, 4535-7
Anson, Leo 860
Anthon, Charles 11
Anthony, John 304
Antonaccio, Carla M. 3054
Aoki, Paul N. 6558

Aperghin, Makis 5231
Aperghis, G. G. 5232
Apostolou, Eva 3309, 4165, 4444, 4931-4
Appleton, William Sumner 12, 2896
Arbuthnot, Charles 1558
Arena, Valentina 3310
Argyropoulou-Evelpidou, Rena 861
Ariel, Donald T. 481-2, 505, 1357a, 5648, 5722
Arif, Aida Sulayman 1872
Arkan, Ali Reza 6078
Arkan, Faezeh 6078
Arnold, T. J. 1632, 3723, 4398, 4445
Arnold-Biucchi, Carmen 105, 483, 1141, 1937, 2630, 2826, 2897-8, 3014a-b, 3074-6, 3114, 3311, 3550, 3662, 4081, 5074, 5914
Arslan, Ermanno A. 1864, 2173, 2899
Arslan, Melih 484-5, 4935, 4956, 5012-3, 5042, 5132a-3, 5233, 6559, 6561
Artemis, Dimitris N. 4458-9
Artemis-Gyselen, L. 4446
Ashmole, Bernard 1142
Ashmolean Museum 1833
Ashton, N. G. 4219
Ashton, Richard H. J. 13-4, 159a, 486-92, 1774, 1972, 1986, 3312-3, 3686, 3753, 3924, 4399, 4489-91, 4667, 4855-63, 4919-20, 4930, 4936-56, 5014-5, 6031, 6560-1
Askew, Gilbert 305, 368, 862
Assar, Gholamreza R. F. 6032-7, 6168-72, 6225, 6524
Atlan, Sabahat 15, 5050-1
Attas, Michael 2836
Attianese, Pasquale 2631-2, 2768-2768a
Attwood, T. W. 5649
Audouin, Rémy 6263
Augé, C. 4166, 5233a
Austin, M. M. 16
Avaldi, L. 1480
Aydarus, U. 6004
Aydemir, P. 4189
Aydrus, M. Omar 6005
Azizipoure, Tahereh 6056, 6079

B

Babelon, Ernest Charles François 17-21, 369, 493, 1237, 1755, 2018, 3231, 3970, 4154, 4529, 5234, 6157, 6180-1
Babelon, Jean 22, 140, 1238-9, 1756, 3804, 3971, 6777
Babington, Churchill 2020, 3314, 3663, 5128
Badecca, H. 1372
Badian, Ernst 3972
Bagloo, Morteza Ghassem 6037
Bagnall, Roger S. 6562

Baker, Donald Gray 863
Baker, F. Brayne 2021
Bakes, James R. 1842
Bakhoum, Soheir 1987
Bakos, Miklos 1999
Bakoum, S. 1987
Balcer, Jack Martin 3837-9, 4741-2
Baldus, Hans Roland 5235-6
Baldwin, Agnes (see Brett, Agnes Baldwin)
Baldwin's, Dmitry Markov, and M&M Numismatics Ltd. 2022
Balmuth, Miriam S. 370-9, 1240, 1925, 3973
Balog, Paul 1358
Balty, Jean Charles 5008
Banerji, J. N. 3551
Bank Leu & Co. (also see Leu Numismatics) 2023-8
Banks, Florence Aiken 5650
Banning, Theodore 864
Bar, M. 494
Barag, Dan P. 5164a, 5237, 5651-9
Baramki, Dimitri C. 1873
Barclay, Kent B. 1143
Barkay, Rachel 4921, 5238, 5660-1, 5915-7, 5940
Barker, A. L. 6038
Barnett, R. D. 495
Barr Sage, Shirley 5662
Barralis, Jean 1483
Barrandon, Jean-Noël 3759, 4851, 5579-80
Barron, John Penrose 4843-5, 4922
Barry, Kevin 306-7, 865-8, 6771
Barth, Henry 2900
Bartlett, R. G. 6039
Barton, John L. 869
Barton, John P. 5663
Basch, Lucien 5569
Basu, S. P. 6264
Batchvarov, I. E. 3775
Bates, Michael 514, 1938, 1950, 1952
Bates, William N. 23
Bateson, Donal 2029
Baty, Kurt 6744
Baty, Roger M. 380
Bauer, George F. 24
Baumann, Hellmut 870
Baumheckel, Ken 5688-9
Baur, Paul Victor Christopher 871
Bauslaugh, Robert A. 1144, 3315, 3569-70, 4167, 4668-9
Baydur, Nezahat 5051a
Bayley, J. 2398
Baynham, E. J. 267
Bean, G. E. 4864
Bean, Simon C. 2174, 2251-7
Beasley, Zachary 306-7, 865-8, 6771
Beaumont, R. L. 3816
Beazley, J. D. 872
Becker, F. 496
Beckman, Martin 497, 3974, 5874

Index of Authors

Bedoukian, Paul Zareh 5459-72
Beer-Tobey, A. G. 1467
Beer-Tobey, Leslie 483, 1359, 1467, 1481-2, 4220
Behrens, Gustav 2175
Bell, Benjamin R. 6169-70
Bell, H. W. 498
Bellinger, Alfred R. 268, 499, 504, 873, 1933, 3232-3, 3316-8, 3511, 3975, 4168, 4250, 4699-701, 5239-46, 6040, 6158-9
Beltran Martinez, Antonio 2124-6a
Bendall, Simon 2901, 5093, 5134
Ben-David, Arye 5664
Ben-Dor, Stella 5247
Ben-Eli, Arie L. 874
Benford, Timothy B. 875
Benner, Steve M. 3234, 3781, 3789, 3840, 4300-1, 4340
Benson, Frank Sherman 25, 2633
Benson, I. 4822
Benton, Sylvia 876, 4341
Bérend, Denyse 26, 877, 1962, 3006, 3115-6, 4957-8
Berg, Joseph 27, 4355
Berger, F. 1763
Berk, Harlan J. 308-9, 1145, 1360, 2901, 3319, 4169, 4577-8, 4980-1, 6265
Berkhout, Nina H. 6772
Berlincourt, Marjorie Alkins 873
Berman, A. 505
Bernard, Dominique 1483
Bernard, Paul 710, 3552, 5473, 6263, 6266-8a
Bernhard, O. 3077-8
Bernhart, Max 878-9, 2992
Berrol, Ronn 5665-7, 5900
Berry, Burton Yost 2030
Bertino, Antonio 2902
Bertman, Stephen 1146
Besom, Tom 6269
Betancourt, Philip P. 4743
Betlyon, John Wilson 5570-1
Beulé, Charles Ernest 3976
Bevan, E. R. 5248-9
Bhattacharyya, Asoke K. 6270
Bicknell, Peter James 2769-70, 2830-1, 2886, 3015, 3977-9, 4221
Biddle, M. 6563
Bidyabinude, B. B. 6271
Bieber, Margarete 880, 1147, 1241-2
Biglaki-Sophianou, M. 4846
Bijovsky, G. 5250
Bing, J. Daniel 3320, 5075
Bingen, J. 506
Birch, Samuel 2762, 2837, 2867, 3841, 4400, 5251
Bird, Roger 5930
Bird, Susan 881
Bishop, J. David 1959
Bitner, John W. 882

Bivar, A. David H. 381, 6182-3, 6272-8
Blamakis, G. 3390
Blamberg, Jan 310
Blanchet, Jules Adrien 2525, 3925-6
Bland, Roger 190
Blankley, Jack 3980
Bloesch, Hansjörg 1905, 3235, 5076-7
Blomberg, Peter E. 4251
Bluyssen, H. 1484
Bodenstedt, Friedrich 1485, 4718, 4744-7
Bodzek, Jaroslaw 2004, 5901-2
Boeckh, August 3981
Boehringer, Christof 269, 2903-5, 2985, 3016, 3042, 3050-1, 3117-9, 3215, 3321, 4302-3, 4865, 4959, 5252
Boehringer, Erich 3120
Bogaert, Raymond 1361, 6537
Bolden, Ron 5768
Bolshakov, A. O. 6538
Bompois, H. Ferdinand 3236
Bonačić Mandinić, Maja 1753
Bon, Anne-Marie 3236a
Bone, Anne 2258
Bonelou, Elena 507
Boneschi, Paulo 5572, 5918
Boon, George C. 5225
Booth, James 2259
Bopearachchi, Osmund 508, 1962, 3561, 4532a, 5253, 6279-95
Borba-Florenzano, Maria Beatriz 28, 171, 883, 2906-8, 2924, 3121
Borrell, H. P. 29, 3842, 4304, 4325, 4748, 4982
Borrell, Maximilian 4719, 5135, 5254
Boston Museum of Fine Arts (see Museum of Fine Arts)
Bosworth, A. B. 884
Boudeau, E. 2526
Boudet, Richard 2527
Bour, R. 5592
Boutin, Serge 2031, 4446a
Boutkowski-Glinka, Alexandre 30
Bower, Nathan 5717a
Bowsher, J. M. C. 5919-20
Boyne, William 2032
Brace, Bruce R. 1633, 3322, 4492
Brace, Dorte 1742
Brandis, Johannes 1559
Brauer, George C., Jr. 885-6, 1148, 1956, 2176, 2838
Brake, Cindy 3982
Bray, Thom 311-2
Breccia, Ev 6564
Breckenridge, James D. 2127
Breglia, Laura 31, 2634-5, 2832, 2887, 3017, 3055, 4983
Breitenstein, Niels 3323
Breitsprecher, Marc 887, 2528
Breitsprecher, Melissa 887

Brenner, Sandy 5668-9
Brenot, Claude 2529-30
Bresc, C. 5503-4
Bressett, Kenneth 5670
Bresson, A. 270, 4960-2
Breton, J.–F. 5921
Brett, Agnes Baldwin 888-91, 1917, 2250, 3122, 3324, 3983, 4576, 4614, 4621-3, 4823, 5255, 6296, 6565-7
Bridge, R. N. 4538
Briggs, Daphne (also see Nash, Daphne) 2260
Briggs, Sherry 892
Brimelow, William 5671
Brin, Howard B. 5672-4
Brindley, James C. 5078-82, 5675, 6041, 6184
Bringmann, Klaus 32, 6661
Briscoe, Lady 2261
Broneer, Oscar 893, 6185
Brooke, G. C. 2262-5
Broshi, M. 509
Broughton, T. Robert S. 4749, 6568
Brousseau, Louis 2802
Brown, Blanche R. 1243-5
Brown, Brian A. 3984
Brown, I. D. 6609
Brown, R. 894
Brown, W. Llewellyn 4222, 4252
Browne, Gerald M. 6297
Brunetti, Lodovico 2636, 2839-41, 2888, 2993
Brunk, Gregory G. 313
Brunnsåker, Sture 895
Bubelis, William S. 5165
Buchanan, James J. 3985
Buckler, W. H. 4984
Buckley, J. A. 1486
Budde, Adelaide M. 3123
Bugno, Maurizio 2778a-b
Bulatovich, S. A. 4624
Bunbury, Edward Herbert 3018, 3325-6, 3664, 3986, 4493, 5257
Burelli, Laura 4720
Burgess, Michael 5258
Burgon, Thomas 896, 1775, 2266, 3216, 5129
Burgos, Fernando Alvarez 2128
Burke, Bryan O., Jr. 382
Burkhardt, A. 2177
Burnett, Andrew M. 180, 271, 1487, 1500, 2258, 2267-70, 2287, 2637-40, 2738, 2798, 2889, 3086, 3124, 3327, 3542, 3571, 4702
Burns, Arthur Robert 33
Burns, Craig Alden 2531
Burrer, F. 3327a
Burstein, Stanley M. 3665
Bush, Joseph E. 897
Butcher, Kevin 510, 6018, 6186
Butler, J. D. 3706
Buttrey, S. E. 1362

Index of Authors

Buttrey, Theodore V.   511-4, 1362-4, 2909, 3056, 3087-8, 3987-9, 6539
Buxton, Richard Fernando   3990
Byrne, S. G.   1317

C

Cabral, J. M. Peixoto   1488, 1886
Cadalvène, E. de.   34
Cahill, Nicholas   515
Cahn, Herbert Adolph   35-6, 314, 516, 898, 1149-52, 2641-2, 2771, 2827, 2842, 3062, 3089, 3125-7, 3337-8, 3991-2, 4750-2, 4866-7, 4918, 4963, 5016
Cain, James   383
Cairns, D.   4625
Calciati, Romolo   2910, 3128-9a, 4253
Caley, Earle Radcliffe   1489-94, 1560-1, 6042
Calhoun, George M.   37
Calicó, Ferran Xavier   2129
Callander, T.   5083
Calliari, Irene   5017
Callot, Olivier   5922-3
Callu, J.–P.   2529
Caltabiano, Maria Caccamo   2129a, 2642a, 2785, 2817, 3130, 3217-8
Cameron, J. S.   4401
Cammann, Jean B.   899, 4254
Cammann, Schuyler V. R.   6298-9
Cammarata, Enzo   3131
Camp, John M.   3993
Campbell, Ian   2029
Campbell, William   1365
Cancio, Leopoldo   1366, 3328, 3994-6, 4155, 4170, 6187, 6714
Canessa, C.   2720
Cantilena, R.   2643
Caramessini-Oeconomides, Mando (see Oeconomides)
Cardwell, Edward   38
Carlson, Carl W. A.   3927, 3997
Carlton, Walker   900, 3012, 5259
Carlyon-Britton, P. W. P.   2271
Carmey, A.   5260
Carnig, Paul (see Toros, Haji)
Carroccio, B.   3130, 3131a-3131b
Carollo, Salvatore   3218a
Carpenter, Rhys   1153
Carradice, Ian A.   39-40, 272, 1246, 3998, 6188-90, 6715
Carratelli, Giovanni Pugliese   2720
Carruba, O.   4985
Carson, Robert Andrew Glindinning   41-3, 112, 773, 2261, 2272
Carter, C.   3790
Carter, Giles F.   1367-9, 1390, 1495
Cary, M.   1496
Casabonne, O.   5083a, 6191
Casagrande, Armonde   3724
Case, Ralph E.   6300
Casey, John   1910

Caskey, Lacey D.   1918, 3132, 4494
Caspari, M. O. B.   45
Casson, Stanley   1370-1
Castelin, Karel O.   2532-4
Castellus, Gabriele Lancilloto   2911
Castrizia, Daniele   2817a, 2912
Catalli, Fiorenzo   2734-6, 2002a
Cavafy, C. P.   2623, 2815, 4379, 5136, 5147, 5219, 5261, 5981, 6145, 6301, 6427
Cavallaro, Giuseppe   3090
Cawkwell, G. L.   4868-9
Ceka, Hasan   3817
Centro Internazionale di Studi Numismatici   3019
Cesano, S. L.   ,2644
Chabouillet, Anatole   2584, 6302
Chadburn, Amanda   2273-5
Chamberlain, V. E.   1497
Chambers, James T.   3999, 4380
Chambers, Mortimer   4000
Chandler, Tertius   901
Chantraine, Heinrich   3133, 3928-9, 4290, 4305
Chapman, Anne E. (also see Anne E. Jackson)   4402
Charrier, L.   6773
Chatterjee, A. K.   1552
Chatziprokopiou, K.   3644
Chaudhary, K.   6303
Chauveau, M.   6540
Chaves Tristan, Francisca   2130
Chaya, Gil   5903
Cheek, Kevin R.   902, 1154, 1247, 3329
Cheng, C. F.   1498, 6443
Cheshire, Wendy A.   6569
Chevillon, Jean-Albert   2535
Chimirri-Russell, Geraldine   2535a
Chittenden, Jacqueline   905, 1155, 2645, 4326
Chiszar, David   384, 903-4
Christ, Karl   2178, 2913-4, 3134
Christie's   1922
Chrysanthaki, Katerina (also Chrysanthaki-Nagle)   3687-8
Chugg, Andrew M.   3553
Ciani, Lewis   2041
Cirami, Giacomo   2915
Clain-Stefanelli, Elvira Eliza   46, 2108, 2818, 2916
Clain-Stefanelli, Vladimir   1634
Claringbull, Maggie   1769
Clark, Cathy L.   4001
Clark, Hyde   1312, 4626
Clarke, G. W.   517
Clarke, R. Rainbird   2277
Clarysse, W.   6570
Classical Numismatic Group, Inc.   2033-5, 2131, 3843, 3894, 4223, 4291, 4824, 5474-6, 6043-4, 6251b, 6304
Clayton, Peter A.   906, 1156, 4403

Clement, Paul A.   518, 3239-40
Clerk, Malcolm G.   4306
Cloke, Christian   1768
Coddrington, K. de B.   385
Coe, John I.   1248
Cohen, Edward E.   47-8, 1313-4, 4224
Cohn, G.   5736
Coin Galleries   2036
Colbert de Beaulieu, Jean-Baptists   2179-81, 2536-8
Colin, H. J.   5052
Collis, John   6571
Colonna, Giovanni   519
Colvin, S.   3844
Combe, Taylor   1776a
Comparette, Thomas Louis   2037, 3135
Comstock, Mary Bryce   1919
Conder, Francis Roubiliac   5676
Confalonieri, L.   1480
Congden, Lenore O. Keene   1157
Conn, Robert   1635-6
Connor, P. J.   517
Conophagos, C.   1372
Cook, A. B.   907-8
Cook, David D.   1522
Cook, J. M.   386-7, 4381
Cook, Peter   4586
Cook, R. M.   4864, 4870
Cope, Stephen N.   1562
Cordova, Simon   3330-1
Corsten, T.   1317
Cottam, Elizabeth   2281
Cottam, G. L.   2282-5
Counts, Derek B.   2917
Courbin, Paul   388
Cowell, Michael R.   1538, 2270, 2286-7, 4832, 4986-7, 5997-8
Cox, Dorothy Hannah   520-3, 5084
Cozzolino, Michael   3079, 4255
Craddock, Paul T.   1487, 1499-1500, 1543-4, 2738, 4987
Crawford, Michael Hewson   49, 273, 524, 1373, 2646-8, 2798, 2803, 3958, 4002
Creighton, John   2288-9
Crewe, L.   517
Cribb, Joe   363, 1769, 6306-7
Croon, J. H.   909
Crosby, Margaret   1592, 4307
Crowfoot, J. W.   5085
Cubelli, Vincenzo   6308
Cuddeford, Michael J.   2290-2
Cuhaj, George   1444
Cumberland, Richard   5677
Cummings, Prentiss   910
Cunliffe, Barry   2293-4
Cunnally, John   1158
Cunningham, Alexander   6192-3, 6309-13
Cunningham, C. J. K.   1501
Curiel, Raoul   525, 6194, 6314
Curteis, Mark   2296

INDEX OF AUTHORS

Curtis, James W.   6541-2
Curtis, Vesta Sarkosh   6045
Curtius, Ernst   911
Cutting, John   2297
Cutroni, Aldina Tusa   1867, 2918, 3020-1, 3067

D

Dabrowa, Edward   6046
Daburon, C.   1965
da Costa, Kate   526, 913
da Costa, Virginia
Daehn, William Eugene   51-2, 389, 914, 1564, 2649, 6195-6
Dahmen, Karsten   3332
Dale, L. J.   5678
D'Alexeieff, G.   4539
Dalton, O. M.   527
Dani, A. H.   6315
Darling, John   315
D'Arms, Edward F.   1928
Das, H. A.   1502-3
Dattari, Giovanni   528, 6543
Daubersy, Bernard   915
Daumas, F.   6544-5
Davesne, Alain   529-30, 4166, 5262, 6572
Davidde, B.   5924
Davidson, G. R.   531
Davies, Glyn   53
Davies, John K.   54
Davis, Gil   4003, 4532a
Davis, Mark   2739
Davis, Norman   55, 274
Davis, Phillip   2539
Davisson, Allan   316
Dawdy, David R.   6316-7
Dawkins, R. M.   4382
Dayet, Maurice   6047-8
Dayton, John   390
De, Gaurisankar   6318
Déchelette, Joseph   1565-6
Deebel, Wallace H.   1494
de Callataÿ, François   56, 159a, 171, 274a-5, 532-3, 723, 912, 1159, 1374-80, 1739, 2986, 3333-5, 3572-3, 3587, 3724a, 3757-8, 3805, 4171, 4501, 4579-80a, 4614a, 4702a-3, 5018, 5086, 5360, 5477, 5573, 6049-50
de Ciccio, Giuseppe   3136
de Hirsch de Gereuth, L.   2919
de Jersey, Philip   2182, 2281, 2294, 2298-315, 2540-1
de Koehne, Baron B.   2038, 4570
de la Houssaye, Noël   2650
de Laix, Roger A.   3782
de la Tour, Henri   2542-3
Delamare, François   1381, 1400
Delestrée, Louis-Pol   2544-7
Del Mar, Alexander   57
Delrieux, Fabrice   4871-2, 4964

de Luynes, LeDuc   5574-5, 5925
Dembski, Günther   2132, 2548, 5926
Demeester, Anne   915
Demetriadi, Vassili (Basil) C.   1638, 3241-2, 3845-6, 3895
de Morgan, Jacques   58, 6171
Demortier, Guy   4018
Dengate, James Andrew   4342, 4753-4
Dengis, Jean-Luc   2549
Denis, Paul   1744
Denkler, Kirk   6573
Denzler, J.-M.   1382
Depeyrot, Georges   275, 1437, 2527, 2550-8, 5495, 5502-4
Deppert-Lippitz, B.   4755
de Renner, Victor   1758
Dervisagaoglu, Ali   4956, 5042, 6561
deSaulcy, Louis Félicien J. C.   2133, 5678a
Descat, Raymond   6197
DeShazo, Alan S.   3336
Desnier, Jean-Luc   1437
Desneux, Jules   916, 3243
Destrooper-Georgiades, Anne   534-5, 5053-4, 5166-72, 6574-5
de Tabley, John B. L. (see Warren, J.B.L.)
Deutsch, R.   5679-80
Dever, William   536
De Villenoisy, F.   1383
De Vogüé, M.   5927
DeWaele, F. J.   3337
Deyell, John S.   6319
Dickens, Guy   1250
Diebolt, Jean   4005
di Floristella, Orazio Pennisi   3119, 3219
Dikaios, P.   5173-4
Dillon, John B.   1384
Dilmaghani, J.   6051
Dimitrov, Dimitar   537-9, 1639, 3342b, 3592, 3699-702, 3704
Dimitrov, Kamen   3338-40, 3588-91a, 3707-8, 3733
Dinsmoor, W. B.   1385, 4006
Dittrich, K.   3741-2
Djukov, Jurij L.   1549, 3341
Dobbins, Ed   6160-1, 6172
Dobbins, K. Walton   6052-3, 6320-3
Dobson, Rosemary   59
Dodd, C. H.   3220
Dodson, G. Derk   917-8
Dodson, Oscar H.   60, 541, 1640, 3342
Dolley, R. H. M.   2261, 2316-8
Donabedian, Asbed H.   5478-80
Donop, Baron de   2559
Dorsey, P. F.   3342a
Douglas, E. M.   4007
Douglass, Summer   919
Dow, Joseph A.   5681
Doyen, Charles   1567, 4670
Doyen, Jean-Marc   2560, 5263, 6123

Draganov, Dimitar   1981, 3244, 3342a, 3592a-b, 4627, 5264-5
Dreni, Stella   542, 4447
Dressel, Heinrich August Edgar Felix   543, 6054
Dreyer, Boris   4172
Driega, A. W.   920
Drougou, S.   60a
Droysen, H.   4495
Duane, Matthew   3343
Du Chastel de la Howardries, Comte Albéric   3137
Dukat, Zdenka   1754, 3427
Dumersan, Théophile Marion   61, 2040, 4496
Dunbabin, T. J.   921
Duncan, Charles   391
Duncan, Jim   1641
Dundua, G. F.   4571
Dunger, G. T.   2319
Dunn, William   904
Dunning, Mark   5682
Dürr, Nicholas   3554-5
Dussaud, R.   5928
Duyrat, Frédérique   5233a, 5576-8, 6576-7

E

Eaglen, Robin J.   2786, 2873, 3091, 3221, 3344-7, 3725, 3791, 3847-8, 3953, 4225, 4756, 5055, 5087-8, 5266-7
Earle-Fox, Harry Bertram   392, 2044, 3799, 4008
Easson, Alison Harle   1750-1
Ebeyan, A.   5481
Ebner, Pietro   2804, 2890
Eckhel, Johann Joseph Hilarius   62
Economou, George   3407
Eddy, Samuel K.   4628
Edgar, C. C.   6578
Edwards, G. Roger   3348
Edwards, Jonathan   1934
Edwards, Katherine May   544-5
Ehrenberg, Victor   2874
Ehrhardt, Christopher T. H. R.   546, 1875-81, 3349-50
Eidswick, Dick   2733
Eiland, Murray L.   6055
Eitan, A.   1356
Elagin, Vladimir   3593
Elam, C. F.   1504
Elayi, Alain G.   4009, 5268, 5579-80, 5583-92
Elayi, Josette   3351, 4009, 4532a, 5268, 5579-92, 5612
Elazin, W.   5019
Elbers, G. C. A.   922
Elder, Thomas L.   3352
Elsen, Jean   1568, 4010
Emeleus, Vera M.   1526
Emerson, A.   2875, 3353-4

Index of Authors

Emmons, Brooks 6580
Emory, Marc 1642-3
Eph'al, I. 5875
Ergeç, R. 4166
Erhart, Katherine Patricia 923
Erim, Kenan T. 3056-9, 3355
Errington, Elizabeth 263, 1769
Esdaile, K. A. 1251
Eshel, Hanan 5876
Estes, J. Worth 1043
Estrada, Rudolph I. 4873, 6743
Esty, Warren W. 40, 546a, 1386-90
Étienne, Roland 4448
Evans, Arthur John 924, 1569, 2787, 2843, 2868, 2920-3, 3138-40
Evans, John 1505, 2320-6
Evans, Jane DeRose 547, 5683
Evelpidis, Réna H. 1994
Evgenidou, Desponia 60a, 548, 925, 1107, 4847

F

Fabretti, A. 1869
Fabricius, Knud 2833
Fagerlie, Joan 926
Faintich, Marshall 927
Faizkhah, Said 6056
Falbe, C. F. 6535
Falkland, Warren 550
Fallani, Carlo Maria 1871
Falter, Reinhard 928
Faucher, Thomas 6581
Favorito, Emilio N. 3141-2, 6744
Fellows, Charles 5020
Fernández Gomez, Jorge H. 2134
Feuardent, Felix Bienaimé 6582
Feuardent, G. L. 393, 2801
Feuardent, Robert 929
Feuardent Frères (Brothers) 2045
Feyel, M. 3896
Figueira, Thomas J. 4011
Figulla, H. H. 6198
Fink, C. M. 930
Finlay, George 4308
Finn, D. J. 3356
Fiorelli, Giuseppe 1865
Fischer, Brigitte 2001, 2181, 2561
Fischer, Calista 2328
Fischer, Thomas 1644, 5269-5269a, 5684
Fischer-Bossert, Wolfgang 159a, 1645, 2844, 3143-4, 3666, 4012-a, 5877
Fischer-Heetfeld, G. 1990
Fisher, Joan E. 551-6, 1962
Fisher, Roger S. 3574
Fitikides, T. J. 5175
Fitzpatrick, A. 2183
Flament, Christophe 62a, 557, 4013-8
Flandrin, Philippe 508
Flegler, Stanley L. 1646-50
Fleischer, Robert 1252
Flight, Walter 6324
Florance, A. 1315-6
Florange, Jules 2041
Floristella, Pennisi di (see di Floristella)
Florenzano, Maria Beatriz Borba (see Borba-Florenzano)
Flower, Michael A. 2876, 3145
Fontana, Alan F. 5270
Fontana, Jeffrey M. 5270
Fontanille, Jean-Philippe 5685-91, 5696
Foraste, D. D. 3792
Forrer, Leonard Steyning 931, 1160-1, 1253, 2042, 2788, 2877-8, 2891, 3043, 3245-8, 3693, 4019, 4256, 4327, 4449, 4540, 4615, 5271, 6199, 6745
Forrer, Robert 2562-3
Fort, E. Tomlinson 394
Foss, Clive 5482-3
Foster, C. W. 4020
Fowler, Barbara Hughes 3897
Fowler, Harold N. 63-4
Fox, Charles R. 2043, 4450
Fox, H. B. Earle (see Earle-Fox)
Fox, Robin Lane 3556
Francfort, Henri-Paul 6324a
Franke, Peter Robert 65-6, 932-3, 1162, 1336, 1536, 1988-9, 3146, 3246, 3357, 3793, 3806, 3849-51, 4356, 4721
Franklin, C. W. 67
Fraser, Peter M. 934, 1317
Freeman, Edward Augustus 3147
Freeman, Kathleen 4021
Freeman, Sarah Elizabeth 1914
Freeman & Sear 4404
Fremont, C. 1383
Frenkel, R. 558
Frey, Imre 1777
Frey-Kupper, Suzanne 2715
Fried, Sallie 559, 3800
Friedberg, Arthur L. 5692
Friedlaender, Julius 1651, 2651, 4309
Friends of the Numismatic Museum 3851a
Froelich, E. 5272
Frolich, B. 517
Frölich, Christine 6057
Frolova, Nina A. 4534, 4541-6a
Frossard, Edward 1652-3
Fulco, William J. 560, 5009
Furtwängler, Adolf 1163
Furtwängler, Andreas E. 395, 2564
Fuscagni, Stefania 2720
Fussman, Gérard 6314

G

Gabrici, Ettore 1391, 1866, 2869, 2925-7, 3022, 4357
Gaebler, Hugo 239a, 1654, 2872, 3247-8, 3359, 3575, 2696
Gainor, John R. 1392, 1655-7
Gaj-Popovic, Dobrila 1960
Galani-Krikou, Mina 60a, 1843
Gale, Noel H. 1482, 1497, 1506-8, 3759
Gale, W. L. 2772-3, 2805, 2828-9
Gallatin, Albert 3148
Galst, Jay M. 5904
Gans, Edward 68, 2184, 3149
Gansiniec, Zofia 4383
Gantz, Timothy 1913
Garcia y Bellido, María Paz 2135-6
Gardiakos, Soterios 3360
Gardiner, Edward Norman 935-6, 4923
Gardner, Percy 69-72, 396, 937-43, 972, 1164, 1254, 1318, 1776, 1778-9, 2652, 2928, 2968, 3601, 3760, 3852-3, 3930, 4199, 4257, 4292, 4358-9, 4630, 4722, 4757, 4825, 4848, 5208, 5273-5, 5484, 6058-9, 6325-8
Gargali, Nomiki 4915
Garlaschelli, M. 5276
Garoufalis, P. 3807
Garraffo, Salvatore 1870, 2653-4, 2773a, 3150
Garrucci, P. Raffaele 2655, 2819
Gatzolis, Christos 561, 3593a-b
Gauba, K. 6329
Gauthier, Ph. 1382
Gebhard, R. 2209, 2565
Gedai, István 1863
Gemmill, Chalmers L. 944
Gentner, W. 1507-8, 1547-8, 4239
Georges, Pericles B. 4758
Georgiades, A. 4200
Georgiou, Evangelia 3793a
Gera, D. 5277
Gerassimov, Theodore D. 397, 3249-50, 3594-6, 3703, 3709, 4631
Gerin, Dominique 912, 1393, 1658, 4344, 4751
Gerojannis, Constantin 945, 2046
Gerson, Stephen N. 946, 5694, 6583
Gesche, Helga 3954, 5176
Geva, H. 5695
Ghaleb, Abbu O. 5913
Ghirshman, Roman 6060-1
Giacchero, Marta 4723
Giacosa, Giorgio 947, 2778c
Giannikouri, A. 4924
Gibbs, William T. 562
Gibson, Carrol 948
Gibson, Thomas L. 3361, 3597
Giedroyc, Richard F. 73-4, 317-8, 563-5, 949, 1319, 1659-63, 3023, 6330, 6584
Gielow, Hertha Edith 3222
Giesecke, Walther 1570, 2656, 2929, 6585
Gil Farrès, Octavio 2137
Gilkes, Paul 1509, 2185
Gill, D. 4328
Gilles, K. J. 614, 1664
Gillespie, J. 4759

INDEX OF AUTHORS

Gillilland, Herbert   2138, 4704
Gillilland, Cora Lee   1165
Gilmore, Starr   3151
Giovanni, Santelli   2632
Giovannini, Adalberto   4022
Gitin, Seymour   569
Gitler, Haim   566-8, 1510, 2986, 4023, 4090a, 5592a, 5693, 5878-80, 5929, 5961-2, 6586-8
Giubba, A.   2845
Gjerstad, Einar   5177
Gjongecaj, Shpresa   713, 3818
Glass, James C.   1511, 4874
Glendining & Co.   2047-8
Glew, Dennis G.   4616
Glytsi, Elena   925
Göbl, Robert   75, 570, 2566-7, 2591
Goddard, John P.   1394, 1979
Göktürk, M. Tevfik   4497, 5088a
Gökyldirim, Turan   571, 3598
Golani, Amir   569
Goldman, Hetty   951
Goldsborough, Reid   319, 398-9, 952, 1665-6, 3362, 3761
Goldstein, Elliott S.   1320
Goldstein, Isadore   5696
Goldstein, Paul   953-4, 5593, 5697
Golenko, Konstantin V.   1657, 4547-8, 4572, 4581-3, 5278
Gomer, John L.   3363
Gomme, A. W.   4024
Gonnella, Robert   6061a-4
Goodall, John A.   955
Goodchild, R. G.   572
Gordon, Thomas   2049
Gordus, A. A.   6064a
Gore, Damian B.   4109a
Gorelick, Leonard   1395
Goring, Elizabeth   1896
Gorini, Giovanni   573, 2657-60, 2930, 3599
Gosline, Sheldon Lee   5690
Gottschewski, Gerhard   3364
Gough, R.   5279
Gow, A. S. F.   956
Gowers, William   957
Goyal, Shankar   6331
Grace, Emily   4307
Grace, Virginia Randolph   958-60, 1396, 4849, 4965
Gramaticu, Steluta   3600
Grandjean, Catherine   4025, 4293, 4310, 4329, 4388-a
Grandjean, Yves   3762
Granger, Lewis G.   961
Grave, Peter   5930
Gray, P. H. K.   2329
Green, Benjamin Richard   78-80
Green, Miranda   2186
Greenwalt, William S.   3365
Greenwell, William (Rev. Canon)   575-6, 2050-4, 4632
Gresham, Carling   4226

Grierson, Philip   400, 2330, 4966
Grigo, Klaus   6291-2
Grigorakis, G.   6589
Grigorova, Valentina   1904
Grinsell, L. V.   2331-2
Grose, Sidney William   1397, 1770, 1834, 2661, 2756, 2774
Grossman, Lee   5698
Grotefend, G. T.   401
Grout, Derek   1744
Grove, L. R. A.   2333
Groves, Thomas G.   3056
Grubb, Steven W.   4258
Grueber, Herbert Appold   2784, 2994
Gruel, Katherine   1483, 2187, 2568
Grunauer von Hoerschelmann, Susanne   1764, 1989, 2012, 2806, 4227, 4384-5
Guadan, Antonio Manuel de   2139
Gubel, Eric   5594
Guépin, J. P.   81, 5209
Guido, Francesco   2002, 6716
Guillaume, Olivier   6268a, 6332-3
Gunstone, Antony John Harris   2334-5
Gupta, Parmeshwari Lal   6334
Gurnet, F.   5503-4
Gutman, Friederike   3024
Gwinnet, John A.   1395

H

Haatvedt, Rolfe A.   577
Habicht, C.   4173
Hackens, Tony   82, 578, 1382, 1398-1400, 1994, 2740, 2931, 3898, 4293a, 4330, 4405, 4451, 5595
Hadji, Athena   4200a
Hadley, Robert A.   276, 5280-1
Haerinck, E.   5931-2
Hahn, W.   5959
Hainzmann, Manfred   579
Halbherr, Federico   4406-7
Hall, E. T.   1512
Hall, H. P.   6590
Hamilton, R.   3025
Hammond, Nicholas Geoffrey L.   3366-8, 4026
Handa, D.   6335
Hands, Alfred Watson   83-5, 2662-3, 2846, 2932, 3369-71, 3899, 4228-9, 4259, 4311, 5881
Hanfmann, George Maxim Anossov   1925
Hansen, Peter   1668, 1925, 3152
Hanse, Richard S.   5828
Hansman, John   6173
Hardwick, Nicholas   490, 3251, 4826-32
Hardy, David B.   3092, 3372
Harl, K.   4671
Harlick, Robert M.   4672
Harris, Josephine M.   580, 4260
Harris, W. V.   86
Harrison, C. M.   6200-1

Harrison, R.   5699
Hart, Gerald D.   962, 1255-7, 6065-6
Hartmann, John E.   1321-4
Harvard University   2055
Harwood, E.   87
Haselgrove, Colin   2244, 2260, 2336-44, 2569-70
Hasluck, F. W.   4633
Hatzopoulos, M. B.   3252
Haughton, Henry Lawrence   6336-41
Hauptmann, A.   614
Havelock, Christine Mitchell   1166-7
Haverfield, F.   581
Haymes, Christopher   4156
Hazelton, James R.   6067
Hazzard, Michael   5591
Hazzard, Richard A.   582, 6592-609
Hazlitt, William Carew   320
Head, Barclay Vincent   88-92, 137, 226- 321, 583-4, 963, 1513, 1572-3, 1776, 1780-3, 2140, 2933, 2968, 2988, 3153, 3253-5, 3373, 3601, 3900-1, 3916, 3931, 3955, 4027, 4157, 4174, 4261, 4634-5, 4760-3, 4875, 4988-9, 5010, 5933-4, 6202, 6342, 6746
Headlam, Arthur C.   3154
Healy, John F.   964-5, 1401, 1514-7, 1974, 4636, 4724-7
Healy, Lawrence P.   3093
Heath, Sabastian   1938-9, 1950, 1952
Hebert, Raymond J.   4498, 5089, 6343
Heckel, Waldemar   93
Heckman, Malcolm W.   73-4, 949, 1319, 3023
Hedges, E. S.   2345
Heeren, Inge   2215
Heichelheim, Fritz Moritz   94, 1771, 1971, 3374, 5282
Heintges, E. R.   3375
Heipp-Tamer, C.   5021
Heiss, Aloïss   2141-2
Hellenic Ministry of Culture and Tourism   585
Helly, Bruno   3853a
Heltzer, M.   5700
Hemmy, A. S.   1574
Hendin, David   323, 1402-3, 1575-8, 1669, 5090-1, 5283, 5596-7, 5701-17a, 5882-4, 5905
Henig, Martin   2346
Henkelman, Wouter   6203
Henry, Alan   4201
Hepworth, R. G.   3895, 3902-3
Herbert, Kevin   1957
Herbert, Sharon C.   586-7
Herbst, Jonathan A.   5718
Heritage Auctions   5717b
Herman, Daniel   5598
Herman, Ira   3376
Hermitage Museum   4549
Herrmann, Fritz   3854-5
Herrmann, John J., Jr.   4028

INDEX OF AUTHORS

Hersh, Charles Austin   3060, 3327, 3377-83, 5599
Herzfeld, E.   6204
Herzfelder, Hubert   2820
Hettger, Joel   5935
Heurgon, Jacques   2741-2
Heyman, Carlo   3856, 4764
Heywood, N.   2347
Higgins, R. A.   966
Hildebrandt, Han Joachim   1579
Hill, B. H.   4029
Hill, D. K.   6610
Hill, George Francis   91, 95-8, 402, 588, 967, 1168-9, 1404, 1580-1, 1670, 1776, 1784-1800, 2056, 2118, 2143, 2348, 2571, 2934, 3384-5, 3557, 3602, 4030, 4158, 4312, 4345, 4390, 4401, 4408-9, 4499, 4876, 5022-4, 5092, 5178-80, 5226, 5600-3, 5719, 5936-7, 6162, 6202, 6205-6, 6546, 6547
Hill, Paul   2022
Hiller, John   403
Hind, John G. F.   3094, 3710-1, 3734, 3763, 3801, 4500, 4550, 4573, 4603
Hingley, R.   2349
Hinks, Roger P.   1258-9
Hipólito, Mário Castro   1884-5, 1886, 1889
Hirmer, Max   65-6, 1162
Hirsch, Herbert   5720
Hirsch, Jacob   2057-8
Hirschfeld, Y.   5722
Hirst, G. M.   3743
Hitchner, R. B.   513
Hixenbaugh, Randall   3386
Hobbs, Richard   2350
Hoberman, Gerald   1170-1
Hobson, Burton   99, 199
Hodder, Michael   6717
Hodgson, T. V.   2351
Hoffmann, Henri   2059
Hoge, Robert W.   968, 1938, 1950, 1952, 2144, 2807, 3026, 3155, 3256, 3744, 4360, 4584, 4705, 4713, 6344-5
Hogg, John   4410
Höghammar, Kerstin   4916, 4925
Hohlfelder, Robert L.   590, 1915-6
Holle, Bruce Fredric   404
Hollis, A. S.   6506
Holloway, R. Ross   405, 591, 1926, 1955, 1959, 1961, 2644-5, 2808, 2870, 2936-41, 3056, 3156-66, 3223, 3387, 4030a, 4230-1, 4331, 4452-3
Hollstein, Wilhelm   3558, 6610a
Holm, Adolf   2942
Holman, David J.   2352
Holmes, Nicholas   2353
Holt, Frank Lee   1260, 3559-61, 6346-54, 6611
Holt, Walter C.   277

Holzer, Hans   2060, 5284
Hook, D. R.   2640
Hooker, John   2572
Hooper, Joseph   2188-9, 5723
Hoover, Oliver D.   322, 592-4, 1405, 2743, 4294, 4454, 4501, 4786, 5210, 5285-99, 5334, 5348, 5375, 5485, 5724-6, 5938-40, 6225, 6612
Hopkins, Chris   1325
Hopper, R. J.   1518, 4031, 4159
Horne, Lauren   4532a, 4764a
Horr, William D.   1406
Horvitz, Peter S.   5604
Hosgören, Ugur   3313
Houghton, Arthur   100, 159a, 323, 595, 663, 1222, 2000, 3388, 5093, 5211, 5265, 5297, 5300-38, 5348, 5365-6, 6019, 6476
Hourmouziadas, J.   4551
Houser, Caroline   969
Howe, Laurence Lee   1261-2
Howe, T. P.   406, 2573
Howgego, Christopher J.   101-2, 407, 5941
Howorth, Henry H.   3932, 4160, 5094, 5339, 6020, 6068-70, 6207
Hrbas, Milos   3742
Hu, Di   1407
Huber, Christian G.   596
Hübner, Ulrich   103
Hulin, P.   6208
Hultsch, Friedrich Otto   1582-3, 6613
Humphreys, Henry Noel   104, 324
Humphris, J. Morineau   597
Hunkin, J. W.   1519
Hunter, Fraser   2354
Hunter, Virginia Joyce   2190
Hurter, Silvia Mani   6, 14, 100, 105, 598-601, 970, 1671-3, 2027, 2069, 2078, 2943, 3068-70, 3095, 3389, 4638, 4728, 4765-6, 4976, 5025-6, 6209
Hussey, Robert   1584
Huston, Stephen M.   6614
Hutchinson, T. P.   4625
Huth, Martin   5942-56
Hutt, Cecelia   6615
Hyne, K.   4986-7

I

Iacovou, Maria   5181
Iashvili, I.   4506
Icard, Severin   1326
Ierardi, Michael   3166a
Iliescu, Octavian   3712-3
Imhoof-Blumer, Friedrich W.   106-7, 971-4, 1263-4, 2062, 2666, 3096, 3167, 3257, 3794, 3904-5, 3933, 4502-3, 4585, 4673, 4877, 4990, 5095-6, 6021
Ingvaldsen, Håkon   602, 4532a, 4674, 4926

International Bureau for the Suppression of Counterfeit Coins   1674
International Nickel Company   6355
Ionita, Virgil   3600
Iossif, Panagiotis P.   5298, 6022
Ireland, Stanley   1839, 1907, 1972, 4546-a, 4586, 4604, 4675, 4967
Irvine, A. K.   5957
Isik, E.   4504, 4767
Israel Numismatic Society   5727
Istituto Italiano di Numismatica   108, 2809, 2944, 3167a
Isvoranu, T.   1895

J

Jackson, Anne E. (also see Anne E. Chapman)   4411-2
Jackson, H.   517
Jacobsthal, Paul   408
Jahn, J.   6530
Jakobsson, Jens   6356-9
Jameson, Robert   4455
Jamgochian, Nicholas   975, 5486
Janis, Edward   5340, 5605, 5885
Jaunzems, Ava C.   1962, 3718
Jenkins, Gilbert Kenneth   109-12, 128, 145, 278, 604-6, 976, 1801-7, 1886, 1982, 2145-50, 2847-8, 2870, 2945-8, 3009-11, 3027, 3036-7, 3040-a, 3097, 3168-9, 3808, 4262, 4413, 4505, 4768, 4878, 4968, 5097, 5341, 6360-5, 6531-3, 6547, 6616, 6718-21, 6748
Jenkins, Michael R.   6617
Jentoft-Nilsen, Marit   1265, 2849
Jesselsohn, D.   5728-30
Jevons, F. B.   113
Jha, Amiteshwar   6366
Jidejian, Nina   279, 1266
Jobert, Louis   114
Johnston, Alan   4263
Johnston, Ann Elizabeth M.   514, 607, 977-8, 2667, 2789-90, 4879
Johnston, Joseph   4032, 4639
Jones, Doran A.   409
Jones, Francis Follin   4232
Jones, H. Stuart   3603
Jones, John Ellis   1520
Jones, John Richard Melville   115-6, 280, 410-1, 1328-35, 1585-7, 3934, 4033, 4972
Jones, Mark   1675
Jones, Nicholas F.   4769
Jones, T.   4034
Jongkees, Jan Hendrik   1408, 3170, 3224, 4035-6, 4175, 4361-2, 4991
Jörgensen, Christian   2879
Josifovski, P.   3257a, 3265
Jucker, Hans   4313
Jungfleisch, Marcel   4037, 6618
Jurukova, J. (see Y. Youroukova)

Index of Authors

K

Kadman, Leo   5731-6
Kaenel, Hans-Markus   608
Kagan, Donald   412, 979, 2880, 4233
Kagan, Jonathan H.   609-11, 835, 3689, 3857, 4264, 4456, 4706, 4880, 5068
Kagan, Ute Wartenberg (see Wartenberg)
Kagin, Don   413
Kahanov, Y.   568
Kahn, Jeff   980
Kakhidze, Amiran   4506, 4575
Kala, Satish Chandra   6367
Kallithrakas-Kontos, N.   3390
Kalligas, Peter G.   1409
Kaltsas, N.   60a
Kambanis, M. L.   4176
Kampmann, Ursula   4295, 4363, 4640, 4676
Kan, Richard W. C.   159
Kanael, Baruch   5737-40
Kanitz, L. El   981
Kapossy, Balázs   1903, 2012
Karadima, Chryssa   3729
Karageorghis, Jacqueline   5182
Karageorghis, Vassos   5182
Karayotov, Ivan   3735-6
Kardara, Chrysoula   3604
Karlsson, Lars   3171
Karo, G.   5098
Karouzos, C. J.   2949
Karweise, Stefan   4770-1, 4881
Karydas, A.   3888-9
Karyshkovski, P. O.   3745-7, 4548
Kastner, W.   414
Katsanos, A.   3390
Katsarova, G.   3764
Kaufman, J. Chaim   5741-2
Kaylan, Melik   476
Keall, E. J.   6071-2
Keary, Charles Francis   1172
Keller, Otto   973
Kent, John Philip Cozens   2172, 2355
Keppel, Derek H. E.   4265
Kern, Jonathan K.   415, 1676
Kerr, David   117
Keyser, Paul T.   1521-2
Khairy, N. I.   5958
Khurshudian, E.   5468a
Kiang, Dawson   6619
Kibbey, Mead B.   325
Kiechle, Franz   4641
Kienast, Dietmar   1988, 4507, 4772-3
Kiernan, Philip   1743
Kim, Henry S.   118-20, 612-3, 1482
Kind, H. D.   614
Kindler, Arie   615, 5606-8, 5736, 5743-52, 5886-7, 6620
King, Cathy E.   1972, 2260
Kinns, Philip   491, 616, 1677-8, 3959, 4508, 4774-82, 4833
Kirkby, Todd   2151-2
Kirkpatrick, C.   6368-72

Kissyov, Kostadin   1701
Kitchell, K. F.   3802
Kiyonaga, S.   416
Klausewitz, Wolfgang (see Noeske under Egypt)
Klawans, Zander H.   326-7
Kleeb, Alvin A.   281, 617, 1410-1, 1679-81, 5650, 5753
Klein, Dieter   2063
Kleiner, Fred S.   618-9, 3391, 4038-40, 4177, 4509-11, 4677, 4783, 5011
Kleiner, Gerhard   1988, 3392-3, 4587-8
Klimowsky, Ernst Werner   5736, 5752, 5754-7
Klose, Dietrich O. A.   982, 3858, 5342-3
Knapp, Jamie   2153, 4041
Knapp, Robert C.   417, 620, 6534
Knauf, Ernst Axel   103
Kneusel, Ronald T.   1523
Knight, Richard Payne   3172
Knoblauch, Ann-Marie   982a
Knobloch, Frederick S.   2064
Knoepfler, Denis   3173, 3906
Koch, Heidemarie   6073
Koch, W.   6621
Koenig, Marie E. P.   2191-2
Koerper, Henry C.   6749
Kogan, Howard   621, 5758-60, 5888
Köhler, U.   4042
Köker, Hüseyin   622, 2016a
Kokkinos, N.   5761
Kolb, Frank   5027
Kolb, P.   4589
Kolev, Boyko   1639
Kolitsida-Makri, I.   623
Kollgaard, Ron   282, 2154-5, 2744, 4234, 4266, 4834, 4969
Kolls, A. L.   6749
Kolníková, Eva   2574-5
Kombou, M.   4732
Kontes, Zoë   4200a
Konuk, Koray   159a, 490-1, 2013, 2065, 4850, 4881a-5a
Kool, Robert   5762
Koppersmith, Daniel   328
Korpe, Funda   2015
Kos, Peter   121, 2005, 2576-7
Kosmetatou, Elizabeth   624, 4678, 5028, 5070
Kosmidou, Elpida   625
Kostial, Michaela   2578
Koumanoudes, Stephanos N.   3907
Kourebanas, T.   3859
Kourempanas, Theodoros   3576
Kourouniotes, K.   626
Kourtzellis, I.   627
Koutsoukos, Eduardo A. M.   6622
Kouymijian, Dickran   5487
Kovacs, Frank L.   1682-3, 2073, 5488-90, 6632
Kovalenko, Sergei A.   4552-3
Koychev, Atanas   3605
Kozik, Vic   3012

Kozolubski, Julius   345, 6373
Kraay, Colin Mackennal   55, 122-8, 274, 418, 628-36, 800, 1524-6, 1588, 1890, 1972, 2066, 2668-70, 2763-4, 2776, 2791, 2810, 2821, 2834, 3028-30, 3098, 3174-7, 3809-10, 3908, 4043-7, 4267, 4457, 4784, 5056, 5183, 6374
Kraft, Konrad   1684, 1988, 4048
Kravchenko, A. A.   4642
Kreindler, Herb   5717b
Kremydi-Sicilianou, Sophia   1995, 3258, 3394
Krengel, Elke   5344
Kretz, Rainer   2356-60, 2579, 3259
Kreuzer, Matthew   6623
Krishnamurthy, R.   637, 5609
Kritt, Brian   1589, 4880, 5345-8, 6375
Kritzas, Ch.   60a
Kroh, Dennis J.   129-30, 1685
Kroll, John H.   131, 159a, 419, 515, 613, 638, 1590, 1844, 1989, 4049-59, 4058a, 4082, 4161, 4927
Kromann, Anne   1982, 5610, 6652
Kropp, M.   5959
Krupp, Michael   5763-4
Kubitschek, J. W.   5960
Kuhner, Max H.   132
Kumpikevicius, Gordon C.   1772
Künker, Fritz Rudolf   133
Kuritzky, Simcha   983
Kurke, Leslie   134
Kuschel, B.   6624
Kushnir-Stein, Alla   283, 5592a, 5765, 5889-90, 5961-2, 6586
Kutajsov, V. A.   3606
Kutcher, Robert R.   1412, 3099, 4554
Küthmann, Harald   1988-9
Kvist, Kjetil   1267
Kyrieleis, H.   6625
Kyrou, Adonis K.   135, 4458

L

LaBaume, Peter   2193
Lacroix, Léon   984-90, 2765, 2850, 2950-1, 3909, 3960, 4060, 4391
Ladd, Raymond   329
Laffaille, Maurice   2067
Lagos, Constantinos   639, 3395, 3910, 4555, 4733, 4835-7
Lahiri, Amarendra Nash   6376-82
Laing, Lloyd Robert   136, 1413, 2194, 2361
Lakakis-Marchetti, Maria   705
Laloux, Monique   4643-4
Lamb, James   1923
Lamb, William Eliot   5349
Lambert, C.   640, 5611, 5766
Lambros, J. P.   4414
Lambros, Paul   3260
Lampinen, Peter   4886
Lanciers, E.   6570

Index of Authors

Lanckoronski, Leo   1173
Lanckoronski, Maria   1173
Landon, C. P.   61
Lane-Poole, Stanley   137
Lang, David Marshall   4574
Lang, Mabel   1591-2, 4061
Lang, R. Hamilton   641-2, 5184
Lange, Kurt   138, 991, 1268-9
Langher, S. Consolo   2952
Langlois, Victor   5491, 5963
Langton, Neville   3961
LaNiece, Susan   1527, 6715
Lanzone, R. V.   1869
Larizza, Pietro   2780, 2822
Laronde, André   6750
Larozas, Christian   2580
Larson, Charles M.   1414, 1686
Lassen, Christian   6383
Lateano, O.   4018
Lattimore, Steven   992
Laum, Bernhard   3748
Laver, Henry   2362
Lavva, Stella   3860
Lawson, A. J.   4785
Lawson, Barbara   1748
Lawton, Carol L.   993, 1270, 1912
Lazarenki, I.   3607
Lazarov, Latchezar   3737
Lazzarini, Lorenzo   2953, 2791a, 4706a, 4729
Leake, William Martin   1593, 2068
Lederer, Philipp   1902, 2881, 3071, 3178-9, 3396, 3608, 5099, 5350
Lee, Ian   3005-6, 3100
Lehman, Phyllis Williams   994-5
Lehmann, Clayton M.   3225
Lehmann-Hartleben, Karl   1271
Lehrberger, G.   2209, 2565
Leigh, T. Gordon   420
Leith, M. J. W.   5906
Lemaire, André   5612, 5767, 6572
Lemaire, V.   1415
Lemburg-Ruppelt, Edith   6384
Lempriere, J.   139
Lengyel, Lancelot   140, 2581
Lenormant, Charles   141-2
Le Rider, Georges   7, 36, 143-5, 284, 421, 530, 570, 595, 643-5, 1416-7, 2671, 3397-402, 3696, 3765, 4415-6a, 4678a-4679, 4887, 5057, 5099a, 5351-60, 6023, 6163, 6173a
Leschhorn, Wolfgang   146, 996, 1336, 1988, 1993, 4970
Leu Numismatics (also see Bank Leu & Co.)   2069-70, 2195, 4364
Levante, Edoardo   1987, 2010-1, 5100-2
Levi, Doro   4417
Levy, Brooks   5613-5
Levy, G. Rachel   997
Lewis, Bart   1418
Lewis, David M.   1528, 4062, 4178, 4202, 6210

Lewis, Peter E.   5071, 5768
Lewis, R. B.   646, 6721-2
Lhotka, John F.   1687, 2123
LHS Numismatics Ltd.   4296
Liampi, Katerini   647-8, 1989, 3261-4, 3403-5, 3546, 3783, 3861-2, 4461
Liebert, David   5769-70
Liegle, Josef   1174
Liewald, Hans-Joachim   4638
Lightfoot, Chris   484, 5013
Lilcic, V.   3265
Lindberg, J. C.   6535
Linders, Tullia   147
Lindgren, Henry Clay   422, 998, 2071-3
Lindsay, John   4314, 6074
Linecar, Howard   2363
Linzalone, Joseph   423
Lipinski, Edouard   424, 6548
Lis, Akio   3749
Lis, L. J.   4235
Lister, Clem W.   2364-5
Littlejohn, J.   517
Lloyd, A. H.   2672, 2954-5, 3080, 3101, 3180
Lloyd, William Watkiss   999, 2766, 2777, 3081
Loginov, S. D.   6074a
Long, A. L.   1594
Longo, Anna Maria   3031
Lönnqvist, Kenneth   649, 4063
Lönnqvist, Minna   649
Lorber, Catharine Custis   159a, 425, 649a-650, 664, 1222, 2000, 2027, 2074, 2956-7, 3266-7, 3863-6, 4786, 5331-4, 5344, 5361-6, 5691, 6022, 6581, 6587-8, 6614, 6626-33, 6702a, 6723
Lordkipanidze, G. A.   4571
Lorimer, H. L.   1000
Losada, Luis A.   651
Lovette, James B.   5771
Lubbock, John   148
Lueke, Jorg   1595
Lukanc, Ivo   2582
Luynes, Duc de   2673, 2851, 5130
Lykiardopoulou-Petrou, Marina   3406-7
Lyrou, F.   4738

M

Mabbott, Thomas Ollive   330, 426, 4236
MacDonald, David J.   1419, 2674, 3268, 3355, 3577-8, 3726, 3766, 3911, 4179, 4418, 4556, 4578, 4787-8, 4888-9, 5299, 6385-7, 6477
Macdonald, George   149-50, 581, 1001, 1272, 1324, 1337, 1420, 1898-9, 2675, 3032, 4180, 4419, 5367, 5492, 6211, 6388
Macdonald, Janet M.   1002
Macdonald, Michael C. A.   5964

MacDowall, David William   652, 6212, 6389-96b
MacFadden, George H.   1273
MacIsaac, John D.   620, 653, 4389
Mack, Richard P.   2366-7
Mackay, James Alexander   151
MacKay, Pierre A.   3579-82
Mackensen, Michael   2583
MacKenzie, Kenneth M.   514, 6397
Mackil, Emily   152
Madden, Frederick W.   5772-8
Madsen, Eardley   427, 1529-31, 2852, 3102, 3269, 3667, 3784, 3867, 3912, 4268, 4365, 4557, 4617, 4789, 4971, 5058
Madsen, Ethel   2852, 3013, 3102, 3269, 3667, 3784, 3867, 3912, 4268, 4617, 4971, 5058
Maffre, Frédéric   4645
Magalhaes, Marici Martins   1967
Magen, Y.   654
Magie, David   1003
Magness, J.   5616
Maharian, E.   5368
Mahler, Arthur   3935
Maier, A.   3819
Mainjonet, Monique   2196, 2592
Makrypodi, S.   1107
Maksudian, William   5493
Malaise, Oscar   3049
Malkmus, William   1421-2
Malloy, Alex G.   2075, 4590
Malter, Joel   2076, 6059, 6075
Maltiel-Gerstenfeld, Jacob   5779-80
Mamroth, Alfred   3408-11, 6634
Mandel, Siegfried   5869
Manfredi, Lorenzo-Ilia   3102a, 6723a
Manganaro, Giacomo   2958-60, 3044, 3052, 3181, 6751
Mangieri, Giuseppe Libero   2892-3
Manning, J. G.   6635
Manning, William A.   428
Mannsperger, Dietrich   1990, 4752
Manov, R.   1702
Manton, Gavin   3412
Mantzouka, E.   3889
Maraqten, Mohammed   5965
Marathaki, Irini   933
Marchetti, Patrich   171, 705, 2745, 3103, 3868, 4646
Marco, Jindrich   3742
Marcos, Carmen   1
Marinescu, Constantin A.   1274, 3668-9, 4512
Maris, Edward   1004
Markham, D.   1911
Markoe, Glenn E.   5617
Markou, Evangéline   5184a-b
Markov, A. de   6075a
Marmorstein, Arthur   5581
Marotta, Michael E.   429-31, 1005, 1275, 1338, 1423, 1532, 3820, 4064, 4605, 4730, 4790-2, 5029, 6752

INDEX OF AUTHORS

Marshall, F. H.   4420
Martin, Erik   1276, 3913, 6636
Martin, J. P.   1688-90
Martin, M. F. C.   6398
Martin, Thomas R.   153-4, 432, 655, 1533, 3869-70, 4065
Martin Valls, Ricardo   2156
Martini, Rodolfo   2001
Masson, Charles   6399-401
Masson, O.   1338a-9
Master, Daniel   6588a
Mathews, George D.   155
Mathiesen, Hans Erik   1984-5
Mathisen, Ralph W.   3413-7, 4237
Matiossian, V.   5494
Matsson, G. O.   1006
Mattheeuws, C.   3757
Matthews, Elaine   1317
Mattingly, Harold   4, 2961, 6637
Mattingly, Harold B.   156-7, 656-8, 797, 1596, 3182, 3727, 4066, 4181-2, 4203-8, 4591, 4680, 4793, 4838, 5369
Matzke, Michael   1990, 4794
Mavrogordato, J. A.   2077, 4839-41, 6549
May, Jeffrey   2368-72
May, John Maunsell Frampton   3609, 3690, 3694, 3728, 3821-2, 5185
Mayer, Leo Ary   5782
Mays, Melinda   2172, 2373-4
Mazard, Jean   6774-8
McAlee, Richard G.   5370
McCartney, E. S.   1007
McClean, John Robinson   1597-8, 2676
McCredie, J. R.   816
McDaniel, W. B.   2853
McDonald, William H.   1657, 1691
McDowall, Katharine A.   4731
McDowell, Robert Harbold   659, 5371
McEwen, H. D.   3104
McFadden, Eric J.   4795
McGovern, Wayne E.   1424
McGregor, Kaelyn Ann   836, 5186
McIntyre, Andrew P.   5030, 5059
McIvor, Robert S.   1008, 2197
McKenna, Thomas P.   1425, 1692
McKinney, Larry E.   5103, 5372
McLean, Mark D.   5783
McMenamin, Mark   6724-6
Meadows, Andrew   158-9, 285, 489-91, 594, 660-5, 1425a, 1774, 1939, 1976, 2144, 2995, 3767, 4707, 4796, 4890-1, 4914, 5060-1, 6638-9
Meaghar, John   4992
Mecquenem, R. de   480
Medvedeva, L. I.   3610
Meeks, N. D.   4986
Megaw, Vincent   2183
Meier, Barry   666
Meiggs, Russell   4209-10
Meir, Cecilia   5618
Meischner, Jutta   5373

Mellink, M. J.   1534
Mel'Nikov, A. V.   3341
Melville Jones, J. R. (see Jones)
Mendelssohn, Edwin   5784
Mensitieri, Marina Taliercio   2714
Mercieri, Dennis J.   1009
Merker, Irwin L.   1961, 3418-21
Merritt, Benjamin Dean   4029, 4067-8, 4211
Meshorer, Ya'akov   433-4, 587, 667-8, 1426-7, 1962, 5619-20, 5785-801, 5828, 5842, 5891, 5907-9, 5966
Metcalf, David Michael   286, 1512, 2441, 6640
Metcalf, William E.   159a, 3422-3
Metropolitan Museum of Art (New York)   1940
Meyer, Casper   3714
Meyers, Robert J.   2746
Meyshan, Joseph   5736, 5802-3
Michaelidou, Lefki   5206a
Michaelidou-Nicolaou, Ino   669, 695, 5187-8, 6656-8
Michaux-Van der Mersch, Françoise   1381, 1400, 3269a
Michell, Humfrey   160, 4386
Middleton, J. H.   1010
Mielczarek, Mariusz   670, 2003, 4162, 4512a, 6402
Mihailescu, Barliba   3424
Milavic, Anthony F.   1011-5, 4332
Milazzo, M.   1480
Milbank, Samuel R.   4238
Mildenberg, Leo   103, 161, 1175-7, 1428, 2078, 2099, 2642, 3072, 3105-8, 3183, 4647, 5031-2, 5621, 5736, 5804-6, 5856, 5892-6, 6213-9, 6727-8
Miles, George Carpenter   570
Milik, J. T.   5967
Militký, Jiri   671
Miller, M. C. J.   1340, 3425-6, 3562
Miller, Michael F.   331
Miller, Richard P.   672-3, 4069, 5374-5
Miller, Stephen G.   620
Millingen, James   2079-80
Milne, Joseph Grafton   162-4, 435, 674-6, 1016, 1429-31, 1535, 1599, 1972, 2666-8, 2962, 4070-4, 4163, 4333, 4346, 4366, 4421, 4462-3, 4513-4, 4714-5, 4797-803, 4892-3, 4928, 5189, 5622, 6174, 6220, 6641-3
Minc, Henryk   5807-11
Mini, Adolfo   2963, 3184
Ministry of Culture (Athens)   1845
Minkova, Mariana   1741
Minns, E. H.   6076
Mionnet, Théodore Edme   165
Mirnik, Ivan   677, 2577, 3427, 3823
Miron, A.   146
Miron, A. V. B.   146
Mirone, Salvatore   2964, 3045
Mirza, S.   6478

Mitchell Havelock, Christine (see Havelock)
Mitchell, Richard E.   2679
Mitchell, Stephen   2375
Mitchiner, Michael B.   436, 5212-3, 5968, 6403
Mitrea, Bucur   4183
Mitsos, M. T.   4334
Mittag, Peter Franz   5376
Mixter, John R.   1017, 4606, 5104
Moesta, Hasso   1536
Mogelonsky, Marcia K.   437
Mohan, Mehta Vasishtha Dev   6404
Molchanov, Arcady A.   4553
Moledor, Victoria Stone   4075
Molinari, C.   3033
Molinari, Nicholas   1178
Molnar, Michael R.   4592
Mommsen, H.   1537
Mommsen, Theodor   1600
Monney, Pierre R.   1018, 4593
Monov, Metodi   3611
Montagu, Hyman   2081, 2376
Montenegro, E.   2680
Montero, Joaquin   1277
Montgomery, Hugo   166, 3428
Moon, George Washington
Moon, Warren G.   4076-7, 4367
Moore, John W.   1368
Moore, Nancy J.   3428a-30
Moore, Wayne   5265, 5335-6, 5377-81
Moorey, P. R. S.   635-6
Moosavi, Sadrodin   6080
Morawiecki, L.   3431
Morcom, John   2681, 3072a, 3185
Mordtmann, J. H.   5969
Morello, Antonio   3218a
Morin, Eric   2187
Morineau-Humphris, J.   678
Mørkholm, Otto   167-9, 287-9, 679-84, 707, 800, 1278, 1432-3, 1601, 1988, 3432, 4184, 4515, 4681, 5033-6, 5105, 5137-43, 5190, 5227, 5382-97, 6077, 6164, 6221, 6644-52, 6658, 6753
Moro, Gotbert   1964
Morris, Robert   6165
Morteani, G.   2209, 2565
Mosher, Stuart   170
Moss, A. A.   6405
Mosser, Sawyer McArthur   1941
Mossop, Henry R.   2377-87
Mossop, J. C.   5062
Mottahedeh, Patricia Erhart   100
Moucharte, Ghislane   171, 5595
Moulakis, Christophoros M.   1693-6
Mousheghian, Anahit   5495, 5502-4
Mousheghian, Khachadour A.   5496-504
Moushmov, Nikola A.   3612-3
Moustaka, Aliki   3871-2, 4804
Mowat, Robert   5063
Moysey, Robert A.   5106, 6222

INDEX OF AUTHORS

Mudd, Douglas   439, 3186
Mukherjee, Bratindra Nath   6406-9
Mullaly, Terence   5191
Müller, Carl Ludwig   3433-6, 3670-3, 6535
Müller, D. H.   5960
Müller, Jörg W.   4804a
Müller, Otto   1508, 1546-8, 4239
Munro-Hay, Stuart C.   5921, 5970-5
Münsterberg, Rudolf   1341
Münzen und Medaillen AG   2025-6, 2082-3, 3795
Münzer, Friedrich   3614
Murphy, Barry P.   4594
Muret, Ernest   2584
Murray, A. S.   1602
Murray, Hugh Alexander   1019-20, 1882
Müseler, Wilhelm   3615, 5336a, 5343, 6225
Museum of Fine Arts (Boston)   1021, 1279, 1920
Myers, Robert J.   3437
Mylonas, George Emmanuel   1022
Myres, John C.   4422

N

Nadooshan, Farhang Khademi   6056, 6078-80
Narain, Awadk Kishore   6410-9
Narain, Sudha   6420
Nash, Daphne (also see Briggs, Daphne Nash)   685, 2198-9, 2585-8
Nasir, M. J.   2210
Naster, Paul   1434, 1603-4, 1740, 4078, 4516, 4993-5, 5107, 5397a-8, 5623-5, 5976, 6223-4, 6251c-2
Naveh, J.   5812
Naville, Lucien   2084-6, 6081, 6754
Nawotka, Krzysztof   4558
Negev, Avraham   5977
Negishi Equine Museum   1023
Nelson, Bradley R.   322, 686, 4294, 4454, 4501, 5210, 5296, 6225
Nercessian, Yeghia T.   5487, 5505-43
Neuburger, Albert   1179
Neumann, Günter   5034
Neupert, Paul E.   2200
Newell, Adra Marshall   5399
Newell, Edward Theodore   290, 687-94, 1280, 1942, 3438-50, 3674, 3936, 4682-3, 5192, 5214-5, 5246, 5400-7, 5626, 6085-4, 6653-5
Newman, John   2313-4
Newman, R. W.   332
Newton, Charles Thomas   172, 1024, 3451, 4423, 4805, 5144
Niah, Sabir Hassan   6056
Nick, Michael   2201, 2588a
Nicolae, E.   1895
Nicolaou, Ino (see Michaelidou)
Nicolaou, K.   1435, 6659

Nicolau Kormikiari, Maria Cristina   6729, 6779
Nicolet-Pierre, Hélène   173, 696, 1342, 1605, 1987, 3563, 3802a, 4005, 4079-82, 4185, 4240-1, 4368-70a, 4464-8, 4684, 4851, 6024, 6421, 6550-1
Nicorescu, Paul   5627
Nielsen, Thomas Heine   4347
Nikitin, A. B.   6074a, 6084a
Nilsson, Harald   174, 2009
Nimchuk, Cindy L.   4997, 6226
Nivaille, J.   1024a
Nixon, C. E. V.   517, 697-8, 1737
Noble, W. J.   6422
Nock, A. D.   1025
Nodelman, S. A.   6166
Noe, Sydney Philip   699-702, 1436, 1943-4, 2682, 2767, 2792-3, 2811, 2882, 3270, 3452, 3937, 4511, 4517, 5037, 5408, 6227
Noehden, George Henry   2683-4
Noeske, Hans-Christoph   6660-1
Nollé, Johannes   1991, 4518, 4806-7, 4998
Nollé, M. K.   4998
Nomos A.G.   3873
Nord, R. S.   1369
Nordbø, Jan H. A.   2087, 4607, 4894-5, 5978-9
Northover, J. P.   2388
Norton, Charles E.   1180
Nouyon, Bernard   1437
Nubar, H.   3716
Numismatic Fine Arts, Inc.   2027-8
Numismatic Museum (Athens)   1026, 3851a
Numismatica Ars Classica   2685, 3956
Numismatik Lanz München   3938, 4269, 4896
Nurpetlian, Jack   5544
Nussbaum, Harold J.   5813

O

Oakley, John H.   4716
O'Bee, Michael   2389-91
Ober, William B.   1027
Oddy, Andrew   5980
Oddy, W. A.   1538, 2287
Oeconomides, Mando Caramessini   703-5, 1846-7, 3453-4, 4084-6, 4242-4, 4852
Oeconomides, Mando L.   175-6, 291, 706, 1843, 1996, 4370a, 5628
Oestreicher, Bruno   5814-5
Oguz, Tekin   4518a
O'Hea, M.   517
Oikonomides, Alcibiades N.   1028, 1281-7, 1539, 3455-8, 3811, 4315, 5981, 6423-8
Olçay, Nekriman   707-8
Oleson, John   1182

Oliver, Graham   4087
Olshausen, Eckert   4595
Olson, Richard Alfred   6085-7
Oman, Charles William Chadwick   3459, 4270-2, 4808, 5409-10
O'Neill, J.   1029
Oraiopoulos, Zacharias L.   4335, 4469
Orati, Irene   1223
Orsi, Paolo   2965
Ortega Galindo, Julio   2157
Orville, Jacob Philipp d'   2966
Osborne, M. J.   1317
Ostermann, Siegfried   5816
Oteri, E.   3130
Otero, Paloma   1
Otto, Brinna   2757
Overbeck, Bernhard H.   2589
Özbek, Osman   4186
Özen, Ayça   6559

P

Paasch, Kasper M.   1438
Pafford, Isabelle   3063, 4249a
Paléothodoros, Dimitri   3768
Palmer, Hazel   1439
Palmer, Thomas A., Jr.   333, 4336
Paltrinieri, E.   1480
Panagopoulou, Katerina   3460
Pandey, Deena Bandhu   3565, 6429
Panvini Rosati, Franco   2686, 2748
Paolini, E. Pozzi   2691, 2781
Paonessa, Joe   1444
Papadopoulos, John K.   2687
Papaeufymiou, Eleni   2088, 3461-2, 4088
Papaevangelou, Cleopatra E.   3874
Papageorgiadou-Banis, Charikleia   219, 4470-1, 4481
Parente, Anna Rita   1987, 2687a
Parise, Nicola Franco   2688, 2782, 2967
Parke-Bernet Galleries, Inc.   2089, 3271
Paruck, Furdoonjee D. J.   6088-9
Paton, W. R.   4897
Patrillo Serafin, Patriza   2747
Paunov, Eugeni   1701, 1703
Pauwels, Ghislaine   2590
Pavlovska, Eftimija   3272
Pásztóry, Emmerich   601, 1540, 4089
Peacock, M. S.   440
Pegan, Efrem   3463
Pegge, Samuel   2392
Pellerin, Joseph   177
Pemberton, Elizabeth G.   709
Pendleton, Elizabeth J.   3875
Penhallurick, R. D.   2393
Penn, R. G.   1030
Penna, Vasso   60a, 1843
Pennington, Paul   334, 1183, 1343
Perala, Adrew   1031
Perdigão, José De Azeredo   1888
Peristeri, Katerina   648

Index of Authors

Perkins, Jonathan   3273
Perlman, S.   3464
Pernice, Erich   1606
Persson, Axel W.   441
Petac, Emanuel   1892-4, 3674a, 3737a
Peter, Ulrike   178, 3617
Peters, Ken   2394
Peterson, Enoch E.   577
Petitot-Biehler, Claire Yvonne   710
Petrányi, Gyula   3824-7a
Petrie, Alfred Edward Hathaway   179, 6228
Petrova, Eleonora   3273a-4a
Petrowicz, Alexander Ritter (see Von Petrowicz)
Pfeiler, Bärbel   4809
Pfeiler, Hasso   2689
Phillips, Henry, Jr.   1032, 4392
Phillips, Wayne C.   3188-90, 4273, 5145, 5411, 6662, 6730
Phoungas, A.   3914
Picard, Olivier   180, 3275-9, 3465-a, 3618-9, 3759, 3768a-72, 3939-40, 4090, 4187, 6577
Pichikyan, I.   711
Pick, Behrend   3620-1, 5817
Pieper, Wilfried   5216, 6393-4, 6430-1
Pierides, D.   5193-4
Pilakouta, M.   3888-9
Pincock, Richard   6663
Pinder, Moritz Eduard   1697
Pink, Karl   2591, 3675
Pinkerton, John   181
Piras, Enrico   3108a
Pitchfork, Colin E.   6664
Pitsillides, Andreas   5181
Plant, Richard J.   1033-5, 1344-6, 2835, 5228, 5412, 5629, 5818-9
Plantzos, Dimitris   5413
Plenderleith, H. J.   6174
Ployart, Brigitte   2592
Poetto, Massimo   4898
Pokorney, Ted   2794
Pokras, Yuri   4648
Pollak, Phyllis   712
Pollard, Graham   1891
Ponting, Matthew J.   159a, 1510, 4023, 4090a
Pontrandolfo, A. G.   2894
Poole, Reginald Stuart   1184-5, 1776, 2690, 2731, 2968, 3038, 4424, 5108, 5414, 6665-6, 6755
Pope, Spencer   2969
Porada, Edith   1036
Porteous, John   182
Porter, Gerald S.   1037
Portolos, Dimitris   3466
Poste, Beale   2395-7
Postel, R.   1762
Postolakos, Achilles   1848
Potts, Dan T.   5630, 5930, 5941, 5953, 5985-9, 6252a
Poulios, V.   3593a

Pozzi, E. (see Paolini, E. Pozzi)
Prakash, Satya   6432
Prasad, Hari Kishore   6433-4
Preda, Constantin   1894, 3622, 3715-6
Preka, Kalliopi   713
Prentzas, Kostas   3876
Preston, K.   1487, 1500
Price, Martin Jessop   40, 183-90, 442, 485, 714-21, 836, 1038, 1541, 1699, 1808-9, 1973, 1976, 3082, 3467-75, 3566, 3691, 4099, 4188-9, 4425, 4596, 4899, 4999, 5820, 5999, 6025, 6231, 6552, 6667-8
Prieto Martinez, J. J.   1440
Prime, William C.   191, 5821
Prinsep, Henry Thoby   6435
Prinsep, James   6436-8
Pritchett, W. Kendrick   4200
Prokopov, Ilya (Ilja) S.   533, 722-4, 1639, 1700-3, 1741, 3279a, 3335, 3583, 3623-5, 3758, 3773-5
Pryer, Charles   192
Psoma, Selene   159a, 193, 1038a-9, 1347, 1997, 3280-4, 3406, 3593b, 3625a-3626, 3697, 3719-20, 3729
Pudill, Rainer   3627
Puetz, Bill   1704
Puglisi, Mariangela   3191, 4273a
Purefoy, Peter Bagwell   1976

Q
Qanbari, Batul   6079
Qedar, Shraga   5658, 5908-9, 5954, 6232
Queyrel, François   4685-6
Quinnell, A.   6090-1
Quiggin, Mary Alison Hingston   443

R
Rahman, Aman Ur   6295
Rahmani, Levi Y.   725-6, 3476, 5822
Rakicic, Mark   292, 1040-2, 1849, 3477-9, 3676, 3915, 4810, 4900, 5415-6
Ralli-Photopoulou, Euterpe   60a, 3796, 4732-3
Ramage, Andrew   1542-4, 2090, 2692, 5000
Ramsay, W. M.   5064
Rant, A.   2593
Raoul-Rochette, Désiré   194
Raoul-Rochette, M.   2854
Raper, Matthew A.   195
Rappaport, Uriel   5823-6, 5897
Rapson, Edward James   6092, 6439-40
Ratto, Rodolfo   2091, 2855
Raub, Charles   2565
Raubitschek, A. E.   1441
Rauch, Hans   2202-3
Ravel, Oscar E.   727, 1186, 1705, 2856, 3192, 3812, 4274-8

Raven, E. J. P.   728, 3193, 3962, 4091
Rawlings, Gertrude Burford   196
Rawson, A. L.   5827
Rawson, Beryl   1736
Ray, John D.   4901
Raymond, Doris   3285, 3480
Raymond, Wayte   335-7, 2092-3
Raynor, Joyce Toby   5828
Rea, John   6506
Reade, Julian   729-30
Ready, W. Talbot   6756
Rebuffat, François   197, 444
Reding, Lucien   2594
Reeds, Brian   2375
Reekmans, Tony   6669-71
Regling, Kurt Ludwig   198, 543, 1187, 2094, 2871, 3194, 3286-8, 3621, 3628, 3797, 4687, 4812-3, 5417
Reichardt, Henry C.   5830-1
Reid, Matthew S.   6672
Reifenberg, Abraham   5832
Reifenberg, Adolph   5832-5
Reifler, E.   1607
Reimers, P.   1485
Reinach, A. J.   3481, 3785, 3877
Reinach, Theodore   4529, 4597, 4688, 5836-7
Reinders, H. Reinder   3878
Reinfeld, Fred   199
Reis, Bob   6757
Reppeteau, L. V.   200
Requier, P.   4337, 4929
Retsinas, G. A.   5418
Rhezakhani, Khodadad   6225, 6252a
Rhodes, P. J.   4092-4
Richard, L.   2595
Richardson, Arthur W.   445
Richter, Gisela Marie Augusta   1188-90, 1288-93, 1442
Riddle, John M.   1043, 6758
Ridgeway, William   1545, 1608-11
Riederer, Josef   2626
Rigsby, Kent J.   4519, 6673
Ripollès, Pere Pau   2009, 2161
Rivero, Casto Maria del   2158
Rives, Robert G.   6093
Rizack, Martin A.   5990
Rizzo, Giulio Emanuele   1191, 2970-2, 3014
Roach, Steven R.   4095
Robbins, K.   2398
Robert, Louis   201-2, 1044, 1348, 3629, 3941-2, 4708, 5038
Roberts, P.   446
Roberts, W. Rhys   3916
Robin, Christian   5991-2
Robins, D. A.   2345
Robinson, C. A., Jr.   1045
Robinson, David Moore   731-41, 1096, 1294, 2758, 3289, 3879, 4096, 4212, 6674
Robinson, Edward Stanley Gotch   4, 447-8, 742-53, 1706, 1776, 1810-3,

Index of Authors

1889, 1969, 1971, 2095-6, 2159, 2693-4, 2883, 2973, 3007, 3226, 3750, 3776, 4097-9, 4213, 4426, 4520, 4608-9, 4689, 4709, 4902, 5001, 5039, 5109, 5195, 5993, 6234-6, 6675, 6759-63
Robinson, Henry S.   449, 754
Robinson, Paul H.   2399-401
Rodee, H. David   1192
Rodger, William   1047-8, 3482-4, 5419, 6676-8
Roebuck, Carl   4814
Rogers, Charles James   6441-2
Rogers, Edgar   3880, 5420-3, 5838
Rogers, G. B.   2596
Rohner, John R.   1443
Roland, Hans   1989
Rolland, Henri   2597
Romano, David Gilman   1921
Romano, Irene Bald   1921
Romanoff, Paul   5839
Ronde, André   6552a
Ronen, Yigal   5840-1, 5910
Rönne, Tullia   934
Root, Margaret Cool   6237-8
Ropel, Harold   1295
Rosati, Francesco Panvini   203
Rosen, Jonathan P.   2097
Rossi, F.   1869
Rossini, Fabrizio   2973a
Rostovtzeff, Michael Ivanovitch   293-4, 6779
Roth, Bernard   2402-6, 2598
Rotroff, S. I.   755
Rottinghaus, Scott   1444
Rougou, K.   4734
Rouse, W. H. D.   1049
Rouvier, Jules   5631
Roux, Alain   1483
Rowe, Clement E.   1445
Rowlandson, Jane   295
Royal Coin Cabinet (The Hague)   1874
Royal Numismatic Society   756
Royal Ontario Museum   1752
Rudd, Chris   2204-7, 2281, 2407-36, 2599-601, 3290
Russel, Josiah C.   1043
Russeva, Boriana   757
Russo, Roberto   2642
Rutter, Nicholas Keith   159a, 204, 1897, 2695-700, 3073-a, 3195-7, 4100
Rynearson, Paul   338, 758, 2783, 4735, 5842, 5856

S

Saatsoglu-Paliadeli, C.   3485
Sacks, K. S.   4717
Sadeghi, Hussain   6080
Saffari, Mohammad   6078
Sage, Shirley Barr (see Barr Sage)
Sagir, Enver   2016
Sakellarakis, Yanni S.   1458
Salinas, Antonio   2974
Salisbury, F. S.   1900
Sallery, Robert D. H.   759
Sallusto, Federico   2812-3
Salmon, J.   4279
Salton, M. M.   3486
Salvesen, Harald   4101, 5146-7
Salviat, François   3762
Sambon, Arthur   2701, 3198
Sambon & Co., Arthur   3199
Sambon, Luigi   2702-3
Samuel, D. H.   6679
Samuels, Claudia Wallack   5842
Sandstrom, Faith Ford   4649
Sarfatti, Gad B.   5843
Särström, Margit   3227
Saryan, Leon A.   760, 1707, 5543, 5546-56
Sasianu, Alexandru   3777, 3828
Saslow, Arnold R.   1708-9
Saussaye, L. de la   2602
Saves, Georges   2603
Savio, Adriano   2704
Sawaya, Ziad   5424-5, 5632-3, 6094
Sayles, Wayne G.   339-43, 1050-69, 1193-1205, 1296, 1446-50, 1710-5, 1932, 2705, 3957, 4610, 5110-8, 5426, 6175
Scaros, Dean   344
Schachter, Albert   3917-8
Schaps, David M.   205-6, 450-1,
Schaeffer, C. F. A.   761
Scheers, Simone   762, 2437, 2530, 2602-16
Schefold, Karl   1206
Schell, James A.   3487-8
Scheu, Frederick   2706-9, 3786
Schlösser, Eckart   5427-9
Schlumberger, Daniel L.   525, 6194, 6239
Schlumberger, Gustave Leon   5994-5
Schlüter, M.   1765
Schmittinger, T.   1537
Schmitt-Korte, Karl   5996-9
Schönert-Geiss, Edith   3630-7, 3698, 3730-1, 3754, 4102, 5430
Schönhammer, Maria   4214
Schroll, Wayne K.   3919
Schubert, Helmut   5065
Schubiger, P. A.   1546-8
Schultz, Han-Dietrich   1759
Schultz, Sabine   1760, 1983, 1992, 4348
Schulze, W.   6680
Schwabacher, Willy   207-10, 452, 763, 1070, 1207, 1451, 2098, 2795, 3024, 3046, 3083-4, 3200-1, 3227a, 3291, 3489, 3738, 3755-6, 3798, 3829, 3881, 4280, 4371, 5040, 5196-7
Schwarz, Dietrich   2099
Schwentzel, C.-G.   6000
Schwitter, C. M.   1498, 6443
Scott, Jane Ayer   100
Scott, William H.   3490, 6095, 6781
Scullard, Howard Hayes   957, 1071-2
Scyphers, John   1716
Seaby, Herbert A.   345
Seaby, Peter   2438
Seaby, Wilfred   1839
Seaby's   21
Seaford, Richard   212-4
Seager, Richard Berry   4427
Sear, David R.   346-8, 353, 2975-6, 3491, 4190, 4372, 4690, 5119, 6240, 6444-5, 6681
Sebring, Thomas H.   764
Secord, Paul R.   238
Sedov, Alexander V.   5913, 6001-5
Seeger, John A.   1717, 5431-2
Segrè, Angelo   6682
Seibert, Robert   215, 1453
Sekulich, Lawrence   1073, 3202
Sekunda, Nicholas V.   5015
Seldarov, Kolekcija   3292
Seldarov, Nikola   3292, 3492-3
Sellers, O. R.   765
Sellwood, David G.   1454-6, 1612, 2108, 5217, 6029, 6031, 6096-121, 6132, 6253
Sellwood, Lyn   2208, 2439-41
Sellwood, P. H.   2442
Seltman, A. J.   5198
Seltman, Charles Theodore   216-7, 766-8, 1074-7, 1155, 1208-11, 2710-2, 2823-4, 2884, 2997, 3494, 4103-5, 4373-4, 4472, 4611, 6782
Seltman, E. J.   1457, 2977, 2998, 3034, 3813, 4106, 4387, 4393, 4691, 5433
Seltman, John   5434
Semrov, Andre   2005
Senior, Robert C.   6005a, 6122, 6225, 6387, 6446-78, 6506
Sergueenkova, Valeria   3495
Servet, Jean-Michel   453
Sestini, Domenico   218, 1718
Severeano, G.   3638
Sey, Katalin B.   1863
Seyrig, Henri   296-9, 708, 769-70, 3677, 4650, 5435-8, 5557, 5634, 5967, 6006, 6241, 6683
Shachar, Ilan   5717, 5844
Shahar, Charles   3882
Shahin, M.   6684
Shapiro, H. A.   4107
Shaw, Carol   6685
Shear, Josephine P.   771, 4108
Shear, Theodore Leslie   4109, 5002
Sheedy, Kenneth A.   159a, 219, 772-3, 1297, 1738, 1774, 1963, 2100, 4003, 4109a, 4473-81, 4532a, 5199
Shelov, Dimitrii B.   4559-60
Sheridan, Walter W.   774, 4973
Sherozia, Medea   6123
Sherwood, Earle D.   349

Index of Authors

Shipton, Kirsty   158, 220
Shlosser, Franziska E.   1745-8
Shore, A. F.   6242
Shore, Fred B.   5120, 6124-7
Shortt, Hugh de S.   2443-5, 6479
Sicurella, Nicholas A.   3678-80
Sievers, Joseph   5845
Sigler, Phares O.   454, 1212
Sikora, Michael A.   2999
Sills, John   2281, 2446-50
Sim, George   2101
Simon, Lilly   2450a
Simonetta, Alberto M.   5148a, 6121, 6128-33, 6480-2
Simonetta, Bono   5149-58, 6133-8c
Simpson, A. J.   3963
Sines, George   1458
Singh, Jai Prakash   6483
Singh, Milan   6484
Singh, Rajendra U.   6432, 6485
Sinisi, Fabrizio   159a
Sippel, Donald V.   4428, 4974
Six, Jean Pieter   4110, 4612, 5121-2, 5635
Sjöqvist, Erik   775, 784, 1298, 3061, 3496
Slabaugh, Arlie R.   1213
Smekalova, T. N.   1549, 3341
Smith, A. H.   1078
Smith, Amy   1078a
Smith, Cecil   1079-80
Smith College   1953
Smith, Charles F.   4281
Smith, David Spencer   3778, 6486-8
Smith, Derek R.   4282-3, 4815
Smith, Douglas   1459
Smith, Helen Wade   6686
Smith, Hobart M.   384, 903-4
Smith, Michael N.   3721-2
Smith, P. B.   1484
Smith, R. A.   2451
Smith, R. Morton   6489-90
Smith, R. R. R.   1299
Smith, Sidney   455
Smith, Vincent A.   6491
Smolderen, L.   171
Smyser, Donald S.   5846
Smyth, Melissa D.   4111
Snible, Ed   1081
Snowden, Frank M., Jr.   1082, 5847
Snowden, James Ross   1954
Sofia Press Agency   3639
Sohoni, S. V.   6492
Sokolovska, Viktorija   3830
Sokolowski, F.   4215
Solé, J. M. Solá   6783
Sosin, Joshua D.   1350, 3920
Sotheby & Co. (and variants)   1084, 1945, 2103-9, 3203, 3293
Sotheby Parke Bernet A.G. (also see Parke Bernet Galleries)
Souchleris, L.   776
Soutzo, Prince Michel C.   1613, 2713

Spaer, Arnold   777-80, 2000, 3497-8, 5337, 5439-42, 5848-50, 5898
Spagnoli, Emanuela   2714
Sparkes, G.   3204
Spengler, William F.   809, 3499
Sperber, Daniel   5851
Spiegel, Sam   4112
Spier, Jeffrey   5003, 5041-2
Spratt, T.   4429
Spring, John   350
Springschnitz, Leopoldine   1964
Spyridakis, C.   5200
Srivastava, A. K.   5493
Srivastava, Prashant   6494
Stancomb, William M.   3640, 4521, 4618-20
Stannard, Clive   2160, 2715
Stanton, Earle Kezartee   1085, 3500
Starck, Jeff   351, 456, 1086-7, 2989-90, 3064, 3883, 4113-4, 4816, 6495
Starr, Chester G.   1088, 4115-8
Stauffer, D. E.   3568
Stazio, Attilio   2716-9, 2732, 2796, 2814
Stecchini, Livio C.   457
Steele, D.   517
Stefanaki, Vasiliki E.   4430-1a, 4924, 4975, 4979
Stefanakis, Manolis I.   221, 1300, 4432-4b
Steffgen, U.   2209, 2565
Stein, Alla   5751
Stein, Harry J.   1214, 5201, 5852-3, 6687
Stein, Jacob K.   3205, 6139
Stein, Louise   5201
Stein, Peter   5955, 6007
Steinberg, Arthur   816
Steinbüchel von Rheinwald, Anton   1719
Stephanakis, Manolis I. (see Stefanakis)
Stern, Ephraim   458, 5636
Sternberg, Heinz-Rainer   2779
Stevens, Gorham P.   4119
Stevens, M. K.   1089
Stevens, Susan T.   222
Stewart, Andrew   5338
Stieglitz, Robert R.   5202, 6784
Stillman, William J.   1215
Stillwell, Richard   781-4
Stills, John   2617-9
Stingl, Timo   459, 4245
Stolba, Wladimir F.   3641, 4561-2
Stoliar, Steven   1090
Stoller, Steve   3501
Stolyarik, Elena   1938, 1946-7, 1950, 1952, 4563-5, 4598
Stos-Gale, Zofia A.   1482, 1550, 4832
St. Pasteur, Julian   4120
Strack, Max L.   3612
Strøm, Ingrid   460
Strauss, Pierre   785, 2110, 2720

Stronach, David B.   6243
Stroud, Ronald S.   786-7, 4216
Stross, F. H.   1557
Stumpf, Gerd   982
Sturdivant, H. H.   788
Stylow, Armin U.   1988
Sugden, Keith F.   1975, 2111, 4817
Sukenik, Eleazar L.   5854-5
Sullivan, Richard D.   93, 1091, 5558
Sunde, C. H.   1092
Superior Galleries, Inc.   5856
Suter, Charles   2721, 4435
Sutherland, Carol Humphrey Vivian   223-4, 352, 1216-7, 1460, 2452, 2722, 2797
Sutton, R. F.   2749
Svoronos, Joannes Nikolous   225-6, 461, 1093-4, 1461-2, 1720-1, 3294, 3884, 3964, 4121-4, 4349, 4436-8, 6688
Swift, R. H.   6140
Swiney, J.   6496
Swinton, John   6141
Sydenham, Edward Allen   2453, 5443
Symons, David   2111, 2454-63
Syon, Danny   789-91, 5637-8
Szaivert, Eva   353
Szaivert, Wolfgang   353, 1965
Szego, Paul S.   354, 1218

T

Taceva, Margarita   3642
Tache, Marcel   2544-7
Tahberer, Bekircan   5123
Tal, Oren   159a, 4023, 4090a, 5693, 5857, 5880
Talbert, R. J. A.   3206
Talfourd, Ely   1463
Talierco Mensitieri, Marina   2798a-b
Talmatchi, Gabriel   3717
Tameanko, Marvin   1095-1102, 1219, 1301, 1464-6, 3085, 3207, 3295, 3568a, 3643, 3965, 4439, 4522, 4710, 4736, 4818, 4903, 5072, 5203, 5639, 5858, 6008, 6536, 6553, 6764-5, 6785-6
Tanabe, Katsumi   2112
Tandy, David W.   462
Tarn, William Woodthorpe   3502, 6497-501
Tasaklaki, M.   3644
Tatman, John   6731, 6766
Tatscheva, Margarita   3296
Tatton-Brown, T.   2464
Taylor, George   1722, 5159-61, 6767
Taylor, J. Edward   355
Tazedakis, Panos   1723
Tebben, Gerald   4125-6
Tebbs, H. V.   227
Tekin, Oguz   228, 1908-9, 2014-6, 3681, 4599, 5066-7, 5559
Terzian, Gregory   3732

Index of Authors

Terzopoulou, Domna 3593a, 3645, 3729
Testi, R. 1480
Thallon, Ida Carleton 1103
Theodorou, Jerry 1220-1, 4127
Thirion, Marcel 2621
Thomas, Edward 1104, 5560, 6142-4, 6502-4
Thomas, Georges 6787
Thompson, Christine M. 463
Thompson, Dorothy Burr 531, 1302, 4128, 6689
Thompson, F. C. 1551-2, 2210, 2465
Thompson, Homer A. 626, 792, 4129-32
Thompson, H. O. 5640
Thompson, J. A. 3047
Thompson, Margaret 793-801, 1553, 1948, 1961, 3504-11, 3682-3, 4133-7, 4191-6, 4651, 5445, 6690
Thompson, Wesley E. 1614, 4138-41, 4652-3, 4842
Thonemann, Peter 4692
Thurlow, Bradbury K. 2723
Tibet, Cihan 5012
Tietz, Werner 1615, 5027
Tiratsian, G. A. 5561
Tobey, A. G. (see Beer-Tobey, A. G.)
Tobey, Leslie (see Beer-Tobey, Leslie)
Tod, James 6505
Tod, Marcus N. 1351-2, 4197
Tompkins, Janice Firth 1222
Tompa, Peter K. 802
Topalov, Stavri 3646-51b, 3739-40, 3779
Torbágyi, Melinda 1999, 2622, 3780
Toros, Haji 5562-7
Torremuzza, Gabriel L. Castellus (see Castellus)
Torrey, Charles C. 3512
Touratsoglou, Yannis (John/Ioannis) P. 803-6, 1105, 1843, 1997, 3390, 3512a-5, 4142, 4198, 4316, 4482, 4853
Traeger, Burkhard 4434b
Travis, Gar 5204
Trell, Bluma 5641
Trevett, Jeremy 4143
Trifiró, Maria Daniela 807, 1998
Tripp, David Enders 2750
Trokay, Madeleine 4523
Troxell, Hyla A. 809, 1962, 2113, 3383, 3516-22, 4524-5, 4654, 4904-5, 5043, 5068, 5073, 6691
Tsangari, Dimitra I. 193, 1106-7, 1223, 1850-9, 3546, 3787, 4483
Tsaîmou, C. 1372
Tsakos, Alexander 1901
Tselekas, Panagiotis 810, 1107-8, 3297-8, 4484, 4737, 4804
Tsotselia, Medea 811
Tsoukanelis, Kimon 3814

Tsourti, Eos 60a, 1843, 1998, 3943, 4316, 4482, 4485
Tuck, Anthony S. 2917
Tudeer, Lauri Oskar Theodore 3208
Tufnell, R. H. C. 5218
Tuplin, Christopher 6244-5
Turnbull, M. I. 1883
Tye, Robert 1616
Tylecote, R. F. 2211
Tyler-Smith, S. 6254
Tzamali, Marion J. A. 230, 5219, 6145, 6506
Tzamalis, Anastasios P. 230, 1109, 1860-1, 2623, 2815, 3299-301, 4144, 4906, 5261
Tziambazis, Elias 5205

U

Ujes, Dubravka 812, 3302
Underhill, Randall M. 5859
Ure, Percy N. 464
Üyümez, Mevlut 3313, 6031

V

Vagel, Jürgen 1617
Vagi, David L. 231-5, 300-1, 356-63, 465-6, 1110-8, 1224-6, 1303-6, 1353, 1468, 1618, 1725-7, 2724-5, 2857, 2978-9, 3048, 3065, 3209-11, 3524-5, 3584, 3684, 3788, 4145, 4284-5, 4375, 4440, 4526-8, 4613, 4655, 4693-4, 4711, 4819, 5446, 5911, 6633, 6692-3
Vaillant, J. Foy 5447
Valassiadis, Chrysanthos 1119, 3526a
Vallet, G. 2825
van Alfen, Peter G. 152, 159a, 236, 467-8, 813-5, 1120-1, 1469, 1728, 1938-9, 1949-50, 1952, 2161, 3969, 4146-a, 4907, 5124, 5693, 5912, 5956, 6009-11, 6554-5
Van Arsdell, Robert D. 2212-4, 2466-501
Van Buchem, H. J. H. 1122
Van Buren, A. W. 2980
Van der Dussen, J. W. 237, 1470
Vanderpool, Eugene 816, 3944
Van der Werf, Greg 238
Van Driessche, Véronique 1618a, 3526
Van Heesch, Johan 1739, 2215
VanHorn, D. Scott 322, 4294, 4454, 4501, 5210, 6254a
Van Keuren, Frances 2759-60, 2858
Van Meter, David 364-5
Van Steen, Gonda 3732
Van't Haaff, P. A. 6176, 6254a
Vardanyan, Ruben E. 5568, 6146-7
Vargyas, Péter 6246-7
Varoufakis, George J. 1554
Varshalomidze, Irine 4575
Vassiliou, John 6507

Vaux, W. S. W. 1814, 2981, 3527, 5220-1, 5448, 6508-10, 6732
Vavliakis, G. 4738
Vecchi, Italo G. 2723, 2751-3
Vecherukhin, N. M. 3341
Vermeule, Cornelius C. 239, 817, 1123-5, 1227-8, 1439, 1471-2, 1919, 1924, 1953, 5206, 6694
Veselý, Petr 5297
Vesely, Zdenek 1229
Vickers, Michael 469, 818, 4217, 4506, 4575, 6248
Vidal-Naquet, P. 16
Viedebantt, Oskar 1619-20
Vilcu, A. 1895
Villard, François 2624
Villaronga, Garriga Leandre 275, 819-20, 1621, 2162-4, 2624a, 6733
Vinchon, Jean 2114-5
Virr, Richard 1748
Vismara, Novella 470, 2001, 5017, 5044-6
Visonà, Paolo 2029, 2726, 2754, 3109-11, 3528, 3803, 3831-5a, 4147, 4486, 5047, 6148, 6695-7, 6734-40a, 6788
Vives y Escudero, Antonio 2165
Vlachogianni, Elena 3921
Vladimirova-Aladzova, Dochka 724
Vlasto, Michel P. 2859-65, 3815
Voegtli, Hans 2642, 3795
Volk, T. R. 1354, 6741
Volkmann, Hans 5449
Von Aulock, Hans 1988, 3692, 3695, 5125
Von Fritze, Hans 239a, 2872, 4657-62
Von Hoerschelmann (see Grunauer von Hoerschelmann)
Von Matt, Leonard 2982
Von Petrowicz, Alexander Ritter 6149
Von Post, Erik 2008
von Prokesch-Osten, Anton 3529, 6149a
Von Reden, Sitta 240-3, 6698-700
Von Sallet, Alfred Friedrich Constantin 1761, 4567
Voulgaridis, Georges 5450

W

Waage, Dorothy B. 821
Waage, Frederick O. 822
Wace, Alan John Bayard 823, 1126, 1307, 4663
Wacks, Mel 5642-3, 5860-1
Waddingham, Gary 244, 5229, 6701
Waddington, William Henry 4529, 5222
Wade-Gery, H. T. 1622, 3885, 4148, 4211
Waggoner, Nancy M. 145, 169, 483, 721, 824-5, 1127, 1951, 1962, 2116,

Index of Authors

3303-4, 3530-1, 3945, 4059, 4525, 4530, 4908, 6026-8, 6150
Wagner, G. A.   1507-8
Wagner, U.   2565
Waites, M. C.   1128
Walburg, R.   5004
Waldstein, Charles   1230-2
Walker, Alan Stuart   826-9, 1473-4, 1729, 1862, 2117, 3873, 4376, 4909, 6150a
Walker, C. T.   2502
Walker, F. G.   830
Walker, John   570, 6012-6
Walker, Obadiah   245
Walker, Ralph   6511-2
Walker, Raymond J.   1129, 2983
Wallace, Malcolm B.   1623-4, 2727, 3946, 3966, 4246, 4531
Wallace, Mary   1929
Wallace, Robert W.   471, 1625-6, 4532, 5005-6
Wallace, William P.   246, 541, 831, 1928-9, 3923, 3944, 3947-52, 4149, 4164, 4350
Walmsley, Alan   773
Walsh, P. G.   6789
Walston, Charles   1130, 1233
Walters, Henry Beauchamp   1234
Ward, John   2118, 6768
Warden, William B., Jr.   2755
Warren, Jennifer A. W.   492, 832-3, 3886, 4286, 4297-9a, 4317-22, 4351-2, 4377, 4394-7
Warren, John Byrne Leicester DeTabley   247, 4323, 5048
Wartenberg, Ute (Kagan)   248-9, 594, 665, 834-5, 1774, 1952, 2144, 3305, 3327, 3532, 3887, 3922, 4917
Washington University   1958
Waters, K. H.   1906
Wear, Ted G.   366
Weber, Charles E.   1131, 1555-6, 1627
Weber, Hermann   837, 2119-21, 3306
Weber, Shirley H.   838
Webster, T. B. L.   1235
Wedig, Harold   250
Weidauer, Liselotte   472-3
Weier-Krystallis, L.   3888-9
Weil, Rudolf   1236, 4324, 4378, 4820, 5644
Weiller, Raymond   82
Weinberg, Gladys Davidson   251
Weinberg, Saul S.   839
Weir, Robert   840
Weiser, Wolfram   3048a, 4910, 6702
Weisgerber, G.   614
Weiskopf, Michael   6151
Weiss, Arnold-Peter C.   3114, 4955, 4976
Weisser, B.   4551
Weissl, Michael   841
Welch, F. B.   4338
Wellington, Imogen   2503

Wells, Henry Bartlett   1475-8, 1730-1, 3533-5, 3652-4, 3751, 4247-8, 4568, 4600, 4977, 5451, 6249
Welz, Karl   2728, 4821
Wenger, Otto Paul   252
Wenninger, A.   4807
Wernicke, I.   2625
West, Allen Brown   3536, 3655
West, Louis C.   253
Westermark, Ulla   145, 254-9, 842-3, 1986, 2008-9, 2729, 2866, 3000-3a, 3035, 3039-40a, 3307, 3537-41, 4695-8, 5223
Westlake, H. D.   3890
Weston, Stephen B. D.   260
Wetterstrom, Kerry K.   1308, 1732, 3891, 4150, 6556
Wharton, Ralph N.   1027
Wheatley, Pat V.   5645
Wheeler, J. R.   64
White, Donald   3212
White, M.   2730
Whitehead, Richard Bertram   6513-8
Wickenden, N.   2315
Wickens, Jere M.   1479
Widawski, Maciej   4569
Wideman, François   1483, 6518a-20
Wiesinger, H.   3213
Wigg-Wolf, David G.   2344, 2626
Wightman, Edith Mary   2627-8
Wihnyk, Joseph   1132, 2778, 2799-800, 2885, 3008, 4249
Wilkenson, Richard H.   1133
Wilkinson, John S.   261, 1970, 2112, 4151
Will, Édouard   262, 474-5, 4287
Williams, D. J. R.   844
Williams, Daniela   4601
Williams, Jonathan H. C.   263, 2504-9, 3542
Williams, Roderick T.   2895, 3214, 3967, 4152, 4353-4
Williamson, George C.   5862
Wilson, Horace Hayman   6525
Wilson, Ladislav   3543
Wilson, Lyn   1733
Wilson, L. M.   1134, 6521-4
Wilson, Professor   6526
Wilson, Thomas   1135
Wilson, William   1734
Winkelmann, Sylvia   6152
Winnington-Ingram, R. P.   966
Winsemann-Falghera, E.   1480
Winter, Jeff   3004
Winter, W. Jeffrey   3544
Winzer, Axel   1309
Virgin, Wolf   3545, 5452, 5863-9
Wise, Philip J.   2510-1
Witschonke, Richard   845, 3327
Wolenik, Robert   1735
Woloch, G. Michael   1748-9
Wood, Bryant G.   5870
Wood, H. G.   1628

Woodward, Arthur M.   1355, 3968, 4153, 4218
Work, Eunice   2761, 3041
Worland, David   1310
Wray, David M.   1136, 2984
Wright, Nicholas L.   4532a, 5453
Wright, William S.   6769
Wroth, Warwick William   846, 1137, 1776, 1815-32, 3892, 4441-3, 4602, 4664-5, 4712, 4911, 5131, 6153-6
Wüthrich, Gottlieb   2629

X

Xella, P.   3112
Xenou, Argyro-Alexandra   264

Y

Yao, T. C.   1557
Yannopoulos, P.   171
Yarbrough, Bill   6703
Yarkin, Ural   3656, 4912-3, 5162
Yarkon, Barry J.   5163, 5646
Yeoman, Richard S.   5871
Yorke, V. W.   847
Young, Rodney S.   848, 5007
Youroukova, Yordanka   3657-61, 3705
Yousef, F. A. A.   6017
Yvon, Jacques   140

Z

Zabel, B.   4914
Zacani-Montuoro, Paola   2827a
Zacharas, Andreas A.   4978
Zachos, Konstantinos   3546
Zagami, Leopoldo   3053
Zahle, Jan   1983, 5035, 5049, 5454, 6250
Zakelj, Ann M.   1275
Zancani Montuoro, Paola   2816
Zapiti, Eleni   5206a
Zayadine, Fawzi   560
Zemke, Jeff   367
Zerman, Percy   5872
Zervos, Orestes H.   849-56, 3547-9, 6557, 6704-8
Zeuner, F. E.   1138-9
Ziegaus, Bernward   2216
Ziegler, Ruprecht   5126-7
Zimmerman, Jeremiah   1140
Zlotnik, Yehoshua   5873
Zobel de Zangroniz, J.   2166
Zodda, Daniela   3008a
Zograph, Alexander Nikolaevich   265-6, 1311, 3685, 3752, 4288, 4533, 4666, 6527
Zolotnikova, Olga   5455
Zonderhuis, J.   1503
Zournatzi, Antigoni   857
Zwicker Ulrich   1766-7
Zygman, Edmund   6528

INDEX OF REVIEWERS

A

Adelson, H. L. 821
Akrigg, Ben 236
Allan, John 164, 6514
Amandry, Michel 1985, 2009
Archibald, Zosia 3617
Arnold-Biucchi, Carmen 39, 530, 2699,
Ashton, Richard H. J. 145, 804, 836, 1317, 1909, 1983, 1995, 3474

B

Balesteri, Lou 1714
Banning, E. B. 6601
Barker, Harold 1512
Barron, J. P. 127, 1971, 6721
Bauslaugh, R. A. 101, 3474, 4579
Bedoukian, Paul 5500, 5508
Bellemare, P. M. 101
Bellinger, Alfred R. 700, 1961, 2792, 2882, 3655, 3812, 5405, 5407, 6498
Bendall, Simon 1170
Bérend, Denyse 3266
Berk, Harlan J. 5702
Billow, R. 153
Bivar, A. D. H. 6404
Boardman, John 972
Boon, George C. 347, 2171
Bowshers, Julian 773
Brace, Bruce 1714, 5286, 5690
Breglia, Laura 721
Breitsprecher, Marc 2544
Brendel, O. 995
Brett, Agnes Baldwin 1970-1, 4514
Bridge, R. N. 4536
Briggs, Daphne Nash 2172, 2497
Brindley, James C. 6104
Bubelis, William 3264
Burn, L. 1222
Burnett, Andrew M. 13, 153, 1963, 2003, 2073, 2199, 2340, 2374, 2790, 3130, 3998, 5579
Butcher, Kevin 695, 1981, 1986, 1991, 1999, 4889
Butcher, Marguerite Spoerri 1336, 1991
Buttrey, S. E. 1374
Buttrey, Theodore V. 190, 1374

C

Caine, Edward 5690, 5800
Cancio, Leopoldo 5305
Cargill-Thompson, J. 620
Carradice, Ian 174, 1299, 2010, 4054
Carson, R. A. G. 55, 127, 136, 345, 352, 500, 1217, 2235, 2366, 3318, 3742, 6721
Carter, Martha L. 6295
Casey, John 136
Chadburn, A. 2172

Chapman, Anne E. 55
Christianian, Jirair 5534
Christiansen, Erik 1987
Clayton, Peter 484, 2171, 3690
Cox, D. H. 6227
Crawford, Michael H. 136, 1976, 4011
Cribb, Joe 6332-3
Curtis, Thomas 1030

D

de Guadan, A. M. 3967
DeJersey, Philip 2289, 2350
Dennis, Megan 2257
Devine, A. M. 1299
Dieudonnè, A. 1315
Draganov, Dimitar 1978
Dunstan, Peter 5768

E

Eddy, S. 4115
Ehling, K. 1965
Elderkin, G. W. 3270
Evans, A. J. 90
Evans, D. Ellis 2181
Evans, DeRose 1245

F

Fanning, David F. 5690
Feaver, D. 934
Fischer-Bossert, Wolfgang 6, 14, 103, 158, 379, 508, 1905, 2699, 3617, 3860, 4321, 5816, 5880
Foraboschi, D. 4011
Forrer, Leonard 4990
Frere, S. S. 2235

G

Gardner, Percy 90, 369
Garner, J. 5512
Gerin, D. 721
Gerson, Stephen N. 5909
Goldsborough, Reid 1702, 3332, 3402, 3774
Goldstein, P. 5662
Grueber, H. A. 196, 1899
Guépin, J. P. 6721

H

Hacken, Tony 3967, 4115
Hawkes, F. C. 2366
Hazzard, Richard A. 274
Head, Barclay V. 1611, 1899, 2118, 2325,
Healy, J. F. 522, 873, 972, 1526, 1975, 4194
Hendin, David 309, 5842, 5857, 5880
Hersh, Charles 3056
Hill, C. W. 55

Hill, George F. 33, 72, 860, 1770, 2042, 3440, 4021, 4306, 4373
Hind, J. G. F. 127, 1891
Hobbs, Richard 2289, 2374
Holloway, R. Ross 721, 873, 2767, 3690, 4194
Hopper, R. J. 3010, 4194, 4843
Hoover, Oliver D. 21, 32, 350, 510, 1577, 1714, 1907, 1983, 2000, 2544, 3311, 3332, 3460, 4388, 4556, 5231, 5534, 5690, 5708, 5768, 5800, 5975, 6176, 6623, 6661
Hurter, Silvia M. 190, 248, 1996

I

Ireland, Stanley 1987, 3332, 4544

J

Jackson, Anne E. 1971
James, T. M. 6601
Jameson, Shelagh A. 109, 122, 128, 3159
Jamgochian, Nicholas 5465
Jenkins, G. Kenneth 124, 216, 500, 522, 676, 821, 1076, 1208, 1210, 1833, 1917, 1961-2, 1970-2, 1982, 2008-9, 2856, 3318, 3452, 3694, 3949, 4194, 4701, 5803, 6227, 6415
Jeselsohn, D. 5779
Johnston, Alan 800, 4011
Johnston, Ann 1965, 1990-1, 2010, 2116, 4889

K

Kagan, Jonathan H. 4456
Kent, J. P. C. 2482
Kiernan, Philip 5702
Kim, H. S. 240
Kindler, Arie 5828
Kinns, Philip 289, 1886, 1974, 1985
Kleeb, Alvin A. 124, 1327, 3447
Konuk, Koray 1986
Kosmetatou, Elizabeth 379, 4686
Kraay, Colin M. 91, 216, 472, 721, 1242, 1961, 3010, 4115, 4843, 6721
Kroh, Dennis 1725, 2078
Kroll, John H. 158, 173, 421, 721, 5869
Kumpikevicius, Gordon C. 39, 6601

L

Lerner, Jeffrey D. 6520
Lewis, David M. 4194
LeRider, Georges 115, 388, 3518
Lightfoot, C. S. 1907
Leschhorn, Wolfgang 2000, 4579
Lorber, Catharine C. 530, 3860, 5305, 6601

Index of Reviewers

M

Mannsperger, D. 3967
Marinescu, C. A. 1639
Markowitz, Mike 423, 2281
Marotta, Michael 309, 338, 927, 3386
Mathisen, Ralph 5043
Mattingly, H. 153
Mattingly, H. B. 40, 1317, 1489, 2895, 2897, 4011
May, Jeffrey 216-7, 2172, 2482
May, J. M. F. 1917, 3480, 3949
Mays, Melinda 2350
McIvor, Robert S. 927
McKay, A. G. 4038
Meadows, Andrew 1317, 2009, 2013-4, 4484, 5716
Metcalf, William 13, 1987, 2330
Middleton, J. H. 90
Mielczarek, Mariusz 1978
Milne, J. G. 72, 1210
Mitchiner, Michael 514, 1616
Moesgaard, J. C. 2259
Molinari, M. C. 3056
Monney, P. 3760
Moorhead, T. S. N. 1334
Morcom, John 39, 171, 248, 1962, 2071, 2700, 2910
Mørkholm, Otto 2695, 3939, 6104

N

Nash, Daphne 400, 2170, 2179
Negev, A. 5773
Nelson, D. K. 115
Newell, Edward T. 659, 1770, 1970, 5936
Newton, C. 2690, 2968
Nicolet, H. 809, 2113, 3581
Noble, J. V. 1217
Nony, D. 2586
Noe, Sydney 1968-9
Noland, C. 384
Nolte, Vincent 2080
North, J. J. 41

O

Oddy, Andrew 5975, 6176
Oeconomides, Mando 2003
Oeconomides-Caramessini, Mando 1992
Overbeck, B. 2172

P

Parks, D. 695
Papaefthymiou, Eleni G. 4484
Pavel, Catalin 2917
Plantzos, Dimitris 3515
Price, Martin J. 55, 124, 266, 274, 289, 304, 472, 800, 1222, 1317, 1334, 1875, 1962, 1972, 3266, 3510, 3967, 4353, 5908, 5966

R

Rambach, Hadrien 3401
Rapson, E. J. 6491
Rauch, Hans 2171
Raven, E. J. P. 3690
Rieske, J. 901
Robinson, David M. 838, 3148
Robinson, E. S. G. 1770, 1917, 2792, 3148, 4103, 6721
Robinson, Frank 384
Rudd, Chris 2215, 2289
Rutter, N. K. 1962, 1972, 2113, 2793, 2895, 3998

S

Saryon, Leon A. 5520
Saslow, Arnold R. 1629
Sawaya, Ziad 5578
Sayles, Wayne G. 1739, 4301, 5708
Scarborough, John 122
Schaps, David M. 421
Schönert-Geiss, Edith 4054
Schulze, C. 6601
Schwabacher, Willy 216, 385, 418, 1917, 1920, 3318, 3694, 4353
Seaford, Richard 379, 421
Sellwood, David 1512, 6073
Seltman, Charles T. 995, 3289, 3821
Sheedy, Kenneth A. 176, 1543, 1906, 2790
Shortt, Hugh de S. 2232, 2366, 6379
Sperber, Daniel 5782, 5803
Spier, Jeffrey 2116
Staffieri, G. M. 1987
Stancomb, William M. 4546
Stewart, Andrew 3311
Sutherland, C. H. V. 1210, 2366

T

Thompson, F. C. 1526, 6042
Thompson, Margaret 274, 6721
Touchette, L. A. 1299
Touratsoglou, Yannis 3401
Tristan, F. C. 1976
Tye, Robert 436
Tzamali, M. J. A. 508

V

Vagi, David L. 48, 339, 1419, 1577, 5702
van Alfen, Peter 1618a, 4017
Vermeule, Cornelius C. 216, 1217
Visonà, Paolo 6529, 6712-3

W

Waage, F. O. 5832
Waggoner, Nancy 3967
Walker, Alan S. 13, 14, 144, 171, 230, 339, 590, 705, 803, 901, 1178, 1447, 1912, 1955, 1966, 1979, 1983, 1987, 1989, 1995, 2000, 2013, 3166, 3341, 3894, 4269, 4301, 4321, 6176
Wallace, M. B. 800, 1891, 1962, 3289
Wallace, William 1941, 4803, 5244
Warren, J. A. W. 115, 127, 153, 204, 2071, 3467, 3967, 4353, 5043
Wartenberg, Ute 286, 1886, 3266, 4771
Weber, S. H. 2792
Webster, T. B. L. 1208
Weigel, R. 101
Westermark, Ulla 4511, 5384
Whitting, P. D. 41, 6721
Wilkinson, J. S. 109
Will, Édouard 153
Williams, J. H. C. 101, 2540
Williams, R. T. 124, 1891, 1962, 1971-3
Wilson, Antony 14, 230
Witschonke, Richard 1981, 3760
Woloch, Michael 151
Wroth, Warwick W. 4292

Z

Zahle, Jan 5043

INDEX OF COLLECTORS AND COLLECTIONS

A

Aarhus University 1984-5
Aberdeen 1968
Académie Roumaine 1892-4
Adana Museum 5084
Adolf, King Gustaf VI 1207, 2008, 2098
Afyon Museum (Turkey) 3312-3, 6031, 6189
Albany Museum 1900
Almeida, António de 1887
al-Mukalla Museum 6004
Alpha Bank (Athens) 5, 858, 1106, 1223, 1840, 1849-62, 1995, 3299, 3546
Amasya Museum 1907
American Numismatic Association 2807, 3026, 3155, 3186, 3744, 4584, 4713
American Numismatic Society 10, 99, 655, 716, 1120-1, 1937-9, 1941-4, 1946-52, 1961-2, 2030, 2037, 2074, 2093, 2144, 2161, 2826, 3076, 3303, 3336, 3516, 3559, 3756, 3945, 3969, 4146, 4524-5, 4574, 4651, 4907-8, 5124, 5149, 5165, 5716, 5801, 5912, 5939, 6150, 6296, 6351, 6554, 6619, 6706-7, 6720
American University of Beirut 1873
Amman Museum 1872
Anamur Museum 2014
Antalya Archaeological Museum 484, 5013
Antikenmuseum Basel 2642, 2685
Araratian Collection 5474, 5551, 5553
Archaeological and Ethnographical Museum (Lódz, Poland) 2003
Archaeological Museum (Chieti, Italy) 6723a
Archaeological Museum (Florence, Italy) 2002a, 4601, 6738
Archaeological Museum (Istanbul, Turkey) 584, 6027
Archaeological Museum (Split, Croatia) 1753
Archaeological Museum (Zagreb, Croatia) 1754, 3822, 4486
Armenian Library and Museum of America 5555
Artemis, Demetrios 4482
Ashmolean Museum 632, 636, 685, 752, 1833, 1835-8, 1972, 3714, 3834, 4421, 4430
Asiatic Society of Bombay 6366
Athens—Numismatic Museum (see Numismatic Museum)
Australian Centre for Ancient Numismatics 1963
Australian National University 1736

B

Baker, F. Brayne 2021
Ball State University 1932
Ballen, Todd A. 6044
Balliol College 1834
Bank of Canada 1743
Bank of Cyprus Cultural Foundation 5181, 5191, 5206a
Bank of England 1773
Bank of Israel 5661, 5749
Banque Centrale de Tunisie 6713
Bar, Marc 1966
BCD 1854, 1939, 1946, 3795, 3843, 3873, 3883, 3894, 3938, 3956, 4269, 4291, 4295, 4296, 4363, 4364
Bedoukian, Paul Z. 5555
Bement, Clarence Sweet 2037, 2086, 2117
Benner, Steve M. 3840
Benson, Frank Sherman 2106, 2633
Bernischen Historischen Museum 2012
Berry, Burton Y. 1673, 1915-6, 1961, 2030, 5559, 6619
Biassono Civic Museum (Italy) 1864
Bibliothèque de l'Académie Roumaine 1892-4
Bibliothèque Nationale (Paris) 144, 1105, 1755-7, 1987, 2018-9, 2196, 2584, 3563, 3936, 4851, 5234, 6057, 6181, 6281, 6420-1
Bibliothèque Royal de Belgique 1739-40, 1966
Bissen, E. 6081
Blackburn Museum 1975
Bobokov, Atanas and Plamen 1981
Bodleian Library 4808
Borrell, H. P. 1773
Boyne, William 2032
Brandis, Augusto 1870
Bretagne, Musée (Paris) 2187
British Museum 18, 39, 76, 88, 91, 172, 248-9, 263, 347-8, 490, 584, 685, 716, 730, 746, 768, 1023, 1168, 1246, 1602, 1631, 1675, 1773-1832, 1882, 1976, 2112, 2170, 2172, 2235, 2350, 2469, 2690, 2947, 2968, 3007, 3216, 3254, 3310, 3384, 3435, 3467-8, 3474, 3557, 3567, 3601, 3680, 3750, 3759, 3799, 3853, 3955, 4012, 4027, 4071, 4144, 4155, 4261, 4292, 4312, 4408-9, 4413, 4420, 4423-4, 4442, 4505, 4602, 4665, 4696, 4709, 4712, 4731, 4763, 4798, 4875, 4988, 5010, 5020, 5023, 5092, 5122, 5131, 5149, 5178, 5273, 5601, 5627, 5656, 5679, 5719, 5804, 5936, 6068, 6102, 6155, 6182, 6233, 6242, 6327-8, 6342, 6363-5, 6406, 6417, 6508, 6547, 6559, 6666, 6721, 6732, 6755, 6760
Bromberg, Abraham 5856
Brown University 4331

Bryn Mawr College 1922-4
Buerger, Ottilia 1912
Bunbury, Edward H. 1773, 2105, 5257
Burdur Museum 2016a
Burton, Irving Frederick 2039

C

Camedda, Salvatore 6723a
Cameron, J. S. 1813, 4401, 4413
Çanakkale Museum 2015
Canessa, C. 2720
Canterbury Museum 1876, 2228
Casden, Alan I. 5842
Castellus, Gabriel Lancilloto (Prince of Torremuzza) 2911, 3070
C.C. (see Canessa, C.)
Chittenden, Jacqueline 1155
Christiansen, Hunt 2087
Christomanos, Antoine 1996
Civic Museum of Biassono (Italy) 1864
Civic Museum—Reggio Emilia 1868
Civiche Raccolte Numismatische (Milan) 470, 2001, 2899, 6711
Civici Musei di Udine (Italy) 1870
Cornell University 2090
Corpus Christi College 1768, 1973
Correr Museum 5047
Costilhes, Alain J. 2924
Côte, Claudius 2855
Courtauld, Stephen 1890-1
Crowe, F. H. 6755
Cyprus Museum (Jacksonville, N.C.) 5204

D

Danicourt, A. 2610
Danish National Museum (see Royal Coin Cabinet, Denmark)
Dartmouth College Museum 1931
Dattari, Giovanni 6696
Davis, Newnham 1968
Davis, Norman 2113
de Ciccio, Giuseppe 3199
de Hirsch, Lucien 1740, 3225
de Hirsch de Gereuth, L. 2919, 2986, 2988
de Lagarde, Bertier 4593
Delepierre, Jean and Marie 1987
de Luynes 1756
Demetriadi, Vassili (Basil) C. 3845-6
de Nanteuil, H. 2041
Detroit Institute of Arts 2039
Deutsche Bundesbank 2017
Deutsches Archäologisches Institut 1988
Dewing, Arthur Stone 1182, 2078, 2692, 3212
di Demetrio, Giovanni 6582
Donat, Karl Eduard Reinhard 1991, 2088

Index of Collectors and Collections

Dreer 1964
Duane, Matthew 3343, 5279
du Chastel de la Howardries, *Comte* Albéric 1739
Durmaz 485

E

Earle-Fox, Harry Bertram 2044
Eddé, Michael 279, 1266
Elliott Classics Museum, John 1906
Emmet, Beulah H. 1931
Empédoclès, Grégoire 4852
Endicott, F. Munroe 1941
Evans, Arthur John 1972, 2085, 2117, 2923, 4421, 6081
Evans, John 2348, 2469, 2543
Evelpidis, Réna H. 1994

F

Fabricius, Knud 1985
Falghera, Donazione Winsemann 470, 5044
Fels, Willi 1875, 1883
Feret, Daniel 2115
Fethiye Archaeological Museum (Turkey) 484, 3312, 4956, 5012, 5042, 6189, 6560-1
Finney, Ian D. 2111, 2252, 2455-7, 2459, 2461
Fitzwilliam Museum 1768-72, 1971, 1973, 2020, 2068, 2330, 6186
Flesche, Christian 2216
Fogg Art Museum 969, 1157, 1182, 1925-6, 2055, 2078, 2692
Forbat, Fred 2008
Forteleoni, Lorenzo 6716
Foundation of the Hellenic World 2088
Fox, Charles 2043
Franke, Peter R. 1935
Freedman, David 2034-5
Freund, Herman Ernst 1984

G

Gale, W. L. 1963, 2772
Gallatin, Albert 2078
Gans, Edward 68
Garrett, John Work (and family) 2027-8, 3995, 3997
Georgia Museum of Art 1913
Gerojannis, Constantin 2046
Getty Museum, J. P. 2097, 5304, 6073, 6695
Ghertsos, Athanasios 3300-1
Gilbertson, Charles 1882
Gilbertson, Edward 3310
Gillet, Charles 2026, 2117
Gisborne Museum 1879
Glencairn Museum 1921
Golden Gate 2036
Goldman, Hetty 5084

Gordon, Thomas 2049
Gorringe, Henry H. 6742
Greene, Henry Augustus 1955, 3123
Greenwell, William (Canon) 320, 2050-4, 4632
Griner, Ned H. and Gloria A. 1932
Gulbenkian, Calouste Sarkis 1168, 1488, 1884-6, 1888-9, 2045
Güterbock, Alfred 1974

H

Hamburger Kunsthalle 1762
Harland, J. Penrose 4232
Hart, Edward 1975
Harvard University (see Fogg Art Museum)
Haughton, A. C. 6341
Haughton, Henry Lawrence 1803, 2107
Hauteroche, M. Louis Allier de 2040
Heberden Coin Room (see Ashmolean Museum)
Hecht Museum 5798
Heckett, Greta S. 1084
Hendin, David 1577, 5939
Hermitage Museum 3341, 3685, 4549
Hersh, Charles 3310
Herzog Anton Ulrich Museum (Braunschweig) 1993
Hirayama 2112
Hispanic Society of America 2144
Historisches Museum (Frankfurt) 6661
Historischen Museums von Stara Zagora 1741
Hosking, Jon Martin 6664
Houghton, Arthur 5294, 5305, 5361
Huber, Christian G. 2103
Hungarian National Museum 1863, 1999
Hunt, Nelson Bunker 1222, 2061, 2108, 4126
Hunt, William Herbert 1222
Hunter, William 204, 1898-9, 1979
Hunterian Museum (see University of Glasgow)
Huntington, Archer M. 2144
Huth, Martin 5947

I

Imhoof-Blumer Friedrich W. 107, 2062
Indian Museum of Calcutta 6264, 6271, 6441, 6491
Indiana University 1915-6, 2030
Institut d'Archéologie de Bucarest 1895
Instituts für Alertumskunde der Universität zu Köln 6702
Israel Museum 2989

J

Jackson, Samuel 2029
Jameson, Robert 1168, 1887-9, 2045, 2117, 3756
Jenks, William J. 2102
Jesuit School of Theology (Berkeley) 5009
Jewish Museum (London) 5851
Johns Hopkins University 1914, 2027-8, 3997
Johnson Museum of Art 2090
Joy, James H. 2083
Judd, J. Hewitt 2023

K

Kabul Museum 6273, 6275-6
Kadman Numismatic Pavillion 5607, 5618, 5887
Kan, Richard 159
Käppeli, Robert 2066
Karl, Erich 4896
Kaufman, J. Chaim 5741-2
Khartoum (see National Archaeological Museum)
Kayhan, Muharrem 2013, 2065
Keckman, Erkki 1986
Kelley, Robert F. 1952, 4525
Kelsey Museum of Archaeology 3528, 4147, 6696
Kestner Museum (Hannover) 1763-5
Khan, Khurshid Ahmad 6295
King, Elisabeth Washburn 1922-4
Klagenfurt Landesmuseum 1964
Klein, Dieter 2063
Knight, Richard P. 1773
Knoepke, Olga H. 2048
Knox 170
Kocabas, Hüseyin 1909
Königliche Museen zu Berlin 1761
Koninklijk Penning Kabinet (The Netherlands) 1874, 4396
Kopp, Josef Vital 1904
Kotschoubev, Basile 2038
Kredi, Yapi 1908
Kungliga Myntkabinettet 2008
Kunstfreundes (see Gillet, Charles)
Kunsthistorisches Museum Wien (Vienna) 2132
Kunstmuseum des Landes Niederachsen 1993
Kurashiki Ninagawa Museum 1871

L

Laffaille, Maurice 2067, 2082, 2110
Lahore Museum (see Punjab Museum)
Lampson, Godfrey Locker 2095
Landesmuseum (see Klagenfurt)
Lanz, Hermann 2578
Lawrence University 1912

INDEX OF COLLECTORS AND COLLECTIONS

Leake, William Martin   1768, 1771, 1971, 2020, 2068
Leiden University   4396
Levante, Edoardo   2010-1
Lewis, R. B.   6763
Lewis, Samuel Savage   1768, 1973
Leypold, Franz   1965
Lindren, Henry Clay   2071-3
Ljubljana, Naradni Muzej (Slovenia)   2005
Lloyd, A. H.   1813, 1969, 2672
Lockett, Richard Cyril   1155, 1970, 2047, 5149
Lorichs, G. D.   2009
Lucic, L. Berualdi   4486
Ludwig   2642, 2685
Lulliri, Giuseppe   6723a

M

Mabbott, Thomas Ollive   2060
Macquarie University Museum of Ancient Cultures   1737, 1963, 2100, 4003
Magyar Nemzeti Múseum   1863, 1999, 6392
Mavrogordato, J. A.   2077
Manchester University   1974
Marshall College   1968
McClean, John R.   1768, 1770, 2661, 4106
McGill University   1745-9, 2836
Metropolitan Museum of Art (New York)   1189, 1936, 1940, 1945, 3586, 3994
Miho Museum (Japan)   711
Mikhailovitch, Grand Duke Alexander   1893, 2085
Minc, Henryk   5809
Montagu, Hyman   320, 1773, 2081, 2104, 6351
Montreal Museum of Fine Arts   1744
Morcom, Christopher   1946, 1977
Morcom, John   1977
Morcom, R. K.   1977
Morgan, J. Pierpont   1945, 2092-3
Morris, J. T.   3212
Münster University   1645
Murray, Margaret   1748
Musée Bretagne (Paris)   2187
Musée des Beaux-Arts de Lyon   2530
Musée Guimet (Paris)   6270
Musée Tbilissi (Georgia)   6123
Museo Archeologica Nazionale (Napoli)   2829, 6712
Museo Archeologico di Siracusa   2965
Museo Archeologico Nazionale, Firenze (Florence)   2002a, 4601, 6738
Museo Archeologico "G.A. Sanna"   2002
Museo Arqueológico Nacional (Madrid)   2006, 2158
Museo Civico Biassono (Italy)   1864
Museo Nazionale di Cagliari   6709
Museo Nazionale di Napoli   1865-6, 2635
Museo Nazionale di Palermo   1867
Museo Numismatico Athenarum Publico (see Athens, Numismatic Museum)
Museu Eng. António de Almeida   1887
Museu Histórico Nacional (Brazil)   1967
Museum of Alexandria   6564
Museum of Applied Arts and Sciences (Sydney)   1738
Museum of Art and Archaeology—University of Missouri   1927
Museum of Fine Arts (Boston)   44, 1021, 1279, 1439, 1917-20, 2094, 3132, 4494, 6694
Museum of Macedonia   3273a-4
Museum of Meshkinshar   6079

N

National Archaeological Museum of Khartoum   1901
National Archaeological Museum (Sofia)   757
National Bank of Detroit Money Museum   60, 1930
National Bank of the Republic of Macedonia   3257a, 3272, 3292
National Historical Museum (Sofia)   1682
National Museum, Aden (Yemen)   5970
National Museum, Afghanistan   6330
National Museum, Belgrade   1960
National Museum, Cracow (Poland)   2004
National Museum of Monetary History (Stockholm)   2009
Newell, Adra M.   1959
Newell, Edward T.   1153, 1188, 1959, 2089, 3756, 5214-5, 6351
Nicholson Museum   6664
Niggeler, Walter   2025
Nercessian, Y. T.   5537
Newdigate, Roger   1839
Northwick, Lord   2684, 2911
Numismatic Museum, Athens   544, 548, 585, 704, 706, 732, 1107, 1841-8, 1996-8, 3282, 4142, 4243, 4482, 4847

O

Odessa Archaeological Museum   4624
Oesterreichische Nationalbank   1965
Okray, Cafer S.   484
Oman, Charles   1813
Osijek Slavonian Museum   677
Oslo University   4607
Otago Museum (Dunedin, New Zealand)   1875, 1879, 1883, 3094, 4500

P

Pauri Museum   6367
Pasha, Ioannis Photiades   2059, 2117
Patna Museum   6366, 6433
Paulson, Richard E.   1913
Pennsylvania Academy of Fine Arts   3212
Pergamon Museum (Berlin)   1759, 5009
Perkins, Catherine Page   44, 1920
Peshawar Museum   6295
Peterson, William   1748
Petrie, Alfred Edward Hathaway   1743
Pfälzer   1991
Pitchfork, Colin E.   4532a
Post, F. Martin   4404
Pozzi, Samuel-Jean   2031, 2084, 2117
Princeton University Museum   3212, 4232, 5458, 5545
Prinsep, James   6435
Prospero   2022
Punjab Museum   6514

Q

Quam, Maurice   6085, 6087

R

"R. A." Collection   5476
Raby, Harold   1974
Rawlinson, Major   5220
Read, Thomas   2029
Ready, Talbot   4841
Reggio Emilia—Civic Museum   1868
Regio Museo di Torino (Italy)   1869
Rhode Island School of Art and Design   1955, 3123, 3223
Rhodesia—University College of   1890-1
Rhousopoulos, Athanasios   2057, 2117
Riegel Memorial Museum, Ella   1924
Righetti, Jean-Pierre   2012
Robinson, Henry S.   449
Rogers, Edgar   5420
Römer, Hans A.   2099
Romanian Academy   1892-4, 3674a, 3737a, 5627
Romano, Luigi E.   2631a
Rosen, Jonathan P.   425, 2097, 2116
Royal Coin Cabinet (Copenhagen, Denmark)   289, 1982-3, 1985, 3200, 3323, 4681, 6651
Royal Coin Cabinet (The Hague, The Netherlands)   1874, 2523
Royal Coin Cabinet (Stockholm, Sweden)   2009, 2168, 2521, 3200, 4355
Royal Cornwall Museum   2434
Royal Library of Belgium   1739-40, 1965

Index of Collectors and Collections

Royal Ontario Museum   1750-2, 2627-8
Royal Scottish Museum   1896-7
Rüpell, Eduard   6661

S

Sadberk Hanin Museum   1909
Sallusto, Federico   2813
Salting   1968
Samsun Museum   4595
Sardar Museum   6255
Saroglos, Petros Z.   1997
Saryan, Leon A.   5546-9
Schuster, Marion   2026
Schweizerischen Landesmuseum (Zürich)   2534
Seager, Richard B.   4408-9
Seattle Art Museum   55
Seldarov Collection   3292
Seltman, Charles T.   1155, 6351
Shapero, Nate S.   60, 1930
Shore, Fred B.   5120, 6043, 6126-7
Shoshana Collection   5717b
Sim, George   2101
Simonetta   5148a
Simpson, David   2090
Sinop Museum (Turkey)   484, 1910
Skopbank   1986
Smith College Museum of Art   1953
Smithsonian Institution   1954, 5089, 6282
Society Historia Numorum   3141
Society of Antiquaries   1980
Sofaer, Abraham D.   5703, 5716, 5801, 5939
Southland Museum   1876-7
Soutzos, A. G.   1998
Spaer, Arnold   2000
Spencer-Churchill, Edward George   1968
Split Museum (Croatia)   1753
Staatliche Münzsammlung (München)   1989, 2216, 2578
Staatlichen Museen (Berlin)   1174, 1187, 4144, 4245
Stancomb, William M.   1978, 3714
State Museum (Lucknow)   6493
Stevenson, George & Robert   2033
Storrs, Ronald   1944
Stroganov, S. G.   4666
Strozzi, M. C.   2093, 3007, 3029
Strutt, Col.   6351
Sunrise Collection   6225
Sutzu, Mihail Constantin   1892-3

T

Tabriz Museum (Iran)   6056
Tasmanian Museum and Art Gallery   4830
Tbilissi Musée (Georgia)   6123
Theodorou, Jerry   2090
Tire Museum (Turkey)   2016
Torino—Regio Museu   1869
Torremuzza (see Castellus)
Tübingen Universität   1990
Turnbull Library, Alexander   1882

U

Udine Civic Museum (Italy)   1870
Ulrich Museum, Herzog Anton   1993
United States Mint   1954, 5753
Università di Pavia   2173
Universität Tübingen   1990
Universität zu Köln   6702
Universitätsbibliothek Erlangen-Nürnberg   1766-7
Universitätbibliothek Leipzig   1992
University College of Rhodesia   1890-1
University of Auckland   1876
University of Cologne (Köln)   6702
University of Colorado   1928-9
University of Indiana   1915-6
University of Fribourg   1904, 5816
University of Glasgow   204, 1979, 1898-9, 4948
Univesity of Haifa   5798
University of Michigan   1911, 3528, 4147, 6696
University of Missouri   1927
University of Leipzig   1992
University of Tasmania   1906
University of Zimbabwe   1890-1

V

Vedat Nedim Tör Museum   1908
Velkov, James and Sneja   2115
Victoria and Albert Museum   1968
Viola, Mauro   6723a
Virzi, Ignazio   2877
Virzi, Tom   2024, 2075
Vlasto, Michel P.   2856
Von Aulock, Hans   1988
Von Petrowicz, Alexander Ritter   6030, 6081, 6149
Von Post, Eric   2008
von Prokesch-Osten, Anton   3529, 4144, 6149a, 6075a

W

Waddington, William H.   2018-9
Wagner, J. S.   5475
Walkhoff-Jordan, K.-D.   6304
Wallace, William P.   3945
Wanganui Regional Museum   1878
Ward, John   1936, 1940, 1945, 2056, 2118
Warren, Edward P.   1917-8, 2094, 2865
Warwickshire Museum   1839
Washington University   1957-8
Watkins, Frederick M.   1926
Weber, Charles E.   1556
Weber, *Consul* Eduard Friedrich   2058
Weber, Hermann   1773, 2042, 2095, 2119-21, 4841
Wertheim, J.   6081
Westmoreland Collection   267, 884, 2100
Wheaton College   1959
Whitehead, Richard B.   6513
Wigan, Edwards   1773, 1783
Wigan, J. A.   2395
Wilbour, Theodora   1917
Wilkinson, John S.   2076, 2122
Wilson College   1968
Winterthur Münzkabinett   1905, 4313
Wirgin, Wolf   5864
Woodhouse, James   1773
Woodward, William Harrison   1168, 2096
Wriston Art Center   1912
Wulfing, John Max   1957

Y

Yale University   1933-5, 3511, 4250

Z

Zagreb (see Archaeological Museum)
Zhuyuetang   159
Zimbabwe University   1890-1
Zwicker, Ulrich   1766-7